PORTUGAL

KT-385-693

V. Castelo

Braga

Bragança

Vila Real

Porto

Aveiro

Viseu

Guarda

Coimbra

Castelo Branco

Leiria

Santarém

Portalegre

Lisboa

Setúbal

Évora

Beja

Faro

0   60 Km

DICIONÁRIO
DE
PORTUGUÊS-INGLÊS
INGLÊS-PORTUGUÊS

2.ª edição | PT-289-99 • Abril 99

© PLÁTANO EDIÇÕES TÉCNICAS
Av. de Berna, 31, 2.º Esq. — 1069-054 LISBOA
Telefone: (01) 797 92 78 — Telefax: (01) 795 40 19

DISTRIBUIÇÃO:
PARALELO EDITORA, LDA.
LISBOA: Rua João Ortigão Ramos, 29-B
☎ (01) 764 98 94 — 1500-363 LISBOA
CENTRO: Rua Manuel Ferreira, 365 Pedrulha
☎ (039) 82 09 45 — 3020-303 COIMBRA
NORTE: Alicerce Editora, Lda.
Rua Guerra Junqueiro, 456
☎ (02) 609 99 79 — 4150-387 PORTO

título | DICIONÁRIO DE PORTUGUÊS-INGLÊS / INGLÊS-PORTUGUÊS

capa
arranjo gráfico
fotocomposição
e montagem | GABINETE TÉCNICO DA PLÁTANO EDITORA

impressão
e acabamento | GRAFO, S.A.

ISBN-972-707-119-8

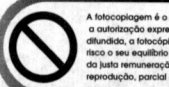

DICIONÁRIO
DE
PORTUGUÊS-INGLÊS

PLÁTANO
Edições Técnicas

ABREVIATURAS UTILIZADAS

adj.	adjectivo	*indef.*	indefinido
adv.	advérbio	*interj.*	interjeição
agric.	agricultura	*jur.*	jurídico
Amer.	América	*loc. adv.*	locução adverbial
amer.	americano	*loc. prep.*	locução prepositiva
anat.	anatomia	*mar.*	marítimo
arc.	arcaico	*mat.*	matemática
arit.	aritmética	*mec.*	mecânica
arq.	arquitectura	*med.*	medicina
art.	artilharia	*meteo.*	meteorologia
art. def.	artigo definido	*mil.*	militar
astro.	astronomia	*mús.*	música
biol.	biologia	*náut.*	náutica
bioq.	bioquímica	*num.*	numeral
bot.	botânica	*pl.*	plural
Bras.	Brasil	*pol.*	política
bras.	brasileiro	*pop.*	popular
carp.	carpintaria	*prep.*	preposição
com.	comercial	*pron.*	pronome
cul.	culinária	*quím.*	química
conj.	conjunção	*rel.*	religião
cont.	contracção	*s.f.*	substantivo feminino
dem.	demonstrativo	*s.m.*	substantivo masculino
dep.	depreciativo	*v.i.*	verbo intransitivo
ecol.	ecologia	*v.refl.*	verbo reflexo
econ.	economia	*v.t.*	verbo transitivo
elect.	electricidade	*vet.*	veterinária
fig.	figurativo	*zool.*	zoologia
fís.	física		
fisiol.	fisiologia		
fot.	fotografia		
geol.	geologia		
geom.	geometria		
gram.	gramática		
hist.	história		

DICIONÁRIO
PORTUGUÊS-INGLÊS

A

a, the first letter of the Portuguese alphabet.

a,aba, *s.f. (de chapéu)* brim; *(de vestuário)* lap, skirt; *(de mesa)* leaf.

abacate, *s.m.* avocado-pear.

abacaxi, *s.m.* pineapple.

ábaco, *s.m.* abacus.

abada, *s.f.* the female of a rhinoceros; a great deal.

abade, *s.m.* abott.

abadessa, *s.f.* abbess.

abadia, *s.f.* abbey.

abafação, *s.f.* suffocation; choke; opression.

abafadiço, *adj.* smothery, not aired, opressive.

abafado, *adj.* suffocating, well clothed.

abafador, *s.m.* choker, damper *(de um piano)*, muffler *(de som)*, cozy *(para bule)*.

abafar, *v.t.* to choke, to suffocate, to smother.

abafo, *s.m.* stuffiness, muffler *(roupa)*.

abainhar, *v.t.* to hem; to hedge.

abaixamento, *s.m.* abasement, lowering.

abaixar, *v.t.* to lower, to bring down, to reduce.

abaixo, *adv.* down, below, under.

abaixo-assinado, *s.m.* undersigned.

abajur, *s.m.* lamp shade.

abalada, *s.f.* sudden departure.

abalado, *adj.* shaken, troubled.

abalançar, *v.t.* to balance, to dare.

abalar, *v.t.* to shake, to disturb, to move *(comover)*; to depart.

abalaustrar, *v.t.* to rail, to enclose with rails.

abalizado, *adj.* competent.

abalizar, *v.t.* to demarcate *(terras)*.

abalo, *s.m.* shake, sock, commotion.

abalroamento, *s.m.* collision, shock.

abalroar, *v.t.* to collide, to board a ship.

abanadela, *s.f.* fanning, shake, joggling.

abanador, *s.m.* fire-fan, fanner.

abananado, *adj.* amazed, astonished, wonder struck.

abananar, *v.t.* to amaze, to astonish.

abanão, *s.m.* a strong shake.

abanar, *v.t.* to shake, to agitate, to wave *(a mão)*.

abancar, *v.t.* to sit down.

abandalhamento, *s.m.* degradation, the act of degrading oneself.

abandalhar-se, *v.r.* to debase oneself.

abandonado, *adj.* abandoned, forsaken, isolated.

abandonar, *v.t.* to abandon, to forsake, to leave, to give up.

abandono, *s.m.* abandonment, abandoning, forsaking, desertion.

abanico, *s.m.* fan.

abano, *s.m.* fan, fanner.

abarbatar, *v.t.* to steal.

abarcador, *s.m.* grasper, embracer, monopolist.

abarcamento, *s.m.* monopoly, embracement.

abarcar, *v.t.* to grasp, to embrace, to include, to monopolise.

abarracamento, *s.m.* camp, quarters for soldiers.

abarracar, *v.t.* to encamp, to lodge into tents.

abarrancar, *v.t.* to ditch.

abarrotado, *adj.* full up, overstocked.

abarrotar, *v.t.* to fill up, to overstock.

abastado, *adj.* wealthy, well of.

abastamento, *s.m.* provisioning, the act of supplying.

abastança, *s.f.* wealth.

abastar, *v.t.* to supply with.

abastardado, *adj.* debased, degraded.

abastardamento, *s.m.* debasement, degradation.

abastardar, abastardear, *v.t.* to debase, to degrade, to spoil.

abastecedor, *s.m.* supplier.

abastecer, *v.t.* to supply, to provide.

abastecido, *adj.* supplied with, provided with.

abastecimento, *s.m.* supply, provisioning.

abatatado, *adj.* potato like, bulbous.

abate, *s.m.* slaughter.

abater, *v.t.* to slaughter *(animais)*, to abate, to reduce.

abatido, *adj.* discouraged, spiritless, sad, weak.

abatimento, *s.m.* discount, deduction, reduction, discouragement, low spirits weakness.

abaulado, *adj.* bulged, bulgy, convex, arched.

abaular, *v.t.* to arch, to vault, to make convex or bulged.

abcesso, *s.m.* abcess, tumour.

abcissa, *s.f.* abcissa (pl. abcissae).

abdicação, *s.f.* abdication.

abdicador, abdicante, *s.m.* abdicatour, renouncer.

abdicar, *v.t.* to abdicate, to renounce.

abdicável, *adj.* that may be abdicated.

abdómen, *s.m.* abdomen.

abdominal, *adj.* abdominal.

abdutor, *s.m.* abductor.

abduzir, *v.t.* to abduce, to abduct, to take away (by fraud or violence).

abeberar, *v.t.* to water, to absorb.

abecedário, *s.m.* abecedary, the alphabet.

abegão, *s.m.* a farmer's servant, manager, land steward.

abegoa, *s.f.* the wife of a farmer's servant.

abegoaria, *s.f.* place where farm implements or tools are kept.

abeirar, *v.t.* e *v.r.* to approach, to come near.

abelha, *s.f.* bee.

abelhal, *s.m.* swarm of bees.

abelha-mestra, *s.f.* queen-bee.

abelhão, *s.m.* drone.

abelhudo, *adj.* nosy, indiscreet.

a bel-prazer, *loc. adv.* leisurely, at ease.

abençoado, *adj.* blessed.

abençoador, *s.m.* blesser.

abençoar, *v.t.* to bless.

aberração, *s.f.* aberration, deviation.

aberrante, *adj.* aberrant.

aberrar, *v.t.* to wander, to deviate.

aberta, *s.f.* opening.

abertamente, *adv.* openly, frankly, sincerely.

aberto, *adj.* open, opened, sincere, open minded; *em aberto,* incomplete, in suspense.

abertura, *s.f.* opening, inauguration, overture (mús.).

abespinhado, *adj.* angry, irritated.

abespinhamento, *s.m.* anger.

abespinhar, *v.r.* to get angry.

abeto, *s.m.* fir.

abetumar, *v.t.* to coat with bitumen.

abichar, *v.t.* to get, to obtain.

abiscoitar, *v.t.* to make like a biscuit, to get, to obtain.

abismado, *adj.* amazed, surprised.

abismal, *adj.* abysmal.

abismar, *v.t.* to amaze, to surprise.

abismo, *s.m.* abysm.

abissal, *adj.* abyssal.

abissínio, *s.m.* Abyssinian, Ethiopian.

abjecção, *s.f.* abjection, vileness.

abjecto, *adj.* abject, vile, contemptible.

abjudicação, *s.f.* abjudication.

abjudicar, *v.t.* to abjudicate.

abjuração, *s.f.* abjuration.

abjurar, *v.t.* to abjurate.

ablação, *s.f.* ablation, amputation, cutting off.

ablactar, *v.t.* to ablactate, to wean.

abnegação, *s.f.* abnegation, renunciation, self sacrifice.

abnegado, *adj.* abnegated, self sacrificing.

abnegar, *v.t.* to abnegate, to renounce.

abóbada, *s.f.* vault, dome *(cúpula).*

abobadado, *adj.* arched, vaulted, dome shaped.

abobadar, *v.t.* to vault, to arch, to dome.

abobado, *adj.* silly, foolish.

abóbora, *s.f.* gourd, pumpkin *(abóbora-menina).*

aboboral, *s.m.* a gourd field.

aboboreira, *s.f.* gourd vine.

abocanhar, *v.t.* to take with the mouth, to slander *(difamar).*

abocar, *v.t.* to take with the mouth.

aboiar, *v.t.* to buoy, to mark with buoys, to moor, to fasten by anchor, to drift about aimless.

abolachado, *adj.* biscuit like, flat.

abolachar, *v.t.* to make like a biscuit, to flatt.

aboletamento, *s.m.* billeting, quartering soldiers.

aboletar, *v.t.* to billet, to lodge soldiers.

abolição, abolimento, s.f. e s.m. abolition, abolishment, surpression.
abolicionismo, s.m. abolitionism.
abolicionista, s.m. abolitionist.
abolir, v.t. to abolish, to cancel.
abolorecer, abolorentar, v.t. to grow mouldy.
abolorecimento, s.m. mouldyng.
abominação, s.f. abomination, extreme aversion.
abominado, adj. detested.
abominador, s.m. abominator.
abominar, v.t. to abominate, to detest, to hate.
abominável, adj. abominable, detestable.
abominavelmente, adv. abominably, detestably.
abominoso, adj. abominable.
abonação, s.f. bail, guaranty, advance payment.
abonadamente, adv. with security, richly.
abonado, adj. rich, well-to-do.
abonador, s.m. guarantor, sponsor, bondsman.
abonatório, adj. guaranteeing.
abonecado, adj. doll-like, dressed smartly.
abono, s.m. bail, guarantee, subsidy; 1) em abono da verdade. 2) to tell the truth; falar em abono de alguém. 3) to speak on someone's behalf.
abordagem, s.f. boarding.
abordar, v.t. to board, to adress (pessoa) to tackle or to approach (assunto).
abordável, adj. accessible.
aborígene, s.m. Aborigene; adj. aboriginal.
aborrascar, v.r. to become stormy.
aborrecer, v.t. to bore, to annoy, to bother.
aborrecido, adj. bored, tedious, annoying.
aborrecimento, s.m. boredoam, tedium, annoyance, inconvenience.
abortar, v.t. e v.i. to abort, to miscarry, to fail.
abortivo, adj. abortive.
aborto, s.m. abortion, miscarriage; aborto da natureza, monster, freak.
abotinado, adj. boot-shaped.
abotinar, v.t. to give the shape of a boot.
abotoadeira, s.f. buttonhook.
abotoadura, s.f. cuff link, cuff button.
abotoar, v.t. to button. v.r. abotoar-se, to snaffle.
abra, s.f. bay, creek.
abracadabrante, adj. eccentric, extraordinary.
abraçador, s.m. embracer.

abraçar, v.t. to embrace, to hug, to encircle (circundar), to contain, to include (conter).
abraço, s.m. hug, embrace.
abrandamento, s.m. softening, relentig.
abrandar, v.t. to relent, to soften, to appease; v.i. to abate (a tempestade).
abranger, v.t. to enfold, to encircle, to embrace, to include, to comprise (incluir).
abrasado, adj. ablaze, glowing, on fire.
abrasador, adj. burning, torrid.
abrasamento, s.m. burning, ardor.
abrasar, v.t. to burn, to inflame.
abrasear, v.t. to reduce to ashes, to become red-hot.
abrasileirado, adj. with the manners of a Brazilian.
abrasileirar, v.t. to brazilianize, to make in the brazilian way.
abrasivo, adj. abrasive.
abrasoar, abrasonar, v.t. to give or to concede a coat of arms.
abre-latas, s.m. can opener.
abreviação, s.f. shortening, abbreviation.
abreviar, v.t. to abbreviate, to shorten.
abreviatura, s.f. abbreviation, abridgement.
abricó, s.m. mammee apple.
abridor, s.m. opener.
abrigado, adj. sheltered.
abrigar, v.t. to shelter, to give shelter.
abrigo, s.m. shelter, refuge, protection.
Abril, s.m. April; o 1º de Abril, all fool's Day.
abrilhantar, to brighten, to grace (com a sua presença).
abrir, v.t. to open, to unlock, to break open; v.i. to bloom (as flores), to clear (desimpedir), to dig (abrir um buraco, escavar); v.i. unblossom oneself (com alguém).
abrochar, v.t. to clasp, to fasten with a brooch.
ab-rogação, s.f. abrogation, suppresion, annulment.
ab-rogar, v.t. (jur.) to abrogate, to annul.
ab-rogativo, adj. (jur.) abrogative.
abrolhar, v.i. to blossom, to bud, to sprout.
abrolho, s.m. thorn (espinho), pl.(fig.) troubles.
abrunho, s.m. sloe.
abruptamente, adv. abruptly, suddenly.
abrupto, adj. abrupt, sudden.
abrutado, adj. brutal, rude.
abrutalhado, adj. brutish, rude.
absentismo, s.m. absenteeism.
absentista, adj. e s.m. absentee.
abside, s.m. apse.

absinto, *s.m.* absinth.
absolutamente, *adv.* absolutely, completely; *absolutamente nada,* nothing at all.
absolutismo, *s.m.* absolutism, despotism.
absolutista, *s.m.* absolutist.
absoluto, *adj.* absolute, total, complete, utter, despotic, autocratic.
absolver, *v.t.* to absolve.
absolvição, *s.f.* absolution, acquital, exculpation.
absorção, *s.f.* absorption, assimilation.
absorto, *adj.* absorbed, contemplative.
absorvência, *s.f.* absorbency.
absorvente, *adj.* absorbent, absorbing.
absorver, *v.t.* to absorb, to soak, to assimilate. *v.r.* to concentrate on something.
abstémio, *adj.* abstemious, sober, *s.m.* teetotaler.
abstenção, *s.f.* abstention, avoidance.
abster, *v.t.* to restrain, to abstain (from).
abstinência, *s.f.* abstinence, temperance.
abstinente, *adj.* abstinent, sober, temperate; *s.m.* abstainer.
abstracção, *s.f.* abstraction.
abstracto, *adj.* abstract.
abstrair, *v.t.* to abstract, to separate; *v.i.* to consider separately; *v.r.* to withdraw (from something).
abstruso, *adj.* abstruse, obscure.
absurdamente, *adv.* absurdly.
absurdo, *adj.* absurd, ridiculous; *s.m.* absurdity, nonsense.
abular-se, *v.r.* to obtain a bull.
abulia, *s.f.* lack or weakness of will.
abundância, *adj.* abundance, profusion.
abundante, *adj.* abundant, plentiful.
abundar, *v.i.* to abound, to exist in great quantity.
aburguesado, *adj.* like one of the middle class.
aburguesar, *v.t.* to give the manners of a burgeois.
abusador, *s.m.* abuser.
abusão, *s.f.* abuse, superstition, illusion.
abusar, *v.t.* to abuse, to go too far.
abusivo, *adj.* abusive.
abuso, *s.m.* abuse, misuse, outrage *(ultrage); abuso de confiança,* breach of confidence.
abutre, *s.m.* vulture.
acabado, *adj.* finished, complete, done.
acabadote, *adj.* oldish.
acabamento, *s.m.* finishing.
acabar, *v.t.* to end, to finish, to complete, to

accomplish *(levar a cabo); v.i.* to end, to cease; *v.r.* to be finished.
acabrunhadamente, *adv.* depressedly, sadly.
acabrunhado, *adj.* dejected, sorrowfull, depressed.
acabrunhar, *v.t.* to opress, to deject, to humble *(humilhar);* **acabrunhar-se,** to lose courage, to become discouraged.
acaçapado, *adj.* crouching *(agachado),* squat *(atarracado).*
acaçapar, *v.t.* to shrink, to crouch, to squat, to lie squat.
acácia, *s.f.* acacia.
academia, *s.f.* academy, college, society.
academia, *s.f.* academy, figure, a drawin of a nude model, a plastic model.
académico, *adj.* academic, scholastic; *s.m.* academician, student in an academy.
açafata, *s.f.* maid of honour.
açafate, *s.m.* small basket.
açafrão, *s.m.* saffron.
açafroa, *s.f.* safflower.
açafroado, *adj.* saffron-coloured, seasoned with saffron.
açafroal, *s.m.* saffron-ground.
açafroar, *v.t.* to season with saffron.
açaimar, *v.t.* to muzzle, to put a muzzle on, *(fig.)* to repress.
açaime, *s.m.* muzzle.
acaju, *s.m.* acajou.
acajueiro, *s.m.* mahogany.
acalcanhar, *v.t.* to tread on, to crush with the heel.
acalentador, *s.m.* lulling, soothing.
acalentar, *v.t.* to rock or lull a child to sleep, to soothe *(acalmar).*
acalento, *s.m.* rocking or lulling to sleep.
acalmar, *v.t.* to calm, to appease, to soothe; *v.i.* to calme down; *v.r.* to grow calm, to quiet down.
acalmia, *s.f.* lull respite.
acalorado, *adj.* heated, excited.
acalorar, *v.t.* to warm, to heat up, to excite.
acamado, *adj.* confined to bed.
acamar, *v.t.* to put in bed, to arrange in layers *(dispor em camadas); v.i.* to fall sick a bed *(cair à cama).*
acamaradar, *v.t.* to become friends.
açambarcador, *s.m.* monopolizer.
açambarcamento, *s.m.* monopolizing, corner.
açambarcar, *v.t.* to monopolize, to corner, to buy up.

11

acampamento, camping, camp.

acampar, *v.t.* to camp, to encamp.

acamurçado, *adj.* chamois coloured.

acamurçar, *v.t.* to dress chamois leather.

acanalar, *v.t.* to channel, to flute.

acanalhar, *v.t. e v.r.* to debase, to debase oneself.

acanhado, *adj.* narrow, poky, shy, timid.

acanhamento, *s.m.* bashfulness, shyness.

acanhar, *v.t.* to make narrow, to inspire with fear; *v.r.* to become bashfull, to be ashamed.

acanto, *s.m.* acanthus.

acantoar, *v.t.* to force into a corner, to sequester, to set apart. *v.r.* to stand in a corner, to live apart.

acantonamento, *s.m.* cantonment.

acantonar, *v.t.* to canton, to quarter, lodge in specific quarters.

acanular, *v.t.* to give the form of a cannula.

acapitular, *v.t.* to divide into chapters.

acardumar, *v.t.* to gather in shoals; *v.r.* to shoal, *(fig.)* to swarm.

acareação, *s.f.* confrontation.

acarear, *v.t.* to confront.

acariciador, *adj.* caressing, tender.

acariciar, *v.t.* to caress, to fondle, to cherish *(uma ideia).*

acaridar-se, *v.r.* to compassionate, to feel pity for.

acarinhar, *v.t.* o mesmo que acariciar.

acarídeos, *s.m. e adj.* acaridan, acaridians.

ácaro, *s.m.* acarrus.

acarraçado, *adj.* sticking like a thick or mite.

acarrapatado, *adj.* like a thick.

acarretar, *v.t.* to carry in a cart, to cart, to cause, to give rise to.

acasalamento, *s.m.* mating.

acasalar, *v.t.* to couple; to mate.

acaso, *s.m.* chance, hazard, accident, *(por acaso),* by accident; luck, fortune *(sorte)*; *adv.* perchance, by chance.

acastanhado, *adj.* brownish, of chestnut colour, reddish brown.

acastelar, *v.t.* to build as a castle, to fortify with castles; *v.r.* to fortify oneself.

acatadamente, *adv.* respectfully.

acatável, *adj.* respectable.

acatitar, *v.t.* to make pretty, to embellish.

acatólico, *s.m.* non-Catholic.

acaudilhar, *v.t.* to command, to lead.

acaule, *s.m. (bot.)* acaulous, acaulescent.

acauteladamente, *adv.* cautiously.

acautelado, *adj.* cautious, prudent.

acautelar, *v.t.* to caution, to warn, to look after *(resguardar);* *v.r.* to be cautious; *acautele-se!,* take care!

acavalado, *adj.* like a horse, to coarse *(praguejar).*

acavalar, *v.t.* to cover with a mare, to put on horseback.

acção, *s.f.* action, act, deed *(feito);* *(jur.)* lawsuit, suit; *(econ.)* share, stock; *acção de graças,* thanksgiving.

accionado, *s.* the person sued at law.

accionar, *v.t. (jur.)* to sue at law, to move, to set in motion.

accionista, share holder.

acedência, *s.f.* accedence, acquiescence, agreement.

aceder, *v.t.* to accede (to), to comply (with), to grant *(conceder).*

acédia, *s.f.* laziness, negligence.

acefalia, *s.f.* acephalia.

acéfalo, *s.m.* acephalous, headless, *(fig.)* without a leader.

aceitabilidade, *s.f.* acceptability.

aceitação, *s.f.* acceptance, approbation.

aceitar, *v.t.* to accept, to receive, to admit.

aceitável, *adj.* acceptable.

aceite, *s.m.* acceptance.

aceito, *adj.* accepted of, well received.

aceleração, *s.f.* acceleration.

aceleradamente, *adv.* speedly, in a hurry.

acelerado, *adj.* accelerated, quickened.

acelerador, *s.m.* accelerator.

acelga, *s.f. (bot.)* swiss chard-beet.

acém, *s.m.* loin, sirloin.

acenar, *v.i.* to wave *(com a mão),* to nod *(com cabeça).*

acendalha, *s.f.* chip, lighter.

acendedor, *s.m.* lighter.

acender, *v.t.* to light, to set on fire.

acendimento, the act of lighting.

acendível, *adj.* inflammable.

acendrado, *adj.* cleansed, greyish.

aceno, *s.m.* nod, beck on, wave of the hand.

acento, *s.m.* accent, tone, note.

acentuação, *s.f.* accentuation, accent.

acentuado, *adj.* stressed *(a sílaba),* striking *(evidente).*

acentuar, *v.t.* to accentuate, to stress, to emphasize.

acepção, *s.f.* acception, meaning.

acepilhador, *s.m.* planer.

acepilhar, *v.t.* to plane, to smoothen, to polish.

acepipe, *s.m.* tidbit, morsel.

ace

acéquia, *s.f.* gutter, canal, dam *(açude)*.

ácer, *s.m. (bot.)* acer.

acerado, *adj.* sharp.

acerar, *v.t.* to steel, temper.

acerbamente, *adv.* bitterly, sharply.

acerbidade, *s.f.* acerbity, bitterness, roughness.

acerbo, *adj.* bitter, harsh, severe.

acerca, *adv.* near, about, *acerca de*, about, on, concerning.

acercar, *v.t.* to approach, to surround.

aceroso, *adj.* acerous, without horns.

acérrimo, *adj.* very sour, very bitter.

acertadamente, *adv.* rightly, wisely, right.

acertado, *adj.* right, correct, wise.

acertar, *v.t.* to do rightly, to set right *(relógio); v.i.* to succeed.

acerto, *s.m.* wisdom, prudence, justness.

acervo, *s.m.* heap, a great quantity, a lot of.

aceso, *adj.* lighted, lit, switched on, *(fig.)* hot, fiery.

acessão, *s.f.* acession, increase.

acessibilidade, *s.f.* accessibility.

acessível, *adj.* accessible, approchable.

acesso, *s.m.* access, approach, admittance, attack, fit.

acessoriamente, *adv.* accessorily.

acessório, *s.n.* accessory, *pl.* fittings; *adj.* accessory, additional.

acetato, *s.m.* acetate.

acético, *adj.* acetic.

acetificação, *s.f.* acetification.

acetificar, *v.t.* to acetify.

acetileno, *s.m.* acetylene.

acetímetro, *s.m.* acetimeter.

acetinado, *adj.* smooth like satin, soft.

acetinar, *v.t.* to make soft, to soften.

acetona, *s.f.* acetone.

acetoso, *adj.* acetous.

acevadar, *v.t.* to feed with barley.

acha, *s.f.* billet, log, a small log of wood.

achacadiço, *adj.* unhealthy.

achacado, *adj.* unhealthy, sick.

achacar, *v.t.* to become sick.

achacoso, *adj.* sickly.

achado, *adj,* found; *s.m.* find, discovery.

achador, *s.m.* finder.

achamento, finding.

achaque, *s.m.* ailment, cronic ilness, indisposition.

achar, *v.t.* to find, to hit on, to come across, to discover, to think, to find out, to remark; **achar-se,** to find oneself.

achatadela, *s.f.* flattening.

achatar, *v.t.* to flatten.

achavascar, *v.t.* to bungle, to make clumsly.

achega, *s.f.* addition; *(fam.)* help, aid.

achegado, *adj.* near; *s.m.* of the same family, relative.

achegamento, *s.m.* approach, approximation.

achegar, *v.t.* to approach.

achincalhação, *s.f.* mocking, degrading, debasement.

achincalhar, *v.t.* to mock, to ridicule to, scoff, to debase.

achinelar, *v.t.* to give the form of a slipper.

achinesar, *v.t.* to make like a Chinese.

achocalhado, *adj.* provided with a cattle bell.

achocalhar, *v.t.* to give the form of a cattle bell, *(fig.)* to divulge, to make public.

achumbado, *adj.* lead coloured, leaden.

acicate, *s.m.* a Moorish spur with a short point.

acicolado, *adj.* acicolar, sharp-pointed.

acidar, *v.t.* to make acid, to acidify.

acidentado, *adj.* irregular, uneven, bumpy, eventfull *(cheio de peripécias)*.

acidental, *adj.* accidental, casual.

acidentalmente, *adv.* casually, occasionally.

acidentar, *v.t.* to produce accident in, to interrupt.

acidente, *s.m.* accident, casualty *(infortúnio)*.

acidez, *s.f.* acidity.

acídia, *s.f.* laziness.

acidificação, *s.f.* acidification.

acidificar, *v.t.* to acidify.

acidificável, *adj.* acidifiable.

acidimetria, *s.f.* acidimetry.

acidímetro, *s.m.* acidimeter.

ácido, *s.m.* acid; *adj.* acid, sour.

acidulado, *adj.* acidulous.

acidulante, *adj.* acidulating.

acidular, *v.t.* to acidulate.

acídulo, *adj.* acidulous.

acima, *adv.* above, up. 1) *acima de, por cima de,* above, over; 2) *acima mencionado,* above mentioned. 3) *pela rua acima,* up the street. 4) *mais acima,* higher up.

acinte, *s.m.* malice, indignity; *adv.* on purpose.

acintosamente, *adv.* maliciously, purposely.

acintoso, *adj.* spiteful, malicious.

acinzentado, *adj.* greyish.

acipreste, *s.m.* cypress.

acirrante, *adj.* irritating.

acirrar, *v.t.* to irritate, to incite, to excite.

aclamação, *s.f.* acclamation, acclaim, applause; *por aclamação,* unanimously.
aclamador, *s.m.* applaudor, proclaimer.
aclamar, *v.t.* to acclaim, to proclaim.
aclaração, *s.f.* clearing up, elucidation.
aclaramento, *s.m.* clearing up, explanation.
aclarar, *v.t.* to make clear, to clarify, to illuminate; *v.i.* to clear up, to become clear.
aclimação, *s.f.* acclimation.
aclimatar, *v.t.* to acclimate, to adapt one self to a new climate.
aclive, *s.m.* acclivity, slope; *adj.* acclivous, steep.
acne, *s.f.* acne.
aço, *s.m.* steel, *aço temperado,* hardened steel.
acobardadamente, *adv.* cowardly.
acobardamento, *s.m.* cowardice.
acobardar, *v.t.* to intimidate; **acobardar--se,** to lose courage, to flinch.
acobertado, *adj.* clad, protected, disguised.
acobertar, *v.t.* to cover, to protect, to disguise.
acobreado, *adj.* coppery.
acobrear, *v.t.* to copper, to give a coppery appearance.
acocorar-se, *v.r.* to crouch, to squat.
açodadamente, *adv.* in haste, in a hurry.
açodar, *v.t.* to hurry, to urge, to instigate.
açofeita, *s.f.* (bot.) jujube.
acogular, *v.t.* to fill up, to heap up.
acoimar, *v.t.* to fill up, to heap up, to reproach.
açoutador, *s.m.* scourger, whipper.
açoitar, *v.t.* to whip, to lash, to scourge.
açoite, *s.m.* whip, lash, whipping, lashing.
acolá, *adv.* there, over there, down there.
acolchetar, *v.t.* to clasp.
acolchoado, *adj.* wadded; *s.m.* quilting.
acolchoador, *s.m.* one who wads.
acolhedor, *adj.* cozy, warm, hospitable; *s.m.* one who welcomes or receive.
acolher, *v.t.* to welcome, to receive.
acolhida, *s.f.* reception, welcome, protection.
acolhimento, *s.m.* welcome, reception, honour.
acolitado, *adj.* accompanied, attended, assisted; *s.m.* a member of the minor orders of the roman Catholic Church.
acolitar, *v.t.* to attend, to assist, to follow.
acólito, *s.m.* acolyte.
acometedor, *s.m.* aggressor, assailant; *adj.* attacking, bold.

acometer, *v.t.* to attack, to assault; *v.i.* to undertake, *ser acometido por uma doença,* to be seized by an illness.
acometida, *s.f.* attack, assault, undertaking.
acomodação, *s.f.* accomodation, arrangement.
acomodadamente, *adv.* accommodatingly, suitably.
acomodar, *v.t.* to accommodate, to suit, to harmonize; *v.r.* to conform oneself.
acomodatício, *adj.* easily accommodating, adaptable, compromising.
acompadrar, *v.t.* to make a person a godfather; **acompadrar-se,** to make friends.
acompanhador, *s.m.* companion, attendant.
acompanhamento, *s.m.* attendance, escort.
acompanhante, *s.m.* escort.
acompanhar, *v.t.* to accompany, to attend, to escort, to keep up with *(progressos); vou acompanhá-lo até à porta,* I'll see you to the door.
aconchegar, *v.t.* to bring close, to cuddle *(uma criança),* to tuck in *(as cobertas).*
aconchego, *s.m.* comfort, relief, shelter.
acondicionação, *s.f.* packing.
acondicionado, *adj.* packed, in a good disposition, placed in good order.
acondicionamento, *s.m.* packing, packaging.
acónito, *s.m.* aconite, monk's hood.
aconselhado, *adj.* prudent, wise.
aconselhador, *s.m.* adviser, mentor.
aconselhar, *v.t.* to advise, to counsel; **aconselhar-se,** to consult.
aconselhável, *adj.* advisable.
acontecer, *v.i.* to happen, to occur, to come about, to take place; *aconteça o que acontecer,* whatever happens.
acontecido, *s.m.* event, occurrence.
acontecimento, *s.m.* event, occurrence.
acoplamento, *s.m.* coupling.
acoplar, *v.i.* to couple.
açor, *s.m.* goshawk.
açorar, *v.t.* to excite a vehement desire.
açorda, *s.f.* a dish made of bread and water, seasoned with garlic and oil.
acordado, *adj.* awake, agreed.
acordante, *adj.* accordant, agreeing.
acórdão, *s.m.* sentence.
acordar, *v.t.* to awake, to rouse, to agree.
acorde, *s.m.* (mús.) accord, harmony; *adj.* conformable.
acordeão, *s.m.* accordion.

acordeonista, s.m. e s.f. accordionist.
acordo, s.m. accord, agreement, pact.
açoriano, s.m. e adj. a native of the Azores, belonging to the Azores.
acoroçoamento, s.m. encouragement.
acorrentado, adj. in chains, enchained.
acorrentar, v.t. to chain.
acorrer, v.t. to come running.
acorrilhar, v.t. to force into a corner.
acortinar, v.t. to enclose with curtains.
acossar, v.t. to pursue, to hound (perseguir), to harass, to torment (atormentar).
acostar, v.t. to approach the coast; v.i. to coast along, to run ashore (dar à costa); **acostar-se** to lean back against.
acostumado, accustomed, used (to).
acostumar, v.t. to accustom; **acostumar--se,** to get used to.
açoteia, s.f. small terrace at the top of a house.
acotiar, v.t. to frequent daily, to wear every day.
acotiledóneo, adj. (bot.) acotyledonous.
acotovelar, v.t. to nudge (fazer sinal), to elbow (empurrar); **acotovelar-se,** to jostle one another.
açougada, s.f. brawling, riot.
açougue, s.m. butcher's shop.
açougueiro, s.m. butcher.
acre, adj. acrid, sour, pungent, biting, scathing (mordaz); s.m. acre.
acreditado, adj. accredited, recognized, trustworthy.
acreditar, v.t. to give credit to, to credit; v.i. to believe.
acreditável, adj. believable, credible.
acre-doce, adj. sourish, sour-sweet.
acrescentamento, s.m. increase, supplement.
acrescentar, to increase, to add to.
acrescento, s.m. augmentation, increase.
acrescer, v.t. e v.i. to add, to increase.
acrescido, adj. increased, enlarged, amplified.
acréscimo, s.m. increase, addition, extension.
acriançado, adj. childish.
acriançar, v.t. to render infantile.
acridez, s.f. acridness, sourness.
acrídio, s.m. locust.
acrimónia, s.f. acrimony, sourness, animosity, bitterness.
acrimonioso, adj. acrimonious, bitter, sarcastic.

acrisolado, adj. perfect, refined, pure.
acrisolar, v.t. to refine, to purify.
acrobacia, s.f. acrobacy, acrobatics.
acrobata, s.m. acrobat.
acrobático, adj. acrobatic.
acrobatismo, s.m. acrobatism.
acromático, adj. achromatic.
acromatização, s.f. achromatization.
acromatizar, v.t. to achromatize, to deprive of colour.
acrópole, s.f. acropolis.
acróstico, s.m. acrostic.
acta, s.f. act, record.
activa, s.f. active; adj. active, dynamic.
activação, s.f. activeness, activation.
activamente, adv. actively.
activante, adj. activating.
activar, v.t. to activate, to stimulate, to hasten.
actividade, s.f. activity; em actividade, at work.
activo, adj. active, dynamic, lively; s.m. assets; activo e passivo, assets and liabilities.
acto, s.m. act, action, deed, feat.
actor, s.m. actor, performer.
actriz, s.f. actress.
actuação, s.f. actuation, performance.
actual, adj. actual, present.
actualidade, s.f. actuality, reality, novelty.
actualização, s.f. actualization.
actualizar, v.t. to actualize, to bring up to date.
actualmente, adv. at present, now, nowadays.
actuante, adj. actuating.
actuar, v.i. to act, to perform, to proceed.
actuário, s.m. actuary.
acuar, v.t. to bring to bay; v.i. to crouch (agachar-se), to back up.
açúcar, s.m. sugar.
açucarado, adj. sugared, sweet.
açucarar, v.t. to sugar, to sweeten with sugar.
açucareiro, sugar-bowl.
açucena, s.f. white lily.
açudar, v.t. to dam.
açude, s.m. dam.
acudir, v.i. to come running, to come to the rescue (vir em socorro), to help, to succor, to answer (responder a um chamado).
acuidade, s.f. acuity, shappness.
açulador, s.m. one who instigate dogs in hunting.

açular, *v.t.* to instigate, to set a dog on someone.

aculeado, *adj.* acute, prickly, thorny.

acúleo, *s.m.* thorn *(espinho)*, prick, incentive.

acume, *s.m.* acumen, sharp point, sharpness.

acuminado, *adj.* acuminate.

acuminar, *v.t.* to acuminate, to sharpen.

acumulação, *s.f.* accumulation.

acumulador, *s.m.* accumulator.

acumular, *v.t.* to accumulate, to pile up, to store up *(armazenar)*.

acumulativamente, *adv.* accumulatively.

acumulativo, *adj.* accumulative,

acumulável, *adj.* accumulative.

acunhar, *v.t.* to wedge.

acupunctura, *s.f.* acupuncture.

acurado, *adj.* accurate, careful, painstaking.

acurar, *v.t.* to treat with care, to improve.

acurvar, *v.t.* to bend, to curve; *v.i.* to give way, to submit.

acurvilhar, *v.i.* to bend, to kneel *(animais)*.

acusação, *s.f.* accusation, charge, incrimination, imputation, indictment, reproach *(censura)*, prosecution (num julgamento).

acusado, *adj.* accused; *s.m.* defendant, culprit *(réu)*.

acusador, *s.m.* accuser, prosecutor *(num julgamento)*.

acusar, *v.t.* to accuse, to charge with, to incriminate, to reproach *(censurar)*, to acknowledge *(acusar o recebimento)*.

acusativo, *s.m. e adj.* accusative.

acusatório, *adj.* accusatory.

acusável, *adj.* accusable, indictable.

acústica, *s.f.* acoustics.

acústico, *adj.* acoustic.

acutangular, *adj.* acutangular.

acutilador, *s.m.* slasher.

acutilar, *v.t.* to slash, to gash *(com espada)*.

acuto, *adj.* acute, sharp pointed.

adáctilo, *adj.* adactylous, fingerless.

adaga, *s.f.* dagger.

adagada, *s.f.* stab, a blow with a dagger.

adagial, *adj.* proverbial.

adagiar, *v.i.* to quote adages.

adagiário, *s.m.* collection of adages.

adágio, *s.m.* adage, proverb, saying.

adail, *s.m.* leader, guide.

adamado, *adj.* effeminate, delicate, soft.

adamantino, *adj.* adamantine.

adamar-se, *v.t.* to adorn oneself like a lady, to become effeminate.

adamascado, *adj.* damasked.

adamascar, *v.t.* to damask.

adaptabilidade, *s.f.* adaptability,

adaptação, *s.f.* adaptation, adjustement.

adaptado, *adj.* adapted, adjusted.

adaptar, *v.t.* to adapt, to adjust, to suit; **adaptar-se,** to adjust oneself to.

adaptável, *adj.* adaptable, adjustable.

adarga, *s.f.* oval target made of hide, a shield made of leather.

adega, *s.f.* cellar.

adegar, *v.t.* to keep in a cellar.

adejar, *v.t.* to flutter, to flit, to flap the wings.

adejo, *s.m.* flap of the wings, fluttering.

adeleiro, *s.m.* fripper, second hand dealer.

adelgaçado, *adj.* thin, slender, slim.

adelgaçamento, *s.m.* thinning.

adelgaçar, *v.t.* to thin.

adelo, *s.m.* o mesmo que "adeleiro".

ademanes, *s.m., pl.* manners, mannerisms.

adenda, *s.f.* addendum, appendix.

adenóide, *adj.* adenoid.

adensado, *adj.* dense, thick.

adensar, *v.t.* to thicken, to concentrate, to condense.

adentado, *adj.* indented, toothed.

adentar, *v.t.* to indent, to tooth.

adentro, *adj.* to the inside, indoors.

adepto, adept.

adequação, *s.f.* adaptation, fitness.

adequadamente, *adv.* fitly, suitably.

adequado, *adj.* fit, suitable.

adequar, *v.t.* to adapt, to fit, to suit.

adereçar, *v.t.* to adorn, to embellish, to bedeck, to equip, to adress *(uma carta)*.

aderecista, *s.m.* decorator, decker.

adereço, *s.m.* ornament, attire, set of jewels, adress *(morada)*.

aderência, *s.f.* adherence, sticking, adhesion.

aderente, *adj.* adherent, sticking; *s.m.* adherent partisan.

aderir, *v.i.* to adhere, to join, to subscribe *(aderir a uma doutrina)*.

adernar, *v.t.* (náut.) to lower, to sink.

adesão, *s.f.* adhesion, adherence.

adesivo, *adj.* adhesive; *s.m.* sticking-plaster.

a desoras, *loc. adv.* very late.

adestrado, *adj.* dexterous.

adestrador, *s.m.* trainer.

adestramento, *s.m.* training.

adestrar, *v.t.* to instruct, to train, to coach.

adeus, *adv.* e *s.m.* good bye, farewell, so long; *dizer adeus,* to say goodbye.

adiamento, *s.m.* adjourning, postponent.

adiantadamente, *adv.* in advance.

adiantado, *adj.* advanced, forward; fast *(o relógio)*, ahead *(chegar adiantado); adv.* in advance.

adiantamento, *s.m.* advancement, progress, advance payment *(pagamento).*

adiantar, *v.t.* to advance, to improve, to pay in advance (dinheiro), to set ahead (relógio); *que adianta isso?,* what is the use of this? **adiantar-se,** to advance, to go forward, to run fast *(relógio).*

adiante, *adv.* before, forward, ahead, further on; *adiante!,* go on!

adiável, *adj.* delayable.

adição, *s.f.* addition.

adicionação, *s.f.* addition.

adicional, *adj.* additional.

adicionar, *v.t.* to add, to join, to sum up, to make an addition.

adicionável, *adj.* that may be added.

adido, *s.m.* attaché.

adietar, *v.t.* to put someone on a diet.

adipe, *s.m.* fat (of animals), obesity.

adipose, *s.f.* adiposis.

adiposidade, *s.f.* adiposity.

adiposo, *adj.* adipose, fatty.

adir, *v.t.* to adjoin, to add.

aditamento, *s.m.* additament, addition; *em aditamento.* in addition to.

aditar, *v.t.* to add, to adjoin, to make happy *(tornar ditoso).*

adivinha, *s.f.* ridule, guess, fortuneteller.

adivinhação, *s.f.* divination, fortelling.

adivinhador, *s.m.* fortuneteller, guesser.

adivinhar, *v.t.* to divine, to guess, to unriddle.

adivinho, *s.m.* o mesmo que adivinhador.

adjacência, *s.f.* adjacency, contiguty, proximity.

adjacente, *adj.* adjacent, adjoining, contiguous.

adjacer, *v.t.* to be contiguous, to lie near.

adjectivação, *s.f.* use of adjectives.

adjectivado, *adj.* adjectival, accompanied by an adjective.

adjectivamente, *adv.* adjectively.

adjectivar, *v.t.* to use as an adjective.

adjectivo, *adj.* adjective.

adjudicação, *s.f.* adjudication, adjudgement, award.

adjudicador, *s.m.* adjudicator.

adjudicar, *v.t.* to adjudicate, to adjudge, to award to someone.

adjudicatário, *s.m.* purchaser at a public sale.

adjudicativo, *adj.* adjudicative.

adjudicatório, *adj.* adjudicative, adjudging.

adjunção, *s.f.* adjunction.

adjunto, *s.m.* assistant, adjoint; *adj.* annexed, adjoining.

adjuração, *s.f.* adjuration.

adjurar, *v.t.* to adjure someone to do something *(rogar).*

adjutor, *s.m.* adjutant, assistant.

adjutório, *s.m.* help, assistance.

adjuvante, *adj.* adjuvant, helping.

administração, *s.f.* administration, management.

administrador, *s.m* administrator, manager, director.

administrar, *v.t.* to administer, to manage, to direct.

administrativamente, *adv.* administratively.

administrativo, *adj.* administrative.

admiração, *s.f.* admiration, wonder, amazement, surprise.

admirado, *adj.* admired, amazed, surprised.

admirador, *s.m.* admiror.

admirar, *v.t.* to admire, to esteem highly, to surprise; **admirar-se,** to wonder at, to be astonished; *não admira que...,* no wonder that...

admirativo, *adj.* admirative.

admirável, *adj.* admirable, wonderful.

admiravelmente, *adv.* admirably, wonderfully.

admissão, *s.f.* admission, admittance.

admissível, *adj.* admissible.

admitir, to admit, to accept, to assume *(supor).*

admoestação, *s.f.* admonition, admonishment.

admoestador, *s.m.* admonisher.

admoestar, *v.t.* to admonish, to warn, to reprimand *(censurar).*

admonição, *s.f.* admonition, warning.

admonitório, *adj.* admonitory, admonishing.

adobe, adobo, *s.m.* adobe.

adoçamento, sweetening, softening *(suavização).*

adoçante, *adj.* sweetening; *s.m.* assuaging medicament.

adoçar, *v.t.* to sweeten, to sugar, to soften *(suavizar).*

adocicado, *adj.* sweetish, sugared.

adocicar, *v.t.* to sweeten lightly.

adoecer, *v.i.* to fall sick, to sicken, to be taken ill.

adoentado, *adj.* indisposed, ailing, unwell.

adoentar, *v.t.* to sicken, to make sick.
adolescência, *s.f.* adolescence.
adolescente, *adj.* e *s.* adolescent.
adopção, *s.f.* adoption.
adoptante, *adj.* adopting.
adoptar, *v.t.* to adopt, to father, to embrace *(uma opinião).*
adoptivo, *adj.* adoptive, adopted, foster; *pai adoptivo,* foster father.
adoração, *s.f.* adoration, worship.
adorador, *s.m.* adorer, worshiper.
adorar, *v.t.* to adore, to worship.
adorável, *adj.* adorable, lovable.
adoravelmente, *adv.* adorably.
adormecer, *v.t.* to put to sleep, to benumb *(entorpecer),* to soothe *(acalmar);* *v.i.* to fall asleep, to become numb *(entorpecer--se).*
adormecido, *adj.* dormant, asleep.
adormecimento, *s.m.* benumbedness, torpor, dormancy.
adormentar, *v.t.* o mesmo que adormecer.
adornar, *v.t.* to adorn, to bedeck, to ornament, to embellish.
adorno, *s.m.* ornament, adornment, decoration.
adquirente, *s.m.* acquirer.
adquirir, *v.t.* to acquire, to get, to purchase *(comprar).*
adquirível, *adj.* acquirable.
adrede, *adv.* purposely, intentionally.
adregar, *v.i.* to happen by chance; *v.i.* to deceive, to cheat.
adrenalina, *s.f.* adrenaline.
Adriático, adriatic; *mar Adriático,* Adriatic sea.
adriça, *s.f. (mar.)* halyard.
adro, *s.m.* yard, churchyard.
ad-rogar, *v.t.* to adopt.
adscrito, *adj.* adscript, enrolled.
adstrição, *s.f.* adstriction, compression.
adstringência, *s.f.* astringency.
adstringente, *adj.* astringent.
adstringir, *v.t.* to astringe, to compress.
adstritivo, *adj.* astringent.
aduana, *s.f.* customs, customhouse.
aduanar, *v.t.* to enter goods at the customhouse.
aduaneiro, *adj.* customs; *direitos aduaneiros,* customs duties.
aduar, *s.m.* a Moorish camp or village; *v.t.* to distribute water for irrigation.
adubação, *s.f.* fertilizing, manuring.
adubar, *v.t.* to fertilize, to manure.

adubo, *s.m.* fertilizer, manure.
adução, *s.f.* adduction.
adueiro, *s.m.* herdsman, scout.
aduela, *s.f.* stave; *(arq.)* intrados, voussoir; *ter uma aduela a menos,* to be crack-brained.
adufa, *s.f.* shutter *(de janela),* flood gate *(comporta).*
adufe, *s.m.* trimbrel, small drum.
adufeiro, *s.m.* trimbrel player.
adulação, *s.f.* flattering, adulation.
adulador, *s.m.* flatterer, adulator, toady.
adular, *v.t.* to adulate, to flatter, to toady.
adulatório, *adj.* adulatory, flattering.
adúltera, *s.f.* adulteress.
adulteração, *s.f.* adulteration.
adulteradamente, *adv.* adulteratedly.
adulterador, *s.m.* adulterator.
adulterar, *v.t.* to adulterate, to corrupt, to falsify; *v.i.* to commit adultery.
adultério, *s.m.* adultery.
adúltero, *adj.* adulterous; *s.m.* adulterer.
adulto, *adj.* e *s.* adult, grown up.
adunar, *v.t.* to join, to unite, to assemble.
adunco, *adj.* adunc, aduncous, crooked.
adurência, *s.f.* causticity, ardency.
adurente, *adj.* caustic, burning, ardent.
adustão, *s.f.* adustion.
adustivo, *adj.* adustive.
adusto, *adj.* adust, burnt, scroched.
aduzir, *v.t.* to adduce, to allege, to present, to bring forward.
adventício, *adj.* adventitious, adventive, accidental *(casual),* foreign *(estrangeiro).*
advento, advent, coming, arrival.
adverbial, *adj.* adverbial.
adverbialmente, *adv.* adverbially.
adverbiar, *v.t.* to use as an adverb.
advérbio, *s.m.* adverb.
adversamente, *adv.* adversely, unfortunately.
adversão, *s.f.* adverseness, opposition, misfortune.
adversar, *v.t.* to oppose, to deny.
adversário, *s.m.* adversary, opponent, antagonist; *adj.* adversative, opposing.
adversidade, *s.f.* adversity, misfortune.
adverso, *adj.* adverso, contrary.
advertência, *s.f.* advice, remark, advertence.
advertidamente, *adv.* advisedly, prudently.
advertido, *adj.* advised, warned.
advertir, *v.t.* to advise, to warn, to remark.

advir, *v.i.* to redound *(os benefícios),* to arrive, to happen.

advocacia, *s.f.* advocateship.

advogado, *s.m.* lawyer, attorney, advocate, defender.

advogar, *v.t.* to advocate, to plead, to defend; *v.i.* to practice law.

aeração, *s.f.* aeration.

aereamente, *adv.* aerially.

aéreo, *adj.* aerial, airy, air; *ataque aéreo,* air raid.

aerífero, *adj.* aeriferous.

aerificação, *s.f.* aerification.

aerificar, *v.t.* to aerify, to aerate.

aeriforme, *adj.* aeriform.

aerização, *s.f.* aerification.

aeróbio, *adj.* aerobic.

aerodinâmica, *s.f.* aerodynamics.

aerodinâmico, *adj.* aerodynamic, streamlined.

aeródromo, *s.m.* aerodrome, airport.

aerofagia, *s.f.* aerophagy.

aerofobia, *s.f.* aerophobia.

aerografia, *s.f.* aerography.

aerograma, *s.m.* aerogram.

aerólito, *s.m.* aerolite.

aerologia, *s.f.* aerology.

aeromodelismo, *s.m.* model-aeronautics.

aeronauta, *s.m.* aeronaut.

aeronáutica, *s.f.* aeronautics.

aeronáutico, *adj.* aeronautic.

aeronave, *s.f.* airship, dirigible, aircraft.

aeronavegação, *s.f.* aerial-navigation.

aeroplano, *s.m.* aeroplane, airplane, plane.

aeroporto, *s.m.* airport.

aeroposta, *s.f.* airmail.

aeroscopia, *s.f.* aeroscopics.

aerostação, *s.f.* aerostation.

aerostática, *s.f.* aerostatics.

aeróstato, *s.m.* aerostat.

afã, *s.m.* eagerness, care, anxiety.

afabilidade, *s.f.* affability, good nature.

afadigar, *v.t.* to fatigue, to tire; **afadigar-se,** to toil, to hasten.

afadigoso, *adj.* fatiguing, tiring, toilsome.

afagador, *s.m.* fondler; *adj.* caressing.

afagamento, *s.m.* caressing, fondling.

afagar, *v.t.* to caress, to fondle, to stroke *(um animal).*

afago, *s.m.* caress, stroke.

afagoso, *adj.* caressing, fondling.

afamado, *adj.* celebrated, nenowned, famous.

afamar, *v.t.* to make famous; **afamar-se,** to become famous.

afanar, *v.t., i.* e *r.* to labour, to toil, to work hard.

afanoso, *adj.* laborious, hardworking.

afasia, *s.f.* aphasia.

afasta, *interj.* get off! clear the way!

afastado, *adj.* distant, far.

afastamento, *s.m.* removing, removal, seclusion.

afastar, *v.t.* to push aside, to take away, to withdraw; **afastar-se,** to go away, to withdrawn, to deviate.

afável, *adj.* kind, affable, good-natured.

afavelmente, affably, kindly.

afazendar-se, *v.i.* to acquire, to grow rich.

afazer, *v.t.* to habituate.

afazeres, *s.m. pl.* affairs, duties.

afazimento, *s.m.* inuring, habit.

afeamento, *s.m.* defacing, disfigurement.

afear, *v.t.* to make ugly.

afecção, *s.f.* affection.

afectação, *s.f.* affectation, presumption, artificial manners.

afectadamente, *adv.* artificially, pretentiously.

afectado, *adj.* affected, artificial.

afectar, *v.t.* to affect, to simulate, to harm.

afectivamente, *adv.* kindly.

afectivo, *adj.* affective, affectionate.

afecto, *s.m.* affection, tenderness, love; *adj.* dependent on.

afectuosamente, *adv.* kindly.

afectuoso, *adj.* affectionate, kind, tender.

afegã, *s.m.* inhabitant of Afghanistan, Afghan; *adj.* afghan.

afeição, *s.f.* affection, love.

afeiçoadamente, *adv.* affectionately.

afeiçoado, *adj.* afectionate, loving.

afeiçoar, *v.t.* to shape, to form; **afeiçoar--se,** to become attached to.

afeito, *adj.* accustomed, inured to.

afélio, *s.m.* aphelion.

afemia, *s.f.* aphasia.

afeminado, *adj.* V. "efeminado".

aferente, *adj.* afferent.

aférese, *s.f.* apheresis.

aferição, *s.f.* calibration, checking (de pesos e medidas).

aferido, *adj.* calibrated, checked.

aferidor, *s.m.* gauger, checker.

aferir, *v.t.* to gauge, to check, to compare, to judge *(julgar).*

aferradamente, *adv.* obstinately.

aferrado, *adj.* obstinate.

aferramento, *s.m.* obstinacy.

aferrar, v.t. to grapple, to hold; v.i. to cast anchor, to moor; v.r. to stick.

aferroar, v.t. to prick, to sting, to irritate.

aferrolhar, v.t. to bolt, to lock up.

aferventar, v.t. to parboil, to excite.

afervoradamente, adv. fervently, eagerly.

afervorado, adj. fervent, eager, zealous.

afervorar, v.t. to excite, to inflame.

afervorizar, v.t. to inflame.

afestoar, v.t. to festoon, to addorn with garlands.

afiação, s.f. sharpening.

afiado, adj. sharp, pointed.

afiador, s.m. sharpener, grinder.

afiambrado, adj. prepared like ham.

afiambrar-se, v.r. to dress smartly.

afiançado, adj. warrantee.

afiançador, s.m. bailsman, guarantor.

afiançar, v.t. to bail, to guarantee, to stand for, to answer for, to assure.

afiar, v.t. to sharpen, to whet, to grind (na mó), to strap (amolar).

aficionado, s.m. enthusiast, fan; adj. enthusiastic, amateur.

afidalgado, adj. aristrocatic, gentle, of noble birth.

afidalgar, v.t. to ennoble, to dignify; v.r. to become noble, to give oneself airs.

afiguração, s.f. fancy imagination, appearance.

afigurar-se, v.r. to seem, to appear, to think.

afilado, adj. slender, tapering.

afilar, v.t. to thin, to taper, to incite.

afilhada, s.f. god-daughter, protégée.

afilhado, s.m. godson, protégé.

afilhar, v.t. to bud, to sprout (planta).

afiliação, s.f. affiliation, connection.

afiliar, v.t. to affiliate, to incorporate, to admit.

afim, adj. affine, related, similar; s.m. relation by marrriage.

a fim de, loc. prep. in order to.

afinação, s.f. tuning.

afinadamente, adv. in harmony, in tune, harmonically.

afinado, adj. tuned.

afinador, s.m. tuner.

afinagem, s.f. refining (metais).

afinal, adv. finally, after all.

afinar, v.t. to tune, to refine (metais), to perfect; v.i. to get angry.

afincadamente, adv. obstinately, diligently.

afincamento, s.m. tenacity, persistence.

afincar, v.t. e v.r. to fix, to drive, to insist on, to persist.

afinco, s.m. tenacity, perseverance, obstinacy.

afinidade, s.f. affinity, relationship by marriage.

a fio, loc. adv. uninterruptedly, in sucession.

afirmação, s.f. affirmation, statement.

afirmar, v.t. to affirm, to state.

afirmativa, s.f. affirmative.

afirmativamente, adv. affirmatively.

afirmativo, adj. affirmative.

afistular, v.t. e v.i. to cover with fistulas, to corrupt.

afivelar, v.t. to buckle, to clasp on.

afixação, s.f. affixing, sticking; afixação proibida, stick (or post) no bills.

afixar, v.t. to fix to stick, to post.

afixo, s.m. affix; adj. affixed.

afleumar, v.r. to become phlegmatic.

aflição, s.f. affliction, anguish, distress.

afligir, v.t. to afflict, to distress, to worry; v.r. to worry, to afflict oneself.

aflitivamente, adv. afflictively.

aflitivo, adj. afflicting.

aflito, adj. afflicted, distress, worried, anxious, in trouble.

afloração, s.f. levelling, (geol.) outcrop.

afloramento, s.m. levelling.

aflorar, v.t. to level, to make level; v.i. to appear.

afluência, s.f. affluence, abundance.

afluente, s.m. affluent, tributary; adj. abundant.

afluir, v.i. to flow, to converge, to stream, to flock to.

afluxo, s.m. afflux, affluxion, affluence, concourse.

afobado, adj. in a hurry.

afocinhar, v.t. to root, to strike with the snout; v.i. to rout, to snout.

afofado, adj. soft, smooth.

afofar, v.t. to soften, to smooth.

afogadilho, s.m. haste; de afogadilho, in hurry.

afogado, adj. drowned.

afogamento, s.m. drowning.

afogar, v.t. to drown, to choke, to suffocate; v.r. to be drowned.

afogo, s.m. opression, affliction, haste, hurry.

afogueado, adj. burning, aglow, glowing.

afoguear, v.t. to redden, to blush.

afoitamente, adv. daringly, boldly, coura-geously.

afoitar, v.t. to encourage; v.r. to dare, to venture.

afoito, s.m. bold, daring, courageous.

afolhamento, s.m. distribution of crops.

afolhar, v.t. to distribute the crops; v.i. to shoot out leaves.

afonia, s.f. aphony, aphonia.

afónico, adj. aphonic.

afora, prep. besides, except, beyond; adv. throughout.

aforador, s.m. lord of a manor.

aforamento, s.m. long-term lease.

aforar, v.t. to take lease of, to let by lease, to lease; v.r. to arrogate to oneself.

aforismo, s.m. aphorism, adage, proverb.

aforístico, adj. aphoristic.

aformoseamento, s.m. embellishment.

aformosear, v.t. to embellish, to adorn, to beautify.

aforquilhado, adj. forky, forked.

aforrado, adj. saved, economized, free (escravos).

aforrar, v.t. to save, to economize, to free (escravos).

afortalezado, fortified, with the shape of a fortress.

afortalezar, v.t. to fortify, to give the shape of a fortress.

afortunadamente, adv. fortunately, luckily.

afortunado, adj. fortunate, lucky.

afortunar, v.t. to make happy.

afrancesado, adj. frenchified.

afrancesar, v.t. to frenchify; v.r. to become frenchified.

afreguesado, adj. having a good clientele.

afreguesar, v.t. to get costumers; v.r. to become a costumer.

afreimado, adj. angry.

afreimar-se, v.r. to become impacient.

afretar, v.t. to freight, to charter.

África, s.f. Africa.

africanismo, s.m. the study of African things.

africano, s.m. African.

áfrico, s.m. south-wind.

afrodisia, s.f. aphrodisia.

afrodisíaco, s.m. e adj. aphrodisiac.

afrodita, s.m. acryptogamic plant.

afronta, s.f. affront, outrage, insult, offense.

afrontado, adj. outraged, insulted, offended.

afrontamento, s.m. exhaustion.

afrontar, v.t. to affront, to face, to confront.

afrontosamente, adv. affrontingly, outrageously.

afrontoso, adj. affronting, insulting, offensive.

afrouxamento, s.m. slackening, loosening, slowing.

afrouxar, v.t. e v.i. to slacken, to loosen, to slow, to weaken.

afta, s.f. aphta; pl. aphtae.

aftoso, adj. aphtous.

afugentar, v.t. to chase, to drive away.

afumadura, s.f. filling with smoke.

afumar, v.t. to smoke, to fill with smoke.

afundamento, s.m. sinking, submersion.

afundar, v.t. to sink, to submerge; v.i. to sink, to founder.

afundir, v.t. e v.i. to sink, to cause to sink, to deepen.

afunilado, adj. funnel-shaped.

afunilar, v.t. to shape like a funnel, to narrow.

afusão, s.f. affusion, aspersion.

afusar, v.t. to taper, to sharpen.

agachar-se, v.r. to crouch, to squat.

agadanhar, v.t. to scratch, to scrape.

agaiatado, adj. childish.

agalegado, adj. boorish, rude.

agaloar, v.t. to adorn or trim with gold lace.

agâmico, adj. agamic.

ágape, s.m. agape, banquet.

agareno, adj. Moorish.

agárico, s.m. agaric, a fungus of the mushroom family; adj. agaric.

agarotado, adj. roguish, mischievous.

agarotar-se, v.r. to become roguish.

agarrado, adj. caught, seized, niggardly (avarento).

agarrar, v.t. to catch, to hold, to seize; **agarrar-se,** to cling, to hold on.

agarrochar, v.t. to goad, to drive with a goad.

agarrotar, v.t. to garrote.

agasalhado, adj. warmed, well wrapped up, sheltered.

agasalhar, v.t. to warm, to muffle, to shelter.

agasalho, s.m. warm clothes, shelter, comfort.

agastadamente, adv. angrily.

agastadiço, adj. irritable, irascible.

agastado, adj. angry, mad, sore.

agastamento, s.m. tiff, bad-humor.

agastar, v.t. to irritate, to provoke; **agastar--se,** to get angry.

ágata, s.f. agate.

agatanhadura, s.f. scratch, scratching.

agatanhar, v.t. to scratch, to wound superficialy.

agência, s.f. agency.

agenciador, s.m. agent, arranger; adj. active, promotive.

agenciar, v.t. to negotiate, to manage, to solicit, to promote.

agencioso, adj. active, diligent.

agenda, s.f. agenda, note-book.

agenesia, s.f. agenesia, impotence.

agente, s.m. agent, broker, solicitor; adj. acting.

agerasia, s.f. agerasia.

agermanar, v.t. to match, to pair; v.r. to associate oneself fraternally.

agigantado, adj. gigantic, giant.

agigantar, v.t. to give gigantic proportions to; to exaggerate.

ágil, adj. agile, swift.

agilidade, s.f. agility, nimbleness.

agilmente, adv. agilely, swiftly.

ágio, s.m. agio, premium.

agiota, s.m. moneylender, speculator, usurer (usurário), stockjobber.

agiotagem, s.f. agiotage, usury, speculation.

agiotar, v.i. to job, to speculate, to gamble.

agir, v.i. to act, to behave.

agitação, s.m. agitation, disturbance, tumult, perturbation, excitement.

agitado, adj. agitated, excited, restless.

agitador, s.m. agitator, trouble-maker.

agitar, v.t. to agitate, to shake, to stir, to excite.

agitável, adj. agitable, excitable.

aglomeração, agglomeration.

aglomerado, s.m. an agglomeration, a mass, agglomerate; adj. agglomerated.

aglomerar, v.t. to agglomerate, to gather together.

aglutição, s.f. inability to swallow.

aglutinação, s.f. agglutination.

aglutinado, adj. agglutinated.

aglutinar, v.t. to agglutinate, to unite with glue.

aglutinativo, adj. agglutinative.

aglutinável, adj. agglutinable.

agnação, s.f. agnation.

agnado, adj. agnate.

agnome, s.m. agnomen.

agnosticismo, s.m. agnosticism.

agnóstico, s.m. agnostic.

agoirar, v.t. to presage, to augur, to foretell.

agoirento, adj. ominous, threatening.

agoiro, s.m. augury, divination, presage.

agonia, s.f. agony, affliction, sea-sickness (náuseas).

agoniado, adj. anguished, sick (indisposto), seasick (nauseado).

agoniar, v.t. to afflict, to sicken, to turn the stomach (causar náuseas).

agónico, adj. agonizing.

ágono, adj. agonic.

ágora, s.f. an assembly, a market-place.

agora, adv. now, at present. 1) agora mesmo, just now. 2) por agora, for the time--beeing, for the moment.

agorafobia, s.f. agoraphobia.

agostinho, s.m. Augustine, Austin friar; adj. augustinian.

Agosto, s.m. August.

agouro, s.m. o mesmo que "agoiro".

agra, s.f. field, bog, fen.

agraciar, v.t. to award, to endow with grace, to invest with a title.

agradado, adj. pleased, glad.

agradar, v.i. to please, to oblige; v.t. to level a field.

agradável, adj. agreeable, pleasant, pleasing, gratifying.

agradavelmente, adv. pleasantly, agreeably.

agradecer, v.t. e v.i. to thank, to acknowledge (um favor).

agradecido, adj. thankful, obliged.

agradecimento, s.m. thanks, gratitude, acknowledgement.

agrado, s.m. pleasure, liking. 1) com agrado, with pleasure. 2) creio que será do seu agrado, I believe it will be to your liking.

agrafar, v.t. to clasp, to staple.

agrafo, s.m. clasp, clip.

agrário, adj. agrarian, agricultural.

agravação, s.f. aggravation, worsening.

agravamento, s.m. o mesmo que "agravação".

agravante, adj. aggravating.

agravar, v.t. to aggravate, to make worse.

agredir, v.t. to attack, to aggress, to hit, to strike.

agregação, s.f. aggregation, association, assembly.

agregado, s.m. aggregate; adj. aggregated.

agregar, v.t. to aggregate, to bring together, to assemble, to add.

agremiação, s.f. association.

agremiar, v.t. to associate, to join, to assemble.

agressão, s.f. aggression, to assault.

agressivo, aggressive, offensive.

agressor, s.m. aggressor, attacker.

agreste, adj. wild, rough.

agrião, s.m. water-cress.

agrícola, *adj.* agricultural.

agricultar, *v.t.* to till the ground, to plough.

agricultor, *s.m.* farmer, agriculturist.

agricultura, *s.f.* agriculture, farming.

agridoce, *adj.* bittersweet.

agrilhoar, *v.t.* to chain.

agrimensor, *s.m.* measurer of the land, surveyor.

agrimensura, *s.f.* surveying.

agro, *s.m.* tilled ground, field; *adj.* bitter, acrid.

agronomia, *s.f.* agronomy.

agronómico, *adj.* agronomic.

agrónomo, *s.m.* agronomist, agriculturist; *engenheiro agrónomo,* agriculturist.

agrosseirado, *adj.* rather coarse, rude.

agrumelar, *v.t.* to coagulate, to curdle.

agrupamento, *s.m.* gathering.

agrupar, *s.f.* sourness, bitterness, sorrow.

água, *s.f.* water. 1) *água benta,* holy water. 2) *água-forte,* aqua-fortis. 3) *água-furtada,* attic, garret. 4) *água-marinha,* aquamarine. 5) *água-pé,* thin wine. 6) *água potável,* drinking water. 7) *água salobra,* brackish water. 8) *ir por água abaixo,* to come to nothing.

aguaceiro, *s.m.* shower, downpour, squall *(com vento).*

aguada, *s.f.* water-supply, watering place;

aguadeiro, *s.m.* water-carrier.

aguado, *adj.* watered, watery, wishy-washy.

aguagem, *s.f.* backwater, dead water.

aguamento, *s.m.* foundering.

aguar, *v.t.* to water, to irrigate, to tone down *(cores).*

aguardar, *v.t.* to await, to wait for, to look forward to.

aguardente, *s.f.* brandy, aqua-vitae.

aguarela, *s.f.* aquarelle.

aguarelar, *v.t.* e *v.i.* to paint in water colours.

aguarelista, *s.m.* e *s.f.* aquarellist, water-colourist.

aguarentar, *v.t.* to cut round, to murur about.

aguarrás, *s.m.* essence of turpentine.

aguçadeira, *s.f.* grindstone.

aguçado, *adj.* pointed, sharp, sharp-pointed.

aguçador, *s.m.* grinder, sharpener; *adj.* sharpening.

aguçadura, *s.f.* grinding, sharpening.

aguçar, *v.t.* to grind, to sharpen, to whet, to stimulate.

agudez, agudeza, *s.f.* sharpness, acuteness, perspicacity.

agudo, *adj.* sharp-pointed, acute.

agueiro, *s.m.* water furrow, gutter, drain.

aguentar, *v.t.* e *v.r.* to support, to hold, to bear, to sustain.

aguerrido, *adj.* brave, intrepid, inured to war.

aguerrir, *v.t.* to accustom to war, to make valiant.

águia, *s.f.* eagle.

aguieta, *s.f.* eaglet.

aguilhada, *s.f.* goad, sting, spur.

aguilhão, *s.m.* goad, sting, *(fig.)* incitement.

aguilhoada, *s.f.* stinging.

aguilhoar, *v.t.* to goad, to sting; *(fig.)* to incite.

agulha, *s.f.* needle, switch point (de linha férrea); *enfiar a agulha,* to thread the needle.

agulhada, *s.f.* needle prick.

agulhão, *s.m.* large needle.

agulhar, *v.t.* to prick, to goad.

agulheiro, *s.m.* needle-case, needle-holder, switchman, poinstman *(linha férrea).*

agulheta, *s.f.* aglet, aiglet, nozzle.

ah!, *interj.* ha! indeed!

ai, *interj.* oh! woe!; *s.m.* sigh, moan; *ai de mim!,* dear me!

aí, *adv.* there, over there, then; *por aí,* around there.

aia, *a.f.* chamber maid, nurse.

ainda, *adv.* still, yet; also *(também).* 1) *ainda assim,* even so. 2) *ainda bem,* so much the better. 3) *ainda mais que,* the more so that. 4) *ainda não,* not yet. 5) *ainda por cima,* in addition. 6) *ainda que,* ever though.

aio, *s.m.* tutor, perceptor.

aipo, *s.m.* celery.

airado, *adj.* airy, unsteady, distracted.

airosamente, *adv.* with grace.

airosidade, *s.f.* grace, elegance, comeliness.

airoso, *adj.* graceful, elegant, comely.

aiveca, *s.f.* earth-board, mould-bourd *(do arado).*

ajaezar, *v.t.* to adorn, to harness *(arrear).*

ajanotado, *adj.* dandysh.

ajanotar-se, *v.r.* to dress like a dandy.

ajantarado, *adj.* hearty.

ajardinado, *adj.* garden-like.

ajardinar, *v.t.* to make into a garden.

ajeitar, *v.t.* to arrange, to dispose, to set right.

ajoelhação, *s.f.* genuflection.

ajoelhar, *v.t.* to kneel down.

ajoujamento, *s.m.* the act of coupling or leashing.

ajoujar, to leash, to couple, to overload.

ajoujo, *s.m.* leash, team *(parelha).*

ajuda, *s.f.* help, aid, assistance; *ajuda de custo,* allowance for expenses.

ajudante, *s.m.* helper, assistant, aid; *ajudante-de-campo,* aide-de-camp.

ajudar, *v.t.* to help, to aid, to assit, to succour; *ajudar à missa,* to serve at mass.

ajuizado, *adj.* wise, judicious, reasonable, sensible.

ajuizar, *v.t.* to judge, to form an opinion about.

ajuntadeira, *s.f.* a woman that stitches together the uppers of a boot.

ajuntador, *s.m.* collector.

ajuntamento, *s.m.* gathering, collection, assemblage.

ajuntar, *v.t.* to join, to gather, to collect, to attach.

ajuramentado, *adj.* sworn, bound by oath.

ajuramentar, *v.t.* e *v.r.* to swear, to bind by oath.

ajustado, *adj.* proper, just, reasonable, tight *(apertado); s.m.* agreed.

ajustamento, *s.m.* adjustment, fitting, agreement.

ajustar, *v.t.* to adjust, to fit, to adapt, to agree on; *ajustar-se,* to adapt oneself to.

ajuste, *s.w.* adjustment, settlement, agreement; *ajuste de contas,* settlement of accounts.

ala, *s.f.* wing, file, row *(fileiras); abrir alas,* to make way.

alabarda, *s.f.* halberd.

alabardeiro, *s.m.* halberdier.

alabastrino, *adj.* white as alabaster.

alabastro, *s.m.* alabaster.

álacre, *adj.* gay, merry, cheerful.

alacridade, *s.f.* alacrity, gaiety.

alado, *adj.* winged.

alagadiço, *adj.* marshy, boggy.

alagado, *adj.* waterlogged, flooded, marshy.

alagamento, *s.m.* an overflow, inundation.

alagar, *v.t.* to overflow, to flood.

alamar, *s.m.* frog.

alamares, *s.m. pl.* ornamental doubling for trimming or buttoning clothes.

alambazar-se, *v.r.* to eat or drink or do with excess.

alambicar, *v.t.* to distill, to polish, to refine.

alambique, *s.m.* alembic, still.

alameda, *s.f.* tree-lined street, row.

alamiré, *s.m.* diapason, tuning fork, *(fig.)* reproach.

álamo, *s.m.* poplar.

alanceador, *s.m.* mortifier, distressing.

alanceamento, *s.m.* wounding with a lance, pain, distress.

alancear, *v.t.* to wound with a lance, to spear, to mortify.

alandro, *s.m. (bot.)* oleander, rosebay.

alandroal, *s.m.* wood of oleanders.

alanos, *s.m. pl.* Alani.

alão, *s.m.* mastiff.

alapado, *adj.* crouching, squat.

alapar, *v.t.* to hide in a cave; *v.r.* to squat down, to crouch.

alapardar-se, *v.r.* o mesmo que "alapar".

alar, *v.t.* to pull up, to haul, to give wings.

alaranjado, *adj.* orange-colored.

alarde, *s.m.* show, ostentation, boasting *(jactância).*

alardeador, *s.m.* boaster.

alardear, *v.t.* to display with ostentation, to show off, to boast of, to vaunt.

alargamento, *s.m.* enlargement, widening.

alargar, *v.t.* e *v.r.* to enlarge, to widen, to spread; *alargar-se nas despesas,* to spend freely.

alarido, *s.m.* clamor, uproar, hullabaloo, whining *(choradeira).*

alarmante, *adj.* alarming, disturbing.

alarmar, *v.t.* to alarm, to frighten.

alarme, *s.m.* alarm, alert, fright; *dar o alarme,* to raise the alarm.

alarmista, *s.m.* alarmist.

alarve, *s.m.* boor, lout, brute, savage, glutton.

alastramento, *s.m.* ballasting, spreading.

alastrar, *v.t.* e *v.i.* to ballast *(pôr lastro),* to scatter, to strew, to spread.

alatinado, *adj.* latinized.

alatinar, *v.t.* to latinize, to give a latin form.

alaúde, *s.m.* lute.

alavanca, *s.f.* lever; *alavanca de mudanças:* gearshift lever.

alazão, *s.m.* e *adj.* sorrel.

albanês, *s.m.* e *adj.* Albanian.

Albânia, *s.f.* Albania.

albarda, *s.f.* pack-saddle; a clumsy clot.

albardão, *s.m.* a large pack-saddle.

albardar, *v.t.* to put a pack-saddle upon a beast.

albardeira, *s.f.* wild rose.

albardeiro, *s.m.* maker of pack-saddles; a bad tailor; *adj.* clumsy, awkward.

albatroz, *s.m.* albatross.

albergamento, *s.m.* lodging.

albergar, *v.t.* to lodge, to give shelter, to harbor.

albergaria, *s.f.* inn.

albergue, *s.m.* lodging-house, inn.

albergueiro, *s.m.* innkeeper, host.

albinismo, *s.m.* albinism.

albino, *s.m.* albino.

albite, *s.f.* albite.

alburcar, *v.t.* to barter, to exchange.

albornoz, *s.m.* burnoose, a mantel with a hood worn by the Arabs.

alborque, *s.m.* exange, truck, a meal given when an agreement is made.

albricoque, *s.m.* apricot.

albufeira, *s.f.* lagoon, shallow lake, dam.

albugem, *s.f.* albugo, leucoma.

albugínea, *s.f.* albuginea.

álbum, *s.m.* album.

albúmen, *s.m.* albumen.

albumina, *s.f.* albumin.

albuminóide, *adj.* albuminoid.

albuminoso, *adj.* albuminous.

albuminúria, *s.f.* albuminuria.

albuminúrico, *adj.* albuminuric.

alburno, *s.m.* alburnum, sapwood.

alça, *s.f.* handle, grip, tab *(presilha)*.

alcaçaria, *s.f.* tannery.

alcácer, *s.m.* alcazar, royal moorish palace, fortress.

alcachofra, *s.f.* artichoke.

alcaçuz, *s.m.* licorice.

alçada, *s.f.* jurisdiction, power.

alçado, *s.m.* vertical projection.

alcaide, *s.m.* alcaide, governor of a fortress.

alcaiote, *s.m.* telltale.

álcali, *s.m.* alkali.

alcalificar, *v.t.* to alkalify.

alcalimetria, *s.f.* alkalimetry.

alcalimétrico, *adj.* alkalimetrical.

alcalímetro, *s.m.* alkalimeter.

alcalino, *adj.* alkaline.

alcalinidade, *s.f.* alkalinity.

alcalóide, *s.m.* alkaloid.

alçamento, *s.m.* lift, raising, *(arq.)* stilting.

alcançado, *adj.* reached, obtained, in arrear *(atrasado nas contas).*

alcançar, *v.t.* e *v.i.* to reach, to obtain, to arrive at, to get, to attain, to gain; **alcançar-se,** to run into debt *(endividar-se).*

alcance, *s.m.* reach, attainment. 1) *ao alcance da mão,* within reach. 2) *arma de longo alcance,* long-range weapon.

alcandorado, *adj.* lofty, towering.

alcandorar-se, *v.r.* to perch on high, to tower, to become exalted *(sublimar-se).*

alcantil, *s.m.* steep, precipice, pinnacle.

alcantilado, *adj.* steep, precipitous, sheer.

alcantilar-se, *v.r.* to rise steeply.

alcantiloso, *adj.* full of precipices.

alçapão, *s.m.* trap-door.

alcaparra, *s.f.* caper.

alçapé, *s.m.* snare used by sportsmen; trap.

alçaprema, *s.f.* lever, crowbar, pincers.

alçapremar, *v.t.* to lift with the lever.

alçar, *v.t.* to lift up, to raise higher, to elevate; *v.i.* e *v.r.* to rise, to get off.

alcateia, *s.f.* pack.

alcatifa, *s.f.* carpet.

alcatifado, *adj.* carpeted.

alcatifar, *v.t.* to carpet.

alcatra, *s.f.* rump of beef.

alcatrão, *s.m.* tar, pitch.

alcatraz, *s.m.* albatross, frigate bird.

alcatroado, *adj.* tarred, tarry.

alcatroamento, *s.m.* tarring.

alcatroar, *v.t.* to tar.

alcatroeiro, *s.m.* tar-maker.

alcatruz, *s.m.* trough, bucket.

alcatruzar, *v.t.* to furnish with buckets, to bend, to crook.

alcavala, *s.f. (arc.)* duty laid on sales of eatables and liquors, supplement dues.

alce, *s.m.* moose.

álcea, *s.f.* holly-hock *(bot.).*

alcear, *v.t.* to arrange the leaves of a book, to be bound.

alcíone, *s.m.* halcyon.

alcofa, *s.f.* basket.

álcool, *s.m.* alcohol.

alcoolato, *s.m.* (med.) alcoholate.

alcoólico, *adj.* e *s.m.* alcoholic.

alcoolismo, *s.m.* alcoholism.

alcoolização, *s.f.* alcoholization.

alcoolizado, *adj.* alcoholized.

alcoolizar, *v.t.* to alcoholize.

alcoometria, *s.f.* alcoholometry.

alcoómetro, *s.m.* alcoholometer.

Alcorão, *s.m.* the Koran.

alcouce, *s.m.* brothel.

alcova, *s.f.* alcove, bed-chamber.

alcovitar, *v.t.* to pander, to bawd.

alcoviteira, *s.f.* bawder.

alcoviteiro, *s.m.* pander, pimp.

alcoviteirice, *s.f.* pimping, bawdiness, gossip.

alcunha, *s.f.* nickname.

alcunhar, *v.t.* to nick name.

aldeã, *s.f.* country-woman, villager.

aldeamento, *s.m.* rural-settlement.

aldeão, *s.m.* country-man, villager.
aldeia, *s.f.* village.
aldeola, *s.f.* small village.
aldraba, *s.f.* latch (da porta), knocker.
aldrabado, *adj.* bungled, cheated.
aldrabão, *s.m.* a large knocker; swindler; liar.
aldrabar, *v.t.* to latch, to lie, to deceive, to cheat.
aldrabice, *s.f.* cheat, lie.
álea, *s.f.* alley.
aleatório, *adj.* aleatory.
alecrim, *s.m.* rosemary.
alegação, *s.f.* allegation, assertion.
alegar, *v.t.* to allege, to affirm, to assert, to plead *(como mérito)*.
alegoria, *s.f.* allegory.
alegoricamente, *adv.* allegorically.
alegórico, *adj.* allegoric.
alegorismo, *s.m.* allegorism.
alegrador, *s.m. e adj.* one who cheers, amusing.
alegrão, *s.m.* great joy.
alegrar, *v.t.* to cheer, to rejoice, to gladden, to animate.
alegre, *adj.* merry, glad, gay, cheerful, joyfull, happy.
alegremente, *adv.* gladly, merrily, cheerfully.
alegro, *s.m. (mús.)* allegro.
alegrote, *adj.* somewhat merry, a little tipsy.
aleijado, *adj.* lame, crippled; *s.m.* cripple.
aleijão, *s.m.* deformity.
aleijar, *v.t.* to cripple, to hurt, to lame.
aleirar, *v.t.* to divide into glebes or ridges.
aleitamento, *s.m.* milk-feeding, lactation.
aleitar, *v.t.* to milk-feed, to suckle.
aleive, aleivosia, *s.m. e s.f.* perfidy, slander, falseness.
aleivoso, *adj.* perfidious, treacherous.
aleluia, *s.f.* alleluiah, hallelujah.
além, *adv.* over there, yonder, further on, beyond. 1) *além de,* beyond. 2) *além-mar,* over-seas. 3) *além disso,* besides that. 4) *além de que,* moreover.
alemão, *s.m. e adj.* German.
alentado, *adj.* stout, robust.
alentar, *v.t.* to animate, to encourage, to cheer.
alento, *s.m.* courage.
alergia, *s.f.* allergy.
alérgico, *adj. e s.m.* allergic.
alerta, *adv.* on the alert, watchfully, vigilantly; *s.m.* alarm; *interj.* attention!
aletria, *s.f.* vermicelli, a very slender macaroni.

alevantadiço, *adj.* seditious, riotous, noisy.
alevantado, *adj.* haughty, proud, thoughtless.
alevantar, *v.t.* to lift up, to raise, to heave, to rebel, to revolt.
alevante, *s.m.* raising, rebellion.
alexandrino, *adj.* alexandrine.
alfa, *s.f.* alpha, the first letter of the Greek alphabet.
alfabetação, alphabetizing, arranging alphabetically.
alfabético, *adj.* alphabetic.
alfabetista, *s.m.* alphabetist.
alfabetização, *s.f.* alphabetization.
alfabetizar, *v.t.* to teach to read and write.
alfabeto, *s.m.* alphabet.
alface, *s.f.* lettuce.
alfacinha, *s.m. e s.f.* a native of Lisbon.
alfafa, *s.f.* alfalfa, lucerne.
alfageme, *s.m.* sword-cutler, armourer, gunsmith.
alfaia, *s.f.* furniture (móveis), household utensils; *alfaias agrícolas,* agricultural implements.
alfaiar, *v.t.* to adorn, to furnish.
alfaiataria, *s.f.* tailor's shop, tailor's.
alfaiate, *s.m.* tailor.
alfândega, *s.f.* custom-house, customs.
alfandegagem, *s.f.* the act of paying custom duties.
alfandegar, *v.t.* to pay custom duties; to store in warehouses.
alfandegário, *adj.* belonging to the custom-house.
alfange, *s.m.* scimitar.
alfanjada, *s.f.* stroke with a scimitar, slash.
alfaque, *s.m.* heap of sand, shoal *(no mar).*
alfarrábio, *s.m.* old book.
alfarrabista, *s.m.* second-hand book seller.
alfarroba, *s.f.* carob.
alfarrobal, *s.m.* carob-tree plantation.
alfarrobeira, *s.f.* carob-tree.
alfavaca, *s.f.* basil.
alfazema, *s.f.* lavender.
alfena, *s.f. (bot.)* privet.
alfenim, *s.m.* sugar paste made with oil of almonds; *(fig.)* mollycoddle *(efeminado),* sissy.
alferes, *s.m.* second lieutenant, ensign.
alfim, *adv.* at last.
alfinetada, *s.f.* prick, dig *(dito mordaz).*
alfinetar, *v.t.* to prick with a pin, to satirize.
alfinete, *s.m.* pin.
alfineteira, *s.f.* pincushion.

alfineteiro, *s.m.* pin-maker.

alfobre, *s.m.* hotbed, place where young plants are cullivated for transplantation.

alfombra, *s.f.* carpet, sward *(relva)*.

alfombrado, *adj.* carpet.

alforge, *s.m.* saddlebag, wallet.

alforra, *s.f.* mildew, rust.

alforrar, *v.t.* to blast, to blight.

alforreca, *s.f.* jellyfish.

alforria, *s.f.* enfranchise, to liberate.

alforva, *s.f. (bot.)* fennu-greek.

alfurja, *s.f.* inner yard, den, cave.

alga, *s.f.* alga, seaweed.

algáceo, *adj.* algal, algoid.

algália, *s.f.* bougie, catheter, probe, civet.

algaliar, *v.i.* to probe, to draw off fluid from the bladder, to catheterize.

algar, *s.m.* pit, cave, precipice, gully *(ravina)*.

algaravia, *s.f.* Arabic language, jargon, gabbling talk.

algaraviada, *s.f.* bawling, hubbub.

algaraviar, *v.t.* to jabber.

algarismo, *s.m.* figure, arithmetic character, cipher.

algarvio, *s.m. e adj.* a native of Algarve, of Algarve.

algazarra, *s.f.* noise, clamor, uproar, racket, hubbub.

álgebra, *s.f.* algebra.

algebricamente, *adv.* algebraically.

algébrico, *adj.* algebraical.

algebrista, *s.m.* algebraist.

algemar, *v.t.* to handcuff, to manacle.

algemas, *s.f.pl.* handcuffs, manacles.

algeroz, *s.m.* gutter.

algia, *s.f.* pain.

algibe, *s.m.* cistern.

algibebe, *s.m.* seller of ready-made clothes.

algibeira, *s.f.* pocket.

algidez, chilliness, iciness.

álgido, *adj.* cold, chilly.

algo, *pron.* somewhat, something; *adv.* a little, rather.

algodão, *s.m.* cotton. 1) *algodão em rama,* raw cotton. 2) *algodão-pólvora,* guncotton.

algodoal, *s.m.* cotton plantation.

algodoaria, *s.f.* cotton manufacture.

algodoeiro, *s.m.* cotton plant, cotton manufacturer.

algor, *s.m.* algor.

algoso, *adj.* algous, full of seaweeds.

algoz, *s.m.* hangman, executioner, torturer, cruel man.

alguém, *pron. indef.* somebody, someone, anyone, anybody.

alguidar, *s.m.* basin, bowl.

algum, *adj. e pron.* some, any. 1) *alguma coisa,* something. 2) *algum dinheiro,* some money. 3) *algumas vezes,* sometimes. 4) *algum tempo,* for some time, for a while. 5) *coisa alguma,* nothing at all. 6) *de modo algum,* not at all. 7) *em algum lugar,* somewhere. 8) *em lugar algum,* nowhere.

algures, *adv.* somewhere.

alhada, *s.f.* dish of garlic; mess *(confusão)*.

alheado, *adj.* oblivious.

alheamento, *s.m.* absent-mindedness, withdrawal *(afastamento)*, alienation *(de bens)*.

alhear, *v.t.* to separate, to withdraw, to estrange, to alienate, **alhear-se,** to turn away from.

alheável, *adj.* alienable.

alheio, *adj.* of others, belonging to other people, unaware, inattentive; *s.m.* other people's property.

alheira, *s.f.* a kind of sausage seasoned with garlic.

alheta, *s.f. (náut.)* quarter; *pôr-se na alheta,* to run away.

alho, *s.m.* garlic; *alho-porro,* leek.

ali, *adv.* there, younder, in that place; *por ali,* that way.

aliáceo, *adj.* alliaceous.

aliado, *adj.* allied, associate; *s.m.* ally, confederate.

aliança, *s.f.* alliance, union.

aliar, *v.t.* to ally, to associate, to combine.

aliás, *adv.* alias, besides, otherwise *(de outro modo)*.

aliável, *adj.* alliable.

álibi, *s.m.* alibi.

alicantina, *s.f.* trickery, fraud.

alicate, *s.m.* pliers.

alicerçar, *v.t.* to lay the foundations, to consolidate.

alicerce, *s.m.* foundation, basis, support.

aliciação, aliciamento, *s.f.* allurement, seduction, enticement.

aliciador, *s.m.* allurer, seductor, enticer.

aliciante, *adj.* alluring, enticer.

aliciar, *v.t.* to allure, to entice, to seduce.

alidade, *s.f.* alidad.

alienabilidade, *s.f.* alienability.

alienação, *s.f.* alienation, transference, separation, insanity *(alienação mental)*.

alienado, adj. alienated, transfered; s.m. lunatic, mad.

alienar, v.t. to alienate, to transfer.

alienável, adj. alienable.

alienismo, s.m. alienism.

alienista, s.m. e s.f. alienist.

alífero, adj. aliferous, winged.

aliforme, adj. aliform.

aligátor, s.m. alligator.

aligeirar, v.t. to lighten, to alleviate, to mitigate.

alígero, adj. aligerous, winged.

alijamento, s.m. jettison, throwing overboard.

alijar, to throw overboard, to lighten (um barco), to jettison.

alimária, s.f. beast, stupid person.

alimentação, s.f. alimentation, feeding, nourishment.

alimentador, adj. feeding; s.m. feeder.

alimentar, adj. alimentary, nourishing.

alimentar, v.t. to feed, to nourish, to cherish (esperanças).

alimentício, adj. nutritive, nourishing.

alimento, s.m. food, aliment, nourishment, nutriment.

alimpa, s.f. cleaning, cleansing.

alimpador, s.m. cleaner.

alimpadura, s.f. cleansing, screenings (de cereais).

alindar, v.t. to beautify, to embellish.

alínea, s.f. paragraph, item.

alinhado, adj. in line, neat (bem vestido).

alinhamento, s.m. alignment, in line, ranging.

alinhar, v.t. to align, to line up.

alinhavar, v.t. to baste, to tack, to sketch (esboçar); to improvise.

alinhavo, s.m. basting, sketch.

alinho, s.m. aligning, neatness.

alisado, adj. smoothed, polished.

alisador, s.m. smoother, smoother machine.

alisar, v.t. to smooth, to even, to polish.

alísio, s.m. e adj. ventos alisios, trade winds.

alistamento, s.m. enrolment.

alistar, v.t. to enlist, to enrol, to join (no exército).

aliteração, s.f. alliteration.

aliterar, v.t. to alliterate.

aliviado, adj. relieved.

aliviador, s.m. alleviator, assuager; adj. alleviating, soothing.

aliviar, v.t. to lighten (a carga), to relieve (libertar), to alleviate (atenuar), to mitigate; **aliviar-se,** to relieve oneself.

alívio, s.m. relief, alleviation, comfort, mitigation.

alizar, s.m. door-case, window-frame, wainscoting.

aljava, s.f. quiver.

aljôfar, aljofre, s.m. seed-pearl, (fig.) tears.

aljube, s.m. prison.

alma, s.f. soul.

almaço, s.m. e adj. a kind of paper, fools-cap paper.

almagre, s.m. red-ochre.

almanaque, s.m. almanac.

almandina, s.f. almandine.

almejar, v.t. to long for, to desire.

almenara, s.f. beacon, watchlight.

almirantado, s.m. admiralty.

almirante, s.m. admiral. 1) vice-almirante, vice admiral. 2) navio almirante, flagship.

almíscar, s.m. musk.

almiscarar, v.t. to perfume with musk.

almiscareira, s.f. musk plant.

almiscareiro, s.m. (zool.) musk-deer; rato- -almiscareiro, musk-rat.

almo, adj. (poét.) cherishing, genial.

almoçadeira, s.f. a large breakfast cup.

almoçar, v.t. e v.i. to have lunch.

almoço, s.m. lunch.

almocreve, s.m. mule driver.

almoeda, s.f. auction.

almoedar, v.t. to auction.

almofaça, s.f. curry comb.

almofada, s.f. pillow, cushion.

almofadar, v.t. to cushion, to pad, to panel (portas).

almofariz, s.m. mortar.

almôndega, s.f. meat-ball.

almotolia, s.f. oil-can.

almoxarife, s.m. (arc.) superintendent of the royal domains.

almude, s.m. almudo; a measure of capacity.

alô!, interj. hello!

alocução, s.f. allocution, address.

alodial, adj. allodial.

aloés, s.m. aloes.

aloirar, alourar, v.t. to render fair or golden; v.i. to become brown (cul.).

alojamento, s.m. lodging, lodgment, accommodation.

alojar, v.t. to lodge, to accommodate, to billet (as tropas).

alombamento, s.m. breaking or bending one's back, crooking.

alombar, *v.t.* to break the hip, to bend one's back.

alongamento, *s.m.* lengthening, elongation.

alongar, *v.t.* to lengthen, to enlarge, to stretch out.

alopata, *s.m.* allopath.

alopatia, *s.f.* allopathy.

alopático, *adj.* allopathic.

alopecia, *s.f.* alopecia, baldness.

aloquete, *s.m.* padlock.

alotropia, *s.f.* allotropy.

alótropo, alotrópico, *adj.* allotropic.

aloucado, *adj.* foolish.

alpaca, *s.f.* alpaca.

alparca, alparcata, alpercata, *s.f.* a sort of sandal.

alpendre, *s.m.* porch, shed.

alperce, *s.m.* apricot.

alperceiro, *s.m.* apricot-tree.

alpestre, *adj.* alpine, mountainous.

alpinismo, *s.m.* alpinism, mountain climbing, mountaineering.

alpinista, *s.m.* alpinist, mountain climber, mountaineer.

alpino, *adj.* alpine.

alpista, *s.f.* canary seed.

alquebrado, *adj.* worn out, weakened, broken down, *(náut.)* hogged, broken--backed.

alquebramento, *s.m.* weakness, debility, *(náut.)* cambering, hogging.

alquebrar, *v.t. e v.i.* to weaken; *v.i.* to become bent, *(náut.)* to become broken--baked, to hog.

alqueire, *s.m.* a measure for grain.

alqueivar, *v.t.* to fallow.

alqueive, *s.m.* fallow.

alquilador, *s.m.* horse-hirer, jobber.

alquilar, *v.t.* to hire horses.

alquilaria, *s.f.* stables where horses are hired.

alquime, *s.m.* tombac, an alloy of copper with a little zinc, prince's metal.

alquimia, *s.f.* alchemy.

alquimista, *s.m.* alchemist.

Alsácia, *s.f.* Alsace.

alsaciano, *adj. e s.m.* Alsatian.

alta, *s.f.* increase *(aumento)*, rise *(subida de preços)*, discharge *(de hospitais, etc.)*. 1) *alta-roda,* high-life, jet-set. 2) *alta sociedade,* high society. 3) *ter alta,* to be discharged.

altanado, *adj.* haughty, inconsiderate.

altanaria, *s.f.* pride, arrogance, haughtiness.

altaneiro, *adj.* lofty, towering *(alto)*, high flying *(que voa alto)*, proud, haughty *(soberbo)*.

altar, *s.m.* altar; *altar-mor,* high altar.

alteamento, *s.m.* raising, heightening, elevation.

altear, *v.t.* to raise, to heighten, to lift up.

alteia, *s.f. (bot.)* marshmallow.

alterabilidade, *s.f.* alterability.

alteração, *s.f.* alteration, change, modification, disorder *(desordem)*.

alterado, *adj.* disturbed, upset.

alterador, *s.m.* one who alters; *adj.* altering, alterative.

alterar, *v.t.* to change, to modify, to alter, to disturb; **alterar-se,** to become altered, to suffer alteration, to become upset, to grow angry *(ficar perturbado ou irado)*.

alterável, *adj.* alterable, changeable.

altercação, *s.f.* altercation, quarrel.

altercador, *s.m.* quarreler, wrangler.

altercar, *v.i.* to altercate, to quarrel, to wrangle.

alternadamente, *adv.* alternately, by turns.

alternado, *adj.* alternate, alternating. 1) *corrente alternada,* alternating current. 2) *em dias alternados,* every other day.

alternador, *s.m.* alternator.

alternância, *s.f.* alternation.

alternante, *adj.* alternating, alternant.

alternar, *v.t. e v.i.* to alternate, to take turns; *v.r.* to come one after the other.

alternativa, *s.f.* alternative, option.

alternativamente, *adv.* alternatively.

alternativo, *adj.* alternative, alternate.

alterno, *adj.* alternate.

alterosamente, *adv.* loftily, majestically.

alteroso, *adj.* high, proud, majestic, lofty.

alteza, *s.f.* highness (título), elevation.

altibaixos, *s.m.pl.* uneven places, ups and downs.

altifalante, *s.m.* loud-speaker.

altiloquência, *s.f.* grandiloquence, pompous language.

altiloquente, *adj.* grandiloquent, bombastic.

altilóquo, *s.m.* o mesmo que "altiloquência".

altimetria, *s.f.* altimetry.

altímetro, *s.m.* altimeter.

altipotente, *adj.* very powerful.

altíssimo, *adj.* very high; *s.m.* The Almighty.

altissonante, *adj.* altisonant, pompous, bombastic, lofty.

altista, *s.m. (com.)* bull.

altitonante, *adj.* altitonant, thundering.
altitude, *s.f.* altitude.
altivamente, *adv.* proudly, haughtly.
altivez, *s.f.* pride, haughtiness, arrogance.
altivo, *adj.* proud, haughty.
alto, *adj.* high, lofty, elevated, tall *(estatura),* loud *(som),* upper *(geografia, ex. Alto Nilo,* Upper Nile). 1) *alto-forno,* blast furnace. 2) *alto-relevo,* alto-relievo, high relief. 3) *a altas horas da noite,* late in the night. 4) *em voz alta,* aloud; *s.m.* top *(topo),* elevation *(elevação).* 5) *de alto a baixo,* from top to bottom. 6) *mãos ao alto,* hands up!. 7) *por alto,* superficially.
altruísmo, *s.m.* altruism.
altruísta, *s.m.* e *s.f.* e *adj.* altruist.
altruístico, *adj.* altruistic.
altura, *s.f.* height, altitude, tallness *(estatura),* point, time *(momento); nas alturas:* aloft.
aluado, *adj.* moonstruck, lunatic, crack-brained.
alucinação, *s.f.* hallucination.
alucinado, *adj.* hallucinated.
alucinador, *adj.* hallucinating.
alucinante, *adj.* hallucinating.
alucinar, *v.t.* to hallucinate.
alucinatório, *adj.* hallucinatory.
alude, *s.m.* avalanche.
aludir, *v.i.* to allude to, to refer to, to mention.
alugar, *v.t.* to let, to hire *(veículos ou animais),* to rent *(imóveis).*
aluguel, aluguer, *s.m.* rent *(renda),* letting, hirei hiring.
aluimento, *s.m.* shaking, slide, landslip, landslide.
aluir, *v.t.* e *v.i.* to shake, to collapse, to slide, to ruin.
alúmen, *s.m.* alum.
alumiar, *v.t.* to illuminate, to light.
alumina, *s.f.* alumina.
alumínio, *s.m.* aluminium.
aluminoso, *adj.* aluminous.
aluno, *s.m.* pupil; *aluno interno,* boarding pupil or student.
alusão, *s.f.* allusion, reference.
alusivo, *adj.* allusive, hinting at, topical, referring to.
aluvial, *adj.* alluvial.
aluvião, *s.f.* alluvion, alluvium.
alva, *s.f.* dawn, daybreak, alb *(paramento).*
alvacento, alvadio, *adj.* whitish.
alvado, *s.m.* socket *(de dente),* entrance *(de colmeia),* eye *(de ferramenta).*

alvaiade, *s.m.* white-lead.
alvar, *adj.* whitish, stupid.
alvará, *s.m.* charter, writ *(judicial).*
alvedrio, *s.m.* will, free will.
alveiro, *adj.* of a white color; *s.m.* white landmark, milestone a linen cloth used to cover the bread after it is baked.
alveitar, *s.m.* veterinary, farrier.
alveitaria, *s.f.* farriery.
alvejante, *adj.* looking white.
alvejar, *v.t.* e *v.i.* to aim, to shot.
alvela, *s.f.* kite.
alvenaria, *s.f.* masonry.
alvéola, *s.f.* wag-tail
alveolado, *adj.* alveolate.
alveolar, *adj.* alveolar.
alvéolo, *s.m.* alveolous, alveole, cocoon, cell *(de colmeia).*
alverca, *s.f.* pool, pond, fen-land.
alvião, *s.m.* mattock.
alvinitente, *adj.* white and bright.
alvino, *adj.* alvine.
alvíssaras, *s.f. pl.* reward, tip.
alvissareiro, *s.m.* someone that brings good news; *adj.* bringing good news.
alvitrador, *s.m.* suggestor, contriver, projector, proposer.
alvitrar, *v.t.* to suggest, to propose, to give a hint.
alvitre, *s.m.* expedient, suggestion, hint, proposal.
alvo, *s.m.* target, aim, purpose; *adj.* white, clear.
alvor, *s.m.* dawn, whiteness, brightness.
alvorada, *s.f.* dawn, reveille *(toque de alvorada).*
alvorecer, *s.m.* dawn; *v.i.* to dawn.
alvoroçado, *adj.* anxious, restless, alarmed.
alvoroçar, *v.t.* e *v.r.* to incite, to alarm, to become excited.
alvoroço, *s.m.* excitement, alarm, enthusiasm, eagerness, commotion.
alvorotar, *v.t.* to disturb, to trouble, to incite.
alvoroto, *s.m.* o mesmo que "alvoroço".
alvura, *s.f.* whiteness, purity.
ama, *s.f.* nurse, mistress *(patroa).*
amabilidade, *s.f.* kindness, friendliness.
amacacado, *adj.* monkeyish, monkey-like.
amachucar, *v.t.* to crumple, to wrinkle.
amaciar, *v.t.* to smooth, to soften.
amada, *s.f.* a beloved woman; *adj.* loved, beloved.
amado, *adj.* loved, beloved, dear; *s.m.* sweetheart.

amador, *s.m.* amateur.
amadorismo, *s.m.* amateurism.
amadurar, amadurecer, *v.t.* e *v.i.* to ripen, to mature, to grow ripe.
amadurecido, *adj.* ripe, mature.
amadurecimento, *s.m.* ripening, maturing, ripeness.
âmago, *s.m.* heart, core, essence, substance.
amainar, *v.t.* e *v.i.* (*náut.*) to lower, to furl (*as velas*), to abate, to relent (*a tempestade*).
amaldiçoado, *adj.* cursed, damned.
amaldiçoador, *s.m.* curser.
amaldiçoar, *v.t.* to curse.
amálgama, *s.f.* amalgam, mixture.
amalgamação, *s.f.* amalgamation.
amalgamar, *v.t.* to amalgamate, to mix, to mingle.
amalhar, *v.t.* to catch in the net, to fold (*ovelhas*).
amalucado, *adj.* foolish, silly, crazy.
amamentação, *s.f.* breast feeding, suckling.
amamentar, *v.t.* to suckle, to nurse.
amancebado, *adj.* concubinary; *viver amancebado,* to live in concubinage.
amancebar-se, *v.t.* to take a mistress, to live in concubinage, to contract an illicit union.
amaneirado, *adj.* affected, priggish (*presumido*).
amaneirar-se, *v.r.* to become affected.
amanhã, *adv.* tomorrow; *depois de amanhã,* the day after tomorrow.
amanhar, *v.t.* to till, to cultivate (*cultivar a terra*), to arrange (*arrumar*).
amanhecer, *v.i.* to dawn, to awake (*acordar*); *s.m.* dawn, daybreak.
amanho, *s.m.* repairing, tillage, cultivation (*cultivo*) to trim, to prepare (*enfeitar*).
amansadela, *s.f.* the act of taming or subduing.
amansador, *s.m.* tamer (*de animais*), subduer.
amansar, *v.t.* to tame, to domesticate (*animais*), to subdue, to calm, to pacify (*acalmar*); *v.i.* to abate, to be tamed.
amante, *s.m.* e *s.f.* lover, mistress; *adj.* loving, fond of.
amanteigado, *adj.* buttery, soft, creamy.
amanteigar, *v.t.* to butter.
amanuense, *s.m.* amanuensis, clerk.
amar, *v.t.* to love, to adore, to be fond of.
amaragem, *s.f.* landing on water.
amarar, *v.t.* e *v.i.* e *v.r.* to land on water, to alight on water.

amarelado, *adj.* yellowish.
amarelecer, *v.t.* e *v.i.* to yellow, to become or to render yellow, to grow yellow.
amarelecido, *adj.* yellowish, faded, withered.
amarelecimento, *s.m.* yellowing.
amarelejar, *v.i.* to grow yellow or pale.
amarelento, *adj.* yellowish, pale.
amarelo, *adj.* yellow; *s.* yellow. 1) *amarelo-canário,* canary yellow. 2) *amarelo pálido,* light or pale yellow.
amarfanhar, *v.t.* to crumple, to wrinkle, to maltreat (*maltratar*).
amargamente, *adv.* bitterly, painfully (*dolorosamente*).
amargar, *v.t.* to embitter, to suffer for (*pagar caro*); *v.i.* to taste bitter.
amargo, *adj.* bitter, painful (*penoso*).
amargor, *s.m.* bitterness.
amargoso, *adj.* bitter.
amargura, *s.f.* bitterness, grief, sorrow (*pesar*).
amargurar, *v.t.* to grieve, to afflict, to distress; *v.r.* to mourn, to grieve.
amaricado, *adj.* effeminate.
amaricar-se, *v.r.* to become effeminate.
amarinhar, *v.t.* to man, to equip (*tripular*); to climb (*trepar*).
amaríssimo, *adj.* very bitter.
amaro, *adj.* bitter, grievous.
amarra, *s.f.* (*náut.*) a cable, chain.
amarração, *s.f.* mooring, anchoring.
amarradouro, *s.m.* (*náut.*) mooring.
amarrar, *v.t.* to fasten, to tie (*atar*), to moor (*ancorar*); *v.i.* to moor.
amarrecado, *adj.* humpbacked.
amarrecar, *v.t.* e *v.i.* to hump.
amarrotado, *adj.* crumpled, wrinkled.
amarrotar, *v.t.* to crumple, to wrinkle.
amarujar, *v.t.* to taste bitter.
amásia, *s.f.* mistress, concubine.
amassadeira, *s.f.* kneading-machine.
amassadela, *s.f.* squashing, embossment.
amassador, *s.m.* kneader.
amassadouro, *s.m.* kneading-trough.
amassadura, *s.f.* kneading, baking, squashing, mixture.
amassar, *v.t.* to knead (*massa*), to paddle (*barro*), to crush (*amolgar*).
amassaria, *s.f.* bake-house.
amaurose, *s.f.* (*med.*) amaurosis.
amaurótico, *adj.* e *s.m.* amaurotic.
amável, *adj.* amiable, kind, lovely.
amavelmente, *adv.* kindly, affably.

amavios, *s.m.pl.* philters, allurements *(encantos).*

amavioso, *adj.* amorous.

amazona, *s.f.* Amazon; *traje de amazona,* riding-habit.

Amazonas, *s.m.* Amazon *(rio).*

amazónico, *adj.* amazonian.

ambages, *s.m.pl.* ambages, circumlocutions, roundabout ways.

âmbar, *s.m.* amber.

ambárico, ambarino, *adj.* amber-coloured.

ambição, *s.f.* ambition.

ambicionar, *v.t.* to ambition, to long for, to aspire to.

ambiciosamente, *adv.* ambitiously.

ambicioso, *adj.* ambitious.

ambidextria, *s.f.* ambidexterity.

ambidextro, *s.m.* ambidexter; *adj.* ambidextrous.

ambientar-se, *v.r.* to adapt oneself to an environment.

ambiente, *s.m.* environment, ambient, atmosphere.

ambiguidade, *s.f.* ambiguity, double meaning.

ambíguo, *adj.* ambiguous, obscure.

âmbito, *s.m.* ambit, sphere of action, scope, range.

ambos, *adj.* e *pron.* both, the two.

ambrear, *v.t.* to amber.

ambrósia, *s.f.* ambrosia (the food of the Greek gods.)

ambrosíaco, *adj.* ambrosian.

âmbula, *s.f.* ampulla.

ambulância, *s.f.* ambulance.

ambulante, *adj.* walking, wandering, moving; *vendedor ambulante,* peddlar.

ambulatório, *adj.* ambulatory; *s.m.* clinic.

ameaça, *s.f.* menace, threat.

ameaçado, *adj.* threatened, menaced.

ameaçador, *s.m.* threatener; *adj.* threatening, menacing.

ameaçadoramente, *adv.* threateningly.

ameaçar, *v.t.* to threaten, to menace.

ameaço, *s.m.* a threat, symptom, sign.

ameado, *adj.* battlemented, castellated.

amealhar, *v.t.* to save, to lay aside *(poupar).*

amedrontado, *adj.* frightened, intimidated.

amedrontar, *v.t.* to frighten, to scare, to intimidate

ameia, *s.f.* battlement.

ameigar, *v.t.* to fondle, to caress, to pet.

amêijoa, *s.f.* cockle.

ameixa, *s.f.* plum, prune.

ameixoal, *s.m.* an orchard of plum-trees.

ameixoeira, *s.f.* plum-tree.

ameloado, *adj.* melon-like.

amém, *interj.* amen!; *s.m.* consent.

amêndoa, *s.f.* almond; the edible part of a fruit: kernel.

amendoado, *adj.* almond-like.

amendoal, *s.m.* field of almond-trees.

amendoeira, *s.f.* almond-tree.

amendoim, *s.m.* peanut.

amenidade, *s.f.* amenity, pleasantness.

ameninado, *adj.* childish.

ameninar, *v.t.* to acquire the manners of a child.

amenizar, *v.t.* to soften, to render pleasant.

ameno, *adj.* agreeable, pleasant, mild.

amenorreia, *s.f.* amenorrhea.

amercear, *v.t.* e *v.r.* to pardon, to pity.

americanismo, *s.m.* americanism.

americanizar, *v.t.* to americanize.

americano, *adj.* e *s.m.* american.

amesendar-se, *v.r.* to sit down, to recline lazily.

amesquinhado, *adj.* depressed, humiliated.

amesquinhar, *v.t.* to disparage, to humiliate, to depreciate.

amestrado, *adj.* trained.

amestrador, *s.m.* trainer.

amestrar, *v.t.* to train, to teach.

ametista, *s.f.* amethyst.

amial, *s.m.* alder-grove.

amiantino, *adj.* amiantine.

amianto, *s.m.* amianthus, asbestos.

amiba, *s.f.* amoeba; *pl.* amoebae.

amibóide, *adj.* amoeboid.

amicíssimo, *adj.* most friendly.

amicto, *s.m.* amice.

amido, *s.m.* starch.

amieiro, *s.m.* alder.

amigalhaço, *s.m.* good friend, old chap.

amigar-se, *v.r.* to live in concubinage.

amigável, *adj.* friendly.

amigavelmente, *adv.* friendlily.

amígdala, *s.f.* amygdala, tonsil.

amigdalite, *s.f.* amygdalitis.

amigo, *s.m.* friend.

amiláceo, *adj.* starchy.

amílico, *adj.* amylic.

amimado, *adj.* fondled, spoiled.

amimar, *v.t.* to fondle, to pet, to spoil *(estragar com mimos).*

amistoso, *adj.* friendly, amicable.

amiudadamente, *adv.* frequently, often.

amiudado, *adj.* frequent.

amiudar, *v.t.* to often, to repeat, to do the same thing many times.
amiúde, *adv.* often, many times.
amizade, *s.f.* friendship, affection.
amnésia, *s.f.* amnesia, loss of memory.
amnésico, *adj.* amnesic.
amnistia, *s.f.* amnesty.
amnistiar, to amnesty, to pardon.
amo, *s.m.* master, owner.
amodorrado, *adj.* drowsy, sleepy.
amodorrar, *v.t.* to become drowsy.
amoedação, *s.f.* coining.
amoedar, *v.t.* to coin.
amofinação, *s.f.* annoyance, vexation, worry.
amofinado, *adj.* grieved, vexed, worried.
amofinar, *v.t.* to annoy, to tease, to vex, to worry; **amofinar-se** to grow angry, to fret.
amojar, *v.t.* to milk, to fill with milk.
amojo, *s.m.* abundance of milk.
amolação, *s.f.* grinding, sharpening, whetting.
amoladeira, *s.f.* grindstone, grinding-machine.
amolador, *s.m.* grinder, whetter.
amolar, *v.t.* to grind, to sharpen, to whet, *(fig.)* to harass, to bother *(importunar).*
amoldar, *v.t.* to mould, to cast in a mould, to adapt, to fit.
amoldável, *adj.* mouldable, adaptable.
amolecedor, *s.m.* e *adj.* softener, softening, assuaging.
amolecer, *v.t.* to soten, to assuage, to grow soft, to melt.
amolecido, *adj.* softened, melt.
amolecimento, *s.m.* softening, assuaging.
amolgadela, *s.f.* squashing, flattening, crushing.
amolgar, *v.t.* to squash, to flatten, to crush, to smash.
amónia, *s.f.* ammonia.
amoniacal, *adj.* ammoniacal.
amoníaco, *s.m.* ammonia, liquid ammonia.
amontoado, *adj.* heaped up, piled up; *s.m.* heap, pile.
amontoador, *s.m.* heeper.
amontoamento, *s.m.* heap, pile, accumulation.
amontoar, *v.t.* to heap up, to accumulate, to pile up, to mass.
amor, *s.m.* love, affection.
amora, *s.f.* blackberry.
amorado, *adj.* blackberry-couloured.

amoral, *adj.* amoral, non-moral, un-moral.
amoralidade, *s.f.* amorality, unmorality.
amorável, *adj.* loving, caressing.
amordaçar, *v.t.* to gag, to muzzle *(açaimar).*
amoreira, *s.f.* mulberry-tree.
amoreiral, *s.m.* mulberry-trees plantation.
amorfia, *s.f.* amorphism.
amorfo, *adj.* amorphous.
amormado, *adj.* *(vet.)* glandered, affected with glanders.
amornado, *adj.* warmed.
amornar, *v.t.* to warm.
amorosamente, *adv.* amorously, lovingly.
amoroso, *adj.* amorous, loving, kind, sweet.
amor-perfeito, *s.m.* pansy.
amor-próprio, *s.m.* self-esteem.
amorrinhar-se, *v.r.* to be taken with murrain, to weaken.
amortalhador, *s.m.* a layer out, a man who shrouds corpses.
amortalhar, *v.t.* to shroud.
amortecedor, *s.m.* a shock-absorber, pad, muffler *(de som).*
amortecer, *v.t.* e *v.i.* to benumb, to deaden, to muffle *(som),* to absorb *(choques).*
amortecimento, *s.m.* weakening, deadening, torpidity, absorption.
amortizaçao, *s.f.* amortization.
amortizar, *v.t.* to amortize.
amortizável, *adj.* amortizable.
amostra, *s.m.* sample, indication *(indício).*
amostrar, *v.t.* o mesmo que "mostrar".
amotinação, *s.f.* mutiny, riot, insurrection.
amotinador, *s.m.* mutineer, rioter.
amotinar, *v.t.* to revolt; *v.r.* to revolt, to mutiny, to rebel.
amouriscado, *adj.* resembling the Moors.
amover, *v.t.* to remove, to withdraw.
amovível, *adj.* removable.
amovibilidade, *s.f.* removability.
amparador, *s.m.* protector, supporter.
amparar, *v.t.* to protect, to support, to help, to sustain.
amparo, *s.m.* protection, assistance, support, shelter.
amperagem, *s.f.* amperage.
ampere, *s.m.* ampere.
amperímetro, *s.m.* ammeter.
amplexo, *s.m.* embrace.
ampliação, *s.f.* amplification, enlargement.
ampliador, *s.m.* amplifier.
ampliar, *v.t.* to amplify, to enlarge, to increase.
ampliativo, *adj.* amplifying, enlarging.

amplidão, *s.f.* ampleness, amplitude, largeness, width.

amplificação, *s.f.* amplification, enlargement.

amplificador, *s.m.* amplifier.

amplificar, *v.t.* to amplify, to enlarge, to increase.

amplificável, *adj.* amplifying.

amplitude, *s.f.* amplitude, extent, range.

amplo, *adj.* ample, large, spacious.

ampola, *s.f.* blister, phial, ampoule.

ampulheta, *s.f.* hourglass, sandglass.

amputação, *s.f.* amputation.

amputar, *v.t.* to amputate, to cut off.

amuado, *adj.* sulky, sullen.

amuar, *v.t. e v.i.* to sulk, to spout.

amulatado, *adj.* like a mulatto.

amuleto, *s.m.* amulet, talisman.

amuo, *s.m.* sulleness, sulkiness, ill-humour.

amurada, *s.f. (náut.)* bulnark, side, gunwall.

anã, *s.f.* dwarf.

anabaptismo, *s.m.* anabaptism.

anabaptista, *s.m. e s.f.* anabaptist.

anabolismo, *s.m.* anabolism.

anacarado, *adj.* nacreous.

anacoreta, *s.m. e s.f.* anachoret.

anacrónico, *adj.* anachronic.

anacronismo, *s.m.* anachronism.

anaeróbio, *s.m. e adj.* anaerobe.

anafa, *s.f. (bot.)* melilot.

anafado, *adj.* fat.

anafar, *v.t.* to fatten.

anáfega, *s.f.* jujube.

anafrodisíaco, *adj.* anaphrodisiac.

anafrodita, *s.m. e s.f.* anaphrodisiac.

anagrama, *s.m.* anagram.

anagramático, *adj.* anagrammatic.

anais, *s.m.pl.* annais.

anal, *adj.* anal, annual.

analepsia, *s.f.* analepsis.

analéptico, *adj.* analeptic.

analfabetismo, *s.m.* illiteracy.

analfabeto, *s.m. e adj.* illiterate, analphabet.

analgesia, *s.f.* analgesia.

analgésico, *adj. e s.m.* analgesic.

analisador, *s.m.* analyser.

analisar, *v.t.* to analyse.

analisável, *adj.* analysable.

análise, *s.f.* analysis, parsing (gramática); *em última análise*, in conclusion.

analista, *s.m.* analyst.

analiticamente, *adv.* analytically.

analítico, *adj.* analytical.

analogia, *s.f.* analogia, similarity.

analógico, *adj.* analogical.

analogismo, *s.m.* analogism.

analogista, *s.m.* analogist.

análogo, *adj.* analogous, similar.

anamnésia, *s.f.* anamnesia.

ananás, *s.m.* pineapple.

ananaseiro, *s.m.* pineapple-plant.

anão, *s.m.* dwarf.

anapesto, *s.m.* anapest.

anarquia, *s.f.* anarchy.

anárquico, *adj.* anarchical.

anarquismo, *s.m.* anarchism.

anarquista, *s.m. e s.f.* anarchist.

anarquizar, *v.t.* to anarchise.

anástrofe, *s.f.* anastrophe.

anatar, *v.t.* to cover with cream, to render cream-like.

anátema, *s.m.* anathema.

anatematização, *s.f.* anathematization.

anatematizar, *v.t.* to anathematize.

anatomia, *s.f.* anatomy.

anatomicamente, *adv.* anatomically.

anatómico, *adj.* anatomical.

anatomista, *s.m.* anatomist.

anatomizar, *v.t.* to anatomize, to dissect.

anavalhar, *v.t.* to knife, to cut with a knife.

anca, *s.f.* hip, haunch, rump *(de animais)*.

ancestral, *adj.* ancestral.

ancho, *adj.* broad, wide, ample, *(fig.)* vain, proud.

anchova, *s.f.* anchovy.

anciã, *s.f.* old woman.

anciania, ancianidade, *s.f.* ancientry, old age.

ancião, *s.m.* old man, an elder; *adj.* very old, ancient.

ancila, *s.f.* a servant maid, slave.

ancilostomíase, *s.f.* hookworm disease.

ancinho, *s.m.* rake.

âncora, *s.f.* anchor, support *(apoio)*, *(fig.)* last resource of hope.

ancoradouro, *s.m.* anchorage, anchorage grouns.

ancoragem, *s.f.* casting of the anchor, archorage dues *(direitos)*.

ancorar, *v.t.* to anchor; *v.i.* to cast anchor, to base oneself *(fundamentar-se)*.

ancoreta, *s.f.* small anchor.

ancudo, *adj.* big-haunched.

andaço, *s.m.* epidemic disease.

andada, *s.f.* journey, long walk.

andadeiras, *s.f.pl.* pleading-strings.

andador, *s.m. e adj.* good walker, fast walker.

andadura, *s.f.* going, pacing, walking.

andaime, *s.m.* scaffold, staging.

andaina, *s.f.* row, range.

andamento, *s.m.* progress, movement, gait *(de cavalo),* tempo *(mús.).*

andança, *s.f.* adventure.

andante, *s.m.* andante *(mús.); adj.* errant, wandering.

andar, *s.m.* walk, manner of walking, step, course *(do tempo),* floor *(de edifício); v.i.* to walk, to go, to work *(máquina),* to wander *(vaguear),* to travel *(viajar),* to progress *(progredir),* to go by *(o tempo),* to behave, to do *(proceder),* to be *(estar).* 1) *andar a pé,* to go on foot. 2) *andar a cavalo,* to ride. 3) *andar de bicicieta, automóvel, etc.,* to ride a bycicle, etc. 4) *andar de comboio, de avião, de barco,* to travel by train, by air, by ship.

andarilho, *s.m.* runner, errand boy.

andas, *s.f.pl.* stilts.

andebol, *s.m.* handball.

andeiro, *adj.* walking.

andejar, *v.t.* to ramble, to wander.

andino, *adj.* andean, andine.

andor, *s.m.* litter.

andorinha, *s.f.* swallow; *andorinha-do-mar,* tern.

andorino, *adj.* swallow coloured.

andrajo, *s.m.* rag, tatter, dout.

andrajoso, *adj.* ragger, tattered.

androceu, *s.m.* androecium.

andrógino, *adj.* androgynous.

andróide, *s.m.* android.

Andrómeda, *s. f.* Andromeda.

andrómina, *s. f.* story, tale, fable.

anedota, *s.f.* anecdote, joke.

anedotário, *s.m.* collection of anecdotes.

anedótico, *adj.* anecdotic.

anedotista, *s.m. e s.f.* anecdotist.

anegrar, *v.t.* to darken, to blacked.

aneiro, *adj.* eventual, uncertain.

anel, *s.m.* ring, link *(de corrente).*

anelação, *s.f.* short breath, panting, anhelation.

anelado, *adj.* curled, curly.

anelante, *adj.* panting.

anelar, *v.t. e v.i.* to long for, to desire, to curl *(encaracolar); adj.* annular.

anelídeo, *adj. e s.m.* annelidan.

anelo, *s.m.* eager desire, ambition.

anemia, *s.f.* anaemia.

anemiar, *v.t.* to make anaemic, to weaken.

anémico, *adj.* anaemic, pale *(pálido).*

anemofilia, *s.f.* anemophily.

anemómetro, *s.m.* anemometer.

anémona, *s.f.* anemone.

anemoscópio, *s.m.* anemoscope.

aneróide, *adj.* aneroid.

anervia, *s.f.* aneuria.

anestesia, *s.f.* anaesthesia, anesthesia.

anestesiante, *adj.* anesthesiant.

anestesiar, *v.t.* to anesthetize.

anestésico, *adj. e s.m.* anesthetic.

aneurisma, *s.m.* aneurism.

anexação, *s.f.* annexation, incorporation.

anexar, *v.t.* to annex, to incorporate, to join.

anexim, *s.m.* byword, adage, saying.

anexo, *adj.* annexed, joined, attached; *s.m.* anaex, additament, appendix.

anfíbio, *s.m.* anphibian, *adj.* anphibious.

anfibiografia, anfibiologia, *s.f.* amphibiology.

anfibiológico, *adj.* amphibiological.

anfiteatro, *s.m.* amphitheatre.

anfitrião, *s.m.* host, amphitryon.

ânfora, *s.f.* amphora.

anfractuosidade, *s.f.* anfractuosity, sinuosity.

anfractuoso, *adj.* anfractuous, sinuous.

angariador, *s.m.* solicitor, recruiter, canvasser.

angariar, *v.t.* to solicit, to allure *(atrair),* to recruit *(recrutar),* to canvass *(votos, contribuições).*

angélica, *s.f. (bot.)* angelica.

angelical, *adj.* angelical.

angélico, *adj.* angelic.

angina, *s.f.* angina; *angina de garganta,* quinsy.

angiospérmico, *adj.* anguiospermous.

anglicanismo, *s.m.* anglicanism.

anglicano, *s.m. e adj.* anglican.

anglicismo, *s.m.* anglicism.

anglofilia, *s.f.* anglomania.

anglófilo, *s.m.* anglophil, pro-English.

anglofobia, *s.f.* anglophobia.

anglófobo, *s.m. e adj.* anglophobe.

anglo-saxão, *s.m. e adj.* Anglo-saxon.

anglo-saxónico, *adj.* anglo-saxonic.

angolano, *s.m.* a native of Angola. *adj.* of Angola.

angora, *s.m.* Angora cat.

angra, *s.f.* bay, creek, inlet.

anguiforme, *adj.* anguiform.

anguilliforme, *adj.* anguilliform, eel-like.

angulado, *adj.* angulated, eith angles.

angular, *adj.* angular.

ângulo, *s.m.* angle, corner *(canto);* ângulo agudo, recto, obtuso, acute, right, obtuse angle.

anguloso, *adj.* angulous.

angústia, *s.f.* anguish, anxiety.

angustiado, *adj.* in anguish, anxious.

angustiante, *adj.* agonizing, afflicting.

angustiar, *v.t.* to anguish, to distress, to afflict.

angustioso, *adj.* anguishing, distressful, oppressive.

anho, *s.m.* lamb.

anichar, *v.t.* to place in a niche.

anídrico, *adj.* anhydrous.

anidrido, *s.m.* anhydride.

anidro, *adj.* anhydrous.

anil, *s.m.* indigo, anil.

anilado, *adj.* indigo-coloured.

anilar, *v.t.* to dye with indigo.

anileira, *s.f.* indigo-tree.

anilha, *s.f.* ring.

animação, *s.f.* animation, liveliness, vivacity.

animado, *adj.* animated, encouraged, lively.

animador, *s.m.* animator, entertainer; *adj.* animating, encouraging.

animadversão, *s.f.* animadversion, aversion.

animal, *s.m.* animal; *animal de estimação,* pet.

animálculo, *s.m.* animalcule, a small animal.

animalejo, *s.m.* animal, beast.

animália, *s.f.* beast.

animalidade, *s.f.* animality.

animalização, *s.f.* animalization.

animalizar, *v.t.* to animalize, to brutalize.

animar, *v.t.* to animate, to encourage, to comfort.

anímico, *adj.* of the soul, psychological.

animismo, *s.m.* animism.

animista, *adj.* animistic. *s.m.* animist.

ânimo, *s.m.* courage, spirit, disposition *(índole)* mind *(mente).*

animosidade, *s.f.* animosity, bitterness, rancor.

aninhar, *v.t.* to nest, to shelter, to cuddle *(aconchegar);* *v.r.* to nestle, to cuddle up.

aniquilação, *s.f.* annihilation, destruction, extinction.

aniquilador, *s.m.* destroyer, annihilator; *adj.* annilhilative.

aniquilar, *v.t.* to annihilate, to destroy, to extinguish; *v.r.* to come to nothing, to break down.

anis, *s.m.* anise; *licor de anis,* anisette.

aniseira, *s.f.* anise plant.

aniseta, *s.f.* anisette.

aniversário, *s.m.* anniversary, birthday *(de nascimento).*

anjinho, *s.m.* a little angel, cherub *(querubim).*

anjo, *s.m.* angel; *anjo-da-guarda,* guardian angel.

ano, *s.m.* year; *ano-luz,* light year.

anódino, *adj.* anodyne.

anódio, *s.m.* anode.

ânodo, *s.m.* anode.

anoitecer, *v.i.* to become night, to grow dark; *s.m.* nightfall, dusk.

anojado, *adj.* grieved, in mourning, sad, nauseated *(nauseado).*

anojar, *v.t.* to make sick, to mourn, to annoy.

anojo, *s.m.* disgust.

anomalia, *s.f.* anomaly, irregularity.

anómalo, *adj.* anomalous, irregular, abnormal.

anona, *s.f.* anona.

anonimato, *s.m.* anonymity.

anónimo, *adj.* anonymous; *s.m.* anonym; *sociedade anónima,* joint stock acompany.

anorexia, *s.f.* anorexy.

anormal, *adj.* abnormal, irregular.

anormalidade, *s.f.* abnormality, irregularity.

anormalmente, *adv.* abnormally.

anosidade, *s.f.* old age.

anoso, *adj.* advanced in years, aged, old.

anotação, *s.f.* annotation, remark, note.

anotador, *s.m.* annotator, commentator.

anotar, *v.t.* to annotate, to comment on, to write down *(tomar nota).*

anquilose, *s.f.* anchylosis.

anquinhas, *s.f.pl.* puffs, padding, pannier.

anseio, *s.m.* anguish, grief, desire.

ânsia, *s.f.* anxiety, affliction, anguish, worry.

ansiar, *v.t.* to cause anguish, to desire eagerly, to long for.

ansiedade, *s.f.* anxiety, anguish, eager desire.

ansioso, *adj.* anxious, impatient, eager, longing for.

anta, *s.f.* dolmen, cromlech; *(zool.)* tapir.

antagonicamente, *adv.* antagonistically.

antagónico, *adj.* antagonical, opposed to.

antagonismo, *s.m.* antagonism, opposition, hostility.

antagonista, *s.m.* antagonist, opponent, rival.

antálgico, *adj.* antalgic, analgesic.

antanho, *adv.* of yore, last year, in olden times.

antárctico, adj. antarctic; s.m. Antarctic.

ante, prep. before.

antebraço, s.m. forearm.

antecâmara, s.f. antechamber, waiting-room.

antecedência, s.f. antecedence, anticipation; com antecedência, in anticipation.

antecedente, adj. antecedent, foregoing, previous, precedent; s.m. antecedent.

anteceder, v.t. to precede, to go before.

antecessor, s.m. antecessor, predecessor.

antecipação, s.f. anticipation, prevention.

antecipadamente, adv. in advance, in anticipation.

antecipar, v.t. to anticipate, to prevent; v.r. to precede, to forestall.

antecoro, s.m. ante-choir.

antedata, s.f. antedate.

antedatar, v.t. to antedate.

antediluviano, adj. antediluvian.

antedizer, v.t. to foretell, to predict.

anteface, s.f. veil that covers the face, mask.

antegostar, v.t. to foretaste.

antegozar, v.t. to enjoy, to look forward, to anticipate with pleasure.

antegozo, s.m. anticipation of pleasure.

anteguarda, s.f. vanguard.

antelóquio, s.m. prologue.

antemão, adv. beforehand, in advance.

antemeridiano, adj. antemeridian, before noon.

antemurado, adj. surrounded with walls.

antena, s.f. antena, pl. antenae, acrial (de rádio, TV, etc.).

antenado, adj. provided with antennas or aerials.

antenal, adj. antennal; s.m. albatross.

antenome, s.m. a title prefixed to a Christian name.

antenupcial, adj. antenuptial, before marriage.

anteontem, adv. the day before yesterday.

antepara, s.f. (náut.) bulkhead.

anteparar, v.t. e v.i. to defend, to protect, to shelter.

anteparo, s.m. fence, screen, defense, protection.

antepassado, adj. e s.m. ancestor, fore-father, bygone.

antepasto, s.m. antispast.

antepenúltimo, adj. antepenultimate.

antepor, v.t. to set before, to prefix, to prefer.

anteporta, s.f. double-door, screen.

anteposição, s.f. precedence, preficion, preference.

anteprojecto, s.m. scheme, preliminary plant.

antera, s.f. anther.

anterior, s.m. adv. anterior, previous, preceding.

anterioridade, adj. anteriority, precedence.

anteriormente, adv. previously, before.

antes, adv. before, previously, rather, better. 1) quisera antes ficar, I would rather stay. 2) antes tarde do que nunca, better late thannever. 3) antes pelo contrário, on the contrary. 4) antes de, before. 5) antes de tudo, first of all.

antessala, s.f. antechamber, waiting-room.

antestreia, s.f. preview.

antever, v.t. to foresee.

anteversão, s.f. inversion of the matrix.

antevéspera, s.f. the day before the eve.

antevidência, s.f. V. "previdência".

antiaéreo, adj. anti-aircraft.

antiapopléctico, adj. antiapopletic.

antiaristocrático, adj. antiaristocratic.

antiartístico, adj. antiartistic.

antiartrítico, adj. antiarthritic.

antiasmático, adj. antiasthmatic.

antibiótico, s.m. e adj. antibiotic.

anticanceroso, adj. anti-cancerous.

anticatólico, adj. anticatholic.

anticiclone, s.m. anticyclone.

anticiclónico, adj. anticyclonic.

anticívico, adj. anticivic.

anticlerical, adj. anticlerical.

anticlericalismo, s.m. anticlericalism.

anticlímax, s.m. anticlimax.

anticomercial, adj. anticommercial.

anticonstitucional, adj. anti constitutional.

anticoncepcional, adj. anticonceptional.

anticorrosivo, adj. anticorrosive.

anticorpo, s.m. antibody.

anticristão, s.m. antichristian.

Anticristo, s.m. Antichrist.

antidemocrático, adj. anti-democratic.

antidiftérico, adj. anti-diftheric.

antidinástico, adj. antidynastic.

antidogmático, adj. antidogmatic.

antídoto, s.m. antidote.

antiepiléptico, adj. antiepileptic.

antiescorbútico, adj. antiescorbutic.

antiespasmódico, adj. antispasmodic.

antiestético, adj. antiaesthetic.

antifebril, adj. antifebrile.

antifilosófico, adj. antiphilosophic.

antifisiológico, *adj.* antiphisiological.

antífona, *s.m.* antiphon.

antifonário, *s.m.* antiphonary.

antífrase, *s.f.* antiphrasis.

antigamente, *adv.* anciently, formerly, in the past, in olden times.

antigermânico, *adj.* antigermanic.

antigo, *adj.* old, ancient, olden, antique; *s.m.pl.* the ancients.

antigovernamental, *adj.* antigovernmental.

antigualha, *s.f.* old thing.

antiguidade, *s.f.* antiquity *(época),* ancientness *(qualidade),* seniority *(deposto),* antiques *(peças antigas).*

anti-hemorrágico, *adj.* antihaemorragic.

anti-higiénico, *adj.* anti-hygienic.

antiliberal, *adj.* antiliberal.

antilogaritmo, *s.m.* antilogarithm.

antilogia, *s.f.* antilogy.

antílope, *s.m.* antelope.

antimilitarismo, *s.m.* antimilitarism.

antimilitarista, *s.m.* antimilitarist.

antimonacal, *adj.* antimonacal.

antimonárquico, *adj.* antimonarchical.

antimoniato, *s.m.* antimoniate.

antimónico, *adj.* antimonic.

antimónia, *s.m.* antimony.

antinacional, *adj.* antinational.

antinomia, *s.f.* antinomy.

antinómico, *adj.* antinomian.

antipapa, *s.m.* antipope.

antiparlamentar, *adj.* antiparliamentary.

antipatia, *s.f.* antipathy, dislike.

antipático, *adj.* antipathetic, disagreeable, uncongenial.

antipatizar, *v.t.* to antipathize, to dislike, to feel antipathy for.

antipatriota, *s.m.* e *s.f.* antipatriot.

antipatriótico, *adj.* antipatriotic, unpatriotic.

antipatriotismo, *s.m.* antipatriotism.

antipedagógico, *adj.* antipedagogical.

antipestilencial, *adj.* antipestilential.

antipirina, *s.f.* antipyrine.

antípoda, *s.m.* e *s.f.* antipode.

antipolítico, *adj.* antipolitical.

antiquado, *adj.* antiquated, obsolete, old-fashioned.

antiquar, *v.t.* to antiquate, to make old.

antiquário, *s.m.* antiquary.

antiquíssimo, *adj.* most ancient.

anti-religioso, *adj.* e *s.m.* antireligious.

anti-semita, *adj.* e *s.m.* e *s.f.* anti-Semite, anti-Semitic.

anti-semitismo, *s.m.* antisemitism.

anti-séptico, *adj.* e *s.m.* antiseptic.

anti-sifilítico, *adj.* antisyphilitic.

antissocial, *adj.* antissocial.

antispasmódico, *adj.* antispasmodic.

antiste, *s.m.* pontiff, prelate.

antístrofe, *s.f.* antistropbe.

antítese, *s.f.* antithesis; opposition.

antitóxico, *adj.* e *s.m.* antitoxic.

antivariólico, *adj.* antivariolar.

antófago, *adj.* flower eating.

antografia, *s.f.* description of flowers.

antojar, *v.t.* to place before the eyes, to picture *(em imaginação); v.r.* to fancy, to desire.

antojo, *s.m.* earger desire, longing, whim *(capricho).*

antolhos, *s.m.pl.* blinders, blinkers.

antologia, *s.f.* anthology.

antológico, *adj.* anthological.

antologista, *s.m.* e *s.f.* anthologist.

antomania, *s.f.* antomania.

antomaníaco, *adj.* e *s.m.* anthomaniac.

antonímia, *s.f.* antonymy.

antónimo, *s.m.* antonym.

antonomásia, *s.f.* antonomasia.

antonomástico, *adj.* antonomastic.

antracífero, *adj.* anthracitous.

antracite, *s.f.* anthracite, stone-coal.

antraz, *s.m.* anthrax, carbuncle.

antro, *s.m.* cave, den *(de fera, de ladrões, etc.),* sink *(de vício).*

antropofagia, *s.f.* anthropophagy, canibalism.

antropófago, *adj.* anthropophagous, canibal; *s.m.* anthropophagist, a anthropophagos, canibal.

antropóide, *adj.* e *s.m.* anthropoid.

antropologia, *s.f.* anthropology.

antropologista, antropofágo, *s.m.* antropologist.

antropometria, *s.f.* anthropometry.

antropométrico, *adj.* anthropometric.

antropomórfico, *adj.* anthropomorphic.

antropomorfismo, *s.m.* anthropomorphism.

antropomorfo, *adj.* anthropomorphous.

anual, *adj.* yearly, annual.

anualidade, *s.f.* annulity.

anualmente, *adv.* annualy, yearly.

anuário, *s.m.* annual, year-book.

anuência, *s.f.* assent, acquiescence, agreement, consent.

anuente, *s.m.* assentor.

anuidade, *s.f.* annuity.

anuir, *v.i.* to accede, to aquiesce, to assent, to agree.

anulação, *s.f.* annulment, cancellation.

anulado, *adj.* annuled, cancelled.

anulador, *s.m.* annuller.

anular, *v.t.* to annul, to cancel, to rescind.

anulatório, *adj.* annuling.

anulável, *adj.* annullable, revokable.

anunciação, *s.f.* annunciation.

anunciada, *s.f.* annunciation.

anunciador, *s.m.* announcer.

anunciante, *s.m.* e *s.f.* advertiser; *adj.* announcing, advertising.

anunciar, *v.t.* to advertise, to announce, to annunciate, to proclaim.

anúncio, *s.m.* advertisement, announcement, notice, proclamation.

ânuo, *adj.* annual.

ânus, *s.m.* anus.

anuviar, *v.t.* to cloud; *v.r.* to become cloudy.

anverso, *s.m.* observe.

anzol, *s.m.* hook, fish-hook.

ao, *contr.* da *prep.* "a" e do artigo "o"; to, the, at, etc. V."a".

aonde, *adv.* where.

aoristo, *s.m.* aorist.

aorta, *s.f.* aorta.

aórtico, *adj.* aortic, aortal.

apache, *s.m.* apache.

apadrinhar, *v.t.* to act as a godfather, to sponsor *(patrocinar),* to protect.

apagado, *adj.* out, switched off, rubbed off, erased *(com borracha),* extinguished, faded *(a cor),* obscure *(pessoa apagada).*

apagador, *s.m.* eraser.

apagar, *v.t.* to extinguish, to put out *(a luz)* to switch off, to erase, to fade, to pass away *(morrer).*

apainelado, *adj.* panel-like.

apainelar, *v.t.* to panel.

apaixonado, *adj.* in love, passionate, enthusiastic, ardent, infatuated; *s.m.* lover.

apaixonar, *v.r.* to fall in love; *v.t.* to impassion.

apalaçado, *adj.* palace-like.

apalaçar, *v.t.* to give the aspect of a palace.

apaladado, *adj.* tasty.

apalavrado, *adj.* settled, agreed.

apalavrar, *v.t.* to agree upon.

apalermado, *adj.* silly, foolish.

apalhaçado, *adj.* clownish.

apalpação, *s.f.* touching, feeling.

apalpadeira, *s.f.* woman searcher.

apalpadela, *s.f.* touching; *às apalpadelas:* gropingly.

apalpar, *v.t.* to touch, to feel, to grope for, to probe *(sondar).*

apanágio, *s.m.* apanage, peculiarity.

apanha, *s.f.* gathering, harvest, crop.

apanhado, *adj.* caught, collected, taken; *s.m.* summary.

apanhar, *v.t.* to catch, to gather, to pick *(colher),* to take up *(levantar do chão); v.i.* to be beaten *(apanhar pancada).*

apaniguado, *s.m.* follower, dependant.

apaniguar, *v.t.* to protect, to patronise.

apaparicar, *v.t.* to coddle, to fondle.

a par, *loc. adv.* side by side, parallely, in paralel; *loc. prep.* near.

apara, *s.f.* chip, scrap, fragment; *pl.* parings, fillings *(limalha).*

aparador, *s.m.* sideboard, buffet.

aparafusar, *v.t.* to screw.

apara-lápis, *s.m.* pencil-sharpener.

aparar, *v.t.* to pare, to cut, to trim *(cortar),* to sharpen *(aguçar),* to parry *(aparar um golpe).*

aparatar, *v.t.* to bedeck with pomp.

aparato, *s.m.* pomp, ostentation, display.

aparatoso, *adj.* pompous, showy, sumptuous.

aparceirar, *v.t.* to enter into a partnership, to become a partner.

aparcelar, *v.t.* to parcel out, to divide into parcels.

aparecer, *v.i.* to appear, to emerge, to come out, to arise, to turn out.

aparecimento, *s.m.* appearing, appearance.

aparelhado, *adj.* ready, harnessed *(um cavalo).*

aparelhador, *s.m.* work-master, preparer.

aparelhagem, *s.f.* equipment.

aparelhamento, *s.m.* equipping.

aparelhar, *v.t.* to prepare, to equip, to harness *(um cavalo).*

aparelho, *s.m.* device, instrument, contrivance, gear, set *(de porcelana).*

aparência, *s.f.* appearance, aspect, look.

aparentado, *adj.* related.

aparentar, *v.t.* e *v.r.* to to pretend, to simulate, to seem *(parecer).*

aparente, *adj.* apparent, similar, seeming.

aparentemente, *adv.* apparently, seemingly.

aparição, *s.f.* apparition.

aparo, *s.m.* nib.

aparta, *s.f.* separation, division.

apartado, *adj.* separated, retired, different.

apartamento, *s.m.* separation, seclusion, flat or apartement *(casa)*.

apartar, *v.t.* to separate, to remove, to set apart, to part *(separar adversários); v.r.* to get away, to withdraw from.

à parte, *loc. adv.* apart, aside, separately.

aparte, *s.m.* an aside, side remark.

aparvalhado, *adj.* foolish, idiot, silly.

aparvalhar, *v.t.* to confound, to puzzle, to make silly.

apascentador, *s.m.* herder, herdsman, shepherd.

apascentamento, *s.m.* the act of feeding the cattle.

apascentar, to feed the cattle, to pasture, to lead to pasture, to herd.

apassamanar, *v.t.* to embroider with lace-work, to lace.

apassivação, *s.f.* the act of putting in the passive voice.

apassivar, *v.t.* to put into the passive form.

apatetado, *adj.* silly, foolish, crack-brained.

apatetar, to make silly, to puzzle.

apatia, *s.f.* apathy.

apático, *adj.* apathetic, nonchalant.

apavonar, *v.t.* to trim, to adorn; *apavonar-se,* to falunt oneself, to grow proud.

apavorar, *v.t.* to terrify, to frighten.

apaziguador, *s.m.* pacifier.

apaziguamento, *s.m.* pacification, pacifying.

apaziguar, *v.t.* to pacify, to appease, to quiet, to calm.

apeadeiro, *s.m.* wayside-station, halt.

apear, *v.t.* to dismount; apear-se: to alight, to come off a horse, a bus, etc.

apedrejamento, *s.m.* stoning.

apedrejar, *v.t.* to stone, to throw stones at.

apegadamente, *adv.* affectionately, devotedly.

apegadiço, *adj.* sticky, viscous, importunate.

apegado, *adj.* attached, joined, fastened to, devoted *(afeiçoado).*

apegar, *v.t.* e *v.r.* to attach, to adhere, to sitck to, to become attached to, to grow fond of *(afeiçoar-se).*

apego, *s.m.* attachment, dedication, devotion, affection, fondness.

apelação, *s.f.* appeal.

apelante, *s.m.* appealer.

apelar, *v.t.* to appeal, to have recourse to *(recorrer).*

apelativo, *adj.* common *(gram.); s.m.* appelative.

apelidação, *s.f.* naming.

apelidar, *v.t.* to surname, to nickname *(alcunhar).*

apelido, *s.m.* surname; *apelido de solteira,* maiden name.

apelo, *s.m.* appeal, call.

apenas, *adv.* just, hardly, only, merely; *conj.* as soon as.

apêndice, *s.m.* appendix, addition, supplement.

apendicite, *s.f.* appendicitis.

apendiculado, *adj.* appendiculate.

apendicular, *v.t.* to apendiculate.

apensar, *v.t.* to append, to annex.

apenso, *adj.* appended, annexed; *s.m.* appended document.

apepinar, *v.t.* to laugh at *(troçar).*

apepsia, *s.f.* apepsy.

apequenar, *v.t.* to make smaller.

aperaltado, *adj.* well dressed, spruce, neat.

aperaltar, *v.t.* to dress smartly, to spruce up.

aperceber, *v.t.* to perceive, to notice, to provide *(prover);* to to become aware.

apercebimento, *s.m.* preparation, equipment.

apercepção, *s.f.* apperception.

aperfeiçoado, *adj.* perfected, improved, bettered.

aperfeiçoador, *s.m.* improver, perfecter.

aperfeiçoamento, *s.m.* improvement.

aperfeiçoar, *v.t.* to improve, to perfect, to better; *aperfeiçoar-se,* to grow better, to improve.

aperitivo, *s.m.* apéritif, appetiser

aperolado, *adj.* pearled, pearly.

aperrar, *v.t.* to cock fire-arms.

aperreação, *s.f.* harassment, teasing, vexation.

aperreadamente, *adv.* under restraint, vexingly.

aperreador, *s.m.* teaser, vexer.

aperreamento, *s.m.* o mesmo que "aperreação".

aperrear, *v.t.* to harass, to vex, to tease, to put under restraint.

apertado, *adj.* narrow, tight *(justo),* strict *(rigoroso),* pressed for money *(em dificuldades financeiras).*

apertão, *s.m.* squeeze, oppression.

apertar, *v.t.* to squeeze, to compress, to clasp, to grip *(segurar com força),* to tighten *(ajustar),* to crowd *(multidão),* to restrict *(restringir),* to shake hands *(apertar a mão),* to press *(pressionar alguém).*

aperto, *s.m.* pressure, squeeze, tightness, trouble, danger *(perigo, dificuldades),* pressure, urgency *(urgência).*

apesar de, *loc. prep.* despite, in spite of, notwithstanding; *apesar disso,* neverthless, for all that.

apessoado, *adj.* having a good stature judicious, wise.

apétalo, *adj.* apetalous.

apetecedor, *adj.* appetising.

apetecer, *v.t.* to wish for, to feel an appetite for, to desire; *v.i.* to tempt the appetite. 1) *apetece-me uma laranja,* I should like to have an orange. 2) *apetece-me sair,* I feel like going out. 3) *quando bem lhe apetece,* whenever he pleases.

apetecível, *adj.* desirable, appetising, tempting.

apetência, *s.f.* appetence, appetite.

apetite, *s.m.* appetite.

apetitoso, *adj.* appetising, tasty.

apetrechar, *v.t.* to equip, to fit out.

apetrechos, *s.m. pl.* equipment, outfit, tools *(ferramentas),* implements.

apiário, *s.m.* apiary; *adj.* apiarian, apian.

apical, *adj.* apical, terminal.

ápice, *s.m.* apex, top, summit; *num ápice,* in an instant.

apícola, *s.m.* bee-keeper; *adj.* apicultural.

apiculado, *adj.* pointed.

apicultor, *s.m.* apiculturist, bee-keeper.

apicultura, *s.f.* apiculture, bee-keeping.

apiedado, *adj.* pitying, moved to pity.

apiedar-se, *v.r.* to pity, to feel sorry for.

apimentado, *adj.* peppered, peppery, malicious.

apimentar, *v.t.* to pepper, to spice.

apinhado, *adj.* full, crowded, heaped up.

apinhar, *v.t.* to crowd, to heap up, to over-crowd; *apinhar-se,* to crowd together, to swarm.

apitar, *v.t.* to whistle, to blow the whistle.

apito, *s.m.* whistle, pipe.

aplacação, *s.f.* appeasement.

aplacar, *v.t.* to appease, to calm.

aplacável, *adj.* appeasable, placable.

aplainado, *adj.* smoothed, planed.

aplainar, *v.t.* to plane, to smooth, to make even.

aplanar, *v.t.* to level.

aplaudir, *v.t.* to applaud, to cheer, to acclaim.

aplausível, *adj.* praisewothy, plausible.

aplauso, *s.m.* applause, cheer, acclamation.

aplicação, *s.f.* application, enforcement *(da lei).*

aplicar, *v.t.* to apply, to use, to employ, to enforce *(uma lei),* to inflict *(multas);* aplicar-se: to apply oneself to *(a uma tarefa).*

aplicável, *adj.* appliable, applicable, suitable, adjustable.

Apocalipse, *s.m.* Apocalipse.

apocalíptico, *adj.* apocalyptical.

apócope, *s.f.* apocope.

apócrifo, *adj.* aprocryphal, fabulous.

apodador, *s.m.* jester.

apodar, *v.t.* to jest, to mock.

ápode, *s.m.* apod; *adj.* apodal, apodous.

apodengado, *adj.* like a basset.

apoderar-se, *v.r.* to seize, to take possession of, to lay hold of.

apodia, *s.f.* absence of feet.

apodíctico, *adj.* apodictical.

apodo, *s.m.* nickname, mockery, taunt *(zombaria).*

apodrecer, *v.t. e v.i.* to rot, to decompose, to putrify, to decay.

apodrecido, *adj.* rotten, putrefied.

apodrecimento, *s.m.* rotteness, putre-faction, decay.

apófise, *s.f.* aphphysis.

apogeu, *s.m.* apogee, peak, culmination.

apógrafo, *s.m.* apograph, copy.

apoiado, *interj.* bravo! hear, hear! well said!; *adj.* leaning (against), based (upon).

apoiar, *v.t.* to support, to second, to back; *apoiar-se,* to lean on, to rest, to base oneself *(basear-se).*

apoio, *s.m.* support, prop, basis, approval, backing; *apoio para os pés,* foothold.

apólice, *s.m.* policy.

apolítico, *adj.* nonpolitical.

apologética, *s.f.* apologetics.

apologético, *adj.* apologetic.

apologia, *s.f.* apology, apologia, defense.

apologista, *s.m. e s.f.* apologist, defender.

apólogo, *s.m.* apologue, fable.

apontado, *adj.* pointed, observed, aimed at.

apontador, *s.m.* marker, timekeeper *(de trabalhadores),* gun pointer *(de canhão).*

apontamento, *s.m.* note, remark, anno-tation.

apontar, *v.t.* to aim, to point, to point out, to indicate, to note.

apontoar, *v.t.* to prop *(no teatro)* to support.

apopléctico, *adj.* apopletic.

apoplexia, s.f. apoplexy.

apoquentação, s.f. worry, bother, affliction, vexation.

apoquentado, adj. worried, distressed, vexed.

apoquentar, v.t. to vex, to tease, to trouble, to afflict, to worry.

apor, v.t. to set, to apply, to add, to append.

aportamento, s.m. arrival at a port.

aportar, v.t. to arrive at a port, to anchor.

aportilhar, v.t. to make a breach in a rampart, to open loop-holes in a wall.

aportuguesar, v.t. to make portuguese; aportuguesar-se, to behave like a Portuguese.

após, prep. after; adv. afterwards.

aposentação, s.f. retirement (reforma), lodging (hospedagem).

aposentado, adj. retired; s.m. retired, pensioner.

aposentadoria, s.f. o mesmo que "aposentação".

aposentar, v.t. to lodge (hospedar), to retire.

aposento, s.m. dwelling, room.

aposição, s.f. apposition, juxtaposition, application of the seal.

apossar-se, v.r. to take possession of, to seize, to appropriate.

aposta, s.f. bet, wager.

apostadamente, adv. on purpose.

apostado, adj. determined.

apostador, s.m. bettor.

apostar, v.t. to bet, to wager.

apostasia, s.f. apostasy.

apóstata, s.m. e s.f. apostate, renegade, apostatic.

apostatar, v.i. to apostatize, to abjure, to turn one's coat.

apostema, s.m. abscess.

apostemar, v.t. to form an abscess.

apostila, s.f. apostil, annotation, comment.

apostilar, v.t. to apostil, to comment, to annotate.

aposto, s.m. noun or sentence in apposition; adj. added, appended, affixed.

apostolado, s.m. apostolate.

apostolar, v.t. e v.i. to preach, to evangelize.

apostolicamente, adv. apostolically.

apostolicidade, s.f. apostolicity.

apostólico, adj. apostolical, apostolic.

apostrofar, v.t. to apostrophize, to upbraid.

apóstrofe, s.f. apostrophe, invective.

apóstrofo, s.m. apostrophe.

apotegma, s.m. apothegm.

apótema, s.m. apothem; (quim.) precipitate.

apoteose, s.f. apotheosis, glorification.

apoteótico, adj. apotheotic.

apoucadamente, adv. poorly, meanly.

apoucado, adj. scanty (escasso), timid, feeble-minded (imbecil), mean, narrowminded (mesquinho).

apoucamento, s.m. meanness, timidity, narrow-mindedness, cowardice.

apoucar, v.t. to lessen, to minimize, to discourage, to lower oneself (subestimar-se).

aprazamento, s.m. appointment, summons.

aprazar, v.t. to appoint, to summon, to fix a date.

aprazer, v.t. to please.

aprazibilidade, s.f. affableness, agreeableness.

aprazimento, s.m. pleasure, satisfaction, approbation, consent.

aprazível, adj. agreeable, pleasant.

aprazivelmente, adv. agreeably, pleasantly.

apre!, interj. by jove! good gracious!

apreçador, s.m. inquirer of prices, appraiser.

apreçar, v.t. to price, to appraise, to estimate.

apreciação, s.f. appreciation, value, estimation, valuation.

apreciador, s.m. appreciator, appraiser.

apreciar, v.t. to appreciate, to estimate, to evaluate (avaliar), to like, to enjoy (gostar de).

apreciativo, adj. appreciative.

apreciável, adj. appreciable, estimable.

apreço, s.m. esteem, consideration, regard; a pessoa em apreço, the person in question.

apreender, v.t. to apprehend, to understand, to perceive.

apreensão, s.f. apprehension.

apreensível, adj. apprehensible.

apreensivo, adj. aprehensive, fearful, preoccupied.

apreensor, s.m. apprehender, seizer.

apregoador, s.m. crier, barker.

apregoar, v.t. to annouce, to cry, to advertise.

aprender, v.t. to learn.

aprendiz, s.m. apprentice.

aprendizagem, s.f. apprenticeship, learning.

apresamento, s.m. capture, seizure.

apresar, *v.t.* to seize, to capture.

apresentação, *s.f.* apresentation, introduction, deportment *(aparência).*

apresentador, *s.m.* presenter, introducer.

apresentante, *s.m.* bearer *(de uma letra de câmbio).*

apresentar, *v.t.* to introduce, to present, to offer *(desculpas, etc.),* to pay *(respeitos, etc.),* to lay *(uma petição),* to produce *(provas, etc.).*

apresentável, *adj.* presentable.

apresilhar, *v.t.* to put loops, to fasten with loops.

apressadamente, *adv.* hastly, in a hurry.

apressado, *adj.* hasty, speedy, hurried, in a hurry.

apressar, *v.t.* to hasten, to hurry, to accelerate, to quicken *(o passo);* **apressar-se,** to hasten, to make haste, to hurry. 1) *apressa-te!,* make haste! be quick!. 2) *não se apresse,* take your time!

apressurar, *v.t.* to hasten, to hurry.

aprestar, *v.t.* to prepare, to make ready, to equip.

apresto, *s.m.* preparation, equipment; *pl.* tools, implements.

aprimorar, *v.t.* to perfect, to improve.

aprisco, *s.m.* sheepfold, sheepcote, pen.

aprisionado, *adj.* imprisioned, captured, locked up.

aprisionamento, *s.m.* capture, imprisonment.

aprisionar, *v.t.* to imprison, to capture.

aprobativo, *adj.* approbative, approving.

aprofundamento, *s.m.* deepening.

aprofundar, *v.t.* to deepen.

aprontar, *v.t.* to prepare, to make ready, to finish; *aprontar-se,* to get ready, to prepare oneself, to dress *(vestir-se).*

apropinquação, *s.f.* approach, proximity.

apropinquar-se, *v.r.* to come near, to approach.

apropositado, *adj.* convenient, adequate, suitable, opportune.

a propósito, *loc. adv.* by the way, opportunely, to the purpose.

apropriação, *s.f.* appropriation, seizure.

apropriadamente, *adv.* adequately, suitably.

apropriado, *adj.* suitable, adequate, appropriate.

apropriar, *v.t.* to appropriate, to adapt, to suit; *v.r.* to appropriate, to misappropriate *(indevidamente).*

aprovação, *s.f.* approval, approbation.

aprovado, *adj.* approved, accepted.

aprovador, *s.m.* approver.

aprovar, *v.t.* to approve, to sanction, to pass *(em exame).*

aprovativo, *adj.* approbative, approving.

aprovável, *adj.* approvable.

aproveitador, *s.m.* utilizer, profiteer, oportunist.

aproveitamento, *s.m.* utilization, use, improvement.

aproveitar, *v.t.* to utilize, to profit, to benefit; *v.i.* to take advantage of, to profit by.

aproveitável, *adj.* profitable, useful.

aprovisionamento, *s.m.* supply, provisioning.

aprovisionar, *v.t.* to provide, to stock, to supply with.

aproximação, *s.f.* approach, aproximation *(cálculo).*

aproximadamente, *adv.* approximately, about, roughly.

aproximar, *v.t.* to approach, to bring near; *aproximar-se,* to approach, to come near or close.

aproximativo, *adj.* approximative, approximate.

aprumado, *adj.* upright, vertical, neatly dressed *(bem vestido).*

aprumar, *v.t.* to set upright; *aprumar-se,* to stand up, to spruce oneself up.

aprumo, *s.m.* uprightness, haughtiness *(altivez).*

ápside, *s.f. (arq.)* apse, vault; *(astr.)* apsis.

áptero, *adj.* wingless.

aptidão, *s.f.* aptitute, aptness, ability, fitness.

apto, *adj.* apt, fit, capable, able.

apuado, *adj.* pierced all over.

apunhalar, *v.t.* to stab.

apupada, *s.f.* hiss, shout.

apupar, *v.t.* to hiss, to boo.

apupo, *s.m.* hoot, jeer, boo.

apurado, *adj.* refined, select, rich *(comida).*

apuramento, *s.m.* inquiry, refinement, settlement *(de contas).*

apurar, *v.t.* to purify, to refine, to select *(escolher),* to find out, to investigate *(verificar),* to settle *(contas),* to thicken *(um molho).*

apuro, *s.m.* purifying, refiment; *pl.* trouble.

apurpurado, *adj.* purplish, purple.

aquadrilhar, *v.t.* to form bands, to gather in bands.

aquando, *adv.* when.

aquário, *s.m.* aquarium.

aquartelamento, *s.m.* quartering of troops, quarters, lodging.

aquartelar, *v.t.* to quarter or to lodge troops; *aquartelar-se,* to take quarters.

aquático, *adj.* aquatic.

aquatinta, *s.f.* aquatint.

aquecedor, *s.m.* heater.

aquecer, *v.t.* to warm, to heat; *v.i.* to get warm or hot; *aquecer-se,* to warm oneself.

aquecimento, *s.m.* heating.

aqueduto, *s.m.* aqueduct.

aquela, aquele, *adj.* e *pron.* that; *pl.* those; that one, *pl.* those ones.

àquela, àquele, to that, to that one.

aqueloutro, *comb.* do *adj.* ou *pron. demonst.* aquele com o *adj.* ou pron. indef. *outro,* the other one, that other.

aquém, *adv.* on this side.

aquentar, *v.t.* to warm, to heat.

aqui, *adv.* here, here in, in this place. 1) *aqui dentro,* in here. 2) *aqui em baixo,* down here. 3) *aqui por perto,* hereabout. 4) *por aqui,* this way.

aquiescência, *s.f.* acquiescence, assent.

aquiescente, *adj.* acquiescent.

aquiscer, *v.i.* to acquiesce, to accede, to assent, to agree.

aquietação, *s.f.* appeasing, pacification, calm, tranquility.

aquietar, *v.t.* to quiet, to calm, to appease; *aquietar-se,* to get quiet.

aquilão, *s.m.* the north wind.

aquilatador, *s.m.* assayer, appraiser.

aquilatar, *v.t.* to assay *(metais),* to value, to appraise, to find out, to weigh *(factos).*

aquilino, *adj.* aquiline.

aquilo, *pron. dem.* that, that thing; *aquilo que,* what, that wich.

aquinhoamento, *s.m.* division.

aquinhoar, *v.t.* to divide, to share.

aquisição, *s.f.* acquisition, acquirement.

aquosidade, *s.f.* aqueousness, wateriness.

aquoso, *adj.* aqueous, watery.

ar, *s.m.* air, atmosphere; breeze *(aragem);* air, look, aspect *(aparência),* manner (modos). 1) *ao ar livre,* outdoors, in the open air. 2) *ar condicionado,* air conditioning. 3) *ar de família,* family likeness. 4) *dar ares,* to resemble. 5) *dar-se ares,* to put on airs.

ara, *s.f.* an altar stone.

árabe, *s.m.* e *adj.* Arab, Arabian.

arabesco, *s.m.* arabesque.

arábico, *adj.* arabic.

arabismo, *s.m.* arabic idiom or locution.

arabista, *s.m.* arabist, a student of Arabic.

aracnídeos, *s.m.pl.* arachnida.

aracnóide, *s.f.* e *adj.* arachnoid.

arada, *s.f.* ploughing, ploughed ground.

arado, *s.m.* plough.

aragem, *s.f.* breeze, a gentle gale.

aragonês, *s.m.* e *adj.* Aragonese.

aralha, *s.f.* a two year old calf, the stalk of garlic.

Aramaico, *s.m.* Aramaic.

arame, *s.m.* wire; *arame farpado,* barbed wire.

arandela, *s.f.* candle-guard.

araneiforme, *adj.* araneiform, spider-like.

aranha, *s.f.* spider.

aranhão, *s.m.* large spider.

aranhiço, *s.m.* field-spider.

aranhol, *s.m.* a spider's hole.

aranzel, *s.m.* long-winded speech; rigmarole, fustain.

arão, *s.m. (bot.)* arum.

arar, *v.t.* to plough.

arara, *s.f.* macaw.

araruta, *s.f.* arrowroot.

aratório, *adj.* relating to husbandry.

araucária, *s.f.* araucaria.

arauto, *s.m.* herald.

arável, *adj.* arable, good for phloughing.

aravela, *s.f.* plough-handle.

aravia, *s.f.* jargon, slang, confused talk.

arbitragem, *s.f.* arbitrage, arbitration.

arbitral, *adj.* arbitral.

arbitramento, *s.m.* arbitration, arbitrage.

arbitrar, *v.t.* to arbitrate, to judge as arbiter, to referee *(no futebol).*

arbitrariamente, *adv.* arbitrarily.

arbitrariedade, *s.f.* arbltrariness, despotism, wilfulness *(capricho),* offense *(abuso).*

arbitrário, *adj.* arbitrard, despotic, wilful.

arbítrio, *s.m.* freedom of choice, will. 1) *livre arbítrio,* free will. 2) *ao arbítrio de,* at the will of.

árbitro, *s.m.* arbitrator, arbiter, judge, referee *(de futebol).*

arbóreo, *adj.* arboreous, arborescent, arboreal.

arborescência, *s.f.* arborescence.

arborescente, *adj.* arborescent.

arborícola, *adj.* arboreal.

arboricultor, *s.m.* arboriculturist.

arboricultura, *s.f.* arboriculture.

arborização, *s.f.* arborization.

arborizado, *adj.* tree-planted, wooded.

arborizar, *v.t.* to wood, to plant with trees.

arbustiforme, *adj.* shrub-like.

arbustivo, *adj.* shrubby.

arbusto, *s.m.* shrub.

arca, *s.f.* chest, coffer, ark. 1) *a arca de Noé,* Noah's Ark. 2) *arca de peito,* thorax.

arcaboiço, *s.m.* skeleton, chest *(tórax),* framework *(armação).*

arcabuz, *s.m.* arquebus.

arcabuzar, *v.t.* to shoot with an arquebus.

arcabuzeiro, *s.m.* arquebusier.

arcada, *s.f.* arcade, arch.

árcade, *s.m.* Arcadian.

arcádico, *adj.* arcadic.

arcado, *adj.* arched.

arcaico, *adj.* archaic, ancient.

arcaísmo, *s.m.* archaism.

arcanjo, *s.m.* archangel.

arcano, *s.m.* arcanum, secret, mystery; *adj.* secret, misterious.

arcão, *s.m.* saddle-bow.

arcar, *v.t.* to arch, to bow; *arcar com,* to shoulder, to bear the burden, to take.

arcaria, *s.f.* arcade.

arcaz, *s.m.* a big chest.

arcebispado, *s.m.* archbishopric.

arcebispal, *adj.* archiespiscopal.

arcebispo, *s.m.* archbishop.

arcediagado, *s.m.* archdeaconry.

arcediago, *s.m.* archdeacon.

archa, *s.f.* halberd.

archeiro, *s.m.* halberdier.

archote, *s.m.* torch.

arciforme, *adj.* arciform.

arcipreste, *s.m.* archpriest.

arco, *s.m.* arc *(geom.),* arch *(arq.),* bow *(de flechas, violino, etc.),* hoop *(brinquedo).*

arcobotante, *s.m.* arch, butress.

arco-íris, *s.m.* rainbow.

árctico, *adj.* arctic.

ardência, *s.f.* ardency, ardour.

ardente, *adj.* ardent, burning, glowing.

ardentemente, *adv.* ardentely, passionately.

arder, *v.i.* to burn, to be on fire, to glow, to flame.

ardido, *adj.* burnt, fermented *(fermentado).*

ardil, *s.m.* stratagem, artifice, ruse.

ardiloso, *adj.* cunning, artful, tricky.

ardimento, *s.m.* o mesmo que "ardência".

ardina, *s.m.* a seller of newspapers.

ardor, *s.m.* ardour, ardency, fervency, heat.

ardósia, *s.f.* slate.

árduo, *adj.* arduous, hard, difficult.

are, *s.m. are,* a hundred square meters.

área, *s.f.* area, zone, surface.

areado, *adj.* sandy, scoured with sand, clean.

areal, *s.m.* sandy ground or beach, sands.

arear, *v.t.* to scour with sand, to refine *(açúcar).*

areeiro, *s.m.* sand-box, sand-pit.

areento, *adj.* sandy.

areia, *s.f.* sand; *areia movediça,* quick sand.

arejado, *adj.* airy, aired.

arejamento, *s.m.* airing, ventilation.

arejar, *v.t.* to air, to ventilate, to expose to the air, to take the air, to go for an airing *(espairecer).*

arejo, *s.m.* airing, ventilation.

arena, *s.f.* arena, ring *(de circo).*

arenáceo, *adj.* arenaceous, sandy.

arenga, *s.f.* harangue, declamation, tirade.

arengador, *s.m.* haranguer.

arengar, *v.t.* to harangue, to make sumptuous speeches, to quarrel *(discutir).*

arengueiro, *s.m.* haranguer, quarreler.

arenícola, *s.m. e s.f. (zool.)* lug-worm; *adj.* arenicolous.

areniforme, *adj.* sand-shaped.

arenito, *s.m.* sandstone.

arenoso, *adj.* sandy.

arenque, *s.m.* herring.

aréola, *s.f.* areola.

areolado, *adj.* areolate.

areometria, *s.f.* areometrics.

areómetro, *s.m.* araeometer.

areopagita, *s.m.* areopagite.

areópago, *s.m.* areopagus, the court.

aresta, *s.f.* edge, corner, ridge, awn *(de espiga),* groin *(de abóbada),* tack *(prego sem cabeça).*

aresto, *s.m.* judgement, decision, sentence.

arfada, *s.f. (náut.)* pitching, palpitation, throbbing.

arfar, *v.i.* to pant, to gasp for breath, to throb; *(náut.)* to pitch.

argamassa, *s.f.* mortar.

argamassar, *v.t.* to join or plaster with mortar.

arganaz, *s.m.* vole, dormouse.

arganel, *s.m.* a small brass ring.

Argélia, *s.f.* Algeria.

argelino, *s.m. e adj.* Algerine, Algerian.

argentar, *v.t.* to silver, to whiten.

argentaria, *s.f.* plate, silver-plate, embroidery in silver.

argentário, *s.m.* a rich man; a cupboard for silver-plate.

argênteo, *adj.* silvery, argent.

argentífero, *adj.* argentiferous.

Argentina, *s.f.* Argentina; *(bot.)* silver-weed.

argentino, *s.m.* Argentine; *adj.* argentine, belonging to Argentina.

argila, *s.f.* argil, clay.

argiláceo, *adj.* argillaceous, clayey.

argileira, *s.f.* clay pit.

argiloso, *adj.* argillous, clayey.

argola, *s.f.* ring, hoop, ear-rings *(brincos)*, knocker *(argola de porta)*.

argolar, *v.t.* to fasten with rings or small hoops.

argoleiro, *s.m.* ring-maker.

argonauta, *s.m.* argonaut.

argúcia, *s.f.* subtlety, sagacity, acumen.

argucioso, *adj.* subtle, shrewd.

argueiro, *s.m.* mote, a particle of dust, trifle *(ninharia)*.

arguente, *s.m.* arguer, opponent, contender.

arguição, *s.f.* arguing, pleading, accusation.

arguidor, *s.m.* blamer, impugner.

arguir, *v.t.* to argue, to accuse, to discuss, to prove, to infer.

arguitivo, *adj.* demonstrative, argumentative, controversial, accusing.

argumentação, *s.f.* argumentation, controversy, discussion.

argumentador, *s.m.* arguer, reasoner, disputant.

argumentar, *v.t.* to argue, to dispute, to prove, to infer *(tirar conclusões)*, to allege, to plead *(argumentar com)*.

argumentativo, *adj.* argumentative, controversial.

argumento, *s.m.* argument, arguing, controversy, proof, plot or script *(de um filme, etc.)*.

arguto, *adj.* sharp, subtle, shrewd, keen.

ária, *s.f.* aria *(de ópera)*, melody, song.

arianismo, *s.m.* arianism.

ariano, *s.m.* arian.

aridez, *s.f.* dryness, aridity.

árido, *adj.* arid, dry, waterless, sterile.

Aries, *s.m. (astrol.)* Aries, Ram.

ariete, *s.m.* battering ram.

arisco, *adj.* shy, indocile, unsociable, wild.

aristarco, *s.m.* aristarch, a severe critic.

aristocracia, *s.f.* aristocracy.

aristocrata, *s.m. e s.f.* aristocrat.

aristocrático, *adj.* aristocratic.

aristocratizar, *v.t.* to aristocratize.

aristotélico, *adj.* aristotelian, relating to Aristotle.

aritmética, *s.f.* arithmetic.

aritmético, *adj.* arithmetical.

aritmo, *adj.* arythmous.

aritmómetro, *s.m.* arithmometer.

arlequim, *s.m.* harlequin.

arlequinada, *s.f.* harlequinade.

arma, *s.f.* arm, weapon; *armas de fogo*, firearms.

armação, *s.f.* framework, structure, bedstead *(armação de cama)*, antlers *(armações de veado)*.

armada, *s.f.* fleet; *a Armada*, the Navy.

armadilha, *s.f.* trap, snare.

armado, *adj.* armed; *à mão armada*, by the force of arms.

armador, *s.m.* ship-owner, outfitter *(de navios)*, undertaker *(cangalheiro)*.

armadura, *s.f.* armour, suit of arms.

armão, *s.m.* futchel.

armar, *v.t.* to arm, to set up *(armar uma armadilha)*, to mount, *(uma máquina)*, to equip, to rig *(um navio)*. 1) *armar alguém cavaleiro*, to dub someone a knight. 2) *armar-se*, to arm oneself with. 3) *armar-se de cora-gem*, to gather courage.

armaria, *s.f.* armoury, heraldry.

armário, *s.m.* cupboard, locker, chest.

armazém, *s.m.* warehouse, store.

armazenagem, *s.f.* warehousing, storage.

armazenar, *v.t.* to store, to stock.

armazenista, *s.m.* storekeeper, warehouseman.

armeiro, *s.m.* armourer, gunsmith; *(náut.)* armrack.

armela, *s.f.* small cramp, cramp-iron.

Arménia, *s.f.* Armenia.

arménio, *s.m. e adj.* Armenian.

armilar, *adj.* armillary.

arminho, *s.m.* ermine; title of nobility.

armistício, *s.m.* armistice.

armorial, *s.m. e adj.* armorial.

arnado, arneiro, *adj.* barren, sandy ground.

arnela, *s.f.* stump.

arnês, *s.m.* harness, armour.

arnica, *s.f. (bot.)* arnica, leopard's vane.

arnoso, *adj.* barren, sandy ground.

aro, *s.m.* ring, hoop, rim *(de óculos)*, tire *(de roda)*, frame *(de janela, etc.)*.

aroeira, *s.f.* lentisk.

aroma, *s.m.* aroma, perfume, scent, smell, flavour *(sabor)*.

aromático, *adj.* aromatic, fragrant.
aromatização, *s.f.* aromatization.
aromatizador, *adj.* aromatizing.
aromatizante, *adj.* aromatizing.
aromatizar, *v.t.* to aromatize, to perfume, to scent.
arpão, *s.m.* harpoon, spear.
arpar, *v.t.* to harpoon, to spear.
arpejar, *v.i.* (*mús.*) to arpeggiate, to play arpeggios.
arpejo, *s.m.* (*mús.*) arpeggio.
arpéu, *s.m.* grappling-iron, grapnel.
arpoação, *s.f.* harpooning.
arpoador, *s.m.* harpooner.
arpoar, *v.t.* to harpoon, to spear.
arqueação, *s.f.* arching, vaulting, gauging (*medição de capacidade*).
arqueado, *adj.* arched, vaulted, gauged.
arqueadura, *s.f.* incurvation, curvature, vault.
arquear, *v.t.* to arch, to give the form of an arch, to curve, to gauge.
arqueiro, *s.m.* hoop-maker (*o que faz arcos para pipas*), archer.
arquejante, *adj.* panting, gasping.
arquejar, *v.t.* to pant, to gasp.
arquejo, *s.m.* panting, gasping, quick-breathing.
arqueologia, *s.f.* archaeology.
arqueológico, *adj.* archaeologic.
arqueólogo, *s.m.* archaeologist.
arquétipo, *s.m.* archetype, model.
arquidiocese, *s.f.* archidiocese.
arquiducado, *s.m.* archduchy.
arquiducal, *adj.* archducal.
arquiduque, *s.m.* archduke.
arquiduquesa, *s.f.* archduchess.
arquiepiscopado, *s.m.* archiepiscopacy, archiepiscopate.
arquiepiscopal, *adj.* archiepiscopal.
arquipélago, *s.m.* archipelago, group of islands.
arquitectar, *v.t.* to plan, to draw plans, to imagine.
arquitecto, *s.m.* architect.
arquitectónica, *s.f.* architecture.
arquitectónico, *adj.* architectonic.
arquitectura, *s.f.* architecture.
arquitrave, *s.f.* architrave.
arquivar, *v.t.* to file, to record (*registar*).
arquivista, *s.m.* archivist, file clerck.
arquivo, *s.m.* archives, file, record, filer (*móvel*).
arquivolta, *s.f.* archivolt.

arrabalde, *s.m.* suburb, environs, neighbourhood.
arraçoar, *v.t.* to ration, to supply with rations.
arraia, *s.m.* ray, skate (*peixe*); frontier, border; *arraia-miúda*, populace, mob.
arraial, *s.m.* country festivity, camp (*acampamento*).
arraiano, *adj.* borderer.
arraigado, *adj.* rooted, inveterate.
arraigar, *v.t.* e *v.i.* to root, to gain roots, to fix deeply, to fix the root.
arrancada, *s.f.* pulling out.
arrancador, *s.m.* drawer.
arrancadura, *s.f.* plucking out, digging up.
arrancar, *v.t.* to pull out, to pluck off, to draw, to pull strogly; *v.i.* to rush out, to depart, to start.
arranchar, *v.t.* to mess; *v.r.* to mess together, to lodge oneself.
arranhadela, *s.f.* scratch, a slight wound.
arranhão, *s.m.* scratch.
arranhar, *v.t.* scratch, to scrape, to have a smattering of (*um assunto*).
arranjado, *adj.* tidy, arranged.
arranjar, *v.t.* to arrange, to set in order, to tidy up, to settle (*conciliar*), to find, to get (*obter*); *arranjar-se,* to take care of oneself, to manage.
arranjista, *s.m.* an active person.
arranjo, *s.m.* arrangement, ordering, good order.
arranque, *s.m.* starter (*de automóvel*).
arrás, *s.m.* arras.
arrasado, *adj.* destroyed, in ruins, exhausted, ruined.
arrasador, *s.m.* demolisher, destroyer; *adj.* ruining, shattering.
arrasar, *v.t.* to dismantle, to destroy, to demolish, to raz to the ground.
arrastado, *adj.* dragged, drawn, drawling (*voz*), carried (*levado*), slow (*lento*).
arrastamento, *s.m.* dragging, drag, drawling.
arrastão, *s.m.* tug, jerk, trawl (*rede*).
arrastar, *v.t.* to draw, to drag, to draggle, to carry, to drive (*forçar*). 1) *arrastar os pés,* to shuffle. 2) *arrastar os "rr",* to burr. 3) *arrastar-se,* to crawl, to creep, to drag on (*o tempo*).
arrasto, *s.m.* trawl (*rede*).
arrátel, *s.m.* pound weight.
arrazoado, *adj.* reasonable, moderate; *s.m.* plea, pleadings, defense.

arrazoamento, *s.m.* reasoning, argument, debate, answer.

arrazoar, *v.t. e v.i.* to plead, to argue, to defend, to upbraid, to discourse.

arre!, *interj.* gee!

arrear, *v.t.* to harness *(um cavalo)*, to adorn.

arreata, *s.f.* halter, hitching rope.

arreatar, *v.t.* to hitch.

arrebanhar, *v.t.* to gather *(o rebanho)*, to monopolize.

arrebatadamente, *adv.* impetuously, suddennly, passionately.

arrebatado, *adj.* rash, hasty, impetuous, hot-headed.

arrebatador, *adj.* ravishing, charming, delightful.

arrebatamento, *s.m.* snatching, frenzy, rapture, ravishment *(enlevo)*.

arrebatar, *v.t.* to snatch, to pull violently, to sweep off, to ravish, to delight *(enlevo)*; *deixar-se arrebatar pelas paixões,* to give over oneself to passions.

arrebentação, *s.f.* bursting *(explosão)*, breaking of the waves *(ondas)*.

arrebentamento, *s.m.* bursting.

arrebentar, *v.t.* to burst, to break.

arrebicado, *adj.* embellished, trimmed, affected *(afectado)*.

arrebicar, *v.t.* to embelish, to trim.

arrebique, *s.m.* paint, cosmetic; *pl.* frippery *(enfeites)*.

arrebitado, *adj.* turned up, snub *(nariz)*, ill-tempered *(mau génio)*.

arrebitar, *v.t.* turn up; *arrebitar-se,* to become haughty.

arrebol, *s.m.* red sky.

arrecadação, *s.f.* deposit, room, storehouse, collection *(de impostos)*.

arrecadado, *adj.* kept, locked up.

arrecadamento, *s.m.* keeping in a safe place.

arrecadar, *v.t.* to keep in a safe place, to deposit, to collect *(impostos)*.

arrecuas, *s.f.pl.* usa-se na *loc. adv.* às *arrecuas,* backward, towards the back.

arreda!, *interj.* get back!

arredamento, *s.m.* removing, removal, retirement.

arredar, *v.t.* to remove, to put aside, to withdraw, to get out of the way, to step aside *(afastar-se)*.

arredio, *adj.* strayed, lonesome, unsociable.

arredondamento, *s.m.* rounding.

arredondar, *v.t.* to round, to round off. *(uma conta)*.

arredores, *s.m.pl.* environs, outskirts, surroundings.

arrefecer, *v.t. e v.i.* to cool, to make cool, to get cold.

arrefecimento, *s.m.* cooling, refrigeration.

arregaçada, *s.f.* lapful.

arregaçar, *v.t.* to tuck up, *(as calças),* to roll up *(as mangas)*.

arregalar, *v.t.* to stare, to open one's eyes wide.

arreganhar, *v.t.* to grin *(os dentes),* to snarl *(como ameaça)*.

arreganho, *s.m.* grin, arrogance, daring *(intrepidez)*.

arregimentar, *v.t.* to enlist in a regiment, to regiment, to recruit.

arreigar, *v.t.* o mesmo que "arraigar".

arreio, *s.m.* harness, array, trappings.

arrelia, *s.f.* annoyance, worry, trouble, contrariety.

arreliado, *adj.* annoyed, teased.

arreliador, *s.m.* teaser; *adj.* teasing, annoying, troublesome.

arreliante, *adj.* annoying, teasing.

arreliar, *v.t.* to tease, to annoy, to trouble; *arreliar-se,* to get angry.

arrelvar, *v.t.* to sward.

arrematação, *s.f.* sale by auction.

arrematado, *adj.* bought at an auction.

arrematante, *s.m.* highest bidder.

arrematar, *v.t.* to buy or sell at an auction, to finish; *v.i.* to end.

arremate, *s.m.* knot, end, finishing touches.

arremedar, *v.t.* to ape, to mimic, to imitate.

arremedo, *s.f.* mimic, imitation, mimicry.

arremessão, *s.f.* impulse, pushing.

arremessar, *v.t.* to throw, to fling, to cast away, to toss; *arremessar-se,* to rush, to throw oneself into, to dash.

arremesso, *s.m.* throw, cast, throwing, fling, toss. 1) *aos arremessos,* in jerks. 2) *arremesso de dardo,* javelin throwing.

arremetedor, *s.m.* assailant, assaulter.

arremeter, *v.t. e v.i.* to assail, to attack, to dash at, to strike at.

arremetida, *s.f.* attack, onslaught, charge.

arrendado, *adj.* let out, leased out, lace-like *(lavores)*.

arrendador, *s.m.* hirer, renter, lessor.

arrendamento, *s.m.* renting, lease, rent.

arrendar, *v.t.* to let, to rent, to lease, to hire (to or from someone).

arrendatário, s.m. lesse, renter, tenant.

arrendável, adj. rentable.

arrenegação, s.f. apostasy, abjuration, denial.

arrenegado, adj. renegade, perjurious.

arrenegar, v.t. to abjure, to deny, to repudiate; v.i. to have an aversion to, to abhor, to dislike; arrenegar-se, to get angry.

arrenego, s.m. execration, abhorrence, anger, blasphemy.

arrepanhar, v.t. to crease, to wrinkle.

arrepelação, s.f. dishevelling, tugging.

arrepelar, v.t. to dishevel, to disorder, to ruffle the hair.

arrepender-se, v.r. to repent, to feel sorry for.

arrependido, adj. repentant, sorry, penitent.

arrependimento, s.m. repentance, sorrow, regret.

arrepiado, adj. creepy (pele), shivering (com frio), frightened (assustado).

arrepiar, v.t. to dishevel (cabelo), to horrify, to frighten; arrepiar-se, to shiver (sentir calafrios).

arrepio, s.m. shiver, chill; isto dá-me arrepios, this gives me the creeps.

arrestado, adj. distrained, arrested.

arrestar, v.t. to arrest, to distrain, to confiscate, to attach (jur.).

arresto, s.m. arrestation, arrest, seizure, attachment (jur.).

arrevesado, adj. reversed, obscure, intricate, difficult, crooked.

arrevesar, v.t. to make intricate, to complicate.

arriar, v.t. (náut.) to lower, to lower or to strike (bandeira); v.i. to give way (afrouxar), to give up (desistir).

arriba, s.f. cliff; adv. above, up, upwards; interj. up!

arribação, s.f. migration, arrival; aves de arribação, migratory birds.

arribada, s.f. landing, arrival; ir de arribada, to sail landward.

arribar, v.i. to arrive, to put into a port, to come to land.

arrieiro, s.m. muleteer.

arrimar, v.t. to prop, to uphold, to put aside, to protect.

arrimo, s.m. support, protection.

arriosca, s.f. trick, artifice, trap.

arriscado, adj. dangerous, risky, daring.

arriscar, v.t. to risk, to dare, to venture, to hazard. 1) arriscar a sorte, to try one's luck. 2) arriscar-se, to run a risk, to venture oneself.

arritmia, s.f. arrhythmia.

arroba, s.f. arroba; equivalent to 25 or 32 pounds.

arrochada, s.f. blow with a cudgel.

arrocho, s.m. tightener, tourniquet, cudgel.

arrogância, s.f. arrogance.

arrogante, adj. arrogant, haughty, supercilious.

arrogar, v.t. to arrogate, to claim unduly as one's own, to lay claim to something; arrogar-se, to arrogate to oneself, to claim unduly.

arroio, s.m. brook, creek, stream.

arrojadamente, adv. audaciously, boldly, daringly.

arrojado, adj. bold, daring, interpid.

arrojar, v.t. to fling, to cast, to throw, to drag (arrastar); arrojar-se, to throw oneself, to dash, to dare to do something (ousar).

arrojo, s.m. boldness, courage, audacity, intrepidity; arrojos do mar, jetsam.

arrolador, s.m. enroller.

arrolamento, s.m. enrolment, enlistment, inventory.

arrolar, v.t. to enrol, to enlist, to inventory, to roll up, to lull to sleep (embalar).

arrolhar, v.t. to cork.

arromba, s.f. de arromba, grand, swell, wonderful.

arrombado, adj. broken into, smashed.

arrombador, s.m. housebreaker, burglar, safebreaker (de cofres).

arrombamento, s.m. breaking open, forcing open, forcible entry, housebreaking, burglary (roubo com arrombamento).

arrombar, v.t. to force open, to brack open, to break into (uma casa).

arrostar, v.t. to defy, to provoke, to face; arrostar com, to cope with.

arrotar, v.i. to belch, to boast about (alardear).

arroteamento, s.m. clearing up.

arrotear, v.t. to clear a piece of ground, (náut.) to woold.

arroteia, s.f. a land newly cleared up.

arroto, s.m. belch.

arroubamento, arroubo, s.m. ecstasy, rapture, transport, ravishment.

arroubar, v.t. to ravish, to enrapture, to entrance.

arroxeado, arroxado, *adj.* violaceous.

arroz, *s.m.* rice; *arroz doce,* rice-pudding.

arrozal, *s.m.* rice-plantation, rice-field.

arruaça, *s.f.* tumult, riot, uproar.

arruaçar, *v.t.* to riot in the streets.

arruaceiro, *s.m.* rioter, hooligan.

arruado, divided into streets.

arruamento, *s.m.* alignement of buildings, laying out of streets.

arruar, *v.t.* to divide into streets, to gad about *(vadiar).*

arruçado, *adj.* blond.

arruda, *s.f. (bot.)* rue.

arruela, *s.f. (mec.)* washer.

arrufada, *s.f.* cake made of flour, eggs and sugar.

arrufadiço, *adj.* peevish, fretful.

arrufar, *v.t.* to ruffle; *arrufar-se,* to sulk *(amuar),* to become ruffled.

arrufo, *s.m.* spat *(de namorados),* peevish mood, sulkiness.

arrugamento, *s.m.* wrinkling, crisping.

arrugar, *v.t.* to crisp, to wrinkle.

arruído, *s.m.* noise, uproar, tumult.

arruinado, *adj.* ruined, ruinous.

arruinador, *s.m.* ruiner, destroyer; *adj.* ruining, destroying.

arruinamento, *s.m.* ruin.

arruinar, *v.t.* to ruin, to destroy, to ravage; *v.r.* to go to ruin, to ruin oneself, to fall to pieces.

arruivado, *adj.* reddish.

arrulhar, *v.i.* to coo.

arrulho, *s.m.* cooing.

arrumação, *s.f.* arrangement, ordering, setting in order, tidying up, packing (malas).

arrumadeira, *s.f.* chambermaid, housemaid.

arrumador, *s.m.* arranger, usher *(no teatro ou no cinema).*

arrumar, *v.t.* to arrange, to set in order, to tidy up, to dispose, to pack *(as malas).*

arrumo, *s.m.* order, ordering, arrangement.

arsenal, *s.m.* arsenal, armory; *Arsenal de Marinha,* Navy Yard.

arseniado, *adj.* combined with arsenic.

arsenical, *adj.* arsenical.

arsénico, *s.m.* arsenic.

arsenioso, *adj.* arsenious.

arte, *s.f.* art, skill *(habilidade),* craft *(ofício),* cunning *(astúcia).* 1) *belas artes,* the fine arts. 2) *malas artes, s.f. pl.* dangerous tricks. 3) *de tal arte que,* in such a way that.

artefacto, *s.m.* artefact.

arteirice, *s.f.* craft, artifice, subtleness.

arteiro, *adj.* artful, cunning, tricky.

artelho, *s.m.* anklebone.

artemísia, *s.f.* artemisia, mugwort.

artéria, *s.f.* artery.

arterial, *adj.* arterial; *tensão arterial,* blood pressure.

arterialização, *s.f.* arterialization.

arterializar, *v.t.* to arterialize, to render arterial *(o sangue).*

arteriografia, *s.f.* arteriography.

arteriosclerose, *s.f.* arteriosclerosis.

arterioso, *adj.* arterial.

arteriotomia, *s.f.* arteriotomy.

arterite, *s.f.* artritis.

artesanato, *s.m.* craftsmanship.

artesão, *s.m.* craftsman, artisan.

artesiano, *adj.* artesian.

artético, *adj.* arthritic.

articulação, *s.f.* articulation *(de ossos),* joint, enunciation.

articulado, *adj.* articulate, joined; *s.m.* article, a juridical statement in articles and paragraphs.

articular, *v.t.* to articulate, to joint, to utter, to pronounce, to link together, to article, to set fourth in articles; *adj.* articular.

articulista, *s.m.* author of an article in a newspaper, newspaper writer.

artículo, *s.m.* joint, knucle, *(bot.)* internode.

artífice, artificer, craftsman, author, inventor.

artificial, *adj.* artificial, synthetic, unnatural, simulated.

artificialidade, *s.f.* artificiality.

artificialmente, *adv.* artificially.

artificializar, artificiar, *v.t.* to arrange with art, to intrigue.

artifício, *s.m.* artifice, art, trick, ruse.

artificioso, *adj.* artful, crafty, cunning.

artigo, *s.m.* article, item *(de uma lista, etc.),* good, merchandise, article *(mercadoria),* paragraph *(de uma lei).*

artiguelho, *s.m.* insignificant article.

artilhar, *v.t.* to mount artillery, to arm with artilery.

artilharia, *s.f.* artillery, gunnery.

artilheiro, *s.m.* artilleryman, gunner, cannoneer.

artimanha, *s.f.* ruse, trick, stratagem.

artista, *s.m. e s.f.* artist; *adj.* skilful.

artístico, *adj.* artistical, artistic.

artrite, *s.f.* arthritis.
artrítico, *adj.* arthritic.
artritismo, *s.m.* arthritism.
artrópode, *s.m.* arthropod.
artrose, *s.f.* arthrosis.
arúspice, *s.m.* haruspex.
aruspício, *s.m.* prognostic made by a haruspex: haruspicy.
arvense, *adj.* growing on tilled ground.
arvícola, *s.m.* e *s.f.* tiller, peasant, country-man; *adj.* rural.
arvorado, *adj.* hoisted, planted with trees; *s.m.* a private soldier who performes the duties of a corporal.
arvorar, *v.t.* to raise, to lift, to set up, to hoist *(bandeira)*, to mast *(navio); arvorar-se em:* to pretend to be.
árvore, *s.f.* tree; shaft, beam *(eixo).*
arvoredo, *s.m.* grove.
as, *art. def. pl.* the; *pron. demo. e pes.* the ones, them.
ás, *s.m.* ace *(cartas),* champion, hero.
às, *contr. da prep. a com o art. ou pron. as,* to the, to those, to them.
asa, *s.f.* wing, handle *(pega).*
asado, *adj.* winged.
asar, *v.t.* to wing.
asca, *s.f.* aversion, disgust.
ascáride, *s.f.* round-worm.
ascendência, *s.f.* ancestry, parentage, origin, influence *(domínio).*
ascendente, *adj.* ascending, rising; *s.m.* ascendant, influence; *pl.* ancestors.
ascender, *v.t.* to ascend, to rise.
ascensão, *s.f.* ascension, ascending.
ascensional, *adj.* ascensional.
ascensor, *s.m.* lift, elevator.
asceta, *s.m.* e *s.f.* ascetic, hermit.
ascética, *s.f.* ascetics.
ascético, *adj.* ascetic, austere, secluded.
ascetismo, *s.m.* asceticism.
ascite, *s.f.* ascites, dropsy.
asco, *s.m.* aversion, repugnance, repulsion.
ascoroso, *adj.* detestable, repulsive.
áscua, *s.f.* live coal, ember.
aselha, *s.f.* loop.
asfaltar, *v.t.* to asphalt, to pave with asphalt.
asfalto, *s.m.* asphalt.
asfixia, *s.f.* asphyxia.
asfixiante, *adj.* choking, suffocating.
asfixiar, *v.t.* to choke, to suffocate, to asphyxiate.
asiático, *adj.* e *s.m.* asian, asiatic.

asilar, *v.t.* to shelter, to give shelter; *asilar--se,* to take shelter.
asilo, *s.m.* asylum *(hospício),* shelter, home *(lar).*
asinário, *adj.* asinary.
asma, *s.f.* asthma.
asmático, *adj.* e *s.m.* asthmatic.
asna, *s.f.* she-ass, truss *(do telhado).*
asnada, *s.f.* drove of asses, big mistake.
asnal, *adj.* silly, stupid.
asnear, *v.i.* to talk nonsense, to play the fool.
asneira, *s.f.* nonsense, folly, blunder.
asneirada, *s.f.* o mesmo que "asneira".
asneirento, *s.m.* fool, silly, awkward.
asneirola, *s.f.* nonsense, little mistake.
asno, *s.m.* ass.
aspa, *s.f.* St. Andrew's cross; *pl.* inverted commas *(sinal ortográfico).*
aspar, *v.t.* to crucify, to tie, to put inverted commas, to erase.
aspárago, aspargo, *s.m.* asparagus.
aspecto, *s.m.* aspect, appearance, look, air.
asperamente, *adv.* harshly, roughly, coarsely.
aspereza, *s.f.* harshness, roughness, rudeness.
asperges, *s.m.* sprinkling with holy water.
aspergir, *v.t.* to sprinkle (with something).
áspero, *adj.* harsh, rough, grained, rugged, coarse.
aspérrimo, *adj.* very rough.
aspersão, *s.f.* sprinkling, aspersion.
aspersório, *s.m.* aspergil.
áspide, *s.f.* asp, viper.
aspiração, *s.f.* aspiration, inhalation.
aspirado, *adj.* aspirate, inhaled.
aspirador, *s.m.* vaccuum cleaner (de pó), inhaler, ventilator.
aspirante, *adj.* aspirant; *s.m.* aspirante, candidate, cadet.
aspirar, *v.t.* e *v.i.* to inspire, to suck, to long for (desejar), to aspirate (fonética).
aspirina, *s.f.* aspirin.
asquerosidade, *s.f.* filthiness, repulsi-veness.
asqueroso, *adj.* repulsive, filthy, dirty.
assacar, *v.t.* to imput calumniously.
assado, *adj.* roasted.
assador, *s.m.* roaster.
assadura, *s.f.* roasting, intertrigo *(de crianças).*
assa-fétida, *s.f.* assafoetida.
assalariado, *adj.* engaged; *s.m.* employee.

assalariamento, *s.m.* engagement of an employee.

assalariar, *v.t.* to engage, to hire, to pay wages to.

assaltada, *s.f.* assault, surprise.

assaltante, assailant, assaulter.

assaltar, *v.t.* to assail, to assault, to attack.

assalto, *s.m.* assault, attack, agression.

assanhadiço, *adj.* irritable, irascible.

assanhado, *adj.* enraged, exasperated.

assanhamento, *s.m.* anger, rage, excitement.

assanhar, *v.t.* to irritate, to provoke, to excite.

assar, *v.t.* to roast, to toast, to burn, to grill *(na grelha).*

assarapantado, *adj.* frightened, astonished.

assarapantar, *v.t.* to frighten, to astonish, to perplex, to disconcert; *assarapantar-se,* to get frightened or astonished.

assassinar, *v.t.* to murder, to assassinate, to slaugter.

assassínio, *s.m.* murder, assassination.

assassino, *s.m.* murderer, assasin.

assaz, *adv.* rather, enough.

assazonado, *adj.* seasoned, ripe, matured.

assazonar, *v.t.* to season, to ripe, to mature.

asseado, *adj.* clean, neat, proper, tidy.

assear, *v.t.* to clean up.

assedar, *v.t.* to heckle, to comb, to render smooth like silk.

assediado, *adj.* besieged, haunter.

assediar, *v.t.* to besiege, to surround, to haunt *(perseguir).*

assédio, *s.m.* siege, blockade, importunity, insistence.

asseguradamente, *adv.* assuredly.

assegurador, *s.m.* assurer, insurer.

assegurar, *v.t.* to assure, to guarantee, to ensure; *assegurar-se,* to make sure of, to assure oneself.

asseio, *s.m.* cleanliness, tidiness, neatness.

asselvajadamente, *adv.* wildly, savagely, coarsely.

asselvajado, *adj.* wild, savage.

asselvajar-se, *v.t.* to become wild or unsociable.

assembleia, *s.f.* assembly, meeting, gathering; *assembleia constitucional,* assembly, Parliament.

assemelhar, *v.t.* to make similar; *assemelhar-se,* to look alike, to resemble.

assenhoreamento, *s.m.* appropriation.

assenhorear-se, *v.r.* to take possession of.

assenso, *s.m.* assent, agreeing.

assentada, *s.f.* sitting, session; *de uma assentada,* all at once, without interruption.

assentadamente, *adv.* steadily, quietly.

assentado, *adj.* seated, steady, quiet, agreed.

assentador, *s.m.* one who notes down, recorder.

assentamento, *s.m.* sitting, laying, record.

assentar, *v.t.* to seat, to place on a seat, to lay *(alicerces, tijolos, etc.)* to make a note *(tomar nota),* to record *(registar),* to settle *(combinar); v.i.* to be based *(basear-se),* to settle down *(tomar juízo),* to look well *(roupa); assentar-se,* to sit down.

assente, *adj.* placed, settled, agreed upon.

assentimento, *s.m.* assent, consent.

assentir, *v.i.* to consent, to assent.

assento, *s.m.* seat, chair; *ter assento,* to sit; *tomar assento,* to take a seat.

assepsia, *s.f.* asepsis.

asséptico, *adj.* aseptic.

asserção, *s.f.* assertion, affirmation.

assertivo, *adj.* assertive, affirmative.

asserto, *s.m.* assertion.

assertoado, *adj.* double-breasted.

assertoar, *v.t.* to make a double-breasted coat.

assessor, *s.m.* assessor, adviser.

assessorar, *v.t.* to assist, to advise.

assessorial, assessório, *adj.* assessorial.

assestar, *v.t.* to point, to aim, to direct against.

assesto, *s.m.* aim, pointing.

asseveração, *s.f.* asseveration, assertion.

asseverador, *s.m.* asserter.

asseverar, *v.t.* to asseverate, to assert, to assure.

assexuado, *adj.* asexual.

assiduamente, *adv.* often, frequently.

assiduidade, *s.f.* assiduity.

assíduo, *adj.* assiduous, diligent, constant.

assim, *adv.* so, thus, in this manner, like this, this way, therefore *(portanto). 1) assim como,* just as; as well as. 2) *ainda assim,* even so. 3) *por assim dizer,* so to say. 4) *assim na terra como no céu,* both on earth and in heaven. 5) *assim Deus me ajude,* so help me God. 6) *assim por diante,* and so on . 7) *assim-assim,* so so.

assimetria, *s.f.* assymmetry.
assimétrico, *adj.* asymmetric.
assimilação, *s.f.* assimilation.
assimilador, *s.m.* assimilator.
assimilar, *v.t.* to assimilate.
assimilativo, *adj.* assimilative.
assimilável, *adj.* assimilable.
assinado, *adj.* signed, subscribed.
assinalação, *s.f.* marking, signalizing.
assinalado, *adj.* marked, distinguished, noted.
assinalar, *v.t.* to mark, to signalize, to signal, to point out.
assinalável, *adj.* remarkable.
assinante, *s.m.* subscriber *(de publicação).*
assinar, *v.t.* to sign, to subscribe; *assinar de cruz:* to make one's mark.
assinatura, *s.f.* signature, subscription.
assírio, *s.m.* e *adj.* Assyrian.
assizado, *adj.* prudent, wise.
assistência, *s.f.* assistance, help, audience, public.
assistente, *s.m.* assistant, attendant, spectator; *adj.* assisting; *médico-assistente:* attending physician.
assistir, *v.i.* to assist (ajudar), to nurse (um doente), to be present to (estar presente); *assiste-lhe o direito:* he has the right to do...
assoalhado, *s.m.* floor; *adj.* floored, exposed to the sun.
assoalhar, *v.t.* to floor, to expose to the sun.
assoante, *adj.* assonant.
assoar, *v.t.* to blow the nose.
assoberbado, *adj.* haughty, proud, overwhelmed *(de trabalho).*
assoberbar, *v.t.* to treat with contempt, to offend, to overwhelm with work; *assoberbar-se:* to become haughty.
assobiador, *s.m.* whistler.
assobiar, *v.t.* e *v.i.* to hiss, to whistle.
assobio, *s.m.* whistle, hiss.
assobradar, *v.t.* to floor, to plank.
associação, *s.f.* association, union, combination, partnership *(sociedade).*
associado, *adj.* associated; *s.m.* associate, partner.
associar, *v.t.* to associate, to join, to unite; *associar-se:* to associate, to join in partnership, to become partners; *associar-se a:* to join.
assolação, *s.f.* devastation, wasting.
assolador, *adj.* devasting, wasting; *s.m.* ravager, wasted.

assolar, *v.t.* to ravage, to waste, to destroy.
assomada, *s.f.* slow, summit (cume), appearance.
assomado, *adj.* angry, irascible.
assomar, *v.i.* e *v.t.* to peep (espreitar), to appear *(aparecer)*, to irritate; *assomar-se:* to get angry .
assombrado, *adj.* haunted *(com fantasmas)*, shady, astonished *(espantado).*
assombramento, *s.m.* shading, astonishment, amazement.
assombrar, *v.t.* to haunt *(com fantasmas)*, to shadow, to astonish, to amaze.
assombroso, *adj.* amazing, astonishing.
assomo, *s.m.* indication, sign, fit (de cólera, de paixão, etc.).
assonância, *s.f.* assonance.
assopradela, *s.f.* blowing.
assoprar, *v.t.* to blow, to whisper *(murmurar).*
assopro, *s.m.* blowing, puff.
assoreamento, *s.m.* silting.
assorear, *v.t.* to silt, to obstruct with silt; *v.i.* to become silted.
assovelar, *v.t.* to prick with an awl, to needle, to irritate.
assuada, *s.f.* tumult, riot, uproar, gang (bando), hooting (vaia).
assumir, *v.t.* to assume, to take on, to take charges of, to take upon oneself *(responsabilidade)*, to put on (ares).
assumptível, *adj.* assumable, admissible.
assumptivo, *adj.* assumptive.
assunção, *s.f.* assumption, elevation (de um cargo).
assunto, *s.m.* subject, matter, topic, theme, business, affair.
assustadiço, *adj.* easily frightened, timid.
assustado, *adj.* frightened, afraid, fearful.
assustador, *adj.* alarming, frightening, startling.
assustar, *v.t.* to frighten, to alarm, to scare; *assustar-se,* to get scared, to be alarmed or frightened.
astenia, *s.f.* asthenia.
astéria, *s.f.* star-stone; *(zool.)* starfish.
asterisco, *s.m.* asterisk.
asteróide, *s.m.* asteroid.
astigmático, *adj.* astigmatic.
astigmatismo, *s.m.* astigmatism.
astracã, *s.f.* Astrakhan *(cidade)*, astrakhan wool *(pele).*
astral, *adj.* astral; *s.m.* astral influence.

ástreo, *adj.* astral.

astro, *s.m.* star, heavenly body.

astróide, *s.m.* asteroid.

astrolábio, *s.m.* astrolabe.

astrolatria, *s.f.* star-worship, astrolatry.

astrologia, *s.f.* astrology.

astrológico, *adj.* astrological.

astrólogo, *s.m.* astrologer.

astronauta, *s.m.* astronaut.

astronáutica, *s.f.* astronautics.

astronomia, *s.f.* astronomy.

astronómico, *adj.* astronomic.

astrónomo, *s.m.* astronomer.

astúcia, *s.f.* astuteness, artfulness, cunning, craft.

astucioso, *adj.* crafty, cunning, artful, astute.

asturiano, *adj.* e *s.m.* Asturian.

astutamente, *adv.* artfully, cunningly, craftily.

astuto, *adj.* astute, cunning, crafty.

atabacado, *adj.* tobacco-coloured.

atabafado, *adj.* stuffy, hushed up, smothered.

atabafar, *v.t.* to smother, to cover, to muffle.

atabalhoadamente, *adv.* disorderly, confusedly, helter-skelter.

atabalhoado, *adj.* confused, hot-headed, reckless.

atabalhoar, *v.t.* to do things in a hurry, to muddle; *atabalhoar-se,* to get mixed up.

atacado, *adj.* attacked, assailed; *por atacado,* wholesale.

atacador, *s.m.* lace, shoe-lace.

atacante, *s.m.* attacker, assailant; *adj.* attacking, insulting.

atacar, *v.t.* to attack, to assail, to strike, to seize *(por doença),* to affect *(um órgão do corpo).*

atacoar, *v.t.* to put a heel.

atadinho, *adj.* timid, awkward.

atado, *adj.* tied, fastened, timid, bashful.

atadura, *s.f.* tie, band, bandage, union, connection.

atafal, *s.f.* crupper.

atafona, *s.f.* horse-mill.

atafoneiro, *s.m.* miller.

atafulhar, *v.t.* to cram, to stuff.

atalaia, *s.f.* watch-tower, sentinel; *estar de atalaia,* to be on the lookout.

atalaiar, *v.t.* to watch, to stand watch over, to spy on.

atalhamento, *s.m.* stop, stoppage, disadvantage, obstacle.

atalhar, *v.t.* to stop, to intercept, to prevent *(impedir),* to abreviate; *v.i.* to take a short cut *(tomar um atalho),* to interpose *(falar).*

atalho, *s.m.* by-path, short cut, crosscut.

atamancar, *v.t.* to bungle, to mend clumsyly, to repair badly.

atanado, *s.m.* tan, tanned leather; *adj.* tanned.

atanar, *v.t.* to tan leather.

atazanar, *v.t.* to tease, to afflict, to plague.

atapetar, *v.t.* to carpet.

atapulhar, *v.t.* to fill up, to cram.

ataque, *s.m.* attack, assault, charge, seizure, fit *(doença).* 1) *ataque aéreo,* air-raid. 2) *ataque cardíaco,* heart attack.

atar, *v.t.* to tie, to bind, to fasten, to lace up *(sapatos),* to unit, to join.

atarantação, *s.f.* perplexity, confusion.

atarantado, *adj.* perplexed, confused, disconcerted.

atarantar, *v.t.* to perplex, to confuse, to puzzle, to disconcert.

atarefado, *adj.* busy.

atarefar, *v.t.* to assign a task to, to overload with work; *atarefar-se,* to flounder, to be busy.

ataroucado, *adj.* silly.

atarracado, *adj.* squat, short, thickset.

atarrafado, *adj.* covered with a casting--net.

atarraxar, *v.t.* to screw up, to tighten up (a screw), to rivet.

atascadeiro, *s.m.* slough, quamire, marshland.

atascar-se, *v.r.* to be bogged, to stick in the mud.

atassalhadura, *s.f.* tearing.

atassalhar, *v.t.* to tear, to rend, to slander, to defame.

ataúde, *s.m.* coffin, casket, tomb *(sepulcro).*

ataviamento, *s.m.* attire, dress, ornament, trim.

ataviar, *v.t.* to dress, to adorn, to trim, to bedeck; *v.r.* to spruce, to dress up.

atávico, *adj.* atavic.

atavio, *s.m.* o mesmo que "ataviamento".

atavismo, *s.m.* atavism.

ataxia, *s.f.* ataxy, ataxia.

atáxico, *adj.* ataxical.

até, *prep.* to, up to, till, until, as far as. 1) o *até agora,* up to now, till now. 2) *até altas horas da noite,* far into the nigh. 3) *até amanhã,* see you tomorrow, until tomorrow.

4) *até certo ponto,* to a certain point. 5) *até que,* till, untill. 7) *até que enfim,* at last; *adv.* even, also.

ateador, *s.m.* lighter, instigator.

atear, *v.t.* to light, to set on fire, to inflame, to kindle.

atediar, *v.t.* to tire, to annoy, to trouble; *atediar-se,* to become tired.

ateísmo, *s.m.* atheism.

ateísta, *s.m. e s.f.* atheist, a godless person.

ateístico, *adj.* atheistical, godless.

atemorizador, *s.m.* alarmist; *adj.* frightening.

atemorizar, *v.t.* to frighten, to alarm; *atemorizar-se,* to become frightened.

atenazar, *v.t.* to tease, to importune, to annoy.

atenção, *s.f.* attention, care, regard *(consideração).* 1) *em atenção a,* in regard to. 2) *prestar atenção,* to pay attention. 3) *chamar a atenção,* to call the attention, to admonish *(advertir).*

atenciosamente, *adv.* kindly, truly; yours truly *(como despedida).*

atencioso, *adj.* kind, polite, obliging, thoughtful.

atender, *v.t.* to attend *(um cliente),* to take care of *(cuidar de),* to answer *(a porta, o telefone, etc.),* to meet *(necessidades).*

atendível, *adj.* deserving attention.

ateneu, *s.m.* Athenaeum.

atentado, *adj.* prudent, careful, wise; *s.m.* crime, assault, attempt, outrage.

atentamente, *adv.* attentively, carefully; *de V. Exa. "atentamente":* yours truly.

atentar, *v.t.* to pay attention, to consider. 1) *atentar contra,* to attempt against. 2) *atentar contra a moral,* to commit a moral outrage.

atentatório, *adj.* offensive.

atento, *s.m.* attentive, diligent, careful.

atenuação, *s.f.* attenuation, reduction.

atenuante, *s.f.* attenuating circumstance; *adj.* attenuating.

atenuar, *v.t.* to attenuate, to reduce, to mitigate, to soften, to make thin.

atérmano, *adj.* athermanous.

atérmico, *adj.* o mesmo que "atérmano".

aterrado, *adj.* frightened, awe-struck, terrified, landed *(o avião).*

aterrador, *adj.* appalling, startling, terrifying.

aterragem, *s.f.* landing.

aterrar, *v.t.* to frighten, to terrify, to appal, to land *(o avião).*

aterro, *s.m.* embankment.

aterrorizar, *v.t.* to terrify.

ater-se, *v.r.* to cling to, to depend on (fiar-se).

atestação, *s.f.* attestation, testemony.

atestado, *s.m.* certificate, testemony; *adj.* filled.

atestar, *v.t.* to attest, to certify, to testify to in writing, to confirm, to fill up.

ateu, *s.m.* atheist; *adj.* atheistic, godless.

atiçador, *s.m.* poker, instigator.

atiçar, *v.t.* to poke, to fan *(o fogo),* to incite, to instigate, to excite.

aticismo, *s.m.* atticism.

ático, *adj.* attic, pure, classical.

atiçoar, *v.t.* to burn with firebrands.

atigrado, *adj.* striped *(listado),* spotted *(sarapintado).*

atilamento, *adv.* wittily, carefully, cleverly.

atilado, *adj.* wise, clever, smart, careful.

atiladamente, *s.m.* correction, refinement.

atilar, *v.t.* to make smart, clever, to perform with care, to perfect.

atilho, *s.m.* band, tie, string.

atinado, *adj.* cautious, clever, wise.

atinar, *v.t.* to execute with care, to guess right, to find out.

atinente, *adj.* concerning, regarding.

atingir, *v.t.* to attain, to get, to obtain, to reach, to understand.

atingível, *adj.* attainable, reachable, conceivable.

atiradiço, *adj.* adventurous, bold, daring, forward.

atirador, *s.m.* shooter, marksman, rifleman.

atirar, *v.t.* to throw, to cast, to fling, to toss, to shoot *(arma de fogo, flecha, etc.),* to fire *(arma de fogo);* atirar-se: to throw oneself, to rush; *atirar-se a,* to venture, to rush into.

atitude, *s.f.* attitude, pose.

Atlântico, *s.m. e adj.* Atlantic.

Atlas, *s.m.* Atlas.

atleta, *s.m.* athlete.

atlética, *s.f.* athletics.

atlético, *adj.* athletic.

atletismo, *s.m.* athletics.

atmosfera, *s.f.* atmosphere.

atmosférico, *adj.* atmospheric.

à toa, *loc. adv.* at random.

atoada, *s.f.* report, rumour.

atoar, *v.t. (náut.)* to tow, to warp; *v.i.* to refuse, to reject.

atochar, *v.t.* to fasten, to fix firmly, to beat, to drive, to force in, to fill up.

atol, *s.m.* atoll.

atolado, *adj.* stuck in the mud, bogged.

atoladouro, *s.m.* slough, mudhole.

atolar, *v.t.* to stick in the mud; *atolar-se,* to stall, to sink.

atoleimado, *adj.* silly, foolish.

atoleimar-se, *v.r.* to stultify oneself.

atoleiro, *s.m.* o mesmo que "atoladouro".

atomicidade, *s.f.* atomicity.

atómico, *adj.* atomic.

atomismo, *s.m.* atomism.

atomista, *s.m.* atomist.

átomo, *s.m.* atom.

atonia, *s.f.* atony, debility.

atónico, *adj.* atonic.

atónito, *adj.* astonished, amazed, surprised.

átono, *adj.* atonic.

atontar, *v.t.* to stupefy, to dull.

atorácico, *adj.* without thorax.

atordoado, *adj.* stunned, dizzy.

atordoador, *adj.* stunning.

atordoar, *v.t.* to stun, to astound, to make dizzy.

atormentação, *s.f.* torment.

atormentado, *adj.* tormented, worried.

atormentador, *adj.* tormenting, harassing; *s.m.* tormenter.

atormentar, *v.t.* to torment, to vex, to worry, to harass; *atormentar-se,* to fret at, to grieve over.

atoucinhado, *adj.* fat, lardaceous, fatty.

atóxico, *adj.* non toxic.

atrabiliário, *adj.* melancholic, badtempered, irascible, violent.

atracação, atracadura, *s.f. (náut.)* grappling, boarding, mooring.

atracar, *v.t.* e *v.i.* to moor, to grapple *(um navio a outro);* to come alongside *(aproximar-se de terra); v.r.* to grapple, to come to blows with someone.

atracção, *s.f.* attraction, allurement, enticement, seduction.

atractivo, *adj.* attractive, catching, alluring; *s.m.* attraction, allurement.

atraente, *adj.* attracting, attractive, alluring.

atraiçoado, *adj.* betrayde, deceived.

atraiçoar, *v.t.* to betray, to deceive, to double-cross.

atrair, *v.t.* to attract, to draw, to catch (a atenção), to allure, to entice.

atrancar, *v.t.* to bar, to bolt.

atrapalhação, *s.f.* embarrassment, confusion, perplexity, bewilderment.

atrapalhado, *adj.* mixed-up, confused, perplexed, embarrassed.

atrapalhar, *v.t.* to mix up, to embarass, to disturb, to stand in the way *(estorvar); atrapalhar-se,* to flounder, to be upset, to become confused.

atrás, *adv.* behind, after. 1) *atrás de,* behind. 2) *cinco anos atrás,* five years ago. 3) *não ficar atrás de,* to keep up with.

atrasado, *adj.* behindhand, late, in arrears *(no pagamento),* backward *(pouco desenvolvido),* slow *(o relógio).*

atrasar, *v.t.* to retard, to delay, to set back *(o relógio); atrasar-se,* to remain behind, to lag, to be late, to go slow *(o relógio),* to get in arrears *(no pagamento).*

atraso, *s.m.* delay, lateness, slowness, backwardness, retardement *(mental).*

atravancar, *v.t.* to obstruct, encumber, to clog.

através, *adv.* through, across.

atravessado, *adj.* laid across, traversed, oblique.

atravessar, *v.t.* to cross, to traverse, to hinder *(estorvar),* to pierce *(trespassar),* to lay across *(pôr de través).* 1) *atravessar-se,* to get stuck *(na garganta, etc.).* 2) *atravessar-se no caminho de alguém,* to thwart someone.

atreito, *adj.* used to, inclined, subject, acostumed.

atrelar, *v.t.* to leash *(o cão),* to yoke *(os bois),* to couple *(vagões),* to put the horses to a carriage ou to get the carriage ready *(atrelar uma carruagem).*

atrever-se, *v.r.* to dare, to venture.

atrevidamente, *adv.* daringly, boldly.

atrevido, *adj.* bold, audacious, daring.

atrevimento, *s.m.* boldness, audacity, impudence.

atribuição, *s.f.* attribution, privilege, competence.

atribuir, *v.t.* to attribute, to ascribe, to impute.

atribuível, *adj.* attributable, imputable.

atribulação, *s.f.* tribulation, affliction, distress.

atribuladamente, *adv.* afflictively.

atribulado, *adj.* afflicted.

atribulador, *s.m.* afflicter; *adj.* afflicting, distressing.

atribular, *v.t.* to afflict, to distress, to torment; *atribular-se,* to worry.

atributivo, *adj.* attributive.

atributo, *s.m.* attribute, quality.

atrição, s.f. attrition, friction, regret.

atrigado, adj. corn-coloured, busy.

átrio, s.m. yard, hall, lobby, vestibule.

atrito, s.m. friction, attriction, disagreement (desentendimento).

atroada, s.f. thundering, noise, clamour.

atroador, adj. thundering, noisy, clamorous; s.m. thunderer.

atroamento, s.m. thundering, resounding, crack.

atroar, v.t. to thunder, to roar; v.i. to thunder, to sound as a thunder.

atrocidade, s.f. attrocity, cruelty.

atrofia, s.f. atrophy.

atrofiar, v.t. to atrophy.

atropelado, adj. run over.

atropelamento, s.m. running over, trampling, confusion.

atropelar, v.t. to run over, to trample (espezinhar).

atropelo, s.m. o mesmo que "atropelamento".

atroz, adj. atrocious, cruel, horrible.

atrozmente, adv. atrociously, cruely.

atulhar, v.t. to fill up, to over fill, to cram, to heap up, (amontoar).

atum, s.m. tuna.

aturadamente, adv. unceasingly, constantly, patiently.

aturado, adj. constant, unceasing, continued, ceaseless.

aturar, v.t. to bear, to endure, to support, to undergo.

aturdido, adj. stunned, dizzy, amazed.

aturdimento, s.m. dizziness, amazement, confusion, bewilderment.

aturdir, v.t. to stun, to astound, to astonish, to make dizzy.

audácia, s.f. audacity, boldness.

audacioso, adj. audacious, bold, daring, fearles.

audaz, adj. o mesmo que "audacioso".

audazmente, audaciosamente, adv. audaciously, boldly.

audição, s.f. audition, hearing.

audiência, s.f. audience, auditory, a judicial hearing, session.

audio visual, s.m. audio-visual.

auditivo, adj. auditory.

auditor, s.m. judge, magistrate, hearer (ouvinte).

auditoria, s.f. auditorship, judgeship.

auditório, s.m. auditorium (recinto), audience (ouvintes).

audível, adj. audible.

auferir, v.t. to get, to obtain, to gain, to receive.

auge, s.m. summit, culmination, climax, zenith, apogee.

augural, adj. augural.

augurar, v.t. to augur, to presage, to foretell.

áugure, s.m. augur, diviner.

augúrio, s.m. augury, omen.

augusto, adj. august, sacred, venerable, solemn.

aula, s.f. class, classroom, lesson, lecture; as aulas acabaram, the school is over.

áulico, adj. aulic; s.m. courtier.

aulido, s.m. roar, howl, yelling.

aumentar, v.t. to augment, to increase, to enlarge, to amplify , to extend; v.i. to increase, to grow.

aumentativo, adj. e s.m. augmentative.

aumento, s.m. increase, enlargement, amplification, growth, raise (de preços), accrestion, increment (acréscimo).

aura, s.f. breath of air, gale, light breeze, fame, popularity.

áureo, adj. golden.

auréola, s.f. aureola, halo, glory.

aureolar, v.t. to glorify, to surround with a halo.

aurícula, s.f. auricule.

auriculado, adj. auriculate.

auricular, adj. auricular; testemunha auricular, ear-witness.

aurífero, adj. auriferous.

aurificar, v.t. to aurify, to turn into gold.

aurífice, s.m. goldsmith.

aurifício, adj. that manufactures gold.

aurífico, adj. aurific, gold-coloured.

aurifulgente, adj. shining like gold.

auriga, s.m. coachman; the constelation Auriga.

auriverde, adj. gold-and-green.

aurora, s.f. dawn, daybreak, sunrise; aurora boreal, aurora borealis.

auroral, adj. auroral, aurorean.

auscultação, s.f. auscultation, sounding, probing (sondagem).

auscultador, s.m. auscultator, receiver (do telefone).

auscultar, v.t. to auscultate, to sound, to probe (sondar).

ausência, s.f. absence, lack (falta).

ausentar-se, v.r. to ausent oneself; ausentar-se de, to leave, to depart.

ausente, adj. absent, away, missing.

áuspice, *s.m.* auxpex, augur.

auspiciar, *v.t.* to augur, to presage, to foretell.

auspício, *s.m.* auspice, omen, prediction, protection.

auspicioso, *adj.* auspicious, promising, favorable, lucky.

austeridade, *s.f.* austerity, severity.

austero, *adj.* austere, severe, rigid.

austral, *adj.* austral, southern.

Austrália, *s.f.* Australia.

australiano, *s.m.* e *adj.* Australian.

Áustria, *s.f.* Austria.

austríaco, *s.m.* e *adj.* Austrian.

autarquia, *s.f.* autarchy, autonomous department.

autárquico, *adj.* autarchical.

autenticação, *s.f.* authentication.

autenticar, *v.t.* to authenticate, to attest, to confirm, to legalize *(documento)*.

autenticidade, *s.f.* authenticity.

autêntico, *adj.* authentic, genuine, real.

auto, *s.m.* act, public cerimony, solemnity, written statement, document. 1) *auto controlo,* self controle. 2) *auto-de-fé,* auto da fé.

autobiografia, *s.f.* autobiography.

autobiográfico, *adj.* autobiographic(al).

autocarro, *s.m.* bus.

autocéfalo, *adj.* autocephalous.

autoclave, *s.f.* autoclave.

autoclismo, *s.m.* flushing cistern.

autocracia, *s.f.* autocracy, despotism.

autocrata, *s.m.* autocrat, despot.

autocrático, *adj.* autocratic, despotic.

autocrítica, *s.f.* autocritics.

autóctone, *adj.* autochthonous, aboriginal; *adj.* aborigenes, natives.

autodidacta, *s.m.* self-taught person.

auto disciplina, *s.f.* self-discipline.

auto domínio, *s.m.* self-control.

auto-educação, *s.f.* self-education.

auto-estrada, *s.f.* highway.

autogiro, *s.m.* autogyro.

autografar, *v.t.* to autograph.

autografia, *s.f.* autography.

autográfico, *adj.* autographic(al).

autógrafo, *s.m.* autograph.

automaticamente, *adv.* automatically.

automático, *adj.* automatic.

automatismo, *s.m.* automatism.

automatização, *s.f.* automatization.

autómato, *s.m.* automaton, robot.

automobilismo, *s.m.* automobilism, automobile racing.

automobilista, *s.m.* e *s.f.* automobilist.

automotora, *s.f.* a self-moving car that goes on rails.

automóvel, *s.m.* car, motor-car.

autonomia, *s.f.* autonomy, self-government.

autonómico, *adj.* autonomic.

autónomo, *adj.* autonomous, independent.

autópsia, *s.f.* autopsy, post-mortem examination.

autopsiar, *v.t.* to autopsy.

autor, *s.m.* author.

autora, *s.f.* authoress.

auto-retrato, *s.m.* self-portrait.

autoria, *s.f.* authorship.

autoridade, *s.f.* authority, power.

autoritário, *adj.* authoritative, despotic, overbearing.

autoritarismo, *s.m.* authoritarianism.

autorização, *s.f.* authorization, permission.

autorizado, *adj.* authorized, authoritative.

autorizar, *v.t.* to authorize, to permit, to allow, to give permission, to approve, to warrant.

autorizável, *adj.* warrantable, permissible.

auto-suficiente, *adj.* self-sufficient.

auto-sugestão, *s.f.* autosuggestion.

autuação, *s.f.* proceedings; the drawing up of a written statement.

autuar, *v.t.* to draw up a written statement of, to sue, to prosecute *(processar)*.

auxiliador, *s.m.* helper, assistant; *adj.* auxiliar, auxiliary, helping.

auxiliar, *v.t.* to help, to aid, to assist.

auxiliar, *adj.* auxiliar, auxiliary, helping, subsidiary *(livros)*.

auxílio, *s.m.* aid, assistance, help.

aval, *s.m.* guarantee.

avalancha, *s.f.* avalanche, snowslide.

avaliação, *s.f.* valuation, evaluation, estimation, assessment, appraisal.

avaliador, *s.m.* appraiser, valuer, assessor.

avaliar, *v.t.* to appraise, to evaluate, to value, to estimate, to set a value on, to prize, to appreciate *(dar valor a)*, to assess *(para tributação)*, to judge (by something); *avaliar para mais:* to overestimate.

avalista, *s.m.* guaranter.

avançada, *s.f.* onset, assault (investida).

avançado, *adj.* advanced, forward, late *(horas)*; avançado em idade: aged; *s.m.* forward *(em futebol)*.

avançamento, *s.m.* advancement, furthering.

avançar, *v.i.* to advance, to proceed, to move on, to progress, to go ahead; *v.t.* to move forward, to carry on *(prosseguir),* to put forward *(uma opinião).*

avanço, *s.m.* advance, advancement, progress, *(náut.)* lead.

avantajado, *adj.* big, huge, larger than average, corpulent, stout.

avantajar, *v.t.* to give an advantage; *v.i.* to progress; *avantajar-se,* to excel, to surpass, to exceed, to surmount.

avante, *adv. e interj.* forward, onward, ahead; *avante!,* go on!, forward!

avantesma, *s.f.* monster, phantom.

avarento, *adj.* avaricious, niggard, greedy; miser, skinflint.

avareza, *s.f.* avarice, greediness, niggardliness, greed.

avaria, *s.f.* damage, average.

avariado, *adj.* damaged.

avariar, *v.t.* to damage, to spoil, to injure; *v.i.* to suffer damage.

avaro, *adj.* o mesmo que "avarento".

avassalador, *s.m.* subduer, conqueror; *adj.* overwhelming, crushing.

avassalar, *v.t.* to subdue, to subjugate, to enslave, to overwhelm; *avassalar-se,* to subject oneself to someone.

avatar, *s.m.* avatar, incarnation.

ave, *s.f.* bird, fowl. 1) *ave canora,* song bird. 2) *aves de arribação,* migratory birds. 3) *ave de rapina,* bird of prey. 4) *aves domésticas,* poultry. 5) *ave de mau agouro,* ominous bird; *interj.* hail! . 6) *Ave Maria,* Hail Mary.

aveal, *s.f.* oat-field.

aveia, *s.f.* oat; *flocos de aveia,* oatmeal.

avelã, *s.f.* hazelnut.

avelanado, *adj.* hazel-coloured.

avalanal, *s.m.* wood of hazelnut.

aveleira, *s.f.* hazel, filbert.

avelhacado, *adj.* knavish, rascally.

avelhado, avelhentado, *adj.* oldish.

aveludado, *adj.* velvety.

aveludar, *v.t.* to make like velvet.

avena, *s.f.* reed.

avenca, *s.f.* maiden-hair.

avença, *s.f.* agreement, franking duty.

avençar, *v.t.* to agree, to pay in advance.

avenida, *s.f.* avenue, alley.

avental, *s.m.* apron.

aventar, *v.t.* to air, to fan, to winnow, to enunciate, to suggest *(uma opinião).*

aventura, *s.f.* adventure, exploit *(proeza).* 1)

aventura amorosa, love affair. 2) *à aventura,* aimlessly.

aventurar, *v.t.* to venture, to risk; *v.r.* to venture oneself, to dare.

aventureiro, *s.m.* adventurer; *adj.* bold, daring, adventuresome.

aventuroso, *adj.* adventurous, daring.

averbamento, *s.m.* registration, registring; marginal note.

averbar, *v.t.* to register, to record, to use as a verb *(gramática).*

avergoar, *v.t.* to lash.

averiguação, *s.f.* inquiry, investigation, verification.

averiguado, *adj.* proved.

averiguador, *s.m.* inquirer, investigator.

averiguar, *v.t.* to inquire, to investigate, to find out, toverify.

avermelhado, *adj.* reddish.

aversão, *s.f.* aversion, dislike, repugnance.

avessas, *s.f.pl.* às avessas, inside out, upside down, backwards.

avesso, *s.m.* wrong side, other side, reverse; *adj.* contrary, adverse, reluctant (to do something).

avestruz, *s.f.* ostrich.

avezar, *v.t.* to accustom, to inure; *avezar-se,* to become used (to).

aviação, *s.f.* aviation.

aviador, *s.m.* aviator, airman, flier.

aviamento, *s.m.* execution, preparation; *aviamentos,* implements, utensils.

avião, *s.m.* airplane, aeroplane, plane. 1) *avião a jacto,* jet plane. 2) *por avião,* by air mail; by plane.

aviar, *v.t.* to prepare, to dispatch, to put up *(uma receita).* 1) *aviar-se,* to bestir oneself, to hurry. 2) *aviar os fregueses,* to attend the customers.

aviário, *s.m.* aviary.

avícola, *s.m.* aviarist, bird-fancier.

avicultor, *s.m.* aviarist.

avicultura, *s.f.* aviculture, bird-rearing.

avidamente, *adv.* avidly, eagerly, greedily.

avidez, *s.f.* avidity, eagerness, greed.

ávido, *adj.* avid, eager, greedy.

avigorar, *v.t.* to invigorate, to strengthen, to fortify.

aviltação, *s.f.* abasement, degradation.

aviltador, *s.m. e adj.* debaser, debasing.

aviltante, *adj.* debasing, humiliating.

aviltar, *v.t.* to abase, to degrade, to debase, to humiliate; *aviltar-se,* to debase oneself.

avinagrado, *adj.* sourish, vinegar-like.

avinagrar, *v.t.* to sour, to irritate.

avindo, *adj.* agreed.

avindor, *s.m.* mediator, arbiter.

avinhado, *adj.* wine-like, mixed with wine, tipsy, drunk *(bêbedo).*

avinhar, *v.t.* to mix with wine; *avinhar-se,* to get drunk.

avioneta, *s.f.* light plain, hedgehopper.

avir, *v.t.* to reconcile, to harmonize; *avir-se,* to come to an agreement, to manage *(arranjar-se).*

avisadamente, *adv.* wisely, prudently.

avisado, *adj.* wise, prudent.

avisar, *v.t.* to advise, to warn, to give notice.

aviso, *s.m.* advise, warning, notice, notification.

avistar, *v.t.* to sight, to catch the sight of, to see; *avistar-se com,* to have an interview with.

avitaminose, *s.f.* avitaminosis.

avitualhar, *v.t.* to victual, to provide with victuals.

avivamento, *s.m.* waking, vivification, enlivening, revival.

avivar, *v.t.* to wake, to rouse, to vivify, to hasten *(apressar),* to heighten *(cores),* to stir, to fan *(o fogo); avivar a memória,* to remind someone.

aviventar, *v.t.* to put life into, to vitalize, to vivify, to reanimate.

avizinhar, *v.t. e v.r.* to bring near or closer, to approach, to come near.

avo, *s.m.* (arit.) fraction; *um doze avos, um treze-avos, etc.,* one twelfth, one thirteenth, etc.

avô, *s.m.* grandfather; *pl.* grand-parent.

avó, *s.f.* grandmother.

avocação, *s.f.* avocation, to call to a higher court.

avocar, *v.t.* to attract, *(jur.)* to transfer to a higher court; *avocar a si,* to arrogate to oneself.

avoengo, *adj.* ancestral; *s.m.* ancestor.

avolumar, *v.t.* to enlarge, to make bigger, to add to; *v.r.* to increase, to swell.

avulsão, *s.f.* avulsion, forcible separation.

avulso, *adj.* separate, detached, unconnected.

avultado, *adj.* voluminous, bulky, big, large, considerable.

avultar, *v.t.* to augment, to enlarge, to increase; *v.i.* to grow, to be proeminent, to expand.

axadrezado, *adj.* chequered.

axadrezar, *v.t.* to checker.

axila, *s.f.* armpit *(bot.)* axila, axil.

axilar, *adj.* axillar, axillary.

axioma, *s.m.* axiom.

axiomático, *adj.* axiomatic.

az, *s.m.* edge *(de uma ferramenta).*

azabumbado, *adj.* astonished, amazed.

azabumbar, *v.t.* to astonish, to stun.

azado, *adj.* suitable, opportune, propitious, fit (for something).

azáfama, *s.f.* hurry, bustle, fuss.

azafamado, *adj.* busy.

azagaia, *s.f.* assagai, javelin.

azálea, *s.f.* azalia.

azambuado, *adj.* confused, dizzy.

azambuja, *s.f.* wild-olive.

azambujeiro, *s.m.* o mesmo que "azambuja".

azar, *s.m.* bad luck, hazard, chance *(acaso).*

azarado, *adj.* unlucky, luckless, out of luck.

azarar, *v.t.* to jin, to bring bad luck to.

azarento, *adj.* hoodoo.

azebre, azevre, *s.m.* verdigris, trick, mischivousness.

azeda, *s.f.* (bot.) sorrel; *adj.* sour.

azedado, *adj.* sour.

azedar, *v.t.* to sour, to turn sour *(o leite); v.r.* to get angry.

azedia, *s.f.* acidity, sourness.

azedo, *adj.* sour, acrid, harsh.

azedume, *s.m.* sourness, acrimony, peevishness.

azeitado, *adj.* oily.

azeitar, *v.t.* to oil.

azeite, *s.m.* olive-oil.

azeiteira, *s.f.* olive-oil jar.

azeiteiro, *s.m.* oil-man, oil-seller.

azeitona, *s.f.* olive.

azeitonado, *adj.* olive-like.

azeitoneira, *s.f.* a dish where olives are served; a woman that gathers or sells olives.

azelha, *s.f.* ring-handle.

azémola, *s.f.* beast of burden, pack-mule.

azenha, *s.f.* water-mill.

azevém, *s.m.* rye-grass.

azevia, *s.f.* dab, a kind of sole *(peixe).*

azevichado, *adj.* jetty, jet-black.

azevicho, *s.m.* jet.

azevieiro, *adj.* crafty, clever, cunning.

azevinho, *s.m.* holly.

azia, *s.f.* heartburn, sour stomach.

aziago, *adj.* unlucky, ominous, sinister.

ázimo, *adj.* unleavened.

azimute, *s.m.* azimuth.

azinhaga, *s.f.* a long and narrow path.

azinhal, *s.m.* a grove of holm-oaks.

azinheira, *s.f.* holm oak, holly oak.

aziomar, *v.t.* to render sour.

aziume, *s.m.* sourness, peevishness, sulkiness.

azo, *s.m.* occasion, motive, pretext, opportunity; *dar azo a*, to give occasion to.

azoado, *adj.* stunned, amazed, dizzy.

azoar, *v.t.* to stun, to amaze.

azoinar, *v.t.* to stun, to make dizzy, to dim.

azoratado, *adj.* hare-brained, wild, silly.

azoratar, *v.t.* to render stupid or silly, to stun.

azorragada, *s.f.* a blow with a whip.

azorragar, *v.t.* to scourge, to whip.

azorrague, *s.m.* scourge, whip.

azotado, *adj.* azotized, nitrogenised.

azotado, *s.m.* nitrate, a salt of nitric acid.

azótico, *adj.* azotic, nitric.

azoto, *s.m.* nitrogen, azote.

azougado, *adj.* light-headed, restless *(inquieto)*.

azougar, *v.t.* to overlay with quick-silver, to make unsteady.

azougue, *s.m.* quicksilver, mercury, a lively person.

azul, *s.m.* blue. 1) *azul-celeste*, sky-blue. 2) *azul claro*, light-blue. 3) *azul da Prússia*, Prussian blue. 4) *azul- escuro*, dark-blue. 5) *azul-ferrete*, dark-blue. 6) *azul marinho*, navy-blue.

azulado, *adj.* bluish.

azular, *v.t.* to blue.

azulejador, *s.m.* one who makes or addorns with tiles.

azulejar, *v.t.* to addorn with glazed tiles.

azulejo, *s.m.* Dutch tile, glazed tile.

azulina, *s.f.* azuline.

azumbrado, *adj.* curved.

azumbrar, *v.t.* to curve.

B

b, the second letter of the Portuguese alphabet.

baba, *s.f.* drivel, slaver, slobber, slime *(de caracóis)*.

babado, *adj.* slavered, slobbered.

babadouro, *s.m.* bib.

babão, *s.m.* driveller, slaverer, idiot.

babar, *v.t.* to slaver, to drivel, to slobber; *babar-se*, to drivel, to slobber, to be nuts on *(gostar muito de qualquer coisa)*.

babeiro, *s.m.* o mesmo que "babadouro".

Babel, *s.m.* Babel, confusion.

Babilónia, *s.f.* Babylone, confusion.

babilónico, *adj.* Babylonish.

babilónio, *s.m. e adj.* babylonian, gigantic.

baboseira, *s.f.* nonsense, drivel.

baboso, *adj.* drivelling, slavering, infatuated *(apaixonado)*.

babugem, *s.f.* slobber, spume, foam, froth.

babujar, *v.t.* to slobber, to smear with slobber.

bacalhau, *s.m.* cod, cod-fish.

bacalhoada, *s.f.* codfish stew.

bacalhoeiro, *s.m.* ship used in cod-fishery, codfisher.

bacamarte, *s.m.* blunderbuss.

bacanal, *s.m.* bacchanal, orgy.

bacante, *s.f.* bacchant.

bacará, *s.m.* baccarat.

bacelada, *s.f.* newly planted vineyard.

baceleiro, *s.m.* vine-dresser.

bacelo, *s.m.* newly planted vine, grapevine cutting.

bacharel, *s.m.* bachelor, graduate.

bacharelato, *s.m.* bachelorship, bachelor's degree.

bacharelar, *v.t.* to confer the degree of bachelor.

bacharelice, *s.f.* chitchat, prattle.

bacia, *s.f.* basin, pelvic cavity *(anatomia)*.

baciada, *s.f.* the liquid contained in a basin.

baciado, *adj.* discoloured, dim, obscure.

bacífero, *adj.* bacciferous.

baciforme, *adj.* bacciform.

bacilar, *adj.* bacillar.

baciliforme, *adj.* bacilliform.

bacilo, *s.m.* bacillous; *pl.* bacilli.

bacinete, *s.m.* basinet, *(anat.)* pelvish.

bacio, *s.m.* chamber-pot.

baço, *s.m.* spleen; *adj.* dim, tarnished.

bacoco, *s.m. e adj.* fool.

bacorejar, *v.t.* to forebode, to divine, to suspect.

bacorejo, *s.m.* presentiment, premonition, hunch.

bacorinho, *s.m.* o mesmo que "bácoro".

bácoro, *s.m.* young pig, suckling pig.

bactéria, *s.f.* bacterium; *pl.* bacteria.

bactericida, *s.m.* bactericid.

bactérico, *adj.* bacteric, bacterian.

bacteriologia, *s.f.* bacteriology.

bacteriológico, *adj.* bacteriological.

bacteriologista, *s.m.* bacteriologist.

bacterioscopia, *s.f.* bacterioscopy.

báculo, *s.m.* staff *(bordão)*, crosier *(de bispo)*.

badalada, *s.f.* stroke of a bell.

badalar, *v.t.* to ring, to blab *(tagarelar)*, to noise abroad *(divulgar)*.

badaleira, *s.f.* a ring to which the clapper is fixed.

badalo, *s.m.* clapper.

badameco, *s.m.* puppy, nobody.

badana, *s.f.* dressed sheep leather.

badejo, *s.m.* haddock.

baderna, *s.f. (náut.)* racking, seizing, a thing without value.

baeta, *s.f.* baize.

baetão, *s.m.* thick baize.

baetilha, *s.f.* flannel.

bafagem, *s.f.* waft, whiff.

bafejador, *s.m.* puffer; *adj.* puffing.

bafejar, *v.t.* to breath upon, to warm with one's breath, to inspire.

bafejo, *s.m.* breath, light breeze.

bafiento, *adj.* mouldy, musty.

bafio, *s.m.* moul, mustiness, musty smell.

bafo, *s.m.* breath, whiff.

baforada, *s.f.* puff, whiff, blast, boast *(bravata)*.

baforar, *v.i.* to whiff, to puff, to blow.

baga, *s.f.* berry *(fruta)*, drop *(de suor)*.

bagaceira, *s.f.* brandy, bagasse pit *(lugar)*.

bagaço, *s.m.* bagasse; *bagaço das uvas*, husk.

bagada, *s.f.* big tear, a lot of berries.

bagageiro, *s.m.* porter, baggageman.

bagagem, *s.f.* baggage, luggage.

bagalhoça, *s.f. (pop.)* a lot of money.

baganha, *s.f.* hull.

bagatela, *s.f.* trifle, a very cheap thing.

bago, *s.m.* grain *(de cereal)*, grape *(uvas)*.

bagulho, *s.m.* grapestone seeds, *(pop.)* chink.

baia, *s.f.* pillar, column.

baía, *s.f.* bay.

baila, *s.f.* ball, dance, perch (peixe); *trazer à baila,* to bring up for discussion.

bailadeira, *s.f.* woman dancer.

bailado, *s.m.* dance, ballet.

bailador, *s.m.* dancer.

bailar, *v.t. e v.i.* to dance.

bailarico, *s.m.* popular ball.

bailarino, *s.m.* dancer, ballet dancer.

baile, *s.m.* ball, dance.

bailéu, *s.m.* scaffold, *(náut.)* gangway.

bainha, *s.f.* sheat, scabbard, hem *(em costura)*.

baio, *adj.* bay; *s.m.* bay horse.

baioneta, *s.f.* bayonet.

baionetada, *s.f.* a bow! with a bayonet, bayonet thrust.

bairrismo, *s.m.* parochialism, sectionalism.

bairrista, *s.m.* parochial, defender of the interests of one's parish.

bairro, *s.m.* quarter, district.

baiuca, *s.f.* gorgot, small tavern.

baiuqueiro, *s.m.* the keeper of a tavern.

baixa, *s.f.* decrease, reduction, drop, fall *(de preços)*, discharge *(do serviço)*, casualty *(em combate)*, downtown *(parte baixa da cidade)*; baixa-mar, low tide.

baixada, *s.f.* download (rádio).

baixar, *v.t. e v.i.* to lower, to bring down, to cut down *(preços)*, to decrease, to ebb *(a maré)*, to deflate *(desinflacionar)*.

baixela, *s.f.* table-ware.

baixeza, *s.f.* baseness, lowness, meaness.

baixio, *s.m.* shoal.

baixista, *s.m.* bear *(na bolsa de valores)*.

baixo, *adj.* e *adv.* low, short, small, shallow *(pouco profundo); baixo-relevo,* bas-relief.

baixote, *adj.* short, dumpy.

bajoujar, *v.t.* to adulate, to coax.

bajoujice, *s.f.* nonsense.

bajoujo, *s.m.* e *adj.* silly.

bajulação, *s.f.* flattering, adulation.

bajulador, *s.m.* flatterer; *adj.* flattering, fawning.

bajular, *v.t.* to flatter, to adulate.

bala, *s.f.* bullet, ball.

balaio, *s.m.* hamper, small basket.

balança, *s.f.* balance, scale, weighing-machine.

balançar, *v.t.* to balance, to swing; *v.i.* to hesitate, to waver.

balancé, *s.m.* balance *(dança),* seesaw *(baloiço).*

balanceamento, *s.m.* balancing, balance-ment, swinging, hesitation.

balancear, *v.t.* o mesmo que "balançar".

balanceiro, *s.m.* swingle-tree.

balancete, *s.m.* trial-sheet, balance-sheet.

balanço, *s.m.* swinging, oscilation, *(com.)* balance, balance-sheet.

balandrau, *s.m.* a garment worn by members of certain cofraternities.

balanite, *s.f.* balanitis.

balão, *s.m.* balloon. 1) *balão de ensaio,* trial balloon. 2) *balão-sonda,* sounding ballon.

balar, *v.t.* to bleat, to baa.

balastragem, *s.f.* ballasting.

balastrar, *v.t.* to fill with ballast.

balastro, *s.m.* ballast.

balata, *s.f.* balata.

balaustrada, *s.f.* balustrade, fence.

balaustrar, *v.t.* to provide with balustres or banisters.

balaústre, *s.m.* baluster, banister.

balázio, *s.m.* large ball, cannon shot.

balbuciação, *s.f.* stammering, babble.

balbuciante, *adj.* balbutient, stammering.

balbuciar, *v.t.* to stammer, to babble.

balbúrdia, *s.f.* mess, confusion, disorder.

balça, *s.f.* coppice *(arvoredo).*

balcão, *s.m.* balcony, counter *(de loja).*

balda, *s.f.* defect, bald, bad habit.

baldadamente, *adv.* uselessly, vainly.

baldado, *adj.* void, frustrated.

baldão, *s.m.* stroke of luck, misfortune, reproach, outrage.

baldaquim, baldaquino, *s.m.* baldachin, canopy.

baldar, *v.t.* to frustrate, to hinder; *v.r.* to discard *(no jogo de cartas).*

balde, *s.m.* bucket.

balde, (de), *loc. adv.* in vain.

baldeação, *s.f.* transhipment, transfer, washing *(lavagem).*

baldear, *v.t.* to tranship, to decant, to wash with buckets of water.

baldio, *adj.* common, untilled; *s.m.* a fallow ground.

baldroca, *s.f.* cheat, fraud; *trocas e baldro-cas,* fraudulent contracts.

baldrocar, *v.t.* to deceive, to cheat.

baleato, *s.m.* whalecalf.

baleeira, *s.f.* whaler, whale-boat.

baleia, *s.f.* whale.

balela, *s.f.* lie, fib.

baleote, *s.m.* whalecalf, a young whale.

balha, *s.f.* barrier, arena.

balido, *s.m.* bleat.

balir, *v.t.* to bleat.

balista, *s.f.* (mil.) balista.

balística, *s.f.* ballistics.

balístico, *adj.* ballistic.

baliza, *s.f.* landmark, boundary, limit, goal *(futebol).*

balizador, *s.m.* setter of marks.

balizagem, *s.f.* setting of landmarks.

balizar, *v.t.* to set up a landmark, to mark out.

balnear, *adj.* balneal, balneary, bathing; *estância balnear,* bathing resort.

balneário, *s.m.* balneary, bathing-place.

balneoterapia, *s.f.* balneotherapy.

balofo, *adj.* swollen, empty, apparent.

baloiçador, *s.m.* balancer.

baloiçar, *v.t.* to swing, to rock, to balance.

baloiço, *s.m.* seesaw, swing.

balsa, *s.f.* vat *(dorna),* raft, ferry *(embar-cação).*

balsâmico, *adj.* balsamic, balmy, aromatic.

balsamina, *s.f.* balsamine.

balsamita, *s.f.* (bot.) costmary.

balsamizar, *v.t.* to aromatize, to soothe, to balsam.

bálsamo, *s.m.* balsam, balm.

balseiro, *s.m.* bush, ticket, ferry-man.

Báltico, *adj.* Baltic.

baluarte, *s.m.* bulwark, rampart, fortress, defence.

bamba, *s.m.* tough *(fanfarrão),* crack *(hábil).*

bambaleante, *adj.* reeling, staggering.

bambalear, *v.t.* e *v.r.* to swing, to shake.

bambaleio, *s.m.* swinging.

bambalhão, *adj.* indolent, lazy, negligent.

bambinelas, *s.f. pl.* window-curtains.

bambo, *adj.* slack, loose.

bamboar, *v.i.* e *v.r.* o mesmo que "bambolear".

bambochata, *s.f.* painting representing scenes of gaiety, farce, comic opera.

bambolear, *v.i.* e *v.r.* to swing, to wag, to reel.

bamboleio, *s.m.* swinging, wagging, swaying.

bambolina, *s.f.* the upper part of the scenes in theatres.

bambu, *s.m.* bamboo.

bambual, *s.m.* bamboo plantation.

bamburral, *s.m.* marshy pasture ground.

bambúrrio, *s.m.* good luck, stroke of luck.

banabóia, *s.m.* e *s.f.* a spiritless person.

banal, *adj.* common, futile, trivial.

banalidade, *s.f.* banality, triviality.

banalizar, *v.t.* to render vulgar or trivial.

banana, *s.f.* banana.

bananal, banana-plantation.

bananeira, *s.f.* banana tree.

banazola, *s.f.* a lazy fellow.

banca, *s.f.* writing-desk, sink *(de cozinha),* stand *(de mercado),* banks.

bancada, *s.f.* long bench, row of benches, bench.

bancal, *s.m.* cloth, *(mec.)* plummer block.

bancário, *adj.* banking, bank; *s.m.* bank employee.

bancarrota, *s.f.* bankruptcy, failure.

banco, *s.m.* bench, seat *(assento),* bank *(instituição bancária); banco de areia, de coral,* sand-bank, coral-bank or coral reef.

banda, *s.f.* side, band *(faixa),* stripe *(lista),* band *(de música).* 1) *ficar de cara a banda,* to be disconcerted. 2) *pôr de banda,* to cast aside; *(chapéu)* to cock.

bandada, *s.f.* flock of birds, covey.

bandalheira, *s.f.* shameless behaviour.

bandalho, *s.m.* shameless fellow.

bandarilha, *s.f.* banderilla.

bandear, *v.t.* e *v.r.* to join a party, to band together.

bandeira, *s.f.* flag, banner, colours, transom *(de porta).*

bandeirinha, *s.m.* linesman *(no futebol).*

bandeirola, *s.f.* streamer, pennant, pennon, banderold.

bandeja, *s.f.* tray, salver.

bandidismo, banditismo, *s.m.* banditry, brigandage.

bandido, *s.m.* bandit, brigand, robber, thief.

bando, *s.m.* band, flock, swarm, gang *(de malfeitores).*

bandola, *s.f.* cartridge-belt.

bandoleira, *s.f.* sholder-belt.

bandoleiro, *s.m.* bandit, brigand, highwayman.

bandolim, *s.m.* mandolim.

bandolinista, *s.m.* mandolin-player.

bandulho, *s.m. (pop.)* belly, guts.

bandurra, *s.m.* mandora, mandolla.

bangaló, *s.m.* bungalow.

banha, *s.f.* fat, lard.

banhado, *adj.* watered, bathed.

banhar, *v.t.* to bathe, to wash.

banheira, *s.f.* bathtub, tub.

banheiro, *s.m.* bath-keeper, bathing-attendant.

banhista, *s.m.* e *s.f.* bather.

banho, *s.m.* bath, bathing. 1) *banhos de casamento,* marriage banns. 2) *banho-maria,* double-boiler.

banido, *adj.* banished, outlawed.

banimento, *s.m.* banishment, exile, expulsion.

banir, *v.t.* to banish, to exile, to expel, to outlaw.

banível, *adj.* deserving banishment.

banqueiro, *s.m.* banker, croupier *(no jogo).*

banquete, *s.m.* banquet.

banqueteador, *s.m.* banqueter.

banquetear, *v.t.* to banquet, to feast; *banquetear-se,* to banquet, to regale oneself.

banquinho, *s.m.* stool.

banza, *s.f.* residence of a black king in Africa.

banzado, *adj.* astonished, perplexed, amazeded.

banzar, *v.t.* to astonish, to amaze, to surprise; *v.i.* to wonder.

banzé, *s.m.* noise, riot, tumult.

banzeiro, *adj.* choppy.

banzo, *s.m.* nostalgia, homesickness (of negro slaves); uprights *(de escada).*

baobá, *s.m.* baobab.

baptismal, *adj.* baptismal.

baptismo, *s.m.* baptism, christening; *nome de baptismo,* Christian name.

Baptista, *s.m.* Baptist.

baptispério, *s.m.* baptistery.

baptizado, *adj.* baptized; *s.m.* christening, baptism.

baptizar, *v.t.* to baptize, to christen.

baque, *s.m.* fall, shock, throb.

baquear, *v.i.* to fall, to tumble down.

baqueta, *s.f.* drum stick.

báquico, *adj.* bacchic.

bar, *s.m.* bar, pub, public house.

baraça, baraço, *s.f.* strap, string.

barafunda, *s.f.* mess, bustle, fuss, confusion.

barafustar, *v.i.* to make a fuss, to gesticulate.

baralha, *s.f.* dispute, quarrel, mess.

baralhada, *s.f.* confusion, mess, fuss.

baralhadamente, *adv.* in confusion, disorderly.

baralhador, *s.m.* shuffler, entangler.

baralhar, *v.t.* to shuffle *(cartas)*, to disorder, to entangle, to confuse.

baralho, *s.m.* pack *(de cartas)*.

barão, *s.m.* baron.

barata, *s.f.* cockroach.

barateamento, *s.m.* cheapening, reduction.

baratear, *v.t.* to cheapen, to sell cheap.

barateiro, *s.m.* one who sells cheap.

barateza, *s.f.* cheapness.

baratinho, *adj.* rather cheap.

barato, *adj.* cheap; *dar de barato,* to admit without argument; *adv.* cheap, cheaply, at a low price.

báratro, *s.m.* gulf, abyss, vortex, precipice.

barba, *s.f.* beard, barb *(anzol)*, silk *(de espiga de milho)*. 1) *fazer a barba,* to shave. 2) *dar água pela barba,* to give a great deal of trouble. 3) *pôr as barbas de molho,* to be on one's guard.

barbacã, *s.f.* barbican.

barbaças, *s.m.* long-bearded man.

barbado, *adj.* bearded.

barbante, *s.m.* twine; string.

barbar, *v.t.* to grow a beard.

barbaramente, *adv.* cruelly, barbarously.

barbaria, *s.f.* barbarism.

barbaridade, *s.f.* barbarity, atrocity, cruelty.

bárbarie, *s.f.* barbarity, barbarism.

barbarismo, *s.m.* barbarism, savageness, cruelty.

barbarizar, *v.t.* to barbarize, to make barbarous.

bárbaro, *adj.* barbarous, barbarian, barbaric, cruel.

barbatana, *s.f.* fin.

barbeação, *s.f.* shaving.

barbear, *v.t.* to shave.

barbearia, *s.f.* barber's shop.

barbeiro, *s.m.* barber.

barbela, *s.f.* dewlap *(do boi)*, double chin *(duplo queixo)*.

barbeta, *s.f.* barbette.

barbicacho, *s.m.* halter, big trouble, confusion.

barbicha, *s.f.* small beard.

barbilhão, *s.m.* barbel *(de peixe)*, wattle *(de ave)*.

barbilho, *s.m.* muzzle, obstacle.

barbirruivo, *adj.* red-bearded.

barbiteso, *adj.* hard-bearded, stour, robust.

barbitúrico, *s.m.* barbituric.

barbo, *s.m.* barbel.

barbotina, *s.f.* wormseed, santonin.

barbudo, *adj.* bearded.

barca, *s.f.* bark, boat, barge.

barcaça, *s.f.* barge, pontoon.

barcada, *s.f.* boatful.

barcagem, *s.f.* ferriage.

barcarola, *s.f.* barcarole.

barco, *s.m.* boat, ship. 1) *barco a motor,* motorboat. 2) *barco a vapor,* steamboat. 3) *barco à vela,* sailboat. 4) *barco a remos,* rowboat. 5) *barco-farol,* lightship.

barda, *s.f.* fence, hedge; *em barda,* in profusion, in great quantity.

bardar, *v.t.* to surround with hedges.

bardo, *s.m.* bard, poet.

barga, *s.f.* straw-hut, fishing-net.

barganha, *s.f.* barter, swap, deal, trickery.

barganhar, *v.t.* to barter, to swap.

bargantaria, *s.f.* debauchery, dishonesty, infamy.

bargante, *s.m.* loafer, vagabond, rascal.

bargantear, *v.i.* to ramble, to wander, to loaf.

bário, *s.m.* barium.

barítono, *s.m.* barytone.

barlaventar, *v.i.* to ply to the windward, to sail against the wind.

barlavento, *s.m.* windward, weather side; *a barlavento,* to windward.

baroado, *s.m.* barony, baronage.

barógrafo, *s.m.* barograph, recording barometer.

baronato, *s.m.* barony, baronage.

baronesa, *s.f.* baroness.

baronete, *s.m.* baronet.

baronia, *s.f.* barony.

baroscópio, *s.m.* baroscope.

barqueiro, *s.m.* boatman, bargeman, ferryman.

barquejar, *v.i.* to to steer a boat, to go in a boat, to sail about in a boat.

barquinha, *s.f.* small boat.

barra, *s.f.* bar, ingot *(de ouro ou prata)*, strip *(faixa)*, crowbar *(alavanca)*, mouth *(foz de um rio)*.

barraca, *s.f.* hut, tent.

barracão, *s.m.* large tent, shed.

barraco, *s.m.* hut, shack.

barragem, *s.f.* dam *(represa)*, embankment *(contra inundações)*, barrage *(militar)*.

barranco, *s.m.* ravine, gully.

barrancoso, *adj.* full of gullies.

barrar, *v.t.* to bar, to obstruct, to thwart *(impedir)*, to cover with.

barrear, *v.t.* to cover with clay, to coat.

barregã, *s.f.* concubine, mistress.

barreira, *s.f.* barrier, bar, hindrance, blockade, obstacle, hurdle *(em corrida)*, toll gate *(fiscal)*.

barrela, *s.m.* lye, buck.

barrento, *adj.* clayey, argillous, muddy.

barretada, *s.f.* the act of lifting one's hat in salutation.

barrete, *s.m.* cap, skull cap *(de clérigo)*.

barretina, *s.f. (mil.)* shako.

barrica, *s.f.* barrel, cask.

barricada, *s.f.* barricade.

barricar, *v.t.* to barricade.

barriga, *s.f.* belly, stomach, abdomen, paunch, bulge *(saliência)*; barriga da perna, calf.

barrigada, *s.f.* bellyfull.

barrigudo, *adj.* big-bellied.

barril, *s.m.* barrel, cask.

barrilete, *s.m.* rundlet, bench-hook *(de carpinteiro)*.

barro, *s.m.* clay.

barroca, *s.f.* gutter.

barroco, *s.m.* e *adj.* baroque, grotesque, extravagant.

barroso, *adj.* clayey, argillaceous.

barrote, *s.m.* rafter, beam.

barulheira, *s.f.* noise, racket.

barulhento, *adj.* noisy, turbulent, boisterous.

barulho, *s.m.* noise, riot, racket, clamour.

basal, *adj.* basal.

basalto, *s.m.* basalt.

basbaque, *s.m.* dolt, idiot, silly.

basbaquice, *s.f.* foolery, silliness, stupidity.

basco, *s.m.* e *adj.* Basque.

báscula, *s.f.* decimal balance, platform scale.

base, *s.f.* base, basis, foundation, support, bottom.

basear, *v.t.* to base, to found, to ground; basear-se, to base oneself on.

basicamente, *adv.* basically.

básico, *adj.* basic, basal, fundamental, basic or alkaline *(quím.)*.

basilar, *adj.* basal, basic, fundamental, essential.

basílica, *s.f.* basilica.

basilicão, *s.m.* basilicon.

basilisco, *s.m.* basilisk.

basta, *s.f.* quilting-stitch; *interj.* enough! stop! that's enough!

bastante, *adj.* e *adv.* enough, sufficient, rather, quite.

bastão, *s.m.* staff, baton, stick.

bastar, *v.i.* to suffice, to be sufficient, to be enough, to do.

bastardia, *s.f.* bastardy, bastardism.

bastardo, *s.m.* bastard, illegitimate.

bastear, *v.t.* to quilt a matress.

bastião, *s.m.* bastion.

bastida, *s.f.* palisade, a fence of stakes.

bastidão, *s.f.* thickness, density, multitude, crowd.

bastidor, *s.m.* embroidering frame, side scenes *(teatro)*; atrás dos bastidores, behind the scenes.

basto, *adj.* thick, compact, plentiful; *s.m.* the ace of clubs in the game of ombre.

bastonada, *s.f.* bastinado, bastinade.

bastonete, *s.m.* small rod, rod-sharped bacillus.

bata, *s.f.* gown, dressing-gown.

batalha, *s.f.* battle, fight, combat.

batalhador, *s.m.* fighter, champion.

batalhão, *s.m.* battalion.

batalhar, *v.i.* to battle, to fight, to combat, to contend.

batata, *s.f.* potato. 1) *batata-doce*, sweet potato. 2) *batatas fritas*, chips.

batatal, *s.m.* potato-field.

batateira, *s.f.* potato-plant.

batateiral, *s.m.* o mesmo que "batatal".

batateiro, *s.m.* potato-plant, an impolite individual.

batedeira, *s.f.* beater.

batedor, *s.m.* beater, scout *(tropa)*.

batedoiro, *s.m.* the persistent act of beating, place of beating.

batedura, *s.f.* beating.

bate-estacas, *s.m.* pile-driver.

bátega, *s.f.* shower, downpour.

bateira, *s.f.* small boat.

batel, *s.m.* small boat.

batelada, *s.f.* boatload, a great deal.

batelão, *s.m.* heavy barge, hopper-barge.

bateleiro, *s.m.* boatman.

batente, *s.m.* doorpost, jamb, door leaf, knocker *(aldrava).*

bater, *v.t.* e *v.i.* to beat, to strike, to hit, to knock *(à porta),* to flutter *(as asas),* to defeat *(derrotar),* to break *(um recorde),* to slam *(bater a porta com estrondo),* to beat up *(ovos, claras, etc.),* to click *(os calcanhares).* 1) *bater o queixo,* to chatter with cold or fear. 2) *bater palmas,* to cap one's hands. 3) *bater em retirada,* to beat a retreat. 4) *bater em,* to strike, to pound, to run into *(chocar).*

bateria, *s.f.* battery, utensils, percussion instruments *(música).*

batida, *s.f.* battue, beat, konck, tap, stroke, bang, raid *(da polícia).*

batido, *adj.* beaten, vulgar, worn; *s.m.* milk-shake.

batimetria, *s.f.* bathymetry.

batímetro, *s.m.* batymeter.

batina, *s.f.* cassock.

batocar, *v.t.* to bung, to close up.

batoque, *s.m.* bung, stopper.

batota, *s.f.* cheating, trickery; *fazer batota,* to cheat.

batotar, batotear, *v.i.* to cheat.

batoteiro, *adj.* cheater.

batráquio, *s.m.* amphibian; *pl.* amphibia.

batuque, *s.m.* a Negro dance; hammering, banging.

batuta, *s.f.* conductor's baton.

baú, *s.m.* trunk, chest.

bauleiro, *s.m.* trunk-maker.

baunilha, *s.f.* vanilla.

bávaro, *s.m.* e *adj.* Bavarian.

Baviera, *s.f.* Bavaria.

bazar, *s.m.* bazar, market.

bazófia, *s.f.* boast, bragging, vaunting.

bazofiar, *v.i.* to boast, to swagger, to bully.

bazófio, *s.m.* e *adj.* boaster, bully, swaggerer, boastfull, swaggering.

bazuca, *s.f.* bazooka.

bazulaque, *s.m.* a big-bellied man, a short and stout person; a stupid person; a cosmetic.

bdélio, *s.m.* bdelium.

beata, *s.f.* the stump of a cigar.

beatice, *s.f.* bigotry, hipocrisy.

beatificação, *s.f.* beatification.

beatificar, *v.t.* to beatify.

beatífico, *adj.* beatific.

beatilha, *s.f.* linen cloth, a nun's white veil.

beatismo, *s.m.* beatitude.

beatíssimo, *adj.* most blessed; *o Beatíssimo Padre,* the Pope.

beatitude, *s.f.* beatitude.

beato, *adj.* blessed, bigoted, hipocritical; *s.m.* bessed, bigot.

bêbado, *adj.* drunk, drunken, ebriated; *s.m.* drunk.

bebé, *s.m.* e *s.f.* baby.

bebedeira, *s.f.* drunkenness, ebriety, intoxication.

bebedice, *s.f.* drunknness.

bêbedo, *s.m.* o mesmo que "bêbado".

bebedouro, *s.m.* watering-place.

beber, *v.t.* to drink; *dar de beber,* to water *(aos animais).*

beberagem, *s.f.* beverage, drink, brew, potion.

beberete, *s.m.* drinking party, cocktail.

bebericar, *v.t.* e *v.i.* to sip, to drink in small quantities.

beberrão, *s.m.* drunkard.

beberricar, *v.t.* o mesmo que "bebericar".

bebes, *s.m.pl.* drinks; *comes e bebes,* eatables and drinkables.

bebida, *s.f.* drink, beverage. 1) bebidas alcoólicas, liquors. 2) bebidas sem álcool, soft drinks.

bebível, *adj.* drinkable.

beca, *s.f.* a magistrate's gown, toga.

beco, *s.m.* alley, a narrow street; *beco sem saída,* a blind alley; cul-de-sac; deadlock.

bedame, *s.m.* o mesmo que "badame".

bedel, *s.m.* beadle.

bedelhar, *v.i.* to meddle, to intrude.

bedelho, *s.m.* latch *(tranqueta),* bolt *(ferrolho); meter o bedelho,* to stick one's nose in.

beduíno, *s.m.* Bedouin.

bege, *s.m.* beige, tan.

begónia, *s.f.* begonia.

begoniáceas, *s.f.pl.* begoniaceae.

beguino, *s.m.* beguin, béguin, beghard, medicant friar.

bei, *s.m.* bey.

beiça, *s.f.* pout; *fazer beiça,* to pout.

beiçada, *s.f.* blobber-lip.

beicinho, *s.m.* little-lip; *fazer becinho,* to pout.

beiço, *s.m.* lip; *trazer alguém pelo beicinho,* to lead someone by the nose.

beiçudo, *adj.* thick-lipped.

beijado, *adj.* kissed; *de mão beijada,* gratuitously, for nothing.

beija-flor, *s.m.* humming-bird.
beija-mão, *s.m.* hand-kissing.
beijar, *v.t.* to kiss.
beijinho, *s.m.* kiss, little kiss.
beijo, *s.m.* kiss.
beijoca, *s.f.* kiss, a noisy kiss, smack.
beijocar, *v.t.* to kiss often.
beijoqueiro, *s.m.* a person fond of kissing; *adj.* fond of kissing, caressing.
beira, *s.f.* brink, edge, brim, rim, margin, bank, border. 1) *beira de estrada,* wayside, roadside. 2) *à beira de,* on the edge of. 3) *à beira-mar,* at the seaside. 4) *à beira do rio,* on the bank of the river. 5) *não ter eira nem beira,* to have neither house nor home.
beirado, beiral, *s.m.* eaves.
bela, *s.m.* beauty; *bela adormecida,* sleeping-beauty.
beladona, *s.f.* belladonna.
belbute, *s.m.* coton velvet.
beldade, *s.f.* beauty.
beldroega, *s.f.* purslane.
beleguim, *s.m.* bailiff's official, cop *(policial).*
beleza, *s.f.* beauty, fineness, good looks.
belga, *s.m.* e *s.f.* e *adj.* Belgian.
Bélgica, *s.f.* Belgium.
belho, *s.f.* bolt.
beliche, *s.m.* berth, bunk.
bélico, *adj.* warlike, bellicose, martial.
belicosidade, *s.f.* bellicosity.
belicoso, *adj.* warlike, bellicose, martial, contentious.
belida, *s.f.* filme, speck on the eye, leu-coma.
beligerância, *s.f.* belligerancy.
beligerante, *s.m.* e *adj.* belligerent.
belígero, *adj.* belligerous.
beliscadura, *s.f.* pinch, scratch.
beliscão, *s.m.* pinch.
beliscar, *v.t.* to pinch.
belo, *adj.* beautiful, fair, fine, nice, pretty, lovely; *o belo sexo,* the fair sex.
beltrano, *s.m.* an indefinite person, Mr. so--and-so.
belvedere, *s.m.* belvedere.
belzebu, *s.m.* Beelzebub.
bem, *adv.* well, right, much, very; *interj.* well! good! well done!. 1) *bem pouco,* very little. 2) *bastante bem,* well enough. 3) *bem--amado,* beloved. 4) *bem-comportado,* well-behaved. 5) *a bem dizer,* as it were. 6) *estar de bem com alguém,* to be on good terms with someone; *s.m.* good, benefit,

advantage; *pl.* goods, possessions, belongings. 7) *bens corpóreos,* tangible goods. 8) *bens de consumo,* consumer goods. 9) *bens de raíz,* fixed real property. 10) *bens imóveis,* real estate. 11) *bens móveis,* movables. 12) *a bem de,* for the sake of. 13) *o bem e o mal,* good and evil. 14) *pessoa de bem,* honest person. 15) *por bem ou por mal,* willy- nilly.
bem-amado, *adj.* e *s.m.* beloved.
bem-aventurado, *adj.* blessed; *s.m.* the blest.
bem-aventurança, *s.f.* blessedness, happiness.
bem-dizente, *adj.* that speaks well of, praising.
bem-dizer, *v.t.* to bless, to praise.
bem-educado, *adj.* well-bred.
bem-encarado, *adj.* good-looking.
bem-estar, *s.m.* welfare.
bem-fadado, *adj.* fortunate, lucky, blissful.
bem-falante, *adj.* glib, fluent, well-spoken.
bem-fazer, *v.t.* to benifit, to do good to; *s.m.* charity, beneficience.
bem-humorado, *adj.* good-humored.
bem-intencionado, *adj.* well-meaning.
bem-me-quer, *s.m. (bot.)* daisy.
bem-nascido, *adj.* well-born.
bemol, *s.m. (mús.)* a flat.
bem-parecido, *adj.* good-looking.
bem-posto, *adj.* well-dressed.
bem-querer, *v.t.* to wish well; *s.m.* good will.
bem-soante, *adj.* harmonious.
bem-te-vi, *s.m.* flycatcher.
bem-vindo, *adj.* welcome.
bem-visto, *adj.* welcome, well-esteemed.
bênção, *s.f.* blessing, benediction.
bendito, *adj.* blessed, fortunate.
bendizente, *adj.* blessing, laudatory.
bendizer, *v.t.* to bless, to praise.
beneditino, *s.m.* e *adj.* Benedictine.
beneficiência, *s.f.* beneficence, charity.
beneficiente, *adj.* beneficent, charitable.
beneficiação, *s.f.* beneficiation, inpro-vement.
beneficiado, *adj.* beneficied, benetifed; *s.m.* beneficed, clergyman.
beneficiador, *adj.* beneficent, kind, benevolent.
beneficiar, *v.t.* to benefit, to improve, to better.
beneficiário, *s.m.* beneficiary.
benefício, *s.m.* benefit, benefice, favour,

service, profit, gain, advantage, help, improvement, betterment.

benéfico, *adj.* beneficent, beneficial, benign, favorable, salutary.

benemerente, *adj.* welldeserving.

benemérito, *s.m.* benefactor, patron; *adj.* worty, meritorious.

beneplácito, *s.m.* consent, permision, approval.

benesse, *s.f.* altarage, emolument, favour, donation.

benevolamente, *adv.* kindly, generously.

benevolência, *s.f.* benevolence, kindness.

benevolente, *adj.* benevolent, kind, generous.

benévolo, *adj.* benevolent, generous, kind.

benfazejo, *adj.* beneficent, kind, generous, charitable.

benfeitor, *s.m.* benefactor.

benfeitora, *s.f.* benefactress.

benfeitoria, *s.f.* improvement, betterment.

benfeitorizar, *v.t.* to improve, to better, to ameliorate.

bengala, *s.f.* cane, walking stick.

bengalada, *s.f.* stroke with a cane.

bengaleiro, *s.m.* umbrella stand.

benignidade, *s.f.* benignity, lenity, mildness, kindness.

benigno, *adj.* benign, kind, mild, lenient.

benjamim, *s.m.* youngest son, benjamin.

benjoeiro, *s.m.* benzoine-tree.

benjoim, *s.m.* gum benzoine.

benquerença, *s.f.* well-wishing, benevolence, affection.

benquistar, *v.t.* to ingratiate (with someone), to conciliate; *v.r.* to win friends.

benquisto, *adj.* well-liked, well-esteemed.

bentino, *s.m.* scapular.

bento, *adj.* holy, consecrated.

benzedeira, *s.f.* witch, sorceress, woman healer.

benzedura, *s.f.* conjuring, incantantion, the act of blessing or consecrating.

benzeno, *s.m.* benzene.

benzer, *v.t.* to bless, to hallow, to consecrate, to sanctify; *benzer-se,* to cross oneself, to make the sign of the cross.

benzido, *adj.* blessed, hallowed.

benzina, *s.f.* benzine.

benzoato, *s.m.* benzoate.

benzóico, *adj.* benzoic.

benzol, *s.m.* benzol.

beócio, *adj. e s.m.* Bocotian.

bequadro, *s.m. (mús.)* a natural sign or note.

berbequim, *s.m.* breast drill.

berbere, *s.m.* Berber.

berbicacho, *s.m.* trouble, confusion.

berbigão, *s.m.* a sort of mussel, cockle.

berço, *s.m.* cradle, birthplace, origin.

bergantim, *s.m.* brigantine.

beribéri, *s.m.* beriberi.

berilo, *s.m.* beryl.

berimbau, *s.m.* jew's harp.

beringela, *s.f.* mad-apple, eggplant.

berlinda, *s.f.* berlin, berline; *estar na berlinda,* to be in the order of the day.

berlinde, *s.m.* marble.

berloque, *s.m.* trinket, gewgaws; *por artes de berliques e bedoques:* hocus-pocus.

berma, *s.f.* berm, road margin.

bernarda, *s.f.* tumult, riot, disorder.

bernardo, *s.m.* a Cistercian monk; *adj.* Bernardine, Cistercian.

berra, *s.f. andar na berra,* to be very popular.

berrante, *adj.* garish, gaudy, loud.

berrar, *v.t.* to shout, to cry, to yell, to bellow, to scream.

berraria, *s.f.* screaming, bawling.

berregar, *v.i.* to cry, to bleat, to bellow, to cry.

berro, *s.m.* scream, shout, yell.

besouro, besoiro, *s.m.* beetle.

besta, *s.f.* crossbow *(arma),* beast, blockhead.

besteiro, *s.m.* cross-bowman, cross-bower, archer.

bestiaga, *s.f.* a worthless beast, blockhead, stupid.

bestial, *adj.* beastly, brutish; *interj.* great!

bestialidade, *s.f.* bestiality, brutality.

bestializar, *v.t.* to bestialize, to make stupid.

bestunta, *s.m.* noodle, brains, dull mind.

besuntadela, *s.f.* the act of besmear.

besuntão, *s.m.* greasy man or boy.

besuntar, *v.t.* to besmear, to grease, to bedaub.

beta, *s.f.* beta, (the second letter of the Greek alphabet); a small metallic vein.

betão, *s.m.* concrete.

beterraba, *s.f.* garden-beet, beet, beetroot.

betesga, *s.f.* narrow street.

betonar, *v.t.* to concrete, to cover with concrete.

bétula, *s.f.* birch.

betumar, *v.t.* to bituminate, to cover or fix with putty.

betume, *s.f.* bitumen, putty.

bexiga, *s.f.* bladder.

bexigas, *s.f.pl.* smallpox *(doença)*, pockmarks *(marcas); bexigas doidas:* chickenpox.

bexigoso, *adj.* pockmarked.

bezerra, *s.f.* heifer.

bezerro, *s.m.* calf, bullock.

biangular, *adj.* biangulated, with two angles.

biatómico, *adj.* biatomic.

bibe, *s.m.* pinafore, little apron for children.

biberão, *s.m.* feeding bottle, sucking--bottle.

Bíblia, *s.f.* Bible.

bíblico, *adj.* biblical.

bibliófilo, *s.m.* bibliophil.

bibliografia, *s.f.* bibliography.

bibliográfico, *adj.* bibliographical.

bibliógrafo, *s.m.* bibliographer.

bibliologia, *s.m.* bibliology.

bibliólogo, *s.m.* bibliologist.

bibliomania, *s.f.* bibliomania.

bibliómano, *adj.* bibliomaniac.

biblioteca, *s.f.* library.

bibliotecário, *s.m.* librarian, library-keeper.

bica, *s.f.* waterspout, water-pipe, spring *(nascente); correr em bica,* to flow.

bicada, *s.f.* peck.

bical, *adj.* beaked.

bicar, *v.t.* to peck.

bicarbonado, *adj.* bicarbonated.

bicarbonato, *s.m.* bicarbonate.

bicéfalo, *adj.* bicephalous, two-headed.

bicelular, *adj.* bicellular.

bíceps, *s.m.pl.* biceps.

bicha, *s.f.* leech (sanguessuga), worm, *(lombriga, etc.),* queue (fila); *bicha-de--rabear,* squib.

bichado, *adj.* wormy, maggoty.

bichanar, *v.t.* to whisper.

bichano, *s.m.* pussy, kitten.

bicharada, *s.f.* vermin, animals, lots of animals.

bicharoco, *s.m.* ugly or repulsive animal.

bicheiro, *s.m.* fish-hoop; *adj.* quibbling, minutious.

bichento, *adj.* wormy.

bicho, *s.m.* animal, bug, insect, worm, grub. 1) *bicho-careta, todo o bico-careta,* every human being. 2) *ter bicho carpinteiro,* to have fidgets. 3) *bicho de sete cabeças,* tough nut to crack. 4) *bicho do mato,* solitary or shy person.

bicho-da-seda, *s.m.* silk-worm.

bichoso, *adj.* wormy.

bicicleta, *s.f.* bicycle, bike.

bicipital, *adj.* bicipital

bicípite, *s.m.* biceps.

bico, *s.m.* beak, bill, point *(ponta),* toe, *(do sapato).* 1) *bico de Bunsen,* Bunsen burner. 2) *calar o bico,* to shut up. 3) *bico-de-obra,* a difficult thing to do. 4) *jogar um pau de dois bicos,* to play a double game.

bicolor, *adj.* bicolour.

bicôncavo, *adj.* biconcave.

biconvexo, *adj.* biconvex.

bicorne, *adj.* bicorn.

bicudo, *adj.* beaked, pointed, sharp; *um caso bicudo,* an intricate matter.

bidão, *s.m.* big can for oil or petrol.

bidé, *s.m.* bidet.

bidentado, *adj.* bidental.

biela, *s.f.* piston rod.

bienal, *adj.* biennial, lasting two years.

biénio, *s.m.* biennium.

bifar, *v.t.* to pilfer, to steal.

bife, *s.m.* steak, beafsteak.

bifendido, *adj.* bifid, cleft in two.

bífido, *adj.* bifid.

biforme, *adj.* biform.

bifronte, *adj.* bifronted, with two faces, double-faced.

bifurcação, *s.f.* bifurcation, forking.

bifurcar, *v.t.* to bifurcate, to divide into branches of forks.

bigamia, *s.f.* bigamy.

bígamo, *s.m.* bigamist.

bigémeo, *adj.* bigeminate.

bigode, *s.m.* moustache, whiskers, *(de gato); dar um bigode,* to suepass, to win.

bigorna, *s.f.* anvil.

bigorrilha, *s.f.* a worthless man.

bigota, *s.f. (náut.)* dead-eyes.

bigúmeo, *adj.* ancipital.

bijutaria, *s.f.* trinkets, costume jewelry.

bilabiado, *adj.* bilabiate.

bilabial, *adj.* bilabial.

bilateral, *adj.* bilateral.

bilha, *s.f.* jar, jug, waterpot.

bilhar, *s.m.* billiards.

bilharda, *s.f.* tipcat.

bilharista, *s.m.* billiard-player.

bilhete, *s.m.* ticket, billet, note *(cartinha).* 1) *bilhete de ida e volta,* return ticket. 2) *bilhete postal,* postcard.

bilheteira, *s.f.* ticket-office, box-office *(numa sala de espectáculos);* card-tray or card-case *(caixa para cartões de visita).*

bilheteiro, *s.m.* ticket-clerk, box-office clerk.

bilião, *s.m.* billion; em Inglaterra: a milliard, a million million.

biliar, *adj.* biliary.

bilingue, *adj.* bilingual.

bilioso, *adj.* bilious.

bílis, *s.f.* bile.

bilobado, *adj.* bilobed, bilobular.

bilro, *s.m.* bobbin, lace bobbin *(renda)*.

biltre, *s.m.* scoundrel, rascal.

bímano, *adj.* bimanous.

bimbalhar, *v.i.* to ring continually, to jingle.

bimensal, *adj.* by-monthly, bimensal.

bimestral, *adj.* by-monthly, bimonthly.

bimestre, *s.m.* the space of two months.

bimotor, *adj.* with two motors.

binar, *v.i.* to say two masses on the same day.

binário, *adj.* binary.

binocular, *adj.* binocular.

binóculo, *s.m.* binocle, binoculars, field glasses, opera glasses.

binómio, *adj.* binomiac; *s.m.* binomiac.

bínubo, *adj.* married twice.

bioco, *s.m.* veil.

biogénese, *s.f.* biogenesis.

biogenia, *s.f.* biogeny.

biografar, *v.t.* to write the biography of someone.

biografia, *s.f.* biography.

biográfico, *adj.* biographic.

biógrafo, *s.m.* biographer.

biologia, *s.f.* biology.

biológico, *adj.* biological.

biologista, *s.m.* biologist.

biólogo, *s.m.* biologist.

biombo, *s.m.* screen.

bioquímica, *s.f.* biochemistry.

bioscópio, *s.m.* bioscope.

bióxido, *s.m.* dioxide.

bíparo, *adj.* biparous.

bipartição, *s.f.* bipartition, division in two parts.

bipartido, *adj.* bipartite.

bípede, *adj.* biped, two-footed; *s.m.* a biped.

bípene, *adj.* bipennate, two-winged; *s.m.* double edged battle-axe.

bipétalo, *adj.* bipetalous.

biplano, *s.m.* biplane.

biplume, *adj.* with two feathers.

bipolar, *adj.* with two poles.

bipolaridade, *s.f.* bipolarity.

biquadrado, *adj.* biquadratic.

biqueira, *s.f.* toe *(de sapato)*, toe-cap *(biqueira de bota)*.

birmanês, *adj.* e *s.m.* Burmese.

Birmânia, *s.f.* Burma.

birra, *s.f.* will foolness, obstinacy, caprice, whim.

birreme, *s.f.* bireme.

birrento, *adj.* stubborn, obstinate, ill-humo-red.

bis, *adv.* bis, twice, encore, again.

bisanual, *adj.* bisannual, half-yearly.

bisão, *s.m.* bison.

bisar, *v.t.* to repeat.

bisavô, *s.m.* great-grandfather.

bisavó, *s.f.* great-grandmother.

bisbilhotar, *v.i.* to meddle, to gossip; *v.t.* to snoop around.

bisbilhoteiro, *s.m.* gossip, meddler, snooper.

bisbilhotice, *s.f.* meddlesomeness, snooping, meddling.

bisca, *s.f.* scoundrel; a game of cards.

biscate, *s.m.* odd job.

biscoito, *s.m.* cookie, biscuit.

bisegre, *s.m.* shoemaker's burnishing stick.

bisel, *s.m.* bevel edge.

bismute, *s.m.* bismuth.

bisnaga, *s.f.* a tube for holding liquids, or paste.

bisnal, *adj.* cunning, sly.

bisneta, *s.f.* great-granddaugther.

bisneto, *s.m.* great-grandson.

bisnetos, *s.m.pl.* great-grandchildren.

bisonharia, *s.f.* inexperience, awkwardeness.

bisonho, *adj.* inexperienced, green, raw.

bisonte, *s.m.* bison.

bispado, *s.m.* bishopric, diocese.

bispar, *v.t.* to act as a bishop, to bishop, to see in the distance, to descry.

bispo, *s.m.* bishop.

bispote, *s.m.* chamber-pot.

bissecção, *s.f.* bisection.

bissector, *adj.* bisecting.

bissectriz, *s.f.* bisector.

bissemanal, *adj.* by-weekly.

bissemanário, *s.m.* bi-weekly, a periodical issued twice a week.

bisseriado, *adj.* biseriate.

bissextil, *adj.* bissextile.

bissexto, *adj.* bissextile; *ano bissexto,* leap year.

bissexual, bissexuado, *adj.* bisexual, hermaphrodita.

bisso, *s.m.* byssus.

bistre, *s.m.* bistre, bister.

bisturi, *s.m.* bistury.

bitácula, *s.f.* bittacle, binnacle.

bitola, *s.f.* standard mesure, size, gauge *(de via férrea).*

bivacar, *v.i.* to bivouac, to camp.

bivalência, *s.f.* bivalence.

bivalente, *s.m.* e *adj.* bivalent.

bivalve, *s.m.* e *adj.* bivalve, bivalbular.

bivaque, *s.m.* bivouac.

bizantinice, *s.f.* futility, trifle, extravagance.

bizantino, *adj.* e *s.m.* Bizantine.

bizarrear, *v.i.* to act in a gallant manner, to boast, to brag of.

bizarria, *s.f.* gallantry, nobleness, courtesy, pomp, bravery.

bizarro, *adj.* gallant, courteous, generous, noble, odd *(esquisito).*

blandícias, *s.f.pl.* caresses, blandishment, endearments.

blandicioso, *adj.* caressing, endearing, loving.

blasfemador, *s.m.* blasphemer.

blasfemar, *v.t.* e *v.i.* to blaspheme.

blasfémia, *s.f.* blasphemy.

blasfemo, *adj.* blasphemous; *s.m.* blasphemer.

blasonador, *s.m.* boaster, bragger, braggart.

blasonar, *v.i.* to boast, to brag of; *v.t.* to blazon, to show of, to display.

blastocarpo, *s.m.* blastocarpous.

blastoderme, *s.f.* blastoderm.

blastodérmico, *adj.* blastodermic.

blindado, *adj.* armor-plated, armor-clad, armored, ironclad, shielded *(electricidade).*

blindagem, *s.f.* armor-plating, shielding *(electricidade).*

blindar, *v.t.* to armor, to armor-plate, to shield.

bloco, *s.m.* block, wtiting pad *(bloco de escrever).*

bloqueante, *adj.* blocking.

bloquear, *v.t.* to blockade *(militar),* to obstruct.

bloqueio, *s.m.* blockade, obstruction.

blusa, *s.f.* blouse.

blusão, *s.m.* jacket.

boa, *s.f.* boa *(serpente).*

boa, *adj.* good.

boataria, *s.f.* false reports.

boateiro, *s.m.* newsmonger, rumor spreader, alarmist.

boato, *s.m.* rumor, report, hearsay.

bobina, *s.f.* coil *(electricidade),* bobbin, reel, spool.

bobinador, *s.m.* coil-winder.

bobinar, *v.t.* to wind, to reel.

bobo, *s.m.* buffooin, jester; *adj.* foolish, silly, simple.

boca, *s.f.* mouth, opening *(abertura),* beam *(largura de navio).* 1) à boca cheia, loudly, freely. 2) à boca pequena, in whispers. 3) andar na boca do povo, to be much talked about or to be the talk of the town. 4) de boca aberta, open-mouthed.

boça, *s.f. (náut.)* stopper, painter.

bocaça, *s.f.* a wide mouth.

bocadinho, *s.m.* a little bit, tiny bit.

bocado, *s.m.* bit, morsel *(pedaço),* mouthful, bite *(alimento).*

bocal, *s.m.* mouth *(de recipiente),* mouthpiece *(de telefone ou instrumento musical),* socket *(de castiçal).*

boçal, *adj.* rude, ignorant, coarse.

bocarra, *s.f.* large mouth.

bocejar, *v.i.* to yawn.

bocejo, *s.m.* yawn, yawning.

bochecha, *s.f.* cheek.

bochechar, *v.t.* to rinse, to gargle, to wash the mouth.

bochecho, *s.m.* mouthful, rinsing the mouth.

bochechudo, *adj.* cheeky, fat-cheeked.

boches, *s.m.pl.* the heart and lungs of animals; *(gíria)* the German people.

bócio, *s.m.* goitre, goiter.

boda, *s.f.* wedding, wedding feast; bodas de ouro, golden wedding.

bode, *s.m.* male goat, billy-goat.

bodega, *s.f.* bodega, low tavern, cheep eating place, rubbish, filthiness.

bodegão, *s.m.* a dirty fellow.

bodeguice, *s.f.* filthiness.

bodo, *s.m.* money or food freely bestowed; dar um bodo aos pobres, to distribute money or food to the poor.

bodum, *s.m.* rank-smell, a disagreable smell.

Boémia, *s.f.* Bohemia; loose living.

boémio, *s.m.* e *adj.* Bohemian; vagabond, vagrant, playboy.

bofe, *s.m.* lung; *s.m.pl.* the lungs, light *(fressura).*

bofetada, *s.f.* slap in the face.

bofetão, *s.m.* slap, blow.

bofete, *s.m.* light slap.

boga, *s.f.* boce or boga.

boi, *s.m.* ox *(pl.* oxen), bull.

bóia, *s.f.* buoy.

boiada, *s.f.* a herd of oxen.

boião, *s.m.* jam-pot.

boiar, *v.i.* to float; *v.t.* to tie a buoy.

boicotagem, *s.f.* boycott, boycotting.

boicotar, *v.t.* to boycott.

boicotear, *v.t.* o mesmo que "boicotar".

boieira, *s.f.* morning star.

boieiro, *s.m.* herdsman.

boina, *s.f.* beret.

boiz, *s.f.* springe noose.

bojador, *adj.* proeminent, jutting, outstanding.

bojar, *v.t.* e *v.i.* to swell, to bulge, to stand out.

bojarda, *s.f.* silly saying, fib, lie.

bojo, *s.m.* bulge, proeminence, protuberance, capacity.

bojudo, *adj.* big-bellied, bulgy.

bola, *s.f.* ball, globe, sphere; *ora bolas!,* shucks!

bolacha, *s.f.* biscuit, cracker, slap in the face *(bofetada).*

bolachudo, *adj.* chubby-faced, round-cheeked.

bolada, *s.f.* a stroke of a ball.

bolandas, *s.f.pl. andar em bolandas,* to blunder on, to tumble about.

bolar, *v.t.* e *v.i.* to serve *(ténis).*

bolbiforme, *adj.* bulbiform.

bolbo, *s.m.* bulb, bulbous root.

bolboso, *adj.* bulbous.

bolçar, *v.t.* to vomit, to bring up milk.

bolchevique, *s.m.* bolshevik.

bolchevismo, *s.m.* bolshevism.

bolchevista, *s.m.* bolshevist.

boldrié, *s.m.* belt, sword-belt.

boleado, *adj.* rounded, well-turned.

bolear, *v.t.* to make round, to round of.

boleeiro, *s.m.* coachman, driver.

boleia, *s.f.* the driver's seat on a carriage; *andar à boleia,* to hitchhike.

boletim, *s.m.* bulletin, report. 1) *boletim de voto,* ballot-paper. 2) *boletim meteorológico,* weather report.

boletineiro, *s.m.* distributer of bulletins or telegrams.

boleto, *s.m.* billet *(mil.).*

boléu, *s.f.* fall, tumble.

bolha, *s.f.* bubble.

bólide, *s.m.* bolide, meteor.

bolina, *s.f. (náut.)* bowline, meteor.

bolinar, *v.i.* to sail close-hauled, to luff.

bolinete, *s.m.* windlass.

boliviano, *s.m.* e *adj.* Bolivian.

bolo, *s.m.* cake.

bolor, *s.m.* mould, mouldiness, must.

bolorecer, *v.i.* to grow mould.

bolorento, *adj.* mouldy.

bolota, *s.f.* acorn.

bolsa, *s.f.* purse, bag, handbag, pouch. 1) *bolsa de estudos,* scholarship. 2) *bolsa de valores,* stock market.

bolsar, *v.t.* to wrinkle.

bolseiro, *s.m.* scholar, holder of a scholarship.

bolso, *s.m.* pocket.

bom, *adj.* good, kind *(bondoso).* 1) *bom--serás,* simple, goodman, good-natured man. 2) *bom-tom,* politeness, distinction.

bomba, *s.f.* bomb, pump *(hidráulica ou pneumática).*

bombarda, *s.f.* bombard.

bombardeamento, *s.m.* bombardment, shelling.

bombardear, *v.t.* to bombard, to shell, to bomb.

bombardeio, *s.m.* o mesmo que "bombardeamento".

bombardeira, *s.f.* embrasure, port-hole.

bombardeiro, *s.m.* bomber, bombing plane.

bombardino, *s.m.* bombardon.

bombástico, *adj.* bombastic, high-sounding, inflated.

bombazina, *s.f.* bombazine.

bombear, *v.t.* to pump.

bombeiro, *s.m.* fireman.

bombice, *s.m.* silkworm.

bombo, *s.m.* large drum.

bombom, *s.m.* bonbon, sugarplum.

bombordo, *s.m.* port, larboard.

bonacheirão, *adj.* e *s.m.* good-natured, patient.

bonacheirice, *s.f.* good nature.

bonança, *s.f.* calm weather, lull, peace, quiet.

bonançar, *v.i.* to be calm (o tempo).

bonançoso, *adj.* calm, quiet, serene.

bondade, *s.f.* goodness, kindness.

bonde, *s.m. (bras.)* tramcar.

bondoso, *adj.* kind, good, kind-hearted, gentle.

boné, *s.m.* cap.

boneca, *s.f.* doll, puppet.

boneco, *s.m.* doll.

bonificação, *s.f.* bonus, premium.

bonificar, *v.t.* to give a bonus.

bonifrate, *s.m.* puppet, marionette.

bonina, *s.f.* daisy.

boniteza, *s.f.* prettiness, beauty, charm.

bonito, *adj.* pretty, beautiful, nice, attractive.

bonomia, *s.f.* good-nature, goodness.

bónus, *s.m.* bonus, premium.

bonzo, *s.m.* bonzo, a Buddhist priest.

boqueirão, *s.m.* gulf, wide opening, river mouth, gorge, canyon.

boquejar, *v.t.* e *v.i.* to blame, to yawn.

boquiaberto, *adj.* open-mouthed, astonished.

boquilha, *s.f.* cigar holder.

borato, *s.m.* borate.

bórax, *s.m.* borax.

borboleta, *s.f.* butterfly.

borboletear, *v.i.* to flutter, to wander *(vaguear)*, to daydream *(devanear)*.

borbotão, *s.m.* gush, spurt, spout.

borbotar, *v.t.* to gush, to spout.

borbulha, *s.f.* blister, boil *(espinha)*.

borbulhagem, *s.f.* great quantity of blisters or spots.

borbulhão, *s.m.* large blister.

borbulhar, *v.t.* to bubble, to sprout *(jorrar)*.

borbulhoso, *adj.* bubbling, having blisters.

borco, *s.m. de borco,* face down, upside-down.

borda, *s.f.* edge, border, brink, shore. 1) *à borda de,* on the edge of. 2) *pela borda fora,* overboard. 3) *à borda de água,* at the seaside, at the sea shore.

bordada, *s.f. (náut.)* tack, lag.

bordadeira, *s.f.* embroideress.

bordado, *s.m.* em broidery.

bordador, *s.m.* embroiderer.

bordadura, *s.f.* edge, rim, hem, fringe.

bordalengo, *adj.* ignorant, coarse, stupid.

bordalês, *s.m.* an inhabitant of Bordeaux.

bordão, *s.m.* staff, stick, bass string *(música)*.

bordar, *v.t.* to embroider, to border *(orlar)*.

bordejar, *v.i.* to tack.

bordel, *s.f.* brothel.

bordo, *s.m. (náut.)* board. 1) *a bordo,* aboard. 2) *subir a bordo,* to go aboard.

bordo, *s.m.* small maple.

bordoada, *s.f.* stroke with a stick, drubbing *(surra)*.

boreal, *adj.* northern, boreal.

bóreas, *adj.* boreas, the north wind.

borga, *s.f.* frolic, merry-making.

Borgonha, *s.f.* Burgundy.

borgonhês, *s.m.* e *adj.* Burgundian.

bórico, *adj.* boric.

borla, *s.f.* tassel *(pó de arroz)*, puff, doctor's cap; *de borla,* gratis, gratuitously.

borlista, *s.m.* one who enjoys privileges without paying.

bornal, *s.m.* haversack, provision bag.

borne, *s.m.* terminal.

bornear, *v.t.* to level.

borneio, *s.m.* turn, the end of a lance.

borra, *s.f.* dregs, sediments.

borra-botas, *s.m.* squirt.

borracha, *s.f.* rubber, caoutchouc.

borracheira, *s.f.* drunkness, a fiasco.

borracho, *s.m.* drunkard; *adj.* drunk.

borrada, *s.f.* stupidity, nonsense.

borrado, *adj.* dirty, badly painted.

borrador, *s.m. (com.)* waste book, a bad painter or writer.

borradura, *s.f.* blot.

borragem, *s.f. (bot.)* borage.

borralheira, *s.f.* ash leap.

borralheiro, *adj.* one who likes to sit by the fireplace.

borralho, *s.m.* embers, fire-place.

borrão, *s.m.* blot, ink-spot, a rough draft *(esboço)*.

borrar, *v.t.* to blot, to stain.

borrasca, *s.f.* tempest, storm.

borrascoso, *adj.* stormy, tempestuous, violent.

borrega, *s.f.* ewe-lamb.

borregada, *s.f.* a flock of lambs.

borrego, *s.m.* lamb.

borregueiro, *s.m.* lamb driver.

borreguice, *s.f.* indolence, foolishness.

borrifadela, *s.f.* sprinkling.

borrifador, *s.m.* sprinkler.

borrifar, *v.t.* to sprinkle, to wet.

borrifo, *s.m.* sprinkling, drizzle.

borzeguim, *s.m.* buskin.

bosque, *s.m.* wood, forest.

bosquejar, *v.t.* to sketch, to outline.

bosquejo, *s.m.* sketch, outline.

bossa, *s.f.* bump, hump, lump, swelling *(inchaço)*.

bosta, *s.f.* dung, excrement.

bostela, *s.f.* pustule, pimple.

bota, *s.f.* boot; *bota-de-elástico,* an antiquated person.

bota-fora, *s.m.* good-bye party.

botânica, *s.f.* botany.

botânico, *adj.* botanic; *s.m.* botanist.

botão, *s.m.* button, bud *(de planta)*, kong *(de trinco)*. 1) *botão de colarinho,* collar stud. 2) *botão de punho,* cuff-links. 3) *caiu um botão,* a button came off.

botar, *v.t.* to put, to place, to cast *(lançar)*.

botaréu, *s.m.* buttress, abutement.

bota-selas, *s.m. (mil.)* signal to saddle.

bote, *s.m.* boat.

botelha, *s.f.* bottle.

botequim, *s.m.* coffee-shop, bar.

botica, *s.f.* pharmacy, drugstore, aphotecary's shop.

boticário, *s.m.* apothecary, pharmacist.

botija, *s.f.* earthenware bottle.

botim, *s.m.* half-boot.

botina, *s.f.* bottine, lady's boot.

boto, *adj.* blunt, dull, pointless.

botoaria, *s.f.* button-factory.

botoeira, *s.f.* button-hole.

botulismo, *s.m.* botulism.

bouça, *s.f.* copse.

bovídeos, *s.m.pl.* bovidae, cattle.

bovino, *adj.* bovine.

boxe, *s.m.* boxing.

braça, *s.f.* fathom.

braçada, *s.f.* armfull, stroke *(na natação).*

braçadeira, *s.f.* tieback *(de cortina),* arm strap *(alça para segurar-se),* arm band *(distintivo).*

braçado, *s.m.* armful.

braçal, *adj.* brachial, manual *(trabalho); s.m.* brassart *(peça de armadura).*

bracejar, *v.t. e v.i.* to wave the arms, to gesticulate, to struggle *(debater-se).*

bracelete, *s.f.* bracelet.

braço, *s.m.* arm, lever *(de alavanca),* beam *(de balança).* 1) a braços com, at grips with. 2) braço de mar, arm of the sea; inlet. 3) de braços cruzados, with folded arms. 4) de braço dado, arm in arm.

bráctea, *s.f.* bract.

bractéola, *s.f.* bracteole.

bradar, *v.t. e v.i.* to cry out, to scream; bradar aos céus, to cry out to heaven.

brado, *s.m.* cry, shout, scream.

braga, *s.f.* shackle, fetter.

bragal, *s.m.* linen.

braguilha, *s.f.* trousers slit, flap.

brâmane, *s.m.* Brahman.

bramanismo, *s.m.* Brahmanism.

bramar, *v.i.* to roar, to bellow, to cry out.

bramido, *s.m.* roar, bellow, howl.

bramir, *v.i.* to roar, to howl, to yell, to rage, to shout.

branca, *s.f.* white hair.

branco, *adj. e s.m.* white, blank *(espaço em branco).*

brancura, *s.f.* whiteness.

brandal, *s.m. (náut.)* stay, backstay.

brandamente, *adv.* softly, gently.

brandão, *s.m.* torch.

brandir, *v.t.* to brandish, to shake, to wave, to swing.

brando, *adj.* soft, gentle, mild.

brandura, *s.f.* softness, mildness.

branqueação, *s.f.* whitening, bleaching.

branqueado, *adj.* whitened.

branqueador, *s.m.* whitener, bleacher.

branquear, *v.t.* to whiten, to bleach; *v.i.* to grow white.

branquejar, *v.i.* to become white, to gleam white.

branquiado, *adj.* blanched.

brânquias, *s.f.pl.* gills.

braquial, *adj.* brachial.

braquicéfalo, *adj.* brachycephalous.

braquigrafia, *s.f.* brachygraphy.

braquígrafo, *s.m.* brachygrapher.

braquilogia, *s.f.* brachylogy.

braquiópodes, *s.m.pl.* brachiopoda.

brasa, *s.f.* ember, live coal, burning coal. 1) em brasa, incandescent, red-hot. 2) sentir--se sobre brasas, to be on pins and needles.

brasão, *s.m.* coat of arms, escutcheon.

braseiro, *s.m.* fire-pan, brazier.

brasido, *s.m.* embers, burning-coals.

brasileirismo, *s.m.* Brazilianism.

brasileiro, *s.m. e adj.* Brazilian.

brasonar, *v.t. e v.i.* to emblazon, to boast *(vangloriar-se).*

brassicáceas, *s.f.pl.* brassicaceae.

bravata, *s.f.* bravado, boasting, bluster.

bravateador, *s.m.* boaster, bully.

bravatear, *v.i.* to boast, to bluster.

bravateiro, *s.m.* boaster, bully, fanfaron.

bravejar, *v.i.* to rage, to cause disturbance.

braveza, *s.f.* bravery, valour, intrepidity.

bravio, *adj.* wild, untilled, coarse, savage; *s.m.* barren ground.

bravo, *adj.* brave, valiant, intrepid, courageous, wild, savage; *interj.* bravo!

bravura, *s.f.* bravery, valour, courage.

breadura, *s.f.* tarring, pitching.

brear, *v.t.* to tar, to smear or coat with tar, to pitch.

breca, *s.f.* cramp; ser levado da breca, to play the devil; to be turbulent; to be mischievous.

brecha, *s.f.* breach, gap, rift, opening.

brejeirice, *s.f.* knavery, roguery.

brejeiro, *adj.* roguish, mischievous, saucy, malicious.

brejo, *s.m.* march, bog, fen, swamp.

brejoso, *adj.* fenny, marshy, boggy.

brenha, *s.f.* bush, ticket, confusion.

brenhoso, *adj.* bushy, woody, brambly.

Bretanha, *s.f.* Britain, Brittany (França).

bretão, *s.m.* e *adj.* a native of Britain, British; Breton (de França).

breu, *s.m.* pitch, tar.

breve, *s.m.* brief, breve (música); *adj.* brief, short.

brevemente, *adv.* soon, briefly, shortly.

breviário, *s.m.* breviary.

brevidade, *s.f.* brevity, briefness, shortness; *com a possível brevidade,* at your earliest convenience.

brial, *s.m.* a silk dress; tunic worn by ancient knights.

brica, *s.f.* the place of the crescent on the field.

bricabraque, *s.m.* bric-a-brac.

briche, *s.m.* a coarse kind of woollen cloth.

brida, *s.f.* bridle; *a toda a brida,* at full speed.

bridão, *s.m.* snaffle-bit, bridoon.

bridar, *v.t.* to bridle; to restrain.

briga, *s.f.* quarrel, fighting.

brigada, *s.f.* brigade.

brigadeiro, *s.m.* brigadier.

brigão, briguento, *adj.* quarrelsome; *s.m.* quarreler, contender.

brigar, *v.t.* to quarrel, to fight, to contend.

brigue, *s.m.* brig.

brilhante, *adj.* brilliant, bright, shining; *s.m.* diamond, brilliant,

brilhantemente, *adv.* brightly.

brilhar, *v.i.* to shine, to glitter, to sparkle, to twinkle (cintilar).

brilho, *s.m.* shine, brightness, brilliancy, glamour, glitter.

brim, *s.m.* duck.

brincadeira, *s.f.* fun, play, amusement, game, joke.

brincalhão, *s.m.* joker, a merry fellow; *adj.* merry, gay, playful.

brincar, *v.t.* to play, to frolic, to amuse oneself, to joke.

brinco, *s.m.* ear-ring; *brincos-de-princesa,* fuchsia.

brindar, *v.t.* to offer; *v.i.* to toast, to make a toast.

brinde, *s.m.* present, gift, toast.

brinquedo, *s.m.* toy, plaything.

brio, *s.m.* self-respect, pride, dignity.

brioche, *s.m.* bun.

briol, *s.m. (náut.)* brail, buntline.

briologia, *s.m.* bryology.

briosamente, *adv.* proudly, bravely.

brioso, *adj.* proud, brave, zealous.

brisa, *s.f.* breese.

brita, *s.f.* small pieces of stone, macadam.

britador, *s.m.* stone-breaker.

Britânia, *s.f.* Britannia.

britânico, *adj.* British.

britar, *v.t.* to break stone into small pieces, to crush.

broa, *s.m.* corn bread; *broas,* Christmas gift.

broca, *s.f.* drill, auger, perforator, central bit.

brocado, *s.m.* brocada.

brocar, *v.t.* to drill, to bore.

brocatel, *s.m.* brocatelle.

brocha, *s.f.* tack, a painter's brush.

brochado, *adj.* stitched.

brochador, *s.m.* stitcher.

brochar, to stitch, to tack on (pregar).

broche, *s.m.* brooch.

brochura, *s.f.* brochure, stitching, pamphlet.

brócolos, *s.m.pl.* broccoli.

bródio, *s.m.* banquet, feasting.

bromato, *s.m.* bromate.

bromatologia, *s.f.* bromatology.

brometo, *s.m.* bromide.

brómico, *adj.* bromic.

brómio, *s.m.* bromine.

bronco, *adj.* stupid, rude, course.

broncopneumonia, *s.f.* bronchopneumonia.

bronquial, *adj.* bronchial.

brônquico, *adj.* bronchial.

brônquio, *s.m.* bronchus; *pl.* bronchi.

bronquite, *s.f.* bronchitis.

bronze, *s.m.* bronze.

bronzeado, *adj.* bronzed, tanned (pelo sol).

bronzear, *v.t.* to bronze, to tan (pelo sol).

brônzeo, *adj.* bronzy, made of bronze.

broquel, *s.m.* buckler, small shield, protection.

brossa, *s.f.* painter's brush, horse brush.

brotar, *v.i.* to sprout, to shoot, to spring, to break out.

brotoeja, *s.f.* rash-blotches.

broxa, brush.

bruços, *loc. adv. de bruços,* face down.

brulote, *s.m.* fire-ship.

bruma, *s.f.* haze, fog, haziness, mist.

brumoso, *adj.* brumous, foggy, misty.

brunideira, *s.f.* ironer, laundrees.

brunido, *adj.* ironed, burnished, polished.

brunidor, *s.m.* burnisher, polisher.

brunidura, *s.f.* burnishing, ironing.

brunir, *v.t.* to burnish, to polish, to iron.

bruno, *adj.* brown, dark.

bruscamente, *adv.* abruptly, suddenly, unexpectedly, roughly.

brusco, *adj.* blunt, abrupt, sudden, rough.

brutal, *adj.* brutal, brutish.

brutalidade, *s.f.* brutality, brutishness, impoliteness.

brutalizar, to brutalize, to treat roughly, to maltreate.

brutalmente, *adv.* brutally.

brutamontes, *s.m.* brute, gorilla, boor.

brutesco, *adj.* rough, coarse, unpolished.

bruto, *s.m.* brute, rude, coarse; *em bruto,* rough, raw, in the rough.

bruxa, *s.f.* witch, sorceress.

bruxaria, *s.f.* witchcraft, witchery, sorcery.

bruxedo, *s.m.* o mesmo que "bruxaria".

bruxo, *s.m.* wizard, sorcerer.

bruxuleante, *adj.* flickering, wavering.

bruxulear, *v.i.* to flicker, to wave.

bubão, *s.m.* bubo.

bubónico, *adj.* bubonic.

bucal, *adj.* buccal.

bucéfalo, *s.m.* bucephalus.

bucha, *s.f.* wad, wadding; hunk of bread *(de pão); adj.* fat.

bucho, *s.m.* maw, stomach.

buço, *s.m.* down on the upper lip.

bucólica, *s.f.* bucolic.

bucólico, *adj.* bucolic, rural, pastoral.

Buda, *s.m.* Buddha.

budismo, *s.m.* buddhism.

budista, *s.m.* e *s.f.* Buddhist.

bueiro, *s.m.* draintrap, sewer.

buena-dicha, *s.f.* fortune, good-fortune.

búfalo, *s.m.* buffalo.

bufão, *s.m.* buffoon, jester.

bufar, *v.i.* to puff, to blow, to protest.

bufarinheiro, *s.m.* peddler.

bufete, *s.m.* buffet, sideboard, cupboard.

bufo, *s.m.* puff, snort, bufffoon; *adj.* grotesque, comic; *ópera bufa,* comic opera.

bufonaria, *s.f.* buffoonery.

bugalho, *s.m.* oak-apple.

bugalhudo, *adj.* like a gall-nut, prominent.

bugia, *s.f.* wax-candle, candlestick.

bugiar, *v.t.* e *v.i.* to ape, to mimic, to imitate, to grimace.

bugiarias, *s.f.pl.* trifles, toys.

bugigangas, *s.f.pl.* trifles, trinkets.

bugio, *s.m.* monjey, ape.

bujão, *s.m. (náut.)* wooden-peg, plug, stopper.

bujarrona, *s.f.* jib.

bula, *s.f.* bull, an edict from the Pope.

bulário, *s.m.* bullary.

bulboso, *adj.* bulbous.

bulcão, *s.m.* thick fog, black cloud.

buldogue, *s.m.* bulldog.

bule, *s.m.* tea-pot.

bulevar, *s.m.* boulevard.

búlgaro, *s.m.* e *adj.* Bulgarian.

bulha, *s.f.* quarrel, fight.

bulhar, *v.i.* to quarrel, to fight.

bulhento, *adj.* quarrelsome, irascible.

bulício, *s.m.* noise, bustle, stear.

buliçoso, *adj.* turbulent, restless, naughty.

bulir, *v.t.* e *v.i.* to move, to stear, to meddle with *(interferir).*

buraca, *s.f.* large gap, cavity.

buraco, *s.m.* hole, opening, cavity, pit, cave, hallow, high *(da agulha).*

burburinho, *s.m.* noise, murmur, disorder, tumult.

burel, *s.m.* monk's habit, a coarse wooden cloth.

burgo, *s.m.* borough, burg, village.

burgomestre, *s.m.* burgomaster.

burguês, *s.m.* bourgeois, *(pertencente a burguesia),* burgess *(cidadão); adj.* bourgeois.

burguesia, *s.f.* bourgeoisie; the middle class.

buril, *s.m.* burin, chisel.

burilador, *s.m.* engraver.

burilar, *v.t.* to engrave, to chisel.

burla, *s.f.* fraud, swindle, deceit, deception.

burlado, *adj.* duped.

burlão, *s.m.* swindler, defrauder, cheater.

burlar, *v.t.* to swindle, to cheat, to dupe, to defraud, to deceive.

burlesco, *adj.* burlesque, comic.

burlista, *s.f.* e *s.m.* o mesmo que "burlão".

burocracia, *s.f.* bureaucracy, red-tape *(formalidade excessiva).*

burocrata, *s.m.* bureaucrat.

burocrático, *adj.* bureaucratic.

burra, *s.f.* she-ass, safe *(cofre).*

burricada, *s.f.* drove of asses; nonsense, stupidity.

burrice, *s.f.* stupidity, foolishness, obstinacy.

burriqueiro, *s.m.* ass-driver.

burro, *s.m.* ass, donkey; *adj.* dumb, stupid.

busca, *s.f.* search, quest, pursuit.

buscar, *v.t.* to seach, to look for, to seek. 1) *ir buscar,* to fetch, to go for. 2) *mandar buscar,* to send for.

busílis, *s.m.* the vital question; *aí é que está o busílis,* there's the rub!

bússola, *s.f.* compass, magnetic needle.
busto, *s.m.* bust.
butano, *s.m.* butane.
buxo, *s.m. (bot.)* box.

buzina, *s.f.* horn.
buzinar, *v.t.* to honk, to sound a horn, to hoot.
búzio, *s.m.* whelk, trumpet shell.

C

c, the third letter of the Portuguese alphabet.
cá, *adv.* here, over here, hither; *para cá e para lá,* back and forth.
cã, *s.m.* khan *(título mongol).*
cabaça, *s.f.* gourd, calabash.
cabaceira, *s.f.* bottle-gourd.
cabaço, *s.m.* bottle-gourd, chub *(peixe).*
cabal, *adj.* exact, correct, complete, convincing.
cabala, *s.f.* cabala, intrigue, plot.
cabalista, *s.m. e s.f.* cabalist.
cablístico, *adj.* cabalistic.
cabalmente, *adv.* exactly, perfectly, correctly, completely.
cabana, *s.f.* hut, cot, shack.
cabaré, *s.m.* cabaret, night-club.
cabaz, *s.m.* hamper, pannier, basket.
cabeça, *s.f.* head, intellect, judgement, top *(parte mais alta),* leader *(chefe).* 1) *da cabeça aos pés,* from head to foot. 2) *de cabeça para baixo,* upside down, head first. 3) *cabeça-de-alho-chocho,* feather-brained. 4) *cabeça-de-casal,* the head of the family. 5) *cabeça-de-vento,* giddy person, scatter-brain.
cabeçada, *s.f.* blow with the head, headgear *(peça de arreio).*
cabeçalho, *s.m.* headline, tittle page.
cabeção, *s.m.* clerical collar, large collar.
cabecear, *v.i.* to nod.
cabeceira, *s.f.* head; *à cabeceira de alguém,* at the beside of.
cabecilha, *s.m.* ringleader, leader.
cabeço, *s.m.* round top *(cume),* knoll *(outeiro), (náut.)* mooring.

cabeçorra, *s.f.* big head.
cabeçote, *s.m.* headstock.
cabeçudo, *adj.* with a large head, obstinate, pig-headed.
cabedal, *s.m.* leather *(couro),* stock, fund.
cabedelo, *s.m.* sandbank.
cabeleira, *s.f.* hair, wig *(peruca).*
cabeleireiro, *s.m.* hair-dresser.
cabelo, *s.m.* hair. 1) *cortar o cabelo,* to have one's hair cut, to have a haircut. 2) *em cabelo,* bareheaded.
cabeludo, *adj.* hairy; *couro cabeludo,* scalp.
caber, *v.i.* to fit, to go into, to concern *(competir),* to have a place, to have room. 1) *cabe-lhes fazer isso,* it's up to them to do that. 2) *caber em sorte,* to fall to someone's lot. 3) *não caber em si de contente,* to be overjoyed.
cabide, *s.m.* rack, peg, coat hanger.
cabido, *s.m.* chapter of a cathedral.
cabimento, *s.m.* fitness, suitableness; *ter cabimento,* to be suitable, to make sense.
cabina, *s.f.* cabin, booth *(telefónica).*
cabisbaixo, *adj.* downcast, sorrowfull, sad, worried.
cabo, *s.m.* handle, grip *(lugar por onde se pega),* cable, rope *(corda),* cable *(eléctrico),* corporal *(militar),* cape, promontory *(promontório),* end *(extremidade).* 1) *cabo de vassoura,* broomstick. 2) *levar a cabo,* to carry out, to accomplish. 3) *ao cabo de,* at the end of, after.
caboclo, *s.m.* civilized Brazilian indian, Brazilian half-breed (indian and white).
cabograma, *s.m.* cablegram, cable.

cabotagem, *s.f.* cabotage, coasting, costwise navigation.

cabotar, *v.i.* to coast, to coast along.

cabotino, *s.m.* bad actor, strolling actor.

caboucar, *v.t.* e *v.i.* to dig trenches or foundations.

cabouco, *s.m.* ditch, trench, foundation.

cabouqueiro, *s.m.* navvy.

caboz, *s.m.* chub.

cabra, *s.f.* she-goat, bad-tempered woman, bitch *(mulher de má conduta).* 1) cabra--cega, blindman's buff. 2) cabra loura, stag-beetle.

cabrão, *s.m.* billy-goat, he-goat.

cábrea, *s.f.* crab, winch, derrick, crane.

cabreiro, *s.m.* goatherd.

cabrestante, *s.m. (náut.)* capstan, windlass.

cabresto, *s.m.* halter, *(náut.)* bobstay.

cabriola, *s.f.* caper, gambol, leap, jump.

cabriolé, *s.m.* cabriolet.

cabrite, *s.f.* small female kid; a sort of catapult.

cabrito, *s.m.* kid goat.

cábula, *adj.* lazy, slothful; *s.m.* e *s.f.* truant, a lazy student; *cábula de estudante,* crib, horse.

cabular, *v.i.* to slack, to cheat, to play truant.

caça, *s.f.* hunt, hunting, chase, chasing, game *(presas).* 1) *caça grossa,* big game fishing. 2) *ir a caça,* to go hunting.

caçada, *s.f.* hunt, hunting party.

caçadeira, *s.f.* hunting-gun.

caçador, *s.m.* hunter; *caçador furtivo,* poacher.

caçadora, *s.f.* huntress.

caça-minas, *s.m.* mine-sweeper.

cação, *s.m.* shark.

caçapo, *s.m.* young rabbit.

caçar, *v.t.* to hunt, to chase, to pursue.

cacarejar, *v.i.* to cackle, to cluck.

cacarejo, *s.m.* cackle, cluck.

cacaréu, cacareco, *s.m.* old piece of furniture.

cacaria, *s.f.* a heap of posherds.

caçarola, *s.f.* casserole, pan.

cacatua, *s.f.* cockatoo.

cacau, *s.m.* cocoa.

cacaual, *s.m.* cocoa plantation.

cacaueiro, cacauzeiro, cocoa palm, cocoa plant.

cacetada, *s.f.* a blow with a club.

cacete, *s.m.* club, stick.

caceteiro, *s.m.* clubman, quarreler.

cachaça, *s.f.* white rum.

cachação, *s.m.* a blow on the neck.

cachaço, *s.m.* nape, the back of the neck.

cachalote, *s.m.* cachalot, sperm whale.

cachamorra, cachaporra, *s.f.* club, a short stick with a heavy striking end.

cachão, *s.m.* bubbles of boiling water; *ferver em cachão,* to foam.

cacharolete, *s.m.* cocktail.

cachecol, *s.m.* neck scarf.

cacheira, *s.f.* club, cudgel, stick.

cacheirada, *s.f.* a blow with a club.

cacheiro, *adj.* sly, wily.

cachené, *s.m.* muffler, comforter.

cachimbada, *s.f.* a pipe full of tobacco, a puff of smoke; *fumar uma cachimbada,* to smoke a pipe.

cachimbar, *v.i.* to smoke a pipe; *v.t.* to deceive.

cachimbo, *s.m.* pipe.

cachimónia, *s.f. (pop.)* head, wits.

cacho, *s.m.* bunch, cluster.

cachoar, *v.i.* to bubble, to foam.

cachoeira, *s.f.* waterfall.

cachola, *s.f.* pate, nut, noodle.

cachopa, *s.f.* lass, girl.

cachopo, *s.m.* lad, boy.

cachorra, *s.f.* a little bitch.

cachorrada, *s.f.* pack of dogs, dirty trick *(má acção).*

cachorro, *s.m.* pup, puppy, cub *(filhote de animal);* hot-dog *(salsicha no pão).*

cachucha, *s.f.* cachucha *(dança).*

cacifo, *s.m.* locker, file-case.

cacimba, *s.f.* drizzle, dew.

cacique, *s.m.* local political boss, tribal chief.

caco, *s.m.* potsherd, piece of broken pottery, fragment.

caçoada, *s.f.* mockery, jest, scoff.

caçoador, *s.m.* jester, jocker, mocker; *adj.* jesting, scoffimg.

caçoar, *v.t.* to jest, to mock, to scoff.

cacofonia, *s.f.* cacophony.

cacofónico, *adj.* cacophonic.

cacografia, *s.f.* cacography, bad spelling.

cacográfico, *adj.* cacographic.

caçoleta, *s.f.* hammer, pan.

cacto, *s.m.* cactus.

cada, *adj.* each, every. 1) *cada qual,* each one. 2) *cada semana,* each or every week. 3) *cada três dias,* every three days. 4) *cada vez mais,* more and more. 5) *cada vez mais barato,* cheaper and cheaper. 6) *cada vez* *melhor,* better and better. 7) *cada vez menos,* less and less. 8) *de cada vez:* at a time.

cadafalso, *s.m.* scaffold.

cadarço, *s.m.* floss slick, cappadine.

cadastrado, *s.m. adj.* with cadastre, with a criminal record.

cadastral, *adj.* cadastral.

cadastro, *s.m.* cadastre, criminal record.

cadáver, *s.m.* corpse, dead body.

cadavérico, *adj.* cadaveric.

cadeado, *s.m.* padlock, chain.

cadeia, *s.f.* chain, prison, jail, sucession, series.

cadeira, *s.f.* chair, seat, professional post (*disciplina*). 1) *cadeira de balanço,* rocking chair. 2) *cadeira de rodas,* wheel-chair. 3) *a cadeira de Geografia,* the chair of Geography.

cadeirinha, *s.f.* sedan, sedan-chair.

cadela, *s.f.* bitch.

cadência, *s.f.* cadence, rythm.

cadenciado, *adj.* rythmical.

cadenciar, *v.t.* to give rythm to.

cadente, *adj.* falling: *estrela-cadente,* shooting star.

caderneta, *s.f.* pass-book (*nos bancos*), register (*na escola*), notebook.

caderno, *s.m.* exercise-book, copy-book, notebook.

cadete, *s.m.* cadet.

cadilhos, *s.m.pl.* fringues, loose ends, troubles (*sarilhos*).

cadimo, *adj.* expert, clever, usual.

cadinho, *s.m.* crucible, melting-pot.

cádmio, *s.m.* cadmium.

caducante, *adj.* decrepit, worn out, expiring.

caducar, *v.i.* to become decrepit, to dote, to lapse, to expire.

caducidade, *s.f.* caducity, decrepitude, expiration.

caduco, *adj.* decrepit, decaying, (*jur.*) lapsed, extinct, null and void; (*biol.*) deciduous.

café, *s.m.* coffee, coffee house (*estabelecimento*).

cafeeiro, *s.m.* coffee-tree.

cafeína, *s.f.* caffeine.

cafeteira, *s.f.* coffee-pot.

cafezal, coffee plantation.

cafezeiro, *s.m.* coffee-tree.

cáfila, *s.f.* caravan, drove of camels, band, gang (*de ladrões*).

cafre, *s.m.* Kaffir.

cafua, *s.f.* dungeon, cavern, cave, den.

cagaço, *s.m.* (*pop.*) fear, fright.

cágado, *s.m.* fresh water tortoise, fresh water turtle.

caiação, caiadela, *s.f.* whitewashing.

caiador, *s.m.* whitewasher.

caiar, *v.t.* to whitewash.

cãibra, *s.f.* cramp.

caibro, *s.m.* rafter, beamlet.

caída, *s.f.* fall, decline.

caído, *adj.* fallen, decayed, ruined.

caídos, *s.m.pl.* arrears.

caimão, *s.m.* caiman.

caínça, caínçada, *s.f.* a pack of dogs.

caipira, *s.m.* backwoodsman, yokel.

caipora, *adj.* unhappy, unlucky; *s.m.* goblin; *s.f.* ill-luck, bad luck.

caíque, *s.m.* caique, ketch (*embarcação turca*).

cair, *v.i.* to fall, to fall down, to drop, to drop down, to tumble, to decrease (*baixar*). 1) *cair de cama,* to fall sick. 2) *cair em si,* to come to one's senses.

cairelar, *v.t.* to lace, to braid.

cairo, *s.m.* coir, coconut fibre used for ropes.

cais, *s.m.* quay, wharf, dock; *cais flutuante,* floater.

caixa, *s.f.* box, chest, case, safe (*cofre*), well (*caixa de elevador*), cashier (*funcionário que faz pagamentos*). 1) *caixa económica,* savings bank. 2) *caixa de pensões,* pensions fund.

caixão, *s.m.* coffin.

caixeira, *s.f.* saleswoman.

caixeiro, *s.m.* salesman; *caixeiro-viajante,* travelling salesman.

caixilharia, *s.f.* framework.

caixilho, *s.m.* frame, window sash.

caixote, *s.m.* large box, packing case; *caixote do lixo,* dust-bin.

cajadada, *s.f.* blow with a staff or club.

cajado, *s.m.* shepherd's staff or crook, club.

caju, *s.m.* cashew-nut.

cajueiro, *s.m.* cashew-tree.

cal, *s.f.* lime.

calaboiço, calabouço, *s.m.* dungeon, jail, prison.

calabre, *s.m.* cable.

calabrês, *s.m.* native of Calabria.

calaça, *s.f.* laziness, idleness.

calacear, *v.i.* to idle, to loaf away.

calaceiro, *adj.* lazy, idle; *s.m.* idler.

calada, *s.f.* 1) *pela calada da noite,* in the death of the night. 2) *pela calada,* secretely, stealthily.

calado, *adj.* quiet, silent, reserved; *s.m.* (*náut.*) draught.

calafate, *s.m.* caulker.

calafetagem, *s.f.* caulking.

calafetar, *v.t.* to caulk.

calafrio, *s.m.* shiver, chill; *sentir calafrios,* to shiver.

calamidade, *s.f.* calamity.

calamitoso, *adj.* calamitous, disastrous.

cálamo, *s.m.* calamus.

calandra, *s.f.* calender.

calandrar, *v.t.* to calender.

calandreiro, *s.m.* calenderer.

calão, *adj.* lazy; *s.m.* slang, jargon.

calar, *v.t.* to silence, to hush, to omit. 1) *cale a boca!,* shut up!; *v.i.* to keep silent, to keep quiet. 2) *calar-se,* to stop talking.

calçada, *s.f.* pavement, sidewalk.

calçadeira, *s.f.* shoehorn.

calçado, *s.m.* footwear; *adj.* shod, paved, with shoes on.

calcador, *s.m.* rammer, tamper.

calcâneo, *s.m.* (*náut.*) calcaneum, heel-bone.

calcanhar, *s.m.* heel.

calção, *s.m. calções,* breeches, shorts.

calcar, *v.t.* to tread, to trample, to crush, to press.

calçar, *v.t.* to put on shoes; to pave (*pavimentar*).

calcário, *adj.* calcareous; *s.m.* limestone.

calças, *s.m.pl.* trousers.

calceta, *s.f.* shackles.

calcetamento, *s.m.* paving.

calcetar, *v.t.* to pave.

calceteiro, *s.m.* paver.

calcificação, *s.f.* calcification.

calcificar, *v.t.* to calcify, to convert into lime, to petrify.

calcinação, *s.f.* calcination.

calcinar, *v.t.* to calcine, to burn ashes.

calcinhas, *s.f.pl.* slip.

cálcio, *s.m.* calcium.

calcite, *s.f.* calcite.

calço, *s.m.* chock, block, wedge.

calcografia, *s.f.* calcography.

calcopirite, *s.f.* calcopyrite.

calcorrear, *v.t.* to walk, to go by foot.

calçudo, *adj.* wearing too long trousers.

calculador, *s.m.* calculator.

calculadora, *s.f.* calculating machine.

calcular, *v.t.* to calculate, to reckon, to estimate, to figure.

calculável, *adj.* calculable, computable.

calculista, *s.m.* a calculating person.

cálculo, *s.m.* calculation, estimate, reckong, (*mat.*) calculus, (*med.*) calculus, stone.

calda, *s.f.* sirup; *pl.* hot springs (*termas*).

caldeação, caldeamento, *s.f.* welding.

caldear, *v.t.* to weld.

caldeira, *s.f.* boiler, kettle.

caldeirada, *s.f.* fish-stew.

caldeirão, *s.m.* caldron, a large kettle or pot.

caldeiraria, *s.f.* copper-smith's trade; copper ware; brazier's shop.

caldeireiro, *s.m.* coppersmith, brazier.

caldeu, *s.m.* Chaldean.

caldo, *s.m.* broth, pottage.

caleça, *s.f.* calash.

calefacção, *s.f.* heating.

caleidoscópio, *s.m.* kaleidoscope.

caleira, *s.f.* gutter.

calejado, *adj.* hardened, accustomed, horny (*com calos*).

calejar, *v.t.* to harden, to accustom; *v.i.* to harden, to grow hard.

calema, *s.f.* ground sea, swell.

calembur, *s.m.* pun, play upon words.

calendário, *s.m.* calender.

calendas, *s.f.* calends; *para as calendas gregas,* in a blue moon; never.

calfe, *s.m.* leather.

calha, *s.f.* gutter, channel.

calhamaço, *s.m.* big old book.

calhambeque, *s.m.* an old coach or car, any worthless object.

calhandra, *s.f.* lark.

calhar, *v.i.* to fit, to be suitable (*convir*), to happen (*acontecer*). 1) *se calhar,* probbably. 2) *calha bem,* it suits perfectly.

calhau, *s.m.* stone, pebble.

calibrador, *s.m.* calibers, gauge.

calibragem, *s.f.* calibration.

calibrar, to calibrate, to gauge.

calibre, *s.m.* caliber, gauge.

caliça, *s.f.* debris.

cálice, *s.m.* cup, chalice, small glass, (*bot.*) calix.

calicida, *s.m.* cornkiller.

cálido, *adj.* calid, hot, warm.

califa, *s.m.* caliph.

califado, *s.m.* caliphate.

caligem, *s.f.* dimness, gloom, darkness.

caliginoso, *adj.* caliginous, dark, dim, gloomy.

caligrafia, *s.f.* calligraphy, handwriting.
caligráfico, *adj.* calligraphic.
calígrafo, *s.m.* penman, calligrapher.
calinada, *s.f.* nonsense.
calino, *s.m.* dunderhead, silly fellow; *adj.* stupid, silly.
calista, *s.m.* chiropodist, corn-cutter.
calistenia, *s.f.* callisthenics.
calma, *s.f.* quietness, calmness, stillness, peace, heat *(calor).*
calmante, *s.m.* sedative; *adj.* calming, soothing.
calmaria, *s.f.* calm, lull, tranquility.
calmo, *adj.* calm, peaceful, quiet, still.
calmoso, *adj.* very hot.
calo, *s.m.* corn.
caloiro, *s.m.* fresher, novice, beginner, newly-arrived.
calomelanos, *s.m.pl.* calomel.
calor, *s.m.* heat, warmth, hotness.
caloria, *s.f.* calorie.
calórico, *adj. e s.m.* caloric.
calorífero, *s.m.* heater, heating stove.
calorificação, *s.f.* calorification.
calorífico, *s.m.* heater; *adj.* calorific.
calorimetria, *s.f.* calorimetry.
calorímetro, *s.m.* calorimeter.
calorosamente, *adv.* warmly, vehemently, heartily.
caloroso, *adj.* warm, ardent, vehement, energetic, enthusiastic.
calosidade, *s.f.* callosity, callousness.
caloso, *adj.* calous, hardened, horny.
calote, *s.m.* debt, swindle, trick; *pregar um calote,* not to pay a debt.
caloteiro, *s.m.* swindler, bad payer.
caluda, *interj.* hush!; quiet!
calúnia, *s.f.* slander, calumny.
caluniar, *v.t.* to slander, to calumniate, to defame.
caluniosamente, *adv.* slanderously, falsely.
calunioso, *adj.* salumnious, slanderous.
calva, *s.f.* baldness.
Calvário, *s.m.* Calvary.
calvejar, *v.i.* to become bald.
calvície, *s.f.* baldness.
calvinismo, *s.m.* calvinism.
calvinista, *s.m.* Calvinist; *adj.* calvinistic.
Calvino, *s.m.* Calvin.
calvo, *adj.* bald, hairless.
cama, *s.f.* bed. 1) *cama de casal,* double bed. 2) *cama de solteiro,* single bed. 3) *estar de cama,* to be sick a bed.

camada, *s.f.* layer, stratum, coat *(de tinta, etc.).*
camafeu, *s.m.* cameo.
camaleão, *s.m.* chameleon.
câmara, *s.f.* chamber room, camera *(de fotografar ou filmar).* 1)*Câmara Alta,* House of Lords. 2) *Câmara baixa,* House of Commons. 3) *câmara ardente,* funeral chamber, mourning chamber. 4) *câmara de ar,* inner-tube. 5) *câmara lenta,* slowmotion *(no cinema).*
camarada, *s.m.* comrade, mate.
camaradagem, *s.f.* comradeship, companionship, fellowship.
camarão, *s.m.* shrimp.
camarata, *s.f.* dormitory.
camareira, *s.f.* chambermaid.
camareiro, *s.m.* chamberlain, room servant *(de hotel).*
camarilha, *s.f.* camrilla, clique.
camarim, *s.m.* dressing room.
camarinha, *s.f.* drop.
camarista, *s.m.* chamberlain.
camaroeiro, *s.m.* shrimpnet.
camarote, *s.m.* box *(no teatro),* cabin *(no navio).*
camaroteiro, *s.m.* steward.
camartelo, *s.m.* bricklayer's hammer, sledge hammer *(de demolição).*
camba, *s.f.* felly *(de roda).*
cambada, *s.f.* band, gang, pack, rabble.
cambado, *adj.* bowlegged; *sapatos cambados,* shoes down at the heels.
cambalacho, *s.m.* swindle, plot, fraud.
cambaleante, *adj.* staggering, tottering.
cambalear, *v.i.* to totter, to stagger, to reel.
cambaleio, *s.m.* tottering, staggering.
cambalhota, *s.f.* sumersault.
cambão, *s.m.* beam to which oxen are yoked; speculative buyer at auctions.
cambapé, *s.m.* trip.
cambar, *v.t.* to wear down at the heels, to bandy one's legs.
cambial, *s.f. e adj.* bill of exchange; relating to exchange.
cambiante, *s.m.* shade, hue; *adj.* shot-colored.
cambiar, *v.t.* to change, to exchange.
câmbio, *s.m.* change, exchange; câmbio do dia: current exchange; câmbio livre, free trade.
cambismo, *s.m.* exchange.
cambista, *s.m.* money-changer, cambist.

cambo, s.m. a hooked or forked pole to gather fruit from trees.

cambota, s.f. rim (de roda), arch frame (em arquitectura).

cambraia, s.f. cambric.

cambulhada, s.f. a collection of things strung together; de cambulhada, pell-mell, in confusion.

cameleiro, s.m. camel driver.

camélia, s.f. camelia.

camelo, s.m. camel.

camerlengo, s.m. camerlingo, papal, treasurer.

camião, s.m. truck, lorry, van (carrinha).

caminhada, s.f. long walk, stroll.

caminhante, s.m. walker, hiker.

caminhão, s.m. o mesmo que "camião".

caminhar, v.t. to walk, to march.

caminho, s.m. way, path, track, road, trail, course. 1) abrir caminho, to make way, to clear the way. 2) a caminho de, on the way to. 3) seguir o seu caminho, to go one's way. 4) caminho de ferro, railway.

camionagem, s.f. transport by truck, truckage.

camioneta, s.f. truck, lorry, van.

camisa, s.f. shirt, chemise (de mulher). 1) camisa de noite, night gown, night shirt. 2) camisa de forças, straightjacket. 3) camisa-de-onze-varas, predicament, troubles.

camisaria, s.f. horsier`s shop.

camiseiro, s.m. shirt, shirt maker.

camiseta, s.f. chemisette.

camisola, s.f. vest, pullover, jersey.

camoeca, s.f. intoxication.

camomila, s.f. camomile.

campa, s.f. grave, tomb, tomb-stone.

campainha, s.f. bell; (bot.) bluebell, bellflower.

campainhada, s.f. ring of a bell.

campal, adj. rural. 1) batalha campal, pitched battle. 2) missa campal, open-air celebration of mass.

campanário, s.m. campanile, steeple.

campanha, s.f. campaign.

campanólogo, s.m. bell-ringer.

campanudo, adj. bell-shaped, swollen, inflated.

campânula, s.f. (bot.) campanula, bell jar (recipiente).

campanulado, adj. campanulate, bell-shaped.

campeão, s.m. champion.

campear, v.i. to scour the countryside (bater campo), to excel (sobressair), to flaunt, to display (ostentar).

campeche, s.m. log-wood.

campeonato, s.m. championship.

campesinho, campesino, adj. rural, rustic, country-like.

campestre, adj. rural, rustic, bucolic, country.

campina, s.f. meadow, plain, field.

campino, s.m. countryman, cowboy.

campo, s.m. field (também de desportos), country, countryside (o oposto de cidade), camp (acampamento), sphere (alcance), room (espaço). 1) campo de acção, scope, sphere of action. 2) campo de batalha, battlefield. 3) em campo aberto, in the open.

camponês, s.m. countryman, peasant.

campónio, s.m. countryman; adj. rustic.

camuflado, adj. camouflaged, disguised.

camuflagem, s.f. camouflage, disguise.

camuflar, v.t. to camouflage, to disguise.

camurça, s.f. chamois.

cana, s.f. cane, reed; cana de pesca, fishing rod.

canada, s.f. a blow with a cane; lane.

cana-de-açúcar, s.f. sugar cane.

canadiano, canadense, s.m. Canadian.

canal, s.m. channel, canal (de navegação).

canalha, s.f. rabble, mob, rascal (patife).

canalhice, s.f. dirty trick, rascality.

canalização, s.f. canalization, piping.

canalizador, s.m. plumber.

canalizar, v.t. to canalize, to pipe (água, gás, etc.), to direct into.

canalizável, adj. that can be canalized.

canapé, s.m. sofa, couch.

canário, s.m. canary.

canasta, s.f. canasta.

canastra, s.f. a shallow basket.

canastrão, s.m. ham, bad actor.

canastro, s.m. basket; (pop.) the human body.

canavial, s.m. cane plantation.

canção, s.f. song, ballad.

cancela, s.f. gate, wicket.

cancelamento, s.m. cancellation, rescission, annulment.

cancelar, v.t. to cancel, to annul.

câncer, s.m. (astr.) Cancer.

cancerar, v.i. to become cancerous.

canceroso, adj. cancerous.

cancioneiro, s.m. song-book.

cancionista, *s.m.* song-writer.
cançoneta, *s.f.* chansonette.
cançonetista, *s.m. e s.f.* singer.
cancro, *s.m.* cancer.
candeeiro, *s.m.* lamp.
candeia, *s.f.* oil lamp.
candeio, *s.m.* torch.
candelabro, *s.m.* candelabrum, chandelier.
Candelária, *s.f.* Candelemas.
candência, *s.f.* candescence.
candente, *adj.* candescence, glowing.
candidamente, *adv.* candidly, sincerely.
candidato, *s.m.* candidate, applicant.
candidatura, *s.f.* candidature.
candidez, *s.f.* candidness, simplicity, cander.
cândido, *adj.* candid, sincere.
candonga, *s.f.* contraband, smuggling.
caneca, *s.f.* mug, can.
caneco, *s.m.* large jug.
caneiro, *s.m.* dike, narrow channel.
canela, *s.f.* cinnamon *(especiaria)*, shin *(da perna)*.
canelada, *s.f.* kick on the shin.
canelado, *adj.* grooved, fluted.
caneleira, *s.f.* shin guard.
caneta, *s.f.* pen; *caneta de tinta permanente,* fountain pen.
cânfora, *s.f.* camphor.
canforado, *adj.* camphorate.
canforeira, *s.f.* camphor-tree.
canga, *s.f.* yoke for oxen, opression, tirany.
cangalhada, *s.f.* old objects.
cangalho, *s.m.* old and worthless object.
cangosta, *s.f.* a narrow lane.
canguru, *s.m.* kangaroo.
cânhamo, *s.m.* hemp.
canhão, *s.m.* cannon, cuff *(de manga)*, top *(de bota)*.
canhenho, *s.m.* note-book.
canhestro, *adj.* left-handed, clumsy.
canhonhaço, *s.m.* cannon shot.
canhonhada, *s.f.* cannonade.
canhoneio, *s.m.* cannonade.
canhoneira, *s.f.* embrasure, port-hole, gun-boat.
canhoto, *adj.* left-handed.
canibal, *s.m.* cannibal.
canibalismo, *s.m.* cannibalism.
caniçada, *s.f.* fence with reeds or canes.
caniçal, *s.m.* plantation of reeds.
canície, *s.f.* the age of grey hairs.
caniço, *s.m.* reed.
canícula, *s.f.* summer heat; *(astro.)* dog-star.

canicular, *adj.* canicular.
canil, *s.m.* kennel.
canilha, *s.f.* weaver's quill.
canino, *adj.* canine.
canivete, *s.m.* penknife, pocket knife.
canja, *s.f.* chicken-soup.
cano, *s.m.* pipe, tube, conduit, barrel *(de arma de fogo)*, bootleg *(de bota)*.
canoa, *s.f.* canoe, barge.
cânon, cânone, *s.m.* canon.
cânones, *s.m. pl.* canon law.
canonicato, *s.m.* canonry, canonship.
canónico, *adj.* canonical.
canonista, *s.m.* canonist.
canonização, *s.f.* canonization.
canonizar, *v.t.* to canonize.
canoro, *adj.* canorous; *ave canora,* song-bird.
canoura, *s.f.* mill-hopper.
cansaço, *s.f.* fatigue, weariness.
cansado, *adj.* tired, weary, fatigued.
cansar, *v.t.* to tire, to fatigue, to weary; *cansar-se,* to get tired, to grow tired.
canseira, *s.f.* fatigue, toil, drudgery.
cantadeira, *s.f.* singer.
cantante, *adj.* singing.
cantão, *s.m.* canton *(cidade)*, canton *(distrito)*.
cantar, *v.t.* to sing, to chant, to crow *(o galo)*, to chirp *(o grilo)*.
cantareira, *s.f.* stand for jars, pitchers, etc.
cantaria, *s.f.* squared stone, masonry.
cantárida, *s.f.* spanish fly.
cântaro, *s.m.* water-pot, pitcher.
cantarolar, *v.t.* to hum.
cantata, *s.f.* cantata.
canteiro, *s.m.* flower bed, stone mason.
cântico, *s.m.* hymn, canticle.
cantiga, *s.f.* song.
cantil, *s.m.* canteen, flask.
cantilena, *s.f.* ditty, chant, song.
cantina, *s.f.* canteen, mess.
canto, *s.m.* corner, angle, singing, vocal music, canto *(parte de um poema)*.
cantochão, *s.m.* plain chant.
cantonal, *adj.* cantonal.
cantoneira, *s.f.* corner cupboard *(peça de mobiliário)*.
cantoneiro, *s.m.* road mender.
cantor, *s.m.* singer.
cantora, *s.f.* singer.
canudo, *s.m.* tube.
cânula, *s.f.* clyster-pipe, canula.
canzoada, *s.f.* pack of dogs.

cão, *s.m.* dog, hound, hammer, cock *(arma de fogo).* 1) *cão raivoso,* mad dog. 2) *cão de guarda,* watch dog. 3) *cão-polícia,* police-dog.

caos, *s.m.* chaos.

caótico, *adj.* chaotic.

capa, *s.f.* cloak, mantle, cape, cover *(de um livro),* covering *(camada).* 1) *capa impermeável,* raincoat, mackintosh. 2) *romance de capa e espada,* cloak and dagger novel, novel of chivalry.

capação, *s.f.* gelding.

capacete, *s.m.* helmet, casque.

capachinho, *s.m.* peruke, wig.

capacho, *s.m.* mat, door mat, servile person.

capacidade, *s.f.* capacity, content, ability, competency, talent.

capacitar, *v.t.* to enable, to convince.

capado, *adj.* castrated, gelded *(animais).*

capador, *s.m.* gelder.

capadura, *s.f.* gelding, castration.

capão, *s.m.* capon, castrated cock.

capar, *v.t.* to geld, to castrate.

caparrosa, *s.f.* copperas.

capataz, *s.m.* foreman.

capaz, *adj.* capable, able, fit, competent.

capazmente, *adv.* fitly, capably.

capcioso, *adj.* captious, deceitful.

capear, *v.t.* to cloak, to cover with cloak, to enclose, to deceive; *v.i.* to make signs with a cloak or banner; *(náut.)* to lie to.

capela, *s.f.* chapel.

capelania, *s.f.* chaplaincy.

capelão, *s.m.* chaplain.

capelista, *s.m. e s.f.* linen-draper.

capelo, *s.m.* hood, cardinal's hat, cap *(de doutor).*

capilar, *adj.* capillary.

capilaridade, *s.f.* capillarity.

capilé, *s.m.* a syrup flavored with orange-flower water.

capim, *s.m.* grass.

capinha, *s.f.* little cloak, bullfighter.

capinzal, *s.m.* pasture land.

capitação, *s.f.* capitation, census, poll tax.

capital, *s.m.* capital, funds; *s.f.* capital, metropolis; *adj.* capital, main, leading, essential.

capitalismo, *s.m.* capitalism.

capitalista, *s.f.* capitalist.

capitalização, *s.f.* capitalization.

capitalizar, *v.t.* to capitalize.

capitalizável, *adj.* that can be capitalized.

capitalmente, *adv.* capitally.

capitanear, *v.t.* to command, to lead, to direct.

capitania, *s.f.* captaincy.

capitânia, *s.f.* admiral-ship.

capitão, *s.m.* captain, commander. 1) *capitão de fragata,* commander. 2) *capitão de porto,* harbour-master.

capitel, *s.m.* capital.

capitolino, *adj.* capitoline.

Capitólio, *s.m.* Capitol.

capitoso, *adj.* heady, obstinate, inebriant.

capitulação, *s.f.* capitulation.

capitular, *adj. e s.f.* capitular; *v.i.* to capitulate, to surrender; *v.t.* to reduce to chapters, to qualify.

capítulo, *s.m.* chapter.

capoeira, *s.f.* poultry house, hencoop.

capota, *s.f.* hood *(de carro).*

capotar, *v.i.* to nose over, to overturn.

capote, *s.m.* cloak, *(mil.),* capote.

caprichar, *v.i.* to do something with great care, to pride oneself on.

capricho, *s.m.* whim, fancy, caprice.

caprichosamente, *adv.* capriciously.

caprichoso, *adj.* capricious, whimsical, moody, fanciful, careful *(zeloso).*

capricórnio, *s.m.* Capricorn.

caprídeo, *adj.* caprid.

caprino, *adj.* caprine.

cápsula, *s.f.* capsule, cap *(de armas de fogo).*

captação, *s.f.* captation.

captar, *v.t.* to captivate, to impound *(águas),* to pick up *(rádio).*

captor, *s.m.* captor, capturer.

captura, *s.f.* capture, seizure, arrest.

capturar, *v.t.* to capture, to arrest, to seize.

capuchinho, *s.m.* Capuchin, small hood *(capuz); menina do capuchinho vermelho,* Little Red riding Hood.

capuz, *s.m.* hood.

caquéctico, *adj.* cachectic.

caquexia, *s.f.* cachexy.

caqui, *s.m.* persimon *(fruta).*

cáqui, *s.m.* khaki; *adj.* khaki coloured.

cara, *s.f.* face, visage, look, expression, aspect; *caramente,* better-half.

carabina, *s.f.* rifle.

carabineiro, *s.m.* rifleman.

caraça, *s.f.* mask.

caracol, *s.m.* snail; *escada de caracol,* winding staircase.

caracolar, caracolear, *v.i.* to wind, to trance.

carácter, *s.m.* character, nature.
característica, *s.f.* characteristic.
característico, *adj.* characteristic.
caracterização, *s.f.* characterization, make up.
caracterizado, *adj.* characterized.
caracterizar, *v.t.* to characterize, to distinguish, to mark, to make up.
Caraíbas, *s.f.pl.* Caribbean.
caramanchão, *s.m.* bower, porch.
caramba!, *interj.* shucks!, my goodness!
carambola, *s.f.* red ball, trickery.
carambolar, *v.i.* to trick, to cheat (aldrabar).
carambolim, *s.m.* damage.
caramelo, *s.m.* caramel, candy.
caramujo, *s.m.* periwinkle.
caramunha, *s.f.* grimace, whimper; *fazer o mal e a caramunha,* to add insult to injury.
caranguejo, *s.m.* crab, crab fish.
caranguejola, *s.f.* large crab, jalopy, rattletrap (calhambeque).
carantonha, *s.f.* mask, grimace, ugly face.
carão, *s.m.* a large face.
carapaça, *s.f.* carapace.
carapau, *s.m.* small saurel.
carapeta, *s.f.* fib (mentira), whirligig (pião).
carapetão, *s.m.* a great lie.
carapeteiro, *s.m.* liar, story-teller.
carapinha, *s.f.* curly hair, wooly hair, kinky hair.
carapuça, *s.f.* pointed cap, cap, hood.
carapuço, *s.m.* cap, hood.
caravana, *s.f.* caravan.
caravansarai, caravansará, *s.m.* caravan-serai, caravansary.
caravela, *s.f.* carvel, caravel.
carbonatado, *adj.* carbonated.
carbonatar, *v.t.* to carbonate.
carbonato, *s.m.* carbonate.
carboneto, *s.m.* carbide.
carbónico, *adj.* carbonic.
carbonífero, *adj.* carboniferous.
carbonização, *s.f.* carbonization.
carbonizar, *v.t.* to carbonize.
carbono, *s.m.* carbon.
carbúnculo, *s.m.* carbuncle.
carbunculoso, *adj.* carbuncled, carbuncular.
carburador, *s.m.* carburettor.
carburante, *s.m.* carburettant.
carburar, *v.t.* carburate.
carbureto, *s.m.* o mesmo que "carboneto".
carcaça, *s.f.* carcass, frame (armação), hull (casco).

carcás, *s.m.* quiver.
carcela, *s.f.* lap.
cárcere, *s.m.* jail, gaol.
carcereiro, *s.m.* jailer, jailor.
carcinóide, *adj.* carcinoid.
carcinoma, *s.f.* carcinoma, cancer.
carcoma, *s.m.* wood-fretter, woodworm.
carcomer, *v.t.* to fret, to eat away, to corrode.
carcomido, *adj.* worm-eaten, decayed.
carda, *s.f.* card, flax-comb.
cardação, *s.f.* wool-combing, carding.
cardador, *s.m.* wool-comber.
cardagem, *s.f.* carding.
cardamina, *s.f.* (bot.) meadow bittercress.
cardar, *v.t.* to card, to comb.
cardeal, *s.m.* cardinal; *adj.* cardinal; *pontos cardeais,* cardinal points.
cárdia, *s.f.* cardia.
cardíaco, *adj.* cardiac; *s.m.* cardiac, person with heart troubles.
cardialgia, *s.f.* cardialgia, cardialgy.
cardiálgico, *adj.* cardialgic.
cardinal, *adj.* cardinal, principal.
cardinalato, *s.m.* cardinalate, cardinal-ship.
cardiograma, *s.m.* cardiogram.
cardiologia, *s.f.* cardiology.
cardiologista, *s.f.* cardiologist.
cardite, *s.f.* carditis.
cardo, *s.m.* thistle.
cardume, *s.m.* shoal, school of fish.
careca, *s.m.* bald; *s.f.* baldness.
carecer, *v.i.* to want, to need, to recquire, to be in need of, to be short of.
carecido, *adj.* short of, lacking.
careiro, *adj.* someone that sells things with high prices.
carência, *s.f.* need, lack, want, shortage.
carestia, *s.f.* dearness, high prices, high cost.
careta, *s.f.* grimace.
carga, *s.f.* load, burden, cargo (de um navio), charge (eléctrica, de arma de fogo, etc.).
cargo, *s.m.* post, position, office, duty (encargo); *a cargo de,* in charge of.
cargueiro, *s.m.* cargo-boat, cargo-ship, freighter.
cariado, *adj.* carious, decayed.
cariar, *v.i.* to make or become carious, to decay.
cariátide, *s.f.* caryatid.
caricato, *adj.* grotesque, ridiculous.

caricatura, s.f. caricature.

caricatural, adj. grotesque.

caricaturar, v.t. to caricaturate, to represent by a caricature.

caricaturista, s.m. caricaturist.

carícia, s.f. caress, endearment.

caridade, s.f. charity, mercy.

caridoso, adj. charitable, merciful.

cárie, s.f. caries, decay; *cárie dentária,* dental caries.

caril, s.m. curry.

carimbador, s.m. rubber-stamper.

carimbagem, s.f. rubber-stamping, sealing.

carimbar, v.t. to stamp, to rubber-stamp, to seal.

carimbo, s.m. rubber-stamp, seal.

carinho, s.m. affection, caress, love, fondness, kindness.

carinhosamente, adv. kindly, fondly.

carinhoso, adj. kind, loving, caressing.

carioca, s.m. e s.f. a native of Rio de Janeiro.

carioso, adj. carious, decayed.

carisma, s.f. charism.

caritativamente, adv. charitably.

caritativo, adj. charitable, benevolent.

cariz, s.m. aspect, countenance, appearance, look; *(bot.)* caraway seed.

carlinga, s.f. step of the mast, mast step, cockpit *(aviação).*

carlovíngio, adj. carlovingian.

carmelita, s.f. e s.m. Carmelite.

carmesim, s.m. crimson.

carmim, s.m. carmine.

carminativo, adj. carminative.

carnação, s.f. carnation.

carnadura, s.f. complexion, flesh.

carnal, adj. carnal, sensual.

carnalidade, s.f. sarnality, sensuality.

carnalmente, adv. carnally, sensually.

carnaval, s.m. carnival.

carnavalesco, adj. of the carnival.

carne, s.f. flesh, meat, beef *(de boi ou de vaca).* 1) *carne verde,* fresh meat. 2) *em carne viva,* flayed. 3) *carne crua,* raw meat.

carneira, s.f. sheep-leather.

carneirada, s.m. flock of sheep.

carneiro, s.m. sheep, mutton *(a carne).*

carnição, s.f. core.

carniçaria, s.f. butchery, butcher`s shop.

carniceiro, s.m. butcher; adj. carnivorous, cruel.

carnificina, s.f. slaughter, massacre.

carnívoro, adj. carnivorous, carnivore, flesh-eating; s.m. carnivore.

carnoso, adj. fleshy, carnous.

carnudo, s.m. fleshy, plump, pulpous, pulpy.

caro, adj. dear *(querido),* expensive, costly; adv. at a high price, dearly.

carocha, s.f. cockroach, beetle.

carochinha, s.f. little beetle; *histórias da carochinha,* nursery tales, fairy tales.

caroço, s.m. stone *(da fruta),* lump *(endurecimento).*

carola, s.f. *(pop.)* head; adj. fanatic, fan.

carolice, s.f. devotion, fanaticism, enthusiasm.

carolo, s.m. blow in the head.

carótida, s.f. carotid.

carpa, s.f. carp.

carpelo, s.m. carpel.

carpideira, s.f. weeper, mourner.

carpidor, s.m. weeper.

carpidos, s.m.pl. mournings.

carpintaria, s.f. carpentry, carpenter's shop.

carpinteirar, v.i. to carpenter.

carpinteiro, s.m. carpenter.

carpir, v.t. e v.i. to lament, to mourn, to weep.

carpo, s.m. *(anat.)* wrist; *(bot.)* any fruit.

carqueja, s.f. a kind of broom.

carraça, s.f. tick.

carrada, s.f. cart-load.

carranca, s.f. grimace, ugly face, sullen look.

carrancudo, adj. sullen, sulky.

carrapata, s.f. embroilment, mischief.

carrapato, s.m. tick.

carrapito, s.m. bun of hair, toupee.

carrascão, s.m. e adj. rough wine, rough.

carrasco, s.m. hangman, executioner.

carraspana, s.f. *(pop.)* booze, drunkness.

carrear, v.t. to cart, to convey in a cart.

carregação, s.f. cargo, lading, freight.

carregado, adj. charged, loaded, laden, oppressed, surly *(carrancudo),* dark *(escuro),* threatening *(ameaçador).*

carregamento, s.m. cargo, shipment, load.

carregar, v.t. to load, to charge, to carry *(levar),* to deepen *(cores, etc.).* 1) *carregar o sobrolho,* to scowl; v.i. to charge against *(o inimigo),* to bear *(suportar),* to press *(fazer pressão).* 2) *carregar-se,* to become dark, cloudy or sad.

carrego, s.m. burden, load, weight.

carreira, course, route, line *(de navegação),* race *(corrida),* rank *(fileira),* career *(profissão); navio de carreira:* liner.

carreiro, *s.m.* path, track, trail.

carrejão, *s.m.* porter.

carreta, *s.f.* cart, wagon.

carretagem, *s.f.* carriage, cartage.

carrete, *s.m.* pinion, cog-wheel.

carreteiro, *s.m.* cartman, wagonner.

carretel, *s.m.* bobbin, coil, reel.

carreto, *s.m.* carting, cartage, reel.

carriça, *s.f.* wren.

carriçal, *s.m.* plantation of corn-flag.

carriço, corn-flag.

carril, *s.m.* rail.

carrilar, *v.t.* to put on rails.

carrilhador, *s.m.* carrillonner.

carrilhão, *s.m.* carillon.

carrilho, *s.m.* ear of maize without its kernels.

carrinho, *s.m.* little cart. 1) *carrinho de mão,* wheel-barrow. 2) *carrinho de bebé,* baby carriage.

carro, *s.m.* car, motor-car, automobile.

carroça, *s.f.* cart, wagon.

carroçada, *s.f.* cart-load.

carroceiro, *s.m.* carter, wagoner.

carrossel, *s.m.* merry-go-round.

carruagem, *s.f.* carriage, coach; *carruagem-cama,* sleeping car.

carta, *s.f.* letter, missive, map, chart, card *(de jogar),* menu *(cardápio).* 1) *dar cartas (ao jogo),* to deal. 2) *dar carta branca,* to give free hand. 3) *carta de condução,* driving license.

cartada, *s.f.* the act of playing a card; *jogar a última cartada,* to play one's last card.

cartaginês, *s.m. e adj.* Cartaginian.

Cartago, *s.m.* Carthage.

cartão, *s.m.* card, card-board, carton; *cartão de visita,* calling card.

cartapácio, *s.m.* old and big book.

cartaz, *s.m.* bill, poster, placard, sticker, popularity.

cartear, *v.t.* to mark the ship's place on a chart; *v.i.* to play cards, to deal; *cartear-se,* to correspond (with someone).

carteira, *s.f.* wallet *(de dinheiro),* desk *(secretária).*

carteirista, *s.m.* pickpocket.

carteiro, *s.m.* postman.

cartel, *s.m.* cartel, trust.

cartesiano, *adj.* Cartesian.

cartilagem, *s.f.* cartilage, gristle.

cartilagíneo, *adj.* cartilaginous.

cartilaginoso, *adj.* cartilaginous, gristly.

cartilha, *s.f.* spelling-book.

cartografia, *s.f.* cartography, mapping.

cartográfico, *adj.* cartographic.

cartógrafo, *s.m.* cartographer.

cartola, *s.f.* top-hat.

cartolina, *s.f.* cardboard, light cardboard.

cartomancia, *s.f.* cartomancy, fortune--telling.

cartomante, *s.m. e s.f.* fortune-teller.

cartonado, *adj.* in boards *(livro).*

cartonagem, *s.f.* boarding, bookbinding.

cartonar, *v.t.* to bind in boards.

cartorário, *s.m.* clerk.

cartório, *s.m.* notary's office, registry.

cartuchame, *s.m.* provision of cartridges.

cartucheira, *s.f.* cardtrige-belt.

cartucho, *s.m.* cardtrige, paper-bag *(saco de papel).*

cartulário, *s.m.* cartulary.

cartuxa, *s.f.* Carthusian order.

caruma, *s.f.* pine-needles.

carunchar, *v.i.* to become worm-holed or worm-eaten.

caruncho, *s.m.* wood-fretter, wood-mite, worm-hole.

carunchoso, *adj.* wormy, worm-eaten.

carvalhal, *s.m.* oak-grove.

carvalho, *s.m.* oak; *madeira de carvalho,* oak wood.

carvão, *s.m.* coal, charcoal *(carvão de madeira),* carbon *(de arco voltaico).*

carvoaria, *s.f.* coal dealers shop.

carvoeiro, *s.m.* coal dealer; *navio carvoeiro,* coal ship.

cãs, *s.f.pl.* white hair.

casa, *s.f.* house, home, place, buttonhole *(de botão),* square *(de tabuleiro),* (com.) shop, establishement. 1) *dentro de casa,* indoors. 2) *fora de casa,* outdoors. 3) *mudar de casa,* to move.

casaca, *s.f.* dress-coat.

casacão, *s.m.* great coat.

casaco, *s.m.* coat, jacket, blazer.

casadoiro, casadouro, *adj.* marriageable, at a proper age for marriage.

casal, *s.m.* couple, farmhouse.

casamata, *s.f.* casemate.

casamenteiro, *s.m.* match-maker.

casamento, *s.m.* marriage, matrimony, wedding.

casão, *s.m.* a large house, regimental clothing shop.

casar, *v.t.* e *v.i.* to marry, to get married, to wed, to join, to match.

casarão, *s.m.* a very large house.

casario, *s.m.* a block of houses.

casca, *s.f.* bark *(de uma árvore)*, peel, skin *(de fruta)*, peel, hull *(de leguminosas)*, shell, husk *(de nozes, ovos, etc.)*, rind *(de queijo)*.

cascalho, *s.m.* gravel, crushed stones.

cascalhoso, *adj.* gravelly, pebbly.

cascão, *s.m.* crust, scab *(de ferida)*.

cascar, *v.i.* to give *(um golpe)*, to beat.

cascaria, *s.f.* casks.

cascata, *s.f.* waterfall, cascade.

cascavel, *s.f.* small bell, rattlesnake *(serpente)*.

casco, *s.m.* hull *(de navio)*, skull *(crânio)*, hoof *(de um animal)*, cask *(barril)*.

cascudo, *adj.* hard-shelled, thick-skinned; *s.m.* beetle *(insecto)*, rap on the head *(pancada)*.

casear, *v.t.* to make button-holes.

casebre, *s.m.* hovel, shanty.

caseiforme, *adj.* cheesy.

caseína, *s.f.* casein.

caseiro, *s.m.* farm-manager, tenant; *adj.* domestic, home-made.

caseoso, *adj.* caseous, cheesy.

caserna, *s.f.* barracks.

casimira, *s.f.* cashmere.

casinhola, *s.f.* **casinhoto,** *s.m.* hovel.

casino, *s.m.* casino.

caso, *s.m.* case, event, matter. 1) *caso ele venha*, in case he comes. 2) *em caso de*, in case of. 3) *em todo o caso*, anyway, at any rate. 4) *fazer caso de*, to mind, to pay attention. 5) *não fazer caso de*, to ignore. 6) *não vir ao caso*, to be irrevelant.

casório, *s.m.* *(pop.)* marriage.

caspa, *s.f.* dandruff.

caspento, casposo, *adj.* dandruffy.

casqueiro, *s.m.* place where wood is barked; brown bread.

casquete, *s.m.* an old hat.

casquilho, *s.m.* brass, beau, fop.

casquinada, *s.f.* burst of laughter.

casquinar, *v.t.* to laugh loudly.

casquinha, *s.f.* plated metal, silver plated.

cassa, *s.f.* musslin.

cassação, *s.f.* cessation, annulment.

cassar, *v.t.* to anull, to cancel.

cassetete, *s.m.* billy, truncheon.

cássia, *s.f.* cassia.

Cassiopeia, *s.f.* Cassiopeia.

cassiterite, *s.f.* cassiterite.

casta, *s.f.* caste, race, breed, kind, sort.

castamente, *adv.* chastely.

castanha, *s.f.* chestnut.

castanhal, grove of chestnut-trees.

castanheiro, *s.m.* chestnut-tree.

castanho, *s.m.* chestnut-tree, chestnut--tree wood *(madeira de castanho)*; *adj.* brown.

castanholas, *s.f.pl.* castanets.

castão, *s.m.* knob.

castelão, *s.m.* castellan.

castelhano, *s.m.* e *adj.* Castilian.

castelo, *s.m.* castle.

castiçal, *s.m.* candlestick.

casticismo, *s.m.* purquess.

castiço, *adj.* genuine, pure.

castidade, *s.f.* chastity, purity, virginity.

castigador, *s.m.* chastiser, punisher; *adj.* punishing.

castigar, *v.t.* to chastise, to punish.

castigável, *adj.* chastisable, punishable.

castigo, *s.m.* chastisement, punishment, penalty.

casto, *adj.* chaste, pure.

castor, *s.m.* beaver.

castração, *s.f.* castration, gelding.

castrado, *adj.* castrated.

castrador, *s.m.* gelder; *adj.* castrating.

castrar, *v.t.* to castrate, to geld.

castrense, *adj.* castrensian, castral.

casual, *adj.* casual, accidental, fortituos, occasional.

casualidade, *s.f.* casualness, chance, accident.

casualmente, *adv.* casualy, occasionally, by chance, accidentally.

casuar, *s.m.* cassowary.

casuísta, *s.m.* casuist.

casuística, *s.f.* casuistry.

casuístico, *adj.* casuistic.

casula, *s.f.* chasuble.

casulo, *s.m.* cocoon, chrysalis.

cata, *s.f.* *andar a cata de*, to search for.

catabolismo, *s.m.* catabolism.

cataclismo, *s.m.* cataclysm.

catacrese, *s.f.* catachresis.

catacumba, *s.f.* catacomb.

catadupa, *s.f.* cataract, waterfall.

catadura, *s.f.* aspect, look.

catafalco, *s.m.* catafalque.

catalão, *s.m.* e *adj.* Catalan.

cataléctico, *adj.* catalectic, incomplete.

catalepsia, *s.f.* catalepsy.

cataléptico, *adj.* cataleptic.

catalisar, *v.i.* to catalyse.

catálise, *s.f.* catalysis.

catalítico, *adj.* catalytic.

catalogação, *s.f.* cataloguing.

catalogar, *v.t.* to catalogue.

catálogo, *s.m.* catalogue, list.

catana, *s.f.* cutlass.

catanada, *s.f.* a blow with a cutlass.

Catão, *s.m.* Cato.

cataplasma, *s.m.* cataplasm, plaster.

cataplexia, *s.f.* cataplexy.

catapulta, *s.f.* catapult.

catar, *v.t.* to search, to look for, to delouse (*piolhos*).

catarata, *s.f.* waterfall, cataract *(também nos olhos).*

catarina, *s.f.* balance-wheel *(do relógio).*

catarral, *adj.* catarrhal.

catarreira, *s.f.* cold.

catarro, *s.m.* catarrh, bronchitis.

catarroso, *adj.* catarrhous.

catarse, *s.f.* catharsis.

catártico, *adj.* cathartic.

catástrofe, catastrophe, calamity.

catatua, *s.f.* cackatoa.

catecismo, *s.m.* catechism.

catecúmeno, *s.m.* catechumen.

cátedra, *s.f.* cathedra, chair.

catedral, *s.f.* cathedral.

catedrático, *s.m.* professor *(numa universidade),* head-professor; *adj.* cathedratic.

categoria, *s.f.* category, class, rank, standing.

categoricamente, *adv.* categorically, positively, point-blank.

categórico, *adj.* categorical, unconditional, plain, absolute.

categorizar, *v.t.* to put in classes, to class, to classify, to categorize.

catequese, *s.f.* catecmism, sunday school.

catequista, *s.f. e s.m.* catechist, sunday school teacher.

catequizar, *v.t.* to catechise.

caterva, *s.f.* crowd, mob, gang.

cateter, *s.m.* catheter.

cateto, *s.m.* cathetus.

catilinária, *s.f.* tirade, a long vehement harangue, diatribe.

catinga, *s.f.* rank, smell; *s.m.* miser.

catita, *adj.* pretty, neat, spruce.

catitismo, *s.m.* neatness, nicety, spruceness, dandyism.

cativante, *adj.* captivating, charming, fascinating.

cativar, *v.t.* to captivate, to seduce, to attract, to charm, to fascinate.

cativeiro, *s.m.* captivity, slavery, bondage.

cativo, *adj. e s.m.* captive, slave, prisoner.

catódio, *s.m.* o mesmo que "cátodo".

cátodo, *s.m.* cathode.

catolicidade, *s.f.* catholicity, universality, liberality of view.

catolicismo, *s.m.* catholicism.

católico, *s.m. e adj.* Catholic; *Igreja Católica,* Roman Catholic Church.

catorze, *adj.* fourteen.

catraia, *s.f.* smal boat, a little girl.

catraio, *s.m.* little boat, little boy.

catre, *s.m.* folding bed, small bed.

caturra, *s.f. e s.m.* pig-headed person.

caturrice, *s.f.* obstinacy, stubbonness.

caução, *s.f.* bail, caution.

caucasiano, caucásico, *adj.* caucasian.

cauchu, *s.m.* caoutchouc, rubber.

caucionar, *v.t.* to bail, to let out on bail, to give bail.

cauda, *s.f.* tail, train *(de vestido),* rear *(retaguarda).*

caudal, *s.m.* torrent, stream, current; *adj.* caudal, abundant, torrential.

caudaloso, *adj.* torrential, carrying much water, mighty.

caudatário, *s.m.* train-bearer.

caudato, *adj.* caudate.

caudelaria, *s.f.* stud.

caudilho, *s.m.* leader, chief, commander.

caule, *s.m.* stalk, stem.

caulescente, *adj.* caulescent.

caulículo, *s.m.* caulicle.

caulífero, *adj.* cauliferous.

caulino, *s.m.* kaolin, china clay.

causa, *s.f.* cause, reason, motive, *(jur.)* lawsuit, case, action; *por causa de,* because of, on account of.

causador, *adj.* causing; causer, author, begetter.

causal, *adj.* causal; *s.f.* reason, motive.

causalidade, *s.f.* causality.

causar, *v.t.* to cause, to originate, to provoque, to occasion, to give rise to, to produce, to give.

causativo, *adj.* causative.

causídico, *s.m.* advocate, barrister, lawyer.

cáustica, *s.f.* caustic curve.

causticante, *adj.* caustic, biting, scathing, vitriolic.

causticar, *v.t.* to apply cauteries, to annoy, to tease.

causticidade, *s.f.* causticity.

cáustico, *adj.* caustic, biting, cutting; *s.m.* caustic; an annoying person.

cautamente, *adv.* cautiously, prudently.

cautela, *s.f.* caution, precaution, care, prudence, fraction of a lottery ticket, warrant *(documento).*

cauteleiro, *s.m.* lottery ticket seller.

cautelosamente, *adv.* cautiously, prudently.

cauteloso, *adj.* cautious, prudent, careful.

cauterização, *s.f.* cauterization.

cauterizar, *v.t.* to cauterize, to sear.

cauto, *adj.* cautious, prudent.

cava, *s.f.* digging, ditch.

cavaca, *s.f.* chip, wood splinter.

cavaco, *s.m.* chip, wood splinter; *não dar cavaco:* to not give answer, to say nothing.

cavadela, *s.f.* digging, stroke with a hoe.

cavado, *adj.* hollowed, dug out, concave.

cavador, *s.m.* digger, ploughman.

cavadora, *s.f.* ploughing machine.

cavala, *s.f.* mackerel.

cavalão, *s.m.* big horse, someone that runs and leaps about.

cavalar, *adj.* equine.

cavalaria, *s.f.* cavalry, chivalry, knighthood *(instituição medieval) soldado de cavalaria,* horse-soldier.

cavalariça, *s.f.* stables.

cavaleiro, *s.m.* horseman, rider, knight; *cavaleiro andante,* knight errant.

cavalete, *s.m.* easel *(de pintor),* trestle *(de mesa),* sawhorse *(de serrador).*

cavalgada, *s.f.* cavalcade.

cavalgadura, *s.f.* beast, mount.

cavalgar, *v.t.* to ride.

cavalheiresco, *adj.* gentlemanly, noble, chivalrous.

cavalheirismo, *s.m.* gentlemanliness, gentlemanship, chivalry.

cavalheiro, *s.m.* gentleman, nobleman; *adj.* polite, gentlemanly.

cavalicoque, *s.m.* small horse.

cavalinha, *s.f. (bot.)* field equiserum.

cavalitas, *s.f.pl.* às cavalitas, pick-a-back.

cavalo, *s.m.* horse, knight *(no xadrez), cavalo de batalha,* charger; *cavalo-vapor:* horse-power.

cavalo-marinho, *s.m.* sea-horse.

cavaqueador, *s.m.* chatterer.

cavaquear, *v.t.* to chat, to talk.

cavaqueira, *s.f.* chat.

cavaquinho, *s.m.* a sort of little guitar.

cavar, *v.t.* to dig, to excavate, to hollow, to hoe; *v.i.* to dig.

cavatina, *s.f.* cavatina.

caveira, *s.f.* skull.

caveiroso, *adj.* skulled.

caverna, *s.f.* cavern, cave.

cavername, *s.m. (náut.)* frame, framework.

cavernoso, *adj.* cavernous.

caviar, *s.m.* caviar.

cavidade, *s.f.* cavity, hollow.

cavilação, *s.f.* cavillation.

cavilador, *s.m.* caviller.

cavilar, *v.i.* to cavil, to quibble.

cavilha, *s.f.* bolt, peg, dowel, pin.

cavilhosamente, *adv.* cavillously, cunningly.

caviloso, *adj.* cavillous, cunning.

cavo, *adj.* hollow, concave, cavernous.

cavoucar, *v.t.* e *v.i.* to open trenches, to dig foundations.

cavouco, *s.m.* hollow, ditch, trench.

cavouqueiro, *s.m.* navvy.

caxemira, *s.f.* cashmere.

cear, *v.t.* e *v.i.* to sup.

cebola, *s.f.* onion.

cebolada, *s.f.* onion stew or sauce.

cebolar, *s.m.* onion bed.

cebolinha, small onion.

cebolinho, *s.m.* onion-seed.

cebolo, *s.m.* onion-seed.

ceca, *s.f.* 1) *Ceca e Meca,* many undetermined countries. 2) *andar Ceca e Meca,* to go on a long journey.

cecal, *adj.* caecal.

cecear, *v.i.* to lisp.

cecém, *s.m.* white lily.

ceceoso, *adj.* lisping.

cecília, *s.f.* coecilia.

ceco, *s.m.* caecum.

cedência, *s.f.* giving up, yielding.

cedente, *adj.* yielding.

ceder, *v.t.* to yield, to give up, to cede; *v.i.* to surrender, to condescende.

cediço, *adj.* rotten, stale, musty, old.

cedilha, *s.f.* cedilla.

cedilhado, *adj.* that has a cedilla.

cedilhar, *v.t.* to place a cedilla below.

cedinho, *adv.* very early in the morning.

cedível, *adj.* that may be ceded, yieldable, transferable.

cedo, *adv.* soon, early; *cedo ou tarde,* sooner or later.

cedro, *s.m.* cedar.

cédula, *s.f.* schedule, ballot *(eleitoral),* bond *(apólice).*

cefalalgia, *s.f.* cephalalgia.

cefálico, *adj.* cephalic.

cefalite, *s.f.* cephalitis.

cefalóide, *adj.* cephaloid.

cefalópodes, *s.m.pl.* cephalopoda.

cegada, *s.f.* party of masquerades.

cegamente, *adv.* blindly, inconsiderately.

cegar, *v.t.* to blind; *v.i.* to become blind; *v.r.* to become blind, to be enraged.

cegarrega, *s.f.* grasshopper, balm cricket, rattle *(barulho).*

cegas, *adv.* às cegas, blindly, in the dark, gropingly.

cego, *s.m.* blind man; *adj.* blind.

cegonha, *s.f.* stork.

cegueira, *s.f.* blindness, fascination.

cegueta, *s.m.* e *s.f.* short-sighted person.

ceia, *s.f.* supper.

ceifa, *s.f.* harvest, crop, reaping.

ceifar, *v.t.* to reap, to crop, to harvest.

ceifeira, *s.f.* reaper, reaping-machine.

ceifeiro, *s.m.* reaper, harvester.

ceitil, *s.m.* old Portuguese coin.

cela, *s.f.* cell.

celebérrimo, *adj.* most remarkable, most famous.

celebração, *s.f.* celebration, commemoration.

celebrador, *s.m.* celebrant.

celebrante, *s.m.* celebrant.

celebrar, *v.t.* to celebrate, to commemorate. 1)*celebrar missa,* to say Mass. 2) *celebrar um contrato,* to make a contract.

celebrável, *adj.* praiseworthy, laudable.

célebre, *adj.* celebrated, famous, renowned.

celebridade, *s.f.* celebrity.

celebrização, *s.f.* the process of becoming famous.

celebrizar, *v.t.* to render famous, to make known; *celebrizar-se,* to become famous.

celeiro, *s.m.* barn, granary.

celerado, *s.m.* malefactor, bandit.

célere, *adj.* swift, rapid, quick.

celeridade, *s.f.* celerity, rapidity, quickness.

celeste, *adj.* celestial, heavenly.

celestial, *adj.* o mesmo que "celeste".

celestialmente, *adv.* celestially, heavenly.

celeuma, *s.f.* clamor, uproar, fuss, controversy.

celha, *s.f.* tub, bucket.

celibatário, *s.m.* e *adj.* bachelor, single, unmarried, celibate.

celibato, *s.m.* celibacy, singleness.

celofane, *s.m.* cellophane.

celta, *adj.* celtic; *s.m.* Celt.

céltico, *adj.* Celtic.

célula, *s.f.* cell.

celular, *adj.* cellular.

celulóide, *s.f.* celulloid.

celulose, *s.f.* cellulose.

celuloso, *adj.* celulose.

cem, *adj.* num. e *s.m.* a hundred, one hundred.

cementação, *s.f.* cementation, cementing.

cementar, *v.t.* to cement, to join closely.

cemento, *s.m.* cement.

cemitério, *s.m.* cemetery, graveyard, churchyard.

cena, *s.f.* scene, scenery, stage *(palco).*

cenáculo, *s.m.* cenacle, cenaculum.

cenário, *s.m.* scenery, setting.

cendrado, *adj.* ash-coloured.

cenho, *s.m.* scowl, frown.

cénico, *adj.* scenical.

cenóbio, *s.m.* coenobium.

cenobita, *s.f* e *s.m.* coenobite.

cenobítico, *adj.* coenobitical.

cenografia, *s.f.* scenography.

cenógrafo, *s.m.* scenographer.

cenosidade, *s.f.* filth, dirty place.

cenoso, *adj.* muddy, miry.

cenotáfio, *s.m.* cenotaph.

cenoura, *s.f.* carrot.

censo, *s.m.* census.

censório, *adj.* censorial.

censura, *s.f.* censure, blame, reprobation, reprimand, censorship.

censurável, *adj.* censurable, reproachable.

centáurea, *s.f.* cornflower.

centauro, *s.m.* centaur.

centavo, *s.m.* centavo, penny.

centeal, *s.m.* field of rye.

centeio, *s.m.* rye.

centelha, *s.f.* spark.

centena, *s.f.* a hundred; *às centenas,* by hundreds.

centenário, *s.m.* centenary, hundreth anniversary, centenarian; *adj.* centenarian, centennial.

centesimal, *adj.* centesimal.

centésimo, *adj.* hundredth.

centiare, *s.m.* centiare, the hundredth part of an are.

centígrado, *adj.* centigrade.

centigrama, *s.m.* centigram.

centilitro, *s.m.* centilitre.

centímetro, *s.m.* centimeter.

cêntimo, *s.m.* centime.

cento, *s.m.* one hundred; *por cento:* per cent.

centopeia, *s.f.* centipede.

central, *adj.* central. 1) *central telefónica,* telephone exchange. 2) *central de polícia,* headquarters.

centralista, *s.m.* centralist.

centralização, *s.f.* centralization.

centralizador, *s.m. e adj.* centralizing.

centralizar, *v.t.* to centralize, to concentrate.

centrar, *v.t.* to center.

centrífuga, *s.f. força centrífuga,* centrifugal force.

centrifugação, *s.f.* to separate by means of the centrifugal force.

centrifugar, *v.t.* to centrifugate.

centrífugo, *adj.* centrifugal.

centrípeta, *s.f. força centrípeta,* centripetal force.

centrípeto, *adj.* centripetal.

centro, *s.m.* centre, center, middle, core, heart, downtown *(de uma cidade).*

centunviral, *adj.* centumviral.

centunvirato, *s.m.* centumvirate.

centúnviro, *s.m.* centumvir.

centuplicar, *v.t.* to centuplicate.

cêntuplo, *s.m.* hundredfold; *adj.* centuple.

centúria, *s.f.* century.

centurião, *s.m.* centurian.

cepa, *s.f.* vine-plant, vine.

cepilhar, *v.t.* to plane, to smooth, to improve.

cepilho, *s.m.* plane.

cepo, *s.m.* stump, block, log.

cepticismo, *s.m.* scepticism, doubt.

céptico, *adj.* sceptic, skeptic, doubtful, incredulous; *s.m.* sceptic.

ceptro, *s.m.* sceptre.

cera, *s.f.* wax.

ceráceo, *adj.* ceraceous, waxen.

cerâmica, *s.f.* pottery, ceramics.

cerâmico, *adj.* ceramic.

ceramista, *s.f. e s.m.* ceramist, potter.

cerasta, *s.f.* cerastes.

cerato, *s.m.* cerate.

cérbero, *s.m.* cerberus.

cerca, *s.f.* enclosure, fence; *adv.* about, near.

cercado, *s.m.* enclosure.

cercadura, *s.f.* border, rim, edging.

cercanias, *s.f.pl.* surroundings, suburbs.

cercar, *v.t.* to enclose, to surround, to encircle, to envelop, to environ, to wall, to hedge, to fence in *(pôr cerca em),* to besiege *(pôr cerco a).*

cerce, *adv.* short.

cerceadura, *s.f.* retrenchment, cutting short.

cercear, *v.t.* to retrench, to cut short, to diminish, to lessen.

cerceta, *s.f.* teal.

cerco, *s.m.* siege, circle.

cerdas, *s.f.pl.* wildboar's bristles.

cerdo, *s.m.* wild boar, hog.

cerdoso, *adj.* bristly.

cereal, *s.m.* cereal, grain.

cerealífero, *adj.* relating to cereals.

cerebelo, *s.m.* cerebelum.

cerebração, *s.f.* cerebration.

cerebral, *adj.* cerebral.

cerebrino, *adj.* cerebral, eccentric, extravagant.

cérebro, *s.m.* cerebrum, brain, mind *(espírito).*

cerefólio, *s.m.* chervil.

cereja, *s.f.* cherry.

cerejal, *s.m.* cherry-orchard.

cerejeira, *s.f.* cherry tree.

céreo, *adj.* waxen, waxy; *s.m.* cerium.

cerieiro, *s.m.* wax-chandler.

cerimónia, *s.f.* ceremony; *traje de cerimónia,* evening dress.

cerimonial, *s.m.* ceremonial, ceremony; *adj.* ceremonial, formal.

cerimoniosamente, *adv.* ceremoniously.

cerimonioso, *adj.* ceremonious, formal.

cernar, *v.t.* to lay bare the heart of a tree; to cut to its heart, to remove the heart of a tree.

cerne, *s.m.* heart of a tree, duramen.

cernelha, *s.f.* withers of an animal.

cerol, *s.m.* shoemaker's wax.

ceroso, *adj.* waxen, waxy.

ceroulas, *s.f.pl.* drawers.

cerração, *s.f.* fog, mist.

cerrado, *adj.* shut, closed, thick *(o nevoeiro),* dark, gloomy *(escuro).*

cerrar, *v.t.* to close, to shut, to lock, to enclose. 1) *cerrar os dentes,* to set one's teeth. 2) *cerrar fileiras,* to close ranks.

cerro, *s.m.* small hill, hillock.

certame, *s.m.* contest, competition, exhibition, show.

certamente, *adv.* certainly, surely, of course.

certeiro, *adj.* well-aimed, infallible, sure.

certeza, *s.f.* certainty, certitude, assurance; *ter a certeza,* to be sure.

certidão, s.f. certificate. 1) *certidão de idade,* birth certificate. 2) *certidão de óbito,* death certificate.

certificação, s.f. certifcation.

certificado, s.m. certificate; adj. certificatory.

certificar, v.t. to certify, to assure, to attest, to vouch for; *certificar-se,* to make sure.

certificativo, adj. certificatory.

certo, adj. certain, sure, true, right, exact; adv. certainly, of course, indeed, for sure; *ao certo,* exactly.

certo, s.m. certainty, certitude.

cerúleo, adj. cerulean.

cerume, cerúmen, s.m. cerumen.

ceruminoso, adj. ceruminous.

cerva, s.f. hind, deer.

cervato, s.m. young deer.

cerveja, s.f. beer, ale.

cervejaria, s.f. beer-house.

cervejeiro, brewer.

cervical, adj. cervical.

cervino, adj. relating to deer.

cerviz, s.f. neck, nape of neck.

cervo, s.m. deer.

cerzideira, s.f. fine-drawer, darner.

cerzidura, s.f. fine-drawing, darning.

cerzir, v.t. to fine-draw, to darn.

César, s.m. Caesar.

cesariano, adj. Caesarean; *operação cesariana,* caesarean operation.

cesarismo, s.m. caesarism.

cesarista, s.m. caesarist.

cessação, s.f. cessation, ceasing, suspension.

cessante, adj. ceasing.

cessão, s.f. cession, assignment, yielding up, giving up, transfer.

cessar, v.t. e v.i. to cease, to stop, to end, to come to an end; *sem cessar,* unceasingly, continually.

cessionário, s.m. cessionary, transference.

cesta, s.f. basket.

cestada, s.f. basketful.

cesteiro, s.m. basket-maker.

cesto, s.m. basket, pannier; *cesto da gávea,* crow's nest.

cesura, s.f. caesura.

cetáceo, s.m. e adj. cetaceon, cetaceous; pl. cetacea.

cetim, s.m. satin.

cetinoso, adj. satiny, like satin.

céu, s.m. sky, heaven, firmament; céu-da--boca, palate, roof of the mouth.

ceva, s.f. hogwash.

cevada, s.f. barley.

cevadal, s.m. barley-plantation.

cevadilha, s.f. cevadilla.

cevado, s.m. pig; adj. fattened.

cevar, v.t. to fatten, to feed up.

cevar-se, v.t. to grow fat.

cevo, s.m. bait, enticement.

chá, s.m. tea.

chã, s.f. plain.

chacal, s.m. jackal.

chácara, s.f. farm.

chacina, s.f. slaughter, massacre.

chacinar, v.t. to slaughter, to massacre, to kill.

chaço, s.m. driver.

chacota, s.f. jest, jesting, mockery, fun; *fazer chacota,* to laugh at, to mock.

chacotear, v.i. to mock, to laugh at.

chafarica, s.f. small shop.

chafariz, s.m. fountain, public fountain.

chafurda, s.f. pigsty, mudhole.

chafurdar, v.i. to wallow, to roll in the mud, to thrive.

chaga, s.f. ulcer, wound, affliction; (bot.) garden climber.

chagado, adj. ulcerated.

chagar, v.t. e v.r. to wound, to ulcerate, to become ulcerated.

chalaça, s.f. jest, joke.

chalaceador, s.m. jester, joker.

chalacear, v.i. to jest, to joke.

chalado, adj. water with tea, insipid, nuts (doido).

chalé, s.m. cottage.

chaleira, s.f. kettle.

chalrar, v.t. to chatter.

chalreta, s.f. pool-snipe, redshank.

chalupa, s.f. sloop.

chama, s.f. flame.

chamada, s.f. call, marginal note, roll-call (militar).

chamado, adj. called, named, said.

chamamento, s.m. calling, summons, convocation.

chamar, v.t. to call, to convoke, to summon, to name. 1) *chamar a atenção,* to draw the attention. 2) *chamar a si a responsabili- dade,* to take the responsability. 3) *mandar chamar,* to send for.

chamariz, s.m. decoy, bait, allurement, enticement.

chambão, s.m. slender leg, beef of bad quality.

chambre, s.m. morning-gown.

chamejante, *adj.* flaming, glowing.

chamejar, *v.i.* to flame, to sparkle, to glow; *v.t.* to dart.

chaminé, *s.f.* chimney.

champanhe, *s.m.* champagne.

chamuscadela, *s.f.* singeing.

chamuscar, *v.t.* to singe, to burn slightly.

chamusco, *s.m.* singeing; *cheirar a chamusco,* to smell of burning.

chanca, *s.f.* clog.

chance, *s.f.* chance, opportunity.

chancela, *s.f.* seal, signet.

chancelaria, *s.f.* chancellery, chancellorship.

chanceler, *s.m.* chancellor.

chanfalho, *s.m.* old sword.

chanfana, *s.f.* badly cooked food.

chanfrado, *adj.* canted, bevelled, grooved, foolish *(apatetado).*

chanfradura, *s.f.* chamfer, bevel, groove.

chanfrar, *v.t.* to bevel, to chamfer, to groove.

chanfro, *s.m.* bevel, groove, chamfer.

chantagem, *s.f.* blackmail; *fazer chantagem,* to blackmail.

chantagista, *s.m.* blackmailer.

chantre, *s.m.* chanter, singer.

chão, *s.m.* ground, earth, floor; *adj.* level, smooth, flat.

chapa, *s.f.* plate, metal sheet.

chapada, *s.f.* blow with the hand.

chapado, *adj.* perfect, downright.

chapar, *v.t.* to plate.

chaparia, *s.f.* plating, plates.

chaparral, *s.m.* wood of young cork-oak--trees.

chaparro, *s.m.* young cork-oak.

chapear, *v.t.* to plate, laminate.

chapejar, *v.t. e v.i.* to paddle.

chapelada, *s.f.* salute with the hat.

chapelaria, *s.f.* hattery, hatter's shop.

chapeleira, *s.f.* hat-box.

chapeleiro, *s.m.* hatter.

chapéu, *s.m.* hat. 1) *chapéu-de-chuva,* umbrella. 2) *chapéu-de-sol,* parasol.

chapim, *s.m.* slipper; *(zool.)* titmouse.

chapinhar, *v.t. e v.i.* to paddle the water, to splash about, to flounder.

charada, *s.f.* charade, riddle.

charadista, *s.m.* guesser or maker of charades.

charamela, *s.f.* bagpipe.

charanga, *s.f.* brass-band, fanfare.

charão, *s.m.* japanese lacquer.

charco, *s.m.* stagnant pool, mud puddle, swamp *(pântano).*

charivari, *s.m.* charivari, hubbub.

charla, *s.f.* prattle, chatter.

charlatanesco, *adj.* quackish.

charlatanismo, *s.m.* quackery, charlatanry.

charlatão, *s.m.* quack, charlatan.

charlateira, *s.f.* epaulet.

charneca, *s.f.* moor.

charneira, *s.f.* hinge, joint.

charola, *s.f.* litter.

charro, *s.m.* rustic.

charrua, *s.f.* plough.

charuteira, *s.f.* cigar-case.

charuteiro, *s.m.* cigar-maker.

charuto, *s.m.* cigar.

chasco, *s.m.* biting jest, sarcasm.

chasquear, *v.t.* to mock.

chatear, *v.t.* to annoy, to bore, to tease.

chateza, *s.f.* lowness.

chatice, *s.f.* boredom, nuisance.

chatim, *s.m.* crooked dealer.

chato, *adj.* flat, tiresome, boring, dull, tiresome.

chauvinismo, *s.m.* chauvinism.

chauvinista, *s.m.* chauvinist.

chavascal, *s.m.* filthy place, mess.

chave, *s.f.* key. 1) *chave de fendas,* screw-driver. 2) *chave-inglesa,* screw-wrench.

chaveiro, *s.m.* key-keeper, key ring *(porta--chaves).*

chavelho, *s.m.* horn.

chavelhudo, *adj.* horned.

chávena, *s.f.* cup, tea-cup.

chaveta, *s.f.* axle pin, cotter pin.

chavo, *s.m.* brass farthins; *não valer um chavo,* to be worthless.

chazeiro, *adj.* fond of tea.

checo, *s.m. e adj.* Czech.

chefe, *s.m.* chief, leader, head, commander, master.

chefia, *s.f.* leadership, command.

chefiar, *v.t.* to lead, to command, to conduct.

chegada, *s.f.* arrival, coming.

chegado, *adj.* close, near, arrived.

chegar, *v.t. e v.i.* to arrive *(from a place at another),* to come, to get to, to suffice, to be enough *(ser suficiente),* to bring near *(aproximar),* to reach *(alcançar).* 1) *chegou a dizer que,* he even said that. 2) *chegar-se,* to come close, to approach.

cheia, *s.f.* overflow, flood, inundation.

cheio, *adj.* full (of something), filled (with something), replete, crowded *(de gente),* well-fed *(bem nutrido).*

cheirar, *v.t. e v.i.* to smell, to nose, to sniff. 1)

cheirar a, to smell of. 2) *cheirar mal,* to smellbad, to stink.

cheirete, *s.m.* stink, very bad smell.

cheiro, *s.m.* smell, odor, fragrance, scent.

cheiroso, *adj.* odorous, fragrant, perfumed.

cheque, *s.m.* cheque, check. 1) *passar um cheque, cheque em branco,* blank cheque. 2) *cheque cruzado,* crossed cheque. 3) *cheque ao portador,* cheque to the bearer;

cherne, *s.m.* black grouper.

cheta, *s.f.* brass farthing; *não ter cheta,* to be penniless.

cheviote, *s.m.* Cheviot.

chiada, *s.f.* creaking, squeaking.

chiadeira, *s.f.* creaking, squeaking.

chiado, *s.m.* chirping.

chiador, *adj.* chirping; *s.m.* squeaker.

chiar, *v.i.* to creak, to squeak, to chirp.

chibante, *s.m.* boaster, braggart, fanfarron.

chibarro, *s.m.* young gelded he-goat.

chibata, *s.f.* switch.

chibatada, *s.f.* blow with a switch.

chibatar, *v.t.* to switch.

chibato, *s.m.* male kid.

chibo, *s.m.* kid.

chicana, *s.f.* chicane, chicanery, cavil, quibble.

chicanar, *v.i.* to chicane, to cavil, to quibble.

chicaneiro, *s.m.* quibbler, pettifogger.

chícara, *s.f.* cup, mug.

chicha, *s.f.* meat.

chicharro, *s.m.* horse-makerel.

chichisbéu, *s.m.* one who flirts with a married woman; gallant, suitor.

chicória, *s.f.* endive.

chicotada, *s.f.* blow with a whip, lash.

chicote, *s.m.* whip.

chicotear, *v.t.* to whip.

chieira, *s.f.* squeaking.

chifre, *s.m.* horn.

Chile, *s.m.* Chile.

chileno, *s.m.* e *adj.* Chilean, of Chile.

chilreada, *s.f.* chirping.

chilreador, *s.m.* chirper, warbler; *adj.* chirping, warbling.

chilrear, *v.i.* to chirp, to warble, to twitter.

chilreio, *s.m.* chirping, warble, twitter.

chilro, *adj.* insipid, tasteless.

chimpanzé, *s.m.* chimpanzee.

China, *s.f.* China.

chinchila, *s.f.* chinchilla.

chinela, *s.f.* slipper.

chinelada, *s.f.* blow with a sweeper.

chinelo, *s.m.* slipper.

chinês, *s.m.* e *adj.* chinese.

chinesice, *s.f.* something peculiar, extravagance.

chinfrim, *s.m.* uproar, tumult, shindy.

chinfrinada, chinfrineira, *s.f.* hubbub, uproar.

chinó, *s.m.* wig, peruke.

chinquilho, *s.m.* game of quoits.

chio, *s.m.* creak.

chique, *adj.* chic, smart.

chiqueiro, *s.m.* pigsty.

chiquismo, *s.m.* smartness.

chispa, *s.f.* spark.

chispar, *v.i.* to sparkle, to flash, to glitter.

chispe, *s.m.* pig's trotters.

chiste, *s.m.* jest, witticism, smart saying.

chistoso, *adj.* wittyfacetious, given to jesting.

chita, *s.f.* printed cotton.

choca, *s.f.* cow's bell; *adj.* broody, sitting *(galinha).*

choça, *s.f.* small hut, hovel, joint *(prisão).*

chocadeira, *s.f.* incubator, hatchery.

chocalhar, *v.i.* to rattle, to shake *(agitar).*

chocalheiro, *s.m.* blabber.

chocalho, *s.m.* cowbell, rattle.

chocar, *v.t.* e *v.i.* to hatch, to brood, to incubate, to shock, to offend; to collide, to bump against, to crash into; *chocar-se,* to be shocked by.

chocarrear, *v.i.* to jest.

chocarreiro, *s.m.* jester, scoffer; *adj.* jesting, scoffing.

chocarrice, *s.f.* vulgar or coarse jesting.

chocho, *adj.* empty, dry, worthless; *(pop.)* kiss.

choco, *s.m.* brooding, hatching; *(zool.)* cuttle fish; *adj.* broody, addled.

chocolate, *s.m.* chocolate.

chocolateira, *s.f.* chocolate-pot, an old and noisy car.

chocolateiro, *s.m.* chocolate maker.

chofre, *s.m.* sudden blow or shot; *de chofre,* suddenly, all of a sudden.

choldra, *s.m.* mob.

choque, *s.m.* shock, impact, collision, crash, conflict.

choradeira, *s.f.* crying, whining, complaint.

choramingar, *v.i.* to whine, to whimper, to cry.

choramingas, *s.m.* whimperer, sniveler, crybaby.

chorão, *s.m.* weeper, whimperer; *(bot.)* weeping-willow.

chorar, *v.i.* to cry, to weep, to wail; *v.t.* to cry over, to lament, to mourn, to mourn over.

choro, *s.m.* weeping, crying, tears.

chorona, *s.f.* weeper.

chorosamente, *adv.* weepingly.

choroso, *adj.* crying, weeping, in tears.

chorrilho, *s.m.* series.

chorudo, *adj.* substantial, lucrative.

chorume, *s.m.* juice, sap, fat, abundance.

choupa, *s.f.* blade of boar spear; a kind of fish.

choupal, *s.m.* grove of poplar-trees.

choupana, *s.f.* hut, hovel, shack.

choupo, *s.m.* poplar-tree.

chouriça, *s.f.* a kind of sausage.

chouriço, *s.m.* sausage.

choutar, *v.i.* to jog along *(o cavalo).*

chouto, *s.m.* jog-trot.

chover, *v.i.* to rain, to pour *(a cântaros).*

chuçada, *s.f.* thrust with a pike.

chucha, *s.f.* sucking.

chuchadeira, *s.f.* sucking; *(pop.)* mockery, sport.

chuchar, *v.t.* to suck; *(pop.)* to mock, to jeer.

chuço, *s.m.* boar-spear, pike, spear.

chufa, *s.f.* mockery, scoffing.

chufar, *v.t.* e *v.i.* to banter, to scoff.

chula, *s.f.* country dance.

chulé, *s.m.* smell of dirty feet, cheesy feet.

chulear, *v.t.* to sew with large stitches, to tack.

chuleio, *s.m.* tacking.

chulice, *s.f.* a low jest, scurrility.

chulipa, *s.f.* slipper.

chumaçar, *v.t.* to pad, to stuff.

chumaceira, *s.f.* bushing.

chumaço, *s.m.* padding, stuffing.

chumbada, *s.f.* shot, load of gunshot *(carga de chumbo),* sinker *(de pesca).*

chumbado, *adj.* filled with lead.

chumbadouro, *s.m.* stone-bolt.

chumbar, *v.t.* to fill or solder with lead, to lead, to reject *(um aluno).*

chumbo, *s.m.* lead, gunshot *(de caça),* failure to pass an examination. 1) *chumbo grosso,* buckshot. 2) *chumbo miúdo,* bird shot.

chupadela, *s.f.* suck, sucking, suction.

chupado, *adj.* sucked, lean, bony.

chupar, *v.t.* to suck, to absorb, to draw, to wring *(extorquir).*

chupeta, *s.f.* rubber nipple, pacifier *(de criança),* sipper *(canudo).*

chupista, *s.m.* sponger, cadger *(parasita).*

churrasco, *s.m.* grilled meat, barbecue.

churrião, *s.m.* cart.

churro, *s.m. adj.* dirty; *s.m.* villain.

chusma, *s.f.* crowd, throng, multitude, lot *(grande quantidade).*

chuva, *s.f.* rain, shower *(aguaceiro); chuva de pedra,* hailstorm.

chuvada, *s.f.* downpour, shower.

chuveiro, *s.m.* shower.

chuviscar, *v.i.* to drizzle, to rain gently.

chuvisco, *s.m.* drizzle, fine rain.

chuvoso, *adj.* rainy.

cianeto, *s.m.* cyanide.

cianogénio, *s.m.* cyanogen.

cianose, *s.f.* cyanosis.

ciar, *v.i. (náut.)* to back water.

ciática, *s.f.* sciatica.

ciático, *adj.* sciatic.

cibato, *s.m.* food for birds.

cibório, *s.m.* ciborium.

cicatriz, *s.f.* scar, cicatrice.

cicatrização, *s.f.* cicatrization.

cicatrizante, *adj.* cicatrizant, healing.

cicatrizar, *v.i.* to heal, to cicatrize.

cicatrizável, *adj.* cicatrisive, that can be lealed.

cicerone, *s.m.* cicerone, guide.

ciceroniano, *adj.* ciceronian, eloquent.

ciciar, *v.i.* to rustle, to murmur, to lisp.

cicioso, *adj.* lisping, rustling.

cíclico, *adj.* cyclical.

ciclismo, *s.m.* cycling.

ciclista, *s.m.* e *s.f.* cyclist, bicycle rider.

ciclo, *s.m.* cycle.

cicloidal, *adj.* cycloidal.

ciclóide, *s.m.* cycloid.

ciclone, *s.m.* cyclone.

ciclónico, *adj.* cyclonic.

Ciclope, *s.m.* Cyclop.

ciclópico, *adj.* cyclopan.

cicuta, *s.f.* hemlock.

cidadã, *s.f.* citizen.

cidadania, *s.f.* citizenship.

cidadão, *s.m.* citizen.

cidade, *s.f.* city, town.

cidadela, *s.f.* citadel.

cidra, *s.f.* cider; *(bot.)* cedrate, citron.

cidreira, *s.f.* citron-tree; *erva-cidreira,* balm--mint.

cieiro, *s.m.* chap.

ciência, *s.f.* science, knowledge.

ciente, *adj.* scient, learned, aware, cognizant, acquainted; *estar ciente de,* to be aware of.

científico, *adj.* scientific.

cientista, *s.m.* scientist, man of science.

cifra, *s.f.* zero, cipher; code, cipher *(escrita em código); cifras,* figures, accounts, arithmetic.

cifrão, *s.m.* dollar sign.

cifrar, *v.t.* to cipher, to code, to abridge; *cifrar-se a,* go no farther than.

cigana, *s.f.* gipsy.

ciganice, *s.f.* trickery, cheating.

ciganada, crowd of gipsies, trickery.

cigano, *s.m.* e *adj.* gipsy.

cigarra, *s.f.* cicala.

cigarrada, *s.f.* puff of smoke from a cigarette.

cigarreira, *s.f.* cigarette-case.

cigarrilha, *s.f.* little cigar, cheroot.

cigarro, *s.m.* cigarette.

cilada, *s.f.* trap, ambush, snare; *armar uma cilada:* to ambush: to set a trap.

cilha, *s.f.* girth.

cilhar, *v.t.* to girth.

ciliar, *adj.* ciliary, ciliated.

cilício, *s.m.* cilice, hair shirt.

cilindrar, *v.t.* to roll, to press.

cilíndrico, *adj.* cylindrical.

cilindro, *s.m.* cylinder, roller.

cílio, *s.m.* cilium, eyelash.

cima, *s.f.* top, summit: *(bot.)* cyme. 1) *de cima,* upper *(superior).* 2) *de cima,* from above *(proveniência).* 3) *de cima para baixo,* from top to bottom. 4) *em cima,* above, up, overhead, upstairs. 5) *em cima de,* on, on top of. 6) *para cima,* up, upwards, upstairs. 7) *para cima e para baixo,* up and down. 8) *por cima,* overhead, superficially. 9) *por cima de,* over, on top of.

cimalha, *s.f.* *(arq.)* cyma.

címbalo, *s.m.* cymbal.

cimbre, *s.m.* *(arq.)* form, center of an arch.

cimeira, *s.f.* crest *(de capacete),* top, summit *(cume),* reunion.

cimeiro, *adj.* uppermost, top.

cimentação, *s.f.* cementing, cementation.

cimentar, *v.t.* to cement, to strengthen.

cimento, *s.m.* cement.

cimitarra, *s.f.* scimitar.

cimo, *s.m.* top, summit.

cinabre, *s.m.* cinnabar, vermilion.

cinamomo, *s.m.* cinnamon.

cinchar, *v.t.* to press, to cinch up.

cincho, *s.m.* cheese-press.

cinco, *adj. num.* card, five.

cindir, *v.t.* to split, to cut, to divide.

cineasta, *s.m.* e *s.f.* motion-picture technician.

cinéfilo, *s.m.* film man.

cinegética, *s.f.* hunting.

cinegético, *adj.* hunting.

cinema, *s.m.* cinema, movies, motion pictures, theatre *(recinto).*

cinemática, *s.f.* kinematics.

cinematografar, *v.t.* to film, to cinematograph.

cinematografia, *s.f.* cinematography.

cinematográfico, *adj.* cinematographic.

cinematógrafo, *s.m.* motion-picture projector.

cineração, *s.f.* cineration.

cinerar, *v.t.* to incinerate, to reduce to ashes.

cinerária, *s.f.* cineraria.

cinerário, *adj.* cinerary.

cinestesia, *s.f.* kinesthesis.

cinestésico, *adj.* kinesthetic.

cingalês, *s.m.* e *adj.* Cingalese.

cingido, *adj.* girded, belted.

cingidouro, *s.m.* girdle.

cingir, *v.t.* to gird *(pôr à cintura),* to bind *(apertar),* to restrict, to confine *(restringir); cingir-se,* to gird oneself, to restrict oneself.

cíngulo, *s.m.* cingulum.

cinicamente, *adv.* cyniclly.

cínico, *adj.* cynic, cynical, impudent.

cinismo, *s.m.* cynicism, impudence.

cinquenta, *adj. num.* fifty.

cinta, *s.f.* girdle, waistband, belt, band *(de jornal, etc.); à cinta,* fastened to one's belt.

cintado, *adj.* fitted to the waist.

cintar, *v.t.* to belt, to girdle, to band, to fit to the waist.

cintilação, *s.f.* sparkling, scintilation, twinkle.

cintilante, *adj.* scintilant, sparkling, brilliant, starlike.

cintilar, *v.t.* e *v.i.* to scintilate, to sparkle, to twinkle, to gleam.

cinto, *s.m.* belt; *cinto de segurança,* safety belt.

cintura, *s.f.* waist.

cinturado, *adj.* belted.

cinturão, *s.m.* belt, sword-belt.

cinza, *s.f.* ash, cinder.

cinzeiro, *s.m.* ashtray.

cinzel, *s.m.* chisel, graver, buin.

cinzelador, *s.m.* engraver, carver, chaser *(de metais).*

cinzeladura, cinzelagem, *s.f.* graving, carving.

cinzelar, *v.t.* to grave, to chisel, to engrave, to carve.

cinzento, *adj.* grey, ashy.

cio, *s.m.* rut, heat.

ciosamente, *adj.* jealously.

cioso, *adj.* jealous, envious, solicitous.

ciprestal, *s.m.* plantation of cypresses.

cipreste, *s.m.* cypress.

ciranda, *s.f.* ring dance *(dança),* screen *(joeira).*

cirandar, *v.t.* to screen; *v.i.* to dance in a ring.

circense, *adj.* circensian, circus.

circo, *s.m.* circus.

circuito, *s.m.* circuit.

circulação, *s.f.* circulation.

circulante, *adj.* circling.

circular, *v.t.* e *v.i.* to circulate, to go round, to move; *adj.* circular: round; *s.f.* circular, document, circular-letter.

circulatório, *adj.* circulatory.

círculo, *s.m.* circle, compass, sphere *(âmbito),* set, circle, club *(social); círculo vicioso,* vicious circle.

circum-navegação, *s.f.* circumnavigation.

circum-navegar, *v.t.* to circumnavigate.

circuncidar, *v.t.* circumcize.

circuncisão, *s.f.* circumsision.

circundação, *s.f.* surrounding, encircling.

circundar, *v.t.* to encircle, to surround, to encompass, to circle, to enclose.

circunferência, *s.f.* circumference.

circunflexo, *adj.* circumflex.

circunjacente, *adj.* circumjacent, lying around, surrounding.

circunlocução, *s.f.* circumlocution.

circunlóquio, *s.m.* o mesmo que "circun-locução".

circunscrever, *v.t.* to circumscribe, to limit, to confine.

circunscrição, *s.f.* circumscription.

circunscrito, *adj.* circumscribe, limited, restricted.

circunspecção, *s.f.* circumspection.

circunspecto, *adj.* circumspect, cautious, discreet.

circunstância, *s.f.* circumstance, condition, cause, situation.

circunstancial, *adj.* circumstancial.

circunstancialmente, *adv.* circumstantially.

circunstanciar, *v.t.* to circumstantiate, to describe exactly.

circunstante, *adj.* surrounding; *s.m.* e *s.f.* bystander, onlooker.

circunvagar, *v.i.* e *v.t.* to walk around, to move about.

circunvalação, *s.f.* circumvallation.

circunvalar, *v.t.* to circumvallate, to surround with trenches.

circunvizinhança, *s.f.* neighbourhood, vicinity, suburbs.

circunvizinho, *adj.* neighbouring, adjacent, adjoining.

circunvolução, *s.f.* circumvolution.

cirenaico, cireneu, *s.m.* helper, assitant, mate; *adj.* Cyrenaic.

círio, *s.m.* wax taper, wax candle.

cirro, *s.m.* cirrhus.

cirrose, *s.f.* cirrhosis.

cirroso, *adj.* cirrous.

cirurgia, *s.f.* surgery.

cirurgião, *s.m.* surgeon.

cirúrgico, *adj.* surgical.

cisalha, *s.f.* parings *(de metal).*

cisalpino, *adj.* Cisalpine.

cisão, *s.f.* scission, separation.

cisco, *s.m.* swepings, coal dust *(de carvão).*

cisma, *s.m.* schism; *s.f.* whim, suspicion, pondering, meditation.

cismar, *v.i.* to meditate, to ponder, to wonder, to think over.

cismático, *adj.* schismatic.

cisne, *s.m.* swan.

cissão, *s.f.* scission, cutting, split.

cissiparidade, *s.f.* scissiparity; *(biol.)* reproduction by fission.

cissura, *s.f.* scissure.

cistalgia, *s.f.* cystalgia.

cistercience, *adj.* Cistercian.

cisterna, *s.f.* cistern, water-tank, reservoir.

cistite, *s.f.* cystitis.

cisto, *s.m.* cyst.

cistocele, *s.f.* hernia of the urinary bladder.

cita, *s.f.* citation.

citação, *s.f.* citation, quotation, excerpt, summons *(convocatória judicial).*

citadino, *adj.* urban; *s.m.* city dweller, townsman.

citar, *v.t.* to quote, to cite, to mention, to summon *(convocar).*

cítara, *s.f.* zither.

citarista, *s.m.* zitherist.

citável, *adj.* quotable.

citologia, *s.f.* cytology.
citologista, *s.m.* cytologist.
citrato, *s.m.* citrate.
cítrico, *adj.* citric.
citrino, *s.m.* citrous fruit; *adj.* lemon-cou-loured.
ciúme, *s.m.* jealousy, envy.
ciumeira, *s.f.* jealousy, envy.
ciumento, *adj.* jealous.
cível, *adj.* civil.
cívico, *adj.* civic; *s.m.* policeman.
civil, *adj.* civil, courteous, polite, civilian; *s.m.* civilian.
civilidade, *s.f.* civility, politeness, courtesy.
civilização, *s.f.* civilisation.
civilizado, *adj.* civilised, polite, well-bred.
civilizador, *adj.* civiliser.
civilizar, *v.t.* to civilize, to educate, to humanize.
civilizável, *adj.* civilizable.
civilmente, *adv.* civilly, politely.
civismo, *s.m.* civism, good citizenship, civic pride.
cizânia, *s.f.* discord, disharmony; *(bot.)* darnel.
clã, *s.m.* clan.
clamador, *s.m.* e *adj.* bawler, implorer.
clamar, *v.t.* e *v.i.* to cry out, to clamour, to shout, to beseech *(implorar)*, to demand *(exigir)*.
clamor, *s.m.* clamour, outcry, uproar, complaint *(queixa)*.
clamoroso, *adj.* clamorous, vociferous, noisy, flagrant.
clandestinamente, *adv.* clandestinely.
clandestinidade, *s.f.* clandestineness, clandestinity, secrecy.
clandestino, *adj.* clandestine, secret, underhanded; *passageiro clandestino,* stowaway.
clangor, *s.m.* clangour, clangor, blare *(de trombetas)*.
clangoroso, *adj.* clangorous, blaring.
claque, *s.f.* claque.
clara, *s.f.* white of egg; *às claras,* openly, straightforwardly.
clarabóia, *s.f.* skylight, bull's eye, glass-roof.
claramente, *adv.* clearly.
clarão, *s.m.* flash of light, glimmer, gleam, glare.
clarear, *v.t.* e *v.i.* to clear, to make or become clear, to clear up *(o tempo)*.
clareira, *s.f.* glade, clearing.
clarete, *s.m.* claret.

clareza, *s.f.* clearness, limpidiness.
claridade, *s.f.* clearness, clarity, brightness, light.
clarificação, *s.f.* clarification.
clarificador, *adj.* clarifying.
clarificar, *v.t.* to clarify, to purify; *clarificar--se:* to settle.
clarim, *s.m.* clarion, bugle *(militar)*.
clarinete, *s.m.* clarinet.
clarividência, *s.f.* clear-sightedness, insight, discernement, clairvoyance *(telepática)*.
clarividente, *adj.* farseeing, sagacious, discerning, clairvoyant.
claro, *adj.* clear, bright, light *(cor)*, limpid, cloudless *(sem nuvens)*, evident, manifest, plain, explicit, intelligible, convincing. 1) *claro que não,* of course not. 2) *é claro, está claro, pois claro,* of course; *adv.* clearly, plainly; *s.m.* clear or open space, blank space. 3) *passar em claro,* to omit.
classe, *s.f.* class, category, group, rank, type, classroom *(sala de aulas)*.
classicismo, *s.m.* classicism.
clássico, *adj.* classic; *s.m.* classic, classicist.
classificação, *s.f.* classification.
classificado, *adj.* classified, classed, qualified.
classificador, *s.m.* classifier.
classificar, *v.t.* to class, to classify, to qualify, to assign to a class, to label *(rotular)*.
classificável, *adj.* classifiable.
claudicação, *s.f.* claudication, limping.
claudicante, *adj.* limping, halting, shaky *(vacilante)*.
claudicar, *v.i.* to walk lamely, to limp, to halt, to fail.
claustral, *adj.* claustral, monastic.
claustro, *s.m.* cloister, convent, monastery.
cláusula, *s.f.* clause, stipulation, article, condition.
clausular, *v.t.* to article, to restrict.
clausura, *s.f.* seclusion, reclusion, closure *(recinto)*.
clausurar, *v.t.* to cloister, to confine.
clava, *s.f.* club, mace.
clave, *s.f.* clef.
clavicórdio, *s.m.* clavichord.
clavícula, *s.f.* clavicle.
claviculado, *adj.* claviculated.
clavicular, *adj.* clavicular.
claviculário, *s.m.* key-keeper, turnkey.
claviforme, *adj.* club-shaped.

clavina, *s.f.* rifle.

cláxon, *s.m.* claxon.

clematite, *s.f.* clematis.

clemência, *s.f.* mercy, clemency, indulgence.

clemente, *adj.* merciful, clement, indulgent.

clepsidra, *s.f.* clepsydra.

cleptomania, *s.f.* kleptomania.

cleptomaníaco, *s.m.* kleptomaniac.

clerezia, *s.f.* clergy.

clerical, *adj.* clerical.

clericalismo, *s.m.* clericalism.

clérigo, *s.m.* clergyman, priest.

clero, *s.m.* clergy.

cliché, *s.m.* cliché, plate.

cliente, *s.m.* customer, client.

clientela, *s.f.* clientele, customers, clientage.

clima, *s.m.* climate, clime.

climatérico, *adj.* climatic.

climático, *adj.* climatic.

climatologia, *s.f.* climatology.

climatológico, *adj.* climatological.

clímax, *s.m.* climax, culmination, acme.

clínica, *s.f.* clinic, medical practice; *fazer clínica,* to practize.

clínico, *adj.* clinical.

clinómetro, *s.m.* clinometer.

clister, *s.m.* clyster.

clítoris, *s.m.* clitoris.

clivoso, *adj.* sloping, declivitous.

cloaca, *s.f.* cloaca.

clorato, *s.m.* chlorate.

cloreto, *s.m.* chlorine.

clorofila, *s.f.* chlorophyl.

clorofórmio, *s.m.* chloroform.

cloroformização, *s.f.* chloroformization.

cloroformizar, *v.t.* to chlorofor, to administer chloroform to.

clorose, *s.f.* chlorosis.

clorótico, *adj.* clorotic.

clube, *s.m.* club.

clubista, *s.m.* member of a club.

coabitação, *s.f.* cohabitation.

coabitar, *v.t. e v.i.* to cohabit, to live together, to dwell together.

coacção, coaction, compulsion, coercion.

coactar, *v.t.* o mesmo que "coagir".

coacto, *adj.* compelled, forced.

coadjutor, *s.m.* coadjutor, assistant.

coadjutoria, *s.f.* coadjutorship, collaboration.

coadjuvação, *s.f.* coadjuvancy, collaboration.

coadjuvante, *adj.* coadjutant, helping; *s.m.* helper.

coadjuvar, *v.t.* to assist, to help, to support.

co-administração, *s.f.* joint-administration.

co-administrar, *v.t.* to administrate in common.

coado, *adj.* strained, filtered.

coador, *s.m.* strainer, colander, percolator, filter.

coadquirir, *v.t.* to acquire in common with another.

coadunação, *s.f.* coadunation, combination, adaptation.

coadunado, *adj.* coadunate.

coadunar, *v.t.* to coadunate, to adapt, to combine, to conciliate.

coagir, *v.t.* to coact, to compel, to force, to coerce.

coagulação, *s.f.* coagulation.

coagulador, *adj. e s.m.* coagulatior.

coagulante, *adj.* coagulative.

coagular, *v.t.* to coagulate, to curdle, to congeal.

coágulo, *s.m.* coagulated mass, clot *(de sangue).*

coalescência, *s.f.* coalescence.

coalescente, *adj.* coalescent.

coalescer, *v.t.* to join, to unite, to combine.

coalhada, *s.f.* curdled milk.

coalhar, *v.t. e v.i.* to curdle, to clot.

coalheira, *s.f.* coagulator.

coalho, *s.m.* curdling.

coalizão, *s.f.* coalition, alliance.

coalizar-se, *v.r.* to form a coalition, to ally oneself with.

coaquisição, *s.f.* the act of acquiring together.

coar, *v.t.* to strain, to filter, to filtrate.

coarctação, *s.f.* coarctation, restraint, limitation.

coarctar, *v.t.* to restrain, to limit.

co-autor, *s.m.* co-author.

co-autoria, *s.f.* co-authorship.

coaxar, *v.i.* to croak.

cobaia, *s.f.* guinea-pig.

cobalto, *s.m.* cobalt.

cobarde, *s.m. adv.* coward; *adj.* coward, cowardly, dastardly, faint-hearted.

cobardemente, *adv.* cowardly.

cobardia, *s.f.* cowardice, pusillanimity.

coberta, *s.f.* cover, covering, bed-cover *(de cama),* covered deck *(de navio).*

coberto, *adj.* covered, hidden *(oculto);* a *coberto de,* safe from.

cobertor, *s.m.* blanket.

cobertura, *s.f.* covering, cover, roof *(tecto)*, shelter *(abrigo)*.

cobiça, *s.f.* covetousness, avidity, greed, cupidity.

cobiçar, *v.t.* to covet, to be greedy for.

cobiçável, *adj.* covetable.

cobiçosamente, *adv.* covetously.

cobiçoso, *adj.* covetous, avid, greedy.

cobra, snake, cobra.

cobrador, *s.m.* collector, receiver.

cobrança, *s.f.* collecting, receiving.

cobrar, *v.t.* to collect, to receive, to charge money for.

cobrável, *adj.* collectable, payable.

cobre, *s.m.* copper.

cobrear, *v.t.* to cover with copper.

cobrição, *s.f.* covering, copulation.

cobrir, *v.t.* to cover, to top, to spread *(espalhar)*, to clothe *(vestir)*, to coat *(revestir)*, to envelop *(envolver)*, to roof *(uma casa)*, to fill with *(de vergonha, etc.)*, to cloack *(disfarçar)*; *cobrir-se,* to cover oneself, to get undercover, to put on one's hat.

cobro, *s.m.* end, stop; *pôr cobro,* to put an end to.

coca, *s.f. (bot.)* coca; *estar à coca,* to pry.

coça, *s.f.* thrashing, drubbing.

coçadela, *s.f.* scratching.

coçado, *adj.* scratched, worn out *(o vestuário)*.

cocaína, *s.f.* cocaine.

cocainomania, *s.f.* cocainomania.

cocainómano, *s.m.* cocainomaniac.

cocar, *v.t.* to spy on.

coçar, *v.t.* to scratch.

cócaras, *s.f.pl.* squatting.

cocção, *s.f.* coction.

coccinela, *s.f.* coccinella.

cóccix, *s.m.* coccyx.

cócegas, *s.f.pl.* tickling, tickle; *fazer cócegas,* to tickle.

coceira, *s.f.* itching.

cochar, *v.t. (náut.)* to lay a cable, to draw water.

coche, *s.m.* coach.

cocheira, *s.f.* coach-house.

cocheiro, *s.m.* coachman, driver.

cochichar, *v.i.* to whisper.

cochicho, *s.m.* whisper, whispering; *(zool.)* skylark.

cochinilha, *s.f.* cochineal.

cocleária, *s.f.* cochlearia.

coco, *s.m.* coconut; *chapéu de coco,* derby hat.

cócoras, *s.f.pl.* 1) *de cócoras,* squatting. 2) *pôr-se de cócoras,* to squat.

cocorocó, *interj.* cock-a-doodle, the crow of a cock.

cocuruto, *s.m.* top.

côdea, *s.f.* crust *(de pão)*, rind *(de queijo)*.

codeína, *s.f.* codeine.

códice, *s.m.* codex, old manuscript.

codiciliar, *adj.* codicillary.

codicilo, *s.m.* codicil.

codificação, *s.f.* codification.

codificador, *s.m.* codifier.

codificar, *v.t.* to codify, to put into code.

código, *s.m.* code.

codilhar, *v.t.* to cheat, to deceive.

codilho, *s.m.* codile, cheat.

codorniz, *s.f.* quail.

coeducação, *s.f.* co-education.

coeficiente, *s.m.* coefficient.

coelha, *s.f.* doe-rabbit.

coelheira, *s.f.* rabbit burrow, warren.

coelheiro, *s.m.* rabbit hunter.

coelho, *s.m.* rabbit.

coempção, *s.f.* coemption.

coentro, *s.m.* coriander.

coerção, *s.f.* coercion, restraint.

coercibilidade, *s.f.* coercibility.

coercivamente, *adv.* coercively, by force.

coercivo, *adj.* coercive, restraining, compulsory.

coerência, *s.f.* coherence.

coerente, *adj.* coherent.

coesão, *s.f.* cohesion.

coesivo, *adj.* cohesive.

coeso, *adj.* cohesive, united.

coessência, *s.f.* the same essence.

coessencial, *adj.* co-essential.

coetâneo, *adj.* coetaneous, contemporary.

coeterno, *adj.* co-eternal.

coevo, *adj.* coeval, of the same age; *s.m.* contemporary.

coexistência, *s.f.* coexistence.

coexistente, *adj.* coexistent.

coexistir, *v.i.* to coexist.

cofiar, *v.t.* to stroke *(a barba)*.

cofre, *s.m.* safe chest; *cofre-forte,* steel safe.

cogitabundo, *s.m.* thoughtful, meditative.

cogitação, *s.f.* cogitation, meditation.

cogitar, *v.t.* to cogitate, to meditate, to ponder, to reflect upon.

cogitativo, *adj.* cogitative, meditative.

cognação, *s.f.* cognation.

cognado, cognato, *s.m.* cogante, kindred.

cognição, *s.f.* cognition, knowledge.

cognitivo, *adj.* cognitive.

cógnito, *adj.* known.

cognome, *s.m.* cognomen, surname.

cognominar, *v.t.* to cognominate, to surname, to name.

cognoscibilidade, *s.f.* cognoscibility.

cognoscível, *adj.* cognoscible, knowable, cognissable.

cogula, *s.f.* monk's cowl.

cogumelo, *s.m.* mushroom.

co-herdeira, *s.f.* co-heiress.

co-herdeiro, *s.m.* co-heir.

coibição, *s.f.* cohibition, restraint.

coibir, *v.t.* to cohibit, to restrain, to repress; *coibir-se,* to abstain (from doing).

coice, couce, *s.m.* kick *(de animal),* recoil *(recuo de arma);* dar coices, to kick.

coicear, *v.i.* to kick.

coiceira, couceira, *s.f.* hinge.

coifa, *s.f.* coif, hair net; *(bot.)* root cap.

coima, *s.f.* fine, penalty.

coimar, *v.t.* to fine.

coincidência, *s.f.* coincidence.

coincidente, *adj.* coincident.

coincidir, *v.i.* to coincide, to be conmensurate.

coió, *adj.* simple, foolish; *s.m.* boob, simpleton.

coiote, *s.m.* coyote.

coiro, couro, *s.m.* leather, hide *(de um animal inteiro); couro cabeludo:* scalp.

coisa, *s.f.* thing, object, something, stuff, matter *(assunto); de coisa alguma:* nothing; *coisa de uma hora:* about an hour; *coisa que o valha:* something like it; *qualquer coisa:* anything, something.

coitado, *adj.* poor, pitiful, unlucky; *coitado!* poor fellow!

coito, *s.m.* coitus, copulation, sexual intercourse.

cola, *s.f.* glue, gum; *ir na cola de:* to follow closely.

colaboração, *s.f.* collaboration.

colaborador, *s.m.* collaborator.

colaborar, *v.t.* to collaborate, to cooperate.

colação, *s.f.* collation, light meal *(refeição).*

colaço, *s.m.* foster-brother.

colado, glued, gummed, stuck.

colagem, *s.f.* gluing.

colapso, *s.m.* collapse, breakdown; *colapso cardíaco:* heart failure.

colar, *v.t.* to glue, to stick, to gum.

colar, *s.m.* necklace, collar.

colarinho, *s.m.* collar.

colateral, *adj.* collateral.

colcha, *s.f.* bedspread, quilt.

colchão, *s.m.* mattress.

clolcheia, *s.f.* quaver.

colchete, *s.m.* clasp.

colchoaria, *s.f.* mattress factory.

coldre, *s.m.* holster.

coleante, *adj.* sinous, winding.

colear, *v.i.* to wind, to wiggle, to move the neck.

colecção, *s.f.* collection, assemblage, assortment, set.

coleccionador, *s.m.* collector.

coleccionar, *v.t.* to collect, to assemble.

colecta, *s.f.* collect *(na missa),* collection, gathrering.

colectar, *v.t.* to collect, to tax, to assess *(tributar).*

colectável, *adj.* collectable, assessable, taxable.

colectivamente, *adv.* collectively.

colectividade, *s.f.* collectivity, community.

colectivismo, *s.m.* collectivism.

colectivista, *s.m. e adj.* collectivist.

colectivo, *adj.* collective, corporate.

colector, *s.m.* collector, gatherer; *adj.* collecting.

colega, *s.m.* colleague, classmate *(de escola),* comrade.

co-legatário, *s.m.* co-legatee, joint legatee.

colegiada, *s.f.* collegiate church.

colegial, *adj.* collegiate, school; *s.m.* schoolboy, schoolgirl.

colégio, *s.m.* college, school.

coleira, *s.f.* collar; *coleira de cão,* dog collar.

coleópetros, *s.m.pl.* coleoptera.

cólera, *s.f.* anger, wrath, fury, cholera *(doença); cólera morbo:* cholera.

colérico, *adj.* choleric, furious, passionate, enraged.

colerina, *s.f.* cholerina, summer cholera.

colesterol, *s.m.* cmolestrol, cliolestrine.

colete, *s.m.* waistcoat, vest, corset *(de senhora).*

colgadura, *s.f.* drapery, hangings.

colgar, *v.t.* to hang, to ornament with hangings.

colheita, *s.f.* harvest, crop, picking.

colher, *v.t.* to pick, to gather, to harvest.

colher, *s.f.* spoon, ladle *(grande).*

colherada, *s.f.* spoonful.

colhimento, *s.m.* gathering, picking.

colibacilo, *s.m.* colibacil.

colibacilose, *s.f.* colibacilose.

colibri, *s.m.* hummingbird.

cólica, *s.f.* colic.

colidir, *v.i.* to collide, to clash (with something), to run into, to bump (against), to interfere (with).

coligação, *s.f.* colligation, alliance, union.

coligar, *v.t.* to colligate, to ally, to unite; *coligar-se,* to ally oneself with; to become allied.

coligir, *v.t.* to gather, to compile, to infer *(concluir).*

colimação, *s.f.* collimation.

colimador, *s.m.* collimator.

colimar, *v.t.* to collimatex, to adjust the line of sight of a telescope, to aim at *(visar).*

colina, *s.f.* hill.

colinoso, *adj.* hilly.

colisão, *s.f.* collision, crash, clash, bump, impact, conflict.

coliseu, *s.m.* coliseum, colosseum.

colite, *s.f.* colitis.

colmado, *adj.* thatched.

colmar, *v.t.* to thatch, to cover with straw, palm-leaves, reeds or something like it.

colmeal, *s.m.* apiary.

colmeia, *s.f.* beehive.

colmilho, *s.m.* tusk.

colmo, *s.m.* thatch, straw.

colo, *s.m.* neck, throat *(pescoço),* bosom *(peito),* lap *(regaço).*

colocação, *s.f.* place, situation, position, job *(emprego),* placing *(acto de colocar).*

colocar, *v.t.* to place, to put, to set, to instal, to place in a job *(empregar); colocar-se,* to place oneself.

colódio, *s.m.* collodion.

coloidal, *adj.* colloidal.

cólon, *s.m.* colon.

colónia, *s.f.* colony; settlement, camp *(de férias);* Cologne *(cidade da Alemanha); água-de-colónia,* Cologne water, eau de Cologne.

colonial, *adj.* colonial.

colonialismo, *s.m.* colonialism.

colonialista, *s.m.* colonialist.

colonização, *s.f.* colonization.

colonizador, *s.m.* colonizer; *adj.* colonizing.

colonizar, *v.t.* to colonize.

colonizável, *adj.* colonizing, that can be colonized.

colono, *s.m.* colonist, settler.

coloquial, *adj.* colloquial.

colóquio, *s.m.* colloquy, dialogue.

coloração, *s.f.* coloration, colour pattern.

colorar, *v.t.* to colour, to dye, to tinge.

colorau, *s.m.* red pepper powder.

colorido, *adj.* coloured.

colorir, *v.t.* to colour, to dye.

colossal, *adj.* colossal, huge, enormous, splendid.

colosso, *s.m.* colossus.

colostro, *s.m.* colostrum.

colubrina, *s.f.* culverin, *(bot.)* serpentary.

columbino, *adj.* columbine, dove-like.

columbofilia, *s.f.* pigeon-fancying.

columbófilo, *s.m.* pigeon-fancier.

coluna, *s.f.* column, pillar.

colunata, *s.f.* colonnade.

coluro, *s.m.* colure.

colza, *s.f.* colza.

com, *prep,* with; formando expressão adverbial com um substantivo traduz-se normalmente por um advérbio; ex. *com segurança,* safely; *com que então,* so.

coma, *s.f.* head of hair *(cabeleira de cometa),* mane *(juba), (med.)* coma; comma *(sinal de pontuação).*

comadre, *s.f. minha comadre,* the god-mother of my child; midwife *(parteira).*

comandante, *s.m.* commander, commanding officer, leader; *comandante-chefe,* commander in chief.

comandar, *v.t.* to command, to lead.

comandita, *s.f.* limited partnership.

comanditário, *s.m.* silent partner.

comando, *s.m.* command, leadership, control.

comarca, *s.f.* district, division of a judicial district, jurisdiction.

comarcão, *adj.* neighbouring, contiguous.

comatoso, *adj.* comatose.

combalido, *adj.* weak, enfeebled, sickly, infirm.

combalir, *v.t.* to weaken, to debilitate, to enfeeble.

combate, *s.m.* combat, fight, battle, conflict; *em combate,* in action.

combatente, *s.m.* fighter, combatant; *adj.* fighting.

combater, *v.i.* to fight; *v.t.* to fight, to combat, to oppose, to battle with.

combatível, *adj.* that can be fought.

combatividade, *s.f.* combativity, combativeness.

combativo, *adj.* combative, pugnacious.

combinação, *s.f.* combination, agreement, arrangement, slip *(peça de vestuário).*

combinado, *adj.* combined, settled, agreed.

combinar, *v.t.* e *v.i.* to combine, to join, to agree, to settle, to match.

comboio, *s.m.* train, convoy.

comburente, *adj.* comburent.

combustão, *s.f.* combustion.

combustibilidade, *s.f.* combustibility.

combustível, *s.m.* fuel; *adj.* combustible.

começar, *v.t.* e *v.i.* to begin, to start, to commence.

começo, *s.m.* beginning, start, commencement, origin.

comédia, *s.f.* comedy, play, farce.

comediante, *s.m.* e *s.f.* comedian, player.

comedido, *adj.* moderate, discreet, modest, prudent.

comedimento, *s.m.* moderation, discretion, prudence.

comediógrafo, *s.m.* writer of comedies.

comedir, *v.t.* to moderate, to regulate, to repress, to restrain, to control; *comedir-se,* to control oneself.

comedor, *s.m.* eater, glutton.

comedouro, *s.m.* feeding place, feed through.

comemoração, *s.f.* commemoration.

comemorar, *v.t.* to commemorate, to celebrate.

comemorativo, *adj.* commemorative, commemoratory.

comemorável, *adj.* commemorable.

comenda, *s.f.* insignia, emblem.

comendador, *s.m.* commandar, comendator.

comenos, *s.m.* instant, moment.

comensal, *s.m.* e *s.f.* commensal, table fellow, fellow boarder.

comensurabilidade, *s.f.* commensurability.

comensurar, *v.t.* to make commensurate, to proportion.

comensurável, *adj.* commensurable.

comentador, *s.m.* commentator, commentor.

comentar, *v.t.* to comment on, to annotate, to remark.

comentário, *s.m.* commentary, comment.

comentarista, *s.m.* e *s.f.* commentator, commenter.

comento, *s.m.* commentary.

comer, *v.t.* to eat, to have, to consume, to devour, to corrode *(corroer),* to jump *(no jogo de damas).* 1) *o que é que comeste ao almoço?,* what did you have for lunch?. 2) *comer as palavras,* to clip one's words. 3) *comer com os olhos,* to ogle. 4) *dar de comer a,* to feed. 5) *comer-se,* to be consumed *(de raiva, inveja, etc.).*

comercial, *adj.* commercial, trading.

comercialista, *s.m.* e *s.f.* commercialist.

comercialização, *s.f.* commercialization.

comercializar, *v.t.* to commercialize.

comerciante, *s.m.* merchant, trader, dealer.

comerciar, *v.t.* e *v.i.* to trade, to deal (in), to engage in business.

comerciável, *adj.* marketable, commerciable.

comércio, *s.m.* commerce, trade, trading, business, traffic. 1) *comércio externo,* foreign trading. 2) *comércio interno,* home trade.

comes, *s.m. pl. comes e bebes,* eatables and drinkables or food and drinks.

comestíveis, *s.m.pl.* eatables.

comestível, *adj.* eatable, comestible.

cometa, *s.m.* comet.

cometer, *v.t.* to commit, to perpetrate.

cometimento, *s.m.* perpetration, undertaking.

comezaina, *s.f.* abundant meal.

comezinho, *adj.* modest, simple.

comichão, *s.f.* itch, itching.

comichoso, *adj.* itchy.

comicidade, *s.f.* comicalness, jocularity.

comício, *s.m.* meeting, assembly.

cómico, *adj.* comic, funny; *s.m.* comedian, comic.

comida, *s.f.* food, fare.

comigo, *loc. pron.* with me.

comilão, *s.m.* glutton, gourmandiser; *adj.* greedy, gluttonous, voracious.

cominação, *s.f.* commination, threatening.

cominador, *s.m.* comminator, threatener; *adj.* cumminatory, threatening.

cominar, *v.t.* to comminate, to threaten.

cominativo, *adj.* comminative, threatening.

cominho, *s.m.* cummin.

comiseração, *s.f.* commiseration, pity, compassion.

comiserar, *v.t.* to commiserate, to feel pity for, to pity.

comiserativo, *adj.* commiserative, merciful.

comissão, *s.f.* commission, committee.

comissariado, *s.m.* commissariat, commissioner's office.

comissário, *s.m.* commissioner, commissary (representante).

comissionado, *adj.* commisioned.

comissionar, *v.t.* to commission, to empower.

comissionista, *s.m.* commission-agent, commission-merchant.

comisso, *s.m.* fine, forfeit.

comissura, *s.f.* commissure, juncture, joint.

comité, *s.m.* committee.

comitente, *s.m.* commitent; *adj.* commiting to the charge of another.

comitiva, *s.f.* retinue, attendance, train.

como, *adv.* how. 1) *como disse?,* I beg your pardon?. 2) *como assim?,* how so?. 3) *como é que?,* how is that?. 4) *como que assustado,* kind of frightened. 5) *como quer que seja,* however it may be. 6) *seja como for,* in any case; *conj.* as, like, as soon as *(logo que).* 7) *como sempre,* as always, as usual. 8) *tão... como...,* as... as...

comoção, *s.f.* commotion, shock, emotion, disturbance, upset.

cómoda, *s.f.* chest of drawers.

comodidade, *s.f.* comfort, cosiness, ease.

comodista, *s.m.* e *adj.* selfish, self-seeking.

cómodo, *adj.* comfortable, cozy, convenient, suitable; *s.m.* room, apartment.

comodoro, *s.m.* commodore.

cômoro, *s.m.* hillock, knoll, hummock, mound *(artificial).*

comovedor, *adj.* moving, touching.

comovente, *adj.* moving, touching.

comover, *v.t.* e *v.i.* to move, to touch, to disturb, to stir.

compaticidade, *s.f.* compactness.

compacto, *adj.* compact, dense, close.

compadecer, *v.t.* to pity, to be compassionate; *compadecer-se,* to have mercy, to take pity (on someone), to feel sorry (for).

compadecido, *adj.* pitying, compassionate, merciful.

compadecimento, *s.m.* pity, commiseration.

compadre, *s.m. meu compadre,* my child's godfather; pal *(amigo).*

compadrio, *s.m.* political favoritism, companionship.

compaixão, *s.f.* compassion, pity, mercy.

companha, *s.f.* crew of a ship.

companheirismo, *s.m.* companionship, fellowship.

companheiro, *s.f.* companion, mate, friend, pal, chum.

companhia, *s.f.* company, gathering, society, firm *(empresa); fazer companhia,* to bear (someone) company.

comparação, *s.f.* comparision.

comparar, *v.t.* to compare, to confront (with); *comparar-se,* to compare oneself, to compare.

comparativamente, *adv.* comparatively.

comparativo, *adj.* comparative; *s.m.* comparative, the comparative degree.

comparável, *adj.* comparable.

comparecer, *v.i.* to appear, to attend *(numa reunião).*

comparecimento, *s.m.* appearance, attendance, presence.

comparência, *s.f.* o mesmo que "comparecimento".

comparsa, *s.m.* e *s.f.* bit player, figurant.

comparte, *s.m.* copartner; *adj.* participant.

compartilhar, *v.t.* to share, to partake of, to participate in.

compartimento, *s.m.* compartment, division, room.

compassadamente, *adv.* slowly, by rule and mesure.

compassado, *adj.* measured, slow, unhurried.

compassar, *v.t.* to measure, to space, to beat time for *(música).*

compassivo, *adj.* compassionate, kindhearted, merciful.

compasso, *s.m.* compasses *(instrumento),* measure, bar, time, rythm *(música); bater o compasso,* to beat time.

compatibilidade, *s.f.* compatibility.

compatível, *adj.* compatible.

compatriota, *s.m.* e *s.f.* compatriot, fellow countryman, or countrywoman.

compelir, *v.t.* to compell, to force, to oblige.

compendiado, *adj.* abridged, epitomized, condensed.

compendiar, *v.t.* to abridge, to epitomize, to condense.

compêndio, *s.m.* compendium, text-book.

compendioso, *adj.* compendious, succint, concise.

compenetração, *s.f.* compenetration, conviction.

compenetrar, *v.t.* to persuade, to convince (of something); *compenetrar-se,* to convince oneself of.

compensação, *s.f.* compensation, reparation, amends, recompense: *em compensação,* on the other hand.

compensador, *adj.* compensating, worthwhile, rewarding.

compensar, *v.t.* to compensate, to counterbalance, to recompense, to make amends, to make up (for something to someone).

compensatório, *adj.* compensatory.

competência, *s.f.* competence, fitness, aptitude.

competente, *adj.* competent, qualified, fit, suitable.

competição, *s.f.* competition, rivalry, contest.

competidor, *s.m.* competitor, rival, opponent.

competir, *v.i.* to compete, to contend (for), to rival, to behoove *(cumprir),* to be due *(caber); compete-lhe a si decidir,* it's up to you to decide.

compilação, *s.f.* compilation, collection.

compilador, *s.m.* compilator, compiler.

compilar, *v.t.* to compile, to collect.

compita, *s.f.* emulation, rivalry, contest, competition.

complacência, *s.f.* complaissance, obligingness, condescension.

complacente, *adj.* compaisant, obliging, kind, willing.

compleição, *s.f.* constitution, build, temperament.

complementar, *adj.* complementary.

complemento, *s.m.* complement.

completamente, *adv.* completely, entirely, quite.

completar, *v.t.* to complete, to finish, to accomplish.

completas, *s.f.pl.* compline.

completo, *adj.* complete, finished, accomplished, perfect, entire.

complexão, *s.f.* complexity, union, sucession.

complexidade, *s.f.* complexity.

complexo, *adj.* complex, intricate, difficult; *s.m.* assemblage, complex whole.

complicação, *s.f.* complication.

complicado, *adj.* complicate, complicated, intricate, difficult.

complicador, *s.m.* complicator.

complicar, *v.t.* to complicate, to entangle, to mix up: *complicar-se,* to become complicated, to thicken.

componedor, *s.m.* composing-stick.

componente, *s.m. e adj.* component.

compor, *v.t.* to compose, to compound, to form, to write *(música),* to conciliate *(disputas),* to arrange, to trim *(arranjar).*

comporta, *s.f.* floodgate, sluice gate, lock *(de canal).*

comportado, *adj. bem-comportado,* well-behaved.

comportamento, *s.m.* behaviour, conduct.

comportar, *v.t.* to bear, to admit, to allow, to contain; *comportar-se,* to behave, to behave oneself *(ter bons modos).*

comportável, *adj.* bearable, tolerable.

composição, *s.f.* composition, composing, piece *(obra musical),* essay *(escolar).*

compositor, *s.m.* composer, writer, typesetter *(tipográfico).*

composto, *adj.* composed, compound, sober, modest; *s.m.* compound, composition, amalgam.

compostura, *s.f.* composition, modesty, decorum, composure.

compota, *s.f.* jam.

compoteira, *s.f.* jam dish.

compra, *s.f.* purchase, buying; *fazer compras,* to go shopping.

comprador, *s.m.* buyer, purchaser.

comprar, *v.t.* to buy, to purchase, to bribe *(subornar).*

comprazer, *v.i.* to please, to comply with; *comprazer-se,* to delight in, to be delighted with.

comprazimento, *s.m.* complaissance, compliance.

compreender, *v.t.* to understand, to comprehend, to make out, to realize, to include *(incluir).*

compreensão, *s.f.* understanding, comprehension, awareness.

compreensibilidade, *s.f.* comprehensibility.

compreensível, *adj.* comprehensible, understandable, intelligible.

compreensivo, *adj.* comprehensive, understanding.

compressa, *s.f.* compress.

compressão, *s.f.* compression.

compressibilidade, *s.f.* compressibility.

compressível, *adj.* compressible.

compressivo, *adj.* compressive.

compressor, *s.m.* compressor, road roller *(de estradas); adj.* compressive.

comprido, *adj.* long; *ao comprido,* lengthwise.

comprimento, *s.m.* length.

comprimido, *adj.* compressed, pressed, condensed; *s.m.* tablet.

comprimir, *v.t.* to compress, to press, to condense, to repress.

comprometedor, *adj.* compromising, suspicious.

comprometer, *v.t.* to compromise, to endanger *(pôr em perigo),* to damage *(prejudicar); comprometer-se,* to engage oneself, to commit oneself, to become involved in.

comprometido, *adj.* engaged, compromised, involved, ashamed *(envergonhado).*

comprometimento, *s.m.* engagement, compromise.

compromisso, *s.m.* compromise, engagement, liability.

comprovação, *s.f.* confirmation, corroboration, proof.

comprovador, *adj.* confirming, that confirms.

comprovar, *v.t.* to confirm, to prove, to corroborate, to prove.

comprovativo, *adj.* confirming, confirmatory, verifying.

compulsação, *s.f.* examination.

compulsão, *s.f.* compulsion, constraint.

compulsar, *v.t.* to examine, to consult.

compulsivo, *adj.* compulsive, compulsory, compelling.

compulsório, *adj.* compulsory.

compunção, *s.f.* compuction, repentance, contrition, remorse.

compungido, *adj.* contrite, repentant, remorseful.

compungir, *v.t.* to move to compunction, to afflict, to distress.

computação, *s.f.* computation, calculation.

computador, *s.m.* computer.

computar, *v.t.* to compute, to calculate, to reckon.

computável, *adj.* computable, calculable.

cômputo, *s.m.* computation, reckoning, estimate.

comum, *adj.* common, usual, ordinary, general, public, habitual, current, frequent, vulgar. 1) *em comum,* in common. 2) *fora do comum,* uncommon. 3) *o comum de gente,* the averago person. 4) *a Câmara dos Comuns,* The House of Commons.

comumente, *adv.* commonly, usually, frequently, generally.

comuna, *s.f.* commune.

comunal, *adj.* communal.

comunalismo, *s.m.* communalism.

comungante, *s.m.* e *s.f.* communicant.

comungar, *v.t.* e *v.i.* to communicate, to commune, to share, to take part, to receive Holy Communion.

comunhão, *s.f.* communion, sharing, participation, Holy Communion; *comunhão de bens,* joint property.

comunicabilidade, *s.f.* communicability, communicativeness.

comunicação, *s.f.* communication, information, announcement, notice, connection, contact.

comunicado, *s.m.* communication, comuniqué.

comunicante, *adj.* communicatory.

comunicar, *v.t.* to communicate, to announce, to make known, to transmit, to report, to connect; *v.i.* 1) *comunicar com,* to correspond with. 2) *comunicar-se,* to communicate with.

comunicativo, *adj.* communicative, expansive, talkative.

comunicável, *adj.* communicable.

comunidade, *s.f.* community, society, communion.

comunismo, *s.m.* communism.

comunista, *s.m.* e *s.f.* communist.

comunitário, *adj.* e *s.m.* communitarian.

comutação, *s.f.* commutation, change.

comutador, *s.m.* commutator, switch.

comutar, *v.t.* to commute, to change, to substitute.

comutativo, *adj.* commutative.

comutável, *adj.* commutable.

conatural, *adj.* connatural.

conca, *s.f.* quoit, woiden bowl, pavillion of the ear.

concatenação, *s.f.* concatenation, chain.

concatenar, *v.t.* to concatenate, to link together.

concavidade, *s.f.* concavity, hollow.

côncavo, *adj.* concave, hollow; *s.m.* hollow, concavity.

conceber, *v.t.* to conceive, to imagine; *v.i.* to become pregnant.

concebível, *adj.* conceivable, imaginable.

conceder, *v.t.* to grant, to bestow, to confer, to award, to give, to concede.

concedido, *adj.* granted, allowed, permitted, given.

concedível, *adj.* grantable, allowable.

conceição, *s.f.* conception.

conceito, *s.m.* thought, opinion, idea, notion, concept.

conceituado, *adj.* esteemed, highly regarded, respected.

conceituar, *v.t.* to judge, to esteem, to consider, to regard.

conceituosamente, *adv.* ingeniously, wisely.

conceituoso, *adj.* ingenious, witty, clever.

concelebrar, *v.t.* to celebrate together.

concelhio, *adj.* municipal.

concelho, *s.m.* municipality, division of a district, council.

concentração, *s.f.* concentration.

concentrado, *adj.* concentrated.

concentrar, *v.t.* to concentrate, to centralize; *concentrar-se,* to concentrate, to focus.

concentricidade, *s.f.* concentricity.

concêntrico, *adj.* concentric.

concepção, *s.f.* conception, concept, notion.

conceptibilidade, *s.f.* conceptibility.

conceptível, *adj.* conceptible, conceivable, imaginable.

conceptivo, *adj.* conceptive.

conceptualismo, *s.m.* conceptualism.

concernente, *adj.* concerning, regarding, relating.

concernir, *v.i.* to concern, to relate to, to regard.

concertadamente, *adv.* prudently, wisely, rightly.

concertado, *adj.* set in order, serene.

concertar, *v.t.* to concert, to settle, to set in order, to dispose, to agree on.

concertina, *s.f.* concertina.

concertista, *s.m.* performer in a concert, concert artist.

concerto, *s.m.* consonance, harmony, concert *(sessão musical),* concerto *(composição).*

concessão, *s.f.* concession, granting.

concessionário, *s.m.* grantee, concessionaire; *adj.* concessionary.

concessivo, *adj.* concessive.

concessor, *s.m.* granter.

concha, *s.f.* shell, conch *(de molusco),* scale *(de balança),* auricle *(do ouvido),* ladle *(de sopa); pôr em concha,* to cup (the hands).

conchado, *adj.* shelled, shelly.

conchavar, *v.t.* to insert, to adjust, to unite; *conchavar-se,* to conspire.

conchavo, *s.m.* plot, conspiracy.

conchegado, *adj.* cosy, comfortable, near, close.

conchegar, *v.t.* to bring close, to cuddle *(uma criança),* to tuck in *(as roupas da cama); conchegar-se,* to approach, to cuddle, to snuggle.

conchego, *s.m.* comfortableness, snugness, support *(amparo).*

concho, *adj.* self-sure, vain.

concidadão, *s.m.* fellow-citizen.

conciliábulo, *s.m.* secret meeting or conversation, conspiracy.

conciliação, *s.f.* conciliation, reconciliation, settlement, adjustment.

conciliador, *adj.* conciliating; *s.m.* conciliator, peace-maker.

conciliar, *v.t.* to conciliate, to reconcile, to pacify, to harmonize; *conciliar o sono,* to manage to sleep, to go to sleep.

conciliatório, *adj.* conciliatory.

conciliável, *adj.* reconciliable, compatible.

concílio, *s.m.* council.

concisão, *s.f.* concision, conciseness, briefness, succintness.

conciso, *adj.* concise, brief, laconic, succint.

concitação, *s.f.* instigation, agitation, excitement, stirring up.

concitador, *s.m.* instigator, inciter; *adj.* exciting, stirring.

concitar, *v.t.* to incite, to excite, to instigate.

conclamação, *s.f.* conclamation.

conclamar, *v.t.* to acclaim together; *v.i.* to shout together.

conclave, *s.m.* conclave.

concludente, *adj.* concluding, conclusive.

concluir, *v.t.* to conclude, to end, to finish, to complete, to infer *(deduzir).*

conclusão, *s.f.* conclusion, end, close, deduction, inference.

conclusivo, *adj.* conclusive, final.

concluso, *adj.* concluded, finished, determined.

concomitância, *s.f.* concomitance, simultaneity.

concomitante, *adj.* concomitant, simultaneous.

concordância, *s.f.* concordance, agreement, conformity, consonance; *(gram.)* concord.

concordante, *adj.* concordant, agreeing, harmonious.

concordar, *v.t. e v.i.* to agree, to concur (with), acquiesce (to).

concordata, s.f. concordat.

concorde, adj. unanimous, agreed to, similar to.

concórdia, s.f. concord, harmony, peace.

concorrência, s.f. concourse (afluência), competition.

concorrente, s.m. e s.f. competitor, candidate, opponent; adj. concurrent, coincident.

concorrer, v.i. to compete, to contribute.

concreção, s.f. concretion.

concretização, s.f. realization.

concretizar, v.t. to make real, to accomplish.

concreto, adj. e s.m. concrete.

concubina, s.f. concubine.

concubinagem, s.f. concubinage.

concunhada, s.f. sister-in-law of one consort in relation to the other.

concunhado, s.m. brother-in-law of one consort in relation to other.

concupiscência, s.f. concupiscence, lust.

concupiscente, adj. concupiscent, lustful.

concurso, s.m. competition, contest, concourse (afluência).

concussão, s.f. concussion, peculation (crime).

concussionário, s.m. peculator.

condado, s.m. county.

condão, s.m. privilege, gift, faculty; varinha de condão, magic wand.

conde, s.m. earl (em Inglaterra), count (noutros países).

condecoração, s.f. decoration, medal.

condecorar, v.t. to decorate, to invest with a medal or an order.

condenação, s.f. condemnation, conviction, blame, reproof.

condenado, adj. condemned, convicted, balmed; s.m. convict.

condenar, v.t. to condemn, to sentence, to dom, to find guilty, to blame (censurar).

condenatório, adj. condemnatory.

condenável, adj. blamable.

condensabilidade, s.f. condensability.

condensação, s.f. condensation, abridgement.

condensador, s.m. condenser.

condensar, v.t. to condense, to compress, to concentrate, to abridge.

condescendência, s.f. condescendence, compliance, acquiescence.

condescendente, adj. condescending, compliant, consenting.

condescender, v.i. to condescend, to comply with, to acquiesce, to assent.

condessa, s.f. countess.

condestável, s.m. constable.

condição, s.f. condition, situation, state, stipulation, clause, rank (social). 1) condições, terms. 2) com a condição de que, provided that. 3) em boas condições, in order, in good shape.

condicional, adj. e s.m. conditional.

condicionalmente, adv. conditionally.

condicionar, v.t. to condition, to subject to conditions.

condignamente, adv. condignnly, adequately.

condigno, adj. condign, adequate, suitable, fitting.

côndilo, s.m. condyle.

condimentação, s.f. seasoning.

condimentado, adj. seasoned, spicy.

condimentar, v.t. to season, to flavour, to spice.

condimento, s.m. condiment, seasoning, flavouring.

condiscípulo, s.m. school fellow, fellow student, condisciple.

condizente, adj. suitable, appropriate, matched, matching.

condizer, v.i. to suit, to match.

condoer-se, v.r. to be sorry for, to feel pity for.

condoído, adj. compassionate, moved.

condolência, s.f. condolence.

condolente, s.m. condolent.

condomínio, s.m. condominium.

condor, s.m. condor.

condução, s.f. conduction, transmission, transportation, management (direcção), driving (de veículos).

conducente, adj. conductive, inductive.

conduta, s.f. conduct, behaviour.

condutividade, s.f. conductivity.

conduto, s.m. duct, conduit, channel, tube, pipe.

condutor, s.m. conductor (também fís. e electr.), leader, driver; adj. conducting, leading.

conduzir, v.t. to conduct, to drive, to lead, to guide, to manage (um negócio); conduzir-se, to behave, to conduct oneself.

cone, s.m. cone.

cónego, s.m. canon.

conexão, s.f. connection, connexion.

conexo, adj. connected, joined.

conezia, *s.f.* canonship.

confabulação, *s.f.* confabulation.

confabular, *v.t.* e *v.i.* to confabulate, to chat, to talk.

confecção, *s.f.* confection, making, preparation, ready-made *(de roupa)*.

confeccionar, *v.t.* to make, to manufacture.

confederação, *s.f.* confederation, league.

confederado, *adj.* confederate, associate, allied.

confederar, *v.t.* e *v.r.* to confederate, to associate, to league.

confederativo, *adj.* confederative.

confeitaria, *s.f.* confectionery, confectioner's shop, sweetshop.

confeiteiro, *s.m.* confectioner.

confeito, *s.m.* comfit, sweetmeat.

conferência, *s.f.* conference, lecture, meeting, checking *(verificação), fazer uma conferência:* to deliver a lecture.

conferenciar, *v.i.* to confer, to hold a conference, to parley.

conferencista, *s.m.* lecturer.

conferir, *v.t.* to compare, to confront, to check, to verify, to confer *(conceder).*

confessado, *adj.* confessed, converted, avowed.

confessar, *v.t.* to confess, to acknoledge, to avow; *confessar-se,* to confess, to make a confession.

confessional, *adj.* confessional.

confessionário, *s.m.* confessional.

confesso, *s.m.* confessed, that pleads guilty *(o réu).*

confessor, *s.m.* confessor.

confiado, *adj.* confident, hopeful, bold, impertinent.

confiança, *s.f.* confidence, reliance, trust, faith, credit, boldness *(impertinência).* 1) *confiança em si próprio,* self-confidence. 2) *digno de confiança,* trustworthy, reliable. 3) *ele não merece confiança,* he's not to be trusted.

confiante, *adj.* confident, trustful, reliant, secure.

confiar, *v.i.* to trust, to rely, to believe (in); *v.t.* to entrust (to someone).

confidência, *s.f.* confidence; *fazer confidências,* to impart confidences.

confidencial, *adj.* confidential, private.

confidencialmente, *adv.* confidentially, privately.

confidente, *adj.* confident, reliant; *s.m.* confidant.

configuração, *s.f.* configuration, shape, form.

configurar, *v.t.* to shape, to represent, to depict; *configurar-se:* to take shape.

confinante, *adj.* confinning, bounding, adjacent, adjoining.

confinar, *v.t.* e *v.i.* to confine, to limit, to restrain; *confinar com,* to adjoin.

confins, *s.m.pl.* limits, boundaries, confines; *lá para os confins do mundo,* in the remotest parts of the world.

confirmação, *s.f.* confirmation.

confirmado, *adj.* confirmed, corroborated, ratified, settled.

confirmador, *s.m.* confirmer; *adj.* confirming.

confirmante, *adj.* confirming.

confirmar, *v.t.* to confirm, to ratify, to corroborate, to support; *confirmar-se,* to prove true: to receive Confirmation *(em religião).*

confirmativo, *adj.* confirmative.

confiscação, *s.f.* confiscation.

confiscar, *v.t.* to confiscate, to seize.

confiscável, *adj.* confiscable.

confissão, *s.f.* confession, avowal, acknowledgement; *confissão de fé,* profession of faith.

confitente, *s.m.* e *adj.* confitent, penitent.

conflagração, *s.f.* conflagration.

conflagrar, *v.t.* to conflagrate.

conflito, *s.m.* conflict, contest, strife, struggle, fight, quarrel, discord.

conflituoso, *adj.* contentious, pugnacious.

confluência, *s.f.* confluence.

confluente, *adj.* e *s.m.* confluent, tributary *(afluente).*

confluir, *v.i.* to flow together.

conformação, *s.f.* conformation, shape.

conformado, *adj.* shaped, resigned.

conformar, *v.t.* to conform, to adapt, to adjust, to fit, to shape; *conformar-se,* to resign oneself to .

conforme, *adj.* conformable, similar, like. 1) *estar conforme com,* to agree with; *prep.* according to; *conj.* as. 2) *conforme me disseram,* as i was told; *adv.* according to circumstances.

conformidade, *s.f.* conformity, similarity, resemblance, accordance; *em conformidade com,* in compliance with, according to.

conformismo, *s.m.* compliance.

conformista, s.m. conformist.
confortador, adj. comforting.
confortante, adj. comforting.
confortar, v.t. to comfort, to soothe, to cheer, to console.
confortável, adj. comfortable, cozy, snug.
conforto, s.m. comfort, coziness, ease, well-being, consolation, relief.
confrade, s.m. colleague, brother.
confrangedor, adj. heart-breaking, distressing.
confranger, v.t. to torment, to distress, to afflict; *confranger-se,* to be distressed, to break one's heart.
confrangimento, s.m. constraint, opression, embarrassment.
confraria, s.f. brotherhood, fraternity.
confraternidade, s.f. fraternity, brotherhood.
confraternização, s.f. fraternization.
confraternizar, v.i. to fraternize.
confrontação, s.f. confrontation, confronting; pl. limits, bounds.
confrontar, v.t. e v.i. to confront, to compare, to collate, to face.
confronto, s.m. confrontation, comparision, parallel.
confundido, adj. confused.
confundir, v.t. to confuse, to confound, to mix, to perplex; *confundir-se,* to become confused.
confusamente, adv. confusedly, in confusion, vaguely.
confusão, s.f. confusion, disorder, mess.
confuso, adj. confused, perplexed, bewildered.
confutação, s.f. confutation, disproof.
confutar, v.t. to confute, to disprove.
congelação, s.f. freezing, congealing.
congelado, adj. frozen, chilled.
congelador, s.m. freezer.
congelar, v.t. to freeze, to congeal.
congeminação, s.f. double and simultaneous formation.
congeminar, v.t. to meditate, to ponder, to think, to muse.
congénere, adj. congenerous, similar, akin.
congenial, adj. congenial.
congénito, adj. congenital, innate, inborn.
congestão, s.f. congestion; *congestão cerebral,* cerebral attack, stroke.
congestionado, adj. congested, bloodshot (olhos).
congestionar, v.t. e v.i. to congest; *congestionar-se,* to become congested.
congestivo, adj. congestive.

conglobação, s.f. conglobation.
conglobado, adj. conglobate.
conglobar, v.t. to conglobate, to conglobe.
conglomeração, s.f. conglomeration.
conglomerado, adj. e s.m. conglomerate.
conglomerar, v.t. to conglomerate, to lump together.
congosta, s.f. narrow lanc.
congraçar, v.t. to reconcile (with).
congratulação, s.f. congratulation.
congratulador, adj. congratulating.
congratular, v.t. to congratulate, to felicitate; *congratular-se,* to congratulate oneself, to rejoice with.
congratulatório, adj. congratulatory, congratulating.
congregação, s.f. congregation, fraternity.
congregado, adj. member of a congregation.
congreganista, s.m. e s.f. congreganaist.
congregar, v.t. to congregate, to gather.
congressista, adj. member of a congress, congressman.
congresso, s.m. congress, assembly, parliament.
congro, s.m. conger-eel.
côngrua, s.f. ecclesiastical revenue paid by the parishioners to their parish minister.
congruência, s.f. congruence, congruity.
congruente, adj. congruent, congruous.
côngruo, adj. congruous, conformable, suitable.
conhaque, s.m. cognac, brandy.
conhecedor, s.m. connoisseur, expert (at); adj. aware, informed.
conhecer, v.t. to know, to be aware of, to meet (pessoas).
conhecido, adj. known, notorious, familiar; s.m. acquaintance.
conhecimento, s.m. knowledge, cognizance, awareness, acquaintance, familiarity; *chegou ao meu conhecimento,* it came to my knowledge.
conhecível, adj. knowable.
cónico, adj. conic.
conifera, s.f. conifer, evergreen; pl. coniferae.
conífero, adj. coniferous.
conivência, s.f. connivance.
conivente, adj. convivent.
conjectura, s.f. conjecture, supposition, guessing.
conjectural, adj. conjectural, tentative.

conjecturar, *v.t.* to conjecture, to suppose, to guess.

conjecturável, *adj.* conjecturable.

conjugação, *s.f.* conjugation.

conjugado, *adj.* congate.

conjugal, *adj.* conjugal, matrimonial: married life.

conjugar, *v.t.* to conjugate, to join, to co-ordinate.

conjugável, *adj.* conjugable.

cônjuge, *s.m.* consort, husband or wife.

conjugicida, *s.m. e s.f.* murderer of wife.

conjugicídio, *s.m.* murder of one's wife or husband.

conjúgio, marriage, matrimony.

conjunção, *s.f.* conjunction, union.

conjuntamente, *adv.* jointly, together.

conjuntiva, *s.f.* conjunctive.

conjuntivite, *s.f.* conjunctivitis.

conjuntivo, *adj.* conjunctive; *s.m.* subjunctive *(gramática).*

conjunto, *s.m.* assemblage, collection, aggregation, whole, body, set, group: *adj.* conjoined, joint, united, collective; *em conjunto,* altogether.

conjura, *s.f.* conjuration, plot.

conjunção, *s.f.* conjuration, plot.

conjurado, *s.m.* conspirator.

conjurar, *v.t.* to plot, to conspire, to prevent *(prevenir males).*

conjuro, *s.m.* conjuration, exorcism.

conluiar, *v.t.* to collude, to plot, to conspire.

conluio, *s.m.* collusion, conspiracy, plot.

connosco, *loc. pron.* with us.

conotação, *s.f.* connotation, denotation, inference implication, signification.

conotado, *adj.*connotative.

conquanto, *conj.* though, although.

conquista, *s.f.* conquest, conquering.

conquistador, *s.m.* conqueror.

conquistar, *v.t.* to conquer, to overcome *(subjugar),* to win *(alcançar).*

conquistável, *adj.* conquerable.

consagração, *s.f.* consecration.

consagrado, *adj.* consecrated, renowned.

consagrante, *s.m.* consecrator; *adj.* consecrating.

consagrar, *v.t.* to consecrate, to devote, to dedicate, to snction; *consagrar-se,* to devote oneself.

consanguíneo, *adj.* consanguineous, related by blood; *parente consanguíneo,* blood relative.

consanguinidade, *s.f.* consanguinity, blood-relationship.

consciência, *s.f.* conscience, consciousness, awarenesss. 1) *em consciência,* in all conscience. 2) *ter consciência de,* to be aware of.

conscienciosamente, *adv.* conscientiously.

consciencioso, *adj.* conscientious, scrupulous.

consciente, *adj.* conscious, aware.

cônscio, *adj.* conscious, aware, cognizant.

conscrição, *s.f.* conscription.

conscrito, *adj.* conscript, enrolled; *s.m.* conscript.

consecução, *s.f.* consecution, attainment.

consecutivamente, *adv.* consecutively, in sucession.

consecutivo, *adj.* consecutive, sucessive.

conseguimento, *s.m.* attainment.

conseguinte, *adj.* consequent; *por conseguinte,* consequently, as a consequence, therefore.

conseguir, *v.t.* to get, to obtain, to attain, to manage, to succeed in.

conseguível, *adj.* obtainable.

conselheiral, *adj.* (pop.) becoming.

conselheiro, *s.m.* counsellor, adviser.

conselho, *s.m.* counsel, advise, admonition, suggestion council *(corporação).* 1) *conselho de guerra,* court-martial. 2) *conselho de ministros,* cabinet.

consenso, *s.m.* consensus, consent.

consentâneo, *adj.* consentaneous, accordant to, in accord (with).

consentimento, *s.m.* consent, assent, permission.

consentir, *v.t. e v.i.* to allow, to permit, to accede, to assent, to consent, to comply (with).

consequência, *s.f.* consequence, result, effect, outcome; *em consequência,* consequently, therefore.

consequente, *adj.* consequent, logic, resulting.

consequentemente, *adv.* consequently, therefore.

consertar, *v.t.* to repair, to mend, to fix, to put right.

conserto, *s.m.* repair, mending.

conserva, *s.f.* conserve, preserve. 1) *conservas em lata,* canned goods. 2) *fábrica de conservas,* cannery.

conserção, *s.f.* conservation, preservation, maintenance.

conservador, *adj.* conservative; *s.m.* curator *(de museus),* conservative *(em política).*

conservantismo, *s.m.* conservantism.

conservar, *v.t.* to conserve, to preserve, to maintain, to retain, to keep *(manter).*

conservativo, *adj.* conservative.

conservatória, *s.f.* registry of deeds of purchase.

conservatório, *s.m.* conservatory.

conservável, *adj.* that can be preserved.

consideração, *s.f.* consideration, regard, respect, esteem, reflection, pondering. 1) *por consideração para com,* for the sake of. 2) *tomer em consideração,* to take in account. 3) *não tomar em consideração,* to ignore.

considerado, *adj.* considered, respected.

considerando, *s.m.* preamble, motive, reason.

considerar, *v.t.* to consider, to ponder, to think over, to esteem, to respect; *v.i.* to reflect, to mediate.

considerável, *adj.* considerable, remarkable, important, substantial.

consideravelmente, *adv.* considerably.

consignação, *s.f.* consignment, deposit; *receber à consignação,* to take on consignment.

consignador, consignante, *s.m.* consigner, shipper.

consignar, *v.t.* to consign, to entrust, to deposit, to ship *(expedir),* to devote (to something), to record.

consignatário, *s.m.* consignee, receiver, trustee, shipping agent *(de navios).*

consigo, *loc. pron.* with himself (herself, itself, yourself, yourselves, themselves, oneself).

consistência, *s.f.* consistency, firmness, stability.

consistente, *adj.* consistent, firm, steady, stable.

consistir, *v.i.* consist (in or of), to be composed of, to lie (in).

consistório, *s.m.* consistory.

consoada, *s.f.* Christmas supper.

consoante, *s.f.* e *adj.* consonant; *prep.* according to .

consoar, *v.i.* to sound together, to have a Christmas supper.

consociar, *v.t.* to consociate, to associate.

consócio, *s.m.* co-partener, associate.

consola, *s.f.* console.

consolação, *s.f.* consolation, comfort, solace.

consolador, *adj.* consoling, comforting; *s.m.* consoler, comforter.

consolar, *v.t.* to console, to comfort, to solace, to cheer up.

consolável, *adj.* consolable.

consolidação, *s.f.* consolidation, strengthening.

consolidado, *adj.* consolidated, strengthened.

consolidar, *v.t.* to consolidate, to solidify.

consolo, *s.m.* consolation, comfort.

consonância, *s.f.* consonance, agreement, harmony; *em consonância,* in harmony.

consonante, *adj.* consonant, harmonious, concordant.

consorciar-se, *v.r.* to get married.

consórcio, *s.m.* marriage, association, *(com.)* trust.

consorte, *s.m.* e *s.f.* consort, spouse, associate.

conspicuidade, *s.f.* conspicuity, distinction, respectability.

conspícuo, *adj.* conspicuous, illustrious, distinguished.

conspiração, *s.f.* conspiracy, plot, conspiration.

conspirador, *s.m.* conspirator, conspirer.

conspirar, *v.t.* to conspire, to plot.

conspurcação, *s.f.* defilement.

conspurcar, *v.t.* to defile, to smear.

constância, *s.f.* constancy, firmness.

constante, *adj.* constant, steady, invariable, continual.

constantemente, *adv.* constantly, continually.

constar, *v.i.* to consist of, to be mentioned *(estar escrito).* 1) *consta-me que,* I hear that.... 2) *que me conste...,* as far as I know...

constatação, *s.f.* ascertainment, verification.

constatar, *v.t.* to ascertain, to verify.

constelação, *s.f.* constellation.

constelado, *adj.* starry, starlit.

consternação, *s.f.* consternation, dismay, dejection *(desalento).*

consternado, *adj.* aghast, dejected, brokenhearted.

consternar, *v.t.* to consternate, to dismay, to desolate, to deject.

constipação, *s.f.* cold, constipation *(prisão de ventre).*

constipado, *adj.* suffering from a cold, constipated.

constitucional, *adj.* constitutional.

constitucionalidade, *s.f.* constitutionality.

constitucionalismo, *s.m.* constitutionalism.

constitucionalista, *s.m.* constitutionalist.

constitucionalmente, *adv.* constitutionally.

constituição, *s.f.* constitution, composition, formation, temperament, bodily strength or constitution.

constituinte, *adj. s.m. e s.f.* constituent.

constituir, *v.t.* to constitute, to form, to compose, to appoint *(nomear).*

constitutivo, *adj.* constitutive.

constrangedor, *adj.* constraining.

constranger, *v.t.* to constrain, to restrain, to bind.

constrangido, *adj.* constrained, uneasy.

constrangimento, *s.m.* constraint, restraint, uneasiness.

constrição, *s.f.* constriction.

constringir, *v.t.* to constrict.

constritor, *s.m.* constrictor; *adj.* constrictive.

construção, *s.f.* construction, building, structure, erection.

construir, *v.t.* to build, to construct, to erect.

construtivo, *adj.* constructive.

construtor, *s.m.* builder, constructor; *adj.* building.

consubstanciação, *s.f.* consubstantiation.

consubstancialidade, *s.f.* consubstantiality.

consubstanciar, *v.t.* to consubstantiate, to cause to unite, to unite.

consuetudinário, *adj.* consuetudinary, customary; *direito consuetudinário,* consuetudinary law.

cônsul, *s.m.* consul.

consulado, *s.m.* consulate.

consular, *adj.* consular.

consulente, *s.m.* consulter; *adj.* consulting.

consulesa, *s.f.* the consul's wife.

consulta, *s.f.* consultation, conference.

consultador, *s.m.* consulter.

consultante, *s.m. e s.f. e adj.* consultant.

consultar, *v.t. e v.i.* to consult, to take counsel, to take advice; *consultar o travesseiro,* to sleep on a matter.

consultivo, *adj.* consultative, advisory.

consultor, *s.m.* consultant, adviser.

consultório, *s.m.* consulting-room, doctor's office.

consumação, *s.f.* consummation, completion, fullfillment.

consumado, *adj.* consummated, accomplished.

consumar, *v.t.* to consummate, to accomplish, to complete.

consumição, *s.f.* vexation, grief, distrees.

consumido, *adj.* consumed, spent, afflicted, distressed.

consumidor, *s.m.* consumer; *adj.* vexing, afflicting, distressing.

consumir, *v.t.* to consume, to use up, to spend; *consumir-se,* to waste away, to languish, to fret.

consumível, *adj.* consumable.

consumo, *s.m.* consumption, use, waste.

consumpção, *s.f.* consumption.

consumptivo, *adj.* consumptive.

conta, *s.f.* account, bill, count, number, calculation, bead *(de colar).* 1) *conta corrente,* current account. 2) *dar conta de,* to account for. 3) *dar conta do recado,* to manage the job. 4) *fazer de conta,* to pretend, to make believe. 5) *levar em conta,* to take into account. 6) *não é da sua conta,* it's none of your business. 7) *pôr na conta de,* to charge (something) to. 8) *ter em conta,* to bear in mind. 9) *pedir a conta,* to ask for the bill.

contabilidade, *s.f.* accounting.

contabilista, *s.m.* accountant.

contactar, *v.t. e v.i.* to contact, to get in touch with.

contacto, *s.m.* contact, touch.

contado, *adj.* counted, computed, reported, told.

contador, *adj.* counter, meter (de gás, etc.); *contador de histórias,* story-teller.

contadoria, *s.f.* accounting department.

contagem, *s.m.* counting.

contagiar, *v.t.* to contaminate, to infect.

contágio, *s.m.* contagion, infection.

contagioso, *adj.* contagious, infectious, catching.

conta-gotas, *s.m.* drop-tube.

contaminação, *s.f.* contamination, infection.

contaminador, *adj.* infectious, infective, contaminative.

contaminar, *v.t.* to contaminate, to infect.

contaminável, *adj.* contaminable.

contanto que, *loc. conj.* provided that, on condition, as long as.

conta-quilómetros, *s.m.* speedometer.

contar, *v.t. e v.i.* to count, to enumerate, to reckon, to calculate, to tell, to narrate, to have, to possess, to expect; *conto voltar esta semana,* i expect to come back this week.

contemplação, s.f. contemplation, meditation, regard, consideration, *sem contemplações,* relentlessly.

contemplador, adj. contemplating.

contemplar, v.t. e v.i. to contemplate, to gaze at, to consider, to muse over; *contemplar alguém com alguma coisa,* to bestow something upon someone.

contemplativo, adj. contemplative.

contemporaneidade, s.f. contemporaneity.

contemporâneo, adj. contemporaneous, contemporary; s.m. contemporary.

contemporizador, s.m. complier.

contemporizar, v.t. e v.i. to comply with, to temporize.

contenção, s.f. contention, dispute, debate.

contencioso, adj. contentious, litigious, controversial.

contenda, s.f. contention, quarrel, dispute.

contender, v.i. to contend, to fight, to dispute, to quarrel, to compete *(rivalizar).*

contendor, s.m. contender, opponent, competitor, rival.

contentamento, s.m. contentment, pleasure, satisfaction, joy.

contentar, v.t. ro content, to satisfy, to please; *contentar-se,* to be satisfied with.

contente, adj. happy, pleased, satisfied, glad, content.

contento, s.m. a contento: satisfactorily.

conter, v.t. to contain, to hold, to comprise, to include, to restrain, to repress; *conter-se,* to contain or to restrain oneself.

conterrâneo, s.m. fellow countryman.

contestação, s.f. contestation, dispute, denial, controversy.

contestador, s.m. contestant.

contestar, v.t. to contest, to dispute, to deny, to reply, to contradict, to question.

contestável, adj. contestable, questionable.

conteúdo, s.m. contents.

contexto, s.m. context.

contextura, s.f. texture, stucture.

contido, adj. contained, held, enclosed, incauoed, prudent, moderate.

contigo, loc. pron. with you.

contiguidade, s.f. contiguity, adjacency.

contíguo, adj. contiguous, close, adjacent, adjoining.

continência, s.f. continence, purity, military salute: *fazer a continência,* to salute.

continental, adj. continental.

continente, s.m. continent, mainland; adj. continent, temperate, *(med.)* unremitting.

contingência, s.f. contingence, chance, eventuality.

contingente, s.m. contingent, quota, share; adj. contingent, uncertain.

continuação, s.f. continuation, prolongation, going on.

continuado, adj. continued, continuous, unceasing.

continuador, s.m. continuer, follower.

continuar, v.t. e v.i. to continue, to prolong, to go on, to proceed, to keep on, to remain, to persist, to carry on.

continuidade, s.f. continuity.

contínuo, s.m. continuous, continual, incessant, never-ending; s.m. attendant, office-boy.

contista, s.m. e s.f. story-teller, story-writer.

conto, s.m. tale, fable, short story.

contorção, s.f. contortion, distortion, twisting, twitch *(dos músculos).*

contorcer, v.t. to contort, to twist, to distort.

contorcionista, s.m. contortionist.

contornar, v.t. to round, to turn round, to flank, to by-pass *(uma dificuldade),* to outline *(desenhar o contorno).*

contorno, s.m. contour, outline, profile, circuit.

contra, prep. against, opposed to, versus; s.m. objection, obstacle. 1) *contra vontade,* against one's will. 2) *os prós e os contras,* the pros and cons.

contra-almirante, s.m. rear-admiral.

contrabaixo, s.m. contrabass.

contrabalançar, v.t. to counter-balance, to compensate.

contrabandear, v.i. to smuggle.

contrabandista, s.m. smuggler, contrabandist.

contrabando, s.m. smuggling, contraband, illegar traffic.

contracção, s.f. contraction, shrinking.

contracifra, s.f. the key to a cipher.

contracosta, s.f. coast opposite to another.

contráctil, adj. contractile.

contractilidade, s.f. contractility.

contracto, adj. contracted, abbreviated.

contradança, s.f. square dance, quadrille.

contradição, s.f. contradiction, opposition.

contradita, s.f. objection.

contraditar, v.t. to contradict, to refute.

contraditório, adj. contradictory.

contradizer, v.t. to contradict, to oppose, to refute.

contraente, *s.m.* e *s.f.* bridgeroom; *adj.* contracting.

contra-espionagem, *s.f.* counter-espionage.

contrafacção, *s.f.* counterfeiting, forgery, simulation.

contrafactor, *s.m.* counterfeiter, forger.

contrafazer, *v.t.* to counterfeit, to forge.

contrafé, *s.f.* copy of a summons.

contrafeito, *adj.* constrained, uneasy.

contraforte, *s.m.* buttress, counterfort, spur *(de montanha).*

contraído, *adj.* contracted.

contra-indicação, *s.f.* contra-indication.

contrair, *v.t.* to contract, to draw together, to constrict, to catch *(uma doença)*, to acquire *(um hábito); contrair-se,* to contract, to shrink.

contralto, *s.m.* contralto.

contraluz, *s.f.* false-light.

contramarcha, *s.f.* countermarch.

contramarchar, *v.t.* to countermarch.

contramaré, *s.f.* counter-tide, ebb tide.

contramestre, *s.m.* foreman, quartermaster.

contramina, *s.f.* countermine.

contraminar, *v.t.* to countermine.

contra-ofensiva, *s.f.* counter-offensive.

contra-ordem, *s.f.* countermand.

contra-ordenar, *v.t.* to countermand.

contrapartida, *s.f.* counterpart; *em contrapartida,* on the other hand.

contrapeso, *s.m.* counterpoise, counterweight.

contrapontista, *s.m.* contrapuntist.

contraponto, *s.m.* counterpoint.

contrapor, *v.t.* to oppose, to compare (with).

contraposição, *s.f.* contraposition, opposition, contrast.

contraposto, *adj.* opposite.

contraproducente, *adj.* self-defeating.

contraproposta, *s.f.* counterproposal.

contraprova, *s.f.* counter-proof.

contraprovar, *v.t.* to prove to be false ro wrong.

contra-regra, *s.m.* stage manager.

contrariamente, *adv.* contrarily.

contrariador, *adj.* annoying, opposing.

contrariar, *v.t.* to contradict, to oppose, to thwart, to contest, to annoy.

contrariedade, *s.f.* contrariety, opposition, obstacle, hindrace.

contrário, *s.m.* adversary, opponent, antagonist, rival; *adj.* contrary, opposite. 1) *ao contrário de,* unlike. 2) *em contrário,* to the contrary. 3) *pelo contrário,* on the contrary.

contra senha, *s.f.* password.

contra senso, *s.m.* nonsense.

contrastar, *v.t.* e *v.i.* to contrast, to oppose.

contrastaria, *s.f.* assayer's office.

contraste, *s.m.* contrast, assay *(de ouro ou prata).*

contratador, *s.m.* contractor, bargainer.

contratante, *s.m.* contractor; *adj.* contracting.

contratar, *v.t.* to contract, to stipulate, to engage *(assalariar).*

contratempo, *s.m.* drawback, hindrance, reverse, mischance.

contrato, *s.m.* contract, deed, pact, agreement.

contratorpedeiro, *s.m.* torpedo boat, destroyer.

contratual, *adj.* contractual, implying or connected with a contract.

contravapor, *s.m.* reverse steam pressure.

contravenção, *s.m.* transgression, infrigement.

contraveneno, *s.m.* antidote.

contraventor, *s.m.* contravener, transgressor.

contravir, *v.t.* e *v.i.* to contravene, to infringe, to break *(uma lei, um costume, etc.),* to transgress.

contribuição, *s.f.* contribuition, tax, subscription.

contribuinte, *s.m.* tax-payer, contributor.

contribuir, *v.i.* to contribute, to concur, to subscribe.

contributivo, *adj.* contributive.

contributo, *s.m.* help, cooperation.

contrição, *s.f.* contriction, remorse, repentance.

contristador, *adj.* afflicting, distressing, grieving.

contristar, *v.t.* to grieve, to make sad.

contrito, *adj.* contrite, sorrowfull, penitent.

controlador, *s.m.* controller, manager, supervisor, checker.

controlar, *v.t.* to control, to handle, to direct, to check.

controlável, *adj.* controllable.

controlo, *s.m.* control, management, supervision, verification.

controvérsia, *s.f.* controversy, debate.

controversista, *s.m.* e *s.f.* controversialist.

controverter, *v.t.* to controvert, to dispute, to oppose.

controvertível, *adj.* controvertible, disputable.

contubérnio, *s.m.* cohabitation, companionship.

contudo, *adv.* e *conj.* nevertheless, however, yet, still.

contumácia, *s.f.* contumacy, obstinacy, stubborness.

contumaz, *adj.* obstinate, stubborn, pertinacious.

contumélia, *s.f.* contumely, reproach, affront, bow salutation.

contumelioso, *adj.* contumellious, violent, insulting.

contundente, *adj.* contusive, blunt.

contundir, *v.t.* to contuse, to bruise, to pound.

conturbação, *s.f.* agitation, disturbance, riot.

conturbar, *v.t.* to agitate, to perturb, to disturb; *conturbar-se,* become upset.

contusão, *s.f.* contusion, bruise.

conubial, *adj.* connubial.

conúbio, *s.m.* matrimony, union.

convalescença, *s.f.* convalescence.

convalescente, *adj.* convalescent.

convalescer, *v.i.* to convalesce, to recover.

convenção, *s.f.* convention, agreement, pact.

convencer, *v.t.* to convince, to persuade, to talk (someone into doing something).

convencido, *adj.* convinced, certain, sure, smug *(presumido).*

convencimento, *s.m.* conviction, persuasion, conceit, smugness.

convencional, *adj.* conventional, formal.

convencionalismo, *s.m.* conventionalism.

convencionar, *v.t.* to agree upon, to stipulate.

convencível, *adj.* convincible.

conveniência, *s.f.* convenience, suitability, advisability; *conveniências sociais,* proprieties.

convenientemente, *adv.* conveniently, suitably.

convénio, *s.m.* convention, agreement, pact.

conventículo, *s.m.* conventicle.

convento, *s.m.* convent.

conventual, *adj.* conventual.

convergência, *s.f.* convergence.

convergente, *adj.* convergent, converging, confluent.

convergir, *v.i.* to converge.

conversa, *s.f.* talk, conversation, chatter.

conversação, *s.f.* conversation.

conversador, *s.m.* talker; *adj.* talkative.

conversão, *s.f.* conversion, transformation.

conversar, *v.i.* to talk, to converse, to chat.

conversável, *adj.* sociable, tractable.

conversível, *adj.* convertible.

conversivo, *adj.* converting.

converso, *adj.* converted.

conversor, *s.m.* converter.

converter, *v.t.* to convert, to turn (into), to win over (to a cause, etc.), to transform, to change; *converter-se,* to be converted, to turn (into).

convertido, *adj.* converted; *s.m.* convert.

convertível, *adj.* convertible.

convés, *s.m.* deck, upper deck.

convexidade, *s.f.* convexity.

convexo, *s.m.* convex.

convicção, *s.f.* conviction, persuasion, belief, assurance, certitude.

convicto, *adj.* convinced, certain, sure.

convidado, *s.m.* guest; *adj.* invited.

convidar, *v.t.* to invite, to ask (to something), to attract.

convidativo, *adj.* inviting, tempting.

convincente, *adj.* convicing.

convir, *v.i.* to suit, to fit, to agree (to something with someone that...), to be convenient, to become *(ficar bem); quando lhe convir,* at your convenience.

convite, *s.m.* invitation, request.

conviva, *s.m.* guest.

convivência, *s.f.* living together, sociability, intimacy.

convivente, *adj.* sociable, affable, kind.

conviver, *v.i.* to live together, to be familiar (with).

convívio, *s.m.* living together, sociability, companionship, intercourse.

convizinhança, *s.f.* neighbourhood.

convizinhar, *v.i.* to live next door to, to be neighbour to.

convizinho, *adj.* neighbouring, contiguous.

convocação, *s.f.* convocation, summons.

convocar, *v.t.* to convoke, to call together, to summon.

convocatória, *s.f.* convocation, calling-up letter.

convocatório, *adj.* convoking.

convolvuláceas, *s.f.pl.* convolvulaceae.

convosco, *loc. pron.* with you.

convulsão, *s.f.* convulsion, agitation.

convulsionar, *v.t.* to convulse, to agitate.

convulsivo, *adj.* convulsive.

convulso, *adj.* convulsed, shaking; *tosse convulsa,* whooping-cough.

coonestação, *s.f.* extenuation, palliation.

coonestar, *v.t.* to extenuate, to palliate, to mitigate.

cooperação, *s.f.* co-operation, collaboration.

cooperador, *s.m.* cooperator, collaborator.

cooperar, *v.i.* to co-operate, to collaborate.

cooperativa, *s.f.* co-operative association.

cooperativismo, *s.m.* co-operativism.

cooperativista, *s.m.* co-operativist.

cooperativo, *adj.* co-operative.

coordenação, *s.f.* co-ordination.

coordenada, *s.f.* coordinate, co-ordinate.

coordenador, *s.m.* co-ordinator.

coordenar, *v.t.* to co-ordinate.

coordenativo, *adj.* co-ordinative.

coorte, *s.f.* cohort, band, crowd.

copa, *s.f.* pantry *(divisão),* crown *(de árvore ou chapéu), copas:* hearts *(nas cartas).*

copado, *adj.* leafy, bushy.

copaíba, *s.f.* copauba.

copal, *s.m.* copal, gum-copal.

copar, *v.t. e v.i.* to top, to branch out *(as árvores).*

copázio, *s.m.* large glass.

copeira, *s.f.* dresser.

copeiro, *s.m.* butler.

cópia, *s.f.* copy, reproduction, duplicate, abundance; *tirar cópias,* to duplicate.

copiador, *s.m.* coyst, copier, imitator, copy book.

copiar, *v.t. e v.i.* to copy, to imitate, to make a copy, to transcribe.

copiografar, *v.t.* to duplicate.

copiógrafo, *s.m.* copying press.

copiosamente, *adv.* copiously, abundantly, plentifully.

copiosidade, *s.f.* abundance, copiousness.

copioso, *adj.* copious, abundant.

copista, *s.m.* copyist.

copla, *s.f.* couplet, song.

copo, *s.m.* glass, guard *(de espada),* goblet *(copo de pé).*

copra, *s.f.* copra.

co-proprietário, *s.m.* joint-owner, co--owner.

copta, *s.f. e adj.* copt.

cóptico, *adj.* Coptic.

cópula, *s.f.* copula.

copulativo, *adj.* copulative.

coque, *s.m.* coke *(carvão),* knot *(de cabelo).*

coqueiral, *s.m.* coco-tree plantation.

coqueiro, *s.m.* coco-tree, coconut-tree.

coqueluche, *s.f.* whooping cough.

coquete, *s.f. e adj.* coquette.

coquetismo, *s.m.* coquetry, flirtation.

cor, *s.f.* colour, hue, tint, dye, pigment.

cor, *s.m. de cor,* by heart.

cora, *s.f.* bleaching.

coração, *s.m.* heart, center, core, kernel, generosity, 1) *de todo o coração,* wholeheartedly. 2) *de bom coração,* kindhearted.

corado, *adj.* ruddy, ruddy-cheeked, blushing.

coradouro, *s.m.* bleaching place.

coragem, *s.f.* courage, bravery, heart, boldness; *encher-se de coragem,* to man oneself, to pluck up one's courage.

corajosamente, *adv.* courageously, bravely.

corajoso, *adj.* courageous, brave, daring, bold.

coral, *s.m.* coral, choral *(canto); adj.* choral.

coralíneo, *adj.* coralline.

coralino, *adj.* coral-red.

corante, *s.m.* colouring, dyestuff; *adj.* colouring.

corar, *v.t.* to colour, to dye, to tinge, to bleach *(branquear),* to blush *(ficar com o rosto corado).*

corbelha, *s.f.* corbeille.

corça, *s.f.* doe, hind.

corcel, *s.m.* steed, courser, charger.

corço, *s.m.* roebuck.

corcova, *s.f.* hump, hunch, humpback, hunchback.

corcovado, *adj. e s.m.* humpbacked, hunchbacked.

corcovar, *v.t.* to bend, to hump, to curve.

corcunda, *s.f. e s.m.* hump, hunch.

corda, *s.f.* rope, cord, *(geom.)* chord, string *(musical),* bowstring *(de arco),* line *(de estender a roupa),* tighrope *(de acrobata); cordas vocais,* vocal cords.

cordame, *s.m.* cordage, *(náut.)* rigging.

cordão, *s.m.* string, twine, cord, row *(fileira).*

cordato, *adj.* prudent, wise, cautious, sober.

cordeiro, *s.m.* lamb.

cordel, *s.m.* string.

cor-de-rosa, *s.f.* pink.

cordial, *adj.* cordial, sincere.

cordialidade, *s.f.* cordiality, sincerity, heartiness.

cordialmente, *adv.* cordially, warmly.

cordiforme, *adj.* cordiform.

cordilheira, *s.f.* chain, ridge.

cordoaria, *s.f.* rope factory.

cordoeiro, *s.m.* rope maker.

cordovão, *s.m.* cordovan.

cordoveias, *s.f.pl.* jugular veins.

cordovês, *s.m.* e *adj.* Cordovan.

cordura, *s.f.* discretion, prudence, wisdom, circumspection.

coreano, *s.m.* e *adj.* Corean, Korean.

coreografia, *s.f.* choreography.

coreógrafo, *s.m.* choreographer.

coreto, *s.m.* band-stand.

co-réu, *s.m.* accomplice.

corgo, *s.m.* o mesmo que "córrego".

coriáceo, *adj.* coriaceous.

coriandro, *s.m.* coriander.

corifeu, *s.m.* coryphaeus.

coríntio, *adj.* e *s.m.* Chorithian.

coriscante, *adj.* coruscant, glittering.

coriscar, *v.i.* to spark, to flash, to glitter.

corisco, *s.m.* flash of lightning, spark.

corista, *s.f.* chorus girl, member of a chorus.

coriza, *s.f.* coryza.

corja, *s.f.* rabble, mob, crowd.

cornaca, *s.m.* elephant-driver.

cornadura, *s.f.* horns.

cornamusa, *s.f.* bagpipe.

córnea, *s.f.* cornea.

corneta, *s.f.* horn, bugle, trupet.

cornetada, *s.f.* sound of trumpets.

corneteiro, *s.m.* bugler, horn-blower, trumpeter.

cornetim, *s.m.* French horn.

cornígero, *adj.* cornigerous, horned.

cornija, *s.f.* cornice.

corno, *s.m.* horn.

cornucópia, *s.f.* cornucopia, horn of plenty.

cornudo, *adj.* horned.

cornúpeto, *s.m.* e *adj.* bull.

coro, *s.m.* chorus, choir *(de igreja); em coro,* in unison.

coroa, *s.f.* crown, garland *(de flores),* tonsure *(de padre), (ast.)* corona, summit *(cume); coroa de louros,* laurel wreath.

coroação, *s.f.* coronation, crowning.

coroado, *adj.* crowned.

coroamento, *s.m.* crowning, capping, climax.

coroar, *v.t.* to crown, to top, to wreathe, to complete, to finish.

corografia, *s.f.* chorography.

corográfico, *adj.* chorographic.

corógrafo, *s.m.* chorographer.

corola, *s.f.* corolla.

corolário, *s.m.* corollary, result, deduction.

coronária, *s.f.* coronary artery.

coronário, *adj.* coronary.

coronel, *s.m.* colonel.

coronha, *s.f.* butt-end of a musket, gunstock, butt, stock.

coronhada, *s.f.* blow with a riffle butt.

corpanzil, *s.m.* big body, stout person.

corpete, *s.m.* corsage, bodice, waistcoat.

corpo, *s.m.* body, assembly, corporation, consistency, volume, *(mil.)* corps. 1) *corpo de bombeiros,* fire brigade. 2) *de corpo e alma,* heart and soul.

corporação, *s.f.* corporation, body, association.

corporal, *adj.* corporal, bodily, physical.

corporalidade, *s.f.* corporality.

corporalmente, *adv.* corporally, bodily.

corporativismo, *s.m.* corporativism.

corporativista, *s.m.* corporativist.

corporativo, *adj.* corporative.

corporeidade, *s.f.* corporeity.

corpóreo, *adj.* corporeal, corporeous, material.

corpulência, *s.f.* corpulence, bulk, stoutness.

corpulento, *adj.* corpulent, stout, voluminous.

corpuscular, *adj.* corpuscular.

corpúsculo, *s.m.* corpuscle.

correada, *s.f.* belting, strapping.

correame, *s.m.* straps, belts.

correaria, *s.f.* saddle's shop.

correcção, *s.f.* correction, emendation, improvement, punishment; *casa de correcção,* reformatory.

correcional, *adj.* correctional.

correctamente, *adv.* correctly, rightly.

correctivo, *adj.* corrective.

correcto, *adj.* correct, proper, right.

corrector, *s.m.* corrector, mender, reformer.

corrediça, *s.f.* slide.

corrediço, *adj.* sliding, running.

corredio, *adj.* running, sliding; *nó corredio,* slip-knot.

corredor, *s.m.* runner, racer, corridor, gangway, passage, gallery; *adj.* running.

correiro, *s.m.* sadler.

corregedor, *s.m.* corregidor.

côrrego, *s.m.* ravine, gutter.

correia, *s.f.* leather strap, strap, belt, thong.

correio, *s.m.* post, mail, post-office *(local)*, messenger, courier. 1) *correio aéreo,* air mail. 2) *por correio,* by mail.

correlação, *s.f.* correlation, inter-relation.

correlacionar, *v.t.* to correlate, to establish a relation between.

correlatar, *v.t.* to establish a mutual relation.

correlativo, *adj.* correlative.

correligionário, *s.m.* coreligionist, fellow beliver.

corrente, *adj.* current, running, flowing, fluent, ordinary, common, present *(mês, ano, etc.); s.m.* current, stream, torrent, draft *(de ar),* chain *(cadeia),* fetter *(de prisioneiro).* 1) *a favor da corrente,* downstream. 2) *contra a corrente,* agaist the stream, upstream. 3) *pôr ao corrente,* to inform.

correntemente, *adv.* fluently, currently, commonly.

correnteza, *s.f.* current, stream, row *(fileira).*

correntio, *adj.* fluent, easy, current, usual.

correr, *v.i.* to run, to race, to scurry *(precipitadamente),* to hasten, to hurry, to dash *(às pressas),* to go by *(o tempo),* to flow *(líquido),* to circulate *(boatos).* 1) *os tempos que correm,* the present times. 2) *nos dias que correm,* nowadays; *v.t.* to run, to be exposed (to risks), to traverse *(viajar por),* to run after *(perseguir),* to drive of *(expulsar),* to draw *(uma cortina),* to undergo *(padecer).* 3) *correr mundo,* to travel around the world. 4) *com o correr do tempo,* in the course of time.

correria, *s.f.* running about, scampering, scurriyng, raid.

correspondência, *s.f.* correspondence, correlation, parallelism, letter-writing, mail.

correspondente, *adj.* corresponding, correspondent, suitable; *s.m.* correspondent.

corresponder, *v.i.* to correspond, to be in harmony with, to be equivalent, to agree; *v.t.* to match; *corresponder-se,* to correspond with.

corretagem, *s.f.* brokerage.

corretor, *s.m.* broker.

corrida, *s.f.* run, race, course, rush, trip *(táxi).*

corrido, *adj.* driven off *(expulso),* ashamed *(envergonhado).*

corrigenda, *s.f.* corrigenda, erratum.

corrigir, *v.t.* to correct, to amend, to rectify.

corrigível, *adj.* corrigible.

corrilho, *s.m.* conventicle, clandestine meeting, conspiracy, plot.

corrimão, *s.m.* handrail.

corrimento, *s.m. (med.)* flux, discharge.

corriola, *s.f. (bot.)* bindweed, riot, hoot.

corriqueiro, *adj.* trivial, common, vulgar.

corroboração, *s.f.* corroboration.

corroborante, *adj.* corroborant.

corroborar, *v.t.* to corroborate.

corroer, *v.t.* to corrode, to eat away.

corroído, *adj.* corroded, pitted, rusted.

corromper, *v.t.* to corrupt, to spoil, to pevert.

corrompido, *adj.* corrupted.

corrosão, *s.f.* corrosion, erosion, rusting.

corrosivo, *adj.* corrosive.

corrupção, *s.f.* corruption, corruptness.

corrupio, *s.m. andar num corrupio,* to be on the run.

corruptibilidade, *s.f.* corruptibility.

corruptível, *adj.* corruptible.

corruptivo, *adj.* corruptive.

corrupto, *adj.* corrupt, rotten, depraved, vicious.

corruptor, *s.m.* corrupter, misleader.

corsário, *s.m.* corsair.

corso, *s.m.* piracy, privateering, parade of carriages, Corsican *(da Córsega).*

cortadeira, *s.f.* pastry-cutter.

cortadela, *s.f.* cut.

cortado, *adj.* cut.

cortador, cutter, butcher.

cortante, *adj.* cutting, biting, sharp.

corta-papel, *s.m.* paper-knife.

cortar, *v.t.* e *v.i.* to cut, to sever, to chop, to incise, to slit, to cut of, to pare *(unhas),* to carve *(trinchar),* to sever *(relações).* 1) *cortar a palavra a,* to cut short. 2) *cortar em fatias,* to slice. 3) *cortar na casaca,* to backbite. 4) *cortar pela raiz,* to cut off at the roots. 5) *vou cortar o cabelo,* I'm going to have my hair cut.

corte, *s.m.* cut *(também de fazenda),* cutting, incision, slit. 1) *corte de cabelo,* haircut. 2) *corte de madeiras,* lumbering. 3) *corte nas despesas,* retrench.

corte, *s.f.* court, courtship *(namoro).*

cortejador, *s.m.* courtier, gallant, flatterer.

cortejar, *v.t.* to court, to woo.

cortejo, *s.m.* procession, parade, retinue.

cortelho, *s.m.* pigsty.

cortês, *adj.* courteous, polite, considerate, well-bred.

cortesã, *s.f.* courtesan.

cortesia, *s.f.* courtesy, politeness, civility, bow *(vénia).*

córtex, *s.m.* cortex, *(bot.)* bark.

cortiça, *s.f.* cork.

cortiçada, *s.f.* a great quantity of cork.

cortical, *adj.* cortical.

cortiçeiro, *s.m.* cork-stripper, corkdealer.

cortiço, *s.m.* beehive.

cortina, *s.f.* curtain.

cortinado, *s.m.* curtain, drapery.

coruchéu, *s.m.* spire, conical cap.

coruja, *s.f.* owl.

coruscante, *adj.* coruscant, brilliant.

coruscar, *v.i.* to coruscate, to flash, to glitter.

coruta, *s.f.* summit, top.

corveta, *s.f.* corvette.

corvídeo, *s.m.* corvide.

corvina, *s.f.* croaker.

corvo, *s.m.* crow, raven.

cós, *s.m.* waistband, nackband.

coscurão, *s.m.* fritter, pancake.

coscuvilhar, *v.i.* to gossip, to pratel idly, to tittle-tattle.

coscuvilheiro, *s.m.* tell-tale, intriguer, gossiper, tittle-tattle.

coscuvilhice, *s.f.* gossip, tittle-tattle, intrigue, gossip.

co-secante, *s.f.* co-secant.

cosedura, *s.f.* sewing, *(náut.)* lacing, lashing.

co-seno, *s.m.* co-sine.

coser, *v.t.* e *v.i.* to sew, to stich; *coser-se com a parede,* to hug the wall, to flatten oneself against the wall.

cosido, *adj.* sewed, stiched.

cosmético, *s.m.* cosmetic.

cósmico, *adj.* cosmic.

cosmogonia, *s.f.* cosmogony.

cosmogónico, *adj.* cosmogonic.

cosmogonista, *s.m.* e *s.f.* cosmogonist.

cosmografia, *s.f.* cosmography.

cosmográfico, *adj.* cosmographic.

cosmógrafo, *s.m.* cosmographer.

cosmologia, *s.f.* cosmology.

cosmológico, *adj.* cosmological.

cosmólogo, *s.m.* cosmologist.

cosmopolita, *s.m.* e *s.f.* cosmopolite; *adj.* cosmopolitan.

cosmopolitismo, *s.m.* cosmopolitanism, cosmopolitism.

cosmorama, *s.m.* cosmorama.

cosmos, *s.m.* cosmos.

cossaco, *s.m.* Cossack.

costa, *s.f.* coast, shore, seashore. 1) *costas,* back, shoulders. 2) *às costas,* on the back, on the shoulders. 3) *dar à costa,* to be washed ashore. 4) *virar as costas,* to turn one's back on. 5) *de costas,* backwards. 6) *em direcção à costa,* landward.

costado, *s.m.* side, broadside *(de navio).*

costal, *adj.* e *s.m.* coastal.

costaneiro, *adj.* outward, coarse paper.

costear, *v.t. (náut.)* to coast along, to follow the coast.

costeiro, *adj.* coasting, coast, maritime.

costela, *s.f.* rib.

costeleta, *s.f.* chop, cutlet.

costumado, *adj.* usual, habitual.

costumar, *v.t.* e *v.i.* to be accustomed (to do something), to be in the habit (of doing); *ele costumava vir,* he used to come.

costumário, *adj.* costumary, usual, common.

costume, *s.m.* custom, habit, usage. 1) *costumes,* behaviour, manners. 2) *como de costume,* as usual. 3) *de costume,* usual. 4) *segundo o costume,* according to the custom. 5) *ter o costume de,* to be in the habit of. 6) *é costume,* it is usual.

costumeiro, *adj.* usual, habitual, customary.

costura, *s.f.* seam, sewing, stitching, scar *(cicatriz).*

costurar, *v.i.* to sew, to seam, to do needlework.

costureira, *s.f.* seamstress, dressmaker.

cota, *s.f.* coat of mail *(de malha),* quota *(quinhão),* annotation *(nota).*

cotação, *s.f.* quotation *(de preços),* price-list; *cotação de câmbios,* course of exchange.

co-tangente, *s.f.* co-tangent.

cotão, *s.m.* fuzz, fluff.

cotar, *v.t.* to quote, to assess, to fix the value, to annotate, to rate.

cotejar, *v.t.* to compare, to confront, to collate (with), to confer.

cotejo, *s.m.* comparing, comparison, collation, confrontation.

cotica, *s.f.* cotise.

cotícula, *s.f.* touchstone.

cotilédone, *s.m.* cotyledon.

cotiledóneo, *adj.* cotyledonous.

cotilhão, *s.m.* cotillon.

cotim, *s.m.* drill.

cotio, *adj.* daily; *s.m.* daily use.

cotização, *s.f.* assessment, quota.

coto, *s.m.* stump, stub, butt.

cotovelada, *s.f.* poke with the elbow, nudge.

cotovelo, *s.m.* elbow, turning bend *(curva)*.

cotovia, *s.f.* skylark.

couce, *s.m.* kick.

coudelaria, *s.f.* stud-farm.

couraça, *s.f.* cuirass, armor plating *(de navio)*.

couraçado, *adj.* iron-clad; *s.m.* battleship.

couraçar, coiraçar, *v.t.* to fit with a cuirass, to cuirass.

couraceiro, *s.m.* cuirassier.

courela, *s.f.* a long and narrow tip of cultivated land.

couro, *s.m.* leather, hide *(de um animal inteiro)*; *couro cabeludo,* scalp.

cousa, *s.f.* thing, matter.

coutada, *s.f.* game preserve.

coutado, *adj.* enclosed, surrounded.

couteiro, *s.m.* gamekeeper, park-keeper.

couve, *s.f.* cabbage.

couve-flor, *s.f.* cauliflower.

couve-lombarda, *s.f.* kale.

cova, *s.f.* hole, ditch, hollow, cavity, pit, grave *(sepultura)*.

côvado, *s.m.* cubit.

coval, *s.m.* graveyard.

coveiro, *s.m.* grave digger.

covil, *s.m.* den, lair.

covilhete, *s.m.* small dish.

covinha, little hole, dimple *(no queixo ou nas bochechas)*.

covo, *adj.* hollow, concave, deep.

coxa, *s.f.* thigh.

coxear, *v.i.* to limp, to hobble, to halt.

coxia, *s.f.* aisle, gangway, wings *(bastidores)*.

coxim, *s.m.* cushion.

coxo, *s.m.* lame, cripple.

cozedura, *s.f.* baking, boiling.

cozer, *v.t.* to cook *(cozinhar),* to boil, to bake.

cozido, *adj.* baked, boiled, cooked.

cozimento, *s.m.* boiling, baking.

cozinha, *s.f.* kitchen, cooking *(arte)*.

cozinhar, *v.t.* o mesmo que "cozer".

cozinheira, *s.f.* cook, female-cook.

cozinheiro, *s.m.* cook, chef.

craniano, *adj.* cranial.

crânio, *s.m.* skull, cranium.

craniologia, *s.f.* craniology.

crápula, *s.f.* licentiousness, debauchery; *s.m.* debauched person, scoundrel.

crapuloso, *adj.* crapulous, licentious, dissolute.

crase, *s.f.* crasis.

crasso, *adj.* crass, gross, thick, coarse.

cratera, *s.f.* crater.

cravação, *s.f.* setting *(de pedras preciosas)*, nailing.

cravador, *s.m.* gem setter, punch *(furador)*.

cravagem, *s.f. (bot.)* ergot.

cravar, *v.t.* to nail, to drive in *(pregos, etc.)*, to set *(pedras)*; *cravar os olhos em,* to stare.

craveira, *s.f.* mesuring stick, size.

craveiro, *s.m.* carnation.

cravejador, *s.m.* gem setter, blacksmith.

cravejar, *v.t.* to set (pedras), to stud with nails.

cravelha, *s.f.* tuning peg.

cravina, *s.f.* small pink.

cravista, *s.m.* harpsichord player.

cravo, *s.m.* nail *(prego)*, blackhead *(da pele)*, harpsichord *(instrumento musical)*, carnation *(flor)*; *cravo-da-Índia,* cloves.

cré, *s.m.* chalk.

creche, *s.f.* day nursery.

credência, *s.f.* credence.

credencial, *s.f.* credential.

credibilidade, *s.f.* credibility.

creditar, *v.t.* to credit.

crédito, *s.m.* credit, reputation, trust, reliance, prestige; *digno de crédito,* reliable.

credível, *adj.* credible, reliable.

credo, *s.m.* the creed.

credor, *s.m.* creditor, worther *(merecedor)*.

credulidade, *s.f.* credulity, credulousness.

crédulo, *adj.* credulous.

cremação, *s.f.* cremation, incineration.

cremador, *s.m.* cremator, incinerator.

cremalheira, *s.f.* rack, cog rail, pothook *(de lareira)*.

cremar, *v.t.* to cremate, to incinerate, to burn.

crematório, *s.m.* crematory.

creme, *s.m.* cream, custard *(doce)*; *adj.* cream-coloured.

cremona, *s.f.* bascule-bolt.

cremor, *s.m.* cremor.

cremoso, *adj.* creamy.

crença, *s.f.* belief, faith, conviction.

crendice, *s.f.* superstition.

crente, *s.m.* e *s.f.* believer; *adj.* believing.

creolina, *s.f.* creosote.

creosotagem, *s.f.* creosoting.

creosote, *s.m.* creosote.

crepe, *s.m.* crepe, crape.

crepitação, *s.f.* crepitation, crackling.

crepitar, *v.i.* to crepitate, to crackle.

crepuscular, *adj.* crepuscular, twilight.

crepúsculo, *s.m.* twilight, crepuscle, dusk.

crer, *v.t.* e *v.i.* to believe, to think, to suppose, to fancy. 1) *creio que sim,* I think so. 2) *fazer crer,* to cause (someone) to believe. 3) *é de crer,* it's likely that.

crescença, *s.f.* growth, increase, development, overplus.

crescendo, *s.m.* crescendo, progression.

crescente, *adj.* crescent, increasing, growing; *s.m.* crescent *(da lua).*

crescer, *v.i.* to grow, to increase, to rise, to mount, to develop, to expand; *deixar crescer a barba,* to grow a beard.

crescido, *adj.* grown up, developed, big.

crescimento, *s.m.* growth, increase, enlargement, development, improvement.

crespidão, *s.f.* crisping, crispness.

crespo, *adj.* crisp, curly, frizzled.

cresta, *s.f.* singeing.

crestadura, *s.f.* light burn.

crestar, *v.t.* to singe, to burn a little, to tan.

crestomatia, *s.f.* chrestomathy.

cretáceo, *adj.* cretaceous.

cretense, *s.m.* e *adj.* Cretan.

cretino, *s.m.* cretin, idiot.

cretone, *s.m.* cretone.

cria, *s.f.* young (of animals).

criação, *s.f.* creation, invention, formation, breeding *(de animais),* upbringing *(educação): má criação,* ill-breeding; rudeness; bad manners.

criada, *s.f.* sevant, maid.

criadagem, *s.f.* servants.

criado, *s.m.* servant; *adj.* bred, reared, educated.

criador, *s.m.* creator, inventor, founder, breeder *(de gado), adj.* creative.

criança, *s.f.* child.

criançada, *s.f.* children.

criancice, *s.f.* childish behaviour.

criançola, *s.f.* puppy, childish person.

criar, *v.t.* to create, to produce, to invent, to originate, to raise *(obstáculos),* to breed *(animais),* to bring up *(educar).*

criatura, *s.f.* creature.

crime, *s.m.* crime.

criminalidade, *s.f.* criminality.

criminalista, *s.m.* criminalist.

criminologia, *s.f.* criminology.

criminologista, *s.f.* criminologist.

criminosamente, *adv.* criminally.

criminoso, *s.m.* criminal, fellon; *adj.* criminal, felonious.

crina, *s.f.* mane, horse-hair.

crinolina, *s.f.* crinolline.

crioulo, *s.m.* creole.

cripta, *s.f.* crypt.

criptogâmicas, *s.f.pl.* cryptogams.

criptogâmico, *adj.* cryptogamic.

criptografia, *s.f.* cryptography.

criptógrafo, *s.m.* cryptographer.

criptograma, *s.m.* cryptogram.

crisálida, *s.f.* crysalis, crysalid.

crisântemo, *s.m.* chrysanthemum.

crise, *s.f.* crisis, emergency, turning point.

crisma, *s.f.* chrism, confirmation.

crismar, *v.t.* to confirm.

crisol, *s.m.* crucible, trial.

crispação, *s.f.* crispation, contraction.

crispar, *v.t.* to crisp, to curl, to contract.

crista, *s.f.* cock's comb *(de galo),* crest, top, ridge.

cristal, *s.m.* crystal.

cristaleira, *s.f.* crystal cupboard.

cristalino, *adj.* crystalline, crystal-clear.

cristalização, *s.f.* crystallization.

cristalizar, *v.t.* e *v.i.* to crystallize.

cristalizável, *adj.* crystallizable.

cristalografia, *s.f.* crystallography.

cristalográfico, *adj.* crystallographic.

cristalógrafo, *s.m.* crystallographer.

cristalóide, *s.m.* e *adj.* crystalloid.

cristandade, *s.m.* Christedom, Christianity.

cristão, *s.m.* e *adj.* Christian.

cristianismo, *s.m.* Christianism.

cristianização, *s.f.* Christianization.

cristianizar, *v.t.* to Christianize.

Cristo, *s.m.* Christ.

critério, *s.m.* criterion, standard, discretion, judgement.

criterioso, *adj.* judicious, wise.

crítica, *s.f.* criticism, critique, judgement, censure.

criticar, *v.t.* to criticize, to censure, to judge, to blame.

criticável, *adj.* criticizable.

crítico, *adj.* critical, crucial, dangerous; *s.m.* critic, reviewer.

crivado, *adj.* riddled *(de balas, etc.),* spotted; *crivado de dívidas,* debt-ridden.

crivar, *v.t.* to riddled *(de balas, etc.),* to pierce all over.

crível, *adj.* credible, believable.

crivo, *s.m.* sieve, riddle, nozzle *(de regador).*

croata, *s.f.* Croat; *adj.* Croatian.

croché, *s.m.* crochet.

crocitar, *v.i.* to croak.

crocito, *s.m.* croak.

crocodilo, *s.m.* crocodile.

cromado, *adj.* chromium-plated.

cromar, *v.t.* to chromate, to chromatize, to plate with chromiúm.

cromático, *adj.* chromatic.

cromatismo, *s.m.* chromatism.

cromato, *s.m.* chromate.

crómio, *s.m.* chromium.

cromo, *s.m.* chrome.

cromolitografia, *s.f.* chromo-lithography.

cromossoma, *s.m.* chromosome.

cromotipografia, *s.f.* chromotypography.

crónica, *s.f.* chronicle, narrative, record.

cronista, *s.m.* chronicler, annalist.

cronografia, *s.f.* chronography.

cronógrafo, *s.m.* chronographer.

cronograma, *s.m.* chronogram.

cronologia, *s.f.* chronology.

cronológico, *adj.* chronological.

cronologista, *s.m. e s.f.* chronologist.

cronometragem, *s.f.* time keeping, timing.

cronometrar, *v.t.* to time.

cronometria, *s.f.* chronometry.

cronométrico, *adj.* chronometrical.

cronometrista, *s.m.* timekeeper.

cronómetro, *s.m.* timepiece, stop watch.

croque, *s.m.* grapple, hook.

croquete, *s.m.* croquette, meat ball.

crosta, *s.f.* crust.

cru, *adj.* raw, crude, uncooked, fresh, cruel, rude.

cruamente, *adv.* rudely, cruelly.

crucial, *adj.* crucial.

cruciante, *adj.* heart-breaking.

cruciferário, *s.m.* cross-bearer.

crucíferas, *s.f.pl.* cruciferae, cruciferous plants.

crucificação, *s.f.* crucifixion.

crucificado, *adj.* crucified.

crucificador, *s.m.* crucifier.

crucificar, *v.t.* to crucify, to mortify.

crucifixo, *s.m.* crucifix.

cruciforme, *adj.* cruciform.

crudelíssimo, *adj.* most cruel.

cruel, *adj.* cruel, merciless, severe.

crueldade, *s.f.* cruelty.

cruento, *adj.* bloody.

crueza, *s.f.* crudity, rawness, cruelty.

crural, *adj.* crural.

crustáceo, *s.m.* crustacean; *adj.* crustaceous.

cruz, *s.f.* cross, crown *(de uma âncora).*

cruzada, *s.f.* crusade.

cruzado, *s.m.* crusader.

cruzador, *s.m.* cruiser.

cruzamento, *s.m.* crossing *(de estradas),* crossbreeding *(de raças).*

cruzar, *v.t.* to cross, to fold *(os braços),* to intersect, to traverse, to crossbreed *(animais),* to cross-fertilize *(plantas); cruzar- -se,* to cross, to interbreed.

cruzeiro, *s.m.* croiss aisle of a church, large cross set up in public places, cruise *(no mar); Cruzeiro do Sul,* Southern cross.

cruzeta, *s.f.* small cross, crosspiece.

cu, *s.m. (pop.)* arse.

Cuba, *s.f.* Cuba; wine vat.

cubagem, *s.f.* cubage.

cubano, *s.m. e adj.* Cuban.

cubar, *v.t.* to cube, to find the cube of a number.

cubata, *s.f.* hut.

cúbico, *adj.* cubic.

cubículo, *s.m.* cubicle.

cubismo, *s.m.* cubism.

cúbito, *s.m.* cubitus.

cubo, *s.m.* cube, hexahedron, hub *(de roda).*

cubóide, *s.m.* cuboid.

cuco, *s.m.* cuckoo.

cucurbitáceas, *s.f.pl.* cucurbitaceous plants.

cucuritar, *v.i.* to crow *(o galo).*

cuecas, *s.f. pl.* shorts.

cueiro, *s.m.* swaddling band.

cuidado, *s.m.* care, attention, caution, carefulness, worry, concern. 1) *cuidado!,* watch out!. 2) *cuidado com o carro!,* mind the car!. 3) *ter ao seu cuidado!,* to take care of. 4) *ao cuidado de,* care of. 5) *com cuidado,* carefully. 6) *ter cuidado,* to be careful, to take care. 7) *ter cuidado com,* to mind.

cuidadosamente, *adv.* carefully, heedfully.

cuidadoso, *adj.* careful, diligent, heedful.

cuidar, *v.t. e v.i.* to care, to take care, to look after, to imagine, to suppose; *cuidar-se,* to take care of oneself.

cujo, *pron. rel.* whose, of whom, of which.

culatra, *s.f.* breech.

culinária, *s.f.* cookery, cooking.

culinário, *adj.* culinary.

culminação, *s.f.* culmination.

culminante, *adj.* culminant, highest, topmost.

culminar, *v.i.* to culminate, to reach the climax.

culpa, *s.f.* guilt, fault, blame; *ter culpa de,* to be to blame for.

culpabilidade, *s.f.* culpability, guiltness.

culpado, *adj.* guilty, culpable; *s.m.* culprit.

culpar, *v.t.* to blame, to accuse (of), to charge (with).

culpável, *adj.* culpable, blameworthy.

culteranismo, *s.m.* cultism, artificial style.

cultivação, *s.f.* cultivation, culture.

cultivado, *adj.* cultivated, tilled.

cultivador, *s.m.* cultivator, tiller, farmer.

cultivar, *v.t.* to cultivate, to till, to farm, to develop, to educate, to indulge in *(hábitos), cultivar-se,* to acquire culture.

cultivável, *adj.* cultivable, tillable, arable.

cultivo, *s.m.* cultivation, tillage, culture.

culto, *s.m.* cult, worship, respect, adoration, religious service; *adj.* cultivated, refined, polished, civilized, learned.

cultor, *s.m.* cultivator, worshipper.

cultura, *s.f.* culture, culture, learning, tillage *(da terra).*

cultural, *adj.* cultural.

cume, *s.m.* summit, top, climax.

cumeada, *s.f.* mountain ridge.

cumeeira, *s.f.* ridge-piece *(de telhado).*

cúmplice, *s.m.* accomplice, abettor, accessory (to something).

cumplicidade, *s.f.* cumplicity, participation.

cumprido, *adj.* fulfilled, accomplished, executed.

cumpridor, *s.m.* fulfiller, executor; *adj.* duteous, observant.

cumprimentar, *v.t.* to compliment, to salute, to greet, to congratulate (on something).

cumprimento, *s.m.* accomplishment, fulfillment, execution; compliment, greeting, salutation, salute. 1) *apresentar cumprimentos,* to pay one's respects. 2) *transmitalhe cumprimentos,* give him my regard's.

cumprir, *v.t.* to execute, to carry out, to perform, to fulfill, to accomplish, to keep *(palavra),* to serve *(pena).* 1) *fazer cumprir,* to enforce *(a lei).* 2) *cumprir-se,* to be fulfilled, to come true.

cumular, *v.t.* to cumulate, to heap up, to overwhelm *(de atenções, favores, etc.).*

cumulativo, *adj.* cumulative.

cúmulo, *s.m.* accumulation, heap, highest point, extremity, cumulus *(nuvem); é o cúmulo,* that's the limit!

cuneiforme, *adj.* cuneiform, cuniform.

cunha, *s.f.* wedge, *à cunha,* jammed, crowded, replete.

cunhada, *s.f.* sister-in-law.

cunhado, *s.m.* brother-in-law.

cunhagem, *s.f.* coinage.

cunhal, angle, corner.

cunhar, *v.t.* to coin, to stamp.

cunhete, *s.m.* amunition-case.

cunho, *s.m.* stamp, die, mark, seal, imprint.

cunicultor, *s.m.* rabbit breeder.

cunicultura, *s.f.* rabbit breeding.

cupão, *s.m.* coupon.

cupidez, *s.f.* cupidity, covetousness.

Cupido, *s.m.* Cupid.

cúprico, *adj.* cupric.

cúpula, *s.f.* dome, cupola.

cura, *s.f.* cure, healing, recovery, treatment, curing *(de carnes, etc.); s.m.* parish priest, curate.

curabilidade, *s.f.* curability.

curado, *adj.* healed.

curador, *s.m.* trustee, tutor, guardian.

curadoria, *s.f.* trusteeship, guardianship.

curandeiro, *s.m.* quack, medicine man.

curar, *v.t.* e *v.i.* to cure, to heal, to set right, to treat, to cure *(carnes); curar-se,* to recover.

curativo, *adj.* healing, curative; *s.m.* treatment, dressing.

curável, *adj.* curable, healable, recoverable.

curcuma, *s.f.* e *s.m.* curcuma.

cúria, *s.f.* Curia.

curial, *adj.* curial, appropriate, convenient.

curiosidade, *s.f.* curiosity, inquisitiveness, oddity.

curioso, *adj.* curious, inquisitive, odd, strange; *s.m.* snooper, amateur.

curral, *s.m.* corral, pen, fold *(de ovelhas).*

currículo, *s.m.* curriculum.

curro, *s.m.* pen for bulls.

cursar, *v.t.* to follow, to attend, *(aulas), v.i.* to travel, to cruise.

cursista, *s.m.* student.

cursivo, *s.m.* cursive.

curso, *s.m.* couse *(também de estudos),* way, track, direction, current, progress, circulation. 1) *curso de água,* watercourse, stream. 2) *de longo curso, (náut.) viagem de longo curso,* long voyage; seasoning. 3) *em curso,* current, in progress.

cursor, *s.m.* slide.

curteza, *s.f.* shortness, brevity, narrowness *(de ideias).*

curtidor, *s.m.* tanner.

curtimento, *s.m.* tanning.

curtir, *v.t.* to tan, to harden; to suffer, to undergo *(padecer).*

curto, *adj.* short, brief, narrow-minded *(de ideias),* short-sighted *(de vistas); curto- - circuito,* short-circuit.

curtume, *s.m.* tanning.

curva, *s.f.* curve, bend, turning.

curvado, *adj.* bent, curved, arched.

curvar, *v.t.* to curve, to bend, to arch; to subdue, to bend (sujeitar-se); *curvar-se,* to bow, to bend over, to stoop, to submit.

curvatura, *s.f.* curvature, curving.

curveta, *s.f.* curvet.

curvetear, *v.i.* to curvet, to prance.

curvilíneo, *adj.* curvilinear.

curvo, *adj.* curved, bent, arched, crooked.

cuspidela, *s.f.* spittle, spit.

cuspir, *v.t.* e *v.i.* to spit, to expectorate; *ser cuspido do cavalo,* to be thrown off.

cuspo, *s.m.* spittle, saliva.

custa, *s.f.* cost, expense. 1) *custas,* costs. 2) *á custa de,* at the expense of. 3) *viver à custa de,* to sponge on.

custeamento, *s.m.* expense, defraying.

custear, *v.t.* to defray, to finance.

custo, *s.m.* cost, price. 1) *a custo,* hardly, with difficulty. 2) *a todo o custo,* at any rate, at any cost.

custódia, *s.f.* custody.

custodiar, *v.t.* to guard, to keep in custody.

custoso, *adj.* costly, expensive, difficult, painful.

cutâneo, *adj.* cutaneous, skin.

cutelaria, *s.f.* cutlery.

cuteleiro, *s.m.* cutler.

cutelo, *s.m.* cutlass, chopping knife, chopper.

cutícula, *s.f.* cuticle.

cuticular, *adj.* cuticular.

cutilada, *s.f.* cut, slash.

cutileiro, *s.m.* cutler.

cútis, *s.f.* skin, complexion.

czar, *s.m.* tzar, czar.

czarina, *s.f.* tsarina, czarina.

czarista, *s.m.* tsarist, czarist.

D

d, *s.m.* the fourth letter of the Portuguese alphabet.

da, *cont. prep.* of the, of that; *pron. dem.* from the, from that.

dacolá, *cont. prep.* from there, from yonder.

dactílico, *adj.* dactylic.

dactilografar, *s.f.* typewriting; typing.

dactilografia, *v.t.* to typewrite.

dactilógrafo, *s.m.* typist.

dactilologia, *s.f.* dactylology.

dactiloscopia, *s. f.* dactiloscopy.

dádiva, *s.f.* gift, present, donation; boon.

dadivoso, *adj.* generous; liberal, bountiful, open-handed.

dado, adj. affable; kind; given to; s. m. die (small cube for gaming; pl. dice); datum, figure; basis, fundamental principle; conj. in view of, considering that. 1) dado que, provided that; as, because. 2) dados conhecidos, known data. 3) em dado momento, at a given moment.

dador, *s.m.* giver; donor, donator; dealer (*nas cartas*).

daí, *prep.* from there; *adv.* thence; therefore, for that reason. 1) *daí a dias*, days later. 2) *daí a pouco*, a little later. 3) *daí em diante*, from then on; ever since; thereafter. 4) *daí para cá*, since then, from then on. 5) *e daí?*, and what then?, what of this (of that, of it?).

dalém, *prep., adv.* from beyond.

dali, *prep. adv.* thence, therefrom, from there. 1) *dali a pouco*, a little later. 2) *dali por diante*, from then on, thereafter.

dália, *s.f.* dahlia.

dálmata, *s.m., adj.* Dalmatian.

dalmática, *s.f.* dalmatic (*veste religiosa*).

daltónico, *adj.* daltonic; *s.m.* daltonist, daltonian, colour-blind.

daltonismo, *s.m.* daltonism, colour-blindness.

dama, *s.f.* lady; queen (*cartas*); female partner (*num baile*); *dama de honor, de companhia*, lady-in-waiting.

damasco, *s.m.* damask; apricot (*fruto*).

damasqueiro, *s.m.* apricot-tree, damson-tree.

damasquino, *adj.* damancene; damask.

danação, danamento, *s.f., s.m.* damnation; condemnation, fury, rage, anger; rabies.

danado, *adj.* damned; wicked; irritated; angry; mad; rabid; clever, keen; valiant, courageous.

danar, *v.t.* to make mad; to irritate; *danar-se*, to become mad, angry, furious, exasperated; to injure, to damage.

dança, *s.f.* dance; ball. 1) *dança de roda*, round dance. 2) *meter-se ou entrar na dança*, to be involved in trouble, to join the dance.

dançadeira, *s.f. v.* **dançarina**.

dançador, *adj., s.m.* dancing, dancer.

dançante, *adj.* dancing; *chá dançante*, a tea dance.

dançar, *v.i.* to dance; to go round; *dançar conforme a música (fig.)*, to adapt oneself to the situation.

dançarina, *s.f.* dancing-girl, ballerina, dancer (*profissional*).

dançarino, *s.m.* dancer; ballet dancer.

dândi, *s.m.* dandy, fop, coxcomb.

dandismo, *s.m.* dandyism.

danificação, *s.f.* damnification; damage, damaging, injury.

danificador, *s.m., adj.* damnifier; damnifying, damaging, imparing, injuring.

danificar, *v.t.* to damnify; to damage, to harm, to hurt, to injure, to impair.

daninho, *adj.* harmful; wicked, prejudicial, injurious.

dano, *s.m.* loss; wrong; hurt, damage, harm, injury; prejudice, impairment.

danoso, *adj.* hurtful; injurious, damaging, prejudicial, noxious, detrimental.

dantes, *adv.* formerly.

dantesco, *adj.* Dantesque, awful, horrible.

daquele, (*prep. de* and *dem. adj.* or *pron. aquele*; the *fem.* is *aquela*) of that; from that; of him who.

daquém, (*prep. de* and *adv. aquém*) this side; on this side.

daqui, (*prep. de* and *adv. aqui*) hence; from here; within; from now; henceforth. 1) *daqui a pouco*, in a little while, shortly, in a few minutes, soon. 2) *daqui a três dias*, within three days, three days from now. 3) *daqui a um ano*, a year hence. 4) *daqui até lá*, between now and then. 5) *daqui em diante*, from now on, henceforth.

daquilo, (*prep. de* and *dem. pron. aquilo*) of that; from that.

dar, *v.t.* to give; to grant; to bestow; to supply; to deliver; to deal (*cartas*). 1) *dar-se*, to happen, to come to be, to occur; to agree, to live in harmony, to be on good terms. 2) *dar a César o que é de César*, to give the devil his due. 3) *dar a mão à palmatória*, to admit one's mistake, to admit to being wrong. 4) *dar a conhecer*, to make known. 5) *dar as boas-vindas*, to welcome. 6) *dar à costa* to run ashore. 7) *dar à língua*, to wag one's tongue. 8) *dar às de vila-diogo*, to take to one's heels. 9) *dar de si*, to give way (*prédio*), to result in, to bring about. 10) *dar em nada*, to fail. 11) *dar nas vistas*, to strike the eye. 12) *dar passagem*, to step aside, to make away for. 13) *dar-se bem com*, to get on well with. 14) *dar-se por vencido*, to give in. 15) *dar um passeio*, to take a walk, to take the air. 16) *dar uma volta (um giro)*, to take a stroll. 17) *dar alta*, to discharge (*um doente*). 18) *dar andamento*, to get something going. 19) *dar ares de*, to resemble (*parecer-se com outra pessoa*). 20) *dar atenção*, to pay attention. 21) *dar aula*, to teach, to lecture (*na universidade*). 22) *dar cabo de*, to put an end to, to do away with, to destroy, to ruin. 23) *dar com a cabeça na parede*, to strike one's head against the wall. 24) *dar com a porta na* *cara*, to slam the door in someone's face; 25) *dar com o nariz na porta*, to find the door closed. 26) *dar conta do recado*, to do the job. 27) *dar corda*, to wind up (*um relógio*), to encourage. 28) *dar crédito a*, to believe in. 29) *dar de cara com*, to bump into someone. 30) *dar de comer*, to feed. 31) *dar em droga*, to come to a bad end; 32) *dar no alvo*, to hit the mark. 33) *dar parabéns*, to offer congratulations. 34) *dar parte de*, to inform, to report. 35) *dar por isso*, to become aware of, to catch on. 36) *dar provimento*, to admit, to receive. 37) *dar que fazer*, to make trouble. 38) *dar razão a*, to agree with, to support. 39) *dar tempo ao tempo*, to bide one's time. 40) *dar trela*, to encourage. 41) *dar um ataque*, to suffer an attack. 42) *dar um passo*, to take a step. 43) *dar uma queda*, to take a tumble. 44)*dar uma satisfação*, to apologize, to offer an explanation. 45)*dar uma vista de olhos*, to glance at. 46)*dar volta à chave*, to turn the key.

dardejante, *adj.* darting.

dardejar, *v.t., v.i.* to dart (*olhares zangados*) at; to shoot out (*raios de calor ou luz*); to throw darts at; to pierce with a dart or spear; to sparkle; to hurl, to let fly.

dardo, *s.m.* dart, javelin, spear; shaft.

dares e tomares, *s.m.pl.* quarrel, give-and-take disputes.

dartro, *s.m.* dartre; herpes, tetter, eczema.

dartroso, *adj.* dartrous.

darwinismo, *s.m.* Darwinism.

darwinista, *s.m.* Darwinist.

dasimetria, *s.f.* dasymetry.

dasímetro, *s.m.* dasymeter.

data, *s.f.* date; large quantity; *de longa data*, of old, from former times.

datador, *s.m.* date stamp.

datar, *v.t., v.i.* to date; to reckon from, to count from.

dataria, *s.f.* dataria, datary.

datário, *s.m.* datary.

dativo, *s.m.* dative case.

de, *prep.* of; from; on; upon; in; out of, for, by, with. 1) *de acordo com*, in accordance with. 2) *de agora em diante*, from now on. 3) *de boa vontade*, with good will. 4) *de comum acordo*, by mutual agreement. 5) *de dia*, by day. 6) *de fora*, on the outside.

deado, *s.m.* deanship, deanery.

dealbação, *s.f.* whitening, bleach, bleaching.

dealbar, *v.t.* to whiten; to dawn.

deambulação, *s.f.* deambulation, walking about, digression, stroll, ramble; promenade.

deambulante, *adj.* wandering.

deambular, *v.i.* to stroll, to ramble.

deambulatório, *adj.* deambulatory, errant, rambling.

deão, *s.m.* dean.

debaixo, *adv.* underneath; under; below, beneath. 1) *debaixo de*, under, beneath, subject to. 2)*debaixo de telha*, indoors. 3) *debaixo de terra*, beneath the ground; in the grave. 4) *debaixo de forma*, in military formation.

debalde, *adv.* in vain, vainly, to no purpose, useless.

debandada, *s.f.* disbandment; dispersing, rout, flight, escape.

debandar, *v.t., v.i.* to disband; to disperse; to take flight, to put to flight, to scatter.

debate, *s.m.* debate; dispute; discussion, contention, contest (*argumentos*); *encerrar o debate*, to close the debate.

debater, *v.t.* to argue; to debate; to contend for; to discuss; *debater-se*, to fight, to struggle.

debatido, *adj.* debated, discussed.

debelação, *s.f.* extinction; suppression; cure, healing.

debelador, *s.m., adj.* suppresser; subduer, conqueror; subduing; healing, curing.

debelar, *v.t.* to extinguish; to overcome; to destroy; to conquer; to defeat, to vanquish; to cure, to heal; *a febre foi debelada*, fever was overcome.

debicador, *adj.* nibbling, pecking, picking.

debicar, *v.t.* to peck, to pick, to nibble (*comida*), to pick at or on (*outra pessoa*).

débil, *adj.* weak, feeble; anemic, frail; irresolute; soft, delicate; *débil mental*, a feebleminded person.

debilidade, *s.f.* debility; weakness, feebleness; fragility; frailty.

debilitação, debilitamento, *s.f., s.m.* enfeeblement, debilitation, weakening.

debilitador, *adj.* weakening.

debilitante, *adj.* debilitating.

debilitar, *v.t.* to debilitate; to enfeeble; to weaken, to lose strenght, to grow weak or feeble; to prejudice, to harm.

debilmente, *adv.* weakly; feebly.

debitar, *v.t.* to debit, to bill, to charge, to enter as a debt.

débito, *s.m.* debit, debt, obligation.

debochado, adj. debauched, dissolute.
debochar, v.t. to debauch, to corrupt, to pervert, to deprave.
deboche, s.m. debauchery.
debruar, v.t. to hem, to bind (bainhas), to border and sew; to adorn, to trim.
debruçado, adj. leaned, bent.
debruçar-se, v. refl. to lean (sobre), to stoop, to lean on the elbows; debruçar-se à janela, to lean out the window.
de bruços, loc. adv. flat; lying flat.
debrum, s.m. hem; binding, border, edging.
debulhadora, s.f. thrashing-machine.
debulhar, v.t. to thrash, to thresh (grão); to shell (milho); debulhar em lágrimas (em pranto), to dissolve (to melt) into tears, to cry one's eyes out.
debutante, s. debutante.
debuxador, s.m. drawer, sketcher, depicter.
debuxar, v.t. to draw; to sketch; to depict; to outline.
debuxo, s.m. drawing; sketch, outline, rough draft.
década, s.f. decade, set of ten.
decadência, s.f. decadency; wane; decrease; decline, decay.
decadente, adj. decaying; decadent.
decaedro, s.m. decahedron.
decagonal, adj. decagonal.
decágono, s.m. decagon.
decagrama, s.m. decagramme, decagram.
decaído, adj. fallen; decayed; decrepit; ruined.
decaimento, s.m. decay, decline, fall.
decair, v.i. to fall away, to decay, to decline; to pine, to waste away; to droop.
decalcar, v.t. to transfer; to trace; to imitate; to copy; to reproduce (copiando).
decalitro, s.m. decalitre, 10 liters.
decálogo, s.m. decalogue; the Ten Commandments.
decalque, s.m. transfering; tracing; copy.
decâmetro, s.m. decametre, 10 meters.
decampamento, s.m. decampment.
decampar, v.i. to decamp, to break camp.
decanado, s.m. deanery, deanship, decanate.
decania, s.f. deanship.
decano, s.m. dean, senior (empr.).
decantação, s.f. decantation; decanting, separation (por decantação), pouring off.
decantado, adj. sung, belauded, celebrated; decanted.

decantar, v.t. to celebrate, to praise; to decant, to pour out.
decapitação, s.f. decapitation; beheading.
decapitar, v.t. to decapitate; to behead.
decassílabo, s.m. decasyllable.
decastere, s.m. decastere.
decenal, adj. decennial; plano decenal, ten--year plan.
decência, s.f. decency, modesty; propriety; decorum; neatness.
decénio, s.m. decennium, period of ten years.
decente, adj. decent, proper, modest, moderate, respectable, passable, honest, fair; convenient, suitable, befitting; clean, tidy.
decentemente, adv. decently.
decentralização, s.f. v. descentralização.
decentralizar, v.t. v. descentralizar.
decenvirato, s.m. decemvirate.
decênviro, s.m. decemvir.
decepado, adj. cut off; maimed.
decepamento, s.m. cutting off, amputation, severance.
decepar, v.t. to mutilate; to cut off, to amputate, to sever.
decepção, s.f. deception; disappointment, desillusion, disenchantment, let-down.
decepcionante, adj. disappointing.
decepcionar, v.t. to disappoint, to surprise.
decerto, adv. assuredly, surely, certainly.
decididamente, adv. decidedly.
decidido, adj. decided, determined, resolute, bold; settled (um negócio).
decidir, v.t. to decide; to determine; to settle; to convince, to persuade; decidir-se, to make up one's mind.
decifração, s.f. deciphering; decipherment.
decifrador, s.m. decipherer.
decifrar, v.t. to decipher; to explain; to discover; to detect; to interpret; to guess.
decifrável, adj. decipherable.
decigrama, s.m. decigramme, decigram.
decilitro, s.m. decilitre.
décima, s.f. tithe, the 10th part; stanza (de dez versos); decimal fraction; tax, tribute.
decimal, adj. decimal.
decímetro, s.m. decimetre.
décimo, adj. tenth, tenth part; em décimo lugar, in tenth place.
decisão, s.f. decision, resolution; conclusion; judgement, veredict; firmness, courage.
decisivamente, adv. decisively.

decisivo, *adj.* decisive; conclusive, final; clear, evident; positive, final.

decistere, *s.m.* decistere.

declamação, *s.f.* declamation; oratory; speech; recitation; empty talk.

declamador, *s.m.* declaimer; reciter.

declamar, *v.t., v.i.* to declaim; to recite; to inveigh.

declamativo, declamatório, *adj.* declamatory.

declaração, *s.f.* declaration, affirmation, exposition; love-letter; statement; document; announcement; proclamation. 1) *declaração de amor,* a proposal. 2) *declaração de direitos,* bill of rights.

declaradamente, *adv.* declaredly; frankly, openly; *declaradamente inimigo,* sworn enemy.

declarado, *adj.* declared, open, clear, manifest, proved, obvious, evident; confessed, sworn.

declarador, dearante, *s.m., s., adj.* declarant, declaring.

declarar, *v.t.* to declare, to proclaim, to affirm, to assert, to state; to announce; to manifest; to confess, to admit; to appoint; to break out (*doença ou febre*). 1) *declarar-se a favor de,* to declare oneself for. 2) *declarar-se a uma senhora,* to propose to a lady.

declarativo, *adj.* declarative.

declaratório, *adj.* declaratory.

declinação, *s.f.* declination; decay; deviation; declension (*gram.*); inflection.

declinante, *adj.* declining; falling, sinking.

declinar, *v.t., v.i.* to decline; to avoid; to refuse; to decrease; to decay; to inflect; to deviate from; to sink, to fall; to mention (*nomes*).

declinatório, *adj.* declinatory.

declinável, *adj.* declinable.

declínio, *s.m.* decline, decadence, deterioration. decay.

declivar, *v.i.* to decline, to slope down, to incline; to render declivous.

declive, *s.m., adj.* declivity; slope; declivous; sloping.

declivoso, *adj.* declivous, sloping down.

decomponente, *adj.* decomposing.

decomponível, *adj.* decomposable.

decompor, *v.t.* to decompose; to decay; to rot; to resolve; to separate; to alter, to modify; to analyse.

decomposição, *s.f.* decomposition; altera-

tion, desintegration, putrefaction; analysis. 1) *decomposição da luz,* decomposition of light. 2) *decomposição das forças,* resolution of forces.

decoração, *s.f.* decoration, ornament; ornamentation.

decorado, *adj.* memorized; decorated.

decorador, *s.m.* decorator.

decorar, *v.t.* to decorate, to adorn; to learn by heart, to know by heart, to retain, to keep in mind, to memorize.

decorativo, *adj.* decorative, ornamental.

decoro, *s.m.* decorum; decency; propriety; seemliness.

decoroso, *adj.* decorous; decent; seemly, becoming, proper.

decorrente, *adj.* current, elapsing; resulting from; decurrent (*bot.*).

decorrer, *v.i.* to slide; to run away; to elapse; to pass; to happen, to occur; to derive, to originate from.

decorrido, *adj.* elapsed; run out.

decotado, *adj.* low-necked.

decotar, *v.t.* to prune; to top; to uncover one's breast, to cut low (*o decote de um vestido*).

decote, *s.m.* pruning; topping (*de árvores*); low neck.

decrépito, *adj.* decrepit; decayed; worn out; broken down, old, infirm, weak, feeble.

decrepidez, decrepitude, *s.f.* decrepitude, feebleness; infirmity, old age.

decrescença, *s.f.* decrease, lessening, diminution.

decrescente, *adj.* decreasing, decrescent.

decrescer, *v.i.* to decrease; to decay; to become less; to fail; to diminish; to decline; to subside.

decrescimento, *s.m.* decreasing; decrease; decay; lessening.

decréscimo, *s.m.* decrease, diminution.

decretal, *s.f.* decretal.

decretar, *v.t.* to decree; to determine; to order.

decreto, *s.m.* decree; edict; order; *nem por um decreto (pop.),* never, not on your life, on no account.

decúbito, *s.m.* decubitus; a lying position.

decumbente, *adj.* decumbent, reclining.

decuplicar, *v.t.* to decuple, to increase tenfold.

décuplo, *s.m., adj.* tenfold; decuple.

decúria, *s.f.* decury.

decurião, *s.m.* decurion.

decurso, *s.m., adj.* course; lapse (*de tempo*); continuation, succession; duration; passing, going by; elapsed; passed. 1) *no decurso do ano,* during the year. 2) *no decurso de,* in the course of.

dedada, *s.f.* finger-print, finger mark.

dedal, *s.m.* thimble; a small quantity.

dedaleira, *s.f.* fox-glove (*bot.*).

dédalo, *s.m.* labyrinth, maze; confusion, mess.

dedeira, *s.f.* finger-stall.

dedicação, *s.f.* devotion; affection, fondness; dedication; faithfulness; self-abandonment.

dedicado, *adj.* dedicated, devoted; zealous.

dedicar, *v.t.* to dedicate; to devote, to consecrate; to offer. 1) *dedicar-se a,* to apply oneself to, to sacrifice oneself for; to follow (*o mar, a lei, uma carreira*). 2) *dedicar-se aos estudos,* to take study. 3) *dedicar-se de corpo e alma,* to put one's back into.

dedicatória, *s.f.* dedication, inscription.

dedignar-se, *v. refl.* to decline, to refuse, to disdain; to deign, to condescend.

dedilhação, *s.f.* fingering.

dedilhar, *v.t.* to finger (*um instrumento musical*); to mark (*uma partitura*).

dedo, *s.m.* finger. 1) *dedo anelar,* ring finger. 2) *dedo do pé,* toe. 3) *dedo indicador,* forefinger. 4) *dedo médio,* middle finger. 5) *dedo mínimo (mindinho),* little finger. 6) *dedo polegar,* thumb. 7) *ter dedo para,* to be good at, to have skill.

dedução, *s.f.* deduction, inference; abatement, subtraction.

dedutivo, *adj.* deductive, inferential.

deduzir, *v.t.* to deduce; to infer; to deduct, to subtract; to draw as a conclusion.

de facto, *loc. adv.* in fact; actually.

defecação, *s.f.* defecation; purification.

defecar, *v.t.* to defecate, to purify, to rifine (*açúcar*); to clarify (*sumo*).

defecatório, *s.f.* defecating; purifying.

defecção, *a.f.* defection, desertion; apostasy.

defectibilidade, *s.f.* defectibility.

defectível, *adj.* defectible.

defectivo, *adj.* defective, faulty; incomplete, imperfect, deficient.

defeito, *s.m.* defect; fault; failure; imperfection, deficiency; deformity, stain, vice; shortcoming. 1) *todos temos defeitos,* everybody has his shortcomings. 2) *pôr defeitos em,* to find fault with, to impute faults to.

defeituosamente, *adv.* defectively; faultily.

defeituoso, *adj.* defective, faulty, imperfect, marred; incomplete.

defender, *v.t.* to defend, to guard, to protect, to forbid, to prohibir (*entrada*); to shield, to shelter; to resist, to withstand. 1) *defender com unhas e dentes,* to fight tooth and nail. 2) *defender tese,* to maintain or substantiate a thesis.

defenestração, *s.f.* defenestration.

defensável, *adj.* defensible; defendable.

defensiva, *s.f.* defensive, position of defense; *estar na defensiva,* to be on the defensive.

defensivo, *adj.* defensive; protective.

defensor, *s.m.* defender; defendant, protector, upholder; defensor (*jur.*).

defensório, *adj.* defensive, defensory.

deferência, *s.f.* deference, respect, regard, esteem, compliance; *por deferência para com,* out of deference (respect) to.

deferente, *adj.* deferential, complying, respectful.

deferimento, *s.m.* grant, concession; *pedir deferimento,* to ask for granting.

deferir, *v.t.* to confer, to grant, to bestow, to concede, to approve.

deferível, *adj.* grantable, approvable.

defesa, *s.f.* defense; defence; protection; prohibition; tusk (*de um animal*); justification; defender (*jur.*); guard, safeguard; the defensive players (*futebol*). 1) *em legítima (própria) defesa,* in self-defense. 2) *sem defesa,* defenseless.

defeso, *adj., s.m.* prohibited, forbidden; closed season (*para caçar*).

defesso, *adj.* fatigued; weary, tired.

défice, *s.m.* deficit, shortage.

deficiência, *s.f.* deficiency; lack; insufficiency, want, need; shortage; imperfection.

deficiente, *adj.* deficient; defective; wanting, faulty, imperfect.

deficitário, *adj.* deficient, giving deficit, affording loss.

definhado, *adj.* decayed, sickly, meager, thin, weak, feeble, wasted.

definhamento, *s.m.* decay; wasting, emaciation.

definhar, *v.i.* to waste; to pine away; to grow lean; to weaken; to emaciate; to languish; to dry out, to whither.

definição, *s.f.* definition, definement; decision, determination (*daquilo que se tem dúvida*).

definido, *adj.* definite; determined, determinate, limited, fixed, distinct; positive.

definidor, *s.m., adj.* definer; definning.

definir, *v.t.* to define; to limit; to explain; to mark out; to fix, to determine, to decide.

definitivamente, *adv.* definitively, conclusively.

definitivo, *adj.* definitive; conclusive; decisive; real; *resposta definitiva,* definite answer.

definível, *adj.* definable, determinable.

deflação, *s.f.* deflation (*dinheiro*).

deflacionista, *adj.* deflationary.

deflagração, *s.f.* deflagration, outburst (*de guerra*).

deflagrar, *v.i.* deflagrate; to burn, to explode; to infame, to excite; to break out (*guerra*).

deflectir, *v.t.* to deflect.

deflexão, *s.f.* deflexion, deviation.

defluir, *v.i.* to flow down; to emanate from, to issue.

defluxão, *s.f.* defluxion, cold.

defluxo, *s.m.* defluxion; cold, nasal discharge.

deformação, *s.f.* deformation, disfigurement, distortion; perversion; deformity.

deformador, *s.m., adj.* deformer; deforming.

deformar, *v.t.* to deform; to disfigure; to distort; to misrepresent; to become deformed.

deformidade, *s.f.* deformity; malformation, disfigurement; distortion.

defraudação, *s.f.* defraudation, cheating, embezzlement.

defraudador, *s.m., adj.* defrauder, cheater; defrauding, cheating.

defraudamento, *s.m.* defrauding; defraudment.

defraudar, *v.t.* to defraud, to cheat; to embezzle; to deprive of; to rook, to dupe, to swindle.

defrontação, *s.f.* confrontation, facing.

defrontar, *v.t., v.i.* to face, to confront, to stand facing; to meet, to encounter; to come face to face.

defronte, *adv.* opposite to, before, in front of, face to face, facing.

defumação, *s.f.* smoking, curing (*alguns alimentos*).

defumado, *adj.* cured, smoke-dried.

defumador, *s.m., adj.* smoker; smokecuring.

defumadouro, *s.m.* smoker; smoking place, smoke-house.

defumadura, *s.f.* smoking, curing.

defumar, *v.t.* to smoke-cure, to smoke-dry, to cure with smoke (*alguns alimentos*)

defunção, *s.f.* decease; death.

defunto, *s.m., adj.* deceased; late; dead; defunct, dead person; *gastar cera com ruim defunto,* to send good money after bad.

degelar, *v.i.* to thaw; breaking up (*do gelo*); thawing.

degeneração, *s.f.* degeneration, debasement; degradation.

degenerado, *adj.* degenerate, corrupted, degraded, sunk, perverted.

degenerar, *v.i.* to degenerate; to grow worse, to fall off; to decline; to become corrupt.

degenerescência, *s.f.* degeneration; degeneracy.

degenerescente, *adj.* degenerating.

deglutição, *s.f.* deglutition, swallowing.

deglutir, *v.t.* swallow.

degola, degolação, degoladura, *s.f.* beheading, decollation, decapitation, throatcutting.

degolador, *s.m.* beheader; throatcutter

degolar, *v.t.* to behead, to decollate, to decapitate, to cut the throat of.

degradação, *s.f.* degradation; degeneracy; debasement, decay; dishonour; deterioration.

degradado, *adj.* degraded.

degradamento, *s.m.* degradation, deposition, demotion.

degradante, *adj.* degrading, debasing; shameful.

degradar, *v.t.* to degrade; to deprive; to lessen; to debase, to dishonour, to discredit; to depose.

degrau, *s.m.* step; degree (*de progresso*), stair step; rung.

degredado, *s.m., adj.* convict, deportee, exilé, outcast; banished; exiled, expatriated.

degredar, *v.t.* to banish, to exile, to expatriate, to deport.

degredo, *s.m.* banishment; exile, expatriation, deportation; place of exile.

degustação, *s.f.* tasting, degustation.

degustar, *v.t.* to taste, to degust.

deicida, *s.m., adj.* deicide; deicidal.

deicídio, *s.m.* deicide.

deidade, *s.f.* deity; goddess; woman of great beauty.

deificação, *s.f.* deification.

deificador, *s.m., adj.* deifier; deifying.

deificar, *v.t.* to deify.

deiscência, s.f. dehiscence.
deiscente, adj. dehiscent.
deísmo, s.m. deism.
deísta, s. deist.
deitado, adj. lying, streched out; in bed.
deitar, v.t. to lay, to put (down); to pour; to throw; to produce; to cast; to put to bed, to lie down; to spill, to shed (líquido) to exhale, to emit. 1) deitar-se, to lie down; to go to bed; to fall upon, to attack. 2) deitar abaixo, to pull down, to demolish, to destroy. 3) deitar a fugir, to start running, to take to one's heels. 4) deitar água no mar, to carry coals to Newcastle. 5) deitar a mão, to lay hands on, to seize; to help. 6) deitar âncora, to cast anchor. 7) deitar à margem, to cast aside. 8) deitar a perder, to impair, to cause the ruin of, to spoil. 9) deitar cartas, to tell fortunes with cards. 10) deitar fora, to throw away (out). 11) deitar lenha no fogo, to add fuel to the flames. 12) deitar poeira nos olhos, to throw dust in the eyes. 13) deitar raízes, to take roots. 14) deitar sortes, to cast lots. 15)deitar uma criança, to put a child to bed. 16) deitar uma galinha, to set a hen.
deixa, s.f. legacy; cue (no teatro); hint.
deixá-lo, interj. it is all the same.
deixar, v.t. to leave; to let; to permit, to allow; to give up; to forsake; to let alone; to overlook, not to mention; to interrupt; to omit; to leave by will; to desist from; to cease to be. 1) deixar a vida, to leave this life, to die. 2) deixar cair, to drop, to let fall. 3) deixar correr, to let it be, to pay no attention to. 4) deixar de fumar, to give up (to stop) smoking. 5) deixar fugir uma oportunidade, to miss an opportunity. 6) deixar em paz, to let alone (in peace). 7) deixar para outro dia, to put off to another day. 8) deixar muito a desejar, to be quite unsatisfactory. 9) deixar um emprego, to quit a job. 10) deixe-se de conversa, cut the cackle. 11) deixe-se disso, give it a miss. 12) deixa estar!, just wait and see!. 13) deixe-se de tolices, stop being silly, don't be a sucker. 14) deixe isso comigo, leave it to me, that is my business. 15) não deixar de, not to fail to. 16) não posso deixar de (ler, rir, pensar), I can't help (reading, laughing, thinking), I can't but (read, laugh, think), I must not fail to.
dejecção, s.f. dejection, evacuation, defecation.

dejecto, s.m. dejection, defecation; excrements, feces.
dejejua, s.f. first breakfast.
dejejuar, v.t. to break one's fast.
dela, cont. prep. pron. of her; from her; her; hers; from it; its.
delação, s.f. delation, accusation; denouncement, denunciation.
delamber-se, v. refl. to rejoice, to delight; to affect; to purr with selfsatisfaction.
delambido, adj., s.m. affected; prudish; prude, dandy, fop.
delapidação, s.f. dilapidation.
delapidar, v.t. to dilapidate; to ruin; to misappropriate.
delatar, v.t. to delate; to accuse; to denounce; to inform against.
delator, s.m. delator, informer, denouncer.
dele, prep. pron. of him, from him, his, from his, of his. 1) a culpa foi dele, it was his fault, the fault was his. 2) ela estava diante dele, she was before him.
delegação, s.f. delegation; delegacy.
delegacia, s.f. delegateship, commissionership.
delegado, s.m. delegate, agent, commissioner; representative, deputy.
delegante, s.m., adj. constituent; delegating, assigning, appointing.
delegar, v.t. to delegate; to commit to, to depute; to assign, to appoint; to entrust, to charge.
deleitação, deleitamento, s.f., s.m. delectation; joy; pleasure, delight, enjoyment.
deleitante, adj. delightful, pleasing, enrapturing.
deleitar, v.t. to delight, to please, to gratify, to enchant, to transport; deleitar-se, to be delighted, to rejoice, to take pleasure (in).
deleitável, adj. delectable; pleasant, delightful.
deleite, s.m. delight, pleasure, enjoyment.
deleitosamente, adv. delightfully.
deleitoso, adj. delightful, charming, delectable.
deletério, adj. deleterious; poisonous, injurious, noxious, harmful.
deletrear, v.t. to spell; to read poorly, with difficulty.
delével, adj. delible.
délfico, adj. Delphic, Delphian.
delfim, s.m. (zool.) dolphim; dauphin (em França); bishop (xadrez).

delgadeza, *s.f.* thinness, slenderness, slimness.

delgado, *adj.* thin; slender; small; slight; lean; delicate.

deliberação, *s.f.* deliberation, consideration; decision, resolution.

deliberadamente, *adv.* deliberately, purposely, resolutely, intentionally.

deliberado, *adj.* deliberate, intentional, studied, premeditated, willful.

deliberante, *adj., s.* deliberating; deliberator.

deliberar, *v.t., v.i.* to deliberate, to determine, to decide, to ponder; to reflect upon; to resolve; to consider.

deliberativo, *adj.* deliberative.

delicadamente, *adv.* delicately, kindly, courteously, politely.

delicadeza, *s.f.* delicacy, fineness, kindness; fragility; subtility, sensitivity; susceptibility.

delicado, *adj.* delicate, kind, polite; tender; courteous; feeble, weak; fragile, frail; fine; smooth; subtile.

delícia, *s.f.* delight, pleasure, joy, charm. *é uma delícia*, it is delicious.

deliciar, *v.t.* to delight, to please, to charm, to gratify, to enchant; *deliciar-se*, to be pleased, to have pleasure in, to enjoy, to be delighted.

deliciosamente, *adv.* deliciously, delight-fully.

delicioso, *adj.* delicious, lovely, delightful, dainty; entrancing.

delimitação, *s.f.* delimitation, demarcation.

delimitador, *adj., s.m.* limiting, delimitative; delimiter.

delimitar, *v.t.* to delimit; to mark out, to delimitate, to bound; to restrict, to circumscribe.

delineação, *s.f.* delineation; sketch.

delineador, *s.m., adj.* delineator, sketcher; limiting; outlining.

delineamento, *s.m.* delineation; sketch, drawing, outlining, plan.

delinear, *v.t.* to delineate; to trace, to draw, to outline, to sketch out, to design; to describe, to represent; to plan; to delimit, to demarcate; to plot (*num mapa*); to lay out (*estratégia*).

delinquência, *s.f.* delinquency; guilt; fault, transgression.

delinquente, *s.m., adj.* delinquent, offender, criminal, transgressor, miscreant.

delinquir, *v.i.* to transgress (*a lei*), to be delinquent.

deliquescência, *s.f.* deliquescence.

deliquescente, *adj.* deliquescent; diffluent.

delíquio, *s.m.* fainting; faintness; deliquium.

delir, *v.t.* to liquefy; to dissolve, to melt; to wipe out; to efface, to erase, to blot out.

delirante, *adj.* delirious, raving, ecstatic, excited; insane, lightheaded; overjoyed.

delirar, *v.i.* to rave; to be delirious, to talk nonsense; ro rage, to rant; to be overjoyed or very happy.

delírio, *s.m.* delirium; enthusiasm; ecstasy; derangemente, insanity, frenzy.

delito, *s.m.* delict; offence; fault; crime, violation of law, trespass. 1) *corpo de delito*, corpus delicti. 2) *em flagrante delito*, in the very act.

delituoso, *adj.* wrong, criminal, punishable; involving crime.

delonga, *s.f.* delay, postponement, deferment; *sem mais delongas*, without further delay.

delongar, *v.t.* to delay, to defer, to prolong, to tarry; to put off; to retard.

delta, *s.m.* delta.

deltóide, *adj.* deltoid.

demagogia, *s.f.* demagogy, demagogism.

demagógico, *adj.* demagogic.

demagogo, *s.m.* demagogue, political agitator.

demais, *adv.* besides, moreover. 1) *o demais*, the rest (of it). 2) *os demais*, the rest (of them).

de mais, *loc. adv.* too; too much, excessively, more than enough, overmuch. 1) *aquecer, beber, comer, dormir, estudar, falar, ferver, ser zeloso, trabalhar de mais*, to over heat, to overdrink, to overeat, to overtrust, to oversleep, to overstudy, to overspeak, to overboil, to be overzealous, to overwork. 2) *isso é de mais*, that is too much, that is the limit, that takes the cake, that beats the Dutch. 3) *dois é bom, três é de mais*, two is company, three is a crowd. 4) *levar longe de mais*, to go too far. 5) *o que é de mais faz mal*, enough is as good as a feast.

demanda, *s.f.* lawsuit, plea, court action, prosecution; contest; dispute. 1) *em demanda de*, in search of. 2) *andar em demanda*, to be at law. 3) *ganhar a demanda*, to gain one's cause.

demandante, *s., adj.* demandant, litigant, plaintiff; pleading, demanding.

demandar, *v.t.* to demand; to sue at law; to

claim; to want; to go in search of; to require, to call for; to prosecute; to question, to dispute.

demandista, s. litigant, plaintiff, demandant.

demão, s.f. coat, coating, layer (de tinta); assistance; help; última demão, paint finish, final coat, finishing touch.

demarcação, s.f. demarcation; boundary; limit.

demarcado, adj. limited.

demarcador, s.m., adj. demarcator; demarcating, delimiting.

demarcar, v.t. to mark, to limit, to demarcate, to line off, to fix the boundaries of; to separate.

demarcativo, adj. serving to demarcate; denotative.

demarcável, adj. definable, determinable.

demasia, s.f. superfluity, surplus, excess, superabundance; remainder; intemperance; abuse; em demasia, in excess.

demasiadamente, adv. excessively, too much.

demasiado, adj., adv. excessive, excessively, overmuch, too much; superfluous, superabundant; immoderate; exaggerated.

demência, s.f. insanity, madness, dementia; craziness.

dementar, v.t. to madden, to craze, to drive to madness, to make insane.

demente, adj. mad; insane, crazy, lunatic.

demérito, s.m. demerit, unworthiness, want of merit.

demissão, s.f. dismissal; resignation, removal (de um emprego), abdication. 1) pedido de demissão, formal resignation. 2) pedir a demissão, to tender or to sen in one's resignation.

demissionário, s.m. resigner.

demissório, adj. demissory.

demitir, v.t. to dismiss, to send away; to discharge, to fire (emprego); to renounce (direitos); demitir-se, to resign.

demo, s.m. devil, demon.

democracia, s.f. democracy.

democrata, s. democrat.

democraticamente, adv. democratically.

democrático, adj. democratic.

democratismo, s.m. democratism.

democratização, s.f. democratization; democratizing.

democratizar, v.t. to democratize; to popularize.

demografia, s.f. demography.

demográfico, adj. demographic.

demolha, s.f. soaking (na água)

demolhar, v.t. to soak; to steep (na água).

demolição, s.f. demolition, demolishment, destruction.

demolidor, s.m., adj. demolisher, destroyer; demolishing, destroying.

demolir, v.t. to demolish, to throw down; to ruin, to raze, to destroy; to tear down (um prédio).

demoníaco, adj. demoniac, devilish; diabolical.

demónio, s.m. demon, devil; evil spirit; wicked person.

demonismo, s.m. demonism.

demonista, s. demonist.

demonografia, s.f. demonography.

demonólatra, s. demon worshipper.

demonolatria, s.f. demonolatry.

demonologia, s.f. demonology.

demonstrabilidade, s.f. demonstrability.

demonstração, s.f. proof; demonstration; show; evidence; manifestation, exhibition; exposition.

demonstrador, adj., s.m. demonstrative; demonstrator.

demonstrar, v.t. to demonstrate; to exhibit; to prove; to explain by examples; to gove evidence of; to manifest; to make a demonstration; ele demonstrou que era bom aluno, he proved himself a good student.

demonstrativo, adj. demonstrative; proving, evincing; illustrative.

demonstrável, adj. demonstrable.

demora, s.f. delay, retardation; deferment; long wait; postponement; lingering; sem demora, at once.

demorado, adj. long lasting, slow; tardy; dilatory.

demorar, v.t., v.i. to delay; to retard; to differ; to stay; to dwell; to abide. 1) demorar a partir, to be long in leaving. 2) demorar em chegar, to be long in arriving. 3) demorar-se muito, to be late.

demover, v.t. to remove; to dissuade; to displace; to discourage.

demudar, v.t. to changre, to alter (face).

denegação, s.f. denial, denying, refusal, rejection (de um pedido), disavowal.

denegar, v.t. to deny, to refuse; to disown, to abjure, to disavow; to contradict, to refute.

denegrido, adj. blackened; soiled; denigrated.

denegridor, *s.m., adj.* denigrator; defamer, slanderer; denigrating; defamatory, slanderous.

denegrir, *v.t.* to blacken; to stain; to soil; to denigrate; to defame, to slander.

dengoso, *adj.* affected, prudish, finical, effeminate, over-nice, goody-goody.

dengue, *s.m., adj.* prudery, primness; affected, finical; effeminate.

denguice, *s.f.* affectation; coyness, prudery; coquetry.

denodadamente, *adv.* resolutely, boldly.

denodado, *adj.* resolute, intrepid, brave, bold, daring, dauntless, courageous; valiant, stout.

denodo, *s.m.* intrepidity, boldness, bravery, courage; high devotion (*a uma causa*).

denominação, *s.f.* denomination, name, designation.

denominado, *adj.* so-called.

denominador, *s.m.* denominator; *denominador comum,* common denominator.

denominar, *v.t.* to denominate, to name, to call, to designate, to entitle.

denominativo, *adj.* denominative.

denotação, *s.f.* denotation; sign.

denotador, *adj.* denotative.

denotar, *v.t.* to denote, to indicate, to show, to point out; to signify, to mean, to symbolize.

densidade, *s.f.* density; thickness; compactness; *densidade da corrente, demográfica, magnética,* current density, density of population, field strength.

densímetro, *s.m.* densimeter.

denso, *adj.* dense, compact, thick, condensed.

dentada, *s.f.* bite, biting; morsel; biting remark.

dentado, *adj.* toothed; dentate, dentated; serrulate cogged; *roda dentada,* cogwheel, toothed wheel.

dentadura, *s.f.* set of teeth, denture, false teeth.

dental, *adj.* dental

dentalgia, *s.f.* toothache.

dentar, *v.t.* to indent, to engrail; to provide with teeth.

dentário, *adj.* dental.

dente, *s.m.* tooth; fang, tusk (*animal*); cog, gear tooth (*roda*); prong, tine (*forquilha*). 1) *dente canino,* canine tooth. 2) *dente de leite,* milk tooth. 3) *dente de serra,* saw tooth. 4) *dento do siso,* wisdom tooth. 5)

dente incisivo, incisor. 6) *dente molar,* molar, grinder. 7) *dente saliente,* bucktooth. 8) *dente postiço,* false tooth. 9) *dente por dente,* a tooth for a tooth, tit for at. 10) *a cavalo dado não se olha o dente,* one does not look a gift horse in the mouth. 11) *armado até aos dentes,* armed to the teeth. 12) *arrancar um dente,* to have a tooth pulled. 13) *arreganhar os dentes,* to bare the teeth. 14) *com unhas e dentes,* tooth and nail. 15) *dar com a língua nos dentes,* to blab, to spill the beans, to let the cat out of the bag. 16) *obturar um dente,* to fill a tooth, to have a tooth filled. 17) *dor de dentes,* toothache. 18) *falar entre dentes,* to mutter, to mumble, to growl. 19) *olho por olho, dente por dente,* an eye for an eye, a tooth for a tooth.

denteação, *s.f.* dentition; indentation, denting.

denteado, *adj.* indented, jagged, notched; dentate (*bot.*).

dentear, *v.t.* to indent; to tooth to notch, to engrail, to jag.

dentição, *s.f.* dentition; teething.

denticulado, *adj.* denticulated, indented.

denticular, *v.t., adj.* to indent, to notch, to jag, to tooth; denticular, indented.

dentículo, *s.m.* denticule, dentice; dentate leaf margin (*bot.*).

dentificação, *s.f.* dentification.

dentiforme, *adj.* dentiform, toothshaped.

dentifrício, *s.m.* dentifrice; tooth powder, tooth paste.

dentífrico, *adj.* tooth-cleaning.

dentista, *s.* dentist, dental surgeon.

dentre, *prep.* among, amongst, in the midst of; from among.

dentuça, *s.f.* buckteeth.

dentro, *adv.* within; in; inside. 1) *dentro de alguns minutos,* within a few minutes. 2) *dentro em breve,* soon, before long, within a short time. 3) *dentro de casa,* indoors. 4) *aqui dentro,* in here. 5) *de dentro,* from within. 6) *por dentro,* inside. 7) *já para dentro!,* in with you!.

dentudo, *adj.* big-toothed.

denudação, *s.f.* denudation, divestment.

denudar, *v.t.* to denude, to make naked, to divest, to lay bare, to undress, to take off the clothes.

denúncia, denunciação, *s.f.* denunciation, denouncement, accusation, delation; revelation; indictment (*lei*).

denunciante, *adj., s.* denunciatory, informer, denouncer, delator, accuser.

denunciar, *v.t.* to denounce, to denunciate, to accuse; to censure, to informe against; to betray; to reveal; to indict (*lei*); to give notice of termination of (*tratado*); to bring to light.

denunciativo, denunciatório, *adj.* denunciative, denunciatory.

denunciável, *adj.* denounciable.

deontologia, *s.f.* deontology.

deontológico, *adj.* deontological.

deparar, *v.t., v.i.* to cause to appear; to give; to meet, to find, to fall in with, to come upon; to come across, to stumble upon; to encounter.

departamental, *adj.* departmental.

departamento, *s.m.* department.

depauperação, depauperamento, *s.f., s.m.* depauperation; impoverishment; weakening.

depauperado, *adj.* depauperated.

depauperante, depauperador, *adj.* depauperating, pauperizing; enfeebling, debilitating, weakening.

depauperar, *v.t.* to depauperate; to impoverish, to pauperize; to enfeeble, to weaken, to deplete, to exhaust.

depenado, *adj.* deplumed, plucked; penniless, broke, picked clean (*dinheiro*).

depenar, *v.t.* to deplume, to pluck, to pick; to fleece, to skin, to strip (*dinheiro*).

dependência, *s.f.* dependence, subjection, subordination; room; dependency; annex (*de um prédio*).

dependente, *adj.* dependent; depending; to be conditioned on; to be pending.

depender, *v.i.* to depend on, to be dependent on (upon); to be conditioned (based) on; to be sublect (subordinate) to.

dependura, *s.f. estar à dependura*, to be on the rocks, to be broke, to be in a tight spot.

dependurado, *adj.* suspended; hanging, dangling.

dependurar, *v.t.* to suspend; to hang.

depenicar, *v.t.* to pluck at (*com bico ou com boca*); to preen; to nibble at.

deperecer, *v.i.* to decline, to languish, to fade away, to droop, to pine away.

deperecimento, *s.m.* languishment; withering.

depilação, *s.f.* depilation.

depilar, *v.t.* to depilate, to strip of hair.

depilatório, *s.m., adj.* depilatory.

deploração, *s.f.* deploration, lamentation, wail.

deplorar, *v.t.* to deplore, to grieve, to regret; to lament, to bemoan.

deplorativo, deploratório, *adj.* deploring, lamenting; pitiful; lamentable.

deplorável, *adj.* deplorable, lamentable; pitiable, pitiful; abominable; wretched.

deploravelmente, *adv.* deplorably, pitiably, detestably.

deplumar, *v.t.* to pluck, to deplume.

depoente, *adj., s.* deponent.

depoimento, *s.m.* evidence, testimony, deposition, affidavit; statement, declaration.

depois, *adv.* afterwards; next; later on; subsequently, then; besides, moreover. 1) *depois de amanhã*, the day after tomorrow. 2) *depois e não antes*, then and not till then. 3) *dois dias depois*, two days later.

depor, *v.t.* to lay down (*armas*), to set aside, to put down; to depose, to deprive of, to discharge, to dethrone; to testify, to depone, to bear witness, to give evidence; to renounce, to give up, to surrender; to entrust to, to deposit.

deportação, *s.f.* deportation, exile, banishment, expatriation.

deportado, *adj., s.m.* banished, exiled, expatriated; deportee.

deportar, *v.t.* to deport, to banish, to exile, to expatriate.

deposição, *s.f.* deposition, displacement, deposal, dismissal.

depositador, depositante, *s.m., s.* depositor.

depositar, *v.t.* to deposit; to entrust, to lodge with (for safekeeping); to trust, to rely upon. 1) *depositar confiança em*, to place confidence in. 2) *depositar no banco*, to bank.

depositário, *s.m.* depositary, trustee.

depósito, *s.m.* deposit; trust; sediment; pledge, security; storehouse, store, warehouse, depot; reservoir, tank. 1) *depósito de abastecimentos*, supply dump. 2) *depósito de água*, water reservoir. 3) *Caixa-Geral de Depósitos*, Public Savings Bank.

deposto, *adj.* deposed, dismissed, dethroned.

depravação, *s.f.* depravation, corruption, depravity, perversion; turpitude.

depravado, *adj.* depraved, corrupt, wicked, vicious, degenerate.

depravador, *s.m.*, *adj.* depraver, corrupter, defiler; depraving, corrupting, demoralizing.

depravar, *v.t.* to deprave, to corrupt, to vitiate, to pervert; *depravar-se*, to degenerate, to become depraved.

deprecação, *s.f.* deprecation, plea, prayer, entreaty petition.

deprecada, *s.f.* requisition.

deprecar, *v.t.* to implore, to beseech, to suplicate, to entreat; to invoke.

deprecativo, deprecatório, *adj.* deprecatory, deprecative, supplicating, entreating.

depreciação, *s.f.* depreciation; contempt, disparagement, detraction.

depreciador, *s.m.*, *adj.* scorner, depreciator, disparager; depreciating, depreciative, depreciant.

depreciar, *v.t.* to depreciate, to belittle, to decry, to undervalue, to debase, to lower in value, to disparage; to underestimate.

depreciativo, *adj.* depreciative.

depredação, *s.f.* depredation, pillaging, spoliation, brigandage, pillage, plunder.

depredar, *v.t.* to plunder, to despoil, to depredate, to laywaste.

depredatório, *adj.* depredatory, plundering, rapacious.

depreender, *v.t.* to conceive, to perceive, to deduce, to infer, to gather, to conclude.

depressa, *adv.* quickly, fast, swiftly, readily, speedily; hastily; *depressa!*, hurry up!, make haste!

depressão, *s.f.* depression (*em todos os sentidos*); abasement; hollow, cavity, pit; stagnation or reduction (*negócio*); dejection, despondency, low-spiritedness, the dumps, the blues.

depressivo, *adj.* depressive, depressing.

depressor, *s.m.*, *adj.* depressor, depressive, depressing.

deprimente, *adj.* depressing; humiliating, debasing, degrading; discouraging.

deprimido, *adj.* depressed, dejected, dispirited, downcast, low-spirited; heartsick.

deprimir, *v.t.* to depress, to abase; to sink; to lower, to depreciate, to disparage; to enfeeble, to weaken; to deject, to sadden, to dispirit.

depuração, depuramento, *s.f.*, *s.m.* depuration; cleansing; purification, expurgation.

depurador, depurante, *s.m.*, *adj.* depurator, purifying, depurant.

depurar, *v.t.* to depurate, to purify, to cleanse.

depurativo, *adj.*, *s.m.* depurative.

deputação, *s.f.* deputation, delegation.

deputado, *s.m.* deputy, delegate, representative, commissioner, agent; *Câmara dos Deputados*, Chamber of Deputies, House of Representatives.

deputar, *v.t.* to depute, to commit, to delegate.

de repente, *loc. adv.* suddenly, all of a sudden.

derisão, *s.f.* derision, mockery.

derisório, *adj.* derisive; scoffing.

deriva, à deriva, *s.f.* adrift; *andar à deriva*, to drift, to float along.

derivação, *s.f.* derivation; deviation, shift, drift; origin, source; (*elect.*) shunt, branch conductor.

derivada, *s.f.* (*mat.*) derivative.

derivado, *adj.*, *s.m.* derived; derivative, by-product.

derivante, *adj.*, *s.m.* derivational.

derivar, *v.t.* to derive, to proceed from; to deviate; to derive (*palavras*); to turn the course of (*corda*); to switch, to shunt, to branch off; to run, to flow; to originate from, to arise from, to descend.

derivativo, *adj.* derivative, revulsive; deversion, occupation, amusement, pastime.

derivável, *adj.* derivable.

dermatite, *s.f.* dermatitis.

dermatologia, *s.f.* dermatology.

dermatológico, *adj.* dermatologic.

dermatologista, *s.* dermatologist.

dermatose, *s.f.* dermatosis.

derme, *s.f.* skin, derma, dermis, cutis.

dérmico, *adj.* dermic, dermal.

dermóide, *adj.* dermoid, dermatoid.

derrabado, *adj.* docked, bobtailed.

derrabar, *v.t.* to dock, to bobtail, to cut off the tail.

derradeiro, *adj.* last, final, conclusive, ultimate.

derrama, *s.f.* local tax, levy; lopping, pruning (of branches).

derramado, *adj.* shed, spread.

derramamento, derrame, *s.m.* scattering, effusion, dispersion; overflowing, shedding; dissemination; lopping pruning (of trees). 1) *derramamento cerebral*, brain hemorrhage. 2) *derramento de sangue*, bloodshed.

derramar, *v.t.* to scatter, to spread; to disperse, to pour out, to diffuse, to shed (*água, lágrimas, sangue*); to disseminate; to distribute; to prune (*árvores*).

derrancado, *adj.* corrupted, depraved; ruined.

derrancamento, *s.m.* corruption; putrescence.

derrancar, *v.t.* to deprave; to spoil, to mar, to deteriorate; to corrupt, to pervert; to grow rancid; to ruin.

derrapagem, *s.f.* skidding, sideslip.

derrapar, *v.i.* to skid, to sideslip.

derreado, *adj.* broken-backed, bowed down, worn out, done in.

derreamento, *s.m.* exhaustion, prostration.

derrear, *v.t.* to exhaust, to wear out; to bend down, to stoop; to jade; to discredit.

derredor, *adv.* around, about.

derreter, *v.t.* to melt, to dissolve, to liquefy, to fuse; to soften, to make gentle; to become tenderhearted; to vex, to torment.

derretido, *adj.* melted, molten, drawn (*manteiga*); depely in love.

derretimento, *s.m.* melting, dissolution, liquefaction, fusion (*fig.*) affectation; tenderheartedness.

derribamento, *s.m.* demolition; destruction; knocking down.

derribar, *v.t.* to demolish; to throwdown, to knock down, to strike down, to cut down; to destroy.

derriçar, *v.t.* to disentangle; to untangle, to untwine; to banter; to wrangle; to quarrel, to contend; (*pop.*) to flirt, to court, to woo.

derriço, *s.m.* love-making; sweetheart; flirtation, dalliance, courtship.

derrocada, *s.f.* destruction; downfall, collapse, debacle, ruin.

derrocar, *v.t.* to demolish, to destroy, to ruin; to overthrow, to overturn; to abase, to subdue; to fall down, to cave in.

derrogação, *s.f.* annulling, derogation.

derrogador, *s.m.* annuller; derogator, detractor.

derrogante, *adj.* annulling, derogative (to or of).

derrogar, *v.t.* to annul (in part) to derogate; to suppress; to detract.

derrogatório, *adj.* annulling; derogatory.

derrota, defeat, rout; overthrow; beating; course (*percurso*).

derrotado, *adj.* routed, defeated, beaten; down and out; downcast, dispirited.

derrotador, *adj., s.m.* defeating; defeater.

derrotar, to defeat, rout; to beat, floor, worst discomfit, lick (*gír.*); to overthrow.

derrotismo, *s.m.* defeatism.

derrotista, *adj., s.* defeatist.

derrubamento, *s.m. v.* derribamento.

derrubar, *v.t. v.* derribar.

derrube, *s.m.* felling (*de árvores*).

derruir, to overthrow, demolish, pull down, destroy.

dervixe, *s.m.* dervish, fakir.

desabado, *adj.* slouch, with a slouched brim (*chapéu*).

desabafar, *v.t.* to free from obstructions; to air, ventilate; to clear, disentangle; to ease, losen (*a roupa*); to give vent to (*sentimentos*).

desabafo, *s.m.* relief, ease, disencumbering; free expression.

desabaladamente, *adv.* unmeasurably; precipitadely.

desabalado, *adj.* enormous, huge, immense, vast, unmeasurable; precipitate, hurried, rash, headlong.

desabalar, *v.t.* to run away rashly.

desabamento, *s.m.* crumbling, falling, collapse.

desabar, *v.t.* to pull down, to turn down; to crumble down, to fall down; to collapse, to topple.

desabitado, *adj.* uninhabited, unoccupied, empty; desert, secluded, solidariry.

desabitar, *v.t.* to disoccupy, to quit (*uma casa*).

desabituação, *s.f.* break of a habit, disaccustoming, disuse.

desabituado, *adj.* unaccustomed.

desabituar, *v.t.* to disaccustom (to do something); to wean (from a habit). 1) *desabituar-se,* to give up, to leave off. 2) *desabituar-se de,* to become disaccustomed to. 3) *desacostumar-se de fumar,* to break the smoking habit, to wean from smoking.

desabonado, *adj.* discredited, ill-reputed; penniless, destitute.

desabonador, *adj., s.m.* discreting; depreciator.

desabonar, *v.t.* to discredit, to disbelieve, to destroy the credit, to bring into descredit, to depreciate.

desabonatório, *adj.* discreditable, disgraceful, disreputable.

desabono, *s.m.* discredit; prejudice, harm,

damage; *falar em desabono de alguém*, to speak ill of somebody.

desabotoar, *v.t.* to unbutton, to lose the buttons; to unloosen; to unfold, to blow *(flores)*

desabridamente, *adv.* rudely, sharply, severely, unfriendly, violently.

desabrido, *adj.* rude, sharp, harsh; brusque, gruff; cross-grained; unfriendly; violent, severe; insolent; stormy *(tempestuoso)*; unbridled, unrestrained *(desenfreado)*.

desabrigado, *adj.* unsheltered, exposed, unprotected, open; abandoned, forsaken.

desabrigar, *v.t.* to uncover, to unshelter; to rob of shelter; *desabrigar-se*, to leave the shelter.

desabrimento, *s.m.* rudeness, sharpness; unclemency; bitterness, harshness, roughness; severety *(do tempo)*.

desabrochar, desabrolhar, *v.t.* to bloom, to blossom, to put forth; to unbutton, to unfasten, to unclasp.

desaçaimar, *v.t.* to unmuzzle, to remove the muzzle.

desacampar, *v.i.* to break camp.

desacatamento, *s.m.* disrespect, disregard, discourtesy; insolence; profanation.

desacatar, *v.t.* to disrespect, to disregard, to slight; to affront, to insult; to vex, to annoy.

desacato, *s.m.* disrespect, insolence, discourtesy; irreverence; contempt *(da autoridade)*.

desacauteladamente, *adv.* carelessly.

desacautelado, *adj.* careless, incautious, heedless, nigligent; improvident.

desacautelar-se, *v. refl.* to be improvident, to be careless; to be heedless.

desaceleração, *s.f.* deceleration.

desacelerar, *v.t.* to decelerate, to decrease speed, to slow down; to retard.

desacentuar, *v.t.* to take the accents away.

desacertadamente, *adv.* inconsiderately, wrongly, imprudently.

desacertado, *adj.* inconsiderate, wrong, imprudent, unwise, ill-advised.

desacertar, *v.i.* to be inconsiderate; to bungle; to miss, to err; to act imprudently; *desacertar o passo*, to break step.

desacerto, *s.m.* fault, mistake, error, blunder; nonsense.

desaclimatar, *v.t.* to unclimatize.

desacolchetar, *v.t.* to unhook, to unfasten a hook; to unclasp.

desacomodar, *v.t.* to displace, to disturb; to dislodge.

desacompanhado, *adj.* alone, unaccompanied, lonely, solitary, single.

desaconchegar, *v.t.* to discomfort, to disturb the comfort.

desaconselhar, *v.t.* to dissuade, to divert *(de um propósito)*; to advise against.

desaconselhável, *adj.* inadvisable.

desacordado, *adj.* unconscious, not aware.

desacordar, *v.t., v.i.* to render discordant; to disagree, to disaccord, to differ.

desacordo, *s.m.* disagreement; dissension; unfitness, dissent, difference, unconformity, disharmony; conflict; *estar em desacordo*, to be at variance.

desacoroçoamento, *s.m.* discouragement.

desacoroçoar, *v.t., v.i.* to discourage, to dishearten; to lose heart.

desacorrentar, *v.t.* to unchain, to unfetter, to free, to unfasten.

desacostumado, *adj.* unaccustomed; unusual, uncommon, non-habitual.

desacostumar, *v.t.* to dishabituate; *desacostumar-se*, to lose the habit of, to break off a habit; to leave off.

desacreditado, *adj.* discredited, disreputable.

desacreditar, *v.t.* to discredited, to slander, to disparage, to defame; *desacreditar-se*, to lose face, prestige, reputation.

desactualizado, *adj.* old, antiquated, antique, outmoded, outdate, out of date, obsolete; old-fashioned.

desactualizar, *v.t.* to outdate, to render antique, to fall in disuse.

desacumular, *v.t.* to unpile, to unstack.

desadorar, *v.t.* to detest, to hate; to disapprove.

desafectação, *s.f.* unaffectedness, frankness, simplicity.

desafectadamente, *adv.* unaffectedly.

desafectado, *adj.* unaffected, unsophisticated.

desafecto, *adj., s.m.* disaffected; rival, enemy.

desafeição, *s.f.* disaffection, dislike, aversion, antipathy; disinclination.

desafeiçoado, *adj.* disaffected; unfriendly, contrary, adverse.

desafeiçoar, *v.t.* to take a dislike to; *desafeiçoar-se*, to become disaffected.

desafeito, *adj.* unaccustomed.

desaferrar, *v.t.* to unhook, to unlose, to untie, to free; to dissuade; to weigh anchor.

desaferrolhar, *v.t.* to unbolt, to unlock.

desafiar, *v.t.* to defy, to challenge, to provoke, to dare, to tempt; to invite *(para um jogo)*.

desafinação, *s.f.* dissonance, disharmony, discord.

desafinado, *adj.* dissonant, discordant, out of tune, tuneless.

desafinar, *v.t.* to untune, to get out of tune, to discord, to sing or to play out of tune.

desafio, *s.m.* challenge, competition, match; provocation, defy; *aceitar o desafio*, to pick up the gauntlet, to take up the glove.

desafivelar, *v.t.* to unbuckle, to unclasp, to unfasten.

desafogadamente, adv. freely; at ease, easily.

desafogado, *adj.* easy; ample; cleared; free from cares.

desafogar, *v.t.* to ease; to clear; to relieve, to disencumber; to free from pain.

desafogo, *s.m.* relief, ease; release; abundance, wealth; space; *viver com desafogo*, to live at ease.

desafoguear, *v.t.* to cool, to refresh *(a cara)*.

desaforadamente, *adv.* impudently, insolently, rudely, abusively.

desaforado, *adj.* impudent, insolent, impertinent, rude, shameless, abusive.

desaforamento, *s.m.* exemption from ground-rent.

desaforar, *v.t.* to make insolent; to become insolent; to exempt from rent payment; to disfranchise; to renounce a privilege.

desaforo, *s.m.* insolence, impudence, impertinence; insult, outrage; shamelessness, brazeness; *que desaforo!*, what a creep!

desafortunado, *adj.* unlucky, luckless, unhappy, unfortunate.

desafreguesar, *v.t.* to take away customers.

desafronta, *s.f.* revenge, retaliation, requital; redress, amends.

desafrontamento, *s.m.* revenge, redress.

desafrontar, *v.t.* to revenge, to avenge, to retaliate; to requite, to repay; to replease, to free, to relieve; *desafrontar-se*, to take vengeance.

desagarrar, *v.t.* to detach, to unfix, to unloosen; to eradicate.

desagasalhado, *adj.* unsheltered, unhoused, roofless, homeless; insufficiently dresses.

desagasalhar, *v.t.* to clothe lightly, to uncover; to deprive of clothes or home; *desagasalhar-se*, to take off the warm clothes.

desagasalho, *s.m.* want of shelter, of clothing of welcome.

desagastar, *v.t.* to quiet down, to appease, to calm.

desagradar, *v.i.* to displease, to discontent, to dislike, to dissatisfy.

desagradável, *adj.* unpleasant, displeasing, disagreeable; ungracious; grating *(uma música)*; unpalatable *(ao paladar)*.

desagradavelmente, *adv.* disagreeably.

desagradecido, *adj.* ungrateful.

desagrado, *s.m.* displeasure; disagreeableness, distaste, dislike; disaproval; *cair em desagrado*, to lose someone's favour.

desagravar, *v.t.* to repair an affront; to relieve; to redress *(injúria)*; to avenge; to make amends to.

desagravo, *s.m.* reparation; satisfaction, redress, requital, retaliation.

desagregação, *s.f.* disaggregation, dissolution, disintegration; separation.

desagregar, *v.t.* to disaggregate; to break up; to dissolve, to separate, to disintegrate, to disunite; *desagregar-se*, to crumble, to decompose.

desagregável, *adj.* separable.

desagrilhoar, *v.t.* unfetter; to set free.

desaguadouro, *s.m.* ditch; drain.

desaguamento, *s.m.* drainage.

desaguar, *v.i.* to discharge, to flow into; to drain, to draw off.

desaguisado, *s.m.* dispute, quarrel, clash, conflict, wrangle.

desaire, *s.m.* inconvenience; taint; blemish; reverse, ill luck; gaucherie.

desairoso, *adj.* without grace; awkward, inelegant; graceless; inconvenient.

desajeitado, *adj.* awkard, clumsy, unskillful; left-handed, uncouth, fumbling.

desajeitar, *v.t.* to disfigure or to disarrange; to deform.

desajoujar, *v.t.* to unyoke, to unharness *(animais)*.

desajudado, *adj.* unhelped, unaided, unassisted; helpless.

desajuizado, *adj.* unwise; foolish; senseless, thoughtless.

desajuntar, *v.t.* disjoin, to separate, to disunite, to uncouple.

desajustamento, *s.m.* inadaptation, maladjustment.

desajustar, *v.t.* to separate; to break off; disadjust, to disarrange; to disunite.

desajuste, *s.m.* disagreemente, breaking of an agreement.

desalagar, *v.t.* to drain *(terra)*, to dry; to set afloat *(um barco)*.

desalastrar, *v.t.* to remove the ballast from.

desalbardar, *v.t.* to unsaddle, to take off (remove) the packsaddle.

desalentadamente, *adv.* despondently, without courage.

desalentado, *adj.* discouraged, depressed, dejected, downhearted.

desalentador, *adj.* discouraging, depressing, dejecting; gloomy.

desalentar, *v.t.* to discourage, to dishearten; to lose one's heart.

desalento, *s.m.* discouragement; despondency, disheartening; dejection; hopelessness.

desalgemar, *v.t.* to unshackle, to unfetter, to lose from shackles; to set free.

desalinhado, *adj.* sluttish; untidy; disheveled, disorderly, slipshod; careless, frowzy; out of line.

desalinhar, *v.t.* to put out of line; to disorder, to dishevel, to disarrange.

desalinhavar, *v.t.* to remove basting stitches from

desalinho, *s.m.* negligence, slovenliness, disorder, disarray, dishevelment, untidiness; carelessness, unkemptness; trouble, affliction.

desalmadamente, *adv.* cruelly, inhumanly.

desalmado, *adj.* inhuman, cruel, perverse, ruthless, merciless.

desalojamento, *s.m.* dislodgement, removal, dislodging.

desalojar, *v.t.* to dislodge, to drive out.

desalugado, *adj.* unoccupied (not rented).

desamarrar, *v.t.* to unbind, to lossen, to untie, to unfasten; to detach; to unmoor *(uma embarcação, etc.)*.

desamarrotar, *v.t.* to unwrinkle, to smooth.

desamassar, *v.i.* to smooth out.

desambientado, *adj.* strange, unadapted *(a um novo ambiente)*.

desamodorrar, *v.t.* to stir up, to quicken, to excite, to enliven.

desamolgar, *v.t.* to smooth out.

desamor, *s.m.* aversion, hatred, hate; disaffection, antipathy, unkindness.

desamorável, *adj.* unlovely, harsh, unkindly, disagreeable.

desamortalhar, *v.t.* to unshroud.

desamortizar, *s.f.* disentailing, exemption from entail.

desamortizável, *s.f.* disentailable.

desamparadamente, *adv.* forlornly, helplessly.

desamparado, *adj.* forlorn, helpless, abandoned, forsaken.

desamparar, *v.t.* to forsake, to desert, to abandon, to quit.

desamparo, *s.m.* abandonmente, forsaking, destituition, distress; helplessness.

desamurar, *v.t.* to put in good humor, to make merry again.

desancar, *v.t.* to beat, to thrash, to drub, to maul, to maltreat.

desancorar, *v.t.* to weigh anchor.

desanda, *s.f.* reprimand, rebuke.

desandador, *s.m.* tap-wrench; screwdriver.

desandar, *v.t.* to pull; to turn back; to unlock; to unscrew; to go bad, to deteriorate.

desanexação, *s.f.* desunion, disjunction, disconnection.

desanexar, *v.t.* to disunite, to disconect, to dissolve.

desanimação, *s.f.* discouragement, dejection, depression, dismay.

desanimado, *adj.* low-spirited, discouraged, dispirited, downhearted, hopeless, depressed, dejected, crestfallen, downcast.

desanimar, *v.t.* to discourage; to lose courage, to dishearten, to despair.

desaninhar, *v.t.* to remove from the nest; to dislodge, to drive out.

desânimo, *s.m.* discouragement, despondency, disheartenment, doldrums; dejection, depression, dismay, prostration, hopelessness.

desanuviado, *adj.* clear; cloudless, unclouded.

desanuviar, *v.t.* to clear up, to uncloud, to disperse clouds; *desanuviar-se,* to grow calm.

desapaixonadamente, *adv.* dispassionately, impartially.

desapaixonado, *adj.* dispassionate, unmotional, passionless, unconcerned, umbiased, detached.

desaparafusar, *v.t.* to unscrew, to screw off; *desaparafusar-se,* to get loose .

desaparecer, *v.i.* to disappear, to vanish, to be lost, to get out of sight; to die, to pass away *(fig.)*; *desaparecer a olhos vistos,* to disappear before one's very eyes.

desaparecido, *adj.* disappearance, lost, missing, absent.

desaparecimento, *s.m.* disappearance, vanishing.

desaparelhado, *adj.* unequipped; unprepared, unprovided with; uncoupled.

desaparelhar, *v.t.* to unrig, to strip, to dismast; to dismantle; to unharness *(um cavalo)*, to disarm, to disgarnish; to uncouple.

desaparição, *s.f.* disappearance.

desapartar, *v.t.* to part, to separate.

desapegado, *adj.* unattached, detached, indifferent; free.

desapegar, *v.t. v.* despegar.

desapego, *s.m.* indifference, detachmente, unconcern.

desapercebidamente, *adv.* unexpectedly.

desapercebido, *adj.* unprovided; devoid of, unprepared, destitute, unequipped, unfurnished; careless, negligent, unguarded.

desapercebimento, *s.m.* improvidence, destitution.

desapertar, *v.t.* to unlace, to loosen; to untie; to unbutton, to unfasten; to unscrew; *desapertar-se,* to get loose.

desaperto, *s.m.* unfastening; ease, relief.

desapiedadamente, *adv.* unmercifully, ruthlessly.

desapiedar, *v.t.* to make pitiless, to render cruel; *desapiedar-se,* to grow merciless.

desaplaudir, *v.t.* to disapprove, to reject.

desaplicado, *adj.* careless; negligent.

desapoderado, *adj.* deprived, dispossessed.

desapoderar, *v.t.* to dispossess, to deprive.

desapoiar, *v.t.* to unprop, to disapprove, to deprive of support.

desapoio, *s.m.* helplessness.

desapontado, *adj.* disappointed, frustrated; thwarted.

desapontamento, *s.m.* disappointment, frustration, letdown.

desapontar, *v.t.* to disappoint, to frustrate, to baffle, to thwart.

desaportuguesar, *v.t.* to deprive of the peculiar Portuguese aspect.

desapossar, *v.t.* to dispossess; to dislodge; to deprive of.

desapreço, *s.m.* disparagemente, lack of esteem.

desaprender, *v.t.* to unlearn, to forget.

desapropriação, *s.f.* expropriation, dispossession.

desapropriar, *v.t.* to dispossess, to deprive, to expropriate, to divest.

desaprovação, *s.f.* disapproval, dislike, disapproving, censure, criticism; disfavour, reproval.

desaprovador, *adj.* disapproving, reproving, disliking.

desaprovar, *v.t.* to disapprove, to reject, to disallow, to reprove; to condemn, to censure, to criticize.

desaproveitado, *adj.* squandered, wasted; unimproved *(terras).*

desaproveitamento, *s.m.* squandering; unimprovement.

desaproveitar, *v.t.* to make no use of; to waste, squander.

desaprumar, *v.t.* to put or to get out of plumb.

desaprumo, *s.m.* lack of verticality, inclination, list.

desaquartelar, *v.t.* to dislodge.

desarborizar, *v.t.* to clear of trees.

desarmado, *adj.* disarmed, unarmed, unprotected.

desarmamento, *s.m.* disarmament.

desarmar, *v.t.* to disarm; to disassemble, take apart, dismantle *(desmontar)*; to unship *(remos).*

desarmonia, *s.f.* disharmony; dissonance; discord, disunion.

desarmónico, desarmonioso, *adj.* inharmonious, discordant.

desarmonizar, *v.t.* to set at variance.

desarraigar, *v.t.* to root out; to unroot, to uproot, to erradicate, to extirpate.

desarranjado, *adj.* out of order; upset, disturbed *(mentalmente).*

desarranjar, *v.t.* to disarrange, to disorder; to trouble, to put out of order, to disturb; to upset; *desarranjar-se,* to get out of order.

desarranjo, *s.m.* confusion, disarrangement, disorder, derangement, distemper, disarray, mental disturbance; diarrhea *(pop.)*

desarrazoado, *adj.* unjust, unreasonable; senseless, absurd, without rhyme or reason, thoughtless.

desarrazoar, *v.i.* to talk nonsense; to rave.

desarrear, *v.t.* unharness, to remove the harness; to unsaddle.

desarrolhar, *v.t.* to unclrk.

desarrumação, *s.f.* disturbance, disorder, disarray, confusion, jumble, mess, untidiness.

desarrumar, v.t. to disarange, disorder; to mess; to unpack (malas).

desarticulação, s.f. disarticulation

desarticular, v.t. to disarticulate; to disjoint; to break up (desorganizar).

desarvorado, adj. dismasted (navio); adrift (sem rumo).

desarvorar, v.t. to dismast; to bolt, run away (fugir).

desasseio, s.m. uncleanliness, dustiness.

desassimilação, s.f. catabolismo.

desassisado, adj. foolish, crazy.

desassombrado, adj. sunny; frank, open; fearless.

desassombro, s.m. frankness; fearlessness; intrepidity, resolution.

desassossegado, adj. unquiet, uneasy, restless; fidgety

desassossegar, v.t. to disquiet, trouble, disturb, perturb.

desassossego, s.m. unquietness, unrest, restlessness, disquiet, uneasiness.

desastradamente, adv. awkwardly, disastrously.

desastrado, adj. awkward, clumsy, bungling; tactless, disastrous, calamitous; unlucky.

desastre, s.m. disaster, calamity; misfortune, mishap; accident; plane crash (acidente de aviação); desastre financeiro, smash, bankruptcy.

desastrosamente, adv. disastrously.

desastroso, adj. disastrous, calamitous; unfortunate, unlucky; ruinous.

desatado, adj. untied, undone; loose, free, open.

desatar, v.t. to untie, unfasten, unlace, unbind; to undo (um nó); to unfurl (desfraldar); to loose, release (soltar); to unravel, untangle (resolver, explicar). 1) desatar a chorar, a rir, to burst into tears, to burst out laughing. 2) desatar-se, to come (get) loose; to free oneself; to detach oneself.

desatarraxar, v.t. to unscrew, unbolt.

desatascar, v.t. to pull out of the mud.

desataviado, adj. simple, unadorned; bare.

desataviar, v.t. to strip of ornament; to undeck.

desatenção, s.f. inattention; absent-mindedness; neglect; negligence; disregard, discourtesy, slight.

desatencioso, adj. inattentive; thoughtless, inconsiderate; disobliging, unmannerly.

desatender, v.t. to pay no attention to, take no notice of; to ignore, disregard; to disoblige.

desatento, adj. inattentive, heedless, thoughtless; absent-minded; negligent; unmindful (of something).

desaterrar, v.t. to excavate; to raze (um monte).

desatinado, adj. desperate; crazy; desatinado de dor, beside oneself with pain.

desatinar, v.t. to madden, render insane.

desatino, s.m. folly, madness, extravagancy, crazy action.

desatolar, v.t. to pull out of the mud.

desatracar, v.t. to unmoor; to weigh anchor, get under way (partir).

desatravancar, v.t. to clear, disencumber.

desatrelar, v.t. to unhitch, unharness (cavalo); to unleash (cão).

desautorizado, adj. deprived of authority; unauthorized; unwarranted.

desautorizar, v.t. to deprive of authority; to unauthorize, disallow, disavow; to discredit, degrade.

desavença, s.f. quarrel; disagreement, dissention; falling-out; em desavença, at variance, at loggerheads.

desavergonhado, adj. shameless, impudent, brazen, unblushing, barefaced.

desavindo, adj. at variance (with).

desavir-se, v. refl. to quarrel, fall out (with someone); to differ, dissent.

desavisado, adj. ill-advised, unwise, imprudent.

desbancar, v.t. to break the bank; to supplant, outshine, throw into the shade.

desbaratamento, desbarato, s.m. defeat, rout; ruin, havoc; waste.

desbaratar, v.t. to defeat, rout, put to rout; to discomfit; to ruin; destroy, make havoc of; to waste, squander (desperdiçar).

desbarretar, v.t. to deprive, to cap, to take off one's hat, to greet someone.

desbastação, desbaste, desbastamento, s.m. rough-hewing; thinning; pruning, lopping (árvores).

desbastar, v.t. to rough-hew; to trim, pare down.

desbloquear, v.t. to raise the blockade, to cease to blockade.

desbocado, adj. foul-mouthed; unruly (cavalo), runaway (desenfreado).

desbocamento, s.m. foul or abusive language.

desbocar-se, v.refl. to use abusive language; to run away (cavalo).

desbordante, *adj.* overflowing.

desbordar, *v.i.* to outflank.

desbotado, *adj.* discolored; pale, colorless.

desbotamento, *s.m.* discoloration, fading.

desbotar, *v.t.* to fade.

desbragado, *adj.* immoderate, loose; indecorous; dissolute.

desbragamento, *s.m.* impudence, shamelessness.

desbragar-se, *v. refl.* to become dissolute, indecent.

desbravador, *s.m.* reclaimer; pioneer, pathfinder.

desbravar, *v.t.* to tame, break in *(amansar)*; to break up, reclaim, cultivate, *(terra)*.

desbulhar, *v.t.* to trash *(milho)*; to peel.

descabelado, *adj.* hairless; disheveled; huge, whopping *(enorme)*; descabelar-se, to pull out one's hair.

descabido, *adj.* improper; irrelevant; untoward, preposterous; foolish.

descaída, *s.f.* slip, oversight, fault.

descaidela, *s.f.* indiscretion.

descaído, *adj.* inclined, sloping.

descaimento, *s.m.* falling down; decline, decadence; droop; sag.

descair, *v.i.* to decay, to decline, to fall, to sink, to droop; toworsen, to weaken *(nos estudos)*; to drift off *(de um barco)*; to deviate, to drive from *(do caminho certo)*.

descalabro, *s.m.* disaster, calamity; misfortune; ruin, ravage.

descalçadeira, *s.f.* boot-jack.

descalçadela, *s.f.* reprimand, reproof, reprehension *(pop.)*

descalçar, *v.t.* to take or pull out *(calçado)*; to remove the chock from *(roda)*; to unpave *(rua, etc.)*.

descalcificar, *v.t.* to descalcify.

descalço, *adj.* unshod, barefoot.

descamar, *v.t.* to scale *(peixe)*; dewcamar--se, to flake.

descambar, *v.i.* to drop, fall (from a place); ro sink *(o sol)*; to sink, lapse, degenerate (into) *(fig.)*.

descaminho, *s.m.* disappearance; embezzlement.

descampado, *s.m.* desert, open field, wild prairie land.

descansadamente, *adv.* easily, quietly.

descansado, *adj.* rested; calm, care-free; unhurried *(vagaroso)*.

descansar, *v.i.* to rest, give rest to; to lay, place *(depositar)*. 1) *descansar armas,* to slope arms. 2) *descansar no cemitério,* to rest in the churchyard. 3) *sem descansar,* continually.

descanso, *s.m.* rest; repose; pause, tranquility; stay, halt; support. 1) *descanso para livros,* book-rest. 2) *sem descanso,* without interruption, without letup.

descante, *s.m.* song sung by two.

descaracterizar, *v.t.* to take away the character of.

descaradamente, *adv.* impudently, barefacedly.

descarado, *adj.* impudent, bareface, insolent, fresh.

descaramento, *s.m.* impudence, sauciness, insolence.

descarar-se, *v. refl.* to grow impudent, to grow bold.

descarbonizar, *v.t.* to descabonize.

descarga, *s.f.* discharge, unloading; dischargement; flight; exhaust; evacuation; excretion *(med.)*. 1) *descarga atmosférica,* atmospheric discharge. 2) *descarga de artilharia,* discharge of guns, volley. 3) *cano de descarga,* eduction pipe. 4) *dar uma descarga,* to fire a round, to fire a volley. 5) *proceder à descarga,* to discharge.

descargo, *s.m.* acquittal; discharge; excuse; *por descargo de consciência,* for the acquittal of my conscience, for conscience's sake.

descarnado, *adj.* fleshless, lanky, gaunt.

descarnar, *v.t.* to cut the meat from the bone, to make lean, to waste away.

descaro, *s.m. v.* descaramento.

descaroável, *adj.* uncharitable, pitiless.

descaroçador, *s.m.* machine for removing seeds; *descaroçador de algodão,* cotton gin.

descaroçar, *v.t.* to seed, to stone, to pit; to tell in detail, to tell one's beads *(pop.)*.

descarregado, *adj.* discharged.

descarregador, *s.m.* discharge, unloading.

decarregar, *v.t.* to discharge, to unload; to acquit *(consciência)*; to fire (to shot) off (a gun); to relieve, to exonerate; to gove vent to; ; to strike (a blow); to empty; to grow calm. 1) *descarregar a bataria,* to discharge the battery, to run the battery down. 2) *descarregar a consciência,* to clear the conscience. 3) *descarregar a culpa sobre,* to put the blame on.

descarrilamento, *s.m.* derailment.

descarrilar, *v.t.* to derail, to jump the rails; to make a slip, to run ruin *(fig.)*.

descartar, *v.t.* to discard, to remove, to reject; *descartar-se de,* to get rid of, to cut up.

descarte, *s.m.* discarding; discar *(jogo)*; excuse, evasion.

descasar, *v.t.* to unmarry; to disunite, to separate *(um par de qualquer coisa).*

descascadeira, *s.f.* hulling machine.

descascadela, *s.f.* reprehension, reprimand.

descascador, *s.m.* husker, peeler, peeling machine.

decascamento, *s.m.* barking, peeling.

descascar, *v.t.* to bark; to peel; to skin; to censure; to talk ill of someone.

descasque, *s.m.* v. descascamento.

descavalgar, *v.i.* to dismount.

descendência, *s.f.* descent, lineage; issue, descendants *(crianças)*. 1) *de baixa descendência,* lowborn. 2) *de ascendência ilustre,* highborn.

descendente, *s.*, *adj.* descendant; progeny, descendants *(pl.)*; descending, descendent.

descender, *v.i.* to proceed from, to come from.

descensão, *s.f.* descent, descension; lowering.

descentralização, *s.f.* decentralization.

descentralizador, *adj.* decentralizing.

descentralizar, *v.t.* decentralize, to separate.

descentrar, *v.t.* to decenter.

descer, *v.i.* to come down; to descend; to dismount *(cavalo)*; to step down; to get off *(de um transporte)*; to get out; to sink; to lower; to humble. 1) *descer na consideração,* to sink in someone's estimation. 2) *descer a cortina,* to drop the curtain. 3) *descer a escada,* to come downstairs. 4) *descer a miudezas,* to enter into particulars. 5) *sem descer a pormenores,* without going into details. 6) *os preços estão a descer,* prices are falling.

descerramento, *s.m.* unveilling

descerrar, *v.t.* to unveil; to unseal; to discover.

descida, *s.f.* going down, descent; fall; decay; slope; *descida da maré,* ebb of the tide.

descimento, *s.m.* descent; descension.

descingir, *v.t.* to ungird; to undo; to unclasp; to loosen.

desclassificação, *s.f.* disqualification.

desclassificado, *adj.* disqualified.

desclassificar, *v.t.* to disqualify, to discredit.

descoagulação, *s.f.* decoagulation.

descoagular, *v.t.* to decoagulate.

descoalhar, *v.t.* to melt, to dissolve.

descoberta, *s.f.* discovery; find; discovered land; detection.

descoberto, *adj.* uncovered, bare-headed, open, divulged.

descobridor, *s.m.* discoverer, explorer.

descobrimento, *s.m.* discovery; finding.

descobrir, *v.t.* to discover; to find out; to descry; to notice; to disclose; to reveal; to detect; to grow clear. 1) *descobrir-se,* to cap, to take the cap off. 2) *descobrir o rosto,* to unmask. 3) *descobrir o fio,* to be threadbare. 4) *descobrir a verdade,* to catch the truth.

descocado, *adj.* wanting in sense; insolent, impudent.

descoco, *s.m.* audacity, nerve.

descolagem, *s.f.* unglueing; taking off *(aeron.).*

descolar, *v.t.* to unglue; to undo; to unpaste.

descoloração, *s.f.* discolouring; discoloration.

descolorido, *adj.* uncoloured, faded, drab.

descolorir, *v.t.* to discolour; to tan; to fade; *descolorir-se,* to change the colour, to grow pale.

descomandar, *v.t.* to deprive from the command, to make lose the command; to lose the direction; *descomandar-se,* to go to excess, to forget oneself (language, anger).

descomedidamente, *adv.* immoderately.

descomedido, *adj.* immoderate, enormous, exorbitant, unreserved; ungovernable, unbridled; rude.

descomedimento, *s.m.* excess; unmannerliness, want of good manners ; immoderacy; extravagance, impoliteness, insolence, rudeness, impudence.

descomedir-se, *v. refl.* to be rash; to become immoderate, to behave immoderately.

descompassadamente, *adv.* excessively, disproportionately, immensely.

descompassado, *adj.* out of measure, immense, excessive, disorderly.

descompassadamente, *adv.* excessively, disproportionately, immensely.

descompassado, *adj.* out of measure, immense, excessive, disorderly.

descompassar, *v.t.* to exaggerate, to overstate, to get out of time; *descompassar-se,* to get out of step; to behave without moderation.

descompor, *v.t.* to discompose, to unsettle; to disorder, to derange, to jumble; to trouble, to irritate; to insult; to scold, to rebuke; *descompor-se,* to get upset, to lose one's composure.

descompostamente, *adv.* insolently; disorderly.

descomposto, *adj.* disorderly; immodest; disarranged; confused, perplexed; indecorous.

descompostura, *s.f.* immodesty; reprehension, scold, reprimand, censure; injury; insult, abuse; *passar uma descompostura,* to give a tongue lashing.

descomprazer, *v.i.* to displease, to be unpleasing to; to dissatisfy, not to comply with.

descompressão, *s.f.* lack of compression; low pressure.

descomunal, *adj.* excessive, enormous, uncommon, rare, extraordinary, strange, unusual; huge, colossal, gigantic; outsize.

desconcertadamente, *adv.* disorderly, confusedly, out of order.

desconcertado, *adj.* perplexed, upset, confused, disturbed, in confusion.

desconcertador, desconcertante, *adj.* disconcerting; disturbing, perplexing, baffling.

desconcertar, *v.t.* to disorder, to disconcert, to disarrange, to derange; to trouble, to confound, to upset, to puzzle, to embarass, to perplex; *desconcertar-se,* to get confused, to be perplexed, bewildered, puzzled or confounded; to lose one's composure.

desconcerto, *s.m.* misconduct; disorder; disharmony, discord.

desconchavar, *v.t.* to disjoint, to disconnect; to set at variance; *desconchavar-se,* to talk or act foolishly.

desconchavo, *s.m.* nonsense, misconduct, foolishness; *dizer desconchavos,* to talk nonsense.

desconchegar, *v.t.* to separate, to disunite.

desconchego, *s.m.* abandonment, without protection.

desconexão, *s.f.* disconnection, disunion.

desconexo, *adj.* disconnected, incoherent, disconnect; fragmentary; unrelated, rambling.

desconfiado, *adj.* suspicious, diffident, distrustful, defiant.

desconfiança, *s.f.* diffidence, suspicion, distrust, doubt, misgiving; shyness; jealousness.

desconfiar, *v.t.* to suspect, to distrust, to mistrust, to doubt, not to rely on.

desconforme, *adj.* discordant; stupendous, enormous, uncommon, unusual; huge; at variance, contrary, disagreeing.

desconformidade, *s.f.* discordance, disconformity; disproportion; dissidence, disagreement.

desconfortante, *adj.* troublesome; distressing, discomforting.

desconfortar, *v.t.* to discomfort; to discourage, to dishearten, to distress; to afflict, trouble.

desconfortável, *adj.* uncomfortable.

desconforto, *s.m.* discomfort; discouragement.

descongelação, *s.f.* thawing, melting.

descongelar, *v.t.* to thaw, to melt, to defrost.

descongestionamento, *s.m.* clearance.

descongestionar, *v.t.* to release; to relieve; to clear, to free of.

desconhecedor, *adj.* ignorant.

desconhecer, *v.t.* to ignore, not to know, to be ignorant of; to be ungrateful.

desconhecido, *adj., s.m.* unknown, anonymous, unheard of, unfamiliar, strange; anonymus, stranger. 1) *ilustre desconhecido,* an obscure individual. 2) *o soldado desconhecido,* the unknown soldier.

desconhecimento, *s.f.* ignorance, want of knowledge, unfamiliarity; obscurity.

desconjuntamento, *s.m.* luxation, dislocation, disarticulation; separation, disunion.

desconjuntar, *v.t.* to dislocate, to disunite, to disjoin, to disarticulate; to wrench; *desconjuntar-se,* to come apart.

desconsertar, *v.t.* to disarrange, to damage, to waste.

desconserto, *s.m.* disorder, ruin.

desconsideração, *s.f.* disesteem, offence, disrespect, disregard, slight, impoliteness.

desconsiderado, *adj.* disesteemed, offended; discredited.

desconsiderar, *v.t.* to disesteem, to offend, to disrespect, to disregard, to slight, to ignore; to pay no attention.

desconsoladamente, *adv.* inconsolably; insipidly.

desconsolado, *adj.* inconsolable, cheerless, disconsolate, desolate, sad, sorry; insipid, dull.

desconsolador, *adj.* sad, grievous, desolating.

desconsolar, *v.t.* to discomfort; to discourage; to sadden, to depress, to dishearten.

desconsolação, desconsolo, *s.f.,s.m.* disconsolation, discomfort, distressing, suffering, sorrow; desolation.

descontar, *v.t.* to discount *(dinheiro),* to deduct, to deduce; to make allowance; to leave out, to disregard.

descontentamento, *s.m.* displeasure, discontent, dissatisfaction, disgust; trouble, sorrow; disaffection.

descontentar, *v.t.* to discontent, to displease, to dissatisfy, to disgust; to disaffect, to disgruntle.

descontente, *adj.* dissatisfied, discontented, unsatisfied, malcontent, ill-pleased, disgruntled.

descontinuação, *s.f.* discontinuance, discontinuation, interruption.

descontinuar, *v.t.* to discontinue, to stop, to cease, to interrupt, to break off.

descontinuidade, *s.f.* discontinuance, descontinuity.

descontínuo, *adj.* discontinuous, intermittent, disconnected.

desconto, *s.m.* discount, reduction, abatement, deduction, allowance, compensation; *dar o desconto,* to discount.

descontrair, *v.t.* to stop the contraction; 1) *descontrair-se,* to relax.

descontrolado, *adj.* uncontrolled, unrestrained, ungoverned; mad, crazy *(pop).*

desconvencer, *v.t.* to dissuade.

desconversar, *v.t., v.i.* to change the subject of a conversation; to dissimulate.

desconvidar, *v.t.* to withdraw an invitation, to disinvite.

desconvir, *v.i.* to discord; to be unsuitable.

descoordenação, *s.f.* discoordination; lack of coordination.

descoordenar, *v.t.* to disarrange, to disorganize.

descorado, *adj.* pale, discoloured.

descoramento, *s.m.* paleness, discolourment; discolouring.

descorante, *adj., s.m.* discolouring, decolourizing; descolourizer, descolourant.

descorar, *v.t.* to discolour; to tarnish; to fade.

descorçoado, descoroçoado, *adj.* disheartened, downcast, crestfallen, dejected, depressed, discouraged, despondent.

descorçoamento, descoroçoamento, *s.m.* discouragement.

descorçoar, descoroçoar, *v.t.* to dishearten; to discourage, to depress, to deject, to lose heart.

descortês, *adj.* impolite, discourteous, rude, uncivil; ill-mannered, disobliging, ungentle, ungracious.

descortesia, *s.f.* impoliteness, discourtesy, rudeness, incivility, coarseness, disrespect, disregard.

descorticamento, *s.m.* decortication, barking, stripping off.

descorticar, *v.t.* to bark, to decorticate, to strip off; to peel.

descortinar, *v.t.* to discover; to unveil, to reveal, to expose, to pull the curtain; to see, to understand, to penetrate.

descortinável, *adj.* discernible, noticeable, visible.

descoser, *v.t.* to unsew, unstitch, to rip out; to take or to rip apart ; to separate; *descoser-se,* to come unstitched, to tear, to rend apart; to lose heart, to reveal a secret.

descosido, *adj.* unstitched, unsewed; incoherent, disconnected.

descravar, *v.t.* to pull out nails, to unnail; to turn away the eyes.

descravejar, *v.t.* to unnail; to unrivet; to remove horseshoe nails; to remove a jewel from its setting.

descrédito, *s.m.* discredit, dishonour, disgrace, disrepute, defame, disesteem.

descrença, *s.f.* incredulity, disbelief, unbelief, want of faith, doubt.

descrente, *adj., s.* incredulous, unbelieving, infidel; disbeliever, unbeliever, infidel.

descrer, *v.t., v.i.* to disbelieve; to be incredulous, to disbelieve.

descrever, *v.t.* to describe, to portray, to depict, to detail, to relate, to explain, to make a description of; to draw, to trace, to outline.

descrição, *s.f.* description, report, portrayal, narration, picture, depiction; delineation; enumeration, specification. 1) *descrição completa,* full description. 2) *descrição de uma paisagem,* portrayal of a landscape.

descriminar, *v.t.* to absolve *(de um crime),* to justify, to acquit.

descristianização, *s.f.* dechristianization.

descristianizar, *v.t.* dechristianize, to paganize.

descritivo, *adj.* descriptive.

descruzar, *v.t.* to uncross *(as pernas).*

descuidadamente, *adv.* negligently, carelessly, incautiously.

descuidado, *adj.* careless, negligent, heedless, thoughtless, regardeless; inattentive, absentminded, carefree; untidy, slipshod; lazy, idle.

descuidar, *v.t.* to neglect; to disregard, to overloick, to slight, to forget; *descuidar-se*, to become careless or neglectful *(hábitos, saúde),* to forget oneself.

descuido, *s.m.* negligence, carelessness, inattention, inadvertency; lapse, overslip; *por descuido*, through negligency.

desculpa, *s.f.* excuse, apology, pardon; evasion, pretext, subterfuge; absolution, exoneration, exculpation. 1) *apresentar desculpas*, to offer excuses. 2) *arranjar uma desculpa*, to find an excuse. 3) *não há desculpa alguma*, there is no excuse whatsoever. 4) *peço desculpa*, I beg your pardon. 5) *pedir desculpa*, to apologize, to ask (or beg) pardon.

desculpar, *v.t.* to excuse, to exculpate, to pardon, to forgive; to acquit, to justify, to exonerate to condone. 1) *desculpar-se*, to apologize, to excuse oneself. 2) *desculpe*, sorry.

desculpável, *adj.* excusable, pardonable.

descurado, *adj.* negligent, neglected, disregarded, forgotten.

descurar, *v.t.* to neglect, to disregard; to omit, to slight.

desde, *prep.* from, since; after. 1) *desde agora*, henceforth, from thence, from now. 2) *desde aqui*, from this place on. 3) *desde cedo*, early. 4) *desde criança*, from (since) childhood. 5) *desde então*, thenceforth, from that time, ever since. 6) *desde há muito*, for a long time past. 7) *desde já (logo)*, at once, immediately, directely. 8) *desde ontem*, since yesterday. 9) *desde quando?*, since when? how long ago?. 10) *desde sempre*, ever since.

desdenhador, *s.m., adj.* disdainer, scorner, despiser; disdaining, scorning.

desdenhar, *v.t.* to disdain, to scorn, to despite, to look down upon; to disregard, to depreciate; to spurn, to slight.

desdenhosamente, *adv.* disdainfully, superciliously, scornfully.

desdenhoso, *adj.* disdainful, scornful, supercilious, contemptuous.

desdentado, *adj., s.m. (pl.)* toothless; Edentata *(zool.).*

desdentar, *v.t.* to draw the teeth.

desdém, *s.m.* disdain, contempt, scorn, despite; haughtiness, pride, arrogance.

desdita, *s.f.* misfortune, distress, adversity; disaster, mischance; misery.

desditosamente, *adv.* unfortunately, miserably.

desditoso, *adj.* unfortunate, ill-fated, wretched, unhappy, unlucky.

desdizer, *v.t.* to contradict, to deny, to gainsay; to differ from; *desdizer-se*, to retract, to disavow.

desdobramento, *s.m.* unfolding, unrolling, development, evolution.

desdobrar, *v.t.* to unfold *(jornal),* to unroll; to develop, to expand, to extend; to disintegrate; to redouble *(esforços);* to deploy *(tropas).*

desdourar, *v.t.* to ungild, to darken; to stain, to blot *(reputação);* to discredit, to dishonour.

desedificação, *s.f.* bad example, demoralization; scandal.

desedificante, *adj.* demoralizing.

desdouro, *s.m.* discredit; blemish, stain, blot.

desedificar, *v.t.* to demoralize, to give a bad example.

deseducação, *s.f.* want of education, poor education, uncivility, impoliteness.

deseducado, *adj.* uneducated, ill-mannered, uncivil, impolite.

desejar, *v.t.* to desire, to want, to wish for; to covet. 1) *desejar com ânsia*, to pine after. 2) *desejar ardentemente*, to rave, to suspire. 3) *como desejar*, as you please. 4) *deixar muito a desejar*, to be far from being what we might expect.

desejável, *adj.* desirable.

desejo, *s.m.* desire, wish, aspiration, longing, will; appetite, hunger, thrist; *à medida dos desejos*, according to the wishes.

desejoso, *adj.* desirous, eager, avid, anxious.

deselegância, *s.f.* inelegance.

deselegante, *adj.* inelegant, ungraceful, ungainly, unhandsome.

desemaçar, *v.t.* unbundle, to unpack, to open a bundle *(documentos ou dinheiro em notas).*

desemalar, *v.t.* to unpack.

desemaranhar, v.t. to disentangle, to unsnarl; to unravel, to unriddle, to solve (problema); to unknit, to untwine.

desembaciar, v.t. to untarnish, to demist, to clean.

desembainhar, v.t. to unsheath; desembainhar a espada, to draw the sword.

desembalagem, s.f. unpacking.

desembalar, v.t. to unbale, to unpack, to unwrap.

desembaraçadamente, adv. speedily, rapidly, easily.

desembaraçado, adj. quick, prompt, easy, agile, unencumbered, unrestrained.

desembaraçar, v.t. to disembarass, to clear, to disengage, to disentangle, to set free. 1) desembaraçar-se, to get rid of, to rid oneself of. 2) desembaraçar-se de alguém, to get rid of someone.

desembaraço, s.m. promptness, ease, riddance, freedom, facility, sell-assurance; unreserve, famliarity, unrestraint; vivacity, quickness, liveliness.

desembaralhar, v.t. to disentangle, to disintricate, to set in order.

desembarcadoiro, desembarcadouro, s.m. landing-place, wharf, quay, dock.

desembarcar, v.t. disembark, to unship, to discharge, to unload; to land, to set on shore, to go ashore. 1) desembarcar mercadoridas, to unship or unload goods. 2) desembarcar passageiros, to land passengers.

desembargador, s.m. judge.

desembargar, v.t. to clear, to rid; to take off, to free.

desembargo, s.m. restraint, deliverance, replevin.

desembarque, s.m. unloading; landing, disembarkation, debarkation

desembarrancar, v.t. to take out of the mire, to draw out of mud.

desembarrilar, v.t. to take out ol a barrel, to empty; to tell the plain truth.

desembebedar, v.t. to make sober, to sober up.

desembestado, adj. unbridled, unrestrained, unruled, ungoverned; run away (cavalo).

desembestar, v.t. to shoot, to run away (cavalo).

desembocadura, s.f. mouth (de um rio).

desembocar, v.i. to discharge into (um rio); to lead to (rua), to disembark; to issue, to flow out.

desembolsar, v.t. to disburse, to expend, to spend, to lay out, to make payments.

desembolso, s.m. disbursement, outlay, expenditure, payment.

desemboscar, v.t. to dislodge, to turn out, to displace.

desembotar, v.t. to make sharp, to sharpen.

desembraiar, desembrear, v.t. to declutch, to ungear.

desembravecer, v.t. to tame, to calm, to make tame; desembravecer-se, to grow calm or gentle, to become tame.

desembrenhar, v.t. to draw forth, to drive out from the woods (jogo).

desembriagar, v.t. to make sober, to sober up.

desembridar, v.t. to unbridle, to remove the bridle.

desembrulhado, adj. unpacked, unwrapped; untangled, made clear.

desembrulhar, v.t. to unfold, to unpack, to unwrap, to unroll, to unravel; to disentangle, to disenroll; to explain, to clear up.

desembrutecer, v.t. to polish, to retine, to civilize, to educate; to humanize.

desembruxar, v.t. to disenchant, to free from witchcraft or sorcery.

desembuçar, v.t. to unmuffle; to unveil, to uncover, to take off to throw open.

desembuchar, v.t. to speak frankly; to disgorge, to throw out; to reveal (um segredo); desembuche, out with it, spit it out.

desemburradela, s.f. rudimental lesson.

desemburrar, v.t. to render less ignorant, to polish, to civilize, to educate.

desemoldurar, v.t. to take out ol a frame, to unframe.

desempacotamento, s.m. unpacking, unwrapping.

desempacotar, v.t. to unpack, to unwrap.

desempalhar, v.t. to remove the straw packing from.

desemparelhar, v.t. to unmatch, to separate (um casal).

desempastar, v.t. to unpaste, to dissolve.

desempatar, v.t. to resolve, to clear up; to break a tie, to cast the deciding vote.

desempate, s.m. clearing up ; breaking of a tie; decision, resolution; settling ol a matter. 1) partida (jogo) de desempate, play off game. 2) ponto de desempate, vantage. 3) voto de desempate, casting vote.

desempecer, v.t. to disentangle, to disencumber, to disembarass, to remove hindrances.

desempecilhar, *v.t.* to free from hindrances, to disentangle, to disencumber.

desempedernir, *v.t.* to soften, to mollify, to make less hard.

desempedrar, *v.t.* to unpave, to clear from stones.

desempenado, *adj.* straight, unwarped, upright; strong; robust; gallant; *indivíduo desempenado*, upstanding person.

desempenar, *v.t.* to unwarp, top straighten.

desempenhar, *v.t.* to redeem; to take out of a pawn; to fulfill, to discharge, to perform, to carry out *(dívidas)*, to make good *(promessa, obrigação)*, to free of debt, to pay off. 1) *desempenhar-se*, to acquit oneself. 2) *desempenhar um papel*, to play a rôle, to act a part.

desempenho, *s.m.* performance; fulfilment, execution, discharge; redemption.

desempeno, *s.m.* straightening, gracefulness, dignified appearance, graceful posture.

desemperrar, *v.t.* to loosen.

desempestar, *v.t.* to desinfect, to purifiy, to cleanse from infection.

desempilhar, *v.t.* to unpile, to unstack, to put in disorder.

desempoado, *adj.* frank, sincere; modest.

desempoar, *adj.* to clean, to shake off.

desempoeirado, *adj.* without dusty; modest; unconceited.

desempoeirar, *v.t.* v. desempoar.

desempolar, *v.t.*, *v.i.* to smooth, to level.

desempoleirar, *v.t.* to unroost; to expulse from a high position.

desempossar, *v.t.* to dispossess, to deprive, to divest.

desempregado, *adj.*, *s.m.* unemployed, out of work, unoccupied, unengaged; an unemployed person.

desempregar, *v.t.* to dismiss (do emprego); *desempregar-se*, to lose one's job.

desemprego, *s.m.* unemployment.

desencabar, *v.t.* to unhaft, to lose the handle of.

desencabrestar, *v.t.* to unhalter, to unyoke; to render ungovernable *(fig)*; *desencabrestar-se*, to give oneself over to passions, to run riot.

desencadeamento, *s.m.* breaking out.

desencadear, *v.t.* to unchain, to let loose, to unfetter, to unloose; to burst forth or to break out *(tempestade)*.

desencadernação, *s.f.* unbinding of books.

desencadernado, *adj.* unbound, missing the covers *(livros)*.

desencadernar, *v.t.* to unbind.

desencaixar, *v.t.* to dislocate, to put out of joint, to disjoint, to disarticulate; *desencaixar-se*, to come loose, to get out of a place.

desencaixilhar, *v.t.* to unframe, to remove from its frame or molding.

desencaixotar, *v.t.* to unpack, to unbox, to uncase, to take out of a boxe or case.

desencalacrar, *v.t.* to free of dificulties.

desencalhar, *v.t.* to set afloat, to set going.

desencalhe, *s.m.* setting afloat, bringing off.

desencaminhado, *adj.* astray, lost, misguide, perverted, out of the right way

desencaminhador, *s.m.*, *adj.* perverter, misleader, seducer, corruptor; misguiding, misleading, corrupting.

desencaminhamento, *s.m.* deviation, misconduct.

desencaminhar, *v.t.* to lead astray, to mislead, to pervert, to misguide, to deviate, to corrupt, to misappropriate *(fundos)*; *desencaminhar-se*, to go astray, to take a bad course.

desencanastrar, *v.t.* to take out of a basket; to untwist.

desencantamento, *s.m.* disenchantment, disillusionment, break of spell.

desencantar, *v.t.* to disenchant, to disillusion, to decharme; to discover, to find *(alguma coisa perdida)*.

desencanto, *s.m.* ver desencantamento.

desencapar, *v.t.* uncover, to unwrap.

desencapelar, *v.t.* to grow calm *(mar)*; to appease, to calm.

desencapotar, *v.t.* to uncloak, to take off the cloak; to reveal, to discover.

desencaracolar, *v.t.* to uncurl.

desencarapinhar, *v.t.* to unkink *(cabelo)*; to untangle *(lã)*.

desencarcerar, *v.t.* to free, to liberate, to release from prison, to set free, to discharge *(um prisioneiro)*.

desencardir, *v.t.* to clean, to cleanse, to wash, to bleach, to free from dirt and spots.

desencarecer, *v.t.* to reduce the price; to underestimate, to depreciate.

desencarnar, *v.t.* to leave the body *(alma)*.

desencarquilhar, *v.t.* to unwrinkle, to smooth, to remove the wrinkles.

desencarregar, *v.t.* to relieve, to exempt, to discharge, to disburden.

desencarreirar, *v.t.* to lead astray, to mislead, to misguide, to put on a wrong way.

desencasacar-se, *v.refl.* to take (one's dress-coat) off.

desencasquetar, *v.t.* to dissuade *(pop).*

desencastelar, *v.t.* to throw down.

desencastoar, *v.t.* to unset, to remove a stone from its setting.

desencerar, *v.t.* to take the wax off, to dewax.

desencharcar, *v.t.* to drain, to dry out.

desencolerizar, *v.t.* to placate, to appease, to calm, to pacify; *desencolerizar-se,* to grow calm.

desencolher, *v.t.* to stretch *(pernas);* to unshrink.

desencontrado, *adj.* opposite *(direcção);* in disagreement; divergent.

desencontrar-se, *v. refl.* to fail to meet; to disagree; to diverge.

desencontro, *s.m.* failure in meeting; disagreement; clash *(ideias),* conflict *(opiniões).*

desencorajar, *v.t.* to discourage, to deject, to dishearten, to throw cold water on.

desencordoar, *v.t.* to unstring *(guitarra, raqueta de ténis);* to take off the strings.

desencorpar, *v.t., v.i.* to make meager; to reduce the volume.

desencorporar, *v.t.* to detach, to separate.

desencortiçar, *v.t.* to unwrinkle, to smooth, to polish.

desencostar, *v.t.* to remove, to take away the support; *desencostar-se,* to straighten up, to stop leaning against some-thing.

desencovar, *v.t.* to dig out, to dig up, to ferret out, to discover, to find out, to bring to light.

desencravar, *v.t.* to unnail; to get out of a fix.

desencrencar, *v.t.* to straighten out, to settle a problem.

desencrespar, *v.t.* to smooth; to uncurl; to grow calm *(mar).*

desencurralar, *v.t.* to bring out, to let out of the stable; to set at liberty.

desendividar, *v.t.* to pay someone's debts; *desendividar-se,* to get out of debt.

desenevoar, *v.t.* to clear *(nuvens ou nevoeiro),* to clear up, to brighten; to make glad, to cheer.

desenfadadamente, *adv.* at leisure.

desenfadado, *adj.* merry; pleasant.

desenfadar, *v.t.* to recreate, to cheer, to amuse, to entrain; to please, to put in good humour; *desenfadar-se,* to amuse oneself, to have a good time.

desenfado, *s.m.* diversion, pleasantness, amusement, recreation, pleasure; relaxation, calmness, tranquility.

desenfaixar, *v.t.* unswaddle, to unwind, to unroll.

desenfardamento, *s.m.* unpacking.

desenfardar, *v.t.* unpack, to open a pack.

desenfardelar, *v.t.* to unpack.

desenfarpelar-se, *v. refl.* to undress, to take the clothes off.

desenfastiadamente, *adv.* smartly; wittily.

desenfastiar, *v.t.* to whet the apetite; to divert, to amuse, to entertain, to recreate.

desenfastioso, *adj.* appetizing; pretty, graceful, witty.

desenfeitar, *v.t.* to take away the ornaments, to disfigure.

desenfeitiçar, *v.t.* to disenchant, to unbewitch, to free of a spell; to deliver from a passion.

desenfeixar, *v.t.* to untie, to unsheaf.

desenferrujado, *adj.* rustless, free of rust.

desenferrujar, *v.t.* to remove the rust; to polish; *desenferrujar a língua,* to pratre, to chatter, to blab.

desenfiar, *v.t.* to unthread, to unstring; *desenfiar a agulha,* to unthread the needle.

desenformar, *v.t.* to take out of a mould.

desenfreadamente, *adv.* licentiously, ungovernably; wildly, riotously.

desenfreado, *adj.* unbridled, unruled, ungoverned, unrestrained, unchecked; reinless, wild.

desenfreamento, *s.m.* unruliness; immo-deration, excess, intemperance.

desenfrear, *v.t.* to unbridle, to let loose; *desenfrear-se,* to lose, all restraint, to throw off the bridle, to lose self-control.

desenfurecer, *v.t.* to appease, to placate; *desenfurecer-se,* to grow calm.

desenfuscar, *v.t.* to clear up, to brighten.

desengaçadeira, *s.f.* grape picker.

desengaçar, *v.t.* to strip off the grapes.

desengaiolar, *v.t.* to set free, to uncage, to release; to release from a prison (fig.).

desengajar, *v.t.* to dismiss, to disengage, to relase.

desenganado, *adj.* undeceived, disillusioned. 1) *desenganado dos médicos,* given over (or up) by the physicians. 2) *desenganado do mundo,* disgusted with the world.

desenganador, *s.m.* undeceiver; *adj.* undeceiving.

desenganar, *v.t.* to undeceive, to disillusion, to open a person's eyes; to give up a case *(med.).* 1) *desenganar-se,* to see clearly, to see one's mistake, to come to reason.

desenganchar, *v.t.* to unhook, to unclasp; to unfasten, to untie.

desengano, *s.m.* undeceiving; disillusion.

desengarrafar, *v.t.* to draw out *(das garrafas).*

desengasgar, *v.i.* to clear the throat (fig.); to disentangle, to disembarras.

desengastar, *v.t.* to take out *(uma pedra)* of a ring, to unset a stone, to take a precious stone out of its setting.

desengatar, *v.t.* to uncouple, to disconnect, to uncramp, to unlink.

desengatilhar, *v.t.* to pull; to fire, to uncock.

desengonçado, *adj.* unhinged, tottering, disjoint, out of joint, gangling, loose.

desengonçar, *v.t.* to dislocate, to unhinge, to disjoint, to loosen; *desengonçar-se,* to fall apart.

desengordar, *v.t.* to loose fatness, to grow thin.

desengordurar, *v.t.* to scour, to clean, to degrease, to remove the grease.

desengraçado, *adj.* ungraceful, insipid, inelegant, awkward; flat, dull.

desengraçar, *v.t.* to dislike, to take a dislike to.

desengrenar, *v.t.* to ungear, to uncouple.

desengrossar, *v.t.* to make thin, to make less thick, to rough-hew.

desenguiçar, *v.t.* to free from with craft; to disentangle, to free.

desenhador, desenhista, *s.m., s.* draughtsman, draftsman, designer, drawer.

desenhar, *v.t.* to draw; to delineate, to sketch, to outline, to design, to draft, to trace; to picture, to depict, to show, to figure; to project, to plan, to scheme; *desenhar-se,* to take form or shape.

desenho, *s.m.* drawing, design, sketch, delineation, draft, outline, pattern; picture, figure, project, plan. 1) *desenho a carvão,* charcoal drawing. 2) *desenho à mão,* freehand sketching. 3) *estojo de desenho,* drawing set.

desenjoar, *v.t.* to relieve of nausea.

desenjoativo, *adj.* appetizing, tasty; *s.m.* aperitif, appetizer.

desenlaçado, *adj.* untied, unlaced.

desenlaçar, *v.t.* to unlace, to disentangle, to unknot, to loose, to untie.

desenlace, *s.m.* issue, event, upshot, epilogue, outcome, end, conclusion.

desenlamear, *v.t.* to clear, to take the mud off, to clean .

desenlear, *v.t.* to untie, to disantangle, to unsnarl, unravel; to loose *(a língua);* to disencumber, to release; to relieve from difficulties; *desenlear-se,* to get free from difficulties.

desenleio, *s.m.* disentanglement, disembarrassment, loosening.

desenodoar, *v.t.* to clean; to remove stains or spots.

desenovelar, *v.t.* to undo a ball of thread, to unravel, to unwind.

desenraizar, *v.t.* to unroot, to uproot, to pluck, to eradicate.

desenredar, *v.t.* to disentangle; to unravel, to untwine, to unknot, to unsnarl; to explain, to clear up. 1) *desenredar-se,* to get rid of a trouble; to become clear. 2) *desenredar um mistério,* to solve a mystery.

desenredo, *s.m.* denouement, outcome, solution, clearing up, explanation.

desenregelar, *v.t.* to thaw, to unfreeze, to melt.

desenriçar, *v.t.* to comb out, to smooth, to uncurl.

desenrodilhar, *v.t.* to unroll, to develop, to uncoil.

desenrolar, *v.t.* to unroll, to unwind, to develop, to unfold; to come to pass or to be *(tragédia, acontecimentos).*

desenroscar, *v.t.* to unscrew; to uncoil.

desenroupar, *v.t.* to undress, to deprive of colthes.

desenrouquecer, *v.i.* to cease to be hoarse, to relieve of hoarseness.

desenrugar, *v.t.* to unwrinkle; to smooth.

desensaboar, *v.t.* to remove the soap, to rinse of a soap.

desensacar, *v.t.* to unsack, to take out of a sack.

desensanguentar, *v.* to wipe off the blood, to clean from blood.

desensarilhar, v.t. to unstack.

desensebar, v.t. to scour; to cleanse.

desensoberbecer, v.t. to humble, to humiliate, to break one's pride; *desensoberbecer-se,* to lose the pride, to become humble or modest.

desensombrar, v.t. to clear; to brighten.

desensopar, v.t. to dry.

desentaipar, v.t. to unpen, to relieve.

desentalar, v.t. to take away; to deliver; *desentalar-se,* to get out of a tight spot, to get free from troubles or difficulties.

desentaramelar, v.t. to loosen one's tongue.

desentender, v.t. to misunderstand; to feign ignorance; *desentender-se,* to come to grips.

desentendido, adj. fazer-se desentendido, to feign ignorance, to turn a deaf ear to.

desentendimento, s.m. misunderstandig, misapprehension; disagreement, dissension.

desentenebrecer, v.t. to clear up, to scatter the darkness.

desenterrado, adj. exhumed; dug up; unearthed; discovered.

desenterramento, desenterro, s.m. exhumation, disinterment, unburying.

desenterrar, v.t. to exhume, to unbury, to disinter; to unearth, to dig up, to excavate; to find, to bring to light, to discover; to bring to light *(fig.).*

desentesar, v.t. to loosen, to unbend, to unstiffen, to render less tense.

desentoadamente, adv. out of tune, dissonantly.

desentoado, adj. dissonant, out of tune, discordant, inharmonious.

desentoar, v.i. to be out of tune, to sing off key, to untune, to discord; to speek or act in a discordant manner.

desentorpecer, v.t. to remove stiffness, to revive, to free of numbness; to reanimate, to comne to life, to regain vigour.

desentorpecimento, s.m. quickening.

desentortar, v.t. to unbend, to make straight, to straighten.

desentrançar, v.t. to unplait *(o cabelo).*

desentranhar, v.t. to lay bare one's bosom, to draw from the bowels of the earth, from the depts of the soul, to disembowel; *desentranhar-se,* to do one's best for another person, to disclose one's feelings.

desentrelaçado, adj. unbraided, unplaited.

desentrelaçar, v.t. to unbraid, to unplait.

desentrincheirar, v.t. to dislodge from the trenches; to drive out.

desentristecer, v.t. to make merry, to drive away the sadness.

desentrouxar, v.t. to unpack, to open a truss or bundle, to untruss.

desentulhar, v.t. to empty, to clear away rubbish or debris.

desentupimento, s.m. unstopping, opening, clearing.

desentupir, v.t. to unstop, to cleanse, to open, to clear, to free from obstructions.

desenvasilhar, v.t. to take out of a cask, to pour *(óleo, leite, vinho)* from a vessel.

desenvencilhar, v.t. to loosen to disengage, to disentangle, to untie, to unfasten. *desenvencilhar-se,* to free oneself *(de obrigações, deveres, dificuldades)* to get rid of.

desenvernizar, v.t. to remove the varnish, to unpolish.

desenvoltamente, adv. expeditiously, nimbly, licentiously.

desenvolto, adj. speedy, brisk, nimble, agile, light; unrestrained; wanton.

desenvoltura, s.f. nimbleness, agility, briskness; insolence, brazenness, boldness.

desenvolver, v.t. to develop, to cause to grow, to bring out, to expound; to unfold *(uma ideia); desenvolver-se,* to grow, to ripen; to untold, to expand.

desenvolvido, adj. developed, grown up; advanced; instructed; ripe, mature.

desenvolvimento, s.m. development, growth, progress, improvement, evolution; explanation, unfolding.

desenxabidamente, adv. insipidly.

desenxabido, adj. insipid, dull, banal, spiritless, unsavoury, tasteless.

desenxamear, v.t. to disperse or break up a sworm.

desenxovalhar, v.t. to clean to wash, to cleanse; to smooth, to unbrinkle.

desequilibrado, adj. unbalanced, unsteady; crazy, top-heavy (fig.).

desequilibrar, v.t. to unbalanced. 1) *desequilibrar-se,* to lose one's balance. 2) *desequilibrar a conta,* to unbalance an account. 3) *desequilibrar os nervos,* to shatter one's nerves.

desequilíbrio, s.m. instability, unbalanced, disequilibrium, distemper.

deserção, *s.f.* desertion, defection, dereliction, abandonment.

deserdação, *s.f.* disinheritance.

deserdado, *adj.* disinherited; ungifted, untalented.

deserdamento, *s.m.* disinheritance.

deserdar, *v.t.* to disinherit; to dispossess, to deprive of heritage.

desertar, *v.i.* to desert, to run away, to leave, to quit, to abandon a post, to fly.

desértico, *adj.* wild, solitary.

deserto, *s.m.* desert, wilderness, waste; desolation, solitude; *adj.* solitary, desert, uninhabited.

desertor, *s.m.* deserter, run away, fugitive, transfuge, renegade.

desesperação, *s.f.* despair, desperation, anger, fury, rage, indignation.

desesperadamente, *adv.* desperately.

desesperado, *adj.* desperate; hopeless; mad, furious, rash.

desesperador, *adj.* hopeless, despairing.

desesperança, *s.f.* despair, hopelessness, desperation.

desesperançar, *v.t.* to discourage, to dishearten, to depress; *desesperançar-se,* to lose hope.

desesperante, *adj.* despairing, hopeless, desponding.

desesperar, *v.t.* to torment; to anger; to despair, to drive to despair; to grow desperate; *desesperar-se,* to rave, to rage, to become impatient.

desespero, *s.m.* despair, loss of hope, hopelessness; desperation, rage.

desestima, desestimação, *s.f.* disesteem, contempt, disregard, disgrace, despise.

desestimar, *v.t.* to disesteem; to dispise, to disregard, to disrespect; to undervalue, to depreciate, to disparage.

desfaçatez, *s.f.* effrontery, impudence, sauciness, insolence, brass, shamelessness, barefacedness.

desfalcamento, *s.m.* defalcation.

desfalcar, *v.t.* to defalcate, to embezzle, to diminish, to misappropriate; to steal, to rob, to plunder.

desfalecente, *adj.* faint, swooning, fainting, decaying.

desfalecer, *v.i.* to fail, to swoon, to grow weak, to faint, to weaken, to fade; to collapse.

desfalecimento, *s.m.* faintness, weakness, breakdown; exhaustion; slowing down.

desfalque, *s.m.* defalcation, embezzlement, peculation; stealing.

desfanatizar, *v.t.* to free from fanaticism.

desfardar, *v.t.* to put off the uniform.

desfasado, *adj.* out of phase.

desfasagem, desfasamento, *s.f., s.m.* dephasing, phase displacement.

desfasar, *v.t.* to put out of phase.

desfastio, *s.m.* cheerfulness; pastime, appetite; good humour, entertainment.

desfavor, *s.m.* disfavour, dislike, disregard, disgrace, disesteem; disdain, aversion, antipathy.

desfavorável, *adj.* unfavourable, adverse, unpropitious, disadvantageous, contrary, unfriendly.

desfavoravelmente, *adv.* unfavourably, unfriendly, adversely.

desfavorecer, *v.t.* to disfavour, to discountenance, to disapprove; to reject, not to accept or support.

desfavorecido, *adj.* ill-favoured, unprotected, not endowed with.

desfazer, *v.t.* to undo, to unmake, to break up *(encontro),* to dilute, to destroy *(uma cidade);* to annul *(um contrato);* to dissolve; to scatter *(nuvens);* to dispel *(dúvidas);* to give up *(projecto);* to unpack; to depreciate, to find fault with, to undervalue; to defeat *(exército);* to rout, to beat; to disjoint, to dismount *(máquina).* 1) *desfazer-se de,* to get rid of, to sell, to dispose of; to disappear, to melt *(gelo).* 2) *desfazer-se em pranto,* to melt into tears. 3) *desfazer um erro (engano),* to clear up (undo) a mistake. 4) *desfazer o casamento,* to break up the marriage. 5) *desfazer-se em bocados,* to go to pieces. 6) *desfazer-se dos criados,* to dismiss the servants. 7) *desfazer-se em desculpas,* to ask a thousand pardons, to offer many excuses. 8) *desfazer-se em pó,* to crumble into dust. 9) *fazer e desfazer,* to do and undo. 10) *ele desfez-se do que tinha,* he disposed of all his possessions. 11) *o homem faz e Deus desfaz,* man proposes and God disposes.

desfear, *v.t.* to deface, to disfigure, to make ugly.

desfechar, *v.t.* to discharge, to fire, to shoot off; to finish, to conclude, to end.

desfecho, *s.m.* issue, outcome, conclusion, solution, result; upshot.

desfeita, *s.f.* outrage, insult, affront, slur, slight.

desfeiteador, *s.m.* insulter, offender.

desfeitear, *v.t.* to affront, to offend, to insult, to abuse; to slight, to disregard, to flout.

desfeito, *adj.* undone; dissolved, melted; violent, furious, dreadful, fierce *(tempestade)*.

desferir, *v.t.* unfurl; to strike *(instrumentos musicais)*; to let fly.

desferrar, *v.t.* unshoe *(cavalo)*; to unfurl; *desferrar-se,* to cast a shoe *(animal)*.

desferrolhar, *v.t.* to unbolt, to withdraw a latch; to open.

desfiado, *adj.* unwoven, unspun, shredded, frayed.

desfiar, *v.t.* to unweave, to unravel, to untwist, to unthread, to fray out, separate into threads; to enumerate, to relate in detail.

desfibração, desfibramento, *s.f., s.m.* shredding, removal of the fibres.

desfibrador, *s.m.* shredder.

desfibrar, *v.t.* to shred; to defiber; to analyse; to relate in details.

desfiguração, *s.f.* disfigurement, deface-ment, deformation.

desfigurar, *v.t.* to disfigure, to distort; to disguise, to alter, to dissemble, to change; to transform.

desfilada, *s.f.* à *desfilada,* at full speed.

desfiladeiro, *s.m.* gorge, defile, ravine, col narrow pass; bottleneck.

desfilar, *v.i.* to defile, to file, to march *(em filas)*; to succeed; to parade.

desfile, *s.m.* parade, review, pageant, procession; a marching by.

desfitar, *v.t.* to turn away the eyes, to cease staring.

desfloração, desfloramento, *s.f., s.m.* defloration, violation.

desflorador, *s.m.* deflowerer; ravisher.

desflorar, *v.t.* to deflower, to strip of flowers; to deflorate; to violate, to deprive of virginity.

desflorescer, desflorir, *v.t.* to cease flowering; to lose blossoms; to fade, to wither.

desflorescimento, *s.m.* fall or loss of the blossoms or flowers.

desflorestar, *v.t.* to deforest.

desfolha, desfolhação, *s.f.* fall *(folhas)*; depriving, defoliation.

desfolhada, *s.f.* husking *(trigo ou milho)*.

desfolhamento, *s.m.* stripping, defoliation.

desfolhar, *v.t.* to strip, to pull off *(folhas)*; to husk; to take way the leaves or petals, to pick *(flor)* apart; to shed leaves.

desforçar-se, *v.refl.* to revenge oneself, to redress.

desforço, *s.m.* revenge, redress, requital, retaliation.

desforra, *s.f.* revenge, redress, satisfaction, avengement; *tirar a desforra,* to get even, to take revenge.

desforrar, *v.t.* to revenge, to avenge, to requite; to compensate, to repay; to win one's money back *(jogo)*; to unline *(casaco)*; *desforrar-se,* to get even, to recoup one's losses; to be revenged of.

desfortuna, *s.f.* misfortune, mischance, ill luck; disaster; adversity.

desfraldar, *v.t.* to unfurl *(vendas)*; to hoist *(bandeira)*.

desfranzir, *v.t.* to undo, to unwrinkle.

desfrechar, *v.t.* to shoot, to let fly; to throw, to cast.

desfrisar, *v.t.* to uncurl.

desfrutação, *s.f.* enjoyment of, delight in; ridicule, derision.

desfrutador, *s.m.* enjoyer, usufruituary; parasite; jester.

desfrutar, *v.t.* to enjoy; to jest at, to mock, to make fun of, to gibe at; to sponge on.

desfrutável, *adj.* enjoyable, open to ridicule.

desfrute, *s.m.* jesting, mockery, derision, scorn; enjoyment, usufruit; *dar-se ao desfrute,* to lend oneself to ridicule.

desgabar, *v.t.* to depreciate; to disparage, to belittle, to undervalue, to underrrate.

desgadelhar, *v.t.* to dishevel, to put in disorder *(cabelo)*.

desgalhar, *v.t.* to lop *(árvore)*, to cut off the branches.

desgarrada, *s.f.* popular song; *cantar à desgarrada,* to sing impromptu in competition.

desgarrado, *adj.* gone astray, lost; off course, strayed.

desgarrar-se, *v. refl.* to miss one's way, to straggle, to take to bad courses; to go off course *(barco)*.

desgasificar, *v.t.* to degas, to degasify.

desgastar, *v.t.* to consume, to wear away, to waste, to destroy.

desgaste, *s.m.* abrasion, wear, wear and tear, wastage.

desgostar, *v.t.* to displease, to disgust, to grieve, to annoy, to vex; to loathe; *desgostar-se de,* to lose one's liking for.

desgosto, *s.m.* dislike, sorrow, displeasure, annoyance; shock, grief; trouble; disappointment.

desgostoso, *adj.* displeased, sad, discontent, dissatisfied; regretful.

desgovernado, *adj.* wasteful; misgoverned, ungoverned, unruled, uncontrolled.

desgovernar, *v.t.* to misgovern, to mismanage; *desgovernar-se,* to lose self-control; to drift at the mercy of the waves.

desgoverno, *s.m.* misgovernment, mismanagement, misrule; wastefulness.

desgraça, *s.f.* misery; misfortune, calamity; disfavour; adversity, trouble; disaster, fatality, catastrophe. 1) *cair em desgraça,* to be out of favour. 2) *uma desgraça nunca vem só,* misfortunes seldom come alone, troubles never come singly, it never rains but it pours. 3) *valer-se da desgraça alheia,* to take advantage of another's misfortune. 4) *por desgraça,* unfortunately.

desgraçadamente, *adv.* unfortunately, unhappily.

desgraçado, *adj.* unfortunate, unhappy, luckless, wretched, unlucky, miserable, ill-fated; *s.m.* poor fellow, rascal, scoundrel; *desgraçado de mim,* poor me.

desgraçar, *v.t.* to ruin; to make unhappy, to bring misfortune to.

desgracioso, *adj.* awkward, ungainly, clumsy, ungraceful; inelegant.

desgranar, *v.t.* to beat or shake out the grain from cereals; to thrash; to flail; to shell.

desgrenhado, *adj.* dishevelled, shaggy, tousled, unkempt, frowzy; in disorder *(cabelo).*

desgrenhar, *v.t.* to dishevel, to tousle, to rumple, to loosen the hair, to disorder the hair.

desgrudar, *v.t.* to unglue, to deglutinated, to come off.

desguarnecer, *v.t.* to unman, to deprive, to disgarnish; to strip, to remove the garrisons from.

desiderativo, *adj.* desiderative.

desiderato, *s.m.* desideratum, aim, purpose, goal.

desidratação, *s.f.* dehydration, removal of water.

desidratar, *v.t.* to dehydrate, to anhydrate.

designação, *s.f.* designation, denomination, indication; appointment.

designadamente, *adv.* namely.

designar, *v.t.* to designate; to appoint; to mean, to denote, to indicate, to select, to name; to signify. 1) *designar para deputado,* to deputize. 2) *designar uma hora,* to set a time.

designativo, *adj.* indicative, distinctive, characteristic.

desígnio, *s.m.* design, intention, meaning, purpose, aim; project, plan.

desigual, *adj.* unequal, unlike, uneven; different, irregular; variable, changeable; rough, rugged; ill-matched.

desigualar, *v.t.* to make unequal, to render unequal to, or different from.

desigualdade, *s.f.* inequality, disparity, disproportion, dissimilarity, difference; unevenness.

desigualmente, *adv.* unequally, unevenly.

desiludido, *adj.* undeceived, disabused, disappointed, disillusioned, disenchanted; realistic.

desiludir, *v.t.* to disillusion, to disabuse; to disappoint; *desiludir-se,* to lose illusions; to give up hope.

desilusão, *s.f.* disillusion, disappointment, deception, disenchantment.

desimpedimento, *s.m.* clearing up; riddance.

desimpedir, *v.t.* to clear up, to disencumber, to disengage, to disembarrass.

desinçar, *v.t.* to extirpate, to root out.

desinchar, *v.i.* to become less swollen, to reduce a swelling.

desinclinar, *v.t.* to straighten up.

desincorporação, *s.f.* disincorporation; detachment of a body, disembodiment.

desincorporar, *v.t.* to disincorporate, to disembody; to detach, to separate.

desincumbir-se, *v. refl.* to discharge, to carry out, to execute *(dever).*

desindividualizar, *v.t.* to generalize; to lose individualism.

desinência, *s.f.* ending *(de uma palavra),* termination.

desinfecção, *s.f.* disinfection, decontamination.

desinfectante, *s.m.* disinfectant; adj. disinfecting, antiseptic.

desinfectar, *v.t.* to disinfect, to purify, to decontaminate; to cleanse.

desinfestar, *v.t.* to disinfest, to clear off, to free from.

desinflação, *s.f.* deflation.

desinflamação, *s.f.* assuagement, reduction or cure of an inflammation.

desinflamar, *v.t.* to remove or cure an inflammation.

desinquietação, *s.f.* disquiet, disquietude, disturbance, uneasiness, anxiety, restlessness.

desinquietador, *s.m.* disturber, disquieter; *adj.* turbulent, disquieting.

desinquietar, *v.t.* to disturb, to disquiet, to trouble, to annoy, to bother, to worry.

desinquieto, *adj.* restless, impatient, fidgety, unquiet, turbulent, disturbing, agitated, uneasy.

desintegração, *s.f.* disintegration; disassociation, decomposition, dissolution, breakup.

desintegrar, *v.t.* to disintegrate; to separate, to decompose, to split; *desintegrar-se,* to dissolve, to break off in pieces, to split.

desinteligência, *s.f.* misunderstanding; disagreement, variance, dissension, rupture, friction, difference.

desinteressadamente, *adv.* uninterestedly, unselfishly.

desinteressado, *adj.* disinterested; detached, unconcerned; unbiased; unselfish.

desinteressante, *adj.* uninteresting.

desinteressar, *v.t.* to disinterest, to neglect, to divest of interest; *desinteressar-se,* to lose interest in, to cease to concern oneself.

desinteresse, *s.m.* disinterest, unconcern, indifference, nonchalance; aloofness; self-denial; abnegation, detachment, unselfishness.

desintoxicar, *v.t.* to free of poison, to unpoison.

desintrincar, *v.t.* to disentangle, to disembarrass; to make clear, to clear up.

desintumescer, *v.t.* to reduce a swelling, to become less swollen.

desipotecar, *v.t.* to pay off a mortgage.

desirmanado, *adj.* unmatched; odd, asunder.

desirmanar, *v.t.* to break a set; to unmatch, to divide a pair, to separate.

desistência, *s.f.* desistance, cessation; giving up.

desistente, *adj.* desisting, renouncing.

desistir, *v.i.* to desist, to leave off, to give up, to cease, to stop; to renounce, to abdicate; to quit, to desert. 1) *desistir de fazer,* to desist from doing. 2) *desistir de uma herança,* to forsake an inheritance. 3) *desistir de uma pretensão,* to give up a claim.

desjejua, desjejum, *s.f., s.m.* first breakfast.

desjejuar, *v.i.* to break one's fast.

desjungir, *v.t.* to unyoke; to unteam, to unharness.

deslaçar, *v.t.* to unlace, to untie, to unfasten; *deslaçar-se,* to get loose.

deslacrar, *v.t.* to unseal, to break the seal *(carta).*

desladrilhar, *v.t.* to remove the tiles from; to unpave.

deslajear, *v.t.* to remove the flagstones from.

deslanar, *v.t.* to shear *(carneiro),* to clip, to remove the wool.

deslassar, *v.t.* to make slack or loose.

deslastrar, *v.t.* to unballast, to take the ballast away.

deslavado, *adj.* discoloured, faded; insipid; shameless, saucy, brazen faced *(fig.).*

desleal, *adj.* disloyal, false; unfair, dishonest, unfaithful, treacherous.

deslealdade, *s.f.* disloyalty, falseness, unfaithfulness, disaffection, treachery.

desleixado, *adj.* careless; negligent, neglectful, untidy, slovenly, unkempt, slipshod, remiss, sloppy, disordered.

desleixar, *v.t.* to neglect, to disregard, to slight, to omit; *desleixar-se,* to become lax or careless, to be negligent.

desleixo, *s.m.* negligence, laxity, carelessness, indifference, nonchalance, disregard; untidiness.

desligado, *adj.* untied, disconnected, loose; indifferent, detached, disinterested.

desligar, *v.t.* to loosen, to separate, to untie, to disconnect, to undo, to disjoint, to detach; to stop, to switch off or out, to turn off *(luz, rádio); desligar-se,* to detach oneself from.

deslindado, *adj.* cleared up, explained.

deslindar, *v.t.* to clear up; to extricate, to unravel; to explain, to investigate; to demarcate.

deslizamento, *s.m.* sliding, slipping, gliding.

deslizar, *v.i.* to slide, to slip, to glide, to skid.

deslize, *s.m.* sliding, slip, gliding, skidding; fault, error, misstep, lapse, false step.

deslocação, deslocamento, *s.f., s. m.* dislocation; luxation; dislodgment, displacement.

deslocado, *adj.* dislocated, out of joint; displaced; misplaced; strange.

deslocar, *v.t.* to dislocate, to luxate, to disjoint *(braço ou perna);* to displace, to remove, to move, to shift (de um local para outro).

deslombar, v.t. to break the back, to beat, to thrash.

deslumbrador, deslumbrante, adj. dazzling, fascinating, blinding; fulgent.

deslumbramento, s.m. dazzling; fascination; blindness.

deslumbrar, v.t. to dazzle, to blind (por excesso de luz), to astonish, to overpower; to fascinate, to tempt; deslumbrar-se com, to be fascinated by.

deslustrar, v.t. to dull, to tarnish; to blemish, to sully, to stain (reputação), dishonour.

deslustre, s.m. tarnishing (reputação), blemish, stain, note of infamy.

desluzido, adj. graceless, obscure, dim, dull.

desmagnetização, s.f. demagnetization.

desmagnetizar, v.t. to demagnetize.

desmaiado, adj. fainted, pale, colourless, unconscious.

desmaiar, v.i. to faint, to swoon, to collapse; to discolour, to turn pale.

desmaio, s.m. fainting, swoon, collapse, faint, fit.

desmalhar, v.t. to undo the meshes.

desmama, desmame, desmamo, s.f., s.m. weaning.

desmamar, v.t. to wean.

desmanchado, adj. taken to pieces, out of joint; upset, surprised.

desmancha-prazeres, s. kill-joy, wetblanket, dog in the manger, damper, spoil-sport.

desmanchar, v.t. to undo, to take to pieces, to rip up, to tear down; to break up; to cancel (contrato). 1) desmanchar-se, to become deranged; to become undone, to spoil (bolo); to misbehave. 2) desmanchar a casa to disarrange the house.

desmancho, s.m. abortion, miscarriage.

desmandado, adj. immoderate; disobedient, indisciplined.

desmandar-se, v.refl. to go beyond one's limits, to go to extremes, to commit excesses, to go too far, to swerve from duty.

desmando, s.m. disorder, immoderation; insubordination; excess, disregard for rules; outrage.

desmantelado, adj. dismantled, demolished; unrigged, unmasted (barco).

desmantelamento, s.m. dismantlement; unrigging.

desmantelar, v.t. to dismantle, to demolish, to throw down, to raze (paredes) to unrig, to

unmast (barco); to clear out; desmantelar-se, to tumble down, to come down, to fall in.

desmarcadamente, adv. excessively.

desmarcado, adj. immoderate, enormous, excessive; outsize, colossal.

desmarcar, v.t. to remove the marks or signs; to remove the boundary stones; demarcar-se, to become excessive.

desmarear, v.t. to clean of stains; desmariar-se, to go out of control (barco).

desmascarar, v.t. to unmask, to remove the mask; to expose, to reveal, to bring, to light; desmascarar-se, to take off the mask.

desmastreamento, s.m. dismasting, removal or loss of the masts.

desmastrear, v.t. to dismast.

desmaterializar, v.t. to dematerialize, to turn immaterial.

desmazeladamente, adv. negligently.

dasmazelado, adj. negligent, careless, untidy, slipshod, indolent, slack.

desmazelar-se, v. refl. to become negligent, to be careless or slipshod, to neglect one's affairs.

desmazelo, s.m. negligence, carelessness, frowziness.

desmedidamente, adv. excessively, immensely, unduly.

desmedido, adj. excessive, enormous, immense, immoderate, colossal, huge.

desmedir-se, v. refl. to behave immoderately, to be impolite or rash.

desmembração, s.s. dismembering, detaching, dividing; partition.

desmembrado, adj. separated, divided, destitute, cast down (fig.).

desmembramento, s.m. dismemberment.

desmembrar, v.t. to dismember, to dislimb, to disjoint; to separate, to disunite.

desmemória, s.s. forgetfulness, obliviousness.

desmemoriado, adj. forgetful, unretentive, deprived of memory.

desmemoriar, v.t. to cause loss of memory, to lose the memory.

desmentido, s.m. contradiction, denial, negation, recantation; adj. contradicted, denied.

desmentir, v.t. to contradict, to deny, to refute, to gainsay.

desmerecedor, adj. undeserving, unworthy, ill-merited.

desmerecer, v.i. to become undeserving, to

demerit, not to deserve; to depreciate, to discredit; not to be inferior to.

desmerecido, *adj.* unworthy, unmerited, undeserved.

desmerecimento, *s.m.* demerit, unworthiness; depreciation.

desmesura, *s.f.* discourtesy, inciviliy, impoliteness, unkindness.

desmesuradamente, *adv.* excessively.

desmesurado, *adj.* immoderate, excessive, huge, enormous, colossal, immense.

desmilitarização, *s.f.* demilitarization.

desmilitarizar, *v.t.* to demilitarize, to demobilize.

desmiolado, *adj.* harebrained, rattlebrained, shallowbrained, rattlehead, brainless.

desmiolar, *v.t.* to take out the insides; to render crazy.

desmobilado, *adj.* unfurnished, disgarnished.

desmobilar, *v.t.* to unfurnish, to remove the furniture from *(casa, apartamento),* to disgarnish.

desmobilização, *s.f.* demobilization, disarmament.

desmobilizar, *v.t.* to demobilize, to disband, to disarm.

desmontar, *v.t.* to dismount, to alight *(de um cavalo),* to unhorse, to throw from the saddle; to undo, to take to pieces, to dismantle, to disassemble.

desmontável, *adj.* dismountable, removable.

desmoralização, *s.f.* demoralization, disparagement, corruption.

desmoralizador, *adj.* demoralizing.

desmoralizar, *v.t.* to demoralize, to corrupt, to pervert, to deprave; to dishearten, to discourage.

desmoronamento, *s.m.* downfall, falling down, collapse *(paredes, prédios);* cave-in *(túnel);* landslide; wash-out.

desmoronar, *v.t.* to throw down, to demolish; *desmoronar-se,* to collapse, to fall to pieces.

desnacionalização, *s.f.* denationalization.

desnacionalizar, *v.t.* to denationalize.

desnarigar, *v.t.* to cut off one's nose.

desnasalação, *s.f.* elimination of nasal sounds.

desnasalar, *v.t.* to rid of nasal sounds.

desnatação, *s.f.* skimming, creaming *(leite).*

desnatadeira, *s.f.* cream separator, milk-skimmer *(máquina).*

desnatar, *v.t.* to separate, cream *(de leite);* to take away the best of a thing *(fig.).*

desnaturado, *adj.* denatured (álcool); inhuman, unnatural, heartless, disnatured, monstrous, cruel.

desnaturalizar, *v.t.* to denaturalize; to change the citizenship.

desnaturar, *v.t.* to denature; to pervert; to misrepresent; to render cruel.

desnecessariamente, *adv.* unecessarily, uselessly.

desnecessário, *adj.* unnecessary, useless, needless, superfluous, uncalled for.

desniquelar, *v.t.* to deprive of nickel.

desnível, *s.m.* unlevelling, unevenness, difference in levels.

desnivelado, *adj.* unlevelled.

desnivelamento, *s.m.* unlevelling.

desnivelar, *v.t.* to unlevel, to make uneven.

desnorteado, *adj.* lost, off course, bewildered, perplexed, confused, muddled; crazy, dizzy, foolish; distempered.

desnorteador, desnorteante, *adj.* confusing, bewildering.

desnorteamento, *s.m.* disorientation, confusion.

desnortear, *v.t.* to desorientate; to mislead, to lead astray, to misguide, to throw off course; to bewilder, to confuse, to perturb; *desnortear-se,* to lose the way, to be lost; to lose one's bearings *(fig.).*

desnublado, *adj.* cloudless; diaphanous.

desnublar, *v.t.* to uncloud, to clear up; *desnublar-se,* to become clear.

desnudação, desnudamento, *s.f., s.m.* denudation, undressing, unclothing.

desnudar, *v.t.* to denude, to undress, to unclothe, to strip; to bare; to lay bare.

desnudez, *s.f.* nudity, nakedness.

desnudo, *adj.* naked, denuded, undressed, uncovered; bare.

desnutrição, *s.m.* malnutrition, undernourishment.

desnutrir, *v.t.* to undernourish, to nourish poorly.

desobedecer, *v.t.* to disobey, to transgress, to be disobedient, to violate *(uma ordem).*

desobediência, *s.f.* disobedience, insubordination, rebellion, indiscipline.

desobediente, *adj.* disobedient, contumatious, insubordinate, ungorvenable.

desobriga, desobrigação, *s.f.* dispensation, exemption, release from; discharge of.

desobrigado, *adj.* unpledged, disengaged, free, exempt of.

desobrigar, *v.t.* to discharge, to exempt, to free, to release, to exonerate, to dispense; to unbind; to disengage. 1) *desobrigar-se,* to discharge a duty, to free oneself of obligation. 2) *desobrigar-se da promessa,* to fulfill the promise.

desobscurecer, *v.t.* to clarily, to enlighten; to clear up.

desobstrução, *s.f.* clearance, unstopping, removal of obstruction.

desobstruir, *v.t.* to remove the obstructions, to free of, to unstop, to desobstruct, to unbar, to clear.

desocupação, *s.f.* leisure, idleness; unemployment; emptiness.

desocupado, *adj.* unoccupied; idle; empty; unemployed; free, vacant, untenanted.

desocupar, *v.t.* to evacuate; to empty; to clear, to disoccupy, to vacate *(casa).*

desodorante, desodorizante, *adj.* deodorizing, disinfecting; *s.m.* deodorant.

desodorizar, *v.t.* to disinfect, to deodorize, to make scentless.

desoficializar, *v.t.* to make unofficial or informal.

desofuscar, *v.t.* to clear up *(atmosfera),* to enlighten.

desolação, *s.f.* desolation; solitude; ravage; affliction, unhappiness, wretchedness.

desolado, *adj.* desolate, solitary; comfortless, afflicted, inconsolable; desolated, devastated, ruined.

desolador, *adj.* desolating, distressing, afflicting, grievous.

desolar, *v.t.* to desolate, to lay waste, to ruin, to destroy; to distress, to afflict, to torment, to depress.

desolhado, *adj.* with hollow eyes, downcast, tired-eyed.

desoneração, *s.f.* disínvesting of a charge, dispensation, exoneration.

desonerar, *v.t.* to exonerate, to free from a charge *(pessoa).*

desonestamente, *adv.* dishonestly.

desonestar, *v.t.* to dishonour; to deflower.

desonestidade, *s.f.* dishonesty, crookedness, knavery, fraud, corruption; immorality, indecency.

desonesto, *adj.* dishonest; unchaste; indecent; corrupt, crooked, foul, unfair; dishonourable, immoral.

desonra, *s.f.* dishonour; ignominy; disgrace, disrepute, defame; shame, baseness, dishonesty.

desonrador, *s.m.* disgracer, disparager; violator; *adj.* shameful.

desonrar, *v.t.* to dishonour; to degrade; to seduce; to discredit, to disgrace, to defame; to violate, to deflower; to spot, to defile.

desonroso, *adj.* dishonourable, disgraceful, shameful.

desopilação, *s.f.* deoppilation; purgation; cheering up, exhilaration.

desopilante, *adj.* relieving, stimulating; purgative; exhilarating, laugh-provoking.

desopilar, *v.t.* to deoppilate, to deobstruct, to free of; to purge; to cheer up, to enliven, to exhilarate; *desopilar o fígado,* to expand, to cheer up, to laugh roarily.

desopressão, *s.f.* relief, ease, freeness from opression.

desoprimir, *v.t.* to free *(da opressão)* to liberate, to ease, to lighten.

desoras, *loc. adv.* very late, untimely, at late *(da noite);* in the small hours.

desordeiro, *s.m.* rioter, brawler, ruffian, rowdy, hooligan; *adj.* quarrel-some, rowdy, turbulent, rough, riotous.

desordem, *s.f.* disorder, riot, tumult, dispute, quarrel, turmoil, commotion, uproar, brawl; confusion, jumble, disarrangement, disarray; muddle, shindy, untidiness. 1) *em desordem,* topsy-turvy, upside down, pell-mell. 2) *estar em desordem,* to lie about. 3) *pôr em desordem,* to pell-mel. 4) *provocar a desordem,* to riot.

desordenadamente, *adv.* disorderly.

desordenado, *adj.* unruly, disordered, untidy, deranged, confused; trouble-some, tumultuary; disordinate.

desordenador, *adj.* disturbing, disordering, disarranging; *s.m.* disturber, rioter, disorderly fellow.

desordenar, *v.t.* to disorder, to disturb, to disarrange, to derange, to put out of order.

desorelhado, *adj.* earless.

desorelhar, *v.t.* to cut off the ears.

desorganização, *s.f.* disorganization, disorder, confusion, chaos, disarrangement.

desorganizador, *adj.* confusing; *s.m.* disorganizer.

desorganizar, *v.t.* to disorganize, to disorder, to unsettle, to disturb, to muddle, to subvert.

desorientação, *s.f.* bewilderment, disorientation, perplexity, confusion, foolishness.

desorientado, *adj.* bewildered, foolish, disorientated, perplexed, confused; lost.

desorientador, *adj.* perplexing, bewildering, leading astray; *s.m.* disorientator.

desorientar, *v.t.* to lead astray, to throw off course; to bewilder, to confuse, to throw into confusion; *desorientar-se,* to become confused, bewildered, lost, to lose one's way.

desossado, *adj.* boned.

desossamento, *s.m.* boning.

desossar, *v.t.* to bone, to remove the bones.

desova, desovamento, *s.f., s.m.* spawn, spawning *(peixes),* egglaying.

desovar, *v.i.* to spawn, to lay eggs.

desoxidação, *s.f.* deoxidation, deoxidization.

desoxidante, *adj.* deoxidizing.

desoxidar, *v.t.* to deoxidize.

desoxigenação, *s.f.* deoxygenation.

desoxigenante, *adj.* deoxigenating.

desoxigenar, *v.t.* to deoxygenate.

despachado, *adj.* resolved, settled; quick, expedite, swift; posted, dispatched; frank, sincere; courageous; put to death *(fig.).*

despachante, *s.m.* customs clearing agent, customhouse broker.

despachar, *v.t.* to dispatch, to dispose of, to render decision on; to register; to label; to clear; to dismiss, to fire, to deprive of employment; to kill; to hasten. 1) *despachar-se,* to conclude the affairs, to make haste, to hurry. 2) *despachar bagagem,* to book the luggage. 3) *despachar uma encomenda,* to express a parcel.

despacho, *s.m.* dispatch; judgement; clearing; decision, resolution; clearance; haste, diligence; writ, order; *despacho ministerial,* ministerial dispatch.

despalmilhar, *v.t.* to take out the inner sole.

desparamentar, *v.t.* to take off vestments *(sacerdotais).*

desparrar, *v.t.* to lop off.

despautério, *s.m.* nonsense, absurdity, foolishness, stupidity.

despedaçar, *v.t.* to tear to pieces, to smash, to shatter, to break, to crash, to destroy; to rend, to rip, to lacerate.

despedida, *s.f.* farewell, leave-taking, departure ; discharge, dismissal; separation; end, conclusion *(fig.).* 1)*jantar de despedida,* farewell dinner. 2) *despedida afectuosa,* friendly send-off.

despedido, *adj.* dismissed, discharged.

despedimento, *s.m.* discharge, dismissal.

despedir, *v.t.* to dismiss, to discharge, to send away; to fire, to shoot, to let off. 1) *despedir-se,* to take leave, to say farewell, to say good-bye, to part with. 2) *despedir-se à francesa,* to take French leave. 3) *despedir alguém,* to give someone the sack.

despegado, *adj.* unattached, free, detached, unfixed, unglued.

despegar, *v.t.* to unglue; to detach, to unfix, to unstick; to stop, to finish *(fig.).*

despego, *s.m.* indifference, detachment, unconcern, apathy.

despeitado, *adj.* spiteful, resentful, offended, hurt.

despeitar, *v.t.* to spite, to vex, to pique, to rile, to fret, to worry.

despeito, *s.m.* spite, displeasure, pique, resentment, umbrage; rage, anger. 1) *por depeito,* out of spite. 2) *a despeito de,* in spite of, despite, notwithstanding.

despejado, *adj.* emptied; clear; licentious, shameless, indecent, obscene.

despejar, *v.t.* to empty; to pour out; to throw away or out; to remove; to evacuate, to oust; to evict, to dispossess.

despejo, *s.m.* emptying, removing; spillilng, pouring out; evacuation, eviction; litter, garbage, rubbish; boldness, impudence; *mandado de despejo,* notice to quit.

despender, *v.t.* to spend *(dinheiro);* to waste; to expend *(tempo e energia);* to dissipate, to squander, to use.

despendurar, *v.t.* to unbook; to unhang; to take down.

despenhadeiro, *s.m.* precipice, steep, crag, slope.

despenhar, *v.t.* to hurl down, to precipitate, to cast down, to fall headlong; to bring low; *despenhar-se,* to fall headlong, to plunge (to ruin); to crash (airplane).

despensa, pantry, larder, buttery, storeroom.

despenseira, *s.f.* stewardess.

despenseiro, *s.m.* steward, butler, prantryman, cellarist.

despenteado, *adj.* disheveled, uncombed, unkempt, rough.

despentear, *v.t.* to undress *(cabelo),* to dishevel, to tousle.

desperceber, *v.t.* not to perceive, to disregard, to pay no attention.

despercebidamente, *adv.* unnoticed, unperceived.

despercebido, *adj.* unnoticed, unobserved, unfelt, unseen, unheeded.

desperdiçado, *adj.* wasted, wasteful, lost, spendthrift; prodigal.

desperdiçador, *adj. s.m.* waster, spendthrift, prodigal.

desperdiçar, *v.t.* to waste, to lavish, to squander, to throw away, to scatter, to fritter away, to dissipate.

desperdício, *s.m.* waste, lavishness, wastage, squandering, loss, dissipation.

despersonalização, *s.f.* depersonalization, loss of personality.

despersonalizar, *v.t.* to depersonalize, to deprive of personality.

despersuadir, *v.t.* to dissuade, to advise to the contrary, to divert from.

despersuasão, *s.f.* dissuasion, diversion from a purpose.

despertador, *s.m.* alarm-clock, alarm-bell.

despertar, *v.t.* to waken, to wake, to awake; to excite; to rouse from sleep; *s.m.* awakening; *despertar interesse,* to arouse interest.

desperto, *adj.* awake, roused from sleep.

despesa, *s.f.* expense, cost, expenditure, outlay, charge, payment. 1) *despesa adicional,* additional charges. 2) *despesa da alfândega,* customs duty. 3) *despesas de porte,* carrying charges. 4) *despesas gerais,* overhead expenses. 5) *despesas miúdas,* petty charges. 5) *despesas de representação,* representation fees. 6) *não olhar a despesas,* not to spare money.

despicar, *v.t.* to revenge, to avenge, to vindicate.

despiciendo, *adj.* worhless.

despido, *adj.* undressed, nude, naked, uncovered, unclothed; bare; free, exempt, stripped.

despiedoso, *adj.* unmerciful, inhuman, pitiless, cruel, merciless, fierce.

despigmentação, *s.f.* lack of pigmentation.

despique, *s.m.* revenge, redress, satisfaction, spite.

despir, *v.t.* to undress, to unclothe, to take off, to strip, to disrobe to divest, to dispossess.

despistagem, *s.f.* the at of misleading or throwing off the track.

despistar, *v.t.* to mislead, to throw off the track.

desplante, *s.m.* impudence, cheek, insolence, sauciness.

desplumar, *v.t.* o pluck, to strip of leathers, to deplume, to unfeather.

despoetizar, *v.t.* to render unpoetical, to make prosaic.

de'spojar, *v.t.* to spoil, to strip; to shear; to deprive, to divest; *despojar-se,* to renounce to.

despojo, *s.m.* booty; spoils; plunder, robbing, despoliation. 1) *despojos,* leftovers, scraps. 2) *despojos mortais,* mortal remains.

despolarização, *s.f.* depolarization.

despolarizante, *adj.* depolarizing.

despolarizar, *v.t.* to depolarize.

despolir, *v.t.* to take the polish away, to render dull, unpolished.

despontar, *v.t.* to blunt, to take the points away, to sprout, to appear, to come to view, to rise, to emerge.

desportista, *s.* sportsman, athlete; *adj.* sportive.

desportivismo, *s.m.* loyalty, desportive.

desportivo, *adj.* sportive, sporting, athletic.

desporto, *s.m.* sport; play, game; recreation, amusement.

desposar, *v.t.* to marry; *desposar-se,* to get married.

desposório, *s.m.* marriage.

déspota, *s.* despot, tyrant, oppressor.

despoticamente, *adv.* despotically.

despótico, *adj.* despotic; absolute, oppressive, tyrannic.

despotismo, *s.m.* despotism, tyranny, dictatorship, oppression.

despovoação, despovoamento, *s.f., s.m.* depopulation.

despovoado, *s.m.* desert; *adj.* depopulated, deserted, uninhabited, empty.

despovoar, *v.t.* to depopulate, to dispeople, to lay waste; *despovoar-se,* to become deserted or depopulated.

despratear, *v.t.* to scrape the silver off, to desilverize.

desprazer, desprazimento, *s.m.* displeasure; grief; *v.i.* to displease, to disgust, to discontent.

desprecatado, *adj.* improvident, careless, heedless.

desprecatar-se, *v. refl.* to be unwary, to neglect.

desprecaver-se, *v. refl.* to be unwary, to be heedless.

despregado, *adj.* loose, unfastened, unnailed; unfurled.

despregar, *v.t.* to unnail, to unfold, to unhook, to unfasten, to unfix, to unpin; to remove; to unfurl.

desprender, *v.t.* to unfasten, to looser, to release, to unfix; to disengage; to detach; to throw off; *desprender-se,* to get loose, to become disengaged.

desprendido, *adj.* loose, untied; unselfish, indifferent.

desprendimento, *s.m.* unfastening; landslide; detachment, indifference; unselfishness, altruism, self-denial.

despreocupação, *v.t.* carelessness, unconcern, nonchalance.

despreocupadamente, *adv.* at ease.

despreocupado, *adj.* careless; thoughtless, carefree, light, unconcerned.

despreocupar, *v.t.* to free from care, to relieve of concern.

desprestigiar, *v.t.* to depreciate, to discredit, to lessen prestige; *desprestigiar-se,* to lose one's prestige or reputation or standing.

desprestígio, *s.m.* depreciation, discredit, loss of authority or reputation.

despretensão, *s.f.* modesty, unpretentiousness.

despretensiosamente, *adv.* unpretentiously.

despretensioso, *adj.* unassuming, modest, unpretentious, simple, modest, humane.

desprevenido, *adj.* unprovided, unwary, unprepared, unaware; off-guard; without money, penniless.

desprevenir, *v.t.* to neglect ; *desprevenir-se,* to be heedless.

desprezador, *s.m.* scorner, despiser; *adj.* scornful, contemptuous, disdainful.

desprezar, *v.t.* to despize, to scorn, to condemn, to disdain, to slight, to look down upon; to neglect, to reject; to disregard, to detest; to undervalue, to underrate.

desprezível, *adj.* contemptible; mean, vile, worthless; sordid, dirty, paltry; miserable, poor; negligible.

desprezivelmente, *adv.* despicably, meanly.

desprezo, *s.m.* disdain, contempt, scorn, slightness; disregard, defiance; carelessness.

desprimor, *s.m.* unfairness, impoliteness, incivility.

desprimoroso, *adj.* impolite, unpolished, ungentle, unkind, discourteous; mean, base, vile.

despronúncia, *s.f.* annulling *(acusação),* acquittal.

despronunciar, *v.t.* to annul, to cancel *(uma acusação);* to acquit, to absolve.

desproporção, *s.f.* disproportion, inadequacy, disparity, inequality.

desproporcionado, desproporcional, *adj.* disproportionate, unsuitable, unequal, inadequate, unbalanced; unshaped, oversize, outsize.

desproporcionar, *v.t.* to disproportion.

despropositadamente, *adv.* unreasonably, nonsensically.

despropositado, *adj.* unreasonable, absurd, nonsensical, inopportune, irrelevant; foolish, impertinent.

despropositar, *v.i.* to talk at random; to be out of the way.

despropósito, *s.m.* nonsense, absurdity, preposterousness, irrelevance; impertinence.

desprotecção, *s.f.* want of protection.

desproteger, *v.t.* to deprive of protection, to fail to protect ; to abandon.

desprotegido, *adj.* unprotected, undefended, unarmed; exposed, uncovered.

desprover, *v.t.* to deprive of.

desprovido, *adj.* unprovided with, destitute of, stripped ol, lacking, without, devoid of.

despudor, *s.m.* shamelessness, impudence.

despudorado, *adj.* impudent, shameless, insolent; *s. m.* shameless fellow.

desqualificação, *s.f.* disqualification, elimination.

desqualificado, *adj.* disqualided, eliminated; worthless.

desqualificar, *v.t.* to disqualify, to eliminate.

desquitação, desquite, *s.m.* divorce, separation, disunion, dissolution of marriage; weaning *(pop).*

desquitar, *v.t.* to divorce, to separate, to release from *(uma obrigação); desquitar-se,* to get rid of; to have done with; to be revenged of; to wean *(uma criança) (pop).*

desramar, *v.t.* to disbranch, to lop a tree.

desrazoável, *adj.* unreasonable.

desregradamente, *adv.* immoderately, intemperately, disorderly; dissolutely.

desregrado, *adj.* intemperate, dissolute, unruly, unrestrained, extravagant.

desregramento, *s. m.* immorality; excess, dissipation; immoderatin, intemperance, unrestraint.

desregrar-se, v. refl. to go astray, to dissipate, to lead a loose life.

desrespeitador, adj. disrespectful.

desrespeitar, v. t. to disrespect, to disregard; to affront.

desrespeito, s. m. disrespect, slight, defiance; impoliteness, incivility.

desrespeitoso, adj. disrespectful, regardless, flippant, fresh.

dessalgar, v. t. to desalt, to deprive of salt.

desse, prep. de e pron. dem. esse; of that; from that.

dessecação, dessecamento, s. f., s. m. desiccation; drying; drainage.

dessecar, v. t. to desiccate, to dry; to drain.

dessedentar, v. t. to quench the thirst; to water (animais).

desselar, v. t. to unsaddle (cavalo); to unseal (cartas).

dessemelhança, s.f. v. dissemelhança.

dessemelhante, adj. ver dissemelhante.

dessemelhar, v.t. v. dissemelhar.

desserviço, s. m. disservice, ill turn.

desservlr, v. t. to disserve, to serve badly.

dessimetria, s. f. dissymmetry, asymmetry.

dessimétrico, adj. dissymmetric, asymmetric.

dessoldar, v. t. to unsolder, to separate.

dessorado, adj. weak, feeble.

dessorar, v. t. to weaken; to make serous.

desta, prep. de e pron. dem. esta; of this, from this. 1) desta sorte, thus. 2) desta vez, this time.

destacado, adj. outstanding.

destacamento, s. m. detachment (de um exército).

destacar, v. t. to detach (tropas); to make salient, to make stand out, to put in relief; destacar-se, to distinguish oneself, to stand out.

destampatório, s. m. nonsense; uproar; loud argument.

destapar, v. t. to uncover, to open; to unstop.

destaque, s. m. prominence, distinction, eminence, notability; pessoa de destaque, person of note.

deste, prep. de e pron. dem. este; of this; from this.

destelhamento, s. m. untiling.

destelhar, v. t. to untile, to unroof, to remove the tiles from the roof.

destemido, adj. fearless, courageous, dauntless, daring, bold, intrepid, brave.

destemor, s. m. fearlessness, daringness, boldness, intrepidity.

destemperadamente, adv. immoderately.

destemperado, adj. intemperate; unreserved, violent; dissonant; excessive, exorbitant; crazy, insane, mad.

destemperança, s. f. intemperance, excess.

destemperar, v. t. to untemper; to untune; to disconcert; to upset, to disturb (estômago); to distemper, to spoil the temper; to comit excesses.

destempero, s.m. disorder; passion; transport; absurdity; fit of anger.

desterrar, v. t. to exile, to banish, to expatriate, to deport; desterrar-se, to emigrate.

desterro, s. m. exile, banishment, expatriation; place of exile.

desterroador, s. m. harrower.

desterroar, v. t. to harrow, to drag, to break up clods.

destilação, s. f. distillation; distillery.

destilador, s. m. distiller; still, retort.

destilar, v. t. to distil, to exude; to pour out in drops.

destilaria, s. f. distillery, boilery.

destinado, adj. intended; determined.

destinar, v. t. to destine; to appoint, to determined to mean, to consign, to allot; destinar-se a, to devote oneself to; to be meant for; to be addressed to.

destinatário, s. m. addressee, receiver, consignee.

destingir, v. t. to discolour, to bleach; to fade, to lose colour.

destino, s. m. destiny; destination; fate; purpose; lot; fatality; future, fortune; com destino a, (barco) bound for.

destituição, s. f. destitution, dismissal, deposing.

destituído, adj. dismissed, deposed, deprived of an office; devoid; needy, destitute, wanting; stupid.

destituir, v. t. to dismiss, to deprive of, to depose, to oust, to fire.

destoante, adj. inharmonious, dissonant, discordant, untunely; harsh.

destoar, v. i. to discord, to sound discordantly; to jar, to clash; to differ, to diverge; to be unsuitable.

destorcer, v. t. to untwist, to untwine; to turn around.

destorroar, v. t. to break up clumps of soil.

destra, s. f. the right hand.

destrambelhado, adj. giddy, foolish, silly.

destrambelhamento, s. m. disorder; disarray; folly, nonsense.

destrambelhar, v. i. to get out of fix, to behave crazily.

destramente, adv. skilfully; adroitly.

destrancar, v. t. to unbar, to unlock.

destravar, v. t. to unfetter; to unshackle; to release the break.

destreinado, adj. unaccostumed, lacking training, untrained, unprepared, ignorant.

destreinar, v. t. to lose training, to forget the training.

destreza, s. f. dexterity, skill; cunning, cleverness; ingenuity, ability; facility, art; readiness, quickness.

destrinça, s. f. specification, detail, particularization.

destrinçar, v. t. to specify, to disentangle, to particularize, to treat in detail.

destro, adj. skilful, dexterous, clever, habile, artful, handy, agile.

destroca, s. f. a changing back.

destrocar, v. t. to change again, to swap (alguma coisa) back.

destroçar, v. t. to break into pieces, to raze, to devastate, to wreck, to destroy; to defeat; to disperse, to disband (um exército).

destroço, s. m. destruction; spoil; havoc; wreckage, rack, ruins (pl.); destroços de um navio, the remains of a ship.

destronamento, s. m. dethronement, deposition.

destronar, v. t. to dethrone; to take down, to humble.

destroncar, v. t. to truncate; to maim, to cut down the trunk (de uma árvore).

destruição, s. f. destruction, ruin, devastation, rack and ruin, ravage; extermination , extinction.

destruidor, adj. destructive, demolishing, ruinous; s. m. destroyer.

destruir, v. t. to destroy, to waste, to annihilate, to demolish, to throw down, to crush, to raze, to blast; to devastate, to shatter, to ruin; to undo; to extirpate, to kill. 1) destruir um forte, to raze a fortress. 2) destruir totalmente, to raze to the ground.

destrunfar, v. t. to force trumps (jogo de cartas).

destrutibilidade, s. f. destructibility.

destrutível, adj. destructible.

destrutivo, adj. destructive, ruinous; wasteful.

desumanidade, s. f. inhumanity, cruelty, barbarism.

desumano, adj. inhuman, cruel, brutal, bararous, savage, pitiless, ruthless.

desunhar, v. t. to pluck off the nails; desunhar-se, to put oneself to work, to work hard.

desunião, s. f. disunion, separation; breach, quarrel; dissension, discord, variance.

desunificar, v. t. to disunify.

desunir, v. t. to disunite, to disjoin, to separate, to divided to set at variance, to alienate.

desusado, adj. unusual, disused; obsolete, unused; uncommon.

desusar-se, v. refl. to gow out of use, to fall into disuse.

desuso, s. m. disuse; cair em desuso, to fall out of use.

desvairado, adj. confused; hallucinated, deranged, wild, frenetic; crazy, crackbrained; de olhar desvairado, wild eyed.

desvairamento, s. m. hallucination; frenzy; bewilderment.

desvairar, v. t. to hallucinate, to make crazy.

desvairo, s. m. v. desvario.

desvalido, adj. helpless, disgraced, abandoned, forsaken.

desvalimento, s. m. disgrace; dereliction; worthlessness; disfavour.

desvalorização, s. f. depreciation, devaluation.

desvalorizar, v. t. to depreciate, to devaluate, to depress; to undervalue, to underrate, to belittle.

desvanecedor, adj. that puffs up; causing pride.

desvanecer, v. t. to disperse; to dissipate.

desvanecido, adj. dissipated, dispelled, vanished; vain, proud, grateful.

desvanecimento, s. m. dissipation; presumption; pride; gratification; complacency.

desvantagem, s. f. disadvantage, handicap; inconvenience; inferiority.

desvantajosamente, adv. disadvantageously.

desvantajoso, adj. disadvantageous, prejudicial, inconvenient, unprofitable, unfavourable.

desvão, s. m. attic, garret, corner; hide-out.

desvario, s. m. raving; incongruity; madness; extravagance, caprice.

desveladamente, adv. carefully.

desvelado, adj. careful, watchful, cautious, zealous, solicitous, unveiled, uncovered.

desvelar-se, v. refl. to be careful or diligent.

desvelo, s. m. care, zeal, attention, diligence, devotion, solicitude.

desvendar, v. t. to discover, to reveal, to uncover, to unveil, to remove the blindfold from *(dos olhos)*; to unriddle; *desvendar um mistério,* to solve a mistery.

desventura, s.f. misfortune, misadventure, unhappiness, ill fortune, bad luck, disaster.

desventurado, adj. unfortunate, unhappy, unlucky, miserable; s.m. a wretch, a miserable creature.

desventurar, v.t. to make unhappy.

desventuroso, adj. unfortunate, unhappy, unlucky.

desvergonha, s.f. shamelessness, impudence, sauciness.

desvergonhado, adj. shameless, unblushing; s.m. shameless fellow.

desvestir, v.t. to undress.

desviado, adj. removed, apart, distant; put out of the way.

desviamento, s. m. removing; deviation.

desviar, v.t. to remove, to put out ol the way, to turn aside; to lead astray; to divert; to mislead, to put in the wrong. 1) *desviar-se,* to miss the way, to straggle. 2) *desviar-se de,* to avoid; to wander, to stray from; to keep clear of. 3) *desviar-se do assunto,* to digress. 4) *desviar o olhar,* to look away. 5) *desviar um golpe,* to parry a blow. 6) *desviar do estudo,* to divert from studying. 7) *desviar dinheiro,* to misappropriate (purloin, embezzle) money. 8) *desviar o pensamento,* to withdraw. 9) *desviar-se de um perigo,* to shun a danger. 10) *desviar-se da verdade,* to deviate from the truth.

desvidrar, v. t. to lose the glaze.

desvincar, v. t. to unwrinkle, to smooth.

desvinculação, s. f. disentail.

desvincunlar, v. t. to disentail, to free from entail; to free from connection; *desvincular--se,* to disengage oneself from; to become separated.

desvio, s.m. deviation; declination; deflection; diversion; detour; bypass; switch, side-track *(caminho de ferro);* dissuation; embezzlement (money); subterfuge, evasion, escape; aberration, misguidance; *desvio da agulha magnética,* deflection of the compass needle.

desvirar, v.t. to unturn, to turn back to a former position.

desvirilizar, v.t. to unman, to destroy the virility.

desvirtuação, s.f. depreciation, disrepute; misrepresentation.

desvirtuar, v.t. to depreciate; to deccry; to misrepresent.

desvitalizar, v. t. to devitalize, to deprive of vitality; to sap.

detalhadamente, adv. particularly, fully, minutely, from point to point.

detalhado, adj. detailed, circumstantial.

detalhar, v.t. to detail, to give full account, to particularize, to specify.

detalhe, s.m. detail, particulirity. 1) *detalhes técnicos,* techncalities. 2) *dar todos os detalhes,* to give full details. 3) *entrar em detalhes,* to go (enter) into particulars. 4) *para mais detalhes dirija-se a,* for further details apply to.

detecção, s.f. detection, discovery.

detectar, v.t. to detect, to uncover, to find out, to discover.

detective, s.m. detective.

detector, s.m. detector.

detença, s.f. delay, stay, retardation, demurrage, detainment.

detenção, s.f. detention, imprisonment, confinement, arrest.

detentor, s.m. detainer; holder, owner, proprietor.

deter, v.t. to detain, to retain, to retard; to hold, to back, to withhold, to stop; to hinder, to check; to retain in custody, to keep in arrest.

detergente, adj. detergent.

deterioração, s.f. deterioration, waste, decay.

deteriorar, v.t. to deteriorate, to impair; to damage; to rot, to putrify; to decay; *deteriorar-se,* to become rotten, to grow worse.

deteriorável, adj. deteriorative, decayable.

determinação, s.f. determination, resolution, decision; instruction; order; firmness, courage, boldness.

determinadamente, adv. determinately.

determinado, adj. determined; definite; bold; courageous; with definite limits, bound; certain, concrete.

determinante, s.f. determinant; adj. determinative; decisive, definite.

determinar, v.t. to determine, to order, to command; to define; to settle, to decide, to regulate; to limit, to fix, to bound, to mark; to cause, to effect; to influence, to impel.

determinativo, adj. determinative, conclusive.

determinável, adj. determinable.

determinismo, *s.m.* determinism.

determinista, *s.* determinist.

detersão, *s.f.* cleansing; detersion.

detersivo, *adj.* detersive, detergent.

detestação, *s.f.* detestation, abhorrence, horror, hatred.

detestar, *v.t.* to detest, to abhor, to loathe, to abominate, to hate, to dislike greatly.

detestável, *adj.* detestable, abominable, odious, execrable, hateful; mean, vile.

detestavelmente, *adv.* detestably.

detidamente, *adv.* minutely, attentively, slowly.

detido, *adj.* detained, retarded, delayed; stopped; in custody; hindered.

detonação, *s.f.* detonation, explosion.

detonador, *s.m.* detonator; exploder.

detonante, *adj.* detonating.

detonar, *v.i.* to detonate, to explode.

detracção, *s.f.* detraction, disparagement; slander, calumny, defamation.

detractivo, *adj.* detractive, derogative.

detractor, *s.m.* detractor, slanderer, maligner, blackmouth, backbiter.

detrair, *v. t.* to detract, to derogate, to malign; to slander, to backbite, to defame.

detrás, *adv.* after, behind, back; *por detrás,* from behind, behind one's back, in the absence of.

detrição, *s.f.* detretion.

detrimento, *s.m.* prejudice, detriment, injury, loss, damage; *em detrimento de,* to the detriment of.

detrito, *s.m.* remains, detritus, debris, dreg.

deturpação, *s.f.* disfigurement, corruption, adulteration, falsification, alteration, distortion.

deturpador, *s.m.* distorter; corrupter.

deturpar, *v.t.* to disfigure, to deform, to distort, to adulterate, to falsify, to misrepresent; to corrupt, to defile.

Deus, *s.m.* God, Lord. 1) *Deus me livre,* god forbid. 2) *Deus permita,* God grant. 3) *Deus queira,* would to God. 4) *meu Deus!,* Good Lord!. 5) *graças a Deus,* thank heavens. 6) *pelo amor de Deus,* for God's sake. 7) *se Deus quiser,* God willing. 8) *vá com Deus,* God speed you. 9) *Deus Todo-Poderoso,* All Mighty God. 10) *estar bem com Deus e com o Diabo,* to make the best of both worlds. 11) *o homem põe e Deus dispõe,* man proposes, but God disposes.

deusa, *s.f.* goddess, deity.

deus-dará, used in the expression, *ao deus-dará,* at random, haphazardly.

Deuteronómio, *s.m.* Deuteronomy.

devagar, *adv.* slowly, at leisure, softly; *interj.* steady!, hold your horses!; *devagar se vai ao longe,* fair and softly goes far.

devaneador, *s.m.* daydreaming; daydreamer, castle builder.

devanear, *v.i.* to rave, to muse, to meditate, to daydream, to dote.

devaneio, *s.m.* fancy, dream, daydream, reverie, illusion, wool-gatherng, chimera.

devassa, *s.f.* inquest, official inquiry, exhaustive investigation.

devassado, *adj.* overlooked; exposed to view, obvious to the sight.

devassador, *s.m.* divulger.

devassar, *v.t.* to view; to divulge; to make licentious; to invade, to enter, to penetrate; to inquire, to examine.

devassidão, *s.f.* licentiousness, lechery, dissoluteness, debauchery, libertinism, prostitution.

devasso, *adj.* licentious, libertine, debauched, dissolute, wanton, immoral, lecherous; *s. m.* debauchee, libertine, rake.

devastação, *s. f.* devastation, havoc, ravage, destruction.

devastador, *adj., s. m.* devastating; devastator, destroyer, waster.

devastar, *v.t.* to devastate, to destroy, to ravage, to lay waste, to destruct.

deve, *s.m.* debit ; *deve e haver,* debit and credit.

devedor, *s.m.* debtor; *adj.* owing, in debt.

dever, *s.m.* obligation, duty; task, job, burden, business; *v. t.* to owe; ought; must; to be obliged; to have to do; to be in debt. 1) *dever os olhos da cara,* to be in head over heels in debt. 2) *dever a vida,* to owe one's lite to.

deveras, *adv.* indeed, truly, in truth, in earnest, really, certainly, in fact.

devesa, *s.f.* alley; farm.

devidamente, *adv.* duly, properly, orderly.

devido, *adj.* due, just, owing to; *devido a,* owing to, due to, on account of.

devoção, *s.f.* devotion, piety; attachment; religious fervour; dedication; fidelity; affection.

devocionário, *s. m.* prayer-book.

devolução, *s. f.* devolution, restitution, return; reversion; refund.

devolutivo, *adj.* devolutive, reversional, returnable.

devoluto, *adj.* vacant, empty, uninhabited, unoccupied.

devolver, *v. t.* to return, to devolve, to give back, to send back.

devorador, *adj.* devouring, consuming, wolfish, voracious, avid, ravenous; *s. m.* devourer.

devorar, *v. t.* to devour; to consume; to waste; to eat up greedily, to eat hungrily.

devorismo, *s. m.* squandering, wasting of money; embezzlement of public funds.

devorista, *s.* squanderer, waster; *adj.* wasteful.

devotação, devotamento, *s.m.* devotement, dedication, fidelity.

devotado, *adj.* devoted, dedicated.

devotar, *v.t.* to devote, to dedicate, to consecrate.

devoto, *s.m.* devotee, bigot, zealot; *adj.* devout, pious, religious, devoted.

dez, *num.* ten.

dezanove, *num.* nineteen.

dezasseis, *num.* sixteen.

dezassete, *num.* seventeen.

Dezembro, *s. m.* December.

dezena, *s.f.* ten; half a-score, ten days; *às dezenas,* by tens.

dezoito, *num.* eighteen.

dia, *s.m.* day. 1) *dia a dia,* daily, day by day. 2) *dia de abstinência, jejum,* fast day, fish day. 3) *dia de Ano Novo (ano Bom),* New Year's Day. 4) *dia de anos (aniversário),* birthday, anniversary. 5) *dia dos enganos,* all fools' day. 6) *dia feriado,* holiday. 7) *dia de finados,* All Souls' Day. 8) *dia de folga,* day of rest, playday, a day off. 9) *dia de gala,* collar-day. 10) *dia de juízo,* doomsday. 11) *dia lectivo,* schoolday. 12) *Dia de Natal,* Christmas Day. 13) *dia de Páscoa,* Easter Day. 14) *dia de Reis,* Epiphany. 15) *um dia de rosas,* a clear, windless day. 16) *dia santo,* holiday. 17) *dia de são nunca,* at the calends. 18) *dia sim, dia não,* every other day. 19) *dias a fio,* days on end. 20) *ao romper do dia,* at daybreak. 21) *bom dia (bons dias),* good morning. 22) *de dois em dois dias,* every two days. 23) *é dia claro,* it is broad daylight. 24) *de dia,* in the day time, by day. 25) *estar em dia,* to be up-to-date. 26) *fazer do dia noite,* to turn day into night. 27) *há dias,* some days ago. 28) *daqui a dias,* some days hence. 29) *hoje em dia,* nowadays. 30) *mais dia menos dia,* sooner or later. 31) *no dia seguinte,* next day. 32) *todo o dia,* all day long. 33) *todos os dias,* every day.

diabetes, *s.m., s. f.* diabetes.

diabético, *adj., s.m.* diabetic.

Diabo, *s.m.* devil, demon, fiend, satan, Beelzebub, Old Nick. 1) *diabo a quatro,* to play the devil. 2) *aí é que está o diabo,* there lies the difficulty. 3) *anda o diabo à solta,* the hell is broken loose. 4) *o diabo não é tão mau como o pintam,* the devil is not so black as he is painted. 5) *por artes do diabo,* devilish tricks. 6) *pintar o diabo,* to raise the devil. 7) *pobre diabo,* poor devil, poor wretch. 8) *que diabo quer?,* what the devil do vou want?. 9) *enquanto o diabo esfrega um olho,* in two shakes of a dog's tail. 10) *valha-te o diabo,* the devil take you.

diabolicamente, *adv.* diabolically, devilishly.

diabólico, *adj.* devilish; diabolical, hellish, infernal, satanic, fiendish, demoniacal; very wicked; intrincate.

diabrete, *s.m.* imp, little devil; mischievous child; sprite; hobgoblin, game at cards.

diabrura, *s.m.* deviltry, devilish trick, prank, mischief; *fazer uma diabrura,* to act up.

diaconado, diaconato, *s.m.* deaconate, deaconry.

diaconisa, *s.f.* deaconess.

diácono, *s.m.* deacon.

diacritico, *adj.* diacritic.

diadema, *s.m.* diadem, crown.

diafaneidade, *s.f.* transparency, diaphaneity.

diáfano, *adv.* diaphanous, transparent, translucent, clear; lean, meagre *(fig).*

diafragma, *s.m.* diaphragm.

diagnose, *s.f.* diagnosis; analysis.

diagnosticador, *s. m.* diagnostician.

diagnosticar, *v. t.* to diagnose, to diagnosticate.

diagnosticável, *adv.* that can be diagnosed.

diagnóstico, *adj.* diagnostic; *s. m.* diagnosis.

diagonal, *s.f., adj.* diagonal.

diagrama, *s.m.* diagram, graph, chart, sketch.

dialectal, *adj.* dialectal.

dialéctica, *s.f.* dialectics.

dialéctico, *adj., s.m.* dialectical; dialectician.

dialecto, *s. m.* dialect.

dialectologia, *s.f.* dialectology.

diálise, *s.f.* dialysis.

dialogado, *adj.* in fom of dialogue, dialogued.

dialogador, *s.m.* dialoguer.

dialogal, *adj.* dialogic.

dialogar, *v.t.* to dialogue; to converse, to talk.

dialogismo, *s.m.* dialogism.

dialogista, *s.* dialogist.

diálogo, *s.m.* dialogue; colloquy; conversation.

diamante, *s.m.* diamond. 1) *damante bruto*, rough diamond. 2) *diamante de vidraceiro*, glazier's diamond. 3) *bodas de diamante*, diamond wedding.

diamantifero, *adj.* diamantiferous, diamond-bearing.

diamantino, *adj.* adamantine, diamantine; diamond-hard; diamond-bright.

diametral, *adj.* diamatrical.

diametralmente, *adv.* diametrically.

diâmetro, *s.m.* diameter.

diante, *adv.* before, in front; *prep.in front of.* 1) *daqui em diante*, hereafter, henceforth, from now on. 2) *dali em diante*, from then on, thereafter, thenceforth. 3) *de trás para diante*, backwards, reversely. 4) *e assim por diante*, and so on, and so forth. 5) *ir por diante*, to go on, to go ahead, to keep on.

dianteira, *s. f.* forepart; front; the lead, vanguard. 1) *dianteira do exército*, the van of an army. 2) *na dianteira*, ahead, leading. 3) *to mar a dianteira*, to overrun, to outpace.

dianteiro, *adj.* leading, fore, foremost, first, front; *s.m.* front line player *(futebol).*

diapasão, *s.m.* diapason; tuning fork; standard *(fig).*

diapositivo, *s.m.* lantern slide, diapositive, a transparency.

diária, *s.f.* daily income; daily expense.

diariamente, *adv.* daily, every day.

diário, *adj.* daily, quotidian, everyday; *s.m.* diary; daily paper; day-book; daily record; *diário de bordo*, log-book, ship's log.

diarreico, adj. diarrheal, lax.

diáspora, *s.f.* diaspora.

diástole, *s.f.* diastole.

diatermia, *s.f.* diathermy.

diatérmico, *adj.* diathermic.

diátese, *adj.* diathesis.

diatónico, *adj.* diatonic.

diatribe, *s.f.* invective, diatribc, violent criticism, banter.

dicacidade, *s.f.* causticity, dicacity, satiricalness.

dicaz, *adj.* caustic, satiric, sarcastic, jeering, bantering.

dicção, *s.f.* diction, expression.

dicéfalo, *adj.* dicephalous, two-headed.

dichote, *s.m.* jest, scoff, scorn, disdain.

dicionário, *s.m.* dictionary; word-book, lexicon, vocabulary, glossary; *dicionário de bolso (algibeira)*, pocket dictionary.

dicionarista, *s.* lexicographer.

dicionarizar, *v.t.* to include in a dictionary.

dicotiledóneas, *s.f. pl.* Dicotyledones.

dicotomia, *s.f.* dichotomy (any sense).

dicromático, *adj.* dichromatic.

didáctica, *s.f.* didactics.

didáctico, *adj.* didactic.

didáctilo, *adj.* two-fingered, didactyl, two-toed.

didascálico, *adj.* didascalic.

diedro, *s.m.* dihedron; *adj.* dihedral.

diérese, *s.f.* diaeresis, dieresis.

dieta, *s.f.* diet; assembly, meeting of delegates. 1) *fazer dieta* to be on diet. 2) *devo fazer dieta?*, must I be on diet?

dietética, *s.f.* dietetics.

dietético, *adj.* dietetic.

difamação, *s.f.* defamation, slander, calumny, backbiting, detraction.

difamador, *s.m.* slanderer, delamer, detractor; *adj.* defamatory, slanderous, defaming.

difamante, *adj.* defaming, slanderous, calumnious.

difama, *v.t.* to defame, to slander, to calumny, to malign, to discredit, to smear, to sully.

difamatório, defamatory; calumnious, slanderous.

diferença, *s.f.* difference; dissimilarity; unlikeness; divergence; discrepancy; distinction; disagreement; diversity; subtraction; mishap. 1) *diferença de preço*, difference in price. 2) *pagar a diferença*, to pay the difference. 3) *fazer diferença (diferenciar)*, to difference, to distinguish, to be different; to make a difference. 4) *faz pouca diferença*, it matters little. 5) *há muita diferença*, there wants a great deal. 6) *partir a diferença ao meio*, to split the difference.

diferençar, *v. t.* to distinguish, to discriminate; to differentiate (um do outro); to differ (de).

diferenciação, *s.f.* differentiation, discrimination.

diferencial, *adj.* differential. 1) *cálculo diferencial*, differential calculus. 2) *quociente diferencial*, differential quotient.

diferenciar, *v.t.* to difference, to discriminate, to differentiate; *diferenciar-se*, to differ, to contrast.

diferente, *adj.* different, unlike, dissimilar, unequal, distinct, particular; other, another; several, various, sundry *(pl.)*. 1) *diferente um do outro*, unlike each other. 2) *o caso é diferente*, it is quite another story.

diferentemente, *adv.* differently.

diferimento, *s.m.* deferment, delay, postponement, putting off.

diferir, *v.i.* to differ; to be unlike; to defer, to postpone, to delay, to retard, to put off, to prolong.

difícil, *adj.* difficult, hard, uneasy; arduous, painful, toilsome, laborious; intricate, complicated, obscure.

dificílimo, *adj.* very difficult.

dificilmente, *adv.* hardly, with difficulty; scarcely; probably not.

dificuldade, *s.f.* difficulty; hardness; objection; complication, trouble, embarrassment; obstacle, obstruction; distress, dilemma. 1) *criar dificuldades*, to raise objections. 2) *desembaraçar-se da dificuldade*, to get out of a scrape.

dificultação, *s.f.* making difficult, difficultating.

dificultar, *v.t.* to make difficult, to difficultate, to raise difficulties or objections; to encumber, to embarrass, to handicap.

dificultoso, *adj.* difficult, hard, laborious, troublesome.

difidência, *s.f.* diffidence, distrust, suspicion; shyness; timidity, modesty.

difidente, *adj.* diffident, suspicious; shy, timid, reserved, modest.

difracção, *s.f.* diffraction.

difractar, *v.t.* to diffract.

difractivo, *adj.* diffractive.

difteria, *s.f.* diphteria.

diftérico, *adj.* diphteric.

difundido, *adj.* spread, widespread; broadcast.

difundir, *v.t.* to diffuse, to spread about, to divulge, to publish; to broadcast; to disseminate, to propagate, to pour out.

difusamente, *adv.* diffusively.

difusão, *s.f.* diffusion, expansion, dissemination, divulgation, propagation; broadcasting.

difusibilidade, *s.f.* diffusibility.

difusível, *adj.* diffusible.

difusivo, *adj.* diffusive.

difuso, *adj.* diffuse, copious, prolix.

difusor, *s.m.* diffuser *(em todos os sentidos)*.

difusora, *s.f.* radio or T.V. station.

digerir, *v.t.*, *v.i.* to digest, to assimilate; to tolerate, to endure, to suffer; to meditate, to work upon, to think hard; to understand.

digerível, *adj.* digestible.

digestão, *s.f.* digestion.

digestibilidade, *s.f.* digestibility.

digestível, *adj.* digestible.

digestivo, *adj.* digestive; *aparelho digestivo*, digestive system.

digitado, *adj.* digitate, digitiform, fingerlike.

digital, *adj.* digital; *s.f.* foxglove; *impressão digital*, fingerprint.

digitalina, *s.f.* digitalin.

digitiforme, *adj.* digitate; finger-shaped, fingerlike.

digitígrado, *adj.*, *s.m.* digitigrade.

dígito, *adj.* digital.

digladiação, *s.f.* digladiation; a dispute, a quarrel.

digladiar, *v.i.* to fight, to struggle, to quarrel, to digladiate, to wrangle.

dignamente, *adv.* worthily, deservingly, honourably.

dignar-se, *v. refl.* to deign; to condescend, to be pleased.

dignidade, *s.f.* dignify, honour, merit, nobleness, elevation of mind, worthiness, excellence; rank, title; dignified behaviour.

dignificação, *s.f.* dignification, elevation, enoblement.

dignificante, *adj.* dignifying.

dignificar, *v.t.* to dignify, to honour, to ennoble, to exalt, to elevate; to raise to dignity.

dignitário, *s.m.* dignitary.

digno, *adj.* worthy; honest; honourable; deserving, meritorious, respectable. 1) *digno de confiança*, trust-worthy, reliable. 2) *digno de louvor*, praiseworthy.

digrafo, *s.m.* digraph.

digressão, *s.f.* digression; deviation; excursion, walk.

digressivo, *adj.* digressive.

dilação, *s.f.* delay, deferring, deferment, postponement, putting off.

dilaceração, dilaceramento, *s.f., s. m.* laceration, tearing asunder.

dilacerante, *adj.* lacerating, pungent, piercing, cruel.

dilacerar, *v.t.* to tear to pieces, to lacerate; to pierce; to torment, to afflict.

dilapidação, *s.f.* dilapidation, waste; embezzlement, squandering.

dilapidador, s.m. dilapidator, waster, spendthrift; adj. dilapidating.

dilapidar, v.t. to dilapidate; to squander, to waste; to ruin, to decay; to defraud.

dilatabilidade, s.f. dilatability, elasticity.

dilatação, dilatamento, s.f., s.m. dilation, expansion, stretching, distension, extension; prorogation, prolongation.

dilatado, adj. delated; vast; diffuse; deferred; expanded, enlarged.

dilatar, v.t. to dilate; to extend; to expand, to enlarge, widen, to swell; to spread abroad, to diffuse; to delay, to put off, to defer.

dilatável, adj. dilatable, elastic, distensible.

dilatório, adj. dilatory, slow, tardy, long.

dilecção, s.f. esteem, affection, dilection, preference; love.

dilecto, adj. dear, beloved, preferred, favourite.

dilema, s.m. dilemma; problem, difficult choice, predicament.

diletante, adj. dilettante; amateur.

diletantismo, s.m. dilettantism, amateurism.

diligência, s.f. diligence, speed, expedition; proceeding, assiduity, application, industry, activity; care, attention, caution, vigilance; judicial proceeding; stage-coach; investigation; *oficial de diligencias,* bailiff.

diligenciar, v. t. to endeavour, to solicit, to make efforts, to do one's best.

diligente, adj. diligent; careful; expeditious, hard-working, assiduous, active; quick, swift; cautious.

diligentemente, adv. carefully; diligently.

dilucidação, s.f. dilucidation, explanation, illustration.

dilucidar, v.t. to elucidate, to explain, to illustrate, to make clear.

dilúculo, s.m. dawn, day-break.

diluente, ad., s.m. diluent.

diluição, s.f. dilution, diluteness; attenuation.

diluído, adj. dilute, thin, waterish, attenuated; weak, poor.

diluir, v.t. to dilute, to thin, to make thin, to render more liquid; to attenuate; *diluir-se,* to dissolve, to become thinner.

diluvial, adj. diluvial.

diluviano, adj. diluvian, torrential, overflowing.

dilúvio, s.m. deluge, food, inundation, overflowing; abundance, large quantity; heavy rainfull, torrent.

diamanação, s.f. emanation, issuing, coming from, derivation, flowing.

dimanante, adj. proceeding, issuing, rising.

diamanar, v.i. to emanate, to proceed from; to stream, to come from, to flow; to derive, to result; to originate, to start from.

dimensão, s.f. dimension, measure, size, volume, magnitude.

dimensional, adj. dimensional.

diminuendo, s.m. minuend.

diminuição, s.f. diminution, decrease; decay; subtraction; reduction, abridgement.

diminuidor, s.m. subtrahend; adj. diminishrig, diminutive.

diminuir, v.t. to diminish, to subtract; to lower, to lessen; to decrease, to abate, to fall off, to reduce, to shorten, to make smaller.

diminutivo, s.m. diminutive.

diminuto, adj. small, diminutive, minute, very small, tiny; reduced.

dimorna, dimorfismo, s.f., s.m. dimorphism.

dimorfo, adj. dimorphic, dimorphous.

dinamarquês, adj. Danish; s.m. Dane.

dinâmica, s. f. dinamics.

dinamico, adj. dynamiic, active, vigorous, energetic.

dinamismo, s.m. dynamism, energy; rush, push.

dinamista, s. dynamist; adj. dynamistic.

dinamitar, v.t. to dynamite, to destroy witb dynamite.

dinamite, s.f. dynamite, blasting, powder, explosive.

dinamitista, s. dynamiter.

dinamizar, v.t. to dynamize, to increase the power.

dínamo, s.m. dynamo, generator.

dinamometria, s.m. dynamometry.

dinamómetro, s.m. dynamometer.

dinasta, s. dynast.

dinastia, s.f. dynasty.

dinástico, adj. dynastic.

dinheiro, s.m. money; cash; currency; capital. 1) *dinheiro a juros,* money at interest. 2) *dinheiro adiantado,* money in advance. 3) *dinheiro a rodos (em barda),* money to burn, plenty of money. 4) *dinheiro apurado,* money realized (numa venda). 5) *dinheiro de contado ,* ready money, cash. 6) *dinheiro em caixa,* cash in hand. 7) *dinheiro empatado,* money tied up. 8) *dinheiro miúdo,* small change. 9) *vender a dinheiro,* to sell for cash. 10) *dinheiro é a mola real,* money makes the mare go. 11) *ter falta de* *dinheiro*, to be short of money. 12) *ganhar dinheiro*, to make money. 13) *levantar dinheiro*, to take out money (de um banco). 14) *nadar em dinheiro*, to be rolling in money.

dinossauro, *s. m.* dinosaur.

dintel, *s.m.* lintel, a beam.

diocesano, *adj.; s. m.* diocesan.

diocese, *s.f.* diocese.

dionisiaco, *adj.* dionysian.

dioptria, *s.m.* dioptric; diopter.

dióptrica, *s.f.* dioptrics.

dióptrico, *adj.* dioptrical.

diorama, *s.m.* diorama.

diorito, *s.m.* diorite, green stone.

diplococo, *s.m.* diplococcus.

diploma, *s.m.* diploma; charter; patent; docent; degree, certificate.

diplomacia, *s.f.* diplomacy ; adroitness, tact, skill; foreign service; diplomatic body.

diplomado, *adj.* certificated, licensed; *s. m.* graduate.

diplomar, *v.t.* to grant a certificate or diploma; 1) *diplomar-se*, to graduate, to receive a diploma.

diplomata, *s.* diplomat, diplomatist; tactful person.

diplomática, *s.f.* diplomatics.

diplomaticamente, *adv.* tactfully.

diplomático, *adj.* diplomatic, tactful, skilful; corteous, well-mannered; *corpo diplomático*, diplomatic corps, diplomatic body.

dípode, *adj.* two-footed, biped, walking on two feet.

dipsáceas, *s.f. (pl) (bot.)* Dipsacaceae.

díptero, *adj.* dipterous; *s. m. (pl) (zool.)* Diptera.

dique, *s.m.* dam; dike; barrier, obstacle, defence; *romper os diques*, to break (open) the dikes.

direcção, *s.f.* direction; address *(em cartas)*; management; directorship; board of directors; course, route; govermnent, control; order, instruction; guidance. 1) *assumir a direcção*, to take the lead. 2) *caixa de direcção*, steering box. 3) *em direcção a*, toward. 4) *em direcção a casa*, homeward. 5) *engrenagem de direcção*, steering gear. 6) *volante de direcção*, steering wheel.

directamente, *av.* directly, direct.

directivo, *adj.* directive.

directo, *adj.* direct; straight; immediate; clear, evident; unambiguous; 1) *comboio directo*, through train. 2) *discurso directo*, direct speech.

director, *s.m.* director; manager; headmaster; editor; superintendent; guide; administrator; headmaster, principal (na escola); adj. ruling, guiding, managing. 1) *director de cena*, stage director. 2) *director espiritual*, spiritual guide. 3) *director de orquestra*, orchestra leader.

directora, *s.f.* directress; headmistress *(na escola)*.

director-geral, *s.m.* general manager.

directoria, *s.f.* directorship; board of directors; administration management; director's office.

directório, *s.m.* directory; board of directors; directorate; executive committee.

directriz, *s.f.* directrix; directive, route, rule, standard of behaviour.

direita, *s.f.* right hand; right side; conservative party. 1) *à direita*, on the right. 2) *às direitas*, as it should be, honest, upright. 3) *seguir pela direita*, to keep to the right . 4) *virar à direita*, to turn to the right.

direiteza, *s.f.* straightness, righteousness, honesty.

direitinho, *adv.* quite correct. just like; *andar direitinho*, to go straight.

direitista, *adj.* rightist *(em política)*.

direito, *adj.* right; upright; straight, even, flat; honest, loyal, righteous, correct, true; fit, suitable; just, equitable; s.m. right, law; justice, equity; rectitude, honesty; prerogative, privilege; authority, power; right side. 1) *direitos aduaneiros (alfandegários)*, custom duties. 2) *direito civil*, civil law. 3) *direito comercial*, commercial law. 4) *direito comum*, common law. 5) *direito como um fuso*, as straight as a die. 6) *direito consuetudinário*, unwritten law. 7) *direito penal*, penal law. 8) *a torto e a direito*, by hook or by crook, at random. 9) *dar direito a*, to entitle. 10) *doutor em direito*, doctor of law. 11) *estudar direito*, to read fof the Bar. 12) *isento de direitos*, duty-free. 13) *seguir sempre a direito*, to follow one's nose. 14) *sujeito a direitos*, liable (subject) to duties. 15) *ter direito a*, to be entitled to.

direitura, *s.f.* uprightness, integrity, honesty; straightness, rightness; *em direitura a*, straight on, directly.

dirigente, *s.* director, manager, leader; *adj.* directing, leading; *as classes dirigentes*, the ruling classes.

dirigido, adj. directed, ruled, managed; pointed, aimed; *dirigido a*, pointed towards.

dirigir, v.t. to direct, to lead, to manage, to govern, to rule, to superintend, to head, to preside; to regulate, to control; to conduct *(orquestra);* to address *(uma carta);* to guide, to drive *(um carro);* to pilot *(avião).* 1) *dirigir-se*, to address oneself to, to apply to, to go up to. 2) *dirigir os passos*, to turn one's steps towards. 3) *dirigir um apelo*, to direct an appeal to. 4) *dirigir um hotel*, to run a hotel. 5) *dirigir-se para casa*, to make one's way home. 6) *queira dirigir-se ao Sr...*, please, apply to Mr...

dirigível, s.m. dirigible, zeppelin; adj. controllable, dirigible.

dirimente, adj. diriment; nullifying.

dirimir, v.t. to annul, to break off, to impede, to nullify, to cancel; to prevent; to dissolve, to put an end to; to decide, to settle, to determine.

discente, adj. learning; *corpo discente*, student body.

discernente, adj. discerning, penetrating, distinguishing, discriminating.

discernimento, s.m. discernment, judgement, criterion; discretion, perception.

discernir, v.t. to discern, to perceive, to distinguish, to discriminate; to discover, to see.

discernível, adj. discernible, distinguishable.

disciforme, adj. disciform, discoidal.

disciplina, s.f. discipline, order, instruction, correction; education, branch of knowledge, course of study scourges *(pl.).*

disciplinador, adj. disciplinarian.

disciplinar, v.t. to discipline, to regulate, to train, to educate, to correct; to punish; adj. disciplinary.

discipulado, s. m. discipleship.

discípulo, s.m. disciple, pupil, student, scholar; follower (de uma doutrina.

disco, s. m. disk; record, discus. 1) *de longa duração*, long-play record. 2) *disco de telefone*, telephone dial. 3) *disco voador*, flying saucer. 4) *arremessar o disco*, to thow the discus. 5) *mudar o disco (pop)*, to change the subject.

discóbolo, s.m. discobolus, discus thrower.

discoidal, discóide, adj. discoid.

díscolo, s. m. rough, rowdy, rioter.

discordância, s.f. discordance, disagreement, discord, divergence, variance.

discordante, adj. discordant, dissonant; disagreeing, opposite, contrary.

discordar, v.i. to disagree, to discord, to disaccord, to differ, to dissent.

discorde, adj. at variance, disagreeing; incongruous.

discórdia, s.f. discord; disagreement; quarrel, contention, wrangling; *pomo da discórdia*, the bone of contention, the apple of discord.

discorrer, v.i. to reason, to discourse, to discuss, to argue; to tell, to relate.

discoteca, s.f. record cabinet; record collection.

discrepância, s.f. discrepancy, difference, disagreement, unconformity, divergence, incongruity.

discrepante, adj. discrepant, different, disagreeing, dissenting, jarring.

discrepar, v.i. to differ, to disagree, to discord, to dissent.

discretamente, adv. discreetly, prudently.

discretear, v.t. to discourse (upon), to converse, to hold forth in speech; to chat.

discreto, adj. cautious, prudent, discreet, circumspect; tactful, wise; reserved.

discrição, s.f. discretion, caution, prudence, circumspection, tactfulness, reserve; *à discrição*, at one's discretion, at will, at one's own pleasure.

discricionário, adj. discretionary, arbitrary, unconditional, capricious, optional.

discriminação, s.f. discrimination; discerning; distinction, separation, selection.

discriminadamente, adv. discriminately, differentiately.

discriminador, adj. discriminatory, discriminating, distinguishing.

discriminnr, v.t. to discriminate, to distinguish; to select, to differentiate, to separate, to discern.

discriminável, adj. discriminable, distinguishable, discernible.

discursar, v. i. to discourse, to make a speech, to hold forth, to orate; to preach, to deliver an address.

discursivo, adj. discursive; desultory.

discurso, s.m. speech, discourse, address, oration, sermon; lecture, dissertation. 1) *discurso de despedida*, valedictory. 2) *discurso de estreia*, maiden speech.

discussão, s.f. discussion, contention, debate, disputation; altercation, quarrel, controversy; *sem discussão*, out of the question, without question.

discutidor, s.m. discusser.

discutir, v.i. to discuss, to argue, to dispute, to reason, to debate; to wrangle, to quarrel.

discutível, adj. discussible, doubtful, disputable, problematic.

disenteria, s.f. dysentery, looseness.

disentérico, adj. dysenteric.

diserto, adj. eloquent, clear, selected.

disfarçadamente, adv. dissemblingly, disguisedly.

disfarçado, adj. dissembled, disguised, masked, veiled; simulated, false, feigned; in fancy dress.

disfarçar, v.t. to disguise, to dissemble, to conceal, to cloak, to mask, to veil; to simulate, to shift; disfarçar-se de, to disguise oneself as.

disfarce, s. m. disguise, mask, veil, cloak; dissimulation, pretense.

disfasia, s.f. dysphasia.

disfonia, s.f. dysphonia.

disforme, adj. deformed, disfigured; enormous, huge, colossal, monstrous; hideous, ugly, misshappen.

disformidade, s.f. deformity, disfigurement; ugliness.

disjunção, s.f. disjunction, separation, disconnection.

disjungir, v.t. to unyoke; to separate, to disjoin, to disconnect, to disunite.

disjuntar, v.t. to separate, to disconnect.

disjuntivo, adj. disjunctive.

disjunto, adj. disjoined, disjunct, disconnected, separated, distinct.

disjuntor, s.m. circuit breaker.

dislalia, s.f. dyslalia.

dislate, s.m. nonsense, absurdity, folly, blunder.

díspar, adj. unequal, unlike, dissimilar, disparate.

disparador, s.m. shooter, trigger; shutter release (numa máquina fotográfica); disparador automático, self-timer.

disparar, v.t. to shoot, to fire, to discharge; to let fly, to cast, to throw. 1) disparar-se, (uma arma), to go off. 2) disparar uma salva, to thunder a salute.

disparatadamente, adv. foolishly, nonsensically, absurdly.

disparatado, adj. extravagant; foolish, absurd, silly, senseless, nonsensical; ridiculous.

disparatar, v.i. to talk foolishly; to blunder, to

blurt out; to play the fool; to rave, to rant; to commit faults.

disparate, s.m. nonsense, folly, absurdity; blunder, silly action, indiscretion. 1) dizer disparates, to talk nonsense. 2) que disparate!, what a thrash!

disparidade, s.f. disparity, inequality, unlikeness; dissimilitude, disproportion, difference.

disparo, s.m. shot, discharge, shooting (com uma arma); detonation.

dispartir, v.t. to distribute, to divide; to scatter.

dispêndio, s.m. expense, disbursement, expenditure; waste, prodigality, loss, damage.

dispendiosamente, adv. expensively.

dispendioso, adj. expensive, dear, costly.

dispensa, s.f. dispensation, exemption; leave, license; dismissal.

dispensabilidade, s.f. dispensability.

dispensação, s.f. dispensation, exemption, remission.

dispensado, adv. exempted, released, free.

dispensar, v.t. to dispense, to grant a dispensation, to exempt, to release, to excuse, to free from; to dismiss, to discharge; to distribute, to bestow; to dispeme with, to do witbout, not to need. 1) dispensar os serviços de, to dispense with a person's services. 2) ser dispensado de comparecer, to be excused from attendance.

dispensário, s.m. dispensary.

dispensável, adj. dispensably, unnecessary, unessential, needless, superfuous.

dispepsia, s.f. dyspepsia, dispepsy, indigestion.

dispéptico, adj. dyspeptic.

dispersão, s.f. dispersion, scattering, diffusion, disbandment, breakup.

dispersar, v.t. to disperse, to scatter, to dispel, to dissipate; to break up, to disband, to put to flight.

dispersivo, adj. dispersive; diffusive.

disperso, adj. dispersed, scattered; disbanded.

displicência, s.f. displeasure, annoyance; carelessness, negligence, indifference, boredom.

displicente, adj. displeasing, unpleasant, disagreeable; negligent, indifferent.

dispneia, s.f. dyspnoea, laboured respiration.

dispneico, adj. dyspneal, dyspneic.

disponibilidade, *s.f.* availability, disposability; reserve.

disponível, *adj.* disposable, available, ready for use; spare; unoccupied. 1) *fundo disponível,* ready money. 2) *não ter dinheiro disponível,* to have no spare cash.

dispor, *s.m.* disposal, disposition; *v. t.* to dispose, to regulate, to order adjust, to arrange; to determine, to decide, to settle, to resolve; to place, to put, to lay out; to prepare, to plan; to rank, to group, to range; to alienate, to bestow. 1) *dispor-se a,* to be disposed to, to get ready to. 2) *dispor de,* to dispose of, to make free use of. 3) *dispor de si,* to be free. 4) *dispor árvores,* to plant trees. 5) *dispor as duas coisas,* to settle the the affairs. 6) *ao seu dispor,* at your disposal, at your service. 7) *não dispor de tempo,* to be pushed for time. 8) *o homem põe e Deus dispõe,* man proposes, God disposes.

disposição, *s.f.* disposition, disposal; arrangement, classification, order; guidance, control; clause (num contrato); aptitude, inclination, tendency; temper, mood, nature; state (de saúde); predisposition, willingness. 1) *à sua disposição,* at your disposal. 2) *estar à disposição,* to be available.

dispositivo, *s.m.* gear; apparatus; device; *dispositivo de protecção,* safety device.

disposto, *s.m.* determination, rule, precept; *adj.* disposed; prepared; ordered; alert; inclined, bent; arranged, settled; willing, eager.

disputa, *s.f.* dispute; quarrel; controversy; struggle; difference, disagreement, debate, altercation.

disputado, *adj.* disputed, sought after; *muito disputado pelos amigos,* eagerly sought by friends.

disputador, *s.m.* arguer, disputer, debater; quarreler, squabbler.

disputante, *adj.* disputing, disputant.

disputar, *v.t.* to contend for; to dispute, to debate, to discuss, to argue; to quarrel, to squab, to brawl, to contest, to fight; to try to win; to altercate; to contend; to challenge. 1) *disputar uma corrida,* to run a race. 2) *disputar alguma coisa a alguém,* to vie with someone for something. 3) *disputar a coroa,* to contend for the crown.

disputável, *adj.* disputable, controvertible, debatable, controversial, questionable, uncertain.

dissabor, *s.m.* displeasure, annoyance, vexation, disgust, contrariety.

dissecação, dissecção, *s.f.* dissection, anatomization; rigorous examination *(fig.).*

dissecar, *v.t.* to dissect, to anatomize; to analize, to examine part by part.

dissector, *s.m.* dissector, anatomist; dissecting knife, scalpel.

dissemelhança, *s.f.* dissimilitude, unlikeness, dissimilarity, diverseness , disparaty, difference.

dissemelhante, *adj.* unlike, dissimilar, disparate, diverse, distinct, different.

disseminação, *s.f.* dissemination, diffusion, propagation, spreading.

dissseminador, *s.m.* desseminator, diffuser; *adj.* disseminating, diffusing.

disseminar, *v.t.* to disseminate, to diffuse, to scatter, to propagate, to spread.

dissensão, *s.f.* dissension, discord, disagreement, variance, difference, divergence, dispute.

dissentimento, *s.m.* dissent, disagreement, dissidence, difference, dissension.

dissentir, *v.i.* to dissent, to disagree, to differ.

dissépalo, *adj. (bot.)* disepalous.

dissertação, *s.f.* dissertation; essay, thesis, treatise.

dissertador, *s.m.* dissertator.

dissertar, *v.i.* to dissert, to discourse, to dissertate, to talk, to discurs, to examine.

dissidência, *s.f.* dissent, dissidence, disagreement, difference.

dissidente, *adj.* dissident, dissenting, disagreeing.

dissódio, *s.m.* dissension; division.

dissilábico, *adj.* dissulabic.

dissílabo, *s.m.* dissyllable.

dissimetria, *s.f.* dissymmetry.

dissimétrico, *adj.* dissymmetric(al); unsymmetric(al) .

dissímil, *adj.* dissimilar, different.

dissimilação, *s.f.* dissimilation.

dissimilar, *adj.* dissimilar, unlike, dilfferent.

dissinulitude, *s.f.* dissimilitude, dissimilarity, unlikeness, difference.

dissimulação, *s.f.* dissimulation, feigning, hypocrisy, disguise, deceit, falseness.

dissimuladamente, *adv.* dissemblingly, covertly.

dissimulado, *adj.* dissembling, sly, secretive, feigned, dissembled; cuning; crafty.

disssimulador, *s.m.* dissembler, dissimulator, disguiser; adj. dissimulating, dissimulative.

dissimular, *v.t., v.i.* to dissimulate, to desguise, to conceal, to feign, to deceive, to pretend.

dissipação, *s.f.* dissipation, waste; dispersion; dissoluteness; expenditure, prodigality, squandering.

dissipadamente, *adj.* dissipatedly.

dissipado, *adj.* dissipated, wasted, consumed; dissolute, wasteful.

dissipador, *s.m.* prodigal, spendthrift, waster, lavisher, dissipator; *adj.* dissipating, wasting.

dissipar, *v.t.* to dissipate, to dispel, to waste, to misspend; to squander; to dissolve, to melt away. 1) *dissipar-se,* to vanish, to disappear. 2) *dissipar as dúvidas,* to remove the doubts. 3) *dissipar uma fortuna,* to waste (dissipate) a fortune.

disso, *prep.* de e *pron. dem.* isso of that; about that; thereirom, there of. 1) *além disso,* thereto, besides, furthermore. 2) *apesar disso,* even so. 3) *nada disso,* nothing of the sort (of the kind).

dissociabilidade, *s.f.* dissociability.

dissociação, *s.m.* dissociation, separation, disunion.

dissociar, *v.t.* to dissociate, to disunite, to disconnect, to separate; to decompose.

dissociativo, *adj.* dissociative.

dissociável, *adj.* dissociable.

dissolubilidade, *s.f.* dissolubility, dissolvability, solubility.

dissolução, *s.f.* dissolution, liquefaction; decomposition, breakup, disintegration; dissoluteness, depravation; dismissal *(de uma reunião).*

dissoluto, *adj.* dissolute, licentious, debauched, vicious, wanton.

dissolúvel, *adj.* dissoluble, dissolvable.

dissolvencia, *s.f.* ver *dissolução.*

dissolvente, *adj., s.m.* dissolvent; depraving, corrupting; solvent.

dissolver, *v.t.* to dissolve, to liquefy, to melt, to fuse, to thaw, to annul, to rescind, to put an end to; to vanish, to consume; to break up, to separate.

dissolvido, *adj.* dissolved, melted, liquified; broken up, separated.

dissonância, *s.f.* dissonance, discord; disagreement, incongruity, disproportion, impropriety *(fig.).*

dissonante, *adj.* dissonant, discordant, harsh, grating, tuneless; disagreeing.

dissuadir, *v.t.* to dissuade, to advise against, to deter, to divert from; to discourage, to bring (call) off; *dissuadir-se,* to change one's mind.

dissuasão, *s.f.* dissuasion, diversion (from), dehortation.

dissuasivo, dissuasório, *adj.* dissuasive, dissuasory.

dissuasor, *s.m.* dissuader, dehorter; *adj.* dissuading, dissuasive.

distância, *s.f.* distance, interval; remoteness; extension; space; reserve of manners, coldness. 1) *distância focal,* focal length (or distance). 2) *à distância,* distantly, aloof, aside. 3) *a curta distância,* a little way off, near. 3) *a grande distância daqui,* a long way off, far-from. 4) *a pouca distância,* at close range. 5) *a que distância?,* how far?. 6) *guardar as distâncias,* to avoid familiarity.

distanciado, *adj.* distant, reserved, not cordial; apart, asunder; set at intervals.

distanciar, *v.t.* to distance; to space; to move away, to get in advance of, to outdo, to excel; to set at intervals; *distanciar-se,* to withdraw, to keep away from.

distante, *adj.* distant, far, remote, far-off, far away; reserved, cool, not cordial; aloof.

distar, *v.i.* to be distant, to be away; to differ, to be dissimilar *(fig.).*

distender, *v.t.* to distend, to enlarge, to expand, to dilate, to swell; to stretch out, to relay *(nervos).*

distensã, *s.f.* distension; a sprain, wrench; extension, expansion; *sofrer de uma distensão no pé,* to give the foot a sprain.

distenso, *adj.* distended, dilated, wide; sprained, wrenched.

distensor, *s.m.* distender, expander; *adj.* distending, distensive.

dístico, *s.m.* inscription, label, sing, lettering; distich, couplet.

distinção, *s.f.* distinction; difference, discrimination, discernment; honour; superiority; eminence; rank, name, dignity, renown, respectability; good-breeding; highest grade *(exame).*

distinguir, *v.t.* to distinguish, to note, to discern, to discriminate, to differentiate; to perceive; to honour, to make famous; to separate, to differ. 1) *distinguir-se,* to differ from; to take the first-class honours *(exame);* to distinguish oneself, to stand out, to win the spurs. 2) *distinguir o bem do mal,* to discern good from evil. 3) *distinguir uma coisa da outra,* to know which is which.

distinguível, *adj.* distinguishable, discernible.

distintamente, *adv.* distinctly, clearly.

distintivo, *adj.* distinctive; *s.m.* decoration, badge, sign, distinctive, atribute, emblem, symbol.

dIistinto, *adj.* distinct, different, separate, diverse, special; eminent, distinguished, famous, remarkable, illustrous, high-bred; fine, elegant; clear, explicit, well-marked, unmistakable.

disto, *prep.* de e *pron. dem.* isto of this; about this, of it, hereof.

distorção, *s.f.* distortion; deformation, malformation.

distorcer, *v.t.* to distort; to deform.

distracção, *s.f.* distraction, absent-mindedness; amusement; inadvertence; irreflection, inattention; pastime, recreation.

distractivo, *adj.* diverting, entertaining.

distraidamente, *adv.* inattentively, thoughtless.

distraído, *adj.* inattentive, absent-minded, thoughtless; amused, entained.

distair, *v.t.* to distract, to diivert, to draw away *(a atenção)* to amuse, to entertain; *distrair-se,* to amuse oneself; to be inattentive, to commit a mistake; to have a good time.,

distratar, *v.t.* to cancel, to annul *(um contrato),* to break *(um pacto).*

distrate, distrato, *s.m.* rescission, dissolution, annulling, cancelling *(um acordo).*

distribuição, *s.f.* distribution; deliver *(de cartas);* dividing, parcelling, sharing, division; arrangement; classification; *quadro de distribuição (elect.),* switchboard.

distribuidor, *s.m.* distributer; post-man.

distribuir, *v.t.* to distribute, to divide, to apportion, to allot; to arrange, to classify, to dispose; to spread, to scatter, to deliver *(cartas).*

distributivamente, *adv.* distributively.

distributivo, *adj.* distributive, distributional, expressing division.

distrital, *adj.* belonging to a district.

distrito, *s.m.* district; region, area, territory, section, zone; *sede de distrito,* county town.

distrofia, *s.f.* dystrophy.

distúrbio, *s.m.* disturbance, trouble, disorder, agitation, affray, riot, tumult, uproar. 1) *distúrbio mental,* mental disorder.2) *provocar distúrbios,* to cause disturbance, to riot.

dita, *s.f.* good luck, fortune, happiness, chance.

ditado, *s.m.* dictation; saying, proverb, sentence, adage; *adj.* dictated, inspired by.

ditador, *s.m.* dictator, despot, tyrant.

ditadura, *s.f.* dictatorship; despotism, absolutism, tyranny.

ditame, *s.m.* dictate, order, direction, precept, maxim, rule, principle; *obedecer aos ditames do coração,* to follow the dictates of the heart.

ditar, *v.t.* to dictate; to impose, to command, to decree, to prescribe; to suggest, to inspire, to teach.

ditatorial, *adj.* dictatorial, absolute; dogmatic, authoritative.

ditério, *s.m.* jest, witticism, scoff, quirk.

ditinho, *s.m.* intrigue; insinuation, hint.

ditirâmbico, *adj.* dithyrambic; lyrical.

ditirambo, *s. m.* dithyramb.

dito, *adj.* aforesaid, named, said; *s.m.* dictum, aphorism, maxim, sentence, saying. 1) *dito e feito,* no sooner said than done. 2) *dar o dito por não dito,* to retract oneself.

ditongo, *s.m.* diphthong; *ditongo crescente (decrescente),* rising (falling) diphthong.

ditoso, *adj.* fortunate, happy, lucky, prosperous.

diurese, *s.f.* diuresis.

diurético, *adj.* diuretic.

diurno, *adj.* daily, diurnal.

diuturnidade, *s.f.* diuturnity, length of time.

diuturno, *adj.* lasting, durable, diuturnal.

diva, *s.f.* goddess; diva.

divã, *s.m.* couch; divan.

divagação, *s.f.* divagation, wandering, deviation, digression.

divagante, *adv.* wandering, rambling; discursive, digressive; dreaming.

divagar, *v.i.* to divagate, to wander; to stray, to rave, to ramble, to digress; to daydream.

divergência, *s.f.* divergence, discordance; deviation, divarication; variance, discrepancy, difference, dissension, disagreement.

divergente, *adj.* divergent; devious; opposite, discrepant; different; disagreeing. *lente divergente,* diverging lens.

divergir, *v. i.* to diverge, to differ; to discord, to disagree, to dissent.

diversamente, *adj.* diversely.

diversão, *s. f.* diversion, pastime, entertaimnent, amusement, recreation; deviation.

diversidade, *s. f.* diversity; difference; variance; variety; unlikeness.

diversificacão, *s. f.* diversification, variation, change, alteration.

diversificar, *v. t.* to diversify, to make different; to vary, to modify.

diversificável, *adj.* diversifiable, variable.

diversivo, *adj.* diversive; revulsive.

diverso, *adj.* different; varied; various; diverse; several, sundry, divers *(pl)*.

divertido, *adj.* amusing, playful, entertaining, diverting, pleasing, funny, merry, gay, comical.

divertimento, *s. m.* diversion, amusement, pastime, entertainment; play, game, festival; enjoyment.

divertir, *v. t.* to divert; to amuse, to please; to distract. 1) *divirta-se,* have a good time, have fun, enjoy yourself. 2) *divertir-se à custa alheia,* to be amused at people's expense. 3) *divertir-se a valer,* to have a high old time.

dívida, *s. f.* debt; duty, obligation. 1) *dívida de honra,* debt of honour. 2) *dívida flutuante,* floating debt. 3) *dívida de jogo,* play debt. 4) *contrair dívidas,* to run into debts. 5) *em dívida,* in debt. 6) *estar crivado de dívidas,* to be deep in debts, to be debt-ridden.

dividendo, *s. m.* dividend; share, portion, bonus.

dividir, *v. t.* to divide, to distribute, to share; to separate; to limit. 1) *dividir em partes iguais,* to go shares. 2) *dividir em duas partes,* to halve. 3) *dividir em parcelas,* to parcel, to branch.

divina (à), *loc. adv.* penniless.

divinação, *s. f.* divination; perception, intuition.

divinal, *adj.* divine, holy, heavenly, celestial; excellent, extraordinary, supreme, admirable', supernatnral.

divinamente, *adv.* divinely.

divinatório, *adj.* divinatory, divining.

divindade, *s. f.* divinity, sanctity, deity; God, divinity.

divinização, *s. f.* divinization, deification, apotheosis.

divinizador, divinizante, *adj.* deifying, divinizing.

divinizar, *v. t.* to deify, to divinize, to regard as divine; to adore, to worship.

divino, *adj.* divine, godlike; sublime; holy, heavenly, celestial; excellent, supreme, admirable. 1) *ofícios divinos,* divine services. 2) *o Divino Espírito Santo,* the Holy Ghost.

divisa, *s. f.* device; emblem; motto, slogan; stripe *(num uniforme militar);* exchange value, foreign exchange credits *(pl.).*

divisão, *s. f.* division; distribution; separation, section, partition; compartment; discord, disunion; classification, category; dividing line, demarcation; district, department; portion, share, parcel. 1) *tomar o comando de uma divisão,* to take the head of a division. 2) *general de divisão,* general of division, major general.

divisar, *v. t.* to see, to discern, to descry, to perceive, to behold.

divisibilidade, *s. f.* divisibility, divisibleness, partibility.

divisional, *adj.* divisional, divisionary.

divisionário, *adj.* divisionary, divisiona; *moeda divisionária,* divisional coin.

divisível, *adj.* divisible, partible.

diviso, *adj.* divided, parted, separated, distributed, disunited.

divisor, *s. m.* divisor; *adj.* dividing; *máximo divisor comum,* greatest common divisor.

divisória, *s. f.* demarcation, separating line; partition, screen, division.

divisória, *s. f.* dividing, divisory, decisive, parting.

divorciar, *v.* to divorce; to separate, to disunite *(fig.); divorciar-se,* to get divorced.

divórcio, *s. m.* divorce, divorcement; separation; *requerer o divórcio,* to sue for divorce.

divulgação, *s. f.* divulgation, propagation, diffusion, disclosure.

divugador, *s. m.* divulger, propagandist; *adj.* divulging, making public.

divulgar, *v. t.* to divulge, to make public, to reveal, to disclose, to publish; *divulgar em segredo,* to spill the beans.

dizedor, *s. m.* teller; talker.

dizer, *v. t.* to say, to tell, to relate, to talk, to speak; to utter, to express; to declare, to assert, to pronounce. 1) *dizer adeus,* to take leave, to say good-bye, to bid farewell. 2) *dizer amen,* to say yes to everything. 3) *dizer bem de,* to speak well of. 4) *dizer cobras e lagartos,* to have no good word to say of, to criticize unreservedly. 5) *não dizer coisa com coisa*, to talk nonsense, to be unintelligible. 6) *dizer com os seus botões*, to say to oneself. 7) *dizer missa*, to say (celebrate) mass. 8) *dizer respeito a*, to be part of, to concern. 9) *a bem dizer*, to tell the truth, so to speak, properly speaking. 10) *como se costuma dizer*, as the sayingng goes. 11) *diz-me com quem andas...*, a man is known by the company he keeps. 12) *escusado é dizer*, needless to say, suffice it to say. 13) *ele disse o que tinha a dizer*, he said his say. 14) *isso não quer dizer nada*, that signifes (means) nothing. 15) *quer dizer*, that is to say. 16) *ouvi dizer*, I was told. 17) *por assim dizer*, so to say.

dize-tu-direi-eu, *s.m.* hot discussion, endless altercation.

dízima, *s.f.* tithe; tax, contribution of a tenth.

dizimação, *s.f.* decimation, restriction, reduction; destruction, devastation.

dizimar, *v.t.* to decimate, to tithe, to levy tithes; to reduce; to destroy, to devastate.

dízimo, *s.m.* tithe, n tenth.

do, *prep.* de e *art.* ou *pron. dem.* o of the, from the, of that, of this.

dó, *s. m.* pity, mourning, compassion; do, C (mús.). 1) *fazer (meter) dó*, to arouse pity. 2) *ter dó de*, to have compasion on,

doação, *s.f.* donation, grant, git, present, endowment, benefaction; *doação por morte*, a bequest.

doador, *s.m.* donor, donator, giver, endower, benefactor.

doar, *v.t.* to bestow, to give, to donate, to endow.

dobadoura, *s.f.* reely, hurry, rush ; *andar numa dobadoura*, to be always stirring.

dobar, *v.t.* to reel, to wind.

doble, *adj.* double; two-faced, deceitful.

doblez, *s.f.* duplicity; doubleness; falsety, hypocrisy.

dobra, *s.f.* fold, plait, plication; *dobra na página do livro*, dog's ear.

dobrada, *s.f.* tripe, tripe stew; ondulation in the ground; descend.

dobradiça, *s.f.* hinge, joint.

dobradiço, *adj.* flexible, supple, easily bent.

dobradinha, *s. f.* tripe stew or ragout.

dobrado, *adj.* folded, doubled; double, bent.

dobradura, *s.f.* a fold, folding, plication; doubling.

dobramento, *s.m.* folding, curvature; fold (geol.).

dobrão, *s.m.* doubloon.

dobrar, *v.t.* to double; to make double, to increase, to extend; to fold, to plait, to ply, to plicate; to round, to curve, to bow, to bend; to sail; to go around; to toll. 1) *dobrar-se*, to humble oneself, to bow, to stoop, to yield. 2) *dobrar a cerviz*, to bow one's head (submissamente). 3) *dobrar uma carta*, to fold a letter. 4) *dobrar um cabo*, to turn a cape. 5) *dobrar uma esquina*, to turn a corner. 6) *dobrar a finados*, to toll the funeral knell. 7) *dobrar a língua*, to hold the tongue. 8) *dobrar a parada*, to double the stake (or the bet).

dobrável, *adj.* bending; folding; pliable; flexible; foldable.

dobre, *adj.* double, double-dealing; double-faced; *s. m.* knell.

dobro, *s.m.* double, duplication. 1) *pagar o dobro*, to give double the price. 2) *a soma em dobro*, twice the sum. 3) *ele tem o dobro da força*, he has twice the strength.

doca, *s.f.* dock, quay, basin. 1) *doca flutuante*, floating dock. 2) *doca seca*, dry dock.

doçaria, *s.f.* confectioner's *(loja)*; confectionery *(pl.)*.

doce, *adj.* sweet, soft, gentle, mild; agreeable, pleasant; harmonious, melodious; *s.m.* sweetmeat; confectionery *(pl.)*. 1) *doce de frutas*, tutti-frutti. 2) *de falas doces*, honey-tongued. 3) *palavras doces*, flattering speech, sugared words. 4) *água doce*, fresh water.

doceira, *s.f.* confectioner, woman who makes or sells sweets.

doceiro, *s.m.* confectioner, candy-maker or seller.

docemente, *adv.* sweetly, mildly, softly.

docência, *s.f.* teaching, the teaching profession.

docente, *s.m.* teacher, professor; *adj.* teaching; *corpo docente*, teaching body, teaching staff.

dócil, *adj.* docile, tractable, easily managed; pliant, ductile, submissive, gentle.

docilidade, *s.f.* docility, suppleness, pliancy, flexibleness, tameness.

docilizar, *v.t.* to make docile, to tame, to soften.

docimasia, *s.f.* docimasy.

documentação, *s.f.* documentation, documents.

documentado, *adj.* proved by documents, supported by documents.

documental, *adj.* documental, documentary.

documentar, *v.t.* to document, to prove, to bring evidence; to provide with documents.

documentário, *s.m.* documentary, set of documents; documentary film, news reel *(cinema).*

documento, *s.m.* document. 1) *documento falso* , pseudograph. 2) *documento legal* , act and deed. 3) *juntar um documento,* to attach a document.

doçura, *s.f.* sweetness; smoothness, meekness, gentleness, mildness.

dodecaédrico, *adj.* dodecahedral.

dodecaedro, *s. m.* dodecahedron.

dodecagonal, *adj.* dodecagonal.

dodecágono, *s. m.* dodecagon.

doença, *s.f.* sickness, infirmity, illness, disease, affection, ailment, malady, complaint. 1)*doença contagiosa,* contagious disease. 2) *doença crónica,* chronic disease. 3)*doença hereditária,* hereditary disease. 4)*doença incurável,* incurable disease. 5)*doença mortal,* fatal illness. 6) *doença do sono,* sleeping sickness. 7)*doença simulada,* feigned illness. 8) *doença tropical,* tropical disease. 9) *doença venérea,* venerial disease. 10) *apanhar uma doença,* to catch a disease. 11) *licença por doença,* sick-leave.

doente, *adj.* sick, ill, diseased, ailing, invalid, indisposed, unwell; *s.* patient. 1)*dar parte de doente,* to report sick. 2) *estar muito doente,* to be seriously ill. 3)*ter aspecto de (parecer) doente,* to look ill.

doetio, *adj.* sickly, unwholesome, unhealthy, morbid; weak, feeble.

doer, *v.i.* to ache, to hurt, to cause pain, to suffer pain; to feel distressed, to be sorry for.

doestador, *s.m.* injurer, offender, affronter; *adj.* injuring, affronting.

doestar, *v.t.* to injure, to offend, to insult, to affront, to reproach.

doesto, *s.m.* injury, affront, offence, insult, blame, vituperation.

doge, *s.m.* doge.

dogma, *s.m.* dogma, principle, maxim, doctrine.

dogmaticamente, *adv.* dogmatically.

dogmático, *adj.* dogmatical.

dogmatismo, *s.m.* dogmatism.

dogmatista, *s.* dogmatist; *adj.* dogmatic.

dogmatizador, *s.m.* dogmatizer; *adj.* dogmatic, dogmatizing.

dogmatizar, *v.t.* to dogmatize, to set down as a dogma.

doidamente, *adv.* crazily, madly; very much.

doidejar, *v.i.* to play the fool, to act crazily; to trifle, to jest.

doidice, *s.f.* silliness, madness, craziness, foolishness; stupidity.

doidinho, *adj.* quite crazy; crazily in love.

doidivanas, *s.* hare-brained, rattle. brained, madcap, fool, windbag.

doido, *adj.* maniac, mad, insane, crazy, out of mind, foolish; enthusiastic, merry, impassioned; *s.m.* a crack pot, madman. 1) *completamente doido,* stark (staring) mad. 2) *doido por,* crazy about. 3) *doido varrido,* downright fool.

doido, *adj.* hurt, aggrieved; aching, painful.

doirador, *s.m. vd.* dourador.

doiradura, *s.m. vd.* douradura.

doirar, *v.t. vd.* dourar.

dois, *num.* two; deuce, two-spot (card, die, domino). 1) *a dois,* by twos, two by two, by pairs. 2) *os dois,* both, the two. 3) *dois é bom, três é demais,* two is company, three is a crowd (is none). 4) *jogar com um pau de dois bicos,* to hunt with the hounds and run with the hare. 5) *tão certo como dois e dois serem quatro,* as sure as eggs are eggs. 6) *homem prevenido vale por dois,* forewarned is forearmed. 7) *dois pontos,* colon.

dóla, *s.m.* dollar.

dolência, *s.f.* melancholy, depression; sorrow, distress.

dolicocefalia, *s.f.* dolichocephalism, dolichocephaly.

dolicocéfalo, *adj.* dolichocephalous, long-headed.

dolente, *adj.* mournful, sorrowful, painful; plaintive, grieved.

dólman, *s.m.* hussar's coat; dolman *(uniforme).*

dólmen, *s.m.* dolmen, cromlech.

dolo, *s.m.* treachery, fraud, deceit, deception, swindling, duplicity; foul dealing.,

dolorido, *adj.* aching, dolorous, painful; sorrowful.

dolorosamente, *adv.* painfully, grievously.

doloroso, *adj.* distressing, doleful, painful, sorrowful, cruel, bitter.

dolosamente, *adv.* fraudulently.

doloso, *adj.* fraudulent, deceitful, crooked, crafty.

dom, *s.m.* donation, gift, present; talent, ability, endowment, qualification; *dom da palavra*, a natural gift.

domação, *s.f.* break-in *(cavalo)*.

domador, *s.m.* tamer, horse-breaker, animal trainer.

domar, *v.t.* to tame; to domesticate.

domável, *adj.* tamable, domesticable.

domesticação, *s.f.* domestication, break-in, taming.

domesticador, *s.m.* tamer, breaker, subduer.

domesticar, *v.t.* to domesticate; to tame.

domesticável, *adj.* domesticable, tamable.

domesticidade, *s.f.* domesticity, homeliness, familiarity.

doméstico, *adj.* domestic, familiar; homemade, household; *s.m.* domestic, servant.

domiciliado, *adj.* resident, residing, domiciled.

domiciliar, *v.t.* to domicile, to domiciliate; to dwell; *domiciliar-se em* , to settle in, to take up residence in.

domiciliário, *adj.* domiciliary.

domicílio, *s.m.* dwelling , residence, home, domicile; *entrega ao domicílio*, home delivery.

dominação, *s.f.* domination, dominance, dominancy, sovereignty.

dominado, *adj.* dominated, governed. 1) *dominado pela mulher*, hen-pecked. 2) *dominado pelo medo*, terror-stricken.

dominador, *s.m.* master, ruler, dominator; *adj.* dominating, ruling, over-bearing.

dominante, *adj.* dominant, ruling, prevailing, predominant, commanding; dictatorial.

dominar, *v.t.* to dominate, to govern; to predominate; to repress; to sway, to control; to overcome; to subdue; to cornmand, to rule, to. reign over; to triumph; to overlook (from above). 1) *dominar-se*, to control oneself, to restrain oneself. 2) *dominar as dificuldades*, to master the dificulties.

dominável, *adj.* controllable.

domingo, *s. m.* Sunday. 1) *Domingo da Paixão*, Passion Sunday. 2) *Domingo de Páscoa*, Easter Sunday. 3) *Domingo de Pascoela*, Low Sunday. 4) *Domingo de Ramos*, Palm Sunday. 5) *Domingo Gordo* , Shrove Sunday.

domingueiro, *adj.* belonging to Sunday; *traje domingueiro*, Sunday best.

dominical, *adj.* dominical.

dominicano, *s.m. e adj.* Dominican.

domínio, *s.m.* domination, rule, control, authority; estate, property, domain, dominion, territory; field of action. 1) *domínio público*, public domain. 2) *estar sob o domínio de* , to be under the lash (or the thumb) of. 3) *perder o domínio de si*, to lose the balance.

dominó, *s.m.* domino *(máscara)*; dominoes *(jogo)*.

dona, *s.f.* mistress, lady; proprietress; *dona de casa*, housewife.

donaire, *s.m.* grace; elegance, gracefulness, comeliness.

donairoso, *adj.* graceful, genteel, debonair, gentle.

donatário, *s.m.* donee.

donativo, *s.m.* donation, gift, present; alms, dole; contribution.

donato, *s.m.* lay-brother.

donde, *(prep.* de and *adv.* onde) from where, whence.

doninha, *s.f.* weasel, ferret; kind of polecat.

dono, *s.m.* master; owner, proprietor; lord, landlord. 1) *dono da casa*, head of the house, landlord. 2) *mudar de dono*, to change hands. 3) *sem dono*, unowned.

donosamente, *adv.* gracefully.

donoso, *adj.* pleasant, graceful, pretty, gracious, charming; gentle, polite.

donzel, *s.m.* young nobleman.

donzela, *s.f.* young lady, girl, maid, maiden, damsel; virgin.

dor, *s.f.* ache, pain, sorrow, suffering; grief; affliction. 1) *dor de alma*, heart-ache. 2) *dor de barriga*, bellyache. 3) *dor de cabeça*, headache. 4) *dor de cotovelo*, jealousy. 5) *dor de dentes*, tooth-ache. 6) *dores de parto*, labour pains. 7) *dor de garganta*, a sore throat. 8) *trespassado pela dor*, pierced with sorrow.

doravante, *adv.* hencelorth, from now on.

dórico, *adj.* Dorian, Doric *(dialecto)*.

dorido, *adj.* aching, painful; doleful; sore.

dormência, *s. f.* dormancy, torpidity.

dormente, *adj.* sleeping, dormant; torpid, stiff, benumbed, insensible; *s.m.* floor beam; sleeper.

dormida, *s.f.* lodging *(noite)*.

dormideira, *s.f. (bot.)* poppy.

dorminhão, dorminhoco, *s.m.* lie-a-bed, sleepyhead; adj. fond of sleep.

dormir, *v.i.* to sleep; to be asleep; to be numb; to repose, to rest, to lie; to be still, to neglect. 1)*dormir a sesta*, to take a siesta;

2) *dormir a sono alto*, to sleep soundly. 3) *dormir ao relento*, to sleep in the open air. 4) *dormir como uma pedra*, to sleep like a log (or top). 5) *dormir sobre o caso*, to sleep on a matter. 6) *dormir sobre os louros*, to rest on laurels. 7) *dormir o sono eterno*, to sleep the eternal sleep. 8) *dormir uma soneca*, to take a nap. 9) *a bom dormir*, sound asleep. 10) *são horas de dormir*, it is bedtime. 11) *quarto de dormir*, bedroom. 12) *ter vontade de dormir*, to feel drowsy (sleep)

dormitar, *v.i.* to slumber, to doze, to drowse, to nap.

dormitório, *s.m.* dormitory.

dorna, *s.f.* vintage tub, vat.

dorsal, *adj.* dorsal; *espinha dorsal*, spine, backbone.

dorso, *s.m.* back; reverse.

dosagem, *s.f.* dosage; dosing.

dosar, *v.t.* to dose, to portion.

dose, *s.f.* dose; portion, quantity.

doseamento, *s.m. vd.* dosagem.

dosear, *v.t.; vd.* dosar.

dosificar, *v.t.* to divide into doses.

dosimetria, *s.f.* dosimetry, dosology.

dosimétrico, *adj.* dosimetric.

dossel, *s.m.* canopy, dossel, tester.

dotação, *s.f.* donation, gift, bestowal, provision, endowment.

dotado, *adj.* endowed, gifted, talented; equipped *dotado de qualidades*, endowed with qualities.

dotal, *adj.* concerning a dowry, dotal.

dotar, *v.t.* to endow; to portion; to give a dowry, to dot, to dower.

dote, *s.m.* dowry, endowment, gift, marriage portion; talent, natural gift.

doudice, *s.f.; vd. doidice.*

doudo, *adj.; vd. doido.*

dourado, *adj.* golden, gilt, gilded; *prata dourada*, gilded silver.

dourador, *s.m.* gilder.

douradura, douramento, *s.f., s.m.* ; gilding; gold leaf.

dourar, *v.t.* to gild; to gilt, to cover with a thin gold layer; to brighten, to adorn; *dourar a pílula*, to gild a pill, to sugarcoat the bitter pill.

douto, *adj.* learned, erudite.

doutor, *s.m.* doctor. 1) *doutor da mula ruça*, a quack. 2) *doutor de borla e capelo*, the highest degree at the University. 3) *doutor da Igreja*, doctor of the Church.

doutora, *s.f.* lady doctor.

doutorado, *s.m.* doctorate, having a doctor's degree.

doutoral, *adj.* doctoral.

doutoramento, *s.m.* taking of a doctor's degree *(exame).*

doutorando, *s.m.* candidate to a doctor's degree.

doutorar, *v.t.* to confer the degree of doctor, to doctorate, to graduate; *doutorar-se*, to receive a doctor's degree (na universidade).

doutorice, *s.f.* airs of a know-it-all.

doutrina, *s.f.* doctrine; formula, dogma, maxim, precept.

doutrinação, *s.f.* indoctrination, catechesis; instruction, teaching.

doutrinador, *s.m.* teacher, instructor.

doutrinal, *adj.* doctrinal.

doutrinar, *v.t.* to indoctrinate, to teach, to instruct, to doctrinize.

doutrinário, *adj.* doctrinal, doctrinaire, theoretical.

doutrinável, *adj.* teachable, docile.

doxologia, *s.f.* doxology.

doze, *num.* twelve.

dracma, *s.f.* drachma.

draconiano, *adj.* Draconian, Draconic, rigorous, harsh, cruel, barbarously, severe.

draga, *s.f.* dredge, drag, dredger, dredging machine.

dragador, *s.m.* dredger.

dragagem, *s.f.* dredging, dredging operation.

dragão, *s.m.* dragon *(animal)*; dragoon (soldier); Draco (constellation).

dragar, *v.t.* dredge, to drag.

dragoeiro, *s.m.* dragon-tree *(bot.).*

dragona, *s.f.* epaulet, shoulder strap.

drama, *s.m.* drama; dramatic literature; catastrophe, horrible event.

dramalhão, *s.m.* melodrame.

dramaticamente, *adv.* dramatically.

dramaticidade, dramatismo, *s.f., s.m.* dramatic quality or nature.

dramático, *adj.* dramatic, striking, tragic; *autor dramático*, playwright.

dramatização, *s.f.* dramatization, dramatizing, dramatic construction.

dramatizar, *v.t.* to dramatize, to make a drama of, to put into a dramatic form.

dramaturgia, *s.f.* dramaturgy, dramatic art .

dramaturgo, *s.m.* dramaturge, dramatist, playwright.

drapejar, *v.i.* to drape; to fly, to wave.
drástico, *adj.* drastic, rigorous, violent, powerful.
drenagem, *s.f.* drainage.
drenar, *v.t.* to drain, to exhaust, to draw off gradually.
dreno, *s.m.* drain, drain pipe, drainage ditch; drain, tent *(med.).*
driça, *s.f.* halyard, halliard *(náut.).*
droga, *s.f.* drug, ingredient; worthless thing, thrash, junk *(pop.); dar em droga,* to come to naught.
drogaria, *s.f.* drug trade; druggist's shop.
droguista, *s.* druggist.
dromedário, *s.m.* dromedary, Arabian camel.
druida, *s.m.* druid *(padre).*
druídico, *adj.* druidical.
druidismo, *s.m.* druidism *(religião).*
drupa, *s.f.* drupe, stone-fruit *(cereja, pêssego).*
dual, *adj.* dual, dualistic, double.
dualidade, *s.f.* duality.
dualismo, *s.m.* dualism.
dualista, *s., adj.* dualist.
duas, *num.* two. 1) *duas vezes* , twice. 2) *duas vezes por dia,* twice a day. 3) *de duas uma,* one of two things.
dubiamente, *adv.* doubtfully, dubiously.
dúbio, *adj.* doubtful, dubious, hesitating, vague, uncertain, hesitant,ambiguous
dubitativo, *adj.* dubitative. doubting.
dubitável, *adj.* doubtful, uncertain, dubitable.
ducado, *s.m.* dukedom; duchy; ducat *(moeda).*
ducal, *adj.* ducal.
ducentésimo, *num.* two hundredth.
ducha, duche, *s.f., s.m.* douche; shower-bath; public bathhouse *(pl.).*
dúctil, *adj.* ductile, flexible, malleable, docile, supple, soft; tractable.
ductilidade, *s.f.* ductility, flexibility, malleability; compliance.
ducto, *s.m.* duct; canal.
duelista, *s.* duelist.
duelo, *s.m.* duel.
duende, *s.m.* hobgoblin, goblin, elf; sprite, pixy.
duetista, *s.* duetist, duet singer.
dueto, *s.m.* duet.
dulcamara, *s.f.* dulcamara *(bot.).*
dulcífero, *adj.* dulciferous.
dulcificação, *s.f.* dulcification, sweetening.
dulcificante, *adj.* dulcifying, sweetening.

dulcificar, *v.t.* to dulcify, to sweeten; ro mollify, to soften.
dulcineia, *s.f.* sweetheart *(pop.).*
dulcíssimo, *adj.* very sweet, most sweet.
dulia, *s.f.* dulia.
dum, *(prep. de* and *art. um)* of a, from a, of one, from one.
duma, *(prep. de* and *art. uma)* of a, from a, of one, from one.
duna, *s.f.* down; sand-hill, dune.
duo, *s.m.* duet, duo, duetto.
duodecimal, *adj.* duodecimal.
duodécimo, *num.* twelfth; duodecimal.
duodécuplo, *adj.* twelvefold, duodecuple.
duodenal, *adj.* duodenal.
duodenite, *s.f.* duodenitis.
duodeno, *s.m.* duodenum.
duplamente, *adv.* doubly.
duplicação, *s.f.* duplication, doubling; duplicating; repeating.
duplicado, *adj.* duplicate, twofold, double; *s.m.* duplicate, copy, transcript.
duplicador, *s.m.* duplicator; duplicating machine.
duplicar, *v.t.* to duplicate, to double; to repeat; to copy.
duplicata, *s.f.* duplicate, counterpart, double, copy.
dúplice, *adj.* duplicate, double, duplex, twofold.
duplicidade, *s.f.* duplicity, double-dealing, doubleness.
duplo, *adj.* double, duplex, twofold, twice as much; dual. 1) *duplo comando,* dual control. 2) *duplo efeito,* double acting. 3) *pneumonia dupla,* double pneumonia. 4) *via dupla,* double line *(caminho de ferro).*
duque, *s.m.* duke; deuce *(cartas).*
duquesa, *s.f.* duchess.
dura, *s.f.* duration, durability. 1) *coisa de muita dura,* resistant or (lasting) thing. 2) *sol de pouca dura,* a flash in the pan.
durabilidade, *s. f.* durability duration
duração, *s.f.* duration, continuance, length of time, term.
duradoiro, duradouro, *adj.* lasting, enduring, durable.
duramente, *adv.* harshly, hardly, unkindly, severely.
durante, *prep.* during, for, while, in the time of, in the course of. 1) *durante a noite,* during the night. 2) *durante a próxima semana,* over the next week. 3) *durante a minha estadia,* during my stay. 4) *durante*

algum tempo, for some time. 5) *durante horas,* for hours. 6) *durante muitos séculos,* for ages. 7) *durante o voo,* on the flight. 8) *durante todo o ano,* throughout the year.

duraque, *s.m.* calamanco.

durar, *v.i.* to last, to last for; to wear well; to continue, to remain; to be resistent; to endure; to live. 1) *durar mais tempo que,* to outwear. 2) *isto está para durar,* that will go far.

durável, *adj.* durable, firm, stable, lasting.

durázio, *adj.* hard; oldish; elderly; *mulher durázia,* middle-aged woman

dureza, *s.f.* hardness; rudeness; callosity; resistance, consistency; compactness, solidity; toughness; severety, harshness, sharpness.

durindana, *s.f.* sword, dagger.

duro, *adj.* hard; firm; solid; cruel; rude; consistent, compact; strong, vigorous; difficult, painful; severe, unkind; *s.m.* Spanish coin. 1) *duro como rocha (calhau),* as hard as flint. 2) *duro de boca,* hard-mouthed (cavalo). 3) *duro de ouvido,* hard of hearing. 4) *duro de roer,* hard to take, hard to swallow. 5) *água mole em pedra dura tanto bate até que fura,* constant dripping wears away the stone. 6) *de casca dura,* hardshelled. 7) *um osso duro de roer,* a hard nut to crack.

duunvirato, *s.m.* duumvirate.

duúnviro, *s.m.* duumvir.

dúvida, *s.f.* doubt, hesitation; distrust; uncertainty; misgiving; suspicion; scrouple; irresolution, indecision. 1) *fora de dúvida,* beyond doubt, doubtless, indubitable. 2) *é fora de dúvida que,* there is no question but. 3) *não resta dúvida,* there is no doubt. 4) *estar em dúvida,* to hang, to halt. 5) *pôr dúvidas,* to raise doubts. 6) *sem dúvida,* doubtless, no doubt, certainly, out of question, surely. 7) *surge uma dúvida,* a doubt arises. 8) *tenho as minhas dúvidas,* I call it in to question.

duvidar, *v.t.* to doubt, to hesitate; to disbelieve, to discredit; to question; to suspect. 1) *duvidar de,* to have doubts about, to distrust.

duvidosamente, *adv.* doubtfully, dubiously.

duvidoso, *adj.* dubtful, questionable, suspicious, dubious, uncertain; problematic, unsettled; ambiguous. 1) *deixar o certo pelo duvidoso,* to grasp at the shadow and lose the substance.

duzentos, *num.* two hundred.

dúzia, *s.f.* dozen; *meia dúzia,* half a dozen.

E

e, the fifth letter of the Portuguese alphabet.

ebano, *s.m.* ebony.

ebonite, *s.f.* ebonite.

ebriedade, *s.f.* drunkness, inebriatuion, intoxication.

ébrio, *adj.* drunk, intoxicated.

ebulição, *s.f.* boiling, ebullition.

ebúrneo, *adj.* eburnean, ivory like.

echarpe, *s.f.* neck scarf.

eclampsia, *s.f.* eclampsia.

ecléctico, *s.m.* e *adj.* eclectic.

eclectismo, *s.m.* eclecticism.

eclesiástico, *adj.* ecclesiastic; *s.m.* clergyman.

eclímetro, *s.m.* eclimeter, clinometer.

eclipsar, *v.t.* to eclipse, to outshine *(ultrapassar em brilho),* to darken *(escurecer);* eclipsar-se: to disappear, to vanish.

eclipse, *s.m.* eclipse.

eclíptica, *s.f.* ecliptic.

eclíptico, *adj.* ecliptic.

eclodir, *v.i.* to hatch.

écloga, *s.f.* eclogue.

eclusa, *s.f.* flood-gate, dam.

eco, *s.m.* echo.

ecoar, *v.t.* e *v.i.* to echo, to resound.

ecologia, *s.f.*

economato, *s.m.* office of a steward.

economia, *s.f.* economy, parsimony, frugality, economics *(ciência).* 1) *economias.* 2) savings, *fazer economias,* to save.

económico, *adj.* economic, sparing, thrifty.

economista, *s.m.* economist.

economizador, *s.m.* sparer, saver, thrifty person; *adj.* economical, saving.

economizar, *v.t.* to economise, to save, to spare.

ecónomo, *s.m.* steward, house-keeper.

ecúleo, *s.m.* rack.

ecuménico, *adj.* aecumenic, universal.

eczema, *s.m.* eczema.

edema, *s.m.* edema.

edematoso, *adj.* edematous.

éden, *s.m.* Eden, paradise.

edénico, *adj.* edenic.

edição, *s.f.* edition.

edicto, *s.m.* edict, court order.

edificação, *s.f.* building, construction, edification.

edificante, *adj.* edifying.

edificar, *v.t.* to build, to construct, to erect, to raise, to edify.

edificativo, *adj.* edifying.

edifício, *s.m.* building, edifice, structure.

edil, *s.m.* aedile, councilman *(vereador).*

edilidade, *s.f.* town council.

edital, *s.m.* bill, placard, proclamation, public notice.

editar, *v.t.* to publish, to edit.

édito, *s.m.* notice, proclamation.

editor, *s.m.* publisher, editor.

editorial, *s.f.* editorial, leading article; *adj.* editorial.

edredão, *s.m.* eider-down.

educação, *s.f.* education, upbringing, politeness.

educado, *adj.* educated, polite. 1) *bem educado,* well-bred. 2) *mal educado,* ill-bred.

educador, *s.m.* educator, teacher, master.

educando, *s.m.* pupil.

educar, *v.t.* to educate, to bring up, to instruct, to teach.

educativo, *adj.* educative, instructive.

educável, *adj.* educable, teachable.

edulcoração, *s.f.* edulcoration.

eduzir, *v.t.* to educe, to deduce.

éfebo, *s.m.* ephebus.

efectivação, *s.f.* effectivation, accomplishment, realization.

efectivamente, *adv.* effectively, really.

efectivar, *v.t.* to effect, to execute, to accomplish, to realize.

efectivo, *adj.* effective, real, actual; *s.m.* *(mil.)* effective.

efectuação, *s.f.* realization, accomplishment, effectuation.

efectuar, *v.t.* to effect, to accomplish, to perform, to realize.

efeito, *s.m.* effect, result, outcome, consequence. 1) *com efeito,* null and void, without effect. 2) *levar a efeito,* to carry into effect. 3) *produzir efeito,* to work.

efeméride, *s.f.* ephemeride.

efémero, *adj.* ephemerous, ephemeral, short-lived, fleeting.

efeminação, *s.f.* effeminacy.

efeminado, *adj.* effeminate, womanish, prissy.

efeminar, *v.t.* to render effeminate.

eferente, *adj.* eferent.

efervescência, *s.f.* effervescence, ebullience; excitement.

efervescente, *adj.* effervescent, bubbling; restless, irascible.

eficácia, *s.f.* efficacy, efficiency.

eficaz, *adj.* efficacious, effective, operative.

eficazmente, *adv.* efficiently.

eficiência, *s.f.* efficiency, efficacy.

eficiente, *adj.* efficient, efficatious.

eficientemente, *adv.* efficiently.

efígie, *s.f.* effigy, image; head *(numa moeda).*

eflorescência, *s.f.* efflorescence.

eflorescente, *adj.* efflorescent.

eflorescer, *v.i.* to effloresce, to blossom, to bloom.

efluência, *s.f.* effluence, efflux.

efluente, *adj.* effluent, flowing out.

eflúvio, *s.m.* effluvium, exhalation.

efundir, *v.t.* to effuse, to shed.

efusão, *s.f.* effusion; shedding.

efusivo, *adj.* effusive, expansive, exuberant.

égide, *s.f.* shield, protection.
egípcio, *s.m.* e *adj.* Egyptian.
egiptologia, *s.f.* egyptology.
egiptólogo, *s.m.* egyptologist.
égloga, *s.f.* eclogue.
ego, *s.m.* ego.
egocêntrico, *adj.* egocentric, self-centered.
egocentrismo, *s.m.* egocentrism.
egoísmo, *s.m.* egoism, selfishness.
egoísta, *adj.* selfish, egoistic.
egotismo, *s.m.* egotism, egoism.
egotista, *s.m.* e *s.f.* egotist; *adj.* selfish.
egrégio, *adj.* egregious, noble, eminent.
égua, *s.f.* mare.
eguariço, *s.m.* breeder of horses.
eia!, *interj.* now! come on! cheer up!
eira, *s.f.* treshing-floor, barn-floor; *sem eira nem beira,* to have neither house, nor home.
eirado, *s.m.* terrace.
eiró, *s.f.* e a kind of eel.
eis, *adv.* eis aqui: here it is.
eito, *s.m.* sucession, sequence; *a eito,* in sucession, one after another.
eivado, *adj.* cracked, tainted, contaminated.
eivar, *v.t.* to stain, to taint, to spot, to contaminate.
eixo, *s.m.* axle, shaft, spindle; *(geom.)* axis. 1) *pôr nos eixos,* to straighten out. 2) *salto ao eixo,* leapfrog.
ejaculação, *s.f.* ejaculation, ejection, discharge.
ejaculador, *s.m.* ejaculator.
ejacular, *v.t.* to ejaculate, to eject, to discharge.
ejecção, *s.f.* ejection.
ejector, *s.m.* ejector.
ela, *pron. pess.* she, her, it; elas: they, them.
elaboração, *s.f.* elaboration, preparation.
elaborado, *adj.* elaborated, carefully worked out.
elaborar, *v.t.* to elaborate, to work out, to prepare, to evolve.
elanguescer, *v.t.* to languish, to grow feeble.
elasticidade, *s.f.* elasticity, springiness.
elástico, *adj.* elastic, springy, flexible; *s.m.* elastic cord.
elatério, *s.m.* elaterium.
ele, *pron. pess.* he, him, it; eles: they, them.
electivo, *adj.* elective.
electrão, *s.m.* electron.
electricidade, *s.f.* electricity.
eletrecista, *s.m.* electrician.

eléctrico, *adj.* eletric, electrical; *s.m.* tramway-car, tram.
electrificação, *s.f.* electrification.
electrificar, *v.t.* to electrify.
electriz, *s.f.* electoress.
electrização, *s.f.* electrization, electrification.
electrizador, *adj.* electrifier; *s.m.* electrizer.
electrizar, *v.t.* to electrize, to electrify.
electrizável, *adj.* electrifiable.
electrocardiograma, *s.m.* electrocardiogram.
electrocussão, *s.f.* electrocussion.
electrocutar, *v.t.* to electrocute, to kill by electricity.
electrocutor, *s.m.* electrocuter, executioner (EUA.)
electrodinâmica, *s.f.* electrodynamics.
elétrodoto, *s.m.* electrode.
elecroforo, *s.m.* electrophorus.
electroíman, *s.m.* electro-magnet.
electrólise, *s.f.* electrolysis.
electrólito, *s.m.* electrolyte.
electromagnetismo, *s.m.* electromagnetism.
electromecânica, *s.f.* electromechanics.
electrómetro, *s.m.* electrometer.
electromotor, *s.m.* electromotor.
eléctron, *s.m.* electron.
electrónica, *s.f.* electronics.
electrónico, *adj.* electronic.
electroquímica, *s.f.* electrochemistry.
electroscópio, *s.m.* electroscope.
electrotecnia, *s.f.* electrical engineering.
electroténico, *s.m.* electrotechnic.
electroterapêutica, *s.f.* electrotherapeutics.
electroterapia, *s.f.* electrotherapy.
electrotipia, *s.f.* electrotypy.
electuário, *s.m.* electrovitalism.
elefante, *s.m.* elephant.
elefantíase, *s.f.* elephantiasis.
elefantino, *adj.* elephantine.
elegância, *s.f.* elegance, grace, smartness.
elegante, *adj.* elegant, smart, fashionable.
eleger, *v.t.* to elect, to choose, to select, to pick up.
elegia, *s.f.* elegy.
elegíaco, *adj.* elegiac, mournful.
elegibilidade, *s.f.* eligibility.
elegível, *adj.* eligible.
eleição, *s.f.* election, choice, selection, preference.
eleito, *adj.* elected, elect.
eleitor, *s.m.* elector, voter; *fem.* electress.

eleitorado, s.m. electorate, body of electors or voters.

eleitoral, adj. electoral.

elementar, adj. elementary, rudimentary.

elemento, s.m. element; ingredient, component, (elect.) cell; elementos, rudiments, first principles.

elenco, s.m. cast.

elevação, s.f. elevation, lifting, raising, height, altitude, rise (aumento).

elevado, adj. elevated, raised, lifted up, lofty, sublime.

elevador, s.m. lift, elevator.

elevar, v.t. to raise, to elevate, to lift up to dignify, to exalt, to increase. 1) elevar uma potência, to to raise to a power. 2) elevar-se, to rise, to mount, to tower.

elfo, s.m. elf.

elidir, s.m. to elide, to cut off, to omit, to eliminate.

eliminação, s.f. elimination, removal.

eliminador, s.m. eliminator.

eliminar, v.t. to eliminate, to remove, to exclude, to cancel.

eliminatório, adj. eliminatory.

elipse, s.m. ellipse, (gram.) ellipsis.

elipsoidal, adj. ellipsoidal.

elipsóide, s.m. ellipsoid.

elíptico, adj. elliptic.

elisão, s.f. elision.

élitro, s.m. elytron, elytrum.

elixir, s.m. elixir.

elmo, s.m. helmet.

elo, s.m. link.

elocução, s.f. elocution.

eloendro, s.m. oleander.

elogiador, s.m. praiser, eulogist.

elogiar, v.t. to praise, to eulogise, to commend, to applaude, to exalt.

elogio, s.m. eulogy, praise, commendation, applause.

elogioso, adj. laudatory, commendatory, appreciative.

eloquência, s.f. eloquence.

eloquente, adj. eloquent.

elucidação, s.f. elucidation, explanation.

elucidar, v.t. to elucidate, to explain.

elucidativo, adj. elucidative, explanatory, illustrative.

elucubração, s.f. lucubration.

elucubrar, v.t. to lucubrate.

em, prep. in, at, on, upon, into, under. 1) em tratamento, under treatment. 2) em que, in which, in what, where, when.

ema, s.f. emu.

emaçar, v.t. to bundle, to tie in.

emaciação, s.f. emaciation, attenuation.

emaciado, adj. emaciated, thin.

emadeiramento, s.m. planking.

emadeirar, v.t. to plank, to cover with planks.

emagrecer, v.t. to make thin, to emaciate; v.i. to grow thin, to reduce weight.

emagrecimento, s.m. growing thin, reduction of weight.

emalar, v.t. to pack.

emanação, s.f. emanation, effluence.

emanar, v.i. to emanate, to issue, to originate (from).

emancipação, s.f. emancipation.

emancipado, adj. emancipated.

emancipar, v.t. to emancipate; emancipar-se: to emancipate oneself.

emaranhamento, s.m. entanglement, intricacy.

emaranhar, v.t. to entangle, to tangle.

emaçadela, s.f. trick, cheat; embarrassment, uneasiness.

embaçado, adj. embarased, confused.

embaçar, v.t. to dim, to shade, to embarrass, to confuse, to perplex.

emaciar, v.t. to dim, to tarnish; v.i. to grow dim.

embaidor, s.m. coaxer, flatterer; adj. coaxing, deceiving, flattering.

embainhar, v.t. to hem, to sheathe (pôr na bainha).

embair, v.t. to allure, to coax, to deceive.

embaixada, s.f. embassy, mision.

embaixador, s.m. ambassador.

embaixatriz, s.f. ambassadress.

embalador, s.m. packer.

embalagem, s.f. packing, package.

embalar, v.t. to lull (uma criança), to pack (acondicionar).

embalo, s.m. lulling.

embalsamador, s.m. embalmer.

embalsamamento, s.m. embalming, embalmment.

embalsamar, v.t. to embalm, to stuff.

embandeirar, v.t. to flag, to adorn with flags.

embaraçado, adj. embarrassed, disconcerted, perplexed, disturbed; tangled, intricate.

embaraçar, v.t. to embarrass, to perplex; to entangle (enlear).

embaraço, s.m. embarrassment, hindrance, obstacle.

embaraçoso, adj. embarrassing, difficult.

embarcação, s.f. boat, vessel, ship, craft.

embarcadiço, s.m. seafaring man.

embarcadoiro, embarcadouro, s.m. landing-place, pier, quay.

embarcar, v.t. to embark, to ship, to put aboard; v.i. to embark, to go aboard; embarcar em, to board, to take.

embargado, adj. seized, under an embargo.

embargador, s.m. one who lays an embargo; adj. embarrassing.

embargamento, s.m. o mesmo que "embargo".

embargante, adj. embarrassing, arresting, seizing, laying an embargo.

embargar, v.t. to embargo, to stay the execution off (a sentença), to hinder (impedir).

embargo, s.m. embargo, hindrance.

embarque, s.m. embarkation (de pessoas), shipment (de mercadorias).

embarrar, v.t. to daub with clay.

embarrilar, v.t. to barrel, to deceive (aldrabar).

embasbacado, adj. gasping, agape.

embasbacar, v.t. e v.i. to amaze, to astonish, to gape, to stare.

embate, s.m. collision, shock, clash, striking.

embater, v.i. to dash against, to strike, to collide with.

embatocar, v.i. to bung.

embatucar, v.t. to dumbfound, to perplex.

embebedar, v.t. to intoxicate, to inebriate; embebedar-se, to get drunk.

embeber, v.t. to imbibe, to absorb, to soak in, to plunge into (cravar); embeber-se, to be soaked in, to become absorbed.

embeiçado, adj. fallen in love.

embeiçar, v.t. to fall in love.

embelezador, adj. beautifying.

embelezamento, s.m. embellishment.

embelezar, v.t. to embellish, to beautify, to smarten up.

embevecedor, adj. moving.

embevecer, v.t. to enrapture; embevecer-se: to become enraptured.

embevecido, adj. enraptured.

embevecimento, s.m. rapture, ravishment, amazement.

embezerrado, adj. sulky, sullen.

embezerrar, v.i. to sulk, to frown, to become sullen.

embicar, v.i. to stumble, to have a tiff with somebody.

embirração, s.f. aversion, deslike, tiff, obstinacy.

embirrante, adj. obstinate, pig-headed, annoying.

embirrar, v.i. to sulk, to persist in, to insist on; embirrar com, to take a strong dislike to.

embelema, s.m. emblem, symbol, insignia.

emblemático, adj. emblematic, symbolical.

embocadura, mouth (de rio), mouthpiece (de instrumento musical).

embocar, v.t. e v.i. to apply the first coat of plaster to.

emboço, s.m. first coat of plaster.

embófia, s.f. presumption.

embolar, v.t. to pad the horns of a bull.

embolia, s.f. embolism.

êmbolo, s.m. piston.

embolsar, v.t. to pocket.

embolorecer, v.i. to grow mouldy.

embolso, s.m. pocketing; reimbursment.

embonecar, v.t. to trim, to embellish, to dress like a doll.

embora, adv. conj. e interj. though, although; ir (levar, mandar, vir) embora: to go (send, take, come) away; muito embora: even though.

emborcar, v.t. to turn upside down, to overturn, to swig (beber).

embornal, s.m. feed bag, (náut.) scupper.

emborrachar, v.t. to intoxicate; emborrachar-se, to get drunk.

emborralhar, v.t. to cover with ashes.

emborrascar, v.t. to make stormy, to overcloud, to darken; v.i. to grow dark, to grow stormy.

emboscada, s.f. ambush, ambuscade; armar emboscada a: to waylay.

emboscar, v.t. to ambush; emboscar-se, to lurk, to lie in wait (for).

embotadura, s.f. dubling, blunting.

embotar, v.t. to blunt, to dull, to deaden.

embraiagem, s.f. clutch.

embraiar, v.t. to engage the clutch.

embranquecer, v.t. to whiten.

embravecer, v.t. to enrage; v.i. to get angry.

embravecido, adj. enraged, angry.

embravecimento, s.m. enragement, anger, fury.

embrechado, s.m. rock-work, shell-work.

embrechar, v.t. to adorn with pebbles and shells.

embrenhar, v.t. to hide; embrenhar-se, to hide, to disappear.

embriagado, *adj.* drunk, drunken, intoxicated, tipsy; enraptured.

embriaguez, *s.f.* drunkness, intoxication; rapture. *(entusiasmo).*

embrião, *s.m.* embryo.

embriologia, *s.f.* embryology.

embriológico, *adj.* embryological.

embriologista, *s.m.* embryologist.

embrionário, *adj.* embryonic; rudimentary.

embrulhada, *s.f.* imbroglio, entanglement, confusion, difficult situation, mess.

embrulhar, *v.t.* wrap up; to complicate, to tangle, to embroil, to deceive *(lograr).*

embrulho, *s.m.* package, parcel.

embrutecer, *v.t.* to brutify, to render stupid.

embrutecimento, *s.m.* the act of becoming stupid or brutish.

embruxar, *v.t.* to bewitch, to enchant.

embuçado, *adj.* wrapped up, muffled up.

embuçar, *v.t.* to muffle, to wrap up, to conceal; *embuçar-se,* to muffle oneself, to disguise oneself.

embuchado, *adj.* fed up, full-fed.

embuchar, *v.t.* to stuff, to tuck in; *v.i.* to choke with one's food.

emburrar, *v.i.* to sulk; to make an ass of.

embuste, *s.m.* stratagem, trick, cheat.

embusteiro, *s.m.* tale-teller. liar, impostor, humbug.

embutido, *s.m.* inlaidwork, inlay work; *adj.* inlaid, built-in *(armário, etc.).*

embutidor, *s.m.* inlayer.

embutir, *v.t.* to inlay, to incrust, to embed.

emenda, *s.f.* correction, emendation, amendment *(a uma lei); não ter emenda,* to be incorrigible.

emendar, *v.t.* to correct, to rectify, to amend, to mend, to piece *(roupa); emendar-se,* to mend one's ways.

emendável, *adj.* repairable, amendable.

ementa, *s.f.* menu.

emergência, *s.f.* emergency.

emergente, *adj.* emergent.

emergir, *v.t.* to emerge (from), to rise out (of), to surface *(submarino).*

emérito, *adj.* emeritus.

emersão, *s.f.* emersion.

emerso, *adj.* floating, emergent.

emético, *adj.* emetic, emetical; *s.m.* emetic.

emigração, *s.f.* emigration.

emigrado, *adj.* e *s.m.* emigrant.

emigrante, *s.m.* e *s.f.* emigrant.

emigrar, *v.i.* to emigrate, to migrate.

eminência, *s.f.* eminece; elevation, height, prominence, distinction; *Vossa Eminência,* Your Eminence.

eminente, *adj.* eminent, distinguished, sublime, remarkable.

eminentemente, *adv.* eminetly.

eminentíssimo, *adj.* most eminent.

emir, *s.m.* emir.

emissão, *s.f.* emission, issue.

emissário, *s.m.* emissary, agent, messenger.

emissível, *adj.* issuable.

emissor, *s.m.* emitter, sender, transmitter; *adj.* issuing *(banco).*

emissora, *s.f.* broadcasting station.

emitir, *v.t.* to emit, to send, to issue *(moeda, etc.),* to broadcast *(rádio).*

emoção, *s.f.* emotion, excitement, thrill.

emocionante, *adj.* exciting, thrilling, moving.

emoldurar, *v.t.* to frame.

emoliente, *adj.* emollient, soothing.

emolumento, *s.m.* emolument, fee.

emotividade, *s.f.* emotiveness.

emotivo, *adj.* emotive.

emouquecer, *v.t.* e *v.i.* to deafen, to grow deaf.

empa, *s.f.* propping of viness.

empacotamentel, *s.m.* packing.

empacotar, *v.t.* to pack, to wrap.

empada, *s.f.* pie.

empadão, *s.m.* pie, large pie.

empáfia, *s.f.* self-importance, haughtiness.

empalação, *s.f.* impalement.

empalado, *adj.* impaled.

empalar, *v.t.* to impale.

empalhação, *s.f.* stuffing *(de animais),* packing in with straw *(louça, etc.).*

empalhado, *adj.* stuffed, packed with straw.

empalhar, *v.t.* to stuff, to pack up with straw.

empalidecer, *v.t.* to pale, to to turn or to grow pale.

empalmação, *s.f.* hiding in the palm of the hand, robbing *(surripiar).*

empalmar, *v.t.* to palm, to filch *(surripiar).*

empanada, *s.f.* window-sash.

empanado, *adj.* dull, tarnished, dim; wraped in cloth.

empandeirar, *v.t.* to swell *(as velas);* to send away.

empandilhar, *v.t.* e *v.i.* to cheat, to swindle.

empanque, *s.m.* packing.

empanturrado, *adj.* overfull.

empanturrar, *v.t.* e *v.refl.* to gorge oneself, to cram with food.
empapado, *adj.* soaked.
empapar, *v.t.* to soak, to imbibe, to drench; *empapar-se:* to get soaked.
empar, *v.t.* to prop a vine.
emparceirar, *v.t.* to join, to match, to associate; *v.i.* to be similar.
emparedamento, *s.m.* walling in, immurement.
emparedar, *v.t.* to wall in, to immure.
emparelhado, *adj.* mached, in pairs, yoked.
emparelhamento, *s.m.* matching, pairing.
emparelhar, *v.t.* to match, to couple, to yoke, to team up; *emparelhar-se,* to match, to be equal to.
empastado, *adj.* paste like, plastered.
empastamento, *s.m.* pasting up, plastering up, impasting *(pintura).*
empastar, *v.t.* e *v.i.* to paste, to plaster, to glue, to impaste.
empatado, *adj.* drawn *(jogo).*
empatar, *v.t.* e *v.i.* to draw, to tie, to hinder *(impedir),* to tie up *(dinheiro).*
empate, *s.m.* draw, tie, stalemate *(no xadrez).*
empavesar, *v.t.* to dress a ship with pennants; to hang with shields.
empavonear-se, *v.refl.* to flaunt, to strut about.
empeçar, *v.t.* to embarass, to entangle, to hinder; *v.i.* to stumble against.
empecer, *v.t.* to hinder, to embarass, to prevent, to thwart; *v.i.* to stand in someone's way.
empecilho, *s.m.* impediment, obstacle, hindrance, snag.
empeçonhamento, *s.m.* poisoning.
empeçonhar, *v.t.* to poison, to infect.
empedernido, *adj.* stony, hard-hearted.
empedernir, *v.t.* to harden; *empedernir-se,* to become hard-hearted, to turn into stone *(o coração).*
empedrado, *s.m.* paving, pavement.
empedrar, *v.t.* to pave with stone, to harden.
empena, *s.f.* warping.
empenachar, *v.t.* to adorn with plumes, to trim.
empenar, *v.t.* to warp; to feather, to adorn with feathers.
empenhamento, *s.m.* zeal, devotion; pawning.
empenhar, *v.t.* to pawn; pledge, to engage

(comprometer), to risk *(arriscar); empenhar-se:* to bind oneself; to run into debt; to struggle (for something), to engage; to use one's influence.
empenho, *s.m.* pawning; diligence, zeal, devotion; support, patronage; *com empenho:* diligently.
empeno, *s.m.* warping; hindrance, obstacle.
emperrado, *adj.* stiff, hard to open *(uma fechadura);* obstinate, stubborn.
emperramento, *s.m.* stiffness; stubborness.
emperrar, *v.t.* e *v.i.* to stiffen, to stick, to be stiff, to become blocked.
empertigado, *adj.* stiff-necked, vain, proud.
empertigar-se, *v.refl.* to stand upright, to become haughty, to stiffen.
empestado, *adj.* infected, contaminated.
empestar, *v.t.* to infect, to contaminate.
emppilhamento, *s.m.* pilling up, stacking.
empilhar, *v.t.* to heap up, to pile up, to stack; *empilhar-se:* to pile up.
empinado, *adj.* reared *(cavalo);* proud.
empinar, *v.t.* to raise, to uplift, to prick up *(orelhas); empinar-se,* to rear *(cavalo).*
empíreo, *adj.* empyreal; *s.m.* empyrean.
empírico, *adj.* empiric; *s.m.* empiric, charlatan, quack.
empirismo, *s.m.* empiricism.
emplastramento, *s.m.* plastering, coating.
emplastrar, *v.t.* to plaster.
emplastro, *s.m.* plaster.
emplumar, *v.t.* to addorn with feathers.
empoado, *adj.* powdered, dusty.
empoar, *v.t.* powder, to dust.
empobrecer, *v.t.* to impoverish; *v.i.* to grow poor.
empobrecimento, *s.m.* impoverishment.
empoçar, *v.t.* to put in a well; to form a puddle.
empoeirado, *adj.* dusty.
empoeirar, *v.t.* to dust, to cover with dust.
empola, *s.f.* bubble, *(de água fervente),* blister *(na pele),* ampoule *(de medicamento).*
empolado, *adj.* swollen; bombastic.
empolar, *v.t.* e *v.i.* to blister; to make proud; *empolar-se,* to swell, to blister; to become bombastic.
empoleirar, *v.t.* to perch, to roost.
empolgante, *adj.* exciting, thrilling.
empolgar, *v.t.* to grip, to grasp, to clutch; to thrill, to charm.
empontar, *v.t.* to dismiss, to send away.
emporcalhar, *v.t.* to dirty, to soil, to defile.

empório, *s.m.* emporium, market.

empossar, *v.t.* to put in possesion, to install (in office); *empossar-se,* to take possesion (of), to assume office.

emprazamento, *s.m.* summons.

emprazar, *v.t.* to summon, to call, to cite, to fix a term.

empreendedor, *adj.* enterprising, aggresive, venturesome; *s.m.* entrepreneur.

empreender, *v.t.* to undertake, to tackle, to embark upon.

empreendimento, *s.m.* undertaking, enterprise.

empregado, *adj.* employed; *s.m.* employee, clek, servant.

empregador, *s.m.* employer.

empregar, *v.t.* to employ, to utilize, to make use of; to apply, to invest *(dinheiro)*, to hire *(contratar); empregar-se,* to get a job.

emprego, *s.m.* employment; use, application; job; investment *(dinheiro).*

empreitada, *s.f.* contract, work, job work, piece-work.

empreiteiro, *s.m.* contractor.

emprenhar, *v.t. (pop.)* to make pregnant; *v.i.* to become pregnant.

empresa, *s.f.* entreprise, undertaking; firm, company.

empresário, *s.m.* entrepreneur, entrepriser; *empresário (de teatro).*

emprestado, *adj.* lent; *pedir emprestado,* to borrow (from someone).

emprestar, *v.t.* to lend, to loan, to impart *(qualidades).*

empréstimo, *s.m.* loan, lending, borrowing.

emproado, *adj.* haughty, proud.

emproar, *v.i. (náut.)* to steer for; *emproar-se,* to grow haughty.

empubescer, *v.i.* to reach puberty.

empubescido, *adj.* pubescent.

empunhar, *v.t.* to grasp or hold by the handle, to grasp, to grip.

empurrão, *s.m.* push, shove, jostle, hustle.

empurrar, *v.t.* to push, to shove, to jostle, to hustle.

empuxar, *v.t. o mesmo que "empurrar".*

emudecer, *v.t. e v.i.* to silence, to grow mute or silent, to become speechless.

emudecimento, *s.m.* silencing, speechlessness.

emulação, *s.f.* emulation, rivalry, envy.

emulador, *s.m.* emulator, rival, competitor; *adj.* emulating, competing.

emular, *v.t. e v.i.* to emulate, to rival, to strive to equal; to imitate.

émulo, *adj.* emulous, emulating; *s.m.* emulator, rival, competitor.

emulsão, *s.f.* emulsion.

emulsionar, *v.t.* to emulsify.

emulsivo, *adj.* emulsive.

emurchecer, *v.t.* to wilt, to wither, to fade.

enálage, *s.f.* enallage.

enaltecer, *v.t.* to exalt, to extol, to praise.

enaltecimento, *s.m.* exaltation.

enamorado, *adj.* enamoured, amorous, in love, infatuated (with).

enamorar-se, *v.refl.* to fall in love with.

enartrose, *s.f.* enarthrosis.

enastrar, *v.t.* to tie with a ribbon.

encabar, *v.t.* to halve.

encabeçamento, *s.m.* tax-roll; census-taking; heading.

encabeçar, *v.t.* to lead, to head, to be at the head of, to butt *(unir pelo topo).*

encabrestamento, *s.m.* haltering *(cavalo).*

encabrestar, *v.t.* to halter, to put a halter on.

encabritar-se, *v.refl.* to prance, to rear *(cavalo).*

encadeamento, *s.m.* chaining, connection, linking, chain.

encadear, *v.t.* to enchain, to link together.

encadernação, *s.f.* binding.

encadernador, *s.m.* bookbinder.

encadernar, *v.t.* to bind.

encafuar, *v.t.* to conceal, to hide; *encafuar-se:* to hide, to shut oneself up.

encaixar, *v.t.* to incase, to fit, to insert; *v.i.* to fit perfectly.

encaixe, *s.m.* fitting; groove; socket; mortise *(carpintaria).*

encaixilhar, *v.t.* to frame, to enclose, as in a frame.

encaixotamento, *s.m.* packing up, encasement.

encaixotar, *v.t.* to encase, to pack up, to put in a case or box.

encalacrar, *v.t.* to put in a tight corner, to be in a difficult situation; *encalacrar-se,* to run into debt.

encalço, *s.m.* pursuit, chase, trail; *ir no encalço:* to chase.

encalhar, *v.t.* to run ashore; *v.i.* to strand, to be driven on shore.

encalhe, *s.m.* stranding, running ashore; hindrance, obstacle.

encalmar, *v.t.* to heat, to stifle with heat.

encalvecer, *v.i.* to grow bald.

encamar, *v.t.* to place in layers.

encaminhamento, *s.m.* guiding.

encaminhar, *v.t.* to guide, to lead, to show the right way, to direct; *encaminhar-se,* to make one's way, to make for.

encanamento, *s.m.* canalization, piping, plumbing.

encanar, *v.t.* to canalize, to put in pipes, to set *(fracturas).*

encanastrado, *adj.* plaiting; basket-work.

encanastrar, *v.t.* to pack up in baskets; to plait.

encandenar, *v.t.* to dazzle.

encanecer, *v.i.* to grow-headed, to turn gray.

encanecido, *adj.* gray, white-haired.

encaniçar, *v.t.* to fence, to surround with canes, to fence with canes.

encantado, *adj.* enchanted, charmed, fascinated, delighted.

encantador, *adj.* charming, enchanting, lovely, ravishing; *s.m.* enchanter, charmer, sorcerer.

encantamento, *s.m.* enchantment, spell, charm, witchery, sorcery.

encantar, *v.t.* to charm, to enchant, to fascinate, to delight.

encanudado, *adj.* curled; tubular.

encanudar, *v.t.* to curl, to plait.

encanzinar, *v.t.* to anger, to enrage; *encanzinar-se,* to grow obstinate; to become enraged.

encapar, *v.t.* to cloak; to put a cover on *(um livro).*

encapelado, *adj.* rough *(mar).*

encapelar-se, *v.refl.* to get rough.

encapotado, *adj.* concealed, disguised.

encapotar, *v.t.* to conceal, to disguise; to muffle.

encaprichar-se, *v.refl.* to be obstinate, to get an idea into one's head.

encapuzar, *v.t.* to hood.

encaracolado, *adj.* curled, curly.

encaracolar, *v.t.* to curl, to crisp.

encarado, *adj. bem encarado:* good-looking; *mal-encarado,* ill-looking.

encarapinhado, *adj.* kinky *(cabelo).*

encarapinhar, *v.t.* to kink.

encarar, *v.t.* to face, to stare at, to consider.

encarceramento, *s.m.* incarceration, imprisonment.

encarcerar, *v.t.* to incarcerate, to imprison, to jail, to shut up.

encardido, *adj.* dingy, grimy, dirty.

encardir, *v.t.* e *v.refl.* to foul, to soil, to make dingy.

encarecimento, *s.m.* increase, raise in prices.

encarecer, *v.t.* to raise the price of, to exaggerate; *v.i.* to grow dear.

encarecidamente, *adv.* earnestly

encargo, *s.m.* charge, commission, assignement, duty, task, obligation, responsability.

encarnação, *s.f.* incarnation; embodiment; personification.

encarnado, *adj.* red *(cor);* incarnate; *s.m.* red.

encarnar, *v.t.* to incarnate, to embody, to personify; *v.i.* to become incarnate.

encarneirar-se, *v.refl.* to become choppy *(o mar).*

encarniçadamente, *adv.* fiercely, furiously.

encarniçado, *adj.* fierce, furious, cruel, pitiless.

encarniçamento, *s.m.* fierceness, fury.

encarniçar-se, *v.refl.* to rage, to grow cruel.

encaroçado, *adj.* lumpy.

encaroçar, *v.i.* to become lumpy.

encarquilhar, *v.t.* to wrinkle.

encarrapitar, *v.t.* to put on the top, to perch; *encarrapitar-se,* to perch oneself.

encarregado, *adj.* charged with; *s.m.* manager, foreman, person in charge.

encarregar, *v.t.* to charge, to entrust with; *encarregar-se de:* to take charge of, to see to.

encarreirar, *v.t.* to put on the right way; *v.i.* to go right.

encartação, *s.f.* registration.

encartar, *v.t.* to register, to invest with an office.

encarte, *s.f.* installation, registration, investiture.

encartuchar, *v.t.* to make cartridges.

encarvoar, *v.t.* to blacken with coal dust.

encasacar-se, *v.refl.* to dress up.

encascar, *v.t.* to set (something) in its place, to adjust.

encasquetar, *v.t.* to put something into a person's head.

encastelado, *adj.* castled.

encastelar, *v.t.* to fortify, to heap up *(amontoar); encastelar-se,* to withdraw to a fortified place.

encastelamento, *s.m.* confinement in a castle; pile, heap.

encastoar, *v.t.* to set *(pedras preciosas),* to put a knob on *(uma bengala).*

encatarroado, *adj.* having a cold; hoarse.

encatarroar-se, *v.refl.* to catch a cold; to get hoarse.

encavacar, *v.i.* to become embarrassed.

encavilhar, *v.t.* to fix with wooden or metal pins; to spike.

encefálico, *adj.* encephalic.

encefalite, *s.f.* encephalitis.

encéfalo, *s.m.* encephalon.

enceleirar, *v.t.* to store in a barn.

encenação, *s.f.* staging, showing off *(fingimento).*

encenador, *s.m.* stage manager.

encenar, *v.t.* to stage.

encerado, *s.m.* oil-cloth, linoleum, polished-floor; *adj.* polished, waxed.

enceradora, *s.f.* waxing machine.

encerar, *v.t.* to wax.

encerramento, *s.m.* closing, enclosing, end, conclusion.

encerrar, *v.t.* to close, to shut up, to lock, to include *(incluir).*

encetar, *v.t.* to begin, to start, to begin to cut *(um bolo, etc.).*

encharcadiço, *adj.* swampy, marshy.

encharcado, *adj.* drenched, soaked, wet through.

encharcar, *v.t.* to soak, to drench, to flood, to swamp; *encharcar-se:* to get drenched.

enchedeira, *s.f.* little funnel.

enchente, *s.f.* flood, inundation, deluge, swelling *(de um rio),* full house *(num teatro, etc.).*

encher, *v.t.* to fill, to fill up (with something), to load, to occupy; to cram; *v.i.* to come in *(a maré);* enchers-se, to fill, to become full.

enchido, *s.m.* sausage.

enchimento, *s.m.* filling, stuffing, quilting *(para acolchoados).*

enchova, *s.f.* anchovy.

enchumaçar, *v.t.* to stuff, to pad.

encíclica, *s.f.* encyclical.

enciclopédia, *s.f.* encyclopaedia.

enciclopédico, *adj.* encyclopedic.

enciclopedista, *s.m.* encyclopedist.

encimar, *v.t.* to top, to crown.

enclaustrar, *v.t.* to cloister.

enclausurar, *v.t.* to imprison, to shut up.

enclavinhar, *v.t.* to interlock *(os dedos),* to clasp *(as mãos).*

enclítica, *s.f.* enclitic.

enclítico, *adj.* enclitic.

encoberto, *adj.* concealed, hiden, secret, dissimulated, foggy *(o tempo).*

encobridor, *s.m.* concealer, accomplice.

encobrimento, *s.m.* hiding, concealing.

encobrir, *v.t.* to conceal, to hide, to dissimulate; *v.i.* to become cloudy *(o tempo).*

encolerizado, *adj.* angered, angry, irate, furious.

encolerizar, *v.t.* to anger, to enrage, to infuriate; *encolerizar-se,* to get angry, to grow angry.

encolha, *s.f.* shrinking.

encolher, *v.t.* to shrink, to shorten, to shrug *(os ombros); encolher-se,* to hudle, to shrink.

encolhido, *adj.* shrunk; bashful.

encolhimento, *s.m.* shrinking, contraction; timidity.

encomenda, *s.f.* order, charge, commission. 1) *encomenda postal,* parcel sent by post. 2) *feito de encomenda,* made to order. 3) *fazer uma encomenda,* to order.

encomendação, *s.f.* order, commendation *(num enterro).*

encomendar, *v.t.* to order, to commission (someone to do something), to commend, to recommend *(num serviço religioso); encomendar-se,* to entrust oneself to.

encomiar, *v.t.* to praise, to laud.

encomiasta, *s.m.* encomiast, eulogist.

encomiástico, *adj.* encomiastic, laudatory.

encómio, *s.m.* encomium, praise, eulogy.

enconchar-se, *v.refl.* to restrain oneself; to take shelter.

encontrão, *s.m.* push, shove, jostle; *dar encontrões em,* to hustle.

encontrar, *v.t.* to find, to come accross; to meet *(pessoas); encontrar-se,* to meet; to find oneself, to be.

encontro, *s.m.* meeting; collision; *ir ao encontro de,* to meet, to go to meet; to anticipate.

encorajamento, *s.m.* encouragement.

encorajar, *v.t.* to encourage, to embolden, to hearten.

encordoamento, *s.m.* sringing *(de instrumento musical).*

encordoar, *v.t.* to string.

encorpado, *adj.* bulky, stout, corpulent, thick, full-bodied *(vinho),* close-woven *(tecido).*

encorpar, *v.t.* to thicken; *v.i.* togrow stout or corpulent.

encorrear, *v.t.* to fasten with a strap.

encorrilhar, *v.t. e v.i.* to enclose, to shut up; to wrinkle.

encortiçar, *v.t.* to put into a bee-hive, to make rough like cork; *v.i.* to grow rough like cork.

encoscorar, *v.t.* to shrivel, to crisp.

encosta, *s.f.* slope, hillside. 1) *encosta a baixo,* downhill. 2) *encosta acima,* uphill.

encostado, *adj.* leaning against.

encostar, *v.t.* to lean, to prop (against or upon something), to place (against); *encostar-se,* to lean (against), to lean back.

encosto, *s.m.* prop, support, back *(de cadeira).*

encourar, *v.t.* to cover with leather; *v.i.* to grow a new skin.

encovado, *adj.* sunk, sunken; hollow.

encovar, *v.t.* to bury, hide in the ground.

encravado, *adj.* stuck, ingrowing *(unha).*

encravação, *s.f.* nailing.

encravar, *v.t.* to embed, to set, to nail *(pregar); encravar-se,* to get stuck.

encrenca, *s.f.* difficulty, trouble, row *(desordem).*

encrespado, *adj.* curled, crisp, rough *(mar).*

encrespar, *v.t.* to curl, to crisp, to frizzle, to wrinkle *(papel),* to ripple *(superfície da água); encrespar-se,* to curl, to become rough *(mar).*

encristar-se, *v.refl.* to crest, to erect the crest.

encrostado, *adj.* crusty.

encrostar, *v.i.* to crust, to form into a crust.

encruado, *adj.* badly baked, hardened.

encruar, *v.i.* to become tough; *v.t.* to harden, to make crude.

encruzilhada, *s.f.* crossroads, crossing.

encubar, *v.t.* to cask liquids.

encurralado, *adj.* driven into a corner, with no escape.

encurralar, *v.t.* to pen up, to corner, to drive into a corner.

encurtamento, *s.m.* shortening, abridgement, lessening.

encurtar, *v.t.* to shorten, to abridge, to lessen, to diminish.

encurvadura, *s.f.* incurvation, curving, bending.

encurvar, *v.t.* to incurve, to bend, to arch.

endecha, *s.f.* dirge.

endemia, *s.f.* endemic disease.

endémico, *adj.* endemical.

endemoninhado, *adj.* demoniac, devilish.

endemoninhar, *v.t.* to bedevil; to infuriate; to play the devil with.

endentar, *v.t.* to indent, to dent.

endereçar, *v.t.* to address.

endereço, *s.m.* address; direction.

endeusamento, *s.m.* deification.

endeusar, *v.t.* to deify, to make a god of.

endiabrado, *adj.* devilish, naughty, mischievous.

endinheirado, *adj.* rich, wealthy.

endireita, *s.m. (pop.)* bone-setter.

endireitar, *v.t.* to straighten, to put in order, to set right; *endireitar-se,* to stand upright, to straighten up.

endividado, *adj.* in debt.

endividar, *v.t.* indebt, to run into debt.

endocárdio, *s.m.* endo-cardium.

endocardite, *s.f.* endocarditis.

endócrino, *adj.* endocrine.

endocrinologia, *s.f.* endocrinology.

endoderme, *s.f.* endoderm.

endoenças, *s.f. pl.* pangs, afflictions.

endógeno, *adj.* endogenous.

endoidecer, *v.t.* to madden; *v.i.* to become mad, to go mad.

endomingado, *adj.* dressed in one's best clothes.

endoplasma, *s.m.* endoplasm.

endoscópio, *s.m.* endoscope.

endosmose, *s.f.* endosmosis.

endosmótico, *adj.* endosmotic.

endosperma, *s.m.* endosperm.

endossado, *s.m. (com.)* endorsee; *adj.* endorsed.

endossante, *s.m.* indorser.

endossar, *v.t.* to endorse, to indorse.

endosso, *s.m.* endorsement.

endovenoso,

endrómina, *s.f.* stratagem, artifice, trick.

endurecer, *v.t.* to harden; *v.i.* to become hard; to become insensitive.

endurecido, *adj.* hardened; hard-hearted, insensitive.

endurecimento, *s.m.* hardening, hardness; hard-heartedness.

eneágono, *s.m.* enneagon.

enegrecer, *v.t.* to blacken, to darken; *v.i.* to grow dark.

enegrecimento, *s.m.* blackening, darkening.

energético, *adj.* energitic.

energia, *s.f.* energy, vigour, force, power.

energeticamente, *adv.* energetically.

enérgico, *adj.* energetic, active, vigorous, powerful.

energúmeno, *s.m.* energumen.

enervação, *s.f.* enervation.

enervado, *adj.* enervate, excited.

enervante, *adj.* enervating.

enervar, *v.t.* to enervate, to unnerve, to exasperate; *enervar-se:* to become enervated, to get excited.

enevoado, *adj.* cloudy, foggy, dim, misty, gloomy, overcast.

enevoar, *v.t.* to cloud, to dim, to darken; *enevoar-se:* to grow misty, to become cloudy or overcast.

enfadar, *v.t.* to bore, to annoy, to tire, to bother, *enfadar-se:* to get bored or tired.

enfado, *s.m.* tediousness, boredom, annoyance, tedium.

enfadonho, *adj.* tiresome, annoying, tedious, dull, boring.

enfaixar, *v.t.* to swaddle, to bind, to bandage.

enfardador, *s.m.* baler, packer.

enfardamento, *s.m.* packing, baling.

enfardar, *v.t.* to pack, to bale.

enfarinhar, *v.t.* to cover with flour.

enfarpelado, *adj.* dressed in one's best clothes.

enfarpelar-se, *v.refl.* to dress in one's best clothes.

enfarruscar, *v.t.* to soot, to blacken.

enfartado, *adj.* overfull.

enfartar, *v.t.* to glut, to fill, to cram.

enfarte, *s.m.* infarct.

ênfase, *s.f.* emphasis.

enfastiadamente, *adv.* wearisomely.

enfastiar, *v.t.* to loathe, to cause loathing; to weary, to tire.

enfastioso, *adj.* tiresome, wearisome.

enfaticamente, *adv.* emphatically.

enfático, *adj.* emphatic.

enfatuado, *adj.* vain, self-complacent.

enfatuar, *v.t.* to infatuate, to make vain, to become vain.

enfeitar, *v.t.* to embellish, to adorn, to deck, to trim, to ornament.

enfeite, *s.m.* attires, ornament, trimming, decoration.

enfeitiçar, *v.t.* to bewitch, to charm, to enchant, to cast a spell (on somebody).

enfermagem, *s.f.* nursing.

enfermar, *v.t.* to make ill, to become sick.

enfermaria, *s.f.* ward.

enfermeira, *s.f.* nurse.

enfermeiro, *s.m.* male nurse.

enfermidade, *s.f.* illness, sickness, infirmity.

enfermo, *adj.* sick, ill, ailing, infirm; *s.m.* sick person.

enferrujado, *adj.* rusty.

enferrujamento, *s.m.* rusting.

enferrujar, *v.t.* to rust; *v.i.* to rust, to become rusty, to go rusty.

enfestar, *v.t.* to fold lengthwise.

enfeudar, *v.t.* to enfeudal.

enfezado, *adj.* scrubby, rachitic, grouchy *(irritado)*.

enfezar, *v.t.* to stunt, to dwarf, to annoy *(irritar)*.

eniada, *s.f.* string, file, chain, series, sucession.

enfiamento, *s.m.* threading *(agulha)*, stringing.

enfiar, *v.t.* to thread *(agulha)*, to string *(um colar)*, to put on *(vestuário)*, to insert *(introduzir)*; *v.i.* to make one's way *(dirigir--se)*; *enfiar-se,* to slip (into or through) *(amedrontar-se)*.

enfileirar, *v.t.* to range, to align, to set in rows; *enfileirar-se:* to line up.

enfim, *adj.* finally, at last.

enfisema, *s.m.* emphysema.

enfistular, *v.t.* to make fistulous; *v.i.* to become fistulous, to form a fistula.

enfiteuse, *s.f.* emphiteusis.

enfiteuta, *s.m. e s.f.* emphyteuta.

enflorar, *v.t. e v.i.* to flower, to make flower grow on, to cover with flowers.

enfolar, *v.t.* to bag *(vestuário)*, to crease, to swell.

enforcado, *adj.* hanged; *s.m.* hanged man.

enforcamento, *s.m.* hanging.

enforcar, *v.t.* to hang; *enforcar-se,* to hang oneself.

enformar, *v.t. e v.i.* to put on the last *(os sapatos)*, to put a mould.

enfornar, *v.t.* to put into the oven.

enfraquecer, *v.t.* to enfeeble, to weaken; *v.i.* to grow weak.

enfraquecimento, *s.m.* enfeeblement, weakening.

enfrascar, *v.t.* to bottle; *enfrascar-se:* to steep oneself *(em perfume, etc.)*.

enfrear, *v.t.* to bridle.

enfrentar, *v.t.* to face, to confront, to dare, to stand up to.

enfronhado, *adj.* well-versed (num assunto).

enfronhar, *v.t.* to put a case on *(almofada)*; *enfronhar-se em,* to study, to become versed in.

enfunado, *adj.* filled *(velas)*, swollen, puffed up.

enfunar, *v.t.* to swell, to puff up, to fill.

enfurecer, *v.t.* to enrage, to make furious;

enfurecer-se, to grow mad, to become furious, to be enraged, to rage *(mar)*.

enfurecido, *adj.* enraged, furious, angered.

enfurnar, *v.t.* to hide away.

enfuscar, *v.t.* to blacken, to darken.

engaço, *s.m.* stalk of a bunch of grapes.

engadanhado, *adj.* stiff with cold.

engaiolar, *v.t.* to cage, to imprision.

engajamento, *s.m.* engagement.

engajar, *v.t.* to engage, to contract, *(mil.)* to enlist.

engalado, *adj.* trimmed, decorated.

engalanar, *v.t.* to adorn, to beautify, to trim, to bedeck.

engalfinhar-se, *v.refl.* to grapple, to wrestle (with someone).

engalinhar, *v.t. (pop.)* to have an aversion to, to dislike.

enganado, *adj.* mistaken, wrong, deceived.

enganador, *adj.* deceiving, false, misleading.

enganar, *v.t.* to deceive, to delude, to dupe, to mislead; *enganar-se*, to be mistaken, to make a mistake, to be wrong.

engachar, *v.t.* to hook.

engano, *s.m.* mistake, error, deceit, cheat, misleading.

enganosamente, *adv.* bottling.

engarrafar, *v.t.* to bottle, to bottle up.

engasgamento, **engasgo**, *s.m.* choking, suffocation.

engasgar, *v.t.* to choke, to suffocate; *engasgar-se*, to choke.

engastar, *v.t.* to set *(pedras preciosas)*, to mount.

engaste, *s.m.* setting, mounting.

engatar, *v.t.* to cramp, to couple.

engate, *s.m.* cramp, hooking, coupling *(de carruagem)*.

engatilhar, *v.t.* to cock *(arma)*, to prepare.

engatinhar, *v.i.* to creep on all fours.

engavetar, *v.t.* to put in a drawer.

engelha, *s.f.* wrinkle, crease.

engelhar, *v.t.* to wrinkle, to crease, to shrivel.

engendrar, *v.t.* to beget, to engender, to originate.

engenhar, *v.t.* to devise, to conceive, to invent.

engenharia, *s.f.* engineering.

engenheiro, *s.m.* engineer; *engenheiro agrónomo*, agriculturist.

engenho, *s.m.* skill, talent; cleverness, inventiveness; wit; engine, contrivance. 1) *um homem de engenho*, a man of wit, a man of talent. 2) *engenho de guerra*, engine of war.

engenhoca, *s.f.* contraption, contrivance, gadget.

engenhoso, *adj.* ingenious, inventive, witty; clever, cunning.

engessar, *v.t.* to plaster, to put in a plaster.

englobar, *v.t.* to conglomerate, to include.

engodar, *v.t.* to bait, to allure, to decoy.

engodo, *s.m.* bait, allurement, enticement.

engolfar-se, *v.refl.* to gain the open sea, to plunge into.

engolir, *v.t.* to swallow, to gulp down; *engolir em seco*, to swallow hard.

engomadeira, *s.f.* ironer.

engomado, *adj.* starched and ironed.

engomadela, *s.f.* ironing.

engomar, *v.t.* to iron, to starch and iron.

engonçar, *v.t.* to hinge.

engoço, *s.m.* hinge.

engorda, *s.f.* fattening.

engordar, *v.t.* to fatten, *v.i.* to put on weight, to grow fat.

engordurar, *v.t.* to grease, to smear with grease.

engra, *s.f.* corner.

engraçado, *adj.* cute, funny, amusing.

engraçar, *v.t.* to beautify; *v.i.* to like, to take a liking to; to take a fancy to.

engradar, *v.t.* to rail, to grate.

engrampar, *v.t.* to ceceive.

engrandecer, *v.t.* to enlarge, to augment; to exalt, to aggrandise; *v.i.* to increase, to exalt oneself, to rise.

engrandecimento, *s.m.* enlargement, increase; elevation, exaltation, glorification.

engravatar-se, *v.refl.* to deck oneself; to put on a neck-tie.

engravidar, *v.i.* to become pregnant.

engraxadela, *s.f.* shining.

engraxador, *s.m.* shoe shiner, bootblack.

engraxar, *v.t.* to shine, *(sapatos)*, to grease.

engrenagem, *s.g.* gear, gearing.

engrenar, *v.t.* to gear, to throw into gear *(automóvel)*.

engrinaldar, *v.t.* to adorn with garlands.

engripado, *adj.* affected with influenza or flu.

engripar-se, *v.refl.* to catch influenza, to catch the flu.

engrolado, *adj.* entangled.

engrolar, *v.t.* to to undercook *(cozer mal)*, to cheat *(vigarizar)*.

engrossamento, *s.m.* swelling, thickening, increase.

engrossar, *v.t.* to thicken, to swell, to make big; *v.i.* to become bigger.

engrunhido, *adj.* stiff with cold, benumbed.

engrunhir, *v.t.* to benumb.

enguia, *s.f.* eel.

enguiçar, *v.t.* to bring someone ill luck, to break down *(avariar)*.

enguiçamento, enguiço, *s.m.* evil eye, bad luck, snag *(empecilho)*, breakdown *(avaria)*.

engulho, *s.m.* nausea, qualm; temptation.

enigma, *s.m.* ridle, enigma.

enigmaticamente, *adv.* enigmatically.

enigmático, *adj.* enigmatic, puzzling, mysterious.

enjaular, *v.t.* to jail, to imprison, to pen up.

enjeitado, *adj.* rejected, abandoned, forsaken; *s.m.* foundling.

enjeitamento, *s.m.* rejection, abandoning.

enjeitar, *v.t.* to reject, to abandon, to forsake.

enjoado, *adj.* sick, sea-sick.

enjoar, *v.t.* to nauseate, to make sick; to reject food; *v.i.* to get sick.

enjoativo, *adj.* nauseous, sickening, disgusting; tiresome.

enjoo, *s.m.* sea-sickness, nausea, disgust.

enlaçar, *v.t.* to bind, to lace, to entangle; to tie, to link, to unite.

enlace, *s.m.* enlacement, union, marriage.

enladeirado, *adj.* steep sloping.

enlambuzar, *v.t.* to soil, to slobber.

enlameado, *adj.* muddy.

enlamear, *v.t.* to soil, to dirty, to splash with mud; *enlamear-se,* to get muddy.

enlanguescer, *v.i. e v.refl.* to languish, to become languid; to weaken.

enlatado, *adj.* canned.

enlatamento, *s.m.* canning.

enlatar, *v.t.* to can.

enleado, *adj.* entangled; confused.

enlear, *v.t.* to tie, to entangle, to puzzle, to perplex; *enlear-se,* to become entangled (in something).

enleio, *s.m.* entanglement, confusion, perplexity.

enlevação, *s.f.* rapture, transport, ecstasy.

enlevado, *adj.* enraptured, absorbed.

enlevar, *v.t.* to charm, to delight, to enchant, to transport, to enrapture, to ravish.

enlevo, *s.m.* rapture, transport, ecstasy, enchantment, absorption.

enlouquecer, *v.t.* to madden, to drive mad; *v.i.* to become mad, to run mad, to go mad.

enlouquecimento, *s.m.* madness, insanity.

enlutado, *adj.* in mourning, bereaved.

enlutar, *v.t.* to drape in mourning, to mourn, *v.i.* to go into mourning.

enluvado, *adj.* wearing gloves, covered with gloves.

enobrecer, *v.t.* to ennoble, to dignify.

enobrecimento, *s.m.* ennobling.

enodar, *v.t.* to knot, to make a knot.

enófilo, *s.m.* oenophilist.

enofobia, *s.f.* oenophobia.

enofóbio, *s.m.* one who has aversion to wine.

enojado, *adj.* disgusted.

enojar, *v.t.* to disgust, to cause nausea; to annoy; to put into mourning *(enlutar)*.

enologia, *s.f.* oenology.

enológico, *adj.* oenological.

enólogo, *s.m.* oenologist.

enorme, *adj.* enormous, huge, very large, immense.

enormemente, *adv.* enormously.

enormidade, *s.f.* enormity, hugeness, immensity; atrocity.

enovelar, *v.t.* to wind into a ball, to coil; *enovelar-se,* to curl; to roll.

enquadramento, *s.m.* framing.

enquadrar, *v.t.* to frame *(emoldurar)*; to fit (into something) *(ajustar)*; *enquadrar-se,* to fit (into).

enquanto, *conj.* while, whilst, as long as, so long as, whereas. 1) *enquanto isso,* meanwhile, in the mean time. 2) *enquanto ele não vem,* till he comes. 3) *por enquanto,* as yet, for the present, for the time being.

enquistado, *adj.* encysted.

enquistamento, *s.m.* encystment.

enquistar, *v.t. e v.refl.* to encyst.

enraivecer, *v.t.* to enrage, to infuriate; *v.i. e v.refl.* to rage, to be furious, to become furious.

enraivecido, *adj.* enraged, furious, angry.

enraizado, *adj.* rooted, ingrained.

enraizar, *v.t. e v.refl.* to root, to take root.

enramalhetar, *v.t.* to adorn with a nosegay; to garland.

enramar, *v.t.* to shelter or addorn with branches.

enrascada, *s.f.* jam, trouble.

enrascadela, *s.f.* jam, embarssment, predicament.

enrascar, *v.t.* to entangle, to bring into trouble; *enrascar-se,* to become entangled, to get into trouble.

enredador, *s.m.* intriguer, entangler.

enredar, *v.t.* to entangle, to net; to involve, to foul *(uma corda, etc.)*.

enredo, *s.m.* entanglement; intrigue, plot *(drama)*.

enregelado, *adj.* freezed, stiff with cold.

enregelamento, *s.m.* freezing, congealing.

enregelar, *v.t. e v.i.* to freeze, to congeal, to chill.

enriçar, *v.t. e v.refl.* to tangle, to entangle; to be infuriated.

enrijar, *v.t.* to harden, to toughen.

enriquecer, *v.t.* to enrich, to make rich; *v.i.* to grow rich, to become rich.

enriquecimento, *s.m.* enrichment.

enristar, *v.t.* to couch *(lança, etc.)*; *enristar com,* to tilt at, to charge.

enrodilhar, *v.t.* to roll up, to entangle; *enrodilhar-se,* to curl up.

enrolado, *adj.* rolled up, curled up; coiled.

enrolamento, *s.m.* rolling up, coiling, winding.

enrolar, *v.t.* to roll up, to wrap up; to wind; to coil; *enrolar-se,* to roll, to curl, to wrap oneself.

enroscado, *adj.* twisted; curled up *(aninhado)*.

enroscamento, *s.m.* twining, twisting, winding up.

enroscar, *v.t.* to coil, to twist, to twine; *enroscar-se,* to wind on to twine (around something), to coil, to curl up.

enroupar, *v.t.* to clothe.

enrouquecer, *v.t.* to make hoarse; *v.i.* to becme hoarse.

enrouquecimento, *s.m.* hoarseness.

enrubescer, *v.t.* to redden, to flush; *v.i.* to blush, to become red.

enrubescimento, *s.m.* blushing.

enrugado, *adj.* wrinkled.

enrugamento, *s.m.* wrinkling.

enrugar, *v.t.* to wrinkle, to crease, to ruffle; *enrugar-se,* to wrinkle, to become wrinkled.

ensaboadela, *s.f.* soaping; scolding *(reprimenda)*.

ensaboado, *adj.* soapy.

ensaboar, *v.t.* to soap.

ensacado, *adj.* bagged.

ensacamento, *s.m.* bagging, sacking.

enscar, *v.t.* to bag, to sack.

ensaiador, *s.m.* rehearser *(no teatro)*, tester.

ensaiar, *v.t.* to rehearse; to test, to try, to attempt; *ensaiar-se,* to prepare oneself (to do something).

ensaibrar, *v.t.* to gravel.

ensaio, *s.m.* rehearsal *(teatro);* test, trial, attempt, essay *(literário)*.

ensaísta, *s.m.* essayist, writer of essays.

ensambladura, *s.f.* joining.

ensamblar, *v.t.* to join, to fit together.

ensancha, *s.f.* surplus width.

ensandecer, *v.t.* to make mad; *v.i.* to grow mad, to become mad.

ensanguentado, *adj.* bloody.

ensanguenrar, *v.t.* to make bloody, to stain with blood.

ensaque, *s.m.* sacking, bagging.

ensarilhar, *v.t.* to reel *(fio)*, to stack *(armas)*.

enseada, *s.f.* inlet, cove, creck.

ensebado, *adj.* greasy.

ensebar, *v.t.* to smear with gease, to smear with tallow.

ensejo, *s.m.* opportunity, occasion, chance; *dar ensejo,* to give cause (to do something).

ensiforme, *adj.* ensiform.

ensilagem, *s.f.* ensilage.

ensilar, *v.t.* to ensile.

ensimesmar-se, *v.refl.* to concentrate one self in meditation.

ensinado, *adj.* taught, trained.

ensinadela, *s.f.* scolding.

ensinamento, *s.m.* teaching, lesson, instruction.

ensinar, *v.t.* to teach, to instruct (in a subject); to show (how to do something).

ensino, *s.m.* teaching, schooling, training, instruction, education.

ensoberbar, ensoberbecer, *v.t.* to make proud or hauhty; *ensoberbar-se,* to become proud er haughty.

ensombar, *v.t.* to shade, to shadow, to overshadow.

ensonado, *adj.* sleepy.

ensopado, *adj.* soaked, drenched, dripping; *s.m.* stew.

ensopar, *v.t.* to soak, to drench.

ensosso, *adj.* insipid, tasteless.

ensurdecedor, *adj.* deafening, stunning.

ensurdecimento, *s.m.* deafening.

ensurdecer, *v.t.* to deafen, to make deaf; *v.i.* to grow deaf.

entablamento, *s.m.* entablature.

entabuar, *v.t.* to plank, to floor, to board up.

entabular, *v.t.* to begin, to start, to undertake *(empreender)*, to broach *(assunto)*.

entaipar, *v.t.* to wall in or out; to enclose.

entaladela, *s.f.* tightening, squeezing; difficulty.

entalado, *adj.* sqeezed, pinched; in trouble *(em apuros).*

entalar, *v.t.* to splint, to sqeeze, to pinch *(os dedos, etc.),* to drive someone into a corner; *o casaco ficou entalado na porta,* the coat got trapped in the door.

entalhador, *s.m.* carver in wood, wood engraver.

entalhar, *v.t.* to carve, to engrave, to chisel.

entalhe, *s.m.* carving, carved work; notch, cut.

entanguido, *adj.* benumbed with cold.

entanto, *adv.* no entanto, nevertheless, however, yet.

então, *adv.* then, at that time, by that time; after that, afterwards; *interj..* 1) *então!* what! How! well then!. 2) *até então,* till then. 3) *desde então,* since then.

entaramelar, *v.t.* e *v.refl.* to make one stutter, to stammer.

entardecer, *s.m.* evening, nightfall; *v.i.* to grow dark, to draw on (evening).

ente, *s.m.* being, creature.

enteada, *s.f.* stepdaughter.

enteado, *s.m.* stepson.

entediar, *v.t.* to cause tedium, to bore.

entendedor, *s.m.* connoisseur.

entender, *v.t.* to understand, to comprehend, to perceive; to catch, to get; to mean *(querer dizer).* 1) *entender-se mal,* to misunderstand. 2) *no meu entender,* in my opinion. 3) *entender-se,* to come to an agreement.

entendido, *adj.* understood; skilled, well-versed (in); *s.m.* expert, connoisseur.

entendimento, *s.m.* understanding, apprehension, intelligence; agreement.

entenebrecer, *v.t.* to darken; *v.i.* to become dark.

entérico, *adj.* enteric.

enterite, *s.f.* enteritis.

enternecedor, *adj.* touching, moving.

enternecer, *v.t.* to move, to touch; *enternecer-se,* to be moved, to reln.

enternecidamente, *adv.* tenderly, movingly.

enternecido, *adj.* touched, moved.

enternecimento, *s.m.* compassion, tenderness.

enterocolite, *s.f.* enterocolitis.

enterozoário, *s.m.* enterozoon.

enterramento, *s.m.* burying, burial.

enterrar, *v.t.* to bury, to inter, to plunge *(uma faca, etc.)* (into); *enterrar-se,* to bury oneself; to sink.

enterro, *s.m.* burial, funeral.

entesado, *adj.* stiff.

entesar, *v.t.* to stiffen; to stretch; *entesar-se com,* to bully.

entesourar, *v.t.* to hoard, to treasure; to store up *(bens, dinheiros, etc.).*

entestar, *v.t.* to border upon, to confine with.

entibiamento, *s.m.* lukewarmness; indecision.

entibiar, *v.t.* to cool, to make lukewarm; *v.i.* to become lukewarm.

entidade, *s.f.* entity, being, institution *(corporação).*

entimena, *s.f.* enthymena.

entisicar, *v.t.* e *v.i.* to cause consumption; to become consumptive.

entoação, *s.f.* intonation, tone; accant; tuning.

entoar, *v.t.* to intone, to sing.

entomologia, *s.f.* entomology.

entomológico, *adj.* entomologic.

entomologista, *s.m.* entomologisst.

entonação, *s.f.* intonation.

entonar, *v.t.* to raise up; *entonar-se,* to strut, to look big, to give oneself airs.

entono, *s.m.* pride, haughtiness, arrogancy.

entontecer, *v.t.* to make dizzy; to stupefy, to stun; *v.i.* to become dizzy.

entontecimento, *s.m.* dizziness; stunning.

entornar, *v.t.* to overturn *(recipiente),* to spill, to pour out *(derramar).*

entorpecer, *v.t.* to numb, to be numb; *entorpecer-se,* to grow numb.

entorpecido, *adj.* numb, benumbed, torpid; stiff.

entorpecimento, *s.m.* numbness, torpor.

entorse, *s.m.* sprain.

entortar, *v.t.* to twist, to make crooked; to wrap. 1) *entortar os olhos,* to squint. 2) *entortar-se,* to become crooked; to twist oneself, to warp.

entozoário, *s.m.* entozoon; *pl.* entozoa.

entrada, *s.f.* entrance, ingress, entry, admittance, acces; door, gate, doorway; down payment *(pagamento inicial); entradas,* receipts *(receitas).*

entrançada, *adj.* braided, interlaced.

entrançar, *v.t.* to braid, to interlace, to twist.

entranhado, *adj.* deeply rooted, ingrained; deep.

entranhar, *v.t.* to implant, to drive in; *entranhar-se,* to penetrate, to enter deeply, to take root (in).

entranhas, *s.f pl.* entrails, bowels; *entranhas da terra,* underground.

entrapar, *v.t.* to wrap in rags.

entrar, *v.t.* e *v.i.* to go (come, walk, run, drive, march, step, get) in. 1) *entrar em,* to go etc. into. 2) *entrar para (uma organização),* to join. 3) *deixar entrar,* to let in.

entravar, *v.t.* to impede, to hinder, to obstruct.

entrave, *s.m.* encumbrance, hindrance, obstacle.

entre, *prep.* among, amongst, between.

entreaberto, *adj.* partly open, half-open, ajar.

entreabrir, *v.t.* to half-open, to set ajar.

entreacto, *s.m.* interlude, intermission.

entrecasca, *s.f.* liber, bast, inner bark.

entrecasco, *s.m.* the upper part of a hoof.

entrecho, *s.m.* plot.

entrecochar-se, *v.refl.* to collide, to crash together, to clash.

entrecortado, *adj.* interrupted, broken *(voz).*

entrecortar, *v.t.* to intersect, to interrup.

entrecosto, *s.m.* rib.

entrecruzar-se, *v.refl.* to cross each other, to intercross.

entrefolha, *s.f.* interleaf.

entrega, *s.f.* delivery, handing over, transmission; commitment; presentation, surrender.

entregar, *v.t.* to deliver, to hand, to hand over; to entrust, to commit; to give back *(restituir),* entregar-se, to give oneself up, to surrender, to abandon oneself *(ao sofrimento, etc.);* to adict oneself *(ao vício),* to devote oneself oneself *(dedicar-se).*

entregue, *adj.* delivered, busy (with something), absorbed (in), abandoned.

entrelaçado, *adj.* interlaced.

entrelaçamento, *s.m.* interlacing, network; web.

entrelaçar, *v.t.* to interlace, to interweave, to wreathe.

entrelinha, *s.f.* space between lines, *ler nas entrelinhas,* to read between lines.

entrelinhar, *v.t.* to interline, *(tip.)* to lead.

entreluzir, *v.t.* to glimmer, to shine through something.

entremeado, *adj.* intermingled, interposed.

entremear, *v.t.* to intermingle, to interlead.

entremeio, *s.m.* interval.

entrementes, *adv.* e *s.m.* in the mean time.

entremeter, *v.t.* to interpose, to place between.

entremetido, *adj.* meddlesome.

entremez, *s.m.* farce, interlude, intermezzo.

entremostrar, *v.t.* to show indistinctly.

entreolhar-se, *v.refl.* to look at each other, to exchange glances.

entrepor, *v.t.* to put between.

entreposto, *s.m.* emporium; large warehouse; trading post.

entretanto, *adv.* meanwhile, in the meantime; nevertheless, however.

entretecer, *v.t.* to interweave.

entretela, *s.f.* buckram, *(arq.)* counterfort.

entretelar, *v.t.* to stiffen with buckram.

entretenimento, *s.m.* amusement, entertainement, diversion.

entreter, *v.t.* to entertain, to amuse, to recreate; *entreter-se,* to amuse oneself, to occupy oneself (with).

entretenimento, *s.m.* amusement, entertainement.

entrevação, *s.f.* paralysis.

entrevado, *adj.* paralytic, crippled.

entrevar, *v.t.* to paralyse, to affect with paralysis, *v.i.* to become paralitic.

entrever, *v.t.* to see indistinctly, to get a glimpse of; to calculate; *entrever-se,* to catch a glimpse of each other.

entrevista, *s.f.* interview, meeting, appointment.

entrevistar, *v.t.* to interview.

entrincheiramento, *s.m.* entrenchment.

entrincheirar, *v.t.* to entrench, to fortify, *entricheirar-se,* to barricade oneself.

entristecer, *v.t.* e *v.i.* to sadden, to make sad, to become sad.

entristecimento, *s.m.* sadness, gloominess, unhappiness.

entroncado, *adj.* corpulent, stout, broad-shouldered.

entroncamento, *s.m.* junction *(de estradas).*

entroncar, *v.t.* to join, *v.i.* e *v.refl.* to be descended from, to converge.

entulho, *s.m.* rubble, debris.

entumecer, *v.t.* e *v.i.* to swell, to puff up.

entronização, *s.f.* enthronement.

entronizar, *v.t.* to enthrone, to place on a throne, to enthronise.

entrouxar, *v.t.* to make a bundle, to put in a bundle, to pack up; *entrouxar-se,* to dress hurriedly.

entrouxo, *s.m.* bundle.

entroviscar, *v.t.* to catch fish by poisoning them with spurge-flax; *entroviscar-se,* to become cloudy.

entrudada, *s.f.* revelry.

Entrudo, *s.m.* Carnival, Shrovetide.

entufado, *adj.* inflated, swollen.

entufar, *v.t.* to inflate, to swell.

entulhar, *v.t.* to heap up, to fill up, to fill with rubble.

entulho, *s.m.* rubble, debris.

entumecer, *v.t.* e *v.i.* to swell, to puff up.

entumecimento, *s.m.* swelling; puffing up with pride.

entupido, *adj.* obstructed; choked.

entupimento, *s.m.* choking, stopping up, obstruction.

entupir, *v.t.* to obstruct, to stop up, to block up, to choke.

enturvar, *v.t.* to make muddy, to soil; to sadden.

entusiasmar, *v.t.* to fill with enthusiasm; *entusiasmar-se,* to become enthusiastic.

entusiasmo, *s.m.* enthusiasm, ardor, fervor, eagerness, rapture.

entusiasta, *s.m.* e *s.f.* enthusiast, devotee; *adj.* enthusiastic.

entusiástico, *adj.* enthusiastic.

enublado, *adj.* cloudy.

enublar, *v.t.* e *v.i.* to overcast, to cloud; to grow or become cloudy.

enumeração, *s.f.* enumeration.

enumerar, *v.t.* to enumerate, to number, to recount.

enumerável, *adj.* numerable.

enunciação, *s.f.* enunciation; expression; statement.

enunciado, *s.m.* enunciation, statement.

enunciar, *v.t.* to enunciate, to express, to state.

enunciativo, *adj.* enunciative, declaratory; foretelling.

envaginado, *adj.* (bot.) sheated, vaginated.

envaidecedor, *adj.* flattering.

envaidecer, *v.t.* to make vain or proud, to puff up; *envaidecer-se,* to become vain, to pride oneself (on something).

envasamento, *s.m.* base of a pillar.

envasilhamento, *s.m.* bottling, barreling.

envasilhar, *v.t.* to bottle, to barrel.

envelhecer, *v.t.* to age; *v.i.* to grow old.

envelhecido, *adj.* old, aged.

envelhecimento, *s.m.* aging, oldness.

envelope, *s.m.* envelope.

envenenador, *s.m.* poisoner.

envenenamento, *s.m.* poisoning.

envenenar, *v.t.* to poison, to envenom; to corrupt; *envenenar-se,* to poison oneself, to take poison.

enveredar, *v.t.* e *v.i.* to turn into, to take, to head for.

envergadura, *s.f.* spread (de vela ou asas de uma ave), span (asas de avião); stature (moral); de grande envergadura, large-scale (empreendimento).

envergar, *v.t.* to bend (vela), to put on (roupa).

envergonhado, *adj.* ashamed, bashful, shy, timid.

envergonhar, *v.t.* to make ashamed, to bring shame; *envergonhar-se,* to be ashamed.

envernizamento, *s.m.* varnishing.

envernizar, *v.t.* to varnish, to polish.

enverrugar, *v.t.* e *v.i.* to wrinkle; to become warty.

envés, *s.m.* ao envés, the wrong way.

envesgar, *v.t.* to make squint, to squint.

enviado, *s.m.* messenger, envoy.

enviar, *v.t.* to send, to dispatch, to forward.

envidar, *v.t.* to exert, to try hard; envidar todos os esforços, to do one's utmost.

envidraçado, *adj.* glazed.

envidraçar, *v.t.* to glaze.

enviesadamente, *adv.* obliquely.

enviesado, *adj.* aslant, askew, awry, oblique, sidelong (olhar).

enviesar, *v.t.* to slant, to set awry, to cut on the bias.

envilecer, *v.t.* to abase, to vilify; *v.i.* to grow vile; to degrade oneself.

envilecimento, *s.m.* abasement, degradation.

envinagrado, *adj.* vinegary, sour.

envinagrar, *v.t.* to vinegar, to sour, to make sour like vinegar.

envio, *s.m.* remittance, sending.

enviuvar, *v.t.* to make a widow or widower of; *v.i.* to become a widow or widower.

envolta, *s.f.* company, confusion; bandage.

envolto, *adj.* wrapped up, involved, enveloped, entangled.

envoltório, *s.m.* wrapper, cover.

envoltura, *s.f.* enveloping, wrapping up, covering.

envolvente, *adj.* involving, including, implying, encircling.

envolver, *v.t.* to wrap, to involve, to envelop; to encircle, to environ; to imply, to entangle; *envolver-se,* to wrap oneself up, to involve oneself, to engage (in).

envolvido, *adj.* enveloped; concerned.

envolvimento, *s.m.* envelopment.

enxabido, *adj.* insipid.

enxada, *s.f.* hoe.

enxadão, *s.f.* mattock.

enxadrezar, *v.t.* to checker.

enxaguar, *v.t.* to rinse.

enxaimel, *s.m.* frame-work.

enxame, *s.m.* swarm.

enxamear, *v.t.* to hive bees; *v.i.* to swarm.

enxaqueca, *s.f.* migraine.

enxárcia, *s.f.* the shrouds of a ship.

enxerga, *s.f.* pallet, mattress.

enxergar, *v.t.* to discern, to perceive, to distinguish.

enxertadeira, *s.f.* grafting-knife.

enxertador, *s.m.* grafter.

enxertar, *v.t.* to graft on, to insert.

enxertia, *s.f.* grafting, engrafting.

enxerto, *s.m.* grafting, graft; slip.

enxó, *s.f.* adze.

enxofração, *s.f.* sulphuring.

enxofrado, *adj.* sulphured; angry.

enxofrar, *v.t.* to sulphur, to powder with sulphur, to treat with sulphur; *enxofrar-se,* to get angry.

enxofre, *s.m.* sulphur.

enxota-moscas, *s.m.* fly-swat.

enxotar, *v.t.* to drive away, to shoo.

enxoval, *s.m.* trousseau, outfit, layette *(de bebé).*

enxovalhado, *adj.* ruffling; untidiness; affront, insult.

enxovalhar, *v.t.* to soil, to foul, to befoul; to insult; *enxovalhar-se,* to disgrace oneself.

enxovia, *s.f.* dungeon, prison.

enxugar, *v.t.* to dry, to wipe.

enxúndia, *s.f.* fat.

enxundioso, *adj.* obese, fat.

enxurrada, *s.f.* torrent, current; abundance.

enxurro, *s.m.* torrent.

enxuto, *adj.* dryed, dry.

enzima, *s.f.* enzime.

eoceno, *s.m. e adj.* eocene.

eólico, *adj.* Eolic, aeolian.

eólio, *s.m.* Aeolian, Eolian.

epacta, *s.f.* epact.

epanáfora, *s.f.* anaphora.

epêntese, *s.f.* epenthesis.

epicarpo, *s.m.* epicarp.

epicédio, *s.m.* epicedium.

epiceno, *adj.* epicene.

epicentro, *s.m.* epicenter, epicentre.

épico, *adj.* epic, heroic.

epicrânio, *s.m.* epicranium.

epicurismo, *s.m.* epicureanism.

epicurista, *s.m.* epicure.

epidemia, *s.f.* epidemic.

epidémico, *adj.* epidemical.

epiderme, *s.f.* epidermis.

epidérmico, *adj.* epidermic.

Epifania, *s.f.* Epiphany.

epigástrico, *adj.* epigastric.

epigastro, *s.m.* epigastrium.

epiglote, *s.f.* epiglotis.

epígrafe, *s.f.* epigraph.

epigrafia, *s.f.* epigraphy.

epigráfico, *adj.* epigraphic.

epigrama, *s.m.* epigram.

epigramático, *adj.* epigrammatic.

epilação, *s.f.* epilation, depilation.

epilatório, *adj.* depilatory.

epilepsia, *s.f.* epilepsy.

epiléptico, *adj. e s.m.* epiletic.

epilogação, *s.f.* epilogation.

epilogar, *v.t.* to epilogize.

epílogo, *s.m.* epilogue.

epiploo, *s.m.* epiploon.

episcopado, *s.m.* episcopacy.

episcopal, *adj.* episcopal.

episódico, *adj.* episodic.

episódio, *s.m.* episode.

episperma, *s.m.* episperm.

epistaxe, *s.f.* epistaxis.

epistílio, *s.m.* epistyle.

epístola, *s.f.* epistle; a letter.

epistolar, *adj.* epistolary.

epistolário, *s.m.* collection of epistles.

epistolografia, *s.f.* epistolography.

epistológrafo, *s.m.* epistolographer.

epistológráfico, *adj.* epistolographic.

epístrofe, *s.f.* epistrophe.

epitáfio, *s.m.* epitaph.

epitalâmico, *adj.* epithalamic.

epitalâmio, *s.m.* epithalamium.

epítase, *s.f.* epitasis.

epitelial, *adj.* epithelial.

epitélio, *s.m.* epithelium.

epíteto, *s.m.* ephitet.

epitema, *s.m.* epithem, epithema.

epitomar, *v.t.* to emitomise; to shorten.

epítome, *s.m.* epitome; summary.

epizoário, *s.m.* epizoon; *pl.* epizoa.

epizootia, *s.f.* episooty.

época, *s.f.* era, time, period.

epodo, *s.m.* epode.

epopeia, *s.f.* epopee, epic poem.

equação, *s.f.* equation.

equacionar, *v.t.* equate.

equador, *s.m.* equator; Ecuador *(país).*

equânime, *adj.* equanimous.

equanimidade, s.f. equanimity.

equatorial, adj. equatorial.

equestre, adj. equeatrian.

equevo, adj. of the same age, contemporary.

equiângulo, adj. equiangular.

equidade, s.f. equity, impartiality.

equídeo, adj. horse-like; relating to the horse.

equidistância, s.f. equidistance, equal distance.

equidistante, adj. equidistant.

equidistar, v.i. to be equidistant.

equidna, s.f. echidna.

equilateral, adj. equilateral.

equilátero, adj. equilateral.

equilibração, s.f. equilibration.

equilibrado, adj. equilibrated, well-balanced; judicious.

equilibrante, adj. equilibratin.

equilibrar, v.t. to equilibrate, to balance; to counter balance; *equlibrar-se*, to balance oneself; to become even.

equilíbrio, s.m. equilibrium, balance, equipoise.

equilibrista, s.m. e s.f. equilibrist, ropewalker.

equimose, s.f. echymosis.

equino, adj. equine.

equinocial, adj. equinoctial.

equinócio, s.m. equinox.

equinodermes, s.m. pl. echinodermes.

equipa, s.f. team.

equipagem, s.f. crew *(de navio, etc.)*, equipage *(carruagem, etc.)*.

equipamento, s.m. equipment, outfit.

equipar, v.t. to equip, to rig, to man *(um navio, etc.)*.

equiparação, s.f. equilization.

equparar, v.t. to equalise, to compare, to make equal.

equiparável, adj. that may be equalized or balanced.

equipolência, s.f. equipollence.

equipolente, adj. equipollent.

equitação, s.f. equitation, horsemanship, riding.

equtativo, adj. equitable, fair, just, impartial.

equivalência, s.f. equivalence.

equivalente, adj. equivalent.

equivaler, v.i. to be equivalent; to amount to.

equivocação, s.f. equivocation.

equivocar, v.t. to equivocate, to mislead *(iludir)*, to mistake *(confundir)*; *equivocar-se*, to be mistaken, to make a mistake.

equívoco, s.m. equivoque, mistaken, misunderstanding; adj. equivocal, ambiguos.

era, s.f. era, age, time.

erário, s.m. exchequer, public treasure.

erecção, s.f. erection.

eréctil, adj. erectile.

erecto, adj. erect, upright, raised.

erector, s.m. erector, s.m. erector; adj. erective.

eremita, s.m. hermit, eremite.

eremitério, s.m. hermitage.

eremítico, adj. eremitic.

eretismo, s.m. erethism.

ergástulo, s.m. dungeon, prision.

erguer, v.t. to raise, to lift, to uplift, to erect, to build; *erguer-se:* to arise (from), to stand up, to get up.

erguido, adj. lifted up, raised up, erect.

eriçado, adj. bristling, bristly.

eriçar, v.t. to bristle, to set on the end.

erigir, v.t. to erect, to build.

erisipela, s.f. erysipelas.

ermida, s.f. hermitage; little chapel.

ermitão, s.m. eremite, hermit; anchorite.

ermo, s.m. waste land, wilderness; adj. solitary, desolate, abandoned.

erosão, s.f. erosion.

erosivo, adj. erosive, corroding, consuming.

erótico, adj. erotic.

erotismo, s.m. erotism.

erotomania, s.f. eretomania.

erradamente, adv. erroneously, wrongly.

erradicação, s.f. eradication.

erradicante, adj. eradicative.

erradicar, v.t. to eradicate, to root out.

erradio, adj. wandering, vagrant.

errado, adj. mistaken, erroneous, wrong.

errante, adj. errant, wandering, vagrant, nomadic; *cavaleiro errante*, knight errant.

errar, v.t. e v.i. to mistake, to miss *(o alvo, etc.)*, to make a mistake in *(uma conta, etc.)*, to err, to make a mistake, to be wrong, to blunder, to go astray, to wander, to roam *(vaguear)*.

errata, s.f. erratum; pl. errata.

errático, adj. erratic, wandering, errant, irregular.

erro, s.m. error, mistake, fault, blunder *(erro crasso)*. 1) *erro de cálculo, de pronúncia, ortográfico,* miscalculation, mispronunciation, misspelling. 2) *em erro,* mistake, wrong. 3) *salvo erro,* errors excepted.

errôneo, adj. erroneous, false, wrong.

eructação, s.f. eructation, belching.

erudição, s.f. erudition, learning.

erudito, adj. erudite, learned; s.m. scholar, savant.

erupção, s.f. eruption; skin eruption (da pele); outbreak.

eruptivo, adj. eruptive.

erva, s.f. grass, herb, herbage; erva daninha, weed.

ervaçal, s.f. pastureland, grass-land.

erva-cidreira, s.f. balm.

ervanário, s.m. herbalist.

ervar, v.t. to poison (setas, etc.).

ervilha, s.f. pea.

ervilhaca, s.f. vetch.

ervilhal, s.m. plantation of peas.

ervoso, adj. herbous, grassy.

esbaforido, adj. panting, gasping.

esbaforir-se, v.refl. to get out of breath.

esbandalhado, adj. disarranged.

esbandalhar, v.t. to break to pieces, to disarrange.

esbanjador, s.m. squanderer, spendthrift; adj. squandering, prodigal, extravagant.

esbanjamento, s.m. squandering, waste.

esbanjar, v.t. to squander, to dissipate, to waste.

esbarrar, v.t. e v.i. to strike against, to dash against, to bump against, to pull (before an obstacle).

esbater, v.t. to attenuate, to shade off, to tone down.

esbatido, adj. subdued, faint.

esbatimento, s.m. toning down, subduinf.

esbelteza, s.f. slenderness, elegance.

esbelto, adj. slender, elegant, graceful.

esbirro, s.m. bailiff, henchman.

esboçar, v.t. to sketch, to outline, to draft; esboçar-se, to appear in outline.

esboço, s.m. sketch, outline, draft.

esbodegado, adj. exhausted.

esbodegar-se, v.refl. to get tired.

esbofetear, v.t. to slap on the face.

esboroamento, s.m. crumbling, downfall.

esboroar, v.t. e v.refl. to crumble to dust.

esborrachar, v.t. to crush, to smash; esborrachar-se, to be smashed.

esborratar, v.t. e v.i. to blot, to make blots.

esbracejar, v.i. to wave one's arms, to gesticulate.

esbranquiçado, adj. whitish.

esbrasear, v.t. to make red-hot, to set aglow.

esbravejar, v.t. to rage, to bluster.

esbugalhado, adj. goggle, bulging, protuberant (olhos).

esbugalhar, v.t. to remove the gall-nuts from; to goggle (os olhos).

esbulhar, v.t. to dispossess of, to strip of, to deprive of.

esbulho, s.m. usurpation.

esburacado, adj. filled with holes, pierced.

esburacar, v.t. to fill with holes, to pierce.

esburgar, v.t. to shell, to skin.

escabeçear, v.t. to nod, to let the head drop in weariness.

escabeche, s.m. sauce for fish; uproar, riot.

escabelo, s.m. footstoll.

escabichador, adj. inquisitive, curious; s.m. investigator.

escabichar, v.t. to investigate, to inquire.

escabrosidade, s.f. roughness, difficulty, coarseness.

escabroso, adj. rough, coarse, improper, indecent, scandalous.

escabujar, v.i. to struggle, to strive.

escabulhar, v.t. to husk, to remove husk from, to shell.

escascar, v.t. to break into pieces.

escachoar, v.i. to boil, to bubble.

escada, s.f. stairs, staircase, stairway, steps, ladder (de mão). 1) escada de incêndio, fire escape. 2) escada rolante, escalator. 3) subir a escada, to go upstairs. 4) descer a escada, to go downstairs.

escadaria, s.f. staircase.

escadote, s.m. small ladder.

escafandrista, s.m. diver.

escafandro, s.m. diving-suit.

escafóide, adj. scaphoid; s.m. scaphoid bone.

escaiola, s.f. scagliola.

escala, s.f. scale, gradation; port of call; stop; gamut (música). 1) escala de serviço, roster. 2) fazer escala em, to make call at. 3) sem escala, nonstop.

escalada, s.f. escalade.

escalamento, s.m. scaling.

escalão, s.m. step, (mil.) echelon.

escalar, v.t. to escalade, to climb, to ascend; to assign for duty (para tarefa).

escalavradura, s.f. injury, affront, bruise.

escalavrar, v.t. to scratch, to bruise, to hurt, to scar.

escaldadela, s.f. burning, scalding, rebuke (repreensão).

escaldado, adj. scalded, rendered wise by experience.

escaldão, s.m. burning, scalding.

escalda-pés, s.m. hot foot-bath.

escaldar, *v.t. e v.i.* to scald, to burn; *escaldar-se:* to scald oneself.

escaleno, *adj.* scalene.

escaler, *s.m.* ship's boat.

escalfador, *s.m.* water-heater.

escalfar, *v.t.* to poach *(ovos).*

escalfeta, *s.f.* foot-warmer.

escalpar, *v.t.* to scalp.

escalpelizar, *v.t.* to dissect with a scalpel.

escalpelo, *s.m.* scalpel.

escalpo, *s.m.* scalp.

escalracho, *s.m.* couch-grass.

escalvado, *adj.* bare, arid, sterile, barren.

escalvar, *v.t.* to make bald, to bare, to render sterile.

escama, *s.f.* scale.

escamação, *s.f.* scaling.

escamado, *adj.* without scales, angry *(furioso).*

escamar, *v.t.* to scale; escamar-se: to get angry.

escambar, *v.t.* to exchange, to trade by exchange.

escambo, *s.m.* barter, exchange.

escamoso, *adj.* scaly; flaky.

escamoteação, *s.f.* palming off, sleight of hand.

escamoteador, *s.m.* palmer; juggler, conjurer.

escamotear, *v.t.* to palm, to palm off, to snatch *(furtar).*

escâncara, *s.f.* display, evidence, manifestation; *às escâncaras,* in public.

escancarado, *adj.* wide-open.

escancarar, *v.t.* to open wide, to throw open; *escancarar-se,* to open wide.

escandaleira, *s.f.* scandal.

escandalizador, *adj.* scandalizing.

escandalizar, *v.t.* to scandalize, to shock; *escandalizar-se,* to be shocked, to take offense.

escândalo, *s.m.* scandal, shame, offence, outrage.

escandalosamente, *adv.* scandalously.

escandaloso, *adj.* scandalous, shocking, outrageous.

escandescência, *s.f.* incandescence.

escandescente, *adj.* incandescent.

escandescer, *v.t. e v.i.* to incandesce, to set aglow, to inflame, to redden.

escandinavo, *adj. e s.m.* Scandinavian.

escangalhado, *adj.* broken, out of order, busted.

escangalhar, *v.t.* to break, to ruin.

escanhoar, *v.t.* to shave closely.

escanifrado, *adj.* skinny, weedy.

escaninho, *s.m.* pigeonhole; corner, hiding place.

escano, *s.m.* bench with a back.

escantilhão, *s.m.* gauge.

escanzelado, *adj.* skinny.

escapada, escapadela, *s.f.* escape, escapade *(leviandade).*

escapar, *v.t.* to escape *(from),* to break loose or free *(from),* to run away, to evade. 1) *escapar por um triz,* to have a narrow escape. 2) *deixar escapar,* to miss *(oportunidade, etc)* 3) *escapar-se,* to run away, to flee (from).

escapatória, *s.f.* subterfuge, excuse.

escape, *s.m.* exhaust *(de gases);* outlet, escape; *tubo de escape,* exhaust pipe.

escapo, *s.m.* shaft *(de uma pena); adj.* free, safe.

secápula, *s.f.* tenter-hook, hook.

escapulário, *s.m.* scapular.

escapulir, *v.i. e v.refl.* to slip, to sneak away.

escaqueirar, *v.t.* to break to pieces, to shatter.

escara, *s.f.* scab, scurf.

escarafunchar, *v.t.* to poke into, to dig into.

escaramuça, *s.f.* skirmish, scrimage.

escaramuçar, *v.t.* to skirmish.

escaravelho, *s.m.* beetle.

escarcéu, *s.m.* roughness *(do mar),* hullabaloo *(gritaria).*

escarchar, *v.t.* to cover with snow.

escarduçador, *s.m.* carder, carding machine.

escarduçar, *v.t.* to card wool.

escarlate, *adj.* scarlet.

escarlatina, *s.f.* scarlet fever.

escarmentado, *adj.* warned, made wise by experience.

escarmentar, *v.t. e v.i. e v.refl.* to punish, to blame, to make wise, to repent.

escarmento, *s.m.* lesson learned at one`s expenses; warning.

escarnecedor, *s.m.* mocker, scoffer.

escarnecer, *v.t. e v.i.* to mock, to scoff, to make fun of.

escarnecimento, *s.m.* mockery, scoffing; contempt.

escarninho, *adj.* jeering, mocking, scoffing.

escárnio, *s.m.* mock, mockery, scoffing, fun.

escarolar, *v.t.* to beat out the grain (of cereals); to pick.

escarpa, *s.f.* scarpe, steep slope.

escarradeira, *s.f.* spitoon.

escarrador, *s.m. o mesmo que "escarra-deira".*

escarranchar, *v.t.* to sit astride something, to straddle *(as pernas).*

escarrapachado, *adj.* sprawling.

escarrapachar, *v.t.* to sprawl.

escarrar, *v.t.* to spit, to expectorate.

escarro, *s.m.* spiotle, spit.

escarumba, *s.m.* e *s.f.* black man or woman.

escarva, *s.f.* scarf, calmp.

escarvar, *v.t.* to scarf; to corrode.

escassear, *v.i.* to become scarce, to grow scarce, to run short.

escassez, *s.f.* scarcity, shortage, lack, want.

escasso, *adj.* scarce, short, rare, scanty, lacking, meager, poor.

escavação, *s.f.* excavation, digging.

escavacar, *v.t.* to brak to pieces, to ruin.

escavador, *s.m.* digger.

escavar, *v.t.* to dig, to excavate, to hollow, to dig out.

escaveirado, *adj.* skinny, emaciated.

escaveirar-se, *v.refl.* to grow skinny or very thin.

esclarecer, *v.t.* to clarify, to elucidate, to clear up, to explain, to enlighten; *esclarecer-se,* to become clear.

esclarecido, *adj.* clarified, enlightened.

esclarecimento, *s.m.* clearing up, elucidation, explanation, enlightenment.

esclerose, *s.f.* sclerosis.

esclerótica, *s.f.* sclerotic.

escoadouro, *s.m.* drain, sewer, gutter, ditch.

escoamento, *s.m.* draining, drainage, sewage.

escoar, *v.t.* to drain, to drain off, to discharge; *escoar-se:* to flow off, to vanish, to pass *(o tempo).*

escocês, *s.m.* e *adj.* Scottish, Scotch.

escol, *s.m.* prime choice, the best of anything, cream.

escola, *s.f.* school, college. 1) *escola primária,* elementary school. 2) *escola secundária,* high school. 3) *escola superior,* university college.

escolar, *adj.* school, of school; *s.m.* e *s.f.* scholar, student, pupil.

escolástica, *s.f.* scholasticism.

escolástico, *adj.* scholastic; *s.m.* scholastic, schoolman.

escolha, *s.f.* choice, selection; preference, option, pick; *à escolha,* at will.

escolher, *v.t.* to choose, to pick out, to select; to prefer.

escolhido, *adj.* chosen, select.

escolho, *s.m.* rock, reef; obstacle.

escólio, *s.m.* scholium.

escoliose, *s.f.* escoliose.

escolopendra, *s.f.* scolopendra.

escolta, *s.f.* escort.

escoltar, *v.t.* escort, to attend as escort, to accompany.

escombro, *s.m.* scomber *(peixe); escombros:* rubbish, debris, ruins.

esconder, *v.t.* to hide, to conceal, to occult; *esconder-se,* to hide oneself.

esconderijo, *s.m.* hiding place.

escondidas, *s.f. pl. às escondidas,* secretely, furtively; hide and seek *(jogo).*

esconjuração, *s.f.* exorcism, conjuration.

esconjurador, *s.m.* exorcist, exorcizer, conjurer.

esconjurar, *v.t.* to exorcize, to conjure.

esconjuro, *s.m. o mesmo que "esconjuração".*

esconso, *s.m.* corner, angle, recess; *adj.* sloping, slanting.

escopeta, *s.f.* musket, carbine.

escopeteiro, *s.m.* carabineer.

escopo, *s.m.* scope, aim, purpose.

escopro, *s.m.* chisel.

escora, *s.f.* prop, propping, support.

escorar, *v.t.* to prop, to bear up, to sustain, to support.

escorbútico, *adj.* scorbutic.

escorbuto, *s.m.* scurvy.

escorchar, *v.t.* to flay, to skin, to fleece, to wound *(ferir).*

escorço, *s.m.* foreshortening.

escória, *s.f.* scoria, slag, scum.

escoriação, *s.f.* excoriation, abrasion.

escoriar, *v.t.* to excoriate, to peel off skin.

escorificar, *v.t.* to scorify.

escornar, escornear, *v.t.* to gore, to perce with anything pointed.

escorpião, *s.m.* scorpion.

escorraçar, *v.t.* to drive away, to expel.

escorralhas, *s.f. pl.* dregs, dross.

escorregadela, *s.f.* slip. slipping, sliding.

escorregadio, *adj.* slippery.

escorregadouro, *s.m.* slide.

escorregamento, *s.m.* slipping, sliding.

escorregar, *v.t.* to slide, to slip, to glide.

escorreito, *adj.* healthy.

escorrer, *v.t.* e *v.i.* to drain, to flow, to run off.

escorrimento, *s.m.* draining, dropping, dripping.

escorripichar, *v.t.* to drink till the last drop.

escorva, *s.f.* touch-hole.

escota, *s.f. (náut.)* the sheet of a sail.

escoteiro, *s.m.* scout, boy scout.

escotilham, *s.f.* hatchway.

escotilhão, *s.f.* scuttle.

escotismo, *s.m.* scouting.

escoucear, *v.t.* to kick.

escova, *s.f.* brush. 1) *escova de cabelo,* hairbrush. 2) *escova de dentes,* tooth brush.

escovadela, *s.f.* brushing.

escovar, *v.t.* to brush, to clean with a brush.

escoveiro, *s.m.* brush dealer, brush maker.

escovém, *s.m.* hawse hole.

escovilhão, *s.m.* sponge, long and cylindrical brush.

escravatura, *s.f.* slavery, slave trade.

escravidão, *s.f.* slavery, servitude, serfdom.

escravizar, *v.t.* to enslave.

escravo, *s.m.* slave.

escrevaninha, *s.f.* writing-desk.

escrever, *v.t.* to write; to compose; *escrever à máquina,* to typewrite.

escrevinhador, *s.m.* scribbler.

escrevinhar, *v.t.* to scribble.

escriba, *s.m.* scribe.

escrínio, *s.m.* jewel case, escritoire.

escrita, *s.f.* writing, handwriting; *escrita comercial,* book keeping.

escritor, *s.m.* writer, author.

escritório, *s.m.* office, study.

escritura, *s.f.* deed, indenture *(de contrato).* 1) *Sagrada Escritura,* holy writ. 2) *as Escrituras,* the Scriptures.

escrituração, *s.f.* book keeping, accounting.

escriturar, *v.t.* to register, to enter, to book.

escriturário, *s.m.* clek, amanuensis.

escrivaninha, *s.f.* writing desk.

escrivão, *s.m.* clerk, notary, registrar.

escrófula, *s.f.* scrofula.

escrofuloso, *adj.* scrofulous.

escroque, *s.m.* swindler, crook.

escrupulizar, *v.t. e v.i.* to scruple, to have scruples about; to hesitate.

escrúpulo, *s.m.* scruple; hesitation. 1) *escrúpulos,* scruples, pricks of conscience. 2) *sem escrúpulos,* uncrupulous.

escrupuloso, *adj.* scrupulous, conscientious.

escrutador, *s.m.* scrutator, examiner.

escrutar, *v.t.* to search, to examine carefully, to scan.

escrutinador, *s.m.* vote counter; teller.

escrutinar, *v.t.* to count (votes).

escrutínio, *s.m.* balloting, voting, poll, counting of votes, scrutiny *(exame).*

escudar, *v.t.* to shield, to protect; *escudar-se,* to shield oneself.

escudeiro, *s.m.* squire, valet.

escudela, *s.f.* wooden bowl.

escudete, *s.m.* a small escutcheon.

escudo, *s.m.* shield, escutcheon *(de armas);* portuguese coin.

esculápio, *s.m.* physician.

esculpir, *v.t.* to sculpture, to carve.

escultor, *s.m.* sculptor.

escultora, *s.f.* sculptress.

escultura, *s.f.* sculpture, carving.

escultural, *adj.* sculptural.

escuma, *s.f.* scum, foam.

escumadeira, *s.f.* skimmer.

escumalha, *s.f.* scum, mob.

escumante, *adj.* foaming, frothy.

escumar, *v.t. e v.i.* to skim, to scum, to foam, to froth.

escumilha, *s.f.* small shot.

escumoso, *adj.* foamy, frothy, scummy.

escuna, *s.f.* schonner.

escuras, *loc. adv.* *às escuras:* in the dark.

escurecedor, *adj.* darkening.

escurecer, *v.t. e v.i.* to darken, to grow dark.

escuridão, *s.f.* darkness, gloominess.

escuro, *adj.* dark, dim, gloomy, obscure, dusky, cloudy; *s.m.* dark, darkness.

escusa, *s.f.* excuse, justification; dispensation, exemption.

escusado, *adj.* useless.

escusar, *v.t. e v.i.* to excuse, to expt, to spare; to do without, to have no need of; *escusar-se,* to refuse (to do something), to evade (an obligation).

escusável, *adj.* excusable, dispensable.

escuso, *adj.* hidden, secret.

escuta, *s.f.* listening; *à escuta:* at listening, all ears.

escutar, *v.t.* to listen, to hear.

escuteiro, *s.m.* scout, boy scout.

esdrúxulo, *adj.* accented on the antepenultimate syllable; extravagant, odd.

esfacelado, *adj.* corrupted, ruined; sphacelated.

esfacelar, *v.t.* to sphacelate; to ruin, to destroy.

esfacelo, *s.m.* sphacelation, ruin, collapse.

esfaimado, *adj.* hungry, starving, famishing.

esfaimar, *v.t.* to famish, to starve, to hunger.

esfalfado, *adj.* exhausted, dog-tired, worn out.

esfalfamento, *s.m.* exhaustion.

esfalfar, *v.t.* to exhaust, to overtire, to wear out; *esfalfar-se,* to exhaust oneself, to tire oneself out.

esfanicar, *v.t.* to break into pieces.

esfaquear, *v.t.* to knife, to stab.

esfarelar, *v.refl. e v.t.* to crumble.

esfarrapado, *adj.* ragged, shred, tattered.

esfarrapar, *v.t.* to tear up, to tear apart, to tear to pieces.

esfenoidal, *adj.* shenoidal.

esfenóide, *s.m.* shpenoid; *adj.* sphenoid, wedge-shaped.

esfera, *s.f.* sphere; globe; ball; environement; field of action.

esfericidade, *s.f.* sphericity.

esférico, *adj.* spheric, globular.

esferográfica, *s.f.* ballpen.

esferoidal, *adj.* spheroidal.

esferóide, *s.m.* spheroid.

esferómetro, *s.m.* spherometer.

esférula, *s.f.* spherule.

esfiapar, *v.t.* to fray.

esfíncter, *s.m.* sphincter.

esfinge, *s.f.* sphinx.

esfoladela, *s.f.* flaying, skinning, excoriation.

esfolar, *v.t.* to skin, to flay, to fleece *(nos preços).*

esfolhada, *s.f.* husking.

esfolhar, *v.t.* to husk.

esfoliação, *s.f.* exfoliation.

esfoliar, *v.t.* to exfoliate.

esfomeado, *adj.* hungry, starving.

esfomear, *v.t.* to starve, to famish.

esforçadamente, *adv.* bravely, resolutely.

esforçado, *adj.* stout, brave, resolute, courageous.

esforçar, *v.t.* to encourage, to incite; *esforçar-se:* to strive, to struggle, to exert oneself , to do one's best (to do something).

esforço, *s.m.* effort, exertion, endeavor, *(mec.)* stress.

esfrangalhar, *v.t.* to tear to pieces, to shred.

esfrega, *s.f.* scrubbing, rubbing.

esfregão, *s.m.* mop, scrub cloth.

esfregar, *v.t.* to mop, to scrub.

esfriamento, *s.m.* cooling.

esfriar, *v.t.* to cool, to chill; *v.i.* to grow cold, to cool down.

esfumado, *adj.* shaded, toned down, stumped.

esfumar, *v.t.* to stump, to tone down, to shade off.

esfuminho, *s.m.* stump.

esfuziante, *adj.* hissins, whistling, whizzing, sibilant.

esfuziar, *v.i.* to hiss, to whistle.

esgadanhar, *v.t.* to scratch.

esgalgado, *adj.* thin, lanky.

esgalha, *s.f.* shoot; twig.

esgalhado, *adj.* looped, pruned.

esgalhar, *v.t.* to lop, to prune, to strip off branches; v.i. to branch out.

esgalho, *s.m.* sprig *(de árvore),* antler *(de veado).*

esgana, *s.f.* destemper.

esganado, *adj.* stangles; greedy; famished.

esganar, *v.t.* to strangle, to choke; *esganar-se:* to be greedy (for something).

esganiçado, *adj.* piercing *(voz),* strident.

esganiçar-se, *v.refl.* to sream, to shriek.

esgar, *s.m.* grimace, face.

esgarçar, *v.t.* to rend, to tear; *v.i.* to open, to fray *(pano).*

esgazeado, *adj.* wild *(olhos);* glaring.

esgazear, *v.t.* to gaze at, to glare at.

esgotado, *adj.* exhausted, worn out; out of print *(um livro).*

esgotamento, *s.m.* exhaustion; *esgotamento nervoso,* nervous breakdown.

esgotante, *adj.* exhausting.

esgotar, *v.t.* to exhaust, to tire out; to empty, to use up; *esgotar-se,* to become exhausted; to run out, to run dry.

esgotável, *adj.* drainable, exhaustible.

esgoto, *s.m.* drain, gutter, sewer.

esgrima, *s.f.* fencing.

esgrimir, *v.t.* to brandish, to wield; *v.i.* to fence, to argue, to fight.

esgrimista, *s.m. e s.f.* fencer.

esgrouviado, *adj.* lanky, scraggy, disheveled *(desgrenhado).*

esguedelhado, *adj.* disheveled.

esguedelhar, *v.t.* to tousle.

esgueirar-se, *v.refl.* to sneak away, to slip away.

esguelha, *s.f. de esguelha:* obliquely, askew, askance; *olhar de esguelha:* sidelong look.

esguichadela, *s.f.* spout, squirt, spurt.

esguichar, *v.t. e v.i.* to spout, to squirt, to spurt.

esguicho, *s.m.* spout, jet, squirt.

esguio, *adj.* slim, tall and slender.

esladroamento, *s.m.* cutting off.

esladroar, *v.t.* to cut off.

eslagartar, *v.t.* to clear trees of caterpillars.

eslavo, *s.m. e adj.* Slav.

esmaecer, *v.i.* to fade away, to grow faint.

esmaecimento, *s.m.* fainting.

210

esmagado, *adj.* crushed, pressed, smashed, overwhelmed.

esmagador, *adj.* crushing, overwhelming, overpowering.

esmagamento, *s.m.* crushing, smashing.

esmagar, *v.t.* to crush, to squash, to press, to smash, to overwhelm.

esmaltado, *adj.* enamelled.

esmaltador, *s.m.* enameller.

esmaltar, *v.t.* to enamel.

esmalte, *s.m.* enamel.

esmerado, *adj.* perfect, skilled.

esmeralda, *s.f.* emerald.

esmeraldino, *adj.* emerald green.

esmerar, *v.t.* to elaborate, to perfect; *esmerar-se,* to take great care (with something); to do one's best.

esmeril, *s.m.* emery.

esmerilador, *s.m.* one who polishes with emery.

esmerilar, *v.t.* to polish with emery.

esmerilhão, *s.m.* merlin *(ave)*.

esmero, *s.m.* care, accuracy, perfection.

esmigalhar, *v.t.* to crush, to crumble; *esmigalhar-se,* to fall into small pieces.

esmiolado, *adj.* brainless, foolish.

esmiuçar, *v.t.* to investigate or explain in detail, to examine closely.

esmo, *s.m.* rough calculation; *a esmo,* at random, aimless.

esmoer, *v.t.* to grind, to pound, to digest.

esmola, *s.f.* alms; charity; dole.

esmolar, *v.t.* e *v.i.* to give alms. to ask for alms, to beg.

esmoler, *adj.* almsgiving, charitable; *s.m.* almoner, almsgiver.

esmorecer, *v.t.* to discourage; *v.i.* to lose heart, to droop, to become faint.

esmorecido, *adj.* discouraged, disaponted.

esmorecimento, *s.m.* flagging, drooping, discouragement, despondency, faintness.

esmurrar, *v.t.* to cuff, to punch, to pound.

esofágico, *adj.* oesophageal.

esófago, *s.m.* oesophagus, gullet.

esotérico, *adj.* esoteric.

esoterismo, *s.m.* esoteric doctriness.

espaçado, *adj.* spaced, occasional.

espaçamento, *s.m.* spacin, postponement.

espaçar, *v.t.* to space, to set at intervals, to postpone.

espacejar, *v.t.* to space out.

espaço, *s.m.* space; room; distance, interval; *a espaços,* from time to time.

espaçoso, *adj.* spacious, vast, ample, broad.

espada, *s.f.* sword; spades *(nas cartas).*

espadachim, *s.m.* swashbuckler.

espadana, *s.f.* spout *(de líquido);* flame *(labareda).*

espadanar, *v.t.* e *v.i.* to spout out, to spurt.

espadarte, *s.m.* swordfish.

espadaúdo, *adj.* stout, broad-shouldered.

espadeirada, *s.f.* sword-stroke.

espadeirar, *v.t.* to strike with a sword.

espadela, *s.f.* brake, swingle.

espadelar, *v.t.* to break, to swingle.

espadilha, *s.f.* spadille.

espadim, *s.m.* dress-sword.

espádua, *s.f.* shoulder-blade; shoulder.

espairecer, *v.t.* to distract, to divert; *v.i.* to amuse oneself, to relax.

espairecimento, *s.m.* amuseemnt, recreation.

espalda, *s.f.* the shoulder; back of a chair.

espaldar, *s.m.* back of a chair.

espalha-brasas, *adj.* hothead.

espalhado, *adj.* scattered, spread.

espalhafato, *s.m.* fuss, bustle, commotion.

espalhafatoso, *adj.* noisy, showy, garish.

espalhar, *v.t.* to scatter, to spread, to shed, to disseminate, to outspread; *espalhar-se:* to spread.

espalmar, *v.t.* to flatten.

espanador, *s.m.* duster.

espanar, *v.t.* to dust.

espancamento, *s.m.* beating, thrashing.

espancar, *v.t.* beat, to thrash.

espanejar, *v.t.* to dust; *espanejar-se,* to flap wing.

espanhol, *s.m.* Spanish; *adj.* Spaniard.

espanholada, *s.f.* swaggering, gasconade.

espantadiço, *adj.* easily frightened, shy, timid.

espantado, *adj.* amazed, astonished.

espantalho, *s.m.* scarecrow.

espantar, *v.t.* to scarer away, to frighten, to astonish, to amaze; *espantar-se,* to be amazed, astonished or suprised.

espanto, *s.m.* astonishment, amazement, surprise.

espantosamente, *adv.* astonishingly, amazingly.

espantoso, *adj.* amazing, astonishing, startling.

espapaçado, *adj.* soft, slack, indolent.

espapaçar, *v.t.* e *v.refl.* to make pasty, to make soft, to become soft, to fall at full lenght.

espargimento, *s.m.* scattering, dissemination, shedding, sprinkling.

espargir, *v.t.* to scatter, to spread, to shed, to sprinkle.

espargo, *s.m.* asparagus.

esparregado, purée of green vegetables.

esparrela, *s.f.* snare, trap, cheat; *cair na esparrela,* to fall in the trap.

esparso, *adj.* scattered, spread, dispersed.

espartano, *adj. e s.m.* Spartan.

espartilhar, *v.t.* to put on a corset.

espartilho, *s.m.* corset, stays.

esparto, *s.m.* esparto.

espasmo, *s.m.* spasm.

espasmódico, *adj.* spasmodic.

espatifar, *v.t.* to break to pieces, to smash.

espátula, *s.f.* spatula.

espaventar, *v.t.* to frighten, to astonish, to amaze; *espaventar-se,* to show off.

espavento, *s.m.* fright, astonishment, ostentation, show.

espaventoso, *adj.* ostentatious, pompous, showy.

espavorido, *adj.* frightened, terrified.

espavorir, *v.t. e v.refl. e v.i.* to prop, to shore.

especial, *adj.* special, particular, peculiar.

especialidade, *s.f.* speciality, particularity, line *(ramo de actividades).*

especialista, *s.m. e s.f.* specialist, expert.

especialização, *s.f.* specialization.

especializado, *adj.* specialized.

especializar, *v.t.* to specialize, to particularize. 1) *especializar-se,* to specialize (in something). 2) *especializar-se em,* to major in *(estudo).*

especiaria, *s.f.* spice.

espécie, *s.f.* species; kind, sort. 1) *causar a espécie a,* to surprise. 2) *gente de toda a espécie,*all kinds of people.

especificação, *s.f.* specification.

especificar, *v.t.* to specify, to particularize.

específico, *adj.* specific, particular; *s.m.* specific.

espécime, *s.m.* specimen, sample.

especioso, *adj.* specious, deceptive, seductive.

espectacular, *adj.* spectacular.

espectáculo, *s.m.* spectacle, show, performance; sight, scene.

espectaculoso, *adj.* spectacular, grand.

espectador, *s.m.* spectator, onlooker, observe, by-stander.

espectral, *adj.* spectral.

espectro, *s.m.* spectre, spectrum.

espectroscopia, *s.f.* spectroscopy.

espectroscópio, *s.m.* spectroscope.

especulação, *s.f.* speculation, conjecture.

especulador, *s.m.* speculator.

especular, *v.t.* to speculate; to ponder, to meditate.

especulativo, *adj.* speculative, theoretical.

espéculo, *s.m.* speculum.

espeleologia, *s.f.* speleology, the scientific study of caues.

espelhado, *adj.* polished.

espelhar, *v.t.* to polish, to reflect an image of, to mirror.

espelhento, *adj.* polished, crystalline.

espelho, *s.m.* mirror, looking-glass.

espelunca, *s.f.* den, joint, hovel.

espeque, *s.m.* prop, support.

espera, *s.f.* expectation, waiting, wait, ambush *(emboscada).* 1) *à espera de,* waiting for. 2) *sala de espera,* waiting-room.

esperança, *s.f.* hope, expectation.

esperançar, *v.t. e v.refl.* to give hope, to trust.

esperançoso, *adj.* hopeful, promising.

esperantista, *s.m. e s.f.* Esperantist.

Esperanto, *s.m.* Esperanto.

esperar, *v.t. e v.refl.* to expect, to await, to wait for, to abide, to anticipate, to look for, to look forward to, to hope, to hope for. 1) *espero que sim,* I hope so. 2) *fazer alguém esperar,* to keep someone waiting. 3) *o comboio é esperado às 5,* the train is due at 5. 4) *quando menos se esperava,* when least expected.

esperável, *adj.* probable, likely.

esperdiçado, *adj.* prodigal, wasteful, extravagant.

esperdiçar, *v.t.* to waste, to spend.

esperdício, *s.m.* waste.

esperma, *s.m.* sperm.

espermático, *adj.* spermatic.

espermatozóide, *s.m.* spermatozoid.

espernear, *v.t.* to fidget with one's legs.

espertalhão, *s.m.* hot-shot, slicker.

espertar, *v.t. e v.i.* to awake, to become alive, to wake up.

esperteza, *s.f.* cleverness, vivacity, cunning.

espertina, *s.f.* insomnia, sleeplessness.

esperto, *adj.* clever, sharp, talented, acute, shrewd, smart, cunning.

espessar, *v.t.* to thicken.

espesso, *adj.* thick, dense.

espessura, *s.f.* thickness, density.

espetada, *s.f.* prick.

espetadela, *s.f.* prick, jab.

espetado, *adj.* sticking out, stabbed.

espetar, *v.t.* to spit, to impale, to pierce, to stick, to prick, to stab.

espeto, *s.m.* spit.

espevitado, *adj.* lively, cocky.

espevitar, *v.t.* to snuff, to trim (*uma chama*), to stimulate.

espezinhar, *v.t.* to trend on, to trample under foot.

espia, *s.f.* spy; hawser (*cabo*).

espião, *s.m.* spy.

espiar, *v.t.* to spy, to spy on, to pry into, to have a peep at; *v.i.* to peep.

espicaçar, *v.t.* to peck, to instigate, to incite.

espicha, *s.f.* string of small fishes; (*náut.*) sprit of a sail.

espichar, *v.t.* to string fish, to pierce, to prick.

espiche, *s.m.* plug, peg, spigot.

espiga, *s.f.* ear (*de gamínea*), spike (*inflorescência*), tang (*de ferramenta*), nuisance (*contratempo*).

espigado, *adj.* bearing ears or spikes; tall (*alto*).

espigão, *s.m.* sharp point; hip (*de telhado*), crest (*de montanha*).

espigar, *v.t.* to bear spikes or ears, to shoot up.

espigueiro, *s.m.* granary.

espiguilha, *s.f.* purl of lace.

espinafre, *s.m.* spinach.

espinal, *adj.* spinal, dorsal; medula espinal, spinal cord.

espíneo, *adj.* thorny.

espingarda, *s.f.* rifle, shotgun.

espingardada, *s.f.* shot.

espingardão, *s.m.* musket, large gun.

espingardear, *v.t.* to shoot with a rifle.

espingardeira, *s.f.* loophole.

espingardeiro, *s.m.* gunsmith.

espinha, *s.f.* spine, backbone; fishbone (*de peixe*), pimple (*da pele*).

espinhaço, *s.m.* mountain ridge.

espinhal, *adj.* spinal; *s.m.* thornbush.

espinheiro, *s.m.* thornbush.

espinhela, *s.f.* gristle of the strenum.

espinho, *s.m.* thorn, prickle.

espinhoso, *adj.* thorny, prickly, difficult.

espinotear, *v.i.* to jump, to leap, to luck (*cavalo*).

espinoteio, *s.m.* leap, bound, jump.

espiolhar, *v.t.* to delouse; to dive into (*examinar*).

espionagem, *s.f.* spying, espionage.

espionar, *v.t.* to spy on, to pry into; *v.i.* to snoop.

espique, *s.m.* stiple.

espira, *s.f.* spire, twist, turn, coil; thread (*de parafuso*).

espiral, *s.m.* spiral; *adj.* winding like thread of a screw.

espiralado, *adj.* spiral, spiral-shaped.

espirante, *adj.* breathing.

espirar, *v.t.* e *v.i.* to breathe, to blow.

espírita, *s.f.* e *s.m.* spirit medium, spiritist.

espiritismo, *s.m.* spiritism.

espiritista, *s.m.* e *s.f.* spiritist, spiritualist.

espírito, *s.m.* spirit, soul, mind, ghost; wit, humour, vivacity; *Espírito Santo,* Holy Ghost.

espiritual, *adj.* spiritual.

espiritualidade, *s.f.* spiritualism.

espirirtualista, *s.m.* spiritualist.

espiritualizar, *v.t.* to spiritualize, to purify.

espirituoso, *adj.* witty, funny, generous (*vinho*); alcoholic.

espirómetro, *s.m.* spirometer.

espirra-canivetes, *s.m.* e *s.f.* spitfire.

espirrar, *v.t.* to sneeze.

espirro, *s.m.* sneeze.

esplanada, *s.f.* esplanade.

esplendecência, *s.f.* brilliancy, resplendecy.

esplendente, *adj.* brilliant, resplendent.

esplendidamente, *adv.* splendidly, very well.

esplêndido, *adj.* splendid, magnificient, great, excellent, superb.

esplendor, *s m.* splendour, magnificence, greatness.

esplenderoso, *adj.* splendid, magnificent.

esplénico, *adj.* splenic.

esplénio, *s.m.* splenius.

esplenografia, *s.f.* splenography.

esplenologia, *s.f.* splenology.

espojar-se, *v.refl.* to wallow, to roll, to flounder.

espoleta, *s.f.* cap; fuze.

espoliação, *s.f.* spoliation, plunder, robbery.

espólio, *s.m.* spoils, loot, booty.

espongiários, *s.m. pl.* Spongiaria.

esponja, *s.f.* sponge, eraser (*de apagar*).

esponjosidade, *s.f.* sponginess.

esponjoso, *adj.* spongy; porous.

esponsais, *s.m. pl.* betrothal, espousals.

espontaneamente, *adv.* spontaneously.

espontaneidade, *s.f.* spontaneity.

espontâneo, *adj.* spontaneous, voluntary.

espontar, *v.t.* to clip, to trim (*o cabelo*).

espora, *s.f.* spur.

esporádico, *adj.* sporadic, occasional.

esporângio, *s.m.* sporangium.

esporão, *s.m.* spur (*de aves*), (*náut.*) ram.

esporear, *v.t.* to spur; to stimulate, to incite.

esporim, *s.m.* small spur.

esporo, *s.m.* spore.

espórtula, *s.f.* tip, gratuity, retribution.

esportular, *v.t.* to tip.

esposa, *s.f.* wife, spouse.

esposar, *v.t.* to epouse, to take in marriage.

esposo, *s.m.* husband, spouse, consort.

esposório, *s.m.* wedding, espousals.

espostejar, *v.t.* to chop, to slice, to quarter *(esquartejar).*

espraiamento, *s.m.* overflowing; foreshore; spreading out.

espraiar, *v.t.* e *v.i.* to cast ashore, to spread, to expand; *espraiar-se,* to spread out, to spread, to expand.

espreguiçadeira, *s.f.* couch, lounge, deck chair.

espreguiçar-se, *v.refl.* to stretch oneself.

espreita, *s.f.* peep, furtive glance; *estar à espreita,* to be on the lookout.

espreitadela, *s.f.* peep, sly look.

espreitar, *v.t.* to peep, to lurk, to spy on.

espremedor, *s.m.* presser, squeezer.

espremadura, *s.f.* squeezing, pressing, pression.

espremer, *v.t.* to squeeze, to press.

espuma, *s.f.* foam, froth, scum.

espumadeira, *s.f.* skimmer.

espumante, *adj.* foamy, frothy, sparkling *(vinho).*

espumar, *v.t.* e *v.i.* to skim, to foam, to froth; *espumar de raiva,* to foam with rage.

espumoso, *adj.* foamy, frothy.

espúrio, *adj.* spurious, illegitimate, false.

esquadra, *s.f.* squad *(militar),* squadron *(naval),* police-station *(de polícia).*

esquadrão, *s.m.* squadron.

esquadrar, *v.t.* to square, to quarter.

esquadrejar, *v.t. o mesmo que "esquadrar".*

esquadria, *s.f.* right angle, square, stone block *(pedra);* frames *(de janelas).*

esquadriar, *v.t.* to square.

esquadrilha, *s.f.* flotilla, squadron *(de aviões).*

esquadrinhador, *s.m.* investigator, searcher.

esquadrinhar, *v.t.* to search, to investigate, to examine, to scan.

esquadro, *s.m.* square, T-square.

esqualidez, *s.f.* squalor, dirt.

esquálido, *adj.* squalid, dirty, filthy.

esqualo, *s.m.* squalus, dog-fish, shark.

esquartejamento, *s.m.* quartering.

esquartejar, *v.t.* to quarter.

esquecer, *v.t.* to forget, to overlook, to neglect, to omit, to remember; *esquecer-se:* to forget.

esquecido, *adj.* forgotten, forgetful, oblivious.

esquecimento, *s.m.* forgetfulness, oblivion, omission.

esquelético, *adj.* skeletal.

esqueleto, *s.m.* skeleton, framework *(arcabouço),* outline *(esboço).*

esquema, *s.m.* scheme, plan; outline.

esquemático, *adj.* schematic, diagramatic.

esquematizar, *v.t.* to schematise, to form a scheme, to arrange according to a scheme.

esquentação, *s.f.* heating.

esquentado, *adj.* heated.

esquentador, *s.m.* heater; warming pan.

esquentar, *v.t.* to heat, to warm.

esquerda, *s.f.* left hand or side; *à esquerda:* to the left.

esquerdista, *s.m.* leftist.

esquerdo, *s.m.* left-handed *(canhoto);* adj. left.

esqui, *s.m.* ski.

esquiador, *s.m.* skier.

esquiar, *v.t.* to ski.

esquife, *s.m.* coffin, casket; skiff *(barco).*

esquilo, *s.m.* squirrel.

esquimó, *s.m.* Eskimo.

esquina, *s.f.* corner, angle, edge.

esquinado, *adj.* cornered, angled, angular.

esquinar, *v.t.* to cut obliquely, to cut on an angle.

esquinência, *s.f.* quinsy.

esquipamento, *s.m.* equipment.

esquipático, *adj.* extravagant, odd, queer.

esquírola, *s.f.* splinter.

esquisitice, *s.f.* queerness, oddity, extravagance, whim *(capricho).*

esquisito, *adj.* odd, queer, strange, funny, extravagant.

esquivamente, *adv.* unwillingly, coyly.

esquivar, *v.t.* to avoid, to evade, to shun, to keep away from; *esquivar-se,* to keep away; to duck, to slip away.

esquivo, *adj.* shy, aloof, unsociable; elusive.

esquizofrenia, *s.f.* schizophrenia.

esquizofrénico, *adj.* e *s.m.* schizophrenic.

essa, *s.f.* cataphalque.

esse, essa, *adj.* e *pron. demo.* that, that one; *esses,* those, those ones.

essência, *s.f.* essence, substance, nature.

essencial, *adj.* essential, indispensable, necessary, vital, principal; *o essencial,* the main point.

essencialidade, *s.f.* essentiality.

essencialmente, *adv.* essentially.

estabelecer, *v.t.* to establish; to found, to institute; to set up; to settle, *estabelecer-se,* to set up (in business) *(em negócio)*, to settle, to establish oneself.

estabelecimento, *s.m.* establishment, settlement, setting up, institucion, shop *(loja).*

estabilidade, *s.f.* stability, steadiness.

estabilização, *s.f.* stabilization.

estabilizador, *s.m.* stabilizer.

estabilizar, *v.t.* to stabilize, to balance; *estabilizar-se,* to become stable.

estabulação, *s.f.* stock raising or breeding.

estábulo, *s.m.* stable, cow-shed.

estaca, *s.f.* prop, stake, pole.

estacada, *s.f.* stockade, palisade.

estação, *s.f.* station, post, resort, season *(do ano).* 1) *estação ferroviária,* railway station. 2) *estação balneária,* seaside resort. 3) *estação de rádio,* broadcasting station.

estacar, *v.t.* to stake, to prop with stakes; *v.i.* to halt, to stop, to stand still.

estacaria, *s.f.* stakes, stockade, palisade.

estacionamento, *s.m.* parking.

estacionar, *v.i.* to park *(veículo)*, to stay *(permanecer)*, to remain stationary.

estacionário, *adj.* stationary, motionless, static.

estada, *s.f.* stay, permanence, sojourn.

estadão, *s.m.* pomp, luxury, splendor.

estadear, *v.t.* e *v.i.* to display, to show off.

estadia, *s.f.* o mesmo que *"estada".*

estádio, *s.m.* stadium *(campo de desportos)*, stage.

estadista, *s.m.* statesman.

estado, *s.m.* state, condition, situation, position; state; status *(jurídico).* 1) *em bom estado,* in good condition. 2) *neste estado de coisas,* in this state of affairs. 3) *conselho de Estado,* council of State. 4) *estado de sítio,* state of siege. 5) *golpe de estado,* coup d'état. 6) *o terceiro estado,* the Third Estate.

Estado-Maior, *s.m.* General-Staff.

estadual, *adj.* state.

estafa, *s.f.* fatigue, weariness.

estafadeira, *s.f.* o mesmo que *"estafa".*

estafado, *adj.* tired out, exhausted.

estafante, *adj.* wearing, toilsome.

estafar, *v.t.* to tire, to weary, to tire out, to exhaust; *estafar-se:* to tire oneself out, to work oneself to death.

estafermo, *s.m.* scarecrow, good-for-nothing.

estafeta, *s.f.* e *s.m.* courier, messenger; *corrida de estafetas,* relay race.

estagiário, *s.m.* probationer.

estágio, *s.m.* apprenticeship, practical training.

estagnação, *s.f.* stagnation.

estagnado, *adj.* stagnant.

estagnar, *v.t.* e *v.refl.* to stagnate.

estai, *s.m.* stay.

estalactite, stalactite.

estalactítico, *adj.* stalactitic.

estalada, *s.f.* slap.

estalagem, *s.f.* inn.

estalagmite, *s.f.* stalagmite.

estalajadeira, *s.f.* hostess.

estalajadeiro, *s.m.* host, innkeeper.

estalado, *adj.* cracked.

estalão, *s.m.* gauge, standard, pattern, scale.

estalar, *v.t.* to crack, to break, to split, to snap *(os dedos)*; *v.i.* to crack, to break, to snap, to split, to burst, to break out *(revolução, etc.).*

estaleiro, *s.m.* shipyard, dockyard; *estaleiro naval,* navy yard.

estalido, *s.m.* crack, clap, clapping, click, crackle, smack *(com os lábios).*

estalo, *s.m.* o mesmo que *"estalido".*

estambre, *s.m.* fine wollen yarn.

estame, *s.m.* stamen.

estaminado, *adj.* staminate.

estampa, *s.f.* printed picture, picture, engraving; *dar à estampa,* to publish.

estampado, *adj.* printed.

estampador, *s.m.* printer.

estampagem, *s.f.* printing.

estampar, *v.t.* to print, to stamp *(metais, etc.)*, to ingrave, to imprint; *estampar-se,* to show itself.

estamparia, *s.f.* print shop, printing.

estampido, *s.m.* crash, crack, detonation.

estampilha, *s.f.* stamp.

estampilhar, *v.t.* to stamp.

estancamento, *s.m.* stanching, stopping.

estancar, *v.t.* e *v.i.* to stanch, to stop the flow, to stop, to dry up.

estância, *s.f.* stock farm, stanza, resort, lumber yard *(de madeiras); estância balnear,* seaside resort.

estanciar, *v.i.* to stop, to sojourn, to dwell for a time.

estanco, *s.m.* tobacconist's shop.

estandardização, *s.f.* standardization.

estandardizar, v.t. to standardize.

estandarte, s.m. standard, banner, flag.

estanhado, adj. tinned, tin-coated.

estanhagem, s.f. tinning, plating.

estanhar, v.t. to tin, to coat with tin.

estanho, s.m. tin.

estanque, adj. tight, waterlight, hermetic.

estanqueiro, s.m. tobacconist.

estanque, s.f. bookcase, bookshelf, music stand (de música).

estapafúrdio, adj. extravagant, eccentric, odd.

estar, v.i. to be; to stand; to lie. 1) estar a fazer, to be doing. 2) estar para fazer, to be about to do. 3) estar por fazer, still to be done. 4) ora aí está!, there you are!. 5) o seu pai está?, Is your father in?

estardalhaço, s.m. bustle, noise, fuss.

estarola, s.f. e s.m. reckless person.

estarrecer, v.t. to frighten, to scare, to appal; estarrecer-se, to be struck with terror, to waver.

estatal, adj. state.

estatelado, adj. laid flat on the ground.

estatelar, v.t. to knock down; estatelar-se: to fall flat.

estática, s.f. statics.

estático, adj. static, at rest, motionless.

estatística, s.f. statistics.

estatístico, adj. statistical; s.m. statiscian.

estátua, s.f. statue.

estatuária, s.f. statuary, sculpture.

estatuário, adj. statuary; s.m. sculptor.

estatueta, s.f. statuette.

estatuir, v.t. to establish, to settle, to decree.

estatura, s.f. stature, height.

estatuto, s.m. statute; bylaw.

estavanado, adj. crackbrained, foolish.

estável, adj. stable, steady, firm.

este, s.m. east.

este, esta, adj. e pron. demo. this, this one; pl. these, these ones.

estear, v.t. to stay, to support, to prop.

esteárico, adj. stearic.

estearina, s.f. stearin.

esteio, s.m. prop, support.

esteira, s.f. mat, wake (de navio), slip stream (de avião); ir na esteira de alguém, to follow in another's wake.

esteirão, s.m. coarse mat.

esteirar, v.t. to mat; v.i. to sail.

esteiro, s.m. salt-marsh, branch (de um rio).

estela, s.f. stele, monolith.

estelar, adj. stellar.

estelífero, adj. stelliferous.

estema, s.m. garland; genealogical tree.

estendal, s.m. drying ground.

estender, v.t. to extend, to stretch, to spread out, to widen, to enlarge, to lengthen, to unfold, to hold out (a mão), to hang out (roupa), to roll (massa); estender-se, to be floored (num exame, etc.).

estenderete, s.m. fiasco, sorry figure.

estendido, adj. stretched, spread, extended.

estendível, adj. extendible, extensible.

esteno dactilógrafo, s.m. shorthand typist.

estenografar, v.t. to take down in shorthand.

estenografia, s.f. stenography, shorthand.

estenógrafo, s.m. stenogrpher, tachygrapher.

estentor, s.m. stentor.

estentório, adj. stentorian.

estepe, s.f. steppe.

estercar, v.t. to manure.

esterco, s.m. dung, manure.

estercorário, adj. stercoral.

estercoreiro, s.m. dung-beetle; adj. stercoral.

estere, s.m. stere.

estereografia, s.f. stereography.

estereográfico, adj. stereographic.

estereometria, s.f. stereometry.

estereoscopia, s.f. stereoscopy.

estereoscópio, s.m. stereoscope.

estereotipagem, s.f. stereotyping.

estereotipar, v.t. to stereotype.

estereotipia, s.f. stereotypography.

estereótipo, s.m. stereotype.

estereotomia, s.f. stereotomy.

estéril, adj. sterile, barren, fruitless, arid.

esterilidade, s.f. sterility, barrenness.

esterilização, s.f. sterilisation.

esterilizar, v.t. to sterilise.

esterlino, adj. sterling; s.m. libra esterlina, pound sterling.

esterno, s.m. sternum, breastbone.

esternutação, s.f. sneeze, sternutation.

esternutatório, adj. sternutatory.

esterqueira, s.f. dunghill, manure-heap.

esterroar, v.t. to harrow.

estertor, s.m. death-rattle, stertor.

estertoroso, adj. stertorous, snoring.

esteta, s.f. e s.m. aesthete; esthetician.

estética, s.f. aesthetics.

estético, adj. aesthetical.

estetoscópio, s.m. stethoscope.

esteva, s.f. ploughtail, plough-handle; (bot.) cistus.

esteval, *s.m.* rock rose plot.

estiagem, *s.f.* dryness, aridity, drought.

estiar, *v.i.* to cease raining, to become serene (*o tempo*).

estibordo, *s.m.* starboard.

estica, *s.m.* e *s.f.* very thin person; vine producing very sweet grapes.

esticador, *s.m.* stretcher.

esticar, *v.t.* to stretch, to pull, to draw, to crane (*o pescoço*); *esticar o pernil*, to kick the bucket.

estigma, *s.f.* stigma.

estigmatizar, *v.t.* to stigmatize.

estilar, *v.t.* e *v.i.* e *v.refl.* to distil.

estilete, *s.m.* stylet, stilleto; (*bot.*) styel.

estilha, *s.f.* chip, scrap, fragment.

estilhaçar, *v.t.* to splinter, to break into long thin pieces.

estilhaço, *s.m.* splinter, fragment.

estilista, *s.f.* stylist.

estilística, *s.f.* stylistics.

estilo, *s.m.* style; fashion; manner.

estilóbato, *s.m.* stylobate.

estilómetro, *s.m.* stylometer.

estima, *s.f.* esteem, affection, regard; valuation.

estimação, *s.f.* estimation, valuation; *animal de estimação*, pet animal.

estimado, *adj.* esteemed; dear; valued.

estimar, *v.t.* to esteem, to prize, to value, to like, to appreciate, to respect; to estimate, to rate, to value.

estimativa, *s.f.* estimation, appraisal, valuation, estimate, guess.

estimativo, *adj.* estimative.

estimável, *adj.* likable, lovable; estimable, valuable.

estimulação, *s.f.* o mesmo que "estímulo".

estimulador, *adj.* stimulating, encouraging; stimulator, promoter.

estimulante, *adj.* stimulating.

estimular, *v.t.* to stimulate, to brace, to incite, to encourage, to promote, to arouse (*apetite, curiosidade, etc.*).

estímulo, *s.m.* stimulus, incentive, inducement.

estio, *s.m.* summer.

estiolado, *adj.* etiolated, faded; weak, wasted.

estiolamento, *s.m.* etiolation, decline.

estiolar, *v.t.* e *v.i.* to etiolate, to wither away, to decline, to decay.

estipendiar, *v.t.* to hire, to pay a stipend to.

estipêndio, *s.m.* stipend, salary.

estipulação, *s.f.* stipulation; condition, caluse.

estipulado, *adj.* stipulate.

estipular, *v.t.* to stipulate, to agree upon, to recquire as a condition.

estiraçar, *v.t.* o mesmo que "estirar".

estirada, *s.f.* long journey, long way; stretch (*trecho*).

estirado, *adj.* stretched; lengthy.

estirão, *s.m.* o mesmo que "estirada".

estirar, *v.t.* to stretch, to pull, to draw out, to extend; *estirar-se*: to stretch out.

estirpe, *s.f.* stock, breed, race; pedigree; lineage, origin.

estiva, *s.f.* hold (*porão*), stowage (*arrumação de carga*); loading and unloading of ships.

estivador, *s.m.* stevedore, longshoreman.

estivagem, *s.m.* stowing, stowage.

estival, *adj.* estival, summer.

estivar, *v.t.* to stow (*carga*), to trim (*navio*).

estocada, *s.f.* stab, thrust, prod, jab.

estofador, *s.m.* upholsterer.

estofar, *v.t.* to upholster, to pad, to stuff.

estofo, *s.m.* stuffing, padding.

estoicismo, *s.m.* stoicism.

estóico, *adj.* stoic, stoical; *s.m.* Stoic.

estoirar, *v.t.* to burst, to explode, to blow out; *v.i.* to burst, blow up.

estoira-vergas, *s.m.* hot-head.

estoiro, estouro, *s.m.* burst, bursting, crash.

estojo, *s.m.* case, set, kit.

estola, *s.f.* stole.

estolho, *s.m.* shoots.

estolhoso, *adj.* provided with shoots.

estolidez, *s.f.* stupidity.

estoma, *s.f.* stoma; *pl.* stomata.

estomacal, *adj.* stomachic, stomachal.

estomagar, *v.t.* to irritate, to offend; *estomagar-se*, to resent (something).

estômago, *s.m.* stomach.

estomatite, *s.f.* stomatitis.

estomatologia, *s.f.* stomatology.

estomatologista, *s.m.* e *s.f.* stomatologist.

estomentar, *v.t.* to scotch hemp, to swingle.

estonar, *v.t.* to peel, to bark, to strip off the skin or the bark.

estonteado, *adj.* dizzy, stunned.

estonteamento, *s.m.* stunning, dizzyness.

estonteante, *adj.* stunning, bewildering, dazzling.

estontear, *v.t.* to stun, to daze, to bewilder.

estopa, *s.f.* oakum, tow, cotton waste.

estopada, *s.f.* annoyance, nuisance, bore.

estopinha, *s.f.* fine flax; *suar as estopinhas:* to sweat blood.

estoque, *s.m.* stock, store, supplies; rapier *(arma).*

estoquear, *v.t.* to thrust, to stab, to pierce.

estoraque, *s.m.* storax.

estorcegar, *v.t.* to dislocate, to twist.

estorcer, *v.t.* to distort, to contort, to twist; *estorcer-se,* to squirm.

estore, *s.m.* window shade, blind.

estornar, *v.t.* (com.) to transfer an item from one account to another.

estorno, *s.m.* (com.) cross entry; compensation.

estorricar, *v.t.* to dry up.

estorvar, *v.t.* to hinder, to hamper, to impede, to encumber, to obstruct, to disturb.

estorvo, *s.m.* hindrance, obstacle, impediment, encumbrance; inconvenience.

estourar, *v.t.* o mesmo que "estoirar".

estouvado, *adj.* light headed, reckless.

estouvamento, *s.m.* ligh headness.

estrábico, *adj.* squint, cross eyed.

estrabismo, *s.m.* cross eye, squint, strabismus.

estraçalhar, *v.t.* to split into small bits, to tear apart.

estrada, *s.f.* road, highway.

estrado, *s.m.* platform, floor, stand.

estragado, *adj.* spoiled, damaged, out of order.

estragão, *s.m.* tarragon.

estragar, *v.t.* to spoil, to damage, to deteriorate, to squander, to ruin.

estrago, *s.m.* damage, deterioration, ravage.

estrambólico, *adj.* odd, queer, eccentic.

estramónio, *s.m.* stramonium.

estrangeirado, *adj.* denationalized; fond of foreign ways.

estrangeirismo, *s.m.* foreign word or expression; foreign ways.

estrangeiro, *s.m.* foreigner; *adj.* foreign, strange; *no estrangeiro,* abroad.

estrangulador, *s.m.* strangler.

estrangulamento, *s.m.* strangulation, strangling.

estrangular, *v.t.* to strangle, to strangulate, to throttle.

estranhar, *v.t.* to find strange, to wonder at, to shy away from *(uma pessoa).*

estranhável, *adj.* strange.

estranheza, *s.f.* strangeness, wonder, surprise, oddness.

estranho, *adj.* strange, odd, queer, peculiar, weird, foreign, unfamiliar; *s.m.* stranger, outsider.

estranja, *s.f.* foreign countries, abroad.

estratagema, *s.m.* stratagem, artifice, trick.

estratega, *s.m.* e *s.f.* strategist.

estratégia, *s.f.* strategy.

estratégico, *adj.* strategic.

estratificação, *s.f.* stratification.

estratificado, *adj.* stratified.

estratificar, *v.t.* to stratify.

estratiforme, *adj.* stratiform.

estratigrafia, *s.f.* stratigraphy.

estrato, *s.m.* stratum; layer; stratus *(nuvem).*

estratosfera, *s.f.* stratosphere.

estreante, *s.m.* e *s.f.* beginner; debutante.

estrear, *v.t.* to use, wear or try for the first time; to inaugurate; *estrear-se,* to make one's debut.

estrebaria, *s.f.* stables.

estrebuchar, *v.i.* to struggle, to toss about.

estreia, *s.f.* debut, first appearence, premiere *(de um espétáculo);* inauguration.

estreitamento, *s.m.* narrowing, constriction.

estreitar, *v.t.* to narrow, to straiten, to contract, to strengthen *(relações).*

estreiteza, *s.f.* narrowness; intimacy.

estreito, *adj.* narrow, tight, scanty; *s.m.* strait.

estrela, *s.f.* star. 1) *estrela cadente,* shooting star. 2) *estrela d'alva,* morning star. 3) *estrela-do-mar,* starfish.

estrelado, *adj.* fried *(ovos),* starry, starlit.

estrelar, *v.t.* to star, to fry *(ovos).*

estrelinha, *s.f.* asterisk.

estrema, *s.f.* landmark.

estremado, *adj.* demarcated, limited.

estremadura, *s.f.* confines, borders, limit.

estremar, *v.t.* to demarcate, to mark the limits of a land; to distinguish.

estreme, *adj.* pure, genuine, unadulterated.

estremeção, *s.m.* shaking, shock, shiver, tremor.

estremecer, *v.t.* e *v.i.* to shake, to tremble, to shudder, to shiver *(de frio ou de medo).*

estremecido, *s.m.* shake, shudder, start, shock, extreme love.

estremenho, *adj.* bordering upon; relating to the providence of Estremadura *(Portugal);* *s.m.* a native of Estremadura.

estremunhado, *adj.* started from sleep, half-awake.

estremunhar, *v.t.* e *v.i.* to start up from sleep; to startle.

estrénuo, *adj.* strenuous, energetic, bold, vigorous.

estrépito, *s.m.* noise, rattle, clatter, burst.

estrepitoso, *adj.* noisy, clattering, resounding.

estreptococo, *s.m.* streptococcus; *pl.* streptococci.

estreptomicina, *s.f.* streptomycin.

estria, *s.f.* groove, fluting, streak, line, rifling *(nas armas de fogo)*.

estriado, *adj.* striated, groove, fluted.

estriamento, *s.m.* grooving, fluting, striation.

estriar, *v.t.* to groove, to flute; to streak; to rifle.

estribar-se, *v.refl.* to rest one's feet on the stirrups; to base oneself (on); to rest.

estribeira, *s.f.* stirrup; *perder as estribeiras,* to lose one's head.

estribeiro, *s.m.* stableman; hostler.

estribilho, *s.m.* refrain, burden, catchword.

estribo, *s.m.* stirrup, step *(de carruagem).*

estricnina, *s.f.* strychnine.

estridência, *s.f.* shillness, harshness, stridency.

estridente, *adj.* strident, shrill, piercing, harsh.

estridor, *s.m.* piercing sound.

estrídulo, *adj.* stridulous, sharp, shrill, harsh.

estriga, *s.f.* a portion of flax wound on a distaff; lock of hair.

estripação, *s.f.* disembowelment.

estripar, *v.t.* to disembowel, to rip up.

estrito, *adj.* strict, exact, rigorous.

estro, *s.m.* inspiration, rapture, enthusiasm; poetic ardour.

estrofe, *s.f.* strophe, stanza.

estrófico, *adj.* strophic.

estroina, *adj.* hare-brained, wild; *s.m.* dissipated person, playboy; *andar na estroina,* to lead a fast life; to squander.

estroinice, *s.f.* fast living, frolic, folly spree.

estrôncio, *s.m.* strontium.

estrondar, estrondear, *v.i.* to thunder, to boom, to roar, to make a great noise.

estrondo, *s.m.* roar, blare, rattle, bang, clangor, thunder; ostentation.

estrondosamente, *adv.* noisily, sumptuosly.

estrondoso, *adj.* noisy, clamorous, resounding, pompous.

estropiado, *adj.* maimed, lame.

estropiar, *v.t.* to maim, to cripple, to mutilate.

estropo, *s.m.* strop.

estrugido, *s.m.* stew, brown sauce.

estrugir, *v.t.* to stew, to boil slowly; *v.i.* to resound, to thunder.

estruma, *s.f.* scrofula.

estrumação, *s.f.* manuring.

estrumar, *v.t.* to manure.

estrume, *s.m.* manure.

estrumeira, *s.f.* dung-hill, manure pile.

estrutura, *s.f.* structure; frame; constitution; tecture; skeleton.

estrutural, *adj.* structural.

estruturar, *v.t.* to to organize, to form the structure of.

estuação, *s.f.* great heat, hotness; nausea.

estuante, *adj.* ardent, burning, boiling, fiery.

estuar, *v.i.* to boil, to glow, to be hot.

estuário, *s.m.* estuary, firth, inlet.

estucador, *s.m.* plasterer, stucco plasterer.

estucar, *v.t.* to plaster, to stucco.

estudado, *adj.* studied, affected *(modos).*

estudantada, *s.f.* students.

estudante, *s.m. e s.f.* student.

estudantil, *adj.* student.

estudar, *v.t.* to study, to learn, to consider, to think over, to analyse.

estúdio, *s.m.* studio.

estudioso, *adj.* studious; diligent; *s.m.* scholar, student.

estudo, *s.m.* study; learning; consideration; research.

estufa, *s.f.* stove, heater; greenhouse *(para plantas),* sterilizer *(de laboratório).*

estufado, *adj.* stewed; *s.m.* stew.

estufar, *v.t.* to stew.

estugar, *v.t.* to quicken, to hasten.

estultícia, *s.f.* folly, silliness.

estulto, *adj.* foolish, silly.

estupefacção, *s.f.* stupefaction, amazement, astonishment.

estupefaciente, *s.m.* narcotic; *adj.* stupefying, amazing.

estupefacto, *adj.* stupefied, amazed, astounded.

estupendo, *s.m.* stupendous, great, wonderful.

estupidez, *s.f.* stupidity.

estupidificar, *v.t.* to stupefy, to make stupid.

estúpido, *adj.* stupid, silly.

estupor, *s.m.* stupor; froght *(pessoa feia),* rotter *(pessoa má).*

estuprador, *s.m.* raper, ravisher.

estuprar, *v.t.* to rape, to ravish.

estupro, *s.m.* rape, ravishment.

estuque, *s.m.* stucco, plaster.

estúrdia, *s.f.* frolic, folly, dissipation.

esturdiar, *v.i.* to frolic, to lead a fast life.
estúrdio, *adj.* frolicsome, dissipated.
esturjão, *s.m.* sturgeon.
esturrado, *adj.* scorched, nearly burned.
esturrar, *v.t.* to scorch, to overcook.
esturro, *s.m.* burniing.
esvaecer, *v.t.* e *v.i.* to efface, to dissipate, to vanish away, to disappear; *esvaecer-se,* to vnosh.
esvaecimento, *s.m.* vanishing, evanescence.
esvaído, *adj.* faint, weak, exhausted; *esvaído em sangue:* faint from loss of blood.
esvaimento, *s.m.* fainting.
esvair-se, *v.refl.* to vanish, to fade away; *esvair-se em sangue,* to bleed to death.
esvaziamento, *s.m.* emptying.
esvaziar, *v.t.* to empty, to drain, to evacuate, to deflate *(balão, etc.), esvaziar-se,* to become empty, to collapse *(balão, etc.).*
esverdeado, *adj.* greenish.
esverdear, *v.t.* e *v.i.* to green, to make or become green.
esvoaçar, *v.i.* to flutter, to flit.
esvurmar, *v.t.* to squeeze *(feridas),* to lay bare *(revelar).*
etapa, *s.f.* halting place, stage, stop.
etc. (et cetera), *loc. lat.* et cetera, etcetera, and so on.
éter, *s.m.* ether.
etéreo, *adj.* ethereal, aereal.
eternamente, *adv.* eternally, forever.
eternidade, *s.f.* eternity, perpetuity.
esternizar, *v.t.* to eternize, to perpetuate, to immortalize.
eterno, *adj.* eternal, everlasting, perpetual, immortal, endless; *o Eterno,* the Eternal, God.
ética, *s.f.* ethics.
ético, *adj.* ethical, moral.
etílico, *adj.* ethylic.
étimo, *s.m.* etymo, origin of a word.
etimologia, *s.f.* etymology.
etimológico, *adj.* etymological.
etimologista, *s.f.* e *s.m.* etymologist.
etiologia, *s.f.* etiology.
etíope, *s.m.* e *adj.* Ethiopian.
etiqueta, *s.f.* etiquette, ceremonial, ceremonny, formality, label *(rótulo).*
etiquetar, *v.t.* to label.
etmóide, *s.m.* ethmoid.
étnico, *adj.* ethnic, ethnical.
etnografia, *s.f.* ethnography.
etnográfico, *adj.* ethnographic.

etnógrafo, *s.m.* ethnographer.
etnologia, *s.f.* ethnology.
etnológico, *adj.* ethnological.
etnólogo, *s.m.* ethnologist.
etrusco, *s.m.* Etruscan, Etrurian.
eu, *pron. pes.* I; *eu mesmo:* I myself; *sou eu:* it is me.
eucaliptal, *s.m.* eucalyptus plantation.
eucalipto, *s.m.* eucalyptus.
Eucaristia, *s.f.* Eucharist, the Holy communion.
eucarístico, *adj.* eucharistical.
eucológio, *s.m.* euchologion, prayer-book.
eudiometria, *s.f.* eudiometry.
eufemismo, *s.m.* euphemism.
eufonia, *s.f.* euphony.
eufónico, *adj.* euphonious; *s.m.* sweet sound; euphonium.
euforbiáceas, *s.f. pl.* Euphorbiaceae.
eufórbio, *s.m.* euphorbia.
euforia, *s.f.* euphoria.
eufórico, *adj.* in good spirits.
eufuísmo, *s.m.* euphuism.
eugenia, *s.f.* eugenics.
eunuco, *s.m.* eunuch.
eupepsia, *s.f.* eupepsy, good digestion.
eurasiano, *adj.* e *s.m.* Eurasiano.
euritmia, *s.f.* eurhythmic.
europeização, *s.f.* europenization.
europeizar, *v.t.* to europeanize.
europeu, *adj.* e *s.m.* European.
eutanásia, *s.f.* euthanasia.
eutaxia, *s.f.* good order.
eutimia, *s.f.* cheerfulness of mind.
evacuação, *s.f.* evacuation.
evacuar, *v.t.* to evacuate; *v.i.* to defecate.
evadir, *v.t.* to evade, to elude; *evadir-se,* to escape (from); to break loose.
evanescente, *adj.* evanescent.
Evangelho, *s.m.* Gospel.
evangélico, *adj.* evangelical.
evangelista, *s.m.* evangelist; preacher.
evangelização, *s.f.* evangelization.
evangelizador, *s.m.* evangelist.
evangelizar, *v.t.* to evangelize.
evaporação, *s.f.* evaporation.
evaporador, *v.t.* evaporator.
evaporar, *v.t.* to evaporate, to vaporize; *evaporar-se,* to evaporate, to vanish.
evasão, *s.f.* evasion, escape; subterfuge.
evasiva, *s.f.* evasion; evasive answer, excuse.
evasivo, *adj.* evasive, elusive.
evento, *s.m.* event, occurence, happening.

eventual, *adj.* eventual, casual, accidental.

eventualidade, *s.f.* eventuality.

eventualmente, *adv.* eventually.

eversão, *s.f.* overthrow, downfall, destruction.

eversivo, *adj.* eversive, destructive, subversive.

evicção, *s.f.* eviction.

evidência, *s.f.* evidence, obviousness.

evidenciar, *v.t.* to evidence, to prove, to establish by evidence; *v.refl. evidenciar-se,* to become evident; to show off.

evidence, *adj.* evident, obvious, clear.

evidentemente, *adv.* evidently, of course, obviously.

evisceração, *s.f.* to evisceration.

eviscerar, *v.t.* to eviscerate, to disembowel.

evitar, *v.t.* to avoid, to shun; to escape; to elude; to prevent; to help; *não pude evitá-lo,* I could not help it.

evitável, *adj.* avoidable.

evo, *s.m.* aeon, eon, age.

evocação, *s.f.* evocation, evoking.

evocar, *v.t.* to evoke, to call up.

evocativo, *adj.* evocative.

evolar-se, *v.refl.* to fly away, to disappear.

evolução, *s.f.* evolution; maneuver.

evolucionar, *v.i.* (*mil.* e *náut.*) to perform evolutions; to evolve.

evolucionário, *adj.* evolutionary.

evolucionismo, *s.m.* evolutionism.

evolucionista, *s.m.* e *adj.* evolutionist.

evoluir, *v.t.* o mesmo que "evolucionar".

evolutivo, *adj.* evolutive.

evulsão, *s.f.* evulsion, rooting out.

exabundância, *s.f.* superabundance.

exabundante, *adj.* superabundant.

exabundar, *v.i.* to superabound.

exacção, *s.f.* exaction; levy; accuracy.

exarcebação, *s.f.* exacerbation.

exacerbador, *adj.* exacerbating.

exacerbar, *v.t.* to exacerbate, to irritate, to exasperate; *exacerbar-se,* to become irritated.

exactamente, *adv.* exactly, precisely, just.

exactidão, *s.f.* exactness, exactitude, preciseness, accuracy.

exacto, *adj.* exact, accurate, correct, rigorous.

exactor, *s.m.* exactor, tax-collector.

exagerado, *adj.* exaggerated, over-enhaced.

exagerar, *v.t.* to exaggerate, to over-enhace, to magnify.

exagero, *s.m.* exaggeration, overstatement.

exalação, *s.f.* exhalation, emanation, vapour.

exalar, *v.t.* to exhale, to breathe out, to evaporate, to emit.

exaltação, *s.f.* exhaltation, excitement, frenzy, passion, anger.

exaltado, *adj.* overexcited, impassioned, heated.

exaltar, *v.t.* to exalt, to excite, to irritate.

exame, *s.m.* examination, exam, test, trial; inspection, survey. 1) *exame de admissão,* entrance examination. 2) *exames finais,* final exams. 3) *fazer um exame,* to take an exam.

examinador, *s.m.* examiner.

examinando, *s.m.* examinee.

examinar, *v.t.* to examine; to investigate, to look into, to inspect.

exangue, *adj.* bloodless; exhausted.

exâmine, *adj.* exanimate, lifeless, spiritless.

exantema, *s.m.* exanthema.

exantemático, *adj.* exanthematous.

exarar, *v.t.* to register, to set down in writing, to mention, to record.

exasperação, *s.f.* exasperation, irritation.

exasperador, *adj.* exasperating.

exasperar, *v.t.* to exasperate, to irritate, to provoke; *exasperar-se,* to become exasperated.

exaurir, *v.t.* to exhaust, to weaken, to tire out.

exaustão, *s.f.* exhaustion.

exaustivo, *adj.* exhaustive, intensive.

exausto, *adj.* exhausted, tired out; prostrate.

exaustor, *s.m.* exhaust, ventilator.

exautoração, *s.f.* depriving of authority.

exautorar, *v.t.* to deprive of authority.

excedente, *adj.* surplus, exceeding; *s.m.* excess, surplus.

exceder, *v.t.* to exced, to surpass, to transcende, to outdo; *exceder-se,* to overdo, to carry matters too far, to overreact.

excedível, *adj.* surpassable.

excelência, *s.f.* excellence, superiority. 1) *por excelência,* par excellence. 2) *Vossa Excelência,* Your Excellency, Your Honour.

excelente, *adj.* excellent, fine, superior.

excelso, *adj.* high, eminent, sublime.

excentricidade, *s.f.* eccentricity, oddity, extravagance.

excêntrico, *adj.* eccentric, extravagant, odd.

excepção, *s.f.* exception. 1) *à excepção de,* except, save, with the exception of. 2) *abrir uma excepção,* to make an exception.

excepcional, *adj.* exceptional, rare.

excepto, *prep.* except, excepting, save, but; *todos excepto um,* all but one.

exceptuar, *v.t.* to except, to make an exception, to exclude

excerto, *s.m.* excerpt, extract, quotation.

excessivamente, *adv.* excessively, too much.

excessivo, *adj.* excessive, overmuch, too much.

excesso, *s.m.* excess, overplus, surplus, remainder; immoderation; *em excesso,* in excess.

excisão, *s.f.* excision, cutting off.

excitabilidade, *s.f.* excitability.

excitação, *s.f.* excitation, excitement, agitation, disturbance.

excitado, *adj.* excited, animated; irritated.

excitamento, *s.m.* excitement.

excitante, *adj.* exciting, stimulating.

excitar, *v.t.* to excite, to rouse up, to incite, to stimulate.

excitável, *adj.* excitable.

exclamação, *s.f.* exclamation.

exclamar, *v.t.* e *v.i.* to exclaim, to cry out.

exclamativo, exclamatório, *adj.* exclamatory.

excluir, *v.t.* to exclude, to leave out; to except, to eliminate.

exclusão, *s.f.* exclusion, exception.

exclusivamente, *adv.* exclusively.

exclusividade, *s.f.* exclusiveness.

exclusivismo, *s.m.* exclusivism.

exclusivista, *s.m.* e *s.f.* exclusivist.

exclusivo, *adj.* exclusive.

excluso, *adj.* excluded.

excogitação, *s.f.* excogitation, invention.

excogitar, *v.t.* to excogitate, to discover.

excomungado, *adj.* excommunicated; *s.m.* excommunicated person.

excomungar, *v.t.* to excommunicate, to deprive of church privileges.

excomunhão, *s.f.* excommunication.

excreção, *s.f.* excretion.

excrementício, *adj.* excrementitious.

excremento, *s.m.* excrement, dung.

excrescência, *s.f.* excrescence, outgrowth.

excrescente, *adj.* excrescent, growing out.

excrescer, *v.i.* to swell, to outgrow.

excretar, *v.t.* to excrete, to eject; to evacuate.

excretor, *adj.* excretory.

excruciante, *adj.* excruciating, extremely painful.

excruciar, *v.t.* to excruciate, to torture.

excursão, *s.f.* excursion, trip, tour; digression.

excursionar, *v.i.* to go on an excursion.

excursionista, *s.m.* excursionist; tourist; hiker.

excurso, *s.m.* digression.

execração, *s.f.* execration, imprecation.

execrar, *v.t.* to execrate, to curse, to detest, to abhor.

execrável, *adj.* execrable, abominable.

execução, *s.f.* execution, accomplishment, doing, performance; enforcement *(da lei);* foreclosure *(de hipoteca);* pôr em *execução,* to carry into execution; to put in practice.

executado, *adj.* executed; *s.m.* a person executed.

executante, *s.m.* executor, executioner.

executar, *v.t.* to execute, to perform, to accomplish, to carry out, to play *(música),* to enforce *(lei),* to foreclose *(hipoteca).*

executável, *adj.* executable, achievable.

executivo, *s.m.* e *adj.* executive.

executor, *s.m.* executor, performer; executioner *(carrasco).*

executora, *s.f.* executrix, executress.

executório, *adj.* executory.

exegese, *s.f.* exegesis, interpretation.

exegeta, *s.m.* exegete, exegetist.

exegética, *s.f.* exegetics.

exemplar, *adj.* exemplary; *s.m.* exemplar, model, type; specimen, copy *(de jornal, etc.).*

exemplaridade, *s.f.* exemplariness, exemplarity.

exemplarmente, *adv.* exemplarily.

exemplificação, *s.f.* exemplification.

exemplificativo, *adj.* exemplifying.

exemplificar, *v.t.* to exemplify, to give an example of.

exemplificável, *adj.* exemplifiable.

exemplo, *s.m.* example; model, illustration; instance. 1) *por exemplo,* for example, for instance. 2) *sem exemplo,* unexampled.

exequente, *adj.* that executes; *s.m.* e *s.f.* one who promotes a judicial execution.

exéquias, *s.f. pl.* exeques, obsequies.

exequibilidade, *s.f.* practicability.

exequível, *adj.* executable, achievable, practicable.

exercer, *v.t.* to exercise *(também escolar);* exertion; practice. 1) *exercícios militares,* military drill. 2) *em exercício,* in office, acting.

exercitação, *s.f.* exercitation, exercize, practice.

exercitar, *v.t.* to exercize, to train, to discipline, to drill; *exercitar-se em,* to practice.

exército, *s.m.* army.

exergo, *s.m.* exergue.

exibição, *s.f.* exhibition, display, showing.

exibicionismo, *s.m.* exhibitionism.

exibicionista, *s.m.* e *s.f.* exhibitionist.

exibidor, *s.m.* showman.

exibir, *v.t.* to exhibit, to show, to display; *exibir-se,* to show off.

exibitivo, exibitório, *adj.* exhibitory.

exício, *s.m.* ruin, destruction.

exigência, *s.f.* exigence, demand.

exigente, *adj.* exigent, demanding, hard to please, finical.

exigir, *v.t.* to require, to demand, to exact.

exigível, *adj.* exigible, demandable.

exiguidade, *s.f.* exiguity, scantiness.

exíguo, *adj.* exiguous, small, scanty, narrow.

exilado, *adj.* exiled, banished; *s.m.* exile.

exilar, *v.t.* to exile, to banish, to expatriate, to deport.

exílio, *s.m.* exile, banishment, expatriation; *ir para o exílio,* to go into exile.

exímio, *adj.* excellent, distinguished, eminent.

eximir, *v.t.* to exempt from, to free from; to release (from something); *eximir-se,* to evade, to shirk.

exinanição, *s.f.* exhaustion.

existência, *s.f.* existence; life.

existencialismo, *s.m.* existentialism.

existencialista, *s.f.* e *s.m.* e *adj.* existentialist.

existente, *adj.* existent, existing; living; actual.

existir, *v.i.* to exist; to be; to live.

êxito, *s.m.* issue, result, success.

ex-líbris, *s.m.* ex-libris.

êxodo, *s.m.* exodus.

exoneração, *s.f.* exoneration, discharge; release.

exonerar, *v.t.* to exonerate, to release, to free (from something); to dismiss, to discharge (from office).

exorar, *v.t.* to entreat, to implore.

exorbitância, *s.f.* exorbitance, excess.

exorbitante, *adj.* exorbitant, excessive, unreasonable.

exorbitar, *v.i.* to go beyond the limit, to exceed.

exorcismar, *v.t.* to exorcize, to conjure up a spirit.

exorcism, *s.m.* exorcism.

exorcisar, *v.t. o mesmo que "exorcismar".*

exorcista, *s.f.* e *s.m.* exorcist.

exórdio, *s.m.* exordium, preface, beginning.

exornar, *v.t.* to decorate, to adorn.

exortação, *s.f.* exhortation; admonishment.

exortar, *v.t.* to exhort, to admonish.

exortativo, *adj.* exhortative.

exortatório, *s.m.* exhortatory.

exosmose, *s.f.* exosmosis, exosmose.

exotérico, *adj.* exoteric.

exótico, *adj.* exotic, extravagant, odd.

expandir, *v.t.* to expand, to extend, to spread, to develop; *expandir-se,* to espand, to swell; to become loquacious.

expansão, *s.f.* expansion, spreading, development.

expansibilidade, *s.f.* expansibility.

expansível, *adj.* expansible.

expansivo, *adj.* expansive, communicative, unreserved.

expatriação, *s.f.* expatriation, exile, banishment.

expatriado, *s.m.* expatriate.

expatriar, *v.t.* to expatriate, to exile, to banish.

expectação, *s.f.* expectation.

expectador, *s.m.* one who expects.

expectante, *adj.* expectant.

expectativa, *s.f.* expectation, anticipation, prospect.

expectoração, *s.f.* expectoration.

expectorante, *adj.* e *s.m.* expectorant.

expectorar, *v.t.* to expectorate, to cough out.

expedição, *s.f.* expedition, dispatchment *(remessa).*

expedicionário, *adj.* expeditionary; s.m. expeditionist.

expedidor, *s.m.* sender, forwarder, forwarding agent, shipper.

expediente, *adj.* active, diligent, efficient; *s.m.* expedient, contrivance means; *viver de expedientes,* to live by one's wits.

expedir, *v.t.* to dispatch, to forward, to send, to ship.

expedito, *adj.* expeditious, active, diligent, prompt.

expelir, *v.t.* to expel, to eject, to throw out, to discharge.

expender, *v.t.* to expound, to set forth, to spend.

expensas, *s.f. pl. a expensas de,* at expenses of.

experiência, *s.f.* experience, experiment, trial, test, proof.

experiente, *adj.* experienced, expert, skilled, practised.

experimental, *adj.* experimental; tentative.

experimentar, *v.refl.* to try, to test, to experience, to experiment.

experimento, *s.m.* experiment, trial, test, proof.

expiação, *s.f.* to expiate, to atone for.

expiatório, *adj.* expiatory, atoning.

expiração, *s.f.* expiration, breathing out, exhalation; conclusion, termination.

expirador, expirante, *adj.* expiratory.

expirar, *v.t.* to expire, to breathe out, to exhale; *v.i.* to expire, to die, to come to an end, to end.

explanação, *s.f.* explanation, exposition.

explanador, *s.m.* explainer, expositor, interpreter.

explanar, *v.t.* to explain, to expose, to interpret.

explanatório, *adj.* explanatory.

explectivo, *adj.* expletive.

explicação, *s.f.* explication, explanation.

explicador, *s.m.* explainer, coach, private teacher.

explicar, *v.t.* to explain, to elucidate, to expound; *explicar-se,* to explain oneself.

explicativo, *adj.* explanatory.

explicável, *adj.* explainable.

explícito, *adj.* explicit, express, clear.

explodir, *v.i.* to explode, to burst, to go off.

exploração, *s.f.* exploration, search, exploitation.

explorador, *s.m.* explorer, scout; *adj.* exploring, exploiting.

explorar, *v.t.* to explore, to search; to exploit, to probe *(sondar),* to operate *(uma indústria),* to overcharge *(cobrar de mais),* to sponge on *(parasitar).*

explorável, *adj.* explorable, exploitable; workable.

explosão, *s.f.* explosion, burst, blast, outburst.

explosivo, *s.m. e adj.* explosive.

expoente, *s.m.* exponent.

exponencial, *adj.* exponential.

expor, *v.t.* to expose, to expound, to state, to present, to exhibit; *expor-se,* to expose oneself, to run (a risk).

exportação, *s.f.* export, exportation.

exportador, *s.m.* exporter; *adj.* exporting.

exportar, *v.t.* to export.

exportável, *adj.* exportable.

exposição, *s.f.* exposition, exhibition, show, display, exposure; statement.

expositivo, *adj.* expository.

expositor, *s.m.* exhibitor, expositor.

exposto, *adj.* exposed; open *(ao tempo).*

expressamente, *adv.* expressly, purposely.

expressão, *s.f.* expression; enunciation; phrase, saying; look; expressiveness.

expressar, *v.t.* to express, to manifest, to show, to state; *expressar-se:* to express oneself, to talk.

expressivo, *adj.* expressive, significative, significant.

expresso, *adj.* express; explicit, definitive; *s.m.* express, express-train.

exprimir, *o mesmo que "expressar".*

exprimível, *adj.* expressible.

exprobração, *s.f.* upbraiding, censure, blame.

exprobrar, *v.t.* to upbraid, to blame, to reproach.

exprobratório, *adj.* reproachful.

expropriação, *s.f.* expropriation.

expropriador, *s.m.* expropriator.

expropriar, *v.t.* to expropriate, to dispossess.

expugnação, *s.f.* assault, attack, conquest.

expugnar, *v.t.* to take by storm, to overcome, to conquer.

expugnável, *adj.* expugnable.

expulsão, *s.f.* expulsion, ejection, banishment, eviction.

expulsar, *v.t.* to expel, to drive out, to force out, to eject, to banish.

expulso, *adj.* expelled, driven out.

expunção, *s.f.* expunction.

expungir, *v.t.* expunge, to delete, to erase.

expurgação, *s.f.* expurgation, purging, purification.

expurgar, *v.t.* to expurgate, to purify, to purge.

expurgatório, *adj.* expurgatorial, expurgatory.

exsudação, *s.f.* exudation.

exsudar, *v.t. e v.i.* to exude, to sweat.

êxtase, *s.f.* ecstasy, rapture, ravishment, transport; trance.

extasiado, *adj.* enraptured, in ecstasy, transported, ravished.

extasiar, *v.t.* to enrapture, to ravish, to transport, to entrance; *extasiar-se:* to be enraptured.

extático, adj. ecstatic, entranging, overjoyed.

extemporaneamente, adv. extemporaneously.

extemporaneidade, s.f. extemporaneousness.

extemporâneo, adj. extemporaneous, inopportune.

extensão, s.f. extension, stretching out, extent, lengthening, expansion, range; enlargement, amplification; fullmeaning (uma palavra).

extensibilidade, s.f. extensibility.

extensivamente, adv. extensively.

extensível, adj. extensible.

extensivo, adj. extensive, large, ample, spacious; por extenso, in full.

extensor, s.m. extensor.

extenuação, s.f. weakening; wearing out, prostration.

extenuado, adj. exhausted, worn-out.

extenuante, adj. exhausting, debilitating.

extenuar, v.t. to exhaust, to wear out, to tire out; extenuar-se, to tire out, to overwork, to enfeeble.

exterior, adj. exterior, outside, external, outer; s.m. exterior, outside, outdoors; do exterior, from abroad.

exterioridade, s.f. exteriority, outside.

exteriorização, s.f. exteriorization.

exteriorizar, v.t. to exteriorize, to manifest, to give outward expression to.

exterminação, s.f. extermination, destruction.

exterminador, s.m. exterminator, destroyer; adj. exterminatory, destroying.

exterminar, v.t. to exterminate, to destroy.

exterminável, adj. exterminable.

extermínio, s.m. extermination, destruction.

externato, s.m. day-school.

externo, adj. extern, external, outward; aluno externo, day pupil.

extinção, s.f. extinction, destruction, suppression.

extinguir, v.t. to extinguish, to put out (fogo), to suppress, to destroy; extinguir-se, to die away, to be extinguished, to go out (luz).

extinguível, adj. extinguishable.

extinto, adj. extinguished, extinct, out (fogo).

extintor, s.m. fire extinguisher.

extirpação, s.f. extirpation, rooting out.

extirpador, s.m. extirpator.

extirpar, v.t. to extirpate, to root out. to destroy.

extirpável, adj. extirpable, removable.

extorquir, v.t. to extort, to exact (from someone), to wring.

extorsão, s.f. extortion.

extorsivo, adj. extorsive.

extra, adj. extra; s.m. extra.

extracção, s.f. extraction, pulling out; drawing (da lotaria).

extractivo, adj. extractive.

extracto, s.m. extract, summary, abridgement, statement (de conta).

extractor, s.m. extractor.

extradição, s.f. extradition.

extraditar, v.t. to extraditate.

extradorso, s.m. extrados.

extrair, v.t. to extract (from), to draw (out); to pull out; to remove; to get.

extrajudicial, adj. extra-judicial.

extramural, adj. extramural.

extraordinário, adj. extraordinary, exceptional, uncommon, remarkable.

extraterritorial, adj. extraterritorial.

extravagância, s.f. extravagance, eccentricity, folly, excess, whim, fancy.

extravagante, adj. extravagant, odd, singular, strange, eccentric.

extravagar, v.i. to extravagate.

extravasamento, s.m. extravazation.

extravasar, v.t. to extravazate, to let out.

extraviado, adj. astray, stray, lost.

extraviar, v.t. to lead astray, to mislead, to mislay (fazer desaparecer); extraviar-se, to go astray, to get lost, to stray.

extravio, s.m. loss, disappearance, deviation, embezzlement, miscarriage.

extrema-direita, s.f. right-end (no futebol).

extremado, adj. extraordinary, distinguished.

extremamente, adv. extremely.

extremar, v.t. to demarcate, to separate, to keep apart; extremar-se, to distinguish oneself, to excel.

extrema-unção, s.f. extrem unction.

extremidade, s.f. extremity, end, edge, tip.

extremismo, s.m. extremism, radicalism.

extremista, s.m. e s.f. extremist, radical.

extremo, adj. extreme, last, utmost, highest, excessive; s.m. extreme, extremity, end, excess.

Extremo Oriente, s.m. Far East.

extremosamente, adv. tenderly, fondly, lovingly.

extremoso, adj. extreme, excessive; loving, attached.

extrinsecamente, adv. extrinsically.

extrínseco, *adj.* extrinsic, external; not essential.

exuberância, *s.f.* exuberance, luxuriance. exuberante; *adj.* exuberant; luxuriant, lavish, profuse, overflowing.

exuberantemente, *adv.* exuberantly, luxuriantly, abundantly.

exuberar, *v.t. e v.i.* to have in excess, to abound, to overflow; to exuberate, to be exuberant.

exúbere, *adj.* weaned.

exul, *s.m.* exile; *adj.* banished.

exular, *v.i.* to emigrate.

exulceração, *s.f.* superficial ulceration; exasperation.

exulcerante, *adj.* tending to produce ulceras.

exulcerar, *v.t.* to exulcerate; to vex, to annoy.

exultação, *s.f.* exultation, rejoicing, jubilation, glee.

exultante, *adj.* exultant, jubilant, gleeful, triumphant.

exultar, *v.i.* to exult, to rejoice, to be jubilant, to triumph.

exumação, *s.f.* exhumation, disinterment.

exumar, *v.t.* to exhume, to disinter, to unbury.

ex-voto, *s.m.* ex-voto.

F

f, the sixth letter of the Portuguese alphabet.

fá, *s.m.* fa.

fã, *s.m. e s.f.* fan.

fábrica, *s.f.* factory, mill, plant, workshop *(oficina)*. 1) *fábrica de conservas,* cannery. 2) *fábrica de papel, de tecidos...* paper mill, textile mill.

fabricação, *s.f.* manufacture; production.

fabricante, *s.m. e s.f.* manufacturer, maker, producer.

fabricar, *v.t.* to manufacture, to make, to produce; to fabricate *(engendrar)*.

fabrico, *s.m. o mesmo que "fabricação".*

fabril, *adj.* manufacturing.

fabriqueiro, *s.m.* churchwarden.

fábula, *s.f.* fable, fiction, myth legend.

fabulação, *s.f.* fantastic report, fiction, tale.

fabulador, *s.m.* fabulist.

fabular, *v.t. e v.i.* to invent *(fábulas)*, to fable.

fabulário, *s.m.* collection of fables.

fabulista, *s.m.* fabulist.

fabuloso, *adj.* fabulous, fantastic.

faca, *s.m.* knife. 1) *faca de mato,* jackknife. 2)

faca de trinchar, carving knife. 3) *faca de dois gumes,* two-edged knife.

facada, *s.f.* stab, cut with a knife.

facalhão, *s.m.* large knife.

façanha, *s.f.* deed, feat, exploit, achievement.

façanhudo, *adj.* rowdy; swaggering.

facão, *s.m.* large knife.

facção, *s.m.* faction; political party; side; clique.

faccionar, *v.t.* to divide into factions.

faccionário, *adj.* factionary.

facciosidade, *s.m.* factiousness.

facciosamente, *adv.* factiously.

facciosismo, *s.m.* factiousness, sectarianism.

faccioso, *adj.* factious, sectarian.

face, *s.f.* face, visage; cheek; right side *(de tecido)*. 1) *face a face,* face to face. 2) em face de, in view of. 3) fazer face a, to face, to meet.

facear, *v.t.* to face, to square *(pedra)*.

facécia, *s.f.* jest, joke, witticism, wisecrack.

facecioso, *adj.* facetious, jocose, witty.

faceira, *s.f.* chap, plump cheeks; double chin; prig.

faceiro, *adj.* coquettish; dandyish; cheerful.

facejar, *v.t.* to face, to square *(pedra)*.

faceta, *s.f.* facet.

facetado, *adj.* faceted.

facetar, *v.t.* to facet.

facetear, *v.t.* o mesmo que "facetar".

faceto, *adj.* faceious; merry, jocose.

facha, *s.f.* torch; axe; battle-axe.

fachada, *s.f.* façade, front, frontage; mug *(cara)*; sham *(fingimento)*.

facho, *s.m.* torch, flambeau; beacon; firebrand.

facial, *adj.* facial.

fácies, *s.f.* facies, general aspect.

fácil, *adj.* easy; facile; fluent; light; smooth; simple.

facilidade, *s.f.* ease, easiness, facility; smoothness.

facilitação, *s.f.* facilitation.

facilitar, *v.t.* to facilitate, to make easy; to promote.

facilmente, *adv.* easily, readly, smoothly.

facínora, *s.m.* criminal, thug, malefactor.

facinoroso, *adj.* wicked, atrocious; *s.m.* bandit, ruffian, thug.

fac-símile, *s.m.* facsimile.

factício, *adj.* facticious, got up, artificial.

factível, *adj.* feasible, practicable, possible.

facto, *s.m.* fact, event, action, happening, deed; *de facto:* indeed, really.

factótum, *s.m.* factotum.

factor, *s.m.* factor, element, part; coefficient; agent.

factorial, *adj.* factorial.

factura, *s.f.* invoice, bill.

facturar, *v.t.* to invoice, to make an invoice of.

faculdade, *s.f.* faculty, ability, capability; power; school; *faculdade de direito,* law school.

facultar, *v.t.* to facilitate, to permit, to allow, to grant *(conceder)*.

facultativo, *adj.* optional, elective; *s.m.* physician.

facúndia, *s.f.* eloquence, fluency of speech.

facundo, *adj.* eloquent, facund.

fada, *s.f.* fairy.

fadado, *adj.* fated, doomed.

fadar, *v.t.* to fate, to destine (to something), a to doom.

fadário, *s.m.* fate, destiny; troubles, hardship.

fadiga, *s.f.* fatigue, tiredness, weariness, toil.

fadigoso, *adj.* troublesome, tiresome.

fadista, *s.m. e s.f.* singer of *fados.*

fado, *s.m.* fate, destiny, lot.

fagote, *s.m.* bassoon.

fagueiro, *adj.* caressing, fondling, gentle.

fagulha, *s.f.* spark.

fagulhento, *adj.* that emits sparks; turbulent.

faia, *s.f.* beech-tree, beech-wood *(madeira)*.

faial, *s.m.* plantation of beech-trees.

faiança, *s.f.* faience, glaze earthenware.

faim, *s.m.* small word.

faina, *s.f.* toil, labour, work, routine work.

faisão, *s.m.* phesant.

faísca, *s.f.* spark, flash.

faiscante, *adj.* sparkling.

faiscar, *v.t. e v.i.* to sparkle, to glitter, to scintilate, to flash.

faixa, *s.f.* strip, band, waistband *(para a cintura)*, belt; lane *(numa estrada)*; faixa de segurança para peões, safety zone.

fajardice, *s.f.* pilfering; knavery, cheat, swindle.

fajardado, *s.m.* scoundrel, rascal, swindler.

fala, *s.f.* speech, talk, utterance, discourse, language, voice; *ficar sem fala,* to stand speechless.

falácia, *s.f.* fallacy, fallaciousness, deceptiveness.

falacioso, *adj.* fallacious.

faladeira, *s.f.* talkative woman, gossip.

falado, *adj.* spoken; famous, notable.

falador, *adj.* talkative, chatty, talking; *s.m.* talker, gabbler, prattler, chatterbox.

falange, *s.f.* phalanx.

falangeta, *s.f.* terminal or third phalanx.

falanginha, *s.f.* second or middle phalanx.

falansteriano, *adj.* phalansterian.

falanstério, *s.m.* phalanstery.

falante, *adj.* speaking, talking; *bem-falante:* well spoken.

falar, *v.t. e v.i.* to speak, to talk (to or with someone; of or about something). 1) *falar mal de,* to backbite. 2) *não falar mais de,* to drop. 3) *por falar nisso,* by the way. 4) *sem falar em,* apart from.

falatório, *s.m.* babbling; gossip, tittle-tattle.

falaz, *adj.* fallacious, deceptive.

falcão, *s.m.* hawk.

falcatrua, *s.f.* cheat, trickery, fraud.

falcatruar, *v.t.* to cheat, to hoax, to swindle.

falcoaria, *s.f.* falconry.

falcoeiro, *s.m.* falconer.

falconete, *s.m.* falconet.

falconídeo, *adj.* falconine.

falda, *s.f.* foot, base (of a hill).

faldistório, *s.m.* faldstool.

falecer, *v.i.* to die, to pass away, to decease, to perish.

falecido, *adj.* deceased, late.

falecimento, *s.m.* death, decease.

falência, *s.f.* bankrupt, failure. 1) *abrir falência,* to declare oneself bankrupt. 2) *levar à falência,* to bankrupt.

falésia, *s.f.* cliff.

falha, *s.f.* crack, fissure; flaw, blemish, defect, imperfection; missing, gap, omission; *(geol.)* fault.

falhado, *adj.* cracked; imperfect; s.m. looser.

falhar, *v.t.* e *v.i.* to fail; to miss *(o alvo); falhar redondamente,* to fall flat.

falho, *adj.* faulty, defective; lacking; short (of something); deficient (in).

falibilidade, *s.f.* fallibility, liability to err.

falido, *adj.* failed; bankrupt.

falir, *v.i.* to fail; to go bankrupt.

falível, *adj.* fallible; unreliable.

falsar, *v.t.* to falsify, to forge, to deceive; *v.i.* to lie.

falsário, *s.m.* falsifier, forger, counterfeiter.

falsear, *v.t.* to play false to, to distort, to pervert; *v.i.* to give way.

falsete, *s.m. (mús.)* falsetto.

falsetear, *v.t.* to sing in falsetto.

falsidade, *s.f.* falseness, falsity, untruth; deceitfulness; deception.

falsificação, *s.f.* falsification, forgery, counterfeit, adulteration.

falsificador, *s.m.* falsifier, forger, counterfeiter.

falsificar, *v.t.* to falsify, to forge, to counterfeit, to adulterate.

falsificável, *adj.* falsifiable.

falso, *adj.* false, untrue, wrong, forged, counterfeit, fake.

falta, *s.f.* lack, want, shortage, need; failing; defect; fault, offense, misdeed; absence (from work, etc.); foul *(no futebol).* 1) *falta de ar,* shortness of breath. 2) *falta de cuidado,* carelessness. 3) *dar pela falta, sentir a falta,* to miss. 4) *estar em falta,* to be in default. 5) *sem falta,* without fail. 6) *ter falta de,* to want, to be short of.

faltar, *v.i.* to be lacking; to be missing; to fail. 1) *falta-nos dinheiro,* we lack money. 2) *falta-nos tempo,* we are pressed for time. 3) *faltar a uma aula,* to miss a class, to be absent from class. 4) *faltar a palavra,* to go back on one's word. 5) *falta pouco tempo para ele chegar,* it won't be long before he arrives. 6) *faltam duas páginas a este livro,* there are two pages missing (or lacking) in this book.

falto, *adj.* in short, deficient, lacking, wanting.

faltoso, *adj.* guilty; needy; faulty, absent.

falua, *s.f.* barge.

falueiro, *s.m.* bargeman.

fama, *s.f.* fame, renown, celebrity, notoriety; reputation, report. 1) *má fama,* bad reputation, ill repute. 2) *ele tem fama de valente,* he is reputed as valiant.

famélico, *adj.* hungry, famishing.

famigerado, *adj.* notorious.

família, *s.f.* family, kindred, kin.

familiar, *adj.* familiar; domestic, home, intimate; well-known, common; *s.m.* member of a family; relative.

familiaridade, *s.f.* familiarity.

familiarizado, *adj.* acquainted (with), familiar (with).

familiarizar, *v.t.* to familiarize, accustom; *familiarizar-se,* to get accustomed (to), to acquaint oneself with, to become familiar (with).

faminto, *adj.* hungry, starving, famished.

famoso, *adj.* famous, renowned, celebrated.

fâmula, *s.f.* servant girl.

fâmulo, *s.m.* a bishop's attendant.

fanal, *s.m.* lighthouse, lantern.

fanático, *adj.* fanatical, rabid, bigoted, *s.m.* fanatic; bigot; devotee.

fanatismo, *s.m.* fanaticism, bigotry.

fanatizar, *v.t.* to fanaticize.

fancaria, *s.f.* drapery, ready made clothes.

fandangoso, *s.m.* fandango.

faneca, *s.f.* without pout.

fanerogâmicas, *s.f. pl.* phanerogams.

fanerogâmico, *adj.* phanerogamic.

fanfarra, *s.f.* brass band; fanfare.

fanfarrão, *s.m.* braggart, bully, boaster, swaggerer.

fanfarrear, *v.i.* to brag, to boast, to swagger.

fanfarrice, fanfarronada, *s.f.* brag, boast, swaggering, boasting.

fanfarronar, *v.i.* to bluster, to swagger.

fanfarronice, *o mesmo que "fanfarrice".*

fanga, *s.f.* corn measure.

fanhoso, *adj.* snuffling, nasal.

fanico, *s.m.* fainting; small piece; *fazer em fanicos:* to break into pieces.

fanqueiro, *s.m.* draper, dealer with cloth.

fantasia, *s.f.* fantasy, fancy, whim; illusion; dream; *traje de fantasia,* fancy dress.

fantasiador, *s.m.* fancier; *adj.* fantastic, fanciful.

fantasiar, *v.t.* to fancy, to imagine, to dream.

fantasista, *adj.* fanciful, imaginative.

fantasma, *s.f.* ghost, phantom, spook, specter, apparition.

fantasmagoria, *s.m.* phantasmagoria.

fantasmagórico, *s.m.* phantasmagorical.

fantástico, *adj.* fantastic, fanciful.

fantochada, *s.f.* puppet-play, puppet-show.

fantoche, *s.m.* puppet, marionette.

faqueiro, *s.m.* knife-case.

faquir, *s.m.* fakir.

faquirismo, *s.m.* fakirism.

faquista, *s.m.* cut-throat, ruffian.

farádio, *s.m.* farad.

faradização, *s.f.* faradization.

faramalha, *s.f.* empty talk, pretentiousness.

farândola, *s.f.* farandole *(dança),* gang *(bando).*

faraó, *s.m.* Pharaoh.

faraónico, *adj.* Pharaonic.

farda, *s.f.* uniform, livery *(de criado).*

fardado, *adj.* in uniform.

fardamento, *s.m.* uniform, regimentals.

fardar, *v.t.* to clothe in uniform; to provide with a uniform; *fardar-se,* to put on a uniform.

fardeta, *s.f.* fatigue uniform.

fardo, *s.m.* burden, bundle, bale, pack, load.

farejar, *v.t.* scent, to smell; to have a presentiment; *v.i.* to get the scent, to sniff.

fareláceo, *adj.* branny.

farelada, *s.f.* a portion of bran.

farelento, *s.m.* branny.

farelo, *s.m.* bran; triffle, bagatelle.

farfalha, *s.f.* noise, rustling; swaggering; empty talk; farfalhas: filings.

farfalho, *s.m.* boast, brag; idle talk.

farfalhudo, *adj.* showy; flashy.

farináceo, *adj.* farinaceous.

farinar, *v.t.* to reduce to flour; to mill.

faringe, *s.f.* pharynx.

faríngeo, faríngico, *adj.* pharyngeal.

faringite, *s.f.* pharyngitis.

faringologia, *s.f.* pharyngolgy.

farinha, *s.f.* flour; meal.

farinhento, *adj.* mealy, crumbly.

farisaico, *adj.* Pharisaic.

farisaísmo, *s.m.* Pharisaism.

fariseu, *s.m.* Pharisee.

farmacêutico, *s.m.* chemist, pharmacist, druggist, apothecary; *adj.* pharmaceutic.

farmácia, *s.f.* pharmacy.

farmacologia, *s.f.* pharmacology.

farmacológico, *adj.* pharmacological.

farmacopeia, *s.f.* pharmacopeia.

farnel, *s.m.* provisions.

faro, *s.m.* sense of smell *(de um animal);* scent, smell.

farofa, *s.f.* boast, bragging.

farofeiro, *s.m.* boaster, blusterer.

farófia, *s.f.* meringue; boast, ostentation.

farol, *s.m.* lighthouse, beacon; headlight *(de veículo); (náut.)* lantern.

faroleiro, *s.m.* lighthouse keeper.

farolim, *s.m.* small headlight.

farpa, *s.f.* banderilla *(na tourada);* splinter, barb.

farpado, *adj.* barbed.

farpão, *s.m.* harpoon.

farpar, *v.t.* to barb; to harpoon.

farpear, *v.t.* to prick with a pike; to goad; to thrust a banderilla into the bull.

farpela, *s.f. (pop.)* suit of clothes.

farra, *s.f.* revelry, carousal, merrymaking, fun, frolic.

farrageal, *s.m.* corn field.

farragem, *s.f.* medley; rubbish, trash, litter.

farrapada, *s.f.* heap of rags.

farrapeira, *s.f.* rag-picker.

farrapilha, *s.f. e s.m.* ragamuffin, tatter-demalion.

farrapo, *s.m.* rag, tatter.

farripa, *s.f.* thin hair.

farrista, *s.f.* reveler, carouser, merrymaker.

farroupilha, *s.f. e s.m.* ragamuffin, taterde-malion.

farrusca, *s.s.* mut on the face; old rusty sword.

farrusco, *adj.* dirty, stained with smuts; black.

farsa, *s.f.* farce, burlesque; buffoonery; lie.

farsada, *s.f.* farce.

farsante, *s.m. e s.f.* low comedian; joker, wag, trifler.

farsista, *s.f. e s.m.* farce-player; impostor; *adj.* untrustworthy.

farsola, *s.m. e s.f.* humbug, impostor, boaster; jest.

farta, *s.f.* à *farta,* as much as one wants.

fartadela, *s.f.* satiation, surfeit.

fartar, *v.t.* to sataite, to surfeit, to cloy, to fill, to cram, to gorge. 1) *fartar-se,* to gorge, to surfeit; to become fed up (with), to have enough of. 2) *fartar-se de rir,* to laugh one's fill. 3) *ele nunca se farta de ler,* he never tires of reading, he is never tired of reading.

farto, *adj.* satiated, fed up, full, satisfied;

complete, abundant. 1) *farto de*, tired of. 2) *estou farto disso*, I have had enough of that. 3) *estou farto dessa gente*, I am sick of those people.

fartum, *s.m.* rancid smell.

fartura, *s.f.* repletion, abundance, plenty.

fasciculado, *adj.* fasciculated.

fascículo, *s.m.* fascicle.

fascinação, *s.f.* fascination, enchantment; charm.

fascinante, *adj.* fascinating, charming, entrancing, glamorous.

fascinar, *v.t.* to fascinate, to enchant, to dazzle.

fascínio, *s.m.* fascination.

fascíola, *s.f.* fluke, fluke-worm.

fascismo, *s.m.* fascism.

fascista, *s.m.* e *adj.* Fascist.

fase, *s.f.* phase, stage, state, period.

faseolar, *adj.* bean-shaped.

fasímetro, *s.m.* phasemeter.

fasquia, *s.f.* lath, slat.

fasquiado, *adj.* lathed; *s.m.* lathing.

fasquiar, *v.t.* to lathe, to board.

fastidiosamente, *adv.* tediously.

fastidioso, *adj.* fastidious, tiresome, tedious, annoying.

fastiento, *adj.* disgusting, fastidious, hard-to please.

fastígio, *s.m.* fastigium, top, summit, apex; zenith.

fastigioso, *adj.* fastigious.

fastio, *s.m.* lack of appetite; tedium; disgust, dislike.

fasto, *adj.* happy, fortunate.

fastos, *s.m. pl.* annals.

fatal, *adj.* fatal, fateful; inevitable; deadly, mortal, lethal.

fatalidade, *s.f.* fatality; fate, destiny; disaster, calamity.

fatalismo, *s.m.* fatalism.

fatalista, *s.m.* e *s.f.* fatalist.

fatalmente, *adv.* fattaly.

fateixa, *s.f.* grapnel, grappling iron, creeper.

fatia, *s.f.* slice.

fatídico, *adj.* fateful; ominous.

fatigado, *adj.* tired, weary.

fatigante, *adj.* tiring, fatiguing, wearying.

fatigar, *v.t.* to fatigue, to tire, to weary; *fatigar-se*, to get tired.

fatiota, *s.f.* suit of clothes.

fato, *s.m.* suit; *fato-macaco*, overalls.

fatuidade, *s.f.* fatuity, infatuation, vanity; foolishness.

fátuo, *adj.* fatuous, foppish; conceited, foolish; *fogo fátuo*, will-o'the wisp, jack-o'lantern.

fauce, *s.f.* fauces.

faúlha, *s.f.* spark.

faulhar, *v.t.* e *v.i.* to sparkle.

fauna, *s.f.* fauna.

fauno, *s.m.* faun.

fausto, *s.m.* pomp, ostentation; *adj.* lucky, prosperous.

faustoso, *adj.* pompous, ostentation, gaudy, magnificent.

fautor, *s.m.* promoter, furtherer, abettor, supporter; cause; *adj.* supporting, promoting.

fava, *s.f.* broad bean.

faval, *s.m.* field of broad beans.

favela, *s.f.* slum; shantytown.

favo, *s.m.* honeycomb.

favónio, *s.m.* favonious, zephyr, west-wind; *adj.* mild, favonian.

favor, *s.m.* favour, kindness, service, benefit; protection. 1) *a favor de,* in favour (in behalf) of. 2) *faça o favor de vir,* please come. 3) *fazer um favor a alguém,* to oblige, to do a favour. 4) *por favor,* please.

favorável, *adj.* favourable, advantageous (to), propitious.

favorecedor, *adj.* favourable.

favorecer, *v.t.* to favour; to aid, to support, to sponser, to patronize; to promote; to further; to benefit.

favorecido, *adj.* favoured; flattering (*uma fotografia*).

favorita, *s.f.* e *adj.* favourite; esteemed, preferred.

favoritismo, *s.m.* favouritism.

favorito, *s.m.* favourite, darling, minion; *adj.* favourite, beloved, preferred, chosen; *favorito do rei:* king's minion.

favoso, *adj.* covered with yellow scabs.

faxina, *s.f.* fascine, faggot; *estar de faxina:* to be on fatigue duty.

faxinar, *v.t.* to tie into bundles.

faxineiro, *s.m.* soldier on fatigue duty.

fazedor, *s.m.* maker; doer.

fazenda, *s.f.* estate, property, farm, plantation; wealth (*bens*).

fazendeiro, *s.m.* farmer; planter; rancher.

fazer, *v.t.* to make; to produce; to create; to do; to perform; to execute; to render. 1) *isto faz-me feliz,* this makes me happy; to make, to induce; to cause, to compel, to oblige. 2) *isso fê-los recuar,* that made them (cause them to) draw back; to get. 3) *faça-os trabalhar*, get them working; to put forth *(esforços)*; to cause *(causar)*; to ask *(perguntas)*; to take *(um curso)*; to pretend *(fazer de conta)*. 4) *ele faz que não ouve*, he pretends not to listen. 5) *fazer bem*, to do (someone) good, to be good (for), to be right *(agir correctamente)*. 6) *fazer com que*, to cause (something to happen), to make: to do (someone) harm, to hurt, to harm (someone), to be wrong (agir mal). 7) *fazer por*, to strive. 8) *fazia por aprender*, he strove to learn. 9) *fazer saber*, to announce, to let (someone) know. 10) *faz um ano*, a year ago. 11) *faz um ano que*, it's a year since. 12) *não faz mal*, never mind. 13) *por fazer*, undone, still to be done. 14) *tanto faz*, it is all the same. 15) *fazer-se*, to become. 16) *fazer-se ao mar*, to put to sea. 17) *isso fazia-me jeito*, I would just do with that. 18) *fazer-se de parvo*, to act the fool, to play the fool. 19) *faz-se tarde*, it is getting late.

fé, *s.f.* faith, belief, creed; religion; faithfulness, fidelity; credit, confidence, trust. 1) *à fé de quem sou*, on my word of honour. 2) *dar fé de*, to notice. 3) *de boa fé*, in good faith. 4) *de má fé*, maliciously, with bad intent. 5) *fazer fé*, to be trustworthy. 6) *ter fé em*, to have faith in, to trust.

fealdade, *s.f.* ugliness; deformity.

febra, *s.f.* fibre, boneleness meat.

febrão, *s.m.* violent fever.

febre, *s.f.* fever. 1) *febre amarela*, yellow fever. 2) *febre tifóide*, typhoid fever. 3) *febre do feno*, hay-fever. 4) *febre aftosa*, aphtous fever. 5) *febre palustre*, malaria. 6) *estar com febre*, to be burning with fever. 7) *um acesso de febre*, a fit of fever. 8) *estar com febre*, to be feverish.

febricitante, *adj.* feverish; excited.

febrícula, *s.f.* slight fever.

febrífugo, *s.m.* febrifuge; *adj.* febrifugal.

febril, *adj.* febrile, feverish.

febriologia, *s.f.* treatize on fever.

fecal, *adj.* faecal.

fechado, *adj.* closed, shut, locked; reserved, taciturn; close *(vogal)*.

fechadura, *s.f.* lock.

fechar, *v.t.* to close, to shut; to lock *(a chave)*; to conclude; to close up *(uma loja)*; to close *(um negócio)*. 1) *fechar-se*, to close *(um negócio)*. 2) *fechar-se*, to close: to close one self up.

fecho, *s.m.* bolt; fastening; clasp; lock; hasp

(de cadeado); close, conclusion *(término)*; *fecho éclair*, zipper.

fécula, *s.f.* starch.

feculência, *s.f.* feculence.

feculento, *adj.* starchy.

fecundação, *s.f.* fertilization; fecundation.

fecundador, *s.m.* fecundator, fertilizer; *adj.* fertilizing.

fecundante, *adj.* fertilizing.

fecundar, *v.t.* to fertilize, to fecundate; to impregnate.

fecundidade, *s.f.* fecundity, fertility; fruitfulness; productiveness.

fecundo, *adj.* fruitful, fertile, productive; prolific.

fedelho, *s.m.* brat.

feder, *v.i.* to stink.

federação, *s.f.* federation; union.

federado, *adj.* federated.

federal, *adj.* federal.

federalismo, *s.m.* federalism.

federalista, *s.m.* federalist.

federativo, *adj.* federative; federal.

fedor, *s.m.* stench, stink; fetidness.

fedorento, *adj.* stinking, fetid, evil-smelling.

feição, *s.f.* form, shape, figure; feature, aspect; look; manner, nature, character. 1) *vento de feição*, fair wind. 2) *feições grosseiras*, rough features.

feijão, *s.m.* bean; *feijão verde*, French bean.

feijoada, *s.f.* bean stew.

feijoal, *s.m.* fields of beans.

feijoeiro, *s.m.* bean.

feio, *adj.* ugdly; deformed; ill-looking; plain; *fazer feio*, to cut a sorry figure.

feira, *s.f.* fair; market.

feirante, *s.m.* merchant.

feirar, *v.i.* to sell or buy at a fair.

feita, *s.f.* occasion, act; *desta feita*, this time.

feitiçaria, *s.f.* witchcraft, sorcery.

feiticeiro, *s.m.* wizard, sorcerer; *adj.* charming, bewitching.

feiticismo, *s.m.* fetichism.

feiticista, *adj.* e *s.m.* fetichist.

feitiço, *s.m.* sorcery, witchery, hoodoo; spell, charm; *ele lançou-lhe um feitiço*, he put a spell on him.

feitio, *s.m.* shape, form, figure, configuration; tailoring *(de roupa)*; temperament, character *(temperamento)*; *ter mau feitio*, to have a bad temper.

feito, *adj.* made, done; finished; ready; grown-up *(adulto)*. 1) *feito á mão*, hand-made. 2) *bem feito*, well done. 3) *bem feito!*, it serves you right!. 4) *mal feito,* badly done; *conj. feito criança:* like a child; *s.m.* feat, exploit, achievement, deed.

feitor, *s.m.* land-steward, administrator, superintendent.

feitora, *s.f.* land-stewardess.

feitoria, *s.f.* factory, trading post; stewardship.

feitura, *s.f.* making, production, execution.

feiura, *s.f.* ugliness, plainess.

feixe, *s.m.* bundle, bunch *(fís.)* bea; *feixe de lenha,* fagot.

fel, *s.m.* gall, bile; bitterness, rancor.

feldspato, *s.m.* feldspar, felspar.

féleo, *adj.* fellic.

felga, *s.f.* clod.

felgueira, *s.f.* gound where ferns grow.

felicidade, *s.f.* happiness, felicity, bliss.

felicitação, *s.f.* congratulation, felicitation.

felicitar, *v.t.* to congratulate, to compliment.

felídeo, *s.m.* felid.

feliz, *adj.* happy, lucky, fortunate, blissful.

felizardo, *adj.* lucky chap.

felizmente, *adv.* happily, fortunately.

felonia, *s.f.* felony, treachery.

felpa, *s.f.* nap *(de tecido);* pile, shag *(de veludo);* fuzz *(de folha ou fruto);* down *(penugem).*

felpudo, *adj.* nappy, shaggy; downy; fuzzy.

feltradeira, *s.f.* felting-machine.

feltragem, *s.f.* felting.

feltrar, *v.t.* to felt.

feltro, *s.m.* felt.

felugem, *s.f.* soot, grime.

felugento, *adj.* sooty.

fêmea, *s.f.* female.

femeeiro, *s.m.* woman chaser, D. Juan.

fementido, *adj.* perfidious; perjured.

fêmeo, *adj.* female.

feminil, *adj.* womanish; womanly, feminine.

feminilidade, *s.f.* feminility, womanliness.

feminino, *adj.* feminine, womanly; female; *sexo feminino,* the female sex.

feminismo, *s.m.* feminism.

feminista, *s.f.* e *s.m.* feminist.

feminizar, *v.t.* to feminise; *feminizar-se,* to become feminine.

fémoral, *adj.* femoral.

fémur, *s.m.* femur.

fenação, *s.f.* hay-making.

fenda, *s.f.* fissure, crack, split, crevice.

fender, *v.t.* to crack, to split, to slit, to break; to cleave; to fissure; *fender-se,* to crack, to split.

fendido, *adj.* cracked, shaky.

fenecer, *v.i.* to end, to finish; to die; to wither, to fade.

fenecimento, *s.m.* withering; death.

fenestrado, *adj.* fenestrate.

fenestragem, *s.f.* fenestration.

feniano, *adj.* e *s.m.* Fenian (Ireland); fainéant *(France).*

fenício, *s.m.* e *adj.* Phenician.

fénico, *adj.* phenic; *ácido fénico,* carbolic acid, phenel.

Fénix, *s.m.* Phoenix.

feno, *s.m.* hay.

fenomenal, *adj.* phenomenal; amazing, prodigious.

fenómeno, *s.m.* phenomenon; prodigy.

fenomenologia, *s.f.* phenomenology.

fera, *s.f.* wild beast, wild animal; cruel or bloodthirsty person.

feracidade, *s.f.* feracity, fertility.

feracíssimo, *adj.* very fertile.

feraz, *adj.* feracious, fertile.

féretro, *s.m.* bier, coffin.

fereza, *s.f.* fierceness, ferocity; cruelty.

féria, *s.f.* daily or weekly wage; intake *(receita); férias:* holidays, vacation; *férias parlamentares,* recess.

feriado, *s.m.* holiday.

ferida, *s.f.* wound; sore; offense.

ferimento, *s.m.* wound, injury.

ferino, *adj.* fierce, savage, feral; cruel; rude.

ferir, *v.t.* to wound; to hurt, to injure; to harm; to hurt the feeling of; to strike *(corda);* to sound *(nota);* to grate upon *(ouvidos); ferir-se,* to hurt oneself; to get hurt.

fermentação, *s.f.* fermentation.

fermentáceo, *adj.* fermenting.

fermentar, *v.t.* e *v.i.* to ferment, to leaven *(pão).*

fermento, *s.m.* ferment, yeast, leaven; *fermento em pó,* baking powder.

fermentável, *adj.* fermentable.

fero, *adj.* fierce, cruel, wild, savage.

ferocidade, *s.f.* ferocity, savageness; cruelty.

feroz, *adj.* ferocious, fierce, cruel, savage.

ferra, *s.f.* shovel *(pá);* branding *(marcação).*

ferrabrás, *s.m.* braggart, bully.

ferrado, *adj.* ironshod; branded *(gado),* shod *(cavalo); ferrado no sono,* sound asleep.

ferrador, *s.m.* horseshoer, farrier.

ferradura, *s.m.* horseshoe.

ferragem, *s.f.* hard ware; iron fittings.

ferrajaria, *s.f.* iron mill, ironwork.

ferramenta, *s.f.* tool; set of tools; implements.

ferrão, *s.m.* goad, prick; stinger *(de animal)*, sting *(de animal ou planta)*.

ferrar, *v.t.* to spike; to shoe *(cavalo)*; to brand *(gado)*, to inflict *(golpes)*; to thrust, to dig (into something) *(cravar)*, to furl *(velas)*.

ferraria, *s.f.* smith's shop.

ferreiro, *s.m.* blacksmith.

ferrenho, *adj.* iron-coloured, hard as iron; inflexible, firm, relentless.

férreo, *adj.* ferrous, ferruginous; pertinacious, firm, inflexible; *água férrea,* chalybeate water.

ferrete, *s.m.* marking-iron, branding-iron; brand, mark; *adj.* dark.

ferretar, ferretear, *v.t.* to brand, to mark with a branding iron.

férrico, *adj.* ferric.

ferrífero, *adj.* ferriferous.

ferrinhos, *s.m. pl. (mús.)* triangle.

ferro, *s.m.* iron; iron tool or weapon; anchor; flatiron *(de engomar)*. 1) *ferros,* fetters, chains. 2) *ferro de frisar,* curling iron. 3) *ferro de soldar,* soldering iron. 4) *ferro forjado,* wrought iron. 5) *ferro fundido,* cast iron. 6) *ferro-velho,* junk. 7) *a ferro e fogo,* at all coasts. 8) *artigos de ferro,* ironwork. 9) *pôr a ferros,* to put on irons. 10) *ferro-velho, s.m.* junk dealer, junkman.

ferroada, *s.f.* sting, prick; twinge, *dar ferroadas,* to sting.

ferrolho, *adj.* bolt; latch; fastening.

ferroso, *adj.* ferrous, ferruginous.

ferrovia, *s.f.* railroad, railway, *s.m.* railwayman.

ferrugem, *s.f.* rust.

ferrugento, *adj.* rusty.

ferruginoso, *adj.* ferruginous.

fértil, *adj.* fertile, fruitful, productive, abundant.

fertilidade, *s.f.* fertility, fruitfulness, productivity.

fertilização, *s.f.* fertilization.

fertilizador, *s.m.* fertilizer; *adj.* fertilizing.

fertilizante, *adj.* fertilizing.

fertilizar, *v.t.* to fertilize, to fecundate.

fertilizável, *adj.* fertilizable.

férula, *s.f.* ferule.

fervedouro, *s.m.* boiling, bubbling up; agitation, stirring.

fervente, *adj.* fervent; boiling; hot, seething.

ferver, *v.t.* e *v.i.* to boil, to bubble *(borbulhar)*; to seethe *(espumar)*; to rage *(enraivecer-se)*.

férvido, *adj.* fervid, eager, ardent; violent.

fervilhar, *v.i.* to simmer, to swarm with, to be excited.

fervor, *s.m.* fervour, ardour, eagerness, devotion.

fervoroso, *adj.* fervent, ardent, zealous; earnest; impassioned, vehement.

fervura, *s.f.* bubbling up, boiling, ebullition. 1) *dar uma fervura,* to parboil. 2) *levantar fervura,* to boil up, to bubble up.

festa, *s.f.* feast, party, festival; festivity; celebration. 1) *festas,* caresses *(carícias).* 2) *festa móvel,* movable feast. 3) *boas festas!,* Merry Christmas and a Happy New Year! 4) *dar uma festa,* to give a party. 5) *fazer festas,* to caress, to fondle.

festança, *s.f.* revelry, merrymaking.

festão, *s.m.* festoon, wreath.

festeiro, *adj.* merrymaking, party-going; *s.m.* feaster, merrymaker.

festejador, *s.m.* feaster; *adj.* merry, lively.

festejar, *v.t.* to celebrate, to commemorate, to feast, to make merry (over an event).

festejo, *s.m.* celebration, festivity.

festim, *s.m.* banquet, feast.

festival, *s.m.* festival.

festividade, *s.f.* festivity, religious feast; celebration; solemnity.

festivo, *adj.* festive, festal; feast, joyful, merry, gay.

festo, *s.m.* fold, crease.

festoar, *v.t.* to festoon, to decorate with festoons.

fetal, *adj.* fetal.

fetiche, *s.m.* fetish; mumbo jumbo.

fetichismo, *s.m.* fetishism.

fétido, *adj.* fetid, stinking.

feto, *s.m.* fetus, *(bot.)* fern.

feudal, *adj.* feudal.

feudalidade, *s.f.* feudality.

feudalismo, *s.m.* feudalism.

feudalista, *s.m. e s.f.* feudalist, *adj.* feudalistic.

feudatário, *adj.* feudal, feudatory.

feudo, *s.m.* feudal estate, fief.

Fevereiro, *s.m.* February.

fez, *s.m.* fez.

fezes, *s.f. pl.* lees, dregs; dross *(de metal)*; feces, excrement, fecal matter.

fiação, *s.f.* spinning; spinning mill *(fábrica)*.

fiacre, *s.m.* fiacre, hackney coach.

fiada, *s.f.* layer *(de tijolos ou pedras)*; row, line *(fileira)*.

fiado, *adj.* spun; bought on credit, sold on credit, *comprar ou vender fiado,* to buy or sell on credit.

fiador, *s.m.* bailsman, bail, surety, guarantor, warrantor; *servir de fiador,* to stand surety for; to act as a guarantee for; sword-kont *(de espada);* safety chain *(de engate).*

fiadoria, *s.f.* guarantee, guaranty, surety.

fiadura, *s.f.* spinning; guaranty.

fiambre, *s.m.* ham.

fiança, *s.f.* bail, bond, security.

fiandeira, *s.f.* spinner.

fiar, *v.t.* to spin; to draw *(metal);* to entrust (to someone) *(confiar);* to sell on credit; *fiar-se em,* to trust; to rely on; to believe in.

fiasco, *s.m.* fiasco, flop, failure.

fibra, *s.f.* fibre; thread, sting, filament; energy.

fibrila, *s.f.* fibril.

fibrina, *s.f.* fibrin.

fibrino, *adj.* fibrillate, fibrillar.

fibrinoso, *adj.* fibrinous.

fibrocelular, *adj.* fibrocellular.

fibróide, *adj.* fibroid.

fibroma, *s.m.* fibroma, fibrous tumour.

fibroso, *adj.* fibrous, stringy.

fíbula, *s.f.* fibula, brooch, clasp.

fibulação, *s.f.* infibulation, fastening with a fibula.

ficar, *v.i.* to remain; to stay; to become, to grow, to get. 1) *está a ficar escuro,* it is getting (growing, becoming) dark. 2) *o meu cabelo ficou branco,* my hair turned white. 3) *ficou louco,* he went crazy; to continue; to be; to endure, to hold out, to last *(durar);* to stop, to halt *(parar);* to linger *(demorar-se);* to be left *(sobrar);* to be; to be pleased *(ficar contente);* to be moved *(ficar emocionado).* 4) *ficar mais barato,* to be cheaper. 5) *ficar bem,* to be proper, to look right, to suit. 6) *ficar curado,* to get well, to recover. 7) *ficar com,* to stay with; to keep *(conservar)* to get, to have *(obter).* 8) *ficar com fome, medo, etc.:,* to get hungry, frightened, etc.. 9) *ficar para trás,* to drop behind. 10) *ficar por fazer,* to remain to be done, to be left undone. 11) *ficámos sem açúcar,* we ran out of sugar. 12) *eles ficaram de vir,* they promised to come.

ficção, *s.f.* fiction.

ficha, *s.f.* chip, counter *(de jogo);* card, index card *(de arquivo);* record *(registo).*

ficheiro, *s.m.* file, card index.

fictício, *adj.* fictitious, imaginary; fictional; false, pretendend.

fidalgaria, *s.f.* nobility; gentry.

fidalgo, *s.m.* nobleman; *adj.* noble.

fidalgote, *s.m.* insignificant nobeman.

fidalguia, *s.f.* nobility; nobleness.

fidalguice, *s.f.* haughtiness, arrogance.

fidedigno, *adj.* trustworthy, credible, reliable.

fideicomissário, *s.m.* trustee; *adj.* in trust.

fideicomisso, *s.m.* fidei-comissum; trust.

fidelidade, *s.f.* fidelity, loyalty; devotion; exactness, accuracy; truth.

fidúcia, *s.f.* confidence, trust; intimacy.

fiduciário, *adj.* fiduciary; *s.m.* fiduciary; trustee.

fieira, *s.f.* drawplate *(para metais);* string, rope *(enfiada);* row, line *(fileira).*

fiel, *adj.* faithful, loyal, true; exact, accurate; constant; store-keeper *(de armazém);* pointer *(de balança); os fiéis,* the faithful.

fífia, *s.f.* discordant or harsh-toned voice; discordance.

figa, *s.f.* fico; *fazer figas,* to detest, to loathe.

figadal, *adj.* deep *(ódio, etc);* deadly *(inimigo).*

figadeira, *s.f.* disease of the liver.

fígado, *s.m.* liver; *ter maus fígados,* to be quick tempered.

fígaro, *s.m.* barber.

figo, *s.m.* fig.

figueira, *s.f.* fig-tree.

figueiral, *s.m.* orchard of fig-trees.

figura, *s.f.* figure, form, shape; person; appearance, looks; design, picture, illustration; face card *(no baralho); fazer figura,* to make a fine figure, to cut a dash.

figuração, *s.f.* figuration; aspect.

figurado, *adj.* figured; figurative, metaphorical.

figurante, *s.m.* e *s.f.* figurante.

figurão, *s.m.* figure; impressive person.

figurar, *v.t.* to represent, to depict, to paint; to imagine, to visualize; to figure; *v.i.* to figure, to appear; to be included.

figurativo, *adj.* figurative, symbolical, representative, metaphorical.

figurino, *s.m.* fashion plate; fashion magazine; model.

fila, *s.f.* file, row, line, rank; *fila indiana:* single file; *fazer fila,* to stand in line.

filaça, *s.f.* weaver's yarn.

filamentar, *adj.* filamentary.

filamento, *s.m.* filament, fibre, thread.

filamentoso, *adj.* filamentous.

filantropia, *s.f.* philanthropy.

filantrópico, *adj.* philanthropic.

filantropo, *s.m.* philantropist, philantrope.

filão, *s.m.* vein, lode.

filar, *v.t.* to catch, to grasp.

filarmónica, *s.f.* band, philarmonic society.

filarmónico, *adj.* philarmonic.

filatelia, *s.f.* philately.

filatélico, *adj.* philatelic.

filatelista, *s.f.* e *s.m.* philatelist, stamp collector.

filatório, *adj.* relating to spinning.

filáucia, *s.f.* conceit, selfishness; presumption.

filé, *s.m.* wish, desire; filet laces *(renda)*.

fileira, *s.f.* row, rank, line; fileiras *(mil.)* ranks; military service.

filete, *s.m.* *(arq.)* filler, listel; narrow ham *(bife);* filament *(de estame).*

filha, *s.f.* daughter.

filharada, *s.f.* many children.

filho, *s.m.* son; child; filhos: children; offspring; young *(de animal).*

filhó, *s.f.* fritter.

filhote, *s.m.* young *(de animal);* pup *(de cão);* nestling *(de ave).*

filiação, *s.f.* filiation, affiliation.

filial, *adj.* filial; *s.f.* branch, branch office.

filiar, *v.t.* to adopt as a child; to affiliate; to join, to incorporate *(numa associação).*

filicida, *s.f.* e *s.m.* murderer of his or her own child.

filicídio, *s.m.* murder of one's own child.

filiforme, *adj.* filiform.

filigrana, *s.f.* filigree, filigrane.

filipino, *s.m.* Filipino; *adj.* Philippine.

filisteu, *s.m.* Philistine.

filmagem, *s.f.* filming.

filmar, *v.t.* to film.

filme, *s.m.* film, motion picture, movie. 1) *filme sonoro,* talking picture, sound film, talkie. 2) *filme mudo,* silent movie, silent picture.

filó, *s.m.* net-lace.

filodendro, *s.m.* philodendron.

filodérmico, *adj.* philodermic.

filogenia, *s.f.* phylogeny.

filóide, *adj.* philloid, leaflike.

filologia, *s.f.* philology.

filológico, *adj.* philological.

filólogo, *s.m.* philologist.

filosofal, *adj.* philosophical; *pedra filosofal:* philosopher's stone.

filosofar, *v.i.* to philosophise.

filosofia, *s.f.* philosophy.

filosoficamente, *adv.* philosophiclaly.

filosófico, *adj.* philosophic.

filosofismo, *s.m.* philosofism.

filósofo, *s.m.* philosopher.

filotécnico, *adj.* philotecnic.

filoxera, *s.f.* phylloxera.

filtração, *s.f.* *o mesmo que "filtragem".*

fltrador, *adj.* filtering.

filtragem, *s.f.* filtration, filtering.

filtrar, *v.t.* to filtrate; to strain; *filtrar-se,* to ooze, to seep.

filtrável, *adj.* filterable.

filtro, *s.m.* filter, strainer; philter *(de amor).*

fim, *s.m.* end; close, termination, conclusion, expiration, finish; aim, purpose *(objectivo).* 1) *a fim de,* in order to. 2) *a fim de que,* so that, in order that. 3) *no fim de contas,* after all. 4) *por fim,* at last, finally. 5) *que fim levou ele?,* what became of him?. 6) *sem fim,* endless.

fímbria, *s.f.* fringe, hem, edging.

fim-de-semana, *s.m.* weekend.

finado, *s.m.* deceased; *dia de finados,* all souls day.

final, *adj.* final, terminal; *s.m.* the end; *(gram.)* last syllable; *as finais,* the finals.

finalidade, *s.f.* finality, aim, purpose.

finalista, *s.m.* e *s.f.* finalist.

finalizar, *v.t.* to finish, to end, to conclude.

finalmente, *adv.* finally, at last.

finança, *s.f.* finance, management of money affairs. 1) *finanças,* finances, public funds; money matters. 2) *ministro das Finanças,* Chancellor of the Exchequer.

financeiro, *adj.* financial; *s.m.* financier.

financiamento, *s.m.* financing.

financiar, *v.t.* to finance.

financista, *s.f.* e *s.m.* financier.

finar, *v.i* e *v.refl.* to pine away; to pass away, to die; to long for *(desejar).*

finca-pé, *s.m.* foothold; obstinacy; *fazer finca-pé,* to put one`s foot down, to persist in.

fincar, *v.t.* to stick (in or into something); to drive; to fix.

findar, *v.t.* to finish, to end, to conclude.

findo, *adj.* finished; last; *o mês findo,* last month.

fineza, *s.f.* fineness; refinement; courtesy.

fingido, *adj.* feigned, sham; counterfeit, make believe; assumed; false.

fingidor, *s.m.* feigner, simulator.

fingimento, *s.m.* feigning, dissimulation, counterfeiting; falsness.

fingir, *v.t.* to feign, to pretend, to assume; to put on; to fake; to simulate; *fingir-se de,* to pretend to be; to play.

finito, *adj.* finite; limited.

finlandês, adj. Finnish; s.m. Finn, Finlander; Finnish (língua).

fino, adj. thin, slender, slim; delicate; elegant; refined, courteous, polite; sharp; subtle, acute, clever; shrill (voz).

finório, adj. sly, cunning, shrew; s.m. cunning fellow.

finta, s.f. feint, dodge (negaça); dribble (no futebol).

fintar, v.t. to feint, to dodge; to dribble.

finura, s.f. fineness; cunning, artfulness, craft; courtesy, urbanity; slenderness.

fio, s.m. thread, yarn; filament; string, cord; (electr.) wire; cord (de tomada); line (telefónico); rivulet (de líquido que corre); edge (gume). 1) da espessura de um fio, hairbreadth. 2) fio de prumo, plum line. 3) a fio, together, on end. 4) de fio a pavio, from beginning to end. 5) estar por um fio, to hang by a thread. 6) sem fios, wireless.

fiorde, s.m. fiord, fjord.

firma, s.f. firm, commercial house; signature.

firmador, s.m. one who signs.

firmal, s.m. broock.

firmamento, s.m. firmament, sky.

firmar, v.t. to make steady; to steady, to stabilize; to fix, to fasten; to tighten; to sign (assinar); to base, to establish, to ground (on something); firmar-se, to be based or grounded on.

firme, adj. steady, firm, stable; tight, fast, solid; erect; sure; resolute; terra firme: main land, dry land.

firmemente, adv. firmly, steadly, decidedly.

firmeza, s.f. firmness; stability; solidity; consistency; resoluteness, determination, assurance.

fiscal, adj. fiscal; s.m. controller, supervisor, surveyor, inspector, revenue agent (de impostos).

fiscalização, s.f. inspection, supervision, control.

fiscalizador, adj. controling.

fiscalizar, v.t. to inspect, to control, to survey; to check, to supervise.

fisco, s.m. exchequer; tax collection.

fisga, s.f. gaff.

fisgar, v.t. to gaff; to hook.

física, s.f. physics.

físico, s.m. physicist; adj. physical; material, corporeal, bodily.

físico-química, s.f. physicochemistry.

físico-químico, adj. physicochemical.

fisiocracia, s.f. phisiocracy.

fisiocrata, s.m. physiocrat.

fisiocrático, adj. physiocratic.

fisiogenia, s.f. physiogeny.

fisiografia, s.f. phisiography, physical geography.

fisiográfico, adj. physiographical.

fisiógrafo, s.m. physiographer.

fisiologia, s.f. physiology.

fisiológico, adj. physiological.

fisiologista, s.m. physiologist.

fisionomia, s.m. physiognomy, face, countenance.

fisionómico, adj. physiognomist.

fisionomista, s.m. physiognomist.

fisioterapia, s.f. physioterapy.

fisioterápico, adj. physiotherapic.

físsil, adj. fissile, cleavable.

fissiparidade, s.f. fissiparism.

fissíparo, adj. fissiparous.

fissípede, adj. fissiped, cloven-footed, cloven-hoofed.

fissirrostros, s.m. pl. Fissirostres (aves); fissirostral.

fissura, s.f. fissure, crack, split, crevice, anal fistule.

fissuração, s.f. fissuration.

fissurado, adj. fissured.

fístula, s.f. fistula.

fistular, adj. fistulated, fistulous, fistular.

fita, s.f. ribbon; tape; band; movie (filme); make-believe, showing off. 1) fita métrica, measuring tape, tapeline. 2) fazer fitas, to pretend, to show off.

fitar, v.t. to stare at, to gaze at; to prick up (as orelhas).

fitilho, s.m. narrow ribbon.

fito, s.m. aim, purpose, intention; adj. fixed; pricked up.

fitofagia, s.f. phytophagy.

fitófago, s.m. phytofogan; adj. phytophagous.

fitogenia, s.f. phytogeny.

fitogénico, adj. phytogenic.

fitogeografia, s.f. phytogeography.

fitografia, s.f. phytography.

fitologia, s.f. phytology.

fitólogo, s.m. phytologist.

fitopatologia, s.f. phytopatology.

fitopatologista, s.m. phytopathologist.

fitonomia, s.f. phytotomy, vegetable anatomy.

fitozoários, s.m. pl. Phytozoa, Phytozoaria.

fiúza, s.f. hope, trust, faith.

fivela, s.f. buckle; clasp.

fixa, *s.f.* plug.

fixação, *s.f.* fixation, fixing; fastening; determination.

fixador, *s.m.* hair cream; fixing bath *(em fotografia);* fixature; *adj.* fixing.

fixamente, *adv.* fixedly; attentively.

fixar, *v.t.* to fix; to fasten; to locate; to implant; to define; to specify; to set, to appoint *(data);* to concentrate *(atenção);* to settle; to stare at *(fitar);* fixar-se, to fasten oneself; to settle.

fixe, *adj.* fixed, steady; *s.m.* chassis.

fixidez, *s.f.* fixedness, fixity.

fixo, *adj.* fixed; fast; settled; firm; stable, permanent; imovable; set.

flabelação, *s.f.* flabellation; fanning.

flabelado, *adj.* flabellate, fan-shapped.

flabelar, *v.t.* e *v.i.* to fan; to blow.

flabeliforme, *adj.* flabelliform, fan-like.

flabelo, *s.m.* flabellum, fan.

flacidez, *s.f.* flacidity, flabbiness.

flácido, *adj.* flaccid; flabby; lax.

flagelação, *s.f.* flagellation, scourging.

flagelado, *adj.* tortured, afflicted, tormented.

flagelador, *s.m.* flagellator; *adj.* flagellant, scourging.

flagelar, *v.t.* to flagellate, to scourge, to whip; to plague, to afflict.

flagelo, *s.m.* scourge; calamity, plague, affliction; *(bot.)* flagellum.

flagrância, *s.f.* glaring evidence, flagrancy.

flagrante, *adj.* flagrant, glaring; obvious, evident, manifest; *s.m. (fot.)* snapshot; *apanhar em flagrante,* to catch in the act.

flagrar, *v.i.* to inflame, to deflagrate.

flama, *s.f.* flame, blaze; ardour; liveliness.

flamante, *adj.* flaming, bright, resplendent.

flamejante, *adj.* flaming, blazing, flamboyant.

flamejar, *v.i.* to flame, to blaze.

flamengo, *s.m.* Fleming; *adj.* Flemish.

flâmine, *s.m.* flamen.

flamingo, *s.m.* flamingo.

flâmula, *s.f.* streamer, pennant.

flanar, *v.i.* to saunter, to stroll, to loaf *(vadiar).*

flanco, *s.m.* flank, side; wing.

flanela, *s.f.* flannel.

flanquear, *v.t.* to flank, to outflank.

flato, *s.m.* flatus.

flatulência, *s.f.* flatulence.

flatulento, *adj.* flatulent.

flauta, *s.f.* flute.

flautear, *v.t.* to play the flute; to relax

(espairecer), to shuffle, to prevaricate, to hoodwink *(lograr).*

flautim, *s.m.* piccolo, small flute.

flautista, *s.m.* e *s.f.* flutist, flute player.

flavescente, *adj.* yellow.

flavescer, *v.i.* to become golden-yellow.

flavo, *adj.* flavous, goldenyellow.

flébil, *adj.* weeping; mournful.

flebite, *s.f.* phlebitis.

flecha, *s.f.* arrow, dart, spire *(de torre),* *(arquit.)* rise (of an arch).

flechada, *s.f.* arrow shot or wound.

flectir, *v.t.* e *v.i.* to flex, to bend; *(geol.)* to fold, to be bent.

flegmasia, *s.f.* phlegmasia.

fleimão, *s.m.* phlegmon.

fleimoso, *adj.* phlegmonic.

fleuma, *s.f.* phleugma, sluggishness; coolness.

fleumático, *adj.* phlegmatic, sluggish, cool.

flexão, *s.f.* flexion, flection, bending, *(gram.)* inflexion.

flexibilidade, *s.f.* flexibility.

flexibilizar, *v.t.* to make flexible.

flexional, *adj.* flexional.

flexionar, *v.t.* to inflect.

flexível, *adj.* flexible, pliant, ductile.

flexivo, *adj. (gram.)* flexional.

flexuosidade, *s.f.* flexuosity, winding.

flexuoso, *adj.* flexuos, sinuous.

flexura, *s.f.* flexure, flexibility, sluggishness.

flibusteiro, *s.m.* flibuster, bucanneer.

floco, *s.m.* flake; flock *(de lã).*

flóculo, *s.m.* floccule.

floema, *s.m.* phloem.

flor, *s.f.* flower; blossom; cream, elite *(o melhor).* 1) *estar na flor da idade,* to be in the prime of life. 2) *em flor,* a bloom, in bloom. 3) *a flor da pele,* on the surface of water. 4) *fina flor,* cream *(da sociedade, etc.).*

flora, *s.f.* flora.

floração, *s.f.* blooming, blossoming, flowering.

floral, *adj.* floral.

florão, *s.m.* floral piece *(de abóbada).*

flor-de-lis, *s.f.* "fleur-de-lis", lily.

floreado, *adj.* florid; *s.m. (mús.)* flourish, fantasy.

florear, *v.t.* to flower; *(mús.)* to flourish; to ornament.

floreio, *s.m.* flourishing.

floreira, *s.f.* flower vase.

florejar, *v.t.* e *v.i.* to adorn with flower; to flower.

florentino, s.m. e adj. Florentine.
flóreo, adj. flourishing.
florescência, s.f. florescence.
florescente, adj. florescent, flourishing; prosperous.
florescer, v.i. to flower to bloom, to blossom; to flourish, to prosper.
floresta, s.f. forest.
florestal, adj. forest.
florete, s.m. foil.
floricultor, s.m. floriculturist.
floricultura, s.f. floriculturist.
florido, adj. in flower, abloom; flowery; florid.
flórido, adj. flourishing; florid; brilliant.
floriforme, adj. floriform.
florilégio, s.m. florilegium.
florim, s.m. florin.
florir, v.i. to flower, to bloom, to blossom; v.t. to adorn with flowers.
florista, s.f. florist.
flotilha, s.f. flotilla.
fluência, s.f. fluency, smoothness; facility.
fluente, adj. fluent; flowing, running; facile.
fluidez, s.f. fluidity.
fluido, adj. flowing, mobile; liquid; s.m. fluid, liquid.
fluir, v.i. to flow, to run; to stream.
fluminense, adj. fluvial; s.m. e s.f. native of Rio de Janeiro.
flúor, s.m. fluorine.
fluorescência, s.f. fluorescence.
fluorescente, adj. fluorescent.
fluoreto, s.m. fluoride.
flutuabilidade, s.f. buoyancy.
flutuação, s.f. floating, fluctuation; unsteadiness.
flutuador, s.m. float; floating platform.
flutuante, adj. floating; buoyant; unfunded (dívida).
flutuar, v.i. to float; to hove (no ar); to fluctuate, to waver, to vacillate; to oscillate, fazer flutuar, to set afloat, to buoy up.
flutuável, adj. floatable.
fluvial, adj. fluvial; river.
fluxão, s.f. fluxion, flux.
fluxibilidade, s.f. fluxibility.
fluxível, adj. fluxional, fluxionary, variable.
fluxo, s.m. flux, flowing, flow; current, flood (da maré).
fobia, s.f. phobia.
foca, s.f. seal.
focagem, s.f. focalization.
focal, adj. focal.
focar, v.t. to focus; to focalize.

focinhada, s.f. blow with the snout.
focinhar, v.t. e v.i. to fall upon one's nose; to snout, to nose.
focinheira, s.f. muzzle.
focinho, s.m. muzzle, snout; nose.
focinhudo, adj. long-snouted; sullen, sulky.
foco, s.m. focus; adjustment; focal point, center; foco de infecção, pesthole.
fofo, adj. soft, fluffy, puffy.
fogacho, s.m. little flame, flare-up.
fogagem, s.f. rash.
fogão, s.m. stove.
fogareiro, s.m. portable stove; brazier (de brasas).
fogaréu, s.m. bonfire.
fogo, s.m. fire; combustion, blaze, flame, ardour. 1) fogo de artifício, fireworks. 2) à prova de fogo, fire-proof. 3) em fogo, afire, aglow. 4) fazer fogo, to make a fire (uma fogueira); to shoot, to open fire (arma de fogo). 5) pôr fogo a, to set fire to. 6) fogo-fátuo, s.m. ignis fatuus, will-o'-the-wisp, jack-o'-lantern.
fogosidade, s.f. fierriness, impetuosity.
fogoso, adj. fiery, ardent, impetuous.
fogueira, s.f. fire, bonfire.
foguete, s.m. rocket, skyrocket.
fogueteiro, s.m. firework-maker, pyrotechnist.
foiçada, a blow with a scythe.
foice, s.f. scythe, sickle.
fojo, s.m. pitfall; pit.
folar, s.m. Easter-gift, Easter pudding.
folclore, s.m. folklore.
folclórico, adj. folkloric.
fole, s.m. bellows.
fôlego, s.m. breath, ficar sem fôlego, to be out of breath.
folga, s.f. rest, relaxation, recreation; looseness; clearance (espaço livre), play, backlash (num mecanismo).
folgado, adj. loose, loose-fitting; slack; ample; unhampered; easygoing.
folgança, s.f. o mesmo que "folguedo".
folgar, v.t. to loosen, to slacken, to relax; v.i. to rest, to relax; to rejoice (in something), to be glad, to amuse oneself; to play.
folgazão, s.m. frolicsome, sportive, gamesome, playful, jolly, jovial; frisky, fun-loving.
folguedo, s.m. merrymaking, revelry; frolic, prank.
folha, s.f. leaf (de planta, metal, porta, mesa, etc.); leaf, sheet (de papel). 1) folha de rascunho, tinfoil. 2) folha de pagamento,

payroll. 3) folha de serviço, record. 4) artigos de folha, tinware. 5) novo em folha, brand new. 6) *folha-de-flandres, s.f.* tinplate.

folhado, *adj.* leaf-covered; foliate; *massa folhada,* pull paste.

folhagem, *s.f.* foliage, leaffage, leaves.

folheado, *adj.* veneered *(madeira); folheado a ouro,* gold-plated.

folhear, *v.t.* to turn the pages of *(livro);* to veneer, to plate.

folhedo, *s.m.* foliage, leaves *(no chão).*

folhetim, *s.m.* feuilleton; serial publication.

folhetinista, *s.m. e s.f.* feuilletonist; serialist.

folheto, *s.m.* leaflet, pamphlet; brochure; prospectus.

folhinha, *s.f.* calendar; leaflet.

folho, *s.m.* flounce *(de vestido);* frill.

folhoso, *adj.* leafy; *s.m.* manyplies.

folia, *s.f.* merrymaking, revelry, prank, frolic.

folião, *s.m.* reveler, merrymaker.

foliar, *v.i.* to revel, to make merry, to frolic.

folicular, *adj.* follicular.

foliculário, *s.m.* pamphleteer; hack journalist.

folículo, *s.m.* leaflet; *(anat.)* follicule.

foliculoso, *adj.* folliculous.

foliforme, *adj.* leaf-shaped.

fólio, *s.m.* folio.

foliolado, *adj.* foliolate.

folíolo, *s.m.* foliole.

fome, *s.f.* hunger; appetite; famine; starvation. 1) *matar a fome,* to starve to death. 2) *morrer de fome,* to starve, to die of starvation. 3) *passar fome,* to starve. 4) *ter fome,* to be hungry.

fomentação, *s.f.* fomentation; instigation.

fomentador, *s.m.* instigator; promoter.

fomentar, *v.t.* to foment; to instigate, to promote, to encourage.

fomento, *s.m.* fomentation, encouragement, promotion, fostering.

fona, *s.f.* spark; bustle; *s.m. e s.f.* miser, niggard; *andar numa fona,* to be on the move, to be bustling about.

fonação, *s.f.* phonation.

fonador, *adj.* producing sound.

fonema, *s.m.* phoneme, speech-sound.

fonética, *s.f.* phonetics.

foneticismo, fonetismo, *s.m.* phoneticism, phonetism.

fonético, *adj.* phonetic.

fónico, *adj.* phonic.

fonografia, *s.f.* phonography.

fonográfico, *adj.* phonographic.

fonógrafo, *s.m.* phonograph.

fonologia, *s.f.* phonology.

fonológico, *adj.* phonological.

fonólogo, *s.m.* phonologist.

fonometria, *s.f.* phonometry.

fonométrico, *adj.* phonometrical.

fonómetro, *s.m.* phonometer.

fonomímico, *adj.* phonomimic.

fonoscópio, *s.m.* phonoscope.

fontainha, *s.f.* little fountain.

fontal, fontanal, *adj.* original, primary.

fontanário, fontenário, *s.m.* public fountain; *adj.* fontal.

fontanela, *s.f.* fontanel.

fonte, *s.f.* fountain, spring; source, origin; temple *(têmpora); de fonte segura,* from a reliable source.

fora, *adv.* out; on the outside; off; away. 1) *fora de,* out of, outside of; away from; beyond; foreign to. 2) *fora de si,* out of one's mind. 3) *de fora,* outer, outside; from the outside. 4) *para fora,* out, outwards, to the outside, off. 5) *por fora,* outside, outwardly; *s.m..* 6) *dar o fora,* to get out, to go away; *prep.* except, save; *interj.* out! get out!

foragido, *adj. e s.m.* fugitive; outlaw, wanderer.

foragir-se, *v.refl.* to emigrate, to leave one's native country.

foral, *s.m.* charter.

forasteiro, *s.m.* stranger.

forca, *s.f.* gallows, gibbet.

força, *s.f.* strength, force, power, might; vigor, energy; potency; intensity *(mil.)* force, troops. 1) *força aérea,* air force. 2) *força de vontade,* willpower, determination. 3) *força electromotriz,* electromotive force. 4) *força hidraulica,* water power. 5) *força motriz,* motive power. 6) *a força,* by force. 7) *a força de,* by dint of. 8) *a viva força,* by main force. 9) *com força,* vigorously, hard. 10) *com toda a força,* with might and main. 11) *fazer força,* to strive, to try hard *(esforçar-se).*

forcado, *s.m.* pitchfork.

forçadamente, *adv.* forcedly.

forçado, *s.m.* galley-slave, convict; *adj.* forced, compulsory; affected. 1) *trabalhos forçados,* hard labour. 2) *aterragem forçada,* forced landing.

forçamento, *s.m.* forcing; coercion, compulsion.

forçar, *v.t.* to force, to compel, to constrain

(someone to do something); to strain; to force open *(porta, etc.);* to twist *(o sentido de uma palavra);* **forçar-se,** to force oneself.

forcejar, *v.i.* to struggle, to endeavour, to try, to do one's outmost; to exert oneself, to resist.

forcejo, *s.m.* struggle, endeavour, affort.

fórceps ou fórcipe, *s.m.* forceps.

forçosamente, *adv.* forcibly.

forçoso, *adj.* forcible, forceful; compulsory; inevitable, unavoidable.

foreiro, *s.m.* tenant on a long lease, lessee; *adj.* under lease.

forense, *adj.* forensic; judiciary.

forja, *s.f.* forge; smithy; foundry, ironworks.

forjado, *adj.* forged; wrought; *ferro forjado,* frought iron.

forjador, *s.m.* smith, forger.

forjadura, *s.f.* forging, forgery.

forjar, *v.t.* to forge *(metais);* to forge, to falsify, to fabricate, to invent.

forma, *s.f.* form, shape; figure; conformation; make; manner, way. 1) *da mesma forma,* likewise. 2) *dar forma,* otherwise. 3) *de forma que,* so that. 4) *de qualquer forma,* anyway. 5) *desta forma,* (in) this way. 6) *estar em forma,* to be in good shape. 7) *fora de forma, (mil.)* dismiss!

forma(ô), *s.f.* mold; matrix; pan *(de bolo);* block *(de chapéu);* last *(de calçado);* loaf *(pão de forma).*

formação, *s.f.* formation *(também mil. e geol.);* forming; array; composition, constitution; background *(antecedentes).*

formado, *adj.* formed; graduated *(por uma faculdade);* ser formado por: to consist of.

formador, *s.m.* former, shaper; *adj.* forming, shaping.

formal, *adj.* formal; manifest, positive; explicit; peremptory.

formalidade, *s.f.* formality; form, ceremony, conventionality.

formalismo, *s.m.* formalism; ceremoniousness; stiffness; primness.

formalista, *s.m.* formalist; *adj.* formal; ceremonious; stiff; prim.

formalizar, *v.t.* to formalize; to draw up in due form.

formão, *s.f.* chisel.

formar, *v.t.* to form, to fashion, to shape, to mold; to make, to create; to compose; to educate, to train; *v.i. (mil.)* to fall in; *formar-se,* to form; to graduate (in law, medicine, etc.).

formativo, *adj.* formative.

formato, *s.m.* format, shape.

formatura, *s.f.* graduation; *(mil.)* muster, formation.

formicação, *s.f.* formication.

formicante, *adj.* formicating.

formicida, *s.f.* formicide, ant poison.

fórmico, *adj.* formic.

formidável, *adj.* formidable, terrible; huge, immense; amazing, stupendous.

formidoloso, *adj.* fearful, formidable, awful.

formiga, *s.f.* ant.

formigamento, *s.m.* itching, tingle.

formigante, *adj.* itching, tickling.

formigar, *v.i.* to tingle; to itch; to swarm *(abundar).*

formigo, *s.m. (vet.)* thrush.

formigueiro, *s.m.* ant hill, antsnest; itching, tingling; swarn, throng *(multidão).*

formol, *s.m.* formol.

formoso, *adj.* beautiful, handsome, fair.

formosura, *s.f.* beauty, handsomeness, fairness.

fórmula, *s.f.* formula.

formulação, *s.f.* formulation.

formular, *v.t.* to formulate; to state; to set forth.

formulário, *s.m.* formulary; form.

formulista, *s.f. e s.m.* formuliste.

fornada, *s.f.* batch.

fornalha, *s.f.* furnace.

fornecedor, *s.m.* furnisher, supplier, purveyor.

fornecer, *v.t.* to furnish, to supply, to porvide (someone with something), to purvey; to give.

fornecimento, *s.m.* supply, furnishing.

forneiro, *s.m.* oven-keeper; *forneiro de cal,* lime-burner.

fornilho, *s.m.* small oven.

forno, *s.m.* oven; kiln; furnace.

foro, *s.m.* court of justice; the bar; jurisdiction; rent money; *foros,* privileges, rights, prerrogatives; claims.

forqueadura, *s.f.* bifurcation.

forquear, *v.t.* to bifurcate.

forqueta, *s.f.* fork *(árvore);* forked branch.

forquilha, *s.f.* fork; forked stick; three-pronged pitchfork; oarlock *(de remo).*

forra, *s.f. (náut.)* tabling; *forra de vela:* sail band.

forrado, *adj.* lined, covered.

forrageador, *s.m.* forager.

forragear, *v.t.* to forage; to rummage; to ravage; *v.i.* to cut fodder.

forragem, s.f. forage, fodder.

forrar, v.t. to line, to cover; to spare, to save *(poupar); forrar com papel:* to paper; *forrar- -se,* to avoid; to keep away from.

forreta, s.m. e s.f. skinflint, niggard.

forro, s.m. lining; padding; adj. freed, emancipated.

fortalecedor, adj. strengthening, fortifying, invigorating.

fortalecer, v.t. to strengthen, to fortify, to invigorate; to thicken; *fortalecer-se:* to grow strong.

fortalecimento, s.m. strengthening, invigoration.

fortaleza, s.f. fortress, stronghold; fortitude, endurance.

forte, adj. strong; vigourous, stout, robust; hardy, tough; powerful; intense; vivid; loud *(voz);* s.m. fort, stronghold; *ponto forte,* strong point.

fortificação, s.f. fortification.

fortificador, adj. fortifying.

fortificante, adj. fortifying, invigorating; s.m. fortifier; tonic.

fortificar, v.t. to fortify, to strenghten; to invigorate; *fortificar-se: (mil.)* to fortify oneself.

fortim, s.m. small fort.

fortuito, adj. fortuitous, casual, accidental, chance.

fortuna, s.f. fortune; chance, luck; fate; wealth.

fortunar, v.t. to give luck; to make happy.

fortunoso, adj. lucky, fortunate.

fosca, s.f. mummery, grimace.

foscagem, s.f. tarnishing, dimming.

fosco, adj. dull, dim, mat; unpolished; opaque.

fosfatado, adj. phosphated.

fosfatar, v.t. to treat with phosphates.

fosfato, s.m. phosphate.

fosfóreo, adj. phosporeous.

fosforescência, s.f. phosphorescence.

fosforescente, adj. phosphorescent.

fosfórico, adj. phosphoric.

fosforífero, adj. phosphorescent.

fósforo, s.m. *(quím)* phosphorus; match *(pau de fósforo).*

fosforoso, adj. phosphorous.

fosquinha, s.f. mummery; wheediling.

fossa, s.f. ditch, pit; *(anat.)* fossa.

fossar, v.t. e v.i. to root, to nuzzle; to nose.

fóssil, s.m. e adj. fossil.

fossilífero, adj. fossiliferous.

fossilização, s.f. fossilization.

fossilizar, v.t. to fossilize.

fosso, s.m. moat; ditch; pit.

fotismo, s.m. photism.

fotocromático, adj. photocromatic.

fotocromia, s.f. photocromy.

fotofobia, s.f. photofobia.

fotoeléctrico, adj. photo-electric.

fotocópia, s.f. photostat; xerox copy, photocopy.

fotogénico, adj. photogenic.

fotografar, v.t. to photograph.

fotografia, s.f. photograph, photo, picture.

fotográrifo, adj. photographic.

fotógrafo, s.m. photographer.

fotogravura, s.f. photo-engraving.

fotolitografia, s.f. photolitography.

fotometria, s.f. photometry.

fotómetro, s.m. photometer.

fotosfera, s.f. photosphere.

fotossíntese, s.f. photosynthesis.

foz, s.f. mouth.

fracalhão, s.f. weakling, coward; adj. faint-hearted.

fracassado, adj. unsuccessful.

fracassar, v.t. e v.i. to fail, to miscarry; to go wrong; to flop, to flunk.

fracasso, s.m. failure, collapse, miscarriage; flop.

fracção, s.f. fraction.

fraccionamento, s.m. breaking up.

fraccionar, v.t. to divide into fractions; to parcel, to break up.

fraccionário, adj. fractional.

fraccionável, adj. fractionable.

fraco, adj. weak, feeble, frail; delicate; faint, dim; poor *(medíocre);* *ter um fraco (por alguém ou por alguma coisa),* to have a crush on.

fractura, s.f. fracture, break; *(geol.)* fault.

fracturar, v.t. to fracture, to break.

frade, s.m. monk, friar.

fradesco, adj. monkish, monklike.

fraga, s.f. crag, rock, cliff.

fragata, s.f. frigate; *(zool.)* frigate bird.

fragateiro, s.m. boatman.

frágil, adj. fragile; weak, delicate.

fragilidade, s.f. fagility, frailty; weakness.

fragmentação, s.f. fragmentation.

fragmentar, v.t. to break up, to shatter, to break to pieces; *fragmentar-se,* to crumble, to break up.

fragmentário, adj. fragmentary.

fragmento, s.m. fragment, piece; scrap; fraction.

fragor, *s.m.* din, crash; roar.

fragoroso, *adj.* noisy, clamorous.

fragosidade, *s.f.* cragginess, craggedness.

fragoso, *adj.* craggy, cragged.

fragrância, *s.f.* fragrance, fragrancy.

fragrante, *adj.* fragrant, sweet-scented, sweet-smelling.

fralda, *s.f.* tail, shirttail *(de camisa);* diaper *(de bebé);* foot *(de monte).*

fraldejar, *v.t.* to flap.

fraldiqueiro, *adj.* effeminate.

framboesa, *s.f.* raspberry.

francamente, *adv.* frankly, openly, honestly.

franças, *s.f. pl.* tops.

francês, *adj.* French; *s.m.* Frenchman; French *(língua).*

francesismo, *s.m.* gallicism.

franciscano, *adj. e s.m.* Franciscan.

franco, *adj.* frank, sincere, open, staight-forward; honest; blunt; free of duties. 1) *porto-franco,* free port; *s.m.* franc *(moeda francesa).* 2) *franco-atirador,* sniper.

francófilo, *s.m.* Francophile.

franga, *s.f.* pullet.

frangalho, *s.m.* rag, tatter.

frangível, *adj.* frangible, breakable, brittle.

frango, *s.m.* chicken; cockerel.

franja, *s.f.* frinje; bang *(de cabelo).*

franjado, *adj.* fringed.

franjar, *v.t.* to frinje.

franquear, *v.t.* to throw open *(portas, etc.);* to give free entrance to *(lugar);* to clear *(caminho, etc.),* to exempt from duties, postage, *etc;* to frank, to reveal, to disclose.

franqueza, *s.f.* frankness, sincerity, staightforwardness; bluntness.

franquia, *s.f.* exemption (from duties, taxes, etc.); immunity; franchise; postage *(correio).*

franquiar, *v.t.* to stamp letters.

franzido, *adj.* plaited; shrunk; *s.m.* plaits, shirr.

franzino, *adj.* slender, thin; frail.

franzir, *v.t.* to plait, to shirr *(em costura);* to wrinkle *(o sobrolho);* to curl *(os lábios); franzir o sobrolho:* to wrinkle the forehead, to frown; *franzir-se,* to wrinkle; to knit.

fraque, *s.m.* cutway coat.

fraquear, fraquejar, *v.i.* to weaken, to grow weak; to flag; to give up.

fraqueza, *s.f.* weakness, feebleness, debility; frailty; infirmity; faintness; *sentir fraqueza,* to be starving, to be hungry.

frascário, *adj.* dissolute, lewd.

frasco, *s.m.* bottle; flask.

frase, *s.f.* phrase; sentence; *frase feita,* stock phrase, cliché.

fraseado, *s.m.* wording, phrasing, diction; style.

frasear, *v.i.* to phrase, to express in words.

fraseologia, *s.f.* phraseology.

frasqueira, *s.f.* cellaret.

fraternal, *adj.* fraternal.

fraternidade, *s.f.* fraternity; brotherhood.

fraternização, *s.f.* fraternization.

fraternizar, *v.i.* fraternization.

fraternizar, *v.i.* to fraternize.

fraterno, *adj.* fraternal.

fratricida, *s.m. e adj.* fratricide.

fratricídio, *s.m.* fratricide.

fraudador, *s.m.* defrauder; smuggle.

fraudar, *v.t.* to defraud, to cheat.

fraude, *s.f.* fraud, deceit, trickery; cheat; fake.

fraudulento, *adj.* fraudulent, dishonest, crooked, underhanded.

frecha, *s.f. o mesmo que "flecha".*

frechal, *s.m.* plate *(de telhado).*

freguês, *s.m.* customer, client; parishioner *(religião).*

freguesia, *s.f. (rel.)* parish; clientele, customers.

frei, *s.m.* friar.

freio, *s.m.* bridle; *(anat.)* fraenum; *(mec.)* brake; *tomar o freio nos dentes:* to take the bit between one's teeth.

freira, *s.f.* nun; sister.

freixo, *s.m.* ash.

fremente, *adj.* quivering; fluttering; tremulous; vibrating; roaring.

fremir, *v.i.* to roar; to quiver; to tremble; to flutter.

frémito, *s.m.* quivering; roaring; thrill.

frenesi, *s.m.* frenzy; fury; excitement; rapture.

frenético, *adj.* frantic, frenzied; raving.

frennologia, *s.f.* phrenology.

frenologista, *s.m.* phrenologist.

frente, *s.f.* front; face; frontage; façade. 1) *frente a frente,* face to face. 2) *à frente,* in front; at the front. 3) *em frente de,* in front of, facing, before. 4) *ir a frente,* to lead. 5) *fazer frente a,* to face. 6) *para a frente,* ahead, forward, onward.

frequência, *s.f.* frequency; commoness; attendance *(clientes); com frequência,* often, frequently.

frequentador, *s.m.* frequenter, attender.

frequentar, *v.t.* to frequent; common, habitual.

fresca, *s.f.* cool breeze.

fresco, *adj.* cool; breezy; new, fresh, recent; new-laid *(ovos)*; crisp *(pão)*, wet *(tinta)*; *s.m..* 1) *fresco*, painting *(pintura).* 2) *ao fresco*, in the open air. 3) *ir tomar fresco*, to go for an airing. 4) *pôr-se ao fresco*, to take to one's heels, to beat it.

frescor, *s.m. o mesmo que "frescura".*

frescura, *s.f.* coolness; freshness; crispness.

fressura, *s.f.* pluck and tripe.

fresta, *s.f.* loophole; gap, aperture; cranny.

fretador, *s.m.* freighter.

fretamento, *s.m.* freightage.

fretar, *v.t.* to freight, to charter.

frete, *s.m.* freight, freightage; transportation; cargo.

friabilidade, *s.f.* friability.

friagem, *s.f.* cold; chill; coldness.

friável, *adj.* friable, crumbly.

fricassé, *s.m.* fricassee.

fricativa, *s.f.* cricative consonant.

fricativo, *adj.* fricative.

fricção, *s.f.* friction, rubbing; massage.

friccionar, *v.t.* to rub; to massage.

frieira, *s.f.* chilblain.

frieza, *s.f.* coldness; chilliness; coollness, indifference; frigidity.

frigideira, *s.f.* frying pan.

frigidez, *s.f.* frigidity, frigidness, iciness.

frígido, *adj.* frigid; chilling; icy.

frigir, *v.t.* to fry.

frigorificar, *v.t.* to freeze, to refrigerate.

frigorífico, *s.m.* freezer, refrigerator.

frincha, *s.f.* crack, chink, cranny; slit; crevice.

frio, *s.m.* cold, chill; *adj.* cold; frigid; lifeless; cool, indifferent. 1) *morrer de frio*, to freeze to death. 2) *ter frio*, to be cold.

frioleira, *s.f.* nonsense, silly remark; triffle; nothing.

friorento, *adj.* sensitive cold.

frisa, *s.f.* frieze *(tecido);* lower box *(no teatro).*

frisador, *s.m.* curling iron.

frisante, *adj.* significant; striking.

frisar, *v.t.* to frizzle, to curl; to emphasize.

friso, *s.m. (arquit.)* frieze.

fritada, *s.m.* dish of fried fish.

fritar, *v.t.* to fry.

frito, *adj.* fried; *estar frito (pop.):* to be done for.

fritura, *s.f.* fritter.

frivolidade, *s.f.* frivolity, futility, trifle.

frívolo, *adj.* frivolous, futile, trifling.

fronde, *s.f.* frond, foliage.

frondejante, *adj.* leafy, thick-foliaded.

frondejar, *v.t. e v.i.* to burst into leaf, to grow a foliage.

frondoso, *adj.* thick-foliage, leafy, frondose.

fronha, *s.f.* pillow-case.

frontal, *adj.* frontal; *s.m.* frontalet; frontal bone *(osso).*

frontão, *s.m.* pediment.

frontaria, *s.f.* façade, frontispiece.

fronte, *s.f.* forehead, brow, front.

fronteira, *s.f.* frontier, border; limits, boundary, line.

fronteiriço, *adj.* frontier, bordering; *linha fronteiriça*, border line.

fronteiro, *adj.* facing, opposite.

frontispício, *s.m.* frontispiece *(de casa);* title page *(de livro).*

frota, *s.f.* fleet.

frouxel, *s.m.* down; fluff *(lanugem).*

frouxidão, *s.f.* looseness; slackness; remissness.

frouxo, *adj.* loose; slack; flalbby; spiritless; cowardly; lax, remiss; dull, inactive; glimmering *(luz).*

frufru, *s.m.* rustling.

frugal, *adj.* frugal; economical; moderate.

frugalidade, *s.f* frugality, frugalness.

fruição, *s.f.* fruition, enjoyment.

fruir, *v.t.* to enjoy; *v.i.* to feel enjoyment.

frustração, *s.f.* frustration; defeat; disappointment.

frustrado, *adj.* frustrated; unsuccessful.

frustrar, *v.t.* to frustrate, to thwart, to counteract; to foil, to disappointment; to defeat; *frustrar-se*, to fail.

fruta, *s.f.* fruit.

fruteira, *s.f.* fruit basket.

fruteiro, *s.m.* fruiterer; fruit vender.

fruticultor, *s.m.* fruitgrower.

fruticultura, *s.f* fruitgrowing.

frutífero, *adj.* fruit-bearing; fruitful.

frutificar, *v.t.* to bear fruit; to be fruitful.

fruto, *s.m.* fruit; product, result; effect; profit.

frutuoso, *adj.* fruitful; profitable, useful.

fúcsia, *s.f.* fuchsia.

fuga, *s.f.* flight; escape; elopement *(de namorados);* *(mús.)* fugue; *(eléct. e mec.)* leak; *pôr-se em fuga*, to take to one's heels.

fugacidade, *s.f.* transiency, transitoriness.

fugaz, *adj.* fugitive, transitory, fleeting, ephemeral.

fugida, *s.f.* flight; escape; *de fugida:* on passing, hurriedly.

fugidio, *adj. o mesmo que "fugaz".*

fugir, *v.i.* to flee, to fly, to escape, to run away; to elope *(namorados);* to evade; to shun, to avoid *(esquivar-se);* to slip from *(da memória).*

fugitivo, *adj.* e *s.m.* fugitive, runaway.

fuinha, marten.

fulano, *s.m.* Mr. So-and-So.

fulcro, *s.m.* fulcrum; support.

fulgência, *s.f.* effulgence.

fulgente, *adj.* effulgent, refulgent, resplendent.

fúlgido, *adj.* o mesmo que "fulgente".

fulgir, *v.i.* to shine, to radiate; to be conspicuous.

fulgor, *s.m.* fulgency, splendor, effulgence; radiance; glare.

fulguração, *s.f.* flash of lightning; flashing.

fulgurante, *adj.* flashing, resplendent.

fulgurar, *v.i.* to shine; to flash; to glow; to coruscate.

fuligem, *s.f.* soot; grime, smut.

fuliginoso, *adj.* sooty.

fulminação, *s.f.* fulmination.

fulminado, *adj.* struck by lightning; thunderstruck.

fulminante, *adj.* fulminating; scathing, withering.

fulminar, *v.t.* to fulminate, to strike or kill by lightning; to destroy, to blast; to apall, to petrify.

fulminato, *s.m.* fulminate.

fulo, *adj.* furious, very angry.

fulvo, *adj.* fulvous, tawny.

fumaça, *s.f.* smoke; fume; puff of smoke.

fumaceira, *s.f.* a great deal of smoke.

fumador, *s.m.* smoker.

fumagem, *s.f.* fumage; smoking *(de carnes).*

fumar, *v.t.* e *v.i.* to smoke.

fumarada, *s.f.* a great deal of smoke.

fumarento, *adj.* smoky.

fumeganta, *adj.* smoking, steaming, fuming.

fumegar, *v.i.* to smoke, to steam.

fumeiro, *s.m.* chimney.

fumigação, *s.f.* fumigation.

fumigar, *v.i.* to fumigate.

fumo, *s.m.* smoke; vapour, fume; tobacco; crape.

fumoso, *adj.* smoky.

funambolismo, *s.m.* ropewalking, funambulism.

funâmbulo, *s.m.* funambulist, ropewalker.

função, *s.f.* function; role, office, duty; performance *(teatral, etc.);* celebration *(festividade);* em função de, in terms of.

funcho, *s.m.* fennel.

funcional, *adj.* functional.

funcionalismo, *s.m.* public servants; civil service.

funcionamento, *s.m.* functioning, operation, working; *pôr em funcionamento,* to put in motion.

funcionar, *v.i.* to function; to operate, to work, to run.

funcionário, *s.m.* officeholder; employee, clerk; *funcionário público,* civil servant.

funda, *s.f.* sling; truss *(para hérnia).*

fundação, *s.f.* foundation; fouding, establishment; basis; endowment; institution.

fundador, *s.m.* founder.

fundamental, *adj.* fundamental; basic; vital; essential; elemental.

fundamento, *s.m.* foundation, grounds, basis, support; motive; *sem fundamento,* groundless, unfounded.

fundar, *v.t.* to found, to establish, to institute; to build; to base, to ground (on something); *fundar-se,* to base oneself; to be based, to rest (on something).

fundear, *v.i.* to cast anchor.

fundeadouro, *s.m.* anchorage.

fundente, *adj.* melting.

fundição, *s.m.* melting, fusion *(processo);* foundry, ironworks *(estabelecimento).*

fundido, *adj.* molten; cast *(ferro, aço).*

fundidor, *s.m.* melter, caster; foundryman.

fundilho, *s.m.* seat.

fundir, *v.t.* to melt, to cast; to fuse, to liquefy; to merge, to blend, to amalgamate; *fundir--se,* to fuse, to melt; to merge.

fundível, *adj.* fusible.

fundo, *s.m.* bottom; depths; depth, profundity; fund, capital; back *(parte traseira);* background *(pano de fundo).* 1) *fundos,* funds, stocks; capital; *adj.* deep; profound. 2) *fundo comum,* pool. 3) *fundo de cena,* backdrop. 4) *fundos públicos,* public funds. 5) *artigo de fundo,* leading article.

fúnebre, *adj.* funeral; mournful; lugubrious, sepulcral.

funeral, *s.m.* funeral, obsequies, burial.

funerário, *adj.* funerary, mortuary; *casa funerária,* undertaker's.

funéreo, *adj.* funeral, funereal; gloomy.

funesto, *adj.* fatal, fateful; disastrous, ruinous.

fungar, *v.t.* to sniff, to sniffle, to snuffle.

fungicida, *s.f.* fungicide.

fungo, *s.m.* fungus.

fungosidade, *s.f.* fungosity.

funicular, *adj.* funicular.

funil, *s.m.* funnel.

funileiro, *s.m.* tin-man, tinker.

fura-bolos, *s.m.* forefinger.

furacão, *s.m.* hurricane, tornado.

furado, *adj.* bored, pierced.

furador, *s.m.* perforator, borer; bradawl.

fura-greves, *s.m.* strikebreaker, scab.

furão, *s.m.* ferret.

furar, *v.t.* to bore, to perforate; to punch, to puncture; to pierce; *furar uma greve,* to break to strike, to scab.

furgão, *s.m.* van.

furgoneta, *s.f.* delivery van.

fúria, *s.f.* fury, rage, wrath; impetuosity, fierceness, violence; *as Fúrias, (mit.)* the Furies.

furibundo, *adj.* furious, enraged.

furioso, *adj.* furious, enraged; mad (at someone).

furna, *s.f.* cave, den, cavern.

furo, *s.m.* hole, perforation; orifice; scoop *(jornalístico).*

furor, *s.m.* furor, fury; frenzy; *fazer furor:* to be the rage.

furriel, *s.m.* lance-corporal.

furta-cor, *s.m.* shot colour; *adj.* irridescent.

furtadela, *s.f.* stealth purloining, pilfering; as furtadelas: stealthily.

furtar, *v.t.* to steal (from someone); to pinch, to pilfer, to purloin; *furtar-se,* to avoid, to shun; to shirk; to dodge.

furtivo, *adj.* furtive, stealthy surreptitious; secret.

furto, *s.m.* theft, larceny; thieving.

furúnculo, *s.m.* furuncle, boil.

furunculose, *s.f.* furunculosis.

fusa, *(mús.),* demi-semiquaver.

fusão, *s.f.* fusion, melting; blnding; liquefaction; coalition.

fusco, *adj.* brown, dark, dusky.

fuselagem, *s.f.* fuselage.

fusibilidade, *s.f.* fusibility.

fusiforme, *adj.* fusiform, spindle-shaped.

fusível, *adj.* fusible; *s.m.* fuse.

fuso, *s.m.* spindle; *fuso horário,* time zone.

fustão, *s.m.* fustian, dimity.

fuste, *s.m.* shaft.

fustigação, *s.f.* thrashing

fustigar, *v.t.* to flog, to thrash, to lash, to whip; to cane; to chatize.

futebol, *s.m.* soccer; football *(americano).*

futebolista, *s.m.* soccer player; football player.

fútil, *adj.* futile, trivial, petty; trifling, frivolous.

futilidade, *s.f.* futility; vainness; trifle; frivolity.

futurismo, *s.m.* futurism.

futurista, *s.m.* e *adj.* futurist.

futuro, *s.m.* future; time to come; *(gram.)* future tense; *adj.* future; to be next; to come; prospective.

futuroso, *adj.* promising, hopeful.

fuzil, *s.m.* link *(elo);* rifle *(arma);* steel *(de fazer fogo);* flash of lightening *(relâmpago).*

fuzilamento, *s.m.* execution by shooting; shooting.

fuzilante, *adj.* flashing, shooting.

fuzilar, *v.t.* to shoot dead, to execute by shooting; *v.i.* to flash.

fuzilaria, *s.f.* fusilade; musketry; shooting.

fuzilante, *adj.* flashing, shooting.

fuzilar, *v.t.* to shoot dead, to execute by shooting; *v.i.* to flash.

fuzilaria, *s.f.* fusilade; musketry; shooting.

fuzileiro, *s.m.* rifleman; *fuzileiro naval,* marine.

fuzilhão, *s.m.* tongue *(de fivela).*

G

g, the seventh letter of the Portuguese alphabet.

gabação, gabadela, *s.f.* boast, praising, eulogy, commendation.

gabador, *s.m.* adj. boaster, praiser, commender; bragging, boastful.

gabamento, *s.m.* praising, laudation, commendation; boasting.

gabão, s.m. cloak; praiser; boaster; eulogy.

gabar, v.t. praise, to laud, to eulogize; to flatter, to cajole; *gabar-se de,* to boast of *(acerca),* to brag, to show off; to pride oneself on.

gabardina, s.f. gabardine *(roupa);* raincoat, waterproof.

gabardo, s.m. a hooded cloak.

gabarola, s.m. boaster, braggart, swaggerer, self-praiser.

gabarolar, v.i. to boast, to brag, to talk big.

gabarolice, s.f. boasting, swank, brag.

gabela, s.f. sheaf, handful, bunch.

gabião, s.f. gabion; vintage-basket; hamper.

gabinardo, s.m. gaberdine; scoundrel *(pop.)*

gabinete, s.m. cabinet, office; study room, private room, consulting room; ministry, body of ministers. 1) *gabinete de leitura,* reading room. 2) *o gabinete delibera,* the cabinet decides. 3) *gabinete do director,* manager's room. 4) *gabinete de imprensa,* editorial office.

gabiru, s.m. scoundrel, crook.

gabo, s.m. praise, eulogy; boasting; vanity.

gadanha, s.f. scythe; reaping hoop; soup ladle; hand *(pop.).*

gadanhada, s.f. stroke with the scythe; grasping with the claws.

gadanhar, v.t. to scythe, to reap, to seize with the claw.

gadanheira, s.f. reaper, reaping machine.

gadanho, s.m. claw, talon; pitchfork; finger hand *(pop).*

gaditano, s.m., adj. a native of Cadiz.

gado, s.m. cattle, livestock, herd, flock. 1) *criação de gado,* cattle raising; stock farming. 2) *gado asinino,* mules and donkeys. 3) *gado bovino,* oxen. 4) *gado bravo,* wild cattle. 5) *gado cavalar,* horses. 6) *gado suíno,* swine.

gaélico, adj., s.m. Gaelic *(língua ou habitantes).*

gafa, s.f. gaff; hook; leprosy.

gafado, adj. infected with scabies, mange, mildew or rot.

gafanhoto, s.m. locust, grasshopper, jumper.

gafar, v.t. to infect with mange or leprosy; to contaminate.

gafaria, s.f. hospital for lepers.

gafe, s.f. blunder, involuntary indiscretion; *cometer uma gafe,* to commit a faux-pas; to put one's foot in one's mouth, to drop a brick.

gafeira, s.f. mange; rot.

gafeirento, gafeiroso, gafento, adj. infected with scabies, itch or mange, leprous.

gafo, adj. leprous, mangy; contaminated, corrupt.

gaforina, s.f. dishevelled hair; curled hair *(negros).*

gagá, adj. decrepit, doting.

gago, s.m., adj. stammerer, falterer, stutterer; stammering, faltering, stuttering; *ver-se gago,* to be embarrassed.

gaguejar, v.i. to stammer, to stutter, to falter (num discurso); to hum and haw.

gaguez, stammering, stuttering.

gaiatada, s.f. gang of urchins, young scamps; prank, escapade, mischievous trick.

gaiatice, s.f. mischief, knavery, roguishness.

gaiato, s.m., adj. urchin, boy, young scamp; wag; gay, joyous, merry; roguish.

gaifona, gaifonice, s.f. face, grimace, antic, monkey pranks.

gaio, adj., s.m. bright; light, gay, jovial, merry, cheerful; jay *(pássaro).*

gaiola, s.f. cage; prison, jail *(fig.);* frame of a building; crate; elevator box; small lodgings.

gaioleiro, s.m. cage-maker or seller.

gaiolim, s.m. small cage *(para pássaros).*

gaiolo, s.m. bird's snare or trap.

gaita, s.f. pipe, reed, flute; mouth organ, harmonica; any worthless thing; *ir-se à gaita,* to fail, to come to nothing.

gaitada, s.f. blowing of a tune on a pipe or flute; rebuke, upbraiding *(pop.)*

gaita-de-foles, s.f. bagpipe.

gaitear, v.i. to play on a pipe, mouth-organ or flute.

gaiteirice, s.f. foppishness, foppery, smartness.

gaiteiro, s.m., adj. bag-piper; playful, lively, smart, merry, gay.

gaiuta, s.f. companion.

gaivina, s.f. tern, sea swallow.

gaivota, s.f. sea-gull, gull.

gajeiro, s.m. topman, lookout-man, topwatch.

gajo, s.m. bloke, chap, guy *(pop.);* rogue

gala, s.f. pomp, show, ornament; gala; festive dress, formal dress; national festivity; rejoicing, delight; treadle *(de um ovo).* 1) *fazer gala de,* to show off, to pride oneself on. 2) *uniforme de gala,* full-dress uniform. 3) *vestido de gala,* gala dress, court-dress.

galã, s.m. gallant, beau, lover, suitor; leading man *(numa peça ou num filme).*

galactite, *s.f.* galactite.

galadura, *s.f.* gallature, tread.

galanice, *s.f.* elegance, smartness, gracefulness, gallantry, courteous, manners.

galantaria, *s.f.* gallantry, flattery, genteelness, courteous behaviour.

galante, *adj.* gallant, gaceful; gay; well dressed, handsome, gentle, courtly, polite.

galanteador, *s.m., adj.* gallant, beau, lover, suitor, philanderer; gallant, courteous, polite; flattering.

galantear, *v.t.* to court, to woo, to make love to; to flatter.

galanteio, *s.m.* gallantry, courtship, courtesy, flattering remark (*a uma senhora*).

galantemente, *adv.* gallantly, politely, courteously.

galantina, *s.f.* galantine (*de fígado de galinha*).

galão, *s.m.* lace; gallon (*medida*); stripe (militar); gallon, braid, trimming; glass of white coffee; *galão imperial,* imperial (ou British) gallon (4,55 l).

galapo, *s.m.* saddle-pad, bandage, ligature.

galar, *v.t.* to tread, to cover (*pássaros*).

galardão, *s.m.* reward, prize, recompense; glory, honour.

galardoador, *s.m.* rewarder, awarder.

galardoar, *v.t.* to reward, to recompense.

galarim, *s.m.* pinnacle of glory, highest point, top, summit; influence, opulence; power.

galáxia, *s.f.* galaxy; the milk way.

galdrope, *s.m.* tiller rope.

galé, *s.f., s.m.* galley (*barco*); printer's galley; galley slave; forced labour (*pl.*); *condenar às galés,* to send to the galleys.

galeão, *s.m.* galleon; compositor's board.

galegada, *s.f.* many Galicians; coarseness; disrespect, vulgar expression.

galego, *s.m., adj.* Galician, boor, uncouth or uneducated fellow.

galena, *s.f.* galena, lead-glance.

galénico, *adj.* Galenical.

galenismo, *s.m.* Galenism.

galeno, *s.m.* a physician.

galeota, *s.f.* galliot, small galley.

galeote, *s.m.* galley-slave, convict; small galley.

galera, *s.f.* lorry, truck, freight-car; galley (*com dois ou três mastros*); fire wagon, foundry furnace.

galeria, *s.f.* gallery, arcade, colonnades; corridor; collection of works of art; gallery in a theatre; covered porch; tunnel; the spectators in a gallery; *dirigir-se à galeria,* to play to the gallery.

galês, *adj.* Welsh (*língua ou habitante*).

galezia, *s.f.* rascality; cheat; roguery; fraud.

galfarro, *s.m.* glutton, voracious, greedy person.

galga, *s.f.* greyhound bitch; lie, fib (*pop.*); mill stone in an olive oil press.

galgar, *v.t.* to jump; to cross; to spring, to leap over (*obstáculos*); to leave behind (*correndo*); to attain; to reach, to arrive at; to cover a distance.

galgo, *s.m.* greyhound, harrier, courser.

galha, *s.f.* gall, gallnut.

galhada, *s.f.* antlers; branches.

galhardamente, *adv.* gracefully; gallantly, bravely.

galhardear, *v.t., i.* to show off, to make a display, to exibit, to parade; to shine, to excel; to show courage.

galhardete, *s.m.* pennant, streamer, banderole, banner.

galhardia, *s.f.* grace, elegance, gallantry.

galhardo, *adj.* genteel, generous, gallant, chivalrous; brave; courageous.

galhas, *s.f.pl.* antlers; horns; branches.

galheta, *s.f.* burette; cruet, vial; slap (*pop*).

galheteiro, *s.m.* cruet-stand, caster.

galho, *s.m.* horn, branch (*de árvores*), arm, twig, offshoot, bough.

galhofa, *s.f.* frolic, mirth, merriment, antics, fun; jest, joke; friksness.

galhofa, *v.i.* to frolic; to jest, to joke, to make merry; to poke fun at, to make fun of.

galhofeiro, *adj., s.m.* frolicsome, jesting, merry, playful, jovial; merry-maker, wag, jester, frolicker.

galhudo, *adj.* branchy, beamy; antlered, pronged.

galicismo, *s.m.* Galicism.

galicista, *s.* gallicizer.

gálico, *adj.* Gallic; gallic acid; Gallic (*nativo da Gália em França*).

galileu, *s.m.; adj.* Galilean.

galináceo, *adj., s.m.* gallinaceous; a gallinacean.

galinha, *s.f.* hen, chicken, fowl; titbit (*pop*); ill luck, misfortune. 1) *galinha choca,* brooding hen. 2) *galinha poedeira,* layer. 3) *pele de galinha,* goose-flesh.

galinheiro, *s.m.* poultry-yard, hen house, chicken coop, pen; poultry dealer, poulterer.

galinhola, *s.f.* woodcock, snipe, gallinule.

galispo, *s.m.* sockalorum, a little cock.

galo, *s.m.* cock, rooster; a lump on the head, bump, protuberance. 1) *ao cantar do galo*, at dawn, at daybreak, very early. 2) *cantar de galo em casa*, to be the master at home. 3) *crista de galo*, cock's comb. 4) *missa do galo*, Christmas night mass *(à meia-noite)*. 5) *outro galo me cantaria se...*, I should be better off if..., things would be different.

galocha, *s.f.* galosh; overshoe.

galopada, *s.f.* gallopade, riding at a gallop, galloping run.

galopador, *s.m.* galloper.

galopante, *adj.* galloping.

galopar, *v.t., v.i.* to gallop, to ride at a gallop; to move very fast.

galope, *s.m.* gallop, rapidity, haste, hurry. 1) *a galope*, at a gallop. 2) *a todo o galope*, at full gallop. 3) *a meio galope*, canter.

galopim, *s.m.* errand boy, street-boy, messenger, canvasser, electioneer.

galopinagem, *s.f.* canvassing, electioneering.

galopinar, *v.i.* to tout (for votes).

galrar, *v.i.* to prattle, to babble; to boast, to brag.

galreador, *s.m., adj.* talker, prattler, tattler; prattling.

galrear, *v.i.* to babble, to prattle *(como as crianças)*.

galucho, *s.m.* raw recruit; beginner *(no exército)*.

galvânico, *adj.* galvanic, voltaic.

galvanismo, *s.m.* galvanism.

galvanização, *s.f.* galvanization.

galvanizador, *s.m., adj.* galvanizer; galvanizing.

galvanizar, *v.t.* to galvinize, to plate; to excite, to stimulate.

galvanografia, *s.f.* galvanography.

galvanómetro, *s.m.* galvanometer.

galvanoplastia, *s.f.* galvanplasty.

gama, *s.f.* gamut, scale; range or series *(de ideias ou tamanhos); raios gama*, gamma rays.

gamacismo, *s.m.* gammacism, guttural stammering.

gamado, *adj.* hook-shaped, hooked; *cruz gamada*, swastika, gammadion

gamão, *s.m.* backgammon *(jogo)*.

gamarra, *s.f.* martingale; checkrein.

gamba, *s.f.* bass viol.

gambarra, *s.f.* two-masted cattle barge.

gambérria, *s.f.* a tripping up *(de outra pessoa)*; trick, fraud; quarrel, dispute.

gâmbia, *s.f.* leg *(pop)*; *dar às gâmbias*, to run away.

gambiarra, *s.f.* stage lights, foot lights.

gambito, *s.m.* gambit *(xadrez)*; feint, trick.

gamboa, *s.f.* quince *(fruto)*.

gamboeiro, *s.m.* quince-tree.

gamela, *s.f.* wooden bowl, trough, porringer, tray, wooden trough.

gamelada, *s.f.* troughful.

gamelão, *s.m.* a large trough.

gâmeta, *s.f.* gamete.

gamo, *s.m.* fallow-deer; stag, buck.

gamopétalo, *adj.* gamopetalous.

gamossépalo, *adj.* gamosepalous.

gana, *s.f.* desire, wish, craving; hate, spite, rancour; hunger, appetite; *ter gana a alguém*, to be enraged at someone.

ganadaria, *s.f.* cattle raising *(para touros)*.

ganância, *s.f.* ambition, covetousness, greed, greediness, rapacity, usury.

ganancioso, *adj., s.m.* covetous, ambitious, greedy, avaricious; greedy fellow *(por dinheiro)*.

gancho, *s.m.* hook; hair-pin; grapple, crook, cramp, clasp; part-time job. 1) *ir a gancho*, to go to jail. 2) *tirar a gancho*, to get something with difficulty.

gandaia, *s.f.* idleness, loose living, vagrancy, dissolute life, rag picking or gathering; *andar na gandaia*, to lead an idle or dissolute life.

gandaiar, *v.i.* to loiter, to loaf about, to roam, to gad about.

gandaieiro, *s.m.* vagrant, vagabond, loafer, idler; ragpicker.

gândara, *s.f.* sandy land, wasteland; moor.

ganga, *s.f.* gangue *(de minerais)*; cotton cloth, jean; *ganga azul*, denim.

gânglio, *s.m.* ganglion.

ganglionar, *adj.* ganglionic, ganglial.

gangrena, *s.f.* gangrene, necrosis; cause of destruction *(fig.)*.

gangrenar, *v.t., v.i.* to gangrene, to become gangrenous; to pervert, to corrupt; to be seized with gangrene.

gangrenoso, *adj.* gangrenous.

ganhança, *s.f.* greed for gain, gain profit, lucre.

ganhão, *s.m.* day labourer, journey man, woorkman.

ganha-pão, *s.m.* means of living, livelyhood, bread.

ganhar, *v.t.* to gain, to obtain, to reach, to get, to earn, to win, to acquire; to prevail, to succeed; to vanquish. to get the better of; to profit. 1) *ganhar a partida*, to win the game. 2) *ganhar a vida*, to earn (to make) a living, to keep the pot boiling. 3) *ganhar juízo*, to get sense. 4) *ganhar tempo*, to stall for time. 5) *ganhar terreno*, to gain ground. 6) *ganhar uma aposta*, to win a bet.

ganho, *s.m., adj.* gain, profit, earning, lucre; gained, acquired, won, earned.

ganhuça, *s.f.* profit, gain *(pop).*

ganido, *s.m.* bark, yelp, whine, yelping, howling.

ganir, *v.i.* to yelp, to bark, to whine, to howl.

ganso, *s.m.* goose, gander.

garagem, *s.f.* garage.

garagista, *s.m. e f.* garageman, garage-woman.

garanhão, *s.m.* stallion, steed, studhorse.

garante, *s.* warrantor, guarantee.

garantia, *s.f.* guarantee, warrant, security, surety, bond; assurance.

garantir, *v.t.* to warrant, to shield, to protect; to guarantee, to vouch for, to avow; to secure; to affirm, to assure.

garatuja, *s.f.* scrawl, scribble, doodle; a grimace.

garatujar, *v.t.* to scribble, to scrawl, to doodle.

garavato, gravato, *s.m.* hook, pole with a hook *(para apanhar frutos);* faggot, dry brushwood.

garbo, *s.m.* garb, countenance, gallantry, distinction, gacefulness; dignity, nobility.

garbosidade, *s.f.* elegance, garb, gracefulness; gallantry, valour.

garboso, *adj.* genteel, graceful, elegant, smart; brave, courageous.

garça, *s.f.* heron.

garço, *adj.* bluish-green, light-blue.

gardénia, *s.f.* gardenia.

gare, *s.f.* railway-station *(plataforma).*

garfada, *s.f.* forkful.

garfo, *s.m.* fork; a saddle graft *(de palnatas).* 1) *almoçar de garfo*, to take a substancial meal. 2) *ser um bom garfo*, to be a hearty eater, to play a good knife and fork.

gargalhada, *s.f.* burst of laughter, laughter, horse-laugh, guffaw.

gargalhar, *v.t.* to laugh loudly, to guffaw.

gargalheira, *s.f.* neck chain *(para escravos),* fetter; dog collar oppression *(fig).*

gargalo, *s.m.* neck *(de uma garrafa),* bottleneck.

garganta, *s.f.* throat; gullet; narrow pass, ravine, desfile; boaster, braggart; voice. 1) *ter boa garganta*, to have a fine voice. 2) *estar com a corda na garganta*, to be hardpressed for money. 3) *ter dores de garganta*, to have a sore throat. 4) *estar pela garganta*, to be fed up.

gargantear, *v.t.* to make roulades; to warble, to trill, to quaver; to brag, to boast, to bluster, to talk big *(pop).*

garganteio, *s.m.* trill, quavering *(voz),* warble.

gargantilha, *s.f.* necklace, collar. neckband.

gargarejar, *v.i.* to gargle, to rinse the throat; to court, to make love *(pop).*

gargarejo, *s.m.* gargle, gargling; courting.

gárgula, *s.f.* gargoyle, water-spout.

garimpagem, *s.f.* prospecting *(ouro, diamantes).*

garimpar, *v.i.* to search for diamonds or gold.

garimpeiro, *s.m.* diamond or gold prospector.

garimpo, *s.m.* diamond mine, gold fields.

garlopa, *s.f.* trying-plane, jointer plane, lack-plane.

garnacha, *s.f.* gown *(dos juízes ou padres).*

garnacho, *s.m.* cloak

garnisé, *s.m.* bantam *(galinha).*

garotada, garotagem, *s.f.* group of young-sters.

garotice, *s.f.* boy's mischief, waggery; pranks.

garoto, *s.m., adj.* boy, lad, urchin, youngster, kid, teen-ager; mischievous, roguish, waggish.

garoupa, *s.f.* grouper.

garra, *s.f.* claw, talon, pounce; nail, fingernail, finger, hand, paw, foot; clutch, grab, fang; *estar nas garras de alguém*, to be in somebody's clutches.

garrafa, *s.f.* bottle, flask. 1) *garrafa térmica*, thermos bottle, hot-water bottle. 2) *garrafa de Leyde*, Leyden jar.

garrafal, *adj.* round, big; bottleshaped.

garrafão, *s.m.* demijohn, carboy; large bottle.

garrafeira, *s.f.* wine-cellar, cellaret.

garraiada, *s.f.* bullock-fight; a lot of bullocks.

garraio, *s.m.* bullok; greenhorn, inexpe-rienced man *(fig.)*

garrano, *s.m.* nag, a sturdy pony; a rogue.

garrar, *v.i.* to drift, to float *(barco);* to drag the anchor.

garridamente, *adv.* gracefully, foppishly, ostentatiously.

garridice, garridismo, *s.f., s.m.* elegance, smartness, dressiness; dandysm, foppery.

garrido, *adj.* showy, elegant, gay, bright-coloured; smart, dressy; dandyish, foppish.

garrocha, *s.f.* goad, goad stick.

garrochada, *s.f.* jab with a goad stick.

garrochar, *v.t.* to prick (with a goad), to prod, to goad.

garrotar, *v.t.* to garrotte, to execute with garrotte.

garrote, *s.m.* garrotte.

garrotilho, *s.m.* croup.

garrular, *v.i.* to gabble, to prattle, to cackle, to chat.

garrulice, *s.f.* garrulity, loquacity, prattle, cackel.

gárrulo, *adj.*, *s.m.* garrulous, loquacious, talkative; chatterbox, cackler.

garupa, buttocks; croup, hindquarters, crupper *(de um cavalo).*

gás, *s.m.* animation, liveliness; flatulence, windiness. 1) *gás carbónico,* carbonic-acid gas. 2) *gás de iluminação,* illuminating gas. 3) *gás hilariante,* laughing gas. 4) *gás lacrimogéneo,* tear gas.

gasalhar, *v.t.* to shelter, to lodge; to warm; to welcome; to wrap up.

gasalho, *s.m.* lodging, shelter; kind reception; warm clothes, wrapper.

gascão, *s.m.*, *adj.* Gascon; gascon, boaster, braggart.

gasconada, *s.f.* gasconade, boasting, bravado.

gasear, *v.t.* to gasify, to gas.

gaseificação, *s.f.* gasification, transformation into gas.

gaseificar, *v.t.* gasify.

gaseificável, *adj.* gasifiable.

gaseiforme, *adj.* gasiform.

gasganete, *s.m.* throat, gullet; neck.

gasogénio, *s.m.* gasogene.

gasolina, *s.f.* petrol; gas, gasoline (USA); a motor boat; *bomba de gasolina,* petrol pump, filling station, gasoline pump (USA).

gasómetro, *s.m.* gasometer.

gasosa, *s.f.* soda, soda water, soda lemonade.

gasoso, *s.f. adj.* gaseous, gassy.

gáspea, *s.f.* vamp *(de um sapato).*

gaspeadeira, *s.f.* woman who sews the uppers *(de um sapato).*

gaspear, *v.t.* to vamp, to provide with vamps.

gastador, *s.m.*, *adj.* spendthrift; waster, prodigal, squanderer, dissipater; prodigal, wasteful, lavish.

gastar, *v.t.* to spend; to expend; to waste; to wear out, to consume; to reduce in size; to decay; to use, to employ; to dissipate, to squander; to efface, to blot out; to exhaust. 1) *gastar-se,* to wear oneself out, to get worn out; to sell well, to be in vogue; to become spoiled. 2) *gastar cera com ruim defunto,* to pay for a dead horse, to throw pearls before swine. 3) *gastar à larga, à toa,* to fritter away, to spend money lavishly. 4) *gastar palavras,* to speak in vain, to waste words. 5) *gastar o tempo,* to waste time.

gasto, *s.m.*, *adj.* wear; cost; expense; worn; spent; used up, exhausted; bare, threadbare; tired, decrepit.

gastralgia, *s.f.* gastralgia.

gástrico, *adj.* gastric. 1) *indisposição gástrica,* gastric upset. 2) *suco gástrico,* gastrice juice.

gastrite, *s.f.* gastritis.

gastroduodenite, *s.f.* gastroduodenitis.

gastrologia, *s.f.* gastrology

gastronomia, *s.f.* gastronomy, epicurism.

gastronómico, *adj.* gastronomical epicurean.

gastrónomo, *s.m.* gastronome, gourmet, epicure.

gastrópodes, *s.m. pl.* Gasteropoda.

gata, *s.f.* she-cat, pussy-cat; failure *(num exame);* low mizzen topsail *(náut.); andar de gatas,* to crawl on all fours.

gata-borralheira, *s.f.* Cinderella, a stay-at-home.

gatafunhos, *s.m. pl.* scrawls, scribblings.

gataria, *s.f.* great number of cats; too many failures *(num exame).*

gatear, *v.i.* to claw, to cramp, to fasten with clamps.

gateira, *s.f.*, *adj.* cat's hole in a door or in a wall for a cat to creep in or out; fond of cats

gaticida, *s.* cat-killer.

gatilho, *s.m.* trigger.

gatinhar, *v.i.* to go on all fours.

gatinhas, *s.f.pl.; andar de gatinhas,* to go on all fours, to creep, to crawl *(com as mãos e os joelhos).*

gato, *s.m.* cat, tom-cat; cramp, hook, clamp; misprint, mistake. 1) *gato escaldado da água fria tem medo,* a burnt child dreads the fire, a scalded cat dreads cold water. 2) *comer gato por lebre,* to buy a pig in a poke, to be cheated. 3) *vender gato por lebre,* to sell goods bricks. 4) *viver como o cão e o gato,* to live like a cat and a dog.

gatunagem, *s.f.* gang of thieves; robbery, thievery, pilferage.

gatunar, *v.i.* to steal, to pilfer, to finger.

gatunice, *s.f.* stealing, theft, pilferage.

gatuno, *s.m.* thief, pick-pocket, stealer, pilferer, robber.

gauchada, *s.f.* a lot of gauchos.

gaúcho, *s.m.* gaucho.

gáudio, *s.m.* pleasure, joy rejoicing, merrymaking, fun; mockery, hilariry.

gaulês, *adj., s.m.* Gaulish; Gaul.

gávea, *s.f.* top, round-top, topsail; *cesto de gávea*, crow's nest, round top of a master.

gavela, *s.f.* sheaf of corn or grain.

gaveta, *s.f.* drawer.

gavetão, *s.m.* large drawer.

gaveto, *s.m.* curved piece of wood; piece of ground at the corner of two streets.

gavião, *s.m.* sparrow-hawk

gavinha, *s.f.* clasper, tendril.

gavota, *s.f.* gavotte *(dança francesa)*.

gaze, *s.f.* gauze, chiffon, tissue.

gazeador, *s.m.* warbler, chirper, truant, runaway.

gazear, *v.i.* to play truant, to shirk *(uma lição ou trabalho)*; to loiter about; to chirp, to twitter.

gazela, *s.f.* gazelle.

gazeta, *s.f.* gazette; newspaper; truancy; *fazer gazeta*, to cut classes; to play truant.

gazetear, *v.i.* to play truant, to cut school; to loiter about.

gazeteiro, *s.m.* hack-writer; truant; newsboy.

gazetilha, *s.f.* section of a newspaper *(pessoas, notícias, aniversários, casamentos, etc.)*; also a satirical section.

gazetista, *s.* gazetteer.

gazua, *s.f.* picklock, skeleton-key, false key, double key.

geada, *s.f.* frost, hoar-frost.

gear, *v.i.* to frost, to chill, to freeze

geba, *s.f.* hunch, hump, hunchback

gebo, *s.m.* shabby person, ragamuffin.

geboso, *adj.* gibbous, hunchbacked; shabby.

geena, *s.f.* gehenna; hell.

geento, *adj.* frosty, rimy, freezing; subject to hoar-frost.

géiser, *s.m.* geyser.

geladeira, *s.f.* refrigerator, freezer, ice-box.

gelado, *adj.* congealed, frozen, icy, glacial, gelid; frosty, covered with ice.

gelador, *s.m., adj.* freezer; freezing, chilly.

gelar, *v.t., v.i.* to freeze, to chill, to congeal; to

paralyse *(de medo)* to cause terror; to be extremely cold; to become unfeeling.

gelatina, *s.f.* gelatine, jelly.

gelatinoso, *adj.* gelatinous, sticky, gummy.

geleia, *s.f.* jelly.

geleira, *s.f.* glacier, ice cream freezer; freezing machine.

gelha, *s.f.* wrinckle, crease; fold pleat.

gelo, *s.m.* ice; frigidity, indifference *(fig.)*.

gelosia, *s.f.* window blind, lattice, trellis; lattice window, venetian blind.

gema, *s.f.* yolk *(de um ovo)*; bud, shoot *(bot.)*; gem, jewel, precious stone; vital or essential part, pith, essence; *de gema*, genuine, pure, through-and-through.

gemação, *s.f.* budding; gemmation.

gemada, *s.f.* egg-flip, eggnog.

gemagem, *s.f.* the tapping of a tree *(para resina ou cola)*.

gemar, *v.i.* to bud, to sprout, to shoot; to graft.

gemebundo, *adj.* groaning, wailing, moaning, complaining.

gemedor, *s.m., adj.* moaner, wailer, groaner; groaning.

gemente, *adj.* moaning, wailing, groaning, sighing.

gémeo, *adj., s.m.* twin, double; alike, identical; gemini (pl.); 1) *irmãos gémeos*, twin brothers.

gemer, *v.i.* to moan, to wail, to groan, to lament; to sob and sigh *(o vento)*; to creak, to rattle, to grate *(porta, janela)*.

gemido, *s.m.* groan, moan, lamentation, wailing, wail, whimpering.

gemífero, *adj.* gemmiferous; producing buds.

geminação, *s.f.* gemination, coupling, pairing.

geminado, *adj.* geminate, in pairs, coupled; double, duplicate.

geminar, *v.t.* to geminate, to double *(consoantes)*; to arrange in pairs.

gémino, *adj.* geminate.

gemiparidade, *s.f.* gemniparity.

gemíparo, *adj.* gemmiparous.

gémula, *s.f.* gemmule.

genciana, *s.f.* gencian *(bot.)*.

gendarmaria, *s.f.* gendarmerie, gendarmery.

gendarme, *s.m.* gendarme; policeman.

gene, *s.m.* gene *(biol.)*

genealogia, *s.f.* genealogy, filiation, pedigree.

genealógico, *adj.* genealogical.

genealogista, *s.* genealogist

genebra, *s.f.* gin.

genebrês, genebrino, *s.m., adj.* Genevan.

general, *s.m.* general; leader, commander, chief.

generalato, *s.m.* generalship; leadership.

generalidade, *s.f.* generality, universality; the greater part, main body; rudiments, elementary principles *(pl)*.

generalíssimo, *s.m.* generalissimo; commander-in-chief, supreme commander.

generalização, *s.f.* generalization, general indiference.

generalizador, *adj., s.m.* generalizing; generalizer.

generalizar, *v.t.* to generalize, to vulgarize, to diffuse, to spread about; *generalizar-se,* to become generalized, to become widespread.

genericamente, *adj.* generically.

genérico, *adj.* generical, generic, general, common.

género, *s.m.* kind, sort; class; gender *(de palavras);* style, manner; provisions *(pl.).* 1) *géneros alimentícios,* foodstuff. 2) *único no género,* unique, sui generis.

generosamente, adv. generously, liberally.

generosidade, *s.f.* generosity, liberality, generous deed, magnanimity, munificence.

generoso, *adj.* generous, liberal; kind; openhanded, magnanimous; unselfish; noble, loyal; daring, courageous; fertile, fruitful *(terra);* bounteous, charitable.

genesíaco, genésico, genético, *adj.* genetic, genic.

genetlíaco, *adj.* genethliac.

gengibre, *s.m.* ginger.

gengiva, *s.f.* gum *(dentes).*

gengivite, *s.f.* gengivitis.

genial, *adj.* genial, of genius, talented, brilliant, ingenious.

genialidade, *s.f.* creative genious.

génio, *s.m.* genius, talent; disposition, nature, humour, temper.

genital, *adj.* genital, reproductive, procreative.

genitivo, *s.m.* genitive, the genitive case.

génito, *adj.* begotten.

genitor, *s.m.* genitor; father.

genovês, *s.m., adj.* Genoese.

genro, *s.m.* son-in-law.

gentalha, *s.f.* mob, populace, rabble, riff-raff.

gente, *s.f.* people, folk, persons; population; humanity; hands, employees; family; nation. 1) *gente de bem,* gentle folk. 2) *gente do mar,* sailors. 3) *gente moça,* young people. 4) *gente da mesma laia,* birds of a feather. 5) *gente grande,* grown-ups. 6) *toda a gente,* everybody.

gentil, *adj.* gentle, courteous, kind; graceful; genteel; pretty; refined; charming; handsome, elegant.

gentileza, *s.f.* kindness, politeness, courtesy; grace; gallantry; favour; gracefulness, elegance.

gentil-homem, *s.m.* gentleman, nobleman, noble, well-bred man.

gentílico, *adj.* heathen, pagan.

gentilidade, *s.f.* paganism, heathenism; pagan faith; pagans.

gentilmente, *adv.* kindly; softly; nicely, politely, gracefully, amiable.

gentinha, *s.f.* low people, the common people. mob.

gentio, *s.m., adj.* gentile, pagan, heathen; populace, crowd *(pop.);* savages; infidel.

genuflectir, *v.i.* to kneel down, to bend the knee.

genuflexão, *s.f.* genefluxion, genuflection.

genuflexório, *s.m.* kneeling desk, praying-chair, praying-stool, hassock.

genuinidade, *s.f.* genuineness, anthenticity.

genuíno, *adj.* genuine, pure, original, authentic; true, real, honest.

geocêntrico, *adj.* geocentric.

geodesia, *s.f.* geodesy

geodésico, *adj.* geodesical.

geofagia, *s.f.* geophagy

geófago, *adj., s.m.* geophagous;earteater, geophagist.

geofísica, *s.f.* geophysics.

geofísico, *adj., s.m.* geophisycal; geophysicist.

geogenia, *s.f.* geogeny.

geografia, *s.f.* geography.

geográfico, *adj.* geographic(al).

geógrafo, *s.m.* geographer.

geologia, *s.f.* geology.

geológico, *adj.* geological.

geólogo, *s.m.* geologist.

geomancia, *s.f.* geomancy.

geómetra, *s.* geometrician.

geometria, *s.f.* geometry. 1) *geometria analítica,* analytic geometry. 2) *geometria descritiva,* descriptive geometry. 3) *geometria no espaço,* space geometry.

geometricamente, *adv.* geometrically.

geométrico, *adj.* geometric(al).

geomorfologia, *s.f.* geomorphology, physiography.

georama, *s.m.* georama.

georgiano, *adj., s.m.* Georgian.

geotermia, *s.f.* geothermy.

geotérmico, *adj.* geothermic.

geotrópico, *adj.* geotropic.

geotropismo, *s.m.* geotropism.

geração, *s.f.* generation *(em todos os sentidos)*, production; family; formation; creation, procreation; offspring; period of a generation; descent; kind, race; conception; development. 1) *geração espontânea,* autogenesis. 2) *a geração vindoura,* the rising generation.

gerador, *adj., s.m.* generative, geberating, procreative, reproductive; generator, creator, author.

geral, *adj., s.m.* general, common, public; universal; usual; generic; generality, majority, the greater part. 1) *em geral, de um modo geral,* generally speaking. 2) *opinião geral,* current opinion. 3) *regra geral,* as a general rule.

geralmente, *adv.* generally, usually, ordinarily, commonly.

gerânio, *s.m.* geranium, crain's bill; crowfoot.

gerar, *v.t.* to beget; to generate; to produce; to create *(novas ideias);* to develop, to form; to originate, to cause.

geratriz, *s.f., adj.* generator; generatrix *(mat.);* geberating.

gerência, *s.f.* management, managership, administration; direction, control.

gerente, *s.m.* manager, administrator; supervisor.

gergelim, *s.m.* sesame *(plante ou semente).*

gerifalte, *s.m.* gerfalcon.

gerigonça, *s.f.* jargon, gibberish; contraption; badly executed work.

gerir, *v.t.* to manage, to administrate; to supervise; to run.

germânico, *adj.* Germanic.

germanismo, *s.m.* Germanism.

germanista, *s., adj.* Germanist.

germanizar, *v.t.* to Germanize.

germano, *s.m., adj.* german; true, pure.

germanófilo, *s.m., adj.* Germanophile.

germanófobo, *s.m., adj.* Germanophobe.

germe, gérmen, *s.m.* germen, sprout; seed-bud, embryo; cause, origin, source; undeveloped state, rudimentariness.

germinação, *s.f., adj.* germination; germinating.

germinador, *s.m.* germinator; evolution.

germinal, *adj.* germinal, germinative.

germinar, *v.i.* to germinate; to sprout, to bud; to begin to grow or develop, to put forth shoots; to generate, to engender.

germinativo, *adj.* germinative, germinant.

gerúndio, *s.m.* gerund.

gerundivo, *s.m.* gerundive

gessal, *s.m.* chalk-pit, gypsum pit.

gessar, *v.t.* to plaster, to cover with plaster.

gesso, *s.m.* gypsum, plaster of Paris, parget; a plaster model; *revestimento de gesso,* plaster cast.

gesta, *s.f.* historical feat; exploit, heroic deed.

gestação, *s.f.* gestation, pregnancy; eleboration, development.

gestante, *adj.* pregnant, gravid.

gestão, *s.f.* management, administration.

gestatório, *adj.* gestatory.

gesticulação, *s.f.* gesticulation.

gesticulador, *s.m., adj.* gesticulator; gesticulating.

gesticular, *v.i.* to gesticulate, to make gestures; to mimic, to mime

gesto, *s.m.* gesture; countenance; motion; signal, beckon; look, appearance, expression; air, mien.

gestor, *s.m.* manager; supervisor, director.

giba, *s.f.* gibbosity, protuberance; hunch, hunchback.

gibão, *s.m.* doublet; kind of overall, jerkin.

gibelino, *s.m.* Ghibelline.

gibosidade, *s.f.* gibbosity, protuberance.

giboso, *adj.* gibbous; humped, hunched.

giesta, *s.f.* genista, woodwaxen, dyer's weed, broom.

giestal, *s.m.* broom plantation.

giesteira, *s.f.* genista, broom

giga, *s.f.* flat and wide wicker basket.

giganta, *s.f.* giantess.

gigante, *s.m., adj.* giant, colossus, titam; gigantic, giant, enormous.

gigantesco, *adj.* gigantic, huge, enormous, extraordinary.

gagantismo, *s.m.* giantism, gigantism.

gigantomaquia, *s.f.* gigantomachy.

gigo, *s.m.* basket, wicker basket, pannier.

gilete, *s.f.* safety razor.

gilvaz, *s.m.* scar, slash *(face).*

gim, *s.m.* rail bender, jim-crow, gin, corn whisky.

gimnasiarco, *s.m.* gymnasiarch.

gimnocarpo, *adj.* gymnocarpous.

gimnocéfalo, *adj.* gymnocephalous

gimnospérmico, *adj.* gymnospermous.

ginasial, *adj.* gymnasial *(universidade).*

ginásio, *s.m.* gymnasium.

ginasta, *s.* gymnast.

ginástica, *s.f.* gymnastics; exercise drill.

ginástico, *adj.* gymnastic(al).

gincana, *s.f.* gymkhana.

ginceu, *s.m.* gynaeceum; gynoecium *(bot.).*

ginecologia, *s.f.* gynaecology.

ginecológico, *adj.* gynaecologic(al).

ginecologista, *s.* gynaecologist.

gineta, *s.f.* genet; style of riding with short stirrups; *montar à gineta,* to ride with short stirrups.

ginete, *s.m.* jennet; rider; a fine small horse.

gingão, *s.m., adj.* loafer, idler; brawler; pitching, balancing.

gingar, *v.i.* to scull *(barco)* to waddle along *(como uma pessoa muito gorda),* to sway *(de um lado para o outro enquanto anda);* to roll, to pitch.

ginja, *s.f.* morello cherry.

ginjal, *s.m.* morello orchard.

ginjeira, *s.f.* morello tree; *conhecer alguém de ginjeira,* to know someone very well, to have a thorough knowledge of.

ginjinha, *s.f.* cherry brandy.

gipso, *s.m.* gypsum, plaster of Paris.

gipsófila, *s.f.* gypsophila.

gira, *s.f., adj.* stroll, walk; gyration; lunatic; crazy, nuts.

giração, *s.f.* turning, gyration, rotation.

girafa, *s.f.* giraffe; tall and long-neckeed person *(fig).*

girândola, *s.f.* girandole.

girante, *adj.* turning round, gyrant, gyranting.

girar, *v.i.* to go round, to circulate; to walk; to move in a circle; to rotate, to wheel; to labour, to toll.

girassol, *s.m.* sunflower.

giratório, *adj.* gyretory, rotative, gyrating, rotary; circulatory; spinning; swinging. 1) *ponte giratória,* turn bridge. 2) *porta giratória,* revolving door.

gíria, *s.f.* jargon; slang; dialect; cant, patois.

girino, *s.m.* tadpole, polliwog.

giro, *s.m.* turn, rotation, circuit; trade; walk, stroll, trip, funny (pop); *dar um giro,* to take a stroll, to go for a walk.

giromancia, *s.f.* giromancy.

girondino, *s.m., adj.* Girondist.

giroscópio, *s.m.* gyroscope.

gitano, *s.m.* gypsy; Spanish gypsy.

giz, *s.m.* chalk.

gizar, *v.t.* to deliniate, to project, to plan.

glabro, *adj.* glabrous, bald, hairless, beardless.

glacial, *adj.* glacial; frozen, icy, freezing, frigid; cold, indifferent.

glacialmente, *adv.* glacially, icily.

glaciar, *s.m.* glacier.

glaciário, *adj.* glacial, relative to glaciers; *período glaciário,* glacial period.

gladiador, *s.m.* gladiator.

gladiar, *v.i.* to fight with sword.

gládio, *s.m.* sword, dagger; power energy *(fig.).*

gladíolo, *s.m.* gladiolusm; sword-lily.

glande, *s.f.* acorn, mast; gland.

glandífero, *adj.* glandiferous, bearing acorns.

glandiforme, *adj.* glandiform.

glandívoro, *adj.* gladivorous, feeding on acorns.

glândula, *s.f.* gland *(anat. e bot.).* 1) *glândula endócrina,* endocrine gland. 2) *glândula lacrimal,* lachrymal gland. 3) *glândula mamária,* mammary gland. 4) *glândula pituitária,* hypophysis pituitary gland. 5) *glândula salivar,* salivary gland. 6) *glândula sebácea,* sebaceous gland. 7) *glândula supra-renal,* adrenal gland.

glandular, *adj.* glandular, glandulous.

glandulífero, *adj.* glanduliferous, bearing, small glands.

glanduliforme, *adj.* gladuliform, acornshaped.

glanduloso, *adj.* glandulous.

glauco, *adj.* glaucous, bluish-green, greenish-blue.

glaucoma, *s.m.* glaucoma.

gleba, *s.f.* land, soil, earth, field, piece of farming land.

glena, *s.f.* glenoid cavity *(anat.)*

glenoidal, glenóide, glenóideo, *adj.* glenoidal.

glicerina, *s.f.* glycerin(e)

glicerol, *s.m.* glycerol, glycerin(e)

glicerose, *s.f.* glycerose.

glicínia, *s.f.* Chinese wistaria.

glicol, *s.m.* glycol.

glicólise, *s.f.* glycolysis.

glicómetro, *s.m.* glucometer.

glicose, *s.f.* glucose, dextrose; grape sugar.

glifo, *s.m.* glyph *(ornamento).*

glíptica, *s.f.* glyptics.

gliptografia, *s.f.* glyptography.

global, *adj.* global, whole, entire, total, over-all; spherical.

globalização, s.f. globalization.

globo, s.m. globe, sphere, ball; earth, terrestrial globe.

globosidade, s.f. globosity, sphericity.

globoso, adj. globous, spherical, globular, round.

globular, adj. globular, spherical, globe-shaped, round, orbicular.

globulina, s.f. globulin

glóbulo, s.m. globule, little globe; blood corpuscle (anat.)

globuloso, adj. globulous, globular, globulose.

glória, s.f. glory; honour, fame, renown; boast, pride; magnificence, pomp, splendour; areole, halo. 1) glória a Deus nas alturas, glory to God in the highest. 2) ir à glória, to lose all, to go to pot (jogo). 3) levar a banca à glória, to break the bank (no jogo).

gloriar, v.t. to glorify, to parise, to extol.

glorificação, s.f. glorification, praise, exaltation.

glorificador, s.m., adj. glorifier, praiser; glorifying, laudatory.

glorificante, adj. glorifying, praising.

glorificar, v.t. to glorify, to praise, to extol, to exalt, to honour, to worship, to bless.

gloríola, s.f. gloriole.

gloriosamente, adv. gloriously.

glorioso, adj. glorious, renowned, ilustrious, victorious, honourable, praiseworthy; blessed.

glosa, s.f. gloss, comment, explanation, annotation; footnote.

glosador, s.m. glosser, commentator, glossarist.

glosar, v.t. to gloss, to explain, to comment upon, to note down, to annotate, to interpret.

glossário, s.m. glossary, vocabulary.

glossarista, s. glossarist, commentator.

glóssico, adj. glossal, lingual.

glossite, s.f. glossitis, inflammation of the tongue.

glossografia, s.f. glossography

glossográfico, adj. glossographical.

glossógrafo, s.m. glossographer

glossóide, adj. glossoid, tonguelike.

glossologia, s.f. glossology, linguistics, glottology.

glossológico, adj. glossological.

glossologista, s. glossologist.

glossotomia, s.f. glossotomy.

glote, s.f. glottis

glotologia, s.f. glottology, linguistics.

glotologista, glotólogo, s.m. glottologist.

gluglu, s.m. gobble-gobble (de um peru); gurgle-gurgle (quando se enche uma garrafa).

glutão, s.m., adj. glutton, devourer, gormandizer; gluttonous, voracious.

glúten, s.m. glutten.

glúteo, adj. gluteal.

glutina, s.f. glutin, gliadin.

glutinar, v.t. to glue, to fasten with glue, to glutinate.

glutinosidade, s.f. glutinosity.

glutinoso, adj. glutinous, viscous, sticky, adhesive.

glutonaria, s.f. gluttony, gulosity, voracity.

gnomo, s.m. gnome, goblin, elf.

gnomologia, s.f. gnomology.

gnómon, s.m. gnomon, sun-dial.

gnomónica, s.f. gnomonics.

gnomónico, adj. gnomonic.

gnose, s.f. gnosis; cognition.

gnosticismo, s.m. Gnosticism.

gnóstico, adj., s.m. gnostic.

godé, s.m. small pan of water colour; godet.

godo, s.m., adj. Goth; Gothic.

goela, s.f. throat, gorge, gullet, esophagus; gulf; molhar a goela, to moisten the throat.

goense, goês, s., s.m. Goanese.

gogo, s.m. pip.

gogoso, goguento, adj. suffering from pip.

goiaba, s.f. guava.

goiabada, s.f. guava jam.

goiabeira, s.f. guava-tree.

goiva, s.f. gouge, hollow-chisel.

goiveiro, s.m. wallflower, gillflower blossom.

goivo, s.m. wallflower.

gola, s.f. collar; grove; pegar pela gola, to collar.

golada, s.f. gulp, swallow, swig.

gole, s.m. gulp, swallow, draught, swig; de um gole, at a draught.

goleada, s.f. great number of goals (futebol).

goleador, s.m. football player who scores many goals.

golear, v.t. to score many goals in a football game.

goleta, s.f. inlet; schooner.

golfada, s.f. gush, spout, spew; all that is vomited at one time.

golfão, gólfão, s.m. water-lily (bot.).

golfar, v.t. to spout out, to vomit, to spew; to expel, to spurt, to gush.

golfe, *s.m.* golf.

golfinho, *s.m.* dolphin, porpoise, cow-fish.

golfo, *s.m.* gulf.

Gólgota, *s.m.* Golgotha, Calvary.

golilha, *s.f.* iron-collar.

golo, *s.m.* goal.

golpe, *s.m.* cut; blow, stroke; slash; throw; incision; stab, thrust; shock, crisis, misfortune; impetus, rush. 1) *golpe de mão*, surprise attack. 2) *golpe de mar*, heavy sea. 3) *golpe de mestre*, master stroke. 4) *golpe de misericórdia*, finishing stroke. 5) *golpe de morte*, death blow. 6) *golpe de vento*, gust of wind. 7) *golpe de vista*, quick glance.

golpeado, *adj.* hit, struck; slashed, cut.

golpear, *v.t.* to cut; to slash; to stab.

goma, *s.f.* gum, glue; starch.

goma-arábica, *s.f.* gum arabic.

gomado, *adj.* gummy, sticky.

goma-laca, *s.f.* shellac, French polish.

gomar, *v.i.* to bud, to sprout, to shoot; to starch, to stiffen with starch.

gomeleira, *s.f.* sucker; shoot.

gomil, *s.m.* jar, jug, pitcher with handle.

gomo, *s.m.* bud, shoot, sprout, gemma; pulpy segment of citrus fruits; division, section.

gomosidade, *s.f.* gummosity.

gomoso, *adj.* gummy, gumous.

gôndola, *s.f.* gondola.

gondoleiro, *s.m.* gondolier.

gongo, *s.m.* gong.

gongórico, *adj.* Gongoresque, Gongoristic.

gongorismo, *s.m.* Gongorism.

gongorista, *s.* Gongorist.

goniógrafo, *s.m.* goniograph.

goniometria, *s.f.* goniometry.

goniométrico, *adj.* goniometric(al).

goniómetro, *s.m.* goniometer.

gonococo, *s.m.* gonococcus.

gonorreia, *s.f.* gonorrhoea, clap *(pop)*.

gonorreico, *adj.* gonorrhoeal.

gonzo, *s.m.* hinge.

gorar, *v.t.* to frustrate, to disappoint; to end in failure; to grow addle *(ovos)*.

goraz, *s.m.* sea-bream.

gordaço, gordalhaço, gordalhão, *adj.* very fat, plump, paunchy.

gordinho, *adj.* plump, chubby.

górdio, *adj.* Gordian; *nó górdio*, Gordian knot.

gordo, *adj.* fat; stout, obese; corpulent, rotund; oily, greasy. 1) *Domingo Gordo*, Shrove Sunday. 2) *leite gordo*, whole milk. 3) *nunca o vi mais gordo*, I never saw him in my life.

gorducho, *adj.* ver "gordaço".

gordura, *s.f.* fatness; fleshiness; obesity, plumpness; grease, fatty matter. 1) *gordura de leite*, butterfat. 2) *gordura de porco*, lard. 3) *gordura vegetal*, vegetable fat. 4) *sem gordura*, fatless. 5) *mancha de gordura*, a grease-spot.

gordurento, *adj.* greasy, unctuous, fatty, oily.

gorduroso, *adj.* greasy, unctuous, lardy oily.

gorgolão, *s.m.* gush, gulp; bubbling.

gorgomilo, *s.m.* gullet, throat.

gorgorão, *s.m.* grosgrain.

gorgulho, *s.m.* weevil.

gorila, *s.m.* gorilla.

gorja, *s.f.* throat, gullet, gorge.

gorjal, *s.m.* gorjet.

gorjeador, *adj., s.m.* warbling, trilling; warbler, caroler.

gorjear, *v.i.* to warble, to quaver, to trill; to chirp, to twitter; to sing.

gorjeio, *s.m.* warbling, chirping, warble, trill; children's babble.

gorjeira, *s.f.* tucker.

gorjeta, *s.f.* drink-money, gratuity, tip; reward, gratification; *dar uma gorjeta*, to tip.

gorra, *s.f.* cap.

gorro, *s.m.* round cap.

gosma, *s.f.* strangles *(de cavalos)*; pip.

gosmar, *v.t.* to hawk up; to have the strangles.

gosmento, *adj.* having the strangles; spitting.

gostar, *v.t.* to taste; to like; to be fond of; to consider tasteful or graceful; to enjoy, to feel pleasure or affection; to sympathize with. 1) *gostar mais*, to like better. 2) *gostar muito*, to love, to hold dear. 3) *não gostar*, to dislike.

gosto, *s.m.* taste, flavour, relish, savour; liking, pleasure, enjoyment; good taste or manners; aesthical discernment. 1) *a seu gosto*, to one's liking. 2) *com todo o seu gosto*, gladly with pleasure. 3) *gostos não se discutem*, there is no accouting for tastes. 4) *brincadeira de mau gosto*, a bad joke. 5) *sem gosto*, in bad taste; insipid, tasteless. 6) *tomar gosto por*, to get a taste for.

gostosamente, *adv.* gladly, willingly, pleasantly.

gostoso, *adj.* savoury; pleasing; tasty, palatable, sapid; tasteful; delicious, delightful.

gota, *s.f.* drop; gout *(med.)*; gutta. 1) *gota a*

gota, by drops. 2) *uma gota no oceano*, an insignificant matter, a drop in the ocean.

goteira, *s.f.* gutter, eaves, down-spout; a leak *(no telhado)*.

gotejamento, *s.m.* a dripping, dropping.

gotejante, *adj.* dropping.

gotejar, *v.i.* to drop, to drip, to trickle, to dribble.

gótico, *adj.* Gothic; black-letter *(tip.)*.

goto, *s.m.* glottis; *dar (cair) no goto*, to go down the wrong throat; to attract one's attention; to take one's fancy; to become popular.

gotoso, *adj.* gouty.

governação, *s.m.* government, administration, direction.

governado, *adj.* ruled, governed; saving, frugal.

governador, *s.m.* governor, ruler.

governamental, *adj.* governmental.

governança, *s.f.* ver governo.

governanta, *s.f.* governess, house-keeper.

governante, *s.m., s.f.* ruler; governess, house-keeper.

governar, *v.t.* to govern, to rule; to steer *(barcos)*. 1) *governar-se*, to manage oneself. 2) *governar bem o barco*, to manage well one's affairs.

governativo, *adj.* governmental.

governável, *adj.* governable, guidable; tractable, docile.

governo, *s.m.* government, direction, management, authority, domination; ministry, steerage *(de um barco)*. 1) *governo autónomo*, self-government. 2) *governo da casa*, household. 3) *governo fantoche*, puppet government. 4) *para seu governo*, for your guidance.

gozador, *s.m., adj.* enjoyer, idler; easy-going.

gozar, *v.t.* to enjoy; to possess; to be pleased with; to take delight in; to profit; to benefit; to take advantage of; *gozar de boa saúde*, to enjoy good health.

gozo, *s.m.* enjoyment, pleasure, delight, satisfaction; *em gozo de férias*, on vacation.

gozoso, *adj.* joyous, merry, delightful.

grã, *adj.* short for *grande* (used in compounds). 1) *Grã-Bretanha*, Great Britain. 2) *Grã-Cruz*, Grand Cross, etc.)

grabato, *s.m.* pallet. miserable couch, straw bed.

graça, *s.f.* grace, favour; mercy; elegance; jest; thankfulness; charm, loveliness; wit, esprit, witticism; humour, drollery, fun, joke; divine, mercy, grace; thanks *(pl.)*. 1) *graças a*, thanks to. 2) *graças a Deus*, thanks be to God, thank God. 3) *acção de graças*, thanksgiving. 4) *de graça*, gratis, gratuitous, for nothing. 5) *nem de graça*, not even as a gift. 6) *quase de graça*, for next to nothing. 7) *estar nas graças de*, to be in someone's favour. 8) *não estar para graças*, to be in bad humour. 9) *não ser para graças*, not to be trifled with. 10) *qual a sua graça?*, your name, please. 11) *sem graça*, insipid, stale, tasteless. 12) *ter graça*, to be funny, amusing.

gracejador, *s.m., adj.* jester, joker, wag; frolic, bantering.

gracejar, *v.i.* to jest, to joke, to banter, to droll, to frolic, to trifle.

gracejo, *s.m.* jest, joke, witticism, fun, drollery, play; jocosity, good humour; pleasantry.

grácil, *adj.* gracile, slender, thin, delicate, frail.

gracilidade, *s.f.* gracility, slenderness, slimness, frailty; delicateness.

graciosamente, *adv.* graciously, kindly, charmingly; gratuitously.

graciosidade, *s.f.* graciousness, gracefulness; elegance, beauty; benevolence.

gracioso, *adj.* gracious, facetious, graceful, elegant, comely, pleasing; witty.

graçola, *s.f.* stupid joke, sorry pleasantry.

grã-cruz, *s.f.* grand cross.

gradação, *s.f.* gradation.

gradador, *s.m.* harrower, harrow, grader.

gradadura, gradagem, *s.f.* harrowing, grading.

gradar, *v.t.* to harrow, to grade, to level; to grow, to swell.

gradativo, *adj.* gradual, gradational.

grade, *s.f.* grating; frame; harrow, grader *(instrumento)*; rail, barrier; locutory (*num convento)*; *grade da janela*, window grating.

gradeamento, *s.m.* railing, a fence of railing and posts.

gradear, *v.t.* to rail, to fence in, to bar, to enclose with a rail; to grate.

gradiente, *s.m.* gradient.

gradil, *s.m.* low fence or railling.

gradim, *s.m.* gradine, sculptor's chisel.

gradiómetro, *s.m.* gradiometer.

grado, *adj., s.m.* filled-out, well-developed; big, important *(pessoas)*; grade *(geom.)*. 1) *de bom grado*, willingly, readily. 2) *de mau grado*, unwillingly. 3) *de bom ou mau grado*, willy-nilly. 4) *mau grado*, in spite of.

graduação, *s.f.* graduation (division into, admission to a degree at the university); rank, grade, hierarchy.

graduado, *adj., s.m.* graduated, graduate.

gradual, *adj., s.m.* gradual, progressive slow; the gradual.

gradualmente, *adv.* gradually, by degrees, slowly, progressively.

graduar, *v.t.* to graduate, to calibrate, to gauge, to divide into grades; to mark with degrees; to classify, to arrange in groups; to regulate by degrees; to confer a degree, to give a diploma to; *graduar-se,* to graduate, to take a university degree.

graduável, *adj.* adjustable.

grafar, *v.t.* to spell, to write *(uma palavra).*

grafia, *s.f.* orthography, spelling.

graficamente, *adv.* graphically.

gráfico, *adj, s.m.* graphic(al); graph; diagram, chart.

grafite, *s.f.* graphite, plumbago, black lead.

grafítico, *adj.* graphitic, plumbaginous.

grafito, *s.m.* graphite, inscription.

grafologia, *s.f.* graphology.

grafológico, *adj.* graphlogic(al).

grafólogo, grafologista, *s.m., s.* grapho-loger, graphologist, handwritting expert.

grafómetro, *s.m.* graphometer.

grafoscópio, *s.m.* graphoscope.

grainha, *s.f.* grape-stone, pip, grape seed.

gral, *s.m.* mortar, pounder.

gralha, *s.f.* jackdaw; misprint; garrulous woman, chaterbox.

gralhada, *s.f.* cawing of rooks, croaking, confused noise.

gralhar, *v.i.* to caw, to croak; to gossip, to babble; to make much noise.

grama, *s.m., s.f.* gramme; dog's tooth, gramma, grass, carpet grass.

gramado, *s.m.* lawn, grass-plot, turf; grass, green.

gramão, *s.m.* Bermuda grass.

gramar, *v.t.* to scratch, to flax, to hemp; to swallow, to gulp down *(pop.);* to bear, to suffer, to undergo, to endure *(pop).*

gramática, *s.f.* grammar, grammar-book.

gramatical, *adj.* grammatical.

gramaticão, *s.m.* petty grammarian.

gramático, *s.m.* grammarian.

gramíneas, *s.f., pl.* Gramineae, gramineous plants.

gramíneo, *adj.* gramineous, grassy.

graminho, *s.m.* scribing-block; carpenter's gauge.

graminiforme, *adj.* graminiform.

graminoso, *adj.* grassy, covered with grass.

gramofone, *s.m.* gramophone, phonograph.

grampo, *s.m.* clamp, cramp, holdfast, brace, dog, clasp.

granada, *s.f.* hand grenade, grenade, bomb, shell; garnet *(pedra preciosa).*

granadeiro, *s.m.* grenadier.

granadina, *s.f.* grenadine, thin silk.

granadino, *adj., s.m.* garnet-red; native of Granada *(em Espanha).*

granador, *s.m.* granulating machine.

granal, *adj.* granular, granulate.

granalha, *s.f.* small shot; granulated metal.

granar, *v.t.* to granulate, to reduce to grains.

granate, *s.m.* garnet, grossularite.

grandalhão, *s.m.* huge, very stout, enormous.

grande, *adj., s.m.* large, great; tall; big; high; chief; huge; stout, bulky; wide, ample. broad; noble, famous, ilustrious; grandee, Spanish or Portuguese nobleman; influential person. 1) *fazer à grande,* to do things in style or magnificently. 2) *viver à grande,* to live in clover. 3) *em ponto grande,* on a big scale.

grandemente, *adv.* greatly, extremely, very much.

grandevo, *adj.* of a great age, longlived, very old.

grandeza, *s.f.* size, vastness, largeness; bulk, bigness; length, extent, hugeness; dignity; generosity; quantity, value *(mat.);* magnificence, greatness, splendour, pomp; majesty; sublimity; *grandeza de alma,* greatness of soul.

grandiloquência, *s.f.* grandiloquence, loftiness of speech, lofty language.

grandiloquente, *adj.* grandiloquent, bombastic, high-sounding.

grandiosidade, *s.f.* greatness, grandeur, splendour, pomp, magnificence, stateliness, sublimity; vastness; grandiosity.

grandioso, *adj.* grand, fine, magnificent, imposing, pompous, grandious, stately, sublime.

granel, *s.m.* granary, barn, corn loft; galley proof *(tip.); a granel,* in bulk, loose; in great quantity, mixed, by heaps.

granífero, *adj.* graniferous, producing grain.

graniforme, *adj.* graniform, granular.

granir, *v.t.* to stipple, to draw, to engrave.

granitar, *v.t.* to granulate, to reduce to grains.

granítico, granitoso, adj. granitical.

granito, s.m. granite.

granitóide, adj. granitoid.

granívoro, adj. granivorous.

granizada, s.f. hail-storm; a shower (of bullets, questions).

granizar, v.i. to hail.

granizo, s.m. hail, hail stone.

granja, s.f. farm; grange, ranch.

granjeador, adj. one who labours hard; granger, tiller.

granjear, v.t. to cultivate, to farm, to till (the soil); to get, to obtain, to win, to acquire; to attract, to conquer.

granjeio, s.m. cultivation, tillage, culture, husbandry, farming; profit, gain, earnings.

granjeiro, s.m. farmer, granger.

granoso, adj. granulous, grainy, granular.

granulação, granulagem, s.f. granulation, graining.

granulado, adj. granulated, grainy, grained.

granular, adj., v.t. granular; to granulate.

grânulo, s.m. granule; corn, small grain.

granuloma, s.m. granuloma, tumour.

granulosidade, s.f. granulosity.

granuloso, adj. granulous, granular, corny, grainy, lumpy.

grão, s.m. grain, corn, cereals; particle. 1) *grão de chumbo*, pellet. 2) *ter um grão na asa*, to be in life`s cups. 3) *grão a grão enche a galinha o papo*, many a little makes a mickle, little and often fills the purse, little strokes fell great oaks.

grão-de-bico, s.m. chick-pea.

grão-ducado, s.m. grand-duchy.

grão-ducal, adj. grand-ducal.

grão-duque, s.m. grand duque.

grão-mestre, s.m. grand master.

grão-turco, s.m. grand turk.

grão-vizir, s.m. grand vizir.

grasnada, s.f. croaking; crawing, quacking.

grasnar, v.t. croak, to caw, to quack; to cackle (ganso).

grasnido, s.m. quack, loud cawing.

grassar, v.i. to spread, to develop gradually (notícias, doenças), to rage (epidemias).

gratamente, adv. gratefully, thankfully; charmingly; pleasantly.

gratidão, s.f. gratitude, thankfulness, gratefulness.

gratificação, s.f. reward, tip, gratuity, recompense; fee, bonus.

gratificador, s.m. rewarder, gratifier.

gatificar, v.t. to reward; to favour with; to gratify; to tip, to give a gratuity to; to remunerate, to pay a fee.

grátis, adv. gratis, for nothing, gratuitously, free, costless; *entrada grátis*, entrance free.

grato, adj. grateful, thankful; pleasing, agreeable, gratifying, comforting; delightful.

gratuitamente, adv. gratis, free, for nothing, graciously.

gratuitidade, s.f. gratuitousness.

gratuito, adj. gratuitous, free, costless, frank; for next to nothing.

gratulação, s.f. congratulation, felicitation, well-wishing.

gratular, v.t. to congratulate, to gratulate, to rejoice at.

gratulatório, adj. gratulatory, congratulatory.

grau, s.m. degree, grade, step, rank, order; measure, extent, length; accademical degree, unit of measurement; degree of kinship; *em alto grau*, to a high degree.

graúdo, adj. big, great, large; distinguished, important; grown, matured.

gravação, s.f. engraving; recording, canned music.

gravado, adj. engraved, cut; canned (música).

gravador, s.m. engraver; recorder, tape recorder.

gravadura, s.f. engraving.

gravame, s.m. charge, burden, hardship; vexation, grievance, molestation; heavy tax; gravamen (leis).

gravanço, s.m. chick-pea; meal, food.

gravar, v.t. to engrave, to impress, to grave; to record; to stamp, to print; to perpetuate; to fix (na memória); to oppress, to burden.

gravata, s.f. neck-tie, cravat, tie; *alfinete de gravata*, scarf-pin, tie-pin.

gravataria, s.f. neck-tie shop or work shop.

gravateiro, s.m. neck-tie manufacturer or retailer.

gravato, s.m. hook, dry brushwood.

grave, adj. grave, serious; solemn; dangerous; grievous; important, momentous; severe, austere; aprehensive; bass, deep (música); parosytone (palavra), with acute accent.

gravemente, adv. gravely, seriously.

gravetos, s.m., pl. brushwood, faggots, bundle of sticks.

graveza, s.f. gravity; grievousness.

grávida, adj., s.f. pregnant, gravid, expectant, heavy; *estar grávida*, to be in the family way.

gravidade, s.f. gravity, terrestrial gravitation;

graveness, importance, seriousness; solemnity; severity; danger. 1) *a gravidade da situação*, the gravity of the situation. 2) *gravidade absoluta*, weight. 3) *gravidade específica*, specific gravity. 4) *centro de gravidade*, the center of gravity.

gravidar, *v.t., v.i.* to make pregnant; to become pregnant, to get into trouble.

gravidez, *s.f.* pregnancy.

gravímetro, *s.m.* gravimeter.

gravitação, *s.f.* gravitation.

gravitante, *adj.* gravitative, gravitational, gravitating.

gravitar, *v.i.* to gravitate, to move or to tend by force of gravity; to be attracted toward.

gravoso, *adj.* grievous; painful; annoying; onerous; troublesome.

gravura, *s.f.* engraving; illustration; art of engraving; picture, print, plate.

graxa, *s.f.* blacking, shoe polishing; flattery *(pop).*

grazina, *s.* prattler, chatterbox; grumbler.

grazinada, *s.f.* prattling, noise; grumbling.

grazinador, *s.m., adj.* chatterbox, prattler; prattling, grumbling.

grazinar, *v.i.* to prattle, to babble; to pester, to importune; to grumble, to complain at.

grecismo, *s.m.* Grecism.

grecizar, *v.t.* to Grecize.

greco-latino, *adj.* Greco-Latin.

greco-romano, *adj.* Greco-Roman.

greda, *s.f.* clay; soapstone; argil, chalk.

gredoso, *adj.* chalky, marly, argillaceous.

grega, *s.f.* fretwork, greek freets.

gregário, *adj.* gregarious, aggregative, sociable.

gregarismo, *s.m.* gregariousness. gregarianism.

grego, *s.m., adj.* Greek; obscure, unumtelligible *(fig.).* 1) *isso é grego para mim*, it is Greek to me. 2) *agradar a gregos e troianos*, to please both sides. 3) *ver-se grego*, to find oneself in difficulties; to be puzzled.

gregoriano, *adj.* Gregorian.

grei, *s.f.* people, nation, herd, flock; society group; party, clique.

grelar, *v.i.* to sprout, to germinate; to thrive, to grow.

grelha, *s.f.* gridirion; grate, grill, fire grate; roaster, toaster, broiler.

grelhar, *v.t.* to broil, to grill.

grelo, *s.m.* sprout, shoot, sprig; greens, spring greens *(pl.)*

gremial, *s.m., adj.* gremial *(para bispos);* gremial.

grémio, *s.m.* club; society; corporation, body; assembly; guild; bosom. lap.

grenha, *s.f.* entangled hair; mane.

grés, *s.m.* sandstone, gritstone, grés.

greta, *s.f.* cleft, crack, crevice, chink, fissure, opening.

gretado, *adj.* cracked, fissured, chapped. cleft, split, creviced.

gretadura, *s.f.* crack, fissure, chink, rent.

gretar, *v.i.* to crack, to chap, to open, to spilt.

grevas, *s.f., pl.* greaves.

greve, *s.f.* strike, industrial action; walkout *(pop); fazer greve*, to strike.

grevista, *s.* striker.

grifa, *s.f.* claw, talon, paw.

grifado, *adj.* in italics.

grifar, *v.t.* to italicize, to print in italics.

grifo, *s.m.* italic type, bastard type; enigma, puzzle; griffin, griffon.

grilhão, *s.m.* chain; fetters, shackles, bonds *(pl.).*

grilheta, *s.f., s.m.* fetter; convict.

grilo, *s.m.* cricket.

grimpa, *s.f.* weather-cock, summit, crest, top. 1) *levantar a grimpa*, to ride the high horse. 2) *baixar a grimpa*, to lower one's flag.

grinalda, *s.f.* wreath, garland.

gripado, *adj.* taken with grippe, seized with flu.

gripal, *adj.* grippal.

gripar, *v.t.* to stick, to pam or to grip *(um motor); gripar-se*, to come down with the grippe, to be taken ill with flu.

gripe, *s.f.* influenza, flu,m bad cold, grippe.

gris, *adj.* gray, blueish-grey.

grisalho, *adj.* greyish, grizzled, hoary, silver-haired.

griseta, *s.f.* lamp, burner of oil lamps.

grisu, *s.m.* march gras; methane gas; fire-lamp.

grita, *s.f.* cry, cries; shouts; clamour, noise, uproar.

gritada, *s.f.* bawling, shouting, noise; altercation.

gritador, *s.m., adj.* crier, clamourer, shouter, bawler; crying, shouting, yelling.

gritante, *adj.* chiding, crying.

gritar, *v.i.* to cry, to shout; to clamour, to call out, to scream out, to vociferate; to shriek; to cry for help.

gritaria, *s.f.* clamour, shouting, bawling; screaming, shrieking; vociferation, uproar;

uma gritaria dos diabos, an infernal din, a frightful row.

grito, *s.m.* cry, shout, yell, scream, shriek, a call. 1) *grito de alegria*, a shout of joy. 2) *grito de dor*, wail, scream of pain. 3) *grito de guerra*, war or battle cry.

grogue, *s.m., adj.* grog *(bebida)*; groggy, tipsy.

grosa, *s.f.* gross; wood-rasp, rasp file.

grosar, *v.t.* to rasp, to smooth with a rasp.

groselha, *s.f.* currant, gooseberry; gooseberry syrup.

groselheira, *s.f.* currant plant, red currant bush.

grossaria, *s.f.* sack-cloth; coarseness.

grosseiramente, *adv.* coarsely, rudely, roughly, vulgarly.

grosseirão, *s.m., adj.* lout, boor, uncouth, uneducated fellow; coarse, crude, rough rustic.

grosseiro, *adj.* coarse; uncivil, crude, unpolished, illmannered; rough, gross; common quality.

grosseria, *s.f.* coarseness, rudeness, impoliteness, uncivility, boorishness; vulgarity.

grossista, *s., adj.* wholesale dealer; wholesale.

grosso, *adj., s.m.* stout; bulky; big; great; thick; the main body or part. 1) *o grosso do exército*, the body of the army. 2) *por grosso e a retalho*, wholesale and retail. 3) *falar grosso*, to boss the show. 4) *fazer vista grossa*, to shut one's eyes to. 5) *voz grossa*, full or thick voice.

grossura, *s.f.* size; bigness; swelling; thickness.

grotesco, *adj.* grotesque, bizarre, extravagant, ridiculous, freakish, eccentric.

grou, *s.m.* crane.

grua, *s.f.* pulley; derrick; crane.

grudador, *s.m.* gluer.

grudadura, *s.f.* gluing, pasting.

grudar, *v.t.* to glue, to stick, to paste; to joint, to unite.

grude, *s.m.* glue; paste.

grugulejar, *v.i.* to gobble.

grulha, *s.m.* babbler, chaterbox, prattler.

grulhada, *s.f.* bawling, noise, calmour; cry of the crane; babbling, prattling.

grulhar, *v.i.* to prattle, to chatter, to babble.

grulhento, *adj.* prating, babbling.

grumete, *s.m.* ordinary seaman; cabin-boy.

grumo, *s.m.* grume; clot, granule; coagulation.

grumoso, *adj.* clotted, grumous; granulated; lumpy.

grunhido, *s.m.* grunt.

grunhidor, *s.m., adj.* grunter, growler, grumbler; grunting, grumbling.

grunhir, *v.i.* to grunt, to grumble, to growl.

grupelho, *s.m.* small group; insignificant faction.

grupo, *s.m.* group; cluster, bunch, collection *(de objectos)*; party, clique, clan; gang, band; *grupo sanguíneo*, blood group.

gruta, *s.f.* den; grotto; cavern, cave.

guache, guacho, *s.m.* gouache.

gualdra, *s.f.* handle, ring.

gualdrapa, *s.f.* saddle-cloth; shabrack.

guano, *s.m.* guano, artificial manure.

guante, *s.m.* gauntlet, iron glove.

guapo, *adj.* brave, bold, valiant; graceful, elegant, handsome.

guarda, *s.m.* keeper; custody; guard; watchman; hilt (of a sword); escort, sentinel, sentry; watchfulness, caution, vigilance; defender, guardian; policeman. 1) *anjo-da--guarda*, guardian angel. 2) *guarda avançada*, outguard. 3) *guarda de honra*, guard of honour. 4) *guarda da ponte*, parapet. 5)*guarda pessoal*, bodyguard. 6) *guarda de armazém*, store-keeper. 7) *guarda de portaria*, gate-keeper. 8)*guarda real*, gentleman-at-arms. 9) *cão de guarda*, housedog, watchdog. 10) *de guarda*, on the lookout. 11) *entrar de guarda*, to mount guard. 12) *estar de guarda*, to keep guard. 13) *render a guarda*, to relieve guard.

guarda-chuva, *s.m.* umbrella.

guarda-costas, *s.m.* coast-guard vessel; bodyguard.

guardador, *s.m.* keeper; watchman, warden; *guardador de cabras*, goat-herdsman.

guarda-fatos, *s.m.* wardrobe.

guarda-fios, *s.m.* wireman.

guarda-fiscal, *s.m.* coast guard.

guarda-florestal, *s.m.* keeper of a forest.

guarda-freio, *s.m.* brakeman, braker *(caminho de ferro)*; tram-driver, tram-car driver.

guarda-jóias, *s.m.* jewel case, casket.

guarda-lamas, *s.m.* mudguard, fender; splashboard.

guarda-livros, *s.m.* book-keeper, accountant.

guarda-loiça, *s.m.* cupboard; sideboard.

guarda-marinha, *s.m.* midshipman.

guarda-mor, *s.m.* high usher, warder.

guardanapo, s.m. napkin, serviette.

guarda-nocturno, s.m. night watchman.

guarda-pó, s.m. dust-coat.

guarda-portão, s.m. porter, doorkeeper, gatekeeper.

guarda-pratas, s.m. sideboard, silver-cup board.

guardar, v.t. to keep; to watch; to guard; to preserve; to retain; to defend; to save up; to observe; to celebrate; to take care of, to look after. 1) guardar-se, to be cautious, to be on one's guard; to avoid, to abstain from. 2) guardar castidade, to live in chastity. 3) guardar a sete chaves, to keep under lock and key. 4) guardar o leito, to lay up. 5) guardar segredo, to keep a secret. 6) guarda que comer não guardes que fazer, never put off till to morrow what you can do today. 7) guarde-o Deus, God save you.

guarda-redes, s.m. goalkeeper.

guarda-rios, s.m. kingfisher; river watcher.

guarda-roupa, s.m. wardrobe; cloak room.

guarda-sol, s.m. sunshade, parasol; umbrella.

guarda-soleiro, s.m. sunshade maker.

guarda-vento, s.m. windscreen, folding screen.

guarda-vestidos, s.m. wardrobe; clothes press.

guardiania, s.f. guardianship.

guardião, s.m. guardian, custodian, warden; goalkeeper (desp.).

guarida, s.f. shelter; place of refuge, protection; cave, den, lair; dar guarida, to protect, to give shelter.

guarita, s.f. sentry-box, watch-box.

guarnecer, v.t. to furnish, to supply, to provide with, to garnish, to adorn, to trim; to fringe, to hem; to line, to face; to fortify, to garrison.

guarnecimento, s.m. provision, supply; decoration, ornament; trimming.

guarnição, s.f. packing; ornament; garrison (de tropas); trimming; crew (de um barco de guerra); hilt and basket; garniture, edging; guarnição da porta, door linning.

guedelha, s.f. tuft of hair, dishevelled hair.

guedelhudo, adj. hairy, long-haired, shaggy.

gueixa, s.f. geisha.

guelra, s.f. gill.

guerra, s.f. war, warfare; struggle, fight, conflict, strife, battle; hostility. 1) em guerra, at war. 2) declarar guerra, to declare war on. 3) fazer guerra, to wage war on. 4)

guerra relâmpago, lightning war blitz. 5) em pé de guerra, on a war footing, on the warpath. 6) teatro de guerra, seat of war. 7) Ministério da Guerra, war office. 8) ministro da Guerra, Secretary of State for War.

guerrear, v.t., v.i. to fight, to make war, to wage war upon, to combat, to struggle, to persecute; to oppose; to invade, to assail.

guerreiro, s.m., adj. warrior, soldier, combatant; warlike; combative.

guerrilha, s.f. guerila, guerilla band.

guerrilhar, v.i. to fight as a guerilla.

guerrilheiro, s.m. guerilla fighter, partisan, bushfighter.

guia, s.m., s.f. guide, leader, cicerone; conductor; guide-book, handbook; delivery bill; way bill, permit; safe-conduct; official mail register; vine-stake; guia comercial, directory.

guiador, s.m. leader, guide; handlebar (bicicleta).

guiamento, s.m. guiding.

guião, s.m. banner, standard, guidon; standard-bearer.

guiar, v.t. to lead, to direct, to conduct, to guide, to govern; to advise, to counsel; to show the road; to drive, to steer; to manage; to regulate; to control.

guieira, s.f. very cold wine (pop).

guiga, s.f. gig, outrigger.

guilherme, s.m. rabbet-plane, grooving-plane.

guilho, s.m. pivot, pin, swivel.

guilhotina, s.f. guillotine; sashwindow.

guilhotinar, v.t. to guillotine, to behead, to cut off.

guinada, s.f. twinge; yaw; deflection (de um barco); sting, sharp pain; dodging leap (de um cavalo); pitching (avião); twist (do corpo).

guinar, v.i. to yaw, to slue (um barco), to dodge, to evade.

guinchar, v.i. to shriek, to squeal, to scream.

guincho, s.m. shriek, squeal, screech, scream, shrill; crab; winch (máquina); swift (pássaro).

guindagem, s.f. hoisting, winding up.

guindar, v.t. to hoist, to lift, to crane; to raise, to elevate (para uma posição mais elevada).

guindaste, s.m. crane; winch, hoist, derrick, jack.

guinéu, adj., s.m. of Guinea; guinea (moeda).

guisa, s.f. mode, way manner; 1) à guisa de, like, just as, by way of.

guisado, *s.m., adj.* stew, ragout, fricasse; stewed.

guisar, *v.t.* to stew.

guita, *s.f.* string, twine, pack thread.

guitarra, *s.f.* guitar; *guitarra havaiana*, ukulele.

guitarrada, *s.f.* guitar concert, guitar palying.

guitarreiro, *s.m.* guitar maker.

guitarrista, *s.* guitar-palyer, guitarist.

guizalhada, *s.f.* jingle, tinkling sound *(de pequenas campainhas).*

guizalhar, *v.i.* to jingle.

guizo, *s.m.* little bell, ball-bell, rattle.

gula, *s.f.* gluttony, voracity, greediness.

gulodice, *s.f.* sweets, delicacy, dainty, titbit.

guloseima, *s.f.* daintiness; dainty, delicatessen, delicacy.

guloso, *adj., s.m.* glutonous; gormandizer; *ser guloso*, to have a sweet tooth.

gume, *s.m.* edge; *espada de dois gumes*, two-edged sword.

gumífero, *adj.* gummiferous, resiniferous.

gumoso, *adj.* gummy.

gurupés, *s.m.* bowsprit.

guruttl, *s.m.* luff.

gusa, *s.f.* cast-iron, pig-iron.

gusano, *s.m.* shipworm, teredo, woodworm.

gustação, *s.f.* gustation, tasting.

gustativo, *adj.* gustative.

guta, *s.f.* gutta, gamboge, latex.

guta-percha, *s.f.* gutta-percha.

gutural, *adj.* guttural.

guturalização, *s.f.* gutturalization.

guturalizar, *v.t.* to gutturalize, to speak gutturally.

H

h, the eighth letter of the Portuguese alphabet.

hábil, *adj.* skilful, able, clever, adroit, capable, ingenious, apt, skilled, fit, dexterous, competent; *hábil em*, skilful at, skilled in.

habilidade, *s.f.* ability, skill cleverness, cunning, competence, talent, skilfulness, ingeniousness, dexterity; *ter habilidade para tudo*, to be a general handyman to be a good hand at everything.

habilidosamente, *adv.* skillfully, ingeniously, cunningly.

habilidoso, *adj.* adroit, dexterous, able, skillful, handy skilled, ingenious, witty; talented.

habilitação, *s.f.* habilitation, capacity, qualification, fitness, competence; legal evidence *(lei).*

habilitado, *adj.* qualified, competent, entitled.

habilitador, *s.m., adj.* qualifier; qualifying.

habilitante, *adj., s.m.* habilitating; plaintif.

habilitar, *v.t.* to enable, to qualify, to prepare, to make able; to entitle. 1) *habilitar-se*, to become able for; to habilitate oneself; to buy a lottery ticket. 2) *estar habilitado para*, to be qualified for.

habilmente, *adv.* ably, skillfully, ingeniously, dexterously, subtly, artfully.

habitabilidade, *adv.* habitableness.

habitação, *s.f.* habitation, dwelling, abode, residence, house, domicile.

habitacional, *adj.* habitational.

habitador, habitante, *s.m., s.* inhabitant, dweller, resident; colonist; people (pl).

habitar, *v.t.* to inhabit; to live, to dwell; to occupy.

habitável, *adj.* inhabitable, fit for habitation.

hábito, *s.m.* habit, custom, manner, use, practice, usage, dress, costume, garb. 1) *o hábito faz o monge*, fine feathers make fine birds. 2) *tomar o hábito*, to take the religious habit, to become a monk, to take the veil (freira). 3) *adquirir um mau hábito*, to get into a bad habit.

habituação, *s.f.* habituation.

habituado, *adj.* accustomed, used.

habitual, *adj.* habitual, customary, frequent, usual, common.

habitualmente, *adv.* usually, habitually, commonly, frequently, normally.

habituar, *c.t.* to habituate, to accustom, to familiarize; *habituar-se*, to get accustomed, to get used, to accustom oneself to, to make familiar with.

habitudinário, *adj.* habitual, customary; incorrigible, incurable.

hagiografia, *s.f.* hagiography.

hagiográfico, *adj.* hagiographic.

hagiógrafo, *s.m.* hagiographer.

hagiolatria, *s.f.* hagiolatry.

hagiologia, *s.f.* hagiology.

hagiólógio, *s.m.* hagiology.

hagiólogo, *s.m.* hagiologist.

hálito, *s.m.* halitus, exhalation, smell; breath, respiration; *mau hálito*, halitosis, foul breath.

halo, *s.m.* halo, aureole, corona; glory, aura.

halogénio, *adj., s.m.* halogeneous; halogen, salt-former.

halografia, *s.f.* halography, descriptions of salts.

halógrafo, *s.m.* expert in salts.

halóide, *adj.* haloide, salt like.

halometria, *s.f.* halometry.

halómetro, *s.m.* halometer.

haltere, *s.m.* dumb-bell, bar-bell.

halterofilismo, *s.m.* dumb-bell exercises.

hangar, *s.m.* shed, hangar.

hanseático, *adj.* Hanseatic.

haplologia, *s.f.* haplology.

haraquiri, *s.m.* hara-kiri.

harém, *s.m.* harem, seraglio.

harmonia, *s.f.* harmony; agreement; accord; consonancy; harmonics *(música)*; concordance of style; due proportion; friendship, understanding.

harmónica, *s.f.* harmonica, concertina, accordion.

harmónico, *adj.* harmonic, tuneful; concordant, consonant; coherent; proportionate.

harmónio, *s.m.* harmonium.

harmoniosamente, *adv.* harmoniously, melodiously.

harmonioso, *adj.* harmonious, tuneful; musical, melodious; concordant.

harmonista, *s.* harmonist.

harmonização, *s.f.* harmonization; arrangement.

harmonizador, *adj., s.m.* harmonizing; harmonizer; mediator.

harmonizar, *v.t.* to harmonize; to arrange, to adjust; to reconcile, to conciliate; to be in conformity.

harpa, *s.f.* harp.

harpear, harpejar, *v.t., v.i.* to harp, to play on the harp.

harpejo, *s.m.* harping.

harpia, *s.f.* harpy, winged monster.

harpista, *s.* harper, harpist.

hasta, *s.f.* lance; pike, auction, public sale; *vender em hasta pública*, to sell by public auction, to put up for auction.

haste, *s.f.* staff; spindle, rod, shaft; stem, trunk *(de uma árvore)*; stipe, stalk *(bot.)*; young shoot, sprout; the horn.

hasteamento, *s.m.* hoist, hoisting.

hastear, *v.t.* to hoist, to raise up, to heave; to fly or to display; to stick at the end of a staff; *hastear a bandeira*, to fly the flag.

haurir, *v.t.* to exhaust; to absorb, to sip, to suck; to derive; to draw off.

haurível, *adj.* exhaustible, drinkable, absorbable.

hausto, *s.m.* draught, gulp. swallow.

havaiano, *s.m.* Hawaiian.

havanês, *s.m., adj.* Havanese.

havano, *s.m.* Havana *(charutos)*.

haver, *v.t., s.m.* to have, to possess; to hold; to get, to obtain; to happen, to occur; to exist; there to be; to judge, to decide; to succeed in; to behave oneself; credit; wealth, riches, fortune *(pl)*. 1) *haver falta de*, to fail. 2) *haver por bem*, to deign. 3) *há anos*, years ago; for years. 4) *há um ano*, a year ago. 5) *há muito tempo*, long, long ago. 6) *há pouco tempo*, lately. 7) *bem haja!*, thanks, thank you!

haxixe, *s.m.* hashish.

hebdómada, *s.f.* hebdomad; week.

hebdomadário, *adj., s.m.* hebdomadal, weekly; weekly-paper, weekly publication.

hebraico, *adj., s.m.* Hebraic; Hebrew.

hebraismo, *s.m.* Hebraism.

hebraizar, *v.t.* to Hebraize.

hebreia, *s.f.* Jewess, Hebrew woman.

hebreu, *s.m., adj.* Hebrew, an Israelite, a jew; the language; Hebrew, Hebraic, Jewish.

hecatombe, *s.f.* hecatomb, massacre, slaughter.

hectare, *s.m.* hectare.

héctica, *s.f.* hectic, comsumption.

héctico, *s.m., adj.* hectic.

hectograma, *s.m.* hectogram *(=100 grams).*

hectolitro, *s.m.* hectolitre *(=100 litres).*

hectómetro, *s.m.* hectometer *(=100 metres).*

hediondez, *s.f.* hideousness, horrible deed, atrocity, dreadfulness.

hediondo, *adj.* hideous, vicious, repugnant, vile, base, mean, monstrous, shocking, revolting, horrible, dreadful.

hedónico, *adj.* hedonic.

hedonismo, *s.m.* hedonism.

hedonista, *s.* hedonist.

hegelianismo, *s.m.* Hegelianism.

hegeliano, *adj.* Hegelian.

hegemonia, *s.f.* hegemony, predominance, leadership, preponderance.

hegemónico, *adj.* hegemonic.

hegemonizar, *v.t.* to hegemonize.

Hégira, *s.f.* Hegira.

helénico, *adj.* Hellenic.

helenismo, *s.m.* Hellenism.

helenista, *s., adj.* Hellenist.

helenístico, *adj.* Hellenistic(al).

helenização, *s.f.* Hellenization.

helenizar, *v.t.* to Hellenize.

heleno, *adj., s.m.* Hellenic; Hellene, Greek.

hélice, *s.f.* helix; propeller, screw *(de um barco); pá da hélice,* propeller blade.

helicoidal, *adj.* helicoid, helicoidal, screw-shaped.

helicóptero, *s.m.* helicopter, autogiro.

hélio, *s.m.* helium.

heliocêntrico, *adj.* heliocentric.

heliocromia, *s.f.* heliochromy, colour photography.

heliocrómico, *adj.* heliochromic.

heliocromo, *s.m.* a colour photograph.

heliografar, *v.t.* to heliograph.

heliografia, *s.f.* heliography.

heliográfico, *adj.* heliographic(al); *cópia heliográfica,* photographic printing.

heliógrafo, *s.m.* heliograph.

heliogravura, *s.f.* heliogravure, photo-engraving.

heliómetro, *s.m.* heliometer.

helioscopia, *s.f.* helioscopy.

helioscópico, *adj.* helioscopic.

helioscópio, *s.m.* helioscope.

helioterapia, *s.f.* heliotherapy.

helioterápico, *adj.* heliotherapic.

heliotermómetro, *s.m.* heliothermometer.

heliotropia, *s.f.* heliotropism, heliotropy.

heliotrópico, *adj.* heliotropic(al).

heliotrópio, *s.m.* heliotrope; blood-stone.

heliotropismo, *s.m.* heliotropism, heliotropy.

helminto, *s.m.* helminth, intestinal horm.

helvécio, helvético, *adj., s.m.* Helvetian, Helvetic; Helvetian; Swiss.

hematite, *s.f.* hematite, iron oxide.

hematófago, *adj.* hematophagous.

hematófilo, *adj.* hematophile.

hematofobia, *s.f.* hematophobia.

hematóide, *adj.* hematoid, blood-like.

hematologia, *s.f.* hematology.

hematológico, *adj.* hematologic(al).

hematoma, *s.m.* hematoma.

hematose, *s.f.* hematosis.

hematozoários, *s.m., pl.* Hematozoa.

hematúria, *s.f.* haematuria.

hemiciclo, *s.m.* hemicycle, semicircle.

hemiplegia, *s.f.* hemiplegia.

hemiplégico, *adj.* hemiplegic.

hemisférico, *adj.* hemispheric.

hemisfério, *s.m.* hemisphere

hemisferoidal, *adj.* hemispheroidal.

hemisferóide, *s.m.* hemispheroid.

hemistíquio, *s.m.* hemistich.

hemofilia, *s.f.* hemophilia.

hemofílico, *adj.* hemophilic.

hemoglobina, *s.f.* hemoglobin.

hemólise, *s.f.* hemolysis.

hemopatia, *s.f.* hemopathy, blood-disease.

hemoptise, *s.f.* haemoptysis, spitting of blood.

hemorragia, *s.f.* haemorrhage, bleeding. 1) *hemorragia cerebral,* cerebral hemorrhage. 2) *hemorragia nasal,* nosebleed, epistaxis.

hemorrágico, *adj.* haemorrhagic.

hemorroidal, *adj.* haemorrhoidal.

hemorróidas, *s.f., pl.* haemorrhoids.

hemostase, *s.f.* hemostasis, stoppage of bleeding; stanching.

hemostático, *adj., s.m.* hemostatic, styptic; hemostat.

hemotórax, *s.m.* hemothorax.

hendecagonal, *adj.* hendecagonal.

hendecágono, *s.m.* hendecagon.

hendecassilábico, *adj.* hendecasyllabic.

hendecassílabo, *s.m.* hendecasyllable.

hepatal, *adj.* epatic.

hepatalgia, *s.f.* liver pain, hepatalgia.

hepática, *s.f.* hepatica, liver-wort, liver-leaf.

hepático, *adj.* hepatic.

hepatismo, *s.m.* hepatism, liver disease.

hepatite, *s.f.* hepatite *(pedra);* hepatitis *(med.).*

hepatogastrite, *s.f.* hepatogastritis.
hepatografia, *s.f.* hepatography.
hepatologia, *s.f.* hepatology.
hepatológico, *adj.* hepatologic.
hepatopatia, *s.f.* hepatopathy.
hepatotomia, *s.f.* hepatotomy.
heptacórdio, *s.m.* heptachord.
heptaédrico, *adj.* heptahedral.
heptaedro, *s.m.* heptahedron.
heptagonal, *adj.* heptagonal.
heptágono, *s.m.* heptagon.
heptâmetro, *s.m.* heptameter.
heptarca, *s.m.* heptarch.
heptarquia, *s.f.* heptarchy.
heptassílabo, *s.m.* heptasyllabic verse.
Heptateuco, *s.m.* Heptateuch.
hera, *s.f.* ivy.
heráldica, *s.f.* heraldry, heraldic art, armoury.
heráldico, *adj.* heraldic, armorial.
herança, herdança, *s.f.* inheritance, heritage, legacy, bequest; family estate, hereditary property; heredity; birthright, succession.
herbáceo, *adj.* herbaceous.
herbanário, *s.m.* herb shop; herb dealer.
herbário, *s.m.* herbarium.
herbífero, *adj.* herbiferous.
herbívoro, *adj., s.m.* herbivorous; herbivore.
herbolário, *s.m.* herbalist, herborist.
herbóreo, *adj.* herbal, herbaceous.
herborista, *s.* herborist, herbalist.
herborização, *s.f.* herborization; botanizing.
herborizador, *s.m.* herborist, herbalist.
herborizar, *v.t.* to herborize, to botanize.
herboso, *adj.* herbous, herby, grassy.
herculano, *adj.* Herculean.
hercúleo, *adj.* Herculean; strong, vigorous, robust.
herdade, *s.f.* farm; estate, landed property.
herdar, *v.t.* to inherit, to get by succession, to come into a fortune, to be the heir.
herdeira, *s.f.* heiress.
herdeiro, *s.m.* heir; heritor, inheritor, successor. 1) *príncipe herdeiro*, crown prince. 2) *herdeiro da coroa*, heir to the crown. 3) *herdeiro presuntivo*, heir presumptive. 4) *herdeiro legítimo*, rightful heir. 5) *herdeiro universal*, residuary legatee.
hereditariedade, *s.f.* heredity, hereditariness.
hereditário, *adj.* hereditary, ancestral; inherited, transmitted.
herege, *adj., s.m.* heretical; heretic, misbeliever.

heresia, *s.f.* heresy, erroneous belief; heterodoxy.
heresiarca, *s.* heresiarch.
herético, *adj.* heretical.
hermafrodita, *s.m., adj.* hermaphrodite; hermaphroditic, bisexual, androgynous.
hermafroditismo, *s.m.* hermaphroditism, androgyny.
hermeneuta, *s.* hermeneutic scholar, hermeneut, exegete.
hermenêutica, *s.f.* hermeneutics.
hermenêutico, *adj.* hermeneutical, explanatory, exegetical.
hermeticamente, *adv.* hermetically, airtightly; *hermeticamente fechado*, air-tight, hermetically sealed.
hermeticidade, *s.f.* air-tightness.
hermético, *adj.* hermetic, air-tigmt; abstruse.
hérnia, *s.f.* hernia, rupture breach; *hérnia estrangulada*, strangulated hernia.
herniado, hernioso, *adj.* herniated, affected by hernia.
hernial, *adj.* hernial; herniary.
herniotomia, *s.f.* herniotomy.
herói, *s.m.* hero.
heroicamente, *adv.* heroically, valliantly, epically.
heroicidade, *s.f.* heroism, valour, bravery.
heróico, *adj.* heroic, heroical, valiant, dauntless, daring.
heróico-cómico, *adj.* hero-comic, mockheroic.
heroificar, *v.t.* to heroify, to make heroic, to glorify, to exalt.
heroína, *s.f.* heroine; heroin *(narcótico)*.
heroísmo, *s.m.* heroism, courage, bravery, valour, boldness intrepidity.
herpes, *s.m., pl.* herpes, skin desease.
herpético, *adj.* herpetic.
herpetismo, *s.m.* herpetism.
herpetografia, *s.f.* herpetography.
herpetógrafo, *s.m.* herpetographer, herpetologist.
herpetologia, *s.f.* herpetology.
hertziano, *adj.* Hertzian.
hesitação, *s.f.* hesitation; perplexity; vacillation; doubt, indecision, pause; faltering, wavering.
hesitante, *adj.* hesitant, vacillating; dubious, undecided, wavering, pausing, irresolute, faltering.
hesitar, *v.i.* to hesitate, to waver; to be reluctant; to linger, to vacillate, to falter, to pause.

heteróclito, *adj.* heteroclite, anomalous, irregular; strange, peculiar.

heterodoxia, *s.f.* heterodoxy, dissent; heterodox opinion.

heterodoxo, *adj.* heterodox, heretical.

heterogeneidade, *s.f.* heterogeneity, dissimilarity, diversity.

heterogéneo, *adj.* heterogeneous, dissimilar, different, unlike.

heterogenesia, *s.f.* heterogenesis.

heterogenia, *s.f.* heterogeny.

heteromorfia, heteromorfismo, *s.f., s.m.* heteromorphism, heteromorphy.

heteromorfo, *adj.* heteromorphic, heteromorphous.

heteromorfose, *s.f.* heteromorfosis.

heteronímia, *s.f.* heteronymy.

heteronomia, *s.f.* heteronomy.

heterónomo, *adj.* heteronomous.

heurística, *s.f.* heuristic.

hexacorde, *s.m.* hexacord.

hexaédrico, *adj.* hexahedral.

hexaedro, *s.m.* hexahedron.

hexagonal, *adj.* hexagonal.

hexágono, *s.m.* hexagon.

hexagrama, *s.m.* hexagrama.

hexâmetro, *s.m.* hexameter.

hexandro, *adj.* hexandrous.

hexapétalo, *adj.* hexapetalous.

hexápode, *adj, s.m.* hexapod; hexapodous.

hexáptero, *adj.* hexapterous.

hexassépalo, *adj.* hexasepalous.

hexassílabo, *adj.* hexasyllabic.

hexavalente, *adj.* hexavalent.

hiacintino, *adj.* hyacinthine.

hiacinto, *s.m.* hyacinth.

Híades, *s.f., pl.* Hyades.

hialino, *adj.* hyaline, glassy, crystal-line, transparent.

hialite, *s.f.* hyalite.

hialografia, *s.f.* hyalography.

hialógrafo, *s.m.* hyalograph.

hialóide, *adj., s.f.* hyaloid, vitriform.

hialoplasma, *s.m.* hyaloplasm.

hiante, *adj.* gaping, wide open, open-mouthed.

hiato, *s.m.* hiatus, grap, lacuna; interval, interruption.

hibernação, *s.f.* hibernation, winter-sleep.

hibernal, *adj.* hibernal, wintry.

hibernante, *adj.* hibernant, hinbernating.

hibernar, *v.i.* to hibernate.

hibridação, *s.f.* hybridization, crossbreeding.

hibridez, *s.f.* hybridity, anomaly, irregularity.

hibridismo, *s.m.* hybridism, a hybrid word.

hibridista, *s.* hybridist.

híbrido, *adj.* hybrid; cross-bred.

hidra, *s.f.* hydra.

hidrácido, *adj.* hydracid.

hidragogo, *s.m.* hydragogue, diuretic.

hidrângea, *s.f.* hydrangea.

hidrante, *s.m.* hydrant.

hidrargírio, *s.m.* mercury, hydrargyrum, quicksilver.

hidratação, *s.f.* hydratation, hydration.

hidratar, *v.t.* to hydrate.

hidratável, *adj.* capable of being hydrated.

hidrato, *s.m.* hydrate.

hidráulica, *s.f.* hydraulics.

hidráulico, *adj.* hydraulic. 1) *força hidráulica*, hydraulic power. 2) *energia hidráulica*, water power. 3) *travão hidráulico*, hydraulic brake. 4) *macaco hidráulico*, hydraulic jack. 5) *pressão hidráulica*, hydraulic pressure.

hidremia, *s.f.* hydremia.

hidreto, *s.f.* hydride.

hídrico, *adj.* hydric.

hidroavião, *s.m.* hydroplane, seaplane, flying boat.

hidrocefalia, *s.f.* hydrocephaly.

hidrocéfalo, *adj.* hydrocephalic.

hidrodinâmica, *s.f.* hydrodynamics.

hidrodinâmico, *adj.* hydrodynamical.

hidroeléctrico, *adj.* hydroelectric.

hidrófilo, *adj.* hydrophil; *algodão hidrófilo*, absorbent cotton.

hidrofobia, *s.f.* hydrophobia; rabies, dread of water.

hidrófobo, *adj.* hydrophobia; rabid, mad.

hidrofone, *s.m.* hydrophone.

hidrófugo, *adj.* hydrofuge.

hidrogenação, *s.f.* hydrogenation; hydrogenization.

hidrogenar, *v.t.* to hydrogenate; to hydrogenize.

hidrogénio, *s.m.* hydrogen; *bomba de hidrogénio*, hydrogen bomb, H-bomb.

hidrografia, *s.f.* hydrography.

hidrográfico, *adj.* hydrographical.

hidrógrafo, *s.m.* hydrographer.

hidrólise, *s.f.* hydrolysis.

hidrologia, *s.f.* hydrology.

hidrológico, *adj.* hydrological.

hidrólogo, *s.m.* hydrologist.

hidromania, *s.f.* hydromania.

hidromecânico, *adj.* hydromechanical.

hidromel, *s.m.* hydromel.

hidrometria, *s.f.* hydrometry.

hidrométrico, *adj.* hydrometrical.

hidrómetro, *s.m.* hydrometer, water-meter.

hidromineral, *adj.* hydromineral.

hidromotor, *s.m.* hydromotor.

hidropata, *s.* hydropath(ist).

hidropatia, *s.f.* hydropathy.

hidropático, *adj.* hydropathic(al).

hidrópico, *adj.* hydropical, hydropic, dropsical, endematous.

hidropisia, *s.f.* dropsy, hydropsy.

hidroplano, *s.m.* hydroplane, flying-boat, water-plane.

hidropneumático, *adj.* hydropneumatic.

hidrópota, *s.* water-drink, hydropot.

hidroquinona, *s.f.* hydroquinone.

hidroscopia, *s.f.* water-divining

hidróscopo, *s.m.* hydroscope, hydrometer; water-finder.

hidrosfera, *s.f.* hydrosphere.

hidrossolúvel, *adj.* water-soluble.

hidrossulfato, *s.m.* hidrosulfate.

hidrossulfito, *s.m.* hidrosulfite.

hidrossulfúrico, *adj.* hydrosulfuric.

hidrostática, *s.f.* hidrostatics.

hidrostático, *adj.* hydrostatic(al).

hidróstato, *s.m.* hydrostat.

hidrotecnia, *s.f.* hydrotechnique.

hidrotécnico, *adj.* hydrotechnic(al).

hidroterapia, *s.f.* hydrotherapy, hydrotherapeutics.

hidroterápico, *adj.* hydrotherapeutic(al).

hidrotérmico, *adj.* hydrothermal.

hidrotórax, *s.m.* hydrothroax, dropsy of the chest.

hidrotrópico, *adj.* hydrotropic.

hidrotropismo, *s.m.* hydrotropism.

hidróxido, *s.m.* hydroxide.

hiemação, *s.f.* heimation, wintering.

hiemal, *adj.* hiemal, hibernal.

hiena, *s.f.* hyena.

hierarquia, *s.f.* hierarchy.

hierárquico, *adj.* hierarchic(al)

hierarquização, *s.f.* hierarchization.

hierarquizar, *v.t.* to hierarchize.

hierático, *adj.* hieratic, religious, sacred.

hieroglífico, *adj.* hieroglyphic.

hieróglifo, *s.m.* hieroglyph.

hierografia, *s.f.* hierography.

hierográfico, *adj.* hierographic(al).

hierologia, *s.f.* hierology.

hierológico, *adj.* hierologic(al).

hífen, *s.m.* hyphen, dash.

higiene, *s.f.* hygiene; hygienics, cleanliness, neatness.

higienicamente, *adv.* hygienically.

higiénico, *adj.* hygienical; clean, neat.

higienista, *s.* hygienist.

higienizar, *v.t.* to hygienize, to make hygienic.

higrometria, *s.f.* hygrometry

higrométrico, *adj.* hygrometric.

higrómetro, *s.m.* hygrometer.

higroscópico, *adj.* hygroscopic (al).

higroscópio, *s.m.* hygroscope.

hílare, *adj.* merry, cheerful, hilarious; satisfied, content.

hilariante, *adj.* exhilarating, hilarious, gay, merry, cheering; *gás hilariante,* laughing gas.

hilaridade, *s.f.* hilarity, merriment, mirth, cheerfulness, high spirits.

hilarizar, *v.t.* to exhilarate, to gladden, to enliven, to cheer up, to make merry.

hilo, *s.m.* hilum; scar, mark.

hilota, *s.m.* helot, slave *(em Esparta).*

hímen, *s.m.* hymen.

himeneu, *s.m.* marriage, wedlock.

himenóptero, *adj., s.m.* hymenopterous, himenopteral; hymenopter.

hinário, *s.m.* hymnal, hymn-book.

hindu, *s., adj.* Hindu, Indian, Hindoo.

hindustânico, *adj.* Hindustani.

hinista, *s.* hymnist, writer of hymns.

hino, *s.m.* hymn, anthem; religious song; *hino nacional,* national anthem.

hinografia, *s.f.* himnography.

hinógrafo, *s.m.* hymnographer.

hinologia, *s.f.* hymnology.

hinólogo, *s.m.* hymnologist. hymnist.

hióide, *adj., s.m.* hyoid; hyoidean bone, tongue bone.

hiperacidez, *s.f.* hiperacidity.

hiperácido, *adj.* hisperacid.

hipérbato, *s.m.* hyperbaton.

hipérbole, *s.f.* hiperbola *(geom.);* hyperbole, exaggeration.

hiperbólico, *adj.* hyperbolic *(geom);* hyperbolical.

hiperbolismo, *s.m.* hyperbolism.

hiperbolóide, *adj.* hyperboloid.

hiperbóreo, *adj.* hyperborean of the far north; very cold.

hipercriticismo, *s.m.* hypercriticism, excessive criticism.

hipercrítico, *adj., s.m.* hypercritical; hyper-critic.

hiperestesia, *s.f.* hyperesthesia.

hipergenesia, *s.f.* hypergenesis, hypertrophy.

hipericão, s.m. St. John's wort.

hipermetropia, s.f. hypermetropy, far-sightedness.

hipermiopia, s.f. hypermyopia, short-sightedness.

hipermnésia, s.f. hypermnesia.

hipersensibilidade, s.f. irritability, hyper-sensitiveness.

hipersensível, adj. hypersensitive.

hipertensão, s.f. hypertension.

hipertenso, adj. hypertensive.

hipértese, s.f. hyperthesis, metathesis.

hipertiroidismo, s.m. hyperthyroidism.

hipertonia, s.f. hypertonia.

hipertrofia, s.f. hypertrophy, excessive growth; exaltation.

hipertrofiar, v.t. to hypertrophy.

hípico, adj. hippic; concurso hípico, horse-race; jumping; steeplechase.

hipismo, s.m. horsemanship.

hipnose, s.a., f. hypnosis, hypnotic state; hypnotism.

hipnótico, adj., s.m. hypnotic, soporific, narcotic.

hipnotismo, s.m. hypnotism, fascination

hipnotista, s. hypnotist.

hipnotização, s.f. hypnotization.

hipnotizador, s.m., adj. hypnotist, hipnotizer; hypnotizing, fascinating.

hipnotizar, v.t. to hypnotize, to fascinate, to entrance.

hipnotizável, adj. hypnotizable.

hipobrânquio, adj. hypobranchial.

hipocampo, s.m. hippocampus, seamonster (mito).

hipocárpio, s.m. hypocarp.

hipocondria, s.f. hypochondria; spleen, melancholy.

hipocondríaco, adj., s.m. hypochondriac, melancholic.

hipocôndrio, s.m. hypochondrium.

hipocorístico, adj., s.m. hypocoristic; pet name (Billy, Mama, etc.).

hipocrático, adj. Hippocratic.

hipocrisia, s.f. hypocrisy, dissimulation, simulation, pretence, falseness; double-dealing.

hipócrita, s., adj. hypocrite, dissembler, double-dealer, tartuffe; hypocritical.

hipoderme, s.f. hypodermis.

hipodérmico, adj. hypodermic, subcuta-neous; hypodermal (bot.)

hipódromo, s.m. hypodrome, race-course.

hipoestesia, s.f. hypoesthesia.

hipófise, s.f. hypophysis, pituitary gland.

hipofosfato, s.m. hypophosphate.

hipogástrico, adj. hypogastric.

hipogastro, s.m. hypogastrium.

hipogeu, s.m. hypogeum, catacomb.

hipologia, s.f. hyppology.

hipólogo, s.m. hyppologist.

hipopótamo, s.m. hippopotamus, river-horse; corpulent person (fig).

hipossulfito, s.m. hyposulphite.

hipostático, adj. hypostatic(al).

hipostenia, s.f. hyposthenia, weakness.

hiposténico, adj. hyposthenic.

hipostilo, s.m. hypostyle.

hipoteca, s.f. mortgage.

hipotecar, v.t. to mortgage; to bond, to pledge.

hipotecário, adj. hypothecary.

hipotensão, s.f. hypotension.

hipotenusa, s.f. hypotenuse.

hipótese, s.f. hypothesis, supposition, theory, assumption, conjecture. 1) na melhor hipótese, at best. 2) na hipótese de, assuming that.

hipoteticamente, adv. hypothetically.

hipotético, adj. hypothetic, conjectural; assumed.

hipotonia, s.f. hypotonia.

hipotónico, adj. hypotonic.

hipotrofia, s.f. hypotrophy, atrophy.

hipsografia, s.f. hypsography.

hipsográfico, adj. hypsographical.

hipsometria, s.f. hypsomeytry.

hipsométrico, adj. hypsometric(al).

hipsómetro, s.m. hypsometer.

hircino, adj. hircine, goatish.

hirsuto, adj. hirsute, rough, unshorn.

hirteza, s.f. stiffness, rigidity, uprightness, immobility.

hirto, adj. stiff, rigid; erect, upright; hairsute, hairy.

hirundino, adj. hirundine.

hispânico, hispano, adj. Hispanic, Spanish.

hispanismo, s.m. Hispanism.

hispanista, s. Hispanist.

hispidez, s.f. hairiness, hairsuteness, bristliness, hispidity.

híspido, adj. hispid, rough, hairsute, bristly, shaggy.

hissope, s.m. aspergillum, sprinkler, aspersorium.

histerectomia, s.f. hysterectomy.

histeria, s.f. hysteria, morbid excitement.

histérica, s.f. hysteric, hysterical woman.

histericamente, adv. hysterically.

histérico, *adj., s.m.* hysterical; hysteriac.

histerismo, *s.m.* hysteria, hysterical state.

histogenia, *s.f.* histogeny, hystogenesis.

histografia, *s.f.* histography.

histográfico, *adj.* histografic(al).

histógrafo, *s.m.* hystographer.

histologia, *s.f.* histology.

histológico, *adj.* histologiac(al).

histologista, *s.* histologist.

história, *s.f.* history; story, tale; narrative, narration; fable, legend; description, fake, sham. 1) *passar à história*, to become history. 2) *história da carochinha*, fairy tale, nursery tale. 3) *a história de sempre*, the same old story. 4) *que história é essa?*, what do you mean?, what are you talking about?

historiador, *s.m.* historian, chronicler.

historial, *s.m.* the history of something or event.

historiar, *v.t.* to chronicle, to tell, to write or tell the history of, to describe, to relate.

historicamente, *adv.* historically.

historicidade, *s.f.* historicity.

histórico, *adj.* historical, true, veracious; famous in history.

historieta, *s.f.* short story; tale.

historiografia, *s.f.* historiography.

historiográfico, *adj.* historiographical.

historiógrafo, *s.m.* historiographer, chronicler, historian.

histrião, *s.m.* histrian, buffoon, clown; impostor.

histriónico, *adj.* histrionical, theatrical; artificial, unreal.

hitlerismo, *s.m.* Hitlerism.

hodiernamente, *adv.* nowadays, today.

hodierno, *adj.* hodiernal, contemporary, present day, of this day.

hodómetro, *s.m.* hodometer.

hoje, *adv.* today; nowadays, at the present time. 1) *hoje em dia*, nowadays, at the present time, in these days. 2) *hoje mesmo*, this very day. 3) *de hoje em diante*, from this day on. 4) *até hoje*, to this day, till now, up to this date.

holanda, *s.f.* Holland, linen fabric.

holandês, *s.m., adj.* Dutchman, Hollander; Dutch, Hollandish.

holocausto, *s.m.* holocaust, sacrifice.

holoédrico, *adj.* holohedral.

holoedro, *s.m.* holohedron.

holofote, *s.m.* holophote, searchlight, projector, spotlight.

hombridade, *s.f.* manliness, nobleness, virility, noble courage.

homem, *s.m.* man; husband; human being; person; human race; mankind; adult male. 1) *homem de negócios*, businessman. 2) *homem de palavra*, a man of his word. 3) *homem do leme*, steersman. 4) *homem do povo*, commoner. 5) *homem importante*, bigwig. 6) *homem prevenido vale por dois*, forwarned is forearmed. 7) *o homem põe e Deus dispõe*, man proposes, God disposes.

homenagear, *v.t.* to homage, to pay homage to.

homenagem, *s.f.* homage; deference; reverence, respect; obeisance; compliments *(pl.)*. 1) *prestar homenagem*, to do homage, to pay tribute. 2) *a última homenagem*, the last honours.

homenzarrão, *s.m.* big man, tall, stout man; a giant.

homenzinho, *s.m.* a little man, dot, a nobody; lad, young.

homeopata, *s.* hemeopathist, homoeopath.

homeopatia, *s.f.* homoeopathy.

homeopático, *adj.* homoeopathic.

homérico, *adj.* Homeric; epic, great.

homicida, *s., adj.* homicide, manslaughter. murder; murderous, homicidal.

homicídio, *s.m.* homicide, manslaughter.

homilia, *s.f.* homily, sermon.

homiliar, *v.i.* to preach homilies, to exhort, to admonish.

homiliário, *s.m.* book of homilies.

homiliasta, *s.* homilist, preacher, composer of homilies.

hominal, *adj.* hominal.

homiziação, *s.f.* refuge, retreat, shelter.

homiziado, *s.m., adj.* refugee, fugitive; hidden, concealed.

homiziar, *v.t.* to conceal, to shelter; *homiziar-se*, to escape, to take refuge, to abscond.

homízio, *s.m.* sheltering, refuge, protection; concealment, hiding.

homocêntrico, *adj.* homocentric, concentric(al).

homofonia, *s.f.* homophony, sameness of sound.

homofónico, *adj.* homophonic, homophonous, unisonant.

homófono, *adj.* homophonous.

homogeneidade, *s.f.* homogeneity, homogeneousness.

homogeneização, *s.f.* homogenization.

homogeneizar, v.t. to homogenize, to make homogeneous.

homogéneo, adj. homogeneous, congenial, uniform, of the same kind.

homogenesia, s.f. homogenesis.

homogenia, s.f. homogeny.

homografia, s.f. homography.

homográfico, adj. homographic(al).

homógrafo, s.m. homograph.

homologação, s.f. homologation, ratification, confirmation, sanction; agreement.

homologar, v.t. to homologate, to ratify, to confirm.

homologia, s.f. homology, correspondence.

homólogo, adj. homologous, corresponding, agreeing.

homomorfismo, s.m. homomorphism.

homomorfo, adj. homomorphous.

homonímia, homonymy, sameness of name.

homonímico, adj. homonymic.

homónimo, adj., s.m. homonymous; homonym.

homopétalo, adj. homopetalous.

homoplasia, s.f. homoplasy.

homoplástico, adj. homoplastic.

homúnculo, s.m. homunculus, little man, dwarf.

honestamente, adv. honestly; frankly, sincerely.

honestar, v.t. to honour; to make honest; to beautify; to justify, to defend.

honestidade, s.f. honesty, integrity; chastity; uprightness, proibity; justice.

honesto, adj. honest, virtuous, just, truthful, upright, conscientious, scrupulous; sincere, reliable, competent; proper, decent; reputable.

honor, s.m. dama do honor, maid of honour.

honorabilidade, s.f. integrity, honourableness, reputability, worthiness.

honorário, adj., s.m. pl. honorary, conferring honour; unpaid; fees, salaries.

honorificar, v.t. to honourify, to confer honour to or upon.

honorificência, s.f. mark of honour or distinction.

honorífico, adj. honorary, honorific.

honra, s.f. honour; reverence; probity; honesty; chastity; reputation, good name; fame, renown, eminence; courtesies, rendered (pl.); funeral ceremonies. 1) código de honra, code of honour. 2) em honra de, in honour of. 3) pela minha honra, on my honour. 4) dar a palavra de honra, to give one's word of honour. 5) fazer as honras da casa, to do the honours of the house.

honradamente, adv. honourably, honestly; sincerely; virtuously.

honradez, s.f. honour, probity, honesty, integrity.

honrado, adj. honest, honourable, reputable; sincere; respected; sound; virtuous, chaste.

honrar, v.t. to honour, to glorify, to exalt, to respect, to revere; to distinguish; to give credit to, to rely on.

honraria, s.f. honour; distinction, privilege, rank.

honrosamente, adv. honourably, honestly, decently.

honroso, adj. honourable, praiseworthy, distinguished, creditable; fair decent.

hóquei, s.m. hockey; hóquei em patins, rink hockey.

hora, s.f. hour, opportunity; time; hours (prayers at certain hours of the day) (pl.); last hour. 1) hora do chá, tea-time. 2) hora de dormir, bedtime. 3) hora de ponta, rush hours. 4) hora de jantar, dinner-time. 5) hora de recolher, curfew. 6) hora de expediente, business hour. 7) hora H, the eleventh hour. 8) de hora a hora, from hour to hour. 9) esperar horas e horas, to wait a long time. 10) está na (deu a) hora, it is time, time is over (up). 11) fora de horas, ill-timed. 12) hora marcada, fixed time. 13) màesmo á hora, just in time. 14) a altas horas, far on in the night. 15) de hora a hora, hourly.

horaciano, adj. Horatian.

horário, s.m., adj. time-table; hourly; horary.

horda, s.f. hord, gang, multitude, troop, rough crowd, band, mob.

horizontal, adj. horizontal; even, flat.

horizontalidade, s.f. horizontality.

horizontalmente, adv. horizonrally, evenly, flatly.

horizonte, s.m. horizon, sky-line; limits, experience, intelligence; horizonte visual, visible horizon.

hormona, s.f. hormone.

horografia, s.f. horography.

horográfico, adj. horographic(al).

horoscópio, s.m. horoscope.

horóscopo, s.m. horoscope, prediction, prophecy.

horrendamente, adv. horribly, horrendously, frightfully, hideously.

horrendo, horrente, adj. horrible, dreadfull, shocking, fearful, frightful, appalling; ugly, monstrous.

horribilidade, s.f. horribleness, horridness, hideousness, dreadfulness.

hórrido, adj. horrible, horrid, fearful, terrible, dreadful, hideous.

horrífico, adj. horrific, horrifying.

horripilação, s.f. horripilation, gooseflesh.

horripilante, adj. horrifying, shocking, hair-raising, heinous, terrifying.

horripilar, v.t. to horrify, to frighten, to produce horripilation; to shudder, to shiver.

horríssono, adj. horrisonous, horrisonant, sounding horribly.

horrível, adj. horrible, dreadful, shocking; revolting, abominable, hideous.

horrivelmente, adv. horribly, frigthfully, grimly.

horror, s.m. horror, dread, horridness, terror; repulsion, aversion; pain, agony; shudder, shiver. 1) *que horror!,* how awful!. 2) *ter horror a,* to abhor, to loathe. 3) *causar horror,* to inspire with horror.

horrorizado, adj. horror-struck, terrified, horrified.

horrorizar, v.t. frighten, to terrify, to horrify; to scandalize, to shock.

horrorosamente, adv. horribly, dreadfully.

horroroso, adj. dreadful, horrible, terrible, frightful, appalling, hideous.

horta, s.f. kitchen-garden, vegetable-garden, truck-farm.

hortaliça, s.f. vegetables, greens, pot-herbs.

hortaliceira, hortaliceiro, s.f., s.m. greengrocer.

hortelã, s.f. mint.

hortelão, s.m. kitchen-gardener, truck-gardener.

hortelã-pimenta, s.f. peppermint.

horteloa, s.f. kitchen-gardener, woman gardener.

hortense, adj. hortensial, hortensian.

hortênsia, s.f. hydrangea.

hortícola, adj. horticultural.

horticultor, s.m. horticulturist, expert gardener.

horticultura, s.f. horticulture.

horto, s.m. kitchen-garden; plant nursery; calvary.

hosana, s.m. hosanna.

hóspeda, s.f. hostess; guest.

hospedagem, s.f. lodging; hospitality, accomodation.

hospedar, v.t. to lodge, to house, to accomodate, to receive as a guest. 1) *hospedar-se,* to take lodgings. 2) *hospedar-se num hotel,* to put up at the hotel.

hospedaria, s.f. inn lodging-house; hostelry, boarding-house.

hóspede, s.m., adj. guest; paying-guest, boarder; stranger; ignorant (fig); guest house.

hospedeira, s.f. hostess, innkeeper, landlady.

hospedeiro, s.m., adj. host, inn-keeper; hospitable.

hospício, s.m. hospice, asylum, refuge.

hospital, s.m. hospital.

hospitalar, adj. of a hospital; hospitable.

hospitalário, s.m. hospitaller; knight Hospitaller.

hospitaleiro, adj. hospitable, friendly, kind.

hospitalidade, s.f. hospitality, friendly reception of guests or strangers.

hospitalização, s.f. hospitalization, admission in a hospital (para tratamento).

hospitalizar, v.t. to hospitalize, to intern in a hospital.

hoste, s.f. host; troop, army; large number of people.

hóstia, s.f. Host; wafer, holy bread; Eucharist.

hostiário, s.m. wafer-box.

hostil, adj. hostile, unfriendly, adverse, inimical, opposed; aggressive, provocative.

hostilidade, s.f. hostility, enmity; antagonism, opposition, animosity; acts of warfare (pl.).

hostilizar, v.t. to oppose; to war, to fight against; to show ill, to persecute, to set against.

hostilmente, adv. hostilely, inimacally, unfriendly.

hotel, s.m. hotel. 1) *hotel para automobilistas,* motel. 2) *gerente de hotel,* hotel manager.

hoteleiro, s.m. hotel-keeper; proprietor of a hotel.

hotentote, adj., s. Hottentot.

huguenote, s. Huguenot.

hulha, s.f. pit-coal, black-coal, stone coal; *hulha branca,* water-power.

hulheira, s.f. colliery; coal-pit, coal-mine.

hulhífero, adj. carboniferous, coalbearing.

humanal, adj. human.

humanamente, adv. humanly, kindly, gently.

humanar, *v.t.* to humanize, to make human; to become man (*o Filho de Deus*).

humanidade, *s.f.* humanity; mankind; human nature; the human race; benevolence, kindness, mercy, compassion; human or classical learning (*pl*).

humanismo, *s.m.* humanism, study of classical learnings and culture.

humanista, *adj., s.* humanist; scholar of classic culture.

humanístico, *adj.* humanistic.

humanitário, *adj., s.m.* humanitarian, philanthropic; philanthropist, humanitarian.

humanitarismo, *s.m.* humanitarianism.

humanização, *s.f.* humanization, humanizing.

humanizar, *v.t.* to humanize, to make human; to render humane or gentle; to make manageable; to civilize.

humano, *adj.* human; tender, compassionate, kind, humane, gentle.

humedecer, *v.t.* to dampen, to moisten; to wet; to humidify, to render humid; to soak.

humedecimento, *s.m.* moistening, wetting, dampening.

humidade, *s.f.* humidity, moisture, dampness.

húmido, *adj.* humid, moist, wet.

húmil, *adj. ver "humilde".*

humildação, *s.f.* humiliation.

humildade, *s.f.* humility, humbleness, modesty, meekness; submission; poverty.

humildar-se, *v. refl.* to humble oneself; to stoop.

humilde, *adj.* humble, modest, meek; submissive; poor.

humildemente, *adv.* humbly, obscurely; 1) *de condição humilde,* low borne, of humble origin.

humilhação, *s.f.* humiliation; humbling; abasement; submission.

humilhante, *adj.* humiliating, humbling, depressing, mortifying; abasing, degradins.

humilhar, *v.t.* to humiliate, to humble; to abase, to debase; to mortify; to lower the pride of, to abash, to crush.

humílimo, *adj.* humble.

humo, húmus, *s.m.* humus.

humor, *s.m.* humour, disposition, mood, temper, feeling; fancy, whim; wit, fun; bofily fluid. 1) *de bom humor,* good-humoured, in a good temper, in high spirits. 2) *de mau humor,* out of humour, in a bad temper, ill-humoured.

humorado, *adj.* humoured, tempered; humorous, comic.

humorismo, *s.m.* humour, drollery, humorism.

humorista, *s.* humorist, wit, witty person.

humoristicamente, *adv.* humoristically, comically.

humorístico, *adj.* humorist, humorous, funny, comical, witty.

humoroso, *adj.* humoral.

humoso, *adj.* humous, rich in humus.

húngaro, *s.m., adj.* Hungarian.

huno, *s.m., adj.* Hun; Hunnish.

huri, *s.f.* houri; beautiful woman.

hurra!, *interj.* hurrah!, cheerio!.

hússar, hussardo, *s.m.* hussar.

I

i, the ninth letter of the Portuguese alphabet.

iâmbico, *adj.* iambic.

iambo, *s.m.* iamb.

ianque, *s., adj.* Yankee.

ião, *s.m.* ion.

iate, *s.m.* yatch.

ibérico, *adj.* Iberian.

iberismo, *s.m.* Iberism.

ibero, *s.m., adj.* Iberian.
ibero-americano, *s.m., adj.* Ibero-American.
ibidem, *adv.* ibidem, in the same place.
íbis, *s.* ibis *(pássaro).*
içar, *v.t.* to hoist, to haul up, to lift; *içar a bandeira,* to hoist the flag.
icebergue, *s.m.* iceberg.
ichó, *s.f.* trap, snare.
icnografia, *s.f.* ichnography.
icnográfico, *adj.* ichnographical.
icnógrafo, *s.m.* ichnographer, draughtsman.
ícone, *s.m.* icon, image, sacred portrait, statue.
icónico, *adj.* iconic(al).
iconismo, *s.m.* iconism.
iconista, *s.* iconist.
iconoclasia, *s.f.* iconoclasm.
iconoclasmo, *s.m.* iconoclasm.
iconoclasta, *adj., s.* iconoclastic; iconoclast, image-breaker.
iconófilo, *s.m.* iconophile.
iconografia, *s.f.* iconography.
iconográfico, *adj.* iconographic(al).
iconógrafo, *s.m.* iconographer.
iconólatra, *s.* iconolater, image worshipper.
iconolatria, *s.f.* iconolatry
iconologia, *s.f.* iconology.
iconológico, *adj.* iconologic(al).
iconologista, iconólogo, *s.m.* iconologist.
iconómaco, *s.m.* iconoclast.
iconomania, *s.f.* iconomania.
icosaedro, *s.m.* icosahedron.
icterícia, *s.f.* jaundice; yellows *(pop).*
ictérico, *adj.* icterical, jaundiced.
ictiofagia, *s.f.* ichthyophagy.
ictiófago, *s.m., adj.* ichthyophagist; ichthyophagous.
ictiografia, *s.f.* ichthygraphy.
ictiográfico, *adj.* ichthygraphic
ictiógrafo, *s.m.* ichthygrapher.
ictiologia, *s.f.* ichthyology.
ictiológico, *adj.* ichthyologic (al).
ictiólogo, *s.m.* ichthyologist.
ictiose, *s.f.* ichthyosis.
ida, *s.f.* going, departure, setting off; starting, leaving; journey. 1) *idas e vindas,* comings and goings. 2) *ida por vinda (bilhete de),* a return ticket. 3) *de ida e volta,* out and home.
idade, *s.f.* age, years; epoch, time; maturity, stage (civilização, arte). 1) *Idade do Bronze,* bronze, iron, stone age. 2) *Idade Média,* Middle Ages. 3) *menor idade,* underage. 4) *de tenra idade,* of tender age;

5) *ter 10 anos de idade,* to be 10 years old, to be 10 years of age. 6) *ter mais de 18 anos de idade,* to turn eighteen. 7) *estar na flor da idade,* to be in the prime of life. 8) *de idade avançada,* advanced in years. 9) *não mostrar a idade,* not to look one's age. 10) *passar da idade,* to be over age. 11) *certidão de idade,* birth certificate. 12) *homem de idade,* old man.
ideação, *s.f.* ideation, conceprion, notion.
ideal, *adj., s.m.* ideal; mental; fanciful; ideal, perfect type, supreme perfection.
idealidade, *s.f.* ideality.
idealismo, *s.m.* idealism.
idealista, *s., adj.* idealist, unpratical, person, daydreamer; idealistic.
idealístico, *adj.* idealistic.
idealização, *s.f.* idealization.
idealizador, *s.m., adj.* idealizer, idealist; creator, organizer; idealizing.
idealizar, *v.t.* to idealize, to imagine, to fancy, to dream, to picture; to organize.
idealmente, *adv.* ideally.
idear, *v.t.* to plan, to imagine, to sketch, to ideate, to invent, to project; *idear um plano,* to form a plan.
ideário, *s.m.* idearium.
ideativo, *adj.* ideative, ideational.
ideável, *adj.* conceivable.
ideia, *s.f.* idea, notion, conception, belief; opinion; intention, design; project, invention, plan. 1) *tirar da ideia,* to put out of one's head. 2) *que ideia!,* the idea!. 3) *mudar de ideias,* to change one's mind. 4) *não ter (não fazer) a menor ideia,* not to have the remotest idea. 5) *fazer ideia,* to imagine. 6) *ideia genial,* brain-wave. 7) *ideia fixa,* fixed idea. 8) *não passar pela ideia,* not to enter one's thoughts. 9) *dar a ideia de,* to look as if it were.
idem, *adv.* idem, ditto, the same, the afore said.
idêntico, *adj.* identical, alike, similar, analogous.
identidade, *s.f.* identity, sameness, exacteness; *bilhete de identidade,* identity card.
identificação, *s.f.* identification; *placa (chapa) de identificação,* identification tag.
identificar, *c.t.* to identify, to establish the identity of, to recognize, to prove to be the same; *identificar-se com,* to identify oneself with, to be associated with.
identificável, *adj.* identifiable, recognizable.
ideografia, *s.f.* ideography.

ideográfico, *adj.* ideographic(al).

ideógrafo, *s.m.* ideographer.

ideograma, *s.m.* ideogram.

ideologia, *s.f.* ideology, faith, opinions, ideas *(políticas, religiosas, etc.)*, principles.

ideológico, *adj.* ideological.

ideólogo, *s.m.* ideologue, ideologist..

idílico, *adj.* idyllic, pleasing; mild.

idílio, *s.m.* idyll, amorous talking.

idilista, *s.* idyllist.

idiocromático, *adj.* idiochromatic.

idiólatra, *s.* self-worshipper, idiolater.

idiolatria, *s.f.* self-worship, idiolatry.

idioma, *s.m.* language, idiom, tongue; dialect, vernacular.

idiomaticamente, *adv.* idiomatically.

idiomático, *adj.* idiomatic; *expressão idiomática,* idiomatic expression.

idiomografia, *s.f.* idiomography.

idiomórfico, *adj.* idiomorfic.

idiossincratia, *s.f.* idiosyncrasy, temperament, mental constituition; antipathy; distinctive mental quality.

idiossincrásico, *adj.* idiosyncratic, peculiar.

idiota, *s., adj.* idiot, stupid, imbecile, cretin, foool, simpleton; idiot, idiotic, foolish, silly.

idiotia, *s.f.* idiocy, mental imbecility.

idiotice, *s.f.* silliness, foolishness, madness.

idiótico, *adj.* idiotic, utterly foolish, senseless.

idiotismo, *s.m.* idiom, peculiarity of speech; idiotism, idiocy.

idiotizar, *v.t.* to idiotize, to make a fool of.

idólatra, *adj., s.* idolatrous, pagan; idolater, pagan.

idolatrar, *v.t.* to idolize, to adore; to be very fond of, to worship, to deify; to admire.

idolatria, *s.f.* idolatry, admiration, excessive devotion; paganism.

idolátrico, *adj.* idolatrous.

ídolo, *s.m.* idol, false god, object of devotion or love; heathen deity; favourite.

idoneidade, aptness, suitableness, finess, competence, capacity, aptitude.

idóneo, *adj.* apt, suitable, fit, competent, incorrupt, taintless.

Idos, *s.m.pl.* ides *(de Março, etc.)*.

idoso, *adj.* aged, old advanced in years.

ignaro, *adj.* ignorant, stupid, unlearning.

ignávia, *s.f.* idleness; cowardice.

ignavo, *adj.* idle, indolent, lazy; weak, feeble, cowardly.

ígneo, *adj.* igneous, hery.

ignescência, *s.f.* ignescent satet.

ignescente, *adj.* igneous, ignescent, alight.

ignição, *s.f.* ignition.

ignífero, *adj.* producing fire, igniferous.

ignificação, *s.f.* combustion.

ignívomo, *adj.* belching out fire, ignivomous.

ignívoro, *adj.* fire-eating, ignivorous.

ignizar-se, *v. refl.* to ignite; to take fire, to kindle; to set on fire, to inflame.

ignóbil, *adj.* ignoble, dishonourable, mean, base, degraded, shameful, abject.

ignobilidade, *s.f.* ignobility, baseness, meansess.

ignobilmente, *adv.* ignobly, debasingly, abjectly.

ignomínia, *s.f.* ignominy, infamy, dishonour, disgrace, discredit; opprobrium, infamy.

ignominiar, *v.t.* ignominious, dishonourable, shameful, mean, infamous.

ignominiosamente, *adj.* ignominiously.

ignominioso, *adj.* ignominious, dishonourable, shameful, mean, infamous.

ignorado, *adj.* unknown, ignored, obscure

ignorância, *s.f.* ignorance, inexperience, illiteracy. 1) *ignorância crassa*, gross ignorance. 2) *alegar ignorância*, to plead ignorance.

ignorantão, *s.m.* ignoramus, block-head, dunce.

ignorante, *adj., s.* ignorant, unlearned; ignoramus, ignorant, illiterate; ass, clodpate *(pop)*.

ignorantismo, *s.m.* ignorantism, obscurantism *(filosofia, religião)*.

ignorantista, *s.* ignorantist, obscurantist.

ignorar, *v.t.* to ignore; to disregard; nor to know, to be ignorant of; to pass over; not to be acquainted with, not to be versed in.

ignoto, *adj.* unknown, obscure; concealed, hidden.

igreja, *s.f.* church, temple; *igreja matriz.*, mother church, parish church.

igrejeiro, *s.m.* church-goer.

igrejinha, *s.f.* collusion, trick; intrigue, group of plotters; little church, chapel.

igual, *adj., s.* equal, equable; uniform, smooth, even; identical, alike, same; equal, peer, fellow. 1) *sem igual*, matchless. 2) *nunca se viu uma coisa igual*, I never saw the like. 3) *de igual para igual*, between equals. 4) *por igual*, equally. 5) *em partes iguais*, in equal shares, fity-fifty. 6) *ser praticamente igual*, to be much the same. 7) *cada qual com seu igual*, birds of a feather flock together.

igualação, *s.f.* equalization, equalizing, levelling.

igualado, *adj.* equalled; levelled.

igualador, *s.m., adj.* equalizer; equalizing, levelling.

igualamente, *s.m.* equalization; levelling.

igualar, *v.t.* to equalize, to make equal; to level with; to equal, to be equal to; to come up to; to be as good as; to compare.

igualável, *adj.* that can be equalized or compared to.

igualdade, *s.f.* equality, equalness; uniformity; equity; equation, expression of equality *(mat.);* parity. 1) *estar em pé de igualdade com,* to be on equal terms with. 2) *em igualdade de circunstâncias,* under the same circumstances.

igualha, *s.f.* equality of rank, equality in station. 1) *não é da minha igualha,* he is not of my class. 2) *pessoa da sua igualha,* a person of the same station.

igualitário, *adj.* equalitarian.

igualitarismo, *s.m.* equalitarianism.

igualitarista, *s.* protagonist of social equality.

iguaria, *s.f.* dish, dainty, delicacy; food; choice viands.

ilação, *s.f.* illation, deduction, inference, conclusion.

ilaqueação, *s.f.* illaqueation.

ilaquear, *v.t.* to entangle, to entrap, to insnare, to illaqueate.

ilativo, *adj.* illative, inferential, conclusive.

ilegal, *adj.* illegal, unlawful, illicit.

ilegalidade, *s.f.* illegality, unlawfulness, illicitness.

ilegalmente, *adv.* illegally.

ilegibilidade, *s.f.* illegibility.

ilegitimar, *v.t.* to bastardize.

ilegitimidade, *s.f.* illegitimacy; spuriousness, bastardy.

ilegítimo, *adj.* illegitimate, illegal; unlawful; illicit, unauthorized; spurious, bastard, natural; wrongly deduced.

ilegível, *adj.* illegible; unreadable, undepcipherable, hard to read.

ilegivelmente, *adv.* illegibly; unreadably.

íleo, *s.m.* ileum *(anat.)*

ileocecal, *adj.* ileocaecal.

ileso, *adj.* unhurt, safe and sound, uninjured, unharmed, undamaged.

iletrado, *adj.* illiterate, unlettered, unlearned; uneducated, rude.

ilha, *s.f.* island; isle.

ilhal, *s.m.* flank.

ilhar, *v.t.* to isolate, to insulate, to separate; to confine.

lharga, *s.f.* flank, side. 1) *de mão na ilharga,* with arms akimbo. 2) *de ilharga,* laterally.

ilheta, *s.f.* islet.

ilhéu, *s.m.* islander; islet, small uninhabited island.

ilhó, *s.m.* eyelet, lacing-hole, eyehole.

ilhoa, *s.f.* female islander.

ilhota, *s.f.* islet.

ilhote, *s.m.* islet.

ilíaco, *adj., s.m.* iliac; ilium, thighbone.

ilibação, *s.f.* rehabilitation, innocence.

ilibado, *adj.* blameless, innocent, guiltless; rehabilitated.

ilibar, *v.t.* to rehabilitate, to clear from guilt; to establish in good repute.

iliberal, *adj.* illiberal; sordid; petty, mean; intolerant.

iliberalidade, *s.f.* illiberality, niggardliness, meaness.

iliberalismo, *s.m.* illiberalism, illiberality.

ilicitamente, *adv.* illicitly, unlawfully, illegitimately, foul.

ilícito, *adj.* illicit, unlawful, illegaly, prohibited; illigitimate,

ilídimo, *adj.* illegitimate, illegal; unlawful.

ilidir, *v.t.* to refute, to confute, to deny, to destroy, to prove to be false.

ilidível, *adj.* refutable.

ilimitação, *s.f.* illimitation.

ilimitadamente, *adv.* unlimitedly.

ilimitado, *adj.* unlimited, infinite, limitless; unrestrained; boundless; absolute, universal.

ilimitável, *adj.* illimitable, immeasurable.

ilíquido, *adj.* not liquid; gross, total, global.

ilogicamente, *adv.* illogically.

ilógico, *adj.* illogical, absurd, irrational, inconsequent, inconsistent,

ilogismo, *s.m.* illogicality.

iludente, *adj.* illusory, illusive, deceitful.

iludir, *v.t.* to ilude, to deceive; to dupe, to trick, to bluff, to cheat; to mislead, to delude; to ensnare. 1) *iludir a resposta,* to beg the question. 2) *iludir a lei,* to evade the law.

iludível, *adj.* deceptible, that can be deceived.

iluminação, *s.f.* lightning; illumination; decoration by means of many lights; *iluminação eléctrica,* electric light.

iluminado, *adj., s.m.* lighted, illuminated; inspired; illuminate, visionary, prophet.

iluminador, *s.m., adj.* illuminator, decorator; illuminating, illuminative.

iluminante, *adj.* illuminating, enlightening, illuminant.

iluminar, *v.t.* to illuminate, to light up; to enlighten; to adorn with lights; to elucidate, to make clear; to adorn with designs.

iluminismo, *s.m.* illuminism; enlightenment.

iluminista, *s.* illuminist.

iluminura, *s.f.* adornment of books or manuscripts, illumination.

ilusão, *s.f.* illusion, fallacy, delusion, deceiving, deception, vision, chimera, fantasy, fancy, mirage; error, mistake. 1) *que grande ilusão!*, what a delusion!. 2) *ilusão de óptica*, a trick of the eye.

ilusionismo, *s.m.* ilusionism; prestidigitation.

ilusionista, *s.* illusionist, prestidigitation.

ilusivo, *adj.* illusive, deceptive, illusory.

ilusor, *s.m.* deceiver, deluder.

ilusório, *adj.* illusory, deceptive, illusive, deceitful, fallacious, false.

ilustração, *s.f.* illustration, engraving; learning; magazine; erudition, knowledge; periodical, publication; picture *(num livro)*, drawing.

ilustrado, *adj.* learned; illustrated; erudite, cultured; illustrious.

ilustrador, *s.m.* illustrator.

ilustrar, *v.t.* to illustrate; to glorify; to adorn; to teach, to impart knowledge; to enlighten; *ilustrar-se*, to distinguish oneself.

ilustrativo, *adj.* illustrative, elucidative.

ilustre, *adj.* illustrious, renowned, famous, distinguish, celebrated, eminent, worthy, honourable.

ilustríssimo, *adj.* most illustrious, most eminent.

imã, *s.m.* imam; imaum.

imaculabilidade, *s.f.* immaculacy, purity, immaculateness.

imaculado, *adj.* immaculate; pure, spotless, unsoiled; *Imaculada Conceição*, Immaculate Conception.

imaculável, *adj.* that cannot be defiled.

imagem, *s.f.* image; effigy; conception; metaphor; likeness, semblance; mental picture; statue; apparition; idol.

imaginação, *s.f.* imagination; fancy, fantasy, invention; idea, thought; spirit, wit; mania.

imaginador, *s.m.* imaginer, schemer.

imaginante, *adj.* imagining, conceiving.

imaginar, *v.t.* to image, to conceive, to conjecture, to suppose, to fancy, to scheme, to create, to invent, to devise; *imagine!*, just imagine!

imaginária, *s.f.* collection of images.

imaginariamente, *adv.* chimerically, unreally.

imaginário, *adj., s.m.* imaginary, illusory, deceptive, fantastic, illusive, visionary, chimerically, unreal, fanciful; carver.

imaginativa, *s.f.* imaginativeness, imagination, imaginative power.

imaginativo, *adj.* imaginative, inventive, creative; fainful.

imaginável, *adj.* imaginable, thinkable, contrivable.

imaginoso, *adj.* imaginative, fanciful, fantastic; showing imagination.

imaleabilidade, *s.f.* immalleability.

imaleável, *adj.* nom-malleable, immaleable.

íman, *s.m.* magnet; loadstone.

imanar, *v.t.* to magnetize; to attract.

imane, *adj.* huge, enormous.

imanência, *s.f.* immanence, immanancy.

imanente, *adj.* immanent, intrinsic, inherent, present, indwelling.

imanentismo, *s.m.* immanentism.

imanidade, *s.f.* hugeness, enormousness; cruelty, brutality.

imanização, *s.f.* magnetization.

imanizar, *v.t.* to magnetize.

imarcescibilidade, *s.f.* unfadingness.

imarcescível, *adj.* unfading, imperishable, incorruptible.

imarginado, *adj.* having no margin; immarginate.

imaterial, *adj.* immaterial, spiritual, incorporeal, unsubstantial.

imaterialidade, *s.f.* immateriality, immateralness, incorporeity.

imaterialismo, *s.m.* immaterialism.

imaterialista, *s.* immaterialist.

imaterializar, *v.t.* to immaterialize, to make incorporeal.

imaturidade, *s.f.* immaturity, unripness; precocity.

imaturo, *adj.* immature; premature; unripe; precocious, undeveloped, imperfecto; early; young; green, tender; unseasoned; crude, cllous.

imbecil, *adj., s.* stupid, imbecile, silly, idiotic, foolish, feeble-minded; idiot, imbecile, fool, simpleton.

imbecilidade, *s.f.* imbecility, idiocy, foolishness, stupidity, dulness, feeble-minded.

imbecilizar, *v.t.* to render imbecile, to become feeble.

imbele, *adj.* timid, unwarlike, pacific; fearful, weak.

imberbe, *adj.* beardless; immature, young, youthful.

imbibição, *s.f.* imbibition, absorption, imbibing.

imbicar, *v.i.* to land, to cast anchor; to pick a quarrel; to tease.

imbricação, *s.f.* imbrication.

imbricar, *v.t.* to imbricate, to overlap.

imbróglio, *s.m.* imbroglio, confusion *(de ideias)*, intricacy, intricate situation.

imbuir, *v.i.* to imbue, to imbibe, to soak, to moisten, to deep; to pervade; to instil into.

imediação, *s.f.* contiguity, proximity, vicinity, neighbourhood; surroundings, environs *(pl).*

imediatamente, *adv.* immediately, at once, right away, right off, directly, without delay, now.

imediato, *adj., s.m.* immediate, next, near close, contiguous; instantaneous; urgent, prompt; chief officer, first mate *(num barco).*

imedicável, *adj.* immedicable, incurable, irremediable.

imemorado, *adj.* unremembered, forgotten.

imemorável, *adj.* nor memorable.

imemorial, *adj.* immemorial, very ancient, remote, long forgotten.

imensamente, *adv.* immensely.

imensidade, *s.f.* immensity, vastness; immeasurablemess, infinite space, infiniteness; very great amount, quantity; hugeness.

imensidão, *s.f.* ver imensidade.

imenso, *adj., adv.* immense, enormous, vast, immeasurable, infinite, boundless, unlimited; huge, great, big; very, very much.

imensurabilidade, *s.f.* immeasurability, limitless, extent.

imensurável, *adj.* immeasurable, immense, limitless, vast, very great.

imerecidamente, *adv.* undeservedly.

imerecido, *adj.* unmerited, undeserved, not merited; undue.

imergente, *adj.* immersing, immergent, plunging.

imergir, *v.i.* to immerse, to dip, to submerge, to plunge, to dive; to penetrate, to enter.

imérito, *adj.* unmerited, undeserved.

imersão, *s.f.* immersion, submersion, plunge, dip; sinkage.

imersivo, *adj.* immersive, suitable for immersion; involving immersion.

imerso, *adj.* immersed, submerged; absorbed.

imersor, *s.m.* immerger.

imigo, *s.m.* enemy, foe *(poético).*

imigração, *s.f.* immigration.

imigrado, *s.m.* immigrant.

imigrante, *s., adj.* immigrant; immigrating.

imigrar, *v.t.* to immigrate, to settle in a foreign country.

imigratório, *adj.* immigratory, migratory.

iminência, *s.f.* imminence; immenency; nearness; *na iminência de,* on the very edge of.

iminente, *adj.* imminent; impending; soon to happen, threatening, menacing.

iminentemente, *adv.* imminently, impendingly.

imiscibilidade, *s.f.* immiscibility.

imiscível, *adj.* immicible.

imiscuir-se, *v. refl.* to interfere, to meddle with, to intrude upon; to be involved in.

imitação, *s.f.* imitation, copy; likeness, resemblance; counterfeit; mimicry; fake.

imitador, *s.m., adj.* imitador; imitating.

imitante, *adj.* artificial, apish.

imitar, *v.t.* to imitate, to copy, to follow the example of; to mimic, to simulate; to falsify; to resemble.

imitativo, *adj.* imitative, imitational. imitating.

imitável, *adj.* imitable, quota of imitation.

imo, *adj.* inmost; deepest.

imóbil, *adj.* immovable, motionless, firm.

imobiliário, *adj., s.m.* immovable; immovables, real estate *(pl.).*

imobilidade, *s.f.* immobility; impassibility, serenity.

imobilismo, *s.m.* immobilism, opposition to progress.

imobilização, *s.f.* immobilization.

imibilizador, *adj.* immobilizing.

imobilizar, *v.t.* to immobilize; to stop, to make immobile; to fix; to impede, to hamper, to retain.

imoderação, *s.f.* immoderation, immoderateness; excess; extravagance; intemperance.

imoderadamente, *adv.* immoderately.

imoderado, *adj.* immoderate, excessive, exaggerated, unreasonable, intemperate.

imodéstia, *s.f.* immodesty; indecency; arrogance; impudence.

imodesto, *adj.* immodest; indecent, impudent, shameless.

imodicidade, *s.f.* exorbitance, excess, exaggeration.

imódico, *adj.* excessive, exorbitant, exaggerated.

imolação, *s.f.* immolation, sacrifice, sacrificial, offering.

imolador, *s.m., adj.* immolator; immolating.

imolar, *v.t.* immolate, to sacrifice, to kill in sacrifice; to offer.

imoral, *adj.* immoral, vicious, unscrupulous, depraved, loose, corrupt, dissolute; obscene.

imoralidade, *s.f.* immorality, wickedness, depravity, wantonness, obscenity.

imoralismo, *s.m.* immoralism.

imoralmente, *adv.* immorally, dissolutely.

imorigerado, *adj.* libertine, dissolute, licentious; illmannered.

imorredoiro, imorredouro, *adj.* immortal, imperishable, everlasting, undying.

imortal, *adj.* immortal, undying, everlasting, eternal; indestructible.

imortalidade, *s.f.* immortalitym eternity.

imortalização, *s.f.* immortalization.

imortalizador, *adj.* immortalizing.

imortalizar, *v.t.* to immortalize, to render immortal, to perpetuate; to make famous, to eternalize.

imortalmente, *adv.* immortally.

imoto, *adj.* immovable, stationary.

imóvel; *adj., s.m.* immovable; still, unalterable; motionless, firm, steadfast, quiet, unmoving; real estate, a building.

impaciência, *s.f.* impatience, eagerness, anxiety, irritability; haste; restlessness.

impacientar, *v.t., v. refl.* to make impatient; to grow impatient.

impaciente, *adj.* impatient, anxious, eager, restless, hasty; fretful.

impacientemente, *adv.* impatientçy.

impacte, *s.m.* impact; discharge, shot; shock, hit; crash.

impagável, *adj.* priceless, invaluable, inestimable, precious, impayable; ridicolous, funny, comic, queer.

impalpável, *adj.* impalpable, immaterial; intangible.

impaludação, *s.f.* infection with malaria.

impaludar, *v.t.* to infect with malaria.

impaludismo, *s.m.* paludism, malaria.

impar, *v.t.* to pant, to sob, to breathe with difficulty; to glut, to feed to satiete; to behave arrogantly.

ímpar, *adj.* odd, uneven, single, unmatched, sole, unique, unpaired, unrivalled; *número ímpar,* odd number.

imparcial, *adj.* impartial, equitable, just, desinterested, unbiassed, unprejudicial; objective, independent.

imparcialidade, *s.f.* impartiality, fairness, justice, equity; objectiveness, neutrality, evenness.

imparcializar, *v.t.* to make impartial.

imparcialmente, *adv.* impartially, fairly, equitably.

imparidade, *s.f.* oddness; disparity; unevenness, singleness.

impartível, *adj.* indivisible, impartible.

impasse, *s.m.* impasse, dilemma, trouble difficulty.

impassibilidade, *s.f.* impassibility. indifference, phlegm; dispassion.

impassível, *adj.* impassible, insensible; placid, quiet, indifferent, phlegmatic, unaffected.

impassivelmente, *adv.* impassibly.

impavidamente, *adv.* fearlessly, intrepidly.

impavidez, *s.f.* intrepidity, courage, bravery, boldness.

impávido, *adj.* intrepid, fearless, brave. courageous.

impecabilidade, *s.f.* impeccability, faultlessness.

impecável, *adj.* impeccable, faultless, perfect; innocent, pure, sinless, immaculate; spotless, irreproachable.

impedição, *s.f. ver "impedimento".*

impedido, *s.m., adj.* batman; hindered, prevented; blocked, interrupted, obstructed; engaged *(telefone).*

impedimento, *s.m.* obstacle, impediment, hindrance, obstruction; embargo, stoppage; inhibition; determent; opposition; difficulty.

impedir, *v.t.* to impede, to obstruct; to prevent, to hinder, to stop; to retard, to delay; to interrupt, to block, to bar, to check; to oppose; to discourage. 1) *impedir de fazer qualquer coisa,* to prevent from doing. 2) *impedir a entrada,* to shut out. 3) *impedir a ferrugem,* to preserve from rust. 4) *impedir o tráfico,* to hinder the traffic.

impeditivo, *adj.* impeditive, impedimental, preventive.

impelente, *adj.* impellent, driving.

impelir, *v.t.* to impel, to push forward, to force on; to incite, to spur on, to stimulate, to urge, to encourage.

impendente, *adj.* inependent, imminent, threatening, about to happen.

impender, *v.t.* to impend, to be immminent, to hang over, to threaten, to be about to happen.

impene, *adj.* plumeless, wingless.

impenetrabilidade, *s.f.* impenetratibility.

impenetrável, *adj.* impenetrable; inscrutable; uncomprehensible, imprevious; dense, obscure; unfathomable.

impenhorável, *adj.* unseizable, undistrainable.

impenitência, *s.f.* impenitency, obscuracy, unrepentence.

impenitente, *adj.* impenitent, unrepenting, obdurate, incorrigible.

impensadamente, *adv.* thoughtlessly; unexpectedly; heedlessly.

impensado, *adj.* thoughtless, unexpected, heedless, inconsiderate, rash.

imperador, *s.m.* emperor.

imperante, *adj., s.* reigning, ruling; sovereign, ruler.

imperar, *v.t.* to reign, to rule, to command, to govern, to prevent.

imperativamente, *adv.* imperatively, peremptorily.

imperativo, *adj., s.m.* imperative, peremptory; imperative mood.

imperatório, *adj.* imperatorial, categorial, absolute.

imperatriz, *s.f.* empress.

impercebível, *adj. ver "imperceptível".*

imperceptibilidade, *adv.* imperceptibility.

imperceptível, *adj.* imperceptible, undiscernible, very slight, almost invisible; gradual, subtle.

imperceptivelmente, *adv.* imperceptibly, gradually.

imperdível, *adj.* unloseable.

imperdoável, *adj.* unpardonable, inexcusable, unforgivable.

imperecedouro, *adj.* imperishable, immortal, everlasting.

imperecível, *adj.* imperishable, permanent, indestructible; eternal.

imperecivelmente, *adv.* imperishably.

imperfectibilidade, *s.f.* imperfectibility.

imperfectível, *adj.* imperfectible.

imperfeição, *s.f.* imperfection, defect, deficiency, blemish; incorrectness, incompleteness.

imperfeitamente, *adv.* imperfectly.

imperfeito, *adj., s.m.* imperfect, incomplete; defective, faulty, deficient, rough; incorrect; imperfect tense.

imperfuração, *s.f.* imperforation; occlusion.

imperfurado, *adj.* imperforate.

imperfurável, *adj.* imperforable.

imperial, *adj.* imperial; arrogant, haughty; majestic, royal, august; authoritative, proud.

imperialismo, *s.m.* imperialism.

imperialista, *s., adj.* imperialist; imperialistic.

imperícia, *s.f.* unskilfulness; rawness; ineptitude, incompetence, incapacity.

império, *s.m.* empire; rule, sway; supremacy, government; power, command.

imperiosamente, *adv.* imperiously; pressingly.

imperiosidade, *s.f.* imperiousness; arrogance, haughtiness; urgency.

imperioso, *adj.* imperious; arbitrary, arrogant; urgent, pressing; peremptory, absolute, commanding.

imperito, *adj.* unskilful, raw, unexpert, unskilled; ignorant.

impermanência, *s.f.* impermanence; instability; inconstancy.

impermanente, *adj.* impermanent, instable, inconstant; temporary, not enduring.

impermeabilidade, *s.f.* impermeability; impenetrability.

impermeabilização, *s.f.* process od making impermeable, waterproofing.

impermeabilizante, *adj.* proofing.

impermeabilizar, *v.t.* to render impermeable, to waterproof, to make waterproof.

impermeável, *adj., s.m.* impermeable, impervious; waterproof, rain-coat, mackintosh.

impermissível, *adj.* unallowable.

impermutabilidade, *s.f.* unchangeableness, impermutability.

impermutável, *adj.* unchangeable, impermutable.

imperscrutável, *adj.* inscrutable, mysterious, impenetrable, untraceable, unfathomable.

impersistente, *adj.* inconstant, fickle.

impersonalidade, *s.f.* impersonality.

impertérrito, *adj.* fearless, brave, dauntless, intrepid.

impertinência, *s.f.* impertinence, preevishness, irrelevance, insolence, petulance, sauciness.

impertinente, *s.f.* impertinent, peevish, irrelevant, insolent, petulant, importune, fretful, saucy, intrusive.

impertinentemente, *adv.* impertinently.

imperturbabilidade, s.f. imperturbability, steadiness, clamness, serenity.

imperturbável, adj. imperturbable, unmoved, serene, calm, cool; unembarrassed; unshakable.

impérvio, adj. impervious, impenetrable.

impessoal, adj. impersonal, objective.

impessoalidade, s.f. impersonality.

impessoalmente, adv. impersonally.

ímpeto, s.m. impetus, impulse, force, vehemence; fury; rushing, haste; frenzy, fieriness.

impetração, s.f. impetration, entreat, petition, suplication.

impetrante, s., adj. supplicant, petitioner; supllication, entreating.

impetrar, v.t. to impetrate, to entreat, to supplicate.

impetrativo, adj. impetrative, supplicatory.

impetratório, adj. impetratory.

impetuosamente, adv. impetuously; impulsively.

impetuosidade, s.f. impetuosity, violence, vehemence, impetuousness; fury, anger.

impetuoso, adj. impetuous, violent; precipitate, hasty; passionate; furious, angry, fierce; temperamental.

impiamente, adv. impiosly, mercilessly, wickedly.

impiedade, s.f. impiety, ungodliness, piyilessness, cruelty, mersilessness.

impiedosamente, adv. pitilessly, mercilessly, cruelly.

impiedoso, adj. pitiless, unmerciful, merciless, cruel, harsh, ruthless.

impigem, s.f. tetter, impetigo, eczema.

impingir, v.t. to compel to accept; to foist on; to sell dear; to palm off on; to fob off, to trick.

ímpio, adj. impious, irreverent, wicked, profane, ungodly.

implacabilidade, s.f. implacability, relentlessness, inflexibility, inexorability; insensibility.

implacável, adj. implacable, relentless, inexorable. pitiless, harsh, merciless; inflexible, insensible, ruthless.

implacavelmente, adv. implacably, inexorably.

implantação, s.f. implanting, implantation.

implantar, vc.t. to implant, to set in, to establish, to fix firmly; to instil, to insert.

implemento, s.m. implement; tool, utensil; fulfilment, execution.

implicação, s.f. implication, entanglement; involvement; indeference; complication; incompatibility.

implicado, adj. implicated, involved, implied.

implicador, adj. implicating, implying, involving; teasing.

implicância, s.f. implication, involvement; incompatibility.

implicante, adj. implicating, implicative, captious.

implicar, v.t. to implicate, to entangle, to envolve; to annoy, to pick a quarrel, to tease; to embarrass; to emply, to enfer; to include, to give rise to; to be incompatible.

implicativo, adj. implicative; teasing.

implicitamente, adv. implicitly.

implícito, adj. implicit, inferable, understood, tacit, involved in.

imploração, s.f. imploration, supplication, earnest entreaty.

implorador, s.m., adj. implorer; imploring, beseeching.

implorante, adj., s. imploring; implorer.

implorar, v.t. to implore, to ask for, to crave, to beseech, to entreat, to beg, to supplicate, to pary.

implorativo, adj. imploring, entreating, appalling.

implume, adj. unfeathered, featherless, unfledged.

implúvio, s.m. impluvium.

impolidez, s.f. impoliteness, indelicacy, rudeness, incivility, coarseness.

impolido, adj. impolite, indelicate, rude, uncivil, ill-manered.

impolítica, s.f. inexpediency; bad policy, impolicy; incivility, impoliteness.

impolítico, adj. impolitic; inexpedient, unwise, injudicious.

impoluível, adj. impollutable, immaculate, unblemished.

impoluto, adj. stainless, spotless, immaculate, unstained, undefiled; virtuous.

imponderabilidade, s.f. imponderability.

imponderação, s.f. inconsideration, irreflection, heedlessness.

imponderado, adj. thoughtless, heedless, rash, precipitate.

imponderável, adj. imponderable; very light, very subtle.

imponência, s.f. magnificence, splendour, brilliance. majesty, pomp, imposingness.

imponente, adj. imposing, imponent, sumptuous, grande, majestic, impressive; stately; arrogant, commanding; superb, gallant.

impontar, *v.t.* to send away or out.

impontual, *adj.* unpunctual, not punctual, inexact.

impopular, *adj.* unpopular, out of popular favour or fashion.

impopularidade, *s.f.* unpopularity, popular disfavour.

impor, *v.t.* to impose; to attach; to compel; to order; to make to accept; to lay on or upon; to burden; to restrain; to establish; to decide; to command, to force; to inflict; to palm off, to foist; *impor-se,* to impose oneself.

importação, *s.f.* importation, entry, influx *(de bens);* imports. 1) *importação e exportação,* import and export. 2) *direitos de importação,* import duties.

importador, *s.m., adj.* importer; importing.

importância, *s.f.* importance; amount, sum, cost; consequence, consideration, authority, significance, interest, value; repute, fame; presumption, arrogance. 1) *dar-se ares de grande importância,* to put on airs. 2) *até à importância de,* to the amount *(extent)* of.

importante, *adj.* important, considerable, essential; serious, significant; momentous, weighty, capital; *dar-se ares de importante,* to ride the high horse.

importar, *v.t.* to import, to bring *(bens)* from; to amount, to cost; to concern; to be interested, to matter; to imply. 1) *importar--se,* to mind. 2) *não se importar nada,* not to care a fig (a pin). 3) *pouco importa,* no matter, it matters little. 4) *não importa,* it doesn't matter. 5) *que importa?,* what does it matter?. 6) *importa muito,* it matters a lot. 7) *importar em,* to amount to, to total. 8) *importar-se com,* to care for.

importável, *adj.* importable.

importe, *s.m.* amount, cost, sum, price.

importunação, *s.f.* importunity, molestation, annoyance; disturbance, molestation.

importunador, *s.m., adj.* importuner, disturber; troublesome, importunate.

importunamente, *adv.* importunately.

importunar, *v.t.* to importune, to worry, to annoy, to pester, to require urgently; to molest, to disturb, to trouble; to tease, to vex.

importunidade, *s.f.* importunity; molestation, annoyance; disturbance, inconvenience.

importuno, *adj., s.m.* importune, insupportable, troublesome, wearisome, importunate, impertinent, pesterous; annoyer, molester, player, obtruder, pesterer.

imposição, *s.f.* imposition; imposing; order.

impositivo, *s.f.* exacting, imposing, commanding.

impossibilidade, *s.f.* impossibility, incapability.

impossibilitar, *v.t.* to render impossible; to disable, to incapacitate, to deprive of power to.

impossível, *adj.* impossible; impracticable, unattainable; intolerable, insufferable; incredible; *pedir o impossível,* to cry for the moon.

impossivelmente, *adv.* impossibly.

imposto, *s.m.* tax, duty, tribute, taxation, levy. 1) *imposto profissional,* profit-tax. 2) *imposto do selo,* stamp duty. 3) *imposto de rendimento,* revenue tax, income tax. 4) *isento de imposto,* tax-free, tax-exempt.

impostor, *s.m.* impostor, deceiver, swindler; charlatan, humbug.

impostura, *s.f.* imposture, fraude, cheat, deceit, farce, take-in; presumption; calumny.

imposturar, *v.i.* to deceive, to cheat; to brag, to boast; to pass off.

imposturice, *s.f.* pretence, feigning; hypocrisy; fraud.

impotabilidade, *s.f.* impotability.

impotável, *adj.* impotable, unfit for drinking.

impotência, *s.f.* impotence, impotency; weakness, inability, disability.

impotente, *adj.* impotent, powerless; feeble, weak unable; helpless.

impraticabilidade, *s.f.* impraticability, impossibility.

impraticável, *adj.* impraticable, inexecutable, impossible, unworkable.

imprecação, *s.f.* imprecation, curse, malediction.

imprecar, *v.t.* to beseech; to swear, to invoke, to pray for.

imprecatado, *adj.* unwary; unguarded, unprepared; incautious.

imprecativo, *adj.* imprecatory; maledictory.

imprecatório, *adj.* imprecatory, invoking evil.

imprecaução, *s.f.* imprudence, carelessness.

imprecisão, *s.f.* inaccuracy, imprecision, inexacteness, inexactitude.

impreciso, *adj.* inaccurate, indefinite, undefinite, inexact; vague, undetermined.

impreenchível, *adj.* unfillable; irreplaceable.

impregnação, *s.f.* impregnation, permeation, saturation.

impregnar, *v.t.* to impregnate, to saturate; to taint; to absorb; to instil into; to imbue; to steep, to soak; to fill up.

impremeditação, *s.f.* unpremeditation.

impremeditado, *adj.* unpremeditated, unprepared, spontaneous, instinctive.

imprensa, *s.f.* printing press; printing; press *(jornais);* art, business of printing; personnel employed in the newspaper business.

imprensar, *v.t.* to press, to print, to impress.

impresciência, *s.m.* imprescience.

imprescindível, *adj.* vital, necessary, indispensable.

imprescritibilidade, *s.f.* imprescriptibility.

imprescritível, *adj.* imprescriptible.

impressão, *s.f.* impression; printing; feeling; shake; disturbance; vague idea, notion; opinion, belief; illusion; impress, stamping, mark. 1) *impressão digital,* finger-print. 2) *erro de impressão,* misprint. 3) *impressão em relevo,* relief-print. 4) *impressão a cores,* colour printing. 5) *ter a impressão de que,* to be under the impression that.

impressionabilidade, *s.m.* impressionability, sensibility, sensitiveness.

impressionante, *adj.* moving, affecting, touching, impressing, shocking, stiking; awful; solemn.

impressionar, *v.t.* to impress, to move, to affect, to touch; to mark, to stamp in; to expose, to shoot film *(fotog.); impressionar-se,* to be impressed, to become nervous.

impressionável, *adj.* impressionable, impressible; sensitive, susceptible, receptive.

impressionismo, *s.m.* impressionism.

impressionista, *s., adj.* impressionist; impressionistic.

impressivo, *adj.* impressive, imposing; moving, touching, stirring.

impressor, *s.m.* printer, pressman; presser, pressworker.

impreterível, *adj.* unavoidable, unfailing; not to be put off, unsurpassable; essential.

impreterivelmente, *adv.* absolutely, unfailing, without any further delay.

imprevidência, *s.f.* improvidence, imprudence, incautiousness.

imprevidente, *adj.* improvident, careless, heedless, imprudent.

imprevisão, *s.f.* improvidence, carelessness, negligence, imprudence.

imprevisível, *adj.* unexpected, unforeseeable.

imprevistamente, *adv.* unexpectdly, of a sudden.

imprevisto, *adj.* unforeseen, unexpected.

imprimir, *v.t.* to print, to imprint, to impress, to press, to stamp; *imprimir movimento,* to set in motion.

improbabilidade, *s.f.* improbability, unlikeliness, implausibility.

improbidade, *s.f.* improbity, dishonest, unfairness, falseness.

improbo, *adj.* dishonest; wicked, base, foul; unfair.

improcedência, *s.f.* want of basis, groundlessness; unfairness, injustice; illogicalness.

improcedente, *adj.* unjust; groundless; unfounded; illogical, irrelevant.

improceder, *v.i.* to be irrelevant.

improdutivamente, *adv.* improductive.

improdutível, *adj.* improductible.

improdutividade, *s.f.* unproductiveness, fruitlessness.

improdutivo, *adj.* unproductive, unfruitful, barren, unprofitable, ineffective, useless.

improferível, *adj.* unutterable.

improficiência, *s.f.* unskilfulness. incompetence, unefficiency.

improficiente, *adj.* incompetent, unskilful, inefficient.

improficuamente, *adv.* vainly; fruitlessly, unprofitably.

improfícuo, *adj.* unprofitable, fruitless, in vain, ineffectual.

improgressivo, *adj.* unprogressive, stationary.

improlífero, *adj.* unprolific; sterile, unfertile.

improperar, *v.t.* to insult; to upbraid, to reproach.

impropriamente, *adv.* improperly.

impropriedade, *s.f.* impropriety, inaccuracy, incorrectness; inadequacy.

impróprio, *adj.* improper, unfit, unsuitable, inopportune; incorrect, inexact, wrong; inadequate, inconvenient.

improrrogabilidade, *s.f.* impossibility of being protracted or delayed.

improrrogável, *adj.* that cannot be postponed, undelayable, unpostponable.

improvável, *adj.* improbable, unlikely, problematic, doubtful.

improvidência, *s.f.* ver imprevidência.

improvidente, *adj.* ver imprevidente.

improvisação, *s.f.* improvisation.

improvisadamente, *adv.* impromptu; offhandedly, unexpectedly.

improvisado, *adj.* improvised, unprepared, offhand, extempore.

improvisador, *s.m., adj.* improviser: improviser; improvising, improvisatory.

improvisar, *v.t.* to improvize, to improvizate.

improviso, *s.m.* improvization, impromptu; *de improviso,* suddenly, of hand; on the spur of the moment.

imprudência, *s.f.* imprudence; indiscretion; rashness, heedlessness; unwise, foolish, ill-divesed.

imprudente, *adj.* imprudent; indiscreet; rash, precipitate, incautious, hasty; thoughtless, heedless.

imprudentemente, *adv.* imprudently.

impuberdade, *s.f.* impuberty.

impúbere, *adj.* impuberal, impubescent, under age.

impubescência, *s.f.* impuberty, immaturity.

impubescente, *adj., s.* impubic, impuberal, impubescent; adolescent.

impublicável, *adj.* unprintable.

impudência, *s.f.* impudence, shamelessness, sauciness, insolence, brazeness.

impudente, *adj.* impudent, shameless, insolent, brazen, bold-faced.

impudentemente, *adv.* impudently, shamelessly, brazenly.

impudicícia, *s.f.* impudicity, impuruty.

impudico, *adj.* immodest; lascivious, indecent, shameless. lewd.

impudor, *s.m.* immodesty; lasciviousness; shamelessness, impudence, insolence.

impugnabilidade, *s.f.* refutability.

impugnação, *s.f.* impugnment; contestation, refutation; opposition, contradiction.

impugnador, *s.m.* impugner, contester, opposer.

impugnar, *v.t.* to impugn; to contest, to contradict, to attack, to gain say, to refute, to oppose, to call in question.

impulsão, *s.f.* impulse, push, impulsion; stimulation, incentive.

impulsar, *v.t.* to give impulse, to impel; to push, to force on; to encourage, to stimulate.

impulsionador, *s.m., adj.* impeller, propeller, propulsor; impelling, driving.

impulsionar, *v.t.* to push, to impel; to urge; to drive; to animate, to stimulate.

impulsividade, *s.f.* impulsiviness, impetuosity, rashness.

impulsivo, *adj.* impulsive; rash, impetuous, precipitate.

impulso, *s.m.* impulse; instigation; impetus; impelling force, push; stimulation; spur.

impulsor, *s.m., adj.* impeller, propeller, propulsor; impelling, driving.

impune, *adj.* unpunished, unavenged; scot-free.

impunemente, *adv.* with impunity.

impunidade, *s.f.* impunity, exemption from punishment.

impunível, *adj.* unpunishable, impunible.

impureza, *s.f.* impurity; uncleanness; immodesty; unchastity, lewdness; filtchiness; lees, dregs.

impuridade, *s.f.* impurity, impureness.

impurificar, *v.t.* to make impure or dirty; to defile.

impuro, *adj.* impure; unclean; unchaste; adulterated, contaminated, polluted, lewd, sensual.

imputabilidade, *s.f.* imputability.

imputação, *s.f.* imputation; attribution; accusation, charge, reproach.

imputar, *v.t.* to impute, to ascribe, to attribute, to charge with, to accuse, to blame, to reproach.

imputável, *adj.* imputable, ascribable.

imputrescibilidade, *s.f.* imputrescibility, incorruptibility.

imputrescível, *adj.* imputrescible, incorruptible.

imudável, *adj.* immutable, unalterable.

imundície, *s.f.* dirt, rubbish, filth, filthiness, foulness, sordidness.

imundo, *adj.* foul, unclean, filthy, nasty, dirty; indecent, indecorous; immoral, obscene.

imune, *adj.* immune, exempt, protected *(doença).*

imunidade, *s.f.* immunity, exemption; prerogative, particular privilege.

imunização, *s.f.* immunization.

imunizador, imunizante, *s.m., adj.* immunizing agent; immunizing.

imunizar, *v.t.* immunize, to protect from *(doença).*

imutabilidade, *s.f.* immutation, transformation.

imutação, *s.f.* immutation, transformation.

imutável, *adj.* immutable, unalterable, uwchangeable; steady, constant.

inabalável, *adj.* immovable, steadfast, unshaken, enexorable; constant, firm; unbreakable.

inábil, *adj.* inapt, enexpert, unskilful, clumsy; tactless; unqualified, unskilled.

inabilidade, *s.f.* inability, incompetence, incapacity; unskilfulness, clumsiness.

inabilitar, *v.t.* to disable, to incapacitate; to render unable *(fazer alguma coisa).*

inabitado, *adj.* deserted; uninhabited, unoccupied, untenanted *(casa).*

inabitável, *adj.* uninhabitable, unfit to live in.

inabordável, *adj.* inaccessible unapproachable; uncommunicative.

inacabado, *adj.* unfinished, uncompleted; unachieved.

inacabável, *adj.* unfinishable, interminable.

inacção, *s.f.* inaction; idleness, sloth; inactivity.

inaceitável, *adj.* unacceptable, inadmissible.

inacessibilidade, *s.f.* inaccessibility.

inacessível, *adj.* inaccessible, unapproachable.

inacreditável, *adj.* incredible, unbelievable; extraordinary; impossible.

inactividade, *s.f.* inactivity, inertness; passivity.

inactivo, *adj.* inactive, indolent, inert, passive, idle; unemployed; paralytic.

inadaptação, *s.f.* inadaptation.

inadaptável, *adj.* inadaptable, unsuitable.

inadequado, *adj.* inadequate, unsuited, unfit; improper; unqualified.

inaderente, *adj.* inadherent.

inadiável, *adj.* urgent, pressing, undelayable, not postponable.

inadmissão, *s.f.* non-admission, exclusion.

inadmissibilidade, *s.f.* inadmissibility.

inadmissível, *adj.* inadmissible, unpermissible.

inadquirível, *adj.* unattainable, not acquirable, unacquirable.

inadvertência, *s.f.* inadvertence; oversight, inconsiderateness, improvidence; *por inadvertência,* inadvertently.

inadvertidamente, *adv.* inadvertently.

inadvertido, *adj.* inadvertent, unintentional, inconsiderate.

inajustável, *adj.* inadjustable.

inalação, *s.f.* inhalation.

inalador, *s.m.* inhaler.

inalante, *adj.* inhalant.

inalar, *v.t.* to inhale; to breath in.

inalcançável, *adj.* unattainable, unapproachable.

inaliável, *adj.* unalliable; unalloyable.

inalienabilidade, *s.f.* inalienability.

inalienável, *adj.* inalienable, unalienable.

inalterabilidade, *s.f.* inalterability, immutability.

inalterado, *adj.* unaltered, unchanged, unmodified; the same; pure; unmoved.

inalterável, *adj.* unalterable, inalterable, unchangeable; imperturbable; constant.

inamistoso, *adj.* unfriendly, unamiable; hostile.

inamolgável, *adj.* indeformable, uncrushable.

inamovibilidade, *s.f.* irremovability.

inamovível, *adj.* unremovable.

inane, *adj.* inane, void, fautous, worthless, vain, futile, frivolous.

inanição, *s.f.* inanition, starvation, exhaustion, famishment.

inanidade, *s.f.* inanity, emptiness; vacuit, frivolity.

inanimado, inânime, *adj.* inanimate, lifeless; spiritless.

inanir, *v.t.* to famish.

inapagável, *adj.* unerasable, ineffaceable.

inapelável, *adj.* unappealable; inescapable.

inapetência, *s.f.* inappetence.

inaplicabilidade, *s.f.* inapplicability, irrelevancy.

inaplicável, *adj.* inapplicable, unsuitable, irrelevant.

inapreciável, *adj.* inappreciable, inestimable.

inapropriado, *adj.* improper, unbecoming, inadequate.

inaproveitado, *adj.* unused, waste.

inaproveitável, *adj.* unusual, useless; ineffectual, inapplicable.

inaptidão, *s.f.* inaptitude, inaptness, inability, disbility, incapacity.

inapto, *adj.* inapt; unsuitable, unfit; unable, incapable, unskilful, unhandy.

inarrável, *adj.* indescribable, inexpressible, unspeakable.

inarticulado, *adj.* inarticulate; not jointed.

inassimilável, *adj.* unassimilable, non-assimilable, inassimilable.

inatacável, *adj.* unassailable; unobjectionable, unimpeachable, incontestable.

inatendível, *adj.* unworthy of attention.

inatingido, *adj.* unattained, unequaled.

inatingível, *adj.* unattainable, inaccessible.

inato, *adj.* unborn; innate, inborn, inbred; congenital.

inaudito, *adj.* unexampled, unprecedented, inconceivable, unheard of, extraordinary.

inaudível, *adj.* inaudible.

inauferível, *adj.* inherent, intrinsic.

inauguração, *s.f.* inauguration; inaugurating, beginning, opening; initiation.

inaugurador, *s.m., adj.* inaugurator; inaugurating.

inaugural, *adj.* inaugural, initial.

inaugurar, *v.t.* to inaugurate; to initiate, to begin ; to open, to start; to establih.

inautenticidade, *s.f.* unauthenticity.

inautêntico, *adj.* unauthentic, not genuine, untrue.

inavegabilidade, *s.f.* unnavigability.

inavegável, *adj.* unnavigable, innavigable.

incalculado, *adj.* unexpected, unforeseen.

incalculável, *adj.* incalculable; countless; incomputable.

incandescência, *s.f.* incandescence; glowing heat.

incandescente, *adj.* incandescent, fiery; red hot, white hot.

incandescer, *v.t., v.i.* to incandesce, to glow with heat.

incansável, *adj.* indefatigable, untiring, tireless; laborious.

incansavelmente, *adv.* tirelessly.

incapacidade, *s.f.* incapacity, inability, incompetence, disbility, inaptitude; impotence.

incapacitar, *v.t.* to incapacitate, to disable, to make incapable or unfir; to cripple.

incapaz, *adj.* incapable, unable, incompetent; unfit, inapt, unqualified; ignorant; impotent.

inçar, *v.t.* to crowd; to fill *(insecots),* to contaminate, to infect; to infest, to beset.

incaracterístico, *adj.* uncharacteristic, confoundable.

incauto, *adj.* incautious, unwary, unsuspecting; heedless, careless; improvident; credolous.

incender, *v.t.* to fire, to light; to inflame, to set on fire.

incendiado, *adj.* afire.

incendiar, *v.t.* to fire, to set light, to set fire, to inflame; to excite; to irritate; *incendiar-se,* to catch fire.

incendiário, *adj., s.m.* incendiary; exciting, inciting, inflammatory; incendiary, arsonist.

incêndio, *s.m.* fire; conflagration. 1) *boca de incêndio* fire hydrant, fire plug. 2) *bomba de incêndio,* fire pump, fire engine. 3) *extintor de incêndio,* fire extinguisher.

incensação, *s.f.* incensation; perfuming, with incense; flattery, adulation.

incensador, *s.m.* incenser, flatterer, adulator.

incensar, *v.t.* to incense; to flatter, to pefume with incense; to flatter, to fawn, to overpraise.

incensário, *s.m.* thurible; censer.

incenso, *s.m.* incense.

incensório, *s.m.* ver incensário.

incensurável, *adj.* uncensurable; correct, right.

incentivar, *v.t.* to stimulate, to encourage, to incite.

incentivo, *s.m., adj.* incentive, incitement, impulse, stimulus, encouragement; incentive, stimulative, inciting.

incerteza, *s.f.* incertitude, uncertainty, doubt; hesitation, indecision; insecurity, vagueness.

incerto, *adj.* uncertain; undecided; changeable; doubtful; dubious; unreliable, insecure, problematic; unsteady; variable, inconstant.

incessante, *adj.* incessant; perpetual, continual, ceaseless, continuous, constant.

incessantemente, *adv.* continually, constantly, incessantly.

incesto, *s.m.* incest.

incestuosamente, *adv.* incestuously.

incestuoso, *adj.* incestuous, infamous, base.

inchação, inchamento, *s.f., s.m.* tumefaction; swelling; anasarca; pride.

inchaço, *s.m.* tumour, swelling, lump, bulge.

inchar, *v.t., v.i.* to swell, to swell up; to grow proud, to puff up, to flush with success.

incidência, *s.f.* incidence, incidency; occurrence.

incidentado, *adj.* chanceful, casual, incidental; full of incidents.

incidente, *s.m., adj.* incident, occurrence; incident; occasional.

incidir, *v.t.* to fall; to strike; to happen, to occur, to chance.

incineração, *s.f.* incineration, cineration; cremation.

incinerador, *s.m., adj.* incinerator; crematory; incinerating.

incinerar, *v.t.* to incinerate, to cremate, to burn to ashes.

incinerável, *adj.* that may be incinerated.

incipiente, *adj.* incipient, inchoate, beginning, initial; crude.

incisão, *s.f.* incision, cut.

incisivo, *adj.* incivise; sharp, acute; *dente incisivo,* incisor, foretooth.

inciso, *adj.* incised, cut.

incisório, *adj.* incisive, incisory.

incisura, *s.f. ver "incisão".*

incitabilidade, *s.f.* incitability; excitability, irritability.

incitação, *s.f.* incitation, stimulus, incentive, incitement, provocation; stimulation, encouragement.

incitador, *s.m., adj.* inciter, instigator; prompter, rouser; provoker; inciting, stimulating.

incitamento, *s.m.* ver incitação.

incitante, *adj.* inciting, stimulating, stimulative.

incitar, *v.t.* to incite; to urge; to stimulate, to encourage, to instigate, to rouse to action; to encourage, to inspire; to stir, to impel.

incivil, *adj.* uncivil, unpolished, rude, discourteous; rough, boorish.

incivilidade, *s.f.* incivility, rudeness, impoliteness, discourtesy, ill manners.

incivilizado, *s.f.* uncivilized, uncultured, rude, rough, impolite, barbarous.

incivismo, *s.m.* incivism.

incivilizável, *adj.* uncivilizable, uneducable.

inclassificável, *adj.* unclassifiable, unclassable.

inclemência, *s.f.* inclemency, mercilessness; asperity, severity; harshness, rudeness.

inclemente, *adj.* inclement; severe; boisterous; stormy; unmerciful, harsh; cruel.

inclinação, *s.f.* inclination, incline, slope, dip, gradient; bow, nod; bending; proclivity; propension, affection, fondness, linking; vocation, disposition; tendency, leaning, penchant.

inclinado, *adj.* inclined; bent, bowed down; predisposed, willing, prone to; fond of.

inclinar, *v.t.* to incline; to bow, to bend; to dispose; to turn, to predispose; to lean, to slope; *inclinar-se,* to be inclined toward; to bow before; to stoop.

ínclito, *adj.* famous, illustrious, distinguish, prominent, egregious.

incluído, *adj.* included, enclosed, involved, comprised.

incluir, *v.t.* to include, to comprise, to embrace, to embodt, to take in; to contain, to enclose; to insert, to introduce.

inclusão, *s.f.* inclusion, incorporation; comprisal.

inclusivamente, *adv.* inclusively.

inclusive, *adv.* inclusively.

inclusivo, *adj.* inclusive; coantaining, including, included.

incluso, *adj., adv.* enclosed; included; herein; herewith.

incoação, *adj.* inchoation, beginning, inception.

incoadunabilidade, *s.f.* incompatibility.

incoadunável, *adj.* incompatible, uncombinable.

incoativo, *adj.* inchoative, inceptive; beginning.

incoagulável, *adj.* incoagulable.

incobrável, *adj.* unrecoverable, uncollectable.

incoercibilidade, *s.f.* incoercibility.

incoercível, *adj.* incoercible, irrepressible, uncontrollable.

incoerência, *s.f.* incoherence, disconnected, inconsistent, disjointed, illogical, contadictory.

incoerente, *adj.* incoherent, disconnected, inconsistent, disjointed, illogical, contadictory.

incoerentemente, *adj.* incoherently.

incoesão, *s.f.* incohension.

incógnita, *s.f.* unknown quantity.

incógnito, *adj.* unknown; incognito, disguised.

incognoscível, *adj.* incognoscible, unknowable.

íncola, *s.* inhabitant, dweller *(poético).*

incolor, *adj.* colourless.

incólume, *adj.* safe and sound, unharmed, unhurt, uninjured; entire.

incolumidade, *s.f.* invulnerability; safety; security.

incombinável, *adj.* uncombinable.

incombustibilidade, *s.f.* incombustibility.

incombustível, *adj.* incombustible, unburnable, fire-proof.

incomensurabilidade, *s.f.* incommensurability.

incomensurável, *adj.* incommensurable, immeasurable, measureless; vast, immenrse.

incomensuravelmente, *adv.* incommensurably, immeasurably.

incomodado, *adj.* indisposed; upset; annoyed.

incomodador, *s.m., adj.* importuner, troubler; troublesome, annoying, importunate.

incomodar, *v.t.* to incommode, to disturb, to trouble, to annoy, to molest, to vex, to bother, to be troublesome. 1) *não se incomode,* never mind, don't bother. 2) *não o incomode,* let him alone.

incomodativo, *adj.* troublesome, importunate, bothersome, troubling, annoying.

incomodidade, *s.f.* incommodity, incommodiousness.

incómodo, *adj., s.m.* incommodious,

inconvenient, troublesome, annoying, uncomfortable; ailing; trouble, disturbance; slight illness; nuisance.

incomparável, *adj.* incomparable, unequalled, unrivalled, matchless, peerless, unique,

incomparavelmente, *adj.* incomparably, matchlessly.

incompassível, *adj.* pitiless, merciless, implacable.

incompassivo, *adj.* pitiless.

incompatibilidade, *s.f.* incompatibility, unconformity, unsuitability.

incompatibilizado, *adj.* on bad terms.

incompatibilizar, *v.t.* to make incompatible; *incompatibilizar-se,* to become incompatible.

incompatível, *adj.* incongruous, incompatible, inharmonious; irreconcilable, unconformable.

incompensado, *adj.* not compensated, unrewarded.

incompensável, *adj.* irreparable, irrecovertable; that cannot be compensated.

incompetência, *s.f.* incompetence, inability, incapacity, unfitness.

incompetente, *adj.* incompetent; inapt.

incomplacência, *s.f.* incompliance.

incomplacente, *adj.* incompliant, unyielding.

incompletamente, *adv.* incompletely, fragmentarily.

incompleto, *adj.* incomplete, uncompleted; unfinished, undone; imperfect; fragmentary.

incomplexidade, *s.f.* incomplexity, simplicity.

incomplexo, *adj.* incomplex, simple, uncomplicated.

incomportável, *adj.* insufferable, intolerable, unbearable.

incompreendido, *adj.* misunderstood, uncomprehended.

incompreensão, misunderstanding, incomprehension.

incompreensibilidade, *s.f.* incomprehensibility.

incompreensível, *adj.* incomprehensible, inconceivable, incredible; unintelligible, impenetrable.

incompreensivelmente, *adv.* incomprehensibly, inconceivably.

incompressibilidade, *s.f.* incompressibility.

incompressível, *adj.* incompressible.

incomprovado, *adj.* unproved.

incomputável, *adj.* incomputable.

incomum, *adj.* uncommon, unusual; abnormal, rare.

incomunicabilidade, *s.f.* incommunicability.

incomunicação, *s.f.* lack of communication.

incomunicante, *adj.* not communicating.

incomunicável, *adj.* incommunicable; unsociable *(fig).*

incomutabilidade, *s.f.* incommutability.

incomutável, *adj.* incommutable.

inconcebível, inconceptível, *adj.* inconceivable, incredible, extraordinay; unthinkable.

inconcepto, *adj.* inconceivable *(poético).*

inconcessível, *adj.* unallowable *(poético).*

inconciliação, *s.f.* irreconciliation.

inconciliável, *adj.* irreconcilable, incompatible; inconsistent.

inconcludente, *adj.* inconclusive, indeterminate.

inconclusivo, *adj.* inconclusive.

inconcluso, *adj.* unfinished, incomplete.

inconcordável, *adj.* irreconcilable, uncordable, incompatible.

inconcusso, *adj.* incorruptible, austere, incontestable.

incondicionado, *adj.* absolute, unconditioned,

incondicional, *adj.* unconditional; absolute.

incondicionalidade, *s.f.* unconditionality, absoluteness.

incôndito, *adj.* incondite; disordered; irregular; confused; rude.

onconexão, *s.f.* inconnexion, disconnexion.

inconexo, *adj.* unconnected; disengaged; discordant.

inconfessado, *adj.* inconfessed.

inconfessável, *adj.* unconfessable, not confessable.

inconfesso, *adj.* unconfessed, unacknowledged.

inconfidência, *s.f.* unfaithfulness; disloyalty; infidelity, treachery; unconfidence, lack of confidence.

inconfidencial, *adj.* unconfidential.

inconfidente, *adj.* unfaithful, false, disloyal; treacherous, indiscreet.

inconformação, *s.f.* unconformity, disagreement.

inconformado, *adj.* unsubmissive; not acquiescent.

inconformidade, *s.f.* disagreement, divergence.

inconfortável, *adj.* uncomfortable, uneasy.

inconfundível, *adj.* unmistakable, distinct.

incongelado, *adj.* uncongealed.

incongelável, *adj.* uncongealable.

incongruência, *s.f.* incongruity, incongruence, inconsistency, inconsequence.

incongruente, *adj.* incongruous, improper, unsuitable.

incongruidade, *s.f.* incongruity.

inconjugável, *adj.* inconjugable.

inconquistado, *adj.* unconquered; untamed.

inconquistável, *adj.* unconquerable, unsubduable, invincible.

inconsciência, *s.f.* unconsciousness; inconsiderateness.

inconsciencioso, *adj.* unconscientious; unscrupulous.

inconsciente, *adj.* unconscious; inconscient; senseless; automatic; unaware.

inconscientemente, *adv.* unconsciously, unwittingly.

incônscio, *adj.* ver *"inconsciente"*.

inconsequência, *s.f.* inconsequence, incongruence, contradiction.

inconsequente, *adj.* inconsequent, illogical, disconnected, inconsistent, irrelevant.

inconsequentemente, *adv.* inconsequentially.

inconsideração, *s.f.* inconsideration, inconsiderateness, thoughlessness, carelessness; rashness, precipitation.

inconsiderado, *s.f.* inconsiderate, incautious, thoughtless, imprudent, rash, precipitate.

inconsistência, *s.f.* inconsistency, incongruity, contradiction, contradictory.

inconsitente, *adj.* inconsistent, incongruous, discrepant, incoherent, contradictory.

inconsolado, *adj.* unconsoled, uncomforted.

inconsolável, *adj.* inconsolable, disconsolate.

inconsolavelmente, *adv.* inconsolably.

inconsonância, *s.f.* inconsonance, discordance, want of harmony.

inconsonante, *adj.* inconsonant, inharmonious.

inconstância, *s.f.* inconstancy, unstableness, unsteadiness, fickleness; instability, variability, mutability.

inconstante, *adj.* inconstant, variable, unsteady, changeable, fickle, capricious, mutable, wavering; unfaithful.

inconstantemente, *adv.* inconstantly.

inconstitucional, *adj.* unconstitutional, unstatutable.

inconstitucionalidade, *s.f.* unconstitutionality.

inconstitucionalmente, *adv.* uncosntitutionally.

inconsulto, *adj.* unconsulted; thoughtless, inconsiderate.

inconsumível, incomsumptível, *adj.* inconsumable; indestructible.

inconsumpto, *adj.* unconsumed, undestroyed.

inconsútil, *adj.* seamless; whole of one piece.

incontaminado, *adj.* unpolluted, uncontaminated, pure, undegiled.

incontável, *adj.* countless, innumerable, incalculable.

incontentável, *adj.* uncontentable, hard to please, difficult.

incontestabilidade, *s.f.* incontestability, incontrovertibility.

incontestado, *adj.* undisputed, uncontested, unrefuted.

incontestável, *adj.* incontestable, indisputable, undeniable, unquestionable; certain, sure.

incontestavelmente, *adj.* incontestably, undoubtedly.

incontido, *adj.* uncheked, unrestrained, unrestricted; not included.

incontinência, *s.f.* incontinence; lust; lack of self-restraint; unchasteness.

incontinente, *adj., adv.* incontinent; licentious, unchaste; immediatelly, at once, forthwith, instantly.

incontingente, *adj.* certain, not contingent.

incontinuidade, *s.f.* incontinuity.

incontínuo, *adj.* incontinuous.

incontrariável, *adj.* incontradictable.

incontrastável, *adj.* insuperable, irresistible, irrevocable; firm, stable.

incontrito, *adj.* uncontrite, unrepentant.

incontrlável, *adj.* uncontrollable, ungovernable, unruly.

incontroverso, *adj.* unquestioned, incontestable, undisputed.

incontrovertível, *adj.* inconvertible, incontestable, undisputable.

inconvencível, *adj.* unconvincible.

inconveniência, *s.f.* discrepancy; impropriety; impoliteness; inconvenience.

inconveniente, *adj., s.m.* improper; innoportune; awkward; inconvenience, trouble, nuisance.

inconversibilidade, *s.f.* unconvertibility.

inconversível, inconvertível, *adj.* unconvertible.

inconvicto, *adj.* unconvonced, not persuaded.

incoordenação, *s.f.* incoordination.

incorporação, *s.f.* incorporation, embodiment; grouping; affiliation; annexation.

incorporal, *adj. ver "incorpóreo".*

incorporalidade, *s.f. ver "incorporeidade".*

incorporar, *v.t.* to incorporate, to embody; to unite, to blend; to connect, to link; to consolidate; to congregate, to affiliate, to associate; *incorporar-se,* to become part of, to share in, to join, to take part in.

incorporeidade, *s.f.* incorporeity, immateriality.

incorpóreo, *adj.* incorporeal, immaterial, spiritual, bodiless.

incorrecção, *s.f.* incorrecteness, inacuracy, impropriety; error, mistake; uncivility, impoliteness.

incorrectamente, *adv.* incorrectly; impolitely.

incorrecto, *adj.* incorrect, innacurate, wrong, inexact, improper, impolite, uncivil; false.

incorrer, *v.i.* to incur, to run into, to fall within.

incorrigibilidade, *s.f.* incorrigibility.

incorrigível, *adj.* incorrigible, hopeless, unregenerate indurate.

incorrigivelmente, *adv.* incorrigibly, unregenerately.

incorrimento, *s.m.* incurring; incurrence.

incorrupção, *s.f.* incorruption.

incorruptibilidade, *s.f.* incorruptibility, integrity, probity, honesty, uprightness.

incorruptível, *adj.* incorruptible, unbribable; just, righteous.

incorruptivelmente, *adv.* incorruptibly.

incorrupto, *adj.* incorrupt, pure, unblemished; honest.

incredibilidade, *s.f.* incredibility.

incredulidade, *s.f.* incredulity; unbelief, disbelief; distrust; doubt.

incrédulo, *adj., s.m.* incredulous; sceptical; impious, godless; sceptic, agnostic, unbeliever.

incrementar, *v.t.* to increase, to augment, to develop.

incremento, *s.m.* increment, increase, enlargement, developement, growth.

increpação, *s.f.* blame, reproof, reprimand, rebuke, chiding.

increpador, *s.m.* rebuker, reprover.

increpante, *adj.* rebuking.

increpar, *v.t.* to blame, to rebuke, to reprimand, to chide.

incréu, *s.m.* unbeliever, agnostic.

incriado, *adj.* uncreated.

incriminação, *s.f.* accusation, imputation, incrimination.

incriminar, *v.t.* to incriminate, to accuse, to charge, to inculpate.

incristalizável, *adj.* uncrystallizable.

incriticável, *adj.* uncriticisable, above criticism.

incrível, *adj.* incredible, astounding, unbelievable, inconceivable; extraordinary, remarkable; strange.

incrivelmente, *adv.* incredibly, remarkably.

incruento, *adj.* bloodless, without bloodshed.

incrustação, *s.f.* incrustation, encrustment, inlay.

incrustador, *adj., s.m.* incrusting; inlay worker.

incrustar, *v.t.* to incrust, to inlay; to coat, to plate.

incubação, *s.f.* incubation; hatching, brooding; eleboration, preparation *(fig).*

incubadora, *s.f.* incubator.

incubar, *v.t.* to incubate, to hatch; to plan, to project.

íncubo, *adj., s.m.* incubous; incubus; nightmare.

inculca, *s.f.* inculcation; search, quest; research; information, inquiry.

inculcadeira, *s.f.* a go-between or telltale *(mulher).*

inculcador, *adj., s.m.* inculcating; inculcator.

inculcar, *v.t.* to inculcate; to comment; to reveal; to warn; to point out, to indicate; to propose; *inculcar-se,* to ingratiate oneself; to show oneself.

inculcas, *s.f. pl.* informations, investigations.

inculpabilidade, *s.f.* want of culpability, nonculpability.

inculpação, *s.f.* inculpation, imputation, accusation, charge.

inculpado, *adj.* inculpable, blameless, innocent.

inculpar, *v.t.* to incriminate; to inculpate, to blame.

inculpável, *adj.* inculpable, blameless, innocent, faultless

incultivável, *adj.* uncultivable, untillable.

inculto, *adj.* uncultivated, untilled; rude, uncultured; wild, savage, desert.

incultura, *s.f.* inculture, lack of culture, wildness.

incumbência, *s.f.* incumbency; charge, mission, task; errand.

incumbente, *adj.* incumbent.

incumbir, *v.t., v.i.* to charge, to entrust, to commit, to assign, to put in charge of; to be the duty; *incumbir-se,* to take upon oneself, to undertake to.

incunábulo, *s.m.* incunabulum.

incurabilidade, *s.f.* incurability.

incurável, *adj.* incurable, irremediable, past cure; hopeless; incorrigible.

incúria, *s.f.* carelessness, remissness, neglect, negligence; disregard.

incurial, *adj.* irregular, unlawful.

incuriosidade, *s.f.* incuriosity, incuriousness.

incurioso, *adj.* incurious; heedless, careless, negligent; indifferent.

incursão, *s.f.* incursion, raid, irruption, foray, attack, invasion.

incurso, *adj.* liable to, subject to.

incurvado, *adj.* curved inward, incurvate.

incuso, *adj.* incuse, stamped on one side only.

incutir, *v.t.* to inspire, to infuse, to suggest, to instil; to inculcate.

indagação, *s.f.* indagation, inquiry, search, quest, investigation.

indagador, *s.m.* inquirer, searcher.

indagar, *v.t.* to seek out, to search out, to investigate; to enquire, to ask, to question.

indagável, *adj.* enquirable.

indébito, *adj.* undue; not right, unjust.

indecência, *s.f.* indecency; immodesty; obscenity, immorality.

indecente, *adj.* indecent, immodest, obscene, offensive, shameful, immoral, indecorous.

indecentemente, *adv.* indecently, shamefully.

indecidido, *adj.* undecided, unsettled; vacillating.

indecifrável, *adj.* indecipherable, illegible; intricate, obscucure.

indecisamente, *adv.* indecidedly.

indecisão, *s.f.* indecision, hesitation, perplexity, vacillation, irresolution; doubt.

indeciso, undecided, irresolute, vacillating, hesitating, hesitant; unconfirmed, dubious, doubtful.

indeclarável, *adj.* undeclarable.

indeclinabilidade, *s.f.* indeclinability; inevitability.

indeclinável, *adj.* indeclinable; inevitable, irrecusable.

indeclinavelmente, *adv.* indeclinably.

indecomponível, *adj.* indecomposable.

indecoro, *s.m.* indecorum; indecency; shamelessness.

indecorosamente, *adv.* indecorously.

indecoroso, *adj.* indecorous, indecent; improper, unseemly, shameful.

indefectibilidade, *s.f.* indefectibility.

indefectível, *adj.* indefectible, faultness; infallible.

indefensável, indefensível, *adj.* indefensible, unsustainable, untenable.

indefenso, *adj.* defenceless, undefended, unarmed; weak, helpless.

indeferido, *adj.* rejected, refused, denied, not granted.

indeferimento, *s.m.* refusal, denial, rejection *(de um pedido).*

indeferir, *v.t.* to reject, to refuse, to deny, to disallow, not grant *(petição).*

indeferível, *adj.* ungrantable, not allowable.

indefeso, *adj.* undefended, defenceless, unprotected, unarmed; helpless.

indefesso, *adj.* indefatigable, unarmed.

indeficiente, *adj.* undeficient; enough.

indefinidamente, *adv.* indefinitely, vaguely; unlimitedly.

indefinido, *adj.* indefinite, vague; undefined, non-descript; unlimited, indeterminate.

indefinível, *adj.* indefinable, vague.

indeiscência, *s.f.* indehiscence.

indeiscente, *adj.* indehiscent.

indelebilidade, *s.f.* indelebility.

indelével, *adj.* indelible, ineffaceable.

indelevelmente, *adv.* indelibly, ineffaceably, for ever.

indeliberação, *s.f.* indeliberation, irresolution, indecision.

indelicadamente, *adv.* indelicatly, unkindly, impolitely, discourteously.

indelicadeza, *s.f.* indelicacy, discourtesy, incivility, rudeness.

indelicado, *adj.* coarse; indelicate, impolite, gross, ill-mannered.

indelineável, *adj.* that cannot be delineated, indistinct, vague.

indemne, *adj.* uninjured, safe and sound, unhurt, undamaged.

indemnidade, *s.f.* indemnity; forgiveness.

indemnização, *s.f.* indemnity, compensation, reparation, restitution, reimbursement.

indemnizador, *s.m., adj.* indemnifier, reimburser; indemnifying.

indemnizar, *v.t.* to indemnify, to compensate for, to reimburse, to make amends to.

indemnizável, *adj.* indemnifiable.
indemonstrado, *adj.* undemonstrated.
indemonstrável, *adj.* undemonstrable; self-
evident.
independência, *s.f.* independence; freedom; autonomy.
independente, *adj.* independent, free;
autonomous; undependable.
independentemente, *adv.* independently,
autonomically.
indescritível, *adj.* indescribable; extraordinary, remarkably; unutterable.
indesculpável, *adj.* inexcusable, unpardonable; unjustifiable.
indesculpavelmente, *adv.* inexcusably.
indesejado, *adj.* undesired, unwished,
uncalled for, not welcome.
indesejável, *adj.* undesirable, unwelcome.
indestronável, *adj.* undethronable.
indestrutibilidade, *s.f.* indestructibility.
indestrutível, *adj.* indestructible, undes-
troyable.
indestrutivelmente, *adv.* iindestructibly.
indesvendável, *adj.* not to be unveiled or
revealed.
indeterminação, *s.f.* indetermination;
indecision, vacillation, irresoluteness.
indeterminadamente, *adv.* indeterminatly.
indeterminado, *adj.* indeterminate; indecisive; undefined; irresolute, vacillating,
wavering; indefinite, vague; uncertain.
indeterminar, *v.t.* to make vague or
uncertain.
indeterminável, *adj.* indeterminable,
undefinable; indecisive.
indeterminismo, *s.m.* indeterminism.
indeterminista, *s.* indeterminist.
indeturpável, *adj.* undefilable.
indevassável, *adj.* unfathomable, inaccessible.
indevidamente, *adv.* unduly, wrongly.
indevido, *adj.* undue; improper; not due;
unjustified; inconvenient.
indevoção, *s.f.* indevotion, impiety.
indevoto, *adj.* undevout; impious.
index, *s.m.* index finger, forefinger. 1) *Index
Librorum Prohibitorum,* Prohibitiry Index. 2)
pôr no Index, to forbid something; to point
out as dangerous *(alguma coisa ou alguma
pessoa).*
indianismo, *s.m.* Indianism.
indianista, *s.* Indianist.
indiano, *adj., s.m.* Indian.
indicação, *s.f.* indication, indicating;

manifestation, sympton; hint, due, sign,
token; appointment.
indicado, *adj.* convenient, right.
indicador, *adj., s.m.* indicating; indicator;
index; forefinger; guide or hand-book; dial,
gauge.
indicar, *v.t.* to indicate, to point out, to show,
to denote, to manifest; to appoint to office;
to reveal, to disclose.
indicativo, *adj., s.m.* indicating; indicatory;
indicative; mark, sign; indication; indicative
mood.
indicatório, *adj.* indicatory.
indicção, *s.f.* indiction; prescription.
índice, *s.m.* index; contents; the forefinger;
table (of contents); catalogue; register;
alphabetical list. 1) *índice de mortalidade,*
death rate. 2) *índice de preços,* price index.
3) *índice remissivo,* cross-index.
indiciação, *s.f.* circumstancial evidence.
indiciado, *s.m., adj.* criminal; indicted
person, indictee; indicted.
indiciador, *s.m.* informer, indicter, accuser.
indiciar, *v.t.* to indict, to denounce, to
charge, to accuse.
indício, *s.m.* indicium, sign, token, mark,
vestige, trace; symptom.
indico, *adj.* Indian.
indiferença, *s.f.* indifference; inattention,
negligence; apathy, unconcern; aloofness;
carelessness; stoicism; scorn, contempt;
insnsitiveness.
indiferenciado, *adj.* indiscriminate; without
distinctions.
indiferente, *adj.* indifferent, apathetic,
careless, negligent, desinterested, neutral,
unconcerned; scornful, contemptuous; *é-me
indiferente,* that's all the same to me.
indiferentemente, *adv.* indifferently, without
distinction.
indiferentismo, *s.m.* indifferentism.
indígena, *s., adj.* indigene, native; natural;
indigenous.
indigenato, *s.m.* indegenousness.
indigência, *s.f.* indigence; want, distress,
proverty, penury, pauperism.
indigente, *adj., s.* indigent, poor, needy;
pauper, beggar, poor.
indigentemente, *adv.* indigently.
indigerível, *adj.* indogestible, indigestive.
indigestão, *s.f.* indigestion.
indigesto, *adj.* undigested; indigestible;
incomprehensible; unendurable,
indígete, *s.m.* venerated hero, demigod.

indigitado, *adj.* designated, indicated, pointed out.

indigitação, *s.f., s.m.* a pointing out.

indigitar, *v.t.* to point out, to designate, to indicate; to suggest, to recommend.

indignação, *s.f.* indignation, anger, resentement.

indignado, *adj.* indignant, vexed, exasperated, angry.

indignar, *v.t.* ro cause indignation; to provoke; to make angry; to offend; *indignar--se,* to be offended, to be angry with.

indignidade, *s.f.* indignity; insult, affront; unworthiness; shamelessness,

indigno, *s.m.* unworthy, ignoble, base, low, despicable, shameful; undeserving.

indigo, *s.m.* indigo, anil, Indian blue.

indigueiro, *s.m.* indigo plant.

indiligência, *s.f.* indiligence, negligence.

indiligente, *adj.* indiligent, idle, negligent.

índio, *s.m., adj.* Indian.

indirectamente, *adv.* indirectly, circuitously.

indirecto, *adj.* indirect; disguised, simulated, circuitous, roundabout.

indirigível, *adj.* ungovernable, unmanageable.

indescernível, *adj.* undiscernible; indistinguishable, imperceptible.

indisciplina, *s.f.* indiscipline, insubordination, disobedience, rebellion, insurrection.

indisciplinado, *adj.* undisciplined, disobedient, unruly, ungovernable, insubordinate.

indisciplinar, *v.t.* to render undisciplined; to stir up.

indisciplinável, *adj.* indisciplinable, insubmissive.

indiscretamente, *adv.* indiscreetly. injudiciously, imprudently.

indiscreto, *adj.* indiscreet, incautions; unguarded, imprudent, foolish, tactless.

indiscrição, *s.f.* indiscretion; imprudence; blunder, misstep.

indiscriminadamente, *adv.* indiscriminately.

indiscriminado, *adj.* indiscriminate; confused; promiscuous; not detailed.

indiscriminável, *adj.* indistinguishable.

indiscutibilidade, *s.f.* indisputability.

indiscutido, *adj.* unquestioned.

indiscutível, *adj.* unquestionable; undeniable; incontestable, positive, certain.

indiscutivelmente, *adv.* unquestionably, undeniably.

indisfarçado, *adj.* undisguished.

indisfarçável, *adj.* undisguisable, uncononcealable.

indispensabilidade, *s.f.* indispensability.

indispensável, *adj.* indispensable, necessary, essential.

indispensavelmente, *adv.* indispensably.

indisponibilidade, *s.f.* unavailability.

indisponível, *adj.* unavailable. inalienable.

indispor, *v.t.* to indispose; to make ill; to render unfavourable; to set against, to disaffect; to irritate.

indisposição, *s.f.* indisposition; unsuitableness; ailment; slight illness, disturbance.

indisposto, *adj.* indisposed; unwilling; slightly ill, unwell, sick; hostile.

indisputabilidade, *s.f.* indisputability.

indisputado, *adj.* undisputed, undoubted, unquestioned.

indisputável, *adj.* undisputable, incontestable, unquestionable.

indissimulável, *adj.* that cannot be dissembled.

indissolubilidade, *s.f.* indissolubility; indissolubleness.

indissolução, *s.f.* the sate of that which is not dissolved.

indissolúvel, *adj.* indissoluble, not dissolvable.

indissoluvelmente, *adv.* indissolubly.

indistinção, *s.f.* indistinctness, indistinction, indiscrimination.

indistinguível, *adj.* undistinguishable, confused.

indistintamente, *adv.* indistinctly, indiscriminately, vaguely.

indistinto, *adj.* indistinct, confused, obscure, ill-defined, vague; unclear, dim, promiscuous.

inditoso, *adj.* unfortunate, unlucky, ill-fated.

individuação, *s.f.* individuation.

individuador, *adj.* individualizing.

individualidade, *s.f.* individuality, personality, person.

individualismo, *s.m.* individualism; selfishness, egoism.

individualista, *s., adj.* individualist; individualistic.

individualização, *s.f.* individuant, characteristic.

individuar, *v.t.* to individualize, to individuate, to specify, to particularize, to single out.

indivíduo, *s.m., adj.* individual; person; undivided, indivisible.

indivisão, *s.f.* indivision.

indivisibilidade, *s.f.* indivisibility.

indivisível, *adj.* indivisible, impartible.

indiviso, *adj.* undivided, whole.

indizível, *adj.* unutterable, unspeakable, inexpressible; indescribable.

indizivelmente, *adv.* unspeakably.

indobrável, *adj.* inflexible, unbending.

indochinês, *adj.* Indochinese.

indócil, *adj.* indocile, unruly, headstrong, unmaneageable, difficult, intractable.

indocilidade, *s.f.* indocility, waywardness, intractability.

indocilizar, *v.t.* to render indocile or stubborn.

indo-europeu, *adj., s.m.* Indo-European.

indo-germânico, *adj.* Indo-Germanic.

índole, *s.f.* character, temper, nature; propensity, bent.

indolência, *s.f.* indolence; idleness, negligence; apathy; laziness, sloth.

indolente, *adj.* indolent, idle, negligent, lazy, slothful; easy-going.

indolentemente, *adv.* indolently, idly.

indolor, *adj.* painless, pangless.

indomado, *adj.* undomesticated, untamed; unsubdued, wild.

indomável, *adj.* indomitable, untameable, invencible; implacable, unruly.

indomesticado, *adj.* undomesticated, wild.

indomesticável, *adj.* ferocious, wild, savage.

indominável, *adj.* ver indomável.

indómito, *adj.* indomitable, untameable, indefatigable.

indonésio, *adj., s.m.* Indonesian.

indo-português, *adj., s.m.* Indo-Portuguese.

indostânico, *adj.* Hindustani.

indouto, *adj.* unlearned, ignorant.

indubitavelmente, *adv.* indubitably, unquestionably, assuredly.

indução, *s.f.* induction; inducting; suggestion; inference, conclusion.

indúcias, *s.f., pl.* armistice; moratorium; indulgence.

indúctil, *adj.* inductile.

inducto, *adj.* induzid.

inductilidade, *s.f.* inductility.

indulgência, *s.f.* indulgence, indulging, tolerance, forbearance, clemency, forgiviness, remission.

indulgenciar, *v.t.* to treat with indulgence; to pardon, to forgive.

indulgente, *adj.* indulgent, indulging, clement, lenient, mild; tolerant, kind.

indultado, *adj.* exempted.

indultar, *v.t.* to grant a pardon or exemption, to pardon.

indultário, *adj.* exempt, pardoned.

indulto, *s.m.* indult, pardon, exemption, remission; grace, favour.

indumentar, *v.t. ver "vestir".*

indumentária, *s.f.* clothes, dresses, apparel, raiment, garments.

indumentário, *adj.* relative to clothes.

indumento, *s.m.* clothing, garment.

induração, *s.f.* induration.

indústria, *s.f.* industry; diligence; assiduity; dexterity; craft; skill. 1) *indústria base*, key industry. 2) *indústria de pesca*, fishery. 3) *cavalheiro de indústria*, a sharper.

industriador, *s.m.* instructor, trainer.

industrial, *adj., s.* industrial, industrialist, manufacturer.

industrialismo, *s.m.* industrialism.

industrialização, *adj., s.* industrialization.

industrializar, *v.t.* to industrialize.

industriar, *v.t.* to instruct, to train, to teach; to coach, to prepare.

industriosamente, *adv.* industriously.

industrioso, *adj.* industrious, skilful, clever; dexterous.

indutância, *s.f.* inductance.

indutivo, *adj.* inductive.

indutor, *adj., s.m.* inducing; inductor; induction coil; inducer.

induzido, *adj., s.m.* induced; armature.

induzidor, *s.m.* inducer, instigator.

induzimento, *s.m.* inducement; inducing, instigation, incentive.

induzir, *v.t.* to induce; to bring about; to lead; to influence, to instigate; to cause; to incite.

inebriação, *s.f.* inebriation.

inebriador, *adj.* ver inebriante.

inebriamento, *s.m.* ver inebriação.

inebriante, *adj.* inebriant; intoxicating; inebriating.

inebriar, *v.t.* to inebriate, to make drunk; to enrapture, to delight.

inédia, *s.f.* inedia; starvation.

ineditismo, *s.m.* newness; novelty.

inédito, *adj., s.m.* inedit, unpublished; original, novel; unprecedented, unexampled; an unpublished work.

inefabilidade, *s.f.* ineffability.

inefável, *adj.* ineffable, inexpressible, indescribable; delicious.

inefavelmente, *adv.* ineffably.

ineficácia, *s.f.* inefficacy, ineffectiveness; powerlessness.

ineficaz, *adj.* inefficacious, ineffectual, ineffective, inoperative.

ineficiência, *s.f.* inefficiency, incompetency.

ineficiente, *adj.* inefficient, ineffective.

inegável, *adj.* undeniable, indisputable; incontrovertible, irrefutable; evident, positive.

inegociável, *adj.* unnegotiable.

inegulável, *adj.* matchless.

inelegância, *s.f.* inelegancy.

inelegante, *adj.* inelegant.

inelegibilidade, *s.f.* ineligibility.

inelegível, *adj.* ineligible.

ineloquente, *adj.* ineloquent.

inelutável, *adj.* ineluctable, inevitable, unavoidable; irresistible.

inenarrável, *adj.* unspeakable, indescribable, innarrable.

inépcia, ineptidão, *s.f.* ineptitude, stupidity; absurdity, nonsense; unfitness.

inepto, *adj.* inept, stupid; absurd, nonsencical; unfit, unsuitable.

inequivocamente, *adv.* unequivocally, unmistakably.

inequívoco, *adj.* unequivocal, manifest, clear, unmistakable, unambiguous.

inércia, *s.f.* inertia *(física);* idleness, indolence, inactivity, inaction; laziness; lethargy.

inerência, *s.f.* inherence.

inerente, *adj. adj.* inherent, innate, intrinsic, inborn; organic.

inerme, *adj.* unarmed, defenseless.

inerrância, *s.f.* inerrancy.

inerrante, *adj.* inerrant, unerring.

inerte, *adj.* inert; slow; motionless; inactive, passive; torpid, lethargic.

inervação, *s.f.* innervation.

inervar, *v.t.* to innervate; to innerve; to invigorate.

inescrutabilidade, *s.f.* inscrutability, impenetrableness.

inescrutável, *adj.* inscrutable, mysterious, impenetrable, enigmatic.

inescurecível, *adj.* that cannot be darkened; memorable; evident.

inescusável, *adj.* inexcusable, indispensable.

inesgotável, *adj.* inexhaustible; unceasing; copious, abundant; unfailing; indefatigable.

inesgotavelmente, *adj.* inexhaustibly.

inesperadamente, *adv.* unexpectedly, suddenly, surprisingly, all of a sudden.

inesperado, *adj.* unexpected, sudden, unforeseen, unlooked for; abrupt.

inesquecível, *adj.* unforgettable.

inesquecivelmente, *adv.* unforgettably.

inestancável, *adj.* that cannot be stopped or stanched *(sangue).*

inestético, *adj.* inaesthetic.

inestimado, *adj.* unesteemed.

inestimável, *adj.* inestimable, invaluable, precious, priceless.

inevidência, *s.f.* inevidence, obscurity.

inevidente, *adj.* inevident, not clear, obscure.

inevitabilidade, *s.f.* inevitability, unavoidableness.

inevitável, *adj.* inevitable, unavoidable, unpreventable.

inevitavelmente, *adv.* inevitably, unavoidably, infallibly, necessarily.

inexactidão, *s.f.* inexactitude, inexactness; inaccuracy, incorrectness; falseness.

inexacto, *adj.* inexact, incorret, inaccurate; false, faulty.

inexaminável, *adj.* unexaminable.

inexaurível, *adj.* unexhaustible, unfailing, abundant.

inexausto, *adj.* unexhausted.

inexcedível, *adj.* unexcelled, unsuperable, unsurpassable, unbeatable.

inexcedivelmente, *adv.* unsuperably, unsurpassably.

inexcitabilidade, *s.f.* inexcitability.

inexcitável, *adj.* unexcitable.

inexecução, *s.f.* inexecution.

inexecutável, *adj.* inexecutable; impraticable.

inexequibilidade, *s.f.* inexecutableness; impraticability.

inexequível, *adj.* inexecutable, impraticable.

inexigível, *adj.* unclaimable, undemandable.

inexistência, *s.f.* inexistence, non-existence; lack, deficiency.

inexistente, *adj.* inexistent, non-existent; absent.

inexorabilidade, *s.f.* inexorability, inflexibility; relentlessness.

inexorável, *adj.* inexorable, inflexible, relentless, rigorous, ruthless, merciless, severe, implacable.

inexoravelmente, *adv.* inexorable.

inexpedito, *adj.* awkward; not active, slow; clumsy.

inexperiência, *s.f.* inexperience; awkwardness; youngness.

inexperiente, inexperto, *adj.* unexperienced; awkward; fresh, young; unskilled, untrained, green, inexpert, unskilful, clumsy.

inexpiado, *adj.* untoned for, unpardoned, unexpiated.

inexpiável, *adj.* inexpiable.

inexplicável, *adj.* inexplicable; obscure; incomprehensible; mysterious, srtange.

inexplicavelmente, *adv.* inexplicably.

inexplícito, *adj.* unexplicit.

inexplorado, *adj.* unexplored; unworked *(mina);* uncultivated *(terra).*

inexplorável, *adj.* inexplorable.

inexpressão, *s.f.* lack of expression

inexpressividade, *s.f.* inexpressiveness.

inexpressivo, *adj.* inexpressive, unexpressive; unutterable; meaningless.

inexprimível, *adj.* inexpressible, unspeakable, indescribable.

inexprimivelmente, *adv.* inexpressibly.

inexpugnabilidade, *s.f.* inexpugnability, impregnability, invincibility.

inexpugnável, *adj.* inexpugnable, impregnable, unconquerable, invincible, insuperable, unassailable.

inexpugnavelmente, *adv.* inexpugnably.

inextensão, *s.f.* inestension.

inextensibilidade, *s.f.* inextensibility.

inextricavelmente, *adv.* inextricably.

inextensível, *adj.* inextensible.

inextenso, *adj.* unextended.

inexterminável, *adj.* inexterminable.

inextinguível, *adj.* inextinguishable, unquenchable, indestructible.

inextinto, *adj.* unextinguished.

inextirpável, *adj.* inextirpable.

inextricável, *adj.* inextricable, entangled, intricate.

infactível, *adj.* impracticable, unfeasible, unrealizable.

infacundo, *adj.* ineloquent.

infalibilidade, *s.f.* infallibility, certainty; inevitability.

infalibilismo, *s.m.* infallibilism.

infalibilista, *adj., s.* infallibilist.

infalível, *adj.* infallible; inevitable; neverfailing, unfailing, sure, certain.

infalivelmente, *adv.* infallibly, unfalingly, doubtlessly, sure as death.

infalsificável, *adj.* unfalsifiable, unadulterable.

infamação, *s.f.* defamation, calumny, slander, detraction.

infamador, *adj., s.m.* slanderous, defamatory; defamer, slanderer.

infamante, *adj.* ignominious, defamatory; slanderous, injurious.

infamar, *v.t.* to infamize, to defame, to slander, to blacken; to discredit, to dishonour.

infamatório, *adj.* defamatory, infamous, opprobious.

infame, *adj.* infamous, vile; scandalous, shameful, abominable, ignominious.

infamemente, *adv.* infamously.

infâmia, *s.f.* infamy, dishonour, discredit; villainy, ignominy.

infância, *s.f.* infancy; childhood, boyhood, girlhood; early period *(de uma instituição, arte, ect.).*

infando, *adj.* abominable, execrable, accursed, horrible, odious, nefarious.

infanta, *s.f.* Infanta (Spanish or Portuguese princess of royal blood, except the eldest); wife of an infant.

infantador, *s.m.* an infant's estate.

infantaria, *s.f.* infantry, foot soldiers.

infante, *s.m.* infant; foot soldier, infantrymen; child, baby; Infant *(príncipe de sangue real em Espanha e Portugal).*

infanticida, *s., adj.* infanticide; infanticidal.

infanticídio, *s.m.* infanticide.

infantil, *adj.* infantile, childish, puerile; innocent.

infantilidade, *s.f.* childishness, infantile act.

infantilismo, *s.m.* infantilism, puerilism.

infantilizar, *v.t.* render infantile; *infantilizar-se,* to become pueril.

infatigabilidade, *s.f.* indefatigability, tirelessness.

infatigável, *adj.* indefatigable, untiring, tireless, unweariable; persevering, zealous.

infatigavelmente, *adv.* indefatigably, assiduously.

infausto, *adj.* unlucky, unhappy, fatal, unfrortunate, ill-fated.

infecção, *s.f.* infection, contagion, corruption, contamination.

infeccionado, *adj.* infected, contaminated, corrupt.

infeccionar, *v.t.* to infect, to corrupt; to taint; to contaminate, to pollute.

infeccioso, *adj.* infectious, infecting, contaminating, contagious.

infectado, *adj. ver "infeccionado".*

infectar, *v.t. ver "infeccionar".*

infecto, *adj.* infected.

infectuoso, *adj.* infectious.

infecundidade, *s.f.* sterility, infertility; unfruitfulness.

infecundo, *adj.* sterile; barren; unproductive, infertile, fruitless.

infelicidade, *s.f.* infelicity; unhapiness; misery; disaster, misfortune, iil-luck, calamity; adversity.

infelicitar, *v.t.* to make unhappy; to cause unhappiness to.

infeliz, *adj.* unhappy, unfortunate, unlucky; deplorabe, disastrous; unsucessful.

infelizmente, *adv.* unhappily, unfortunately, unluckily.

infenso, *adj.* inimical, unfriendly, hostile, contrary to.

inferência, *s.f.* inference, conclusion, deduction; consequnece, induction.

inferior, *adj., s.m.* lower, inferior, ordinary, common, second-rate, mediocre, poor quality; subordinate, person of lower rank, subaltern; *não ser inferior a ninguém,* to be second to none.

inferioridade, *s.f.* inferiority, disadvantage; poorness, ordinariness.

inferiorizar, *v.t.* to make inferior, to abase; *inferiorizar-se,* to become inferior.

inferiormente, *adv.* inferiorly, below.

inferir, *v.t.* to infer, to deduce, to conclude, to draw conclusions; to presume, to guess.

infermentescível, *adj.* unfermentability.

infernação, *s.f.* annoyance.

infernal, *adj.* infernal, diabolical; hellish, devilish, satanic; horrible, cruel; *barulho infernal,* a hell of a noise.

infernar, *v.t.* to harass, to plague, to pester, to torment, to afflict.

inferneira, *s.f.* hubbub, tumult, uproar, turmoil, confusion, disorder.

inferno, *s.m.* hell; torment, torture; remorse.

ínfero, *adj., s.m.* inferior, lower; hell, inferno.

inferovariado, *adj.* infraovarian.

infértil, *adj.* infertile, barren, unfruitful, sterile, unproductive.

infertilidade, *s.f.* infertility, barrenness; sterility.

infertilizar, *v.t.* to make infertile; to sterilize.

infertilizável, *adj.* unfertilizable.

infestação, *s.f.* infestation, molestation.

infestador, *adj., s.m.* infesting; infester.

infestante, *adj.* infesting.

infestar, *v.t.* to infest, to swarm in.

infesto, *adj.* hostile, prejudicial, pernicious; annoying.

infibulação, *s.f.* infibulation.

infibular, *v.t.* infibulate, to attach a ring to.

inficionar, *v.t.* ver *"infeccionar".*

infidelidade, *s.f.* infidelity, deceit, disloyalty.

infiel, *adj., s.* infidel, disloyal, unfaithful, false, treacherous, perfidious, inaccurate, inexact; atheist, unbeliever.

infiltração, *s.f.* infiltration.

infiltrador, *adj.* infiltrating, pervasive.

infiltrar, *v.t.* to infilter, to infiltrate, to pass through, to penetrate, to percolate.

ínfimo, *adj.* lowest; meanest.

infindável, *adj.* endless, unending, boundless, infinite, never-ending, interminable.

infindo, *adj.* endless, unlimited, countless, interminable, infinitem innumerable.

infinidade, *s.f.* infinity, infinitude, infiniteness, infinite number, immensity.

infinitamente, *adv.* infinitely.

infinitésima, *s.f.* infinitesimal, infinitesimal quantity.

infinitesimal, *adj.* infinitesimal, minute, very small.

infinitésimo, *adj.* infinitesimal, infinitesimal quantity.

infinitivo, *adj. s.m.* infinitive.

infinito, *adj., s.m.* infinite, endless, unlimited; boundless, immeasurable; infinite, infinitive, space.

infirmar, *v.t.* to lessen. to weaken, to enfeeble; to invalidate, to annul.

infirmativo, *adj.* infirmative, invalidating.

infixação, *s.f.* infixing.

infixar, *v.t.* to infix, to fix; to insert.

infixidez, *s.f.* inconsistency, unsteadiness, unfixedness.

infixo, *s.m.* infix.

inflação, *s.f.* inflation; swelling; haughtiness; conceit; excessibe increase.

inflacionismo, *s.m.* inflationism.

inflacionista, *adj., s.* inflationist.

inflado, *adj.* inflated; tumid, turgid; swollen, puffed up, puffy, conceited.

inflamabilidade, *s.f.* inflammability, combustibility.

inflamação, *s.f.* inflammation, swelling.

inflamado, *adj.* inflamed, excited, exacerbated; fiery, vehement, ardent, passionate, enthusiastic.

inflamador, *adj., s.m.* inflaming, inflamtory; inflamer.

inflamar, *v.y.* to inflame; to excite; to exarcerbate; to rouse; to set afire; *inflamar-se,* to become inflamed.

inflamativo, inflamatório, *adj.* inflammatory, inflammative.

inflamável, *adj.* inflammable, combustible; excitable.

inflar, *v.t.* to inflate; to puff out; to elate.

inflectir, *v.t.* to inflect, to bend, to curve, to incline; to modulate *(som, voz).*

inflexão, *s.f.* inflexion; bending, curving; variation, modulation *(voz);* intonation; inclination.

inflexibilidade, *adv.* inflexibly.

inflexível, *adj.* inflective, inflectional.

inflexivelmente, *adj.* inflexed, curved, bent.

inflexivo, *adj.* inflecive, inflectional.

inflexo, *adj.* inflexed, curved, bent.

inflicção, *s.f.* infliction.

infligir, *v.t.* to inflict, to impose *(um penalty).*

inflorar, *v.t.* to flower, to bloom, to blossom; *inflorar-se,* to blossom.

inflorescência, *s.f.* inflorescence, flowering.

inflorescente, *adj.* inflorescent.

influença, *s.f.* influenza, flu.

influência, *s.f.* influence; ascendency; power, authority; importance, prestige.

influenciação, *s.f.* influence; influencing.

influenciar, *v.t.* to influence; to bias; to sway; to presdispose; to affect, to touch, to impress.

influenciável, *adj.* easy to influence.

influente, *adj., s.m.* influent, influential, powerful, persuading, important; person of influence, big-wig, big shot.

influenza, *s.f.* flu, grippe.

influição, *s.f.* flowing in; inflowing.

influidor, *adj., s.m.* influential, influencing; influencer.

influir, *v.i.* to inflow; to predominate, to influence, to induce, to persuade; to instil, to infuse, to inspire; to impel; to prevail upon.

influxo, *s.m.* influx, affluence; high tide, full tide; influence, power; infusion.

in-fólio, *s.m.* folio *(livro).*

informação, *s.f.* information, informing, notice; knowledge; news; intelligence, report; communication; judicial inquiry. 1) *agência de informações,* inquiry office. 2) *dar boas informações,* to give good references. 3) *colher informações,* to make inquiries. 4) *informação meteorológica,* weather report.

informador, *s.m., adj.* informer; informing.

informante, *adj.* informant, informational.

informar, *v.t.* to inform, to tell; to impart knowledge, to acquaint with, to let know, to notify, to give notice; to give form to; to give shape to; *informar-se,* to inform oneself about, to inquire about.

informativo, *adj.* informative.

informe, *adj., s.m.* shapeless; deformed; formless, monstrous; information, report; advice.

informidade, *s.f.* shapelessness, deformity.

infortificável, *adj.* unfortifiable.

infortuna, *s.f.* adversity, misfortune, unhappiness; misery, distress.

infortunadamente, *adv.* unfortunately.

infortunado, *adj.* unfortunate, unhappy, ill-fated.

infortunar, *v.t.* to make unfortunate, to cause ill fortune to.

infortúnio, *s.m.* misfortune, ill-luck, adversity, unhappiness, bad fortune; misery, distress.

infortunoso, *adj.* unfortunate, unhappy.

infracção, *s.f.* infraction, violation, breaking, infringement, transgression, breach.

infracitado, *adj.* mentioned, below, undermentioned.

infractor, *s.m.* infringer, transgressor, violator.

infra-estrutura, *s.f.* substructure.

infravermelho, *adj.* infra-red.

infrene, *adj.* unbridled, uncontrolled, unrestrained.

infrequência, *s.f.* infrequency, rarity.

infrequente, *adj.* infrequent, uncommon, rare.

infringir, *v.t.* to infringe; to transgress, to violate, to break; to overstep.

infringível, *adj.* infrigible, unbreakable, inviolable.

infrutescência, *s.f.* infructescence.

infrutescente, *adj.* infructescent.

infrutífero, *adj.* unfruitful, unfructuous, fruitless, vain, useless; unsuccessful.

infrutuosidade, *s.f.* infructuosity, fruitlessness.

infrutuoso, *adj.* unfruitful, vain, fruitless, useless.

infundadamente, *adv.* groundlessly, unfoundedly, baselessly.

infundado, *adj.* unfounded, groundless, baseless, causeless.

infundir, *v.t.* to infuse, to instill, to inspire, to implant, to pour in; to impress.

infusa, *s.f.* pitcher; jug.

infusão, *s.f.* infusion; instillation; steeping; *pôr de infusão,* to steep, to soak.

infusibilidade, *s.f.* infusibility.

infusível, *adj.* infusible.

infuso, *adj.* steeped, infused; of natural virtues, inbred.

infusórios, *s.m., pl.* infusoria.

ingénito, *adj.* innate, inborn, congenital, hereditary.

ingente, *adj.* enormous, huge, great, immense, large.

ingénua, *s.f.* ingénue; inexperienced girl; actress who fills that role.

ingenuamente, *adv.* ingenuously, credulously, naively.

ingenuidade, *s.f.* ingenuousness, candour, naivety simplicity innocence, frankness.

ingénuo, *adj.* ingenuous, candid, frank, open, simple, artless, innocent.

ingerência, *s.f.* meddling; interference, intervention.

ingerir, *v.t.* to ingest, to swallow.

ingestão, *s.f.* ingestion, swallowing.

inglês, *adj., s.m.* English; Englishman, the English language. 1) *inglês incorrecto, macarrónico,* broken English. 2) *inglês correcto,* king's English. 3) *para inglês ver,* merely for show.

inglesada, *s.f.* group of English people.

inglesar, *v.t.* to Anglicize, to render English.

inglesismo, *s.m.* Anglicism.

inglório, *adj.* inglorious, modest, obscure, renowness.

inglorioso, *adj.* inglorious.

ingovernável, *adj.* ungovernable, unruly, uncontrollable, unmanageable.

ingracioso, *adj.* ungraceful, awkward.

ingratamente, *adj.* ungratefully.

ingratatão, *s.m.* ungrateful man.

ingratidão, *s.f.* ingratitude, ungratefulness.

ingrato, *adj.* ungrateful, thankless; sterile, barren *(fig)*.

ingrediente, *s.m.* ingredient, component, constituent.

íngreme, *adj.* steep, abrupt, precipitous.

ingremidade, *s.f.* steepness.

ingresia, *s.f.* uproar, fuss, clamour.

ingressão, *s.f.* ingression, entrance.

ingressar, *v.i.* to enter, to go in; to join *(como membro)*.

ingresso, *s.m.* ingress, entering, admission, entrance.

íngua, *s.f.* bubo.

inguinal, *adj.* inguinal.

ingurgitação, ingurgitamento, *s.m.* ingurgitation, swelling; distension.

ingurgitar, *v.t.* to ingurgitate; to swallow, to gulp, to engorge.

inibição, *s.f.* inhibition, inhibiting, restraint; prohibition.

inibidor, *adj., s.m.* inihibiting; inhibitor.

inibir, *v.t.* to inhibit, to repress, to hinder, to restrain; to prohibit.

inibitivo, *adj.* inhibitory; inhibitive.

inibitória, *s.f.* difficulty; hindrance, obstruction.

inibitório, *adj.* inhibitory.

iniciação, *s.f.* initiation, beginning, star; admission; indoctrination.

iniciado, *s.m.* initiate, nocive, adept, neophyte.

iniciador, *adj., s.m.* initiating; initiator, founder, starter, beginner.

inicial, *adj., s.m.* initial; beginning; incipient; initial.

iniciar, *v.t.* to initiate, to begin, to commence, to start; to inaugurate; to admit; to instruct; to introduce; to inform.

iniciativa, *s.f.* iniciative, energy, activity, enterprise; *por iniciativa,* on one's own initiative.

iniciativo, *adj.* initiative, initiatory, initial.

início, *s.m.* initiation, beginning, start, opening.

inigualável, *adj.* uneequalled, unique, peerless, unmatchable, unrivalled.

iniludível, *adj.* unmistakable; plain, manifest, undeceivable, undoubtful, evident.

inimaginável, *adj.* unimaginable inconceivable, unthinkable.

inimicícia, *s.f.* enmity, hostility.

inimicíssimo, *adj.* most inimical, most hostile.

inimigo, *adj., s.m.* inimical, hostile, unfriendly, adverse, unfavourable; enemy; adversary; the Evil One.

inimistar, *v.t.* to make an enemy of, to set at variance; *inimistar-se,* to become an enemy of.

inimitável, *adj.* inimitable, unrivalled, unique.

inimitavelmente, *adv.* inimitably.

inimizade, *s.f.* enmity, hostility, hatred, animosity, antagonism, rancour, hate, disaffection.

inimizar, *v.t.* to make an enemy of, to arouse enemity.

ininteligente, *adj.* unintelligent, unwise witless.

ininteligível, *adj.* unintelligent, obscure.

ininterrupção, *s.f.* continuity, uninterruption.

ininterruptamente, *adv.* uninterruptedly.

ininterrupto, *adj.* uninterrupted, constant, continuous, ceaseless, unceasing.

iniquamente, *adv.* iniquitously, wrongly.

iniquidade, *s.f.* iniquity, unrighteousness, injustice, misdeed, unjustness.

iníquo, *adj.* iniquos, unrighteous, wicked, inequitable, unfair, unjust, perverse.

injecção, *s.f.* injection; injecting *(o acto ou a substância);* tedious discourse; *injecção hipodérmica, intramuscular, intravenosa, subcutânea,* hypodermic, intramuscular, intravenous, subcutaneous injection.

injectado, *adj.* injected, bloodshot *(olhos).*

injectar, *v.t.* to inject, to introduce, to drive in, to insert.

injector, *s.m.* injector.

injucundo, *adj.* disagreeable, unpleasant.

injudicioso, *adj.* injudicious, ill-judged.

injunção, *s.f.* injunction, order, command, mandate, instruction.

injúria, *s.f.* injury, wrong, harm; affront, offense, insult, invective, grievance, abuse.

injuriador, *s.m.* insulter, injurer, slanderer.

injuriante, *adj.* insulting, offending, injurious.

injuriar, *v.t.* to insult, to injure, to abuse, to do harm to, to defame, to revile.

injurioso, *adj.* injurious, insulting, abusive, offensive, calumnious, defamatory.

injustamente, *adv.* unjustly.

injustiça, *s.f.* injustice; unfairness, wrong, harm, unjust action, injury, grievance; *reparar uma injustiça,* to right a wrong.

injustificação, *s.f.* unjustification.

injustificado, *adj.* unjustified, not defensible; unjust, illegal, untenable.

injustificável, *adj.* unjustifiable, not defensible; unjust, illegal, untenable.

injustificavelmente, *adv.* unjustifiably.

injusto, *adj.* unjust, unfair, not equitable, dishonest, unrighteous.

inobediência, *s.f.* disobedience, insubordination.

inobediente, *adj.* disobedient.

inobliterável, *adj.* ineffaceable, indelible.

inobscurecível, *adj.* inobscurable.

inobservado, *adj.* unobserved, unregarded, unperceived, unseen.

inobservância, *s.f.* inobservance, nonobservance.

inobservante, *adj.* inobservant, not attentive.

inobservável, *adj.* unobservable, unnoticeable.

inocência, *s.f.* innocence; candour; guitlessness; simplicity, purity.

inocentar, *v.t.* to declare innocent, to acquit.

inocente, *adj., s.* innocent; candid, pure; guiltless; inoffensive, harmless; simple, ingenuous; baby, young child.

inocentemente, *adv.* innocently, ingenuously.

inocuidade, *s.f.* innocuousness, innocuity, harmlessness.

inoculabilidade, *s.f.* inoculability.

inoculação, *s.f.* inoculation.

inoculador, *s.m., adj.* noculator; inoculating.

inocular, *v.t.* to inoculate; to imbue; to impregnate; to insert, to engraft.

inoculável, *adj.* inoculable.

inócuo, *adj.* innocuous, innoxious, harmless, innofensive.

inocupado, *adj.* unoccupied, free.

inodoro, *adj.* odourless, inodorous, scentless.

inofensivo, *adj.* inoffensive, harmless, innocuous, unoffending; unobjectionable.

inoficioso, *adj.* inoficious *(testamento).*

inolente, *adj.* odourless.

inolvidável, *adj.* unforgettable.

inominado, *adj.* innominate; nameless.

inominável, *adj.* unnamable, unfit to be named; base object.

inoperante, *adj.* inoperative, inert.

inoperável, *adj.* inoperable, that cannot be operated.

inópia, *s.f.* want, need, indigence, penury, poverty.

inopinadamente, *adv.* unexpectedly.

inopinado, *adj.* unexpected, unforeseen, unlooked for.

inopinável, *adj.* surprising, unforeseeable, unappreciable.

inoportunamente, *adv.* inopportunely, untimely, inconveniently.

inoportunidade, *s.f.* inopportunity; unfitness; irrelevnace; inconvenience.

inoportuno, *adj.* inopportunity; unseasonable, ill-timed; inconvenient, inappropriate.

inorgânico, *adj.* inorganic.

inorganismo, *s.m.* inorganic, substance.

inorganizado, *adj.* unorganized; inorganic.

inospitaleito, *s.f.* inhospitable, unwelcoming, uninviting.

inospitalidade, *s.f.* inhospitableness, inhospitaly.

inóspito, *adj.* inhospitable, desolate, uninhabitable; barren, wild.

inovação, *s.f.* innovatio; change, alteration, novelty.

inovador, *adj., s.m.* innovative, innovatory; innovator.

inovar, *v.t.* to innovate, to change, to make changes in; to renovate.

inoxidável, *adj.* inoxidable; stainless, rustproof.

inóxio, *adj.* innoxious, innocuous; inoffensive, harmless.

inqualificável, *adj.* unqualified, shameless, vile.

inqualificavelmente, *adv.* shamelessly; vilely.

inquebrantável, *adj.* inflexible, unbending; unbreakable, unfailing.

inquebrável, *adj.* unbreakable, adamantine; *vidro inquebrável,* safety glass.

inquérito, *s.m.* inquiry, search, inquest, investigation; *fazer um inquérito,* to hold an inquest.

inquestionável, *adj.* unquestionable, indisputable, certain; irrefutable, incontestable.

inquestionavelmente, *adv.* unquestionably.

inquietação, *s.f.* inquietude; restlessness; uneasiness; anxiety, apparehension, concern; unrest, disturbance.

inquietador, *adj., s.m.* disturbing; alarmimg, troubling; disquieter, disturber.

inquietamento, *s.m. ver "inquietação".*

inquietante, *adj.* disturbing, troubling, alarming; worrisome.

inquietar, *v.t.* to disturb, to disquiet, to trouble, to alarm; to worry, to molest; *inquietar-se,* to be uneasy.

inquieto, *adj.* disquiet, unquiet, restless, anxious, uneasy, troubled, unrestful; troublesome, turbulent.

inquietude, *s.f.* inquietude, uneasiness, apprehension; unrest.

inquilinato, *s.m.* tenancy.

inquilino, *s.m.* lodger, tenant, occupant.

inquinação, inquinamento, *s.f., s.m.* pollution; corruption; infection.

inquinar, *v.t.* to pollute, to contaminate, to corrupt, to infect.

inquirição, inquirimento, *s.f., s.m.* inquest, inquiry; investigation, examination.

inquiridor, *s.m., adj.* inquirer, inquisitor; inquisitive; inquiring.

inquirir, *v.t.* to inquire; to search; to find out; to interrogate, to ask, to question, to investigate.

inquisição, *s.f.* inquisition; the Holy Office.

inquisidor, *s.m.* inquisitor.

inquisitivo, *adj.* inquisitive.

inquisitorial, *adj.* inquisitorial.

inquisitorialmente, *adv.* inquisitorially.

inrestaurável, *adj.* unrestorable, irreparable.

insaciabilidade, *s.f.* insatiability; greediness.

insaciado, *adj.* unsatiated.

insaciável, *adj.* insatiable, greedy, voracious, rapacious; unquenchable.

insaciavelmente, *adv.* insatiably.

insaciedade, *s.f.* insatiety.

insalivação, *s.f.* insalivation.

insalivar, *v.t.* to insalivate.

insalubérrimo, *adj.* most unhealthful.

insalubre, *adj.* insalubrious, unhealthy.

insalubridade, *s.f.* insalubrity, unhealthfulness.

insalutífero, *adj. ver "insalubre".*

insanabilidade, *s.f.* incurability.

insanável, *adj.* incurable, irremediable, irreparable.

insânia, *s.f.* insanity, madness, dementia, lunacy, craziness.

insanidade, *s.f.* insanity.

insaponificável, *adj.* unsaponifiable.

insano, *adj.* insane, mad, fool; difficult; senseless; excessive, hard, fatiguing, exhaustive.

insarável, *adj.* incurable.

insatisfação, *s.f.* dissatisfaction.

insatisfatório, *adj.* unsatisfactory, insufficient.

insatisfeito, *adj.* dissatisfied, discontented.

insaturável, *adj.* unsaturable.

insciência, *s.f.* inscience, ignorance.

insciente, ínscio, *adj.* inscient, ignorant.

inscrever, *v.t.* to inscribe, to register; to engrave; to enrol; *inscrever-se,* to sign up, to enlist.

inscrição, *s.f.* inscription *(em monumentos)*; registering, enrolment, registration, matriculation; signing up; legend; epitaph.

inscritível, *adj.* inscribable.

inscrito, *adj.* incribed, registered, enroled.

insculpir, *v.t.* to engrave, to carve; to inscribe.

inscultor, *s.m.* engraver.

inscultura, *s.f.* engraving, inscription.

insecável, *adj.* undryable.

insecticida, *adj., s.m.* insecticidal; insecticide, insect-powder.

insectífugo, *adj.* insectifuge.

inséctil, *adj.* indivisible.

insectívoro, *adj. s.m. pl.* insectivorous; Insectivora.

insecto, *s.m.* insect; insignificant person *(fig).*

inseduzível, *adj.* unseducible.

insegurança, inseguridade, *s.f.* insecurity, unsafeness, instability.

inseguro, *adj.* unsafe, insecure; unstable, unreliable, doubtful.

inseminação, *s.f.* insemination.

inseminar, *v.t.* to inseminate.

insensatamente, *adv.* foolishly, unwisely, stupidity.

insensatez, *s.f.* imprudence, foolishness; stupidity; nonsense.

insensato, *adj.* insensate, follish, unwise, stupid.

insensibilidade, *s.f.* insensibility; indifference; apathy; hardness, callousness.

insensibilização, *s.f.* insensibilization.

insensibilizar, *v.t.* to insensibilize, to render insensible; to numb.

insensitivo, *adj.* insensitive.

insensível, *adj.* insensible; imperceptivel; unware; indifferent, hard, callous, cold-hearted, unfeeling.

insensivelmente, *adv.* insensibly; imperceptibly.

inseparabilidade, *s.f.* inseparability.

inseparável, *adj.* inseparable.

inseparavelmente, *adv.* inseparably.

insepulto, *adj.* unburied.

inserção, *s.f.* insertion, intercalation.

inserir, *v.t.* to insert; to introduce, to put in; to intercalate.

inserto, *adj.* insert, inserted.

inservível, *adj.* useless; unsuitable, unfit.

insexoado, *adj.* sexless.

insídia, *s.f.* insidiousness; treachery, snare, ambush, statagem, perfidy.

insidiador, *s.m.* insidiator, waylayer.

insidiar, *v.t.* to waylay, to plot, to ambush.

insidiosamente, *adv.* insidiously.

insidioso, *adj.* insidious, treacherous; subtle, double-minded.

insigne, *adj.* notable, egrigious, remarkable, eminent, renowned, famous, distinguished, celebrated, illustrious.

insígnia, *s.f.* emblem, badge; sign, mark; symbol; insignia *(pl.)*.

insignificância, *s.f.* insignificance, insignificancy, triviality, a trifle.

insignificante, *adj.* insignificant, trivial, unimportnat, petty, trifling, meaningless.

insignificativo, *adj.* insignificative, unmeaning.

insinceridade, *s.f.* insincerity, dissimulation.

insincero, *adj.* insincere, untruthful.

insinuação, *s.f.* insinuation, hint, allusion, suggestion, cue, inuendo.

insinuador, *s.m., adj.* insinuator; insinuating.

insinuante, *adj.* insinuative, insinuating, ingratiating, engaging, charming, attractive.

insinuar, *v.t.* to insinuate, to hint, to suggest; *insinuar-se*, to worm oneself into, to force its way.

insinuativo, *adj.* insinuative.

insipidamente, *adv.* insipidly, unsavourily, monotonously.

insipidez, *s.f.* insipidity, staleness, dullness.

insípido, *adj.* insipid, tasteless, savourless; falt; stale, uninteresting, tedious.

insipiência, *s.f.* foolishness, insipience, ignorance.

insipiente, *adj.* insipient, foolish, senseless, stupid.

insistência, *s.f.* insistence, stubborness, obstinacy, persistence, perseverance.

insistente, *adj.* insistent, obstinate, stubborn, persistent.

insistentemente, *adv.* insistently, pressingly.

insistir, *v.i.* to insist on; to emphasize; to press hard, to be obstinate.

insito, *adj.* innate, inborn, natural.

insobriedade, *s.f.* insobriety, intemperance.

insóbrio, *adj.* intemperate.

insociabilidade, *s.f.* unsociability; aloofness.

insocial, *adj.* unsocial, reserved.

insociável, *adj.* unsociable, reserved, misanthrophical.

insofismável, *adj.* insubitable, unmistakable, undeniable.

insofismavelmente, *adv.* indubitably.

insofrido, *adj.* impatient, restless.

insofrimento, *s.m.* impatience, intolerance.

insofrível, *adj.* insufferable, intolerable, unbearable.

insolação, *s.f.* sunstroke, insolation.

insolçar, *v.t.* to expose to sun's rays.

insoldável, *adj.* unweldable.

insolência, *s.f.* insolence, insult, offence, sauciness, impertinence; arrogance.

insolente, *adj.* insolent, offensive, insulting, impertinent, saucy; cocky, petulant.

insolentemente, *adv.* insolently.

insolidariedade, *s.f.* lack of solidarity.

insólito, *adj.* unusual, uncommon, extraordinary, strange; incredible.

insolubilidade, *s.f.* insolubility.

insolúvel, *adj.* insoluble, insolvable; unrecoverable.

insolvabilidade, *s.f.* insolvenbcy, bankruptcy.

insolvência, s.f. insolvency.

insolvente, adj. insolvent.

insolvível, adj. insolvable.

insondável, adj. unsoundable, incomprehensible, unfathomable, impenetrable.

insónia, s.f. insomnias, sleplessness.

insonoro, adj. soundless, insonorous, voiceless.

insonso, adj. ver "insosso".

insopitável, adj. unquenchable, irrepressible.

insosso, adj. unsalted, insipid, saltless, tasteless.

inspecção, s.f. inspection, overseeing, examination, surveying, supervision, control, superintendence; visit; check-up, review; inspecção médica, medical examination.

inspeccionar, v.t. to inspect, to survey, to examine, to oversee, to superintend, to supervise, to control, to check, to visit.

inspector, s.m. inspector, overseer, superintendent, supervisor.

inspectoria, s.f. inspectorship, inspectorate.

inspiração, s.f. inspiration; breathing; enthusiasm, exaltation, divine, influence, creative impulse.

inspirador, s.m., adj. inspirer, stimulator; inspiring, dynamic.

inspirar, v.t. to inspire, to breathe into; to instil; to suggest.

inspirativo, adj. inspirative, inspiring.

inspiratório, adj. inspiratory

inspirável, adj. inspirable.

instabilidade, s.f. instability, inconstancy, inconsistence, unsteadiness.

instalação, s.f. installation; fitting; accomodation, arrangement; plant; equipment (de escola, hospital). 1) instalação eléctrica, electric installation, the electric fittings. 2) instalação de água quente, hot water connections.

instalado, adj. installed, settled.

instalador, s.m., adj. installer; installing.

instalar, v.t. to install, to establish, to set; to erect, to construct; to fit out, to equip; instalar-se, to set down, to lodge oneself.

instaminado, adj. unstamened, without stamens.

instância, s.f. instance, urgency, sollicitation, urgent entreaty, insistency. 1) primeira instância, court of first instance. 2) a instâncias de, at the instance of. 3) em última instância, as a last resort.

instantaneamente, s.f. instantaneously.

instantaneidade, s.f. instantaneity, instantaneousness.

instantâneo, adj., s.m. instantaneous, rapid, momentary, immediate; snapshot (fotog.); tirar um instantâneo, to take a snapshot.

instante, adj., s.m. instant, urgent, pressing; instant, moment, second, falsh. 1) num instante, in a second, in a flash, in a tice, in a trick. 2) num instante, in no time. 3) naquele mesmo instante, at that very moment. 4) neste instante, this instant. 5) a cada instante, every minute, continually, all the time. 6) a todo o instante, at any moment. 7) de instante a instante, from moment to moment.

instantemente, adv. instantly, urgently.

instar, v.t. to insist, to press, to urge, to request insistently, to drive.

instauração, s.f. instauration, renewal, restoration, institution.

instaurador, s.m., adj. restorer, founder; founding, establishing.

instaurar, v.t. to restore, to establish, to constitute; to begin; instaurar um processo, to bring an action against.

instável, adj. unstable, inconsistent, changeable, moving, unsteady, unreliable, fickle.

instavelmente, adv. unstably, unsteadily, insecurely.

instigação, s.f. instigation, urging, inciting; persuasion, encouragement, stimulation, inducement; a instigação dele, at his instigation.

instigador, s.m., adj. instigator, setter-on. inducer, prompter; instigating.

instigar, v.t. to incite, to instigate, to press, to stimulate, to supur, to urge, to goad; to prompt, to induce.

instilação, s.f. instillation, instilment.

instilador, s.m., adj. instiller; instilling.

instilar, v.t. to instill, to infuse, to implant.

instintivamente, adv. instinctively.

instintividade, s.f. instinctiveness.

instintivo, adj. instinctive; impulsive; natural, spontaneous, intuitive.

instinto, s.m. instinct, tendency, intuition; impulse, propensity. 1) instinto de conservação, instinct of self-preservation. 2) agir por instinto, to act on (by) instinct.

institucional, adj. institucional.

instituição, s.f. institution, act of instituting; creation; society, organization; established custom or usage, order, principle.

instituidor, *s.m.* institutor, founder.

instituir, *v.t.* to establish, to set up, to institue, to found, to creat; to appoint (as heir); to originate, to begin.

instituto, *s.m.* institue; precept, law; academy; organization *(científica, social, educacional);* building used by this.

instrução, *s.f.* instruction, teaching, learning, education, training, knowledge; orders, directions *(pl).*

instruído, *adj.* leaned, lettered, erudite, educated; informed.

instruir, *v.t.* to instruct, to teach, to educate; to inform; to appraize; to train, to drill; to direct, to give orders; *instruir um processo,* to prepare an action or suit.

instrumentação, *s.f.* instrumentation.

instrumental, *adj., s.m.* instrumental; instruments of an orchestra collectively.

instrumentar, *v.t.* to instrument, to arrange *(composição musical).*

instrumentista, *s., adj.* instrumentalist.

instrumento, *s.m.* instrument, implement, tool; machine; agent, medium, human tool; legal document, deed.

instrutivamente, *adv.* instructively.

instrutivo, *adj.* instructive, educative; informative.

instrutor, *adj., s.m.* instructional; instructor, trainer, teacher, drill-master.

instrutura, *s.f.* structure, frame *(de um edifício).*

ínsua, *s.f.* islet, river island; fenland.

insuave, *adj.* unpleasant, disagreeable.

insuavidade, *s.f.* roughness.

insubmergível, insubmersível, *adj.* unsinkable, insubmergible, insubmersible.

insubmissão, *s.f.* disobedience, unsubmissiveness.

insubmisso, *adj.* unsubmissive; unruly, disobedient, refractory.

insubordinação, *s.f.* insubordination, mutiny, revolt, rebellion, insurrection.

insubordinado, *adj.* insubordinate, disobedient, mutinous, ungovernable, rebellious.

insubordinador, *s.m., adj.* one who promotes insubordination; rebelling.

insubordinar, *v.t.* to make insubordinate, to incite against; *insubordinar-se,* to rise, to rebel, to revolt against.

insubordinável, *adj.* rebellious, insubordinate, unruly, indocile, intractable.

insubornável, *adj.* unbribable, incorruptible.

insubsistência, *s.f.* inability to subsist.

insubsistente, *adj.* unable to subsist, ineffectual.

insubstancial, *adj.* unsubstancial.

insubstancialidade, *s.f.* unsubstantiality.

insubstituível, *adj.* irreplaceable.

insucesso, *s.m.* failure, unsuccess.

insueto, *adj.* unusual, uncommon, disused, *(palavras, expressões).*

insuficiência, *s.f.* insufficiency, poorness, deficiency; inaptitude, incompetence; indequacy.

insuficiente, *adj.* insufficient, poor, deficient; inadequate; incapable, incompetent.

insuficientemente, *adv.* insufficiently.

insuflação, *s.f.* insufflation; breathing.

insuflador, *s.m., adj.* insufflator; insufflating.

insuflar, *v.t.* to insufflate; to blow; to breathe into; to insinuate, to instil; to instigate; to incite.

ínsula, *s.f.* islet, island *(poético).*

insulação, insulamento, *s.f., s.m.* segregation; solitude, loneliness; isolation.

insulador, *s.m., adj.* insulator; insulating.

insulano, *adj., s.m.* insular; islander.

insular, *v.t., adj., s.* to insulate, to isolate; insular; islander.

insularidade, *s.f.* insularity.

insulina, *s.f.* insulin.

insulsez, insulsidade, *s.f.* insipidity.

insulso, *adj.* insipid, dull, spiritless; prosaic, flat; saltless.

insultador, *s.m., adj.* offender, insulter; insulting, offending.

insultante, *adj.* insulting, offensive, insolent, abusive.

insultar, *v.t.* to insult, to abuse, to offend, to affront, to abuse, to wound.

insulto, *s.m.* insult, affront, offence; stroke, fit.

insultuosamente, *adv.* insultingly.

insultuoso, *adj.* insulting, offensive, provocative, scurrilous.

insuperável, *adj.* insuperable, unsurmountable, unexcelled, invincible.

insuperavelmente, *adv.* insuperably.

insuportável, *adj.* insupportable, insufferable, intolerable, unbearable; annoying, bothersome.

insuportavelmente, *adv.* insupportably, unendurably, intolerably.

insuprimível, *adj.* unsuppressible.

insuprível, *adj.* irreplaceable; that cannot be supplied.

insurdescência, *s.f.* deafness.

insurgência, *s.f.* insurgency.

insurgente, *adj., s.m.* insurgent, rebellious; insurgent.

insurgir, *v.t.* to rouse, to stir up; *insurgir-se*, to rebel, to revolt, to rise up against.

insurreccional, *adj.* insurrectional, rebellious.

insurreccionar, *v.t., v. refl.* ver insurgir.

insurrecto, *s.m.* insurrectionist, insurgent, rebel.

insurreição, *s.f.* insurrection, rebellion, uprising, revolt.

insusceptibilidade, *s.f.* insusceptibility.

insusceptível, *adj.* insusceptible.

insuspeição, *s.f.* unsuspicion, unsuspiciousness.

insustentável, *adj.* untenable, undefendable, insupportable, unsustainable.

intáctil, *adj.* intactile, impalpable, intangible.

intacto, *adj.* intact, untouched; entire; safe; whole, complete; sound, uninjured, woundless.

intangibilidade, *s.f.* intangibility.

intangível, *adj.* intangible, untouchable.

integérrimo, *adj.* most upright, most honourable.

íntegra, *s.f.* totally; *na íntegra*, in full, integrally.

integração, *s.f.* integration.

integrador, *adj., s.m.* integrating; integrator.

integral, *adj.* integral, complete; entire, whole, total, unabridged. 1) *pão integral*, whole bread. 2) *cálculo integral*, integral calculus.

integralidade, *s.f.* integrality, completeness.

integralista, *s., adj.* integralist.

integralizar, *v.t.* to integrate, to complete.

integralismo, *s.m.* integralism

integralmente, *adv.* integrally.

integrante, *adj.* integrant, constituent, component.

integrar, *v.t.* to integrate, to complete; to aggregate.

integrável, *adj.* integrable.

integridade, *s.f.* integrity, probity, rectitude, honesty, uprightness; wholeness, entirety.

íntegro, *adj.* whole, complete, entire, intact, inviolate; just, upright, righteous, incorruptible; impartial, virtuous.

inteirado, *adj.* aware, informed.

inteiramente, *adv.* entirely, completely, fully, quite, altogether.

inteirar, *v.t.* to complete; to certify, to assure, to inform; *inteirar-se*, to inform oneself in detail.

inteireza, *s.f.* entireness, entirety; integrity; uprightness, honorability, probity, moral integrity.

inteiriçado, *adj.* rigid, stiff.

inteiriçar, *v.t.* stiffen, to benumb, to paralyse; *inteiriçar-se*, to become stiff, to grow rigid.

inteiriço, *adj.* entire, whole, of one piece; stiff, inflexible.

inteirinho, *adj.* every bit, all of it.

inteiro, *adj.* entire, whole, complete, perfect, undivided, unbroken, intact; honest, upright, righteous; sound, safe. 1) *retrato de corpo inteiro*, wholelength portrait. 2) *número inteiro*, whole number.

intelecção, *s.f.* intellection; activity of the intellect.

intelectivo, *adj.* intellective, rational; mental.

intelecto, *s.m.* intellect, understanding, intelligence, mind, reason.

intelectual, *adj., s.* intellectual, mental.

intelectualidade, *s.f.* intellectually.

intelectualismo, *s.m.* intellectualism.

intelectualista, *s., adj.* intellectualist; intellectualistic.

intelectualização, *s.f.* intellectualization.

intelectualizar, *v.t.* to intellectualize.

intelectualmente, *adv.* intellectually.

inteligência, *s.f.* intelligence, comprehension, understanding, ability, sagacity, penetration, sharpness; intellect, aptitude.

inteligente, *adj.* intelligent, clever, sagacious, quick, acute, bright, talented, sharp-witted.

inteligentemente, *adv.* intelligently, wisely, cleverly.

inteligibilidade, *s.f.* intelligibility.

inteligível, *adj.* intelligible, plain, clear, understandable.

inteligivelmente, *adv.* intelligibly.

intemerato, *adj.* undefiled, incorruptible, pure, honest, spotless.

intemperado, *adj.* intemperate, immoderate, unrestrained, excessive; hard-drinking.

intemperança, *s.f.* intemperancy, excess, over-indulgence, gluttony.

intemperante, *adj.* intemperate, immoderate, excessive, inordinate, dissolute, uncontrolled.

intempérie, *s.f.* inclemency *(do tempo)*, bad weather.

intempestivamente, *adv.* inopportunely.

intempestividade, *s.f.* untimeliness, inopportunity.

intempestivo, *adj.* inopportune, ill-timed, unseasonable, untimely.

intenção, *s.f.* intention, intent, design, purpose, object, aim, end, deliberation. 1) *ter intenção de*, to intend to, to mean to. 2) *com segunda intenção*, with a second motive. 3) *de boas intenções está o inferno cheio*, the way to hell is paved with good intentions. 4) *não ter má intenção*, to mean no harm.

intencionado, *adj.* intentional, deliberate.

intencional, *adj.* intentional, willful, deliberate, designed, premeditated.

intencionalidade, *s.f.* intentionality.

intencionalismo, *s.m.* intentionalism.

intencionalmente, *adv.* intentionally, on purpose, deliberately, purposely.

intendência, *s.f.* intendancy; administration, management.

intendente, *s.m.* intendant, superintendent, manager, administrator.

intender, *v.t.* to superintend, to manage, to oversee, to control.

intensamente, *adv.* intensely, acutely, ardently, violently.

intensão, *s.f.* intensity, intenseness, vehemence.

intensidade, *s.f.* intensity, force, power, strength, vehemence.

intensificação, *s.f.* intensification.

intensificar, *v.t.* to intensify, to amplify; to exalt; to concentrate.

intensivamente, *adv.* intensily.

intensivo, *adj.* intensive, intense, vehement.

intenso, *adj.* intense, vehement, ardent, eager, strong, acute, profound, fervent, violent, vivid.

intentar, *v.t.* to intend; to attempt; to design, to project, to plan, to scheme; to try, to endeavour; *intentar uma acção*, to bring an action against.

intento, *s.m. ver "intenção".*

intentona, *s.f.* rebellion, riot, revolt; conspiracy.

interacção, *s.f.* interaction.

interaliado, *adj.* interallied.

intercadência, *s.f.* interruption; intermittence, intercadence.

intercadente, *adj.* intermittent, irregular, intercadent.

intercalação, *s.f.* intercalation, insertion.

intercalar, *v.t., adj.* to intercalate, to insert; intercalary.

intercâmbio, *s.m.* interchange, reciprocity.

intercedente, *adj.* interceding, pleading.

interceder, *v.i.* to intercede, to intervene, to mediate, to plead for, to pray for.

intercelular, *adj.* intercellular.

intercepção, interceptação, *s.f.* interception, interruption, obstruction.

interceptar, *v.t.* to intercept, to obstruct, to cut off, to impede, to stop on the way.

interceptor, *adj., s.m.* intercepting; interceptor.

intercessão, *s.f.* intercession, interceding, pleading, mediation, intervention, solicitation.

intercessor, *s.m.* intercessor, mediator, pleader, interceder.

intercisão, *s.f.* interruption.

interciso, *adj.* cut through, truncated.

intercolonial, *adj.* intercolonial, intercurrence.

intercolúnio, *s.m.* intercolumniation.

intercomunicação, *s.f.* intercomunication, reciprocal intercourse.

intercontinental, *adj.* intercontinental.

intercorrência, *s.f.* intercurrence

intercorrente, *adj.* intercurrent; intervening.

intercorrer, *v.i.* to run between *(como um rio).*

intercósmico, *adj.* intercosmic.

intercostal, *adj.* intercostal.

intercutâneo, *adj.* subcutaneous.

interdependência, *s.f.* interdependence, mutual, dependence.

interdependente, *adj.* interdependent.

interdepender, *v.i.* to interdepend.

interdição, *s.f.* interdiction, forbidding, prohibition, poscription.

interdigital, *adj.* interdigital.

interditar, *v.t.* to interdict, to forbid; to procribe; to stop, to restrain.

interdito, *adj., s.m.* interdicted, prohibited, forbidden; interdiction, interdict, ban.

interdizer, *v.t.* to interdict, to forbid, to prohibit, to restrain; to cut off from ecclesiastical functions and privileges.

interessadamente, *adv.* interesredly, concernedly.

interessado, *adj., s.m.* interested, concerned; sharer, patry, partner.

interessante, *adj.* interesting, attractive, engaging, pleasing; *estado interessante*, in the family way, pregnant.

interessar, *v.t., v.i.* to interest, to concern; to be interesting, to please; to be of interest to; to engage the attention of, to attract; to stimulate; to be profitable to; to give a share in; *interessar-se*, to take an interest in, to show interest, to concern oneself.

interesse, *s.m.* interest; advantage; profit; concern; share; attention, regard, curiosity.

interesseiro, *adj.* self interested, egoistical, self-seeking; calculating.

interestadual, *adj.* interstate.

interestelar, *adj.* interstellar *(espaço).*

interferência, *s.f.* interference, intervention; interruption, obstruction; jamming *(rádio).*

interferente, *adj.* interferent, interferential.

interferir, *v.i.* to intervene, to interfere, to jam *(rádio);* to obstruct.

interfixo, *adj.* interfixed.

interfoliação, *s.f.* interleaving.

interfoliáceo, *adj.* interfoliaceous.

interfoliar, *v.t.* to interleave.

interfone, *s.m.* interphone.

interglaciário, *adj.* interglacial.

interim, *s.m.* interim, interval; *neste interim,* meanwhile, in the meantime.

interinado, interinato, *s.m.* temporary office, provisional arrangement.

interinamente, *adv.* provisionally, temporarily.

interinidade, *s.f.* provisionality.

interino, *adj.* interim, temporary, provisional.

interinsular, *adj.* interinsular.

interior, *adj., s.m.* interior, inner; internal, inward; inside, inner nature.

interioridade, *s.f.* interiority.

interiormente, *adv.* interiorly, inwardly, internally.

interjeccional, interjectivo, *adj.* interjectional, interjectory.

interjeição, *s.f.* interjection, exclamation.

interligação, *s.f.* interconnection.

interlinear, *adj.* interlineal, interlinear.

interlocução, *s.f.* interlocution, conversation, dialogue.

interlocutor, *s.m.* interlocutor.

interlocutória, *s.f.* interlocution, interlocutory, decree.

interlocutório, *adj.* interlocutory.

interlúdio, *s.m.* interlude.

interlunar, *adj.* interlunar.

interlúnio, *s.m.* interlunar period, new moon.

intermaxilar, *adj.* intermaxillary.

intermediar, *v.t.* to intermediate, to intervene, to interpose; to intermingle.

intermediário, *adj., s.m.* intermediate, intervening; intermediary, mediator, go--between.

intermédio, *s.m., adj.* intermezzo, interlude; intervention; means, way; intermediate; interposed; *por intermédio de,* through, by means of.

intermeter, *v.t.* to interpose, to place between; to interfere.

interminável, *adj.* endless, interminable, unending, infinite; wearisome; long, vast, limitless.

interminavelmente, *adv.* interminably.

intérmino, *adj. ver "interminável".*

intermissão, *s.f.* intermission, pause, interval, interruption.

intermitência, *s.f.* intermittence, intermission, interruption.

intermitente, *adj.* intermittent; alternating; recurrent.

intermitentemente, *adv.* intermittently, intermittingly.

intermitir, *v.i.* to entermit, to cease; to relax; to suspend, to interrupt, to pause.

intermuscular, *adj.* intermuscular.

internação, *s.f.* internment *(hospital, asilo).*

internacional, *adj.* international.

internacionalidade, *s.f.* internationality.

internacionalismo, *s.m.* internationalism.

internacionalista, *s., adj.* internationalist.

internacionalização, *s.f.* internationalization.

internacionalizar, *v.t.* to internationalize.

internacionalmente, *adv.* internationally.

internado, *s.m., adj.* inmate, internee; impatient *(hospital);* interned.

internamente, *adv.* internally, inwardly.

internamento, *s.m.* internment, interning.

internar, *v.t.* to intern, to place in a boarding school.

internato, *s.m.* boarding-school; orphanage.

interno, *adj., s.m.* interned, internal, interior, inward; domestic; resident; boarder; intern.

internúncio, *s.m.* internuncio.

interoceânico, *adj.* interoceanic.

interocular, *adj.* interocular.

interósseo, *adj.* interosseous.

interparlamentar, *adj.* interparliamentary.

interpelação, *s.f.* interpellation.

interpelador, *s.m.* interpellator.

interpelante, *s.m.* interpellant.

interpelar, *v.t.* to interpellate, to question; to summon; to demand offical explanations; to interrupt.

interpenetração, *s.f.* interpenetration.

interpenetrar, *v.i.* to interpenatrate.

interpeninsular, *adj.* interpeninsular.

interplanetário, adj. interplanetary.

interpolação, s.f. interpolation.

interpolador, s.m., adj. interpolator; interpolating.

interpolar, v.t., adj. to interpolate, to insert, to introduce, to intercalate; interpolar.

interpor, v.t. to interpose; to intervene, to intercede; to intercalate, to insert; to oppose; to mediate; to interrupt; interpor recurso, to lodge an appeal.

interposição, s.f. interposition, intervention, mediation; interruption, interference.

interposto, s.m., adj. emporium, market-place, store, bonded warehouse; interposed, intermediary.

interpretação, s.m. interpretation, explanation, version, elucidation.

interpretador, s.m., adj. interpreter; interpreting.

interpretar, v.t. to interpret, to expound, to explain, to elucidate, to make clear; to translate.

interpretativo, adj. interpretative.

interpretável, adj. interpretable.

intérprete, s.m. interpreter.

inter-regional, adj. interregional.

interregno, s.m. interregnum, interval,

interrogação, s.f. interrogation, question, query; 1) ponto de interrogação, note (mark) of interrogation, question mark.

interrogador, adj., s.m. interrogating; interrogator.

interrogar, v.t. to interrogate, to inquire, to put questions to, to examine, to cross-examine.

interrogativamente, adv. interrogatively.

interrogativo, adj. interrogative, inquiring.

interrogatório, s.m. interrogatory, inquiry, examination, questionnaire.

interromper, v.t. to interrupt, to stop, to suspend, to break in upon, to cut off; to disturb; to disconnect.

interrupção, s.f. interruption, suspension, stoppage; disturbance; disconnected.

interrupto, adj. interrupted, suspended, broken off; discountinued.

interruptor, adj., s.m. interrupting; interruptory;interrupter; circuit breaker, switch, cut out (eléctrica). 1) abrir o interruptor, to switch on. 2) fechar o interruptor, to switch off.

intersecção, s.f. intersection; cutting; crossing.

interseccional, adj. intersectional.

intersectar, v.t. to cut (duas linhas).

interseriar, v.t. to insert, to interpose.

interstelar, adj. interstellar.

intersticial, adj. interstitial.

interstício, s.m. interstice, opening, crevice, chink, crack.

intertrigem, intertrigo, s.f., s.m. intertrigo.

intertropical, adj. intertropical.

interurbano, adj. interurban.

intervaladamente, adv. at intervals.

intervalado, adj. intervaled; spaced at intervals.

intervalar, v.t., adj. to interval; to alternate; to intermix; to space, to interrupt at intervals; intervallic.

intervalo, s.m. interval, gap, period; pause; interspace; break (na escola).

intervenção, s.f. intervention; mediation; interference; interposition; intercession; intervenção cirúrgica, surgical operation.

intervencionismo, s.m. interventionism.

intervencionista, adj. interventionist.

interveniente, adj. intervenient, intervening, interposing.

interventivo, adj. interventive.

interventor, s.m. intervener, mediator.

interversão, s.f. inversion, reversal (da ordem natural).

intervertebral, adj. intervertebral.

interverter, v.t. to invert, to reverse (a ordem ou a posição).

intervir, v.i. to intervene, to interfere, to intercede; to take part, to step in.

intervocálico, adj. intervocalic.

intestado, adj. intestate, without a will.

intestinal, adj. intestinal.

intestino, s.m., adj. bowel; intestine; gut; intestine, domestic, internal; intestino delgado, grosso, small, large intestine.

intimação, s.f. notification, summons, criation.

intimador, s.m. intimater, summoner.

intimamente, adv. intimaly.

intimar, v.t. to intimate, to summon, to notify, to inform, to cite; to order, to urge.

intimativa, s.f. arrogance, forceful statement, imperious gesture or command.

intimativo, adj. forceful, energetic, imperious, authoritative.

intimidação, s.f. intimidation, threat.

intimidade, s.f. intimacy, privacy, closeness, friendship.

intimidador, s.m., adj. intimidator; intimidating.

intimidar, *v.t.* to intimidate, to frighten, to dishearten.

intimidativo, *adj.* intimidating.

íntimo, *adj.*, *s.m.* intimate, innermost, deepseated; very dear; familiar; soul, heart, core, the inner soul; the intimate *(amigo)*; *no íntimo,* at heart.

intimorato, *adj.* fearless, bold, intrepid.

intitulação, *s.f.* titling.

intitular, *v.t.* to entitle, to name, to denominate, to designate; to give a title to; *intitular-se,* to call oneself.

intocável, *adj.*, *s.* untouchable, of the lowest cast *(Índia).*

intolerância, *s.f.* intolerance, intransigence, bigotry.

intolerante, *adj.* intolerant, intransigent, bigoted.

intolerantemente, *adv.* intolerantly.

intolerantismo, *s.m.* intolerance, dogmatism, narrowness.

intolerável, *adj.* intolerable, unendurable, unbearable, plagued.

intoleravelmente, *adv.* intolerably, unbearably.

intonação, *s.f.* intonation, tone, modulation of tone.

intonso, *adj.* unshorn, unshaven, hirsute.

intorção, *s.f.* intorsion, twining.

intragável, *adj.* uneatable; unreadable.

intoxicação, *s.f.* intoxication, poisoning.

intoxicante, *s.m.*, *adj.* poison; poisoning.

intoxicar, *v.t.* to intoxicate, to poison.

intracelular, *adj.* intracellular.

intradérmico, *adj.* intradermic.

intraduzível, *adj.* untranslatable, inexpressible.

intramuros, *adj.* intramural.

intramuscular, *adj.* intramuscular.

intranquilidade, *s.f.* intranquility, uneasiness, restlessness.

intranquilo, *adj.* uneasy, perturbed, anxious, restless, unsettled.

intransferível, *adj.* untransferable.

intransigência, *s.f.* inflexibility, austerity, intransigence, intolerance.

intransigente, *adj.* intransigent, inflexible, irreconcilable; intolerant, austere, strict.

intransitável, *adj.* impassable, pathless, invious.

intransitivo, *adj.* intransitive.

intransmissibilidade, *s.f.* untransmissibility.

intransmissível, *adj.* intransmissible, not negotiable, untransferable.

intransplantável, *adj.* not transplantable.

intransponível, *adj.* insurmountable, impassable.

intransportável, *adj.* untransportable.

intra-ocular, *adj.* intraocular.

intrapulmonar, *adj.* intrapulmonary.

intratável, *adj.* intractable, indocile, refractory, unmanageable; stubborn; unsociable.

intravascular, *adj.* intravascular.

intravenoso, *adj.* intravenous.

intrepidamente, *adv.* intrepidly, bravely, fearlessly.

intrepidez, *s.f.* intrepidity, fearlessness, boldness, courage, dauntlessness.

intrépido, *adj.* intrepid, fearless, bold, daring, brave, dauntless, courageous.

intricado, *adj.* ver intrincado.

intricar, *v.t.* ver intrincar.

intriga, *s.f.* intrigue, plot, scheme, machination, wile, ruse.

intrigado, *adj.* puzzled at, intrigued; piqued.

intrigalhada, *s.f.* gossip, intriguery.

intrigante, *adj.* intriguing; *s.* intriguer, troublemaker; talebearer.

intrigar, *v.t.* to intrigue; to perplex, to upset, to puzzle; to plot, to scheme; to rouse the interest of, to pique the curiosity.

intriguista, *s.* intriguer, schmer, troublemaker.

intrincado, *adj.* intricate, entangled, complicated, involded, perplexing.

intrincar, *v.t.* to render intricate; to perplex, to confuse.

inrinsecamente, *adv.* intrinsically.

intrínseco, *adj.* intrinsic, inherent; inward, inborn, natural, native; essential; real, true.

introdução, *s.f.* introduction; preface; foreward; prelude; presentation.

introdutivo, *adj.* introductive.

introdutor, *s.m.* introducer, announcer; adj. introductory, preliminary.

introdutório, *adj.* introductory, preliminary.

introduzir, *v.t.* to introduce; to lead in; to insert; to bring in; to establish, to initiate, to begin with; to inoculate, to inject; to penetrate.

intróito, *s.m.* beginning; preface; introit *(religião).*

intrometediço, *adj.* meddler, intruder.

intrometer, *v.t.* to intromit, to admit; 1) *intrometer-se,* to meddle, to interfere, to intervene, to intrude.

intrometido, *adj.* meddlesome, bold,

intrusive, nosey, impertinent; *s.m.* meddler, busybody.

intromissão, intrometimento, *s.m.* intromission, interference.

introspecção, *s.f.* introspection, self-examination; self-analysis.

introspectivamente, *adv.* introspectively.

introspectivo, *adj.* introspective.

introversão, *s.f.* introvert.

introverter, *v.* to introvert.

introvertido, *adj.* introverted.

intrujão, *adj.* delusive, deceitful; *s.m.* deceiver, impostor, tricker, cheater, swindler.

intrujar, *v.t.* to deceive, to cheat, to delude, to take in, to dupe, to swindle.

intrujice, *s.f.* cheat, humbug, trickery, fraud, hoax.

intrusão, *s.f.* intrusion, invasion; encroachmente; trespass.

intruso, *s.m.* usurper, intruder; adj. intrusive.

intuição, *s.f.* intuition, instinct, perception, insight; feeling, anticipation; presentiment.

intuitivamente, *adv.* intuitively.

intuitivo, *adj.* intuitive.

intuito, *s.m.* design, intention, aim, purpose, idea, end, object.

intumescência, *s.f.* intumescence, swelling, tumidity, tumefaction.

intumescente, *adj.* intumescent, swollen.

intumescer, *v.i.* to untumesce, to become turgid, to swell up.

intumescimento, *s.m.* ver intumescência.

inturgescência, *s.f.* turgescence, turgidity.

inturgescente, *adj.* turgescent, turgid, swollen.

inturgescer, *v.t., v.i.* to swell up, to grow turgid.

inultrapassável, *adj.* unsurpassable.

inumação, *s.f.* inhumation; burial.

inumanidade, *s.f.* unhumanity, cruelty, barbarity, brutality.

inumano, *adj.* inhuman, cruel, unfeeling, brutal.

inumar, *v.t.* to inhume, to bury.

inumerável, *adj.* innumerable, countless, numberless.

inúmero, *adj.* numberless, countless.

inundação, *s.f.* inundation, flood, deluge, overflow,

inundante, *adj.* overflowing, inundating.

inundar, *v.t.* to inundate, to flood, to overflow, to deluge.

inundável, *adj.* floodable.

inusitado, *adj.* unusual, unwanted; strange.

inútil, *adj.* useless, inutile; needless, unnecessary; unworthy; ineffectual, vain, unprofitable, good-for-nothing.

inutilidade, *s.f.* inutility, uselessness.

inutilizar, *v.t.* to make useless; to disable, to frustrate, to nullify, to render effectless; to incapacitate.

inutilizável, *adj.* unavailable, unserviceable.

inutilmente, *adv.* uselessly, vainly, ineffectually.

invadeável, *adj.* unfordable, impassable.

invadir, *v.t.* to invade; to violate; to overrun, to raid; to spread over, to throng; to attack, to assail.

invaginação, *s.f.* invagination.

invaginante, *adj.* invaginating.

invalidação, *s.f.* invalidation, annulment, cancellation.

invalidade, *s.f.* invalidity, nullity.

invalidar, *v.t.* to invalidate, to annul, to nullify, to deprive of legal force.

invalidez, *s.f.* invalidity, infirmity, disability, illness.

inválido, *adj., s.m.* invalid, infirm, weak, ill, feeble; sick or disabled person.

invariabilidade, *s.f.* invariability, unchangeableness.

invariável, *adj.* invariable, constant, firm, unchangeable, unalterable.

invariavelmente, *adv.* invariably.

invasão, *s.f.* invasion, raid, incursion, inroad.

invasivo, *adj.* invasive; aggressive, hostile.

invasor, *s.m.* invader.

invectiva, *s.f.* invective, vituperation, diatribe.

invectivador, *s.m.* vituperator, inveigher; adj. vituperative.

invectivar, *v.t.* to vituperate, to abuse, to censure, to inveigh against, to rail at.

invectivo, *adj.* invectibe, abusive, vituperartive; aggressive.

inveja, *s.f.* envy, jealousy. 1) *ter inveja*, to be envious of. 2) *fazer inveja*, to arouse envy,

invejar, *v.t.* to envy; to desire, to covet; to grudge.

invejável, *adj.* enviable, very desirable, covetable; valuable.

invejoso, *adj.* envious, covetous, jealous; grudging *(pessoa)*.

invenção, *s.f.* invention, discovery, finding, creation, contrivance; fiction.

invencibilidade, *s.f.* invincibility, insuperability.

invencionar, *v.t.* to adorn artfully.

invencionice, s.f. fabrication, falsehood; artifice, trick.

invencível, adj. invincible, unconquerable, insuperable, irresistible.

invendável, invendível, adj. unsalable, unmarketable.

inventar, v.t. to invent, to find out, to devise, to conceive, to discover, to create; to fake, to forge.

inventariação, s.f. inventotring.

inventariante, s.m. one who makes inventories.

inventariar, v.t. to inventory, to register, to take stock, to catalogue, to make an inventory.

inventário, s.m. inventory, catalogue, register; fazer um inventário, to take stock.

inventiva, s.f. inventiveness, ingeniousness, imagination.

inventivo, adj. inventive, ingenious, imaginative, creative.

invento, s.m. invention, discovery, contrivance.

inventor, s.m. inventor, discoverer, originator, framer; liar (pop).

inventora, s.f. inventress.

inverdade, s.f. untruth, untruthfulness.

inverídico, adj. untruthful, untrue, false, inexact.

inverificável, adj. unverifiable.

invernada, s.f. hard winter, winter season, rainy weather.

invernage, s.f. wintering.

invernal, adj. wintry, winterly, hibernal.

invernar, v.i. to hibernate.

inverneira, invernia, s.f. hard winter, cold weather, wintriness.

Inverno, s.m. Winter.

invernoso, adj. wintry, cold, rainy, stormy.

inverosímil, adj. unlikely, improbable.

inverosimilhança, s.f. unlikeliness, improbability.

inverosimilhante, adj. ver "in iverosímil".

inverisimilmente, adj. untrhthfully.

inversamente, adv. inversely.

inversão, s.f. inversion, reversal, reversing; transposition; investment (de dinheiro).

inversivo, adj. inversive.

inverso, adj. inverse, contrary; s.m. inverse, reverse, contrary. 1) na razão inversa de, in the inverse ratio to. 2) ao inverso, inversely; inreverse. 3) ao inverso de, contrary to.

inversor, s.m. inverter, reverser; adj. inverting, inversive.

invertebrado, adj., s.m. invertebrate; Invertebrata (pl).

inverter, v.t. to invert, to turn upside-down, to reverse; to invest (capital).

invertido, adj. inverted; upside-down.

invertível, adj. invertible.

invés, s.m. reverse side, wrong side; the opposite.

investida, s.f. charge, assault, attack, rush.

investidura, s.f. investiture.

investigação, s.f. investigation, inquiry, examination, research, scrutiny.

investigador, s.m. investigator, researcher, detective; adj. investigating.

investigante, adj. investigating.

investigar, v.t. to investigate, to inquire into, to explore, to scrutinize, to study; to trace.

investigável, adj. investigable.

investimento, s.m. investment.

investir, v.t. to invest, to install (num escritório); to attack, to assault, to fall upon; to invest, to lay out (dinheiro).

inveteração, s.f. inveteracy.

inveterado, adj. inveterate, obstinate, persistent, chronic; deep-rooted.

inveterar, v.t. to implant (um hábito); inveterar-se, to grow inveterate.

inviabilidade, s.f. impracticableness, unfeasibility.

inviável, adj. impracticable, unfeasible; inaccessible, trackless.

invicto, adj. unvanquished, invincible, unbeaten.

ínvio, adj. impassable; trackless, pathless.

inviolabilidade, s.f. inviolability.

inviolado, adj. inviolate; pure; whole; unhurt.

inviolável, adj. inviolable, sacred.

inviolavelmente, adv. inviolably, sacredly.

invisibilidade, s.f. invisibility, invisibleness.

invisível, adj. invisible, unseen, hidden, concealed, imperceptible.

invisivelmente, adj. invisibly.

invisual, adj., s. blind; a blind person.

invocação, s.f. invocation, supplication, prayer; appeal (às Musas).

invocador, s.m., adj. implorer, supplicant; invoking.

invocar, v.t. to invoke; to summon; to call upon; to appeal to; to implore, to supplicate.

invocativo, adj. invocatory, invocative.

invocatória, s.f. invocation.

involução, s.f. involution, degeneration.

invólucro, s.m. covering, wrapper, packing; envelope.

involuntariamente, *adv.* involuntarily.

involuntário, *adj.* involuntary, unintentional, unwilling; automatic, instinctive.

invulgar, *adj.* rare, unusual, uncommon, exceptional.

invulnerabilidade, *s.f.* invulnerability.

invulnerável, *adj.* invulnerable; unassailable.

inzoneiro, *adj.* intriguer *(pop.).*

iodar, *v.t.* to iodize, to treat or impregnate with iodine.

iodato, *s.m.* iodate.

iodeto, *s.m.* iodide.

iodo, *s.m.* iodine; *tintura de iodo,* tincture of iodine.

iodofórmio, *s.m.* iodoform.

iodoterapia, *s.f.* iodotherapy.

iogurte, *s.m.* yoghurt, yogurt.

ion, ionte, *s.m.* ion.

ionização, *s.f.* ionization.

ionizar, *v.t.* to ionize.

ionosfera, *s.f.* ionosphere.

ipecacuanha, *s.f.* ipecacuanha.

ir, *v.i.* to go; to depart; to start; to move; to pass away; to be about to; to walk; to march; to travel; to pass, to elapse (tempo); to retire. 1)*ir-se* to go away. 2) *ir adiante* to lead the way, to go first. 3) *ir atrás* to go behind, to go after. 4) *ir abaixo* to fail. 5) *ir por água abaixo* to go to the dogs; to fall through *(planos).* 6) *ir ao encontro de* to go to meet. 7) *ir a pé* to go on foot. 8) *ir a pique* to sink. 9) *ir avante* to go ahead. 10) *ir bem* to be well, to be all right. 11) *ir com Deus* to go in peace. 12) *ir no conto* to be duped. 13) *ir para os anjinhos* to go west. 14) *ir de vento em popa* to proceed under favourable circumstances. 15) *ir embora* to go away, to leave; to die. 16) *ir a caminho* to be on the way to. 17) *ir à cena* to be staged. 18) *ir à deriva* to drift,to go astray. 19) *ir à praça* to be put up for public sale. 20) *ir a terra* to fall to the ground; to fail (an enterprise). 21) *ir andando* to keep going, to keep moving; to be so-so *(saúde).* 22) *ir aos ares* to hit the ceiling. 23) *ir desta para melhor* to die. 24) *ir direito a* to go straight to. 25) *ir na onda* to make no resistance; to be fooled. 26) *ir no embrulho* to be taken in. 27) *ir por partes* to proceed by steps.

ira, *s.f.* anger, rage, wrath; passion, fury, indignation. 1) *acesso de ira,* fit of rage. 2) *ter um acesso de ira,* to fly into a passion.

iracúndia, *s.f.* irascibility.

iracundo, *adj.* angry, enraged, iracund, irritable, irascible.

iradamente, *adv.* angrily, furiously.

irado, *adj.* irate, angry, enraged, furious, choleric, wrathful.

iraniano, irânico, *adj.,s.m.* Iranian.

irar, *v.t.* to make angry, to irritate; to enrage to infuriate; *irar-se,* to grow angry, to fly into a passion.

iraquiano, *s.m., adj.* Iraki; Iraquian.

irascibilidade, *s.f.* irascibility, irritability.

irascível, *adj.* irascible, passionate, angry, irritable, hot-tempered; quarrelsome.

irascivelmente, *adv.* irascibly.

iriante, *adj.* iridescent.

iriado, *adj.* iridescent.

iriar, *v.t.* to make irisdescent,to iridize.

iridescente, *adj.* iridescent.

irídico, *adj.* iridic.

irídio, *s.m.* iridium.

íris, *s.m.* iris.

irisação, *s.f.* irisation.

irisar, *v.t.* to iridize; to make iridescent.

irlandês, *s.m., adj.* Irishman; Irish.

irmã, *s.f.* sister; *irmã de caridade,* sister of charity.

irmãmente, *adv.* fraternally.

irmanar, *v.t.* to match, to pair, to couple; to join, to link.

irmandade, *s.f.* brotherhood; fraternity; community; sisterhood; a religious order.

irmão, *s.m.* brother; fellow-member; equal; *adj.* alike, similar, equal; *(pl.)* brothers; brother and sister; brethren. 1) *irmão colaço* foster brother. 2) *irmão de armas* brother in arms. 3) *irmão gémeo* twin brother. 4) *irmão germano* brother german. 5) *irmão uterino* brother on the mother'side.

ironia, *s.f.* irony; sarcasm, mockery.

ironicamente, *adv.* ironically.

irónico, *adj.* ironical, sarcastical, derisive.

ironista, *s.* ironist, ironical writer.

ironizar, *v.t.,i.* to use irony, to speak or write ironically.

iroso, *adj.* angry, furious, raging.

irra!, *interj.* zounds!, egad!

irracional, *adj., s.* irrational, absurd, unreasonable, illogical, foolish; irrational being; animal, brute.

irracionalidade, *s.f.* irrationality.

irracionalismo, *s.m.* irrationalism.

irracionalizar, *v.t.* to irrationalize.

irracionalmente, *adv.* irrationally.

irradiação, *s.f.* irradiation; splendour,

irradiancy; radiation, emission; broadcasting (*rádio*).

irradiador, *s.m., adj.* radiator; radiating.

irradiante, *adj.* irradiant.

irradiar, *v.t.* to irradiate, to beam, to shed light on, to emit rays, to shine; to broadcast (*rádio*).

irreal, *adj.* unreal, imaginary, visionary, illusive, fanciful.

irrealidade, *s.f.* unreality, imagination, unsubstantiality; falseness.

irrealizável, *adj.* unrealizable, illusory.

irreclamável, *adj.* irreclaimable.

irreconciliável, *adj.* irreconcilable, incompatible.

irreconciliavelmente, *adv.* irreconcilably.

irreconhecível, *adj.* unrecognizable.

irrecorrível, *adj.* unavoidable, inescapable; unappealable (*lei*).

irrecuperável, *adj.* irrecoverable, irretrievable.

irrecuperavelmente, *adv.* iirrecoverably.

irrecusável, *adj.* irrecusable, irrefragable.

irredimível, *adj.* irredeemable.

irredutibilidade, *s.f.* irreducibility.

irredutível, *adj.* irreducible; unbending, tough.

irredutivelmente, *adv.* irreducibly.

irreduzível, *adj. vd.* irredutível.

irreflectidamente, *adv.* inconsiderately, unthinkingly.

irreflectido, *adj.* inconsiderate, unthinking, thoughtless, rash, heedless.

irreflexão, *s.f.* irreflection; inconsideration, rashness; imprudence.

irreflexivo, *adj. vd.* irreflectido.

irreformável, *adj.* irreformable; unalterable.

irrefragável, *adj.* irrefragable, undeniable, irrefutable,unquestionable.

irrefrangível, *adj.* irrefrangible.

irrefreável, *adj.* irrepressible, uncontrollable, unrestrainable.

irrefutabilidade, *s.f.* irrefutability, incontestability.

irrefutado, *adj.* not refuted, uncontested.

irrefutável, *adj.* irrefutable, indisputable, unquestionable, cogent, incontestable.

irrefutavelmente, *adv.* irrefutably, unanswerably.

irregular, *adj.* irregular, abnormal, deviating, not uniform; uncertain; variable; abnormal; illegal.

irregularidade, *s.f.* irregularity, deviation, unevenness; anomaly, abnormality.

irregularmente, *adv.* irregularly.

irreligião, *s.f.* irreligion; unbelief.

irreligiosidade, *s.f.* irreligiosity, irreligiousness.

irreligioso, *adj.* irreligious, impious.

irremediável, *adj.* irremediable; incurable; irreparable; inevitable, fatal.

irremediavelmente, *adv.* irremediably.

irremissibilidade, *s.f.* irremissibility, irremissibleness.

irremissível, *adj.* irremissible, unpardonable; incurable; unfailing.

irremível, *adj.* unredeemable.

irremovível, *adj.* irremovable; firm, stable; unremovable; unavoidable, inevitable.

irremunerado, *adj.* unpaid, unremunerated.

irremunerável, *adj.* irremunerable.

irreparabilidade, *s.f.* irreparableness, irreparability.

irreparável, *adj.* irreparable, irremediable, past cure, irretrievable.

irreparavelmente, *adv.* irreparably, irretrievably.

irrepartível, *adj.* indivisible, infrangible.

irreplicável, *adj.* irrefutable, unanswerable, unrepliable.

irrepreensibilidade, *s.f.* irreproachability, irreprehensibleness.

irrepreensível, *adj.* irreprehensible, irreproachable, blameless, faultless, impecable.

irrepreensivelmente, *adv.* irreprehensibly, impeccably.

irrepresentável, *adj.* unplayable.

irrepressível, irreprimível, *adj.* irrepressible, uncontrollable, invincible.

irreprimivelmente, *adv.* irrepressibly.

irrequietismo, *s.m.* restlessness.

irrequieto, *adj.* turbulent, unsteady, restless; fidgety, fussy, unquiet.

irresgatável, *adj.* unredeemable.

irresignável, *adj.* unrenounceable.

irresistência, *s.f.* nonresistance

irresistente, *adj.* unresisting

irresistibilidade, *s.f.* irresistibility, irresistibleness.

irresistível, *adj.* irresistible, overpowering, cogent, convincing.

irresistivelmente, *adv.* irresitibly, overwhelmingly, cogently.

irresolução, *s.f.* irresolution, hesitation, lack of decision, indecision.

irresolutamente, *adv.* irresolutely.

irresoluto, *adj.* irresolute, undecided, vacillating, unsure, hesitant.

irresolúvel, irresolvível, *adj.* insoluble, irresolvable.

irrespeito, *s.m.* lack or respect, impoliteness; contempt.

irrespeitoso, *adj.* irreverent, disrespectful.

irrespirável, *adj.* irrespirable, unfit for respiration.

irrespondível, *adj.* unanswerable, irrefutable.

irresponsabilidade, *s.f.* irresponsability, unaccountable.

irresponsável, *adj.* irresponsible.

irrestringível, *adj.* unrestrictable, unrestrainable.

irretorquível, *adj.* irrefutable, unanswerable.

irretratável, *adj.* irreversible, irrevocable.

irrevelado, *adj.* unrevealed.

irreverência, *s.f.* irreverence, disrespect, insolence.

irreverente, *adj.* irreverent, disrespectful.

irreverentemente, *adv.* irrevocable.

irreversível, *adj.* irreversible, reverseless.

irrevogabilidade, *s.f.* irrevocability.

irrevogável, *adj.* irrevocable, final, unalterable.

irrevogavelmente, *adv.* irrecably.

irridente, *adj.* scoffing, mocking.

irrigação, *s.f.* irrigation, watering.

irrigador, *s.m., adj.* irrigator, water sprinkler; irrigational.

irrigar, *v.t.* to irrigate, to water.

irrigável, *adj.* irrigable.

irrisão, *s.f.* mockery, derision, ridicule; scorn, contempt.

irrisor, *s.m.* derider, scoffer, mocker.

irrisoriamente, *adv.* derisively, ridiculously.

irrisório, *adj.* derisive, scoffing, deriding, scornful; ridiculous, petty.

irritabilidade, *s.f.* irritability.

irritação, *s.f.* irritation, anger, excitement; exasperation; itching, burning *(da pele)*.

irritadiço, *adj.* querulous, peevish, craky, crabby.

irritado, *adj.* irritated, exasperated; resentful; furious, angry.

irritante, *adj.* irritant, irritating, provoking.

irritar, *v.t.* to irritate, to anger, to excite, to annoy, to exacerbate, to vex, to enrage, to provoke, to put out of temper; *irritar-se,* to grow angry.

irritativo, *adj.* irritative, irritant.

irritável, *adj.* irritable, irascible, touchy, excitable, fiery.

írrito, *adj.* null, invalid; useless, ineffectual.

irrogação, *s.f.* imposition *(de um dever).*

irrogar, *v.t.* to impose; to stigmatize; to impute; to inflict.

irromper, *v.t.* to spring, to surge; to rise; to spout out, to rush in, to burst into; to come into view.

irrupção, *s.f.* irruption; incursion, invasion, inroad, raid.

irruptivo, *adj.* irruptive.

isca, *s.f.* bait; allurement; enticement; *morder a isca,* to take the bait.

iscar, *v.t.* to bait, to allure, to entice.

isco, *s.m.* bait *(para pescar).*

isenção, *s.f.* exemption; abnegation, desinterestedness; independence, impartiality; immunity.

isentar, *v.t.* to exempt, to free from; to release, to dispense, to let off.

isento, *adj.* exempt, free, released; immune; excused. 1) *isento de selo* free of postage. 2) *isento de direitos* free of customs duties.

islâmico, *adj.* Islamic; Islamitic.

islamismo, *s.m.* Islamism.

islamita, *s.* Islamite.

islamítico, *adj.* Islamitic, Islamic.

islandês, *adj., s.m.* Icelandic; Icelander.

islão, *s.m.* Islam.

ismaelita, *s.* Ismaelite.

isobárico, *adj.* isobaric; isobarometric.

isóbaro, *adj.* isobar.

isocromático, *adj.* isochromatic.

isocromia, *s.f.* lithochromy.

isocronamente, *adv.* isochronously.

isocronismo, *s.m.* isochronism.

isócrono, *adj.* isochronous.

isolação, *s.f.* isolation, separation, solitude; dissociation.

isolacionismo, *s.m.* isolationism.

isolacionista, *s.* isolationist.

isoladamente, *adv.* separately.

isolado, *adj.* isolate, separated, solitary; dissociated, disconnected.

isolador, *adj., s.m.* isolating; isolator; insulator.

isolamento, *s.m.* isolation; separation, solitude; insulation.

isolante, *adj.* insulating, isolating.

isolar, *v.t.* to isolate, to insulate; to separate, to dissociate; to segregate; *isolar-se,* to live by oneself, to withdraw.

isómero, *adj.* isomerous; isomerical.

isométrico, *adj.* isometric.

isomórfico, *adj.* isomorphic, isomorphous.

isomorfismo, *s.m.* isomorphism.

isomorfo, *adj.* isomorphic; isomorphous.

isósceles, *adj.* isosceles.

isotérico, isótero, *adj.* isotheral.

isotérmico, *adj.* isothermal.

isótopo, *s.m.* isotope.

isotropia, *s.f.* isotropism, isotropy.

isotrópico, *adj.* isotropic, isotropous.

isqueiro, *s.m.* lighter.

ísquio, ísquion, *s.m.* ischium.

israeliano, *s.m., adj.* Jew, Hebrew; Jewish.

israelita, *s.* Israelite.

isso, *dem. pron.* that; it. 1) *só isso?,* is that all?. 2) *isso mesmo,* just so *(that).*

ístmico, *adj.* isthmian.

istmo, *s.m.* isthmus, strait.

isto, *dem. pron.* this; *isto é,* that is to say.

italianismo, *s.m.* Italianism.

italianizar, *v.t.* to italianize.

italiano, *s.m., adj.* Italian.

itálico, *adj.,s.m.* italic; italics, italic type.

italiota, *s.* Italiot.

ítalo, *adj., s.m.* Italian.

iteração, *s.f.* iteration, repetition.

iterar, *v.t.* to iterate, to repeat, to say over again.

iterativo, *adj.* iterative.

itinerante, *adj.* itinerant.

itinerário, *s.m., adj.* itinerary, route.

J

j, the tenth letter of the Portuguese alphabet.

já, *adv.* already; this moment, at once, now, presently, immediately, right now. 1) *já que,* now that. 2) *já então,* even then. 3) *já não,* no longer, no more. 4) *já que assim quer,* since you will have it so. 5) *já há muito,* a long while ago. 6) *já se vê,* it is evident, to be sure. 7) *já vou,* I am coming. 8) *já estiveste em Londres?,* have you ever been to London?. 9) *já venho,* I'll be back in a jiffy.

jaça, *s.f.* stain, spot, blemish; fault, imperfection (numa pedra preciosa); *sem jaça,* perfect, flawless.

jacaré, *s.m.* cayman, alligator.

jacente, *adj., s.m.* lying, recumbent, resting; girder of a bridge.

jacintino, *adj.* hyacinthine.

jacinto, *s.m.* hyacinth.

jacobinismo, *s.m.* Jacobinism, radicalism.

jacobino, *s.m., adj.* Jacobin, extreme nationalist.

jactância, *s.f.* pride, boastfulness, vanity, self-love, self-conceit, brag,vaunt.

jactanciar-se, *v.refl.* to boast, to brag.

jactanciosidade, *s.f.* boastfulness, braggartism.

jactancioso, *adj.* proud, boastful, vain, ostentatious.

jactante, *adj.* boasting.

jactar-se, *v.refl.* to boast, to pride oneself, to swagger, to vaunt, to brag, to talk big.

jacto, *s.m.* cast, throw, impetus; jet gush, flush, rush. 1) *jacto de água,* jet of water. 2) *avião a jacto,* jet plane. 3) *jacto de areia,* sand-blast. 4) *de um jacto,* at one stretch.

jaculação, *s.f.* jaculation.

jacular, *v.t.* to throw, to dart, to hurl, to cast.

jaculatória, *s.f.* prayer.

jaculatório, *adj.* ejaculatory.

jade, *s.m.* jade, nephrite.

jaez, *s.m.* harness; kind, sort, condition, quality; *do mesmo jaez,* of the same kind, alike.

jaezar, *v.t.* to harness.

jagodes, *s.m.* lout, boor, clumsy fellow, dunce *(pop).*

jaguar, *s.m.* jaguar.

jaleca, *s.f.* short jacket.

jaleco, *s.m.* jacket.

jalne, *adj.* golden yellow.

jamais, *adv.* never; ever; at no time.

jâmbico, *adj.* iambic; satirical.

jambo, *s.m.* iambus.

janeiras, *s.f. pl.* new year's carols of gifes (*em Portugal*).

Janeiro, *s.m.* January; years of age (*pl.*).

janela, *s.f.* window; any opening or hole (pop). 1) *janela de correr*, sash-window. 2) *janela de sacada*, bay window. 3) *janela de guilhotina*, guillotine window.

janelo, *s.m.* small window.

jangada, *s.f.* raft, float, float of planks.

jangadeiro, *s.m.* rafstman.

janizaro, *s.m.* janizary, Turkish soldier.

janota, *s.m., adj.* dandy, coxcomb; foppish, dandyish, smart, elegant.

janotar, *v.i.* to dress well, to play the galant.

janotice, *s.f.* dandyism.

janotismo, *s.m.* dandyism, foppery.

jansenismo, *s.m.* Jansenism.

jansenista, *s., adj.* Jansenist; Jansenistic.

janta, *s.f.* dinner (pop).

jantar, *s.m., v.t.* dinner; to dine, to have dinner. 1) *hora de jantar*, dinner-time. 2) *sala de jantar*, dinning-room. 3) *serviço de jantar*, dinner-service.

jantarada, jantarão, *s.f., s.m.* big dinner, sumptuous dinner.

japoneira, *s.f.* camelia.

japonês, *s.m., adj.* Japanese.

japónico, *adj.* Japonic.

japonizar, *v.t.* to Japonize.

jaqueta, *s.f.* short jacket.

jaquetão, *s.m.* double-breasted coat.

jarda, *s.f.* yard (0,9144 m).

jardim, *s.m.* garden, flower-garden. 1) *jardim botânico*, botanical garden. 2) *jardim zoológico*, zoological garden.

jardinagem, *s.f.* gardening.

jardinar, *v.i.* to garden, to cultivate a garden; to walk idly, to lounge.

jardineira, *s.f.* flower-stand; woman gardener.

jardineiro, *s.m.* gardener.

jargão, *s.m.* jargon, slang; gibberish.

jarra, *s.f.* pitcher, jar; vase, flower-pot.

jarrão, *s.m.* large vase.

jarreta, *s., adj.* old person, old fashioned man, ridiculous person.

jarretar, *v.t.* to hamstring; to cripple; to disable.

jarrete, *s.m.* hamstring.

jarreteira, *s.f.* garter, the Order of the Garter.

jarretice, *s.f.* something oldfashioned.

jarro, *s.m.* jug, pitcher, water-jar, water-pot; arum lilly (*bot.*)

jasmim, *s.m.* jasmine (*a flor e o perfume*).

jasmineiro, *s.m.* jasmine shrub.

jaspe, *s.m.* jaspe.

jaspear, *v.t.* to speckle,. to marble, to give the appearance of jasper.

jáspeo, *adj.* jaspideous, jasperous.

jau, *s.* Javanese.

jaula, *s.f.* cage, jail.

javali, *s.m.* wild boar.

javalina, *s.f.* wild pig (*fêmea*).

javalino, *adj.* like a wild boar.

javanês, *s.m., adj.* Javanese.

javardo, *s.m.* ver Javali; a rascal, nasty fellow.

javradeira, javradoura, *s.f.* croze.

javrar, *v.t.* to croze.

javre, *s.m.* croze, groove.

jazer, *v.i.* to lie to be buried.

jazida, *s.f.* resting-place.

jazigo, *s.m.* tomb, grave, vault; filed, bed (*de minerais*). 1) *jazigo de carvão*, coal-field. 2) *jazigo de família*, family vault.

jecoral, jecorário, *adj.* jecoral (*anat.*)

jeira, *s.f.* yoke of land; a day's work; a day's wages; *à jeira*, by the day.

jeiteira, *s.f.* skill, ability, knack (pop).

jeito, *s.m.* way, rule; aptitude, skill, leaning, bent, dexterity; propensity, adroitness. 1) *com jeito*, gently, carefully. 2) *dar um jeito*, to manage. 3) *dar um mau jeito*, to strain. 4) *de qualquer jeito*, at any rate, by hook or by crook. 5) *falta de jeito*, clumsiness.

jeitoso, *adj.* apt, handy, skilled, dexterous; clever; handsome.

jejuador, *s.m.* faster.

jejuar, *v.i.* to fast, to abstain from something.

jejum, *s.m.* fast; fasting; a time of fasting. 1) *em jejum*, fasting. 2) *quebrar o jejum*, to break one's fast. 3) *dia de jejum*, day of fasting.

jejuno, *s.m.* jejunum (*anat.*).

jeovismo, *s.m.* Jehovism, Judaism.

jeovista, *adj.* Jehovistic.

jerarca, *s.m.* hierarch.

jerarquia, *s.j.* hierarchy.

jerárquico, *adj.* hierarchical.

jeremiada, *s.f.* jeremiad, lamentation, mournful complaint.

jeremiar, *v.i.* to lament, to complain.

jericada, *s.f.* group of donkeys; stupidity, nonsense.

jerico, *s.m.* ass, donkey.

jeronimita, jerónimo, *adj.* Hieronymian *(a Ordem).*

jeropiga, *s.f.* unfermented wine, poor wine.

jesuíta, *s.m., adj.* Jesuit; Jesuitical; cunning *(fig);* fanatical.

jesuítico, *adj.* Jesuitical.

jesuitismo, *s.m.* Jesuitism.

Jesus, *s.m.* Jesus; *ai Jesus!,* mercy on me!

jibóia, *s.f.* boa constrictor.

jiga, *s.f.* jig, lively dance.

jigajoga, *s.f.* swindle, cheat; *andar numa jigajoga,* to go from pillar to post.

jipe, *s.m.* jeep.

joalharia, *s.f.* jewellery, jeweller's *(loja).*

joalheiro, *s.m.* jeweller.

joanete, *s.m.* topsail; bunion.

joaninha, *s.f.* lady-bird, lady-bug.

joanino, *adj.* refering to D. João I, III or V, or to São João.

joão-fernandes, *s.m.* a nobody.

joão-ninguém, *s.m.* a pygmy, a nobody.

joão-pestana, *s.m.* sleep *(pop).*

job, *s.m.* a very patient or poor man.

joco-sério, *adj.* partaking of mirth and sadness; half serious, half joking.

jocosidade, *s.f.* jocosity, joviality, cheerfulness, jocularity.

jocoso, *adj.* jocose, humorous, playful.

joeira, *s.f.* fan sieve.

joeiramento, *s.m.* winnowing, sieving, screening.

joelhada, *s.f.* stroke with the knee.

joeirar, *v.t.* to fan, to winnow; to separate, to select.

joeireiro, *s.m.* winnower, sifter, screener.

joeiro, *s.m.* winnowing.

joelheira, *s.f.* kneepiece, knee-pad; baggy knees.

joelho, *s.m.* knee. 1) *de joelhos,* on one's knees. 2) *cair ou pôr-se de joelhos,* to fall on one's knee. 3) *até aos joelhos,* knee-deep in.

joelhudo, *adj.* having thick knees.

jogada, *s.f.* play; move, throw, cast, stroke, hit, shot; *bela jogada,* well played, good shot.

jogador, *s.m.* player; gambler, gamester *(dinheiro); jogador de primeira categoria,* a first-rate player *(desp.).*

jogão, *s.m.* very good cards; *fazer um jogão,* to play very well.

jogar, *v.t.* to play, to play at; to venture; to gamble, to risk, to stake; to take part *(num jogo);* to make a move *(num jogo);* to throw, to cast, to hit, to fling. 1) *jogar a última cartada,* to sink or swim. 2) *jogar uma partida,* to play a game. 3) *jogar forte,* to play high. 4) *jogar a dinheiro,* to play for money. 5) *jogar com um pau de dois bicos,* to hunt with the hounds and run with the hare, to play both ends against the middle, to double-cross.

jogata, *s.f.* game *(de cartas).*

jogatina, *s.f.* gambling.

jogo, *s.m.* game, play, match; pastime; gambling; trick, cheat; set, equipment, collection *(de brinquedos).* 1) *jogo de azar,* game of chance. 2) *jogo de empurra,* passing the buck. 3) *jogo de palavras,* play on words, pun quibble. 4) *jogo de salão,* parlour game. 5) *Jogos Olímpicos,* Olympic games. 6) *jogo franco,* fair play. 7) *jogo da macaca,* hopscotch. 8) *jogo das escondidas,* hide-and-seek. 9) *jogo da vermelhinha,* three-card monte. 10) *jogo da cabra-cega,* blindman's buff. 11) *jogo das damas,* checkers. 12) *jogo das prendas,* forfeits. 13) *jogo dos quatro cantinhos,* puss-in-the-corner. 14) *jogo de sala de jantar,* dinning-room set. 15) *casa de jogo,* gambling-house. 16) *ter bom jogo,* to have good cards. 17) *ter mau jogo,* to have a bad hand. 18) *abrir o jogo,* to open the pot *(no poker).* 19) *estar em jogo,* to be at stake. 20) *pôr em jogo,* to risk, to stake.

jogral, *s.m.* jester, buffoon, scoffer.

jogralice, jogralidade, *s.f.* jesting, buffoonery.

joguete, *s.m.* plaything, toy; laughing-stock; fool, dupe, cat's paw; *ser um joguete,* to be a fool.

joguetear, *v.i.* to jest.

jóia, *s.f.* jewel; entrance fee *(clube);* person of great esteem; darling.

joio, *s.m.* darnel; *separar o trigo do joio,* to separate the wheat from the chaff.

jónico, *adj.* Ionic.

jónio, *s.m.* Ionian.

jóquei, *s.m.* jockey.

jorna, *s.f.* daily wage, pay *(pop).*

jornada, *s.f.* journey; a day's work or travel; battle; trip, tour; expedition.

jornadear, *v.i.* to journey, to travel.

jornal, *s.m.* newspaper, paper; day-wages; day-book; diary.

jornaleco, *s.m.* a rag, paper of no importance.

jornaleiro, *s.m.* day-labourer, journey-man.

jornalismo, *s.m.* journalism, the press.

jornalista, *s.* journalist, newspaper-man.

jornalístico, *adj.* journalistic.

jorra, *s.f.* pitch; slag; dross.

jorrão, *s.m.* lorry, truck, sledge.

jorrar, *v.i.* to spout out, to gush out, to pour, to spring forth, to flow.

jorro, *s.m.* gush, spate, spout, jet, flow, stream, gush; *a jorros,* in torrents.

jovem, *s.,* *adj.* young person youth; young youthful.

jovial, *adj.* jovial, merry, gay, joyous.

jovialidade, *s.f.* joviality, jolliness, merriment, gaiety, good humour.

jovializar, *v.t.* to render jovial; to be jovial.

jovialmente, *adv.* jovially.

juba, *s.f.* mane.

jubado, *adj.* maned.

jubilação, *s.f.* jubilation, exultation, great joy, retirement.

jubilado, *adj.* retired.

jubilar, *v.t.,* *adj.* to rejoice, to cheer, to jubilate, to exult; to retire; referring to a jubilee.

jubileu, *s.m.* jubilee, fiftieth anniversary *(de um acontecimento).*

júbilo, *s.m.* joy exultation, triumph, gladness.

jubilosamente, *adv.* joyfully, joyously.

jubiloso, *adj.* joyful, gay, glad, exultant, eleated rejoicing.

jucundidade, *s.f.* jocundity, cheerfulness, gaiety, gladeness.

jucundo, *adj.* jocund; gay, cheerful.

judaico, *adj.* Judaic, Jewish.

judaísmo, *s.m.* Judaism.

judaísta, *s.* Judaist.

judaizante, *adj.* Judaizing.

judaizar, *v.t.* to Judaize.

judas, *s.m.* Traitor, false friends; Judas.

judeu, *s.m.,* *adj.* Jew, Hebrew, Israelite; Jewish, greedy, avaricious.

judia, *s.f.* Jewness.

judiar, *v.t.* to mock, to deride; to torment, to mistreat.

judiaria, *s.f.* Jewry ghetto, Jewish quarter in a city; mockery, derision, dirty trick; cruelty, ill-treatment.

judicativo, *adj.* judicial, judicative.

judicatório, *adj.* judicatory.

judicatura, *s.f.* judicature (the judges collectivelt; court of justice; judge's office).

judicial, *adj.* judicial.

judiciar, *v.t.* to judge, to decide judicially.

judiciário, *adj.* judiciary, judicial, forensic.

judiciosamente, *adv.* judiciously, wisely.

judicioso, *adj.* judicious, wise, prudent; sagacious, discerning, sensible, clearsighted.

judo, *s.m.* judo, jujitsu.

jugada, *s.f.* yoke of land.

jugo, *s.m.* yoke, servitude, obedience, authority, domination, oppression; a yoke of oxen. 1) *estar sobre o jugo de,* to be dominated by. 2) *sacudir o jugo,* to shake off the yoke.

jugoslavo, *adj.,* *s.m.* Jugoslav.

jugulação, *s.f.* jugulation.

jugular, *v.t.,* *adj.* to jugulate, to subjugate, to dominate; jugular.

juiz, *s.m.* judge. 1) *juiz de instrução,* examining magistrate. 2) *juiz de linha,* linesman. 3) *juiz de paz,* justice of the peace. 4) *juiz do supremo,* judge of the supreme court. 5) *ser juiz em causa própria,* to be the judge and party.

juíza, *s.f.* female judge.

juízo, *s.m.* judgement, discernment, good sense; criticism; opinion; prediction; understanding; sense. 1) *juízo perfeito,* sound mind. 2) *chamar a juízo,* to summon to court. 3) *juízo final,* doomsday. 4) *perder o juízo,* to go mad, to lose one's mind. 5) *dia de juízo,* doomsday. 6) *tenha juízo,* be sensible.

jujuba, *s.f.* jujube *(bot.).*

julepo, *s.m.* julep, soothing drink.

julgado, *s.m.,* *adj.* jurisdiction of a judge. judgeship; judged, decided, sentenced.

julgador, *s.m.,* *adj.* judge, judger; judging.

julgamento, *s.m.* judgment; sentence, decision; trial; appreciation, opinion, discernment; *submeter-se a julgamento,* to stand trial.

julgar, *v.t.* to judge, to decide, to pass sentence upon, to try; to consider, to criticize, to suppose, to think; to esteem; to imagine, to believe. 1) *julgo que sim,* I think so. 2) *julgo que não,* I don't think so.

Julho, *s.m.* July, seventh month of the year.

juliana, *s.f.* julienne *(sopa).*

juliano, *adj.* Julian *(calendário).*

jumenta, *s.f.* she-ass, she-donkey, jenny-ass.

jumentada, *s.f.* stupidity, foolishness.

jumental, *adj.* asinine, stupid.

jumento, *s.m.* jack-ass, donkey-ass.

junça, *s.f.* galingale, the chufa.

juncáceas, *s.f. pl.* juncaceae.

juncada, *s.f.* a quantity of rushes.

juncal, *s.m.* rush-bed.

juncal, *s.m.* field of galingale.

junção, *s.f.* junction, joining, union, linking, connection.

juncar, *v.t.* to strew, to spread, to cover with *(folhas ou flores).*

junceira, *s.f.* ver *"junça".*

junco, *s.m.* rush, bulrush; junk *(na China).*

juncoso, *adj.* rusky.

jungir, *v.t.* to yoke; to couple; to link, to join.

Junho, *s.m.* June, sixth month of the year.

júnior, *adj.,* *s.m.* junior, younger; junior

junqueira, *s.f.* ver juncal.

junquilho, *s.m.* jonquil.

junta, *s.f.* joint, articulation, knuckle; junction (madeira, paredes); board; council; pair, team. 1) *Junta de Saúde,* Medical Board. 2) *Junta Nacional da Educação,* Board of Education. 3) *Junta do Comércio,* Board of Trade. 4) *junta de bois,* yoke of oxen.

juntamente, *adv.* jointly, together, closely; enclosed.

juntar, *v.t.* to join, to unite, to couple; to associate; to assemble, to connect, to link, to combine; *juntar-se,* to come together, to associate oneself with.

junteira, *s.f.* jointer, plane for joining.

junto, *adj.,* *adv.* united; close; together, jointly, closely.

juntoira, juntoura, *s.f.* bonder, bond-stone, header.

juntura, *s.f.* juncture, junction, articulation.

Júpiter, *s.m.* Jupiter *(planeta ou deus).*

jura, *s.f.* ver *"juramento".*

jurado, *s.m.* juryman, juror, member of a jury; *inimigo jurado,* sworn enemy.

jurador, *s.m., adj.* swearer, curser; swearing, cursing.

juramento, *s.m.* oath; curse; swearing; *prestar juramento,* to take an oath, to swear.

jurar, *v.t., v.i.* to swear, to take an oath; to promise, to testify, to make a solemn vow; to declare, to affirm.

júri, *s.m.* jury.

juridicamente, *adv.* juridically.

jurídico, *adj.* juridical, judicial, legal.

jurisconsulto, *s.m.* jurisconsult, jurist.

jurisdição, *s.f.* jurisdiction; power, authority, control; competence.

jurisdicional, *adj.* jurisdictional.

jurisperito, *s.m.* jurisprudent, jurist, expert in law.

jurisprudência, *s.f.* jurisprudence.

jurista, *s.* jurist, jurisconsult, lawyer.

juro, *s.m.* interest *(dinheiro).* 1) *juro de mora,* interest on deferred payment. 2) *juros compostos,* compound interest. 3) *juros simples,* simple interest. 4) *juros atrasados,* back interest. 5) *pôr dinheiro a juros,* to put money to interest. 6) *juros vencidos,* interest due.

jus, *s.m.* right; 1) *ter jus a,* to have a right to, to be entitled to, to merit,

jusante, *s.m.* ebb tide; *a jusante,* downstream.

justa, *s.f.* joust, just, tournament; fight, dispute; *à justa,* exactly.

justador, *s.m.* jouster, titler, competitor.

justamente, *adv.* exactly, justly, precisely.

justapor, *v.t.* juxtapose, to place side by side.

justaposição, *s.f.* juxtaposition, contiguity, proximity.

justaposto, *adj.* juxtaposed, contiguous.

justar, *v.i.* to agree on, to wire for wages, to ascertain *(o preço);* to joust, to tilt.

justeza, *s.f.* justness, exactness, accuracy, exactitude; correctness, precision.

justiça, *s.f.* justice, uprightness, rectitude, equity, impartiality, integrity; the law; the lawyers; magistrates.

justiçado, *adj.* executed, punished.

justiçar, *v.t.* to execute, to punish.

justificadamente, *adv.* rightly, justifiably.

justiceiro, *adj.* severe, inflexible; righteous, impartial, just.

justificação, *s.f.* justification, excuse.

justificador, *adj., s.m.* justifying; justifier.

justificante, *adj., s.* justifying; warrant, voucher.

justificar, *v.t.* to justify, to prove; to exculpate, to excuse, to vindicate; to explain; *justificar-se,* to clear oneself.

justificativa, *s.f.* justification.

jsutificativo, *adj.* justificative, justifying, explanatory.

justificatório, *adj.* justificatory.

justificável, *adj.* justifiable, defensible.

justilho, *s.m.* corset; stays.

justo, *adj.* just, equitable, upright; precise; fit; proper; merited; sinless; tight, too small, close-fitting.

justura, *s.f.* adjustment.

juta, *s.f.* jute.
juvença, *s.f.* heifer.
juvenco, *s.m.* steer.
juvenil, *adj.* young, juvenile; youthful.

juvenilidade, *s.f.* juvenility.
juvenilmente, *adv.* juvenilely.
juventude, *s.f.* youth, youthfulness, adolescence, young people.

L

l, the eleventh letter of the Portuguese alphabet.
lá, *adv.* there; over there; yonder; thither; *lá dentro, lá em baixo, lá em cima, lá fora, lá longe,* inside, down there, up there, outside there, way off there. 1) *de lá,* from there. 2) *de lá para cá,* back and forth, to and from. 3) *por lá,* that way; around there.
lã, *s.f.* wool.
labaça, *s.f.* dock.
labaçal, *s.f.* dock plantation.
labareda, *s.f.* flame, blaze; enthusiasm, ardour.
lábaro, *s.m.* labarum.
labelo, *s.m.* labellum.
labéu, *s.m.* shame; stigma; dishonour.
lábia, *s.f.* smooth talk, blarney; cunning; *ter lábia:* to have the gift of the gab.
labiado, *adj.* labiate, labiated.
labial, *adj.* labial, lip; *s.f.* labial consonant.
labializar, *v.t.* to labialize, to render labial.
lábio, *s.m.* lip; *lábio leporino,* harelip.
labiríntico, *adj.* labyrinthine.
labirinto, *s.m.* labyrinth, maze; tangle, intricacy.
labor, *s.m.* labour, work, toil.
laboração, *s.f.* working.
laborar, *v.t.* to labour, to work; to function; laborar em erro: to labour under mistake.
laboratório, *s.m.* laboratory, lab.
laboriosidade, *s.f.* laboriousness; diligence; effort.
laborioso, *adj.* laborious, hard-working, industrious; diligent; busy.

labrego, *s.m.* rustic, lout, boor; awkward fellow.
labuta, *s.f.* drudgery, toil.
labutar, *v.t.* to toil, to drudge, to grind, to work hard.
labutador, *s.m.* toiler, drudger.
laca, *s.f.* lac *(resina);* lacquer *(verniz).*
laçada, *s.f.* bow; slipknot *(nó corredio);* loop *(aselha).*
lacado, *adj.* lacquered.
lacaio, *s.m.* lackey, footman.
laçar, *v.t.* to lasso; to bind, to tie; to lace.
laçaria, *s.f. (arq.)* tracery, lacelike work.
laçarote, *s.m.* rosette; gay knot; knot ribbons.
lacedemónio, *s.m.* e *adj.* Lacedaemonian, Laconian.
laceração, *s.f.* laceration; tearing.
lacerante, *adj.* lacerant; lacerating, dilacerating, pungent; piercing.
lacerar, *v.t.* to lacerate, to dilacerate, to rend, to tear.
lacerável, *adj.* lacerable.
lacertiforme, *adj.* lizard-shapped.
laço, *s.m.* knot, bow; noose; lasso; snare, trap *(armadilha);* tie *(de amizade, etc.).* 1) *cair no laço,* to fall into the trap. 2) *dar um laço,* to make a bow.
lacólito, *s.m.* laccolith.
laconicamente, *adv.* laconically.
lacónico, *adj.* laconic; curt; brief, succint.
laconismo, *s.m.* laconism; curtness; brevity.
laconizar, *v.t.* to laconize.
lacrador, *s.m.* sealer.

lacrar, *v.t.* to seal (with wax).

lacrau, *s.m.* scorpion.

lacre, *s.m.* sealing wax.

lacrimação, *s.f.* lachrymation; flow of tears.

lacrimal, *adj.* lachrymal, tear.

lacrimejante, *adj.* tearful, in tears.

lacrimejar, *v.i.* to water, to shed tears.

lacrimogéneo, *adj.* lachrymatory, causing tears; *gás lacrimogénio,* tear gas.

lacrimoso, *adj.* lachrymose, tearful; weeping; watery.

lactação, *s.f.* lactation, suckling.

lactante, *adj.* suckling, feeding on milk.

lactar, *v.t.* to nurse.

lactário, *s.m.* milk dispensary; *adj.* lactiferous.

lactato, *s.m.* lactate.

lácteo, *adj.* lacteous, lacteal, milky.

lactescência, *s.f.* lactescence.

lactescente, *adj.* milky.

lacticínio, *s.m.* dairy product.

láctico, *adj.* lactic.

lacticolor, *adj.* milky.

lactífago, *adj.* feeding on milk.

lactífero, *adj.* lactiferous, secreting milk.

lactiforme, *adj.* milk-like.

lactígeno, *adj.* lactigenic.

lactobutirómetro, *s.m.* lactobutyrometer.

lactose, *s.f.* lactose, milk suger.

lacuna, *s.f.* lacuna, gap, blank; hiatus; omission.

lacunar, *adj.* lacunal.

lacunoso, *adj.* full of gaps; discontinous; desultory.

lacustre, *adj.* lacustrine, lake; *casas lacustres,* lacustrine dwellings.

ladainha, *s.f.* litany; rigmarole.

ládano, *s.m.* ladannum, labdanum.

ladeamento, *s.m.* warping; deviation; shift.

ladear, *v.t.* to flank, to lie or stand alongside of; to escort; to get around, to bypass *(contornar);* to dodge, to side-step *(evadir).*

ladeira, *s.f.* slope, rise; hillside; *ladeira acima,* uphill.

ladeirento, *adj.* sloping; steep.

ladeiro, *adj.* sloped, declivous.

ladino, *adj.* cunning, sly, artful, crafty, astute.

lado, *s.m.* side, flank; face, way, direction. 1) *lado a lado,* side by side. 2) *lado de dentro,* inside. 3) *lado de fora,* outside. 4) *lado direito,* right hand side. 5) *ao lado,* close by, next. 6) *ao lado de,* at the side of, beside, close to, next to. 7) *de lado,* aside, sideways, sidelong. 8) *de lado a lado,* from side to side; across. 9) *de um lado para o outro,* back and forth. 10) *para o lado de,* toward. 11) *ser parente pelo lado materno,* on one`s mother's side. 12) *pôr de lado,* to set aside. 13) *por outro lado,* on the other hand. 14) *por um lado..., pelo outro lado...,*on the one hand..., on the other hand.... 15) *por todo o lado,* everywhere.

ladra, *s.f.* woman thief.

ladrado, *s.m.* barking.

ladrador, *adj.* barking.

ladrão, *s.m.* thief, robber; burglar.

ladrar, *v.i.* to bark; to bay.

ladrido, *s.m.* barking.

ladrilhador, *s.m.* tile setter, tile paver.

ladrilhar, *v.t.* to tile, to pave with tiles.

ladrilho, *s.m.* floor tile, brick.

ladroagem, *s.f.* robbery; the thieves.

ladroar, *v.t.* to steal, to rob; swindle.

ladroeira, *s.f.* robbery; swindle.

ladroíce, *s.f.* robbery; extortion.

lagamar, *s.m.* pond, basin, lagoon.

lagar, *s.m.* press; olive press; win press.

lagarada, *s.f.* pressful.

lagaragem, *s.f.* fruit-pressing.

lagareiro, *s.m.* pressman.

lagarta, *s.f.* caterpillar; track *(de tractor).*

lagartear, *v.i.* to sun oneself.

lagartixa, *s.f.* small lizard.

lagarto, *s.m.* lizard.

lago, *s.m.* lake; pond *(artificial).*

lagoa, *s.f.* lagoon, small lake, pool.

lagosta, *s.f.* spiny lobster.

lagostim, *s.m.* crayfish; Norway lobster.

lágrima, *s.f.* tear.

lagrimal, *adj.* o mesmo que "lacrimal".

laguna, *s.f.* lagoon.

laia, *s.f.* kind, sort. 1) *gente da mesma laia,* birds of feather. 2) *à laia de,* like, in the manner of.

laicado, *s.m.* state of layman.

laical, *adj.* laical, laic, secular.

laicidade, *s.f.* laity, laicity.

laicismo, *s.m.* laicality, secularism.

laicizar, *v.t.* to laicize, to secularize.

laico, *adj.* laic, secular.

laís, *s.m.* yard arm.

laivar, *v.t.* to stain, to spot.

laivo, *s.m.* stain, spot; mark, trace; *laivos,* smattering, superficial knowledge.

laje, *s.f.* flagstone, stone, slab.

lajeado, *adj.* paved, flagged.

lajeador, *s.m.* paver, flagger.

lajeamento, *s.m.* paving with flagstones.

lalação, *s.f.* lallation.

lama, *s.f.* mud, mire, sludge, dirt; lama *(sacerdote)*: llama *(animal)*.

lamaçal, *s.m.* slough, quagmire, mud hole.

lamacento, *adj.* muddy, miry; oozy, sloppy.

lambada, *s.f.* blow; slap in the face.

lambão, *s.m.* glutton, gorger.

lambareiro, *adj.* gluttonous; *s.m.* glutton.

lambarice, *s.f.* greediness.

lambaz, *s.m.* mop; swab.

lambazar, *v.t.* to mop, to swab.

lambedela, *s.f.* licking, fawning.

lambedor, *s.m.* licker; flatterer.

lamber, *v.t.* to lick; *lamber-se,* to be delighted.

lambidela, *s.f.* licking; lap; flattery.

lambiscar, *v.t.* to nibble; to pick at.

lambisco, *s.m.* morsel, snack, bite.

lambisgóia, *s.f.* prig; busybody *(intrometida)*.

lambril, *s.m.* wainscoting.

lambugem, *s.f.* dainties, titbits.

lambuzar, *v.t.* to smear, to besmear; to daub.

lamecha, *adj.* sentimental, soft.

lameirão, *s.m.* large marsh.

lameiro, *s.m.* slough, quagmire, mud hole, marsh.

lamela, *s.f.* lamella.

lamelado, *adj.* lamellate, composed in thin plates.

lamelar, *adj.* lamellar.

lamelibrânquio, *s.m.* bivalve, lamellibranch.

lameliforme, *adj.* lamellar.

lameloso, *adj.* lamellose, lamellate.

lamentação, *s.f.* lamentation, lament, wail; mourning.

lamentar, *v.t.* to lament; to mourn for, to bewail; to weep over; to regret; to feel sorry for; *lamentar-se,* to wail, to sorrow; to cry, to weep.

lamentável, *adj.* lamentable, regrettable, deplorable; pitiful; sad; unfortunate.

lamento, *s.m.* lament, lamentation, moaning, wail, wailing, complaint; whine.

lamentoso, *adj.* mournful, plaintive, wailing; whining; woebegone.

lâmina, *s.f.* thin plate; blade *(de instrumento cortante ou de barbear)*; shear *(de tesoura)*; slide *(para microscópio)*; *(bot.)* lamina.

laminação, *s.f.* lamination; rolling *(de aço, etc.)*.

laminado, *adj.* laminated.

laminar, *v.t.* to laminate; to roll; *adj.* laminar.

lamiré, *s.m.* diapason, tuning fork.

lâmpada, *s.f.* lamp; bulb *(eléctrica)*; lâmpada piloto, pilot lamp.

lampadário, *s.m.* chandelier.

lampadejar, *v.i.* to shine, to flare, to flash up.

lampana, *s.f.* lie; slap.

lamparina, *s.f.* night lamp; taper.

lampeiro, *adj.* bold; forward; lively, jaunty.

lampejante, *adj.* sparkling, flashing, shining.

lampejar, *v.i.* to flash, to shine, to sparkle.

lampejo, *s.m.* glimpse, ray; flash; flare; gleam.

lampião, *s.m.* lantern; street lamp.

lampo, *s.m.* early ripe; premature.

lampreia, *s.f.* lamprey.

lamúria, *s.f.* lamentation, complaint, whining, whimper.

lamuriador, *adj.* lamenter.

lamuriar, *v.i.* to lament, to complain, to whimper, to whine.

lamuriento, *adj.* lamenting, whinig, whipe-ring.

lana-caprina, *s.f.* trifle, triviality, insigni-ficance.

lanar, *adj.* wool, lanigerous.

lança, *s.f.* lance, spear; shaft, pole *(de veículo)*; jib *(de guindaste)*.

lança-chamas, *s.m.* flame thrower.

lançada, *s.f.* spear thrust.

lançadeira, *s.f.* shuttle.

lançador, *s.m.* thrower.

lança-granadas, *s.m.* mortar.

lançamento, *s.m.* throw, throwing, cast, casting; launching *(de navio)*; entry *(em livro comercial)*; publication *(de livro)*.

lançar, *v.t.* to throw, to cast, to fling; to pitch *(basebol)*; to project; to lanuch *(navio, etc.)*; to emit; to publish *(livro)*; to lay *(fundações)*; to impose *(imposto)*; to bid *(num leilão)*; to make an entry *(num livre comercial)*; lançar--se: to throw oneself; to rush; to jump; to plunge; lançar ferro, to cast anchor.

lança-torpedos, *s.m.* torpedo tube.

lance, *s.m.* casting, throwing; move *(no xadrez)*; episode; scene, situation; bid *(num leilão)*.

lanceiro, *s.m.* lancer.

lanceolado, *adj.* lanceolate.

lanceta, *s.f.* lancet.

lancetada, *s.f.* lancer-cut.

lancetar, *v.t.* to lance.

lancha, *s.f.* launch; longboat; motor-boat *(a gasolina)*.

lanchão, *s.m.* barge-lighter.

lanchar, *v.t.* to eat a snack; to have tea.

lanche, *s.m.* snack; afternoon tea.

lancheira, *s.f.* small suit-case for a snack.

lancinante, *adj.* poignant, harrowing, distressing; stabbing (*dor*).

lancinar, *v.t.* to lancinate, to pierce, to stab, to sting; to harrow, to afflict.

lanço, *s.m.* throw, cast; flight (*de escadas*); bid (*em leilão*).

landa, *s.f.* moor, barren sandy land.

landau, *s.m.* landau.

lande, *s.f.* acorn; moor.

landegrave, landegrávio, *s.m.* landegrave.

langor, *s.m.* langour, languidness, lassitude; listlessness.

langoroso, *adj.* languorous, languid; feeble.

languento, *adj.* ailing, sickly.

languescente, *adj.* languising.

languescer, *v.i.* to languish; to weaken, to fade.

languidez, *s.f.* languour, lassitude, languidness; weakness, feebleness.

lânguido, adj. languid, langurous; faint, feeble.

languinhento, *adj.* clammy, viscous; slack.

lanhar, *v.t.* to cut; to slash, to tear up, to wound.

lanho, *s.m.* cut, slash, gash.

lanífero, *adj.* laniferous, fleecy.

lanifício, *s.m.* wollen manufacture; woolen cloth; *lanifícios*, woolen goods.

lanígero, *adj.* woolbearing.

lanolina, *s.f.* lanolin.

lanosidade, *s.f.* woolliness.

lanoso, *adj.* wooly; fleecy.

lantejoula, *s.f.* spangle, sequin.

lanterna, *s.f.* lantern, flashlight (*eléctrica*).

lanternim, *s.m.* lantern, clerestory.

lanudo, *adj.* wooly, wolen; fleecy.

lanugem, *s.f.* down, fluff.

lanuginoso, *adj.* downy, wooly, lanuginous.

lapa, *s.f.* den, grotto, small cave; limpet (*molusco*).

lapada, *s.f.* slap on the face.

lapão, *s.m.* Laplander.

láparo, *s.m.* young rabbit.

laparotomia, *s.f.* laparotomy.

lapela, *s.f.* lapel, flap.

lapidação, *s.f.* cutting, stonecutting.

lapidado, *adj.* cut, polished, lapidated.

lapidar, *v.t.* to cut (precious stones), to polish; *adj.* lapidary.

lapidário, *s.m.* lapidary, stonecutter.

lápide, *adj.* stony, lapideous.

lapidificação, *s.f.* lapidification, petrification.

lápis, *s.m.* pencil; *lápis-lazúli*, *s.m.* lapis-lazuli, lazulite, azure-stone.

lapiseira, *s.f.* pencil case; pencil box (*caixa*).

lapónio, *adj.* boor, bumpkin.

lapso, *s.m.* lapse, slip (*de linguagem, memória*), lapse, space (*de tempo*).

lapuz, *adj.* boor, rustic.

laqueação, *s.f.* lacquering; ligature (*de vaso sanguíneo*).

laquear, *v.t.* to lacquer; to ligature, to tie off.

lar, *s.m.* home; heart; fireplace.

laracha, *s.f.* joke, jest.

larada, *s.f.* embers; spot, stain.

laranjada, *s.f.* orangeade.

laranjal, *s.m.* orange-grove.

laranjeira, *s.f.* orange-tree.

larápio, *s.m.* thief, filcher, pilferer.

larário, *s.m.* lararium; home.

lardear, *v.t.* to lard; to interlard (*entremear*); to interperse (with).

lardo, *s.m.* lard, bacon.

laré, *s.m.* bad dancer; *andar no laré,* to gad about, to idle.

lareira, *s.f.* fireplace, hearth; fireside.

laréu, *loc. adv.* ao laréu, exposed, bare.

larga, *s.f.* à larga: freely, lavishly; in grand style; *dar largas a,* to give free rein to.

largada, *s.f.* start (*em corrida*); (*náut.*) sailing, sea-going.

largamente, *adv.* largely, widely; to a great extent.

largar, *v.t.* to let go, to let loose, to set free, to release; to put down; to give up, to leave, to abandon; to drop (*deixar cair*); *v.i.* to start; to depart; to put to sea.

largo, *s.m.* square (*praça*); *ao largo,* offshore, in the offing; *fazer-se ao largo,* to put off; *passar ao largo,* to overlook, not to care much; *adj.* broad, wide, ample, spacious; *adv.* largely.

largueza, *s.f.* width, breadth (of mind, views); liberality.

largura, *s.f.* width, breadth; *tem 2 metros de largura,* it is 2 meters wide.

larica, *s.f.* darnel; (*pop.*) hunger.

laringe, *s.f.* larynx.

laríngeo, *adj.* laryngeal.

laringite, *s.f.* laryngitis.

laringologia, *s.f.* laryngology.

laringologista, *s.m.* laryngologist.

laringotomia, *s.f.* laryngotomy.

larva, *s.f.* larva; grub; wriggler (*de mosquito*).

larval, *adj.* larval.

larviforme, *adj.* larviform.

lasca, s.f. splinter, chip, fragment. bit.

lascar, v.t. to splinter; to split; to take a chip off (something).

lascivamente, adv. lasciviously.

lascívia, s.f. lasciviousness, wantonness, lewdness, lust.

lascivo, adj. lascivious, wanton, lewd, lustful.

lassidão, lassitude, s.f. lassitude, prostration, weariness, languour.

lasso, adj. loose, slack; tired, weary, worn out.

lástima, s.f. compassion, pity; grief, sorrow.

lastimar, v.t. to deplore, to lament; to regret, to be sorry for; to feel sorry for, to pity; lastimar-se, to moan, to wail; to complain (of something).

lastimável, adj. deplorable, lamentable, regrettable.

lastimosamente, adv. pitifully; regrettably.

lastimoso, adj. pitiful, deplorable, pitiable.

lastra, s.f. flagstone.

lastração, lastragem, s.f. ballasting.

lastrar, v.t. to ballast.

lastro, s.m. ballast.

lata, s.f. tin, can, tin can; tin plate (material).

latada, s.f. trellis.

latagão, s.m. strong man, stout man.

latão, s.m. brass.

lategada, s.f. stroke, slash.

látego, s.m. scourge, whip.

latejante, adj. throbbing, beating.

latejar, v.i. to throb; to pulsate; to beat.

latejo, s.m. throbbing; beating; pulsation.

latência, s.f. latency.

latente, adj. latent, hidden, concealed.

later, v.i. to lie hidden.

lateral, adj. lateral; side; sideways; porta lateral, side door.

lateralidade, s.f. state of being sideways.

lateralmente, adv. laterally; sideward.

látex, s.m. latex.

latíbulo, s.m. hiding place.

latido, s.m. barking, baying.

latifundiário, s.m. large landowner.

latifúndio, s.m. latifundium, large landed estate.

latim, s.m. Latin.

latinada, s.f. mistake in Latin; a speech in Latin.

latinismo, s.m. latinism.

latinista, s.m. latinist.

latinização, s.f. latinization.

latinizar, v.t. to latinize.

latino, adj. Latin.

latino-americano, s.m. e adj. Latin-American.

latinório, s.m. bad Latin; flowery speech.

latir, v.t. to bark, to bay, to yelp.

latitude, s.f. latitude; breadth, scope, amplitude, extent.

latitudinário, adj. latitudinarian, liberal.

lato, adj. wide, broad, ample, extensive: em sentido lato, in a broad sense.

latoaria, s.f. tin-smith; tinker.

latria, s.f. latria.

latrina, s.f. latrine, water-closet.

latrinário, adj. sordid, repulsive.

latrocinar, v.t. to rob.

latrocínio, s.m. robbery, theft.

lauda, s.f. page; sheet of paper.

laudabilidade, s.f. laudability.

laudanizar, v.t. to prepare with laudanum.

láudano, s.m. laudanum.

laudativo, adj. laudative, laudatory.

laudatório, adj. laudatory, commendatory.

laudémio, s.m. dues, tax.

laudes, s.f. pl. lauds.

laudo, s.m. report; findings; laudo arbitral, arbiter's award.

laureado, adj. laureate.

laurear, v.t. to reward; to praise, to crown with laurel; (pop.) to gad about, to idle.

laurel, s.m. laurel, prize, reward, premium; homage.

láureo, adj. of laurel.

lauréola, s.f. small crown of laurel; aureole.

lauto, adj. sumptuous; plentiful, lavish.

lava, s.f. lava.

lavabo, s.m. wash-basin.

lavadeira, s.f. laundress, washerwoman.

lavadoiro, lavadouro, s.m. washing-place.

lavadura, s.f. dish-wash, kitchen refuse.

lavagante, s.m. kind of lobster.

lavagem, s.f. washing; hogwash, dishwater (água de lavagem).

lava-louças, s.m. sink.

lavandaria, s.f. laundry.

lavandisca, s.f. pied wagtail.

lava-pés, s.m. foot-washing (on Maundy Thursday).

lavar, v.t. to wash; to cleanse; lavar-se, to wash; to bathe.

lavatório, s.m. wash-basin; wash-stand.

lavável, adj. washable.

laverca, s.f. skylark, laverock.

lavor, s.m. embroidery, needlework.

lavoso, adj. lavatic, lavalike.

lavoura, *s.f.* tillage; farming, agriculture, field work.

lavra, *s.f.* tillage, farming; working, production; making, authorship.

lavradio, *adj.* arable, fit for ploughing.

lavrado, *adj.* ploughed, tilled; *s.m.* embroidery.

lavrador, *s.m.* farmer, tiller; ploughman, agricultural worker.

lavrante, *s.m.* chaser, enchaser; goldsmith.

lavrar, *v.t.* to plough, to till, to cultivate; to chisel, to carve, to engrave; to draw up *(acta).*

laxação, *s.f.* laxity, laxation, lassitude.

laxante, *adj.* e *s.m.* laxative, purgative.

laxar, *v.t.* to loose, to slacken; to purge.

laxativo, *adj.* laxative, purgative.

laxidão, *s.f.* lassitude.

lazão, *s.m.* sorrel.

lazarento, *adj.* score-covered, leprous; *s.m.* leper, lazar.

lazareto, *s.m.* lazaret, lazaretto, quarantine.

lázaro, *s.m.* lazar, leper.

lazeira, *s.f.* misery, misfortune; leprosy; junger.

lazer, *s.m.* leisure, spare time.

lázudo, *adj.* boor, brute.

lazulite, *s.f.* lazulite.

leal, *adj.* loyal, faithful; true; trustworthy.

lealdade, *s.f.* loyalty, faithfulness; fidelity; sincerity.

lealmente, *adv.* loyally, faithfully.

leão, *s.m.* lion.

leão-marinho, *s.m.* sea-lion.

lebracho, *s.m.* leveret, bunny.

lebrão, *s.m.* male-hare.

lebre, *s.f.* hare.

lebreiro, *adj.* hare-hunting dog.

lebréu, *s.m.* harrier *(cão).*

leccionar, *v.t.* to teach; to instruct; to lecture (pupils on a subject).

leccionista, *s.m.* teacher, lecturer.

lectivo, *adj. ano lectivo,* school year.

ledice, *s.f.* joy, joyfulness, merriment.

ledo, *s.f.* joy, gay, jovial, happy.

legação, *s.f.* legation.

legacia, *s.f.* legateship.

legado, *s.m.* legate *(do Papa);* legacy *(herança);* envoy *(diplomático).*

legal, *adj.* legal, lawful; legitimate.

legalidade, *s.f.* legality, lawfulness.

legalismo, *s.m.* legalism.

legalista, *s.m.* legalist.

legalização, *s.f.* legalization.

legalizar, *v.t.* to legalize, to render legal.

legalmente, *adv.* lawfully, legally.

legar, *v.t.* to legate, to bequeath, to leave *(em testamento).*

legatário, *s.m.* legatee.

legatório, *adj.* legatorial.

legenda, *s.f.* inscription, legend *(lenda);* subtitle *(em cinema e televisão).*

legendário, *adj.* legendary, fabulous, mythical; *s.m.* legendary.

legião, *s.f.* legion.

legionário, *s.m.* legionary.

legislação, *s.f.* legislation.

legislador, *s.m.* legislator, lawmaker; *adj.* legislating.

legislar, *v.t.* to legislate, to make laws.

legislativo, *adj.* legislative.

legislatório, *adj.* legislatory.

legislatura, *s.f.* legislature.

legislável, *adj.* that can be enacted into law.

legista, *s.f.* e *s.m.* legist, jurisconsult, lawyer.

legitimação, *s.f.* legitimation.

legitimar, *v.t.* to legitimate, to legitimatize.

legitimidade, *s.f.* legitimacy, lawfulness; authenticity.

legitimismo, *s.m.* legitimism.

legitimista, *s.m.* legitimist.

legítimo, *adj.* legitimate; legal; fair; real, true, authentic. 1) *em legítima defesa,* in self-defense. 2) *filho legítimo,* legitimate.

legível, *adj.* legible, readable.

legra, *s.f.* xyster, chisel.

legrar, *v.t.* to scrape a bone.

légua, *s.f.* league (5 kilometers in Portugal).

legume, *s.m.* vegetable, legume.

legumina, *s.f.* legumin.

leguminívoro, *adj.* vegetarian.

leguminosas, *s.f. pl.* Leguminosae.

leguminoso, *adj.* leguminous.

lei, *s.f.* law; rule; act (of Parliament). 1) *projecto de lei,* bill. 2) *prata de lei,* sterling silver; *previsto na lei,* statutory.

leicenço, *s.m.* furuncle, boil.

leigo, *s.m.* layman; *os leigos,* the laity; *adj.* lay, secular; non-professional; ignorant, unacquainted (with).

leilão, *s.m.* auction, public sale; *vender em leilão,* to outcry.

leiloar, *v.t.* to auction, to sell by auction, to outcry.

leiloeiro, *s.m.* auctioneer.

leira, *s.f.* bed *(canteiro de jardim);* narrow piece of cultivated land.

leitão, *s.m.* sucking pig.

leitaria, *s.f.* milk-bar, dairy.

leite, *s.m.* milk; *leite em pó,* dried milk. 1) *leite condensado,* condensed milk. 2) *leite coalhado,* sour milk. 3) *leite desnatado,* skim milk. 4) *leite-creme,* custard. 5) *leite--de-cal,* whitewash; linewater.

leiteira, *s.f.* milkmaid; milk pot *(recipiente).*

leiteiro, *s.m.* milkman.

leito, *s.m.* bed.

leitoado, *adj.* fat.

leitor, *s.m.* reader; lecturer.

leitorado, *s.m.* lectureship, post of lecturer *(numa universidade).*

leitoso, *adj.* milky, lacteous.

leituga, *s.f.* hawk's beard.

leitura, *s.f.* reading, perusal; reading matter; *livro de leitura,* reader.

leiva, *s.f.* clod *(gleba);* furrow *(sulco);* ploughed land.

lema, *s.m.* motto; slogan.

lembrado, *adj.* remembered; mindful (of something); *se estou bem lembrado,* if I remember well.

lembrança, *s.f.* remembrance, memory, recollection, souvenir; suggestion, idea; *lembranças a todos:* remember me to the folks!

lembrar, *v.t.* to remind, to recall, to recollect; to suggest; to call to mind; *lembrar-se,* to remember, to recollect; to think of.

lembrete, *s.m.* note, memorandum; reprimand.

leme, *s.m.* rudder; helm; direction, steerage. 1) *ir ao leme,* to steer, to guide, to be at the helm. 2) *leme de profundidade,* elevator.

lémure, *s.m.* lemure.

lenço, *s.m.* handkerchief; neckerchief *(de pescoço).*

lençol, *s.m.* sheet.

lenda, *s.f.* legend; myth, popular tale.

lendário, *adj.* legendary; mythical; fabulous.

líndea, *s.f.* nit.

lendroeira, *s.f.* oleander.

lengalenga, *s.f.* rig,arole; litany.

lenha, *s.f.* wood, firewood.

lenhador, *s.m.* woodcutter.

lenheiro, *s.m.* dealer in firewood.

lenhificação, *s.f.* lignification.

lenhificar, *v.t.* to harden, to lignify.

lenho, *s.m.* trunk; block, log; *Santo Lenho,* the Holy Cross.

lenhoso, *adj.* ligneous; woody.

lenimento, *s.m.* liniment.

lenir, *v.t.* to mitigate, to alleviate, to lenify.

lenitivo, *s.m.* lenitive; relief; balm, salve; *adj.* palliative; mitigating.

lenocínio, *s.m.* pandering, white slavery.

lentamente, *adv.* slowly.

lente, *s.m.* professor, college professor; *s.f.* lens; glass.

lenteiro, *s.m.* marsh.

lentejar, *v.t.* e *v.i.* to moisten, to damp, to wet.

lenticular, *adj.* lenticular.

lentidão, *s.f.* slowness, lentitude; sluggishess.

lentigem, *s.f.* lentigo.

lentiginoso, *adj.* lentiginous, freckled.

lentilha, *s.f.* lentil.

lentisco, *s.m.* lentisk.

lento, *adj.* slow; sluggish; tardy.

lentura, *s.f.* moisture, humidity; slowness.

leoa, *s.f.* lioness.

leônculo, lion club.

leonês, *s.m.* Leonese.

leónico, *adj.* lionesque.

leonino, *adj.* leonine, lion-like.

leopardo, *s.m.* leopard.

lépido, *adj.* quick, swift; cheerful, gay; lively, jovial.

lepidóptero, *s.m.* lepidopteran; *pl.* Lepidoptera.

leporino, *adj.* leporine.

lepra, *s.f.* leprosy.

leprosaria, *s.f.* leper-hospital.

leproso, *adj.* leprous; *s.m.* leper, lazar.

leque, *s.m.* fan.

ler, *v.t.* to read; to peruse; to perceive, to discern; to decipher; to skim over or through *(superficialmente).*

lerdice, *s.f.* slowness, sluggishness.

lerdo, *adj.* slow, sluggish, tardy; dull, stupid.

léria, *s.f.* verbiage; idle talk, verbosity; rigmarole.

lés, *s.m. de lés a lés,* thoroughly, from end to end.

lesa-majestade, *s.f.* lese-majesty.

lesão, *s.f.* lesion, injury, damage; wound.

lesar, *v.t.* to injure, to hurt; to damage; to cheat (someone out of a sum).

lesivo, *adj.* offensive, injurious, damaging, prejudicial.

lesma, *s.f.* slug; lazy fellow.

lesmento, *adj.* slow, indolent.

leso, *adj.* hurt; damage, injured, wounded.

lestada, *s.f.* east wind.

leste, east.

lesto, *adj.* smart, clever; quick, agile; expeditious.

letal, *adj.* lethal, deadly, mortal.

letalidade, *s.f.* lethelity, deadliness.

letargia, *s.f.* lethargy; apathy; torpidity; inactivity.

letárgico, *adj.* lethargical, drowsy; torpid.

letargo, *s.m.* lethargus; lethargy, apathy, torpor, indolence.

letífero, *adj.* lethiferal, lethiferous, deadly.

letificante, *adj.* rejoicing, deadly.

letificar, *v.t.* to rejoice, to gladden, to cheer up.

letra, *s.f.* letter; handwriting; hand; literal sense; *(com.)* promisory note; lyrics *(de uma canção).* 1) *letras,* letters, literature. 2) *letra de câmbio,* bill of exchange. 3) *letra de forma,* print. 4) *ao pé da letra,* literally, to the letter.

letrado, *adj.* learned, literate, erudite; *s.m.* learned man; man of letters.

letreiro, *s.m.* inscription, lettering; label.

letria, *s.f.* vermicelli.

léu, *s.m. ao léu,* exposed, bare.

leucemia, *s.f.* leukemia.

leucito, *s.m.* leucite; *(bot.)* leucoplast.

leucócito, *s.m.* leucocyte.

leucocitose, *s.f.* leucocytosis.

leucoma, *s.m.* leucoma, albugo.

leucorreia, *s.f.* leucorrhoea.

leucose, *s.f.* leucosis.

leva, *s.f.* weighing of an anchor; mustering; levy; band, crowd.

levada, *s.f.* stream; waterfall, mill stream.

levadiça, *s.f. ponte levadiça,* drawbrige.

levado, *adj.* mischievous; unruly.

levandisca, *s.f.* pied wagtail.

levantado, *adj.* upright, lifted, raised; high, elevated, lofty; up *(acordado);* hare-brained.

levantamento, *s.m.* lifting, raising; uprising, insurrection; elevation; survey *(topográfico).*

levantar, *v.t.* to raise, to lift up; to upraise; to draw up, to rear; to hoist; to heave; to elevate, to uplift, to exalt; to erect, to build; to heighten; to suspend *(sessão),* to levy *(angariar);* to moot *(uma questão);* to jack up *(com macaco);* to break (camp) *(o acampamento); levantar-se,* to get up, to rise, to stand up; to rise up; to rebel.

levante, *s.m.* Levant; mutiny *(revolta).*

levantino, *adj.* Levantine.

levar, *v.t.* to carry, to take (away); to convey; to bear; to bring; to get; to lead, to conduce (to); to induce, to impel, to drive (someone to do something); to gain, to win; to take, to require *(tempo);* to suffer, to undergo

(golpes); to lead *(uma boa vida, etc.); v.i.* to lead (to a place). 1) *levar a bem,* to take in good part. 2) *levar avante,* to carry forward; to go ahead with. 3) *levar a mal,* to take ill or amiss. 4) *levar a melhor,* to get the upper hand; to win. 5) *levei vários dias para o conseguir,* it took me several days to get it.

leve, *adj.* light; slight; mild; tenuous; faint; *ao de leve,* lightly; slightly, gently.

levedação, *s.f.* leavening.

levedar, *v.t.* to leaven, to raise; *v.i.* to rise.

lêvedo, *adj.* leavened.

levedura, *s.f.* leaven, yeast.

levemente, *adv.* lightly, slightly, gently.

leves, *s.m. pl.* lights *(de um animal).*

leveza, *s.f.* lightness, levity; airiness.

leviandade, *s.f.* levity, frivolity, folly; giddiness; inconsiderate action; trifling; escapade.

leviano, *adj.* inconsiderate, thoughtless; frivolous, flippant; giddy, rattlebrained.

levita, *s.m.* Levite; parson.

levitação, *s.f.* levitation.

levitar-se, *v.refl.* to levitate, to raise.

levítico, *adj.* levitical.

levulose, *s.f.* laevoulose, fructose, fruit sugar.

lexical, *adj.* lexical.

léxico, *s.m.* lexicon.

lexicografia, *s.f.* lexicography.

lexicógrafo, *s.m.* lexicographer, compiler of a dictionary.

lexicologia, *s.f.* lexicology.

lexicólogo, *s.m.* lexicologist.

lezíria, *s.f.* marshy land, marsh, river meadowland.

lhama, *s.f.* llama.

lhaneza, *s.f.* affability; sincerity, candor, frankness; plainness.

lhano, *adj.* sincere, frank; plain; affable.

lhanura, *s.f.* o mesmo que "lhaneza".

lhe, *pron pes.* him; her, it; to him, to her, to it; you or to you.

lia, *s.f.* dregs, lees.

liame, *s.m.* bond, tie; connection.

liar, *v.t.* to bind, to tie; to link.

libação, *s.f.* libation; potation, drinking.

libanês, *s.m. e adj.* Lebanese.

libar, *v.i.* to ship, to drink.

libelinha, *s.f.* dragon-fly.

libelista, *s.f.* libelant.

libelo, *s.m.* booklet; lampoon, pasquinade; *(jur.)* accusation, bill of indictment.

libélula, *s.f.* dragon-fly.

liber, *s.m.* liber, phloem, innermost bark.

liberação, *s.f.* quittance, discharge.

liberado, *adj.* free on parole, liberated.

liberal, *adj.* liberal; generous, openhanded; broadminded.

liberalidade, *s.f.* liberaty; generosity, bountifulness.

liberalismo, *s.m.* liberalism.

liberalista, *s.f.* e *adj.* e *s.m.* liberalist, liberal.

liberar, *v.t.* to liberate; to release, to discharge; to set free.

liberativo, *adj.* liberating; acquitting.

liberatório, *adj.* suitable as legal tender.

liberdade, *s.f.* freedom, liberty; frankness; imunity; boldness; *liberdade condicional,* parole.

liberiano, *adj.* e *s.m.* Liberian.

libertação, *s.f.* liberation; delivrance, release; discharge.

libertador, *s.m.* liberator, deliverer; *adj.* liberating, releasing.

libertar, *v.t.* to liberate, to set free, to release; to rescue, to save; to discharge; *libertar-se,* to break loose, to free oneself.

libertário, *s.m.* anarchist.

libertinagem, *s.f.* libertinism, licentiousness, debauchery, profligacy.

libertino, *adj.* dissolute, licentious, profligate; rakish; wanton; *s.m.* libertine, rake.

liberto, *adj.* emmancipated; free, at liberty; *s.m.* freedman.

libidinagem, *s.f.* lust, lewdness, lechery.

libidinoso, *adj.* libidinous, lustful, lewd, lecherous.

líbido, *s.m.* the libido.

líbito, *s.m.* will, choice.

libra, *s.f.* pound; *libra esterlina,* pound sterling.

libração, *s.f.* oscillation.

librar, *v.t.* to librate, to balance.

libré, *s.f.* livery.

libretista, *s.m.* librettist.

libreto, *s.m.* libretto.

liça, *s.f.* lists, scene of contest; fight, combat; *entrar na liça,* to enter the lists (for or against).

licanço, *s.m.* worm lizard.

lição, *s.f.* lesson; lecture; reprimand.

liceal, *adj.* relating to a lyceum or lycée.

licença, *s.f.* leave, permission; license, permit; authorization; *(mil.)* leave. 1) *com licença,* excuse me, allow me. 2) *dar licença,* to permit, to allow. 3) *de licença,* on leave.

licenciado, *s.m.* licenciate, graduate; *adj.* licensed; discharged.

licenciamento, *s.m.* licensing; discharge; disbandment (of troops).

licenciar, *v.t.* to license; to grant leave of absence to; to dismiss temporarily; to discharge; *licenciar-se,* to take a degree (of licenciate).

licenciatura, *s.f.* licenciate's degree.

licenciosidade, *s.f.* licentiousness, dissoluteness.

licencioso, *adj.* licentious, dissolute.

liceu, *s.m.* state secondary school; grammar-school; lycée; high-school.

licitação, *s.f.* bidding.

licitador, *s.m.* bidder.

licitante, *s.m.* bidder; seller at auction.

licitar, *v.t.* to bid, to offer, to make an offer (at an auction).

lícito, *adj.* licit, lawful, legal.

licor, *s.m.* liqueur; liquor *(líquido).*

licoreira, *s.f.* liqueur set.

licoroso, *adj.* luscious, sweet fortified *(vinho).*

lictor, *s.m.* lictor.

lida, *s.f.* toil, labour, work, chore; housework.

lidador, *s.m.* fighter; champion.

lidar, *v.i.* to labour, to toil; to fight *(touros);* to deal with.

lide, *s.f.* toil, fatigue; bull-fighting.

líder, *s.m.* leader, chief, guide.

liderança, *s.f.* leadership.

liderar, *v.t.* to lead, to guide.

lidimar, *v.t.* to legitimate.

lídimo, *adj.* legitimate, legal; genuine, real.

lido, *adj.* read; learned, erudite.

liga, *s.f.* ligation, alliance, league, union; garter *(de meia);* alloy *(metálica).*

ligação, *s.f.* binding, joining, junction; bond; connection *(também eléct.);* relation; attachment; liaison *(amorosa).*

ligado, *adj.* tied, joint; connected; *(eléct.)* on.

ligadura, *s.f.* ligature; bandage.

ligame, ligâmen, *s.m.* connection; obstacle to marriage.

ligamento, *s.m. (anat.)* ligament; binding, joining, tie, bond.

ligamentoso, *adj.* ligamentous, fibrous.

ligar, *v.t.* to tie, to bind, to fasten; to join, to link, to connect, to unite; to attach; to associate (with); to alloy *(metais);* to turn on *(gás, elect., etc.);* to switch on, to plug in, to connect *(elect.).* 1) *ligar importância,* to pay attention, to mind. 2) *ligar para* *(telefonar),* to call. 3) *ligar-se,* to become associated (with).

ligeiramente, *adv.* lightly, slightly; superficially.

ligeireza, *s.f.* lightness; levity; promptness, agility; unsteadiness.

ligeiro, *adj.* light, slight; swift, quick; agile; superficial.

lígneo, *adj.* woody, ligneous.

lignificação, *s.f.* lignification.

lignificar-se, *v.refl.* to lignify.

ligniforme, *adj.* ligniform.

lignite, *s.f.* lignite, brown coal.

lignívoro, *adj.* lignivorous.

lígula, *s.f.* lugela; ligule.

ligulado, *adj.* ligulate.

liguliforme, *adj.* liguliform.

ligúrico, *adj.* Ligurian.

lilás, *s.m.* lilac; lilac, mauve *(cor).*

liliáceas, *s.f. pl.* Liliaceae.

liliáceo, *adj.* liliaceous, lilylike.

liliforme, *adj.* lilyshaped.

liliputiano, *adj.* Liliputian.

lima, *s.f.* file; sweet lime *(fruto).*

limadura, *s.f.* filing.

limalha, *s.f.* filings.

limão, *s.m.* lemon.

limar, *v.t.* to file; to trim.

limatão, *s.m.* round file.

limbo, *s.m.* limb; blade *(de uma folha);* edge, border.

limeira, *s.f.* lime.

limiar, *s.m.* threshold, doorstep; entrance; beginning.

liminar, *adj.* preliminary, introductory.

limitação, *s.f.* limitation; restriction.

limitado, *adj.* limited; narrow, small.

limitar, *v.t.* to limit; to restrict, to confine; to reduce; to retrench; *limitar-se,* to confine oneself (to), to limit oneself.

limitativo, *adj.* limitative, limiting; restrictive.

limite, *s.m.* limit, boundary; border; limitation.

limnologia, *s.f.* limnology.

limnólogo, *s.m.* limnologist.

limo, *s.m.* slime, mud; ooze; silt; conferva *(alga).*

limoal, *s.m.* lemon-orchard.

limoeira, *s.m.* lemon tree.

limonada, *s.f.* lemonade.

limonite, *s.f.* limonite, brown hematite.

limosidade, *s.f.* sliminess, ooziness, muddiness.

limoso, *adj.* slimy, muddy; oozy; silty.

limpa-chaminés, *s.m.* chimney-sweep.

limpador, *s.m.* cleaner; wiper.

limpadura, *s.f.* cleansing; cleaning; *limpaduras,* table scraps.

limpa-neves, *s.m.* snowplough.

limpar, *v.t.* to clean, to scour; to wipe; to mop up; to cleanse, to clear (of something); to purify.

limpeza, *s.f.* cleaning; neatness; washing; scouring.

limpidez, *s.f.* limpidity, clearness; pureness; serenity.

límpido, *adj.* limpid, clear, transparent, crystaline; cloudless *(o céu).*

limpo, *adj.* clean; neat; tidy; clear; aboveboard *(honesto).* 1) *passar a limpo,* to make a clean copy of. 2) *tirar a limpo,* to clear up, to find out.

limusina, *s.f.* limousine.

linácea, *s.f.* plant of the family Linaceae.

lináceo, *adj.* flax-like, linen-like.

linária, *s.f.* toadflax.

lince, *s.m.* lynx.

linchamento, *s.m.* lynching.

linchar, *v.t.* to lynch.

lindar, *v.t.* to demarcate, to limit, to border (upon something).

linde, *s.f.* limit, landmark, boundary.

lindeira, *s.f.* lintel; doorpost.

lindeiro, *adj.* limitrophe, bordering.

lindeza, *s.f.* beauty; perfection; handsomeness; prettiness, grace.

lindo, *adj.* beautiful, pretty; handsome, elegant, charming, lovely.

lineamento, *s.m.* outlining; *lineamentos,* lineaments, features, contours; outlines.

linear, *adj.* linear.

líneo, *adj.* linen, flaxy, flaxen.

linfa, *s.f.* lymph.

linfático, *adj.* lymphatic.

linfatismo, *s.m.* lymphatism.

linfócito, *s.m.* limphocyte.

linga, *s.f.* sling.

lingar, *v.t.* to sling.

lingote, *s.m.* ingot.

língua, *s.f.* tongue; language, idiom; speech. 1) *língua de areia,* sand spit. 2) *língua de terra,* strip of land. 3) *língua de trapos,* stammerer. 4) *língua materna,* mother tongue. 5) *puxar pela língua a,* to pump.

linguado, *s.m.* sole; strip of paper.

linguafone, *s.m.* recorder (to study languages).

linguagem, *s.f.* language; speech.

linguajar, *v.i.* to talk, to speak; *s.m.* dialect, mode of speech.

lingual, *adj.* lingual.

linguareiro, *adj.* babbling, chatty; *s.m.* chatterbox; back-biter.

linguarudo, *adj.* talkative, gossiping, evil-speaking; *s.m.* prattler, gossip.

lingueta, *s.f.* bolt *(de fechadura);* tong *(de sapato).*

linguiça, *s.f.* suasage.

linguiforme, *adj.* linguiform, tongueshaped.

linguista, *s.m.* e *s.f.* linguist.

linguística, *s.f.* e *s.m.* linguistics, philology.

linguístico, *adj.* linguistic.

linguodental, *adj.* linguadental.

linguopalatal, *adj.* linguapalatal.

linha, *s.f.* line; thread; streak, stripe; row, file, rank; string; limit, boundary; lineage; direction, course; self control, decorum; line, track *(férrea); linhas:* (mil.) lines, fortifications. 1) *linha aérea,* airline, air route. 2) *linha de água,* (náut.) water line. 3) *linha de montagem,* assembly line. 4) *linha de pescar,* fishing line. 5) *'linha de tiro,* target range. 6) *linha recta:* straight line. 7) *perder a linha,* to loose one's decorum.

linhaça, *s.f.* linseed.

linhagem, *s.f.* lineage, ancestry, descent; pedigree; genealogy; *de alta linhagem,* high horn.

linhagista, *s.f.* e *s.m.* genealogist.

linhal, linhar, *s.m.* flax-field.

linho, *s.m.* flax *(planta);* linen *(tecido).*

linhol, *s.m.* cobbler's thread.

linhoso, *adj.* flaxen, flaxy, linen-like.

linimento, *s.m.* liniment, ointment.

linóleo, *s.m.* linoleum.

linotipia, *s.f.* linotype.

linotipista, *s.f.* e *s.m.* linotypist.

linótipo, *s.m.* linotype machine.

lintel, *s.m.* lintel.

lioz, *s.f.* lias, blue limestone.

lípase, *s.f.* lipase.

lipemania, *s.f.* melancholy; sadness.

lipóide, *adj.* fatlike, fatty, lipoid.

lipoma, *s.m.* lipoma.

lipomatoso, *adj.* lipomatous.

lipossolúvel, *adj.* fat-soluble.

lipotimia, *s.f.* fainting-fit; syncope.

liquefacção, *s.f.* liquefaction.

liquefacto, *adj.* o mesmo que "liquefeito".

liquefazer, *v.t.* to liquefy.

liquefeito, *adj.* liquefied; molten, melted.

líquen, *s.m.* lichen.

liquescer, *v.i.* to liquefy, to liquesce.

liquidação, *s.f.* liquidation; settling, settlement *(de contas);* clearance sale *(de mercadorias).*

liquidado, *adj.* liquidated; finished; done for.

liquidar, *v.t.* to liquidate, to settle; to sell off *(mercadorias);* to pay off *(dívida);* to wind up *(negócio).*

liquidatário, *s.m.* liquidator.

liquidável, *adj.* liquidable.

liquidez, *s.f.* liquidity, liquidness.

liquidificação, *s.f.* liquefaction.

liquidificador, *s.m.* liquidizer, liquefier *(aparelho).*

liquidificante, *adj.* liquefactive, liquefacient.

liquidificar, *v.t.* to liquefy.

líquido, *s.m.* liquid, fluid; liquor; *adj.* liquid, fluid *(com.)* net.

lira, *s.f.* lyre; lira *(moeda).*

lírica, *s.f.* lyric poem.

lírico, *s.m.* lyric, lyrical; *s.m.* lyric poet.

lírio, *s.m.* lily.

lirismo, *s.m.* lirycism.

lis, *s.m.* lily, Iris flower.

lisboeta, *s.m.* e *adj.* Lisbonian.

liso, *adj.* smooth; flat, even; bare; straight, lank *(cabelo);* blind *(parede).*

lisonja, *s.f.* flattery; adulation; blandishment.

lisonjeador, *adj.* flattering, fawning; *s.m.* flatterer, cajoler, fawner.

lisonjear, *v.t.* to flatter, to cajole, to fawn; to adulate, to blandish.

lisonjeiro, *adj.* flattering; complimentary; pleasing.

lista, *s.f.* list, roll, roster, register, catalogue; band, bar, stripe, streak; bill of fare *(menu); lista telefónica,* telephone book, telephone directory.

listel, *s.m.* listel, fillet, rim.

listra, *s.f.* stripe.

listrar, *v.t.* to stripe, to trim.

lisura, *s.f.* smoothness; flatness; frankness, sincerity; honesty.

litania, *s.f.* litany.

liteira, *s.f.* litter, sedan.

liteireiro, *s.m.* litter carrier.

literal, *adj.* literal; exact, precise.

literalmente, *adv.* literally.

literário, *adj.* literary.

literatice, *s.f.* trashy literature, bad writing.

literatismo, *s.m.* mania for literature; pedantic writing.

literato, *s.m.* man of letters.

literatura, *s.f.* literature.
litíase, *s.f.* lithiasis.
lítico, *adj.* lithic.
litigação, *s.f.* litigation.
litigante, *adj. e s.m.* litigant.
litigar, *v.i.* to litigate, to go to law; to contend; to fight.
litigável, *adj.* litigable, contestable.
litígio, *s.m.* litigation, lawsuit; dispute, contest.
litigiosamente, *adv.* litigiously.
litigioso, *adj.* litigious, disputable; contentious.
lítio, *s.m.* lithium.
litófago, *adj.* lithophagous.
litografar, *v.t.* to lithograph.
litografia, *s.f.* lithographic.
litógrafo, *s.m.* lithographer.
litóide, *adj.* lithoid, stonelike.
litologia, *s.f.* lithology.
litologista, *s.m. e s.f.* lithologist.
litoral, *s.m. e adj.* littoral; coastland, seaside, seashore.
litosfera, *s.f.* lithosphere.
litragem, *s.f.* quantity expressed in litres.
litro, *s.m.* litre.
lituano, *adj. e s.m.* Lithuanian.
liturgia, *s.f.* liturgy.
litúrgico, *adj.* liturgic.
liturgista, *s.m. e s.f.* liturgist.
lividez, *s.f.* lividness, lividity; ghastly pallor.
lívido, *adj.* livid, pale, ashy; black and blue.
livra!, *interj.* heaven forbid!
livrador, *s.m.* liberator, deliverer.
livralhada, *s.f.* pile of books.
livramento, *s.m.* liberation, release.
livrança, *s.f.* promissory note.
livrar, *v.t.* to deliver; to liberate, to set free, to release; *livrar-se,* to get rid of, to escape from; to free oneself of.
livraria, *s.f.* bookshop, bookstore.
livre, *adj.* free; independent; at liberty, released; clear, rid (of something): imune (from); disengaged; spare *(tempo).* 1) *livre arbítrio,* free will. 2) *livre de perigo,* safe, secure. 3) *ao ar livre,* in the open air, out doors. 4) *livre-câmbio,* free trade.
livreiro, *s.m.* bookseller.
livremente, *adv.* freely.
livre-pensador, *s.m.* freethinker.
livre-pensamento, *s.m.* freethinking.
livrete, *s.m.* note-book; booklet.
livro, *s.m.* book; volume, tome. 1) *livro de cheques,* checkbook. 2) *livro de leitura,* reader. 3) *livro de orações,* prayer-book. 4)

livro de ponto, time book. 5) *livro-razão,* ledger.
lixa, *s.f.* sandpaper; dogfish *(peixe).*
lixadeira, *s.f.* sandpapering machine.
lixadela, *s.f.* sandpapering.
lixar, *v.t.* to sandpaper.
lixeira, *s.f.* rubbish or garbage heap.
lixeiro, *s.m.* garbage collector.
líxivia, *s.f.* lye.
lixiviar, *v.t.* to leach.
lixo, *s.m.* garbage, litter; trash; refuse; rubbish.
ló, *s.m.* gauze; luff.
loa, *s.f.* encomium, laudatory speech; prologue *(numa peça de teatro).*
loba, *s.f.* she-wolf.
lobacho, *s.m.* wolf cub.
lobado, *adj.* lobate, lobed.
lobisomem, *s.m.* werewolf.
lobo, *s.m.* wolf.; *lobo do mar,* old sea dog *(marinheiro);* *lobo-marinho,* sea wolf.
lôbrego, *adj.* dark, gloomy.
lobrigar, *v.t.* to perceive, to notice, to catch a glimpse of, to discern.
lobulado, *adj.* lobulated.
lobular, *adj.* lobular.
lóbulo, *s.m.* lobule; lobe; *lóbulo de orelha,* ear-lap, ear lobe.
loca, *s.f.* hiding place *(de um peixe).*
locação, *s.f.* location; leasing, renting.
locador, *s.m.* lessor, hirer.
local, *s.m.* place, locality, spot, site; *adj.* local.
localidade, *s.f.* locality, place, village.
localista, *s.m. e s.f.* writer of local news.
localização, *s.f.* localization.
localizar, *v.t.* to localize, to locate, to place; to spot, to trace.
localizável, *adj.* localizable.
locanda, *s.f.* public house; inn; small shop.
locandeiro, *s.m.* inn-keeper, publican.
loção, *s.f.* lotion, wash.
locar, *v.t.* to let, to lease; to hire.
locatário, *s.m.* tenant; lessee; renter.
locativo, *adj.* locative.
locomobilidade, *s.f.* locomobility.
locomoção, *s.f.* locomotion.
locomotiva, *s.f.* locomotive; railway engine.
locomotor, *adj.* locomotor.
locomóvel, *adj. e s.m.* locomobile, self-propelling.
locomover-se, *v.refl.* to move about.
locução, *s.f.* locution; speech; *(gram.)* phrase.
loculado, *adj.* loculate.

locular, *adj.* locular.

lóculo, *s.m.* loculus.

locupletar, *v.t.* to enrich; *locupletar-se,* to get rich, to make money; to get one's fill *(saciar-se).*

locutor, *s.m.* speaker, announcer.

locutório, *s.m.* locutory, visiting room.

lodaçal, *s.m.* slough, quagmire, mud hole.

lodacento, *adj.* muddy, swampy.

lódão, *s.m.* nettle-tree.

lodo, *s.m.* mud, mire, slush, sludge; slime; silt.

lodoso, *adj.* muddy, miry; slimy; turbid.

loendral, *s.m.* oleander-grove.

logarítmico, *adj.* logarithmic(al).

logaritmo, *s.m.* logarithm.

lógica, *s.f.* logic; reasoning.

lógico, *adj.* logical, rational.

logística, *s.f.* logistics.

logo, *adv.* soon, immediately, right away; straight; before long; right. 1) *logo no começo,* right at the beginning. 2) *logo mais,* later on. 3) *logo que,* as soon as, *conj.* so, therefore, hence.

logografia, *s.f.* logography, stenography, shorthand.

logógrafo, *s.m.* logographer.

logradouro, *s.m.* public park or playground; common ground.

lograr, *v.t.* to enjoy; to gain, to obtain, to attain; to achieve; to succeed (in doing something); to cheat, to deceive, to humbug, to outwit, to fool.

logro, *s.m.* cheat, deceit, fraud, swindle, trickery, bluff.

loiça, *s.f.* o mesmo que "louça".

lóio, *s.m.* friar of the Order of St. John the Evangelist; *adj.* silly, foolish.

loira, *s.f.* o mesmo que "loura".

loisa, *s.f.* o mesmo que "lousa".

loja, *s.f.* shop, store; lodge *(maçónica).*

lojista, *s.m.* shopkeeper, storekeeper.

lomba, *s.f.* upland; crest, ridge, slope.

lombada, *s.f.* long ridge; back *(de livro ou animal).*

lombar, *adj.* lumbar.

lombarda, *s.f.* variety of cabbage.

lombardo, *s.m.* Lombard; *adj.* Lombardic.

lombo, *s.m.* loin; back; sirloin *(de vaca).*

lombriga, *s.f.* roundworm.

lona, *s.f.* canvas; sail cloth.

londrino, *adj.* London; *s.m.* Londoner.

longada, *s.f.* a long way.

longânime, *adj.* longanimous, forbearing, tolerant.

longanimidade, *s.f.* longanimity, forbearance, patience.

longarina, *s.f.* stringe; longitudinal bar *(num carro).*

longe, *adj.* far, far off, a long way off, far away, in the distance; *longe de,* far from; a long way from, wide of; *ao longe,* far off, in the distance. 1) *de longe,* from afar, from a distance. 2) *mais longe,* farther, farther on. 3) *para longe,* far away, off.

longes, *s.m. pl.* background; slight resemblance.

longevidade, *s.f.* longevity, long life.

longevo, *adj.* long-lived, very old, macrobian.

longímano, *adj.* longimanous, long-handed.

longínquo, *adj.* distant, remote, far off, far away.

longípede, *adj.* long-footed.

longitude, *s.f.* longitude.

longitudinal, *adj.* longitudinal; lenghtwise.

longitudinalmente, *adv.* lenghtwise.

longo, *adj.* long; lengthy; *ao longo de,* along, alongside.

lonjura, *s.f.* great distance.

lontra, *s.f.* otter.

loquacidade, *s.f.* loquacious, talkative, garrulous.

loquazmente, *adv.* loquaciously.

loquela, *s.f.* speech, verbosity; fluency.

loquete, *s.m.* padlock, detachable lock; bolt.

lora, *s.f.* burrow.

lorde, *s.m.* lord.

lordose, *s.f.* lordosis.

loriga, *s.f.* loriga, cuirass.

lornhão, *s.m.* lorgnette, lorgnon.

loro, *s.m.* stirrup strap.

lorpa, *adj.* imbecile, stupid, silly; boorish.

losango, *s.m.* lozenge, rhombus.

lota, *s.f.* place where fish is sold by auction.

lotação, *s.f.* holding capacity; *(náut.)* tonnage; jitney *(automóvel).* 1) *lotação esgotada,* sold out, filled up, full house. 2) *lotação de vinhos,* blending of wines.

lotador, *s.m.* auctioneer, valuer, estimator.

lotar, *v.t.* to divide into lots; to fill up; to blend *(vinhos).*

lotaria, *s.f.* lottery.

lote, *s.m.* allotment, portion, share; parcel, lot *(de terra);* lot, batch *(grupo);* shipment *(mercadorias).*

loto, *s.m.* lotus; lotus flower; lotto *(jogo).*

louça, *s.f.* tableware; china; dishes, plates; earthenware *(de barro).*

louçainha, *s.f.* finery; ornaments, pomp, attire, gala dress.

louçainho, *adj.* adorned, ornamented, elegant.

louçania, *s.f.* finery, attire; gaiety.

loução, *adj.* fine, gay, smart, goodlooking, elegant, smart.

louçaria, *s.f.* crockery-shop; amount of crockery.

louceiro, *s.m.* cupboard for china.

louco, *adj.* crazy, mad, insane, out of one's mind; rash, reckless, wild; *louco-varrido,* raving mad, stark crazy; *s.m.* mad man, lunatic; maniac.

loucura, *s.f.* madness, craziness, insanity, lunacy, derangement; folly, crazy action.

louquejar, *v.t.* to act foolish.

loura, *s.f.* blonde.

lourar, louriar, *v.t.* to make yellow or brown.

loureiro, *s.m.* laurel; bay tree.

lourejante, *adj.* yellowing, growing yellow.

lourejar, *v.t. e v.i.* to yellow; to make yellow; to turn yellow.

lourejo, *s.m.* golden colour; the proccess of browning.

louro, *s.m.* laurel, bay; bay leaf *(folha);* parrot *(papagaio); adj.* blond; fair; yellow.

lousa, *s.f.* slate *(ardósia);* flagstone *(laje);* tombstone *(tumuilar).*

louseira, *s.f.* slate quarry .

louva-a-deus, *s.m.* mantis, praying mantis.

louvação, *s.f.* appraisement, praising, laudation, valuation.

louvado, *adj.* praised; *s.m.* appraiser; valuer, assessor, expert, judge, arbit, arbiter.

louvaminha, *s.f.* coaxing, flattering, adulation.

louvaminhar, *v.t.* to coax, to flatter, to fawn.

louvaminheiro, *s.m.* sycophant; *adj.* flattering, sycophantic.

louvar, *v.t.* to praise, to laud, to extol; to commend, to applaud.

louvável, *adj.* praiseworthy, laudable, commendable.

louvor, *s.m.* praise, eulogy, encomium. laudation, commendation; *digno de louvor,* praiseworthy.

lua, *s.f.* moon. 1) *lua cheia,* full moon. 2) *lua--de-mel,* honey moon. 3) *lua nova,* new moon. 4) *andar no mundo da lua,* to moon about.

luar, *s.m.* moonlight.

luarento, *adj.* moonlit, flooded with moonlight.

lubricar, *v.t.* to make lewd; to lubricate.

lubricidade, *s.f.* lubricity, lewdness, lasciviousness.

lúbrico, *adj.* lubricous, lascivious, lewd.

lubrificação, *s.f.* lubrication, greasing, oiling.

lubrificador, *s.m.* lubricator; *adj.* lubricating.

lubrificar, *v.t.* to lubricate, to oil, to grease.

lucarna, *s.f.* lucarne, garret-window, skylight.

lucerna, *s.f.* lucerne.

lucidar, *v.t.* to pounce or trace *(um desenho).*

lucidez, *s.f.* lucidity, clearness; discernment, keenness; transparence.

lúcido, *adj.* lucid; clear, bright; clearheaded, keen, discerning.

Lúcifer, *s.m.* Lucifer, Satan.

luciférico, luciferino, *adj.* luciferian, satanic, diabolic, devilish.

lucífero, *adj.* luciferous, illuminating.

lucífugo, *adj.* lucifugous, avoiding light.

lucilação, *s.f.* gleam, glimpse, glare, glimmering.

lucilante, *adj.* gleaming, glimmering, flickering.

lucilar, *v.i.* to gleam, to twinkle, to glitter, to flicker.

luciluzir, *v.i.* to sparkle, to twinkle.

lúcio, *s.m.* pike *(peixe).*

lucrar, *v.t.* to gain; to make (money); to profit (from or by something); to benefit (by).

lucrativo, *adj.* lucrative, profitable, advantageous.

lucro, *s.m.* profit, gain; winnings, proceeds, returns. 1) *lucro líquido,* net profit. 2) *lucros e perdas,* profit and loss. 3) *lucros extraordinários,* excess profits.

lucubração, *s.f.* lucubration, laborious study.

lucubrar, *v.i.* to lucubrate, to work or study at night, to burn the midnight oil.

lúcula, *s.f.* granule, bright spot on the sun's disk.

luculento, *adj.* shining, bright.

luculiano, *adj.* Lucullean.

ludibriante, *adj.* deceiving, cheating; derisive.

ludibriar, *v.t.* to dupe, to cheat, to deceive; to mock, to ridicule, to deride.

ludíbrio, *s.m.* deception, deceit, dupery; mockery, derision.

ludibrioso, *adj.* scornful, mocking.

ludreiro, *s.m.* mud hole, quagmire.

lúdrico, *adj.* ludricous, comical, laughable.

ludroso, *adj.* dirty, foul.

lues, *s.f.* lues, syphilis.

luético, *adj.* luetic, syphilitic.

lufa, *s.f. lufa-lufa:* bustle, hurry-scurry; fuss.

lufada, *s.f.* gust (of wind); blast; puff.

lugar, *s.m.* place; spot; position; post; locality; job, employment; opportunity; seat *(num teatro, etc.).* 1) *dar lugar a,* to make way for, to give place to. 2) *em lugar algum,* nowhere. 3) *em lugar de,* instead of. 4) *em qualquer lugar,* anywhere. 5) *fora do lugar,* in the wrong place, misplaced. 6) *ele chegou em primeiro lugar,* he arrived in first place. 7) *lugar-comum,* common-place, cliché.

lugarejo, *s.m.* hamlet, small village.

lugar-tenente, *s.m.* substitute.

lugente, *adj.* plangent, mournful, plaintive.

lugre, *s.m.* lugger.

lúgubre, *adj.* lugubrious; mournful, doleful; gloomy, glum; dreary; funereal.

lugubridade, *s.f.* lugubriousness.

lula, *s.f.* squid; cuttlefish.

lumaréu, *s.m.* bonfire; little flame.

lumbago, *s.m.* lumbago.

lumbrical, *adj.* lumbrical.

lumbricida, *s.m.* e *adj.* vermicide.

lume, *s.m.* fire; light; *trazer a lume,* to bring to light. 1) *vir a lume,* to become known. 2) *acender o lume,* to light the fire. 3) *lume, se faz favor,* a light please.

lúmen, *s.m.* lumen.

lumieira, *s.f.* skylight; torch; candlestick.

luminar, *s.m.* luminary; illustrious person.

lumináría, *s.f.* light, lamp, torch; luminary; *luminárias,* illuminations.

luminescência, *s.f.* luminescence.

luminescente, *adj.* luminescent.

luminosamente, *adv.* luminously.

luminosidade, *s.f.* luminosity; brilliance.

luminoso, *adj.* luminous, bright, shining, brilliant, clear.

lunação, *s.f.* lunar month.

lunar, *adj.* lunar, moon; *s.m.* birthmark.

lunário, *s.m.* lunar calendar.

lunático, *adj.* lunatic, insane, moonstruck; *s.m.* lunatic, madman.

luneta, *s.f.* eyeglass, pince-nez, *(arq.)* lunette.

lunícola, *adj.* lunarian, selenite.

luniforme, *adj.* luniform, crescentshaped.

lunissolar, *adj.* lunisolar.

lúnula, *s.f.* lunule *(numa unha);* a crescent-shaped figure.

lupa, *s.f.* magnifying glass.

lupino, *adj.* lupine, wolfish.

lúpulo, *s.m.* hop.

lúpus, *s.m.* lupus.

lura, *s.f.* burrow.

lurar, *v.t.* to burrow, to hollow out.

lúrido, *adj.* lurid, gloomy, pale; dark.

lusco, *adj.* squinting, squint-eyed, cross-eyed; *lusco-fusco,* dusk, nightfall, twilight.

lusíada, *adj.* e *s.m.* e *s.f.* Lusitanian, Portuguese.

lusismo, *s.m.* Lusitanism.

lusitanismo, *s.m.* Portuguesism.

lusitano, *adj.* e *s.m.* Lusitanian, Portuguese.

luso, *adj.* e *s.m.* Lusitanian, Lusian.

luso-brasileiro, *s.m.* Luso-Brazilian.

lustração, *s.f.* lustration, purification; polishing.

lustradela, *s.f.* glossing, polishing.

lustrador, *s.m.* polisher; *adj.* glossing, polishing.

lustral, *adj.* lustral.

lustrar, *v.t.* to gloss, to polish, to purify.

lustre, *s.m.* lustre; brilliancy, radiance; chandelier of crystal or glass.

lustrina, *s.f.* lustrine, glossy silk fabric.

lustrino, *adj.* glossy, sheeny.

lustro, *s.m.* lustrum, quinquennium; polishing, shine.

lustroso, *adj.* lustrous, glossy, bright, shining.

luta, *s.f.* fight; struggle; strife; wrestle; fighting; conflict, contest, dispute; combat, battle. 1) *luta armada,* warfare. 2) *luta livre,* catch-as-catch-can. 3) *luta romana,* wrestling.

lutador, *s.m.* fighter; wrestler; scuffer; contender; *adj.* fighting.

lutar, *v.t.* to fight; to wrestle; to battle; to scuffle; to struggle, to strive (to do something); *lutar pela vida,* to struggle for life.

luteranismo, *s.m.* Lutheranism.

luterano, *adj.* e *s.m.* Lutheran.

luto, *s.m.* mourning; sorrow, grief. 1) *estar de luto,* to be in mourning. 2) *luto aliviado,* half mourning. 3) *luto fechado,* full mourning.

lutulência, *s.f.* muddiness, mud, mire.

lutulento, *adj.* muddy, miry, dirty.

lutuoso, *adj.* mournful, sad, doleful.

luva, *s.f.* glove. 1) *luvas,* gratuity, tip, bribe. 2) *assentar como uma luva,* to fit like a glove.

luvaria, *s.f.* glover's shop.

luveiro, *s.m.* glover, glove maker.

luxação, *s.f.* luxation, dislocation (of joints); wrench.

luxar, *v.t.* to luxate, to dislocate; *v.i.* to luxuriate, to live high.

luxemburguês, *adj*. Luxemburgian; *s.m*. Luxemburger.

luxento, *adj*. showy, pretentious.

luxo, *s.m*. luxury, sumptuousness; magnificence. 1) *dar-se ao luxo de,* to permit oneself the luxury of. 2) *de luxo,* de luxe. 3) *não posso dar-me ao luxo,* I can not afford (to do something).

luxuosamente, *adv*. luxuriously, sumptuously.

luxuoso, *adj*. luxurious, sumptuous, costly, magnificent.

luxúria, *s.f*. luxuriance, lust, lasciviousness, lechery; dissolution, corruption.

luxuriante, *adj*. luxuriant, lush, rank, exuberant.

luxuriar, *v.i*. to luxuriate, to indulge in luxury.

luxuriosamente, *adv*. luxuriously.

luxurioso, *adj*. luxurious, lustful, lascivious, lewd.

luz, *s.f*. light; brightness; glare; elucidation; knowledge, understanding, enlightenment. 1) *dar à luz,* to give birth to. 2) *à média luz,* in semiobscurity, dimly. 3) *à luz de,* in the light of. 4) *abrir a luz,* to switch on the light. 5) *fechar a luz,* to switch off the light. 6) *ter umas luzes,* to have some notions. 7) *luze--cu, s.m.* glow-worm, firefly.

luzeiro, *s.m*. light.

luze-luze, *s.m*. glow-worm, firefly.

luzerna, *s.f*. alfafa.

luzidio, *adj*. shining, glistening, bright.

luzido, *adj*. pompous, showy; shining, brilliant.

luzir, *v.i*. to glitter, to gleam, to shine, to sparkle.

M

m, the twelfth letter of the Portuguese alphabet.

maca, *s.f*. hammock; strecher *(padiola)*.

maça, *s.f*. club; club; Indian club *(de ginástica);* tamper *(de calceteiro)*.

maçã, *s.f*. apple; *maçã-de-adão,* Adam's apple; *maçã de rosto,* cheek.

macabeu, *adj*. Maccabean.

macabro, *adj*. macabre, horrible, gruesome; *dança macabra,* dance of death.

macaca, *s.f*. she-monkey; bad-luck.

macacada, *s.f*. band of monkeys; monkey trick.

macacal, *adj*. apish; monkeyish.

macacão, *s.m*. big monkey; shifty person.

macacaúba, *s.f*. timber for fine furniture and inlay work.

macaco, *s.m*. monkey, ape, simian; jack *(mecânico)*.

macacoa, *s.f*. slight disease.

maçada, *s.f*. worry; bother; bore; nuisance, annoyance; tedious talk.

macadame, *s.m*. macadam.

macadamização, *s.f*. macadamization.

maçador, *s.m*. tiresome person, bore, pest; *adj*. boring, tiresome.

maçadura, *s.f*. massage, rubbing; bruise, contusion.

macaense, *adj*. e *s.m*. e *s.f*. native of Macao.

maçagem, *s.f*. beating or dressing of flax.

maçal, *s.m*. whey, milk serum.

macambúzio, *adj*. melancholic, sad, handle; pommel *(de sela)*.

mação, *s.m*. freemason.

maçapão, *s.m*. marzipan.

macaqueação, *s.f*. mimicking, aping; mockery.

macaquear, *v.t*. to ape, to mimic; to mock.

macaquice, *s.f*. mimicry; monkey trick, monkeyshine.

macaquinho, *s.m.* little monkey.

maçar, *v.t.* to pound; to bore, to weary.

macaréu, *s.m.* bore, tidal wave.

maçarico, *s.m.* blow-torch, blowpipe; plover, curlew *(ave).*

maçaroca, *s.f.* spindleful of thread *(no fuso);* sheaf *(feixe);* ear corn *(de milho).*

macarrão, *s.m.* macaroni.

macarronete, *s.m.* thin macaroni.

macarrónico, *adj.* macaronic.

macarronismo, *s.m.* macaronic style.

macarronista, *s.m.* writer in the macaronic style.

macavenco, *s.m.* eccentric, an eccentric fellow; an oddity; *adj.* eccentric, odd, singular.

macedónico, *adj.* Macedonian.

macedónio, *s.m.* Macedonian.

macega, *s.f.* weed.

maceiro, *s.m.* verger, mace bearer, beadle.

macela, *s.f.* camomile.

maceração, *s.f.* maceration; mortification; softening.

macerado, *adj.* macerated; softened; mortified.

macerar, *v.t.* to macerate; to soak; to soften; to mortify.

maceta, *s.f.* mallet *(de cantoneiro);* muller *(para tintas);* drumstick *(de bombo).*

macetar, *v.t.* to pound, to maul.

macete, *s.m.* mallet.

machacaz, *s.m.* brutish or bulky man.

machada, *s.f.* hatchet.

machadada, *s.f.* blow with an axe.

machado, *s.m.* axe.

machear, *v.t.* to plait *(em costura).*

machete, *s.m.* sword; hunting-knife; matchet.

machial, *s.m.* uncultivated pasture; barren land.

machiar, *v.i.* to become barren, to degenerate.

machila, *s.f.* palanquin; litter.

machão, *s.m.* virago; macho.

macheado, *s.m.* plait.

machileiro, *s.m.* palanquin-bearer.

machilo, *adj.* barren, unfertyile, dried.

macho, *s.m.* male; mule *(animal);* box plait *(em costura);* tenon *(em carpintaria);* pintle *(de gonzo);* male; masculine; manly; virile.

machucadura, *s.f.* bruise, contusion; crushing.

machucar, *v.t.* to bruise; to crush, to mash; to hurt; to crumple *(amarrotar).*

machucho, *adj.* sly, cunning, astute; rich, powerful.

maciço, *s.m.* thicket *(de vegetação);* (geol.) massif; *adj.* massive, solid, thick; bulky, voluminous.

macieira, *s.f.* apple-tree.

macieza, *s.f.* softness, smoothness; mildness.

macilência, *s.f.* emanciation, gauntness.

macilento, *adj.* emaciated, gaunt; haggard.

macio, *adj.* soft, smooth, supple; mild, agreeable.

macla, *s.f.* macle.

maço, *s.m.* mallet; maul; gavel; bundle, stack *(de papéis);* packet *(de cigarros).*

maçom, *s.m.* Freemason.

maçonaria, *s.f.* Freemasonry.

maçónico, *adj.* Masonic.

macrobia, *s.f.* longevity, old age, macrobiosis.

macróbio, *adj.* long lived, macrobian; *s.m.* macrobiote.

macrocefalia, *s.f.* macrocephaly.

macrocefálico, *adj.* macrocephalical.

macrocéfalo, *adj.* macrocephalous.

macrocosmo, *s.m.* macrocosm.

macruro, *adj.* macruran, with a long tail.

maçudo, *adj.* tiresome, boring, dull, tedious.

macroscópio, *s.m.* macroscopic.

mácula, *s.f.* macula, stain, spot, blot; dishonour, discredit.

maculado, *adj.* maculate, spotted, stained; impure, dishonoured.

macular, *v.t.* to maculate, to stain, to spot; to dishonour, to discredit.

maculável, *adj.* stainable; discreditable.

maculoso, *adj.* spotted, stained.

macumba, *s.f.* voodoo.

madagascarense, *adj.* e *s.m.* Malagasy, Madagascan.

madeira, *s.f.* wood; timber, lumber. 1) *Madeira (vinho).* 2) *cortar madeira,* to log. 3) *de madeira,* wooden. 4) *trabalho de madeira,* woodwork.

madeirame, *s.m.* large quantity of wood.

madeiramento, *s.m.* timberwood; framework.

madeirar, *v.t.* to do wood-work; to set up a wooden frame.

madeireiro, *s.m.* lumber or timber dealer.

medeirense, *s.m.* native of Madeira; *adj.* Madeiran.

madeiro, *s.m.* log, timber; beam; the cross of our Lord.

madeixa, s.f. lock (de cabelo); skein (de fio).

mádido, adj. moistened, soaked, wet.

madona, s.f. Madonna; the Virgin Mary.

madraçaria, s.f. idleness, laziness, sloth, indolence.

madraceador, s.m. e adj. lazy, lazy fellow, truant.

madracear, v.i. to loaf, to loiter, to idle; to slounch.

madraço, adj. lazy; s.m. loafer, idler, sluggard.

madrasta, s.f. stepmother.

madre, s.f. nun; mother; matrix; madre superiora, Mother Superior.

madrepérola, s.f. mother of pearl, nacre.

madrépora, s.f. madrepore.

madrepórico, adj. madreporic.

madressilva, s.f. woodbine, honeysuckle.

madrigal, s.m. madrigal.

madrigalista, s.m. e s.f. madrigalist.

madrigoa, s.f. burrow, hole, hiding-place (de ladrões).

madrileno, s.m. a native of Madrid.

madrinha, s.f. godmother; patroness; ser madrinha, to stand godmother to a child.

madrugada, s.f. dawn, day-break.

madrugador, s.m. early riser; adj. rising early.

madrugar, v.i. to rise early, to get up in the morning; to be ahead of time.

maduração, s.f. ripening, maturation.

maduramente, adv. maturely; wisely.

madurar, v.i. to ripen; to mature; to become ripe.

madurecer, v.t. to ripen, to become ripen.

madureza, s.f. maturity, ripeness; eccentricity, oddity.

maduro, adj. mature, ripe; mellow; wise, judicious.

mãe, s.f. mother. 1) mãe adoptiva, foster-mother. 2) mãe-d`água, s.f. well-head. 3) mãe pátria, s.f. mother land.

maestria, s.f. mastrery, skilfulness, skill.

maestrino, s.m. maestrino.

maestro, s.m. maestro, conductor.

mafamético, adj. Mohammedan.

mafarrico, s.m. deuce, devil, demon.

maga, s.f. witch, sorceress.

magala, s.m. private (no exército); tommy.

maganão, s.m. mischievous person, rogue, rascal; adj. playful, prankish; mischievous.

magano, adj. artful; roguish; jovial; s.m. rogue, rascal, scoundrel.

magarefe, s.m. butcher.

magazine, s.m. magazine.

magenta, s.f. magenta.

magia, s.f. magic; enchantment; sorcery, wichtcraft.

magiar, s.m. e adj. Magyar; Hungarian.

mágica, s.f. magic; witch; trick, conjuration.

magicar, v.t. to brood, to think; to devise.

mágico, s.m. magician, enchanter, sorcerer, conjurer; adj. magic, magical.

magistério, s.m. teaching profession, professorship; staff of teachers.

magistrado, s.m. magistrate, judge.

magistral, adj. magisterial; masterly; perfect, excellent; masterful.

magistralmente, adv. magisterially; in a master manner.

magistratura, s.f. magistrature, magistracy; the bench.

magma, s.m. magma.

magmático, adj. magmatic.

magnanimidade, s.f. magnanimity; nobleness, generosity.

magnânimo, adj. magnanimous, generous, noble, greathearted.

magnata, magnate, s.m. magnate; tycoon; lord.

magnésia, s.f. magnesia.

magnesiano, magnésico, adj. magnesian.

magnésio, s.m. magnesium.

magnete, s.m. magnet; loadstone (íman).

magnético, adj. magnetic.

magnetismo, s.m. magnetism; attractiveness, charm.

magnetite, s.f. magnetite.

magnetização, s.f. magnetization.

magnetizador, s.m. magnetizer; adj. magnetising.

magnetizar, v.t. to magnetize; to attract, to charm.

magnetizável, adj. magnetizable.

magneto, s.m. magneto.

magnetofone, s.m. magnetophone.

magnetógrafo, s.m. magnetograph.

magnetologia, s.f. study of magnetism.

magnetómetro, s.m. magnetometer.

magnetoscópio, s.m. magnetoscope.

magnificação, s.f. magnification; exaltation.

magnificar, v.t. to magnify; to extol, to glorify; to amplify, to enlarge.

magnificência, s.f. magnificence, grandeur, splendour, pomp.

magnificente, adj. magnificent, lordly, royal; grand, imposing.

magnífico, adj. magnificent, majestic,

sumptuous; generous; extraordinary, superb; sublime, wonderful.

magniloquência, *s.f.* magniloquence.

magníloquo, *adj.* eloquent; pompous; bombastic.

magnitude, *s.f.* magnitude, greatness; importance, consequence.

magno, *adj.* great, grand, important.

magnólia, *s.f.* magnolia.

mago, *s.m.* wizard, magician; *os reis magos,* the Magi; the Three Wise Men from the East.

mágoa, *s.f.* grief, sorrow, woe; regret, complaint; envy.

magoado, *adj.* sorrowful, offended; hurt, agrieved.

magoar, *v.t.* to hurt, to bruise, to injure; to grieve, to distress; to offend; *magoar-se,* to hurt oneself.

magote, *s.m.* band; cluster; crowd, swarm; heap.

magreza, *s.f.* thriness, leaness; meagerness.

magricela, *s.f.* skinny, scrawny, lanky, weedy.

magriço, *s.m.* knight of the ladies; ridiculous defender of futile things.

magro, *adj.* thin, lean; slender, slim; meager, scanty.

magrote, *adj.* rather thin.

magusto, *s.m.* roasting of chestnuts in St. Martin's Eve.

maia, *s.f.* May-Day.

maiêutica, *s.f.* maieutic method (Socratic).

mainel, *s.m.* hand-rail.

Maio, *s.m.* May.

maionese, *s.f.* mayonnaise.

maior, *adj.* larger, bigger, greater; of age, adult *(de idade)*; *s.m.* adult.

maioral, *s.m.* chief, headman; foreman *(capataz).*

maioria, *s.f.* majority, greater number, major part; generality; bulk. 1) *a maioria,* most. 2) *por maioria de votos,* by a plurality of votes.

maioridade, *s.f.* majority; full legal age; *atingir a maioridade,* to come of age.

maiorquino, *adj.* native of Maiorca.

mais, *adv.* more; also; over; besides; further; moreover; *adj.* more, further; *s.m.* greater part; the remnant, the surplus. 1) *mais de,* more than; over. 2) *mais nada,* nothing more. 3) *mais ou menos,* more or less; about. 4) *mais uma vez,* once more. 5) *a mais,* in excess. 6) *alguém a mais,* somebody else. 7) *as mais das vezes,* mostly. 8) *de mais a mais,* moreover, besides. 9) *não mais do que,* no more than. 10) *não posso esperar mais,* I can not wait any longer. 11) *nem mais nem menos,* neither more nor less. 12) *o mais,* the rest. 13) *por mais que,* howevermuch. 14) *quanto mais melhor,* the more the better. 15) *sem mais nem menos,* for no reason, just llike that, without warning.

maisena, *s.f.* maizena, corn-starch.

mais-que-perfeito, *s.m. (gram.)* past perfect.

maiúscula, *s.f.* capital letter.

maiúsculo, *adj.* capital.

majestade, *s.f.* majesty, grandeur, loftiness; dignity; *Vossa Majestade,* Your Majesty; *lesa-majestade,* lese-majesty.

majestático, *adj.* majestic, imposing.

majestosamente, *adv.* majestically.

majestoso, *adj.* majestic, imposing, august, lofty, stately.

major, *s.m.* major.

mal, *s.m.* evil; wrong, harm, injury; wrong-doing; illness, disease; trouble, misfortune, grief. 1) *dizer mal de,* to speak ill of. 2) *fazer mal a,* to harm, to hurt, to disagree with *(indispôr).* 3) *levar a mal,* to take amiss, to take offense at. 4) *não faz mal,* never mind, no matter. 6) *que mal tem isso?,* what is wrong with that? *adv.* badly, poorly; ill; scarcely; scarcely, hardly, barely; wrong; as soon as. 7) *mal o vi,* I hardly see him, as soon as I saw him, barely; wrong *(logo que o vi).* 8) *mal chegámos, ele partiu,* we had no sooner arrived he went away. 9) *de mal a pior,* from bad to worse, worse and worse. 10) *estar mal,* to turn out badly. 11) *sentir--se mal,* to feel bad.

mala, *s.f.* trunk; bag *(de viagem),* handbag *(de mão).* 1) *malas,* bags, luggage, baggage. 2) *fazer as malas,* to pack.

malabar, *adj.* Malabar.

malabarismo, *s.m.* uggling, jugglery; *fazer malabarismos,* to juggle.

malabarista, *s.m.* juggler.

malacia, *s.f.* calm, calmness; weakness, feebleness.

mal-agradecido, *adj.* ungrateful.

malaguenha, *s.f.* Spanish song and music.

malaguenho, *s.m.* native of Malaga.

malagueta, *s.f.* chili; cayenne pepper.

malaio, Malay; *adj.* Malayan.

mal-amanhado, *adj.* ill-dressed; clumsy.

malandragem, *s.f.* gang of rascals, rascality; truancy; vagrancy.

malandrão, *s.m.* scoundrel.

malandrar, *v.i.* to loaf, to rove; to lead the life of vagabond.

malandrice, *s.f.* rascality, roguery; idleness.

malandrim, *s.m.* vagabond; thief; rascal.

malandro, *s.m.* scoundrel, rogue, rascal; loafer.

malapeira, *s.f.* pearmain-tree.

malápio, *s.m.* pearmain.

mala-posta, *s.f.* mail-coach.

malaquite, *s.f.* malachite.

malar, *s.m.* malar bone, cheek bone; *adj.* malar.

malária, *s.f.* malaria.

mal-aventurado, *adj.* unlucky, unhappy.

mal-avindo, *adj.* disagreed, discordant.

malaxação, *s.f.* malaxation; mollification; kneading.

malaxador, *s.m.* kneader, machine for grinding; mixing mill.

malaxar, *v.t.* to knead, to molify; to malax.

malbaratador, *s.m.* squanderer, dissipator, prodigal.

malbaratar, *v.t.* to waste, to squander, to fritter away.

malbarato, *s.m.* squandering; underselling.

malcasado, *adj.* ill-matched.

malcheiroso, *adj.* stinking, bad-smelling.

malcomido, *adj.* illfed; thin.

malcriado, *adj.* ill-bred, unmannerly, rude.

maldade, *s.f.* badness; wickedness; malice; meanness, venom; mischief, devilry.

maldição, *s.f.* curse, malediction.

maldito, *adj.* cursed, damned, accursed.

malditoso, *adj.* unhappy, unlucky.

maldizente, *adj.* slanderous, evil-speaking, backbiting; *s.m.* slanderer; backbiter.

maldizer, *v.t.* to slander; to curse; to execrate.

maldoso, *adj.* wicked; mean, vicious, malicious, malevolent.

maleabilidade, *s.f.* malleability, ductility.

maleável, *adj.* malleable; ductile; tractable.

maledicência, *s.f.* evil-speaking, slander, calumny, defamation.

mal-educado, *adj.* ill-bred, rude.

maleficência, *s.f.* maleficence, evildoing.

malefício, *s.m.* misdeed; damage, evil; evil spell.

maléfico, *adj.* maleficent, harmful, injurious, evil; malignat.

maleiro, *s.m.* trunk maker or seller.

maleita, *s.f.* ague, malaria.

mal-encarado, *adj.* evil-looking; grim-looking; surly.

mal-enjorcado, *adj.* badly dressed.

mal-entendido, *s.m.* misunderstanding, misapprehension.

maleolar, *adj.* malleolar.

maléolo, *s.m.* malleolus.

mal-estar, *s.m.* indisposition; discomfort; uneasiness.

maleta, *s.f.* valise, handbag.

malevolência, *s.f.* malevolence; malice.

malevolente, malévolo, *adj.* malevolent, malignant.

malfadado, *adj.* unlucky, ill-fated, unfortune.

malfadar, *v.t.* to curse; to disgrace.

malfazejo, *adj.* evil-doing, maleficent.

malfeitor, *s.m.* malefactor, criminal; gangster.

malfeitoria, *s.f.* malefaction, delict, misdeed, felony.

malferido, *adj.* badly wounded.

malga, *s.f.* porriger, bowl.

malgastar, *v.t.* to misspend, to squander.

malgaxe, *s.m.* e *s.f.* e *adj.* Madagascan.

mal-grado, *s.m.* ill will.

malha, *s.f.* mesh *(de rede);* mail *(de armadura);* stitch *(no tricô);* quoit *(no jogo da malha);* threshing *(acto de malhar);* artigos de malha, hosiery.

malhada, *s.f.* threshing; shepherd's hut; enclosure for cattle.

malhadela, *s.f.* slight threshing.

malhadiço, *adj.* dull, indolent; stupid.

malhado, *adj.* spotted, speckled, mottled; beaten, threshed.

malhar, *v.t.* to thresh *(o grão);* to hammer, to pound, to beat.

malhetar, *v.t.* to mortise.

malhete, *s.m.* mallet, mortise joint.

malho, *s.m.* mallet, hammer; sledge hammer.

malhoada, *s.f.* plot, intrigue.

mal-humorado, *adj.* ill-humoured, ill-tempered, sulky, sullen, grumpy.

malícia, *s.f.* malice; malevolence; cunning; evil intention.

maliciar, *v.t.* to suspect maliciously.

maliciosamente, *adv.* maliciously.

malicioso, *adj.* malicious; artful; roguish.

málico, *adj.* malic.

maligna, *s.f.* malignant fever.

malignidade, *s.f.* malignity, ill-nature.

maligno, *adj.* malign, pernicious, malignant, malevolent; ill-natured; deadly, *fatal; s.m.* the devil.

malina, *s.f.* spring tide.
má-língua, *s.f.* slanderer; gossip.
mal-intencionado, *adj.* evil-minded, malicious; ill-meaning, ill-intentioned.
malmequer, *s.m.* daisy, pot marrigold.
malnascido, *adj.* ill-starred; low-born.
malogrado, *adj.* unlucky, unhappy; abbortive, frustrated.
malograr, *v.t.* to fustrate, to fail; to miscarry; to wreck.
malogro, *s.m.* failure, frustration; miscarriage, disappointment.
malquerença, *s.f.* malevolence, ill-will, animosity, aversion.
malquerente, *adj.* malevolent, ill-disposed (towards others).
malquerer, *v.t.* to wish ill to, to detest; *s.m.* animosity, aversion.
malquistar, *v.t.* to disunite, to render inimical, to indispose, to cause animosities; *malquistar-se com,* to fall out with.
malquisto, *adj.* hated, disliked, detested; odious.
malsão, *adj.* sickly; unhealthy, noxious.
malsim, *s.m.* informer, spy.
malsinação, *s.f.* denounciation, slanderous information.
malsinar, *v.t.* to accuse; to slander; to denounce; to defame.
malsoante, *adj.* ill-sounding, jarring, harsh, dissonant.
malsofrido, *adj.* impacient, unresigned, disquiet.
malsonância, *s.f.* dissonance.
malsonante, *adj.* ill-sounding.
malta, *s.f.* gang, band; mob.
maltar, *v.t.* to malt.
máltase, *s.f.* maltase.
malte, *s.m.* malt, barley.
maltês, *s.m.* e *adj.* Maltese.
malthusianismo, *s.m.* Maltusianism.
malthusiano, *s.m.* Malthusian.
maltose, *s.f.* maltose.
maltrapilho, *s.m.* ragamuffin; *adj.* ragged, in tatters; beggarly.
maltratado, *adj.* maltreated.
maltratar, *v.t.* to ill-treat, to ill-use; to victimize, to abuse, to outrage, to isuse, to injure.
maluco, *adj.* crazy, insane; crackbrained; *s.m.* madman.
maluquice, *s.f.* madness; folly; eccentricity.
malva, *s.f.* mallow.
malvadez, *s.f.* wickedness, meanness, malignity, cruelty.

malvado, *adj.* wicked, cruel, mean.
malvaísco, *s.m.* marsh-mallow.
malvar, *v.t.* to mallow-bed.
malva-rosa, *s.f.* rose-mallow.
malvasia, *s.f.* malmsey, sweet white wine.
malversação, *s.f.* malversation; embezlement.
malversar, *v.t.* to embezzle, to dilapidate *(fundos).*
malvisto, *adj.* dislikled; distrusted.
mama, *s.f.* breast; teat, dug.
mamã, *s.f.* mammy.
mamada, *s.f.* act of sucking.
mamadeira, *s.f.* nursing bottle.
mamal, *adj.* mammiferous.
mamão, *s.m.* papaya; *adj.* suckling.
mamar, *v.t.* e *v.i.* to suck, to suckle; *dar de mamar,* to nurse.
mamário, *adj.* mammary.
mamarracho, *s.m.* grotesque figure.
mamelão, *s.m.* mamelon; rounded hillock.
mameliforme, *adj.* melon shaped.
mameluco, *s.m.* Mameluke.
mamífero, *s.m.* mammifer, mammal, mammalian; *adj.* mammalian.
mamilar, *adj.* mammilary.
mamilo, *s.m.* nipple.
mamiloso, *adj.* nipple-shaped, mamillated.
mamute, *s.m.* mammoth.
mana, *s.f.* sister.
maná, *s.m.* manna; delicious food.
manada, *s.f.* herd.
manancial, *s.m.* fountain, spring, source.
manante, *adj.* flowing, running.
manápula, *s.f.* large hand.
manar, *v.i.* to flow, to spring, to proceed from; to emanate.
mancal, *s.m.* plumber, block hinge.
mançanilha, *s.f.* manzanilla olive.
mancar, *v.i.* to limp, to walk lamely, to cripple.
manceba, *s.f.* concubine.
mancebia, *s.f.* concubinage.
mancebo, *s.m.* lad, boy, young man.
mancenilha, *s.f.* manchineel.
mancha, *s.f.* stain, spot, speck, fleck; disgrace, defect; *mancha solar,* sunspot.
manchar, *v.t.* to stain, to spot; to maculate; to sully, to tarnish.
mancheia, *s.f.* handful; *às mancheias,* by the handful.
manchete, *s.f.* newspaper.
manchil, *s.m.* chopping-knife.
manco, *adj.* crippled, lame; *s.m.* cripple.

mancomunação, *s.f.* connivance, conspiracy, plot.

mancomunar-se, *v.refl.* to act in concert with.

manda-chuva, *s.m.* big-shot, bigwig; political boss.

mandado, *s.m.* order, command, injunction, mandate; *(jur.)* writ, warrant. 1) *mandado de prisão,* warrant for someone's arrest. 2) *mandado de despejo,* notice to quit. 3) *mandado judicial,* judge's order.

mandamento, *s.m.* commandment; order.

mandante, *s.m.* chief, boss; instigator.

mandão, *s.m.* domineering person, despot, bully; *adj.* bossy, domineering.

mandar, *v.t.* to command, to order, to direct; to tell (someone to do something); to send, to envoy. 1) *mandar buscar, pedir ou chamar:* to send for. 2) *mandar embora:* to send away. 3) *mandar entrar:* to show in. 4) *mandar fazer:* to have something made.

mandarete, *s.m.* errand-boy.

mandarim, *s.m.* mandarin.

mandatário, *s.m.* mandatary, agent, delegate, representative.

mandato, *s.m.* mandate; order; charge, injunction; delegation.

mandíbula, *s.f.* jaw, mandible.

mandinga, *s.f.* witchcraft, sorcery.

mandioca, *s.f.* manioc, cassava.

mando, *s.m.* command; power, authority; *a mando de,* by order of.

mandrágora, *s.f.* mandrake.

mandrião, *s.m.* idler, loafer, sluggard; *adj.* idle, lazy.

mandriar, *v.t.* to idle, to loiter, to loaf, to dawdle.

mandril, *s.m. (zool.)* mandrill; *(mec.)* broach, reamer.

manducar, *v.t.* to manducate, to chew, to eat.

maneabilidade, *s.f.* handiness, manageability.

manear, *v.t.* to handle, to manage, to manipulate; to hobble *(cavalo).*

maneável, *adj.* handy, workable.

maneio, *s.m.* handiness, handling; management.

maneira, *s.f.* manner, method, way, fashion; style; pl. manners, behavior, demeanor. 1) *à maneira de,* like, in the manner of, after. 2) *da mesma maneira,* in the same manner or way, likewise. 3) *de maneira a,* so as to. 4) *de maneira alguma,* not at all, not in the least, in no way. 5) *de maneira que,* so that.

6) *de qualquer maneira,* in one way or another. 7) *desta maneira,* this way. 8) *maneira de falar:* way of speech.

maneirinho, *adj.* easy to carry, small.

maneirismo, *s.m.* mannerism.

maneiroso, *adj.* mannerly, well-mannered, polite.

manejar, *v.t.* to handle, to wield, to manipulate; to manage; to deal with.

manejável, *adj.* handy, manageable.

manejo, *s.m.* handling, wielding; manipulation; management.

manequim, *s.m.* mannequin; dummy; model.

maneta, *s.* one-handed or one-harmed person.

manga, *s.* sleeve; mango *(fruto).*

manga-de-alpaca, *s.m.* white collar worker; bureaucrat.

manganês, *s.m.* manganese.

mangar, *v.i.* to joke, to banter, to make fun of.

mangra, *s.f.* blight, rust; mildew.

mangual, *s.m.* flail.

mangue, *s.m.* marshy ground; mangrove.

mangueira, *s.f.* hose; *(bot.)* mango-tree.

mangueiral, *s.m.* mango-grove.

manguito, *s.m.* muff; mitten.

manha, *s.f.* cunning, artfulness, craftiness; ruse, trick.

manhã, *s.f.* morning, forenoon; *de manhã cedo,* early in the morning.

manhoso, *adj.* crafty, cunnung, wily, tricky.

mania, *s.f.* mania; madness; obsession; fixed idea; peculiarity.

maníaco, *adj.* maniac, maniacal, lunatic, cranky.

manicómio, *s.m.* asylum, madhouse.

manietar, *v.t.* to manacle, to shacke; to restrain.

manifestação, *s.f.* manifestation; demonstrastion, display; exhibition.

manifestante, *s.m.* manifestant, demonstrator.

manifestar, *v.t.* to manifest; to show, to display, to exhibit; to express, to reveal, to declare.

manifesto, *adj.* manifest, obvious, visible; *s.m.* manifesto, proclamation, public declaration.

manigância, *s.f.* underhand dealing; trick, stratagem.

manilha, *s.f.* manilla; bracelet; shackle.

maninho, *adj.* barren, uncultivated, unproductive, waste.

manipanso, *s.m.* fetish, mumbo jumbo.

manipulação, *s.f.* manipulation, handling.

manipular, *v.t.* to manipulate, to handle, to operate; to process.

manípulo, *s.m.* handle, knob, lever; maniple *(estola usada pelos sacerdotes).*

maniqueísmo, *s.m.* Manicheism.

manivela, *s.f.* crank, handle.

manjar, *s.m.* delicious food, delicacy, titbit.

manjedoura, *s.f.* manger, crib.

manjericão, *s.m.* basil.

manjerico, *s.m.* basil.

mano, *s.m.* brother.

manobra, *s.f.* maneuver; handling; tactic, stratagem.

manobrar, *v.t.* to maneuver, to handle, to operate; to switch *(comboios).*

manómetro, *s.m.* manometer, pressure gauge.

manopla, *s.f.* iron glove, gauntlet.

manqueira, *s.f.* lameness, hobble.

manquejar, *v.i.* to limp, to lame, to hobble.

mansão, *s.f.* mansion, residence.

mansarda, *s.f.* garret, mansard, attic.

mansidão, *s.f.* tameness; gentleness, mildness, docility.

mansinho, *adj.* very mild; *de mansinho,* quietly, softly.

manso, *adj.* mild, gentle, meek; tame.

manta, *s.f.* rug, blanket.

manteiga, *s.f.* butter; *(pop.)* flattery.

manteiqueira, *s.f.* butter dish.

manteigueiro, *s.m.* butter maker; *(pop.)* flatterer.

mantel, *s.m.* altar-cloth.

mantença, *s.f.* nourishment, sustenance; maintenance.

mantenedor, *s.m.* maintainer; supporter; champion.

manter, *v.t.* to maintain; to sustain, to support; to keep up; to hold; to keep; to retain; to carry on, to continue. 1) *manter--se,* to supoort oneself, to subsist, to keep, to live by. 2) *manter a palavra,* to keep, to live by. 3) *manter a palavra,* to keep one's word. 4) *manter-se firme,* to hold out.

mantilha, *s.f.* mantilla; head scarf.

mantimento, *s.m.* maintenance; *pl.* provisions.

manto, *s.m.* mantle; cloak; robe.

manual, *adj.* manual, hand; *s.m.* manual, handbook.

manufactor, *s.m.* manufacturer.

manufactura, *s.f.* manufacture, manu-facturing.

manufacturar, *v.t.* to manufacture.

manuscrever, *v.t.* to write by hand.

manuscrito, *adj.* e *s.m.* manuscript.

manusear, *v.t.* to handle, to manipulate.

manuseio, *s.m.* handling.

manutenção, *s.f.* maintenance; keeping, preservation; subsistence.

mão, *s.f.* hand; coat, layer *(de tinta, etc.);* lead *(precedência em jogo de cartas);* round *(jogada);* side *(lado por onde os carros devem circular).* 1) *mãos ao alto!,* hands up!. 2) *estar à mão,* at hand. 3) *feito á mão,* hand made. 4) *à mão armada,* by armed force. 5) *a quatro mãos, (mús.)* for four hands. 6) *com as mãos a abanar,* empty-handed. 7) *em contra mão,* on the wrong side of the road. 8) *deitar mãos à obra,* to set to work. 9) *de mão beijada,* for nothing, gratuitously. 10) *de mãos dadas,* hand in hand. 11) *em primeira mão,* firsthand. 12) *em segunda mão,* second-hand. 13) *enquanto estamos com a mão na massa,* while we are at it. 14) *lançar mão de,* to resort to. 15) *não ter mãos a medir,* to have one's hands full. 16) *de mão em mão,* from hand to hand. 17) *pedir a mão de,* to ask the hand of. 18) *pôr as mãos no fogo por alguém,* to swear for someone's integrity.

mão-cheia, *s.f.* handful. 1) *de mão-cheia,* perfect, excellent. 2) *às mãos-cheias,* by handfuls.

mão-de-obra, *s.f.* workmanship, labour force.

maometano, *s.m.* e *adj.* mohammedan.

maometismo, *s.m.* mohammedism.

mãos-largas, *s.* generous person.

mãos-rotas, *s.* spendthrift; open-handed.

mão-travessa, *s.f.* hand's breadth.

mãozorra, *s.f.* big hand.

mapa, *s.m.* map; chart.

mapa-múndi, *s.m.* world map.

maqueiro, *s.m.* stretcher bearer; ambulance man.

maquia, *s.f.* corn measure; amount of money; profit, money.

maquiavélico, *adj.* Machiavellian; cunning, astute, crafty.

maquiavelismo, *s.m.* machiavellism; craftiness.

maquilhagem, *s.m.* make-up.

maquilhar-se, *v.refl.* to make-up; to paint.

máquina, *s.f.* machine, engine, mill; machinery. 1) *máquina a vapor,* steam engine. 2) *máquina de calcular,* calculator, calculating machine. 3) *máquina de costura,* sewing machine. 4) *máquina fotográfica,* camara.

maquinação, *s.f.* machination; scheme; plot, intrigue, conspiracy.

maquinal, *adj.* mechanical, automatic; unconscious.

maquinar, *v.t.* to contrive, to plan; to plot, to scheme.

maquinaria, *s.f.* machinery.

maquinismo, *s.m.* machinery, mechanism, gear; machine, apparatus.

maquinista, *s.m.* machinist, operator; engine driver, engineer *(de locomotiva).*

mar, *s.m.* sea, ocean. 1) *alto mar,* open sea, high sea. 2) *fazer-se ao mar,* to sail, to put to sea. 3) *por mar,* by sea.

marabu, *s.m.* marabou.

maracujá, *s.m.* passion fruit.

marafona, *s.f.* rag-doll; prostitute.

marajá, *s.m.* maharaja.

marasmo, *s.m.* marasmus, apathy, indifference.

marasquino, *s.m.* maraschino.

maratona, *s.f.* marathon.

marau, *s.m.* rascal, swindler.

maravalhas, *s.f. (pl.)* wood shavings; needles of pine-trees; trifles.

maravilha, *s.f.* marvel, wonder; *às mil maravilhas,* splendidly, wonderfully.

maravilhado, *adj.* amazed, astonished, wonder-stricken.

maravilhar, *v.t.* to amaze, to astonish, to surprise; *maravilhar-se,* to wonder (at something), to marvel, to be surprised at.

maravilhoso, *adj.* marvellous, wonderful, amazing.

marca, *s.f.* mark, stamp; sign; caracteristic; imprint, impress; trace. 1) *marca registada, marca de fábrica,* trade mark. 2) *de marca maior,* first-rate. 3) *passar das marcas,* to go too far.

marcação, *s.f.* marking; demarcation; booking *(reserva de lugares).*

marcador, *s.m.* marker, scorer; scoreboard.

marcar, *v.t.* to mark, to stamp; to register, to record; to label; to indicate, to point out; to brand *(gado);* to set *(data, reunião, etc.);* to dial *(um número de telefone); o termómetro marca zero,* the termometer reads zero.

marcela, *s.f.* camomile.

marcenaria, *s.f.* cabinet-marker`s shop, joinery.

marceneiro, *s.m.* cabinet-maker, joiner.

marcha, *s.f.* march; course, progress; advance; walking; pace, speed. 1) *marcha atrás,* reverse gear. 2) *marcha forçada,* forced march. 3) *em marcha,* on the march. 4) *pôr em marcha,* to start.

marchante, *s.m.* cattle-dealer.

marchar, *v.t.* to march, to walk.

marchetar, *v.t.* to inlay, to incrust.

marchetaria, *s.f.* inlaid work, marquetry.

marcial, *adj.* martial, military; warlike.

marciano, *s.m.* e *adj.* martian.

marco, *s.m.* boundary mark, landmark; mark *(moeda alemã), marco de correio,* pillar-box.

Março, *s.m.* March.

maré, *s.f.* tide. 1) *maré alta,* high tide. 2) *maré baixa,* low tide. 3) *maré viva,* spring-tide. 4) *a maré está a encher,* the tide is rising. 5) *a maré está a vazar,* the tide is falling. 6) *estar de maré,* to be well disposed. 7) *remar contra a maré,* to be against the stream. 8) *aprovar a maré,* to ride the tide.

mareado, *adj.* seasick.

marear, *v.t.* to sail, to steer; to trim *(velas);* to become seasick; to lose lustre.

marechal, *s.m.* marshal.

marechalato, *s.m.* marshalship.

marejado, *adj. marejado de lágrimas,* brimming with tears, filled with tears.

marejar, *v.t.* to exude; to ooze; *marejar-se,* to become filled with tears.

maremoto, *s.m.* seaquake.

maresia, *s.f.* sea smell at low tide.

marfim, *s.m.* ivory.

marga, *s.f.* marl.

margarida, *s.f.* daisy.

margarina, *s.f.* margarine.

margear, *v.t.* to border, to marginate; to run alongside of.

margem, *s.g.* margin; border; riverside; edge; borderline, limit; bank, shore. 1) *à margem,* aside. 2) *pôr à margem,* to put to lay aside.

marginal, *adj.* marginal; side.

margueira, *s.f.* marl-pit.

mariano, *adj.* e *s.m.* Marian.

maricas, *adj.* e *s.m.* sissy, milksop.

marido, *s.m.* husband, spouse.

marimba, *s.f.* marimba.

marinha, *s.f.* navy; marine; salt-pit *(salina).* 1) *marinha de guerra,* navy. 2) *marinha mercante,* merchant marine.

marinhagem, *s.f.* crew.

marinhar, *v.i.* to sail, to navigate, to man *(um navio)*; to climb.

marinheiro, *s.m.* sailor, mariner, seaman.

marinho, *adj.* marine, maritime; sea *(atr.)*.

mariola, *s.m.* porter; rascal, scoundrel.

marioneta, *s.f.* marionette, puppet.

mariposa, *s.f.* moth, butterfly.

marisco, *s.m.* shell-fish.

marisma, *s.f.* marshy area on the seashore.

marital, *adj.* marital.

maritalmente, *adv.* maritally.

marítimo, *adj.* maritime, marine; sea *(atr.)*; *s.m.* sailor, seaman.

marmanjo, *s.m.* rough man, brute.

marmelada, *s.f.* quince jam, quince marmalade.

marmeleiro, *s.m.* quince-tree.

marmelo, *s.m.* quince.

marmita, *s.f.* pot, lunch pail; mess kit.

mármore, *s.m.* marble.

marmoreira, *s.f.* marble-quarry.

marmóreo, *adj.* marmoreal, marble-like.

marmoriasta, *s.* marble-cutter.

marmota, *s.f.* marmot.

marosca, *s.f.* trick, trickery, plot.

maroteira, *s.f.* rascality, knavish trick.

maroto, *s.m.* rascal, scoundrel, rogue; *adj.* knavish, roguish, malicious.

marquês, *s.m.* marquis.

marquesa, *s.f.* marquise; settee *(móvel)*.

marquise, *s.f.* marquee.

marrada, *s.f.* butt; thrust with a horn.

marrano, *adj.* cursed; unclean, impure.

marrão, *s.m.* weaned pig.

marrar, *v.i.* to butt.

marreca, *s.f.* hump; hunchback.

marreco, *s.m.* duck; *adj.* hunchbacked.

marreta, *s.f.* stonemason`s hammer, stone hammer.

marretada, *s.f.* blow with a stonemason`s hammer.

marroquino, *s.m.* e *adj.* Moroccan.

marsupial, *s.m.* e *adj.* marsupial.

marsúpio, *s.m.* marsupial pouch.

marta, *s.f.* marten.

Marte, *s.m.* Mars.

martelada, *s.f.* blow with a hammer.

martelagem, *s.f.* hammering.

martelar, *v.t.* to hammer.

martelo, *s.m.* hammer.

martinete, *s.m.* steam hammer; hammer *(de piano)*.

mártir, *s.* martyr.

martírio, *s.m.* martyrdom; torment, pain.

martirizar, *v.t.* to martyrize, to torment.

marujo, *s.m.* sailor, seaman.

marulhar, *v.i.* to surge, to roar.

marulho, *s.m.* pounding of the surf; noise.

marxismo, *s.m.* marxism.

marxista, *s.* marxist.

mas, *conj.* but, however, yet, only, still, even; *s.m.* objection, hindrance; *não há mas nem meio mas,* but me no buts.´

mascar, *v.t.* to chew; to mumble *(palavras)*.

máscara, *s.f.* mask; disguise; veil; *baile de máscaras,* fancy dress ball.

mascarada, *s.f.* masquerade.

mascarado, *adj.* masked, disguised.

mascarar, *v.t.* to mask, to disguise; *mascarar-se,* to disguise oneself; to dress as; to put on a mask.

mascarilha, *s.f.* half-mask.

mascarra, *s.f.* stain, spot.

mascarrar, *v.t.* to stain, to soil, to taint.

mascate, *s.m.* hawker, street peddler.

mascavado, *adj.* unrefined, raw.

mascote, *s.m.* mascot.

masculinidade, *s.f.* masculinity, virility; manhood.

masculinizar, *v.t.* to render masculine.

masculino, *adj.* masculine, male; virile; mannish.

másculo, *adj.* robust, strong, manly.

masmorra, *s.f.* dungeon.

masoquismo, *s.m.* masochism.

masoquista, *s.* e *adj.* masochist.

massa, *s.f.* mass, volume, bulk; paste *(alimentícia),* dough *(de pão, bolos, etc.)*; mortar *(para paredes)*. 1) *massa de vidraceiro,* putty. 2) *as massas,* the masses. 3) *em massa,* in a mass, altogether.

massacrar, *v.t.* to massacre, to slaughter.

massacre, *s.m.* massacre, slaughter.

massagem, *s.f.* massage.

massagista, *s.* masseur, masseuse *(fem.)*.

masseira, *s.f.* kneading trough.

massudo, *adj.* voluminous, bulky; massive, compact.

mastaréu, *s.m.* small mast, topmast.

mastigação, *s.f.* mastication, chewing.

mastigar, *v.t.* to masticate, to chew; to ruminate.

mastim, *s.m.* watch-dog, mastiff.

mastite, *s.f.* mastitis.

mastodonte, *s.m.* mastodon.

mastreação, *s.f.* masting of ships, masts.

mastrear, *v.t.* to mast.

mastro, *s.m.* mast; pole; staff.

masturbação, *s.f.* masturbation.

masturbar-se, *v.refl.* to masturbate.

mata, *s.f.* wood, thicket.

mata-borrão, *s.m.* blotting-paper.

matacão, *s.m.* boulder.

matador, *s.m.* killer; murderer; matador *(na tourada).*

matadouro, *s.m.* slaughterhouse.

matagal, *s.m.* thicket, brushwood.

matalotagem, *s.f.* provisions, food supplies; jumble *(mixórdia).*

matança, *s.f.* killing; slaughter, butchery.

matar, *v.t.* to kill; to put to death; to murder; to quench *(sede);* to satisfy *(fome);* to while away *(o tempo); matar-se,* to kill oneself, to commit suicide.

mata-ratos, *s.m.* rat poison.

mate, *s.m.* mate *(no xadrez);* casting off *(no tricô); adj.* dim, unpolished, dull.

mateiro, *s.m.* forest keeper.

matemática, *s.f.* mathematics.

matemático, *s.m.* mathematician; *adj.* mathematical.

matéria, *s.f.* matter; material, stuff; subject, affair.

material, *adj.* material; phisical; concrete; earthly; bodily, corporeal; *s.m.* material; stuff; substance.

materialidade, *s.f.* materiality.

materialismo, *s.m.* materialism.

materialização, *s.f.* materialization.

materializar, *v.t.* to materialize.

matéria-prima, *s.f.* raw material.

maternal, *adj.* maternal, motherly.

maternidade, *s.f.* maternity, motherhood; maternity hospital.

materno, *adj.* maternal, motherly; *língua materna,* native language, mother tongue.

matias, *s.* simpleton, foolish person; *adj.* foolish, stupid.

matilha, *s.f.* pack.

matinal, *adj.* matinal, matutine, morning *(atr.).*

matinas, *s.f. pl.* matins.

matiz, *s.m.* shade, tinta; hue; tinge; blend of colours.

matizado, *adj.* variegated, many hued, many-coloured.

matizar, *v.t.* to shade, to tint, to tinge; to blend.

mato, *s.m.* brushwood, scrub; bush; woods.

matraca, *s.f.* rattle.

matraquear, *v.t.* to rattle; to clatter.

matreirice, *s.f.* craftiness, cunning, slyness.

matreiro, *adj.* cunning, crafty, wily, sly.

matriarca, *s.f.* matriarch.

matriarcado, *s.m.* matriarchy.

matriarcal, *adj.* matriarchal.

matricial, *adj.* original, primordial, main.

matricida, *s.* matricide.

matricídio, *s.m.* matricide.

matrícula, *s.f.* matriculation; registration; enrolment; matriculation fee.

matriculado, *adj.* matriculated, registered.

matricular, *v.t.* to matriculate, to register, to enroll.

matrimonial, *adj.* matrimonial; conjugal.

matrimónio, *s.m.* matrimony, marriage.

matriz, *s.f.* matrix, womb; origin, source; *igreja-matriz,* mother church; *adj.* principal, original.

matroca, *s.f. à matroca,* at random.

matrona, *s.f.* matron.

matulagem, *s.f.* gang; vagrancy.

matulão, *s.m.* vagrant; strong man.

maturação, *s.f.* maturation, ripening; development.

maturar, *v.t.* e *v.i.* to mature, to ripen.

maturidade, *s.f.* maturity, ripeness.

maturo, *adj.* o mesmo que "maduro".

matutar, *v.i.* to muse, to ponder, to think, to brood.

matutino, *adj.* matutinal; morning *(atr.)* early-rising; *s.m.* morning paper.

matuto, *s.m.* backwoodman, simpleton; rustic person.

mau, *adj.* bad; evil; wicked; mean; malignant; foul; nasty; vile; poor, inferior; wrong; mis (misconduct, misbehaviour, etc.)

mau-olhado, *s.m.* evil-eye.

mauritano, *s.m.* e *adj.* Mauretanian.

mausoléu, *s.m.* mausoleum.

maviosidade, *s.f.* tenderness, gentleness, softness; harmony.

mavioso, *adj.* tender, soft, gentle; melodious, harmonious.

maxila, *s.f.* maxilla, jaw.

maxilar, *s.m.* maxillary bone; jawbone; *adj.* maxillary.

máxima, *s.f.* maxima, aphorism, proverb.

máximo, *adj.* greatest; maximum; *s.m.* maximum; top; *no máximo,* at most.

mazela, *s.f.* wound, sore; disease, illness; blemish.

mazurca, *s.f.* mazurka.

me, *pron. pess.* me, myself; to me.

meada, *s.f.* skein; hank.

meado, *adj.* halved, divided; *s.m.* middle; *nos meados de,* in the middle of.

mealheiro, *s.m.* piggy bank, money box.

meandro, *s.m.* meander(ing), winding, sinuosity.

meão, *adj.* medium, average; mediocre.

mear, *v.t.* to divide into two equal parts, to halve; to reach the middle.

mecânica, *s.f.* mechanics.

mecanicismo, *s.m.* mechanicism.

mecânico, *s.m.* mechanician, mechanic; *adj.* mechanical.

mecanismo, *s.m.* mechanism, gear, machinery.

mecanização, *s.f.* mechanization.

mecanizar, *v.t.* to mechanize.

meças, *s.f. (pl.)* measuring; comparision; *pedir meças,* to ask for a verification, to demand proofs.

mecha, *s.f.* wick, fuse; cotton plug *(para ferida); (carp.)* tenon.

meda, *s.f.* heap; rick *(de feno);* stack *(de palha).*

medalha, *s.f.* medal.

medalhão, *s.m.* medallion, locket.

medalhar, *v.t.* to engrave on a medal; to reward with a medal.

medalhista, *s.m.* an expert on medals, medal maker.

medalhística, *s.f.* study of medals.

média, *s.f.* average; mean *(aritmética, geométrica, etc.); em média,* on an average.

mediação, *s.f.* mediation; intervention.

mediador, *s.m.* mediator, intermediary; *adj.* mediating.

medial, *adj.* medial.

mediana, *s.f.* median.

medianeiro, *adj.* e *s.m.* o mesmo que "mediador".

mediania, *s.f.* mediocrity; moderation; average conditions.

mediano, *adj.* median, medium, common.

mediante, *adj.* intervening; *prep.* by means of, through.

mediar, *v.t.* to mediate; to intervene; to occur in the meantime; to lie between, to be in the middle.

mediato, *adj.* mediate, indirect, secondary.

mediatriz, *s.f.* mediatrix.

médica, *s.f.* woman physician.

medicação, *s.f.* medication, medical treatment.

medicamentar, *v.t.* to prescribe, to medicate.

medicamento, *s.m.* medicine, remedy.

medicamentoso, *adj.* medicamental, medicinal.

medição, *s.f.* measurement; measuring.

medicar, *v.t.* to medicate, to prescribe.

medicastro, *s.m.* quack.

medicável, *adj.* medicable.

medicina, *s.f.* medicine.

medicinal, *adj.* medicinal.

médico, *s.* physician, doctor, practitioner; *adj.* medical. 1) *médico de clínica geral,* general practitioner. 2) *médico assistente,* family doctor. 3) *médico legista,* coroner.

medida, *s.f.* measure; measurement; extent, size, quantity; proportion. 1) *medidas de comprimento,* long measure. 2) *medidas de superfície,* square measure. 3) *medidas de volume,* solid measure. 4) *à medida que:* while, at the same time that, according as. 5) *encher as medidas,* to fill the bill. 6) *feito por medida,* tailor made *(vestuário),* made to order. 7) *tomar medidas,* to take steps, to take measures.

medieval, *adj.* mediaeval.

medievo, *adj.* mediaeval.

médio, *adj.* medial, intermediate, median, middle, average, mean; *s.m.* halfback *(fut.).*

mediocre, *adj.* mediocre, common, ordinary; insignificant, second-rate.

mediocridade, *s.f.* mediocrity, commonness.

medir, *v.t.* to measure; to gauge; to size up; to weigh; to judge *(as palavras);* to survey *(terrenos).*

meditabundo, *adj.* meditative, musing; melancholic, thoughtful.

meditação, *s.f.* meditation, cogitation.

meditadamente, *adv.* calmly, well-thought.

meditar, *v.t.* to meditate, to think, to ponder, to cogitate, to reflect.

meditativo, *adj.* meditative.

médium, *s.* medium.

medo, *s.m.* fear, fright, dread, awe; *ter medo de,* to be afraid of.

medonho, *adj.* awful, frightful, horrible, fearful, hideous.

medrança, *s.f.* growth, development.

medrar, *v.i.* to grow, to increase, to progress, to thrive, to flourish, to prosper.

medricas, *adj.* chickenhearted.

medronheiro, *s.m.* arbutus.

medronho, *s.m.* arbutus.

medroso, *adj.* fearful, timorous, chickenhearted.

medula, *s.f. (anat.)* medulla; marrow *(de osso); (bot.)* medulla, pith; heart, core, essence; *espinal medula,* spinal cord.

medular, *adj.* medullary, pithy.

medusa, *s.f.* jellyfish.

meeiro, *s.m.* profit-sharer.

mefistofélico, *adj.* Mephistophelian, diabolic.

mefítico, *adj.* mephitic; noxious.

megafone, *s.m.* megaphone.

megalítico, *adj.* megalithic.

megálito, *s.m.* megalith.

megalomania, *s.f.* megalomania.

megalómano, *s.m. e adj.* megalomaniac.

megera, *s.f.* harridan, vixen, termagant.

meia, *s.f.* stocking *(de senhora);* sock *(meia curta); a meias,* fifty-fifty.

meia-idade, *s.f.* middle-age.

meia-lua, *s.f.* crescent, half-moon.

meia-noite, *s.f.* midnight.

meias-palavras, *s.f. (pl.)* subterfuges.

meia-volta, *s.f.* half-turn; *meia-volta volver!* about face!

meia-voz, *s.f. a meia-voz:* undertone.

meigo, *adj.* tender, gentle, meek, affectionate.

meiguice, *s.f.* tenderness, meekness, gentleness.

meio, *s.m.* middle; midst; center; medium; element, environment, surrounding; instrument, means, way, resource; *(pl.)* wealth, resources. 1) *meio de vida,* living, livelihood. 2) *dividir ao meio,* to divide in half. 3) *no meio de,* among, between. 4) *no meio do Verão,* in mid-summer. 5) *por meio de,* by means of. 6) *meio de transporte,* means of transport; *adj.* half; *adv.* a little, somewhat, half; *(fam.)* kind of. 7) *meio morto,* half dead. 8) *meio assustado,* kind of scared.

meio-corpo, *s.m.* bust.

meio-dia, *s.m.* midday, noon.

meio-soprano, *s.* mezzo-soprano.

meio-termo, *s.m.* middle course; compromise.

meio-tom, *s.m.* half-tone.

meirinho, *s.m.* bailiff.

mel, *s.m.* honey.

melaço, *s.m.* molasses.

melado, *adj.* honey-coloured, sweet as honey; sticky.

melancia, *s.f.* watermelon.

melancolia, *s.f.* melancholy; sadness, gloominess; the blues.

melancólico, *adj.* melancholic, gloomy, sad, low-spirited.

melanina, *s.f.* melanine.

melão, *s.m.* melon.

melena, *s.f.* long and disheveled hair; lock of hair.

melga, *s.f.* gnat, midge.

melhor, *adj.* better, best. 1) *levar a melhor,* to get the best. 2) *cada vez melhor,* better and better. 3) *tanto melhor,* so much the bettet. 4) *era melhor ficar em casa,* you had bette to stay at home. 5) *quanto mais melhor,* the more the better. 6) *o melhor,* the best.

melhora, *s.f.* improvement, amelioration, betterment.

melhoramento, *s.m.* improvement, amelioration; progress, benefit.

melhorar, *v.t.* to ameliorate, to improve, to make better; to get better, to recover; to get fine *(o tempo).*

melhoria, *s.f.* improvement; betterment; rise.

meliante, *s.m.* scoundrel, rascal.

melifluidade, *s.f.* mellifluence, mildness.

melífluo, *adj.* mellifluous; smooth-tongued.

melindrar, *v.t.* to offend, to vex, to hurt; *melindrar-se,* to resent, to take offense.

melindre, *s.m.* susceptibility, delicacy.

melindroso, *adj.* susceptible, sensitive; resentful; coy; prudish.

melissa, *s.f.* balm.

melodia, *s.f.* melody, tune.

melódico, *adj.* melodic, melodious.

melodioso, *adj.* melodious, harmonious; musical.

melodista, *s.* melodist.

melodrama, *s.m.* melodrama.

melodramático, *adj.* melodramatic.

melomania, *s.f.* melomania.

melomaníaco, *s.m.* melomaniac.

melopeia, *s.f.* singsong.

meloso, *adj.* sweet; sticky.

melquetrefe, *s.m.* rascal.

melro, *s.m.* blackbird.

membrana, *s.f.* membrane; *membrana interdigital,* web.

membranoso, *adj.* membranous; filmy.

membro, *s.m.* member; limb *(do corpo).*

memento, *s.m.* momento; reminder, memorandum; note-book.

memorando, *s.m.* memorandum, note; *adj.* memorable, worth remembering.

memorável, *adj.* memorable, remarkable.

memória, *s.f.* memory; remembrance, recollection; fame, renown; record; memoir.

memorial, *s.m.* memorial.

memorização, *s.f.* memorization.

memorizar, *v.t.* to memorize.

menagem, *s.f.* homage; *torre de menagem,* main tower of a mediaeval castle.

menção, *s.f.* mention, reference, citation; indication. 1) *fazer menção de,* to make as if. 2) *menção honrosa,* honourable mention.

mencionar, *v.t.* to mention, to refer, to allude to, to name.

mendacidade, *s.f.* mendacitiu, untruthfulness.

mendaz, *adj.* mendacious, lying, untruthful.

mendicância, *s.f.* mendicity, begging.

mendicante, *adj.* mendicent, begging; *s.* beggar.

mendicidade, *s.f.* o mesmo que "mendicância".

mendigar, *v.t.* e *v.i.* to beg.

mendigo, *s.m.* beggar, mendicant.

mendinho, *s.m.* little finger.

menear, *v.t.* to wag; to swing; to toss *(a cabeça).*

meneio, *s.m.* swaying; wagging; wiggle.

menestrel, *s.m.* minstrel, poet, troubadour.

menina, *s.f.* miss, young lady, girl. 1) *menina do olho,* pupil. 2) *ser a menina dos olhos de alguém,* to be the apple of someone`s eye.

menineiro, *adj.* childlike, childish.

meninge, *s.f.* meninx; *(pl.)* meninges.

meningite, *s.f.* meningitis.

meninice, *s.f.* childhood.

menino, *s.m.* little boy; *menino de coro,* choir boy.

menisco, *s.m.* meniscus.

menopausa, *s.f.* menopause.

menor, *adj.* smaller; less, lesser; *s.* minor, underage.

menoridade, *s.f.* minority.

menorreia, *s.f.* menorrhoea.

menos, *pron. ind.* less; *adv.* less. 1) *a menos,* lacking, wanting. 2) *a menos que,* unless. 3) *ao menos,* at least; *prep.* except, save, but, lest; *s.m.* the least, minus.

menosprezar, *v.t.* to despise, to hold in contempt; to understimate, to undervalue.

menosprezo, *s.m.* contempt, scorn, disdain.

mensageiro, *s.m.* messenger, courier; herald.

mensagem, *s.f.* message communication.

mensal, *adj.* monthly.

mensalidade, *s.* montlhy payment.

mensário, *s.m.* monthly publication.

menstruação, *s.f.* menstruation, menses.

menstruada, *adj.* menstruant.

menstrual, *adj.* menstrual.

menstruar, *v.i.* to menstruate.

mensurável, *adj.* measurable.

mental, *adj.* mental; intellectual.

mentalidade, *s.f.* mentality, mind.

mente, *s.f.* mind, intellect, understanding; disposition; intention, purpose. 1) *ter em mente,* to keep in mind. 2) *vir à mente,* to occur.

mentecapto, *adj.* mad, demented; foolish.

mentir, *v.i.* to lie, to deceive, to tell a lie.

mentira, *s.f.* lie; falsehood.

mentiroso, *s.m.* lier; *adj.* lying, untruthful, false.

mento, *s.m.* chin.

mentol, *s.m.* menthol.

mentolado, *adj.* mentholated.

mentor, *s.m.* mentor, guide, adviser.

menu, *s.m.* menu.

meramente, *adv.* merely, simply, only.

mercadejar, *v.i.* to trade, to traffic.

mercado, *s.m.* market; market place; trade center; commerce.

mercador, *s.m.* merchant, trader, dealer.

mercadoria, *s.f.* merchandise, commodity; goods.

mercante, *adj.* merchant, mercantile, commercial; *marinha mercante,* merchant marine.

mercantil, *adj.* mercantile, commercial.

mercantilismo, *s.m.* mercantilism.

mercantilista, *adj.* e *s.* mercantilist.

mercar, *v.t.* to buy, to purchase; to trade.

mercê, *s.f.* grace, mercy; benefit; favor; gift. 1) *mercê de,* thanks to, owing to. 2) *à mercê de,* at the mercy of.

mercearia, *s.f.* grocery, grocer`s.

merceeiro, *s.m.* grocer.

mercenário, *s.m.* e *adj.* mercenary.

mercenarismo, *s.m.* mercenariness; greed.

mercerização, *s.f.* mercerization.

mercerizar, *v.t.* to mercerize.

mercúrio, *s.m.* mercury; Mercury *(deus ou planeta).*

mercurocromo, *s.m.* mercurochrome.

merda, *s.f. (pop.)* excrement; *interj.* shit!

merecedor, *adj.* worthy, deserving.

merecer, *v.t.* to deserve, to be worthy of, to merit.

merecido, *adj.* due, just, deserved.

merecimento, *s.m.* merit, desert.

merenda, *s.f.* snack, light meal.

merendar, *v.t.* to have a snack, to picnic.

merengue, s.m. meringue.

meretriz, s.f. prostitute, whore.

mergulhador, s.m. diver.

mergulhante, adj. diving.

mergulhão, s.m. grebe.

mergulhar, v.i. to dive, to plunge, to dip; to submerge.

mergulho, s.m. dive, plunge, dip.

meridiana, s.f. meridian line.

meridiano, s.m. e adj. meridian.

meridional, adj. meridional, southern, austral.

merino, s.m. e adj. merino.

meretíssimo, adj. most-worthy; Your Honour (dirigindo-se a um juiz).

mérito, s.m. merit, worthiness, desert.

meritório, adj. meritorious, worthy, deserving.

mero, adj. mere, simple, shere.

mês, s.m. month.

mesa, s.f. table; board (de assembleia). 1) pôr a mesa, to set the table. 2) tirar a mesa, to clear the table. 3) servir à mesa, to wait at table.

mesada, s.f. monthly allowance.

mesário, s.m. board member.

mescla, s.f. mixture; jumble; medley.

mesclado, adj. mixed; motley, variegated.

mesclar, v.t. to mix, to mingle, to variegate.

mesets, s.f. small plateau.

mesmerismo, s.m. mesmerism, magnetism.

mesma, s.f. Ver "mesmo". 1) na mesma, unchanged, just the same. 2) o estado do doente continua na mesma, the patient`s condition is still the same.

mesmíssimo, adj. the very same.

mesmo, adj. e pron. same, identical, unchanged, equal. 1) eu mesmo o fiz, I did it myself. 2) este mesmo homem, this very man; adv. exactly, right, just; even; indeed; really; the same (pessoa ou coisa). 3) agora mesmo, right now. 4) mesmo assim, even so. 5) mesmo que, even if, even though. 6) nem mesmo, not even.

mesocarpo, s.m. mesocarp.

mesolítico, adj. mesolithic.

mesquinhez, s.f. stinginess; perriness; meanness; trifle.

mesquinho, adj. stingy, mean, niggardly, narrow-minded.

mesquita, s.f. mosque.

messe, s.f. harvest, crop; officer`s mess.

messiânico, adj. messianic.

messianismo, s.m. messianism.

messias, s.m. Messiah; liberator.

mestiçagem, s.f. miscegenation, crossbreading, interbreeding.

mestiçar, v.i. to crossbreed, to interbreed.

mestiço, s.m. half-breed, crossbred; hybrid; mongrel; mestizo; adj. crossbred, half-blooded; of mixed blood.

mestra, s.f. schoolmistress, teacher; forewoman.

mestre, s.m. master; teacher, schoolmaster; foreman; (mar.) boat swain. 1) mestre-de--cerimónias, master of ceremonies. 2) mestre-de-armas, fencing master. 3) mestre-de-obras, foreman; adj. chief, principal, main.

mestria, s.f. mastery, expertness.

mesura, s.f. bow, reverence, curtsy.

mesureiro, adj. obsequious, servile.

meta, s.f. limit, goal; finish-line.

metabolismo, s.m. metabolism.

metacarpo, s.m. metacarpus.

metade, s.f. half.

metafísica, s.f. metaphysics.

metafísico, adj. metaphysical, trancendental; s.m. metaphysician.

metáfora, s.f. metaphor.

metal, s.m. metal; pl. (mús.) brass instruments; metal sonante, hard cash.

metálico, adj. metallic.

metalífero, adj. metalliferous.

metalizar, v.t. to metallize.

metalóide, s.m. nonmetal, metalloid.

metalurgia, s.f. metallurgy.

metalúrgico, adj. metallurgic(al); s.m. metallurgist.

metamorfismo, s.m. metamorphism.

metamorfose, s.f. metamorphosis.

metamorfosear, v.t. to metamorphose; to transform; to turn into.

metano, s.m. methane.

metástase, s.f. metastasis.

metatarso, s.m. metatarsus.

metazoários, s.m. metazoa.

metediço, adj. meddlesome, intrusive.

meteórico, adj. meteoric.

meteorismo, s.m. meteorism.

meteorito, s.m. meteorite.

meteoro, s.m. meteor.

meteorologia, s.f. meteorology.

meteorológico, adj. meteorological; boletim meteorológico, weather forecast.

meteorologista, s.m. meteorologist.

meter, v.t. to put in, to introduce, to insert; to lay, to set; to thrust, to stick, to tuck in; to inspire *(medo).* 1) *meter-se,* to interfere, to intrude; to penetrate, to pierce; to get, to get oneself into. 2) *meter-se em trabalhos,* to get into trouble. 3) *meter-se ondse não é chamado,* to meddle with other`s affairs. 4) *meter-se com alguém,* to provoke someone, to pick a quarrel with, to get involved with.

meticulosamente, *adv.* meticulously.

meticulosidade, *s.f.* meticulousness, meticulosity; precision.

meticuloso, *adj.* meticulous, precise.

metido, *adj.* meddlesome; put in, introduced.

metileno, *s.m.* methylene.

metilo, *s.m.* methyl.

metódico, *adj.* methodical, systematic.

metodismo, *s.m.* methodism.

metodista, *s.* methodist.

metodizar, *v.t.* to methodize, to arrange with method.

método, *s.m.* method, manner, way, procedure; rule, order.

metodologia, *s.f.* methodology.

metonímia, *s.f.* metonymy.

metralha, *s.f.* grapeshot, shrapnel; rubble *(entulho).*

metralhadora, *s.f.* machine-gun.

metralhar, *v.t.* to machine-gun.

métrica, *s.f.* metrics.

métrico, *adj.* metric(al); *fita métrica,* tape measure.

metrificação, *s.m.* versification.

metro, *s.m.* meter; *(meio de transporte)* subway, underground, tube *(em Lisboa).*

metrópole, *s.f.* metropolis, capital; mother country.

metropolitano, *adj.* metropolitan; *s.m.* ver "metro".

meu, *pron. poss.* mine; *adj.* my.

mexedela, *s.f.* stirring.

mexer, *v.t.* e *v.i.* to stir; to move; to wag *(abanar),* to shake; to touch; to bidge; to meddle; to mix up; *mexer os cordelinhos:* to pull the strings.

mexericar, *v.i.* to gossip, to tittle-tattle, to intrigue.

mexerico, *s.m.* gossiping, talebearing, intrigue.

mexeriqueiro, *s.m.* talebearer, telltale, intriguer, busybody; *adj.* gossiping, tattling, talebearing.

mexeriquice, *s.f.* gossip, intrigue.

mexicano, *s.* e *adj.* mexican.

mexida, *s.f.* disorder, confusion, mess, jumble.

mexido, *adj.* active, lively; stirred, mixed; *ovos mexidos,* scambled eggs.

mexilhão, *s.m.* mussel.

mezena, *s.f. (náut.)* mizen.

mezinha, *s.f.* household medicine.

mi, *s.m.* mi.

miado, *s.m.* miaow.

miar, *v.i.* to mew, to miaow.

miasma, *s.m.* miasma.

miau, *s.m.* miaow.

mica, *s.f.* mica, isinglass.

micção, *s.f.* urination.

mico, *s.m.* small monkey.

micose, *s.f.* mycosis.

micro, *s.m.* micron.

microbiano, *adj.* microbial.

microbicida, *s.m.* microbicide, bactericide; *adj.* microbicidal.

micróbio, *s.m.* microbe, bacterium.

microbiologia, *s.f.* microbiology.

microcefalia, *s.f.* microcephaly.

microcéfalo, *adj.* microcephlous.

microcósmico, *adj.* microcosmic.

microcosmo, *s.m.* microcosm.

microfilme, *s.m.* microfilm.

microfone, *s.m.* microphone.

micrologia, *s.f.* micrology.

micrómetro, *s.m.* micrometer.

mícron, *s.m.* micron.

micro onda, *s.f.* microwave.

micro organismo, *s.m.* microorganism.

microscópico, *adj.* microscopic.

microscópio, *s.m.* microscope.

mictório, *s.m.* public urinal; *adj.* diuretic.

miga, *s.f.* bread-soup.

migalha, *s.f.* crumb; bit, particle, fragment; scraps *(da mesa).*

migar, *v.t.* to crumble; to crush.

migração, *s.f.* migration.

migrador, migrante, *adj.* migrating, migrant.

migrar, *v.i.* to migrate.

migratório, *adj.* migratory.

mija, *s.f. (pop.)* urine, pissing; *fazer uma mija,* to piss.

mijão, *s.m.* bed-wetter; coward.

mijar, *v.t.* to urinate, to piss.

mijo, *s.m. (pop.)* urine, pissing.

mil, *num.* thousand.

milagre, *s.m.* miracle, wonder, prodigy. 1) *fazer um milagre,* to work a miracle. 2) *por milagre,* miraculously.

milagreiro, *s.m.* wonder-worker.

milagroso, *adj.* miraculous; supernatural.

milanês, *s. adj.* Milanese.

míldio, *s.m.* mildew.

milenário, *adj.* millennial; age-old.

milénio, s. m. millenium.

milésimo, *adj.* millesimal, thousandth; *s.m.* millesimal, thousand part.

milha, *s.f.* mile.

milhafre, *s.m.* kite.

milhão, *num.* million.

milhar, *num.* a thousand; *aos milhares,* by the thousand.

milheiral, *s.m.* maize-field, corn-field.

milheiro, *s.m.* a thousand.

milhentas, *s.f. pl.* too many.

milho, *s.m.* maize, Indian corn, (E. U.) corn.

milícia, *s.f.* militia, military force.

miliciano, *s.m.* militiaman,

miligrama, *s.m.* milligramme.

mililitro, *s.m.* millilitre.

milímetro, *s.m.* millimetre.

milionário, *s.m.* millionaire.

milionésimo, *adj.* e *s.m.* millionth.

militância, *s.f.* militancy.

militante, *adj.* militant.

militar, *adj.* military; soldier; *s.* military man, soldier; *v.t.* to serve as a solldier; to militate.

militarismo, *s.m.* militarism.

militarista, *adj.* militaristic; *s.* militarist.

militarização, *s.f.* militarization.

militarizar, *v.t.* to militarize.

milorde, *s.* milord, lord.

mim, *pron. pess.* me.

mimalho, *adj.* spoilt; *s.m.* pet, mollycoddle.

mimar, *v.t.* to caress, to fondle, to pet; to spoil.

mimetismo, *s.m.* protective mimicry; simulation.

mímica, *s.f.* mimicry, mimicking, dumb-show.

mímico, *adj.* mimic, imitative.

mimo, *s.m.* mime *(o que faz mímica);* caress, tenderness, petting, fondling.

mimosa, *s.f. (bot.)* mimosa.

mimosear, *v.t.* to offer, to present (someone with something).

mimoso, *adj.* delicate, gentle, sensitive.

mina, *s.f.* mine; lead *(de lapiseira);* source, fountain.

minar, *v.t.* to mine; to dig; to undermine, to destroy, to subvert.

minarete, *s.m.* minaret.

minaz, *adj.* menacing.

mindinho, *s.m.* the little finger.

mineiro, *s.m.* miner; *adj.* mining.

mineração, *s.f.* mining; purification of ores.

mineral, *s.* e *adj.* mineral.

mineralogia, *s.f.* mineralogy.

mineralógico, *adj.* mineralogical.

mineralogista, *s.* mineralogist.

minério, *s.m.* ore.

míngua, *s.f.* lack, want, need shortage. 1) *à míngua de,* for want of. 2) *morrer à míngua,* to die of starvation.

minguado, *adj.* wanting, locking; scant, thin.

minguante, *adj.* waning, decreasing; 1) *quarto minguante:* last quarter.

minguar, *v.i.* to decrease, to wane, to become scace, to diminish; to lack, to miss; to fall off.

minha, *pron. pess.* mine; *adj.* my.

minhoca, *s.f.* earthworm, angleworm.

miniatura, *s.f.* miniature.

miniaturizar, *v.t.* to miniature.

miniaturista, *s.* miniature painter.

minifúndio, *s.m.* minifundium, small estate.

mínima, *s.f. (mús.)* minim.

minimizar, *v.t.* to minimize.

mínimo, *adj.* least; smallest; slightest; *s.m.* minimum, the least; the little finger; *no mínimo,* at least.

ministerial, *adj.* ministerial.

ministério, *s.m.* ministry cabinet: department; trade, profession; cabinet, body of ministers. 1) *Ministério do Interior,* Home Office. 2) *Ministério do Exército,* War Office. 3) *Ministério dos Negócios Estrangeiros,* Foreign Office. 4) *Ministério do Comércio,* Board of Trade. 5) *Ministério das Finanças,* the Exchequer, Treasurey Department. 6) *Ministério da Justiça,* Supreme Court of Justice. 7) *Ministério da Educação,* Ministry of Education. 8) *Ministério Público,* Prosecuting Office. 9) *Delegado do Ministério Público,* public prosecutor.

ministrar, *v.t.* to minister, to administer; to furnish, to supply; to give *(remédios).*

ministro, *s.m.* minister, secretary; priest.

minorar, *v.t.* to diminish, to lessen; to mitigate, to assuage, to soften.

minoria, *s.f.* minority.

minoritário, *adj.* of the minority.

minúcia, *s.f.* detail; trifle.

minuciosamente, *adv.* minutely; thoroughly.

minuciosidade, *s.f.* minuteness; thoroughness.

minucioso, *adj.* minute, detailed, thorough; precise, careful.

minudência, *s.f.* minuteness, preciseness, detail.

minuete, *s.m.* minuet.

minúscula, *s.f.* small letter.

minúsculo, *adj.* minuscule, small, tiny.

minuta, *s.f.* rough draft, minute; sketch.

minuto, *s.m.* minute.

miocárdio, *s.f.* miocardium.

mioleira, *s.f.* brains.

miolo, *s.m.* crumb *(de pão);* the brain; core; kernel.

míope, *s.m.* myope, short-sighted person; *adj.* myopic, short-shighted.

miopia, *s.f.* myopia, short-sightedness.

miose, *s.f.* myosis.

miosótis, *s.f.* forget-me-not.

mira, *s.f.* sight; aim, intent, purpose; view. 1) *linha de mira,* sight line. 2) *ter em mira,* to have in view.

mirabolante, *adj.* showy; gaudy.

miraculoso, *adj.* miraculous, wonderful, supernatural.

mirada, *s.f.* gaze, glance, view.

miradouro, *s.m.* belvedere.

miragem, *s.f.* mirage, illusion, vision.

mirante, *s.m. o mesmo que "miradouro".*

mirar, *v.t.* to look closely at; to stare at, to observe; *mirar-se,* to look at oneself.

miríade, *s.f.* myriad.

miriápode, *adj. e s.* myriapod.

mirífico, *adj.* marvelous, wonderful, amazing.

mirone, *s.m.* onlooker, spectator, bystander.

mirra, *s.f.* myrrh.

mirrado, *adj.* withered, dried up; lean.

mirrar, *v.t.* to dry up, to wither, to waste away.

mirto, *s.m.* myrtle.

misantropia, *s.f.* misanthropy.

misantrópico, *adj.* misanthropic(al).

misantropo, *adj. e s.m.* misanthrope.

miscelânea, *s.f.* miscellanny, medley; confusion; mixture.

miscigenação, *s.f.* miscigenation.

miserável, *adj.* miserable; poverty; unhappiness.

miséria, *s.f.* mercy, mercifulness, compassion.

misericordioso, *adj.* merciful, compassionate.

mísero, *adj.* miserable, unhappy, pitiable.

misogamia, *s.f.* misogamy.

misógamo, *s.m.* misogamist.

misoginia, *s.f.* misogyny.

misógino, *s.m.* misogynist.

missa, *s.f.* mass.

missal, *s.m.* missal, mass-book

missanga, *s.f.* glass-beads.

missão, *s.f.* mission; charge, comission; errand; delegation.

míssil, *s.m.* missile.

missionar, *v.t.* to preach, to evangelize.

missionário, *s.m.* missionary.

missiva, *s.f.* missive, letter.

mistela, *s.f.* hotchpot, mixture.

mister, *s.m.* business, occupation; want, need; *haver mister de,* to be in need of; to require.

mistério, *s.m.* mistery, secrecy.

misterioso, *adj.* misterious, secret.

mística, *s.f.* mysticism.

misticidade, *s.f.* mysticism.

místico, *adj.* mystic(al); occult, esoteric; *s.m.* mystic.

mistificação, *s.f.* mystification; fraud, deception.

mistificador, *s.m.* mystifier, cheater, deceiver; *adj.* mystifying.

mistificar, *v.t.* to mystify, hoax, to deceive.

misto, *adj.* mixed; *s.m.* mixture, compound.

mistral, *s.m.* mistral.

mistura, *s.f.* mixture, blend; compound; combination; medley.

misturada, *s.f.* jumble, mixture.

misturar, *v.t.* to mix, to blend; to mingle, to combine, to compound.

misturável, *adj.* miscible, blendable.

mísula, *s.f.* bracket, corbel.

mitene, *s.m.* mitten.

mítico, *adj.* mythic(al), fabulous, legendary.

mitificar, *v.t.* to mythicize, to mythify.

mitigação, *s.f.* mitigation, palliation, relief; moderation.

mitigador, *adj.* mitigating.

mitigar, *v.t.* to mitigate, to assuage, to ease, to relieve; to soften.

mitigativo, *adj.* mitigating, soothing.

mitigável, *adj.* mitigable.

mito, *s.m.* myth.

mitologia, *s.f.* mythology.

mitológico, *adj.* mythological.

mitólogo, *s.m.* mythologer.

mitose, *s.f.* mitosis.

mitra, *s.f.* mitre.

miudeza, *s.f.* smallness, minuteness; exactness; *(pl.)* trifles, details.

miudinho, *adj.* minute; stingy.

miúdo, *adj.* small, little; slender, slim; *s.m.* little boy, kid.

mixórdia, *s.f.* jumble, hodgepodge, hotchpotch, mixture.

mnemónica, s.f. mnemonics.

mnemonizar, v.t. to mnemonize.

mnemotecnia, s.f. mnemotechny.

mó, s.f. grindstone, mill-stone.

moageiro, s.m. miller.

moagem, s.g. milling, grinding.

móbil, v.t. to furnish, to provide with furnish.

mobília, s.f. furniture.

mobiliário, s.m. furniture.

mobilidade, s.f. mobility; changeableness.

mobilização, s.f. mobilization.

mobilizar, v.t. to mobilize; to put in circulation (capitais).

moca, s.f. club, cudgel; mocha (café).

moça, s.f. girl, young woman; lass; maiden.

moção, s.f. motion; proposal.

moçárabe, adj. mozarabic; s. mozarab.

mocetão, s.m. stout young fellow.

mochar, v.t. to cutt off the horns.

mochila, s.f. knapsack, rucksack; pack.

mocho, s.m. owl (ave); stool (assento); adj. hornless; polled.

mocidade, s.f. youth, youthfulness; young people.

moço, s.m. young man; adj. young.

moda, s.f. fashion; mode, stile; manner, way; custom; vogue; popular song. 1) à moda antiga, old-fashioned. 2) estar na moda, to follow the laest fashion, to be the fashion, to be fashionable. 3) fora de moda, old-fashioned, out of fashion. 4) loja de modas, dress shop. 5) à minha moda, in my own way.

modal, adj. modal.

modalidade, s.f. kind, form; aspect, manner, way.

modelagem, s.f. modelling, moulding.

modelar, v.t. to model, to shape, to fashion; to mold; to pattern; adj. model, exemplary.

modelarmente, adv. exemplarily.

modelo, s.m. model (de moda, de arte, etc.); mannequin; pattern; type; design; prototype; standard; example; original.

moderação, s.f. moderation, temperance; restraint; prudence.

moderado, adj. moderate, temperance; prudent, judicious; sparing.

moderador, s.m. moderator; regulator; adj. moderating, restraining.

moderar, v.t. to moderate; to temper; to reduce; to restrain; to control; moderar-se, to restrain oneself.

modernice, s.f. excessive modernism.

modernidade, s.f. modernity.

modernismo, s.m. modernism.

modernista, s. e adj. modernist.

modernização, s.f. modernization.

modernizar, v.t. to modernize; modernizar-se: to become modernized.

moderno, adj. modern; recent; up-to-date.

modéstia, s.f. modesty; demureness; plainness; simplicity.

modesto, adj. modest; simple,humble.

modicamente, adv. moderately.

modicidade, s.f. moderateness; lowness.

módico, adj. moderate, reasonable; small.

modificação, s.f. modification, change.

modificado, s.f. modified, changed, altered.

modificador, s.f. modifying.

modificar, v.t. to modify, to change, to alter.

modismo, s.m. idiom.

modista, s.f. dressmaker, modiste.

modo, s.m. manner, way; mode; fashion; method; means; disposition; humour, temper; (gram.) mood. 1) modo de falar, way of speaking. 2) modo de ver, point of view, way of thinking. 3) modo de vida, way of life. 4) de modo geral, generally speaking. 5) de modo que, so that, so, in order to. 6) de algum modo, de certo modo: somehow. 7) de modo algum, not at all, by no means. 8) de qualquer modo, anyhow, anyway. 9) desse modo, in that way. 10) de tal modo que, in such a manner that. 11) do mesmo modo, likewise, in the same way. 12) de mau modo, with a bad glance. 13) com bons modos, politely, with a good grace. 14) maus modos, bad manners.

modorra, s.f. torpor, lethargy, sleepiness, drowsiness.

modorrar, v.t. to drowse; to doze.

modulação, s.f. modulation; intonation; inflexion of voice.

modulador, adj. modulating.

modular, v.t. to modulate; to intone; to inflect.

módulo, s.m. (arquit.) module; modulus.

moeda, s.f. coin; piece; currency; money; Casa da Moeda, The Mint.

moedagem, s.f. coinage; mintage.

moedeiro, s.m. coiner, minter; moedeiro falso, counterfeiter.

moedura, s.f. grinding.

moela, s.f. gizzard.

moenda, s.f. grinder, mill; millstone, grinstone.

moer, v.t. to grind, to mill, to crush, to triturate; to harass, to annoy; to tire; moer de pancada, to beat black and blue.

mofa, *s.f.* mockery, scoffing, derision, scorn.

mofado, *v.t.* to muck, to scoff at, to deride; to grow musty, to mold.

mofino, *adj.* unhappy; mean, niggard; stingy.

mofo, *s.m.* mold, mustiness. 1) *cheirar a mofo,* to smell musty. 2) *criar mofo,* to grow mouldy.

mogno, *s.m.* mahogany.

moído, *adj.* ground, crushed; worn out.

moinha, *s.f.* chaff.

moinho, *s.m.* mill; grinder. 1) *moinho de água,* water mill. 2) *moínho de café,* coffee mill. 3) *moinho de vento,* windmill.

moirama, *s.f.* the Moors.

moiro, *s.m.* Moor; *adj.* moorish.

moita, *s.f.* thicket, bush; tussock *(de capim),* tuft.

mola, *s.f.* spring.

molar, *adj. e s.m.* molar.

moldador, *s.m.* moulder.

moldagem, *s.g.* moulding, casting.

moldar, *v.t.* to mould, to shape, to form; to cast *(ferro);* to adapt.

molde, *s.m.* mould; pattern; model.

moldura, *s.f.* frame.

mole, *adj.* soft; flabby, flaccid; slack; weak; *s.m.* enormous volume; a huge thing; bulk.

molécula, *s.f.* molecule.

molecular, *adj.* molecular.

moleirinha, *s.f.* fontanel.

moleiro, *s.m.* miller.

moleja, *s.f.* pancreas of animals.

molenga, *adj.* lazy, indolent.

molengão, *s.m.* stuggard; slacker; lazy-bones.

moleque, *s.m.* black boy; ragamuffin.

molestador, *s.m.* molester, harass; *adj.* molesting, disturbing.

molestar, *v.t.* to molest, to harass, to annoy; to trouble, to disturb; to hurt, to offend.

moléstia, *s.f.* disease, illness; annoyance.

molesto, *adj.* molesting, troublesome, annoying.

moleza, *s.f.* softness; lassitude; slackness; laziness; weakness.

molha, *s.f.* wetting; bath; *apanhar uma molha,* to get all wet through.

molhado, *adj.* wet; moist, damp.

molhar, *v.t.* to wet; to moisten; to soak; *molhar-se,* to get wet.

molhe, *s.m.* pier, jetty; quay; breakwater.

molheira, *s.f.* sauce-boat, gravy-boat.

molho, *s.m.* bundle; bunch; sheaf *(de trigo);* faggot *(de lenha).*

molho, *s.m.* suuce, gravy.

moliço, *s.m.* seaweed used as manure.

molificar, *v.t.* to mollify, to soften; to appease, to calm.

molinete, *s.m.* windlass; reel.

molosso, *s.m.* mastiff, big hound.

molusco, *s.m.* mollusk, mollusc.

momentâneo, *adj.* momentary, transitory; instantaneous.

momento, *s.m.* moment, instant.

momentoso, *adj.* momentous, important, serious.

momice, *s.f.* grimace, face.

momo, *s.m.* buffoon; mime.

mona, *s.f.* she-ape; doll.

monacal, *adj.* monachal, monastic.

monarca, *s.m.* monarch, sovereign, king.

monarquia, *s.f.* monarchy.

monárquico, *adj. e s.m.* monarchic.

monástico, *adj.* monastic(al).

monção, *s.f.* monsoon; opportunity.

monco, *s.m.* snivel, snot; wattle *(de perú).*

monda, *s.f.* weeding.

mondador, *s.m.* weeder.

mondar, *v.t.* to weed, to hoe; to trim; to cut out; to expurgate.

monetário, *adj.* monetary.

monge, *s.m.* monk, friar.

mongol, *s.* Mongol; *adj.* mongolian.

mongólico, *adj.* mongolina.

mongolismo, *s.m.* mongolism.

mongolóide, *adj.* mongoloid.

monismo, *s.m.* monism.

monitor, *s.m.* monitor; adviser.

monitória, *s.f.* monition, summons.

monja, *s.f.* nun.

mono, *s.m.* ape, monkey; dummy; simpleton; unsaleable article.

monociclo, *s.m.* monocycle.

monocórdico, *adj.* monochordic.

monocotiledóneas, *s.f. (pl.)* monoco-tyledons.

monocotiledóneo, *adj.* monocotyledonous.

monocromático, *adj.* monochromatic.

monóculo, *s.m.* monocle; eye-glass.

monogamia, *s.f.* monogamy.

monogâmico, *adj.* monogamic.

monógamo, *s.m.* monogamist.

monografia, *s.f.* monograph.

monograma, *s.m.* monogram.

monolítico, *adj.* monolithic.

monolito, *s.m.* monolith.

monologar, *v.i.* to soliloquize, to monologue.

monólogo, *s.m.* monologue, soliloquy.

monomania, s.f. monomania.
monomaníaco, s.m. monomaniac.
monómio, s.m. monomial.
monoplano, s.m. monoplane.
monopólio, s.m. monopoly.
monopolista, s. e adj. monopolist.
monopolização, s.f. monopolization.
monopolizador, adj. monopolistic; s.m. monopolist.
monopolizar, v.t. to monopolize.
monossilábico, adj. monosyllabic.
monossílabo, s.m. monosyllable.
monoteísmo, s.m. monotheism.
monoteísta, s. monotheist; adj. monotheistic.
monótipo, s.m. monotype.
monotonia, s.f. monotony; sameness; dullness.
monótono, adj. monotonous, tedious, dull.
monovalente, adj. monovalent.
monsenhor, s.m. monsignor.
monstro, s.m. monster; freak.
monstruosidade, s.f. monstrosity; monster; abortion.
monstruoso, adj. monstrous; enormous; hideous, shocking.
monta, s.f. amount, sum; cost, price. 1) de monta, important. 2) de pouca monta, of little importance, trifling.
montada, s.f. riding horse.
montado, adj. mounted; equipped; assembled; on horseback (a cavalo); oak grove.
montador, s.m. assembler; editor (de filmes).
montagem, s.g. mounting; fitting up; assembly; editing (de filme).
montanha, s.f. mountain.
montanha-russa, s.f. roller-coaster.
montanhês, adj. mountain s.m. mountaineer.
montanhismo, s.m. alpinism, mountaineering.
montanhoso, adj. mountainous.
montante, s.m. amount, sum; rising tide; big sword; a montante, upstream.
montar, v.t. to mount, to ride (a cavalo); to amount to; to assemble, to put together; to set up (loja, casa, etc.); to stage (peça de teatro); to edit (filme). 1) montar a, to amount to. 2) montar guarda, to mount guard.
montaria, s.f. riding horse, mount; hunting (caçada).
monte, s.m. mount, mountain, hill; heap, pile. 1) por montes e vales, up hill and down

dale. 2) andar a monte, to live like an outlaw.
montepio, s.m. mutual pension society.
montês, adj. mountain (atr.); wild.
montesino, adj. wild, rustic; simple.
montículo, s.m. small heap; mound; knoll.
montra, s.f. window.
monturo, s.m. dughill, garbage heap.
monumental, adj. monumental, majestic, huge, grand.
monumento, s.m. monument.
mor, adj. chief, principal; grand; major.
mora, s.f. delay, respite; extension of time.
morada, s.f. residence, dwelling, domicile, adress.
moradia, s.f. house, residence.
morador, s.m. dweller, resident; tenant; occupant; adj. dwelling.
moral, s.f. morals, ethics; morality; moral (de uma história); adj. moral, ethical.
moralidade, s.f. morality.
moralismo, s.m. moralism.
moralista, s.m. moralist; adj. moralistic.
moralização, s.f. moralization.
moralizador, adj. moralizing; s.m. moralizer.
moralizar, v.t. to moralize.
morango, s.m. strawberry.
morar, v.i. to live, to dwell, to reside.
moratória, s.f. moratorium.
morbidez, s.f. mobidity, moridness.
mórbido, adj. morbid, diseased; unhealthy.
morcego, s.m. bat.
morcela, s.f. blood-sausage, blood-pudding.
mordaça, s.f. gag; muzzle (açaime).
mordacidade, s.f. mordancy, causticity; sarcasm; bitterness; sharpness.
mordaz, adj. mordacious, mordant, caustic, sarcastic; bitter; pungent.
mordedor, adj. biting.
mordedura, s.f. bite.
mordente, adj. biting, mordant; sarcastic.
morder, v.t. to bite; to snap; to corrode; morder-se de inveja, to grow green with envy.
mordiscar, v.t. to nibble, to gnaw, to pick at.
mordomia, s.f. stewardship.
mordomo, s.m. major-domo; butter, steward.
moreia, s.f. moray.
morena, s.f. brunett; (geol.) moraine.
moreno, adj. brunet; dar tawny.
morfeia, s.f. leprosy.
morfina, s.f. morphine.
morfómano, s.m. morphine addict.
morfologia, s.f. morphology.

morfológico, *adj.* morphologic.

morfologista, *s.m.* morphologist.

morfose, *s.f.* morphosis.

morgadio, *s.m.* enteiled estate.

morgado, *s.m.* first-born son.

morganático, *adj.* morganatic.

morgue, *s.f.* morgue, mortuary.

moribundo, *adj.* moribund, dying; *s.m.* dying person.

morigerado, *adj.* of good morals, wellmannered.

morigerar, *v.t.* to educate; to moralize; to reform; *morigerar-se,* to mend one`s ways.

moringa, *s.* jar, pitcher, jug.

mormacento, *adj.* sultry, muggy, sweltering.

mormaço, *s.m.* sultry weather.

mormente, *adv.* mainly, chiefly.

mormo, *s.m.* glanders.

mórmon, *s.* e *adj.* mormon.

morno, *adj.* warm, tepid, lukewarm.

morosamente, *adv.* slowly.

morosidade, *s.f.* slowness, tardiness.

moroso, *adj.* slow, tardy, dilatory.

morra! *interj.* down with!

morrão, *s.m.* fuse; snuff *(de vela).*

morrer, *v.i.* to die, to perish, to pass away, to expire; to wither; to end, to cease; to disappear.

morrião, *s.m.* scarlet pimpernel.

morrinha, *s.f.* murrain *(doença);* mizzle, drizzle.

morro, *s.m.* hill; mound.

morsa, *s.f.* walrus.

mortal, *s.m.* mortal; *adj.* mortal; lethal, deadly, fatal.

mortalha, *s.f.* shroud, winding sheet; smoking paper.

mortalidade, *s.f.* mortality; death rate.

mortandade, *s.f.* massacre, slaughter, carnage.

morte, *s.f.* death; extinction, end; expiration; passing.

morteiro, *s.m.* mortar.

morticínio, *s.m.* massacre, slaughter, carnage.

mortiço, *adj.* dim, lifeless, dull; pale, spiritless.

mortífero, *adj.* deadly, mortal, lethal.

mortificação, *s.f.* mortification; torment.

mortificante, *adj.* mortifying, afflicting.

morto, *s.m., adj.* dead; deceased; gone; lifeless, inert; extinct; killed. 1) *morto de cansaço,* dead tired, tired to death. 2) *morto de acção,* killed in action. 3) *estar morto por,* to be dying for. 4) *natureza morta,* still life.

mortuário, *adj.* mortuary.

mosaico, *s.m.* mosaic.

mosca, *s.f.* fly; bull`s eye *(centro do alvo);* mosca varejeira, blue-bottle.

moscardo, *s.m.* horsefly.

moscatel, *s.m.* muscatel.

moscovita, *s.* e *adj.* Muscovite.

mosqueado, *adj.* spotted, mottled, speckled.

mosquear, *v.t.* to spot, to speckle, to fleck, to dot.

mosquedo, *s.m.* swarm of flies.

mosquetão, *s.m.* musket.

mosquetaria, *s.f.* musketry.

mosquete, *s.m.* musket.

mosquetear, *v.t.* to shoot with a musket.

mosqueteiro, *s.m.* musketeer.

mosqueteiro, *s.m.* fly trap.

mosquiteiro, *s.m.* mosquito net, mosquito curtain.

mosquito, *s.m.* mosquito.

mossa, *s.f.* dent, indentation; notch.

mostarda, *s.f.* mustard.

mostardeira, *s.f.* mustard plant.

mosteiro, *s.m.* monastery, convent.

mosto, *s.m.* must.

mostra, *s.f.* show, showing, display, exhibition; demonstration; signs. 1) *dar mostras de,* to show, to give signs of. 2) *pôr à mostra,* to expose, to reveal. 3) *à mostra,* bare, uncovered, visible.

mostrador, *s.m.* dial.

mostrar, *v.t.* to show; to exhibit, to display, to expose, to disclose; to point out; to manifest; to prove; *mostrar-se,* to show oneself, to appear; to show off *(dar nas vistas).*

mostrengo, *s.m.* lubber, slob; ugly person, scarecrow.

mostruário, *s.m.* show-case; show window; collection of samples.

mote, *s.m.* motto; theme.

motejador, *s.m.* scoffer, mocker; *adj.* scoffing, mocking.

motejar, *v.t.* to mock, to scoff at; to jeer.

motejo, *s.m.* mockery, flout, jest, joke.

motilidade, *s.f.* motility.

motim, *s.m.* riot, mutiny, revolt, rebellion.

motivação, *s.f.* motivation.

motivar, *v.t.* to motivate, to cause; to induce; to be the motive of.

motivo, *s.m.* motive, cause, reason; ground; intent, purpose; *por motivo de,* by reason of.

moto, *s.m.* motion. 1) *de moto próprio,* of one`s own accord. 2) *moto contínuo,* continual motion; *s.f. abrev. de motocicleta.*

motocicleta, *s.f.* motorcycle, motor-bike.

motococlismo, *s.m.* motor-cycling.

motociclista, *s.* motor-cyclist.

motociclo, *s.m.* motor-cycle.

motor, *s.m.* motor; engine; *motor de arranque,* starter; *adj.* motor, motive, moving.

motorista, *s.* motorist, driver.

motorizar, *v.t.* to motorize.

motricidade, *s.f.* motricity.

motriz, *adj.* motive, moving; driving; *força motriz,* motive power.

mouco, *s.m.* e *adj.* deaf.

mouraria, *s.f.* moorish quarter.

mourejar, *v.i.* to toil, to work hard, to slave.

mourisco, *adj.* moorish.

mouro, *s.m.* Moor; *adj.* moorish.

movediço, *adj.* moving, movable, mobile; unstable; *areias movediças,* quicksand. **móvel,** *adj.* movable, moving; *bens móveis,* movables; *s.m.* piece of furniture; cause, motive.

movente, *adj.* moving.

mover, *v.t.* to move; to shift; to drive, to propel; to affect; to induce. 1) *mover uma acção,* (*jur.*) to bring suit (against somebody). 2) *movido a electricidade,* electrically driven.

movimentação, *s.f.* movement, moving.

movimentado, *adj.* active; busy.

movimentar, *v.t.* move; to set in motion; to activate; to enliven.

movimento, *s.m.* motion, movement, moving; agitation; activity.

movível, *adj.* movable, changeable.

muar, *adj. gado muar,* mules.

mucilagem, *s.f.* mucilage.

muco, *s.m.* mucus.

mucosa, *s.f.* mucous membrane, mucosa.

mucosidade, *s.f.* mucus.

mucoso, *adj.* mucous; slimy, viscous.

muçulmano, *adj.* e *s.* Mohammedan, Moslem.

muda, *s.f.* change, shift; stage *(em viagem);* seedling *(de planta);* moult *(de pena ou pele);* a mute woman.

mudado, *adj.* changed; different.

mudança, *s.f.* change, shift; modification; alteration; removal, removing.

mudar, *v.t.* to change; to alter; to move, to remove; to shift, to transfer; to moult *(de pena);* to shed its skin *(de pele);* to crack *(de voz); mudar de casa,* to move away, to move.

mudável, *adj.* changeable, mutable, variable; mobile, unstable.

mudez, *s.f.* muteness, dumbness; silence.

mudo, *adj.* dumb, mute; speechless, voiceless.

mugido, *s.m.* bellowing, mooing.

mugir, *v.i.* to moo, to bellow.

mui, *adv.* very; too.

muito, *adj. pron.* e *s.* much; a lot of, a great deal of, plenty of; many, too many, a lot; long. 1) *muita gente,* many people. 2) *muito tempo,* a long time. 3) *muitas vezes,* often. 4) *há muito,* long ago; *adv.* very; much, a lot, too, most, considerably; long. 5) *muito belo,* very beautiful. 6) *muito agradecido,* much obliged. 7) *muito melhor,* much better. 8) *muito antes,* long before. 9) *por muito que,* however much. 10) *por muito que se esforce ...,* whatever efforts he makes .... 11) *quando muito,* at most.

mula, *s.f.* mule.

mulato, *s.m.* e *adj.* mulatto.

muleta, *s.f.* crutch; support.

muleteiro, *s.m.* muleteer.

mulher, *s.f.* woman; wife *(esposa).*

mulherengo, *s.m.* woman chaser.

mulheril, *adj.* womanish; womanly.

mulherido, *s.m.* large number of women; womenfolk.

multa, *s.f.* fine, penalty.

multar, *v.t.* to fine.

multicelular, *adj.* multicellular.

multicolor, *adj.* multicoloured, many--coloured.

multidão, *s.f.* crowd, multitude, throng.

multiface, *adj.* multifaced.

multiforme, *adj.* multiform, diversified.

multimilionério, *s.m.* multimillionaire.

multipartidário, *adj.* multiparty.

multiplicação, *s.f.* multiplication; reproduction.

multiplicador, *s.m.* multiplier, *adj.* multiplying.

multiplicando, *s.m.* multiplicating.

multiplicar, *v.t.* to multiply; to increase; *multiplicar-se,* to multiply; to reproduce.

multiplicativo, *adj.* multiplicative, multiplying.

multiplicável, *adj.* multipliable.

multiplicidade, *s.f.* multiplicity; variety.

múltiplo, *s.m.* multiple; *menor múltiplo comum,* least common multiple; *adj.* multiple, manyfold.

múmia, *s.f.* mummy.

mumificação, *s.f.* mummification.

mumificar, *v.t.* to mummyfy, to embalm.

mundana, *s.f.* harlot, dissolute woman.

mundanismo, *s.m.* worldliness.

mundano, *adj.* wordly, mundane; earthly.

mundial, *adj.* world-wide; world *(atr.),* universal.

mundo, *s.m.* world; universe; earth, globe, planet.

mungidura, *s.f.* milking.

mungir, *v.t.* to milk.

munheca, *s.f.* wrist.

munição, *s.f.* ammunition; munition; military supplies.

municiamento, *s.m.* munitioning, provisions, supplies.

municiar, *v.t.* to provide with munitions, to munition.

municipal, *adj.* municipal.

municipalidade, *s.f.* municipality; town hall, city hall.

munícipe, *s.m.* townsman; citizen.

município, *s.m.* municipality; town hall.

munido, *adj.* provided with.

munificência, *s.f.* munificence, generosity, bounty.

munificente, *adj.* munificent, generous, magnanimous.

munir, *v.t.* to provide, to supply, to equip.

murado, *adj.* walled, enclosed with walls.

mural, *adj.* e *s.m.* mural.

muralha, *s.f.* wall; rampart.

muralhar, *v.t.* to wall in; to enclose, to fortify.

murar, *v.t.* to wall, to wall in, to immure, to enclose; to fortify.

murchar, *v.i.* to wither, to wilt; to fade; to dry up; to decay.

murcho, *adj.* withered, wilted, dry; faded; sad, pensive, dispirited.

muriático, *adj.* muriatic.

murmulhante, *adj.* rustling.

murmulhar, *v.i.* to rustle *(árvores);* to ripple *(ondas);* to whisper.

murmulho, *s.m.* rustling; rippling.

murmurante, *adj.* whispering; rustling.

murmurar, *v.t.* to murmur; to whisper; to mutter; to rustle *(árvores);* to ripple *(ondas);* to mumble *(resmungar).*

murmurejar, *v.i.* to murmur, to rustle, to whisper.

murmúrio, *s.m.* murmur; whisper(ing); grumble, mumble; rustling.

muro, *s.m.* wall.

murro, *s.m.* punch, blow with the fist.

murta, *s.f.* myrtle.

musa, *s.f.* muse.

musaranho, *s.m.* shrew-mouse.

muscoso, *adj.* mossy.

musculado, *adj.* muscled, muscular; strong.

muscular, *adj.* muscular.

musculatura, *s.f.* musculature.

músculo, *s.m.* muscle.

musculoso, *adj.* brawny, strong, athletic, sturdy, robust, muscular.

museu, *s.m.* museum.

musgo, *s.m.* moss.

musgoso, *adj.* mossy.

música, *s.f.* music; tune.

musical, *adj.* musical; tuneful, melodious.

musicalidade, *s.f.* musicality; harmony.

musicar, *v.t.* to set to music, to music.

músico, *s.m.* musician.

musselina, *s.f.* muslin.

mussitar, *v.i.* to whisper, to murmur, to mumble.

mustelídeo, *adj.* musteline; *s.m. pl.* mustelidae.

mutabilidade, *s.f.* mutability, changeableness, variability.

mutação, *s.f.* mutation; change, alteration.

mutante, *s.* mutant.

mutável, *adj.* mutable, changeable, variable.

mutilação, *s.f.* mutilation, maiming; defacement.

mutilado, *adj.* mutilated, maimed; diminished.

mutilar, *v.t.* to mutilate, to maim, to mangle, to cripple; to deface, to disfigure.

mutismo, *s.m.* mutism, muteness, dumbness, silence.

mutualidade, *s.f.* mutuality; reciprocity; *(com.)* system of mutual insurance.

mutualismo, *s.m.* mutualism.

mutualista, *s.* e *adj.* mutualist.

mutuamente, *adv.* mutually, reciprocally.

mutuante, *adj.* lending; *s.* lender, loaner.

mutuar, *v.t.* to mutualize; to exchange; to lend, to borrow.

mutuário, *s.m.* borrower.

mútuo, *adj.* mutual, reciprocal; *s.m.* loan; exchange; *Associação de Socorros Mútuos,* benefit society.

N

n, the thirteenth letter of the Portuguese alphabet.

nababesco, *adj.* rich, opulent.

nababo, *s.m.* nabab, opulent person.

nabada, *s.f.* dish of turnips.

nabal, *s.m.* turnip field.

nabiça, *s.f.* turnip greens

nabiçal, *s.m.* filed with turnip rootlets.

nabo, *s.m.* turnip

nacada, *s.f.* a big slice

nação, *s.f.* nation, country, land, state; people, race, folk; nationality; origin; species, sort.

nácar, *s.m.* nacre, mother-of-pearl; carmine, pink.

nacarado, *adj.* nacreous, pearly.

nacarar, *v.t.* to cover with nacre; to give a nacreous appearance.

nacarino, *adj.* ver "nacarado".

nacional, *adj.* national. 1) *bandeira nacional,* national flag. 2) *fabrico nacional,* home--made. 3) *economia nacional,* home economy. 4) *hino nacional,* national anthem.

nacionalidade, *s.f.* nationality, nation.

nacionalismo, *s.m.* nationalism, patriotism.

nacionalista, *adj., s.* nationalistic; nationalist.

nacionalização, *s.f.* nationalization.

nacionalizador, *adj.* nationalizing.

nacionalizar, *v.t.* to nationalize.

naco, *s.m.* piece, chunk, slice, morsel, portion.

nada, *s.m.* nothing, naught, notingness; insignificant, trifle; *pron. ind.* nothing; *adv.* nothing, not at all. 1) *nada disso,* nothing of the kind. 2) *nada mais,* nothing else. 3) *acabar em nada,* to end in smoke. 4) *dar em nada,* to come to naught. 5) *antes de mais nada,* first of all. 6) *quase nada,* next to nothing. 7) *não ter nada a ver com,* to have nothing to do with. 8) *nada feito,* nothing doing. 9) *nada mai que,* nothing but, only. 10) *ou tudo ou nada,* all or nothing. 11) *não valer nada,* to be good for nothing, not worth a whoop. 12) *nada*

absolutamente, not at all. 13) *daqui a nada,* in a moment. 14) *daí a nada,* soon after. 15) *não me é nada,* he is no relative of mine. 16) *não sobrou nada,* nothing was left over. 17) *por nada desta vida,* for love or money, not for the world. 18) *de nada, (agradecimento)* don't mention it, you are welcome.

nadador, *s.m.* swimmer.

nadante, *adj.* swimming.

nadar, *v.i.* to swim, to overflow, to float. 1) *nadar de costas,* to swim on one's back. 2) *nadar em dinheiro,* to roll in wealth. 3) *nadar como um prego,* to swim like a stone, to float like a brick. 4) *ficar a nadar,* to be at a loss. 5) *filho de peixe sabe nadar,* like father, like son.

nádega, *s.f.* buttock; rump.

nadegada, *s.f.* blow on the buttocks.

nadegudo, *adj.* large-buttocked.

nadegueiro, *adj.* pertaining to the buttock.

nadinha, *s.f.* just a little, insignificance; *adv.* absolutely nothing.

nadir, *s.m.* nador; the lowest point.

nado, *adj.* born; *s.m.* swimming.

nado morto, *adj.* stillborn.

nafta, *s.f.* naphta.

naftalina, *s.f.* naphatline.

naftol, *s.m.* naphotol.

nagalhé, *s.m.* stingy man.

nagalho, *s.m.* neckerchief.

náiade, *s.f.* naiad, water nymph.

naifa, *s.f.* pocket knife.

naifada, *s.f.* cut with a knife.

naipe, *s.m.* suit *(de cartas)*.

naja, *s.f.* hooded snake; spittoon.

nalga, *s.f.* buttock.

namorada, *s.f.* sweetheart.

namoradeira, *s.f.* coquette; *adj.* coquettish.

namorado, *s.m.* lover, sweetheart; adj. enamoured, in love.

namorador, *adj.* flirtatious; *s.m.* lover flirter.

namorar, *v.t.* to love; to seduce; to make love to; to make love, to pay court to.

namoricar, *v.i.* to flirt with, to philander.

namorico, *s.m.* flirt, flirtation.

namoriscar, *v.i.* ver "namoricar".

namorisco, *s.m.* ver "namorisco".

namoro, *s.m.* love-making; courtship; lover, sweetheart.

nana, *s.f.* lullaby to lull to sleep.

nanar, *v.i.* (criança) to sleep.

nanismo, *s.m.* nanism, dwarfishness.

nanja, *adv.* no, not (pop.); nanja eu, not me.

nanquim, *s.m.* China ink; nankeen.

não, *adv.* no; not; s.m. no, refusal, denial. 1) ainda não, not yet. 2) a não ser que, unless. 3) pois não, certainly. 4) quer queira quer não, willing or not. 5) não obstante, in spite of. 6) não apoiado, not approved.

não-me-deixes, *s.m.* groundsel (bot.).

não-te-esqueças, *s.m.* forget-me-not, myositis.

napeiro, *adj.* drowsy, sleepy; indolent, lazy.

napelina, *s.f.* aconitine.

napelo, *s.m.* monk's hood.

napoleão, *s.m.* napoleon (moeda de ouro).

napoleónico, *adj.* Napoleonic.

napolitano, *adj., s.m.* Napolitan.

naquele, em aquele, in that (one), on that (one), at that.

naquilo, em aquilo, in that, on that, at that.

narceína, *s.f.* narceine.

narceja, *s.f.* snipe.

narcisar-se, *v.refl.* to grow fond of oneself, to admire oneself (num espelho), to adorn oneself excessively.

narcisismo, *s.m.* narcissism.

Narciso, *s.m.* Narcissus; a vain young man.

narcose, *s.f.* narcosis; narcotism.

narcótico, *s.m., adj.* narcotic, drug.

narcotina, *s.f.* narcotine.

narcotismo, *s.m.* narcotism.

narcotização, *s.f.* narcotization.

narcotizar, *v.t.* to narcotize.

nardo, *s.m.* nard, spikernard.

narícula, *s.f.* nostril.

narigada, *s.f.* blow on the nose or with nose.

narigão, *s.m.* large nose.

narigudo, *adj.* long-nosed.

narina, *s.f.* nostril.

nariz, *s.m.* nose. 1) meter o nariz onde não é chamado, to poke one's nose into another's bussiness. 2) torcer o nariz, to turn up one's nose at. 3) nariz arrebitado, snub-nose, pug-nose.

nariz-de-cera, *s.m.* common-place.

narração, *s.f.* narration, narrative, tale; report, account, description.

narrador, *s.m.* narrator, describer.

narrar, *v.t.* to relate, to narrate, to tell, to report, to describe.

narrativa, *s.f.* narration, narrative, tale, story, account.

narrativo, *adj.* narrative, descriptive, expository.

narrável, *adj.* describable.

nartece, nártex, *s.m.* narthex.

narval, *s.m.* narwhal, unicornfish.

nasal, *adj.* nasal; s.f. nasal letter.

nasalação, *s.f.* nasalization.

nasalar, *v.t.* to nasalize.

nasalidade, *s.f.* nasality.

nasalização, *s.f.* ver "nasalação".

nasalizar, *v.t.* ver "nasalar".

nascedoiro, nascedouro, *s.m.* birth-place.

nascença, *s.f.* birth; nascency; rise; origin, source, beginning, spring. 1) de nascença, by birth. 2) cego de nascença, born blind.

nascente, *adj.* nascent; rising; growing; s.f. spring, fountain, source, origin; s.m. East, Orient.

nascer, *v.i.* to be born; to rise; to dawn (o dia); to spring; to come into the world, to see the light; to shoot, to germinate. 1) ao nascer do Sol, at sunrise. 2) o nascer do dia, daybreak, the dawn.

nascida, *s.f.* boil, swelling, abscess.

nascido, *adj.* born.

nascimento, *s.m.* birth, nativity; beginning, origin, source; rise, formation.

nascituro, *adj.* unborn, embryolan; s.m. unborn child.

nassa, *s.f.* wicker fish trap.

nastro, *s.m.* tape, ribbon.

nata, *s.f.* cream; the best of anything.

natação, *s.f.* swimming, natation; art of swimming.

natadeira, *s.f.* creamer, a shallow milk pan.

natado, *adj.* creamy.

Natal, *s.m.* Christmas, Noel; adj. natal, native. 1) dia de Natal, Christmas Day. 2) árvore de Natal, Christmas tree. 3) terra natal, birthplace.

natalício, *adj.* natal; aniversário natalício, birthday.

natalidade, *s.f.* natality, birth-rate.

natátil, *adj.* floating, floatable, natant.

natatório, *adj.* natatorial, natatory.

nateirado, *adj.* muddy, slimy.

nateiro, *s.m.* slime, mud, soft river mud.

natio, *s.m.* a ground which produces plants without culture.

natividade, *s.f.* Nativity; Christmas.

nativismo, s.m. nativism.

nativista, s., adj. nativist.

nativo, adj. native, born; innate; natural, home-born; vernacular; original.

nato, adj. born, innate, congenital,ingrained.

natural, adj. natural; ordinary; inborn; normal; instinctive; illegitimate; spontaneous, unaffected, genuine; congenital, inherent; original; human; elemental; s.m. nature, character. 1) *natural de,* born in. 2) *ser natural de,* to be of, to be born in, to be a native of. 3) *ao natural,* from life (painting).

naturalidade, s.f. naturalness, simplicity; birth-place, nationality.

naturalismo, s.m. naturalism, realism; materialism, positivism.

naturalista, s. naturalist; adj. naturalistic.

naturalização, s.f. naturalization, nationalization.

naturalizar, v.t. to naturalize, to nationalize; *naturalizar-se,* to become naturalized.

naturalmente, adv. naturally; of course; probably.

natureza, s.f. nature; constitution; kind, class, sort; character, temper, disposition, mood.

natureza-morta, s.f. still life.

naturismo, s.m. naturalism.

naturista, s. naturalist; adj. naturalistic.

nau, s.f. ship, vessel.

naufragar, v.i. to shipwreck, to be shipwrecked; to fail, to frustrate, to suffer failure.

naufrágio, s.m. shipwreck; ruin, loss; failure.

náufrago, s.m. wrecked person.

naufragoso, adj. dangerous, wreckful.

náusea, s.f. nausea; loathing; seasickness; repugnance, repulse.

nauseabundo, adj. nauseating, loathing, nauseous, repulsive, repugnant.

nauseante, adj. ver nauseabundo.

nausear, v.t. to nauseate; to abhor; to feel nausea, to cause vomit; to make sick; to bore, to disgust.

nauseativo, adj. ver nauseabundo.

nauseoso, adj. nauseous.

nauta, s.m. sailor, mariner, seaman.

náutica, s.f. seamanship, navigation, nautics.

náutico, adj. nautical, naval, maritime.

náutilo, s.m. nautilus *(molusco).*

naval, adj. naval.

navalha, s.f. knife, pocket knife; *navalha de barba,* razor, cutthroat.

navalhada, s.f. cut with a knife.

navalhar, v.t. to knife, to cut, to stab, to slash.

navalhista, s. one who slashes with a knife.

nave, s.f. nave, temple, church; ship, vessel.

navegabilidade, s.f. navigability.

navegação, s.f. navigation, shipping, sailing, seafaring; nautics; maritime commerce; *navegação aérea,* aerial navigation.

navegador, s.m. navigator, sailor, seafarer.

navegante, s.m. navigator.

navegar, v.i. to navigate, to sail, to steer; to journey by water.

navegável, adj. navigable, passable.

naveta, s.f. shuttle bobin; small boat.

navicular, adj. navicular, boat-shaped.

naviforme, adj. ver navicular.

navigabilidade, s.f. navigability.

navio, s.m. ship, vessel, boat, steamer. 1) *navio almirante,* flagship. 2) *navio de carga,* cargo boat, freighter. 3) *navio de guerra,* warship, man-of-war.

navio-cisterna, s.m. tanker.

navio-escola, s.m. training ship.

navio-hospital, s.m. hospital-ship.

nazareno, s.m. e adj. Nazarene.

nazi, s., adj. Nazi.

nazismo, s.m. Nazi.

nazista, adj., s. Nazi.

neblina, s.f. mist, haze, fog.

nebulosa, s.f. nebula.

nebulosidade, s.f. nebulosity, mistiness, haziness, fogginess.

nebuloso, adj. nebulous; cloudy; vague; uncertain; gloomy; indistinct, obscure; misterious.

necear, v.i. to talk nonsense.

necedade, s.f. nonsense, silliness; ignorance, stupidity, nescience.

necessária, s.f. water-closet; privy *(pop).*

necessariamente, adv. necessarily, inevitably.

necessário, adj. necessary, needful, indispensable; useful; compulsory.

necessidade, s.f. necessity, need; indispensability; poverty; distress; exigence, requirement. 1) *a necessidade não tem lei,* necessity knows no law. 2) *géneros de primeira necessidade,* essential commodities. 3) *na necessidade se conhecem os amigos,* a friend in need is a friend indeed.

necessitado, adj. necessitous, in need, indigent, poor.

necessitante, adj. necessitous, needy.

necessitar, *v.t., v.i.* to need, to want; to be in need of; to demand, to require; to be necessary.

necessitoso, *adj.* ver necessitante.

necrologia, *s.f.* necrology, obituary.

necrológico, *adj.* necrological.

necrológio, *s.m.* necrology.

necromancia, *s.f.* necromancy, sorcery, witchcraft, conjuration.

necromante, *s.m.* necromancer, wizard, sorcerer.

necromântico, *adj.* necromantic.

necrópole, *s.f.* necropolis, cemetery.

necrose, *s.f.* necrosis, mortification, gangrene.

necrotério, *s.m.* morgue, dead-house, mortuary.

néctar, *s.m.* nectar; anything delicious *(wines)*.

nectarífero, *adj.* nectariferous.

nectário, *s.m.* nectary.

nediez, *s.f.* fatness, plumpness.

nédio, *adj.* fat, fleshy, sleek, plump, well-fed.

neerlandês, *adj.* netherlandish; *s.m.* Netherlander.

nefando, *adj.* nefarious, abominable, wicked, heinous, execrable, villainous.

nefário, *adj.* ver nefando.

nefas, *s.m. por fás e por nefas,* by hook or by crook, by fair means or by foul.

nefasto, *adj.* beleful, ill-omened, ominous, fatal, disastrous.

nefelibata, *s.* nepheliad, dreamer.

nefralgia, *s.* nephralgia.

nefrite, *s.f.* nephritis, Bright's disease.

nefrítico, *adj.* nephritic, renal.

nega, *s.f.* negation, denial, refusal.

negaça, *s.f.* lure, decoy, bait, enticement, allurement; trap; provocation.

negação, *s.f.* negation, denial, refusal; want of inclination; lack of some quality.

negaceador, *adj., s.m.* alluring, enticing; decoyer, enticer.

negacear, *v.t.* to allure, to entice, to deceive, to decoy, to lure; to provoke.

negado, *adj.* denied, refused; rejected.

negador, *s.m.* denier.

negalho, *s.m.* skein.

negar, *v.t.* to negate, to deny, to refuse, to reject; to say no; to contradict; to betray.

negativa, *s.f.* negative, refusal, prohibition.

negativamente, *adv.* negatively.

negatividade, *s.f.* negativity.

negativismo, *s.m.* negativism.

negativista, *s., adj.* negativist.

negativo, *adj.* negative, denying, refusing; *s.m.* negative *(foto.).*

negável, *adj.* deniable.

negligência, *s.f.* negligence, carelessness; disregard, omission; indolence; indifference.

negligenciar, *v.t.* to neglect, to disregard; to omit, to fail to do; to oversee.

negligente, *adj.* negligent, careless, neglectful, heedless, inattentive, thoughtless; slipshod.

negligentemente, *adv.* negligently.

negociação, *s.f.* negotiation, transaction; arrangement; treaty, deal.

negociador, *s.m.* negotiator; member of one of two parties in conference.

negociante, *s.m.* merchant, trader, dealer, businessman or woman; shopkeeper.

negociar, *v.t., v.i.* to negotiate; to trade or to deal in, to by or to sell, to transact; 1) *negociar um empréstimo,* to negociate a loan.

negociarrão, *s.m.* splendid deal, very lucrative business.

negociata, *s.f.* shady transaction.

negociável, *adj.* negotiable, sellable.

negócio, *s.m.* business, commerce, trade, affair; transaction; deal, affair, matter; bargain; shop; enterprise. 1) *negócio da China,* fine bargain. 2) *negócio de ocasião,* bargain. 3) *fazer bom negócio,* to do a good stroke of business. 4) *fazer mau negócio,* to drive a bad bargain.

negocioso, *adj.* very busy, active, dilligent; careful; commercial.

negra, *s.f.* negress.

negrada, negralhada, *s.f.* great number of negroes.

negralhão, *s.m.* stout negro.

negregado, *adj.* unlucky, disgraceful, unhappy, wretched; troublesome.

negreiro, *s.m.* slaver; slave-ship.

negrejante, *adj.* blackish, dark.

negrejar, *v.i.* to look black; to grow black.

negridão, *s.f.* blacness, obscurity, darkness.

negrilho, *s.m.* black poplar; negrillo.

negro, *adj.* black; gloomy; dark-skinned; Africam; dark; *s.m.* negro. 1) *ver tudo negro,* to look on the black side. 2) *negro retinto,* jet-black.

negrófilo, *s.m.* negrophile; abolitionist.

negróide, *s., adj.* negroid.

negror, *s.m.* darkness, obscurity, blacness.

negrume, s.m. darkness; gloomy weather; sadness, gloom.

negrura, s.f. blackness, darkness, obscurity.

nela, prep. em e ela, in her, in it; on her, on it.

nele, prep. em e ele, in him, on him; in it, on it.

nem, conj. nor, neither; not, not even. 1) nem por isso, not much, not at all. 2) nem a bem nem a mal, neither well nor badly. 3) nem mais nem menos, that it just it. 4) nem peixe nem carne, neither fish nor fowl. 5) nem por isso deixo de ir, I'll go just the same. 6) nem sequer, not even. 7) nem sempre, not always. 8) sem pés nem cabeça, without rhyme or reason. 9) nem por sombras, not a chance. 10) nem que, even though.

nematelminte, s.m. nemathelminth.

nematóide, s.m. nematode, thread worm; adj. nematoid.

nembo, s.m. pier, solid masonry between windows.

nemésia, s.f. retaliator.

nemoral, adj. pertaining to a wood.

nemoroso, adj. woody, abounding in woods; tree-shaded.

nenhum, adj., pron. ind. no, not any, neither; none, no one, nobody, nothing, neither. 1) nenhum de nós, none (neither) of us. 2) nenhum dos dois, neither of the two. 3) não é nenhum tolo, he is no fool. 4) de modo nenhum, by no means, on no account, not at all. 5) em parte nenhuma, nowhere. 6) tenho pouco dinheiro, talvez nenhum, I have little money, if any. 7) nenhum outro, nobody (no one) else.

nenhures, adv. nowhere.

nénia, s.f. dirge, elegy.

nenúfar, s.m. nenuphar, water-lily.

neocatolicismo, s.m. neo-Catholicism.

neocatólico, s.m., adj. neo-Catholic.

neoclássico, adj. neoclassic.

neófito, s.m. neophyte; novice, beginner.

neofobia, s.f. neophobia.

neófago, s.m. neophobic person.

neogótico, adj. neo-Gothic.

neolatino, adj. neo-Latin.

neolítico, adj. neolitic.

neologismo, s.m. neologism.

neologista, s., adj. neologist.

néon, s.m. neon.

neoplasia, s.f. neoplasia.

neoplasma, s.m. neoplasm, tumour, growth.

neoplastia, s.f. neoplasty.

neoplástico, adj. neoplastic.

neoplatónico, adj. neo-Platonic.

neoplatonismo, s.m. neo-Platonism.

neo-realismo, s.m. neo-realism.

neo-romantismo, s.m. neo-romantism.

neotomismo, s.m. neo-Thomism.

neozelandês, s.m. New Zealander.

neozóico, adj. neozoic.

nepote, s.m. favourite.

nepotismo, s.m. nepotism, favouritism.

nepotista, s. nepotist.

neptuniano, adj. Neptunian.

neptunino, adj. Neptunian.

nequícia, s.f. badness, perversity, malice, wickedness.

nereida, nereide, s.f. Nereid, sea nymph.

nervação, s.f. nervation, venation.

nervado, adj. nervate, veined, ribbed.

nerval, adj. nerval.

nérveo, adj. nervous.

nervino, adj., s.m. nervine.

nervo, s.m. nerve, tendon, sinew; power, force, energy, vigour, courage. 1) nervo óptico, ciático, optic, ciatic nerve. 2) ataque de nervos, fit of nerves. 3) pilha de nervos, a bundle of nerves.

nervosidade, s.f. nervousness; nervous energy.

nervosismo, s.m. nervousness, excitability, jitters; flurry.

nervoso, adj. nervous; excitable. irritable; apprehensive; jumpy, fussy; sinewy; muscular, vigorous; s.m. hysteria, nerves. 1) esgotamento nervoso, nervous breakdown. 2) muito nervoso, highly-strung. 3) sistema nervoso, nervous system.

nervudo, adj. strong, vigorous, robust.

nervura, s.f. nervure; rib (de um insecto, livro, etc.); vein.

néscio, adj. nescient, ignorant, stupid, silly.

nesga, s.f. bit, piece; small piece of land, of cloth; small space.

nêspera, s.f. loquat.

nespereira, s.f. loquat-tree.

nesse, prep. em e esse, in (on) that.

neste, prep. em e este, in (on) this.

neta, s.f. grand-daughter, grand-child.

neto, s.m. grandson; grandchildren (pl); descendants, posterity.

neural, adj. neural, of the nerves.

neuralgia, s.f. neuralgia.

neurálgico, adj. neuralgic.

neurastenia, s.f. neurasthenia.

neurasténico, adj. neurasthenic.

neurastenizar, *v.* to make or become neurasthenic.

neurite, *s.f.* neuritis.

neurologia, *s.f.* neurology.

neurológico, *adj.* neurologic.

neurologista, neurólogo, *s., s.m.* neurologist.

neuroma, *s.m.* neuroma *(tumour).*

neurónio, *s.m.* neuron.

neurose, *s.f.* neurosis.

neurótico, *adj.* neurotic.

neutral, *adj.* neutral; impartial; non-belligerant, neuter.

neutralidade, *s.f.* neutrality.

neutralização, *s.f.* neutralization.

neutralizador, *s.m.* neutralizer; *adj.* neutralizing.

neutralizante, *adj.* neutralizing.

neutralizar, *v.t.* to neutralize, to counteract; to destroy, to render ineffectual.

neutrão, *s.m.* neutron *(física).*

neutro, *adj.* neuter; neutral.

nevada, *adj.* snow-fall.

nevado, *adj.* snowy, snow-covered.

nevão, *s.m.* snow-fall.

nevar, *v.i.* to snow.

nevasca, *s.f.* snow-storm, blizzard.

neve, *s.f.* snow; 1) *neve carbónica,* dry ice.

nêveda, *s.f.* calamint *(bot.)*

névoa, *s.f.* fog, mist; obscurity, dimness.

nevoar(-se), *v.* to fog, to become foggy; to darken.

nevoeirento, *adj.* foggy.

nevoeiro, *s.m.* fog, mist, obscurity.

nevoento, *adj.* foggy, mist; obscure.

nevoso, *adj.* snowy.

nevralgia, *s.f.* neuralgia.

nevrálgico, *adj.* neuralgic.

nevrite, *s.f.* neuritis.

nevrítico, *adj.* neuritic.

nevrologia, *s.f.* neurology.

nevrológico, *adj.* neurologic.

nevrologista, *s.* neurologist.

nevroma, *s.m.* neuroma.

nevropata, *s.* neuropath.

nevropatologia, *s.f.* neuropathology.

nevrose, *s.f.* neurosis.

nevrótico, *adj.* neurotic.

nexo, *s.m.* nexus; link, bond, connexion; coherence.

nica, *s.f.* trifle; impertinence.

nicada, *s.f.* pecking.

nicar, *v.t.* to peck.

nicho, *s.m.* niche; sinecure; small home.

nicles, *adv.* nothing at all, nothing whatsoever *(pop).*

nicotina, *s.f.* nicotine.

nicotino, *adj.* nicotian.

nicromancia, *s.f. ver "necromancia".*

nictação, *s.f.* nictation, winking, blinking.

nidificação, *s.f.* nidification, nesting.

nidificar, *v.t.* to nidificate, to nidify, to nest.

nidor, *s.m.* bad breath, halitosis.

nidoroso, *adj.* nidorous.

nigela, *s.f.* love-in-a-mist, fennelflower; niellowork.

nigelador, *s.m.* niellist.

nigelagem, *s.f.* nielloing.

nigelar, *v.t.* to decorate with niello.

nigérrimo, *adj.* very black.

nigrícia, *s.f.* nigritude, blackness.

nigromancia, *s.f.* necromancy.

nigromante, *s.m.* necromancer.

niilismo, *s.m.* nihilism.

niilista, *s., adj.* nihilist.

nimbar, *v.t.* to surround with a nimbus, to adorn with halo.

nimbo, *s.m.* nimbus, rain-cloud, light rain; halo, aureole.

nimboso, *adj.* stormy, rainy.

nimiamente, *adv.* excessively.

nimiedade, *s.f.* excess; redundancy; superfluity.

nímio, *adj.* excessive, overmuch, superfluous.

ninfa, *s.f.* nymph.

ninfeia, *s.f.* water-lily.

ninfeu, *adj.* nymphish, nymphean.

ninfóide, *adj.* nymphean, nymphlike.

ninfómana, *s.f.* nymphomaniac.

ninfomania, *s.f.* nymphomania.

ninfomaníaca, *s.f.* nymphomaniac.

ninguém, *pron. ind.* no one, nobody, no man, no person; *um joão-ninguém,* a mere nobody.

ninhada, *s.f.* brood, offspring; nestful, covey, litter. 1) *ninhada de leitões,* farrow, litter of pigs. 2) *ninhada de pintos,* a brood of chikens. 3) *ninhada de ratos,* a litter of mice.

ninharia, *s.f.* trifle, bauble, insignificance; small amount.

ninheiro, *s.m.* nest where hens unsually lay eggs.

ninho, *s.m.* nest; shelter; hole, den; hiding-place; home.

nipónico, *adj.* Japanese, Nipponese.

niqueiro, *adj.* whimsical, faddy.

níquel, *s.m.* nickel *(metal e moeda).*

niquelagem, *s.f.* nickel-plating.

niquelar, *v.t.* to nickel, to nickel-plate, to coat with nickel.

niquelina, *s.f.* nickeline.

niquento, *adj.* fussy; peevish; punctilious, whimsical.

niquice, *s.f.* fussiness, faddiness, punctiliousness.

nirvana, *s.m.* nirvana.

nisso, *prep. em* e *isso,* in, on that.

nisto, *prep. em* e *isto,* in, on this; at this moment.

nitente, *adj.* bright, shining; clear, distinct; resistant.

nitescência, *s.f.* brightness, splendour.

nitidamente, *adv.* clearly.

nitidez, *s.f.* clearness, neatness, distinctness; vividness *(memória).*

nítido, *adj.* clear, bright, neat, distinct, well-marked; explicit, vivid *(memória);* brilliant, shining.

nitrado, *adj.* nitrated.

nitrato, *s.m.* nitrate.

nitreira, *s.f.* nitre-bed, manure-heap.

nítrico, *adj.* nitric.

nitrido, *s.m.* neighing.

nitrificação, *s.f.* nitrification.

nitrificar, *v.t.* to notrify.

nitrir, *v.i.* to neigh, to whinny.

nitrito, *s.m.* nitrite.

nitro, *s.m.* nitre; saltpetre.

nitrobenzeno, *s.m.* nitrobenzene.

nitrobenzina, *s.f.* nitrobenzene.

nitrocelulose, *s.f.* nitrocellulose.

nitrogénio, *s.m.* nitrogen.

nitroglicerina, *s.f.* nitro-glycerine.

nitrosidade, *s.f.* nitrousness.

nitroso, *adj.* nitrous.

niveal, *adj.* winterly; niveous, nival.

nível, *s.m.* level, water-level, balance-level; horizontality; level surface; moral or intellectual standard, position. 1) *nível de bolha de ar,* spirit level. 2) *nível de vida,* standard of life. 3) *nível do mar,* sea-level. 4) *passagem de nível,* level crossing.

nivelado, *adj.* even, flush, flat.

nivelador, *adj., s.m.* levelling; leveller.

nivelamento, *s.m.* levelling; equalizing.

nivelar, *v.t.* to level; to raze; to destroy; to even, to flatten; to equalize, to flush.

níveo, *adj.* niveous; snowy.

nivoso, *adj.* snowy.

no, *prep. em* e *art.* o, in the, on the.

nó, *s.m.* knot; node (de uma planta); bow; kurl (da madeira);tie union *(fig.);* joint, articulation. 1) *nó cego,* dead knot. 2) *nó górdo,* Gordian knot. 3) *dar o nó,* to tie the knot, to marry. 4) *nó na garganta,* a lump in the throat. 5) *não dar ponto sem nó,* not to do anything for nothing. 6) *nó dos dedos,* knuckles, joints. 7) *nó de milha, knot.*

noa, *s.f.* nones.

nobiliário, *adj.* nobiliary; *s.m.* peerage book.

nobiliarista, *s.* author of nobiliary history.

nobiliarquia, *s.f.* nobiliary history, peerage book.

nobiliárquico, *adj.* referring to blazonry.

nobilíssimo, *adj.* most noble.

nobilitação, *s.f.* ennoblement.

nobilitante, *adj.* ennobling; dignifying.

nobilitar, *v.t.* to ennoble, to raise to nobility; to dignify, to exalt, to praise.

nobre, *adj.* noble, illustrious, aristocratic, high-bred; generous; high, elevated, grand splendid, magnificent; fine; *s.m.* noble, nobleman, aristocrat, peer, lord.

nobrecer, *v.t.* to ennoble.

nobremente, *adv.* nobly.

nobreza, *s.f.* nobleness, nobility; dignity; the nobles, peerage, aristocracy; excellence, distinction.

noção, *s.f.* notion, idea, conception, concept.

nocente, *adj.* harmful; mischievous, noxious, hurtful.

nocional, *adj.* notional; abstract.

nocivamente, *adv.* noxiously.

nocividade, *s.f.* noxiousness, harmfulness.

nocivo, *adj.* noxious, pernicious, harmful, hurtful, poisonous, bad, malign.

noctambulação, *s.f.* noctambulation, sleep-walking.

noctambular, *v.i.* to sleep-walk.

noctambulismo, *s.m.* noctambulism, somnambulism, sleep-walking.

noctâmbulo, *adj.* noctambulous; *s.m.* noctambulist, sleep-walker.

nocticolor, *adj.* dark, somber, black.

noctígeno, *adj.* that producers darkness.

noctívago, *adj.* noctivagous, night-wandering, nocturnal; *s.m.* night-walker.

nocturnal, *adj.* nocturnal.

nocturno, *adj.* nocturnal; *s.m.* nocturne *(música).*

nodal, *adj.* nodal.

nó-de-adão, *s.m.* Adam's apple.

nodo, *s.m.* node.

nódoa, *s.f.* spot, stain, speck, blot, blur; dishonour, ignominy.

nodoar, *v.t.* to spot, to stain.

nodosidade, *s.f.* nodosity, knottiness.

nodoso, *adj.* nodose, knotty.

nódulo, *s.m.* nodule.

noduloso, *adj.* nodulous, nodular.

nogada, *s.f.* flower of a walnut-tree.

nogal, *s.m.* orchard of walnut-trees.

nogueira, *s.f.* walnut *(a árvore ou a madeira).*

nogueiral, *s.m.* a grove of walnut-trees.

noitada, *s.f.* evening-party; a night out; night work; sleepless night, vigil, watch.

noite, *s.f.* night; evening; darkness; ignorance *(fig.)* 1) *de noite,* by night. 2) *durante a noite,* in the night. 3) *a noite passada, ontem à noite,* last night. 4) *amanhã à noite,* tomorrow night. 5) *alta noite, pela calada da noite,* in the dead of the night. 6) *hoje à noite,* tonight. 7) *ao cair da noite,* at dusk, at nightfall. 8) *boa noite,* good evening, good night. 9) *fazer-se noite,* to grow late. 10) *pela noite fora,* far into the night. 11) *a noite dos tempos,* the dark ages. 12) *a noite eterna,* the death. 13) *noite fechada,* dark night. 14) *noite velha,* late at night.

noitecer, *v.i.* to grow dark.

noitibó, *s.m.* nighthawk, nightjar.

noitinha, *s.f.* à *noitinha,* at nightfall.

noiva, *s.f.* bride, fiancée. 1) *ficar noiva,* to engage herself with. 2) *vestido de noiva,* bridal (wedding) dress. 3) *véu de noiva,* bridal veil.

noivado, *s.m.* wedding, engagement. 1) *anel de noivado,* wedding-ring. 2) *romper o noivado,* to break off the engagement.

noivar, *v.i.* to become engaged; to court.

noivo, *s.m.* bridegroom, fiancé; *os noivos,* the bridal pair, newlyweds.

nojento, *adj.* nauseating, repulsive, repugnant, sordid; disgusting.

nojo, *s.m.* nausea, loathing, disgust, aversion, repugnance; sorrow, grief, mourning.

nojoso, *adj.* disgusting, loathing.

nolição, *s.f.* unwillingness.

nómada, nómade, *s.m., adj.* nomad, wanderer; wandering, vagrant, vagabond.

nomadismo, *s.m.* nomadism.

nome, *s.m.* name; repute, fame; nickname; denomination, designation; renown; noun, substantive. 1) *nome de baptismo,* Christian name. 2) *nome de família,* surname, family name. 3) *de nome,* by name. 4) *bom nome,* reputation. 5) *dar nome,* to make famous.

nomeação, *s.f.* nomination, appointment.

nomeada, *s.f.* fame, reputation, name, renown.

nomeadamente, *adv.* namely.

nomeado, *adj.* appointed, designated; named, nominated.

nomear, *v.t.* to name; to nominate, to designate; to call; to appoint; to denominate, to mention.

nomenclatura, *s.f.* nomenclature, terminology.

nómina, *s.f.* relics-bag; amulet; brass stud.

nominação, *s.f.* denomination.

nominal, *adj.* nominal, not actual or real; *valor nominal,* face value.

nominalismo, *s.m.* nominalism.

nominalista, *s.* nominalist.

nominalmente, *adv.* nominally.

nominativo, *s.m., adj.* nominative; nominatival.

nomografia, *s.f.* nomography.

nomograma, *s.m.* nomogram.

nomologia, *s.f.* nomology.

nonada, *s.f.* trifle, bagatelle.

nonagenário, *s.m., adj.* nonagenarian.

nonagésimo, *adj.* nonagesimal; nonetieth.

nonas, *s.f. (pl.)* nones.

nongentésimo, *adj.* nine-hundredth.

nónio, *s.m.* nonious, vernier.

nono, *adj.* ninth.

nónuplo, *adj.* ninefold.

nora, *s.f.* daughter-in-law; noria *(para tirar água).*

nordeste, *s.m.* north-east; northeaster *(vento).*

nordestear, *v.i.* to swing northeast; to steer northeast.

nordestina, *s.f.* cold northeast wind.

nordestino, *s.m.* Brazilian northeasterner.

nórdico, *adj.* Nordic.

norma, *s.f.* norm, standard, model, pattern; type rule, percept; principle.

normal, *adj.* normal, usual, regular, natural; *s.f.* normal perpendicular line.

normalidade, *s.f.* normality.

normalista, *s.* student of a normal school.

normalização, *s.f.* normalization; adjustment.

normalizar, *v.t.* to normalize, to return to normal, to make normal.

normalmente, *adv.* normally.

normando, *adj.* Norman; *s.m.* Norseman, Norman; a printing type.

normativo, *adj.* regular, as usual, normative, perceptive; standard.

nor-nordeste, *s.m.* north-northeast.

nor-noroeste, *s.m.* north-northwest.

noroeste, *s.m.* north-west.

nortada, *s.f.* north wind.

norte, *s.m.* north; direction guide *(fig)*.

norteador, *adj.* guiding, directing.

norte-americano, *adj., s.m.* North American.

nortear, *v.t.* to guide, to lead, to direct; to regulate; to show the way.

nortenho, *adj.* relating to the North *(de Portugal)*.

nortista, *s., adj.* pertaining to the North *(no Brasil)*.

norueguês, *s.m., adj.* Norwegian *(língua ou habitante)*.

nós, *pron. pess.* we; us; ourselves.

nos, *pron. pess.* us; *prep. em e art. os,* in the, on the.

nosocómio, *s.m.* hospital.

nosofobia, *s.f.* nosophobia.

nosografia, *s.f.* nosography.

nosologia, *s.f.* nosology.

nosológico, *adj.* nosological.

nosso, *adj. poss.* our; *pron. poss.* ours.

nostalgia, *s.f.* nostalgia, homesickness.

nostálgico, *adj.* nostalgic, homesick.

nota, *s.f.* note, memorandum, annotation; comment; repute; sound; mark *(na escola)*; regard, attention; observation, remark; bank-note; musical note. 1) *de má nota,* noteworthy. 2) *tomar nota,* to commit to paper.

notabilidade, *s.f.* notability; remarkableness.

notabilizar, *v.t.* top make notable; to shine; *notabilizar-se,* to become notable, famous.

notação, *s.f.* notation.

notado, *adj.* notable, conspicuous; noted.

notar, *v.t.* to note, to mark; to observe; to set down, to record; to notice, to regard; to keep in mind.

notariado, *s.m.* notary's office, the profession or function.

notarial, *adj.* notarial.

notário, *s.m.* notary.

notável, *adj.* notable, remakable, eminent, distinguished, famous, extraordinary, important; strange, amazing.

notavelmente, *adv.* notably.

notícia, *s.f.* information, news; report, word, notice.

noticiador, *s.m.* informer, reporter; advertiser.

noticiar, *v.t.* to announce, to publish; to inform, to notify, to tell, to make known.

noticiário, *s.m.* news section; news service.

noticiarista, *s.* reporter, news writer.

noticioso, *adj.* well informed; informative; newsy.

notificação, *s.f.* notification, communication; announcement; summons, citation.

notificador, *s.m.* notifier, informer; *adj.* notifying.

notificante, *adj.* notifying.

notificar, *v.t.* to notify, to summon.

notificativo, notificatório, *adj.* that notifies, notifying.

notificável, *adj.* notifiable.

noto, *s.m.* south wind; *adj.* notorious, known.

notoriamente, *adv.* notoriously.

notoriedade, *s.f.* notoriety, publicity, proeminency.

notório, *adj.* notorious, evident, patent, well known, public.

nótula, *s.f.* comment, brief note.

noute, *s.f.* ver noite.

nova, *s.f.* news, novelty, piece of news; intelligence, tidings, account.

novação, *s.f.* novation, change; renewal *(contrato)*.

nova-iorquino, *s.m.* New Yorker.

novamente, *adv.* newly, again, once more, over and again.

novato, *s.m.* novice, tyro, beginner, apprentice; freshman *(universidade)*; new-comer; *adj.* inexperienced, untrained, raw.

nove, *num.* nine.

novecentos, *num.* nine hundred.

novedio, *s.m.* shoot, sprout, bud, sprig, gem; *adj.* young.

nove-horas, *s.f. (pl)* airs, ceremonies, overpoliteness.

novel, *adj.* novel, new, fresh, young, beginning, raw, untrained.

novela, *s.f.* shortnovel, tale, story, narrative; plot. 1) *novela de rádio,* feature. 2) *novela policial,* detective story.

novelesco, *adj.* novel-like, novelistic, romantic.

novelista, *s., adj.* novelist.

novelo, *s.m.* ball of thread or yarn, skein; plot; tangle.

Novembro, *s.m.* November.

novena, *s.f.* novena, nine days; devotion repeated during nine days *(católicos)*; group of nine.

novenal, *adj.* of nine days.

novenário, *s.m.* prayer book of novenas.

novénio, *s.m.* period of nine years.

noveno, *adj.* ninth.

noventa, *num.* ninety.

noviciado, *s.m.* noviciate *(numa ordem religiosa);* apprenticeship.

noviciar, *v.i.* to be a novice; to start.

noviciaria, *s.f.* section assigned to novices.

noviciário, *adj.* relating to novices.

noviço, *s.m.* novice; beginner apprentice; *adj.* inexperienced, green.

novidade, *s.f.* novelty, newness, news, tidings; latest fashion; new fruit, crops; early vegetables.

novilatino, *adj.* New-Latin.

novilha, *s.f.* heifer.

novilhada, *s.f.* herd of steers; bullfight.

novilheiro, *s.m.* herdsman; bullfighter.

novilho, *s.m.* steer. bullock.

novilunar, *adj.* novilunar.

novilúnio, *s.m.* new moon.

novinho, *adj.* quite new, brand new.

novíssimo, *adj.* very new, latest, most recent.

novo, *adj.* new, modern, recent, fresh, green, original; not worn out, unused; strange; inexperienced; young *(pessoas ou animais).* 1) *os novos,* young people. 2) *novo em folha,* fire new, brand new. 3) *de novo,* anew, over again.

novocaína, *s.f.* novocaine.

nóxio, *adj.* noxious, harmful, poisonous.

noz, *s.f.* nut, walnut; *miolo de noz,* kernel of a walnut.

noz-moscada, *s.f.* nutmeg.

noz-vómica, *s.f.* nut vomica, poison nut.

nu, *adj.* bare, naked, unclothed, undressed, uncovered; barren *(vegetação);* drawn; simple, sincere; plain, artless. 1) *nu em pêlo,* stark-naked. 2) *a olho nu,* with the naked eye.

nuamente, *adv.* plainly.

nuamça, *s.f.* nuance, shade, hue.

nubente, *adj., s.* betrothed.

nubífero, *adj.* nubiferous, cloudy.

núbil, *adj.* nubile, marriageable.

nubilidade, *s.f.* nubility.

nubiloso, *adj.* cloudy, foggy, misty.

nublado, *adj.* cloudy, overcast, dark, gloomy, obscure, somber.

nublar, *v.t.* to cloud, to overcast, to become cloudy.

nubloso, *adj.* cloudy, misty; gloomy, sullen.

nuca, *s.f.* nape; neck.

nução, *s.f.* assent, consent.

nuciforme, *adj.* nuciform, nut-shaped.

nucífrago, *adj.* nutcracking.

nucívoro, *adj.* nucivorous, nut-eating.

nucial, nuclear, *adj.* nucleal, nuclear.

núcleo, *s.m.* nucleus; kernel, core; center, essential part.

nucléolo, *s.m.* nucleolus.

nuculoso, *adj.* that contains nuts.

nudação, *s.f.* undressing, stripping; nudity.

nudez, *s.f.* nudity, bareness, nudeness.

nudeza, *s.f. ver "nudez".*

nudismo, *s.m.* nudism.

nudista, *s.* nudist.

nuelo, *adj.* new-born; featherless.

nueza, *s.f. ver* nudez.

nuga, *s.f.* trifle, frivolity.

nugação, *s.f.* futility; vain argument.

nugacidade, *s.f.* frivolity, futility, triviality.

nugativo, nigatório, *adj.* nugatory, trifling, frivolous, futile, trivial, vain; ridiculous.

nulidade, *s.f.* nullity, nothingness, insignificance; negation; nobody.

nulificação, *s.f.* nullification, nullifying.

nulificar, *v.t.* to nullify; to cancel.

nulípara, *s.f.* nulliparous.

nulo, *adj.* null, void, useless; worthless; unable, inept; zero, nought.

num, *prep. em e art. um,* in a, on a, at a (one).

numária, *s.f.* numismatics.

numário, *adj.* nummary.

nume, númen, *s.m.* deity.

numeração, *s.f.* numeration; numbering.

numerador, *s.m.* numerator, numberer; numbering machine, *adj.* numerative.

numeral, *adj., s.m.* numeral.

numerar, *v.t.* to number; to count; to enumerate; to expose.

numerário, *adj.* nummary; *s.m.* money, cash; coin.

numerativo, *adj.* numbering.

numerável, *adj.* numerable.

numericamente, *adv.* numerically.

numérico, *adj.* numerical.

número, *s.m.* number; multitude, plurality, quantity, amount, sum. 1) *número par,* even number. 2) *número ímpar,* odd number. 3) *número atrasado (jornal, revista, etc.),* back number. 4) *fazer número,* to fill the number, to be an «also». 5) *número fraccionário,* fractional number. 6) *número primo,* prime number. 7) *número de ordem,* reference number. 8) *ser um bom número,* to be a laughing stock.

numerosamente, *adv.* numerously.

numerosidade, *s.f.* numerousness.

numeroso, *adj.* numerous, plentiful; harmonious, melodious *(verso ou prosa)*.

númida, *s., adj.* Numidian.

numismata, *s.* numismatist.

numismática, *s.f.* numismatics.

numismático, *adj.* numismatic.

numulite, *s.f.* nummulite.

numulítico, *adj.* nummulitic.

nunca, *adv.* never, at no time. 1) *quase nunca,* hardly ever. 2) *nunca se sabe,* you can never tell. 3) *mais do que nunca,* more than ever. 4) *melhor do que nunca,* better than ever. 5) *é um nunca acabar,* there is no end to it. 6) *nunca mais,* nevermore, never again, no more.

nunciatura, *s.f.* nunciature *(dignidade ou residência do núncio).*

núncio, *s.m.* nuncio, papal legate.

nuncupação, *s.f.* nuncupation.

nuncupativo, nuncupatório, *adj.* nuncupative; oral, not written.

nunes, *adj.* odd (not even).

nupcial, *adj.* nuptial, bridal.

núpcias, *s.f. (pl.)* nuptials, wedding, wedding ceremonies.

nutação, *s.f.* nutation; vacillation.

nutar, *v.i.* to nod; to nutate, to oscillate.

nuto, *s.m.* nod (of the head).

nutrição, *s.f.* nutrition, nourishment, feed.

nutrício, *s.f.* nutritious, nourishing.

nutrido, *adj.* well-fed, strong, robust, corpulent; continual *(fogo).*

nutridor, *s.m.* nourisher, feeder.

nutriente, *adj.* nutrient, nourishing, nutritive, nutritious.

nutrimento, *s.m.* nutriment, nourishment; food.

nutrir, *v.t.* to nourish, to feed; to maintain; to cherish; to entertain; to fatten.

nutrítício, *adj.* nutritive; nourishing.

nutritivo, *adj.* nourishing, nutritive, nutrient.

nuvem, *s.f.* cloud; haze; gloom; shadow, shade; multitude. 1) *cair das nuvens,* to be flabbergasted. 2) *ir às nuvens,* to see red, to be exasperated, to explode.

O

o, the fourteenth letter of the Portuguese alphabet.

oaristo, *s.m.* dialogue; intercourse.

oasiano, *adj. s.m.;* relative to an oasis; oasis dweller.

oásico, *adj., v.* oasiano.

oásis, *s.m.* oasis; resting place *(fig.).*

obcecação, *s.f.* obduracy; blindness, obstinacy, stubborness, contumacy.

obcecado, *adj.* unreasoning; blind; stubborn; bewildered.

obcecador, obcecante, *adj.* obsessing.

obcecar, *v.t.* to obfuscate; to obscure (the understanding); to blind; to obsess; to fascinate, to bewilder.

obduração, *s.f.* obduracy, inflexibility, obstinacy; hardness (of heart).

obdurar, *v.t.* to obdurate, to harden; to persist; to indurate; to make or to become unfeeling.

obedecer, *v.i.* to obey, to execute, to comply with; to follow; to submit; to listen to; to yield.

obediência, *s.f.* obedience, submission, compliance.

obediente, *adj.* obedient, submissive, respectful, compliant; docile, humble.

obedientemente, *adv.* obediently.

obeliscal, *adj.* obeliscal.

obelisco, *s.m.* obelisk.

obesidade, *s.f.* obeseness, obesity; fatness, corpulence.

obeso, *adj.* obese; fat, fleshy, corpulent.

óbice, *s.m.* hinderance, impediment, obstacle.

óbito, *s.m.* obit, death, decease.

obituário, *s.m., adj.* obituary.

objecção, *s.f.* objection, opposition; obstacle; disapproval.

objectar, *v.t.* to object, to oppose, to disaprove; to refute; to contest.

objectiva, *s.f.* objective, lens; objective-glass.

objectivação, *s.f.* objectification.

objectivamente, *adv.* objectively.

objectivar, *v.t.* to objectify.

objectividade, *s.f.* objectivity.

objectivismo, *s.m.* objectivism.

objectivo, *adj.* objective, impartial; s.m. end, aim, purpose, intent, object.

objecto, *s.m.* object, thing; purpose; matter, subject, topic; motive, reason.

objurgação, *s.f.* objurgation, reproof, blame, rebuke, reproach.

objurgar, *v.t.* to objurgate, to chide, to blame, to reproof, to rebuke.

objurgatória, *s.f.* ver objurgação.

objurgatório, *adj.* objurgatory, reproachful, upbraiding, rebuking.

oblação, *s.f.* oblation; offering *(a Deus)*; gift, donation.

oblata, *s.f.* ver oblação.

oblatar, *v.t.* to offer.

oblativo, *adj.* oblational, oblatory.

oblato, *s.m.* oblate *(padres seculares)*.

oblíqua, *s.f.* oblique line.

obliquamente, *adc.* obliquely.

obliquângulo, *adj.* oblique-angled.

obliquar, *v.i.* to oblique, to slant, to move forward half-right or half-left.

obliquidade, *s.f.* obliquity, slanting, position.

oblíquo, *adj.* oblique; evasive; ambiguous.

obliteração, *s.f.* obliteration, effacement, extinction.

obliterado, *adj.* obliterated, forgotten; extinguished, effaced.

obliterante, *adj.* obliterating.

obliterar, *v.t.* to oblitearte, to efface, to blot out, to destroy, to extinguish; not to remember.

oblívio, *s.m.* oblivion, forgetfulness.

oblongo, *adj.* oblong, oval, elongated.

obnóxio, obnoxious, offensive.

obnubilação, *s.f.* obnubilation, mental derangement.

obnubilar, *v.t.* to obnubilate, to cloud, to obscure.

oboé, *s.m.* oboe, hautboy.

oboísta, *s.* oboe-player, oboist.

óbolo, *s.m.* obolus, alms, donation.

obra, *s.f.* work; action, deed; achievement, performance; composition *(musical ou literária)*; painting, artistic creation; task; undertaking, engineering structure; reairs *(de um prédio)*. 1) *obra de arte*, work of art. 2) *obra em madeira*, timber work. 3) *obra clássica*, classic (work). 4) *obra de cantaria*, stonework. 5) *obra de consulta*, reference work. 6) *obra de empreitada*, contract work. 7) *mãos à obra*, let us get to work. 8) *obra de fancaria*, shoddy work. 9) *obra de misericórdia*, act of charity. 10) *meter mãos à obra*, to set to work.

obra-prima, *s.f.* masterpiece.

obrar, *v.t.* to work; to carry on; to effect; to bringabout; to make, to execute, to put into practice; to defecate.

obreia, *s.f.* wafer.

obreira, *s.f.* worker, workwoman; workerbee.

obreiro, *s.m.* worker; workman, labourer.

obrigação, *s.f.* obligation; engagement; favour; gratitude; responsability; duty; bond, debenture; task work. 1) *obrigação do Estado*, Government bond. 2) *ter obrigação de*, to be obliged to. 3) *fazer a sua obriga-ção*, to perform one's duty. 4) *primeiro a obrigação depois a devoção*, duty before pleasure.

obrigacional, *adj.* obligational.

obrigacionista, *s.* bondholder.

obrigado, *adj.* obliged, bound; compelled, forced; thankful, grateful; *interj.* thanks, thank you; *muito obrigado!*, many thanks!, thank you very much!.

obrigador, obrigante, *adj.* obliging, binding, imposing.

obrigar, *v.t.* to oblige; to compel, to constrain, to force; to put under an obligation; to incite, to urge; *obrigar-se*, to bind oneself, to assume an obligation.

obrigatoriamente, *adv.* compulsorily.

obrigatoriedade, *s.f.* obligatoriness, compulsiveness.

obrigatório, *adj.* compulsory; obligatory, binding.

ob-rogação, *s.f.* derogation.

ob-rogar, *v.t.* derogate.

obscenamente, *adv.* obscenely, bawdly, indecently.

obscenidade, *s.f.* obscenity, bawdiness, indecency.

obsceno, *adj.* obscene, repulsive, indecent, bawdy, filthy; vulgar, foul.

obscuração, *s.f.* obscuration.

obscuramente, *adv.* obscurely.

obscurante, *adj.* darkening, obscurant.

obscurantismo, *s.m.* obscurantism.

obscurantista, *s., adj.* obscurantist.

obscurecer, *v.t.* to obscure; to make dark; to grow dark; to render unintelligible, to confuse.

obscurecimento, *s.m.* obscuratio; darkening.

obscuridade, *s.f.* obscurity; darkness, dimness; unnintelligibility; humble position in life.

obscuro, *adj.* obscure, dark, dim, dusky; indistinct; remote; unnoticed; secluded; doubtful; hidden; lowly; humble.

obsecração, *s.f.* obsecration, imploring, entreaty, supplication.

obsecrar, *v.t.* to implore, to obsecrate, to beseech, to supplicate.

obsequente, *adj.* obedient, yielding, compliant, docile; obsequious, serviceable.

obsequiador, *adj.* obsequious, oblinging, kind, polite; *s.m.* kind person.

obsequiar, *v.t.* to oblige; to a favour; to offer as a gift; to display courtesy.

obséquio, *s.m.* kindeness, favour, service, courtesy.

obsequiosamente, *adv.* obligingly, politely.

obsequiosidade, *s.f.* kindliness, politeness, complaisance.

obsequioso, *adj.* kind, obliging, serviceable; courteous.

observação, *s.f.* observation; notice, note; remark, comment; examination, investigation.

observador, *s.m.* observer; watcher; spectator; astronomer, weather observer; *s.m.* observant, watchful, heedful.

observância, *s.f.* observance, execution, accomplishment, fulfilment; discipline, ritual.

observante, *adj.* observant, obedient; loyal.

observar, *v.t.* to observe, to take notice, to perceive, to examine, to perform; to remark, to comment; to respect, to be observant of, to obey, to follow *(uma regra);* to keep.

observatório, *s.m.* observatory.

observável, *adj.* observable.

obsessão, *s.f.* obsession, fixed idea, mania.

obsessionante, obsessivo, *adj.* obsessive, troublesome.

obsesso, *s.m.* person possessed; *adj.* harassed, hunted *(por um espírito maligno).*

obsessor, *s.m.* obsessor; *adj.* obsessive, obsessing.

obsidente, *adj.* besieging, obsessive.

obsidiante, *adj.* besieging.

obsidiar, *v.t.* to besiege; to haunt; to watch; to spy; to molest, to annoy.

obsolência, *s.f.* obsolescence.

obsoletismo, *s.m.* obsoletism, obsoluteness.

obsoleto, *adj.* obsolete, out of date, old-fashioned, archaic, outmoded.

obstáculo, *s.m.* obstacle, impediment; obstruction, hindrance; difficulty; objection; drawback; jump, hurdle *(desporto);* stumbling block; snag.

obstante, *adj.* hindering, obstructive; *não obstante,* in spite of, nevertheless; although, notwithstanding, however.

obstar, *v.i.* to be opposed, to oppose, to hinder, to prevent; to resist, to bar.

obstativo, *adj.* hindering, obstructive.

obstetra, *s.* obstetrician.

obstétrica, *s.f.* obstetrics.

obstetrícia, *s.f. ver "obstétrica".*

obstetrício, *adj.* obstetric.

obstétrico, *adj. ver "obstetricio".*

obstinação, *s.f.* obstinacy; obduracy, tenacity, persistance, stubbornness, pertinacity, contumacy.

obstinadamente, obstinately, stubbornely.

obstinado, *adj.* obstinate, obdurate, persistent, stubborn, pigheaded, inflexible; headstrong; resolute, contumacious.

obstinar-se, *v.refl.* to stick to, to persist in, to preserve, to be stubborn.

obstipação, *s.f.* obstipation.

obstipar, *v.t.* to cause obstipation.

obstringir, *v.t.* to constrain, to press, to force, to compel.

obstrito, *adj.* constrained, bound, forced, obliged.

obstrução, *s.f.* obstruction, hindrance, blockage; opposition.

obstrucionismo, *s.m.* obstructionism, filibuster.

obstrucionista, *s.* obstructionist, filibuster; *adj.* obstrucionist.

obstruir, *v.t.* to obstruct, to hinder, to impede, to block, to bar, to hamper, to stop up.

obstrutivo, *adj.* obstructive.

obstrutor, adj. obstructive, obstructing; s.m. hinderer, obstructor.

obstupefacção, s.f. amazement, stupefaction, surprise.

obstupefacto, adj. amazed, astonished.

obstúpido, adj. amazed, surprised.

obtemperação, s.f. obedience, submission, compliance.

obtemperar, v.t. to obtemper, to submit to, to comply with; to repley mildly; to agree.

obtenção, s.f. obtaining, obtainment, aquisition, attainment, acquirement.

obtenível, adj. obtainable.

obtentor, s.m. obtainer, acquirer.

obter, v.t. to obtain, to get; to procure; to reach, to acquire; to win, to achieve; to buy.

obtestação, s.f. obtestation.

obtestar, v.t. to obtest; to supplicate; to adjure.

obtundente, adj. obtundent, blunting.

obtundir, v.t. to obtund, to blunt, to deaden, to bruise.

obturação, s.f. obturation, stopping up, plugging, filling (um dente).

obturador, s.m. obturator; shutter (de uma máquina fotográfica); plug, stopper; adj. obturating.

obturante, adj. obturing.

obturar, v.t. to obturate, to close; to stop up; to plug; to fill (um dente).

obtusamente, adv. obtusely, bluntly.

obtusângulo, adj. obtuse-angular, obtused-angled.

obtusão, s.f. obtuseness, dullness; stupidity.

obtusidade, s.f. obtusity; dullness; bluntness.

obtuso, adj. obtuse; dull, stupid, slow.

obumbrante, adj. overshadowing.

obumbrar, v.t. to darken, to overshadow, to shade; to overcast; to grow cloudy.

obus, s.m. howitzer.

obvenção, s.f. profit, gain.

obviamente, adv. obviously, plainly.

obviar, v.t. to obviate; to remove; to prevent; to remedy; to get rid of.

óbvio, adj. obvious, manifest, evident, clear, visible.

obvir, v.i. to accrue, to come to, to fall to (lei, direitos, etc.).

oca, s.f. ochre (cor): the goose (jogo).

ocar, v.t. to hollow, to excavate, to make hollow; to empty.

ocarina, s.f. ocarina.

ocasião, s.f. occasion, opportunity; reason, motive, cause; time, spare time. 1) em qualquer ocasião, at any time. 2) aproveitar a ocasião enquanto é tempo, to make hay while the sun shines. 3) aproveitar a ocasião, to take advantage. 4) a ocasião faz o ladrão, opportunity makes the thief.

ocasionado, adj. occasioned, caused incidentally.

ocasionador, s.m. causer.

ocasional, adj. occasional, incidental, casual, eventual.

ocasionalidade, s.f. occasionality.

ocasionalismo, s.m. occasionalism.

ocasionalista, s.m., s.f. occasionalist.

ocasionalmente, adv. occasionally, eventually, sometimes, row and then, at times.

ocasionar, v.t. to occasion, to cause, to give rise to, to bring about, to originate.

ocaso, s.m. sunset; occident; west; end; death, decline, decay.

occídio, s.m. murder.

occipício, s.m. occiput, back of the head.

occipital, adj. occipital.

occipúcio, s.m. icciput, hindhead.

occiput, s.m. occiput.

occisão, s.f. killing, slaying.

oceânico, adj. oceanic.

Oceânides, s.f. (pl.) Oceanides, ocean nymphs.

oceano, s.m. ocean; the sea.

oceanografia, s.f. oceanography.

oceanográfico, adj. oceanographic(al).

oceanógrafo, s.m. oceanographer.

oceanologia, s.f. oceanology.

ocelado, adj. ocellated; spotted.

ocelo, s.m. ocellus; spot.

ocidental, adj. wester, occidental.

ocidentalidade, s.f. occidentality.

ocidentalismo, s.m. occidentalism.

ocidentalização, s.f. occidentalization.

ocidentalizar, v.t. to occidentalize.

ocidente, s.m. west, occident.

ócio, s.m. idleness, leisure, time, laziness, inactivity, spare time.

ociosidade, s.f. idleness, laziness, indolence; a ociosidade é a mãe de todos os vícios, idleness is the root of all evils.

ocioso, adj. idle, lazy, vain; s.m. idler, idle man, loafer, lazybones.

oclusão, s.f. occlusion, shutting up.

oclusivo, adj. occlusive; consoante oclusiva, explosive consonant.

ocluso, adj. occluded, closed.

oco, adj. empty, hollow; vain, futile.

ocorrência, *s.f.* occurrence, event, happening, fact.

ocorrente, *adj.* occuring, happening, occurrent.

ocorrer, *v.i.* to occur, to take place, to happen; to come to the mind.

ocra, *s.f.* ochre.

ocráceo, *adj.* ochraceous, ochreous.

ocre, *s.m.* ver ocra.

octacordo, *s.m.* octachord.

octaédrico, *adj.* octahedral.

octaedro, *s.m.* octahedron.

octana, *s.f.* octane.

octante, *s.m.* octant.

octilião, *s.m.* octillion.

octingentésimo, *adj.* eighthundredth.

octogenário, *s.m.* octogenarian; *adj.* octo-genary.

octogésimo, *adj.* eightieth.

octogonal, *adj.* octagonal.

octógono, *s.m.* octagon.

octossilábico, *adj.* octosyllabic.

octossílabo, *s.m.* octosyllable; adj. octossyllabic.

octuplicar, *v.t.* to octuple, to make eightfold.

óctuplo, *s.m., adj.* octuple; eightfold.

oculação, *s.f.* the grafting of a bud on a tree.

oculado, *adj.* oculate, having eyes; spotted.

ocular, *adj.* ocular, visual; *s.m.* eyepiece *(de um instrumento óptico)*. 1) *globo ocular,* eyeball. 2) *testemunha ocular,* eyewitness.

oculiforme, *adj.* oculiform, eye-like *(na forma ou na aparência).*

oculista, *s.* occulist *(o médico);* optician.

óculo, *s.m.* eye-glass; bull's-eye window; circular window; spectacles, glasses *(pl).* 1) *óculo de alcance,* spy-glass. 2) *óculos de protecção,* goggles.

ocultação, *s.f.* occultatio, concealment.

ocultador, *s.m.* cancealer; *adj.* concealing.

ocultamente, *adv.* secretely.

ocultante, *adj.* cancealing.

ocultar, *v.t.* to occult, to conseal, to hide; to cover; to keep secret; to disguise, to dissemble; *ocultar a verdade,* to hold back the truth.

ocultas, *s.f. (pl.) às ocultas,* secretely, by stealth, in an underhand manner.

ocultismo, *s.m.* occultism.

ocultista, *s., adj.* occultist.

oculto, *adj.* occult, hidden, concealed; recondite; veiled; secret; invisible; misterious.

ocupação, *s.f.* occupation; employment, business, work, job, position.

ocupado, *adj.* busy; occupied; engaged; taken *(casa).*

ocupador, ocupante, *s.m.* occupier; tenant; *adj.* occupying.

ocupar, *v.t.* to occupy; to hold in possession; to fill; to engage; to employ; to live in, to inhabit; to take up, to capture, to invade; to keep busy; 1) *ocupar um bom lugar,* to hold a good position.

odalisca, *s.f.* odalisque, odalisk.

ode, *s.f.* ode.

odiar, *v.t.* to hate, to detest, to dislike, to abhor, to, loathe, to execrate.

odeão, *s.m.* odeum *(teatro).*

odiável, *adj.* hatable.

odiento, *adj.* hateful, spiteful, rancorous, odious.

ódio, *s.m.* hate, aversion, dislike; enmity; animosity; hatred; rancour, hostility, spite; *ódio de morte,* deep-seated; hatred.

odiosamente, *adv.* odiously, hatefully.

odioso, *adj.* odious, repulsive, hateful, rancorous; abominable, spiteful.

odisseia, *s.f.* Odyssey.

odometria, *s.f.* odometry.

odómetro, *s.m.* odometer.

odontalgia, *s.f.* odontalgia, toothache.

odontálgico, *adj.* odontalgic.

odontíase, *s.f.* odontiasis, dentition.

odontite, *s.f.* odontitis.

odontogenia, *s.f.* odontogeny.

odontografia, *s.f.* aodontography.

odontógrafo, *s.m.* odontograph.

odontóide, *adj.* odontoid, like a tooth.

odontologia, *s.f.* odontology.

odontológico, *adj.* odontoligic(al).

odontologista, *s.* odontologist, dentist.

odontólogo, *s.m.* ver odontologista.

odor, *s.m.* odour, smell, fragrance, scent, perfume, aroma, sweet smell.

odorante, *adj.* odorant, odoriferous, fragrant, perfumed.

odorar, *v.i.* to scent, to perfume; to emit odour.

odorífero, *adj.* odotiferous, odorous, sweet-smelling.

odorífico, *adj.* odoriferous.

odoroso, *adj.* odoriferous, perfumed.

odre, *s.m.* wine-skin; leather-bottle; drunkard *(fig).*

oés-noroeste, *s.m.* west-northwest.

oés-sudoeste, *s.m.* west-southwest.

oeste, *s.m.* west, occident; west wind; *adj.* western.

ofegante, *adj.* panting, breathless, gasping, puffing, out-of-breath.

ofegar, *v.i.* to pant for breath; to breath quickly; to long for; to breath hard, to gasp.

ofego, *s.m.* panting; breathlessness.

ofendedor, *s.m.* offender.

ofender, *v.t.* to offend; to hurt; to annoy; to shock, to affront, to insult; to disrespect, to transgress, to sin; to scandalize; to harm, to injure; *ofender-se com,* to resent, to take amiss, to feel hurt; to be offended by (with).

ofendido, *adj.* offended, insulted; hurt; *s.m.* offended person.

ofensa, *s.f.* offence, affront, insult; misdeed.

ofensão, *s.f.* offensiveness; offence.

ofensiva, *s.f.* offensive, assault; attack; *tomar a offensiva,* to take the offensive.

ofensivamente, *adv.* offensively.

ofensivo, *adj.* offensive; aggressive; vexing, annoying; insulting; injurious.

ofensor, *s.m.* offender, injurer.

oferecedor, *s.m.* offerer.

oferecer, *v.t.* to offer, to present, to proffer; to exibit, to expose; to bid *(preço);* to devote, to consecrate. 1) *oferecer-se para,* to volunteer. 2) *oferecer resistência,* to stand up against. 3) *oferecer garantia,* to stand security. 4) *oferecer uma vista bonita,* to command a fine view.

oferecimento, *s.m.* offer, proposal, tender.

oferenda, *s.f.* offering; sacrifice, oblation.

oferendar, *v.t.* to offer, to present, to make an offering.

oferente, *s. ver "oferecedor", "ofertante".*

oferta, *s.f.* gift; promise; oblation; offering, donation, present; bidding *(preço); oferta e procura,* supply and demand.

ofertamento, *s.m.* offering.

ofertante, *s.* proffer, offerer.

ofertar, *v.t.* to offer, to give, to present, to bestow.

ofertório, *s.m.* offertory.

oficiador, *s.m.* officiant, officiator; officiating.

oficial, *adj.* official, formal, authorized; authentic; s.m.official, artisan, artifice, skilled workman; craftsman; journeyman; officer (militar). 1) *oficial de dia,* officer of the day. 2) *oficial de ligação,* liaison officer. 3) *oficial do Estado-Maior,* general staff officer. 4) *oficial subalterno,* non-commissioned officer. 5) *oficial às ordens,* attached *(ao pessoal do general)* officer. 6) *oficial de diligências,* a minor court official.

oficialato, *s.m.* officership.

oficialidade, *s.f.* the officers, body or staff of officers.

oficialismo, *s.m.* officialism, officialdom; bureaucracy.

oficialização, *s.f.* officialization.

oficializar, *v.t.* to make official, to officialize; to sanction.

oficialmente, *adv.* officially.

oficiante, *s.m.* officiant, celebrant.

oficiar, *v.t.* to officiate.

oficina, *s.f.* workshop; factory; *oficina de encadernação,* bookbinder`s.

oficinal, *adj.* officinal.

ofício, *s.m.* office; duty, charge; function, employment, service; letter; art, trade; occupation, job. 1) *ofício divino,* divine office. 2) *artes e ofícios,* arts and crafts. 3) *Santo Ofício,* Holy office. 4) *são ossos de ofício,* it is all in a day's work.

oficiosamente, *adv.* officiously.

oficiosidade, *s.f.* officiousness.

oficioso, *adj.* officious; gratuitous, obsequious; obliging, friendly; unofficial, informal.

ofídio, *adj.* ophidian; *s.m. (pl.)* Ophidia *(cobra).*

ofidismo, *s.m.* study of the poison of serpents.

ofiografia, *s.f.* ophiography.

ofiolatria, *s.f.* ophiolatry, serpent worship.

ofiologia, *s.f.* ophiology.

ofiologista, *s.* ophiologist.

ofite, *s.f.* serpentine marble.

ofítico, *adj.* ophitic.

ofiurídeos, *s.m. (pl.)* Ophiuroidea.

oftalgia, *s.f.* eye-ache.

oftalmia, *s.f.* ophthalmia.

oftálmico, *adj.* ophthalmic.

oftalmologia, *s.f.* ophthalmology.

oftalmológico, *adj.* ophthalmologic(al)

oftalmologista, oftalmólogo, *s., s.m.* ophthalmologist.

oftalmocospia, *s.f.* ophthalmoscopy.

oftalmoscópio, *s.m.* ophthalmoscope.

ofuscação, *s.f.* darkening, dazzling, obfuscation, darkness, obscuration.

ofuscamento, *s.m.* obfuscation, darkness; bewilderment.

ofuscante, *adj.* blinding, flaring, dazzling.

ofuscar, *v.t.* to darken; to dazzle, to daze; to obfuscate, to overshadow, to obscure; to eclipse, to hide; to lower the prestige of, to outshine; to blind, to blear.

ogiva, *s.f.* ogive, pointed arch.

ogival, *adj.* ogival.

oh!, *interj.* oh! oh my!

ohm, *s.m.* ohm *(resistência eléctrica).*

oídio, *s.m.* oidium, powdery mildew.

oira, *s.f. ver* "oura."

oirar, *v.i.* to feel dizzy.

oiriçar, *v.t. ver* "ouriçar".

oiriço, *s.m. ver* "ouriço".

oiro, *s.m. ver* "ouro".

oitante, *s.m.* octant.

oitava, *s.f.* octave *(música, poesia).*

oitavado, *adj.* eight-sided; octogonal.

oitavar, *v.t* to make eight-sided.

oitavário, *s.m.* religious festival of eight days; octavarium *(livro).*

oitavo, *s.m., adj.* eighth.

oiteiro, *s.m., adj. ver* outeiro.

oitenta, *num.* eighthy.

oitentão, *s.m.* octogenarian.

oito, *num.* eight.

oitocentos, *num.* eight hundred.

olá!, *interj.* ho!, hello!, hey!.

olaia, *s.f.* Judas-tree.

olaria, *s.f.* pottery, earthenware, potter's ware.

olé!, *interj.* halloo!

oleáceo, *adj.* oleaceous, oleaginous.

oleado, *s.m.* oil-skin, oil-cloth; linoleum; *adj.* oily, greasy, containing oil.

oleagíneo, *adj. ver* oleaginoso.

oleaginoso, *adj.* oleaginous; oily; unctuous.

oleandro, *s.m.* oleander.

olear, *v.t.* to oil, to smear or rub over with oil; to impregnate with oil.

olearia, *s.f.* oil factory.

oleento, *adj.* oily, greasy.

oleico, *adj.* oleic.

oleícola, *adj.* pertaining to the culture of olive-trees.

oleicultor, *s.m.* olive grower.

oleicultura, *s.f.* olive growing.

oleífero, oleígeno, *adj.* oleiferous, oil-producing.

oleína, *s.f.* olein.

oleiro, *s.m.* potter; pottery worker.

olência, *s.f.* fragrance.

olente, *adj.* olent, smelling, odorous, fragrant.

óleo, *s.m.* oil. 1) *óleo canforado,* campho-rated oil. 2) *óleo de rícino,* castor oil. 3) *óleo de fígado de bacalhau,* cod-oliver oil. 4) *óleo de amendoim,* peanut oil. 5) *óleo de linhaça,* linseed oil. 6) *óleo de baleia,* whale oil. 7) *óleo de palma,* palm oil.

oleoduto, *s.m.* pipe-line, oleoduct.

oleografia, *s.f.* oleography, oleograph.

oleográfico, *adj.* oleographic.

oleogravura, *s.f.* oleograph.

oleómetro, *s.m.* oleometer.

oleosidade, *s.f.* oiliness.

oleoso, *adj.* oily, greasy; fat, fatty.

olfacção, *s.f.* olfaction, smelling.

olfactar, *v.t.* to smell.

olfactivo, *adj.* olfactive, olfactory.

olfacto, *s.m.* smell, the sense of smell.

olga, *s.f.* strip of land; plain between hills.

olha, *s.f.* hotchpotch.

olhada, *s.f.* glimpse, glance, look, squint.

olhadela, *s.f. ver* olhada.

olhador, *s.m.* seer, looker, observer.

olhadura, *s.f.* olhada.

olhal, *s.m.* the span of an arch, archway, arch of a bridge; ring.

olhar, *v.t.* to look at, to stare at, to observe, to behold; to look, to gaze; to look after, to care for; to give attention to, to consider; to beware of; to look into; to contemplate; to study, to examine, to inspect; to face. 1) *olhar-se,* to look at oneself *(num espelho).* 2) *olhar de esguelha,* to look askance at.

olhar, *s.m.* look, mien, aspect, expression of the eyes; countenance.

olheiras, *s.f. (pl.).* ter olheiras, to have rings round the eyes.

olheirento, *adj.* having dark circles under the eyes.

olheiro, *s.m.* overseer, foreman, superin-tendent, informer; spring, water-jet.

olhento, *adj.* eyed; porous, full of holes.

olho, *s.m.* eye; eyeball; pupil; care, attention; bud *(bot).* 1) *olho clínico,* clinical eye. 2) *olho da rua,* the middle of the street. 3) *a olho nu,* with the naked eye. 4) *olho por olho,* an eye for an eye. 5) *abrir os olhos a,* to undeceive someone. 6) *custar os olhos da cara,* to be excessively expensive. 7) *enquanto o diabo esfrega um olho, num abrir e fechar de olhos,* in the twinkling of an eye. 8) *fechar os olhos a,* to connive at. 9) *levantar os olhos,* to look up. 10) *lançar uma vista de olhos,* to cast a glance at. 11) *trazer debaixo de olho,* to keep an eye on. 12) *ver com bons olhos,* to see with pleasure. 13) *comprar a olho,* to buy on sight. 14) *fechar os olhos a,* to pretend not ro see. 15) *piscar os olhos,* to wink. 16) *pelos seus lindos olhos,* for his fair face. 17) *pôr no olho da rua,* to turn out, to throw out. 18) *bons olhos o vejam!,* well met!. 19) *fechar os olhos*, to die. 20) *saltar aos olhos*, to stare in the face. 21) *olho do queijo*, hole in the cheese. 22) *não ver com bons olhos*, to take a dim view of. 23) *olho do cu*, arsehole.

olho-d'água, *s.m.* water spring.

olho-de-boi, *s.m.* bull's eye, deck light.

olho-de-cabra, *s.m.* kind of rib grass.

olho-de-perdiz, *s.m.* phesant's eye, garden pink; a small corn on the toe.

olhudo, *adj.* goggle-eyed, big-eyed.

olíbano, *s.m.* olibanum, frankincense.

oligarca, *s.m.* oligarch.

oligarquia, *s.f.* oligarchy.

oligárquico, *adj.* oligarchic.

olimpíada, *s.f.* Olympiad.

olímpico, *adj.* Olympic; divine.

Olimpo, *s.m.* Olympus.

olissiponense, *adj.* referring to Lisbon, Lisbonese.

oliva, *s.f.* olive; olive-tree; olive shell.

oliváceo, *adj.* olivaceous, olive-green *(cor)*.

olival, *s.m.* olive grove, olive yard.

olivar, *adj.* olivary; olive shaped.

olivedo, *s.m.* ver *"olival"*.

oliveira, *s.f.* olive-tree.

oliveiral, *s.m.* ver *"olival"*.

olivicultor, *s.m.* olive grower.

olivicultura, *s.f.* olive growing.

olmedal, *s.m.* elm-grove.

olmedo, *s.m.* ver olmedal.

olmeiro, *s.m.* elm-tree.

olmo, *s.m.* elm-trees.

olor, *s.m.* aroma, fragrance, perfume, odour, scent.

oloroso, *adj.* odorous, fragrant, aromatic, perfumed.

olvidar, *v.t.* to forget; to overlook, to omit, to neglect, to leave out.

olvidável, *adj.* forgettable.

olvido, *s.m.* oblivion, forgetfulness.

omagra, *s.f.* gout in the shoulder.

omalgia, *s.f.* omalgia, pain in the shoulder.

omaso, *s.m.* omasum.

ombrear, *v.i.* to rival, to equal, to match, to be comparable to, to vie with.

ombreira, *s.f.* jamb, door post.

ombro, *s.m.* shoulder. 1) *ombro a ombro*, side by side, shoulder to shoulder. 2) *ombro armas!*, slope arms!. 3) *encolher os ombros*, to shrug the shoulders. 4) *olhar por cima do ombro*, to look down upon, to despise, to disdain. 5) *meter ombros a*, to put your shoulder to the wheel.

ómega, *s.m.* omega; the end, the last of a series.

omeleta, *s.f.* omelet.

ominar, *v.t.* to omen; to prognosticate; to hate; to augur ill, to presage, to forebode, to foretell.

ominoso, *adj.* ominous, inauspicious; hateful; portentous, foreboding.

omissão, *s.f.* omission; neglect, oversight, negligence; fault, lacuna; exclusion; 1) *salvo erro ou omissão*, errors and omission excepted.

omisso, *adj.* omitted, neglectful, excluded, remiss, suppressed.

omitir, *v.t.* to omit, to leave out, to neglect, to overlook, to forget, to fail to do, to disregard; to supress, to skip, to pass without notice.

omnicolor, *adj.* omnicoloured, multicoloured.

omniforme, *adj.* omniform.

omnimodo, *adj.* omnimodus.

omnipotência, *s.f.* omnipotence, almightiness.

omnipotente, *adj.* omnipotent, almighty, all-powerful; *s.m.* the Omnipotent, God himself, the Almighty.

omnipresença, *s.f.* omnipresence, ubiquity.

omnipresente, *adj.* omnipresent, ubiquitous.

omnisciência, *s.f.* omniscience, infinite knowledge.

omnisciente, *adj.* omniscient, all-knowing.

omnívoro, *adj.* omnivorous.

omoplata, *s.f.* omoplate; shoulderblade; scapula.

onagro, ónagro, *s.m.* onager, wild ass.

onanismo, *s.m.* onanism, masturbation.

onanista, *s.* onanist, masturbator.

onça, *s.f.* ounce (28,69 g); jaguar, ounce; *amigo da onça*, false friend.

oncologia, *s.f.* oncology.

oncologista, *s.* oncologist.

onda, *s.f.* wave, undulation, surge; vibration, oscillation *(radio)*; agitation, confusion, tumult. 1) *onda de calor*, heat wave. 2) *onda curta*, short wave. 3) *onda média*, medium wave. 4) *onda ultracurta*, ultra-short wave. 5) *onda sonora*, sound wave. 6) *onda ertziana*, Hertzian wave. 7) *comprimento de onda*, wave-length. 8) *ao sabor das ondas*, at the mercy of the waves. 9) *ir na onda*, to be swept along by others; to be taken in.

onde, *adv.* where; in which. 1) *onde quer que seja*, wherever it may be. 2) *até onde?*, as far as. 3) *de onde?*, where from?. 4) *de onde em onde*, from time to time, now and then. 5) *por onde?*, which way?

ondeado, *adj.* wavy; undulating.

ondeante, *adj.* undulating, waving.

ondear, *v.t., v.i.* to wave; to billow; to roll; to serpentine; to ripple.

ondejante, *adj.* ver *"ondeante".*

ondejar, *v.t., v.i.* ver *"ondear".*

ondina, *s.f.* undine.

ondulação, *s.f.* undulation, waviness; vibration.

ondulado, *adj.* wavy; undulated, rippled, crisp.

ondulante, *adj.* wavy; undulated; waving.

ondular, *v.i.* to undulate; *v.t.* to wave *(ar).*

ondulatório, *adj.* undulatory, wavy.

onduloso, *adj.* undulous, undulating; wavy, undulant.

oneração, *s.f.* taxation.

onerado, *adj.* overburdened, able to a tax.

onerar, *v.t.* to burden, to charge, to tax, to load.

onerosamente, *adv.* onerously.

onerosidade, *s.f.* onerousness.

oneroso, *adj.* onerous; heavy.

onglete, *s.m.* graver, burn.

ónibus, *s.m.* omnibus.

onicofagia, *s.f.* nail biting.

onicófago, *s.m.* nail-biter.

ónix, *s.m.* onyx.

onomástica, *s.f.* onomasticon.

onomástico, *adj.* onomastic.

onomatologia, *s.f.* onomatology, terminology.

onomatológico, *adj.* onomatological.

onomatólogo, *s.m.* onomatologist.

onomatopaico, *adj.* onomatopoeic.

onomatopeia, *s.f.* onomatopoeia.

onomatopeico, *adj.* ver onomatopaico.

ontem, *adv.* yesterday. 1) *ontem à noite,* last night. 2) *ontem de manhã,* yesterday morning.

ontogénese, *s.f.* ontogenesis.

ontogenia, *s.f.* ontogeny.

ontogénico, *adj.* ontogenic.

ontologia, *s.f.* ontology.

ontológico, *adj.* ontological.

ontologista, *s.* ontologist.

ónus, *s.m.* onus; burden; obligation, responsability; heavy taxes.

onusto, *adj.* overburdened, surcharged, overloaded, full.

onze, *num.* eleven.

onzena, *s.f.* usury.

onzenário, *s.m.* usurer, money-lender.

onzeneiro, *s.m.* usurer; intriguer, telltale; *adj.* gossiping, intriguing; usurious.

onzenice, *s.f.* intrigue, plot; gossip, talebearing.

onzeno, *num.* oogenesis.

oogenia, *s.f.* oogenesis.

oolítico, *adj.* oolitic.

oólito, *s.m.* oolite.

oologia, *s.f.* oology.

oosfera, *s.f.* oosphere.

opa, *s.f.* sleeveless surplice.

opacidade, *s.f.* opacity; darkness, obscurity.

opaco, *adj.* opaque; dark, obscure; not transparent.

opado, *adj.* swollen.

opala, *s.f.* opal, gem, precious stone; fine muslin.

opalescência, *s.f.* opalescence, milky iridescence.

opalescente, *adj.* opalescent, opaline, iridescent.

opalino, *adj.* opaline.

opalizar, *v.i.* to opalize, to make opalescent.

opção, *s.f.* option, choice.

ópera, *s.f.* opera; opera-house; *ópera cómica,* comic-opera

operação, *s.f.* operation; action, work, performance.

operacional, *adj.* operational.

operador, *s.m.* operator, surgeon; *operador cinematográfico,* cinematographer, projectionist.

operar, *v.t.* to operate on *(um doente); v.i.* to work, to produce; to accomplish; to perform an operation *(de qualquer tipo); operar-se,* to take place.

operariado, *s.m.* the workers, working classes, proletariat.

operário, *s.m.* worker, workman, artisan. 1) *operário especializado,* skilled workman. 2) *sindicato operário,* trade union.

operativo, *adj.* operative.

operatório, *adj.* operative, operating.

operável, *adj.* operable.

operculado, *adj.* operculate.

opercular, *adj.* opercular.

opérculo, *s.m.* operculum, cover, lid, calyx *(bot);* gill cover.

opereta, *s.f.* operetta.

operosidade, *s.f.* operoseness, toil, labour.

operoso, *adj.* laborious, wearisome; operose, active, productive.

opiáceo, adj. opiate.

opiar, v.t. to opiate, to narcotize, to mix with opium.

opiato, s.m. opiato, narcotic.

opilação, s.f. oppilation, obstriction, stopping up.

opilar, v.t. to oppilate, to obstruct; to hinder, to block.

opimo, adj. excellent, abundant, rich, productive, fertile.

opinante, adj. opining; s. person who holds an opinion.

opinar, v.t., v.i. to opine, to judge; to give or express an opinion.

opinativo, adj. opinative.

opinável, adj. conjectural, probable, disputable.

opinião, s.f. opinion, judgement, conviction, view; impression, feeling; thinking, idea; conjecture, point of view; reputation. 1) *mudar de opinião*, to change one's mind. 2) *na minha opinião*, in my opinion, to my thinking, as I take it. 3) *sou da opinião que*, I hold the opinion that.

opiniático, adj. opiniated, obstinate; conceited, arrogant.

opinioso, adj. opinionative; dogmatic, stubborn, obstinate, self-willed.

ópio, s.m. opium.

opiofagia, s.f. opium-eating.

opiófago, s.m. opium-eater.

opiomania, s.f. opiumism.

opiomaníaco, opiómano, s.m. opium-eater, opium-smoker.

opíparo, adj. sumptuous, abundant, magnificent, rich, abounding.

opodeldoque, s.m. opodeldoc.

opoente, oponente, adj. opponent, opposing, adverse, antagonistic; s. antagonist, adversary, rival, opponent.

oponibilidade, s.f. opposibility.

oponível, adj. opposable.

opor, v.t. to oppose, to set against; to object; to dispute; *opor-se*, to set oneself against, to resist, to withstand.

oportunamente, adv. opportunely, on occasion, apropos, seasonably.

oportunidade, s.f. opportunity, occasion, chance, favourable time. 1) *aproveitar a oportunidade*, to take an opportunity. 2) *dar uma oportunidade*, to give a chance.

oportunismo, s.m. opportunism.

oportunista, s. opportunist, timeserver; adj. opportunistic.

oportuno, adj. opportune, seasonable, suitable, appropriate, timely, favourable, propitious; *no momento oportuno*, in the nick of time.

oposição, s.f. opposition; hostility, resistance, obstacle; antagonism; contrast. 1) *em oposição a*, in opposition to, against. 2) *o chefe da oposição*, the leader of the opposition. 3) *encontrar oposição*, to meet with opposition.

oposicionismo, s.m. obstructionism.

oposicionista, s., adj. oppositionist.

opositivo, adj. oppositive, opposed.

opositor, adj. opposing, opponent; s.m. opposer, opponent, antagonist; competitor *(para um emprego)*; rival.

oposto, adj. opposed; facing, fronting; contrary; over against; antagonistic; s.m. the contrary, the opposite.

opressão, s.f. oppression, tyranny; suffocation, stifling, pressure; cruelty, persecution.

opressivo, adj. oppressive; tyrannical, severe.

opresso, adj. oppressed.

opressor, s.m. oppressor, despot, tyrant; adj. oppressing, oppressive.

oprimido, s.m. oppressed *(pessoa)*; adj. oppressed, persecuted.

oprimir, v.t. to oppress; to overcome; to overburden; to persecute, to torment, to scourage; to tyrannize, to enslave.

opróbrio, s.m. opprobrium; infamy, ignominy, shame, dishonour, disgrace.

oprobrioso, adj. opprobrious, shameful, defamatory, base, vile.

optação, s.f. optation, choice.

optante, s., adj. optant.

optar, v.i. to choose, to opt, to make a choice, to select, to decide for.

optativo, adj. optative.

óptica, s.f. optics.

óptico, adj. optic; s.m. optician.

optimamente, adv. very well. excellently.

optimismo, s.m. optimism.

optimista, s. optimist; adj. optimistic.

óptimo, adj. very good, excellent, fine.

optometria, s.f. optometry.

optómetro, s.m. optometer.

opugnação, s.f. oppugnancy. opposition, resistance; disputation, controversy.

opugnador, adj. oppugnant, opposing, antagonostic, contrary; s.m. opposer, oppugner, opponent, adversary.

opugnar, v.t. to oppugn, to oppose, to refute, to reject; to contradict.

opulência, opulence, wealth; abundance, riches.

opulentamente, adv. opulentcy.

opulentar, v.t. to make opulent; to enrich.

opulento, adj. opulent, rich, wealthy; abundant, profuse.

opúsculo, s.m. opuscule; pamphlet.

ora, conj. but, therefore, neverthless, however; adv. now, at present; interj. well!, well now!; why!; pooh, bah!. 1) *ora bem ora mal,* sometimes well, sometimes badly; up and down. 2) *por ora,* for the present. 3) *ora um ora outro,* now one then the other.

oração, s.f. prayer, supplication; sentence, clause, proposition, discourse, speech.

oracional, adj. clausal, propositional.

oracular, adj. oracular; oraculous.

oráculo, s.m. oracle.

orador, s.m. orator, speaker; preacher; to supplicate, to beseech.

orago, s.m. patron saint.

oral, adj. oral, spoken, verbal, vocal; 1) *exame oral,* oral examination.

oralidade, s.f. orality.

oralmente, adv. orally, verbally, by word of mouth.

orangotango, s.m. orangoutang, orangutan.

orar, v.i. to pray; to orate; to preach; to supplicate, to beseech.

orate, s.m. madman, lunatic, maniac, insane; *casa de orates,* bedlam, lunatic asylum.

oratória, s.f. oratory, eloquence, rhetoric.

oratoriano, s.m., adj. Oratorian *(Oratory Congregation).*

oratório, adj. oratorical; s.m. oratory, small chapel, shrine.

orbe, s.m. orb, globe, the world; sphere.

orbícola, adj. cosmopolitan.

orbicular, adj. orbicular, circular, round, spherical.

órbita, s.f. orbit, course *(de um planeta);* orbit, eye socket; scope, orbit (range field) of activity.

orbital, orbitário, adj. orbital.

orca, s.f. a killer whale, grampus.

orça, s.f. guess, estimate.

orçador, s.m. estimator; adj. estimating, estimative.

orçamental, adj. budgetary.

orçamentar, v.t. to estimate, to calculate.

orçamento, s.m. budget; estimate, cost, valuation. 1) *equilibrar o orçamento,* to balance the budget. 2) *fazer um orçamento,* to draw up an estimate.

orçar, v.t. to budget for; to estimate, to compute, to reckon.

orchata, s.f. orgeat *(bebida doce).*

ordálio, s.m. ordeal.

ordeiro, adj. orderly; peaceful, peaceable, fond of order.

ordem, s.f. order; arrange, disposition, regularity, method; rule, regulation, mandate; rank, degree; kind, sort; row; peace, discipline; category, group; religious order; succession; sequence; writ *(lei).* 1) *ordem de despejo,* eviction notice. 2) *ordem de pagamento,* banker's order. 3) *ordem de prisão,* warrant for arrest. 4) *ordem do dia,* order of the day. 5) *ordem social,* social order. 6) *ordem de terceira,* third order of Saint Francis. 7) *ordens maiores,* the major orders. 8) *ordens menores,* the minor orders. 9) *chamar à ordem,* to call to order. 10) *de primeira ordem,* first-rate. 11) *em perfeita ordem,* in due order, shipshape. 12) *pôr em ordem,* to put (to set) to right. 13) *por ordem,* in order, in succession. 14) *por ordem de,* by order (authority) of. 15) *até nova ordem,* until further orders. 16) *ordem do Banho,* Order of the Bath. 17) *Ordem da Jarreteira,* Order of the Garter. 18) *às ordens de,* under the orders of, at the disposal of. 19) *às suas ordens,* at your service, at your command.

ordenação, s.f. ordination, arrangement, disposition, order; ordination *(igreja);* classification, ordering; rule, law, ordinance.

ordenada, s.f. *(geom)* ordinate.

ordenadamente, adv. orderly, methodically.

ordenado, s.m. salary, wages, stipend, pay; adj. orderly, arranged; methodical; ordained *(igreja).*

ordenador, adj. ordering, regulating, directing; s.m. orderer, ordainer.

ordenamento, s.m. ver ordenação.

ordenança, s.f. ordinance, order, regulation, orderly *(no exército).*

ordenar, v.t. to order, to put in good order; to arrange, to organize; to comand, to bid to give an order, to enjoin, to regulate; to decree, to establish; to ordain, to confer holy orders; *ordenar-se,* to take (holy) orders.

ordenável, adj. orderable; ordainable.

ordenha, s.f. milking *(vaca).*

ordenhador, s.m. milker; milkmaid *(fem.).*

ordenhar, v.t. to milk.

ordinal, adj. ordinal.

ordinando, *s.m.* ordinand (about to be ordained).

ordinante, *s.m.* ordinant, ordainer.

ordinariamente, *adv.* ordinarily, commonly, usually; basely.

ordinário, *adj.* usual, habitual, common; mediocre; *s.m.* ordinary.

ordinarismo, *s.m.* baseness.

oréade, *s.f.* oread (mountain nymph).

orégão, *s.m.* marjoran.

orelha, *s.f.* ear; flap; volute; lug *(âncora);* claw.

orelhado, *adj.* eared.

orelhão, *s.m.* parotitis, mumps.

orelheira, *s.f.* pig's ears.

orelhudo, *adj.* large-eared; long-eared.

orexia, *s.f.* orexis, appetite; desire.

órfã, *s.f.* orphan-girl.

orfanar, *v.t.* to orphan, to orphanize.

orfanato, *s.m.* orphanage, orphan asylum; state of being an orphan.

orfandade, *s.f.* orphanhood.

orfanológico, *adj.* relating to orphans.

órfão, *s.m.* orphan. 1) *órfão de pai,* fatherless. 2) *órfão de mãe,* motherless.

orfeão, *s.m.* choral society; choir.

orfeico, *adj.* musical, orphean, melodious.

orfeónico, *adj.* relating to a choral society; choral.

orfeonista, *s.* orpheonist, choral singer.

organicamente, *adv.* organically.

organicismo, *s.m.* organicism.

orgânico, *adj.* organical; fundamental, vital, basic.

organismo, *s.m.* organism; body; constitution; authority.

organista, *s.* organist, organ player.

organização, *s.f.* organization; arrangement, order; organic structure; organism; institution.

organizado, *adj.* organized, structured; methodical, orderly.

organizador, *adj.* organizing; s.m. organizer.

organizar, *v.t.* to organize; to draw up; to order, to arrange; to give organic structure to; to put in order; to systematize; to promote *(um festival); organizar-se,* to get organized.

organizável, *adj.* organizible.

organografia, *s.f.* organography.

organográfico, *adj.* organographic(al).

organologia, *s.f.* organology.

organsim, organsina, *s.m., s.f.* organzine *(tecido).*

órgão, *s.m.* organ; agent; instrument; newspaper; part *(de uma máquina);* harmonium.

orgasmo, *s.m.* orgasm.

orgástico, *adj.* orgastic.

orgia, *s.f.* orgy, revelry, debauch, bacchanals; disorder, confusion, anarchy.

orgíaco, *adj.* orgiastic, bacchanal; anarchic.

orgulhar-se, *v. refl.* to be proud of, to take a pride in; to become proud.

orgulho, *s.m.* arrogance; pride; insolence; conceit; vanity; haughtiness.

orgulhosamente, *adv.* proudly.

orgulhoso, *adj.* proud, arrogant, haughty, lofty, conceited.

orientação, *s.f.* orientation; guidance, direction, bearings; *orientação profissional,* professional *(vocational)* guidance.

orientador, *adj.* orienting, guiding, directing; *s.m.* guide, leader; orientator.

oriental, *adj.* Oriental, eastern.

orientalidade, *s.f.* Orientality.

orientalismo, *s.m.* Orientalism.

orientalista, *s.* Orientalist.

orientalizar, *v.t.* to make Oriental, to give an Oriental shape.

orientar, *v.t.* to orient, to direct, to guide, to lead; *orientar-se,* to find the way, to get one's bearings; to take stock of (a situation).

Oriente, *s.m.* orient, east; the Orient, the eastern countries. 1) *Extremo Oriente,* Far East. 2) *Próximo Oriente,* Near East. 3) *Médio Oriente,* Middle East.

orifício, *s.m.* orifice, opening, mouth, hole, aperture.

oriflama, *s.f.* oriflamme.

oriforme, *adj.* mouth-shaped, oriform.

origem, *s.f.* origin, beginning; source, spring; derivation; ancestry, ascendance; extraction; cause, motive, root; *dar origem a,* to give rise to.

originador, *s.m.* originator; *adj.* originating.

original, *adj.* original; primitive; initial; odd; creative, inventive; new, fresh; singular, eccentric; *s.m.* original, pattern; archetype; model; manuscript.

originalidade, *s.f.* originality.

originalmente, *adv.* originally.

originar, *v.t.* to originate; to cause to begin; to rise, to start; to occasion, to bring about; *originar-se,* to arise from; to proceed, to derive.

originário, *adj.* native, natural of; derived from; descended, descending.

orilha, s.f. edge, brim, border.

oriundo, adj. native, natural of; derived from; originating in, resulting from.

orizícola, adj. relating to rice.

orizicultor, s.m. rice grower.

orizicultura, s.f. rice growing.

orizívoro, s.m. orvyzivorous.

orla, s.f. border; skirt; edge, rim, fringe; margin; orle, fillet (arquitectura).

orladura, s.f. edging, border, fringe, hemming.

orlar, v.t. to border, to edge, to hem, to fringe; to outline.

ornador, s.m. decorator; adj.ornamenting.

ornamentação, s.f. ornamentation, decoration, adornment, embellishment.

ornamentador, s.m. decorator; adj. ornamenting.

ornamental, adj. ornamental, decorative, adorning.

ornamentar, v.t. to ornament, to adorn, to decorate, to attire, to garnish.

ornamentista, s. ornamentalist, interior decorator, decorative artist.

ornamento, s.m. ornament, decoration, adornment, embellishment; eminent person (fig.).

ornar, v.t. to adorn, to ornament, to embellish, to decorate; to attire; to embroider, to trim.

ornato, s.m. ornament, garnisment, decoration, adornment.

ornear, v.i. to bray, to heehaw.

orneio, s.m. bray, heehaw.

ornejador, adj. braying, s.m. brayer.

ornejar, v. ver "ornear".

ornejo, s.m. ver "orneio".

órnis, s.m. Indian muslin.

ornitologia, s.f. ornithology.

ornitológico, adj. ornithologic(al).

ornitologista, s. ornithologist.

ornitorrinco, s.m. ornithorhynchus, duckbill.

oroesfera, s.f. lithosphere.

orogenia, s.f. orogeny.

orografia, s.f. orography.

orográfico, adj. orographic(al).

orógrafo, s.m. orograph.

orologia, s.f. orology, orography.

orquestra, s.f. orchestra.

orquestração, s.f. orchestration.

orquestrador, s.m. orchestrator; adj. orchestrating.

orquestral, adj. orchestral.

orquestrar, v.t. to orchestrate.

orquídea, s.f. orchid.

orquite, s.f. orchitis.

ortiga, s. ver "urtiga".

orto, s.m. rising (de um planeta ou de uma estrela).

ortocentro, s.m. orthocenter.

ortoclásio, s.m. orthoclase.

ortodoxia, s.f. orthodoxy.

ortodoxo, adj. orthodox.

ortodromia, s.f. orthodromy, great-circle route.

ortodrómico, adj. orthodromic.

ortoépia, s.f. orthoepy.

ortoépico, adj. orthoepic(al).

ortofonia, s.f. orthogenesis.

ortofónico, adj. orthogonal, right-angled.

ortogénese, v.t. to write, to spell correctly.

ortogonal, ortógono, adj. orthogonal, right-angled.

ortografar, v.t. to write, to spell correctly.

ortografia, s.f. orthography, correct spelling.

ortográfico, adj. orthographic(al).

ortógrafo, s.m. orthographer.

ortolexia, s.f. ortholexy, correct expression.

ortologia, s.f. orthology; correct speaking.

ortopedia, s.f. orthopaedics.

ortopédico, adj. orthpaedic.

ortopedista, s., adj. orthopaedist.

ortóptero, s.m. orthopteran; orthopterous.

ortorrômbico, adj. orthorhombic.

orvalhada, s.f. dewfall, morning dew.

orvalhado, adj. dewy.

orvalhar, v.t., v.i. to dew, to bedew, to fall dew, to wet; to drizzle.

orvalheira, s.f. a heavy dew.

orvalho, s.m. dew, mist, drizzle.

orvalhoso, adj. dewy, misty.

oscilação, s.f. oscillation; hesitation, vacillation; perplexity; swinging; fluctuation; variation.

oscilador, adj. oscillating; s.m. oscillator.

oscilante, adj. oscillating, swinging.

oscilar, v.i. to oscillate, to swing; to vacillate; to vibrate; to waver, to fluctuate; to hesitate.

oscilatório, adj. oscillatory.

oscilógrafo, s.m. oscillograph.

oscilograma, s.f. oscillogram.

oscilometria, s.f. oscillometry.

oscilómetro, s.m. oscillometer.

osciloscópio, s.m. oscilloscope.

oscitar, v.i. to gape, to yawn.

osculação, s.f. osculation, kissing.

osculador, s.m. kisser, adj. osculatory, kissing.

oscular, *v.t.* to kiss, to osculate.
osculatório, *adj.* osculator, kissing.
ósculo, *s.m.* kiss.
osga, *s.f.* gecko; hatred *(pop)*.
ósmico, *adj.* osmic.
ósmio, *s.m.* osmium.
osmose, *s.f.* osmose, osmosis.
osmótico, *adj.* osmotic.
ossada, *s.f.* bones; skeleton; ruins, mortal remains; carcass.
ossamenta, *s.f.* skeleton; bony structure.
ossaria, *s.f.* large quantity of bones.
ossário, *s.m.* ossuary, bone house, charnel-house; bone-vault.
ossatura, *s.f.* bones; skeleton, osseous framework; ossature.
osseína, *s.f.* ossein, ostein.
ósseo, *adj.* osseous, bony.
óssicos, *s.m. (pl.)* vomer *(cavalo)*.
ossiculado, *adj.* bony, with ossicles.
ossicular, *adj.* ossicle-like, relating to ossicles.
ossículo, *s.m.* ossicle, small bone.
ossífero, *adj.* ossiferous.
ossificação, *s.f.* ossification.
ossificar, *v.t., v.i.* to ossify.
ossífico, *adj.* ossific.
ossiforme, *adj.* bone-shaped.
ossívoro, *adj.* ossivorous.
osso, *s.m.* bone; difficulty, rub, nut *(fig.)* 1) *osso ilíaco*, ilium, hip-bone. 2) *osso difícil de roer*, a hard nut to crack. 3) *ossos do ofício*, the seamy side of a job, the headaches, difficulties. 4) *carne sem osso*, profit without pain. 5) *em carne e osso*, in flesh and blood *(boné)*; in person. 6) *só pele e osso*, nothing but skin and bones. 7) *até aos ossos*, to the very bones.
ossuário, *s.m.* ossuary, charnel-house; a common grave.
ossudo, *adj.* bony, big.boned; gaunt.
ostealgia, *s.f.* bone-ache.
osteíte, *s.f.* osteitis.
ostensivamente, *adv.* ostensively, apparently.
ostensível, *adj.* ostensible.
ostensivo, *adj.* ostensive, showing, manifest, exhibiting.
ostensor, *adj.* ostensive; *s.m.* exhibitor.
ostensório, *adj.* ostensory.
ostentação, *s.f.* ostentation; parade; boasting; pomp, display, magnificence.
ostentador, *s.m.* displayer, boaster; *adj.* ostentatious.

ostentar, *v.t.* to display; to boast; to exhibit, to make a show of, to parade; to flaunt; to sport.
ostentativo, *adj.* ostentatious, boastful.
ostentosamente, *adv.* ostentatiously.
ostentoso, *adj.* ostentatious; sumptuous; showy; magnificent, splendid.
osteogenia, *s.f.* osteogenesis.
osteogénico, *adj.* osteogenic.
osteografia, *s.f.* osteography.
osteográfico, *adj.* osteographic.
osteologia, *s.f.* osteology.
oeteológico, *adj.* osteological.
osteologista, osteólogo, *s.m.* osteologist.
osteoma, *s.m.* osteoma *(tumor)*.
osteomalacia, *s.f.* osteomalacia *(fraqueza nos ossos)*.
osteomielite, *s.f.* osteomyelitis.
osteoplastia, *s.f.* osteoplasty.
osteoplástico, *adj.* osteoplastic.
osteose, *s.f.* calcification.
osteotomia, *s.f.* osteotomy.
ostiário, *s.m.* ostiary.
ostra, *s.f.* oyster.
ostráceo, *adj.* ostraceous.
ostracismo, *s.m.* ostracism, banishment, exclusion *(da sociedade)*.
ostracista, *s.* adherent to ostracism.
ostracita, *s.f.* ostracite, fossil oyster.
ostraria, *s.f.* large quantity of oysters, oyster bed.
ostreicultor, *s.m.* oyster-farmer, breeder of oysters.
ostreicultura, *s.f.* oysterculture, oyster-breeding.
ostreira, *s.f.* oyster-bank, oyster-bed.
ostreiro, *s.m.* oyster-man.
ostrífero, *adj.* that produces oysters, ostriferous.
ostro, *s.m.* purple dye.
ostrogodo, *adj.* Ostrogothic; *s.m.* Ostrogoth.
otalgia, *s.f.* ear-ache, otalgia.
otálgico, *adj.* otalgic.
ótico, *adj.* otic.
otite, *s.f.* otitis.
otologia, *s.f.* otology.
otológico, *adj.* otological.
otomana, *s.f.* ottoman.
otomano, *adj.* Ottoman, Turkish; *s.m.* Ottoman, Turk.
otorrinolaringologia, *s.f.* otorhinolaryngology.
otorrinolaringologista, *s.* otorhinolaringologist.

otoscopia, *s.f.* otoscopy.

otoscópio, *s.m.* otoscope.

ototerapia, *s.f.* ototherapy.

ototerápico, *adj.* ototherapic.

ou, *conj.* or. 1) *ou...ou...ou,* either... or. 2) *ou oito ou oitenta,* all or nothing.

oução, *s.m.* cheese-mite.

oura, *s.f.* giddiness, vertigo, dizziness.

ourar, *v.i.* to feel dizzy.

ourela, *s.f.* list, brim; border, edge, margin.

ourelo, *s.m.* list.

ouriçar, *v.t.* to bristle, to frizzle.

ouriço, *s.m.* hedgehog; chestnut bur.

ouriço-cacheiro, *s.m.* hedgehog; coendu (Brasil).

ouriço-do-mar, ouriço-marinho, *s.m.* sea-urchin.

ourives, *s.m.* goldsmith; jeweller, dealer in jewellery.

ourivesaria, *s.f.* gosldsmithery; goldsmith's and silversmith's shop.

ouro, *s.m.* gold; wealth, riches, money; diamonds *(cartas de jogar)*; golden-yellow colour *(pl).* 1) *ouro de lei,* standard gold. 2) *ouro em pó,* gold-dust. 3) *a preço de ouro,* at a very high price. 4) *naipe de ouros,* suit of diamonds. 5) *nem tudo o que luz é ouro,* all that glitters is not gold.

ouropel, *s.m.* tinsel; sham splendour, pinchbeck.

ousadia, *s.f.* boldness, daring, courage, audacity; shamelessness, insolence; temerity.

ousado, *adj.* bold, fearless, courageous, audacious, daring, intrepid; insolent.

ousar, *v.t.* to dare, to venture, to attempt, to risk; to have the courage for.

ousio, *s.m. ver "ousadio".*

outão, *s.m.* side wall.

outar, *v.t.* to winnow, to sift, to fan *(grão).*

outeiro, *s.m.* hillock.

outiva, *s.f.* 1) *de outiva,* from hearsay.

outonada, *s.f.* fall harvest, autumn harvest.

outonal, *adj.* autumnal, fall.

outoniço, *adj.* autumnal, growing in autumn.

Outono, *s.m.* autumn, fall *(Amer.).*

outorga, *s.f.* grant, bestowal; charter; warrant.

outorgador, *s.m.* granter.

outorgamento, *s.m.* grant, granting.

outorgante, *s.m.* grantor.

outorgar, *v.i.* to grant; to consent; to declare by deed; to approve; to bestow, to confer; to allow, to concede, to consent.

outrem, *pron. ind.* somebody else; other people.

outro, *adj., pron. ind.* other; another; different, not the same; following. 1) *outro tanto,* twice as much. 2) *outra vez,* again, once more. 3) *um ao outro,* each other, one another. 4) *outro que tal,* another such. 5) *nenhum outro,* nobody else. 6)*um e outro,* both. 7) *de outro modo,* otherwise.

outrora, *adv.* formerly, once, long ago, of old.

outrossim, *adv.* also, likewise, furthermore, moreover.

Outubro, *s.m.* October.

ouvida, *s.f.* hearing.

ouvido, *s.m.* ear, hearing, audition; touch-hole *(de uma arma).* 1) *de ouvido,* by ear. 2) *entrar por um ouvido e sair pelo outro,* in at one ear and out at the other. 3) *fazer ouvido de mercador,* to turn a deaf ear. 4) *chegar aos ouvidos,* to come to the knowledge. 5) *ser todo ouvidos,* to be all ears. 6) *dar ouvidos a,* to listen to. 7) *apurar o ouvido,* to prick up the ear.

ouvidor, *s.m.* auditor.

ouvidoria, *s.f.* auditorship.

ouvinte, *s.* listener, hearer; auditor *(numa aula).*

ouvir, *v.t.* to hear, to listen to; to understand; to pay attention to, to heed.

ova, *s.f.* spawn, roe, eggs of fishes.

ovação, *s.f.* ovation, applause.

ovacionar, *s.t.* to acclaim, to cheer, to applaud.

ovado, *adj. ver "oval".*

oval, *adj.* oval, ovate; *s.f.* oval.

ovalar, *v.t.* to ovalize, to make oval.

óvalo, *s.m.* ovolo, quarter round.

ovante, *adj.* triumpahnt, victorious, exultant, rejoicing.

ovar, *v.t.* to lay eggs *(pássaros);* to spawn *(peixes).*

ovariano, *adj.* ovarian.

ovário, *s.m.* ovary.

ovariotomia, *s.f.* ovariotomy.

oveiro, *s.m.* bird ovary; egg-cup.

ovelha, *s.f.* ewe, sheep; member of a spiritual flock; *ovelha-ronhosa, tinhosa,* black sheep.

ovelhada, *s.f.* flock of sheep.

ovelheiro, *s.* shepherd.

ovelhum, ovelhuno, *adj.* ovine; wooly, laniferous.

ovém, *s.m. (naut.)* shroud.

óveo, *adj.* having eggs; oval, ovate, egg-shaped.

oviário, s.m. ver "ovil".

ovículo, s.m. small egg-shaped ornament, oviculum.

ovídeos, s.m. (pl.) Ovidae.

ovificação, s.f. ovification, ovogenesis.

oviforme, adj. oviform, egg-shaped.

ovil, s.m. sheepfold, sheep-pen; flock of sheep.

ovino, adj. ovine.

oviparidade, s.f. oviparity.

oviparismo, s.m. oviparidade.

ovíparo, adj. oviparous.

ovíporo, adj. oviorous.

ovo, s.m. egg; germ; origin. 1) ovo choco, addle egg. 2) ovo fresco, new-laid egg. 3) ovo cozido, hard boiled egg. 4) ovo escalfado, poached egg. 5) ovo estrelado, fried egg. 6) ovo mexido, scrambled egg. 7) ovo quente, soft boiled egg. 8) ovo podre, rotten egg. 9) clara do ovo, the white of the egg. 10) gema do ovo, the yolk of the egg. 11) casaca do ovo, egge-shell.

ovócito, s.m. ovocyte.

ovogénese, s.f. ovogenesis.

ovóide, adj. ovoid, egg-shaped.

ovologia, s.f. ovology.

ovoviviparidade, s.f. ovoviviparity.

ovovivíparo, adj. ovoviviparous.

ovulação, s.f. ovulation.

ovulado, adj. ovulate, having ovules.

ovular, adj. ovukar, resembling an egg.

ovuliforme, adj. ovule-shaped.

óvulo, s.m. ovule, small ovum; ovum, egg-cell; see-bud.

oxácido, s.m. oxy-acid.

oxalá!, interj. God grant!, let's hope!, would to God!, may it please God!. 1) oxalá assim seja!, let's wait for the best!, may it be so!. 2) oxalá assim fosse!, would that it were so!

oxalato, s.m. oxalate.

oxálico, adj. oxalic.

oxidabilidade, s.f. oxidability.

oxidação, s.f. oxidation.

oxidante, adj. oxidizing; s.m. oxidizing agent.

oxidar, v.t., v. refl. to oxidize, to oxidate; to rust; to become rusty.

oxidase, s.f. oxidase.

oxidável, adj. oxidizable.

óxido, s.m. oxide.

oxigenação, s.f. oxygenation.

oxigenado, adj. oxygenated; água oxigenada, oxygenated water, hydrogen peroxide.

oxigenador, s.m. oxygenator; adj. oxygenating.

oxigenar, v.t. to oxygenate, to oxygenize, to oxidize; oxigenar o cabelo, to bleach or to peroxidize the hair.

oxigenável, adj. oxygenizable.

oxigénio, s.m. oxygen.

oxítono, adj. oxytone.

oxiúre, oxiúro, s.m. pinworm.

ozonização, s.f. ozonization.

ozonizador, s.m. ozonizer.

ozonizar, v.t. ozonize.

ozono, s.m. ver ozone.

ozonometria, s.f. ozonometry.

ozonómetro, s.m. ozonometer.

ozonoscópio, s.m. ozonoscope.

ozotipia, s.f. ozotype.

P

p, the fifteenth letter of the Portuguese alphabet.

pá, s.f. spade, shovel; shoulder. 1) pá do forno, ovenpeel. 2) pá de remo, peel. 3) pá de carvão, coal shovel.

pabulagem, s.f. fatuity, pride; boasting; trick, deceit.

pábulo, s.m. pabulum, food, nourishment, sustenance.

paca, s.f. paca.

pacatez, s.f. peacefulness, tranquillity, quietness, clamness.

pacato, adj. peaceful, quiet, pacific; tranquil, placid, gentle.

paceiro, adj. courtly.

pacho, s.m. compress (fria ou quente).

pachola, s.m. clumsy fellow; idler, loafer.

pacholice, s.f. idleness.

pachorra, s.f. sluggishness; calmness; phlegm; apathy, slowness.

pachorrento, adj. sluggish, calm, phlegmatic; slow; easy-going

pachouchada, s.f. nonsense, absurdity; obsecene remark; gross blunder.

paciência, s.f. patience; endurance, forbearance; resignation; persistence, pertinacity; a card game. 1) tem paciência, calm down. 2) paciência!, it can't be helped!.

paciente, adj. patient; persevering; s.m. patient, sufferer, sick person.

pacientemente, adv. patiently, with patience.

pacificação, s.f. pacification, reconciliation.

pacificador, adj. pacifying; s.m. pacifier, pacificator, peacemaker.

pacificar, v.t. to pacify, to appease, to calm, to conciliate.

pacífico, adj. pacific; peaceful; conciliatory, peaceable.

pacifismo, s.m. pacifism.

pacifista, s., adj. pacifist; pacifistic.

paço, s.m. palace, court; residence (real ou episcopal); the courtiers. 1) paço episcopal, bishops palace. 2) Paços do Concelho, Town, Hall.

pacote, s.m. parcel, pack; bundle; packet, package.

pacotilha, s.f. passenger's luggage, private goods; shoddy work; poor quality articles.

pacovice, s.f. silliness, foolishness.

pacóvio, s.m. simpleton; silly person, dunce, imbecile, blockhead.

pacto, s.m. pact, agreement; alliance.

pactuante, adj. pact-making, contracting; s. pact-maker.

pactuar, v.t. to make a pact with, to agree with, to side with.

pactuário, s.m. party to a pact, convenanter.

pada, s.f. small bread.

padaria, s.f. bakery, baker's shop.

padecedor, adj. ver "padecente".

padecente, adj. suffering; s. sufferer, one condemned to death.

padecer, v.t., v.i. to suffer, to endurece; to undergo; to tolerate.

padecimento, s.m. suffereing, pain, distress; illness; disease.

padeira, s.m. woman-baker.

padeiro, s.m. baker.

padejador, s.m. shoveller.

padejar, v.t. to shovel; to work as a baker.

padejo, s.m. shovelling, panification, baking.

padieira, s.f. lintel (porta ou janela).

padiola, s.f. handbarrow, strecher. litter.

padioleiro, s.m. stretcher-bearer.

padrão, s.m. patterm, standard, model, sample; guidance; stone monument; measure.

padrasto, s.m. stepfather.

padre, s.m. priest, clergyman; father.

padreação, s.f. act of covereing.

padreador, adj. stud; s.m. studhorse.

padrear, v.i. to cover (stallion).

padre-cura, s.m. parish priest.

padre-mestre, s.m. priest-teacher.

padre-nosso, s.m. Lord's prayer; ensinar o padre-nosso ao vigário, to teach grandmother to suck eggs.

padre santo, s.m. Holy Father; the Pope.

padrinho, s.m. godfather, sponsor (baptismo); patronizer, protector.

padroado, s.m. ecclesiastical patronage.

padroeiro, s.m. patron, patron saint.

padronizar, v.t. to standardize.

paduano, s.m., adj. Paduan.

paga, s.f. pay, salary, wages; reward.

pagador, s.m. payer, paymaster, pay-clerk.

pagadoria, s.f. pay-office.

pagamento, s.m. pay, payment. 1) pagamento à vista, payment in cash. 2) pagamento adiantado, payment in advance. 3) pagamento a prestações, payment by instalments. 4) pagamento por conta, payment on account. 5) condições de pagamento, terms of payment. 6) dia de pagamento, pay-day. 7) folha de pagamento, pay roll, pay sheet. 8) mediante pagamento, on payment of. 9) pronto pagamento, cash, cash down.

paganismo, s.m. paganism, idolatry, heathenism.

paganização, s.f. paganization; paganizing.

paganizador, paganizante, adj. paganizing.

paganizar, v.t. to paganize, to heathenize, to turn pagan.

pagante, adj. paying; s. payer.

pagão, *s.m.* pagan, heathen; *adj.* pagan, idolatrous.

pagar, *v.t.* to pay; to compensate; to bestow; to requite, to discharge *(dívida);* to retaliate; to expiate, to atone for. 1) *pagar a prestações,* to pay by instalments. 2) *pagar adiantado,* to prepay. 3) *pagar a pronto,* to pay cash down. 4) *pagar na mesma moeda,* to pay in his own coin, to do (return) like for like.

pagável, *adj.* payable; *pagável ao portador,* payable to the bearer.

pagela, *s.f.* small page.

página, *s.f.* page; *a páginas tantas,* at a certain moment.

paginação, *s.f.* pagination, paging; arrangement of pages.

paginador, *s.m.* maker-up, pager.

paginadora, *s.f.* paging machine.

paginar, *v.t.* to paginate, to page.

pago, *adj.* paid; *s.m.* reward.

pagode, *s.m.* pagoda; spree, merry-making; feasting *(pop.).*

pagodear, *v.i.* to go on the spree, to revel.

pagodeira, *s.f.* feasting, revelry, spree, frolic.

pagodeiro, *s.m. ver "pagodeira".*

pagodice, *s.f. ver "pagodeira".*

pagodista, *s.* gay dog, merrimaker, reveller.

paguro, *s.m.* (zool.) pagurian.

pai, *s.m.* father; parents, progenitors *(pl.)* 1) *pai de família,* family man, head of a family. 2) *pai adoptivo,* foster-father. 3) *o Pai Nosso,* the Lord's prayer. 4) *tal pai, tal filho,* like father, like son. 5) *pai de todos,* the middle finger *(pop).*

painço, *s.m.* millet; groundsell.

painel, *s.m.* panel, picture, painting.

Pai-nosso, *s.m.* the Lord's Prayer.

paio, *s.m.* variety of pork sausage.

paiol, *s.m.* powder-magazine.

paioleiro, *s.m.* gunner's mate; store-keeper.

pairar, *v.i.* to hover; to heave to *(barco);* to soar *(pássaro);* to be imminent, to impend.

país, *s.m.* country; nation; territory; fatherland; *por todo o país,* all over the country.

paisagem, *s.f.* scenery, landscape, view, scene, prospect.

paisagista, *s.* landscape-painter.

paisagístico, *adj.* referring to a landscape.

paisana, *s.* civilian; *à paisana* in civillian clothes, in mufti.

paisanada, *s.f.* civilian collectively.

paisano, *s.m.* civilian; not military.

paivante, *s.m.* cigarteete *(pop).*

paixão, *s.f.* passion; fondness; grief; anger; hallucination; enthusiasm, deep love; ardour, vehemence, zeal; martyrdom, suffering. 1) *domingo da Paixão,* Passion Easter Sunday. 2) *semana da Paixão,* Passion holy Week.

paixoneta, *s.f.* slight passion, love affair.

paje, pajem, *s.m.* page, attendant.

pala, *s.f.* peak; bezel *(jóia);* eye-shade; pall, cover on the chalice; visor.

palacete, *s.m.* small palace, stately house.

palacianismo, *s.m.* court etiquette.

palaciano, *adj.* palatioal, aristocratic, polite, courteous; *s.m.* courtier.

palácio, *s.m.* palace, stately house; large public building; *palácio da justiça,* court--house.

paladar, *s.m.* palate; taste, flavour, savour.

paladino, *s.m.* paladin; knight-errant; a champion, strenuous defender.

paládio, *s.m.* palladium; safeguard.

palafita, *s.f.* palafitte, lake-dwelling built on plies.

palafrém, *s.m.* palfrey, saddle-horse *(para senhoras).*

palafreneiro, *s.m.* ostler; undergroom; palefrenier, stable servant.

palanca, *s.f.* pile; platform; palisade.

palanco, *s.m.* tackle *(náut.).*

palancar, *v.t.* to pile; to palisade, to defend.

palanfrório, *s.m.* ver palavreado.

palangana, *s.f.* large dish; bowl; platter for roasts.

palanque, *s.m.* platform; scaffold; raised stage.

palanquim, *s.m.* palanquin; palankeen; covered litter.

palatal, *adj.* palatine; palatal.

palatalização, *s.f.* palatalization *(sons).*

palatatizar, *v.t.* to palatalize *(som).*

palatina, *s.f.* palatine.

palatinado, *s.m.* palayonate.

palatino, *adj.* palatino, palatal.

palatite, *s.f.* palatitis.

palatização, *s.f. ver "palatalização".*

palatizar, *v.t. ver "palatalizar".*

palato, *s.m.* palate, roof of the mouth; taste savour.

palavra, *s.f.* word, term; affirmation; assurance; vocable, expression, signal, speech; promise, warrant; permission to talk; faith, doctrine. 1) *palavra!* (I give you) my word. 2) *palavra de honra!,* upon my honour!, upon my word!. 3) *palavra de ordem,* word of command. 4) *palavra que não sei*, I don't know. 5) *faltar à palavra*, to break one's word. 6) *cumprir (ter, honrar) a palavra*, to keep one's word. 7) *ter uma só palavra*, to be as good as one's word. 8) *passar palavra*, to pass on word. 9) *pegar na palavra*, to take on at his word. 10) *pedir a palavra*, to catch the speaker's eye. 11) *não dar (dizer) palavra*, to make no words about, to say nothing. 12) *não entender palavra*, not to understand anything. 13) *dar a palavra a*, to give permission to speak. 14) *usar da palavra*, to address a meeting. 15) *homem de palavra*, a man of his word. 16) *palavras cruzadas*, crossword puzzle. 17) *a bom entendedor meia palavra basta*, a word to the wise is sufficient. 18) *palavras leva-as o vento*, words are but wind.

palavrada, *s.f.* coarse expression; boast; insulting language.

palavrão, *s.m.* obscenity, base language; long word of difficult pronunciation; bombastic term.

palavreado, *s.m.* babbling, rigmarole, verbiage, idle talk; talkativeness; gabble, gibberish.

palavrear, *v.i.* to prattle, to babble, to talk idle.

palavrinha, *s.f., interj.* short word, message; my word.

palavrório, *s.m. ver "palavreado".*

palavroso, *adj.* verbose, prolix, long-winded, talkative.

palco, *s.m.* platform; stage.

paleio, *s.m.* idle chatter or talk, prattle, chat.

paleografia, *s.f.* palaeography.

paleográfico, *adj.* palaeographic.

paleógrafo, *s.m.* palaeographer.

paleolítico, *adj.* palaeolithic *(período).*

paleologia, *s.f.* palaeology.

paleólogo, *s.m.* palaeologist.

paleontografia, *s.f.* palaeontography.

paleontologia, *s.f.* palaeontology.

paleontológico, *adj.* palaeontological.

paleontologista, paleontólogo, *s.m.* palaeontologist.

paleozóico, *adj.* palaeozois *(era).*

palerma, *adj., s.* silly, foolish, idiotic, stupid; simpleton, silly person, fool, idiot, imbecile, blockhead.

palermice, *s.f.* silliness, stupidity, imbecility, foolishness.

palestino, *s.m., adj.* Palestinian.

palestra, *s.f.* talk, chat; discussion; conversation; informal lecture.

palestrador, palestrante, *s.m., s.* talker, one who chats or talks.

palestrar, palestrear, *v.i.* to chat; to talk, to converse.

paleta, *s.f.* palette.

paletó, *s.m.* singlebreasted jacket, man's coat.

palha, *s.f.* straw; dry grass; trifle, bagattele. 1) *palha de aço*, steel wool. 2) *palha de milho*, corn husk. 3) *chapéu de palha*, straw hat. 4) *muita palha e pouco grão*, much cry and little wool. 5) *por dá cá aquela palha*, (to lose one's temper) for little or no reason.

palhabote, *s.m.* schooner.

palhaçada, *s.f.* buffonery; mummery; clowning; group of clowns.

palhaço, *s.m.* clown, buffoon; quack, jester.

palhada, *s.f.* a mixture of straw and bran; mere talk, boring talk.

palhal, palhar, *s.m.* thatched hut.

palheira, *s.f.* straw.

palheiro, *s.m.* hay-loft, haystack; hay rick; wooden house *(ao pé do mar).*

palheta, *s.m.* reed *(de um instrumento);* racket; pallet.

palhetada, *s.f.* blow with a racket; *numa palhetada*, quick, in a moment.

palhetão, *s.m.* key-bit.

palhete, *adj.* straw-coloured; *vinho palhete*, pale wine.

palhiça, palhiço, *s.f., s.m.* slender straw, chopped straw.

palhinha, *s.f.* straw for chair seats; straw hat.

palhoça, palhota, *s.f.* thatched cottage; negro-hut.

paliação, *s.f.* palliation, extenuation, excuse.

paliar, *v.t., v.i.* to palliate, to mitigate; to extenuate, to excuse; to moderate; to cloak, to disguise.

paliativo, *adj., s.m.* palliative, mitigating; a palliative agent or medicine.

paliçada, *s.f.* palisade, fence, stockade.

palidamente, *adv.* palelym faintely, wanly.

palidez, *s.f.* paleness, pallor, clourlessness, wanness.

pálido, *adj.* pale, wan, pallid, faint; colourless.

palimpsesto, *s.m.* palimpsest.

palingenesia, *s.f.* palingenesis, rebirth, regeneration.

palinódia, *s.f.* palinode; recantation.

palinódico, *adj.* palinodic.

palinuro, *s.m.* pilot, guide.

pálio, *s.m.* canopy; pallium, pall.

palitar, *v.t.* to pick the teeth.

paliteiro, *s.m.* toothpick-case or holder.

palito, *s.m.* toothpick; a match; a very thin person.

palma *s.f.* palm-leaf; palm-tree; victory, laurels, triumph. 1) *palmas,* hand-clapping. 2) *bater palmas,* to clap hands. 3) *levar a palma a,* to cry off the palm, to win the prize, to take the cake.

palmada, *s.f.* stroke with the palm of the hand; slap, rap, smack, cuff.

palmar, *s.m.* grove of palm-trees; adj. palmar, relating to the palm of the hand; clear, big; *v.t.* to pilfer, to purloin *(pop); erro palmar,* gross blunder.

palmatoada, *s.f.* a blow with a ferule on the palm of the hand.

palmatoar, *v.t.* to punish by a striking the palm of the hand with a ferule.

palmatória, *s.f.* ferule; rod; candlestick; *dar a mão à palmatória,* to acknowledge one's mistake.

palmeador, *s.m.* traveller, explorer.

palmear, *v.t.* to applaud, to clap hands; to travel on foot.

palmeira, *s.f.* palm-tree.

palmeiral, *s.m.* palm-wood, palm-grove.

palmeiro, *adj.* about a span long; *s.m.* palmer foreigner.

palmeta, *s.f.* spatula.

palmiforme, *adj.* palmiform, resembling a palm.

palmilha, *s.f.* inner sole *(de sapato).*

palmilhadeira, *s.f.* woman who wears stockings.

palmilhar, *v.t.* to put feet; to foot; to walk.

palminérveo, *adj.* palminervate.

palminhas, *s.f. (pl); trazer nas palminhas,* to take great care of.

palmípede, *s.m., adj.* palmiped, web-footed bird; web-footed.

palmiste, *s.m.* kind of palm-tree; palm-fruit; palm-oil.

palmito, *s.m.* palm leaf; palmetto; palm cabbage.

palmo, *s.m.* palm; span *(de mão);* lineal measure; *palmo a palmo,* inch by inch, step by step, foot by foot.

paloma, *s.f.* sailmaker's twine.

palomba, *s.f.* bolt-rope; hank.

palonço, *s.m., adj.* lout, simpleton, fool; bumpkin; stupid, foolish.

palor, *s.m.* paleness, wanness.

palpabilidade, *s.f.* palpability.

palpação, *s.f.* palpation, act of touching or feeling.

palpadela, *s.f.* touch, touching.

palpar, *v.t.* to palpate, to feel, to touch; to grope.

palpável, *adj.* palpable; plain, evident, obvious, manifest.

palpavelmente, *adv.* palpably.

pálpebra, *s.f.* eyelid.

palpebrado, *adj.* palpebrate.

palpitação, *s.f.* palpitation, pulsation *(do coração).*

palpitante, *adj.* palpitating, throbbing, panting; exciting, thrilling.

palpitar, *v.i.* to palpitate; to pulsate; to throb; to vibrate; to conjecture, to guess.

palpite, *s.m.* presentiment, foreboding; tip *(para um cavalo numa corrida),* suggestion.

palpo, *s.m.* palpus; *em palpos de aranha,* in the soup, in a difficult situation, in a fine pickle, in a spot, in hot water, in a fix.

palra, *s.f.* speech, talk; chatter, babble; garrulity.

palração, *s.f. ver "palra".*

paradeiro, palrador, *adj.* prattling, talkative; *s.m.* prattler, chatterer, tattler.

palrar, *v.i.* to prattle, to chatter *(como um papagaio);* to babble, to tattle; to talk; to reveal.

palraria, *s.f. ver "palra".*

palratório, *s.m.* locutory; chatter, idle talk, prattle, gossip.

palreiro, *adj.* ver palrador.

palrice, *s.f.* chattiness, babble.

palude, *s.m.* lagoon, pool; marsh, swamp.

paludial, *adj.* paludal, marshy.

palúdico, *adj.* malarial, marshy.

paludismo, *s.m.* paludism, malarial disease.

paludoso, *adj.* paludous, paludal, marshy, malarial.

palurdice, *s.f.* stupidity, nonsense, silliness.

palúrdio, *s.m., adj.* blockhead, fool; silly, foolish, simple, stupid.

palustre, *adj.* swampy, marshy, paludal; *febre palustre,* malarial fever.

pampa, *s.f.* pampas.

pâmpano, *s.m.* vine-shoot.

pampilho, *s.m.* goad, prod.

panaceia, *s.f.* panacea, cure-all; allheal *(a planta).*

panado, *adj.* breaded.

panal, *s.m.* cloth; sail.

panarício, *s.m.* whitlow.

panariz, *s.m. ver "panarício".*

panascal, *s.m.* cockfoot fielf, waste land.

panasco, *s.m.* cocksfoot, wild parsnip.

panásio, *s.m.* a kick or blow *(pop)*.

panasqueira, *s.f. ver "panascal".*

panca, *s.f.* wooden lever.

pança, *s.f.* paunch; belly.

pancada, *s.f.* blow, stroke; shock; knock; hit; beat, pulsation; impact; drubbing; mania; sudden downpour. 1) *às três pancadas,* slovenly. 2) *ter pancada na mola,* to be crackbrained. 3) *espera-lhe pela pancada,* you will see what is the end of it.

pançada, *s.f.* bellyful; slap.

pancadaria, *s.f.* brawl, tumult, affray, fracas; pounding.

pancrácio, *s.m.* simpleton, fool, idiot, nitwit.

pâncreas, *s.m.* pancreas.

pancreático, *adj.* pancreatic.

pancreatina, *s.f.* pancreatin.

pancreatite, *s.f.* pancreatitis.

pancromático, *adj.* panchromatic.

pançudo, *adj.* big-bellied, potbellied, paunchy; *s.m.* sponger, parasite.

panda, *s.f.* cork float.

pandarecos, *s.m.* *(pl.)* bits, crumbs, scraps, chips, fragments.

pândega, *s.f.* spree, feast; frolic; lark; revelry, high jinks; *andar na pândega,* to go on the spree, to have a jolly good time.

pandegar, *v.i.* to feast, to revel, to carouse, to paint the town red.

pândego, *adj., s.m.* fond of feasting; gay; merrymaker; gay, dog, reveller, carouser, funny person.

pandeireta, *s.f.* tambourine *(pequena).*

pandeiro, *s.m.* timbrel.

pandemónio, *s.m.* pandemonium, confusion, infernal noise, tumult.

pandilha, *s.f.* gang; *s.m.* knave, rogue, scoundrel; gangster.

pandilhar, *v.i.* to swindle, to live by cheating; to loaf.

pandilheiro, *s.m.* rogue, loafer.

pando, *adj.* puffed, swollen; full, inflated, stretched; broad, wide.

pandora, *s.f.* pandor, abnore.

pandorca, *s.f.* corpulent, woman; discordant music.

pandorga, *s.f. ver "pandorca".*

panegírico, *s.m.* panegyric; eulogy, encomium.

panegirista, *s.* panegyrist.

paneiro, *s.m.* basket; pannier, hamper; seats *(num barco).*

panejamento, *s.m.* drapery; flapping.

panejar, *v.t., v.i.* to drape; to flap.

panela, *s.f.* pot, pan; *panela de pressão,* pressure cooker.

panelada, *s.f.* potful, panful.

panelinha, *s.f.* clique, political insiders; small pot; intrigue, plot; *ser da mesma panelinha,* to be in a plot.

panfletário, *s.m.* pamphleteer.

panfleteiro, panfletista, *s.m., s.* pamphletter.

panfleto, *s.m.* pamphlet.

pangaio, *s.m.* reveller, merrymaker; loafer; Arabian coastal vessel.

pangermanismo, *s.m.* Pan-Germanism.

pânico, *s.m.* panic, alarm.

panícula, *s.f.* panicle.

panículo, *s.m.* panniculus, tela.

panificação, *s.f.* panification, breadmaking; bakery.

panificador, *s.m.* breadmaker, baker.

panificar, *v.t.* to bake, to make into bread *(farinha).*

panificável, *adj.* that can be converted into bread.

paninho, *s.m.* calico.

pano, *s.m.* cloth; sails *(de um barco)* skin blemish; curtain *(teatro).* 1) *pano cru,* unbleached cloth. 2) *pano da chaminé,* manteltree of a chimney. 3) *pano de boca,* stage curtain. 4) *pano de fundo,* backcloth, backdrop. 5) *pano de mesa,* table cloth or cover. 6) *pano para mangas,* more then enough, plenty to spare. 7) *panos quentes,* half-measures. 8) *a todo o pano,* under full sail.

panóplia, *s.f.* panoply; armour.

panorama, *s.m.* panorama; landscape, scenery, view.

panorâmico, *adj.* panoramic(al).

pantafaçudo, *adj.* chubby-faced, fat-cheecked.

pantagruélico, *adj.* Pantagrielian.

pantagruelismo, *s.m.* Pantagruelism.

pantalha, *s.f.* lamp-shade; screen.

pantalonas, *s.f.* *(pl.)* pantaloons, trousers.

pantana, *s.f. dar em pantanas,* to go to the dogs, to go broke.

pantanal, *s.m.* large swamp, swampland, marshy place.

pântano, *s.m.* marsh, bog, swamp, mudhole, morass, mire.

pantanoso, *adj.* marshy, swampy, boggy, fenny, miry.

panteão, *s.m.* pantheon.

panteísmo, *s.m.* pantheism.

panteísta, *adj.* pamtheistic; *s.* pantheist.

pantera, *s.f.* panther.

pantografia, *s.f.* pantography.

pantógrafo, *s.m.* pantograph.

pantomima, *s.f.* pantomime; swindle, fraud; farce.

pantomimeiro, *s.m.* pantomimist; cheater, swindler, trickster.

pantomina, *s.m.* ver "pantomima".

pantomineiro, *s.m.* ver "pantomimeiro".

pantominice, *s.f.* ver "pantomima".

pantorrilha, *s.f.* calf; false calf.

pantufa, *s.f.* slipper.

pantufo, *s.m.* slipper.

panturra, *s.f.* potbelly, paunch; pride, vanity, conceit.

pão, *s.m.* loaf; bread; food. 1) *pão fresco,* new bread. 2) *pão duro,* stale bread. 3) *pão caseiro,* home-made bread. 4) *pão ázimo,* unleavened bread. 5) *pão ralado,* breadcrumbs. 6) *pão mole,* soft bread. 7) *côdea de pão,* crust of the bread. 8) *pão bolorento,* mouldy bread. 9) *um pão,* a loaf. 10) *o pão nosso de cada dia,* the daily bread; something very usual. 11) *pão de forma,* thin loaf. 12) *pão integral,* whole bread. 13) *pão, pão, queijo, queijo,* frankly, forthrightly. 14) *a pão e água,* on bread and water, hard-up. 15) *ganhar o pão,* to earn living.

pão-de-ló, *s.m.* sponge cake.

pãozinho, *s.m.* roll.

papa, *s.m.* Pope, the Bishop of Rome, supreme pontiff; pap, soft food for babies; *não ter papas na língua,* to be outspoken.

papá, *s.f.* father; daddy, dad, papa.

papa-açorda, *s.* slacker.

papada, *s.f.* mumps, double chin; gills; dewlap.

papado, *s.m.* papacy.

papa-figo, *s.m.* beccafico, figpecker, garden-warbler.

papa-fina, *adj.* tasty, excellent delicious, savoury; *s.* ridiculous person.

papagaia, *s.m.* female parrot.

papagaio, *s.m.* parrot; kite.

papa-gente, *s.m.* hobgoblin, cannibal.

papaguear, *v.i., v.t.* to parrot, to repeat like a parrot, to chatter.

papagueador, *s.m.* parroter; *adj.* parroting.

papa-hóstias, *s.m.* bigot, very devout person.

papai, *s.m.* papa, dad, pappy.

papa-jantares, *s.m.* parasite, sponge, hanger-on.

papal, *adj.* papal, pontifical.

papa-léguas, *s.m.* great walker, fast walker, hiker.

papalvice, *s.f.* stupidity, silliness; naivety.

papalvo, *s.m.* simpleton, tomfool, boob.

papa-missas, *s.m.* bigot, sanctimonious person.

papa-moscas, *s.m.* fly-catcher; simpleton, silly person, ninny.

papança, *s.f.* food, things to eat, eatables, vittles.

papa-novenas, *s.* sanctimonious person.

papão, *s.m.* bug-bear, hobgoblin, bogey, ogre.

papar, *v.t., v.i.* to eat; to cheat, to extort *(por fraude).*

paparicar, *v.t.* to nibble.

paparicos, *s.m. (pl.)* dainties; petting; caresses.

paparoca, *s.f.* food, eating, meal.

papas, *s.f. (pl.)* cereal food, pap for children. 1) *papas de linhaça,* linseed poultice. 2) *papas de aveia,* porridge.

papável, *adj.* papable; eatable.

papear, *v.i.* to chatter, to jaber.

papeira, *s.f.* mumps.

papel, *s.m.* paper; part *(de um actor),* role *(no teatro);* documents *(pl.).* 1) *papel higiénico,* toilet paper. 2) *papel de rascunho,* scrap paper. 3) *papel pautado,* ruled paper. 4) *papel químico,* carbon paper. 5) *papel selado,* stamped paper. 6) *desempenhar (fazer) o papel de,* to play the part of. 7) *fazer um triste papel,* to cut a sorry figure.

papelada, *s.f.* heap of papers or documents.

papelão, *s.m.* pasteboard, cardboard.

papelaria, *s.f.* stationery; stationer's *(loja).*

papeleira, *s.f.* bureau, standing desk.

papeleiro, *s.m.* paper-maker; stationer.

papeleta, *s.f.* bill; notice; placard.

papelinho, *s.m.* slip of paper; confetti *(pl.).*

papelista, *s.* recorder; filling clerk, archivist.

papel-moeda, *s.m.* paper currency.

papelotes, *s.m. (pl.)* curl-papers *(para o cabelo).*

papelucho, *s.m.* wrapping-paper; slip of paper *(pouco importante).*

papila, *s.f.* papilla; nipple.

papilar, *adj.* papillary.

papilonáceo, *adj.* papilionaceous, like a butterfly.

papiro, *s.m.* papyrus, ancient manuscript; aquatic plant.

papisa, *s.f.* popess.

papismo, *s.m.* papism.

papista, *s., adj.* papist.

papo, *s.m.* goitre; craw; crop *(dos pássaros);* stomach *(pop);* double chin. 1) *bate papo,* talk, chatter. 2) *de grão a grão enche a galinha o papo,* little strokes fell great oaks. 3) *falar de papo,* to put on airs.

papoila, *s.f.* poppy.

papo-seco, *s.m.* a roll; a dandy.

papoula, *s.f. ver "papoila".*

papua, *s.* Papuan.

papudo, *adj.* swollen, turgid, protuberant, large cropped.

pápula, *s.f.* papule pimple.

paqueta, *s.f.* errand-girl.

paquete, *s.m.* mail-boat, liner, steamer; packet; errand-boy.

paquiderme, *s.m.* pachyderm; *adj.* pachydermous.

paquidérmico, *adj.* pachydermatous.

par, *s.m.* pair; couple; partner *(na dança);* peer; two of a kind; adj. similar. like, equal, equivalent, even (a number). 1) *par e ímpar,* even and odd. 2) *a par de,* informed about; along with; at the same time as. 3) *ao par,* at par. 4) *aos pares,* in pairs. 5) *de par em par,* wide open (janelas). 6) *sem par,* peerless, unmatched. 7) *a par,* abreast. 8) *andar a par com,* to keep pace with.

para, *prep.* for; to; in order to; about to. 1) *para baixo,* downwards. 2) *para cima,* upwards. 3) *para diante,* forward. 4) *para lá e para cá,* to and fro, hither and thither. 5) *para quê?,* what for?. 6) *para sempre,* for ever. 7) *para a vida e para a morte,* come life, come death. 8) *para inglês ver,* just for show. 9) *estar para,* to be about to.

parabéns, *s.m. (pl.)* congratulations, felicitations; *dar os parabéns,* to congratulate.

parábola, *s.f.* allegory; parable; parabola *(geom).*

parabólico, *adj.* parabolic(al).

parabolismo, *s.m.* parabolicalism.

parabolóide, *adj.* paraboloid(al).

pára-brisas, *s.m.* windscreen, windshield; *limpa-brisas,* windscreen wiper.

pára-choque, *s.m.* buffer, bumper *(de um carro).*

pára-chuva, *s.m.* umbrella.

Paracleto, *s.m.* Paraclete, Holy Ghost.

paracronismo, *s.m.* parachronism.

parada, *s.m.* parade /tropas); halt; stopping-place; ostentation, display, pomp; pompous show; bet, stake *(no jogo).*

paradeiro, *s.m.* whereabouts, destination; stopping-place.

paradigma, *s.m.* paradigm; example, pattern, model.

paradisíaco, paradísico, *adj.* paradiciac(al), paradisian, celestial.

parado, *adj.* stopped; still, motionless; quiet, spiritless; stagnant.

paradoiro, paradouro, *s.m.* ver paradeiro.

paradoxal, *adj.* paradoxical, contradictory.

paradoxalmente, *adv.* paradoxically.

paradoxar, *v.i.* to paradox.

paradoxo, *s.m.* paradox, absurd.

paraense, *s.m.* native of Pará.

parafina, *s.f.* paraffin.

parafinagem, *s.f.* paraffining.

parafinar, *v.t.* to coat with paraffin.

paráfrase, *s.f.* paraphrase, exposition.

parafraseador, *s.m.* paraphraser.

parafrasear, *v.t.* to paraphrase.

parafrasticamente, *adv.* paraphrastically.

parafrástico, *adj.* paraphrastic(al).

parafusar, *v.t., v.i.* to screw, to meditate, to ponder, to cogitate, to muse.

parafuso, *s.m.* screw; bolt.

paragem, *s.f.* stopping, halt, pause, suspension, break; stoppage; *nestas paragens,* in these parts, hereabouts.

paragoge, *s.f.* paragoge.

paragrafar, *v.t.* paragraph.

parágrafo, *s.m.* para graph.

paragrama, *s.f.* paragram; pun.

paraguaiano, paraguaio, *adj., s.m.* Paraguayan.

paraíso, *s.m.* paradise; heaven; Eden, delightful place.

pára-lamas, *s.m.* mudguard.

paralaxe, *s.f.* parallax.

paralela, *s.f.* parallel; parallel bars *(ginástica).*

paralelamente, *adv.* parallelly.

paralelepípedo, *s.m.* parallelipiped; paving blocs.

paralelismo, *s.m.* parallelism, resemblance *(informação ou ideias).*

paralelizar, *v.t.* to render parallel.

paralelo, *adj.* parallel, similar, corresponding; *s.m.* parallel; comparison, confrontation.

paralelogramo, *s.m.* parallelogram.

paralipse, *s.f.* paralipsis.

paralisação, *s.f.* paralyzation; stoppage, interruption, suspension.

paralisar, *v.t., v.i.* to suspend, to stop; to paralyse; to become paralised; to render powerless or inoperative; to neutralize.

parálise, *s.f.* paralysis.

paralisia, *s.f.* paralysis, palsy; numbness, torpor marasmus. 1) *paralisia infantil,* infantil paralysis, poliom-elitis. 2) *ataque de paralisia,* paralytic stroke.

paralítico, *s.m., adj.* paralytic.

paralogia, *s.f.* paralogy.

paralogismo, *s.m.* paralogism.

pára-luz, *s.m.* lamp-shade.

paramagnético, *adj.* paramagnetic.

paramagnetismo, *s.m.* paramagnetism.

paramécia, *s.f.* paramecium.

paramentado, *adj.* adorned, ornamented; wearing liturgical vestments.

paramentar, *v.t.* to adorn, to embellish; to cover with hangings, to vest, to attire; *paramentar-se,* to clothe oneself with liturgical vestments *(padre).*

paramenteiro, *s.m.* maker of church-vestments.

paramento, *s.m.* church-vestments; hanging, trappings.

parâmetro, *s.m.* parameter.

paramnésia, *s.f.* paramnesia, false memory.

paramnésico, *adj.* paramnesic.

páramo, *s.m.* firmament; desert plain.

parança, *s.f.* stop, rest, pause; repose.

parangona, *s.f.* paragon; two-line long primer.

paraninfar, *v.t.* to stand as paranymph, to sponsor.

paraninfo, *s.m.* paranymph; godfather; sponsor; best man, groom`s-man; protector.

paranóia, *s.f.* paranoia.

paranóico, *adj.* paranoiac.

parapeito, *s.m.* parapet, rampart, breastwork, windowsill.

paraplegia, *s.f.* paraplegia.

paraplégico, *adj.* paraplegic.

pára-quedas, *s.m.* parachute.

pára-quedismo, *s.m.* parachutism.

pára-quedista, *s.* parachutist.

parar, *v.t., v.i.* to stop, to halt; to check; to cease; to leave off; to cease, to move, to come to an end.

pára-raios, *s.m.* lightning-rod.

parasceve, *s.f.* parasceve; Good Friday.

parasita, *s.m.* parasite, hanger-on, sponger; *adj.* parasitic.

parasitar, *v.i.* to live like a parasite, to sponge.

parasitário, *adj.* parasitic(al).

parasiticida, *s.m.* parasiticide.

parasítico, *adj.* parasitic.

parasitismo, *s.m.* parasitism.

parasitologia, *s.f.* parasitology.

pára-sol, *s.m.* umbrella, parasol, sunshade.

parasselénio, *s.m.* paraselene.

parassintético, *adj.* parasynthetic.

paratifo, paratifóide, *s.m., s.f.* paratyphoid fever.

paratireóide, *s.f., adj.* parathyroid glands.

paravante, *s.m.* foredeck.

pára-vento, *s.m.* wind-screen.

parcas, *s.f.* *(pl.)* Parcae; the Fates, the Witches, the weird sisters.

parceiro, *s.m.* partner, associate, copartner; *adj.* similar, alike.

parcel, *s.m.* shoal, reef, shelf.

parcela, *s.f.* fragment, part, portion, share, piece, parcel; item, entry.

parcelado, *adj.* shoaly; parcelled, made in parcels.

parcelar, *adj.* divided into parts; *v.t.* to divide into parts, to parcel out.

parceria, *s.f.* partnership.

parche, *s.m.* pledget, compress.

parcial, *adj.* partial biassed; not complete; prejudiced; *s.* partisan.

parcialidade, *s.f.* partiality, bias, descriminatuon, prejudice.

parcialista, *s.* partialist.

parcialmente, *adv.* partially, partly; unfairly.

parcimónia, *s.f.* frugality, parsimony, economy.

parcimoniosamente, *adv.* parsimoniously.

parcimonioso, *adj.* parsimonious, frugal, sparing, sober, economic.

parco, *adj.* sober, frugal, economic(al), saving; scanty, poor.

parda, *s.f.* lentil.

pardacento, *adj.* dark-grey, dusky.

pardal, *s.m.* sparrow.

pardalada, *s.f.* a flight of sparrows.

pardalão, *s.m.* rascal, foxy person.

pardalejo, *s.m.* ver *"pardoca".*

pardejo, *s.m.* ver *"pardal".*

pardelha, *s.f.* a kind of sea-fish.

pardieiro, *s.m.* hovel, hut, squalid dwellin, the ruins of a house.

pardo, *adj.* grey, cloudy, dull, overcast, dark.

pardoca, *s.f.* hen-sparrow.

pardusco, *adj.* greyish.

parear, *v.t.* to gauge casks, barrels, etc.

parecença, *s.f.* likeness, resemblance, similarity; analogy.

parecente, *adj.* resembling, like similar.
parecer, *v.i.* to seem, to look, to appear, to resemble; *s.m.* aspect, look, appearance, mien; opinion, concept, idea, judgment, impression; *parecer-se com,* to resemble, to look like, to be similar to.
parecido, *adj.* like, resembling, similar.
paredão, *s.m.* big wall; breakwater; pier.
parede, *s.f.* wall. 1) *parede meia,* party-wall. 2) *parede mestra,* main wall. 3) *entre a espada e a parede,* in a tight corner, between the devil and the deep blue sea. 4) *paredes meias com,* next door to. 5) *ir à parede,* to go to the wall. 6) *pôr os pés à parede,* to put your foot down. 7) *fazer parede,* to strike.
paredista, *s.* striker; picket.
parelha, *s.f.* couple; pair; team *(de cavalos)* match; running mate; couplet. 1) *correr parelha com,* to run neck-and-neck with. 2) *uma parelha de bois,* a yoke of oxen.
parelho, *adj.* similar, like, equal; mated, matched.
parélio, *s.m.* parhelion, mock sun.
parémia, *s.f.* allegory, proverb, saying.
paremiologia, *s.f.* a set of proverbs.
parencéfalo, *s.m.* the cerebellum.
parénese, *s.f.* parenesis, exhorbitation, admonition.
parenética, *s.f.* holy eloquence.
parenético, *adj.* exhorbiting to moral.
parênquima, *s.m.* parenchyma; tissue.
parenquimático, parenquimato, *adj.* parenchymatous.
parenta, *s.f.* kinswoman, female relation.
parente, *s.* relation, relative, kinswoman; *adj.* related. 1) *parente chegado (próximo),* near relation, close kin. 2) *parente mais próximo,* next of kin. 3) *parente afastado (remoto),* distant (remote) relative. 4) *ser parente de,* to be related to. 5) *parente por afinidade,* relation by marriage (in-laws). 6) *os meus parentes,* my folks.
parentela, *s.f.* kindred; the relatives, kinsfolk, relations.
parenteral, parentérico, *adj.* parenteral.
parentesco, *s.m.* relationship, kinship, consanguinity, affinity; connection; similarity, likeness.
parêntese, parênteses, *s.m.* parenthesis; round brackets *(pl.).*
ᵖᵃʳᵉᵉⁿtético, *adj.* parenthetic(al).
ᵖᵃʳᵉᵉˢ᙭ᵃ, *s.f.* paresis.
ᵖᵃʳᵃˢᵗᵉˢᵃ, *s.f.* paresthesia.

parga, *s.f.* stack of straw, grain or hay; heap, pile.
pargo, *s.m.* sea-bream.
pária, *s.m.* pariah; a social outcast.
pariambo, *s.m.* pyrrhic foot *(medida).*
pariato, *s.m.* peerage.
parição, parturition *(dos animais);* foaling; calving.
paridade, *s.f.* parity; analogy; equality; likeness, similirity.
parideira, *adj.* old enough to bear young *(animais).*
paridura, *s.f.* ver parto.
parietal, *adj.* parietal; mural.
parietária, *s.f.* wall-pellitory.
parietário, *adj.* parietal, growth on walls *(plantas).*
pariforme, *adj.* alike, similar, equal, resembling.
parir, *v.t.* to bring forth; to produce; to give birth to; to deliver *(animais).*
parisiense, *s., adj.* Parisian.
parissílabo, *adj.* parisyllabic.
parla, *s.f.* talk conversation, palaver.
parlamentação, *s.f.* parleying; negotiation.
parlamentar, *adj.* parliamentary; *v.i.* to parley, to treat, to negotiate; *s.m.* deputy, Member of Parliament, M.P.
parlamentário, *adj.* parliamentary; *s.m.* messenger.
parlamentarismo, *s.m.* parliamentary system, parliamentarism.
parlamentarista, *s.* supporter of the parliamentary system.
parlamento, *s.m.* parliament.
parlapatão, *s.m.* swaggerer, braggart; impostor, liar.
parlapatice, *s.f.* swaggering, boasting, vaunting; rubbish.
parlar, *v.i.* to prattle, to chatter, to jabber.
parlatório, *s.m.* parlour, parlatory *(nos conventos);* chat.
parlenda, parlenga, *s.f.* verbiage, idle talk; speech; quarrel.
parmesão, *adj., s.m.* Parmesan.
parnão, *adj.* odd, not divisible by two.
parnasianismo, *s.m.* Parnassianism.
parnasiano, *s.m., adj.* Parnassian.
parnaso, *s.m.* Parnassus.
pároco, *s.m.* parson; parish priest.
paródia, *s.f.* parody, travesty; burlesque imitation; feasting, revel.
parodiador, parodiante, *s.m., s.* ver parodista.

parodiar, *v.t.* to parody, to imitate, to travesty; to mimic.

parodista, *s.* parodist.

parola, *s.f.* loquacity, verbiage, garrulity.

parolador, *s.m.* prattler, chatterer, fond of chatting.

parolagem, *s.f.* palaverment; gabbling.

parolar, *v.i.* to chat, to prattle.

parolice, *s.f.* chatter, babbling, gossip; action of a boor.

parolo, *s.m.* boor, bumpkin, rustic fellow.

paronímia, *s.f.* paronymy.

paronímico, *adj.* paronymous.

parónimo, *s.m.* paronym; *adj.* paronymous.

paronomásia, *s.f.* paronomasia.

paróquia, *s.f.* parish; parish church.

paroquial, *adj.* parochial.

paroquiano, *s.m.* parishioner; *adj.* parochial.

paroquiar, *v.t.* to discharge the duties of a parish priest, to be in charge of a parish.

parótida, parótide, *s.f.* parotid *(glândula).*

parotídeo, parotidiano, *adj.* parotid.

parotidite, *s.f.* parotiditis, mumps.

paroxismal, paroxísmico, *adj.* paroxysmal.

paroxismo, *s.m.* paroxysm, spasm, attack, fit *(dor, raiva , riso).*

paroxítono, *adj., s.m.* paroxytone.

parque, *s.m.* park, public square, garden; game reserve.

parqué, parquete, *s.m.* parquet floor, parquetry.

parra, *s.f.* vine-leaf; *muita parra, pouca uva,* much cry and little wool.

parrado, *adj.* full of vine leaves; trellised vine.

parrana, *s.m.* slob; slow poke; *adj.* slovenly, slipshod; slow; slack.

parranice, *s.f.* slackness, laziness.

parreira, *s.f.* vine; grape-vine; trellis.

parreiral, *s.m.* vine-arbour, trellised vines.

parrésia, *s.f.* parrhesia.

parricida, *s.* parricide *(o criminoso).*

parricídio, *s.m.* parricide *(o crime).*

partazana, *s.f.* partizan, partisan.

parte, *s.f.* part, portion; side; place; share; lot; interest; account; information; role; fragment, fraction; plaintiff. 1) *em parte alguma,* nowhere, anywhere. 2) *parte dianteira (traseira),* front (rear) end. 3) *à parte,* apart, separately, by itself. 4) *a maior parte,* the most of. 5) *da parte de,* on the part of, from, in the name of. 6) *dar parte de,* to impart, to disclose, to inform, to report. 7) *de parte a parte,* reciprocally. 8) *em parte,* partly. 9) *em qualquer parte,* anywhere, somewhere. 10) *em toda a parte,* everywhere. 11) *em grande parte,* largely. 12) *fazer parte de,* to be a constituent of. 13) *tomar parte em,* to participate. 14) *pôr de parte,* to put aside. 15) *fazer a parte,* to make a show of doing something, to pretend. 16) *chamar de (à) parte,* to call aside. 17) *ter parte em,* to have a share. 18) *parte integrante,* part and parcel. 19) *em partes iguais,* share and share alike.

parteira, *s.f.* midwife.

parteiro, *s.m.* obstetrician, accoucheur.

partejamento, *s.m.* midwifery.

partejar, *v.t.* to deliver *(mulher)* of a child, to give birth to; to act as miwife.

partenogénese, *s.f.* parthenogenesis.

partição, *s.f.* partition, division.

participação, *s.f.* participation, communication, imparting, notification; sharing, partaking; information, announcement. 1) *participação de casamento,* wedding announcement. 2) *participação nos lucros,* profit sharing.

participador, *s.m.* participator, informer, participant; *adj.* informing, participant.

participante, *adj.* participant; *s.* participator; sharer.

participar, *v.t.* to communicate, to inform, to impart, to report; to partake; to have a share; to take part.

participável, *adj.* participable.

participe, *s.m.* sharer, partaker.

participial, *adj.* participal, of a participle.

particípio, *s.m.* participle.

partícula, *s.f.* particle, bit, very small part; atom, element; the small Host given to each lay communicant; a fragment of a consacrated Host.

particular, *adj.* particular; peculiar; private; personal; intimate; specific, special; separate; *em particular,* privately, in private.

particularidade, *s.f.* particularity, peculiarity; detail.

particularismo, *s.m.* particularism.

particularista, *a., adj.* particularist.

particularização, *s.f.* particularization.

particularizar, *v.t.* to particularize, to specify, to itemize, to individualize.

particularmente, *adv.* particularly; privately; specially, specifically; distinctly.

partida, *s.f.* departure, leaving; start; party; match, game; hoax, trick, joke; shipment, lot; entry. 1) *pregar uma partida,* to pl⌐

trick on. 2) *ponto de partida*, starting point, place of departure. 3) *estar de partida*, to be about to start.

partidário, *s.m., adj.* partisan; supporter, adherent; sectarian.

partidarismo, *s.m.* proselytism; partisanship.

partidarista, *adj., s.* strong partisan.

partidismo, *s.m.* ver "*partidarismo*".

partidista, *adj., s.* ver "*partidarista.*"

partido, *s.m.* party *(organização ou conjunto de pessoas)*, faction, profit; advantage; *adj.* broken; divided; gone; 1) *um bom partido*, excellent match; 2) *mudar de partido*, to change side; 3) *tomar o partido de*, to make common cause with; 4) *tirar o melhor partido de*, to make the most of, to turn to advantage; 5) *dar partido*, to give odds; 6) *filiar-se num partido*, to join a party; 7) *partido trabalhista*, Labour Party; 8) *partido no poder e na oposição*, the ins and outs.

partilha, *s.f.* partition, division; portion; lot; apportionment.

partilhar, *v.t., v.i.* to share; to divide, to distribute; to partake; to particicpate, to have a share, to share with.

partimento, *s.m.* division, partition, distribution.

partir, *v.t.* to divide, to part, to break; to split, to rend, to fracture, to cleave; to sever; to depart, to go away, to start, to set off, to leave; to arise from, to emanate. 1) *a partir de hoje*, from today on, beginning today. 2) *partir a meio*, to halve, to divide into halves.

partitivo, *adj.* partitive.

partitura, *s.f.* score *(mús.).*

partível, *adj.* partible, divisible.

parto, *s.m.* delivery, chilbirth, parturition, labour.

parturejar, *v.t.* to bring forth; to produce.

parturição, *s.f.* parturition.

parturiente, *s.f.* woman in labour; *adj.* parturient.

parva, *s.f.* snack *(antes do almoço).*

parvajão, parvajola, *s.m., s.* fool, numbskull, noodle.

parvalhão, *s.m.* big fool.

parvalheira, *s.f.* country life; the country.

parvalhice, *s.f.* silliness, nonsense, idiotic, remark.

~vidade, *s.f.* stupidity; littleness.

~, *adj., s.m.* idiotic, stupid, foolish; ~ad, fool, nitwit; *fazer figura de ~ke* an ass of oneself.

parvoíce, *s.f.* silliness, imbecility, nonsense.

parvónia, *s.f.* small village in the country *(pop).*

parvulez, parvuleza, *s.f.* childnood; purility; child's trick.

párvulo, *s.m.* child.

pascacice, *s.f.* silliness, stupidity.

pascácio, *s.m.* idiot, stupid, lout.

pascal, *adj.* pascal.

pascer, *v.t.* to pasture, to graze, to take to pasture.

pascigo, *s.m.* pasturage, pasture, grassland.

Páscoa, *s.f.* Easter *(para os Cristãos);* Passover *(para os Judeus).*

pascoal, *s.f.* Low Sunday.

Pascoela, pasmaceira, *s.f.* astonishment, gaping; amazement; apathy.

pasmado, *adj.* astonished, amazed, stupefied, star-gazing.

pasmar, *v.t., v.i.* to amaze, to astound; to gape, to wonder, to be amazed at, to stare at.

pasmo, *s.m.* astonishment, amazement, surprise, stupefaction, admiration, wonder.

pasmosamente, *adv.* wonderfully, amazingly.

pasmoso, *adj.* astonishing, surprising, wonderful, strange, marvellous, astounding.

paspalhão, *s.m.* silly, person, scarecrow, simpleton.

paspalhice, *s.f.* foolishness, nonsense, stupidity, silliness.

paspalho, *s.m.* dunce, fool, oaf.

pasquim, *s.m.* lampoon, pasquinade; cheap newspaper; yellow journal.

pasquinada, *s.f.* pasquinade, lampoon.

pasquinagem, *s.f.* lampoonery.

pasquinar, *v.t.* to pasquinate; to lampoon, to satirize, to ridicule.

pasquineiro, *s.m.* lampooner, yellow journalist.

passa, *s.f.* raisin, dried grape.

passa-culpas, *s.f.* indulgent person.

passada, *s.f.* step, pace, stride; diligences, efforts *(pl.).*

passadeira, *s.f.* stepping-stone; runner; stair-carpet, runner; zebra-crossing.

passadiço, *s.m.* way; foot-bridge; side-walk.

passadio, *s.m.* daily food; *bom passadiço*, good table.

passado, *adj.* gone, past; dried; done *(comida).*

passadoiro, *s.m.* passage, crossing-place.

passador, *s.m.* atrainer, colander; smuggler.

passadouro, *s.m.* ver passadoiro.

passageiro, *s.m.* passenger; traveller; *adj.* transitory, momentary, ephemeral, passing, fugitive; *passageiro clandestino*, stowaway.

passagem, *s.* passage, way; corridor; transit; migration; fare; act of passing; episode; portion of a writing or speech; a repair by darning. 1) *passagem de nível*, grade (level crossing). 2) *abrir passagem*, to make way. 3) *de passagem*, in passing, on the way, passing through. 4) *dar uma passagem*, to darn.

passajar, *v.t.* to stitch, to darn, to mend.

passal, *s.m.* ground adjoining a presbytery.

passamanaria, *s.f.* passementerie, lace-work, lace-making, trimmimg for dresses; lace-shop.

passamaneiro, *s.m.* lacemaker; laceseller.

passamanes, *s.m. (pl.)* trimmings, lace, braid.

passamento, *s.m.* death, decease, passing.

passante, *adj.* passing, exceeding; *s.m.* passer-by, walker; *passante de*, surpassing.

passaporte, *s.m.* passport, pass; safe-conduct.

passar, *v.t., v. refl.* to pass; to go beyond, to cross; to pass through; to carry; to spend (tempo); to excuse; to endure; to undergo, to suffer; to overpass; to omit; to filter; to cross over; to die, to pass away; to pass (exames); to kick (a bola); to forget; to circulate; to dry (fruta). 1) *passar-se*, to happen to occur. 2) *passar a ferro*, to iron, to press. 3) *passar a limpo*, to make a clean copy of. 4) *passar a fio de espada*, to put to the sword. 5) *passar à frente*, to outrun. 6) *passar de largo*, to by-pass. 7) *passar as raias (os limites)*, to overpass the bounds, to exceed. 8) *passar desta para melhor*, to die. 9) *passar por alto*, to omit, to overlook. 10) *passar mal*, to feel bad. 11) *passar de moda*, to go out of fashion. 12) *passar fome*, to go hungry, to starve. 13) *passar os olhos por*, to glance over. 14) *passar por*, to pas as (bom, virtuoso); to endure, to suffer. 15) *passar por cima de*, to break a rule, to overlook. 16) *passar revista*, to pass in review. 17) *passar sem*, to do without, to dispense with. 18) *passar a vau*, to ford. 19) *passar pelas armas*, to shoot. 20) *passar de memória*, to slip from the memory. 21) *passar uma lição*, to set a lesson. 22) *não passar de ano*, to be left back. 23) *passar uma certidão*, to give a certificate. 24)

passar palavra, to pass word. 25) *passar pela ideia*, to cross one's mind. 26) *passar de ideia*, to forget. 27) *passar pela tangente*, to scrape through (exames).

passarada, *s.f.* the birds; crowd of birds.

passarão, *s.m.* big bird; a crafty person, cunning fox.

passaredo, *s.m.* ver "passarada".

passareira, *s.f.* aviary.

passareiro, *s.m.* bird.catcher.

passarinhada, *s.f.* flock of birds.

passarinhar, *v.i.* to catch birds; to loaf, to gad about.

passarinheiro, *s.m.* birdcatcher, bird trapper; bird fancier; bird-seller.

passarinho, *s.m.* little bird, any small bird, birdie.

pássaro, *s.m.* bird; cunning fellow; *mais vale um pássaro na mão do que dois a voar*, a bird in the hand is worth two in the bush.

passatempo, *s.m.* pastime; sport; diversion, amusement, recreation, entertainment; *passatempo predilecto*, hobby, favourite pastime.

passavante, *s.m.* pursuivant; herald.

passável, *adj.* tolerable, not too bad, so-so.

passe, *s.m.* pass, permission, leave, licence, permit, free ticket, season-ticket.

passeadoiro, *s.m.* promenade, public walk.

passeador, *adj.* much given to promenading.

passeadouro, *s.m.* ver "passeadoiro".

passeante, *s., adj.* walker, promenader; idling, strolling.

passear, *v.t., v.i.* to walk, to promeande, to stroll, to go for a walk; to show; to display; to take for a walk; *mandar passear*, to send someone packing or about his business.

passeata, *s.f.* stroll, tour, promenade, little walk, trip.

passeio, *s.m.* walk, stroll, trip, excursion; pavement, side-walk; *ir dar um passeio*, to go for a walk.

passeira, *s.f.* place where grapes are spread to dry.

passeiro, *adj.* negligent, slow.

passento, *adj.* absorbent, porous, permeable, pervious (papel, etc.)

passibilidade, *s.f.* possibility.

passional, *adj., s.m.* passional.

passionário, *s.m.* ver "passional".

passiva, *s.f.* passive voice.

passivar, *v.t.* to change to the passive.

passível, *adj.* passible, susceptible of, liable of.

passividade, s.f. passivity, apathy, inactivity.

passivo, adj. passibe, inert, inactive, apathetic, submissive, indifferent; s.m. liabilities.

passo, s.m. pace, step, footstep; manner of walking; march; narrow passage; passage of a book. 1) *passo a passo*, step by step. 2) *a passo*, slowly. 3) *passo de gigante*, giant stride. 4) *a cada passo*, every now and then. 5) *a dois passos de*, a short distance from. 6) *a um passo de*, on the verge of. 7) *acertar o passo*, to get in step with. 8) *ao passo que*, while, whereas. 9) *dar um passo*, to take a step. 10) *marcar passo*, to mark time, to stay in the same place, to make no progress. 11) *passo ariscado*, a leap in the dark. 12) *passo em falso*, wrong move. 13) *dar o primeiro passo*, to break the ground; situation; condition; affair; act.

pasta, s.f. paste; portfolio *(de um Ministério)*; briefcase; *pasta dentrífica*, tooth paste.

pastagem, s.f. pasture, pasturage, grazing ground; herbage.

pastar, v.t., v.i. to pasture, to feed; to graze, to browse.

pastel, s.m. pastry, pie, tart; pastel *(desenho)*; mixture of types *(tipografia)*; indolent person *(fig)*.

pastelão, s.m. big pie; indolent person *(fig)*.

pastelaria, s.f. pastry, confectionery; confectioner's.

pasteleiro, s.m. pastrycook, pastrymaker.

pastelista, s. pastellist.

pasteurização, s.f. pasteurization.

pasteurizador, s.m. pasteurizer *(aparelho)*.

pasteurizar, v.t. to pasteurize, to sterilize *(leite)*.

pastilha, s.f. lozenge, pastille.

pastinaca, pastinaga, s.f. *(bot)* parsnip.

pastinhar, v.i. to nibble at food.

pastio, s.m. pasturage, grazing.

pasto, s.m. pasturage, pasture, grass; food, nourishment; *casa de pasto*, eating house.

pastor, s.m. shepherd; parson, parish-priest; pastor, minister, vicar, clergyman *(na Igreja Protestante)*.

pastora, s.f. shepherdess.

pastorado, s.m. pastorship, pastorate.

pastoral, s. pastoral *(carta)*; pastorale *(música)*; eclogue, idyl; adj. pastoral, rural.

pastoreação, s.f. act of pasturing or tending a flock.

pastorear, v.t. to keep; to act as a pastor, to pasture, to put to graze, to herd; to guide, to direct, to lead *(fig)*.

pastoreio, s.m. pasturing of cattle.

pastorejar, v.t. ver pastorear.

pastorela, s.f. pastorale, pastoral poem; an eclogue.

pastorícia, s.f. ver pastoreio.

pastorício, adj. pastoral.

pastoril, adj. pastoral, rustic, bucolic.

pastosidade, s.f. viscousiness.

pastoso, adj. clammy; sticky; viscous, pasty, gummy; husky *(voz)*.

pata, s.f. duck; paw; foot.

pataca, s.f. silver coin *(Brasil)*.

patacão, s.m. ancient copper coin *(em Portugal)*.

patacho, s.m. brigantine, twomasted pinnace.

pata-choca, s.f. lazy or clumsy woman.

pataco, s.m. ancient coin *(em Portugal)*; *não valer um pataco*, to be good for nothing, of little value.

patacoada, s.f. nonsense; boasting.

patada, s.f. kick, taping with paw or foot; blunder, foolishness.

patagão, patagónio, adj., s.m. Patagonian.

patamar, s.m. landing; paltform.

pataqueiro, adj. common, ordinary, poor; cheap, low-priced.

patarata, s. braggart, blusterer; non-sensical talk; fib.

pataratice, s.f. nonsense, fib.

patau, s.m. *pagar o patau*, to pay the piper, to abide the consequences.

patavina, s.f. nothing. 1) *não perceber patavina*, to make neither head nor tail. 2) *nem patavina*, not the least, nothing at all.

pateada, s.f. hissing; hooting; stamping with the feet.

pateadura, s.f. ver "pateada".

patear, v.t. to hiss; to hoot; to stamp with the feet *(para expressar desaprovação)*.

pategada, s.f. stupidity, act of a simpleton.

patego, s.m., adj. simpleton, fool, blockhead, bumpkin; foolish, stupid.

pateguice, s.f. ver "pategada".

pateiro, s.m. duck-breeder, duck raiser.

patela, s.f. knee-cap, patella; quoit; quoits *(jogo)*; iron-disk.

patena, s.f. paten.

patente, s.f. patent, privilege, exclusive grant; military rank; adj. patent, obvious, manifest, palin, evident; open.

patentear, v.t. to manifest; to patent *(uma invenção)*; to show, to unfold, to reveal.

pátera, *s.f.* patera.

paternal, *adj.* paternal; fatherly.

paternalismo, *s.m.* paternalism.

paternalista, *adj.* paternalist.

paternalmente, *adv.* paternally.

paternidade, *s.f.* paternity; authorship; fatherhood; fathership.

paterno, *adj. ver "paternal".*

pateta, *s.m., adj.* simpleton, ninny, fool, imbecile, idiot.

patetar, patetear, *v.i.* to speak nonsense.

pateticamente, *adv.* pathetically.

patetice, *s.f.* nonsense, silliness, dotage, stupidity.

patético, *adj.* pathetic, sad, moving, touching; *s.m.* pathetic; pathos, deep emotion.

patetóide, *adj.* somewhat dotard.

patibular, *adj.* of the gallows, criminal.

patíbulo, *s.m.* scaffold, gibbet, gallows.

patifaria, *s.f.* knavery, mischief, rascality, roguery, knavish behaviour, villany, scoundrelism.

patife, *s.m.* knave, rogue, rascal, scoundrel, scamp.

patifório, *s.m. (pop)* sly rogue.

patilha, *s.f.* spangle; cantle; brake *(bicicleta).*

patim, *s.m.* skate; landing, stair-landing.

pátina, *s.f.* patina.

patinação, *s.f. ver "patinagem".*

patinador, *s.m.* skater.

patinagem, *s.f.* skating.

patinar, *v.i.* to skate, to glide over the ice; to slide, to skid; to become covered with a patina.

patinhar, *v.i.* to paddle, to dabble, to splash *(na água);* to skid.

patinheiro, *s.m.* slough, puddle.

patinho, *s.m.* duckling; simpleton, foll.

pátio, *s.m.* yard; courtyard, inner court; *pátio de recreio,* playground.

pato, *s.m.* drake; duck; simpleton *(pop).*

patoá, *s.m.* patois, dialect.

patogénese, *s.f.* pathogenesis.

patogenia, *s.f.* pathogeny.

patogénico, *adj.* pathogenic.

patola, *adj.* silly, foolish, stupid, ignorant.

patologia, *s.f.* pathology.

patológico, *adj.* pathologic(al).

patologista, *s.* pathologist.

patorra, *s.f.* big foot.

patranha, *s.f.* fib, lie, untruthful story.

patranheiro, *s.m.* liar, fibber, story-teller.

patrão, *s.m.* master, employer, boss; chief; skipper *(barco);* coxswain.

pátria, *s.f.* fatherland, mother-country, home, native country.

patriarca, *s.m.* patriarch; venerable old man.

patriacado, *s.m.* patriarch.

patriarcal, *adj.* patriarchal, venerable, respectable; peaceful; *s.f.* patriarchal see.

patriciado, *s.m.* patriciate; the nobility; patrician class.

patrício, *s.m.* patrician, noble; fellow-country-man, nobleman, compatriot, of the same country; adj. patrician, noble.

patrimonial, *adj.* patrimonial.

património, *s.m.* patrimony; family estate; heritage. 1) *património do Estado,* State property. 2) *património hereditário,* birthright.

pátrio, *adj.* native; paternal.

patriota, *s.* patriot; adj. patriotic.

patrioteiro, *s.m.* jingo, chauvinist; *adj.* chauvinistic.

patrioticamente, *adv.* patriotically.

patriotice, *s.f.* false patriotism.

patriótico, *adj.* patriotic.

patriotismo, *s.m.* patriotism.

patrística, *s.f.* patristics, patrology.

patroa, *s.f.* lady, mistress *(de casa, loja, etc.).*

patrocinador, *adj.* patronizing, supporting, favouring, sponsoring; *s.m.* patronizer, patron, sponsor, protector.

patrocinar, *v.t.* to patronize, to support, to aid, to sponsor, to back up.

patrocínio, *s.m.* patronage, sponsorship, help, support, protection.

patrologia, *s.f.* patrology.

patrológico, *adj.* patrologic(al).

patrona, *s.f.* patroness; cartridge-box.

patronal, *adj.* patrinal.

patronato, *s.m.* patronage; the employers; child-welfare instituition.

patronímico, *adj., s.m.* patronymic.

patrono, *s.m.* patron; advocate; protector; patron saint; sponsor, supporter.

patrulha, *s.f.* patrol.

patrulhar, *v.t.* to patrol, to go the rounds.

patudo, *adj.* broad-footed, big-pawed.

patuscada, *s.f.* spree, lark, revelry, carousal; banquet.

patuscar, *v.i.* to go on the spree; to have a light meal *(pop).*

patusco, *s.m., adj.* merry maker, joker, roisterer; feaster; joyful, funny; queer.

pau, *s.m.* piece of wood; timber; stick, staff, rod, cudgel, club clubs *(naipe de cartas)* *(pl.);* Portuguese money *(escudos) (pop).* 1) *pau de bandeira,* flagstaff, flagpole. 2) *jogar comn pau de dois bicos,* to hunt with the hounds and run with the hare, to play a double game. 3) *servir de pau-de-cabeleira,* to play gooseberry, a go-between for lovers. 4) *dar por paus e por pedras,* to go off the deep end. 5) *pau para toda a obra (colher),* Jack-of-all-trades. 6) *a dar com um pau,* in great quantity. 7) *pau de virar tripas,* very skinny person.

pau-brasil, *s.m.* brazil-wood, red wood.

pau-de-cabeleira, *s.m.* pander, pimp.

pau-ferro, *s.m.* ironwood.

paul, *s.m.* marsh, swamp, fen, bog; quagmire.

paulada, *s.f.* blow; a drubbing, cudgeling, stroke.

paulatinamente, *adv.* alowly, gradually.

paulatino, *adj.* slow, gradual, by degrees.

paulista, *s., adj.* Paulist, native of S. Paulo, Brazil; of or pertaining to the city of S. Paulo.

paulistano, *s.m., adj.* paulista.

paulito, *s.m.* little stick, peg.

pau-mandado, *s.m.* servile person, tool; cat's paw.

paupérie, *s.f.* pauperism; absolute poverty.

pauperismo, *s.m.* pauperism, poverty; the poor.

paupérrimo, *adj.* most poor, very poor.

pau-preto, *s.m.* blackwood.

pau-rosa, *s.m.* rosewood.

pausa, *s.f.* pausa, cessation, stop, rest; intermission, interruption, break, interval; rest *(música).*

pausadamente, *adv.* slowly, pausingly.

pausado, *adj.* paused; leisurely, slow-moving.

pau-santo, *s.m.* lignum viate, holy wood.

pausar, *v.t., v.i.* to pause; to stop, to delay, to rest, to linger; to make a pause.

pauta, *s.f.* stave *(música);* register; tariff; roll, list; guide-lines; *pauta alfandegária,* customs tariff.

pautado, *adj.* ruled; moderate; methodic, measured; *papel pautado,* ruled paper.

pautador, *s.m.* rulled; ruling machine.

pautal, *adj.* relative to tariffs; indicated in the tariffs.

pautar, *v.t.* to rule *(papel);* to direct; to moderate, to regulate; to include in a list, to enroll.

pauzinho, *s.m.* little stick, twig; *mexer os pauzinhos,* to pull strings.

pavana, *s.f.* pavan *(música ou dança); tocar a pavana a alguém,* to give a thrashing.

pavão, *s.m.* peacock.

paveia, *s.f.* bundle.

pavês, *s.m.* pavese, large shield.

pavesado, *adj.* lined with paveses.

pavesar, *v.t.* to line with paveses.

pávido, *adj.* fearful, timid, frightened, afraid; astonished.

pavilhão, *s.m.* pavilion; turret; canopy; flag; auricle; division of a hospital; exhibition building.

pavimentação, *s.f.* paving, flooring.

pavimentar, *v.t.* to pave.

pavimento, *s.m.* pavement; floor.

pavio, *s.m.* wick; *de fio a pavio,* from beginning to end, from soup to nuts.

pavoa, *s.f.* pea-hen.

pavonaço, *adj.* violet-coloured.

pavonada, *s.f.* boasting, ostentation.

pavonear, *v.t.* to display; to boast; to brag.

pavoneio, *s.m.* displaying; boasting.

pavor, *s.m.* dread, awe, terror, fear, fright, horror.

pavorosamente, *adv.* dreadfully, fearfully.

pavoroso, *adj.* frightful, horrid, dreadful, terrible, fearful, appalling.

paxá, *s.m.* pasha.

paz, *s.f.* peace, tranquility, calmness, repose; concord, harmony; silence. 1) *deixa-me em paz,* let me alone, leave me in peace. 2) *fazer as pazes,* to make peace, to bury the hatchet. 3) *descansar em paz,* justice of the peace.

pazada, *s.f.* shovelful; blow with a shovel.

pé, *s.m.* foot; paw; support; bottom, base; pedestal; pretext; reason; opportunity; stem; state of affairs; a single vine, shrub or plant; excuse; lineal measure; leg *(cadeira, mesa).* 1) *pé ante pé,* on tiptoe. 2) *a pé,* on foot, afoot; out of bed, up. 3) *a pé firme,* resolutely, firmly. 4) *a pé coxinho,* hopping. 5) *ao pé da letra,* literally, to the letter. 6) *bater o pé,* to put one's foot down. 7) *em (com) pés de lã,* stealthily. 8) *com o pé no estribo,* about to depart. 9) *com os pés para a cova,* with one foot in the grave, very old. 10) *de pé para a mão,* at a moment's notice, on the spur of the moment. 11) *dos pés à cabeça,* from head to toe, from top to bottom. 12) *em pé de guerra,* on a war footing. 13) *entrar com o pé direito,* to make a good start, to begin luckily. 14) *fazer pé atrás,* to step back, to hesitate. 15) *estar de* *pé (um convite)*, to stand. 16) *ficar (estar) de pé atrás*, to be on guard against. 17) *meter os pés pelas mãos*, to go haywire, to get hopelessly confused. 18) *peito do pé*, instep. 19) *perder o pé*, to loose one's footing *(na água)*. 20) *planta do pé*, sole of the foot. 21) *ponta do pé*, toe tip. 22) *pôr-se de pé*, to stand up, to jump up. 23) *sem pés nem cabeça*, without head or tail, without rhyme or reason. 24) *tomar pé*, to touch bottom. 25) *fazer pé-de-alferes*, to court. 26) *perder o pé*, to go out of one's depth. 27) *ver em que pé está*, to see how the wind blows or land lies. 28) *em pé de igualdade*, on equal terms. 29) *ao pé de*, close to. 30) *ao pé*, near by. 31) *um pé lá e outro cá*, in a minute.

peanha, *s.f.* pedestal, stand.

peão, *s.m.* walker; pedestrian; foot-soldier; plebeian; pawn *(xadrez)*.

pear, *v.t.* to hinder, to embarass; to fetter; to impede *(progresso);* to hobble *(cavalos)*.

peça, *s.f.* piece; part, portion; cannon, gun; coin; play, drama, musical composition; man (xadrez); prank, trick. 1) *peça antia-érea*, antiaircraft gun. 2) *peça de artilharia*, piece of ordenance. 3) *peça em um acto*, one-act play. 4) *peça sobresselente*, spare part. 5) *pregar uma peça*, to play a practical joke on, to play a trick on. 6) *peça de linho*, piece of linen.

pecadilho, *s.m.* peccadillo, slight offence, trifling sin.

pecado, *s.m.* sin; misdeed, offence. 1) *os sete pecados mortais*, the seven deadly *(mortal)* sins. 2) *pecado original*, original sin.

pecador, *s.m.* sinner, offender, wrongdoer; *adj.* sinful, sinning.

pecaminosamente, *adv.* sinfully.

pecaminoso, *adj.* sinful.

pecante, *adj.* peccant, sinful.

pecar, *v.i.* to sin, to offend, to trespass, to commit a sin.

pecável, *adj.* peccable, liable, sinful.

pecha, *s.f.* fault; blemish; defect, failing.

pechincha, *s.f.* bargain; find; godsend.

pechinchar, *v.t.* to gain; to profit; to bargain.

pechincheiro, *s.m.* bargainer, bargainhunter.

pechisbeque, *s.m.* pinchbeck; tombac.

pechoso, *adj.* faulty, faultfinding; particular; whimsical; scruoulous.

peciolado, *adj.* petiolate, petiolated.

peciolar, *adj.* petiolar.

pecíolo, *s.m.* petiole, leafstalk.

peco, *adj.* blighte, withered *(vegetais);* stunned; nescinet, stupid, dull; *s.m.* plant, blight.

peçonha, *s.f.* poison, venom; malice; malevolence.

peçonhento, *adj.* poisonous, venomous, baneful, nausious; malignat.

pécora, *s.f.* prostitute, drab, wench.

pé-coxinho, *s.m.* act of walking only on one foot.

pectina, *s.f.* pectin.

pectíneo, *adj.* pectinate; pectinal.

pectoral, *adj.* pectoral.

pecuária, *s.f.* cattle breeding, cattle raising.

pecuário, *adj.* relating to cattle; *s.m.* cattle breeder, cattleman.

peculador, *s.m.* peculator, embezzler.

peculato, *s.m.* peculation, embezzlement *(fundos públicos)*.

peculiar, *adj.* peculiar, particular; private; special, characteristic.

peculiaridade, *s.f.* peculiarity.

peculiarmente, *adv.* peculiarly.

pecúlio, *s.m.* savings, nestegg, money reserve.

pecúnia, *s.f.* money, funds.

pecuniário, *adj.* pecuniary, monetary.

pecunioso, *adj.* pecunious, rich, opulent, moneyed.

pedaço, *s.m.* bit, piece; morsel; fragment, fraction; portion, slice; a long time. 1) *pedaço de asno*, ass, fool. 2) *fazer em pedaços*, to tear (to smash) to pieces, to break. 3) *estar em pedaços*, to be very tired.

pedagogia, *s.f.* pedagogy.

pedagogicamente, *adv.* pedagogically.

pedagógico, *adj.* pedagogic(al).

pedagogismo, *s.m.* pedagogism.

pedagogista, *s.* pedagogist.

pedagogo, *s.m.* pedagogue *(professor)*.

pedal, *s.m.* foot-lever, pedal, treadle; *pedal da embraiagem*, clutch pedal.

pedalada, *s.f.* pedal-pushing, act of pedalling.

pedalar, *v.i.* to pedal; to ride a bicycle.

pedaleiro, *s.m.* main axle, the pedals of a velociped.

pedantaria, *s.f.* pedantry *(maneiras, actos, carácter)*, pedantism.

pedante, *adj.* pedantic, conceited, priggish; *s.* pedant, prig.

pedantear, *v.i.* to be a pedant, to pedantize; to display, to parade.

pedantesco, *adj.* pedantic, affected.

pedantice, *s.f.* pedantism.

pedantismo, *s.m.* pedantry.

pé-de-alferes, *s.m.* courtship.

pé-de-altar, *s.m.* altarahe, altar fees *(casamento, baptismo)*.

pé-de-cabra, *s.m.* crow-bar, pinch-bar.

pé-de-chumbo, *s.m.* a plodder, someone walking slowly and heavily.

pé-de-galinha, *s.f.* crow's foot; bird's foot.

pé-de-galo, *s.m.* hop; *mesa de pé-de-galo,* pedestal-table, round-table.

pé-de-meia, *s.m.* savings, nest-egg.

pederasta, *s.m.* pederast.

pederastia, *s.f.* pederasty, sodomy.

pedernal, pederneira, *s.m., s.f.* firestone; flint.

pedestal, *s.m.* base, support, pedestal, socle.

pedestre, *adj.* pedestrian; *corrida pedestre,* foot race.

pedestrianismo, *s.m.* pedestrianism, walking, hiking.

pedestrianista, *s.* pedestrian.

pé-de-vento, *s.m.* puff, blast, whirl-wind; tumult.

pediatra, *s.m.* pediatrician, pediatrist.

pediatria, *s.f.* pediatrics.

pediátrico, *adj.* pediatric.

pedicelado, *adj.* pedicellate.

pedicelo, *s.m.* pedicel.

pediculado, *adj.* pediculate.

pedicular, *adj.* pedicular.

pedículo, *s.m.* pedicel, pedicle, peduncle.

pedicuro, *s.m.* pedicure; chiropodist.

pedido, *s.m.* petition; prayer, supplication; demand, request; order, requisition. 1) *pedido de casamento,* marriage proposal. 2) *pedido de demissão,* resignation. 3) *a pedido,* on demand, upon (by) request. 4) *a pedido de,* at the request of.

pedidor, *s.m.* demander, applicant, petitioner.

pediforme, *adj.* foot-like, foot-shaped, pediform.

pedilúvio, *s.m.* foot-bath.

pedímano, *adj.* pedimanous.

pedincha, *s.f.* begging.

pedinchão, *s.m.* beggar; *adj.* whining, begging, always begging.

pedinchar, *v.t., v.i.* to beg importunately.

pedinchice, *s.f.* begging; beggary.

pedintão, *adj., s.m.* always begging.

pedintar, *v.t., v.i.* to beg (importunately).

pedintaria, *s.f.* beggary, begging.

pedinte, *s.* beggar; petitioner, mendicant, pauper; *adj.* begging.

pedir, *v.t.* to beg; to pray, to beseech; to ask, to supplicate; to demand, to request; to apply for; to order. 1) *pedir a mão (em casamento),* to ask the hand, to ask in marriage. 2) *pedir a palavra,* to ask for the floor. 3) *pedir contas,* to demand an accounting, an explanation. 4) *pedir a demissão,* to resign. 5) *pedir desculpa,* to apologize (for). 6) *pedir emprestado,* to borrow (from). 7) *pedir licença (vénia),* to ask permission of. 8) *pedir misericórdia,* to beg for mercy. 9) *pedir por,* to intercede, to plead for.

pé-direito, *s.m.* height *(de um quarto);* headway, headroom.

peditório, *s.m.* public collection; begging alms *(esmolas);* importunate begging.

pedófilo, *adj.* fond of children.

pedologia, *s.f.* pedology.

pedómetro, *s.m.* pedometer.

pedra, *s.f.* stone, rock, pebble, cobble; gravel; jewel, gem; kidney stone, calculus; flint; blackboard; tombstone; hail. 1) *pedra angular,* cornerstone. 2) *pedra de amolar,* whetstone, grindstone. 3) *água mole em pedra dura...,* constant dripping wears away a stone. 4) *ter pedra no sapato,* to smell a rat. 5) *dormir como uma pedra,* to sleep like a top *(pop).* 6) *de pedra e cal,* firm, steadfast. 7) *ser de pedra,* to be stony-hearted. 8) *pôr uma pedra em cima de,* to bury in oblivion, to forget. 9) *não deixar pedra sobre pedra,* to leave no stone unturned.

pedrada, *s.f.* stone's throw; stoning; insult, offence.

pedra de ara, *s.f.* altar-stone.

pedra de cevar, *s.f.* loadstone.

pedra-de-toque, *s.f.* touchstone.

pedrado, *adj.* speckled, spotted *(pedra branca e preta);* paved.

pedra-íman, *s.f.* loadstone.

pedral, *adj.* stony.

pedranceira, *s.f.* heap of stones, rock pile.

pedra-pomes, *s.f.* pumicestone.

pedraria, *s.f.* precious stones, gems, jewels; freestone.

pedra-ume, *s.f.* alum.

pedregal, *s.m.* place full of stones; stony ground.

pedregoso, *adj.* stony rocky.
pedregulhento, *adj.* stony gravelly.
pedregulho, *s.m.* big stone, block of rock.
pedreira, *s.f.* stone quarry, stone-pit.
pedreiro, *s.m.* mason, bricklayer; martinet *(zool.)*
pedreiro-livre, *s.m.* freemason.
pedrês, *adj.* spotted, speckled, mottled *(preto e branco).*
pedrisco, *s.m.* hail, sleet.
pedroiço, *s.m. ver "pedrouço".*
pedroso, *adj.* stony, rocky.
pedrouço, *s.m.* heap of stones.
pedunculado, *adj.* pedunculate.
peduncular, *s.m.* peduncular.
pedúnculo, *s.m.* peduncle.
pedunculoso, *adj. ver "pedunculado".*
pega, *s.f.* hold, seizing, handle; quarrel, clash, discussion; setting; hardening.
pega, *s.f.* magpie; parting woman, chatterbox.
pegada, *s.f.* footprint, footmark, track, trace, vestige.
pegadeira, *s.f.* handle, ear, catch.
pegadiço, *adj.* sticky, clammy, contagious; importunate.
pegadilha, *s.f.* quarrel, dissension, dispute.
pegado, *adj.* close to; stuck; contiguous, next door, near to, near by.
pegadoiro, *s.m.* haft, handle.
pegador, *s.m.* carcher; remora *(peixe).*
pegadouro, *s.m. ver "pegadoiro".*
pegadura, *s.f.* holding; sticking.
pegajento, pegajoso, *adj.* clammy, viscous, sticky, gummy; contagious, catching.
pegamasso, *s.m.* glue, paste, loam.
pegamento, *s.m. ver "pega".*
peganhento, *adj. ver "pegadiço, pegajoso".*
pegão, *s.m.* abutment pier; gust of wind, wind-storm.
pegar, *v.t., v.i.* to hold, to seize; to take up; to join, to unite; to infect; to stick; to be contagious; to take root *(plantas);* to become generalized, to spread; to begin. 1) *pegar-se*, to cling to; to be catching; to quarrel, to fall out with. 2) *pegar em armas*, to take upon arms. 3) *pegar na palavra*, to take at one's word. 4) *pegar fogo*, to catch fire. 5) *pegar no sono*, to fall asleep. 6) *pegar-se com alguém*, to pick a quarrel with. 7) *o motor não pega*, the engine doesn't start up. 8) *não pega!*, a lie, I don't believe it!
Pégaso, *s.m.* Pegasus.

pegmatite, *s.f.* pegmatite.
pego, *s.m.* whirlpool, pit, abyss, chasm, vortex; the deep sea, lake.
pegueiro, *s.m.* pitch-marker.
peguilha, *s.f.* quarrel, the beginning of a dispute.
peguilhar, *v.i.* to quarrel, to squable, to provoke a dispute.
peguilhento, *adj.* quarrelsome, contentious.
peguilho, *s.m.* obstacle, hinderance; motive, pretext *(para uma disputa).*
peguinhar, *v.t., v.i.* to trample; to provoke.
pegulho, *s.m.* savings, nest-egg.
pegural, *adj.* pastoral.
pegureiro, *s.m.* shepherd, herdsman; sheep dog; hunting dog.
peia, *s.f.* embarrass, hinderance; shackle, fetter.
peita, *s.f.* subordination, bribe.
peitaça, *s.f.* strong chest.
peitar, *v.t.* to suborn, to bribe.
peitilho, *s.m.* shirt-front, bosom; bib.
peito, *s.m.* breast, chest; shirt-front, bosom; valour; courage. 1) *peito do pé*, instep. 2) *criança de peito*, suckling. 3) *tomar a peito*, to take to heart. 4) *a peito descoberto*, defenceless, with bared breast.
peitoral, *adj.* pectora; *s.m.* pectoral; breastband; chest or lung medicine.
peitoril, *s.m.* parapet, windswill.
peitudo, *adj.* big-bosomed *(mulher)*, big-chested.
peixão, *s.m.* big fish; comely woman or girl *(pop).*
peixaria, *s.f.* fish market.
peixe, *s.m.* fish. 1) *peixe fumado*, smoked fish. 2) *nem carne nem peixe*, neither fish nor fowl. 3) *viveiro de peixes*, fish pond. 4) *como peixe na água*, a pig in clover, perfectly at ease. 5) *filho de peixe sabe nadar*, like father, like son. 6) *vender o seu peixe*, to look out for one's interests.
peixe-agulha, *s.m.* needle-fish.
peixe-aranha, *s.m.* greater weever; stingbull.
peixe-espada, *s.m.* swordfish; sutlass fish.
peixe-galo, *s.m.* moonfish.
peixeira, *s.f.* fishwoman, fishwife.
peixeiro, *s.m.* fishmonger.
peixelim, *s.m.* sea-fish generally to be dried.
peixe-lua, *s.m.* sunfish.
peixe-martelo, *s.m.* hammerhead shark.
peixe-sapo, *s.m.* toadfish, frogfish.
peixe-serra, *s.m.* saw-fish.

peixota, s.f. whiting, hake, sea luce.

pejado, adj. filled, replete, overcharged; pregnant; bashful.

pejamento, s.m. impediment, obstacle, hindrance.

pejar, v.t. to hinder, to obstruct, to encumber, to fill up, to charge, to overload; to become pregnant; pejar-se, to be bashful or ashamed.

pejo, s.m. prudency, modesty, shame, bashfulness; timidity, shyness.

pejorar, v.t. to render, worse, to disparage, to depreciate, to underrrate, to debase.

pejorativo, adj. pejorative, depreciatory, disparaging.

pejoso, adj. bashful, shy, timid; ashamed.

pela, prep. por e art. a, by, through, for the, as for, about. 1) pela janela, through the window. 2) pela manhã, in the morning. 3) pela segunda vez, for the second time. 4) pela força, by force. 5) pela calada, on the sly.

péla, s.f. ball; sport; toy.

pelada, s.f. baldness; alopecia; bald spot.

pelado, adj. bald, hairless.

pelador, s.m. hair-remover; skinner.

peladura, s.f. baldness; hair-removal.

pelagem, s.f. pelage; fur.

pelágico, adj. pelagic, of the deep sea, oceanic.

pélago, s.m. high-sea; abyss, profundity, deepness.

pelagra, s.f. pellagra (doença).

pelame, s.m. hides, tanning; curring; fur, hair; pelts.

pelangana, s.f. porringer, wrinkled skin.

pelar, v.t. to pull off (cabelo); to peel; to bark. 1) pelar-se, to grow bald, to lose hair; to shiver with fright. 2) pelar-se por, to be crazy about, to long for, to be very fond of.

pelargónio, s.m. pelargonium.

pelaria, s.f. tanning; portion of hides; fur shop; peltry, furs.

pele, s.f. skin, epidermis; leather. 1) pele-de--galinha, gooseflesh. 2) só pele e osso, only skin and bone. 3) não queria estar-lhe na pele, I would not want to be in his shoes. 4) salvar a pele, to save one's skin; pelt, fur, hide (de animais).

peleiro, s.m. skinner; furrier.

peleja, s.f. fight, battle, combat, strife; contest.

pelejador, s.m. fighter, struggler; adj. fighting, struggling.

pelejar, v.i. to fight, to struggle; to quarrel, to dispute, to contend; to combat; to struggle with.

pelém, s.m. skinny person, spindle-shanks.

pele-vermelha, s. a redskin.

pelica, s.f. kid leather.

peliça, s.f. pelisse.

pelicano, s.m. pelican.

pelicaria, s.f. furriery; industry of furs.

peliceiro, s.m. tanner.

película, s.f. pellicle; film; motion picture reel.

pelicular, adj. pellicular.

pelintra, adj. penniless; poor but pretentious fellow.

pelintragem, s.f. poverty, penury, shabby-genteel people collectively.

pelintrão, s.m. ragamuffin.

pelintraria, s.f. ver pelintragem.

pelintrice, s.f. shabbiness, poverty, misery, penury.

peliqueiro, s.m. dealer in kid leather.

pelitrapo, s.m. ragamuffin.

pelo, prep. por e art. o, by the, at the, for the, in the, through the, over the, among the. 1) pelo que, in view of which, wherefore. 2) pelo que respeito a, as regards, in respect to. 3) pelo sim pelo não, on account of this or that.

pêlo, s.m. hair, down, flue, pile; em pêlo, naked.

peloirinho, s.m. ver "pelourinho".

peloiro, s.m. ver "pelouro".

peloso, adj. hairy, shaggy, furry.

pelota, s.f. leather pad; pellet; pelota (jogo); any small ball; a football.

pelotada, s.f. blow with a ball.

pelotão, s.m. platoon.

pelote, s.m. a jerkin made of sheepskin; em pelote, naked.

pelotica, s.f. prestidigitation; sleight of hand.

pelotiqueiro, s.m. juggler.

pelourinho, s.m. pillory, whipping-post.

pelouro, s.m. cannon ball, musket ball; departmente (de estado).

pelta, s.f. pelt.

peltado, adj. peltate.

pelúcia, s.f. plush,

peludo, adj. hairy, shaggy; timid; shy (pop).

pelugem, s.f. down, flue, fluff.

peluginoso, adj. downy, hairy, shaghgy.

pelve, s.f. pelvis.

pélvico, adj. pelvic.

pélvis, s.f. ver "pelve".

pena, s.f. pen, penholder; pain, pity, grief;

feather, plume; penalty, punishment; sorrow, compassion. 1) *pena de morte*, capital punishment, pain of death. 2) *não vale a pena*, it is not worth while. 3) *que pena!*, what a pity!. 4) *ter pena de*, to feel (to be) sorry for.

penáceo, *adj.* pennaceous, resembling a feather.

penacho, *s.m.* feather-bunch, plume, panache; a crest; government, power *(fig.)*.

penada, *s.f.* stroke of type pen; penful, a dip of ink.

penado, *adj.* feathered; suffering; painful.

penal, *adj.* penal; punitive.

penalidade, *s.f.* penalty, punishment.

penalizar, *v.t.* to distrees, to pain, to afflict, to penalize, to torment, to torture; *penalizar-se*, to feel pity for.

penão, *s.m.* penon, pennant.

penar, *v.i.* to be in pain; to suffer.

penates, *s.m. (pl.)* Penates, household gods; family, home.

penca, *s.f.* cabbage; big nose *(pop)*.

pencudo, *adj.* long-nosed.

pendão, *s.m.* pennon, banner, flag, pennant, ensign, standard.

pendência, *s.f.* quarrel, dispute; contention, strife; fight, fray.

pendenciar, *v.i.* to quarrel; to dispute, to wrangle.

pendente, *adj.* pendent, pending, suspended; undecided, undetermined; inclined, slanting, sloping.

pender, *v.i.* to be suspended; to hang; to bend, to drop; to impend, to incline, to be inclined; to decline, to fall; to lean, to slope; to be favourably disposed to; to verge, to verge, to tend.

pendericalho, *ver "penduricalho".*

pendoar, *v.i.* to put forth tassels.

pendor, *s.m.* declivity, slope; inclination; disposition, propensity, propension.

pêndula, *s.f.* pendulum clock.

pendular, *adj.* pendular; swinging, oscillatory.

pêndulo, *s.m.* pedulum.

pendura, *s.f.* hanging, suspended thing.

pendurar, *v.t.* to hang up, to suspend.

penduricalho, *s.m.* pendant; badge, medal, decoration.

penedia, *s.f.* cliff, cluster of rocks.

penedo, *s.m.* rock, big stone.

peneira, *s.f.* sieve, sifting machine, riddle.

peneiração, *s.f.* sifting, screening, bolting.

peneirada, *s.f.* quantity sifted at a time.

peneirador, *s.m.* sifter.

peneiramento, *s.m.* screening, sifting; selection.

peneirar, *v.t.* to sift, to bolt, to sieve, to screen, to drizzle.

peneireiro, *s.m.* sieve-maker, sieve-seller; kite *(pássaro)*.

peneiro, *s.m.* big sieve.

penejar, *v.t.* to write; to draw.

penela, *s.f.* hillock; little rock.

peneplanície, *s.f.* peneplain.

penetra, *adj.* saucy, insolent.

penetrabilidade, *s.f.* penetrability.

penetração, *s.f.* penetration; acuteness, sagacity, perspicacity, discernment.

penetrador, *adj.* piercing, penetrative.

penetrais, *s.m. (pl.)* penetralia.

penetrante, *adj.* piercing, penetrative, keen, sharp; discerning, sagacious, astute, acute, deep.

penetrantemente, *adv.* penetratively; sharply.

penetrar, *v.t., v.i.* to penetrate, to pierce; to enter, to invade, to go in, to pass; to perforate; to discern, to see into, to understand.

penetrativo, *adj.* ver "penetrante".

penetrável, *adj.* penetrable.

penha, *s.f.* cliff, rock, crag.

penhascal, *s.m.* succession of cliffs.

penhasco, *s.m.* cliff, crag, steep rock.

penhascoso, *adj.* cliffy, rocky, cragged.

penhasqueira, *s.f.* ver "penhascal".

penhor, *s.m.* pawn, pledge, guarantee, bail; warrant; proof. 1) *casa de penhores*, pawnshop. 2) *cautela de penhores*, pawn ticket. 3) *dar em penhor*, to pawn; token.

penhora, *s.f.* seizure, confiscation, restraining, attatchment.

penhorado, *adj.* seized, confiscated; thankful, grateful, obliged.

penhorante, *adj.* obliging, captivating, charming, kind..

penhorar, *v.t.* to seize, to confiscate; to distrain; to give, in pawn, to mortgage; to captivate, to fascinate; to oblige, to engage; *penhorar os bens de*, to seize someone's property.

penhorável, *adj.* seizable, distrainable.

penhorista, *s.* pawnbroker.

penicilina, *s.f.* penicillin.

pénico, *adj.* Punic, Carthagian.

penico, *s.m. (pop)* chamber pot.

penífero, *adj.* penniferous, feathered.

peniforme, *adj.* penniform.

penígero, adj. pennigerous.
peninervado, adj. penninervate, penni-nerved.
peninérveo, adj. penninervate.
península, s.f. peninsula.
peninsular, adj., s. peninsular.
pénis, s.m. penis.
peniscar, v.t., v.i. to ear little bits; to nibble.
penisco, s.m. pine-seed.
penitência, s.f. repentence; penitence, penance; contrition, regret for sin.
penitencial, adj., s.m. penitential.
penitenciar, v.t. to penance; penitenciar-se, to repent, to make penance, to regret.
penitenciária, s.f. penitentiary, prison.
penitenciário, adj., s. penitentiary; prisoner.
penitente, adj., s. penitent; contrite.
penol, s.m. arm of a yard, peak.
penosamente, adv. painfully, arduously.
penoso, adj. painful, difficult, toilsome, hard, arduous.
pensabundo, adj. ver "pensativo".
pensado, adj. deliberate, intentional, purposed, thought of, studied. 1) bem pensado, well thought. 2) de caso pensado, deliberately, on purpose.
pensador, s.m. thinker, philosopher; livre--pensador, freethinker.
pensamento, s.m. thought; meaning; understanding; reflection; cogitation, thinking, idea; view; fancy; opinion, belief; transmissão de pensamento, thought-transference.
pensante, adj. thinking, reflecting.
pensão, s.f. boarding-house; allowance, pension.
pensar, v.t., v.i. to think, to meditate, to cogitate, to consider, to ponder, to imagine, to conceive; to judge; to suppose, to believe; to dress; to groom (cavalos); s.m. "ver pensamento". 1) a pensar morreu um burro, a penny for your thoughts. 2) pensar no futuro, to look ahead. 3) caso para pensar, food for thought. 4) depois de pensar bem, on second thoughts.
pensativamente, adv. pensively, thought-fully; musingly.
pensativo, adj. thoughtful; pensive, sad, meditative; contemplative; melancholic.
pênsil, adj. hanging, suspended, pensile; ponte pênsil, suspension bridge.
pensionar, v.t. to pension, to grant or pay a pension; to impose a burden, to overload with work.

pensionário, s.m., adj. pensionary.
pensionato, s.m. boarding-school; orpha-nage.
pensionista, s. pensionary; pensioner, border in a boarding.house or school.
penso, s.m. ration, food ration; dressing.
pentacarpo, adj. pentacarpellary.
pentacórdio, s.m. pentachord.
pentadáctilo, adj. pentadactyl.
pentadecágono, s.m. pentadecagon.
pentaedro, s.m. pentahedron.
pentagonal, adj. pentagonal.
pentágono, s.m. pentagon.
pentagrama, s.m. pentagram, pentacle.
pentâmetro, s.m. pentameter.
pentassílabo, adj. pentasyllabic.
Pentateuco, s.m. Pentateuch.
pentatlo, s.m. pentathlon.
pentavalente, adj. pentavalent.
pente, s.m. comb; car; reed; clip.
penteação, s.f. combing.
penteadela, s.f. combing, careless hasty combination.
penteado, s.m. hairdressing.
penteador, s.m. dressing-gown.
penteadura, s.f. combing, hairdressing.
pentear, v.t. to comb, to dress the hair.
pentearia, s.f. comb-works, comb shop.
Pentecostes, s.m. Pentecost, Whitsunday.
penteeiro, s.m. comb-maker or seller.
penudo, adj. feathered.
penugem, s.f. down.
penugento, adj. downy.
penujoso, adj. downy.
penúltimo, adj. penultimate, the last but one.
penumbra, s.f. penumbra, half-light; partial shadow, shade.
penumbroso, adj. dimly lit, penumbral; penumbrous; shadowy.
penúria, s.f. penury, scarcity, want, misery, indigence, need, poverty.
penurioso, adj. penurious, stingy; indigent, very poor.
peonagem, s.f. infantry, peonage, foot soldiers.
peónia, s.f. peony.
pepinal, s.m. plantation of cucumbers.
pepineira, s.f. field of cucumbers; rotten show (pop); hopeless muddle.
pepineiro, s.m. cucumber-plant.
pepino, s.m. cucumber.
pepita, s.f. nugget, lump.
pepónio, s.m. (bot) pepo (fruto).
pepsina, s.f. pespsin.

péptico, *adj.* peptic, digestive.
peptona, *s.f.* peptone.
pequena, *s.f.* girl, young woman; sweetheart.
pequenada, *s.f.* children.
pequenez, pequeneza, *s.f.* smallness; lowness; childhood.
pequenino, *adj.* very little; very small; *s.m.* little one.
pequenitates, *s.* small person.
pequenito, *adj.* ver "pequenino".
pequeno, *adj.* small, little; short; *s.m.* child, boy.
pequenote, *adj.* smallish; *s.m.* boy, lad, youngster.
pequerrucho, *s.m.* baby.
pequice, *s.f.* nonsense, stupidity.
pêra, *s.f.* pear *(fruto);* beard.
perada, *s.f.* pear-jam, stewed pears; wine pear.
peral, *s.m.* pear orchard; *adj.* pearlike, pear-shaped.
peralta, *s.* dandy, coxcomb, fop, beau.
peraltear, *v.i.* to play the swell.
peraltice, *s.f.* dandyism, foppishness.
peraltismo, *s.m.* ver peraltice.
peralvilhada, peralvilhice, *s.f.* ver peraltice.
peralvilho, *s.m.* fop, coxcomb, spark.
perambulação, *s.f.* perambulation.
perambular, *v.i.* to perambulate; to roam, to wander.
perambulatório, *adj.* perambulatory.
perante, *prep.* in the presence of, before, in front of.
perborato, *s.m.* perborate.
perca, *s.f.* loss, damage, waste; perch *(peixe).*
percal, *s.m.* percale *(algodão).*
percalço, *s.m.* mishap; annoyance, profit, gain.
percalina, *s.f.* percaline.
perceba, percebe, *s.f., s.m.* goosebarnacle.
perceber, *v.t.* to understand; to perceive; to think; to discern; to conceive, to apprehend, to grasp; to notice; to hear, to listen; to receive *(salário).*
percebimento, *s.m.* perceiving; perception.
percebível, *adj.* perceptible.
percentagem, *s.f.* percentage, rate, interest.
percepção, *s.f.* perception, insight; discernment, comprehension, understanding, feeling.
perceptibilidade, *s.f.* perceptibility.
perceptível, *adj.* perceptible, visible.

perceptivo, *adj.* perceptive.
perceve, *s.m.* ver "perceba".
percevejo, *s.m.* bedbug; drawing-pin.
percha, *s.f.* perch; pole; bar.
percluso, *adj.* crippled, maimed, lamed.
percorrer, *v.t.* to go through; to traverse; to travel over, to cover a distance; to look over *(com os olhos);* to examine; to investigate.
percuciente, *adj.* percussive, percutient, striking.
percurso, *s.m.* course, route, distance; journey.
percussão, *s.f.* percussion, shock, collision.
percussor, *s.m.* firing-pin; hammer, percussor; *adj.* percussibe, striking.
percutidor, *s.m., adj.* ver percussor.
percutir, *v.t.* to percuss, to strike.
percutor, *s.m.* ver percussor.
perda, *s.f.* loss; failure; waste, damage; detriment; ruin; destruction, calamity; disappearance; casuality *(na guerra).*
perdão, *s.m.* pardon, forgiveness, mercy, grace; indult.
perder, *v.t.* to lose; to waste; to miss; to ruin; to fail to gain. 1) *perder-se,* to lose oneself; to lose one's way; to become confused; to lose; to disappear; to bring misfortune upon; to lose meritor value. 2) *perder a cabeça (as estribeiras),* to lose one's head (temper). 3) *perder a oportunidade,* to miss the opportunity. 4) *perder de vista,* to lose sight of. 5) *perder terreno,* to fall behind. 6) *deitar a perder,* to ruin, to corrupt. 7) *perder o comboio,* to miss the train. 8) *fazer perder a cabeça,* to drive one mad.
perdição, *s.f.* perdition; ruin, destruction; calamity; disgrace; damnation.
perdida, *s.f.* lost woman, prostitute.
perdidamente, *adv.* fondly, madly.
perdidiço, *adj.* easily lost.
perdidinho, *adj.* madly in love with.
perdido, *adj.* lost; ruined; depraved; undone; disappeared, gone; immoral; perplexed.
perdigão, *s.m.* male partridge.
perdigoto, *s.m.* young partridge; droplet of saliva, sputter.
perdigueiro, *adj.* that hunts partridges, setter-dog. pointer, setter.
perdimento, *s.m.* ver perdição.
perdível, *adj.* losable.
perdiz, *s.f.* partridge.
perdoador, *s.m.* pardoner, forgiver.
perdoar, *v.t.* to forgive, to pardon, to excuse; to absolve, to overlook; to spare.

perdoável, *adj.* pardonable, forgivable, excusable.

perdulário, *adj.* prodigal, lavish, wasteful, large-handed; *s.m.* prodigal, lavisher, spendthrift.

perdurabilidade, *s.f.* perdurability.

perduração, *s.f.* perdurability, duration, length.

perdurar, *v.i.* to last long; to persist, to endure; to remain.

perdurável, *adj.* everlasting, perdurable, durable, lasting.

perduravelmente, *adv.* perdurably, eternally.

perecedoiro, perecedouro, *adj.* perishable, mortal.

perecer, *v.i.* to die, to perish; to end, to finish.

perecimento, *s.m.* perishing, decay; extinction.

perecível, *adj.* perishable, mortal, ephemeral.

peregrinação, *s.f.* pilgrimage; peregrination.

peregrinador, *s.m.,* *adj.* pilgrim, traveller; wandering, peregrinating.

peregrinante, *adj.* peregrinating.

peregrinar, *v.i.* to pilgrim; to wander; to go on a pilgrimage, to travel.

peregrinismo, *s.m.* barbarism, foreign word or expression.

peregrino, *s.m.* pilgrim, traveller, wonderer; *adj.* foreign; excellent, rare; pilgrim, peregrine.

pereira, *s.f.* pear-tree.

pereiral, *s.m.* orchard of pear-trees.

perempção, *s.f.* prescription.

perempto, *adj.* prescribe, extinct, null.

peremptoriamente, *adv.* peremptorily, formally.

peremptório, *adj.* peremptory, absolute, decisive, imperious, categorical, final.

perenal, *adj. ver "perene".*

perene, *adj.* perennial, unceasing, lasting, enduring, continual, permanent, perpetual, undying.

perenemente, *adv.* perennially, eternity, perpetually.

perenidade, *s.f.* perenniality, eternity, perpetuity.

perfazer, *v.t.* to finish, to complete, to perfect, to conclude; to amount to.

perfazimento, *s.m.* completion, finishing, perfecting.

perfectibilidade, *s.f.* perfectibility.

perfectível, *adj.* perfectible.

perfectivo, *adj.* perfective.

perfeição, perfection, excellence; handsomeness, beauty, faultlessness; purity, refinement, mastery.

perfeitamente, *adv.* perfectly, completely, accuratly; fine.

perfeito, *adj.* perfect; finished; faultless; spotless; fine, excellent; correct; beautiful.

perficiente, *adj. ver "perfeito".*

perfidamente, *adv.* perfidiously, treacherelously.

perfídia, *s.f.* perfidy, treachery, guile; faithlessness; falseness, disloyalty.

pérfido, *adj.* perfidious, treachereous, faithless, unfaithful, false, disloyal.

perfil, *s.m.* profile; outline, contour; sideface; aspect, appearance.

perfilar, *v.t.* to profile; to straighten; to draw the profile of; to outline; to draw up in a line *(soldados).*

perfilhação, *s.f.* adoption, affiliation.

perfilhador, *s.m.* adopter; *adj.* adpting.

perfilhamento, *s.m. ver "perfilhação".*

perfilhar, *v.t.* to adopt, to affiliate; to espouse *(uma cause),* to defend.

perfloração, *s.f.* florescence.

perfolhado, *adj.* perfoliate.

perfoliação, *s.f.* perfoliation.

perfulgência, *s.f.* prefulkgence, splendour.

perfulgente, *adj.* fulgent, brilliant, shining, splendant, radiant.

perfumado, *adj.* perfumed, fragant, scented, odorous, sweet-smelling.

perfumador, *adj.* perfuming; *s.m.* perfuming-pan.

perfumadura, *s.f.* perfuming.

perfumante, *adj.* perfuming.

perfumar, *v.t.* to perfum, to scent, to impregnate, to embalm.

perfumaria, *s.f.* perfumery; perfumer's *(loja);* perfumes in general.

perfume, *s.m.* perfume, odour, aroma, scent, fragrance.

perfumista, *s.* perfumer *(o que faz ou o que vende).*

perfumoso, *adj.* perfumed, aromatic, odoriferous.

perfunctoriamente, *adv.* perfunctorily.

perfunctório, *adj.* perfunctory, negligent, careless, superficial, mechanical.

perfuração, *s.f.* perforation; boring, hole.

perfurador, *adj.* perforating, piercing; *s.m.* perforator; drill, boring machine.

perfurante, *adj.* perforating, piercing, penetrant.

perfurar, *v.t.* to perforate, to pierce; to drill, to bore; to penetrate into; to make holes in.

perfurativo, *adj.* perforative.

perfusão, *s.f.* perfusion.

pergamináceo, *adj.* pergameneous.

pergaminharia, *s.f.* parchment-making.

pergaminheiro, *s.f.* parchment-maker; parchment-seller.

pergaminho, *s.m.* parchment; *(pl.)* honours, titles.

pérgula, *s.f.* pergola.

pergunta, *s.f.* question, interrogation, inquiry, demand *(informações).* 1) *pergunta de algibeira,* tricky question. 2) *fazer uma pergunta,* to ask (or put) a question.

perguntador, *adj., s.m.* questioning, inquiring; curious, inquisitive; questioner, inquirer.

perguntante, *adj., s.* questioning, inquiring; curious, inquisitive; questioner, inquirer.

perguntar, *v.t.* to ask; to question; to query; to inquire, to demand.

perianto, *s.m.* perianth, floral envelopes.

pericárdio, pericardino, *adj.* pericardial.

pericárdio, *s.m.* pericardium.

pericardite, *s.f.* pericarditis.

pericárpio, pericarpo, *s.m.* pericarp, seed-vessel.

perícia, *s.f.* expertness, skill, ability, dexterity, mastery, mastership, art.

pericial, *adj.* skilful, cleverly.

periciclo, *s.m.* pericycle.

periclitante, *adj.* hesitating, wavering; risky, in danger.

periclitar, *v.i.* to be in danger; to stagger, to waver.

pericrânio, *s.m.* pericranium.

perídio, *s.m.* peridium.

periecos, *s.m. (pl.)* perioeci.

periélio, *s.m.* perihelion.

periferia, *s.f.* periphery, circumference; surrounding region, country or area; suburb.

periférico, *adj.* peripheral, peripherical.

periforme, *adj.* pear-shaped.

perífrase, *s.f.* periphrasis; circumlocution.

perifrasear, *v.i.* to periphrase.

perifrasticamente, *adv.* periphrastically.

perifrástico, *adj.* periphrastic.

perigar, *v.i.* to run a risk, to be in danger.

perigeu, *s.m.* perigee.

perigínico, *adj.* perigynous.

perigo, *s.m.* danger, risk, hazard, peril.

perigosamente, *adv.* dangerously, perilously.

perigoso, *adj.* dangerous, perilous, hazardous.

perilha, *s.f.* ornament in form of a perimeter.

perimetria, *s.f.* measuring of a perimeter.

perimétrico, *adj.* perimetrical.

perímetro, *s.m.* perimeter.

perimir, *v.t.* to put an end; to cancel, to annul.

perimísio, *s.m.* perimysium.

perineal, *adj.* perineal.

períneo, *s.m.* perineum.

periodicamente, *adv.* periodically.

periodicidade, *s.f.* periodicity.

periodista, *s.* periodicalist.

periódico, *adj.* periodic, periodical, regular, cyclic; *s.m.* periodical, magazine, paper.

periodismo, *s.m.* journalism.

periodista, *s.* journalist.

periodização, *s.f.* division into periods.

periodizar, *v.t.* to divide into periods; to set forth in periods.

período, *s.m.* period; age, era; sentence; length of time, epoch, cycle; term *(escola).*

periósteo, *s.m.* periosteum.

periostite, *s.f.* periostitis.

peripatético, *adj., s.m.* peripatetic.

peripatetismo, *s.m.* peripateticism.

peripécia, *s.f.* peripetia, incident; vicissitude.

périplo, *s.m.* periplus, circumnavigation.

periquito, *s.m.* parakeet.

periscópico, *adj.* periscopic.

periscópio, *s.m.* periscope.

perissodáctilo, *s.m. (zool.)* perissodactyl.

perissologia, *s.f.* roundabout sentence; pelonasm.

peristáltico, *adj.* peristaltic.

peristaltismo, *s.m.* peristalsis.

peristilo, *s.m.* peristyle.

perístole, *s.f.* peristole.

perístomo, *s.m.* peristome.

peritagem, *s.f.* examination made by experts.

perito, *adj.* skilful, expert; clever; proficient; dexterous; specialist, apt; *s.m.* expert.

peritoneal, *adj.* peritoneal.

peritoneu, peritónio, *s.m.* peritoneum.

peritonite, *s.f.* peritonitis.

perjurar, *v.t.* to perjure, to forswear; to swear falsely.

perjúrio, *s.m.* perjury, false oath; oath-breaking, breach of oath.

perjuro, *s.m.* perjurer, forswearer, oath-breaker.

perlar, *v.t.* to pearl, to form peals like drops.
perlenda, perlanga, *s.f.* idle talk.
perlífero, *adj.* pearl-bearing.
perliquitetes, *adj.* assuming, conceited, pretentious, vain.
perlonga, *s.f.* delay, postponement, putting off.
perlongar, *v.t.* to lengthen, to elongate; to retard, to prolong.
perlustrador, *adj., s.m.* observing, examining; observer, examiner.
perlustrar, *v.t.* to look over; to inspect, to search, to scrutinize; to look at, to look into, to examine thoroughly, to survey.
perluxo, *adj.* prolix, diffuse, verbose, tedious; conseited, presumptuous.
permanecente, *adj.* lasting; remaining; permanent; fixed, stable, unchangeable.
permanecer, *v.i.* to remain, to stay; to persist; to insist; to preserve; to amint; to delay, to retard; to stand.
permanência, *s.f.* permanency; perseverance, persistent; durability; stability; constancy.
permanente, *adj.* permanent; lasting, continuous, durable; constant; continuous, unchangeable; *s.f.* perm, permanent wave *(cabelo).*
permanentemente, *adv.* permanently.
permanganato, *s.m.* permanganate.
permeabilidade, *s.f.* permeability.
permeabilização, *s.f.* permeabilization.
permeabilizar, *v.t.* to render impermeable.
permeação, *s.f.* permeation.
permear, *v.t.* to permeate, to pass through, to pervade, to penetrate, to pierce; to place between.
permeável, *adj.* permeable, penetrable, pervious.
permeio, *adv.* in the middle. 1) *de permeio,* between, among. 2) *meter-se de permeio,* to come between.
permissão, *s.f.* permission, leave, consent, licence, allowance.
permissível, *adj.* permissible, admissible, allowable.
permissivo, *adj.* permissive, permiting.
permissório, *adj.* ver *"permissivo".*
permisto, *adj.* mixed, blended.
permitir, *v.t.* to permit, to allow, to consent; to make possible; to authorize, to give permission; to admit, to concede; to suffer, to tolerate, to indulge; *se o tempo o permitir,* weather permitting.

permuta, *s.f.* exchange, permutation, barter, truck, interchange.
permutabilidade, *s.f.* permutability.
permutação, *s.f.* ver *"permuta".*
permutador, *adj.* permuting; *s.m.* exchanger.
permutar, *v.t.* to permute, to exchange, to barter, to truck, to interchange; to substitute.
permutável, *adj.* permutable, exchangeable.
perna, *s.f.* leg. 1) *perna-de-pau,* woodenleg. 2) *perna torta,* bowleg. 3) *barriga da perna,* calf of the leg. 4) *com uma perna às costas,* easily. 5) *dar à perna,* to walk fast, to dance. 6) *de perna cruzada,* cross-legged. 7) *de pernas para o ar,* topsyturvy, upside down. 8) *ter alguém à perna,* to be harassed by someone. 9) *passar a perna a,* to get ahead of, to trick someone.
pernaça, *s.f.* thick leg.
pernada, *s.f.* stride, long step; bough *(de uma árvore).*
pernaltas, *s.f. (pl.)* waddingbirds.
pernalto, *adj.* long-legged.
pernambucano, *s.m., adj.* of the Pernambuco, in Brazil.
pernão, *adj.* ver *"parnão".*
pernear, *v.i.* to gambol; to frisk; to kick the legs.
pernegudo, *adj.* big-legged.
perneira, *s.f.* disease.
perneta, *s.f.* little leg; obstinacy, stubbornness.
pernície, *s.f.* destruction, damage, ruin.
perniciosamente, *adv.* perniciously, dangerously.
perniciosidade, *s.f.* pernisiousness.
pernicioso, *adj.* pernicious, noxious; dangerous; bad, ruinous, malign; destructive.
pernicurto, *adj.* short-legged.
pernil, *s.m.* slender leg; thghbone of a quadruped; *esticar o pernil, (pop)* to kick the bucket, to die.
pernilongo, *adj.* long-legged.
perno, *s.m.* bolt, pin, stud, dogstay.
pernoita, pernoitamento, *s.f., s.m.* an overnight stay.
pernoitar, pernoutar, *v.i.* to stay overnight, to pass the night anywhere.
pernosticismo, *s.m.* insolence; presumptuousness.
pernóstico, *adj.* pedantic, assuming, pretentious, affected.
pernudo, *adj.* thick-legged, long-legged.

pêro, *s.m.* pearmain, sort of apple.

pérola, *s.f.* pearl, dewdrop, bead; a kind person. 1) *pérolas a porcos,* pearls before swine. 2) *pescador de pérolas,* pearl-fisher.

peroleira, *s.f.* pearl-oyster; olive-pot.

perolífero, *adj.* pearl-bearing.

perolino, *adj.* pearly, pearled.

perolizar, *v.t.* pearl, to cause to resemble pearls.

peronial, *adj.* peroneal, fibular.

perónio, *s.m.* perone, fibula.

peroração, *s.f.* peroration; epilogue; the conclusion of *(discurso, poema, sinfonia).*

perorador, *s.m.* orator, haranguer.

perorar, *v.i.* to perorate.

peroxidar, *v.t.* to peroxidize, to oxidize.

peróxido, *s.m.* peroxide.

perpassar, *v.i.* to pass by, to gilde over, to pass over.

perpassável, *adj.* passable, tolerable.

perpendicular, *adj.* perpendicular; upright; vertical.

perpendicularidade, *s.f.* perpendicularity.

perpendicularmente, perpendicularly.

perpendículo, *s.m.* plumb-line.

perpetração, *s.f.* perpetration; act of committing an evil action.

perpetrador, *adj.* perpetrating; *s.m.* perpetrator.

perpetrar, *v.t.* to perpetrate; to perform; to commit, to execute.

perpétua, *s.f.* immortelle, everlasting *(planta ou flor).*

perpetuação, *s.f.* perpetuation.

perpetuador, *adj.* perpetuating; s.m. perpetuator.

perpetuamente, *adv.* perpetually, for ever, eternally.

perpetuar, *v.t.* to perpetuate, to make perpetual; to immortalize, to gain immortal fame.

perpetuidade, *s.f.* perpetuity, endless duration.

perpétuo, *adj.* perpetual, everlasting, unending; perennial; constant, continual, endless; eternal, immortal, lifelong.

perpianho, *s.m.* bon-stone, perpendstone.

perplexão, *s.f.* ver perplexidade.

perplexidade, *s.f.* perplexity; hesitation, indecison; amazement, astonishment, bewilderment, embarrassment.

perplexo, *adj.* perplexed; hesitating, irresolute, uncertain; confused, embarrassed.

perquirição, *s.f.* search, inquiry, minute investigation, quest, scrutiny.

perquirir, *v.t.* to investigate, to inquire into, to examine minutely.

perquisição, *s.f.* ver perquirição.

perquisitivo, *adj.* inquisitive, sifting.

perraria, *s.f.* spite, teasing; trick; affront, insult.

perreiro, *s.m.* dog-keeper.

perrexil, *s.m.* samphire.

perrice, *s.f.* obstinacy, teasing, stubbonness.

perro, *s.m.* dog; knave; adj. stubborn; stiff.

persa, *adj., s.* Persian *(a língua dos nativos).*

perscrutação, *s.f.* scrutiny, investigation, minute inquiry.

perscrutador, *adj.* scrutinizing; *s.m.* investigator.

perscrutar, *v.t.* to scrutinize; to examine, to search, to probe, to sound out; to inquire into; to peer into the future; to analize, to study.

perscrutável, *adj.* that can be investigated or looked into.

persecução, *s.f.* ver perseguição.

persecutório, *adj.* persecutory, demandable, demandative.

perseguição, *s.f.* persecution, importuning, harassing; oppression; pursuit, chase.

perseguidor, *adj.* persecuting; *s.m.* persecutor.

perseguimento, *s.m.* ver *"perseguição".*

perseguir, *v.t.* to persecute, to pursue; to annoy; to harass, to oppress, to worry; to run after; to follow closely.

perseverança, *s.f.* perseverance, persistence, constancy, steadiness, tenacity, determination.

perseverante, *adj.* persevering, constant, steady, firm, tenacious, persistent.

perseverar, *v.i.* to persevere, to persist in, to go on; to last; to be persistent.

persiana, persienne, Persian blind, Venetian blind.

pérsico, *adj.* Persian.

persigal, *s.m.* hog cote, hogsty, pigsty.

persignação, *s.f.* act of crossing oneself.

persignar-se, *v. refl.* to cross oneself.

persistência, *s.f.* persistence, persistency, perseverance, constancy, tenacity, obstinacy.

persistente, *adj.* persistent, persisting, persevering, constant, firm, steady, obstinate.

persistentemente, *adv.* persistently, persevereringly, insistently.

persistir, *v.i.* to persist, to remain; to perse-vere, to insist; to last, to endure to survive.

persolver, *v.t.* to pay off.

personado, *adj.* personate, masklike.

personagem, *s.f.* personage; character *(numa novela, peça, etc.);* person of importance.

personalidade, *s.f.* personality; individuality; personage; character.

personalismo, *s.m.* personalism.

personalização, *s.f.* personalization.

personalizar, *v.t.* to personalize.

personificação, *s.f.* personification, impersonation, embodiment.

personificar, *v.t.* to personify, to perso-nalize; to symbolize; to exemplify.

perspectiva, *s.f.* perspective, view, prospect; sight, vista, panorama. 1) *ter algo em perspectiva,* to have something in prospect. 2) *desenho de perspectiva,* perspective drawing.

perspectivação, *s.f.* act of putting in perspective.

perspectivar, *v.t.* to put in perspective.

perspectivo, *adj.* perspective.

perspectógrafo, *s.m.* perspectograph.

perspicácia, *s.f.* perspicacity; acumen; insight, discernmet; sagacity, acutness.

perspicaz, *adj.* perspicacious, discerning, penetrating, sagacious, keen, astute, quick-eyed, sharp-witted.

perspicazmente, *adv.* perspicaciously, quick-sightedly.

perspicuidade, *s.f.* perspicuity, clearness, lucidity, distinctness.

perspícuo, *adj.* perspicuous, clear, lucid, transparent, distinct, manifest, obvious.

perspiração, *s.f.* perspiration, sweating.

perspirar, *v.i.* to perspire, to sweat.

perspiratório, *adj.* perspiratory.

persuadir, *v.t.* to persuade, to induce; to advise; to influence, to convince, to move; to counsel; *persuadir-se,* to persuade oneself; to be convinced.

persuadível, *adj.* persuadable, persuadible.

persuasão, *s.f.* persuasion, conviction, opinion.

persuasiva, *s.f.* persuasiveness, induce-ment.

persuasivamente, *adv.* persuasively.

persuasivo, *adj.* persuasive, persuading, convincing, enticing.

persuasor, *adj.* persuading; *s.m.* persuader.

persuasória, *s.f.* persuasive motive, inducement.

persuasório, *adj.* persuasive.

pertença, *s.f.* property; belongings, estate.

pertence, *s.m.* accessory.

pertencente, *adj.* belonging, pertaining; proper, relating to, concerning.

pertencer, *v.i.* to belong, to appertain; to relate to, to concern, to be due to; to be fitting to; to be one's duty.

pértiga, *s.f.* pole, long stick.

pertinácia, *s.f.* pertinacity, obstinacy, stubbornness.

pertinaz, *adj.* pertinacious, tenacious, persistent, persevering, obstinate, stubbor.

pertinazmente, *adv.* pertinaciously.

pertinência, *s.f.* pertinence, relevancy.

pertinente, *adj.* pertinenet, relevant.

pertinho, *adv.* quite near, at hand.

pertíssimo, *adv.* very near hard by.

perto, *adv.* near, close, at a short distance. 1) *perto de cem,* about a hundred. 2) *conhecer de perto,* to know intimately. 3) *perto das 5 horas,* about five o'clock. 4) *muito perto,* next, close by.

pertransir, *v.t.* to pierce through.

perturbabilidade, *s.f.* perturbability.

perturbação, *s.f.* perturbation, disturbance, agitation of mind; disorder, confusion.

perturbado, *adj.* perturbed, confused, upset, worried, excited, troubled.

perturbador, *adj.* perturbatibve, disturbing, turbulent, troublesome; *s.m.* perturber, disturber; troubler, rioter, disquieter.

perturbante, *adj.* ver "perturbador".

perturbar, *v.t.* to perturb, to disturb, to disquiet, to trouble, to molest; to confuse, to perplex, to upset to disorder, to disarrange; to worry, to vex.

perturbativo, peturbatório, *adj.* pertur-bative.

perturbável, *adj.* perturbable.

peru, *s.m.* turkey, turkey-cock.

perua, *s.f.* turkey-hen.

peruano, *adj., s.m.* Peruvian.

peruca, *s.f.* wig, peruke, perwig.

peruviano, *adj., s.m.* ver "peruano".

perversão, *s.f.* perversion, corruption, depravation.

perversidade, *s.f.* perversity, wickedness, perverseness.

perverso, *adj.* perverse, vicious, wicked, bad, devilish; corrupted.

perversor, *adj.* perverting; *s.m.* perverter, corrupter.

pervertedor, *s.m.* ver perversor.

perverter, *v.t.* to pervert, to corrupt, to deprave; to mislead, to lead astray; to distort, to misrepresent; to adulterate.

pervicácia, *s.f.* pertinacity, obstinacity.

pervicaz, *adj.* pertinacious, persistent, obstinate.

pervinca, *s.f.* periwinkle.

pérvio, *adj.* pervious, accessible, permeable, open; frank, sincere.

pesa-cartas, *s.m.* letter-balance.

pesadamente, *adv.* heavily; slowly; soundly.

pesadão, *adj.* very heavy; slow-moving.

pesadelo, *s.m.* nightmare.

pesado, *adj.* heavy, ponderous, weighty; hard; fastidious; dull, difficult, laborious; boresome, tedious, slow, slow-machine; costly, expensive; fat, corpulent.

pesador, *s.m.* weigher.

pesadora, *s.f.* weighing-machine.

pesadume, *s.m.* burden; grief.

pesa-espíritos, *s.m.* alcoholometer.

pesagem, *s.f.* weighing.

pesa-leite, *s.m.* lactometer, milk-gauge.

pêsames, *s.m. (pl.)* condolences; *dar os pêsames a,* to condole with.

pesa-mosto, *s.m.* hydrometer.

pesa-papéis, *s.m.* paper-weight.

pesar, *v.t.* to weigh, to ponder; to estimate, to poise, to balance; to consider, to examine; to influence; to oppress; to be sorry; *s.m.* sorrow, grief, regret; sadness.

pesarosamente, *adv.* sorrowfully.

pesaroso, *adj.* sorrowful, sorry, grievous; sad, distressed.

pesca, *s.f.* fishing, fishery, angling; search, investigation.

pescada, *s.f.* whiting.

pescadinha, *s.f.* whiting *(pequena).*

pescado, *s.m.* fish, caught, fishery.

pescador, *s.m.* fisherman, angler.

pescar, *v.t.* to fish; to catch fish; to have some knowledge of, to perceive, to understand.

pescaria, *s.f.* fishing, fishery; fishing trade or industry; great quantity of fish.

pescoçada, *s.f.* blow on the neck.

pescoceira, *s.f.* nape, large neck.

pescoço, *s.m.* neck.

percoçudo, *adj.* thick-necked, long-necked, bull-necked.

pesebre, *s.m.* crib, manger.

peseta, *s.f.* peseta.

peso, *s.m.* weight; burden, load; pressure; importance, influence, power; peso *(moeda).* 1) *peso atómico,* atomic weight. 2) *peso bruto,* gross weight. 3) *peso líquido,* weight. 4) *em peso,* entire, whole, in full.

pespegar, *v.t.* to apply; to strike, to hit; *pespegar-se,* to fix, to settle.

pespego, *s.m.* tiresome person; impediment, obstacle, difficulty.

pespita, *s.f.* wagtail.

pespontar, *v.t.* to quilt, to nackstitch.

pespontear, *v.t.* ver pespontar.

pesponto, *s.m.* quilting-stitch, back-stitch.

pesqueira, *s.f.* fishing net; ground for fishery-stakes.

pesqueiro, *s.f.* fishing ground; fish hatchery.

pesquisa, *s.f.* search, inquiry, examination, investigation; prospecting.

pesquisador, *s.m.* searcher, examiner, investigator, researcher; *adj.* searching, examining, investigating.

pesquisar, *v.t.* to search, to inquire, to examine, to seek after, to investigate, to inquire about; to explore, to prospect.

pessegada, *s.f.* peach-jam; muddle, mess, confusion.

pessegal, *s.m.* peach orchard, peachgrove.

pêssego, *s.m.* peach.

pessegueiro, *s.m.* peach-tree.

pessimamente, *adv.* very badly, detestably.

pessimismo, *s.m.* pessimism.

pessimista, *s., adj.* pessimist.

péssimo, *adj.* very bad.

pessoa, *s.f.* person, individual, personage; individuality, someone, one, fellow; *(pl.)* people.

pessoal, *adj.* personal, individual, private; *s.m.* personnel, staff, workers, employees, officials.

pessoalidade, *s.f.* personality, individuality.

pessoalismo, *s.m.* personalism.

pessoalmente, *adv.* personally, in person.

pestana, *s.f.* eye-lash; flap *(de um bolso); queimar as pestanas,* to burn the midnight oil.

pestanejante, *adj.* blinking, twinkling, winkling.

pestanejar, *v.i.* to blink, to wink, to twinkle.

pestanejo, *s.m.* blinking, winking, twinkling.

pestanudo, *adj.* that has long eye-lashes.

peste, *s.f.* plague, pestilence, pest; trouble, vexatious person; calamity, epidemic disease.

pestífero, *adj.* pestiferous, malign; dangerous.

pestilência, *s.f.* pestilence, plague, pest.

pestilencial, pestilencioso, *adj.* pestilential, pernicious, baleful, pestiferous, infectious.

pestilento, *adj.* pestilent, noxious.

pestoso, *adj.* ver pestífero.

peta, *s.f.* fib, lie, story.

pétala, *s.f.* petal.

petalado, *adj.* petalled, petalous.

petaliforme, *adj.* petaliform, petaline, petal-shaped.

petalino, *adj.* petaline, petaliform.

petalóide, *adj.* petaloid.

petar, *v.i.* to fib, to lie.

petardar, petardear, *v.t.* to blow up *(com um petardo).*

petardo, *s.m.* petard, bomb.

petear, *v.i.* to lie, to tell fibs.

peteiro, *s.m.* liar, fibber.

petéquia, *s.f.* blood spot.

petição, *s.f.* petition, request; prayer, supplication; suit, appeal; entreaty, application.

peticego, *s.m.* very short-sighted person; *adj.* near-sighted.

peticionar, *v.t.* to petition to address a petition to, to entreat.

peticionário, *s.m.* petitioner, applicant.

petimetre, *adj., s.m.* dandy, beau, fop.

petinga, *s.f.* small sardine; bait.

petipé, *s.m.* measuring-scale, scale, map-scale.

petisca, *s.f.* game *(para rapazes).*

petiscador, *s.m.* nibbler.

petiscar, *v.t.* to eat; to taste; to eat dainties; to strike fire.

petisco, *s.m.* dainty, tidbit, morsel; very good food; steel.

petisqueira, *s.f.* dainty dish.

petitório, *adj.* petitory, petitionary; *s.m.* petition, rqeust.

petiz, *s.m.* boy, child, little one.

petizada, *s.f.* little children, the little ones, boys, kids.

peto, *s.m. (zool.)* woodpecker.

petrechar, *v.t.* to supply with, to furnish, to equip, to provide.

petrechos, *s.m. (pl.)* ammunition; tools; supplies, implements; equipment.

pétro, *adj.* stony, rocky, petrous; insensible, pitiless, hard-hearted.

petrificação, *s.f.* petrification.

petrificador, petrificante, *adj.* petrifying.

petrificar, *v.t.* to petrify, to turn into a stone; to stupefy, to stun, to paralyse.

petrificável, *adj.* petrifyable.

petrífico, *adj.* petrifying, petrific.

petrografia, *s.f.* petrography.

petrográfico, *adj.* petrographic(al).

petrolaria, *s.f.* oil refinery, petroleum works.

petroleiro, *s.m.* oil tanker, petroler.

petróleo, *s.m.* petroleum; oil.

petrolífero, *adj.* petrolife; *s.f.* petrology; *campo petrolífero,* oil-field.

petrolina, *s.f.* petrolin.

petrologia, *adj.* petrology.

petrológico, *adj.* petrologic(al).

petrologista, *s.* petrologist.

petroso, *adj.* stony.

petulância, *s.f.* petulance, insolence, sauciness, peevishness.

petulante, *adj.* petulant, insolent, peevish, saucy.

petulantemente, *adv.* petulantly.

petúnia, *s.f.* petunia *(flor).*

peúga, *s.f.* sock.

peugada, *s.f.* track, footprint; vestige, sign, trace, trail.

pevide, *s.f.* pip, seed *(laranja, maçã, pêra).*

pevidoso, *adj.* pippy.

pexotada, *s.f.* bad playing, bungle, clumsy performance.

pexote, *s.m.* novice; bungler; beginner, bad player.

pexotice, *s.f.* ver "pexotada".

pez, *s.m.* pitch, tar, bitumen, asphalt.

pezudo, *adj.* big-footed.

pezunho, *s.m.* pig's foot, large foot.

pia, *s.f.* stone-cistern; sink; wash basin; *pia baptismal,* font.

piaçá, piaçaba, *s.m.* piassava, brush made with piassava fibers.

piada, *s.f.* joke, witticism, anecdote, quio, gag, biting jest; peep, chirp *(pássaros).*

piadeira, *s.f.* ver "pieira".

piadético, *adj.* funny.

piadinha, *s.f.* little joke.

piadista, *s.* wisecracker, jester, scoffer.

piadoiro, *s.m.* ver "piadouro".

piador, *adj.* chirping.

piadouro, *s.m.* frequent chirping.

pia-máter, *s.f.* pia mater.

pianinho, *adj.* soft.

pianíssimo, *adj.* very soft.

pianista, *s.* pianist.

piano, *s.m.* piano, pianoforte; *adv.* softly. 1)

piano de cauda, grand piano. 2) piano vertical, upright piano.

pianola, *s.f.* pianola.

pião, *s.m.* top.

piar, *v.i.* to peep, to chirp.

piara, *s.f.* multitude of people; band, gang; herd; drove.

piasca, *s.m.* little top.

piastra, *s.f.* piastre, plaster.

pica, *s.f.* pricking.

picada, *s.f.* prick *(de um espinho)*, sting *(de uma abelha)*, bite *(de um insecto)*, peck *(com um bico)*; puncture *(com uma agulha epidérmica)*; narrow trail in a forrest; peak, summit, dive.

picadeira, *s.f.* pickaxe; scaling hammer; fire-picker.

picadeiro, *s.m.* riding-school.

picadela, *s.f.* ver *"picada"*.

picado, *adj.* pricked, punctured; provoked; irritated; pinked; choppy; sourish *(comida)*; minced meat; *s.m.* hash.

picador, *s.m.* riding-master, horse-master; *(touro)* picador.

picadura, *s.f.* ver *"picada"*.

pica-flor, *a.m.* humming-bird; colibri.

picanço, *s.m.* woodpecker.

picante, *adj.* pricking; piquant; pungent; spicy; biting, caustic, sharp; stimulating; malicious.

picão, *s.m.* pickaxe.

pica-pau, *s.m.* woodpecker.

pica-peixe, *s.m.* kingfisher.

picar, *v.t.* to prick; to stab; to sting (abelha) to pierce; to mince, to hash, to chop *(alimentação)*; to bite; to stimulate, to spur, to incite; to provoke, to tease; to raise *(preços)*; to dive ; to become sour *(vinho)*; *v.i.* to prickle; to be sharp; *picar-se*, to take offence, to feel hurt, to be offended or angry; to prick oneself.

picarço, *adj.* ver *"pigarço"*.

picardia, *s.f.* knavery, roguery, malicious-ness, knavish trick.

picaresco, *adj.* picaresque, burlesque, comic, funny, ludicrous.

picareta, *s.f.* pickaxe, pick.

picaria, *s.f.* horsemanship; riding-school.

pícaro, *adj.* knavish, artful; ludicrous, roguish, astute, crooked; ridiculous.

picaroto, *s.m.* vertex, top, summit.

piçarra, *s.f.* shale, gravel, slate, clay rock.

piçarroso, *adj.* shaly, slaty, gravelly, stony.

piche, *s.m.* pitch, tar, asphalt.

pichel, *s.m.* pewter-tankard.

pichelaria, *s.f.* tinsmith's shop or trade.

picheleiro, *s.m.* plumber; tinsmith, tinker; pewterer.

pichelim, *s.m.* dried, salted fish.

picho, *s.m.* ver pichel.

pichorra, *s.f.* ver pichel.

picles, *s.m. (pl.)* pickles.

pico, *s.m.* peak; sharp point; summit, top; thorn, small quantity. 1) *uma semana e pico*, a week and a bit. 2) *ele tem 30 anos e pico*, he is thirty odd.

picoso, *adj.* prickly, thorny.

picota, *s.f.* pillory, stake, post.

picotagem, *s.f.* perforation *(de papéis)*; punching *(de bilhetes)*.

picotar, *v.t.* to perforate *(papel)*, to punch *(bilhetes)*.

picote, *s.m.* coarse cloth.

picotilho, *s.m.* cloth of goat's hair.

picoto, *s.m.* peak, pinnacle, top of a high mountain.

pícrico, *adj.* picric *(ácido)*.

pictografia, *s.f.* pictography.

pictográfico, *adj.* pictographic.

pictórico, *adj.* pictorial.

pictural, *adj.* picturesque.

picuinha, *s.f.* peep *(pássaro jovem)*; taunt, fussiness; rifle; someone very particular.

piedade, *s.f.* piety, pity, compassion, mercy, commiseration; devotion, religiousness. 1) *por piedade!* , for mercy's sake. 2) *sem dó nem piedade*, pitilessly. 3) *Senhor, tende piedade de nós*, Lord, have mercy on us.

piedosamente, *adj.* piously.

piedoso, *adj.* pious, religious, devout; pitiful, merciful.

piegas, *adj.* maudlin, sentimental, womanish, effeminate; *s.m.* milksop, crybaby.

pieguice, *s.f.* effeminacy, sentimentality.

pieira, *s.f.* wheezing, wheeze, wheezy, breathing.

piela, *s.f.* drunkenness, intoxication *(pop)*.

piemontês, *adj., s.m.* Piedmontese.

pietismo, *s.m.* pietism.

pietista, *s.* pietist.

pífano, *s.m.* ver *"pífaro"*.

pifão, *s.m.* *(pop)* drunkenness.

pifar, *v.t.* to steal, to rob.

pífaro, *s.m.* fife.

pífio, *adj.* coarse, vulgar, poor, rough.

pigarço, *adj.* piebald *(cavalo)*, dapple-grey; speckled *(cavalo)*.

pigarrar, pigarrear, *v.i.* to clear the throat; to hawk.

pigarrento, *adj.* raucous, phlegmy.

pigarro, *s.m.* raucouness, a frog in the throat, thick phlegm.

pigarroso, *adj. ver "pigarrento".*

pigmentação, *s.f.* pigmentation, coloration.

pigmentar, *v.t.* to give the colour of the skin to, to colour, to pigment.

pigmantário, *adj.* pigmentary.

pigmento, *s.m.* pigment; colouring matter.

pigmeu, *s.m.* pygmy, dwarf.

pijama, *s.m.* pyjamas, pajama.

pilado, *adj.* bruised; peeled.

pilador, *s.m.* peeler, crusher.

pilão, *s.m.* pestle, stamper, crusher.

pilar, *s.m.* pillar, pier, column, post, stanchion; *v.t.* to pund; to peel; to bray, to bruise, to beat *(grão).*

pilarete, *s.m.* pillaret, a little pillar.

pilastra, *s.f.* pilaster, square pillar.

pilé, *adj.* grannulated *(açúcar).*

pileca, *s.f.* jade, broken-down horse, worn-out horse.

píleo, *s.m.* pileus.

pilha, *s.f.* pile, heap, accumulation; electric battery. 1) *estar como uma pilha,* to be very salted. 2) *pilha seca,* dry battery.

pilhagem, *s.f.* pillage, plundering; looting.

pilhanço, *s.m. ver "pilhagem".*

pilhante, *s.* plunderer, marauder, pillager.

pilhar, *v.t.* to loot; to plunder, to pillage, to catch; to rob, to steal, to sack.

pilheiro, *s.m.* water-cistern.

pilhéria, *s.f.* fun, jest, wit, salt, joke.

pilhérico, *adj.* sportive, jesting, playful.

pilífero, *adj.* hairy.

piliforme, *adj.* piliform.

pilo, *s.m.* javelin, dart.

piloada, *s.f.* blow with a pestle.

piloro, *s.m.* pylorus.

pilosidade, *s.f.* pilosity, hairiness.

piloso, *adj.* pilose, hairy, pilous.

pilota, *s.f.* fatigue, tiredness; rout, defeat.

pilotagem, *s.f.* pilotage.

pilotar, *v.t.* to pilot, to lead, to steer.

pilotear, *v.t.* to pilot.

piloto, *s.m.* pilot; guide, leader. 1) *piloto de provas,* test pilot. 2) *segundo-piloto,* second mate.

pilrete, *s.m.* little or insignificant man; turbulent child.

pilriteiro, *s.m.* hawrhorn.

pilrito, *s.m.* haw.

pílula, *s.f.* pill; pilule.

pilular, *adj.* pilular.

pimenta, *s.f.* pepper.

pimental, *s.m.* pepper field.

pimentão, *s.m.* red pepper.

pimenteira, *s.f.* pepper-shrub; pepper-box.

pimenteiro, *s.m.* pepper-box.

pimento, *s.m.* pimento; green pepper.

pimpão, *s.m.* swaggerer, boaster, dandy.

pimpar, *v.i.* to bluster, to boast, to show off, to flaunt.

pimpinela, *s.f.* burnet.

pimpolho, *s.m.* young shoot; youngster.

pimponar, pimponear, *v.i.* to boast, to swagger, to bluster, to show off.

pimponice, *s.f.* swaggering, boasting, boast, bluster.

pina, *s.f.* felly *(de uma roda).*

pinaça, *s.f.* pinnace.

pinacoteca, *s.f.* pinacotheca, picture-galery.

pináculo, *s.m.* pinnacle, culmination, the top, gable; the highest point, peak; small turret.

pinar, *v.t.* to put pegs in, to set pins.

pinázio, *s.m.* mullion; sash bar; cross-bar of a window frame.

pinça, *s.f.* pincers, nippers *(cirurgia);* tongs; tweezers.

píncaro, *s.m.* pinnacle, apex, peak, summit, top, zenith; *pôr nos píncaros da lua,* to laud to the skies.

pincel, *s.m.* brush, a painter's brush; shaving-brush; a painter.

pincelada, pincelagem, *s.f.* stroke *(com um pincel).*

pincelar, *v.t.* to paint, to daub *(com um pincel).*

pinceleiro, *s.m.* brush-maker; brush-seller; brush-box.

pincha, *s.f.* cruet.

pinchar, *v.i.* to leap, to jump; to pitch, to hurl; to tumble.

pincho, *s.m.* to leap, to jump, bound; crowbar, a pinch bar.

pindárico, *adj.* Pindaric.

pindarismo, *s.m.* Pindarism *(estilo).*

pindarizar, *v.t.* to praise highly.

pineal, *adj.* pineal.

píneo, *adj.* spinny, of pines.

pinga, *s.f.* drop; booze *(pop);* gulp, swallow; wine. 1) *gostar da pinga,* to be fond of the bottle *(vinho).* 2) *estar com a pinga,* to be drunk.

pingadeira, *s.f.* dripping-pan; small but continuous receipts; constant expense.

pingado, *adj.* wet; sprinkled, spotted; *gato-pingado*, pallbearer.

pingalim, *s.m.* thin whip, stick.

pingante, *adj.* dripping.

pingão, *s.m.* dirty person; simpleton.

pingar, *v.i.* to drop, to drip, to fall in drops; to drizzle; to trickle; to give profit little by little; to pour drop by drop; to leak.

pingarelho, *s.m.* poor fellow; *armar ao pingarelho*, to complain (to obtain something of a favour).

pingente, *s.m.* ear-ring.

pingo, *s.m.* drop; dripping; snivel, mucus.

pingoleta, *s.f.* drop; small draught of wine.

pingona, *s.f.* alttern, sluttish woman; sloven.

pingoso, *adj.* dripping, drippy.

pingue, *s.m.* fat *(de porco)*; *adj.* fat; fertile, rich, fruitful; profitable.

pinguela, *s.f.* small wooden bridge; little stick.

pingue-pongue, *s.m.* ping-pong.

pinguim, *s.m.* pinguin.

pinha, *s.f.* pine-cone; heap, crowd of people, bunch; the head *(pop)*.

pinhal, *s.m.* pine-wood, pine-grove, pine forest.

pinhão, *s.m.* pine-seed, pine-nut; pinion.

pinheira, *s.f.* sugar-apple; sweet-sop.

pinheiral, *s.m. ver "pinhal".*

pinheiro, *s.m.* pine, pine-tree.

pinheiro-bravo, *s.m.* pinaster, wild pine-tree.

pinheiro-manso, *s.m.* stone pine, parasol pine.

pinho, *s.m.* pine-wood; pine-tree; pine timber.

pinhoada, *s.f.* candied pine nut kernel.

pinífero, *adj.* producing pine-tress.

piniforme, *adj.* piniform.

pinígero, *adj.* pinífero.

pino, *s.m.* peg; summit, pinnacle, height, top, apex, pitch, zenith. 1) *no pino do Inverno,* in the depth of winter. 2) *no pino do Verão,* in the height of summer. 3) *fazer o pino,* to stand on the hands.

pinoco, *s.m.* summit of a mountain geodetical landmark; vagrant.

pinóia, *s.* elegant *(homem ou mulher).*

pinote, *s.m.* jump, lead; kick.

pinotear, *v.i.* to jump, to caper, to leap; to curvet *(cavalo).*

pinta, *s.f.* spot, mark, mole (on the body); appearance, expression *(cara);* complexion; young pullet.

pintada, *s.f.* Guinea fowl.

pintadela, *s.f.* light painting; a coat of paint.

pintado, *adj.* painted; exactly alike; tricked, taken in. 1) *é o pai pintado,* he is the spitting image of of this father. 2) *ao mais pintado,* to the wisest. 3) *pintado de fresco,* newly painted; wet paint.

pintainho, *s.m.* chicken, young chicken.

pintalegrete, *s.m.* dandy, fop, coxcomb; man about town.

pintalgar, *v.t.* to speckle, to spot; to variegate.

pinta-monos, *s.m.* bad painter, dauber.

pintar, *v.t.* to paint; to depict; to colour, to tinge; to portray; to describe, to represent; to make up; to begin, to ripen. 1) *pintar a manta,* to paint the town red. 2) *pintar a óleo,* to paint in oil. 3) *vir ao pintar,* to come in handy, to come in the nick of time.

pintarroxo, *s.m.* robin.

pintassilgo, *s.m.* goldfinch.

pinto, *s.m.* chicken; ancient Portuguese coin.

pintor, *s.m.* painter.

pintora, *s.f.* paintress.

pintura, *s.f.* painting, picture, paint; figure, image; face makeup; description.

pintural, *adj.* pictorial.

pinturesco, *adj.* picturesque.

pínula, *s.f.* pinnule.

pio, *s.m.* cry; peep; chirp; *adj.* pious, devout, religious; charitable.

piolhada, piolharia, *s.f.* great quantity of lice.

piolheira, *s.f.* lousiness; filthy place; misery.

piolhento, *adj.* lousy, infested with lice.

piolhice, *s.f.* meanness.

piolho, *s.m.* louse, *(pl.)* lice.

piolhoso, *adj. ver "piolhento".*

pioneiro, *s.m.* pioneer; scout; explorer; percursor.

pior, *adj., adv.* worse, the worst. 1) *pior a emenda que o soneto,* the remedy is worse than the disease. 2) *cada vez pior,* worse and worse. 3) *de mal a pior,* from bad to worse. 4) *na pior das hipóteses,* at the worst. 5) *tanto pior,* so much the worse. 6) *o pior é o resto,* the sting is in the tail.

piora, *s.f.* worsening, change for the worse, a growing worse.

piorar, *v.i.* to grow worse, to make worse, to become worse.

pioria, *s.f.* aggravation.

piorno, *s.m.* wild furze, broom.

piorra, *s.f.* small top, whirligig.

piorreia, *s.f.* pyorrhea.

piorreico, *adj.* pyorrheal.

pipa, *s.f.* cask, pipe, barrel, hogshead; drunkard *(pop)*.

piparote, *s.m.* fillip, flick.

pipeta, *s.f.* pipette.

pipi, *s.m.* children's name for chickens or pullets.

pipiar, *v.i.* to chirp, to peep.

pipilante, *adj.* peeping, chirping.

pipilar, *v.i.* ver pipiar.

pipilo, pipio, *s.m.* chirp, chirping.

pipo, *s.m.* keg, cask, small barrel.

pipoca, *s.f.* popcorn.

pique, *s.m.* pike; quarrel; stubbornness; pique; grudge. 1) *a pique*, vertically. 2) *ir a pique*, to sink, to founder *(barco)*. 3) *meter a pique*, to sink a ship.

piqué, *s.m.* piqué *(algodão)*.

piquenique, *s.m.* picnic.

piqueta, *s.f.* picket, stake, peg.

piquetagem, *s.f.* the act of picketing.

piquetar, *v.t.* to demarcate with pickets.

piquete, *s.m.* picket, guard.

pira, *s.f.* pyre.

piramidal, *adj.* pyramidal; colossal, huge.

pirâmide, *s.f.* pyramid.

piranga, *adj.* poor, miserable; stingy.

pirangueiro, *adj.* poor, shabby; ridiculous.

piranha, *s.f.* caribe *(peixe)*.

pirar-se, *v. refl.* to steal away *(pop)*.

pirata, *s.m.* pirate, robber, searobber, corsair.

piratagem, *s.f.* piracy, robbery *(no mar)*.

pirataria, *s.f.* piracy, robbery, extorsion.

piratear, *v.t., v.i.* to pirate, to rob, to plunder *(um barco)*.

pirático, *adj.* piratica(al).

pirenaico, pirenéu, *adj.* of the Pyrenees, Pyrenean.

pires, *s.m.* saucer.

pirético, *adj.* pyretic, pyrexial, feverish febrile.

pirexia, *s.f.* pyrexia, fever.

pírico, *adj.* referring to fire.

piriforme, *adj.* pyriform, pear-shaped.

pirilampo, *s.m.* glow-worm, firefly.

pirite, *s.f.* pyrites, sulphide of iron.

piritífero, piritoso, *adj.* pyritiferous.

pirliteiro, *s.m.* hawthorn.

pirlito, *s.m.* haw *(fruta)*.

pirofobia, *s.f.* pyrophobia.

piróforo, *s.m.,* *adj.* pyrophorus.

piroga, *s.f.* pirogue, canoe.

pirogálhico, pirogálico, *adj.* pyrogallic *(ácido)*.

pirógénese, *s.f.* pyrogenesis, production of heat.

pirogenético, pirogénico, *adj.* pyrogenic.

pirogravar, *v.t.* to pyrograph.

pirogravura, *s.f.* pyrogravure, pyrography.

pirolatra, *s.* pyrolater.

pirolatria, *s.f.* pyrolatry, fire worship.

pirolito, *s.m.* fizzy drink.

pirologia, *s.f.* pyrology.

piromancia, *s.f.* pyromancy.

piromania, *s.f.* pyromania.

piromaníaco, *adj.* pyromaniac.

pirometria, *s.f.* pyrometry.

pirómetro, *s.m.* pyrometer.

piropo, *s.m.* pyrope; gallantry, madrigal.

piroscópio, *s.m.* pyroscope.

pirose, *s.f.* pyrosis, heartburn.

pirosfera, *s.f.* pyrosphere.

perotecnia, *s.f.* pyrotechny *(aplicação)*; pyrotechnics *(arte)*.

periotécnico, *s.m.* pyrotechnist; *adj.* pyrotechnic(al).

pirótico, *adj.* pyrotic, caustic.

pirraça, *s.f.* teasing; trick. 1) por pirraça, spitefully, purposely.

pirraça, *v.t., v.i.* to spite, to thwart.

pírrica, *s.f.* pyrrhic.

pirríquio, *s.m.* metrical foot.

pirronice, *s.f.* Pyrrhonism; obstinacy, stubbornness.

pirrónico, *adj.* Pyrrhonic; obstinate, stubbor.

pirronismo, *s.m.* Pyrrhonism, scepticism; stubbornness.

pírtiga, *s.f.* long strick, pole, shaft.

pírtigo, *s.m.* swingle of a flail.

pirueta, *s.f.* piroutte; whirl.

piruetar, *v.i.* to pirouette, to whirl round, to perform pirouettes.

pisa, *s.f.* pressing, treading *(uvas)*.

pisada, *s.f.* footstep, track, trace; pressing, treadin Uvas).

pisadela, *s.f.* treading, stamping; slight bruise.

pisador, *s.m.* wine-press.

pisadura, *s.f.* bruise; treading, trampling.

pisa-flores, *s.m.* fop, coxcomb.

pisão, *s.m.* fulling-mill.

pisar, *v.t.* to tread, to trample, to step on; to walk over; to offend, to hurt; to despise; to crush; to press; to squeeze; to subdue; to bruise, to contuse.

pisca, *s.f.* very samll thing; particle, spark.

piscadela, *s.f.* twinkle, wink, blink.

pisca-pisca, *s.* flasher; blinker *(de um*

carro).

piscar, *s.f.* twinkle, to wink, to blink; 1) *piscar o* olho, to tip (a person) the wink; to give a wink.

piscatório, *adj.* piscatory, piscatorial.

písceo, *adj.* piscine.

pisces, *s.m. (pl)* Pisces (dos signos do zodíaco).

piscícola, *adj.* pisciaultural.

piscicultor, *s.m.* pisciculturist.

piscicultura, *s.f.* pisciculture, fish breeding.

pisciforme, *adj.* fish-like, pisciform.

piscina, *s.f.* swimming-pool, bathing-pool.

piscívoro, *adj.* piscivorous, fish-eating.

pisco, *s.m.* bullfinch; *adj.* winking, blinking, half-open (olho).

piscoso, *adj.* fishy.

pisgar-se, *v. refle.* to steal away.

piso, *s.m.* pavement floor, ground; manner of walking, gait.

pisoada, *s.f.* cloth-fulling.

pisoador, *s.m.* fuller.

pisoagem, *s.f.* cloth-fulling.

pisoar, *v.t.* to full cloth.

pisoeiro, *s.m.* fuller.

pista, *s.f.* trail, trace, track; runway (aeroporto). 1) *piata de corridas,* race--course, race-ground. 2) *ir na pista de,* to track down (uma pessoa). 3) *estar na pista de,* to follow up the scent.

piatão, *s.m.* piston.

pistilar, *adj.* pistillary; pistillate.

pistilo, *s.m.* pistil.

pistiloso, *adj.* pistillate.

pistola, *s.f.* pistol.

pistolada, *s.f.* pistol-shot.

pistolão, *s.m.* big pistol.

pistoleiro, *s.m.* pistoleer, gunman.

pistolete, *s.m.* pistolet.

pita, *s.f.* agave; aloe; pita.

pitada, *s.f.* pinch; small quantity; stench, bad smell.

pitadear, *v.i.* to take snuff.

pitagórico, *adj.* Pythagorean; *s.m.* Pythagorist, Paythagorean.

pitagorismo, *adj.* Pythagorean.

pitagorista, *s.* Pythagorist.

pitança, *s.f.* pittance; small portion, small allowance (comida).

pitão, *s.m.* screw-ring.

pitecantropo, *s.m.* pithecanthrope.

piteira, *s.f.* agave; aloe; drunkness.

pitéu, *s.m.* dainty, dedicacy, choice, morsel.

pítia, *s.f.* Pythia (sacerdotisa).

pítico, *adj.* Pythian, Pythic.

pito, *s.m.* young chicken; pipe (para fumar); reprimed, scolding.

pitonisa, pitonissa, *s.f.* pythoness; sorceress, witch; soothsayer.

pitoresco, *adj.* pictorial; picturesque; creative.

pitorra, *s.f.* little top; small person.

pitisga, *adj.* short-sighted.

pituíta, *s.f.* phelem, mucus.

pituitária, *s.f.* pituitary membrane, nasal mucosa.

pituitário, *adj.* pituitary.

pituitoso, *adj.* pituitous.

pivete, *s.m.* smart child; bad smell.

piveteiro, *s.m.* perfuming pan.

píxide, *s.f.* pyx, ciborium.

pixídio, *s.m. (bot)* capsule of which the top comes off like lid of a box.

placa, *s.f.* plate; plaque; badge. 1) *placa comemorativa,* memorial tablet.

placabilidade, *s.f.* placability.

placar, *v.t.* placate, to soothe, to appease.

placável, *adj.* placable, appeasable, reconciliable.

placenta, *s.f.* placenta.

placentação, *s.f.* placentation.

placentário, *adj.* placentary.

placidamente, *adv.* placidly.

placidez, *s.f.* placidity, calmness, tranquility, serenity.

plácido, *adj.* placid, calm, tranquil, quiet, serene, peaceful.

plácito, *s.m.* placet, sanction, assent, approval, consent.

placitude, *s.f.* ver placidez.

plaga, *s.f.* region, country.

plagiador, *s.m.* plagiarist, plagiary.

plagiar, *v.t.* to plagiarize.

plagiário, *s.m.* ver plagiador.

plagiato, *s.m.* plagiarism, literary theft.

plágio, *s.m.* plagiarism.

plaina, *s.f.* plane.

plaino, *adj.* flat, plane, level; *s.m.* plane, plain; prairie.

plana, *s.f.* category; order, clas, rank, reputation, fame.

planador, *s.m.* glider (aeroplano).

planáltico, *adj.* marked by plataux.

planalto, *s.m.* uplnad, table-land, plateau.

planar, *v.i.* to plane, to glide.

plancto, plâncton, *s.m.* plankton.

planeamento, *s.m.* projection, planing, scheming.

planear, *v.t.* to project; to desin, to plan.
planejamento, *s.m.* ver planeamento.
planejar, *v.t.* ver planear.
planeta, *s.m.* planet.
planetário, *adj.* planetary; *s.m.* planetarium.
planetóide, *s.m.* planetoid, a minor planet.
planeza, *s.f.* fletness, plain, an eve, open ground.
plangência, *s.f.* plangency, sadness, moaning.
plangente, *adj.* plangent, sad, mournful, mourning.
planger, *v.i.* to lament, to mourn; to toll (bells).
planície, *s.f.* plain, flat country.
planificação, *s.f.* planning.
planificar, *v.t.* to plan, to design, to delineate.
planificar, *adj.* capable of being planned.
planiforme, *adj.* planiform, flat, level.
planiglobo, *s.m.* planisphere.
planimetria, *s.f.* planimetry.
planímetro, *s.m.* planimeter.
planisférico, *adj.* planispheric(al).
planisfério, *s.m.* palnisphere.
plano, *adj.* plane, even, level, flat; smooth; *s.m.* plane; plain; project, scheme, plain; intention, idea, intent, purpose, design. 1) plano inclinado, slide-way, inclines plane. 2) no primeiro plano, in the foreground. 3) último plano, background.
plano-côncavo, *adj.* plano-concave.
plano-convexo, *adj.* plano-convex.
planografia, *s.f.* planography.
planta, *s.f.* palnt; plan, draft *(prédio, cidade, etc.)*. 1) planta do pé, sole of the foot.
plantação, *s.f.* plantation, planting; planted ground.
plantador, *s.m.* planter.
plantão, *s.m.* sentry, guard, duty, service; orderly. 1) estar de plantão, to be on the duty.
plantar, *v.t.* to plant; to set, to fix; to establish to build, to found, to settle; to lay, to place; to cultivate.
plantígrado, *adj., s.m.* plantigrade.
plantio, *s.m.* ver plantação.
plântula, *s.f.* plantule, an embryo plant.
planura, *s.f.* ver planície.
plaqueta, *s.f.* booklet with few pages.
plasma, *s.m.* pasma.
plasmar, *v.t.* to mould, to shape, to model.
plasmático, *adj.* plasmatic, plasmic.
plasmódio, *s.m.* plasmodium.

plástica, *s.f.* plastic art; figure. 1) cirurgia plástica, plastic surgery.
plasticidade, *s.f.* plasticity.
plasticina, *s.f.* plasticine.
plasticização, *s.f.* plasticization.
plasticizae, *v.t.* to plasticize.
plástico, *adj.* plastic, moldable, pliable, ductile, soft; *s.m.* plastic material; plastics.
plastilina, *s.f.* plastilina, modelling clay.
plastrão, *s.m.* plastron; large cravat.
plataforma, *s.f.* platform, terrace; semblance; agreement. 1) plataforma de embarque, loading ramp. 2) plataforma giratória, turntable.
plátano, *s.m.* plane-tree; platan.
plateia, *s.f.* stalls and pit *(de um teatro);* the audience.
platelminta, *s.m.* platyhelminth.
platibanda, *s.f.* platband.
platina, *s.f.* platinum; stage of a microscope; shoulder-strap.
platinado, *s.m.* platinum-point, platinum-contact *(carro).*
platinador, *s.m.* platinizer.
platinagem, *s.f.* platinization, platinum coating.
platinar, *v.t.* to platinize.
platinífero, *adj.* platiniferous.
platinotipia, *s.f.* platinotype.
platonicamente, *adv.* Platonically.
platónico, *adj.* Platonic; ideal; harmless.
platonismo, *s.m.* Platonism.
plausibilidade, *s.f.* plausibility.
plausível, *adj.* plausible; reasonable, sensible.
plausivelmente, *adv.* plausible.
plebe, *s.f.* the common people, mob, rabble, populace.
plebeidade, *s.f.* plebeianism.
plebeismo, *s.m.* plebeianism, vulgarity, vulgarism.
plebeizar, *v.t.* to plebeianize.
plebeu, *s.m.* plebeian; *adj.* plebeian, vulgar.
plebiscitário, *adj.* plebiscitary.
plebiscito, *s.m.* plebiscite, referendum.
plectro, *s.m.* plectrum; poetry, inspiration.
plêiada, **plêiade**, *s.f.* Pleiad *(estrelas);* group of illustrious people.
pleiteador, *s.m.* pleader, litigant, demandant; *adj.* pleading, disputing, demanding.
pleiteante, *s.* litigant.
pleitear, *v.t.* to plead, to litigate, to dispute, to contest, to demand; to vie with; to sue, to

prosecute.

pleito, *s.m.* suit, action *(lei)*, lawsuit, plea, prosecution; contest, dispute.

plenamente, *adv.* fully, completely, entirely, absolutely.

plenário, *adj.* plenary, complete, entire; *s.m.* plenary assembly; court, jury. 1) *sessão plenária,* plenary sitting.

plenidão, *s.f.* fullness, abundance, plenitude, completeness.

plenificar, *v.t.* to fill, to complete.

plenilunar, *adj.* plenilunal, plenilunar, plenilunary.

plenilúnio, *s.m.* plenilune, full moon.

plenipotênciário, *s.f.* plenipotence, full power.

plenitude, *s.m., adj.* plenipotentiary.

pleno, *s.f.* plenitude, completeness, fullness.

pleonasmo, *adj.* full, complete, entire.

pleonástico, *s.m.* pleonasm, redundancy.

pletora, *adj.* plethora, superabundance.

pletórico, *adj.* plethoric.

pleura, *s.f.* pleura.

pleural. *adj.* pleural.

pleuris, pleurisia, *s.m., s.f.* pleurisy.

pleurite, *s.f.* pleuritis.

pleurítico, *adj.* pleuritic.

pleurodinia, *s.f.* pleurodynia.

pleuropneumonia, *s.f.* pleuropneumonia.

plexo, *s.m.* plexus.

plica, *s.f.* accent; plica, fold.

plicar, *v.t.* to fold, to plicate; to mark with an accent.

plicatura, *s.f.* plicature, plication, fold.

plito, *s.m.* plinth; pedestal, socle *(de uma estátua).*

plissado, *adj.* pleated, folded, crimped.

plissagem, *s.f.* pleating, crimping.

plissar, *v.t.* to pleat, to crimp, to fold.

plombagina, *s.f.* to pelat, to crimp, to fold.

pluma, *s.f.* ver plumbagina.

plumaceiro, *s.f.* feather, plume, bunch of feathers.

plumagem, *s.m.* plumassier.

plumar, *s.f.* plumage, feathers, birds, feathers, plume; crest.

plumbagina, *s.f.* plumbago, graphite, black-lead.

plumbagíneo, plumbaginoso, *adj.* plumbaginous.

plumbaria, *s.f.* plumbery, lead-work.

plumbear, *v.t.* to lead, to give a leaden appearance.

plúmbeo, *adj.* plumbeous, plumbic leaden; lead-coloured.

plúmbico, *adj.* plumbic.

plumbífero, *adj.* plumbiferous.

plumboso, *adj.* plumbeous.

plúmeo, *adj.* feathered, plumose.

plumiforme, *adj.* featherlike.

plumilha, *s.f.* plumelet.

plumista, *s.* plumassier; plumist *(negociante).*

plumitivo, *s.m.* journalist; scribbler.

plumoso, *adj.* plumous, feathery, plumose, feathered.

plúmula, *s.f.* plumule.

plural, *s.m., adj.* plural.

pluralidade, *s.f.* plurality; multiplicity.

pluralismo, *s.m.* pluralism.

pluralização, *s.f.* pluralization.

pluralizar, *v.t.* to plurtalize, to multiply.

pluricarpelar, *adj.* pluricarpellar.

pluricelular, *adj.* plericellular.

pluriforme, *adj.* plurishaped.

purilinque, *adj.* plurilinqual.

plurilobulado, *adj.* plurilobulate.

plurilicular, *adj.* plurilocular.

pluripartido, *adj.* pluripartite.

plurisseriado, *adj.* pluriseriated.

plurivalve, *adj.* plurivalve, multivalve.

plutão, *s.m.* Pluto.

plutocracia, *s.f.* plutocracy.

plutocrata, *s.* plutocrat.

plutocrático, *adj.* plutocratic.

plutónico, *adj.* plutonic, igneous.

plutónio, *s.m.* plutonium.

plutonismo, *s.m.* Plutonism.

plutonista, *s.* Plutonist.

plutonomia, *s.f.* political economy, plutonomy.

pluvial, *adj.* rainy, pluvial; *s.m.* prit`s cope, pluvial.

pluviátil, *adj.* puvial.

pluviógrafo, *s.m.* pluviograph.

pluviometria, *s.f.* pluviometry.

pluviométrico, *adj.* pluviometric(al).

pluviómetro, *s.m.* pluviometer.

pluvioso, *adj.* pluvial, rainy, pluvious.

pneu, *s.m.* tyre, tire.

pneuma, *s.m.* pneuma, breath.

pneumática, *s.f.* pneumatics.

pneumático, *adj.* pneumatic: *(pneumatic)* tyre.

pneumatologia, *s.f.* pneumatology.

pneumatológico, *adj.* pneumatological.

pneumatologista, *s.* pneumatologist.

pneumatose, *s.f.* pneumatosis.

pneumobacilo, *s.m.* pneumobacillus.
pneumococo, *s.m.* pneumococcus.
pneumogástrico, *adj.* pneumogastric.
pneumografia, *s.f.* pneumography.
pneumologia, *s.f.* pneumology.
pneumonalgia, *s.f.* pain in the lungs.
pneumonia, *s.f.* pneumonia.
pneumónico, *adj.* pneumonic.
pneumopleurisia, *s.f.* pneumopleuritis.
pneumorragia, *s.f.* pneumorrhagia.
pneumoscópio, *s.m.* penumoscope.
pneumotomia, *s.f.* pneumonotomy.
pneumotárax, *s.m.* pneumothorax.
pó, *s.m.* powder; dust. 1) *pó-de-arroz,* rice powder. 2) *leite em pó,* powdered milk.
poalha, *s.f.* fine dust.
pobre, *adj.* poor, indigent, needy, miserable; wretched; worthless; scanty, meagre; barren, unproductive *(solo);* unsatisfactory, deficient. 1) *pobre como job,* as poor as a church mouse. 2) *pobre diabo,* devil, poor fellow. 3) *pobre de mim!,* poor me!; *s.* pauper, beggar.
pobremente, *adv.* poorly.
pobreta, pobretana, pobretão, *s.m.* poor person, wretch.
pobrete, *adj.* rather poor.
pobreza, *s.f.* poverty, indigence; want, scarcity, need, penury; the poor.
poça, *s.f.* pool, pond, puddle.
poção, *s.f.* potion, dose; drink, draught.
poceiro, *s.m.* digger of wells; large basket.
pocilga, *s.f.* pigsty, pigpen; dirty room or house.
poço, *s.m.* well; pit-shaft; abysm, chasm. 1) *poço artesiano,* artesian well; 2) *poço sem fundo,* widow`s cruse; 3) *poço sem ar,* air-pocket; 4) *poço de ciência,* deeply learned person.
poda, *s.f.* lopping, pruning.
podadeira, *s.f.* pruning-hook, pruning-knife; pruning-shears.
podador, *s.m.* pruner.
podadura, *s.f.* ver poda.
podagra, *s.f.* podagra, gout.
podágrico, *adj.* podagric, gouty.
podão, *s.m.* prunning-hook, vine-knife; a clumsy awkward man.
podar, *v.t.* to lop, to prune, to trim; to dress *(vinhas);* to cut.
podengo, *s.m.* setter, rabbit hound.
poder, *v.t.* may; can, to be able; to be allowed; *s.m.* power, capacity, force; authority; energy, strenght; command,

sway, influence; ability, faculty, possibility; government. 1) *em poder de,* in the hands of, in possession of. 2) *plenos poderes,* full powers.
poderio, *s.m.* power, authority, might, force.
poderosament, *adv.* powerfully.
poderoso, *adj.* powerful, strong, potent, mighty; intense, vigorous; influential. 1) *Deus Todo-Poderoso,* God Almighty.
podoa, *s.f.* ver podadeira.
podologia, *s.f.* description of the foot, podology.
podómetro, *s.m.* podometer.
podre, *adj.* putrid, fetid, rotten; decayed; carious; perverted, corrupt; *s.m.* rotten part of something; blemishes, vices, defects, bad habits *(pop).* 1) *podere de rico,* rich as Croesus, very rich.
podricalho, *adj.* indolent, lazy, slothful; weak.
podrião, *s.f.* rottenness, putrefaction; corruption, demoralization.
podrido, *adj.* putrefied, putrid.
poedeira, *s.f.* laying hen.
poedoiro, poedouro, *s.m.* nesting box.
poeira, *s.f.* dust; presumption, self-conceit.
poeirada, *s.f.* cloud of dust, dust cloud.
poeirento, *adj.* dusty.
poema, *s.m.* poem.
poemeto, *s.m.* little poem.
poente, *s.m.* occident, west; adj. setting *(sol).*
poesia, *s.f.* poetry, poesy; verse, poetical work; poem.
poeta, *s.m.* poet, bard.
poetaço, *s.m.* poetaster, inferior poet.
poetar, *v.i.* to poetize, to make poetry or verses.
poetastro, *s.m.* poeataster, scribbler of verses.
poética, *s.f.* poetics, theory of poetry.
poeticamente, *adv.* poetically.
poético, *adj.* poetic, poetical.
poetisa, *s.f.* poetess.
poetismo, *s.m.* the poets collectively.
poetizar, *v.t., v.i.* ver poetar.
poia, *s.f.* large loaf.
poial, *s.m.* stone bench.
pois, *conj.* because; then; so; since, for, as, morever. 1) *pois bem,* well. 2) *pois de certo,* why yes.
poisa, *s.f.* ver pousa.
poisada, *s.f.* ver pousada.
poisadoiro, *s.m.* ver pousadouro.
poisar, *v.t., v.i.* ver pousar.

poisio, *s.m.* ver pousio.

poiso, *s.m.* ver pouso.

pojadoiro, pojadouro, *s.m.* top round *(bife)* flesh of ox leg.

pojante, *adj.* sailing before wind.

pojar, *v.i.* to land, to touch land, to cast anchor; to swell, to raise, to elevate.

pojo, *s.m.* landing-place.

póla, *s.f.* scuffle, brawl, thrashing.

pôla, *s.f.* branch, sprout, shoot; bough.

polaca, *s.f.* polacca, tree-masted vessel.

polaco, *adj.* Polish; *s.m.* Pole.

polainas, *s.f.* (pl) gaiters.

polainitos, *s.m.* (pl) spats.

polar, *adj.* polar.

polaridade, *s.f.* polarity.

polarímetro, *s.m.* polarimeter.

polarização, *s.f.* polaization.

polarizador, *s.m.* polarizer; *adj.* polarizing.

polarizar, *v.t.* to polarize.

polarizável, *adj.* polarizable.

polca, *s.f.* polka.

polcar, *v.i.* to polk, to dance the polka.

pólder, *s.m.* polder.

poldra, *s.f.* filly; stepping-stone.

poldro, *s.m.* colt, young horse.

polé, *s.m.* pulley. 1) *dar tratos de polé à cabeça,* to cudgel the brains.

poleame, *s.m.* blocks; tackle *(de um barco).*

polear, *v.t.* to strappado.

poleeiro, *s.m.* block-maker or seller.

polegada, *s.f.* inch; the twelfth part of a foot.

polegar, *s.m.* thumb.

poleiro, *s.m.* roost, perch, hen-roost, pole; domineering position; pigeonhole *(teatro),* the top gallery.

polémica, *s.f.* polemic, controversy, dispute, debate.

polemicar, *v.i.* to polemize.

polémico, *adj.* polemic, controversial.

polemista, *s., adj.* polemist.

polemizar, *v.i.* to polemize.

pólen, *s.m.* pollen.

polenta, *s.f.* polenta *(comida).*

pólex, *s.m.* thumb, pollex.

polha, *s.f.* pullet, chicken.

polhastro, *s.m.* big chicken; sturdy youngster.

polia, *s.f.* pulley, sheave.

poacanto, *adj.* thorny.

poliadelfia, *s.f.* polyadelphia.

poliadelfo, *adj.* polyadelphous.

poliandria, *s.f.* polyandry.

poliandro, *adj.* polyandrous.

polianto, *adj.* polyanthous.

poliarquia, *s.f.* polyarchy.

policárpico, *adj.* polycarpic.

policarpo, *adj.* polycarpous; *s.m.* polycarp.

policelular, *adj.* policellular.

policêntrico, *adj.* polycentric.

polichinelo, *s.m.* Punch; buffon; Merry-
-Andrew.

polícia, *s.f.* police *(organização, corpo da polícia).* 1) *polícia marítima,* coast-guard. 2) *polícia-secreta,* detective force. 3) *esquadra da polícia,* police station; *s.m.* policeman.

policial, *adj.* police. 1) romance policial, detective story.

policiamento, *s.m.* policing, watching, patrolling, police supervision.

policiar, *v.t.* to police, to patrol, to keep vigil.

policlínica, *s.f.* polyclinic.

policlínico, *adj.* polyclinical; *s.m.* physician for general medicine.

policónico, *adj.* polyconic.

policórdio, *s.m.* polychord.

policresto, *s.m.* polychrestic.

policromático, *adj.* polychromatic.

policromia, *s.f.* polichromy.

policromo, *adj.* polychromous, polychromatic, multicoloured.

policultura, *s.f.* mixed farming.

polidáctilo, *adj.* polydactil.

polidamente, *adv.* politely; smoothly, brightly.

polidez, *s.f.* politness, civility, courtesy, urbanity.

polido, *adj.* polite, courteous, genteel, well-bred, civil; polished, smooth, glossy; shining, bright.

polidor, *s.m.* polisher, burnisher.

polidura, *s.f.* polishing.

poliédrico, *adj.* polyhedral, polyhedric.

poliedro, *s.m.* polyhedron.

polifagia, *s.f.* polyphagia, voracity.

polífago, *s.m.* polyphagous.

polifilo, *adj.* polyphyllous.

polifonia, *s.f.* polyphony, polyphonic compo-sition.

polifónico, *adj.* polyphonic.

polífono, *adj.* polyphonic, polyphonnous.

poligania, *s.f.* polygamy.

poligâmico, *adj.* polygamic, poligamous.

polígamo, *s.m.* polygamist; *adj.* polygamous.

poligástrico, *adj.* polygastric.

poligenia, *s.f.* polygenesis.

polígeno, *adj.* polygenous.

poliglota, *s., adj.* polyglot.

poliglótico, *adj.* polyglottic, polyglottal.

poliglotismo, *s.m.* polyglottism.

poligonal, *adj.* polygonal.

polígono, *s.m.* polygon.

poligrafia, *s.f.* polygraphy.

poligráfico, *adj.* polygraphic.

polígrafo, *s.m.* polygraph; polygrapher.

polimento, *s.m.* polishing; polish, burnish, shine.

polimetria, polimerismo, *s.f., s.m.* polymerism.

polimerização, *s.f.* polymerization.

polimerizar, *v.t.* to polymerize.

polímero, *adj.* polymeric, polymerous.

polimorfia, polimorfismo, *s.f., s.m.* polymorphism.

polimórfico, *adj.* polymorphic, polymorphous.

polimorfismo, *s.m.* polymorphism.

polimorfo, *adj.* polymorphic, multiform.

polinésico, polinésio, *s.m., adj.* Polynesian.

polínico, *adj.* pollinic.

polinífero, *adj.* pollineferous.

polínio, *s.m.* pollinium.

polinização, *s.f.* pollination.

polinizador, *adj.* pollinating.

polinizar, *v.t.* to pollinate.

polinómio, *s.m.* polynomial.

polinoso, *adj.* pollinose.

pólio, *s.m.* poly.

poliomielite, *s.f.* poliomyelitis.

poliónimo, *adj.* polyonymous.

poliopia, *s.f.* polyopia.

poliose, *s.f.* polyose.

polipeiro, *s.m.* polypary.

polipétalo, *adj.* polypetalous.

poliforme, *adj.* polypiform.

pólipo, *s.m.* polypus; polyp *(animal).*

polipódio, *s.m.* polypody; *adj.* polypod.

poloposo, *adj.* polypose; polypous.

poloprismo, *s.m.* poliprism.

polir, *v.t.* to polish; to civilize, to refine, to cultivate.

polissépalo, *adj.* polysepalous.

polissilábico, *adj.* polysyllabic.

polissílabo, *s.m.* polysyllable; *adj.* polysyllabic.

polissintético, *adj.* polysynthetic(al).

polístilo, *s.m.* polystile.

politécnica, *s.f.* polytechnic; scool.

politécnico, *adj.* polytechnic; *s.m.* polytechnical student.

politeísmo, *s.m.* polytheism.

politeísta, *s.* polytheist; *adj.* polytheisric(al).

politeístico, *adj.* polytheistic.

política, *s.f.* politics, political science; policy.

politicagem, *s.f.* petty politics.

politicamente, *adv.* politically.

politicante, *s.* politicaster.

politicão, *s.m.* great politican; who is very fond of politics.

politicar, *v.i.* to politicize, to talk politics.

político, *s.m.* politician, statesman; *adj.* political, politic.

politiqueiro, *s.m.* politicaster, petty politician; *adj.* given to petty politics.

politiquice, *s.f.* ver politicagme.

polítrico, *s.m.* maidenhair spleenwort.

polivalente, *adj.* polyvalent.

polmão, *s.m.* swelling, tumour.

polme, *s.m.* pap, pulp.

pólo, *s.m.* pole *(Norte ou Sul);* the North; the pole *(de um magneto);* polo *(jogo).* 1) *pólo aquático,* waterpolo.

pôlo, *s.m.* yearling hawk or falcon.

polonês, *s.m., adj.* Polish.

polonesa, *s.f.* polonaise *(música).*

polpa, *s.f.* pulp; pap, aquash; marrow.

polposo, *adj.* pulpous, pulpy.

polpudo, *adj.* ver polposo.

poltrão, *adj.* cowardly, craven; *s.m.* poltroon; coward.

poltrona, *s.f.* armchair, easy-chair, elbow chair.

poltronaria, *s.f.* poltroonery, cowardice.

poltronear, *v.i.* to show cowardice, to act as a coward.

poluição, *s.f.* pollution, corruption, contamination.

poluir, *v.t.* to pollute, to defile; to stain; to corrupt, to contaminate.

poluível, *adj.* corruptible.

poluto, *adj.* polluted; stained; corrupted, foul, tained, soiled.

polvilhação, *s.f.* powdering, dusting, spraying.

polvilhamento, *s.m.* ver polvilhação.

polvilhar, *v.t.* to powder, to dust, to cover with dust; to sprinkle, to spray; to flour.

polvilho, *s.m.* powder, hairpowder.

polvo, *s.m.* octupus.

pólvora, *s.f.* powder; gunpowder. 1) *não é homem para descobrir a pólvora,* he is rather dull. 2) *ele está como pólvora,* he is quick-tempered.

polvorada, *s.f.* explosion of gunpowder; powder smoke.

polvorento, *adj.* powdery, pulverulent.

polvorim, *s.m.* gunpowder.

polvorinho, *s.m.* powder-horn, powder-flash.

polvorista, *s.* gunpowder-maker.

polvorosa, *s.f.* bustle, flurry, uproar fuss, disorder.

polvoroso, *adj.* powdery, dusty.

poma, *s.f.* breast, teat; sphere, globe, ball.

pomáceo, *adj.* pomaceous.

pomada, *s.f.* pomade, pomatum; salve, ointment; cream; balm, balsam.

pomar, *s.m.* orchard.

pomareiro, *s.m.* orchardman, orchardist, fruit-grower, fruit-farmer; *adj.* relating to orchards.

pomba, *s.f.* female dove.

pombal, *s.m.* dove-cot, pigeon-house, pigeonry.

pobalino, *adj.* relative to the first Marquis of Pombal and his time.

pombo, *s.m.* dove, pigeon. 1) *pombo-bravo,* wood (wild-pigeon). 2) *pombo-torcaz,* ringdove.

pombo-correio, *s.m.* carrier-pigeon, homing pigeon.

pomes, *adj.* pumice-stone.

pomicultor, *s.m.* pomiculturist, fruitgrower.

pomicultura, *s.f.* pomiculture, fruit-growing.

pomífero, *adj.* pomiferous, fruit-bearing.

pomo, *s.m.* pome, fruir; apple. 1) *pomo de discórdia,* apple of discord, bone of contention.

pomologia, *s.f.* pomology.

pomológico, *adj.* pomological.

pomologista, *s.* pomologist.

pomólogo, *s.m.* pomologist, friut-grower.

pompa, *s.f.* pomp, ostentation state, splendour, magnificence.

pompeante, *adj.* pompous, ostentatious, boastful.

pompear, *v.t.* to exhibit, to parade; to show off, to display riches.

pompeiano, *adj.* Pompeian.

pompom, *s.m.* pompon.

pomposamente, *adv.* pompously, showily, spectacularçy.

pomposidade, *s.f.* pomposity.

pomposo, *adj.* pompous, ostentatios, magnificent; solemn, sumptuous, splendid; sounding, bombastic *(linguagem).*

pómulo, *s.m.* cheek bone.

ponche, *s.m.* punch *(bebida).*

poncheira, *s.f.* punch-bowl.

ponderabilidade, *s.f.* ponderability.

ponderação, *s.f.* ponderation, gravity, importance; reflection, judiciousness, consideration.

ponderadamente, *adv.* advisedly, ponderously.

ponderado, *adj.* considerate, weighed; well-advised; cool judicious.

ponderador, *s.m.* pondere; *adj.* pondering.

ponderal, *adj.* ponderal.

ponderar, *v.t.* to ponder, to think over, to cogitate, to weigh, to reflect, to consider; to examime, to study.

ponderativo, *adj.* ponderative.

ponderável, *adj.* ponderable.

ponderoso, *adj.* ponderous, heavy, important, weighty notable.

pónei, *s.m.* pony, small horse.

pongo, *s.m.* a chimpanzee.

ponta, *s.f.* extremity, end, point; horn; peak, top, summit; edge *(de uma mesa);* fag-end *(de um cigarro);* tip *(da língua ou dos dedos).* 1) *ponta de Paris,* wire-nail. 2) *de ponta a ponta,* from end to end. 3) *à ponta da espada,* at the point of the sword. 4) *andar de ponta com,* to bear someone a grudge. 5) *saber na ponta da língua,* to have something at the finger tips. 6) *tomar de ponta,* to dislike.

pontada, *s.f.* stitch; twinge sharp pain; pang.

ponta-direita, *s.m.* outside-right *(futebol).*

pontado, *adj.* basting-thead, stitched.

ponta-esquerda, *s.m.* outside-left.

pontal, *s.m.* depth of hold, small point of land.

pontalete, *s.m.* prop. stay, shore, stanchion.

pontão, *s.m.* prop; pontoon, float-bridge; viaduct; brace; support.

pontapé, *s.m.* kick; insult, offence *(fig.).*

pontapear, *v.t., v.i.* to kick, to give a kick.

pontar, *v.t., v.i.* to prompt *(teatro).*

pontarelo, *s.m.* long stitch.

pontaria, *s.f.* aim, aiming, sight; target. 1) *fazer pontaria,* to sight, to aim at. 2) *errar a pontaria,* to miss the aim.

ponte, *s.f.* brodge; deck *(de um barco);* pverpass. 1) *ponte-cais,* jetty, pier, wharf. 2) *ponte de comando,* commandingbridge. 3) *ponte pênsil (suspensa),* chain (suspension), bridge. 4) *ponte giratória,* swingbridge. 5) *ponte de barcas,* pontoon-bridge. 6) *ponte levadiça,* draw-bridge.

ponteado, *s.m.* stipple; dotting; stitching.

pontear, *v.t.* to dot; to stitch; to staple; to baste; to sew.

ponteira, *s.f.* tip.

ponteiro, *s.m.* rod; pointer; chisel, puncheon; style; plectrum *(música)*; hand *(de relógio)*; *adj.* contraru *(vento)*.

pontel, *s.m.* glass blower's pipe.

pontiagudo, *adj.* sharp pointed, pointed, peaky, sharp.

pontícula, *s.m.* small bridge.

pontículo, *s.m.* small point, puncule.

pontificado, *s.m.* pontificate; papacy.

pontifical, *adj., s.m.* pontifical.

pontificar, *v.i.* topontoficate, to pontify; to speak as a great authority.

pontífice, *s.m.* pontiff; the Pope. 1) *Sumo Pontífice,* Pontifex Maximus.

pontifício, *adj.* ver pontifical.

pontilha, *s.f.* sharp point; purl of lace.

pontilhão, *s.m.* small bridge.

pontilhar, *v.t.* to dot, to stipple.

pontinha, *s.f.* small peak or point; a trifle, a little bit; quarrel. 1) *nas pontinhas dos pés,* on tiptoe.

pontinho, *s.m.* small point; small stitch; *(pl)* dots.

ponto, *s.m.* point; dot; stitch; position; instant; verge; aim; purpose; object; full stop; test *(na escola);* prompter *(no teatro);* matter, subject; register, roll; speck, spot; place; end, conclusion; *(pl)* score *(jogo)*. 1) *ponto ajour,* hem stitch. 2) *ponto culminante,* culminating point. 3) *ponto de apoio,* point of support, fulcrum. 4) *ponto de cruz,* cross-stitch. 5) *ponto de espinha,* herringbone-stitch. 6) *ponto de exclamação,* exclamation mark, note of exclamation. 7) *ponto de fusão,* emlting point. 8) *ponto de interrogação,* note (mark) of interrogation, question marks. 9) *ponto de partida,* starting point. 10) *ponto de rebuçado,* sugardegree. 11) *ponto final,* full stop. 12) *ponto de vista,* point of view, view poit, angle, opinion. 13) *ponto e vírgula,* semicolon. 14) *ponto morto,* dead center, out of gear, neutral. 15) *ponto nevrálgico,* punctilio. 16) *pôr ponto a,* to put a stop to. 17) *de ponto em branco,* dressed up to the nines. 18) *assinar o ponto,* to sign the register. 19) *estar a ponto de,* to be about to. 20) *pôr os pontos nos ii,* to make things clear. 21) *até certo ponto,* to a certain extent. 22) *concordo até certo ponto,* I agree in a sense. 23) *às duas horas em ponto,* upon the stroke of two, at two sharp. 24) *chegar a um ponto morto,* to come to a

deadlock. 25) *ele foi a ponto de,* he went so fas as.

pontoar, *v.t.* to dot, to point, to mark with points; to punctuate.

pontonerio, *s.m.* pontoneer, pontoon builder.

pontoso, *adj.* punctilious, scrupulous, very particular, exact.

pontuação, *s.f.* punctuation.

pontual, *adj.* punctual; exact; strict; prompt; precise.

pontualidade, *s.f.* punctuality; exactitude; preciseness; promptutude.

pontualmente, *adv.* in due time, punctually.

pontuar, *v.t.* to punctuate, to put in punctuation marks.

pontudo, *adj.* sharp, pointed, peaked; aggressive, caustic.

popa, *s.f.* poop, stern *(barco)*. 1) *à popa,* astern, abaft. 2) *de vento em popa,* before the wind.

pope, *s.m.* pope *(bispo de Alexandria)*.

popelina, *s.f.* poplin.

popinha, *s.f.* lark.

populaça, *s.f.* populace, common people, the mob, the masses, the rabble.

população, *s.f.* population, the inhabitants *(de uma região);* the people *(de um país)*.

populacho, *s.m.* ver populaça.

popular, *adj.* popular, common, public; agreeable, well-liked; sympathetic.

popularidade, *s.f.* popularity; vogue.

popularização, *s.f.* popularization.

popularizar, *v.t.* to popularize, to make popular, to spread; to vulgarize.

popularmente, *adj.* popularly.

populina, *s.f.* populin.

populoso, *adj.* populous.

póquer, *s.m.* poker *(jogo)*.

por, *prep.* by; though; for; out of; about. 1) *por assim dezer,* so to speak. 2) *por causa de,* because of on account of, for. 3) *por conseguinte,* therefore. 4) *por enquanto,* for the time being. 5) *por escrito,* in writting. 6) *por extenso,* in full. 7) *por fim,* lastly, at last. 8) *por isso mesmo,* for that very reason. 9) *por mar,* by sea. 10) *por meio de,* by means of. 11) *por ora,* for the present. 12) *por outro lado,* on the other hand. 13) *por quanto tempo?,* for how long?. 14) *por sua vez,* in his turn. 15) *por volta de,* about, around.

pôr, *v.t.* to put; to set; to place; to deposit; to render; to produce; to impose; to submit; to lay *(ovos);* to fix; to put on, to dress; to translate into; to include.

porão, *s.m.* hold, bilge, bottom.

porca, *s.f.* sow; screw-nut; dirty woman. 1) *apertar a porca,* to tighten the nut.

porcada, *s.f.* a herd of swine.

porcalhão, *adj.* dirty; *s.m.* dirty fellow.

porção, *s.f.* portion, share, part, lot, morsel; dose; amount; a goof deal.

porcaria, *s.f.* dirtiness; filth; dirty work, patchwork; obscenity.

porcelana, *s.f.* china, china-ware, porcelain.

porcelanite, *s.f.* porcellanite.

porcino, *adj.* porcine.

porcionário, *s.m.* portioner.

porcionista, *s.* portionist, boarder *(escola).*

porciúncula, *s.f.* small portion; fest of the Franciscan order.

porco, *adj.* dirty, filthy; obscene, indecent; *s.m.* swine, pig, hog. 1) *carne de porco,* pork.

porco-espinho, *s.m.* porcupine.

porco-marinho, *s.m.* porpoise.

porco-montês, *s.m.* wild-boar.

porejar, *v.t., v.i.* to exude, to perspire, to sweat out; to distil.

porém, *conj.* but; however; yet; nevertheless, notwithstanding.

porfia, *s.f.* obstinacy, insistence; contention, strife, dispute, debate. 1) *à porfia,* in competition with.

porfiadamente, *adv.* tenaciously.

porfiado, *adj.* obstinate, stubborn, pertinacious; disputed, eargerly sought.

porfiador, *adj.* obstinate, stubborn, insistent.

pofiar, *v.i.* to persist, to insist on, to be obstinate, to discuss, to contend.

porfioso, *adj.* obstinate, stubborn, contentious, persistent, constant; quarrelsome.

porfírico, *adj.* porphyritic.

porfirito, *s.m.* porphyrite.

pofirizar, *v.t.* to porphyrize; to grind, to pulverize.

pórfiro, *s.m.* porphyry.

porífero, *adj.* poriferous, poriferal.

poriforme, *adj.* poriform.

pormenor, *s.m.* detail; a particular; an item; particuçarity. 1) *entrar em pormenores,* to go into details.

pormenorização, *s.f.* detailing, detailled report or account.

pormenorizadamente, *adv.* in detail; minutely.

pormenorizar, *v.t.* to detail, to describe in detail, to particularize.

pornografia, *s.f.* pornography, licentiousness.

pornográfico, *adj.* pornographic, obscene, licentious.

pornógrafo, *s.m.* pornographer, pornographist.

poro, *s.m.* pore.

por ora, *loc. adv.* for the present, for now.

porosidade, *s.f.* porosity, porousness.

poroso, *adj.* porous, full of pores.

poquanto, *conj.* since; seeing that, considering that.

porque, *conj., adv,* because; as; for; why;, for what reason.

porquê, *s.m.* cause, reason; adv. why.

porqueira, *s.f.* pigsty, hovel, pig-pen; woman swineherd, dirty place.

poequeiro, *s.m.* swineherd; *adj.* porcine.

porquice, porquidade, porquidão, *s.f.* dirt, filth, dirtiness.

porquinho, *s.m.* piglet; bundle of hemp. 1) *porquinho-da-Índia,* Guinea-pig.

porrada, *s.f.* blow with a cudgel, hit, knock.

porrete, *s.m.* club, cudgel, truncheon, stick.

porro, *adj.* 1) *alho-porro,* leek.

porta, *s.f.* door; entrance, entry, gate, gateway. 1) *porta principal,* front door. 2) *porta giratória,* revolving door. 3) *porta de vaivém,* swing door. 4) *empurrar a porta,* to push the door. 5) *à porta fechada,* in private. 6) *por portas e travessas,* by foul practices.

porta-aviões, *s.m.* aircraft-carrier.

porta-bagagem, *s.m.* parcel-rack, luggage carrier.

porta-bandeira, *s.m.* ensign-bearer, standard-bearer, flag-bearer.

porta-chaves, *s.m.* key-ring, key holder.

poratada, *s.f.* portal, porch, doorway; frontispiece, façade.

potador, *s.m.* bearer; porter; carrier; messenger; holder *(títulos);* vehicle. 1) *ao portador,* to the bearer.

porta-escovas, *s.m.* brush-case.

porta-estandarte, *s.m.* ensign-bearer, flag-bearer.

porta-ferramenta, *s.m.* tool-holder.

portageiro, *s.m.* exciseman, toll-collector.

portagem, *s.f.* toll, tollgate, tollbridge, tollroad; tax.

portal, *s.m.* portal; gateway.

porta-lápis, *s.m.* pencil-case.

portaló, *s.m.* gangway, entering-port, gangway port.

porta-machado, *s.m.* sapper.

porta-moedas, *s.m.* purse.

portanto, *conj.* therefore; so, consequently, for that reason.

portão, *s.m.* gate; gateway; garden gate.

portar-se, *v. refl.* to behave; to conduct oneself. 1) *portar-se bem,* to behave well, to act correctly.

portaria, *s.f.* main gate *(num convento, escola, etc.);* doorkeeper's box; entrance; reception desk *(hotel);* governmental order, decree.

portátil, *adj.* portable, easily carried; handy, small; light.

porta-voz, *s.m.* speaking-tube, magaphone; spokesman, voice.

porte, *s.m.* behaviour, manners, air, gait, bearing, carriage, transport; charge, transport fee; loading capacity, tonnage; postage.

portear, *v.t.* to stamp *(carta).*

porteira, *s.f.* woman door-keeper, portress.

porteiro, *s.m.* porter, door-keeper.

portela, *s.f.* narrow passage *(entre montanhas),* gorge.

portelo, *s.m.* small door or gate.

portento, *s.m.* prodigy, marvel, portent, wonder, miracle.

portentosamente, *adv.* portentouslt, marvellously.

portentoso, *adj.* portentous, marvellous, prodigious, wonderfull, extraordinary, amazing, unusual.

pórtico, *s.m.* porch; portico, colonnade; portal.

portilha, *s.f.* loophole.

portilho, *s.m.* small port.

portinhola, *s.f.* small door; cariiage door; flap of a pocket; porthole, scuttle *(barco).*

porto, *s.m.* port, harbour, haven; port-wine; refuge, shelter. 1) *porto de escala,* port of call. 2) *porto fluvial,* river harbour. 3) *porto de mar,* seaport. 4) *porto franco,* free port. 5) contas do Porto, Dutch treat.

portuário, *adj.* relative to a port. 1) *direitos portuários,* port charges, port dues.

portucalense, *adj.* Portuguese.

portucha, *s.f.* reef hole.

portuchar, *v.t.* to reef sails.

portuensa, *s.m.* born in Oporto; *adj.* relative to Oporto.

português, *adj., s.m.* Portuguese.

portuguesa, *s.f.* Portuguese national anthem.

portuguesismo, *s.m.* Portuguese mode of thought or feeling; Portuguese behaviour and mannerism.

portuguesmente, *adv.* in a Portuguese way.

portulano, *s.m.* portolano.

portuoso, *adj.* having many sea-sport.

porventura, *adv.* by chance, perhaps, perchance, possibly.

porvindoiro, porvindouro, *adj.* future.

porvir, *s.m.* future, the time to come.

posar, *v.i.* to pose *(como modelo),* to sit for *(modelo).*

poscénio, *s.m.* postcenum, backstage.

pós-clássico, *adj.* postclassic(al).

pós-data, *s.f.* post-date.

pós-datar, *v.t.* to post-date.

pós-diluviano, *adj.* postdiluvian.

pose, *s.f.* pose, position, posture, assumed attitude; posing *(modelo);* time exposure *(quadro).*

pós-escrito, *s.m.* postscript; P.S.

posfácio, *s.m.* postface.

posição, *s.f.* position; situation; disposition; attitude; office; post; appointment; rank; condition.

posicional, *adj.* positional.

positivamente, *adv.* positively, absolutelt, decidedly.

positivar, *v.t.* to make positive, real.

positividade, *s.f.* positiviness, positivity.

positivismo, *s.m.* positivism.

positivista, *adj.* positivisstic; *s.* positivist.

positivo, *adj.* positive, express, definite, actual, real; certain; evident, clear, obvious; formal; dogmatic; objective; affirmative; categorical; *s.m.* positive degree *(gram.);* positive print *(quadro).*

pós-nupcial, *adj.* post-nuptial.

posologia, *s.f.* posology, dosology.

pós-operatório, *adj.* post-operative.

pospasto, *s.m.* dessert.

pospelo, *s.m.* direction, aginst the fur, the hair or the grain. 1) *a pospelo,* against the grain and the fur.

pospontar, *v.t.* to backstitch.

posponto, *s.m.* backstitch.

pospor, *v.t.* to postpone, to defer, to delay, to put off, to place after.

posposição, *s.f.* postposition, postponement.

pospositivo, *adj.* postpositive; pospositional *(partícula).*

posposto, *adj.* postponed, deferred, placed after.

pós-romano, *adj.* post-Roman.

possança, *s.f.* power, might, strength; bravery, courage.

possante, *adj.* powerful, vigorous, mighty, strong, stout.

posse, *s.f.* possession; occupancy; retention, ownership, tenure; *(pl)* wealth, riches, property, state. 1) *dar posse,* to invest. 2) *tomar posse de,* to take over.

possessão, *s.f.* possession; dominion, colony. 1) *possessão ultramarina,* over-seas possession.

possessivo, *adj.* possessive.

possesso, *adj.* possessed, mad, crazy, demoniac.

possessor, *s.m.* possessor.

possessório, *adj.* possessory.

possibilidade, *s.f.* possibility, chance; feasibility; *(pl)* means, money; propects, potentialities.

possibilitar, *v.t.* to make possible, to enable.

possível, *adj.* possible; feasible, praticable. 1) *fazer o possível,* to do one`s best.

possivelmente, *adv.* possibly, maybe, perchance.

possuidor, *adj.* possessing; *s.m.* possessor, owner, master, holder.

possuir, *v.t.* to possess, to own, to be in possession of, to have, to hold *(proprie-dades);* to occupy.

posta, *s.f.* slice *(peixe);* portion, share; lucrative job; post, mail.

postal, *adj.* postal; *s.m.* postcard. 1) *postal ilustrado,* picture postcard. 2) *encomenda postal,* parcel post.

postar, *v.t.* to station, to post. 1) *postar-se,* to place oneself.

posta-restante, *s.f.* poste retante; to be called for.

poste, *s.m.* pole; stake; pillar, post.

postejar, *v.t.* to cut up, to slice, to cut into slices.

postema, *s.f.* aposteme.

postergação, *s.f.* postponement, preterition; carelessness.

postergador, *adj., s.m.* postponing; postponer.

postergar, *v.t.* to omit; to pass over; to postponer.

posteridade, *s.f.* posterity, future generations, descendants; the coming ages.

posterior, *adj.* posterior; later; hinder; ulterior; after.

posterioridade, *s.f.* posteriority.

posteriormente, *adv.* posteriorly; later on; subsequently, afterwards.

póstero, *adj.* future; coming; *s.m. (pl)* posterity.

postiço, *adj.* superadded; false, artificial, counterfeit; imitated.

postigo, *s.m.* wicket; scuttle; peep-window.

postilhão, *s.m.* postilliom, post boy; messenger.

posto, *adj.* placed, put; set *(sol);* disposed, arranged; *s.m.* post, station; situation; place, position; military post; office; duty; rank, grade; dignity. 1) *ao sol posto,* at sunset. 2) *bem-posto,* well-groomed *(vestido).* 3) *posto de socorros,* first-aid station.

postónico, *adj.* posttonic.

posto que, *conj.* although, though, even if.

post, *s.m.* dessert.

postremo, *adj.* last, extreme.

postulação, *s.f.* postulation, suplication; petition, application.

postulado, *s.m.* postulate, principçe, assumprion, supposition.

postulador, *s.m.* postulator.

postulante, *s.* postulator, postulant, petitioner, candidate; *adj.* postulating.

postular, *v.t.* to postulate, to claim, to demand, to require; to take for granted.

postumamente, *adv.* posthumously.

póstumo, *adj.* posthumous.

postura, *s.f.* posture; attitude; arrangement; by-law, municipal bylaw; laying of egges, number of eggs laid; a city ordinance.

potabilidade, *s.f.* potability, potableness.

potamologia, *s.f.* potamology.

potamológico, *adj.* potamological.

potassa, *s.f.* potash. 1) *potassa cáustica,* caustic potash.

potássico, *adj.* potassic.

potássio, *s.m.* potassium.

potável, *adj.* potable, drinkable.

pote, *s.m.* pot, water-jug, vessel, water-jar; squat person; chamberpot.

potência, *s.f.* power, potency, strength; working power; a power *(nação);* horse power, potence *(mat.).* 1) *potência ao freio,* brake horse-power. 2) *potência calorífica,* heating power. 3) *potência luminosa,* candlepower.

potenciação, *s.f.* raising to a power, potentiation.

potencial, *adj.* potential, powerful, potent; *s.m.* potential.

potencialidade, *s.f.* potentiality.

potenciar, *v.t.* to raise the power of a number.

potenciómetro, *s.m.* potentiometer.

potentado, *s.m.* potentate, sovereign, ruler, great nation.

potente, *adj.* powerful, potent, mighty, strong, vigorous.

poterna, *s.f.* postern, back-door.

potestade, *s.f.* divide power; authority, power.

potra, *s.f.* filly, foal; rupture, hernia.

potreia, *s.f.* bad drink; trash.

potreio, *s.m.* colt-dealer.

potro, *s.m.* colt, foal, young horse; rack.

pouca-vergonha, *s.f.* sauciness, a great shame; knavery.

pouco, *pron., adv., s.,.* little, small quantity, somewhat; not much; *(pl)* few. 1) *pouco a pouco,* little by little, by degrees. 2) *pouco se me dá,* I don't care. 3) *melhor pouco que nada,* half a loaf is better than no bread. 4) *a pouca distância,* near. 5) *aos poucos,* little by little, by inches. 6) *há pouco,* a while ago. 7) *muitos poucos, fazem muito,* many a pickle a mickle. 8) *por pouco,* almost, about. 9) *pouco depois,* soon after. 10) *fazer pouco de,* to make fun of, to mock. 11) *até há pouco,* till recently. 12) *daqui a pouco,* soon. 13) *por pouco que seja,* however little.

poucochinho, *adj., adv.* very little; *s.m.* a little bit.

poupa, *s.f.* hoopoe; crest, tuft; topknot.

poupador, *adj.* frugal, economical, saving, thrifty.

poupança, *s.f.* economy, thrift, savings.

poupar, *v.t.* to save, to husband, to spare, to economize; to preserve, to retain; to lay by *(dinheiro),* to be economical. 1) *poupar-se,* to spare oneself, to care for oneself. 2) *não se poupar a trabalhos ou esforços,* to spare no trouble or pains.

poupudo, *adj.* tufted, crested.

pouquidade, pouquidão, *s.f.* smallness, small amount.

pouquinho, *s.m.* a little, trifle, snatch; *adj.* very little.

pouquíssimo, *adj.* very little.

pousa, *s.f.* stop; resting-place, lodge.

pousada, *s.f.* inn, country-house hotel, lodging-house.

pousadouro, *s.m.* resting-place.

pousar, *v.t.* to put down, to place; to lodge; to perch; to land.

pousio, *s.m.* fallow.

pouso, *s.m.* resting-place.

poviléu, *s.m.* populace, mob, rabble.

povo, *s.m.* people; inhabitants; crowd; nation, race, community.

póvoa, *s.f.* hamlet, small village.

povoação, *s.f.* village, settlement; population.

povoado, *s.m.* village, place, settlement; *adj.* populated, populous.

povoador, *adj.* populating, *s.m.* settler; colonist; colonizer.

povoamento, *s.m.* act of peopling; part of a forest.

povoar, *v.t.* to people, to colonize, to popilate, to settle. 1) *povoar-se,* to become populated.

povoléu, *s.m.* populace, mob, rabble, low people, rank and file.

pozolana, *s.f.* pozzolana.

potaça, *s.f.* squere; market-place; soldier; fortified place, fortress; bull-ring; the merchants of a town, auction. 1) *carro de praça,* taxi. 2) *assentar praça,* to enlist *(no exército).* 3) *pôr em praça,* to put up tp auction.

pracear, *v.t.* to sell by auction, to auction off.

praceiro, *adj.* local; public; known.

praceta, *s.f.* small square.

pracista, *s.* salesman.

pradaria, *s.f.* prairie, meadow.

prado, *s.m.* meadow, pasture ground, grassy land.

pradoso, *adj.* meadoy, abounding in meadows, grassy.

praga, *s.f.* imprecation, curse, laediction; blasphemy; plague, calamity. 1) *rogar pragas,* to curse, to imprecate.

pragal, *s.m.* wasteland, heath.

pragana, *s.f.* awn, beard.

praganoso, *adj.* awned, bearded.

pragmática, *s.f.* etiquette; rules for state occasions; formalities.

pragmático, *adj.* pragmatic(al); customary, usual.

pragmatismo, *s.m.* pragmatism.

pragmatista, *s., adj.* pragmatist.

praguedo, *s.m.* volley of oaths or curses.

praguejador, *adj.* cursing; *s.m.* curse, blasphemer.

praguejamento, *s.m.* cursing, imprecation, swering.

praguejar, *v.i.* to curse, to swear, to imprecate, to blaspheme.

praguento, *adj.* cursing, inprecatory.

praia, *s.f.* seashore, seaside; beach, stand, coast.

pralina, *s.f.* praline *(guloseima)*.

prancha, *s.f.* plank, board; stage.

pranchada, *s.f.* blow with the flat side of a sword.

pranchão, *s.m.* plank, thick board.

prancheta, *s.f.* plane-table; drawing-board.

prandial, *adj.* relating to meals.

prândio, *s.m.* repast.

prantar, *v.t.* (pop) to place, to put; to plant.

pranteadeira, *s.f.* mourner, weeper.

prateador, *s.m.* mourner, weeper; *adj.* mourning, weeping.

prantear, *v.t.* to mourn, to grive for, to lament; to cry, to weep.

pranto, *s.m.* weeping; tears.

prásimo, *s.m.* emerald *(pedra preciosa)*.

prásio, *s.m.* prase *(quartzo)*.

prata, *s.f.* silver. 1) *prata de lei,* sterling. 2) *prata dourada,* silver-gilt. 3) *bodas de prata,* silver wedding.

pratada, *s.f.* plateful.

prataria, *s.f.* silver-plate, silverware; lots of plates.

prateação, *s.f.* silvering, silver-plating.

prateado, *adj.* silvery; silver-coloured; silver--plated, argenteous; silver-grey.

prateador, *s.m.* silver player.

prateadura, *s.f.* ver prateação.

pratear, *v.t.* to silver, to plate with silver; to make silvery.

prateleira, *s.f.* case for keeping silver-ware.

prateleiro, *s.m.* silversmith.

parteleira, *s.f.* shelf; rack.

prateleiro, *s.m.* ver prateleira.

pratense, *adj.* meadowy, growing in meadows.

prática, *s.f.* practice, experience; habit; skill; discourse; drill, training; dexterity; exhortation, speech; lecture.

praticabilidade, *s.f.* praticability.

praticador, *s.m.* practician.

praticamente, *adv.* pratically.

praticante, *s.* practitioner, probationer, apprentice.

praticar, *v.t., v.i.* to practise, to exercise; to exercise; to talk, to preach; to perform; to train, to work at, to drill.

praticável, *adj.* practicable, possible, attainable.

prático, *adj.* practical, skilled, experienced; *s.m.* practician; pratique.

pratícola, *adj.* living in the meadows.

praticultor, *s.m.* cultivator of meadows.

praticultura, *s.f.* culture of meadows.

pratilheiro, *s.m.* cymbalist, cymbal player.

pratinho, *s.m.* small plate; *(fig)* laughing--stock. 1) *servir de pratinho,* to be the laughing-stock.

prato, *s.m.* dish; plate; course (ao jantar); pan; *(pl)* cymbals. 1) *jantar de dois pratos,* two-course dinner. 2) *pôr em pratos limpos,* to clear up a matter.

pravidade, *s.f.* perversity, depravity.

pravo, *adj.* perverse, wicked.

praxe, *s.f.* praxis, practice, custom, tradition. 1) *ser da praxe,* to be customary, usual, the rule.

praxista, *s.* stickler for tradition; *adj.* traditional, conventional.

prazeiro, *s.m.* flaterry, balndishment.

prazenteiramente, *adv.* joyfully, merily, jovially.

prazenteiro, *s.m.* joyful, merry, amusing, jovual, gay, cheerful.

prazer, *s.m.* pleasure delight, enjoyment, amusement, joy, happiness, satisfaction. 1) *ter prazer em,* to take pleasure in.

prazimento, *s.m.* pleasure, delight.

prazo, *s.m.* term, time. 1) *a curto prazo,* at short notice or term. 2) *acabar o prazo,* to fall due. 3) *a longo prazo,* at long term.

pré, *s.m.* daily pay *(soldados)*.

prealegar, *v.t.* to allege before.

preambular, *adj.* preambulary, introductory; *v.t.* preamble, to preface, to precede.

preâmbulo, *s.m.* preamble, perface, introduction, foreword.

preanunciação, *s.f.* preannouncement.

preanunciador, *adj.* preannouncing.

preanunciar, *v.t.* to preannounce, to announce previously.

prear, *v.t.* to seize, to take, to catch, to grab.

pré-aviso, *s.m.* pre-warning, prior notice.

prebenda, *s.f.* prebend, benefice, sinecure, stipend.

prebendar, *v.t.* to bestow a prebend, to prebendate.

prebendaria, *s.f.* prebendship.

prebendário, *s.m.* prebendary.

prebostade, *s.m.* rank of a provost, provostship.

preboste, *s.m.* provost.

precação, *s.f.* supplication, entreaty.

precariamente, *adv.* precariously.

precaridade, *s.f.* uncertainty, precariousness.

precário, *adj.* precarious, hazardous, uncertain, insecue, risky, unsafe; doubtful.

preçário, *s.m.* price-list.

precatadamente, *adv.* warily, cautiously.

precatado, *adj.* cautious, prudent, wary, careful.

precatar, *v.t.* to precaution, to warn, to forewarn. 1) *precaver-se,* to beware, to be prepared for, to take care, to be on guard.

precatória, *s.f.* rogatory, letter, deprecative letter, mandamus.

precatório, *adj.* precatory.

precaução, *s.f.* precaution, cuation, care, forethought, foresight.

precaucionar-se, *v. refle.* to be one`s guard, to take care.

precaver, *v.t.* to prevent, to obviate. 1) *precaver-se,* to take precautiion, to guarf against.

precavido, *adj.* precautions, wary, vigilant, on guard.

prece, *s.f.* prayer.

precedência, *s.f.* precedence, priority, superiority, preeminence.

precedente, *adj.* precedence, preceding, going before *(ordem do tempo, lugar, etc.):* anterior, previous, former; *s.m.* precedent.

preceder, *v.t.* to precede, to go before: to anticipate, to excel, to prevail; to have preference, to be superior.

preceito, *s.m.* precept, maxim; order, principle, rule, commandment.

preceituação, *s.f.* ordering, ruling.

preceituador, *adj.* ordering.

preceituar, *v.t.* to order, to establish; to prescribe, to give precepts.

preceituário, *s.m.* collection of precepts or maxims.

preceptivo, *adj.* preceptive, instructive.

preceptor, *s.m.* preceptor, teacher, tutor, instructor.

preceptora, *s.f.* preceptress, governess.

preceptorado, *s.m.* preceptorship.

preceptoral, *adj.* preceptorial.

preceptoria, *s.f.* preceptorate.

precessão, *s.f.* precession, precedence, anticipation, advance.

precingir, *v.t.* to gird; to strap; to enclose, to lace, to encircle.

precinta, *s.f.* band; strap.

precintar, *v.t.* to strap up, to fasten with a strap.

precinto, *s.m.* precint.

preciosamente, *adv.* preciously.

preciosidade, *s.f.* preciousness; preciosity; anything of great value.

preciosismo, *s.m.* preciosity; affectedness, euphuism; excessive refinement.

precioso, *adj.* precious, valuable, costly; splendid, excellent; affected, over-refined, pedantic; beloved, dear.

precipício, *s.m.* precipice, abyss, crag; ruin, danger, perdition.

precipitação, *s.f.* precipitation, haste, hurry, rush; ill-considered action.

precipitadamente, *adv.* precipitately, hastily, rashly.

precipitado, *adj.* precipitate, hurried, hasty, heedless; sudden; ill-judged; *s.m.* precipitate, sediment.

precipitante, *adj., s.m.* precipitant; causing the precipitation of a solution.

precipitar, *v.t.* to precipitate; to throw headlong; to hasten, to rush, to hurry up, to fly; to hurl down; to deposit, to subside. 1) *precipitar-se,* to rush headlong; to act hastly.

precípite, *adj.* precipitated, hasty, speedy, hurried; danger of falling.

precipitoso, *adj.* precipitous, very steep; rash, inconsiderate, abrupt.

precípuo, *adj.* principal, essential, aim, foremost, paramount.

precisado, *adj.* needy, poor.

precisamente, *adv.* precisely, exactly, quite so, absolutely.

precisão, *s.f.* want, need, lack, necessity, poverty; preciseness, exactness, accuracy.

precisar, *v.i.* to need, to want, to necessitate, to be short of, to stand in need; to state exactly, to particularize, to fix; to require, to demand. 1) *criada, precisa-se,* servant wanted.

preciso, *adj.* necessary, needful, indispensable, required; exact, definite, accurate, precise, just, correct.

precito, *s.m.* reprobate; *adj.* condemned to hell, damned.

preclaro, *adj.* famous, notable, illustrious, renowned; pre-eminent, bright, brilliant.

pré-clássico, *adj.* preclassic(al).

preço, *s.m.* price, cost, value; estimation; worth, charge, compensation, reward, prize; expense, rate. 1) *preço de custo,* cost-price. 2) *preço médio,* average price. 3) *preço de fábrica,* manufacturer`s price. 4) *preço corrente,* ruling price. 5) *preço de concorrência,* competitive price. 6) *preço justo,* fair price. 7) *preço de factura,* invoice price. 8) *preço fixo,* set price. 9) *preço de venda,* sale price. 10) *preço de revenda,* trade (or wholesale) price. 11) *o mínimo preço,* the lowest price. 12) *preço líquido,* net price. 13) *preço de ocasião,* bargain price. 14) *preço com tudo incluído,* inclusive terms.

precoce, *adj.* precocious, premature, untimely; *adv.* precociously, too early.

precocemente, *adj.* precociously, prematurely.

precocidade, *s.f.* precocity; precociousness, prematurity.

precogitar, *v.t.* to precogitate, to plan, to premeditate, to contrive.

precognição, *s.f.* precognition.

precógnito, *adj.* known before, foreseen.

preconceber, *v.t.* to plan befoehand, to preconceive.

preconceito, *s.m.* preconceit, prejudice; superstition; bias *(contra ou a favor de);* preconceived opinion.

preconização, *s.f.* preconization.

preconizador, *s.m.* preconizer.

preconizar, *v.t.* to preconize, to proclaim; to praise, to commend.

precursor, *s.m.* precursor, forerunner, precessor, pioneer; herald; *adj.* preceding, precursory.

predatório, *adj.* predatory, pillaging, plundering.

predecessor, *s.m.* predecessor, antecessor.

predefinição, *s.f.* predifinition, predetermination, prognostication.

predefinir, *v.t.* to predefine.

predestinação, *s.f.* predestination, fate, destiny.

predestinado, *adj.* predestinate, predestined; *s.m.* elect.

predestinar, *v.t.* to predestinate, to foredoom, to foredain, to predestine.

predeterminação, *s.f.* predetermination, foreordainment, preordination.

predeterminar, *v.t.* to predetermine, to preordain, to preorder.

predial, *adj.* predial. 1) *contribuição predial,* land *(propriedades, casa)* tax.

prédica, *s.f.* sermon, preaching, preachment.

predicação, *s.f.* preachmente; predication, assertion.

predicado, *s.m.* predicate; virtue, quality, attribute, capacity; aptitude.

predicador, *s.m.* preacher.

predicamental, *adj.* predicamental.

predicamentar, *v.t.* to class, to classify.

predicamento, *s.m.* predicament, category, class, order, degree.

predicante, *s.m.* predicant, preacher; *adj.* preaching.

perdição, *s.f.* prediction; forecast; prophecy, vatication.

predicar, *v.t.* to preach, to predicate; to admonish, to counsel.

predicativo, *adj.* predicative.

predicatório, *adj.* predicatory, laudatory, encomiastic, flattering.

predicável, *adj.* predicable.

predilecção, *s.f.* predilection, preferencve, inclination, liking, leaning.

predilecto, *adj., s.m.* favourite, beloved, dear.

pré-diluviano, *adj.* antediluvian.

prédio, *s.m.* house, builfing, edifice; estate, property.

predisoinência, *s.f.* predisponency, predisposition.

predisponente, *adj.* predisponent, predisposing, predetermining.

predispor, *v.t.* to predispose, to prepare, to prearrange, to adapt previously; to prepossess, to prejudice *(contra).*

predisposição, *s.f.* inclination, predisposition, bent, tendency, vocation, inclination.

predisposto, *adj.* predisposed, prone.

predizer, *v.t.* to foretell, to predict, to presage, to prophesy, to vaticinate.

predominação, *s.f.* predominancy, ascendeancy, preponderance, prevalence.

predominador, *adj.* predominant, predominating.

predominância, *s.f.* predominance, preponderance, influence.

predominante, *adj.* predominant, predominating.

predominantemente, *adv.* predominantly.

predominar, *v.i.* to predominate, to prevail, to exceed, to preponderate, to surpass.

predomínio, *s.m.* preponderance, predominance, supremacy, power, supriority.

preeminência, *s.f.* pre-eminence, distinction, superiority.

preeminente, *adj.* pre-eminent, superior, remakable, distinguished.

preempção, *s.f.* pre-emption.

preencher, *v.t.* to fill; to ccupy, to perform, to fulfill. 1) *preencher um cheque,* to fill out a cheque. 2) *preencher uma vaga,* to fill a vacancy. 3) *preencher uma lacuna,* to fill a gap.

preenchimento, *s.m.* fulfilling, filling in; performance, accomplishment.

preesão, *s.f.* prehension, seizing, grasping, understanding.

preênsil, *adj.* prehensile, seizing, grasping.

pré-escolar, *adj.* precollege.

preestabelecer, *v.t.* to pre-establish, to predeterminate, to arrange preciously, to settle beforehand.

preexcelência, *s.f.* superexcellence.

preexcelente, *adj.* surpexcellent.

preexcelso, *adj.* eminent, sublime, grand.

preexistência, *s.f.* pre-existence.

preexistente, *s.f.* pre-existence, preceding.

preexistir, *v.i.* to pre-exist.

prefabricação, *s.f.* prefabrication.

prefabricar, *v.t.* prefabricate.

prefação, *s.f.* prologue, preface, premble.

prefaciador, *s.m.* prefacer.

prefaciar, *v.t.* to preface; to introduce.

prefácio, *s.m.* preface, exordium, introduction, foreword, preamble.

prefeito, *s.m.* prefect, monitor; mayor.

prefeitoral, *adj.* prefectoral.

prefeitura, *s.f.* prefecture; office, state or jurisdiction of a perfect; city hall.

preferência, *s.f.* preference, predilection, liking; priority; option, alternative; 1) *de preferência,* prefarably, in preference.

preferente, *adj.* preferring; *s.m.* preferrer.

preferir, *v.t.* to prefer, to like better, to give preference to, to choose; to be preferred; to have rather.

preferível, *adj.* preferable, better, more desirable.

preferivelmente, *adv.* prefarably, rather.

prefiguração, *s.f.* prefiguration, prefigurement, foreshadowing.

prefigurar, *v.t.* to prefigure, to foreshadow.

prefixação, *s.f.* prefixion, prefixation; pre-appointment.

prefixar, *v.t.* to prefix; to appoint in advance, to fix or to set at the beginning.

prefixo, *s.m.* prefix; *adj.* prefixed.

prefloração, **preflorescência,** *s.f.* prefloration, aestivation.

prefoliação, *s.f.* prefoliation, vernation.

prefulgência, *s.f.* brightness; resplendence.

prefulgente, *adj.* bright, replendent, outshining.

prefulgir, *v.i.* to shine, to glitter; to be resplendent, to sparkle.

prega, *s.f.* fold, plait, crease, pleat.

pregação, *s.f.* nailing.

pregação(é), *s.f.* preaching, sermon, lecture.

pregadeira, *s.f.* pincase, pincushion.

pregador, *s.m.* nailer, fastener.

pregador, *s.m.* preacher.

pregadura, *s.f.* quantity of nails; nailwork.

pregão, *s.m.* street cry; proclamation; *(pl)* banns *(casamento);* the cries of the street venders.

pregar, *v.t.* to nail, to rivet, to spike, to fix, to fasten, to peg, to stick in; to sew on *(botão).* 1) *pregar um prego,* to fix a nail. 2) *pregar uma partida,* to play a trick on. 3) *não pregar olho,* not to sleep a wink. 4) *pregar os olhos em,* to fix someone. 5) *pregar uma peta,* to teel a lie. 6) *pregar uma bofetada,* to slap or to box someone´s ears or face. 7) *pregar um susto,* to give a fright to.

pregar(é), *v.t., v.i.* to preach; to proclaim; to discourse; to sermonize, to exhort, to lecture. 1) *pregar um sermão a alguém,* to lecture a person. 2) *pregar no deserto (aos peixes)* to preach in vain, to cry out in the desert.

pregareta, *s.f.* Dominican nun.

pregaria, *s.f.* lot of nails; nailworks; nail-factory.

pré-glacial, pré-galciário, *adj.* pre-glacial.

prego, *s.m.* nail, spike; *(pop)* pawnshop. 1) *pôr no prego,* to pawn, to leave at uncle`s . 2) *carta de prego,* sealed orders.

pregoar, *v.t.* to cry; to proclaim, to publish, to divulge.

pregoeiro, *s.m.* crier, proclaimer; auctionnier, bidder.

pregresso, *adj.* prior, previous, antecedent, former.

pregueadeira, *s.f.* crisping-iron; crimper, former.

pregueado, *s.f.* pleated, tucked; *s.m.* pleat, folding.

preguear, *v.t.* to fold, to plait, to crimp, to pleat.

pregueiro, *s.m.* nail-maker or seller.

preguiça, s.f. laziness, idleness, indolence; (zool) sloth.

preguiça, v.i. to idle, to laze, to lounge; to lie abed.

preguiceira, s.f. couch, sofa, easy-chair, deck-chair.

preguiceiro, s.m., adj. couch, lounge, sofa; lazy, idle.

preguicento, adj. idle, lazy, indolent, laggard, slothful, sluggush; s.m. idler, lazy-bones, lie-a-bed, do-nothing.

preguilha, preguinha, s.f. small pleat, tuck.

preguista, s. pawnbroker.

pregustação, s.f. foretasting, forestaste, pregustation.

pregustar, v.i. to foretaste.

pré-história, s.f. prehistory.

pré-histórico, adj. prehistoric(al).

praia-mar, s.f. high-water, high-tide.

preitear, preitejar, v.t. to do, to play or to render homage to.

preito, s.m. homage, respect, reverence.

prejudicador, s.m. mischief-maker.

prejudicar, v.t. to prejudice; to damage; to injure, to hurt, to impair, to harm.

prejudicial, adj. prejudicial, injurious, hurtful, harmful, detrimental, ill; mischievous.

prejuízo, s.m. prejudice; damage, wrong, detriment, loss, impairment, injury; prejudgement, bias, leaning.

prelação, s.f. prelation, preference, preferment.

prelacia, s.f. prelacy, prelateship.

prelada, s.f. prelatedd, abbess, prioress.

prelado, s.m. prelate (bispo ou arcebispo).

prelatício, adj. prelatical, prelatial.

prelatura, s.f. prelature.

prelazia, s.f. prelacy.

prelecção, s.f. prelection, lecture, lesson, dissertation; sermon.

preleccionar, v.i. to prelect, to lecturer.

prelector, s.m. prelector, lecturer.

prelevar, v.t. to surmount, to outdo, to raise; to excuse.

prelibação, s.f. prelibation, foretaste; antecipatio.

prelibador, s.m. foretaster; adj. foretasting.

prelibar, v.t. to foretaste, to antecipate the enjoyment.

preliminar, adj. preliminary, introductory, prefatory, preparatory; s.m. preliminary.

prélio, s.m. fight, battle, conflict, combat, struggle.

prelo, s.m. press, printing press.

prelucidação, s.f. preliminary explanation, previous elucidation.

prelúcido, adj. shining, bright, very clear.

preludiar, v.t. to prelude; to preface; to introduce by a prelude; to play a prelude; to foreshadow.

prelúdio, s.m. prelude, introduction, preface; ouverture.

preluzente, adj. very bright.

preluzir, v.i. shine intensely, to be very bright.

prema, s.f. constraint, oppression.

premar, v.t. to oppress.

prematuração, s.f. prematurity, precocity, earliness.

prematuramente, s.f. prematurely.

prematuridade, s.f. ver prematuração.

prematuro, adj. premature, precocious, untimely; too easy.

premedeura, s.f. treadle.

premeditação, s.f. premeditaion, forethought.

premeditadamente, adv. deliberately.

premeditado, adj. deliberate, studied.

premeditar, v.t. to premeditate, to scheme, to plan, to contrive, to design.

premência, s.f. pressure, urgency.

premente, adj. pressing, urgent, forcing.

premer, v.t. to press; to oppress, to squeeze, to urge, to hasten.

premiador, sm. rewarder; adj. rewarding.

premiar, v.t. to reward, to recompense, to remunerate, to give a prize to, to repay.

pré-militar, adj. premilitary (treino).

prémio, s.m. prize, reward; bonus; premium; gain, profit, interest. 1) prémio de seguro, premium of insurance. 2) prémio de consolação, booby prize.

premir, v.t. ver premer.

premissa, s.f. premiss, premise, reason, supposition.

pré-molar, s.m. adj. premolar (dente).

premonitório, adj. premonitory, premonitive.

premunição, s.f. premonition, forewarning.

premunir, v.t. to forewarn; to prevent, to avert. 1) premunir-se, to be prepared, to be on one´s guard.

pré-natal, adj. prenatal, previous to birth.

prenda, s.f. gift, present, favour; talent, ability, token, proof; bad person (irónico); (pl) talents, endowments. 1) jogo das prendas, game of forefeits.

prendado, adj. talented, endowed, gifted.

prendar, v.t. to present with, to give a present to, to bestow on.

prendedor, s.m. fastener, staple, clasp, clip.

prender, v.t. to size, to hold; to hinder; to capture; to attach, to fasten, to arrest, to imprison, to lock in; to fascinate, to charm; to stick to.

prenhe, adj. pregnant, gravid; full, replete.

prenhez, s.f. pregnancy, gestation, child-bearing.

prenhidão, s.f. ver prenhez.

prenoção, s.f. foreknowledge, prenotion, preconception.

prenome, s.m. prenomen, Christian name, first name.

prenotação, s.f. prenotation.

prenotar, v.t. to note beforehand.

prensa, s.f. press.

prensador, s.m. presser, pressman.

prensagem, s.f. pressing, squeezing.

prensar, v.t. to crush; to press, to compress, to squeeze.

prenseiro, s.m. presser.

prensista, s. presser.

prenunciação, s.f. foreboding, prenunciation, prophecy, prediction.

prenunciador, s.m. foreteller, predictor, foreshadower; adj. foretelling, foreboding.

prenunciar, v.t. to foretell, to vaticinate, to forebode, to predict, to presage, to prophesy.

prenunciativo, adj. predictive, presaging, prophetic.

prenúncio, s.m. foretelling, prognostic, foreboding, presage, prediction, prophecy, forewarning, sign.

preocupação, s.f. preoccupation; anxiety; care, concern, worriment, apprehension, prepossession.

preocupado, adj. preoccupied, troubled, worried, uneasy, anxious, concerned.

preocupante, adj. worrying; s. preoccupier, previous occupant.

preocupar, v.t. to preoccupy, to absorb, to worry, to disturb, to cause anxiety. 1) preocupar-se, to become aprehensive, to be worried.

pré-operatório, adj. preoperative.

preopinante, adj. speaking before; s. previous speaker.

preopinar, v.t. to speak before.

preordenação, s.f. preordination, foreordination; predetermination.

preordenar, v.t. to preordain; to predetermine, to preestablish.

preparação, s.f. preparation; training; confection, manufacture.

preparado, s.m. preparation; adj. prepared, ready.

preparador, s.m. assistant; preparer, adj. preparing, preparatory.

preparar, v.t. to prepare; to fit; to make ready; to arrange; to instruct, to teach; to equip; to dispose. 1) preparar-se, to get ready; to prepare oneself.

preparativo, s.m. (pl) preparatives; adj. preparatory.

preparatório, adj. preparatory; s.m. (pl) preparatory studies.

preparo, s.m. preparation; (pl) first coast; notions for dressing.

preponderância, s.f. preponderance, predominance, superiority, supremacy, power, prevalence.

preponderante, adj. preponderant, prevailing, predominant, superior, prevalent.

preponderar, v.i. to predominate, to prevail, to exceed; to overbear, to overweigh.

preponente, adj. preposing, undertaking; s. proposer, enterpriser.

prepor, v.t. to prefix; to place before; to prefer; to preplace.

preposição, s.f. preposition.

preposicional, adj. prepositional.

prepositivo, adj. prepositive, placed before, prefixed.

prepósito, s.m. purpose, intention, design, aim, end.

preposteração, s.f. preposterousness, absurdity.

preposterar, v.t. to preposterate, to invert, to reverse.

preposteridade, s.f. ver preposteração.

prepóstero, adj. preposterpous, reversed; absurd; foolish.

preposto, adj. prefixed, preferred.

prepotência, s.f. prepotency, oppresion, despotism, absolutism, tirany.

prepotente, adj. prepotent, powerful; oppressing, overbearing, despotic, tyrant.

prenupcial, adj. prepuptial.

prepúcio, s.m. prepice.

pré-romano, adj. pre-Roman.

pré-romântico, adj. pre-romantica.

pré-romantismo, s.m. pre-romanticism.

prerrogativa, s.f. prerogative, privilege.

presa, *s.f.* capture, seizure, booty; fang, claw; dam *(água)*.

presbíope, *s.m.* presbyope.

presbiopia, *s.f.* presbyopia.

presbita, *s.* presbyope, presbyte; *adj.* presbyopic, long-sighted.

presbiterado, *s.m.* presbyterate.

presbiteral, *adj.* presbyterial.

presbiteranismo, *s.m.* ver presbiterianismo.

presbiterano, *adj.* ver presbiteriano.

presbiterato, *s.m.* presbyterate.

presbiterianismo, *s.m.* Presbyterianism, Presbyterism.

presbitariano, *adj., s.m.* Presbyterian.

presbitério, *s.m.* presbytery, presbyter`s house.

presbítero, *s.m.* presbyter; priest.

presbitia, *s.f.* presbyopia, far-sightedness.

presbitismo, *s.m.* ver presbitia.

presciência, *s.f.* precience, foresight, foreknowledge, prevision.

presciente, *adj.* prescient, foreknowing, foreseeing.

prescindir, *v.i.* to prescind, to cut off, to leave out; to renounce, to do without, to give up.

prescindível, *adj.* dispensable.

prescrever, *v.t.* to prearrange; to prescribe, to lay down; to become void; to lapse, to exist no more, to fall into disuse.

prescribente, *adj.* prescriptive.

prescrição, *s.f.* prescription, command, order, rule; lapse, forfeiture.

prescritível, *adj.* prescriptible.

prescrito, *adj.* prescribed, ordained, ordered, set down.

presença, *s.f.* presence, being present; aspect, appearance; mien, air.

presencial, *adj.* present. 1) *testemunha presencial,* eye witness.

presenciar, *v.t.* to be present; to witness, to see, to observe.

presente, *adj.* present, existing now, existent, here; *s.m.* actuality, the present time, present; the present tense; gift, present. 1) *ter presente,* to be bear in mind. 2) *ofício de corpo presente,* lying in state.

presenteador, *adj.* presenting; *s.m.* presenter.

presentear, *v.t.* to give presents, to bestow, to offer as a gift.

presentemente, *adv.* presently; at present, now.

presepe, presépio, *s.m.* crib.

prevenção, *s.f.* preservation, conservation, keeping.

preservador, *s.m.* preserver; *adj.* preserving, preservative.

preservar, *v.t.* to preserve, to keep safe, to protect, to keep from decay, to save from injury, to guard; to retain.

preservativo, *adj., s.m.* preservative, prophylatic, preventive.

presidência, *s.f.* presidency, chairmanship.

presidencial, *adj.* presidential.

presidencialismo, *s.m.* presidentialism.

presidencialista, *s., adj.* presidentialist.

presidente, *s.m.* president, chairman. 1) *presidente do Conselho de Ministros,* Prime Minister. 2) *presidente da Câmara Municipal,* Lord Mayor.

presidiar, *v.t.* to garrison, to defend.

presidiário, *s.m.* cpnvict, prisoner; *adj.* presidiary.

presídio, *s.m.* prison; garrison, fortress; penitentiary.

presidir, *v.i.* to presid, to superintend, to manage, to administer; to take the chair.

presigo, *s.m.* anything eaten along with bread alone *(presunto, bacon).*

presilha, *s.f.* loop; starp.

preso, *adj.* arrested, imprisoned, captive, jailed; *s.m.* prisoner.

pressa, *s.f.* haste, hurry, urgency, celerity, speed. 1) *a toda a pressa,* in great haste. 2) *estar com pressa,* to be in a hurry.

pressagiador, *s.m.* presager, foreboder; *adj.* foreboding, ominous.

pressagiar, *v.t.* to presage, to forebode, to foretell, to portend; to vaticinate; to prophesy, to prognosticate, to betoken.

presságio, *s.m.* presage, prognostic, pressentiment, sign, augury, foreboding, prophecy.

pressagioso, *adj.* presageful.

pressago, *adj.* presageful, foreboding, ominous, presagious.

pressão, *s.f.* pressure; pression, compulsion; strain, stress. 1) *pressão de água,* water pressure. 2) *pressão atmosférica,* air pressure. 3) *panela de pressão,* pressure cooker.

pressentido, *adj.* foreseen; having a presentiment.

pressentimento, *s.m.* presentiment, foreboding; apprehension; suspicion.

pressentir, *v.t.* to foresee; to forebode, to have a presentiment, to suspect.

pressupor, v.t. to presuppose, to imply, to involve; to assume, to take for granted.

pressuposição, s.f. presupposition; surmise; presumption, conjecture.

pressuposto, s.m. presupposition; design, purpose; adj. presupposed, assumed.

pressurosamente, adv. hastily, hurriedly; eagerly.

pressuroso, adj. hasty, hurried, speedy, swift, quick; impatient, eager, keen.

prestabilidade, s.f. unsefulness.

prestação, s.f. instalment; leading; contribution.

prestadio, adj. serviceable.

prestamista, s. money-lender; pawn-broker.

prestança, prestância, s.f. utility, usefulness; comvinience; kindness.

prestante, adj. obliging; useful; excellent.

prestar, v.i. to be useful, to be good for; to give, to render; to lend. 1) prestar-se, to be of use, to be willing. 2) prestar atenção, to listen to. 3) prestar auxílio, to render assistance. 4) prestas contas, to render account. 5) prestar juramento, to take an oath. 6) não prestar para nada, to be good for nothing.

prestável, adj. obliging; useful; kind; helpful.

prestes, adj. ready to, prepared; about to, on the point of.

presteza, s.f. quickness, promptitude, promptness; rapidity, celerity, agility.

prestidigitação, s.f. prestidigitation, magic, juggkery, sleight of hand.

prestidigitador, s.m. pretidigitator, juggler, conjurer, magician.

prestigiação, s.f. conjuring, sorcery, wirchcraft.

prestigiafor, s.m. conjurer, juggler, impostor.

prestigiante, adj. prestigious, influential.

prestigiar, v.t. to give prestige to, to render important.

prestígio, s.m. prestige, reputation; influence, credit.

prestigioso, adj. respected; prestigious, important, influential.

prestímano, s.m. pretidigitator.

préstimo, s.m. utility, usefulness; merit; service.

pretimoso, adj. useful, serviceable.

préstito, s.m. train; procession.

presto, adj., adv. quick, speedy, agile, ready; quickly, soon, immediately.

presumido, adj. presuming; presumptuous, self-conceited, arrogant, vain.

presumidor, s.m. conjecturer, presumer.

presumir, v.t. to presume; to suppose; to conjecture, to think, to imagine.

presumível, adj. presumable, probable, surmisable.

presumivelmente, adv. presumably.

presunção, s.f. presumption, suspicion, conjecture, guess; arrogance, self-conceit, affectation, vanity.

presunçoso, adj. presumptuous, arrogant, self-conceited, uppish.

presunho, s.m. dewclaw.

presuntivo, adj. presumptive, probable.

presunto, s.m. smoked ham.

presúris, s.f. dam, dike.

preta, s.f. negro woman, negress.

pretalhada, s.f. crowd of negroes.

pretalhão, s.m. stout negro.

pretaria, s.f. ver pretalhada.

pretendente, s.m. pretender, candidate, suitor, claimant; adj. pretending.

pretender, v.t. to pretend, to claim; to aspire to, to endeavour, to attempt; to mean, to assume; to suit, to woo; to intend.

pretendida, s.f. intended (mulher); sweetheart, fiancée.

pretensão, s.f. pretence, claim, pretension, aim, design; intention, sumption; ambition.

pretensiosamente, adv. pretensiously, ostentatiously.

pretensioso, adj. pretensious, affected; arrogant; vain, self-conceited, presuming.

pretenso, adj. supposed, alleged, assumed, false.

preterição, s.f. preterition, omission, disregard; protponement.

preterir, v.t. to pass over, to omit, to pretermin; to defer, to postpone.

pretérito, s.m. past tense; adj. past. preterit, bygone. 1) pretérito mais-que-perfeito, pluperfect tense.

preterível, adj. that may be pretermitted.

pretermissão, s.f. pretermission, omission, preterition.

pretermitir, v.i. to pretermit, to omit, to overlook, to neglect.

preternatural, adj. preternatural, supernatural, miraculous.

pretextar, v.t. to pretext, to allege; to pretend, to feign.

pretexto, s.m. pretext, excuse, pretence,

cover, reason, motive; simulation, subterfuge.

pretidão, s.f. blackness.

preto, adj., s.m. black; negro. 1) *preto no branco,* in cold print, in black and white.

pretor, s.m. praetor.

pretoriano, adj., s.m. praetorian.

pretório, s.m. praetorium.

prevalecente, adj. prevalent, prevailing, current.

prevalecer, v.i. to prevail, to predominate. 1) *prevalecer-se,* to take advantage of, to avail oneself of.

prevalência, s.f. prevalence, predominance, superiority.

prevaicação, s.f. prevarication, embezzlement, forfeiture, maversation.

prevaricador, s.m. prevaricator, transgressor, quibbler.

prevaricar, v.i. to prevaricate, to sin, to transgress, to trespass; to violate or break a law; to prevert, to abase.

prevenção, s.f. prevention, precaution; prejudice, preconception; warning.

prevenido, adj. forewarned; advised, informed; cautions, on one`s guard.

preveniente, adj. prevenient, precedent; preventive.

prevenir, v.t. to forestall; to anticipate; warn; to caution, to alarm. 1) *prevenir-se,* to provide against, to be on one`s guard. 2) *mais vale prevenir do que remediar,* a stitch in time saves nine, prevention is better than cure.

preventivo, adj. preventive, prophylactic.

prever, v.t. to foresee, to antecipate; to reckon, to suppose, to expect.

previamente, adj. previously.

previdência, s.f. providence; prevision, foresight, forethought; precaution, prudence.

previdente, adj. cautious, prevident, prudent, far-seeing.

previdentemente, adv. providently, cautiously.

prévio, adj. previous, prior; former; earlier; preliminary. 1) *aviso prévio,* previous notice.

previsão, s.f. prevision, foresight; forecast (weather).

previsibilidade, s.f. previsibility.

previsível, adj. previsible, foreseeable.

previsto, adj. foreseen, anticipated; fixed; expected.

prezado, adj. dear, esteemed.

prezar, v.t. to esteem, to cherish, to consider highly, to value, to respect; to appreciate, to prize, to honour.

prezável, adj. estimable, respectable, praiseworthy.

prima, s.f. female-cousin; *(mús)* first string; first canonical hour.

primacial, adj. primatial, superior; essential, fundamental.

primado, s.m. primateship, primacy, priority, supremacy.

prima-dona, s.f. prima donna *(ópera).*

primar, v.i. to surpass; to take the lead of; to excel, to rank first; to do the very best.

primariamente, adv. firstly; primarily.

primário, adj. primary, fundamental, first, principal; narrowminded, limited; primitive; chief.

primatas, primates, s.m. *(pl)* Primates.

Primavera, s.f. spring; primrose (bot); youth; *(pl)* years *(aniversário).*

primaveral, primaveril, adj. vernal.

primaz, s.m. primate; adj. prime.

primazia, s.f. primateship, primacy, priority, superiority, preference.

primeira, s.f. 1) *à primeira vista,* at first sight.

primeiramente, adv. firstly, in the first place.

primeiranista, s. a first year student *(universidade).*

primeiro, adj. first; earliest; chief; primitive; fundamental, principal, main. 1) *primeiro plano,* foreground. 2) *primeiro que tudo,* first of all. 3) *de primeira (qualidade),* tiptop, firstrate.

primeiro-ministro, s.m. prime minister.

primeiro-sargento, s.m. segeant-major.

primeiro-tenete, s.m. first lieutenant.

primevo, adj. primeval, primitive, original.

primícias, s.f. *(pl)* primitiae, first-lings; the first fruits; firstproduction of anything.

primigénio, primígeno, adj. primigenial, primitive, primordial.

primina, s.f. primine *(bot).*

primípara, adj. primiparous.

primitiva, s.f. *(pop)* the ancient times; beginning.

primitivamente, adv. primitively, at the beginning, originally, formerly.

primitivo, adj. primitive, original; primordial; rudimental, simple, rude; old-fashioned.

primo, s.m. cousin, male-cousin; adj. first; prime *(número).* 1) *matéria-prima,* raw material. 2) *obra-prima,* masterwork, masterpiece.

primogénito, adj. primogenital, first-born, eldest.

primogenitor, s.m. primogenitor, ancestor, forefather.

primogenitura, s.f. primogeniture.

primor, s.m. perfection, excellence; beauty, nicety, delicacy; exectness, accuracy; skilfulness.

primordial, adj. primordial, primeval, original, primitive.

primórdio, s.m. origin, beginning.

primorosamente, adv. perfectly, nicely, excellently; elegantly; precisely.

primorose, adj. perfect, nice, excellent; masterly; accurate, precise; neat, impeccable.

primceps, adj. first (edição).

princesa, s.f. princess. 1) princesa real, princess royal.

principado, s.m. princedom; principality.

principal, adj. principal, chief, main; s.m. principal, headmaster, leader, chief.

principalidade, s.f. primacy, preeminence, principalness.

principalmente, adv. principally, chiefly, mainly.

príncipe, s.m. primnce; adj. principal, first, prime. 1) príncipe consorte, prince consort. 2) príncipe herdeiro, crown prince. 3) edição príncipe, first edition.

principescamente, adv. in a princely manner.

principesco, adj. princely, stately, magnificent.

principiante, s.m. beginner, novice, principiant, apprentice, tyro.

principair, v.t. to begin, to commence, to start, to initiate.

princípio, s.m. beginning, start, commencement; starting-point; maxim, axiom; principale, the first cause. 1) a (ao) princípio, at first, at the beginning. 2) desde o princípio, from the very beginning. 3) por princípio, on principle. 4) os princípios, the rudiments; source, origin.

prior, s.m. parish-priest, prior.

priora, s.f. prioress.

priorado, priorato, s.m. priorate, priorship, dignity of a prior or prioress; period of a priorship.

prioresa, s.f. prioress.

prioridade, s.f. priority, primacy, preference, precedence.

prisão, s.f. capture, detention; prison, jail; imprisonment, arrest, seizure. 1) sob prisão, under arrest. 2) ordem de prisão, warrant. 3) prisão de venter, constipation.

prisca, s.f. cigarette end.

prisco, adj. pristine, ancient.

prisional, adj. relating to prison.

prisioneiro, s.m. prisoner, captive. 1) prisioneiro de guerra, prisoner of war. 2) prisioneiro político, prisoner of state. 3) fazer prisineiro, take prisoner.

prisma, s.m. prism.

prismático, adj. prismatic.

pristino, adj. ancient, pristine, primitive, original, primeval.

privação, s.f. privation, lack, want, need, destitution; (pl) hardships.

privada, s.f. water-closet, latrine, privy, toilet, lavatory, bathroom.

privadamente, adv. privately.

privado, adj. private; retired; secret, confidential, not public, familiar, personal; deprived, destituted; s.m. favourite. 1) conselho privado, privy counsellor. 2) selo privado, privy seal. 3) vida privada, personal life.

privança, s.f. intimacy, favour. 1) ter privança com, to be in favour with.

privar, v.t. to deprive, to dispossess, to strip of, to debar from; to hinder; to be in favour of, to be intimate with. 1) privar-se, to deprive oneself of, to abstain from.

privadamente, adv. exclusively.

privativo, adj. exclusive, peculiar, proper, privative.

privilegiadamente, adv. with privilege.

privilegiado, adj. pribileged, favoured.

privilegiar, v.t. to privilege, to grant a privilege; to exempt from.

privilégio, s.m. privilege, advantage, immunity, prerogarive.

pró, s.m. pro, advantage, reason; adv. por, for, in favour of. 1) os prós e os contras, the pros and cons. 2) nem prá nem contra, neither for nor against.

proa, s.f. head, stem, prow, bow; swank, airs, pride, presumption, vanity.

probabilidade, s.f. probability, likelihood; chance, prospect.

probabilismo, s.m. probabilism.

probabilista, s. probabilist.

probante, adj. probative, proving, authentic, evidential, convincing.

probatório, adj. probative, probational, affording proof.

probidade, *s.f.* probity, honesty, integrity.
problema, *s.m.* problem; doubt, quiz.
problematicamente, *adv.* problematically.
problemático, *adj.* problematical; doubtful, uncertain, questionable.
problematizar, *v.t.* to put in doubt, to render problematic.
probo, *adj.* honest, upright, trusrworthy, good.
probóscida, *s.f.* proboscis.
proboscídeo, *adj.* proboscidean; *s.m. (pl)* Proboscidea.
procace, *adj.* ver procaz.
procacidade, *s.f.* petulance, forwardness, pertness, insolence, impudence.
procaína, *s.f.* procaine.
procaz, *adj.* procacious, petulent, saucy, insolent.
procedência, *s.f.* provenance, origin, source, provenience.
procedente, *adj.* precceding, coming, from, sprung, arising from; consequent; valid.
proceder, *v.i.* to proceed to go on; to behave, to act, to deal; to spring from, to arise from; to proceed against; to take legal action. 1) *proceder de boa-fé,* to act in good faith. 2) *proceder honestamente,* to play fair. 3) *proceder de má-fé,* to play foul.
procedimento, *s.m.* behavious, proceeding, conduct, manners.
procela, *s.f.* storm, tempest.
procelária, *s.f.* procellaria, petrel, strom-bird.
proceloso, *adj.* stromy, tempestuous.
prócer, prócere, *s.m.* magnate, chief, head.
proceridade, *s.f.* procerity.
prócero, *adj.* procere, high, lofty.
processamento, *s.m.* making up (*um processo*), processing.
processão, *s.f.* proceeding, origin.
processar, *v.t.* to process; to proceed aginst; to sue, to prosecute, to take action against.
processional, *adj.* processional.
processionário, *s.m.* processional book.
processo, *s.m.* process, way, method, procedure, manner; course, cycle; documents; lawsuit. 1) *instaurar um processo,* to take proceedings against. 2) *processo disciplinar,* disciplinary proceeding.
processual, *adj.* processual.
procissão, *s.f.* procession; train.
proclama, *s.m.* banns; proclamation.
proclamação, *s.f.* proclamation, announcement; declaration.

proclamador, *adj., s.m.* proclaiming; proclaimer.
proclamar, *v.t.* to proclaim; to publish, to promulgate, to announce officially, to declare publicly.
proclamatório, *adj.* proclamatory.
próclise, *s.f.* proclisis.
proclítica, *s.f.* proclitic.
proclítico, *adj.* proclitic.
proclive, *adj.* proclive, proclivous, inclined.
proclividade, *s.f.* proclivity, inclination.
procônsul, *s.m.* proconsul.
proconsulado, *s.m.* proconsulate, proconsulship.
proconsular, *adj.* proconsular.
procrastinação, *s.f.* delay, procrastination, deferment, putting off.
procrastinador, *adj.* procrastinating dilatory; *s.m.* procrastinator.
procrastinar, *v.t.* to procrastinate, to defer, to delay, to postpone; to be dilatory.
procriação, *s.f.* procreation, generation, breeding.
procriador, *adj.* procreative, progenitive; *s.m.* procreator.
procriar, *v.t.* to procreate, to beget, to generate; to produce, to germinate.
procura, *s.f.* search, quest, demand, pursuit, inquiry. 1) *lei da oferta e da procura,* law of supply and demand. 2) *à procure de,* in search of.
procuração, *s.f.* procuration, proxy, power of attorney, mandate. 1) *por procuração,* by proxy.
procurador, *s.m.* procurator; solicitor, sttorney, proxy, agent, mandatary, trustee. 1) *procurador-geral,* attorney General.
procuradoria, *s.f.* procuratorship; procuracy; procurato`s fees.
procurar, *v.t.* to search, to look for, to seek for; to try, to attempt; to rey to obtain; to endeavour; to visit, to call on.
procuratório, *adj.* procuratory.
prodigalidade, *s.f.* prodigality, extravagance, lavishness; profusion, plenty, abundance, copiousness.
prodigalizador, *adj.* prodigal, profuse, lavish; *s.m.* prodigal, spendthrift, waster.
prodigalizar, *v.t.* to prodigalize, to waste, to lavish, to dissipate.
pordigamente, *adv.* prodigally, wastefully.
prodigar, *v.t.* ver prodigalizar.
prodígio, *s.m.* prodigy, wonder, marvel, poetent; miracle, phenomen.

prodigiosamente, *adv.* prodigiously, marvellously.

prodigioso, *adj.* prodigious, wonderful, astounding, marvellous, amazing, portentous, extraordinary; immense, vast, enormous.

pródigo, *s.m., adj.* prodigal; wasteful, lavish, spendthrift.

proditor, *s.m.* traitor, betrayer.

porditório, *adj.* treacherous, perfidous.

prodrómico, *adj.* prodromal, preliminary.

pródromo, *s.m.* prodrome; prodromus, warning.

produção, *s.f.* production, product; work; output. 1) *produção em série,* mass production.

producente, *adj.* producing, causing; conclusive, logical.

produtibilidade, *s.f.* productiveness, productivity.

produtível, *adj.* producible, fertile.

produtividade, *s.f.* productivity, productiveness, fertility.

productivo, *adj.* productive, fertile, fruitful, fecund.

produto, *s.m.* production, produce; output; fruit, result.

produtor, *adj.* productive, creative; *s.m.* producer, creator, manufacturer.

produzir, *v.t.* to produce, to originate, to bring forth; to cause; to make, to manufacture, to create.

produzível, *adj.* producible.

proejar, *v.i.* to steer towards, to head for, to row against the wind.

proemial, *adj.* proemial, introductory, preliminary.

proemiar, *v.t.* to preface, to make a preamble.

proemoência, *s.f.* prominence, salience; eminence, distinction, importance.

proeminente, *adj.* prominent, conspicuous, eminent, distinguished.

proémio, *s.m.* proem, preface, preamble, prelude, introduction.

proençal, *adj.* ver provençal.

proeza, *s.f.* exploit, deed, achievement; bravery, prowess.

profanação, *s.f.* profanation, desecration, sacrilege, violation.

profanador, *adj.* sedecrating, sacrilegious; *s.m.* profaner, desecrater, violator, defiler.

profanar, *v.t.* profane, to violate; to pollute; to desecrate.

profanidade, *s.f.* profanity, blasphemy, irreverence.

profano, *adj.* profane; secular; blasphemous; irreligious, sacrilegious.

prófase, *s.f.* prophase, mitosis.

profecia, *s.f.* prophecy, prediction, vatication.

proferir, *v.t.* to utter, to say, to pronounce, to declare.

professar, *v.t.* to profess, to avow, to declare, to confess, to acknowledge; *v.i.* to take religious vows, to take the veil.

professo, *adj.* professed; expert, skilled; s.m. one who has taken a vow.

professor, *s.m.* teacher, master, scoolmaster; professor; educator, pedagogue.

professora, woman teacher, schoolmistress.

professorado, *s.m.* teachership; professorship; teaching staff.

professoral, *adj.* professorial.

professar, *v.i.* to teach, to be a teacher.

profeta, *s.m.* prophet, predictor, foreteller.

profético, *adj.* prophetical.

profetisa, *s.f.* prophetess.

profetismo, *s.m.* prophetism.

profetisador, *s.m.* prophesier; *adj.* prophesying.

profetizar, *v.t.* to prophesy, to predict, to foretell, to vaticinate.

proficiência, *s.f.* proficiency, expertness, skill, competence, efficiency.

proficiente, *adj.* proficient, expert, skilled, competent, qualified.

proficientemente, *adv.* proficiently.

profícuamente, *adv.* usefully, profitably.

proficuidade, *s.f.* utility, profitableness, profitability, usefulness.

profícuo, *adj.* useful, profitable, advantageous.

profiláctico, *adj.* prophylactic, preventive, preservative.

profilaxia, *s.f.* prophylaxis, preventive treatment.

profissão, *s.f.* profession, calling, occupation; career, office, employment; confessional *(de fé); avowal (lealdade, etc.).*

profissional, *s., adj.* professional.

profissionalismo, *s.m.* professionalism.

profitente, *adj.* professing.

profligação, *s.f.* profligacy; waste; overthrowing; defeat; destruction, extermination.

profligador, *adj.* overthrowing, destructive, destroyer, depraver.

profligar, *v.t.* to overthrow; to cast down; to destroy.

pró-forma, *s.m.* for form`s sake, a matter of form.

prófugo, *adj.* fugitive, deserter; vagabond.

profundamente, *adv.* profoundly, soundly; deeply; thoroughly.

profundar, *v.t.* to deepen; to fathom; to sound; to grow deeper; to sink; to examine thoroughly; to investigate, to explore, to enter deeply.

profundas, *s.f. (pl)* the depths; hell.

profundeze, *s.f.* ver profundidade.

profundidade, *s.f.* profundity, depth, deepness; abyss; thoroughness, sagacity.

profundo, *adj.* profund, deep; enormous; recondite, impenetrable, fathomless; obscure; complete, sagacious, penetrating.

profundura, *s.f.* ver profundidade.

profusamente, *adv.* profusely, plentifully, copiously.

profusão, *s.f.* profusion; exuberance; superabundance.

profuso, *adj.* profuse, exuberant, copious; prodigal, pelntiful; wasteful.

progénie, *s.f.* progeny, offspring; issue; lineage; children, descendants.

progenitor, *s.m.* progenitor, ancestor; father, forefather.

progenitura, *s.m.* progeniture, progeny; issue; birth.

prognatismo, *s.m.* prognathism.

prógnato, *adj.* prognathic; *s.m.* prognathic person.

prognose, *s.f.* prognosis, prognostication.

prognosticador, *adj.* prognosticative; *s.m.* prognosticator.

prognosticar, *v.t.* to prognosticate; to foretell, to predict; to warn, to presage, to prophesy.

prognóstico, *s.m.* prognostic; omen, token; prognosis; prediction, warning.

programa, *s.m.* programme, program; schedule, plan; syllabus.

programação, *s.f.* programming.

programador, *s.m.* programmer.

programar, *v.t.* to plan, to program, to schedule.

programático, *adj.* programmatic.

programatizar, *v.t.* to program, to plan.

progredimento, *s.m.* progress, advance.

progredir, *v.i.* to progress, to proceed, to advance, to develop, to improve, to go on, to move forward; to go on (in life).

progressão, *s.f.* progression; advance, progress.

progressismo, *s.m.* progressism, progressionism.

progressista, *s.* progressist, progressionist; *adj.* progressive, making progress.

progressivamente, *adv.* progressively.

progressividade, *s.f.* progressiveness.

progressivo, *adj.* progressive, advancing; increasing.

progresso, *s.m.* progress, development; advance, improvement, growth; forward move.

proibição, *s.f.* prohibition, forbidding, interdiction.

proibido, *adj.* forbidden, prohibited, unlawful; taboo.

proibidor, *s.m.* prohibiter, forbidder.

proibir, *v.t.* to prohibit, to forbid, to interdict; to prevent.

proibitivo, *adj.* prohibitive.

proibitório, *adj.* prohibitory.

projecção, *s.f.* projection, plan, scheme; protuberance, bulge; projecting; prominence.

projectante, *adj.* projectin.

projectar, *v.t.* to project, to plan, to contrive, to skerch, to scheme out; to propel, to thow, to cast.

projéctil, *s.m.* projectile, missile, bullet, bomb.

projectista, *s.* projector, schemer, planner.

projectibo, *adj.* projective, projecting.

projecto, *s.m.* project, plan, scheme, design, draft, sketch. 1) *projecto de lei,* bill. 2) *fazer um projecto,* to draw up a plain.

projector, *s.m.* projector, searchlight.

prol, *s.m.* advantage, benefit, profit.

prolação, *s.f.* prolation, pronunciation, utterance.

prolapso, *s.m.* prolapsus, prolapse.

prole, *s.f.* offspring, children, issue, progeny, descendants.

prolegómenos, *s.m. (pl)* prolegomena, introductory part, preface.

prolepse, *s.f.* prolepsis.

proléptico, *adj.* proleptic(al).

proletariado, *s.m.* prolateriat, labouring classes.

proletário, *s.m., adj.* proletarian.

proletarização, *s.f.* proletarization.

proletarizar, *v.t.* to proletarize.

proleferação, *s.f.* proliferation.

proliferar, *v.i.* to proliferate, to reproduce.

prolífero, adj. proliferous, prolific, fertile, fruitful, fecund.

prolificação, s.f. prolification, fertility, fruitfulness.

prolificar, v.i. to proliferate, to generate, to reproduce, to breed.

prolífico, adj. prolific, productive, fruitful, fertile.

prolígero, adj. proligerous, productive.

prolixamente, adv. prolixly, diffusely.

prolixidade, s.f. prolixity, verbosity, deffuseness.

prolixo, adj. prolix, diffuse, long-winded; tiresmoe, wearisome, tedious.

prologar, v.t. to prologize, to prologue, to preface.

prólogo, s.m. prolongue, preamble, introduction.

prolonga, s.f. delay, deferment, retardation, prolong.

prolongação, s.f. prolongation, extension; delay, postpoment.

prolongadamente, adv. lengthily, extendedly.

prolongado, adj. prolonged, extended, long-drawn; delayed; longish, oblong.

prolongamento, s.m. prolongation; continuation; extension.

prolongar, v.t. to prolong, to extend, to lenthen; to delay, to put off; to continue.

prolongável, adj. prolongable.

proloquial, adj. relating to a maxim.

prolóquio, s.m. proverb, maxim, adage.

prolusão, s.f. propulsion, introduction.

promanar, v.i. to proceed, to come forth, to emanate from, to originate.

promessa, s.f. promise, word, assurance, pledge; vow; votive offer. 1) *fazer uma promessa,* to make a vow. 2) *promessa de casamento,* bethrothal.

prometedor, adj. promising, hopeful.

prometer, v.t. to promise, to make a promise, to assore, to pledge; to vow; to bethroth, to engage. 1) *prometer mundos e fundos,* to promise wonders, to promise mountains and marvels (or the moon).

prometida, s.f. intended (mulher) fiancée.

prometido, adj. promised, pledged; vowed; engaged; s.m. thing promised; fiancé. 1) *o prometido é devido,* promise is binding.

prometimento, s.m. promise.

promiscuamente, adv. promiscuously.

promiscuidade, s.f. promiscuity; confusion.

pormiscuir-se, s. reflex. to mingle with.

promíscuo, adj. promiscuous, mixed, mingled.

promissão, s.f. promise.

promissivo, adj. promissory, promissive.

promissor, s.f. promising; s.m. promiser.

promissória, s.f. promissory note.

promissório, adj. promissory.

promitente, s., adj. ver promissor.

promoção, s.f. promotion, advencement, elevation, rise; progress.

promontório, s.m. promontory, headland.

promotor, s.m. promotor, supporter; inciter, instigator; adj. promotive. 1) *promotor de justiça,* prosecutor.

promovedor, s.m. promoter.

promover, v.t. to promote; to advance; to cause; to encourage; to foment; to further, to foster.

promulgação, s.f. promulgatuon, publication; declaration.

promulgador, s.m. promulgator.

promulgar, v.t. to promulgate, to publish, to announce, to declare, to make known.

pronome, s.m. pronoun.

pronominal, adj. pronominal.

pronominalmente, adv. pronominally.

pronéstico, s.m. *(pop)* pretentious, petulant, affected.

prontamente, adv. readily, promptly.

prontidão, s.f. promptitude, promptness, readiness, quickness alacrity.

pronteficar-se, v. refl. to offer oneself, to be ready for.

pronto, adj. ready, prompt, prepared; inclined, disposed to; handy; available; swift. 1) *a pronto pagamento,* cash down, cash payment.

pronto-socorro, s.m. ambulance station; breakdown-car.

prontuário, s.m. handbook; reference book.

pronúncia, s.f. pronunciation, pronouncing; indictment, formal accusation.

pronunciação, s.f. pronunciation, utterance.

pronunciado, pronounced, articulate, distinct, well-marked; indicted.

pronunciamento, s.m. pronouncement, revolt, rebellion, insurrection.

pronunciar, v.t. to pronunce, to utter, to speak, to articulate; to declare *(opinião).* 1) *pronunciar-se,* to declare, to speak; to revolt.

pronunciável, adj. pronounceable.

pronúncio, s.m. deputy papel nuncio.

propagação, s.f. propagation, diffusing,

dissemination, spreading; procreation, breeding.

propagador, *adj.* propagative; *s.m.* propagator, breader, diffuser, promoter.

propaganda, *s.f.* propaganda.

propagandista, *s.* propagandist.

propagar, *v.t.* to propagate, to diffuse, to spread abroad, to disseminate; to multiply, to reproduce.

propagativo, *adj.* propagative.

propalador, *s.m.* divulger; *adj.* divulging.

propalar, *v.t.* to divulge, to publish.

propano, *s.m.* *(chem)* propane.

proparoxítono, *adj.* proparoxytone.

propedêutica, *s.f.* propaedeutics.

propedêutico, *adj.* propaedeutic.

propelir, *v.t.* to propel, to impel forward, to drive forward.

propendente, *adj.* inclining, bent, leaning forward.

propender, *v.i.* to tend; to aim; to incline.

propensão, *s.f.* propensity, inclination, tendency, disposition.

propenso, *adj.* inclined, disposed, minded to.

propiciação, *s.f.* propitiation, expiation, atonement.

propiciador, *adj.* propitiatory; s.m. propitiator.

propiciar, *v.t.* to propitiate, to make propitious, to render favourable; to appease, to conciliate.

propiciatório, *adj.* propitiatory, favourable.

proícío, *adj.* propitious, favourable, auspicious, benevolent; opportune, timely.

propileu, *s.m.* propylaeum, entrance.

propina, *s.f.* reward; fees; gratuity.

propinação, *s.f.* propination.

propinar, *v.t.* to pledge in drinking; to minister.

propinquidade, *s.f.* propinquity, nearness, proximity *(tempo ou espaço)*.

propínquo, *adj.* near, approaching, neighbouring.

proplasma, *s.m.* proplasm, mold.

proplástica, *s.f.* proplastics (arte).

proplástico, *adj.* proplastic.

própole, própolis, *s.f.* propolis, bee-glue.

proponente, *s.m.,* *adj.* proponent; proposer.

propor, *v.t.* to propose, to offer, to suggest, to recommend; to intend, to mean, to have in view.

proporção, *s.f.* proportion, relation, ratio, rate; harmony; dimension, form, shape.

proporcionado, *adj.* proportionate, propor-

tioned, proportional; harmonic, adapted, harmonious.

proporcionador, *adj.* proportioning.

proporcional, *adj.* proportional, proportionate.

proporcionalidade, *s.f.* proportionality.

proporcionalmente, *adv.* proportionally.

proporcionar, *v.t.* to proportionate, to proportion, to adapt, to adjust; to regulate, to present, to provide, to offer.

proporcionável, *adj.* proportionable.

proposição, *s.f.* proposition; assertion; sentence; proposal.

propositadamente, *adv.* on purpose, intentionally, willfully.

propositado, *adj.* purposive, purposeful, intentional, deliberate, willful.

propósito, *s.m.* purpose, aim, intent, determination, design; end, object, intention; fitness, convenience; circumspection. 1) *a propósito,* by the way. 2) *a que propósito?,* for what purpose?. 3) *de propósito,* purposely, on purpose. 4) *falar de propósito,* to speak to the purpose. 5) *fora de propósito,* irrelevant, ill-timed. 6) *a propósito de,* with regard to. 7) *muito a propósito,* much to the purpose.

proposta, *s.f.* proposal, promise; offer; offer of marriage; plan, scheme; motion.

proposto, *adj.* proposed, offered; s.m. locum tenens, deputy.

propriamente, *adv.* properly, suitable, justly, rightly, correctly. 1) *propriamente dito,* properly so-called.

propriedade, *s.f.* propriety, fitness, correctness; particularity; property; ownership; real estate, land; wealth.

proprietário, *s.m.* proprietaor, owner, landlord, holder.

próprio, *adj.* proper, own, peculiar, suitable, just, exact; very; *s.m.* express messenger.

propugnação, *s.f.* propugnation.

propugnador, *s.m.* defender, protector, vindicator.

propugnar, *v.t., v.i.* to defend, to vindicate, to contend for, to fight for.

propulsão, *s.f.* propulsion, propelling. 1) *propulsão a jacto,* jet propulsion.

propulsar, *v.t.* to propel, to driveforward, to impel.

propulsionador, *adj.* propelling, driving.

propulsionar, *v.t.* to propel.

propulsivo, *adj.* propulsive.

propulsor, *adj.* propulsive, propelling, driving; *s.m.* propeller, pusher.

prorrogação, *s.f.* prorogationm, adjournment, extension, putting off, deferment, extension, putting off, deferment. 1) *prorrogação do contrato,* renewal of the contract.

prorrogar, *v.t.* to prorogue, to postpone, to extend, to put off, to adjourn.

prorrogativo, *adj.* prorogative.

prorrogável, *adj.* that may be prorogued, postponable.

prorromper, *v.i.* to break out, to burst.

prosa, *s.f.* prose.

prosador, *s.m.* proser, prose-writer, prosaist.

prosaicamente, *adv.* prosaically.

prosaico, *adj.* prosaic, commonplace, dull, tedious, monotonous.

prosaísmo, *s.m.* prosaism, prosaicness, mere prose.

prosaísta, *s.* prosaist, prose writer.

prosápia, *s.f.* progency, race, ancestry, generation, arrogance, conceit, pride, haughtiness.

prosar, *v.i.* to prose, to write in prose.

proscénio, *s.m.* proscenium.

proscrever, *v.t.* to proscribe, to outlaw, to banish; to forbid, to interdict, to prohibit.

proscrição, *s.f.* proscription, banishment, exile.

proscrito, *adj.* proscribed, exiled, outlawed; *s.m.* exile, outlaw.

proscritor, *s.m.* proscriber.

proselítico, *adj.* proselytical.

proselitismo, *s.m.* proselytism.

prosélito, *s.m.* proselyte, convert, neophyte.

prosista, *s.m.* prose-writer.

prosódia, *s.f.* prosody.

prosódico, *adj.* prosodic; prosodical.

prosopopeia, *s.f.* prosopopoeia.

prospecção, *s.f.* prospecting *(ouro, etc.).*

prospectar, *v.i.* to prospect.

prospectivo, *adj.* prospective.

prospecto, *s.m.* prospect, outlook, plan, outline, view; prospectus, handbill, circular.

prospector, *s.m.* prospector.

prosperamente, *adv.* prosperously, successfully.

prosperar, *v.i.* to prosper, to thrive, to succeed, to flourish, to develop, to improve, to be fortunate.

prosperidade, *s.f.* prosperity, succedd, fortune, welfare, wealth, good luck.

próspero, *adj.* prosperous; successful, auspicious, thriving, lucky, favourable, fortune.

prossecução, *s.f.* prosecution, pursuit; continuation.

prossecutor, *s.m.* prosecutor.

prosseguição, prosseguidor, *s.f.* ver prossecução.

prosseguimento, *s.m.* prosecutor; *adj.* prosecuting.

prosseguir, *s.m.* pursuit, continuation, prosecution.

próstata, *v.t.* prosecute, to follow, to continue, to proceed, to go on, to carry on to pursue.

prostático, *s.f.* prostate.

prostatite, *s.f.* proststitis.

prosternação, *s.f.* prostration.

prosternamento, *s.m.* porstration.

prosternar, *v.t.* to prostrate, to cast down, to throwdow; to humiliate, to humble.

próstese, *s.f.* prosthesis.

prostíbulo, *s.m.* brothel, boadyhouse.

prostilo, *s.m.* prostyle.

prostituição, *s.f.* prostitution, harlotry, perversion, degradation.

prostituidor, *s.m.* prostitutor; *adj.* prostituing.

prostituir, *v.t.* to prostitute; to revile, to corrupt, to degrade.

prostituta, *s.f.* prostitute, coutesan, whore, harlot.

prostração, *s.f.* prostration, exhaustion, debility, depression.

prostramento, *s.m.* ver prostração.

prostrar, *v.t.* to prostrate, to throw; to exhaust, to depress.

protagonista, *s.* protagonist, figurant, leading person.

protão, *s.m.* proton.

prótase, *s.f.* protasis.

protático, *adj.* protatic.

protecção, *s.f.* protection; help; defence; patronage, support; security, safeguard; shelter, cover.

proteccional, *adj.* protective.

proteccionismo, *s.m.* protectionism, protective system.

proteccionista, *s., adj.* protectionist.

protector, *s.m.* protector, patron; *adj.* proteting, protective, sheltering.

protectora, *s.f.* protectress.

protectorado, *s.m.* protectorate; protectorship.

protectoral, *adj.* protectoral.

protectoria, *s.f.* protectorship.

protectório, *adj.* protecting, favouring, sheltering.

protegedor, *s.m., adj.* protector; protecting.

proteger, *v.t.* to protect, to shield, to guard; to shelter; to favour, to support; to defend, to preserve; to take under one`s wing.

protegido, *s.m.* protegee; *adj.* protected.

proteico, *adj.* albuminoid, proteinic, proteinaceous.

proteiforme, *adj.* proteiform.

proteína, *s.f.* protein.

protelação, *s.f.* protraction, delay, prostponement, deferment.

protelador, *s.m.* protractor, delayer; *adj.* delaying, putting off.

protelar, *v.t.* to protract, to delay, to adjourn, to put off.

protelatório, *adj.* protractive, dilatory, tardy.

protérvia, *s.f.* pertness, petulance, insolence, impudence, sauciness.

protervo, *adj.* petulant, insolent, impudent, brazen-faced.

prótese, *s.f.* prosthesis.

protestação, *s.f.* protestation, protest; asseveration.

protestador, *s.m.* protester; *adj.* protesting.

protestante, *s., adj.* Protestant.

protestantismo, *s.m.* Protestantism.

protestar, *v.t.* to protest, to declare; to raise objections, to disagree, to object; to swear. 1) *protestar uma letra,* to protest a bill.

protestatório, *adj.* protesting.

protesto, *s.m.* protest, protestation, disapproval; solemn declaration. 1) *protesto por falta de pagamento,* protest for nonpayment.

protético, *adj.* prosthetic.

protista, *s.m.* prostist.

protocolar, *adj.* relative to protocol, protocolar.

protocolo, *s.m.* protocol, etiquette, official formulas; register, record *(conferência, audiência).*

protógino, *s.m.* protogine.

protomártir, *s.m.* protomartyr.

protónico, *adj.* pretonic.

protonotário, *s.m.* prothonotary.

protoplasma, *s.m.* protoplasm.

protopasmático, protoplásmico, *adj.* protoplasmatic.

protoplasto, *s.m.* protoplast.

protóptero, *s.m* protopterus.

protótipo, *s.m.* prototype, archetype, model, patter, protoxido, *s.m.* protoxide.

protozoário, *adj.* protozoan; *s.m.* protozoan; *s.m. (pl)* Protozoa.

potraimento, *s.m.* protracting; delay; prostponement; adjournment.

protrair, *v.t.* to protract, to delay, to put off, to prolong.

protrusão, *s.f.* protrusian.

protruso, *adj.* protruded.

protuberância, *s.m.* protuderance, prominence, bump, bulge.

protuberante, *adj.* protuberant, prominent, bulging, protruding.

protutela, *s.f.* protutotry, guardinship.

protutor, *s.m.* protutor, guardian.

prova, *s.f.* proof, test, trial; evidence; verification; taste; examination; sample; fitting; demonstration; sign, mark; confirmation; proof sheet; copy (fotografia). 1) *prova escrita,* written test or paper. 2) *prova oral,* oral test. 3) *à prova de água,* waterproof. 4) *à prova de bala,* bulletproof. 5) *pôr à prova,* to put to the test. 6) *resistir à prova,* to stand the trial. 7) *tirar uma prova,* to pull a proof.

provação, *s.f.* probation, trial; misfortune, distress, hardship, suffering; novitiate.

provador, *s.m.* taster.

provadura, *s.f.* tasting.

provar, *v.t.* to prove, to demonstrate, to testify. to try, to attempt; to taste; to evince, to show; to experiment; to check, to verify; to try on *(vestido).*

provatório, *adj.* probatory.

provével, *adj.* probable, likely; provable, demonstrable. 1) *pouco provável,* unlikely.

provavelmente, *adv.* probably.

provecto, *adj.* old, aged; experienced, versed; well on *(em anos).*

provedor, *s.m.* proveyor; head of a charitable instituition, superintent.

provedoria, *s.f.* proveyor`s office.

proveito, *s.m.* profit, gain, benefit, advantage; progress, improvement; utility. 1) *bom proveito,* may you enjoy it. 2) *tirar proveito de,* to make good use of, to turn to account. 3) *tirar o maior proveito de,* to male the most of.

proveitoso, *adv.* profitably.

proveitoso, *adj.* profitable, advantageous, useful, lucrative, gainful.

provençal, *adj., s.* Provençal.

proveniência, s.f. provenance, provenience, origin, source.

proveniente, adj. preceeding, from, originating in, derived from, coming from.

provento, s.m. profit, gain, revenue.

prover, v.t. to provide, to furnish, to supply; to give, to grant; to appoint; to look after, to care for; to confer, to see to.

proverbial, adj. proverbial; notorious, well-known.

proverbialmente, adv. proverbially.

provérbio, s.m. proverb, maxim, adage, saying.

proveta, s.f. test-tube.

provete, s.m. areometer.

providência, s.m. Providence; God; (pl) measure, ateps, arrangements, precautions.

providencial, adj. providential fortunate, lucky; opportune, welcome.

providencialmente, adv. providentially, luckily, fortunately.

providenciar, v.i. to take measures, provide for, to make arrangements for; to look after.

providente, adj. provident, prudent, wise, cautious, careful; farseeing.

providamente, adv. providently.

próvido, adj. provident.

provigário, s.m. provicar.

provimento, s.m. providing; appointment; equipment. 1) dar provimento, to grant a petition.

província, s.f. province; country district or region.

provincial, adj., s.m. provincial.

provincialado, provincialato, s.m. dignity or office of a provincial.

provincialismo, s.m. provincialism, provincial manner, fashion, word, phrase, etc.

provinciano, s.m., adj. provincial.

provindo, adj. proceeding, coming from, arising from.

provir, v.i. to proceed, to come from, to arise, to spring, to result (from).

provisão, s.f. provision, supply, storage; stock; (pl) provisions, victuals.

provisão, adj. provisional.

provisor, s.m. purveyor, provisor.

provisorado, s.m. provisorship.

provisoriamente, adv. provisorily, provisionally, temporarily.

provisório, adj. provisory, provisional, temporary, transitory.

provocação, s.f. provocation, provoking; affront; challenge; incitement, temptation.

provocador, adj. provoking, insolent, provocative; s.m. provoker.

provocante, adj. provocarive, provoking, tempting, irritating, vexatious.

provocantemente, adv. provokingly.

provocar, v.t. to provoke, to instigate, to incite, to stimulate, to tempt; to insult, to affront; to irritate; to stir up, to give rise to; to arouse.

provocativo, adj. provocative, provoking.

provocatório, adj. provoking, tempting.

proxeneta, s. pender, procurer, go-between, intermediary, pimp.

proxenetismo, s.m. profession of a procurer.

proximamente, adv. in the near future.

proximidade, s.f. proximity, nearness, contiguity; (pl) surroundings, neighbourhood.

próximo, adj. near, next, neighbouring, close by, adjacent; coming, impending, imminent; s.m. felow-creature. 1) parente próximo, next of kin. 2) próximo da praia, near the shore. 3) no próximo mês, next month.

prudência, s.f. prudence, caution, discretion, wisdom, judiciousness.

prudencial, adj. prudential, discreet, wise, prudent.

prudente, adj. prudent, cautious, discreet, wise, judicious, circumspect; careful.

prudentemente, adv. prudently, carefully, cautiously, discreetly.

pruído, s.m. ver prurido.

pruir, v.t., v.i. to itch.

prumada, s.f. plumb line; casting of the lead. 1) tirar uma prumada, to cast the lead, to take a cast of the lead.

prumador, s.m. leadsman.

prumagem, s.f. sounding, plumbing.

prumar, v.i. to sound, to take sounding.

prumo, s.m. plummet, plumb bob, sounding-lead, sounding-line. 1) a prumo, vertically, perpendiculary.

prurido, s.m. pruritus, itch, prurigo, itching (pele); craving, burning, desire, impatience.

pruriente, adj. pruriginous, itching.

prurigem, s.f. prurigo, pruritus, violent itching.

pruriginoso, adj. pruriginous.

prurigo, s.m. ver prurigem.

prurir, v.i. to itch; to long for; to cause itching to.

prussiano, *adj., s.m.* Prussian.

prussiato, *s.m.* prussiate.

prússico, *adj.* prussic.

pselismo, *s.m.* stammering.

pseudo, *pref.* false psellism.

pseudónimo, *s.m.* pseudonym, penname.

pseudópode, *s.m.* pseudopodium.

pseudoprofeta, *s.m.* false prophet.

pseudo-sábio, *s.m.* false scientist.

psicanálise, *s.f.* psychoanalyst.

psicanalista, *s.* psychoanalyst.

psicastenia, *s.m.* psychasthenia, phobias.

psicasténico, *adj.* psychasthenic.

psiché, *s.m.* dressing-table.

psicofísica, *s.f.* psychophysics.

psicofísico, *adj.* psychophysic.

psicofisiologia, *s.* psychophysiology.

psicogenia, *s.m.* psychogenesis.

psicogénico, *adj.* psychogenic.

psicognosia, *s.f.* psychognosis.

psicognóstico, *adj.* psychognostic.

psicografia, *s.f.* psychography.

psicogéfico, *adj.* psichographic.

psicógrafo, *s.m.* psychograph.

psicologia, *s.f.* psychology.

psicologicamente, *adv.* psychologically.

psicológico, *adj.* psychological.

psicologista, *s.* psychologist.

psicólogo, *s.m.* psychologist.

psicometria, *s.f.* psychometry.

psicometrico, *adj.* psychometrical.

psicómetro, *s.m.* psychometer.

psiconeurose, *s.f.* psychoneurosis.

psiconeurótico, *adj.* psychoneurotic.

psicomotor, *adj.* psycho-motor.

psicopata, *s.* psychopath.

psicopatia, *s.f.* psychopathy, mental disorder.

psicopático, *adj.* psychopathic.

psicopatológico, *adj.* psychopathological.

psicopatologia, *s.f.* psychopathology.

psicopedagogia, *s.f.* psychopedagogy.

psicose, *s.f.* psychosis.

psicotécnica, *s.f.* psychotechnology.

psicotecnológico, *adj.* psychotechnological.

psicoterapia, *s.f.* psycho-therapy.

psicoterápico, *adj.* psychotherapic.

psicrometria, *s.f.* psychrometry.

psicrómetro, *s.m.* psychrometer.

psique, *s.f.* psyche, soul.

psiquiatria, *s.m.* psychiatrist.

psiquiatria, *s.f.* psychiatry.

psiquiátrico, *adj.* psychiatric(al).

psiquicamente, *adv.* psychically.

psíquico, *adj.* psychic.

psiquismo, *s.m.* psychism.

psitacismo, *s.m.* psittacism, parrotlike speech, vain talk.

psitacista, *s.m.* psittacistic.

psitacose, *s.f.* parrot fever, psittacosis.

psiu!, *interj.* pst!, hush!.

ptérmico, *adj.* ptarmic, sternitative, causing sneezing.

pteridófictas, *s.f. (pl)* Pteridophyta.

pterígio, *s.m.* pterygium.

pterodáctilo, *s.m.* pterodactyl.

pterópodo, *s.m., adj.* pteropod.

ptialina, *s.f.* ptyalin *(saliva).*

ptialismo, *s.m.* ptyalism, excessive salivation.

ptolemaico, *adj.* Ptolomaic.

ptomaína, *s.f.* ptomaine.

ptose, *s.f.* ptosis.

pua, *s.f.* auger-bit, gimlet, sharp point. 1) *arco de pua,* brace (for a bit).

pube, *s.f.* ver púbis.

puberdade, *s.f.* puberty.

púbere, *adj.* relating to the puberty.

puebertário, *s.f.* pubescence.

pubescência, *adj.* pubescent.

pubescente, *v.i.* to reach puberty.

púbico, *adj.* pubic.

púbis, *s.f.* pubis.

publicação, *s.f.* publication; thing published *(livro, etc.);* announcement.

publicador, *adj.* publishing; *s.m.* publisher.

púbica-forma, *s.f.* authentic copy *(de um documento).*

publicamente, *adv.* publicly, openly.

publicano, *s.m.* publican.

publicarm, *v.t.* to publish; to proclaim, to announce, to divulge; to issue; to reveal; to advertise.

publicidade, *s.f.* publicity; advertising.

publicismo, *s.m.* publicism, journalism.

publicista, *s.* publicist, writer.

publicitério, *s.m.* advertising man; *adj.* relating to publicity or advertising.

público, *adj.* public, notorious, not private, open to all; *s.m.* public, audience. 1) *cargo público,* public office. 2) *do domínio público,* common knowledge.

púcara, *s.f.* earthenup, mug, small pot.

púcaro, *s.m.* earthenup, mug.

pudendo, *adj.* shy; shameful, prudish, modest, chaste. 1) *partes pudendas,* the pudenda.

pudente, *adj.* pudibundo.

pudera!, *interj.* no wonder! why!.
pudibundo, *adj.* shameful, bashful, modest, pudic.
pudicamente, *adv.* bashfully.
pudicícia, *s.f.* pudency, bashfulness, modesty, shyness, chastity.
pudico, *adj.* bashful, vhaste, modest, shy.
pudim, *s.m.* pudding.
pudor, *s.m.* modest, shame, pudency, shyness.
puerícia, *s.f.* childhood, boyhood.
puericultor, *s.m.* one who practiced pueri-culture.
puericultura, *s.f.* child welfare, child care, puericulture.
pueril, *adj.* puerile, childish; silly, foolish.
puerilidade, *s.f.* puerility; foolishness; futility, futile action or talk.
puerilizar-se, *v. ref.* to grow childish, to become puerile.
puerilmente, *adv.* childishly.
puérpera, *s.f.* lying-in woman, parturient woman.
puerperal, *adj.* puerperal.
puerpério, *s.m.* puerperium.
púgil, *s.m.* pugilist, boxer.
pugilar, *v.i.* to fight.
pugilato, *s.m.* boxing, pugilism.
pugilismo, *s.m.* pugilism, boxing.
pugilista, *s.* pugilist, boxer.
pugna, *s.f.* fight, struggle, combat, strife, battle.
pugnace, *adj.* pugnacious.
pugnacidade, *s.f.* pugnacity, fighting mood, combativeness.
pugnador, *s.m.* fighter; *adj.* pugnacious, combative.
pugnar, *v.i.* to fight, to struggle, to contend, to strive *(for)*, to defend vigorously.
pugnaz, *adj.* pugnacious, combative.
puideira, *s.f.* polishing powder.
puído, *adj.* theadbare.
puir, *v.t.* to wear out, to use up; to polish.
pujança, *s.f.* puissance, vitality, exuberance, force, vigour, strngth.
pujante, *adj.* puissant, vigorous, magnificent; strong, powerful.
pujar, *v.t.* to surpass, to excel, to exceed; to strive for, to endeavour.
pular, *v.i.* to jump, to leap; to spring; to beat, to throb *(o coração)*. 1) *pular de contente,* to leap for joy; to bound; to skip.
pulcritude, *s.f.* pulchritude, beauty, grace, loveliness.

pulcro, *adj.* pulchritudinous.
pulga, *s.f.* flea.
pulga-do-mar, *s.f.* sand-hopper.
pulgão, *s.m.* plant-louse.
pulgoso, *adj.* full of fleas.
pulguedo, *s.m.* large quantily of fleas.
pulguento, *adj.* flea-bitten; full of fleas.
pulha, *s.f.* joke, lie, fib, jest; *s.m.* knave, rotter; *adj.* roguish, knavish, contemptible.
pulhastra, pulhastro, *s.m.* rotter, blackguard.
pulhice, *s.f.* roguery, knavery, nasty trick, mean action.
pulmão, *s.m.* lung. 1) pulmão d eaço, iron lung.
pulmonar, *adj.* pulmonary.
pulo, *s.m* leap, rebound, spring jump. 1) *aos pulos,* by leaps. 2) *dar um pulo,* to take a leap. 3) *de um pulo,* at a leap.
púlpito, *s.m.* pulpit; preaching.
pulquérrimo, *adj.* most beautiful.
pulsação, *s.f.* pulsation; throbbing; pulse; beat.
pulsar, *v.i.* to pulse; to throb; to impel; to pulsate.
pulsátil, *adj.* pulsatile, throbbing, pulsating.
pulsatila, *s.f.* pulsatilla, the pasque-flower.
pulsativo, *adj.* pulsatory, pulsative.
pulseira, *s.f.* bracelet, wristband.
pulsímetro, *s.m.* pulsimeter, shygmograph.
pulso, *s.m.* wrist; pulse; beat; *(fig)* strength, vigour, energy. 1) *ter pulso,* to have a command. 2) *tomar o pulso,* to feel the pulse; *(fig)* to obsreve.
pululação, *s.f.* pullulation.
pululante, *adj.* pullulating, swarming, teeming.
pulular, *v.i.* to pullulate, to bud, to swarm; to breed; to spread, to sprout, to multiply quickly.
pulvéreo, *adj.* dusty, like dust.
pulverescência, *s.f.* pulverulence, dustiness.
pulverização, *s.f.* pulverization; spraying; *(fig)* destruction.
pulverizador, *s.m.* pulverizer; sprayer; pulverizing, spraying.
pulverizar, *v.t.* to pulverize, to spray; to destroy completely; to atomize.
pulverizável, *adj.* pulverizable, pulverable.
pulveroso, *adj.* pulverous, powdery, pulverlent, dusty.
pulverulência, *s.f.* pulverulence, dustiness.

pulverulento, *adj.* pulverulent, dusty, dust-covered.

pum!, *interj.* bang! boom!.

puma, *s.m.* puma, wildcat.

pumba!, *interj.* bang!, cras!.

puna, *s.f.* higher Andes; mountain sickness.

punção, *s.f.* punch; die; puncture, prick.

punçar, *v.t.* ver puncionar.

punceta, *s.f.* steel punch.

puncionar, *v.t.* to punch; to puncture; to perforate.

punctura, *s.f.* puncture.

pundonor, *s.m.* dignity; pride; point of honour, decour, self-respect.

pundonoroso, *adj.* proud, honour-loving, gentlemanly.

pungente, *adj.* pungent, keen, trilling, piercing, poignant; painful, bitter.

pungimento, *s.m.* pungency, stimulation; distress.

pungir, *v.i.* to begin to grow; to prick, to pierce, to hurt; to vex, to torment; to stimulate, to incite.

pungitivo, *adj.* ver pungente.

punhada, *s.f.* thump, punch, blow, cuff.

punhado, *s.m.* handful, a few, a small number.

punhal, *s.m.* dagger, dirk.

punhalada, *s.f.* stab; *(fig)* serious offence.

punho, *s.m.* wrist, fist, cuff *(de camisa)*; handle, hilt. 1) *punho cerrado,* clenched first. 2) *de seu próprio punho,* in his own hand-writing. 3) *botão, de punho,* sleeve-link, cufflink.

punibilidade, *s.f.* punishability.

punição, *s.f.* punishment, chastisement, penalty.

púnico, *adj.* Punic, Carthaginian; treacherous.

punidor, *adj.* punishing; *s.m.* punisher.

punir, *v.t.* to punish, to chastise, to inflict a penalty; to fight or to struggle for.

punitivo, *adj.* punitive, punishing.

punível, *adj.* punishable, deserving punishement.

puntura, *s.f.* puncture; point.

pupila, *s.f.* pupil *(do olho);* ward, protegée, underage girl in charge of a tutor.

pupilagem, *s.f.* tutelage; minority.

pupilar, *adj.* pupillary; *v.i.* to cry.

pupilo, *s.m.* pupil; ward, underage boy, protegé.

puramente, *adv.* purely, simply, merely.

puré, *s.m.* purée. 1) *puré de batatas,* mashed potatoes.

pureza, *s.f.* purity, chastity; pureness; innocence; perfection.

purga, *s.f.* purgative, purge, laxative.

purgação, *s.f.* purgation, purification, cleansing.

purgador, *s.m.* purger, purifier, refiner.

purgante, *adj.* purging; *s.m.* purge, purgative, aperient.

purgar, *v.t.* to clean; to purify; to give a purgative; to discharge.

purgativo, *adj., s.m.* purgative; aperient.

purgatório, *s.m.* purgatory.

puridade, *s.f.* purity; secret. 1) *à puridade,* in secret.

purificação, *s.f.* purification; cleansing.

purificador, *adj., s.m.* purifying; purifier.

purificante, *adj.* purifying.

purificar, *v.t.* to purify; to cleanse; to clear.

purificativo, *adj.* purifying, purificative.

purificatório, *adj.* purifying, purificatory.

purismo, *s.m.* purism, puruty of language, style, etc.

purista, *s., adj.* purist.

puritanismo, *s.m.* Puritanism.

puritano, *s.m.* Puritan; *adj.* puritain, puritanic.

puro, *adj.* pure, clear, clean; innocent, chaste; mere, sheer, genuine; stainless, undefiled, unspoiled; correct, exact.

púrpura, *s.f.* purple; purpura *(doença);* cardinalate.

purpurado, *adj.* clad in purple; *s.m.* a cardinal.

purpurar, *v.t.* to purple; to dye purple; to raise to the cardinalate.

purpurear, *v.t., v.i.* to purple, to make red. 1) *purpurear-se,* to blush.

purpurejar, *v.t.* ver purpurear.

purpúreo, *adj.* purple, purplish, red, crimson red.

purpurina, *s.f.* purpurin.

purpurino, *adj.* ver purpúreo.

purpurizar, *v.t., v.i.* ver purpurear.

purelência, *s.f.* purulence, purulency, suppuration.

purulento, adj. purulent, suppurating.

pus, *s.m.* pus; matter.

pusilânime, *adj.* pusillanimous, faint-hearted, cowardly, timid.

pusilanimidade, *s.f.* pusillanimity, cowardice, faintheartedeness, timidity.

pústula, *s.f.* purtule, simple, blister.
pustulento, *adj.* pustulous, postular.
pustuloso, *adj.* pustulous.
putativo, *adj.* putative, supposed, reputed.
putredinoso, *adj.* putrid, rotten; corrupt.
putrefacção, *s.f.* putrefaction, putridity, decomposition, rotting; decay, corruption.
putrefaciente, *adj.* putrefactive.
putrefactivo, *adj.* ptrefactivo.
putrefacto, *adj.* putrid, putrefied, rotten; corrupt.
putrefazer, *v.t., v. refl.* to putrefy; to make putrid; to rot.
putrescência, *s.f.* putrescence.
putrescente, *s.f.* putrescent.
putrescibilidade, *s.f.* putrescibility.
putrescível, *adj.* putrescibe.
pútrido, *adj.* putrid, rotten, corrupted, putrefied; pestilential.
putrificar, *v.t., v.i.* putrefazer.
puxada, *s.f.* drawing, pull; a lead card, first play *(jogo de cartas).*
puxadeira, *s.f.* loop, handle, knob, band, string, etc. for pulling something.
puxadela, *s.f.* a pulling.

puxado, *adj.* drawn, pulled; high, exorbitant *(preço);* exhaustive (trabalho).
puxador, *s.m.* door-handle, knob, handle, puller.
puxante, *adj.* pulling, drawing; piquant, sharp *(sabor);* stimulating.
puxão, *s.m.* push, shove, jerk, pull.
puxar, *v.t.* to draw, to drag, to pull, to haul, to tug; to attract, to impel, to urge; to resemble, to look after. 1) *puxar conversa,* to strike up a conversation. 2) *puxar pela espada,* to draw the sword. 3) *puxar pela língua,* to make one speak. 4) *puxar as orelhas,* to pull (twist) a person`s ears. 5) *puxar pela memória,* to cudgel one`s brains. 6) *puxar pela bolsa,* to dip into the pocket. 7) *puxar certo,* to pull together. 8) *puxar os cordelinhos,* to pull the strings. 9) *puxar a brasa à sua sardinha,* to draw water to one`s mill. 10) *puxar um assunto,* to bring up a matter. 11) *puxar à mãe,* to take after one`s mother.
puxativo, *adj.* stimulating.
puxavante, *s.m., adj.* driving rod *(locomotiva);* butteris; thirstarousing; stimulant, piquant.
puxo, *s.m.* tenesmus; labour.

Q

q, the sixteenth letter of the Portuguese alphabet.
quacre, *s.m.* Quaker *(sociedade religiosa).*
quacrismo, *s.m.* Quakerism.
quaderna, *s.f.* the four spot face of a die or dice.
quadernado, *adj.* quaternate *(folhas).*
quadra, *s.f.* square room, place, yard, enclosure; season; four *(no jogo de cartas);* quatrain.
quadrado, *adj.* square; *s.m.* square.

quadragenário, *s.m., adj.* quadragenarian.
Quadragésima, *s.f.* Quadragesima; Lent.
quadragesimal, *adj.* quadragesimal, Lenten.
quadragésimo, *num.* fortieth; *s.m.* the fortieh part.
quadrangulado, *adj.* quadrangular.
quadrangular, *adj.* ver quadrangulado.
quadrângulo, *s.m.* quandrangle.
quadrante, *s.m.* quadrant; dial *(de um relógio).*
quadrar, *v.t.* to square, to make square, to

give a square shape to; v.i. to agree, to correspond; to suit, to fit, to harmonize, to match.

quadrático, adj. quadratic, square.

quadratim, s.m. quadrat (impressão).

quadratriz, s.f. quadratix.

quadratura, s.f. quadrature.

quadrela, s.f. section of a wall; piece of land.

quadribásico, adj. quadribasic.

quadricolor, adj. four-coloured, quadri-colour.

quadricórneo, adj. quadricorn.

quadrícula, s.f. small square.

quadriculado, adj. squared; cross-ruled paper; cross-line, square lined; chequered. 1) papel quadriculado, graph paper.

quadricular, v.t. cross-rule; adj. cross-ruled.

quadricúspide, adj. quadricuspidal.

quadridentado, adj. quadridentate.

quadridigitado, adj. four-fingered, quadri-digitate.

quadrienal, adj. quadriennial.

quadriénio, s.m. quadriennium.

quadrifendido, quádrifído, adj. quadrifid.

quadrifólio, adj. quadrifoliate.

quadriforme, adj. qaudriform.

quadriga, s.f. quadriga; set of four horses.

quadrigémeo, adj. quadrigeminal.

quadrigeminado, adj. quadrigeminate.

quadril, s.m. haunch; hip.

quadrilateral, adj. quadrilateral, foursided.

quadrilátero, s.m., adj. quadrilateral.

quadrilha, s.f. gang, band; quadrille (dança); quadrilha de ladrões, gang of theives.

quadrilheiro, s.m. gangster, bandit, high-wayman, hoodlum.

quadrilobado, quadrilobulado, adj. quadribolate.

quadriloculado, quadrilocular, adj. quadrilocular.

quadrilongo, adj. oblong.

quadrímano, adj. quadrimanous.

quadrimembre, adj. quadrimembral.

quadrimestral, adj. four-monthly.

quadrimestre, s.m. a period of four months.

quadrimotor, s.m. four-motored.

quadrigentenário, s.m. commemoration of an event that took place four hundred years before; quatercentenary, quadricen-tennial.

quadringentésimo, num. four-hundredth.

quadrinómio, s.m. quadrinomial.

quadripartição, s.f. quadripartition.

quadripartido, adj. quadripartite.

quadripétalo, adj. having four petals.

quadrirreme, s.f. quadrireme.

quadrissilábico, adj. quadrisillabic.

quadrissílabo, adj. quadrisyllable.

quadrivalente, adj. quadrivalent, tetravalent.

quadrivalve, adj. quadrivalve.

quadrivalvulado, quadrivalvular, adj. quadrivalvular.

quadrívio, s.m. the meeting of four ways; cross-way, cross-roads; quadrivivium (geometria, aritmética, astronomia, música).

quadro, s.m. square; picture-frame; board; table; picture; staff; scene; tableau; sight; view; image, portrait; card, map; list, roll; panel, dashboard. 1) quadro a óleo, oil painting. 2) quadro preto, negro, black-board. 3) quadro de pessoal, working staff. 4) quadro de distribuição, switchboard. 5) quadro sinóptico, synoptic chart. 6) quadro vivo, living tableau.

quadrúmano, adj. quadrumanous; s.m. (pl.) Quadrumana.

quadrunvirato, s.m. quadriumvirate.

quadrúnviro, s.m. quadrumvir.

quadrupedante, adj. quadrupedal, four-footed.

quadrupedar, v.i. to go on four feet.

quadrúpede, adj. quadruped; s.m. quadru-ped; stupid person (fig).

quadruplicação, s.f. quadruplication.

quadruplicad, adj. quadruplicate.

uqdruplicar, v.t. to quadruplicate, to quadruple, to double twice.

quádruplo, s.m., adj. quadruple, fourfold.

qual, pron. which; what; who; whom; that; adj. which, what; conj. as like as; interj. nonsense!; fiddlesticks.

qualidade, s.f. quality; condition; charac-teristic; kind, class; feature, trait, rank, standing; importance; capacity.

qualificação, s.f. qualification; qualifying, ability, capacity; classification, denomi-nation.

qualificado, adj. qualified, able, competent; appropriate.

qualificador, adj. qualificative, qualifying; s.m. qualifier.

qualificar, v.t. to qualify; to class; to ennoble; to desigante, to denominate; to describe; to regard, to repute.

qualificativo, adj. qualificative, qualifying.

qualificável, adj. qualifiable.

qualitativo, adj. qualitative.

qualquer, pron., adj. whoever, whichever;

whatever; any (pessoa, coisa); a, an; every, either (of two).

quando, conj. when; though; although; at what time, as soon as; while; even if; whereas; adv. how soon?; how long ago?.; 1) quando muito, at the most, at best. 2) até quando?, till when?. 3) de quando em quando, from time to time, now and then, occasionally. 4) desde quando?, since when? how long?. 5) ainda quando, although, even if. 6) quando mais não seja, at the very least, if for no other reason. 7) quando menos se espera, when least expected.

quantia, s.f. sum, amount; quantity.

quantiar, v.t. to count, to estimate.

quantidade, s.f. quantity, measure; extent; size; greatness; amount; number; portion.

quantioso, adj. numerous; valuable; copious, abundant.

quantitativo, adj. quantitative.

quanto, adv., pron. all that; what; how much?; whatever. 1) quanto a isso, for that matter, as to that. 2) quanto a mim, as for me. 3) quanto a, with regard to. 4) a quantos está (jogo), what is the score. 5) tanto quanto sei, as far as I know. 6) quanto antes, as soon as possible. 7) quanto mais barato melhor, the cheaper the better. 8) quantos?, how many?. 9) quanto?, how much?. 10) quanto tempo?, how long?. 11) quanto mais depressa mais devagar, more haste less speed.

quantum, s.m. (fís.) quantum.

quão, adv. how; as.

quarenta, num. forty.

quarentão, adj., s.m. quadragenarian.

quarentena, s.f. quarantine; de quarentena, in quarantine.

quarentenar, v.t. to quarantine; to be in quaratine.

quarentona, s.f. quadragenarian womam.

Quaresma, s.f. Lent.

quaresmal, adj. Lenten.

quaresmar, v.i. to keep lent.

quarta, s.f. the four part; quarter.

quartã, adj., s.f. quartan (febre).

quartado, adj. quartered.

quarta-feira, s.f. wednesday.

quartanista, s. fourth-year student (universidade).

quartear, v.t. to quarter, to divide into four parts.

quarteio, s.m. act of dodging in bullfight.

quarteirão, s.m. quarter-hundred; block (de casas).

quartejar, v.t. to quarter.

quartel, s.m. barracks; quarter; period. 1) quartel-mestre, quarter master. 2) sem quartel, merciless. 3) não dar quartel, to give no quarter.

quarteleiro, s.m. store-keeper (de um quartel).

quartel-general, s.m. general headquarters.

quarteto, s.m. quatrain; quartet (mús.); any group of four.

quartil, adj. quartile (planetas).

quartilho, s.m. pint.

quarto, num. fourth; s.m. room; quarter; quarto (forma de um livro). 1) quarto crescente, first quarter. 2) quarto minguante, last quarter. 3) quarto de banho, bathroom. 4) quarto de casal, double bed room. 5) quarto de hóspedes, guest room.

quartola, s.f. cask, small pipe.

quartzífero, adj. quartziferous.

quartzito, s.m. quartzite.

quartzo, s.m. quartz.

quartzoso, adj. quartzose, quarzy.

quase, adv. nearly, almost; all but; approximately, about; scarcely, hardly, barely. 1) quase o mesmo, much the same. 2) quase nada, next to nothing, almost nothing. 3) quase nunca, hardly ever. 4) quase que não, barely. 5) quase impossível, hardly possible.

quasimodal, quasimodesco, adj. monstrous.

quasímodo, s.m. Low Sunday.

quássia, s.f. quassia.

quassina, quassite, s.f. quassin.

quaternado, adj. quaternate, consisting of four (folhas).

quaternário, adj. quaternary (quatro elementos); quadruple (mús.); compasso quaternário, quadruple time.

quaternidade, s.f. quaternity.

quaterno, adj. quatern, fourfold, quadruple.

quatriduano, adj. lasting four days.

quatríduo, s.m. the períod of four days.

quatrienal, adj. quadriennial.

quatriénio, s.m. quadriennium, four-year period.

quatrilião, num quadrillion.

quatro, num. four. 1) a quatro, by fours; on all fours. 2) o diabo a quatro, terrible fuss.

quatro-cantinhos, s.m. (pl.) puss-in-the-corner (jogo).

quatrocentista, *adj.* quattrocentist.

quatrocentos, *num.* four hundred.

que, *pron.* who; whom; which; that; what? which?; *conj.* that; because; for, as; how; *prep.* except, but.

quê, *s.m.* something; why so?. 1) *não há de quê,* its nothing, don`t mention that it, you're welcome. 2) *para quê?,* what for?. 3) *qual o quê!,* no such thing!.

quebra, *s.f.* loss; break; breach; damage; bankruptcy. 1) *quebra fraudulenta,* fraudulent, bankruptcy. 2) *quebra de líquidos,* leakage.

quebra-cabeças, *s.m.* (pop) puzzle, difficult problem, enigma, riddle; a nut to crack.

quebrada, *s.f.* steep; slope; gully, hillside; ravine.

quebradela, *s.f.* breaking, splitting.

quebradiço, *adj.* brittle, friable, fragile, delicate, frail.

quebrado, *s.m.* fraction; *adj.* broken, ruptured; bankrupt; severed; in pieces; tired, exhausted; decrepit.

quebrador, *s.m.* breaker.

quebradura, *s.f.* breaking; hernia, rupture.

quebra-gelo, *s.m.* icebreaker *(navio).*

quebra-luz, *s.f.* shade, lamp-shade.

quebra-mar, *s.m.* break-water, jetty, sea-wall.

quebramento, *s.m.* breaking; depression, dejection; weariness, prostration.

quebrança, *s.f.* the breaking of the waves.

quebra-nozes, *s.m.* nutcracker.

quebrantado, *adj.* broken down; dejected, enfeebled, worn-out.

quebrantador, *adj.* breaking.

quebrantamento, *s.m.* breaking; infrigment; weariness, dpression, prostration, weakness.

quebrantar, *v.t.* to break; to bruise; to grow weak, to despirit, to despond; to weaken.

quebranto, *s.m.* prostration, weariness; exhaustion, relaxation, langour, lassitude; bewitching.

quebrar, *v.t.* to break, to shatter, to smash, to crak; to infringe, to violate; to intercept, to disconnect, to disjoin; to calm down, to mitigate; to tame; to wear out, to exhaust; to subjugate; to bend, to turn. 1) *quebrar a cabeça (fig.),* to cudgel one's brains. 2) *quebrar a palavra,* to break one's word. 3) *quebrar-se em pedaços,* to come asunder. 4) *quebrar o encanto,* to break the spell. 5) *quebrar lanças por,* to break lances with. 6)

quebrar o silêncio, to break the silence. 7) *quebrar a cara,* to smash another's face. 8) *quebrar o jejum,* to break fast.

quebrável, *adj.* breakable.

quebreira, *s.f.* prostration, weariness, lassitude, exhaustion, fatigue.

quebro, *s.m.* modulation *(da voz);* flexion *(do corpo),* intonation, cadence.

queda, *s.f.* fall, tumble; moral lapse; surrender; capitulation; collapse; ruin; decay; disgrace; drop; declivity; downfall; bent, inclination, aptitude; sin; *queda de água,* waterfall.

quedar-se, *s. refl.* to stop, to halt; to be quiet; to remain.

quediva, *s.m.* khedive.

quedo, *adj.* quiet; still, calm, peaceful, tranquil; stopped, motionless; *mudo e quedo como um penedo,* as silent and still as the grave.

quefazer, *s.m.* business, affairs, occupations, job; tasks, duties.

queijada, *s.f.* cheese-cake.

queijadeiro, *s.m.* chesse-cake maker.

queijar, *v.i.* to make cheese, to become cheese.

queijaria, *s.f.* cheese-making; cheese-factory, dairy.

queijeiro, *s.m.* cheese maker, cheese merchant.

queijo, *s.m.* cheese. 1) *queijo flamengo,* Dutch cheese. 2) *ser pão, pão, queijo, queijo,* to be outspoken, to call a spade a spade. 3) *ter a faca e o queijo na mão,* to have the ball at one`s feet, to take the law into one's own hands.

queima, *s.f.* burning, combustion, consuming, cremation; fire. 1) *queima das fitas,* burning of the ribbons *(Festival Universitário Português).* 2) *preço de queima,* low price.

queimação, *s.f.* burning,

queimada, *s.f.* burning, forest fire; burned-over land.

queimadela, *s.f.* burn.

queimado, *adj.* burnt; blasted; sunburnt, tanned; frost-bitten *(plantas);* *s.m.* smell or taste of burnt food.

queimadoiro, queimadouro, *s.m.* burning place.

queimadura, *s.f.* ver queimadela.

queimante, *adj.* burning, scorching; piquant.

queimar, *v.t.* to burn; to scald; to sunburn, to tan; to consume *(com fogo);* to char, to scorch; to sell out at reduced price; to blast, to blight, to nip *(plantas)*. 1) *queimas as pestanas*, to burn the midnight oil. 2) *queimar o último cartucho*, to fire one's last shout.

queima-roupa (à), *loc. adv.* pont-blank, face to face, at close range.

queímo, *s.m.* piquancy, burning taste.

queimor, *s.m.* intense heat.

queimoso, *adj.* burning, hot; piquant, caustic.

queiró, queiroga, queirós, *s.f.* ling, Sctoch heather.

queixa, *s.f.* complaint; accusation; offence; groan, moan; grievance, resentment; lamentation. 1) *razão de queixa*, reason (grounds) for complaint. 2) *apresentar queixa*, to lodge a complaint.

queixada, *s.f.* jaw-bone.

queixal, *s.m.* molar; grinder.

queixar-se, *v. refl.* to complain, to grumble; to groan, to moan; to resent, to take amiss; to lament, to wail; to make a formal accusation.

queixeiro, *adj.* wisdom tooth.

queixo, *s.m.* chin; jaw, jaw-bone; *bater o qeixo*, to chatter (com frio ou medo).

queixoso, *adj.* palintive, mournful; complaing; *s.m.* palintiff; complainer.

queixudo, *adj.* big-chinned, big-jawed.

queixume, *s.m.* complaint, lament, groan, moan, lamentation.

quejando, *adj.* like, alike, such, of the same kind; *e quejandos*, and the like.

quelha, *s.f.* lane, alley, narrow way.

quelho, *s.m.* blind alley.

quelónios, *s.m. (pl.)* Chelonia.

quem, *pron.* who, whom, which. 1) *quem de vocês?*, which of you?. 2) *quem é?*, who is it?. 3) *quem quer que seja*, whoever, whosoever 4) *de quem*, whose. 5) *seja quem for*, whoever it may be.

quemose, *s.f.* chemosis.

quente, *adj.* hot; warm; enthusiastic, fiery, excited; s.m. warm place, the bed.

quentura, *s.f.* heat, warmth.

quépi, *s.m.* kepi.

queque, *s.m.* cake.

quer, *conj.* either; whether. 1) *quer...quer*, either... or, whether... or. 2) *quer queira, quer não*, whether he will or not. 3) *quer este, quer aquele*, either his or that. 4) *onde quer que*, wherever. 5) *o que quer que*, whatever.

querco, *s.m.* oak.

querela, *s.f.* accusation, charge; indictment; lawsuit; dispute, altercation.

querelado, *s.m.* the accused, defendant.

querelador, *s.m.* plaintiff; prosecutor, accuser, demandant.

querelante, *adj.* complaining, querulous; *s.m.* plaintiff; accuser.

querelar, *v.i.* to make a charge; to complain; to sue.

quereloso, *adj.* querulous, complaining.

querena, *s.f.* hull of a vessel.

querenar, *v.t.* to careen.

querença, *s.f.* desire, will; affection, love, fondness.

querençoso, *adj.* desirous; benevolent; longing for; affectionate, fond.

querente, *adj.* willing, desirous of; wanting something.

querer, *v.t.* to want, to will, to desire, to wish; to be fond of, to appreciate, to have an affection for; to prefer; *s.m.* wish, will, desire; affection, love. 1) *sem querer*, by accident, unintenionally. 2) *querer é poder*, where there is a will there is a way. 3) *por querer*, intentionally, on purpose.

querido, *adj.*, *s.m.* dear, beloved, darling, favourite, pet; sweetheart.

quermesse, *s.f.* kermis, charitable bazaar.

querosene, *s.m.* kerosene, coal oil.

querubim, *s.m.* cherub.

querubínico, *adj.* cherubic.

quesito, *s.m.* question; requisite.

questão, *s.f.* question, interrogation, inquiry; subject, matter; controversy, contention; problem; point at issue. 1) *questão de honra*, affair of honour. 2) *uma questão de gosto, de opinião*, a matter of taste, of opinion. 3) *questão de vida ou de morte*, a case of life or death. 4) *eis a questão*, that is the point. 5) *fazer questão de*, to insist on, to make a point of. 6) *ladear a questão*, to dodge the question. 7) *resolver a questão*, to settle the question. 8) *é uma questão de dias*, it is a matter of days. 9) *questão judicial*, lawsuit. 10) *levantar uma questão*, to raise a question. 11) *não ver a questão*, to miss the point; quarrel; dispute.

questionador, *s.m.* quarreler; questioner; *adj.* questioning, quarreling.

questionar, *v.t.* to question, to interrogate; to dispute; to quarrel; to discuss.

questionário, *s.m.* questionary; questionnaire.

questionável, *adj.* questionable, debatable.

questiúncula, s.f. little discussion or dispute; slight difference.

questor, s.m. questor, State-treasurer (em Roma).

questorado, s.m. questorship.

quezilar, v.t. to anger; to irritate, to worry, to tease, to loathe, to annoy, to bore.

quezilento, adj. annoying, quarrelsome.

quezília, s.f. annoyance, repugnace; quarrel, disagreement; aversion, antipathy.

quiasma, s.m. chiasmus; chiasma (anatomia).

quiçá, adv. perhaps, maybe; who knows; possibly, perchance.

quício, s.m. hinge (de uma porta).

quico, s.m. ridiculous small hat (pop).

quiescente, adj. quiescent, still, inert, calm.

quietação, s.f. quietness, placidity; silence; calmness, peace, quietude.

quietar, v.t. to quiet, to appease, to calm, to pacify.

quietismo, s.m. quietism, passive mysticism; peace.

quietista, s. quietist; adj. quietistic.

quieto, adj. quiet, calm, placid, tranquil, still, motionless, peaceful, slient, serene.

quietude, s.f. quietude, quietness, placidity, tranquility, repose, rest, peacefulness, serenity.

quilatação, s.f. assaying.

quilatador, s.m. assayer.

quilatar, v.t. to assay, to value (ouro, prata, pedras preciosas).

quilate, s.m. carat; excellence, perfection.

quilha, s.f. keel.

quilífero, adj. chylific, chyliferous.

quilificação, s.f. chylification.

quilificar, v.t. to chylify.

quilo, s.m. kilo, kilogram; chyle.

quilociclo, s.m. kilocycle.

quilograma, s.m. kilogram(me).

quilogrâmetro, s.m. kilogrammetre.

quilolitro, s.m. kilolitre.

quilometragem, s.f. distance in kilometres.

quilometrar, v.t. to measure in kilometers.

quilométrico, adj. kilometric(al).

quilómetro, s.m. kilometre.

quiloplastia, s.f. plastic surgery of the lip, chiloplasty.

quilópode, s.m. chilopod, centipede.

quiloso, adj. chylous.

quilovático, s.m. kilowatt.

quilovolt, s.m. kilovolt.

quilúria, s.f. chyluria

quimão, quim, s.m. kimono.

quimbundo, s.m. language spoken by natives in Angola.

quimera, s.f. chimera, fancy, reverie, dream, fantasy, illusion.

quimérico, adj. chimerical, fanciful, unreal, fantastic, visionary, imaginary.

química, s.f. chemistry.

quimicamente, adv. chemically.

químico, adj. chemical; s.m. chemist.

quimificação, s.f. chymification.

quimificar, v.t. to chymify, to turn into chyme.

quimo, s.m. chyme.

quimono, s.m. kimono.

quina, s.f. five (jogo de cartas); cinque; sharp edge (de uma mesa); corner (de uma parede); quinquina.

quinado, adj. with quinquina, quinate, cinchonized.

quinaquina, s.f. quinquina.

quinar, v.t. to treat with quinquina, to cinchonize; to win (no loto).

quinário, adj. quinary.

quinau, s.m. correction, corrective.

quichorro, s.m. stable.

quincêncio, s.m. quincunx.

quindecágono, s.m. quindecagon.

quindénio, s.m. set of fifteen; period of five years.

quindim, s.m. difficulty; blandishment.

quineira, s.f. cinchona, quinquina, quinine bush.

quingentésimo, num. five-hundredth; s.m. the five-hundredth part.

quinhão, s.m. share, part, portion; allotment, divison; quota; destiny, fate (fig).

quinhentismo, s.m. cinquecento (estilo, gosto).

quinhentista, adj. of the 16th century; s. cinquencentist.

quinhentos, num. five hundred.

quinhoar, v.t. to apportion, to allot, to share, to partake.

quinhoeiro, s.m. sharer, partner.

quínico, adj. quínic.

quinina, s.f. quinine.

quinino, s.m. quinine.

quinismo, s.m. cinchonism.

quino, s.m. lotto.

quinquagenário, s.m., adj. quinquagenary, quinquagenarian.

Quinquagésima, s.f. quinquagesima; domingo da Quinquagésima, Shrove Sunday.

quinquagésimo, *num.* fiftieth; *s.m.* the fiftieth part.

quinquenal, *adj.* quinquennial.

quinquénio, *s.m.* quinquennium.

quinquilharias, *s.f. (pl.)* ironmongery, trifles, knicknacks, baubles, gewgaws, fripperies.

quinquilheiro, *s.m.* ironmonger.

quinta, *s.f.* farm; country-house; estate; *estar nas suas sete quintas*, to be satisfied with life, as happy as a sandboy.

quintão, *adj.* quintan.

quinta-coluna, *s.f.* fifth column.

quinta-essência, *s.f.* quintessence, the pure essence, the purest part, refinement.

quinta-feira, *s.f.* Thursday; *Quinta-Feira santa*, Maundy Thursday.

quintal, *s.m.* kitchen-garden; quintal; a hundred-weight.

quintalejo, quintalório, *s.m.* little garden.

quintanista, *s.* a fifth-year student *(Universidade)*.

quintarola, *s.f.* small farm.

quinteiro, *s.m.* farmer, farm caretaker.

quinteto, *s.m.* quintet.

quintilha, *s.f.* stanza with five lines.

quintilião, *num.* quintillion.

quinto, *num.* fifth; *s.m.* the fifth part.

quintuplicação, *s.f.* quintuplication.

quintuplicado, *adj.* quintuplicate, fivefold.

quintuplicar, *v.t.* to quintuplicate, to quintuple.

quíntuplo, *s.m., adj.* fivefold, quintuple.

quinze, *num.* fifteen.

quinzena, *s.f.* fortnight, two weeks.

quinzenal, *adj.* fortnightly, biweekly.

quinzenalmente, *adv.* fortnightly.

quinzenário, *s.m.* a fortnightly publication.

quiosque, *s.m.* kiosk, bookstall, news stand.

quiproquó, *s.m.* mistake, misinterpretation.

quiragra, *s.f.* chiragra, gouty pain.

quirografia, *s.f.* chirography, hand-writing.

quirógrafo, *s.m.* chirograph.

quirologia, *s.f.* dactylology.

quiromancia, *s.f.* chiromancy, palmistry.

quiromante, *s.m.* chiromancer, palmist, fortune teller.

quiromântico, *adj.* chiromantic(al).

quironomia, *s.f.* chironomy.

quirópteros, *s.m. (pl.)* Chiroptera.

quisto, *s.m.* cyst, wen; *adj.* well-liked, beloved.

quistoso, *adj.* cystic.

quita, *s.f.* ver quitação

quitação, *s.f.* acquittance, receipt; discharge, release.

quitamento, *s.m.* ver quitação.

quitança, *s.f.* ver quitação.

quitanda, *s.f.* shop, stall, small shop.

quitandeiro, *s.m.* street vender *(vegetais, fruta, ovos, etc.)*.

quitanga, *s.f. ver "quitanda".*

quitar, *v.t.* to acquit, to release from; to exempt from, to liberate, to free from, to relieve.

quite, *adj.* free; quit, discharged, released; *estar quite*, to be quits, to be even with.

quitina, *s.f.* chitin.

quitinoso, *adj.* chitinous.

quixotada, *s.f.* quixotry, vain boast.

quixotesco, *adj.* quixotic.

quixotice, *s.f.* ver quixotada.

quixotismo, *s.m.* quixotism, boasting.

quociente, *s.m.* quotient.

quoro, quórum, *s.m.* quorum.

quota, *s.f.* share, portion, quota, allotmant; contribution.

quota-parte, *s.f.* share, investment.

quotidianamente, *adv.* daily, every day.

quotidiano, *adj.* quotidian, daily.

quotiliquê, *s.m.* person *(ou coisa)* of no importance; trifle.

quotização, *s.f.* contribution; assessment.

quotizar, *v.t.* to assess, to parcel out; *quotizar-se*, to contribute, to club together.

R

r, the seventeenth letter of the Portuguese alphabet.

rã, *s.f.* frog.

rabaça, *s.f.* (bot.) a water parsnip.

rabaçal, *s.m.* (pl. - ais). 1) place where water parsnips grow; 2) a variety of Portuguese cheese.

rabaçaria, *s.f.* (pop.). 1) vegetables, greens. 2) fruits of inferior quality.

rabaceiro, *adj.* fond of fruits and vegetables.

rabada, *s.f.* 1) tail. 2) caudal fin.

rabadão, *s.m.* (pl.- ões) herdsman.

rabadela, rabadilha, *s.f.* the tail or rump of animals.

rabado, *adj.* tailed, caudate.

rabalvo, *adj.* white-tailed.

rabanada, *s.f.* 1) French toast. 2) stroke with the tail.

rabanal, *s.m.* (pl. -ais) growth of radish.

rabanete, *s.m.* (bot.) radish.

rábano, *s.m.* 1) turnip. 2) the root of this plant.

rabão, *s.m.* (pl. - ões) (f. rabona), large behind, posterior.

rabavento, *adj.* flying or sailling before the winds.

rabaz, *s.m.* thief.

rabdóide, *adj. m.f.,* rabdóide m. rhabdoid(al), spindle-shaped, rod-shaped.

rabdologia, *s.f.* rhabdology, art or method of calculating by means of small rods.

rabdológico, *adj.* rhabdological.

rabdomancia, *s.f.* rhabdomancy, divination by rods or wands.

rabdomante, *s.m. e f.* rhabdomancer, dowser.

rabdomântico, *adj.* rhabdomantic.

rabeador, *adj.* wagging, whisking (tail).

rabear, *v.* 1) to wag, whisk (the tail); 2) to move restlessly, fidget; 3) to be restless or uneasy. 4) to wheedle around a person, flatter meanly.

rabeca, *s.f.* 1) fiddle, violin. 2) (billiards) cue rest.

rabecada, *s.f.* 1) fiddling, fiddle music. 2) (fig.) reprimand. 3) slander, backbiting.

rabecão, *s.m.* (pl. -ões). 1) bass fiddle. 2) double bass.

rabeira, *s.f.* 1) track, trace. 2) awn. 3) chaff.

rabejador, *s.m.* bull catcher, one who holds a bull by the tail.

rabejar, *v.* to hold a bull by the tail.

rabelaisiano, *adj.* Rabelaisian, characteristic of Rabelais or his works.

rabela, *s.f.* back part of a plough (from share to handle).

rabelo, *s.m.* 1) plough-tail. 2) handle of a plough.

rabequista, *s.m., f.* fiddler, violinist.

rabeta, *s.m.* white wagtail.

rabi, *s.m.* rabbi, Jewish master of religious law.

rábia, *s.f.* (med.) hydrofobia, rabies.

rabialvo, *adj.* white-tailed.

rabiar, *v.* 1) to rage, rave. 2) to act violently. 3) to grow impatient; 4) to become enraged.

rabiça, *s.f.* plough-tail, plough handle.

rabicão, (pl. -ões), rabicano *adj.* having threads of white hair in the tail (said of horses).

rabicha, *s.f.* back part of a carriage.

rabicho, *s.m.* 1) pigtail. 2) crupper (of a harness). 3) tail. 4) hitch rope of a water-wheel.

rábico, *adj.* rabietic.

rabicó, *adj.* tailless, docked.

rabicurto, *adj.* short-tailed.

rábido, *adj.* 1) rabid. 2) raging, furious. 3) wild, fierce.

rabiforcado, *adj.* (zool.) fork-tailed.

rabigo, *adj.* 1) that wags constantly its tail. 2) (fig.) active, diligent. 3) (fig.) restless, fussy.

rabijunco, *s.m.* pintail.

rabila, *s.f.* gallinule, water hen.

rabilonga, *s.f.* a kind of blue magpie.

rabilongo, *adj.* long-tailed.

rabinice, *s.f.* 1) mischief, prank. 2) crossness, sullenness.

rabínico, *adj.* rabbinic(al).

rabinismo, *s.m.* rabbinism.

rabinista, *s.m., f.* rabbinist.

rabino, *s.m.* rabbi, master and teacher of Jewish religious law.

rabino, *adj.* 1) mischievous, frolicsome. 2) peevish, cross.

rabioso, *adj.* 1) rabid. 2) irritated, furious. 3) wild, fierce.

rabiosque, rabioste, rabiote, *s.m. (pop.)* the posterior, behind.

rabipreto, *adj. (zool.)* black-tailed.

rabirruivo, *adj. (zool.)* red-tailed.

rabisca, *s.f.* scrawl, scribbling.

rabiscado, *adj.* scrawly.

rabiscador, *s.m.* 1) scribbler. 2) scrawler. *adj.* scrawling.

rabiscar, *v.* 1) to scribble, scrawl. 2) to write hastily or carelessly. 3) to draw doodles. 4) to scrabble, scratch.

rabisco, *s.m.* 1) scribble, scrawl. 2) doodle(s). 3) scratch. 4) curlicue, flourish.

rabisseco, adj. unproductive, barren, sterile.

rabisteco, rabistel, *s.m. (fam.)* a child's buttocks.

rabo, *s.m.* 1) tail, brush. 2) tail feathers, tail fin. 3) handle (of certain implements). 4) *(fam., pop.)* buttocks, bottom, posterior. 5) stern.

rabona, *s.f.* 1) short jacket. 2) *(fam.)* dress with a train. 3) dress coat. 4) hoe with a short handle.

rabonar, *v.* 1) to crop an animal's tail. 2) to get ahead of (another horse at a race).

rabo-ruivo, *s.m. (pl. rabos-ruivos) (zool.)* black redstart.

raboso, *adj.* long-tailed.

rabotar, *v.* to plane, smooth.

rabote, *s.m.* jack plane.

rabudo, *adj.* long-tailed, tailed.

rabugem, *s.f. (pl. -ens).* 1) *(vet.)* mange. 2) ill temper, crossness. 3) fretfulness.

rabugento, *adj.* 1) *(vet.)* mangy (said of dogs). 2) morose, sullen. 3) cross, cantankerous. 4) *(fig.)* impertinent. 5) peevish, fretful.

rabugice, *s.f.* 1) peevishness, fretfulness. 2) crossness, petulance. 3) impertinence. 4) chicanery.

rabuja, *s.m., f.* cantankerous or peevish person. *adj.* 1) cross, cantankerous. 2) peevish, fretful. 3) impertinent.

rabujar, *v.* 1) to act morosely. 2) to be impertinent. 3) to grumble. 4) to scold continually. 5) to whimper.

rábula, *s.m.* 1) pettifogger, shyster. 2) talkative man, prattler.

rabujar, *v. (also rabulejar).* 1) to pettifog, shyster. 2) to brag, boast. 3) to act in a petty or tricky manner.

rabularia, rabulice, *s.f.* 1) pettifoggery, chicanery. 2) boast, bragging. 3) empty talk, prattle.

rabulista, *s.m. , f.* trickster, pettifogger. *adj.* pettifogging.

rabujar, *v.* to prepare the bark of cork-tree (for production of stoppers).

raça, *s.f.* 1) race. 2) generation, genealogical group. 3) origin, descent, lineage. 4) tribe, family. 5) stock, breed, strain. 6) mankind. 7) ethnical stock. 8) species, pedigree, ancestry.

ração, *s.f. (pl. -ões)* ration, fixed daily allowance of food served out for man or animal; portion. 1) *ração de reserva,* emergency ration. 2) *ração dobrada,* double allowance. 3) *para um dia,* daily allowance.

racemado, *adj. (bot.)* racemose.

racemico, *adj. (quim.)* racemic.

racemifero, *adj. (bot.)* racemiferous.

racemifloro, *adj. (bot.)* racemiflorous.

racemiforme, *adj., m. e f.* racemiform.

racemo, *s.m. (bot.)* 1) raceme, cluster. 2) a bunch of grapes.

racemoso, *adj. (bot.)* racemose, clustered.

racha, *s.f.* 1) crack, cleft, fissure; 2) splinter, sliver, chip.

rachadeira, *s.f.* cleaver, cleaving tool, grafting knife.

rachado, *adj.* cleft. split, cracked.

rachador, *s.m.* 1) woodcutter. 2) hewer, splitter. *adj.* splitting.

rachadura, *s.f.* 1) cleft, fissure, crack. 2) splitting, cleaving.

rachão, *s.m. (pl. -ões) (bar.).* 1) mountain gorge, defile. 2) a woodman's axe.

rachar, *v.* 1) to split, cleave. 2) to splinter, shiver. 3) to chap, rive.

racial, *adj., m. e f. (pl. -ais)* racial; raciamente *adv.* racially.

racimo, *s.m. (bot.)* 1) raceme, cluster. 2) a bunch of grapes.

raciocinação, *s.f. (pl. -ões)* reasoning, ratiocination.

raciocinador, *s.m.* reasoner, ratiocinator, *adj.* reasoning.

raciocinar, *v.* 1) to reason, ratiocinate. 2) to think. 3) to consider, deliberate. 4) to argue.

raciocinativo, *adj.* ratiocinative, ratiocinatory, discursive.

raciocínio, *s.m.* 1) rationcination, reasoning. 2) thought. 3) judgment, reasoning power. 4) argumentation, inductions. 5) logic.

racionabilidade, *s.f.* rationality, rationalness.

racionado, *adj.* rationed, stinted; ter a comida racionada, to be kept on short commons, rations.

racional, *s.m. (pl. -ais)* a rational being; *adj. m., f.* 1) rational, endowed with reason. 2) reasonable, sensible. 3) logical. 4) laboursaving, methodic(al). 5) sane; *racionalmente adv.* rationally.

racionalidade, *s.f.* rationality, reasonableness, reason.

racionalismo, *s.m.* 1) retionalism. 2) adherence to the supremacy of reason. 3) doctrina that knowledge is exclusively the product of ratiocination.

racionista, *s.m. e f.* rationalist, adj. rationalistic.

racionalização, *s.f. (pl. -ões)* rationalization.

racionalizar, *v.* 1) to rationalize, make conformable to reason. 2) to ratiocinate, reason. 3) to interpret by rational principles. 4) to streamline business procedures or production methods.

racionamento, *s.m.* rationing, ration.

racionar, *v.* 1) to ration. 2) to supply with rations. 3) to divide into rations. 4) to put upon allowance.

racionável, *adj., m. e f. (pl. -áveis)* reasonable.

racismo, *s.m.* racism.

racista, *s.m. e f.* racist; *adj.* racialistic.

raçoeiro, *s.m.* distributer or receiver of rations.

racontar, *v.* to narrate, relate.

raconto, *s.m.* narration, story, report.

radar, *s.m.* radar.

radiação, *s.f. (pl. -ões).* 1) irradiation, emission and diffusion of rays. 2) radiation. 3) radiance, radiancy.

radiado, *s.m. (zool.)* the Radiata: a group of invertebrates. *adj. (bot., zool.)* radiate, radiated.

radiador, *s.m.* radiator.

radial, *adj., m. e f. (pl. -ais)* radial; radial-mente *adv.* radially.

radialista, *s.m. e f.* broadcaster.

radiano, *s.m. (mat.)* radian, unit angle.

radiante, *adj. m. e f.* 1) radiant, brilliant. 2) radiate. 3) beautiful. 4) splendid. 5) gleeful, joyous; radiantemente adv. radiantly.

radiar, *v.* 1) to radiate, emit rays. 2) to sparkle, scintillate. 3) to beam. 4) to broadcast, transmit by wireless. 5) to diffuse, divulge.

radiário, *s.m. (zool.)* the Radiata.

radicação, *s.f. (pl. -ões)* radication, rootage, rootedness.

radicado, *adj.* 1) radicated, rooted. 2) *(fig.)* inveterate.

radical, *s.m. (pl. -ais)* radical. 1) *(pol.)* ultraist, adept of radicalism. 2) *(fil.)* primitive word, root of a word. 3) *(mat.)* radical expression or sign. 4) *(quím.)* fundamental constituent of a compound. *adj., m. e f.* 5) radical: of or pertaining to a root. 6) basic, fundamental. 7) essential. 8) *(pol.)* leftist. 9) thoroughgoing; *adv.* radically. 10) houve uma mudança radical, there was a radical change.

radicalismo, *s.m.* radicalism, ultraism.

radicalista, *s.m. e f.* radical, ultraist; *adj. m. e f.* radical.

radicando, *s.m. (mat.)* radicand.

radicar, *v.* 1) to radicate, take root. 2) to root. 3) to plant deeply and firmly. 4) to settle (down).

radicela, *s.f. (bot.)* radicel, radicle, rootlet.

radicícola, *adj., m. e f.* radicicolous, living upon roots.

radicifloro, *adj. (bot.)* radiciflorous.

radiciforme, *adj., m. e f.* radiciform, rootlike.

radicívoro, *adj.* radicivorous.

radícola, *adj., m. e f.* radicicolous.

radicoso, *adj.* radicose, rooty, full of roots.

radícula, *s.f. (bot.)* radicule, radicle, rootlet.

radiculado, *adj.* radicular, having roots, rooty.

radicular, *adj., m. e f.* radicular, of or pertaining to roots.

rádio, *s.m.* 1) *(anat.)* radius: the shorter of the two forearm or forelimb bones. 2) *(chem.)* radium: a radioactive, metallic element (Ra). 3) radio transmitter or receiver. 4) radiogram, wireless telegram. 5) radiometer.

radioactividade, *s.f.* radioactivity.

radioactivo, *adj.* radioactive.

radiocomunicação, *s.f. (pl. -ões)* radio communication.

radiocondutor, *s.m.* radioconductor.

radiocultura, *s.f.* 1) *(fis.)* branch of physics which deals with the effects of (high-frequency, colour or ultrasonic) radiations on plant growth. 2) the cultural influence of radiobroadcasting.

radiodermite, *s.f. (med.)* radiodermatitis, dermatitis caused by exposure to radiations.

radiodiagnóstico, *s.m. (med.)* radiodiagnosis.

radiofundir, *v.* to radiobroadcast.

radiodifusão, *s.f.* (pl. -ões) broadcasting.

radiodifusor, *s.m.* broadcasting station, broadcaster. *adj.* broadcasting.

radioelectricidade, *s.f.* radioelectricity.

radioemissora, *s.f.* radio broadcasting station.

radiofaixa, *s.f.* radio range.

radiofarol, *s.m.* (pl. -óis) radio beacon.

radiofone, *s.m.* radiophone.

radiofonia, *s.f.* radiophony.

radiofonização, *s.f.* (pl. -ões) adaptation of a script for radiobroadcasting.

radiofonizar, *v.* to adapt a script for radiobroadcasting.

radiofrequência, *s.f.* radio frequency.

radiogoniometria, *s.f.* radiogoniometry, direction finding.

radiogoniómetro, *s.m.* radiogoniometer, direction finder.

radiografar, *v.* 1) to radiograph. 2) to radiotelegraph, radio.

radiografia, *s.f.* radiography, roentgenogram, x-ray photograph or inspection.

radiográfico, *adj.* radiographic(al); radiogra-ficamente, *adv.* radiographically.

rediógrafo, *s.m.* radiographer.

radiograma, *s.m.* radiogram, wireless telegram or message.

radiola, *s.f.* radiophonograph.

radiolário, *s.m.* (zool.) radiolarian, specimen of the Radiolaria; *adj.* radiolarian.

radiologia, *s.f.* radiology, roentgenology, science of radioactive substances and their application.

radiológico, *adj.* radiologic(al).

radiologista, *s.m. e f.* radiologist, roentgenologist.

radiometria, *s.f.* (fis.) radiometry.

radiometro, *s.m.* 1) (náut.) cross-staff. 2) (fís.) radiometer.

radiopatrulha, *s.f.* flying squad, radio patrol.

radioquimografia, *s.f.* (med.) roentgen--kymography.

radioquimógrafo, *s.m.* (med.) radio-kymo-graph.

radioquimograma, *s.m.* (med.) radio-kymogram.

radiorreceptor, *s.m.* radio receiver.

radioscopia, *s.f.* radioscopy, fluoroscopy.

radioscópico, *adj.* radioscopic(al).

radioso, *adj.* 1) radiant, brilliant. 2) ecstatic. 3) jubilant, joyful.

radiossonda, *s.f.* (meteor). radiosonda.

radioteatro, *s.m.* radio theater.

radiotecnica, *s.f.* radiotechnology.

radiotelefonia, *s.f.* radiotelephony, radiophony.

radiotelefónico, *adj.* radiotelephonic(al).

radiotelegrafia, *s.f.* radiotelegraphy, wireless telegraphy.

radiotelegráfico, *adj.* radiotelegraphic(al).

radiotelegrafista, *s.m. e f.* radio operator, wireless operator.

radioterapêutico, *adj.* radiotherapeutic(al).

radioterapia, *s.f.* (med.) radiotherapy.

radioterápico, *adj.* radiotherapeutic(al).

radiouvinte, *s.m. e f.* radio listener.

radónio, *s.m.* (quím) radon (Rn), niton.

raer, *v.* 1) to sweep the (warm) furnace of a bakery after heating. 2) to pile up salt (in a salt bed.)

rafa, *s.f.* 1) hunger. 2) poverty,m penury. 3) (náut). full tide.

rafado, *adj.* 1) hungry, starved. 2) shabby, theadbare. 3) poor, indigent.

rafaelesco, *adj.* Raphaelesque, Raphaelic.

rafaelista, rafaelita, *s.m.* Raphaelite, painter of the Raphaelic school.

raféia, *s.f.* rabble, mob, riffraff.

rafar, *v.* to waste, wear out, fray.

rafeiro, *s.m.* cattle dog, watch-dog.

ráfia, *s.f.* raffia. 1) (bot.) the palm. 2) its fiber.

rafiar, *v.t.* 1) to weave. 2) to pamper, coddle.

ráfide, *s.f.* (bot.) raphides.

rafigrafia, *s.f.* art or system of writing for the blind, in which the letters are represented by raised dots.

rafigráfico, *adj.* of or referring to Braille or similar systems of printing for the blind.

raflesiácea, *s.f.* any plant of the rafflesia family.

raflesiáceo, *adj.* (bot.) rafflesiaceous.

ragóideo, *adj.* aciniform.

ragu, *s.m.* ragout.

raia, *s.f.* 1) line, stroke, streak. 2) line in the palm of the hand. 3) octogonal paper kite. 4) race-course. 5) brand on a horse. 6) limit, boundary, ambit; 7) frontier, border. 8) common European skate; ray. 9) blunder, boner, mistake.

raiado, *adj.* 1) striped, streaked. 2) radiated. 3) veined.

raiano, *s.m.* borderer. *adj.* bordering upon.

raia-pintada, *s.f. (pl. raias-pintadas)* spotted sting ray.

raiar, *v.* 1) to break (the day), dawn. 2) to emit rays, radiate. 3) to shine, sparkle, gleam. 4) to come in sight, appear, peep out. 5) to rifle. 6) to stripe, streak. 7) to cover with strokes or lines. 8) to reach extremes. 9) to come nearer.

raigota, *s.f.* 1) rootlet, radicle. 2) hangnail.

raigotoso, *adj.* radicant.

raineta, *s.f.* 1) reinette, queen apple. 2) *(zool.)* tree toad.

rainha, *s.f.* 1) queen. 2) the principal or first among others. 3) a variety of apples or pears. 4) queen bee.

rainha-cláudia, *s.f. (pl. rainhas-cláudias)* greengage.

raio, *s.m.* 1) ray, beam. 2) heat radiation. 3) *(geom.)* radius. 4) spoke of a wheel. 5) *(fig.)* signal, sign, indication. 6) flash of lightning, thunderbolt. 7) fatality, disgrace, misfortune. 8) turbulent person.

raiva, *s.f.* 1) rage, fury. 2) *(vet.)* hydrophobia, rabies. 3) hate. 4) dislike, aversion. 5) madness.

raivar, raivecer, *v.* 1) to rage, rave. 2) to be extremely angry or furious. 3) to be mad *(dog).* 4) to burn with desire or lust after. 5) to threaten, menace.

raivejar, *v.* to become angry, shout angrily.

raivento, *adj.* 1) furious, angry. 2) choleric.

raivoso, *adj.* angry, furious, raging; raivosa-mente adv. ragefully.

raiz, *s.f. (pl. raízes)* 1) root: subterranean part of a plant; the hidden cause of anything, base; origin, source. 2) *(med.)* radicles of a tumour; 3) original or principal site of a rural property. 4) *raiz aérea,* aerial root. 5) *raiz cubica,* cube root.

rajá, *s.m.* raja, rajah.

rajada, *s.f.* 1) gust of wind, squall, blast. 2) stroke with the tail. 3) *(fig.)* burst of eloquence. 4) impetuousness. 5) rajada forte, a heavy squall of wind.

rajado, *s.m.* rajahship.

rajar, *v.* 1) to stripe, streak. 2) to intermingle. 3) to intersperse.

rajeira, *s.f.* hawser.

rajo, *s.m.* part of a pine tree cut off in order to extract turpentine.

rala, *s.f.* 1) *(med.)* rhonchus. 2) bran, brown flour.

ralação, *s.f. (pl. -ões)* 1) act of grating. 2) worry, vexation. 3) weariness.

ralador, *s.m.* grater, rasper.

raladura, *s.f.* 1) raspings, scrapings. 2) act of grating.

ralar, *v.* 1) to grate, rasp. 2) to worry, annoy. 3) to chafe, fret. 4) to vex, harass.

ralé, *s.f.* 1) common people, riffraff, rabble, populace, mob. 2) animals on which raprapine birds usually prey.

raleadura, *s.f.* raleamento, m. act of thinning out (unripe fruit on trees, foliage) or making less compact.

ralear, *v.* (also *ralentar*) to thin out, make sparse.

raleira, *s.f.* empty spot in a field; glade.

ralhação, *s.f. (pl. -ões)* scolding, rebuke, chiding.

ralhador, *s.m.* scolder, chider. *adj.* scolding.

ralhão, *s.m. (pl. -ões) (f. -ona)* scolder, reprimander.

ralhar, *v.* 1) to scold, rail. 2) to chide. 3) to reprimand, censure. 4) to find fault with. 5) to get angry.

ralho, *s.m.* scolding, chiding, rebuke, reprimand.

ralo, *s.m.* 1) grater, rasper. 2) strainer. 3) sprinkling nozzle. 4) grating. 5) *(med.)* rhonchus. 6) *(zool.)* mole cricket; *adj.* thin, rare, diluted.

rama, *s.f.* 1) branches, boughs (of a tree). 2) foliage. 3) (weav.) tenter. 4) *(tipog.)* printer's chase.

ramada, *s.f.* branches, boughs. 2) foliage. 3) trellis, latticework. 4) shelter for ranging cattle. 5) arbour, bower.

Ramadão, *s.m.* Ramadhan: name of the ninth month of the Moslem year.

ramado, *adj.* branchy, ramate, branched.

ramagem, *s.f. (pl. -ens)* 1) branches, boughs, foliage. 2) *(art.)* floral or leaf pattern.

ramal, *s.m. (pl. -ais)* 1. strands (of a yarn or rope). 2) railroad branch line. 3) string. 4) telephone extension line. 5) ramification. 6) tassel of a doctor's cap.

ramalhada, *s.f.* 1) boughs, branches. 2) rustling of leaves.

ramalhão, *s.m. (pl. -ões) (pop.)* big branch. *adj.* bulky, large in size.

ramalhar, *v.* to rustle, sough.

ramalheira, *s.f.* 1) branches, boughs. 2) *(naút.)* rowlock strap.

ramalhete, *s.m.* 1) little branch. 2) nosegay, little bunch of flowers, bouquet. 3) cluster. 4) hoarding.

ramalheteira, *s.f.* flower-girl, female florist.

ramalho, *s.m.* 1) big branch. 2) dead bough cut from a tree.

ramalhoso, ramalhudo, *adj.* 1) branchy, full of boughs. 2) *(fig.)* long-winded, verbose. 3) having long eyelashes.

ramaria, *s.f.* branches, boughs, foliage.

rambutão, *s.m. (pl. -ões)* rambutan (fruit).

rambuteira, *s.f. (bot.)* rambutan (tree).

rameira, *s.f.* prostitute.

rameiro, *s.m.* best bidder on a part contract.

ramela, *s.f.* = remela.

rameloso, *adj.* bleary-eyed, bleary.

ramento, *s.m.* 1) fragment, particle, remnants. 2) *(bot.)* ramentum.

râmeo, *adj.* growing on branches, rameous.

ramerrão, *s.m. (pl. -ões).* 1) monotonous sound, dull routine; rut. 2) constant use.

rami, *s.m.* ramie (plant and fiber).

ramificação, *s.f. (pl. -ões)* 1) ramification. 2) branching, offshoot. 3) branches of a stem. 4) *(fig.)* propagation, diffusion.

ramificado, adj. 1) ramified, branched. 2) subdivided. 3) forked, furcate.

ramificar, *v.* 1) to divide into branches, ramify. 2) to furcate, subdivide. 3) *ramificar--se,* to branch off. *(fig.)* to propagate, diffuse.

ramifloro, *adj. (bot.)* ramiflorous.

ramiforme, *adj., m. e f. (bot.)* ramiform.

ramilhete, *s.m.* = ramalhete.

ramilho, *s.m.* small bough, twig.

raminho, *s.m.* twig.

ramíparo, *adj. (bot.)* ramiparous.

ramnácea, *s.f.* plant of the buckthorn family (Rhamnaceae).

ramnáceo, *adj. (bot.)* rhamnaceous.

ramo, *s.m.* 1) branch, bough. 2) twig, sprig. 3) offshoot. 4) bunch of flowers, nosegay, bouquet.

ramonadeira, *s.f.* rasp file.

ramosidade, *s.f.* branchiness.

ramoso, *adj.* ramose, ramouse, branchy, twiggy.

rampa, *s.f.* 1) ramp, sloping roadway. 2) stage.

rampadouro, *s.m.* sloping ground.

rampante, *adj., m. e f. (her.)* rampant, combatant.

rampear, *v.* to slope.

ramudo, *adj.* 1) ramose, branchy. 2) dense.

ramúsculo, *s.m.* little branch, twig.

rançado, *adj.* rancid, rank, stale.

rançar, rancescer, *v.* to grow rancid, musty or stale.

ranchada, *s.f.* crowd of people, band, gang.

rancheiro, *s.m.* messmate, regimental cook.

ranchel, *s.m. (pl. -éis)* small mess.

rancheira, *s.f.* rancheiro m. hut camp.

rancho, *s.m.* 1) group of wanderers or revellers. 2) fare, ration, chow, grub, food (for seamen, soldiers, prisoners, etc. 3) crowd of people. 4) soldiers`mess. 5) *(naút.)* crew`s quarters. 6) hut, shelter, lodge, ranch.

râncido, râncio, *adj.* rancid, rank, musty.

ranco, *s.m.* branch of a tree.

ranço, *s.m.* 1) rancidity, rancidness. 2) rank smell. 3) mustiness. 4) *(fig.)* old things or sayings, rubbish. *adj.* rancid, rank. 5) cheirar a ranço, to have a rank smell.

rancor, *s.m.* 1) rancour, deep-seated hate; 2) resentment. 3) spite, grudge, ill blood. 4) enmity.

rancoroso, *adj.* 1) rancorous. 2) resentful, spiteful, hateful. 3) malicious.

rançoso, *adj.* 1) rancid, rusty, rank. 2) stale, musty; 3) *(fig.)* antiquated, old-fashioned.

rasfastídeo, *s.m. (zool.)* specimen of the toucan family (Ramphastidae); *adj.* of or pertaining to this family.

ranfoteca, *s.f. (zool.)* rhamphoteca.

rangedeira, *s.f.* inner sole, piece of leather put between the soles.

rangedor, *adj. m.,* rangente *m. e f.* creaking, grating.

ranger, *v.* 1) to screach, creak. 2) to grate, grit. 3) to cause to creak.

rangido, *s.m.* creaking, gnashing, screach.

rangíter, rangífero, *s.m. (zool.)* reindeer, caribou.

ranhar, *v.* to scratch, scrape.

ranheta, *s.m. e f.* impertinent person, curmudgeon.

ranho, *s.m.* snivel, snot, mucus from the nose.

ranhoso, *adj.* snotty, snivelling, snotty-nosed.

ranhura, *s.f.* 1) groove. 2) notch, rabbet. 3) slot, slit. 4) furrow, trench, chase.

ranicultura, *s.f.* frog breeding.

ranídeo, *s.m. (zool.)* specimen of the family Ranidae *(frogs).*

ranilha, *s.f.* frog of a horse`s hoof.

ranini, *adj. (anat.)* ranine.

ranu, *s.m.* plant of the nettle family (Urtica utilis).

ranu-branco, s.m. (pl. ranus- brancos) (bot.) false nettle.

rânula, *s.f. (med.)* ranula, small cystic tumour on the underside of the tongue.

ranunculácea, *s.f.* plant of the family Ranunculaceae.

ranunculáceo, *adj. (bot.)* ranunculaceous.

ranúnculo, *s.m. (bot.)* lesser spearwort, ranunculus, buttercup, crowfoot.

ranúnculo-aquático, *s.m. (pl. ranúnculos-aquáticos)* water crowfoot.

ranúnculo-dos-jardins, *s.m. (pl. ranúnculos-dos-jardins) (bot.)* Asiatic crowfoot.

ranúnculo-dos-prados, *s.m. (pl. ranúnculos-dos-prados) (bot.)* paigle, meadow crowtoot.

ranzinza, *adj. m. e f.* 1) sullen, sulky. 2) ill-humoured. 3) unruly. 4) impertinent. 5) crabby, crabbed.

ranzinzar, *v.* to be or become sullen, cantankerous or unruly.

rapa, *s.f.* 1) teetotum, small four-sided toy of the top kind marked with letters on each side, which indicate the player's score. 2) *(fam.)* glutton.

rapace, *adj. m. e f.* rapacious, ravening.

rapácio, *adj. (bot.)* resembling a bobtail.

rapacidade, *s.f.* rapacity, rapaciousness, ravenousness.

rapa-cuia, *s.f. (pl. rapa-cuias) (zool.)* 1) a snout beetle. 2) small frog which lives on plants of the pineapple family, (also called rapa-coco).

rapadeira, *s.f.* scraper, rasp, scraping knife.

rapadela, *s.f.* scraping, scratching, rubbing.

rapado, *adj.* 1) scraped, rasped. 2) cropped. 3) clean-shaven.

rapador, *s.m.* 1) scraper. 2) *(Bras.)* completely grazed or short-cropped pasture; *adj.* scraping, rasping.

rapadouro, *s.m.* pasture which has been grazed clean.

rapadura, *s.f.* 1) scraping, scrapings. 2) raspings. 3) block of raw brown sugar.

rapagão, *s.m. (pl. -ões)* strong, healthy lad.

rapalhas, *s.f.* litter of manure which remains in a stable.

rapante, *adj. m. e f. (her.)* represented in the posture of scraping the ground.

rapão, *s.m. (pl. -ões)* 1) person who gathers litter or manure. 2) a saltmaker's rake.

rapapé, *s.m.* 1) curtsy, scrape. 2) servile greeting. 3) flattery, adulation.

rapar, *v.* 1) to scrape, scratch. 2) to wear out. 3) to cut, cut off or short. 4) to rasp, grate. 5) to cause the death of. 6) to shave close

to the skin. 7) to steal, rob. 8) to extort cunningly, cheat. 9) to paw the ground (horses, dogs, etc.).

rapariga, *s.f.* 1) girl, maiden. 2) *(pop.)* lass, filly.

raparigaça, *s.f.* strong, comely girl.

raparigada, *s.f.* a lot of girls.

raparigota, *s.f.* lass, filly.

raparigueiro, *s.m. (Bras.)* woman chaser. *adj.* woman-chasing.

rapa-tábuas, *s.m., pl.* mediocre carpenter.

rapa-tachos, *s.m. e f., pl.* gorger, greedy eater, plate licker.

rapateácea, *s.f.* plant of the family Rapateaceae.

rapaz, *s.m.* 1) boy, lad. 2) youth, youngster. 3) young man, fellow, chap. 4) *(Bras.)* Negro stripling. 5) errand boy, servant. 6) a snipe *(Capella undulata).*

rapazelho, rapazete, *s.m.* little boy, urchin.

rapaziada, *s.f.* 1) a lot of boys, gang of urchins. 2) boyish act or saying, mischievous trick. 3) folly, prank. 4) spree, frolic.

rapazinho, *s.m.* 1) little boy, kid. 2) *(Bros.)* spotted sandpiper. 3) rapazinho de recados, call boy.

rapazinho-dos-velhos, *s.m. (pl. rapazinhos-dos-velhos) (zool.)* puffbird.

rapazio, *s.m.* 1) group of boys. 2) boys or young men collectively.

rapazola, *s.m.* lad, young man.

rapazote, *s.m.* = rapazelho.

rapé, *s.m.* snuff, rappee.

rapeira, *s.f.* spawning ground.

rapezista, *s.m. e f.* snuff-taker.

rapidez, *s.f.* 1) rapidity. 2) quickness, swiftness. 3) speed velocity. 4) haste. 5) a *rapidez das impressões visuais,* the fleetingness of visual impressions.

rápido, *s.m.* 1) rapids, chute, swift current. 2) express or special delivery service. 3) express train, fast day train. *adj.* 4) rapid, quick, swift. 5) speedy. 6) instantaneous, prompt. 7) active, sharp, brisk. 8) hasty. rapidamente, *adv.* rapidly, speedily, apace, double-quick. 9) *rápido como um raio,* quick as lightning.

rapilho, *s.m.* 1) rapilho, volcanic dust; 2) seaweed used as manure.

rapina, *s.f.* rapine, robbery, plunder; ave de rapina.

rapinador, *s.m.* plunderer, robber. *adj.* plundering.

rapinagem, *s.f., (pl. -ens)* robbery, plunder, pillage.

rapinante, *s.m. e f.* robber, plunderer. *adj.* plundering, pillaging, predatory.

rapinar, *v.* 1) to rob, plunder. 2) to take away by force. 3) to commit robbery.

rapineiro, *s.m. (Bras.)* bird of prey. *adj.* rapacious, raptorial.

rapistro, *s.m. (bot.)* a kind of wild turnip.

rapôncio, raponço, *s.m. (bot.).* 1) rampion. 2) horned rampion.

raposa, *s.f.* 1) *(zool.)* fox.

raposada, *s.f.* 1) nap, doze. 2) undisturbed sleep.

raposar, *v.* 1) to play truant, shirk lessons. 2) to idle about. 3) to reproof, reprimand. 4) to reject a student (exami-nation).

raposear, *v. (Bras.)* to reject, plough a student in an examination.

raposeira, *s.f.* 1) deep undisturbed sleep. 2) a nap in the mild sun. 3) intoxication, drunkeness. 4) fox hole.

raposeiro, *s.m.* sly or cunning fellow. *adj.* sly, artful, cunning.

raposeira, raposice, *s.f.* 1) slyness of a fox. 2) artfulness, cunningness. 3) malice, ill will.

raposinho, *s.m.* 1) fox cub. 2) strong, disa-greeable smell (like that of a fox). 3) noxious exhalation.

raposino, *adj.* vixenish, vixenly.

raposo, *s.m. (zool.)* male fox, dog-fox.

rapsódia, *s.f.* rhapsody. 1) *(hist.)* portion of an epic poem (e. g. the iliad or the Odyssey). 2) literary miscellany. 3) excerpt from a poem. 4) *(mús.)* improvisation.

rapsódico, *adj.* rhapsodic(al).

rapsodista, *s.m. e f.* rhapsodist.

rapsodo, *s.m.* 1) rhapsode, itinerant bard. 2) *(fig.)* poet.

rapsodomancia, *s.f.* rhapsodomancy: divi-nation by means of verses.

rapsodomante, *s.m. e f.* rhapsodomancer.

rapsodomântico, *adj.* of or referring to rapsodomancy.

raptor, *s.m.* abductor, kidnapper. *adj.* abduc-ting, ravishing.

raptar, *v.* 1) to ravish, abduct. 2) to kidnap. 3) to rob, plunder. 4) to grab, snatch away.

rapto, *s.m.* 1) abduction, ravishment. 2) kidnapping. 3) pillage, plunder. 4) rapture, ecstasy.

raptor, *s.m.* abductor, ravisher, kidnapper. adj. abducting, ravishing, kidnapping.

rapúncio, *s.m. (bot.)* rampion.

raque, *s.f.* 1) *(anat.)* rachis, spinal column. 2) *(bot.)* central axis of an inflorescence; the principal petal of a pinnately compound leaf. 3) *(zool.)* shaft of a feather.

raquel, *s.f. (pl. -éis) (bot.)* Guernsey lily or flower.

raqueta, *s.f.* 1) racket, racquet. 2) snow-shoe.

raquialgia, *s.f. (med.)* rachialgia, pain in the spine.

raquianestesia, *s.f. (med.)* spinal anes-thesia.

raquidiano, *adj.* rachidian.

raquiocentese, *s.f. (med.)* rachicentesis: puncture into the spinal canal.

ráquis, *s.f.* = raque.

raquítico, *s.m.* rachitic man. *adj.* 1) rachitic, rickety. 2) scrubby, stunted.

raquitismo, *s.m.* 1) *(med.)* rachitis, rickets, inflammation of the spine. 2) *(bot.)* blight, abortion of seeds. 3) *(fig.)* feebleness of intellect, weakness of character.

rarear, *v.* 1) to make rare, rarefy. 2) to dimi-nish in density, quantity or number.

rarefação, *s.f. (pl. -ões)* rarefaction, rarefica-tion, tenuity.

rarefaciente, *adj.* rarefactive, rare-fying, producing rarefaction.

rarefazer, *v.* 1) to rarefy; make thin, rare or scarce. 2) to reduce the density of. 3) to dilate, expand. 4) to spread, disperse.

rarefeito, *adj.* rarefied, less dense, tenuous.

rareza, *s.f.* rareness, rarity, scarcity.

raridade, *s.f.* 1) rareness rarity. 2) infre-quency. 3) thinness. 4) uncommonness, unusualness. 5) scarceness, sparseness. 6) singularity, curiosity. 7) extraordinariness, remarkable success.

rarifloro, *adj. (bot.)* rariflorous.

raro, *adj.* rare. 1) unfrequent, sporadic, seldom. 2) thin, not dense. 3) common unusual. 4) scarce, sparse. 5) singular, unique. 6) subtle, tenuous. 7) extraordinary, exquisite. 8) excellent. 9) small in number or quantity.

rasa, *s.f.* 1) old dry measure; grain strickle. 2) tariff for manuscripts. 3) rock bottom price. 4) loss of reputation, discredit.

rasadura, *s.f.* act of measuring corn with a strickle.

rasante, *adj.* 1) levelling. 2) smoo-thing, skimming.

rasar, *v.* 1) to measure whith a strickle. 2) to

level, raze, equalize. 3) to become full. 4) to overflow. 5) to touch lightly, graze. 6) fill to the brim.

rasca, *s.f.* 1) dragnet, trawl-net. 2) small two--masted fishing boat. 3) *(pop.)* share in the profit.

rascante, *s.m.* strong, cheap wine; *adj. m. e f.*, tart, sour, that scratches the throat, sharp to the taste.

rascão, *s.m. (pl. -ões);* 1) vagabond, vagrant, loiterer. 2) page, manservant. 3) towing-line of a fishing-het. 4) mutton stew.

rascar, *v.* 1) to rasp, grate. 2) to scratch. 3) to splinter, sliver. 4) to pare down, roughhew.

rascasso, *s.m.* a scorpion fish *(Scorpoema scrapo).*

rascoa, *s.f.* 1) nursemaid, governess. 2) cook, kitchen maid.

rascolnismo, *s.m.* faith and religious principles of a Russian orthodox sect.

rasconista, rascolnita, *s.m. e f.* disciple of a Russian orthodox sect. *adj.* of or referring to this sect.

rascunhar, *v.* 1) to sketch, outline, draw the outline of. 2) to jot down, make rough notes of.

rascunho, *s.m.* 1) first plan, draft, sketch. 2) outline, rough copy. 3) minute, memo-randum. 4) rough sketch block.

rasgadela, *s.f.* rending, tearing, ripping, rent.

rasgado, *adj.* 1) torn, rent. 2) frank, open. 3)unconstrained, unreserved.

rasgador, *s.m.* tearer, ripper. *adj.* tearing, ripping.

rasgadura, *s.f.* 1) rent, tear. 2) act of rending or tearing. 3) breach. 4) opening, operture. 5) laceration. 6) gash.

rasgamento, *s.m.* 1) act of rending, tearing or ripping.

rasgão, *s.m. (pl. -ões)* tear, rent, gash, rip.

rasgar, *v.* 1) to tear, rend. 2) to split, cleave. 3) to lacerate. 4) to wound, hurt. 5) to make a hole in, bore. 6) to open, make an opening.

rasgo, *s.m.* 1) rip, tear. 2) split, cleft.

raso, *s.m.* plain, flatland, open country.

rasóforo, *s.m.* rhasophore: novice of a monastic order who has not yet received the little habit.

rasoura, *s.f.* 1) strickle, strike. 2) any instrument which serves to level or equalize.

rasourar, *v.* 1) to level with a strickle. 2) to make even, equalize.

raspa, *s.f.* shaving, scrapings, filings, chips.

raspadeira, *s.f.* 1) scraper, scratcher.

raspadela, *s.f.* 1) act of scraping or rasping. 2) erasure. 3) abrasion.

raspado, *adj.* shaven.

raspador, *s.m.* scraper, scratcher, skimmer.

raspadura, raspagem, *(pl. -ens) s.f.* scraping, filings.

raspança, *s.f.* scrapings, filings.

raspanete, *s.m.* 1) reprimand, censure. 2) scolding.

raspão, *s.m. (pl. -ões)* 1) scratch, slight injury on the skin. 2) chafing, gall, sore caused by friction.

raspar, *v.* 1) to scrape, scratch. 2) to rasp, grate, abrade. 3) to rase, erase. 4) to shave. 5) to destroy.

raspilha, *s.f.* a cooper`s scraper, edging tool.

rasqueta, *s.f. (náut.)* deck scraper.

rasqueteação, *s.f. (pl. -ões)* act of currying horses.

rasquetear, *v.* to currycomb.

rasqueteio, *s.m.* act of currying horses or cattle.

rastear, *v.* to track down, trace, look for something.

rasteira, *s.f. (pop.)* act of tripping a person up, trip.

rasteirinha, *s.f.* a low malvaceous herb (Sida procumbens).

rasteiro, *adj.* 1) creeping, crawling. 2) low. 3)humble, modest. 4) abject, contemptible. 5) vulgar mean.

rastejador, *s.m.* 1) searcher, inquirer. 2) tracer, tracker. 3) creeper.

rastejar, *v.* 1) to trace, track. 2) to follow the track, trace down, pursue.

rastejo, *s.m.* 1) tracing, trailing. 2) act of following by the track.

rastelar, *v.* to hackle, comb, ripple (flax, hemp, etc.).

rastelo, *s.m.* 1) flax-comb, hackle, ripple. 2) harrow.

rastilho, *s.m.* 1) train, line of gunpowder leading to a charge. 2) fuse. 3) *(fig.)* the alleged or real cause of violent social commotion or agitation (strike, revolution, war).

rasto, *s.m.* 1) track, trace. 2) mark, sign. 3) step, footprint. 4) wake. 5) vestige, spoor. 6) clue. 7) scent.

rastolho, *s.m.* 1) stubble, stubble field. 2) noise, din, uproar.

rastrear, *v.* 1) to trace, track. 2) to trace

down, pursue. 3) to investigate. 4 to calculate approximately. 5) to harrow.

rasto, *s.m.* 1) = rasto. 2) *(agric.)* manure rake. 3) dragnet, trawlnet.

rasura, *s.f.* 1) erasure, rasure. 2) scrapings, filings. 3) place in a text where an erasure was made. 4) grated medicinal herbs or drugs. 5) obliteration.

rasurar, *v.* 1) to erase, blot out. 2) to scrape, grate. 3) to reduce to filings or chips.

rata, *s.f.* female rat.

ratado, *adj.* infested with rats, eaten by rats.

ratafia, *s.f.* ratafia: any sweet liqueur flavoured with fruit kernels.

ratão, *s.m.* *(pl. -ões)* 1) a large rat. 2) *(zool.)* a kind of ray *(Miliobatis aquila)*. 3) *(fam.)* queer or eccentric fellow.

rataplã, rataplão, *s.m.* rataplan, sound of drumming.

ratar, *v.* to bite or gnaw like a rat.

rataria, *s.f.* lots of rats.

ratazana, *s.f.* 1) female rat. 2) large rat.

rateação, *s.f.* *(pl. -ões)* apportionment, proration, allotment.

rateador, *s.m.* portioner, distributor of proportional shares.

rateamento, *s.m.* apportionment, allotment.

ratear, *v.* 1) to divide proportionally, prorate, average. 2) to portion out, distribute. 3) to assess and give every one his just share.

rateio, *s.m.* 1) apportionment, proportional distribution. 2) proration. 3) allotment, share. 4) *(náut.)* average.

rateiro, *s.m.* ratter, ratcatcher. *adj.* ratting.

ratel, *s.m. (pl. -éis)* *(zool.)* ratel.

ratice, *s.f.* 1) amusing act or saying. 2) witty remark, joke. 3) oddity, eccentricity, extravagance.

raticida, *s.m.* rat poison, raticide.

ratificação, *s.f.) pl. -ões)* 1) ratification, act of ratifying. 2) confirmation, approbation, sanction. 3) enactment.

ratificado, *adj.* ratified, confirmed, sanctioned.

ratificar, *v.* 1) to ratify. 2) to confirm. 3) to approve or sanction formally. 4) to validate. 5) to corroborate, reaffirm.

ratificável, *adj. m. e f. (pl. -áveis)* ratifiable, confirmable, sanctionable.

ratina, *s.f.* ratteen, coarse woollen fabric, baize.

ratinhar, *v.* 1) to pinch and screw. 2) to be exceedingly parsimonious. 3) to haggle over (prices).

ratinheiro, *adj.* 1) thrifty, parsimonious. 2) haggling, chaffering.

ratinho, *s.m.* 1) small rat or mouse. 2) *(fam.)* a baby`s first tooth.

ratívoro, *adj.* that eats mice or rats.

rato, *s.m.* 1) mouse, rat. 2) *(fig.)* thief, pilferer.

rato-almiscarado, *s.m.* *(pl. ratos--almiscarados)* muskrat.

rato-de-água, *s. m. (pl. ratos-de-água)* water rat.

ratoeira, *s.f.* 1) mouse-trap, rat-trap. 2) artifice, trick. 3) snare.

ratona, *s.f.* 1) female rat. 2) large rat.

ratoneiro, *s.m.* pilferer, filcher, fingerer, petty thief.

ratonice, *s.f.* pilferage, filching, petty theft.

raucíssono, *adj.* raucous.

ravina, *s.f.* 1) mountain stream. 2) ravine, deep gulch. 3) steep riverbank. 4) arroyo.

raxa, *s.f.* coarse cotton fabric.

razão, *s.f. (pl. -ões)* 1) reason, reasoning power. 2) good sense right judgment. 3) justice, right. 4) moral law. 5) cause, motive. 6) argument. 7) proof. 8) knowledge. 9) notice. 10) share, rate. 11) *(mat.)* ratio: relation berween two quantities of the same species, proportion. 12) account. 13) m. *(com.)* ledger book.

razia, *s.f.* razzia. 1) foray, raid. 2) incursion. 3) plundering, looting. 4) *(fig.)* destruction. 5) attack.

razoado, *s.m.* 1) plea, defense. 2) speech, discourse. *adj.* reasonable, rational.

razoamento, *s.m.* 1) reasoning, drawing inferences. 2) argumentation. 3) pleading, defense *(of a lawyer).*

razoar, *v.* 1) to reason, infer, conclude. 2) to argue. 3) to plead a cause, defend. 4) to discourse.

razoável, *adj., m. e f. (pl. -áveis)* 1) reasonable, sensible. 2) rational. 3) sane, sound. 4) moderate, open-minded. 5) tolerant, just. 6) fair, decent.

rasoavelmente, *adv.* reasonably, rightly, justly.

ré, *s.f. (jur.)* 1) female defendant or criminal. 2) stern of a ship. 3) s.m. *(mús)* the second note of the diatonic scale.

reabastecer, *v.* 1) to supply with fresh provisions. 2) to renew the stocks, replenish. 3) revictual or provision abundantly.

reabastecimento, *s.m.* replenishment, restocking, renewal of provisions.

reabertura, *s.f.* reopening.

reabilitação, *s. f. (pl. -ões)* 1. rehabilitation. 2) reinstatement. 3) reacquisition of credit or public recognition. 4) justification.

reabilitado, *adj.* rehabilitated, reinstated, justified.

reabilitador, *s.m.* rehabilitator.

reabilitar, *v.* 1) to rehabilitate. 2) to reinstate. 3) to re-establish former rights or privileges. 4) to white-wash. 5) to right, justify, clear. 6) to reacquire credit or public esteem.

reabitar, *v.* to re-inhabit.

reabrir, *v.* to reopen, open again.

reabsorção, *s.f. (pl. -ões)* reabsorption, resorption.

reabsorver, *v.* to reabsorb, resorb, swallow or suck in again.

reacção, *s.f., (pl. -ões)* 1) reaction. 2) *(mec.)* resistance. 3) *(quím.)* chemical transformation or change. 4) *(med.)* physiological opposition or response. 5) *(pol.)* countertendency, conservativeness.

reacionário, *s.m.* reactionary, conservative or reaction, ary person. *adj.* reactionary, opposing liberty and progress.

reacender, *v.* 1) to light again, relight, rekindle. 2) to activate. 3) to incite, rouse, stir up.

recomodar, *v.* to accommodate again, readap to.

reactivar, *v.* to reactivate, revive, reanimate.

reactividade, *s.f.* reactivity, condition of being reactive.

reactivo, *s.m. (quím)* reagent, reactive agent. *adj.* reactive.

reactor, *s.m.* reactor, reagent. *adj.* reacting, reactive.

reacusação, *s.f. (pl. -ões)* 1) act or effect of accusing again. 2) recrimination, countercharge.

reacusar, *v.* 1) to reaccuse, accuse again. 2) to recriminate, make a counterchange.

readmissão, *s.f. (pl. ões)* readmission, readmittance.

readmitir, *v.* to readmit, admit again.

readormecer, *v.* 1) to fall asleep again. 2) to put to sleep again.

readquirir, *v.* 1) to reacquire. 2) to recover, get back, retrieve. 3) to repurchase, redeem.

reafirmação, *s.f. (pl. -ões)* reaffirmation, reassertment.

reafirmar, *v.* to reaffirm, reassert.

reagente, *s.m.* 1) any substance employed

to detect the presence of other ones, agent. 2) *(quím.)* reagent.

reagir, *v.* 1) to react. 2) to answer, respond. 3) to resist. 4) to act in return, counteract. 5) to be opposed, fight agains. 6) *(mil.)* to make counterattacks.

reagradecer, *v.* to thank again, renew one`s thanks.

reagravação, *s.f. (pl. -ões)* 1) new offense. 2) act or circumstance that aggravates again the seriousness of a situation, exacerbation.

reagravar, *v.* 1) to renew an offense. 2) to make worse or aggravate again, exacerbate.

reagrupamento, *s.m.* reassemblage, rally.

reagrupar, *v.* to regroup, reassemble.

reajuntar, *v.* to reassemble, recollect.

reajustamento, *s.m.* readjustment, rearrangement.

reajustar, *v.* 1) to readjust, adjust anew. 2) to rearrange, readapt.

reajustável, *adj. m. e f. (pl. -áveis)* readjustable.

real, *s.m. (pl. reais)* reality, fact. *adj.* 1) real, actual, factual. 2) true, truthful. 3) honest. 4) genuine. 5) certain.

realçar, *v.* 1) to raise to a higher place. 2) to render conspicuous, enhance. 3) to bring into prominence. 4) to intensify, accentuate, emphasize. 5) to dignify, give distinction to.

realce, *s.m.* 1) distinction. 2) enhancement. 3) high spot. 4) relief. 5) lustre, brilliancy, splendour.

realegrar, *v.* 1) to make happy again. 2) --se to rejoice, become happy again.

realejo, *s.m.* 1) street organ, barrel organ, hurdy-girdy.

realengo, *adj.* 1) royal, regal, kingly. 2) *(prov.)* disorderly, inordinate.

realeza, *s.f.* 1) royalty, regality. 2) kingship. 3) crow. 4) member of the royal family. 5) *(fig.)* magnificence, pomp.

realgar, *s.m. (min.)* realgar, arsenic monosulfide.

realidade, *s.f.* 1) reality, realness. 2) actuality, fact.. 3) truth, verity. 4) *(filos.)* real, positiveness. 5) substantiality.

realimentação, *s.f. (pl. -ões)* 1) *(electr.)* self-excitation. 2) *(radio)* feedback, regeneration.

realismo, *s.m.* realism. 1) *(filos.)* doctrine that universals exist independent of intellectual perception. 2) *(psicol.)* doctrine that we have an immediate perception of things extrenal to us. 3) *(art.)* tendency to represent things in their real forms, fidelity to nature. 4) practical action and/or policy. 5) royalism, affachment to the cause of royalty or monarchic government.

realista, *s.m. e f.* 1) realist: adherent of realism. 2) royalist, supporter of a monarchic government, legitimist. *adj.* royalistic(al), legitimistic.

realístico, *adj.* realistic.

realização, *s.f. (pl. -ões)* 1) realization. 2) realizing, state of being realized. 3) accomplishment, achievement, attainment. 4) execution, consummation. 5) *(com.)* turnover, conversion into money (of goods). 6) holding (of a reunion, assembly, etc.). 7) production, fruition.

realizado, *adj.* realized, accomplished, fulfilled, consummated.

realizador, *sm.* realizer, accomplisher, executor, producer. *adj.* realizing, performing, accomplishing, pushful.

realizar, *v.* 1) to realize. 2) to bring to pass, carry through, put into practice. 3) to fulfil, achieve, accomplish. 4) to consummate. 5) *(com.)* to transact, convert into cash. 6) to perceive, recognize as fact.

realizável, *adj., m. e f. (pl. -áveis)* realizable, achievable, accomplishable, possible.

realugar, *v.* to relet.

reamanhecer, *v.* 1) to awaken again, reawaken. 2) to rejuvenate.

reamar, *v.* to love again.

reanexar, *v.* to reannex, reattach, reincorporate.

reanimação, *s.f. (pl. -ões)* reanimation, revivification.

reanimado, *adj.* reanimated, revived, reinvigorated.

reanimador, *s.m.* encourager, reviver, *adj.* reanimating, reviving, refreshing, stimulating, encouraging.

reanimar, *v.* 1) to reanimate, restore to life. 2) to revive, revivify. 3) to strengthen, reinvigorate. 4) to refresh.

reaparecer, *v.* to reappear, appear again.

reaparecimento, *s.m.* reappearance.

reaparelhamento, *s.m.* re-equipment, refitting.

reaparelhar, *v.* to re-equip, refit, prepare for use again.

reaparição, *s.f. (pl. -ões)* reappearance, act or fact of reappearing.

reaprender, *v.* to learn again.

reapresentar, *v.* to present, perform or play again.

reaquecer, *v.* to reheat.

rearmamento, *s.m.* rearmament, rearming.

rearmar, *v.* to rearm, re-equip with arms.

reassumir, *v.* 1) to reassume, assume again. 2) to reacquire, repurchase. 3) to retake, recover, resume.

reassumível, *adj. m. e f. (pl. íveis)* resumable, recoverable.

reassunção, *s.f. (pl. -ões)* reassumption, act of retaking or recovering.

reata, *s.f.* 1) halter rope, hitching rope. 2) ~s *pl. (náut.)* coils of rope, wooldings.

reatado, *adj.* bound or tied again.

reatadura, *s.f.* rebinding, refastening.

reatamento, *s.m.* 1) act or effect of rebinding, reattachment. 2) continuation, re--establishment.

reatar, *v.* 1) to rebind, reattach. 2) to reassume, re-establish. 3) to renew, recommence. 4) to take up again, proceed.

reaver, *v.* 1) to have again, get back. 2) to reobtain, recover. 3) to retrieve, recuperate.

reaviar, *v.* 1) to bring again in the right way. 2) to orient, redirect. 3) to guide anew.

reavisar, *v.* to advise or warm again.

reaviso, *s.m.* renewed advice or warning.

reavivar, *v.* 1) to revive (memories). 2) to recall, remember well. 3) to renew. 4) to stimulate reminiscences.

rebaixado, *adj.* 1) lowered, let down again. 2) *(fig.)* discredited, debased, defamed. 3) despicable, contemptible.

rebaixador, *s.m.* 1) one who lowers (prices), underseller. 2) *(carp.)* fillister, rabbit plane.

rebaixamento, *s.m.* 1) lowering. 2) reduction. 3) degradation, debasement. 4) depreciation, decrease in value.

rebaixar, *v.* 1) to lower, let down. 2) to reduce the price or value of, cheapen, depreciate.

rebaixe, rebaixo, *s.m.* lowering, act or result of letting down.

rebanhada, *s.f.* 1) a large flock, big herd. 2) *(fig.)* multitude, a crowd.

rebanhar, *v.* 1) to unite in a herd, form a flock. 2) to gather, collect. 3) to reunite. 4) to agglomerate, crowd together.

rebanho, *s.m.* 1) flock of sheep, herd of cattle. 2) drove, bunch, troop. 3) cattle, livestock. 4) *(rel.)* congregation.

rebaptismo, s.m. (rel.) rebaptization, rebaptizing.

rebaptizador, s.m. (rel.) rebaptizer. adj. rebaptizing.

rebaptizar, v. to rebaptize, rechristen.

rebarba, s.f. 1) sharp edge, barb.

rebarbar, v. to remove the burr, trim off, deburr, plane.

rebarbativo, adj. double-chinned, fat.

rebate, s.m. 1) act or effect of striking again. 2) repelling, act of beating back (enemy).

rebatedor, s.m. (com.) discounter, bill broker, exchange broker.

rebater, v. 1) to strike again. 2) to repel, beat back (enemy).

rebatida, s.f. 1) repellence. 2) act of driving back (enemy). 3) (sport) rally, undercut. 4) refutation, disproof.

rebatido, adj. 1) repelled, beaten back.

rebatimento, s.m. 1) striking, beating again. 2) driving away, pushing back, repulsion.

rebatinha, s.f. 1) children`s toy, plaything. 2) any thing much sought after.

rebeijar, v. to kiss again.

rebel, s.m. (pl. -eis) rebel. adj. m. e f. rebe, contumacious.

rebelado, s.m. rebel, mutineer.

rebelador, adj. rebellious, insurgent, defiant.

rebelar, rebelar-se, v. to stand up against, rise against. 2) to oppose, resist.

rebelde, s.m. e f. 1) rebel, insurgent, mutineer. 2) deserter. adj. m. e f. 2) rebel, insurgent, revolutionary. 3) unsubmissive, disobedient. 4) unruly, defiant. 5) (med.) refractory.

rebeldia, s.f. 1) rebellion, insurrection, revolt. 2) rebelliousness. 3) (fig.) opposition, resistance. 4) (med.) refractoriness. 5) defiance, disloyalty. 6) obstinacy, stubbornness.

rebelião, s.f. (pl. -ões) 1) rebellion, revolt. 2) insurrection, mutiny. 3) disobedience, insubordination. 4) (fig.) opposition, resistance.

rebentação, s.f. (pl. -ões) 1) act of bursting, breaking open. 2) pounding of waves, surf.

rebentão, s.m. (pl. -ões) 1) shoot, offshoot, sprout. 2) (fig.) progeny, offspring. 3) scrub vegetation.

rebentar, v. 1) to burst, split open. 2) to blow up, explode. 3) to thrust forward. 4) to roar, resound. 5) to outburst. 6) to break lose. 7) to fall into pieces, crack, split.

rebentina, rebentinha, s.f. (fam.) 1) rage, anger. 2) fit of rage, outburst of fury. 3) passion.

rebento, s.m. 1) shoot, sprout. 2) (bot.) ratoon, sapling. 3) (fig.) offspring. 4) (fig.) product. 5) burgeon, bud.

rebicar, v. to make up, rouge the face.

rebique, s.m. 1) make-up, rouge. 2) excessive affectation of style. 3) extravagant finery, affected elegance.

rebitador, s.m. reviter, reviting machine.

rebitagem, s.f. (pl. -ens), rebitamento m. riveting.

rebitar, v. 1) to rivet. 2) to clinch (bolts, nails) 3) to fasten with rivets or nails.

rebite, s.m. 1) rivet. 2) clinch.

reboante, adj., m. e f. resounding, re--echoing, reverberating.

reboar, v. to resound, re-echo, reverberate.

rebocado, adj. 1) plastered, coated. 2) towed (like a trailer).

rebocado, s.m. tug, towboat.

rebocadura, s.f. act of towing, towage. 2) plastering, roughcast.

rebocar, v. 1) to plaster, coat with stucco. 2) to tow, take in tow.

reboco, s.m. (pl. rebocos) 1) plaster, rough-cast, parget. 2) plasterwork.

rebojo, s.m. (pl. rebojos). 1) foam or froth of swiftly moving water. 2) southwest wind.

rebolado, s.m. swinging movement of the hips, swaying or waddling motion.

rebolar, v. 1) to roll, tumble. 2) to shake the hips, waddle. 3) to shimmy. 4) to twirl around, revolve rapidly.

rebolaria, s.f. 1) bragging, swaggering, boasting. 2) excessive and tawdry finery, affected elegance.

rebolcar, v. 1) to let roll, tumble. 2) to revolve rapidly, twirl. 3) to fling, throw, hurl. 4) to welter, wallow, slosh (animals).

rebolear, v. 1) to swing, twirl and fling like a lasso. 2) to sway, swagger.

reboleira, s.f. 1) the thickes part of a wood, camp or field. 2) dirt which falls from a grindstone, forming muddy residues in the grindstone box.

reboleiro, s.m. 1) great cattle bell. 2) homing (cattle), living and grazing near the farmhouse and stables. 3) said of a shifty steer.

reboliço, adj. 1) resembling a grindstone. 2) revolving, turning around itself.

rebolir, v. 1) to swagger, shake one`s body.

2) to walk rapidly, hurry. 3) to revolve, spin, rotate. 4) to stir up, grow agitated. 5) to sway, waggle. 6) to swing the hips, shake one's body.

rebolo, *s.m.* 1) grindstone, whetstone, abrasive wheel. 2) *(pop.)* cylinder. 3) measles of the olive tree.

reboludo, *adj.* 1) plump, bulky. 2) roundish, rounded. 3) rotund.

rebombar, *v.* 1) to boom, resound. 2) to re-echo.

rebombeação, *s.f. (pl. -ões)* weakness, bad state of health.

reboo, *s.m.* 1) resonance, act of resounding. 2) reverberation, re-echo. 3) reflexion of sound.

reboque, *s.m.* 1) act of towing, towage. 2) trailer, vehicle hauled by another.

reboquear, *v.* to tow, take in tow.

rebordão, *adj. (pl. -ões)* wild, sylvan (said of plants used for living or quickset hedges).

rebordar, *v.* 1) to embroider elaborately. 2) to flange, bevel. 3) to smooth the edges of plate-glass. 4) to embroider again.

rebordo, *s.m.* turned edge, brim, fold.

rebordosa, *s.f.* 1) censure, reprimand, reproof. 2) severe illness, disease. 3) difficult situation, dilemma, serious predicament. 4) relapse, severe recurrence of an illness.

rebotalho, *s.m.* 1) trash, rubbish, junk. 2) refuse, dregs, leavings. 3) trifles. 4) crumbs, morsel, scrap. 5) scum, dross, outcasting.

rebotar, *v.* 1) to make blunt or dull. 2) to take the edge off. 3) to grow tired or wedry, be bored with. 4) to discourage, dishearten. 5) to repel, drive back, beat.

rebote, *s.m.* large wooden jack plane.

reboto, *adj.* 1) blunt, dull. 2) rude, uncouth. 3) stupid, ignorant.

rebraço, *s.m. (ant.)* part of the armour which covered the arm from the elbow to the shoulder.

rebradar, *v.* to roar again, yell.

rebramar, rebramir, *v.* 1) to resound, reverberate. 2) to roar, bellow, low. 3) to shout, vociferate. 4) *(fig.)* to grow angry, flare up.

rebrilhante, *adj., m. e f.* radiant, refulgent, shining again, splendiferous.

rebrilhar, *v.* 1) to shine again. 2) to glitter or sparkle intensely. 3) to radiate, be very bright, be resplendent.

rebrotar, *v.* to sprout again, produce new shoots.

rebuçado, *s.m.* 1) piece of candy wrapped in paper, lollipop. 2) *(fig.)* anything said or done with perfection. 3) a disguised person.

rebuçado, *v.* 1) to hide, conceal. 2) to muffle up, veil, cloak. 3) to disguise, dissemble, dissimulate. 4) rebuçar-se, to keep in hiding, disguise, dissemble, feign.

rebuço, *s.m.* 1) collar of a gown. 2) coat lapel. 3) hood, cowl, large collar of a cloak.

rebuliço, *s.m.* 1) clamour, noise, uproar. 2) tumult, hubbub. 3) fuss, excitement, fluster. 4) confusion, disorder, medley. 5) welter, rumpus, turmoil.

rebusca, *s.f.* act of searching for.

rebuscado, *adj.* 1) searched for, looked after. 2) *(fig.)* highly refined, highly cultured, accomplished. 3) desired.

rebuscar, *v.* 1) to search again. 2) to search thoroughly. 3) to dress with excessive elegance, spruce up. 4) to refine, perfect. 5) to glean. 6) to ransack, rummage.

rebusco, *s.m.* new or repeated search.

rebusque, *s.m.* 1) favourable settlement, arrangement. 2) deal, bargain.

recadeiro, *s.m.* errand-boy, messenger. *adj.* of or referring to errands and messages, relative to, messengers.

recadista, *s.m., f.* person who goes on errands.

recado, *s.m.* 1) verbal communication, word. 2) information, message. 3) errand, commission. 4) scoldings, reprimand. 5) caution, prudence. 6) circumspection.

recados, *s.m. pl.* complete saddle with its trimming.

recaída, *s.f.* (also recaimento) 1. act or effect of falling back. 2) recurrence. 3) *(med.)* relapse, recidivation, setbak. 4) o paciente teve uma recaída, the patient has had a serious relapse.

recair, *v.* 1) to fall again, fall back. 2) to return to a previous state, backslide. 3) to relapse into. 4) to befall, occur, happen again. 5) to revert.

recalcado, *adj.* 1) depressed, trodden down. 2) rammed, beaten down. 3) concentrated, massed. 4) restrained.

recalcador, *s.m.* winepress. *adj.* pressing, squeezing, crushing down.

recalcamento, *s.m.* 1) act or fact of pressing down. 2) repression, suppression. 3) settling (of a building). 4) *(psic.)* exclusion of undesirable impulses from consciousness.

recalcar, *v.* 1) to step on, tread on. 2) to

press down, crush down, trample. 3) to compress, condense, squeeze together. 4) to insist, reiterate. 5) to curb, restrain, check, subdue.

recalcitração, *(pl. -ões),* recalcitrância *s.f.* 1) recalcitrance, recalcitration. 2) reluctance. 3) stubbornness, obstinacy.

recalcitrante, *s.m. e f.* recalcitrant, stubborn or obstinate person. *adj.* recalcitrant, reluctant, renitnent, stubborn, refractory.

recalcitar, *v.* 1) to recalcitrate. 2) to resist, refuse obedience. 3) to manifest stubborn opposition. 4) to insist on, persist in. 5) to retort, talk back rudely. 6) to be or become obstinate. 7) to revolt against. 8) to kick backwards.

recalcular, *v.* to recalculate, recount.

recálculo, *s.m.* recalculation, second account.

recaldear, *v.* to weld again, weld firmly together.

recalescência, *s.f. (met.)* recalescence.

recalmão, *s.m. (pl. -ões) (naút.)* lull between great storms.

recalque, *s.m.* 1) act or fact of pressing down. 2) repression, suppression. 3) settling of a foundation (wall, building). 4) *(psic.)* exclusion of undesirable impulses from conscious mind. 5) stuffing, cramming.

recamado, *adj.* embroidered.

recamador, *s.m.* embroiderer.

recamadura, *s.f.* embroidery, adornment, ornament.

recamar, *v.* 1) to embroider, trim with embroidery. 2) to adorn, decorate. 3) to embroider with raised stitches. 4) to cover, overlay. 5) recamar-se, to line or cover. 6) to fill.

recâmara, *s.f.* 1) wardrobe, closet. 2) dressing room. 3) retreat, place of retirement. 4) household utensils. 5) alcove. 6) gun breech (of firearms).

recambiar, *v.* 1) *(com.)* to return an unaccepted or unpaid bill of exchange. 2) to rechange, change again. 3) to send back. 4) to exchange, interchange. 5) to give back, devolve, pass on.

recâmbio, *s.m.* 1) act or fact of returning. 2) *(com.)* re-exchange, redraft. 3) *(com.)* returning of a bill of exchange. 4) *(com.)* expense incurred when returning an unaccepted or unpaid bill, protest charges.

recamo, *s.m.* 1) raised embroidery, relief

stitch embroidery. 2) ornament, decoration. 3) *(fig.)* adornment, ornate

recantar, *v.* 1) to sing again. 2) to sing emphatically. 3) to retract, recant. 4) to revoke, recall.

recanto, *s.m.* 1) recess, nook, corner. 2) hiding place, place of concealment. 3) cubbyhole, den. 4) retreat.

recapacitar, *v.* 1) to persuade or convince again. 2) to call to mind.

recapitulação, *s.f. (pl. -ões)* 1) recapitulation. 2) act of synthesizing, summary. 3) repetition, review. 4) curso de recapitulação, refresher course.

recapitulante, *adj., m. e f.* recapitulative, recapitulatory.

recapitular, *v.* 1) to recapitulate. 2) to synthesize, summarize, sum up. 3) to repeat, review, enumerate again.

recapitulativo, *adj.* recapitulative, recapitulatory.

receptor, *s.m.* recaptor, one who catches again.

recapturar, *v.* to recapture, capture again, retake.

recarbonização, *s.f. (pl. -ões)* recarbonization, recarburization.

recarbonizar, *v.* to recarbonize, recarburize.

recardar, *v.* to recard, card again *(wool, flax).*

recarga, *s.f.* 1) fresh load, reload. 2) reshipment. 3) *(bullfight)* second charge of a bull.

recargar, *v. (bullfight)* 1) to check the attack of the bull. 2) to repeat the attack, recharge.

recarregar, *v.* to reload, recharge, load excessively.

recartilha, *s.f. (mech.)* index plate.

recartilhar, *v. (mech.)* to knurl, index.

recasar, *v.* to remarry, marry a second time.

recatado, *adj.* 1) modest, moderate. 2) discreet. 3) reserved, restrained. 4) prudent, cautious, circumspect. 5) coy. *recatadamente, adv.* modestly, discreetly, cautiously, coyly.

recatar, *v.* 1) to keep in safety, hide secretly. 2) to guard, safeguard. 3) to shield, protect.

recativar, *v.* to capture again, recapture, catch again.

recativo, *s.m.* subdued or wholly dominated *person. adj.* captive, subdued, subjugated, dominated.

recato, *s.m.* 1) modesty, bashfulness. 2)

honesty. 3) prudence, caution, circumspection. 4) reservedness.

recauchutado, adj. recapped (tires).

recauchutar, v. to recap, retread (tires).

recavar, v. 1) to dig again, dig many times. 2) to insist in, persist on. 3) to extract from (by digging), excavate, unearth.

recavém, s.m. (pl. -énis) the rear end of a cart bed.

receado, adj. feared, dreaded, causing apprehension.

recear, v. 1) to fear, dread. 2) to be afraid of. 3) to apprehend. 4) to distrust, doubt.

recebedor, s.m. 1) receiver. 2) recipient. 3) tax-collector, gatherer.

recebedoria, s.f. 1) office of tax-collector, excise office. 2) treasury. 3) collectorship.- 4) custom office.

receber, v. 1) to accept, take, get. 2) to cash in, take in, collect (money, debts). 3) to admit, harbour, shelter. 4) to greet, welcome. 5) to receive. 6) to give lodging to, take in as guest. 7) to receive communication.

recebimento, s.m. 1) act or fact of receiving. 2) apartment, room, hall, parlour. 3) receivership. 4) reception. 5) receipt. 6) admission. 7) acceptance.

recebível, adj., m. e f. (pl. -íveis) receivable, acceptable, collectable.

receio, s.m. 1) fear, dread, terror. 2) apprehension. 3) apprehensiveness, fearfulness. 4) uncertainty, doubt, misgiving(s). 5) distrust.

receita, s.f. 1) income, revenue, proceeds. 2) taking(s), receipt(s). 3) budget. 4) (med.) recipe, formula, prescription. 5) food. 6) (fig.) counsel, advice.

receitante, adj., m. e f. prescribing, formulating advice.

receitar, v. 1) (med.) to prescribe (a remedy), make out a prescription. 2) to advise, counsel.

receituário, s.m. (farm.) 1) pharmacopoeia. 2) prescription book.

recém, adv. newly recently, lately.

recém-casado, adj. (pl. recém-casados) newly married or wed.

recém-chegado, s.m. (pl. recém-chegados) newcomer. adj. newly arrived, newcomer, fresh.

recém-convertido, adj. (pl. recém-convertidos) newly converted.

recém-falecido, s.m. (pl. recém-falecidos) recently deceased person. adj. recently deceased.

recém-feito, adj. (pl. recém-feitos) recently made or done, fresh.

recém-nado, s.m. (pl. recém-nados), recém--nascido (pl. recém-nascidos) a new-born baby, adj. newborn.

recendência, s.f. 1) fragrance, perfume. 2) strong scent. 3) agreeable odour.

recendente, adj., m. e f. fragrant, odorous, redolent, sweet-smelling.

recender, v. 1) to smell sweetly, be odoriferous. 2) to exhale a strong aroma. 3) to give forth an agreeable scent.

recendor, s.m. fragrance, perfume, strong pleasant aroma.

recensão, s.f. (pl. -ões) 1) census. 2) survey, verification. 3) enumeration, counting. 4) comparing of a published text with the original manuscript, proofreading.

recenseado, s.m. registered voter, person included in a census. adj. registered, polled, included in a census.

recenseador, s.m. census taker, pollster, registrar. adj. registering, polling.

recenseamento, s.m. 1) census. 2) survey, verification. 3) official enumeration, counting (population, animals, demographic density, etc.).

recensear, v. 1) to take a census or poll. 2) to survery, verify. 3) to count, enumerate. 4) (com.) to audit (accounts).

recenseio, s.m. act or result of census-taking or polling.

recental, s.m. (pl. -ais) sucking lamb, lambkin.

recente, adj., m. e f. (abs. sup. -íssimo). 1) recent. 2) modern, new. 3) late, fresh, novel. recentemente, adv. recently, newly.

receoso, adj. 1) afraid, fearful. 2) anxious, apprehensive. 3) distrustful, suspicious. 4) uneasy. 5) timid. receosamente, adv. fearfully, apprehensively, anxiously, distrustfully.

recepagem, s.f. (pl. -ens) lopping of plants close to the ground.

recepção, s.f. (pl. -ões) 1) reception. 2) act or fact of receiving. 3) admittance. 4) receipt. 5) welcome.

recepisse, s.m. (L.) receipt, voucher.

receptação, s.f. (pl. -ões) receiving of stolen goods.

receptacular, adj., m. e f. (bot.) receptacular.

receptáculo, *s.m.* 1) receptacle, container. 2) vessel. 3) place of refuge, retreat, shelter. 4) reservoir, pool.

receptador, *s.m.* receiver of stolen goods, fence. *adj.* receiving, concealing (stolen goods).

receptar, *v.* to receive, conceal (stolen goods).

receptibilidade, *s.f.* receptibility, receptiveness.

receptível, *adj., m. e f. (pl. íveis)* receptive.

receptividade, *s.f.* 1) receptivity, receptiveness. 2) penetrativeness. 3) open-mindedness.

receptivo, *adj.* receptive, receptible, susceptive, open-minded. receptivamente, *adv.* receptively, susceptively.

receptor, *s.m.* receiver. 1) cashier, treasurer. 2) receiver, receptor (of stolen goods), accessory. 3) (telegr., teleph.) receiving instrument. 4) *(rádio)* wireless receiving set.

recessivo, *adj.* recessive, subordinate.

recesso, *s.m.* 1) recess, corner. 2) alcove, niche. 3) retreat, hiding place. 4) retirement.

rechaçar, *v.* 1) to repel, repulse. 2) to throw back, fight off. 3) to resist, oppose. 4) to drive back, beat back. 5) *(fig.)* to contradict, refute.

rechaço, *s.m.* 1) repulsion. 2) a striking back. 3) driving or pushing back. 4) rebound, recoil. 5) *(fig.)* resistance, opposition. 6) old dance and dance melody.

recheado, *adj.* stuffing. *adj.* stuffed, filled, crammed, full, replete. recheadamente, adv. fully, plentifully.

rechear, *v.* 1) to stuff, fill with seasoning. 2) to cram, make full. 3) to make abundant, enrich.

rechegar, *v.* 1) to tap pine trees for resin. 2) (saltmaking) to stir up the brine.

rechego, *s.m.* a hunter's blind, shooting box.

recheio, *s.m.* 1) stuffing, farcing. 2) act of stuffing. 3) filling. 4) dressing.

rechinante, *adj., m. e f.* hissing, creaking, whizzing, squeaky.

rechinar, *v.* to creak, hiss, whiz, frizzle.

rechino, *s.m.* creaking, hissing, whizzing.

rechinchudo, *adj.* thickset, round, rotund, stumpy, crummy.

reciário, *s.m. (Roman hist.)* gladiator, retiary.

recibo, *s.m.* written receipt, acquittance, voucher.

recidiva, *s.f.* 1) return, reappearance. 2) *(med.)* relapse, reincidence.

recidivar, *v.* to return, relapse, suffer a setback.

recidivo, *adj.* relapsing, recidivous.

recife, *s.m.* reef, skerry, key.

recifoso, *adj.* full of reefs, reefy.

recingir, *v.* to gird or encircle again.

recinto, *s.m.* 1) enclosure, enclosed space. 2) verge, precinct, limited area. 3) dooryard. 4) sanctuary.

récipe, *s.m.* recipe, medical prescription.

recipiângulo, *s.m.* recipiangle, instrument for measuring angles.

recipiendário, *s.m.* recipiendary, accepted candidate, new member-elect. *adj.* of or referring to a recipiendary.

recipiente, *s.m.* 1) recipient, receiver. 2) vessel, receptacle, balloon, container. 3) *(mec.)* recipient of an air pump. *adj., m. e f.* recipient.

reciprocar, *v.* 1) to reciprocate, make reciprocal. 2) to act interchangeably. 3) to make a return for something done or given. 4) to compensate. 5) to exchange, interchange. 6) to alternate.

reciprocidade, *s.f.* reciprocity, reciprocalness, reciprocality, mutuality.

recíproco, *s.m.* 1) *(gram.)* reciprocal verb. 2) *(mat.)* reciprocal proportion. *adj.* 2) reciprocal, reciprocative. 4) mutual. 5) interchangeable. 6) alternate.

récita, *s.f.* theatrical performance, recital, declamation.

recitação, *s.f. (pl. -ões)* 1) recitation, recital. 2) declamation.

recitado, *s.m.* recitation, recitative. adj. 1) recited, repeated by heart. 2) declamatory, recitative. 3) rehearsed.

recitador, *s.m.* reciter, recitalist, declaimer.

recital, *s.m. (pl. -ais)* recital, concert, theatrical or musical performance of one artist.

recitante, *s.m. e f.* reciter, recitalist. *adj.* reciting, performing a solo.

recitar, *v.* 1) to recite, declaim. 2) to read with a clear loud voice. 3) to narrate, relate. 4) to rehearse. 5) to perform a recitative.

recitativo, *s.m.* 1) recitative. 2) declamatory passage of an opera or concert. 3) melodramatic performance. *adj.* recitative.

reclamação, *s.f. (pl. -ões)* 1) reclamation. 2) complaint. 3) demand. 4) claim. 5) protest, objection.

reclamado, *adj.* reclaiming, reclaimed, protesting.

reclamador, *s.m.* reclaimer, reclaimant, protester. *adj.* reclaiming.

reclamante, *s.m. e f.* reclaimer, reclaimant, protester. *adj.* claiming, demanding, protesting.

reclamar, *v.* 1) to oppose. 2) to object, impugn. 3) to protest, complain about.

reclamável, *adj., m. e f. (pl. -áveis)* claimable, demandable, redemandable, reclaimable.

reclamista, *s.m. e f.* propagandist.

reclamo, reclame, *s.m.* 1) propaganda. 2) advertisement. 3) birdcall, decoy-whistle or bird. 4) allurement, enticement. 5) act of attracting attention. 6) (newsprint) catchword, direction word. 7) propagandistic activity of a firm.

reclinação, *s.f. (pl. -ões)* leaning back, reclination, reclining.

reclinado, *adj.* 1) turned or curved down or backwards. 2) reclinate, reclining, recumbent. 3) *(bot.)* reclined.

reclinar, *v.* 1) to lean back, recline. 2) to fold, bend back. 3) to recurve, curve downwards. 4) to lie down. 5) to lean against.

reclinatório, *s.m.* any object fit to lean upon; pillow, cushion, headrest.

recluir, *v.* to confine, shut up, seclude.

reclusão, *s.f. (pl. -ões)* 1) reclusion, recluseness. 2) recess. 3) seclusion, continement. 4) cell, prison. 5) restraint.

recluso, *s.m.* recluse, hermit, monk; prisoner. *adj.* recluse, solitary, secluded, cloistered.

recobramento, *s.m.* recovery, recuperation (of something lost).

recobrar, *v.* 1) to acquire again, reacquire. 2) to recover, regain, recuperate. 3) to retrieve, retake. 4) recobrar-se, to be restored to health, rally. 5) to free from (illness, difficulties, etc.), escape from. 6) to be encouraged, cheer up.

recobrável, *adj., m. e f. (pl. -áveis)* recoverable, retrievable.

recobrimento, *s.m. (geol.)* deposition of older rock formations on younger layers.

recobrir, *v.* 1) to cover again, recover. 2) to cover well.

recobro, *s.m.* 1) act or fact of covering again. 2) recuperation, regaining, retrieving. 3) rally, recovery.

recocto, *adj.* 1) cooked over again. 2) overboiled, overdone.

recognição, *s.f. (pl. -ões)* recognition, perception of identity, acknowledgement.

recognitivo, *adj.* recognitory, fit for investigation or identification.

recognoscível, *adj., m. e f. (pl. -íveis)* recognizable, identifiable.

recoitar, *v.* to anneal *(metals)*.

recoleta, *s.f.* 1) nun of the order of St. Francis. 2) monastery of Recollects. 3) *(fig.)* austere mode of life.

recoleto, *s.m.* 1) Franciscan monk. 2) person who leads an ascetic life.

recolha, *s.f.* 1) act of gathering or sheltering. 2) stable. 3) garage.

recolhedor, *s.m.* gatherer, collector.

recolher, *v.* 1) to guard, safeguard, preserve. 2) to take care of, take into custody. 3) to shelter, harbour. 4) to harvest, bring in a crop. 5) to collect, cash in. 6) to receive, accept. 7) to reunite, assemble. 8) to attain, obtain (as recompense).

recolhida, *s.f.* 1) retirement, retreat. 2) withdrawal. 3) recluse, lay sister.

recolhido, *adj.* 1) retired. 2) solitary, secluded. 3) withdrawn. 4) reserved. 5) meditating, dwelling in thought.

recolhimento, *s.m.* 1) act or fact of retiring, retirement. 2) shelter, home, refuge. 3) barn, garage. 4) privacy, secrecy. 5) contemplation, meditation. 6) intensive life. 7) house for recluses, asylum.

recolho, *s.m.* 1) act or fact of gathering, collection. 2) retirement. 3) strong heavy breath. 4) spouting of a whale.

recolocar, *v.* to put back, restore.

recolonização, *s.f. (pl. -ões)* recolonization, re-establishment of a colony, resettlement.

recolonizar, *v.* to recolonize, re-establish a colony, resettle.

recolorir, *v.* to dye or paint again.

recombinação, *s.f. (pl. -ões)* recombination, new combination, *(biol.)* cross over.

recombinar, *v.* to recombine, recompose, rearrange.

recomeçado, *adj.* recommenced, renewed, resumed, continued.

recomeçar, *v.* 1) to recommence, begin again. 2) to renew. 3) *(com.)* reopen. 4) to resume, continue.

recomeçável, *adj., m. e f. (pl. -áveis)* capable of being recommenced, resumable, renewable.

recomeço, *s.m.* 1) act of beginning again, recommencement. 2) restart. 3) reopening (school, business enterprise, etc.)

recomendação, *s.f.* (pl. -ões) 1) act of recommending. 2) recommendation, commendation. 3) recommendableness, commendable qualities. 4) advice, suggestion, counsel. 5) warning.

recomendado, *s.m.* recommendee, one who is recommended. *adj.* recommended.

recomendar, *v.* 1) to recommend. 2) to commend, praise. 3) to counsel, give advice, suggest. 4) to prefer, favour. 5) to order, charge, entrust with.

recomendável, *adj.* (pl. -áveis) recommendable, advisable, commendable. recomendavelmente, *adv.* recommendably, advisably.

recompensa, *f.* 1) act or fact of rewarding. 2) recompense, reward. 3) prize, premium. 4) compensation, pay, remuneration, gratification. 5) award, meed, requital.

recompensado, *adj.* recompensed, rewarded, compensated, requited.

recompensador, *s.m.* rewarder, recompenser, indemnifier. *adj.* rewarding, requiting, compensatory.

recompensar, *v.* 1) to retribute, give an equivalent for. 2) to reward, recompense. 3) to premiate. 4) to compensate, pay, fee, remunerate. 5) to indemnify, repair. 6) to punish. 7) to requite, gratify. 8) to award, crown.

recompensável, *adj., m. e f.* (pl. -áveis) 1) worthy of recompense, deserving reward. 2) awardable, rewardable, requitable, remunerable.

recompilação, *s.f.* (pl. -ões) recompilation, new compilation.

recompilador, *s.m.* recompiler, recollector. adj. recompiling.

recompilar, *v.* to compile or collect again, recompile.

recompor, *v.* 1) to recompose, compose again. 2) to give a new form to, renew. 3) to reset, reframe. 4) to set in order again, reorganize. 5) to re-establish, restore. 6) to reconcile, harmonize.

recomposição, *s.f.* (pl. -ões) 1) recomposition, rearrangement. 2) reconciliation. 3) *(pol.)* recomposition of the cabinet (ministers or governmental advisers).

recomposto, *adj.* recomposed, rearranged, reset.

recomprar, *v.* to repurchase, to buy again.

recôncavo, *s.m.* 1) deep cave, grotto, hollow. 2) fold. 3) den, lair. 4) environs (of a city).

reconcentração, *s.f.* (pl. -ões) act or effect of reconcentrating, reconcentration.

reconcentrado, *adj.* 1) reconcentrated, thoroughly concentrated. 2) very private, intimate. 3) meditative, contemplative. 4) *(quím.)* strongly concentrated or acid.

reconcentrar, *v.* 1) to concentrate again, reconcentrate. 2) to bring or direct to a common center, reunite. 3) to harbour deep in one's heart (feelings, sentiments). 4) to converge upon a common center.

reconciliação, *s.f.* (pl. -ões) 1) reconciliation, reconcilement. 2) restoration of friendship. 3) atonement. 4) *(rel.)* repetition of the confession (out of devotion). 5) reconsecration of a profaned church or temple.

reconciliado, *s.m.* *(ecles., rel.)* reconcilee. *adj.* reconciled, acquitted.

reconciliador, *s.m.* reconciler, conciliator. *adj.* reconciling, reconciliatory.

reconciliar, *v.* 1) to reconcile, conciliate. 2) to establish peace (among, between), appease. 3) to restore friendship. 4) to attain the grace of God. 5) to reach an agreement.

reconciliatório, *adj.* reconciliatory, conciliatory, reconciling.

reconciliável, *adj., m. e f.* (pl. -áveis) reconcilable, capable of reconciliation.

recondicionar, *v.* to recondition, overhaul.

recôndito, *s.m.* 1) corner, recess. 2) hiding place. *adj.* 3) hidden, concealed. 4) recondite. 5) abstruse. 6) unknown. 7) obscure.

reconditório, *s.m.* hiding place, retreat, refuge.

recondução, *s.f.* (pl. -ões) 1) act of leading back or reconducting. 2) devolution, return. 3) renewing, continuation, prorogation. 4) re-election, renomination.

reconduzir, *v.* 1) to lead back, reconduct. 2) to devolve, return. 3) to renew, continue, prorogate. 4) to re-elect, renominate. 5) to reconvey, send again.

reconfessar, *v.* to confess again.

reconfortante, *s.m.* *(med.)* restorative, tonic.

reconfortar, *v.* 1) to recomfort. 2) to refresh. 3) to strengthen, reinvigorate.

reconforto, *s.m.* reinvigoration, comfort, new strength, uplifting.

reconhecedor, *s.m.* 1) acknowledger, recognizer. 2) *(mil.)* runner.

reconhecer, *v.* 1) to recognize, know again. 2) to acknowledge, admit. 3) to verify, ascertain. 4) to understand, comprehend.

reconhecido, *adj.* 1) thankful, grateful. 2) recognized. 3) admitted, acknowledged. 4) avowed.

reconhecimento, *s.m.* 1) recognition, cognizance. 2) acknowledgement, admission. 3) gratitude, thankfulness. 4) recompense, reward, compensation. 5) reconnoitring, reconnaissance.

reconhecível, *adj., (pl. -íveis)* 1) recognizable, cognizable. 2) acknowledgeable, confirmable. 3) knowable, distinguishable, easy to recognize.

reconquista, *s.f.* reconquest, reconquering, aim of conquest.

reconquistar, *v.* 1) to reconquer, conquer again. 2) to recapture, regain. 3) to recover, retake by force. 4) to rewin.

reconsagrar, *v.* to reconsecrate, consecrate again, dedicate again.

reconsertar, *v.* to repair again, remend.

reconsideração, *s.f. (pl. -ões)* 1) reconsideration, reconsidering. 2) reflexion. 3) second consideration, new deliberation. 4) change of mind. 5) reponderation.

reconsiderar, *v.* 1) to reconsider, consider again. 2) to give a second thought, think over again. 3) to redeliberate, change one's mind. 4) to ponder, meditate. 5) to disavow, unsay.

reconsolidar, *v.* to reconsolidate, consolidate again, make firm again.

reconstituição, *s.f. (pl. -ões)* reconstitution, recomposition, reform.

reconstituinte, *s.m. (med.)* reconstituent, restorative, tonic. *adj. m. e f.* 1) reconstituent, restoring. 2)rebuilding. 3) recomposing. 4) *(med.)* restorative, tonic.

reconstituir, *v.* 1) to reconstitute, constitute again. 2) to recompose. 3) to rebuild, re-establish. 4) to strengthen, invigorate.

reconstrução, *s.f. (pl. -ões)* 1) reconstruction, rebuilding. 2) reform. 3) reorganization. 4) something reconstructed.

reconstruído, *adj.* reconstructed, rebuilt, reformed.

reconstruir, *v.* 1) to reconstruct, rebuild. 2) to reorganize. 3) to reform. 4) to restore.

reconstrutor, *s.m.* reconstructor, rebuilder, restorator.

recontado, *adj.* 1) recounted, recalculated. 2) retold, related.

recontar, *v.* 1) to count again, recount. 2) to calculate a new. 3) to retell, relate again, report anew. 4) to retail.

reconto, *s.m.* iron fitting at the butt of a lance.

recontro, *s.m.* 1) encounter, skirmish, brush. 2) combat, battle. 3) conflict, clash. 4) chance meeting.

reconvir, *v.* 1) to counterclaim, countercharge. 2) to file a countersuit. 3) to recriminate, charge back on an accuser. 4) to get back, recover.

recopilação, *s.f. (pl. -ões)* 1) compilation. 2) summary, abstract. 3) abridgment. 4) recapitulation.

recopilador, *s.m.* compiler, summarizer, abridger, collector. *adj.* compiling, summarizing, collecting.

recopilar, *v.* 1) to compile, collect, gather. 2) to abridge, make an abstract of. 3) to recapitulate. 4) to sum up, summarize, epitomize.

recordação, *s.f. (pl. -ões)* 1) remembrance, recollection, recordation. 2) memory, power or faculty of recalling. 3) reminiscence. 4) memento, token, souvenir.

recordador, *s.m.* recorder, reminder, one who remembers or reminds. *adj.* recalling, remembering, reminding.

recordar, *v.* 1) to remember, recall. 2) to recollect. 3) to bear in mind, call to mind. 4) to be similar to. 5) to commemorate, indulge in reminiscence. 6) to relive, reproduce (in our mind).

recorde, *s.m.* record (in sports), special prowess, feat, accomplishment.

recordista, *s.m. e f.* record holder, record breaker, champion. *adj.* record-holding.

reco-reco, *s.m.* musical instrument made of a piece of bamboo with notches cut into it and over which a rod is rubbed to produce a rhytmical sound.

recorrência, *s.f.* recurrence, act or fact of occurring again.

recorrente, *s.m. e f. (jur.)* appellant. *adj.* recurring.

recorrer, *v.* 1) to run over, go through again. 2) to search, scrutinize. 3) to investigate, inquire into. 4) to evoke call forth. 5) *(pog.)* to overrun a page. 6) to ask for help, request protection. 7) to apply, resort to. 8) *(jur.)* to appeal to.

recorrido, *s.m. (jur.)* appellee.

recorrível, *adj., m. e f. (pl. -íveis)* appealable, subject to or admitting appeal.

recortador, *s.m.* cutter, pinker. *adj.* cutting, clipping, pinking.

recortar, *v.* 1) to cut out, trim, clip. 2) to slash, slice. 3) to carve, chisel.

recorte, *s.m.* 1) act or fact of cutting out. 2) indentation, indenture.

recoser, *v.* to resew, sew over again.

recostar, *v.* 1) to recline, lean back. 2) to incline, bend. 3) to lean against. 4) to prop up, rest on.

recosto, *s.m.* 1) resting place, retreat. 2) lounge, sofa, couch.

recova, recovagem, *(pl. -ens) s.f.* 1) payload and business of muleteers. 2) carrier, forwarding business, transporter. 3) transport, conveyance. 4) transport charges.

récua, *s.f.* = récua.

recovar, *v.* 1) to transport, convery (baggage or other goods). 2) to work as a muleteer.

recoveira, *s.f.* 19 female mule driver, female muleteer. 2) fisherman`s yoke (to transport on the shoulder a pole with two baskets).

recoveiro, *s.m.* 1) carrier, transporter. 2) muleteer, mule driver.

recovo, *s.m.* 1) act of reclining or leaning back. 2) act of leaning on one`s elbows.

recozedor, *s.m.* annealer. *adj.* annealing.

recozer, *v.* 1) to cook again. 2) to boil or bake again. 3) to overcook, cook too much, overdo. 4) to anneal, temper.

recozido, *adj.* cooked or boiled again, overcooked, overdone, annealed.

recozimento, *s.m.* 1) cooking, boiling. 2) overcooking, overboiling. 3) *(met.)* annealing.

recravar, *v.* to nail again, nail much.

recreação, *s.f. (pl. -ões)* 1) recreation. 2) amusement, distraction. 3) sport. 4) pastime. 5) enjoyment, relaxation.

recreador, *s.m.* person who takes things easy or looks for amusement. adj. amusing, pleasant, sportive, relaxing.

recrear, *v.* 1) to recreate. 2) to rest, relax. 3) to entertain, divert.

recreativo, *adj.* 1) recreative, refreshing. 2) amusing, exhilarating, diverting. 3) sportive.

recreatório, *adj. e m., recreável m. e f. (pl. -áveis)* recreative, recreational.

recreio, *s.m.* 1) recreation. 2) relaxation, refreshment. 3) diversion, distraction, entertainment. 4) summer-house, playground. 5) interval, school recess time. 6) game, play, sport.

recrementício, *adj. (med.)* recrementitious, recremental.

recremento, *s.m. (med.)* recrement, recrementitious secretion, dross.

recrescência, *s.f.* growth, excrescente, new growth.

recrescente, *adj.,* that grows again, recrescent.

recrescer, *v.* 1) to grow again. 2) to increase, augment. 3) to sprout out, shoot up again. 4) to become more intense. 5) to happen, befall. 6) to be left over, rest, be more than enough.

recrescido, *adj.* that grew again.

recrescimento, *s.m.* 1) regrowth, new growth. 2) increase, augmentation. 3) intensification. 4) happening, occurrence. 5) surplus, rest, leftover. 6) excess, redundancy.

recrestar, *v.* 1) to burn or scorch again. 2) to dry up, parch.

recria, *s.f.* 1) new or late rearing, breeding, hatching. 2) aftergrowth, offshoots, new generation (of animals).

recriação, *s.f. (pl. -ões)* 1) act of creating again. 2) raising or breeding anew. 3) to increase the stock of animals on a farm. 4) new creation or invention.

recriar, *v.* 1) to create again. 2) to raise, breed or bring up again. 3) to restock the farmyard. 4) to reproduce, invent anew.

recriminação, *s.f. (pl. -ões)* 1) act or fact of recriminatimg. 2) countercharge, recrimination. 3) exprobation.

recriminador, *s.m.* recriminador. *adj.* recriminating, recriminatory.

recriminar, *v.* 1) to recriminate, make a counterchange or accusation. 2) to reproach, censure, reprimand.

recriminatório, *adj.* recriminatory, recriminative, recriminating.

recrudescência, *s.f.* 1) recrudescence. 2) renewed or intensified activity. 3) intensification. 4) *(med.)* aggravation (after a remission).

recrudescente, *adj., m. e f.* 1) recrudescent. 2) renewed or intensified (activity). 3) intensifying. 4) *(med.)* aggravating.

recrudescer, *v.* 1) to recrudesce. 2) to renew or intensify activity). 3) *(med.)* to aggravate, break out again, change for the worse. 4) to increase, augment.

recrudescimento, *s.m.* 1) recrudescence, recrudescency. 2) intensification. 3) *(med.)* fresh outbreak (of an illness), relapse, aggravation. 4) increase, augmentation.

recruta, *s.m.* 1) *(mil.)* recruit, newly enlisted soldier or sailor, rookie. 2) novice, beginner. 3) new member (of a school, club, society.

recrutamento, *s.m.* 1) *(mil.)* recruitment, recruiting, recruital. 2) enlistment, conscription.

recrutar, *v.* 1) *(mil.)* to recruit. 2) to enlist, conscribe, draft. 3) to canvass, procure, enlist (new adepts, members, etc.). 4) to levy, collect troops for service.

recruzar, *v.* to recross, cross again, cross repeatedly.

récua, *s.f.* 1) a train of pack animals. 2) herd of pack animals, herd of mules.

recuada, *s.f.* recuamento *m.* = recuo.

recuadeira, *s.f.* breeching (harness).

recuanço, *s.m.* backspin of a billiard ball.

recuar, *v.* 1) to put, pull or draw back. 2) to regress, retrace one's steps. 3) to walk back, move backward, retreat.

recúbito, *s.m.* recumbency, recumbent position or attitude, reclining.

recuidar, *v.* 1) to consider, think over with care. 2) to ponder, resolve in mind. 3) to take everything into account, deliberate, think over thoroughly.

recultivar, *v.* to recultivate, cultivate again.

recumbente, *adj., m. e f.* recumbent, reclining, leaning against.

recumbir, *v.* to be in a recumbent position, recline, lean back, rest upon.

recunhamento, *s.m.* recoinage, remintage.

recunhar, *v.* to recoin, coin anew, mint or stamp again.

recuo, *s.m.* 1) act or fact of moving backwards, retrocession. 2) recoiling, recoil. 3) recession. 4) kick (of firearms). 5) retreat, retirement. 6) *(mec.)* return movement, backing. 7) revulsion. 8) setback. 9) (swimming) backstroke).

recuperação, *s.f.* recuperation, recovery. 2) reconquest. 3) reclamation, salvage. 4) retrieval, regaining.

recuperado, *adj.* recuperated, recovered, reclaimed, redeemed.

recuperador, *s.m.* recuperator, recoverer, rescuer, redeemer. *adj.* recuperative, recuperatory, recuperating.

recuperar, *v.* 1) to recuperate, recover. 2) to

recoup. 3) to re-acquire, repurchase. 4) to retake, retrieve. 5) to reobtain, regain.

recuperável, *adj., (pl. áveis)* 1) recuperable, recoverable. 2) reclaimable. 3) reobtainable, retrievable. 4) that may be recaptured or won back.

recurrência, *s.f. (med.)* recurrence, periodical or frequent returning.

recurrente, *adj., m. e f.* recurrent, returning, running back.

recurso, *s.m.* 1) act and fact of running back or running again. 2) *(jur.)* appeal, recourse (to a superior court). 3) reclamation, claim, complaint. 4) petition, application for help.

recurvação, *s.f. (pl. -ões)* recurvation, recurvature.

recurvado, *adj.* 1) recurvate. 2) curve, bent. 3) twisted, contorted. 4) arched. 5) bowed down, bent over.

recurvar, *v.* 1) to curve again, recurve. 2) to curve back, bend over, bow back, crook. 3) to twist, contort. 4) to form into an arch.

recurvo, *adj.* 1) recurved, crooked. 2) bent backwards. 3) recurvate. 4) twisted, contorted. 5) bowed down, bent over.

recusa, *s.f.* 1) act or fact of refusing. 2) denial, refusal. 3) rejection, declination, non-acceptance. 4) non-compliance, non-cooperation.

recusado, *adj.* refused, rejected, not accepted, snubbed.

recusador, *s.m.* 1) refuser, denier. 2) *(júr.)* challenger. *adj.* refusing.

recusar, *v.* 1) to refuse, deny. 2) to reject, not to accept, decline. 3) to oppose, act against. 4) to deny, not admit. 5) to prohibit, forbid.

recusativo, *adj.* refusing, negative, rejective.

recusável, *adj., m. e f. (pl. -áveis)* refusable, rejectable, exceptionable, deserving refusal. recusavelmente, *adv.* refusably, exceptionably.

redacção, *s.f. (pl. -ões)* 1) act or fact of composing a script, 2) redaction. 3) style or manner of writing. 4) editorship. 5) editorial staff. 6) home office, building of the editorial staff of a newspaper, editorial room.

redactor, *s.m.* 1) editor, newpaper editor, redactor. 2) writer, journalist. 3) redactores, editorial staff.

redactora, *s.f.* editress.

redada, *s.f.* 1) act of casting a fishing-net. 2) draught haul, catch (of fish).

redar, *v.* to cast a fishing-net, catch in a net.

redarguente, *adj.,* retorting, refuting, recriminating.

redarguição, *s.f. (pl. -ões)* 1) retort, retortion, quick sharp reply. 2) rejoinder, rebuttal. 3) refutation. 4) recrimination.

redarguidor, *s.m.* retorter, recriminator. *adj.* retorting, recriminating.

redarguir, *v.* 1) to retort, give a quick sharp reply. 2) to rejoin, refute, return an argument. 4) to recriminate.

rede, *s.f.* 1) net, fishing net. 2) hair net. 3) wire gauze, wire netting. 4) water, gas or sewerage system. 6) electric distribution system.

rédea, *s.f.* reins, bridle.

redeclamar, *v.* to declare again, reaffirm.

redecretar, *v.* to decree again, re-enact.

redeiro, *s.m.* 1) net knitter, netmaker. 2) small fishing net.

redemoinhado, *adj.* whirling, put into or passing through a whirlpool.

redemoinhador, *adj.* whirling, twirling. 2) restless, unquiet (said of cattle).

redemoinho, *s.m.* 1) whirl, swirl. 2) eddy, vortex. 3) whirlwind.

redenção, *s.f. (pl. -ões)* 1) redemption. 2) redeeming. 3) ransom. 4) *(rel.)* salvation, deliverance, atonement.

redente, *s.m.* step like increase of the superstructure of a wall built on sloping ground.

redentor, *s.m.* 1) redeemer, saviour. 2) *(rel.)* the Redeemer, Jesus Christ. adj. redeeming, leading to salvation, redemptive, saving.

redentorista, *s.m. e f.* Redemptorist.

redescender, redescer, *v.* to redescend, descend again.

redescobrimento, *s.m.* rediscovery, discovering anew.

redescobrir, *v.* to rediscover, reveal again, unearth again.

redescontar, *v.* to rediscount, debut again.

redesconto, *s.m.* 1) rediscount. 2) act of rediscounting. 3) rediscounted bill.

redestolar, *v.* to redistil, distil again or anew.

redibição, *s.f. (pl. -ões) (jur.)* redhibition; the act of annulling a sale and devolution of the article to the seller on account of a material defect.

redibir, *v. (jur.)* 1) to avoid or annual a sale (purchase) on account of a material defect. 2) to resell goods to the original seller.

redibitório, *adj. (jur.)* redhibitory.

redigir, *v.* 1) to write, write down. 2) to express one`s thoughts in writing. 3) to compose. 4) to redact, pen, draught. 5) to edit a newspaper or write professionally for a periodical.

redil, *s.m.* 1) corral. 2) sheep-pen or fold. 3) cot(e), coop for small domestic animals. 4) (fig.) flock, congregation.

redimir, *v.* 1) to redeem, regain. 2) to ransom. 3) to buy off, exempt. 4) to atone for. 5) to repurchase, reacquire.

redimível, *adj., m. e f. (pl. -íveis)* redeemable, retrievable, that can and should be redeemed.

redingote, *s.m.* redingote, riding coat, frock coat.

redinha, *s.f.* small net, shrimp net.

redintegrar, *v.* 1) to redintegrate. 2) to restore to integrity, renovate. 3) to renew. 4) to reinstate.

redissolver, *v.* to redissolve, dissolve again.

redistribuir, *v.* to redistribute, distribute again, recast.

redito, *adj.* said again, said many times, repeated.

rédito, *s.m.* 1) act of returning. 2) profit, again. 3) advantage. 4) income, proceeds. 5) product, result. 6) interest.

rediviva, *s.f.* rose of Jericho, resurrection plant.

redivivo, *adj.* redivivus, resuscitated, revived, renewed, *(fig.)* reborn.

redizer, *v.* 1) to say again. 2) to say many times, repeat. 3) to tell again, retell (what other people told us). 4) to relate, narrate over again.

redobrado, *adj.* 1) reduplicate. 2) folded again. 3) redoubled, intensified.

redobramento, *s.m.* 1) redoubling, reduplication. 2) increase, augmentation. 3) *(med.)* periodic aggravation of a disease.

redobrar, *v.* 1) to redouble, reduplicate. 2) to quadruple. 3) to augment, increase considerably. 4) to repeat. 5) to peal (the bells) over again. 6) to intensify. 7) to twitter, chirp. 8) *(med.)* to become severer (illness, attack).

redobro, *s.m.* 1) twice the double. 2) quadruple. 3) redoubling, reduplication. 4) increase, augmentation.

redolente, *adj.,* 1) *(poet.)* fragrant. 2) redolent, aromatic.

redoma, *s.f.* glass shade, vial, bell jar.

redondeado, *adj.* rounded, rotund.

redondear, v. to make round, round off, become round.

redondel, s.m. (pl. -éis) 1) circular arena, bull ring. 2) a kind of havelock.

redondela, s.f. small wheel, ring, washer.

redondeza, s.f. 1) round, roundness, rondure. 2) rotundness, chubbiness. 3) surroundings, environs. 4) suburbs.

redondil, adj., m. e f. (pl. -is) round, spherical, circular.

redondilha, s.f. (poet.) roundel, rondel.

redondo, adj. 1) round, circular. 2) globular, spherical. 3) cylindrical. 4) curved. 5) (fig.) fat, stout, rotund, chubby. 6) outspoken.

redor, s.m. 1) circle, circuit. 2) contour, outline. 3) environs, surroundings. 4) suburb.

redourar, v. 1) to regild, gild again. 2) to illuminate brightly.

redra, s.f. (agric.) second dressing of vines.

redrar, v. (agric.) to dig around vines a second time, to weed a second time (in a vineyard).

redução, s.f. (pl. -ões) 1) reduction, reducing. 2) abbreviation, summary. 3) diminution, abatement. 4) subduing, bringing under subjection. 5) (com.) deduction, cut, cutting (prices). 6) act of bringing back to the original place. 7) (cirur.) setting of bones or joints. 8) redução de despesas, retrenchment of expenses.

reducente, adj., m. f. reducing, tending to reduce, reductive.

redundância, s.f. 1) redundance, redundancy. 2) pleonasm. 3) superfluity, excess (esp. use of more words than needed).

redundante, adj., m. e f. 1) redundant. 2) pleonastic. 3) superfluous, excessive. 4) abounding, exuberant.

redundar, v. 1) to overflow, run over. 2) to be redundant or profuse. 3) to originate from, derive, result from. 4) to redound to 5) to come to pass, happen. 6) to change into.

reduplicação, s.f. (pl. -ões) 1) reduplication, redoubling. 2) repetition. 3) increase, augmentation.

reduplicar, v. 1) to reduplicate, double again. 2) to repeat. 3) to increase, augment. 4) to multiply. 5) to repeat a syllable or word, reiterate.

reduplicativo, s.m. (gram.) reduplicative word, word which indicates repetition. adj. reduplicative, reiterative, double.

redutibilidade, s.f. reducibility, quality of being reducible.

redutível, adj., m. e f. (pl. -íveis) 1) reducible, that may be reduced. 2) (arit.) divisible (said of a fraction).

redutivo, adj. reductive, reducible, reductional.

reduto, s.m. 1) (fort.) redoubt, outwork, temporary fortification. 2) (fig.) key.

redutor, s.m. 1) (mec.) reducer, reducing device. 2) reducent, reducing agent. adj. reducing, reductive.

redúvio, s.m. (zool.) assassin bug.

reduzido, adj. reduced, diminished, cut, bated; reduzido à pobreza, reduced to poverty.

reduzir, v. 1) to reduce. 2) to separate, disaggregate. 3) to bring back to.

reduzível, adj., m. e f. (pl. -íveis) reducible, compressible, diminishable.

reedição, s.f. (pl. -ões) re-edition, new edition, reprint, reissue.

reedificação, s.f. (pl. -ões) re-edification, rebuilding, reconstruction.

reedificado, adj. re-edified, rebuilt, reconstructed.

reedificador, s.m. rebuilder. adj. rebuilding, reconstructing.

reedificar, v. 1) to rebuild, re-edify. 2) to reconstruct. 3) to build or construct again. 4) to reform.

reeditar, v. to re-edit, republish, publish again, reprint, reissue.

reeducação, s.f. (pl. -ões) re-education, rehabilitation through education.

reeducador, s.m. re-educator, rehabilitador.

reeducar, v. 1) to re-educate, educate again. 2) to complete or perfect the education of. 3) to rehabilitate through education.

reelectômetro, reeletometro, s.m. (fisiol.) rheoscope, galvanoscope.

reeleger, v. to chose or elect again, re-elect.

reelegível, adj., m. e f. (pl. -íveis) re-eligible, capable of being elected again, susceptible to re-election.

reeleição, s.f. (pl. -ões) re-election, act of electing again.

reeleito, s.m. a re-elected person. adj. re-elected, elected again.

reembarcar, v. to re-embark, embark again, reship, transship.

reembarque, s.m. re-embarkation, reshipment, transshipment.

reembolsado, adj. reimbursed, refunded, repaid.

reembolsar, v. 1) to reimburse. 2) to pay

back, repay. 3) to indemnify. 4) to be in possession of (on outstanding amount), be refunded for.

reembolsável, *adj., m. e f. (pl. -áveis)* reimbursable, repayable, refundable.

reembolso, *s.m.* reimbursement, repayment, refund, recoupment.

reemenda, *s.f.* 1) new emendation, second correction. 2) remending, repatching. 3) emending over again.

reemendar, *v.* to emend again, recorrect, correct over again.

reemergência, *s.f.* re-emergence, re-emergency.

reemergir, *v.* to re-emerge, emerge again.

reempossar, *v.* to give again possession to, reinstall in office.

reempregar, *v.* to re-employ, use again.

reemprego, *s.m.* renewed employment, repeated use.

reencarcerar, *v.* to reincarcerate, reimprison.

reencarnação, *s.f. (pl. -ões)* reincarnation.

reencarnar, *v.* to reincarnate, incarnate again.

reencenar, *v.* to restage, to play or perform again.

reencher, *v.* to refill, fill up again.

reenchimento, *s.m.* refilling, refill.

reencontrar, *v.* to meet or find again.

reencontro, *s.m.* a new or second meeting.

reendireitar, *v.* to straighten again, rectify or repair anew.

reegajamento, s.m. re-engagement, re-employment.

reengajar-se, *v.* to engage o.s. again, re-employ o.s.

reenlaçar, *v.* to refasten, tie, join or bind again.

reenlace, *s.m.* refastening, binding again.

reentrada, *s.f.* re-entrance, return, comeback.

reentrância, *s.f.* 1) re-entrance, re-entering. 2) re-entering angle or curve. 3) bay, recess.

reentrante, *adj., m. e f.* re-entrant, forming a recess.

reentrar, *v.* 1) to re-enter, again. 2) to go home, go to bed.

reenviar, *v.* 1) to send again, redispatch. 2) to remit. 3) to return, send back again. 4) to rechange, change again.

reenvio, *s.m.* act of sending back, return, reshipping, redispatching.

reerguer, *v.* 1) to re-erect, reconstruct. 2) to raise again. 3) to elevate or exalt again.

reescrever, *v.* to rewrite, write a second time.

reestabelecer, *v.* to re-establish, restore, establish anew.

reexpedição, *s.f.* act of reshipping, transshipment, new dispatching.

reexpedir, *v.* 1) to reship, transship. 2) to dispatch again, re-export. 3) to send off again (what one has received), redirect.

reexportação, *s.f. (pl. -ões)* re-exportation, re-export, exportation of imported goods, transshipment.

reexportador, *s.m.* re-exporter, forwarding agent of a free port.

reexportar, *v.* to re-export, reship, transship, export again imported goods.

refalar, *v.* to speak again, talk anew.

refalsado, *adj.* 1) unsincere, false. 2) disloyal. 3) deceitful, tricky, fraudulent. 4) feigned, deceptive, hypocritical.

refalsamento, *s.m.* falsehood, disloyalty, deceit, fraud, hypocrisy.

refalsear, *v.* 1) to betray, be disloyal to. 2) to deceive, delude. 3) to double-cross, cheat. 4) to mislead, mystify.

refazedor, *s.m.* remaker, repairer, *adj.* remaking, repairing, mending over again, refitting.

refazer, *v.* 1) to make once more, make over again. 2) to reform, remodel. 3) to reorganize, recompose. 4) to repair, mend again. 5) to correct. 6) to renew. 7) to re-establish, recover, refresh, reinvigorate. 8) to indemnify, compensate. 9) to feed, nourish. 10) refazer-se, to supply, furnish. 11) to recover one`s force, rally, gather strength.

refazimento, *s.m.* 1) remaking, remodeling. 2) re-establishment, recovery. 3) repair, remending. 4) compensation, indemnification.

refega, *s.f.* 1) skirmish, fray, brush. 2) whirlwind, gust of wind.

refegado, *adj.* pleated, folded, tucked.

refegar, *v.* 1) to pleat, fold. 2) to wrinkle, crease, furrow. 3) to crumple.

refego, *s.m.* 1) fold, pleat. 2) tuck. 3) crease. 4) wrinkle.

refeição, *s.f. (pl. -ões)* 1) meal, repast. 2) repose. 3) *(fig.)* table.

refeito, *adj.* 1) restored, recovered. 2) mended, repaired. 3) fat, thickset, plump.

refeitório, *s.m.* refectory, dining-hall, mess hall, commons.

refém, *s.m. (pl. -éns)* 1) hostage. 2) open city or fortified place held by the enemy as a pledge. 3) ransom, amount paid for the release of a prisoner. 4) security, pledge.

referência, *s.f.* 1) act of referring. 2) reference, indication. 3) allusion, hint. 4) mention, notice. 5) remark, citation. 6) respect, regard. 7) concern.

referenda, *s.f.* act or effect of counter-signing, countersignature.

referendado, *adj.* countersigned, authorized, authenticated.

referendar, *v.* 1) to countersign, sign in addition to (an other signature). 2) to authenticate, attest. 3) to accept responsability as to the enactment and execution of a decree.

referendário, *s.m.* referendary, minister or chief clerk who countersigns.

referente, *adj., m. e f.* 1) referring to, relating to. 2) relative, regarding. 3) referential. 4) concerning, respecting.

referido, *adj.* 1) above-mentioned, aforesaid. 2) reported. 3) cited quoted.

referimento, *s.m.* 1) act of referring, reference. 2) allusion, hint. 3) remark, observation. 4) report.

referir, *v.* 1) to refer. 2) to narrate, tell, relate. 3) to report. 4) to allude, hint 5) to cite, mention.

refermentação, *s.f. (pl. -ões)* refermentation.

refermentar, *v.* to referment, ferment again.

referrar, *v.* to reshoe, shoe again (horses, mules, etc.).

refervente, *adj., m. e f.* boiling, bubbling again, boiling excessively.

referver, *v.* 1) to reboil, boil again, boil a lot. 2) to ferment.

refervido, *adj.* reboiled, boiled again, spoiled by repeated boiling.

refestelar-se, *v.* 1) to loll, lollop. 2) to recline, lean back. 3) to relax, repose.

refiar, *v.* 1) to respin, spin again. 2) to divide in strands or sheets.

refilão, *s.m. (pl. -ões)* recalcitrant, rebellious person backbiter. *adj.* refractory, stubborn, rebellious, backbiting.

refilar, *v.* 1) to bite back, retort. 2) to attack, assault. 3) to react, counteract, counter. 4) to recalcitrate.

refiltrar, *v.* to refilter, filter again.

refinação, *s.f. (pl. -ões)* 1) act or process of refining or purifying. 2) refining, refinery. 3) building and apparatus for refining, refining plant. 4) refinement, subtlety. 5) sugar refinery.

refinado, *adj.* 1) purified, pure. 2) refined, subtle. 3) polished, cultured. 4) downright, thorough. 5) shrewd, clever. 6) nice, polite, fine. 7) açucar refinado, refined sugar.

refinador, *s.m.* 1) refiner. 2) purifier. 3) *(fig.)* chastener, reformer. adj. refining, purifying.

refinadura, *s.f.* 1) refining, refinery. 2) refinement, culture.

refinamento, *s.m.* 1) refining, refinery. 2) refinement.

refinar, *v.* 1) to refine, purify. 2) to civilize, cultivate. 3) to make stronger, intensify.

refinaria, *s.f.* refinery, sugar refinery, skimming plant; refinaria de petróleo, oil refinery.

refincar, *v.* 1) to thrust or drive in with force (nails, stakes, etc.). 2) to fasten anew, clinch again.

reflectido, *adj.* 1) prudent, cautions. 2) sensible, thoughtful, thinking.

reflectidor, *s.m.* reflector, headlight, searchlight. adj. reflecting.

reflectir, *v.* 1) to reflect. 2) to turn, throw or fall back. 3) to deflect, divert. 4) to give back an image, mirror.

reflectivo, *adj.* 1) reflective, pondering. 2) pensive, thoughtfull. 3) serious, sober. 4) deliberative.

reflector, *s.m.* reflector, searchlight, headlight.

reflexão, *s.f. (pl. -ões)* 1) reflection, reflexion. 2) reflex. 3) contemplation, meditation. 4) reverberation of light. 5) consideration. 6) prudence, caution.

flexibilidade, *s.f.* reflexibility, reflectiveness.

reflexionar, *v.* 1) to ponder, meditate. 2) to object, argue. 3) to reflect, think. 4) to consider, cogitate.

reflexível, *adj., m. e f. (pl. íveis)* reflexible.

reflexivo, *adj.* 1) reflexive, reflective. 2) *(gram.)* referring back to the subject.

reflexo, *s.m.* 1) reflex, reflection. 2) reflected light or image, sheen. 3) imitation. 4) *(fisiol.)* involuntary reaction, reflex action.

reflorescência, *s.f.* reflorescence, blossoming anew.

reflorescente, *adj., m. e f.* reflorescent, reflowering.

reflorescer, *v.* 1) to blossom again,

reflourish, reflower. 2) *(fig.)* to recover, reinvigorate, rejuvenate. 3) to revive, reanimate.

reflorescido, *adj.* reflourished, blooming again.

relorescimento, *s.m.* act or fact of reflowering, reflorescence, second flowering.

reflorestador, *s.m.* person who promotes reforestation, planter of new forests. *adj.* reforesting, replanting (of forests).

reflorestamento, *s.m.* reforestation, reforestment.

reflorestar, *v.* to reforest, forest anew, reafforest, renew forest cover.

reflorido, *adj.* reflourished, blooming anew, covered whith new blossoms.

reflorir, *v.* 1) to flower or blossom again, reflourish. 2) *(fig.)* to recover strength, reinvigorate, rejuvenate. 3) to revive.

refluência, *s.f.* refluence, reflux, flowing back.

refluente, *adj., m. e f.* refluent, flowing back, ebbing.

refluir, *v.* 1) to flow back, reflow. 2) to recede, retrocede *(flood)*. 3) to return, go back to the starting point. 4) to overflow, flood. 5) to regurgitate.

réfluo, *adj.* refluent, flowing back, ebbing.

refluxo, *a.m.* 1) act of flowing back, reflow. 2) refluence, refluency. 3) ebb, ebbing. 4) recess, retrocession.

refocilamento, *s.m.* 1) refreshment, refreshing. 2) restoration of strength, recovery. 3) reanimation, revival. 4) recreation, pleasure.

refocilante, *adj., m. e f.* refreshing, strengthening, recreative.

refocilar, *v.* 1) to refresh, revive. 2) to strengthen, fortify. 3) to restore, reanimate. 4) to recreate.

refogado, *s.m.* butter sauce, meat gravy, any dish fried with butter, onions or herbs.

refogar, *v.* 1) to fry with butter or oil, onions, parsley or other herbs. 2) to stew, boil slowly, simmer.

refolgo, *s.m.* 1) rest, repose. 2) recreation. 3) relief, ease, comfort.

refolhado, *adj.* 1) wrapped in leaves, covered whith leaves. 2) pleated, folded, tucked.

refolhamento, *s.m.* 1) pleat, tuck. 2) fold. 3) disguise, dissimilation.

refolhar, *v.* 1) to wrap in folds or leaves. 2) to disguise, dissemble. 3) to cover up, conceal, hide.

refolho, *s.m.* 1) ruffle, pleat, plait, fold. 2) *(fig.)* dissimulation, dissembling, disguise.

refolhudo, *adj.* 1) pleated, plaited, folded. 2) ramose, having dense foliage.

reforçado, *adj.* 1) reinforced, strengthened. 2) strong, vigorous. 3) robust, stocky, brawny.

reforçado, *v.* 1) to give additional force to. 2) to reinforce, strengthen. 3) to intensify. 4) to amplify.

reforço, *s.m.* 1) reinforcement, reinforcing. 2) supply of additional force, new assistance. 3) succour, relief, help.

reforma, *s.f.* 1) reform, reformation. 2) new form, modification. 3) *(rel.)* Reformation: important religious movement of the 16th century, protestantism. 4) amendment, correction.

reformação, *s.f. (pl. -ões)* reform, reforming, reformation, correction.

reformado, *s.m.* 1) pensioner, retired officer. 2) protestant.

reformador, *s.m.* reformer, redresser, remodeller. *adj.* reformative, reformational.

reformar, *v.* 1) to reform. 2) to give a new or better form, improve. 3) to remodel, make over. 4) to reconstruct, rebuild. 5) to reorganize, renovate. 6) to correct, mend. 7) to repair, rectify.

reformativo, *adj.* reforming, reformative, reformatory.

reformatório, *s.m.* house of correction, reformatory, protectory. *adj.* reformatory, reformative.

reformável, *adj., m. e f. (pl. -áveis)* reformable, renewable.

reformista, *s.m. e f.* reformer, reformist. *adj.* referring to reform.

reformular, *v.* to reformulate, formulate again.

refornecer, *v.* to resupply, furnish again.

refracção, *s.f. (fisic)* refraction, deflection.

refractar, *v.* 1) to refract, deflect. refractar--se, to be reflected or deflected.

refractário, *s.m.* 1) refractory or intractable person. 2) *(mil.)* deserter. *adj.* refractory.

refractivo, *adj.* refractive, refracting, deflective, refringent.

refracto, *adj.* refracted, subject to refraction.

refractómetro, *s.m. (fisic.)* refractometer.

refractor, *adj.* refractive, serving or tending to refract.

refrangência, *s.f.* refraction, refractivity, refractiveness.

refrangente, *adj., m. e f.* refracting, refractive.

refranger, *v.* to refract.

refrangibilidade, *s.f.* refrangibility, refrangibleness.

refrangível, *adj., m. e f. (pl. -íveis)* refrangible, capable of being refracted.

refrão, *s.m.* 1) refrain. 2) adage, saving. 3) proverb. 4) burden of a song.

refreado, *adj.* 1) curbed, restrained. 2) moderate.

refreador, *s.m.* refrainer, coercer, restrainer. *adj.* refraining.

refreamento, *s.m.* 1) restraint. 2) restraining, refraining. 3) moderation. 4) constraint, curbing, rein.

refrear, *v.* 1) to refrain, restrain. 2) to coerce, repress. 3) to curb, check. 4) to subdue, hold in.

refreável, *adj., m. e f. (pl. áveis)* restrainable.

refrega, *s.f.* 1) fight, combat. 2) fray, skirmish.

refregar, *v.* to fight, quarrel, dispute, brawl.

refreio, *s.m.* 1) act of checking, curbing or holding in . 2) bridle, rein(s), bit.

refrescado, *adj.* refreshed, reanimated, revived, comforted.

refrescamento, *s.m.* act or effect of refreshing, comforting, refreshment.

refrescante, *adj., m. e f.* refreshing, cooling, crisp, comforting.

refrescar, *v.* 1) to refresh, freshen. 2) to make cool, refrigerate. 3) to reanimate, revive, reinvigorate. 4) to relieve, soothe, mitigate.

refresco, *s.m.* 1) refreshment. 2) comfort, ease, rest. 3) cooling draught, drink. 4) refrigeration.

refrigeração, *s.f. (pl. -ões)* 1) act or effect of cooling. 2) refrigeration, freezing. 3) cooling, chilling. 4) refrigeration.

refrigerador, *s.m.* refrigerator, freezer, cooler, ice chest, spray-cooler. *adj.* refrigerating, cooling,chilling.

refrigerante, *s.m.* refreshment, refresher, cooling (soft) drink.

refrigerar, *v.* 1) to refresh, cool. 2) to make fresh or cooler. 3) to protect from the heat. 4) to comfort, relieve.

refrigerativo, *s.m.* refrigerant, refreshment, refresher. *adj.* refreshing, refrigerative, refrigeratory, cooling.

refrigério, *s.m.* 1) refrigeration, freezing. 2) well-being produced by coolness.

refringência, *s.f.* 1) *(opt.)* refringency, refringence. 2) *(fis.)* refractivity.

refringente, *adj., m. e f. (fis.)* refringent, refractive, deflecting.

refrondescente, *adj., m. e f.* growing green or verdant again.

refugado, *adj.* 1) disregarded, spurned. 2) refused, rejected. 3) castoff, thrown out.

refugador, *s.m.* 1) rejecter, refuser. *adj.* rejecting.

refugar, *v.* 1) to reject, refuse to accept. 2) to throw aside, cast off.

refugiado, *s.m.* refugee, fugitive, displaced person. *adj.* fugitive.

refugiar-se, *v.* 1) to take refuge, seek shelter. 2) to withdraw from one`s native country, emigrate.

refúgio, *s.m.* 1) refuge. 2) shelter, asylum.

refugir, *v.* 1) to fly again, flee anew. 2) to flow back, reflow.

refugo, *s.m.* 1) refuse, rejection. 2) garbage, sweepings, tailings.

refulgência, *s.f.* refulgence, refulgency, radiance, splendour.

refulgente, *adj., m. e f.* 1) refulgent, fulgent. 2) rediant, brilliant.

refulgir, *v.* 1) to shine resplendently. 2) to shine, glitter, sparkle.

refundição, *s.f. (pl. -ões)* recast, recasting, remelting, new cast.

refundir, *v.* 1) to cast again. 2) to recast, refound. 3) to remelt.

refusar, *v.* 1) to refuse, deny. 2) to reject, decline. 3) to oppose.

refutação, *s.f. (pl. -ões)* 1) refutation, refute. 2) disproof, disproval. 3) confutation. 4) rebuttal.

refutador, *s.m.* refuter, disprover.

refutar, *v.* 1) to refute. 2) to deny the truth of belie.

refutatório, *adj.* refutatory, refutative, disproving.

refutável, *adj., m. e f. (pl. -áveis)* refutable, refutative.

rega, *s.f.* irrigation, watering.

rega bofe, *s.m.* 1) festivity, feast. 2) revelery, merrymaking.

regaçar, *v.* to tuck up, turn or gather up.

regaço, *s.m.* 1) lap. 2) *(fig.)* bosom, bowels. 3) shelter, retreat.

regada, *s.f.* 1) farm, farmyard. 2) irrigated field.

regadio, *s.m.* 1) act of watering. 2) irrigation, watering. *adj.* watered, irrigated.

regador, *s.m.* watering can or pot, sprinkler, waterer. *adj.* watering, sprinkling.

regadura, *s.f.* 1) watering, irrigation. 2) sprinkling. 3) affusion.

regalado, *adj.* 1) delicate, dainty. 2) rich, sumptuous.

regalador, *s.m.* host, entertainer, feaster.

regalar, *v.* 1) to regale, entertain, feast. 2) to please, delight, gratify.

regalardoar, *v.* to reward or recompense again, repay twice the value.

regalengo, *adj.* regal, rayal.

regalia, *s.f.* 1) regal rights or privileges. 2) prerogative, special or exclusive right(s).

regalismo, *s.m.* regalism: doctrine of royal supremacy.

regalista, *s.m. e f.* regalist, upholder of royal sovereignty.

regalo, *s.m.* 1) regalement. 2) pleasure, delight.

reganhar, *v.* 1) to regain, win back. 2) to reacquire, repurchase. 3) to recuperate, recover, rehave.

regar, *v.* 1) to water, irrigate. 2) to sprinkle. 3) to wash, bathe.

regata, *s.f. (sport)* regatta, boat race.

regatão, *s.m. (pl. -ões)* huckster, retail dealer.

regateador, *s.m.* haggler, bargainer. *adj.* haggling, bargaining.

regatear, *v.* 1) to haggle over the price, bargain. 2) to drive a hard bargain.

regateio, *s.m.* haggling, bargaining, wrangling.

regateira, *s.f.* huckstress, itinerant (female) trader.

regateiro, *s.m.* huckster, itinerant vendor.

regateirona, *s.f.* extremely quarrelsome woman (used as a superlative of regateira).

regato, *s.m.* brooklet, creek, rivulet, streamlet, rill.

regedor, *s.m.* 1) administrator. 2) jurat. 3) chairman of the board of parish counsellors.

regedoria, *s.f.* office, authority and jurisdiction of a regedor.

regeira, *s.f. e m.* supporting beam (which props up a ship at launching.

regelação, *s.f. (pl. -ões) (fís.)* phenomenon of recongelation of broken lumps of ice.

regelado, *adj.* congealed, frozen, extremely cold.

regelador, *adj.* freezing, chilling.

regelante, *adj., m. e f.* freezing, chilling, tending to freeze.

regelar, *v.* 1) to freeze, congeal. 2) to chill.

regélido, *adj.* extremely cold, deeply frozen.

regelo, *s.m.* 1) refreezing. 2) glazed frost, white frost.

regência, *s.f.* 1) regency. 2) office, authority and jurisdiction of a ruler.

regencial, *adj., m. e f. (pl. -ais)* of, referring to or relative to regency.

regeneração, *s.f. (pl. -ões)* 1) regeneration. 2) renovation, reform.

regenerado, *adj.* regenerate, renewed, reformed, *(fig.)* spiritually reborn.

regenerador, *s.m.* regenerator.

regenerando, *adj.* regenerating, tending to regenerate, bound to spiritual recreation.

regenerante, *adj., m. e f.* regenerating, tending to regenerate.

regenerar, *v.* 1) to regenerate. 2) to reproduce, build up again what has been destroyed.

regenerativo, *adj.* regenerative, prone to regenerate.

regenerável, *adj., m. e f. (pl. -áveis)* regenerable, regenerative, amendable.

regente, *s.m. e f.* 1) regent, governor, ruler. 2) *(mús.)* maestro, conductor.

reger, *v.* 1) to govern, rule, reign. 2) to manage, administer. 3) to direct, guide. 4) *(mús.)* to conduct.

regerar, *v.* to generate again, regenerate.

régia, *s.f.* a king`s palace, manor-house, castle.

região, *s.f. (pl. -ões)* 1) large tract of land, area. 2) country, province. 3) region, zone, section. 4) realm.

regicida, *s.m. e f.* regicide: killer or murderer of a king or queen.

regicídio, *s.m.* regicide: killing or murdering of a king or queen.

regicidismo, regicismo, *s.m.* doctrine maintaining the elimination of royal sovereignty and monarchic government.

regime, *s.m. (also regímen pl. regimens, regimenes).* 1) regime, regimen. 2) mode or principles of ruling, political system. 3) *(med.)* rational use of food, diet.

regimental, *adj., m. e f. (pl. -ais)* regimental, of or referring to regimentation.

regimentar, *v.* to regulate, bring under control. *adj., m. e f.* regimental, regulating, regulatory.

regimento, *s.m.* 1) act or effect of governing.

2) government, administration. 3) guide rule, direction. 4) regime, form of government. 5) *(mil.)* regiment, body of soldiers, troops.

régio, *adj.* royal, regal. 2) kinglike, kingly.

regional, *adj., m. e f. (pl. -ais)* 1) regional, sectional, local. 2) *(med.)* endemical.

regionalismo, *s.m.* 1) regionalism. 2) provincialism, provinciality.

regionalista, *s.m. e f.* regionalist, provincialist.

registação, *s.f. (pl. -ões)* registration, registering.

registado, *s.m.* 1) registered letter or package. 2) registrant. *adj.* registered, recorded.

registador, *s.m.* 1) registrar, registrary. 2) registrant. 3) recorder, filer. 4) *(mec.)* recording device.

registar, *v.* 1) to register, enregister. 2) to book, list. 3) to write down, inscribe. 4) to record.

registável, *adj., m. e f. (pl. -áveis)* registrable, recordable, enterable.

registo, *s.m.* 1) register, record. 2) registry, registration office. 3) registration, enrol(l)-ment.

rego, *s.m.* 1) channel, duct. 2) gutter, drain.

regolfo, *s.m.* 1) turbine. 2) backwater, backwash. 3) countercurrent, crosscurrent.

regoliz, *s.m.* 1) *(bot.)* licorice, liquorice. 2) the root of this plant.

regorjeado, *adj.* similar to a trill, warble.

regorjear, *v.* to warble very much, trill, utter trilling sounds.

regorjeio, *s.m.* act of warbling or trilling, warble, trill.

regougante, *adj., m. e f.* 1) groaning, moaning. 2) grumbling, mumbling.

regougar, *v.* 1) to groan, moan. 2) to grumble, gripe, mumble. 3) to croak, utter hoarse cries, yelp.

regougo, *s.m.* 1) howl, yelp, yawp. 2) any deep hoarse sound or cry.

regozijado, *adj.* cheerful, merry, gay, rejoicing.

regozijador, *s.m.* one who rejoices or causes merriness, merrymaker. *adj.* joyful, cheerful, exhilarating.

regozijar, *v.* 1) to rejoice, cheer. 2) to cause merriment or pleasure. 3) to delight, please, gladden.

regozijo, *s.m.* 1) great pleasure or joy. 2) mirth, glee. 3) deep satisfaction, gladness.

regra, *s.f.* 1) ruler, metal or wood strip used for measuring. 2) rulings on paper, ruled paper.

regrado, *adj.* 1) sensible, reasonable. 2) moderate, temperate.

regrante, *adj., m. e f.* 1) regulated. 2) observant, observing (any religious law or precept).

regrar, *v.* 1) to rule, draw lines (on paper). 2) to regulate, set in order. 3) to moderate. 4) to guide, direct.

regraxar, *v.* to apply paint so fine in texture as to remain transparent.

regraxo, *s.m.* method and process of application of fine, translucent paint.

regredir, *v.* to retrograde, recede, withdraw.

regressão, *s.f. (pl. -ões)* 1) regression, regressing. 2) retrocession, retrogression. 3) throwback.

regressar, *v.* 1) to return, go back. 2) to come back, return home. 3) to send back, cause to return.

regressivo, *adj.* 1) regressive, retrogressive. 2) reactive.

regresso, *s.m.* 1) return, returning. 2) going or coming back. 3) reversion, regress. 4) throwback.

regreta, *s.f. (tip.)* reglet, small ruler.

regrista, *s.m. e f. (depr.).* 1) precisionist, pedant.

régua, *s.f.* ruler, rule, straight edge.

regueira, *s.f.* regueiro, m. 1) rivulet, creek, small stream. 2) irrigation or drainage ditch.

reguengo, *s.m.* crown land, land belonging to the king, royal domain.

reguengueiro, *s.m.* inhabitant or resident of a royal domain or crown land.

reguingar, *v.* 1) to object, remonstrate. 2) to reply sharply, retort. 3) to contest. 4) to kick back, recalcitrate.

regulação, *s.f. (pl. -ões)* 1) regulation, regulating. 2) rule, principle.

regulado, *adj.* regulated, regular, ruled, ordered, fixed.

regulador, *s.m.* regulator.

regulamentação, *s.f. (pl. -ões)* 1) regulation, act of regulating. 2) publication of rules, bylaws or statutes. 3) adjustment, settlement.

regulamentar, *adj., m. e f.* of, referring to or relative to regulation(s), regulative, regulatory. 1) *v.* to regulate, bring under control. 2) to arrange, settle, order. 3) to subject to order or regulations.

regulamentário, *adj.* regulative, regulatory.

regulamento, *s.m.* 1) regulation, rule. 2) ordinance, statute, bylaw. 3) resolution, determination.

regular, *s.m.* 1) regular occurrence. 2) regular soldier or member of a religious order. 3) habitual customer or frequenter. *v.* 4) to regulate. 5) to subject to rules or laws. 6) to direct, guide.

regularidade, *s.f.* 1) regularity. 2) regulation. 3) punctuality, steadiness.

regularização, *s.f.* (*pl.* *-ões*) regularization, act of regularizing.

regularizador, *s.m.* regulator, evener, regulating device. *adj.* regulating, regulative, regulatory.

regularizar, *v.* 1) to regularize, regulate. 2) to make steady or uniform. 3) to rectify, set right, bring in order. 4) to methodize.

regulável, *adj.*, *m. e f.* (*pl.* *-áveis*) regulable, regulatable, adjustable.

régulo, *s.m.* kinglet, native ruler.

regurgitação, *s.f.* (*pl.* *-ões*) regurgitation, backward flow, a casting up.

regurgitar, *v.* 1) to regurgitate. 2) to overflow, run over. 3) to pour, rush or surge back.

rei, *s.m.* 1) king, monarch sovereign. 2) (fig.) magnate, tycoon. 3) dia dos Reis, Epiphany.

reiforme, *s.m.* ratite, bird of the order Ratitae.

reigada, *s.f.* hollow along the buttock or the rump of certain animals.

reima, *s.f.* olive juice.

reimão, *s.m.* (*pl.* *-ões*) 1) animal without regular dwelling place. 2) (*zool.*) black panther.

reimoso, *adj.* 1) rheumy. 2) bad for the blood. reimpressão, *s.f.* (*pl.* *-ões*) 1) reprint, reprinting. 2) new impression.

reimpressor, *s.m.* reprinter, publisher or editor who reprints. *adj.* reprinting.

reimprimir, *v.* to reprint, republish, make a new impression or edition.

reinação, *s.f.* (*pl.* *-ões*) 1) merrymaking, high jinks. 2) carousal, revelry.

reinaço, *s.m.* (*pop.*) rut, oestrus.

reinadio, *s.m.* merrymaking, revelry, spree.

reinado, *s.m.* 1) reign. 2) duration and jurisdiction of a sovereign. 3) supremacy, predominancy, predominance.

reinador, *adj.* naughty, mischievous, wanton.

reinante, *s.m. e f.* 1) ruler. 2) king, queen.

reinar, *v.* 1) to reign, rule, govern. 2) to be enthroned, be king, queen or regent of. 3) to dominate, control.

reinauguração, *s.f.* (*pl.* *-ões*) reinauguration.

reinaugurar, *v.* to reinaugurate, initiate again.

reincidência, *s.f.* 1) reincidence, reincidency. 2) relapse, recidivation. 3) obstinacy, pertinacy. 4) backsliding, wilfulness.

reincidente, *adj.*, *m. e f.* 1) recidivistic, recidivous. 2) relapsing, backsliding.

reincidir, *v.* to relapse, fall back.

reincitar, *v.* to reincite, rouse, instigate again.

reincorporação, *s.f.* (*pl.* *-ões*) reincorporation.

reincorporar, *v.* to reincorporate, unite, blend or merge again.

reinel, *adj.*, *m. e f.* (*pl.* *-éis*) of the realm.

reineta, *s.f.* reinette, a variety of apple.

reinfecção, *s.f.* (*pl.* *-ões*) reinfection, additional infection.

reinflamar, *v.* 1) to reinflame, set alight again. 2) to rouse, incite again.

reinfundir, *v.* to reinstil, infuse, inculcate again.

reiniciar, *v.* to begin or initiate again, recommence, restart.

reino, *s.m.* 1) kingdom, monarchy. 2) realm, domain, dominion, empire.

reinquirir, *v.* to cross-examine, interrogate anew.

reinscrever, *v.* to reinscribe, sign up again, inscribe anew.

reinstalação, *s.f.* (*pl.* *-ões*) reinstallation, reinstal(l)ment.

reinstalar, *v.* 1) to reinstall, install again. 2) to reinstate. 3) to re-establish, restore.

reintegração, *s.f.* (*pl.* *-ões*) 1) reintegration. 2) restoration. 3) repeated or renewed integration. 4) reposition, reinstatement.

reintegrador, *s.m.* reintegrator, restorator, restorer. *adj.* reintegrating.

reintegrar, *v.* 1) to reintegrate, restore. 2) to renew. 3) to reinstate, reinstall, place again in a (*former*). 4) reintegrar-se, position; to settle or establish o.s. again, become reintegrated.

reintroduzir, *v.* to reintroduce, introduce again or anew.

reinvidar, *v.* 1) to raise once more (*a bet*). 2) to reply, retort, answer sharply. 3) to counterchange, pay back in the same coin.

reira, *s.f. (med.)* pain in the kidneys; diarrhea.

réis, *s.m.* plural of real, former Brazilian monetary unit.

reisado, *s.m.* 1) celebration of Epiphany. 2) popular dramatic dance (usually performed on January 6th, day of the Magi).

reiteração, *s.f. (pl. -ões)* reiteration, repetition, renewal.

reiterado, *adj.* reiterated, repeated; reiteradamente, *adv.* repeatedly, reiteratedly.

reiterar, *v.* 1) to reiterate, repeat. 2) to say over again. 3) to renew. 4) to reaffirm, ingeminate.

reiterativo, *adj.* reiterative, repeated, reiterating.

reiterável, *adj., m. e f. (pl. áveis)* reiterable, apt to be repeated.

reitor, *s.m.* 1) rector, head of a university or college. 2) headmaster, principal. 3) *(ecol.)* pastor, minister, prior. 4) reitor de universidade, president of a university.

reitora, *s.f.* headmistress.

reitorado, *s.m.* 1) rectorship, rectorate. 2) dignity and authority of a rector. 3) duration of the rectorship.

reitoria, *s.f.* 1) rectorship, rectory. 2) office or authority of a rector. 3) duration of a rectorship.

reiuna, *s.f.* 1) flintlock, old-fashioned shotgun.

reiuno, *s.m.* ugly or worn out horse. adj. supplied by the government (said with regard to a soldier's uniform and outfit).

reivindicação, *s.f. (pl. -ões)* 1) act of claiming, reclamation. 2) claim, demand (for rights, compensation or return of property).

reivindicador, *s.m.* claimant, claimer. *adj.* claiming, demanding.

reivindicante, *adj., m. e f.* claiming, demanding, revindicative.

reivindicar, *v.* 1) to revindicate. 2) *(jur.)* to vindicate, assert one's legal right. 3) to recover, regain. 4) to reclaim, demand.

reivindicativo, *adj.* revindicative, concerning revindication or demands.

reivindicável, *adj., m. e f. (pl. -áveis)* claimable, subject to revindication.

reixa, *s.f.* 1) small board or plank. 2) bars, window grate, grating. 3) window blind, venetian blinds. 4) quarrel, brawl, strife.

reixador, *s.m. (pop.)* quarrelsome person.

reizete, reizinho, *s.m. (depr.)* kinglet, native ruler.

rejeição, *s.f. (pl. -ões).* 1) rejection, refusal. 2) exclusion. 3) repulse, repudiation. 4) denial.

rejeitado, *adj.* 1) castoff, castaway. 2) rejected. 3) unsuccessful.

rejeitar, *v.* 1) to reject. 2) to cast or throw away. 3) to refuse, decline to accept. 4) to repudiate, repulse, reprobate.

rejeitável, *adj., m. e f. (pl. -áveis)* rejectable, that may or should be rejected or refused.

rejubilação, *s.f. (pl. -ões)* rejoicing, jubilation, exultation, delight.

rejubilante, *adj., m. e f.* rejoicing, rejubilant.

rejubilar, *v.* 1) to cause great joy, bring happiness to. 2) to jubilate, exult, rejoice. 3) to feel great pleasure or satisfaction. 4) to be very glad. 5) to make merry.

rejúbilo, *s.m.* rejoicing, joyfulness, exultation, delight.

rejubiloso, *adj.* joyful, glad, rejoicing, jubilant.

rejuntado, *adj.* articulate, jointed, segmented.

rejuntamento, *s.m.* tuck pointing: fillet of building cement (used to cover the joints in brickwork).

rejuntar, *v.* to flush. 2) to seal the joints.

rejurar, *v.* to swear again, repeat an oath.

rejuvenescente, *s.m. e f.* rejuvenator. *adj.* rejuvenescent.

rejuvenescer, *v.* 1) to rejuvenate, rejuvenize, make young again. 2) to renew, renovate. 3) to appear to be young or younger.

rejuvenescimento, *s.m.* rejuvenescence, rejuvenation, regeneration.

rela, *s.f.* 1) *(zool.)* tree toad. 2) bird trap.

relação, *s.f. (pl. -ões)* 1) act of reporting. 2) description, report. 3) narrative, recital. 4) roll, list, register.

relacionado, *adj.* related, connected, conversant, having relations with.

relacional, *adj., m. e f. (pl. -ais)* relational, of or pertaining to kinship.

relacionar, *v.* 1) to relate, tell, report. 2) to include in a list, inscribe, register. 3) to expound, explain. 4) to procureconnections, try to enter into relationship with. 5) to enrol, catalogue.

relacrar, *v.* to reseal with wax.

relamber, *v.* to lick again, relick.

relambório, *s.m.* laziness, indolence, idleness.

relâmpago, *s.m.* 1) lightning, flash of lightning, thunderbolt. 2) brilliancy, effulgence, brightness. 3) sudden luminous appearance.

relampagueante, *adj. m. e f.* (also relampeante, relampejante, relampear) flashing (like a thunderbolt), glittering, sparkling.

relampaguear, relampejar, *v.* (also relampadear). 1) to lighten. 2) to glitter, sparkle. 3) to appear like a flash of lightning. 4) to execute or quick and transient occurrence. 5) sheet-lighting.

relançar, *v.* to cast a quick glance upon, glance at.

relance, *s.m.* 1) glance, glimpse. 2) (bullfighting) the second unexpected encounter of the tortador with the charging bull.

relancear, *s.m.* glance, glimpse, quick look. *v.* to glance at, cast a furtive look at.

relapsão, *s.f. (pl. -ões)* relapse, sliding back, reincidence, recurrence.

relapsia, *s.f.* relapse, recurrence, backsliding into crime, vice or error.

relapso, *s.m.* relapser, recidivist, backslider; *adj.* 1) relapsing, backsliding. 2) recidivous. 3) obstinate, refractory, contumacious.

relar, *v.* to grate, scrape.

relasso, *adj.* slack, sloppy, slipshod.

relatar, *v.* 1) to mention, discuss casually. 2) to tell, narrate. 3) to refer to. 4) to expound, explain. 5) to describe. 6) to report.

relatividade, *s.f.* 1) relativity, relativeness. 2) conditionality.

relativismo, *s.m.* relativism, relativity of knowledge.

relativo, *adj.* relative, relating to, concenting; corresponding.

relato, *s.m.* report, account; description.

relator, *s.m.* relater, reporter, narrator.

relatório, *s.m.* report, account, formal statement; *fazer um relatório:* to draw up a report.

relaxação, *s.f.* relaxation, negligence, slackness; lassitude.

relaxadamente, negligently.

relaxado, *adj.* relaxed; loose; dissolute; slack; negligent, careless.

relaxamento, *s.m.* relaxation; laxity, slackness; negligence, carelessness.

relaxante, *adj.* relaxing.

relaxar, *v.t.* to relax, to loesen, to slacken; *v.i.* to become slack ou careless; *relaxar-se:* to become careless.

relaxativo, *adj.* relaxing.

relaxe, *s.m.* compulsory collection of overdue taxes.

relaxidão, *s.f.* relaxation; loosening, slackness: negligence.

relegação, *s.f.* relegation, banishment.

relegar, *v.t.* to relegate, to banish, to exile; to despise, do disdain.

relegável, *adj.* exilable; despisable.

relembrança, *s.f.* rememberance, recollection.

relembrar, *v.t.* to remind; to remember again, to call to mind.

relembrável, *adj.* rememorable.

relentar, *v.t.* to moisten; to bedew.

relento, *s.m.* dew; night air, night dampness; *dormir ao relento,* to sleep in the open.

reler, *v.t.* to read again.

reles, *adj.* worthless, common, shabby, inferior; vulgar.

relevação, *s.f.* forgiveness; remission, absolution.

relevador, *adj.* pardoning, absolving.

relevamento, *s.m.* release; pardon; exemption.

relevância, *s.f.* importance, prominence, significance.

relevante, *adj.* important, outstanding; considerable.

relevar, *v.t.* to relieve, to pardon, to excuse, to forgive; to exempt; *relevar uma falta:* to overlook a fault.

relevável, *adj.* excusable.

relevo, *s.m.* relief; prominence, importance; distinction; emphasis. 1) *dar relevo a,* to bring out; to accentuate, to emphasize. 2) *trabalhar em relevo,* to emboss *(metal).*

relha, *s.m.* ploughshare.

relhador, *s.m.* long whip.

relhar, *v.t.* to lash, to whip.

relheira, *s.f.* furrow.

relho, *adj. velho e relho:* very old.

relicário, *s.m.* reliquary, shrine, tabernacle.

religião, *s.f.* religion; cult; faith; belief; church.

religionário, *s.m.* religionist; reformist.

religiosa, *s.f.* nun.

religiosamente, *adv.* religiously, devoutly; exactly, scrupulously.

religiosidade, *s.f.* religiousness, religiosity; devotion.

religioso, *adj.* religious, pious, devout.

relinchar, *v.i.* to neigh.

relincho, *s.m.* neigh, whinny.

relíquia, *s.f.* relic; treasure; *s.f. pl.* remains; ruins.

relógio, *s.m.* clock, watch, timepiece. 1)

relógio de bolso, pocket watch. 2) *relógio de parede*, wall clock. 3) *relógio de pulso*, wrist watch. 4) *relógio de sol*, sundial. 5) *relógio despertador*, alarm clock.

relojoaria, *s.f.* watchmaker's shop.

relojoeiro, *s.m.* watchmaker.

relutância, *s.f.* reluctance, aversion, unwillingness.

relutante, *adj.* reluctant, unwilling, averse.

relutar, *v.i.* to feel reluctance; to resist.

reluzente, *adj.* refulgent, shining, radiant, glittering.

reluzir, *v.i.* to shine, to glitter, to sparkle, to gleam.

relva, *s.f.* grass, turf, sward.

relvado, *s.m.* lawn, grassplot, sward.

relvar, *v.t.* to cover with grass.

relvejar, *v.i.* to be covered with new grass.

relvoso, *adj.* grassy, swarded, lawny.

remadad, *s.f.* stroke with an oar; act of rowing.

remador, *s.m.* oarsman; rower.

remanência, *s.f.* remanence.

remanescente, *adj.* remaining, residual, remanent, left over, resting; *s.m.* remainder, residue, remnant, rest, surplus.

remanescer, *v.i.* to remain, to be left over.

remansado, *adj.* calm, still; slow; slack, lazy.

remansar-se, *v.refl.* to stand still; to stop flowing (*água*).

remansear, *v.i. e v.refl.* to rest, to repose, to stand still, to grow sluggish.

remanso, *s.m.* stillness, calmness; immobility; quietude; sluggishness.

remansoso, *adj.* still, calm, slow, quiet.

remar, *v.t.* to row; to paddle.

remarcação, *s.f.* relabelling.

remarcar, *v.t.* to re-mark, to tag again, to relabel.

remastigação, *s.f.* remastication, rumination.

remastigar, *v.t.* to ruminate, to remasticate.

rematação, *s.f.* sale by auction; adjudication.

rematado, *adj.* surmounted; complete, perfect; consummate.

rematador, *adj.* finishing, perfecting.

rematar, *v.t.* to finish, to conclude, to complete; to wind up; to crown; to finish off (*costura*); *v.i.* to end (*in*).

remate, *s.m.* conclusion, completion, finish; finishing touch; trimmings; shot at goal. (*desporto*).

remedar, *v.t.* to imitate, to mimic.

remedeio, *s.m.* remedy; stop-gap; resource.

remediado, *adj.* comfortably off, well-off; removed (*um erro*).

remediar, *v.t.* to remedy; to relieve; to mend, to repair; to stop; to put right; *remediar-se com*, to put up with; to eke out a living.

remediável, *adj.* remediable, reparable.

remédio, *s.m.* remedy; medicine, physic medicament; cure; relief. 1) *não há remédio*, it can't be helped. 2) *não há outro remédio senão*, there is nothing for it but .... 3) *não tive outro remédio*, I could not help it.

remedo, *s.m.* imitation; mockery.

remeiro, *s.m.* rower, paddler.

remela, *s.f.* secretion of the eyes, bleary-eye.

remelento, remeloso, *adj.* bleary-eyed.

rememoração, *s.f.* remembrance, recollection.

rememorar, *v.t.* to remember, to recollect, to recall.

remomorativo, *adj.* rememorative.

rememorável, *adj.* rememberable.

remendado, *adj.* mended.

remendagem, *s.f.* patching, mending.

remendão, *s.m.* patcher; botcher, bungler.

remendar, *v.t.* to patch, to mend, to repair.

remendeiro, *adj.* patching; *s.m.* patcher.

remendo, *s.m.* patch; mending, repair, amendment.

remendona, *s.f.* clumsy or unskilled woman.

remessa, *s.f.* sending; shipping; shipment; remittance (*de dinheiro*).

remessão, *s.f.* throw.

remessar, *v.t.* to throw, to hurl, to fling.

remetente, *s.m. e s.f.* sender; remitter; shipper.

remeter, *v.t.* to send, to remit, to forward; to put off, to delay (*atrasar*).

remetida, *s.f.* charge, assault.

remexer, *v.t.* to rummage, to stir, to jumble, to derange.

remexida, *s.f.* bustle, confusion, stir; disorder.

remexido, *adj.* stirred up; restless; bustling, unquiet.

remição, *s.f.* redemption, redeeming; deliverance.

remidor, *s.m.* redeemer; *adj.* redeemer; *adj.* redeeming.

rémige, *s.f.* pen-feather, wing-quill; *adj.* remigial.

remígio, *s.m.* remex, flight-feather, flight guide.

remigração, *s.f.* remigration, repatriation.

remigrar, *v.i.* to remigrate.

reminiscência, *s.f.* reminiscence, remembering, recollection.

remípede, *adj.* remiped.

remir, *v.t.* to redeem; to buy back; to ransom; to save, to rescue, to free from; to compensate, to make up for; to expiate; *remir-se,* to redeem oneself; to pay one's debts.

remirar, *v.t.* to look again.

remissa, *s.f.* adjournment; delay, postponment, putting off.

remissão, *s.f.* remission, forgiveness; remittance.

remissibilidade, *s.f.* remissibility.

remissível, *adj.* remissible, absolvable.

remissivo, *adj.* remissive; forgiving; allusive.

remisso, *adj.* remiss, careless, negligent; lazy, indolent.

remissório, *adj.* remissory, remissive.

remitência, *s.f.* remission, abatement, diminution.

remitente, *adj.* remittent, abating.

remitir, *v.t.* to remit, to pardon, to forgive; to relax.

remível, *adj.* redeemable, recoverable, redemptible.

remo, *s.m.* oar; rowing *(actividade desportiva).*

remobilar, *v.t.* to refurnish.

remoçado, *adj.* rejuvenated; reinvigorated.

remoçador, *adj.* rejuvenating.

remoção, *s.f.* removal, remotion; transfer.

remoçar, *v.t. e v.i.* to make young, to grow young again.

remodelação, *s.f.* remodelling.

remodelador, *adj.* remodelling; *s.m.* remodeller, reformer.

remodelagem, *s.f.* remodelling.

remodelar, *v.t.* to remodel, to recast, to reform.

remoedura, *s.f.* rumination.

remoer, *v.t.* to grind again; to munch; to ruminate; to brood over *(matutar).*

remoinhar, *v.t.* to whirl, to spin, to turn round, to swirl, to flow in circles.

remoinho, *s.m.* whirlwind, whirlpool; eddy; vortex.

remolhar, *v.t.* to soak, to drench.

remolho, *s.m.* soaking again.

remondagem, *s.f.* reweeding.

remondar, *v.t.* to weed again.

remonta, *s.f.* remount, fresh horse; supply for fresh horses; horses for the army.

remontagem, *s.f.* reassemblage, reconstitution.

remontar, *v.t.* to lift up, to raise on high; to remount, to furnish fresh horses to; to refit, to reassemble; *v.i.* to return, to go back (to the past); to take its rise (in, from).

remonte, *s.m.* remounting, ascension; repair.

remoque, *s.m.* scoff, taunt, twit; mockery.

remoquear, *v.t.* to taunt, to twit.

remora, *s.f.* hindrance, delay, postponement, putting off.

remorado, *adj.* delayed, retarded.

remordaz, *adj.* biting, sarcastic.

remordente, *adj.* gnawing.

remorder, *v.t.* to gnaw; to bite again; to afflict; to brood over *(cismar); remorder-se,* to fret oneself; to be consumed.

remoroso, *adj.* delaying, hindering.

remorso, *s.m.* remorse; regret; pricks of conscience.

remoto, *adj.* remote, distant, out of the way; faraway, far off; outlying.

remover, *v.t.* to remove; to shift; to transfer; to clear away; to dispose of.

removimento, *s.m.* removing, removal; displacement.

removível, *adj.* removable; transferable.

remudar, *v.t.* to remove again; to change again.

remuneração, *s.f.* remuneration; pay; salary, wages; fee; reward, recompense.

remunerador, *adj.* remunerating, remunerative; profitable; *s.m.* remunerator.

remunerar, *v.t.* to remunerate; to pay; to reward, to recompensate.

remunerativo, *adj.* remunerative.

remunerável, *adj.* remunerable; rewardable.

remurmúrio, *s.m.* remurmuring.

rena, *s.f.* reindeer.

renal, *adj.* renal.

renano, *adj.* Rhine.

renascença, *s.f.* renascence; rebirth; *(hist.)* Renaissance.

renascente, *adj.* renascent, reviving, renewed.

renascentista, *adj.* Renaissant; *s.m. e s.f.* Renaissancist.

renascer, *v.i.* to be born again; to grow again; to revive, to reappear.

renascimento, *s.m. o mesmo que "renascença".*

renda, *s.f.* income, revenue, profit; rent *(aluguer);* lace *(tecido).*

rendado, *adj.* lace-trimmed; *s.m.* lacework; lace-trimming.

rendar, *v.t.* to trim with lace.

rendedoiro, rendedouro, *adj.* profitable, lucrative, productive.

rendeiro, *s.m.* tenant farmer; tenant; renter; lace-maker.

render, *v.t.* to subdue; to relieve; to yeld; to render; to give up; *v.i.* to rupture; to produce income. 1) *render-se,* to surrender; to capitulate, to fall. 2) *render a guarda,* to relive guard. 3) *render graças,* to render thanks. 4) *render homenagem,* to pay homage. 5) *render pouco,* to pay little. 6) *render juros,* to draw interests.

rendição, *s.f.* surrender, giving up, capitulation, fall.

rendido, *adj.* overcome, subdued *(by)*; ruptured.

rendilha, *s.f.* fine lace.

rendilhado, *adj.* lacy: *s.m.* lacework.

rendilhar, *v.t.* to trim with lace.

rendimento, *s.m.* revenue, income; profit, product, proceeds; interest *(juros)*; efficiency *(de uma máquina)*.

rendoso, *adj.* profitable, lucrative; fruitful; paying.

renegação, *s.f.* renegation; denial, apostasy.

renegado, *s.m.* renegade, apostate, deserter.

renegador, *adj.* faithless; *s.m.* renegade; denier.

renegar, *v.t.* to deny; to renouce; to abjure; to repudiate; to repel.

renhidamente, *adv.* fiercely, relentlessly.

renhido, *adj.* fierce, furious, relentless; hotly contested.

renhimento, *s.m.* quarrel, fight; furry, fierceness.

renhir, *v.t.* to dispute, to debate, to quarrel; to argue, to contest, to contend for.

reniforme, *adj.* reniform; kidney-shaped.

renitência, *s.f.* obstinacy, contumacy; resistance; reluctance.

renitente, *adj.* resistant, obstinate, stubborn; reluctant, renitent.

renitir, *v.i.* to resist, to oppose; to persist in; to be obdurate.

renome, *s.m.* renown, celbrity, fame; reputation, prestige.

renova, *s.f.* new shoot, sprout.

renovação, *s.f.* renewal, renovation; revival.

renovador, *adj.* renewing; *s.m.* renewer, reformer.

renovar, *v.t.* to renew; to renovate; to restore; to revive; to resume; to repeat; to sprout *(lançar renovos).*

renovável, *adj.* renewable.

renovo, *s.m.* sprout, shoot.

renque, *s.m.* file, row, rank.

rentar, *v.i.* to pass close by; to defy: to flirt.

rente, *adj. e adv.* close; close to, near; even with.

renteador, *s.m.* gallant, suitor.

rentear, *v.t.* to cut off, loose; to play the gallant; to make love; to pass close by.

renuir, *v.t.* to renounce; to reject, to refuse.

renúncia, *s.f.* renunciation, renouncing, giving up; resignation; self-denial; *(jur.)* quitclaim.

renunciação, *s.f. o mesmo que "renúncia".*

renunciador, *adj.* renouncing; *s.m.* renouncer; abjurer.

renunciante, *adj.* renouncing; *s.m.* renouncer.

renunciar, *v.t.* to renounce; to repudiate; to abjure, to resign; to abdicate; to renege *(em jogo de cartas).*

renunciatório, *adj.* renunciatory.

renunciável, *adj.* renunciable.

reocupação, *s.f.* reoccupation.

reocupar, *v.t.* to reoccupy; to reconquer.

reóforo, *s.m.* rheophore.

reómetro, *s.m.* rheometer, galvanometer.

reordenação, *s.f.* reordination.

reordenar, *v.t.* to reordain, to rearrange.

reorganização, *s.f.* reorganization.

reorganizador, *s.m.* reorganizer; *adj.* reorganizing.

reorganizar, *v.t.* to reorganize; to rearrange.

reóstato, *s.m.* rheostat.

repa, *s.f.* thin hair.

repagar, *v.t.* to repay; to pay well; to pay back.

repaginação, *s.f.* repagination.

repaginar, *v.t.* to repaginate; to repage.

reparação, *s.f.* reparation; repair; restoration; amends, satisfaction, redress; indemnification.

reparador, *adj.* repairing; restoring, invigorating; *s.m.* repairer.

reparar, *v.t.* to repair, to refit; to restore; to mend, to remedy; to make amends for; to make up for; to notice, to observe. 1) *repara!,* look!. 2) *reparar em,* to notice, to take notice of, to pay attention to.

reparatório, *adj.* reparative, repairing.

reparável, *adj.* repairable; remediable.

reparo, *s.m.* repair; notice, observation, remark; objection.

repartição, *s.f.* partition, allotment, distribution; office, bureau, branch, department.

repartideira, *s.f.* copper pan used in sugar mills.

repartidor, *adj.* dividing, distributing; *s.m.* divider.

repartimento, *s.m.* compartment; distribution, allotment, division.

repartir, *v.t.* to divide; to share, to allot, to parcel out; to split up; to part *(o cabelo); repartir-se,* to branch out; to scatter; to divide one's attention.

repartitivo, *adj.* distributive.

repartível, *adj.* dividable.

repassado, *adj.* soaked, impregnated; saturated.

repassar, *v.t.* to pass again; to go over again; to soak, to drench; to fill; v.i. to ooze, to drip; to soak *(papel).*

repasse, *s.m.* gleaning.

repasto, *s.m.* repast; meal; banquet.

repatriação, *s.f.* repatriation.

repatriado, *s.m.* returning emigrant; *adj.* repatriate.

repatriamento, *s.m.* repatriation.

repatriar, *v.t.* to repatriate; *repatriar-se:* to return to one's country.

repelão, *s.m.* shove, jostle, push; assault; *de repelão:* abruptly, roughly.

repelar, *v.t.* to pull, to push.

repelência, *s.f.* repellency, repulsion, repugnance.

repelente, *adj.* repellent, repulsive, revolting, repugnant.

repelir, *v.t.* to repel, to repulse; to refuse, to reject; to feel aversion.

repelo, *s.m.* pull, push.

repenicar, *v.i.* to tinkle, to clink; to chime *(sinos);* to twang *(viola).*

repensar, *v.t.* to rethink, to ponder.

repente, *s.m.* sudden action; fit, outburst; *de repente,* suddenly, all of a sudden.

repentinamente, *adv.* suddenly, all of a sudden.

repentino, *adj.* sudden, unexpected.

repentista, *s.m.* e *s.f.* improviser, extemporizer.

repercussão, *s.f.* repercussion, reverberation; significance; echo.

repercussivo, *adj.* repercussive.

repercutir, *v.t.* to reverberate, to send back; to recoil; to reflect, to resound; to influence.

repertório, *s.m.* repertory; repertoire.

repes, *s.m.* rep, reps, textile fabric.

repeso, *adj.* contrite, sorry, repentant, regretful.

repetência, *s.f.* repetition.

repetente, *adj.* repeating; *s.m.* repeater.

repetição, *s.f.* repetition; recurrence; reiteration.

repetidamente, *adv.* repeatedly, frequently.

repetido, *adj.* repeated; frequent; repetidas vezes: again and again.

repetidor, *adj.* repeating; *s.m.* repeater; coach *(professor).*

repetir, *v.t.* to repeat; to iterate, to reiterate; to echo; to harp on; to reproduce; *repetir-se,* to recur; to happen again.

repicar, *v.t.* e *v.i.* to ring, to chime, to peal.

repimpadamente, *adv.* in a comfortable way.

repimpado, *adj.* comfortable seated; well-fed.

repimpar-se, *v.refl.* to loll, to settle oneself comfortably; to cram oneself with food.

repimpim, *s.m.* pin-clover.

repinchar, *v.i.* to splash; to rebound.

repique, *s.m.* chime; alarm; pealing of bells.

repisar, *v.t.* to tread again; to repeat over and over.

replantação, *s.f.* replantation, replanting.

replantar, *v.t.* to replant, to plant again.

repleção, *s.f.* repletion, surfeit, fullness.

repletar, *v.t.* to fill to capacity, to cram.

repleto, *adj.* filled up, replete; crammed; surfeited.

réplica, *s.f.* reply, rejoinder, retort; refutation; *réplica,* reproduction *(de obra de arte).*

replicador, *s.m.* replier; *adj.* replying.

replicar, *v.t.* to reply, to answer, to retort; to refute, to object.

repolho, *s.m.* cabbage.

repolhudo, *adj.* round, plum, fat.

repoltrear-se, *v.refl.* to lounge, to recline idly; to linger.

repontão, *adj.* cranky; *s.m.* grambler.

repontar, *v.i.* to grumble, to talk bak, to retort; to recalcitrate.

repor, *v.t.* to replace, to put back; to restore.

reportação, *s.f.* moderation, modesty.

reportado, *adj.* modest, discreet; moderate.

reportagem, *s.f.* newspaper report; story; reporting; report.

reportamento, *s.m.* moderation; modesty.

reportar, *v.t.* to turn back; to refer; to allude; to moderate.

repórter, *s.m.* reporter.

reportório, *s.m.* repertory.

reposição, *s.f.* replacement.

repositório, *s.m.* repository; compilation; store.

reposta, *s.f.* money staked at ombre.

repostada, *s.f.* rude answer.

repostar, *v.i.* to reply or to answer rudely.

reposteiro, *s.m.* drapes, curtains; butler; treasurer.

repousante, *adj.* restful; relaxing.

repousar, *v.t.* to repose, to rest; to relax; to lie; to soothe *(tranquilizar)*.

repouso, *s.m.* repose, rest; relaxation; quiet; *em repouso,* quiet; resting.

repovoar, *v.t.* to repeople, to repopulate.

repreendedor, *s.m.* reprehender, reproacher; *adj.* reprehending.

repreender, *v.t.* to reprehend, to reprimand, to rebuke, to reproach, to censure, to reprove; to admonish, to scold.

repreensão, *s.f.* reprehension, reprimand.

repreensivamente, *adv.* reprehensively.

repreensível, *adj.* reprehensible, blamable, reproachable.

repreensivo, *adj.* reprehensive, admonitory.

represa, *s.f.* dam, dike.

represado, *adj.* repressed, restrained; dammed up.

represália, *s.f.* reprisal, retaliation; revenge; *exercer represálias sobre,* to take reprisals on.

represamento, *s.m.* act or process of restraining or keeping back.

represar, *v.t.* to dam; to repress, to restrain; to hamper.

representação, *s.f.* representation; performance, acting, playing *(teatral)*; picture, image.

representador, *s.m.* representer, actor, player; *adj.* representing, acting.

representante, *adj.* representating; *s.m.* representative; deputy, delegate; substitute.

representar, *v.t.* to represent; to perform, to act, to play; to stand for; to figure, to portray; *v.i.* to lodge a complaint with; to present a petition.

representativo, *adj.* representative; typical.

represo, *adj.* restrained, repressed.

repressão, *s.f.* repression, restraint; suppression.

repressivo, *adj.* repressive.

repressor, *s.m.* represser; *adj.* repressing.

reprimenda, *s.f.* reprimand, rebuke.

reprimir, *v.t.* to repress, to restrain; to suppress; to control; to subdue.

reprimível, *adj.* repressible, restrainable.

reprise, *s.f.* rerun, repeated performance.

reprobatório, *adj.* reprobative, reprobatory.

réprobo, *s.m.* e *adj.* reprobate, outcast, castaway.

reprodução, *s.f.* reproduction, copy; duplicate.

reprodutibilidade, *s.f.* reproducibility.

reprodutível, *adj.* reproductible, reproducible.

reprodutivo, *adj.* reproductive.

reprodutor, *s.m.* reproducer; breeder; studhorse, stallion *(cavalo)*; *adj.* reproducing; breeding.

reproduzir, *v.t.* to reproduce; to multiply, to propagate; to repeat; to copy, to imitate; *reproduzir-se,* to reproduce itself; to breed, to multiply.

reproduzível, *adj.* reproducible.

reprovação, *s.f.* reproval, reproof; disapproval; blame; failure, flank *(em exame)*.

reprovado, *adj.* reproved; failed, flunked *(em exame)*.

reprovador, *adj.* reproving, disapproving; reproachful; *s.m.* reprover.

reprovar, *v.t.* to disapprove, to reprove; to censure, to blame; to fail.

reprovável, *adj.* reprovable, censurable, blameworthy.

reptação, *s.f.* challenge, defiance.

reptor, *s.m.* defier, challenger.

reptante, *adj.* reptant, creeping; reptil; challenger.

reptar, *v.t.* to defy, to challenge; to creep.

réptil, *s.m.* reptile.

repto, *s.m.* challenge, defy, provocation.

república, *s.f.* republic.

republicanismo, *s.m.* republicanism.

republicanização, *s.f.* republicanization.

republicanizar, *v.t.* to republicanize.

republicano, *s.m.* e *adj.* republican.

republicar, *v.t.* to republish.

república, *s.m.* e *adj.* republican.

republiqueta, *s.f.* banana republica.

repudiação, *s.f. o mesmo que "repúdio".*

repudiar, *v.t.* repugnance; to reject; to cast off; to disavow; to abjure.

repúdio, *s.m.* repudiation, disowning; abjuration, denial.

repugnância, *adj.* repugnant, repulsive; repellent; loathsome.

repugnante, adj. repugnant, repulsive; repellent; loathsome.

repugnar, v.t. to reject; to be disgusting; to cause aversion; to disgust.

repulsa, s.f. repulse, rejection, repudiation; hostility; repulsion; repugnance, disgust, abhorrence.

repulsão, s.f. o mesmo que "repulsa".

repulsar, v.t. to repulse, to repel, to reject.

repulsivo, adj. repulsive, repellent; disgusting; odious; revolting.

repulso, s.m. repulsion, repulse; adj. repulsed, repelled.

repululação, s.f. repullulation.

repulular, v.i. to repullulate, to sprout again.

repurgar, v.t. to repurge.

repurificação, s.f. repurification.

reputação, s.f. reputation, prestige; fame, renown; respectabillity.

reputar, v.t. to repute, to consider, to esteem; to regard as; to appraise; reputar--se, to consider oneself; to regard oneself as.

repuxado, adj. draw back, pulled back.

repuxão, s.m. drawing back, pulling back, stron jerk.

repuxar, v.t. to draw back, to pull back; to jerk at.

repuxo, s.m. drawing back; jet of water, waterspout; kick (de arma de fogo).

requebrado, adj. languid, languishing.

requebrar, v.t. to move languidly; requebrar--se, to languish; to walk in a languishing manner.

requebro, s.m. languishing look or movement; (mús.) trill.

requeijão, s.m. curd cheese; cream cheese.

requeima, s.f. burning, parching.

requeimado, adj. burned, parched.

requeimar, v.t. to burn, to parch; to dry up, to scorch.

requeime, s.m. acridity, piquant flavour.

requentado, adj. reheated.

requentar, v.t. to heat again, to reheat.

requerente, s.m. e s.f. petitioner, applicant; adj. petitionrig.

requerer, v.t. to apply for, to petition; to request, to solicit; to demand, to require, to call for.

requerimento, s.m. petition, application; demand.

requesta, s.f. strife, quarrel, dispute; demand; courtship.

requestador, s.m. wooer, suitor; adj. wooing, courting.

requestar, v.t. to request; to woo, to court, to make love to.

requesto, s.f. request, demand; petition; quarrel.

réquiem, s.m. Mass for the dead; requiem.

requife, s.m. trimming, binding.

requinta, s.f. clarinet.

requintado, adj. refined, exquisite; cultivated; perfect.

requintar, v.t. to refine, to perfect; v.i. to perfect oneself; to excel; to outdo oneself (in something).

requinte, s.m. refinement; perfection; elegance.

requisição, s.f. requisition, requirement, request.

requisitante, s.m. requisitioner.

requisitar, v.t. to requisition, to commandeer; to press (into the service of the army, etc).

requisito, s.m. requisite, requirement; qualification.

requisitório, adj. beseeching; s.m. charge, indictment.

rês, s.f. cattle for slaughter; s.f. pl. livestock.

rés, adj. even, even with; adv. close to; rés--do-chão, ground-floor.

resbordo, s.m. port.

rescaldar, v.t. to scald anew, to overheat.

rescaldo, s.m. embers; remains; cinders.

rescendência, s.f. scent, fragrance, redolence.

rescendente, adj. fragrant, redolent, perfumed.

rescender, v.i. to smell sweetly.

rescindir, v.t. to rescind; to annul, to cancel.

rescindível, adj. rescindable, annullable.

rescisão, s.f. rescission, abrogation, cancellation, cancelling.

rescisório, adj. rescissory, revoking, annuling.

rescrever, v.t. to rewrite.

rescrição, s.f. cheque, order for payment.

reseda, s.f. reseda, mignonette.

resenha, s.f. list, summary, description; inventory, enumeration.

resenhar, v.t. to draw up a list of; to report minutely; to enumerate.

reserva, s.f. reserve; store, stock, extra supply; spare; caution; restiction, restraint; shyness (timidez).

reservado, *adj.* reserved; shy; cautions; private; *s.m.* private booth.

reservar, *v.t.* to reserve; to hold back; to keep in store; to set apart; to make a reservation *(hotel, lugar, etc.).*

reservatório, *s.m.* reservoir; tank, vessel.

reservista, *s.m.* e *s.f.* reservist.

resfolegadoiro, resfolegadouro, *s.m.* breathing hole, air hole.

resfolegar, *v.i.* to breathe, to pant, to breath heavily, to puff, to blow.

resfriado, *s.m.* cold; adj. cold, chilly.

resfriador, *s.m.* cooler, resfriator; *adj.* cooling, chilling.

resfriamento, *s.m.* cold; cooling, chill.

resfriar, *v.t.* e *v.i.* to cool, to make cool, to chill; to grow cold, to become cold; to moderate; to catch a cold.

resgatador, *s.m.* ransomer, redeemer; adj. ransoming, redeeming, releasing.

resgatar, *v.t.* to ransom, to redeem, to pay off *(hipoteca, dívida, etc.);* to release, to rescue.

resgatável, *adj.* redcemable, retrievable.

resgate, *s.m.* ransom; deliverance; redemption; liquidation.

resguardado, *adj.* protected, shielded; cautions.

resguardar, *v.t.* to shelter, to defend, to protect, to guard, to shield; to preserve.

resguardo, *s.m.* guard, protection, defense; shelter; security; prudence, caution; secrecy.

residência, *s.f.* residence, dwelling, home, abode.

residential, *adj.* residential.

residente, *adj.* residing, resident; *s.m.* resident.

residir, *v.i.* to reside, to dwell, to live in.

residual, *adj.* residual, residuary, remaining, remanent.

resíduo, *s.m.* residue; remainder; waste; rest; leavings.

resignação, *s.f.* resignation; renouncement; submission; meekness.

resignante, *adj.* resigning, renouncing; *s.m.* e *s.f.* resigner, abdicator.

resignar, *v.t.* to resign, to renounce; *resignar-se:* to resign oneself to, to accept with resignation.

resignatário, *s.m.* resigner; *adj.* resigning, renouncing.

resignável, *adj.* that may be resigned.

resina, *s.f.* resin; rosin.

resinagem, *s.f.* resin-tapping, extraction of resin.

resinar, *v.t.* to resinate, to extract resin from; to rosin.

resineiro, *s.m.* resin extractor.

resinento, *adj.* resinous, resiny.

resinífero, *adj.* resiniferous.

resinificar, *v.t.* to resinify, to convert into resin.

resiniforme, *adj.* resiniform, resinoid.

resinoso, *adj.* resinous, resiny.

resistência, *s.f.* resistence, opposition, hindrance; reaction; strength, force endurance; non-conductivity.

resistente, *adj.* resistant, resisting; strong, tough; enduring.

resistir, *v.i.* to resist, to oppose; to endure, to last; to hold out, to withsland.

resistível, *adj.* resistible.

resistividade, *s.f.* resistivity.

reslumbrar, *v.t.* to shine through.

resma, *s.f.* ream.

resmoneador, *s.m.* grumbler; *adj.* grumbling.

resmungão, *s.m.* grumbler; *adj.* grumbling.

resmungar, *v.t.* e *v.i.* to grumble; to mutter; to grow, to mumble.

resmunguento, *adj.* grumbling.

resmunguice, *s.f.* grumbling.

resolubilidade, *s.f.* resolubility, resolvability.

resolução, *s.f.* resolution; decision, determination, deliberation, courage, firmeness; conclusion, solutiuon.

resolutivo, *adj.* resolutive, dissolvent; *s.m.* resolvent, resolutive drug.

resoluto, *adj.* resolute; decided, firm; bold, courageous.

resolutório, *adj.* resolurory.

resolúvel, *adj.* resoluble, resolvable; soluble.

resolvente, *adj.* resolvent.

resolver, *v.t.* to resolve; to dissolve; to solve; to clear up; to settle; to decide, to make up one's mind; to resolve to convert into; resolver-se: to decide (to do), to make up one's mind.

resolvido, *adj.* resolved, decided; bent, intent (on doing).

resolvível, *adj.* resoluble; soluble.

respaldar, *v.t.* to smooth, to polish, to make palin; to repair; *s.m.* back.

respaldo, *s.m.* back of seat.

respançadura, respançamento, *s.m.* scraping, rasping; erasing.

respançar, *v.t.* to erase, to rub out, to scrape.

respectivamente, adv. respectively.

respectivo, adj. respective, relative, concerning; particular, own.

respeitabilidade, s.f. respectability.

respeitado, adj. respected, considered, esteemed.

respeitador, adj. respectful; respeitador das leis: law-abiding; s.m. respecter.

respeitante, adj. concerning, regarding, referring to.

respeitar, v.t. to respect, to esteem, to honour, to look up to; to consider; respeitar a: to concern, to relate to.

respeitável, adj. respectable, estimable, worthy.

respeito, s.m. respect, esteem, regard, consideration; deference; awe, dread; s.m. pl. respects, regards. 1) apresentar os seus respeitos, to pay one's respects. 2) a este respeito, concerning, about that. 3) a respeito de, about, concerning. 4) com respeito a, in relation to, with refernce to. 5) dizer respeito a, to concern, to have to do with. 6) no que diz respeito a, in what concerns, respecting, regardind.

respeitoso, adj. respectful; reverent, deferent; polite.

respiga, s.g. gleaning; (carp.) mortise.

respigar, s.m. gleaning.

respingador, respingão, s.m. surly person, grumbler; adj. surly, grumbling.

respingar, s.m. aspersion, sparkling; kicking back; resistance.

respirabilidade, s.f. respirability.

respiração, s.f. respiration, breathing.

respiradoiro, respiradouro, air hole, vent; breathing hole, breather.

respirar, v.t. to breathe, to inhale; to respite.

respiratório, adj. respiratory.

respiro, s.m. breath, breathing; air vent.

resplandecência, s.f. resplendence, splendour, brilliance.

resplandecente, adj. resplendent, shining, brilliant, refulgent.

resplandecer, v.t. to shine, to glow, to glitter.

resplendência, s.f. resplendence, brilliance.

resplendente, adj. resplendent, brilliant.

resplêndido, adj. very splendid or bright.

resplendor, s.m. splendour, resplendence, refulgence; blaze, glory.

resplendoroso, adj. splendorous, resplendent, refulgent, glorious.

respondão, s.m. e adj. snappish, saucy; churlish, impolite.

respondência, s.f. respondence; communication; contacts.

responder, v.t. to answer, to reply, to respond; responder por: to account for, to be responsible for.

respondível, adj. answerable.

responsabilidade, s.f. responsability; accountability; liability.

reaponsabilizar, v.t. to hold (someone) responsible for.

responsar, v.t. to pray responsories; to murmur; to slander.

responsável, adj. responsible; answerable; liable, accountable.

responsivo, adj. responsive, replying.

responso, s.m. response; reprimand, rebuke.

responsório, s.m. responsory.

resposta, s.f. answer, response, reply; replication; solution.

respostada, s.f. rude answer.

respostar, v.t. to answer discourteously.

resquício, s.m. vestige, remainder; chink, crack (fenda).

ressaber, v.t. to know very well; to have a strong taste.

ressabiado, adj. suspicious; distrustfull; fearsome; scared; resentful.

ressabiar, v.i. to grow skittish or distrustful; to be resentful; to acquire an unpleasant taste.

ressaca, s.f. hangover (de embriagez); undertow (correnteza); pounding surf.

ressacar, v.t. to redraw (letra).

ressaibo, s.m. bad taste; vestige, trace.

ressaio, s.m. public square; yard.

ressair, v.i. to stand out, to be prominent, to portrude.

ressalga, s.f. resalting.

ressalgar, v.t. resalt.

ressaltar, v.i. to rebound, to bounce; to project, to just out, to stand out; v.t. to cause to stand out; to emphasize.

ressalto, s.m. rebound, jut, projection; ledge; overhang.

ressalva, s.f. exception,reservation; safety clause; rectification; safe-conduct.

ressalvar, v.t. to except; to safeguard; to preserve (from something); to correct.

ressaque, s.m. redraft (de letra).

ressarcido, adj. compensated, repaired, indemnified; recovered.

ressarcimento, *s.m.* amends, reparation, ondenmification.

ressarcir, *v.t.* to compensate, to make up for; to make amends for; to indemnify; *ressarcir-se,* to recover.

ressecar, *v.t.* to dry again; to exsiccate.

ressecção, *s.f.* resection.

rerssegar, *v.t.* to mow again, to reap.

ressegurar, *v.t.* to reinsurance.

resseguro, *s.m.* reinsurance.

ressentido, *adj.* resentful, hurt, offended.

ressentimento, *s.m.* resentment, umbrage, grudge; hardfeeling.

ressentir, *v.i.* to feel again, to be hurt by; *ressentir-se,* to resent, to feel hurt, to take offense; to feel the effects of.

ressequido, *adj.* very dry, dried up; parched.

ressequir, *v.t.* e *v.i.* to dry up, to wither; to become dry.

ressicação, *s.f.* excessive dryness.

ressicar, *v.t.* to dry up, to wither.

ressoador, *s.m.* resonator; *adj.* resounding.

ressoante, *adj.* ressounding, ressounant.

ressoar, *v.i.* to resound, to reverberate, to echo; *v.t.* to sound, to reverberate.

ressobrar, *v.i.* to superabound.

ressoldar, *v.t.* to resolder.

ressonadela, *s.f.* snoring.

ressonância, *s.f.* resonance, echo; vibration; sonority.

ressonante, *adj.* resonant, resounding, sonorous.

ressonar, *v.t.* to snore.

ressono, *s.m.* deep sleep.

ressorção, *s.f.* resorption, reabsorgtion.

ressuar, *v.t.* e *v.i.* to sweat freely.

ressudação, *s.f.* perspiration; resudation.

ressudar, *v.t.* to distil; to exude, to perspire, to transpire, to transure, to sweat.

ressumação, *s.f.* exsudation, distilation.

ressumar, *v.t.* to distill, to exude; to show, evince; *v.i.* to coze, to transude, to percolate; to perspire.

ressunção, *s.f.* resumption; restoration, reintegration.

ressupinação, *s.f.* resupination, inverted position.

ressupinado, *adj.* resupinate, inverted, upside down; bent backward.

ressupino, *adj.* turned upwards; resupinate.

ressurgente, *adj.* resurgent, renewed, reviving.

ressurgimento, *s.m.* resurgence, resurrection, revival; renascence.

ressurgir, *v.t.* to reappear; to resurge, to rise again; to revive.

ressurreição, *s.f.* ressurrection; revival.

ressuscitação, *s.f.* resuscitation, resurrection; revival.

ressuscitamento. *adj.* resusctitated.

ressuscitador, *s.m.* resuscitator, reviver; *adj.* reviving.

ressuscitar, *v.t.* to revive, to resuscitate; to ressorect, to bring back to life; to renew; *v.i.* to ressurect, to raise from the dead; to rise again; to revive.

ressuscitável, *adj.* ressuscitable.

restabelecer, *v.t.* to re-establish; to restore; *restabelecer-se:* to recover, to be restored to health.

restabelecimento, *s.m.* re-establishment; restoration; recovery; recuperation.

restante, *adj.* remaining; *s.m.* remainder, rest.

restar, *v.i.* to remain; to be left over; *restam-lhe algumas horas:* he has some hours left.

restauração, *s.f.* restoration; restoring; renewal; recuperation.

restaurador, *s.m.* restorer; *adj.* restorative, rerstoring.

restaurante, *s.m.* restaurant.

restaurar, *v.t.* to restore, to repair; to renew; to reconstruct; to retrieve.

restaurativo, *adj.* restorative.

restaurável, *adj.* restorable, retrievable.

restauro, *s.m.* o mesmo que "restauração".

restelo, *s.m.* hackle.

resteva, *s.f.* stubble field.

réstia, *s.f.* rope of reeds; ray *(de luz); réstia de cebolas,* string of onions.

restilação, *s.f.* redistillation.

restilar, *v.t.* to redistill.

restinga, *s.f.* reef, sand bank, shoal; thicket *(matagal).*

restituição, *s.f.* restitution, return; devolution.

restituidor, *adj.* returning; *s.m.* restorer.

restituir, *v.t.* to return, to give or send back; to replace, to put back; to repay, to refund; to restore.

restituitório, *adj.* restitutive, restitutory.

restituível, *adj.* returnable; restorable.

resto, *s.m.* rest, remainder; residue; remnant; leavings, surplus. 1) *de resto,* moreover. 2) *quanto ao resto,* as for the rest.

restolhada, *s.f.* uproar, noise, hubbub.

restolhal, *s.m.* stubble-land or field.

restolhar, *v.i.* to make a noise.

restolho, *s.m.* stubble.

restribar, *v.i.* to rest firmly on; to resist.

restrição, *s.f.* restriction, limitation, reserve; shortage.

restrigência, *s.f.* astringency.

restringente, *adj.* astringent.

restringir, *v.t.* to restrict, to limit, to confine; to restrain; to cut down; to modify. 1) *restringir-se,* to be limited; to limit oneself. 2) *restringir-se aos factos,* to stick to the facts.

restringível, *adj.* restrainable, limitable.

restritivo, *adj.* restrictive, limitative.

restrito, *adj.* restricted, limited.

restrugir, *v.i.* to resound, to echo.

resultado, *s.m.* result, outcome; effect, consequence; upshot; conclusion. 1) *dar resultado,* to succeed, to work. 2) *não dar resultado,* to come to nothing.

resultância, *s.f.* result, resultant.

resultante, *adj. e s.f.* resultant.

resultar, *v.i.* to result. 1) *resultar de,* to result from, to follow from. 2) *resultar em,* to result in, to end in.

resumidamente, *adv.* shortly, inshort.

resumido, *adj.* resumed, reduced, condensed, abridged, summarized.

resumir, *v.t.* to summarize, to sum up, to abridge, to shorten, to cut down; *resumir-se,* to be brief; to limit itself to; to consist in.

resumo, *s.m.* summary, résumé; abridgement, condensation; *em resumo,* in short.

resvaladiço, *adj.* slippery.

resvaladio, *adj.* slippery.

resvaladoiro, resvaladouro, *s.m.* slide; slippery place; steep place.

resvaladura, *s.f.* sliding; fault, lapse.

resvalamento, *s.m.* gliding, slipping.

resvalante, *adj.* sliding, slipping; steep.

resvalar, *s.m.* sliping, slide, slope.

resvés, *adj. e adv.* close, even with; exactly, justly.

retábulo, *s.m.* retable, atlar piece.

retaguarda, *s.f.* rear-guard, rear; back, tail end.

retalhado, *adj.* cut into pieces, cut up, shredded.

retalhador, *s.m.* cutter, shredder.

retalhamento, *s.m.* shredding.

retalhar, *v.t.* to cut up, to cut into pieces; to shred; to divide.

retalhista, *s.m. e s.f.* retailer, retail dealer, small trader.

retalho, *s.m.* shred; scrap; little piece; *a retalho,* at retail.

retaliação, *s.f.* retaliation, requital.

retaliar, *v.t.* to retaliate; to revenge; to strike back.

retaliativo, *adj.* retaliatory.

retama, *s.f.* woadwaxen.

retambana, *s.f.* scolding.

retanchar, *v.t.* to replant *(vinha).*

retanha, *s.f.* false key.

retardsação, *s.f.* retardation; delay, postponement.

retardado, *adj.* delayed; retarded *(mentalmente); s.m.* retarded child; moron.

retardador, *s.m.* retarder; *adj.* retarding.

retardamento, *s.m.* retardation, delay; slowdown.

retardar, *v.t.* to retard, to delay; to slow down; to hinder; to keep back.

retardatário, *s.m.* late-comer; lagger, lingere; *adj.* late, lingering.

retardativo, *adj.* retardative, delaying; hindering.

retardio, *adj.* tardy, late; slow; dilatory.

retardo, *s.m.* retard, retardation, delay.

retém, *s.m.* reserve, store, stock; *armazém de retém,* storehouse, depot.

retêmpera, retemperação, *adj.* retempering; strengthening.

retemperante, *adj.* retempering.

retemperar, *v.t.* to retemper; to strengthen, to invitorage; to purify.

retenção, *s.f.* retention, keeping back, delay; retentiveness.

retenida, *s.f.* guy.

retentiva, *s.f.* retentiveness.

retentivo, *adj.* retentive.

retentor, *s.m.* retainer, keeper, *adj.* retaining, retentive.

reter, *v.t.* to retain, to hold back; to restrain, to curb, to detain; to confine, to imprison; to keep in mind, to memorize; to hinder.

retesado, *adj.* stretched, tightened; tight; tense.

retesamento, *s.m.* stretching.

retesar, *v.t.* to stretch, to tighten, to stiffen; to make tense; *retesar-se,* to tighten; to stiffen.

reteso, *adj.* siff, tense, rigid, tight.

reticências, *s.f.* reticence; *s.f. pl.* suspension points.

reticente, *adj.* reticent; reserved.

retícula, *s.f.* small net; reticle.

reticulado, *adj.* reticulate, reticular.

reticular, *adj.* reticular.

retículo, *s.m.* reticule; reticulum *(de animais).*

retiforme, *adj.* retiform, netlike.

retina, *s.f.* retina.

retinente, *adj.* tinkling, resourdling, jingling.

retingir, *v.t.* to dye again, to re-dye.

retiniano, *adj.* retinal, retinian.

retinir, *v.i.* to tinkle, to resound, to ring, to jingle.

retinite, *s.f.* retinitis.

retinto, *adj.* redyed; jet-black; deep, dark.

retiração, *s.f.* printing of the backside of a sheet.

retirada, *s.f.* removal; withdrawal; recassion; departure; *(mil. e fig.)* retreat; *bater em retirada,* to beat a retreat, to decamp.

retirado, *adj.* retired; secluded; far off. remote; solitary.

retiramento, *s.m.* retirement, seclusion, solitude.

retirar, *v.t.* to take off, to pull off; to take away; to remove; to withdraw; to take back; *v.i. (também retirar-se)* to quit, to leave, to depart; to walk off or away; to withdraw (from); *(mil.)* to retreat.

retiro, *s.m.* retreat; refuge; secluded place; privacy; *fazer um retiro,* to go into retreat.

retocador, *s.m.* retoucher, finisher.

retocar, *v.t.* to retouch, to finish, to perfect; to correct.

retoiça, *s.f.* swing; frisking, frolic.

retoiçar, *v.i.* to balance, to swing; to frolic, to romp; to roll.

retomada, *s.f.* retaking, recapturing, recpature, reconquest.

retomar, *v.t.* to retake; to resume; to recapture, to reconquest.

retoque, *s.m.* retouch, finishing touch; improvement.

retorção, *s.f.* retortion, turning.

retorce, *s.m.* twisting.

retorcedeira, *s.f.* twisting machine.

retorcedor, *s.m.* twister.

retorcedura, *s.f.* twisting, winding.

retorcer, *v.t.* to twist; to contort; *retorcer-se,* to wriggle, to squirm, to writhe.

retorcido, *adj.* twisted; gnarled; tourtuous.

retórica, *adj.* rhetoric; oratory; bombastic style.

retórico, *adj.* rethorical; *s.m.* rethorician.

retornar, *v.t.* to give back, to send back; to restore; *v.i.* to return; to go back, to come back; to revert.

retornelo, *s.m.* refrain.

retorno, *s.m.* return; going back, coming back; recurrence; *(com.)* barter, exchange.

retorquir, *v.t.* to retort; to reply.

retorsão, *s.f.* retortion, reply, retort.

retorta, *s.f.* retort, still.

retorto, *adj.* curved, bent, twisted.

retostar, *v.t.* to toast too much.

retouça, *s.f. o mesmo que "retoiça".*

retouço, *s.m.* leap, jump, hop; frisking.

retraçar, *v.t.* to retrace; to shred.

retracção, *s.f.* traction, drawing back, retraction, retracting; withdrawing; shrinkage.

retractação, *s.f.* retractation; disavowal; confession of an error.

retractar, *v.t.* to retract, to withdraw, to unsay; *retractar-se,* to confess one's error, to recant.

retráctil, *adj.* retractile.

retractibilidade, *s.f.* retractility.

retractivo, *adj.* retractive.

retracto, *adj. o mesmo que "retraído".*

retraduzir, *v.t.* to retranslate.

retraidamente, *adv.* reservedly, shyly.

retraído, *adj.* retracted; shy; reticent; unsociable, offish.

retraimento, *adj.* retracted; shy; reticent; unsociable, offish.

retraimento, *s.m.* reserve, shyness.

retrair, *v.t.* to retract; to draw in; to shrink, to contract; *retrair-se,* to become reserved, to go into one's shell.

retranca, *s.f. (náut.)* boom; crupper *(rabicho).*

retrança, *s.f.* dense crown of a tree.

retrancar, *v.t.* to put a boom in.

retranscrever, *v.t.* to retranscribe.

retranscrição, *s.f.* retranscription.

retransferir, *v.t.* to retransfer.

retransir, *v.t.* to trespass; to penetrate, to affect.

retransmissão, *s.f.* retransmission; rebroadcast.

retransmissor, *v.m.* retransmitter.

retransmitir, *v.t.* to retransmit; to rebroadcast.

retratado, *adj.* photographed; portrayed; mirrored, reflected; described.

retratador, *adj.* retracting, disavowing.

retratar, *v.t.* to photograph; to portray, to paint; to mirror; to describe, to depict.

retratista, *s.m.* e *s.f.* portrait painter; photographer.

retrato, *s.m.* portrait, picture, photograph; image.

retravar, *v.t.* to brake again; to begin again.

retreta, *s.f.* retreat; tattoo; chambermaid.

retrete, *s.f.* water-closet.

retribuição, *s.f.* retribution, recompense; return; salary, remuneration; wage, pay.

retribuidor, *s.m.* retributor; *adj.* retributive.

retribuir, *v.t.* to requite; to reward; to pay back; to remunerate; to return; to answer.

retribuível, *adj.* returnable, requitable.

retrincado, *adj.* cunning, artful.

retrincar, *v.t.* to lock up again; to crush *(com os dentes)*; to interpret maliciously; to misunderstand.

retroacção, *s.f.* retroaction, reverse action.

retroactividade, *s.f.* retroactivity.

retroactivo, *adj.* retroactive.

retroagir, *v.t.* to retroact, to act in return; to react.

retroar, *v.i.* to resound, to echo.

retrocedência, *s.f.* retrocedence, retrocession.

retrocedente, *adj.* retrocedent.

retroceder, *v.i.* to retrocede, to recede; to move backwards.

retrocedimento, *s.m.* retrocession.

retrocessão, *s.f.* retrocession, receding.

retrocessivo, *adj.* retrocessive.

retrocesso, *s.m.* retrocession, retrogression; backspacer *(em máquina de escrever)*.

retrodatar, *v.t.* to date back, to antedate.

retroflexão, *s.f.* retroflexion.

retroflexo, *adj.* retroflex.

retrogradação, *s.f.* retrogradation; retrogression.

retrogradar, *v.i.* to retrograde, to retrogress; to recede; to revert.

retrógado, *adj.* retrogade; backward; reactionary.

retrogressivo, *adj.* retrogressive.

retropropulsão, *s.f.* jet propulsion; backward reaction.

retrós, *s.m.* twisted sewing silk.

retrosaria, *s.f.* haberdasher`s shop.

retrospecção, *s.f.* retrospection.

retrospectiva, *s.f.* retrospective.

retrospectivo, *adj.* retrospective, retroactive.

retrospecto, *s.m.* retrospect, review of the past.

retrosseguir, *v.t.* to retrocede, to recede, to go back.

retrotrair, *v.t.* to make retroactive; to retroact.

retroversão, *s.f.* retroversion, translation.

retroverter, *v.t.* to retranslate, to translate; to retrovert.

retrovisor, *s.m.* rear view mirror.

retrucar, *v.t.* to retort, to reply, to answer.

retumbância, *s.f.* repercussion, resounding, reverberation.

retumbante, *adj.* resounding; booming, rumbling.

retumbar, *v.i.* to resound, to reverberate; to rumble, to boom.

retundir, *v.t.* to repress, to supress, to check, to repel; to restrain, to hold back.

réu, *s.m.* culprit, defendant; the accused.

reuma, *s.f.* rheum, catarrh.

reumatalgia, *s.f.* rheumatic pain.

reumático, *adj.* rheumatic; *s.m.* rheumatism.

reumatismal, *adj.* rheumatismal, rheumatic.

reumatismo, *s.m.* rheumatism.

reumatóide, *adj.* rheumatoid.

reumatologia, *s.f.* rheumathology.

reumatologista, *s.m.* e *s.f.* reumathologist.

reumoso, *adj.* rheumy.

reunião, *s.f.* reunion, meeting; gathering; assembly.

reunificação, *s.f.* reunification.

reunificar, *v.t.* to reunify.

reunir, *v.t.* to reunite; to gather; to assemble; to rejoin; to collect; to bring together; *reunir- -se,* to come together, to get together; to meet; to cluster.

revacinação, *s.f.* revaccination.

revacinar, *v.t.* to revaccinate.

revalidação, *s.f.* revalidation, reconfirmation.

revalidador, *adj.* revalidating.

revalidar, *v.t.* to revalidate, to confirm, to ratify.

revalorização, *s.f.* revalorization.

revalorizar, *v.t.* to revalorize.

revel, *s.m.* rebel, rebeller, defaulter; *adj.* rebellious.

revelação, *s.f.* revelation, disclosure, discovery; divine inspiration; *(fot.)* development.

revelador, *adj.* revealing; *s.m. (quím.)* test; *(fot.)* developer.

revelar, *v.t.* reveal, to disclose, to unveil, to uncover; to show, to display; to expose; to divulge; *(fot.)* to develop; *revelar-se,* to reveal oneself; to be disclosed; to turn out.

revelável, *adj.* revealable.

revelho, *adj.* very old.

revelia, *s.f.* (*jur.*) default. 1) *à revelia,* in the absence of the defendant by default (*julgamento*). 2) *à revelia de,* without the knowledge of.

revenda, *s.f.* resale.

revendedor, *s.m.* reseller, middleman; *adj.* reselling.

revender, *v.t.* to resell.

revendível, *adj.* resalable.

rever, *v.t.* to see again; to correct (*provas tipográficas*); to revise. 1) rever provas, to proofread. 2) *rever-se,* to look at oneself (*num espelho*); to see oneself (in).

reverberação, *s.f.* reverberation, reflection.

reverberante, *adj.* reverberating, reflecting.

reverberar, *v.i.* to reverberate, to reflect, to flash back.

reverberatório, *adj.* reverberatory.

revérbero, *s.m.* reverberation, reflection; brightness.

reverdecer, *v.t.* to make verdant; to clothe with verdure; to rejuvenate, to reinvigorate, to give new life to; *v.i.* to become verdant; to grow green, to grow luxuriant; to rejuvenate.

reverdejante, *adj.* verdant, green.

reverdejar, *v.i.* to become green.

reverência, *s.f.* reverence, veneration, respect, deference, homage, courtesy; bow; *Vossa Reverência,* your Reverence.

reverenciador, *s.m.* reverencer, worshipper; *adj.* reverencing.

reverenciar, *v.t.* to revere, to venerate, to honour.

reverencioso, *adj.* reverential, respectful, formal.

reverendas, *s.f. pl.* demissory letters.

reverendíssimo, *adj.* most reverend.

reverendo, *adj.* reverend, venerable; *s.m.* reverend.

reverente, *adj.* reverent, reverential, respectfull.

reverificação, *s.f.* reverification, recheck.

reverificar, *v.t.* to verify again, to recheck.

reversal, *adj.* confirmator.

reversão, *s.f.* reversion; return.

reversar, *v.t. e v.i.* to throw up; to return.

reversibilidade, *s.f.* reversibility.

reversível, *adj.* reversible; revertible, returnable.

reversivo, *adj.* reversive.

reverso, *s.m.* reverso, contrary, opposite, back side; *o reverso da medalha,* the other side of a situation.

reverter, *v.i.* to revert; to return, to go back to.

revertível, *adj.* revertible.

revés, *s.m.* reverse, opposite; backhanded blow; reverse of fortune, setback, hardship, adversity; *s.m. pl.* ups and downs.

revessa, *s.f.* countercurrent; valley of a roof.

revesso, *adj.* reverse, contrary; rough, hard (to work).

revestimento, *s.m.* coating, covering, lining; outside layer; overlay, veneering.

revestir, *v.t.* to don, to put on; to clothe; to coat, to cover, to line, to overlay; to endow (with authority, etc.); *revestir-se de,* to assume, to cover oneself with.

revezadamente, *adv.* by turns, alternatively.

revezado, *adj.* alternate, alternating.

revezamento, *s.m.* alternation, rotation.

revezar, *v.t.* to relieve, to relay, *revezar-se,* to take turns, to alternate.

revigoramento, *s.m.* reinvigoration.

revigorante, *adj.* reinvigorating.

revigorar, *v.t.* to reinvigorate; to grow strong again.

revimento, *s.m.* perspiration, sweat.

revinda, *s.f.* coming back, return.

revindicação, *s.f.* claim, demand.

revindicta, *s.f.* revenge, retaliation, requital.

revir, *adj.* to come again.

reviramento, *s.m.* reversal, sudden change.

revirão, *s.m.* welt (*de sapato*).

revirar, *v.t.* to turn again; to turn inside out; to roll (*olhos*).

reviravolta, *s.f.* sudden change, turn, overturn; about-face.

revisão, *s.f.* revision; review; checking; correction; *revisão de provas,* proofreading.

revisar, *v.t.* to revise, to review, to reexamine; to check; to correct.

revisionismo, *s.m.* revisionism.

revisionista, *adj. e s.m. e s.f.* revisionist.

revisor, *s.m.* reviser; proofreader; ticket-inspector; examiner.

revisório, *adj.* revisory, revisional.

revista, *s.f.* search, investigation; review, magazine, journal; (*mil.*) review, inspection; musical comedy (*teatral*); *passar em revista,* to pass in review; to inspect.

revistador, *s.m.* reviewer.

revistar, *v.t.* to pass in review; to search; to inspect: to ransack.

revisteca, *s.f.* worthless magazine.

revisteiro, *s.m.* wirter of revues.

revisto, *adj.* reviewed; revised; checked; inspected; corrected.

revitalização, *s.f.* revitalization.

revitalizar, *v.t.* to revitalize.

revivência, *s.f.* revival; reviving.

revivente, *adj.* reviving.

reviver, *v.i.* to revivex; to return to life; to recover one's strength; *v.t.* to relive; to revive; to reanimate; to recall *(recordar).*

revivescência, *s.f.* revivescence, revival, reanimation.

revivescente, *adj.* revivescent.

revivescer, *v.t. e v.i.* to revive, to revivify.

revivificação, *s.f.* revivification, revival; reactivation.

revivificador, revivificante, *adj.* reviving.

revivificar, *v.t.* to revivify, to reanimate, to restore to life.

révoa, revoada, *s.f.* flock of birds in flight; flight.

revoar, *v.i.* to fly again; to soar.

revocação, *s.f. o mesmo que "revogação".*

revocatória, *s.f.* revocatory act or document.

revogabilidade, *s.f.* revocability, defeasibility.

revogação, *s.f.* revocation; repeal, recall; annulment, cancellation, withdrawal.

revogador, *s.m.* revoker, canceller; *adj.* revoking.

revogante, *adj.* revoking, revocative.

revogar, *v.t.* to revoke, to repeal, to recall; to annul, to cancel; to rescind; to abolish.

revogatório, *adj.* revogatory, revoking.

revogável, *adj.* revocable.

revolta, *s.f.* revolt, insurrection, uprising, rebelion; mutiny, riot.

revoltato, *adj.* revolted, rebellious, insurgent; *s.m.* mutineer, rebel.

revoltante, *adj.* revolting; shocking, disgusting, repulsive.

revoltar, *v.t.* to revolt, to turn again; to incite to revolt; to shock; *revoltar-se,* to revolt, to rebel, to mutiny; to rise (against).

revoltear, *v.i.* to turn over and over or around and aruond.

revoltado, *adj.* troubled, turbulent; boisterous; excited, agitated.

revoltoso, *adj.* rebellious, mutinous.

revolução, *s.f.* revolution; rotation; revulsion; revot, rebellion.

revolucionamento, *s.m.* revolt, revolution, sub-version.

revolucionar, *v.t.* to revolutionize; to stir up; to turn over; to provoke a tumult.

revolucionário, *adj.* revolutionary; *s.m.* revolutionist, revolutionary.

revoluteante, *adj.* whirling, wheeling, revolving, swirling.

revolutear, *v.i.* to revolver; to turn around; to flutter.

revoluteiro, *s.m.* turning around movement.

revolver, *v.t.* to revolve; to rummage; to stir, to turn over, to move.

revólver, *s.m.* revolver.

revolvido, *adj.* revolved, stirred, disturbed.

revolvimento, *s.m.* revolving, rolling; revolution.

revoo, *s.m.* flying back or around.

revulsão, *s.f.* revulsion.

revulsivo, *adj.* revulsive.

revulsor, *s.m.* revulsor.

revulsório, *adj.* revulsive.

reza, *s.f.* prayer, praying.

rezar, *v.t.* to pray; to say *(missa).*

rezinga, *s.f.* grumbling, growling.

rezingão, *adj.* grumbling, peevish, grumbler.

rezingar, *v.i.* to grumble; to flind fault; to quarrel.

rezingueiro, *adj.* grumbling, grouchy; *s.m.* grumbler.

ria, *s.f.* estuary; mouth.

riacho, *s.m.* creek, brook.

riba, *s.f.* cliff, bank.

ribaldaria, *s.f.* ribaldry, rascality.

ribaldeiro, *s.m.* ribald, rogue.

ribaldo, *adj.* ribald, scurrilous, licentious; *s.m.* ribald, rascal.

ribalta, *s.m.* footlights.

ribamar, *s.f.* seashore; shore land.

ribanceira, *s.f.* ravine, cliff, steep slope.

ribeira, *s.f.* bank, riverside; stream.

ribeirão, *s.m.* wide stream.

ribeirinho, *adj.* riverside, riparian, riverine.

ribeiro, *s.m.* brook, creek, rivulet, streamlet.

ribete, *s.m.* lace, ribbon; hem, border.

ribombância, *s.f.* booming, thundering, resounding.

ribombante, *adj.* booming, thundering, rumbling.

ribombar, *v.i.* to thunder, to resound, to boom, to rumble.

ribombo, *s.m.* thundering; reverberation; boom, roar, rumbling.

riça, *adj.* frizzed, fuzzy.

ricaço, *adj.* very rich; *s.m.* wealthy man.

ricamente, *adv.* richly; finely, prosperously.

riçar, *v.t.* to curl, to frizzle; to become curled. *(cabelo).*

rícino, s.m. ricinus, castor-oil plant.

rico, adj. rich, wealthy; fertile, abundant; plentiful; magnificent.

riço, adj. frizzly, shaggy; s.m. hair-pad.

ricochete, s.m. ricochet.

ricochetear, v.i. to ricochet; to skip.

rico-homem, s.m. grandee, nobleman.

ricto, s.m. rictus.

ridência, s.f. cheerfulness, mirth.

redente, adj. smiling, cheerful, joyfull, gay, merry.

ridicularia, s.f. trifle; trifling sun.

ridicularizador, ridicularizante, adj. ridiculing.

ridicularizar, v.t. to ridicule, to make fun of; to mock, to deride; to chaif.

ridículo, adj. ridiculous; absurd, foolish; grotesque; s.m. ridicule, mockery.

rifa, s.f. raffle.

rifada, s.f. sequence of cards of the same suit.

rifador, s.m. raffler.

rifão, s.m. maxim, proverb, adage, saying.

rifar, v.t. to raffle.

rifle, s.m. rifle, carabine.

rigidamente, adv. rigidly; stiffly.

rigidez, s.f. rigidity, severity, sternness; stiffness; inflexibility; rigidez cadavérica, rigor mortis.

rígido, adj. rigid, hard, rigorous; harsh; austere, severe, stern; stiff.

rigor, s.m. rigour, strictness, severity; hardness; exactness. 1) trajado a rigor, formally dressed. 2) no rigor do Inverno, in coldest winter.

rigorismo, s.m. rigorism, strictness; preciseness.

rigorista, s.m. s.f. e adj. rigorist.

rigorosamente, adv. rigorously; strictly.

rigorosidade, s.f. rigorousness;strictness.

rigoroso, adj. rigorous; strict; stern; harsh, severe; exact, precise, accurate; austere.

rijão, s.m. rasher of bacon.

rijar, v.t. e v.i. to fry, to toast.

rijeza, s.f. hardness; rigidity; stiffness.

rijo, adj. hard, harsh; stiff; tough; solid, firm.

rilada, s.f. kidney stew.

rilhador, s.m. gnawer, chewer; adj. grawing, chewing.

rilhar, v.t. to chew, to gnaw, to grind.

rim, s.m. kidney.

rima, s.f. rhyme; pile, stack (montão); s.f. pl. verses.

rimador, s.m. rhymer, rhymester.

rimance, s.m. tale in verse; popular song.

rimar, v.t. to rhyme, to put into rhyme; to make rhymes; to agree, to fit, to go well together.

rimoso, adj. cracked, rimose.

rímula, s.f. small crack, chink.

rinalgia, s.f. rhinalgia.

rinálgico, adj. rhinalgic.

rincão, s.m. corner, nook, groove, stria; small strip of land.

rinchada, s.f. neighing, neigh.

rinchante, adj. neighing.

rinchão, s.m. yaffle; hedge mustard.

rinchar, v.i. to neigh, to whinny.

ringer, ringir, v.t. e v.i. to creak; to grind (os dentes); to chew.

ringue, s.m. ring.

rinite, s.f. rhinitis.

rinoceronte, s.m. rhinocerous.

rinofaringite, s.f. rhinopharingitis.

rinologia, s.f. rhinology.

rinologista, s.m. e s.f. rhinologist.

rinoplastia, s.f. rhinoplasty.

rinoplástico, adj. rhinoplastic.

rinorragia, s.f. rhinorrhagia, nosebleed.

rinorrágico, adj. rhinorrhagic.

rinorreia, s.f. rhinorrhoea.

rinoscopia, s.f. rhinoscopy.

rinoscópio, s.m. rhinoscope.

rio, s.m. river, stream. 1) rio acima, upstream, up the river. 2) rio abaixo, downstream, down the river.

ripa, s.f. lathe slat, batten.

ripada, s.f. stroke with a lathe; scolding, rebuke.

ripado, s.m. lathing.

ripador, s.m. ripple.

ripadura, ripagem, s.f. flax dressing.

ripanço, s.m. harrow; hackle; indolence, leisure.

ripar, v.t. to lathe; to saw into strips.

ripícola, adj. riparian.

rípio, s.m. rubble, stone chip; pebbles, gravel.

riposta, s.f. riposte.

ripostar, v.i. to make a ripost; to retort.

riqueza, s.f. wealth, riches; richness, wealthiness; abundance; resources.

rir, v.i. to laugh; to smile; to chuckle (silenciosamente); to sneer (com desdém); rir estrondosamente, to shout with laughter.

risada, s.f. laugh.

risca, s.f. stripe, stroke; line; parting line (do cabelo); á risca: to the letter, exactly.

riscado, *s.m.* striped cotton cloth; *adj.* striped.

riscador, *s.m.* scriber; *adj.* scribing, scratching.

riscadura, *s.f.* scratch; dash; stripe, streak.

riscar, *v.t.* to scratch; to mark with lines; to trace, to delineate; to scratch out, to cancel, to expunge; to strike *(um fósforo)*.

risco, *s.m.* stripe; scratch; line; dash; danger, risk, peril, chance; outline, delineation; trace, mark. 1) *com risco de,* at the risk of. 2) *correr risco,* to be in danger; to run a risk. 3) *em risco,* in danger; at stake. 4) *sem risco,* safely.

risibilidade, *s.f.* risibility.

risível, *adj.* risible, ridiculous.

riso, *s.m.* laughter, laugh, loughing; smiling.

risonho, *adj.* smiling, laughing; gay, cheerful.

risório, *s.m.* risorious; laughing muscle.

risota, *s.f.* jeering laugh; mockery.

rispidamente, *adv.* harshly, sharply, sternly, severely.

rispidez, *s.f.* harshness, roughness, severity, sternness.

ríspido, *adj.* harsh, severe, stern, sharp.

rissol, *s.m.* sort pastry with fish or meat inside.

riste, *s.m.* rest; *em riste,* upheld, pointing.

ritmado, *adj.* cadenced, rhythmic.

ritmar, *v.t.* to give rhythm to, to put into rythm.

ritmicamente, *adv.* rhythmically.

rítmico, *adj.* rhythmic, cadenced, measured.

ritmo, *s.m.* rhythm, cadence; rate; beat; time.

rito, *s.m.* rite, ritual; ceremony; cult; observance.

ritornelo, *s.m.* ritornello, prelude, interlude.

ritual, *adj. e s.m.* ritual.

ritualismo, *s.m.* ritualism.

ritualista, *adj.* ritualistic; *s.m. e s.f.* ritualist.

rival, *adj.* rival; emulous; *s.m. e s.f.* rival, emulator, antagonist, opponent, competitor.

rivalidade, *s.f.* rivalry, rivalship, antagonism, opposition; competition; emulation.

rivalizar, *v.i.* to rival; *rivalizar com,* to rival, to emulate, to vie with.

rixa, *s.f.* quarrel, dispute, brawl, fight.

rixador, *s.m.* ruffian, brawler; *adj.* quarrelsome.

rixento, *adj.* quarrelsome, contentious, pugnacious.

rizadura, *s.f.* reef, reefing.

rizar, *v.t. e v.i.* to reef.

rizes, *s.m. pl. (náut.)* reef points.

rizicultor, *s.m.* rice grower.

rizicultura, *s.f.* rice growing.

rizina, *s.f.* rhizine, rhizoid.

rizocárpio, *s.m.* rhizocarp.

rizofagia, *s.f.* rhizophagy.

rizófago, *adj.* rhizophagous.

rizófilo, *adj.* rhizophilous.

rizóide, *s.m.* rhizoid, rootlike filaments.

rizoma, *s.m.* rhizome, rhizoma, rootstock.

rizomatoso, *adj.* rhizomatous.

rizomorfo, *adj.* rhizomorphous.

rizópode, *s.m.* rhizopod.

roaz, *adj.* ravenous.

robalo, *s.m.* snook, robalo.

roble, *s.m.* white oak.

robledo, *s.m.* oak grove.

roboração, *s.f.* corroboration, confirmation.

roborante, *adj.* corroborant, confirming.

roborar, *v.t.* to corroborate, to confirm, to ratify; to strengthen.

roborativo, *adj.* corroborative, confirmatory.

roboredo, *s.m.* oak grove.

roborizar, *v.t.* to fortify, to strengthen.

robustecedor, *adj.* fortifying.

robustecer, *v.t.* to fortify, to make robust, to strengthen, to vitalize.

robustecimento, *s.m.* strengthening, invigoration.

robustez, robusteza, *s.f.* robustness, vigour.

robusto, *adj.* robust, strong, vigorous; hardy, tough, sturdy; stout; powerful.

roca, *s.f.* distaff, spinning-wheel.

roça, *s.f.* plantation; field.

rocada, *s.f.* blow with a distaff; the flax a distaff can hold.

roçadeira, *s.f.* scythe.

roçador, *s.m.* clearer; planter, weeder, farmer.

roçadura, *s.f.* clearing of undergrowth; rubbing.

roçagante, *adj.* trailing; rustling.

roçagar, *v.i.* to rustle.

roçagem, *s.f.* clearing of land.

rocal, *s.m.* string of pearls; *adj.* very hard.

rocalha, *s.f.* a quantity of beads.

rocambolesco, *adj.* entangled; fantastic.

roçar, *v.t.* to clear *(terra);* to cut down; to brush, to skim *(roçar por),* to trail *(pelo chão).*

rocega, *s.f.* dragging, sweeping; drag cable.

rocegar, *v.t.* to drag, to sweep.

roceiro, *s.m.* small planter; peasant; backwoodsman.

rocha, s.f. rock.

rochaz, adj. living or growing on rocks.

rochedo, s.m. cliff.

rochoso, adj. rocky, stony, cragged, craggy.

rociada, s.f. dew-fall.

rociar, v.i. to dew; to wet; to drizzle.

rocim, s.m. jade, nag, small horse.

rocinante, s.m. nag, jade, small weak horse.

rocio, s.m. dew, mist; drizzle.

rocioso, adj. dewy, misty, bedewed.

rococó, adj. rococo; eccentric; antiquated; florid; gaudy; s.m. rococo; rococo ornamentation.

roda, s.f. wheel; circle; circuit, circumference; round (de bebidas); circle, set (agrupamento); turnbox (de convento); lottery wheel (roda da lotaria). 1) à roda, em roda, round, around. 2) em roda de, around, about. 3) alta-roda, high society. 4) andar à roda, to go round and round; to reel. 5) roda-viva, bustle, fuss. 6) andar numa roda--viva, to rush to and fro.

rodada, s.f. round (de bebidas); turn (volta).

rodado, adj. wheeled; wide (vestido) s.m. wheels of a car.

rodagem, s.f. wheels; rolling; breaking-in (de automóvel).

rodante, adj. rolling.

rodapé, s.m. baseboard (de parede); valance (de cama); footnote (em texto).

rodar, v.t. to roll; v.i. to turn, to rotate, to revolve; to spin, to whirl; to drive (ir de automóvel).

rodeamento, s.m. encircling, surrounding.

rodear, v.t. to surround, to encircle; to turn round.

rodeio, s.m. circumlocution, subterfuge, evasion; rodeo (de gado). 1) fazer rodeios, to beat around the bush. 2) sem rodeios, roundly, outspokenly.

rodeira, s.f. gate-keeper (num convento); rut (sulco).

rodela, s.f. round slice.

rodeleiro, s.m. buckler (soldado).

rodilha, s.f. dishcloth; pad (para a cabeça).

rodilhão, s.m. large dishcloth; wheel of a barrow.

rodilhar, v.t. to twist, to curl.

rodilho, s.m. rag, shred of cloth.

ródio, s.m. rhodium.

rodo, s.m. rake; a rodo, abundantly, plentifully.

rododendro, s.m. rhododendron.

rodopelo, s.m. twist of the hair.

rodopiante, adj. swirling, spinning.

rodopiar, v.i. to whirl, to swirl, to twirl, to spin.

rodopio, s.m. whirl(ing), swirl(ing), spin(ning).

rodovalho, s.m. turbot.

rodovia, s.f. highway.

rodoviário, adj. highway.

rodriguinho, s.m. common-place.

roedor, adj. gnawing; corroding; (zool.) rodent; s.m. rodent.

roedura, s.f. gnawing; corrosion; abrasion.

roer, v.t. to gnaw; to gnaw at, to nibble; to corrode, to eat away; to bite (as unhas).

rogação, s.f. rogation, supplication; petition; s.f. pl. rogations, litanies.

rogador, s.m. supplicant; intercessor, mediator.

rogar, v.t. to beseech, to implore, to supplicate; to beg; rogar pragas: to curse.

rogativa, s.f. request, petition, entreaty; supplication.

rogativo, adj. supplicating, beseeching, entreating.

rogatória, s.f. request, petition; entreaty.

rogatório, adj. rogatory.

rogo, s.m. request; prayer; petition; a rogo de: at the request of.

rogador, adj. crawling, creeping; s.m. crawler.

rojão, s.m. roast pork, crackling.

rojar, v.t. to drag, to trail; rojar-se, to drag oneself; to throw oneself to the ground.

rojo, s.m. dragging, trailing; de rojo, crawling, trailing along the ground.

rol, s.m. roll, record, register, list.

rola, s.f. turtle-dove.

rolador, s.m. roller, cylinder; adj. rolling.

rolagem, s.f. rolling, passing a rollerover.

rolamento, s.m. rolling; (mec.) bearing.

rolante, adj. rolling; revolving.

rolão, s.m. brown flour, bran; billow (vaga).

rolar, v.t. to roll; to wheel, to bowl; v.i. to roll; to run (onwheels); to trundle; to coo (arrulhar).

roldana, s.f. pulley, sheave.

roldão, s.m. confusion, turmoil; de roldão, impetuously; headlong; pell-mell.

roleta, s.f. roulette.

rolete, s.m. roller, small wheel; a hatter`s roller.

rolha, s.f. cork; stopper; tirar a rolha, to uncork.

rolhador, s.m. corking machine; bottle corker.

rolhagem, *s.f.* corking.

rolhar, *v.t.* to cork.

rolharia, *s.f.* cork factory.

rolheiro, *s.m.* cork maker; sheaf of grain.

rolhista, *s.m. e s.f.* cork-cutter.

roliço, *adj.* plump, chubby, round.

rolo, *s.m.* roll; roller; rolling pin *(da mesa).*

romã, *s.f.* pomegranate.

romagem, *s.f.* pilgrimage.

romaico, *adj.* Romaic.

romança, *s.f.* ballad.

romance, *s.m.* romance, novel; love affair.

romanceação, *s.f.* the act of writing in form of a novel.

romanceado, *adj.* told in story; exaggerated, fanciful.

romancear, *v.t.* to write novels; to romance; to invent stories; to romanticize, *v.i.* to romance.

romanceiro, *s.m.* collection of novels, poems or popular songs of a nation.

romancista, *s.f.* novelist.

romanço, *s.m.* the Romance languages.

romanesco, *adj.* romanesque; fanciful; romantic; fantastic; Romanesque *(estilo).*

românico, *adj.* Romanic; *s.m.* Romanic *(lingua);* Romanesque *(estilo).*

romanismo, *s.m.* Romanism.

romanista, *s.m. e s.f.* Romanist.

romanístico, *adj.* Romanistic.

romanização, *s.f.* Romanization.

romanizar, *v.t.* to Romanize.

romano, *s.m. e adj.* Roman.

romanólogo, *s.m.* Romanist.

romântico, *adj.* romantic, fanciful, sentimental, dreamy.

romantismo, *s.m.* romanticism.

romantizar, *v.t.* to romanticize, to fancy.

romaria, *s.f.* pilgrimage; popular festival, religious feast.

romãzeira, *s.f.* pomegranate-tree.

rômbico, *adj.* rhombic.

rombiforme, *adj.* rhombiform, rhombic.

rombo, *s.m.* rhomb; hole, breach, gap; *adj.* blunt; dull.

romboédrico, *adj.* rhombohedral, rhombohedric.

romboidal, *adj.* rhomboidal.

romboide, *adj. e s.m.* rhomboid.

rombudo, *adj.* very blunt; not sharp; stupid.

romeira, *s.f.* woman pilgrim; pomegranate-tree.

romeiro, *s.m.* pilgrim.

romeno, *s.m. e adj.* Rumanian.

rompante, *s.m.* impetuosity; fury; bluster, arrogance; outburst *(de cólera, etc.).*

rompedeira, *s.f.* chisel; punch.

romper, *v.t.* to break; to tear, to rend; to sever; to split, to disrupt; to break open, to break through, to pierce; to violate; to interrupt; to plow *(as ondas);* to break off *(relações); v.i.* to burst out; to erupt; to break out; to begin; to apper, to emerge; to rush *(investir); s.m.* 1) *ao romper do dia,* at daybreak. 2) *romper-se,* to break asunder; to part; to be disrupted.

rompimento, *s.m.* breaking, rupture; breaking up of relation.

ronca, *s.f.* shore; snoring; fog-horn.

roncada, *s.f.* snore; snoring.

roncador, *adj.* snoring, roaring; *s.m.* snorer; boaster.

roncante, *adj.* snoring, roaring.

roncar, *v.i.* to snore *(ressonar);* to grunt *(grunhir);* to roar *(fazer estrondo)* to bluster *(bravatear).*

roncaria, *s.f.* bragging, boasting.

ronçaria, *s.f.* slackness, indolence, negligence.

ronceirice, *s.f.* slowness, indolence.

ronceiro, *adj.* slow, sluggish, indolent, laggard.

ronco, *s.m.* snore; roar; grunt; growl, snarl.

ronda, *s.f.* patrol; watch; inspection; *fazer a roda,* to go the rounds.

rondar, *v.t.* to patrol; to go the rounds of ; to prowl about or around; to keep an eye on; *v.i.* to prowl about, to lurk around.

rondó, *s.m.* rondeau.

ronha, *s.f.* scab, mange; cunning *(astúcia).*

ronhento, ronhoso, *adj.* scabby; sly, cunning.

ronqueira, *s.f.* hoarseness; snoring.

ronquejante, *adj.* snoring, roaring.

ronquejar, *v.i.* to snore; to roar; to snort.

ronquenho, *adj.* hoarse, raucous.

ronquidão, *s.f.* hoarseness, wheeziness.

ronrom, *s.m.* purring.

ronronante, *adj.* purring.

ronronar, *v.t.* to purr.

roque, *s.m.* castle *(no xadrez); sem rei nem roque,* without rhyme or reason.

roqueiro, *adj.* built in rocks; rocky.

roquete, *s.m.* ratchet.

roro, *s.m. (pop.)* a great quantity, lots.

rorejante, *adj.* roral, roric.

rorejar, *v.i.* to bedew; to perspire; to let fall.

rosa, s.f. rose; pink (cor); rosa-dos-ventos, compass-card.

rosácea, s.f. rose-window, rosace.

rosáceas, s.f. pl. Rosaceae.

rosáceo, adj. rosaceous; rose, rozy, rose-like.

rosado, adj. rose-coloured, rozy, roseate, pink.

rosal, s.m. rose garden.

rosalgar, s.m. realgar, arsenic mono-sulphide.

rosália, s.f. mountain rose.

rosar, v.t. to rose, to render rosecoloured.

rosário, s.m. rosary; string of beads.

rosar-se, v.refl. to blush.

rosbife, s.m. roast beef.

rosca, s.f. screw thread (de parafuso); spiral; coil (de serpente).

roscar, v.t. to thread.

roseira, s.f. rose-bush.

roseiral, s.m. rose-garden.

róseo, adj. rosy, roseate; rose-coloured, pink.

roséola, s.f. German measles, roseola.

roseta, s.f. rosette; rowel (de espora); red spot (na face).

rosicler, adj. rose-pink; s.m. ruby silver; string of pearls.

rosmaninho, s.m. French lavender; rose-mary.

rosnadela, s.f. snarl, growl.

rosnador, adj. growling, snarling.

rosnar, v.i. to growl, to snarl; to mutter.

rosnido, s.m. o mesmo que "rosnadela".

rosquilha, rosquilho, s.f. ring-shaped biscuit.

rossio, s.m. public square.

rosto, s.m. face; countenance; visage; head (de moeda); title page (página).

rostrado, adj. rostrate, beaked, rostral.

rostriforme, adj. rostriform.

rostro, s.m. rostrum.

rota, s.f. route, course, itinerary; way; de rota batida: posthaste, in full flight.

rotação, s.f. rotation; revolution; gyration; spin, turn.

rotáceo, adj. rotate; wheel shaped.

rotacismo, s.m. rhotacism.

rotacista, adj. rhotacist.

rotador, s.m. rotator (músculo); rotifer.

rotar, v.i. to rotate, to revolve, to move in circles.

rotário, s.m. e adj. rotarian.

rotativa, s.f. rotary press, rotary printing press.

rotativismo, s.m. rotativism.

rotativo, adj. rotary, rotatory; rotating.

rotatório, adj. rotatry.

rotear, v.t. to steer a ship; to go to sea; to clear land for planting.

roteiro, s.m. itinerary; guidebook; schedule, agenda; norm, regulation; script (de um filme, etc.).

rotífero, adj. rotiferous; rotiferal.

rotiforme, adj. rotiform.

rotina, s.f. routine; daily round; custom.

rotineiro, adj. routine; customary, habitual.

roto, adj. broken; torn, rent; tattered; ragged.

rotogravura, s.f. rotogravure.

rotor, s.m. rotor, impeller.

rótula, s.f. lattice; (anat.) kneecap, patella.

rotulagem, s.f. labelling.

rotular, v.t. to label; adj. rotular.

rótulo, s.m. label; tag, mark, inscription.

rotunda, s.f. circus; rotunda.

rotundidade, s.f. rotundity; roundness; obesity.

rotundo, adj. rotund; round.

rotura, s.f. rupture, break; crack.

roubador, s.m. robber, thief.

roubalheira, s.f. swindle, cheat, robbery.

roubar, v.t. to steal, to thieve, to rob; to pinch; to deprive of.

roubo, s.m. theft, robbery, plunder, stealing, thieving.

rouco, adj. hoarse; roucous, husky, gruff.

roufenho, adj. hoarse; nasal; roucous.

roupa, s.f. clothes, clothing, garments.

roupagem, s.f. drapery (em arte); outward appearance; clothes; dress.

roupão, s.m. dressing-gown; bath-robe, robe.

roupar, v.t. e v.i. to dress, to clothe; to drape.

rouparia, s.f. linen room.

roupeira, s.f. woman who takes care of the linen.

roupeiro, s.m. linen cupboard, clothes closet; wardrobe.

roupeta, s.f. cassock.

roupido, adj. dressed; well-provided with clothes.

rouquejante, adj. croaking, hoarse.

rouquejar, v.i. to be hoarse; to croak, to talk hoarsely.

rouquenho, adj. hoarse, twangy; husky, raucous.

rouquidão, s.f. hoarseness, huskiness, raucousness.

rouquido, s.m. hoarse sound.

rouxinol, s.m. nightingale.

roxear, v.t. e v.i. to purple; to become purple.

roxidão, *s.f.* purpleness.

roxo, *adj.* e *s.m.* purple; blue *(de frio)*.

rua, *s.f.* street; walk *(de jardim)*; pôr na rua, to show the door, to dismiss, to kick out; to fire *(despedir)*.

ruão, *s.m.* roan (horse).

rubefacção, *s.f.* rubefaction.

rubefaciente, *adj.* rubefacient.

rubente, *adj.* ruby, red, reddish.

rúbeo, *adj.* ruby-coloured, reddish, ruddy.

rubéola, *s.f.* rubeola, rubbela.

rubescência, *s.f.* rubescence, flush.

rubescente, *adj.* rubescent, flushing.

rubescer, *v.i.* to become red.

rubi, *s.m.* ruby.

rubicão, *s.m.* fifficulty, obstacle, hindrance; Rubicon.

rubicundo, *adj.* rubicund, ruddy, rosy.

rubidez, *s.f.* rubicundity, ruddiness, flush.

rubídio, *s.m.* rubidium.

rúbido, *adj.* reddish, red, rubycoloured.

rubificante, *adj.* rubefacient, rubific.

rubificar, *v.t.* to rubefy, to make red.

rubigine, *s.f.* rustiness, rust.

rubiginoso, *adj.* rubiginous, red, rusty.

rubim, *s.m.* ruby.

rublo, *s.m.* rouble.

rubor, *s.m.* redness, blush; shame.

ruborescer, *v.i.* to become red, to blush.

ruborização, *s.f.* reddening, blushing.

ruborizar, *v.t.* to redden; *ruborizar-se,* to redden, to blush, to become red.

rubrica, *s.f.* rubric; heading; initials, abbreviated signature.

rubricador, *s.m.* rubricator.

rubricar, *v.t.* to rubricate; to mark, to initial.

rubro, *adj.* red, ruddy; red-hot, glowing; *ao rubro,* red-hot.

ruçar, *v.i.* to become grey; to fade.

ruço, *adj.* grey; faded; sandy hair.

rude, *adj.* rude, coarse, rough; impolite, uncivil, ill-mannered; unkind; boorish; rustic.

rudeza, *s.f.* rudeness, coarseness, severity; uncivility; boorishness.

rudimentar, *adj.* rudimentary, elementary, rudimental; primitive.

rudimento, *s.m.* rudiment; beggining; first principles, grounds; notion.

rudo, *adj.* rude, crude, rough.

ruela, *s.f.* by-street, side-street, alley; lane.

rufadela, *s.f.* the act of beating the drum.

rufador, *s.m.* drummer; *adj.* drimming.

rufar, *v.t.* to ruffle, to beat; to ruffle, to frill *(franzir)*; *v.i.* to roll.

rufia, rufião, *s.m.* ruffian, hooligan.

rufo, *s.m.* drum-beat, roll; *num rufo,* in less than no time.

ruga, *s.f.* wrinkle; rumple, crease; furrow.

rugar, *v.t.* wrinkle, to crease; to crumple.

ruge-ruge, *s.m.* restling.

rugido, *s.m.* roaring; bellow.

rugir, *v.i.* to roar, to bellow, to rustle.

rugosidade, *s.f.* rugosity, wrinkle, corrugation.

rugoso, *adj.* wrinkled, rugous, corrugated, creased; rugged, rough.

ruibarbo, *s.m.* rhubarb.

ruído, *s.m.* noise; sound; din, clatter; rumour.

ruidosamente, *adv.* noisily; boisterously.

ruidoso, *adj.* noisy; showy, pompous.

ruim, *adj.* bad, evil; vile, mean, perverse; rotten; wretched.

ruína, *s.f.* ruin; destruction, downfall; overthrow; wreck; *s.f. pl.* remains, ruins.

ruindade, *s.f.* badness, vileness, meanness; wretchedness.

ruinoso, *adj.* ruinous, wasteful, baneful, destructive.

ruir, *v.i.* to crash to earth; to tumble down, to fall; to collapse.

ruiva, *s.f.* dyer`s madder, madderplant; red-haired woman.

ruivo, *adj.* red-haired, red.

rum, *s.m.* rum.

ruma, *s.f.* heap, pile, stack.

rumar, *v.t.* to sterr, to head, to make (for).

ruminação, *s.f.* rumination, chewing; meditation.

ruminante, *adj.* e *s.m.* ruminant; *s.m. pl.* Ruminantia.

ruminar, *v.t.* to ruminate; to meditate, to brood over; to muse.

rumo, *s.m.* course, direction; tendency; point *(da rosa-dos-ventos).* 1) *rumo a,* toward, bound for, headed for. 2) *perder o rumo,* to lose one`s bearings. 3) *sem rumo,* adrift; aimlessly. 4) *tomar o rumo de,* to head for.

rumor, *s.m.* rumour, noise; uproar; murmur; hearsay, report.

rumorejante, *adj.* rustling, murmuring; rumbling.

rumorejar, *v.i.* to rumble; to rustle, to murmur; to whisper; *v.t.* to rumour; no noise abroad.

rumoroso, *adj.* noisy; humming; much talked about.

runa, *s.f.* rune.

rúnico, *adj.* runic.

runrum, *s.m.* rumour, hum.

rupestre, *adj.* rupestral, rupestrian; engraved or growing in rocks.

rupia, *s.f.* rupee *(moeda)*.

rúpia, *s.f.* Ruppia, (marine herbs).

rupícola, *adj.* rupicolous, living on rocks.

rúptil, *adj.* brittle, fragile, breakable, easily broken; dehiscing irregularly (botany).

ruptilidade, *s.f.* brittleness; dehiscence.

ruptura, *s.f.* rupture, disruption; breach, breaking up; fracture, break; crack.

rural, *adj.* rural; country.

ruralidade, *s.f.* rurality.

ruralismo, *s.m.* ruralism.

ruralista, *adj.* e *s.m.* e *s.f.* ruralist.

ruralizar, *v.t.* to ruralize.

rusga, *s.f.* tiff, spat; police raid; quarrel.

russo, *s.m.* e *adj.* Russian.

russófilo, *adj.* Russophile.

russófobo, *s.m.* Russophobe.

rusticamente, *adv.* rustically.

rusticar, *v.i.* to rusticate; to retire to the country.

rusticidade, *s.f.* rusticity; rudeness, coarseness.

rústico, *adj.* rustic; rural, bucolic; country; simple; loutish, boorish; rough; *s.m.* rustic, lout, yoken.

rutênio, *s.m.* ruthenium.

rutilação, *s.f.* o mesmo que "rutilância".

rutilância, *s.f.* brightness, splendour, resplendence.

rutilante, *adj.* blazing; flashing, glittering; radian, resplenden; bright.

rutilar, *v.i.* to shine, to blaze, to flash, to glitter.

S

s, the eighteenth letter of the Portuguese alphabet.

sã, *adj.* fem. de *são*, healthy, vigorous; perfect, entire, undamaged; honest, right; sane.

sabadeador, *adj., s.m.* sabbatarian; sabbat-keeper.

sabadear, *v.i.* to keep the sabbath.

sábado, *s.m.* Saturday; Sabbat *(judeu); Sábado de Aleluia,* Holy Saturday.

sabão, *s.m.* soap; a learned man.

sabático, *adj.* sabbatical.

sabatina, *s.f.* repetition *(das lições);* schoolwork on Saturday; discussion.

sabatinar, *v.t., v.i.* to discuss in detail; to recapitulate.

sabatino, *adj.* sabbatical.

sabatismo, *s.m.* sabbatarianism.

sabatizar, *v.i.* to sabbatize.

sabedor, *adj.* acquaint with; learned; knowing; aware of; proficient.

sabedoria, *s.f.* wisdom, prudence; learning, discretion, sagacity, knowledge.

sabeísmo, *s.m.* Sabaism, star worship.

sabeísta, *s.* Sabaist, starworshipper.

sabeliano, *s.m.* Sabellian.

saber, *s.m.* learning, knowledge, erudition; wisdom; prudence; *v.t., v.i.* to know, to be aware of, to be conscious of; to know how to; to be able, can; to hear, to learn; to taste, to smack, to savour. 1) *saber a*, to taste of to smack of. 2) *saber de cor (e salteado)*, to know by heart or perfectly well. 3) *a saber*, namely. 4) *não saber que fazer*, to be at a loss. 5) *saber a quantas anda*, to know what is what. 6) *saber as linhas com que se cose*, to know what one is doing. 7) *fazer saber*, to inform, to make known. 8) *não saber a quantas anda*, not to know what one is about.

sabeu, *s.m.* Sabaen.

sabiá, *s.m. (zool.)* song-thrush.

sabiamente, *adv.* wisely, discreetly, prudently.

sabichão, *s.m.* wiseacre, learned person; *adj.* clever, erudite.

sabichar, *v.t.* to nose around or about, to pry about.

sabichona, *s.f.* blue stocking *(mulher)*; pedantic woman.

sabidas (às), *loc. adv.* openly, publicly, clearly.

sabido, *adj.* known; wise, prudent; knowing; intelligent, learned; smart, cunning; skilful; *é um tipo muito sabido*, a downy old bird.

sabina, *s.m. (bot.)* savin.

sabinal, *s.m.* plantation of savins.

sabino, *adj., s.m.* Sabine; roan *(cavalo)*.

sábio, *adj.* wise; learned, judicious; *s.m.* sage, wise man; savant, scholar.

sable, *s.m.* sable, black .

saboaria, *s.f.* soap-works, soap-factory; soap warehouse.

saboeira, *s.f.* soapberry, soap-wort.

saboeiro, *s.m.* soap-boiler; soap-maker; soap dealer.

saboiano, *adj. s.m.* Savoyard.

sabonete, *s.m.* toilet-soap, soap-cake, scented soap; scolding, reprimand.

saboneteira, *s.f.* soap-dish, soap bowl, soap-holder.

sabor, *s.m.* savour, taste, relish, flavour, sort, nature; style, character; *ao sabor de*, at the mercy of.

saborear, *v.t.* to relish, to enjoy, to savour; to taste.

saborosamente, *adv.* pleasantry, tastily, appetizingly.

saboroso, *adj.* savoury, pleasant, tasty, palatable, appetising.

sabotagem, *s.f.* sabotage.

sabotar, *v.t.* to damage, to sabotage; to sap, to undermine.

sabre, *s.m.* sabre, sword.

sabugal, *s.m.* plantation of eldertrees, a growth of elders.

sabugo, *s.m.* pith; root *(unhas)*; elder.

sabugueiro, *s.m. (bot)* elder-tree.

sabujar, *v.t.* to flatter, to fawn on, to cajole.

sabujice, sabujismo, *s.f., s.m.* fawing, flattery, cringing.

sabujo, *s.m.* bloodhound, hunting dog; flatterer, fawner, heeler, toady.

sabuloso, *adj.* sandy, gritty; sabulous.

saburra, *s.f.* saburra; fur *(da língua)*.

saburrento, *adj.* furred, coated *(língua)*.

saburroso, *adj.* ver saburrento.

saca, *s.f.* bag, sack.

saca-balas, *s.m.* bullet-extractor, crow's bill.

saca-bocados, *s.m.* punching-machine.

saca-buchas, *s.m.* wad hook.

sacabuxa, *s.f. (mús)* sackbut.

sacada, *s.f.* jogging, jolting *(cavalo)*; pulling, drawing; balcony; bagful, sackful.

sacadela, *s.f.* pulling up, pull jerk.

sacado, *s.m.* drawee *(comercial)*.

sacador, *s.m.* drawer *(letra)*.

saca-molares, *s.m.* tooth-drawer; a bad dentist, tooth-puller.

sacão, *s.m.* jerk, jolt, jump, plunge *(cavalo)*.

sacar, *v.t.* to draw, to pull on, to extract; to draw against credit. 1) *sacar a descoberto*, to overdraw (sem crédito). 2) *sacar sobre*, to draw on *(crédito)*. 3) *sacar a oito dias*, to draw at eight day's date. 4) *sacar à vista*, to draw at sight. 5) *sacar a curto prazo*, to draw at short date. 6) *sacar de*, to draw out quickly *(faca)*.

saca-rabo, *s.m.* a mongoose.

sacaria, *s.f.* a number of sacks, a large quantity.

sacarídeo, *adj.* saccharoid.

sacarífero, *adj.* sacchariferous.

sacarificação, *s.m.* saccharification.

sacarificar, *v.t.* to saccharify, to convert into sugar.

sacarificável, *adj.* saccharificable.

sacarímetro, *s.m.* saccharimeter.

sacarina, *s.f.* saccharin.

sacarino, *adj.* saccharine.

sacaróide, *adj.* saccharoid, christalline.

saca-pilhas, *s.m.* cork-screw.

sacarose, *s.f.* saccharous, sucrose; cane or beet sugar.

sacaroso, *adj.* saccharous, sugary.

casa-trapos, *s.m.* wad-hook, worm-screw.

sacerdócio, *s.m.* priesthood; honourable profession.

sacerdotal, *adj.* sacerdotal; priestly.

sacerdote, *s.m.* priest, clergyman, cleric, ecclesiastic.

sacerdotisa, *s.f.* priestess.

sacha, *s.f.* weeding; hoe.

sachada, *s.f.* weeding, hoeing.

sachadela, *s.f.* weeding, light cultivation with a hoe.

sachador, *s.m.* weeder, raker, hoer.

sachadura, *s.f.* weeding, raking, hoeing.

sachar, *v.t.* to weed, to rake, to hoe, to grub up.

sacho, *s.m.* weeding hoe.

sachola, *s.f.* small hoe.

sacholada, *s.f.* blow *(com um sacho).*

saciar, *v.t.* to satiate, to sate, to quench; to cloy, to glut; to appease.

saciável, *adj.* satiable.

saciedade, *s.f.* satiety, satiation; surfeit.

saco, *s.m.* sack; bag. 1) *despejar o saco,* to say all, to say one's say. 2) *meter a viola no saco,* to hold one's tongue.

sacola, *s.f.* wallet, knapsack, pich.

sacolejar, *v.t.* to shake *(líquido),* to agitate.

sacolejo, *s.m.* shaking up and down *(líquido).*

saco-roto, *s.m.* blabbermouth, chaterer, prattler.

sacra, *s.f.* canon of the mass.

sacralização, *s.f.* to sacralize.

sacramento, *adj.* who received the last sacraments.

sacramental, *adj.* sacramental.

sacramentar, *v.t.* to administer the sacraments, to receive the sacraments.

sacramento, *s.m.* sacrament; *Santíssimo Sacramento,* the Blessed (the Holy) Sacrament, the Eucharist.

sacrário, *s.m.* tabernacle, sanctuary, sacrarium, shrine; refuge.

sacratíssimo, *adj.* most sacred, most holy.

sacrificador, *s.m.* sacrificer; *adj.* sacrificing.

sacrificar, *v.t.* to sacrifice, to devote; to give up; to immolate; *sacrificar-se,* to devote oneself to, to sacrifice oneself for.

sacrificável, *adj.* that can be sacrificed.

sacrificial, *adj.* sacrificial.

sacrifício, *s.m.* sacrifice; abnegation; self-denial; immolation; offering.

sacrilegamente, *adv.* sacrilegiously.

sacrilégio, *s.m.* sacrilege, desecration, profanation.

sacrílego, *adj.* sacrilegious, impious.

sacripanta, *s.m.* vile wretch, rascal, scoundrel; sanctimonious.

sacrista, *s.m.* sexton, sacristan *(pop).*

sacristania, *s.f.* office of a sexton.

sacristão, *s.m.* sexton.

sacrista, *s.f.* sacristy, vestry.

sacro, *adj.* sacred, holy, hallowed; venerable; sacral *(anat.); s.m.* sacrum.

sacrofemoral, *adj.* sacrofemoral.

sacrolombar, *adj.* sacrolumbar.

sacrossanto, *adj.* most holy; sacrosanct, sacred.

sacudida, *s.f.* saking; cleansing.

sacudidamente, *adv.* boldly, roughly; by jerks.

sacudidela, *s.f.* shake, agitation; jolt, jerk; smack; rejection *(popular).*

sacudido, *adj.* shaken; harsh; expeditious, prompt, rapid; unrestrained; determined; rude, tough; expert, capable, skilful.

sacudidura, *s.f.* shaking, shake, shoke, jerk. rejection.

sacudimento, *s.m.* ver sacudidura.

sacudir, *v.t.* to shake; to agitate; to dust, to wag; to jolt, to toss; to get rid of; to rouse, to stir up; to stimulate. 1) *sacudir o jugo,* to shake off the yoke. 2) *sacudir o pó,* to shake off the dust.

sádico, *adj.* sadistic; *s.m.* sadist.

sádio, *adj.* sound, healthy, wholesome.

sadismo, *s.m.* sadism.

saduceísmo, *s.m.* Sadduceism.

saduceu, *s.m.* Sadducee.

safa!, *interj.* out of the way! good gracious! good Heavens!.

safadice, *s.f.* dirty trick; immorality; baseness.

safadismo, *s.m.* low behaviour.

safado, *adj.* worn out, threadbare; barefaced, brazen, shameless.

safanão, *s.m.* jerk, push, shove; fling, yank.

safar, *v.t.* to wear out; to clear; to rub out; to remove, to pull off; to set free; *safar-se,* to sneak away, to run away; to get rid of, to get free from.

sáfara, *s.f.* stony waste, stony desert.

safardana, *s.m.* wretch, rascal, scoundrel, mean person.

sáfaro, *adj.* sterile, wild, rude; waste, barren *(terra).*

sáfico, *adj.* Sapphic.

safio, *s.m.* small conger, large sea-eel.

safira, *s.f.* saphire.

safismo, *s.m.* Sapphism.

safo, *adj.* clear; free, disembarrassed; put afloat.

safões, *s.m. pl.* sheepskin trousers.

safra, *s.f.* smith's anvil; harvest, harvest-fine.

saga, *s.f.* saga.

sagacidade, *s.f.* sagacity, perspicacity, mental acuteness; shrewdness.

sagaz, *adj.* sagacious, intelligent, perspicacious, shrewd, sharp-witted, astute, clever, wise.

sagazmente, *adv.* sagaciously.

sage, *adj.* wise.

sageza, *s.f.* wisdom.

sagitado, *adj.* arrow-shaped; saggitate, saggitated.

sagital, *adj.* saggital; arrow-shaped.

sagitária, *s.f.* sagittaria, arrowhead *(bot).*

sagitário, *s.m.* Sagittarius, Archer.

sagração, *s.f.* coronation *(rei);* consecration *(bispo).*

sagrado, *adj.* sacred, holy, consecrated, sanctified; taboo.

sagrador, *adj.* sanctifying.

sagrante, *adj.* sanctifying.

sagrar, *v.t.* to anoint, to consecrate, to dedicate.

sagu, *s.f.* sago (starch).

saguão, *s.m.* inner yard; porch.

sagueiro, *s.m.* sago-palm *(bot).*

sagui, saguim, *s.m.* sapagou.

saia, *s.f.* skirt.

saião, *s.m.* houseleek *(bot).*

saibo, *s.m.* bad taste; taste flavour.

saibramento, *s.m.* trenching, covering with gravel.

saibrão, *s.m.* gravelly soil.

saibrar, *v.t.* to trench up, to cover with gravel.

saibreira, *s.f.* gravel-pit.

saibro, *s.m.* gravel, gross sand.

saibroso, *adj.* gravelly, sandy.

saída, *s.f.* going out; issue, outlet, exit, way out; utterance; expedient; kick-off *(futebol); beco sem saída,* blind alley, deadlock.

saído, *adj.* jutting out, projecting, salient, sticking out; bold; gone out.

saimel, *s.m.* springer.

saimento, *s.m.* funeral, funeral procession.

sainete, *s.m.* joke, jest; taste, flavour; short farce.

saio, *s.m.* loose coat.

saiote, *s.m.* petticoat.

sair, *v.i.* to go out; to come out; to get out, to go off; to set out for; to leave for; to depart; to jut out, to stick out; to exceed; to be published; to issue from; to slip out; to sally; to turn out. 1) *sair a alguém,* to take after someone, to resemble. 2) *sair-se bem,* to come off well. 3) *sair-se mal,* to come off badly, to fail. 4) *sair mal,* to turn out badly. 5) *sair a lume,* to come out, to be published. 6) *sair dos eixos,* to go beyond the bounds. 7) *sair certo,* to come true. 8) *sair do caminho,* to get out of the way, to stand aside.

sal, *s.m.* salt; piquancy, wit, humour, sparkle *(fig).* 1) *sal amargo,* Epsom salts. 2) *sal refinado,* table salt. 3) *sal-gema,* rock-salt. 4) *sal marinho,* sea-salt. 5) *pedra de sal,* a lump of salt.

sala, *s.f.* room; hall. 1) *sala de estar,* living-room. 2) *sala de jogo,* card-room. 3) *sala de espera,* waiting-room. 4) *sala de armas,* reading-room. 5) *sala de sessões,* assembly room. 6) *sala de visitas,* drawing room. 7) *fazer sala,* to entertain guests.

salada, *s.f.* salad; mess, medley, confusion. 1) *salada de alface,* lettuce salad. 2) *salada de fruta,* fruit salad.

saladeira, *s.f.* salad-bowl, salad dish.

salafrário, *s.m.* rascal, scoundrel, rogue.

salalé, *s.m.* white ant, termite.

salamaleque, *s.m.* bow; affected compliments *(pl.).*

salamandra, *s.f.* salamander; salamander-stove.

salame, *s.m.* salami.

salão, *s.m.* drawing-room or lounge *(hotel);* saloon; parlour; large hall; reception room; salon *(exposição de arte),* picture gallery. 1) *salão de chá,* tea-room. 2) *salão de baile,* dance-hall, ball-room. 3) *salão de beleza,* beauty parlour.

salário, *s.m.* wages, pay, earnings.

salchicha, *s.m. ver salsicha.*

saldar, *v.t.* to balance, to close, ro settle *(conta);* to sell at low price; to pay in full.

saldo, *s.m.* balance; remainder, rest; job-lot; clearing sale. 1) *saldo a favor ou positivo,* credit balance. 2) *saldo negativo,* debit balance.

saleiro, *s.m.* salt-cellar; salt merchant, salt-seller, salter.

salesiano, *adj.* Salesian.

saleta, *s.f.* sitting-room, waiting-room, small hall.

salga, *s.f.* salting, curing.

salgação, *s.f.* salting.

salgadeira, *s.f.* salting-tub, salting-box; salting-place.

salgado, *adj.* salted, salty, brackish; witty *(fig.);* costly, very dear, expensive.

salgador, *s.m.* salter.

salgadura, *s.f.* salting.

salgalhada, *s.f.* hotch-potch, meddley, mixture, mess, confusion.

salgar, *v.t.* to salt, to pickle.

salgueiral, *s.m.* plantation of willows.

salgueiro, *s.m.* willow.

salicilato, s.m. salicylate.
salicílico, adj. salicylic.
saliciloso, adj. salicylous.
salicilina, s.f. salicin.
sálico, adj. Salic.
salícola, adj. salt-producing, saliniferous.
salicórnia, s.f. glasswort (bot.).
salicultura, s.f. salt-production, salt-making.
saliência, s.f. salience, projection, prominence, relief.
salientar, v.t. to point out, to stress; salientar-se, to stand out, to distinguish oneself, to become prominent or conspicuous, to set off, to emphasize.
saliente, adj. salient, projecting, jutting, outstanding; prominent, conspicuous; remarkable.
salífero, adj. saliferous, salt-bearing, containing or producing salt.
salificação, s.f. salification.
salificar, v.t. to salify.
salificável, adj. salifiable.
salina, s.f. saline, salt-spring, salt-mine, salt-pit, saltworks; salt-marsh; salt-pan; saltern.
salinação, salinagem, s.f. salification, salt-making.
salineiro, s.m. salter; one who manufactures, deals or works in the salt industry.
salinidade, s.f. salinity, saltiness.
salino, adj. saline; briny.
salinómetro, s.m. salinometer, salt-gauge.
salitração, s.f. natural formation of saltpetre; nitrification.
salitrato, adj. impregnated of saltpetre, nitrified.
salitrar, v.t. to mix with saltpetre; to nitrify.
salitre, s.m. saltpetre; saltpetre rot, nitre, nitrate.
salitrização, s.f. nitrification.
salitroso, adj. nitrous.
saliva, s.f. saliva, spittle, spit, dribble.
salivação, s.f. salivation.
salivante, adj. salivating, salivant.
salivar, adj. salivary; v.t., v.i., to salivate, to spit.
salivoso, adj. salivous, salivary.
salmão, s.m. salmon.
salmear, v.t., v.i. to chant psalms; to sing-song (fig).
sálmico, adj. psalmodical.
salmista, s., adj. psalmist; psalmodist.
salmo, s.m. psalm.
salmodia, s.f. psalmody.

salmodiar, v.t., v.i. to psalmodize, to sing or recite psalms.
salmoeira, s.f. brine.
salmoeirar, v.t. to salt, to pickle.
salmoeiro, s.m. a vessel for salting.
salmoira, s.f. brine; pickle; salt-water.
salmonado, adj. salmon-like.
salmonete, s.m. red mullet.
salmonídeo, adj. salmonoid.
salmoura, s.f. brine; pickle.
samourar, v.t. to pickle, to salt.
salobre, salobro, adj. brackish, briny.
saloiada, s.f. a lot of rustics; peasants, countrymen.
saloiice, s.f. boorishness, rudeness.
saloio, s.m. peasant, countryman, villager; yokel, rustic; adj. rustic, clumsy, boorish, rude, clownish.
salomónico, adj. Solomonic.
salpicado, adj. sprinkled, mottled, speckled, spotted.
salpicadura, s.f. sprinkle, mottled, speckled, spotted.
salpicão, s.m. pork sausage.
sapicar, v.t. to sprinkle, to spatter; to mottle; to splash, to spot, to speck.
salpico, s.m. speck, spot, speckle, sprinkle, splash.
salpimenta, s.f. salt-and-pepper; adj. greyish, ashcoloured, speckled.
salpimentar, v.t. to salt-and-pepper.
salpresar, v.t. to salt slightly.
salpreso, adj. powdered with salt, salty, salted.
salsa, s.f. garden-parsley.
salsada, s.f. mess, confusion, muddle; intricate affair.
salsaparrilha, s.f. sarsaparilla.
salseira, s.f. sauce-boat, sauce-dish.
salseiro, s.m. heavy shower, downpour.
salsicha, s.f. sausage; hot-dog; Frankfurter.
salsichão, s.m. large-sized sausage.
salsicharia, s.m. pork-butcher; pork-seller.
salsicheiro, s.m. pork-butcher; pork-seller.
salsifré, s.m. dance; small party; hubbub, tumult; confusion; noise.
salso, adj. salty, salted (poét.).
salsugem, s.f. saltness, brine.
salsuginoso, adj. salsaginous; brackish.
saltada, s.f. assault; leap; short visit.
saltador, s.m. jumper, leaper, vaulter; adj. leaping, saltant, jumping.
saltante, adj. saltant, leaping, jumping, dancing.

saltão, *s.m.* grasshopper *(pop).*

salta-pocinhas, *s.m.* affected person, one who minces his steps.

saltar, *v.t., v.i.* to skip over, to omit, to get over; to leap, to jump, to skip, to hop; to burst out, to explode; to shift *(vento).* 1) *saltar à vista aos olhos,* to strike the eye. 2) *saltar da cama,* to jump out of bed. 3) *saltar a corda,* to skip. 4) *saltar palavras,* to skip words. 5) *saltar de alegria,* to jump for joy. 6) *saltar em terra,* to land, to disembark. 7) *saltar do comboio,* to alight from the train. 8) *saltar por cima de,* to overleap. 9) *fazer saltar,* to blow up *(ponte).*

salta-regra, *s.m.* sliding-rule, set square.

saltaricar, saltarilhar, *v.i.* to hop, to skip, to go by little jumps.

salteado, *adj.* assaulted, robbed; intermissive, alternated, interpolated; *de cor e salteado,* by heart, at finger-tips.

salteamento, *s.m.* assault.

saltear, *v.t.* to assault; to overtake; to skip *(páginas);* psalterium, tripe *(animais); v.i.* to rob.

salteiro, *s.m.* heel-maker.

saltério, *s.m.* psalter *(livro);* psaltery *(instrumento).*

saltígrado, *adj.* saltigrade.

saltimbanco, *s.m.* mountibank; quack; juggler.

saltinho, *s.m.* skip, hop.

saltitante, *adj.* skipping, hopping, frisky, lively.

saltitar, *v.i.* to skip, to hop; to digress; to show inconstancy.

salto, *s.m.* leap. jump, hop; omission; heel *(sapatos, etc.);* bound, bounce. 1) *salto com vara,* pole vaulting. 2) *salto em altura,* high jump. 3) *salto de anjo,* swan jump. 4) *salto em comprimento,* broad jump. 5) *salto mortal,* somersault, back flip. 6) *salto em pára-quedas,* parachute jump. 7) *de um salto,* at a jump. 8) *triplo salto,* hop, step and jump. 9) *ir num salto,* to go quickly.

salubérrimo, *adj.* most salubrious, very healthy.

salubre, *adj.* salubrious, healthy, wholesome.

salubridade, *s.f.* salubrity, salubriousness.

salubrificar, *v.t.* to make healthy, to cleanse, to render salubrious.

salutar, *adj.* salutary, beneficial, good, wholesome; moralizing.

salutífero, *adj.* ver salutar.

salva, *s.f.* volley *(tiros, etc.);* salver, tray; gar-den sage *(bot.).* 1) *salva de palmas,* round of applause. 2) *dar uma salva,* to volley.

salvação, *s.f.* salvation; deliverance; salutation; salvage, rescue; redemption.

salvádego, *s.m.* salvage (dinheiro); vessel employed in salvaging another.

salvador, *s.m.* saviour, saver; *adj.* saving.

salvados, *s.m. pl.* salvage, property salvaged; salvaged goods *(fogo, inundações).*

salvaguarda, *s.f.* safeguard; safe-conduct; security, garanty; protection, defence.

salvaguardar, *v.t.* to protect; to secure, to safeguard, to defend; to preserve.

salvamento, *s.m.* safety; salvage, rescue; deliverance, salvation.

salvante, *prep.* saving, except.

salvar, *v.t.* to save, to deliver, to free, to rescue; to reclaim; to salute; to salvage; to redeem; to jump, to leap over; to skip over; *salve-se quem puder!,* everyman for himself!

salvatério, *s.m.* resource, salvation, escape.

salvável, *adj.* savable, redeemable.

salva-vidas, *s.m.* life-buoy, life-belt, life-boat.

salve, *interj.* hail!.

salve-rainha, *s.f.* Hail Mary; *Ave Maria;* Hail, holy Queen.

sálvia, *s.f.* ver *"salva".*

salvo, *adj.* safe, secure, saved; out of danger; *prep.* save, except unless. 1) *salvo seja!,* God forbid!. 2) *a salvo,* in safety. 3) *são e salvo,* safe and sound. 4) *salvo erro,* barring a mistake. 5) *salvo erro ou omissão,* errors and omissions excepted.

salvo-conduto, *s.m.* safe-conduct, passport, pass.

sâmara, *s.f.* samara *(fruto).*

samaritano, *adj., s.m.* Samaritan.

samarra, *s.f.* sheepskin coat; short overcoat.

samba, *s.m.* samba.

sambenito, *s.m.* sanbenito.

samblado, *adj.* joined.

samblador, *s.m.* joiner.

sambladura, *s.f.* assemblage; woodjoint; rabbet; mortise.

samblagem, *s.f.* ver sambladura.

samblar, *v.t.* to join, to mortise, to carve in wood.

samoiedo, *adj., s.m.* Samoyed *(mongóis siberianos).*

samorim, *s.m.* zamorim.

samovar, *s.m.* samovar *(chaleira russa).*

sanação, *s.f.* curing, healting.

sanador, *adj.* sanative; curative.

sanar, *v.t.* to cure, to heal; to remedy.
sanatório, *s.m.* sanatorium, health resort.
sanável, *adj.* curable, sanable.
sanca, *s.f.* cove; cavetto.
sanção, *s.f.* sanction; ratification, confirmation; penalty or reward.
sancionador, *adj.* sanctioning, confirmatory, ratifying; *s.n.* ratifier, sanctioner.
sancionar, *v.t.* to sanction, to ratify; to authorize, to confirm, to approve.
sandália, *s.f.* sandal.
sândalo, *s.m.* sandal-wood.
sandáraca, *s.m.* sandarac *(resina).*
sandejar, *v.* to act foolishly, to act like a fool.
sandeu, *adj.* foolish; *s.m.* fool.
sandice, *s.f.* folly, nonsense, stupidity, foolishness.
sanduíche, *s.f.* sandwich.
saneador, *adj.* sanitizing; curing; improving; *s.m.* improver, sanotationist.
saneamento, *s.m.* santitation, drainage.
sanear, *v.t.* to render salubrious, to make healthy; to remedy.
saneável, *adj.* that can be made healthy.
sanedrim, sanédrio, *s.m.* sanhedrin.
sanefa, *s.f.* pelmet, valance *(para janelas).*
sanfeno, *adj. s.f. s.m. (bot.)* sainfoin.
sanfona, *s.f.* hurdy-gurdy.
sanfonina, *s.f.* small hurdy-gurdy; *s.m.* hurdy-gurdy player, accordionist.
sanfoninar, *s.t.* to paly on the hurdy-gurdy or accordion.
sangradoiro, *s.m.* blood-letting; trench for draining; bleeder valve.
sangrador, *s.m.* bleeder; blood-letter.
sangradouro, *s.m.* blood-letting; drain; bleeder.
sangradura, *s.m.* bleeding; blood-letting; tapping.
sangrar, *v.t.* to bleed; to let bleed; to tap *(árvore);* to fall in drops.
sangrento, *adj.* bloody; bleeding.
sangria, *s.f.* bleeding; blood-letting.
sangue, *s.m.* blood *(fig.)* race, kindred, family, lineage.
sangue-frio, *s.m.* cold blood.
sangueira, *s.f.* pool of blood; bloodshed, slaughter.
sanguento, *adj.* bloody; sanguinary.
sanguessuga, *s.f.* leech; *(fig.)* bloodsucker, extortioner.
sanguífero, *adj.* sanguiferous.
sanguinário, *adj.* bloodthristy, sanguinary, bloody, cruel, inhuman.

sanguínea, *s.f.* red-pencil drawing; knot grass.
sanguíneo, *adj.* sanguine; sanguineous; blood coloured.
sanguinhal, *s.m.* plantation of dogwoods.
sanguinho, *s.m.* dogwood.
sanguinidade, *s.f.* consanguinity, blood-relationship.
sanguino, *adj.* ver sanguíneo.
sanguinolência, *s.f.* blood shedding, cruelty.
sanguinolento, *adj.* bloody, cruel, sanguinary.
sanguinoso, *adj.* ver sanguinário.
sanguissedento, *adj.* bloodthirsty.
sanha, *s.f.* fury, rage, wrath, anger.
sanhoso, *adj.* angry, ill-tempered, enraged; irascible.
sanhudo, *adj.* furious; grim, raging, fierce.
sanidade, *s.f.* sanity, soundness; hygiene, salubrity, sanitation.
sânie, *s.f.* sanies.
sanificação, *s.f.* sanification.
sanificador, *adj.* sanitary; improving.
sanificar, *v.t.* to make healthy; to sanitate; to clear; to sanify.
sanitário, *adj.* sanitary; hygienic.
sanitarista, *s.* sanitarian.
sanja, *s.f.* gutter, drain, sitch.
sanscritismo, *s.m.* Sanskritism.
sanscritista, *s.* Sanskritist.
sânscrito, *s.m.* Sanskrit.
santa-bárbara, *s.f.* powder-room, powder-magazine.
santa-fé, *s.m.* Brazilian grass used for rhatching.
santa-luzia, *s.f.* ferule.
santamente, *adj.* holily; in a holy manner, piously.
santanário, *s.m.* bigot, hypocrite.
santantoninho, *s.m.* favourite, much petted person.
santão, santarrão, *s.m.* bigot, hypocrite.
santeiro, *s.m.* image-maker.
santelmo, *s.m.* St. Elmo's fire; corposant.
santidade, *s.f.* holiness, sanctity, saintliness; *Sua Santidade,* His Holiness *(o papa).*
santificação, *s.f.* sanctification; sanctifying.
santificador, *s.m.* sanctifier; *adj.* sanctifying.
santificante, *adj.* sanctfying.
santificar, *v.t.* to sanctify, to hallow, to glorify, to purify *(de pecado).*
santificável, *adj.* sanctifiable.
santimónia, *s.f.* sanctimony, affected piety, hypocrisy.

santimonial, *adj.* sanctimonious, hipocritic.

santíssimo, *adj.* most holy; *o Santíssimo Sacramento*, the Blessed *(Santo)* Sacrament.

santo, *adj.* holy, saintly, sacred, pure, pious; *s.m.* saint; very virtuous person. 1) *Santo Padre*, the Holy Father, the Pope. 2) *santo padroeiro*, patron saint. 3) *um santo homem*, a very good man. 4) *remedio santo*, wonderful remedy. 5) *santo Deus!*, good Heavens. 6) *dia santo*, holyday. 7) *o Santo Ofício*, the Holy Office; Inquisition. 8) *Espírito Santo*, the Holy Ghost, Holy Spirit.

santo-e-senha, *s.m.* watchword, catchword, password.

santola, *s.f.* spider-crab.

santolina, *s.f.* lavender-cotton, cotton-weed.

santonina, *s.f.* santonica; *(med.)* santonina.

santoral, *s.m.* sermon-book; hagiology.

santuário, *s.m.* sanctuary; shrine; Holy of Holies; holy place; a place of refuge.

sanzala, *s.f.* plantation slave quarters, hamlet of negroes.

são, *adj.* sound, hale, healthy, vigorous, wholesome; perfect, undamaged; reliable, judicious; true, right, honest; *são como um pêro*, as sound as a bell.

sapa, *s.f.* shovel; sap, sapping, undermining.

sapador, *s.m.* sapper.

sapal, *s.m.* toad-hole; marsh, moor.

sapar, *v.t.* to sap, to undermine; to subvert.

sapata, *s.f.* leather slipper; footing of a wall; low shoe.

sapatada, *s.f.* blow *(com um sapato)*; slap.

sapataria, *s.f.* shoemaker's *(loja)*; shoe shop.

sapateada, *s.f.* stamping *(com os pés)*

sapateado, *s.m.* tap-dance, clog-dancing.

sapatear, *v.t.* to keep time *(com o pé)*; to stamp; to tap-dance.

sapateiro, *s.m.* shoemaker; cobbler; shoeseller.

sapatilha, *s.f.* slipper.

sapato, *s.m.* shoe. 1) *sapato de baile*, pump. 2) *sapato de defunto*, doubtful promise, dead-man's shoe. 3) *sapato de salto alto (baixo)*, high (low) heeled shoe. 4) *sapato de ténis*, sneaker. 5) *sapato de polimento (verniz)*, patent leather shoe. 6) *andar com a pedra no sapato*, to smell a rat. 7) *fazer gato-sapato*, to make light of, to make sport of.

sapatorra, sapatorro, *s.f., s.m.* clumsy shoe, barlike shoe.

sape!, *interj.* scat!; scram!, shoo!

sapeca, *s.f.* Chinese coin.

sápia, *s.f.* fir-tree *(bot.)*

sápido, *adj.* sapid, savoury, palatable.

sapiência, *s.f.* sapience; wisdom, knowledge, learning.

sapiencial, *adj.* sapiential.

sapiente, *adj.* sapient, wise, scholary, learned.

sapientemente, *adv.* wisely.

sapinhos, *s.m. pl.* aphtae.

sapo, *s.m.* toad.

sapo-concho, *s.m.* fresh water tortoise.

saponáceas, *s.f. pl.* Saponaceae.

saponáceo, *adj.* saponaceous.

saponária, *s.f.* soapwort.

saponificação, *s.f.* saponification.

saponificador, *adj.* saponifying.

saponificar, *v.t.* to saponify.

saponificável, *adj.* saponifiable.

saporífico, *adj.* saporific, saporous.

saprófago, *s.m.* saprophagan; *adj.* saprophagous.

saprófilo, *adj.* saprophyte, saprophilous.

saprófito, *s.m.* saprophyte.

saprógeno, *adj.* saprogenic, saprogenous.

sapudo, *adj.* thickset; fat.

saque, *s.m.* sack, plunder, pillage; *(com)* draft.

saqueador, *s.m.* plunderer, pillager.

saquear, *v.t.* to sack, to plunder, to pillage; to devastate, to despoil.

saqueio, *s.m.* sack, plunder, pillage.

saquitel, *s.m.* satchel, samll bag.

saquitéu, saquito, *s.m.* ver saquitel.

sarabanda, *s.f.* saraband (Spanish dance); reprehension, reprimand, rebuke; tumult, riot, agitation.

sarabandear, *v.i.* to dance the saraband.

sarabatana, *s.f.* horn, speaking trumpet, megaphone; Indian blow-gun.

sarabulhento, *adj.* full of burs; full of pimples, pimply, rough, rugged.

sarabulho, *s.m.* lump; pimple, blister, blotch.

saracoteador, *s.m.* waddler.

saracotear, *v.t.* to move, to shake, to stir; to waddle.

saracoteio, *s.m.* shaking.

saragoça, *s.f.* brown woolen cloth.

saragoçano, *s.m.* native of Saragossa; *adj.* referring to Saragossa.

saraiva, *s.f.* hail, hailstone.

saraivada, *s.f.* hail-strom.

saraivar, *v.i.* to hail.

saraiveiro, *s.m.* hail-storm.
saramago, *s.m.* wild rape, wild radish.
saramântiga, *s.f.* salamander.
sarambeque, *s.m.* a negro dance.
sarampão, *s.m.* attack of measles.
sarampelo, *s.m.* rubella.
sarampo, *s.m.* measles.
saramposo, *adj.* measled, measly.
sarampanel, *s.m.* baskethandle arch, three-centered arch.
sarapilheira, *a.f.* sarp-cloth.
sarapintado, *adj.* freckled, spotted, speckled; with small spots or specks.
sarapintar, *v.t.* to speckle, to spot; to paint vary-coloured; to dot.
sarar, *v.t.* to cure, to heal, to restore to health; to recover *(de)*
sarau, *s.m.* evening-party, evening concert.
sarça, *s.f.* bramble, bush, thorn.
sarçal, *s.m.* bushy place, brier patch.
sarcasmo, *s.m.* sarcasm, taunt, ironical remark; bitter irony, cutting jest.
sarcástico, *adj.* sarcastic, taunting, ironical, cutting, sardonic, biting.
sarcocarpo, *s.m.* sarcocarp.
sarcocele, *s.m.* *(med.)* sarcocele.
sarcófago, *s.m.* sarcophagus, stone-coffin; *adj.* sarcophagous; flesh-eating.
sarcoma, *s.m.* sarcoma *(pl. sarcomata).*
sarcomatose, *s.f.* sarcomatosis.
sarcomatoso, *adj.* sarcomatous.
sarçoso, *adj.* thorny, bushy, brambled, brambly.
sarda, *s.f.* freckle.
sardanisca, *s.f.* wall lizard.
sardão, *s.m.* lizard, green, lizard.
sardento, *adj.* freckled, freckly.
sardinha, *s.f.* sardine. 1) *como sardinha em canastra,* packed like sardines. 2) *chegar a brasa à sua sardinha,* to bring grist to the mill. 3) *sardinha em conserva,* tinned sardines.
sardinheira, *s.f.* sardine-seller; geranium *(bot).*
sardinheiro, *s.m.* sardine-seller.
sárdio, *s.m.* carnelian, sard.
sardo, *adj., s.m.* Sardinian.
sardónico, *adj.* sardonic, sneering, scornful, derisive.
sardonisca, *s.f. ver "sardanisca".*
sardoso, *adj.* freckled.
sargaça, *s.f.* rock-rose.
sargaçal, *s.m.* plantation of rock-roses.
sargaceiro, *s.m.* sea-weed gatherer.

sargaço, *s.m.* sea-weed, gulf weed, sargasso.
sargento, *s.m.* sergeant.
sargo, *s.m.* sea-bream, sargus.
sarilhar, *v.t.* ver ensarilhar.
sarilho, *s.m.* winder; reel; rack. 1) *sarilho de armas,* arm-stack; *(pop)* mess, confusion, disorder; bustle, agitation. 2) *andar num sarilho,* to be always in motion. 3) *que sarilho!,* here is a pretty kettle of fish. 4) *meter-se em sarilhos,* to get into a mess.
sarja, *s.f.* serge.
sarjado, *adj.* scarified, serge-like.
sarjador, *s.m.* scarifier; *adj.* scarifying.
sarjadura, *s.f.* scarification, scarifying.
sarjar, *v.t.* to scarify; to twill.
sarjeta, *s.f.* gutter.
sármata, *adj., s.* Sarmatian.
sarmentáceas, *s.f. pl.* Sarmentaceae.
sarmentáceo, *adj.* sarmentose, sarmentous.
sarmento, *s.m.* wine-twig, or shoot.
sarmentoso, *adj.* sarmentose, sarmentous.
sarna, *s.f.* itch; *(pop)* bore, tiresome person.
sarnento, *adj.* itchy, mangy.
sarnoso, *adj.* ver sarnento.
sarrabiscar, *v.t.* to scrawl, to scribble.
sarrabisco, *s.m.* scrawl; scribbling.
sarrabulhada, *s.f.* confusion, uproar, tumult, disorder.
sarrabulho, *s.m.* coagulated blood of a hog; *(pop)* uproar, confusion.
sarraceno, *adj., s.m.* Saracen.
sarrafaçal, *s.m.* botcher, bungler.
sarrafo, *s.m.* lathe, batten, shingle.
sarrafusca, *s.f.* riot, uproar, tumult.
sarrazina, *s.f.* tiresome person.
sarrazinar, *v.t.* to bore, to importune; to nag.
sarreiro, *s.m.* dealer in argol.
sarrento, *adj.* tartarous; furred.
sarro, *s.m.* tartar; fur *(na língua).*
saruga, *s.f.* beard *(milho).*
Satã, Satanás, Satan, devil, Lucifer.
satânico, *adj.* satanic, diabolical, devilish, infernal.
satanismo, *s.m.* Satanism.
satélite, *s.m.* satellite; *(fig)* hanger-on, henchman, vassal, dependant.
sátira, *s.f.* satire; lampoon, sarcasm.
satiríase, *s.f.* satyriasis.
satírico, *adj.* satirical, satiric, sarcastic; *s.m.* satirist.
satirizar, *v.t.* to satirize, to scoff at; to lampoon.
sátiro, *s.m.* satyr.

satisdação, *s.f.* bail, security, surety.

satisdar, *v.i.* to bail, to put on bail.

satisfação, *s.f.* satisfaction, pleasure; amends, atonement, excuse; payment *(dívidas)*; apologies, explanations.

satisfatoriamente, *adv.* satisfactorily.

satisfatório, *adj.* satisfactory.

satisfazer, *v.t.* to satisfy, to content, to please; to atone.

satisfeito, *adj.* satisfied, pleased, gratified, content, happy, cheeful; fulfilled, met.

sativo, *adj.* sown; planted.

sátrapa, *s.m.* satrap; despot.

satrapia, *s.f.* satrapy.

saturação, *s.f.* saturation.

saturado, *adj.* saturated, full; sick, tired.

saturador, *s.m.* saturator; *adj.* tired.

saturante, *adj.* saturant, saturating; tedious, tiresome.

saturar, *v.t.* to saturate; to satiate; to imbue, to steep.

saturável, *adj.* saturable.

saturnal, *adj.* saturnal.

saturniano, *adj.* Saturnian.

Saturnais, *s.f. pl.* saturnalia, orgy.

saturnino, *adj.* saturnine.

saturnismo, *s.f. pl.* saturnism, plumbism, lead-poisoning.

saturno, *s.m.* Saturn *(planeta);* lead *(metal).*

saudação, *s.f.* salutation; greeting, welcome; a salute.

saudade, *s.f.* regret, sorrow; longing; home-sickness, nostalgia; ardent desire. 1) *ter saudades da terra,* to be homesick. 2) *tenho saudades dela,* I long to see her, I miss her very much.

saudador, *s.m.* saluter; *adj.* saluting.

saudar, *v.t.* to salute, to greet, to bow to.

saudável, *adj.* wholesome, sound, healthy.

saúde, *s.f.* health; toast. 1) *fazer uma saúde,* to propose a toast. 2) *à tua saúde!,* your health!

saudosamente, *adv.* longingly, ardently.

saudosismo, *s.m.* longing for bygone days.

saudosista, *s.* one who longs for the return of former days.

saudoso, *adj.* longing; sorrowful; homesick; of fond memory.

sáurios, *s.m. pl.* Sauria.

saval, *s.m.* trammel.

savana, *s.f.* savannah, prairie.

saveiro, *s.m.* long and narrow fishing-boat; the fisher.

sável, *s.m. (zool)* shad.

saxão, *adj., s.m.* Saxon.

saxátil, *adj.* saxatile, saxicoline.

saxífraga, *s.f.* saxifrage, a rock plant.

saxofone, *s.m.* saxophone *(homem ou instrumento).*

saxofonista, *s.* saxophonist.

saxónio, *s.m., adj.* Saxon.

saxoso, *adj.* stony, abounding with stones, rocky.

sazão, *s.f.* season, time, opportunity, proper time.

sazonação, *s.f.* ripening, seasoning.

sazonado, *adj.* ripe; seasoned.

sazonador, *adj.* ripening, seasoning.

sazonamento, *s.m.* ver sazonação.

sazonar, *v.t.* to mature, to season; to ripen.

sazonável, *adj.* seasonable; productive.

se, *pron.* himself, herself, itself, oneself; yourself, yourselves; themselves; each other, one another; *conj.* if; provided, in case that, though, supposing. 1) *se ao menos,* if only. 2) *se bem que,* even though, although. 3) *como se,* as if.

sé, *s.f.* see, cathedral; *a Santa Sé,* the Holy See.

seara, *s.f.* corn-filed; harvest.

seareiro, *s.m.* tiller, small farmer.

sabáceo, *adj.* sebaceous, fatty; dirty, greasy.

sebastianismo, *s.m.* Sebastianism.

sebastianista, *s.* Sebastianist.

sebe, *s.f.* hedge, fence; *sebe viva,* quickset hedge.

sebenta, *s.f.* lithographed lecture of a professor *(em Coimbra).*

sebentão, *s.m.* dirty fellow.

sebenteiro, *s.m.* student who duplicates lecture-notes *(em Coimbra).*

sebentice, *s.f.* dirtiness, filthiness.

sebento, *adj.* gresy, dirty.

sebo, *s.m.* tallow, suet, grease.

seborreia, *s.f.* seborrhea.

seborreico, *adj.* seborrheic.

seboso, *adj.* greasy, fatty, suety, tallowish; unclean, filthy.

seca, *s.f.* drying; dryness, drought; *(fig)* bore, long, boring talk.

secação, *s.f.* drying, siccation, airing.

secadoiro, *s.m.* drying place.

secador, *s.m.* drier; *adj.* drying.

secadouro, *s.m.* drying place.

secagem, *s.f.* drying; seasoning.

secamente, *adv.* drily, sharply.

secante, *adj.* drying; *(fig)* boring; *s.m.* dryer; *s.f. (geom)* secant.

secar, *v.t.* to dry, to drain; to season; to dry up, to wither, to pine, to languish; to parch.

secativo, *adj.* siccative, disiccant; *s.m.* siccative drug.

secção, *s.f.* section, division; portion; cutting off; department.

seccional, *adj.* sectional.

seccionamento, *s.m.* partition, division.

seccionar, *v.t.* to divide; to cut off; to part, to section.

secessão, *s.f.* secession, separation.

sécia, *s.f.* coquette; gown *(mulheres); (bot.)* china aster.

seco, *adj.* dry, dried, lean, gaunt; withered, parched; hard; barren, rough; cold, sharp, severe.

secreção, *s.f.* secretion.

secreta, *s.f.* silent prayer.

secretamente, *adv.* secretly, privately, in secret.

secretaria, *s.f.* office; secretaryship, clerkship; bureau, department; ministry.

secretária, *s.f.* desk, writing-desk; woman secretary.

secretariado, *s.f.* secretariat; secretaryship, secrerary's department; secretarial staff.

secretarial, *adj.* secretarial.

secretariar, *v.i.* to act as secretary.

secretário, *s.m.* secretary of State, minister of State; *secretário particular,* private secretary.

secreto, *adj.* secret, concealed; reserved; private.

secretor, *adj., s.m.* secretory; secretor.

secretório, *adj.* secretory, secretive *(órgão, glândula).*

sectário, *adj., s.m.* sectarian, partisan, adherent; proselyte.

sectarismo, *s.m.* sectarianism.

sectarista, *s.* sectarianist.

sector, *s.m.* sector *(em todos os sentidos).*

secular, *adj.* secular, temporal, profane, lay; century-old; *s.m.* layman.

secularidade, *s.f.* secularity.

secularismo, *s.m.* secularism.

secularização, *s.f.* secularization.

secularizar, *v.t.* to desecrate *(igreja);* to secularize.

secularmente, *adv.* secularly.

século, *s.m.* century; age; the world; secular life.

secundar, *v.t.* to second, to assist, to aid, to support; to repeat.

secundariamente, *adv.* secondarily.

secundário, *adj.* secondary; subordinate; unimportant, not essential.

secundina, *s.f.* secundine *(bot).*

secundogénito, *s.m.* second son, second-born.

secura, *s.f.* drought, dryness; harshness, sharpness.

seda, *s.f.* silk; hair, bristle.

sedação, *s.f.* sedation, allaying, mitigation *(dor).*

sedaço, *s.m.* boulting-cloth.

sedar, *v.t.* to dress flax; to allay, to assuage, to calm, to mitigate *(dores).*

sedativo, *adj., s.m.* sedative, calmative.

sede, *s.f.* seat; head office, headquarters *(comercial).*

sede, *s.f.* thrist; strong desire, greediness. 1) *matar a sede,* to quench the thrist. 2) *estar com sede,* to be thristy.

sedeiro, *s.m.* flax-comb, hackle, hemp-comb.

sedenho, *s.m.* seton, rowel.

sedentariedade, *s.f.* sedentariness.

sedentário, *adj.* sedentary; stationary, attached to one place.

sedentarismo, *s.m.* sedentarism, sedentary habits.

sedento, *adj.* thristy; eager, greedy.

sedição, *s.f.* sedition, tumult, insurrection, rebellion, mutiny.

sediciosamente, *adv.* seditiously.

sedicioso, *adj.* seditious, rebellious.

sedimentação, *s.f.* sedimentation; subsidence.

sedimentar, *adj.* sedimentary; *v.i.* to form sediment.

sedimentário, *adj.* sedimentary.

sedimento, *s.m.* sediment, settlings, lees, dregs, deposit.

sedimentoso, *adj.* sedimentary, dreggy.

sedoso, *adj.* silken, silky.

sedução, *s.f.* seduction, allurement, enticement, temptation, charm.

sédulo, *adj.* sedulous, diligent, active.

sedutor, *adj.* seducing, alluring, charming, attractive, fascinating; *s.m.* seducer, misleader, enticer; corrupter.

sedutoramente, *adv.* seductively.

seduzir, *v.t.* to seduce, to charm, to allure, to entice, to tempt; to mislead; to corrupt; to deceive.

seduzível, *adj.* seducible.

sega, *s.f.* harvest, harvest-time, reaping-time.

segada, *s.f. ver "sega".*

segadeira, s.f. mower, harvester, reaper, mowing-machine.

segadoiro, adj. ver sagadouro.

segador, s.m. mower, reaper, harvester.

segadouro, adj. harvesting; ripe, fit to be mowed.

segadura, s.f. reaping, reaping-time.

segar, v.t. to mow, to reap.

sege, s.f. two-wheeled chaise, coach, carriage.

segeiro, s.m. coach-maker; driver.

segmentação, s.f. segmentation.

segamentar, v.t. to segment; adj. segmental, segmentary.

segmentário, adj. segmentary.

segmento, s.m. segment.

segradar, v.t. to whisper, to murmur; to confide, to tell in secret.

segredeiro, adj. confiding, telling secrets; whispering.

segredo, s.m. secret; secrecy; confidence; whisper; safe code; recess.

segregação, s.f. segregation, separation; secretion.

segregar, v.t. to segregate, to separate, to isolate; to secrete.

segregativo, adj. segregative; partitive.

seguida, s.f. em, de seguida, soon after, afterwards.

seguidamente, adv. afterwards; continually, consecutively.

seguido, adj. followed; continuous, without interruption; connected.

seguidor, s.m. follower, adherent, sectarian.

seguimento, s.m. following, pursuing; attendance; continuation, sequence.

seguinte, adj. following, nest, subsequent; s. the nest, the following.

seguir, v.t. to follow; to attend; to pursue; to imitate; to watch, to observe; to walk along; to proceed, to go on; to adhere to, to side with; to engage in (profissão). 1) seguir depressa, to hurry on. 2) seguir o exemplo, to take example of. 3) seguir o rasto, to dog. 4) a seguir, following, next. 5) seguir a carreira de, to take up. 6) quem segue?, who is next?. 7) que se segue?, what next?

segunda, s.f. (mús.) second.

segunda-feira, s.f. Monday.

segundanista, s. second-year student (universidade).

segundo, adj. second; adv. secondly, in second place; prep. according to.

segundogénito, s.m. second son, second-born.

segundo-piloto, s.m. second mate.

segundo-tenente, s.m. second lieutenant.

segurado, adj. insured, assured; s.m. policy holder.

segurador, s.m. insurer, underwriter; adj. insuring.

seguramente, adv. surely, certainly; safely.

segurança, s.f. assurance; safety, security, freedom from danger; protection, safeguard; guarantee, warranty.

segurar, v.t. to seize, to seize upon; to hold; to secure; to assure; to insure, to underwrite, to guarantee, to warrant; to fasten, to bind; to catch, to grasp; to protect, to support.

segurável, adj. insurable.

segurelha, s.f. savory (bot).

segureza, seguridade, s.f. ver segurança.

seguro, adj. safe; steady; trustworthy; solid; protected; firm; cautious, prudent: s.m. insurance, assurance. 1) seguro de vida, life insurance. 2) apólice de seguro, insurance policy. 3) o seguro morreu de velho, prevention is better than cure.

seio, s.m. breast, bosom; womb; midst, heart; belly.

seira, s.f. rush basket; frail; wicker basket.

seirão, s.m. big basket.

seis, num. six; seis avos, the sixth.

seiscentismo, s.m. style and school of the 17th century.

seiscentista, s. writer of the 17th century; adj. referring to this century.

seiscentos, num. six hundred.

seisdobro, s.m. sextuple.

seita, s.f. sect; party, faction; a denomination.

seiva, s.f. sap (plantas); (fig) force, vigour, energy.

seivoso, adj. sappy, juicy, succulent; vigorous.

seixal, s.m. place full of pebbles.

seixo, s.m. pebble, small stone.

seixoso, adj. pebbly, pebbled, full of pebbles.

seja, interj. be it.

sela, s.f. saddle.

selado, adj. saddled (cavalo); sealed, stamped (carta, ect.).

selador, s.m. saddler; sealer.

seladura, s.f. sadding.

selagem, s.f. sealing, stamping.

selar, v.t. to saddle (cavalo); to seal, to stamp; to close up, to finish; to ratify.

selaria, *s.f.* saddlery, harness-trade; sadller's *(loja).*

selecção, *s.f.* selection, choosing; choice; team *(desporto); selecção manual,* hand-sorting.

seleccionador, *adj.* selecting; *s.m.* selector.

seleccionar, *v.t.* to select, to choose, to pick, to select.

selecta, *s.f.* book of select passages; reading-book; text-book; anthology; reader.

selectividade, *s.f.* selectivity.

selectivo, *adj.* selective.

selecto, *adj.* select; choice; chosen, excellent, fine, prime.

selector, *s.m.* selector.

seleiro, *s.m.* saddler; saddle-maker.

selénio, *s.m.* selenium.

selenita, *s.* selenite.

selenitoso, *adj.* selenitic, selenious.

selenografia, *s.f.* selenography.

selenográfico, *adj.* selenographical.

selenógrafo, *s.m.* selelnographer.

selenologia, *s.f.* selelnology.

selha, *s.f.* wooden vessel; wash tub.

selim, *s.m.* English saddle; saddle *(bicicleta).*

selo, *s.m.* seal; stamp, postage-stamp; label; token, guarantee. 1) *selo branco,* embossed seal or stamp. 2) *selo fiscal,* revenue stamp. 3) *imposto do selo,* stamp-duty. 4) *inutilizar um selo,* to cancel a stamp.

selva, *s.f.* jungle.

selvagem, *adj.* savage; wild; cruel; unsociable; uncivilized, barbaric; rude, brutal, barbarous; *s.* a savage, barbarian.

selvageria, *s.f. ver "selvajaria".*

selvajaria, *s.f.* savageness; savagery, cruelty, brutality, barbarity.

selvático, *adj.* wild, rude, savage; of the woods.

sem, *prep.* without, lacking, wanting, destitute of.

semafórico, *adj., s.m.* semaphoric(al); operator of a semaphore.

semáforo, *s.m.* semaphore.

semana, *s.f.* week. 1) *Semana Santa,* Holy Week. 2) *semana dos nove dias,* a week that will never come to pass or when two Sundays come together. 3) *para a semana,* next week. 4) *a semana passada,* last week.

semana-inglesa, *s.f.* a five-and-a-half days work-week.

semanal, *adj.* weekly; hebdomadal.

semanalmente, *adv.* weekly, by the week.

semanário, *s.m.* weekly, paper, weekly publication.

semântica, *s.f.* semantics, semasiology.

semântico, *adj.* semantic(al).

semasiologia, *s.f.* semasiology.

semasiológico, *adj.* semasiologic(al).

sematologia, *s.f.* sematology.

semblante, *s.m.* countenance, face, mien, appearance, visage, aspect, look, expression.

sem-cerimónia, *s.f.* informality, unconventionality; rudeness, abruptness.

sêmea, *s.f.* wheat-flour; bran; bread of bran.

semeação, *s.f.* sowing, scattering.

semeada, *s.f.* sown field; seeding; seed-time.

semeadeira, *s.f.* ver semeadora.

semeado, *adj.* sown; *(fig)* scattered, spread, strewn *(flores);* beset *(perigos);* spangled *(estrelas).*

semeadoiro, *adj.* ver semeadouro.

semeador, *s.m.* sower; sowing machine; *adj.* sowing.

semeadora, *s.f.* sowing-machine.

semeadouro, *adj.* fit for sowing.

semeadura, *s.f.* sowing, seed to be sown.

semear, *v.t.* to sow; to spread, to scatter, to cast *(sementes);* to disseminate, to propagate, to cover all over; *à mão de semear,* within reach of the hand.

semelhança, *s.f.* likeness, resemblance; similarity, similitude, analogy; *à semelhança de,* in the likeness of; similar to.

semelhante, *adj.* like, similar, alike, resembling; *s.m. pl.* our fellow-creatures; *não fiz semelhante coisa,* I didn't do such a thing.

semelhantemente, *adv.* in like manner, similarly, likewise, in the same way.

semelhar-se, *s.* reflex. to be like, to resemble, to look like, to be similar to.

semelhável, *adj.* similar to, alike.

sémen, *s.m.* sperm, seed, semen.

semente, *s.f.* seed; source, origin, germ.

sementeira, *s.f.* seed-time; land sown; sowing.

sementeiro, *s.m.* seed-bag, seed-basket; sower.

semestral, *adj.* half-yearly, semiannual semestral.

semestralidade, *s.f.* semestral allowance or payment.

semestre, *s.m.* half year, semester.

sem-fim, *s.m.* endless quantity or number or space.

semiaberto, *adj.* half-open, ajar.

semiânime, *adj.* half-dead, lifeless.

semianual, *adj.* semiannual half-yearly, semestral.

semianular, *adj.* semi-circular.

semiautomático, *adj.* semiautomatic.

semibárbaro, *adj.* semibarbarous.

semibreve, *s.f.* semibreve.

semicadáver, *s.m.* half-dead person.

semicerrar, *v.t.* to halfshut.

semicircular, *adj.* semicircular, half-round, semi-circled.

semicírculo, *s.m.* semicircle.

semicircunferência, *s.f.* semicircumference.

semicivilizado, *adj.* halfcivilized.

semiclausura, *s.f.* semiclosure.

semicolcheia, *s.f.* semiquaver.

semiconfuso, *adj.* somewhat confused.

semiconsciente, *adj.* half-conscious.

semiconsoante, *s.f.* semi-consoant.

semicúpio, *s.m.* hip-bath.

semidefunto, *adj.* half-dead.

semideira, *s.m.* path, footway.

semideus, *s.m.* demigod.

semideusa, *s.f.* demigodess.

semidiâmetro, *s.m.* semidiameter.

semieixo, *s.m.* hlaf-axle.

semiesfera, *s.f.* hemisphere.

semiesférico, *adj.* hemispheric.

semifusa, *s.f.* *(mús)* double demisemiquaver.

semi-internato, *s.m.* day-boarding school.

semi-interno, *adj., s.m.* day-boarder.

semimorto, *adj.* half-dead.

seminação, *s.f.* semination, sowing.

seminal, *adj.* seminal; productive.

seminário, *s.m.* seminary; training college for the Roman Catholic priesthood.

seminarista, *s.m.* seminarist.

seminífero, *adj.* seminiferous.

semínima, *s.f.* crotchet.

seminu, *adj.* half, naked.

seminudez, *s.f.* semi-nudity, half-nakedness.

semioficial, *adj.* semi-official.

semiografia, *s.f.* semiography.

semiográfico, *adj.* semiographical.

semiologia, *s.f.* semiology; symptomatology; semantics.

semiológico, *adj.* semiological; semiotical; symptomatic.

semiparente, *adj.* kindred, distantly related.

semipenunbra, *s.f.* half shadow.

semipútrido, *adj.* semirotten, half-putrid.

semi-recta, *s.f.* half a straight line.

semi-roto, *adj.* half-broken, half-ragged.

semi-selvagem, *adj.* semisavage, brutal; very rude.

semita, *s.* Semite, Jew; *adj.* Semitic; Jewish.

semítico, *adj.* Semitic; Jewish.

semitismo, *s.m.* Semitism.

semitom, *s.m.* demi-tone, semitone, half--note.

semitónico, *adj.* semi-tonic.

semitrágico, *adj.* almost tragic.

semitranquilo, *adj.* neither tranquil nor agitated.

semitransparência, *s.m.* semitransparency.

semitransparente, *adj.* semitransparent.

semiverdade, *s.f.* half-truth.

semivivo, *adj.* half-alive.

semivocálico, *adj.* semivocal.

semivogal, *s.f.* semivowel.

sem-luz, *s.* blind person.

sem-nome, *s.* anonymous person.

sem-número, *s.m.* a great number innumerable quantity.

sêmola, *s.f.* semolina, semola.

semovente, *adj.* self-moving, self-moved; *bens semoventes,* movables, movable property.

sem-par, *adj.* peerless, unequalled, matchless, unique, incomparable, unrivalled.

sempiterno, *adj.* sempiternal, everlasting, endless; perpetual.

sempre, *adv.* always, still, ever; evermore, forever; constantly, continually, really, in fact. 1) *sempre que,* whenever. 2) *como sempre,* as always, as usual. 3) *história de sempre,* same old story. 4) *nem sempre,* not always. 5) *para todo o sempre,* for ever and ever. 6) *quase sempre,* nearly always. 7) *de uma vez para sempre,* once and for all. 8) *sempre vais?,* are you really going?

sempre-noiva, *s.f.* knot-grass, knot-weed *(bot).*

sem-razão, *s.f.* wrong, injustice.

sem-sabor, sem-sal, *adj.* insipid, tasteless.

sem-segundo, *adj.* unique, matchless.

sem-termo, *s.m.* endless period.

sem tir-te nem guar-te, *loc. adv.* suddenly, wilhour further ado.

sem-vergonha, *s.* chamelessness, shameless person.

sena, *s.f.* six *(cartas).*

senado, s.m. senate; senate-house.

senador, s.m. senator.

senão, s.m. fault, defect; prep. but, except; adv. save, except, else, otherwise; conj. unless, else. 1) *ela não faz senão chorar*, she does nothing but cry. 2) *não há bela sem senão*, there is no rose withour a thorn.

senário, adj. senary, group of six.

senatorial, adj. senatorial.

senatório, adj. senatporial.

senda, s.f. trail, track, path, way.

sendeiroce, s.f. foolishness.

sendeiro, s.m. jade, worn-out horse, sorry nag; despicable person.

senectude, s.m. old age, senility, decrepitude.

senegalês, s.m., adj. Senegalese.

senescal, s.m. seneschal.

sengo, adj. intellignet, wise, witty; grave, judicious, sly.

senha, s.f. watchword, password, sign; check *(teatro);* voucher.

senhor, s.m. lord; master, owner; sir, mister *(seguido do nome); receber o Senhor*, to receive Holy Communion.

senhora, s.f. lady, mistress, miss.

senhoraça, s.f. well-developed woman, a would-be grande dame.

senhoreador, s.m. dominator.

senhorear, v.t. to domineer, to subject, to master; to control, to dominate.

senhoria, s.f. lordship, ladyship; landlady; *Vossa Senhoria* Your Lordship.

senhorial, adj. mannorial.

senhoril, adj. elegant, distinguished, ladylike, grave, majestic.

senhorinha, s.f. young unmarried girl.

senhorio, s.m. dominion, seigniory; landlord.

senhorita, s.m. young lady.

senil, adj. senile, aged, worn-out, old.

senilidade, s.f. senility, old age.

sénior, adj. senior, older elder.

seno, s.m. sine.

sensabor, adj. insipid, tasteless; s. dull person.

sensaborão, s.m. bore, insipid person.

sensaboria, s.m. tastelessness; insipidity, dullness, nuisance, displeasure; trouble.

sensação, s.f. sensation; feeling; a sensational event; impression, perception; excitement, thrilling experience.

sensacional, adj. sensational, thrilling; remarkable.

sensacionalismo, s.m. sensationalism.

sensatamentel, adv. wisely, with sense.

sensatez, s.m. sensibleness; wisdom, good sense, good judgment.

sensato, adj. sensible, discreet, wise, judicious, prudent, levelheaded.

sensibilidade, s.m. sensibility; sensitiveness, delicacy, susceptibility; sensitivity *(rádio).*

sensibilização, s.f. sensitization.

sensibilizador, adj. touching, moving, affecting; s.m. sensitizer.

sensibilizante, adj. ver sensibilizador.

sensibilizar, v.t. to affect, to touch, to move; to sensitize.

sensitiva, s.f. sensitive plant.

sensitivo, adj. sensitive, susceptible, impressible, tender.

sensível, adj. sensitive, tender, impressionable; perceptible, appreciable; compassionate, tender, touchy.

sensivelmente, adj. visibly, perceptibly.

senso, s.m. sense, reason, wisdom, judgment, soundness.

sensorial, adj. sensorial.

sensório, adj. sensorial, sensory; s.m. sensorium.

sensual, adj. sensual, licentious, luxurious, libidinous.

sensualidade, s.m. sensuality, lewdness.

sensualismo, s.m. sensualism.

sensualista, s., adj. sensualist.

sensualizar, v.t. to sensualize.

sentar, v.t. to seat, to place; *sentar-se*, to sit down, to take a seat.

sentença, s.f. sentence; decision, judgment, opinion; verdict, saying, proverb, maxim. 1) *cada cabeça sua sentença*, everyone to his own taste. 2) *dar uma sentença*, to pass sentence or judgment.

sentenciado, adj. sentenced, judged, condemned.

sentenciador, s.m. sentencer, judge.

sentenciar, v.t. to sentence; to doom; to pass judgment upon; to condemn, to judge.

sentenciosamente, adv. sententiously.

sentencioso, adj. sententious, concise, pithy; cocksure.

sentidamente, adv. painfully, feelingly, resentfully.

sentido, adj. sorry, grieved; hurt, offended, sorrowful, sad, shocked; s.m. sense; meaning; direction; attention; heed; purpose, intent; good sense, judgment.

sentimental, *adj.* sentimental, emotional, tender.hearted, romantic; *caso sentimental*, a love affair.

sentimentalidade, *s.f.* sentimentality.

sentimentalismo, *s.m.* sentimentalism, emotionalism.

sentimentalista, *adj., s.* sentimentalist.

sentimentalizar, *v.t.* to sentimentalize.

sentimento, *s.m.* sentiment, sensibility; opinion; feeling, sense; *(pl.)* condolences.

sentina, *s.m.* latrine, lavatory, water-closet; dirty place.

sentinela, *s.f.* sentinel, sentry. 1) *de sentinela*, on sentry-duty, on duty, on guard. 2) *render a sentinela*, to relieve guard.

sentir, *s.m.* sentiment, feeling; *v.t.* to feel, to be conscious of, to be sensible of; to foresee; to be sorry for; to know, to undersatnd, to appreciate; to feel offended; to suffer, to be impressed with. 1) *sentir-se*, to be resent, to take offense. 2) *sentir-se à vontade*, to feel at home. 3) *sentir a falta de*, to miss *(alguém)*.

senzala, *s.f.* plantation slave quarters.

sépala, *s.f.* sepal.

sepalóide, *adj.* sepaloid.

separação, *s.f.* separation; disjunction; divorce.

separadamente, *adv.* separately.

separado, *adj.* separate; apart; divided, disjoined, cut, dissociated.

separador, *adj.* separating; *s.m.* separator *(leite)*.

separar, *v.t.* to separate, to disunite; to sever, to divide, to cut up; to segregate; to sort; to disintegrate; to part from; *separar-se de*, to part with.

separata, *s.f.* offprint; reprint.

separatismo, *s.m.* separartism.

separatista, *s. adj.* separartist.

separativo, *adj.* separative.

separatório, *adj.* separatory.

separável, *adj.* separable, detachable; partible.

sépia, *s.f.* sepia

septena, *s.f.* sevem-lined stanza.

septenal, *adj.* septennial.

septenário, *s.m.* septennary.

septénio, *s.m.* septennium.

septênviro, *s.m.* septemvir.

septicemia, *s.m.* septicaemia.

septicida, *s.f.* septicidal.

séptico, *adj.* septic(al), not aeseptic.

septiforme, *adj.* septiform.

septil, *adj.* septile.

septissilano, *s.m.* septisyllable.

septo, *s.m. (anat)* septum.

septuagenário, *adj.* septuagenary; *s.m.* septuagenarian.

Septuagésima. *s.m.* Septuagesima.

septuagésimo, *adj.* seventieth.

septuplicar, *v.t.* to septuple.

séptulo, *adj., s.m.* sevenfold, septuple.

sepulcral, *adj.* sepulchral, funereal, gloomy, ghastly.

sepulcro, *s.m.* sepulchre, grave, tomb.

sepultado, *adj.* buried; hidden.

sepultador, *s.m.* grave-digger or maker.

sepultamento, *s.m.* burying.

sepultar, *v.t.* to bury, to entomb, to inter; to cover up; to hide, to conceal.

sepulto, *adj.* buried.

sepultura, *s.f.* tomb, grave, resting-place.

sequaz, *s.m.* follower, partisan, adherent.

sequeira, *s.f.* dry land.

sequeiro, *adj.* dry, unirrigated, arid.

sequela, *s.f.* sequel, consequence, result; band, gang.

sequência, *s.f.* sequence, succession, continuation, continuity, series.

sequente, *adj.* sequent, following, subsequent.

sequer, *adv.* at least, even, so much as; 19 *nem sequer*, not even, not so much as; 2) *nem sequer me viu*, he didn't even see me.

sequestração, *s.f.* sequestration, kidnapping.

sequestrador, *s.m.* sequestrator.

sequestrar, *v.t.* to sequester, to set apart, to isolate, to seclude; to confiscate, to seize.

sequestro, *s.m.* sequestration; seizure *(propriedade)*; seclusion, isolation.

sequidão, *s.f.* dryness; frigidity, indifference, unconcern.

sequioso, *adj.* thirsty; thirsting; eager, greedy, avid.

séquito, *s.m.* suite, train, attendance, retinue, entourage.

ser, *s.m.* being; nature; essence; creature; existence; *v.i.* to be, to exist; to come to pass, to happen; to cost.

seráfico, *adj.* sephic, angelic.

serafim, *s.m.* seraph.

serandar, *v.i.* to work at night.

serão, *s.m.* evening; evening-party; night work; overtime.

serapilheira, *s.f.* sackcloth, burlap.

sereia, *s.f.* siren, mermaid; foghorn; hooter; steam-whistle.

serenamente, *adv.* quietly, serenely, calmly.

serenar, *v.t.* to calm, to quiet, to make serene, to pacify; to clear up; to become serene, to get calm.

serenata, *s.f.* serenade.

serenidade, *s.f.* serenity, tranquility, calmness; composure; self-control.

serenim, *s.m.* evening-party; ancient ladies garmant; old Portuguese song.

sereno, *adj.* serene, calm, placid, tranquil, cool, undisturbed; still, peaceful; bright, unclouded; *s.m.* night-dew, mist; open-air, out-of-doors.

seresma, *s.f.* hag, useless woman, indolent woman.

seriação, *s.f.* seriation, arrangment in series; classification.

seriamente, *adv.* seriously, really.

seriar, *v.t.* to seriate, to arrange in series; to order, to file.

sericícola, *adj.* sericicultural; *s.* sericiculturist, breeding silkworms.

sericicultor, *s.m.* sericicultutist.

sericicultura, *s.f.* sericiltuture.

sérico, *adj.* silken, soft as silk.

sericultor, *s.m.* ver "sericicultor".

sericultura, *s.f.* ver "sericicultura".

série, *s.f.* series; order; succession; course, run, train; sequence, row; *produção em série,* mass production.

seriedade, *s.f.* seriousness; integrity; gravity, solemnnity; sternness.

serigaria, *s.f.* silk-factory.

serigueiro, *s.m.* silkman, lace-maker or seller.

seringa, *s.f.* syringe.

seringação, *s.f.* syringing.

seringada, *s.f.* a squirt; bore.

seringadela, *s.f.* syringing.

seringador, *s.m.* who syringes; bore.

seringal, *s.m.* stand of rubber-trees.

seringar, *v.t.* to syringe; to importune, to bore, to annoy.

seringueira, *s.f.* rubber-tree.

seringueiro, *s.m.* rubber-gatherer, exploiter of a rubber plantation.

sério, *adj.* serious, earnest, sober, grave, thoughtful; honest, trust-worthy, reliable; *adv.* really, truly, seriously. 1) *é sério,* it's no joke. 2) *tomar a sério,* to take to heart.

sermão, *s.m.* sermon, preach; tedious harrangue; reprimand; *pregar um sermão,* to give a lecture.

semonário, *s.m.* sermon-book.

seroar, *v.i.* to work in the evening, to burn the midnight oil, to work late, to sit up late, to work.

serôdio, *adj.* tardy, late.

serosa, *s.f.* serosa.

serosidade, *s.f.* serosity.

seroso, *adj.* serous, watery.

seroterapia, *s.f.* serum-therapy.

serpão, *s.m.* wild thyme *(bot.).*

serpe, *s.f.* serpent *(poét.).*

serpeante, *adj.* creeping, winding, coiling, bending, twisting, meandering.

serpear, *v.i.* to meander, to wind about, to turn, to twist, to serpentine; to crawl *(como uma cobra).*

serpejante, *adj.* ver sepeante.

serpejar, *v.i.* ver serpear.

serpentária, *s.f.* serpentaria, snake-root.

serpentário, *s.m.* secretary-bird, serpent-eater.

serpente, *s.f.* snake, serpent; venenous person.

sepenteante, *adj.* winding, twisting.

serpentear, *v.i.* to serpentine, to twist, to wind, to meander, to turn.

serpentina, *s.f.* branched candle-stick, chandelier; carnival paper ribbon, serpentine; dragon-wort *(bot)*; girandole.

serpentino, *adj.* serpentine, twisting, winding, meandering, tortuous; serpent-form.

serpete, *s.m.* pruning-knife.

sepilho, sepol, *s.m.* ver "serpão".

serra, *s.f.* saw; ridge of mountains, mountain. 1) *serra de fita,* band-saw. 2) *ir à serra,* to take umbrage, to get huffed, to become angry.

serração, *s.f.* saw-mill; sawing.

serradela, *s.f.* bird's foot, serradella.

serrador, *s.m.* sawyer.

serradura, *s.f.* sawing; sawdust.

serragem, *s.f.* sawing *(o acto).*

serralha, *s.f.* sowthistle.

serralharia, *s.f.* locksmith's, metal-worker's or mechanic's worshop.

serralheiro, *s.m.* locksmith; metal-worker; mechanic.

serralho, *s.m.* seraglio; harem; brothel.

serrana, *s.f.* mountain dweller *(mulher)*; rustic, simple woman; country dance.

serrania, *s.f.* ridge of mountains, cordillera, chain of mountains.

serranice, *s.f.* custom of a mountaineer.

serrano, *s.m.* mountaineer, highlander;

countryman; peasant; *adj.* mountainous, rustic.

serrar, *v.t.* to saw; to saw off; *serrar de cima,* to be on the top, to call the tune.

serraria, *s.f.* sawer's frame; sawmill.

serrazina, *s.* importunity, bore; nagger, pesterer, to harp on the same string.

serrazinar, *v.i.* to bore, to importune; to nag, to pester, to annoy.

serrear, *v.t.* to serreate, to notch; to make saw-toothed.

sérreo, *adj.* saw-toothed, sawlike, serriform.

serreta, *s.f.* samll saw; hillock.

serridênteo, *adj.* serrated, toothed.

serrilha, *s.f.* milled rim; bridle-bir.

serrilhado, *adj.* serrated, milled.

serrilhador, *s.m.* milling machine.

serrilhar, *v.t.* to mill, to rim, to knurl.

serrim, *s.m.* sawdust.

serro, *s.m.* hillock, knoll.

serrotar, *v.t.* to cut with a hand-saw.

serrote, *s.m.* hand-saw.

sertã, *s.f.* frying-pan.

setanejo, *s.m.* inlander; backwoodsman; rude; rough, rustic; from the back-country.

sertão, *s.m.* back-woods; bush; hinterland, back-country, wilderness; remote interior.

sérum, *s.m.* serum, whey.

serva, *s.f.* servant; woman-slave; attendant.

servente, *s.* servant; under-cook; hodman; helper.

serventia, *s.f.* service, use, utility, usefulness; servitude; passageway, entrance.

serventuário, *s.m.* servant, deputy, substitute.

serviçal, *adj.* serviceable, officious, useful, helpful, willing, obliging; *s.* servant.

serviço, *s.m.* service, duty; work, occupation, employment; course, set *(copos, pratos, etc.).* 1) *serviço religioso,* divine service. 2) *serviço obrigatório,* compulsory service. 3) *estar de serviço,* to be on duty. 4) *lindo serviço!,* fine job!

servidão, *s.f.* servitude; slavery, bondage; right of passage.

servido, *adj.* served; worn, used. 1) *como Deus é servido* as God wills. 2) *é servido de almoçar connosco?,* will you join us for lunch?

servidor, *s.m.* servant; servitor; attendant; *servidor do Estado,* civil servant.

servil, *adj.* servile; slavish; abject.

servilismo, *s.m.* servility, subservience.

servilmente, *adv.* servilely; basely.

sérvio, *adj., s.m.* Serb, Serbian.

servir, *v.t.* to serve, to attend on, to wait upon; to help *(à mesa);* to be useful; to fit, to suit. 1) *servir-se,* to help oneself *(à mesa);* to make use of. 2) *servir à mesa,* to wait at table. 3) *servir um cliente,* to attend a customer. 4) *andar a servir,* to be in service. 5) *não servir de nada,* to be of no use, no good. 6) *servir de lição,* to serve as a lesson.

servitas, *s.m.pl.* Servites *(ordem religiosa).*

servitude, *s.f.* servitude.

servo, *s.m.* servant; slave; serf.

sésamo, *s.m.* sesame *(planta);* a key to a mistery.

sesamóide, sesamóideo, *adj.* sesamoid *(cartilagem).*

sesgo, *adj.* biased, sloped, on a slant; twisted.

sesma, *s.f.* sixth of anything.

sesmar, *v.t.* to portion, to divide land.

sesmaria, *s.f.* division of abandoned lands; allotment.

sesmeiro, *s.m.* distributor of uncultivated lands.

sesmo, *s.m.* uncultivated land for distribution; sixth of anything.

sesquiáltera, *s.f. (mús)* sesqualter, a perfect fifth.

sesquióxido, *s.m.* sesquioxide.

sessão, *s.f.* session; meeting, sitting; performance *(cinema).* 1) *abrir a sessão,* to open the session. 2) *encerrar a sessão,* to close the meeting. 3) *adiar a sessão,* to adjourn the meeting. 4) *estar em sessão,* to be in session, to be sitting. 5) *suspender a sessão,* to recess the meeting.

sessenta, *num.* sixty.

séssil, *adj.* sessile *(bot., zool.).*

sesta, *s.f.* siesta, afternoon nap; *dormir a sesta,* to take a nap *(depois do almoço).*

sestérco, *s.m.* sestertium, sesterce *(moeda romana).*

sestro, *s.m.* fate, lot; humour, fancy, destiny, fortune; bad custom; vice; *adj.* left, sinister.

seta, *s.f.* arrow, dart.

setada, *s.m.* arrowshot, arroa wound or thrust.

sete, *num.* seven.

setear, *v.t.* to wound, to shoot at.

setecentismo, *s.m.* style or school of the writers of the 18th century.

setecentista, *s., adj.* writer of the 18th century; referring to the 18th century.

setecentos, *num.* seven hundred.

sete-e-meio, *s.m.* a card game.

sete-estrelo, *s.m.* the Pleiads, the little bear *(pop).*

seteira, *s.f.* loophole.

seteiro, *s.m.* archer, bowman.

Setembro, *s.m.* September.

sete-mês, sete-mesinho, *adj.* born in the seventh month of pregnancy.

setenta, *num.* seventy.

setentrião, *s.m.* the north; the north wind; North Pole.

setentrional, *adj.* northern, from the north, septentrional.

sétimo, *num.* seventh.

seu, *adj.* his *(dele);* her *(dela);* its *(neutro);* their *(deles, delas);* one's *(indeterminado);* your *(vosso); pron.* his, hers, yours, theirs; *ter de seu,* to be well-off.

sevandija, *s.* contemptible person; vermin, parasite.

sevandijaria, *s.f.* sevility.

sevandijar-se, *s.* refle. to cringe, to fawn, to crawl.

severamente, *adv.* harshly, severely.

severidade, *s.f.* severity, harshness, rigour, inflexibility.

severo, *adj.* severe, grave, stern, strict; harsh, stringent; austere, rigorous, rigid; accurate, exact.

sevícia, *s.f.* ill-treatment, abuse, cruelty *(geralmente plural).*

seviciar, *v.t.* to ill-treat, to treat cruelly, to mal-treat.

sevilhano, *adj., s.m.* Sevillian.

sexagenário, *adj., s.m.* sexagerarian.

sexagésima, *s.f.* Sexagesima Sunday.

sexagesimal, *adj.* sexagesimal.

sexagésimo, *num.* sixtieth.

sexcentésimo, *num.* six hundredth,

sexenal, *adj.* sexennial.

sexénio, *s.m.* sexennian.

sexo, *s.m.* sex. 1) *o belo sexo,* the fair sexo. 2) *o sexo fraco,* the weaker sex.

sexta, *s.f.* sext *(hora canónica);* sixth *(mús);* Friday.

sexta-feira, *s.f.* Friday; *Sexta-Feira Santa,* Good Friday.

sextanista, *s.* a sixth year student.

sextante, *s.m.* sextant *(em todos os sentidos).*

sextavado, *adj.* hexagonal, six-sided.

sexteto, *s.m.* sextette.

sextilha, *s.f.* sextain, six-line satnza.

sextina, *s.f.* sestina.

sexto, *num.* sixth.

sextuplicação, *s.f.* sextuplication.

sextuplicar, *v.t.* to multiply by six.

sêxtuplo, *adj.* sextuple, sixfold.

sexuado, *adj.* with sexual organs.

sexual, *adj.* sexual.

sexualidade, *s.f.* sexuality.

sexualismo, *s.m.* sexualism.

sezão, *s.f.* intermittent fever, ague, malaria, paludism *(geralmente no plural).*

sezoar, *v.i.* to mature, to ripen.

sezonático, *adj.* malarial.

sezonismo, *s.m.* malaria.

si, *s.m. (mús)* si, *pron.* himself; herself, itself; oneself; yourself, yourselves; themselves. 1) *de si para si,* to oneself. 2) *voltar a si,* to come back to one's senses. 3) *fora de si,* besides himself, out of his wits. 4) *ser senhor de si,* to depend upon nobody. 5) *dar sinal de si,* to show signs of life.

sialismo, *s.m.* ptyalism, salivation.

siame, siamês, *adj., s.m.* Siamese.

siba, *s.f.* cuttle-fish.

sibarita, *s.* sybarite; *adj.* sybaritic(al).

sibarítico, *adj.* sybaritic, voluptuous.

sibaritismo, *s.m.* sybaritism.

siberiano, *adj., s.m.* Siberian.

sibila, *s.f.* sibyl; prophetess; witch.

sibilação, *s.f.* sibilation, hissing.

sibilância, *s.f.* sibilance.

sibilante, *adj.* sibilant, hissing, whistling.

sibilar, *v.i.* to hiss, to whistle, to whiz.

sibilino, *adj.* sibylline, mysterious, oracular, enigmatic.

sibilismo, *s.m.* sybillism.

sibilo, *s.m.* hiss, hissing, whistling sound.

sicário, *s.m.* hired murderer, criminal, malefactor.

sicativo, *adj.* siccative, drying substance.

siciliano, *s.m., adj.* Sicilian.

sicofanta, *s.* sycophant; parasite; fawner, flatterer; scoundrel.

sicômoro, *s.m.* sycamore.

sicone, sicónio, *s.m.* syconium *(bot).*

Sicrano, *s.m.* such a one, Mr. So-and-so, indeterminate person.

sicupira, *s.f.* a locust tree.

sideração, *s.f.* sideration, astrological influence; fulmination.

sideral, *adj.* sidereal, starry, astral.

sidéreo, *adj. ver "sideral".*

siderografia, *s.f.* siderography.

siderógrafo, *s.m.* siderographist.

sideroscopia, *s.f.* sideroscopy.

sideroscópio, *s.m.* sideroscope.

siderurgia, *s.f.* siderurgy.

siderúrgico, *adj.* siderurgic, siderurgical.

sidra, *s.f.* cider, apple-wine,

sifão, *s.m.* siphon, trap.

sifiligrafia, *s.f.* syphilography.

sífilis, *s.f.* syphilis.

sifilítico, *adj.* syphilitic.

sifilografia, *s.f.* syphilography.

sifilógrafo, *s.m.* syphilographist.

sigilo, *s.m.* secret, seal.

sigla, *s.f.* sigla, monogram, abbreviature.

sigma, *s.m.* sigma.

sigmático, *adj.* sigmatic.

sigmóide, *adj.* sigmoid.

signa, *s.f.* standard, banner, flag, ensign.

signatário, *s.m.* undersigned; signatory, signer.

significação, *s.f.* signification; meaning; sense.

significado, *s.m.* ver significação.

significante, *adj.* signigicant, significative, expressive, senseful.

significar, *v.t.* to signify; to imply; to mean; to denote; to tell, to express.

significativo, *adv.* significantly.

signo, *s.m.* sign *(do Zodiaco);* fate, destiny *(fig); sob o signo de,* under the spell of.

signo-saimão, *s.m.* Solomon's seal, talisman, amulet.

sílaba, *s.f.* syllable.

silabação, *s.f.* syllabication.

silabada, *s.f.* mispronunciation.

silabar, *v.i.* to syllabize, to spell.,

silabário, *s.m.* syllabary, first reading book.

silábico, *adj.* syllabic.

silabismo, *s.m.* syllabism.

silenciador, *s.m.* silencer, muffler.

silenciar, *v.t.* to remain silent, to be silent; to silence, to reduce to silence.

silêncio, *s.m.* silence, stillness, muteness; oblivion; quiet, calm; secrecy.

silenciosamente, *adv.* silently, in silence.

silencioso, *adj.* silent, still, mute; quiet, noiseless, soundless; voiceless, num; *s.m.* silencer, muffler *(carro).*

silente, *adj.* silent *(poético).*

silepse, *s.f.* syllepsis.

sílex, *s.m.* silex, flint.

sílfide, *s.f.* sylphid, delicate, graceful woman.

silfo, *s.m.* sylph, gnome, elf, air-spirit,

silha, *s.f.* row.

silhal, *s.m.* great number of beehives, apiary.

silhão, *s.m.* sidesaddle *(para senhoras).*

silhar, *s.m.* ashalar.

silharia, *s.f.* ashlar-work.

silhueta, *s.f.* silhouette, outline, figure, profile.

sílica, *s.f.* silica.

silicato, *s.m.* silicate.

silícico, *adj.* silicic.

silificação, *s.f.* silicification.

silificar, *v.t.* to silicify.

silício, *s.m.* silicon.

silicioso, *adj.* silicious, flinty.

silicose, *s.f.* silicosis.

silíqua, *s.f.* silique *(bot.).*

siliquoso, *adj.* siliquous.

silo, *s.m.* silo.

silogismo, *s.m.* syllogism.

silogístico, *adj.* syllogistic.

silogizar, *v.t.* to sillogize.

silúrico, *adj.* Silurian.

silva, *s.f.* bramble, blackberrybush.

silvado, *s.m.* blackberry thicket; hedgerow; brambles.

silvano, *s.m.* sylvan.

silvar, *v.i.* to hiss, to whistle.

silvático, *adj.* wild, savage.

silvedo, *s.m.* thicket of brambles.

silveira, *s.f.* bramble; briar patch.

silvestre, *adj.* wild; woody; silvan.

silvícola, *adj.* silvicolous.

silvicultor, *s.m.* silviculturist; forester.

silvicultura, *s.f.* forestry; silviculture.

silvite, *s.f.* sylvite.

silvo, *s.m.* whistle; hiss.

silvoso, *adj.* brambly, full of briars.

sim, *adv.* yes.

simbiose, *s.f.* symbiosis.

simbiótico, *adj.* symbiotic.

simbólica, *s.f.* symbolics.

simbolicamente, *adv.* symbolically.

simbólico, *adj.* symbolical, symbolic, representative.

simbolismo, *s.m.* symbolism.

simbolista, *s.* symbolist.

simbolístico, *adj.* symbolistic(al).

simbolização, *s.f.* symbolization, representation.

simbolizador, *adj.* symbolizing; *s.m.* symbolizer, symbolist.

simbolizar, *v.t.* to symbolize, to tipify, to represent.

símbolo, *s.m.* symbol, type, emblem, representation; token, sign; mark, note.

simbologia, *s.f.* symbology.

simbológico, *adj.* symbological.

simetria, *s.f.* symmetry; harmony, proportion.

simetricamente, *adv.* symmetrically.

simétrico, *adj.* symmetrical; proportional.

simetrizar, *v.t.* to symmetrize.

simiesco, *adj.* simian, ape-like.

símil, *adj.* like, similar, simile

similar, *adj.* similar, like, alike, resembling.

similaridade, *s.f.* similarity, likeness, resemblance; parallelism, correspondence.

símile, *s.m.* simile, similitude, analogy, comparison.

similitude, *s.f.* similitude, simile, likeness, resemblance, analogy.

símio, *s.m.* ape, monkey.

simonia, *s.f.* simony.

simoníaco, *adj.* simoniacal; *s.m.* simoniac.

simpatia, *s.f.* sympathy, agreement; liking; charm, appeal, attractiveness; affection; admiration.

simpático, *adj.* sympathetic; cahrming, nice; likeable, attractive, pleasing.

simpatizante, *adj.* well-wishing, sympathizing; s. sympathizer, adherent, supporter, follower.

simpatizar, *v.i.* to sympathize; to take a liking to; to feel an affection for; to like.

simpétalo, *adj.* gamopetalous.

simples, *adj.* simple, plain, unpretending; single, unblended; bare, mere; unadorned, artless; naive; clear, intelligible, easy; *s.* a simpleton.

simplesmente, *adv.* simply, merely.

simpleza, *s.f.* simplicity, plainness.

simplicidade, *s.f.* simplicity, plainness, innocence.

simplicíssimo, *adj.* very simple.

simplificação, *s.f.* simplification.

simplificador, *adj.* simplifying; *s.m.* simplifier.

simplificar, *v.t.* to simplify, to make easier.

simplificativo, *adj.* simplificative.

simplificável, *adj.* simplificable.

simplismo, *s.m.* simplism.

simplista, *adj.* simplistic.

simplório, *s.m.* simpleton, fool, silly; greenhorn; *adj.* simple-minded, stupid.

simpósio, *s.m.* symposium.

simulação, *s.f.* simulation, feigning, pretence; disguise; affection.

simulacro, *s.m.* sham, pretence, image; copy, imitation.

simuladamente, *adv.* feignedly, artfully, affected.

simulado, *s.m.* simulator, imitator, faker; *adj.* simulating.

simulador, *v.t.* to simulate, to feign, to sham; to imitate; to assume, to pretend.

simular, *adj.* simulatory.

simulatório, *adv.* simultaneously, all are done, together.

simultaneamente, *s.f.* simultaneity.

simultaneidade, *adj.* simultaneous, concurrent. coincidental.

simultâneo, *adj.* simultaneous, concurrent, coincidental.

simum, *s.m.* simoon.

sina, *s.f.* destiny, fate, lot; 1) *ler a sina,* to tell one's fortune.

sinagoga, *s.f.* synagoge.

sinal, *s.m.* sign, token, mark; proof; signal; mole, patch, spot *(na pele, etc.);* emblem; indication; evidence, vestige; signature; earnest money; presage; seal. 1) *fazer sinal com a mão (chamar),* to beckon. 2) *abrir sinal,* to register one's signature. 3) *em sinal de,* in token of. 4) *sinal horário,* time signal.

sinalar, *v.t.* to mark, to point out, to mention; to signalize.

sinalefa, *s.f.* synalepha.

sinaleiro, *s.m.* signalman; traffic policeman.

sinalização, *s.f.* road-signs.

sinalizar, *v.t.* to signalize, to equip with signs; to mark.

sinapismo, *s.m.* sinapism, mustard plaster.

sinartrose, *s.f.* synarthrosis.

sinceiral, *s.m.* plantation of willows.

sinceiro, *s.m.* willow.

sincelo, *s.m.* icicle.

sinceramente, *adv.* sincerely, frankly, honestly, seriously.

sinceridade, *s.f.* sincerity, ingenuousness, honesty, frankness; simplicity.

sincero, *adj.* sincere; candid, plainhearted; ingenuous, honest; true; real; frank, open.

sincipital, *adj.* relatibe to the sinciput.

sincipúcio, sínciput, *s.m.* sinciput.

sinclinal, *adj.* synclinal.

síncopa, *s.f.* syncopation, syncope.

sincopal, *adj.* syncopal.

sincopar, *v.t.* to syncopate, to syncopize *(música, palavras).*

síncope, *s.f.* syncope, fainting-fit.

sincrético, *adj.* syncretic.

sincretismo, *s.m.* syncreyism.

sincretista, *s.* syncretic, syncretist; *adj.* syncretistic.

sincretizar, *v.t.* to syncretize.

sincrónico, *adj.* synchronous, synchronal, simultaneous.

sincronismo, *s.m.* synchronism.

sincronização, *s.f.* synchronization.

sincronizador, *s.m.* synchronizer.

sincronizar, *v.t.* to synchronize; to time.

síncrono, *adj.* ver sincrónico.

sincronologia, *s.f.* synchronology.

sindáctilo, *adj.* syndactyl.

sindicação, *s.f.* syndication; inquiry.

sindicado, *adj.* syndicated; belonging to a trade union.

sindical, *adj.* syndical.

sindicalismo, *s.m.* syndicalism.

sindicalista, *s.,* *adj.* syndicalist.

sindicalização, *s.f.* syndicalization.

sindicalizar, *v.t.* to syndicalize, to syndicate.

sindicância, *s.f.* inquiry, investigation.

sindicante, *s.* inquirer, investigator, prosecutor.

sindicar, *v.t.* to inquire; to organize into a trade union.

sindicato, *s.m.* syndicate; trade-union; trust.

síndico, *s.m.* syndic; trustee.

síndroma, *s.f.* syndrome.

sinecura, *s.f.* sinecure.

sinecurismo, *s.m.* sinecurism.

sinecurista, *s.* sinecurist.

sinédoque, *s.f.* synecdoche.

sinédrio, *s.m.* Sanhedrin.

sineira, *s.f.* bell-tower, bell-gable.

sineiro, *s.m.* bell-ringer; bell-founder.

sinérese, *s.f.* syneresis.

sinergia, *s.f.* synergy.

sinérgico, *adj.* synergetic, synergic.

sinergismo, *s.m.* synergism.

sínese, *s.f.* synesis.

sinestesia, *s.f.* synesthesia.

sineta, *s.f.* small bell; hand-bell.

sinete, *s.m.* seal; signet.

sínfise, *s.f.* symphysis.

sinfonia, *s.f.* symphony.

sinfónico, *adj.* symphonic.

sinfonista, *s.* symphonist.

singelamente, *adv.* simply, unoretentiously, plainly, sincerely.

singelez, singeleza, *s.f.* simplicity; sincerity; innocence.

singelo, *adj.* simple; light, plain; unpretentious, artless; unfeigned.

singradura, *s.f.* run, say's run or sail, sailing course *(náutico).*

singrar, *v.i.* to steer; to sail; to plow the seas; to make sail for.

singular, *adj.* singular; individual; peculiar, eccentric, extraordinary, unusual, surprising; odd; starnge; *s.m.* singular.

singularidade, *s.f.* singularity, pecularity, oddity; extravagance; eccentricity.

singularizar, *v.t.* to singularize; to single out, to particularize; to specify; *singularizar-se,* to distinguish oneself.

singularmente, *adv.* singularly, unusually; remarkably.

sinistra, *s.f.* the left hand.

sinistrado, *s.m.* victim of an accident; adj. damaged, injured.

sinistramente, *adv.* sinisterly, ominously, fatally.

sinistrar, *v.i.* to suffer an accident.

sinistro, *adj.* sinister, ominous, dreadful, fatal; on the left, unlucky; *s.m.* disaster, accident, casualty; calamity, cataclysm.

sino, *s.m.* bell.

sinodal, *adj.* synodal.

sinódico, *adj.* synodic(al).

sínodo, *s.m.* synod.

sinologia, *s.f.* sinology *(cultura chinesa).*

sinólogo, *s.m.* sinologue.

sinonímia, *s.f.* synonymy.

sinonímica, *s.f.* the study of synonyms.

sinonímico, *adj.* synonymous.

sinónimo, *adj.* synonymous; *s.m.* synonym.

sinople, *s.f.* sinople, vert, green.

sinopse, *s.f.* synopsis, summary.

sinóptico, *adj.* synoptical.

sinóvia, *s.f.* synovia, synovial fluid.

sinovial, *adj.* synovial.

sinovite, *s.f.* synovitis.

sintáctico, *adj.* syntactic(al).

sintagma, *s.m.* syntagam.

sintaxe, *s.f.* syntax.

sintáxico, *adj.* syntactic(al).

síntese, *s.f.* synthesisi, combination, putting together.

sinteticamente, *adv.* synthetically.

sintético, *adj.* synthetical.

sintetização, *s.f.* synthetizing, synthesis.

sintetizar, *v.t.* to synthetize, to abrigde, to epitomize, to sum up.

sintoma, *s.m.* symptom; sign, token.

sintomático, *adj.* symptomatic(al), indicative.

sintomatologia, *s.f.* symptomatology.

sintomatológico, *adj.* symptomatologic(al).

sintonia, *s.f.* syntony; tuning in.

sintonização, *s.f.* syntonization, tuning-in (*rádio*).

sintonizar, *v.t.* to syntonize, to tune in.

sinuosidade, *s.f.* sinuosity, winding, tortuosity; subterfuge.

sinuoso, sinuous, winding, bending, tortuous.

sinusite, *s.f.* sinusitis.

sinusoidal, *adj.* sinusoidal.

sinusóide, *adj.* sinusoid, sino curve.

sionismo, *s.m.* Zionism.

sionista, *adj., s.* Zionist.

sipaio, sipal, *s.m.* Indian soldier, sepoy.

sirga, *s.f.* tow-rope, track-rope.

sirgagem, *s.f.* towing, towage, trackage.

sirgar, *v.t.* to tow, to haul, to warp (*barco*).

sirgaria, *s.f.* lace-trimming.

sirgo, *s.m.* silk-worm.

sigueiro, *s.m.* silk-man, silk spinner, silk thrower.

siríaco, *adj., s.m.* Syriac, Syrian.

sirigaita, *s.f.* restless girl, libely, spirited woman; wren.

sírio, *adj., s.m.* Syrian; Syrius, the dog star.

siroco, *s.m.* sirocco.

sirtes, *s.f. pl.* quicksand.

sisa, *s.f.* conveyance tax, transfer tax.

sisal, *s.m.* sisal, sisal-hemp.

sisar, *v.t.* to collect conveyance tax, to pay the transfer tax.

sísmico, *adj.* seismic, seismal.

sismo, *s.m.* earthquake.

sismografia, *s.f.* seismography.

sismográfico, *adj.* seismographic(al).

sismógrafo, *s.m.* seismograoh.

sismograma, *s.m.* seismogram.

sismologia, *s.f.* seismilogy.

sismológico, *adj.* seismological.

sismólogo, *s.m.* seismologist.

siso, *s.m.* sense, judgement, prudence; *dente do siso,* wisdom tooth.

sistema, *s.m.* system, method; plan, arrangement; rule, theory.

sistemática, *s.f.* systematics, taxonomy.

sistematicamente, *adv.* systematically, regularly, emthdically.

sistemático, *adj.* systematic; methodical, orderly, regular.

sistematização, *s.f.* systematization, classification.

sistematizador, *adj.* systematizing, *s.m.* systematizer.

sistematizar, *v.t.* to systematize; to classify, to arrange.

sistilo, *s.m.* systyle.

sístole, *s.f.* systole.

sistólico, *adj.* systolic.

sistro, *s.m.* sistrum.

sisudamente, *adv.* wisely, gravely, solemnly.

sisudez, sisudeza, *s.f.* circumspection, wisdom, prudence, gravity, discretion.

sisudo, *adj.* serious, sober, wise, sensible, grave, prudent.

sitiado, *adj.* besieged (*pessoa, lugar*).

sitiador, *s.m.* besieger.

sitiante, *s.m.* besieger.

sitiar, *v.t.* to besiege, to beleaguer, to lay siege to, to surround.

sitibundo, *adj.* thirsty.

sítio, *s.m.* ground, soil; place, site, spot; siege.

sito, *adj.* situated, located.

situação, *s.f.* situation; position, site, location; circumstances, condition, job, post, employment.

situacionismo, *s.m.* the dominant political power.

situacionista, *s.* member of the ins (*partido no poder*).

situar, *v.t.* to situate, to place, to site; to assign a place to.

sizígia, *s.f.* syzygy.

snobe, *s.m.* snob; *adj.* snobbish.

snobismo, *s.m.* snobbery, snobism.

só, *adj.* alone, single; lonely; only, sole; *adv.* mere, only.

soada, *s.f.* tone, sound, rumour, report; clap, noise.

soagem, *s.f.* viper's bugloss (*bot.*)

soalhada, *s.m.* floor; flooring.

soalhar, *v.t.* to floor, to plank; to expose, to the sun.

soalheira, *s.f.* noonday heat.

soalheiro, *adj.* sunny; *s.m.* sunny place; gossip.

soalho, *s.m.* floor, wooden floor, ground.

soante, *adj.* sounding; sonorous, resonant, vibrant.

soão, *s.m.* east wind.

soar, *v.i.* to sound; to ring; to strike (*sino, hora*); to be spread or rumoured.

sob, *prep.* under; beneath; below; *sob pena de,* on pain of.

soba, *s.m.* chief (*de uma tribo africana*).

sobado, *s.m.* territory governed by a tribal chief (*em África*).

sobalçar, *v.t.* to raise high, to exalt; to lift, to elevate.

sobejamente, *adv.* exceedingly, excessively.

sobejar, *v.i.* to superabound, to exceed; to be left over; to be more than enough.

sobeijão, *s.f.* superabundance, excess, profusion.

sobejo, *adj.* excessive; *s.m. pl.* left-overs, remains, leavings, surplus.

soberanamente, *adv.* supremely, paramountly, absolutely.

soberania, *s.f.* sovereignity; power, supreme power, supremacy, domination.

soberano, *adj.* sovereign, supreme; *s.m.* sovereign, king, monarch; a gold coin *(em Inglaterra);* ruler.

soberba, *s.f.* haughtiness, pride; arrogance, loftoness, self-exaltation.

soberbia, haughtiness, loftiness, arrogance.

soberbo, *adj.* superb, grand, magnificent; haughty, lofty, disdainful, self-important.

sobernal, *s.m.* overwork, overstarin; exhaustion, overfatigue.

sobestar, *v.i.* ro be below, to be under, to be inferior to.

sobpor, *v.t.* to put under, to underlay.

sobra, *s.f.* overplus, excess, abundance; remainder; *(pl.)* leavings, scraps, remains, rests.

sobraçar, *v.t.* to put or to carry under the arms.

sobradar, *v.t.* to floor, to plank, to board.

sobrado, *s.m.* floor, wooden floor; the first floor, the upper story.

sobral, *s.m.* cork-tree forest.

sobrançaria, *s.f. ver "sobranceria".*

sobrancear, *v.i.* to rise above, to hang over; to tower, to overlook, to over top; to excel, to outdo; to be superior to.

sobranceiramente, *adv.* aloft, high; above; haughtily, with pride, arrogantly *(fig).*

sobranceiro, *adj.* hanging over; *(fig)* haughty, higher, dominant;: proud, arrogant, disdainful.

sobrancelha, *s.m.* eyebrow.

sobranceria, *s.m.* haughtiness, pride, loftiness, disdain, arrogance; contempt.

sobre, *prep.* on; upon; over; about; above; in addition to, besides; towards.

sobreabundar, *v.i.* to superabound.

sobreaquecer, *v.t.* to overheat.

sobreaquecimento, *s.m.* overheating.

sobrearco, *s.m.* lintel.

sobreaviso, *s.m.* precaution, previous care; forethought; *estar de sobreaviso,* to be forewarned, to be on the alert.

sobrecana, *s.f.* splint.

sobrecarga, *s.f.* surcharge, overload, overburden.

sobrecarregar, *v.t.* to surcharge, to overload, to overburden, to overcharge; to increase excessively; to overtax.

sobrecarta, *s.f.* envelope, cover; confirmatory letter.

sobrecasaca, *s.f.* frock-coat.

sobrecenho, *s.m.* frown, sullen look, scowl.

sobrecéu, *s.m.* tester *(de uma cama),* canopy.

sobrecomum, *adj.* of common gender, the same form for both genders.

sobrecoser, *v.* to oversew.

sobrecu, *s.m.* rump *(de um pássaro),* uropygium.

sobrecurva, *s.f.* curb; windgall.

sobredito, *adj.* above-mentioned, aforesaid, forenamed.

sobredoiro, sobredouro, *adj.* overgilded; *s.m.* gilt work.

sobredoirar, sobredourar, *v.t.* to gild anew, to overgild.

sobreentender, *v.i. ver "superintender".*

sobreerguer, *v.* to raise higher.

sobreexaltar, *v.* to superexalt.

sobreexcedente, *adj.* exceeding, surpassing.

sobreexceder, *v.t.* to surpass, to exceed, to excel, to outdo, to outstrip.

sobreexcitação, *s.f.* superexcitation, overexcitement.

sobreexcitar, *v.t.* to superexcite, to overexcite.

sobre-humano, *adj.* superhuman, supernatural, sublime.

sobreiral, *s.m.* cork-oak, plantation.

sobreiro, *s.m.* cork-oak, cork-tree.

sobrejacente, *adj.* overlying, superjacent.

sobrelanço, *s.m.* outbidding.

sobrelevante, *adj.* surpassing, surmounting.

sobrelevar, *v.t.* to surpass, to surmount, to outdo, to rise above, to exceed in height, to surmount; to endure.

sobreloja, *s.f.* entresol, mezzanine.

sobrelotação, *s.f.* overload, overcharge.

sobreluzir, *v.i.* to shine, to gleam.

sobremaneira, *adv.* excessively, greatly, exceedingly.

sobremanhã, *s.f.* dawn, day.break.

sobremão, *s.m.* splint, tumour; *de sobremão,* leisurely, carefully done.

sobremesa, *s.f.* dessert.

sobremodo, *adv.* much, greatly, extremely.

sobrenadar, *v.i.* to swim on the surface, to float.

sobrenatural, *adj.* supernatural, miraculous, transcendental, divine; extraordinary; *s.m.* the supernatural.

sobrenaturalidade, *s.f.* supernaturalness, transcendentality.

sobrenaturalismo, *s.m.* supernaturalism.

sobrenome, *s.m.* surname, family name, patronymic.

sobreolhar, *v.t.* to look down upon; to look arrogantly.

sobreosso, *s.m.* swelling (on the bones); ringbone, splint.

sobrepaga, *s.f.* extra pay, bonus, gratuity.

sobrepairar, *v.i.* to hang or to hover over.

sobrepeliz, *s.f.* surplice.

sobrepensado, *adj.* a forethought, premeditated, intentional, on purpose.

sobrepensar, *v.t.* to think over carefully, to ponder, to reflect on, to meditate.

sobrepesar, *v.t.* to overweigh; to ponder; to weigh upon the heart.

sobrepor, *v.t.* to superpose, to overlay, to overlap; *sobrepor-se a,* to overcome.

sobreposição, *s.f.* superposition; overlapping.

sobreposse (a), *loc. adv.* excessively, too much.

sobrepovoar, *v.t.* to overpopulate.

sobrepujado, *adj.* surpassed, exceeded, topped.

sobrepujamento, sobrepujança, *s.m., s.f.* surpassing, excelling; superabundance.

sobrepujante, *adj.* surpassing, excelling.

sobrepujar, *v.t.* to surpass, to surmount, to excel.

sobrequilha, *s.f.* keelson.

sobrerrena, *adj.* suprarenal.

sobre-ronda, *s.f.* counterround.

sobre-rondar, *v.t., v.i.* to do the counterround, to check on sentinels, to control, to inspect.

sobrescrever, *v.t.* to write on; to address *(carta).*

sobrescritar, *v.t.* to address *(carta).*

sobrescrito, *s.m.* envelope; address.

sobressaia, *s.f.* overskirt.

sobressair, *v.i.* to excel, to surpass; to stand out, to project; to be prominent; to attract attention.

sobresselente, *adj.* salient; supernumerary; spare part *(de alguma coisa).*

sobressaltado, *adj.* surprised; frightened, startled.

sobressaltar, *v.t.* to surprise, to catch unawares, to startle, to shock; *sobressaltar-se,* to be startled at.

sobressalto, *s.m.* start; alarm; fear, fright, shock, surprise; uneasiness.

sobressaturação, *s.m.* supersaturation.

sobressaturar, *v.t.* to supersaturate.

sobresselente, *adj.* ver sibresselente.

sobressinal, *s.m.* device.

sobrestante, *adj.* overseeing, overlooking; s. overseer, superintendent.,

sobrestar, *v.i.* to stop. to cease; to defere; to come to a stop; to forbear; to be imminent; to put a stop to *(trabalho).*

sobrestimar, *v.t.* to overestimate, to overrate, to overvalue.

sobretarde, *s.f.* the late afternoon; dusk, nightfall; adv. at dusk.

sobretaxa, *s.f.* surtax, supercharge; additional charge.

sobretecer, *v.t.* to overweave, to interweave

sobretoalha, *s.f.* cover.

sobretudo, *adv.* above all, chiefly, mainly, especially; *s.m.* overcoat.

sobreveste, *s.f.* upper garment.

sobrevestir, *v.t.* to put on, to wear over.

sobrevindo, *adj.* occuring, happening.

sobrevir, *v.i.* to occur, to turn up, to arise, to befall, to come upon unexpectedelly, to supervene.

sobrevirtude, *s.f.* nun's veil, wimple.

sobrevivência, *s.f.* survival.

sobrevivente, *adj.* surviving; *s.m.* survivor, outliver.

sobreviver, *v.t.* to outline, to survive.

sobrevoar, *v.t.* to fly over.

sobrevoo, *s.m.* flying over.

sobriamente, *adv.* soberly, frugally, moderately.

sobriedade, *s.f.* sobriety, abstemiousness, temperance, frugality, moderation.

sobrinha, *s.f.* niece.

sobrinha-neta, *s.f.* grand-niece.

sobrinho, *s.m.* nephew.

sobrinho-neto, *s.m.* grand-nephew.

sóbrio, *adj.* sober, temperate, abstemious, frugal; economical.

sobro, *s.m.* the cork-oak or its wood.

sobrolho, *s.m.* eyebrow.

socairo, *s.m.* cave, shelter; foot of the mountain.

socalco, *s.m.* terrace; ledge *(montanha).*

socapa(à), *loc. adv.* by stealth, in secrecy, furtively; *rir à socapa,* to laugh up one's sleeve.

socar, *v.t.* to box; to pound, to beat; to strike, to hit *(com o punho).*

socarrão, *adj.* cunning, sly; *s.m.* sly fellow.

socava, *s.f.* underground cave or hole or den.

socavar, *v.t.* to mine, to undermine, to dig up, to sap.

sociabilidade, *s.f.* sociability, good fellowship.

sociabilizar, *v.t.* to make sociable.

social, *adj.* social, sociable, friendly.

socialismo, *s.m.* socialism.

socialista, *s., adj.* socialist.

socialização, *s.f.* socialization.

socializar, *v.t.* to socialize.

socialmente, *adv.* socially.

sociável, *adj.* sociable, communicative, civilized.

sociedade, *s.f.* society; company; partnership, association *(de pessoas);* fashionable world; consortium; social high life.

societário, *s.m.* partner; member, associate.

sócio, *s.m.* member; fellow; sharer; joint owner; partner, associate, copartner *(com).*

sociologia, *s.f.* sociology.

sociológico, *adj.* sociological.

sociólogo, *s.m.* sociologist.

soco, *s.m.* sock; clog, wooden hoe; socle, basis.

soco (ô), *s.m.* blow *(com o punho),* fisticuff, punch, box, stroke.

soçobrar, *v.t., v.i.* to turn upside down, to overturn; to sink, to founder, to go to the bottom, to go down; to lose courage.

soçobro, *s.m.* sinking, foundering, shipwreck; ruin, disaster.

socorrer, *v.t.* to help, to assist, to succour, to relieve, to aid, to protect; to rescue, to relieve; *socorrer-se de,* to have recourse to, to resort to.

socorrimento, *s.m.* assistance, aid, rescue.

socorro, *s.m.* help, relief, assistance, succour, aid.

socrático, *adj.* Socratic.

soda, *s.f.* soda.

sodalício, *s.m.* sodality, fraternity, brotherhood.

sódico, *adj.* sodic.

sódio, *s.m.* sodium.

sodomia, *s.f.* sodomy.

sodomita, *s.* sodomite.

soer, *v.i.* to be wont to.

soerguer, *v.t.* to lift, to raise slightly.

soez, *adj.* vile, base, low, mean.

sofá, *s.m.* sofa, settee, couch.

sofá-cama, *s.m.* sofa-bed, day-bed.

sofisma, *s.m.* sophism; sophistry; fallacy; quibble.

sofismar, *v.* to quibble; to sophistry; to be sophistical.

sofista, *s., adj.* sophist; quibbler.

sofística, *s.f.* sophistry.

sofisticação, *s.f.* sophistication, adulteration, debasement.

sofisticar, *v.t.* to sophisticate, to adulterate, to falsify.

sofístico, *adj.* sophistical; casuistical; misleading, deceptive.

sofraldar, *v.t.* to lift something slightly.

sofreamento, *s.m.* curbing, checking, retraining.

sofrear, *v.t.* to curb, to refrain, ro repress, to bridle, to restrain, to hold back.

sofredor, *adj.* suffering; tolerating; *s.m.* sufferer, endurer.

sofregamente, *adv.* greedily, avidly, impatiently.

sôfrego, *adj.* greedy, voracious, eager, avid, impatient; ambitious.

sofreguidão, *s.f.* greediness, greed, avidity; gluttony; ambition.

sofrer, *v.t.* to suffer, to grieve, to be in pain, to undergo, to endure, to go through; to allow, to permit, to tolerate.

sofrido, *adj.* suffered; patient, uncomplaining.

sofrimento, *s.m.* suffering; pain; distress, anguish; endurance; agony, tribulation, torment.

sofrível, *adj.* tolerable, passable, sufferable, endurabel; so-so; pretty good, fair.

sofrivelmente, *adv.* tolerably, passably, sufferably; decently.

soga, *s.f.* rope of esparto; leather thong (to lead oxen by).

sogra, *s.f.* mother-in-law.

sogro, *s.m.* father-in-law.

soído, *s.m.* sound, noise, tone.

soja, *s.f.* soybean, soja.

sol, *s.m.* sun; aunshine; sol *(musica).* 1) *ao sol,* in the sun. 2) *de sol a sol,* from sunrise to sunset. 3) *pôr do sol*, sunset. 4) *nascer do sol*, sunrise. 5) *sol de pouca dura*, a flash in the pan. 6) *relógio de sol*, sundial.

sola, *s.m.* hide, leather; sole *(do pé)*.

solagem, *s.f.* soling.

solano, *s.m.* nightshade *(botanica)*.

solapa, *s.f.* sap, underminig; a cave; disguise; *à solapa*, secretly, under disguise, furtively.

solapadamente, *adv.* secretly, by stealth.

solapado, *adj.* hidden, secret; undermined, excavated; disguised.

solapador, *s.m.* sapper, excavator; *adj.* undermining, sapping.

solapamento, *s.m.* sap, undermining.

solapar, *v.t.* to undermine; to hide, to conceal; to mine, to sap, to disguise, to dissemble.

solar, *adj.* solar; *s.m.* manor-house; *v.t.* to sole *(sapatos)*. 1) *mancha solar*, sunspot. 2) *sistema solar*, solar system. 3) *hora solar*, solar time.

solarego, solarengo, *adj.* manorial.

solaria, *s.f.* soles *(de sapatos)*; a quantity of leather.

solário, *s.m.* sun-dial; solarium, sun porch.

solavancar, *v.i.* to jolt, to jostle, to bump, to jog.

solavanco, *s.m.* bump, jerk, jolt, jar.

solda, *s.f.* solder.

soldada, *s.f.* wages, salary.

soldadesca, *s.f.* soldiery, rank and file; troops, soldiers collectively.

soldadesco, *adj.* soldierlike, soldierly.

soldado, *s.m.* soldier; private; *soldado raso*, private, common soldier.

soldador, *s.m.* welder, solderer, joiner; soldering iron; *adj.* soldering.

soldadura, *s.f.* soldering; welding.

soldagem, *s.f.* soldering; welding.

soldar, *v.t.* to solder, to weld; to join, to unite, to connect; to fasten, to fix.

soldável, *adj.* weldable.

soldo, *s.m.* soldier's pay; *(moeda francesa)*; salary of officers *(exército ou marinha)*; *a soldo de*, in the pay of.

solecismo, *s.m.* solecism; error, incorrectness of language.

solecista, *s.* solecist.

solecizar, *v.i.* to solecize.

soledade, *s.f.* solitude, loneliness, isolation; seclusion, retiremant.

soleira, *s.f.* threshold; foot-board.

solene, *adj.* solemn; grave, serious, sober, formal, self-important.

solenemente, *adv.* solemnly, emphatically, portentously.

solenidade, *s.f.* solemnity, formal, ceremony, festival, celebration.

solenização, *s.f.* solemnization.

solenizador, *s.m.* solemnizer; *adj.* solmnizing.

solenizar, *v.t.* to solemnize; to celebrate, to commemorate with solemnity.

solércia, *s.f.* cunning, craft, guile, skill, sherewdness; sharp practice.

solerte, *adj.* shrewd, cunning, crafty, guileful, skilful, industrious; *s.* rascal, crook, rogue; sagacious person.

soletração, *s.f.* spelling.

soletrador, *s.m.* speller; *adj.* spelling.

soletrar, *v.t.* to spell out *(oralmente)*; to read slowly and with difficulty.

solevantamento, *s.m.* taking up.

solevantar, *v.t.* to lift, to take up; to raise a little.

solfa, *s.f.* art of sol-faing, solmization.

solfar, *v.t.* to repair the pages of a book, to glue sheets of paper.

solfejar, *v.t.* to sol-fa, to solmizate.

solfejo, *s.m.* sol-fa, solfeggio, solmization.

solfista, *s.* solfaist.

solha, *s.f.* flounder, flat-fish; slap *(pop)*

solhar, *v.t.* to lay a wood floor.

solho, *s.m.* plaice; floor.

solicitação, *s.f.* solicitation, entreaty, request.

solicitador, *s.m.* petitioner, suitor; solicitor *(agente legal)*.

solicitante, *s.* solicitant, petitioner.

solicitar, *v.t.* to solicit, to invite, to apply for, to ask, to request; to court, to woo; to induce to, to incite; to attract.

solícito, *adj.* solicitous; careful; anxious, willing, dilligent, full of zest, obliging.

solicitude, *s.f.* solicitude, carefulness, care, concern; diligence.

solidamente, *adv.* solidly, strongly, durably.

solidão, *s.f.* solitude, seclusion, loneliness, isolation, privacy, exile; lonely place, wilderness.

solidar, *v.t.* to solidify; to confirm, to corroborate.

solidariamente, *adv.* solidarily.

solidariedade, *s.f.* solidarity, friendship, fellowship; community of interests.

solidário, *adj.* linked *(por interesses*

comuns); solidary, sharing, mutual; harmonious; jointly liable.

solidarizar, *v.t.* to make solidary; *solidarizar--se,* to make common cause, to become jointly liable.

solidéu, *s.m.* calotte, skull-cap *(bispos).*

solidez, *s.f.* solidity, strength, resistance, durability, security, consistence.

solidificação, *s.f.* solidification, consolidation; concretion.

solidificador, *s.m.* solidifier, consolidator; *adj.* solidifying.

solidificar, *v.t.* to solidify, to make solid; to become solid.

sólido, *adj.* solid, firm, compact, strong, stout, robust, vigorous, durable; *s.m.* a solid.

solidónia, *s.f. (bot)* columbine.

solilóquio, *s.m.* soliloquy, monologue.

solimão, *s.m.* corrosive sublimate; any deadly poison.

solinhadeira, *s.f.* a quarryman's hammer.

solinhar, *v.t., v.i.* to cut wood or stone along a marked line.

sólio, *s.m.* throne; regal power; papal chair.

solípede, *s.* soliped.

solista, *s.* soloist.

solitária, *s.f.* tapeworm, taenia.

solitariamente, *adv.* solitarily, lonely.

solitário, *adj.* solitary, lonesome, lonely, retired, secluded; unsociable; desert, wild, desolate; *s.m.* hermit, solitarian, cenobite; solitaire *(jóia ou jarra de flores).*

sólito, *adj.* wonted, accustomed, used; usual, habitual.

solo, *s.m.* soil, ground, earth; solo *(música).*

sol-pôr, sol-posto, *s.m.* sunset.

solsticial, *adj.* solstitial.

solstício, *s.m.* solstice.

solta, *s.f.* hobble, shackle, fetter *(para animais);* feed pasture; *à solta,* footloose, on the loose, freely.

soltador, *s.m.* releaser, liberator; *adj.* releasing, loosening.

soltar, *v.t.* to loosen, to untie, to unfasten, to unloose; to let loose, to let go, to free; to unfurl, to let out *(grito);* to slacken. *soltar-se,* to get loose, to escape; to discharge, to release; to utter *(palavras).*

solteira, *s.f.* spinster, single woman, bachelor girl; *adj.* single, unmarried.

solteirão, *s.m.* old bachelor, confirmed bachelor.

solteiro, *adj.* unmarried, single; *s.m.* bachelor; single woman, spinster *(fem).*

solteirona, *s.m.* spinster, old maid.

solto, *adj.* loose; free, unbound, untied, unfastened; released, loberated; licentious, dissolute; audacious; blank *(verso).*

soltura, *s.f.* setting *(para a liberdade),* release, loose, bowels, looseness, diarrhea.

solubilidade, *s.f.* solubility.

solubilizar, *v.t.* to solubilize, to make soluble.

soluçante, *adj.* sobbing, weeping, hiccupy.

solução, *s.f.* solution; explanation; solving *(problema);* conclusion; answer; interruption; key; mixture *(com um dissolvente).*

soluçar, *v.i.* to hiccup, to sob.

solucionar, *v.t.* to solve, to decide, to find a way out, to find a solution for, to work out a solution.

soluço, *s.m.* hiccup, sob.

solutivo, *adj.* laxative; solvent; dissolvable.

soluto, *s.m.* solution, solute.

solúvel, *adj.* soluble, solvable, resolvable.

solvência, *s.f.* solvency, solvability.

solvente, *adj.* solvent, dissolving, soluble, resolvent; capable to play.

solver, *v.t.* to solve, to explain; to liquidate *(obrigações);* to pay.

solvibilidade, *s.f.* solvency, ability to pay the debts.

solvível, *adj.* solvent *(financeiramente).*

som, *s.m.* sound, noise, tone. 1) *alto e bom som,* loud and clear. 2) *sem tom nem som,* withoue rhyme or reason.

soma, *s.f.* sum, amount, total, totality; addition.

somar, *v.t.* to sum, to add up; to totalize, to amount to; to gather.

somático, *adj.* somatic.

somatologia, *s.f.* somatology.

somatológico, *adj.* somatologic(al).

somatório, *s.m.* sum, sum total, total amount, totality.

sombra, *s.f.* shade, shadow; ghost, spirit; trace, vestige; protection, shelter; solour, hue. 1) *à sombra,* in the shade; colour, hue. 2) *fazer sombra,* to eclipse somenone's merit. 3) *nem por sombras,* not in the least. 4) *sem sombra de dúvida,* without the slightest doubt.

sombral, *s.m.* shady place.

sombreado, *s.m., adj.* shading *(num quadro);* shady, shaded.

sombrear, *v.t.* to shade, to obscure, to shadow, to darken, to screen.

sombreiro, *s.m.* umbrella, shady place; broad-brimmed hat.

sombrinha, *s.f.* umbrella *(pequena),* parasol, sunshade.

sombrio, *adj.* dark, gloomy; dismal; sombre; dull; shady, dim; overcast; sullen, grim; frowning, moody.

somenos, *adj.* of little worth, ordinary, inferior; *de somenos,* unimportant, insignificant.

somente, *adv.* only, solely, merely, simply.

somítico, *adj.* stingy, avaricous, closefisted, stingy, mean; *s.m.* miser, niggard.

somitiquice, *s.f.* avarice, greediness.

sonambulismo, *s.m.* somnambulism, sleep-walking, night-walking.

sonâmbulo, *s.m.* somnambulist, sleep-walker, night-walker.

sonância, *s.f.* sonancy; tone, tune.

sonante, *adj.* sonant, sounding; tonic; 1) *em metal sonante,* hard cash.

sonata, *s.f.* sonata.

sonatina, *s.f.* sonatina.

sonda, *s.f.* probe, sound, catheter; lead line, plummet.

sondador, *s.m.* sounder; probe; *adj.* probing, sounding.

sondagem, *s.f.* sounding; boring, drilling *(minas);* exploration.

sondar, *v.t.* to sound; to bore, to drill *(minas);* to probe; to test; to fathom; to explore.

soneca, *s.f.* a nap, forty winks, short sleep, snooze.

sonega, sonegação, *s.f.* concealing, unlawful concealmente; holding back.

sonegador, *s.m.* soncealer, withholder; *adj.* concealing.

sonegamento, *s.m.* ver sonegação.

sonegar, *v.t.* to steal; to hide, to conceal, to supress; to withhold.

soneira, *s.f.* sleepiness, somnolence, drowsiness.

sonetista, *s.* sonneteer, sonetist.

soneto, *s.m.* sonnet.

sonhador, *adj.* dreaming, dreamy; *s.m.* dreamer, visionary.

sonhar, *v.t., v.i.* to dream; to fancy, to imagine.

sonho, *s.m.* dream, reverie, fancy, musing, fantasy, fiction, vision; friedcake, culler.

sónico, *adj.* sonic, phonic.

sonido, *s.m.* sound, tone; noise, murmur, rumour.

sonífero, *adj., s.m.* somniferous, narcotic, soporific.

sono, *s.m.* sleep; slumber. 1) *dormir a sono solto,* to sleep soundly, to sleep like a dog or like a top. 2) *ter sono,* to be (feel) sleepy. 3) *doença do sono,* sleeping sickness. 4) *pegar no sono,* to fall asleep. 5) *tonto de sono,* sleep-drunk.

sonolência, *s.f.* somnolence, drowsiness sleepiness; torpor.

sonolento, *adj.* somnolent, drowsy, sleepy; torpid, sluggish.

sonoridade, *s.f.* sonority, sonorousness, resonance.

sonorização, *s.f.* the act of rendering sonorous.

sonorizar, *v.t.* to render sonorous.

sonoro, *adj.* sonorous, sounding, ringing; harmonious; vibrant, resonant; voiced.

sonoroso, *adj.* sonourous, resounding; melodious.

sonsa, sonsice, *s.f.* slyness, craftiness, artfulness, cunning; dissimulation.

sonsinho, *s.m.* willy, shrewd, crafty.

sonso, *adj.* sly, willy, cunning artful, crafty.

sopa, *s.f.* soup; broth, sop. 1) *como sopa no mel,* just at the right moment. 2) *molhar a sopa, (popular)* to beat, to thrash. 3) *estar numa sopa,* to be wet through.

sopapo, *s.m.* cuff; slap. blow, thrashing, hit.

sopé, *s.m.* foot, base *(de um monte).*

sopeador, *s.m.* represser, suppressor.

sopeamento, *s.m.* repression, subjugation; restraint, check.

sopear, *v.t.* to repress, to restrain, to check, to rein; to hamper, to hinder; to subjugate; to trample under foot.

sopeira, *s.f.* tureen; maid-servant *(pop.)*

sopeiro, *adj.* fond of soup; *prato sopeiro,* soup-plate.

sopesar, *v.t.* to weigh by hand, to estimate the weight of; to keep balance.

sopetear, *v.i., v.t.* to sop, to dunk, to soak; to savour, to relish.

sopitar, *v.t.* to make drowsy, to lull to sleep; to calm; to fill with hopes; to repress.

sopor, *s.m.* sound sleep, sopor, stupor, lethargic, sleep, lethargy.

soporativo, *adj., s.m.* soporific.

soporífero, *adj., s.m.* soporiferous, soporific.

soporífico, *adj., s.m.* soporific.

soporizar, *v.t.* to put to sleep, to calm; to enfeeble.

soporoso, *adj.* sleepy, drowsy; somnolent, torpid; soporific.

soprador, *s.m.* blower; *adj.* blowing.

soprano, *s.m.* soprano.

soprar, *v.t.* to blow; to whisper, to prompt *(estudante)*; ro suggest, to hint.

sopro, *s.m.* blow, blowing; breath, breathing, puff, whiff; moment.

soquear, *v.t.* to give a blow, to sock, to hit with the fist; to box.

soqueiro, *s.m.* wooden-shoemaker.

soqueixado, *adj.* tied under the chin.

soqueixar, *v.t.* to tie under the chin.

soqueixo, *s.m.* bandage under the chin.

soquete, *s.m.* rammer, ramrod; light blow, soft punch; half-length stocking.

soquetear, *v.t.* to ram down; to punch.

sorar, *v.t.* to convert into whey, to change into serum.

sorda, *s.f.* kind of thick soup.

sordícia, sordície, *s.f.* sordidness, paltriness, filthiness, dirtiness; base avarice; depravity.

sordidamente, *adv.* sordidly, nastily, miserably.

sordidez, sordideza, *s.f.* sordidness; stinginess, meanness.

sórdido, *adj.* sordid, filthy, dirty, foul, nasty, low, base, stingy, mean; vile.

sorgo, *s.m.* sorghum *(bot.)*.

sorites, *s.m.* sorites.

sorna, *s.f.* slowness, heaviness; indolence; *s.* lazy person; *adj.* boring.

sornar, *v.i.* to go slowly; to sleep; to be lazy.

sornice, *s.f.* indolence, laziness; slyness, artfulness.

soro, *s.m.* serum; whey.

Soror, *s.f.* sister *(freira)*.

sororicida, *s.* sororicide *(o assassino)*.

sorodicídio, *s.m.* sororicide *(o acto)*.

sorose, *s.f.* sorosisi *(bot)*.

soroso, *adj.* serous, wheyey.

soroterapia, *s.f.* serum-therapy.

sorrateiramente, *adv.* cunningly, stealthily, secretly, furtively.

sorrateiro, *adj.* cunning, crafty; malicious; stealthy, sneaky, sly; underhand.

sorrelfa(à), *loc. adv.* secretly, by stealth, furtively, under disguise.

sorrelfo, *adj.* secretive, on the sly; artful, cunning.

sorridente, *adj.* smiling, cheerful; gay, in good spirits, radiant.

sorrir, *v.i.* to smile, to laugh gently.

sorriso, *s.m.* smile; *sorriso amarelo*, sickly smile.

sorte, *s.f.* chance, lot; condition; sort, kind, species; lottery; fate, destiny; success; share, allotment; lucky strike. 1) *sorte grande*, grand (first) prize. 2) *dar sorte*, to bring good luck. 3) *ter sorte*, to be lucky. 4) *maré de sorte*, wave of good luck. 5) *de tal sorte que*, in such a way that. 6) *por sorte*, luckily. 7) *tirar à sorte*, to draw lots. 8) *deitar sortes*, to cast lotes.

sorteador, *s.m.* caster of lots.

sorteamento, *s.m.* "ver sorteio".

sortear, *v.t.* to draw lots, to raffle, to allot.

sorteio, *s.m.* lottery, raffle.

sortido, *adj.* stocked, assorted, furnished; *s.m.* assortment, stock, supply.

sortilégio, *s.m.* spell, charm, witchcraft, sorcery; sortilege.

sortimento, *s.m.* assortment, stock, supply; variety.

sortir, *v.t.* to supply, to furnish, to provide, to stock, to assort; to blend, to mix; to vary *(cores, etc.)*.

sorumbático, *adj.* gloomy, sullen, dour, sad, somber, moody, dejected; taciturn.

sorvedela, *s.f.* draught, swallow.

sorvedoiro, sorvedouro, *s.m.* gulf, abyss, vortex, whirlpool, pit.

sorver, *v.t.* to suck, to sip, to absorb; to swallow.

sorvete, *s.m.* sherbert; ice-cream.

sorveteira, *s.f.* ice-pail, ice-cream freezer, ice-chest.

sorveteiro, *s.m.* ice-cream, peddler.

sorvo, *s.m.* sip, gulp, draught, swallow.

sós(a), *loc. adv.* alone, by oneself.

sósia, *s.m.* double, counterpart, second self, duplicate.

soslaio, *(de) loc. adv.* askew, aslant, sideways, askance.

sossega, *s.f.* rest, repose; ease, calm.

sossegadamente, *adv.* quietly, calmly.

sossegado, *adj.* quiet; peaceful; still; sleepy; calm.

sossegador, *s.f.* soother, calmer, tranquilizer; *adj.* calming, appeasing.

sossegar, *v.t.* to calm, to still, to appease; to be quiet, to calm down.

sossego, *s.m.* quietness, calmness, tranquility, peace; ease, rest, repose.

sosso, *s.m.* stone.

sota, *s.f.* queen *(no jogo de cartas)*; *s.m.* postillion, coachman, outrider; lull, spell *(período de descanso); (pl.)* the lead horses.

sotaina, *s.f.* cassock, soutane; a priest *(pop).*

sótão, *s.m.* garret, attic; *ter macaquinhos no sótão,* to have bats in the belfry.

sota-piloto, *s.m.* second pilot.

sotaque, *s.m.* accent, brogue.

sotavento, *s.m.* leeward, lee.

soteia, *s.f.* roof terrace, flat roof.

soterração, *s.f.* burying, interment.

soterramento, *s.m.* ver soterração.

soterrar, *v.t.* to bury, to cover up.

sotopor, *v.t.* to put under; to omit, to leave out; to postpone; to neglect.

sotrancão, *adj.* disguised, dissembled.

soturnidade, *s.f.* taciturnity, sullenness, sadness, moroseness.

soturno, *adj.* taciturn, sullen, gloomy, moody; somber; depressed.

souto, *s.m.* grove of chesnut-trees; thicket, coppice.

sova, *s.f.* thrashing, beating, cudgelling.

sovaco, *s.m.* arm-pit, arm-hole, axilia.

sovaqueira, *s.f.* thief *(mulher)* who escapes with stolen goods under her arm.

sovaquinho, *s.m.* smell of the arm pit.

sovar, *v.t.* to knead; to thrash, to beat, to drub, to cudgel, to give a hiding.

sovela, *s.f.* awl; pricker.

sovelão, *s.m.* big awl.

soveleiro, *s.m.* awlmaker; awlseller.

soveral, *s.m.* plantation of cork-trees.

sovereiro, *s.m.* cork-tree.

soviete, *s.m.* soviet.

soviético, *adj.* sovietic, Russian.

sovietismo, *s.m.* sovietism, bolshevism.

sovina, *adj.* mean, niggardly; churlish, sordid; dingy, miserly; *s.* miser skinflint, niggar; a wooden pin.

sovinaria, *s.f.* ver *"sovinice".*

sovinice, *s.f.* avarice, stinginess.

sozinho, *adj.* all alone, quite alone.

sua, *adj. poss.* his, her, its, your, their; *pron. poss.* his, hers, its, yours, theirs.

suã, *s.f.* loin of pork, joint of pork.

suadela, *s.f.* sweating, perspiration.

suado, *adj.* sweaty, perspiring, wet with sweat.

suadoiro, suadouro, *s.m.* sudorific; horses back.

suão, *s.m.* south wind *(quente).*

suar, *v.i.* to sweat, to perspire; to toil, to druge, to work hard; to distil.

suarda, *s.f.* suint; grease.

suarento, *adj.* sweaty, perspiring, sweat-covered.

suasório, *adj.* persuasive, suasive.

suástica, *s.f.* swastika, fylfot.

suave, *adj.* suave, bland, smooth, sweet, mild, soft, gentle, soothing.

suavemente, *adv.* softly, sweetly, mildly, smoothly, gently.

suavidade, *s.f.* suavity, sweetness, gentleness, softness, mildness.

suavização, *s.f.* smoothing, softning; mitigation, relenting.

suavizador, *adj.* smoothing, softening, soothing, relaxative.

suavizar, *v.t.* to smooth, to assuage, to soothe, to soften, to molify, to appease; to mitigate.

subácido, *adj.* subacid.

subaéreo, *adj.* subaerial.

subafluente, *s.m.* subaffluent.

subagência, *s.f.* subagency.

subagente, *s.* subagent.

subalimentação, *s.f.* undernourishment.

subalimentado, *adj.* undernourished, underfeed.

subalimentar, *v.t.* undernourish, to underfeed.

subalternação, *s.f.* subalternation, subordination.

subalternar, *v.t.* to make subaltern, to subordinate, to subject to; to alternate.

subalternidade, *s.f.* dependency; inferiority; subordination.

subalternização, *s.f.* subordination.

subalternizar, *v.t.* ver subalternar.

subalterno, *adj. s.m.* subaltern, inferior, subordinate.

subalugar, *v.t.* to sublet, to underlet.

subaluguer, *s.m.* subrenting, sublettin.

subaquático, *adj.* subaquatic, underwater.

subarbusto, *s.m.* sundershrub, subshrub.

subarrendamento, *s.m.* sub-tenancy, subletting.

subarrendar, *v.t.* to sublet, to underlet, to sublease.

subarrendatário, *s.m.* sublessor, sublessee, underletter; subtenanr.

sub-bibliotecário, *s.m.* assistant librarian.

subchefe, *s.m.* deputy chief, subchief; assistant director.

subclasse, *s.f.* subclass, subdivision.

subclavicular, *adj.* suclavicular.

subclávio, *adj.* subclavian.

subcomissão, s.f. subcommittee, subcommission.

subcomissário, s.m. subcommissioner.

subconsciência, s.f. subconsciousness.

subconsciente, adj. subconscious; s.m. subconscienciousness.

subcutâneo, adj. subcutaneous.

subdelegação, s.f. subdelegation, succursal, branch office or store.

subdelegacia, s.f. ver subdelegação.

subdelegado, s.m. subdelegate.

subdelegar, v.t. to subdelegarte.

subdiaconado, subdiaconato, s.m. subdeaconry, sub-deaconship.

subdiaconisa, s.f. subdeaconess.

subdiácono, s.m. subdeacon.

subdialecto, s.m. subdialect.

subdirecção, s.f. assistant-headmastership, deputy directorship.

subdirector, s.m. subdirector, deputy director, assistant manager.

subdirectoria, s.f. ver subdirecção.

subdirigir, v.t. to subdirect.

súbdito, s.m. subject.

subdividir, v.t. to subdivide.

subdivisão, s.f. subdivision.

subdivisível, adj. subdivisable.

subempreitada, s.f. subcontract.

subenfiteuse, s.f. subemphyteusis.

subenfiteuta, s. subemphyteuta.

subentender, v.t. to understand; to interpret; to assume, to suppose, to infer, to discern.

subentendido, adj. understood; impleid, implicit.

súber, s.m. suber, cork, tissue.

subérico, adj. suberic, of cork.

suberina, s.f. suberine.

suberização, s.f. suberization.

suberizar, v.t., v.i. to suberize.

suberoso, adj. subereous, suberic, suberose, corky.

subespécie, s.f. subspecies.

subertação, s.f. substation.

subestimar, v.t. to underrate, to underestimate.

subfamília, s.f. subfamily.

subgénero, s.m. subgenus.

subgerente, s. assistant manager.

subgrupo, s.m. subgroup.

sub-hepático, adj. sub-hepatic.

subida, s.f. ascension, going up; ascent; slope; rise (preços).

subido, adj. raised, mounted; excessive; sublime, exalted; excellent; dear, expensive.

subimento, s.m. rise; ascent; increase; excess.

subinspector, s.m. subinspector, deputy inspector.

subintendência, s.f. subintendancy.

subintendente, s. subintendant.

subir, v.t. to ascend, to climb, to go up; to carry up, to bring up; to walk up, to walk upstairs.

subitamente, adv. suddenly, on (of a sudden, all of a sudden, unexpectedly).

subitâneo, adj. sudden; hasty; abrupt.

súbito, adj. ver subitâneo; de súbito, ver "subitamente".

subjacente, adj. subjacent; underlying.

subjectivação, s.f. subjectiveness.

subjectivar, v.t. to subjectivize, to render subjective.

subjectividade, s.f. subjectivity.

subjectivismo, s.m. subjectivism.

subjectivista, s., adj. subjectivist.

subjectivo, adj. subjective.

subjugação, s.f. subjugation.

subjugador, s.m. subjugator; adj. subjugating.

subjugante, adj. subjugating, sominating.

subjugar, v.t. to subjugate, to master, to overpower, to subdue, to conquer, to overcome; to subject; to supree; to tame; subjugar-se, to refrain from, to contain oneself.

subjunção, s.f. subjunction.

subjuntivo, s.m. subjunctive.

sublevação, s.f. uprising, insurrection, rebellion, revolt.

sublevador, s.m. insurrectionist, mutineer.

sublevar, v.t. to revolt; sublevar-se, to rise up, to rebel.

sublimação, s.f. sublimation.

sublimado, adj. sublimated; s.m. sublimate.

sublimar, v.t. to sublimate; to exalt, to extol, to glorify, to honour.

sublimatório, adj. sublimatory.

sublimável, adj. sublimable.

sublime, adj. sublime, high, lofty, noble; grandiose, grand; divine; excellent.

sublimidade, s.f. sublimity, perfection, excellence.

sublingual, adj. sublingual.

sublinhar, v.t. to underline, to underscore; to emphasize.

sublocação, s.f. sublease, act of subletting.

sublocador, *s.m.* underletter, subletter, sublessor.

sublocar, *v.t.* to sublet, to sublease, to underlease.

sublocatário, *s.m.* undertenant, sublessee.

sublunar, *adj.* sublunary.

submarino, *adj., s.m.* submarine, sub, U-boat.

submaxilar, *adj.* submaxillary.

submergir, *v.t.* to submerge, to sink; to flood, to deluge, to inundate; to drown.

submergível, *adj.* submergible, sinkable.

submersão, *s.f.* submersion; inundation, deluge; drowning.

submersível, *adj.* submersible; *s.m.* submarine.

submerso, *adj.* submerged, sunken.

submeter, *v.t.* to submit, to subdue, to subject.

submetimento, *s.m.* submission, subjection, surrender.

subministrador, *s.m.* provider, subminister; *adj.* subministring.

subministrar, *v.t.* to provide, to supply, to furnish; to subministrate.

submissão, *s.f.* submission; submissiveness, humility; obedience; conformity, resignation.

submisso, *adj.* submissive; yelding; humble, obedient, dutiful; compliant; docile, tamed.

submúltiplo, *s.m.* submultiple.

subnasal, *adj.* subnasal.

subnormal, *s., adj.* subnormal.

subnutrição, *s.f.* undernourishment.

subnutrir, *v.t.* to underfeed, to undernourish.

subocular, *adj.* subocular.

suborbicular, *adj.* suborbital.

subordem, *s.f.* suborder.

subordinação, *s.f.* subordination. inferiority; subservience; obedience, subjection.

subordinado, *adj.* subordinate; inferior; subject, dependent, secondary, subaltern; *s.m.* subordinate, dependant, subordinador.

subordinador, *s.m.* he who enforces subordination; *adj.* subordinating.

subordinante, *adj.* subordinating, subordinative.

subordinar, *v.t.* to subordinate, to subject; *subordinar-se,* to submit to, to yield.

subordinativo, *adj.* subordinative.

subornação, *s.f.* subornation, bribery.

subornador, *s.m.* suborner, briber, corrupter.

subornar, *v.t.* to suborn, to bribe, to corrupt; to grease, to palm.

subornável, *adj.* bribable, corruptible.

suborno, *s.m.* subornation, bribery, corruption.

subpolar, *adj.* subpolo, subpolar.

subpor, *v.t.* to put under.

subperfeito, *s.m.* sub-perfect.

subperfeitura, *s.f.* sub-perfecture.

subproduto, *s.m.* subproduct, byproduct.

sub-região, *s.f.* subregion.

sub-repção, *s.f.* subreption, concealment.

sub-repticiamente, *adv.* surreptitiously, by stealth.

sub-reptício, *adj.* surreptitious; secret, underhand.

sub-rogação, *s.f.* subrogation, surrogation.

sub-rogador, *s.m.* subrogator.

sub-rogar, *v.t.* to subrogate, to surrogate.

sub-rogatório, *adj.* subtogatory.

subscrever, *v.t.* to subscribe; to sign one's name; to approve, to sanction, to consent; to contribute to; to agree.

subscrição, *s.f.* subscription; contribution, sum subscribed.

subscritar, *v.t.* to subscribe, to sign.

subscrito, *adj.* subscribed; signed; underwritten; *s.m.* subscript.

subscritor, *s.m.* subscriber.

subsecção, *s.f.* subsection, subdivision.

subsecretariado, *s.m.* undersecretaryship; office of an undersecretary.

subsecretariar, *v.t.* to act as undersecretary.

subsecretário, *s.m.* subsecretary.

subsecutivo, *adj.* subsecutive, consecutive.

subseguir, *v.t.* to follow after; to come later.

subsequência, *s.f.* subsequence, continuation, sequel.

subsequente, *adj.* subsequent, succeeding; *subsequente a,* subsequente to, following.

subsequentemente, *adv.* subsequently, afterwards.

subserviência, *s.f.* subserviency, servility, flaterry; compliance.

subserviente, *adj.* subservient, servile, cringing, fawning.

subsidiado, *adj.* subsidized, to assisr, to help, to aid, to support.

subsidiar, *v.t.* to subsidize.

subsidiariamente, *adv.* subsidiarily.

subsidiário, *adj.* subsidiary, additional, auxiliary.

subsídio, *s.m.* subsidy, grant, allowance; help, aid, assistance; subvention.

subsistência, *s.f.* subsistence, maintenance, sustenance, living.

subsistente, *adj.* subsisting, subsistent.

subsistir, *v.i.* to subsist, to remain, to exist; to persist, to endure; to survive.

subsolo, *s.m.* subsoil; underground; layer, startum.

substabelecer, *v.t.* to subrogate, to appoint a deputy, to substitute, to transfer to another.

substabelecimento, *s.m.* substitution.

substância, *s.f.* substance, essence, matter.

substancial, *adj.* substantial, nourishing, essential, important.

substancialidade, *s.f.* substantiality.

substancialismo, *s.m.* substantialism.

substancializar, *v.t.* to substantialize.

substancialmente, *adv.* substantially.

substanciar, *v.t.* to substantiate; to nourish; to fortify.

substancioso, *adj.* substantial, nourishing, nutritive.

substantivação, *s.f.* changing into a substantive or a noun.

substantivar, *v.t.* to use as a substantive, to change into a noun, to substantize.

substantivo, *s.m., adj.* substantive, noun.

substituição, *s.f.* substitution; replacement, change.

substituinte, *adj.* substituting, substitutional; *s.* deputy, substitute.

substituir, *v.t.* to substitute, to exchange, to replace, to take the place of; to succeed to; to change, to displace.

substituível, *adj.* substitutable, replaceable.

substitutivo, *adj.* substitutive.

substituto, *s.m.* substitute, deputy, representative.

substrato, *s.m.* substratum, substract.

substrutura, *s.f.* substructure, understructure.

subtendente, *adj.* subtendent.

subtender, *v.t.* to subtend, to extend under.

subtenente, *s.m.* second lieutenant.

subtensa, *s.f.* subtense, chord of an arc.

subterfúgio, *s.m.* subterfuge, shift, evasion, pretext, excuse.

subterrâneo, *adj.* subterranean, underground; *s.m.* subterranean cave, vault.

subterrar, *v.t.* to put under ground, to bury.

subtérreo, *adj.* subterraneous.

subtil, *adj.* subtle, ingenious, clever, acute, delicate.

subtileza, *s.f.* subtlety, acuteness, quibble, nice distinction; sagacity, keenness.

subtilidade, *s.f.* ver subtileza.

subtilização, *s.f.* subtilization.

subtilizar, *v.t.* to subtilize, to make subtle.

subtipo, *s.m.* subtype.

subtítulo, *s.m.* subtitle.

subtracção, *s.f.* subtraction; a theft.

subtractivo, *adj.* subtractive.

subtraendo, *s.m.* subtrahend.

subtrair, *v.t.* to subtract; to take away; to steal; *subtrair-se* to avoid, to escape.

subtropical, *adj.* subtropical.

subtutor, *s.m.* subtutor.

suburbano, *adj.* suburban, outskirt, outlying.

subúrbio, *s.m.* suburb; *(pl.)* outskirts, environs.

subvenção, *s.f.* subvention, subsidy, grant, pecuniary help.

subvencionar, *v.t.* to subsidize, to grant a subvention, to assist.

subversão, *s.f.* subversion, overthrow, upset, insubordination, rebellion.

subversivo, *adj.* subversive, revolutionary.

subversor, subvertedor, *s.m.* subverter; *adj.* subverting.

subverter, *v.t.* to subvert, to overthrow, to overturn, to destroy; to confuse; to disorganize; to pervert; to rouse to revolt.

subvertimento, *s.m.* subversion.

sucata, *s.f.* scraps, scrap iron.

sucateiro, *s.m.* dealer of scraps.

sucção, *s.f.* sucking, suction.

sucedâneo, *adj., s.m.* succedaneous, substitute.

suceder, *v.i.* to succeed, to follow, to come after, to ensue, to be succesor, to happen, to occur, to come to pass, to take place, to befall.

sucedido, *s.m.* an occurrence, happening, incident, vent. 1) *bem sucedido,* successful. 2) *ser bem sucedido,* to succeed, to get on well.

sucessão, *s.f.* succession; lineage; sequence, series, chain, continuity.

sucessivamente, *adv.* successively, in succession.

sucessivo, *adj.* successive.

sucesso, *s.m.* success; event, fact, occurrence; chilbirth, parturition; luck, fortune; triumph; sensation, hit.

sucessor, *s.m.* successor, follower, heir.

sucessório, *adj.* successional; relating to succession.

súcia, *s.f.* gang, band, mob, rabble *(pop)*; spree, revelry.

suciata, *s.f.* merry, making, revelry.

sucintamente, *adv.* succintly, shortly, briefly, curtly.

sucinto, *adj.* succint, concise, brief, short.

súcio, *s.m.* rascal, scoundrel.

suco, *s.m.* juice; sap, essence.

sucosidade, *s.f.* juiceness, succulence.

sucoso, *adj.* juicy, succulent.

súcubo, *s.m.* succubus.

suculência, *s.f.* succulence; sappiness, juiceness.

suculento, *adj.* succulent, juicy, sappy; pulpy; rich, substantial.

sucumbido, *adj.* defeated, dejected, depressed.

sucumbir, *v.i.* to succumb, to yield, to faint; to be overcome; to die; to despair, to lose heart; to submit.

sucursal, *s.f.* branch *(de um negócio)*; chain store.

sucussão, *s.f.* succussion.

sudação, *s.f.* sweating, sweat, perspiration.

sudanês, *adj., s.m.* Sudanese.

sudário, *s.m.* shroud; winding-sheet; series of misfortunes.

sudatório, *adj., s.m.* sudatory, sudorific.

sudeste, *s.m.* south-east.

sudoeste, *s.m.* south-west.

sudorífero, *adj., s.m.* sudoriferous.

sudorífico, *adj.* sudorific.

sudoríparo, *adj.* sudoriparou.

sudra, sudro, *s.m.* Sudra (Hindu caste).

sueca, *s.f.* game *(cartas)*.

suécia, *s.f.* swage-block.

sueco, *adj.* Swedish; *s.m.* Swede; Swedish *(língua)*.

sueste, *s.m.* south-east.

sueto, *s.m.* holiday, rest, repose, leisure.

suficiência, *s.f.* sufficiency, ability, capacity; aptitude.

suficiente, *adj., s.m.* sufficient, enough; fair, satisfactory *(na escola)*.

suficientemente, *adv.* sufficiently, enough, well.

sufixação, *s.m.* suffixion.

sufixar, *v.t.* to suffix.

sufixo, *s.m.* suffix.

sufocação, *s.f.* soffocation, choking; strangulation; oppressiveness.

sufocador, *adj.* suffocating, chocking.

sufocamento, *s.m.* suffocation, asphyxiation.

sufocante, *adj.* suffocating, stifling; sultry, oppressive.

sufocar, *v.t.* to suffocate, to stifle, to smother, to choke, to strangle; to throttle, to repress; to asphyxiate; to quench, to overcome *(uma revolta)*.

sufocativo, *adj.* suffocative, suffocating.

sufragâneo, *adj.* suffragan.

sufragar, *v.t.* to aprove *(por sufrágio)*; to pray for the soul of.

sufrágio, *s.m.* suffrage, vote; prayer for the soul of; approval, assent.

sufragismo, *s.m.* suffragism.

sufragista, *s.* suffragist, suffragette.

sufumigação, *s.m.* suffumigation, fumigation from below.

sufumigar, *v.t.* to suffumigate, to fumigate from below.

sugação, *s.m.* sucking.

sugadoiro, *s.m.* sucker *(insectos)*.

sugador, *s.m.* sucker; suctorial organ; sucking pipe; *adj.* sucking suctorial.

sugadouro, *s.m.* ver sugadoiro.

sugar, *v.t.* to suck, to absorb; to extort *(dinheiro a)*, to bleed.

sugerir, *v.t.* to suggest; to hint; to imply; to recommend, to propose; to bring into the mind; to insinuate; to prompt.

sugerível, *adj.* suggestible.

sugestão, *s.f.* suggestion; hint, insinuation, indication, cue; proposal.

sugestibilidade, *s.f.* suggestibility.

sugestionador, *s.m.* inpirer; *adj.* suggesting.

sugestionamento, *s.m.* act of suggesting.

sugestionante, *adj.* that suggests.

sugestionar, *v.t.* to influence by suggestion, to inspire.

sugestionável, sugestível, *adj.* sugestible, easily influenced.

sugestivo, *adj.* suggestive.

sugilar, *v.t.* to bruise, to contuse, to hurt; to defame, to vilify.

suíças, *s.f. pl.* whiskers.

suicida, *s.* suicide, self murderer; *adj.* suicidal.

suicidar-se, *v. refl.* to commit suicide; to ruin oneself.

suicídio, *s.m.* suicide, self-murder.

suíço, *s.m., adj.* Swiss.

suídeos, *s.m. pl.* Suidae *(família dos suínos)*.

suíno, *s.m.* swine, hog, pig; *adj.* swinish.

sujamente, *adv.* filthily, dirtily, piggisly.

sujar, *v.t.* to soil, to dirty; to sully, to stain; to pollute, to defile.

sujeição, *s.f.* subjection, servitude, submission, subordination, dependence; bondage.

sujeira, *s.f.* filth, dirt, grime; low behaviour.

sujeitar, *v.t.* to subdue, to subject, to submit, to subordinate; to constrain; *sujeitar-se,* to submit, to yeld; to conform to, to obey.

sujeito, *adj.* subject, liable, subordinate, dependent; *s.m.* fellow, guy, man, chap; person, subject.

sujidade, *s.f.* filth, dirtiness, dirt, foulness, nastiness; excrement.

sujo, *adj.* dirty, unclean, filthy, untidy, foul, nasty, sordid, soiled; mean, abject, vile.

sul, *s.m.* south; *adj.* south, southern.

sulano, *s.m.* south wind.

sulaventear, *v.i.* to make leeway.

sulcar, *v.t.* to furrow, to plough; to wrinkle; to streak; *sulcar os mares,* to plough the seas.

sulco, *s.m.* furrow; groove; track; wake.

sulfamida, *s.f.* sulphamide, sulphnonamide.

sulfatador, *s.m.* sulphate sprayer.

sulfatagem, *s.f.* sulphate spraying.

sulfatar, *v.t.* to spray with sopper-sulphate.

sulfatização, *s.f.* sulphatization.

sulfatizar, *v.t.* to sulphatize, to sulphate.

sulfato, *s.m.* sulphate.

sulfídrico, *adj.* hydrosulphuric.

sulfito, *s.m.* sulphite.

súlfur, *s.m.* sulphur.

sulfuração, *s.f.* sulphuration.

sulfurador, *s.m.* sulpurator.

sulfurar, *v.t.* to sulphurate, to sulphurize.

sulfúreo, *adj.* sulphureous, sulphury.

sulfureto, *s.m.* sulphid.

sulfúrico, *adj.* sulphuric.

sulfuroso, *adj.* sulphurous.

sulista, *adj.* southerm; *s.* southerner *(Brasil).*

sultana, *s.f.* sultana.

sultanado, sultanato, *s.m.* sultanship, sultanate.

sultão, *s.m.* sultan.

suma, *s.f.* abridgement; sum; summary; *em suma,* in short, briefly.

sumagre, *s.m.* sumac(h) *(a planta).*

sumamente, *adv.* extremely, supremely, very highly.

sumarento, *adj.* juicy, succulent, sappy.

sumariamente, *adv.* summarily, briefly, concisely.

sumariar, *v.t.* to summarize, to make a summary of, to sum up; to synthetize.

sumário, *adj.* summary, brief, concise, short; *s.m.* summary, digest, epitome, synopsis.

sumaúma, *s.f.* kapok, silk-cotton tree, ceiba tree.

sumição, *s.f.* disappearance, vanishing.

sumiço, *s.m.* ver sumiço; *levar sumiço,* to disappear, to vanish.

sumidade, *s.f.* prominent person, celebrity, authority, high-standing personality.

sumidiço, *adj.* evanescent.

sumido, *adj.* low; sunk, overwhelmed; disappearing; faint, tenuous; lean, thin; indistinct; hidden.

sumidoiro, sumidouro, *s.m.* sinkhole; drain, gutter, gulf.

sumir, *v.t.* to cause to vanish, to make disappear; *sumir-se,* to disappear, to vanish; to sink, to submerge; to conceal, to fade away.

sumo, *adj.* most excellent, highest, supreme; *s.m.* juice, sap.

sumoso, *adj.* juicy, succulent.

sumpção, *s.f.* sumption, consumption.

sumptuário, *adj.* sumptuary, costly, expensive, rich.

sumptuosamente, *adv.* sumptuously.

sumptuosidade, *s.f.* sumptuosity, magnificence, splendour, state.

sumptuoso, *adj.* sumptuous, splendid, gorgeous; costly, expensive, rich.

súmula, *s.f.* epitome, abridgement, summary.

suor, *s.m.* perspiration, sweat; labour, hard work.

supedâneo, *s.m.* footstool, foot-rest. footboard; pedestal; foundation.

supeditar, *v.t.* to furnish, to provide, to supply.

superabundância, *s.f.* superabundance, excess, superfluity, overflow: exuberance; oversupply.

superabundante, *adj.* superabundant, overflowing, copious, excessive, exuberant.

superabundar, *v.i.* to superabound to be in excess, to be full.

superação, *s.f.* surpassing.

superacidez, *s.f.* excessive acidity.

superácido, *s.m., adj.* superacid.

superar, *v.t.* to surpass, to exceed, to outdo; to overcome; to surmount.

superável, *adj.* surmountable, surpassable.

superavit, *s.m.* surplus.

superciliar, *adj.* superciliary.

supercílio, *s.m.* brow, eyebrow.

supercilioso, *adj.* supercilious; arrogant, austere.

supercivilizado, *adj.* supercivilized.

supereminência, *s.f.* supereminence.

supereminente, *adj.* supereminent.

superficial, *adj.* superficial; shallow; frivolous, slight, external.

superficialidade, *s.f.* superficiality, shallowness.

superficialmente, *adv.* superficially, slightly, perfunctorily.

superfície, *s.f.* surface; area; outside; superficies.

superfino, *adj.* superfine, refined, very fine, of the best quality.

superfluidade, *s.f.* superfluity, superfluousness, excess.

supérfluo, *adj.* superfluous; needless, useless, unnecessary.

super-homem, *s.m.* superman.

super-humano, *adj.* super-human.

superintendência, *s.f.* superintendence; overseeing, management, supervision.

superintendente, *s.* superintendent, overseer, manager.

superintender, *v.i.* to superintend, to oversee, to direct, to manage, to supervise.

superior, *adj.* superior; upper; higher; greater; *s.m.* superior, master, chief.

superiora, *s.f.* mother superior.

superioridade, *s.f.* superiority.

superiorizar, *v.t.* to make superior.

superiormente, *adv.* in a masterly manner, superiorly.

superlativamente, *adv.* superlatively.

superlativar, *v.t.* to render superlative.

superlativo, *s.m.*, *adj.* superlative.

superlotação, *s.f.* overcrowd.

superlotar, *v.t.* to overcrowd, to overload.

supermercado, *s.m.* supermarket.

superno, *adj.* supernal; excellent.

supernumerário, *adj.* supernumerary.

súpero, *adj.* superior.

superpor, *v.t.* to superpose.

superposição, *s.f.* superposition.

superprodução, *s.f.* overproduction.

supersaturação, *s.f.* supersaturation.

supersaturar, *v.t.* to supersaturate.

supersensível, *adj.* supersensible.

supersónico, *adj.* supersonic.

superstição, *s.f.* superstition, credulity.

supersticiosamente, *adv.* superstitiously.

supersticioso, *adj.* superstitious, credulous, fanatical.

superstrutura, *s.f.* superstructure.

supervenção, *s.f.* supervention.

superveniência, *s.f.* supervenience.

superveniente, *adj.* supervenient.

supervisão, *s.f.* supervision.

supervisionar, *v.t.* supervise.

supervisor, *s.m.* supervisor.

supervivência, *s.f.* survival.

supervivente, *adj.* surviving; *s.* surviver.

supetão, *s.m.* only used in the expression: *de supetão,* all of a sudden suddenly.

supinação, *s.f.* supination.

supinador, *s.m.* supinator.

supinamente, *adv.* supinely; indolently.

supino, *adj.* supine; turned up, lying on the back; superior, excessive.

suplantação, *s.f.* supplanting.

suplantador, *s.m.* supplanter.

suplantar, *v.t.* to supplant, to oust, to supersede.

suplementar, *adj.* supplementary, additional, extra.

suplementário, *adj.* supplementary.

suplemento, *s.m.* supplement; extra charge.

suplente, *adj.* substitutive; *s.* substitute, proxy, alternate.

supletivo, *adj.* suppletive.

supletório, *adj.* suppletory.

súplica, *s.f.* supplication, entreaty, prayer; petition, request.

suplicação, *s.f.* ver súplica.

suplicante, *s.* suppliant, petitioner; *adj.* supplicating.

suplicar, *v.t.* to supplicate, to entreat, to bessech, to implore; to pray; to plead.

suplicativo, suplicatório, *adj.* supplicatory.

súplice, *adj.* suppliant, suplicant, beseeching, pleading.

supliciado, *adj.* executed; *s.m.* executed, criminal.

supliciar, *v.t.* to execute, to torture.

suplício, *s.m.* torture, torment, suffering; capital punishment.

supor, *v.t.* to suppose, to imagine; to allege, to infer, to presume; to take for granted; to fancy, to believe; to think.

suportar, *v.t.* to support; to bear, to endure; to stand.

suportável, *adj.* supportable, endurable, bearable.

suporte, *s.m. prop.* stand, bearer. support; rest; stay.

suposição, *s.f.* supposition, conjecture, surmise; assumption.

supositório, *s.m.* suppository.

suposto, *adj.* supposed; *suposto que,* allowing that; supposing, granting that.

supracitado, *adj.* above-mentioned, mentioned before.

supradito, *adj.* ver supracitado.

supramencionado, *adj.* above-mentioned.

supranumerário, *s.m., adj.* supernumerary.

supra-renal, *adj.* suprarenal.

supra-sensível, *adj.* supersensible.

supra-sumo, *s.m.* top, utmost, the highest, the ideal.

supremacia, *s.f.* supremacy, domination, power, preponderance.

supremo, *adj.* supreme, highest, paramount; Supreme Court.

supressão, *s.f.* supression, cancellation, extinction, omission.

supressivo, supressor, *adj.* suppressive.

supressório, *adj.* suppressible.

supridor, *adj.* supplying; *s.m.* supplier, furnisher.

suprimento, *s.m.* supply, loan; suppliment; assistance, aid; advance.

suprimir, *v.t.* to suppress, to do away with; to cancel, to abolish, to eliminate; to omit, not to mention.

suprir, *v.t.* to supply, to furnish, to make up for, to take the place of, to substitute; to fill in or up, to complete.

suprível, *adj.* replaceable; suppliable.

supuração, *s.f.* suppuration.

supurante, *adj.* suppurating.

supurar, *v.i.* to suppurate.

supurativo, *adj.* suppurative.

suputação, *s.f.* reckoning, computation, calculation, estimate.

suputar, *v.t.* to compute, to reckon, to calculate, to value.

surdamente, *adv.* without noise; in secrecy.

surdear, *v.i.* to feign to be deaf, to play deaf.

surdez, *s.f.* deafness.

surdimutismo, *s.m.* deaf-mutism.

surdina, *s.f.* damper, sordine, mute; *em surdina,* silently, softly, in a wisper; on the sly.

surdir, *v.t.* to spring, to issue forth; to emerge, to appear; to result from.

surdo, adj. deaf, insensible; heedless, unattentive; muffled *(som)*; voiceless *(consoante).* 1) *surdo a,* deaf to; indifferent to. 2) *surdo como uma porta,* as deaf as a post, stone-deaf. 3) *fazer-se surdo,* not to listen, not to care for.

surdo-mudez, *s.f.* deaf-muteness.

surdo-mudo, *adj., s.m.* deaf-mute, deaf-and-dumb.

surgir, *v.i.* to emerge, to loom, to appear; to arise; to spring up, to gush out; to come to light.

surpreendente, *adj.* surprising; astonishing, amazing, startling; remarkable, wonderful, extraordinary, marvellous.

surpreender, *v.t.* to surprise, to excite, wonder in, to startle, to amaze, to astonih, to astound; to shock; to catch unwares, to detect; to overhear.

surpreendido, *adj.* astonished, surprised; overtaken, caught; *ficar surpreendido com,* to be surprised at.

surpresa, *s.f.* surprise; amazement; trick; *de surpresa,* by surprise; unawares, unexpectedly.

surpreso, *adj.* ver "surpreendido".

surra, *s.f.* thrashing, beating, cudgelling, spanking.

surrado, *adj.* threadbare, worn-thin, seedy, worn-out; beaten; curried *(pele).*

surrador, *s.m.* currier, tanner.

surramento, *s.m.* tanning, currying *(pele).*

surrão, *s.m.* leather bag.

surrar, *v.t.* to curry *(pele);* to thrash, to beat *surrar-se,* to wear out, to become threadbare.

surrealismo, *s.m.* surrealism.

surrealista, *adj., s.* surrealist.

surriada, *s.f.* hooting, hissing, mockery, scoff; volley *(armas);* spray, foam; *fazer surriada,* to hoot, to hiss, to mock.

surriba, *s.f.* deep digging.

surribar, *v.t.* to dig deeply.

surripiar, *v.t.* to cheat, to swindle: to steal, to pilfer, to purloin, to filch.

surro, *s.m.* dirtiness, filthiness, filth; waste, trash; coal-dust.

surrobeco, *s.m.* coarse, cotton cloth, kind of burel.

surtir, *v.t.* to produce, to bring about, to give rise to, to cause; to succeed, to thrive, to result; *surtir efeito,* to take effect, to produce the desired result.

surto, *adj.* at anchor, moored; *s.m.* outbreak, eruption, impetus.

sus!, *interj.* come!, up!, courage!, go on!, take heart!

susceptibilidade, *s.f.* susceptibility; sensitiveness, touchiness.

susceptibilizar, *v.t.* to offend slightly, to hurt

(sentimentos); susceptibilizar-se, to feel offended, to take offence.

susceptível, *adj.* susceptible; liable to, admitting of; sensitive, touchy.

suscitação, *s.f.* arousal, prompting; instigation, stimulation, incitement.

suscitador, *s.m.* instigator, inciter.

suscitamento, *s.m. ver "suscitação".*

suscitar, *v.t.* to raise, to stir up, to excite; to bring on, to cause, to occasion.

suserania, *s.f.* suzerainty.

suserano, *adj., s.m.* suzerain.

suspeição, *s.f. ver suspeita.*

suspeita, *s.f.* suspicion, doubt, mistrust.

suspeitador, *s.m.* suspecter; *adj.* suspecting.

suspeitar, *v.t.* to suspect, to mistrust, to distrust; to conjecture, to presume.

suspeito, *adj.* suspicious; untrustworthy, doubtful.

suspeitoso, *adj. ver "suspeito".*

suspender, *v.t.* to hang up, to suspend; to stop, to interrupt; to adjourn *(reunião),* to delay, to postpone.

suspensão, *s.f.* suspension; hanging up; adjournment, temporary dismissal *(do emprego);* floating *(partículas).*

suspensivo, *adj.* suspensive.

suspenso, *adj.* suspended, hanging; adjourned; *em suspenso,* in suspense.

suspensor, *adj.* suspending.

suspensório, *adj.* suspensory; *s.m.* suspender; *(pl.)* braces, suspenders.

suspicácia, *s.f.* distrust, suspiciousness.

suspicaz, *adj.* suspicious, questionable.

suspitado, *adj.* sighed for, longed for.

suspirante, *adj.* sighing, craving for.

suspirar, *v.i.* to sigh; to pine for, to long for; to lament.

suspiro, *s.m.* sigh; white of egg; small meringue; sweet scabiosa *(bot.);* vent.

suspiroso, *adj.* sighing; lamenting.

suspirador, *s.m.* sigher.

sussurrante, *adj.* whispering, murmuring, rustling; purling.

sussurrar, *v.i.* to whisper, to rustle, to murmur; to rustle; to ripple, to purl.

sussurro, *s.m.* whisper, murmur; rustle *(folhas)* purl *(água).*

sustância, *s.f.* substance, food; strength, vigour.

sustar, *v.t.* to stop, to halt, to suspend; to cease, to defer.

sustenido, *s.f.* sharp *(música).*

sustentação, *s.f.* support; maintenance, subsistence, livelihood.

sustentáculo, *s.m.* support, stay, prop; supporter.

sustentador, *s.m.* sustainer, supporter; *adj.* sustaining.

sustentar, *v.t.* to sustain; to maintain; to provide for; to bear, to support, to keep, to nourish; to endure; to assert, to affirm; *sustentar-se,* to resist, to defend oneself; to live on.

sustentável, *adj.* sustainable, defensible, supportable.

sustento, *s.m.* sustenance, nourishing, maintenance, food.

suster, *v.t.* to sustain, to hold up; to restrain, to stop.

susto, *s.m.* fright, scare, shock; 1) *pregar um susto,* to scare, to frighten.

su-sudeste, *s.m.* south-southeast.

su-sudoeste, *s.m.* south-southwest.

suta, *s.f.* bevel.

sutura, *s.f.* suture; seam.

suturar, *v.t.* to join, to suture.

T

t, the nineteenth letter of the Portuguese alphabet.

tabacal, *s.m.* tobacco plantation.

tabacaria, *s.f.* tobacconist´s *(loja).*

tabaco, *s.m.* tobacco; tobacco-plant; *levar para tabaco,* to be taught a lesson.

tabagismo, *s.m.* tobaccoism.

tabaquear, *v.i.* to snuff, to smoke tobacco.

tabaqueira, *s.f.* snuff-box; tobacco-pouch.

tabaqueiro, *adj.* relating to tobacco.

tabaquismo, *s.m.* abuse of smoking, over-smoking.

tabardilha, *s.f.* small tabard.

tabardo, *s.m.* tabard.

tabefe, *s.m.* buffet, cuff, slap, blow; whey, eggnog.

tabela, *s.f.* table (of contents); list; legend; chart, schedule; billiard-table cushion. 1) *tabela de preços,* price list. 2) *por tabela,* indirectly. 3) *repreensão por tabela;* indirect rebuke. 4) *chegar à tabela,* to arrive on time or up to the time or schedule. 5) *vender à tabela,* to sell at fixed price.

tabelamento, *s.m.* price-control.

tabelar, *v.t.* to fix, to restrain or to regulate prices.

tabeliado, *s.m.* notary´s profession.

tabelião, *s.m.* notary (public).

tabelionado, tabelionato, *s.m.* office of a notary, notary´s office.

taberna, *s.f.* tavern, inn, public house, pub.

tabernáculo, *s.m.* tabernacle.

taberneiro, *s.m.* tavern-keeper, inn-keeper, publican.

tabique, *s.m.* wood-partition; partition (wall).

tablado, *s.m.* scaffold; stage (of a theatre); raised platform; boxing ring.

tabu, *s.m.* taboo; prohibited, forbidden.

tabua, *s.f. mandar à tabua,* to send one about one´s business.

tábua, *s.f.* board, plank; index, table (of contents); map; list. 1) *tábua de salvação,* last resource. 2) *fazer tábua rasa,* to wipe off the slate. 3) *tábua de logaritmos,* logarithmic table. 4) *tábua de passar a ferro,* ironing board. 5) *tábua de mesa,* leaf of a table.

tabuada, *s.f.* multiplication table.

tabuado, *s.m.* floor; planks; wooden floor.

tabuinha, *s.f.* slat, thin board; *salvar-se numa tabuinha,* to have a narrow escape.

tabulado, *s.m.* wooden partition; wooden floor; wooden fence.

tabulador, *s.m.* tabulator *(tecla)* in a typewriter.

tabulageiro, *s.m.* gaming-house keeper.

tabulagem, *s.f.* gaming-house.

tabular, *adj.* tabular.

tabuleiro, *s.m.* tray; bed *(no jardim);* platform *(de uma ponte);* chessboard; tin to bake cakes on; *tabuleiro de damas,* draught--board.

tabuleta, *s.f.* sign-board *(na frente de um edifício),* plate, name-plate, brass-plate.

taburno, *s.m.* footstool; stairstep; sepulchral cover plate.

taça, *s.f.* cup, champagne plass; trophy cup.

tacada, *s.f.* stroke *(com um taco, golf).*

taçada, *s.f.* cupful.

tacanharia, *s.f.* meanness.

tacanhez, tacanheza, tacanhice, *s.f.* stupidity; avarice; narrow-mindedness; stinginess.

tacanho, *adj.* stupid; covetous; narrow-minded; stingy, miserly.

tacão, *s.m.* heel *(de uma bota ou sapato).*

taceira, *s.f.* showcase.

tacha, *s.f.* blemish, fault; tack, small nail, flat-headed nail, shoestud.

tachada, *s.f.* panful, potful, boilerful; drunken, tipsy *(popular).*

tachado, *adj.* branded, stigmatized, drunk.

tachão, *s.m.* stud; big pot or pan.

tachar, *v.t.* to find fault with; to brand as, to stigmatize; *tachar-se,* to get drunk.

tachinha, *s.f.* small tack; small stain.

tacho, *s.m.* pot, pan .

tachonado, *adj.* studded.

tachonar, v.t. to stud, to adorn with studs; to spot, to speckle.

tacitamente, adv. tacitly, implicitly.

tácito, adj. tacit; silent; understood, implied, implicit, inferred.

taciturnidade, s.f. taciturnity, reserve.

taciturno, adj. taciturn, silent, reserved, uncommunicative.

taco, s.m. cue, billiard cue; golf stick; hockey stick; polo mallet; wooden plug.

tacteante, adj. fumbling, groping; touching, feeling.

tactear, v.t. to feel, to touch; to fumble, to grope; to search blindly.

tacteável, adj. touchable.

táctica, s.f. tactics; policy, diplomacy.

táctico, s.m. tactician; adj. tactical.

táctil, adj. tactile; tangible.

tactilidade, s.f. tactility, tangibility.

tacto, s.m. tact, adroitness, discretion, diplomacy, prudence, alertness, skill, discernment; touch , feeling.

tafetá, s.m. taffeta.

taful, s.m. beau, buck,dandy; adj. dandyish, foppish, affected.

tafular, v.i. to be fashionable, to live dandyishly.

tafularia, s.f. dandyism, smartness; group of gamblers.

tafulhar, v.t. to cram, to stuff.

tafulho, s.m. plug or cork; stopper.

tafulice, s.f. vd. tafularia.

tagantada, s.f. stroke.

tagantar, v.t. to strike, to lash, to flog, to scourge, to whip.

tagante, s.m. lash, whip, scourge, thong.

taganteador, s.m. scourger, flogger; adj. whipping, flogging.

tagantear, v.t. v.d. tagantar.

tagarela, adj. talkative, garrulous, prattling; s. talker, chatterbox, gossip, chatterer, tattler.

tagarelar, v.i. to chatter, to gossip, to jabber, to babble.

tagarelice, s.f. chatter, gossip, prattle, garrulity.

tagaté, s.m. cajolery, caress, pat; fazer tagatés, to wheedle, to cajole.

taina, s.f. feast with excessive eating.

tainha, s.f. grey mullet.

taipa, s.f. lathe-and-plaster wall, wall of mud.

taipal, s.m. outside shutter (de uma loja); plaster or mud wall; wooden mold for concrete; side walls of a truck.

taipar, v.t. to enclose with mud walls.

tal, adj. such, like, similar; adv. so, thus; pron. this, that. 1) tal pai, tal filho, like father, like son. 2) tal qual, just as just like, exactly so. 3) fulano de tal, John Doe. 4) de tal maneira, in such a way. 5) um tal João, a certain John. 6) a tal ponto, to such a degree (or extent). 7) que tal um cigarro?, how about a cigarrete?. 8) é tal e qual, it is exactly the same. 9) em tal caso, in that case; in such a case. 10) outro que tal, another such. 11) que tal ?, well?, what do you think of it ?, what do you say?, how does it strike you ?

tala, s.f. lathe; splint; dilemma, predicament, fix; ver-se em talas, to be in a fix.

talabarte, s.m. baldric, shoulder belt.

talagarça, s.f. canvas.

talamento, s.m. destruction, ravage, devastation.

tálamo, s.m. nuptialbed; wedding; thalamus (botânica, anatomia).

talante, s.m. will, pleasure; a seu bel-talante, at one´s pleasure.

talão, s.m. stock, counterpart, counterfoil, coupon stub.

talar, v.t. to ravage, to spoil, to waste; to trench, to destroy; to till, to plough; adj. relating to a counterfoil; heel, heel-length; hábito talar, priest´s robes.

talassa, s. Portuguese monarchists or reactionists.

talassaria, s.f. group of monarchists.

talássico, adj. thalassic.

talassocracia, s.f. thalassocracy, sea-power.

talassofobia, s.f. thalassophoby.

talassografia, s.f. thalassography, oceano-graphy.

talassográfico, adj. thalassographic, oceanographic.

talassómetro, s.m. thalassometer, tide-gauge.

talassoterapia, s.f. thalassotherapy, sea--bathing.

talco, s.m. talc, talcum powder.

talcoso, adj. talcous, talcose.

taleiga, s.f. wallet, sack (para grão ou farinha).

taleigada, s.f. sackful, bagful.

taleigo, s.m. narrow bag.

talento, s.m. talent, ability, skill. aptitude, faculty, genius, gift, accomplishment.

talentoso, adj. talented, able, gifted, clever.

talha, s.f. vessel (para água), water-pot.

talhada, *s.f.* cut, slice, chop, peirce.

talladeira, *s.f.* chopping knife, cleaver.

talhado, *adj.* able; fit; cut out; chopped; fashioned, proper, apt; carved, shaped; sour *(leite)*.

talhador, *s.m.* cutter, chopper; chopping--knife.

talhadura, *s.f.* cutting, incision, cleaving.

talha-mar, *s.m.* cutwater, stem, forefoot.

talhante, *adj.* cutting, cleaving; *s.* butcher.

talhão, *s.m.* bed *(num jardim);* water-pot.

talhar, v.t. to cut, to cut out, to hew; to carve, to engrave; to tailor, to fashion; to curdle *(leite);* to prevent, to put a stop to.

talhe, *s.m.* cut *(de um casaco),* style; figure; size, form, configuration.

talher, *s.m.* cover *(na mesa);* set of knife, fork and spoon; each of places at table.

talho, *s.m.* butcher's *(loja),* butchery; a cut; act of cutting; tree pruning; butcher's block; a plot of land; shape, form; *vir a talho de foice,* to come to the purpose or at the right time.

talião, *s.m.* retaliation, talion; *pena de talião,* law of retaliation.

talim, *s.m.* shoulder-belt, sash, baldric, sword-belt.

talinga, *s.f.* cable, rope, anchor rope; clinch knot.

talingadura, *s.f.* clinching of a rope.

talingar, *v.t.* to clinch.

tálio, *s.m.* thallium.

talionar, *v.t., .v.i.* to retaliate; to pay back in the same kind.

talionato, *s.m.* talion, the law of retaliation *(de "olho por olho, dente por dente").*

talisca, *s.f.* crevice, chink; fragment, splinter.

talismã, *s.m.* talisman, amulet, fetich, charm.

talismânico, *adj.* talismanic, magic.

Talmude, *s.m.* Talmud.

talmúdico, *adj.* Talmudic(al).

talmudista, *s.* Talmudist; *adj.* Talmudistic.

talo, *s.m* stalk, stem, axis, petiole *(planta);* shaft *(coluna);* shoot *(raiz);* thallus *(botânica).*

talocha, *s.f.* mason's float or mortarboard.

talófita, *s.f.* thallophyte.

taluda, *s.f.* the highest prize *(lotaria).*

talude, *s.m.* slope, embankment, ramp, incline, scarp, shelvung; talus .

taludo, *adj.* stalky, grown-up, stout, well-developed, corpulent, strong.

talvez, *adv.* perhaps; maybe, possibly.

tamanca, *s.f.* clog, wooden-soled shoe.

tamanco, *s.m.* clog, wooden-shoe.

tamanhão, *adj.* vert tall, big, large stout, strong.

tamanhinho, tamanhino, *adj.* very small, little, tiny, short, minute.

tamanho, *adj.* so great, big, large, so remarkable, eminent; *s.m.* size, dimensions, volume, extent, magnitude; *tamanho natural,* life size.

tamanquear, *v.i.* to clatter with clogs.

tamanqueiro, *s.m.* clogger, clogmaker or seller.

tâmara, *s.f.* date.

tamaral, *s.m.* a grove of date palms.

tamareira, *s.f.* date palm.

tamargal, *s.m.* plantation of tamarisks.

tamargueira, *s.f.* tamarisk.

tamarindal, *s.m.* a grove of tamarinds.

tamarindeiro, *s.m.* tamarind-tree.

tamarindo, *s.m.* tamarind.

tamarisco, *s.m.* tamarisk seed.

tamariz, *s.m.* tamarisk.

também, *adv., conj.* also, too, as well, besides, likewise, moreover.

tambor, *s.m.* drum; drummer; barrel *(de uma máquina);* eardrum, the tympanum.

tamborete, *s.m.* low stool, footstool, tabouret.

tamboril, *s.m.* timbrel, tabor, tambourine, monk-fish.

tamborilar, *v.i.* to patter; to drum, to rap *(com os dedos).*

tamborileiro, *s.m.* drummer.

tamborim, *s.m. v.d.* tamboril.

tamiça, *s.f.* thin cord of esparto.

tamiceiro, *s.m.* maker or seller of esparto cords.

tamis, *s.m.* silk sieve, strainer of cloth.

tamisação, *s.f.* sifting, sievimg, straining.

tamisar, *v.t.* to sift, to sieve, to strain; to bolt *(farinha).*

tampa, *s.f.* cover, lid; cap.

tampão, *s.m.* cover; stopper; plug; compress, tampon *(cirurgia).*

tampar, *v.t.* to cover; to top, to shut; to tampon.

tampo, *s.m.* cap, cover; top; toilet seat cover; the back or front of a stringed instrument; head.

tampouco, *adv.* either, neither.

tanado, *adj.* brown, tan-coloured, tanned, chesnut-coloured.

tanagem, *s.f.* tannage, tanning.

tanar, *v.t.* to tan, to make brown.

tanásia, *s.f.* tansy *(botânica).*

tanato, *s.m.* tannate.

tanchagem, *s.f.* ribgrass, platain, roadweed.

tanchão, *s.m.* slip, twig; vine-prop, vine-stick, grapevine stake.

tanchar, *v.t.* to set twigs, to plant sticks or cuttings; to stake *(plantas);* to drive in.

tanchoal, *s.m.* plantation of sapplings; nursery.

tandem, *s.m.* tandem.

tanga, *s.f.* breech-cloth, loin-cloth; *estar (ficar) de tanga,* to be penniless, to be completely run down.

tangedor, *s.m.* player *(instrumentos musicais);* driver *(de animais).*

tangência, *s.f.* tangency.

tangencial, *adj.* tangential.

tangencialmente, *adv.* tangentially.

tangenciar, *v.t.* to touch, to be tangent to, to contact, to graze.

tangente, *adj.* touching, tangent; *s.f.* tangent; *escapar pela tangente,* to have a narrow escape *(na escola).*

tanger, *v.t.* to play on *(musical instruments);* to ring *(as campaínhas);* to drive *(gado); tanger a,* to relate to, to refer to, to concern.

tangerina, *s.f.* tangerine.

tangerineira, *s.f.* tangerine-tree, mandarin orange tree.

tangerino, *adj., s.m.* Tangerine, inhabitant or native of Tangier.

tangibilidade, *s.f.* tangibility.

tangível, *adj.* tangible, tactile, palpable; corporeal.

tango, *s.m.* tango *(uma dança).*

tanho, *s.m.* big basket *(para cereais).*

tânico, *adj.* tannic.

taninizar, *v.t.* to add tannin to.

tanino, *s.m.* tannin.

taninoso, *adj.* containing tannin.

tanjão, *adj.* idle, lazy, indolent, lazy bones.

tanoar, *v.i.* to cooper, to make barrels or casks.

tanoaria, *s.f.* cooper´s *(loja);* cooperage.

tanoeiro, *s.m.* cooper, barrelmaker.

tanque, *s.m.* tank; cistern; pond.

tanso, *adj.* foolish, dum, sluggish; simpleton, booby, fool.

tantã, *s.m.* tom-tom, gong.

tantálico, *adj.* tantalic.

tântalo, *s.m.* tantalum *(química).*

tanto, adv. as much, so much; *(pl.)* as many, so many. 1) *tanto assim que,* as much so that. 2) *tanto como,* as much as. 3) *tanto eu como ele,* both he and. 4) *tanto faz,* it

makes no difference. 5) *tanto melhor,* so much the better, all the better. 6) *tanto quanto,* as much as; as far as. 7) *tanto se me dá,* it´s all the same to me. 8) *tanto um como outro,* both of them. 9) *não é tanto assim,* it´s not as bad as all that. 10) *outro tanto,* as much again. 11) *se tanto,* at most, if that much. 12) *um tanto,* somewhat, a little. 13) *um tanto ou quanto,* more or less. 14) *vinte e tantos livros,* twenty odd books. 15) *tanto mais que,* all the more since.

tão, *adv.* so, such, as, as much; as well; 1) *tão bem como,* as well as; 2) *tão... como...,* as...as.

taoismo, *s.m.* Taoism.

taoista, *s.* Taoist.

tão-só, tão-somente, *adv.* only, merely, simply.

tapa, *s.f.* side wall of a hoof; tampion of a gun; slap, rap, cuff; clincher; blindfold *(para cavalos).*

tapada, *s.f.* park; enclosure.

tapado, *adj.* stopped up; closed; covered, hidden; plugged, tamponed; stupid, dull.

tapador, *s.m.* cover, lid; stopper.

tapadouro, *s.m.* cover; axle end.

tapadura, tapagem, *s.f.* stopping, covering, enclosure, hedgerow.

tapamento, *s.m.* enclosure; screen; act of stopping or plugging.

tapar, *v.t.* to stop, to close, to cover, to screen, to hide; to plug; to shut off *(com uma cancela),* to hedge.

tapear, *v.t.* to fool, to trick, to deceive; to disguise, to dissemble.

tapeçaria, *s.f.* tapestry, hangings, drapery, carpets.

tapeceiro, *s.m.* upholsterer; carpet-maker.

tapetar, *v.t.* to carpet.

tapete, *s.m.* carpet, rug; grassplot, lawn.

tapeteiro, *s.m.* upholsterer; carpet-maker.

tapioca, *s.f.* tapioca.

tapir, *s.m.* tapir.

tapiz, *s.m.* tapis, carpet.

tapizar, *v.t.* to cover with carpets.

tapona, *s.f.* blow, stroke, hit *(popular).*

tapulhar, *v.t.* to stop up, to plug.

tapulho, *s.m.* tampion, plug, stoppre.

tapume, *s.m.* fence, hedge, boarding, palisade, paling.

taqueira, *s.f.* cue rack .

taqueiro, *s.m.* parquet layer, parquetry maker.

taqueógrafo, *s.m.* recording tacheometer.

taqueometria, s.f. tachymetry.

taqueómetro, s.m. tachymeter.

taquicardia, s.f. tachycardia.

taquicardíaco, adj. tachycardiac.

taquigrafar, v.t. to write shorthand, to stenograph.

taquigrafia, s.f. stenography, tachygraphy.

taquigráfico, adj. tachygraphical.

taquígrafo, s.m. tachygrapher, stenographer.

taquímetro, s.m. tachymeter, speedometer.

tara, s.f. flaw; degeneration; defect; tare *(comercial)*.

tarado, adj. tared; ill-famed; degenerate; unbalanced.

taralhão, s.m. bee-bird, fly catcher.

tarambola, s.f. plover.

taramela, s.f. mill-clapper; wooden bolt; gabbler, chatterbox.

taramelagem, s.f. gossip,glibness.

taramelar, taramelear, v.i. to gabble, to chat, to talk idly.

tarameleiro, s.m. talkative person.

taramelice, s.f. idle talking.

tarantela, s.f. tarantella *(dança)*.

tarantismo, s.m. tarantism.

tarântula, s.f. tarantula.

tarar, v.t. to tare *(comercial)*.

tarara, s.f. winnowing-machine.

taraxaco, s.m. taraxacum; dandelion *(bot.)*.

tardador, s.m. delayer; adj. dilatory, tardy.

tardamento, tardança, s.m., s.f. delay, procrastination, tardiness.

tardar, v.i. to delay, to loiter, to be long, to be late in coming; to linger, to tarry.

tarde, adv. late; s.f. afternoon; evening. 1) *à tarde*, in the afternoon. 2) *hoje à tarde*, this afternoon. 3) *mais vale tarde que nunca*, better late than never. 4) *ontem à tarde*, yesterday afternoon. 5) *mais tarde*, later on, afterwards. 6) *fazer-se tarde*, to grow late.

tardego, tardeiro, adj. tardy.

tardeza, s.f. tardiness, lateness.

tardiamente, adv. late, tardly.

tardígrado, adj., s.m. tardigrade, slow-moving.

tardinha, s.f. nightfall, late afternoon.

tardio, adj. late, slow, tardy; inopportune, untimely.

tardívago, adj. moving slowly, sluggish.

tardo, adj. slow, sluggish; lazy, indolent; clumsy, awkward.

tarear, v.t. to tare, to balance; to thrash, to beat, to cudgel.

tareco, s.m. fool, silly person; piece of junk; cat, puss; *(plu.)* sticks of furniture.

tarefa, s.f. task, toil; duty, job, work, labour; assignment.

tarefeiro, s.m. pieceworker, jobber.

tareia, s.m. drubbing, thrashing, spanking, flogging, sound beating; dressing down.

tarelar, v.i. to gossip, to chatter, to prattle.

tarelice, s.f. gabbling, gossip, idle talk.

tarifa, s.f. tariff; rate, price-list; table of charges.

tarifar, v.t. to tariff, to fix a tariff on.

tarima, s.f. platform.

tarimba, s.f. wooden platform, plank-bed; bunk; army life.

tarimbar, v.i. to serve in the army.

tarimbeiro, s.m. officer risen from the ranks; adj. coarse, rude, impolite, rough.

tarja, s.f. border, edging; targe, shield.

tarjar, v.t. to border, to surround with a black border.

tarjeta, s.f. narrow border, mourning stripe.

tarlatana, s.f. tarlatan, fine muslin; buckram.

taró, s.m. cold wind *(popular)*.

tarraçada, s.f. bowful, great quantity of drink.

tarrafa, s.f. sweep-net, fishing net, casting net.

tarraxa, s.f. screw, die, vice.

tarraxar, v.t. to screw, to rivet.

tarro, s.m. milk- pail.

tarso, s.m. tarsus, ankle.

tartamudear, v.i. to stutter, to stammer, to falter.

tartamudez, s.f. stuttering, stammering, faltering, speech difficulty.

tartamudo, adj. stuttering, stammering; s.m. stutterer, stammerer.

tartana, s.f. tartan *(vaso)*.

tartarato, s.m. tartrate.

tartárico, adj. tartaric.

tartarizar, v.t. to tartarize.

tártaro, s.m. tartar *(de vinho, de dentes)*; scale; hell; a Tartar *(na Ásia)*; adj. Tartarian.

tartaroso, adj. tartarous.

tasna, tasneira, s.f. ragwort, ragweed.

tartaruga, s.f. turtle, tortoise.

tartufice, s.f. Tartuffism, hypocrisy, dissimulation.

tartufismo, s.m. Tartuffism.

tartufo, s.m. tartuffe, hypocrite, false friend, dissembler.

taruca, taruga, s.f. vicugna, the wild llama.

tarugar, v.t. to dowel, to fasten with dowels.

tarugo, s.m. dowel; peg, wooden pin.

tasca, s.f. low tavern; cheap eating place.

tascadeira, s.f. woman who beats or scutches flax, hemp.

tascar, v.t. to chew; to masticate; to swingle, to beat, to scutch; to champ (cavalo).

tasco, s.m. scutch, refuse of hemp; tavern, low public house.

tasna, tasneira, s.f. ragwort, ragweed.

tasneirinha, s.f. groundsel.

tasqueiro, s.m. keeper of a eatinghouse, taverner, innkeeper.

tasquinhar, v.t. to chew, to eat, to nibble; to swingle, to beat; to backbite.

tassalho, s.m. cut, slice, piece, lump.

tataraneto, s.m. great-great-great-grandson.

tataranha, s. timid, shy person.

tataranhar, v.i. to stammer, to falter, to stutter; to be at a loss; to be irresolute, bewildered; to make a mess of.

tataranho, s.m. stammerer, falterer.

tatibitate, s. shy, timid person; stammerer.

tato, adj. stammering, stuttering.

tatu, s.m. armadillo.

tatuador, s.m. one who tattoos.

tatuagem, s.m. tattoo, tottooing, tattoo mark.

tatuar, v.t. to tattoo.

taumaturgia, s.m. thaumaturgy; magic.

taumaturgo, s.m. thaumaturge.

táureo, taurino, adj. taurine, bullish, oxlike (poét.).

tauro, s.m. Taurus (constelação).

tauromaquia, s.f. bullfighting, tauromachy.

tauromáquico, adj. relating to a bullfighting, tauromachian.

tautocronismo, s.m. tautochronism, simultaneousness.

tautócrono, adj. tautochronous, synchronous.

tautofonia, s.f. tautophony.

tautologia, s.f. tautology.

tautológico, adj. tautological, tautologic.

tauxia, s.f. damascene, marquetry.

tauxiar, v.t. to damascene, to inlay.

tavanês, adj. active, busy; turbulent, heedless, rash; restless.

tavão, s.m. horse-fly, gad-fly.

taverna, s.f. tavern, inn, pub.

taverneiro, s.m. innkeeper, taverner.

tavolagem, s.f. gambling-house.

taxa, s.f. tax, fee, rate; surcharge, tariff, price; duty, tribute, custums.

taxação, s.f. rate fixing; taxation.

taxador, s.m. rate fixer, valuer.

taxar, v.t. ro tax; to rate; to charge, to accuse of.

taxativamente, adv. restrictedly; positively, decidedly.

taxativo, adj. limitative; limited, circumscribed.

táxi, s.m. taxi-cab.

taxidermia, s.f. taxidermy.

taxidérmico, adj. taxidermic, taxidermal.

taxidermista, s. taxidermist.

taxímetro, s.m. taximeter.

taxinomia, taxionomia, s.f. taxonomy.

taxinómico, taxionómico, adj. taxonomic(cal).

taxinomista, taxionomista, s. taxonomist.

taxologia, s.f. taxology, taxonomy.

te, pron. thee, to thee; you, to you.

teáceas, s.f. (plu.) Theaceae (família do chá).

teada, s.f. piece of linen.

teagem, s.f. web, texture, network.

tear, s.m. oom.

teatrada, s.f. theatricals, a show.

teatral, adj. theatrical; pompous, showy.

teatralidade, s.f. theatricality, theatricalism.

teatralismo, s.m. theatricalism.

teatralizar, v.t. to imitate the theatre.

teatralmente, adv. theatrically.

teatro, s.m. theatre; play-house; stage; scene.

teatrólogo, s.m. playwrite, dramatist.

tebaida, s.f. refuge, retirement, solitude.

tebano, adj., s.m. Theban.

teca, s.f. teak (árvore); money (popular).

tecedeira, s.f. womanweaver.

tecedor, s.m. weaver; (fig.) contriver, schemer, intriguer.

tecedura, s.f. weaving; the textile industry; lacework; weaver´s trade.

tecelão, s.m. weaver.

tecer, v.t. to weave; interwine, to entwine; to contrive, to plot, to scheme; to twist, to spin.

tecido, adj. woven; s.m. cloth; tissue; textile fabric.

tecla, s.f. key (de um piano); bater sempre na mesma tecla, to harp on the same string.

teclado, s.m. keyboard.

técnica, s.f. technique, skill; technics; know-how.

tecnicamente, adv. technically.

tecnicismo, s.m. technicality.

técnico, adj. technical; s.m. technician.

tecnicolor, *adj.* technicolour.

tecnocracia, *s.f.* technocracy.

tecnocrata, *s.* technologist.

tecnografia, *s.f.* technography.

tecnologia, *s.f.* technology.

tecnológico, *adj.* technological.

tecnólogo, *s.m.* technologist.

tecto, *s.m.* ceiling, roof.

tectónica, *s.f.* tectonics.

tectónico, *adj.* tectonic.

tédio, *s.m.* tedium, tediousness, irksomeness, boredom, spleen.

tedioso, *adj.* tedious, irksome; wearisome, boring, tiresome.

tegumentar, tegumentário, *adj.* tegumentary.

tegumento, *s.m.* tegument.

teia, *s.f.* web; plot; railing; *teia de aranha,* cobweb.

teima, *s.f.* stubborness, obstinacy, wilfulness.

teimar, *v.i.* to persist, to insist, to be obstinate, to persevere; to argue.

teimosamente, *adv.* stubborny, obstinately.

teimosia, teimosice, *s.f.* wilfulness, obstinacy, stubbornness, persistance.

teimoso, *adj.* stubborn, headstrong, refractory, inflexible, obstinate, wilful, self-willed; persistent; pigheaded, dour.

teína, *s.f.* theine.

teísmo, *s.m.* theism.

teísta, *adj.* theistic; *s.* theist.

teixo, *s.m.* yem.

teixugo, *s.m.* vd. texugo.

tejadilho, *s.m.* roof, top *(de um veículo).*

tela, *s.f.* gauze; canvas; web *(da roupa);* a painting; screen *(cinema).*

telecomando, *s.m.* remote control.

telecomunicação, *s.f.* telecommunication.

teledinâmica, *s.f.* teledynamics.

teledinâmico, *adj.* teledynamic.

teleférico, *s.m.* teleferic.

telefonadela, *s.f.* telephone call.

telefonar, *v.t., v.i.* to telephone, to ring up, to phone, to call.

telefone, *s.m.* telephone.

telefonema, *s.m.* telephone call.

telefonia, *s.f.* telephony.

telefonicamente, *adv.* telephonically.

telefónico, *adj.* telephonic. 1) *lista telefónica,* telephone directory. 2) *cabina telefónica,* telephone booth or box.

telefonista, *s.* telephonist, operator.

telefoto, *s.m.* telephoto.

telefotografia, *s.f.* telephotography.

telefotográfico, *adj.* telephotographic.

telegrafar, *v.t., v.i.* to telegraph, to wire, to cable.

telegrafia, *s.f.* telegraphy; *telegrafia sem fios,* wireless.

telegraficamente, *adv.* telegraphically.

telegráfico, *adj.* telegraphic, wired, cabled.

telegrafista, *s.* telegraphist, telegrapher.

telégrafo, *s.m.* telegraph, wire; telegraph office.

telegrama, *s.m.* telegram, cable, wire.

teleguiado, *s.m.* guided missile.

teleinterruptor, *s.m.* remote-control switch.

telemetria, *s.f.* telemetry.

telemétrico, *adj.* telemetric.

telémetro, *s.m.* telemeter, range finder.

teleobjectiva, *s.f.* telephoto lens.

teleologia, *s.f.* teleology.

teleológico, *adj.* teleologic(cal).

teleósteo, *adj.* teleostean.

telepatia, *s.f.* telepathy.

telepático, *adj.* telepathic.

telerreceptor, *s.m.* television receiver, television set.

telescopia, *s.f.* telescopy.

telescópico, *adj.* telecopic.

telescópio, *adj.* telescope.

telescritor, *s.m.* telewriter, teletypewriter.

telésia, *s.f.* white sapphire.

telespectador, *s.m.* televiewer.

telestúdio, *s.m.* television studio.

teletipista, *s.* teletypist.

televisão, *s.f.* television.

televisar, *v.t.* to televise.

televisor, *s.m.* television set; television station, telestation.

telha, *s.f.* tile; whim, caprice, mania, kink; *ter uma telha a menos,* to have a screw loose.

telhado, *s.m.* roof, tile roof.

telhal, *s.m.* tile-kiln.

telhão, *s.m.* large tile.

telhar, *v.t.* to tile, to cover *(um telhado)* with tiles.

telheira, *s.f.* tile-works, tilery, tile factory.

telheiro, *s.m.* shed, open tile-covered shed; tile marker.

telhudo, *adj.* eccentric, whimsical, crazy, crackbrained *(popular).*

telim, *s.m.* sword-belt.

telimpressor, *s.m.* teleprinter.

telintar, *v.i.* to chink, to clink, to jingle.

teliz, *s.m.* saddle-cloth.

telurato, *s.m.* tellurate.

telureto, *s.m.* telluride, telluret.

telúrico, *adj.* telluric, terrestrial.

telúrio, *s.m.* tellurium.

telurismo, *s.m.* tellurism.

teluroso, *adj.* tellurous.

tema, *s.m.* theme, subject, topic, motive; exercise, composition; stem *(de uma palavra).*

temão, *s.m.* tiller; beam.

temário, *s.m.* list of topics *(conferência).*

temática, *s.f.* list of themes.

temático, *adj.* thematic.

temente, *adj.* reverent, fearing.

temer, *v.t.* to fear; to dread, to apprehend, to be afraid of; to respect, to reverence.

temerariamente, *adv.* rashly, boldly, daringly.

temerário, *adj.* rash, foolhardy, daring, headstrong, reckless, inconsiderate, risky.

temeridade, *s.f.* temerity, boldness, rashness, audacity.

temerosamente, *adv.* dreadfully, fearfully.

temeroso, *adj.* dreadful, timorous,fearful, appalling; afraid.

temido, *adj.* dreaded, feared.

temível, *adj.* dreadful, terrible, direful, appalling.

temor, *s.m.* dread, fear; awe; anxiety, apprehension.

têmpera, *s.f.* tempering *(metais);* temper, humour, temperament; tempera *(quadro);* hardness, toughness; nature, character.

temperadamente, *adv.* temperately, moderately.

temperado, *adj.* frugal, temperate, moderate, sober; mild; spiced, seasoned; hardened, toughened *(metais).*

temperamental, *adj.* temperamental.

temperamento, *s.m.* temperament, disposition, constitution, nature, mood, humour.

temperança, *s.f.* temperance, moderation, sobriety; soberness.

temperante, *adj.* tempering, seasoning; soothing, sedative, moderating.

temperar, *v.t.* to season, to soften; to anneal *(vidro);* to temper *(metal);* to spice, to flavour; to moderate, to calm.

temperatura, *s.f.* temperature, fever.

tempero, *s.m.* seasoning; flavouring; condiment, spice, zest, sauce.

tempestade, *s.f.* tempest, storm. 1) *tempestade num copo de água,* storm in a tea-cup, much ado about nothing. 2) *após a tempestade vem a bonança,* after a storm comes a calm.

tempestivo, *adj.* opportune, timely, well-timed, suitable.

tempestuosidade, *s.f.* storminess.

tempestuoso, *adj.* tempestuous, stormy, tumultuous, agitated.

templário, *s.m.* Templar.

templo, *s.m.* temple, church.

tempo, *s.m.* time; season; period, age, epoch; duration. 1) *com o tempo,* in the course of time. 2) *dar tempo ao tempo,* to bide one´s time. 3) *a seu tempo,* in due time. 4) *há muito tempo,* long ago. 5) *há pouco tempo,* recently. 6) *não é sem tempo,* it is high time. 7) *no tempo em que,* at the time when.

temporada, *s.f.* a long time; spell, season.

temporal, *s.m.* tempest, gale, storm; temporal bone *(anat.); adj.* temporal, transient, worldly, secular.

temporalidade, *s.f.* temporality.

temporalizar, *v.t.* to secularize.

temporaneidade, *s.f.* temporariness, transitoriness.

temporâneo, *adj.* temporary, transitory, ephemeral.

temporão, *adj.* hasty, premature; early; early ripe.

temporariamente, *adv.* temporarily.

temporário, *adj.* temporary, provisional, transient, fleeting, brief.

têmporas, *s.f. pl.* ember-days; temples *(anatomia).*

temporização, *s.f.* temporization, procrastination, lingering.

temporizador, *s.m.* temporizer, delayer, lingerer; adj. temporizing, lingering.

temporizar, *v.i.* to temporize, to delay, to linger, to gain time; to yield.

temulência, *s.f.* intoxication.

temulento, *adj.* intoxicated, drunk, temulent.

tenacidade, *s.f.* tenacity, perseverance; toughness, obstinacy.

tenacíssimo, *adj.* most tenacious.

tenalha, *s.f.* tenaille.

tenalhão, *s.m.* tenaillon.

tenaz, *adj.* tenacious; tough *(met.);* sticky, adhesive; stubborn, dogged, obstinate; *s.f.* tongs, pincers.

tenazmente, *adv.* tenaciously.

tenca, *s.f.* tench *(peixe).*

tença, *s.f.* pension, annuity.

tenção, *s.f.* intention, aim, intent, purpose, design; emblem, device. 1) *fazer tenção de,* to intend to. 2) *mudar de tenção*, to alter one´s mind.

tencionar, *v.t.* to intend, to purpose; to mean; to design, to have a mind to.

tenda, *s.f.* tent; stall, small shop.

tendal, *s.m.* tilt, awning.

tendão, *s.m.* tendon, sinew.

tendeiro, *s.m.* shopkeeper, grocer, one who keeps a stall; hawker; devil *(popular)*.

tendência, *s.f.* tendency, inclination, propensity, bent, bias; predisposition; vocation, calling; aptitude; trend.

tendencioso, *adj.* tendentious, biassed, partial.

tendente, *adj.* tending, prone, apt.

tender, *v.i.* to tend, to extend; to roll out, to mould; to dispose, to predispose; to have a tendency to; to aim at.

tênder, *s.m.* tendet *(de uma locomotiva)*.

tendilha, *s.f.* tiny shop, stall.

tendinoso, *adj.* tendinous, sinewy.

tenebrosidade, *s.f.* darkness, gloominess, obscurity.

tenebroso, *adj.* dark, gloomy, obscure, dim; terrible, frightful.

tenência, *s.f.* lieutenancy.

tenente, *s.m.* lieutenant.

tenente-coronel, *s.m.* lieutenant-colonel.

tenesmo, *s.m.* tenesmus.

tenesmódico, *adj.* tenesmic.

ténia, *s.f.* taenia, tapeworm.

ténis, *s.m.* tennis, lawn tennis; *tenis de mesa*, table-tennis, ping-pong.

tenista, *s.* tennis player.

tenor, *s.m.* tenor.

tenro, *adj.* tender; soft; weak; delicate; young, immature.

tenrura, *s.f.* tenderness, softness, mildness; affection, love.

tensão, *s.f.* tension, strain. 1) *tensão arterial*, arterial pressure. 2) *alta tensão*, high tension.

tensímetro, *s.m.* tensimeter.

tensivo, *adj.* tensive, tensional.

tenso, *adj.* tense, strained, taut, tight, rigid, stiff.

tensor, *s.m.* tensor; adjusting rod; tie beam; muscle; *adj.* tensive, stretching.

tenta, *s.f.* probe *(cirur.)*.

tentação, *s.f.* temptation; enticement, seduction, bait, attraction.

tentacular, *adj.* tentacular.

tentaculiforme, *adj.* tentaculiform.

tentáculo, *s.m.* tentacle, feeler.

tentador, *s.m.* tempter *(fem.* temptress); *adj.* tempting.

tentame, tentâmen, *s.m.* attempt, essay.

tentar, *v.t.* to attempt, to undertake, to risk, to venture; to try, to endeavour; to essay; to allure, to tempt, to entice, to seduce; to decoy.

tentativa, *s.f.* attempt, trial, essay, experiment, effort.

tentear, *v.t.* to probe, to try, to sound, to explore, to grope.

tenteio, *s.m.* probing, groping.

tentilhão, *s.m.* finch.

tento, *s.m.* counter; care, attention, caution, good sense; goal *(futebol)*; score, point *(nos jogos)*.

ténue, *adj.* tenuous, thin, slender; small, minute; subtle, rarefied; fragile, feeble.

tenuidade, *s.f.* tenuity, thinness, slenderness.

teocracia, *s.f.* theocracy.

teocrata, *s.* theocrat.

teocraticamente, *adv.* theocratically.

teocrático, *adj.* theocratical.

teodoceia, *s.f.* thedicy.

teodolito, *s.m.* theodolite.

teogonia, *s.f.* theogony.

teologal, *adj.* theological.

teologia, *s.f.* theology.

teologicamente, *adv.* theologically.

teológico, *adj.* theological.

teólogo, *s.m.* theologian.

teor, *s.m.* tenor, meaning; manner; wording; contents *(quím.)*.

teorba, *s.f.* theobo.

teorema, *s.m.* theorem.

teorético, *adj.* theoretical, abstract.

teoria, *s.f.* theory.

teoricamente, *adv.* theoretically.

teórico, *adj.* theoretical; *s.m.* theoretician.

teorista, *s.* theorist.

teorização, *s.f.* theorization.

teorizar, *v.t.* to theorize; to speculate.

teosofia, *s.f.* theosophy.

teosófico, *adj.* theosopic.

teosifismo, *s.m.* theosophism.

teosofista, teósofo, *s., s.m.* theosophist.

tepidez, *s.f.* tepidity, tepidness, likewarmness.

tépido, *adj.* tepid; likewarm.

ter, *v.t.* to have, to hold, to keep; to possess; to contain; to get, to obtain; to bear, to give birth to; to suffer from; *ter-se*, to hold oneself, to consider oneself; to keep *(a sua posição).*

terapeuta, *s.m.* therapist, therapeutist.

terapêutica, *s.m.* therapeutics.

terapêutico, *adj.* therapeutic, therapeutical, curative.

terapia, *s.f.* therapy.

teratogenia, *s.f.* teratogeny.

teratogénico, *adj.* teratogenic, teratoid.

teratologia, *s.f.* teratology.

teratológico, *adj.* teratological.

teratologista, *s.* teratologist.

teratólogo, *s.m.* teratologist.

teratoma, *s.f.* teratoma *(tumor).*

térbio, *s.m.* terbium *(metal).*

terça, *s.f.* third part; tierce *(hora canónica);* Tuesday.

terçã, *s.f.* tertian, tertian-ague or fever *(todos os terceiros dias).*

terçado, *s.m.* short broad sword, sabre; machete.

terçador, *s.m.* mediator, intercessor.

terça-feira, *s.f.* Tuesday.

terçar, *v.t.* to cross; to mix *(três coisas):* to divide *(em três partes);* to intercede, to mediate; to fight for; *terçar armas,* to fence, to cross swords.

terceira, *s.f.* third *(mús.);* procuress; mediatrix.

terceiranista, *s.* third year student *(na universidade).*

terceiro, *num.* third; *s.m.* mediator, intercessor.

terceto, *s.m.* tercet, trio, triplet.

tércia, *s.f.* tierce *(hora canónica).*

terciário, *adj.* tertiary.

tercina, *s.f.* tercine *(bot.)*

tércio-décimo, *num.* thirteenth.

terciopelo, *s.m.* variety of velvet.

terço, *s.m.* the third part; third; chaplet.

terçol, terçolho, *s.m.* stye, eyesore; sty.

terebintina, *s.m.* turpentine.

terebinto, *s.m.* turpentine-tree; terebinth *(bot.)*

terebração, *s.f.* a piercing pain; boring with a gimlet.

terebrante, *adj.* piercing, perforating.

terebrar, *v.t.* to bore with a gimlet.

teres, *s.m. pl.* possession, riches, means, money.

tergal, *adj.* tergal, dorsal.

tergeminado, *adj.* tergeminate *(bot).*

tergémino, *adj.* threefold.

tergiversação, *s.f.* tergiversation, evasion, subterfuge, vacillation.

tergiversador, *s.m.* tergiversator; *adj.* tergiversating.

tergiversante, *adj.* tergiversating.

tergiversar, *v.i.* to tergiversate, to quibble, to shuffle, to flinch, to shift.

tergo, *s.m.* tergum; back.

teriaga, *s.f.* theriac *(antídoto).*

termal, *adj.* thermal.

termas, *s.f. pl.* thermae, thermal baths, hot springs spa.

térmico, *adj.* thermic.

Termidor, *s.m.* Thermidor.

terminação, *s.f.* termination, ending, end, conclusion, close.

terminal, *adj.* terminal, ending, limiting, limitative; *s.m.* terminal.

terminante, *adj.* categorical, conclusive, absolute, positive, decisive, definite.

terminar, *v.i.* to end, to terminate, to come to an end, to finish; to close, to conclude; to complete; to expire; to limit, to bound.

terminativo, *adj.* terminative.

término, *s.m.* terminus, end, limit; terminal; limit, boundary.

terminologia, *s.m.* terminology.

terminológico, *adj.* terminological.

térmita, térmite, *s.f.* termite, white ant.

termiteira, *s.f.* nest or hill of white ants, termitary.

termo, *s.m.* end, boundary, limit, term; span, period; tenor, text; word, expression, vocable; termination, ending; term; surrounding *(cidade);* (pl.) manners, ways, behaviour. 1) *pôr termo a,* to put an end to. 2) *meios-termos,* subterfuge. 3) *estar em termos,* to be in due order. 4) *termo médio,* average, median. 5) *ao termo de,* at the end of. 6) *meio-termo,* moderation.

termobarómetro, *s.m.* thermobarometer.

termocautério, *s.m.* thermocautery.

termodinâmica, *s.f.* thermodynamics.

termoelecticidade, *s.f.* thermoelectricity.

termoeléctrico, *s.m.* thermoelectrical.

termogénese, termogenia, *s.f.* thermo-genesis.

termogénico, *adj.* thermogenic.

termogeno, *adj.* thermogenous.

termógrafo, *s.m.* thermograph.

termologia, *s.f.* thermology.

termológico, *adj.* thermological.

termomagnético, *adj.* thermomagnetic.

termomagnetismo, *s.m.* thermomagnetism.

termomecânica, *s.f.* thermomecanics.

termometria, *s.f.* thermometry, heat measuring.

termométrico, *adj.* thermometrical.

termómetro, *s.m.* thermometer.

termonuclear, *adj.* thermonuclear.

termoquímica, *s.f.* thermochemistry.

termoquímico, *adj.* thermochemical.

termoscopia, *s.m.* thermoscopy.

termoscópico, *adj.* thermoscopic(al).

termoscópio, *s.m.* thermoscope.

termostático, *adj.* thermostatic.

termóstato, thermostate.

termoterapia, *s.m.* thermotherapy.

termotipia, *s.f.* thermotype.

ternado, *adj.* ternate *(folhas);* arranged in groups of three.

ternamente, *adv.* tenderly, gently, kindly, lovingly.

ternário, *adj.* ternary, ternal, threefold.

terno, *adj.* tender, fond, tender-hearted, loving gentle mild, affectionate; *s.m.* ternary, triplet, trio; threesome, triad; men's suit *(três peças);* three *(no jogo de cartas).*

ternura, *s.f.* terdenness, fondeness, gentleness, kindness, dearness, affection, love.

terpina, *s.m.* terpene, terpin.

terra, *s.f.* earth; soil; land; ground; country; territory; estate; the world. 1) *terra-a-terra,* commonplace, simple. 2) *terra alheia,* foreign land. 3) *terra natal,* native land, birthplace, mother land. 4) *terra vegetal,* humus leaf mould. 5) *em terra,* ashore. 6) *ir a terra,* to go ashore, to fall. 7) *terra-de--ninguém,* no man's land. 8) *deitar a terra,* to throw, to knock down. 9) *de que terra é?,* where are you from?

terraço, *s.m.* terrace; flat roof.

terracota, *s.f.* terracotte *(cerâmica ou objecto).*

terramicina, *s.f.* terramycin.

terramoto, *s.m.* earthquake.

terra-nova, *s.* newfoundland *(cão).*

terraplenagem, *s.f.* earthwork; ground-levelling.

terraplenar, *v.t.* to level ground, to make even, to embank.

terrapleno, *s.m.* platform, levelled ground; rampart.

terráqueo, *adj.* terraqueous.

terreal, *adj.* terrestrial, earhly; mundane.

terrear, *v.i., v.i.* to be sparsely covered with vegetation; to look earth-like.

terreiro, *s.m.* public square; terrace; yard.

terrenal, terrecho, *adj.* terrestrial, earthly.

terreno, *s.m.* ground, soil; groundplot; site; terrain; filed or branch of activity; *adj.* earthy, mundane, terrestrial. 1) *ceder terreno,* to give way. 2) *perder terreno,* to lose ground. 3) *ganhar terreno,* to gain ground. 4) *apalpar terreno,* to feel someone's way. 5) *preparar terreno,* to pave the way for.

terrento, *adj.* earth-coloured; lusterless.

térreo, *adj.* low, even with the ground; *andar térreo,* ground-flour.

terrestre, *adj.* terrestrial, earthly; overland *(transporte).*

terrícola, *s.* inhabitant of the earth; *adj.* terricolous.

terrificador, terrificante, *adj. ver "terrífico".*

terrificar, *v.t.* to terrify, to frighten, to horrify, to appal, to scare.

terrífico, *adj.* terrific, dreadful, frightful, appaling.

terrígeno, *adj.* terrigenous, earthborn, from the earth.

terrina, *s.f.* tureen.

terríola, *s.f.* hamlet, small village or place.

territorial, *adj.* territorial.

territorialidade, *s.f.* territoriality.

territorialmente, *adj.* territorially.

território, *s.m.* territory, land, country, region, district, dominion, area.

terrível, *adj.* terrible, fearful, frightful, awful, horrible, dreadful; shocking, hideous.

terrivelmente, *adv.* terribly, awfully.

terror, *s.m.* terror, dread, fright, fear, horror; panic, dismay.

terrorismo, *s.m.* terrorism.

terrorista, *s.* terrorist.

terroso, *adj.* earthy, dull, earth-coloured.

terso, *adj.* terse, concise, clear, neat, pure, correct; polished, bright; vernacular.

tertúlia, *s.f.* literary assembly, social gathering, club.

tese, *s.f.* thesis *(pl.* theses); dissertation.

teso, *adj.* tight, rigid; form, stiff; stubborn; tough; strong; courageous; brave; top of the hill, steep; broke, ruined, penniless *(calão).*

tesoira, tesoura, *s.f.* scissors; shears; backbiter, slanderer *(pop.);* truss of a rope; cross-reins. 1) *tesoura de podar,* pruning shears. 2) *tesoura de unhas,* nail scissors.

tesoirada, tesourada, *s.f.* cut *(com tesoura),* backbiting, slander.

tesoirar, tesourar, *v.t.* to cut with scissors, to backbite.

tesoiraria, tesouraria, *s.d.* treasury; treasure house; exchequer; treasureship.

tesoiriro, tesoureiro, *s.m.* treasurer, paymaster; *tesoureiro da universidade ou do liceu,* bursar.

tesoiro, tesouro, *s.m.* treasure; hoard; thing of great value; riches, wealth; exchequer, treasury, public purse; darling.

tessela, *s.f.* tessella.

tesselário, *s.m.* mosaicist; skilled in mosaic decorations.

tessitura, *s.f.* tessitura *(música)*.

testa, *s.f.* forehead; front; brow. 1) *testa-de--ferro,* dumny, man of straw. 2) *estar à testa de,* at the head of. 3) *testa-de-ponte,* bridgehead.

testáceo, *adj.* testaceous; brick-red.

testada, *s.f.* part of a road or street facing a house; *varrer a sua testada,* to decline all responsability.

testador, *s.m.* testador (fem. testatrix); bequeather.

testamental, *adj.* testamental, testamentary.

testamentário, *adj.* testamentary.

testamenteiro, *s.m.* executor (of a will).

testamento, *s.m.* testament; will.

testante, *s.* ver testador.

testar, *v.i.* to make one's will; to bequeath, to legate.

teste, *s.m.* test, examination, research, trial.

testeira, *s.f.* front forepart.

testemunha, *s.m.* witness; *(pl.)* landmarks. 1) *testemunha ocular,* eyewitness. 2) *testemunha presencial,* personal witness. 3) *testemunha de defesa,* witness for the defence. 4) *testemunha de acusação,* witness for the prosecution. 5) *banco das testemunhas,* witness-box.

testemunhador, *s.m.* witness; *adj.* bearing evidence.

testemunhal, *adj.* testimonial.

testemunhar, *v.t.* to testify to, to witness; to bear witness to; to give evidence; to serve as a witness; to confirm; to see, to notice.

testemunhável, *adj.* testimonial; evidential, corroborative.

testemunho, *s.m.* testimony; evidencd, proof, witness; report. 1) *dar testemunho,* give evidence. 2) *em testemunho de que,* witness where of.

testico, *s.m.* sidepieces of a bow saw.

testicular, *adj.* testicular.

testículo, *s.m.* testicle.

testificação, *s.f.* testification, evidence, witness.

testificador, testeficante, *adj.* testifying; *s.m.* testifier.

testificar, *v.t.* to testify, to attest, to attest, to afirm, to give evidence, to declare, to certify.

testilha, *s.f.* quarrel, dispute, brawl, contention; conflict.

testilhar, *v.i.* to quarrel, to dispute, to altercate, to contend.

testo, *adj.* firm, determined, resolute; inflexible, stubborn.

testudo(ê), *s.m.* cover, lid.

tesoura, *adj.* head strong; stubborn, obstinate.

teta, *s.f.* firmness; stiffness.

tetania, *s.f.* tetany.

tetânico, *adj.* tetanic.

tétano, *s.m.* tetanus; lockjaw.

tetérrimo, *adj.* hideous, abominable, dreadful.

tetracordo, *s.m.* tetrachord *(lira).*

tetradáctilo, *adj.* tetradactyl.

tetraédrico, *adj.* tetrahedral

tetraedro, *adj.* tretrahedron.

tetragonal, *adj.* tetragonal.

tetrágono, *s.m.* tetragon.

tetragrama, *s.m.* tetragam.

tetralogia, *s.f.* tetralogy.

tetrâmetro, *s.m.* tetrameter.

tetraneto, *s.m.* great-great-great-grandson.

tetrapétalo, *adj.* tetrapetalous.

tetrápode, *adj.* tetrapod.

tetráptero, *adj.* tetrapterous.

tetrarca, *s.m.* tetrarch.

tetrarcado, *s.m.* tetrarchate.

tetrarquia, *s.f.* tetrarchy.

tetrassilábico, *adj.* tetrasyllabic.

tetrassílabo, *adj.* tetrasullabic; *s.m.* tetrasyllable.

tetrastilo, *adj.* tetrastyle.

tetravalente, *adj.* tetravalent.

tetravó, *s.f.* great-great-great-grandfather.

tétrico, *adj.* horrible, frightful, macabre, gruesome, awful; gloomy, sad, funereal.

tetro, *adj.* black, dark, gloomy, somber; dreadful, horrible.

teu, *adj. pron.* your; yours; thy, thine *(bíbl. ou poét.).*

teurgia, *s.f.* theurgy, miracle; sorcery, magic.

teúrgico, *adj.* theurgic, magic, miraculous.

teutão, *s.m.* Teuton.

teutónico, *adj.* Teutonic, German.

têxtil, *adj.* textile, woven.

texto, *s.m.* text, subjectmatter.

textual, *adj.* textual, literal.

textualista, *s.* textualist.

textualmente, *adv.* textually, literally.

textuário, *s.m.* textuary, textbook.

textura, *s.f.* textura, fabric, structure, arrangement.

texugo, *s.m.* badger; well-fed person *(pop.).*

tez, *s.f.* skin; complexion (the face); cutis.

ti, *pron.* you; thee *(poét.).*

tia, *s.f.* aunt; old maid *(pop)*; ficar para tia, to remain unmarried.

tia-avó, *s.f.* great aunt, grandaunt.

tiara, *s.f.* tiara, triple crown; papal dignity.

tibetano, *adj., s.m.* Tibetan.

tíbia, *s.f.* shinbone; tibia *(pl. tibiae);* flute.

tibial, *adj.* tibial.

tibiamente, *adv.* tepidly.

tibiez, tibieza, *s.f.* lukewarmness; indifference, slakness, remissness.

tíbio, *adj.* lukerwarm; tepid; sluggish; indifferent.

tição, *s.m.* firebrand, piece of burned wood; very dark person.

tiçoeiro, *s.m.* poker.

tido, *adj.* had; reputed, considered, supposed.

tífico, *adj.* typhoid, typhous.

tiflite, *s.f.* typhlitis.

tiflografia, *s.f.* typhlography, Braille.

tiflógrafo, *s.m.* typhlograph, *(instrumento).*

tiflologia, *s.f.* typhlology.

tiflológico, *adj.* pyphological.

tifo, *s.m. (med.)* typhus, typhoid fever.

tifóide, *adj.* typhoid.

tifoso, *adj.* typhous; *s.m.* person affected by thyphus.

tigela, *s.f.* bowl, basin, cup, porringer; de meia-tigela, mediocre, ordinary; small.

tigelada, *s.f.* bowlful.

tigrado, *adj.* spotted like a tiger.

tigre, *s.m.* tiger; cruel person.

tigrino, *adj.* tigrine, tigerish, fierce, cruel.

tijolaria, *s.f.* brick workshop.

tijoleiro, *s.m.* brick-maker; bricklayer.

tijolo, *s.m.* brick.

til, *s.m.* tilde *(acento).*

tília, *s.f.* lime-tree, linden.

tilintante, *adj.* tinkling.

tilintar, *v.i.* to tinkle, to clink, to jingle.

tilose, *s.f.* corn, callus.

timão, *s.m.* tiller, rudder; beam; pole *(de um veículo);* control, command.

timbale, *s.m.* timbal, kettle-drum.

timbaleiro, *s.f.* kettle-drummer; tympanist.

timbrador, *s.m.* stamper.

timbragem, *s.f.* stamping, marking.

timbrar, *v.t.* to stamp, to mark with an emblem or seal; timbrar em, to pride oneself on, to take a pride in.

timbre, *s.m.* timbre, tone *(mús.);* ring; stamp, mark, seal, emblem, ensign; point of honour, justifiable pride.

timbroso, *adj.* punctilious, meticulous, cereful; having timbre.

timidamente, *adj.* timidly, shyly.

timidez, *s.f.* timidity, timidness, bashfulness shyness, lack of courage or self-confidence.

tímido, *adj.* timid, fearful, shy, bashful.

timo, *s.m.* thyme *(bot.);* rhymus *(med.)*

timocracia, *s.f.* tomacracy.

timocrático, *adj.* tomicratic.

timoneiro, *s.m.* helmsman, steersman; guide, leader.

timorato, *adj.* timorous, timid.

timpanal, *adj.* tympanic.

timpanilho, *s.m.* inner tympan.

timpanismo, *s.m.* tympanism, tympanites.

timpanite, *s.f.* tympanitis.

tímpano, *s.m.* tympan; tympanum, ear-drum *(corpo humano);* cimbal kettledrum *(mús.);* tympanum, door panel *(arquit.).*

tina, *s.f.* tub; pail, vat, wooden vessel.

tinada, *s.f.* tubful, vatful.

tinalha, *s.f.* vintage-tub.

tineta, *s.f.* fancy, whim, mania, freak *(pop.)*

tingidor, *s.m.* dyer; *adj.* dyeing.

tingidura, *s.f.* dyeing; tinting.

tingir, *v.t.* to dye; to tinge; to tint.

tingitano, *adj., s.m.* Tangerine.

tingível, *adj.* tingible, colourabel.

tinha, *s.f.* ringworm, scurf, scab, tinea.

tinhoso, *adj.* suffering from ringworm, scurfy, scabby, mangy, repugnant; *s.m.* the devil *(pop.)*

tinido, *s.m.* tinkling, jingling, clinking.

tinir, *v.i.* to tinkle, to jingle, to ring, to clink; to shiver; to tremble; estar a tinir, to be penniless or stony broke.

tino, *s.m.* judgement, prudence, diplomacy.

tinta, *s.f.* ink, dye, painy; shade, nuance, tone.

tinta-da-china, *s.f.* Indian ink.

tinteiro, *s.m.* inkstand, inkpot, inkwell; ficar no tinteiro, to omit, to be forgotten.

tintim por tintim, *loc. adv.* minutely, point for point, particularly. 1) *contar tintim por tintim,* to give full account. 2) *explicar tintim por tintim,* to give chapter and verse.

tintinábulo, *s.m.* tintinnabulum (*pl.* tintinnabula), bell.

tinto, *s.m.* dye, dyeing; *adj.* dyed, tinted; red *(vinho, uvas).*

tintorial, *adj.* tinctorial.

tintura, *s.f.* tincture; dyeing; colour, tint, hue; superficial knowledge, smattering; *tintura de iodo,* tincture of iodine.

tinturaria, *s.f.* dye-house, dye-works; dye's *(loja);* dyeing; cleaner's *(loja).*

tintureiro, *s.m.* dyer.

tio, *s.m.* uncle.

tio-avô, *s.m.* great uncle.

tipicamente, *adv.* typically.

típico, *adj.* typical, typic, representative; symbolic, characteristical.

tiple, *s.* treble, soprano *(música).*

tipo, *s.m.* type; style, model, mould, pattern; class, sort, kind; symbol; printing type; fellow, guy, chap.

tipografar, *v.t.* to print.

tipografia, *s.f.* typography; printing-works, printer's *(loja);* art of printing.

tipograficamente, *adv.* typographically.

tipográfico, *adj.* typographical. 1) *prova topográfica,* proof sheet. 2) *revisor tipográfico,* proof reader.

tipógrafo, *s.m.* typographer, printer, typsetter, compositor.

tipóia, *s.f.* hammock; carriage.

tipolitografia, *s.f.* typolithography.

tipologia, *s.f.* typology.

tipometria, *s.f.* typometry.

tique, *s.m.* tic, bad habit; *tique nervoso,* nervous tic.

tiquetaque, *s.m.* tick-tack; pit-a-pat *(coração).*

tiquetaquear, *v.i.* to make tick-tack.

tira, *s.f.* dtriop, ribbon, band.

tiracolo(a), *adv.* over the shoulder and across the chest.

tirada, *s.f.* long speech, outburst, tirade; stretch; long walk; *de uma tirada,* at one stretch, at one draft.

tiradeira, *s.f.* starp. strip of leather.

tiradela, *s.f.* drawing, pulling.

tirador, *s.m.* drawer; pressman.

tiragem, *s.f.* printing; issue, circulation; draught, draft *(de uma chaminé, etc.);* collection of letters *(correio);* edition.

tira-linhas, *s.m.* drawing-pen, ruling-pen, bow-pen.

tiranete, *s.m.* petty tyrant.

tirania, *s.f.* tyranny, oppression; harshness; despotism, absolutism.

tiranicamente, *adj.* tyrannically.

tiranicida, *s.* tyrannicide.

tiranicídio, *s.m.* tyrannicide.

tirânico, *adj.* tyrannical, despotic, oppressive, cruel, overbearing.

tiranizar, *v.t.* to tyrannize, to oppress.

tirano, *s.m.* tyrant, oppressor, despot, autocrat; *adj.* tyrannical, despotic, oppressive, cruel.

tira-nódoas, *s.m.* spot remover, stain, cleaner.

tirante, *s.m.* joist; trace; tie-rod; tie; stay, rod; *adj.* drawing, inclinning to; *prep.* save, except.

tirão, *s.m.* haul, pull, tug, jerk.

tira-olhos, *s.m.* dragon-fly.

tirapé, *s.m.* shoemaker's stirrup.

tirar, *v.t.* to draw, to draw out; to take away; to take out; to take off *(roupas);* to get out or off; to infer, to deduce; to deprive; to exclude, to suppress; to print; to make copies; to set free; to steal; to deduct, to subtract. 1) *tirar a limpo,* to make a clean copy of, to get to the bottom of. 2) *tirar a mesa,* to clear the table. 3) *tirar boas notas,* to get high marks *(na escola).* 4) *tirar o retrato,* to have one's picture taken. 5) *tirar partido de,* to turn to account, to take advantage of. 6) *tirar um curso,* to take a course. 7) *tirar uma conclusão,* to draw a conclusion. 8) *tirar uma cópia,* to make a copy. 9) *tirar uma factura,* to make out an invoice. 10) *tirar a conta,* to draw up an account. 11) *sem tirar nem pôr,* precisely, for all the world like. 12) *tirar uma dificuldade,* to remove a difficulty. 13) *tirar à sorte,* to draw lots. 14) *tirar a prova,* to check up a calculation. 15) *tirar a falta,* to pardon an absence *(na escola).* 16) *tirar um diploma,* to take a diploma. 17) *tirar informações,* to make inquiries. 18) *tirar licença,* to get licence. 19) *tirar a sardinha com a mão do gato,* to use someone as a cat's paw. 20) *tirar a sorte grande,* to win the great prize, to hit the jackpot.

tira-teimas, *s.m.* decisive argument, final word.

tírio, *adj., s.m.* Tyrian.

tiritação, *s.f.* shivering.

tiritante, *adj.* shivering, trembling, quivering.

tiritar, *v.i.* to shiver, to shake, to tremble.

tiro, *s.m.* shot; shooting, firing, discharge; target range; a cutting remark. 1) *tiro ao alvo*, target practice. 2) *carreira de tiro*, shooting range, shooting gallery. 3) *linha de tiro*, line of sight.

tirocinante, *s.* apprentice.

tirocinar, *v.i.* to make one's apprenticeship.

tirocínio, *s.m.* apprenticeship, military training.

tiróide, *adj.* thyroid *(gland.)*.

tiróideo, *adj.* thyroid.

tiroidismo, *s.m.* thyroidism.

tiroidite, *s.f.* thyroiditis.

tirolês, *adj., s.m.* Tyrolese.

tirotear, *v.i.* to volley, to fire.

tiroteio, *s.m.* firing, volley, shooting, gunfight, musketry.

tirrénio, tirreno, *adj.* Tyrrhenoan, Etruscan.

tirso, *s.m.* thyrsus.

tir-te, *sem tir-te nem guar-te,* suddenly.

tisana, *s.f.* tisane, ptisan.

tísica, *s.f.* consumption, phthisis, tuberculosis; *tísica galopante*, galloping consumption.

tísico, *s.m.* consumptive, hectic.

tisiologia, *s.f.* thisiology.

tisiologista, tisiólogo, *s., s.m.* phthisiologist.

tisna, tisnadura, *s.f.* smut, blackening.

tisnar, *v.t.* to blacken; to soot; to scorch; *tisnar-se*, to become (to get) sunburnt.

tisne, *s.m.* black, spot, soot, smear; lampblack.

titã, *s.m.* Titan, superman, giant.

titânico, *adj.* titanic, gigantic, huge, herculeous.

titânio, *s.m.* titanium.

titanita, *s.f.* titanite, shpene.

titela, *s.f.* breast *(galinha)*.

titeragem, *s.f.* puppetry.

títere, *s.m.* puppet, marionette; jumping Jack.

titereiro, *s.m.* puppet-player.

titilação, titilamento, *s.f., s.m.* titillation, tickling.

titilante, *adj.* tickling, titillating.

titilar, *v.t.* to titillate, to tickle.

titubeação, *s.f.* hesitation, vacillation, titubation.

titubeante, *adj.* hesitating, wavering, faltering.

titubear, *v.i.* to stagger, to reel, to waver, to hesitate, to falter.

titular, *adj.* titular; *s.* titled person; holder; nobleman; *v.t.* to title, to entitle.

título, *s.m.* title; right; title-deed; security; diploma, patent; caption; heading; bond; rank; claim; designation; pretext. 1) *título ao portador*, active bond. 2) *a título de* , on pretence of. 3) *a título de experiência*, by way of trial. 4) *título de renda*, stock certificate.

tmese, *s.f.* tmesis.

toa(à), *loc. adv.* inconsiderately; at random, carelessly.

toada, *s.f.* tune, air, melody; sound, tone, noise, rumour; fashion, style.

toadilha, *s.f.* little melody.

toalha, *s.f.* towel; sheet *(água)*. 1) *toalha de mesa*, table-cloth. 2) *toalha de rosto*, face towel. 3) *toalha de altar*, altar cloth.

toalheiro, *s.m.* towel rack; towel horse.

toalhete, *s.m.* small hand towel.

toante, *adj.* consonant; resounding; sounding, rhyming.

toar, *v.i.* to sound, to resound; to fit, to suit, to match.

toarda, *s.f.* rumour; report.

toca, *s.f.* burrow, hole, den, lair; mean habitation.

tocadela, *s.f.* touch, contact; ringing.

tocado, *adj.* bruised *(fruta)*, somewhat rotten; tipsy, touched *(na cabeça)*.

tocador, *s.m.* player.

tocante, *adj.* touching, moving, affecting; concerning; *no tocante a,* as regards, with respect to, as to.

tocar, *v.t.* to touch, to feel, to impress, to inspire, to move; to hit; to concern; to ring *(campainha)*; to try *(metal)*; to play *(instrumentos)*, to blow *(trompete)*; to meddle with; to belong; to be contiguous; to drive *(animais)*. 1)*tocar a*, to fall to the lot of; to be the turn of; to refer to. 2) *tocar em*, to touch; to call *(a uma porta)*; to strike on; to touch upon *(um objecto)*. 3) *tocar na ferida (corda sensível)*, to touch one's soft spot. 4) *tocar de perto*, to strike closely. 5) *tocar ao de leve*, to slide over. 6) *tocar à missa*, to ring for mass. 7) *tocar de ouvido*, to play by ear.

tocata, *s.f.* toccata, serenade, music.

tocha, *s.f.* torch; large candle; firebrand.

tocheira, tocheiro, *s.f, s.m.* torch-holder, large candle-holder.

toco, *s.m.* stump, stub; butt *(cigarros, lápis, vela)*.

tocologia, *s.f.* tocology; obstetrics; midwifery.

tocológico, *adj.* obstetric(al).

tocologista, tocólogo, *s., s.m.* obstetrician.

todavia, *conj.* neverthless, yet, however, still, though.

todo, *adj.* all; whole, complete, entire, total; every; *s.m.* the whole, entirety, totality; *(pl.)* everybody.

Todo-Poderoso, *s.m.* The Almighty.

toesa, *s.f.* fathom *(medida de seis pés).*

toga, *s.f.* toga; gown, robe; magistracy.

togado, *adj.* gowned, magisterial; *s.m.* judge, magistrate.

toicinho, *s.m.* ver *"toucinho".*

toira, *s.f.* ver *"toura".*

toirada, *s.f.* ver *"tourada".*

toirão, *s.m.* ver *"tourão".*

toireador, *s.m.* ver *"toureador".*

toirear, *v.i., v.t.* ver *"tourear".*

toireiro, *s.m.* ver *"toureiro".*

toiro, *s.m.* touro.

toitiço, *s.m.* ver *"toutiço".*

tojal, *s.m.* place full of furze.

tojeira, *s.m.* furze.bush, gorse-bush.

tojeiro, *s.m.* the man who gathers furze.

tojo, *s.m.* furze, gorse.

tojoso, *adj.* furzy, gorsy.

tola, *s.m.* head, brains, judgement *(pop.);* variety of wood.

tolamente, *adv.* foolishly.

tolda, *s.f.* quarter-deck *(náut.).*

toldado, *adj.* mouldy *(vinho);* overcast *(tempo);* tipsy.

toldar, *v.t.* to hang an awning over; to cloud, to gloom; *toldar-se,* to be spoiled, to get mouldy *(vinho);* to get cloudy *(tempo);* to become tipsy.

toldo, *s.m.* awning; sunblind *(de uma loja).*

toledana, *s.f.* Toled sword blade.

toledano, *adj., s.m.* Toledan.

toledo, toleima, *s.m., s.f.* silliness, foolishness; vanity.

toleirão, *adj.* silly; *s.m.* silly fool.

tolerabilidade, *s.f.* tolerability.

tolerada, *s.f.* harlot, prostitute.

tolerado, *adj.* tolerated.

tolerância, *s.f.* tolerance, toleration, open-mindedness; indulgence.

tolerante, *adj.* tolerant, forbearing, indulgent, broadminded.

tolerantismo, *s.m.* toleration.

tolerar, *v.t.* to tlerate; to suffer, to endure; to bear; to indulge; to sufeer; to allow, to permit.

tolerável, *adj.* tolerable, endurable, supportable, passable, bearable, not too bad.

toleravelmente, *adv.* tolerably, moderately, fairly.

tolete, *s.m.* thole-pin, rowlock, roller *(náut.).*

toleteira, *s.f.* thole-board, rowlock, oarlock.

tolher, *v.t.* to hinder, to check; to stop, to obstruct, to hmaper; to restrain, to oppose; to disable, to injure, to lame, to cripple.

tolhido, *adj.* oaralysed, palsied, disabled, helpless; paralytic; benumbed; hindered.

tolhimento, *s.m.* obstacle, hindrance, impediment; lameness.

tolice, *s.f.* nonsense, silliness, folly, stupidity, foolishness. 1) *dizer uma tolice,* to talk nonsense, to talk rot. 2) *que tolice!,* what rot!

tolo, *adj.* foolish, silly, conceites, ridiculous, stupid, *s.m.* fool, idiot.

tolueno, *s.m.* tolueno.

tom, *s.m.* tone, accent; mode, tone, key; tint, shade *(cores).*

tomada, *s.f.* taking, seizure, capture, conquest; plug, outlet.

tomadia, *s.f.* capture, taking, seizure, catch.

tomadiço, *adj.* peevish, fretful, choleric, excitable.

tomado, *adj.* taken, seized; tipsy, drunk; *tomada de medo,* sezed with fear; frightened.

tomador, *s.m.* taker; seizer; bearer.

tomar, *v.t.* to take *(em todos os sentidos),* to seize, to catch, to grasp, to lay hold of; to drink; to eat; to assume. 1) *tomar a mal,* to take amiss. 2) *tomar a palavra,* to take the floor. 3) *tomar a peito* to take to heart. 4) *tomar a sério,* to take seriously. 5) *tomar cuidado,* to be careful. 6) *tomar de assalto,* to take by storm. 7) *tomar uma bebida,* to have a drink. 8) *tomar vulto,* to grow in size. 9) *tomar por modelo,* to take as model. 10) *tomar ordens,* to be ordained. 11) *tomar o gosto a ,* to find delight in. 12) *tomar posse,* to take up a post. 13) *tomar ao seu cuidado,* to take in hand. 14) *tomar confiança,* to outstrip, to overrun. 19) *tomar conhecimento de,* to take notice of. 16) *tomar conta,* to look after. 17) *tomar uma decisão,* to reach a decision. 18) *tomar a dianteira,* to outstrip, to overrun. 19) *tomar fôlego,* to catch one's breath. 20) *tomar por,* to take for. 21) *tomar posição,* to take one's stand. 22) *tomar providências (medidas),* to take steps, measures. 23) *tomar o pulso*, to feel the pulse.

tomares, *s.m. pl. dares e tomares*, disputes, dealings.

tomatada, *s.f.* tomato paste, tomato juice.

tomatal, *s.m.* tomato plantation.

tomate, *s.m.* tomato.

tomateiro, *s.m.* tomato-plant.

tomba, *s.f.* patch *(sapato)*; leather-back of a book.

tombadilho, *s.m.* quarter-deck, poop, poop-deck.

tombador, *s.m.* stumbler.

tombar, *v.t.* to throw down, to tumble, to turn over; to tumble down, to drop, to fall down; to reel, to stagger.

tombo, *s.m.* tumble, fall; cartulary, register.

tômbola, *s.f.* tombola; lotto.

tomento, *s.m.* tow, hurds; tomentum.

tomentoso, *adj.* downy, tomentose, tomentous.

tomilho, *s.m.* thyme.

tomismo, *s.* Thomism.

tomista, *s., adj.* Thomist.

tomo, *s.m.* tome, volume, book; value, worth.

tona, *s.f.* surface; inner bark; pellicle; skin, peel. 1) *à tona de água*, afloat, awash. 2) *vir à tona*, to emerge. 3) *manter-se à tona*, to keep afloat.

tonal, *adj.* tonal, relating to a tone.

tonalidade, *s.f.* tonality, colour, hue, tint, shade.

tonante, *adj.* thundering, thunderous.

tonar, *v.t., v.i.* to thunder.

tonel, *s.m.* tun, vat, large cask.

tonelada, *s.f.* ton.

tonelagem, *s.f.* load, tonnage, capacity.

tónica, *s.f.* keynote; stresses syllable; tonic.

tonicidade, *s.f.* tonicity.

tónico, *adj.* tonic; bracing, invigorating, strenghtening; key-note, fundamental; voiced, stressed; predominant; *s.m.* invigorating medicine.

tonificação, *s.f.* invigoration.

tonificante, *adj.* tonic, invigorating, streng-thening.

tonificar, *v.t.* to strengthen, to invigorate, to refresh, to tone up.

toninha, *s.f.* porpoise.

tonite, *s.f.* tonite *(explosivo)*.

tonitruante, *adj.* thundering.

tonitruar, *v.i.* to thunder.

tonítruo, *adj.* ver "tonitruante".

tono, *s.m.* tone, aria, song; attitude; muscular tension.

tonsura, *s.f.* tonsure.

tonsurado, *s.m.* priest; monk.

tonsurar, *v.t.* to tonsure, to make a tonsure on.

tontaria, *s.f.* folly, silliness, nonsense, foolishness.

tontear, *v.i.* to be giddy; to act foolishly, to play the fool; to talk nonsense.

tonteira, tontice, *s.f.* nonsense; foolery, dotage.

tontina, *s.f.* tontine.

tonto, *adj.* giddy, dizzy; foolish, crazy, silly, stupid, dull.

tontura, *s.f.* vertigo, diziness, giddiness.

topa-a-tudo, *s.m.* Jack-of-all trades.

topada, *s.f.* stumbling, tripping. *dar uma topada*, to stub one's toe.

topar, *v.t.* to find; to meet with, to come across, to strike against, to collide, to hit.

topázio, *s.m.* topaz.

tope, *s.m.* top; cockade, clash, striking, collision, jar; summmit; masthead.

topetada, *s.f.* butt.

topetar, *v.i.* to butt, to strike.

topete, *s.m.* toupee, forelock; impudence, insolence, sauciness.

tópico, *adj.* topical; *s.m.* topic, subject, theme, heading matter.

topinambo, topinambor, *s.m.* Jerusalem artichoke *(bot)*.

topo, *s.m.* top, summit, peak, highest, point, crest; end, extremity; *topo a topo*, end to end.

topografia, *s.f.* topography.

topográfico, *adj.* topographical.

topógrafo, *s.m.* topographer.

toponímia, *s.f.* toponymy.

toponímico, *adj.* toponymical.

topónimo, *s.m.* toponym, place name.

toque, *s.m.* touch, feeling; stroke; call; blast; playing, sound *(instrumento)*; bouquet *(vinho)*; ringing *(campainhas)*; este *(metais)*; handshake; artist touch; rotten spot *(fruta)*. 1) *toque de alvorada*, reveille, rouse. 2) *toque de caixa*, drumbeat. 3) *toque de silêncio* lights out, last post. 4) *toque de recolher*, call to quarters. 5) *a toque de caixa*, posthaste. 6) *pedra-de--toque*, touchstone.

tora, *s.f.* portion of meat *(calão no exército)*.

torácico, *adj.* thoracic.

torado, *adj.* cut up into logs.

toral, *s.m.* butt end (of spear or lance).

toranja, *s.f.* grapefruit.

toranjeira, *s.f.* grapefruit tree.

torar, *v.t.* to saw *(árvore),* to cut into logs.

tórax, *s.m.* thorax, chest, breast.

torça, *s.f.* lintel.

torçal, *s.m.* twisted, silk, silk cord.

torção, *s.f.* torsion; twist.

torcaz, *adj.* pombo-torcaz, wood-pigeon.

torcedela, *s.f.* twist, wrench.

torcedor, *s.m.* twister; spindle; twisting, machine.

torcedura, *s.f.* ver "torcedela"; torcedura de pé, sprain.

torcegar, *v.t.* to twist; to pinch.

torcer, *v.t.* to twist, to wring; to distort, to writhe; to turn; to wrench; to sprain. 1) torcer a orelha, to repent of. 2) torcer a roupa, to wring out the linen. 3) torcer o fio, to twist thread. 4) torcer o nariz, to turn up one's nose. 5) torcer o sentido, to twist the meaning. 6) aí é que a porca torce o rabo, that is where the shoe pinches. 7) não dar o braço a torcer, to refuse to admit or confess anything. 8) antes quebrar que torcer, rather break than yield.

torcicolo, *s.m.* stiff neck; winding way; subterfuge; ambiguity; wryneck *(pássaro).*

torcida, *s.f.* wick.

torcido, *adj.* crooked, twisted, tortuous, sinuous, winding.

torcimento, *s.m.* twist, tortuosity.

torda, *s.f.* female thrush; torda-mergulheira, razorbill.

tordilho, *s.m.* sapple-grey *(cavalo).*

tordo, *s.m.* thrush.

torêutica, *s.f.* toreutics.

torga, *s.f.* heather, briar.

tório, *s.m.* thorium *(elemento radioactivo).*

tormenta, *s.f.* storm; tempest, gale; turmoil, trouble.

tormento, *s.m.* torment, anguish, torture, anxiety, worry, annoyance, distress.

tormentório, tormentoso, *adj.* stromy, tempestuous.

torna, *s.f.* compensation; return, retitution.

tornada, *s.f.* a returning.

tornado, *s.m.* tornado.

tornar, *v.i.* to return; to turn; to come back; to retort; to give back, to pay back; tornar-se, to become, to grow into, to turn into.

tornassol, *s.m.* sunflower.

torneado, *adj.* turned, weel-turned.

torneador, *s.m.* turner; tool of a gunsmith.

torneamento, *s.m.* turning.

tornear, *v.t.* to turn, to shape, to mold; to surround; to go round.

tornearia, *s.f.* turnery, turner's workshop.

torneio, *s.m.* torney, tornament, joust; contest; competition.

torneira, *s.f.* cock, tap, spigot. 1) abrir a torneira, to turn on the tap. 2) fechar a torneira, to turn off the tap.

torneiro, *s.m.* turner, lathe operator, wood turner.

tornejar, *v.t.* to turn or curve, to go around; to meander *(rio);* to turn a corner.

torniquete, *s.m.* turnstile, turnpike; tourniquet *(médico);* rack *(tortura).*

torno, *s.m.* lathe; vice. 1) em torno de, around, about. 2) em torno da cidade, round about town. 3) olhar em torno, to look about.

tornozelo, *s.m.* ankle.

toro, *s.m.* trunk, stump *(árvore),* log.

torpe, *adj.* dirty, indecorous, obscene, base, vile, sordid, torpid, low, mean.

torpecer, *v.i.* to grow numb.

tropedeamento, *s.m.* torpedoing.

torpedear, *v.t.* to torpedo.

torpedeiro, *s.m.* torpedo-boat.

torpedo, *s.m.* torpedo.

torpemente, *adv.* basely, vilely.

torpeza, torpidade, *s.f.* turpide, obscenity; infamy, baseness, vileness, infamy, dishonesty.

tórpido, *adj.* torpid, numb, lethargic.

torpor, *s.m.* torpor, torpidity, numbness, slugishness.

torquês, *s.f.* pincers; nippers.

torrada, *s.f.* toast.

torradeira, *s.f.* toaster.

torrado, *adj.* toasted.

torragem, *s.f.* toasting.

torrão, *s.m.* clod, lump; country, ground, land; glebe, tract of land. 1) torrão de açúcar, sugar lump. 2) torrão natal, native land.

torrar, *v.t.* to toast, to roast; to brown; to dry, to scorch, to parch.

torre, *s.f.* tower; steeple; rook, castle *(xadrez).* 1) torre de comando, conning. 2) torre de menagem, donjon. 3) alto como uma torre, as tall as a poplar tree, tower

torreada, *adj.* tower-shaped; towered, turreted.

torreão, *s.m.* turret, small tower.

torrear, *v.t.* to surround with towers; to tower.

torrefacção, *s.f.* torrefaction, roasting *(café).*

torrefacto, *adj.* roasted, torrefied.

torrefactor, *s.m.* roaster toaster.

torreira, *s.f.* solar heat, violent heat *(sol).*

torrencial, *adj.* torrential; impetuous, rushing, *chuva torrencial,* pouring rain.

torrencialmente, *adv.* torrentially.

torrente, *s.f.* torrent, flood, rushing stream; downpour; multitude, plenty; outburst *(lágrimas).*

torrentoso, *adj.* torrent, rushing, rapid.

torresmo, *s.m.* small rashers of lard fried or roasted brown.

tórrido, *adj.* torrid, burning, hot, scorching.

torrificar, *v.t.* to torrefy; to roast, to parch, to scorch.

torroada, *s.f.* pile of clods; blow with a clod.

torso, *s.m.* torso, bust, trunk.

torta, *s.f.* tart, pie; *torta de maçã,* apple pie.

torteira, *s.f.* patty-pan.

torto, *adj.* crooked, tortuous, awry; one-eyed; deformed, distorred; wrong, unfair. 1) *a torto e a direito,* right or wrong, right and left, at random, anyhow. 2) *a torto ou a direito,* by hook or by crook.

tortulho, *s.m.* mushroom; a squat person.

tortiosamente, *adv.* tortuously, crookedly, stealthily.

tortuosidade, *s.f.* tortuousity, turnpike; sinuosity, winding.

tortuoso, *adj.* tortuous crooked, winding, twisting, twisted.

tortura, *s.f.* torture; anguish, pain, torment.

torturado, *adj.* totured, afflicted, tormented.

torturante, *adj.* tormenting, torturing, painful, neverracking.

torturar, *v.t.* to torture, to rack, to strain, to harass, to torment, to distress, to grieve, to worry.

torvação, torvamento, *s.f., s.m.* disturbance, upset, perturbation.

torvamente, *adv.* threateningly, sternly, grimily.

torvamento, *s.m.* disturbance, upset, perturbation.

torvar, *v.i.* to trouble, to disturb, to agitate, to upset; *turvar-se,* to become, irritated or sullen.

torvelinhar, *v.i.* to whirl, to eddy, to swirl.

torvelinho, *s.m.* whirlwind; *andar num torvelinho,* to whirl round, to be in a whirl, to be always on the go.

torvo, *adj.* angry; grim, stern, frowning, moody.

tosa, *s.f.* thrashing, drubbing, beating; rebuke, reproof; shearing. 1) *apanhar uma tosa,* to get a thrashing. 2) *dar uma tosa,* to get a dressing down.

tosador, *s.m.* shearer.

tosadura, *s.f.* shearing, sheep-shearing.

tosão, *s.m.* fleece; a net (for fishing).

tosar, *v.t.* to shear; to clip, to fleece; to browse, to crop; to drub, to beat, to thrash, to cudgel.

toscamente, *adv.* roughly, coarsely.

tosco, *adj.* coarse, rude; rough, rugged, unpolished; clumsy, awkward, inept.

tosquia, *s.f.* shearing, clipping; sheep-shearing time; sharp dressing-down.

tosquiadela, *s.f.* slight shearing; rebuke reprimand.

tosquiador, *s.m.* shearer, fleecer, clipper.

toasquiadora, *s.f.* shearing-machine.

toaquiadura, *s.f.* shearing.

toaquiar, *v.t.* to shear *(barco),* to clip *(cães, cavalos),* to cut *(cabelo).*

tosse, *s.f.* cough, coughing; *tosse convulsa,* whooping cough.

tossegoso, *adj.* coughing.

tossicar, *v.i.* to cough slightly.

tossidela, *s.f.* slight coughing.

tossir, *v.i.* to cough.

tosta, *s.f.* toast.

tostadela, *s.f.* toasting, roasting, light roasting.

tostado, *adj.* parched, toasted, roasted; tanned *(pelo sol),* browned, sunburnt.

tostadura, *s.f.* ver *"tostadela".*

tostão, *s.m.* portuguese coin. 1) *sem tostão,* penniless. 2) *não vale um tostão,* it is not worth a toss.

tostar, *v.i.* to tast, to rast, to parch, to tan, to make brown.

total, *adj.* total; entire, absolute, through whole, utter; *s.m.* total, sum total.

totalidade, *s.f.* totality, whole, entirety; *na totalidade,* in all.

totalitário, *adj.* totalitarine.

totalitarismo, *s.m.* totalitarianism.

totalitarista, *s.* totalitarian.

totalização, *s.f.* totalization.

totalizador, *s.m.* totalizer.

totalizar, *v.t.* to totalize.

totalmente, *adv.* totally, wholly; utterly.

touca, *s.f.* coif, cap, hood.

touça, *s.f.* thicket.

toucado, *s.m.* headgear; hair-dressing, head-dress.

toucador, *s.m.* dressing-table; dressing-room.

toucar, *v.t.* to dress *(o cabelo);* to crown; to wreathe; to surmount.

touceira, *s.f.* big stump *(de uma árvore).*

toucinheiro, *s.m.* bacon-dealer; pork-butcher.

toucinho, *s.m.* bacon; lard, salt pork fat.

toupeira, *s.f.* mole.

toura, *s.f.* heifer, young cow.

tourada, *s.f.* bullfight.

tourão, *s.m.* polecat.

toureador, *s.m.* bullfighter.

tourear, *v.t.* to flight bulls.

toureio, *s.m.* bullfighting, art of fighting bulls.

toureiro, *s.m.* bullfighter, toreador.

touril, *s.m.* ox-stall.

touro, *s.m.* bull.

toutiçada, *s.f.* blow on the hindhead.

toutiço, *s.m.* occiput; head, hindhead.

toutinegra, *s.f.* blackcap.

toxicidade, *s.f.* toxiticity.

tóxico, *adj.* toxic, poisonous; *s.m.* toxicant, poison.

toxicologia, *s.f.* toxicology.

toxicológico, *adj.* toxicological.

toxicologista, toxicólogo, *s., s.m.* toxicologist.

toxicomania, *s.m.* toxicomani, drug addiction.

toxicómano, *s.m.* drug, addict.

toxicose, *s.f.* toxicosis.

toxidez, *s.f.* toxicity.

toxina, *s.f.* toxin.

trabalhadamente, *adv.* laboriously.

trabalhadeira, *adj.* diligent, laborious, hard-working *(mulher).*

trabalhado, *adj.* laboured; wrought; well-done, elaborate.

trabalhador, *adj.* industrious, hard-working; *s.m.* worker, workman.

trabalhão, *s.m.* tiring work, heavy work; big brother.

trabalhar, *v.t.* to work; to shape; to toil, to labour; to run, to go, to function *(máquina);* to perform *(no palco); trabalhar para o bispo,* to work for a dead horse, to have a thankless task.

trabalheira, *s.f.* laborious, work, drudgery, toil; bother.

trabalhismo, *s.m.* labourism; labour Party.

trabalhista, *s.* labourite; Labour Party supporter ou member.

trabalho, *s.m.* work; toil, labour; workmanship; industry; task; occupation, employment; result, piece of work. 1) *trabalho escolar (para casa),* homework. 2) *trabalho de sapa,* spadework.

trabalhosamente, *adv.* laboriously.

trabalhoso, *adj.* laborious, toilsome, fatiguing, difficult, arduous, tiring.

trabucador, *s.m.* one who works hard; adj. hard-working, diligent.

trabucar, *v.t.* to work hard; *quem não tabuca não manduca,* no work, no pay.

trabuzana, *s.f.* tempest, storm; disease, sickness; drunkenness.

traça, *s.f.* draft, plan, outline, sketch; aspect; look; clothes-moth.

traçado, *adj.* moth-eaten; outlined, delineated, drawn; *s.m.* outline, sketch.

traçamento, *s.m.* skect, drawing.

tracanaz, *s.m.* a big slice or portion of something.

traçar, *v.t.* to trace, to delineate, to map, to draw; to eat clothes; to cut up, to cut to pieces.

tracção, *s.f.* traction, tension, pull, pulling, stress, tug, hauling.

tracejado, *s.m.* broken line.

tracejamento, *s.m.* sketch, laying out.

tracejar, *v.t.* to sketch; to draw a broken line.

trácio, *adj., s.m.* Thracian.

traço, *s.m.* trace; streak; line; dash; slice; track, sign; feature, trait.

tracoma, *s.m.* trachoma.

tracto, *s.m.* tract, region, area.

tractor, *s.m.* tractor, traction engine.

tradição, *s.f.* tradition.

tradicional, *adj.* traditional.

tradicionalismo, *s.m.* traditionalism.

tradicionalista, *s.* traditionalist; *adj.* traditionalistic.

tradicionalmente, *adv.* traditionally.

trado, *s.m.* auger, boring-tool.

tradução, *s.f.* translation, version.

tradutor, *s.m.* translator.

traduzir, *v.t.* to translate, to render; to interpret; to express.

traduzível, *adj.* translatable.

trafegar, *v.i.* to labour, to toil, to plod.

tráfego, *s.m.* traffic; trade, commerce; transport.

traficância, *s.f.* swindle, roguery, knavery, shifiting.

traficante, *s.m.* swindler, rogue, crook, rascal.

traficar, *v.i.* to trade, to traffic; to swindle.

tráfico, s.m. traffic, trade, shady business.

trafulha, s. impostor, trickster.

trafulhice, s.f. fraud, trickery.

tragadoiro, s.m. ver tragadouro.

tragador, s.m. swallower, devourer, gormandizer; adj. devouring.

tragadouro, s.m. pit, gulf, abyss, vortex.

tragamento, s.m. swallowing.

traga-mouros, s.m. bully; blusterer; ruffian.

tragar, v.t. to swallow; to engulf; to eat; to devour, to absorb; to put up with, to bear, to tolerate.

tragédia, s.f. tragedy; calamity, disaster.

tragicamente, adv. tragically.

trágico, adj. tragical, tragic, fatal, calamitous, sad, fatal, disastrous, s.m. tragedian, (actor ou escritor).

tragicomédia, s.f. tragicomedy.

tragicómico, adj. tragicomic.

trago, s.m. draught, gulp; de um trago, in one gulp.

traição, s.f. treason, treachery, betrayal.

traiçoeiramente, adv. treacherously.

traiçoeiro, adj. treacherous, traitorous, perficous, disloyal.

traidor, adj. treacherous, false, disloyal; s.m. traitor, double-crosser.

traimento, s.m. ver traição.

traineira, s.f. trawlboat, trawler.

trair, v.i. to betray, to deceive, to be false to, to double-cross; to reveal.

trajar, v.t. to dress, to wear, to have on; to put on.

traje, s.m. dress, clothing, clothes, apparel.

trajecto, s.m. way, road, course; journey, distance; passage.

trajectória, s.f. trajectory; way, manner.

trajo, s.m. dress, garment, clothes, garb, attire, suit. 1) trajo à paisana, civilian clothes. 2) trajo de cerimónia ou gala, full dress, formal dress. 3) trajo de fantasia, fancy dress. 4) trajos menores, underclothes. 5) trajo de passeio, street clothes. 6) trajo de rigor, formal evening dress or attire.

tralha, s.f. fishing-net; rubbish; luggage; old household articles.

trama, s.f. woof, texture; plot, intrigue, conspiracy, scheme.

tramador, s.m. weaver; plotter, intriguer.

tramar, v.t. to weave; to plot; (pop) to drive (uma pessoa) into a tight corner; to trick.

trambolhão, s.m. tumble, tumbling down, fall.

trambolhar, v.t. to tumble, to tumble down, to go tumbling along, to stagger, to falter.

trambolho, s.m. clog; hindreance, impediment, burden.

tramela, s.f. wooden latch; gabbler.

tramelo, s.m. little mouse.

trâmites, s.m. (pl.) means; course, procedure, way, channels, formalities.

tramo, s.m. roof frame, the part of a bridge.

tramóia, s.f. intrigue, plot, swindle.

tramontana, s.f. pole-star; direction, course; tramontana (vento norte); perder a tramontana, to lose one's bearings, to be at loss.

trampolim, s.m. spring-board, leaping-board, jumping-board.

trampolinagem, s.f. cheating, trickery; swindle, fraud.

trampolinar, v.i. to cheat, to swindle, to trick, to dupe, to take in.

trampolineiro, s.m. cheat, knave, swindler, deceiver, double-crosser, trickster.

trampolinice, s.f. swindle, trick, cheating, deceit, imposture.

trâmuei, s.m. suburban train.

tranca, s.m. bar, espagnolette, sash-fastner, window fastening; thick stick.

trança, s.f. tress, braid (de cabelo); pigtail.

trancada, s.m. stroke, blow.

trancamento, s.m. barring, bolting.

trancanaz, s.m. a big portion.

trancar, v.t. to bar, to bolt.

trançar, v.t. to plait, to braid, to twist, to tress.

tranca-ruas, s. bully.

trancelim, s.m. thin gold chain, gold braid; ribbon.

tranqueira, s.f. palisade; trench; door-post.

tranqueta, s.f. door-latch; dog; bolt, door-bar.

tranquiberneiro, adj. swindler, trickster, imposter.

tranquibérnia, s.f. trickery, cheating, fraud.

tranquilamente, adv. tranquilly, quietly, peacefully, calmly.

tranquilidade, s.f. tranquility, stillness, calm, quiet.

tranquilizador, adj. tranquilizing, lulling, reassuring; s.m. tranquilizer.

tranquilizar, v.t. to tranquilize, to queit; to calm down, to appease; to reassure.

tranquilo, adj. tranquil, calm, serene, queit, peaceful.

traquitana, s.f. ver "traquitana".

transacção, *s.f.* transaction, business deal; affair.

transaccionar, *v.i.* to transact, to negotiate.

transacto, *adj.* past; former; previous.

transalpino, *adj.* transalpine.

transatlântico, *adj.* transatlantic; *s.m.* ocean steamer, liner.

transbordamento, *s.m.* overflowing.

transbordante, *adj.* overfull, overflowing.

transbordar, *v.i.* to overflow; to spill over.

transbordo, *s.m.* transhipment, transfer, change; overflow.

transcendência, *s.f.* transcendency, transcendence.

transcendental, *adj.* transcendental.

transcendentalismo, *s.m.* transcendentalism.

transcendentalista, *s.* transcendentalist.

transcendente, *adj.* transcendent.

transcender, *v.t.* to transcend, to surmount, to surpass, to excel, to exceed.

transcontinental, *adj.* transcontinental.

transcorrer, *v.i.* to elapse, to go by, to pass (time), to glide away.

transcrever, *v.i.* to transcribe; to copy out.

transcrição, *s.f.* transcription; copy, transcript.

transcrito, *adj.* transcribed, copied out; s.m. transcript, copy.

transcritor, *adj.* transcribing; *s.m.* transcriber.

transcursão, *s.f.* course, lapse *(de tempo)*.

transcursar, *v.t.*, *v.i.* to pass away; to elapse.

transcurso, *s.m.* course, process *(de tempo)*.

transe, *s.m.* anguish, distress, crisis, ordeal; *a todo o transe,* at any cost, by any means.

transepto, *s.m.* transept.

transeunte, *s.* passer-by; pedestrian.

transferência, *s.f.* removal, transference; transfer, conveyance; *pedir transferência,* to ask to be transferred.

transferidor, *s.m.* protractor *(para medir ângulos)*

transferir, *v.t.* to transfer; to remove, to convey; to hand over, to transmit; to postpone, to put off, to defer; to pass.

transferível, *adj.* transferable.

transfiguração, *s.f.* transfiguration.

transfigurado, *adj.* transfigured, changed, transformed.

transfigurador, *adj.* transfiguring, changing; *s.m.* one who transfigures.

transfigurar, *v.t.* to transfigure, to transform, to change; *transfigurar-se,* to change utterly; to be transfigured.

transfigurável, *adj.* transfigured.

transfixação, *s.f.* transfixion.

transfixão, *s.f.* amputation.

transfixar, *v.t.* to transfix, to pierce through.

transformação, *s.f.* transformation, change, alteration.

transformador, *adj.* transforming; *s.m.* transformer *(pessoa ou máquina).*

transformante, *adj.* transforming.

transformar, *v.t.* to transform, to change, to alter to modify.

transformativo, *adj.* transformative.

transformável, *adj.* transformable.

transformismo, *s.m.* transformism.

transformista, *s.f.* transformist.

trânsfuga, *s.m.* deserter, runaway; turncoat.

transfúgio, *s.m.* desertion.

transfugir, *v.i.* to desert.

transfundir, *v.t.* to transfuse; to transfer; to inject.

transfusão, *s.m.* transfusion.

transgredir, *v.t.* to transgress, to break, to violate, to overstep, to infringe, to trespass.

transgressão, *s.f.* transgression, violation, breach, infringement, trespass.

transgressivo, *adj.* transgressive, lawbreaking.

transgressor, *s.m.* transgressor, sinner, offender, law-breaker, infringer, trespasser, violater.

transiberiano, *adj.* trans-Siberian.

transição, *s.f.* transition, passage, change.

transido, *adj.* chilled, frozen, benumbed; shivering *(de medo, frio).*

transigência, *s.f.* compliance, compromise; indulgence, tolerance, consent.

transigente, *adj.* compliant, condescending, broad-minded.

transigir, *v.t.*, *v.i.* to be condescending; to consent, to compromise, to yield, to come to terms, to temporize.

transigível, *adj.* conformable.

transilvano, *adj.*, *s.m.* Transylvanian.

transir, *v.t.* to pass through, to penetrate, to pierce; *transir-se de frio,* to chill, to be paralyzed.

transitar, *v.i.* to pass, to change, to go through; to travel; to be moved up *(na escola).*

transitável, *adj.* passable, usable, practicable.

transitivo, *adj.* transitive.
trânsito, *s.m.* transit, traffic.
transitoriedade, *s.f.* transitoriness.
transitório, *adj.* transitory, perishable; transient, passing, ephemeral, fugacious; brief, temporary, fugitive.
translação, *s.f.* translation; removal; metaphor.
transladação, *s.f.* ver trasladação.
transladar, *v.t.* ver trasladar.
translatício, *adj.* metaphoric.
translato, *adj.* metaphoric, figurative; transferred.
translineação, *s.f.* division of words at the end of a line.
transliteração, *s.m.* transliteration.
transliterar, *v.t.* to transliterate.
translucidez, *s.f.* translucence, translucency.
translúcido, *adj.* translucent, pellucid; transparent.
transluzente, *adj.* translucent, clear.
transluzimento, *s.m.* transparency.
transluzir, *v.t., v.i.* to shine through, to come to light, to become known.
transmigração, *s.f.* transmigration, metempsychosis.
transmigrante, *adj.* transmigrant, transmigratory.
transmigrar, *v.i.* to transmigrate.
transmigratório, *adj.* transmigratory.
transmissão, *s.f.* transmission; transmitting, transmittal. 1) *transmissão radiofónica,* radio broadcasting. 2) *direitos de transmissão,* death duties.
transmissibilidade, *s.f.* transmissibility.
transmissível, *adj.* transmissible, transmittable, communicable.
transmissivo, *adj.* transmissive, transferable.
transmissor, *adj.* transmissive; *s.m.* transmitter *(em todos os sentidos); transmissor de ondas curtas,* short-wave transmitter.
transmitir, *v.t.* to transmit; to send on; to broadcast; to tell, to impart; to pass on, to hand over.
transmontano, *s.m.* native of *Trás-os-Montes.*
transmudação, *s.f.* transmutation; transformation, change.
transmudar, *v.t.* to transmute, to change, to transform.
transmutabilidade, *s.f.* transmutability.

transmutação, *s.f.* transmutation, transformation.
transmutar, *v.t.* to transmute, to transform into.
transmutativo, *adj.* transmutative.
transmutável, *adj.* transmutable.
transoceânico, *adj.* transoceanic.
transpadano, *adj.* transopadane, beyond the river Po *(Itália).*
transparecer, *v.i.* to appear through, to show, to be evident, to reveal itself, to become clear.
transparência, *s.f.* transparency, transparence, limpidity; slide *(fotografia).*
transparente, *adj.* transparent; clear, evident, plain, patent, obvious, manifest.
transpassar, *v.t.* to pass over, to go beyond, to cross; to exceed, to excel; to trespass; to pierce through.
transpiração, *s.f.* transpiration, perspiration, sweat, exudation.
transpirar, *v.i.* to perspire, to transpire, to sweat; to come to light, to become known, to leak out.
transpirável, *adj.* transpirable.
transplantação, *s.f.* transplantation.
transplantador, *s.m.* transplanter *(pessoa, brinquedo ou máquina).*
transplantar, *v.t.* to transplant; to move; to transfer; *transplantar-se para,* to move to.
transponível, *adj.* removable, that can be overcome.
transpor, *v.t.* to transpose *(uma linha);* to change; to remove, to transport, to pass over, to cross over, to pass through; to overcome *(dificuldade);* to leap, to jump over.
transportação, *s.f.* transportation, conveyance.
transportador, *s.m.* transporter, trucker, conveyor.
transportar, *v.t.* to transport, to convey, to transfer, to remove, to carry; to ravish, to enrapture, to delight.
transportável, *adj.* transportable, portable; conveyable.
transporte, *s.m.* transport, conveyance; transfer, rapture, ecstasy; troopship, transport ship; brought forward.
transposição, *s.m.* transposition; change; transposal.
transpositivo, *adj.* transpositional, transpositive.

transposto, *adj.* transposed; overcome, surpassed.

transtagano, *adj.* beyond the river Tagus.

transtornar, *v.t.* to overturn; to upset; to disturb; to trouble; to derange, to unsettle, to throw into disorder.

transtorno, *s.m.* disturbance; upset; inconvenience; trouble; derangement.

transtrocar, *v.t.* to invert, to reverse, to alter; to confuse.

transubstanciação, *s.f.* transubstantiation.

transubstancial, *adj.* transubstantial.

transubstanciar, *v.t.* to transubstantiate, to transform, to transmute.

transudação, *s.f.* transudation, transpiration, perspiration, sweating.

transudar, *v.i.* to transude, to exude.

transumanar, *v.t.* to transhumanize, to make humane.

transumância, *s.f.* transhumance.

transumano, *adj.* transhumane.

transumante, *adj.* said of the cattle that change grazing *(periodicamente)*.

transumar, *v.t., v.i.* to change the grazing grounds.

transunto, *s.m.* copy, transcript, duplicate; image.

transvaliano, *adj., s.m.* Transvaalian.

transvasamento, *s.m.* transfusing.

transvasar, *v.t.* to transfuse *(de uma garrafa para outra)*.

transvazar, *v.t.* to decant, to pour out; to empty.

transverberar, *v.t.* to reflect, to chine; to manifest itself.

transversal, *adj.* transversal, transverse; *s.f.* transversal.

transversalmente, *adv.* transversally, crosswise.

transverso, *adj.* transversal, transverse, lying across, oblique.

transverter, *v.t.* to transform; to convert; to overturn, to overthrow.

transviado, *adj.* wayward.

transviar, *v.t.* to mislead, to lead astray, to corrupt, to pervert; *transviar-se,* to go astray, to stray, to get lost.

transvio, *s.m.* going astray, deviation.

tranvia, *s.f.* local or suburban train.

trapaça, trapaçaria, *s.f.* cheat, fraud, swindle, trick, knavery.

trapacear, *v.i.* to cheat, to defraud, to trick, to swindle, to deceive, to dupe, to take in.

trapaceiro, *adj.* deceitful; *s.m.* cheat, trickster, impostor, deceiver.

trapacice, *s.f.* ver *"trapaça"*.

trapada, trapagem, *s.f.* rag pile, clothes.

trapalhada, *s.f.* confusion; entanglement, imbroglio; complication, disorder; *que trapalhada!,* what a mess!

trapalhão, *s.m.* bungler; blunderer; impostor, liar.

trapalhice, *s.f.* swindle, trick, fraud.

trapeira, *s.f.* dormer, dormer-window; rag-picker *(mulher)*.

trapeiro, *s.m.* rag-gatherer, ragman.

trapejar, *v.i.* to falp, to clap, to clash.

trapeziforme, *adj.* trapeziform, trapezoidal.

trapézio, *s.m.* trapeze; trapezium *(geometria)*.

trapezista, *s.* trapezist *(acrobata)*.

trapezoidal, *adj.* trapezoidal.

trapezóide, *adj.* trapezoid.

trapiche, *s.m.* water-front warehouse.

trapista, *s.* Trappist *(frade ou freira)*.

trapo, *s.m.* rag, tatter; *(pl.)* old clothes.

traqueal, *adj.* tracheal.

traqueano, *adj.* trachean.

traqueia, *s.f.* trachea, windpipe.

traqueíte, *s.f.* tracheitis.

traquejar, *v.t., v.i.* to chase, to pursue; to beat.

traquejo, *s.m.* skill, practice, experience.

traqueotomia, *s.f.* tracheotomy.

traquete, *s.m.* foresail.

traquina, *adj.* troublesome; frolicsome; retless; turbulent, fidgety.

traquinada, *s.f.* frisk, frolic, escapade *(criança)*; turbulent, fidgety.

traquinar, *v.i.* to romp about; to play pranks.

traquinas, *adj., s.* mischievous, fidgety; prankish child.

traquinice, *s.f.* misbehaviour, mischief.

traquitana, *s.f.* rattletrap.

trás, *prep. adv.* after, behind; *interj.* bang! 1) *andar para trás,* to walk backwards. 2) *de trás,* from behind. 3) *de trás para diante,* backward. 4) *de diante para trás,* from front to rear. 5) *deixar muito para trás,* to leave far behind. 6) *por trás de,* behind.

trasantontem, *adv.* the day before the day before yesterday; three days ago.

trasbordamento, *s.m.* overflow, overflowing.

trasbordante, *adj.* overflowing, too full.

trasbordar, *v.t.* to overflow; to tram-ship; to spread, to spill over.

trasbordo, *s.m.* trans-shipment, transfer; change *(pessoas de comboio)*.

trascâmara, *s.f.* backroom.

traseira, *s.f.* back part, rear.

traseiro, *adj.* back, rear, hind, posterior; *s.m.* sit-me-down, the behind, buttocks.

trasfega, *s.m.* racking, drawing off, decantation *(vinho)*.

trasfegador, *s.m.* racker.

trasfegadura, *s.f.* ver trasfega.

trasfegar, *v.t.* to rack, to decant, to pour out *(vinho)*.

trasfego, *s.m.* drawing off.

trasgo, *s.m.* elf, goblin; ghost.

trasladação, *s.f.* removal, conveyance; translation.

trasladador, *adj.* translator; remover.

trasladar, *v.t.* to remove, to convey; to translate; to postpone, to defer.

traslado, *s.m.* copy; transcript; translation; image; model.

trasmontano, *adj.* ver "transmontano".

trasorelho, *s.m.* mumps; parotitis.

traspassação, traspassamento, *s.m.* passing over; piercing through.

traspassar, *v.t.* to pass over; to go beyond; to croo; to copy; to transfer, to sublet; to pine away, to faint; to rend *(o coração);* to pierce; to be struck with.

traspasse, *s.m.* assignment, transfer; death.

traspasso, *s.m.* transfer; violent pain; delay, deferment.

trastalhada, *s.f.* old pieces of furniture, lumber.

trastalhão, *s.m.* scamp, rascal, rogue.

traste, *s.m.* piece *(de mobiliário);* rogue, rascal.

trastejar, *v.t.* to furnish *(uma casa);* to play the rascal.

tratadista, *s.* writer of a treatise.

tratado, *s.m.* treatise; treaty, agreement, pact, convention.

tratador, *s.m.* cattle-feeder; groom; caretaker; horse-breeder.

tratamento, *s.m.* treatment, usage, management; daily food; address; nursing.

tratantada, *s.f.* roguery, swindle, knavery, rascality.

tratante, *s.* dealer, contractor; rogue, crook, rascal, scamp, scoundrel.

tratantice, *s.f.* ver "tratantada".

tratar, *v.t.* to treat; to use; to manage; to conduct; to nurse; to negotiate; to deal with; to look after, to care for, to attend; to consider, to regard; to discuss.

tratável, *adj.* tractable, accessible, accostable, docile, affable, manageable.

trato, *s.m.* treatment; behaviour; address, manner, agreement, pact; handling; trade, traffic, food, table, board.

trauma, *s.m.* trauma, traumatism.

traumático, *adj.* traumatic.

traumatismo, *s.m.* traumatism.

traumatizar, *v.t.* to cause a trauma.

traumatologia, *s.m.* traumatology.

traumatológico, *adj.* traumatologic.

trautear, *v.t.* to hum, to trill, to sing *(em voz baixa);* to scold.

trauteio, *s.m.* humming, trilling.

trava, *s.f.* clog, trammel, fetters; setting.

travação, *s.f.* joining; link; connexion.

travadeira, *s.f.* saw-set.

travado, *adj.* joined, linked; set.

travador, *s.m.* joining, linking; cheking; *s.m.* saw-set.

travadouro, *s.m.* brace; fetlock-joint; pastern *(de cavalos)*.

travadura, *s.m.* junction, union.

travagem, *s.f.* braking.

travamento, *s.m.* stiffening; staying; breaking; locking.

travanca, *s.f.* clog; obstacle, hindrance, impediment; stumbling block.

travão, *s.m.* shackle *(para cavalos);* brake, check. 1) *travão às quatro rodas,* four-wheel brake. 2) *alavanca do travão,* brake lever.

travar, *v.t.* to join, to bind, to tie; to clog *(animais);* to set; to put the drag on; to check, to brake; to lock; to restrain; to impede, to moderate; to taste sour; to engage on. 1) *travar uma batalha,* to engage in battle. 2) *travar combate,* to join combat. 3) *travar conhecimento (relações),* to get acquainted with, to come to know, to make the acquaintance of. 4) *travar-se de razões,* to cross words with.

trave, *s.f.* beam, rafter; cross-bar; tongue-tied *(pop)*.

travejamento, *s.m.* timber work, frameowrk; house-frame.

travejar, *v.t.* to lay the beams, to frame.

travelã, *s.f.* cutworm; wooden doorknocker.

travertino, *s.m.* travertine *(mineral)*.

través, *s.m.* bias; traverse; slant. 1) *de través,* across, crosswise, aslant. 2) *olhar* *de través*, to look down one's nose, to look askew.

travessa, *s.f.* cross-beam; sleeper; transom; dish; crossroad; narrow street; by-street; comb, bar, pin *(para o cabelo)*. 1) *mão--travessa*, a hand's breadth. 2) *por portas travessas*, in secret.

travessão, *s.m.* beam *(de uma balança)*; dash; large dish.

travesseira, *s.m.* pillow; cushion.

travesseiro, *s.m.* bolster; *consultar o travesseiro*, to sleep over something, to take counsel of one's pillow.

travessia, *s.m.* crossing, voyage; passage.

travesso, *adj.* restless, uneasy, playful, frisky, gambol; knavery.

travessura, *s.f.* prank; mischief, frisk, gambol; knavery.

travesti, *s.m.* disguise, any disguise.

travinca, *s.f.* small beam; pin bolt.

travo, *s.m.* acridness, harshness, tartness, bitterness, sourness, acredity; after-taste.

travor, *s.m.* ver "*travo*".

travoso, *adj.* acrid, harsh, sour, bitter.

trazedor, *s.m.* bringer, carrier, messenger.

trazer, *v.t.* to bring, to fetch; to carry; to bear; to wear, to have on *(roupa)*; to take, to convey; to cause; to gain, to receive.

trebelho, *s.m.* folly, joke, jest; dance.

trecentésimo, *adj.* three hundredth.

trecentista, *s.* of the 12th century *(escritor ou artista)*.

trecho, *s.m.* piece *(de música)*; passage, extract; period, space, distance; *a breve trecho*, soon, shortly after.

tredo, *adj.* disloyal, treacherous, false.

trêfego (trefo), *adj.* naughty, stirring, unquiet, turbulent, restless; crafty, deceitful.

trégua, *s.f.* truce; rest, cessation, pause, respite; armistice.

treinador, *s.m.* trainer.

treinamento, *s.m.* training, practice, drill, exercise.

treinar, *v.t.* to train; to exercise; to teach; to drill, to instruct.

treino, *s.m.* training, exercise, drill, practice, preperation.

trejeitador, *s.m.* buffoon, jugler; mocker.

trejeitar, trejeitear, *v.i.* to grimace, to make faces.

trejeito, *s.m.* grimace, antic, wry face.

trejurar, *v.t., v.i.* to swear often *(três vezes)*.

trela, *s.f.* lead, leash, strap *(para cães)*; talk,

chat, gossip *(pop); dar trela*, to encourage to talk, to flirt.

trem, *s.m.* coach; carriage, train, equipage, suite, retinue; kitchen-ware; *trem de aterragem*, landing gear.

trema, *s.f.* diaeresis.

tremar, *v.t.* to mark wirh a diaeresis.

tremebundo, *adj.* trembling, shaking, tremulous; tremendous, dreadful.

tremedal, *s.m.* morass, marsh, quagmire, bog, swamp; moral degradation.

tremedor, *s.m.* quaker, trembler; *adj.* shivering, trembling.

tremelear, *v.t.* to quiver, to shiver; to stammer.

tremelga, *s.m.* torpedo, cramp-fish, electric ray.

tremelica, *adj.* weak, coward, timid; *s.* fainthearted person.

tremelicar, *v.i.* to shiver, to quiver, to tremble.

tremelicas, *adj.* ver "*trmelica*".

tremelique, *s.m.* shiver, tremble.

tremeliquento, *adj.* shivery.

tremeliques, *s.m. pl.* shivering, trembling; *estar com tremeliques*, in fear and trembling.

tremeluzente, *adj.* twinkling, blinking, flickering, sparkling.

tremeluzir, *v.i.* to twinkle, to blink, to flicker, to glimmer, to flare.

tremendamente, *adv.* dreadfully, tremendously.

tremendo, *adj.* trmendous, dreadfull, awful, frightful, terrible, horrible, fearful; formidable.

tremenhos, *s.m. pl.* manners, ways, attitude.

tremente, *adj.* trembling, quivering, shivering, quaking.

tremer, *v.i.* to tremble, to shake, to quake, to shiver; to quiver; to quaver *(voz)*, to vibrate, to oscillate; to be tremulous or shaky; to shudder; to fear, to dread; *tremer como varas verdes*, to shake in one's shoes.

tremês, tremesinho, *adj.* lasting three months.

tremido, *adj.* doubtful; shaky, risky, dubious.

tremó, *s.m.* pier, pier-glass.

tremoçada, *s.f.* large quantity of lupiness.

tremoçal, *s.m.* plantation of lupine.

tremoceira, *s.f.* seller of lupines *(mulher)*.

tremoço, *s.m.* lupine *(planta ou semente)*.

tremonha, *s.f.* hopper.

tremor, *s.m.* tremor, shiver, shaking, quake, quiver; *tremor de terra,* earthquake.

trempe, *s.f.* trivet, tripod; trio *(pessoas).*

tremulação, *s.f.* shivering, wavering, trembling; flicker.

tremulante, *adj.* waving, fluttering, shaking.

tremular, *v.i.* to wave, to fly; to tremble, to flutter; to twinkle, to glimmer, to shimmer.

tremulina, *s.f.* glimmer, shimmer, glister.

trémulo, *adj.* tremulous, trembling, shaking; *s.m.* tremolo *(música).*

tremura, *s.f.* tremor, shivering, tremble, shaking.

trena, *s.f.* hair-ribbon; tape-line.

treno, *s.m.* lament, elegy, dirge.

trenó, *s.m.* toboggan; sledge; sleigh.

trepa, *s.f.* rebuke, scolding, dressing-down; thrashing.

trepadeira, *s.f.* climber, climbing plant, creeper; *adj.* climbing.

trepador, *adj.* climbing, creeping; *s.m.* climber, creeper; scansorial bird.

trepanação, *s.f.* trepanation, trepanning.

trepanar, *v.t.* to trepan, to trephine.

trépano, *s.m.* trepan, trephine *(espécie de serra).*

trepar, *v.t., v.i.* to climb; to ascend; to rise, to become important; to mount, to scale.

trepidação, *s.f.* trepidation; bustle, stir, fuss.

trepidante, *adj.* tremulous, shaking, oscillating.

trepidar, *v.i.* to shake, to tremble, to bustle; to vibrate, to oscillate; to hesitate.

trepidez, *s.f.* tremor, trembling; fright.

trépido, *adj.* trembling, timorous; waving, fluttering.

tréplica, *s.f.* rejoinder, rebutter, answer.

treplicar, *v.i.* to rejoin, to surrebut, to answer.

três, *num.* three; trey *(cartas).*

tresandar, *v.i.* to stink, to have a bad smell; to cause to go back; to upset.

tresantontem, *adv.* the day before the day before yesterday.

trescalar, *v.t, v.i.* to smell strongly.

tresdobrado, *adj.* triplicate, treble, triple, threefold.

tresdobrar, *v.t., v.i.* to treble, to triple, to triplicate.

tresdobro, *s.m.* treble, triple.

tresler, *v.i.* to read backwards; to dote.

tresloucado, *adj.* mad, deranged, crazy, insane; *s.m.* madman, lunatic, crazy person.

tresloucar, *v.t., v.i.* to make mad; to dote, to go crazy.

tresmalhado, *adj.* strayed, lost, off course; runaway.

tresmalhar, *v.t.* to let go *(escapar),* tresmalhar-se, to go astray, to get lost.

tresmalho, *s.m.* trammel; disappearance; escaping.

tresnoitar, tresnoutar, *v.i.* to pass a sleepless night; to stay awake all night; to keep awake.

trespassado, *adj.* transferred, pierced through; violated; breathless.

trespassar, *v.t.* to transfer, to pass over; to violate; to pierce through; to go too far.

trespasse, trespasso, *s.m.* transfer; subletting; death.

tressuar, *v.i.* to sweat, to perspire very much.

tresvariado, *adj.* doting, wild, delirious, raving.

tresvariar, *v.i.* to dote; to rave, to speak wildly; to act foolishly.

tresvario, *s.m.* dotage, raving, delirium, mental disorder, madness.

treta, *s.f.* stratagem, feint; verbiage, pratle.

treteiro, *s.m.* smooth talker; crook.

trevas, *s.f. pl.* darkness, obscurity; night; ignorance.

trevo, *s.m.* clover.

treze, *num.* thirteen.

trezena, *s.f.* thirteen days; a unit of thirteen.

trezeno, *adj.* thirteenth.

trezentos, *num.* three hundred.

tríada, tríade, *s.f.* triad; a group of three.

triaga, *s.f.* theriac.

triandria, *s.f.* triandria *(flores).*

triangulação, *s.f.* triangulation, divison into triangles.

triangulado, *adj.* triangulated, divided into triangles.

triangulador, *s.m.* triangulator.

triangular, *adj.* triangular, three-cornered; *v.t.* to triangulate, to divide into triangles.

triângulo, *s.m.* triangle; *triângulo equilátero, escaleno, rectângulo,* equilateral, isoscels, scalene, right-angled triangle.

triarca, *s.m.* triarch.

triarquia, *s.f.* triarchy, triumvirate.

triásico, *adj.* Triassic; *s.m.* Trias.

triatómico, *adj.* triatomic.

tribal, *adj.* tribal.

tribásico, *adj.* tribasic.

tribo, *s.f.* tribe, clan; race, folk, family.

tríbraco, *s.m.* tribrach.

tribulação, *s.f.* tribulation; distress, affliction, tial, adversity, suffering.

tribulado, *adj.* afflicted.

tribuna, *s.f.* tribune, platform; stand; rostrum; pulpit; eloquence, oratory. 1) *tribuna da imprensa*, reporter's gallery. 2) *subir à tribuna*, to mount the rostrum.

tribunado, *s.m.* tribunate, tribuneship.

tribunal, *s.m.* tribunal, court of justice, forum, bar. 1) *ir para tribunal*, to go to law court. 2) *tribunal de contas*, Audit Department, Audit Office. 3) *tribunal de pequenos delitos*, Police-Court. 4) *Supremo Tribunal de Justiça*, High Court of Justice. 5) *tribunal de primeira instância*, County Court.

tribunício, *adj.* tribunician, tribunicial.

tribuno, *s.m.* tribune; orator.

tributação, *s.f.* tributation, taxation, contribution.

tributado, *adj.* taxed.

tributal, *adj.* concerning tributes.

tributar, *v.t.* to impose, to levy *(taxas, contribuições, etc.)*, to tax; to pay homage, to dedicate; to contribute.

tributário, *adj.* tributary; *s.m.* contributor; tributary stream or river, confluent.

tributável, *adj.* that can pay tribute; taxable.

tributo, *s.m.* tribute, tax; contribution; duty; homage, respect.

trica, *s.f.* chiane, quibble; trick; cheat.

tricana, *s.f.* country-woman *(Coimbra).*

tricéfalo, *adj.* tricephalous.

tricelular, *adj.* three-celled.

tricenal, *adj.* tricennial, lasting thirty years.

tricénio, *s.m.* thirty years.

tricentenário, *s.m.* tricentenary, tercentenary.

tricentésimo, *num.* three hundredth.

triciclo, *s.m.* tricycle.

tricípete, *adj.* three-headed, triceps *(musc.).*

triclínico, *adj.* triclinic *(de cristais).*

triclínio, *s.m.* triclinium.

tricóide, *adj.* trichoid, hair-like, capillary.

tricolor, *adj.* tricolour, tricoloured.

tricoma, *s.m.* trichome *(doença do cabelo).*

tricorde, *adj.* with three cords.

tricórdio, *s.m.* trichord *(música).*

tricorne, *adj.* three-horned, tricorn.

tricórnio, *s.m.* cocked-hat, tricorn.

tricotar, *v.t, v.i.* to knit.

tricotomia, *s.f.* trichotomy.

tricotómico, *adj.* trichotomous.

tricromático, *adj.* trichromatic.

tricromia, *s.f.* three-colour process of printing.

tricrómico, *adj.* trichromic.

tricúspide, *adj.* tricuspid.

tridáctilo, *adj.* tridactyl(ous).

tridentado, *adj.* tridentate.

tridente, *s.m.* trident.

tridentino, *adj.* Tridentine (de Trent).

tridigitado, *adj. vd.* tridáctilo.

tríduo, *s.m.* triduum, triduo *(em rezas).*

triedro, *adj.* trihedral; *s.m.* trihedron.

trienal, *adj.* triennial.

triénio, *s.m.* three years.

trifacial, *adj.* trifacial.

trifásico, *adj.* three-phase.

trifauce, *adj.* having three jaws.

trífido, *adj.* trifid; three-cleft.

trifloro, *adj.* trifloral, triflorous, three-flowered.

trifólio, *adj.* trifoliate, trifolated; *s.m.* clover; trefoil.

trifório, *s.m.* triforium.

triforme, *adj.* triform.

trifurcação, *s.f.* trifurcation.

trifurcar, *v.t.* to trifurcate.

trigal, *s.m.* cornfield, wheat field.

trigar-se, *v. refl.* to hurry up, to haste.

trigémeo, *s.m.* triplet.

trigémino, *adj.* trigeminal.

trigésimo, *num.* thirtieth.

tríglifo, *s.m.* triglyph.

trigo, *s.m.* corn; wheat. 1) *de trigo*, wheaten. 2) *farinha de trigo*, wheat flour. 3) *separar o trigo do joio*, to separate the chaff from the wheat.

trigonal, *adj.* trigonal.

trígono, *adj.* trigonal, triangular; *s.m.* trigon.

trigonometria, *s.f.* trigonometry.

trigonométrico, *adj.* trigonometric, trigonometrical.

trigoso, *adj.* hasty, impatient.

trigueirão, *s.m.* corn bunting *(pássaro).*

trigueiro, *adj.* brownish; swarthy; dark (skinned).

triguenho, *adj.* swarthy, dark; like wheat.

trilado, *adj.* quaver, trill.

trilar, *v.t. v.i.* to trill, to quaver, to warble.

trilateral, *adj.* trilateral, three-sided.

trilátero, *adj. vd.* trilateral.

trilha, trilhada, *s.f.* track, trace, trail, footstep, way; thrashing *(grão)*; example.

trilhadela, *s.f. ver "trilhadura".*

trilhado, *adj.* thrashed; trodden; common, habitual.

trilhador, *s.m.* thrasher, thresher; thrashing-machine.

trilhadura, *s.f.* tthrashing; bruise; trail.

trilhamento, *s.m.* vd. trilhadura.

trilhar, *v.t.* to thrash, to thresh; to beat; to tread; to bruise; to follow *(caminho)*, to travel on foot.

trilho, *s.m.* track, rail; harrow (for thrashing corn); churn-staff.

trilião, *num.* trillion.

trilíngue, *adj.* trilingual.

triliteral, *adj.* triliteral.

trilo, *s.m.* trill, quaver, warble.

trilobado, *adj.* trilobate, trilobal.

trilobite, *s.f.* trilobite.

triloculado, trilocular, *adj.* trilocular.

trilogia, *s.f.* trilogy, triad.

trimensal (trimestral), *adj.* quarterly, trimensual, trimestrial.

trímero, *adj.* trimerous.

trimestre, *s.m.* quarter; trimester.

trimotor, *s.m.* trimotor *(avião).*

trinado, *s.m.* trill, warble, chirp.

trinador, *adj.* trilling.

trinar, *v.i.* to trill, to warble.

trinca, *s.f.* trine, three analogous things; bite, mouthful.

trincadela, *s.f.* mouthful, nibble.

trincado, *adj.* bitten off; sly.

trinca-espinhas, *s.m.* bean pole, spindle-legs *(pop.).*

trincafio, *s.f.* shoemaker´s thread.

trinca-pau, *s.m.* goat-moth.

trincar, *v.t.* to bite, to chew, to crunch.

trincha, *s.f.* broad brush.

trinchador, *s.m.* carver.

trinchante, *s.m.* carver *(na mesa);* carving-knife; dresser; trencher.

trinchar, *v.t.* to carve *(carne).*

trincheira, *s.f.* trench, parapet, barrier; shelter.

trinchete, *s.m.* shoemaker´s knife.

trincho, *s.m.* trencher, cutting- board.

trinco, *s.m.* latch *(para porta ou portão).*

trindade, *s.f.* Trinity; *(pl.)* angelus, angelusbell.

trinervado, trinérveo, *adj.* trinervate; three-nerved.

trineta, *s.f.* great-great-granddaughter.

trineto, *s.m.* great-great-grandson.

trinfar, *v.i.* to chirp, to twitter; *s.m.* chirp, twittering.

trinitário, *adj., s.m.* Trinitarian.

trino, *adj.* trine; *s.m.* triad; Trinitarian; warble, quaver.

trinómio, *s.m.* trinomial.

trinque, *s.m.* coat-peg, coat-hanger; spruceness, elegance, neatness.

trinta, *num.* thirty; *o dia trinta,* the thirtieth.

trintanário, *s.m.* footman, lackey.

trintão, *adj.* thirtyish.

trintar, *v.i.* to reach thirty *(anos).*

trintena, *s.f.* thirty.

trintenário, *adj.* vd. trintão.

trio, *s.m.* trio; group of three.

tríodo, *s.m.* triode.

tripa, *s.f.* tripe, intestine, gut; *(pl.)* bowels, entrails. 1) *comer à tripa-forra,* to have one´s fill. 2) *viver à tripa-forra,* to live on the fat of the land.

tripalhada, *s.f.* entrails, guts.

tripanossomo, *s.m.* trypanosome.

tripartição, *s.f.* tripartition.

tripartido, *adj.* tripartite.

tripartir, *v.t.* to divide into three parts.

tripartível, *adj.* divisable into three parts.

tripé, *s.m.* tripod, trivet.

tripeça, *s.f.* three-legged stool.

tripeiro, *s.m.* tripe-seller; tripe-eater; nickname of those born in Oporto.

tripétalo, *adj.* tripetalous.

triplano, *s.m.* triplane.

triple, *adj.* triple, treble, threefold.

triplicação, *s.f.* triplication.

triplicado, *adj.* triplicate, threefold, tripled.

triplicar, *v.t.* to triple, to trebble, to triplicate.

triplicata, *s.f.* third copy *(papel químico).*

tríplice, *adj.* vd. triple.

triplo, *adj.* vd. triple.

trípode, *s.m., adj.* tripod, three-legged *(banco).*

tríptico, *s.m.* triptych.

tripudiante, *adj.* dancing or lesping for joy.

tripudiar, *v.i.* to dance, to rejoice; to make merry, to exult; to tripudiate.

tripúdio, *s.m.* leaping; rejoicing; libertinism, debauchery.

tripulação, *s.f.* crew.

tripulante, *s.* crew-member; seaman.

tripular, *v.t.* to man *(um barco).*

triques, *adj.* dandy, smart.

trirreme, *s.f.* trireme.

trisanual, *adj.* triennal; lasting three years; every third year.

trisavó, *s.f.* great-great-grandmother.

trisavô, *s.m.* great-great-grandfather.

trissecção, *s.f.* trisection.

trissecular, *adj.* lasting three centuries.

trissilábico, *adj.* trisyllabic.

trissílabo, *s.m.* trisyllable.

triste, *adj.* sad, mournful, gloomy; dejected, sorry, depressed, unhappy, blue; sombre, dark; *fazer um triste papel,* to cut a sorry figure.

tristemente, *adv.* sadly, mournfully.

tristeza, *s.f.* sadness, sorrow, grief, gloom; dreariness, dejection, grief, depression.

tristonho, *adj.* somewhat sad, sad-looking; delected, blue, dull, depressed.

tristura, *s.f. vd.* tristeza.

tritão, *s.m.* triton.

tritongo, *s.m.* triphthong.

trítono, *s.m.* tritone *(mús.).*

tritura, trituração, *s.f.* trituration; crushing; grinding.

triturado, *adj.* triturated, crushed.

triturador, *adj.* triturating, crushing.

trituramento, *s.m. ver "trituração".*

triturar, *v.t.* to triturate; to grind down.

triturável, *adj.* triturable.

triunfador, *s.m.* triumpher, conqueror, vanquisher; triumphant, successful, victorious.

triunfal, *adj.* triumphal.

triunfalmente, *adv.* triumphantly.

triunfante, *adj.* triumphant, exulting, exultant, rejoicing.

triunfar, *v.i.* to triumph; to overcome; to exult, to rejoice; to succeed, to conquer; to win.

triunfo, *s.m.* triumph, victory, success.

triunvirado, *s.m.* triumvirate.

triunviral, *adj.* triumviral.

triunvirato, *s.m.* triumvirate.

triúnviro, *s.m.* triumvir.

trivalência, *s.f.* trivalence.

trivalente, *adj.* trivalent.

trivalve, *adj.* trivalvular.

trivial, *adj.* trivial, trite, commomplace, hackneyed, trifling, unimportant, petty, worthless.

trivialidade, *s.f.* triviality; triteness, vulgarity, banality.

trivializar, *v.t.* to make trivial.

trivialmente, *adv.* trivially.

triz, *s.m.* instant, moment. 1) *por um triz,* on the point of. 2) *escapar por um triz,* to have a narrow escape.

troada, *s.f.* thunder; roar, rumbling.

troante, *adj.* thundering.

troar, *v.i.* to thunder; to rumble, to roar; *s.m.* thunder.

troca, *s.f.* exchange, interchange, barter; permutation, conversion. 1) *em troca de,* in exchange for. 2) *troca de ideias,* exchange of views.

troça, *s.f.* mockery, scoff, derision, ridicule; *fazer troça de,* to make fun of.

trocadilho, *s.m.* pun, quobble, play on words; equivoke, ambiguity.

trocador, *adj.* exchanging; *s.m.* mocker, scoffer.

trocaico, *adj.* trochaic.

trocânter, *s.m.* trochanter.

trocar, *v.t.* to exchange, to truck, to barter; to replace by other; to confuse; to permute, to substitute.

troçar, *v.t.* to mock, to scoff, to jeer, to gibe, to laugh at, to deride, to make fun of.

troca-tintas, *s.* dauber; bungler, humbug, trickster.

trocável, *adj.* exchangeable, convertible, changeable.

trochada, *s.f.* blow *(com um cacete);* stroke.

trocho, *s.m.* cudgel, rough stick.

trocista, *s.* mocker, scoffer, derider, joker; *adj.* mocker, scoffer, mocking.

troco, *s.m.* change, odd money, small coin; pert answer. 1) *a troco de,* in exchange for, at the price of. 2) *dar o troco,* to give tit for tat, to pay back in the same coin.

troço, *s.m.* fragment; pin, stretch *(de uma estrada);* body *(soldados).*

troféu, *s.m.* trophy; victory, triumph.

trófico, *adj.* trophic *(nutrição).*

troglodita, *s.m.* troglodyte, cave-man.

troiano, *adj., s.m.* Trojan.

troixa, *s.f.* bundle, package, truss, fardel; sucker, fool, gull.

troixe-moixe, *loc. adv.* at random, pell-mell.

trólei, *s.m.* trolley, trolly.

troleicarro, *s.m.* trolley bus.

trolha, *s.m.* trowel; mason, bricklayer; mortarboard.

tromba, *s.f.* trunk *(de um elefante);* snout; water-spout.

trombada, *s.f.* blow *(com um tronco);* hit, clash, impact, collision.

tromba-de-água, *s.f.* waterspout.

trombeta, *s.f.* trumpet; trumpetplayer; horn, tuba, bugle.

trombetear, *v.i.* to trumpet; to proclaim.

trombeteiro, *s.m.* trumpet-player, trumpeter.

trombetista, *s.* trumpet-player.

trombone, *s.m.* trombone; tromboneplayer, trombonist.

trombose, *s.f.* thombosis.

trombudo, *adj.* having a trunk; sulky, sullen, grouchy, crabbed.

trompa, *s.f.* horn, trump. 1) *trompa de caça,* hunting horn. 2) *trompa de Eustáquio,* Eustachian tube.

trompaço, *s.m.* bump, collision.

trompejar, *v.i.* to play a horn.

trompeta, *s.f.* good-for-nothing.

trompete, *s.m.* musical instrument.

trompetista, *s.* trumpet player.

tronante, *adj.* thundering, roaring.

tronar, *v.i.* to thunder, to rumble, to roar.

troncar, *v.t.* to truncate, to cut off.

troncas, *s.f.* toll calls *(telefone).*

tronchar, *v.t.* to chop off, to cut short.

troncho, *s.m.* cabbage-stalk; piece cut (or broken).

tronchuda, *s.f.* thick-stalked, variety of cabbage.

tronco, *s.m.* trunk; stem; stock, lineage, race, pedigree, family tree; *tronco de pirâmide,* frustum of pyramid.

troncudo, *adj.* sturdy, strong, vigorous, bulky.

troneira, *s.f.* embrasure *(para uma pistola).*

trono, *s.m.* throne.

tropa, *s.f.* troop; army, military forces; *s.m.* soldier; *tropafandanga,* mob, rabble, crowd.

tropeada, *s.f.* trampling, stamping *(com os pés).*

tropear, *v.i.* to trample; to work as a muleteer.

tropeção, *s.m.* stumble, trip, stumbling.

tropeçar, *v.i.* to stumble; to come across a difficulty.

tropeço, *s.m.* stumble; obstacle, hindrance, impediment.

trôpego, *adj.* hobbling, limping, unsteady, shaky, disabled, tottery.

tropel, *s.m.* crowd; heap, multitude; hubbub, tumult; rush, confusion; clatter. 1) *de tropel,* tumultuously. 2) *em tropel,* pell-mell, in a huddle.

tropelia, *s.f.* confusion, hurry; prank; mischief, damage; trouble; oppression, ill-treatment.

tropical, *adj.* tropical, very hot, burning hot.

tropicalismo, *s.m.* tropicalism.

tropicalista, *s.* tropicalist *(especialista).*

tropicar, *v.i.* to stumble continuously.

trópico, *s.m.* tropic.

tropismo, *s.m.* tropism.

tropo, *s.m.* trope, figure of speech.

tropologia, *s.f.* tropology.

tropológico, *adj.* tropological.

troposfera, *s.f.* troposphere.

troquel, *s.m.* a die for stamping coins or medals.

troqueu, *s.m.* trochee.

trotador, *adj.* trotting; *s.m.* trotter, trotting horse.

trotão, *s.m.* trotter, trotting horse.

trotar, *v.i.* to trot, to ride *(cavalo)* at a trot, to go at a trot.

trote, *s.m.* trot; 1) *a trote,* in haste; trotting.

trotear, *v.i. vd.* trotar.

trouxa, *s.f.* truss; bundle, pack *(roupas); s.m.* sucker, fool, dupe, gudgeon *(popular).* 1) *arrumar a trouxa,* to get going. 2) *sempre de trouxa às costas,* always on the move *(casa).*

trouxe-mouxe, *loc. adv.* helter-skelter, in disorder, pell-mell, at random; without care.

trova, *s.f.* ballad, song.

trovador, *s.m.* troubadour; minstrel; bard; poet.

trovadoresco, *adj.* like a troubadour.

trovão, *s.m.* thunder; thunderbolt, thunder-clap; a peal of thunder.

trovar, *v.i.* to make rhymes, to compose or sing folk tunes; to versify.

trovejante, *adj.* thundering, roaring, rumbling.

trovejar, *v.t., v.i.* to thunder.

troviscal, *s.m.* a growth of spurge flax or spurge-laurel.

troviscar, *v.i.* to thunder lightly.

trovisco, *s.m.* spurge-laurel; *amargo como trovisco,* as bitter as a gall.

trovoada, *s.f.* thunderstorm; tumult, turmoil, uproar.

trovoar, *v.i.* to thunder *(pop.).*

truanear, *v.i.* to play the buffoon *(ou o vadio).*

truanesco, *adj.* funny, clownish, buffoon.

truanice, *s.f.* buffoonery, truancy, drollery.

truão, *s.m.* buffoon, jester, clown.

trucidação, *s.f.* murder, decapitation.

trucidador, trucidante, *adj.* killing, slaughtering.

trucidar, *v.t.* to kill, to murder; to mangle; to slaughter, to savage; to decapitate.

truculência, *s.f.* truculence, truculency, ferocity, fierceness, cruelty.

truculento, *adj.* truculent, cruel, fierce, savage, harsh.

trufa, *s.f.* truffle.

trufar, *v.t.* to stuff with truffles.

trufeira, *s.f.* plantation of truffles.

trufeiro, *s.m.* truffler *(quem vende ou cultiva).*

truísmo, *s.m.* truism.

truncado, *adj.* truncate, truncated, lopped off; garbled, incomplete, mutilated.

truncamento, *s.m.* truncation, truncature.

truncar, *v.t.* to truncate, to lop off; to mutilate; to garble, to cut off; to shorten, to curtail.

trunfa, *s.f.* dishevelled hair; head-dress; mop of hair.

trunfar, *v.i.* to play a trump.

trunfo, *s.m.* trump; trump card; big shot, important person *(pop.).*

truque, *s.m.* trick, wile, dodge, artifice; fake, deceit.

truta, *s.f.* trout; *não se pescam trutas a bragas enxutas,* no grains without pains.

truz!, *interj.* crash!; de truz, excellent, first-rate, splendid, capital.

tsé-tsé, *s.f.* tsetse fly.

tu, *pron.* thou; you.

tua, *pron.* your, yours; thy, thine.

tuba, *s.f.* tuba, bass horn.

tubagem, *s.f.* tubing, pipes, set of tubes.

túbara, *s.f.* vd. túbera.

tubarão, *s.m.* shark.

túbera, *s.f.* truffle.

tuberculado, *adj.* tubercular.

tuberculiforme, *adj.* like a tubercle.

tuberculina, *s.f.* tuberculin.

tuberculização, *s.f.* tuberculization.

tuberculizar, *v.t., v.i.* to tuberculize; to become tuberculous.

tubérculo, *s.m.* tubercle.

tuberculose, *s.f.* tuberculosis; consumption.

tuberculoso, *adj.* tuberculous; tubercular *(bot.); s.m.* a tuberculous person.

tuberiforme, *adj.* tuberiform.

tuberosa, *s.f.* tuberose.

tuberosidade, *s.f.* tuberosity.

tuberoso, *adj.* tuberous.

tubiforme, *adj.* tubiform, tubulate.

tubo, *s.m.* tube, pipe. 1) *tubo de ensaio,* test-tube. 2) *tubo porta-voz,* voice-pipe.

tubulação, *s.f.* tubulation, piping, tubing.

tubulado, *adj.* tubulate, tubulated.

tubuladura, *s.f.* tubulure, piping, tubing.

tubular, *adj.* tubular, tubulous, tubeshaped.

tubuliforme, *adj.* tubuliform.

túbulo, *s.m.* tubule, small tube.

tubuloso, *adj.* tubulous, tubiform.

tucano, *s.m.* toucan.

tudesco, *adj.* Teutonic; *s.m.* Teuton, German.

tudo, *pron.* all, the whole; anything; everything; 1) *tudo menos,* all but. 2) *antes de tudo,* first of all. 3) *depois de tudo,* after all. 4) *ou tudo ou nada,* all or nothing, neck or nothing. 5) *tudo incluído,* all-in, in full. 6) *nem tudo que luz é ouro,* all that glitters is not gold.

tudo-nada, *s.m.* little bit, jot.

tufão, *s.m.* hurricane, typhoon, gale.

tufar, *v.i.* to swell, to puff up; to form into tufts, to flare out.

tufo, *s.m.* flock *(de algodão);* mandrel; puff *(num vestido);* tuft *(cabelo, relva, penas);* bunch.

tufoso, *adj.* tufted, puffed out, puffy, swollen.

tugir, *v.i.* to mutter, to speak in a whisper; *não tugir nem mugir,* not to utter a word.

tugúrio, *s.m.* shack, hut; hideout, mean dwelling.

tule, *s.m.* tulle.

tulha, *s.f.* granary; bin.

túlipa, *s.f.* tulip; lamp-shade .

tumba, *s.f.* bier, tomb, grave; unlucky person *(no jogo).*

tumefacção, *s.f.* tumefaction; swelling.

tumefaciente, *adj.* tumefacient.

tumefacto, *adj.* tumefied, swollen.

tumefazer, *v.t.* to tumefy, to swell, to inflate.

tumefeito, *adj.* tumefied.

tumeficante, *adj.* tumefying.

tumeficar, *v.t.* to tumefy.

tumescência, *s.f.* tumescence, swelling.

tumescente, *adj.* tumescent.

tumescer, *v.t., v.i.* to intumesce, to swell up.

tumescimento, *s.m.* swelling.

tumidez, *s.f.* tumidity.

túmido, *adj.* tumid, swollen, inflated.

tumor, *s.m.* tumour; swelling.

tumoroso, *adj.* tumorous, tumid.

tumular, *adj.* tumular; *pedra tumular,* tombstone.

túmulo, *s.m.* tomb, grave.

tumulto, *s.m.* tumult, commotion, uproar, disturbance.

tumultuador, *adj.* agitating.

tumultuante, *adj.* tumultuous.

tumultuar, *v.t., v.i.* to mutiny, to revolt; to stir.

tumultuariamente, *adv.* tumultuously.

tumultuário, *adj.* tumultuary, tumultuous, disorderly.

tumultuoso, *adj.* vd. tumultuário.

tuna, s.f. student´s musical group; *andar à tuna*, to idle.

tunantaria, s.f. idle life.

tunante, s. vagrant, idler, vagabond.

tunantear, tunar, v.i. to idle, to ramble.

tunda, s.f. a thrashing, sound beating; harsh criticism.

tundra, s.f. tundra.

túnel, s.m. tunnel.

tunesino, adj., s. Tunesian.

tungstato, s.m. tungstate.

tungsténio, s.m. tungsten.

túnica, s.f. tunic.

tunicela, s.f. tunicle, dalmatic.

tuno, s.m. vd. tunante.

tupia, s.f. sharper; jack.

turba, s.f. mob, rabble, crowd, throng.

turbação, s.f. disorder, commotion, confusion.

turbado, adj. disordered, perplexed; cloudy, overcast.

turbador, s.m. disturber; adj. disturbing.

turbamulta, s.f. mob, turbulent multitude, populace.

turbante, s.m. turban.

turbar, v.t. to disturb, to trouble; to darken, to dim, to grow cloudy.

turbativo, adj. disturbing, perturbative.

túrbido, adj. thick, turbid, cloudy.

turbilhão, s.m. whirlwind, whirlpool, vortex; swirl.

turbilhonar, v.i. to whirl, to spin, to swirl.

turbina, s.f. turbine.

turbulência, s.f. turbulence, agitation, turmoil, disorder, uproar.

turbulento, adj. turbulent, troublesome, disturbed, tumultuous.

turco, s.m. davit; adj. Turkish; s.m. Turk.

turdídeo, adj. turdoid, thrushlike.

turfa, s.f. peat, turf.

turfeira, s.f. peat-bog, peatery.

turgência, s.f. turgidity.

turgescência, s.f. ver "turgidez".

turgescente, adj. turgescent, turgid.

turgescer, v.t., v.i. to make turgid, to swell.

turgidez, s.f. turgescence; turgidity.

túrgido, adj. turgid, tumid, swollen, bloated.

turgimão, s.m. dragoman; interpreter.

turibular, v.t. to cense, to fltter, to thurify.

turibulário, s.m. thurifer, acolyte; cajoler, flatterer.

turíbulo, s.m. thurible, censer.

turiferar, v.t. to incense, to thurify.

turiferário, s.m. thurifer.

turífero, adj. thuriferous.

turificação, s.f. thurification, incense-burning.

turificador, s.m. one who burns incense; incensing, perfuming.

turificante, adj. incense-burning.

turificar, v.t. to incense; to flatter.

turino, adj. relating to incense.

turismo, s.m. tourism, touring, pleasure trips.

turista, s. tourist.

turístico, adj. touristic.

turma, s.f. division (de uma classe); band, company.

turmalina, s.f. tourmaline (mineral).

túrnepo, s.m. variety of turnip (para gado).

turno, s.m. turn, group; round; school period; hour. 1) por turnos, in turns; by spells. 2) por seu turno, for his part (or turn), in his (her) turn.

túrpido, adj. sordid.

turpilóquio, s.m. indecent talk.

turpitude, s.f. turpitude, vileness.

turquês, s.f. pincers, nippers.

turquesa, s.f. turquoise.

turquesado, adj. turquoise-coloured.

turqui, adj. deep-blue.

turra, s.f. butt (com a cabeça); stubborn dispute, controversy; andar às turras com, to be at sixes and sevens with.

turrão, adj. obstinate, hard-headed; s.m. blockhead, stubborn person.

turrar, v.i. to knock or to butt with the head, to be obstinate, to persist, to wrangle.

turvação, s.f. disquietude (da mente), disturbance; clouding (vinho).

turvador, adj. disturbing; muddling.

turvamento, s.m. vd. turvação.

turvar, v.t. to disturb, to trouble; to darken, to cloud.

turvo, adj. muddy, turbid, cloudy.

tussilagem, s.f. colt´s foot (botânica).

tuta-e-meia, s.f. triflle; comprar por uma tuta-e-meia, to buy for a song.

tutano, s.m. marrow, pith, medulla; essential part.

tutear, v.t. to thee, to thou; to address familiarly.

tutela, s.f. guardianship, tutelage, protection, care.

tutelado, adj. tutored; under the care of a guardian.

tutelagem, s.f. tutelage; tutorship.

tutelar, *adj.* tutelary, tutelar, guarding, protecting; *v.t.* to tutor, to protect, to defend.
tutor, *s.m.* guardian; tutor.
tutorar, tutorear, *v.t.* to act as a guardian.

tutoria, *s.f.* tutorship, tutelage, guardianship; also the building.
tutório, *adj.* tutorial.
tzar, *s.m.* czar.

U

u, the twentieth letter of the Portuguese alphabet.
uberdade, *s.f.* abundance, fertility, fruitfulness, rich growth.
úbere, *s.m.* udder, teat, dug; *adj.* fertile, fruitful, abundant, uberous.
ubérrimo, *adj.* most fertile, very fruitful.
ubiquidade, *s.f.* ubiquity, omnipresence.
ubiquitário, *s.m.* ubiquitarian; *adj.* omnipresent.
ubíquo, *adj.* ubiquitous, omnipresent.
ucha, *s.f.* grain hutch, box, chest (para abastecimento, provisões).
uchão, *s.m.* pantryman, butler.
ucharia, *s.f.* pantry, store-room, larder; storehouse; granary.
ucraniano, *adj., s.m.* Ukranian.
udometria, *s.f.* udometry.
udométrico, *adj.* pluviometric, udometric.
udómetro, *s.m.* udometer, pluviometer; rain-gauge.
ufa (à), *loc. adv.* at large, copiously.
ufanar, *v.t.* to make proud; *ufanar-se,* to boast, to become proud, to be proud of.
ufania, *s.f.* ostentation, boating; pride, vanity, conceit.
ufano, *adj.* proud, boastful, vainglorious, vain; self-satisfied; showy.
ufanoso, *adj.* proud, conceited; boastful, arrogant.
ui!, *inter.* oh! (dor, surpresa, desgosto).
uísque, *s.m.* whisky.
uivador, *adj.* howling; *s.m.* howler.

uivante, *adj.* howling.
uivar, to howl.
uivo, *s.m.* howl; yelling, bawling.
úlcera, *s.f.* ulcer.
ulceração, *s.f.* ulceration, fester.
ulcerar, *v.t.* to ulcerate.
ulcerativo, *adj.* ulcerative.
ulceroso, *adj.* ulcerous.
uliginário, *adj.* uliginose.
uliginoso, *adj.* marshy, muddy.
ulmária, *s.f.* meadow-sweet.
ulmeiro, ulmo, *s.m.* elm-tree.
ulna, *s.f.* ulna .
ulnar, *adj.* ulnar.
ulterior, *adj.* ulterior; further, later, remoter, subsequent; future.
ulterioridade, *s.f.* remoteness.
ulteriormente, *adv.* afterwards.
ultimação, *s.f.* finishing, completion, final touch; conclusion.
ultimado, *adj.* finished, ended, complete, concluded; closed.
ultimamente, *adv.* lately, of late, recently.
ultimar, *v.t.* to end, to finish, to put an end to, to conclude, to complete; to close (comercial).
últimas, *s.f. pl.* final throes, last moments; agony; extreme poverty.
ultimato, *s.m.* ultimatum.
último, *adj.* last; latest (no tempo); final; ultimate; latter; lowest; *por último,* at last, finally.
ultra-humano, *adj.* preterhuman.

ultrajador, *adj.* reviling, insulting, injurious, offensive; *s.m.* reviler, slanderer, insulter.

ultrajante, *adj.* insulting, outrageous, offending, injurious.

ultrajar, *v.t.* to insult, to outrage, to abuse, to offend, to injure.

ultraje, *s.m.* outrage, insult, offence, affront.

ultrajosamente, *adv.* outrageously.

ultrajoso, *adj.* v.d. ultrajante.

ultraliberal, *adj.* ultra-liberal.

ultraliberalismo, *s.m.* ultra-liberalism.

ultramar, *s.m.* overseas territories.

ultramarino, *adj.* ultramarine; overseas.

ultramoderno, *adj.* ultramodern.

ultramontanismo, *s.m.* ultramontanism.

ultramontano, *adj.* ultramontane.

ultrapassagem, *s.f.* overtaking.

ultrapassar, *v.t.* to surpass; to exceed; to outdo; to go beyond; to overtake *(um carro)*; to get ahead of, to transcend; to outstrip.

ultra-sensível, *adj.* ultra-sensitive.

ultra-som, *s.m.* supersonic sound waves.

ultra-sónico, *adj.* supersonic.

ultravermelho, *adj.* ultrared.

ultravioleta, *adj.* ultra-violet.

ululação, *s.f.* howling, ululation; wailing, moaning *(vento);* screaming, crying.

ululador, *adj.* howling, ululating; s.m. howler.

ululante, *adj.* howling, ululant.

ulular, *v.i.* to howl, to ululate, to whine, to wail, to scream, to cry; to moan *(vento);* to vociferate.

um, uma, *art.* a, an; *adj., pron.* one.

umbela, *s.f.* umbrella, sunshade; umbel *(bot.).*

umbelado, *adj.* umbellate.

umbelíferas, *s.f. pl.* Umbelliferae.

umbelífero, *adj.* umbelliferous.

umbeliforme, *adj.* umbellar.

umbélula, *s.f.* umbellule.

umbigo, *s.m.* navel, umbilicus.

umbilicado, *adj.* umbiliform, like a navel; umbilicate.

umbilical, *adj.* umbilical; *cordão umbilical,* umbilical cord, nave string.

umbral, *s.m.* door-post; entrance; threshold.

umbrático, umbrátil, *adj.* umbratile, obscure; phantastic.

úmbrico, *s.m., adj.* Umbrian

umbroso, *adj.* umbrageous, shady; obscure, dark.

ume, *s.f.* alum.

umeral, *adj.* humeral.

úmero, *s.m.* humerus.

unânime, *adj.* unanimous, of like mind.

unanimemente, *adv.* unanimously.

unanimidade, *s.f.* unanimity, unity, harmony.

unção, *s.f.* unction; suavity; anointment, anointing.

uncial, *adj.* uncial.

unciforme, *adj.* unciform, hook-shaped, uncinate.

uncirrostro, *adj.* hook-billed.

undação, *s.f.* flood.

undante, *adj.* wavy.

undecágono, *s.m.* undecagon.

undecênviro, *s.m.* undecemvir.

undécimo, *num.* elenventh.

undívago, *adj.* floating *(nas ondas),* drifting.

undoso, *adj.* wavy, undulating.

ungido, *adj.* anointed, consecrated.

ungir, *v.t.* to anoint, to consecrate *(com óleos).*

ungueal, *adj.* ungual.

unguentar, *v.t.* to oil with unguent.

unguento, *s.m.* unguent, ointment.

unguiculado, *adj.* unguiculate, clawed.

unguiforme, *adj.* unguiform, nailshaped.

unguinoso, *adj.* unguinous, oily.

únguis, *s.m.* unguis, lachrymal bone.

ungulado, *adj.* ungulate; s.m. *(pl.)* Ungulata.

unha, *s.f.* nail; claw. 1) *à unha de,* with the bare hands. 2) *com unhas e dentes,* tooth and nail. 3) *pegar à unha,* to take by the horns. 4) *ser unha e carne,* to be hand in glove with someone. 5) *enterrar (meter) a unha,* to sell dear. 6) *escapar por uma unha,* to have a hairbreadth escape.

unhada, *s.f.* nail-scratch.

unha-de-fome, *s.* niggard, miser.

unhamento, *s.m.* layering *(das vinhas).*

unhar, *v.t.* to layer *(vinhas);* to scratch *(com as unhas);* to grasp.

unheiro, *s.m.* whitlow.

uniangular, *adj.* uniangulate.

união, *s.f.* union; alliance; coupling, joint; marriage, match; confederation; junction; concord, harmony; fusion, unification; screw cap, screw joint. 1) *a união faz a força,* union is strength. 2) *traço de união,* hyphen.

unicamente, *adv.* only; merely; uniquely; exclusively.

unicarpelar, *adj.* unicarpelar.

unicapsular, *adj.* unicapsular.

unicelular, *adj.* unicellular.

unicidade, *s.f.* uniqueness, unicity.

único, *adj.* only; sole; unique; single, alone; unequalled, peculiar; exclusive; excepcional, rare; incomparable. 1) *filho único*, single child. 2) *preço único*, single price. 3) *o único processo*, the only way. 4) *o único no género*, the only one of its kind. 5) *prato único*, one dish meal. 6) *rua de sentido único*, one-way street.

unicolor, *adj.* unicolour; unicoloured.

unicorne, *adj.* one-horned; s.m. unicorn.

unicórnio, *s.m.* unicorn; *adj.* unicornous.

unicúspide, *adj.* unicuspid, single-pointed.

unidáctilo, *adj.* unidactyl.

unidade, *s.f.* unity; agreement, harmony, concord; military unit; unit; digit.

unido, *adj.* united; allied; joined, joint; tied; connected; wedded.

unificação, *s.f.* unification.

unificador, *adj.* unifying; s.m. unifier.

unificar, *v.t.* to unify, to unite; to concentrate; to incorporate; to standardize.

unifloro, *adj.* uniflorous.

unifoliado, *adj.* unifoliate.

uniforme, *adj.* uniform; regular, constant, unchanging; same, equal; steady; *s.m.* uniform; livery.

uniformemente, *adv.* uniformly.

uniformidade, *s.f.* uniformity; monotony.

uniformização, *s.f.* standardization.

uniformizador, *adj.* standardizing, uniformizing.

uniformizar, *v.t.* to uniformize, to standardize; *uniformizar-se,* to put on a uniform.

unigénito, *adj.* only-begotten.

unijugado, *adj.* unijugate, only one pair.

unilateral, *adj.* unilateral; one-sided.

unilateralidade, *s.f.* one-sidedness.

unilateralmente, *adv.* unilaterally.

unilingue, unilíngue, *adj.* unilingual.

unilobado, *adj.* unilobed.

unilocular, *adj.* unolocular.

uninervado, uninérveo, *adj.* uninerved.

unionismo, *s.m.* unionism.

unionista, *adj., s.* unionist.

uniparidade, *s.f.* one youth at a time *(nascimento).*

uníparo, *adj.* uniparous.

unipessoal, *adj.* unipersonal.

unipétalo, *adj.* unipetalous.

unipolar, *adj.* unipolar, monopolar.

unipolaridade, *s.f.* unipolarity.

unir, *v.t.* to unite; to connect; to join; to couple, to marry; to bind, to fasten; to reconcile; to associate.

unissexuado, *adj.* unisexual.

unissonância, *s.f.* unisonance; concordance; harmony; monotony.

unissonante, *adj.* unisonant; melodious; monotonous.

uníssono, *adj.* unisonal, unisonous; unisonant.

unitário, *adj.* unitary; *s.m.* Unitarian.

unitarismo, *s.m.* Unitarianism.

unitarista, *adj., s.* unitarist.

unitivo, *adj.* unitive.

univalência, *s.f.* univalence.

univalente, *adj.* univalent, monovalent.

univalvular, *adj.* univalvular.

universal, *adj.* universal, general,ecumenic, common.

universalidade, *s.f.* universality, totality.

universalismo, *s.m.* universalism.

universalista, *adj.* universalistic; *s.* universalist.

universalização, *s.f.* universalization.

universalizar, *v.t.* to universalize, to render universal.

universalmente, *adv.* universally, ecumenically.

universidade, *s.f.* university *(instituição, menbros ou edifício);* college, school.

universitário, *adj.* university *(educação, grau);* academic *(honras);* s.m. university student or teacher.

universo, *s.m.*universe, the world.

univocação, *s.f.* univocation.

univocidade, *s.f.* univocity.

unívoco, *adj.* univocal, not equivocal; unisonous; unanimous.

uno, *adj.* sole, only, unique, only one, single.

untadela, *s.f.* greasing, slight anointing, smearing.

untador, *s.m.* dauber, greaser, lubricator; *adj.* greasing.

untadura, *s.f.* greasing, daubing.

untar, *v.t.* to grease; to daub; to besmear; to oil; to bribe *(pop.).*

unto, *s.m.* grease; lard, animal fat.

untuosidade, *s.f.* unctuosity, greasiness.

untuoso, *adj.* unctuous, greasy, oily; mellifluous.

untura, *s.f.* grease, ointment; superficial knowledge.

upa!, *interj.* hop!, jump!, up!

uraliano, *adj.* Uralian.

uralite, *s.f.* uralite.

urânico, *adj.* uranic.

urânio, *s.m.* uranium.

uranografia, *s.f.* uranography.

uranográfico, *adj.* uranographical.
uranógrafo, *s.m.* uranographer.
uranologia, *s.f.* uranology.
uranológico, *adj.* uranologoc.
uranometria, *s.f.* ueranometry.
uranométrico, *adj.* uranometric.
uranómetro, *s.m.* uranometer.
uranoscopia, *s.f.* uranoscopy.
urato, *s.m.* urate *(sal).*
urbanamente, *adv.* courteously, politely.
urbanidade, *s.f.* urbanity; politeness, coutesy, refinement.
urbanismo, *s.m.* town-planning.
urbanista, *s.* town-planner, urbanist; *adj.* urbanistic.
urbanístico, *adj.* urbanistic.
urbanita, *s.* urbanite, city dweller.
urbanização, *s.f.* urbanization.
urbanizar, *v.t.* to urbanize.
urbano, *adj.* urban; polite, courteous, polished.
urbe, *s.f.* city.
urbícola, *s.* urbanite, city dweller.
urdideira, *s.f.* woman warper, weaver; warp frame.
urdidor, *s.m.* warper, weaver; schemer, intriguer.
urdidura, *s.f.* warp; plot, intrigue; chain.
urdimento, *s.m.* warping.
urdir, *v.t.* to warp, to weave; to plot, to scheme, to intrigue.
urdume, *s.m. v.d.* urdidura.
uredo, *s.m.* uredo; itching, nettle-rash.
ureia, *s.f.* uraea.
uremia, *s.f.* uraemia.
urémico, *adj.* uraemic.
urência, *s.f.* ardency; heat.
urente, *adj.* hot, ardent, burning.
uréter, *s.m.* ureter.
uretérico, *adj.* ureteral, ureteric.
ureterite, *s.f.* urethritis.
urético, *adj.* uretic, urinary.
uretra, *s.f.* urethra.
uretral, *adj.* urethral.
uretrite, *s.f.* urethritis.
uretroscopia, *s.f.* urethroscopy.
uretroscópio, *s.m.* urethroscope.
uretrotomia, *s.f.* urethrotomy.
urgência, *s.f.* urgency, pressure, need.
urgente, *adj.* urgent, pressing, imperative, instant.
urgentemente, *adv.* urgently.
urgir, *v.i.* to be urgent, to urge, to press; to drive, to impel.

úrico, *adj.* uric.
urina, *s.f.* urine.
urinação, *s.f.* urination.
urinar, *v.i.* to urinate, to make water; to piddle *(crianças).*
urinário, *adj.* urinary.
urinífero, *adj.* uriniferous.
urinol, *s.m.* urinal.
urna, *s.f.* coffin; ballotbox.
urodelo, *s.m.* uridele.
urogenital, *adj.* urogenital.
urografia, *s.f.* urography.
urologia, *s.f.* urology.
urológico, *adj.* urological.
urologista, *s.* urologist.
uropígio, *s.m.* uropygium.
uroscopia, *s.f.* uroscopy.
urrar, *v.i.* to roar; to bellow; to bawl.
urro, *s.m.* roar; bellow.
ursa, *s.f.* she-bear.
ursino, *adj.* ursine, bear-like.
urso, *s.m.* bear; distinguished student; fazer figura de urso, to cut a poor figure.
ursulina, *s.f.* Ursuline *(freira).*
urticante, *adj.* urticant, itching, acrid.
urticar, *v.t.* to sting.
urticária, *s.f.* nettle-rash, urticaria, hives.
urtiga, *s.f.* nettle.
urtigação, *s.f.* urtication.
urtigar, *v.t.* to nettle, to urticate.
urzal, *s.m.* moorland, fell.
urze, *s.f.* heather.
usado, *adj.* worn out; usual, common; used; second-hand; threadbare, old.
usagre, *s.m.* impetigo, eczema *(nas crianças).*
usança, *s.f.* custom, usage.
usar, *v.t.* to use; to employ; to ressort to; to wear *(roupas),* to dress; to make use of; 1) usar-se, to be in fashion, in use.
usável, *adj.* wearable, usable.
useiro, *adj.* customary, wonted; *ser useiro e vezeiro,* to be addicted to, to be given to doing the same thing repeatedly.
uso, *s.m.* use, custom; wear; practice; usage; habit; mode, fashion; function, utility; form, style; praxis.
ustão, *s.f.* act of burning, com bustion.
ustório, *adj.* burning, having the quality of facilitating combustion.
ustulação, *s.f.* ustulation.
ustular, *v.t* to scorch, to dry, to burn.
usual, *adj.* usual, habitual, customary; ordinary; frequent, familiar, commonplace.

usualmente, *adv.* usually; customarily, as a rule, generally.

usuário, *adj., s.m.* usufructuary, usuary.

usucapião, *s.m.* usucapion, prescription.

usufruição, *s.f.* usufruetion.

usufruidor, *adj., s.m.* usufructuary.

usufruir, *v.t.* to usufruct, to enjoy the usufruct of.

usufruto, *s.m.* usufruct; life interest.

usufrutuário, *s.m.* usufructuary.

usura, *s.f.* usury; avarice.

usurar, *v.i.* to practice usuary.

usurário, *adj.* usurious; *s.m.* usurer.

usurpação, *s.f.* usurpation.

usurpador, *adj.* usurping; *s.m.* usurper.

usurpar, *v.t.* to usurp; *v.i.* to encroach upon.

utensilagem, *s.f.* utensils.

utensílio, *s.m.* utensil, tool, implement.

utente, *adj.* usuary; he or she who uses.

uteralgia, *s.f.* uterus pain.

uterino, *adj.* uterine.

útero, *s.m.* uterus, womb.

útil, *adj.* useful; serviceable; helpful; profitable, beneficial.

utilidade, *s.f.* utility; usefulness; profit.

utilitário, *adj.* utilitarian, practical.

utilitarismo, *s.m.* utilitarianism.

utilitarista, *s.* utilitarian.

utilização, *s.f.* utilization, application.

utilizar, *v.i.* to utilize; to employ; to put to use; to make use of; to take advantage of, to use.

utilizável, *adj.* utilizable, usable; applicable.

utilmente, *adv.* usefully.

utopia, *s.f.* utopia; fancy, chimera, dream.

utópico, *adj.* utopian; fanciful, chimeric, visionary.

utopismo, *s.m.* utopianism.

utopista, *s.* utopian, dreamer, visionary; *adj.* fanciful, utopian.

utricular, *adj.* utricular, baglike.

utrículo, *s.m.* utricle; small bag.

utriculoso, *adj.* utricular.

uva, *s.f.* grape; *cacho de uvas,* bunch of grapes.

uvada, *s.f.* grape jam.

uva-de-cão, *s.f.* bittersweet.

uval, *adj.* grapey, resembling grapes.

uva-passa, *s.f.* raisin; plum.

úvula, *s.f.* uvula.

uvular, *adj.* uvular.

uvulária, *s.f.* double-tongue *(bot.)*.

uvulite, *s.f.* uvulitis *(inflamação)*.

uxoricida, *s.m.* uxoricide.

uxoricídio, *s.m.* uxoricide.

uxórico, uxório, *adj.* uxorious.

V

v, the twenty first letter of the Portuguese alphabet

vaca, *s.f.* cow.

vacância, *adj.* vacant; unoccupied; void.

vacante, *adj.* vacant; unoccupied; void.

vacar, *s.f.* cow barn; herd of cows.

vacilação, *s.f.* vacillation; wavering, tottering; hesitation; oscillation.

vacilante, *adj.* vacillating, unsteady, infirm; tottering; wavering; hesitant.

vacilar, *v.i.* to vacillate; to sway; to totter; to waver; to hesitete; to oscillate.

vacina, *s.f.* vaccine.

vacinação, *s.f.* vaccination.

vacinador, *s.m.* vaccinator.

vacinar, *v.t.* to vaccinate.

vacínico, *adj.* vaccinal, vaccinic.

vacinoterapia, *s.f.* vaccine therapy.

vacuidade, *s.f.* vacuity, emptiness.

vacum, *adj.* relating to oxen, cows or calves; gado vacum: cattle, oxen.

vácuo, *s.m.* vacuum; void, empty space; *adj.* empty, void.

vadear, *v.t.* to wade, to ford.

vadeável, *adj.* fordable.

vade-mécum, *s.m.* vade-mecum.

vadiação, vadiagem, *s.f.* loafing, idleness; truancy; vagrancy.

vadiar, *v.i.* to loaf, to be idle; to loiter; to gad about.

vadio, *adj.* idle; lazy; vagrant, truant; *s.m.* loafer, idler; sluggard; truant.

vaga, *s.f.* wave, billow; surge; vacancy, vacant position *(lugar vago).*

vagabundagem, *s.f.* vagrancy; vagabondage; vagrants, tramps.

vagabundear, *v.i.* to roam, to wander, to loaf.

vagabundo, *s.m.* vagrant, tramp, hobo, vagabond; *adj.* vagabond, vagrant; wandering, roaming, erratic; cheap, shabby *(reles).*

vagalhão, *s.m.* billow; roller.

vaga-lume, *s.m.* glow-worm.

vagante, *adj.* vacant; vagrant.

vagão, *s.m.* car, coach *(de passageiros),* waggon.

vagar, *v.i.* to roam, to wander; to stroll about; to become vacant *(ficar vago); v.t.* to vacate (an office). *s.m.* leisure, spare time, slowness.

vagaroso, *adj.* slow, slow-moving; lingering; leisurely; sluggish.

vagem, *s.f.* shell, pod *(invólucro).*

vagido, *s.m.* cry.

vagina, *s.f.* vagina.

vaginal, *adj.* vaginal.

vaginite, *s.f.* vaginitis.

vagir, *v.i.* to cry.

vago, *adj.* vacant; void; free, unoccupied; vague, indefinite, indistinct; spare *(de lazer); s.m.* vagueness.

vagoneta, *s.f.* small waggon.

vagueação, *s.f.* wandering, rambling.

vaguear, *v.i.* to wander, to roam; to ramble; to stray; to prowl.

vaia, *s.f.* hoot, boo, jeer, scoff.

vaiador, *adj.* mocking, jeering.

vaiar, *v.t.* to hoot, to boo, to jeer (at).

vaidade, *s.f.* vanity, ostentation, pride.

vaidoso, *adj.* vain, proud, puffed up; haughty.

vaivém, *s.m.* to and fro motion; coming and going; vicissitude.

vala, *s.f.* trench, ditch, drain; *vala comum:* common grave.

valada, *s.f.* long ditch, or trench.

valado, *s.m.* hedge; ditch; fence, rampart.

valão, *s.m.* Walloon.

valar, *v.t.* to provide with a ditch or trench; to fortify.

valdevinos, *s.m.* rogue, vagrant, idler; rascam.

vale, *s.m.* valley; *vale postal,* money order.

valedio, *adj.* valid, current.

valedor, *adj.* helping, protecting.

valeira, *s.f.* valeiro, *s.m.* ditch, trench.

valência, *s.f.* valence, valency.

valentaço, *s.m.* valentão, *s.m.* daredevil, braggart, sturdy fellow.

valente, *adj.* valiant, courageous, brave, dauntless, daring, bold.

valentia, *s.f.* bravery, courage, valour, boldness.

valer, *v.t.* to be worth (so much), etc. to cost; to deserve; to carry weight; to be of some avail; to mean; to count *(ter validade). 1) valer a,* to help; to be of use to; to avail. 2) *a valer,* really; a lot; very. 3) *fazer valer,* to assert. 4) *fazer-se valer,* to assert oneself. 5) *não valer nada,* to be worthless. 6) *valer-se,* to avail oneself, to make use, to take advantage of, to resort to.

valeriana, *s.f.* valerian.

valeta, *s.f.* gutter, roadside ditch.

valete, *s.m.* knave, jack.

valetudinário, *adj.* valetudinarian; infirm; *s.m.* invalid.

valhacoito, valhacouto, *s.m.* shelter, asylum, refuge.

valia, *s.f.* value, worth; price; merit; credit, prestige.

validação, *s.f.* validation, confirmation, acknowledgement.

validar, *v.t.* to validate, to ratify, to confirm; to legalize, to authenticate, to give legal force to.

validez, *s.f.* validity; vigour.

válido, *adj.* valid; sound, healthy, strong; legal.

valido, *s.m.* favourite; *adj.* beloved.

valimento, *s.m.* favour; influence, credit; prestige; power.

valiosamente, *adv.* valuably.

valioso, *adj.* valuable, precious, costly, rich.

valo, *s.m.* entrenchment, trench; ravine.

valor, *s.m.* valour; worth; value; courage; merit; *s.m. pl.* securities, bonds; marks *(notas)*.

valorização, *s.f.* valorization; valuation.

valorizar, *v.t.* to value, to valorize, to raise the price of; *valorizar-se,* to increase one`s value.

valoroso, *adj.* valorous, courageous; intrepid, dauntless.

valquíria, *s.f.* valkyrie.

valsa, *s.f.* waltz.

valsador, *s.m.* waltzer.

valsar, *v.t.* to waltz.

valva, *s.f.* valve.

valvar, *adj.* valvar, valvelike.

valverde, *s.m.* summer cypress, mock cypress.

válvula, *s.f.* valve; tube *(de rádio); válvula de segurança,* safety valve.

valvulado, *adj.* valved, having valves.

valvular, *adj.* valvular.

vampírico, *adj.* vampiric.

vampirismo, *s.m.* vampirism.

vampiro, *s.m.* vampire.

vanádio, *s.m.* vanadium.

vandálico, *adj.* vandalic.

vandalismo, *s.m.* vandalism.

vândalo, *s.m.* vandal.

vanglória, *s.f.* vainglory, vanity, boasting.

vangloriar-se, *v.refl.* to boast, to brag, to praise oneself.

vangloriosamente, *adv.* vaingloriously.

vanglorioso, *adj.* vainglorious, boastful, proud.

vanguarda, *s.f.* vanguard, van; forefront; head, lead.

vanguardista, *s.m. e s.f.* pioneer.

vanguejar, *v.i.* to slip, to swing, to vacillate.

vanilina, *s.f.* vanillin.

vaniloquência, *s.f.* bragging, vain talk.

vaniloquente, *adj.* vain, empty.

vantagem, *s.f.* advantage; profit, gain, benefit; odds *(no jogo).* 1) *levar vantagem,* to get the upper hand. 2) *tirar vantagem de,* to take advantage of.

vantajoso, *adj.* advantageous; profitable.

vante, *s.f.* foreship, head, prow.

vão, *adj.* vain, futile, fallacious; false; useless, futile; *s.m.* empty space; recess; span *(de ponte)* embrasure *(de janela);* doorway *(de porta); em vão,* in vain; to no avail; for nothing.

vápido, *adj.* vapid, insipid.

vapor, *s.m.* steam, vapour; steamer, steamship.

vaporação, *s.f.* evaporation.

vaporar, *v.i.* to evaporate; to steam; to turn into vapour.

vaporímetro, *s.m.* vaporimeter.

vaporização, *s.f.* vaporization.

vaporizador, *s.m.* vaporizer; *adj.* vaporizing.

vaporizar, *v.t.* to vaporize, to evaporate; to convert into vapor; to pulverize.

vaporoso, *adj.* vaporous; transparent; misty; ethereal; fanciful.

vaqueiro, *s.m.* cowboy, cow-keeper.

vara, *s.f.* stick; rod; pole; staff; jurisdiction; herd *(de porcos).*

varação, *s.f.* beaching *(de barco);* fording.

varada, *s.f.* blow with a rod.

varado, *adj.* pierced; scared to death.

varador, *s.m.* gauger.

varadouro, *s.m.* beaching place.

varal, *s.m.* shaft, pole *(de cadeirinha).*

varanda, *s.f.* balcony; veranda; terrace.

varandim, *s.m.* narrow balcony; low window railing.

varão, *adj.* male; *s.m.* male; man; rod *(de ferro).*

varapau, *s.m.* pole, stick.

varar, *v.t.* to pierce (through), to run through; to cross, to traverse; to beach *(um barco).*

vareja, *s.f.* bluebottle, blow-fly, meat-fly.

varejador, *s.m.* measurer; beater, fustigator *(árvores).*

varejar, *v.t.* to beat; to knock down fruit; to measure; to search *(revistar);* to fling *(atirar).*

varejeira, *s.f. o mesmo que "vareja".*

varejo, *s.m.* search *(revista);* retail trade *(venda a retalho).*

vareque, *s.m.* sea-weed; wrack.

vareta, *s.f.* rod; stirring rod; rib *(de guarda--chuva);* leg *(de compasso).*

varga, *s.f.* marshy plain.

vargem, *s.f.* meadow, plain.

variabilidade, *s.f.* variability; changeableness.

variação, *s.f.* variation; variance; change; modification, alteration; diversification.

variado, *adj.* varied; various; varying; diverse; miscellaneous; assorted; inconstant.

variante, *adj.* variant, varying; *s.m.* variant, version; branchline *(ferroviária).*

variar, *v.i.* to vary; to differ; to be at variance, to disagree; to deviate; to be delirious; to oscillate; to range (from... to ...); *v.t.* to vary; to alter, to change; to shift (one's position, attitude, etc.); *para variar,* for a change.

variável, *adj.* variable, changeable; inconstant; *s.f.* variable.

varicela, *s.f.* chicken-pox, varicella.

varicocele, *s.m.* varicocele.

varicose, *s.f.* varicose.

varicosidade, *s.f.* varicosity.

varicoso, *adj.* varicose.

variedade, *s.f.* variety, diversity; inconstance; kind, class, sort; *s.f. pl.* variety show.

variegação, *s.f.* variegation, diversity of colours.

variegado, *adj.* variegated, multicoloured.

variegar, *v.t.* to variegate, to diversify; to grade colours, to dapple.

varina, *s.f.* Portuguese fishwife.

varinha, *s.f.* switch; wand, small stick; *varinha de condão,* magic wand.

varino, *s.m.* narrow and long boat; cloak with a hook.

vário, *adj.* various, different; *pl.* several, sundry, some, a number of.

varíola, *s.f.* variola; smallpox.

variolado, *adj.* variolar.

variólico, *adj.* variolic.

variz, *s.f.* varix, varicose vein.

varja, *s.f.* cultivated plain.

varonia, *s.f.* manliness, masculinity, virility, manhood; male line.

varonil, *adj.* manly, virile, masculine, vigorous.

varonilidade, *s.f.* manliness; courage; virility, manhood.

varrão, *s.m.* boar.

varrasco, *s.m.* boar.

varredeira, *s.f.* studding sail.

varredela, *s.f.* sweeping.

varredor, *s.m.* sweeper.

varredura, *s.f.* sweepings.

varrer, *v.t.* to sweep; to clean.

varrido, *adj.* swept; clean; *doido-varrido,* stark mad.

várzea, *s.f.* tilled plain; meadow.

vasa, *s.f.* slime, ooze; mud.

vasca, *s.f.* nausea; convulsion, qualm, spasm.

vascão, vasco, *adj.* Basque.

vascolejador, *adj.* shaking, revolving.

vascolejamento, *s.m.* shaking, agitation.

vascolejar, *v.t.* to shake, to agitate, to stir up.

vasconço, *s.m.* Basque; gibberish *(algaraviada).*

vascongado, *adj.* e *s.m.* Biscayan, Basque.

vascoso, *adj.* convulsive.

vascular, *adj.* vascular.

vascularidade, *s.f.* vascularity.

vascularização, *s.f.* vascularization.

vasculhador, *adj.* sweeping; searching; *s.m.* searcher; sweeper.

vasculhar, *v.t.* to sweep; to search, to ransack.

vasculho, *s.m.* broom, long broom.

vaselina, *s.f.* vaseline.

vasento, *adj.* miry, slimy, muddy.

vasilha, *s.f.* vessel; container; can; barrel, cask.

vasilhame, *s.m.* vessels; containers; cans.

vaso, *s.m.* vase; vessel; flowerpot; *(anat. e bot.)* vessel, duct. 1) *vaso de noite,* chamber pot. 2) *vaso sanguíneo,* blood vessel.

vasoconstrição, *s.f.* vasoconstriction.

vasoconstritor, *s.m.* e *adj.* vasoconstrictor.

vasodilatação, *s.f.* vasodilatation.

vasodilatador, *adj.* e *s.m.* vasodilator.

vasomotor, *adj.* vasomotor.

vasoso, *adj.* muddy.

vasquejante, *adj.* convulsive; trembling; agonizing.

vasquejar, *v.i.* to writhe, to have convulsions; to agonize.

vassalagem, *s.f.* vassalage, servitude; subjection.

vassalo, *s.m.* vassal; bondsman; subject; *adj.* vassal; subordinate.

vassoira, vassoura, *s.f.* broom.

vasaourada, *s.f.* blow with a broom; sweep.

vassoureiro, *s.m.* broommaker; broomseller.

vassouro, *s.m.* oven-broom, broom of twigs.

vasteza, vastidão, *s.f.* vastness; amplitude; largeness; wideness; immensity.

vasto, *adj.* vast; ample; broad, wide; roomy; big.

vate, *s.m.* bard, poet.

Vaticano, *s.m.* Vatican.

vaticinação, *s.f.* vaticination, prediction; prophecy.

vaticinador, *s.m.* vaticinator; prophet; foreteller; *adj.* vaticinating; foretelling; prophetical.

vaticinante, *adj.* vaticinating, foretelling.

vaticinar, *v.t.* to vaticinate; to foretell, to predict; to prophesy.

vaticínio, *s.m. o mesmo que "vaticinação".*

vátua, *s.m.* Vatua.

vau, *s.m.* ford; river crossing; *passar a vau,* to wade through, to ford.

vaza, *s.f.* trick *(em jogo de cartas).*

vazador, *s.m.* bit, boring tool.

vazadouro, *s.m.* refuse pit, drain, sewer.

vazadura, *s.f.* act of emptying or draining.

vazamento, *s.m.* emptying.

vazante, *s.f.* reflux, ebb-tide, low water.

vazão, *s.m.* emptying; solution; outlet.

vazar, *v.t.* to pour; to empty; to gouge *(um olho); v.i.* to leak; to ooze out; to ebb *(a maré).*

vazio, *adj.* empty; void; vacant; blank; *s.m.* vacuum; vacuity; emptiness; void.

veada, *s.f.* hind.

veado, *s.m.* deer; stag *(macho).*

vector, *s.m.* vector.

vectorial, *adj.* vectorial.

veda, *s.f.* close season.

vedação, *s.f.* barrier, fence; enclosure.

vedado, *adj.* fenced in, closed off; forbidden.

vedador, *s.m.* fencer.

vedália, *s.f.* cochineal insect.

vedar, *v.t.* to hinder; to forbid; to shut off; to bar, to block; to stop; *v.i.* to stop running; *mal vedado,* leaky.

vedeta, *s.f.* vedette, mosquito boat; star *(actriz).*

védico, *adj.* Vedaic.

vedismo, *s.m.* Vedaism.

vedor, *s.m.* overseer, inspecto; water finder, dowser.

vedoria, *s.f.* inspectorship.

vedro, *s.m.* enclosure, fence.

veeiro, *s.m.* vein or fissure *(de rocha).*

veemência, *s.f.* vehemence; fervor; heat; impetuosity; intensity.

veemente, *adj.* vehement; impetuous; ardent, eager, keen; passionate; loud.

vegetabilidade, *s.f.* vegetability.

vegetação, *s.f.* vegetation, plants, growth.

vegetal, *s.m.* vegetable; *adj.* vegetable.

vegetalidade, *s.f.* vegetality.

vegetalismo, *s.m.* vegetarianism.

vegetalista, *s.m. e s.f.* vegetarian.

vegetalizar, *v.t.* to give the shape of vegetables to.

vegetante, *adj.* vegetating.

vegetar, *v.i.* to vegetate.

vegetariano, *s.m.* vegetarian.

vegetarismo, *s.m.* vegetarianism.

vegetarista, *s.m. e s.f.* vegetarian.

vegetativo, *adj.* vegetative; fertile, productive.

veia, *s.f.* vein; *(bot.)* vein, nervure; *(fig.),* disposition, mood; talent; veiculador, *s.m.* vehicle; *adj.* transporting, transmitting.

veicular, *adj.* vehicular.

veículo, *s.m.* vehicle; medium.

veiga, *s.f.* lowland; fertile plain.

veio, *s.m.* vein, seam; shaft; spindle *(eixo);* grain *(de madeira);* streamlet *(de água).*

veiro, *s.m.* vair.

vela, *s.f. (de navio);* candle *(de iluminação);* spark plug *(de ignição);* vigil, watch *(vigília).* 1) *navio à vela,* sailing vessel. 2) *navegar á vela,* to sail.

valada, *s.f.* watch, wakefulness.

velado, *adj.* veiled; hidden.

velador, *s.m.* watcher; wooden candlestick.

veladura, *s.f.* glazing *(pintura);* fog *(fotografia).*

velame, *s.m.* sails.

velamento, *s.m.* veiling; hiding.

velar, *v.t.* to veil; to conceal, to hide: to watch over; to keep watch over *(um defunto);* to fog *(fotografia); v.i.* to be awake; to kee vigil; to be watchful; *velar-se,* to become veiled.

veleidade, *s.f.* whim, caprice; mere wish.

veleiro, *s.m.* sailing vessel; sailboat; sailmaker.

velejar, *v.i.* to sail.

veleta, *s.f.* weathercock, weather vane; fickle person.

velha, *s.f.* old woman; crone.

velhacaria, *s.f.* knavery, rascality, roguery.

velhaco, *s.m.* knave, rascal, rogue, crook, swindler; *adj.* knavish, crafty, foxy, tricky.

velhada, lots of old people.

velharia, *s.f.* old thing; rubbish; antique.

velhice, *s.f.* old age; oldness.

velho, *adj.* old, aged; ancient; old-fashioned; *s.m.* old man.

velhote, *s.m.* old man.

velífero, *adj.* carrying sails.

velino, *s.m.* vellum.

velo, *s.m.* fleece.

velocidade, *s.f.* speed; rapidity, velocity, swiftness, fastness; *a toda a velocidade,* at full speed.

velocímetro, *s.m.* speedometer.

velocino, *s.m.* fleece, sheepskin.

velocípede, *s.m.* velocipede, bicycle.

velocipedismo, *s.m.* cycling.

velocipedista, *s.m. e s.f.* cyclist.

velódromo, *s.m.* cycle racingtrack.

veloso, *adj.* downy, wooly, shaggy, fleecy.

veloz, *adj.* swift, quick, speedy, fast.

velozmente, *adv.* swiftly.

veludilho, *s.m.* velveteen.

veludinoso, *adj.* velvety, velveted.

veludo, *s.m.* velvet.

veludoso, *adj.* velvety.

venábulo, *s.m.* javelin, light spear.

venal, *adj.* venal; corrupt.

venalidade, *s.f.* venality, corruption.

venatório, *adj.* venatic.

vencedor, *s.m.* winner; victor; conqueror; *adj.* victorious; winning.

vencelho, *s.m.* sort of straw rope.

vencer, *v.t.* to win; to conquer, to vanquish; to beat, to defeat; to subdue; to overcome; to win *(salário); vencer-se,* to fall due *(chegar ao fim do prazo).*

vencida, *s.f. levar de vencida:* to get the better of.

vencido, *adj.* defeated, vanquished, conquered, overcome; due, overdue *(letra, etc.).*

vencimento, *s.m. (com.)* maturity; salary *(ordenado);* expiration *(fim de prazo).* 1) *pagável no vencimento,* payable when due. 2) *pagar no vencimento,* to discharge at maturity. 3) *dar vencimento a,* to cope with.

vencível, *adj.* conquerable; surmountable; *(com.)* due.

venda, *s.f.* sale; selling; blindfold *(de olhos).* 1) *à venda,* on sale, for sale. 2) *pôr à venda,* to place on sale. 3) *ter à venda,* to keep for sale.

vendar, *v.t.* to blindfold.

vendaval, *s.m.* gale; storm.

vendável, *adj.* saleable, marketable.

vendedeira, *s.f.* woman seller; saleswoman.

vendedor, *s.m.* seller; salesman; *vendedor ambulante,* pedlar, street seller.

vendedouro, *s.m.* market.

vendeira, *s.f.* inn-keeper.

vendeiro, *s.m.* inn-keeper.

vender, *v.t.* to sell; to market; to vend; to peddle; to sell away. 1) *vender fiado,* to sell on credit. 2) *vender a prazo,* to sell on account. 3) *vender a pronto,* to sell for cash.

vendeta, *s.f.* vendetta.

vendibilidade, *s.f.* vendibility.

vendido, *adj.* sold; sold over to; *s.m.* bribed person; traitor.

vendilhão, *s.m.* peddler, hawker.

vendível, *adj.* saleable, vendible.

venefício, *s.m.* poisoning.

venéfico, *adj.* venefical, poisonous; harmful.

veneno, *s.m.* poison, venom; malice.

venenosidade, *s.f.* venomousness.

venenoso, *adj.* poisonous, venomous; malicious, malignant; virulent.

venera, *s.f.* scallop-shell; badge, decoration.

venerabilidade, *s.f.* venerability.

venerabundo, *adj.* reverent.

veneração, *s.f.* veneration, worship; reverence, respect.

venerador, *adj.* venerating, *s.m.* venerator, adorer.

venerando, *adj. o mesmo que "venerável".*

venerar, *v.t.* to venerate; to respect; to worship; to revere, to adore.

venerável, *adj.* venerable, respectable.

venéreo, *adj.* venereal.

venereologia, *s.f.* venereology.

venereologista, *s.f. e s.m.* venereologist.

veneta, *s.f.* fit of madness; fancy, whim.

veneziano, *adj. e s.m.* Venetian.

venezuelano, *adj. e s.m.* Venezuelan.

vénia, *s.f.* leave, permission; bow *(mesura); pedir vénia,* to ask leave (to do); to ask someone`s forgiveness.

veniaga, *s.f.* traffic; swindle, trick, cheat, fraud; commodity.

venial, *adj.* venial, pardonable.

venialidade, *s.f.* veniality, venialness.

venosidade, *s.f.* quality or state of being venous.

venoso, *adj.* venous; veiny.

venta, *s.f.* nostrial; *s.f. pl.* nose; face; *nas ventas de,* right in front of, under the nose of.

ventana, *s.f.* window; fan.

ventanear, *v.t.* to ventilate, to air; to agitate.

ventaneira, *s.f.* high wind.

ventania, *s.f.* gale; high wind.

ventar, *v.i.* to blow *(vento).*

ventarola, *s.f.* fan.

ventilação, *s.f.* ventilation; airing.

ventilador, *adj.* ventilating; *s.m.* ventilator.

ventilante, *adj.* ventilating.

ventilar, *v.t.* to ventilate, to expose to air; to discuss, to debate.

vento, *s.m.* wind; breeze; *de vento em popa,* under a fair wind.

ventoinha, *s.f.* weather vane, weather cock; fan; blower.

ventosa, *s.f.* cupping glass; (zool.) sucker.

ventosidade, *s.f.* flatulence, flatus.

ventoso, *adj.* windy; gusty; windswept.

ventral, *adj.* ventral.

ventre, *s.m.* abdomen, belly; womb, uterus; bulge *(bojo)*; heart *(âmago)*.

ventricular, *adj.* ventricular.

ventrículo, *s.m.* ventricle.

ventriloquia, *s.f.* ventriloquism, *s.m.* ventriloquism.

ventríloquo, *s.m.* ventriloquist.

ventrudo, *adj.* stout; pot-bellied, big-bellied; fat.

ventura, *s.f.* fortune, venture, luck, fate; good luck, good fortune; happiness; hazard, risk; *à ventura,* haphazardly, at random.

venturoso, *adj.* lucky, fortunate; happy, blissful; risky.

Vénus, *s.f.* Venus.

venustidade, *s.f.* gracefulness, beauty.

venusto, *adj.* graceful, beautiful.

ver, *v.t.* to see; to behold; to discern; to look at; to examine; to perceive; to notice, to observe; to find; to witness; to know; to try (if etc.). 1) *a meu ver,* as I see it, in my opinion. 2) *até mais ver,* farewell, au revoir. 3) *bem se vê que ...,* it's plain that .... 4) *fazer ver,* to point out, to remind. 5) *maneira de ver,* point of view, opinion. 6) *vamos ver,* let's see. 7) *ver-se,* to see oneself; to find oneself. 8) *ver-se e desejar-se,* not to know which way to turn.

veracidade, *s.f.* veracity; truthfulness, truth, verity.

vera-efígie, *s.f.* likeness, faithful portrait, exact copy.

veraneante, *s.m.* holiday-maker.

veranear, *v.t.* to spend the summer, to summer.

veraneio, *s.m.* summer vacation; *estância de veraneio,* summer resort.

Verão, *s.m.* summer.

veras, *s.f. pl.* truth, earnestness, sincerity; *com todas as veras,* in all truth.

veraz, *adj.* veracious, truthful, veritable.

verba, *s.f.* item, article; appropriation *(designação de quantia);* sum, fund *(quantia).*

verbal, *adj.* verbal, oral.

verbalismo, *s.m.* verbalism.

verbalista, *s.m.* e *s.f.* verbalist.

verbalização, *s.f.* verbalization.

verbalizador, *s.m.* verbalizer.

verbalizar, *v.t.* to verbalize.

verbalmente, *adv.* verbally, orally.

verbesco, *s.m.* great mullein.

verbena, *s.f.* verbena.

verberação, *s.f.* verberation; striking, beating; reproof, reproach.

verberador, verberante, *adj.* punitive, reproachful.

verberar, *v.t.* to reprove, to censure, to criticize, to reproach; to strike.

verberativo, *adj.* verberative.

verbete, *s.m.* account, bill; note; card.

verbo, *s.m.* verb; word.

verborreia, *s.f.* verbosity, loquacity, prolixity.

verborreico, *adj.* verbose, prolix.

verbosidade, *s.f.* verbosity, wordiness, talkativeness.

verboso, *adj.* prolix, verbose, loquatious, wordy.

verça, *s.f.* sort of cabbage.

verdade, *s.f.* truth, truthfulness. 1) *para dizer a verdade,* to tell the truth. 2) *na verdade,* in fact, indeed. 3) *isso é verdade?,* is that so?

verdadeiro, *adj.* true; truthful; real; sincere; veritable.

verdasca, *s.f.* rod, cane.

verdascada, a blow with a rod.

verdascar, *v.t.* to cane, to lash.

verdasco, *s.m.* sour winc.

verde, *adj.* green; verdant; unripe, immature; young, tender, inexperienced; fresh *(carne).*

verdeal, *adj.* greenish.

verdecer, *v.i.* to become green, to grow green.

verde-claro, *s.m.* light green, grass green.

verde-escuro, *s.m.* dark green.

verde-esmeralda, *s.m.* chromegreen.

verde-gaio, *adj.* e *s.m.* popular dance; light green.

verdejante, *adj.* verdant, green.

verdejar, *v.i.* to become green, to green.

verdelhão, *s.m.* greenfich.

verdete, *s.m.* verdigris.

verdoengo, *adj.* greenish, not quite ripe.

verdor, *s.m.* verdure; greenness, inexperience.

verdoso, *adj.* green, verdant, greeny.

verdugo, *s.m.* executioner; hangman; flange *(de roda de vagão).*

verdum, verdume, *s.m.* the green colour.

verdura, *s.f.* greenness; verdure; herbage; vegetable *(hortaliça).*

vereação, *s.f.* town council.

vereador, *s.m.* councilman; alderman.

verear, *v.t.* to administer (as a town-councilor).

verecúndia, *s.f.* shame.

verecundo, *adj.* shameful.

vereda, *s.f.* path, footpath; walk, lane.

veredito, *s.m.* vercdict, finding; sentence.

verga, *s.f.* switch; wand; lath; lintel *(de porta); (náut.)* yard.

vergado, *adj.* bent, curved; subdued.

vergalhada, *s.f.* lash; stoke with a whip.

vergalhar, *v.t.* to whip, to lash.

vergalho, *s.m.* whip, lash, scourge.

vergame, *s.m.* the yards *(de um navio).*

vergão, *s.m.* wale, weal, welt.

vergar, *v.t.* to bend, to curve; to submit; *vergar-se,* to bow, to bend, to groan (under a weight).

vergasta, *s.f.* switch, whip.

vergastada, *s.f.* lash, cut with a whip.

vergastar, *v.t.* to lash, to whip.

vergel, *s.m.* orchard.

vergonha, *s.f.* shame; disgrace, dishonour; embarrassment, timidity; *ter vergonha,* to be ashamed, to be shy.

vergonhoso, *adj.* shameful, disgraceful; opprobious, ignominious.

vergôntea, *s.f.* shoot, scion; sprig; twig; *(fig.)* offspring.

vergontear, *v.i.* to shoot forth, to sprout.

vergueiro, *s.m.* switch, slender rod.

veridicamente, *adv.* veridically, truthfully.

veridicidade, *s.f.* veracity.

verídico, *adj.* truthful, veracious.

verificação, *s.f.* verification, examination; checking, test; confirmation.

verificador, *s.m.* verifier, checker; *adj.* verifying, controlling, checking.

verificar, *v.t.* to verify, to examine, to check; to control; to ascertain; to happen, to occur, to take place.

verificativo, *adj.* verificative.

verificável, *adj.* verifiable, controllable, checkable.

verme, *s.m.* worm; grub, vermin, larva.

vermelhaço, *adj.* reddish, ruddy.

vermelhão, *s.m.* vermillion, cinnabar; redness.

vermelhar, *v.i.* to redden.

vermelhecer, *v.i.* to grow red.

vermelhidão, *s.f.* redness; clush.

vermelho, *adj.* e *s.m.* red; ruddy.

vermelhuço, vermelhusco, *adj.* somewhat red.

vermicida, *adj.* vermicidal; *s.m.* vermicide, vermifuge.

vermicular, *adj.* vermicular, wormlike.

vermiculária, *s.f.* stone crop.

vermículo, *s.m.* vermicule.

vermiforme, *adj.* vermiform, wormlike, wormshaped.

vermífugo, *adj.* vermifugal; *s.m.* vermifuge.

vermina, *s.f.* vermin.

verminação, *s.f.* vermination.

verminado, *adj.* verminous; vermin-eaten.

verminose, *s.f.* verminosis.

verminoso, *adj.* verminous.

vermívoro, *s.m.* vermivorous.

vermute, *s.f.* vermouth.

vernaculidade, *s.f.* vernacularity.

vernaculismo, *s.m.* vernacularism.

vernaculista, *s.m.* e *s.f.* vernacularist.

vernaculização, *s.f.* vernacularization.

vernaculizar, *v.t.* to vernacularize.

vernáculo, *adj.* vernacular; native; correct, faultless; *s.m.* vernacular.

vernal, *adj.* vernal.

vernalização, *s.f.* vernalization.

vernante, *adj.* flourishing in the spring.

verniz, *s.m.* varnish; polish; patent leather *(couro); (fig.)* gloss, veneer.

verno, *adj.* vernal.

vero, *adj.* true, veracious.

verónica, *s.f.* veronica.

verosímil, *adj.* likely, probable.

verosimilhança, *s.f.* verisimilitude, likeliness.

verosimilhante, *adj.* likely, probable.

verrina, *s.f.* lampoon; diatribe.

verrineiro, *s.m.* lampooner, lampoonist, bitter critic.

verrucal, *adj.* warty.

verruga, *s.f.* wart.

verrugoso, verrugento, *adj.* warty.

verruma, *s.f.* gimlet, wimble; auger, borer.

verrumar, *v.t.* to bore, to bore through; *v.i. (fig.)* to ponder, to rack one`s brains.

versado, *adj.* versed (in a subject), conversant (with); skilled; expert (at, in).

versal, *s.m.* capital letter.

versalete, *s.m.* small capital letter.

versalhada, *s.f.* doggerel verse, bad poetry.

versão, *s.m.* version, translation; reading; account, story.

versar, *v.t.* to study, to search; to practice, to handle, to manipulate; to discuss; to treat of *(versar sobre);* to make verses.

versátil, *adj.* versatile; variable, inconstant; changeable.

versatilidade, *s.f.* versatility; inconstance, fickleness.

versejador, *s.m.* versifier, poetaster.

versejar, *v.i.* to versify; to make verses.

verseto, *s.m.* versicle; verse.

versicolor, *adj.* versicolour, varicoloured, parti-coloured.

versículo, *s.m.* versicle.

versificação, *s.f.* versification.

versificador, *s.m.* versifier, versemaker.

versificar, *v.t.* o mesmo que "versejar".

verso, *s.m.* verse; poetry; line *(cada linha)*; reverse, back *(lado de trás)*.

vértebra, *s.f.* vertebra.

vertebrado, *adj.* vertebrate; *s.m. pl.* vertebrata.

vertebral, *adj.* vertebral.

vertedor, *adj.* spilling, pouring.

vertedouro, *s.m.* spilway; wooden scoop.

vertedura, *s.f.* spilling; overflow.

vertente, *s.f.* slope, hillside; watershed: *adj.* spilling, outpouring; under discussion.

verter, *v.t.* to spill; to pour out; to shed; to translate, to turn; *v.i.* to leak, to ooze; to overflow.

vertical, *adj.* vertical, upright; *s.f.* vertical line.

verticalidade, *s.f.* verticality, uprightness.

vértice, *s.m.* vertex; top, summit; apex.

verticidade, *s.f.* verticity.

verticilado, *adj.* verticillate, whorled.

verticilo, *s.m.* verticil, whorl.

vertigem, *s.f.* vertigo; giddiness, dizziness.

vertiginosamente, *adv.* very quickly, vertiginously.

vertiginoso, *adj.* vertiginous, dizzy; very quick.

verve, *s.f.* verve, energy; bounce.

vesânia, *s.f.* insanity, madness, mental illness.

vesano, *adj.* mad, insane, mental ill, delirious.

vesgo, *adj.* squinting, cross-eyed; *s.m.* squinter.

vesguear, *v.i.* to squint; to be cross-eyed; to look askance.

vesgueiro, *adj.* squint-eyed.

vesguice, *s.f.* strabismus.

vesicação, *s.f.* vesication.

vesical, *adj.* vesical.

vesicante, *adj. e s.m.* vesicant, vesicatory.

vesícula, *s.f.* vesicle; sac, cyst; air bladder *(de peixe)*; blister *(bolha)*; vesícula biliar, gall bladder.

vesicular, *adj.* vesicular.

vesiculoso, *adj.* vesiculose; vesiculous.

vespa, *s.f.* wasp.

vespão, *s.m.* hornet.

vespeiro, *s.m.* wasp's nest.

Vésper, *s.m.* vesper, evening star; Venus; the West.

véspera, *s.f.* eve, day before; evening; *s.f. pl.* vespers; estar em vésperas de, to be about to (do something).

vesperal, *adj.* vesper, vesperian; *s.m.* vesperal.

Véspero, *s.m.* o mesmo que "Vésper".

vespertino, *s.m.* evening paper; *adj.* vespertine.

vessada, *s.f.* fertile land.

vessadela, *s.f.* deep ploughing.

vessar, *v.t.* to plough deeply.

vestal, *s.f.* vestal, vestal virgin.

veste, *s.f.* dress; clothing; garment; vestment.

vestiária, *s.f.* vestry; wardrobe.

vestiário, *s.m.* cloack-room.

vestibular, *adj.* vestibular.

vestíbulo, *s.m.* vestibule; lobby, hallway, entrance, hall; main entrance.

vestido, *s.m.* dress; gown; *adj.* dressed.

vestidura, *s.f.* clothes, clothing, garment.

vestígio, *s.m.* vestige, trace, sign, mark; footprint; remains.

vestimenta, *s.f.* vesture; garment; robe, apparel.

vestimenteiro, *s.m.* vestmentmaker.

vestir, *v.t.* to clothe, to dress; to put on; to wear: vestir-se, to dress, to put on one's clothes.

vestuário, *s.m.* clothing, clothes; garments; costume; wearing apparel.

veterano, *s.m. e adj.* veteran.

veterinária, *s.f.* veterinary science.

veterinário, *s.m.* veterinarian; *adj.* veterinary.

veto, *s.m.* veto; prohibition, interdiction.

vetustez, *s.f.* oldness, antiquity.

vetusto, *adj.* old, ancient; venerable, vetust.

véu, *s.m.* veil; disguise, mask; curtain.

vexação, *s.f.* vexation, annoyance, molestation.

vexador, *adj.* affronting; shameful; vexatious.

vexame, *s.m.* affront, indignity; humiliation, chagrin; shame.

vexante, *adj.* vexing; humiliating.

vexar, *v.t.* to vex, to molest, to annoy; to humiliate; to afront.

vexativo, *adj.* vexing, vexatious.

vexatório, *adj.* vexing; humiliating.

vexilar, *adj.* vexilary.

vexilo, *s.m.* vexillum; banner.

vez, *s.f.* time; occasion; turn *(de fazer alguma*

coisa); move *(no xadrez, damas, etc.).* 1) *uma vez por outra,* now and then; once in a while. 2) *mais uma vez,* once more. 3) *algumas vezes,* sometimes. 4) *às vezes,* sometimes, at times, now and then. 5) *as mais das vezes,* generally, as a rule, mostly. 6) *cada vez mais,* more and more. 7) *cada vez menos,* less and less. 8) *cada vez que,* whenever. 9) *certa vez,* once. 10) *de uma vez por todas,* once and for all. 11) *duas vezes,* twice. 12) *duma só vez,* all at once, at one stroke. 13) *é a minha vez,* it is my turn. 14) *em vez de,* instead of. 15) *fazer as vezes de,* to serve as. 16) *muitas vezes,* often. 17) *pela última vez,* for the last time. 18) *perder a vez,* to miss one's turn. 19) *raras vezes,* seldom, rarely. 20) *uma vez que,* since. 21) *era uma vez,* once upon a time.

vezeiro, *adj.* accustomed (to do); habitual.

vezo, *s.m.* bad habit; custom, use; vice.

via, *s.f.* way; road; track; direction, manner; motive. 1) *Via Láctea,* Milky Way. 2) *chegar a vias de facto,* to come to blows. 3) *em vias de,* about to. 4) *segunda via,* copy. 5) *via pública,* thoroughfare. 6) *via férria,* railway, railroad. 7) *via sacra,* the way of the cross.

viabilidade, *s.f.* viability, feasibility.

viação, *s.f.* means of transportation; public ways; highway system.

viador, *s.f.* traveller, passenger.

viaduto, *s.m.* viaduct.

viageiro, *s.m.* e *adj.* traveller, wanderer; relating to travels.

viagem, *s.f.* travel, journey, voyage; trip, tour. 1) *viagem de ida e volta,* round trip. 2) *viagem de regresso,* return trip. 3) *seguir viagem,* to leave, to depart (for).

viajador, *s.m.* traveller.

viajante, *adj.* travelling; *s.m.* e *s.f.* traveller.

viajar, *v.i.* to travel; to journey; to voyage.

viajata, *s.f.* trip, tour.

vianda, *s.f.* viands; victuals, meat.

viandante, *s.m.* e *s.f.* traveller; wayfarer; *adj.* wayfaring.

viandar, *v.i.* to travel, to roam, to wander.

viandeiro, *s.m.* glutton, gourmand.

viático, *s.m.* viaticum; provisions or money for a journey.

viatura, *s.f.* vehicle; carriage, conveyance.

viável, *adj.* passable, transitable; feasible, practicable, workable; (med.) viable.

víbora, *s.f.* viper; adder, spiteful person.

vibordo, *s.m.* gunwale.

vibração, *s.f.* vibration; oscillation; thrill.

vibrador, *s.m.* vibrator; electric buzzer.

vibrante, *adj.* vibrant, vibrating; thrilling.

vibrar, *v.t.* to vibrate; to brandish *(uma arma, etc.);* to strike *(cordas, etc.);* to deal *(golpe).*

vibrátil, *adj.* vibratile.

vibratilidade, *s.f.* vibratility.

vibratório, *adj.* vibratory; vibrative.

vibrião, *s.m.* vibrio.

vibrissas, *s.f.* vibrissaz; hair in the hostrils.

viburno, *s.m.* viburnum.

viçar, *v.t.* to grow luxuriant.

vicariato, *s.m.* vicarship, vicariate.

vicário, *s.m.* substitute; *adj.* vicarious.

vice, *pref.* vice.

vice-almirantado, *s.m.* vice-admiralty.

vice-almirante, *s.m.* vice-admiral.

vice-cônsul, *s.m.* vice-consul.

vice-consulado, *s.m.* vice-consulate.

vice-governador, *s.m.* vice-governor; lieutenant-governor.

vicejante, *adj.* luxuriant, exuberant, verdant; thriving.

vicejar, *v.i.* to grow luxuriant, to flourish; to thrive.

vicejo, *s.m.* exuberance, rankness.

vicenal, *adj.* vicennial, every twenty years.

vicénio, *s.m.* period of twenty years.

vicentino, *adj.* e *s.m.* pertaining to S. Vincent.

vice-presidência, *s.f.* vice-presidency.

vice-presidente, *s.m.* vice-president.

vice-rei, *s.m.* viceroy.

vice-reinado, *s.m.* viceroyalty.

vice-reitor, *s.m.* vice-rector; assistant headmaster.

vicésimo, *num.* twentieth.

vice-versa, *adv.* vice-versa.

viciação, *s.f.* vitiation, falsification, forgery; corruption.

viciado, *s.m.* addict, fiend; *adj.* vitiated, vicious; foul (ar); perverted, corrupt.

viciador, *adj.* vitiating.

viciar, *v.t.* to vitiate; to corrupt; to adulterate, to contaminate; to debase; to be habit-forming *(criar vício); viciar-se,* to become addicted.

vicinal, *adj.* vicinal, neighbouring.

vicinalidade, *s.f.* vicinity, vicinage.

vício, *s.m.* vice; failing, besetting sin; blemish; bad habit; addction; depravity.

viciosidade, *s.f.* depravity, faultiness.

vicioso, *adj.* vicious; corrupt, depraved; defective, faulty.

vicissitude, *s.f.* vicissitude, change; variation; alternation; reverse (of fortune); *s.f. pl.* ups and downs.

vicissitudinário, *adj.* vicissitudinary.

viço, *s.m.* exuberande, luxuriance; lushness; energy.

viçoso, *adj.* verdant, flourishing; lush, exuberant; fresh; youthful.

vicunha, *s.f.* vicunha.

vida, *s.f.* life; existence; living; lifetime; manner of life; carer; animation, liveliness, vivacity, spirit; biography. 1) *a vida aqui é muito cara,* it costs a lot to live here. 2) *cheio de vida,* full of life, lively, vivid. 3) *com vida,* alive. 4) *estar bem de vida,* to be well off. 5) *ganhar a vida,* to earn a living. 6) *meta-se na sua vida!,* mind your own business!. 7) *nível de vida,* standard of life. 8) *sem vida,* lifeless. 9) *modo de vida,* manner of living, profession. 10) *seguro de vida,* life insurance. 11) *uma vez na vida,* once in a lifetime.

vidão, *s.m.* easy life; opulent life.

vide, *s.f.* vine branch, grape vine.

videira, *s.f.* vine, grape-vine.

videirinho, videiro, *adj.* selfish; industrious; self-seeking.

vidência, *s.f.* clairvoyance.

vidente, *s.m. e s.f.* clairvoyant; seer, prophet; *adj.* clairvoyant.

vidoeiro, *s.m.* white birch.

vidonho, *s.m.* vine-branch.

vidraça, *s.f.* window pane, window sash.

vidraceiro, *s.m.* glazier; *massa de vidraceiro,* putty.

vidraço, *s.m.* glasslike stone.

vidrado, *adj.* glazed; dim; transparent, glassy.

vidragem, *s.m.* glazing.

vidrar, *v.t.* to glaze; to make dim; to make or become glassy.

vidraria, *s.f.* glassmaking; glass factory; glassware; glazier`s shop.

vidreiro, *adj.* glass; *s.m.* glass-maker.

vidrento, *adj.* glassy, vitreous.

vidrilho, *s.m.* glass bead.

vidro, *s.m.* glass; small bottle; pane *(de vidraça);* crystal *(de relógio).*

vidual, *adj.* relating to widowhood.

vieira, *s.f.* scallop-shell.

vieiro, *s.m.* vein *(metálico).*

viela, *s.f.* alley; lane, narrow street.

vienense, *adj. e s.m. e s.f.* Viennese.

viés, *s.m.* obliquity, bias binding; sloping. 1) *de viés,* on the vias, aslant; askance *(olhar).* 2) *um olhar de viés,* a sidelong glance.

viga, *s.f.* beam, girder.

vigamento, *s.m.* beams; frame *(de edifício).*

vigar, *v.t.* to put beams, to place on beams; to frame.

vigariato, *s.m.* vicariate.

vigarice, *s.f.* swindle, gyp.

vigário, *s.m.* vicar.

vigarista, *s.m.* swindler, crook; confidence man.

vigarizar, *v.t.* to swindle, to cheat.

vigência, *s.f.* period of valitiy; operation *(de uma lei); durante a vigência da lei,* while the law is in force.

vigente, *adj.* in force, in effect; present.

vigésimo, *num.* twentieth.

vigia, *s.f.* vigilance, watch; lookout; sentinel; *(náut.)* porthole; *s.m.* watchman; sentinel.

vigiar, *v.t.* to watch; to keep an eye on; to watch over; *v.i.* to watch; to keep vigil; to be on the lookout.

vígil, *adj.* vigilant, watchful, wideawake.

vigilância, *s.f.* vigilance, watchfulness; wakefulness; alertness; caution.

vigilante, *adj.* vigilant; cautious; attentive; watchful, on the alert, wary; *s.m.* watchman, watcher.

vigilar, *v.t.* o mesmo que "vigiar".

vigília, *s.f.* vigil; insomnia, sleeplessness; eve *(de uma festa).*

vigor, *s.m.* vigour, strength, energy, force; activity; power; validity, legality. 1) *entrar em vigor,* to become effective, to come into force. 2) *estar em vigor,* to be in force.

vigorante, *adj.* invigorating, stimulating; in force, effective.

vigorar, *v.t.* to invigorate, to strengthen; to be in force.

vigorizar, *v.t.* to strengthen; to invigorate, to fortify.

vigorosamente, *adv.* vigourously.

vigoroso, *adj.* vigorous, strong, robust, virile, energetic; sturdy, tough; powerful.

vigota, *s.f.* small beam.

vil, *adj.* vile, despicable, base, mean, depraved, abject, shameful.

vila, *s.f.* town; country-house, villa.

vilanagem, *s.f.* peasantry; villains, villainy.

vilancete, *s.m.* pastoral poem.

vilania, *s.f.* villainy, meanness, rascality.

vilão, *s.m.* villager, peasant; villain, rascal; *adj.* rustic; vulgar, coarse, plebeian; vile, sordid, contemptible.

vilegiatura, *s.f.* country holiday, stay in the country.

vileza, *s.f.* meanness; vileness, vaseness, wickedness; villainy.

vilipendiador, *adj.* depreciating; slandering; *s.m.* backbiter, slanderer.

vilipendiar, *v.t.* to vilipend, to vilify, to defame, to slander; to despise.

vilipêndio, *s.m.* contempt, disdain; slander, vilification.

vilipendioso, *adj.* contemptuous; slanderous; vilipendious.

vilória, *s.f.* townlet, village.

vilosidade, *s.f.* villosity; villus.

viloso, *adj.* villous, hirsute, hairy.

vime, *s.m.* osier; withe.

vimeiro, *s.m.* osier.

vimieiro, *s.m.* osier-holt, field of oseiers.

viminoso, *adj.* vimineous, viminal.

vináceo, *adj.* vinaceous, wine-coloured, winelike.

vinagem, *s.f.* wine-making.

vinagrar, *v.t.* to make bitter; to get angry.

vinagre, *s.m.* vinegar.

vinagreiro, *s.m.* vinegar-seller; vinegar-maker.

vinagrete, *adj.* vinegary, sour.

vinário, *adj.* vinous.

vincar, *v.t.* to crease, to make a crease! to crease, to plait; to emphsize.

vincelho, vincilho, *s.m.* osier-string, straw rope.

vinco, *s.m.* crease, plait; weal, wale *(na carne).*

vinculação, *s.f.* entailment.

vinculado, *adj.* entailed; linked; bound.

vinculador, *s.m.* entailer; *adj.* entailing.

vincular, *v.t.* to entail; to bind; *adj.* entailing, binding.

vinculável, *adj.* entailable.

vínculo, *s.m.* entail, link, tie, bond of union; entailed estate.

vinda, *s.f.* coming; arrival, return.

vindicação, *s.f.* vindication, claim, demand.

vindicador, *s.m.* vindicator; *adj.* vindicative.

vindicar, *v.t.* to vindicate, to claim; to recover; to recovar; to assert a right.

vindicativo, *adj.* vindicative, vindicatory; protective.

vindicta, *s.f.* vindictiveness; revenge; punishment.

vindima, *s.f.* vintage, grape crop.

vindimador, *s.m.* vintager, grape-gatherer.

vindimar, *v.t.* to gather grapes; to gather the grapes from.

vindimeiro, vindimo, *adj.* autumnal; late in the season.

vindo, *adj.* come, arrived; vindo de: proceeding from.

vindoiro, vindouro, *adj.* future, forthcoming; *s.m.* newcomer; *s.m. pl.* the future generation.

víneo, *adj.* vinous; wine.

vingador, *s.m.* revenger, avenger; *adj.* avenging.

vingança, *s.f.* revenge, vengeance; retaliation; requital.

vingar, *v.t.* to avenge, to revenge; to reach, to attain to *(alcançar);* to cross *(percorrer); v.i.* to suceed, to be successful; to thrive, to flourish, to grow *(planta): vingar-se,* to take revenge.

vingativo, *adj.* vengeful, revengeful, vindictive; spiteful.

vunha, *s.f.* vineyard.

vinháceo, *adj.* vinous, winy.

vinhal, *s.m.* vineyard.

vinhão, *s.m.* very good wine.

vinhateiro, *s.m.* wine-grower, vine-dresser; *adj.* relating to the viniculture, viticultural.

vinhedo, *s.m.* vineyard.

vinheiro, *s.m.* wine-grower; vineyard keeper.

vinheta, *s.f.* vignette; printer`s flower.

vinho, *s.m.* wine; vinho tinto: red wine; *cor de vinho,* claret.

vinhoca, *s.f.* cheap wine.

vínico, *adj.* vinic.

vinícola, *adj.* wine-growing.

vinicultor, *s.m.* viniculturist, winegrower.

vinicultura, *s.f.* viniculture, viticulture.

vinífero, *adj.* viniferous, wine-producing.

vinificação, *s.f.* wine-making, vinification.

vinificar, *s.f.* to convert into wine.

vinolência, *s.f.* drunkenness, intoxication.

vinolento, *adj.* drunk, intoxicated.

vinosidade, *s.f.* vinosity.

vinoso, *adj.* vinous, winy.

vintavo, *s.m.* a twentieth.

vinte, *num.* twenty; *acertar no vinte,* to guess right.

vintém, *s.m.* ancient Portuguese coin; *não ter vintém,* not to have a penny.

vintena, *s.f.* score.

viola, *s.f.* guitar.

violabilidade, *s.f.* violability.

violação, *s.f.* violation; infringement, trangression; profanation; rape.

violáceo, *adj.* violaceous, violet.

violador, *s.m.* violator; raper; *adj.* violative.

violão, *s.m.* French guitar.

violar, *v.t.* to violate; to break; to trangress, to infringe; to encroach upon, to trespass upon; to profane; to ravish; to rape.

violável, *adj.* violable.

violeiro, *s.m.* guitar-maker.

violência, *s.f.* violence; impetuosity, rage, fierceness, fury; coercion.

violentador, *s.m.* ravisher; *adj.* forcing.

violentar, *v.t.* to force, to do violence to; to coerce; to violate; to break open; to ravish, to rape.

violento, *adj.* violent; brutal; wild, impetuous, furious, fierce, raging; passionate; brutal, rude.

violeta, *s.f.* violet.

violetista, *s.m.* e *s.f.* player of viola.

violinista, *s.m.* e *s.f.* violinist, fiddler.

violino, *s.f.* violin, fiddle.

violoncelista, *s.m.* e *s.f.* cellist, cello player.

violoncelo, *s.m.* violoncello, cello.

violonista, *s.f.* e *s.m.* guitar player.

viperina, *s.f.* viper's bugloss, blue weed.

viperino, *adj.* viperine, venomous; malignant, caustic; viperous.

vir, *v.i.* to come; to proceed from; to arrive; to happen; to come back; to return; to reach; to take place; to result; to grow. 1) *vir a saber,* to find out. 2) *vir a ser,* to become; to amount to. 3) *vir ao mundo,* to be born. 4) *mandar vir,* to order, to send for. 5) *vir a si,* to recover consciousness. 6) *vir a público,* to become known.

vira, *s.f.* welt *(de sapato);* Portuguese popular song.

viração, *s.f.* breeze, sea-breeze, fresh wind.

vira-casaca, *s.m.* e *s.f.* turncoat, weather-cock.

vira-cu, *s.m.* somersault.

viradela, *s.f.* turning, turn.

virador, *s.m.* bow rope, tow cable.

viragem, *s.f.* turning, change of direction; *(fot.)* toning, toning bath.

virente, *adj.* verdant, viridescent, green; flourishing.

virgem, *s.f.* virgin; maiden; *adj.* virgin, maiden, pure, chaste; intact, untouched; unused, untried; *A Virgem,* The Blessed Virgin, The Virgin Mary.

virginal, *adj.* virginal; maiden; maidenly.

virgindade, *s.f.* virginity, maidenhood.

virgíneo, *adj. o mesmo que "virginal".*

vírgula, *s.f.* comma; *ponto e vírgula:* semicolon.

virgulação, *s.f.* the inserting of commas.

virgular, *v.t.* to insert commas.

viridente, *adj.* viridescent, greenish.

viril, *adj.* manly, virile, masculine; vigorous, strong; *idade viril,* manhood.

virilha, *s.f.* groin.

virilidade, *s.f.* virility, manhood; vigour, energy.

virilizar, *v.t.* to strengthen, to invigorate, to fartify.

virilmente, *adv.* in a manly manner.

viripotente, *adj.* strong, robust; manly.

virola, *s.f.* ferrule.

virote, *s.m.* short arrow.

virose, *s.f.* virus disease.

virtual, *adj.* virtual; potential, possible; apparent.

virtualidade, *s.f.* virtuality.

virtude, *s.f.* virtue; uprightness, probity; saintliness; chastity; merit, worth; porperty; efficacy, potency; *em virtude de,* by virtue of, owing to, as a result of.

virtuosidade, *s.f.* virtuousness, virtuosity.

virtuoso, *adj.* virtuous; chaste; honest, exemplary, upright; *s.m.* virtuoso, artist.

virulência, *s.f.* virulence; malignancy, acrimony.

virulento, *adj.* virulent; acrimonious, malignant; poisonous, noxious.

vírus, *s.m.* virus; poison, venom.

visagem, *s.f.* grimace.

visão, *s.f.* vision, sight, eyesight; seeing, view; vision, apparition, shadow.

visar, *v.t.* to aim at; to sight; to visa *(documentos);* to have in view; to certify *(um cheque).*

víscera, *s.f.* visceral organ; *s.f. pl.* viscera; entretails.

visceral, *adj.* visceral.

visceralmente, *adv.* deeply; essentially.

víscido, *adj. o mesmo que "viscoso".*

visco, *s.m.* birdlime *(para apanhar pássaros);* mistletoe *(planta).*

viscondado, *s.m.* viscounty, viscountcy, viscountship.

visconde, *s.f.* viscount.

viscondessa, *s.f.* viscountess.

viscose, *s.f.* viscose.

viscosidade, *s.f.* viscosity; stickiness.

viscoso, *adj.* viscous; viscid; sticky; slimy.

viseira, *s.f.* vidor.

visgo, *s.m. o mesmo que "visco".*

visguento, *adj.* o mesmo que "viscoso".

visibilidade, *s.f.* visibility, perceptibility.

visigodo, *s.m.* Visigoth.

visigótico, *adj.* visigothic.

visionar, *v.t.* to vision; to fancy; to think of, to imagine, to dream.

visionário, *s.m.* visionary, dreamer, idealist, utopian.

visita, *s.f.* visit, call; visitor, caller; guest. 1) *visita de cerimónia,* formal call. 2) *visita de médico,* hurried call. 3) *de visita,* on a visit. 4) *fazer uma visita,* to pay a call. 5) *ter visitas,* to have guests, to have company.

visitação, *s.f.* visitation, visiting.

visitador, *s.m.* visitor, visitant, caller; *adj.* visiting.

visitante, *s.m. e s.f.* visitor, caller, guest; visitant; *adj.* visiting.

visitar, *v.t.* to visit, to call on, to go to see.

visível, *adj.* visible; perceptible, noticeable; discernible; in view; evident manifest.

vislumbrar, *v.t.* to glimpse, to catch a glimpse of, to descry, to see in the distance; to guess at; *v.i.* to glimmer; to emerge, to peep out.

vislumbre, *s.m.* glimmer, gleam; shadow, ghost, appearance; hint, conjecture.

viso, *s.m.* sight; countenance; glimmer; sign; top, summit *(cume).*

visinha, *s.f.* phantom, frightful view.

visor, *s.m. (fot.)* view finder; sight-hole.

vispar-se, *v.refl.* to run away.

vista, *s.f.* sight, vision, eyesight; seeing; the eyes; range of vision; view, outlook; scene. 1) *vista,* aspect; conception; point of view; *s.f. pl.* views intentions, designs, plans. 2) *vista curta,* myopia, nearsightedness, shortsightedness; *vista cansada:* presbyopia. 3) *vista desarmada,* naked eye. 4) *à vista,* in sight, in view; at sight *(comercial).* 5) *à vista de,* in view of, in the presence of. 6) *à vista disso,* in view of that, therefore. 7) *a perder de vista,* as far as the eye can see. 8) *à primeira vista,* at first sight. 9) *até à vista,* I´ll be seeing you, so long. 10) *com vista a,* with the purpose of. 11) *conhecer de vista,* to know by sight. 12) *dar nas vistas,* to be conspicuous, to attract attention. 13) *dar uma vista de olhos,* to glance (something) over. 14) *ter em vista,* to have in mind. 15) *fazer vista grossa,* to overlook. 16) *perder de vista,* to losesight (track) of. 17) *pôr à vista,* to expose, to view, to display, to make visible. 18) *ter vista para*

o mar. 19) to look on to the sea. 20) *aparecer à vista,* to come in sight.

vistão, *s.m. fazer um vistão,* to cut a good figure.

visto, *adj.* seen; *visto que:* seeing that, since, as, considering that; *está visto que:* of course; *s.m.* visa *(em passaporte);* O.K. *(em outros documentos).*

vistoria, *s.f.* inspection, survey.

vistoriar, *v.t.* to inspect; to survey.

vistoso, *adj.* showy, ostentatious; eye-catching; gaudy, flashy; gay, spruce, good-looking.

visual, *adj.* visual.

visualidade, *s.f.* visuality, visibleness; mirage.

visualização, *s.f.* visualization.

visualizar, *v.t.* to visualize.

visualmente, *adv.* visually.

vital, *adj.* vital, essential, indispensable.

vitalício, *adj.* for life, lifelong, life.

vitalidade, *s.f.* vitality; vigour.

vitalismo, *s.m.* vitalism.

vitalista, *s.m. e s.f.* vitalist; *adj.* vitalistic.

vitalização, *s.f.* vitalization.

vitalizador, *adj.* vitalizing.

vitalizar, *v.t.* to vitalize, to put life into; to vivify.

vitamina, *s.f.* vitamin, vitamine.

vitaminar, *v.t.* to give vitamines to.

vitela, *s.f.* heifer; veal *(carne);* calf *(couro).*

vitelino, *adj.* viteline; yolk.

vitelo, *s.m.* calf; *(biol.)* vitellus, yolk.

vitícola, *adj.* viticultural; *s.m. e s.f.* viticulturist, grape-grower.

viticultor, *s.m.* wine-grower, viticulturist.

viticultura, *s.f.* wine-growing, viticulture.

vítima, *s.f.* victim; prey.

vitimar, *v.t.* to victimize; to kill; to cause losses.

vitivinícola, *adj.* winegrowing.

vitivinicultor, *s.m.* winegrower.

vitória, *s.f.* victory; triumph; sucess; conquest.

vitoriano, *s. e adj.* Victorian.

vitoriar, *v.t.* to applaud; to cheer, to acclaim.

vitorioso, *adj.* victorious, triumphant; successful.

vitral, *s.m.* stained glass window.

vítreo, *adj.* vitreous, glassy; transparent.

vitrificação, *s.f.* vitrification.

vitrificar, *v.t.* to vitrify, to convert into glass.

vitrificável, *adj.* vitrifiable.

vitrina, *s.f.* shop-window; showcase.

vitrinista, *s.m.* e *s.f.* window dresser.

vitriolado, *adj.* vitriolated.

vitriólico, *adj.* vitriolic.

vitriolização, *s.f.* vitriolization.

vitriolizar, *v.t.* to vitriolize.

vitríolo, *s.m.* vitriol.

vitualhar, *v.t.* to victual, to supply with provisions.

vitualhas, *s.f. pl.* victuals; provisions, food.

vítulo, *s.m.* calf; seal.

vituperação, *s.f.* vituperation, injury; upbraiding, severe reproach.

vituperador, *adj.* vituperative; *s.m.* vituperator, abuser, insulter.

vituperar, *v.t.* to vituperate; to reprimand; to abuse; to slander; to insult.

vituperativo, *adj.* vituperative.

vituperável, *adj.* vituperable.

vitupério, *s.m.* vituperation; shame, ignominy, infamy; abuse.

viúva, *s.f.* widow.

viuvez, *s.f.* widowhood.

viúvo, *s.m.* widower.

viva, *s.f.* cheer; *interj.* hurra, hurray.

vivacidade, *s.f.* vivacity, vivaciousness; liveliness; sprightliness; buoyancy; alacrity; animation.

vivandeira, *s.f.* vivandiere.

vivandeiro, *s.m.* sutler, canteen man.

vivaz, *adj.* vivacious; lively, animated; *(bot.)* perennial.

viveirista, *s.m.* e *s.f.* owner of a nursery (of trees, fish, flowers, etc.).

viveiro, *s.m.* vivarium, aviary; hatchery *(de peixes);* warren *(de coelhos, etc.)* nursery, hotbed.

vivência, *s.f.* living, way of life.

vivenda, *s.f.* dwelling house, villa, country house, cottage.

vivente, *adj.* alive, living; *s.m.* e *s.f.* mortal, human being.

viver, *v.i.* to live; to be alive; to exist; to subsist, to survive.

víveres, *s.m. pl.* provisions, food, victuals.

vividez, *s.f.* vividness.

vivido, *adj.* experienced (in life).

vívido, *adj.* vivid; bright; lively.

vivificação, *s.f.* vivification.

vivificador, *adj.* vivifying, enlivening; *s.m.* vivifier.

vivificante, *adj.* vivifying, life-giving.

vivificar, *v.t.* to vivify, to animate, to enliven, to revive; to encourage.

vivífico, *adj.* vivifying, vitalizing, life-giving.

viviparidade, *s.f.* viviparity.

vivíparo, *adj.* viviparous.

vivisecção, *s.f.* vivisection.

vivo, *adj.* alive, live, living, animated; active, lively, brisk; bright, vivid; ardent; sharp, intense; *s.m.* piping *(em costura).* 1) *ao vivo,* to the life; alive. 2) *os vivos,* the living.

vivório, *s.m.* cheers, shouts, hurrahs.

vizinhança, *s.f.* vicinity, neighbourhood; nearness, proximity, surroundings; the neighbours.

vizinhar, *v.i.* to neighbour; to come near, to approach, to be near to.

vizinho, *s.m.* neighbour; *adj.* vicinal, bordering, adjoining.

vizir, *s.m.* vizier.

voadoiros, *s.m. pl.* wing feather, remiges.

voador, *adj.* flying; *s.m.* flyer, filer; acrobat; *disco voador,* flying saucer.

voagem, *s.f.* chaff.

voante, *adj.* speedy, fleeting, swift.

voar, *v.i.* to fly; to soar; to flee, to run away; to hurry; to pass quickly *(o tempo).*

vocabular, *adj.* relating to a vocabulary, vocabular.

vocabulário, *s.m.* vocabulary.

vocabularista, vocabulista, *s.m.* e *s.f.* compiler of a vocabulary.

vocábulo, *s.m.* vocable, word, term.

vocação, *s.f.* vocation, calling; inclination; talent (for something).

vocacional, *adj.* vocational.

vocal, *adj.* vocal.

vocálico, *adj.* vocalic.

vocalismo, *s.m.* vocalism.

vocalista, *s.m.* e *s.f.* vocalist, singer.

vocalização, *s.f.* vocalization.

vocalizador, *adj.* vocalizing; *s.m.* vocalizer.

vocalizar, *v.t.* to vocalize; to vowelize.

vocalizo, *s.m.* vocalise, vocalization.

vocativo, *s.m.* vocative *(caso).*

você, *pron. pes.* you.

vociferação, *s.f.* vociferation, shout, outcry.

vociferador, *adj.* vociferous; *s.m.* vociferator.

vociferante, *adj.* vociferant.

vociferar, *s.m.* e *v.i.* to vociferate, to baw, to shout, to cry.

voejar, *v.i.* to flutter; to flicker, to flit; to hover.

voejo, *s.m.* fluttering, flitting.

voga, *s.f.* vogue; fashion; currency; usage; stroke *(remador); estar em voga,* to be in vogue; to be current; to be in great request.

vogal, s.f. (fon.) vowel; s.m. e s.f. voter, member of a board; adj. vocal.

vogante, adj. rowing, sailing, floating.

vogar, v.i. to row; to sail; to float, to glide; to drift; to circulate; to be in vogue.

volante, s.m. fly-wheel (roda reguladora); steering wheel (de direcção); racing driver (automobilista); adj. flying; mobile.

volantim, s.m. rope-dancer, wire-dancer, acrobat.

volataria, s.f. hawking, falconry.

volatear, v.i. to flutter, to flap.

volátil, adj. volatile; fickle, changeable (vilúvel).

volatilidade, s.f. volatility.

volatilização, s.f. volatilization.

volatilizador, s.m. volatilizer.

volatilizar, v.t. to volatilize; to cause to evaporate; volatilizar-se, to evaporate.

volatilizável, adj. volatilizable.

voleibol, s.m. volleyball.

volfrâmio, s.m. wolfram, tungsten.

volframite, s.f. wolframite.

volição, s.f. volition; will.

volitante, adj. fluttering, volitant, flying, flickering; hovering.

volitar, v.i. to flutter, to flap, to flicker.

volitivo, adj. volitive.

volt, s.m. volt.

volta, s.f. turn; turning, revolution; bend; curve; winding, meander; coil; loop; twist; circuit; walk, stroll; detour; return; way back; recurrence, repetition; retort (réplica). 1) volta e meia, every now and then. 2) às voltas com, busy with. 3) dar volta, to turn back. 4) dar volta a, to turn (something) round; to go round (something). 5) dar volta ao juízo, to go crazy. 6) dar uma volta, to go for a stroll, to go for a walk. 7) de volta, back. 8) em volta, around. 9) em volta de, around. 10) levar de volta, to take back. 11) trazer de volta, to bring back. 12) na volta do correio, by return mail. 13) por volta de, around, about.

voltado, adj. turned. 1) voltado para, facing. 2) estar voltado para, to face.

voltagem, s.f. voltage; potential.

voltaico, adj. voltaic.

voltâmetro, s.m. voltameter.

voltar, v.t. to turn; to direct; to turn over (uma página); to return, to give back, to restore; v.i. to return; to go (come, get) back; to revert; to recur; to reappear. 1) voltar a fazer alguma coisa, to do something again.

2) voltar a si, to recover, to come to oneself, to come to life. 3) voltar atrás, to turn back; to change one's mind, to go back on one's word. 4) voltar para junto de, to rejoin. 5) voltar-se, to turn, to turn round, to turn back; to turn over; to resort, to have recourse to; to fall back (on).

voltarete, s.m. omber.

volteador, adj. whirling; s.m. vaulter, rope-dancer.

volteadura, s.f. vaulting; turning, rotating.

voltear, v.i. to turn round, to whirl, to revolve; to fly about in circles; to vault.

volteio, s.m. swing; whirl; vaulting.

volteiro, adj. fluttering; unsteady, changeable, unstable.

voltímetro, s.m. voltmeter.

volubilidade, s.f. volubility, inconstance, fickleness.

volume, s.m. volume (também de som); bulk; mass; tome, book; packet, parcel.

volumétrico, adj. volumetric, volumetrical.

volumoso, adj. voluminous, large, bulky; big, massive; loud.

voluntariado, s.m. volunteering; volunteers.

voluntariamente, adv. willingly, voluntarily.

voluntariedade, s.f. voluntariness; spontaneity.

voluntário, adj. voluntary, willing; free; spontaneous; s.m. volunteer.

voluntariosidade, s.f. willfulness; capriciousness.

voluntarioso, adj. willful, self-willed, headstrong; obstinate; capricious.

voluntarismo, s.m. voluntarism.

volúpia, s.f. voluptuousness; pleasure, delight.

voluptuosamente, adv. voluptuously, sensually.

voluptuosidade, s.f. voluptuousness, pleasure.

voluptuoso, adj. voluptuous; sensual, luxurious.

voluta, s.f. volute, spiral, scroll (também em arquitectura); (zool.) spiral shell.

volutear, v.i. to turn, to rotate, to circle.

volúvel, adj. inconstant, changeable, fickle, unstable, unreliable.

volva, s.f. volva.

volváceo, adj. volvate.

volver, v.t. to turn; to turn over; to turn round;

to roll, to toss; to return, to take back (to a place, etc.); *v.i.* to return, to go or to come back; to reply; to pass by *(o tempo)*; *direita, volver!*, right, turn!

volvido, *adj.* passed.

volvo, *s.m.* volvulus.

vómer, *s.m.* vomer.

vomeriano, *adj.* vomerine.

vomição, *s.f.* vomiting, spew, puke; matter vomited.

vomitado, *s.m. o mesmo que "vomição".*

vomitar, *v.t.* to vomit, to spew; to throw up.

vomitivo, *adj. e s.m.* emetic, vomitory.

vómito, *s.m.* vomit; vomiting.

vomitório, *s.m. e adj. o mesmo que "vomitivo".*

vontade, *s.f.* will; wish; desire; mind, intention. 1) *à vontade,* at will; at discretion, at pleasure; at ease. 2) *à vontade de,* at the will of. 3) *boa vontade,* good will. 4) *com vontade,* resolutely, with a will. 5) *com vontade ou sem ela,* willy-nilly. 6) *contra a vontade de,* against one`s will, unwillingly. 7) *de boa vontade,* willingly, readily. 8) *de má vontade,* relutantly. 9) *esteja à vontade,* make yourself comfortable, make yourself at home. 10) *fazer a vontade de,* to comply with the wish of. 11) *má vontade,* ill will. 12) *ter vontade de,* to want to, to feel like doing something.

voo, *s.m.* flight; flying; soaring; *levantar voo:* to take off *(avião).*

voracidade, *s.f.* voracity, voraciousness, greediness, ravenousness.

voragem, *s.f.* vortex, whirlpool; abyss.

voraginoso, *adj.* voraginous, gulfy.

voraz, *adj.* voracious, greedy, ravenous, rapacious.

vórtice, *s.m. o mesmo que "voragem".*

vos, *pron.* you; to you.

vós, *pron.* you.

vosso, *adj.* your; *pron.* yours.

votação, *s.f.* voting, suffrage; votes, ballot, poll.

votante, *s.m. e s.f.* voter; *adj.* voting.

votar, *v.t.* to approve *(uma lei);* to vow; to commend; to award, to grant; *v.i.* to vote (for a candidate; in favour of a measure, etc.); *votar-se,* to devote oneself to.

votivo, *adj.* votive.

voto, *s.m.* vote; ballot, suffrage; vow, solemn promise; oath; sincere wish. 1) *fazer votos por,* to hope that. 2) *fazer voto de,* to be

under the vow. 3) *com os melhores votos de felicidade,* with best wishes.

vovô, *s.m.* grandpapa, grandpa.

vovó, *s.f.* grandmama, grandma.

voz, *s.f.* voice; speech; tone, expression; word, language. 1) *de viva voz,* verbally. 2) *em voz alta,* aloud, in a loud voice. 3) *em voz baixa,* in a low tone, undertone. 4) *dar voz de prisão,* to arrest, to place someone under arrest.

vozeador, *s.m.* bawler, squaller; *adj.* bawling, hallooing.

vozear, *v.i.* to bawl, to halloo; to cry out, to shout; *s.m.* bawl, cry, clamor.

vozearia, *s.f.* outcry, bawling, uproar, hubbub, clamour.

vozeirão, *s.m.* thundering voice, strong voice.

vozeiro, *adj.* talkative.

vulcânio, *adj.* Vulcanian.

vulcanicidade, *s.f.* volcanicity.

vulcânico, *adj.* volcanic; *(fig.)* violent, impetuous.

vulcaniforme, *adj.* like a volcano.

vulcanismo, *s.m.* volcanism.

vulcanista, *s.m. e s.f.* volcanist.

vulcanite, *s.f.* vulcanite; ebonite.

vulcanização, *s.f.* vulcanization.

vulcanizador, *s.m.* vulcanizer; vulcanizing-machine.

vulcanizar, *v.t.* to vulcanize.

vulcanologia, *s.f.* volcanology.

vulcanologista, *s.f. e s.m.* volcanologist.

vulcão, *s.m.* volcano.

vulgacho, *s.m.* populace, mob, rabble.

vulgar, *adj.* vulgar, ordinary, common; coarse; banal, trivial; *s.m.* the vernacular.

vulgaridade, *s.f.* vulgarity, triviality, banality; coarseness.

vulgarismo, *s.m.* vulgarism, vulgarity.

vulgarização, *s.f.* vulgarization.

vulgarizar, *v.t.* to vulgarize, to make well known; *vulgarizar-se,* to become vulgar or well known.

Vulgata, Vulgata.

vulgo, *s.m.* the vulgar, the common people, the multitude; *adv.* commonly, ordinarily.

vulnerabilidade, *s.f.* vulnerability.

vulneração, *s.f.* wounding.

vulnerador, vulnerante, *adj.* hurting, wounding.

vulnerar, *v.t.* to wound; to offend; to hurt.

vulnerável, *adj.* vulnerable; weak; open to attack.

vulpino, *adj.* vulpine, crafty, foxy, cunning.

vulto, *s.m.* face; appearance; figure, form, shape; shadow; indistinct shape; bulk, size, dimensions; importance, important person. 1) *de vulto,* important, substantial. 2) *tomar vulto,* to grow in size, to increase, to mount, to take shape.

vultoso, *adj.* bulky; large, important.

vultuosidade, *s.f.* congestion of the face; size.

vultuoso, *adj.* attacked by a congestion; voluminous, important.

vulturino, *adj.* vulturine; vulturous.

vulva, *s.f.* vulva.

vulvar, *adj.* vulvar.

vulvite, *s.f.* vulvitis.

vurmo, *s.m.* pus.

vurmoso, *adj.* purulent.

X

x, the twenty-second letter of the Portuguese alphabet.

xá, *s.m.* shah.

xabraque, *s.m.* shabrock.

xácara, *s.f.* romance; ballad.

xadrez, *s.m.* chess *(jogo);* checkered cloth, plaid cloth *(tecido);* checkered pattern, checker *(padrão); (pop.)* jail *(prisão).*

xadrezado, *adj.* checkered.

xadrezista, *s.m. e s.f.* chesser, chess player.

xaile, *s.m.* o mesmo que "xale".

xaimel, *s.m.* timber work, frame work.

xairel, *s.m.* saddle-cloth, horse-cloth.

xale, *s.m.* shawl.

xântico, *adj.* xanthic, yellow.

xantia, *s.f.* xanthine.

xântio, *s.m.* xanthium, cocklebur.

xantofila, *s.f.* xanthophyll.

xantogénico, *adj.* xanthogenic.

xantoma, *s.m.* xanthoma.

xantopsia, *s.f.* xanthopsia.

xaque, *s.m.* check.

xaquear, *v.t.* to check.

xara, *s.f.* wooden-arrow; *(bot.)* rock-rose.

xaroco, *s.m.* sirocco.

xaropada, *s.f.* cough syrup. boring conversation or speech.

xarope, *s.m.* syrup.

xaroposo, *adj.* syrupy.

xarroco, *s.m.* a fish.

xaveco, *s.m.* xebec *(barco do Mediterrâneo);* old boat.

xelim, *s.m.* shilling.

xenofilia, *s.f.* xenophilism; fond of foreigners.

xenófilo, *adj.* xenophile.

xenofobia, *s.f.* xenofobismo, *s.m.* xenophobia.

xenófobo, *s.m.* xenophobe.

xenografia, *s.f.* xenography.

xenógrafo, *s.m.* xenographer.

xenomania, *s.f.* xenomania.

xeque, *s.m.* check *(no xadrez);* sheik *(chefe árabe).* 1) *em xeque,* in check, in danger, at bay. 2) *pôr em xeque,* to put in check, to endanger.

xeque-mate, *s.m.* checkmate.

xerez, *s.m.* sherry.

xerifado, *s.m.* sheriffdom.

xerife, *s.m.* sheriff.

xerofagia, *s.f.* xerophagy.

xerófago, *s.m.* one who professes xerophagy.

xerofilia, *s.f.* xerophily.

xerófilo, *adj.* xerophilous.

xerófita, *s.f.* xerophyte.

xeroftalmia, *s.f.* xerophthalmia.

xeroftálmico, *adj.* xerophthalmic.

xícara, *s.f.* cup, tea-cup, coffee-cup.

xifóide, *adj.* xiphoid.
xilofagia, *s.f.* eating of wood.
xilófago, *adj.* xylophagous.
xilófilo, *adj.* xylophiloud.
xilofone, *s.m.* xylophone.
xilofonista, *s.m.* e *s.f.* xylophonist.
xilografia, *s.f.* xilography, wood carving.
xilógrafo, *s.m.* xylographer.
xilogravura, *s.f.* xilograph; woodcut.
xiloide, *adj.* xyloid; woody.
xiloidina, *s.f.* xyloidin.

xilologia, *s.f.* xylology.
xintoísmo, *s.m.* Shintoism.
xintoísta, *s.m.* e *s.f.* e *adj.* Shintoist.
xístico, *adj.* schistose.
xisto, *s.m.* schist.
xistóide, *adj.* schistoid.
xistosidade, *s.f.* foliation, schistosity.
xistoso, *adj.* schistous.
xofrango, *s.m.* small eagle.
xucro, *adj.* wild, savage, untamed; unbroken *(cavalo);* rax, unskilled, clumsy *(inexperiente).*

Z

z, the twenty-third letter of the Portuguese alphabet
zabumba, *s.m.* bass drum.
zabumbar, *v.t.* to deafen; to beat a bass drum; to spread *(notícias).*
zagaia, *s.f.* assagai, assegai.
zagaiada, *s.f.* wound made by an assagai.
zagal, *s.m.* shepherd, herdsman.
zagala, *s.f.* shepherdess.
zagalote, *s.m.* small bullet.
zaguncho, *s.m.* spear, light spear; dart, javelin.
zaivo, *adj.* squint-eyed, cross-eyed; knock-kneed.
zaino, *adj.* dark, chestnut *(cavalo).*
zambaio, *s.m.* squint; one-eyed.
zambro, *adj.* bandy-legged, bow-legged.
zambujal, *s.m.* wild olive grove.
zambujeiro, *s.m.* wild olive oleaster.
zambulho, *s.m.* wild olive.
zanaga, *adj.* squint-eyed, cross-eyed, one-eyed.
zanga, *s.f.* anger, rage; aversion, dislike; quarrel, tiff.
zangado, *adj.* angry, choleric, exasperated, out of temper, mad.

zângano, *s.m.* parasite; money-jobber; jester.
zângão, *s.m.* drone.
zangar, *v.t.* to anger, to irritate, to annoy; *zangar-se:* to get angry.
zangalhão, *s.m.* ill-shaped fellow.
zangarelho, *s.m.* dragnet, casting net.
zangarrear, *v.t.* e *v.i.* to thrum, to strum, to twang.
zangarreio, *s.m.* strumming.
zanzibarita, *s.m.* e *s.f.* Zanzibari.
zarabatana, *s.f.* blow-pipe, blowgun.
zaragata, *s.f.* disorder, riot, uproar, turmoil, hubbub, bustle.
zaragatear, *v.i.* to quarrel.
zaragateiro, *s.m.* rioter, bustler; *adj.* tumultuous, turbulent.
zaragatoa, *s.f.* swab.
zaranza, *s.f.* e *s.m.* bungler, scatter-brained person; *adj.* scatter-brained.
zaranzar, *v.i.* to loiter, to loaf.
zarcão, *s.m.* red-lead; minium.
zarco, *adj.* light-blue-eyed.
zarelha, *s.f.* busy-body, meddlesome woman.
zarelhar, *v.i.* to meddle; to intrigue, to meddle with.

zarelho, *s.m.* busy-body, meddler; scatter-brain.

zarolho, *adj.* one-eyed; squint-eyed, cross-eyed.

zarpar, *v.t.* e *v.i.* to weigh anchor; to make sail; to sail (for a place).

zarro, *s.m.* headline.

zarzuela, *s.f.* zarzuela.

zás!, *interj.* bang! pop! smack!

zebo, *s.m.* Indian ox.

zebra, *s.f.* zebra.

zebrado, *adj.* striped.

zebrar, *v.t.* to stripe.

zebrino, *adj.* zebrine.

zebu, *s.m.* zebu, the humped Indian ox or cow.

zedoária, *s.f.* zedoary.

zefir, *s.m.* zephyr, zephyr cloth.

zéfiro, *s.m.* zephyr, breeze, West wind, gentle breeze.

zelar, *v.t.* to watch over, to take care, to treat carefully.

zelo, *s.m.* zeal, care, solicitude; caution; devotion; ardour, fervency.

zeloso, *adj.* zealous, careful, solicitous, diligent; watchful, dedicated.

zenital, *adj.* zenithal.

zénite, *s.m.* zenith, culmination, top, summit.

zepelim, *s.m.* zeppelin.

zé-povinho, *s.m.* the people.

zerbo, *s.m.* epiploon.

zero, *s.m.* zero; nothing; nil; nought.

zetacismo, *s.m.* zetacism.

zeugma, zeugma.

zibelina, *s.f.* sable.

zigoma, *s.m.* zygoma, cheekbone.

zigoto, *s.m.* zygote.

ziguezague, *s.m.* zigzag.

ziguezagueante, *adj.* zigzagging.

ziguezaguear, *v.i.* to zigzag; to meander.

zimbório, *s.m.* cupola, dome.

zimbrada, *s.f.* lashing, flogging; rolling, rocking.

zimbral, *s.m.* juniper-grove.

zimbro, *s.m.* juniper.

zímico, *adj.* zymic, zymotic.

zimogenia, *s.f.* zymogenesis.

zimogénico, *adj.* zymogenic.

zimologia, *s.f.* zymology.

zimológico, *adj.* zymological.

zimoscópio, *s.m.* zymoscope.

zimose, *s.f.* zymosis, fermentation.

zimótico, *adj.* zymotic.

zinabre, *s.m.* verdigris.

zincagem, *s.f.* zinc-coating, galvanization.

zincar, *v.t.* to coat with zinc, to zincify.

zinco, *s.m.* zinc.

zincografar, *v.t.* to zincograph.

zincografia, *s.f.* zincography.

zincogravador, *s.m.* zincographer.

zincogravura, *s.f.* zincography.

zingamocho, *s.m.* weathercock; top, summit.

zingar, *v.i.* to scull (um barco).

zingarear, *v.i.* to wander, to roam, to rove.

zíngaro, *s.m.* zingaro, gipsy.

zingração, *s.f.* mockery, derision, scoffing.

zingrar, *v.t.* to mock, to scoff, to deride, to jest; to disdain.

zínia, *s.f.* zinnia.

zirbo, *s.m.* zpiploon (anat.).

zircão, *s.m.* zircon.

zircónio, *s.m.* zirconium.

zirro, *s.m.* sea-swallow, swift.

zizânia, *s.f.* zizania; discord.

zoada, *s.f.* humming, buzzing.

zoadeira, *s.f.* hum, buzz.

zoar, *v.i.* to hum, to buzz, to whiz.

zodiacal, *adj.* zodiacal.

zodíaco, *s.m.* zodiac.

zoeira, *s.f.* whiz, buzz, hum.

zoilo, *s.m.* severe critic, bitter critic.

zoina, *adj.* giddy, dizzy, harebrained.

zombador, *adj.* mocking, sneering, scoffing; *s.m.* mocker.

zombar, *v.i.* to mock, to scoff, to jeer, to sneer; to joke, to jest; to deride; to make jokes; zombar de, to make fun of, to laugh at.

zombaria, *s.f.* derision, mockery, scoffing, derision.

zombetear, *v.i.* o mesmo que "zombar".

zombeteiro, *adj.* o mesmo que "zombador".

zona, *s.f.* zone, area, region; (med.) shingles.

zonal, *adj.* zonal.

zonchadura, *s.f.* pumping.

zonchar, *v.i.* to pump.

zoncho, *s.m.* pump, handle and lever.

zonzo, *adj.* dizzy, giddy.

zobiologia, *s.f.* zoology.

zoófago, *s.m.* zoophagan; *adj.* zoophagous, carnivorous.

zoofilia, *s.f.* zoophilia.

zoófilo, *adj.* zoophilous; *s.m.* zoophilist.

zoófito, *s.m.* zoophyte.

zoofobia, *s.f.* zoophobia.

zoogenia, *s.f.* zoogeny.

zoogeografia, *s.f.* zoogeography.

zoografia, *s.f.* zoography, descriptive zoology.

zoográfico, *adj.* zoographical.

zoógrafo, *s.m.* zoographer.

zoóide, *adj.* zooidal.

zoólatra, *adj.* zoolatrous; *s.m.* e *s.f.* zoolater.

zoolatria, *s.f.* zoolatry, zootheism.

zoólito, *s.m.* zoolite, fossil animal.

zoologia, *s.f.* zoology.

zoológico, *adj.* zoological.

zoologista, *s.m.* e *s.f.* zoologist.

zoólogo, *s.m.* zoologist.

zoomagnético, *adj.* zoomagnetic.

zoomagnetismo, *s.m.* zoomagnetism.

zoomorfia, *s.f.* zoomorphysm.

zoomórfico, *adj.* zoomorphic.

zoomorfismo, *s.m.* zoomorphism.

zoonomia, *s.f.* zoonomy.

zooquímica, *s.f.* zoochemistry.

zooscopia, *s.f.* zooscopy.

zoosperma, *s.m.* zoosperm.

zootaxia, *s.f.* zootaxy.

zootecnia, *s.f.* zootechny, animal husbandry.

zootécnico, *adj.* zootechnic.

zooterapêutica, *s.f.* zootherapy.

zooterápico, *adj.* zootherapeutic, veterinary.

zootomia, *s.f.* zootomy, dissecation of animals.

zootómico, *adj.* zootomic.

zootomista, *s.m.* e *s.f.* zootomist.

zopo, *adj.* lame, sluggish, faltering; *s.m.* totterer, lazybones.

zorate, zorato, *adj.* lunatic, crazy.

zorra, *s.f.* old she fox; dray, sledge *(veículo).*

zorrague, *s.m.* scourge, whipp.

zorral, *s.m.* starling.

zorro, *s.m.* fox; *adj.* sly, cunning, crafty.

zoupeiro, *adj.* sluggish, shy.

zuavo, *s.m.* zouave.

zuca, *adj.* crazy.

zuído, *s.m.* humming, buzzing.

zulu, *s.m.* Zulu.

zumba! *interj.* bang!

zumbaia, *s.f.* profound bow; adulation.

zumbaiar, *v.t.* to bow; to flatter, to adulate.

zumbaieiro, *s.m.* flatterer.

zumbar, *v.i.* to whiz, to hum; to beat, to strike.

zumbido, *s.m.* humming, buzz, buzzing; whirring.

zumbido, *adj.* buzzing, humming.

zumbir, *v.i.* to buzz, to hum, to whir, to drone.

zumbo, *s.m.* buzzing; report, rumour.

zumbrir-se, *v.r.* to stoop, to curve, to bow down.

zunido, *s.m. o mesmo que* "zumbido".

zunir, *v.i.* to whistle, to hum, to buzz.

zunzum, *s.m.* rumour; hum; report.

zupar, *v.i.* to beat; to strike, to thrash.

zurrada, *s.f.* braying, heehaw.

zurrador, *adj.* braying.

zurrapa, *s.f.* cheap wine.

zurrar, *v.i.* to bray, to heehaw.

zurro, *s.m.* bray, braying.

zurvada, *s.f.* shower.

zurzidela, *s.f.* cudgelling, drubbing; lashing, whipping.

zurzidor, *adj.* beating, whipping; *s.m.* flogger, thrasher.

zurzir, *v.i.* to whip; to lash; to thrash, to drub, to strike; to chastise.

DICIONÁRIO
DE
INGLÊS-PORTUGUÊS

ABREVIATURAS UTILIZADAS

abrev.	abreviatura	*geom.*	geometria
adj.	adjectivo	*gír.*	gíria
aeron.	aeronáutica	*gram.*	gramática
agric.	agricultura	*her.*	heráldica
agrim.	agrimensura	*hist.*	história
amer.	americano	*igr.*	igreja
anat.	anatomia	*Ingl.*	Inglaterra
arc.	arcaico	*interj.*	interjeição
arit.	aritmética	*Irl.*	Irlanda
arq.	arquitectura	*joc.*	jocoso
arqueol.	arqueologia	*jur.*	jurídico
art.	artilharia	*liturg.*	liturgia
astrol.	astrologia	*lóg.*	lógica
astron.	astronomia	*magn.*	magnetismo
austral.	australiano	*máq.*	máquina
av.	aviação	*mar.*	marítimo
bibl.	bíblico	*med.*	medicina
bibliol.	bibliologia	*meteo.*	meteorologia
biol.	biologia	*mét.*	métrica
bioq.	bioquímica	*mil.*	militar
bot.	botânica	*miner.*	mineralogia
cal.	calão	*mús.*	música
cal. mil.	calão militar	*musc.*	muscular
cam. de fer.	caminho de ferro	*náut.*	náutica
catól.	católico	*nut.*	nutricionismo
cin.	cinema	*paleo.*	paleontologia
coloq.	coloquial	*pint.*	pintura
com.	comercial	*pl.*	plural
cul.	culinária	*poes.*	poesia
conj.	conjunção	*poét.*	poética
contr.	contracção	*pol.*	política
dep.	depreciativo	*pp.*	particípio passado
desp.	desporto	*prep.*	preposição
dial.	dialéctica	*pret.*	pretérito
ecles.	eclesiástico	*prov.*	provincianismo
econ.	economia	*quim.*	química
electr.	electricidade	*rád.*	rádio
esgr.	esgrima	*rel.*	religião
esp.	espanhol	*s.*	substantivo
fam.	familiar	*suf.*	sufixo
farm.	farmácia	*superl.*	superlativo
fig.	figurativo	*sup. abs.*	superlativo absoluto
filos.	filosofia	*teat.*	teatro
fís.	física	*tecel.*	tecelagem
fisiol.	fisiologia	*teol.*	teologia
for.	forense	*v. defect.*	verbo defectivo
fot.	fotografia	*v.i.*	verbo intransitivo
fr.	francês	*v.t.*	verbo transitivo
fut.	futebol	*vul.*	vulgar
geol.	geologia	*zool.*	zoologia

A

a, primeira letra do alfabeto.

aback, *adv.* atrás, detrás; *taken aback*, surpreendido.

abandon, *s.* à-vontade, naturalidade; despreocupação. *v.t.* abandonar, deixar; *to abandon oneself to*, entregar-se a.

abandoned, *adj.* abandonado; dissoluto, imoral.

abandonee, *s.* segurador (a quem são entregues os salvados de um navio).

abandoner, *s.* abandonador.

abandonment, *s.* abandono, desamparo.

abase, *v.t.* humilhar, rebaixar.

abasement, *s.* humilhação, degradação, desonra; abatimento, aviltamento.

abash, *v.t.* embaraçar, envergonhar, confundir.

abashement, *s.* vergonha, confusão, humilhação.

abate, *v.t., v.i.* abater, diminuir; amainar.

abatement, *s.* abatimento, diminuição, redução; atenuação.

abater, *s.* o que diminui, reduz ou faz abatimento; calmante.

abatis, *s.* trincheira de troncos pontiagudos.

abbaci (ies), *s.* dignidade e direitos de um abade; jurisdição abacial.

abbatial, abbatical, *adj.* abacial.

abbé, *s.* padre, sacerdote.

abbess, *s.* abadessa, superiora de um convento.

abbey, *s.* abadia, mosteiro.

abbot, *s.* abade.

abbotship, *s.* cargo de abade, dignidade de abade.

abbreviate, *v.t.* abreviar; encurtar; (mat.) redução.

abbreviation, *s.* abreviação, abreviamento; (mat.) redução.

abdicant, *adj.* e *s.* abdicante, renunciante.

abdicate, *v.t., v.i.* abdicar, renunciar.

abdication, *s.* renúncia, abdicação, demissão; denegação de paternidade.

abdomen, *s.* abdómen, ventre.

abdominous, *adj.* corpulento, barrigudo; do abdómen, abdominal.

abduct, *v.t.* raptar, sequestrar.

abducent, *adj.* abducente.

abduction, *s.* rapto, sequestro.

abductor, *s.* raptor. (musc.) abdutor.

abeam, *adv.* através (náut.) pelo través; *abeam of us*, pelo nosso través (fora do navio).

abed, *adv.* na cama.

abecedarian, *adj.* disposto alfabeticamente; elementar; ignorante. *s.* aprendiz das primeiras letras.

aberdevine, *s.* verdelhão.

aberrance, *s.* desvio, afastamento; lapso moral; deficiência mental.

aberrant, *adj.* aberrante, que se afasta do tipo considerado normal; com deficiências de ordem moral.

aberration, *s.* aberração; erro; anomalia; *to steal something on a moment of aberration*, roubar num momento de fraqueza.

abet, *v.t.* incitar, instigar, induzir.

abetment, *s.* incitamento; instigação, cumplicidade, apoio.

abetter, *s.* instigador, cúmplice.

abeyance, *s.* suspensão temporária; condição suspensiva; vacatura; falta de possuidor. 1) *to be in abeyance*, em suspensão. 2) *to fall into abeyance*, cair em desuso. *adj.* 3) *lands in abeyance*, bens jacentes.

abhor, *v.t.* odiar, detestar.

abhorrence, *s.* ódio, aversão, horror.

abhorrent, *adj.* em contradição com, incompatível com, contrário. 1) *abhorrent hateful (to a person)*, odioso, repugnante, detestável. 2) *his conduct id abhorrent from his principles*, o seu procedimento está em contradição com os seus princípios.

abhorrer, s. pessoa odienta.

abidance, s. (com in) continuação, residência; (com by) conformidade com.

abide, v.i. pas. e part. pas. de abode, habitar, residir; suportar, tolerar. 1) to abode by one's principles, manter-se fiel às suas convicções. 2) I can't abide that fellow, não posso suportar aquele camarada.

abiding, adj. permanente, duradoiro.

abidingly, adv. de maneira permanente, com duração.

abies, s. abeto.

abigail, s. dama de companhia.

ability, s. habilidade, capacidade, aptidão.

abiogenesis, s. abiogénese, geração espontânea.

abiogenetic, adj. abiogénico.

abiogenist, s. abiogenista.

abiogeneous, adj. produzido por geração espontânea.

abject, adj. vil, baixo.

abkjection, s. abjecção, vileza, baixeza (acto), aviltamento.

abjectness, s. abjecção, vileza, baixeza.

abjuration, s. abjuração.

abjure, v.t. abjurar, repudiar.

abjurer, s. apóstata; repudiante.

ablactation, s. desmame.

ablation, s. ablação.

ablative, s. e adj. ablativo; ablative case, caso ablativo.

ablaut, s. apofonia.

ablaze, adv. em chamas; excitado.

able, adj. apto, hábil, capaz. 1) to be able to, poder, saber. 2) able bodied, robusto, forte.

ablet, ablen, s. peixinho branco do rio.

ablings, ablins, adv. talvez, possivelmente.

abloom, adj., adv. em flor.

ablution, s. ablução; to perform one's ablutions, fazer as suas abluções.

ably, adv. habilmente, com talento.

abnegate, v.t. abnegar, denegar, recusar a si mesmo (alguma coisa), privar-se de, renunciar a.

abnegation, s. abnegação; renúncia; apostasia.

abnormal, adj. anormal, irregular.

abnormally, adv. anormalmente.

abnormality (oes), s. anormalidade.

abnormity (ies), s. monstruosidade; disformidade; irregularidade, anomalia, monstro, criatura ou coisa anormal.

aboard, adv. a bordo. 1) go aboard, embarcar. 2) all abord!, embarquem!. 3) close aboard, perto.

abode, pas., part. pas. de abide, s. residência, casa; to take up (make) one's abode, viver, morar.

aboil, adv. a ferver.

abolish, v.t. abolir, extinguir; revogar (uma lei).

abolishable, adj. abolível.

abolisher, s. abolidor, anulador.

abolishment, a. abolição.

abolition, s. abolição, extinção, revogação, abolição da escravatura dos negros.

abolitionism, s. abolicionismo.

abolitionist, s. abolicionista.

abominable, adj. abominável, odioso.

abominableness, s. qualidade de abominável.

abominate, adj. execrando, abominado; execrável.

abomination, s. abominação; to hold in abomination, odiar, abominar, ter horror.

aboriginal, adj. indígena; s. aborígene, indígena, natural.

aboriginally, adv. primitivamente; desde o princípio.

aborigines, s. pl. aborígenes, indígenas.

abort, v.i. abortar.

aborted, adj. abortado; atrofiado, rudimentar.

aborting, s. aborto.

abortion, s. aborto, aborto provocado, desenvolvimento deficiente; monstro; criatura mal conformada.

abortionist, s. abortadeira.

abortive, adj. abortivo; abortado, prematuro, que é mal sucedido; rudimentar. 1) abortive medicines, remédios abortivos. 2) abortive scheme, esquema que abortou. 3) abortive organ, órgão que não chegou a desenvolver-se completamente.

abortively, adv. abortativamente, prematuramente.

abortiveness, s. aborto; fracasso, estado abortivo.

abound, v.i. abundar. 1) to abound in (with), abundar em. 2) to abound in oil, abundar em depósitos de petróleo.

about, adv. ao redor, em volta; quase; por toda a parte, de um lado para outro; prep. em volta de; pronto a; a respeito de.

above, adv. acima; prep. sobre, por cima de; above all, principalmente.

above-board, *adv.* e *adj.* jogo franco; cartas na mesa.

above ground, *adv.* e *adj.* vivo.

abrade, *v.t.* raspar, desgastar, esfregar; irritar a pele, ferir a pele; (med.) tirar a camada superior dum tecido, desagregar-se.

abraham-man, *s.* falso pedinte, velhaco refinado; *to sham abraham,* fingir doença ou loucura.

abranchial, abranchiate, *adj.* desprovido de brânquias.

abrasion, *s.* desgaste; raspadura; (med.) abrasão.

abreast, *adv.* ombro a ombro, lado a lado; à altura de. (náut.) pelo través de. 1) *they walked two or three abreast; four abreast,* dois ou três da frente; quatro de frente. 2) *abreast with; abreast of the times,* acompanhado; a par dos tempos.

abridge, *v.t.* abreviar, resumir; *a lot of novels were abridged for school use,* muitos romances foram resumidos para fins escolares.

abridg(e)ment, *s.* diminuição, redução; restrição, abolição; epítome, compêndio. (mat.) simplificação.

abroach, *adv.* furado; aberto; furar (pipa) para deixar correr; em andamento. 1) *to set abroach,* abrir ou encetar (pipa, etc.). 2) *the subject was set abroach,* começou a estudar-se o assunto.

abroad, *adv.* largamente, em diferentes direcções; no estrangeiro.

abrogate, *v.t.* anular, revogar, abolir, ab-rogar.

abrogation, *s.* ab-rogação, revogação.

abrupt, *adj.* abrupto, brusco, repentino; escarpado; desconexo.

abruption, *s.* ruptura, separação brusca.

abruptly, *adv.* abruptamente, bruscamente.

abruptness, *s.* escarpamento, talude; brusquidão, falta de cerimónia.

abscess, *s.* abcesso.

absciss, abscissa, *s.* abcissa.

abscission, *s.* amputação, excisão.

abscond, *v.i.* desaparecer, esconder-se; subtrair-se a, escapar-se; safar-se; fugir à acção da justiça.

absconder, *s.* o que se esconde, fugitivo; contumaz.

absence, *s.* ausência; falta; descuido. 1) *absence of mind,* distracção. 2) *leave of absence, licença* (para ausentar-se).

absent, *adj.* ausente; descuidado; *absent-minded,* distraído; *v.t.* ausentar-se.

absentee, *s.* pessoa ausente, absentista, proprietário que não reside nas terras.

absenteeism, *s.* absentismo; acção de estar voluntariamente afastado (do seu posto, país, etc.).

absinth, *s.* absinto.

absinthian, *adj.* absinto, que lembra o absinto.

absolute, *adj.* absoluto; completo; arbitrário.

absolutely, *adv.* absolutamente, completamente, categoricamente.

absoluteness, *s.* poder ilimitado, qualidade de ser absoluto, independência; absolutismo.

absolution, *s.* absolvição, perdão.

absolutism, *s.* absolutismo.

absolutist, *s.* absolutista.

absolve, *v.t.* absolver; perdoar; isentar.

absonant, *adj.* discordante, contrário a; dissonante.

absorb, *v.t.* absorver, embeber; preocupar.

absorbable, *adj.* absorvível.

absorbant, *adj.* absorvente.

absorbed, *pp.* e *adj.* absorvido; absorto.

absorbefacient, *adj.* e *s.* reabsorvente.

absorbent, *adj.* absorvente; *s.* absorvente.

absorbing, *adj.* absorvente, cativante.

absorption, *s.* absorção; concentração.

absorptive, *adj.* absorvente.

absquatulate, *v.i.* (*from*) *to make off,* dar às de vila-diogo.

abstain, *v.i.* abster-se de, privar-se de.

abstainer, *s.* pessoa que se abstém (geralmente de bebidas alcoólicas); abstémio.

abstemious, *adj.* abstémio, sóbrio, frugal; moderado.

abstemiously, *adv.* sobriamente.

abstemiousness, *s.* sobriedade, temperança.

abstention, *s.* abstenção, abstinência; abstenção (de voto); (ecl.) abstinência.

abstentionist, *s.* abstencionista.

abstergent, *s.* e *adj.* abstergente, purificador.

abstersion, *s.* abstersão.

abstersive, *adj.* abstersivo.

abstinence, *s.* abstinência.

abstinency, *v.* hábitos de temperança, jejum, renúncia aos prazeres da mesa.

abstinent, *adj.* abstinente; sóbrio.

abstract, *adj.* abstracto; separado; *s.* resumo, extracto; *in the abstract,* em teoria; *v.t.* abstrair, tirar; resumir; surripiar.

abstracted, *pp.* e *adj.* abstracto; distraído.

abstractedly, *adv.* abstractamente.

abstractedness, *s.* distracção.

abstraction, s. abstracção, distracção; desvio, roubo.
abstractly, adj. abstractamente.
abstruse, adj. obscuro, recôndito.
abstrusely, adv. obscuramente, dificilmente.
abstruseness, s. obscuridade; dificuldade.
absurd, adj. absurdo; ridículo.
absursity, s. absurdo, disparate.
absurdly, adv. absurdamente, disparatadamente.
abundance, s. abundância; riqueza.
abundant, adj. abundante.
abuse, v.t. abusar; enganar; maltratar; seduzir; s. abuso; engano; insulto.
abuser, s. o que abusa ou insulta; enganador.
abusive, adj. abusivo, ofensivo; *abusive language*, linguagem, palavras injuriosas.
abusiveness, s. vitupério, insulto; abuso; insolência.
abusively, adv. abusivamente; de uma maneira injuriosa, grosseiramente.
abut, v.i. (com on, upon) acabar em, confinar com, lindar; (com on) estar topo com topo com, chegar a, entroncar em; (com on, against) apoiar-se sobre, fazer pressão lateral sobre. v.t. entestar com, tocar em; *his field abuts my state*, o seu campo está contíguo à minha propriedade.
abutement, s. (arq.) suporte lateral; encontro (de ponte e abóbada, etc.); sapata do estribo (de uma ponte); muro de suporte; junta de nascença; limite; pé--direito.
abutter, s. proprietário vizinho.
abysm, s. abismo.
abyss, s. abismo: inferno; *abyss of despair*, desespero atroz.
abyssal, adj. insondável, como o abismo; abissal.
acacia, s. acácia.
academic, s. academia; colégio.
academical, adj. académico, universitário. s. pl. vestes, trajes académicos; *in full academical*, a rigor, de cerimónia.
academician, s. académico, membro de uma academia.
Academy, s. Academia; a escola de Platão (discípulos e doutrinas). adj. 1) *young ladies academy*, casa de educação particular, pensionato, colégio de meninas. 2) *Royal Military Academy*, escola de guerra. 3) *fencing academy*, sala de armas, sala de esgrima; academia de ciências, de

belas-artes. 4) *the Royal Academy of Arts*, a Academia Real de pintura e escultura; o salão de exposição anual.
Acadian, adj. e s. da Nova Escócia.
acajou, s. acaju; mogno.
acantha, s. espinho (de planta); aguilhão de animal.
acanthus, s. branca-ursina; acanto.
acaridae, s. zool. acarídeos.
acarpous, adj. bot. acárpico.
acarus, s. ácaro.
acatalectic, adj. e s. acataléctico.
acatalepsy, s. acatalepsia.
acaulous, acaulescent, adj. acaule, acaulescente.
accede, v.i. aceder, concordar; suceder (num cargo).
accelerate, v.t., v.i. acelerar, apressar.
acceleration, s. aceleração.
accelerative, s. acelerativo.
accelerator, s. acelerador.
accent, s. acento; sotaque. v.t. acentuar; salientar.
accentor, s. o que dá a entoação em corpo coral, regente; (zool.) acentor. (vulg.) negrinha, pretinha.
accentual, adj. rítmico, cadenciado, de tonicidade, baseado na acentuação.
accentually, adv. cadenciadamente.
accentuate, v.t. acentuar.
accentuation, s. acentuação.
accept, v.t. aceitar; admitir; aprovar.
acceptability, s. aceitabilidade.
acceptable, adj. aceitável.
acceptably, adv. gostosamente.
acceptance, s. aceitação; bom acolhimento.
acceptation, s. aceitação, acolhimento favorável; acepção, significação, interpretação; *the word in its proper acceptation*, o termo no seu sentido próprio.
accepter, acceptor, s. aceitante. (duma letra comercial).
access, s. acesso; aproximação; entrada.
accessary, ies, s e adj. cúmplice; acessório.
accessibility, s. acessibilidade.
accessible, adj. acessível.
accession, s. acesso, aproximação; elevação ou promoção a uma dignidade; entrada em gozo de, tomada de posse; chegada, acção de atingir; aumento, aquisição; adesão; assentimento, aprovação; acessão.
accessory, s. acessório; cúmplice. adj. acessório, adicional.

accidence, s. morfologia; rudimentos de qualquer assunto.

accident, s. acidente; *by accident*, por acidente, casualmente.

accidental, adj. acidental, casual; *accidentaly*, acidentalmente.

accipitral, adj. rapace; de vista penetrante, de lince.

acclaim, v.t. aclamar, aplaudir. s. aplauso, aclamação.

acclamation, s. aclamação, aplauso.

acclamatory, adj. laudatório.

acclimation, s. aclimação, aclimatação.

acclimatization, s. aclimatização.

acclimatize, v.t., v.i. aclimatar(-se).

acclivity (ies), s. encosta, ladeira, declive, rampa.

acclivous, adj. aclive.

accolade, s. abraço, pancada com a espada; acolada.

accommodate, v.t. acomodar, adaptar; conciliar; reconciliar; ajudar.

accommodating, adj. obsequioso, serviçal, acomodatício, conciliador.

accommodation, s. acomodação, adaptação; reconciliação; alojamento.

accompaniment, s. acompanhamento, acessório.

accompanist, s. acompanhador.

accompany, v.t. acompanhar, escoltar.

accomplice, s. cúmplice.

accomplish, v.t. efectuar, executar, realizar; aperfeiçoar.

accomplished, adj. completo; perfeito; treinado.

accomplishment, s. acabamento, consumação; perfeição, talento; acto realizado, realizações.

accord, s. acordo, consentimento; harmonia, coerência. 1) *of one's own accord*, por sua iniciativa, espontaneamente. 2) *with one accord*, unânime. v.t. conceder; concordar.

accordance, s. acordo, concordância; *in accordance with*, em conformidade com.

accordant, adj. de acordo, conforme, em harmonia com; *accordant to reason*, de acordo com a razão.

according, prep. segundo, conforme; *according to*, de acordo com.

accordingly, adv. em conformidade, consequentemente.

accordion, s. acordeão, harmónica.

accordionist, s. acordeonista.

accost, v.t. dirigir-se a; acercar-se de; molestar.

accosted, adj. (heráld.) colocado lado a lado.

accouchement, s. parto.

accoucheur, s. parteiro

accoucheuse, s. parteira.

account, v.t. considerar, julgar; explicar, dar razão; dar contas de. s. conta, cálculo; relato, estimação. 1) *by all accounts*, segundo dizem todos. 2) *of no account*, de nenhuma importância. 3) *on account of*, por causa de. 4) *on no account*, de modo algum. 5) *on my account*, por mim.

accountability, s. responsabilidade.

accountable, adj. responsável; explicável.

accountableness, s. responsabilidade.

accountancy, s. profissão de contabilista.

accountant, s. guarda-livros, contador.

accountantship, s. ofício de guarda-livros.

account-book, s. livro de contas.

accounting, s. contabilidade.

accoutre, v.t. equipar, ataviar.

accoutrement, s. (pl.) aprestos; atavios, trajos; (milit.) equipamento.

accredit, v.t. autorizar, aceitar, dar valor; acreditar.

accredit, v.t. autorizar, acreditar, revestir de crédito, aceitar, dar valor, abonar; enviar como, dar credenciais, acreditar; atribuir.

accredited, adj. acreditado, abonado; aceite; autorizado.

accrete, v.i. crescer por concreção em volta de um núcleo central, crescer simultaneamente. v.t. amontoar, por concreção em volta de um núcleo.

accretion, s. acreção, crescimento por concreção; crescimento orgânico; agregação; parte da matéria assim agregada; majoração (de uma herança); aumento (de uma propriedade, de uma fortuna), acessão.

accrue, v.i. aumentar, resultar.

accumbent, adj. reclinado, encostado.

accumulate, v.t., v.i. acumular(-se).

accumulation, s. acumulação.

accumulative, adj. acumulativo; acumulado; agenciador, ganacioso.

accumulator, s. acumulador, bateria de acumuladores.

accuracy, s. exactidão; precisão.

accurate, adj. exacto, preciso; *accurate sciences*, ciências exactas.

accurately, adv. com exactidão.

accurateness, s. exactidão, precisão.

accursed, adj. maldito, infame.

accurst, adj. maldito, execrável.

accusation, s. acusação, imputação, denúncia, delação.

accusative, s. e adj. acusativo.

accusatorial, adj. acusatório.

accusatory, adj. acusatório, que envolve acusação.

accuse, v.t. acusar; denunciar. s. acusação, denúncia.

accuser, s. acusador, delator.

accusing, s. acusação, acção de acusar. adj. acusador.

accustom, v.t. acostumar, habituar. 1) to accustom oneself to, acostumar-se. 2) to get accustomed, habituar-se.

accustomed, pp. e adj. (to) habituado a; habitual, familiar.

ace, s. ás (de cartas ou dados); nome dado ao aviador que tenha derrubado aviões inimigos; within an ace of, a um passo de.

Aceldama, s. campo de sangue.

acephalous, adj. acéfalo.

acerb, adj. acerbo, amargo.

acerbity, s. amargura, severidade, aspereza; sabor acre.

acerose, acerous, adj. (bot.) aceroso; palhoso.

acervate, adj. (bot.) que cresce em massas, em cachos.

acescent, adj. acescente.

acetabulum, s. acetábulo.

acetate, s. acetato.

acetated, adj. tratado pelo ácido acético.

acetification, s. acetificação.

acetify, vt. acetificar ou acetificar-se, azedar--se.

acetimeter, s. acetímetro.

acetimetry, s. acetimetria.

acetone, s. acetona.

acetous, adj. acetoso, avinagrado.

acetyl, s. acetilo.

acetylene, s. acetilene.

ache, v.i. doer. s. dor; headache, dor de cabeça.

achene, s. aquénio.

acheron, s. aqueronte.

achieve, v.t. obter, alcançar; executar, fazer.

achievement, adv. realização, execução; façanha.

achilous, adj. alabiado.

aching, s. dor, sofrimento (físico ou moral). adj. dorido.

achromatic, adj. acromático.

achromatically, adv. acromaticamente.

achromatism, s. acromatismo.

achromatize, v.t. acromatizar.

acid, s., adj. ácido, azedo.

acidify, v.t. e v.i. acidificar(-se).

acidimiter, s. acidímetro.

acidity, s. acidez.

acidly, adv. acremente.

acidness, s. acidez.

acidulated, adj. acidulado (coisas); (pessoas) avinagrado, azedado, mal-disposto.

acidulate, v.t. acidular.

acidulous, adj. acídulo; azedado, mal-humo-rado, mordaz, satírico.

acierate, v.t. acerar.

acinus, s. (pl. acini) ácino; glândula acinosa.

ack-ack, adj. (coloq.) antiaéreo; our ack-ack batteries, as nossas baterias antiaéreas.

acknowledge, v.t. reconhecer; admitir; acknowledge receipt of, acusar recebimento de.

acknowledgment, reconhecimento, confissão; confirmação.

aclinic, adj. aclínico.

acme, s. cume, auge; apogeu; crise (duma doença); ponto culminante; the acme of perfection, o auge da perfeição.

acne, s. acne.

acock, adv. com a aba (do chapéu) levantada ou no canto da orelha, à fadista, de maneira provocante.

acockbill, adv. (náut.) âncora prestes a ser lançada; com as vergas oblíquas; à roça (ferro); desmantilhada.

acolyte, s. acólito.

aconite, s. (bot.) acónito.

acorn, s. bolota (fruta).

acotyledon, s. planta acotiledónea.

acoustic, adj. acústico.

acoustics, s. acústica.

acquaint, v.t. informar, comunicar; familiarizar. 1) to acquaint oneself with, inteirar-se de. 2) to be acquainted with, conhecer; ter conhecimento.

acquaintance, s. conhecimento; I am glad to make your acquaintance, prazer em conhecê-lo.

acquaintanceship, s. conhecimento, facto de estar em relações, de conhecer.

acquest, s. aquisição; propriedade adquirida por compra.

acquiesce, v.i. aquiescer, concordar, consentir.

acquiescence, s. aquiescência, consentimento.

acquiescent, *adj.* condescendente, acomodatício.

acquire, *v.t.* adquirir, obter; contrair (hábito ou costume).

acquirement, *s.* aquisição; conhecimentos adquiridos, saber, experiência, prendas.

acquisition, *s.* aquisição.

acquisitive, *adj.* levado a, adquirir, apto para aprender, ávido de.

acquisitiveness, *s.* desejo de adquirir, propensão para adquirir, desejo de possuir; faculdade de adquirir.

acquit, *v.t.* absolver, libertar. 1) *to acquit oneself,* comportar-se. 2) *to acquit oneself of duty,* desempenhar um dever.

acquittal, *s.* absolvição, desempenho.

acquittance, *s.* conhecimento; pessoa do conhecimento de, das relações (geralmente no pl.).

acre, acre; terrenos, campos.

acreage, *s.* superfície, área de um campo (contada em acres).

acred, *adj.* que possui terras; *a many-acred (large-acred) man,* um homem dono de grandes propriedades rurais.

acrid, *adj.* picante, acre; (fig.) mordaz, irritante.

acridly, *adj.* de um modo irritante ou picante.

acridness, *s.* acridez, acrimónia; aspereza.

acrimonious, *adj.* acrimonioso; sarcástico, mordaz.

acrimony (ies), *s.* acrimónia, desabrimento, rudeza, azedume.

acrobat, *s.* acrobata.

acrobatic, *adj.* acrobático.

acrobatics, *s.* acrobacia.

acrobatism, *s.* acrobatismo.

acrocarpous, *adj.* acrocárpico.

acrocephalic (phalous), *adj.* acrocefálico, acrocéfalo.

acrogen, *s.* acrógeno.

acrogenous, *adj.* acrógeno.

acropolis (es), *s.* acrópole.

across, *adv., prep.* através; *to run, come across,* encontrar.

acrostic, *s.* acróstico.

act, *s.* acto, acção; decreto, acto (de uma peça teatral). *v.t., v.i.* representar; executar; funcionar.

acting, *s.* representação, desempenho; acto, feito. *adj.* que desempenha, activo.

actinic, *adj.* actínico.

actinism, *s.* actinismo.

actinium, *s.* actínio.

action, acção, actividade; acto, movimento.

actionable, *adj.* accionável, que pode ser citado em justiça.

active, *adj.* activo; vivo; enérgico.

activity, *s.* actividade; energia.

acton, *s.* pelota; casaco almofadado usado por baixo da armadura.

actor, *s.* actor.

actress, *s.* actriz.

actual, *adj.* real, verdadeiro; presente.

actually, *adv.* realmente, de facto; até mesmo; actualmente, por agora.

actuality (ies), *s.* actualidade, realidade; (pl.) realidade, estado presente das coisas.

actualize, *v.t.* realizar, efectuar, pôr em prática; pintar ao vivo, descrever com cores vivas.

actuary (ies), *s.* actuário.

actuate, *v.t.* mover, pôr em movimento; estimular, incitar; *he was actuated only by ambition,* só a ambição o estimulava.

actuation, *s.* comunicação de movimento; acção de pôr em movimento; impulso, movimento.

acuity, *s.* agudeza; acuidade, gravidade; agudeza, perspicácia.

aculeate, *adj.* (bot.) aculeado, com acúleos; (zool.) munido de picos ou aguilhões.

acumen, *s.* sagacidade, perspicácia.

acute, *adj.* agudo; vivo, perspicaz.

acuteness, *s.* agudeza, subtileza; acuidade, vivacidade, penetração, profundeza.

adage, *s.* adágio, provérbio.

adagio, *s.* adágio (mús.)

Adam, *s.* Adão. 1) *Adam's ale wine,* água. 2) *as old as Adam,* tão velho como a Sé de Braga.

adamant, *s.* substância dura, diamante. *adj.* duro, inflexível.

adamantine, *adj.* adamantino, duro como o diamante.

Adamite, *s.* Filho de Adão; ser humano, humano nu; adamita.

adapt, *v.t.* adaptar. *to adapt oneself to,* adaptar-se a.

adaptability, *s.* adaptabilidade.

adaptable, *adj.* adaptável.

adaptedness, *s.* conformidade.

adaptation, *s.* adaptação.

add, *v.t.* juntar, unir; somar; incluir.

adder, *s.* serpente venenosa; víbora; *flying adder,* libélula.

adder-wort, *s.* retorcida; bistorta.

addict, *v.t.* dedicar-se, consagrar-se. 1)

much addicted to drink, dado à bebida. *s.* pessoa dada a qualquer vício. 2) *drug addict*, morfinómano.

addiction, addictedness, *s.* (to) gosto por, inclinação para.

addition, *s.* adição, soma; *in addition to*, em acréscimo a.

additional, *adj.* adicional.

additionally, *adv.* a mais, em suplemento.

addle, *adj.* (de ovos) um ovo podre, choco; (fig.) chocho, oco, parvo; estéril. 1) *addle-brained, addle-head, addle-pated*, cabeça oca, pateta. *v.i.* 2) *to grow addle*, gorar-se, estragar-se. *v.t.* pôr a cabeça em água, aturdir, perturbar a cabeça.

address, *v.t.* dirigir-se a, falar a; endereçar; aplicar-se a. *s.* endereço; petição; discurso; galanteio.

addressee, *s.* destinatário.

addresser, *s.* peticionário, remetente, expedidor.

adduce, *v.t.* aduzir.

adduceable, adducible, *adj.* aduzível, que pode ser apresentado ou alegado.

adducent, *adj.* (músculo) adutor.

adduct, *vt.* (fisiol.) pôr em adução.

adduction, *s.* adução; apresentação (de provas, de testemunhas), alegação.

adenitis, *adj.* (med.) adenite.

adenoids, *s.* adenóides.

adept, *s.* perito. *adj.* hábil, sabedor.

adequacy, *s.* justa proporção, adequação, suficiência.

adequate, *adj.* adequado; suficiente.

adeundem, *adv.* equiparado (ao mesmo grau de outra universidade).

adhere, *v.i.* ligar, unir; aderir; concordar.

adherence, *s.* adesão, dedicação.

adherent, *adj.* aderente, que adere, pegado, colado; inerente, ligado; *the dificulties adherent to his position*, as dificuldades inerentes à sua situação. *s.* aderente, partidário.

adhesion, *s.* aderência; adesão.

adhesive, *adj.* pegajoso; aderente; tenaz.

adhesiveness, *s.* aderência, adesividade; tendência para se dedicar às pessoas.

adhibit, *v.t.* pôr, apor a assinatura; aplicar, administrar (remédios).

adhibition, *s.* administração, aplicação (de um remédio, etc.)

adiantum, *s.* (bot.) avenca.

adieu, *interj.* adeus.

adipocere, *s.* adipocera.

adipose, *adj.* adiposo, gordo. *s.* gordura animal.

adiposity, *s.* adiposidade.

adit, *s.* acesso, entrada, aproximação.

adjacency, *s.* adjacência.

adjacent, *adj.* adjacente, contíguo.

adjacently, *adv.* dum modo adjacente.

adjectival, *adj.* adjectível.

adjective, *s.* adjectivo.

adjoin, *v.t., v.i.* unir, juntar; confinar.

adjoining, *adj.* contínuo, imediato.

adjourn, *v.t.* adiar, transferir; *to adjourn the meeting*, adiar, suspender a sessão.

adjournment, *s.* adiamento, suspensão.

adjudge, *v.t.* julgar; condenar.

adjudicate, *v.t.* decidir judicialmente, julgar, sentenciar; adjudicar, atribuir; *that is a thing to be adjudicated*, é uma coisa que tem de ser decidida judicialmente. *v.i.* sentenciar, emitir ou pronunciar uma opinião.

adjudicator, *s.* juiz adjudicador.

adjudication, *s.* julgamento, sentença, julgado, decisão judicial.

adjunct, *s.* complemento, acessório; adjunto, auxiliar; epíteto.

adjunction, *s.* adição, adjunção.

adjunctive, *adj.* que junta.

adjuration, *s.* imprecação; súplica.

adjuratory, *adj.* que contém adjuração; imprecatório.

adjure, *v.t.* imprecar; suplicar.

adjust, *v.t.* ajustar; reconciliar; regular.

adjustable, *adj.* adaptável, ajustável. *adjustable spanner*, chave-inglesa.

adjuster, *s.* adaptador; esticador (bicicleta). *average adjuster*, árbitro (em seguros marítimos).

adjustment, *s.* adaptação; regulação, ajustamento.

adjutancy, *s.* cargo, grau de ajudante, auxílio; apoio.

adjutant, *s.* ajudante (militar) 1) *adjudant-general*, ajudante-general, secretário-geral do Ministério da Guerra. 2) *adjutant-bird*, marabu.

adjuvant, *adj.* auxiliar; (med.) adjuvante. *s.* auxiliar.

admeasure, *v.t.* repartir, fazer partilhas, medir a parte de cada um; medir.

admeasurement, *s.* divisão por igual; atribuição, adjudicação dos bens ou direitos numa partilha; medida, processo de medir (tamanho).

administer, *v.t.* administrar; conferir,

ministrar; *to administer an oath*, prestar juramento.

administrable, *adj.* susceptível de ser administrado.

administrant, *s.* e *adj.* director; administrador.

administration, *s.* administração; governo; distribuição. *administration of the oath*, prestação de um juramento.

administrative, *adj.* administrativo.

administrator, *s.* administrador.

administratorship, *s.* funções de administrador ou de curador.

admirable, *adj.* admirável.

admirableness, *s.* excelência de alguma coisa.

admirably, *adv.* admiravelmente.

admiral, *s.* almirante.

admiralship, *s.* cargo, dignidade de almirante.

admiralty, *s.* almirantado.

admiration, *s.* admiração.

admire, *v.t.* admirar, estimar.

admirer, *s.* admirador.

admiring, *adj.* que admira, admirador; cheio de admiração.

admiringly, *adv.* com admiração.

admissible, *adj.* admissível, aceitável; apto, idóneo, que pode ser admitido (a um emprego, etc.).

admission, *s.* admissão; recebimento; aceitação.

admit, *v.t.* permitir, aceitar; reconhecer; dar entrada.

admittable, *adj.* admissível.

admittance, *s.* admissão; entrada.

admittedly, *adv.* por consenso, por comum consentimento, com a confissão da parte adversa. *the man was admittedly drunk*, por confissão própria, o homem estava ébrio.

admix, *v.t.* misturar.

admixture, *s.* mistura.

admonish, *v.t.* advertir; repreender.

admonition, *s.* advertência, aviso; repreensão.

admonitor, *s.* conselheiro, mentor.

admonitory, *adj.* admonitório, de aviso, de advertência. *a few admonitory words*, algumas palavras de advertência.

ado, *s.* tumulto, barulho; trabalho.

adobe, *s.* tijolo cru, adobo; casa feita deste tijolo.

adolescence, *s.* adolescência.

adolescent, *s., adj.* adolescente.

Adonis, *s.* Adónis; (bot.) adónio.

adonize, *v.i.* adonizar-se, aperaltar-se.

adopt, *v.t.* adoptar; escolher; aceitar.

adoptedly, *adv.* por adopção.

adopter, *s.* o ou a que adopta; (quím.) recipiente.

adoption, *s.* adopção; aceitação; escolha.

adoptive, *adj.* adoptivo; adoptado; *apt to adopt*, inclinado a adoptar.

adorable, *adj.* adorável.

adorableness, *s.* qualidade de ser adorável.

adorably, *adv.* adoravelmente.

adoration, *s.* adoração.

adore, *v.t.* adorar, prestar culto.

adorer, *s.* adorador, que adora; (amar) apaixonado, admirador.

adoringly, *adv.* com adoração.

adorn, *v.t.* adornar, decorar.

adornment, *s.* adorno, enfeite.

adresser, *s.* signatário.

adrift, *adj., adv.* sem governo, flutuando ao acaso.

adroit, *adj.* hábil, destro.

adroitness, *s.* habilidade, destreza, esperteza.

adscititious, *adj.* adicional.

adulate, *v.t.* bajular.

adulation, *s.* adulação.

adulator, *s.* adulador.

adulatory, *adj.* adulador.

adult, *s.* adulto.

adulterant, *s.* pessoa ou coisa que adultera ou falsifica; adulterador.

adulterate, *v.t.* adulterar.

adulteration, *s.* adulteração, falsificação, alteração.

adulterator, *s.* falsificador.

adulterer, *s.* adúltero.

adulteress, *s.* adúltera.

adulterine, *adj.* adulterino, espúrio, ilegal.

adulterous, *adj.* adulteroso, falso.

adulterously, *adv.* com adultério.

adultery (ies), adultério.

adumbrate, *v.t.* adumbrar, sombrear; delinear, esboçar.

adumbration, *s.* esboço, bosquejo, plano, previsão de intenções para acção futura, imagem sumária ou vaga, adumbração.

adust, *adj.* adusto, queimado; atrabiliário, rabugento.

advance, *v.t.* avançar; melhorar; progredir; promover; antecipar; pagar adiantado; aumentar (preço). *v.i.* avançar; adiantar-se; subir. *s.* avanço; progresso; aumento; adiantamento (de dinheiro).

advanced, *adj.* avançado; adiantado; *advanced in years*, avançado em anos.

advancement, *s.* progresso; promoção; avanço; impulso.

advantage, *s.* vantagem; superioridade; lucro. 1) *to take advantage of*, tirar proveito de. 2) *to have an advantage over*, ter vantagem sobre. *v.t.* favorecer, auxiliar, promover. *v.i.* ser vantajoso.

advantageous, *adj.* vantajoso, útil.

advantageously, *adv.* vantajosamente.

advantegeousness, *s.* vantagem, utilidade, proveito, conveniência.

advent, *s.* chegada, advento. (Com maiúscula) Advento de Cristo.

adventitious, *adj.* acidental, casual; proveniente de uma sucessão na linha lateral; adventício; *adventitious aids*, auxílios adventícios, fortuitos.

adventure, *s.* aventura; risco; acaso. *v.t., v.i.* aventurar. arriscar; *to adventure upon*, aventurar-se a.

adventurer, *s.* aventureiro.

adventuress, (es), *s.* aventureira.

adventurous, *adj.* aventuroso, arriscado.

adventurousness, *s.* intrepidez, ousadia.

adverb, *s.* advérbio.

adverbial, *adj.* adverbial.

adverbially, *adv.* adverbialmente.

adversary, *s.* adversário, antagonista.

adversative, *s.* adversativo.

adverse, *adj.* adverso, hostil; contrário.

adversely, *adv.* adversamente.

adversity, *s.* adversidade, infortúnio.

advert, *v.i.* referir-se a; chamar a atenção para.

advertence (cy), *s.* advertência.

advertise, advertize, *v.t.* anunciar; informar.

advertisement, *s.* anúncio, aviso.

advertiser, *s.* anunciante; notificador.

advertising, *s.* arte de anunciar.

advice, *s.* conselho, advertência; aviso. 1) *a piece of advice*, um conselho. 2) *a letter of advice*, carta de aviso.

advice-boat, *s.* (náut.) aviso.

advisability, *s.* prudência, conveniência, oportunidade.

advisable, *adj.* aconselhável; prudente; útil.

advisableness, *s.* oportunidade.

advisably, *adv.* prudentemente.

advise, *v.t.* aconselhar: avisar; *to advise with (person) on (something)*, consultar (pessoa) sobre.

advised, *adj.* reflectido, deliberado, com premeditação; avisado, prudente, ajuizado. 1) *it is an advised act*, isso é feito com propósito deliberado. 2) *ill-advised, well-advised*, mal avisado, bem avisado.

advisedly, *adv.* deliberadamente, de caso pensado.

advisedness, *s.* deliberação.

adviser, advisor, *s.* conselheiro; informador.

advisory, *adj.* consultivo, que exprime parecer ou conselho; *adviser board*, junta consultiva.

advocacy, *s.* advocacia, defesa, apoio, discurso em favor de; acção de preconizar.

advocate, *s.* advogado, defensor. *v.t.* defender, advogar.

advowsan, *s.* colação, direito de conferir um benefício eclesiástico.

adynamia, *s.* adinamia.

adynamic, *adj.* adinâmico.

adytum, *s.* ádito, santuário.

adze, *s.* enxó (de tanoeiro); *cooper's adze*, machadinha recurvada (de tanoeiro). *v.t.* cortar, ou aplanar, alisar (com uma enxó), etc.

aedile, *s.* edil.

aedilesdhip, *s.* edilidade.

aeger, *s.* atestado de doença.

aegis, *s.* égide, escudo.

aeolian, *adj.* eólio, eólico, natural da Eólia; Eólio; produzido ou levado pelo vento; *aeolian harp*, harpa eólica.

aeolic, *adj.* e *s.* eólico (dialecto).

aeon, eon, *s.* evo, eternidade, idade do universo.

aerate, *v.t.* arejar, expor à acção do ar; carregar de gás carbónico ou anidrido carbónico; (med.) arterializar; (expressão vulgar) ácido carbónico; *aerated waters*, águas gasosas.

aeration, *s.* aeração, arejamento; gasificação; (med.) arterialização.

aerator, *s.* gaseificador.

aerial, *s.* antena.

aerie, *s.* ninho de ave de rapina (especialmente águia, etc.); edifício alcandorado; ninhada (de ave de presa).

aeriform, *adj.* aeriform, gasoso; (fig.) imaginário.

aero, *s.* (coloq.) (pl.) aeroplano, avião, aviação.

aerobatics, *s.* acrobacia aérea.

aerobus, *s.* (coloq.) aeroplano.

aerodrome, *s.* campo de aviação, aeródromo.

aerodynamics, *s.* aerodinâmica.

aerofoil, *s.* asa, superfície de sustentação.

aerogram, *s.* aerograma, radiograma.

aerohydroplane, *s.* hidroplano.

aerolite, aerolith, *s.* aerólito.

aerometer, *s.* aerómetro; aeromotor.

aero-motor, *s.* motor de aviação.

aeronaut, *s.* aeronauta.

aeronautic, *adj.* aeronáutico.

aeronautics, *s.* aeronáutica.

aeroplane, *s.* aeroplano.

aerostat, *s.* aeróstato.

aerostatics, *s.* aerostática.

aerostation, *s.* aerostação.

aeruginous, *adj.* coberto de verdete.

Aesculapian, *adj.* pertencente à arte de curar.

aesthesis, *s.* estese, estesia.

aesthete, *s.* esteta.

aesthetic, *adj.* estético. *s.* estética (ramo da filosofia). *aesthetically adv.* de uma maneira estética, do ponto de vista estético.

aesthetics, *s.* estética.

aesto-physiology, *s.* estesiofisiologia.

aestival, *adj.* estival.

aestivate, *v.i.* (zool.) passar o Verão em estado de torpor.

aestivation, *s.* torpor estival.

aether, *s.* éter.

aetiological, *adj.* etiológico.

aetiology, *s.* etiologia.

afar, *adv.* longe, ao longe, distante; *from afar*, de longe.

affability, affableness, *s.* afabilidade.

affable, *adj.* afável, amável.

affably, *adv.* com afabilidade.

affair, *s.* negócio; assunto; transacção; *affair of honour*, duelo de honra.

affect, *v.t.* gostar de ; aparentar, simular; comover.

affectation, *s.* afectação; fingimento.

affected, *adj.* afectado; artificial; simulado; comovido.

affectedly, *adv.* afectadamente, com afectação, de maneira simulada ou exagerada.

affectedness, *s.* afectação.

affecting, *adj.* comovedor, terno.

affection, *s.* afeição, amor; afecção (med.).

affectionate, *adj.* carinhoso, afectuoso.

affectionateness, *s.* afecto, carinho, afectuosidade.

affective, *adj.* afectivo, comovedor.

afferent, *adj.* aferente.

affiance, *v.t.* desposar.

affidavit, *s.* declaração debaixo de juramento feito perante um magistrado; *to swear an affidavit*, declarar debaixo de juramento.

affiliate, *v.t., v.i.* filiar, incorporar; afiliar-se; perfilhar.

affiliation, *s.* afiliação, adopção, perfilhação, incorporação; atribuição de paternidade; relação; parentesco.

affinity, *s.* parentesco; afinidade.

affirm, assegurar; confirmar.

affirmation, *s.* afirmação; declaração.

affirmative, *adj.* afirmativo, positivo. *s.* afirmativa.

affirmatory, adj. assertório, afirmativo.

affix, *v.t.* fixar, unir; afixar; assinar.

affixture, *s.* adjução, afixação, aposição, fixação.

afflatus, *s.* aflato, inspiração.

afflict, *v.t.* afligir.

affliction, *s.* aflição, dor, pesar.

afflictive, *adj.* aflitivo.

affluence, *s.* opulência, riqueza, abastança; profusão, abundância.

affluent, *adj.* que corre livremente, copioso, abundante, opulento. *s.* afluente.

afflux, *s.* afluxo, confluência, fluxo; afluência, concorrência de gente.

afford, *v.t.* ter recursos para; proporcionar, prover.

afforest, *v.t.* plantar um bosque ou floresta, povoar de, converter em floresta ou coutadas.

afforestation, *s.* plantação dum bosque ou floresta, povoamento.

affranchise, *v.t.* manumitir, dar alforria, libertar, forrar, isentar da obrigação, dispensar.

affray, *s.* alvoroto, alvoroço, motim, rixa, tumulto, refrega.

affright, *v.t.* assustar, aterrar. *s.* susto, terror.

affront, *v.t.* insultar; encarar. *s.* afronta, insulto.

affusion, *s.* afusão, rega, aspersão.

afield, *adv.* sobre, no, para o campo; fora de casa, longe. 1) *far afield*, muito longe, ao longe. 2) *to go far afield*, afastar-se para muito longe.

afire, *adj., adv.* em fogo.

aflame, *adv.* em chamas; *all aflame with curiosity*, a arder de curiosidade.

afloat, *adj., adv.* à tona da água, flutuando; a bordo; inundado, divulgado.

afoot, *adv.* a pé; em movimento.

aforesaid, *adj.* já citado.

afraid, *adj.* com medo; *to be afraid,* ter medo.

afresh, *adv.* outra vez, novamente.

African, *adj.* e *s.* africano.

africanism, *s.* africanismo.

africanize, *v.t.* africanizar.

Afrikander, *s.* indígena branco da África do Sul, africano branco.

aft, *adv.* à popa; atrás; à ré. 1) *aft of the mast,* atrás do mastro. 2) *he sleeps aft,* ele dorme a ré. *adj.* que está atrás.

after, *prep.* depois de, atrás de, após; *day after day,* dia após dia.

afterbirth, *s.* placenta, secundinas.

afterdamp, *s.* mofeta.

afterglow, *s.* rosicler, resplendor crepuscular.

after-grass, *s.* outonada.

after-life, *s.* período ulterior da vida, continuação da vida; idade madura; vida futura.

aftermost, *adj.* (náut.) o mais à ré possível (de um navio).

afternoon, *s.* tarde.

afterpiece, *s.* entremez.

aftertaste, *s.* ressaibo, travo.

afterthought, *s.* reflexão.

afterwards, *adv.* depois, mais tarde.

again, *adv.* outra vez, de novo. 1) *again and again,* muitas vezes. 2) *once again,* uma vez mais. 3) *now and again,* de vez em quando.

against, *prep.* contra; em oposição a; em face de.

agar-agar, *s.* ágar-ágar.

agape, *s.* ágape. *adv.* e *adj.* de boca aberta, boquiaberto.

agaric, *s.* agárico, nome de vários fungos.

agate, *s.* ágata. *adv.* a caminho, em movimento

agave, *s.* (bot.) agave.

agaze, *adv.* em contemplação, em admiração.

age, *s.* idade; época; velhice. 1) *to become of age,* atingir a maioridade. 2) *under age,* de menoridade. 3) *what is your age?* que idade tens? *v.t., v.i.* envelhecer.

aged, *adj.* velho, idoso.

ageless, *adj.* sempre jovem.

agency, *s.* acção; agência; intervenção.

agent, *s.* agente; instrumento; intermediário.

agenda, *s.* ordem do dia, lista das questões para debater; agenda, memorando.

agglomerate, *v.t.* e *v.i.* aglomerar, aglo-merar-se. *adj.* aglomerado. *s.* aglomerado; (geol.) tufo.

agglomeration, *adj.* aglomeração.

agglomerative, *adj.* aglomerativo.

agglutinate, *v.t.* aglutinar, colar, converter ou transformar-se em cola. *adj.* aglutinado, aglutinante.

agglutination, *s.* aglutinação.

agglutinative, *adj.* aglutinador, aglutinativo.

aggrandize, *v.t.* elevar; exaltar; exagerar.

aggrandizement, *s.* engrandecimento, aumento, enaltecimento.

aggravate, *adj.* agregado; unido. *s.* conjunto; massa; agregado. *v.t.* unir; agregar; associar. *v.i.* associar-se; agregar-se.

aggravating, *adj.* agravante; exasperador.

aggravatingly, *adv.* de maneira irritante, exasperadora, agravante.

aggravation, *s.* agravação, agravamento, circunstância agravante, irritação, vexação.

aggregate, *adj.* agregado unido num todo, tomado num todo, colectivo, total. *s.* massa, agregado, conjunto, total colecção; (fig.) agregado; *in the aggregate,* no todo, no conjunto. *v.t.* agregar, reunir num todo; incorporar; associar, admitir, receber, filiar; orçar, perfazer, somar, ascender a. *v.i.* agregar-se, unir-se num todo, numa massa.

aggregation, *s.* agregação; reunião num todo, colecção, afiliação; massa total, conjunto, associação; (fís.) agregação.

aggregative, *adj.* agregativo.

aggress, *v.i.* ser o primeiro a agredir.

aggression, *s.* agressão.

aggressive, *adj.* agressivo, ofensivo. *s.* ofensiva.

aggressiveness, *s.* agressividade.

aggressor, *s.* agressor.

aggrieve, *v.t.* afligir, incomodar; molestar, entristecer.

aggrieved, *adj.* lesado, prejudicado, ofen-dido.

aghast, *adj.* espantado, horrorizado.

agile, *adj.* ágil, vivo.

agilely, *adv.* agilmente.

agility, *s.* agilidade.

agio, *s.* (pl) ágio.

agiotage, *s.* agiotagem.

agist, *v.t.* receber gado para alimentar, mediante pagamento.

agitate, *v.t.* agitar; perturbar; discutir, debater.

agitation, *s.* agitação; perturbação; debate.

agitator, *s.* agitador.

aglet, aiglet, s. canudilha, agulheta, ponta; agulheta (do uniforme).

aglow, adj. vermelho, excitador; incandescente.

agnail, s. espigão ou espigo (da unha); calo do dedo grande do pé ou no pé.

agnate, adj. agnado; pertencente à mesma raça; (fig.) da mesma espécie, natureza. s. agnato.

agnation, s. agnação.

agnomen, s. agnome.

agnostic, s. e adj. agnóstico.

agnosticism, s. agnosticismo.

ago, adj., adv. passado, há; long time ago, há muito tempo.

agog, adj. impaciente, que não sossega, irrequieto; em movimento; em andamento. 1) they were agog to, ardiam em desejo de. 2) they were all agog to know what happened, estavam todos ansioso por saber o que aconteceu. 3) to set agog, pôr em movimento.

agonic, adj. ágono.

agonistic, adj. agonístico, combativo; afectado, pretensioso.

agonistics, s. agonística.

agonize, v.t., v.i. torturar, atormentar, sofrer; lutar; agonizar.

agonizing, adj. agonizante, doloroso.

agonizingly, adv. em agonia, de modo doloroso.

agony, s. sofrimento, dor violenta; luta; acesso; agony solumn (nos jornais), coluna dos desaparecidos, necrologia.

agorophobia, s. agorafobia.

agrarian, adj. e s. agrário, agrícola.

agrarianism, s. agrarianismo.

agree, v.i. concordar com, aprovar; harmonizar-se; dar-se bem; drink does not agree with her, ela não se dá bem com a bebida.

agreeable, adj. agradável, amável; conveniente.

agreebleness, s. agrado, satisfação, aprazimento, amenidade, encanto; concordância; conformidade com.

agreeably, adv. agradavelmente; conformemente, de acordo com, em conformidade com.

agreement, s. acordo; harmonia; transacção. 1) to be in agreement with, estar de acordo com. 2) to inter into (come to) an agreement, entrar em acordo.

agricultural, adj. agrícola.

agriculturalist, s. agricultor; scientific agriculturalist, agrónomo.

agriculture, s. agricultura.

agriculturist, s. agricultor.

agrimony, s. agrimónia.

agronomic, adj. agronómico.

agronomist, s. agrónomo.

agronomy, agronomics, s. agronomia.

aground, adv. encalhado; to be (run, go) aground, encalhar, dar à costa.

ague, s. sezão, malária, maleita. febre intermitente, calafrio. 1) ague-cake, tumor do fígado. 2) agued, que tem malária.

aguish, adj. palustre, febril, tiritante, intermitente, febricitante.

aha!, interj. ah! (exprimindo surpresa, triunfo ou ironia).

ahead, adv., adj. na frente, avante. 1) go ahead, para à frente! 2) straight ahead, bem em frente.

aheap, adv. em monte; a granel; todo abatido (pelo terror, etc.).

ahem, interj. heim! hem!

ahoy, interj. olé! olá! 1) ship ahoy!, ó do barco!. 2) all hands ahoy, toda a gente para o convés.

aid, v.t., v.i. auxiliar, ajudar. s. ajuda, auxílio; ajudante, auxiliar.

aide-de-camp, aid-de-camp, s. ajudante de campo, ajudante de ordens.

aider, s. auxiliador.

aiding and abetting, s. aprovação e incitamento a um crime.

aigrette, s. graça, tufo de penas ou cabelos; penacho.

aiguille, s. agulha, pico agudo de um monte.

ail, v.t. doer, afligir; what ails you?, que lhe dói?. v.i. estar doente.

ailing, adj. doente.

ailment, s. indisposição; doença.

aileron, s. pequena asa do avião para o conservar em equilíbrio.

aim, v.t. apontar, dirigir. v.i. aspirar a, pretender; to aim to please, desejar agradar. s. alvo; fim; aspiração.

aiming tripod, s. cavalete de mira.

aimless, adj. sem desígnio, sem objectivo.

air, s. ar; atmosfera; aparência, modo; tom, ária. 1) open air, ar livre! 2) to put on airs, fazer de importante. 3) air tight, hermeticamente fechado. adj. aéreo. 4) air-line, linha aérea. 5) air-mail, mala aérea, correio aéreo. v.t. arejar, ventilar. 6) to air one's views, publicar.

aircraft, *s.* qualquer tipo de máquina aérea.

airdrome, *s.* aeródromo.

airier, airiest, *comp.* e *superl.* de airy.

airily, *adv.* ligeiramente; alegremente.

airiness, *s.* ventilação; viveza; actividade.

airing, *s.* ventilação; exposição ao ar; excursão ao ar livre; *to go for a airing*, ir dar uma volta (a pé ou a cavalo).

airless, *adj.* abafado, sem ventilação.

airman, *s.* aviador.

airmanship, *s.* arte do aviador.

airplane, *s.* aeroplano; *air-carrier*, porta-aviões.

airport, *s.* aeroporto.

airpost, *s.* correio aéreo.

airship, *s.* dirigível.

airy, *adj.* aéreo; arejado; alegre; visionário.

aisle, *s.* nave lateral da igreja; passagem entre filas de bancos.

aisled, *adj.* com naves laterais, com passagem entre filas de bancos de igreja.

aitchbone, *s.* osso da rabadilha.

ajar, *adj.* meio aberto.

ajutage, *s.* tubo para vazar líquidos; bica de fonte.

akimbo, *adv.* com as mãos nos quadris.

akin, *adj.* consanguíneo, semelhante.

alabaster, *s.* alabastro.

alack, *interj.* ai de mim!

alacrity, *s.* alegria; vivacidade.

aland, *adv.* em terra; para terra.

alarm, *s.* alarme; sobressalto; *alarm clock*, despertador. *v.t.* alarmar; assustar.

alarming, *adj.* alarmante.

alarmingly, *adv.* de modo assustador.

alarmist, *adj.* assustador.

alarum, *s.* rebate.

alas, *interj.* ah! ai de mim!

alate, *adj.* alado. *adv.* ultimamente.

alb, *s.* alva (veste sacerdotal).

albata, *s.* albata, liga semelhante à prata.

albatross, *s.* albatroz, ave muito voraz; tipo de avião alemão.

albeit, *adv.* não obstante.

albert, *s.* corrente de relógio pequena.

albescent, *adj.* alvejante; esbranquiçado.

albinism, *s.* albinismo.

albino, *s.* albino; indivíduo que tem albinismo; planta ou animal de cor branca, contra o costume.

albugineous, *adj.* albugíneo, albuginoso.

album, *s.* album; *slip-in-album*, passe-partout.

albumen, *s.* albúmen, clara do ovo.

albumin, *s.* albumina.

albuminoid, *adj.* albuminóide.

albuminous, *adj.* albuminoso.

alburnum, *s.* alburno, entrecasco de árvore.

alcaic, *s.* alcaico (verso).

alchemic, *adj.* alquímico.

alchemist, *s.* alquimista.

alchemy, *s.* alquimia, química da Idade Média.

alcohol, *s.* álcool.

alcoholic, *adj.* alcoólico. *s.* alcoólatra.

alcoholism, *s.* alcoolismo.

alcoholometer, *s.* alcoómetro.

alcove, *s.* alcova.

aldehyde, *s.* aldeído, fluido obtido pela oxidação do álcool.

alder, *s.* amieiro.

alderman, *s.* vereador; senador.

aldermanly, *adj.* grave; como vereador.

aldern, *adj.* feito de amieiro.

ale, *s.* cerveja.

alehouse, *s.* cervejaria.

alembic, *s.* alambique.

alert, *adj.* alerta, vigilante; *on the alert*, pronto para o que der e vier.

alertly, *adv.* alerta; activamente.

alertness, *s.* vigilância; actividade.

alewife, *s.* mulher que cuida de uma cervejaria; espécie de peixe americano parecido com o arenque.

Alexandrino, *s.* alexandrino (verso).

alexia, *s.* alexia, impossibilidade patológica de ler.

alfalfa, *s.* alfafa.

alfresco, *ad.* e *adj.* ao fresco, ao ar livre; *an alfresco lunch*, um almoço ao ar livre.

alga, *pl.* algae. *s.* alga.

algebra, *s.* álgebra.

algebraic, *adj.* algébrico.

algebraist, *s.* algebrista.

algid, *adj.* álgido.

algidity, *s.* algidez.

algorism, *s.* algorismo.

alias, *adv.* aliás. *s.* (*pl.*) *aliases,* pseudónimo, nome suposto ou falso.

alibi, *s.* álibi; *to set up an alibi*, apresentar um álibi.

alidade, *s.* alidade.

alien, *adj.* estranho; alheio; estrangeiro. *s.* estrangeiro; forasteiro.

alienable, *s.* alienável.

alienage, *s.* qualidade de estrangeiro.

alienate, *v.t.* ceder; transferir; tornar hostil; malquistar.

alienation, s. afastamento; alheamento; demência.

alienator, s. alienador.

alienee, s. adjudicatário, alienatário.

aliform, adj. aliforme.

alienist, s. alienista.

alight, v.i. descer, desmontar; pousar; to alight on, cair sobre.

align, v.t. alinhar, pôr em linha recta.

alignment, s. alinhamento.

alike, adj. semelhante; igual; it is all alike to me, é-me inteiramente indiferente.

aliment, s. alimento.

alimental, adj. alimentício, nutritivo.

alimentary, adj. alimentar, alimentício; alimentary canal, tubo digestivo.

alimentation, s. alimentação.

alimoby (ies), s. pensão alimentícia.

aliquant, s. aliquanta.

aliquot, s. alíquota. adj. alíquota.

alive, adj. vivo; consciente; depressa. 1) alive to the act, cheio. 2) the lake is alive with fish, o lago está cheio de peixes. 3) look alive!, ande depressa!

alizarin, s. alizarina.

alkahest, s. dissolvent universal, soluto universal; (fig.) panaceira.

alkalescence (cy), s. alcalescência.

alkali, s. álcali.

alkalify, v. alcalificar.

alkaloyd, s. alcalóide.

alkaline, adj. alcalino.

alkalinity, s. alcalinidade.

all, adj. todo, inteiro; todos. s., pron. todos. 1) all of us, todos nós. 2) after all, afinal. adv. inteiramente, todo. 3) all at once, de uma vez. 4) all right, está bem. 5) all over, por toda a parte. 6) all the better, tanto melhor.

allay, v.t. acalmar; aliviar.

allegation, s. alegação.

allege, v.t. alegar; afirmar.

allegiance, s. lealdade; fidelidade.

allegiant, adj. leal. s. súbdito.

allegoric, adj. alegórico.

allegorical, ver allegoric.

allegorically, adv. alegoricamente.

allegorist, s. alegorista.

allegorize, v.t. alegorizar.

allegory, s. alegoria.

allegreto, s. alegreto (mús.).

allegro, s. alegro (mús.).

alleluia, s. aleluia.

allemande, s. alemanda (dança).

allergic, adj. alérgico.

allergy, s. alergia.

alleviate, v.t. aliviar, mitigar.

alleviation, s. alívio.

alleviator, s. pessoa ou coisa que alivia.

alley, s. álea, rua estreita; blind alley, beco sem saída.

all-fools'-day, s. dia dos enganos, 1.º de Abril.

all-fours, s. os quatro naipes; as quatro patas; to go on all-fours, andar de gatas.

all-hallows, s. todos os santos; all--hallows'day, dia de Todos os Santos.

alliance, s. aliança.

allied, adj. aliado.

alligator, s. jacaré.

alliterate, vt. aliterar.

alliteration, s. aliteração.

alliterative, adj. relativo à aliteração.

allocate, v.t. colocar; designar; fixar; distribuir, repartir.

allocation, s. colocação, fixação.

allocution, s. alocução.

allodial, adj. alodial.

allodium, a. alódio, propriedade sem encargos.

allopath, s. alopata.

allopathic, adj. alopático.

allopathist, s. alopata.

allopathy, s. alopatia.

allot, v.t. distribuir, repartir.

allotment, s. lote, parte, quinhão, pensão à família dum soldado, durante a guerra; porção de terra cedida pelo governo, para cultura.

allotee, s. cessionário.

allotropic, s. alotrópico.

allow, v.t. permitir; confessar, admitir; allow for, levar em conta.

allowable, adj. admissível, lícito, tolerável.

allowableness, s. legitimidade, permissão.

allowably, adv. legitimamente.

allowance, s. concessão; permissão; pensão, mesada; desconto; to make allowance for, atenuar, conceder atenuantes.

alloy, s. liga (de metal); mistura. v.t. ligar (metais), misturar.

all-round, adj. completo; all-round education, educção completa.

All-Saints'-Day, s. Dia de Todos os Santos

All-Souls'-Day, s. Dia de Finados.

allspice, pimenta-da-jamaica.

allude, v.t. aludir.

allure, v.t., v.i. seduzir, atrair.

allurement, s. sedução, atractivo, tentação.

alluring, *adj.* sedutor,

allusion, *s.* alusão, referência, insinuação.

allusive, *adj.* alusivo.

allusively, *adv.* alusivamente.

alluvial, *adj.* aluvial, inundação.

alluvion, *s.* aluvião, inundação.

alluvium, *s.* terra de aluvião.

ally, *v.t., v.i.* aliar(-se), unir(-se). *s.* aliado; parente.

almanac, *s.* almanaque.

almightily, *adv.* omnipotentemente.

almightiness, *s.* omnipotência.

almighty, *adj.* omnipotente, todo. poderoso.

almond, *s.* amêndoa; *almond tree,* amendoeira.

almoner, *s.* esmoler; oficial da Casa Real encarregado de dar esmolas.

almost, *adv.* quase.

alms, *s. singl., pl.* esmola, caridade; *alms box,* caixa das esmolas.

almshouse, *s.* hospício; asilo dos pobres.

aloe, *s.* aloés (planta).

aloft, *adv.* em cima, no alto.

alone, *adj.* só, solitário; único. *adv.* somente; *to let alone,* deixar sozinho, em paz.

aloneness, *s.* unicidade; estado de ser só e uno (referindo-se a Deus).

along, *prep., adv.* ao longo; adiante; com; em companhia. 1) *come along,* vamos adiante! 2) *get along with,* progredir. 3) *all along,* do princípio ao fim. 4) *along with,* juntamente com.

alongshore, *adv.* ao longo da praia.

alongside, *adv., prep.* ao lado; junto a.

aloof, *adj.* longe; separado; reservado; indiferente; *to stand aloof from,* manter-se afastado de.

aloofness, *s.* separação; distância.

aloud, *adv.* alto, em voz alta.

alpaca, *s.* alpaca.

alpenstock, *s.* pau com ponta de ferro para subir aos montes elevados.

alpestrian, *adj.* alpestre; alpino.

alpha, *s.* alfa; princípio; *alpha and omega,* o princípio e o fim.

alphabet, *s.* alfabeto.

alphabetic, *adj.* alfabético.

alphabetize, *v.t.* alfabetizar.

alpine, *adj.* alpestre; alpino.

alpinist, *s.* alpinista.

already, *adv.* já.

also, *adv.* também; igualmente.

alt, *adj.* alto, agudo (mús.).

altar, *s.* altar. 1) *high altar,* altar-mor. 2) *to lead a woman to the altar,* casar com.

altar-rail, *s.* grade do altar.

altazimuth, *s.* instrumento para determinar a altitude e azimute de corpos celestes.

alter, *v.t.* alterar, mudar, transformar. *v.i.* modificar-se.

alterable, *adj.* alterável, mudável.

alterant, *adj.* e *s.* alterante.

alteration, *s.* alteração, mudança; inovação.

alterative, *adj.* alterante. *s.* remédio que altera o processo de nutrição.

altercate, *v.i.* altercar, disputar.

altercation, *s.* disputa, discussão.

alternant, *s.* qualidade alternante.

alternate, *adj.* alternado. *s.* substituto. *v.t.* alternar. *v.i.* alternar-se.

alternately, *adv.* alternadamente.

alternateness, *s.* alternação.

alternation, *s.* alternação; turno.

alternative, *adj.* alternativo. *s.* alternativa.

alternatively, *adv.* alternativamente.

although, *conj.* embora, ainda que.

altimeter, *s.* altímetro.

altimetry, *s.* altimetria.

altiscope, *s.* altiscópio.

altitude, *s.* altitude.

alto, *s.* contralto (mús.).

altogether, *adv.* juntamente; totalmente, inteiramente.

alto-relievo, *s.* alto-relevo.

altruism, *s.* altruísmo.

altruist, *s.* altruísta.

altruistic, *adj.* altruísta.

altruistically, *adv.* dum modo altruísta.

alum, *s.* alúmen.

alumina, *s.* alumina.

aluminium, *s.* alumínio.

alumnus, *s. masc. pl.* alumni, alumna; fem. pl. *alumnae,* universitário.

alveolar, *adj.* alveolar.

alveole, *s.* alvéolo.

alveolus, *s.* alvéolo.

always, *adv.* sempre.

am, 1ª. pes. sing. pres. ind. do *v.* to be, sou, estou.

amain, *adv.* com veemência; a toda a pressa.

amalgam, *s.* amálgama; mistura.

amalgamate, *v.t., v.i.* amalgamar, misturar; unir-se.

amalgamation, *a.* amalgamação, acto de amalgamar; fusão de vários negócios.

amanuensis (nses), *s.* amanuense.

amaranth, *s.* amaranto, crista de galo, planta

ervácea; cor encarnada como a flor do amaranto.

amaranthine, *adj.* amarantino; encarnado.

amass, *v.t.* acumular; juntar.

amateur, *s.* amador.

amateurish, *adj.* à maneira de amador; superficial.

amative, *adj.* propenso para o amor; amoroso.

amativeness, *s.* propensão para o amor.

amatory (ies), *adj.* e *s.* amatório, erótico.

amaze, *v.t.* espantar, deixar atónito.

amazed, *adj.* espantado, atónito.

amazedly, *adv.* com espanto.

amazedness, *s.* espanto, estupefacção.

amazement, *s.* espanto, estupefacção.

amazing, *adj.* espantoso.

amazingly, *adv.* assombrosamente.

amazon, *s.* amazona.

amazonian, *adj.* amazónico.

ambage, *s.* circunlóquio, ambages.

ambassador, *s.* embaixador.

ambassadorial, *adj.* relativo a embaixador.

ambassadress, *s.* embaixatriz.

amber, *s.* âmbar. *adj.* de âmbar.

ambergris, *s.* âmbar virgem ou gris.

ambidexter, *s.* ambidextro, hipócrita.

ambidexterity, *s.* ambidestreza; hipocrisia.

ambidextrous, *adj.* ambidestro; hipócrita.

ambient, *adj.* ambiente.

ambiguity, *s.* ambiguidade; incerteza.

ambiguous, *adj.* ambíguo.

ambiguously, *adv.* ambiguamente.

ambiguousness, *s.* ambiguidade.

ambit, *s.* âmbito, limites.

ambition, *s.* ambição; aspiração.

ambitious, *adj.* ambicioso.

ambitiously, *adv.* ambiciosamente.

ambitiousness, *s.* qualidade de ambiciosa.

amble, *s.* marcha a passo travado. *v.i.* marchar a passo.

ambler, *s.* cavalo que marcha a furta-passo.

ambrosia, *s.* ambrósia, manjar delicioso; comida de deuses.

ambrosial, *adj.* delicioso; celestial.

ambrosially, *adv.* deliciosamente.

ambry (ies), despensa; armário; nicho.

ambulance, *s.* ambulância.

ambulant, *adj.* ambulante.

ambulation, *s.* passeio.

ambulatory, *adj.* ambulante; ambulatório.

ambuscade, *s.* emboscada. *v.t., v.i.* atacar de emboscada.

ambush, *s.* emboscada. *v.t.* atacar de emboscada.

ameliorate, *v.t.* melhorar; aperfeiçoar. *v.i.* melhorar-se, aperfeiçoar-se.

amelioration, *s.* melhoramento; aperfeiçoamento.

amen, *adv.* amém, assim seja.

amenability, *s.* responsabilidade.

amenable, *adj.* responsável; tratável.

amenableness, *s.* responsabilidade.

amenably, *adv.* dum modo tratável.

amend, *v.t.* emendar, corrigir; reformar.

amendment, *s.* corecção; emenda.

amends, *s.* recompensa; restituição, compensação.

amenity, *s.* amenidade; brandura.

amerce, *v.t.* multar; punir.

amercement, *s.* multa; privação de privilégios.

American, *adj.* americano. *s.* americano, habitante da América, habitante dos Estados Unidos da América.

americanism, *adj.* americanismo.

americanize, *v.t.* americanizar.

amethyst, *s.* ametista.

amethystine, *adj.* semelhante à ametista.

amiability, *s.* amabilidade.

amiable, *adj.* amável, afável.

amiableness, *s.* amabilidade.

amiably, *adv.* amavelmente.

amicability, *s.* amizade, afecto.

amicable, *adj.* amigável; pacífico.

amice, *s.* amicto.

amid, *prep.* entre, no meio de.

amidship, *adv.* no meio de um navio.

amidst, *prep.* entre, no meio, misturado com, cercado de.

amir, ameer, *s.* título entre os maometanos do Afeganistão.

amiss, *adj.* errado; impróprio. *adv.* erradamente; impropriamente; *to take amiss,* levar a mal.

amity, *s.* amizade.

ammeter, *s.* amperímetro.

ammonia, *s.* amónia; *liquid ammonia,* amoníaco.

ammoniac, *s.* e *adj.* amoníaco; da natureza da amónia.

ammoniacal, *adj.* amoniacal.

ammoniated, *adj.* que contém amónio.

ammonite, *s.* amonite, género fóssil de cefalópodes.

ammonium, *s.* amónio.

ammunitium, *s.* munição.

amnesia, *s.* amnésia.

amnesty, *s.* amnistia.

among, *prep.* entre; no meio de; misturado com.

amorist, *s.* amante, namorado.

amorous, *adj.* amoroso, terno, carinhoso.

amorously, *adv.* amorosamente.

amorousness, *s.* amor, carinho; qualidade de ser amoroso.

amorphism, *s.* amorfia, deformidade.

amorphous, *adj.* amorfo, sem forma; anómalo.

amortization, *s.* amortização.

amortize, *v.t.* amortizar.

amount, *v.i.* somar, importar. *s.* soma, total; *a great amount,* uma grande soma, quantidade.

amour, *s.* amor, namorico; intriga amorosa.

amour propre, *s.* amor-próprio.

ampere, *s.* ampere.

amphibian, *s.* e *adj.* anfíbio.

amphibious, *adj.* anfíbio.

amphibole, *s.* anfíbolo.

amphibology (ies), *s.* anfibologia; sentido ambíguo.

amphiboly (ies), *s.* anfibolia; equívoco.

amphibrach, *s.* anfíbraco.

amphictyons, *s. pl.* anfictiões.

amphigouri, amphigory, *s.* anfiguri.

amphitheater, amphitheatre, *s.* anfiteatro.

amphora, *a.* ânfora.

amphoric, *adj.* anfórico, semelhante ao som que se obtém soprando a uma ânfora vazia.

ample, *adj.* amplo; espaçoso.

ampleness, *s.* amplitude, espaço; abundância.

ampliation, *s.* ampliação (de prazo, etc.); prorrogação.

amplification, *s.* amplificação, desenvolvimento.

amplificatory, *adj.* amplificativo.

amplified, *pret.* e *pp.* de amplify.

amplifier, *s.* amplificador.

amplify, *v.t.* ampliar; dilatar; aumentar.

amplitude, *s.* amplitude, extensão, abundância.

amply, *adv.* amplamente.

ampoule, *s.* ampola.

ampulla, âmbula.

amputate, *v.t.* amputar.

amputation, *s.* amputação.

amuck, *adv.* furiosamente; *to run amuck,* andar tresloucado de um lado para outro com mania sanguinária.

amulet, *s.* amuleto.

amuse, *v.t.* divertir.

amusement, *s.* divertimento, entretenimento.

amusing, *adj.* divertido, engraçado; agradável.

amusingly, *adv.* divertidamente.

amyl, *s.* amilo, amido.

amylic, *adj.* amílico.

an, *artigo indefinido* um, uma.

anabaptism, *s.* anabaptismo.

anabasis, *s.* expedição militar.

anachronism, *s.* anacronismo, erro de data ou facto.

anachronous, *s.* anacrónico.

anacoluthon, *s.* anacoluto.

anaconda, *s.* anaconda.

anacreontic, *adj.* anacreôntico, amatório, erótico.

anaemia, *s.* anemia.

anaemic, *adj.* anémico.

anaesthesia, *s.* anestesia.

anaesthetic, *adj.* anestético.

anaesthetist, *s.* a pessoa que anestesia.

anaesthetize, *v.t.* anestesiar, diminuir a sensibilidade.

anagnorisis, *s.* desenlace de um drama.

anagogic, *adj.* anagógico.

anagogics, *s.* estudo e tratado de vida contemplativa.

anagogy, *s.* anagogia; êxtase; interpretação espiritual ou alegórica.

anagram, *s.* anagrama.

anagramatic (al), *adj.* que forma anagrama.

anal, *adj.* anal, do ânus.

analects, *s.* antologia; analecto.

analgesia, *s.* analgia.

analgesic, *adj.* analgésico.

analogic (al), *adj.* analógico.

analogically, *adv.* analogicamente.

analogist, *s.* analogista.

analogous, *adj.* análogo.

analogously, *adv.* analogamente.

analogousness, *s.* analogia.

analogue, *s.* palavra ou coisa análoga.

analogy, *s.* analogia, semelhança.

analphabetic, *adj.* analfabeto; ignorante.

analphabetically, dum modo que revela ignorância.

analisable, *adj.* analisável.

analyse, *v.t.* analisar, dividir, separar.

analysis, *s., pl. analyses,* análise; divisão, separação.

analyst, *s.* analista, químico analista.

analytic, *adj.* analítico.

analytically, *adv.* analiticamente.

analytics, *s.* ciência da análise; geometria analítica.

analyze, *v.t.* analisar; dividir, separar.

ananas (es), *s.* ananás.

anapaest, *s.* anapesto, pé de verso grego ou latino, formado por duas sílabas breves seguidas duma longa.

anapaestic, *adj.* anapéstico.

anarch, *s.* anarquista.

anarchic, *s.* anárquico.

anarchism, *s.* anarquismo.

anarchist, *s.* anarquista.

anarchy, *s.* anarquia.

anastrophe, *s.* anástrofe.

anathema, *s.* anátema, excomunhão.

anathematization, *s.* anatematização, excomunhão.

anathematize, *v.t.* anatematizar, excomungar.

anatomic, *adj.* anatómico.

anatomically, *adv.* anatomicamente.

anatomist, *s.* anatomista.

anatomize, *v.t.* anatomizar; dissecar.

anatomy, *s.* anatomia.

ancestor, *s.* antepassado.

ancestral, *adj.* hereditário; ancestral.

ancestress, *s.* fem. de ancestor.

ancestry, *s.* linhagem: descendência. *adj.* ancestral, hereditário.

anchor, *s.* âncora. 1) *to wiegh the anchor*, levantar a âncora. 2) *to cast anchor*, lançar a âncora. *v.t.*, *v.i.* ancorar; fixar.

anchorable, *adj.* próprio para ancorar.

anchorage, *s.* ancoradouro.

anchoress, *s.* eremita, mulher que vive numa ermida.

anchorite, anchoret, *s.* anacoreta, ermitão.

anchorhold, *s.* fundo onde a âncora pega; o agarrar da âncora.

anchovy, *s.* anchova.

anchylosis, *s.* anquilose.

ancient, *adj.* antigo, velho. *s.* um ancião; *the ancients*, antepassados.

anciently, *adv.* antigamente.

ancients, *s. pl.* antepassados; antiguidade; *the ancients*, os antigos (as nações antigas civilizadas, especialmente os Gregos e os Romanos).

anciliary, *adj.* subserviente, subordinado.

ancipital, *adj.* ancípite, com dois gumes.

and, *conj.* e. 1) *by and by*, logo. 2) *and so forth*, e assim por diante. 3) *wait and see*, espere e veja.

andante, *s.* andante (mús.)

andiron, *s.* cão de chaminé; trempe (do lar); tripeça de ferro.

androgynous, *adj.* andrógino; hermafrodita.

android, *s.* andróide, fantoche.

anecdote, *s.* anedota.

anecdotic, *adj.* anedótico.

anecdotically, *adv.* em forma de anedota.

anelectric, *adj.* aneléctrico.

anelectrode, *s.* aneléctrodo.

anemia, *s.* anemia.

anemic, anaemic, *adj.* anémico.

anemograph, *s.* anemógrafo.

anemometer, *s.* anemómetro.

anemometric, *adj.* anemométrico.

anemometry, *s.* anemometria.

anemone, *s.* anémona (género de plantas); *sea anemone*, anémona-do-mar.

anent, *prep.* referente a.

aneroid, *adj.* aneróide.

aneurism, *s.* aneurisma.

aneurismal, *adj.* aneurismal.

anew, *adv.* de novo, outra vez.

angel, *s.* anjo.

angeldom, *s.* reino dos anjos.

angelic, *s.* angélico.

angelically, *adv.* angelicamente.

angelica, *s.* angélica (planta).

angelus, *s.* Ângelus, ave-marias.

anger, *s.* raiva, ira, cólera. *v.t.* irritar, enfurecer.

angina, *s.* angina.

angle, *s.* ângulo; esquina; anzol. *v.t.* pescar.

angler, *s.* pescador à cana; (zool.) diabo marinho.

angleworm, *s.* minhoca.

angling, *s.* pesca à cana.

anglican, *s.* e *adj.* anglicano.

anglicanism, *s.* anglicanismo.

anglice, *adv.* em inglês.

anglicism, *s.* anglicismo.

anglicize (ise), *v. t.* inglesar.

Anglo-French, *s.* e *adj.* anglo-francês.

anglomania, *s.* anglomania.

Anglo-Norman, *s.* e *adj.* anglo-normando.

anglophobe, *s.* anglófobo.

anglophobia, *s.* anglofobia.

Anglo-Saxon, *s.* anglo-saxão, língua dos anglo-saxões. *adj.* anglo-saxónico.

angrier, angriest, *comp.* e *sup.* de angry.

angrily, *adv.* colericamente.

angriness, *s.* cólera, ira.

angry, *adj.* irritado, irado; aborrecido.

anguine, *adj.* anguino, semelhante à cobra.

anguish, *s.* dor, ânsia.

anguished, *adj.* angustiado, atormentado.

angular, *adj.* angular; anguloso; magro.

angularity, *s.* angularidade.

angulated, *adj.* angulado.

anhydride, *s.* anidrido.

anhydrite, *s.* anidrite.

anhydrous, *adj.* anídrico.

anil, *s.* anil.

anile, *adj.* anil, relativo a mulher velha; imbecil.

aniline, *s.* anilina.

anility, *s.* velhice de mulher.

animadversion, *s.* animadversão, censura, crítica.

animadvert, *v.i.* animadvertir, censurar, fazer observações; *he animadverts on my conduct,* ele critica a minha conduta.

animal, *s. adj.* animal.

animalcular, *adj.* animalcular, relativo a animálculos.

animalcule, *s.* animálculo, animal microscópico.

animalism, *s.* animalismo; sensualidade.

animate, *v.t.* animar; encorajar. *adj.* animado.

animated, *pret.* e *pp.* de animate e *adj.* animado.

animatedly, *adv.* animadamente.

animation, *s.* animação; vivacidade.

animatograph, *s.* animatógrafo.

animator, *s.* animador.

animosity, *s.* animosidade.

animus, *s.* ânimo, animosidade.

anise, *s.* anis, erva-doce.

aniseed, *s.* grão de anis.

anisette, *s.* aniseta, licor de anis.

anker, *s.* medida de vinho antiga.

ankle, *s.* tornozelo.

anklet, *s.* ornamento ou suporte para o tornozelo.

anna, *s.* aná, moeda de níquel da Índia, correspondente à 16ª parte da rupia.

annalist, *s.* cronista, analista.

annals, *s. pl.* anais.

annatto, *s.* cor amarelada obtida da polpa e sementes do arnoto.

anneal, *v.t.* tornar maleável pela acção do fogo; temperar.

annex, *s.* anexo, dependência. *v.t.* anexar, juntar.

annexation, *s.* anexação.

annexment, *s.* anexação.

annihilate, *v.t.* aniquilar, destruir.

annihilation, *s.* aniquilação.

anniversary, *s., adj.* aniversário.

annotate, *v.t.* anotar.

annotador, *s.* anotador, comentador.

annotation, *s.* anotação.

announce, *v.t.* anunciar, publicar; declarar.

annoucement, *s.* anúncio, publicação; declaração.

announcer, *s.* anunciador.

annoy, *v.t.* aborrecer, importunar.

annoyance, *s.* aborrecimento, incómodo.

annoying, *adj.* importuno, incómodo, fastidioso, vexatório.

annoyingly, *adv.* de um modo importuno; vexatoriamente.

annual, *adj.* anual. *s.* anual; planta que só vive um ano.

annually, *adv.* anualmente.

annuitant, *s.* o que recebe uma anuidade.

annuity, *s.* anuidade.

annul, *v.t.* anular, invalidar.

annular, *adj.* anelado, em forma de anel.

annulate, *adj.* formado de anéis.

annulment, *s.* anulação, rescisão.

annunciate, *v.t.* ver announce.

annunciation, *s.* anunciação, proclamação.

Annunciation, *s.* Anunciação de N. Senhora; *Annunciation day,* Festa da Anunciação.

annunciator, *s.* indicador usado nos hotéis para mostrar onde se reclamam serviços.

anode, *s.* ânodo eléctrodo positivo.

anodyne, *s.* e *adj.* anódino.

anoint, *v.t.* untar, ungir; consagrar.

anomalous, *adj.* anómalo, irregular.

Anointed, *s.* o Messias.

anointment, *s.* unção, consagração.

anomalistic, *adj.* anomalístico.

anomalous, *adj.* anómalo.

anomalously, *adv.* irregularmente.

anomaly, *s.* anomalia, irregularidade.

anon, *adv.* logo, em breve, *ever and anon,* amiúde, a miúdo.

anonaceous, *adj.* anonáceo.

anonym, *s.* anónimo.

anonymity, *s.* anonímia.

anonymous, *adj.* anónimo.

anonymously, *adv.* anonimamente.

anopheles, *s.* anofelíneo.

another, *adj., pron.* outro, um outro; *one another,* uns aos outros.

answer, *s.* resposta; solução. *v.t., v.i.* responder a; satisfazer; *to answer for,* responsabilizar-se por.

answerable, *adj.* responsável.

answerably, *adv.* convenientemente.

answerer, *s.* o que responde, fiador.

ant, *s.* formiga 1) *ant hill,* formigueiro. 2) *anteater,* tamanduá.

antacid, *s.* e *adj.* antiácido.

antagonism, s. antagonismo.
antagonist, s. adversário, antagonista.
antagonistic, adj. antagónico, contrário.
antagonistically, adv. contrariamente; antagonicamente.
antagonize, v.t. competir, disputar. v.i. ser antagónico.
antarctic, s. adj. antárctico.
anteater, s. urso-formigueiro.
antecedence, s. antecedência, precedência.
antecedent, adj. antecedente, precedente. s. antecedente.
antecedently, adv. anteriormente.
antechamber, s. antecâmara.
antedate, v.t. antedatar; preceder.
antediluvian, adj. e s. antediluviano.
antelope, s. antílope.
antemeridian, adj. antemeridiano.
antenatal, adj. pré-natal.
antenna, s. pl. antennae, antena.
antennal, adj. relativo às antenas.
antenuptial, adj. pré-nupcial.
antependium, s. antepêndio.
antepenult, s. antepenúltima sílaba.
antepenuetimate, adj. antepenúltima sílaba.
anteprandial, adj. antes do jantar.
anterior, adj. precedente, anterior.
anteriorly, adv. anteriormente.
anteriorness, s. precedência, anterioridade.
anteriority, s. precedência.
anteroom, s. antessala.
anthem, s. antífona; cântico de alegria ou louvor.
anther, s. antera.
anthill, s. formigueiro.
anthological, adj. antológico.
anthology, s. antologia.
anthracic, adj. relativo a antraz.
anthracite, s. antracite.
anthracitic, adj. que tem as propriedades da antracite.
anthrax, s. antraz.
anthropography, s. antropografia.
anthropoid, s., adj. antropóide.
anthropoidal, adj. antropóide.
anthropologic, adj. antropológico.
anthropologist, s. antropologista.
anthropology, s. antropologia.
anthropometric, adj. antropométrico.
anthropometry, s. antropometria.
anthropomorphic, adj. antropomórfico.
anthropomorphism, s. antropomorfismo.
anthropophagi, s. antropófagos.
anthropaphagy, s. antropofagia.

antiaircraft, adj. antiaéreo.
antibilious, adj. antibilioso.
antic, adj. ridículo, grotesco. s. bobo; bobice; travessura.
anticatholic, s. e adj. anticatólico.
Antichrist, s. Anticristo.
antichristian, s. e adj. anticristão; relativo ao Anticristo.
anticipant, s. anticipador.
anticipate, v.t. prever; antecipar.
anticipation, s. antecipação.
anticipative, adj. que antecipa.
anticipator, s. antecipador.
anticipatorily, adv. antecipadamente.
anticipatory, adj. anticipatório.
anticlimax, s. anticlímax.
anticyclone, s. anticiclone.
anticyclonic, s. anticiclónico.
antidotal, adj. antidotal, contraveneno.
antidote, s. antídoto.
antifat, adj. contra a gordura.
antifebrile, adj. antifebril.
antilogy (ies), s. antilogia.
antimacassar, s. cobertura para cadeiras, sofás, etc., para evitar o pó, gorduras, ou para servir como ornamento.
antimonarchical, adj. antimonárquico.
antimonarchist, s. antimonárquico.
antimonial, adj. antimonial, relativo ao antimónio.
antimonic, s. antimónico.
antimony, s. antimónio.
antinational, adj. antinacional.
antinomian, s. antinomiano. adj. antinómico, contraditório.
antinomic (al), s. adj. antinómico; oposto.
antinomically, adv. de um modo antinómico.
antinomy (ies), s. antinomia.
antipasmin, s. narcótico brando.
antipathy, s. antipatia.
antiphon, s. antífona, versículo que se entoa antes do salmo.
antiphonal, adj. que tem antífonas.
antiphonary (ies), s. antifonário, livro de antífonas.
antiphoner, s. antifoneiro, o que levanta a antífona.
antiphonic (al), adj. antifónico, relativo à antífona.
antiphony (ies), s. antifonia, canto em oitavas entre os gregos.
antiphrasis, s. antífrase.
antipodal, adj. antipodal; contrário; diametralmente oposto.

antipodes, s. antípodas.
antipope, s. antipapa; falso Papa.
antipyretic, s. antipirético.
antipyrin, s. antipirina.
antiquary, antiquarian, s. antiquário.
antiquated, adj. velho; fora de moda.
antique, adj. antigo, s. antiguidade, coisa antiga.
antiquely, adv. antigamente.
antiqueness, s. antiguidade.
antiquity, s. antiguidade; obras dos antigos.
antiscians, s. antecos.
antiscorbutic, s. antiescorbútico.
antiseptic, s., adj. antisséptico.
antislavery, adj. antiescravista.
antisocial, adj. anti-social.
antisocialist, s. anti-socialista.
antistrophe, s. antístrofe.
antithesis, s. pl. antitheses, antítese.
antithetic, adj. antitético.
antitoxin, s. contraveneno.
antler, s. chifre de veado.
ant-lion, s. formiga-leão.
antonym, s. antónimo.
anus (es), s. ânus.
anvill, s. bogorna.
anxiety, s. ansiedade, ânsia; inquietação.
anxious, adj. ansioso, impaciente; que causa ansiedade.
anxiously, adj. ansiosamente.
anxiousness, s. ânsia, ansiedade.
any, adj., pron. algum, alguma, alguns, algumas; qualquer. 1) any further, mais além. 2) at any rate, custe o que custar. adv. de alguma forma.
anybody, pron. alguém; qualquer; is there anybody in? há alguém lá dentro?
anyhow, adv. de qualquer forma.
anyone, pron. qualquer pessoa; alguém.
anything, pron. alguma coisa; qualquer coisa; anything else?, mais alguma coisa?
anyway, adv. de qualquer modo.
anywhere, adv. em qualquer parte; not anywhere, em parte alguma.
anywise, adv. de qualquer modo.
Anzac, s. nome dado às tropas vindas da Austrália e da Nova Zelândia para a Grande Guerra. Palavra formada das iniciais de Australia-New-Zealand Army Corps.
aorist, s. aoristo.
aorta, s. aorta.
aortic, adj. aórtico.
apace, adv. rapidamente.

apache, s. apache.
apagoge, s. apagogia.
apart, adv. à parte; separadamente.
apartness, s. separação; isolamento.
apartment, s. apartamento.
apathetic (al), adj. apático, indiferente, insensível.
apathetically, adv. indiferentemente.
apathy, s. apatia, indiferença.
ape, s. macaco; imitador. v.t. imitar, arremedar; macaquear.
apeak, adv. e adj. quase a pique (náut.), vertical.
apepsia, s. apepsia.
aperient, adj. laxativo. s. laxante.
aperture, s. abertura.
apery, s. macaquice.
apex, s. pl. apexes, apices, ápice; cume.
aphasia, s. afasia.
aphelion, s. afélio.
aphidian, adj. relativo aos afídios.
aphis, s. afídio, pulgão das plantas.
aphonia, s. afonia.
aphonic, adj. afónico.
aphony, s. afonia, perda da voz.
aphorism, s. aforism.
aphorist, s. aforista, o que faz aforismos.
aphoristic, adj. aforístico.
aphrodisiac, adj. e s. afrodisíaco.
aphtha, s. afta.
apiarian, adj. apiário.
apiarist, s. apicultor.
apiary, s. colmeal.
apical, adj. cimeiro.
apices, pl. de apex.
apiculture, s. apicultura.
apiece, adv. por cabeça, cada um.
apish, adj. imitador; macaqueador.
apishly, adv. com macaquices; afectadamente.
apishness, s. arremedo; macaquice.
aplomb, s. aprumo; altivez.
apocalypse, s. apocalipse; revelação.
apocalyptic, adj. apocalíptico.
apocopate, adj. apocopado. v.t. apocopar.
apocope, s. apócope.
apocrypha, s. livros apócrifos.
apocryphal, adj. apócrifo.
apod, s. ápode.
apodosis, s. apodose.
apogee, s. apogeu; auge.
Apollyon, s. Satanás.
apologetic, adj. apologético.
apologetics, s. apologética.

apologetical, adj. apologético.
apologetically, adv. apologeticamente.
apologist, s. apologista.
apologize, v.i. desculpar-se.
apologizer, s. o que pede desculpa.
apologue, s. apólogo, fábula.
apology, s. apologia; desculpa; to demand an apology, exigir satisfações.
apophthegm, s. apotegma.
apopletic (al), adj. apopléctico. 1) apopletic stroke, ataque apopléctico.
apopletically, adv. apoplecticamente.
apoplexy, s. apoplexia.
aposiopesis, s. aposiopese, reticência.
apostasy (ies), s. apostasia.
apostate, s. apóstata.
apostatic (al), adj. apostático.
apostatize, v.i. apostatar.
a posteriori, adv. a posteriori.
apostil, s. apostila.
apostle, s. apóstolo.
apostleship, s. apostolado.
apostolate, s. apostolado.
apostolic, apostolical, adj. apostólico.
apostolically, adv. apostolicamente.
apostrophe, s. apóstrofe; apóstrofo.
apostrophize (ies), v.t. e v.i. apostrofar, interpelar.
apothecary, s. boticário.
apothegm, s. aforismo.
apotheosis, s. apoteose.
apotheosize (ise), v.t. fazer a apoteose, deificar, divinizar.
appall, v.t. aterrar, espantar; desanimar.
appalling, adj. aterrador, espantoso.
appallingly, adv. de um modo aterrador.
appanage, apanage, s. apanágio.
apparatus, apparatuses, s. aparelho; mecanismo.
apparel, s. roupa. v.t. vestir; ornar.
apparent, adj. aparente; manifesto; evidente.
apparently, adv. manifestamente, aparentemente.
apparentness, s. evidência.
apparition, s. aparição; fantasma.
apparitor, s. beleguim.
appeal, v.i. clamar, tomar por testemunha. v.t. aplelar, recorrer. s. apelação, recurso; petição, apêlo.
appealer, s. apelante.
appealing, adj. apelante; suplicante.
appealingly, adv. de modo suplicante.
appear, v.i. aparecer; comparecer; parecer.
appearance, s. aparição; aparência. 1) for appearance sake, para salvar as aparências. 2) to all appearance, ao que parece.
appearer, s. pessoa que aparece ou comparece.
appeasable, adj. reconciliável, aplacável.
appease, v.t. pacificar; aplacar; acalmar.
appeasement, s. apaziguamento, conciliação.
appeasing, adj. pacificador; calmante.
appellant, s. apelante.
appellate, adj. de apelação; Appelate court, Tribunal de apelação.
appelation, s. apelação judicial; denominação, nome.
appellative, s. nome apelativo (gram.). adj. apelativo, comum.
appellatively, adv. apelativamente.
append, v.t. anexar, juntar.
appendage, s. acessório; apêndice.
appendicitis, s. apendicite.
appendix, s. pl. **appendixes, appendices,** apêndice, adição; acessório.
aperception, s. apercepção.
appertain, v.i. pertencer; tocar a, referir a.
appertinent, adj. pertencente, pertinente, concernente.
appetence, s. apetência, desejo, inclinação; afinidade.
appetent, adj. ávido, desejoso (com after ou of).
appetite, s. apetite.
appetize (ise), v.t. abrir o apetite.
appetizer, s. aperitivo.
appetizing, adj. apetitoso, tentador.
appetizingly, adv. de um modo apetitoso, tentador.
applaud, v.t. e v.i. aplaudir.
applauder, s. aplaudidor.
applaudingly, adv. com aplauso.
applause, s. aplauso.
apple, s. maçã. 1) apple of discord, pomo de discórdia. 2) apple-pie, tarte, pastel de maçã. 3) apple-sauce, compota de maçã.
appliable, adj. aplicável, dócil.
appliableness, s. aplicabilidade; docilidade.
appliance, s. utensílio, ferramenta; aplicação.
applicability, s. aplicabilidade.
applicable, adj. aplicável.
applicableness, s. aplicabilidade.
applicably, adv. de modo que se pode aplicar.
applicant, s., adj. pretendente, suplicante.

application, s. aplicação; requerimento; estudo.

applied, adj. aplicado, usado; adoptado; applied for, pedido, solicitado.

apply, v.t. aplicar. 1) to apply to, recorrer a. 2) to apply oneself to, dedicar-se a. v.i. pedir. 3) to apply for a job, pedir um emprego, candidatar-se.

applied, adj. aplicado, usado; adoptado; applied for, pedido.

appoggiatura, s. apogiatura (mús.).

appoint, v.t. designar, nomear; fornecer. 1) well apponted, bem provido. 2) at the apponted hour, à hora marcada.

appointee, s. pessoa nomeada para um cargo.

appointment, s. nomeação; compromisso; entrevista. pl. mobília, acessórios.

apportion, v.t. repartir, dividir; ratear.

apportionment, s. partilha, divisão.

appose, v.t. pôr diante; examinar.

apposite, adj. adaptado, próprio, apropriado.

appositely, adv. adaptadamente, apropriadamente.

appositeness, s. adaptação, propriedade.

apposition, s. aposição, adição.

appositional, adj. relativo a posição.

appraisable, adj. apreciável.

appraisal, s. avaliação; apreciação.

appraise, v.t. avaliar; apreciar, estimar.

appraiser, s. avaliador.

appraisement, s. avaliação, apreciação.

appreciable, adj. apreciável; notável, perceptível.

appreciate, v.t. apreciar, estimar; avaliar.

appreciator, s. apreciador, avaliador.

appreciation, s. apreciação, avaliação.

appreciatingly, adv. com apreciação.

appreciative, adj. apreciativo.

appreciativeness, s. qualidade de ser apreciado.

appreciatory, ver appreciative.

apprehend, v.t. prender; compreender; temer.

apprehensibility, s. apreensibilidade.

apprehensible, adj. compreensível; concebível.

apprehension, s. apreensão, receio; compreensão.

apprenhensive, adj. apreensivo; perspicaz.

apprehensively, adv. apreensivamente.

apprehensiveness, s. receio, apreensão.

apprentice, s. aprendiz; principiante.

apprenticeship, s. aprendizagem.

apprise, apprize, v.t. informar.

apprizer, s. avaliador.

approach, v.t., v.i. aproximar(-se). s. aproximação; acesso.

approachable, adj. acessível.

approaching, adj. próximo, aproximado.

approbate, v.t. aprovar, sancionar.

approbation, s. aprovação.

approbative, adj. aprovativo.

appropinquate, v.t. e v.i. aproxinquar.

appropinquity, s. apropinquação.

appropriate, adj. apropriado; apto. v.t. apropriar(-se); destinar, fixar (uma soma de dinheiro).

appropriately, adv. apropriadamente.

appropriateness, s. propriedade, aptidão.

appropriation, s. apropriação; posse.

appropriator, s. apropriador.

approvable, adj. digno de aprovação.

approval, s. aprovação; adesão.

approve, v.t., v.i. aprovar; confirmar.

approver, s. aprovador.

approving, s. aprovativo.

approvingly, adv. com aprovação.

approximate, adj. aproximação. v.t. aproximar.

approximately, adv. aproximadamente.

approximation, s. aproximação.

approximative, adj. aproximativo; aproximado.

appulse, s. choque, encontro.

appurtenance, s. pertença, acessório.

apricot, s. damasco.

April, s. Abril.

apriori, adv. a priori.

apron, s. avental.

apropos, adv. a propósito; apropos of, a propósito de.

apse, s. abside de uma igreja ou coro.

apsidal, adj. absidal.

apsis, s. aféiio de um astro.

apt, adj. apto; com tendência para; próprio.

aptness, s. aptidão, disposição.

apteral, apterous, adj. áptero, sem asas.

aptitude, s. aptidão, capacidade; disposição.

aptly, adv. com aptidão.

apyretic, adj. apirético.

aqua-fortis, s. água-forte.

aquamarine, s. água-marinha, pedra preciosa. adj. verde-azulado.

aqua-regia, s. água-régia.

aquarelle, s. aguarela.

aquarellist, s. aguarelista.

aquarium, s. aquário.

aquatic, *adj.* aquático.

aquatint, *s.* método de gravar em metal por meio de ácido.

aqua-vitae, *s.* aguardente.

aqueduct, *s.* aqueduto.

aqueous, *adj.* aquoso.

aquiline, *adj.* aquilino.

Arab, *s.* árabe; cavalo árabe; *street arab*, criança sem lar. *adj.* árabe.

arabesque, *s.* e *adj.* arabesco.

Arabia, *s.* Arábia.

Arabian, *s.* e *adj.* árabe; *arabian nights*, as mil e uma noites.

arabic, *s.* língua árabe; *gum arabic*, goma--arábica.

arable, *adj.* cultivável, arável.

arachnida, *s.* aracnídeos.

arachnoid, *s.* aracnóide.

aragonite, *s.* aragonite.

araucaria, *s.* araucária.

arbiter, *s.* árbitro.

arbitrage, *s.* arbitragem.

arbitrament, *s.* arbitramento.

arbitrarily, *adv.* arbitrariamente.

arbitrariness, *s.* arbitrariedade; despotismo.

arbitrary, *adj.* arbitrário; déspotico.

arbitrate, *v.t.* julgar; decidir.

arbitration, *s.* arbitragem.

arbitrator, *s.* árbitro.

arbitress(es), *s.* arbitradora; medianeira.

arbor, arbour, *s.* caramanchão, latada.

arboreal, *adj.* arbóreo.

arboreous, *adj.* arbóreo.

arborescence, *s.* arborescência.

arborescent, *adj.* arborescente.

arboriculture, *s.* arboricultura.

arbor-vitae, *s.* nome de várias plantas vivazes.

arbour, *s.* caramanchel.

arbut, *s.* medronheiro.

arbutus, *s.* árbuto.

arc, *s.* arco; arco de círculo.

arcade, *s.* arcada.

arcanum, *s.* arcano, mistério.

arch, *s.* arco; abóbada; *pointed arch*, arco ogival. *adj.* principal; astuto. *vt.* arquear; cobrir com um arco. *pref.* principal.

archaeological, *adj.* arqueológico.

archaeologist, *s.* arqueólogo.

archaeology, *s.* arqueologia.

archaic, *adj.* antigo, arcaico.

archaism, *s.* arcaísmo.

Archangel, *s.* Arcanjo.

archbishop, *s.* arcebispo.

archbishopric, *s.* arcebispado.

archdeacon, *s.* arcediago.

archdiocese, *s.* arquidiocese.

archduchess, *s.* arquiduquesa.

archduchy, arquiducado.

arched, *adj.* abobadado, construído em arco; arqueado, dobrado em arco.

archer, *s.* archeiro.

archeress, *s.* mulher armada de bestas.

archery, *s.* arte de atirar com flechas.

archetype, *s.* arquétipo.

arch-fined, *s.* o demónio.

arch-heretic, *s.* heresiarca.

archidiaconal, *adj.* pertencente ao arcediago.

archiepiscopacy, *s.* arcebispado.

archiepiscopal, *adj.* arquiepiscopal.

archiepiscopate, *s.* arcebispado.

Archimedean, *adj.* de Arquimedes.

arching, *adj.* arqueado. *s.* curvatura.

archipelago, *s.* arquipélago.

architect, *s.* arquitecto.

architectonic, *adj.* arquitectónico.

architectural, *adj.* arquitectural, arquitectónico.

architecture, *s.* arquitectura.

architrave, *s.* arquitrave.

archival, *adj.* dos arquivos.

archive, *s.* arquivo.

archivist, *s.* arquivista.

archly, *adv.* jocosamente, maliciosamente.

archness, *s.* travessura.

archon, *s.* arconte; governante, presidente.

arch-priest, *s.* arcipreste.

arch-traitor, *s.* o demónio.

archway, *s.* passagem abobadada.

archwise, *adj.* em forma de arco.

arctic, *s.* árctico. *adj.* árctico, setentrional.

arcuate, *adj.* arqueado.

arcuated, *adj.* arqueado.

ardency, *s.* ardência, calor; ardor.

ardent, *adj.* ardent; apaixonado.

ardently, *adv.* ardentemente, apaixonadamente.

ardor, ardour, *s.* ardor, calor; entusiasmo.

arduour, *adj.* árduo, difícil; laborioso; escabroso.

arduous, *adj.* difícil, trabalhoso, árduo.

arduously, *adv.* dificilmente.

are, *pres. pl.* do ind. de *To be*.

area, *s.* área, superfície.

areca, *s.* areca, palmeira da Índia.

arefied, *pret.* e *pp.* de *arefy*.

arefy, *v.t.* secar.

arena, s. arena.

aren't, contracção de are not.

areometer, s. areómetro.

areometry, s. areometria.

Areopagite, s. areopagita, magistrado do Areópago.

areopagitic, adj. pertencente ao Areópago.

Areopagus, s. Areópago, tribunal de Atenas.

argent, adj. prateado.

argentiferous, adj. argentífero.

Argentina, s. Argentina.

argentine, adj. argentino, de prata, argênteo.

argil, s. argila.

argol, s. tártaro (de vinho).

argon, s. árgon.

Argonaut, s. argonauta; navegante ousado; (zool.) náutilo.

argosy (es), s. carraca, grande navio antigo.

argot, s. calão, gíria.

argue, v.i. argumentar; disputar. v.t. debater; provar.

arguable, adj. disputável; impugnável.

arguer, s. argumentador.

argument, s. argumento; debate.

argumentation, s. argumentação.

argumentative, adj. argumentativo; lógico; contencioso.

argumentatively, adj. com argumentos.

argus (es), s. argos; guarda vigilante; argus--eyed, vigilante.

aria, s. ária (mús.).

arian, s. sectário de Ário.

arianism, s. arianismo.

arianize (ise), vt. criar adeptos do arianismo.

arid, adj. árido, seco; desagradável.

aridly, adv. aridamente, com aridez.

ariel, s. espécie de gazela da Ásia e da África.

Aries, s. Áries ou Carneiro (constelação).

arietta, s. pequena ária.

aright, adv. correctamente, acertadamente.

arise, v.i. pas. arose, part. pas. arisen, subir; surgir, aparecer; levantar-se; provir de.

aristocracy, s. aristocracia.

aristocrat, s. aristocrata.

aristocratic, adj. aristocrático.

aristocratically, adv. aristocraticamente.

Aristotelian, adj. aristotélico. s. discípulo de Aristóteles.

arithmetic, s. aritmética.

arithmetically, adv. aritmeticamente.

arithmetician, s. perito em aritmética.

ark, s. arca; Noah`s ark, arca de Noé.

arles, s. sinal de contrato, de assoldadar um criado.

arm, s. braço; ramo de árvore; poder, força; arma. 1) at arm's lenght, a uma braçada. 2) arm in arm, de braço dado. 3) armpit, sovaco. v.t., v.i. armar-se.

armada, s. armada, frota.

armadillo, s. armadilho.

armament, s. armamento.

armature, s. armadura.

armchair, s. poltrona, cadeira de braços.

armed, adj. armado; long armed, que tem braços compridos.

Armenian, s. arménio (habitante e língua). adj. arménico. 1) armenian bole, terra vermelha da Arménia. 2) armenian stone, carbonato azul de cobre.

armful, s. braçada.

armhole, s. abertura de vestido para o braço; sovaco.

armiger, s. armígero, escudeiro.

armipotent, s. armipotente.

armistice, s. armistício.

armless, adj. desarmado; sem um braço.

armlet, s. bracelete.

armor, armour, s. armadura; insígnia. v.t. defender com armadura.

armored, armoured, adj. blindado; armored car, carro blindado.

armorial, adj. heráldico. s. livro sobre heráldica; armorial bearings, brasão de armas.

armory, armoury, s. arsenal. EUA fábrica de armas.

armoured, adj. blindado. 1) armoured train, comboio blindado. 2) armoured motor-car, automóvel blindado.

armour-bearer, s. escudeiro, o que leva o escudo.

armourer, s. armoreiro, espingardeiro.

armour-plate, s. chapas de aço para defesa de um navio.

armoury (ies), s. armaria.

armpit, s. sovaco, axila.

arms, s. pl. armas; serviço militar; hostilidades; brasões. 1) to arms!, às armas! 2) fire-arms, armas de fogo. 3) under arms, pronto para a luta, zangado. 4) present arms!, apresentar armas. 5) pile arms, ensarilhar armas. 6) trail arms!, suspender armas! 7) to lay down arms, cessar hostilidades.

army, s. exército; multidão.

army corps, s. corpo de exército.

arnica, s. arnica.

aroma, s. aroma.

aromatic, adj. aromático.

arose, pas. de to arise.

around, prep., adv. em redor de, em volta de; cerca; to fool around, desperdiçar o tempo.

arousal, s. o acto de despertar.

arouse, v.t. provocar, despertar; animar.

arpeggio, s. arpego (mús.).

arquebus, s. arcabuz.

arquebusier, s. arcabuzeiro.

arrack, s. araca.

arraign, v.t. acusar; processar.

arraigner, s. o acusador num processo criminal.

arraignment, s. processo criminal, acusação.

arrange, v.t. arrumar; ajustar; adaptar.

arrangement, s. arranjo.

arrant, adj. consumado, notório; desavergonhado. 1) an arrant fool, tolo chapado. 2) an arrant knave, um velhaco. 3) an arrant nonsense, tolice rematada.

arrantly, adv. vergonhosamente.

arras, s. pano de arrás.

array, v.t. pôr em ordem de batalha; ataviar, vestir. s. ordem de batalha, vestido, atavio.

arrear, s. a parte de trás.

arrearage, s. atrasos. (pl.) débitos.

arrears, s. pl. débitos; in arrears, atrasado (no pagamento de uma conta).

arrest, s. prisão. v.t. prender; interromper.

arrestable, adj. que pode ser preso ou arrestado.

arrestation, s. prisão.

arrestment, s. prisão, arresto.

arrival, s. chegada, vinda; recém-chegado; the new arrivals, os recém-chegados.

arrive, v.i. chegar; alcançar, conseguir; arrive at a decision, chegar a uma decisão.

arrogance, s. arrogância.

arrogancy, ver arrogance.

arrogant, adj. arrogante.

arrogantly, adv. arrogantemente.

arrogate, v.t. arrogar-se; reclamar.

arrogation, s. arrogação.

arrow, s. flecha.

arrowroot, s. araruta.

arrowy, adj. de flecha; rápido.

arse, s. traseiro (de animais).

arsenal, s. arsenal.

arsenate, s. arseniato.

arsenic, s. arsénico.

arsenious, adj. arsenioso.

arsenite, s. arsenito.

arsis, s. sílaba acentuada.

arson, s. incêndio premeditado.

art, s. arte; destreza, habilidade; astúcia. 1) fine arts, belas-artes. 2) black art, magia negra. 3) master of arts, licenciado em artes.

arterial, adj. arterial.

arterialize, vt. arterializar.

arteriosclerosis, s. arteriosclerose.

arteritis, s. arterite.

artery, s. artéria.

artesian, adj. artesiano; artesian well, poço artesiano.

artful, adj. habilidoso; astucioso.

artfully, adv. astutamente.

artfulness, s. astúcia, habilidade.

arthritic, s. e adj. artrítico.

arthritis, s. artrite.

artichoke, s. alcachofra.

article, s. artigo; cláusula; objecto; (gramaticalmente) artigo a, an, the.

articular, adj. articular.

articulate, adj. articulado; claro. v.t., v.i. articular, pronunciar; unir.

articulately, adv. distintamente; artigo por artigo.

articulateness, s. qualidade de ser articulado.

articulator, s. articulante.

articulation, s. articulação.

artifice, s. artifício; engenho; estratagema.

artificer, s. artífice.

artificial, adj. artificial; falso.

artificially, adv. artificialmente.

artificialness, ver artificiality.

artificiality (ies), s. artificialidade, arte, aparência.

artillerist, s. artilheiro.

artillery, s. artilharia; artillery man, artilheiro.

artisan, s. artesão.

artist, s. artista.

artistic, adj. artístico.

artistically, adv. artisticamente.

artistry, s. habilidade artística.

artless, adj. natural, sem arte, simples; ingénuo.

artlessly, adv. ingenuamente, com naturalidade.

artsman, s. pessoa versada numa arte prática.

Aryan, adj. e s. ariano, indo-europeu, indo--germânico.

as, adv. como; igualmente; por exemplo. 1) as...as, tão...como. 2) as for (to), no que respeita a conj. pois, porque, quando; enquanto. prep. como (he entered the contest as an amateus). Depois de such a forma «as» funciona como pron. rel. 3) in cities such as Lisbon, em cidades tal como Lisboa.

asafoetida, s. assa-fétida (planta).

asbestic, adj. asbestino.

asbestos, s. asbestos, amianto.

ascend, v.t., v.i. ascender, subir, elevar-se.

ascendance, s. ascendência, predomínio, influência.

ascendant, ascendent, s. predomínio; ascendente (pai ou avô). adj. ascendente, predominante.

ascension, s. ascensão, subida.

Ascension, Ascensão do Senhor.

ascensional, adj. ascensional.

Ascension-day, adj. Dia da Ascensão.

ascent, s. subida; elevação.

ascertain, v.t indagar, averiguar.

ascertainable, adj. averiguável.

ascertainment, s. certeza, averiguação.

ascetic, adj. ascético. s. asceta.

ascetical, adj. ascético.

ascetically, adv. asceticamente.

ascetism, s. ascetismo.

ascian, s. áscio.

asclepiad, s. asclepiadeu (verso grego ou latino).

ascribe, v.t. atribuir, imputar.

ascribable, adj. atribuível, imputável.

aseptic, adj. asséptico.

asexual, adj. assexuado.

ash, s. freixo (árvore); cinza. 1) as pale as ashes, pálido como um cadáver. 2) ashtray, cinzeiro. 3) Ash-Wednesday, Quarta-Feira de Cinzas.

ashamed, adj. envergonhado.

ashamedly, adv. vergonhosamente.

ashamedness, s. vergonha.

ashen, adj. cinzento; pálido; his face turned ashen at the news, ele ficou pálido com a notícia.

ashes, s. pl. cinzas; restos mortais.

ashlar, s. silhar.

ashore, adj., adv. em terra. 1) to run ashore, encalhar. 2) to go ashore, desembarcar.

ashy, adj. de cinzas; coberto de cinzas; cinzento-pálido.

Ash-Wednesday, s. Quarta-Feira de Cinzas.

Asia, s. Ásia.

Asiatic, adj., s. asiático.

aside, adv. de lado, de parte; put aside, pôr de lado, abandonar. s. um aparte.

asinine, adj. asinino.

ask, v.t. perguntar; exigir; pedir; convidar. 1) to ask for, pedir; perguntar. 2) to ask after, perguntar sobre.

askance, adv. de soslaio; to look askance, olhar de soslaio.

askew, adv. de lado, obliquamente. 1) to look askew, não olhar de frente. 2) to hang a picture askew, pôr um quadro torto ao pendurá-lo.

asking, s. pergunta, pedido.

aslant, adv. de atravéz, obliquamente.

asleep, adj. adormecido. 1) to fall asleep, adormecer. 2) my foot is asleep, o meu pé está dormente.

aslope, adv. em declive.

asp, s. serpente venenosa do Egipto, áspide; faia preta.

asparagus, s. espargo.

aspect, s. aspecto; aparência.

aspectable, adj. visível.

aspen, s. faia preta. adj. de faia, trémulo como faia.

asper, s. aspre, moeda turca.

asperge, v.t. aspergir.

asperges, s. asperges.

aspergill, s. hissope.

asperity, s. aspereza.

asperse, v.t. aspergir; difamar, caluniar.

aspersion, s. calúnia, difamação.

aspersorium, s. caldeirinha de água benta.

asphalto, s. asfalto.

asphaltic, adj. betuminoso.

asphodel, s. asfódelo.

asphyxia, s. asfixia.

asphyxiate, v.t. sufocar, asfixiar.

asphyxiation, s. asfixia.

asphyxy, s. asfixia.

aspic, s. áspide pequena, cobra; geleia de carne.

aspidistra, s. (bot.) aspidistra.

aspirant, s. aspirante, candidato; pretendente.

aspirate, s. consoante aspirada. adj. aspirado.

aspiration, s. aspiração (de ar); ambição.

aspirator, s. aspirador.

aspire, v.i. aspirar, desejar; subir.

aspirer, s. aspirante.

aspirin, s. aspirina.

aspiring, *adj.* ambicioso, aspirante. *s.* ambição.

aspiringly, *adv.* ambiciosamente.

aspiringness, *s.* aspiração.

asquint, *adv.* e *adj.* com os olhos trocados, de esguelha, como um vesgo.

ass, *s.* asno, burro; pessoa estúpida.

assagal, *s.* azagaia.

assail, *v.t.* atacar, assaltar.

assailable, *adj.* que pode ser assaltado.

assailant, *s.* assaltante.

assassin, *s.* assassino.

assassinate, *v.t.* assassinar.

assassination, *s.* assassínio, assassinato.

assassinator, *s.* assassino.

assault, *s.* assalto; agressão; *to carry by assault,* tomar de assalto. *v.t., v.i.* assaltar; agredir; atacar.

assaulter, *s.* agressor, salteador.

assay, *s.* análise; ensaio de metais. *v.t.* analisar; ensaiar (metais).

assayer, *s.* ensaiador (de metais).

assaying, *s.* método de analisar os metais.

assay-master, *s.* chefe dos ensaiadores.

assegai, *s.* ver *assagai.*

assemblage, *s.* assembleia, reunião; montagem.

assemble, *v.t.* reunir; montar. *v.i.* reunir-se.

assembly, *s.* assembleia; toque de reunir tropas.

assent, *v.i.* consentir; aprovar. *s.* consentimento; aprovação.

assentingly, *adv.* por consentimento.

assert, *v.t.* afirmar, declarar.

assertable, *adj.* sustentável.

assertion, *s.* afirmação; declaração.

assertive, *adj.* assertivo, dogmático.

assertiveness, *s.* asserção, defesa.

asserter, *s.* afirmador, defensor.

assess, *v.t.* taxar; lançar impostos.

assessable, *adj.* sujeito a impostos.

assessment, *s.* taxa; contribuição; avaliação.

assessor, *s.* louvado da Fazenda Nacional; assessor.

asset, *s.* vantagem. *pl.* fundos, bens.

asseverate, *v.t.* asseverar, afirmar.

asseveration, *s.* afirmação, asseveração.

assibilate, *v.t.* assibilar, tornar sibilante.

assibilation, *s.* assibilação, acto de tornar sibilante.

assiduity, *s.* assiduidade, diligência; (*pl.*) atenções constantes.

assiduous, *adj.* assíduo.

assiduously, *adv.* assiduamente.

assiduousness, *s.* assiduidade.

assign, *v.t.* designar; transferir; assinar.

assignable, *adj.* assinável, transferível.

assignat, *s.* assinado; papel-moeda durante a Revolução Francesa.

assignation, *s.* cessão; trespasse, citação.

assignee, *s.* cessionário; administrador duma falência.

assigner, *s.* cessionista, comitente.

assignment, *s.* atribuição; trespasse; cessão.

assimilable, *adj.* assimilável.

assimilate, *v.t., v.i.* assemelhar; assimilar.

assimilation, *s.* assimilação.

assimilative, *adj.* assimilativo.

assist, *v.t., v.i.* auxiliar; estar presente.

assistance, *s.* auxílio, ajuda.

assistant, *adj., s.* auxiliar, ajudante.

assister, *s.* assistente, auxiliar.

assize, *s.* (geralmente pl.) tribunal que se reúne periodicamente nos diversos condados da Inglaterra; sessões deste tribunal.

associable, *adj.* associável.

associate, *v.t.* associar; unir. *v.i.* associar-se. *adj.* associado. *s.* sócio; cúmplice.

association, *s.* associação, sociedade. 1) *deed of association,* documento que dá as particularidades duma companhia de responsabilidade limitada. 2) *association football* (coloq. *soccer, socker*) futebol.

associative, *adj.* associativo.

assonance, *s.* assonância.

assonate, *v.t.* formar assonância.

assort, *v.t.* classificar; sortir.

assorted, *adj.* sortido.

assortment, *s.* classificação.

assuage, *v.t.* aliviar, acalmar; mitigar.

assuagement, *s.* mitigação, alívio.

assume, *v.t.* assumir; fingir; supor.

assumable, *adj.* assumptível.

assumed, *adj.* suposto, afectado, fingido; *assumed name,* nome suposto.

assumedly, *adv.* afectadamente.

assuming, *adj.* arrogante, pretensioso.

assumingly, *adv.* arrogantemente.

assumption, *s.* Assunção de Nossa Senhora; arrogância; suposição.

Assumption, *s.* Festa da Assunção de Nossa Senhora.

assumptive, *adj.* assumptivo, suposto.

assurance, *s.* garantia; segurança; certeza, firmeza; arrogância.

assure, *v.t.* garantir; assegurar, afirmar.
assured, *s.* segurado contra riscos. *adj.* seguro, certo.
assuredly, *adv.* sem dúvida, certamente.
assuredness, *s.* certeza, confiança.
assurer, *s.* assegurador; segurador.
Assyrian, *s.* e *adj.* assírio; indivíduo ou dialecto da Assíria.
assyriology, *s.* assiriologia.
aster, *s.* áster.
asterisk, *s.* asterisco.
astern, *adv.* detrás, à popa.
asteroid, *s.* a *adj.* asteróide.
asthenia, *s.* astenia, fraqueza.
asthenic (al), *adj.* asténico.
asthma, *s.* asma.
asthmatic, *adj.* asmático; eficaz contra a asma.
astigmatic, *adj.* astigmático.
astigmatism, *s.* astigmatismo.
astir, *adj.*, *adv.* activo; em movimento; *you are astir early this morning,* você pulou cedo da cama hoje.
astonish, *v.t.* causar admiração, espantar, surpreender; *to be astonished at,* estar admirado de.
astonished, *adj.* admirado, espantado.
astonishing, *adj.* surpreendente, espantoso.
astonishingly, *adv.* assombrosamente.
astonishment, *s.* admiração, espanto.
astound, *v.t.* aterrar, aturdir.
astounding, *s.* aterrador, espantoso.
astraddle, *adj.* escarranchado, escarrapachado.
astragal, *s.* (anat. e arq.) astrágalo.
astrakhan, *s.* astracã; tecido de lã; de Astrakan (Rússia).
astral, *adj.* astral.
astray, *adv.*, *adj.* desviado; perdido. 1) *to go astray,* extraviar-se. 2) *to lead astray,* desencaminhar, seduzir.
astride, *adj.*, *prep.* escarranchado.
astringe, *v. t.* adstringir, apertar.
astringency, *s.* adstringency.
astringent, *adj.* adstringente; austero; áspero. *s.* adstringente.
astringently, *adv.* de um modo adstringente.
astrolabe, *s.* astrolábio.
astrologer, *s.* astrólogo.
astrologic (al), *adj.* astrológico.
astrologically, *adv.* astrologicamente.
astrology, *s.* astrologia.
astrometry, *s.* astrometria.
astronomer, *s.* astrónomo.

astronomic (al), *s.* astronómico.
astronomically, *adv.* astronomicamente.
astronomy, *s.* astronomia.
astute, *adj.* astuto.
astutely, *adv.* sagazmente, com astúcia, sagacidade.
asunder, *adv.* separadamente; em pedaços.
asylum, *s.* asilo; manicómio.
asymmetric (al), *adj.* assimétrico, irregular, desproporcionado.
asymmetrically, *adv.* irregularmente.
asymmetry, *s.* assimetria.
asymptote, *s.* assíntota.
asymptotic (al), *adj.* assintótico.
asyndeta, plural de *asyndeton.*
asyndeton, *s.* assíndeto.
at, *prep.* a, *at the window;* em, no, na, *at school, at the top of the page;* (em referência a tempo) *at five o'clock;* (ocupação) *at work, at one's studies,* (estado, condição) *at peace, at war,* (modo) *at a gallop;* (direcção) *the dog jumped at the cat;* (preço, quantia) *he sold the book at two dollars.* 1) *at once,* de uma vez, de repente. 2) *at last, at lenght,* finalmente. 3) *at first,* a princípio.
atavism, *s.* atavismo.
atavistic, *s.* atávico.
ataxy (ies), *s.* ataxia.
ate, *pas.* de *to eat.*
atelier, *s.* atelier, oficina.
atheism, *s.* ateísmo.
atheist, *s.* ateu.
atheistic (al), *adj.* ateístico.
atheling, *s.* filho de um nobre; príncipe herdeiro.
Athenaeum, *s.* ateneu.
athirst, *adj.* sedento; sequioso.
athlete, *s.* atleta.
athletic, *adj.* atlético.
athletically, *adv.* atleticamente.
athletics, *s.* atletismo.
at-home, *s.* recepção de visitas íntimas.
at home, *adj.* e *adv.* em casa. 1) *he is at home,* conhecedor, perito. 2) *charity begins at home,* a caridade bem entendida começa por nós.
athwart, *adv.* contrariamente, a torto e a direito. *prep.* através.
atlantic, *s.* a *adj.* atlântico.
atlas, *s.* atlas.
atmosphere, *s.* atmosfera; ambiente.
atmospheric, *adj.* atmosférico.
atoll, *s.* ilhota de coral.

atomic, *adj.* atómico.

atom, *s.* átomo.

atomic, *adj.* atómico; *atomic bomb*, bomba atómica.

atomization, *s.* atomização.

atomize, *v.t.* reduzir a átomos.

atomizer, *s.* pulverizador.

atone, *v.t., v.i.* reparar; expiar.

atonement, *s.* expiação.

atoner, *s.* expiador.

atoning, *adj.* expiatório.

atoningly, *adv.* como expiação.

atonic, *s.* e *adj.* atónico.

atop, *adj., adv.* para cima; para o cume. *prep.* em cima.

atrabilious, *adj.* atrabiliário, acriminoso.

atria, *pl.* de **atrium.**

atrip, *adj.* garrada (âncora); guindada (vela).

atrium, *s.* átrio.

atrocious, *adj.* atroz, cruel.

atrociously, *adv.* atrozmente.

atrociousness, *s.* atrocidade.

atrocity, *s.* atrocidade, crueldade.

atrophic, *s.* atrófico.

atrophy, *v.t., v.i.* atrofiar(-se).

atropine, *s.* atropina.

attach, *v.t.* unir, juntar; embargar; atribuir.

attachable, *adj.* que se pode ligar.

attachment, *s.* união; afecto; embargo.

attaché, *s.* adido a uma embaixada.

attack, *v.t.* atacar, agredir. *s.* ataque, assalto. 1) *counter attack*, contra-ataque. 2) *false attack*, ataque simulado.

attacker, *s.* agressor.

attain, *v.t.* alcançar, atingir, obter.

attainability, *s.* probabilidade de alcançar.

attainable, *adj.* conseguível.

attainder, *s.* proscrição; extinção dos direitos civis, morte civil.

attainment, *s.* obtenção; aquisição; prenda pessoal.

attaint, *v.t.* desonrar; privar dos direitos civis.

attar, *s.* essência de rosas.

attemper, *v.t.* temperar; modificar, adaptar; moderar; afinar.

attempt, *v.t.* tentar, esforçar-se; atacar; *to attempt the life of*, atentar contra a vida de.

attemptable, *adj.* que se pode tentar.

attemptor, *adj.* empreendedor.

attend, *v.t.* cuidar; acompanhar; estar presente. *v.i.* prestar atenção; atender. 1) *to attend to a business*, tratar de um negócio. 2) *to attend on*, servir, acompanhar.

attendance, *s.* presença. serviço; auditório.

attendant, *s.* servidor. *adj.* subordinado, que acompanha; presente.

attention, *s.* atenção, aplicação; *pl.* galanteio; *to pay attentions to a lady*, galantear uma senhora.

attentive, *adj.* atento, cortês.

attentively, *adv.* atentamente.

attentiveness, *s.* atenção, cuidado.

attenuate, *s.* atenuado, enfraquecido, delgado. *v.t.* atenuar, diminuir, adelgaçar.

attenuation, *s.* atenuação, fraqueza.

attest, *v.t.* atestar, certificar, confirmar.

attestation, *s.* atestação, confirmação.

attic, *s.* água-furtada.

atticism, *s.* aticismo, elegância de linguagem.

atticize (ise) *v.i.* usar linguagem elegante.

attire, *v.t., v.i.* vestir, ataviar, adornar. *s.* adorno, atavio.

attirement, *s.* atavio, adorno.

attitude, *s.* atitude; postura.

attitudinize(ise), *v.i.* tomar atitudes; falar, escrever, comportar-se afectadamente.

attorn, *v.t.* e *v.i.* fazer transferência legal.

attorney, *s.* procurador. 1) *letter ou power of*, procuração. 2) *attorney general*, procurador-geral da República ou da Coroa.

attorneyship, *s.* procuradoria.

attract, *v.t.* atrair; cativar; *to attract attention*, chamar a atenção.

atractability, *s.* atractividade, poder ou propriedade de atrair.

attractable, *adj.* que pode ser atraído.

attracting, *adj.* atractivo.

attractingly, *adv.* atractivamente.

attraction, *s.* atracção, simpatia.

attractive, *adj.* atractivo.

attractively, *adv.* atractivamente.

attractiveness, *s.* força atractiva, atracção, graça.

attractor, *s.* o que atrai.

attrahent, *s.* atraente.

attributable, *adj.* imputável, atribuível.

attribute, *v.t.* atribuir, imputar. *s.* característica; atributo.

attribution, *s.* atribuição, atributo; qualidades.

attributive, *adj.* e *s.* atributivo.

attributivelly, *adv.* atributivamente.

attrition, *s.* atrito.

attune, *v.t.* harmonizar, afinar.

auberge, *s.* hospedaria.

aubergine, *s.* beringela.

auburn, *adj.* e *s.* moreno; trigueiro; moreno dourado.
auction, *v.t.* aleiloar.
auctionary, *adj.* relativo a um leilão.
auctioneer, *s.* leiloeiro.
audacious, *adj.* audacioso, insolente.
audaciousness, *s.* audácia, descaramento.
audacity, *s.* audácia.
audibility, *s.* audibilidade.
audible, *adj.* audível.
audibleness, ver *audibility.*
audibly, *adv.* perceptivelmente, em voz alta.
audience, *s.* auditório; audiência; entrevista.
audion, *s.* audião, instrumento para aumentar o som (na telefonia sem fios).
audiphone, *s.* audifone.
audit, *s.* exame de contas. *v.t.* examinar as contas.
auditing, *s.* exame e ajuste de contas.
auditive, *adj.* auditivo.
auditor, *s.* auditor; revisor de contas.
audition, *s.* audição.
auditorium, *s.* auditório, sala.
auditorship, *s.* auditoria.
auditory (ies), *s.* auditório, ouvintes. *adj.* auditivo.
auger, *s.* broca.
aught, *s.* zero, algo. *adv.* de qualquer forma.
augment, *v.t., v.i.* aumentar; acrescentar; ampliar; crescer. *s.* aumento; vogal prefixa os pretéritos em certas línguas antigas.
augmentable, *adj.* capaz de ser aumentado.
augmentation, *s.* aumento.
augmentative, *adj.* aumentativo.
augur, *v.t., v.i.* predizer, pressagiar.
augural, *adj.* augural.
augury, *s.* augúrio.
August, *s.* Agosto.
august, *adj.* augusto.
augustly, *adv.* majestosamente.
augustness, *s.* grandeza, majestade.
auk, *s.* corvo marinho *(Alca torda).*
aula, *s.* a porção anterior do terceiro ventrículo do cérebro; vestíbulo.
aulic, *s.* e *adj.* áulico, cortesão.
aunt, *s.* tia.
aura, *s.* aura; magnetismo animal; influência.
aural, *adj.* auricular.
aurate, *adj.* com orelhas; áureo. *s.* arauto.
aureate, *adj.* áureo; dourado.
aureola, *s.* auréola.
auric, *adj.* áurico.
auricle, *s.* pavilhão da orelha; aurícula (do coração).

auricula, *s.* orelha-de-urso; (planta); aurícula.
auricular, *adj.* auricular; tradicional; confidencial.
auricularly, *adv.* auricularmente; secretamente.
auriculate, *adj.* em forma de orelha.
auriculated, ver *auriculate.*
auriferous, *adj.* aurífero.
auriform, *adj.* auriforme.
aurist, *s.* especialista em doenças dos ouvidos.
aurochs, *s.* boi selvagem.
aurora, *s.* aurora.
auroral, *adj.* auroral.
auscultation, *s.* auscultação.
auscultator, *s.* auscultador.
auspice, *s.* presságio. *pl.* protecção.
auspicious, *adj.* auspicioso, favorável; próspero.
auspiciously, *adv.* prosperamente.
auspiciousness, *s.* prosperidade.
austere, *adj.* severo, austero.
austerely, *adv.* austeramente.
austereness, *s.* austeridade.
austerity, *s.* austeridade, severidade.
austral, *adj.* austral.
Australasia, *s.* Australásia.
Australia, *s.* Austrália.
Australian, *s.* e *adj.* australiano.
Austria, *s.* Áustria.
austrian, *s.* e *adj.* austríaco.
austro-hungarian, *s.* e *adj.* austro-húngaro.
authentic, *adj.* autêntico, genuíno.
autentically, *adv.* autenticamente.
authenticate, *v.t.* autenticar.
authentication, *s.* autenticação.
authenticity, *s.* autenticidade.
author, *s.* autor; escritor.
authoress, *s.* autora.
authoritarian, *adj.* autoritário.
authoritative, *adj.* autoritário; positivo.
authoritatively, *adv.* com autoridade; de um modo positivo.
authoritativeness, *s.* qualidade de autoridade, ou de autoritário; arrogância.
authority, *s.* autoridade; governo. *pl.* as autoridades.
authorization, *s.* autorização; sanção; ordem.
authorize, *v.t.* autorizar; permitir; sancionar.
authorship, *s.* autoria.
auto, prefixo auto.
autobiographer, *s.* autobiográfico.
autobiographic (al), *adj.* autobiográfico.

autobiography, s. autobiografia.
autocar, s. automóvel.
autochthon, s. indígena; aborígena; aborígene.
autocracy, s. autocracia.
autocrat, s. autocrata.
autocratic, adj. autocrático.
autocratically, adv. autocraticamente.
auto-da-fé, s. auto-de-fé.
autogiro (gtro), s. autogiro.
autograph, s. autógrafo. v.t. autografar.
autographic, adj. autográfico.
autography, s. autografia, reprodução fiel de uma escrita.
autointoxication, s. auto-intoxicação.
automatic, adj. automático; involuntário. s. pistola automática.
automatical, adj. automático; involuntário; por força da lei; espontâneo.
automatically, adv. automaticamente.
automatism, s. automatismo.
automatist, s. automatário; sequaz do automatismo.
automaton, s. autómato.
automobile, s. automóvel.
automotive, adj. autopropulsor.
autonomic, adj. autónomo.
autonomous, adj. autónomo.
autonomy, s. autonomia.
autonym, s. autónimo.
autopsy, s. autópsia.
autos-de-fé, s. autos-de-fé.
auto-suggestion, s. auto-sugestão.
autotruck, s. camião.
autotype, s. cópia exacta; autotipia. v.i. tirar fac-símiles.
autotypography, s. autotipografia; zincogravura.
autumn, s. Outono.
autumnal, adj. outonal.
auxiliary, s. auxiliar (verbo); assistente. adj. auxiliar.
avail, v.i. ser útil, servir. v.t. aproveitar, utilizar. s. proveito, benefício. pl. proveitos. 1) to avail oneself of, aproveitar-se de. 2) of on avail, de nenhuma utilidade.
availability, s. utilidade, eficácia.
available, adj. útil; vantajoso; disponível.
availableness, ver availability.
availably, adv. eficazmente, utilmente.
avalanche, s. avalancha.
avant-courier, s. guarda-avançada, escuteiro.
avarice, s. avareza.

avaricious, adj. avaro.
avariciously, adv. avaramente.
avariciousness, s. avareza.
avast, int. Pare! Basta!
avatar, s. avatar, descendente de uma divindade mitológica; encarnação; fase.
avaunt, int. fora daqui!
ave, int. e s. bem-vindo! adeus!
avenge, v.t. vingar; castigar.
avenger, s. vingador.
avengeress, s. vingadora.
avenue, s. avenida; alameda.
aver, v.t. afirmar, assegurar.
average, s. média, parte proporcional; avaria. adj. médio; típico. v.t. avaliar; dar como média.
averment, s. afirmação.
averruncator, s. instrumento para podar árvores.
averse, adj. adverso; contrário.
aversely, adv. com repugnância.
averseness, s. repugnância, má vontade.
aversion, s. aversão.
avert, v.t. desviar, impedir.
avertible, adj. separável.
aviatist, s. avicultor.
aviary, s. aviário.
aviate, v. i. voar em avião.
aviation, s. aviação.
aviator, s. aviador.
avid, adj. ávido.
avidity, s. avidez, ânsia.
avion, s. avião.
aviso, s. aviso (embarcação).
avocado, s. abacate.
avocation, s. distracção, passatempo; ocupação; vocação.
avoid, v.t. evitar; escapar.
avoidable, adj. evitável, iludível, revogável.
avoidance, s. acto e efeito de evitar alguma coisa; anulação.
avoirdupois, s. sistema de pesos de Inglaterra e dos Estados Unidos, usados para todas as mercadorias menos para metais preciosos, pedras preciosas e remédios. A libra «avoirdupois» tem 453,59 gramas.
avouch, v.t. afirmar, declarar; garantir.
avow, v.t. declarar, confessar; admitir.
avowal, s. declaração, confissão.
avowed, adj. manifesto, declarado.
avowedly, adv. declaradamente.
avulsion, s. avulsão, extracção, arranco.
avuncular, adj. avuncular, relativo a um tio.

await, *v.t.* esperar.

awake, awoke, awaked, *v.t., v.i. pas., part. pass.* acordar, despertar.

awaken, *v.t., v.i.* acordar.

awakening, *s.* o despertar. *adj.* despertador.

award, *v.t.* julgar, decidir; premiar. *s.* julgamento; prémio.

aware, *adj.* ciente, sabedor.

awash, *adj.* e *adv.* à flor da água.

away, *adv.* longe, fora. 1) *to go away,* ir-se embora. 2) *to run away,* fugir. 3) *to give away,* presentear, distribuir. 4) *right away,* agora mesmo. 5) *away with you,* fora daqui!

awe, *s.* medo, temor (com respeito), pavor. *v.t.* aterrar; infundir temor, respeito; *to stand in awe,* ficar pasmado.

aweless, *adj.* irreverente; sem receio.

awesome, *adj.* terrível, pavoroso.

awe-striken, awe-struck, *adj.* espantado, aterrado.

awful, *adj.* grande, extremo; terrível, espantoso; grande, considerável.

awfully, *adv.* terrivelmente; muito, excessivamente; *I am awfully fagged,* estou exausto de fadiga.

awhile, *adv.* por um instante.

awkward, *adj.* desalinhado, desajeitado; grosseiro; estúpido.

awkwardish, *adj.* desastrado, inepto.

awkwardly, *adv.* desastradamente, grosseiramente.

awkwardeness, *s.* grosseria, inépcia; estupidez; falta de graça.

awl, *s.* sovela.

awn, *s.* pragana (das espigas).

awning, *s.* toldo.

awoke, pas. part. pass de *to awake.*

awry, *adv., adj.* oblíquo, torto, torcido; perverso; obliquamente.

axe, *s.* machado; *axe head,* ferro de machado.

axial, *adj.* axial, formando eixo; redondo como um eixo.

axil, *s.* axila, sovaco.

axilla, *s.* axila, sovaco; axila de planta.

axiliar, *adj.* axilar.

axillary, *adj.* axilar.

axiom, *s.* axioma.

axiomatic, *adj.* axiomático.

axiomatically, *adv.* de um modo axiomático.

axis, *s., pl. axes,* eixo.

axle, *s.* eixo da roda.

axled, *adj.* com eixo.

axle-tree, ver *axle.*

aye, ay, *adv.* sim. *s.* resposta afirmativa.

ayah, *s.* aia.

aye-aye, *s.* ai-ai; animal semelhante ao lemur.

azalea, *s.* azálea.

azimuth, *s.* azimute.

Azores, *s.* arquipélago dos Açores.

azote, *s.* azote.

azotic, *adj.* azótico.

azure, *s.* azui-celeste. *adj.* azulado. *v.t.* azular.

azurine, *s.* azurina; ave; cor de azul-escuro.

azurite, *s.* azurite, malaquite.

B

b, segunda letra do alfabeto.

baa, *s.* balido de ovela. *v.i.* balir, dar balidos.

baa-lamb, *s.* nome familiar do cordeiro.

babble, *v.i.* balbuciar; tagarelar. *s.* parolagem; murmúrio (das águas).

babblement, ver *babbling.*

babbler, *s.* palrador, tagarela.

babbling, *s.* parolagem; murmúrio das águas. *adj.* falador.

babe, *s.* criança de peito.

bable, *s.* confusão, desordem.

baboon, *s.* bugio, mono.

baboonery, *s.* bugiaria, modos de bugio.

babouche, *s.* babucha.

baby, *s.* criança de peito. *v.t.* mimar.

baby-farm, *s.* dispensário para criação e educação de crianças.

babyhood, *s.* período da infância.

babyish, *adj.* pueril, infantil.

babyishly, *adv.* dum modo pueril.

babyshness, *s.* puerilidade

baccalaureate, *s.* bacharelato.

baccara, *s.* bacará (jogo).

bacchanal, *s.* e *adj.* bacanal; ébrio.

bacchanalian, *s.* bacanal.

bacchant, *s.* bacante.

bacchic, *adj.* báquico, bacanal.

Bacchus, *s.* o deus Baco.

bachelor, *s.* bacharel; solteiro, celibatário.

bachelorship, *s.* estado de solteiro; bacharelato.

bacillus, *s., pl. bacilli,* bacilo.

back, *s.* costas; parte posterior. 1) *the back of a chair, book, knife,* costas de uma cadeira, livro, etc. 2) *behind one's back,* às costas de alguém (sem o seu conhecimento). 3) *to be on one's back,* estar de cama. 4) *to turn one's back on (upon),* dar as costas a. 5) *to fall on one's back,* cair de costas. *adj.* posterior, traseiro. 6) *back door,* porta dos fundos, traseira. 7) *back number,* número atrasado (de revista, jornal, etc.). *adv.* para trás, atrás. 8) *back and forth,* dum lado para o outro. 9) *to pay a man back,* pagar na mesma moeda. *v.t.* fazer recuar; apoiar, ajudar. 10) *to back out of,* abandonar. 11) *to back up,* ajudar.

backache, *s.* dor nas costas.

backbite, *pret.* backbit. *par. pass.* backbitten, *v.t.* murmurar, detrair.

backbiter, *s.* murmurador, detractor.

backbiting, *s.* maledicência.

back-board, *s.* espaldar.

back-door, *s.* porta traseira, porta falsa.

backbone, *s.* espinha dorsal.

backe, *s.* defensor; fiador.

back gammon, *s.* gamão (jogo).

background, *s.* fundo, último plano; experiência.

back-hair, *s.* tranças do cabelo.

backhand, *s.* escrita feita da direita para a esquerda; revés; *backhanded remark,* uma ironia.

backing, *s.* apoio, protecção; reforço; retrocesso.

back-set, *s.* reverso.

backside, *s.* a parte traseira, as nádegas, o assento.

backslide, *v.i.* desviar-se; reincidir.

backstairs, *s.* escada secreta.

backstays, *s.* estais, cabos que partem do mastro dum navio, molas de tesouras.

backstitch, *s.* pesponto.

backward, *adv.* para trás; de costas. *adj.* retrógrado, tardio.

backwardly, *adv.* em pior estado.

backwardness, *s.* negligência, atraso.

backwater, *s.* água represada, água obrigada a retroceder devido a uma obstrução, a uma corrente contrária, ao fluxo da maré; água atirada para trás pela rotação duma roda hidráulica ou pelas pás dum navio de rodas.

backwoods, *s.* região não cultivada; sertão; *nackwoods man,* colono de floresta (América).

back-yard, *s.* pátio das traseiras.

bacon, *s.* toucinho.

bactriologist, *s.* bacteriólogo.

bacteria, *s. pl.* bactérias.

bacteriology, *s.* bacteriologia.

bad, *adj.* mau, perverso; nocivo; indisposto. 1) *from bad to worse,* de mal a pior. 2) *to look bad,* ter má aparência.

baddish, *adj.* um tanto mau; inferior.

bade, *pass.* to bid.

badge, *s.* insígnia; distintivo.

badger, *s.* texugo. *v.t.* atormentar; fatigar.

badly, *adv.* mal 1) *baddly off,* com poucos meios. 2) *to be baddly off for,* ter grande necessidade.

badness, *s.* maldade.

badminton, *s.* refresco (soda, clarete, açúcar); jogo de campo, com rede, raquetas e volante.

baffle, *v.t.* frustrar; confundir; tornar perplexo.

baffler, *s.* enganador.

bag, *s.* saco, bolsa; úbere. 1) *handbag,* bolsa de mão. 2) *bagpipe,* gaita-de-foles. *v.t.* ensacar; agarrar; caçar. *v.i.* inflar; apossar-se de.

bagatelle, *s.* bagatela.

baggage, *s.* bagagem; *baggage car,* vagão de bagagens.

baggy, *adj.* largo como um saco; flácido.

bagnio, *s.* casa de banhos; cadeia oriental; bordel.

bagpipe, *s.* gaita-de-foles.

bagpiper, *s.* gaiteiro.

baignoire, *s.* camarote da última fila.

bail, *s.* fiança; asa de balde ou chaleira; balde. *s.* paliçada; *to let out on bail,* dar liberdade sob fiança. *v.t.* afiançar; pôr em liberdade sob fiança; esvaziar (com um balde).

bailable, *s.* afiançável.

bail-bond, *s.* termo de fiança.

bailee, *s.* depositário.

Bailey, *s.* pátio de castelo; Old Bailey, tribunal criminal de Londres.

bailiff, *s.* beleguim.

bailiwick, *s.* mordomia.

baillie, s. funcionário municipal da Escócia.

bailment, s. depósito; entrega de coisas depositadas.

bailor, s. o que entrega bens a outro em depósito.

bait, s. isca; engodo. v.t. iscar; atrair; atormentar.

bake, v.t. cozer no forno ; calcinar.

baker, s. padeiro.

bakery, s. padaria; ocupação de padeiro.

baking, s. cozedura; fornada.

balance, s. balança; balanço; equilíbrio; saldo de uma conta, pêndulo. v.t. hesitar; contrabalançar; to lose one's balance, perder, o equilíbrio.

balance-sheet, s. balancete.

balcony, s. sacada; balcão (teatro).

bald, adj. calvo; nu; baid head, um calvo.

baldarhash, s. disparate.

bald-headed, adj. calvo.

baldly, adv. grosseiramente, nuamente.

baldness, s. calvície, nudez.

baldric, s. cinturão.

bale, s. fardo. v.t. enfardar; empacotar.

baleful, adj. pernicioso, maligno, funesto.

balefully, adv. dum modo funesto ou maligno; tristemente.

balefulness, s. malignidade; pesar; tristeza.

baler, s. enfardador.

balk, baulk, s. obstáculo, impedimento. v.t. impedir, frustrar; to balk someone's plans, impedir os planos de alguém.

ball, s. bola; bala (de canhão); baile, novelo. 1) eyeball, globo ocular. 2) fancy-ball, baile de máscaras. v.t. fazer um novelo. 3) to ball up, confundir.

ballad, s. balada; canção.

ballast, s. lastro (de navio); balastro (para formar o leito dos caminhos de ferro).

ballerina, s. bailarina.

ballet, s. dança artística, bailado.

ballistics, s. balística.

balloon, s. balão.

balloonist, s. o que faz os balões; aeronauta.

ballot, s. esfera para votos; voto, votação. v.t., v.i. votar.

ball-room, s. sala de baile.

ballyrag, v.t. e v.i. maltratar empurrando, zombando, ou pregando partidas.

balm, s. bálsamo; unguento.

balminess, s. fragrância, aroma.

balmy, adj. balsâmico, calmante.

balsam, s. bálsamo.

balsamic, adj. balsâmico.

baluster, s. balaústre.

balustrade, s. balaustrada.

bamboo, s. bambu.

ban, v.t. proibir; excomungar. s. proibição; excomunhão; mariage bans, banhos de casamento.

banal, adj. banal, trivial.

banality, banalities, s. banalidade; direito do senhor feudal para obrigar os súbditos a usar do seu moinho, etc.

banana, s. banana; bunch of bananas, cacho de bananas.

band, s. faixa; tira; vínculo; banda (de música); bando, multidão. v.t. unir, associar. v.i. associar-se.

bandage, s. atadura. v.t. enfaixar, pôr atadura.

bandana, s. lenço estampado.

bandbox, s. caixa de cartão para chapéus, bonés, etc.

banderole, s. bandeirola.

bandicoot, s. marsupial da Austrália; rato grande da Índia e do Ceilão.

bandit, s. bandido. pl. **bandits** ou **banditti**.

bandmaster, s. mestre de banda.

bandog, s. mastim.

bandoline, s. bandoline.

bands, s. bandas de linho usadas no peito pelos clérigos franceses e pelos funcionários do foro de Inglaterra.

bandsman, s. músico de banda.

bandy, v.t. trocar golpes ou palavras; passar de boca em boca. adj. curvo; bandyleggs, pernas curvas.

bane, s. veneno; ruína; castigo. 1) ruinbaneful, pernicioso; funesto. 2) rat's bane, veneno para ratos.

banefully, adv. perniciosamente.

banefulness, s. perniciosidade.

bang, v.t., v.i. bater (porta); dar pancadas; cortar o cabelo formando franjas. s. pancada; golpe, murro; corte de cabelo formando franja; estouro, estrondo, estrépito.

bangle, s. bracelete.

banish, v.t. desterrar; demitir; exterminar.

banishment, s. desterro, expulsão.

banister, s. balaústre. pl. balaustrada.

banjo, s. banjo.

bank, s. margem; baixio; montão (de terra); banco, casa bancária. 1) savings bank, caixa económica. 2) bank-note, nota de banco. 3) a bank of clouds, uma aglomeração de nuvens. v.t. amontoar (terra ou

areia); inclinar; depositar num banco. *v.i.* ter
conta num banco.

banker, *s.* banqueiro.

banking, *adj.* bancário. *s.* negócio bancário.

bank note, *s.* nota de banco.

bankrupt, *s.* falido. *v.t., v.i.* tornar falido; falir.
adj. falido.

bankruptcy, *s.* bancarrota, falência.

banner, *s.* bandeira; insígnia.

banns, *s. pl.* banhos de casamento.

banquet, *s.* banquete. *v.t., v.i.* banquetear.

banqueting-hall, *s.* sala para banquetes.

banter, *s.* gacejo, ironia, *v.t.* gracejar, zombar.

bantling, *s.* fedelho.

baptism, *s.* baptismo.

baptismal, *adj.* baptismal.

baptist, *s.* baptist.

baptistery, baptisteries, *s.* baptistério.

baptistery, baptistry, *s.* baptistério.

baptize, *v.t.* baptizar.

bar, *s.* barra; faixa; barreira; tribunal, foro;
balcão; loja de bebidas; barra de um porto;
barbell, barra de ginástica. *v.t.* trancar;
impedir; excluir.

barb, *s.* farpa (de arame), ponta de seta.

barbarian, *s.* bárbaro, selvagem.

barbaric, *adj.* bárbaro.

barbarism, *s.* barbarismo, barbárie.

barbarity, barbarities, *s.* barbaridade,
crueldade.

barbarize (ise), *v.t.* e *v.i.* barbarizar; cometer
barbaridades.

barbarous, *adj.* bárbaro, selvagem.

barbarously, *adv.* barbaramente.

barbarousness, *s.* barbarismo.

barbate, *adj.* que tem barbas ou tufos.

barbecue, *s.* animal assado inteiro. *v.t.* assar
um animal inteiro; churrasco; churrasquear.

barbed-wire, *s.* arame farpado.

barber, *s.* barbeiro; *barbershop,* barbearia.

barcarolle, *s.* barcarola.

bard, *s.* poeta, bardo.

bare, *adj.* nu; vazio; simples; descoberto. *v.t.*
descobrir; *to bare one's head,* descobrir a
cabeça.

bareback, *adj.* que monta em pêlo. *adv.* sem
selim.

barefaced, *adj.* descarado.

barefacedly, *adv.* descaradamente.

barefacedness, *s.* descaro.

barefoot, *adj., adv.* descalço; *barefooted,*
descalço.

bareheaded, *adj.* de cabeça descoberta.

barely, *adv.* nuamente; pobremente; simplesmente, apenas, escassamente.

bareness, *s.* nudez; pobreza.

bargain, *s.* acordo; negócio; coisa adquirida
por baixo preço; *to strike a bargain,* concluir um ajuste. *v.t.* contratar, ajustar;
regatear.

bargaining, *s.* regateio.

barge, *s.* barca; lancha.

bargee, *s.* barqueiro.

baritone, barytone, *s.* barítono.

bark, *s.* latido; cortiça, casca de árvore. *v.t.*
descascar (árvore); raspar. *v.i.* latir.

barker, *s.* cão que ladra; o que descasca as
árvores.

barking, *s.* latido.

barley, *s.* cevada.

barleycorn, *s.* grão de cevada; medida da
terça parte de polegada.

barm, *s.* levedura, fermento.

barmaid, *s.* empregada de bar

barman, *s.* empregado de bar

barn, *s.* celeiro.

barnyard, *s.* pátio de quinta.

barometer, *s.* barómetro.

baron, *s.* barão.

baronage, *s.* baronia.

baroness, *s.* baronesa.

barony (ies), *s.* baronia.

baroque, *adj.* grotesco com forma irregular.
s. estilo barroco.

barque, *s.* barca, barco.

barracks, *s. pl.* quartel.

barrage, *s.* barragem; fogo de artilharia
contínuo sobre uma certa área.

barrel, *s.* barril, barrica; cano de espingarda;
parte que contém a tinta de uma caneta de
tinta permanente. *v.t.* embarrilar.

barren, *adj.* árido, estéril; infrutífero; estúpido. *s.* baldio.

barrenly, *adv.* esterilmente.

barreness, *s.* esterilidade, aridez.

barrette, *s.* gancho para os cabelos.

barricade, *s.* barricada, barreira. *v.t.* levantar
barricadas.

barrier, *s.* obstáculo, barreira; limite.

barrister, *s.* advogado.

barrow, *s.* carrinho de mão; padiola.

barter, *s.* troca, permuta. *v.t.* trocar, permutar.

barytone, variante de barítono.

basal, *adj.* básico.

basalt, *s.* basalto.

basaltic, *adj.* basáltico.

basan, s. pele de carneiro curtida, carneira.

bascule, s. báscula; *bascule-bridge*, ponte levadiça levantada e baixada com o contrapeso, como a Tower Bridge de Londres.

base, s. base, fundamento. *adj.* baixo, humilde; vil; ordinário. *v.t.* estabelecer; firmar.

basely, *adv.* vilmente.

baseball, s. jogo feito entre nove jogadores de cada lado.

baseless, *adj.* sem base, infundado.

baselessly, *adv.* infundadamente, temerariamente.

baselessness, s. inconsistência; temeridade; falta de base.

baseness, s. vileza; ruindade; baixeza; profundeza de som.

basement, s. pavimento de uma casa parcial ou completamente abaixo do nível do chão.

bashful, *adj.* tímido, envergonhado.

bashfully, *adv.* timidamente. modestamente, com acanhamento.

bashfulness, s. timidez, acanhamento.

basic, *adj.* básico, fundamental.

basil, s. mangericão; carneira.

basilica, s. basílica.

basilicom, s. basilicão.

basilisk, s. basilisco (animal fabuloso); antiga peça de artilharia.

basin, s. bacia; tigela; dique; prato da balança côncavo.

basis, s. fundamento, base; princípio fundamental. *pl.* bases.

bask, *v.t., v.i.* aquecer (ao sol, etc.).

basket, s. cesto, canastra.

basketball, s. basquetebol.

bas-relief, s. baixo-relevo.

bass, s. perca (peixe).

bass, basses, s. baixo (em música); *basshorn*, trombone. *adj.* baixo, grave.

basset-horn, s. clarinete de tenor.

basso, s. baixo (cantor).

bassoon, s. fagote.

bastard, s. bastardo, filho natural. *adj.* ilegítimo, bastardo.

baste, *v.t.* alinhavar; untar a carne com gordura enquanto assa.

bastille, s. fortaleza, prisão.

bastinado, s. bastonada. *v.t.* dar bastonadas.

bastion, s. baluarte.

bat, s. morcego; bordão, cajado. *v.t.* bater, manejar a pá no jogo de *cricket* ou *baseball*.

batch, s. fornada.

bate, *v.t.* reduzir; baixar (preço). *v.i.* bater as asas.

bath, s. banho; *v.t., v.i.* banhar.

bathe, *v.t.* banhar. *v.i.* banhar-se.

bather, s. banhista; banheiro.

bathing, s. banho. 1) *bathing-hut*, barraca de banho. 2) *bathing beach*, praia de banhos.

bathos, s. anticlímax, passagem do sublime ao ridículo.

bathroom, s. quarto de banho.

batiste, s. musselina.

baton, s. batuta; bastão de comando.

batrachian, *adj.* batráquio.

battalion, s. batalhão.

batten, s. sarrafo. *v.t.* cobrir com sarrafos. *v.i.* engordar.

batter, *v.t., v.i.* bater. 1) *to batter down*, demolir. 2) *batters*, pasta culinária; murro.

battering-ram, s. aríete.

battery, s. bateria; acumulador; ataque; *galvanic battery*, pilha galvânica.

battle, s. batalha. *v.t., v.i.* lutar, batalhar.

battledore, s. raqueta.

battlefield, s. campo de batalha.

battlement, s. ameia.

battleplane, s. avião equipado com metralhadoras.

battleship, s. navio de guerra, couraçado.

battue, s. batida, montaria de caça grossa; matança.

bauble, s. ninharia, frioleira; brinquedo de criança.

bawd, s. alcoviteiro.

bawdry, s. alcovitice; linguagem obscena.

bawdy, *adj.* obsceno.

bawdy-house, s. lupanar.

bawl, s. gritar, apregoar; *bawls*, grito, berro.

bay, s. bais; vão de janelas ou portas; louro (árvore); latido de cão de caça; dificuldade, aperto. *adj.* baio. *v.i.* ladrar.

bayonet, s. baioneta. *v.t.* matar, ferir com baioneta.

baysalt, s. sal marinho.

bay window, s. janela saliente.

bazaar, bazar, s. bazar.

bdellium, s. bdélio (árvore); pedra preciosa.

be, v. pas. *was* part. pas. *been*, part. pres. *being* é um verbo aux. e significa ser ou estar. 1) *he is a student*, ele é um estudante. 2) *he is in England*, ele está em Inglaterra. 3) *to be hungry*, estar com fome. 4) *to be in a hurry*, estar com pressa. 5) *to be about to*, estar para. 6) *to be able*, ser capaz, poder. 7) *to be thirsty*, ter sede. 8) *to* be cold, ter frio. 9) *to be hot, warm*, ter calor. 10) *to be 10 years old*, ter 10 anos de idade. 11) *to be in want of*, ter necessidade de. 12) *to be ashamed*, ter vergonha. 13) *to be shy*, ser acanhado. 14) *to be right*, ter razão. 15) *to be wrong*, não ter razão. 16) *to be afraid*, ter medo. 17) *to be sleepy*, ter sono. 18) *to be desirous*, ter desejo.

beach, s. praia, costa. v.t. arremessar à praia, encalhar.

beacon, s. farol; baliza, sinal para dirigir. v.t. guiar por meio de luz; colocar uma baliza.

bead, s. conta (de rosário, etc.), pl. contas, rosário; gota.

beadle, s. bedel; guarda das igrejas.

beagle, s. sabujo.

beagles, s. caça à lebre e coelho com cães, mas sem armas.

beak, s. bico de ave; qualquer coisa em forma de bico.

beaker, s. copo ou chávena de boca larga.

beam, s. viga de madeira ou ferro; braço de balança; raio de luz; sorriso; *radio beam*, sinal dado pelo rádio num campo de aviação para guiar os pilotos. v.t., v.i. brilhar; sorrir.

beaming, adj. radiante, resplandecente; alegre, vivo.

beamful, adj. luminoso.

beamily, adv. luminosamente.

beaminess, s. luz, brilho.

beaming, adj. brilhante, radiante, alegre, vivo.

beamless, adj. sem luz, sem brilho.

beamy, adj. luminoso.

bean, s. semente como do feijão, fava, etc. 1) *beanpod*, vagem. 2) *coffee bean*, grão de café.

bear, v.t. pas. *bore*, part. pas. *borne* ou *born*, levar; suportar; produzir, dar à luz; aguentar. 1) *to bear in mind*, lembrar-se, ter em conta. 2) *to bear out*, defender, confirmar. 3) *to bear with*, perdoar; 4) *to bear up*, suportar, conservar a coragem. 5) *to bear oneself with dignity*, portar-se com dignidade. 6) *to bear testimony*, prestar testemunho.

bear, s. urso; pessoa grosseira.

bearable, adj. suportável.

bearably, adv. de um modo suportável.

bearableness, s. tolerância.

beard, s. barba; barba de milho, centeio, etc. v.t. insultar audaciosamente

bearded, adj. barbado.

beardless, adj. sem barbas, imberbe.

bearer, s. portador; mensageiro.

bearing, s. porte; ponto de apoio; paciência; situação, posição; frutificação; relação. pl. emblema num brazão; *to lose one's bearings*, desorientar-se, perder o rumo.

bearish, adj. grosseiro.

bearishly, adv. grosseiramente.

bearishness, s. grosseria.

bearskin, s. pele de urso.

beast, s. animal; homem brutal; *wild beast*, fera.

beastly, adj. brutal; indesejável. adv. brutalmente.

beat, v.t. bater, golpear; vencer; derrotar; marcar (o compasso). v.i. pulsar; bater. 1) *to beat about the bush*, ficar-se com rodeios. 2) *to beat about*, procurar dum lado para outro. 3) *to beat away*, afugentar. 4) *to beat the alarm*, bater, tocar o alarme. s. golpe, pancada; pulsação; toque de tambor; compasso.

beaten, part. pass. de *to beat*, adj. batido, vencido; fatigado; gasto, usado; conquistado; exausto.

beater, s. batedor o que levanta a taça; *ggbeater*, batedeira.

beatific, adj. beatífico.

beatifically, adv. beatificamente.

beatification, s. beatificação.

beatify, v.t. beatificar.

beatitude, s. beatitude.

beau, s. pl. **beaux**, galante, janota.

beauteous, adj. belo, lindo.

beauteously, adv. belamente.

beauteousness, s. beleza, encanto; elegância.

beautifier, s. aformoseador.

beautiful, adj. formoso, belo.

beautifully, adv. belamente, lindamente, primorosamente.

beautify, v.t. embelezar, adornar.

beauty, s. beleza; *beauty parlor*, salão de beleza.

beaver, s. castor.

becalm, v.t. acalmar, serenar.

became, pas. do verbo *to become*.

because, conj. porque.

beck, s. sinal, aceno; riacho; *to have someone at one's beck and call*, ter alguém à sua disposição.

beckon, v.t., v.i. acenar. s. aceno.

become, v.i. pas. *became*, part. pas. become, tornar-se; fazer-se 1) *what has be-*

come of him?, que é feito dele? 2) *to become crazy*, enlouquecer. 3) *to become angry*, zangar-se. 4) *to become old*, envelhecer. *v.t.* convir, assentar bem.

becoming, *adj.* próprio, conveniente.

becomingly, *adv.* a propósito, com elegância.

becomingness, *s.* propriedade, conveniência.

bed, *s.* cama; canteiro; leito (de rio); fundo do mar; base. 1) *bedclothes*, roupa de cama. 2) *bedframe*, armação da cama. 3) *bedhanging*, cortinado da cama. 4) *to go to bed*, deitar-se. *v.t.* colocar, deitar; plantar. *v.i.* deitar-se.

bedabble, *vt.* borrifar; humedecer, salpicar.

bedaub, *v.t.* sujar, salpicar, com lama ou óleo.

bedazzle, *v.t.* deslumbrar, ofuscar, confundir.

bedbug, *s.* percevejo.

bedchamber, *s.* quarto de cama.

bedding, *s.* roupas de cama; fundamento.

bedeck, *v.t.* adornar.

bedew, *v.t.* orvalhar.

bedight, *v.t.* ornar, vestir.

bedim, bedimming, bedimmed, *v.t.* obscurecer, ofuscar.

bedizen, *v.t.* adornar.

bedlam, *s.* manicómio; confusão.

bedmaker, *s.* marceneiro de camas; criado dos quartos.

bedraggie, *v.t.* manchar a roupa com lama.

bedridden, *adj.* preso à cama por doença.

bedroom, *s.* dormitório.

bedside, *s.* lado da cama.

bedstead, *s.* armação da cama.

bedtime, *s.* hora de ir para a cama.

bee, *s.* abelha. 1) *beehive*, cortiço. 2) *beeyard*, colmeal. 3) *busy as a bee*, muito ocupado. 4) *to have a bee in one's bonnet*, ter a pulga atrás da orelha.

beech, *s.* faia (árvore).

beef, *s. pl.* **beeves**, carne de vaca; *roast beef*, rosbife.

beefiness, *s.* musculatura; gordura.

beefsteak, *s.* bife, posta de carne assada na grelha.

Beelzebub, *s.* Belzebu.

been, *part. pas.* do verbo *to be*.

beer, *s.* cerveja.

beer-house, *s.* cervejaria.

beeriness, *s.* influência causada pela cerveja, embriaguez causada pela cerveja.

beery, *adj.* de cerveja; com cerveja; influenciado pela cerveja; ébrio.

beeswax, *s.* cera virgem.

beet, *s.* beterraba.

beetle, *s.* escaravelho; barata; pisão.

beetling, *adj.* saliente. *s.* pisoamento.

beetroot, *s.* nabo da beterraba.

beeves, *pl.* de *beef, s.* gado.

befall, *v.t., v.i.* pas. *befell*, part. pas. *befallen*, acontecer, suceder.

befit, *v.t.* convir, ser próprio de.

befitting, *adj.* próprio, conveniente.

befittingly, *adv.* convenientemente.

befog, *v.t.* obscurecer.

before, *prep.* antes de, anterior a; diante de. *adv.* antes, anteriormente. *conj.* antes que.

beforehand, *adv.* de antemão.

beforetime, *adv.* em outro tempo, antigamente; previamente.

befoul, *v.t.* sujar, emporcalhar.

befriend, *v.t.* favorecer, proteger.

befuddle, *v.t.* confundir, estontear, embriagar.

beg, *v.t.* pedir, rogar, suplicar; *I beg your pardon*, desculpe-me! *v.i.* mendigar.

begad, *interj.* por Deus!

began, *pas.* de *to begin*.

beget, *v.t. pas. begot* ou *begat, part. pas. begotten* ou *begot*, gerar, produzir, engendrar.

beggar, *s.* pedinte; mendigo, pobre. *v.t.* reduzir à miséria.

beggarliness, *s.* pobreza, miséria, mediocridade.

beggarly, *adj.* pobre, indigente, miserável; desprezível.

beggary, *s.* penúria.

begin, *v.t.* pas. *began*, part. pas. *begun*, começar; principiar; *to begin with*, em primeiro lugar.

beginner, *s.* principiante.

beginning, *s.* começo, princípio.

begone, *ind.* fora daqui.

begonia, *s.* begónia.

begot, *pas.* e *part. pas.* de *to beget*.

begotten, *part. pas.* de *to beget*.

begrime, *v.t.* enfarruscar.

begrudge, *v.t.* invejar, chorar de raiva.

beguile, *v.t.* enganar; divertir, passar o tempo.

begun, *part. pas.* de *to begin*.

behalf, *s.* em favor de, em nome de; *in my behalf*, a meu favor.

behave, *v.t., v.i.* comportar-se; conduzir-se; *behave yourself*, comporte-se bem!

behaviour, *s.* comportamento.

behead, *v.t.* degolar, decapitar. *beheld pas.* e *part. pas.* de *to behold.*

beheader, *s.* carrasco.

beheading, *s.* decapitação.

behest, *s.* mandado, ordem.

behind, *prep.* atrás de, detrás de. 1) *behind one's back,* sem o seu conhecimento, nas suas costas. 2) *behind the times,* fora de moda. *adv.* atrás, detrás. 3) *to fall behind,* atrasar-se.

behindhand, *adj., adv.* atrasado, com atraso; atrás.

behold, *v.t.* pas. *beheld,* part. pas. *beheld,* ver, observar.

beholder, *s.* contemplador, espectador.

beholden, *adj.* obrigado, devedor.

behoof, *s.* proveito, vantagem.

behoove, behove, *v.t.* ser necessário, convir.

being, *s.* ser, ente; existência; entidade. part. pas. de *to be; for the time be,* por agora, no momento.

beknown, *adj.* reconhecido.

belabor, belabour, *v.t.* espancar; cansar-se com trabalho.

belated, *adj.* atrasado; retardado.

belatedness, *s.* lentidão, retardamento, tardança.

belay, *v.t., v.i.* amarrar (as cordas) aos cabos para tornar seguro; parar, impedir; *belay there!,* pare ai!

belch, *v.t., v.i.* arrotar; vomitar; pôr para fora. *s.* arroto, vómito.

beldam, beldame, *s.* mulher velha e feia.

beleaguer, *v.t.* sitiar, bloquear.

belfry, *s.* campanário.

Belgian, *s., adj.* belga.

Belgium, *s.* Bélgica.

belie, *v.t.* enganar; desmentir.

belief, *s.* fé, crença; credo.

believable, *adj.* crível.

believe, *v.t.* acreditar, crer; supor. 1) *to believe in,* crer em, ter fé em. 2) *to make believe,* fingir.

believer, *s.* crente.

belike, *adv.* provavelmente, talvez.

belittle, *v.t.* depreciar, deprimir.

bell, *s.* sino; campainha, guizo. 1) *bellhanger,* pessoa que faz instalações de campainhas ou que coloca sinos. 2) *chime of bells,* repique de sinos. *v.t.* pôr sinos ou instalar campainhas; dar forma de sinos.

belladonna, *s.* beladona.

belle, *s.* mulher bela.

belles-lettres, *s. pl.* belas-letras, literatura.

bellicose, *adj.* belicoso.

bellicosely, *adv.* belicosamente.

belligerent, *adj.* beligerante. *s.* beligerante.

bellman, *s.* pregoeiro das ruas com campainha.

bellow, *v.* bramir, berrar; mugir; troar; roncar.

bellows, *s. sing. pl.,* fole.

belly, *s.* estômago; barriga, ventre; bojo. *v.t., v.i.* inchar, criar barriga.

belong, *v.i.* pertencer; relacionar-se (com); dizer respeito.

belongings, *s., pl.* pertences; anexos.

beloved, *s.* pessoa amada. *adj.* querido, amado.

below, *prep.* abaixo de, por baixo de; inferior a. *adv.* abaixo, por baixo; inferior.

belt, *s.* cinto, cinturão; faixa; zona; correia. *v.t.* cingir; bater com um cinto.

bemoan, *v.t.* e *v.i.* lamentar, deplorar.

bemoaning, *s.* lamento.

bench, *s.* banco, assento; tribunal.

bend, *v.t.* pas. e part. pas. *bent,* curvar; arquear; inclinar. *v.i.* curvar-se, dobrar-se; submeter-se.

beneath, prep. de baixo de, abaixo de, por baixo de. *adv.* debaixo, abaixo.

benedick, *s.* noivo, recém-casado.

benediction, *s.* bênção.

benefaction, *s.* benefício, favor, contribuição.

benefactor, *s.* benfeitor. *fem. benefactress.*

benefice, *s.* benefício eclesiástico.

beneficence, *s.* caridade; beneficência.

beneficent, *adj.* caritativo, generoso.

beneficently, *adv.* caridosamente.

beneficial, *adj.* benéfico; proveitoso, útil.

beneficially, *adv.* beneficamente.

beneficialness, *s.* utilidade, proveito.

beneficiary, *s.* beneficiário.

benefit, *s.* benefício; vantagem; benefício de teatro. *v.t.* beneficiar. *v.i.* beneficiar-se, ser beneficiado.

benevolence, *s.* benevolência; caridade

benevolent, *adj.* benevolente, bondoso; caridoso; benévolo.

benevolently, *adv.* benignamente.

benighted, *adj.* surpreendido pela noite; em trevas; ignorante.

benign, *adj.* benigno; salutar.

benignly, *adv.* benignamente.

benignancy, *s.* gentileza.

benignant, *adj.* benéfico, benevolente, salutar.

benignantly, *adv.* beneficamente.

benignity, s. benignidade, bondade, gentileza.

bent, pas. e part. pas. de to bend. s. inclinação, tendência; curvatura. adj. curvo, inclinado; determinado a; to be bent on, estar resolvido a.

benumb, v.t. entorpecer.

benzene, s. benzina.

benzoic, adj. benzóico.

benzolin, s. benzolina.

bequeath, v.t. legar; transmitir à posteridade.

bequest, s. legado, doação.

berate, v.t. repreender, reprovar.

bereave, v.t. pass. e part. pas. bereaved ou bereft, despojar, arrebatar; desolar.

beriberi, s. beribéri.

berm, s. berma; espaço entre a base do parapeito e o fosso numa fortificação.

berry, s. baga, grão.

berth, s. beliche; ancoradouro; situação. v.t. ancorar, arranjar para alguém lugar onde durma.

beryl, s. berilo (pedra preciosa).

beseech, v.t. pass. e part. pas. besought ou beseeched, implorar, rogar.

beseeching, s. súplica, rogo. adj. suplicante.

beseem, vt. convir, quadrar. v.i. parecer.

beseemingly, adv. convenientemente.

beset, v.t. assediar, cercar; obstruir.

beshrew, vt. amaldiçoar.

beside, prep. ao lado de, perto de. adv. perto, junto.

besides, prep. além de. adv. além, disso, demais.

besiege, v.t. sitiar, cercar.

besieger, s. sitiante.

besmear, v.t. lambuzar.

besom, s. espanador.

besought, pass. e part. pass. de to beseech.

besotted, adj. embrutecido; estonteado por narcóticos.

bespangle, v.t. adornar com lantejoulas.

bespatter, v.t. salpicar; manchar.

bespeak, v.t. bespoke, pass. bespoken, part. pass., encomendar; indicar; predizer.

besprinkle, vt. borrifar, aspergir; humedecer.

best, adj. superlativo de good, o melhor, o superior. 1) best man, padrinho de casamento; adv. superlativo de well, o melhor, mais a propósito. 2) at best, quando muito. 3) To do one's best, fazer o máximo que se pode. v.t. sobrepujar.

bestial, adj. bestial, brutal.

bestially, adv. bestialmente.

bestiality, s. bestialidade.

bestir, v.t. mover, agitar; v.i. mover-se.

bestow, v.t. conferir, dar, conceder. 1) to bestow gifts upon, dar presentes a. 2) to favors on, dispensar obséquios a.

bestowal, s. concessão, outorga; graça, presente.

bestride, v.t. pass. bestrode, part. pass. bestridden, montar, escarranchar; v.i. andar a passos largos.

bet, v.t. pass. bet ou betted, part. pass. bet ou betted, apostar. s. aposta.

betake, v.t. pass. betook part. pass. betaken, recorrer a; ir.

betaken, part. pass. de to betake.

bête noire, s. a pessoa mais detestada, o nosso pesadelo.

betide, v.t e v.i. acontecer.

betimes, adv. a tempo, cedo.

betook, pass. de to betake.

betray, v.t. trair, enganar, atraiçoar; revelar.

betrayal, s. traição; denúncia.

betrayer, s. traidor, denunciante.

betroth, v.t. desposar.

betrothal, s. esponsais.

better, adj. comp. de good, melhor, superior. adv. compart. de well, melhor. s. vantagem, melhoria; um superior. v.t. melhorar. 1) better half, cara-metade. 2) so much the better, tanto melhor. 3) better and better, cada vez melhor. 4) better alone than in bad company, antes só que mal acompanhado.

betterment, s. melhoria, melhoramento.

betting, s. aposta.

bettor, s. apostador.

between, prep. entre, no meio de. adv. entre.

betwixt, prep. e adv. entre.

beverage, s. bebida.

bewail, v.t. e v.i. chorar, lamentar, deplorar.

beware, v.t. e v.i. acautelar-se; beware of pickpockets, acautelar-se contra os gatunos.

bewilder, v.t. confundir, desnortear.

bewilderingly, adv. perplexamente.

bewilderment, s. confusão, desnorteamento.

bewitch, v.t. fascinar, encantar; enfeitiçar.

bewitchingly, adv. de um modo encantador.

bewitchment, s. feitiço, encanto.

beyond, prep. além de, mais longe que. adv. além, do outro lado, ao longe.

bias, s. viés, direcção oblíqua; preconceito, tendência. v.t. induzir, influenciar.

biaxal, adj. com dois eixos.

bib, *s.* babador.

bibelot, *s.* pequeno objecto de arte.

Bible, *s.* Bíblia.

Biblical, *adj.* bíblico.

bibliographer, *s.* bibliógrafo.

bibliography, *s.* bibliografia.

bibliomania, *s.* bibliomania.

bibliomaniac, *s.* bibliomaníaco.

bibliophile, *s.* bibliófilo.

bibulous, *s.* poroso; absorvente.

bicarbonate, *s.* bicarbonato

bicentenary, *s.* bicentenário.

bicentennial, *adj.* de dois em dois séculos.

biceps, *s.* bicípites.

bichromate, *s.* bicromato.

bicker, *v.i.* e *s.* altercar, discutir; altercação, discussão.

bickerer, *a.* altercador.

bicuspid, *adj.* bicúspide, que tem duas pontas. *s.* bicúspide (dente).

bicycle, *s.* bicicleta. *v.i.* andar de bicicleta.

bicyclist, *s.* ciclista.

bid, *v.t. pass.* de *bade* ou *bid, part. pass. bidden* ou *bid,* ordenar, mandar; saudar, proclamar; lançar em leilão. *v.t.* fazer uma oferta. *s.* lanço em leilão, licitação; convite.

bidder, *s.* lançador em leilão.

bidding, *s.* ordem; convite; *bidding-prayer,* oração dos pregadores, antes de começar o sermão.

bide, *v.t.* e *v.i. pass.* e *part. pass. bode* ou *bided,* esperar; permanecer, ficar; *to bide one's time,* esperar por uma oportunidade.

biennal, *adj.* bienal. *s.* planta bienal.

bier, *s.* carreta fúnebre, ataúde.

bifurcate, *vi.* e *vt.* bifurcar.

bifurcation, *s.* bifurcação.

big, *adj.* grande; importante; imponente; *big heart,* coração generoso.

bigamist, *s.* bígamo.

bigamous, *adj.* bígamo.

bigamously, *adv.* em bigamia.

bigamy, *s.* bigamia.

bigger, biggest, *sup. abs.* simples de *big.*

biggin, *s.* barrete de criança.

biggish, *adj.* presumido, vaidoso.

bight, *s.* pequena baía; laçada numa corda.

bigness, *s.* grossura, volume, grandeza.

bigot, *s.* fanático.

bigotry, *s.* fanatismo, intolerância.

bigwig, *s.* pessoa de importância.

bijou, *s.* jóia.

bike, *s.* abreviatura de *bicycle.*

bilabial, *s.* e *adj.* bilabial.

bilateral, *adj.* bilateral.

bilaterally, *adv.* dum modo bilateral.

bile, *s.* bílis; mau humor, cólera, ira.

bilge, *s.* fundo chato de navio; bojo de barril.

bilgy, *adj.* semelhante em cheiro à água do porão do navio.

biliary, *adj.* biliário.

bilingual, *adj.* bilingue.

bilious, *adj.* bilioso.

biliousness, *s.* temperamento bilioso.

bilk, *v.t.* enganar, lograr, fugir ao pagamento de.

bill, *s.* bico, ponta; projecto de lei; cartaz; conta; aviso; programa (de teatro); letra de câmbio, 1) *bill of exchange,* letra de câmbio. 2) *bill of fare,* cardápio. 3) *bill of credit,* carta de crédito. 4) *bill of lading,* conhecimento de embarque. 5) *bill of rights,* declaração dos direitos dos cidadãos. *v.t.* anunciar, afixar cartazes.

billet, *s.* bilhete, nota, ordem para aboletar soldados; acha de lenha. *v.t.* aboletar.

billet-doux, *s.* carta de namoro.

billiards, *s.* bilhar.

billion, *s.* bilião.

billow, *s.* onda, vaga. *v.t.* crescer, encapelar-se.

bill-sticker, *s.* homem que coloca cartazes nas paredes.

bill-sticking, *s.* afixação.

biltong, *s.* carne magra cortada em pedaços e seca ao sol.

bin, *s.* depósito, celeiro; dispensa.

binary, *adj.* binário.

bind, *v.t., pass.* e *part. pass. bound,* unir, ligar; debruar; encadernar; obrigar moralmente, contratar.

binderq, *s.* encadernador; atador de molhos de trigo, centeio, etc.; faixa para as crianças.

bindery, *s.* oficina de encadernação.

binding, *s.* encadernação; ligadura, faixa; debrum; *cloth binding,* encadernação de pano. *adj.* obrigatório.

bindweed, *s.* uma espécie de trepadeira.

binocle, *s.* binóculo.

binomial, *adj.* binómico, que tem dois termos. *s.* binómio.

biogenesis, *s.* biogénese.

biographer, *s.* biógrafo.

biographic, *adj.* biográfico.

biographical, *adj.* biográfico.

biographically, *adv.* biograficamente.

biography, s. biografia.
biologic, adj. biológico.
biological, adj. biológico.
biologically, adv. biologicamente.
biology, s. biologia.
biometry, s. biometria.
bioplasm, s. protoplasma.
bioscope, bioscópio
bipartite, adj. bipartido.
biped, s. bípede.
bipedal, adj. bípede.
biplane, s. biplano.
birch, s. vidoeiro; vara de vidoeiro. v.t. açoitar, castigar com vara de vidoeiro.
birching, s. açoite.
bird, s. pássaro, ave. 1) *bird cage*, gaiola. 2) *bird lime*, viscoso. 3) *bird of prey*, ave de rapina, 4) *bird seed*, alpista. 5) *a bird in the hand is worth two in the bush*, mais vale um pássaro na mão do que dois a voar.
biretta, s. barrete de clérigo.
birth, s. nascimento; origem; linhagem, descendência. 1) *birth certificate*, certidão de nascimento. 2) *birth rate*, natalidade. 3) *to give birth*, dar à luz.
birthday, s. aniversário natalício.
birthmark, s. sinal congénito no corpo.
birthplace, s. terra natal.
birthright, s. direito de nascimento.
bis, adv. (mús.) outra vez; repetir.
biscuit, s. biscoito, bolacha.
bisect, v.t. dividir em duas partes iguais.
bisector, s. bissector.
bisection, s. bissecação.
bisexual, adj. bissexual.
bishop, s. bispo; peça de xadrez com este nome.
bishopric, s. bispado; diocese.
bismuth, s. bismuto.
bison, s. *sing.* e *pl.* bisão.
bissextile, s. bissexto.
bistoury (ies), s. bisturi.
bisulphate, s. bissulfato.
bit, s. freio de cavalo; pua; bocado; alguma coisa. 1) *I don't care a bit*, não me importa nada. 2) *bit by bit*, gradualmente.
bit, pass. de *to bite*.
bitch, s. cadela.
bite, v.t. pas. bit, *part. pass.* bitten, morder, cortar com os dentes; ferrar; picar; corroer. s. mordedura, dentada, picada; bocado.
biter, s. mordedor.
biting, adj. afiado; cortante; sarcástico.
bitten, *part. pass.* de *to bite*.

bitter, adj. amargo; severo; penoso, aflitivo; mordaz; penetrante.
bitterly, adv. amargamente; severamente; *it is bitterly cold*, está um frio de rachar.
bitterness, s. amargor, severidade; azedu-me; mordacidade.
bitter-sweet, s. doce-amarga (planta).
bitters, s. licor de ingredientes amargos; aperitivos.
bitumen, s. betume.
bituminous, adj. betuminoso.
bi-weekly (ies), s. periódico, quinzenal. adj. quinzenal.
bizarre, adj. bizarro, caprichoso.
blab, v.i. tagarelar; revelar um segredo.
blabber, s. indiscreto.
black, adj. preto; negro; sombrio; sujo; zangado. 1) *black friar*, dominicano. 2) *black flag*, bandeira dos piratas. 3) *black mark*, estigma. s. cor preta; um negro; luto. 4) *in black and white*, por escrito. v.t. pintar ou tingir de negro; engraxar; 5) *to black out*, obliterar; apagar as luzes.
blackamoor, s. negro.
blackball, s. voto contra. v.t. votar contra.
blackberry, s. amora silvestre.
blackbird, s. melro.
blackboard, s. lousa, quadro negro.
blackbook, s. livro negro.
black-cattle, s. gado vacum; pessoas desprezíveis; escravos.
blacken, v.t. escurecer, tingir de preto; difamar. v.i. enegrecer-se.
black-eye, s. olho pisado.
black-eyed, adj. que tem olhos pretos.
blackguard, s. canalha. v.t. insultar indecentemente.
blacking, s. graxa.
blackish, adj. escuro, enegrecido.
blackleg, s. gatuno; operário que trabalha quando os outros estão em greve.
black-list, s. lista negra (firmas que não podiam negociar com a Inglaterra durante a Grande Guerra).
blackly, adj. de um modo escuro.
blackmail, s. chantagem. v.t. fazer chantagem.
blackmailer, s. o que faz chantagem.
blackness, s. negrume, negrura.
black-sheep, s. ovelha ronhosa na família; patife.
blacksmith, s. ferreiro.
blackthorn, s. espinheiro negro.
bladder, s. bexiga, ampola.

blade, *s.* lâmina; folha de planta; pessoa matreira, valente.

blade-done, *s.* omoplata.

blague, *s.* mentira pretensiosa.

blain, *s.* pústula, chaga.

blamable, *adj.* culpável, censurável.

blamably, *adv.* culpavelmente.

blame, *s.* culpa, censura, responsabilidade. *v.t.* culpar, censurar.

blameless, *adj.* sem culpa.

blamelessly, *adv.* inculpavelmente.

blamelessness, *s.* inculpabilidade, inocência.

blameworthy, *adj.* culpável, censurável.

blameworthiness, *s.* culpabilidade.

blanch, *v.t.* branquear. *v.t.* empalidecer.

blanching, *s.* embranquecimento dos vegetais, pela exclusão da luz.

bland, *adj.* brando, suave; calmante.

blandish, *v.t.* acariciar, lisonjear.

blandishment, *s.* carícia, lisonja.

blandly, *adv.* suavemente, ironicamente.

blandness, *s.* suavidade.

blank, *adj.* em branco, não escrito; desanimado; vazio; pálido. 1) *blank cartridge,* cartucho sem bala. 2) *blank cheque,* cheque em branco. 3) *blank verse,* verso branco. *s.* espaço em branco; papel em branco; alvo; vazio.

blanket, *s.* cobertor; manta de cavalo; *to be a wet blanket,* ser um desmancha-prazeres. *adj.* geral, que inclui todos os indivíduos de uma classe. *v.t.* cobrir com manta.

blankly, *adv.* em branco.

blankness, *s.* palidez; confusão, perturbação.

blank-verse, *s.* verso solto.

blare, *s.* estrondo; frémito. *v.t.* e *v.i.* proclamar; soar como as trombetas, fazer estrondo.

blarney, *s.* adulação, intrujice.

blasé, *adj.* saciado, cansado de prazer.

blaspheme, *v.t.* e *v.i.* blasfemar.

blasphemer, *s.* blasfemo, ímpio.

blaspheming, *s.* blasfémia.

blasphemous, *adj.* blasfemo.

blasphemously, *adv.* impiamente.

blasphemy (ies), *s.* blasfémia.

blast, *s.* rajada de vento, vento; som (de instrumento de sopro); sopro de um fole; explosão. *v.t.* destruir com explosivos; arruinar; secar.

blasted, *adj.* maldito; *pret.* e *pp.* de *blast.*

blast-furnace, *s.* fornalha de fundição, alto--forno.

blastine, *s.* blastina (explosivo)

blasting, *s.* acção de fazer voar por meio de explosão.

blast-pipe, *s.* tubo de escape, de tiragem.

blatancy, *s.* barulho, ruído.

blatant, *adj.* ruidoso.

blatantly, *adv.* ruidosamente.

blatherskite, *s.* paroleiro, parlapatão.

blaze, *s.* chama, fogo; luz brilhante; estrela branca na testa de certos animais; explosão de cólera. *v.i.* brilhar, resplandecer; arder com chamas. *v.t.* marcar as árvores para indicar o caminho.

blazer, *s.* fato leve de cores claras usado para desporto.

blazing, *adj.* em chamas; resplandecente.

blazon, *s.* brasão; louvor, descrição de virtudes. *v.t.* descrever o escudo de alguém; adornar; alardear.

bleach, *v.t.* e *v.i.* branquear(-se), distinguir. *s.* produto químico para branquear.

bleacher, *s. pl.* lugar mais barato para os espectadores de jogos, geral.

bleaching, *s.* branqueamento.

bleaching-powder, *s.* pó para branquear, cloreto de cal, etc.

bleak, *adj.* sombrio, deserto, ermo; frio, gelado.

bleakly, *adv.* friamente.

bleakness, *s.* frio, frialdade, intempérie.

blear, *adj.* turvo; remeloso.

bleary-eyed, *adj.* remeloso.

bleat, *s.* balido. *v.i.* balir.

bled, *pass.* e *part. pass.* de *to bleed.*

bleed, *v.i.* sangrar. *v.t.* extrair seiva por corte; tirar dinheiro a alguém.

bleeding, *s.* sangria. *adj.* que sangra, a sangrar.

blemish, *v.t.* manchar; difamar; afeiar. *s.* mancha; defeito; desonra.

blench, *v.t.* e *v.i.* recuar; interromper.

blend, *v.t.* misturar; combinar; fundir. *v.i.* unir--se, combinar-se; fundir-se. *s.* mistura, combinação.

blending, *s.* mistura, combinação.

bless, *v.t. pass.* e *part. pass. blessed* ou *blest,* abençoar, consagrar; santificar; fazer feliz; invocar Deus; *bless me!,* valha-me Deus!

blessed, *adj.* abençoado; santificado; santo; *the whole blessed day,* todo o santo dia.

blessedly, *adv.* ditosamente, bem-aventuradamente.

blessedness, *s.* bem-aventurança, santidade, felicidade.

blessing, *s.* bênção; benefício; graça divina.

blew, *pass.* de *to blow.*

blight, *s.* doença das plantas; ruína. *v.t.* destruir, arruinar; afectar as plantas com doenças.

blimp, *s.* pequeno avião primitivamente usada para a caça aos submarinos.

blind, *adj.* cego; insensato; ignorante; escondido; obscurecido; *the blind,* os cegos; *s.* biombo; evasiva; transparente de janela. *v.t.* cegar; vendar os olhos; confundir; deslumbrar, escurecer, esconder.

blindage, *s.* resguardo, armação coberta de terra para proteger os soldados nas trincheiras, etc.; defesa.

blindfold, *v.t.* vendar os olhos. *adj.* às cegas, com os olhos vendados.

blindly, *adv.* às cegas.

blindness, *s.* cegueira.

blink, *v.i.* pestanejar, piscar os olhos; cintilar. *s.* vislumbre; clarão; piscadela.

blinker, *s.* o que pestaneja; *(pl.)* óculos de cor; antolhos.

bliss, *s.* felicidade; alegria; bem-aventurança.

blissful, *adj.* bem-aventurado, feliz.

blissfully, *adv.* felizmente, bem-aventuradamente.

blissfulness, *s.* suprema felicidade.

blister, *s.* pústula; bolha. *v.t.* e *v.i.* empolar, levantar borbulhas.

blithe, *adj.* alegre, jovial.

blithely, *adv.* alegremente.

blitheness, *s.* alegria, júbilo.

blizzard, *s.* violenta tempestade de neve.

bloat, *v.t.* e *v.i.* inchar, entumecer.

bloatedeness, *s.* inchação, inflamação.

bloater, *s.* arenque defumado.

blob, *s.* gota de líquido; borbulha, ampola.

block, *s.* cepo; bloco de madeira ou pedra; quarterão de prédios; obstáculo; forma de chapéu; pedra de bater (encadernador); pessoa estúpida. *v.t.* obstruir; delinear; apoiar com cepos. 1) *to block the door,* bloquear a passagem. 2) *to block up a door,* tapar uma porta.

blockade, *s.* bloqueio. *v.t.* bloquear, sitiar.

blockader, *s.* bloqueador.

blockhead, *s.* estúpido, tolo, néscio.

blockhouse, *s.* fortim.

blockship, *s.* navio com material para obstruir um canal ou porto.

blocktin, *s.* estanho de qualidade inferior.

bloke, *s.* sujeito; labrego, parolo.

blond, blonde, *adj.* loiro (pele e cabelos). *s.* pessoa loira.

blood, *s.* sangue; vida; linhagem; parentesco; temperamento, paixão; seiva das árvores. 1) *bloodcount,* análise quantitativa de sangue. 2) *blood relative,* parente consanguíneo. 3) *blood vessel,* veia. 4) *in cold blood,* a sangue-frio.

blood-guiltiness, *s.* responsabilidade pela morte de alguém

blood-guilty, *adj.* responsável pela morte de alguém; homicida.

bloodheat, *s.* temperatura do sangue.

bloodhorse, *s.* cavalo de pura raça.

blooded, *adj.* da melhor raça; *half blooded,* degenerado.

bloodily, *adv.* cruamente, barbaramente.

bloodiness, *s.* sanguinolência, crueldade.

bloodless, *adj.* exangue; pálido; sem efusão de sangue.

bloodlessly, *adv.* sem efusão de sangue.

blood-money, *s.* dinheiro ganho por um assassínio.

bloodpoisoning, *s.* envenenamento do sangue.

blood-rain, *s.* chuva avermelhada.

bloodshed, *s.* efusão de sangue; matança.

bloodshot, *adj.* injectado de sangue.

bloodstain, *s.* mancha de sangue.

bloodstained, *adj.* manchado de sangue.

blood-stone, *s.* heliotrópio, hematite.

bloodsucker, *s.* sanguessuga.

bloodthirstiness, *s.* sede de sangue; encarniçamento.

bloodthirsty, *adj.* sanguinário, cruel.

bloody, *adj.* ensanguentado; sanguinário; infame; desprezível.

bloom, *s.* flor; florescimento; beleza, frescura; cor rosada. *v.i.* florescer; ostentar frescura.

bloomer, *s.* vestido de mulher com saia curta e calções; disparate grande (calão).

blooming, *adj.* florescente; fresco, vigoroso.

blossom, *s.* flor (de árvores frutíferas. *v.i.* florescer.

blot, *s.* mancha; borrão; defeito. *v.t.* manchar; borrar; difamar; secar com mata-borrão. 1) *this pen blots,* esta pena deita borrão. 2) *to blot out, destruir,* obliterar. 3) *blotting-paper,* mata-borrão.

blotch, *s.* mancha, borrão; pústula. *v.t.* e *v.i.* cobrir de pústulas.

blotchy, *adj.* com manchas ou pústulas.

blotter, *s.* mata-borrão; borrão (livro).

blouse, *s.* blusa.

blow, *v.t.* e *v.i.* florescer. *v.i* e *v.t. pass* blew, *part. pass.* blown, soprar; ventar; fazer soar (um instrumento de sopro); vangloriar-se; 1) *to blow a fuse*, queimar um fusível, 2) *to blow one's nose*, assoar o nariz. 3) *to blow out*, apagar. 4) *to blow out the brains*, fazer saltar os miolos. *s.* golpe, pancada, bofetada; sopro; desgraça; ostentação; floração.

blower, *s.* soprador; ventilador; fole.

blow-fly (ies), *s.* mosca varejeira.

blown, *part. pass.* de *to blow*.

blowout, *s.* estouro; escape violento de gás,ar, etc.

blowpipe, *s.* maçarico.

blowy, *adj.* ventoso.

blowzed, *adj.* de face vermelha; com aspecto grosseiro; desalinhado.

blubber, *s.* óleo de baleia; choro. *v.i.* chorar muito.

bluchers, *s.* botas baixas.

blue, *adj.* azul; triste, melancólico; coloq. 1) *blue nose*, puritano; 2) *once in a blue moon*; raramente. 3) *sky blue*, azul-celeste. *s.* cor azul; tinta azul; anil.

bluebell, *s.* campainha (flor).

bluejacket, *s.* marinheiro da armada.

blueness, *s.* cor azul.

blues, *s.* depressão moral; *to be in the blues, to get the blues, to look blues*, estar melancólico.

bluff, *adj.* escarpado, íngreme; franco; *v.t.* alardear, bravatear, fanfarronar.

bluffer, *s.* fanfarrão.

bluffly, *adv.* rudemente.

bluffness, *s.* aspereza; rudeza; fanfarronada.

bluish, *adj.* azulado.

blunder, *s.* erro crasso, disparate. *v.t.* e *v.i.* cometer um erro crasso, errar. 1) *to blunder into* (*on, upon*), topar por acaso. 2) *to blunder something out*, dizer algo descuidadamente.

blunderbuss (es), *s.* bacamarte.

blunderer, *s.* desatinado.

blundering, *adj.* disparatado.

blunge, *v.i.* amassar (cal ou gesso) por meio de uma máquina.

blunger, *s.* máquina de amassar (cal ou gesso).

blunt, *adj.* tolo, embotado; sem corte; brusco.

bluntly, *adv.* sem fio; sem ponta; sem artifício; rudemente.

bluntness, *s.* embotadura; aspereza; grosseria; franqueza rude.

blur, *v.t.* e *v.i.* obscurecer, enublar; borrar, manchar. *s.* mancha, nebulosidade.

blurt, *v.t.* proferir abrupta e impulsivamente.

blush, *s.* rubor, vermelhidão. *v.i.* corar, ruborizar; envergonhar-se (com *for, at*).

blushing, *s.* rubor na face. *adj.* corado; modesto.

blushingly, *adv.* corando.

bluster, *v.i.* soprar violentamente; esbravejar. *s.* estrondo; ventania; bravata.

blusterer, *s.* fanfarrão.

boa, *s.* jibóia.

boar, *s.* varrão; *wild boar*, javali.

board, *s.* tábua, prancha; cartão; mesa; comida, junta, conselho; bordo; 1) *board of education*, junta de educação. 2) *on a board*, a bordo; 3) *board and lodging*, cama e comida. 4) *to go over board*, cair ao mar. *v.i.* hospedar-se; bordejar; *v.t.* assoalhar; abordar; dar pensão; ir para bordo.

boarder, *s.* hóspede, pensionista; aluno interno.

boarding, *s.* abordagem; tábuas; cobertura de tábuas; hospedagem.

boardinghouse, *s.* pensão.

boardingschool, *s.* colégio ou escola com internato.

boardwages, *s.* paga de alimentação (aos criados).

boarish, *adj.* brutal, cruel.

boast, *v.t.* e *v.i.* jactar-se, vangloriar-se; ostentar, alardear; *he boasts of being the best player in the town*, ele vangloria-se de ser o melhor jogador da cidade. *s.* jactância, ostentação.

boastful, *adj.* jactancioso.

boastfully, *adv.* jactanciosamente.

boat, *s.* barco, bote, navio. 1) *life boat*, salva--vidas. 2) *boatman*, barqueiro. 3) *boat race*, regata. 4) *to turn one's boat*, fazer algo que impossibilite mudança de ideia.

boating, *s.* passeio de barco; *to go boating*, ir passear de barco.

boatman, *s.* barqueiro.

boatswain, *s.* contramestre de navio.

bob, *s.* pêndulo, flutuador de linha de pesca; aceno, cortesia; corte curto de cabelo para criança ou mulher. (coloq. ingl.) xelim. *v.t.* e *v.i.* bater de leve; balançar-se; cortar o cabelo curto; *to bob up and down*, saltar.

bobbin, s. bobina, carretilha.
bobwhite, s. codorniz.
boche, s. soldado alemão (nome de desprezo usado na Grande Guerra)
bode, pass. de to bide.
bode, v.t. e v.i. predizer; prometer.
bodeful, adj. ominoso.
bodice, s. corpete.
bodily, adv. todos juntos, colectivamente, em
peso. adj. corpóreo, corporal.
bodkin, s. furador (de costura, etc.) punção;
alfinete do cabelo.
body, s. corpo; tronco; substância; corporação; parte principal; grupo. v.t. dar corpo,
corporizar.
bodyguard, s. guarda pessoal, escolta.
body-snatcher, s. o que desenterra cadáveres.
bog, s. pântano, lodaçal. v.t. e v.i. afundar
como num pântano, atolar.
bogey, s. duende; o demónio.
bogginess, s. qualidade de pantanoso.
boggle, v.i. hesitar, vacilar. v.t. confundir,
equivocar. s. hesitação.
boggler, s. pessoa irresoluta.
boggy, adj. pantanoso.
bogie, s. carreta giratória para transportar
carruagens compridas; duende; espectro.
bogie-engine, s. locomotiva com carreta
giratória.
bogle, s. fantasma.
bogus, adj. fictício, falso.
bohemian, s. e adj. boémio; da Boémia;
boémio, valdevinos.
boil, v.t. ferver; cozer; estar agitado. v.t.
ferver (um líquido); cozer. s. fervura,
ebulição; furúnculo.
boiler, s. vasilha para ferver, caldeira a
vapor.
boiling, s. fervura, ebulição. adj. fervente,
escaldante; ardente. 1) boiling spring,
géiser. 2) boiling hot, escaldante; 3) at the
boiling point, no ponto de ebulição; muito
agastado.
boiling-point, s. ponto de ebulição.
boisterous, adj. turbulento, ruidoso, tumultuoso.
boisterously, adv. tumultuosamente.
boisterousness, s. turbulência, tumulto.
bold, adj. arrojado, audacioso; insolente;
íngreme; bold faced, descarado;
boldly, adv. ousadamente.
boldness, s. arrojo, ousadia; descaramento.
bole, s. tronco de árvore.

bolero, s. bolero.
Bolivia, s. Bolívia.
Bolivian, s. e adj. boliviano.
boll, s. cápsula, casulo.
bolled, adj. em casulos.
bolometer, s. bolómetro.
bolshevism, s. bolchevismo.
bolshevist, s. e adj. bolchevista.
bolster, s. travesseiro, almofadão; reforço,
suporte. v.t. sustentar, apoiar; to bolster
someone's courage, dar ânimo a alguém.
bolt, s. dardo; raio; ferrolho, lingueta (de
fechadura); cavilha ou parafuso de ferro;
rolo grosso e compacto de pano ou papel.
v.i. e v.t. fechar com um ferrolho; engolir
sem mastigar; fugir; peneirar; saltar como
um raio; (nos EUA) recusar apoiar o
candidato ou a política do próprio partido. 1) to blot in, fechar; 2) to bolt out,
excluir.
bolting, s. acto de aferrolhar, cavilhar,
peneirar ou de fugir. 1) bolting-cloth, pano
para peneira. 2) bolting-mill, máquina de
peneirar.
bolus (es), s. bolo; pílula grande.
bomb, s. bomba. v.t. bombardear.
bombard, v.t. bombardear, canhonear; (fig.)
importunar com perguntas ou reclamações.
bombardier, s. bombardeiro, oficial de
artilharia.
bombardment, s. bombardeamento, bombardeio.
bombasine, s. bombazina.
bombast, s. linguagem bombástica.
bombastic, adj. bombástico.
bomber, s. soldado ou avião que lança
granadas, bombardeiro.
bon, adj. bom.
bona fide, adj. e adv. boa-fé; genuíno; sincero.
bonanza, s. bonança.
bonbon, s. bombom, doce.
bond, s. laço, vínculo; acordo; fiança; obrigação; bónus; retenção de mercadorias na
Alfândega até que os direitos ou as taxas
sejam pagos; (pl.) cadeias, prisão. adj.
escravizado, cativo. v.t. amarrar; afiançar,
hipotecar.
bondage, s. escravidão, servidão.
bonded, adj. depositado como fiança para
pagamento de direitos; hipotecado;
garantido por escritura.
bondmaid, s. escrava.

bondman, bondsman, s. escravo; fiador.

bondwoman, s. escrava.

bone, s. osso; espinha de peixe; *pl.* esqueleto; objecto feito de osso. 1) *as dry as a bone,* bem seco. 2) *to the bone,* completamente. *v.t.* desossar.

bone-ash, s. cinza de ossos para a confecção de porcelanas.

bone-setter, s. endireita.

bone-shaker, s. bicicleta sem rodas de borracha; carriola sem molas; máquina de sacudir.

bonfire, s. fogueira de festa.

boniness, s. ossatura.

boning, s. acto de desossar; aplicação de adubos em pó.

bonne-bouche, s. acepipe.

bonnet, s. boné, gorro, chapéu de senhora.

bonnily, *adv.* alegremente; formosamente.

bonniness, s. alegria; formusura.

bonny, bonnie, *adj.* formoso, belo; sadio.

bonus, s. prémio, gratificação, bónus.

bony, s. ossudo.

bonze, s. bonzo.

boo, vt. apupar. *int.* expressão de desprezo.

booby, s. bobo, tolo, estúpido.

boobyish, *adj.* estúpido.

booby-hatch, s. escotilhão.

booby-trap, s. armadilha, coisas colocadas no cimo duma porta para caírem sobre o primeiro que entrar.

boodle, s. dinheiro para suborno de actos políticos; multidão; um simplório.

booer, s. escarnecedor.

book, s. livro; tomo; volume. 1) *the Book,* a Bíblia. 2) *day book,* diário. 3) *cash book,* livro-caixa. *v.t.* registar; descrever; reservar lugar para espectáculo.

bookbinder, s. encadernador.

bookbinding, s. encadernação.

bookcase, s. estante para livros.

book-debt, s. dívida registada em livro comercial.

booking, s. registo de bagagens.

booking-office, s. bilheteira (dos caminhos de ferro).

bookish, *adj.* versado em livros; estudioso; teórico; pedante.

bookishly, *adv.* teoricamente.

bookishness, s. aplicação aos livros; falta de senso prático.

bookkeeper, s. guarda-livros, contador.

bookkeeping, s. escrituração comercial, contabilidade.

booklearning, s. conhecimentos obtidos pelos livros.

booklet, s. opúsculo, livreto.

bookman, s. pessoa interessada em livros; sábio, estudioso.

bookmaker, s. pessoa que faz livros; apostador na corrida de cavalos.

bookmaking, s. compilação ou confecção de livros; aposta na corrida de cavalos.

bookmark, s. marca que se coloca entre as páginas dum livro.

bookplate, s. etiqueta com o nome do dono do livro, ex-líbris.

bookseller, s. livreiro.

bookselling, s. venda de livros.

bookself, s. estante de livros.

bookshop, s. livraria.

bookstall, s. quiosque.

bookstore, s. livraria.

booktrade, s. comércio de livros.

bookworm, s. traça que ataca os livros; rato de biblioteca.

boom, *v.t.* e *v.i.* ecoar ou fazer ecoar com grande barulho; tornar-se popular; favorecer; prosperar. s. grande estampido; aumento repentino de valor dos títulos na bolsa; prosperidade.

boomerang, s. bumerangue.

boon, s. benefício; dádiva; favor. *adj.* jovial, alegre; generoso.

boor, s. indivíduo grosseiro, rude; camponês.

boorish, *adj.* rústico, grosseiro.

boorishly, *adv.* rusticamente.

boorishness, s. rusticidade.

boost, s. empurrão; levantamento; *bost in prices,* aumento de preços. *v.t.* e *v.i.* empurrar; levantar.

boot, s. bota, calçado; porta-mala; pontapé; algo que se dá para igualar uma troca. *v.t.* e *v.i.* chutar; calçar as botas; servir; ser proveitoso.

bootee, s. botina; carapim.

booteeblack, s. engraxador.

booth, s. barraca, tenda.

bootleg, s. contrabandista.

bootless, *adj.* inútil, vão.

bootlessly, *adv.* inutilmente.

bootlessness, s. inutilidade.

boots, s. criado de hotel que engraxa botas e faz recados.

booty, s. saque, pilhagem.

booze, *v.i.* embriagar-se. s. bebida alcoólica; bebedeira; *he is on the booze,* ele está com os copos.

boozer, s. ébrio.

boracic, adj. bórico.

borage, s. borragem.

borate, s. borato.

borax, s. bórax.

border, s. borda, margem; fronteira, limite, v.t. e v.i. guarnecer, debruar; limitar; confinar.

borderer, s. confinante; raiano, especialmente o que morava na fronteira da Inglaterra-Escócia.

bore, s. buraco, cavidade; verruma; calibre de arma de fogo; um maçador. v.t. furar, sondar; importunar.

bore, part. de to bear.

borealis, adj. boreal.

Boreas, s. Bóreas (o deus e o vento norte).

boredom, s. tédio, aborrecimento, fastio.

borer, s. broca, verruma.

boring, adj. fastidioso, tedioso.

born, part. pass. de to bear. adj. nascido. 1) to be born, nascer. 2) still born, nascido morto.

borne, part. pass. de to bear (levar, carregar).

borough, s. vila, pequena cidade; distrito de município.

borrow, v.t. pedir emprestado.

borrower, s. aquele que pede emprestado.

borrowing, s. empréstimo.

bosh, s. tolice.

bosk, bosket, s. pequeno bosque; plantação.

bosky, adj. de bosques; nemoroso.

bosom, s. peito, seio; peito de um vestido; coração; amor, carinho. adj. querido, íntimo. 1) bosom friend, amigo íntimo. 2) in the bosom of a family, no seio de uma família.

boss (es), s. (coloq.) chefe, patrão, capataz; (gíria) chefe político; protuberância; botão. v.t. e v.i. trabalhar em relevo; dirigir, chefiar.

bossily, s. de um modo saliente.

bossiness, s. saliência; relevo.

bossy, adj. autoritário, mandão.

botanic, adj. botânico.

botanize, s. estudar as plantas praticamente; herborizar.

botany, s. botânica.

botanical, adj. botânico.

botanist, s. botânico.

botch (es), s. remendo. v.t. remendar mal; estropiar.

botcher, s. remendão (alfaiate).

both, adj. e pron. ambos, os dois. 1) both of us, nós dois. conj. tanto como. 2) both... and, não só... mas também.

bother, s. aborrecimento, enfado. v.t. e v.i. aborrecer, molestar.

botheration, s. aborrecimento, incómodo, enfado.

bothersome, adj. aborrecido.

bottle, s. garrafa, frasco; quantidade contida numa garrafa ou frasco. v.t. engarrafar; bottle up, controlar.

bottler, s. engarrafador.

bottom, s. fundo; base, fundamento; leito de rio; casco de navio. 1) to send to the bottom, afundar. 2) from top to the bottom, de alto a baixo. 3) to be at the bottom of the class, ser o último da classe. adj. fundo; fundamento; ínfimo, v.t. pôr a fundo, firmar, v.i. apoiar-se.

bottomless, adj. sem fundo, insondável, visionário.

bottomry, s. bodemeria.

botuline, s. botulina.

botulism, s. botulismo.

boudoir, s. toucador.

bouffe, adj. cómico.

bough, s. ramo de árvore.

bought, pass. e part. pass. de to buy.

bougie, s. vela de cera; algália.

boulder, s. penhasco; bloco de minério; seixo.

boulevard, s. bulevar; avenida larga e arborizada.

boulter, s. linha de pesca com muitos anzóis.

bounce, s. salto, pulo; estalo; exagero. v.t. e v.i. saltar, estalar; exagerar.

bouncer, s. fanfarrão; coisa exagerada.

bouncing, adj. forte, vigoroso; mexido, vivo, exagerado.

bound, s. limite, fronteira; salto; repercussão. v.t. limitar, confinar; fazer saltar. v.i. saltar.

bound, pass. e part. pass. de to bind. adj. sujeito, obrigado; encadernado.

bound, adj. com destino a, pronto a partir. 1) outward bound, indo. 2) homeward bound, vindo.

boundary (ies), s. limite; fronteira; linha demarcadora.

bounden, adj. obrigatório.

bounder, s. demarcador; indivíduo pretensioso.

boundless, adj. ilimitado.

boundlessness, s. imensidade.

bounteous, adj. generoso; abundante.

bounteously, adv. generosamente.

bounteousness, s. generosidade; liberalidade.

bountiful, adj. generoso, liberal; abundante.

bounty (ies), s. generosidade, bondade; concessão; prémio.

bouquet, s. ramalhete; aroma característico (como do vinho).

bourdon, s. bordão, registo de órgão.

bourgeois, s. masc. fem. sing. pl. burguês.

bourgeoisie, s. burguesia.

bourne, s. limite; meta; arroio; corrente de água.

bourse, s. bolsa, mercado estrangeiro de fundos.

boursocrat, s. magnata de finanças.

bout, s. combate, luta; turno, período; a bout of pneumonia, um ataque de pneumonia.

bovine, adj. bovino.

bovril, s. bovril, extracto de carne.

bow, s. saudação, inclinação, reverência. v.t. e v.i. submeter-se; curvar-se, cumprimentar-se; to bow the neck, submeter-se.

bow, s. arco-íris; arco de flecha; arco de violino; curva; laço; v.t. e v.i. curvar; dobrar; tocar instrumento de corda. 1) to draw the long bow, exagerar. 2) bow-legged, de pernas tortas.

bow, s. proa de navio; o remador que rema desse lado.

bowdlerize (ise), v.t. expurgar (uma composição literária).

bowels, s. pl. intestinos, tripas, entranhas.

bower, s. caramanchão; arvoredo.

bowery, s. viveiro de plantas; sombrio.

bowie-knife, s. faca de mato.

bow-knot, s. laço de nó corredio.

bowl, s. tigela; taça grande; bojo; bola de madeira; pl. jogo de bola. v.t. e v.i. rolar, rodar, rebolar; jogar a bola.

bow-legged, adj. que tem as pernas tortas.

bowler, s. chapéu de feltro; jogador de bola.

bowling-green, s. tabuleiro de relva para o jogo de bolas.

bowman, s. arqueiro.

bowshot, s. arremesso de frecha.

bowsprit, s. gurupés.

bowstring, s. corda do arco.

bow-window, s. janela saliente ou arqueada, ou de sacada.

bow-wow, s. latido de cão.

box, s. bofetada, murro. v.t. esbofetear, esmurrar. v.i. lutar.

box, s. caixa; caixote; conteúdo de uma caixa; camarote de teatro; assento de cocheiro; buxo. 1) box-car, furgão. 2) box-office, bilheteira. 3) in a box, em

apuros. 4) in the same box, na mesma situação. v.t. encaixotar; pôr dentro de caixas.

boxer, s. pugilista.

boxing, s. pugilismo.

Boxing-day, s. dia seguinte ao Natal.

boxing-glove, s. luva para o boxe.

boxing-match (es), s. desafio de boxe.

boxwood, s. madeira de buxo.

boy, s. menino; lacaio.

Boyard, s. boiardo.

boyau, v.t. boicotar, cortar as relações comerciais ou sociais com alguém. s. boicotagem, corte de relações comerciais ou sociais com alguém.

boycott, s. boicotagem. v.t. boicotar; cortar relações.

boyhood, s. meninice, juventude.

boyish, adj. pueril.

boyishly, adv. de um modo pueril.

boyishness, s. puerilidade.

boy-scout, s. escuteiro.

brace, s. braçadeira; tira; par de animais; apoio, reforço; colchetes (sinais usados na escrita); pl. suspensórios. v.t. atar, ligar; retesar; apoiar; estimular; to brace up, animar-se.

bracelet, s. pulseira, bracelete.

brachial, adj. braquial.

bracing, adj. estimulante, fortificante, revigorante, tonificante.

brack, s. falha, defeito, rotura.

bracken, s. (bot.) feto, fetal.

bracket, s. suporte, braço de candeeiro para fixar nas paredes; parênteses ou colchetes de impressão. v.t. juntar, emparelhar; incluir colchetes de impressão.

brackish, adj. salobra (água).

brackishness, s. sabor salobre.

bract, s. bráctea.

brad, s. prego sem cabeça.

bradawl, s. furador.

brae, s. ladeira de monte.

brag, s. jactância, fanfarronada. v.t. e v.i. vangloriar-se, jactar-se.

braggadocio, s. fanfarrão; fanfarrice.

braggart, s. fanfarrão, valentão.

bragging, s. jactância.

Brahman, s. brâmane.

Brahmanism, s. bramanismo.

braid, s. trança; galão; debrum.

brail, s. rizes (náut.). v.t. meter a vela nos rizes.

braille, s. escrita para cegos.

brain, s. cérebro; pl. compreensão, juízo; to blow out the brains, fazer saltar os miolos.

brainless, adj. insensato.

brainlessness, s. insensatez.

brainy, adj. esperto. inteligente

braird, s. primeiro rebento (cereais). v.i. lançar rebentos.

braise, v.t. refogar, guisar.

brake, s. travão, breque; espadela para bater linho; matagal; to apply the brakes, travar. v.t. e v.i. travar, fechar o freio, brecar.

bramble, s. espinheiro, sarça.

brambling, s. tentilhão.

brambly, adj. cheio de abrolhos ou de espinhos, silvoso.

bran, s. farelo.

branch (es), s. galho, ramo de árvore; ramo, secção, divisão; filial, sucursal; branch railway, ramal. v.i. ramificar-se, bifurcar-se.

branching, s. desenvolvimento dos rebentos; ramagem; derivação; ramificação; bifurcação (máq.). adj. ramudo, ramoso, ramificado.

branchia, s. guelras de peixes.

branchy, adj. ramudo, ramoso, ramificação.

brand, s. tição; marca, estigma; marca de fábrica; ferro de marcar reses; brand new, novinho em folha. v.t. marcar; estigmatizar; difamar.

brander, s. grelha. v.t. assar na grelha.

brandied, adj. aguardentado.

branding-iron, s. ferro de marcar a quente.

brandish, v.t. brandir, agitar.

brand-new, adj. novo em folha.

brandy (ies), s. aguardente (de vinho).

brank, s. trigo mourisco; (pl.) espécie de freio para tapar a boca a mulheres turbulentas.

brank-ursine, s. acanto.

brant, s. pato bravo. adj. escarpado; direito; altivo.

brash (es), s. erupção; entulho. adj. impetuoso; temerário.

brasier, s. caldeireiro, braseiro.

brass (es), s. latão, bronze; (coloq.) desfaçatez, descaro; 1) brasses, utensílios de latão; 2) brass band, charanga.

brassard, s. braçal, parte da armadura que defende o braço; banda (no braço).

brassband, s. charanga.

brassy, adj. de latão de cobre; como latão ou cobre (em cor, som, etc.); pretensioso; descarado.

brat, s. criança, fedelho.

brattle, v.i. produzir um som prolongado de matraca.

bravado, s. bravata, fanfarronice.

brave, adj. corajoso, bravo, valente.

bravely, adv. valentemente.

bravery (ies), s. coragem.

bravo, s. assassino assalaiado. interj. bravo!

bravura, s. bravura.

brawl, s. contenda, disputa; alvoroço, v.t. discutir ruidosamente; fazer burburinho.

brawler, s. alvoroçador; disputador.

brawn, s. músculo; preparado em que entra cabeça de porco, chispe e língua, tudo picado, cozido e temperado.

brawniness, s. musculatura; força muscular.

brawny, adj. musculoso; vigoroso.

braxy, s. febre carbuncular.

bray, s. zurro, voz de burro; v.i. zurrar; triturar, moer.

brazen, adj. de bronze; como bronze; descarado.

brazen-faced, adj. descarado; cara-estanhada, lata estanhada.

brazenly, adv. descaradamente.

brazenness, s. descaro.

brazier, s. latoeiro, caldeireiro; braseiro.

brazil, s. pau-brasil.

Brazil, s. Brasil; Brazil-nut, castanha do Maranhão.

Brazilian, s. e adj. brasileiro.

brazing, s. soldadura.

breach (es), s. brecha, abertura; ruptura; violação; rompimento de relações.

bread, s. pão; alimento; to earn one's bread, ganhar a vida.

breadth, s. largura; extensão; amplitude.

breadthways, adv. à largura.

breathwise, adv. à largura.

break, v.t. e v.i. pass. de broke part. pass. broken, quebrar, partir; transgredir; violar; interromper; dispersar; 1) to break news, revelar notícias; 2) to break a horse, domar um cavalo; 3) to break away, escapar, fugir. 4) to break into, entrar por arrombamento. 5) to break out, rebentar. 6) to break loose, escapar. s. rompimento; rotura; interrupção; baixa na bolsa; 7) without a break, sem interrupção, continuamente.

breakable, adj. quebradiço, frágil.

breakage, s. rotura, fractura, indemnização por coisa quebrada.

breakdown, s. colapso; depressão, fadiga; *nervous breakdown*, neurastenia.

breaker, s. quebrador; domador; onda que se quebra na praia ou num rochedo; máquina de quebrar carvão.

breakfast, s. primeira refeição do dia. *v.t.* e *v.i.* tomar a primeira refeição; dar a primeira refeição do dia.

breakfast-set, s. serviço de almoço.

breaking, s. fractura; irrupção; transgressão; bancarrota.

breaking-up, s. colapso; encerramento; dissolução; transgressão; bancarrota.

break-neck, s. despenhadeiro. *adj.* perigoso.

breakwater, s. quebra-mar.

bream, s. sargo (peixe). *v.t.* limpar (o casco do navio).

breast, s. peito; parte de peça de vestuário que cobre o peito; seio, tetas; coração; *to make a clean breast of,* confessar tudo.

breast-bone, s. esterno.

breastplate, s. couraça, armadura que cobre o peito.

breastwork, s. defesa, peitoril baixo.

breath, s. respiração, fôlego; alento; sopro. 1) *to waste one's breath,* falar às paredes. 2) *out of breath,* sem fôlego. 3) *to take breath,* tomar fôlego.

breathe, *v.t.* e *v.i.* respirar; viver; tomar fôlego; descansar; falar brandamente; *to breathe one's last,* morrer.

breather, s. o que respira.

breathing, s. respiração, inspiração. 1) *breathing-space,* pausa. 2) *breathing-hole,* respiradouro.

breathless, *adj.* esbaforido; desalentado; morto.

breathlessness, s. desalento.

breathy, *adj.* aspirado (diz-se das notas de música no canto).

bred, *pass.* e *part. pass.* de *to breed.*

bree, s. caldo; sumo de carne; sobrancelha; desentendimento (diál.).

breech, s. culatra de arma de fogo; nádegas; traseiro.

breeches, s. *pl.* calças, calções.

breeching, s. retranca, corda para segurar as peças de fogo.

breach-loader, s. arma ou peça de carregar pela culatra.

breed, *v.t.* e *v.i. pass.* e *part. pass.* bered, procriar; criar; educar; multiplicar-se. s. casta, raça; espécie; geração; ninhada.

breeder, s. criador, educador.

breeding, s. criação; educação; civilidade; geração.

breeze, s. brisa, viração; rumor.

breezily, s. brisa, vento fresco; agitação; rumor.

breeziness, s. jovialidade.

breezy, *adj.* ventilado; alegre, jovial.

brethren, *pl.* de brother, irmãos (membros de uma igreja ou sociedade).

breve, s. breve (mús,); acento de sílaba breve.

brevet, s. diploma, patente; graduação honorária conferida a um oficial do exército; certificado de piloto de aeronáutica. *v.t.* graduar.

breviary (ies), s. breviário, compêndio.

breviate, s. resumo, sumário.

brevity, s. brevidade

brew, *v.t.* fermentar, misturar, fazer cerveja; *v.i.* preparar-se. s. cerveja.

brewer, f. cervejeiro.

brewing, s. fabricação de cerveja.

brewery (ies), s. fábrica de cerveja.

briar, variante de brier.

bribe, s. suborno, *v.t.* subornar.

briber, s. subornador.

bribery (ies), s. suborno.

bric-à-brac, s. bricabraque, objectos de arte antigos.

brick, s. tijolo; ladrilho. *v.t.* cobrir com tijolos, ladrilhar.

brickbat, s. bocado de tijolo.

brick-dust, s. pó de tijolo.

brick-kiln, s. forno para cozer tijolos ou ladrilhos.

bricklayer, s. assentador de tijolos ou ladrilhos.

bricklaying, s. assentamento de tijolos ou ladrilhos.

brickmaker, s. fabricante de tijolos ou ladrilhos.

brickmaking, s. fabricação de tijolos ou ladrilhos.

brickwork, s. obra de tijolos ou ladrilhos.

bridal, *adj.* nupcial. s. núpcias; *bridaldress,* vestido de noiva.

bride, s. noiva, recém-casada.

bride-chamber, s. câmara nupcial.

bridegroom, s. noivo, recém-casado.

bridesmaid, s. dama de honra, dama de honor.

bridewell, s casa de correcção; cadeia.

bridge, s. ponte; cavalete do nariz; jogo de cartas; plataforma de navio. 1) *draw bridge,* ponte elevadiça. 2) *suspension bridge*, ponte pênsil. *v.t.* construir uma ponte.

bridle, *s.* freio, rédea; restrição. *v.t.* frear, refrear. *v.i.* erguer ou jogar a cabeça em sinal de vaidade, ódio, desprezo.

bridle-path, *s.* caminho para passeio a cavalo.

bridoon, *s.* bridão.

brief, *adj.* breve, curto. *s.* sumário, resumo; breve apostólico.

briefly, *adv.* brevemente, em resumo.

briefless, *adj.* sem clientes (diz-se do advogado).

briefness, *s.* brevidade, concisão.

brier, *s.* sarça, roseira brava.

brig, *s.* brigue.

brigade, *s.* brigada.

brigadier, *s.* brigadeiro.

brigadier-general, *s.* general de brigada.

brigand, *s.* bandido, salteador.

brigandage, *s.* roubo, assalto.

brigantine, *s.* bergantim.

bright, *adj.* brilhante, claro, radiante; alegre, vivo; inteligente.

brightly, *adv.* brilhantemente.

brightness, *s.* brilho, esplendor, claridade; agudeza, vivacidade.

brighten, *v.t.* e *v.i.* polir, lustrar; ilustrar; alegrar-se, animar-se; tornar-se claro.

Bright's disease, *s.* mal de Bright.

brill, *s.* peixe parecido com o rodovalho.

brilliance, *s.* brilho; esplendor.

brilliant, *adj.* brilhante, resplandecente; esplêndido; talentoso. *s.* brilhante, diamante.

brilliantly, *adv.* brilhantemente.

brilliantness, *s.* brilhantismo.

brilliantine, *s.* brilhantina.

brim, *s.* borda, margem, extremidade; orla.

brimful, *adj.* cheio até à borda, completamente cheio.

brimming, *pp.* de rim; *adj.* completamente cheio.

brimstone, *s.* enxofre.

brindled, *adj.* malhado.

brine, *s.* salmoura; mar; lágrimas.

bring, *v.t.* *pass.* e *part. pass.* brought, trazer; conduzir; induzir, persuadir; produzir. 1) *to bring about*, efectuar, produzir. 2) *to bring down*, derrubar, humilhar. 3) *to bring forth*, produzir, dar à luz; 4) *to bring to*, resolver; reanimar uma pessoa desmaiada. 5) *to bring up*, educar, criar. 6) *to bring up the rear*, fechar a retaguarda.

bringer, *s.* portador.

brininess, *s.* sabor a sal ou a água salobra.

brink, *s.* borda, margem; extremidade; *on the brink of*, à beira de.

brinometer, *s.* instrumento para medir a densidade da água salgada.

briny, *adj.* salgado; salobre.

brio, *s.* vivacidade.

briony, *s.* briónia (planta).

briquette, *s.* briquete.

brisk, *adj.* alerta, vivo, animado; forte; rápido.

brisket, *s.* peito (dum animal).

briskly, *adv.* rapidamente.

briskness, *s.* viveza, actividade, desembaraço.

bristle, *s.* cerda, pêlo. *v.i.* eriçar-se, entesar-se; *to bristle with*, estar pleno de.

bristliness, *s.* qualidade de ser hirsuto.

bristly, *adj.* eriçado.

Britain, *s.* Grã-Bretanha.

Britannia, *s.* nome dado pelos romanos à Grã-Bretanha; *britannia metal*, liga de estanho e antimónio metálico parecida com prata.

British, *s.* os ingleses. *adj.* britânico.

Briton, *s.* bretão, nativo ou habitante da Inglaterra ou do Império Britânico.

brittle, *adj.* quebradiço, frágil; fraco.

brittleness, *s.* fragilidade.

broach (es), *s.* espeto, agulheta. *v.t.* abrir uma pipa ou tonel; introduzir um tópico de conversação, mencionar; espetar.

broad, *adj.* largo; espaçoso, amplo; óbvio; grosseiro; tolerante. 1) *broad hint*, insinuação clara. 2) *in broad day-light*, em pleno dia.

broadbrimmed, *adj.* de abas largas.

broadly, *adv.* largamente, francamente; de um modo grosseiro.

broadcast, *s.* radiodifusão; difusão; emissão; transmissão. *adj.* espalhado; difundido; radiodifundido. *v.t.* e *v.i.* espalhar; difundir; emitir; radiodifundir.

broadcloth, *s.* pano de algodão ou lã.

broaden, *v.t.* alargar.

broad-gauge, *s.* via larga (caminho de ferro).

broadminded, *adj.* de visão ampla; tolerante.

broadness, *s.* largura; grosseria.

broadside, *s.* costado de navio; descarga simultânea dos canhões de um dos lados do navio.

brocade, *s.* brocado.

brocaded, *adj.* tecido como brocado.

broccoli, *s.* brócolos.
brochure, *s.* folheto, panfleto.
brock, *s.* texugo.
brock-bullet, *s.* projéctil incendiário anti-aéreo.
broider, *v.t.* bordar.
brogan, *s.* sapato grosseiro.
brogue, *s.* chanca; sotaque irlandês.
broil, *v.t.* e *v.i.* assar; aquecer (ao sol, calor, etc.).
broil, *s.* tumulto; disputa, discussão. *v.i.* discutir, fazer bulha.
broiler, *s.* grelhas; perturbador.
broke, *pass.* do verbo *to break.*
broken, *part. pass.* de *to break. adj.* quebrado, partido; interrompido; arruinado; abatido; *broken English,* inglês mal pronunciado.
brokenly, *adv.* interrompidamente.
broken-down, *adj.* arruinado; desfeito.
broken-hearted, *adj.* esmagado pela dor.
broker, *s.* corretor; agente; bolsista; comissário; *money broker,* corretor de câmbio.
brokerage, *s.* corretagem.
bromate, *s.* bromato.
bromic, *adj.* brómico.
bromide, *s.* brometo.
bromine, *s.* bromina.
bronchia, brônquios.
bronchial, *adj.* bronquial.
bronchitic, *adj.* relativo à bronquite.
bronchitis, *s.* bronquite.
bronchus, *pl.* bronchi.
bronco, *s.* cavalo meio selvagem.
bronze, *s.* bronze; cor de bronze. *v.t.* bronzear.
bronzing, *s.* processo de bronzear.
bronzy, *adj.* bronzeado.
brooch, *s.* broche.
brood, *s.* ninhada, cria; raça. *v.t.* e *v.i.* chocar; ponderar, meditar.
broody, *adj.* choca. (diz-se da galinha).
brook, *s.* riacho, arroio. *v.t.* suportar, tolerar.
brooklet, *s.* regato.
broom, *s.* vassoura; giesta; *broomstick,* cabo de vassoura.
bros., abreviatura de *brothers.*
broth, *s.* caldo.
brothel, *s.* bordel, lupanar.
brother, *s.* irmão; companheiro, colega; irmão de confraria. 1) *half brother,* meio irmão. 2) *foster brother,* irmão colaço. 3) *brother in law,* cunhado.

brotherhood, *s.* irmandade; fraternidade; confraria; sociedade.
brotherly, *adj.* fraternal. *adv.* fraternalmente.
brougham, *s.* carro fechado dum só cavalo (ou eléctrico).
brought, *pass.* e *part. pass.* de *to bring.*
brow, *s.* testa; cume.
browbeat, *v.t.* tratar com arrogância; intimidar; ameaçar.
brown, *s.* cor castanha. *adj.* castanho, trigueiro; pardo. *v.t.* e *v.i.* tostar, tornar ou tornar-se castanho.
brownie, *s.* duende benévolo que, na Escócia, se supõe trabalhar nos campos e em casa; máquina fotográfica.
browning, *s.* tipo moderno de pistola automática; processo de fazer a cor castanha. *p. pr.* de *brown.*
brownish, *adj.* acastanhado, atrigueirado.
browse, *s.* folhas, raminhos próprios para dar ao gado. *v.t.* e *v.i.* comer folhas, raminhos, pastar; (fig.) folhear um livro.
bruin, *s.* urso.
bruise, *s.* contusão, machucadura. *v.t.* contundir, magoar, ferir.
bruiser, *s.* pugilista; máquina de triturar.
bruit, *s.* ruído, rumor. *v.t.* divulgar; publicar.
brume, *s.* bruma, bevoeiro.
brummagem, *adj.* vistoso e barato. *s.* imitação barata de objectos artísticos, feita em Birmingham.
brunet, brunette, *adj.* moreno, trigueiro. *s.* pessoa morena.
brunt, *s.* choque, embate; assalto; *the brunt of the battle,* o auge da luta.
brush, *s.* escova; brocha, pincel; cauda de raposa; escovadela. *v.t.* escovar; rolar; pintar com brocha; tocar de leve. 1) *to brush aside,* não fazer caso. 2) *to brush up,* retocar.
brushwood, *s.* matagal; sarça; gravetos.
brusque, *adj.* abrupto, brusco, rude.
brusquely, *adv.* bruscamente.
brusqueness, *s.* rudeza, brusquidão.
brussels-sprouts, *s.* couve-de-bruxelas.
brutal, *adj.* brutal; cruel; grosseiro.
brutally, *adv.* brutalmente.
brutality (ies), *s.* brutalidade.
brutalize (ise), *v.t.* e *v.i.* embrutecer; bestializar; embrutecer-se.
brute, *s.* besta; bruto. *adj.* brutal, bestial; estúpido; sensual.
brutish, *adj.* brutal, bestial; feroz, selvagem; sensual, estúpido.

brutishly, adv. brutalmente.

brutishness, s. brutalidade.

bryony, s. briónia (planta)

bubble, s. bolha; empola; ilusão, coisa frívola ou insegura. v.t. e v.i. borbulhar; murmurar; fazer espuma; to bubble over with joy, transbordar de alegria.

bubbly, adj. espumoso; bubbly-jock, pavão.

bubo (es), s. bubão.

bubonic, adj. bubónico.

buccal, adj. bucal.

buccanneer, s. pirata, aventureiro.

buck, s. macho de lebre, coelho, gamo, antílope, etc; janota; barrela; to pass the buck, transmitir a outrem a responsabilidade. v.t. e v.i. levantar as patas traseiras; fazer barrela.

bucket, s. balde, cubo, alcatruz; êmbolo de bomba; to kick the bucket, esticar o pernil, morrer.

bucketful, s. porção contida num balde ou cubo.

buckhorn, s. ponta de veado (para cabos de faca, etc.).

buckhound, s. uma raça de cão.

buckle, s. fivela. v.t. afivelar. v.i.; to buckle down, aplicar-se com empenho.

buckler, s. escudo.

buckram, s. bocaxim.

bucksaw, s. serra de mão.

buckshot, s. chumbo para caça grossa.

buckskin, s. anta; pele de gamo, de carneiro, etc.

buckwheat, s. trigo mourisco.

bucolic (al), adj. bucólico.

bucolically, adv. de modo pastoril.

bud, s. botão (de flor); rebento. v.i. brotar, germinar, florescer.

Buddha, s. Buda.

Buddhism, s. budismo.

budding, adj. botão. s. rebento, botão; enxerto de borbulha.

buddle, s. aparelho para separar a terra dos metais.

buddy, s. (coloq.) companheiro, amigo.

budge, v.t. e v.i. mover(-se), agitar(-se).

budget, s. orçamento. v.t. fazer o orçamento; to budget for the coming year, planear o orçamento do ano vindouro.

buff, s. pele de anta ou búfalo; cor laranja-amarelado. v.t. polir com couro; blind-man's buff, jogo de cabra-cega.

buffalo, s. búfalo.

buffer, s. mola para mortecer um choque, tampão. 1) buffer state, estado-tampão. 2)

old buffer, sujeito antiquado ou incompetente.

buffet, s. bofetada, golpe. v.t. bater; lutar.

buffet, s. aparador, balcão para refrescos.

buffoon, s. bufão, palhaço, bobo.

buffoonery (ies), s. chocarrice, zombaria.

bug, s. insecto qualquer, espécie de besouro; percevejo.

bugaboo, bugbear, s. fantasma.

bugger, s. sodomita.

buggery, s. sodomia.

buggy (ies), s. carruagem pequena. adj. cheio de percevejos.

bugle, s. corneta, trombeta, clarim.

bugler, s. trombeteiro, corneteiro.

buhl, adj. e s. embutido, especialmente de tartaruga e madrepérola.

build, v.t. pass. e part. pass. built, construir; fundar; basear; to built up, reconstruir. s. estrutura, forma; construção.

builder, s. construtor, mestre de obras.

building, s. edifício, construção.

built, pret. e pp. de build; squarely built, robusto.

bulb, s. bulbo; planta bulbosa; electric light bulb, lâmpada eléctrica.

bulbous, adj. bulboso.

bulbaceous, adj. bulboso.

bulbul, s. ave canora do Irão, espécie de rouxinol; cantor, poeta.

bulge, s. bojo, protuberância; inchaço. v.t. e v.i. fazer bojo; avultar.

bulginess, s. bojo.

bulgy, adj. bojudo.

bulimy, bulimia, s. bulimia, fome canina.

bulk, s. volume, tamanho; massa; grandeza; 1) the bulk of the army, o grosso do exército. v.i. ser volumoso, grande, importante. 2) in bulk, a granel; 3) to sell in bulk, vender por atacado.

bulk-head, s. tabique, divisão; anteparo (náut.).

bulkier (iest), comp. e superl. de bulky.

bulkiness, s. volume, tamanho.

bulky, adj. volumoso, avultado.

bull, s. touro; macho do elefante, girafa, etc.; altista; bula; bullfighter, toureiro.

bullace, s. abrunho.

bulldog, s. buldogue, cão de fila.

bullet, s. bala, projéctil; bullet proff, à prova de bala.

bulletin, s. boletim, circular.

bullfrog, s. rã grande.

bullion, s. ouro ou prata em barra.

bullish, *adj.* disparatado; estúpido.

bullock, *s.* boi castrado.

bull's eye, *s.* centro do alvo; clarabóia; lanterna.

bully (ies), *s.* valentão, fanfarrão; insolente. *adj.* excelente, magnífico, óptimo. *v.t.* e *v.i.* fazer bravatas; intimidar.

bully-beef, *s.* carne em latas de conserva.

bullyrag, *v.t.* tratar com insolência.

bulrush (es), *s.* junco (planta).

bulwark, *s.* baluarte; defesa; *law is the bulwark of society*, a lei é a defesa da sociedade.

bum, *s.* o assento, as nádegas.

bumblebee, *s.* abelha grande.

bumbledom, *s.* ostentação.

bumble-foot, *s.* inflamação na planta do pé.

bumblepuppy, *s. whist* jogado sem regras.

bumboat, *s.* bote para venda de pequenas mercadorias aos navios.

bummaree, *s.* intermediário na praça de peixe em Billingsgate, Londres.

bump, *v.t.* e *v.i.* bater com força; colidir (com); magoar; machucar. *s.* pancada, sacudidela; inchaço.

bumper, *s.* pára-choques; copo cheio até às bordas. *adj.* grande, excelente; *bumper crop*, colheita abundante.

bumpkin, *s.* rústico, grosseiro, caipira.

bumptious, *adj.* presunçoso, vaidoso.

bumptiously, *adv.* de um modo vaidoso.

bumptiousness, *s.* presunção, vaidade.

bun, *s.* bolo (de pão doce).

bunch (es), *s.* punhado; feixe; molho (de chaves); cacho (de uvas); *bunch of flowers*, ramalhete. *v.t.* e *v.i.* juntar, agrupar.

buncombe, *s.* charlatanice, imposturice, discurso inútil.

bundle, *s.* pacote; trouxa; feixe; maço; fardo. *v.t.* empacotar, atar.

bung, *s.* batoque; tapulho. *v.t.* abatocar.

bungalow, *s.* casa térrea.

bungle, *s.* erro, trabalho mal feito. *v.t.* e *v.i.* estropiar, errar; estragar, pôr a perder.

bungler, *s.* o que trabalha sem cuidado.

bunion, *s.* joanete.

bunk, *s.* leito de trem ou navio; (gír.) charlatanice, disparate.

bunker, *s.* carvoeira de navio; arca de madeira.

bunny (ies), *s.* coelhinho; *bunny-hug,* dança americana.

bunsen-burner, *s.* bico de gás incandescente.

bunt, *s.* inchação; cavidade; bojo de roda ou de vela de navio.

bunting, *s.* tecido próprio para bandeiras; bandeiras (colectivamente).

buntline, *s.* briol, cabo de ferrar velas.

buoy, *s.* bóia. *v.t.* e *v.i.* pôr bóias; boiar; *to buoy up,* boiar, (fig.) sustentar, apoiar.

buoyancy, *s.* flutuação, propriedade de boiar.

buoyant, *adj.* flutuante; animado, alegre.

buoyantly, *adv.* alegremente.

bur, *v. burr.*

burberry, *s.* espécie de pano, casaco, etc., impermeável feito por uma companhia desse nome.

burden, *s.* carga, peso; aflição; responsabilidade; tonelagem de navio. *v.t.* carregar; oprimir.

burdensome, *adj.* pesado; opressivo.

burdock, *s.* bardana.

bureau, *s. pl. bureaus,* ou *bureaux* (EUA) cómoda para dormitórios. Escritórios; departamento do governo. 1) *travel bureau,* agência de turismo. 2) *weather bureau,* observatório meteorológico. 3) secretária; escritório; agência.

bureaucracy (ies), *s.* burocracia.

bureaucrat, *s.* burocrata.

bureaucratic, *s.* burocrático.

burette, *s.* tubo graduado para medir líquidos.

burgeon, *s.* rebento (de árvores); *v.t.* rebentar (árvores).

burgess (es), *s.* cidadão livre; deputado municipal.

burgher, *s.* cidadãos (principalmente de cidades estrangeiras).

burglar, *s.* ladrão, arrombador.

burglary (ies), *s.* roubo.

burgle, *v.t.* arrombar uma casa de noite para roubar.

burgomaster, *s.* burgomestre.

burgundy (ies), *s.* vinho de Borgonha.

burial, *s.* enterramento. 1) *burial ground,* cemitério. 2) *burial-service,* serviço fúnebre (cerimónias religiosas).

burin, *s.* buril, cinzel.

burke, *vt.* encobrir, calar.

burlap, *s.* sarapilheira, tecido grosseiro.

burlesque, *s.* paródia; teatro burlesco. *adj.* burlesco. *v.t.* imitar, ridicularizar.

burliness, *s.* volume, grossura,

burly, *adj.* corpulento; volumoso, grandalhão.

burn, *v.i. pas.* e *part. pass. burned* ou *burnt,* arder, queimar; abrasar-se; escaldar-se. *v.t.*

incendiar; queimar; cauterizar. *s.* queimadura.

burner, *s.* queimador; bico de gás.

burning, *s.* queimadura, fogo; ardor, inflamação. *adj.* abrasador, ardente.

burning-glass (es), *s.* lente convexa para concentrar os raios do sol.

burnish, *v.t.* polir, ilustrar. *s.* lustro, brilho, polimento.

burnisher, *s.* polidor.

burnt, *pass.* e *part. pass.* de *to burn.*

burr, *s.* ouriço (de castanha, cardo, etc); rebarba de metal.

burro, *s.* burro.

burrow, *s.* buraco de coelho, etc. *v.i.* fazer buraco como coelho, escavar.

bursar, *s.* tesoureiro de colégio.

burst, *v.i. pass.* e *part. pass.* burst, explodir, rebentar; irromper. *v.t.* quebrar, fazer em pedaços. *s.* explosão; estouro; ruptura. 1) *to burst into laghter,* cair na gargalhada. 2) *to burst into tears,* debulhar-se em lágrimas.

burthen, *v.* de *burden.*

bury, *v.t.* enterrar; ocultar.

burying, *s.* enterramento; *burying ground on place,* cemitério.

bus (es), *s.* autocarro.

bush (es), *s.* mouta, matagal; arbusto, ramo de louro (nas tabernas); penacho; cauda espessa (raposas, etc.); bucha (mec.). 1) *to beat about the bush,* ficar-se com rodeios. 2) *bush-harrow,* grade ou sebe feita de arbustos. 3) *a bird in the hand is worth two in the bush,* mais vale um pássaro na mão do que dois a voar. *v.t.* e *v.i.* copar, tornar espesso, igualar o terreno com arbustos.

bushel, *s.* medida de capacidade para cereais equivalente ao alqueire.

bushiness, *s.* espessura formada por arbustos.

bushy, *adj.* espesso, cerrado, cheio de arbustos.

busily, *adv.* diligentemente, altivamente.

business, *s.* negócio; ocupação; comércio; assunto. 1) *on a business,* a negócios. 2) *business man,* homem de negócios. 3) *get down to business,* começar a trabalhar.

businesslike, *adj.* eficaz, prático, sistemático.

buskin, *s.* borzeguim.

buss, *s.* beijo (arcaico). *v.t.* beijar.

bust, *s.* busto; peito.

bustard, *s.* abetarda (ave).

buster, *s.* alguma coisa notável.

bustle, *v.t.* e *v.i.* bulir; locomover-se, apressar-se ruidosamente. *s.* ruído, alvoroço, comoção; enchimento usado sob as saias para avolumar as ancas.

busy, *adj.* ocupado; activo, diligente. *v.t.* fazer, manter ocupado; *to be busy,* estar ocupado.

busybody, *s.* intrometido.

busyness, *s.* actividade.

but, *prep.* excepto; *sem. conj.* mas, porém, não obstante; senão. 1) *all but,* quase. 2) *but for you,* não fosse você. 3) *not only ... but also,* não só... mas também. 4) *she is but a child,* ela não passa de uma criança. 5) *the last but one,* o penúltimo.

butcher, *s.* açougueiro; (fig.) sanguinário, verdugo. *v.t.* abater reses; matar cruelmente; destroçar.

butchery, *s.* açougue; carnificina, matança.

butler, *s.* mordomo; despenseiro.

butlery (ies), *s.* despensa.

butt, *s.* pipa grande; parte final ou mais grossa de um objecto; culatra; pessoa alvo de ridículo; marrada (de carneiro, boi, etc.); alvo. *v.t.* e *v.i.* marrar.

butte, *s.* monte escarpado.

butter, *s.* manteiga. *v.t.* passar manteiga.

butterboat, *s.* molheira.

buttercup, *s.* rainúnculo amarelo.

butterfingers, *s.* mãos-de-aranha, pessoa incapaz de segurar as coisas na mão.

butterfly (ies), *s.* borboleta.

buttermilk, *s.* soro de leite.

buttery, *s.* despensa. *adj.* amanteigado.

buttocks, *s. pl.* nádegas, traseiro, assento.

button, *s.* botão; botão de campainha. *v.t.* e *v.i.* pregar botões a; abotoar.

buttonhole, *s.* casa de botão; flor usada na lapela. *v.t.* abrir casas de botões; fazer parar; *to buttonhole someone,* deter alguém.

buttonhook, *s.* abotoador.

buttons, *s.* paquete (de banco, de hotel, etc.).

buttress, *s.* contraforte; reforço. *v.t.* sustentar; reforçar; *to buttress an argument,* reforçar um argumento.

buxom, *adj.* saudável, gordo e corado.

buxomness, *s.* jovialidade, alegria, graça.

buy, *v.t. pass.* e *part. pass.* bought, comprar. *s.* pechincha.

buyer, *s.* comprador.

buzz, s. zumbido; murmúrio. v.i. zumbir; cochichar.
buzzard, s. bútio; mandrião.
buzzer, s. aparelho eléctrico para dar sinais; zunidor, zumbidor.
by, prep. perto, junto; ao lado de; por; através; conforme, segundo; 1) all by oneself, sozinho. 2) by day, de dia. 3) one by one, um de cada vez. 4) step by step, passo a passo. 5) by the way, a propósito. adv. perto, à mão; passado, além; à parte. 6) in days gone by, em tempos passados. 7) by and by, logo.
bye, s. assunto sem importância; lugar (de cada parceiro no jogo). 1) good bye, adeus; 2) bye-bye, até logo.

bygone, s. o passado; let bygones be bygones, esqueça o passado. adj. passado.
bylaw, byelaw, s. regulamento, estatutos.
bypath, s. atalho, vereda.
byplay, s. mímica; passatempo.
by-product, s. produto acessório.
byre, s. aido de vacas.
by-road, s. atalho.
byssus, s. tecido antigo.
bystander, s. espectador, circunstante.
by-strees, s. viela, travessa.
by-the-bye, adv. a propósito; entre parênteses.
byway, s. atalho.
byword, s. provérbio, rifão; objecto de chacota.

C

c, terceira letra do alfabeto.
cab, s. carro de aluguer, táxi; cabina de locomotiva.
cabal, s. cabala, trama, conspiração.
cabalistical, adj. cabalístico.
cabalist, s. cabalista.
cabaret, s. cabaré, café-concerto.
cabbage, s. couve.
cabin, s. cabana, choupana; cabina; camarote; v.t. e v.i. alojar em cabana, camarote ou cabina.
cabinet, s. armário; consultório; gabinete ministerial.
cabinetmaker, s. marceneiro.
cable, s. cabo, amarra; telegrama; cabograma; v.t. e v.i. telegrafar.
cablegram, s. cabograma.
cabman, s. cocheiro; motorista de táxi.
caboodle, s. bando, cambada.
cabotage, s. cabotagem, navegação costeira.
cabriolet, s. cabriolé.
cacao, s. cacau.
cachalot, s. cachalote.
cache, s. esconderijo; v.t. esconder.
cacique, s. cacique.

cackie, s. cacarejo; v.i. cacarejar; rir-se; tagarelar.
cacography, s. cacografia.
cacology, s. cacologia.
cacoon, s. cipó de beira-mar.
cacophonous, adj. cacofónico, dissonante.
cacophony, s. cacofonia.
cactus, s.m. cacto.
cad, s. indivíduo grosseiro, malcriado, grosseirão.
cadastral, adj. cadastral; cadastral survey, levantamento de cadastro.
cadastre, cadaster, s. cadastro.
cadaver, s. cadáver.
cadaveric, adj. cadavérico.
cadaverous, adj. cadavérico, pálido, macilento.
caddie, caddy, s. mensageiro, rapaz que carrega os tacos, no jogo do golfe; v.i. fazer recados.
caddish, adj. grosseiro, mal-educado.
caddence, cadency, s. cadência, ritmo; compasso.
cadenced, adj. cadenciado, compassado.
cadenza, s. cadência.
cadet, adj. cadete; filho mais novo.

cadi, s. cádi, magistrado muçulmano.
cadmium, s. cádmio.
caducity, s. caducidade, senilidade.
caducous, adj. caduco; fugaz, transitório.
Caesarean, Caeserian, adj. cesariano, cesáreo; caesarian operation, cesariana.
caesura, s. cesura.
café, s. café, bar (estabelecimento).
cafeteria, s. restaurante onde cada um se serve por si mesmo.
caffeine, s. cafeína.
cage, s. gaiola; jaula; caixa; v.t. engaiolar, enjaular.
cajole, v.t. e v.i. lisonjear, adular, bajular.
cajolery, s. lisonja, adulação
cake, s. bolo; v.t. e v.i. aglutinar-se; amassar; endurecer.
calabash, s. cabaça.
calamary, s. calamar, lula.
calamitous, adj. calamitoso.
calamity, s. calamidade, desastre, desgraça, flagelo.
calcareous, adj. calcário.
calcic, adj. cálcico.
calciferous, adj. calcífero.
calcification, s. calcificação.
calcify, v.t. e v.i. calcificar, reduzir(-se) a cal; endurecer.
calcination, s. calcinação.
calcine, v.t. e v.i. calcinar(-se), oxidar(-se); derreter (os ingredientes).
calcium, s. cálcio.
calculable, adj. calculável, computável.
calculate, v.t. calcular, estimar, avaliar.
calculating, adj. calculador, interesseiro; calculating machine, máquina de calcular.
calculator, s. calculador, calculista, máquina de calcular.
calculus, s. cálculo.
caldron, s. caldeirão.
calefaction, s. calefacção, aquecimento.
calendar, s. calendário, almanaque; registo cronológico; v.t. inscrever em calendário; registar.
calenderer, s. calendreiro.
calends, s., pl. calendas.
calf, s., pl. calves, bezerro, vitelo; pele de bezerro; barriga da perna.
caliber, calibre, s. calibre; diâmetro; excelência, importância.
calibrate, v.t. calibrar, regular, graduar.
calibration, s. calibragem, calibração.
calico, s., pl. calicoes, tecido de algodão, chita.

caliph, calif, s. califa.
caliphate, califate, s. califado.
calix, s., pl. calices, cálix, cálice.
calk, v.t. calafetar, vedar.
call, v.t. gritar, anunciar, proclamar, invocar; telefonar a; acordar, convocar (reunião, assembleia); chamar, dar nome a; v.i. gritar, bradar. 1) to call for, pedir, exigir, chamar. 2) to call on. 3) fazer breve visita a, telefonar. 3) to call back, mandar voltar, telefonar em resposta a um telefonema; revogar, desdizer; recordar-se de. 4) to call in, mandar entrar; recolher. 5) to call up, recordar, evocar.
call, s. grito, brado; chamado, chamamento, apelo; invocação; convite; chamada; convocação; pio (de ave); grito (de animal); pedido; visita; obrigação.
caller, s. visita, visitante.
calligraphy, s. caligrafia.
calling, s. chamado, convocação; calling card, cartão de visita.
callosity, s. calosidade.
callous, adj. caloso, calejado, endurecido; (fig.) insensível, empedernido.
callousness, s. insensibilidade, dureza, empedernimento.
callus, s. calo, calosidade.
calm, adj. calmo, tranquilo, silencioso, sereno, sossegado; s. calma, calmaria, tranquilidade, sossego; v.t. e v.i. acalmar (-se), serenar, sossegar, apaziguar(-se).
calmative, adj. e s. calmante, sedativo.
calmy, adj. calmo, tranquilo.
caloric, adj. calórico, térmico; s. calórico.
calorie, calory, s. caloria.
calorific, adj. calorífero.
calorimetry, s. calorimetria.
calumniate, v.t. caluniar, difamar.
calumnious, adj. calunioso, difamatório.
calumny, s. calúnia, difamação.
Calvary, s. Calvário.
calve, v.i. partir.
calves, s., pl. de "calf".
Calvinism, s. calvinismo.
calyx, s., pl. calyxes ou calyces. (bot.) cálice.
camarilla, s. pequena câmara; camarilha.
cambist, s. cambista.
cambric, s. cambraia.
came, pret. de "come".
camel, s. camelo.
cameleer, s. cameleiro, condutor de camelos.
camellia, s. camélia.

camion, s. carroção; camião.

camouflage, s. camuflagem; dissimulação; v.t. e v.i. camuflar(-se), disfarçar.

camp, s. acampamento; campo; vida militar; *camp fever,* tifo; v.t. e v.i. acampar.

campaign, s. campanha; v.i servir numa campanha.

camper, s. pessoa acampada.

camphor, s. cânfora.

campus, s. terrenos de colégio ou universidade destinados à prática desportiva.

can, s. lata; vasilha de lata; caneca, cântaro; *can-opener,* abre-latas; v.t. pret. e p.p. *canned,* enlatar.

can, v. def.; pret. could.; poder, ter capacidade de; saber; *I can not swim,* não sei nadar; ser capaz de.

Canadian, adj. e s. canadiano, canadense.

canal, s. canal (artificial); (anat. e zool.) canal; v.t. canalizar, abrir canal ou canais em.

canary, s. canário; vinho das Canárias.

cancel, v.t. cancelar; anular; invalidar; revogar; eliminar.

cancellation, s. cancelamento, anulação.

cancer, s. câncer, cancro;

cancerous, adj. canceroso.

candelabrum, s. candelabro.

candescence, s. incandescência.

candescent, adj. incandescente.

candid, adj. cândido; puro, franco.

candidate, s. candidato.

candidature, s. candidatura.

candle, s. vela, círio.

candlestick, s. castiçal.

candor, candour, s. imparcialidade, sinceridade, pureza.

candy, s. açúcar cristalizado; rebuçado, confeito, bombom; v. cristalizar, açucarar.

cane, s. cana; bastão, bengala; *sugar-cane,* cana-de-açúcar; v.t. vergastar.

canicular, adj. canicular, relativo à canícula.

canine, adj. canino.

canister, s. caixa para guardar chá, tabaco, café, etc.; lata, vasilha; granada com metralha.

canker, s. gangrena, cancro, v.t. e v.i. gangrenar, cancerar.

cankerous, adj. gangrenoso.

canned, adj. enlatado, em conserva; (gír.) bêbedo.

cannery, s. fábrica de conservas.

cannibal, s. canibal, antropófago.

cannibalism, s. canibalismo, antropofagia.

cannon, s. canhão, peça de artilharia; canhões (colectivamente); coroa de sino; canela de boi ou cavalo.

cannonade, s. canhonada; v.t. e v.i. canhonear.

cannoneer, s. canhoneiro, artilheiro.

cannula, s. cânula.

canny, adj. prudente, cauteloso; sagaz; matreiro; hábil, engenhoso; económico.

canoe, s. canoa.

canoeing, s. canoagem.

canon, s. cânone; regra, lei, princípio; *canon law:* direito canónico.

canoness, s. cónega.

canonical, adj. canónico.

canonicals, s. pl. paramentos de sacerdote oficiante.

canonicate, s. canonicato.

canonist, s. canonista, professor de direito canónico.

canonize, v.t. canonizar; glorificar.

canonry, s. canonicato; cónegos.

canonship, s. canonicato.

canopy, s. dossel; pálido; tecto, cobertura; v.t. cobrir com dossel.

canorous, adj. canoro; melodioso, harmonioso.

canteen, s. cantina; cantil; bufete.

canton, s. cantão; divisão administrativa; distrito, v.t. dividir em cantões ou distritos.

canvas, s. lona; tela; tenda.

canvass, v.t. examinar; solicitar votos; averiguar; s. exame, discussão; solicitação de votos.

canyon, s. garganta, desfiladeiro.

cap, s. boné, touca, bóina, tampa, tampo; cápsula, capitel; cobertura. v.t. cobrir, tapar; exceder, suplementar; rematar.

capability, s. capacidade, aptidão; faculdade.

capable, adj. capaz, apto; competente, hábil, dotado.

capacitate, v.t. capacitar; habilitar; tornar capaz.

capacity, s. capacidade, espaço; aptidão; faculdade, possibilidade; qualidade.

cape, s. capa curta; cabo, promontório.

caper, s. alcaparra; cabriola; excentricidade.

capillaceous, adj. capilar, filiforme.

capillarity, s. capilaridade.

capillary, adj. capilar; s. vaso capilar.

capital, adj. capital; principal, essencial, fundamental; s. letra maiúscula; capital (sede do governo); (com.) capital.

capitalism, s. capitalismo.

capitalist, s. e adj. capitalista.

capitalization, s. capitalização; financiamento.

capitalize, v.t. capitalizar, converter em capital; fornecer capital; financiar; v.i. acumular capital; (fig.) tirar partido, aproveitar.

capitular, s. membro de um capítulo; adj. capitular.

capitulary, adj. capitular; s. decreto real.

capitulate, v.i. capitular, render-se.

capitulation, s. capitulação, rendição.

capon, s. capão, galo capado.

caprice, s. capricho; fantasia.

capricious, adj. caprichoso.

capsize, v.t. e v.i. virar de pernas para o ar.

capstan, s. cabrestante.

capsular, adj. capsular.

capsulate, adj. capsulado.

capsule, s. cápsula.

captain, s. capitão, chefe, comandante; v.t. capitanear, chefiar, comandar.

captaincy, captainship, s. capitania, posto de capitão.

caption, s. título; legenda.

captious, adj. capcioso, insidioso, ardiloso.

captivate, v.t. cativar, fascinar, encantar.

captive, adj. cativo, prisioneiro; cativado, fascinado.

captive, s. cativeiro, escravidão.

captor, s. captor.

capture, s. captura, apreensão; v.t. capturar, apanhar, aprisionar, apresar, apreender.

car, s. carro, viatura; carruagem; automóvel.

carabin, s. carabina.

carabineer, s. carabineiro.

caramel, s. caramelo, açúcar queimado.

caramelize, v.t. e v.i. caramelizar.

carapace, s. carapaça, couraça.

carat, s. quilate.

caravan, s. caravana.

caravel, s. caravela.

carbohydrate, s. hidrato de carbono.

carbon, s. carbono; folha de papel carbono, químico; *carbon paper,* papel carbono.

carbonate, s. carbonato; v.t. carbonizar, reduzir a carbono pela acção do fogo.

carbonation, s. carbonização, carbonatação.

carbonic, adj. carbónico.

carboniferous, adj. e s. carbonífero.

carbonize, v.t. carbonizar.

carbuncle, s. carbúnculo.

carburetter, s. carburador.

carcass, s. carcaça; cadáver; casco velho de navio; armação, esqueleto, arcabouço.

carcinogen, s. carcinógeno.

card, s. carta de baralho; cartão (postal ou de visita); carda, instrumento de cardar; v.t. cardar.

cardiac, adj. cardíaco; s. estimulante do coração; cardiaco.

cardinal, adj. cardeal, cardinal, principal, fundamental; de cor escarlate; *cardinal numbers,* números cardinais; s. cardeal; número cardinal; ponto cardeal; cardeal (ave).

cardinalate, s. cardinalato.

carding, s. cardação.

cardiogram, s. cardiograma.

cardiology, s. cardiologia.

cardiologist, s. cardiologista.

carditis, s. cardite.

care, s. cuidado, cautela, atenção, solicitude,; inquietação, preocupação; desvelo; custódia; v.i. e v.t. interessar-se por, importar-se com, mostrar interesse, preocupar-se; cuidar de; gostar de; *to care to,* querer, desejar.

career, s. carreira; profissão.

carefree, adj. livre de inquietação, despreocupado, feliz.

careful, adj. cuidadoso, atento, zeloso, cauteloso, solícito; *to be careful,* ter cuidado.

carefulness, s. cuidado, atenção, desvelo.

careless, adj. descuidado, despreocupado, desatento, negligente; indiferente.

carelessness, s. descuido, negligência, indiferença.

caress, s. carícia, afago, carinho; v.t. acariciar, afagar, mimar, acarinhar.

caressive, adj. meigo, acariciador.

caretaker, s. zelador, guarda.

cargo, s. carga, carregamento, frete (de navio, avião, etc.).

caribou, s. caribu.

caricature, s. caricatura; v.t. caricaturizar, caricaturar.

carillon, s. carrilhão.

carmine, s. carmim.

carnage, s. carnagem, carnificina, mortandade.

carnage, adj. carnal; lascivo, sensual; mundano, material.

carnality, s. carnalidade, sensualidade, concupiscência.

carnation, s. cravo (flor).

carnival, s. carnaval, entrudo: folia; festa ruidosa; parque de diversões.

carnivore, s. carnívoro.

carnivorous, adj. carnívoro.

carol, s. canto de Natal; v.t. cantar alegremente.

carob, s. alfarroba.

carotid, s. carotídeo; carotid artery, carótida.

carousal, s. pândega, farra, patuscada.

carouser, s. farrista, pândego, beberão.

carp, s. carpa (peixe); v.i. criticar, censurar.

carpenter, s. carpinteiro; v.t. carpinteirar.

carpentry, s. carpintaria.

carpet, s. tapete, carpeta, alcatifa; v.t. atapetar, alcafifar.

carpus, s. carpo, pulso.

carriage, s. carruagem, coche, carro; transporte.

carrier, s. portador, carregador; transportador.

carrion, s. carniça, carne putrefacta; carcaça.

carrot, s. cenoura.

carrousel, carousel, s. carrossel.

carry, v.t. levar; transportar; carregar; levar consigo, usar, trazer sobre si. 1) carry on, prosseguir, continuar. 2) carry out, levar a cabo.

cart, s. carroça, carro, carreta; v.t. e v.i. guiar carroça ou carro; acarretar.

cartage, s. carretagem, transporte em carro ou carroça.

cartel, s. cartel; acordo escrito.

carter, s. carroceiro, carreteiro.

cartesian, adj. e s. cartesiano.

cartilage, s. cartilagem.

cartilaginous, adj. cartilaginoso.

cartographer, s. cartógrafo.

cartography, s. cartografia.

carton, s. caixa ou estojo de papelão; papelão.

cartoon, s. desenho animado; caricatura.

cartoonist, s. caricaturista, cartonista.

cartouche, s. cartucho.

cartridge, s. cartucho de arma de fogo; cartridge belt, cartucheira.

cartwright, s. fabricante de carros.

carve, v.t. e v.i. esculpir, cinzelar, entalhar, gravar; trinchar (carne).

carver, s. gravador, escultor, entalhador.

carving, s. gravura, entalhadura, entalhe.

cascade, s. cascata, catarata, queda de água; v.i. e v.t. cair em cascata; ligar em cascata (elect.).

case, s. caso; situação, questão; causa, acção judicial, processo; in any case, seja como for; caixa, estojo, invólucro; casulo (crisálida); v.t. encaixar; envolver.

casemate, s. casamata.

casement, s. batente de janela, caixilho; coberta, armação.

cash, s. dinheiro, numerário, moeda sonante; pronto pagamento; v.t. cobrar, apresentar à cobrança; pagar em dinheiro.

cash-book, s. caixa, livro-caixa.

cashew, s. cajueiro.

cashie, s. caixa, caixeiro, encarregado de caixa; v.t. demitir, despachar; excluir do exército.

cashmere, s. caxemira, lã de caxemira.

casing, s. invólucro, revestimento; armação; caixas; esquadria (de porta ou janela); capa; casing paper, papel de embalagem.

casino, s. casino, casa de jogos.

cask, s. casco, barril, pipa.

casket, s. cofre, guarda-jóias.

casque, s. casco, capacete, elmo.

cassation, cassação, anulação, cancelamento, revogação.

casserole, s. caçarola; guisado.

cassette s. châssis, caixilho de chapa fotográfica.

cassock, s. batina, sotaina.

cast, v.t. pret. e pp. cast. lançar, arremessar, atirar, deitar; moldar, fundir; distribuir papéis em teatro. 1) to cast aside, pôr de lado. 2) to cast away, abandonar, arruinar. 3) to cast out, expelir. 4) to cast lots, deitar sortes; v.i. meditar; moldar-se; vomitar.

cast, s. lanço, arremesso; alcance de coisa arremessada; cálculo, soma; previsão; elenco de peça teatral ou filme.

castanets, s. pl. castanholas.

castaway, adj. rejeitado, deitado fora; s. réprobo, pária; náufrago.

caste, s. casta.

caster, s. aquele que arremessa; fundidor; galheteiro.

castigate, v.t. castigar, punir, emendar.

castigation, s. castigo, crítica ou censura severa; revisão, correcção (de livros, etc.).

casting, s. lanço, arremesso; muda (de penas, pele, etc.); rejeição; vómito; fundição.

castle, s. castelo; praça-forte, fortaleza.

castled, adj. acastelado.

castor, s. vasilha em que se coloca açúcar,

pimenta ou sal para ser servido à mesa; *castor oil*, óleo de rícino.

castrate, *v.t.* castrar, capar.

castration, *s.* castração.

casual, *adj.* casual; fortuito; ocasional, eventual; irregular; despreocupado; negligente, indiferente.

casually, *adv.* casualmente; de passagem.

casualty, *s.* casualidade, acaso; acidente; acidentado; vítima de acidente; (mil.) baixas, perdas de soldados em acção, soldado morto em acção.

casuist, *s.* casuísta; sofista.

casuistry, *s.* casuísmo; sofisma.

cat, *s.* gato; felino.

catabolic, *adj.* catabólico.

catabolism, *s.* catabolismo.

cataclysm, *s.* cataclismo.

catacomb, *s.* catacumba.

catalogue, *s.* catálogo; lista; anuário.

catalyse, *v.t.* catalisar.

catalysis, *s.* catálise.

catalyst, *s.* catalisador.

catalytic, *adj.* catalítico.

cataplasm, *s.* cataplasma, emplastro.

catapult, *s.* catapulta; *v.t.* catapultar.

cataract, *s.* catarata; aguaceiro, inundação; (med.) catarata.

catarrh, *s.* catarro; gripe.

catastrophe, *s.* catrástrofe; desfecho de peça teatral.

catch, *pret.* e *pp.* caught, apanhar, agarrar, capturar; surpreender; compreender; alcançar.1) *to catch a cold*, apanhar uma constipação. 2) *to catch a glimpse*, vislumbrar. 3) *to catch unawared*, apanhar desprevenido. 4) *to catch on*, entender, perceber. 5) *to catch up*, conseguir acompanhar, apanhar. *s.* aquilo que se apanha, presa, captura.

catcher, *s.* aquele que apanha; captor, jogar de que se coloca atrás do *batman* para aparar a bola.

catchword, *s.* chamada (palavra de referência); (teat.) deixa.

catchy, *adj.* atraente, chamativo; contagioso.

catechesis, *s.* catequese; doutrinação.

catechism, *s.* catequismo.

catechist, *s.* catequista.

catechize, *v.t.* catequizar; instruir, doutrinar.

catechumen, *s.* catecúmeno; neófito.

categorical, *adj.* categórico; absoluto; incondicional.

category, *s. f.* categoria.

cater, *v.i.* fornecer comida ou provisões; abastecer, prover do necessário.

caterer, *s.* fornecedor de provisões; abastecedor.

caterpillar, *s.* lagarta; explorador, usurário; tractor.

caterwaul, *v.i.* miar.

catharsis, *s.* catarse.

cathedra, *s.* cátedra.

cathedral, *s.* catedral; *adj.* catedral, oficial, autorizado.

catheter, *s.* cateter, sonda.

cathode, *s.* cátodo.

cathodic, *adj.* catódico.

catholic, *s.* e *adj.* católico.

catholicism, *s.* catolicismo.

catholicity, *s.* catolicidade; universalidade.

catholicize, *v.t.* e *v.i.* catolizar, converter ao catolicismo.

catlike, *adj.* semelhante a gato, felino; furtivo.

cattle, *s.* gado, gado vacum.

catwalk, *s.* passadiço estreito numa ponte.

caught, *pret.* e *pp.* de catch.

cauliflower, *s.* couve-flor.

cauline, *s.* caulino.

causal, *adj.* causal, causativo.

causality, *s.* causalidade.

causeway, *s.* estrada elevada ou passagem em terreno pantanoso ou arenoso.

caustic, *adj.* cáustico; corrosivo; mordaz.

causticity, *s.* causticidade; mordacidade.

cauterize, *v.t.* cauterizar.

caution, *s.* aviso, advertência; prudência, cautela; *caution money*, caução em dinheiro.

cautious, *adj.* cauteloso, prudente, precavido.

cavalcade, *s.* cavalgada; desfile, cortejo, parada.

cavalier, *s.* cavaleiro; soldado de cavalaria; cavalheiro; *adj.* jovial; arrogante.

cavalry, *s.* cavalaria.

cave, *s.* caverna, gruta; antro; *v.t.* escavar; *v.i.* aluir, ruir, desmoronar; entrar em dissidência.

cavern, *s.* caverna, cavidade, subterrâneo; *v.t.* meter em caverna; tornar oco.

cavil, *v.i.* sofismar; recriminar; *s.* sofisma, cavilação.

cavity, *s.* cavidade; cárie (dentária).

caw, *v.i.* grasnar, crocitar; *s.* grasnido, crocito.

cayman, *s.* caimão, jacaré.

cease, v.i. cessar, ter fim, extinguir-se, terminar, acabar; v.t. cessar, pôr fim a, parar; without cease, sem parar, incessantemente.

cecity, s. cegueira.

cedar, s. cedro.

cede, v.t. ceder, conceder.

cedilla, s. cedilha.

ceiling, s. tecto.

celebrant, s. celebrante.

celebrate, v.t. celebrar, comemorar, festejar; realizar (cerimónia); exaltar; v.t. celebrar missa, oficiar.

celebrated, adj. célebre, ilustre, famoso; notório.

celebration, s. celebração, comemoração; festa, festividade, festejo.

celebrity, s. celebridade, fama, renome; pessoa célebre.

celerity, s. celeridade, velocidade, rapidez.

celery, s. aipo.

celestial, adj. celeste, celestial.

celibacy, s. celibato, estado de solteiro.

celibate, s. e adj. solteiro, celibatário.

cell, s. cela de prisão ou de convento; cubículo; cavidade; alvéolo (em favo de mel); (elect.) elemento, pilha, célula; (biol.) célula.

cellar, s. adega, cave, porão.

cello, s. violoncelo.

cellule, s. célula; lóculo, pequena cavidade.

celluloid, s. celulóide.

cellulose, s. celulose.

celt, s. género de machado pré-histórico; celta.

Celtic, adj. céltico; s. celta.

cement, s. cimento; argamassa; v.t. cimentar, tornar firme.

cementation, s. cimentação.

cemetery, s. cemitério.

censer, s. turíbulo, incensório.

censor, s. censor; crítico; v.t. censurar, submeter a censura; criticar.

censorial, adj. censório.

censorious, adj. repreensivo, severo, reprovador.

censorship, s. censura.

censurable, adj. censurável, condenável.

censure, s. censura, repreensão, condenação; crítica hostil; v.t. censurar, repreender, condenar, criticar.

census, s. censo, recenseamento.

cent, s. centavo, centésimo (de dólar); per cent, por cento.

centaur, s. centauro.

centenarian, s. pessoa centenária, centenário.

centenary, s. centénio, século; centenário; adj. centenário, relativo a centena.

centennial, adj. centenário, que tem ou dura cem anos; s. centenário.

center, centre, s. centro; meio; âmago; v.t. centrar, pôr no meio; fixar; v.i. centrar-se, estar no centro.

centering, s. acto de centrar ou centralizar; centragem.

centerpiece, centrepiece, s. centro (de mesa, tecto, etc.); peça central.

centesimal, adj. centesimal, centésimo.

centigrade, adj. centígrado.

centigram, centigramme, s. centigrama.

centiliter, centilitre, s. centilitro.

centime, s. cêntimo.

centimeter, centimetre, s. centímetro.

centipede, s. centopeia.

central, adj. central, fundamental; principal, dominante; s. central telefónica.

centralism, s. centralismo, centralização.

centralize, v.t. e v.i. centralizar(-se), concentrar(-se).

centric, adj. central.

centrifugal, adj. centrífugo.

centrifugation, s. centrifugação.

centripetal, adj. centrípeto.

centurion, s. centurião.

century, s. século; centenário.

ceramics, s. cerâmica.

cereal, s. e adj. cereal.

cerebellum, s. cerebelo.

cerebral, adj. cerebral.

cerebrum, s. cérebro.

ceremonial, adj. cerimonial, ritual, formal; s. cerimonial, ritual; rito.

ceremonious, adj. cerimonioso, formalista, cerimonial, formal.

ceremony, s. cerimónia, solenidade; formalidade, praxe.

ceriferous, adj. cerífero, cerífico.

cerous, adj. ceroso.

certain, adj. certo, fixo, invariável; verdadeiro, exacto.

certainly, adv. certamente, sem dúvida.

certainty, s. certeza, convicção; coisa certa.

certifiable, adj. certificável; interditável (um doente mental).

certificate, s. certificado, certidão, atestado; diploma; v.t. certificar, atestar.

certification, s. certificação.

certificatory, *adj.* certificatório, certificativo, atestatório.

certified, *adj.* certificado, garantido, autenticado; *certified check,* cheque visado.

certify, *v.t.* certificar, atestar; assegurar; autenticar, visar (cheque).

cerulean, *adj.* azul-celeste.

cerumen, *s.* cerúmen, cera dos ouvidos.

ceruminous, *adj.* ceruminoso.

cervical, *adj.* cervical.

cervine, *adj.* cervino.

cessation, *s.* cessação, interrupção.

cession, *s.* cessão; território concedido, concessão.

cesspool, *s.* fossa sanitária.

cetacean, *adj.* e *s.* cetáceo.

chaff, *s.* farelo; palha; ninharia, insignificância; brincadeira; *v.t.* e *v.i.* ridicularizar, troçar, zombar.

chaffer, *v.i.* regatear; discutir, questionar.

chagrin, *s.* mortificação, desgosto, *v.t.* mortificar, vexar, desgostar.

chain, *s.* corrente; cadeia; *s. pl.* grilhões, ferros; *v.t.* acorrentar, agrilhoar, escravizar.

chair, *s.* cadeira; cadeira presidencial; *to take the chair,* presidir; *v.t.* instalar, conduzir em cadeira.

chairman, *s.* presidente (de assembleia, comissão, etc.).

chairmanship, *s.* presidência de uma assembleia.

chaise, *s.* carruagem de duas rodas com capota conversível.

chalice, *s.* taça; cálice.

chalk, *s.* giz; greda; contagem (de pontos); *by a long chalk:* por grande diferença; *v.t.* traçar com giz; branquear.

chalky, *adj.* gredoso; branco como giz.

challenge, *s.* desafio, repto; grito de sentinela; *v.t.* desafiar, provocar; bradar alerta; *v.i.* reivindicar um direito, lançar um desafio.

chamber, *s.* câmara; quarto, aposento; *chamber music,* música de câmara.

chamberlain, *s.* camarista de corte; tesoureiro municipal.

chambermaid, *s.* criada de quarto.

chameleon, *s.* camaleão.

chamois, *s.* camurça.

champ, *v.t.* e *v.i.* mastigar com ruído; *s.* campeão.

champaign, *s.* campina.

champion, *s.* campeão; paladino, defensor; herói; *v.t.* advogar, defender uma causa; *adj.* esplêndido, de primeira ordem.

championship, *s.* campeonato; defesa, advocatura.

chance, *s.* oportunidade, ocasião, possibilidade; probabilidade, hipótese; sorte, acaso. 1) *by chance,* por acaso. 2) *to give someone a chance,* dar uma oportunidade a alguém; *adj.* casual, acidental; *v.i.* acontecer por acaso; *v.t.* arriscar.

chanceful, *adj.* cheio de acontecimentos; acidentado.

chancel, *s.* coro, parte da igreja reservada ao clero.

chancellery, *s.* chancelaria.

chancellor, *s.* chanceler; *Chancellor of the Exchequer,* ministro do Tesouro.

chancellorship, *s.* chancelaria, cargo de chanceler.

chancery, *s.* tribunal do lorde chanceler (uma das divisões do Supremo Tribunal em Inglaterra).

chancy, *adj.* incerto, arriscado.

chandelier, *s.* candeeiro, lampadário, candelabro.

change, *s.* troca, alteração, mudança; troco; muda de roupa; *v.t.* alterar, mudar, trocar; *v.i.* alterar-se, mudar, sofrer alteração.

changeability, *s.* mutabilidade, inconstância.

changeable, *adj.* mutável, variável, alterável, inconstante.

changeful, *adj.* variável, inconstante, incerto.

changeless, *adj.* imutável, inalterável.

channel, *s.* canal (natural ou artificial); leito de rio; tubo; meio ou via de comunicação.

chant, *v.i.* cantar, gorjear; *v.t.* cantar, entoar.

chanter, *s.* cantor.

chaos, *s.* caos; desordem, confusão.

chaotic, *adj.* caótico.

chap, *s.* comprador, freguês, camarada, amigo, companheiro; fenda, greta (na pele) *v.t.* e *v.i.* rachar, gretar, fender, abrir.

chapel, *s.* capela.

chaperon, *s.* dama de companhia; *v.t.* acompanhar, servir de companhia.

chaperonage, *s.* companhia, tutela, protecção.

chapiter, *s.* capitel, remate de coluna.

chaplain, *s.* capelão.

chaplet, *s.* grinalda, festão; colar; terço.

chapter, *s.* capítulo (de livro); assembleia de cónegos.

char, *v.t.* e *v.i.* queimar, carbonizar(-se); tostar, torrar(-se).

character, *s.* sinal, marca; *pl.* caracteres, letras, sinais de escrita; carácter, qualidade, característica de uma pessoa ou espécie;

feitio, personalidade, índole; fama, reputação; personagem de peça teatral ou de romance; pessoa excêntrica, *v.t.* gravar, traçar, inscrever.

characteristic, *adj.* característico, típico; *s.* característica.

characterize, *v.t.* caracterizar, descrever, definir; distinguir, ser característico de.

charade, *s.* charada; enigma.

charcoal, *s.* carvão de lenha, carvão vegetal; desenho a carvão; *v.t.* marcar, escrever ou desenhar a carvão.

charge, *v.t.* carregar; carregar arma de fogo; encarregar, confiar; acusar; atacar, assaltar; cobrar, pedir preço; *v.i.* atacar, acometer; pronunciar uma exortação. *s.* carga, fardo, peso; carga de arma de fogo, bateria; encargo, incumbência, responsabilidade, ónus; guarda, protecção, custódia, tutela; ordem, mandato; acusação; despesa, gasto, custo; carga, assalto, investida, ataque.

chargeable, *adj.* acusável, imputável.

charger, *s.* cavalo de batalha; (elect.) carregador de baterias.

charily, *adv.* parcimoniosamente, com cuidado.

chariot, *s.* carro de guerra ou de corridas; coche ligeiro.

charitable, *adj.* caridoso; generoso, misericordioso.

charity, *s.* caridade, amor cristão, misericórdia; esmola, obra de caridade.

charlatan, *s.* charlatão; impostor, intrujão.

charlatanism, *s.* charlatanismo.

charm, *s.* encantamento, sortilégio, feitiço; amuleto, talismã; encanto, beleza, sedução; *v.t.* encantar, enfeitiçar, facinar, seduzir, deleitar.

charming, *adj.* encantador, fascinante; delicioso, maravilhoso.

charnel, *s.* cemitério; capela mortuária; ossuário; *adj.* sepulcral.

chart, *s.* carta, mapa geográfico, carta marítima; roteiro, itinerário; *v.t.* cartografar, fazer o mapa de, indicar em mapa; representar por gráfico; catalogar.

charter, *s.* título, escritura pública; patente, diploma; decreto; privilégio; *v.t.* conceder patente, alvará, diploma ou privilégio a; fretar, alugar.

chary, *adj.* difícil de contentar, meticuloso, enjoado; cuidadoso; económico.

chase, *v.t.* perseguir, correr atrás de; caçar;

afugentar, escorraçar, repelir; cinzelar, gravar, entalhar; *v.i.* lançar-se em perseguição; *s.* caça, caçada, perseguição; presa; caixilho onde se prendem as letras tipográficas.

chaser, *s.* perseguidor; caçador; gravador, cinzelador.

chasm, *s.* fenda profunda, brecha; abismo; hiato, lacuna, falha.

chassis, *s.* châssis (de automóvel); trem de aterragem.

chaste, *adj.* casto, virtuoso; puro, virginal; decente, decoroso.

chasten, *v.t.* castigar, punir, corrigir; disciplinar; purificar; moderar, temperar, abrandar, atenuar.

chastise, *v.t.* castigar, punir; disciplinar.

chastisement, *s.* punição, castigo.

chastity, *s.* castidade; virgindade; pureza, simplicidade (de estilo, etc.).

chat, *v.i.* cavaquear, conversar, tagarelar; *s.* charla, conversa, cavaqueira.

chatelain, *s.* castelão.

chatelaine, *s.* castelã.

chattel, *s.* escravo, servo; *pl.* bens móveis.

chatter, *v.i.* chilrear; papaguear, tagarelar; *v.t.* pronunciar rapidamente, engrolar. *s.* charla, tagarelice.

chatterbox, *s.* tagarela.

chatterer, *s.* tagarela, palrador.

chatty, *adj.* conversador, loquaz, palrador.

chauffer, *s.* motorista.

chauvinism, *s.* chauvinismo.

cheap, *adj.* barato; de mau gosto, ordinário.

cheapen, *v.t.* negociar, regatear; depreciar; *v.i.* baixar de preço; rebaixar-se.

cheaply, *adv.* barato, por baixo preço, facilmente.

cheapness, *s.* barateza; facilidade, vulgaridade.

cheat, *s.* impostor; escroque; trapaceiro; impostura, fraude, embuste, trapaça; *v.t.* enganar, lograr, defraudar; *v.i.* fazer batota, trapacear.

check, *s.* xeque (no jogo de xadrez); xadrez (padrão de quadrados), tecido axadrezado; obstáculo, impedimento, estorvo, entrave; revés militar; controlo, verificação. 1) *to keep in check*, reprimir, manter em observação; cheque bancário; *v.t.* dar xeque a (no xadrez), pôr em xeque; deter, refrear, impedir; verificar, examinar, controlar. 2) *to check in*, registar entrada num hotel, 3) *to check out*, desocupar o quarto de um hotel.

checkbook, s. livro de cheques.

checker, s. verificador, controlador, inspector.

checker, chequer, s. tabuleiro de xadrez; xadrez ou padrão axadrezado; v.t. quadricular; variar, diversificar; *a checkered life*, uma vida acidentada.

checkerboard, chequerboard, s. tabuleiro do jogo de damas.

checkers, chequers, s. pl. jogo de damas.

checkmate, s. xeque-mate.

cheek, s. face, bochecha; descaramento, audácia; *cheek bone,* osso malar.

cheep, v.i. piar, pipilar.

cheer, s. ânimo, disposição mental; coragem; alegria, animação, jovialidade; provisões, comida; grito de aplauso; v.t. animar, alegrar, confortar, consolar, encorajar; incitar, instigar com gritos; v.i. animar-se, alegrar-se.

cheerful, adj. alegre, bem-disposto, jovial, animado.

cheerless, adj. desalentado, desanimado, triste, melancólico.

cheery, adv. alegremente, animadamente.

cheese, s. queijo.

cheetah, s. (zool.) chita.

chemical, adj. químico; produto químico.

chemist, s. químico; farmacêutico.

chemistry, s. química; composição química.

cherish, v.t. alimentar, nutrir; acariciar, acalentar, tratar com carinho.

cherry, s. cereja; cor de cereja; *cherry tree,* cerejeira.

cherub, s. querubim, anjo.

chess, s. jogo de xadrez.

chest, s. arca, cofre; fundos; haveres; peito, tórax; *chest of drawers,* cómoda.

chestnut, s. castanha (fruta); castanheiro; a cor castanha; adj. castanho.

chevalier, s. cavaleiro; cavalheiro.

chevron, s. divisa.

chew, v.t. e v.i. mastigar, mascar; *to chew over,* matutar, ruminar; s. mastigação.

chewing gum, s. pastilha elástica.

chiasma, s. quiasma.

chicane, s. chicana; v.t. enganar por meio de chicana.

chicanery, s. chicana, cavilação.

chick, s. pinto, pintainho.

chicken, s. galinha, frango; *chicken pox,* varicela, bexigas-doidas.

chicken-hearted, adj. medroso, tímido.

chick-pea, s. grão-de-bico.

chicory, s. chicória.

chide, v.t. e v.i. ralhar, repreender, censurar.

chief, s. chefe, comandante, capitão, líder, cabeça; adj. principal, mais eminente, mais importante, primeiro.

chieftain, s. chefe, capitão, maioral.

chiffon, s. gaze.

child, s. pl. children. criança, filho, menino.

childhood, s. infância, meninice.

childdish, adj. infantil, pueril.

childlike, adj. infantil, próprio de criança.

children, s. pl. de child.

chilean, s. e adj. chileno.

chili, s. pimenta-malagueta.

chill, s. calafrio; frio; resfriamento; friagem, baixa temperatura; adj. frio, gelado; desanimado, indiferente; v.t. e v.i. esfriar, resfriar--se; arrefecer, desanimar.

chillied, adj. frio.

chillness, s. frio desagradável, friagem, frieza, indiferença.

chilly, adj. que sente frio; frio, friorento.

chime, s. carrilhão; repique; harmonia, melodia; v.t. tocar (sino, carrilhão); tocar a rebate.

chimera, chimaera, s. quimera, fantasia.

chimerical, adj. quimérico, fantástico, imaginário.

chimney, s. chaminé; lareira; *chimney sweeper,* limpa-chaminés.

chimp, s. o mesmo que:

chimpanzee, s. chimpanzé.

chin, s. queixo, mento.

china, porcelana; *china-ware,* louça de porcelana.

Chinese, adj. e s. chinês.

chink, s. fenda, racha, fresta, fisga; tinido de metal; v.t. e v.i. tinir.

chintz, s. chita.

chip, s. lasca, apara; fragmento; *chips,* batatas fritas; v.t. lascar, cortar em lascas; v.i. esmigalhar-se.

chipmuck, s. tâmia, espécie de esquilo.

chirk, v.i. ranger (porta); guinchar (rato); v.t. e v.i. *to chirk up,* animar, animar-se, alegrar, alegrar-se.

chirp, v.t. e v.i. piar, pipilar, chilrear; s. pio, chilreio.

chisel, s. cinzel, formão, escopro; v.t. e v.i. cinzelar, esculpir.

chivalrous, adj. cavalheiresco, nobre, valoroso; relativo à cavalaria.

chivalry, s. cavalaria; cavalheirismo, bravura.

chive, s. cebolinho.

chlorate, s. clorato.

chloride, s. cloreto.

chlorine, s. cloro.

chloroform, s. clorofórmio, v.t. cloroformizar.

chlorophyll, s. clorofila.

chock, s. calço, cunha; v.t. calçar, prender com calços.

chocolate, s. chocolate; barra de chocolate; cor de chocolate; adj. de chocolate, cor de chocolate.

choice, s. escolha, opção, selecção, preferência; adj. escolhido, seleccionado.

choir, s. coro de igreja; coro (parte de igreja); v.i. cantar em coro.

choke, v.t. sufocar, abafar, asfixiar; reprimir (emoções); obstruir, engasgar, congestionar; afogar (motor); v.i. sufocar; engasgar-se; s. sufocação, asfixia.

choker, s. aquele ou aquilo que sufoca; rolha; (gír.) gravata apertada, colarinho alto; gargantilha.

choking, adj. asfixiante, sufocante.

choler, s. bílis; cólera, ira.

cholera, s. cólera (doença).

choleric, adj. colérico, bilioso; irascível.

cholesterol, s. colesterol.

choose, v.t. e v.i. escolher, preferir.

chop, s. bocado; costeleta; posta; pl. queixadas; v.t. cortar em pedaços, retalhar.

chopper, s. cortador, talhante.

choppy, adj. gretado, fendido; picado (o mar); variável, instável.

choral, adj. coral, cantado por coro.

choral, chorale, s. (mús.) coral.

chord, s. corda (de instrumento musical); acorde.

chore, s. tarefa; serviço doméstico; biscate.

choreographer, s. coreógrafo.

choreography, s. coreografia.

chosen, adj. escolhido, seleccionado; eleito.

chrism, s. crisma, confirmação.

chrisom, s. chrisom-child, criança no primeiro mês.

Christ, s. Cristo; Jesus Cristo.

christcross, s. sinal-da-cruz.

christen, v.t. e v.i. baptizar; usar pela primeira vez.

Christendom, s. cristandade.

Christening, s. baptismo, baptizado.

Christian, adj. e s. cristão; christian name, nome de baptismo, primeiro nome.

Christianism, s. cristianismo, a religião cristã.

Christianize, v.t. cristianizar.

Christmas, s. Natal; christmas Eve, véspera de Natal, noite de Natal.

chroma, s. (fís.) croma, intensidade de uma cor.

chromatic, adj. cromático.

chrome, s. cromo (metal); v.t. cromar.

chromium, s. cromo (metal).

chronic, adj. crónico; duradouro; contínuo, constante.

chronicle, s. crónica, narração cronológica; relato; v.t. cronicar, narrar.

chronicler, s. cronista.

chronologer, s. cronologista, cronólogo.

chronologist, s. cronologista.

chronometer, s. cronómetro; relógio de precisão.

chrysalid, s. (zool.) crisálida.

chrisanthemum, s. crisântemo.

chubby, adj. gorducho, roliço, rechonchudo, redondo.

chuck, s. carícia; piparote; agulha (parte do boi); cacarejo; v.t. arremessar; acariciar; v.i. cacarejar.

chuckle, v.i. rir-se por entre dentes; s. riso reprimido.

chuff, s. campónio, labrego, rústico.

chum, s. companheiro, camarada, amigo.

chummy, adj. íntimo; sociável, comunicativo.

chump, s. cepo, madeiro, tronco; lombo de carneiro; v.t. e v.i. mascar.

chunk, s. naco, pedaço, cepo.

chunky, adj. atarracado, volumoso.

church, s. igreja.

churchman, eclesiástico, clérigo.

churchyard, s. cemitério; adro de igreja.

churn, s. desnatadeira, batedeira de manteiga; lata para leite; v.t. bater (leite, manteiga ou nata), desnatar; sacudir, agitar, fazer espumar (líquido).

chute, s. queda de águal rápido; escoadouro.

chyle, s. (fisiol.) quilo.

chyme, s. (fisiol.) quimo.

cicada, s. cigarra.

cicala, o mesmo que "cicada".

cicatricle, c. cicatrícula.

cicatrix, s. cicatriz.

cicatrize, v.t. e v.i. cicatrizar.

cicerone, s. cicerone, guia.

cider, s. cidra.

cigar, s. charuto; cigar-case: charuteira.

cigarrette, cigaret, s. cigarro. 1) cigarrete-case, cigarreira. 2) cigarrette-holder, boquilha de cigarro.

cilia, pl. cilium. s. cílios.

cinch, s. cilha; (gír.) coisa certa, "canja"; v.t. apertar a cilha.

cinder, s. escória, escumalha; brasa, carvão apagado; pl. cinzas; v.t. queimar, reduzir a cinzas.

cinema, s. cinema, sala de projecção.

cinematograph, s. cinematógrafo, aparelho de projecção; v.t. e v.i. cinematografar.

cinematographic, adj. cinematográfico.

cinematography, s. cinematografia.

cinerarium, s. cinerário.

cinerator, s. crematório; incinerador.

cinnamon, s. canela.

cipher, s. cifra; número; zero; código; v.t. escrever em código; v.i. fazer cálculos aritméticos.

circle, s. círculo; circunferência; anel; arco; período, ciclo; círculo social, grupo de pessoas; to come full circle, completar o ciclo; v.t. cercar, rodear, circundar, envolver; circular, dar a volta a; v.i. mover-se em círculo, descrever círculos.

circuit, s. circuito, giro, volta; circuito de corrente eléctrica.

circular, adj. circular; redondo; s. circular.

circulate, v.i. circular, mover-se em círculo; v.t. pôr em circulação, divulgar.

circulation, s. circulação; divulgação; tiragem (de uma publicação); dinheiro em circulação.

circumcise, v.t. circuncidar.

circumcision, s. circuncisão.

circumference, s. circunferência; círculo, perímetro, periferia.

circumlocution, s. circunlóquio, perífrase.

circumnavegate, v.t. circum-navegar.

circumscribe, v.t. circunscrever, cercar; limitar, definir.

circumscription, s. circunscrição; limitação; limite; distrito.

circumspect, adj. circunspecto, ponderado, discreto.

circumspection, s. circunspecção.

circumstance, s. circunstância; particularidade, pormenor; caso; cerimónia; s. pl. meio, ambiente.

circumstantial, adj. circunstancial, incidental, acidental; pormenorizado.

circumvallate, adj. circunvalado; v.t. circunvalar.

circumvent, v.t. enredar, prender na rede; enganar, lograr; rodear, fazer o circuito de.

circumvolution, s. circunvolução; revolução, rotação.

circus, s. circo; arena.

cirrhosis, s. cirrose.

cirrus, s. cirro.

cistern, s. cisterna, algibe; reservatório.

citadel, s. cidadela, fortaleza.

citation, s. citação; intimação.

cite, v.t. citar; intimar.

cithara, s. cítara.

citizen, s. cidadão; munícipe.

citizenship, s. cidadania.

citric, adj. cítrico.

citrin, s. citrino.

citrine, s. citrino; adj. citrino, amarelado.

citron, s. cidreira; cidra.

city, s. cidade; parte importante da cidade, baixa.

civet, s. almíscar.

civic, adj. cívico; citadino.

civics, s. sing. ciência dos direitos e deveres do cidadão.

civil, adj. civil (em oposição a militar); (jur.) civil, cível.

civilian, s. civil, paisano; civilista, pessoa versada em direito civil.

civility, s. civilidade, cortesia, delicadeza.

civilization, s. civilização.

civilize, v.t. civilizar; educar.

civism, s. civismo.

clack, v.i. dar à língua, tagarelar, cacarejar; v.t. revelar indiscretamente.

clad, pret. e pp. de clothe.

claim, v.t. reclamar, reivindicar; exigir, requerer; to claim to be, pretender ser; s. pretensão, reclamação, reivindicação.

claimant, claimer, s. reivindicador; pretendente, reclamante.

clairvoyance, s. clarividência.

clairvoyant, adj. e s. clarividente.

clam, s. nome vulgar de alguns mexilhões ou mariscos.

clamber, v.i. trepar, amarinhar, subir.

clammy, adj. húmido, viscoso, pegajoso.

clamor, clamour, s. clamor; gritaria, algazarra, alarido; barulhada, fragor; v.i. clamar, protestar, reclamar; gritar, vociferar; v.t. gritar, expressar em altos brados.

clamorous, adj. clamoroso, ruidoso, vociferante; premente.

clamp, s. grampo, pregador, braçadeira, presilha, colchete; v.t. prender, segurar; v.i. caminhar pesadamente.

clan, s. clã; tribo.

clandestine, adj. clandestino.

clang, *v.i.* retinir, ressoar; *v.t.* fazer ressoar; *s.* som metálico ou agudo.

clangor, clangour, *s.* clangor, estrondo; *v.i.* ressoar, retinir.

clank, *s.* fragor, estrépito; *v.t.* e *v.i.* estrepitar, ressoar.

clap, *v.i.* estalar, estrepitar; bater; bater palmas; *v.t.* bater ruidosamente; *s.* estalo, estrondo, estampido.

clapboard, *s.* ripa.

claque, *s.* claque.

claret, *s.* clarete.

clarification, *s.* clarificação (de um líquido).

clarify, *v.t.* e *v.i.* clarificar(-se), aclarar(-se), esclarecer.

clarinet, *s.* clarinete.

clarion, *s.* clarim, trompeta, *adj.* clarinete; alto e claro (o som).

clarity, *s.* clareza, lucidez; claridade, brilho.

clash, *v.i.* chocar-se, colidir; *v.t.* chocar, bater ruidosamente em; *s.* choque, embate, colisão; estrondo.

clasp, *v.t.* afivelar, prender com colchete, acolchetar; apertar; *s.* broche, fivela, colchete, pregador; abraço, amplexo; aperto de mão.

class, *s.* classe, camada social, posição social, casta; classe escolar; aula; classe, grupo, categoria, espécie, género; excelência, distinção; *v.t.* e *v.i.* classificar(-se).

classic, *adj.* clássico; *s.* clássico, obra clássica, autor clássico; erudito; *pl.* letras clássicas.

classical, *adj.* clássico.

classicism, *s.* classicismo.

classicist, *s.* classicista; clássico; aquele que é versado em estudos clássicos.

classification, *s.* classificação.

classify, *v.t.* classificar; *classified matter,* assunto sigiloso.

classmate, *s.* condiscípulo.

classroom, *s.* aula, sala de aula.

classy, *adj.* fino, distinto, elegante, chique.

clatter, *v.i.* fazer barulho, fazer estardalhaço; tagarelar; *v.t.* agitar ruidosamente, fazer barulho com; *s.* bulha, estardalhaço, tumulto.

clause, *s.* cláusula, artigo; condição, estipulação.

claustral, *adj.* claustral, conventual, monástico.

claustrophobia, *s.* claustrofobia.

clavicle, *s.* clavícula.

clavier, *s.* teclado (de órgão, piano ou harmónio).

claw, *s.* garra, unha; pinça, tenaz (de caranguejo, lagosta, etc.); *claw-bar,* pé-de-cabra; *v.t.* e *v.i.* arranhar, dilacerar, agarrar.

clay, *s.* argila; lodo, barro.

clean, *adj.* limpo, puro, claro, asseado; imaculado; *v.t.* limpar; desobstruir; *v.i.* lavar-se, arranjar-se.

clean-cut, *adj.* bem talhado, limpo, bem definido.

cleaner, *s.* limpador, funcionário de limpeza.

cleanly, *adj.* asseado; *adv.* asseadamente, com limpeza; honestamente.

cleanness, *s.* limpeza, asseio, arranjo; pureza.

cleanse, *v.t.* limpar; purificar.

clear, *adj.* claro, brilhante, nítido, límpido; certo, que tem certeza; franco, honesto; *adv.* claro, claramente. *v.t.* clarear, clarificar, limpar, desanuviar; aclarar, esclarecer, elucidar; limpar, lavar, purificar, inocentar, justificar; desimpedir, desobstruir; saldar, liquidar (contas, dívidas); ganhar como lucro líquido; *v.i.* clarear, limpar (o tempo).

clearance, *s.* esclarecimento, desobstrução; certificado alfandegário para sair um navio.

clearing, *s.* clarificação; clareira, terra desbravada; compensação de contas.

clearinghouse, *s.* câmara de compensação.

cleavage, *s.* rachadura, divisão, separação; clivagem; divisão celular.

cleave, *v.i.* aderir, unir-se; apagar-se.

cleave, *v. pret. cleft, cleaved* ou *clove; pp. cleft, cleaved* ou *cloven; v.t.* e *v.i.* fender (-se), rachar(-se), partir(-se).

cleaver, *s.* machadinha, cutelo, rachador.

clef, *s.* clave.

cleft, *s.* fenda, racha, fissura.

cleft, *pret.* e *pp.* de *cleave. adj.* rachado, fendido.

clemency, *s.* clemência, indulgência.

clement, *adj.* clemente, indulgente, brando; ameno.

clench, *v.t.* pregar, prender com prego; dobrar a ponta (de prego); cerrar, unir, apertar; segurar; decidir, confirmar; *s.* rebite; acto de cerrar ou apertar.

cleptomania, *s.* cleptomania.

clergy, *s.* clero.

clergyman, *s.* clérigo, sacerdote.

cleric, *s.* sacerdote, clérigo.

clerical, *adj.* clerical, eclesiástico, sacerdotal; relativo a amanuense, empregado de escritório, etc.; *s.* sacerdote, clérigo.

clerck, *s.* amanuense, empregado de escritório, escriturário, escrivão; caixeiro, vendedor de balcão; clérigo (em Inglaterra).

clever, *adj.* esperto, inteligente, vivo, talentoso; destro, ágil; hábil.

clew, clue, *s.* indício, pista; novelo de fio; *v.t.* apontar (com *out*); seguir a pista de.

cliché, *s.* cliché; frase ou palavra muito repetida.

click, *s.* estalido; *v.i.* estalar, dar estalidos; (gír.) ser bem sucedido.

client, *s.* cliente; constituinte (de advogado).

clientage, *s.* clientela, freguesia.

clientele, *s.* clientela, freguesia.

cliff, *s.* penhasco, rochedo.

climacteric, *adj.* climactérico, crítico.

climactic, *adj.* relativo a clímax; culminante; ascendente.

climate, *s.* clima.

climatic, *adj.* climático.

climatology, *s.* climatologia.

climax, *s.* clímax; ponto culminante, auge.

climb, *v.t.* e *v.i.* subir, trepar, escalar; *s.* escalada, ascensão, subida.

climber, *s.* trepador, escalador; trepadora (ave).

climbing, *adj.* trepador, ascendente.

clinch, *v.t.* fixar com rebite; prender; rebitar.

cling, *v.i.* aglutinar-se, unir-se, manter-se unido; aderir, colar-se, agarrar-se.

clinging, *adj.* aderente, pegajoso, adesivo.

clinic, *s.* clínica; *adj.* o mesmo que *clinical*.

clinical, *adj.* clínico.

clink, *s.* tinido; prisão, cela; *v.t.* e *v.i.* tinir, tilintar.

clip, *v.t.* e *v.i.* segurar firmemente; atirar-se por trás às pernas de um jogador que não tem a bola no jogo do râguebi; clipe, grampo.

clip, *v.t.* cortar com tesoura; aparar; perfurar um bilhete; abreviar; *v.i.* aparar o cabelo; tirar recortes de jornais; *s.* tosquia, corte de cabelo, tosão, retalho.

clipper, *s.* tosquiador, cortador; tosquiadeira, máquina de cortar o cabelo.

clipping, *s.* tosquia; recorte; retalho; *adj.* cortante; rápido; (gír.) esplêndido.

clique, *s.* facção, parceria, igrejinha.

cloack, *s.* capa, manto, capote; máscara: *v.t.* encapar, encapotar; disfarçar, mascarar.

cloakroom, *s.* vestiário.

clock, *s.* relógio (todos menos os de pulso e de bolso).

clockwise, *adv.* no sentido dos ponteiros do relógio.

clockwork, *s.* mecanismo de relógio; *adj.* cronométrico; automático.

clod, *s.* torrão (de terra); solo; rústico, labrego.

clog, *s.* pedaço de madeira; cepo; embaraço, estorvo, impedimento; tamanco; *v.t.* pear, embaraçar; obstruir; *v.i.* embaraçar-se.

cloggy, *adj.* nodoso, grumoso.

cloister, *s.* claustro; convento; *v.t.* enclausurar.

cloistered, *adj.* solitário, recluso, enclausurado.

close, *adj.* fechado, encerrado; preso; denso, cerrado (o tempo); contíguo; íntimo; estreito; mal ventilado; mesquinho; *adv.* perto, junto, rente, ao pé; firmemente. *s.* recinto fechado; propriedade, cercado; átrio de catedral; recreio de escola.

close, *v.t.* fechar; encerrar; concluir; *v.i.* encerrar-se, cerrar-se, fechar-se; terminar; acabar; cerrar fileiras; aproximar-se; *s.* término, fim, conclusão.

closefisted, *adj.* avarento, sovina, mesquinho.

closely, *adv.* hermeticamente; estritamente; firmemente; atentamente; perto.

closeness, *s.* reclusão; abafamento; densidade; proximidade; intimidade; concisão; avareza.

closet, *s.* gabinete reservado; quarto pequeno; armário; retrete; *v.t.* encerrar, encalusurar.

close-up, *s.* grande plano, plano de pormenor.

closure, *s.* encerramento, fechamento; suspensão; conclusão; encerramento de um debate na Câmara dos Comuns.

clot, *s.* coágulo, grumo; pasta; torrão de terra; *v.t.* e *v.i.* coagular(-se); formar grumos.

cloth, *s.* pano, tecido; toalha de mesa; vestes de sacerdote, a batina.

clothe, *v.t. prest.* e *pp. clothed* ou *clad.* vestir, trajar; cobrir, revestir, forrar.

clothes, *s. pl.* roupa, roupas, vestes, vestuário, vestimentas.

clothesline, *s.* estendal, varal.

clothespin, *s.* mola para estender roupa.

clothing, *s.* roupa, vestuário; revestimento, invólucro.

cloud, *s.* nuvem; *v.t.* nublar, toldar, obscurecer, enevoar; *v.i.* nublar-se.

cloudiness, s. nebulosidade; obscuridade.

cloudy, adj. nebuloso, nublado; obscuro, vago, confuso.

clove, s. dente de alho.

cloven, pp. de cleave, adj. fendido, rachado.

clover, s. trevo.

clown, s. palhaço, cómico, comediante; rústico, campónio.

clownish, adj. apalhaçado; rústico, grosseiro; desajeitado.

cloy, v.t. e v.i. fartar, saciar, saturar, enjoar.

club, s. moca, cacete, cajado, maça, clava, taco (de golfe, etc.); clube, grémio, sociedade; pl. paus (naipe); v.t. bater com uma moca, cacete, etc.; v.i. reunir-se.

clubhouse, s. sede de clube.

cluck, v.i. cacarejar; v.t. chamar os pintos; s. cacarejo.

clue, s. o mesmo que clew.

clump, s. massa, bloco, pedaço, torrão, grumo; grupo, moita, maciço; v.i. caminhar pesadamente; engrumescer; v.t. reunir, agrupar, amontoar.

clumpish, adj. pesado, desajeitado.

clumsy, adj. desajeitado, tosco, desastrado.

clung, prest. e pp. de cling.

cluster, s. cacho, feixe, grupo; bando, magote, multidão; v.t. reunir, agrupar, enfeixar; v.i. crescer em grupos ou em cachos; agrupar-se, reunir-se.

clutch, v.t. prender, agarrar, segurar, deitar a mão a; v.i. agarrar-se a, deitar mão a; s. garra, mão; acto de agarrar; presa; ninhada (de pintos).

clutter, s. grupo desordenado, montão; desordem, confusão; v.t. pôr em desordem, baralhar, atravancar.

clyster, s. clister.

coach, s. coche, carruagem, carro; treinador, professor, explicador; state-coach, diligência; v.t. preparar para exame, treinar; v.i. estudar com preceptor, preparar-se para exame; viajar em diligência.

coachman, s. cocheiro.

coaction, s. colaboração, cooperação; coacção, compulsão, coerção.

coactive, adj. coercivo.

coagulant, s. coagulante; coalho.

coagulate, v.t. e v.i. coagular(-se), coalhar; adj. coagulado.

coagulation, s. coagulação.

coal, s. brasa; tição; carvão; carvão de pedra, carvão mineral. 1) coal gas, gás de carvão. 2) coal oil, querosene; v.t. carbonizar, abastecer de carvão;

coalesce, v.i. fundir-se, unir-se, aglutinar-se; misturar-se.

coalescence, s. coalescência, junção; fusão, aglutinação; mistura.

coalition, s. coalescência, fusão; coligação, aliança.

coarse, adj. grosseiro, rude, ordinário; áspero.

coarsen, v.t. e v.i. agrosseirar(-se), tornar (-se) grosseiro, tosco ou áspero.

coast, s. costa, litoral, praia; coast-guard, guarda-costeira, polícia marítima; v.i. costear, navegar ao longo da costa; v.t. costear.

coastal, adj. costeiro.

coaster, s. navio costeiro; bandeja com rodas (para circular sobre a mesa); trenó.

coastwise, adv. ao longo da costa.

coat, s. casaco; pêlo, pelagem, lã, plumagem, etc. (de animal); camada, demão; coat of arms, brasão, escudo de armas; v.t. vestir com casaco; revestir, cobrir.

coax, v.t. induzir, persuadir; v.i. adular.

coaxer, s. adulador.

cob, s. cisne macho; pedaço arredondado, bloco; cavalo robusto e de pernas curtas, garrano; sabugo de milho.

cobalt, s. cobalto.

cobble, s. carvão em pedaços; v.t. calçar com pedras arredondadas; remendar.

cobbler, s. sapateiro, remendão; (EUA) pastelão de fruta.

cobweb, s. teia de aranha, fio de teia de aranha; (fig.) raciocínio subtil, emaranhado, malha; adj. ténue, frágil; v.t. cobrir com teias de aranha.

cocaine, s. cocaína.

cock, s. galo; macho de qualquer ave; chefe, conquistador; torneira, válvula; fiel de balança; aba levantada de chapéu; v.i. empertigar-se, emproar-se; erguer-se, empinar-se; v.t. engatilhar; pôr perpendicular; arrebitar.

cockade, s. cocar, cocarda.

cock-a-doodle-doo, s. cocorocó.

cockatrice, s. basilisco, serpente fabulosa.

cockney, s. pessoa natural de Londres; o dialecto londrino.

cockpit, s. arena; (av.) carlinga, cabina.

cockroach, s. barata (insecto).

cocktail, s. cavalo que não é de raça pura; pelintra; mistura de bebidas; cacharolete.

cocky, *adj.* atrevido; vaidoso, presunçoso, arrogante.

coco, *s.* coco, coqueiro.

cocoa, *s.* cacau.

coconut, *s.* coco, coqueiro.

cocoon, *s.* casulo.

cod, *s.* bacalhau. *coddle, v.t.* cozer na água a fogo lento (fruta); amimar, acarinhar.

code, *s.* código; cifra; *v.t.* codificar.

codfish, *s.* bacalhau.

codicil, *s.* codicilo; apêndice, suplemento.

codify, *v.t.* codificar; sistematizar, classificar.

coefficient, *s.* coeficiente.

coerce, *v.t.* coagir, compelir, constranger, forçar, obrigar.

coercible, *adj.* coercível.

coercion, *s.* coerção, compulsão, coacção.

coercive, *adj.* coercivo, compulsório.

coeval, *adj.* coevo; *s.* coevo, contemporâneo.

coffee, *s.* café.

coffeepot, *s.* cafeteira.

coffer, *s.* cofre, arca; *pl.* fundos, tesouro; câmara de represa.

coffin, *s.* caixão, esquife.

cogent, *adj.* compulsório, poderoso, irresistível; convincente.

cogitable, *adj.* concebível.

cogitate, *v.i.* cogitar, meditar, reflectir; *v.t.* cogitar em; planear.

cogitation, *s.* cogitação, meditação; ideia.

cogitative, *adj.* cogitativo, pensativo.

cognate, *adj.* cognado; consanguíneo; *s.* cognado; parente consanguíneo; língua irmã.

cognition, *s.* conhecimento; cognição; percepção, ideia; intuição.

cognitive, *adj.* cognitivo.

cognoscible, *adj.* cognoscível.

cohabit, *v.i.* coabitar.

coheir, *s.* co-herdeiro.

cohere, *v.i.* aderir, manter-se unido, ser coerente.

coherent, *adj.* coerente, congruente.

cohesion, *s.* coesão, união.

cohort, *s.* coorte; bando, grupo, magote.

coif, *s.* touca, coifa.

coiffeur, *s.* cabeleireiro.

coil, *v.t.* enrolar, enroscar; espiralar, enovelar; *v.i.* enrolar-se, enroscar-se; serpentear; *s.* rolo, espiral; serpentina (de alambique, etc.); cacho (de cabelos); bobina; rosca, anel, espira, volta de espiral.

coin, *s.* moeda; esquina; pedra de canto, pedra angular; cunha; *v.t.* cunhar, amoedar;

tirar proveito de, ganhar dinheiro rapidamente; *v.i.* cunhar moedas.

coinage, *s.* cunhagem de moedas; sistema monetário.

coincidence, *s.* coincidência.

coincident, *adj.* coincidente.

coiner, *s.* cunhador; falsificador de moeda.

coke, *s.* coque (carvão); (gír.) coca-cola.

colander, *s.* coador, coadouro.

cold, *adj.* frio; frígido; arrefecido; apático, indiferente, insensível; que sente frio; *s.* frio, friagem, frieza; constipação, resfriamento.

coldness, *s.* frieza; insensibilidade, indiferença.

cole, *s.* couve.

colic, *s.* cólica; *adj.* cólico, relativo ao cólon.

coliseum, *s.* coliseu.

colitis, *s.* colite.

collaborate, *v.i.* colaborar.

collaboration, *s.* colaboração.

collaborationist, *s.* colaboracionista.

collaborator, *s.* colaborador.

collagen, *s.* colagénio.

collapse, *v.i.* aluir, desmoronar, desabar, ruir, vir abaixo; ceder; sucumbir; desfalecer; *v.t.* desmoronar, arruinar, aniquilar; *s.* colapso; desfalecimento.

collar, *s.* gola; colarinho; gargantilha; coelheira (parte dos arreios); coleira; aro, colar, argola; *v.t.* agarrar pela gola.

collarbone, *s.* clavícula.

collate, *v.t.* cotejar, conferir, confrontar.

collateral, *adj.* colateral; paralelo; secundário; adicional, subsidiário; concomitante; *s.* colateral, parente colateral.

collation, *s.* colação; confronto, conferência; concessão de benefício eclesiástico; pequena refeição.

collator, *s.* confrontador; colator.

colleague, *s.* colega, confrade.

collect, *v.t.* reunir; arrecadar, recolher; colectar (impostos); angariar, cobrar; refazer-se, recobrar o autocontrolo; coligir, compilar; coleccionar; concluir; *v.i.* reunir-se; amontoar-se; fazer colecta; coleccionar.

collectanea, *s.* colectânea.

collection, *s.* colecção; compilação; colecta.

collective, *adj.* colectivo; conjunto; *s.* corpo colectivo; organização colectivista.

collectivism, *s.* colectivismo.

collectivity, *s.* colectividade.

collector, *s.* colector; cobrador.

college, colégio, corporação, congregação; universidade; faculdade, academia; colégio, escola; grupo, assembleia.

collegial, adj. colegial.

collide, v.i. colidir, embater, chocar-se.

collie, s. raça de cães pastores.

collier, s. carvoeiro; mineiro; barco carvoeiro.

colligate, v.t. unir, ligar, coligar.

colligation, s. coligação; união; aliança.

collision, s. colisão, choque, embate; oposição, conflito.

colloquial, adj. familiar, coloquial.

colloquy, s. colóquio, conversação, palestra, conferência.

collude, v.i. conluiar-se; conspirar; ser convivente.

collusion, s. conluio, trama, conspiração.

collusive, adj. conspiratório, fraudulento.

collyrium, s. colírio.

colon, s. cólon; sinal gráfico composto por dois pontos.

colonel, s. coronel.

colonial, s. adj. colonial; s. colono.

colonist, s. colono, colonial; colonizador.

colonize, v.t. colonizar.

colonnade, s. colunate.

colony, s. colónia.

color, colour, s. cor; colorido, coloração.

coloration, colouration, s. coloração.

color-blind, colour-blind, adj. daltónico; acromatóptico.

color-blindness, colour-blindness, s. daltonismo; acromatopsia.

colored, coloured, adj. colorido; de cor.

colorful, colourful, adj. colorido, cheio de cor.

coloring, colouring, s. colorido, coloração, corante; adj. corante.

colorless, colourless, adj. incolor, pálido, descorado.

colossal, adj. colossal, descomunal, gigantesco.

colosseum, adj. coliseu.

colossus, pl. colossal, colosso, estátua gigantesca.

colostrum, s. colostro.

colt, s. poldro, potro; principiante; revólver ou pistola.

column, s. coluna; coluna de jornal, secção, crónica, artigo.

columnist, s. colunista, pessoa que escreve regularmente uma coluna de jornal.

coma, s. coma; estupor, letargia.

coma, s. pl. comae, coma; coma, cabeleireira de cometa.

comatose, adj. comatoso; letárgico.

comb, s. pente; crista de galo; crista de vaga; carda, pente de cardar; v.t. pentear; cardar; vascular; v.i. rebentar, quebrar-se (as vagas). combat, s. combate, batalha, luta; v.t. e v.i. combater, lutar.

combatant, s. e adj. combatente.

combative, adj. combativo, lutador.

comber, s. penteador, cardador, carda; vaga de rebentação.

combination, s. combinação; junção, união; acordo.

combine, v.t. e v.i. combinar(-se), unir(-se), juntar(-se), associar(-se), conjugar(-se).

combine, s. combinação; conluio; acordo; ceifeira-debulhadora.

combustible, adj. combustível; inflamável; s. combustível.

combustion, s. combustão; oxidação; agitação, tumulto.

come, pret. came, pp. come. v.i. vir; chegar; aproximar-se; acontecer; vir a ser; entrar; to come about: acontecer; conseguir. 1) to come again, voltar. 2) to come along, andar, apressar-se, vir ter com alguém. 3) to come for, vir buscar. 4) to come in, entrar. 5) to come next, seguir-se de imediato. 6) to come out, sair. 7) to come off age, atingir a maioridade. 8) to come to terms, chegar a acordo. 9) to come up, subir. 10) to come upon, descer sobre, cair sobre. 11) the world to come, a vida futura.

comedian, s. comediante, cómico.

comedienne, s. comediante (fem.).

comedist, s. comediógrafo.

comely, adj. bonito, atraente, gracioso.

comer, s. aquele que chega.

comestible, adj. comestível; pl. comestíveis, comida.

comet, s. cometa.

comfort, s. conforto; consolo; alívio; bem--estar, comodidade; (jur.) auxílio; v.t. confortar, consolar; (jur.) auxiliar.

comfortable, adj. confortável; cómodo; suficiente, satisfatório; confortador, consolador.

comforter, s. confortador, consolador; manta de lã para o pescoço.

comforting, adj. consolador, confortador, animador.

comfortless, adj. sem conforto; desolado.

comic, adj. cómico; burlesco, engraçado; s.

comicidade, cómico; histórias ao quadradinhos.

comical, adj. cómico, risível, engraçado; esquisito.

coming, adj. próximo, vindouro; s. chegada, vinda.

comity, s. cortesia, urbanidade.

comma, vírgula.

command, v.t. e v.i. ordenar, mandar; comandar; dominar; controlar; s. ordem, mando.

commandant, s. comandante.

commandeer, v.t. recrutar, compelir ao serviço militar; apoderar-se de.

commander, s. comandante.

commanding, adj. comandante, que comanda; dominante; dominador, imponente.

commandment, s. mandamento.

commemorate, v.t. comemorar, celebrar.

commemoration, s. comemoração, celebração.

commemorative, adj. comemorativo.

commence, v.t. e v.i. começar, principiar, iniciar(-se).

commencement, s. começo, princípio, início; acto de entrega de diplomas.

commend, v.t. encomendar, confiar.

commendable, adj. louvável, recomendável.

commendation, s. encómio, elogio, louvor; homenagem.

commendatory, adj. elogioso, laudatório.

commensal, s. comensal, conviva.

commensurable, adj. comensurável.

commensurate, adj. coincidente; proporcionado, correspondente.

comment, s. comentário, anotação; crítica, observação; v.t. e v.i. comentar, anotar; criticar, observar.

commentary, s. comentário.

commentator, s. comentador, comentarista.

commerce, s. comércio, tráfego.

commisariat, s. comissariado.

commisary, s. comissário; delegado, agente.

commission, s. comissão; delegação; junta; patente militar, posto; v.t. encarregar, comissionar; autorizar; nomear.

commissioner, s. comissário; delegado; membro de uma comissão.

commit, v.t. cometer, confiar, incumbir, encarregar, entregar; comprometer, empenhar; to commit to prison, encarcerar, mandar recolher à prisão.

commitment, s. cometimento, entrega,

incumbência; acto de confiar alguma coisa a alguém; recolhimento à prisão; compromisso.

committee, s. comité, comissão; junta.

commode, s. cómoda (móvel); lavatório.

commodity, s. mercadoria, artigo; (jur.) conveniência.

commodous, adj. cómodo, conveniente.

common, adj. comum, vulgar, frequente; ordinário, inferior; common law, direito comum.

commonly, adv. comummente, habitualmente, geralmente, vulgarmente.

commonness, s. vulgaridade, qualidade do que é comum.

commonplace, s. lugar-comum; adj. comum, vulgar.

commons, s. pl. o povo, o terceiro estado; (com maiúscula) a Câmara dos Comuns; provisões para uma mesa comum; refeitório.

commonweal, s. bem geral, bem público.

commonwealth, s. comunidade; república.

commotion, s. agitação, tumulto; confusão, alvoroço.

communal, adj. comunal, comunitário; popular.

commune, s. povo, plebe; comuna.

communicable, adj. comunicável; contagioso.

communicate, v.t. comunicar, transmitir, participar; v.i. comunicar-se, comungar.

communicative, adj. comunicativo, expansivo.

communion, s. comunhão; participação; união.

communiqué, s. comunicado oficial.

communism, s. comunismo.

communist, s. e adj. comunista.

community, s. comunidade; sociedade; povo; comunhão; paridade.

commutation, s. comutação; permutação, substituição; conversão; abono.

commutator, s. (elect.) comutador.

commute, v.t. comutar; trocar, substituir; converter; liquidar (uma anuidade); v.i. compensar; substituir por outra; fazer as vezes de; viajar com bilhete de assinatura.

compact, adj. compacto, denso, espesso; comprimido, apertado; firme, sólido; condensado; v.t. unir com firmeza; comprimir.

companion, s. companheiro, parceiro, camarada; dama de companhia; sócio.

companionship, s. companhia; camaradagem, companheirismo.

company, s. companhia; sociedade; convivência; *to keep someone company,* fazer companhia a alguém.

comparable, adj. comparável; semelhante.

comparative, adj. comparativo.

compare, v.t. comparar, confrontar; s. comparação; *beyond compare,* sem comparação.

comparision, s. comparação, confronto.

compartment, s. compartimento; divisão, secção.

compass, s. círculo, circuito; âmbito, espaço, alcance; compasso (instrumento); bússola; v.t. planear, maquinar; dar volta a; percorrer; cercar, rodear; alcançar.

compassion, s. compaixão, piedade, dó, comiseração.

compassionate, adj. compassivo, piedoso; v.t. compadecer-se, apiedar-se.

compatibility, s. compatibilidade.

compatible, adj. compatível, conciliável.

compatriot, s. e adj. compatriota, patrício.

compel, v.t. compelir, constranger, obrigar; extorquir, arrancar pela força, forçar.

compelling, adj. coercivo; urgente, premente; imperioso, irresistível.

compendium, s. compêndio; sumário, resumo; epítome.

compensate, v.t. compensar, contrabalançar, equilibrar, recompensar; indemnizar.

compensation, s. compensação; recompensa, remuneração, indemnização.

compensatory, adj. compensatório, compensador.

compete, v.i. competir, concorrer, contender, rivalizar.

competence, competency, s. abastança; competência, capacidade, aptidão, habilidade.

competent, adj. competente, idóneo; apto, hábil, capaz; adequado, suficiente, admissível.

competition, s. competição, rivalidade; competência.

competitive, adj. competitivo.

competitor, s. competidor, concorrente, rival.

compilation, s. compilação.

compile, v.t. compilar, coligir.

complacence, s. complacência.

complacent, adj. complacente, benévolo.

complain, v.i. queixar-se, lamentar-se; apresentar queixa.

complainant, s. queixoso.

complaint, s. queixa, lamento, lamúria; protesto.

complaisance, s. complacência, condescendência, benevolência; cortesia.

complaisant, adj. complacente, condescendente; cortês.

complement, s. complemento; remate, acabamento; acessório; v.t. completar, complementar.

complementary, adj. complementar.

complete, adj. completo, inteiro; preenchido; concluído; v.t. completar, perfazer; preencher; acabar, terminar, concluir.

completion, s. acabamento, conclusão; perfeição.

complex, adj. complexo; complicado; s. complexo.

complexion, s. compleição; carácter, natureza.

complexity, s. complexidade.

compliance, compliancy, s. condescendência, complacência, transigência.

compliant, adj. condescendente, transigente, complacente; obsequioso.

complicate, adj. complicado; v.t. e v.i. complicar(-se), enredar-se.

complicated, adj. complicado, intrincado, enredado, complexo.

complication, s. complicação.

complicity, s. cumplicidade; participação.

compliment, s. cumprimento, cortesia, atenção; pl. cumprimentos, saudações, respeitos, recomendações; v.t. cumprimentar, saudar; felicitar.

complimentary, adj. cortês, lisonjeiro; de felicitações, de cortesia.

comply, v.i. aquiescer, consentir, condescender, anuir, ceder.

component, s. componente, ingrediente, elemento; adj. componente, constituinte.

comport, v.r. portar-se, comportar-se; v.i. concordar, estar de acordo.

compose, v.t. compor, constituir, formar; arranjar; escrever; acalmar.

composed, adj. calmo, sereno, sossegado.

composer, s. compositor; autor.

composite, adj. composto, compósito; s. composto, combinação.

composition, s. composição (também literária, artística ou tipográfica); combinação; constituição, formação.

compositor, s. compositor (em tipografia).

compost, s. composto.

composure, s. compustura; calma, serenidade.

compound, *v.t.* compor, combinar; unir, juntar, misturar; construir, formar; resgatar (dívida); concordar; *v.i.* transigir, pactuar; *adj.* composto; misto, combinado; *s.* composto; composição; mistura; palavra composta.

comprehend, *v.t.* compreender, entender; abranger; constar de, incluir; *v.i.* compreender, entender.

comprehensible, *adj.* compreensível, inteligível, concebível; abrangível.

comprehension, *s.* compreensão, entendimento; inclusão; amplitude.

comprehensive, *adj.* compreensivo.

compress, *v.t.* comprimir, apertar; condensar, resumir; *s.* compressa.

compressed, *adj.* comprimido.

compressible, *adj.* compressível.

compression, *s.* compressão; condensação.

comprise, *v.t.* compreender, abranger, abarcar, conter, incluir; consistir em.

compromise, *s.* compromisso, acordo; concessão, transigência; *v.t.* chegar a acordo; comprometer.

comptroller, *s.* examinador, inspector.

compulsion, *s.* compulsão, coerção, coacção.

compulsive, *adj.* compulsivo, compulsório, coercivo.

compulsory, *adj.* compulsório, obrigatório, coercivo.

compunction, *s.* compunção, arrependimento, remorso; escrúpulo.

compunctious, *adj.* compungido, arrependido.

computable, *adj.* computável, calculável.

computation, *s.* computação, cômputo, cálculo.

compute, *v.t.* computar, calcular.

computer, *s.* computador.

comrade, *s.* camarada, companheiro.

con, *v.t.* estudar, decorar; examinar, considerar.

con, *adv.* contra; *s.* voto ou argumento contrário.

concatenation, *s.* concatenação, encadeamento; cadeia, série.

concave, *adj.* côncavo; cavado, escavado.

concavity, *s.* concavidade.

conceal, *v.t.* ocultar, esconder, encobrir.

concealment, *s.* ocultamento, encobrimento; segredo, sigilo; disfarce.

concede, *v.t.* conceder, admitir, reconhecer; *v.i.* ceder, fazer concessão.

conceit, *s.* vaidade, presunção; conceito; imaginação, fantasia.

conceited, *adj.* vaidoso, presumido.

conceivable, *adj.* concebível, imaginável, compreensível.

conceive, *v.t.* conceber; imaginar, idealizar; pensar, julgar, crer; *v.i.* conceber, ser fecundada; fazer ideia de.

concentrate, *v.t.* concentrar, fixar; intensificar; *v.i.* concentrar-se, fixar-se *s.* produto concentrado.

concentration, *s.* concentração; reunião.

concentric, *adj.* concêntrico.

concept, *s.* concepção, ideia, noção; opinião; conceito.

conception, *s.* concepção.

conceptional, *adj.* conceptual.

concern, *v.t.* dizer respeito a, interessar, afectar; inquietar, afligir; *s.* relação: *I have no concern with that,* não tenho nada a ver com isso; assunto, interesse; ansiedade, peocupação.

concerned, *adj.* ansioso, preocupado, inquieto.

concerning, *prep.* acerca de, a respeito de, respeitante a.

concernment, *s.* assunto, interesse; relação, ligação; participação; ansiedade.

concert, *v.t.* concertar, combinar, pactuar; planear, projectar; *s.* concerto, combinação, acordo; concerto musical.

concession, *s.* concessão; privilégio; licença, permissão.

concessionaire, *s.* concessionário.

concessionary, *adj.* e *s.* concessionário.

conch, *s.* búzio, concha.

conciliable, *adj.* conciliável.

conciliate, *v.t.* conciliar; conquistar; aplacar, apaziguar, reconciliar.

conciliatory, *adj.* conciliatório.

concise, *adj.* conciso, sucinto, resumido, breve.

conclave, *s.* conclave.

conclude, *v.t.* concluir, acabar, terminar; inferir, deduzir; *v.i.* terminar, concluir, chegar a uma resolução.

conclusion, *s.* conclusão; fim, termo; resultado; resolução.

conclusive, *adj.* conclusivo; final, definitivo; concludente.

concoct, *v.t.* preparar, misturar; inventar, engendrar.

concoction, *s.* preparação, mistura; invenção; trama, plano.

concomitance, s. concomitância, simultaneidade.

concomitant, adj. concomitante, simultâneo.

concord, s. concórdia, harmonia, união; acordo, tratado; (gram.) concordância; (mús.) consonância.

concordat, s. concordata; convenção, pacto.

concourse, s. concurso, afluência; confluência, junção, encontro.

concrete, s. cimento; adj. concreto, particular, determinado; real, material; v.t. e v.i. unir numa massa, consolidar(-se).

concubinage, s. concubinato, mancebia.

concubine, s. concubina.

concupiscence, s. concupiscência, luxúria.

concupiscent, adj. concupiscente; libidinoso.

concur, v.i. coincidir; concorrer; convir.

concurrence, s. concorrência, concurso, confluência; coincidência, concomitância.

concurrent, adj. confluente, convergente; concorrente; simultâneo, coincidente; concordante; s. concorrente, rival, oponente.

concussion, s. concussão, abalo, choque.

condemn, v.t. condenar, reprovar, censurar; declarar culpado, sentenciar.

condemnation, s. condenação; censura.

condensation, s. condensação, resumo.

condense, v.t. condensar; comprimir; reduzir; resumir; concentrar; v.i. condensar-se.

condenser, s. condensador.

condescend, v.t. condescender, transigir.

condescendence, s. condescendência.

condescension, s. condescendência.

condiment, s. condimento.

condisciple, s. condiscípulo.

condition, s. condição; requisito, estipulação; v.t. e v.i. estipular, pôr condições.

conditional, adj. condicional.

conditioned, adj. condicionado; an ill conditioned person, uma pessoa de mau génio.

condole, v.i. condoer-se, apresentar condolências.

condolence, s. condolência, manifestação de pesar.

condominium, s. condomínio.

condor, s. condor.

conduce, v.i. levar, concorrer, contribuir.

conducive, adj. conducente, útil; propício.

conduct, s. procedimento, conduta, comportamento; direcção, gerência.

conduct, v.t. conduzir, guiar, levar, dirigir; gerir; reger (orquestra).

conductance, s. condutância.

conductive, adj. condutor.

conductivity, s. condutibilidade.

conductor, s. condutor; guia; director, gerente; maestro.

conductress, s. fem. do anterior.

conduit, s. conduto, canal.

cone, s. cone.

confabulate, v.i. confabular, conversar, cavaquear.

confabulation, s. confabulação, conversa.

confection, s. preparação, feitura, confecção; conserva de fruta, confeito.

confectioner, s. doceiro.

confectionery, s. confeitaria.

confederacy, s. confederação; aliança, liga; conluio, trama, conspiração.

confederate, adj. confederado, aliado; s. confederado; aliado; v.t. e v.i. confederar (-se), aliar(-se), coligar(-se).

confederation, s. confederação; união, aliança.

confer, v.t. conferir, conceder, outorgar, prestar; comparar, confrontar; v.i. conferenciar, consultar.

conference, s. conferência; consulta; colóquio; assembleia anual.

confess, v.t. confessar; reconhecer; admitir; professar; ouvir em confissão; v.i. confessar-se.

confession, s. confissão; admissão.

confessional, adj. confessional; s. confessionário.

confessor, s. confessor.

confetti, s. pl. confeitos.

confidant, s. confidente.

confide, v.i. confiar, ter confiança, fiar-se; v.t. confiar, dizer em confidência.

confidence, s. confiança; segurança; confidência.

confident, adj. confiante; confiado; s. confidente.

confidential, adj. confidencial.

configuration, s. configuração.

confine, v.t. limitar, restringir; prender, encarcerar; reter; v.i. limitar, confinar.

confinement, s. reclusão, clausura; prisão; detenção; restrição, limitação; parto.

confirm, v.t. confirmar; ratificar, corroborar; crismar.

confirmation, s. confirmação, ratificação, comprovação; crisma.

confirmatory, adj. confirmatório, comprovativo.

confirmed, *adj.* confirmado, comprovado.

confiscable, *adj.* confiscável.

confiscate, *v.t.* confiscar, apreender; *adj.* confiscado.

confiscation, *s.* confiscação, confisco.

confiture, *s.* compota; rebuçado.

conflagration, *s.* conflagração, incêndio.

conflict, *s.* conflito, luta, combate, divergência, desacordo, oposição, antagonismo; *v.i.* combater, lutar.

confluence, *s.* confluência.

confluent, *adj.* confluente.

conflux, *s.* confluência.

conform, *v.t.* conformar, ajustar, amoldar; adaptar; *v.i.* conformar-se; adaptar-se.

conformable, *adj.* conforme, semelhante; submisso, dócil.

conformation, *s.* conformação, configuração.

confounded, *adj.* confuso, perplexo; amaldiçoado, detestável.

confront, *v.t.* confrontar, defrontar, enfrentar; comparar, cotejar.

confuse, *v.t.* confundir, misturar; atrapalhar, desconcertar.

confusion, *s.* confusão; perplexidade, perturbação, embaraço; desordem.

confute, *v.t.* refutar, rebater; confundir; derrotar.

congé, *s.* licença para que alguém se retire, despedida; demissão; *v.i.* retirar-se, despedir-se.

congeal, *v.t.* e *v.i.* congelar(-se), gelar; endurecer, coagular(-se).

congelation, *s.* congelação; coagulação; endurecimento.

congenerous, *adj.* congénere.

congenial, *adj.* congenial, compatível, conforme, adequado.

congenital, *adj.* congénito, inato, de nascença.

congest, *v.t.* e *v.i.* congestionar(-se).

congestion, *s.* congestão.

conglomerate, *adj.* conglomerado; heterogéneo; *s.* conglomerado; amontoado; *v.t.* e *v.i.* conglomerar(-se), amontoar(-se).

conglomeration, *s.* conglomeração, aglomeração.

congratulate, *v.t.* congratular, felicitar.

congratulation, *s.* congratulação; *pl.* felicitações, parabéns.

congregate, *adj.* congregado, junto, reunido; *v.t.* e *v.i.* congregar(-se), juntar(-se), reunir (-se).

congregation, *s.* congregação; ajuntamento, reunião, assembleia; paróquia.

congress, *s.* congresso; assembleia; reunião.

congressman, *s.* congressista, membro do Congresso norte-americano.

congruent, *adj.* congruente, coerente; adequado.

congruity, *s.* congruência; harmonia, concordância.

congruous, *adj.* congruente; apropriado, adequado; razoável.

conic, *adj.* cónico.

conifer, *s.* conífera.

coniferous, *adj.* conífero.

conjecture, *s.* conjectura; suposição; *v.t.* e *v.i.* conjecturar.

conjoin, *v.t.* juntar, unir, combinar, associar.

conjoint, *adj.* conjunto, unido, combinado.

conjugal, *adj.* conjugal, matrimonial.

conjugate, *adj.* conjugado, unido; *s.* palavra que tem a mesma derivação de outra; *v.t.* conjugar.

conjugation, *s.* conjugação; união, combinação.

conjunct, *adj.* conjunto, associado, reunido.

conjuction, *s.* conjunção, ligação, junção.

conjunctive, *s.* conjuntiva.

conjure, *v.t.* e *v.i.* conjurar, invocar; *v.t.* rogar, suplicar.

connect, *v.t.* ligar, unir, juntar; encadear; *v.r.* ligar-se, relacionar-se.

connected, *adj.* ligado, unido, associado; relacionado, aparentado.

connecting, *adj.* que liga ou une.

connection, connexion, *s.* ligação, união, junção, relação; nexo, coerência.

connective, *adj.* que liga; *connective tissue*, tecido conjuntivo; *s.* conectivo.

connoiseur, *s.* conhecedor, entendido, perito.

connotation, *s.* conotação.

connubial, *adj.* conubial, matrimonial, nupcial.

conquer, *v.t.* conquistar; vencer, derrotar; subjugar; *v.i.* vencer, saír vencedor.

conquering, *adj.* vitorioso, triunfante.

conqueror, *s.* vencedor, conquistador.

conquest, *s.* conquista; vitória.

consanguineous, *adj.* consanguíneo.

consanguinity, *s.* consanguinidade.

conscience, *s.* consciência.

conscienceless, *adj.* sem consciência, sem escrúpulos.

conscientious, *adj.* conscencioso.
conscious, *adj.* consciente, cônscio; *to be conscious of*, ter consciência de, aperceber-se de.
consciousness, *s.* consciência, percepção; conhecimento.
conscript, *adj.* conscrito, alistado, recrutado; *s.* conscrito; *v.t.* alistar, recrutar.
conscription, *s.* conscrição, alistamento compulsório; sorteio.
consecrate, *adj.* consagrado; *v.t.* consagrar; devotar.
consecration, *s.* consagração; dedicação.
consecutive, *adj.* consecutivo, sucessivo; consequente.
consensual, *adj.* consensual.
consensus, *s.* consenso, acordo.
consent, *v.i.* consentir, anuir, permitir, aquiescer; *s.* consentimento, anuência, aquiescência, permissão.
consentaneous, *adj.* consentâneo, apropriado, congruente.
consequence, *s.* consequência; resultado; encadeamento lógico; inferência; importância, alcance, monta, relevo.
consequent, *adj.* consequente, resultante; *s.* consequência, resultado; conclusão lógica.
consequently, *adv.* consequentemente, por consequência, por conseguinte.
conservancy, *s.* conservação (da natureza), preservação.
conservation, *s.* conservação, preservação.
conservationist, *s.* aquele que luta pela preservação da natureza, conservacionista.
conservatism, *s.* conservantismo, conservadorismo.
conservative, *adj.* conservativo, preservativo; conservador (em política); moderado, cauteloso; *s.* conservador.
conservatoire, *s.* conservatório (de música).
conservator, *s.* conservador; protector, defensor.
conservatory, *s.* estufa (para plantas); conservatório musical.
conserve, *s.* conserva de frutas; *v.t.* conservar, guardar, preservar.
consider, *v.t.* considerar, estudar, apreciar, ponderar; levar em consideração, ter em conta; *v.i.* pensar, reflectir, considerar.
considerable, *adj.* considerável, digno de consideração; importante, notável.
considerate, *adj.* atencioso, cortês, educado, respeitador; ponderado, circunspecto.

consideration, *s.* consideração; reflexão, meditação, ponderação, atenção; observação, comentário; contemplação, estima, deferência; importância.
considered, *adj.* considerado, respeitado; ponderado.
considering, *prep.* em vista de, atendendo a.
consign, *v.t.* entregar; transferir, trespassar, ceder, confiar; destinar; (com.) consignar.
consignation, *s.* consignação.
consignement, *s.* entrega, cessão; (com.) consignação.
consist, *v.i.* consistir, constar, compor-se.
consistency, *s.* consistência, densidade; firmeza.
consistent, *adj.* consistente, espesso, firme, sólido; congruente; uniforme, compatível.
consistory, *s.* consistório; reunião, assembleia.
consolation, *s.* consolação, consolo, conforto.
console, *v.t.* e *v.i.* consolar, confortar; *s.* consola.
consolidate, *v.t.* e *v.i.* consolidar(-se), firmar(-se), fortalecer(-se).
consolidation, *s.* consolidação.
consommé, *s.* consomé.
consonance, consonancy, *s.* consonância.
consonant, *adj.* consonante; conforme, em harmonia; *s.* consonante.
consort, *s.* consorte, cônjuge, esposo(a); sócio, colega, confrade; *v.i.* ter relações, dar-se, privar, ser amigo de; casar-se, combinar; *v.t.* unir, juntar, associar.
conspicuous, *adj.* visível, conspícuo, patente, evidente, manifesto, chamativo.
conspiracy, *s.* conspiração, concluio.
conspirator, *s.* conspirador.
conspire, *v.i.* conspirar; *v.t.* conspirar, tramar, maquinar.
constable, *s.* guarda, polícia.
constancy, *s.* constância, firmeza, estabilidade, perseverança.
constant, *adj.* constante; firme, resoluto, fiel; contínuo, uniforme, permanente; *s.* constante.
constellation, *s.* constelação.
consternate, *v.t.* consternar; apavorar.
consternation, *s.* consternação.
constipate, *v.t.* constipar (os intestinos).
constipation, *s.* constipação intestinal.
constituency, *s.* eleitorado; distrito eleitoral.
constituent, *adj.* constituinte, componente, integrante; *s.* componente; constituinte, eleitor.

constitute, *v.t.* nomear, eleger; constituir-se, arvorar-se em; fundar, criar, instituir; organizar.

constitution, *s.* constituição; compleição; estrutura; nomeação; estatuto.

constitutional, *adj.* constitucional.

constitutionalism, *s.* constitucionalismo.

constitutionalist, *s.* constitucionalista.

constrain, *v.t.* constranger, obrigar, forçar, coagir; comprimir, apertar; aprisionar; cercar; sujeitar, refrear.

constraint, *s.* coacção, coerção; repressão; constrangimento.

constrict, *v.t.* constringir, apertar; contrair.

construct, *v.t.* construir, erigir, edificar; arquitectar, elaborar.

construction, *s.* construção, edificação, elaboração; estrutura; interpretação.

constructive, *adj.* construtivo; proveitoso.

construe, *v.t.* construir; interpretar, explicar.

consubstantial, *adj.* consubstancial.

consul, *s.* cônsul.

consulate, *s.* consulado.

consult, *v.t.* consultar, pedir conselho a; *v.i.* consultar, aconselhar-se.

consultant, *s.* consulente; consultor.

consultation, *s.* consulta.

consume, *v.t.* consumir; absorver; preocupar; usar, gastar, despender; *v.i.* consumir-se, gastar-se.

consumer, *s.* consumidor.

consummate, *adj.* consumado, acabado, perfeito; *v.t.* consumar, completar, terminar, concluir, realizar.

consummation, *s.* consumação, conclusão, realização.

consumption, *s.* consumo, gasto; tuberculose pulmonar.

consumptive, *adj.* destrutivo; definhado; *s.* tuberculoso.

contact, *s.* contacto, proximidade; comunicação, ligação, relação; *v.t.* e *v.i.* pôr em contacto, estabelecer contacto ou ligação, estar ou entrar em contacto com; comunicar-se com.

contagion, *s.* contágio; infecção; epidemia; comunicação, propagação.

contagious, *adj.* contagioso, infeccioso.

contain, *v.t.* conter, incluir, encerrar, compreender; abranger; reprimir, refrear.

container, *s.* recipiente.

contaminate, *v.t.* contaminar, contagiar; perverter, corromper.

contamination, *s.* contaminação.

contemn, *v.t.* desprezar, desdenhar.

contemplable, *adj.* contemplável, digno de atenção.

contemplate, *v.t.* contemplar, considerar; meditar.

contemplation, *s.* contemplação; meditação.

contemplative, *adj.* contemplativo.

contemporaneous, *adj.* contemporâneo.

contemporary, *adj.* contemporâneo, coevo.

contemporize, *v.t.* tornar simultâneo; *v.i.* sincronizar-se.

contempt, *s.* desprezo, desdém; desrespeito, desobediência.

contemptuous, *adj.* desdenhoso; insolente.

contend, *v.i.* lutar, pelejar; competir, contender, rivalizar, argumentar; *v.t.* sustentar, afirmar.

content, *s.* conteúdo (geralmente no pl.); capacidade, volume.

content, *adj.* satisfeito, contente; a favor; *s.* contentamento; *v.t.* satisfazer, cumprir os desejos de, contentar.

contented, *adj.* contente, satisfeito.

contention, *s.* luta, disputa, contenda; alegação, afirmação.

contest, *s.* contenda, competição, disputa; debate; *v.t.* disputar, lutar por; *v.i.* discutir, questionar.

context, *s.* contexto.

contiguity, *s.* contiguidade, proximidade, contacto.

contiguous, *adj.* contíguo, adjacente, pegado; imediato.

continence, continency, *s.* continência; moderação.

continent, *adj.* continente; moderado; *s.* continente.

continental, *adj.* continental.

contingency, *s.* contingência; ocorrência fortuita, casualidade; eventualidade.

contingent, *adj.* contingente, eventual; possível; duvidoso, incerto; *s.* contingente; contingência.

continual, *adj.* contínuo; sucessivo; frequente.

continuance, *s.* continuação, prolongamento; sucessão; constância; duração; adiamento (de actos judiciais).

continuation, *s.* continuação, prosseguimento.

continue, *v.i.* continuar, permanecer, ficar; durar; prosseguir, seguir; *v.t.* continuar, prosseguir; prolongar, alongar; (jur.) adiar.

continuity, *s.* continuidade.

continuous, *adj.* contínuo, continuado.

contort, *v.t.* contorcer, torcer, retorcer.

contortion, *s.* contorção, torcedura.

contortionist, *s.* contorcionista.

contour, *s.* contorno, perfil, delineamento; *v.t.* contornar, traçar o contorno de.

contraband, *s.* contrabando.

contrabandist, *s.* contrabandista.

contrabasse, *s.* contrabaixo.

contraception, *s.* prevenção da gravidez.

contraceptive, *adj.* anticoncepcional; *s.* preventivo contra a gravidez, contraceptivo.

contract, *s.* contrato; acordo; pacto; *v.t.* contratar; contrair, limitar; *v.i.* contratar, fazer contratos.

contractile, *adj.* contráctil.

contraction, *s.* contracção; restrição.

contradict, *v.t.* contradizer, contrariar, desmentir; contestar.

contradiction, *s.* contradição; contestação; oposição, desacordo.

contradictory, *adj.* contraditório; oposto.

contralto, *s.* e *adj.* contralto.

contraposition, *s.* contraposição, oposição, contraste.

contrariety, *s.* contrariedade; oposição, antagonismo; desacordo.

contrary, *adj.* contrário, oposto; *adv.* contrariamente, ao contrário.

contrast, *v.t.* pôr em contraste; *v.i.* contrastar; *s.* contraste.

contravention, *s.* contravenção, transgressão, infracção.

contribute, *v.t.* contribuir; *v.i.* contribuir, concorrer, cooperar.

contribution, *s.* contribuição; cooperação, concurso; colaboração; imposto.

contributor, *s.* contribuidor, contribuinte.

contrite, *adj.* contrito, penitente, arrependido.

contrition, *s.* contrição, penitência, arrependimento.

contrivance, *s.* maquinação; plano; ardil, manha, artifício; invenção, invento, engenhoca.

contrive, *v.t.* idealizar, imaginar, inventar, criar; maquinar, tramar; *v.i.* arquitectar planos.

control, *v.t.* controlar, fiscalizar, verificar; governar, dominar; refrear, limitar. *s.* controlo; direcção; domínio; comando; verificação; restrição.

controller, *s.* controlador; dirigente, inspector.

controversial, *adj.* controverso, polémico.

controversy, *s.* controvérsia, polémica; discussão.

controvert, *v.t.* controverter, rebater, contestar, contradizer.

contumacious, *adj.* contumaz, desobediente.

contumacy, *s.* contumácia; obstinação; desobediência.

contusion, *s.* contusão.

conundrum, *s.* adivinha, enigma.

convalesce, *v.i.* convalescer.

convalescence, *s.* convalescência, convalescença.

convalescent, *adj.* convalescente.

convene, *v.i.* reunir-se; juntar-se; *v.t.* reunir; convocar assembleia; citar.

convenience, *s.* conveniência, comodidade, facilidade, oportunidade; *pl.* confortos materiais.

convenient, *adj.* conveniente, cómodo, oportuno.

convent, *s.* convento.

convention, *s.* convenção, acordo, contrato; reunião, assembleia.

conventional, *adj.* convencional; comum, usual; banal.

converge, *v.i.* convergir; *v.t.* fazer convergir.

convergence, *s.* convergência.

conversant, *adj.* familiar, íntimo; versado, entendido.

conversation, *s.* conversa, conversação, colóquio.

converse, *v.i.* conversar.

conversion, *s.* conversão; transformação.

convert, *v.t.* converter; transformar; *v.i.* converter-se; *s.* convertido.

converter, convertor, *s.* convertedor, conversor.

convertible, *adj.* convertível, conversível.

convex, *adj.* convexo.

convexity, *s.* convexidade.

convey, *v.t.* transportar, carregar, conduzir; transmitir, transferir.

conveyance, *s.* transporte; viatura, meio de transporte; escritura.

conveyer, conveyor, *s.* transportador, transmissor; (jur.) transmitente.

convict, *v.t.* declarar culpado.

convict, *s.* réu convicto, criminoso, condenado.

conviction, *s.* convicção, prova irrefutável; condenação.

convince, *v.t.* convencer, persuadir.

convincing, adj. convincente.

convivial, adj. convivial; festivo, jovial.

convocation, s. convocação, chamada; assembleia.

convoke, v.t. convocar, reunir.

convolution, s. convolução, enrolamento.

convoy, v.t. escoltar; s. comboio; escolta.

convulse, v.t. convulsionar; abalar.

convulsion, s. convulsão.

cony, coney, s. coelho europeu.

coo, v.i. arrulhar.

cook, s. cozinheiro; v.t. cozer, cozinhar; falsificar, tramar.

cookery, s. culinária, cozinha.

cooking, s. cozimento, cozedura; cozinha, arte culinária.

cooky, cookie, s. biscoito, bolinho.

cool, adj. fresco; calmo; to keep cool, manter a calma; v.t. refrescar, arrefecer; v.i. arrefecer; acalmar-se.

cooler, s. refrigerante, refrigerador.

coolness, s. frescura; calma; indiferença.

coom, coomb, s. fuligem.

coon, s. o mesmo que "raccoon" (gír.) negro.

coop, s. capoeira; terreiro; v.t. engaiolar, encurralar, prender.

cooper, s. tanoeiro; v.t. fazer barris; embarrilar; arrumar.

cooperate, v.i. cooperar; colaborar.

cooperation, s. cooperação; colaboração.

cooperative, adj. cooperativo; s. cooperativa.

coordinate, adj. da mesma categoria; coordenado; s. coordenada; v.t. coordenar.

coordination, s. coordenação.

copartnership, s. sociedade.

cope, s. cúpula, capa de asperges; v.t. cobrir, tapar; v.i. lutar, bater-se, enfrentar.

copious, adj. copioso, abundante, profuso; prolixo, verboso.

copper, s. cobre; v.t. revestir de cobre, chapear a cobre.

coppice, s. bosque.

copula, s. cópula.

copulate, v.i. copular.

copulation, s. cópula, coito; união; conjunção.

copy, s. cópia, imitação, reprodução; exemplar de livro, número de um jornal; v.t. copiar, transcrever; imitar.

copyright, s. direitos autorais; propriedade literária ou artística; v.t. registar os direitos autorais de.

coquetry, s. galanteio, namoro.

coquette, s. coquete, namoradeira.

coracle, s. pequeno barco de couro utilizado pelos antigos bretões.

coral, s. coral; adj. coralino, de coral.

cord, s. cordel, cordão; corda; medida para lenha; v.t. encordoar, atar com cordel; empilhar lenha em "corda".

cordage, s. cordame.

cordial, adj. cordial, sincero, amistoso.

cordiality, s. cordialidade.

cordon, s. cordão.

corduroy, s. veludo, belbutina; calças de belbutina.

core, s. coração, centro, parte central, miolo; âmago, essência; v.t. tirar o coração a (fruta); descaroçar.

coreligionary, s. correligionário.

coriaceous, adj. coriáceo; duro, rijo.

cork, s. cortiça; rolha; bóia (de pesca); v.t. tapar com rolha, revestir de cortiça.

corkscrew, s. saca-rolhas.

corky, adj. corticento, encortiçado; frívolo, irrequieto.

corn, s. grão, semente de cereal; cereal; trigo (em Inglaterra); milho (EUA); calo; v.t. salgar, conservar em sal; corned beef, carne enlatada.

cornea, s. córnea.

corner, s. canto, ângulo, esquina; beco sem saída; recanto; to turn the corner, dobrar a esquina; v.t. encurralar, entalar.

cornet, s. cornetim; cartucho cónico de papel; corneta.

cornice, s. cornija; sanefa de cortina; v.t. rematar com uma cornija.

corolla, s. corola.

corollary, s. corolário; consequência, resultado.

corona, s. coroa.

coronary, adj. coronária, coronal.

coronation, s. coroação.

coroner, s. magistrado encarregado de investigar os casos de morte suspeita.

corporal, adj. corporal, corpóreo, físico; s. cabo (na tropa).

corporate, adj. incorporado, unido, associado; colectivo.

corporation, s. corporação; grémio, associação.

corporative, adj. corporativo.

corporeal, adj. corpóreo; material, físico, tangível.

corporeity, s. corporeidade.

corpse, s. cadáver, corpo, defunto.

corps, *s.* corpo, conjunto organizado de pessoas; corpo de exército.

corpulence, *s.* corpulência.

corpulent, *adj.* corpulento.

corpus, *s. pl. corpora.* corpo; conjunto de leis ou obras literárias.

corpuscle, *s.* corpúsculo; molécula, átomo.

corral, *s.* curral, cercado.

correct, *v.t.* corrigir, emendar, rectificar, rever; repreender, censurar; *adj.* correcto; corrigido; esmerado; exacto.

correction, *s.* correcção, rectificação, emenda; repreensão.

correctness, *s.* correcção, exactidão.

corrective, *adj.* e *s.* correctivo.

correlate, *s.* correlativo; *v.i.* ser correlativo; *v.t.* correlacionar; *adj.* correlacionado.

correlation, *s.* correlação.

correspond, *v.i.* corresponder, ajustar-se, adaptar-se; combinar; corresponder-se, cartear-se.

correspondence, *s.* correspondência; correlação, concordância.

correspondent, *adj.* correspondente; correlativo; *s.* correspondente.

corresponding, *adj.* correspondente; conforme.

corridor, *s.* corredor, passagem.

corrigible, *adj.* corrigível, emendável, reformável.

corroborate, *v.t.* corroborar, confirmar.

corroboration, *s.* corroboração, confirmação.

corrode, *v.t.* corroer, roer, carcomer, desgastar, consumir; *v.t.* desgastar-se, decair, consumir-se.

corrosion, *s.* corrosão; desgaste.

corrosive, *adj.* corrosivo; cáustico; *s.* corrosivo.

corrugate, *adj.* enrugado, ondulado, crespo; *v.t.* enrugar, ondular; *v.i.* enrugar-se, franzir-se.

corrugation, *s.* ondulação, enrugamento.

corrupt, *adj.* corrupto, corrompido, podre; depravado, devasso; adulterado; *v.t.* corromper, estragar; poluir; perverter; subornar, viciar; adulterar; *v.i.* corromper-se, apodrecer, estragar-se; perverter-se.

corrupter, corruptor, *s.* corruptor.

corruptible, *adj.* corruptível, perecível.

corruption, *s.* corrupção; depravação; suborno; adulteração.

corsage, *s.* corpo de vestido, corpete; ramalhete de flores usado como adorno.

corsair, *s.* corsário, pirata.

corselet, corslet, *s.* corselete.

corset, *s.* espartilho, colete.

cortege, *s.* cortejo, comitiva, séquito.

cortex, *s. pl. cortices.* córtex, córtice.

coruscate, *v.i.* coruscar, cintilar, faiscar.

corvette, *s.* corveta.

cosine, *s.* co-seno.

cosmetic, *s.* e *adj.* cosmético.

cosmetology, *s.* cosmetologia.

cosmic, cosmical, *adj.* cósmico; universal.

cosmography, *s.* cosmografia.

cosmologist, *s.* cosmólogo.

cosmology, *s.* cosmologia.

cosmopolitan, *adj.* e *s.* cosmopolita.

cosmos, *s.* cosmo, o universo.

cost, *s.* custo, preço; gasto, dispêndio, despesa; *pl.* custas; *at all costs,* custe o que custar; *v.i.* e *v.t.* custar, valer; causar, acarretar, orçar o custo de.

costly, *adj.* dispendioso, caro.

costume, *s.* fato, trajo, indumentária.

cosy, *adj.* o mesmo que *cozy.*

cot, *s.* cabana; cama de lona.

cote, *s.* curral, abrigo de animais.

coterie, *s.* círculo social, roda de amigos.

cottage, *s.* casa de campo, chalé, vivenda.

cotton, *s.* algodão, algodoeiro.

cottonwool, *s.* algodão em rama.

cotyledon, *s.* cotilédone.

couch, *s.* cama, leito; canapé, otomana, divã, sofá; *v.t.* e *v.i.* deitar(-se), recostar-se; encostar; conter, incluir.

cougar, *s.* puma.

cough, *s.* tosse; *v.i.* tossir; *v.t.* tossir, expectorar.

could, *pret.* de *can.*

council, *s.* conselho; assembleia consultiva; concílio; *council city,* conselho municipal.

councilman, *s.* conselheiro; vereador municipal.

councilor, councillor, *s.* conselheiro.

counsel, *s.* conselho; opinião, juízo, parecer; advogado; *v.t.* aconselhar, avisar.

counsellor, *s.* conselheiro; consultor, advogado.

count, *v.t.* contar, somar; calcular; enumerar; julgar, considerar, ter na conta de; *v.i.* contar, fazer contas; contar com, confiar em; ser levado em conta; contar-se, incluir-se; *to count as,* valer, valer por; *s.* conta, contagem, soma; cálculo; conde.

countable, *adj.* contável.

countenance, *s.* semblante; expressão do

rosto; calma, compostura; aprovação, patrocínio; *v.t.* aprovar, sancionar, apoiar, patrocinar.

counter, *s.* contador, computador; ficha (em jogo); balcão (de loja); *adv.* contra, em sentido contrário; *adj.* contrário, oposto; *v.t.* e *v.i.* opor, contradizer.

counteract, *v.t.* contrariar, impedir, neutralizar, opor-se a.

counterbalance, *v.t.* e *v.i.* contrabalançar, compensar.

counterclockwise, *adv.* e *adj.* no sentido inverso ao dos ponteiros do relógio.

counterfeit, *adj.* falso, falsificado; fingido; *s.* imitação, simulação, falsificação; *v.i.* imitar, simular, falsificar; *v.i.* fingir, falsificar dinheiro.

counterfoil, *s.* canhoto (de cheque, etc.).

counterfort, *s.* contraforte.

counterpart, *s.* parte ou peça correspondente; reverso, oposto; duplicata.

counterpoise, *v.t.* e *v.i.* o mesmo que *counterbalance.*

countersign, *s.* senha, contra-senha; assinatura com que se autentica uma outra.

countess, *s.* condessa.

countinghouse, *s.* escritório comercial.

countless, *adj.* incontável, sem conta.

country, *s.* país, região; campo, província; *adj.* campestre, rural, rústico; *country seat,* residência de fidalgo no campo.

countryman, *s.* camponês, provinciano; compatriota.

countryside, *s.* o campo, zona rural.

county, *s.* condado; comarca.

coup, *s.* golpe, rasgão; estratagema.

couple, *s.* par, parelha, casal; laço que ata duas coisas; *v.t.* unir, ligar, juntar; *v.i.* unir-se; acasalar-se.

couplet, *s.* parelha de versos; dístico.

coupling, *s.* união, ligação, junção, conjugação; engate; acasalamento.

coupon, *s.* cupão.

courage, *s.* coragem, ânimo, valor, bravura.

courageous, *adj.* corajoso, valoroso, bravo.

courier, *s.* correio, estafeta, mensageiro.

course, *s.* curso, marcha, andamento, progresso; direcção, rumo, rota; caminho, percurso, trajectória; conduta; método; conjunto de iguarias servidas ao mesmo tempo; *of course,* claro, certamente; *v.t.* e *v.i.* percorrer, transpor; seguir, correr.

court, *s.* pátio; quadra de ténis; corte (de um

soberano), paço real; séquito; tribunal; galanteio; *v.t.* cortejar, namorar, fazer a corte.

corteous, *adj.* cortês, educado, amável, delicado.

courtesan, *s.* cortesã.

court-martial, *s.* conselho de guerra; *v.t.* submeter a conselho de guerra.

courtesy, *s.* cortesia; civilidade, urbanidade; deferência; cumprimento, mesura, reverência; favor, obséquio, gentileza.

courtier, *s.* cortesão, homem da corte.

courtship, *s.* corte, galanteio; acto de cortejar; solicitação.

courtyard, *s.* pátio.

cousin, *s.* primo, prima.

cove, *s.* enseada, angra; recanto, recesso abrigado; vale estreito; moldura côncava, abóbada; *v.t.* e *v.i.* abobadar-se.

covenant, *s.* ajuste, pacto, compromisso; concerto, convenção; escritura de contrato; *v.i* e *v.t.* pactuar, ajustar, combinar; contratar; estipular.

cover, *v.t.* cobrir, tapar, envolver, revestir; vestir; abrigar, proteger, resguardar; encobrir, ocultar; chocar, incubar; cobrir (aposta); abranger, incluir, compreender; *s.* cobertura, coberta, tampa; capa de livro; abrigo, protecção; talher.

coverage, *s.* cobertura; alcance, extensão.

covering, *s.* cobertura, revestimento, invólucro, capa.

coverlet, coverlid, *s.* colcha (de cama).

covert, *adj.* coberto, abrigado; encoberto, oculto, dissimulado; *s.* cobertura, abrigo; coutada.

coverture, *s.* cobertura; abrigo, defesa; disfarce; (jur.) matrimónio.

covet, *v.t.* e *v.i.* cobiçar, ambicionar.

covetous, *adj.* cobiçoso, ambicioso.

covetousness, *s.* cobiça, ganância, avareza.

cow, *s.* vaca; fémea de búfalo, elefante, baleia, etc.; *v.t.* intimidar, acovardar, atemorizar, meter medo a.

coward, *adj.* e *s.* cobarde, covarde.

cowardice, *s.* covardia, cobardia, pusilanimidade.

cowardly, *adj.* covarde, cobarde, pusilânime; *adv.* cobardemente.

cowboy, *s.* vaqueiro.

cower, *v.i.* agachar-se, encolher-se (de medo).

cowhide, *s.* couro de vaca; *v.t.* fustigar, chicotear.

cowl, s. capuz (especialmente de frade); v.t. cobrir com capuz.

coxcomb, s. barrete de bobo; pretensioso, peralvilho.

coy, adj. modesto, recatado, tímido, arisco, melindroso; v.t. acariciar, afagar.

coyote, s. coiote.

cozen, v.t. lesar, lograr, enganar.

cozy, cosy, adj. aconchegado, confortável, cómodo.

crab, s. caranguejo; pessoa rabugenta; crab apple, maçã silvestre.

crabbed, adj. rabugento, impertinente, irritadiço, desabrido; confuso, intricado.

crack, v.i. rachar, fender-se, lascar, rebentar, estalar; falhar (a voz); fraquejar; to crack down someone, dar uma descompostura a alguém; v.t. rachar, fender, gretar; quebrar, partir; estalar; gracejar; s. fenda, racha, ruptura, frincha; falha, defeito; estalo, estalido, estrondo; tiro de arma de fogo; piada, gracejo; dissonância da voz; loucura, maluquice.

cracker, s. o que fende, quebra, etc.; fanfarrão; ponta de chicote; mentira, peta.

crackle, v.i. crepitar, dar estalidos; v.t. partir, quebrar; s. crepitação.

cradle, s. berço; origem; armação, grade, cavalete; gancho de telefone; v.t. deitar ou embalar no berço; criar, educar.

craft, s. habilidade, perícia, destreza, arte; astúcia, manha, esperteza; ofício, profissão, ocupação.

craftsman, s. artífice, artesão; artista.

crafty, adj. astuto, manhoso, esperto, matreiro.

crag, s. fraga, penhasco, rochedo; pescoço, garganta.

cragged, adj. o mesmo que craggy.

craggy, adj. fragoso; escarpado, áspero.

cram, v.t. encher, abarrotar, atestar, apinhar, atulhar; estudar à pressa; v.i. empanturrar-se; s. multidão.

cramp, s. cãibra; grampo, gancho, presilha; obstáculo, estorvo, impedimento; v.t. dar cãibras a; comprimir dentro de um espaço pequeno, apertar, apinhar; restringir, refrear, tolher; adj. difícil, espinhoso, obscuro.

cranberry, s. uva-do-monte.

crane, s. grou (ave); guindaste; v.t. suspender com guindaste, levantar, içar, guindar; v.i. esticar o pescoço; estacar (o cavalo perante um obstáculo).

cranial, adj. craniano.

craniology, s. craniologia.

crank, s. manivela, manípulo; equívoco; fantasia, excentricidade; pessoa excêntrica; cotovelo (no percurso do fio que acciona uma sineta ou campainha); v.t. dobrar em cotovelo; dar à manivela; adj. desconjuntado; instável.

cranky, adj. desconjuntado, vacilante; irritadiço, irascível; excêntrico.

cranny, s. fenda, greta, frincha.

crapulent, crapulous, adj. glutão, beberrão.

crash, v.t. e v.i. desfazer-se, espatifar(-se); fazer estardalhaço; chocar; s. estampido; destruição; choque, colisão; pano de estopa.

crate, s. cabaz, cesto grande; grade; v.t. acondicionar em grades.

crater, s. cratera.

cravat, s. gravata.

crave, v.t. e v.i. rogar, solicitar, implorar; ansiar por suspirar por, almejar.

craven, adj. medroso, cobarde; to cry craven, dar-se por vencido; s. poltrão, cobarde; v.t. acobardar.

craw, s. papo (de ave ou insecto); bucho, estômago.

crawfish, s. o mesmo que crayfish; v.i. recuar, bater em retirada.

crawl, v.i. rastejar, arrastar-se, rojar; andar de gatas; trepar; fervilhar de; arrepiar-se; s. rastejo; viveiro de peixes, etc.; estilo de natação.

crawler, s. animal rastejante; pessoa objecta, sabujo.

crawling, adj. rastejante; servil, abjecto.

crayfish, s. lagostim, lagosta.

crayon, s. lápis de desenho.

craze, v.t. enlouquecer, endoidecer; transtornar; gretar (peça de cerâmica); v.i. endoidecer; s. loucura, demência; capricho, mania; moda.

crazy, adj. louco, doido, maluco; rachado, fendido, estalado; defeituoso.

creak, v.i. ranger, chiar; v.t. ranger, fazer ranger; s. rangido, chiado.

creaky, adj. que range, que chia; frágil.

cream, s. creme, nata; v.i. formar nata. v.t. desnatar, pôr ou misturar com nata.

creamery, s. fábrica de manteiga; leitaria.

creamy, adj. cremoso.

crease, s. prega, dobra, ruga, vinco, sulco; v.t. e v.i. franzir(-se), vincar(-se), dobrar(-se).

create, v.t. criar, produzir, originar, inventar, fazer.

creation, s. criação, produção, invenção; instituição.

creative, adj. criador, criativo.

creator, s. criador; autor, inventor.

creature, s. criatura, ser vivo.

credence, s. crédito, fé, confiança; credência (móvel); to give credence to, acreditar em, dar crédito a.

credent, adj. crente, confiante.

credential, s. e adj. credencial.

credibility, s. credibilidade, verosimilhança.

credible, adj. crível, verosímil, fidedigno.

credit, s. crédito, fé, confiança; reputação; apreço, consideração; influência; honra. 1) credit and debit, activo e passivo. 2) on credit, a crédito; v.t. acreditar em, confiar em, dar crédito a; creditar.

creditable, adj. louvável, honroso, meritório.

creditor, s. credor.

credo, s. credo; doutrina professada por alguém.

credulity, s. credulidade.

credulous, adj. crédulo; ingénuo.

creed, s. credo; doutrina; profissão de fé.

creek, s. angra, enseada; riacho.

creep, v.i. pret. e pp. crept; arrastar-se, rastejar, andar de rastos ou de rojo, mover-se furtiva ou vagarosamente; sentir arrepios, arrepiar-se; escorregar; s. movimento rastejante; arrepio, calafrio.

creeper, s. aquele que rasteja; réptil; planta rasteira; ave trepadeira; fateixa; espora.

creeping, adj. rastejante; furtivo; vagaroso; abjecto, servil; arrepiada (a pele); rastejante ou trepadeira (as plantas).

creepy, adj. rastejante; vagaroso; arrepiado, horrorizado; arrepiante.

cremate, v.t. cremar, incinerar.

cremator, s. incinerador, forno crematório.

crematory, s. crematório, forno crematório.

creole, s. crioulo; mestiço, mulato; adj. crioulo.

creosote, s. creosoto.

crepe, crêpe, s. crepe.

crepitate, v.i. crepitar.

crept, pret. e pp. de creep.

crepuscle, crepuscule, s. crepúsculo.

crepuscular, adj. crepuscular; vago, indistinto.

crescent, s. crescente, emblema da Turquia ou do Islamismo; adj. crescente, em forma de meia-lua.

cress, s. agrião.

crest, s. crista (de ave ou animal); penacho; cimo, topo; pico, aresta; cumeeira; cachaço (de cavalo); timbre; v.t. pôr crista em; timbrar; encimar, coroar; v.i. formar crista, encapelar-se (as vagas).

crestfallen, adj. cabisbaixo, abatido; desconcertado, intimidado, humilhado.

cretaceous, adj. cretáceo, gredoso.

cretonne, s. cretone.

crevasse, s. fenda de icebergue.

crevisse, s. fenda, frincha, greta, fissura.

crew, pret. de crow.

crew, s. tripulação, guarnição; grupo, bando.

crib, s. manjedoura; estábulo; cabana; cesto, cabaz; silo, depósito, armazém; caminha de criança; v.t. encerrar em pequeno espaço; engaiolar; furtar, roubar, plagiar.

cricket, s. grilo; críquete (jogo); jogo limpo, procedimento justo; banquinho para os pés; v.i. jogar o críquete.

crime, s. crime, delito.

criminal, adj. criminoso, criminal; s. criminoso, réu.

criminality, s. criminalidade.

crimp, v.t. franzir, preguear, enrugar; frisar, ondular; torcer; s. onda, friso; adj. crespo; quebradiço.

crimson, s. carmesim; adj. carmesim, vermelho, rubro; v.t. e v.i. enrubescer, tornar-se carmesim.

cringe, v.i. encolher-se, agachar-se; curvar-se; aviltar-se; agachar-se diante de; s. mesura servil, servilismo.

crinkle, v.t. e v.i. serpentear; enrugar(-se), encrespar(-se); rogaçar; murmurejar; s. sinuosidade; ruga, ondulação.

cripple, adj. e s. aleijado, coxo; v.t. aleijar, estropiar, mutilar, inutilizar, incapacitar; frustrar, estragar.

crisis, s. crise.

crisp, adj. crespo; quebradiço; encaracolado; enrugado; a crisp answer, uma resposta firme; v.t. e v.i. encrespar(-se), tornar-se quebradiço; encaracolar(-se).

crispation, s. crispação.

crispy, adj. crespo, encaracolado; quebradiço.

criterion, s. critério.

critic, s. crítico, censor.

critical, adj. crítico; decisivo, crucial; arriscado, perigoso; difícil.

criticism, s. crítica, apreciação; censura, maledicência.

criticize, criticise, v.t. e v.i. criticar, fazer crítica; censurar.

critique, s. crítica.

croack, *v.i.* grasnar; coaxar; crocitar; resmungar, lamentar-se; agourar; (gír.) morrer; *v.t.* proferir em voz lúgubre; agourar; (gír.) matar; *s.* grasnido, crocito.

crochet, *s.* croché; *v.t.* fazer croché.

crock, *s.* vaso de barro; caco de louça de barro; ovelha velha; ferrugem; *v.t.* debilitar, incapacitar; sujar de fuligem; *v.i.* fraquejar.

crockery, *s.* louça de barro.

crocodile, *s.* crocodilo.

crone, *s.* velha.

crony, *s.* amigo íntimo, camarada, companheiro.

crook, *s.* gancho, croque; cajado, báculo; volta, curva; cabo de guarda-chuva; curvatura; vigarista, trapaceiro; *v.t.* e *v.i.* entornar, curvar(-se), vergar(-se).

crooked, *adj.* torto, torcido; deformado; desonesto, mau.

croon, *v.t.* e *v.i.* cantarolar, entoar; *s.* canto em voz baixa, canto sentimental.

crop, *s.* papo (de ave); cabo de chicote; colheita, produção; cultura (espécie vegetal cultivada); cabelo cortado à escovinha; *v.t.* mordiscar, encurtar, cortar o cabelo à escovinha, tosquiar; semear, plantar; *v.i.* dar fruto; surgir à superfície; surgir inesperadamente, revelar-se.

cropper, *s.* cortador; tosquiador, tosador; planta que origina colheita; pessoa que trabalha numa herdade e recebe como pagamento parte da colheita.

cross, *s.* cruz; cruzeiro (monumento); sinal da cruz; cruzamento, encruzilhada; provação, infortúnio; cruzamento de raças; *v.t.* cruzar; cortar, interceptar; atravessar, cruzar-se com; riscar; cruzar um cheque; fazer o sinal da cruz; *v.i.* atravessar; cruzar-se; *adj.* transversal; atravessado; cruzado, em cruz; contrário; oposto, adverso; mal--humorado, rabugento; mestiço, cruzado, híbrido.

crossbar, *s.* barra transversal; travessa, travessão.

crossbow, *s.* besta.

crossbreed, *v.t.* e *v.i.* cruzar, entrecruzar (raças); *s.* cruzamento de raças.

cross-examine, *v.t.* e *v.i.* interrogar (uma testemunha pelo lado contrário).

cross-eye, *s.* estrabismo, vesgueira.

crosse-eyed, *adj.* estrábico, vesgo.

crossing, *s.* travessia, passagem; encruzilhada; cruzamento; contrariedade.

crossroad, *s.* estrada transversal, encruzilhada.

crosswalk, *s.* faixa para peões.

crouch, *v.i.* agachar-se; curvar-se; *v.t.* acaçapar; *s.* mesura servil.

croup, *s.* garupa.

crow, *v.i.* cantar (o galo); gabar-se; *s.* corvo; canto de galo.

crowbar, *s.* alavanca, pé-de-cabra.

crowd, *s.* multidão, turba, ajuntamento; *v.t.* amontoar, apinhar; comprimir, apertar; *v.i.* avançar, apressar a marcha; abrir caminho à força, romper.

crowded, *adj.* apinhado, cheio.

crown, *s.* coroa; grinalda; moeda de cinco xelins; soberania; copa de chapéu; *v.t.* coroar; premiar; completar, acabar; pôr uma coroa num dente.

crowned, *adj.* coroado; *a high crowned hat,* chapéu de copa alta.

crow's nest, *s.* cesto de vigia no alto de um mastro.

crucial, *s.* crucial; crítico, decisivo.

crucible, *s.* cadinho.

crucifix, *s.* crucifixo; cruz.

crucify, *v.t.* crucificar; mortificar.

crude, *adj.* cru; tosco, imperfeito; indigesto; *crude oil,* crude.

crudity, *s.* crueza; imperfeição; rudeza.

cruel, *adj.* cruel, desumano, impiedoso; atroz.

cruelty, *s.* crueldade.

cruet, *s.* galheta.

cruise, *v.i.* cruzar o mar; fazer um cruzeiro; *v.t.* cruzar; *s.* cruzeiro.

cruiser, *s.* cruzador; navio de cruzeiro.

crumb, *s.* migalha; miolo de pão; *v.t.* esmigalhar; fragmentar; *v.i.* esmigalhar-se.

crumble, *v.t.* e *v.i.* esmigalhar(-se), fragmentar(-se), desmoronar(-se), esboroar(-se); *s.* poeira.

crumple, *v.t.* amarrotar, amarfanhar; amachucar; enrugar; *v.i.* amarrotar-se; encolher (tecido); *s.* ruga.

crumpled, *adj.* amarrotado, enrugado; enrolado em espiral.

crunch, *v.t.* mastigar com ruído; triturar; *v.i.* avançar sobre a areia fazendo-a ranger; ranger (a areia sob os pés de alguém); *s.* mastigação ruidosa.

crusade, *s.* cruzada; *v.i.* cruzar-se, partir em cruzada.

crusader, *s.* cruzado.

crush, *v.t.* esmagar; moer, triturar; amarrotar, amachucar; comprimir; meter à força; oprimir; subjugar, derrotar, aniquilar; *v.i.*

esmagar-se; comprimir-se; s. esmagamento, compressão, aperto; acotovelamento.

crust, s. côdea; crosta; crusta; casca; incrustação; v.t. e v.i. incrustar(-se); formar crosta.

crustacean, adj. e s. crustáceo.

crusty, adj. duro, rude; crustáceo, cascudo.

crutch, s. muleta; apoio.

crux, s. cruz; a constelação do Cruzeiro do Sul; dificuldade, enigma; ponto crucial.

cry, v.t. e v.i. gritar, bradar, clamar, exclamar; chorar, lamentar-se, pedir; to cry one's eyes out, debulhar-se em lágrimas; s. grito, brado; exclamação; choro, lamento; pregão de vendedores; proclamação.

crypt, s. cripta.

cryptic, cryptical, adj. secreto, oculto, místico; enigmático.

cryptogram, s. criptograma, escrita em código.

crystal, s. cristal; vidro de relógio; crystal set, galena; adj. de cristal, cristalino.

crystalline, adj. cristalino, claro, límpido, transparente.

cristallization, s. cristalização.

crystallize, v.t. e v.i. cristalizar.

cub, s. filhote, cria de animal.

cubby, cubbyhole, s. lugar confortável, cantinho.

cube, s. cubo; cube root, raiz cúbica; v.t. elevar ao cubo; dar forma cúbica a.

cubic, adj. cúbico; cubiforme.

cubism, s. cubismo.

cuckoo, s. cuco.

cucumber, s. pepino.

cud, s. porção de alimento que volta à boca dos ruminantes; to chew the cud, ruminar.

cuddle, v.t. abraçar, aconchegar, acariciar; v.i. aninhar-se, aconchegar-se; enroscar-se; s. abraço.

cudgel, s. cacete, moca, porrete; v.t. espancar com cacete; to cudgel one's brains, dar tratos à imaginação.

cue, s. deixa (em teatro, música, etc.); insinuação, sugestão; taco de bilhar.

cuff, s. punho (de camisa); canhão (de manga); bofetada; v.t. esbofetear.

cuisine, s. cozinha.

cul-de-sac, s. beco sem saída.

cull, v.t. escolher, seleccionar; s. animal que não serve para a reprodução; mercadoria defeituosa.

cullender, s. variante de colander.

culminate, v.i. culminar; atingir o auge.

culmination, s. culminância, ponto culminante, auge; (astron.) culminação.

culpable, adj. culpável, censurável.

culprit, s. réu, acusado, culpado.

cult, s. culto; ritual; seita.

cultivable, adj. cultivável.

cultivate, v.t. cultivar; plantar; lavrar; aperfeiçoar, educar, desenvolver; cultivar a amizade de.

cultivation, s. cultivo, plantio, amanho; cultura, aperfeiçoamento.

cultivator, s. cultivador; agricultor; máquina agrícola.

cultural, adj. cultural.

culture, s. cultura; cultivo, aperfeiçoamento.

cultured, adj. cultivado; culto, ilustrado.

cumber, v.t. embaraçar, atrapalhar; atravancar, estorvar, obstruir; s. estorvo, embaraço, empecilho, impedimento.

cumbersome, adj. atravancador, desajeitado, incómodo, embaraçoso.

cumbrance, s. estorvo, empecilho.

cumbrous, adj. o mesmo que cumbersome.

cumulation, s. acumulação, amontoamento; pilha, monte.

cunning, adj. astuto, manhoso, ardiloso; engenhoso, habilidoso; atraente, engraçado; s. astúcia, esperteza, manha; habilidade, destreza.

cup, s. taça; chávena; cálice; ventosa; v.t. aplicar ventosas; pôr a mão em concha.

cupboard, s. armário, guarda-louça.

cupidity, s. cupidez, cobiça, ganância, avidez.

cupola, s. cúpula.

cur, s. cão vadio; vilão, cobarde.

curate, s. adjunto.

curator, s. director, superintendente; conservador (de museu); curador.

curb, s. barbela; freio, restrição, repressão, entrave; parapeito de poço; rebordo; v.t. pôr freio em; refrear, sujeitar.

curd, s. coalho, coágulo; v.t. e v.i. coalhar, coagular(-se).

curdle, v.t. e v.i. coalhar, coagular; to curdle the blood, gelar o sangue (de horror).

cure, s. cura; remédio; tratamento; v.t. curar; medicar, tratar; defumar, secar ao sol; v.i. curar, curar-se.

curé, s. cura, pároco.

curial, adj. curial.

curio, s. objecto de arte.

curiosity, s. curiosidade; raridade.

curious, adj. curioso; interessante, raro, estranho.

curl, s. anel de cabelo, caracol; ondulação. 1) curl paper, papelote; v.t. encrespar, encaracolar, frisar; enrolar, enroscar; v.i. encrespar-se, encaracolar-se; revolutear. 2) to curl up, enroscar-se.

curly, adj. crespo, encaracolado; ondulado.

curmudgeon, s. avarento, sovina, forreta.

curr, v.i. arrulhar.

currant, passa de Corinto; groselha.

currency, s. curso, vigência, voga; circulação (de dinheiro); moeda corrente.

current, adj. corrente, em curso, em circulação; comum, geral; actual; s. corrente; correnteza; fluxo, curso.

curriculum, s. currículo.

curse, s. maldição, praga, imprecação; calamidade; v.t. amaldiçoar, maldizer; v.i. praguejar, blasfemar.

cursed, adj. amaldiçoado, maldito; odioso, detestável.

cursive, adj. e s. cursivo.

cursor, s. cursor.

cursory, adj. apressado, rápido, breve; ligeiro, superficial.

curt, adj. lacónico, breve, conciso.

curtail, v.t. cortar, mutilar; cercear, reduzir, restringir; privar.

curtain, s. cortina; v.t. guarnecer com cortinas.

curtsy, curtsey, s. reverência, mesura; v.t. e v.i. fazer uma reverência.

curvature, s. curvatura.

curve, s. curva, linha curva; adj. curvo; v.t. e v.i. curvar(-se), recurvar(-se); dobrar, vergar.

curvilinear, curvilineal, adj. curvilíneo.

cushion, s. almofada, coxim; amortecedor; v.t. almofadar.

cusp, s. cúspide; corno do crescente lunar.

cuspidor, s. escarrador.

cuss, s. praga; v.t. e v.i. praguejar, rogar pragas.

custard, s. leite-creme.

custodian, s. guarda; depositário.

custody, s. custódia, guarda, protecção; detenção, prisão.

custom, s. costume, hábito, uso; norma, praxe; pl. direitos alfandegários.

customary, adj. costumeiro, habitual, usual; comum; consuetudinário.

customer, s. cliente, freguês.

customhouse, s. alfândega.

cut, v.t. pret. e pp. cut. cortar, partir, talhar, retalhar, trinchar; fender; magoar, ofender; decepar, amputar; derrubar, abater (árvores); esculpir; encurtar; lapidar (diamantes); interromper; v.i. cortar, trinchar, ferir, ofender; deixar-se cortar, nascer (dente). 1) to cut back, retroceder. 2) to cut in, intervir, penetrar; s. corte, golpe; ferida; ofensa; talhe, estilo; redução; corte das cartas no jogo; pedaço cortado; entalhe. 3) short cut, atalho.

cutaneous, adj. cutâneo.

cutback, s. corte, redução, diminuição.

cute, adj. engraçado, atraente, bonito; hábil, astuto.

cuticle, s. cutícula; película.

cutis, s. derme.

cutler, s. cuteleiro.

cutlet, s. costeleta.

cutter, s. cortador, aquele que corta; trenó puxado por cavalo; dente incisivo; pequeno navio guarda-costas.

cutting, s. acto de cortar; corte, incisão, entalhe; pedaço cortado; adj. cortante; frio, gélido; mordaz, severo.

cycle, s. ciclo, período; circuito; bicicleta.

cyclic, adj. cíclico.

cyclist, s. ciclista.

cyclone, s. ciclone.

cygnet, s. pequeno cisne.

cylinder, s. cilindro; rolo; tambor.

cylindrical, adj. cilíndrico.

cymbal, s. címbalo, prato.

cyme, s. cima, cimeira.

cynic, s. cínico; crítico; misantropo; adj. cínico.

cynical, adj. cínico; céptico, descrente.

cynism, s. cinismo; sarcasmo; misantropia, descrença.

cypress, s. cipreste.

cyst, s. quisto.

cytology, s. citologia.

cytoplasm, s. citoplasma.

czar, czarevitch, variantes de tsar, tsarevitch.

D

d, quarta letra do alfabeto.

dab, *v.t.* e *v.i.* dar pancadinhas em, bater ao de leve; bicar; *s.* pancadinha; salpico, borrifo; sopapo, estalada; (fam.) pessoa exímia em alguma coisa; *he is a dab at games,* ele é um barra em jogos.

dabble, *v.t.* salpicar, borrifar, aspergir, molhar, humedecer; *v.i.* chafurdar, patinhar; dedicar-se a alguma coisa como amador: *to dabble in poetry,* meter-se na poesia.

dabbler, *s.* amador, diletante.

dace, *s.* bordado; robalinho, nome de alguns peixes de água doce.

dactyl, *s.* (métr.) dáctilo.

dad, *s.* pai, paizinho, papá.

daddle, *v.t.* lograr; calotear.

daddy, *s.* o mesmo que *dad.*

daedal, *a.* inventivo, engenhoso; labiríntico, complexo.

daffodil, *s.* narciso.

daffy, *a.* doido, imbecil.

daft, *a.* tolo, idiota, maluco.

dagger, *s.* adaga, punhal. 1) *to be at daggers drawn,* ser como o cão e o gato, estar a ponto de se pegar. 2) *to look daggers,* deitar olhares furiosos.

dago, *s.* nome depreciativo que se dá a pessoas de raça espanhola, italiana ou portuguesa.

dahlia, *s.* dália.

daily, *a.* diário, quotidiano; *s.* jornal, diário; *adv.* diariamente.

daimio, daimyo, *s.* daimio, antigo senhor feudal japonês.

daintiness, *s.* graça, elegância; esmero, gosto delicado; requinte.

dainty, *a.* delicioso ao paladar, saboroso; gracioso, bonito; elegante; requintado; afectado. *s. pl. ties:* iguaria, acepipe, petisco. *adv. daintily* (delicadamente).

dairy, *s.* leitaria, queijaria, lacticínio.

dairying, *s.* indústria leiteira, indústria de lacticínios.

dairyman, *s.* leiteiro; queijeiro.

dais, *s.* estrado, tablado; plataforma, terraço.

daisied, *a.* cheio de margaridas, enfeitado com margaridas.

daisy, *s.* margarida.

dale, *s.* vale, baixada.

dalesman, *s.* habitante de um vale.

dalles, *s.* paredões de uma garganta ou desfiladeiro.

dalliance, *s.* brincadeira, folguedo; namorico, galanteio; frivolidade, leviandade.

dally, *v.i.* brincar, divertir-se; zombar; *do not dally with her sorrows,* não brinques com os sentimentos dela. *v.t.* desperdiçar, passar o tempo frivolamente.

dam, *s.* represa, dique. *v.t.* represar, açudar; obstruir.

dam, *s.* mãe dos animais.

damage, *s.* dano, estrago, avaria; prejuízo, perda; *pl.* indemnização; *v.t.* prejudicar, avariar; danificar. *v.i.* arruinar-se, avariar-se.

damaging, *a.* prejudicial.

dame, *s.* dama, senhora, dona; mulher idosa, matrona; (com maiúsc.) titular feminina da Ordem do Império Britânico.

damn, *v.t.* condenar; reprovar; blasfemar; amaldiçoar. 1) *damn him,* diabos o levem. *v.i.* praguejar. *s.* praga, imprecação. 2) *it is not worth a damn,* não vale nada. 3) *I don't give a damn,* pouco me importa.

damnable, *a.* condenável; maldito; detestável, odioso.

damnableness, *s.* condenação.

damnation, *s.* condenação, maldição.

damning, *a.* condenador; que traz condenação ou perdição.

damoiselle, damosel, damozel, *s.* variantes de *damsel.*

damp, *s.* humidade; relento; desalento, depressão; *to cast a damp over,* espalhar o desânimo; *a.* húmido; enevoado. *v.t.* abafar, sufocar; amortecer; afogar, apagar; arrefecer, desalentar.

dampen, *v.t.* e *v.i.* desalentar, descoroçoar; humedecer; arrefecer.

dampish, *a.* um tanto húmido.

damsel, *s.* donzela.

damson, *s.* espécie de ameixa pequena e escura.

dance, *s.* dança; baile, reunião dançante; música de dança. 1) *to lead someone a dance,* fazer alguém andar numa roda-viva; *v.t.* e *v.i.* dançar; brincar; saltitar; embalar nos braços. 2) *to dance a baby,* embalar uma criança. 3) *to dance to one's tune*, conformar-se com a vontade de.

dancer, *s.* dançarino, bailarino.

dandelion, *s.* dente-de-leão (planta).

dander, *s.* cólera, ira, irritação; *to get one's dander up*, irritar(-se).

dandify, *v.t.* ajanotar, arrebicar.

dandle, *v.t.* embalar nos braços; acariciar, acarinhar, amimar.

dandruff, *s.* caspa.

dandy, *s.* janota, peralta; excelente.

dandyism, *s.* dandismo, peraltismo.

Dane, *s.* dinamarquês.

danger, *s.* perigo, risco.

dangerous, *a.* perigoso, arriscado. *adv. dangerously* (perigosamente).

dangle, *v.i.* pender, balancear; *to dangle about* ou *to dangle after someone*, seguir alguém como partidário; pretendente. *v.t.* balançar; acenar com, tentar com; *s.* balanceio.

dangler, *s.* galanteador, pretendente. 1) *a dangler after girls*, um cortejador de raparigas. 2) *a dangler after literature*, um devoto da literatura.

Danish, *a.* dinamarquês; *s.* língua dinamarquesa.

danseuse, *s.* bailarina.

dap, *s.* pulo, ressalto; *v.i.* pular, ressaltar.

daphne, *s.* loureiro.

dapper, *a.* vivo, activo, esperto.

dapple, *s.* aspecto malhado ou mosqueado; malhas; *v.t.* malhar, salpicar de manchas, sarapintar; *a.* malhado.

darbies, *s.* algemas.

dare, *v.i.* ousar, atrever-se; *v.t.* desafiar, provocar, fazer frente; *s.* ousadia, desafio; *dare-devill*, atrevido; temerário, afoito.

daren't, contracção de *dare not*; *I daren't do it*, não ouso fazê-lo.

daring, *s.* atrevimento, ousadia; coragem; *a.* atrevido.

dark, *a.* escuro, baço, moreno; obscuro, tenebroso, enigmático, secreto. 1) *to keep something dark*, guardar segredo sobre alguma coisa. 2) *to keep dark*, manter escondido; calado, reservado; triste; mal--humorado. 3) *a dark mood*, carrancudo; ignorante, inculto, desconhecido. 4) *dark horse*, cavalo de corrida cujas qualidades são desconhecidas; candidato ignorado até ao último momento. 5) *dark ages*, Idade Média. 6) *to be in the dark about*, ignorar.

darken, *v.t.* escurecer, cegar, confundir.

darkling, *a.* escurecido; extinto.

darkly, *adv.* obscuramente; cegamente; misteriosamente.

darkness, *s.* escuridão; cegueira, ignorância.

darkroom, *s.* câmara escura.

darksome, *a.* escuro, opaco, sombrio.

darky, *s.* negro, mulato.

darling, *s.* e *a.* querido, amado.

darn, *v.t.* e *v.i.* serzir; *s.* serzidura; *darning needle*, agulha de serzir.

darnel, *s.* joio.

dart, *s.* dardo; seta, flecha; movimento rápido, disparada; arremesso; aguilhão, ferrão. *v.t.* dardejar, desfechar, arremessar; *v.i.* disparar, correr, arremeter; *to dart out*, sair como uma flecha.

darter, *s.* arremessador de dardos, flecheiro.

dartle, *v.t.* e *v.i.* arremessar(-se), dardejar repetidas vezes.

dartre, *s.* impigem, herpes.

dash, *v.t.* despedaçar, destroçar, esmigalhar. 1) *to dash to pieces*, fazer em pedaços; lançar; arremessar. 2) *the storm dashed the ship upon the rocks*, a tempestade lançou o navio contra as rochas; repelir; destruir, frustrar. 3) *his hopes were dashed*, as suas esperanças foram frustradas; diluir, misturar; *v.i.* arremeter, chocar, embater. 4) *to dash off*, escrever apressadamente, rabiscar; golpe, pancada, colisão; pequena quantidade, pitada; arremetida, investida; energia, vigor; traço, linha; ostentação, alarde. 5) *to cut a dash*, fazer figura.

dashboard, *s.* guarda-lamas, painel de instrumentos.

dasher, *s.* o que despedaça; pessoa ostentosa.

dashing, *a.* arrojado, impetuoso, precipitado; ostentoso, pomposo. *adv. dashingly*, impetuosamente.

dashpot, *s.* amortecedor a êmbolo, freio amortecedor.

dastard, *s.* e *a.* cobarde; vilão.

dastardliness, *s.* cobardia; perfídia.

data, *s. pl.* de *datum*, dados, elementos.

date, *s.* data, época; encontro; tâmara. 1) *date palm*, tamareira. 2) *out of date*, antiquado, fora de moda. 3) *up to date*, moderno, actualizado; *v.t.* e *v.i.* datar; ter a sua origem.

dateless, *a.* sem data; eterno; de interesse permanente.

dative, *a.* dativo; de que se pode dispor à vontade.

datum, s. dado, elemento; base, premissa. 1) *datum point*, ponto de referência. 2) *datum level*, nível de referência.

daub, v.t. untar ou cobrir com substância viscosa; pintar toscamente; borrar. s. pintura tosca; borradela.

dauber, s. pintor ordinário, troca-tintas.

daughter, s. e a. filha. 1) *grand-daughter*, neta. 2) *god-daughter*, afilhada. 3) *daughter-in-law*, nora. 4) *step-daughter*, enteada.

daughterly, a. filial, próprio de filha.

daunt, v.t. desencorajar; desalentar; atemorizar, assustar, intimidar.

dauntless, a. destemido, audaz; adv. *dauntlessly*, destemidamente.

dauntlessness, s. intrepidez.

dauphin, s. delfim, herdeiro da Coroa de França.

davenport, s. escrivaninha pequena e elegante.

daw, s. gralha (ave).

dawdle, v.i. perder o tempo com ninharias.

dawdler, s. vadio.

dawn, s. aurora, alvorada; v.i. amanhecer, assomar; *to dawn upon*, começar a ser percebido.

day, s. dia; jornada; horas de trabalho. 1) *day boy*, aluno externo. 2) *day school*, externato. 3) *day man*, jornaleiro. 4) *pay day*, dia de pagamento. 5) *to name the day*, marcar o dia do casamento. 6) *rainy day*, o tempo de adversidade. 7) *to this day*, até hoje. 8) *every other day about*, dia sim, dia não. 9) *to win the day*, ganhar a vitória. 10) *day nursery*, infantário. 11) *day wages*, diária. 12) *fallen on evil days*, caído em desgraça. 13) *to know the time of the day*, ser esperto.

daydream, s. devaneio.

daylight, s. luz do dia. 1) *to let daylight into someone*, meter uma bala em alguém ou dar-lhe uma facada. 2) *daylight saving time*, hora de Verão.

daystar, s. estrela-d'alva.

daytime, s. dia, tempo de luz natural.

daze, v.t. deslumbrar; ofuscar, cegar por excesso de luz; atordoar. s. aturdimento, tontura.

dazzle, v.t. fascinar, maravilhar; encadear, aturdir; s. deslumbramento.

dazzling, a. deslumbrante; adv. *dazzlingly*, deslumbrantemente.

deacon, s. diácono.

deaconry, s. diaconado, diaconato.

dead, a. morto; falecido, defunto; inanimado, sem vida; imóvel, parado. 1) *dead-beat*, exausto de forças. 2) *deadcalm*, calmaria podre. 3) *dead-head*, pessoa que goza privilégios sem pagar. 4) *dead house*, necrotério. 5) *dead language*, língua morta. 6) *dead loss*, prejuízo sem compensação. 7) *dead wall*, parede sem janela. 8) *dead wind*, vento contrário. 9) *dead work*, trabalho inútil. 10) *dead men tell no tales*, morto o bicho acaba a peçonha. 11) *in the dead of night*, na calada da noite.

deaden, v.t. amortecer, atenuar, enfraquecer.

deadliness, s. capacidade de causar a morte; perigo de morte.

deadlock, s. beco sem saída.

deadly, a. fatal; mortal; adv. mortalmente.

deadness, s. morte; marasmo, torpor; insipidez.

deaf, s. surdo, mouco; insensível; *deaf-mute*, surdo-mudo, adv. *deafly*, surdamente.

deafness, s. surdez.

deal, v.t. distribuir, repartir, espalhar; v.i. negociar, servir de intermediário. 1) *to deal with*, tratar com. 2) *to deal in*, ocupar-se em; s. porção, quantidade; pacto secreto; negociação. 3) *a great deal*, muito. 4) *a good deal*, bastante.

dealer, s. negociante; distribuidor. 1) *plain dealer*, homem sincero. 2) *double dealer*, homem de duas caras.

dealing, proceder; conduta; *plain dealing*, boa-fé.

dean, s. deão.

dear, a. amado, querido; caro, custoso; raro; s. pessoa querida, predilecto; adv. *dearly*, caríssimo; carinhosamente.

dearness, s. carinho, afecto;

dearth, s. carestia, escassez.

death, s. morte, falecimento, óbito; extinção, cessação; mortandade, matança. 1) *to catch one's death*, contrair uma doença fatal. 2) *field of death*, campo de batalha. 3) *death warrant*, sentença de morte. 4) *to be death on*, pelar-se por.

deathbed, s. leito de morte; *deathbed repentance*, arrependimento tardio.

deathblow, s. golpe fatal.

deathful, a. mortífero; homicida.

deathless, a. imortal, imorredouro.

deathly, a. e adv. como a morte, cadavérico.

death's-head, s. caveira.

deathwatch, s. velório.

deb, s. o mesmo que debutante.

debar, v.t. excluir, privar.

debark, v.t. e v.i. desembarcar.

debase, v.t. humilhar, depreciar, rebaixar; adulterar, viciar.

debasement, s. humilhação.

debatable, s. discutível.

debate, v.t. e v.i. debater, discutir; s. debate, discussão.

debauch, v.t. corromper, perverter, viciar; seduzir; v.i. cometer excessos, entregar-se aos prazeres; s. devassidão, vida dissoluta; orgia.

debauchee, s. libertino, devasso.

debauchery, s. devassidão, libertinagem.

debenture, s. obrigação; promissória.

debilitate, v.t. debilitar, enfraquecer.

debility, s. debilidade, fraqueza.

debit, v.t. debitar; s. débito; lançamento de débito.

debonair, debonaire, s. afável, cortês; jovial; adv. debonairly, cortesmente.

debonairness, s. cortesia, civilidade.

debouch, v.i. desembocar, emergir; v.t. fazer desembocar, fazer sair: s. desembocadura.

debris, s. escombros, ruínas.

debt, s. dívida; débito. 1) outstanding debt, dívidas a receber. 2) to get into debt, contrair dívidas. 3) to be head over ears in debt, estar cheio de dívidas.

debtor, s. devedor.

début, s. estreia.

debutante, s. estreante; rapariga que faz a sua estreia na sociedade.

decade, s. década.

decadence, decadency, s. decadência, declínio.

decadent, s. decadente.

Decalogue, s. Decálogo, os Dez Mandamentos.

decamp, v.i. desacampar, levantar acampamento; escapar, fugir, abalar.

decant, v.t. decantar.

decantation, s. decantação, trasfego.

decanter, s. frasco para decantar; garrafa de mesa.

decapitate, v.t. decapitar, degolar.

decay, v.i. decair; declinar, cair, diminuir; definhar; piorar, degenerar, v.t. apodrecer, deteriorar, arruinar; s. decadência; apodrecimento, podridão; tecido orgânico em decomposição.

decease, v.i. morrer, falecer; s. morte, óbito, falecimento.

deceased, s. morto, finado, defunto.

deceit, s. engano, fraude, burla.

deceitful, a. enganoso, enganador, falso, embusteiro; adv. deceitfully, falsamente.

deceive, v.t. e v.i. enganar, iludir; frustrar, decepcionar; to deceive one's hopes, acabar com as esperanças de alguém.

deceiver, s. impostor, embusteiro.

decelerate, v.t. e v.i. retardar, desacelerar.

deceleration, s. retardamento; diminuição da velocidade.

December, s. Dezembro.

decency, s. decência, decoro, pudor; the decencies, as regras dos decoro.

decent, a. decente, decoroso, digno; adequado, apropriado; tolerável; adv. decently, decentemente.

decentness, s. decência.

decenter, decentre, v.t. descentralizar.

decentralize, v.t. o mesmo que decenter e decentre.

decentralization, s. descentralização.

deception, s. decepção, engano, desilusão.

deceptive, a. falaz, enganoso, ilusório; adv. deceptively, enganadoramente.

deceptiveness, s. qualidade de ser enganoso.

decern, v.t. julgar; discernir.

decide, v.t. e v.i. decidir, resolver, determinar; to decide on, pronunciar-se por.

decide, a. decidido, determinado, categórico. adv. decidely, decididamente.

decider, s. árbitro.

deciduous, a. caduco.

decimal, a. e s. decimal.

decimate, v.t. dizimar, decimar.

decipher, v.t. decifrar; interpretar; s. decifração (de documento cifrado).

deck, s. convés, coberta de navio; baralho de cartas; to sweep the deck, varrer o convés, ganhar tudo no jogo de cartas; v.t. vestir, ataviar.

deckhouse, s. casota, compartimento levantado no convés de um navio.

declaim, v.t. e v.i. declamar, recitar; discursar, arengar; to declaim against, invectivar.

declamation, s. declamação; discurso; arenga.

declamatory, a. declamatório; enfático; empolado.

declare, v.t. declarar, anunciar; demonstrar;

afirmar. *v.i.* declarar-se, pronunciar-se, tomar partido; *to declare off,* retirar-se, desistir.

déclassé, *a.* desqualificado.

declension, *s.* declinação; inclinação, declive.

declination, *s.* declinação; decadência; inclinação; escusa, renúncia.

decline, *v.t.* escusar, recusar; inclinar, declinar; *v.i.* recusar; inclinar-se, decair. *s.* declinação, decadência; baixa de preço.

declivity, *s.* declive, inclinação do terreno, ladeira.

decoct, *v.t.* cozer, ferver, fazer cozimento.

decoction, *s.* cozimento.

decode, *v.t.* decifrar, traduzir um código.

decollate, *v.t.* degolar.

décolleté, *a.* decotado.

decolorize, decolourize, *v.t.* descorar, descolorar.

decompose, *v.t.* decompor; desintegrar; *v.i.* decompor-se; desintegrar-se; apodrecer.

decomposition, *s.* decomposição, análise; desintegração.

decompound, *v.t.* compor de coisas já compostas.

decorate, *v.t.* decorar, ornamentar, enfeitar; condecorar.

decorated, enfeitado, decorado; estilo de arquitectura inglesa.

decoration, *s.* decoração, ornamentação; condecoração.

decorative, *a.* decorativo, ornamental; *adv. decoratively,* decorativamente.

decorous, *a.* decoroso, digno, correcto.

decorousness, *s.* compostura, dignidade, decência.

decorum, *s.* formalidade, etiqueta; compostura, decoro.

decoy, *v.t.* e *v.i.* atrair, engodar; apanhar no laço; *s.* armadilha, engodo; chamariz.

decrease, *v.t.* e *v.i.* diminuir, decrescer, baixar, cair. *s.* diminuição, redução, baixa, queda; *adv. decreasingly,* cada vez menos.

decree, *v.t.* decretar, mandar, ordenar; *s.* decreto, mandato ou decisão judicial.

decrepit, *a.* decrépito, caduco, gasto.

decrepitate, *v.t.* e *v.i.* decrepitar; crepitar no fogo.

decrepitude, *s.* decrepitude, caducidade.

decry, *v.t.* desacreditar, rebaixar.

decurrent, *a.* que decorre, decorrente.

decussate, *v.t.* interceptar; cruzar(-se).

dedicate, *v.t.* dedicar, consagrar, destinar.

dedication, *s.* dedicação; dedicatória.

deduce, *v.t.* deduzir; derivar; acompanhar o curso de.

deduct, *v.t.* deduzir; abater.

deduction, *s.* dedução, diminuição, desconto.

deed, *s.* acto, acção; façanha, proeza. 1) *we want deeds, not words,* queremos obras, não palavras. 2) *indeed,* na verdade; escritura de venda de uma propriedade. *v.t.* transmitir, passar. 3) *to be taken in the deed,* ser apanhado em flagrante.

deedless, *a.* inactivo, inerte.

deem, *v.t.* julgar, pensar, considerar; *to be deemed,* ser considerado.

deep, *a.* fundo, profundo; íntimo, sincero, intenso; sagaz, astuto. 1) *a deep one,* um finório ou pessoa reservada. 2) *deep in love,* muito apaixonado. 3) *deep sea,* mar alto. 4) *in deep waters,* em situação difícil; abismo, fundão. *adv. deeply,* fortemente, profundamente, muito.

deepen, *v.t.* e *v.i.* profundar, afundar; escurecer, carregar as cores.

deer, *s.* veado, corça, gamo; *deer-skin,* camurça.

deface, *v.t.* desfigurar; mutilar.

defacement, *s.* violação; destruição; mutilação; falsificação.

defacer, *s.* desfigurador.

defalcate, *v.t.* desfalcar, descontar; *v.i.* praticar desfalques.

defalcation, *s.* desfalque.

defalcator, *s.* autor de desfalque.

defamation, *s.* difamação, calúnia, maledicência.

defame, *v.t.* difamar, caluniar, denegrir.

default, *v.t.* faltar a, não cumprir; deixar de pagar; condenar à revelia; *s.* omissão, falta; negligência; mora.

defaulter, *s.* delinquente.

defeasance, *s.* anulação, revogação.

defeat, *v.t.* anular, invalidar; privar; *to defeat someone of his state,* esbulhar alguém; derrotar, vencer; *s.* malogro, frustração; derrota.

defeatism, *s.* derrotismo; *s.* e *a. defeatist,* derrotista.

defecate, *v.t.* defecar, depurar; purificar.

defect, *v.i.* desertar, insurgir-se; *s.* falta, deficiência, defeito.

defection, *s.* deserção, rebelia; defecção.

defective, *a.* deficiente, defeituoso; *a.*

retardado mental; verbo defectivo. *adv.*
defectively, deficientemente.

defectiveness, *s.* deficiência, imperfeição.

defence, *s.* defesa, protecção, apoio; resistência.

defenceless, *s.* indefeso. *adv. defencelessly,* sem poder resistir.

defencelessness, *s.* desamparo, abandono.

defend, *v.t.* defender, amparar, proteger, manter.

defendant, *s.* réu; defensor.

defender, *s.* defensor; protector; advogado.

defensible, *a.* defensável, sustentável, justificável; *adv. defensibly,* dum modo justificável.

defensive, *s.* defensiva; *a.* defensivo; *adv. defensively,* defensavelmente.

defer (deferring, deferred), *v.t.* deferir, dilatar, adiar. *v.i.* demorar-se, consentir; *defered pay,* pensão de invalidez ou morte.

deference, *s.* deferência, consideração.

deferential, *a.* deferente, respeitador, condescendente.

deferment, *s.* demora, delonga; adiamento.

deferrable, *a.* adiável, transferível.

defiance, *s.* desafio, desobediência, desrespeito; *to set at defiance,* desafiar, afrontar; resistir abertamente.

defiant, *a.* desafiador, provocador, arrogante; *adv. defiantly,* desafiantemente, provocantemente.

deficiency, *s.* deficiência, falta, carência.

deficient, *s.* deficiente, falho, carente; *adv. deficiently,* deficientemente.

deficit, *s.* défice, falta.

defile, *v.t.* manchar, sujar, profanar; *v.i.* desfilar, marchar em fila; *s.* desfiladeiro, garganta, passagem.

define, *v.t.* definir; explicar; circunscrever; determinar.

definite, *a.* definido, determinado, exacto; *adv. definitely,* definidamente, decididamente.

definition, *s.* definição, explicação; nitidez, distinção, clareza.

definitive, *a.* definitivo, decisivo, final; distintivo, característico. *adv. definitively,* definitivamente.

deflagrate, *v.t.* e *v.i.* deflagrar, inflamar(-se).

deflate, *v.t.* esvaziar.

deflation, *s.* esvaziamento.

deflect, *v.t.* e *v.i.* desviar(-se), afastar(-se), flectir, curvar(-se).

deflection, *s.* desvio; afastamento; curva, dobra, refracção.

deflector, *s.* desviador, deflector.

defloration, *s.* desfloração, desvirginamento.

deflower, *v.t.* desflorar, desvirginar.

deform, *v.t.* deformar, desfigurar.

deformation, *s.* deformação, desfiguração.

deformed, *a.* deformado, desfigurado; *adv. deformedly,* deformadamente.

deformity, *s.* deformidade, fealdade; aleijão; depravação, vício.

defraud, *v.t.* defraudar, fraudar, lesar; *he was defrauded of his rights,* ele foi lesado nos seus direitos.

defray, *v.t.* custear, pagar.

defrost, *v.t.* degelar, descongelar.

deft, *a.* destro, hábil, jeitoso, capaz, perito. *adv. deftly,* destramente.

defunct, *a.* e *s.* defunto, morto, extinto.

defy, *v.t.* desafiar, desdenhar, resistir a; *s.* desafio.

degeneracy, *s.* degeneração, decadência.

degenerate, *v.i.* degenerar, abastardar-se, decair; *a.* e *s.* degenerado, degradado, corrompido; *adv. degenerately,* degeneradamente.

degeneration, *s.* degeneração, abastardamento, decadência.

deglutinate, *v.t.* desgrudar, despegar.

deglutition, *s.* deglutição.

degradation, *s.* degradação; rebaixamento.

degrade, *v.t.* degradar, destituir, depor; rebaixar, aviltar; *v.i.* degenerar; envilecer-se.

degraded, *a.* degradado, rebaixado, degenerado; *adv. degradedly,* degradadamente.

degrading, *a.* degradante.

degree, *s.* grau, qualidade, condição, graduação, degrau; modo, maneira. 1) *by degrees,* gradualmente, pouco a pouco. 2) *to take one's degrees,* graduar-se, tomar grau universitário.

degust, degustate, *v.t.* provar, saborear.

deification, *s.* deificação; divinização; apoteose.

deify, *v.t.* deificar, divinizar.

deign, *v.t.* conceder, permitir; *v.i.* dignar-se, condescender.

deigning, *s.* condescendência.

deism, *s.* deísmo.

deity, *s.* deidade, divindade.

deject, *v.t.* desalentar, deprimir, abater.

dejected, *a.* desalentado, abatido; *adv. dejectedly,* desalentadamente.

dejection, s. desalento, desânimo, abatimento; dejecção, evacuação das fezes.

delate, v.t. delatar, denunciar; acusar, atacar.

delay, v.t. e v.i. demorar, atrasar, tardar; s. demora, atraso.

delectate, v.t. deleitar.

delectation, deleite, prazer.

delegacy, s. delegação; mandato.

delegate, v.t. delegar, comissionar; confiar; s. delegado, comissário.

delegation, s. delegação, comissão.

delete, v.t. apagar, suprimir; obliterar.

deleterious, a. deletério, nocivo, prejudicial; adv. deleteriously, prejudicialmente.

deletion, s. acção de apagar; obliteração; passagem suprimida.

deliberate, v.t. deliberar, consultar, ponderar. v.i. conferenciar, discorrer; a. deliberado, reflectido, considerado; premeditado, cauteloso, descansado adv. deliberately, deliberadamente.

deliberateness, s. deliberação, reflexão, ponderação, vagar.

deliberation, s. ponderação, reflexão; discussão; calma; determinação.

deliberative, a. deliberativo, reflexivo; adv. deliberatively, deliberativamente.

deliberator, s. deliberante.

delicacy, s. delicadeza, consideração; ternura; bom gosto; acepipe.

delicate, a. delicado, cortês, fino; frágil; efeminado; de bom gosto.

delicatessen, s. iguarias, acepipes; especialidades; fiambres; delicatessen store, charcutaria.

delicious, a. delicioso, saboroso; adv. deliciously, saborosamente.

delict, s. delito.

delight, v.t. deleitar, agradar, encantar; v.i. deleitar-se; I delight in going for a swim, gosto muito de ir nadar; s. deleite, prazer, encanto.

delighted, a. deleitado, encantado; adv. delightedly, deleitadamente.

delightful, a. deleitoso, aprazível, encantador; adv. delightfully, deliciosamente.

delightsome, a. deleitoso.

delimit, v.t. delimitar, demarcar, balizar.

delineate, v.t. delinear, esboçar; retratar.

delineation, s. delineamento; esboço; descrição.

delineator, s. delineador; molde de costura.

delinquency, s. delinquência; culpa; delito; inobservância do dever.

delinquent, s. delinquente; adv. delinquently, delinquentemente.

deliquesce, v.i. liquefazer-se; derreter-se; ramificar-se.

delirious, a. delirante; louco; entusiástico; adv. deliriously, delirantemente.

delirium, s. delírio; desvario; excitação; delirium tremens, delírio tremens ou alcoólico.

deliver, v.t. dar, entregar, ceder; libertar, salvar; transmitir, passar. 1) to deliver over, transmitir. 2) to deliver a ball, lançar uma bola. 3) she was delivered of a child, ela deu à luz uma criança. 4) to deliver the goods, entregar a mercadoria. 5) stand and deliver, a bolsa ou a vida.

deliverance, s. libertação, salvamento; parecer; veredicto.

delivery, s. livramento; parto; entrega; distribuição do correio; acto de pronunciar; enunciação.

dell, s. valeira, pequeno vale.

delude, v.t. iludir, enganar, burlar.

deluge, v.t. inundar, alagar; s. dilúvio, inundação, cheia.

delusion, s. engano, fraude; ilusão.

delusive, a. enganador, falaz, ilusório; adv. delusively, enganosamente.

delve, v.t. cavar; desenterrar; pesquisar; s. cova; depressão de superfície.

demand, v.t. pedir, reclamar; exigir; perguntar; s. exigência; pergunta; pedido. 1) demand draft, letra à vista. 2) payable on demand, pagável à vista. 3) demand deposit, depósito bancário à ordem.

demarcate, v.t. demarcar, delimitar, abalizar; distinguir.

demarcation, s. demarcação, separação.

demean, v.t. portar-se, comportar-se; rebaixar-se; conduzir-se.

dement, v.t. enlouquecer, endoidecer.

demented, a. demente, insano, louco; adv. dementedly, dementemente.

dementia, s. demência, loucura.

demerit, s. demérito, desmerecimento, falta reprovável.

demesne, s. domínio, posse de terras, bem de raiz; solar; região, território; the demesne of knowledge is vast, o campo do conhecimento é vasto.

demijohn, s. garrafão.

demilitarize, v.t. desmilitarizar.

demilune, s. meia-lua.

demise, v.t. e v.i. legar, deixar em testamento; arrendar; s. aforamento, transferência; arrendamento; morte, falecimento; *demise of the crown*, sucessão da coroa.

demission, s. demissão, renúncia.

demit, v.t. e v.i. demitir-se (de); renunciar (a).

demobilize, v.t. desmobilizar.

democracy, s. democracia.

democrat, s. democrata.

democratic, a. democrático.

democratize, v.t. e v.i. democratizar(-se).

demoiselle, s. donzela, menina solteira; libélula.

demolish, v.t. demolir, arrasar, deitar por terra; arruinar, destruir.

demolition, s. demolição, destruição.

demon, s. demónio, espírito mau.

demoniac, s. e a. demoníaco, endemoninhado, possesso; satânico.

demoniacal, a. demoníaco, diabólico; adv. *demoniacally,* demoniacamente.

demonize, v.t. endemoninhar; converter em demónio.

demonstrable, demonstrável; adv. *demonstrably,* de modo demonstrável.

demonstrate, v.t. demonstrar, provar.

demonstration, s. demonstração, prova; manifestação; *to prove to demonstration,* provar concludentemente.

demonstrative, a. demonstrativo, concludente.

demoralize, v.t. desmoralizar; corromper; indisciplinar.

demote, v.t. despromover, baixar de posto.

demotion, s. despromoção.

demount, v.t. desmontar.

demur (demurring, demurred), v.i. objectar; pôr dúvidas; hesitar; criar dificuldades; s. objecção; vacilação.

demure, a. grave, sério; reservado; pudico; adv. *demurely,* gravemente.

demurral, s. objecção; hesitação; demora.

demurrer, s. pessoa hesitante ou escrupulosa; chicana.

den, s. caverna; covil, toca; espelunca; cubículo; *to beard the lion in his den,* arrostar contra uma pessoa temida.

denationalize, v.t. desnacionalizar.

denaturize, v.t. desnaturar; desfigurar.

denial, s. negação; recusa; repúdio; abstinência.

denier, s. negador, o que nega; antiga moeda.

denim, s. ganga; azulão.

denominate, v.t. denominar, dar nome a; intitular; chamar.

denomination, s. denominação, título; categoria.

denote, v.t. marcar, assinalar; caracterizar; designar; adv. *denotable,* marcadamente.

denouement, s. desenlace; fim.

denounce, v.t. denunciar; protestar contra; anunciar.

dense, a. denso, espesso, cerrado; estúpido. adv. *densely,* densamente.

densety, s. densidade; estupidez.

dent, v.t. fazer mossa; abrir boca em instrumento cortante; s. mossa; boca; dente, entalhe.

dental, a. dentário, dental; s. dental.

dentate, a. dentado.

dentifrice, s. dentifrício.

dentist, s. dentista.

dentition, s. dentição.

denture, s. dentadura.

denude, v.t. desnudar, despir; privar; *he was denuded of his rights,* ele foi privado dos seus direitos.

denunciation, s. denúncia; acusação; advertência.

deny, v.t. negar, desmentir; repudiar; *Peter denied Christ,* Pedro renegou Cristo; recusar-se.

deodorant, a. e s. desodorizante, desodorante.

deodorize, v.t. desodorizar, tirar o cheiro.

depart, v.i. partir, ir embora, sair; deixar alguém; morrer; *he departed from life,* ele morreu; desviar-se, divergir.

departed, a. e s. falecido; passado.

department, s. departamento; divisão territorial; repartição pública; *department store,* armazém geral.

departure, s. partida; afastamento, divergência, morte.

depende, v.i. pender, depender, estar sujeito; *she depends upon her work,* ela vive do seu trabalho; confiar, fiar-se, contar com.

dependable, a. digno de confiança; fidedigno; certo.

dependence, s. dependência, subordinação; confiança.

dependency, s. dependência, anexo, sucursal.

dependent, a. e s. dependente; condicionado; subordinado.

depict, v.t. pintar, retratar; descrever.

depilate, v.t. depilar.

deplane, *v.i.* desembarcar de um avião.

deplete, *v.t.* esvaziar, esgotar; desconges-tionar.

deplorable, *a.* deplorável, lamentável; *adv.* deplorably, lamentavelmente.

deplore, *v.t.* deplorar, lastimar; censurar.

deploy, *v.t.* e *v.i.* desenvolver(-se), estender (-se).

deployment, *s.* desenvolvimento.

depone, *v.t.* e *v.i.* depor, testemunhar.

deponent, *s.* e *a.* depoente, testemunha.

deport, *v.t.* deportar, desterrar; *to deport oneself,* comportar-se.

deportation, *s.* deportação, desterro; expulsão.

deportee, *s.* deportado, expatriado.

deportment, *s.* porte, postura, modos; pro-cedimento, conduta.

deposal, *s.* deposição, destituição, demissão.

depose, *v.t.* depor, demitir; *v.i.* depor, teste-munhar.

deposit, *v.t.* depositar, dar a guardar; colocar, pôr; *v.i.* depositar-se; *s.* depósito, coisa depositada; armazém; garantia.

depositor, *s.* depositante.

depot, *s.* armazém, depósito, arrecadação.

depravation, *s.* depravação; perversão.

deprave, *a.* depravado, corrupto, viciado; perverso.

deprecate, *v.t.* deprecar, implorar; *to deprecate someone's anger,* aplacar a cólera de alguém; desaprovar.

deprecating, *a.* suplicar; *adv. deprecatingly,* suplicantemente.

deprecation, *s.* súplica; desaprovação, protesto.

deprecative, *a.* depreciativo; suplicante; desaprovador; *adv. deprecatively,* deprecia-tivamente.

depreciate, *v.t.* depreciar, rebaixar, deprimir; *v.i.* desvalorizar(-se), baratear.

depreciating, *a.* depreciador.

depredate, *v.t.* saquear, pilhar.

depredation, *s.* saque, roubo.

depredator, *s.* saqueador.

depress, *v.t.* deprimir, humilhar; desanimar; desvalorizar.

depressed, *a.* desanimado; abaixado, *depressed classes,* castas inferiores.

depressing, *a.* depressivo; opressivo; desa-lentador; *adv. depressingly,* desalen-tadamente.

depression, *s.* depressão; concavidade; abatimento; crise económica.

deprivation, *s.* privação; carência; perda.

deprive, *v.t.* privar; destituir; excluir.

depth, *s.* profundidade; fundo; altura; abis-mo; sagacidade, agudeza; escuridão; *to be out of one's depth,* estar desnorteado.

deputation, *s.* delegação, missão, comis-são.

depute, *v.t.* delegar, incumbir.

deputy, *s.* deputado, representante.

derange, *v.t.* desarranjar, desconcertar; desarrumar; perturbar; tresloucar.

deranged, *a.* desarranjado; doido, treslou-cado.

derangement, *s.* desarranjo, desordem, transtorno.

derelict, *a.* abandonado, desprezado; sem dono; *s.* coisa abandonada, navio abando-nado; pária; empregado negligente.

dereliction, *s.* abandono, desleixo.

deride, *v.t.* escarnecer, mofar de; ridicu-larizar.

derisive, *a.* escarninho, irrisório.

derivation, *s.* derivação; origem, descen-dência.

derive, *v.t.* derivar; obter; deduzir; *v.i.* derivar-se, descender.

derogate, *v.t.* depreciar, desluzir; degenerar; *this man derogates from his father,* este homem desmente o seu pai.

derogation, *s.* depreciação; deslustre; degradação.

derrick, *s.* guindaste.

descend, *v.i.* descer, baixar, cair; derivar. 1) *he descends from a noble family,* ele descende de uma família nobre; cair sobre, invadir; *v.i.* descer. 2) *to descend a hill,* descer uma colina.

descendant, *s.* descendente.

descent, *s.* descida; queda; baixa; encosta.

describe, *v.t.* descrever; explicar.

description, *s.* descrição, características, tipo; espécie, categoria; *he is a criminal of the worst description,* ele é um criminoso da pior espécie.

descriptive, *a.* descritivo.

descry, *v.t.* observar, avistar; perceber, des-cobrir.

desecrate, *v.t.* dessagrar; profanar.

desecration, *s.* desconsagração; profa-nação.

desert, *v.t.* e *v.i.* desertar; abandonar; *s.* mérito, merecimento.

desert, *s.* e *a.* deserto, ermo, solitário.

deserter, *s.* desertor.

desertion, s. deserção.

deserve, v.t. e v.i. merecer, fazer jus a; *one good turn deserves another,* amor com amor se paga.

deserved, a. merecido, justo; *adv. deservedly,* condignamente.

deserving, a. e s. digno, merecedor; mérito; *adv. deservingly,* condignamente.

design, v.t. e v.i. propor, ter intenção de; projectar, criar; desenhar; s. desígnio, intenção; projecto, desenho, esboço.

designate, v.t. designar; nomear; a. designado.

designation, s. designação; nomeação; título.

designed, a. propositado, intencional; destinado. *adv. designedly,* intencionalmente.

designer, s. planejador; desenhista; inventor.

designing, a. insidioso, intrigante; astuto.

desirability, s. conveniência; ânsia.

desirable, a. apetecível; atraente; conveniente; *adv. desirably,* dum modo agradável.

desire, v.t. desejar, querer; pedir; s. desejo, aspiração.

desirous, a. desejoso; *adv.* desejosamente.

desist, v.t. desistir, renunciar.

desistance, s. desistência.

desk, s. carteira, escrivaninha, secretária; estante.

desolate, v.t. desolar, desvastar, despovoar; a. deserto; desolado.

desolation, s. desolação; solidão; desconsolo.

despair, v.t. desesperar, perder a esperança; s. desespero.

despairing, a. desesperante; *adv. despairingly,* desesperadamente.

desperado, s. malfeitor, facínora.

desperate, a. desesperado, perdido; furioso.

desperately, adv. desesperadamente, *desperately in love,* desesperadamente apaixonado.

desperation, s. desespero; furor, *to be urged to desperation,* ser levado ao desespero.

despise, v.t. desprezar, detestar, menosprezar.

despite, s. despeito, rancor, má vontade, aversão; *in despite of,* a despeito de, apesar de.

despiteful, a. rancoroso, acintoso; *adv. despitefully,* com rancor, com despeito.

despoil, v.t. saquear, pilhar; espoliar, despojar; *to despoil someone of his honor,* desonrar alguém.

despoliation, s. espoliação, saque, roubo.

despond, v.i. desanimar, descoroçoar, desalentar-se; perder a esperança.

despondence, s. desânimo, abatimento.

despondent, a. desalentado, desanimado; *adv. despondently,* desanimadamente.

despot, s. déspota, tirano.

despotic, a. despótico, tirânico, opressivo.

despotism, s. despotismo, tirania.

dessert, s. sobremesa.

destination, s. destino; fim, propósito; paradeiro.

destine, v.t. destinar; reservar, consagrar.

destiny, s. destino, fado, sina.

destitute, a. destituído, falto; carente, pobre; *adv. destitutely,* ao desamparo, pobremente.

destitution, s. miséria; privação, desamparo.

destroy, v.t. destruir, arrasar; exterminar; invalidar.

destroyer, s. destruidor; contratorpedeiro.

destructible, destrutível.

destruction, s. destruição; arrasamento; extermínio; ruína.

destructive, a. destruidor, demolidor, fatal.

destructivity, s. tendência destruidora, capacidade destruidora.

destructor, s. destruidor; forno de incineração.

desuetude, s. desuso.

desultory, s. variável, irregular, vago.

detach, v.t. separar, destacar, arrancar.

detachable, a. destacável, separável; amovível.

detached, a. separado, isolado; desprendido, desapaixonado.

detachment, s. separação, desligamento; indiferença, desprendimento; imparcialidade.

detail, s. detalhe, pormenor; minúcia; *to go into details,* entrar em pormenores.

detailed, a. detalhado, pormenorizado.

detain, v.t. deter; fazer esperar; impedir.

detainer, s. detenção; retenção; processo para reaver bens.

detect, v.t. descobrir, desmascarar, revelar.

detection, s. descoberta.

detective, s. investigador policial; a. que serve para descobrir.

detector, s. descobridor.

detent, s. detentor, alavanca, gatilho; escape de relógio.

detention, s. detenção; prisão.

deter (deterring, deterred), v.t. dissuadir, desviar.

deteriorate, v.t. e v.i. deteriorar(-se), estragar(-se); danificar.

deterioration, s. deterioração, dano.

determinant, a. determinante, decisivo. s. causa determinante.

determinate, a. determinado, decidido; definitivo.

determination, s. determinação, orientação; decisão.

determinative, a. determinativo; decisivo; s. móbil determinante; *determinatively,* determinadamente.

determine, v.t. determinar, decidir; v.i. concluir; resolver-se.

determined, a. resolvido, decidido, *a very determined girl,* uma rapariga determinada; *adv. determinedly,* dum modo resoluto.

determinism, s. determinismo.

deterrence, s. repressão.

deterrent, a. repressivo, dissuasivo; s. coibição, repressão.

detest, v.t. destestar, odiar.

detestable, a. destestável, odioso, insuportável.

detestation, s. ódio, aversão.

dethrone, v.t. destronar, depor.

dethronement, s. destronamento.

detonate, v.t. e v.i. detonar, causar detonação.

detour, s. volta, rodeio; desvio.

detract, v.t. tirar, retirar, diminuir; caluniar, difamar.

detraction, s. detracção, calúnia.

detractive, a. detractivo, difamatório.

detractor, s. detractor, difamador.

detrain, v.t. e v.i. desembarcar dum comboio, descarregar um comboio.

detriment, s. detrimento, prejuízo.

detrimental, a. prejudicial.

detrition, s. detrição, desgaste.

detritus, s. detritos, desperdícios; entulho.

detruncate, v.t. destroncar, podar; mutilar; decapitar.

deuce, s. dois, duque (cartas e dados); dois, iguais, pares (jogo); demónio, diacho, praga; *deuce take it!,* diabos o levem!

deuced, a. dos diabos; *the deuced woman,* o diabo da mulher.

devastate, v.t. devastar, assolar; gastar.

devastation, s. devastação, assolação.

develop, v.t. desenvolver; fomentar; revelar (fot.); v.i. desenvolver-se, progredir.

developer, s. revelador (fot.).

development, s. desenvolvimento; revelação (fot.); crescimento, progresso.

deviate, v.t. desviar, afastar; v.i. desviar-se, divergir.

deviation, s. desvio; divergência.

device, s. plano, projecto, invento, dispositivo; estratagema; lema, divisa; *to leave the child to his own devices,* deixar a criança à sua vontade.

devil (devilling, devilled), v.t. condimentar, apimentar; v.i. apoquentar, fazer o trabalho desagradável; demónio, diabo. 1) *like the devil,* com muita energia. 2) *devil's books,* cartas de jogar. 3) *between the devil and the deep sea,* entre a espada e a parede. 4) *blue devils,* melancolia, tédio. 5) *the devil a bit,* nem pensar!, de modo nenhum. 6) *devil-dodger,* pregador, beato. 7) *devil-fish,* polvo.

deviled, a. apimentado, picante.

devilish, a. diabólico; execrável; endiabrado; excessivo; *adv. devilishly,* diabolicamente, excessivamente.

devilment, s. diabrura; estouvamento.

devilry, s. bruxaria; perversidade, crueldade; obra do demónio.

devious, a. remoto, distante; perdido; tortuoso; errante, vagabundo. *adv. deviously,* errantemente.

devisable, a. imaginável, ideável; legável.

devisal, s. ideia, plano.

devise, v.t. idear, inventar; legar; s. legação.

devoid, a. destituído, carente; isento.

devoirs, s. deveres; civilidade; respeitos.

devolution, s. transmissão; devolução.

devolve, v.t. entregar, transmitir por direito de sucessão; passar.

devote, v.t. devotar, consagrar, dedicar; destinar; condenar.

devoted, a. devotado, dedicado; condenado.

devotee, s. partidário; devoto; fanático.

devotion, s. devoção, dedicação; veneração.

devour, v.t. devorar, tragar; dissipar; devastar.

devouringly, adv. vorazmente.

devout, a. devoto, piedoso, religioso; *adv. devoutly,* devotadamente.

dew, s. orvalho, relento; influência benéfica. 1) *the dew of youth,* no frescor da juventude. 2) *dew point,* ponto de condensação.

3) *dew-berry*, amora. 4) *dewdrop*, gota de orvalho. 5) *dewfall*, orvalhada.

dewy, *a.* orvalhado.

dexter, *a.* destro; auspicioso.

dextery, *s.* destreza, habilidade; tino, esperteza.

dexterous, dextrous, *a.* destro, hábil; esperto; *adv. dextrously,* habilmente.

diabetes, *s.* diabetes.

diabetic, *a.* e *s.* diabético.

diabolic, *a.* diabólico; *adv. diabolically,* diabolicamente.

diadem, *s.* diadema, coroa.

diagnose, *v.t.* diagnosticar.

diagnosis, *s.* diagnose, diagnóstico.

diagnostic, *a.* diagnóstico; *s.* sinal, sintoma.

diagram, *s.* diagrama, gráfico.

dial, *v.t.* medir, indicar; *s.* relógio de sol; mostrador de relógio.

dialect, *s.* dialecto, linguagem.

dialectic, *s.* dialéctica; *a.* dialéctico; *adv. dialectically,* dialecticamente.

dialectician, *s.* versado em dialéctica.

dialogue, *s.* diálogo; palestra.

dialysis, *s.* diálise.

diamond, *s.* diamante, brilhante; ouros (naipe de cartas). 1) *a rough diamond,* pessoa rica e grosseira. 2) *black diamond,* carvão mineral. 3) *diamond black,* diamante não lapidado.

diapason, *s.* diapasão.

diaper, *s.* pano adamascado; toalha; fralda de criança; padrão.

diaphanous, *a.* diáfano; transparente.

diaphragm, *s.* diafragma.

diarist, *s.* jornalista; aquele que escreve um diário.

diarrhea, *s.* diarreia.

diary, *s.* diário, jornal.

diatribe, *s.* discussão prolongada; invectiva.

dib (dibbing, dibbed) *v.t.* mergulhar.

dibble, *s.* instrumento para abrir buracos na terra; plantador; *v.t.* plantar com o *dibble*.

dice, *s.* dados (de jogar); *v.t.* jogar aos dados; cortar em cubos; desperdiçar ao jogo.

dickens, *s.* e *interj.* diabo! diacho!

dicker, *s.* troca, trato; *v.t.* e *v.i.* barganhar; regatear.

dickey, dicky, *s.* peitilho postiço; avental; boleia; lugar do cocheiro; passarinho; inferior.

dictate, *v.t.* ditar, mandar; *s.* ditame; máxima; ditado.

dictation, *s.* ditado; ordem arbitrária; prepotência.

dictator, *s.* ditador.

dictatorial, *a.* ditatorial; prepotente. *adv. dictatorially,* ditatorialmente.

dictatorship, *s.* ditadura.

diction, *s.* dicção; estilo; expressão pela linguagem.

dictionary, *s.* dicionário.

dictum, *s.* dito, máxima; sentença de tribunal.

didactic, *a.* didáctico, instrutivo.

diddle, *v.t.* enganar, burlar.

diddler, *s.* burlão.

didn't, contracção de *did not.*

die (dying, died), *v.t.* morrer, fenecer, extinguir-se. 1) *to die in one's bed,* morrer de velhice. 2) *to die the death,* sofrer as agonias. 3) *to die in harness,* morrer a trabalhar. 4) *to be dying for,* estar ansioso. 5) *to die in one's shoes,* termorte violenta. *s.* dado para jogar; cubo.

die-hard, *s.* político conservador ferrenho.

diet, *s.* dieta, regime alimentar, alimento; *v.t.* pôr a dieta.

differ, *v.t.* diferir, discordar; ser diferente; contender; *he differed with his partner,* ele desentendeu-se com o sócio.

difference, *s.* diferença, distinção; controvérsia, desavença. 1) *to make a difference between two persons,* tratar duas pessoas de modo diferente. 2) *to split the difference,* adoptar um meio-termo. *v.t.* diferenciar, distinguir.

different, *a.* diferente, diverso; incomum.

differentiate, *v.t.* diferenciar, distinguir; *v.i.* diferenciar-se.

differentiation, *s.* diferenciação; diferença.

differently, *adv.* diferentemente.

difficult, *a.* difícil, árduo.

difficulty, *s.* dificuldade; obstáculo; objecção; hesitação, dúvida.

diffidence, *s.* desconfiança, suspeita; timidez, insegurança.

diffident, *a.* tímido, hesitante, acanhado; desconfiado.

diffuse, *a.* difuso, espalhado, disperso; *v.t.* e *v.i.* difundir(-se), espalhar(-se), derramar (-se); *adv. diffusely,* extensivamente, com redundância.

diffusible, *a.* difusível.

diffusion, *s.* difusão, propagação.

diffusive, *a.* difusivo, difuso; propagador; *adv. diffusively,* difusamente.

dig (digging, dug ou **digged),** v.t. cavar, escavar; v.i. trabalhar com enxada, penetrar cavando; pesquisar, esgaravatar. 1) to dig up, desenterrar; s. estocada, empurrão; remoque, censura. 2) the boy is a dig, o rapaz é um estudante brioso.

digest, v.t. classificar, codificar; pensar, meditar; digerir; aguentar, conformar-se com; v.i. digerir, fazer a digestão; assimilar--se; s. sumário, selecção, resumo.

digestant, a. e s. digestivo.

digestible, a. digerível, digestível; adv. digestibly, digerivelmente.

digestion, s. digestão.

digestive, a. digestivo; s. digestivo; medicamento que auxilia a digestão.

digger, s. cavador; cavadeira (instrumento); pessoa trabalhadora.

digging, s. escavação; (pl.) mina de ouro; casa, toca.

digit, s. dígito; algarismo; dedo da mão ou do pé; unidade.

digital, a. digital; digitado; s. tecla.

dignified, a. dignificado; digno, nobre; promovido a uma dignidade.

dignify, v.t. dignificar, honrar; condecorar.

dignitary, s. dignitário. a. eminente; honorífico.

dignity, s. dignidade; valor, mérito; respeitabilidade; cargo, emprego.

digress, v.i. digressar, divagar.

digression, s. digressão, divagação; excursão.

dike, dyke, s. dique, represa; vala, canal; v.t. represar; pôr dique.

dilacerate, v.t. dilacerar, fazer em pedaços.

dilapidate, v.t. dilapidar, arruinar; v.i. arruinar-se.

dilapidation, s. dilapidação; ruína.

dilate, v.t. dilatar; ampliar, aumentar; v.i. dilatar-se; estender-se.

dilation, s. dilatação.

dilemma, s. dilema; embaraço; beco sem saída; to be in a sad dilemma, estar entre a bigorna e o martelo.

dilettante, s. diletante; amador.

diligence, s. diligência; cuidado, atenção; s. diligência (carruagem).

diligent, a. diligente, aplicado, trabalhador; adv. diligently.

diluent, a. diluente; dissolvente; s. diluente; líquido diluidor.

dilute, v.t. diluir; dissolver; enfraquecer; a. diluído; aguado; fraco.

dilution, s. diluição.

diluvium, s. dilúvio.

dim (dimming, dimmed), v.t. e v.i. obscurecer; ofuscar; a. obscuro, opaco; confuso; sombrio.

dime, s. décimo do dólar; novela; dime novel, novela barata.

dimension, s. dimensão, medida, tamanho.

diminish, v.t. e v.i. diminuir, minorar; enfraquecer, debilitar.

diminution, s. diminuição, redução.

diminutive, s. diminutivo; diminuto.

dimity, s. fustão, tecido de algodão.

dimple, s. covinha no queixo ou na face; v.i. formar covinhas no rosto.

dimply, a. que forma covinhas no rosto.

din (dinning, dinned), v.t. aturdir; ensurdecer; repisar; to din into someone's ears, matraquear os ouvidos; v.i. estrondear, fazer alarido; s. barulheira, gritaria; bulha.

dine, v.t. dar de jantar; alimentar; v.i. jantar.

diner, s. aquele que janta; vagão-restaurante.

dingle, s. vale estreito.

dingy, a. escuro; manchado; sujo.

dinner, s. jantar, refeição principal do dia. 1) a farewell dinner, jantar de despedida. 2) dinner-set, serviço de loiça para jantar. 3) dinner-jacket, "smoking".

dint, s. pancada, golpe; força; mossa; by dint of, à força de.

diocese, s. diocese.

dip (dipping, dipped), v.t. mergulhar, emergir; molhar; baixar a vela (dum barco). 1) to dip a sail, baixar a vela. 2) to dip the flag, saudar com a bandeira; v.i. mergulhar--se, enfiar a mão; desaparecer; s. imersão, mergulho, banho.

diphtheria, s. difteria.

diphthong, s. ditongo.

diploma, s. diploma.

diplomacy, s. diplomacia; tacto; circunspecção.

diplomat, s. diplomata.

diplomatic, a. diplomático; diplomatic body ou corps, corpo diplomático; hábil, discreto; adv. diplomatically, diplomaticamente.

diplomatics, s. diplomacia, diplomática.

diplomatize, v.i. exercer funções diplomáticas; proceder com diplomacia.

dipper, s. concha da sopa; mergulhador; mergulhão, torda mergulheira, melro ribeirinho. 1) Big Dipper, Ursa Maior. 2) Little Dipper, Ursa Menor.

dire, *a.* terrível, horrendo; avassalador; *the dire sisters,* as Fúrias.

direct, *v.t.* dirigir, guiar, conduzir; apontar; reger, governar; *v.i.* dar instruções, dar ordens, mandar; *a.* directo, direito, recto; imediato.

direction, *s.* sentido, rumo, lado; tendência; endereço; condução, governo, instrução, *pl.* instruções.

directive, *a.* directivo, regulador; *s.* directiva, directriz.

directly, *adv.* e *conj.* directamente, em linha recta; imediatamente.

director, *s.* director; orientador.

directory, *a.* directório; directoria.

dirge, *s.* canto fúnebre.

dirt, *s.* sujeira, imundície, lama; maledicência. 1) *to fling dirt at,* caluniar. 2) *dirt cheap,* muito barato. 3) *to eat dirt,* suportar humilhações.

dirty, *a.* sujo, porco, imundo; sórdido, desprezível; *v.t.* emporcalhar; manchar.

disability, *s.* inabilidade; incapacidade; invalidez.

disable, *v.t.* incapacitar, inabilitar; inutilizar.

disabled, *a.* incapacitado, incapaz; inválido.

disabuse, *v.t.* desenganar; abrir os olhos.

disaccord, *v.i.* discordar, divergir; *s.* discordância, desacordo.

disaccustom, *v.t.* desacostumar.

disadvantage, *s.* desvantagem, prejuízo.

disadvantageous, *a.* desvantajoso, inconveniente.

disaffect, *v.t.* desafeiçoar; descontentar; indispor-se com.

disaffected, *a.* desafecto; desleal; hostil.

disaffection, *s.* desafeição; deslealdade.

disagree, *vi.* discordar; contender.

disagreeable, *a.* desagradável; mal-humorado, irritadiço; coisa incómoda. *adv. disagreeably,* desagradavelmente.

disagreement, *s.* desacordo, divergência; recusa; desavença.

disallow, *v.t.* desaprovar; negar a autoridade; censurar.

disallowance, *s.* desaprovação; proibição.

disappear, *v.i.* desaparecer.

disappearance, *s.* desaparecimento.

disappoint, *v.t.* desapontar; desiludir; faltar à palavra.

disappointment, *s.* desapontamento; desilusão; contrariedade.

disapprobation, *s.* desaprovação, censura.

disapproval, *s.* reprovação, censura.

disapprove, *v.t.* desaprovar, reprovar, censurar; *township disapproves this building project,* a câmara condena este projecto; *adv. disapprovingly,* com desaprovação.

disarm, *v.t.* desarmar; tornar inofensivo; desguarnecer; *v.i.* depor as armas.

disarmamente, *s.* desarmamento.

disarming, *a.* que desarma; desarmante; conciliatório; cândido.

disarrange, *v.t.* desarranjar, desordenar; desorganizar.

disarray, *v.t.* desordenar, desarranjar; *s.* desarranjo.

disaster, *s.* desastre, desgraça; miséria; calamidade.

disastrous, *a.* desastroso; *adv. disastrously,* desastrosamente.

disavow, *v.t.* negar, repudiar.

disband, *v.t.* debandar; licenciar (tropas); despedir; expulsar; *v.i.* dispersar-se, separar-se.

disbandment, *s.* licenciamento.

disbar (disbarring, disbarred), *v.t.* excluir (advogado) do foro judicial.

disbelief, *s.* descrença, incredulidade.

disbelieve, *v.t.* descrer.

disbeliever, *s.* descrente.

disburse, *v.t.* desembolsar, despender.

disbursement, *s.* desembolso, despesa.

disc, *s.* disco; patena; *disc jockey,* locutor que põe discos a tocar.

discard, *v.t.* e *v.i.* descartar(-se), desfazer(-se); despedir; banir do espírito; *s.* refugo.

discern, *v.t.* perceber, distinguir, discernir; avistar; *v.i.* fazer distinção.

discernible, *a.* discernível, perceptível; visível. *adv. discernibly,* perceptivelmente.

discerning, *a.* penetrante, perspicaz; *adv. discerningly,* penetrantemente.

discernment, *s.* discernimento, percepção; agudeza; critério.

discharge, *v.t.* descarregar; desembarcar; disparar; cumprir; dispensar; despedir; libertar; *v.i.* descarregar(-se); desembocar; destingir; *s.* descarga; resgate, recibo; libertação; quitação.

disciple, *s.* discípulo; apóstolo; adepto; sequaz.

discipline, *v.t.* disciplinar; dominar, educar, corrigir; *s.* disciplina; ensino; castigo.

disclaim, *v.t.* negar, recusar. *v.i.* renunciar a um direito.

disclamation, *s.* renúncia, repúdio.

disclose, v.t. descobrir, pôr à vista; revelar, divulgar; mostrar.

disclosure, s. descoberta, exposição; divulgação.

discolor, discolour, v.t. descolorar.

discoloration, s. descoloração.

discomfit, v.t. desbaratar, destroçar, vencer; transtornar os planos a.

discomfiture, s. derrota; desapontamento.

discomfort, v.t. desconfortar, incomodar, desconsolar; s. desconforto, mal-estar; desconsolo; intranquilidade.

discomfortable, a. sem conforto, incómodo; desassossegado.

discompose, v.t. descompor, desordenar; vexar.

discomposure, s. desordem; transtorno; perturbação.

disconcert, v.t. desconcertar, confundir, embaraçar; transtornar, estragar os planos.

disconcerting, a. desconcertante, perturbador; adv. disconcertingly, desconcertantemente.

disconnect, v.t. desligar, desunir, separar.

disconnected, a. desligado, separado; incoerente, desconexo.

disconnection, s. desconexão; separação; incoerência.

disconsolate, a. desconsolado, triste; desanimado, a disconsolate room: um quarto desanimador; adv. disconsolately, desconsoladamente.

disconsolation, s. desconsolo, tristeza, desolação.

discontent, a. descontente, insatisfeito; s. descontentamento, insatisfação. v.t. descontentar, desagradar.

discontented, a. descontente, desgostoso; adv. discontentedly, de má vontade.

discontentment, s. descontentamento.

discontinue, v.t. interromper; suspender; cessar.

discontinuity, s. descontinuidade; interrupção.

discontinuous, a. descontínuo; interrompido; adv. discontinuously, descontinuadamente.

discord, v.t. discordar; desavir-se; her opinions discord with mine, a opinião dela difere da minha. s. discórdia.

discordance, discordancy, s. desacordo; discordância.

discordant, a. discordante, discrepante; adv. discordantly, discordantemente.

discount, v.t. descontar, deduzir, diminuir; at a discount, com desconto.

discountenance, s. v.t. desfavorecer, desencorajar, desaprovar.

discourage, v.t. desencorajar, desanimar, desaconselhar; desviar.

discouragement, s. desencorajamento; desaprovação; desânimo, desalento.

discouraging, a. desalentador, deprimente; adv. discouragingly, de modo desanimador.

discourse, s. discurso; dissertação; v.i. discursar; discorrer.

discourteous, a. descortês, rude; adv. discourteously, descortesmente.

discourtesy, s. descortesia, indelicadeza.

discover, v.t. descobrir, revelar; inventar.

discovery, s. descoberta; revelação; invenção.

discredit, v.t. descrer, desacreditar; s. descrédito; desconfiança; desonra.

discreditable, a. desabonador, vergonhoso, ignominioso. adv. discreditably, ignominiosamente.

discreet, a. discreto, circunspecto; prudente; adv. discreetly, discretamente.

discrepancy, s. discrepância, disparidade, diferença.

discrepant, discrepante, discordante, diferente.

discrete, a. distinto, individualizado; abstracto; descontínuo; adv. discretely, distintamente.

discretion, s. discrição, prudência; vontade. 1) to eat at discretion, comer à vontade. 2) to surrender at discretion, render-se incondicionalmente.

discriminate, v.t. discriminar, diferenciar, separar; a. discriminado, separado; adv. discriminately, distintamente.

discriminating, a. discriminador; judicioso; adv. discriminatingly, discriminadamente, judiciosamente.

discrimination, s. discriminação, diferenciação, parcialidade; discernimento.

discriminative, a. discriminativo; distintivo, parcial; adv. discriminatively, discriminativamente, distintivamente.

discursive, a. divagador, discursivo, errante; adv. discursively, de modo divagante.

discuss, v.t. discutir, debater; examinar; tratar.

discussion, s. discussão, debate; exame.

disdain, v.t. desdenhar, desprezar; s. desdém, desprezo.

disdainful, *a.* desdenhoso, soberbo, arrogante; *adv. disdainfully,* desdenhosamente.

disease, *s.* doença, enfermidade.

diseased, *a.* doente, enfermo; mórbido, corrompido.

disembark, *v.t.* e *v.i.* desembarcar.

disembarkation, *s.* desembarque.

disembarkment, *s.* desembarque.

disembarrass, *v.t.* desembaraçar, livrar.

disembody, *v.t.* separar do corpo; dispersar, licenciar.

disenable, *v.t.* inabilitar.

disenchant, *v.t.* desencantar.

disenchantment, *s.* desencanto.

disencumber, *v.t.* desincumbir; desembaraçar.

disengage, *v.i.* e *v.t.* desprender(-se), desembaraçar(-se); desocupar.

disengaged, *a.* desprendido; sem compromisso; desocupado, livre.

disengagement, *s.* desprendimento; desocupação; rompimento.

disentagle, *v.t.* desenredar; desligar.

disesteem, *v.t.* desprezar, ter em pouca estima; *s.* desestima, descrédito.

disfavor, *s.* desfavor; desvalimento; *v.t.* desfavorecer, desestimar.

disfeature, *v.t.* desfigurar, deformar.

disfigure, *v.t.* desfigurar, deformar, mutilar; manchar.

disfranchise, *v.t.* privar dos direitos civis ou políticos.

disgorge, *v.t.* vomitar; devolver; desaguar.

disgrace, *s.* ignomínia, desonra; *v.t.* desonrar, desgraçar.

disgraceful, *a.* vergonhoso, desonroso; *adv. disgracefully,* ignominiosamente.

disguise, *v.t.* disfarçar, dissimular, mascarar; *s.* disfarce, máscara.

disguised, *a.* disfarçado, mascarado.

disgust, *v.t.* enojar, repugnar; desgostar, enfadar.

disgusted, enojado, nauseado; *adv. disgustedly,* desgostosamente.

disgustful, *a.* nojento, repugnante, repelente; *adv. disgustfully,* repelentemente.

disgusting, *a.* nojento, asqueroso, desagradável; *adv. disgustingly,* de forma nojenta.

dish, *s.* prato (de servir), travessa; comida. 1) *standing dish,* comida de todos os dias. 2) *dish-cloth,* pano de loiça. 3) *dish of gossip,* cavaqueira.

dishabille, *s.* traje caseiro, roupão.

dishallow, *v.t.* profanar, violar.

dishearten, *v.t.* desanimar.

disherit, *v.t.* deserdar.

dishful, *s.* pratada.

dishonest, *a.* desonesto, infiel; fraudulento; *adv. dishonestly,* desonestamente.

dishonesty, *s.* desonestidade, deslealdade.

dishonor, dishonour, *s.* desonra, vergonha; infâmia; insulto. *v.t.* desonrar, infamar; insultar.

dishouse, *v.t.* desalojar, despejar.

disillusion, *s.* desilusão, desengano; *v.t.* desiludir, desenganar.

disillusive, *a.* desilusivo, desenganador.

disinclination, *s.* desafecto, aversão.

disincline, *v.t.* desinclinar, indispor.

disinfect, *v.t.* desinfectar.

disinfectant, *a. s.* desinfectante.

disinfection, *s.* desinfecção, assepsia.

disinfest, *v.t.* desinfestar.

disinherit, *v.t.* deserdar.

disintegrate, *v.t.* e *v.i.* desintegrar, desagregar.

disinter, *v.t.* desenterrar, exumar.

disinterest, *v.t.* desinteressar(-se).

disinterested, *a.* desinteressado, imparcial.

disjoin, *v.t.* desunir, separar.

disjoint, *v.t.* desconjuntar; deslocar (membro); desmembrar; trinchar (ave).

disjointed, *a.* desconjuntado, deslocado; desconexo; *adv. disjointedly,* desconjuntadamente, desunidamente.

disjunct, *a.* desunido; desconexo.

disjunction, *s.* desunião.

disk, *s.* disco; patena; gravação fonográfica.

dislikable, *a.* desagradável, antipático.

dislike, *v.t.* antipatizar, não gostar de; *s.* antipatia, aversão.

dislocate, *v.t.* deslocar; desconjuntar; perturbar.

dislocation, *s.* deslocação; desconjuntação.

dislodge, *v.t.* desalojar; *v.i.* mudar-se.

disloyal, *a.* desleal; falso; *adv. disloyally,* deslealmente.

dismal, *a.* triste, melancólico; sombrio; *the dismal science,* a economia política. *s.* (pl.) melancolia; coisas tristes.

dismantle, *v.t.* desguarnecer; despir; demolir.

dismay, *v.t.* aterrar; desanimar; *s.* terror; desalento.

dismember, *v.t.* desmembrar; dividir.

dismiss, *v.t.* despedir; licenciar; mandar embora; repudiar; *s.* ordem de debandar.

dismissal, s. demissão; liberação; abandono.

dismount, v.t. desmontar, desarmar; v.i. desmontar-se, descer.

disobedience, s. desobediência, rebeldia.

disobedient, a. desobediente, rebelde; adv. disobediently, desobedientemente.

disobey, v.t. desobedecer, transgredir.

disorder, s. desordem, confusão; irregularidade.

disordered, a. desordenado; doente.

disorderly, a. desordenado, confuso; turbulento; adv. desordenadamente.

disorganize, v.t. desorganizar, pôr em desordem.

disown, v.t. negar, repudiar; this man disowned his child, este homem não reconheceu o filho.

dispair, v.t. separar.

disparage, v.t. rebaixar, desacreditar; escarnecer.

disparagement, s. menosprezo.

disparity, s. disparidade; diferença.

dispatch, v.t. despachar, enviar; matar; s. despacho, envio; pressa; homicídio.

dispel (dispelling, dispelled), v.t. dispersar; espalhar; dissipar; expelir.

dispensable, a. dispensável, prescindível.

dispensary, s. dispensário; farmácia.

dispensation, s. distribuição; disposição; isenção, dispensa.

dispense, v.t. dispensar; distribuir; desobrigar; fazer justiça; to dispense a prescription, aviar uma receita.

disperse, v.t. dispersar, debandar; espalhar; dissipar; v.i. dispersar-se; dissipar-se.

dispersed, a. disperso, espalhado; adv. dispersedly, dispersadamente.

displace, v.t. deslocar, remover; desalojar; demitir.

displacement, s. deslocamento, deslocação; substituição; demissão.

display, v.t. expor, apresentar; estender; arvorar; s. exibição; aparato, ostentação.

displease, v.t. desagradar, antipatizar; ofender.

displeasure, s. desagrado, descontentamento; indignação; desgosto.

dispose, v.t. e v.i. dispor, colocar; predispor; assentar. 1) ill-disposed towards, não estar predisposto em relação a. 2) to be well disposed of, bem assente, bem casado.

disposition, s. disposição, ordem; (pl.) preparativos, plano; tendência; humor.

dispossess, v.t. desapossar, desalojar.

disprove, v.t. refutar, provar a falsidade de.

dispute, v.t. disputar; discutir; s. disputa, contenda.

disqualify, v.t. desqualificar; incapacitar.

disquiet, v.t. desinquietar, desassossegar; a. inquieto; a. desassossego.

disquietude, s. intranquilidade, desassossego.

disregard, v.t. descurar, desconsiderar; s. descuido, desprezo.

disregardful, a. desatento, negligente.

disreputable, a. desonroso, desacreditado; vil; adv. disreputably, ignominiosamente.

disrepute, s. descrédito; mau nome.

disrespect, s. desrespeito, desconsideração, irreverência; v.t. desconsiderar, faltar ao respeito.

disrespectable, a. pouco respeitável, não merecedor de respeito.

disrespectful, a. desrespeitoso, irreverente, grosseiro; adv. disrespectfully, irreverentemente.

disrobe, v.t. e v.i. despir(-se), privar(-se).

disrupt, v.t. despedaçar, dilacerar; a. despedaçado; partido.

disruption, s. rompimento, rotura.

dissatisfaction, s. descontentamento, insatisfação.

dissatisfy, v.t. desagradar, desgostar.

dissect, v.t. dissecar, anatomizar; examinar com minúcia.

dissected, a. dissecado; recortado; dissected puzzle, jogo de paciência.

dissection, s. dissecação, anatomia.

dissemblance, s. dissimulação, hipocrisia.

dissemble, v.t. e v.i. dissimular, fingir.

dissembler, s. hipócrita, fingido.

disseminate, v.t. disseminar, espalhar; divulgar.

dissension, s. dissensão.

dissent, v.i. dissentir, discordar, divergir; s. dissensão, discórdia.

dissenter, s. dissidente, não conformista.

dissentient, a. e s. dissidente, discordante.

dissenting, a. discordante, contrário; adv. dissentingly, discordantemente.

dissentious, a. discordante, faccioso.

dissert, dissertate, v.i. dissertar, discorrer.

dissertation, s. dissertação.

disserve, v.t. prejudicar; servir mal.

disservice, s. dano, prejuízo.

dissever, v.t. e v.i. separar(-se), dividir(-se).

dissidence, s. desacordo, divergência.

dissident, *a.* dissidente, divergente; *s.* dissidente.

dissimilar, *s.* dissemelhante, diferente; *adv. dissimilarly,* dissemelhantemente.

dissimilation, *s.* dissimilação, diferenciação.

dissimulate, *v.t.* e *v.i.* dissimular, disfarçar; fingir.

dissipate, *v.t.* dissipar, dispersar; desfazer; esbanjar; *v.i.* dissipar-se, desaparecer; entregar-se à dissipação.

dissipation, *s.* dissipação; desperdício; libertinagem.

dissociate, *v.t.* dissociar, separar, dividir; decompor.

dissociation, *s.* dissociação, separação.

dissolute, *a.* dissoluto, libertino, devasso; *adv. dissolutely,* de modo dissoluto.

dissolution, *s.* dissolução; ruína.

dissolvable, *a.* dissolúvel; decomponível.

dissolve, *v.t.* dissolver, derreter; separar; anular. *v.i.* dissolver-se; evaporar-se; decompor-se.

dissonance, *s.* dissonância.

dissonant, *a.* dissonante; incongruente; *adv. dissonantly,* com dissonância.

dissuad, *v.t.* dissuadir; desviar.

dissuasion, *s.* dissuasão.

dissuasive, *a.* dissuasivo; *adv. dissuasively,* dissuasivamente.

dissuasiveness, *s.* qualidade de dissuasivo.

distaff, *s.* roca; mulheres; *the distaff side,* ramo feminino da família.

distance, *s.* distância, afastamento; respeito; altivez. 1) *at a distance,* de longe em longe. 2) *to keep one at a distance,* guardar distância, não permitir familiaridades. 3) *to know one's distance,* saber o seu lugar; *v.i.* distanciar, espaçar; distanciar-se de; vencer.

distant, *a.* distante, afastado, distanciado; *adv. distantly,* a distância.

distaste, *v.t.* não gostar de, ter aversão; *s.* aversão, nojo; fastio.

distasteful, *a.* desagradável; repugnante; insípido; *adv. distastefully,* desagradavelmente.

distastefulness, *s.* insipidez; falta de sabor.

distemper, *v.t.* perturbar, indispor; irritar-se; destemperar; pintar; *s.* indisposição; esgana (nos animais); destempero; pintura.

distend, *v.t.* estender, alargar; *v.i.* dilatar-se, expandir-se.

distention, distension, *s.* distensão, dilatação.

distill, distil (distilling, destilled), *v.t.* destilar, submeter à destilação; *v.i.* destilar, gotejar, passar pela destilação.

distillation, *s.* destilação; purificação; essência.

distiller, *s.* destilador, alambique.

distillery, *s.* destilaria.

distilment, *s.* destilação.

distinct, *a.* distinto, diferente; claro, preciso; marcado.

distinction, *s.* distinção, diferença; prerrogativa; excelência, superioridade.

distinctive, *a.* distintivo; *adv. distinctively,* distintivamente.

distinctly, *adv.* distintamente, nitidamente.

distinctness, *s.* distinção, clareza.

distingué, *a.* distinto, elegante.

distinguish, *v.t.* distinguir; enaltecer.

distinguished, *a.* distinto, assinalado.

distort, *v.t.* torcer, contorcer; deturpar.

distortion, *s.* contorção; deturpação.

distortionist, *s.* contorcionista.

distract, *v.t.* distrair; perturbar; enlouquecer, *distracted with fear,* louco de medo.

distractedly, *adv.* loucamente; *he loves her distractedly,* ama-a loucamente.

distraction, *s.* distracção, passatempo, diversão; loucura, demência.

distractive, *a.* perturbador, atordoador.

distrain, *v.t.* embargar.

distraint, *s.* embargo, arresto.

distrait, *a.* distraído.

distraite, *a.* distraída.

distress, *s.* dor, angústia, aflição; dificuldade; perigo; *a ship in distress,* navio em perigo; *v.t.* afligir, angustiar; pôr em dificuldades.

distressful. *a.* aflito, angustiado; aflitivo; *adv. distressfully,* aflitivamente, miseravelmente.

distressing, *a.* aflitivo, penoso; *adv. distressingly,* dum modo aflitivo.

distribute, *v.t.* distribuir; dividir; classificar, dispor.

distribution, *s.* distribuição, divisão; ordem, disposição; classificação.

distributive, *a.* e *s.* distributivo; *adv. distributively,* distributivamente.

destributor, *s.* distribuidor; *distributor point,* platinado.

district, *s.* distrito; comarca; bairro; paróquia; *district-attorney,* promotor público.

distrust, *v.t.* desconfiar de, suspeitar de. *s.* falta de confiança; desconfiança, suspeita.

distrustful, *a.* desconfiado, suspeitoso;

incrédulo. *adv. distrustfully*, desconfia-
damente.

distrustfulness, *s.* desconfiança.

disturb, *v.t.* perturbar; inquietar; desconcertar; incomodar.

disturbance, *s.* perturbação; desassossego;
distúrbio.

disunion, *s.* desunião, separação.

disunite, *v.t.* desunir, separar, dividir; *v.i.*
separar-se.

disuse, *s.* desuso; *v.t.* desacostumar; deixar
de usar.

ditch, *s.* fosso, vala; regato; *the Ditch*, canal
do Panamá; *v.t.* abrir fossos em, valar,
drenar.

ditto, *s.* sinal de repetição. 1) *ditto suit*, fato
de uma só cor ou de uma só fazenda. 2) *to
say ditto to*, apoiar; *adv.* idem.

ditty, *s.* canção; balada; modinha.

diuretic, *a.* e *s.* diurético.

diurnal, *a.* diurno, diário; *s.* diário, jornal.

diva, *s.* cantora; diva; prima-dona.

divagate, *v.i.* divagar; vaguear.

divan, *s.* divã, sofá; tribunal turco; sala de
fumo.

dive, *v.t.* mergulhar; submergir; *s.* mergulho;
antro, espelunca; *dive bomber*, bombardeiro de mergulho.

diver, *s.* mergulhador; escafandrista;
mergulhão (ave).

divergence, *s.* divergência, desacordo.

diverse, *a.* diverso, distinto, diferente; *adv.*
diversely, diversamente.

diversify, *v.t.* diversificar, variar.

diversion, *s.* desvio, afastamento; distracção, divertimento.

diversity, *s.* diversidade, variedade, multiplicidade.

divert, *v.t.* desviar; distrair; divertir; entreter.

diverting, *a.* divertido, recreativo.

divest, *v.t.* despir, despojar, desviar.

divestment, *s.* despojamento, destituição.

divide, *v.t.* dividir, repartir; *v.i.* dividir-se,
separar-se, ramificar-se; *s.* linha divisória;
partilha.

divided, *a.* dividido, separado.

dividend, *s.* dividendo.

divider, *s.* repartidor; distribuidor.

divination, *s.* adivinhação; vaticínio.

divine, *a.* divino; sagrado; sublime; *v.t.* e *v.i.*
adivinhar, profetizar, conjecturar; *divining
rod*, varinha de condão.

diviner, *s.* adivinho, adivinhador.

divinity, *s.* divindade; teologia.

divinize, *v.t.* divinizar.

divisible, *a.* divisível; *adv. divisibly*, dum
modo divisível.

division, *s.* divisão; compartimento; separação; discórdia; *family division*, partilhas
de família.

divisive, *a.* divisório; discordante; desar-
monizador.

divisor, *s.* divisor (mat.).

divorce, *s.* divórcio, separação; repúdio; *v.t.*
divorciar.

divorcé, *s.* divorciado.

divorcée, *s.* divorciada.

divorcee, *s.* divorciado, divorciada.

divorcement, *s.* divórcio.

divulge, divulgate, *v.t.* divulgar, revelar.

divulgeance, *s.* divulgação, revelação.

dizziness, *s.* tontura, vertigem.

dizzy, *a.* tonto, atordoado; confuso; *v.t.*
estontear, atordoar.

do (did, done), *v.t.* fazer, executar, efectuar; preparar, arranjar; traduzir; enganar.
1) *he tried to do me*, ele tentou enganar-
-me; visitar. 2) *I have done all the cities in
Spain*, visitei todas as cidades espanholas;
cozer ou assar. 3) *I like it well done*, gosto
dele bem passado; pagar; *v.i.* proceder;
servir. 4) *the housemaid who did this
house*, a empregada que serviu nesta casa;
bastar. 5) *that will do?*, isto chega?; passar
de saúde. 6) *how do you do?*: como está?;
terminar. 7) *have you done?*: acabou?
como auxiliar, serve para formar as
negativas e interrogações com a maioria
dos verbos; usa-se igualmente para evitar a
repetição de verbos. 7) *do you speak
English? Yes, I do!*, fala inglês? falo.; para
dar ênfase. 8) *I do believe you*, acredito-te.
9) *to do away with*, abolir. 10) *do by*, tratar.
11) do for, ser a propósito. 12) *do into*,
traduzir. 13) *do one's best*, esmerar-se. 14)
do out off, enganar. 15) *do over*, repetir. 16)
do over with, cobrir de. 17) *do time*, cumprir
uma sentença. 18) *do up*, arranjar; limpar;
restaurar; fatigar. 19) *do without*, dispensar.
20) *to do like for like*, pagar na mesma
moeda. 21) *well-to-do*, abastado. 22) *he did
well*, ele foi bem sucedido. 23) *done!*, feito!,
combinado!

do, dos, do's, *s.* fraude, impostura.

do, *s.* dó (mús.).

do-all, *s.* faz-tudo.

doc, *s.* doutor, médico.

docent, *s.* docente, professor.

docile, *a.* dócil, obediente, submisso; *adv.* *docilely:* docilmente.

dock, *s.* doca; estaleiro; rabicho; banco dos réus. 1) *wet dock,* doca de carga e descarga. 2) *dry dock,* doca seca. 3) *dock charges,* encargos de doca. 4) *dock dues,* direitos de doca. 5) *dock master,* mestre de doca; *v.t.* meter o navio na doca; cortar a cauda.

dockage, *s.* entrada de navio numa doca; direito de doca; corte, redução.

docker, *s.* trabalhador das docas, estivador.

docket, *s.* sumário, lista de causas pendentes; *v.t.* registrar; rotular.

dockyard, *s.* estaleiro.

doctor, *s.* doutor, médico; *v.t.* doutorar; medicar; *v.i.* exercer clínica.

doctorate, *s.* doutorado, grau de doutor.

doctrine, *s.* doutrina, dogma; crença.

document, *s.* documento; *v.t.* documentar.

documentary, *a.* documentário, documental; *s.* documentário.

dodge, *v.t.* esquivar(-se), fugir; iludir; fintar; *s.* evasiva, subterfúgio; finta.

dodger, *s.* trapaceiro.

doe, *s.* corça; fêmea (de coelho, lebre ou cabrito).

does, 3ª pess. do sing. do pres. ind. de *to do.*

doesn't, contracção de *does not.*

doff, *v.t.* despir; abandonar.

dog, *s.* cão; macho de vários animais; miserável, velhaco. 1) *to go to the dogs,* arruinar-se, perder-se. 2) *to lead a dog's life,* levar uma vida de cão. 3) *dog in the manger,* desmancha-prazeres. 4) *it is raining cats and dogs,* chove a cântaros. 5) *an artful dog,* um esperto. 6) *to die like a dog,* morrer miseravelmente. 7) *barking dogs don't bite,* cão que ladra, não morde; *v.t.* seguir, perseguir como um cão.

dogged, *a.* obstinado, persistente.

doggedly, *adv.* persistentemente.

doggy, *s.* cãozinho.

doghouse, *s.* canil.

dogma, *s.* dogma, crença.

dogmatic, *a.* dogmático.

dogmatize, *v.t.* e *v.i.* dogmatizar.

doily, *s.* guardanapo.

doing, *s.* feito, acção; acontecimento.

dole, *s.* distribuição; porção; subsídio; esmola; aflição, dor; *v.t.* distribuir, dividir em pequenas porções.

doleful, *a.* pesaroso, aflito; triste; *adv.* *dolefully,* tristemente.

doll, *s.* boneca; mulher bonita e fútil; *v.t.* e *v.i.* enfarpelar(-se), embonecar(-se).

dollar, *s.* dólar (moeda).

dollop, *s.* naco, pedaço; tronco.

dolly, *s.* boneca; mexedor de roupa.

dolor, dolour, *s.* dor, aflição, angústia.

dolorous, *a.* doloroso, aflito.

dolphin, *s.* golfinho.

dolt, *s.* parvo, pateta.

domain, *s.* domínio, território; terras, bens de raiz; soberania.

dome, *s.* domo, cúpula; mansão; tecto abobadado; *v.t.* e *v.i.* cobrir com cúpula; arquear-se.

domesday, *s.* variante de *doomsday;* *Domesday Book,* livro mandado fazer por Guilherme I no qual constava a descrição das terras da Inglaterra.

domestic, *a.* doméstico, caseiro; domesticado; nacional; *s.* doméstico, criado; *adv.* *domestically,* domesticamente.

domesticate, *v.t.* domesticar, amansar; acostumar à vida doméstica.

domesticity, *s.* domesticidade.

domicile, *s.* domicílio, residência, habitação, casa; *v.t.* domiciliar; *v.i.* estabelecer residência.

domiciliary, *a.* domiciliário; *domiciliary visit,* visita domiciliária.

dominance, dominancy, *s.* dominância; domínio; autoridade.

dominant, *a.* dominante; predominante, preponderante.

dominate, *v.t.* e *v.i.* dominar; predominar; governar.

domination, *s.* domínio, império; autoridade; tirania.

dominative, *a.* dominativo, dominador, autoritário.

dominator, *s.* dominador, governador.

domineer, *v.t.* e *v.i.* dominar, tiranizar.

dominion, *s.* domínio, soberania; território; propriedade.

domino, *s.* traje de máscara; jogo de pedras.

don (donning, donned), *v.t.* vestir; *s.* título espanhol; dom; lente de universidade inglesa.

donate, *v.t.* e *v.i.* doar, fazer doação.

donation, *s.* doação; donativo, dádiva.

done, *pp.* de *do.*

donkey, *s.* burro, asno; caldeira; *donkey--engine,* pequeno motor.

donor, *s.* doador.

do-nothing, *a.* ocioso, indolente; vadio, mandrião.

don't, contracção de *do not*.

donzel, *s.* pajem.

doom, *s.* lei, decreto; destino; sentença; *v.t.* sentenciar, condenar.

Doomsday, *s.* Dia do Juízo Final.

door, *s.* porta, entrada. 1) *next door*, na casa vizinha. 2) *to show someone the door*, expulsar alguém de uma casa. 3) *to lay something at someone's door*, imputar alguma coisa a alguém. 4) *at death's door*, às portas da morte. 5) *out of doors*, ao ar livre. 6) *within doors*, em casa.

doorkeeper, *s.* porteiro.

doorknob, *s.* maçaneta.

doorpost, *s.* ombreira.

doorstep, *s.* degrau da porta.

doorway, *s.* vão de escada.

dooryard, *s.* pequeno jardim à frente de casa.

doper, *s.* narcotizador; que toma estupefacientes.

dopey, *a.* intoxicado com estupefacientes; inerte; narcotizante.

dormant, *a.* dormente; em hibernação; em repouso; inactivo; suspenso; não reclamado. 1) *dormant partner*, sócio capitalista. 2) *a dormant title*, título não usado. 3) *dormant warrant*, ordem assinada em branco.

dormer, *s.* quarto de dormir; mansarda.

dormitory, *s.* dormitório, quarto de dormir; subúrbio.

dormouse, *s.* arganaz, rato.

dorsal, *a.* dorsal.

dosage, *s.* dosagem.

dose, *s.* dose, porção.

doss, *s.* cama; pousada; *doss house*, albergue ordinário.

dossal, *s.* dossel (pano que cobre o espaldar de cama ou trono).

dosser, *s.* cesto que se coloca no lombo dos animais.

dossier, *s.* pasta de documentos.

dot, *s.* dote; ponto; pequena mancha; insignificância; *we arrived at the airport on the dot*, chegámos ao aeroporto no momento exacto; *v.t. (dotting, dotted)* pontuar, marcar (com pontos); salpicar; semear.

dotage, *s.* caduquice; imbecilidade; afeição excessiva.

dotard, *s.* pessoa senil, velho caduco.

dote, doat, *v.i.* caducar, desatinar; amar cegamente, idolatrar; *to dote on some one*, apaixonar-se por alguém.

double, *s.* dobro; duplicado; contrafigura; sósia; *a.* duplo; dobrado, duplicado; dúplice; hipócrita; *v.t.* dobrar, duplicar; *v.i.* duplicar-se; dissimular; voltar atrás. 1) *double-edged*, de dois gumes. 2) *double-entry*, partida dobrada. 3) *double face*, hipocrisia. 4) *double-meaning*, ambíguo. 5) *double-minded*, indeciso. 6) *double-tongued*, enganador.

double-barreled, *a.* de dois canos (arma).

double-breasted, *a.* trespassado (casaco).

double-cross, *v.t.* trair, atraiçoar.

double-crosser, *s.* traidor.

double-dealer, *s.* velhaco, pessoa falsa.

double-dealing, *s.* duplicidade.

doubly, *adv.* em duplicado.

doubt, *v.t.* e *v.i.* duvidar, suspeitar, desconfiar; *s.* dúvida, suspeita, incerteza; *no doubt*, sem dúvida.

doubtful, *a.* duvidoso, incerto; ambíguo; discutível; *adv. doubtfully*, duvidosamente.

doubtless, *a.* seguro, certo; indubitável; *adv. doubtlessly*, indubitavelmente.

douche, *s.* duche; *v.t.* tomar duche.

dough, *s.* massa de farinha para fabrico de pão; pasta; dinheiro.

doughnut, *s.* sonho, rosca (bolo).

doughty, *a.* capaz, forte, valente.

dour, *a.* severo, duro, obstinado.

dove, *s.* pombo ou pomba. 1) *dove-cot*, pombal. 2) *my dove*, minha querida.

dovetail, *s.* cauda de andorinha; malhete; *v.t.* malhetar; encaixar.

dowdy, *a.* desalinhado, mal vestido, sujo.

dower, *s.* dote; bens deixados a uma viúva; dom, prenda; *v.t.* dotar, favorecer.

down, *s.* duna, montículo; penugem; (pl.) revés da sorte; *a.* descendente; *(prep.)* abaixo, debaixo, em baixo; *to sit down*, sentar-se; *v.i.* derrubar, vencer; *v.i.* descer, cair.

downdraft, *s.* corrente de ar.

downfall, *s.* aguaceiro; ruína, derrocada.

downhill, *s.* encosta.

downhearted, *a.* abatido, triste.

downpour, *s.* aguaceiro.

downright, *a.* direito; categórico; completo; *adv.* completamente.

downrightness, *s.* sinceridade.

downstairs, *adv.* em baixo, em baixo das escadas; no piso inferior.

downtown, *adv.* ao centro, centro de uma cidade, central.

downward, *a.* inclinado; *adv.* (pl.) para baixo.

downwind, *a.* e *adv.* a favor do vento.

downy, *a.* felpudo, coberto de penugem; fofo, suave.

doxology, *s.* doxologia.

doxy, *s.* doutrina; mulher de maus costumes.

doze, *s.* sono ligeiro, soneca; *v.t.* dormitar.

dozen, *s.* dúzia.

drab, *s.* mulher porca; prostituta; *v.i.* (drabbing, drabbed) andar com prostitutas; *a.* pardacento; monótono, triste; *adv.* drably, monotonamente, insipidamente.

drabble, *v.t.* e *v.i.* emporcalhar(-se), enlamear(-se), arrastar pela lama.

draff, *s.* desperdícios; fezes.

draft, draught, *s.* acto de puxar; tracção; ordem de pagamento; desenho, planta; esquema, projecto; selecção, recrutamento; *v.t.* delinear, traçar; redigir; destacar.

draftsman, *s.* desenhador, delineador.

drag (dragging, dragged), *v.t.* dragar, arrastar; *s.* draga, calço de travão; carruagem pesada; arrasto; corda com que se arrasta uma coisa; âncora.

draggle, *v.t.* e *v.i.* sujar ou sujar-se (arrastando pelo chão); enxovalhar; ficar para trás, retardar-se.

dragnet, *s.* rede de arrasto.

dragon, *s.* dragão; homem feroz; megera; planta; dragontree, dragoeiro.

dragonfly, *s.* libélula.

dragoon, *s.* dragão, soldado de cavalaria.

drain, *v.t.* drenar, escoar; *s.* dreno, escoadouro; cano de esgoto.

drainage, *s.* drenagem.

drake, *s.* pato, cisne, ganso (macho); *to make ducks and drakes of,* desperdiçar.

dram, *s.* trago, pinga, gole.

drama, *s.* drama.

dramatic, *s.* dramático; teatral; comovente; (pl.) arte dramática.

dramatist, *s.* dramaturgo.

dramatize, *v.t.* dramatizar.

dramshop, *s.* bar, botequim.

drape, *v.t.* ornar, enfeitar; *s.* cortina.

draper, *s.* negociante de panos.

drapery, *s.* negócio de panos, fanqueiro; roupagem.

drastic, *a.* drástico, enérgico; violento; *adv.* drastically, drasticamente.

draughts, *s.* jogo de damas.

draw (drew, drawn) *v.t.* arrastar, puxar; extrair, arrancar; persuadir; sacar; *v.i.* içar; atrair; tirar. 1) *to draw asunder,* separar. 2) *draw away,* dissuadir. 3) *draw back,* retirar. 4) *draw breath,* tomar fôlego. 5) *draw in,* atrair. 6) *draw off,* dissuadir. 7) *draw out,* extrair. 8) *draw on,* aproximar-se. 9) *draw a profit,* tirar proveito, lucro. 10) *draw interest,* render juros. 11) *draw up,* puxar para cima, estabelecer. 12) *draw the line,* fixar limites. 13) *draw a line,* passar um traço. 14) *draw the long bow,* exagerar. 15) *draw bridge,* ponte levadiça.

drawback, *s.* reembolso de direitos; desvantagem.

drawee, *s.* sacado.

drawer, *s.* gaveta; *s.* desenhador; sacador.

drawers, *s.* ceroulas.

drawing, *s.* desenho, esboço; sorteio. 1) *drawing board,* prancheta de desenho. 2) *drawing master,* professor de desenho. 3) *drawing pen,* tira-linhas. 4) *drawing-room,* sala de visitas; sala de desenho.

drawl, *v.t.* e *v.i.* balbuciar, arrastar as palavras; *s.* balbuciação.

dray, *s.* carro para transportar cargas.

drayman, *s.* carroceiro.

dread, *v.t.* e *v.i.* temer, recear; *s.* medo, temor.

dreadful, *a.* terrível, medonho; *adv.* dreadfully, terrivelmente; *penny dreadful,* livro de contos de horror.

dream, *v.i.* e *v.t.* sonhar, imaginar, fantasiar; *s.* sonho, fantasia.

dreamer, *s.* sonhador, visionário.

dreaming, *a.* sonhador, fantasiador.

dreamland, *s.* terra dos sonhos, região dos sonhos.

dreamlike, *a.* de sonho, como em sonhos; irreal.

dreamy, *a.* cheio de sonhos; fantasista; lânguido; *adv. dreamily,* sonhadoramente.

drear, dreary, *a.* triste, monótono; fatigante; *adv. drearily,* tristemente.

dredge, *s.* rede para a captura de marisco; draga; *v.t.* dragar; limpar com draga; polvilhar.

drench, *v.t.* ensopar; fazer beber, medicar pela força; *s.* beberagem, remédio; purgante; carga de água.

drencher, *s.* extintor.

dress, *s.* vestido, adorno, trage. 1) *full-dress,* vestido de cerimónia. 2) *dress-coat,* casaca. 3) *evening-dress,* traje de noite. 4) *morning-dress*, traje de passeio. 5) *dress--uniform*, uniforme de gala; *v.t.* vestir, ataviar; preparar; cozinhar; pentear; escovar; curtir couro; temperar; *v.i.* vestir--se, arranjar-se. 6) *to dress a tree*, podar uma árvore. 7) *to dress up*, vestir-se de cerimónia.

dresser, *a.* aparador; armário de cozinha; costureiro de teatro; *hairdresser*, cabeleireiro, *adv. dressily*, elegantemente vestido.

dressing, *s.* adorno; vestimenta, roupa; acto de vestir; condimento; curativo; (pl.) pensos de feridas. 1) *dressing bag*, mala de artigos de toilette. 2) *dressing-case*, toucador. 3) *dressing-gown*, penteador.

dressmaker, costureiro, modista.

dressy, *a.* elegante, chique; à moda.

dribble, *s.* saliva, baba; gota; *v.t.* e *v.i.* gotejar, pingar; babar(-se); diblar no futebol.

dribbler, *s.* jogador de futebol; baboso.

drier, dryer, *s.* secador; secante; *hairdryer*, secador de cabelo.

drift, *s.* impulso; violência; aquilo que é levado por uma corrente; detritos; rumo, direcção; sentido; *v.t.* impelir, levar, amontoar; abrir galerias nas minas.

drifter, *s.* navio caça-minas; arrastão (barco).

driftless, *a.* sem direcção, à deriva.

drill, *s.* broca, berbequim; máquina de semear; instrução militar; treino; *drill-sergeant*, sargento instrutor; *v.t.* furar, brocar; exercitar; treinar; semear em filas.

driller, *s.* perfurador; instrutor; semeador.

drink (drank, drunk), *v.t.* beber; embriagar-se; *s.* bebida, bebida alcoólica, trago. 1) *to drink like a fish*, beber demasiado. 2) *to drink up*, beber dum trago. 3) *to drink a toast*, fazer uma saúde.

drinkable, *s.* potável, bebível; *s.* bebida.

drinker, *s.* bebedor; bêbedo, ébrio.

drip (dripping, dripped), *v.t.* e *v.i.* gotejar, pingar; *s.* gota, goteira.

dripping, *s.* gotejamento; pingue-pongue; *dripping-pan*, panela para aparar a gordura da carne que está a assar.

drive (drove, driven), *v.t.* e *v.i.* impelir, empurrar; atirar; levar, conduzir; tornar, fazer; induzir, compelir, forçar, cravar; guiar; passear; mover. 1) *drive along*, impelir. 2) *drive at*, aspirar a. 3) *drive away*, afugentar, expulsar; andar de carro. 4) *drive a good bargain*, fazer um bom negócio. 5) *drive mad*, exasperar, enlouquecer. 6) *drive*

over, passar por cima de. 7) *drive something to the last moment*, protelar uma coisa para a última hora. 8) *drive*, a caminho!; *s.* passeio (de carro ou automóvel); calçada ou parque para estacionar; exigência. 9) *drive-in*, cinema ao ar livre com estacionamento para automóveis.

drivel, *v.t.* e *v.i.* babar(-se); dizer parvoíces; *s.* baba.

driver, *s.* condutor de veículo; motorista.

drizzle, *v.i.* chuviscar; *v.t.* borrifar, salpicar; *s.* salpico, chuvisco.

droit, *s.* (jur.) direito; direitos; taxa.

droll, *a.* engraçado, cómico; jocoso. *adv. drolly*, dum modo jocoso.

drollery, *s.* chocarrice.

drone, *s.* zângão; gaita-de-foles; zumbido; *v.t.* viver à custa alheia; lengalengar; zumbir.

drop (dropping, dropped), *v.t.* e *v.i.* soltar; deixar; deixar cair; pender, desistir; cair desmaiado, cessar. 1) *drop down*, morrer de repente; cair por terra. 2) *drop in upon*, surpreender. 3) *drop a hint*, dar uma sugestão. 4) *drop the curtain*, descer o pano (teat.); *s.* gota, pinga, queda; descida, baixa; brinco, pingente.

dropper, *s.* conta-gotas.

dropsy, *s.* hidropisia (med.), edema.

dross, *s.* escória, escumalha; refugo; *adv. drossy*, com impurezas, cheio de escumalha.

drought, drouth, *s.* seca, aridez; secura.

droughty, *a.* seco, árido.

drove, *s.* manada, rebanho.

drover, *s.* condutor de rebanho; boieiro.

drown, *v.t.* e *v.i.* afogar, matar por afogamento, afogar-se; morrer afogado; submergir, inundar.

drowse, *v.i.* estar sonolento, dormitar; *v.t.* adormentar, entorpecer. *s.* soneca.

drowsy, *a.* sonolento, adormecido; letárgico, indolente; soporífico; *adv. drowsily*, com sonolência.

drudge, *v.i.* trabalhar muito sem grande proveito; mourejar, afadigar-se; *s.* lacaio, escravo, trabalhador servil.

drudgery, *s.* trabalho penoso; servidão; labuta.

drug (drugging, drugged), *v.t.* misturar com drogas; narcotizar; *v.i.* tomar narcóticos; medicar, prescrever receitas; *s.* droga, remédio.

druggist, *s.* farmacêutico; droguista.

drugstore, *s.* farmácia; drogaria.

drum, *s.* tambor, caixa; rufo; tímpano do ouvido; *v.t.* e *v.i. (drumming, drummed),* tocar tambor, tamborilar; expulsar; aliciar adeptos pela insistência.

drummer, *s.* tambor, tamborileiro.

drunk, *a.* embriagado, bêbedo, ébrio; *s.* embriaguez, bebedeira, bêbedo.

drunkard, *s.* ébrio, bêbedo.

drunken, *a.* ébrio; *adv. drunkenly,* embriagadamente.

dry, *a.* seco, árido; enxuto; sequioso; pobre, estéril; áspero. 1) *dryeyed,* sem lágrimas. 2) *drylodging,* hospedagem sem comida. 3) *dry-nurse,* ama-seca. 4) *dry-clean,* limpar a seco. 5) *dry-rot,* caruncho. *v.t.* e *v.i.* secar, enxugar; ressequir(-se), estancar(-se).

dryad, *s.* dríade.

drying, *a.* secador, secante; *s.* secador, estendal.

dryly, drily, *adv.* secamente, friamente.

dryness, *a.* secura, sequidão; frieza.

dry-salt, *v.t.* salgar e secar a carne.

drysalter, *s.* negociante de produtos salgados.

dryshod, *a.* pé enxuto.

dual, *a.* dual, relativo a dois.

dualism, *s.* dualismo.

dub (dubbing, dubbed), *v.t.* apelidar, baptizar; conferir título; armar cavaleiro; *s.* pancada seca; rufo do tambor.

dubious, *a.* dúbio; equívoco; suspeito; incerto; *adv. dubiously,* duvidosamente.

duchess, *s.* duquesa.

duchesse, *s.* cetim fino.

duchy, *s.* ducado, domínio dum duque.

duck, *s.* pato, pata; carne de pato; mergulho; lona (velas de navio); queridinho; *to make ducks and drakes of,* dissipar, estragar; *v.t.* e *v.i.* mergulhar-se.

duckbill, *s.* ornitorrinco.

ducking, *s.* mergulho.

duckling, *s.* patinho.

duct, *s.* ducto, canal, conduta.

dude, *s.* janota, almofadinha.

due, *s.* dívida, obrigação; direitos alfandegários. 1) *to fall due,* terminar o prazo, vencer-se; *a.* devido, que se deve. 2) *the love due to one's parents,* o amor devido aos pais; cumprido; próprio; oportuno; exacto. 3) *in due course,* no tempo devido; *adv.* exactamente, directamente.

duel, *s.* duelo; combate; *(duelling, duelled) v.i.* bater-se em duelo.

duet, *s.* dueto, duo.

dug, *s.* teta.

duke, *s.* duque.

dull, *a.* estúpido, néscio, obtuso; triste, melancólico, insípido. *v.t.* embotar, entorpecer; *dull season,* estação morta.

dullard, *s.* pessoa obtusa, bronca.

dullish, *a.* estúpido, triste, lento.

dullness, *s.* estupidez; lentidão; sonolência.

dully, *adv.* estupidamente, lentamente.

duly, *adv.* devidamente.

dumb, *a.* mudo; taciturno, calado; pateta, burro. 1) *dumb-show,* cena muda, mímica. 2) *dumb-waiter,* pequeno elevador da cozinha para a sala de jantar.

dumbness, *s.* mudez; mutismo; estupidez, burrice.

dummy, *s.* pessoa muda ou silenciosa; personagem muda numa peça; pateta; manequim para vestidos; espantalho de palha.

dump, *v.t.* esvaziar; descarregar; depositar; deixar cair pesadamente; exportar ou importar em larga escala; *s.* lixeira; depósito.

dumps, *s.* melancolia, depressão, abatimento.

dumpy, *a.* curto e grosso; pessoa atarracada; rabugento.

dun (dunning, dunned), *v.i.* importunar (um devedor); *v.t.* salgar ou curar peixe; *dun--fish,* bacalhau (seco); *s.* credor importuno, credor; cor pardacenta.

dung, *s.* esterco, estrume; *dung-hill,* pilha de estrume.

dungeon, *s.* masmorra, calabouço.

duo, *s.* duo, dueto; dupla de artistas.

dupe, *s.* ingénuo, incauto; *v.t.* lograr, ludibriar.

dupery, *s.* logro, burla.

duple, *a.* duplo.

duplex, *a.* duplo, composto de duas partes; apartamento com dois andares; sistema de telegrafia.

duplicate, *a.* duplicado, duplo, dobrado; *s.* duplicado, duplicata, cópia; reprodução; *v.t.* duplicar, dobrar; fazer uma cópia de.

duplication, *s.* duplicação; duplicado.

duplicity, *s.* duplicidade, má-fé.

durable, *a.* durável, duradouro; resistente.

duress, *s.* encerramento, prisão; constrangimento.

during, *prep.* durante, no decurso de.

dusk, *a.* escuro, obscuro, sombrio; *s.* o anoitecer; *v.i.* escurecer.

dusky, a. fusco, escuro; adv. duskily, obscuramente.

dust, s. pó, poeira; restos mortais; terra, solo. 1) dust-coat, guarda-pó. 2) in the dust, morto. 3) to dust someone's jacket, dar uma tareia em alguém; v.t. limpar, varrer o pó; cobrir ou encher de pó.

duster, s. espanador, pano do pó.

dustman, s. varredor.

Dutch, s. e a. holandês; dutch courage, coragem obtida pelo álcool; língua holandesa.

duteous, a. cumpridor dos seus deveres, obediente, respeitoso; adv. duteously, respeitosamente.

dutiful, a. obediente, submisso, zeloso; adv. dutifully, obedientemente.

duty, s. obrigação, dever; obediência, acatamento; imposto; to be on duty, estar de serviço.

dwarf, s. anão; v.t. impedir o crescimento.

dwell (dwelled, dwelt), v.i. habitar, morar, residir.

dweller, s. habitante, morador.

dwelling, habitação, residência.

dwindle, v.i. diminuir, minguar, reduzir-se.

dye, s. tinta, corante; matriz; dye-works, tinturaria; v.t. (dyeing, dyed), v.t. tingir, pintar, corar.

dyeing, s. tinturaria, tintura; acto de tingir.

dyer, s. tintureiro.

dyestuff, s. corante, matéria corante.

dying, a. moribundo, agonizante.

dynamic, a. dinâmico, activo, enérgico.

dynamism, s. dinamismo.

dynamite, s. dinamite; v.t. dinamitar.

dynamo, s. dínamo, gerador.

dynast, s. dinasta; soberano.

dynastic, a. dinástico.

dynasty, s. dinastia.

dysentery, s. disenteria.

dysfunction, s. (med.) disfunção.

dysphagia, s. disfagia.

dysphasia, s. disfasia.

dysphoria, s. disforia, mal-estar, inquietação.

dyspnea, s. dispneia.

E

e, quinta letra do alfabeto.

each, *adj.* cada; por cada um; *each-other*, mutuamente.

eager, *adj.* ávido, ansioso; vivo, fogoso, impaciente.

eagerly, *adv.* ardentemente.

eagerness, *s.* ânsia, avidez, veemência; impaciência.

eagle, *s.* águia (ave); águia (moeda de 10 dólares); *eagle-eyed*, que tem olhos de lince.

eaglet, *s.* aguieta.

eagre, *s.* macaréu.

ear, *s.* orelha; ouvido; espiga; asa (de cesto). 1) *ear-ache*, dor de ouvidos. 2) *ear-drop*, pingente. 3) *ear-lap*, ponta da orelha. 4) *ear-trumpet*, corneta acústica. 5) *ear-wax*, cerúmen dos ouvidos. 6) *ear witness*, testemunha auricular. 7) *I am all ears*, sou todo ouvidos. 8) *to turn a deaf ear to*, fazer ouvidos de mercador. 9) *over head and ears in*, enfronhado em. *v.i.* espigar.

earache, *s.* dor de ouvidos.

eardrum, *s.* tímpano do ouvido.

eared, *adj.* espigado; com orelhas; *long eraed*, orelhudo.

earing, *s.* pequena corda que prende o punho do gurutil.

earl, *s.* conde (na Inglaterra).

earldom, *s.* condado.

earles-penny, *s.* dinheiro por conta; sinal dum contrato.

earless, *adj.* sem orelhas; sem espigas.

earlier, earliest, *comp. sup.* de *early*.

earliness, *s.* precocidade, antecipação.

earl-marshal, *s.* alto dignitário britânico.

early, *adj.* primitivo; precoce; antecipado; próximo; relativo ao princípio. 1) *early fruit*, fruta temporã. 2) *the early part of the century*, o começo do século. 3) *at your earliest convenience*, logo que possa. 4) *to keep early hours*, deitar-se e levantar-se cedo. *adv.* cedo. 5) *early-riser*, ou early bird, madrugador. 6) *early in the morning*, de madrugada. 7) *early to bed and early to rise, makes a man healthy and wise*, deitar cedo e cedo erguer, dá saúde e faz crescer.

earmark, s. marca ou sinal nas orelhas (dos carneiros, etc.). *v.t.* pôr marca ou sinal; separar para um fim especial.

earn, *v.t.* ganhar, adquirir; merecer.

earnest, *adj.* fervoroso, zeloso, activo, enérgico; cuidadoso; grave, importante. *s.* seriedade; boa-fé; penhor. 1) *earnest-money,* sinal de um contrato. 2) *in good earnest,* seriamente. 3) *are you in earnest?,* estás (a falar) a sério?

earnestly, *adv.* sinceramente.

earnestness, s. fervor; actividade; cuidado.

earning, s. salário, estipêndio, paga; *(pl.)* ganhos, lucros. 1) *net earnings,* lucros líquidos; 2) *gross earnings,* receita bruta.

earring, s. brinco das orelhas.

earshot, s. alcance do ouvido.

earth, s. terra, terreno; globo terrestre; mundo, toca. 1) *earth-board,* aiveca. 2) *earth-flax,* amianto. 3) *earth-nut,* amendoim. 4) *earth-ward,* em direcção à terra. 5) socalco, fortificação militar feita com terra. 6) *earth-worm,* minhoca. 7) *fuller's earth,* greda. 8) *potter's earth,* argila, barro. 9) *why on earth!* por que demónio!. 10) *to put to earth,* ligar à terra. *v.t.* cobrir-se de terra; obrigar a recolher à toca. *v.t.* recolher-se à toca.

earthen, *adj.* de barro, de terra. 1) *earthen-ware,* louça de barro. 2) *earthen-pan,* alguidar.

earthiness, s. qualidade do que é terreno.

earthliness, s. qualidade terrestre; grosseria; vaidade humana.

earthly, *adj.* terrestre; mundano.

earthquake, s. terramoto.

earthy, *adj.* térreo; terroso; grosseiro.

earwig, fura-orelhas (insecto).

ease, s. sossego, repouso; ócio; comodidade; facilidade, desembaraço. 1) *at ease,* à-vontade. 2) *with ease,* com facilidade. 3) *heart's ease,* contentamento; amor-perfeito. 4) *to be ill at ease,* estar inquieto, embaraçado, não estar descansado. *v.t.* aliviar, suavizar, mitigar; afrouxar; tiramolar (náut.); moderar a marcha (de uma máquina). 5) *to ease off,* afrouxar, diminuir, aliviar um peso. 6) *ease her,* pouco a pouco (náut.).

easel, s. cavalete de pintor.

easement, s. alívio; vantagem.

easier, easiest, *comp.* e *sup.* de *easy.*

easily, *adv.* facilmente

easiness, s. facilidade; tranquilidade; desembaraço.

east, s. este, oriente; *East-Indiaman,* navio mercante da Índia.

Easter, s. Páscoa. 1) *Easter-day,* dia de Páscoa. 2) *easter-egg,* ovo pintado que se dá de presente na Páscoa.

easterly, *adj.* e *adv.* oriental, de leste.

eastern, *adj.* e s. oriental.

eastermost, *adj.* o mais oriental.

easting, s. curso feito em direcção a este; direcção de este.

eastward, *adj.* e *adv.* a leste, para o lado do este.

easy, *adj.* fácil, acessível; condescendente; sociável; liso, plano; sossegado; devagar. 1) *easy-chair,* poltrona. 2) *easy rolling,* balanço doce. 3) *easy sail,* pano reduzido. 4) *take it easy,* não se canse, não se atrapalhe. 5) *he is very free and easy,* ele não faz cerimónias. 6) *easy ahead!,* para diante, pouco a pouco! 7) *easy astern!,* para trás, pouco a pouco! (náut.).

easygoing, *adj.* pachorrento, indolente, que não se rala; que tem bom andar (falando de um cavalo).

eat, *pret. ate, pp. eaten. v.t.* e *v.i.* comer; mastigar; roer; consumir. 1) *to eat away,* destruir gradualmente, roer. 2) *to eat into,* corroer, consumir. 3) *to eat one's heart out,* consumir-se, sofrer em silêncio. 4) *to eat up,* devorar. 5) *to eat one's words,* engolir o que se disse.

eatable, *adj.* comestível.

eatables, s. comestíveis, víveres.

eaten, *pp.* de *eat.*

eater, s. comedor.

eating-house, s. casa de pasto.

eaves, s. goteiras do telhado.

eavesdrop, *v.i.* escutar às portas ou janelas.

eavesdropper, s. o que escuta às portas ou janelas.

ebb, *v.i.* baixar (a maré); decair. s. baixa-mar; vazante; decadência. 1) *at a low ebb,* em dificuldades. 2) *ebb and flood,* fluxo e refluxo.

ebonite, s. ebonite.

ebon, *adj.* ébano; negro.

ebonize, *v.t.* fingir de ébano.

ebony, s. ébano.

ebriate, *adj.* embriagado.

ebriety, s. embriaguez.

ebullience, s. ebulição.

ebulliency, ver *ebullience.*

ebullient, *adj.* em ebulição, a ferver.

ebullition, s. ebulição.

eccentric (al), adj. excêntrico, extravagante; raro.

eccentric, s. pessoa excêntrica; roda excêntrica. 1) *eccentric hosp,* ou *strap,* aro do excêntrico. 2) *eccentric-pulley* ou *sheave,* carro de excêntrico. 3) *eccentric rod,* haste ou tirante do excêntrico.

eccentrically, adv. de modo excêntrico.

eccentricity (ies), s. excentricidade.

Ecclesiastes, s. *Eclesiastes* (um livro da Bíblia).

ecclesiastic, s. e adj. eclesiástico.

ecclesiastical, adj. eclesiástico; *ecclesiastical commissioners,* administradores dos bens da Igreja na Inglaterra.

ecclesiastically, adv. eclesiasticamente.

echelon, s. escalão.

echelonned, adj. escalonado.

echidna, s. equidna.

echinoderm, s. equinoderme.

echinus, s. equino (ouriço-do-mar).

echo, s. eco. v.t. e v.i. ecoar, repercutir.

eclectic, s. e adj. ecléctico.

eclectical, adj. ecléctico.

eclectically, adv. eclecticamente.

eclecticism, s. eclectismo.

eclipse, s. eclipse. v.t. eclipsar; nublar. v.i. eclipsar-se.

ecliptic, s. eclíptico (astr.).

eclogue, s. écloga.

economic (al), adj. económico, frugal, moderado.

economically, adv. economicamente.

economics, s. economia (ciência); economia política.

economist, s. economista; pessoa económica; ecónoma.

economizer (ise), v.t. e v.i. economizar.

economizer (ise), s. economizador.

economy (ies), s. economia, parcimónia, frugalidade; ordem moral ou física.

ecstasy (ies), s. êxtase, transporte, arrebatamento.

ecstatic (al), adj. extático, absorto.

ecstatically, adv. de um modo extático.

ecumenic (al), adj. ecuménico.

eczema, s. eczema.

ed, terminação do *pret. perf.* e *pp.* dos verbos fracos regulares, como *to call, called;* sufixo que se junta a *subst.* e que significa «que tem», «que possui» como: *foot,* pé; *footed,* que tem pés.

edacious, adj. voraz, glutão.

eddied, pret. pp. de *eddy.*

eddy, s. redemoinho; refluxo da água ou do ar contra a corrente. v.i. pret. e pp. eddied, redemoinhar.

edleweiss, s. leontopódio.

Eden, s. éden, paraíso.

edge, s. fio, corte, gume; borda, margem; ourela, esquina; orla; acrimónia. 1) *to take off the edge,* embotar. 2) *to set teeth on edge,* embotar os dentes; (fig.) bulir com os nervos. 3) *edge-tools,* instrumentos cortantes. v.t. aguçar, afiar; debruar; irritar, exasperar; voltar, virar; fazer avançar. v.i. avançar de lado. 4) *to edge away,* inclinar-se a sotavento (náut.); ir-se afastando pouco a pouco.

edged, adj. afiado, cortante.

edgeless, adj. embotado, obtuso.

edgeways, adv. de ponta; do lado do fio; do lado da margem; lateralmente.

edgewise, ver *edgeways.*

edging, s. fita, debrum, orla, guarnição, bainha.

edgy, pret. e pp. *edified* v.t. edificar, levar à virtude pelo exemplo, instruir.

edile, s. edil.

edit, v.t. editar (uma obra alheia).

edition, s. edição, publicação.

editor, s. editor; director de um periódico.

editorial, adj. editorial. s. editorial, artigo de jornal (da responsabilidade do editor).

editorially, adv. editorialmente.

editorship, s. cargo e obrigações do editor.

educability, s. educabilidade.

educable, adj. educável.

educate, v.t. educar; instruir; criar.

education, s. educação; instrução; ilustração.

educational, adj. pedagógico.

educationally, adv. pedagogicamente.

educationist, s. pedagogo; educador.

educative, adj. educativo.

educator, s. educador.

educe, v.t. eduzir, deduzir.

eduction, s. edução, dedução; emissão; saída, descarga, escape (máq.); *eduction-pipe,* tubo de descarga.

eel, s. enguia; 1) *eel-pot,* nassa para enguias; 2) *eel-pout,* pequeno peixe parecido com as enguias.

e'en, contracção de *even.*

e'er, contracção de *ever.*

eerie, adj. que inspira medo; temido; extraordinário, sobrenatural.

eerily, adv. timidamente.

eeriness, *s.* timidez.

eery, ver *eerie.*

effable, *adj.* dizível.

efface, *v.t.* apagar, safar.

effaceable, *adj.* que se pode safar ou apagar.

effacement, *s.* acto de safar ou apagar.

effect, *s.* efeito, resultado, trabalho (de máquina, etc.); consequência; impressão; eficácia; realização; *(pl.),* bens, propriedade. 1) *to take effect,* produzir efeito; entrar em vigor (for.). 2) *of no effect,* inútil. 3) *in effect,* efectivamente. 4) *useful effect,* rendimento (mec.). 5) *whole effect,* efeito total. *v.t.* efectuar, realizar; assegurar.

effective, *adj.* efectivo; eficaz; vistoso. *s.* pessoa eficaz; soldado apto para o serviço; eficácia de tensão (elect.)

effectively, *adv.* eficazmente.

effectiveness, *s.* eficiência, eficácia.

effectual, *adj.* eficiente; eficaz; valido.

effectuality, *s.* eficácia, realização.

effectually, *adv.* eficazmente; eficientemente.

effectuate, *v.t.* efectuar, realizar.

effeminacy, *s.* efeminação.

effeminate, *v.t.* efeminar. *v.i.* efeminar-se. *adj.* efeminado.

effeminately, *adv.* efeminadamente.

effeminateness, *s.* efeminação.

effervesce, *v.i.* efervescer.

effervescence, *s.* efervescência.

effervescent, *adj.* efervescente.

effete, *adj.* exausto, usado, gasto; impotente, estéril.

efficacious, *adj.* eficaz.

efficaciously, *adv.* eficazmente.

efficaciousness, *s.* eficácia.

efficacity, efficacy, *s.* eficácia.

efficiency, *s.* eficiência, eficácia; rendimento (máq.).

efficient, *adj.* eficiente; activo.

efficiently, *adv.* eficientemente.

effigy (ies), *s.* efígie, imagem.

effloresce, *v.i.* eflorescer.

efflorescence, *s.* eflorescência.

effluence, *s.* efluência; emanação; emissão.

effluente, *adj.* efluente.

effluvium, *s.* eflúvio.

efflux (es), *s.* fluxo; efusão; emanação.

effort, *s.* esforço.

effortless, *adj.* sem esforço.

effrontery (ies), *s.* descaro, desfaçatez.

effulge, *v.i.* brilhar, resplandecer.

effulgence, *s.* brilho, resplendor.

effulgent, *adj.* brilhante, resplandecente.

effulgently, *adv.* brilhante.

effuse, *adj.* espalhado, derramado.

effuse, *v.t.* derramar, espargir, verter. *v.i.* emanar.

effusion, *s.* efusão, derrame; expansão.

effusive, *adj.* efusivo; expansivo, comunicativo.

effusively, *adv.* de um modo expressivo.

effusiveness, *s.* expansão.

eft, *s.* lagartixa.

e.g., *abrev.* de *exempli gratia,* por exemplo.

egad, *interj.* por Deus!

egg, *s.* ovo. 1) *egg-bag,* ovário. 2) *egg-cup,* oveiro (peça de louça ou metal para segurar o ovo). 3) *egg-dealler,* negociante de ovos. 4) *egg-flip,* gemada (ovos, vinho, cerveja ou leite). 5) *egg-plant,* beringela. 6) *egg-shell,* casca de ovo. 7) *buttered eggs,* ovos mexidos. 8) *poached eggs,* ovos escalfados. 9) *soft-eggs,* ovos quentes. 10) *new laid eggs,* ovo fresco. 11) *to put all one's eggs in one basket,* arriscar toda a fortuna numa empresa. 12) to *teach one's grand mother to suck eggs,* ensinar o padre-nosso ao vigário. *v.t.* misturar ou cobrir com ovos; coleccionar ovos.

eglantine, *s.* roseira brava odorífera.

egoism, *s.* egoísmo.

egoist, *s.* egoísta.

egoistic(al), *s.* egotista.

egoistically, *adv.* egoisticamente.

egotism, *s.* egotismo.

egotist, *s.* egotista.

egotistic (al), *adj.* egotista.

egotize (ise), *v.t.* falar muito de si.

egregious, *adj.* egrégio, insigne; estupendo. 1) *an egregious blunder,* uma tolice tremenda. 2) *an egregious ass,* um burro exímio.

egregiously, *adv.* egregiamente.

egregiousness, *s.* distinção, notabilidade.

egress (es), *s.* egresso.

egression, ver *egress.*

egret, *s.* uma espécie de garça; penacho.

Egiptian, *adj.* e *s.* egípcio.

egyptologist, *s.* egiptólogo, pessoa versada em egiptologia.

egyptology, *s.* egiptologia.

eh, *int.* hein!, quê!

eider, *s.* ganso do norte. 1) *eider-down,* penugem de ganso, edredão. 2) *eider-cloth,* edredão.

eidograph, s. instrumento para ampliar ou reduzir desenhos.

eidolon, s. espectro, fantasma.

eight, adj. oito; eight-sided, octaedro.

eighteen, adj. dezoito.

eighteenth, adj. e s. décimo oitavo.

eightfold, a. óctuplo.

eighth, adj. e s. oitavo.

eighthly, adv. em oitavo lugar.

eightieth, adj. e s. octogésimo.

eighty, adj. oitenta.

eirenicon, s. proposta para conseguir a paz.

eisteddfod, s. reunião de bardos e cantores para promover o amor pela literatura e música.

either, ad. e pron. um de dois; ambos; qualquer (referindo-se a uma grande número). conj. ou; também de nenhum modo, em qualquer caso (depois de uma negação); he could nor speak, and I could nor either, ele pode não falar e eu também não.

ejaculate, v.t. falar com veemência; exclamar; proferir jaculatórias; ejacular.

ejaculation, s. exclamação; jaculatória, ejaculação.

ejaculatory, adj. exclamatório, ejaculatório.

eject, v.t. lançar; expulsar.

ejection, s. expulsão, exclusão.

ejectment, s. expulsão; exclusão; mandato de despejo.

ejector, s. expulsor; ejector.

eke, v.t. suprir; manter ou produzir com dificuldade; alongar. adv. e conj. também; eke out, aumentar; prolongar.

eking, ekeing, s. enchimento.

elaborate, v.t. elaborar; trabalhar com esmero. adj. elaborado, primoroso, feito com esmero.

elaborately, adv. esmeradamente.

elaborateness, s. primor, perfeição.

elaboration, s. elaboração.

elaborative, adj. elaborativo, usado na elaboração.

elaborator, s. elaborador.

eland, s. antílope.

elapse, v.i. passar, decorrer.

elastic, adj. e s. elástico.

elastically, adv. elasticamente.

elasticity, s. elasticidade.

elate, v.t. exaltar, estimular; ensoberbecer. adj. exaltado, entusiasmado, orgulhoso.

elately, adv. altivamente.

elation, s. elação, altivez.

elbow, s. cotovelo; ângulo; meia volta (nas amarras). 1) at elbow, à mão; perto, 2) elbow-chair, cadeira de braços. 3) elbow--grease, trabalho pesado. 4) up to the elbows, muito ocupado. 5) out at elbows, com o casaco roto nos cotovelos. 6) elbow--room, muito espaço, largueza. v.t. acotovelar, abrir caminho usando os cotovelos.

elder, s. chefe de uma tribo; ancião; oficial superior em algumas igrejas protestantes; sabugueiro. adj. mais velho; comp. de old que se emprega falando de duas pessoas (geralmente da mesma família), mas não pode ser seguido de «than».

elder-berry (ies), s. baga de sabugueiro.

elderliness, s. idade madura.

elderly, adj. de idade madura.

eldest, o mais velho. sup. de old (usa-se falando de três ou mais pessoas, sobretudo parentes); eldest-born, o filho mais velho, o primogénito.

elecampane, s. énula-campana.

elect, s. adj. eleito, escolhido, predestinado. v.t. eleger, escolher.

election, s. eleição; predestinação.

electioneer, v.i. solicitar votos, galopinar.

electioneering, s. manobras eleitorais.

elective, adj. electivo.

electively, adj. electivamente.

elector, s. eleitor.

electoral, eleitoral.

electorate, s. eleitorado.

electric (al), adj. eléctrico. 1) electric burner, acendedor eléctrico. 2) electric column, pilha voltaica. 3) electric energy, energia eléctrica. 4) electric fan, ventoinha eléctrica. 5) electric light, luz eléctrica. 6) electric saw, arame incandescente, que serve para cortar.

electrically, adv. electricamente.

electrician, s. electricista.

electricity, s. electricidade; electricity works, fábrica geradora de electricidade.

electrification, s. electrificação.

electrifiable, adj. electrizável.

electrified, pret. e pp. de electrify.

electrify, v.t. pret. e pp. electrified, electrizar; electrificar; entusiasmar.

electro, prefixo que significa «eléctrico».

electro-culture, s. cultura vegetal por meio da electricidade.

electrocute, v.t. electrocutar, matar por meio de electricidade.

electrocution, s. electrocução.
electrode, s. eléctrodo.
electro-dynamic, adj. electrodinâmico.
electrolier, s. grupo de lâmpadas eléctricas, em forma de candeeiro.
electrolysis, s. electrólise.
electrolyte, s. electrólito.
electrolytic, adj. electrolítico.
electro-magnet, s. electromagneto.
electro-magnetism, s. electromagnetismo.
electro-magnetic, adj. electromagnético.
electrometer, s. electrómetro.
electromobile, s. veículo movido por electricidade.
electro-motor, s. motor eléctrico.
electron, s. electrão.
electrophone, s. electrofone.
electrophorus, s. electróforo.
electroplate, v.t. cobrir com metal por meio de electrodeposição.
electroscope, s. electroscópio.
electrostatic, s. electrostático.
electrotype, s. electrótipo.
electrum, s. electro, liga de oiro e prata; âmbar amarelo.
electuary (ies), s. electuário.
eleemosynary, adj. caritativo; s. pobre que vive de esmolas.
elegance, s. elegância, gentileza.
elegant, adj. elegante, gentil.
elegantly, adv. elegantemente.
elegiac (al), adj. elegíaco.
elegist, s. autor de elegias, poeta elegíaco.
elegize (ise), v.t. escrever elegias, lamentar.
elegy (ies), s. elegia.
element, s. elemento, componente; princípio fundamental (pl.) noções, fundamentos, rudimentos; os quatro elementos (terra, água, fogo e ar); *he is in his element*, ele está como peixe na água.
elemental, adj. elementar, que tem natureza de elemento.
elementally, adv. de um modo rudimentar, simples.
elementarily, adv. rudimentarmente.
elementariness, adj. simplicidade.
elementary, adj. elementar, rudimentar.
elemi, s. elemi.
elenchus, s. refutação lógica; sofisma.
elephant, s. elefante. 1) *white elephant*, presente que incomoda mais do que o que vale. 2) *elephant-driver*, cornaca, o que conduz elefantes e trata deles.
elephantiasis, s. elefantíase.

elephantine, adj. elefantino.
elevate, v.t. elevar, levantar, exaltar; excitar; animar; alegrar.
elevated, adj. elevado, alto; exaltado; ébrio.
elevation, s. elevação; altura, exaltação; alçado de um edifício.
elevator, s. elevador, ascensor; armazém de trigo; aparelho regulador do leme de profundidade dos aviões.
elevatory, adj. elevatório.
eleven, adj. onze; *eleven-o'clock*, estrela--de-belém (planta).
eleventh, adj. e s. undécimo.
elf, s. duende, gnomo, trasgo; bruxa. pl. *elves*. 1) *elf-child*, criança que se supunha ter sido substituída por outra pelas bruxas. 2) *elf-fire*, fogo-fátuo. 3) *elf-land*, pátria dos duendes; região encantada
elfin, s. duendezinho; menino travesso. adj. pertencente aos duendes.
elfish, adj. próprio de duende; misterioso; travesso.
elicit, v.t. tirar, deduzir.
elicitation, s. dedução, obtenção gradual.
elidable, adj. elidível.
elide, v.t. elidir (uma vogal ou sílaba).
eligibility, s. elegibilidade.
eligible, adj. elegível.
eligibleness, s. elegibilidade.
eligibly, adv. de um modo elegível.
eliminate, v.t. eliminar, expulsar; excluir.
elimination, s. eliminação; expulsão; exclusão.
elision, s. elisão.
élite, s. o melhor; escol, a fina flor da sociedade.
elixir, s. elixir.
elk, s. alce, espécie de veado do Norte.
ell, s. vara (med. de 45 polegadas); *give him an inch and he'll take an ell*, oferece-lhe um bocado e ele fica logo com tudo.
ellipse, s. elipse (geom.).
ellipsis, s. elipse (gram.).
ellipsoid, s. elipsóide.
ellipsoidal, adj. elipsoidal.
elliptic (al), adj. elíptico.
ellipticity, s. elipticidade.
elm, s. olmo, ulmeiro.
elocution, s. elocução.
elocutionary, adj. declamatório.
elocutionist, s. declamador; professor de declamação.
elongate, v.t. alongar, estender. v.i. alongar--se, estender-se.

elongation, s. prolongação, extensão.

elope, v.i. escapar-se; fugir de casa para casar.

elopment, s. fuga para se casar.

eloquence, s. eloquência.

eloquent, adj. eloquente.

eloquently, adv. eloquentemente.

else, pro. noutro. 1) *nobody else,* nenhuma outra pessoa. 2) *no one else,* nenhum outro. 3) *anything else,* alguma coisa mais. 4) *nothing else,* nada mais. 5) *nowhere else,* em nenhuma outra parte. 6) *what else?,* que mais?; adv. mais, além de. conj. outro modo, senão, ou.

elsewhere, adv. em qualquer outra parte.

elucidate, v.t. elucidar.

elucidation, s. elucidação, explicação.

elucidative, adj. elucidativo,

elucidator, s. elucidador.

elucidatory, adj. elucidativo.

elude, v.t. evitar; eludir; tergiversar; escapar.

elusion, s. ilusão; engano.

elusive, adj. ilusório.

elusively, adv. ilusoriamente.

elusiveness, s. engano, fraude.

elusory, adj. ilusório.

elvan, s. élvano, granito da Cornualha. adj. próprio dos duendes; travesso; disfarçado.

elves, plural de *elf.*

elvish, adj. próprio de duende.

elytron, s. (pl. *elytra*), élitro.

elzevir, adj. elzevirianos, pertencente aos Elzevires (impressores de obras clássicas em Amesterdão). s. elzevir, livro impresso pelos Elzevires.

'em, contracção do pronome *them.*

emaciate, v.t. emagrecer; extenuar. v.i. definhar.

emaciation, s. emagrecimento, emaciação; extenuação.

emanate, v.i. emanar.

emanative, adj. emanante.

emanation, s. emanação.

emancipate, v.t. emancipar, libertar.

emancipator, s. emancipador.

emancipation, s. emancipação, libertação.

emasculate, adj. efeminado, castrado. v.i. castrar.

emasculation, s. castração.

emasculator, s. castrador.

embalm, v.t. embalsamar.

embalmment, s. embalsamamento.

embalmer, s. embalsamador.

embank, v.t. represar; terraplenar.

embankment, s. represa, dique, aterro.

embarcation, ver *embarkation.*

embargo, s. embargo; detenção de navios ou mercadorias: proibição de comércio estrangeiro. 1) *to lay an embargo,* embargar. 2) *to take off an embargo,* levantar um embargo. v.t. embargar a saída de navios ou mercadorias; proibir.

embark, v.t. v.i. embarcar; aventurar-se.

embarkation, s. embarque.

embarras, v.t. embaraçar, dificultar, enredar.

embarrassment, s. embaraço.

embassy(ies), s. embaixada.

embattle, v.t. formar em ordem de batalha; pôr ameias.

embay, v.t. deter numa baía; forçar a entrar numa baía; encerrar.

embed, embedding, embedded, v.t. encaixar, embutir; encastoar, enterrar, incrustar; implantar.

embedment, s. embutidura, encaixe; incrustação.

embellish, v.t. embelezar, aformosear, adornar, enfeitar, decorar.

embellisher, s. decorador, enfeitador.

embellishment, s. embelezamento, adorno.

ember, s. pedaço de carvão incandescente; período regular de tempo; pl. cinzas, borralho.

ember-days, s. as quatro Têmporas. 1) *ember-week,* semana das Têmporas. 2) *ember-fast,* jejum das Têmporas.

embezzle, v.t. apropriar-se de uma coisa que lhe foi confiada.

embezzlement, s. peculato.

embezzler, s. defraudador.

embitter, v.t. amargar.

embitterment, s. acção de tornar amargo.

emblazon, v.t. brasonar, esmaltar com cores brilhantes.

emblazonment, s. acto de brasonar ou esmaltar.

emblazonry, s. brasão; arte de brasonar ou esmaltar.

emblem, s. emblema, símbolo; divisa.

emblematic (al), adj. emblemático, simbólico.

emblematically, adv. emblematicamente.

emblematize (ise), v.t. simbolizar, representar por emblemas.

emblement, s. produto da terra semeada ou plantada; colheita anual do que se semeou ou plantou.

embodied, pret. e pp. de *embody.*

embodiment, s. encorporação; personificação.

embody, pret. e pp. emboided. v.t. encorporar; dar forma de corpo; juntar, englobar.

embolden, v.t. animar, encorajar.

embonpoint, s. corpulência; gordura (sobretudo das mulheres).

embosom, v.t. pôr no seio; ocultar, proteger.

emboss, s. gravar em relevo.

embosser, s. gravador em relevo.

embossing, s. gravura em relevo.

embossment, s. relevo; realce.

embouchure, s. desembocadura; abertura de vale; embocadura (de um instrumento, etc.).

embowel, embowelling, embowelled, v.t. desentranhar, estripar.

embower, v.t. cobrir com folhagem, em forma de caramanchão.

embrace, s. abraço. v.t. abraçar, cingir; aceitar; incluir, abranger.

embracement, s. abraço.

embracer, s. abraçador.

ambranchment, s. ramificação.

embrasure, s. canhoneira; abertura em muralhas para assestar as peças; abertura de uma janela ou porta.

embrocate, v.t. aplicar linimentos; fazer fomentações.

embrocation, s. fomentação, linimento.

embroglio, v. imbróglio.

embroider, v.t. bordar.

embroiderer, s. bordador ou bordadeira.

embroidery (ies), s. bordado; embroidery-frame, bastidor.

embroil, v.t. embrulhar, enredar, confundir, intrigar.

embroilment, s. confusão, enredo, intriga.

embryo, s. embrião; princípio, rudimento.

embryologist, s. embriologista.

embryology, s. embriologia.

embryon, ver embryo.

embryonic, adj. relativo ao embrião.

embus, v.t. (embussing, embussed) carregar veículos a motor com tropas, provisões, etc. v.i. entrar nesses veículos.

emend, v.t. emendar, corrigir.

emendable, adj. emendável.

emendate, v.t. emendar.

emendator, s. emendador.

emendation, s. emenda.

emendatory, adj. próprio para emendar.

emerald, s. esmeralda; cor de esmeralda; tipo de impressão. 1) Emerald isle, Irlanda.

2) emerald copper, dioptase. 3) emerald nickle, zaratite.

emerge, v.i. emergir, aparecer.

emergence, s. emergência, aparição.

emergency (ies), s. emergência, necessidade urgente; in case of emergency, no caso de necessidade absoluta.

emergent, adj. emergente.

emergently, adv. repentinamente.

emeritus, s. e adj. emérito, jubilado, aposentado (professor, pároco, etc.).

emerods, ver hemorrhoid.

emersion, s. emersão.

emery, s. esmeril. 1) emery filleting, fita de esmeril. 2) emery-paper, lixa de esmeril. 3) emery-powder, pó de esmeril. 4) emery-stick, polidor de esmeril. 5) emery-wheel, roda de esmeril.

emetic, s. vomitório. adj. emético, que provoca vómitos.

emetical, adj. ver emetic.

emetically, adv. de um modo emético.

emeute, s. tumulto, sublevação.

emigrant, s. e adj. emigrante.

emigrate, v.i. emigrar.

emigrator, s. emigrante.

emigration, s. emigração.

emigratory, adj. emigratório.

eminence, s. eminência, elevação; título dado aos cardeais.

eminency, ver eminence.

eminent, adj. superior; notável; most eminence, eminentíssimo.

eminently, adv. eminentemente.

emir, s. emir, governador de uma província; chefe independente; título dos descendentes de Mafoma.

emissary (ies), s. emissário, mensageiro. adj. enviado; pertencente ao emissário.

emission, s. emissão; saída.

emissive, adj. emissivo.

emit, emtting, emitted, v.t. emitir, despedir; arrojar; pôr em circulação.

emma gee, s. metralhadora.

emmet, s. formiga.

emollient, s. e adj. emoliente.

emolument, s. emolumento, gratificação.

emotion, s. emoção; comoção; sensação.

emotional, adj. emocional.

emotionally, adv. de modo emocional.

emotionalism, s. sentimentalismo.

emotionless, adj. insensível, sem emoção.

emotive, adj. emotive.

empanel, empanelling, empanelled, *v.t.* fazer a lista ou nomeação dos jurados.

empanelment, *s.* nomeação de jurados.

empennage, *s.* «empinage», aplicação de pequenos planos à extremidade de um dirigível.

emperor, *s.* imperador, variedade de borboletas.

emphasis, *s.* ênfase.

emphasize (ise), *v.t.* dar ênfase; acentuar.

emphatic (al), *adj.* enfático; categórico.

emphatically, *adv.* enfaticamente.

emphaticalness, *s.* vigor, energia.

emphysema, *s.* enfisema.

empire, *s.* império.

empiric, *s.* empírico; charlatão, curandeiro. *adj.* empírico.

empirical, *adj.* empírico.

empirically, *adv.* empiricamente.

empirism, *s.* empirismo.

emplacement, *s.* posição dos canhões numa fortaleza; colocação.

emplane, *v.i.* e *v.t.* ir ou pôr a bordo de um avião.

employ, *s.* emprego, ocupação, cargo. *v.t.* ocupar, dar trabalho; usar, servir-se de, aplicar.

employable, *adj.* que se pode empregar.

employé, ver *employee.*

employee, *s.* empregado.

employer, *s.* patrão, chefe.

employment, *s.* emprego, ocupação, uso, aplicação.

emporium, *s.* empório,

empower, *v.t.* autorizar; dar poderes; comissionar.

empress (es), *s.* imperatriz.

emptied, *pret.* e *pp.* de *empty.*

emptier, *s.* esvaziador. *adj. comp.* de *empty.*

emptiness, *s.* vacuidade, estado do que é oco ou está vazio; futilidade.

emption, *s.* compra.

empty, *v.t. pret. pp.* emptied. esvaziar; desocupar; esgotar. *v.i.* esgotar-se, desembocar. *adj.* vazio; oco; desocupado; vago, 1) *empty-headed,* estúpido. 2) *empty--handed,* sem trazer nem levar nada; de mãos vazias.

empurple, *v.t.* tornar vermelho, avermelhar.

empyreal, *adj.* empíreo.

empyrean, *s.* e *adj.* empíreo.

emu, *s.* ema, avestruz da Austrália.

emulate, *v.t.* emular, competir, imitar.

emulation, *s.* emulação, rivalidade.

emulative, *adj.* emulativo.

emulator, *s.* êmulo, rival.

emulous, *adj.* êmulo, rival.

emulously, *adv.* com emulação.

emulsion, *s.* emulsão.

emunctory (ies), emunctório. *adj.* excretório.

enable, *v.t.* habilitar, facilitar, proporcionar.

enact, *v.t.* estabelecer, determinar, ordenar, executar.

enactive, *adj.* que tem eficácia para ordenar.

enactment, *s.* ordem, lei, determinação.

enactor, *s.* legislador, executor.

enamel, enamelling, enamelled, *v.t.* esmaltar. *s.* esmalte; *enamel-ware,* louça esmaltada.

enameller, *s.* esmaltador.

enamelling, *s.* arte de esmaltar.

enamour, *v.t.* enamorar.

enamoured, *pp.* e *adj.* enamorado.

encage, *v.t.* engaiolar.

encamp, *v.t.* e *v.i.* acampar.

encampment, *s.* acampamento, campo.

encase, *v.t.* encaixotar; forrar.

encasement, *s.* encaixotamento.

encaustic, *s.* encáustica. *adj.* encáustico.

enceinte, *adj.* grávida.

encephalic, *adj.* encefálico.

encephalitis, *s.* encefalite.

enchain, *v.t.* encadear, concatenar.

enchainment, *s.* encanto; feitiço.

enchiridion, *s.* enquirídio.

encircle, *v.t.* cercar, rodear, cingir; acompanhar, escoltar.

enclasp, *v.t.* cingir, abrochar, acolchetar; abraçar.

enclave, *s.* território encravado no meio de domínios estrangeiros.

enclitic, *s.* enclítica (partícula gramatical). *adj.* enclítico.

enclitically, *adv.* encliticamente.

enclose, *v.t.* cercar, murar, tapar, encerrar.

encloser, *s.* o que cerca, muro, cercado.

enclosure, *s.* recinto frechado, encerramento, cerca, tapada; conteúdo.

encomiast, *s.* encomiasta.

encomium, *s.* encómio, elogio, louvor.

encompass, *v.t.* cercar, circundar, abraçar, incluir, encerrar.

encore, *int.* bis!, outra vez! *s.* repetição (teat.). *v.t.* pedir a repetição.

encounter, *s.* encontro, choque, luta, escaramuça. *v.t.* e *v.i.* encontrar, encontrar--se; acometer, vir às mãos.

encourage, *v.t.* animar, encorajar, estimar.

encouragement, s. estímulo, incentivo, incitamento.

encourager, s. animador.

encouraging, adj. animador.

encouragingly, adv. com estímulo; de modo animador.

encroach, v.i. usurpador, invasor.

encroachingly, adv. de um modo usurpador.

encroachment, s. abuso, usurpação; invasão.

encrust, v.t. incrustar, embutir, entalhar.

encumber, v.t. estorvar; sobrecarregar; atravancar.

encumbrance, s. obstáculo; estorvo, embaraço, impedimento.

encyclic, s. encíclica.

encyclical, s. encíclica. adj. encíclico.

encyclopaedia, s. enciclopédia.

encyclopaedic (al), adj. enciclopédico.

enciclopaedist, s. enciclopedista.

end, v.i., v.t. acabar, terminar, concluir, decidir; matar; morrer. 1) all is well that ends well, tudo está bem quando acaba bem. s. fim, extremidade, termo; chicote (de cabo); extremo (de navio, etc.); objecto, objectivo, alvo; conclusão, resultado; 2) end plate, tampo (de caldeira). 3) odds and ends, bagatelas, bocados. 4) there's no end to it, não tem fim. 5) to what end?, com que fim? 6) world without end, para sempre. 7) at one's wits end, todo atarantado. 8) to come to an end, cessar. 9) no end of, muito, um não acabar. 10) to one end, em vão. 11) in the end, afinal. 12) on end, sem interrupção (for three weeks on end). 13) shoemaker's end, linhol. 14) to make an end of, acabar com. 15) to the end that, a fim de que. 16) I have it at my fingers' ends, sei isso muito bem (na ponta da língua). 17) to stand on end, arrepiar-se (o cabelo). 18) to make both ends meet, não gastar mais do que se tem de renda. 19) he is at the end of his tether, já não pode mais.

endanger, v.t. comprometer, sujeitar, expor, arriscar, pôr em perigo, fazer perigar.

endangering, adj. perigoso, arriscado, comprometedor.

endangerment, s. perigo.

endear, v.t. fazer estimar, prender, cativar.

endearing, adj. terno, efectuoso.

endeavour, s. esforço, empenho. v.i. e v.t. esforçar-se; fazer o possível, procurar, tentar.

endemic (al), adj. endémico.

endermic (al), adj. endérmico.

ending, s. fim, termo, conclusão, remate, fecho.

endive, s. chicória, endívia.

endless, adj. sem fim, interminável, contínuo, perpétuo.

endlessly, adv. perpetuamente, sem fim.

endlessness, s. perpetuidade, continuidade.

endlong, adv. ao comprido, estendido, em linha recta.

endmost, adj. o mais afastado; na própria extremidade.

endocrine, adj. endócrino.

endogamy, s. endogamia.

endorse, v.t. endossar; abonar; referendar, sancionar.

endorsee, s. endossado.

endorsement, s. endosso.

endorser, s. endossante.

endow, v.t. dotar, doar.

endower, s. doador.

endowment, s. dote, doação; dotes, talentos.

endue, v.t. dotar, privilegiar; investir; assumir.

endurable, adj. suportável, sofrível, tolerável.

endurance, s. paciência, sofrimento, tolerância; duração.

endure, v.t. tolerar, suportar, sofrer. v.i. durar, preservar; ter paciência, sofrer; what can't be cured must be endured, o que não tem remédio, remediado está.

endurer, s. tolerante.

enduring, adj. tolerante, paciente; constante, permanente.

endways, endwise, adv. com a extremidade virada para o espectador ou para cima ou para a frente; ponta com ponta.

enema, s. enema.

enemy (ies), s. inimigo, adversário, antagonista.

energetic (al), adj. energético, vigoroso, activo.

energetically, adv. energeticamente.

energize (ise), v.t. dar energia, dar vigor. v.i. obrar com energia.

energizer, s. o que dá energia.

energumen, s. energúmeno, endemoninhado, furioso; colérico.

energy (ies), s. energia, vigor, força.

enervate, v.t. enervar, debilitar, enfraquecer; cortar os nervos.

enervating, adj. enervante.

enervation, *s.* enervação, fraqueza, prostração de forças.

enfeeble, *v.t.* enfraquecer, debilitar.

enfeeblement, *s.* enfraquecimento, debilidade.

enfeoff, *v.t.* enfeudar.

enfeoffment, *s.* enfeudação.

enfilade, *v.t.* varrer (com tiros, tropas, etc.). *s.* fogo ou tiros de enfiada; enfiada, porção de coisas postas em linha.

enfold, *v.t.* envolver, embrulhar; cercar, abraçar, incluir.

enfoldment, *s.* acto de envolver.

enforce, *v.t.* forçar; fazer cumprir; pôr em vigor; compelir; reforçar.

enforced, *adj.* forçado.

enforcedly, *adv.* violentamente.

enforcement, *s.* constrangimento, coacção; execução de uma ordem ou lei.

enfranchise, *v.t.* franquear; conceder direitos civis; libertar; emancipar; adoptar.

enfranchisement, *s.* franquia; direito de cidadão; emancipação.

engage, *v.t.* ajustar, encomendar, apalavrar, alugar; assalariar; empregar; travar batalha com. *v.i.* empenhar-se, obrigar-se, dar palavra, comprometer-se; fazer promessa de casamento; ocupar-se; combater; vir às mãos; *to be engaged,* estar ocupado; estar comprometido; ter prometido casamento.

engagement, *s.* ajuste; promessa; compromisso; combate, batalha.

engager, *s.* o que se obriga.

engaging, *adj.* atractivo, insinuante, encantador.

engender, *v.t.* engendrar, procriar, gerar, produzir.

engine, *s.* máquina, motor, engenho, locomotiva; mecanismo; agente, instrumento; ardil. 1) *beam-engine,* máquina de balancim. 2) *carding engine,* carda. 3) *fire engine,* bomba de incêndio. 4) *stationary engine,* máquina fixa. 5) *steam engine,* máquina a vapor. 6) *engine-driver,* maquinista. 7) *engine house,* edifício de máquinas. 8) *engine fitter,* montador de máquinas. 9) *engine room,* casa das máquinas. 10) *engine survey,* inspecção das máquinas. *v.t.* prover de máquinas; usar de máquinas.

engineer, *s.* engenheiro; maquinista; mecânico. *v.i.* exercer a função de engenheiro. *v.t.* dirigir e executar construções; arranjar, inventar.

engineering, *s.* engenharia (ciência e arte de fazer máquinas, construções, etc.); direcção, manejo.

enginery, *s.* manejo de máquinas ou de artilharia; maquinaria.

engird, *v.t.* cingir, cercar.

Englander, *s.* inglês; *Little Englander,* o que se opõe à política imperialista.

English, *adj.* inglês. *s.* os ingleses, o povo inglês; a língua inglesa. 1) *the King's English,* inglês correcto. 2) *to murder the King's English,* falar ou escrever inglês sem correcção.

english, *v.t.* traduzir em inglês.

Englishman, *s.* inglês.

Englishmen, *s.* ingleses.

Englishwoman, *s.* inglesa.

Engliswomen, *s.* inglesas.

engraft, *v.t.* enxertar; gravar.

engraftment, *s.* enxerto.

engrain, *v.t.* tingir com grã.

engrave, *v.t.* gravar, cinzelar, burilar, esculpir; gravar na memória.

engraver, *s.* gravador.

engravery, *s.* gravação.

engraving, *s.* gravura (acto de gravar; trabalho do gravador); lâmina gravada.

engross, *v.t.* escrever em caracteres grandes; monopolizar; absorver; engrossar.

engrosser, *s.* copista; monopolista.

engrossment, *s.* transcrição caligráfica; monopólio.

engulf, *v.t.* engolfar, abismar, imergir; mergulhar.

engulfment, *s.* acto de engolfar; mergulho, imersão.

enhance, *v.t.* encarecer, realçar, aumentar o valor.

enhancement, *s.* encarecimento, realce; melhoria; aumento de valor.

enharmonic (al), *adj.* inarmónico.

enigma, *s.* enigma, mistério.

enigmatic (al), *adj.* enigmático, misterioso.

enigmatically, *adv.* enigmaticamente.

enigmatist, *s.* enigmatista.

enigmatize (ise), *v.t.* usar enigmas; falar enigmaticamente.

enjambment, *s.* continuação duma frase além do fim da linha.

enjoin, *v.t.* mandar, ordenar, impor, proibir.

enjoy, *v.t.* gozar, fruir, desfrutar; gostar de apreciar: *how did you enjoy your visit your excursion?*; divertir-se: *I enjoyed myself thoroughly*; sentir prazer em: *I enjoy* *cycling, bathing,* etc.; ter, possuir: *he enjoys a good reputation,* etc.

enjoyable, *adj.* que se pode gozar, deleitável, agradável.

enjoyableness, *s.* gozo.

enjoyably, *adv.* agradavelmente.

enjoyer, *s.* o que goza.

enjoyment, *s.* gozo, prazer.

enkindle, *v.t.* acender, inflamar.

enlace, *v.t.* enlaçar, entrelaçar.

enlacement, *v.t.* enlaçadura.

enlarge, *v.t.* engrandecer; aumentar, ampliar, alargar.

enlargement, *s.* ampliação, extensão.

enlarger, *s.* ampliador.

enlarging, *s.* ampliação.

enlighten, *v.t.* iluminar, instruir, ilustrar, dar luz.

enlightenment, *s.* ilustração, instrução, esclarecimento.

enlist, *v.t.* e *v.i.* alistar, recrutar, atrair; assentar praça.

enlistment, *s.* alistamento, assentamento de praça.

enliven, *v.t.* animar, divertir.

enlivener, *s.* o que anima, o que vivifica; excitante.

enmesh, *v.t.* enredar.

enmity (ies), *s.* inimizade, antipatia, aversão, ódio, rancor.

ennoble, *v.t.* enobrecer.

ennoblement, *s.* enobrecimento, nobilitação, esclarecimento.

ennui, *s.* aborrecimento; tédio, desgosto.

enormity (ies), *s.* enormidade; demasia; atrocidade.

enormous, *adj.* enorme, excessivo; atroz.

enormously, *adv.* enormemente.

enormousness, *s.* enormidade, grandeza.

enough, *s.* e *adj.* bastante, suficiente. 1) *a word to the wise is enough,* a bom entendedor meia palavra basta. *adv.* assaz, bastante. 2) *well enough,* toleravelmente, sofrivelmente, menos mal; muito bem: *you know well enough what I mean.* Como *adv.* vem sempre depois do *adj.* ou *adv.* que modifica; *ex: cheap enough,* bastante caro; *soon enough,* bastante cedo. Pode dizer-se: *enough of,* mas nesse caso *enough* é *s.* e *of* liga-lhe outro *s.*; *ex: we have enough of wine.*

enounce, *v.t.* pronunciar, enunciar; declarar, anunciar.

enquire, inquire, *v.t.* indagar, informar-se inquirir, averiguar.

enquirer, inquirer, *s.* investigador, indagador, esquadrinhador.

enquiry(ies) inquiry(ies), *s.* investigação, indagação, averiguação; *to make enquiries,* tomar informações.

enrage, *v.t.* enraivecer, irritar.

enrapt, *adj.* arrebatado, extasiado.

enrapture, *v.t.* transportar, arrebatar, enlevar, encantar.

enrigester, *v.t.* registar, inscrever, apontar.

enrich, *v.t.* enriquecer; adornar, ornar; fertilizar.

enrichment, *s.* enriquecimento.

enrol, enrolling, enrolled, *v.t.* registar, inscrever, alistar, recrutar. *v.i.* assentar praça; matricular-se.

enrolment, *s.* alistamento, recrutamento, registo.

enroller, *s.* registador.

ens, *s.* ente, ser. *pl. entia.*

ensanguined, *adj.* ensanguentado.

ensconce, *v.t.* e *v.i.* cobrir, guardar, encobrir.

ensemble, *s.* conjunto; totalidade.

enshrine, *v.t.* guardar num relicário.

enshrinement, *s.* guarda em relicário.

enshroud, *v.t.* cobrir, esconder, encobrir; amortalhar.

ensign, *s.* insígnia, bandeira, sinal; porta-bandeira.

ensign, *v.t.* assinalar, distinguir.

ensigncy (ies), *s.* posto de porta-bandeira; *ensigncy staff,* pau de bandeira.

ensignship, ver *ensigncy.*

ensilage, *s.* ensilagem.

ensile, ensilate, *v.t.* ensilar.

enslave, *v.t.* escravizar.

enslavement, *s.* escravidão.

enslaver, *s.* o que escraviza.

ensnare, *v.t.* armar o laço.

ensnarer, *s.* o que arma o laço.

ensue, *v.t.* seguir, procurar. *v.i.* seguir-se, suceder.

ensuing, *adj.* seguinte.

ensure, ver *ensue.*

entablature, *s.* entablamento.

entail, *s.* vínculo, morgado. *v.t.* vincular; assegurar, perpetuar; impor; acarretar (como consequência).

entailer, *s.* vinculado.

entailment, *s.* vínculo.

entangle, *v.t.* enredar, emaranhar, intrincar.

entanglement, *s.* enredo.

enter, *v.t.* penetrar, introduzir; registar, anotar, inscrever, dar entrada (em livros; na alfândega); alistar; matricular. *v.i.* entrar, introduzir, entrar em cena. 1) *to enter into,* fazer parte de; meter-se em; empenhar; penetrar. 2) *enter on, upon,* começar; entrar de posse.

enteric, *s.* entérico.

entering, *s.* entrada.

enteritis, *s.* enterite.

enterology, *s.* enterologia, tratado dos intestinos.

enterotomy, *s.* enterotomia, incisão nos intestinos.

enterprise, *s.* empresa, empreendimento, iniciativa. *v.t.* empreender, arriscar.

enterprising, *s.* empresa. *adj.* audaz, empreendedor, atrevido.

enterprisingly, *adv.* arrojadamente.

entertain, *v.t.* obsequiar, festejar, hospedar; entreter, divertir, distrair; receber em casa como hóspede ou visita.

entertainer, *s.* o que convida e dá hospitalidade; o que diverte.

entertainment, *s.* hospitalidade, festim; entretenimento, divertimento.

enthral, enthrall, *v.t.* dominar o ânimo; escravizar; encantar.

enthralment, *s.* domínio, escravidão.

enthrone, *v.t.* entronizar.

enthronement, *s.* entronização.

enthuse, *v.t.* e *v.i.* entusiarmar(-se).

enthusiasm, *s.* entusiasmo.

enthusiast, *s.* entusiasta.

enthusiastic (al), *adj.* entusiástico.

enthusiastically, *adv.* entusiasticamente.

entia, *pl.* de *ens.*

entice, *v.t.* tentar, seduzir, atrair, engodar; *to entice away,* raptar (uma donzela).

enticement, *s.* tentação, sedução.

enticer, *s.* tentador, sedutor.

enticing, *adj.* tentador, sedutor.

enticingly, *adv.* de modo sedutor.

entire, *adj.* inteiro, completo, cabal, íntegro; constante, firme.

entirely, *adv.* inteiramente, totalmente, completamente.

entireness, *s.* inteireza.

entirety (ies), *s.* integridade.

entomb, *v.t.* enterrar, sepultar,

entombment, *s.* enterramento.

entomologist, *s.* entomologista, entomólogo.

entomologize (ise), *v.i.* estudar entomologia; coleccionar insectos para estudos científicos.

entomology, *s.* entomologia, tratado dos insectos.

entourage, *s.* companhia, séquito, roda.

entr'acte, *s.* entreacto.

entrails, *s.* entranhas, intestinos.

entrain, *v.t.* meter em comboio (tropas, etc.); arrastar; acarretar.

entrammel, entrammelling, entrammelled, *v.t.* pôr em dificuldades.

entrance, *s.* entrada; porta; embocadura; ingresso; tomada de posse (de um cargo). *v.t.* extasiar, transportar, fascinar, arrebatar; *an entrancing vision,* uma visão arrebatadora.

entrancement, *s.* êxtase, transporte, arrebatamento.

entrancingly, *adv.* extaticamente.

entrap, entrappin, entrapped, *v.t.* prender no laço.

entrapment, *s.* laço, armadilha.

entrapper, *s.* o que lança armadilha.

entreat, *v.t.* rogar, suplicar.

entreatingly, *adv.* de um modo suplicante.

entreatment, ver *entreaty.*

entreaty (ies), *s.* súplica, rogo, petição, instância.

entrée, *s.* direito, privilégio de admissão; prato servido entre o peixe e a carne assada.

entremets, *s.* prato servido depois do assado; entremez.

entrench, *v.t.* entrincheirar.

entrenchment, *s.* entrincheiramento; invasão.

entrepot, *s.* entreposto.

entresol, *s.* andar baixo de uma casa (entre o rés-do-chão e o primeiro andar).

entrust, *v.t.* confiar, depositar.

entry (ies), *s.* entrada, vestíbulo, pórtico; assento, nota, entrada em livro comercial, lançamento; registo de entrada (mar.) 1) *single entry,* partidas simples. 2) *double entry,* partidas dobradas. 3) *entry port,* portaló. 4) *bill of entry,* declarações na Alfândega.

entwine, *s. v.t.* enlaçar, entrelaçar, abraçar.

entwist, *v.t.* torcer, enroscar; cercar, cingir.

enumerate, *v.t.* enumerar.

enumeration, *s.* enumeração; lista; recapitulação.

enumerative, *adj.* enumerativo.

enumerator, *s.* enumerador.

enunciable, *adj.* enunciável.

enunciate, *v.t.* enunciar, expor; articular; pronunciar.

enunciation, s. enunciação, exposição, articulação.

enunciative, adj. enunciativo.

enunciator, s. enunciador.

enure, ver inure.

envelop, v.t. envolver; cobrir.

envelope, s. envelope; sobrescrito; invólucro; balão de gás dos dirigíveis; espaço onde se colocam esses balões.

envelopment, s. envolvimento.

envenom, v.t. envenenar.

enviable, adj. invejável.

enviableness, s. qualidade de excitar inveja.

enviably, adv. de um modo invejável.

envied, pret. e pp. de envy.

envier, s. invejoso.

envious, adj. invejoso.

enviously, adv. invejosamente.

enviousness, s. inveja.

environ, v.t. cercar, rodear.

environment, s. ambiente; arrabaldes; soma das condições e circunstâncias de um organismo.

envirous, d. pl. arredores, cercanias, subúrbios.

envisage, v.t. encarar; considerar; examinar; reflectir.

envoy, s. enviado, mensageiro; embaixador temporário.

envy (ies), s. inveja, emulação, ciúme, objecto ou motivo de inveja. v.t. e v.i. pret. e pp. envied, invejar, cobiçar, apetecer.

enwrap, enwrapping, enwrapped, v.t. envolver, enrolar.

enwreath, v.t. engrinaldar.

eolienne, s. pano de seda e lã.

eolithic, adj. eolítico.

epact, s. epacta.

eparch, s. eparca.

eparchy (ies), s. aparquia.

epaulement, s. parapeito (para proteger uma bateria).

epaulet, s. dragona.

epenthesis, s. epêntese.

epenthetic, adj. epentético.

epergne, s. centro de mesa.

epexecesis, s. epexegese.

ephah, s. efa, antiga medida hebraica.

ephemera, s. (pl.) **ephemeras;** ou então já é plural de ephemeton, efémeras, insectos que nascem e morrem no mesmo dia; coisa efémera.

ephemeron, ver ephemera.

ephemerous, adj. efémero.

ephemeris, pl. **ephemerides.** s. efemérides.

ephod, s. paramento sagrado hebraico.

epiblast, s. epiblasto.

epic, adj. épico. s. poema épico.

epicedium, s. epicédio.

epicene, s. e adj. epiceno.

epicism, s. aptidão para poemas épicos.

epicist, s. poeta épico.

epicure, s. epicúrio; gastrónomo.

epicurean, s. epicurista. adj. epicureu, epicurista.

epicycle, s. epiciclo.

epicyclic, adj. epicíclico.

epicycloid, s. epiciclóide.

epidemic, s. epidemia, peste. adj. epidémico.

epidemical, adj. epidémico.

epidermal, adj. epidérmico.

epidermic, adj. epidérmico.

epidermis, s. epiderme.

epidermoid, adj. semelhante à epiderme.

epigene, adj. epígeno.

epigenesis, s. epigenesia.

epiglottis (es), s. epiglote.

epigram, s. epigrama.

epigrammatic (al), adj. epigramático.

epigrammatist, s. epigramatista.

epigrammatize (ise), v.t. epigramatizar, fazer epigramas.

epigraph, s. epígrafe.

epigrapher, s. o que faz epígrafes.

epigraphic, adj. epigráfico.

epigraphist, s. epigrafista.

epigraphy, s. epigrafia.

epilepsy, s. epilepsia.

epileptic, s. e adj. epiléptico.

epilogic, s. epilógico.

epologize (ise), v.t. epilogar.

epilogue, s. epílogo.

Epiphany, s. Epifania, dia dos Reis Magos.

episcopacy (ies), s. episcopado, bispado.

episcopal, adj. episcopal.

episcopally, adv. de um modo episcopal.

episcopalian, s. membro da seita protestante episcopal.

episcopalianism, s. seita protestante episcopal.

episcopate, s. episcopado.

episcopize (ise), v.t. consagrar um bispo. v.i. exercer função de bispo.

episode, s. episódio.

episodic, adj. episódico, incidente.

episodically, adv. episodicamente.

epispastic, *ad.* epispático.

epistie, *s.* epístola, carta.

epistier, *s.* epistológrafo, pessoa que escreve epístolas.

epistolary, *adj.* epistolar.

epistoler, *v.* epistler.

epistolis, *s.* epistológrafo.

epistolize (ise), *v.i.* escrever cartas.

epistyle, *s.* epistilo, arquitrave.

epitaph, *s.* epitáfio.

epithalamium, *s.* epitalâmio.

epithelium, *s.* epitélio.

epithet, *s.* epíteto.

epithetic, *adj.* epitético.

epitome, *s.* epítome, resumo.

epitomic (al), *adj.* resumido.

epitomist, *s.* autor de um epítome.

epoch, *adj.* época.

epochal, *adj.* relativo a épocas.

epode, *s.* epodo.

eponym, *s.* epónimo, o que dá o seu nome a um novo lugar ou instituição.

eponymous, *adj.* epónimo.

apopee, *s.* epopeia.

epos (es), *s.* epos, poema épico.

epsilon, quinta leta do alfabeto grego.

Epsom-salts, *s.* sais de Epsom, sais purgativos (sulfato de magnésio).

equability, *s.* igualdade.

equable, *adj.* uniforme.

equably, *adj.* igualdade.

equal, *s.* igual; adequado; uniforme; justo; imparcial. 1) *equal to the occasion,* à altura da situação. *v.t. equalling, equalled,* igualar; igualar-se; pôr-se ao nível. 2) *not to be equalled,* sem igual.

equalization, *s.* igualação.

equalize (ise), *v.t.* e *v.i.* igualar.

equally, *adv.* igualmente.

equalness, *s.* igualdade, uniformidade.

equanimity, *s.* equanimidade, serenidade de ânimo, imparcialidade.

equanimous, *adj.* equânime, imparcial

equanimously, *adv.* imparcialmente.

equate, *v.t.* considerar ou representar como equivalente; igualar; uniformizar.

equation, *s.* equação.

equator, *s.* equador.

equatorial, *adj.* equatorial. *s.* equatorial.

equatorially, *adv.* na direcção do equador.

equerry (ies), *s.* eguariço; oficial da Casa Real Inglesa.

equestrian, *s.* cavaleiro. *adj.* equestre.

equiangular, *adj.* equiângulo.

equibalance, *s.* equilíbrio.

equidistantly, *adv.* a igual distância.

equilateral, *adj.* equilateral.

equilibrate, *v.t.* equilibrar.

equilibration, *s.* equilibração, equilíbrio,

equilibrator, *s.* equilibrador (avião).

equilibrist, *s.* equilibrista, funâmbulo, acrobata.

equilibrium, *s.* equilíbrio; *in stable equilibrium,* em equilíbrio estável.

equimultiple, *s.* equimúltiplo.

equine, *adj.* equino.

equinoctial, *s.* linha equinocial. *adj.* equinócio.

equinox (es), *s.* equinócio.

equip, equipping, equipped, *v.t.* equipar, apetrechar, aparelhar, prover, habilitar,

equipage, *s.* equipagem, equipamento; carruagem.

equipment, *s.* equipamento, armamento; vestuário,

equipoise, *s.* equilíbrio; contrapeso. *v.t.* equilibrar.

equitable, *adj.* equitativo, justo, imparcial.

equitableness, *s.* equidade.

equitably, *adj.* imparcialmente.

equitation, *s.* equitação.

equity (ies), *s.* equidade.

equivalence, *s.* equivalência.

equivalent, *s.* equivalente.

equivalently, *adv.* de um modo equivalente.

equivocal, *adj.* equívoco, ambíguo.

equivocally, *adv.* equivocamente.

equivocate, *v.t.* equivocar, usar de palavras ambíguas.

equivocation, *s.* equívoco, equivocação.

equivocator, *s.* o que usa palavras ambíguas.

equivoke (voque), *s.* equívoco; ambiguidade.

era, *s.* era, época, idade.

eradiate, *v.t.* e *v.i.* irradiar.

eradiation, *s.* irradiação.

eradicable, *adj.* o que se pode arrancar, extirpar, destruir.

eradication, *s.* erradicação; extirpação.

eradicative, *adj.* erradicativo.

erasable, *adj.* que se pode safar; delével.

erase, *v.t.* safar, apagar, riscar, raspar, rasurar.

erasement, *s.* rasura.

eraser, *s.* raspador; raspadeira; *ink-eraser,* borracha de tinta.

erasion, *s.* rasura.

erasure, s. rasura.

ere, pre. antes de; conj. antes que.

erect, v.t. erigir, levantar; construir, edificar; to erect an engine, montar uma máquina. adj. erecto, direito, levantado.

erectile, adj. eréctil.

erection, s. erecção; construção; estrutura; montagem (de máquinas, etc.).

erectly, adv. direito, a prumo.

erectness, s. posição erecta.

eremite, s. eremita.

eremitic (al), adj. relativo ao eremita.

ergo, adv. portanto.

ergonic, adj. ergónico.

ergot, s. cravagem de centeio; espécie de esporão nos cavalos.

ergotism, s. ergotismo.

eric, s. indemnização pela morte de alguém.

erica, s. erica, urze.

eristic, s. pessoa que gosta de disputar.

Eri-king, s. ser imaginário da mitologia germânica (para amedrontar as crianças), rei dos álamos.

ermine, s. arminho; pele de arminho; funcionário que usa pele de arminho na toga.

ermined, adj. coberta de arminho.

erne, s. pigargo, águia aquática, de cauda branca.

erode, v.t. roer, corroer. v.i. desgastar-se.

erosion, s. corrosão.

erosive, adj. corrosivo.

erotic, s. e adj. erótico.

eroticism, s. erotismo.

err, v.i. errar, equivocar-se; desviar-se; pecar; to err is human, to forgive divine, errar é próprio dos homens, perdoar é próprio de Deus.

errand, s. mensagem, comissão, recado; errand-boy, moço de recados.

errant, adj. errante, vagabundo, ambulante; knight errant, cavaleiro andante.

errantly, adv. de um modo errante.

errantry, s. vida errante.

errata, pl. de erratum.

erratic (al), adj. errante, irregular, excêntrico, variável.

erratically, adv. sem regra, sem ordem, irregularmente.

erratum, s. errata. pl. errata.

erroneous, adj. erróneo, inexacto, falso, errado.

erroneously, adv. erroneamente.

erroneousness, s. erro; falsidade.

error, s. erro, engano; equívoco; variação da agulha (náut.).

erst, adv. outrora, antigamente.

erstwhile, v. erst.

erubescence, s. vermelhidão, rubor.

erubescency, ver erubescence.

erubescent, adj. vermelho, corado.

eructate, v.t. e v.i. arrotar

eructaction, s. eructação, arroto.

erudite, adj. erudito, letrado.

eruditely, adv. eruditamente.

eruditeness, s. erudição.

erupt, v.i. fazer erupção; sair com força e rapidez.

eruption, s. erupção.

eruptive, adj. eruptivo.

eruptively, adv. de um modo eruptivo.

eruptiveness, s. erupção.

erysipelas, s. erisipela.

erythema, s. eritema.

escalade, s. escalada. v.t. escalar.

escalator, s. escada rolante.

escallop, ver scallop.

escapade, s. correria; fuga; travessura, partida estouvada.

escape, v.t. evitar, iludir v.i. escapar, fugir, salvar-se. 1) to escape by the skin of one's teeth ou to have a narrow escape, escapar por um triz. 2) his named has escaped me, fugiu-me o nome dele, s. fuga, fugida; fuga de gás; derrame de um líquido. 3) escapepipe, tubo de descarga de vapor. 4) escapevalve, válvula de escape.

escapement, s. escape, saída; escapo (do relógio).

escarp, v.t. escarpa, fazer escarpa. s. escarpa.

escarpment, s. escarpa.

eschalot, s. chalota (planta).

escharotic, s. cáustico, adj. escarótico.

eschatological, adj. escatológico.

eschatologist, s. escatologista.

eschatology, s. escatologia.

escheat, s. reversão de bens para o Estado; confiscação de bens. v.t. e v.i. reverter para o Estado os bens dos que falecem ab intestato; confiscar.

eschew, v.t. fugir de; evitar.

escort, v.t. escoltar.

escritoire, s. escrivaninha, secretária.

escudo, s. escudo.

esculent, s. e adj. comestível.

escutcheon, s. escudo de armas; a blot on

his escutcheon, uma mancha na sua reputação.

Eskimo, *s.* esquimó.

esophagus, *s.* esófago.

esoteric (al), *adj.* esotérico.

esoterically, *adv.* secretamente.

espalier, *s.* espaldeira, renque de árvores; latada. *v.t.* formar espaldeira ou latada.

esparto, *s.* esparto.

especial, *adj.* especial.

especially, *adv.* especialmente.

Esperantist, *s.* esperantista.

Esperanto, *s.* esperanto.

espial, *s.* espionagem.

espied, *pret.* de *espy*.

espionage, *s.* espionagem.

esplanade, *s.* esplanada; avenida.

espousal, *s.* esponsal; adesão a uma causa.

espouse, *v.t.* e *v.i.* contrair esponsais; casar-se, sustentar (doutrina, causa, etc.).

espouser, *s.* contraente de esponsais ou matrimónio; defensor.

esprit, *s.* espírito, graça.

esprit-de-corps, *s.* camaradagem.

espy, *pret.* e *pp.* *espied. v.t.* divisar, ver ao longe; descobrir.

Esq., abreviatura de *Esquire*. Usa-se nos sobrescritos das cartas depois do nome, e corresponde a «Ex.mo Sr.».

esquire, *s.* escudeiro que conduzia o escudo de um cavaleiro.

essay, *s.* ensaio, opúsculo; esforço.

essay, *v.t.* ensaiar, tentar, experimentar.

essayer, *s.* ensaiador; escritor de ensaios.

essayist, *s.* escritor de ensaios, ensaísta.

essence, *s.* essência, perfume; substância; gasolina.

essential, *adj.* essencial, substancial, indispensável, constitutivo.

essentiality, *s.* essencialidade.

essentially, *adv.* essencialmente.

essentialness, *s.* essencialmente.

establish, *v.t.* estabelecer, fundar, instituir, confirmar.

establisher, *s.* instituidor.

establishment, *s.* estabelecimento; fundação; instituição; casa de residência ou de negócios; negócio.

estate, *s.* bens, propriedade; herdade, quinta, fazenda; estado, condição, posição, hierarquia. 1) *personal estate*, bens móveis. 2) *real estate*, bens de raiz.

esteem, *s.* estima, consideração, apreço, crédito. *v.t.* estimar, apreciar, considerar.

estimable, *adj.* estimável, apreciável, calculável.

estimableness, *s.* apreço.

estimate, *s.* cálculo, cômputo, orçamento; preço; avaliação; *rough estimate*, orçamento aproximado. *v.t.* calcular, computar, avaliar, apreciar, fazer orçamento.

estimator, *s.* computador.

estimation, *s.* apreciação, cômputo, cálculo; estima, apreço; opinião favorável.

estival, ver *aestival*.

estrade, *s.* estrado, tablado, palco.

estrange, *v.t.* alienar, tornar indiferente.

estrangedness, *s.* indiferença.

estrangement, *s.* indiferença, alienação.

estreat, *s.* extracto (do registo de multas). *v.t.* extrair (do registo de multas).

estuary (ies), *s.* estuário, esteiro.

esurience, *s.* fome, necessidades, penúria.

esuriency, ver *esurience*.

esurient, *adj.* esfomeado, necessitado.

etc., ver etcetera.

etcetera, *s.* o resto. *pl.* extras.

etch, *v.t.* gravar (por meio de ácidos); delinear, traçar.

etcher, *s.* gravador.

etching, *s.* gravura por meio de ácidos; impressão da gravura; bosquejo; rascunho.

eternal, *adj.* eterno, imortal; perdurável, incessante.

eternally, *adv.* eternamente.

eternalize (ise), *v.t.* eternizar, perpetuar.

eternity (ies), *s.* eternidade.

Etesian, *adj.* etésio.

ether, *s.* éter.

ethereal, *adj.* etéreo, aéreo, celestial, espiritual.

ethereally, *adv.* celestialmente.

etherealize (ise), *v.t.* eterificar, misturar com éter; espiritualizar.

etherize (ise), *v.t.* anestesiar por meio de éter.

ethic, *adj.* ético, moral. *s.* ver *ethics*.

ethical, *adj.* relativo à ética ou moral.

ethically, *adv.* moralmente.

ethics, *s.* ética, filosofia moral.

ethnic (al), *s.* étnico.

ethnographer, *s.* etnógrafo.

ethnographic, *adj.* etnográfico.

ethnography, *s.* etnografia.

ethnologic (al), *adj.* etnológico.

ethnologically, *adv.* etnologicamente.

ethnologist, *s.* etnologista.

ethnology, *s.* etnologia.

ethologic (al), *adj.* etológico.
ethologist, *s.* etologista.
ethology, *s.* etologia.
ethos, *s.* espírito característico (de uma comunidade, povo ou estado).
ethyl, *s.* etilo, base de álcool, do éter e do ácido acético.
etiolate, *v.t.* estiolar, branquear, desbotar. *v.i.* estiolar-se.
etiologist, *s.* etiologista.
etiology, *s.* etiologia.
etiquette, *s.* etiqueta, cerimónia.
etui, *s.* estojo, agulheiro.
etymologic (al), *adj.* etimológico.
etymologically, *adv.* etimologicamente.
etymologize (ise), *v.t.* dar ou estudar a derivação das palavras.
etymology (ies), *s.* etimologia.
etymon, *s.* étimo.
eucalyptus (es), *s.* eucalipto.
Eucharist, *s.* Sagrada Eucaristia.
eucharistic (al), *adj.* eucarístico.
eucharistically, *adv.* modo eucarístico.
euchre, *s.* iúcar, um jogo de cartas. *v.t.* ganhar no iúcar; enganar.
Euclid, *s.* Elementos ou tratado de geometria de Euclides, célebre matemático de Alexandre (300 anos antes de Cristo); geometria.
eudemonism, *s.* eudemonismo.
eudemonist, *s.* eudemonistas.
eudiometer, *s.* eudiómetro.
eugenic, *adj.* eugénico.
eugenics, *s.* eugenia.
eulogist, *s.* elogiador.
eulogistic (al), *adj.* laudatório, encomiástico.
eulogistically, *adv.* de um modo elogioso; panegírico.
eulogize (ise), *v.t.* elogiar, encomiar, louvar.
eulogy (ies), ver *elogium.*
eunuch, *s.* eunuco.
eunuchism, *s.* eunuquismo.
euonymus, *s.* evónimo.
eupepsia, *s.* eupepsia.
eupeptic, *adj.* eupéptico.
euphemism, *s.* eufemismo.
euphemistic (al), *adj.* eufémico.
euphemize (ise), *v.t.* e *v.i.* usar eufemismo.
euphonic (al), *adj.* eufónico; suave, melodioso.
euphonically, *adv.* eufonicamente.
euphonious, ver *euphonic.*
euphiously, ver *euphonically.*
euphonium, *s.* eufónio.

euphonize (ise), *v.t.* eufonizar, tornar eufónico.
euphony, *s.* eufonia; suavidade, melodia.
euphorbia, *s.* (bot.) eufórbio.
euphorbium, *s.* eufórbio, goma extraída da *Euphorbia resinifera,* que os veterinários usam hoje como vesicatório.
euphrasy, *s.* eufrásia, planta medicinal.
euphuism, *s.* eufuísmo, estilo afectado, gongórico.
euphuist, *s.* eufuísta.
euphuistic, *s.* eufuístico, gongórico.
eureka, *int.* eureka!, descobri! *s.* descoberta importante.
eurhythmics, *s.* euritmia.
European, *s.* e *adj.* europeu.
europeanize, *v.t.* europeizar.
Euterpean, *adj.* de Euterpe, musa e deusa da música.
euthanasia, *s.* eutanásia.
evacuate, *v.t.* evacuar; desocupar; despejar; abandonar.
evacuation, *s.* evacuação.
evacuator, *s.* o que evacua, desocupa ou abandona.
evade, *v.t.* evadir, fugir, iludir. *v.i.* evadir-se; escapar-se.
evader, *s.* fugitivo.
evaluate, *v.t.* avaliar.
evaluation, *s.* avaliação.
evanesce, *v.i.* esvaecer, dissipar, desaparecer.
evanescence, *s.* esvaecimento.
evanescent, *adj.* evanescente, que se dissipa.
evangel, *s.* evangelho.
evangelic, *adj.* evangélico. *s.* evangélico, da seita dos Evangélicos.
evangelical, *adj.* evangélico.
evangelist, *s.* evangelista.
evangelistic, *adj.* relativo aos evangelistas.
evangelization (isa), *s.* evangelização.
evangelize (ise), *v.t.* evangelizar.
evaporate, *v.t.* evaporar, evaporizar; secar; dissipar. *v.i.* evaporizar-se, dissipar-se.
evaporation, *s.* evaporação.
evaporator, *s.* vaporizador.
evasion, *s.* evasão, fuga; evasiva, escusa, subterfúgio.
evasive, *adj.* evasivo, ambíguo.
evasively, *adv.* de um modo evasivo.
evasiveness, *s.* evasiva, escusa.
eve, *s.* véspera; o anoitecer; *Christmas Eve,* véspera de Natal.

even, *adj.* plano, liso, igual; uniforme; sereno; invariável, no mesmo nível 1) *even-handed*, imparcial. 2) *even tide*, o anoitecer. 3) *to be even with*, estar em paz com; não dever nada. 4) *to make even*, unir, igualar. *adv.* exactamente, precisamente; de um modo igual. 5) *even though*, *even if*, ainda que, mesmo que. 6) *even as*, ainda assim. 7) *not even*, nem mesmo. *v.t.* igualar, nivelar; liquidar contas. *s.* (poét.) noite, o anoitecer.

evener, *s.* nivelador; regulador.

evening, *s.* o anoitecer; noite. *adj.* vespertino. 1) *good evening*, boa tarde; boas noites. 2) *last evening*, ontem à noite. 3) *evening dress*, vestido de noite. 4) *evening party*, sarau.

evenly, *adv.* igualmente, lisamente.

evenness, *s.* igualdade, uniformidade, lisura; imparcialidade.

evensong, *s.* vésperas, oração da tarde.

event, *s.* acontecimento; êxito, conse-quência, resultado. 1) *at all events*, suceda o que suceder; em todo o caso. 2) *in the event of*, no caso de.

eventful, *adj.* cheio de acontecimentos.

eventide, *s.* o anoitecer.

eventual, *adj.* consequente; final; eventual; contingente.

eventually, *adv.* consequentemente, eventualmente.

eventuality (ies), *s.* eventualidade, casuali-dade.

eventuate, *v.i.* acontecer, resultar.

ever, *adv.* sempre; já, alguma vez; nunca, jamais (depois de palavras, ou frases negativas). 1) *have you ever been to Paris?*, já foste a Paris? 2) *for ever and ever*, eternamente. 3) *for ever and a day*, para todo o sempre. 4) *as ever*, como sempre. 5) *ever young*, sempre jovem. 6) *ever and anon*, de vez em quando. 7) *worse than ever*, pior do que nunca. 8) *hardly (scarcely) ever*, quase nunca.

evergreen, *s.* e *adj.* sempre verde; (bot.) persistente.

everlasting, *adj.* perpétuo, eterno; perdurável.

everlastingly, *adv.* sem cessar.

everlastingness, *s.* eternidade.

evermore, *adv.* eternamente.

eversion, *s.* eversão, subversão, destruição; reviramento para fora.

evert, *v.t.* revirar para fora.

every, *adj.* todo; *every other day*, dia sim, dia não.

everybody, *pron.* toda a gente.

everyday, *adj.* diário; usual; comum; *every day*, todos os dias.

everyone, every one, *pron.* toda a gente.

everything, *pron.* tudo.

everyway, *adv.* a todos os respeitos.

everywhere, *adv.* por toda a parte.

evict, *v.t.* desalojar, desapossar, excluir; usurpar.

eviction, *s.* evicção; despejo (de casa).

evidence, *s.* evidência; demonstração; prova; declaração; testemunho. 1) *to give evidence*, dar testemunho. 2) *to turn king's evidence*, depor contra o seu cúmplice. *v.t.* evidenciar, provar, demonstrar.

evident, *adj.* evidente, claro.

evidential, *adj.* comprovativo, evidencial.

evidently, *adv.* evidentemente.

evil, *s.* mal, dano; inconveniente; mal-dade, depravação; pecado. 1) *evil-doer*, malfeitor. 2) *evil-eye*, mau-olhado. 3) *evil--minded*, malicioso. 4) *evil-speaking*, maledicência. 5) *the evil one*, o demónio. *adj.* mau, depravado, pernicioso, prejudi-cial, nocivo.

evilness, *s.* maldade.

evilly, *adv.* mal.

evince, *v.t.* provar, justificar, demonstrar.

evincible, *adj.* demonstrável.

evincibly, *adv.* demonstrativamente.

evincive, *adj.* demonstrável.

evirate, *v.t.* castrar, capar; cortar os rebentos às plantas.

eviscerate, *v.t.* estripar, abrir o ventre.

evisceration, *s.* estripação.

evocate, ver *evoke*.

evocation, *s.* evocação, avocação; intima-ção; apelação.

evoke, *v.t.* evocar; avocar.

evolute, *s.* evoluta, manobra, desenvolvi-mento.

evolutional, *adj.* evolutivo.

evolutionary, ver *evolutional*.

evolutionism, *s.* evolucionismo.

evolutionist, *s.* evolucionista.

evolvable, *adj.* que se pode desenrolar ou despegar.

evolve, *v.t.* desenrolar; produzir por evolução. *v.i.* abrir-se, despegar-se.

evulsion, *s.* arrancamento, evulsão.

ewe, *s.* ovelha.

ewer, *s.* jarro para água.

exacerbate, *v.t.* irritar, exasperar, exacerbar, agravar.

exacerbation, *s.* irritação, exasperação, exacerbação.

exact, *v.i.* exigir, obrigar, extorquir. *adj.* exacto, pontual, rigoroso, justo, correcto, escrupuloso.

exacting, *adj.* exigente.

exaction, *s.* exacção; exigência; extorsão.

exactitude, *s.* exactidão, rigor, precisão, justiça, pontualidade.

exactly, *adv.* exactamente; *exactly so!,* isso mesmo!

exacteness, ver *exactitude.*

exactor, *s.* exactor.

exaggerate, *v.t.* exagerar.

exaggeration, *s.* exageração.

exaggerative, *adj.* exagerativo, exagerado.

exaggerator, *s.* exagerador.

exalt, *v.t.* exaltar, enaltecer, reforçar; intensificar (cores, etc).

exaltation, *s.* exaltação, regozijo, intensificação.

exalted, *pp.* e *adj.* exaltado, elevado, glorificado, sublime.

exaltedly, *adv.* exaltadamente.

exaltedness, *s.* exaltação, glorificação, sublimidade.

exam, *s.* exame; *to do an exam,* fazer exame.

examination, *s.* exame; investigação; inspecção; registo; autópsia. 1) *cross examination,* instância a uma testemunha. 2) *custom-house examination,* visita aduaneira. 3) *written examination,* provas escritas. 4) *viva voce examination,* provas orais.

examine, *v.t.* examinar, investigar, inspeccionar; registar; interrogar.

examinee, *s.* examinando.

examiner, *s.* examinador.

example, *s.* exemplo; modelo; cópia, exemplar, espécime; precedente. *v.t.* exemplificar; ensinar por meio de exemplo. 1) *to make an example of him,* castigá-lo como aviso para os outros. 2) *to give* ou *set a good example,* dar bom exemplo. 3) *to take example by,* copiar. 4) *for example,* por exemplo.

exarch, *s.* exarca; patriarca, bispo da igreja grega.

exarchate, *s.* exarcado.

exasperate, *v.t.* exasperar, provocar, irritar; agravar.

exasperation, *s.* exasperação, provocação, irritação.

exasperator, *s.* exasperador.

excavate, *v.t.* cavar, escavar; esvaziar; fazer oco; profundar.

excavation, escavação; cavidade.

excavator, *s.* escavador.

exceed, *v.t.* exceder, sobressair, avantajar, sobrepujar. *v.i.* exceder-se, preponderar.

exceeding, *adj.* excessivo, excedente. *s.* excesso.

exceedingly, *adv.* excessivamente.

excel, excelling, excelled, *v.t.* e *v.i.* primar, sobressair, avantajar, superar, vencer.

excellence, *s.* excelência.

excelency (ies), *s.* excelência; título de honra; *His Excelency,* Sua Excelência.

excellent, *adj.* excelente, primoroso.

excellently, *adv.* excelentemente.

excelsior, *adj.* mais alto.

except, *v.t.* exceptuar, excluir. *v.i.* objectar; *pret.* excepto, menos, salvo, fora. *conj.* a menos que.

excepting, *prep.* com excepção de, exceptuando.

exception, *s.* excepção; exclusão; recusa; *to take exception to,* objectar.

exceptionable, *adj.* recusável; contestável.

exceptionableness, *s.* qualidade de ser recusável.

exceptionably, *adv.* de um modo recusável.

exceptional, *adj.* exceptional; superior.

exceptionally, *adv.* excepcionalmente.

excerpt, *s.* extracto, excerto. *v.t.* extractar.

excerption, *s.* acto de extractar; extracto.

excess, *s.* excesso, demasia, sobra; transgressão. 1) *excess fare,* sobretaxa nos comboios, etc. 2) *excess-luggage,* excesso de bagagem.

excessive, *adj.* excessivo, demasiado, exorbitante.

excessively, *adv.* excessivamente.

excessiveness, *s.* excesso, demasia.

exchange, *s.* troca; câmbio; Bolsa; letra de câmbio. 1) *sight exchange,* cheque à vista. 2) *bill of exchange,* letra de câmbio. 3) *exchange broker,* corretor de câmbios. 4) *rate of exchange,* taxa de desconto. *v.t.* trocar, permutar, cambiar.

exchangeable, *adj.* trocável; permutável.

exchangeability, *s.* propriedade ou qualidade de ser trocável.

exchanger, *s.* cambista.

exchequer, *s.* tesouro público. 1) *Chancellor of the Exchequer,* ministro das Finanças. 2) *exchequer bill,* bilhete do Tesouro.

excise, *s.* sisa; imposto do consumo. 1) *excise duties,* contribuições indirectas. 2) *excise office,* repartição de finanças. *v.t.* extirpar.

exciseman, *s.* cobrador de contribuições.

excision, *s.* excisão.

excitability, *s.* excitabilidade.

excitable, *adj.* excitável.

excitant, *s.* excitante.

excitation, *s.* excitação.

excitative, *ad.* excitativo.

excitatory, ver *excitative.*

excite, *v.t.* excitar, emocionar, incitar, provocar, animar.

excitement, *s.* incitamento, excitação.

excoter, *s.* incitador; instigador; gerador (da corrente eléctrica nos magnetes de um dínamo).

exciting, *adj.* emocionante.

exclaim, *v.t.* e *v.i.* exclamar.

exclamation, *s.* exclamação; *note of exclamation,* ponto de exclamação.

exclamatory, *adj.* exclamatório.

exclude, *v.t.* excluir, exceptuar, rejeitar.

exclusion, *s.* exclusão.

exclusive, *adj.* exclusivo.

exclusively, *adv.* exclusivamente.

exclusiveness, *s.* estado ou qualidade de ser exclusivo.

excogitate, *v.t.* excogitar, pensar, imitar.

excogitation, *s.* excogitação.

excommunication, *s.* excomunhão, anátema.

excoriate, *v.t.* escoriar.

excoriation, *s.* escoriação.

excrement, *s.* excremento.

excremental, *adj.* excrementoso

excrementitious, *adj.* excrementício.

excrescence, *s.* excrescência.

excrescent, *adj.* supérfluo; que forma excrescência.

excrete, *v.t.* excretar.

excretion, *s.* excreção.

excretive, *adj.* excretório.

excruciate, *v.t.* atormentar, martirizar.

excruciating, *adj.* cruciante, penosíssimo, torturante.

excruciatingly, *adv.* de um modo torturante.

excruciation, *s.* tormento, tortura, martírio.

exculpate, *v.t.* desculpar, justificar.

exculpation, *s.* desculpa, justificação.

exculpatory, *adj.* justificativo.

excursion, *s.* excursão, viagem; correria; desvio.1) *excursion steamer,* vapor de excursionistas. 2) *excursion train,* comboio para excursionistas, geralmente com preços reduzidos.

excursionist, *s.* excursionista.

excursionize (ise) *v.t.* fazer ou tomar parte numa excursão.

excursively, *adv.* de um modo vago ou errante; caprichosamente.

excursiveness, *s.* qualidade de errante.

excursus (es), *s.* dissertação pormenorizada; excurso.

excusable, *adj.* desculpável.

excusableness, *s.* desculpa, qualidade de ser desculpável.

excusably, *s.* desculpavelmente.

excusatory, *adj.* justificativo, apológético,

excuse, *v.t.* escusar, desculpar, justificar; dispensar, isentar.

exeat, *s.* permissão para se ausentar, temporariamente, de um colégio.

execrable, *adj.* execrável.

execrableness, *s.* abominação.

execrably, *adv.* de um modo execrável.

execrate, *v.t.* execrar, abominar, maldizer.

execration, *s.* execração, abominação, maldição.

execrative, *adj.* execratório.

execratively, *adv.* de um modo execratório.

execratory, *adj.* execratório.

executable, *adj.* executável.

executant, *s.* executante.

execute, *v.t.* executar, cumprir; desempenhar (teat.; mús.); matar.

executer, *s.* executor; carrasco.

execution, *s.* execução, cumprimento; mandato do juiz; execução, morte; *writ of execution,* auto de execução.

executioner, *s.* executor; carrasco.

executive, *s.* poder executivo. *adj.* executivo.

executively, *adv.* de um modo executivo.

executor, *s.* testamenteiro; executor.

executorship, *s.* testamentaria.

executory, *adj.* executório.

executrix (es), *s.* testamenteira.

exegesis, *s.* exegese.

exegetic (al), *adj.* exegético.

exegetically, *adv.* exegeticamente.

exemplar, *s.* exemplar, original, modelo.

exemplarily, *adv.* exemplarmente.

exemplariness, *s.* qualidade do que deve servir de exemplo.

exemplarity, *s.* exemplaridade.

exemplary, *adj.* exemplar.

exemplified, *pret. pp.* de *exemplify.*

exemplification, *s.* exemplificação; exemplo; traslado.

exemplify, *v.t.* exemplificar, declarar; trasladar.

exempt, *v.t.* isentar, libertar, dispensar, exceptuar. *adj.* isento, livre.

exemption, *s.* isenção, dispensa.

exequatur, *s.* exequatur.

exequies, *s. pl.* exéquias.

exercise, *s.* exercício, uso; tema; ensaio. 1) *exercise book,* caderno de exercícios. *v.t.* excercitar, pôr em exercício, destrar; exercer, empregar; comunicar. *v.i.* exercitar-se.

exerciser, *s.* exercitante.

exercitation, *s.* exercitação, exercício.

exergue, *s.* exergo.

exert, *v.t.* esforçar; exercer; *exert oneself,* esforçar-se, empenhar-se.

exertive, *adj.* esforçado.

exertion, *s.* esforço, diligência; (pl) meios, passos, diligência; *to use all exertions,* fazer todos os esforços.

exeunt, *s.* locução latina.

exfoliate, *v.i.* esfoliar-se.

exfoliation, *s.* esfoliação.

exhalant, *adj.* exalador.

exhalation, *s.* exalação.

exhale, *v.t.* exalar, evaporar; emitir. *v.i.* dissipar-se, evaporar-se.

exhaust, *v.t.* exaurir, esgotar, consumir; dissipar, empobrecer. *s.* escape, descarga, emissão de vapor. 1) *exhaust fan,* ventilador de aspiração. 2) *exhaust-pipe,* tubo de escape. 3) *exhaust port,* orifício de evacuação (mec.).

exhauster, *s.* esgotador.

exhaustible, *adj.* exaustível.

exhausting, *adj.* fatigante; *exhausting pump,* bomba de esgoto.

exhaustive, *adj.* exaustivo; fatigante; completo.

exhaustively, *adv.* de um modo exaustivo; completamente.

exhaustiveness, *s.* exaustação, esgotamento.

exhibit, *v.t.* exibir, expor. *s.* documento ou objecto apresentado no tribunal; coisas postas em exposição.

exibition, *s.* exibição; exposição; bolsa de estudo a aluno de universidade; *to make an exbition of oneself,* fazer uma figura ridícula.

exhibitioner, *s* estudante bolseiro.

exhibitive, *adj.* representativo. *s.* expositor.

exhilarate, *v.t.* alegrar, divertir, regozijar.

exhilarating, *adj.* divertido, que causa alegria; hilariante.

exhilaration, *s.* alegria, jovialidade, regozijo, bom humor.

exhilarative, *adj.* que causa alegria.

exhort, *v.t.* exortar.

exhortation, *s.* exortação.

exhortative, *adj.* exortativo.

exhortatory, *adj.* exortatório.

exhumation, *s.* exumação, desenterramento.

exhume, *v.t.* enxumar, desenterrar.

exhumer, *s.* o que exuma.

exigence, *s.* exigência, falta, necessidade; urgência.

exigency, ver *exigence.*

exigent, *adj.* exigente.

exiguity, *s.* exiguidade.

exiguous, *adj.* exíguo, escasso, pequeno.

exiguousness, *s.* exiguidade.

exile, *s.* exílio, desterro; exilado, desterrado. *v.t.* exilar, desterrar, banir, expatriar.

exilian, exilic, *adj.* relativo ao exílio dos Judeus na Babilónia.

exility, *s.* finura, tenuidade, subtileza.

exist, *v.i.* existir, subsistir.

existence, *s.* existência; ser, ente; vida; *in existence,* existente; que existe.

existent, *adj.* existente.

existing, *adj.* existente, actual.

exit, *s.* saída; partida, morte; saída (do actor) do palco.

ex libris, *s.* ex-líbris.

exode, *s.* entremez, farsa; êxodo.

exodus (es), *s.* êxodo, saída, emigração.

ex officio, frase latina: «em virtude do cargo».

exonerate, *v.t.* exonerar, desonerar; aliviar; desculpar.

exoneration, *s.* exoneração; desculpa.

exonerative, *adj.* que exonera.

exorbitance, *s.* exorbitância, excesso.

exorbitant, *s.* exorbitante.

exorbitantly, *adv.* exorbitantemente.

exorcise, *v.t.* exorcismar, ler os exorcismos; esconjurar.

exorcism, *s.* exorcismo.

exorcist, *s.* exorcista.

exordium, *s.* exórdio.

exoteric, *adj.* exotérico; vulgar. *s.* exotérico, pessoa não admitida a ensino esotérico.

exoterics, s. exotérica.

exotic, adj. exótico, estrangeiro. s. planta exótica.

expand, v.t. expandir, dilatar, alargar, desenvolver; abrir, despregar. v.t. expandir--se, dilatar-se; abrir-se.

expander, s. pessoa ou coisa que expande; dilatador (das caldeiras a vapor).

expanse, s. extensão, grande superfície; expansão.

expansibility, s. expansibilidade.

expansile, adj. capaz de expansão; capaz de causar expansão.

expansion, s. expansão, dilatação; desenvolvimento; extensão; imensidade. 1) expansion gear, aparelho de expansão variável. 2) expansion hatch, escotilha de expansão. 3) expansion joint, junta de expansão.

expansive, adj. expansivo; extensive; comunicativo.

expansively, adv. de um modo expansivo.

expansiveness, s. qualidade de ser expansivo.

expatiate, v.i. desenvolver (um assunto), discursar desenvolvidamente; espaçar-se; ampliar-se, dilatar-se.

expatiation, s. acção de espaçar-se; desenvolvimento de um assunto.

expatiatory, s. difuso, prolixo.

expatriate, v.t. expatriar, desterrar; exilar.

expatriation, s. expatriação, desterro; exílio.

expect, v.t. esperar, aguardar, contar com; pensar, supor (que).

expectance, s. expectação, expectativa.

expectancy, ver expectance.

expectant, s. e adj. expectante.

expectantly, adv. com esperança.

expectation, s. expectação; expectativa; esperança.

expecter, s. expectador.

expectorant, s. e adj. expectorante.

expectorate, v.t. expectorar.

expectoration, s. expectoração.

expedience, s. aptidão; conveniência, desembaraço, expediente.

expediency, ver expedience.

expedient, s. expediente, recurso. adj. vantajoso, conveniente; oportuno.

expediently, adv. oportunamente.

expedite, v.t. apressar; desembaraçar; expedir; despachar.

expedition, s. expedição, diligência; expedição (militar, etc.).

expeditious, adj. expedito, desembaraçado.

expeditiously, adv. expeditamente.

expeditiousness, s. prontidão, diligência.

expel, expelling, eppelled, v.t. expelir, expulsar; despedir.

expellable, adv. expulsável.

expend, v.t. expender, despender, gastar.

expenditure, s. gasto, desembolso.

expense, s. despesa, custo, desembolso, gasto. 1) discharging expenses, despesas de desembarque, ou de descarga. 2) law expense, despesas de justiça. 3) loading expenses, despesas de carregamento ou de desembarque. 4) free of expense, franco de porte. 5) petty expense, despesas miúdas. 6) travelling expenes, despesas de viagem. 7) working expenses, despesas de exploração. 8) to defray the expenses, custear as despesas. 9) at the expense of, à custa de.

expensive, adj. dispendioso.

expensiveness, s. dispêndio.

experience, s. experiência, conhecimento; perícia; aventura. v.t. experimentar; conhecer.

experiment, s. experimentação, experiência, tentativa, ensaio.

experiment, v.t. experimentar, tentar, ensaiar.

experimental, adj. experimental.

experimentally, adv. experimentalmente.

experimentalism, s. experimentalismo.

experimentalist, s. experimentalista.

experimentalize (ise), v.t. experimentar.

experimentation, s. experimentação, ensaio.

expert, s. perito, sabedor.

expert, adj. perito, experimentado, esperto, prático, hábil, destro.

expertly, adv. destramente, com perícia.

expertness, s. perícia, habilidade, destreza.

expiable, adj. expiável.

expiate, v.t. expiar, reparar um dano.

expiation, s. expiação.

expiator, s. expiador.

expiatory, adj. expiatório.

expiration, s. expiração; termo, terminação; morte.

expiratory, adj. relativo à expiração do ar.

expire, v.t. expirar, respirar. v.i. expirar, morrer, fenecer (com.) terminar um prazo.

expiring, adj. que está a terminar; moribundo.

expiry, *s.* terminação (de um período, tréguas, etc.).

explain, *v.t.* explicar, explanar, interpretar; *to explain away*, modificar, fazer desaparecer por meio de explicações.

explainable, *adj.* explicável.

explainer, *s.* explicador.

explanation, *s.* explicação, esclarecimento, interpretação.

explanatory, *adj.* explicativo.

explanatorily, *adv.* explicativamente,

expletive, *s.* explicativa. *adj.* expletivo.

explicable, *adj.* explicável.

explicate, *v.t.* explicar, aclarar, interpretar.

explication, *s.* explicação, aclaração, interpretação.

explicative, *adj.* explicativo,

explicit, *adj.* explícito, definitivo.

explicitness, *s.* clareza, especificação.

explicity, *av.* explicitamente.

explode, *v.t.* explodir, fazer saltar (uma bomba, etc.); expelir (com violência e ruído); reprovar, causar descrédito de (teoria, etc.). *v.i.* explodir; rebentar 1) *to explode with laughter*, rebentar de riso. 2) *exploded notion*, ideia abandonada.

exploder, *s.* explosivo; pessoa que causa explosão.

exploit, *s.* façanha, proeza. *v.t.* usar, utilizar, (para uso próprio); tirar partido de; explorar; pormenorizar; procurar.

exploitation, *s.* utilização (para uso próprio); exploração.

exploration, *s.* exploração, investigação.

exploratory, *adj.* exploratório, que serve para explorar.

explore, *v.t.* explorar, averiguar, examinar.

explorer, *s.* explorador.

explosion, *s.* explosão.

explosive, *s.* e *adj.* explosivo.

explosively, *adv.* com explosão.

explosiveness, *s.* propriedade explosiva, explosividade.

exponent, *s.* exponente (mat.); expositor; representante; intérprete; executante (de música, etc.).

exponential, *adj.* exponencial (mat.).

export, *s.* exportação; (pl.); artigos de exportação; *export duty*, direitos de exportação. *v.t.* exportar.

exportable, *adj.* exportável.

exportation, *s.* exportação.

exporter, *s.* exportador.

expose, *v.t.* expor; arriscar; exibir, descobrir;

revelar; desmascarar; comprometer; abandonar; *to expose for show, for sale*, expor à vista, à venda.

exposé, *s.* revelação comprometedora; exposição, explicação.

exposedness, *s.* exposição, explicação.

exposition, *s.* exposição, exibição; explicação.

expositive, *adj.* expositivo.

expositor, *s.* expositor.

expository, *s.* expositivo.

expostulate, *v.i.* altercar, contender; queixar-se.

expostulation, *s.* expostulação, debate, disputa; queixa, censura amigável.

expostulator, *s.* altercador.

expostulatory, *adj.* relativo à expostulação.

exposure, *s.* exposição, situação, orientação; revelação.

expound, *v.t.* expor, explicar, comentar, interpretar.

expounder, *s.* expositor, comentador.

express, *v.t.* expressar, exprimir; espremer. 1) *to express oneself*, expressar-se, explicar-se. 2) *not to be expressed*, inexprimível. *adj.* expresso, explícito; claro, categórico; especial; rápido; veloz; exacto. 3) *express steamer*, paquete rápido. 4) *express train*, comboio expresso, rápido. *s.* correio, mensageiro, próprio.

expressible, *adj.* exprimível.

expression, *s.* expressão, atitude; semblante; locução.

expressional, *adj.* relativo à expressão; que tem poder de expressão.

expressionless, *adj.* sem expressão, inexpressivo.

expressive, *adj.* expressivo.

expressively, *adv.* de um modo expressivo.

expressivness, *s.* expressão, significação.

expressly, *adv.* expressamente.

expressness, *s.* exactidão, clareza.

exprobration, *v.t.* exprobração.

expropriate, *v.t.* expropriar, alienar.

expropriation, *s.* expropriação, alienação.

expulsion, *s.* expulsão.

expulsive, *adj.* expulsivo.

expunge, *v.t.* expungir; expurgar.

expurgate, *v.t.* expurgar.

expurgation, *s.* expurgação, purificação.

expurgator, *s.* purificador.

expurgatory, *adj.* expurgatório.

exquisite, *adj.* excelente, primoroso, delicado; excessivo, agudo. *s.* pretensioso.

exquisitely, *adv.* primorosamente.
exquisiteness, *s.* primor, delicadeza, perfeição.
exscind, *v.t.* cortar; excluir.
exsecte, *v.t.* amputar, extirpar.
exsection, *s.* amputação; extirpação.
exsiccate, *v.t.* secar, enxugar.
exsiccation, *s.* dessecação.
exsiccator, *s.* dessecador.
extant, *adj.* existente.
extemporaneous, *adj.* extemporâneo, sem preparação.
extemporaneously, *adv.* extemporaneamente.
extemporaneousness, *s.* extemporaneidade.
extemporay, ver *extemporaneous*.
extempore, *adv.* e *adj.* improvisado; *speak extempore*, falar sem quaisquer notas.
extemporization (isa), *s.* improviso, improvisação.
extemporize (ise), *v.t.* improvisar. *v.i.* falar sem preparação.
extend, *v.t.* estender, ampliar, prolongar; conceder, prorrogar; embargar. *v.i.* estender-se.
extensibility, *s.* extensibilidade.
extensible, *adj.* extensível.
extensile, *adj.* extensível.
extension, *s.* extensão, expansão; prolongação, prorrogação.
extensive, *adj.* extenso, extensivo, grande; *extensive repairs*, reparação importante.
extensively, *adv.* extensivamente.
extensiveness, *s.* extensão; extensibilidade.
extensor, *s.* extensor.
extent, *s.* extensão, dimensão, tamanho, alcance; execução; embargo; *to a certain extent*, até certo ponto.
extenuate, *v.t.* atenuar, diminuir; paliar; extenuar (raro).
extenuating, *adj.* atenuante.
extenuation, *s.* atenuação; paliação.
extenuative, *s.* atenuativo, que serve para atenuar.
extenuatory, *adj.* que atenua.
exterior, *s.* exterior; exterioridade; aspecto. *adj.* exterior, externo; visível.
exteriorize (ise), *v.t.* exteriorizar, manifestar.
exteriorly, *adv.* exteriormente.
exterminable, *adj.* exterminável.
exterminate, *v.t.* exterminar, extirpar, eliminar.

extermination, *s.* extermínio, destruição; eliminação.
exterminative, *adj.* exterminador.
exterminator, *s.* exterminador.
exterminatory, *adj.* exterminador.
extern, *s.* aluno externo; a parte externa; médico ou doente externo de hospital. *adj.* externo.
external, *adj.* externo, exterior. *s.* (pl.) o exterior; exterioridade.
externalism, *s.* externalismo.
externalist, *s.* externalista.
externality, *s.* exterioridade.
externalization (isa), *s.* acto de exteriorizar.
externalize (ise), *v.t.* exteriorizar, dar forma ou corpo.
externally, *adv.* externamente, exteriormente.
exterritorial, *adj.* exterritorial.
exterritoriality, *s.* exterritorialidade.
extinct, *adj.* extinto; abolido.
extinction, *s.* extinção, aniquilamento, apagamento, abolição.
extinctive, *adj.* extintivo.
extinguish, *v.t.* apagar, extinguir; suprimir, aniquilar.
extinguishable, *adj.* extinguível.
extinguisher, *s.* extintor.
extinguishgment, *s.* extinção, abolição, supressão.
extirpate, *v.t.* extirpar; arrancar; exterminar; destruir.
extirpation, *s.* extirpação.
extirpator, *s.* extirpador.
extol, extolling, extolled, *v.t.* exaltar, louvar, enaltecer.
extort, *v.t.* extorquir, obter por violência ou ameaça; arrebatar.
extorter, ver *extortioner*.
extortion, *s.* extorsão.
extortionate, *adj.* extorsivo; exorbitante.
extortioner, *s.* opressor.
extra, *adj.* extra, extraordinário. 1) *extra charge*, taxa suplementar. 2) *extra postage*, sobretaxa. 3) *extra strenght*, reforço. 4) *it is nothing extra*, não é nada fora do vulgar.
extract, *s.* extracto, essência; resumo, sumário.
extract, *v.t.* extrair, arrancar; compendiar, sumariar.
extractable, *adj.* que se pode extrair.
extraction, *s.* extracção, linhagem; origem; extracção (quím.).
extractive, *adj.* que serve para extrair.

extractor, s. extractor.
extraditable, adj. que se pode extraditar, extraditável.
extradite, v.t. extraditar.
extradition, s. extradição.
extra-judicial, adj. extrajudicial.
extra-judicially, adv. extrajudicialmente
extraneous, adj. estranho, extrínseco, externo, exterior.
extraneously, adv. de um modo estranho, extrínseco.
extraordinarily, adv. extraordinariamente.
extraordinariness, s. singularidade.
extraordinary, adj. extraordinário; raro, singular.
extraterritorial, adj. extraterritorial.
extravagance, s. extravagância.
extravagant, adj. extravagante.
extravagantly, adv. extravagantemente.
extravaganza, s. composição literária, dramática ou musical de carácter fantástico; linguagem ou comportamento fantástico.
extravasate, v.t. e v.i. extravasar.
extravasation, s. extravasamento.
extreme, adj. extremo, sumo, supremo, excessivo; rigoroso, severo. 1) extremes meet, os extremos tocam-se. 2) in extreme, ao extremo.
extremely, adv. extremamente; muito. 1) extremely sorry, desolado. 2) extremely glad, encantado.
extremeness, s. qualidade de ser excessivo.
extremism, s. extremismo, radicalismo.
extremist, s. extremista.
extremity (ies), s. extremidade, ponta, cabo; rigor.
extricable, adj. o que se pode aclarar ou deslindar.
extricate, v.t. desembrulhar, deslindar, aclarar; libertar (quím.).
extrication, s. desembaraço, desprendimento, desenredo.
extrinsic (al), adj. extrínseco, externo.
extrinsically, adv. extrinsecamente.
extrude, v.t. expulsar, banir.
extrusion, s. expulsão, exclusão.
extrusive, adj. que serve para expulsar.
extrusory, adj. que expulsa.
exuberance, s. exuberância, superabundância, excesso.
exuberancy, ver exuberance.
exuberant, adj. exuberante.
exuberantly, adv. exuberantemente.

exuberate, v.i. exuberar, superabundar.
exudation, s. exsudação, transpiração, suor.
exude, v.t. e v.i. suar, transpirar.
exult, v.i. exultar, triunfar.
exultance, s. exultação, alegria, triunfo, superioridade.
exultation, ver exultation.
exulting, adj. triunfante, alegre, jubiloso.
exultingly, adv. alegremente; com ar de triunfo.
exuviae, s. pl. exúvias.
eyas (es), s. falcão novo, ainda por acabar de treinar.
eye, s. olho; vista; olhar; atenção, vigilância; aspecto; fêmea (do colchete); furo, buraco; janela redonda; balão (de planta); escapeladura; olhal; escovém; direcção do vento (náut.) 1) eyeball, globo do olho. 2) apple of the eye, menina do olho. 3) eye beam, olhadela. 4) eyebright, eufrásia. 5) eyebrow, sobrancelha. 6) eye-glass, monóculo. 7) eye-glasses, óculos. 8) eyehole, ilhó. 9) eyelash, pestana. 10) eyelid, pálpebra. 11) eye of a stay, garganta de estai (náut.). 12) eye-opener, facto ou história surpreendente. 13) eye-servant, criado que precisa ser vigiado. 14) eyesight, sentido da vista. 15) eyeshot, alcance da vista. 16) eyesore, coisa feia que ofende a vista. 17) eye-tooth, dente canino. 18) eye-wash, colírio. 19) eyewater, loção para os olhos. 20) eye wink, piscadela, sinal com os olhos. 21) eye witness, testemunha ocular. 22) before one's eyes, à vista. 23) as far as the eye can reach, a perder de vista. 24) in my eyes, na minha opinião. 25) in the twinkling of an eye, num abrir e fechar de olhos. 26) in the wind's eye, contra o vento; à trinca. 27) to keep on eye an, olhar por. 28) to give an eye to, vigiar cuidadosamente. 29) to see with half an eye, ver sem dificuldade. 30) eyes front!, olhar, frente!. v.t. olhar, ver contemplar. v.i. parecer.
eyed, adj. que tem olhos; One-eye, que tem um só olho.
eyeless, s. cego, sem olhos.,
eylet, s. cego, sem olhos.
eylet, eylet-hole, s. ilhó; buraco (para espreitar ou fazer fogo através)
eyot (ait), s. ilhota, especialmente num rio.
eyrie (ies), s. ninho de ave de rapina; residência humana no cimo de montanha.
eyry, (ies), ver eyrie.

F

f, sexta letra do alfabeto.

fa, fá (nota musical).

fabian, *adj.* cauteloso, prudente; *Fabian Society,* grupo socialista que advoga métodos cautelosos e prudentes.

fable, *s.* fábula, conto, mentira. *v.t.* fingir; inventar fábulas,

fabric, *s.* tecido, pano; construção, edifício, mão-de-obra.

fabricate, *v.t.* fabricar construir; fingir, inventar.

fabricator, *s.* fabricante; inventor; embusteiro.

fabulise, *v.i.* fabulizar.

fabulist, fabulista; mentiroso.

fabulous, *adj.* fabuloso.

fabulously, *adv.* fabulosamente.

façade, *s.* fachada.

face, *s.* cara, rosto; lado, face, superfície (de um objecto); espelho (de cilindro); frente, fachada; descaro, atrevimento, gesto, careta. 1) *face-ache,* nevralgia facial. 2) *face value,* valor nominal (moedas, notas). 3) *to face,* cara a cara. 4) *in my face,* nas minhas barbas. 5) *to set one's face against,* opor-se tenazmente. 6) *to make faces,* fazer caretas. 7) *to pull a long face,* fazer uma cara feia. *v.t.* e *v.i.* encarar, fazer frente, aparentar, enganar; forrar; tornear uma face (mec.); voltar o corpo. 8) *right face,* direita, volver!. 8) *to face one out,* sustentar descaradamente. 9) *to face out a lie,* sustentar uma mentira. 10) *to face a thing out* ou *to face the music,* arrostar com as consequências.

facecloth, *s.* toalha para cobrir o rosto de um cadáver.

faced, *adj.* forrado, guarnecido; *ill-faced,* mal--encarado.

facer, *s.* bofetão na face.

facet, *s.* faceta. *v.t.* facetar.

facetiae, *s.* facécia, chiste.

facetious, *s.* chistoso, jovial.

facetiously, *adv.* jovialmente.

facetiousness, *s.* chiste, graça.

facia, *s.* tabuleta.

facial, *adj.* facial.

facially, *adv.* de um modo facial.

facile, *adj.* fácil; hábil, vivo; dócil; obediente; cortês.

facilitate, *v.t.* facilitar.

facilitation, *s.* facilitação.

facility, *s.* facilidade, habilidade, docilidade; afabilidade.

facing, *s.* adorno, ou cobertura (na frente); revestimento.

fac-simile, *s.* fac-símile.

fact, *s.* facto, acção; realidade. 1) *in fact,* de facto. 2) *matter of fact person,* sujeito muito prático.

faction, *s.* facção, parcialidade.

factional, *adj.* faccionário.

factious, *adj.* faccioso.

factiously, *adv.* facticiamente, artificial-mente.

factitiousness, *s.* artificialidade.

factitive, *adj.* factitivo.

factor, *s.* factor, agente.

factorage, *s.* corretagem, comissão.

factorial, *adj.* relativo a uma fábrica, ou a um factor.

factorship, *s.* agência.

factory, ies, *s.* fábrica; *actory acts,* leis sobre a segurança dos operários.

factotum, *s.* factótum.

facula, *s.* fécula.

facultative, *adj.* facultativo.

faculty (ies), *s.* faculdade.

fad, *s.* moda, novidade, mania.

faddier, faddiest, *comp. sup.* de *faddy.*

faddily, *adv.* caprichosamente.

faddiness, *s.* moda, capricho.

faddish, *adj.* caprichoso.

faddism, *s.* capricho.

faddist, *s.* pessoa caprichosa.

faddy, *adj.* caprichoso.

faddy, *v.i.* murchar, definhar, desaparecer gradualmente. *v.t.* desbotar, perder a cor.

fading, *adj.* moribundo; lânguido. *s.* extinção ou desaparecimento gradual de imagens ou de sons (cinema, rádio).

faeces, *s.* fezes.

faerie, faery, *s.* fada.

fag, fagging, fagged, *v.t.* fatigar, cansar. *v.i* estafar-se. *s.* cansaço; escravo; aluno obrigado a prestar serviços a outro mais adiantado; nó. 1) *fag-end*, extremidade de uma corda; chicote de cabo sem falcaça (náut.); ourela, orla (de pano); desperdícios. 2) *brain-fag*, cansaço do cérebro.

fagged, *pret.* e *pp.* de *fag*.

fagging, *s.* obrigação dos alunos de prestarem certos serviços e obedecerem a outros mais adiantados.

faggot, fagot, *s.* feixe (de lenha ou de varas de ferro, aço, etc.); faxina. *v.t.* enfeixar.

faggotist, *s.* o que toca fagote.

fagott, *s.* fagote.

Fahrenheit, *s.* nome de um termómetro em que 32° correspondem a zero graus centígrados, e 212° correspondem a 100° centígrados.

faience, *s.* faiança, louça fina.

fail, *v.t.* faltar, não cumprir. *v.i.* falhar, malograr-se, falir (com). 1) *do not fail to come*, não deixes de vir. s. falta, omissão. 2) *without fail*, sem falta.

failing, *s.* falta; fraqueza, imperfeição. *prep.* à falta de; *failing wine I will drink beer*, à falta de vinho, beberei cerveja.

failure, *s.* malogro, falta, quebra, falência.

fain, *adj.* e *adv.* resignado; bem-disposto; de bom grado; *would fain do it, if I could*, de bom grado faria isso, se pudesse.

faint, *v.i.* desmaiar, desfalecer; desanimar. *s.* desmaio. *adj.* abatido, tímido; indistinto. 1) *to grow faint*, desfalecer. 2) *faint hope*, leve esperança. 3) *faint-hearted*, cobarde, medroso. 4) *faint-heartedly*, cobardemente. 5) *faint heart never won faire*, dos fracos não reza a história.

fainting, *s.* desmaio.

faintish, *adj.* fraco.

faintly, *adv.* debilmente.

faintness, *s.* languidez, fraqueza; timidez; inactividade.

fair, *adj.* claro, distinto, sem mancha; *(fair day*, ou *fair name);* imparcial, honesto, justo *(fair play);* loiro de cor clara e com brilho *(fair hair);* regular, favorável *(fair wind);* distinto, compreensível *(fair writing, fair copy).* s. feira, mercado, exposição. *adv.* imparcialmente; cortesmente. *v.t.* acabar (tempo). 1) *fair-haired*, de cabelos loiros. 2) *fair-spoken*, gracioso, cortês. 3) *the fair*, o belo sexo. 4) *to bid fair to*, prometer. 5) *to come a day after the fair*, chegar muito tarde. 6) *fair and solfy goes far*, devagar se vai ao longe.

fairish, *adj.* razoável; claro, regular.

fairlead, *s.* macarrão.

fairleader, ver *fairlead; fairleader truck*, caçoilo (náut.).

fairly, *adv.* regularmente; justamente; claramente; completamente. 1) *fairly good*, razoável, tolerável. 2) *fairly well*, sofrivelmente.

fairness, *s.* beleza, clareza, boa-fé; probidade; jogo franco.

fair-spoken, *adj.* cortês, delicado, polido.

fairway, *s.* curso próprio (num canal ou porto); lugar navegável (de um rio).

fairy (ies), *s.* fada, duende. *adj.* relativo a fadas.

fairyland, *s.* terra das fadas.

fairylike, *adj.* parecido com fadas.

fairy-ring, *s.* círculos nos pastos, onde se supunham que dançavam as fadas.

fairy-tale, *s.* conto de fadas.

faith, *s.* fé, crença, confiança, doutrina. 1) *faith-healing*, cura pela fé ou orações. 2) *in faith*, em verdade. 3) *in good faith*, de boa fé. 4) *to break faith with*, faltar ao prometido.

faithful, *adj.* fiel, leal; crente; exacto; *the faithful*, os verdadeiros crentes, principalmente os maometanos.

faithfully, *adv.* fielmente, firmemente, sinceramente.

faithfulness, *s.* fidelidade, lealdade; constância.

faithless, *adj.* incrédulo; sem fé; falto de lealdade.

faithlessness, *s.* incredulidade, infidelidade, deslealdade.

fake, *s.* (fam.) patranha, falsidade; aducha (de cabo), volta de pandeiro (náut.). *v.t.* enganar; roubar; colher um cabo à manobra.

faker, *s.* enganador, roubador.

fakir, *s.* faquir.

fakirism, *s.* faquirismo.

falcate, *adj.* falcado.

falcated, *adj.* (astrn.) falcado (lua, etc.).

falchion, *s.* cimitarra.

falcon, *s.* falcão.

falconer, *s.* falcoeiro.

falconery, *s.* falcoaria; caça com falcões.

falderal, *s.* ninhada, bagatela.

fall, *pret.* fell, fallen. *v.i.* cair; deixar-se cair; minguar, diminuir; ceder; apostatar; aparecer; principiar uma coisa com entusiasmo; baixar (preço, maré, barómetro); acontecer, suceder. 1) *to fall aboard*, abordar, cair em cima (de um navio). 2) *fall asleep*, adormecer. 3) *fall astern*, cair para trás (náut.) 4) *fall away*, desfalecer; emagrecer; murchar; apostatar; deixar de cumprir o dever; morrer. 5) *fall back*, retroceder; faltar à palavra. 6) *fall back on* ou *upon*, retirar-se (para uma posição ou fortificação); recorrer (a um expediente, auxílio, etc.). 7) *fall backward*, cair de costas. 8) *fall behind*, perder terreno. 9) *fall calm*, ser surpreendido pela calmaria; acalmar. 10) *fall down*, cair por terra; arruinar-se; flutuar à mercê da corrente; abater, derivar. 11) *fall dry*, cair em seco. 12) *fall due*, terminar o prazo, vencer-se. 13) *fall flat*, deixar de produzir o efeito desejado. 14) *fall from*, abandonar. 15) *fall foul off*, questionar. 16) *fall home*, pôr ou cair no lugar devido. 17) *fall in*, desaprumar-se; aceder; coincidir, terminar, tomar uma posição entre outros; tornar-se útil; desfechar; enfileirar-se. 18) *fall in love*, apaixonar-se. 19) *fall in with*, encontrar-se; associar-se; conformar-se. 20) *fall off*, desprender-se; apartar-se; apostatar; diminuir, minguar; arribar-se; desviar-se (náut.). 21) *fall on*, assaltar, acometer; descobrir; descer sobre. 22) *fall out*, inclinar-se para fora (náut.); acontecer; questionar; ficar mal; tirar das fileiras. 23) *fall overboard*, cair ao mar. 24) *fall short*, faltar, ser insuficiente. 25) *fall sick*, adoecer. 26) *fall through*, falhar, fracassar. 27) *fall to*, cair sobre; fechar; começar (a comer ou a fazer alguma coisa com sofreguidão). 28) *fall under*, cair debaixo de; estar sujeito a; ser considerado como; tornar-se objecto de. 29) *fall upon*, cair sobre; atacar; assaltar, descer; recorrer. 30) *she fell acrying*, começou a chorar.

fallacious, *adj.* falaz.

fallaciously, *adv.* falazmente.

fallaciousness, *s.* falácia.

fallacy (ies), *adj.* falácia.

fal-lal, *s.* ornamento insignificante. *adj.* adamado, fátuo.

fallen, *pp.* de *fall* e *adj.* caído, decaído.

faller, *s.* vareta.

fallibility, *s.* falibilidade.

fallible, *adj.* falível.

fallibleness, *s.* falibilidade.

fallibly, *adv.* falivelmente.

falling, *s.* queda, recaída; deserção; baixa (da maré, do barómetro). 1) *falling away*,

emagrecimento, apostasia, abandono. 2) *falling in*, desaprumo. 3) *falling off*, decadência; arribada de governo (náut.). 4) *falling out*, arrufo, desavença. 5) *falling sickness*, epilepsia. 6) *falling star*, estrela cadente.

fallow, *v.t.* arrotear. *s.* terra de pousio. *adj.* fulvo; desocupado, de pousio (terra); *fallow-deer*, gamo vulgar.

fallowness, *s.* pousio (de terra).

false, *adj.* falso, pérfido, desleal; postiço, fingido; ilegal, irregular. 1) *false claim*, queixa infundada. 2) *false imprisionment*, detenção ilegal, 3) *false teeth*, dentes postiços.

falsehood, *s.* falsidade.

falsely, *adv.* falsamente.

falseness, *s.* falsidade.

falsetto, *s.* falsete.

falsification, *s.* falsificação; adulteração.

falsified, *pret.* e *pp.* de *falsify*.

falsifier, *s.* falsificador.

falsify, *pret.* e *pp.* de *falsified. v.t.* falsificar; forjar; adulterar.

falsity (ies), *s.* falsidade.

falter, *v.t.* e *v.i.* gaguejar; hesitar; vacilar; tremer.

falterer, *s.* gago; o que hesita.

faltering, *s.* gaguez; hesitação. *adj.* vacilante, titubeante.

falteringly, *adv.* de um modo vacilante; com hesitação.

fame, *s.* fama, celebridade. *v.t.* afamar, celebrar.

famed, *adj.* afamado, célebre.

familiar, *adj.* familiar, íntimo; *familiar with*, versado em. *s.* amigo íntimo; familiar de um bispo.

familiarly, *adv.* familiarmente, intimamente.

familiarity (ies), *s.* familiaridade, intimidade; *familiarity breeds contempt*, a familiaridade engendra desprezo.

familiarize (ise), *v.t.* familiarizar, acostumar.

family (ies), *s.* família; linhagem; raça. 1) *family man*, homem casado. 2) *family tree*, árvore genealógica. 3) *family divisions*, partilhas (entre pessoas de família). 4) *to be in the family way*, achar-se no seu estado interessante. 5) *in a family way*, sem cerimónia.

famine, *s.* fome, carestia; *cotton-famine*, crise algodoeira.

famish, *v.t.* e *v.i.* matar ou morrer à fome.

famous, *adj.* famoso, célebre.

famously, *adv.* famosamente.

famousness, *s.* celebridade.

fan, *s.* leque; ventilador, aspirador; ventoinha; abano; crivo de joeirar; entusiasta de algum divertimento, *(foot-ball fan, film fan)* 1) *fan-palm*, palmeira, leque. *v.t.* fanning, fanned ventilar; abanar; joeirar. 2) *to fan the flame*, aumentar a excitação.

fanatic, *s.* e *adj.* fanático.

fanatical, *adj.* fanático.

fanatically, *adv.* fanaticamente.

fanaticism, *s.* fanatismo.

fanaticize (ise) *v.t.* fanatizar.

fancied, *pret.* e *pp.* de *fancy. adj.* imaginário.

fancier, *s.* visionário, sonhador; aficcionado; criador e vendedor de aves e animais, ou de outro artigo *(dog-fancier, rose-fancier)*.

fanciful, *adj.* fantástico; imaginário; caprichoso.

fancifully, *adv.* fantasticamente.

fancifulness, *s.* fantasia.

fancy, *s.* fantasia, imaginação; capricho; imagem; afeição. 1) *to take a fancy to a person*, ter simpatia por alguém. 2) *to catch the fancy of*, agradar a, dar no goto a. *adj.* imaginário, caprichoso, ideal; de gosto. 3) *fancy-ball*, baile de fantasia. 4) *fancy-dress*, vestido de fantasia. 5) *fancy-free*, livre do poder do amor. 6) *fancy work*, trabalho de fantasia (costura). 7) *fancy goods*, artigos de fantasia. *v.t.* e *v.i.* imaginar, fantasiar, apaixonar-se. 8) *only fancy*, ora imagina!

fandango, *s.* fandango.

fane, *s.* fano, templo, santuário.

fanfare, *s.* som de trombetas.

fanfaron, *s.* fanfarrão.

fanfaronade, *s.* fanfarronada.

fang, *s.* unha, garra; colmilho, dente de serpente; raiz de dente.

fanged, *adj.* que tem colmilhos.

fangless, *adj.* sem dentes.

fanlight, *s.* bandeira (de janela ou porta).

fanner, *s.* joeirador (pessoa que joeira, ou instrumento para joeirar).

fanning, *p. pr.* de *fan*.

fantail, *s.* pomba de leque; papa-moscas (ave); bico do gás em forma de leque.

fantasia, *s.* fantasia (mús.)

fantast, *s.* fantasista.

fantastic, *adv.* fantástico.

fantastical, *adj.* fantástico.

fantastically, *adv.* fantasticamente.

fantasticalness, *s.* fantasia; capricho.

fantasy (ies), *s.* fantasia, imaginação; capricho; mania.

far, *adv.* longe, distante; em alto grau; muito. *adj.* distante, remoto. 1) *far away*, muito distante. 2) *far and wide*, por toda a parte. 3) *far be it from me*, longe de mim. 4) *far better*, muito melhor. 5) *a far cry*, uma grande distância. 6) *far-famed*, de muita fama. 7) *far-fetched*, forçado; artificial; afectado. 8) *far-flung*, muito estendido. 9) *far from*, longe de. 10) *far gone*, muito doente; muito maluco; muito embriagado; muito endividado. 11) *far off*, a grande distância. 12) *farseeing*, que se vê ao longe. 13) *far-sighted*, presbita. 14) *as far as*, até; tanto quanto. 15) *as far as I am concerned*, pelo que me diz respeito. 16) *as far as I am concerned*, pelo que me diz respeito. 17) *as far as I know*, que eu saiba. 18) *by far*, com muito, em muito; em alto grau. 19) *how far*, a que distância.

farad, *s.* farad.

farce, *s.* farsa, entremez. *v.t.* rechear, temperar.

farcical, *adj.* cómico, burlesco.

farcically, *adj.* jocosamente.

farcy, *s.* gafeira (dos cavalos).

fardel, *s.* fardo, trouxa.

fare, *s.* preço de passagem; frete; comida. 1) *bill of fare*, lista dos pratos, ementa. 2) *single fare*, bilhete de ida. 3) *return fare*, bilhete de ida e volta. *v.i.* ir andar; suceder; comer.

farewell, *s.* despedida. 1) *to bid farewell*, despedir-se. 2) *last farewell*, último adeus. *adj.* de despedida. 3) *farewell song*, canção de despedida. 4) *farewell dinner*, jantar de despedida. *interj.* Adeus!

farina, *s.* farinha de milho; fécula.

farinaceous, *adj.* farináceo.

farinose, *adj.* farinhento, coberto de farinha.

farm, *s.* quinta, herdade. 1) *baby-farm*, dispensário para crianças. 2) *farm buildings*, dependências de quinta. *v.t.* e *v.i.* cultivar, granjear, lavrar terra; arrendar terras; dar de arrendamento (contribuições, foros); contratar para cuidar e sustentar pessoas, especialmente crianças.

farmer, *s.* cultivador, lavrador; rendeiro, cobrador de rendas; pessoa que toma conta de uma criança por paga.

farmhouse, *s.* casal; granja; casa de quinta.

farming, *s.* cultura, agricultura; arrendamento de contribuições, cobrança de rendas ou contribuições. 1) *good, bad farming*, boa, má exploração. 2) *small farming*, cultura em pequena escala.

farmstead, s. quinta com edifícios anexos.

farmyard, s. quinteiro, pátio de uma propriedade rústica.

farrago, s. farragem; mistura de coisas mal ordenadas.

farrier, s. ferrador, alveitar.

farriery, s. oficina de ferrador, alveitaria.

farrow, s. barriga (de uma porca); ninhada. v.t. e v.i. parir (a porca).

farther, comp. de far, mais distante. adv. mais longe; além de; além disso.

farthest, adj. e adv. à maior distância; superl. de far, o mais distante.

farthing, s. a quarta parte de um péni.

farthingale, s. arco para enfunar saias.

fasces, s. pl. fasces, feixes.

fascia, s. faixa, venda; tabuleta de uma loja.

fasciated, adj. enfaixado.

fascicle, s. fascículo; pequeno feixe; paveia.

fascicular, fasciculate, adj. fascicular, fasciculado.

fascinate, v.t. fascinar.

fascinating, adj. fascinador.

fascinatingly, adv. de um modo encantador.

fascination, s. fascinação.

fascinator, s. fascinador.

fascine, s. faxina, feixe de paus usado para estabelecer trincheiras, baterias, etc.

fascism, s. fascismo.

fash, s. incómodo; rebarba. v.t. e v.i. incomodar, aborrecer.

fashion, s. moda, uso, estilo; forma; figura; modo, maneira; alta sociedade, escol. 1) fashion piece, ou timber, manco (náut.). 2) in fashion, à moda. 3) the last fashion, a moda passada. 4) the latest fashion, a última moda, a mais recente. 5) out of fashion, fora de moda. 6) after the English fashion, à inglesa. 7) to bring into fashion, pôr à moda. 8) fashion-plate, gravura ou quadro com as modas do vestuário. 9) to set the fashion, dar o tom, o exemplo. v.t. amoldar, adaptar; talhar.

fashionable, adj. da moda; elegante, de bom gosto; the fashionable world, a sociedade elegante.

fashionableness, s. moda; qualidade, forma (do que é segundo a moda).

fashionably, adv. à moda.

fashioner, s. alfaiate da moda.

fashionmonger, s. pessoa que observa a moda.

fast, s. jejum, abstinência, amarra, cabo. 1) fast-day, dia de jejum. 2) fast sailer, navio de bom andamento. 3) to break one's fast, quebrar o jejum. v.i. jejuar, fazer abstinência. adj. firme, fixo, seguro (a fast intent, a fast knot); fiel, leal (a fast friend); firme, permanente, fixo, durável (fast colour); profundo (fast sleep); rápido (fast train); adiantado (relógios) (a fast watch); dissoluto, de maus costumes (a fast woman). 4) to make fast, amarrar; dar a volta; fazer fixe (náut.). adv. fortemente; duradouramente; profundamente; depressa. 5) fast asleep, profundamente adormecido. 6) hold fast, Segura bem! 7) to play fast and loose, proceder inconstantemente. 8) to live fast, estroinar. 9) fast bind, fast find, fechar à chave o que se não quer perder. 10) fast-by, muito perto.

fasten, v.t. atar, prender, ligar; cavilhar, unir, juntar, segurar; aboçar (náut.) 1) to fasten one's eyes upon, cravar os olhos em. 2) to fasten on (upon), prender, fixar, imputar, agarrar-se a.

fastener, s. pessoa ou objecto que ata ou segura (colchete, etc.).

fastening, s. ligadura, laço, união; cravação, ligação; cavilhamento; fecho, ou ferrolho.

faster, s. jejuador.

fasti, s. pl. fastos, anais.

fastidious, adj. fastidioso.

fastidiously, adv. fastidiosamente.

fastidiousness, s. enfado, tédio.

fasting, s. jejum; fasting-day, dia de jejum.

fastish, adj. inclinado à dissipação.

fastness, s. firmeza; fortaleza; solidez; velocidade; dissipação.

fat, adj. gordo, obeso, corpulento, resinoso; untoso; puro (diz-se da cal); 1) to cut up fat, deixar muito dinheiro. 2) cut it fat, fazer uma exibição. s. gordura, sebo; a parte mais proveitosa de uma coisa. v.t. e v.i. fatting, engordar.

fatal, adj. fatal, mortal.

fatalism, s. fatalismo.

fatalist, s. fatalista.

fatalistic, adj. fatalístico.

fatality (ies), s. fatalidade.

fatally, adv. fatalmente.

fate, s. fado, destino, sorte; predestinação.

fated, adj. predestinado; fadado.

fateful, adj. fatal, funesto.

fathead, s. espécie de peixe da família dos ciprínidas.

father, s. pai; pai espiritual; criador, inventor; Padre (1.ª pessoa da Santíssima Trindade);

no *pl.* antepassados; 1) *adoptive father*, pai adoptivo. 2) *putative father*, pai putativo. 3) *natural father*, pai natural. 4) *step-father*, padrasto. 5) *spiritual father*, pai espiritual, o que promoveu uma conversão, 6) *godfather*, padrinho. 7) *father in God*, bispo. 8) *father-in-law*, sogro. 9) *father of lies*, demónio. 10) *Holy Father*, o Papa. 11) *grand-father*, avô. 12) *great-grand-father*, bisavô. 13) *like father, like son*, tal pai, tal filho. 14) *the sins of the fathers are sometimes visited upon the children*, os filhos muitas vezes sofrem pelas culpas dos pais. 15) *the wish is father to the thought*, acredita-se porque assim se quer. 16) *the child is father to the man*, a criança mostra o que será como homem. 17) *the fathers of the church*, os Santos padres da Igreja, os escritores cristãos dos primeiros cinco séculos. *v.* gerar, dar origem a; governar paternalmente; determinar a paternidade de.

fatherhood, *s.* paternidade.
fatherland, *s.* pátria.
fatherless, *adj.* órfão de pai.
fatherliness, *s.* amor paternal.
fatherly, *adj.* paternal. *adv.* paternalmente.
fathom, *s.* toesa, medida náutica de seis pés; sonda; profundidade. *v.t.* sondar; profundar.
fathomable, *adj.* sondável.
fathomless, *adj.* insondável.
fatom-line, *s.* sonda.
fatidical, *adj.* fatídico.
fatigue, *s.* fadiga, cansaço; *fatigue-duty*, trabalho pesado (de soldados no campo). *v.t.* fatigar, cansar.
fatiguing, *adj.* fatigante.
fatiguingly, *adv.* de um modo fatigante.
fatling, *s.* animal pequeno engordado (próprio para matar). *adj.* gordo.
fatly, *adv.* corpulentamente.
fatness, *s.* gordura, corpulência; fertilidade de solo.
fatted, *adj.* engordado, gordo.
fatten, *v.i.* e *i.* engordar, cevar.
fattener, *s.* o que engorda.
fattening, *s.* engorda.
fatter, fattest, *comp.* e *sup.* de *fat.*
fattness, *s.* gordura.
fatty, *adj.* gordurento; oleoso. *s.* pessoa ou animal gordo.
fatuity, *s.* fatuidade.
fatuous, *adj.* fátuo; insensato.

fatuously, *adv.* fatuamente.
fatuousness, *s.* fatuidade.
faubourg, *s.* subúrbio.
faucal, *adj.* profundamente gutural (som).
fauces, *s.* fauces.
faucet, *s.* batoque; torneira; *faucet joint*, canhão e caixa.
faugh, *interj.* fora!
fault, *s.* falta, culpa, delito; imperfeição, defeito, carência; deslocação de uma rocha (geol.). 1) *fault-finder*, crítico, que só encontra faltas; galvanómetro (para encontrar os defeitos) (mec.). 2) *to find fault with*, queixar-se de; censurar.
faultily, *adv.* defeituosamente.
faultiness, *s.* culpa; falta; imperfeição.
faultless, *adj.* sem falta.
faultlessly, *adv.* inculpavelmente.
faultlessness, *s.* irrepreensibilidade, perfeição, inculpabilidade.
faulty, *adj.* culpável; imperfeito.
faun, *s.* fauno.
fauna, *s.* fauna.
fauteil, *s.* poltrona.
favour, *s.* favor, fineza; obséquio; patrocínio, carta (com.); auxílio; coisa dada ou usada como sinal de favor; roseta; distintivo; aparência, aspecto; *In favour of*, a favor de. 2) *by favour*, por favor. 3) *out of favour*, desaprovado de. 4) *to do a favour*, fazer um favor. 5) *under favour*, com licença. 6) *under favour of night*, favorecido pela escuridão. *v.t.* favorecer; proteger, auxiliar; parecer-se com *(he favours his father)*.
favourable, *adj.* favorável, propício.
favourableness, *s.* benignidade.
favourably, *adv.* favoravelmente, benignamente.
favoured, *adj.* favorecido; bem encarado. 1) *well-favoured*, bem-parecido. 2) *ill-favoured*, mal encarado.
favourer, *s.* favorecedor.
favourite, *s.* e *adj.* favorito, predilecto, amado, protegido.
favouritism, *s.* favoritismo.
favourless, *adj.* desprotegido.
fawn, *s.* cria (de corça ou outro animal semelhante); cor de corça. *v.i.* (com *on*) acariciar, adular; mostrar afeição; comportar-se servilmente. *adj.* da cor da corça, castanho-claro.
fawner, *s.* adulador.
fawning, *s.* lisonja; carícia. *adj.* lisonjeiro, servil.

fawningly, *adv.* servilmente.

fay, *s.* fada, duende.

fealty, *s.* preito, menagem.

fear, *s.* medo, receio, susto; respeito, temor. 1) *to be in fear*, recear. 2) *No fear*, não há perigo! *v.t.* temer, recear. *v.i.* ter medo, estar com cuidado.

fearful, *adj.* medroso; terrível, digno de respeito.

fearfully, *adv.* medrosamente; horrivelmente.

fearfulness, *s.* timidez, medo, pusilanimidade.

fearing, *s.* receio. *adj.* receoso.

fearless, *adj.* intrépido, audaz, destemido.

fearlessly, *adv.* intrepidamente, sem receio.

fearlessness, *s.* intrepidez, bravura, valentia.

fearsome, *adj.* temível, espantoso; tímido, medroso.

fearsomely, *adv.* timidamente.

fearsomeness, *s.* medo.

feasibility, *s.* praticabilidade, possibilidade de fazer uma coisa.

feasible, *adj.* praticável.

feast, *s.* festa, regozijo; festim, banquete. *v.t.* festejar, banquetear. *v.i.* comer regaladamente.

feaster, *s.* festejador; guloso.

feasting, *s.* festim, banquete.

feat, *s.* feito, façanha; proeza.

feather, *s.* pena (de ave); qualquer coisa que se pareça com uma pena; cavalete (náut.). 1) *feather bed*, colchão de penas. 2) *feather-brain*, imbecil. 3) *feather brained*, imbecil. 4) *feather-edge*, chanfro, 5) *feather palm*, palmeira do género das geonomas. 6) *feather-weight*, peso pluma (boxe). 7) *he has feathered his nest*, tem juntado dinheiro. 8) *birds of a feather flock together*, cada qual com o seu igual; diz-me com quem andas, dir-te-ei as manhas que tens. *v.t.* ornar; forrar. *v.i.* suspender os remos (náut.).

feathered, *adj.* coberto de penas.

featheriness, *s.* o ser coberto de penas; tacto suave.

feathering, *s.* plumagem; pêlos encaracolados de certos cães.

featherstich, *s.* renda ou bordado semelhante a uma pena de ave.

feathery, *adj.* coberto de penas ou parecido com penas.

fearherweight, *s.* coisa ou pessoa muito leve; peso pluma.

featle, *adv.* destramente.

feature, *s.* traço, feição ou carácter distintivo; parte essencial de uma coisa; ponto característico; rosto, semblante; *topographical feature*, configuração do terreno. *v.t.* dar importância; fazer sobressair; retratar.

featured, *adj.* bem caracterizado.

featureless, *adj.* sem feições características.

feaze, *v.t.* fazer estopa.

febrifugal, *adj.* febrífugo.

febrile, *adj.* febril.

February, *s.* Fevereiro.

fecal, *adj.* fecal.

feckless, *adj.* ineficiente, fraco, fútil.

fecklessly, *adv.* ineficientemente.

fecklessness, *s.* ineficiência.

feculence, *s.* feculência.

feculent, *adj.* feculento.

fecund, *adj.* fecundo, fértil.

fecundate, *v.t.* fecundar; fertilizar.

fecundation, *s.* fecundação; fertilização.

fecundity, *s.* fecundidade; fertilidade.

fed, *pret.* e *pp.* de *feed.* 1) *under-feed*, mal alimentado. 2) *fed up*, farto, enfastiado.

federal, *adj.* federal.

federalism, *s.* federalismo.

federalist, *s.* federalista.

federate, *v.t.* confederar. *v.i.* confederar-se.

federation, *s.* federação.

federative, *adj.* federativo.

fee, *s.* honorários, salários; propina; cota; feudo. 1) *fee farm*, domínio útil. 2) *fee-simple*, domínio absoluto. 3) *fee-faw-fum*, expressão para amedrontar crianças. 4) *fee-tail*, domínio limitado. *v.t.* pagar; gratificar; alugar; subornar.

feeble, *adj.* fraco, débil, lânguido, ténue, delicado. 1) *to grow* ou *to become feeble*, enfraquecer. 2) *feeble-minded*, imbecil.

feebleness, *s.* debilidade.

feebly, *adv.* debilmente.

feed, *pret.* e *pp.* de *fed.* *v.t.* alimentar, dar de comer, manter; alimentar. *v.i.* comer, alimentar-se, apascentar. 1) *to feed on* ou *upon*, alimentar-se de. *s.* alimento, ração, sustento (especialmente para animais), alimentação. 2) *feed-bag* ou *cloth*, saca donde os cavalos comem o grão. 3) *feed cock*, torneira de alimentação. 4) *feed heater*, aparelho para aquecer a água de alimentação de uma caldeira. 5) *feed pump*, bomba de alimentação das caldeiras. 6) *feed rack*, manjedoura. 7) *feed roller*, rolo alimentar. 8) *feed trunk*, tubo alimentar. 9) *feed valve*, válvula de alimentação.

feeder, *s.* alimentador; babeiro de criança; biberão; o que dá de comer; incitador; afluente de um rio; reserva de estiva; condutor principal de electricidade. 1) *oil-feeder*, almotolia. 2) *feeder switchboard*, quadro de distribuição para alimentadores.

feeding, *s.* alimentação; pastagem. 1) *feeding-bottle*, biberão. 2) *feeding device*, aparelho de alimentação. 3) *feeding stuffs*, alimento para animais.

feel, *pret.* e *pp. felt. v.t.* e *v.i.* sentir; perceber; apalpar; experimentar; examinar; conhecer--se. 1) *to feel one's pulse*, tomar o pulso; sondar alguém; 2) *to feel the way with the lead*, navegar pelo prumo; tentativa (para saber alguma coisa); o que toca ou apalpa. 3) *feel plate*, chapa sensível.

feeling, *s.* tacto; sentido do tacto; sentimento; ternura; sensação. *adj.* sensível, terno, comovedor.

feelingly, *adv.* sensivelmente; com muita expressão.

feet, plural de *foot.*

feign, *v.t.* e *v.i.* fingir, dissimular; pretextar; inventar, imaginar.

feignedly, *adv.* fingidamente.

feignedness, *s.* fingimento, dissimulação.

feint, *s.* ficção; dissimulação; finta.

feldspar, *s.* feldspato.

felicitate, *v.t.* felicitar.

felicitacion, *s.* felicitação.

felicitous, *adj.* feliz, ditoso; bem-aventurado; apropriado.

felicitously, *adv.* felizmente, ditosamente; apropriadamente.

felicity, *s.* felicidade, ventura; bem-aventurança.

feline, *s.* e *adj.* felino; cruel.

fell, *pret.* de *fall. v.t.* derribar, lançar por terra; cortar. *s.* costura, remate (de tecido); cabelo, pêlo; baldio; monte estéril; pele de animal; *fell-monger*, peliqueiro. *adj.* cruel, feroz.

feller, *s.* máquina de fazer costuras; rachador de lenha.

fellah, *s.* felá, aldeão do Egipto.

felloe, felly, *s.* pina (de roda de carro).

fellow, *s.* companheiro, camarada, sócio; membro da universidade; sujeito. 1) *fellow-creature*, o próximo. 2) *fellow-feeling*, simpatia. 3) *fellow man*, o próximo. 4) *fellow-traveller*, companheiro de viagem. 5)

fellow-worker, companheiro de trabalho; colaborador (literário). 6) *school-fellow*, condiscípulo. 7) *matter-of-fact-fellow*, homem prático. 8) *not half a bad fellow*, não é mau de todo. 9) *poor fellow!*, coitado!. 10) *old fellow!*, meu velho!. 11) *my dear fellow!*, meu caro!. 12) *stone dead hath no fellow*, homem morto guarda segredo. *v.t.* irmanar; aparelhar.

fellowship, *s.* companhia, sociedade; associação; participação de lucros e perdas; lugar de colegial nos colégios anexos às universidades; *good fellowship*, sociabilidade, convivência. *v.t.* admitir em sociedade.

felly, *adv.* cruelmente, ferozmente. *s.* pina (de roda de carro).

felo, *s.* suicida.

felon, *s.* réu, criminoso; panarício. *adj.* malvado, criminoso, traidor.

felonious, *adj.* malvado, perverso.

feloniously, *adv.* malvadamente; com intenção criminosa.

feloniousness, *s.* ver *felony.*

felony (ies), *s.* felonia, traição, crime capital.

felspar, ver *feldspar.*

felt, *pret.* e *pp.* de *feel. s.* feltro; *feltcovering*, revestimento de feltro.

felting, *s.* feltro; material ou processo de fazer feltro.

female, *s.* fêmea. *adj.* feminino, feminil; *female thread* ou *screw*, porca de parafuso.

feminility, *s.* feminilidade.

femine, *adj.* feminino; feminil; mulheril; efeminado.

femininely, *adv.* feminilmente.

feminist, *s.* feminista.

femora, *pl.* de *fémur.*

femoral, *adj.* femural.

fen, *s.* pântano, paul.

femur, *s.* fémur.

fence, *s.* guarda; valado; tabela (no hóquei em patins); cerca; barreira; jogo de esgrima. 1) *fence time*, tempo de defeso da caça. 2) *fence stone*, parede construída sem cal. 3) *fence wire*, arame farpado. *v.i.* cercar; fechar com valado; defender. *v.i.* esgrimir, defender-se.

fenceless, *adj.* indefeso; que não está cercado; sem guardas.

fencer, *s.* esgrimista.

fencible, *adj.* que pode ser defendido. *s.* soldado sujeito apenas a serviço de defesa.

fencing, *s.* guarda, cercado; esgrima. 1)

fencing-master, mestre de esgrima. 2) *fencing-school*, escola de esgrima, sala de armas. 3) *fencing-bout*, ou *match*, assalto (esgr.).

fend, *v.t.* aparar, desviar; repelir (com *off*). *v.i.* (com *for oneself*) arranjar a sua vida.

fender, *s.* guarda-fogo (de chaminé ou de fogão); defensa (molhelha feita de cordas para defesa dos navios quando atracam, ou encostam a outros navios).

fenestra, *s.* abertura, fresta.

fenestral, *s.* pertencente às janelas.

Fenian, *s.* feniano, membro de uma associação irlandesa, formada contra o Governo inglês.

fenianism, *s.* associação irlandesa formada contra o Governo inglês.

fennel, *s.* funcho.

fenny, *adj.* pantanoso, palustre.

fent, *s.* fenda.

feoff, *s.* feudo. *v.t.* enfeudar.

feoffee, *s.* feudatário.

feoffer, *s.* senhor feudal.

feoffment, *s.* enfeudação.

ferae naturae, *adj.* de natureza selvagem, não domesticada.

feral, *adj.* selvagem; silvestre.

feretory (ies), *s.* relicário (que se leva nas procissões).

ferial, *adj.* ferial, de férias.

ferine, *adj.* ferino, selvagem.

ferity (ies), *s.* ferocidade.

ferment, *v.t.* e *v.i.* fermentar; fazer fermentar; agitar-se; excitar.

fermentable, *adj.* fermentável.

fermentation, *s.* fermentação; agitação, excitação.

fermentative, *adj.* fermentativo.

fermentativeness, *s.* fermentiscibilidade.

fern, *s.* feto (planta); *fern-owl*, engole-vento (ave).

fernery, *s.* fetal.

ferny, *adj.* cheio de fetos,

ferocious, *adj.* feroz, cruel.

ferociously, *adv.* ferozmente.

ferociousness, *s.* ferocidade; crueldade.

ferocity, *s.* ferocidade.

ferreous, *adj.* férreo.

ferret, *s.* furão; fita de seda. *v.t.* indagar, esquadrinhar; caçar com furão.

ferreting, *s.* caça com furão.

ferriage, *s.* frete (de um barco, para atravessar um rio ou canal).

ferric, *adj.* férrico.

ferried, *pret.* e *pp.* de ferry.

ferriferous, *adj.* ferrífero.

ferro-concrete, *s.* cimento armado.

ferrotype, *s.* fotografia sobre uma chapa de ferro.

ferruginous, *adj.* ferruginoso.

ferrule, *s.* ferrão (de bengala), círculo de ferro; virola.

ferry, *pret.* e *pp.* *ferried.* *v.t.* atravessar, transportar em barco (de uma margem ou costa para a outra). *s.* travessia, passagem, barco de passagem. 1) *ferry-boat*, barco ou navio de travessia ou passagem. 2) *ferryman*, barqueiro.

fertile, *adj.* fértil, fecundo.

fertilely, *adv.* fertilmente.

fertility, *s.* fertilidade; fecundidade; abundância.

fertilization (isa), *s.* fertilização; fecundação.

fertilize, *v.t.* fertilizar.

fertilizer, *s.* fertilizador; adubo químico.

ferule, *s.* férula, palmatória. *v.t.* dar palmatoadas a.

fervency, *s.* fervor, ardor.

fervent, *adj.* ardente, vivo, fervoroso.

fervently, *adv.* ardentemente.

ferventness, *s.* ardor, fervor, zelo.

fervid, *adj.* férvido, ardente.

fervidly, *adv.* ardentemente.

fervidness, *s.* ardor, zelo.

fervour, *s.* fervor, devoção.

fescue, *s.* ponteiro (usado antigamente nas escolas).

fesse, *s.* banda do escudo.

festal, *adj.* festivo, solene.

festally, *v.i.* ulcerar-se; inflamar-se (uma ferida). *s.* úlcera, chaga.

festival, *s.* e *adj.* festival.

festive, *adj.* festive, alegre.

festively, *adv.* festivamente.

festivity, *s.* festividade; regozijo, alegria.

festoon, *s.* festão; grinalda. *v.t.* engrinaldar.

fetch, *v.t.* ir buscar; trazer; alcançar; conseguir, atingir (preço); restaurar; produzir; atrair, encantar; fascinar. *v.i.* mover-se; chegar a. 1) *to fetch away*, soltar-se; cair a sotavento; levar, conduzir. 2) *fetch down*, abaixar; humilhar. 3) *fetch a harbour*, alcançar um porto. 4) *fetch in*, fazer entrar; levar. 5) *fetch out*, mostrar, fazer ressaltar; fazer sair. 6) *fetch a pump*, pôr uma bomba a funcionar deitando-lhe água no tubo. 7) *fetch up*, educar; recuperar; fazer subir, prender. *s.* acto de ir buscar; estratagema.

fetcher, s. o que vai buscar.

fête, s. festa. v.t. festejar; *fête-day*, festa onomástica.

fetial, s. e adj. fecial.

fetid, adj. fétido.

fetidly, adv. com mau cheiro.

fetidness, s. mau cheiro.

fetish (es), s. feitiço.

fetishism, s. feiticismo.

fetlock, s. topete (detrás da pata do cavalo).

fetter, v.t. encadear; lançar cadeias ou grilhões. s. ferros, grilhões, cadeias (usado geralmente no plural).

fettered, adj. preso com cadeias.

fettle, s. situação, condição *(in good fettle)*. v.t. alisar *(to fettle pottery);* cobrir com substância refractária.

fetus, ver *foetus.*

feu, s. aforamento perpétuo.

feud, s. rixa, contenda; feudo.

feudal, adj. feudal.

feudalism, s. feudalismo.

feudality, s. feudalidade.

feudalization, s. enfeudação.

feudalize, v.t. enfeudar.

feudatory, s. feudatário.

feuilleton, s. folhetim (de um jornal).

fever, s. febre; calor; agitação. v.t. causar febre. 1) *yellow-fever*, febre-amarela. 2) *scarlet-fever*, escarlatina.

feverheat, s. temperatura febril.

feverish, adj. febril; febricitante; exaltado.

feverishly, adv. de um modo febril.

feverishness, s. estado febril; desassossego.

few, adj. poucos. 1) *a few*, alguns. 2) *in few*, em poucas palavras, em resumo. 3) *the few*, a minoria.

fewer, fewest, comp. sup. de *few; the few the better,* quanto menos melhor.

fewness, s. pequeno número; escassez.

fez (es), s. fez, barrete turco.

fiacre, s. fiacre.

fiancé, s. noivo.

fiancée, s. noiva.

fiasco, s. fiasco, fracasso.

fiat, s. ordem, mandato.

Fiat, nome de uma marca de automóveis.

fib, fibbing, fibbed, v.i. mentir (levemente); trapacear. s. mentira leve, patarata, embuste.

fibber, s. mentiroso, embusteiro.

fibre, s. fibra, filamento.

fibred, adj. fibroso.

fibreless, adj. sem fibras.

fibril, s. fibrazinha.

fibrillous, adj. composto de fibrazinhas.

fibrin, s. fibrina.

fibrous, adj. fibroso.

fibrously, adv. de um modo fibroso.

fibrousness, s. qualidade de ser fibroso.

fibster, s. mentiroso.

fibula, s. perónio; agulha para coser feridas; gato de ferro para ligar pedras.

fickle, adj. inconstante, volúvel.

fickleness, s. inconstância.

fictile, adj. feito de terra ou barro por oleiro; de olaria; susceptível de ser moldado ou modelado.

fiction, s. ficção, invenção.

fictional, adj. imaginário.

fictionist, s. novelista.

fictitious, adj. fictício.

fictitiously, adv. ficticiamente.

fictitiousness, s. carácter fictício.

fictive, adj. fictício.

fid, s. tarugo; cunha (de mastaréu); *splicing fid,* passador.

fiddle, s. rabeca. 1) *fiddle-bow*, arco de rabeca. 2) *fiddle-bridge*, cavalete de rabeca. 3) *fiddle string,* corda de rabeca. v.i. tocar rabeca; gastar o tempo com ninharias; deitar à cunha um mastaréu. 4) *he plays first fiddle in his family,* ele é o mandão da casa. 5) *to play the second fiddle,* ocupar o segundo lugar.

fiddle-de-dee, s. disparate. *interj.* Bolas! Tretas!

fiddle-faddle, s. bagatela. adj. pequeno, insignificante, bulhento. v.t. dizer disparates. *interj.* disparate!

fiddlestick, s. arco de rabeca; disparate. *fiddler,* s. rabequista.

fidelity, s. fidelidade.

fidget, adj. inquieto, impaciente, nervoso.

fidgetily, adv. impacientemente; com nervoso.

fidgetiness, s. mal-estar; nervosismo.

fidgety, v.t. inquietar. v.i. inquietar-se. s. inquietação.

fiducial, adj. fiducial.

fiducially, adv. confiadamente.

fiduciary (ies), s. fiduciário. adj. de confiança.

fie, interj. fora!

fief, s. feudo.

field, s. campo, campina; campo de batalha; batalha; esfera de actividade; todos os cavalos de uma corrida; conjunto de competidores em jogos de campo. 1) *field day*, dia de exercícios de campo. 2) *field dressing*, boceta com antissépticos, para soldados. 3) *field-glass*, óculo de campo. 4) *field-gun* ou *piece*, peça de campanha. 5) *field hospital*, hospital ambulante. 6) *field-marshal*, marechal de campo. 7) *field-mouse*, arganás. 8) *field-officer*, oficial superior (major, ten.-coronel). 9) *field-sports*, desportos de caça, corrida, etc. 10) *field-works*, trabalhos de campo (de engenheiros, geólogos, etc.). 11) *fields of ice*, bancos de gelo. 12) *to make the field*, entrar em campanha. *v.i.* estar em posição (para apanhar a bola no jogo de *cricket* e *baseball*).

fielder, *s.* jogador de *baseball* e de *cricket* que intercepta a bola.

fieldfare, *s.* tordo.

fieldsman, *s.* o que procura apanhar a bola (no jogo do *cricket, baseball*, etc.)

fiend, *s.* inimigo, demónio.

fiendish, *adj.* diabólico.

fiendishly, *adv.* diabolicamente.

fiendishness, *s.* perversidade diabólica.

fierce, *adj.* feroz, furioso, cruel, violento, impetuoso.

fiercely, *adv.* ferozmente.

fierceness, *s.* ferocidade.

fierily, *adv.* ardentemente, apaixonadamente.

fieriness, *s.* ardor, calor, veemência.

fiery, *adj.* ígneo, ardente; impetuoso, fogoso, vivo; furioso; *fiery cross*, cruz de tinta em sangue, como sinal para chamar às armas.

fife, *s.* pífano. *v.i.* tocar pífano; *fife-major*, sargento que manda nos tocadores de pífano de um regimento.

fifer, *s.* tocador de pífano.

fifteen, *n.* quinze.

fifteenth, *adj.* e *s.* décimo quinto.

fifth, *adj.* e *s.* quinto.

fifthly, *adv.* em quinto lugar.

fiftieth, *n.* cinquenta.

fig, *s.* figo; figueira; bagatela; figa; vestuário (fem.). 1) *Adam's fig*, banana. 2) *figleaf*, folha de figueira. 3) *I do not care a fig*, não me importo nada. *v.t.* fazer figas; vestir, adornar.

fight, *pret.* e *pp.* fought. *v.t.* lutar, batalhar, combater, guerrear; pugnar, disputar. *v.i.* bater-se, defender-se. 1) *to fight hand to hand*, combater corpo a corpo; 2) *to fight*

shy of, evitar por desconfiança. *s.* luta, batalha, combate; pugna, disputa. 3) *sea-fight*, batalha naval.

fighter, *s.* combatente, batalhador, brigão, espadachim.

fighting, *s.* combate, luta. *adj.* combatente, aguerrido; usado na guerra. 1) *fighting men*, combatentes; homens disponíveis. 2) *fighting-cock*, galo de briga. 3) *to live like fighting-cocks*, comer e beber do melhor.

figment, *s.* invenção, ficção.

figtree, *s.* figueira.

figurability, *s.* figurabilidade.

figurable, *adj.* figurável.

figuration, *s.* figuração (acto e efeito de figurar); configuração.

figurative, *adj.* figurativo.

figuratively, *adv.* figurativamente.

figurativeness, *s.* qualidade de ser figurativo.

figure, *s.* figura, forma (de uma pessoa ou coisa); aparência; imagem representada por meio de pintura, desenho, garvura, etc.; figura geométrica; grande personagem; cifra, número, algarismo; figura de gramática ou retórica. 1) *figure-head*, beque, extremo da proa onde está uma figura. 2) *figure of eight*, figura em forma de 8. 3) *figure of speech*, figura de gramática ou retórica. 4) *to cut a poor figure*, produzir fraca impressão, fazer triste figura. *v.t.* passar por; calcular.

figured, *adj.* adornado com figuras; simbolizado.

filament, *s.* filamento, fibra.

filamentous, *adj.* filamentoso, fibroso.

filature, *s.* fiação de seda; fábrica de seda.

filbert, *s.* avelã; aveleira.

filch, *v.t.* tirar, roubar com artifício, surripiar.

filcher, *s.* larápio.

file, *s.* fio ou arame para segurar papéis; colecção ou maço de papéis ou jornais; fila de soldados; lima; instrumento de dentista para limpar os dentes; pano para esfregar o soalho. 1) *bow-file*, lima arqueada. 2) *flat-file*, lima plana. 3) *round-file*, lima redonda. 4) *saw-file*, lima para serras. 5) *threesided-file*, lima triangular. 6) *soft* ou *dead-file*, lima surda. *v.t.* marchar em fila; depositar o balanço, isto é, o livro de «Deve» e «Haver». 7) *to file a schedule*, depositar o seu balanço. 8) *to file one's petition in bankruptcy*, dar-se por falido. 9) *to file off*, desfilar.

filemot, s. e adj. cor de folha seca.

filer, s. limador.

filial, adj. filial.

filially, adv. filialmente.

filialness, s. filiação.

filiation, s. filiação; perfilhação; adopção.

filibeg, s. saiote escocês.

filibuster, s. flibusteiro, pirata. v.t. piratear; fazer obstrução nos trabalhos parlamentares.

filiform, adj. filiforme.

filigrane, s. filigrana.

filigree, s. filigrana.

filing, s. método para ter a correspondência em ordem; limadura.

filings, s. limalha.

fill, v.t. encher; satisfazer; contentar; ocupar; obturar (dentes). v.i. saciar-se; fartar-se. 1) to fill in, terraplenar; preencher. 2) fill out, completar. 3) fill up, encher completamente; ocupar, provar um lugar.

filler, s. funil ou instrumento semelhante próprio para encher; conta-gotas, coisa apropriada para encher uma cavidade.

fillet, s. atadura, faixa; fita; moldura estreita; meia-cana; filete (de vitela, etc.); v.t. atar, enfaixar.

filling, s. adição, complemento; obturação. adj. que enche. 1) filling piece, maciço; enchimento. 2) filling-chock, enchimento do beque.

fillip, s. piparote; estímulo. v.i. dar um piparote; estimular.

filly (ies), s. poldra; rapariga folgazã.

film, s. película, membrana; película fotográfica. v.t. cobrir com película. v.i. formar-se película.

filmness, s. qualidade ou aparência de película.

filoselle, s. filosela.

filter, v.t. filtrar. v.i. filtrar-se. s. filtro; filter bed, filtro (areia no fundo de um lago ou tanque para purificar a água).

filtering, s. filtragem; filtering-paper, papel de filtrar.

filth, s. sujidade, imundície, porcaria; infecção.

filthier, filthiest, comp. sup. de filthy.

filthily, adv. sujamente.

filthiness, s. imundície, sujidade.

filthy, adj. sujo, imundo; corrompido.

filtrate, s. líquido filtrado.

filtrate, v.t. filtrar.

filtration, s. filtração; filtration plant, reser-

vatório onde se purifica a água de uma cidade ou localidade.

fimbria, s. fímbria.

fimbriate, adj. fimbriado; franjado.

fimbriate, v.t. pôr fímbrias ou franjas.

fin, s. barbatanas; barba de baleia; plano vertical fixo da cauda de um avião dando estabilidade lateral de movimento. 1) tip us your fin, estende cá os ossos (apertar a mão). 2) fin-back, espécie de baleia.

finable, adj. sujeito ou exposto a multa.

final, adj. final; decisivo.

finale, s. o final, o fim de qualquer coisa, principalmente de uma peça teatral.

finalism, s. finalismo.

finalist, s. finalista.

finality, s. finalidade.

finally, adv. finalmente.

finance, s. finança; fundos públicos. v.t. meter-se em operações financeiras.

financial, adj. financial, financeiro.

financially, adv. financeiramente.

financier, s. financeiro, banqueiro; capitalista.

financier, v.t. conduzir operações financeiras (muitas vezes em sentido pejorativo).

finch (es), s. ave pequena. 1) chaffinch, tentilhão. 2) bull-finch, verdelhão. 3) goldfinch, pintassilgo.

find, pret. e pp. de found. v.t. encontrar; achar; descobrir; averiguar, saber; (for) julgar, decidir; aprovar, admitir; sortir, fornecer. 1) to find out, descobrir; adivinhar; resolver. 2) to find fault, censurar, repreender. 3) fast bind fast find, o que bem se guarda facilmente se encontra. 4) all found, tudo incluído (falando do ordenado de criadas).

finder, s. descobridor, inventor; descobridor (pequeno telescópio junto a outro para descobrir o objecto que há-de ser examinado por este).

finding, s. descobrimento, invenção; decisão do júri.

fine, adj. belo, formoso; excelente, admirável; primoroso, saboroso; delicado, fino, delgado; refinado; fine-spun, subtil, fútil; teórico. s. multa. v.t. multar; refinar; purificar; clarificar (vinho, cerveja, etc.).

finely, adv. finalmente, primorosamente, subtilmente.

fineness, s. delicadeza; primor; subtileza; proporção (do metal puro contido numa liga de metais).

fine-draw, pret. finedrew, pp. fine-drawn. v.t. cerzir.

fine-drawer, s. cerzideira, cerzidor.

fine-drawing, s. cerzidura.

fine-drawn, pp. de fine-draw. adj. subtil; muito fino.

finelcocking, adj. elegante.

finery, s. adorno, atavio; primor, elegância; fornalha para fundição de ferro.

finesse, s. artifício, astúcia, subtileza. v.t. usar de artifícios.

finger, s. dedo; largura ou comprimento de um dedo. 1) finger-board, teclado; braço de rabeca. 2) finger-mark, mancha ou marca feita pelo dedo. 3) finger-nail, unha. 4) finger-post, poste indicador. 5) finger-print, impressão digital. 6) finger-stall, dedeira. 7) finger ring, anel. 8) to have a finger in the pie, tomar parte em certo negócio. 9) to snap one's finger at, rir-se de. 10) to have at one's finger ends, saber perfeitamente (a lição); saber na ponta da unha. v.t. tocar com os dedos; dedilhar; manusear. v.t. ter destreza nos dedos. 11) light fingered, ligeiro de dedos. 12) clean-fingered, insubornável; íntegro.

fingering, s. dedilhação.

finial, s. remate.

finical, adj. afectado; delicado; melindroso; fastidioso.

finically, adv. afectadamente,

finicalness, s. afectação.

finicking, ver finical.

finikin, ver finical.

fining, s. refinação, purificação; clarificação (do vinho).

finis, s. o fim; o fim de qualquer coisa, especialmente da vida.

finish, v.t. acabar, terminar, concluir, consumar, arrematar; aperfeiçoar; retocar; vencer. s. fim, termo, remate, acabamento.

finished, pp. e adj. completo; perfeito; acabado.

finisher, s. acabador, consumador, aperfeiçoador.

finishing, s. acabamento, consumação; perfeição; última demão, pincelada, toque. adj. último. 1) finishing-stroke, golpe de misericórdia. 2) The finishing touch, o fim da história, remate.

finite, adj. finito, limitado.

finitely, adv. limitadamente.

finiteness, s. limitação.

finitude, ver finiteness.

finsen rays, s. raio finsen, luz intensa, para o tratamento de doenças de pele.

funny, adj. com barbatanas; com uma barbatana; abundante em peixe.

fiord, s. fiorde.

fiorin, s. agróstis.

fir, s. abeto.

fire, s. fogo, lume; incêndio, combustão; chama; descarga (de armas de fogo). 1) fire-ball, granada de mão. 2) fire bars, grelhas. 3) fire bell, campinha de alarme. 4) fire-box, fornalha de máquina a vapor. 5) fire brand, facho, tição. 6) fire brick, tijolo refractário. 7) fire-brigade, corporação de bombeiros. 7) fire crackers, fogo chinês. 8) fire-control, direcção de tiro. 9) fire-lighter, acendedor. 10) fire-clay, barro refractário. 11) fire-damp, hidrogénio carburetado. 12) fire-dog, cão da chaminé. 13) fire-eater, pantomineiro que finge engolir fogo. 14) fire-escape, salva-vidas contra incêndios. 15) fire-engine, bomba de incêndio. 16) fire-fly, pirilampo. 17) fire grate, grelha. 18) fire-hose, mangueira de incêndio. 19) fire-insurance, seguro contra o fogo. 20) firelock, carabina de pederneira. 21) fireman, bombeiro; fogueiro de bordo. 22) fire-pan, braseira. 23) fire-place, fogão; lar, lareira. 24) fire-plug, boca de incêndio. 25) fire proof safe, cofre à prova de fogo. 26) fire quarters, postos de incêndio. 27) fire-screen, pára-fogo. 28) fireside, lar. 29) fire-ship, brulote. 30) fire stick, tição. 31) fire-stone, pedra refractária; pederneira. 32) firewood, lenha. 33) fireworks, fogos de artifício. 34) fire worship, adoração do fogo. 35) heavy fire, fogo intenso. 36) searching fire, fogo progressivo. 37) st. Antony's fire, erisipela. 38) to bank the fires, apagar o fogo (nas caldeiras). 39) to light a fire, acender um lume. 40) to keep the fire in, conservar o fogo. 41) to hang ou miss fire, errar fogo. 42) to poke up the fire, atiçar o fogo. 43) to put the fires out, encostar os fogos. 44) to play with fire, brincar com o fogo. 45) to silence the enemy's fire, calr o fogo do inimigo. 46) to urge the fires, activar mais o fogo (na caldeira). 47) to take fire. incendiar-se. v.t. incendiar, abrasar, queimar; cozer (louça, tijolos); animar, incitar. v.i. incendiar-se; excitar-se; incomodar-se; disparar, descarregar, fazer fogo; arremessar (projécteis). 48) to fire up, activar o fogo da caldeira. 49) fire away!, comece!

firer, s. o que acende o lume, incendiário,

firing, s. fogo, combustível; acto ou processo de aplicar o fogo a qualquer coisa; descarga de fogo. 1) *firing-party*, destacamento que dá as descargas (em funerais) ou que executa a sentença de morte por meio de descargas. 2) *heavy firing*, fogo intenso. 3) *firing-line*, linha de fogo.

firkin, s. pequeno barril para líquidos, manteiga, peixe, etc.; medida (de 9 galões); 55 arráteis (de manteiga).

firm, adj. firme, fixo; sólido; inflexível. s. firma comercial.

firmament, s. firmamento.

firman, s. passaporte ou édito turco ou oriental.

firmly, adv. firmemente.

firmness, s. firmeza, consistência, constância, resolução.

firry, adj. feito de abeto; pertencente ao abeto.

first, adj. primeiro, anterior; primitivo, principal. s. o primeiro; o princípio. adv. antes, primeiro, de preferência. 1) *first aid*, os primeiros socorros. 2) *first-born*, primogénito. 3) *first-class*, primeira classe; muito bem. 4) *first-fruit*, primícias. 5) *first-hand*, em primeira mão. 6) *first-rate*, de primeira ordem, excelente. 7) *first of all*, primeiro que tudo. 8) *first of exchange*, primeira via (de letra). 9) *at first*, primeiramente, a princípio. 10) *from the first*, desde o princípio. 11) *first come, first served*, o primeiro que chega é o primeiro a ser servido.

firstling, s. primogénito; primícias.

firstly, adv. primeiramente.

firth, s. braço de mar.

fisc, s. fisco, erário.

fiscal, s. tesoureiro; procurador fiscal, adj. fiscal.

fish, s. peixe; pescado; reforço; tala; travessão; lambareiro (náut.). 1) *coal-fish*, bacalhau preto. 2) *freshwater fish*, peixe de água doce. 3) *sea fish*, peixe do mar. 4) *shell fish*, testáceo. 5) *fish bone*, espinha. 6) *fish breeder*, piscicultor. 7) *fish cake*, bolinho (de bacalhau, ou doutro peixe). 8) *fish-carver*, trinchante de peixe. 9) *fish crow*, corvo-do-mar. 10) *fish day*, dia de abstinência. 11) *fish davit*, turco do lambareiro. 12) *fish factory*, fábrica de conserva (de peixe). 13) *fish fag*, peixeira; mulher malcriada. 14) *fish farm*, piscina

para cultura de peixe. 15) *fish gig*, fisga de peixe. 16) *fish glue*, cola de peixe. 17) *fish hook*, anzol, bicheiro. 18) *fish line*, linha de pesca. 19) *fish-pond*, viveiro de peixes. 20) *fish pearl*, pérola falsa (de vidro, com uma camada de cera). 21) *fish-sauce*, molho para peixe. 22) *fish skin*, lixa. 23) *fish story*, conto exagerado. 24) *fishwife ou fishwoman*, peixeira. 25) *a pretty kettle of fish*, uma confusão, uma trapalhada dos diabos. 26) *to feed the fishs*, afogar-se; enjoar. 27) *mute as a fish*, calado como um peixe. 28) *to be neither fish nor flesh*, não se inclinar nem para um nem para outro lado. 28) *to have other fish to fry*, ter em vista negócios mais importantes. 29) *to drink like a fish*, beber como uma esponja. 30) *I feel like a fish out of water*, estou fora do meu elemento. v.t. pescar; buscar; alcançar; intentar; reforçar; pôr gêmeas (náut.). 31) *to go fishing*, ir à pesca. 32) *to fish the anchor*, atravessar a âncora; engatar o lambareiro. 33) *to fish for*, procurar obter. 34) *to fish in troubled waters*, pescar em águas turvas. 35) *to fish out*, esgotar a pesca. 36) *to fish up*, suspender (ferro, etc.).

fisher, s. pescador; marta da América.

fisherman, s. pescador.

fishery, s. pesca, pescaria; direito de pesca. 1) *coast fishery*, pesca costeira. 2) *deep-sea fishery*, pesca do alto mar. 3) *drift-fishery*, pesca de arrasto. 4) *inland-fishery*, pesca fluvial.

fishily, adv. relativo a peixe; duvidosamente.

fishiness, s. forma, sabor ou cheiro de peixe; carácter duvidoso.

fishing, s. pesca; acto de pôr gêmeas ou talas. 1) *fishing-frog*, martinho-pescador ou diabo-marinho. 2) *fishing gear*, aprestos de pesca. 3) *fishing ground*, pesqueiro. 4) *fishing line*, linha de pesca. 5) *fishing net*, rede de pesca. 6) *fishing-rod*, cana de pesca. 7) *fishing-tackle*, aparelho de pesca.

fishmonger, s. vendedor de peixe.

fishy, adj. piscoso, de peixe; duvidoso; suspeito.

fissile, adj. fendível, separável.

fission, s. divisão, separação.

fissiparous, adj. fissíparo.

fissure, s. fissura, fenda, greta.

fissured, adj. fendido, gretado, aberto.

fist, s. punho; chamada; letra, caligrafia;

mão; *give us your fist,* = *shake hands*, aperta a mão. *v.t.* socar, bater com o punho.

fistic, al, *adj.* relativo ao punho, ou ao pugilato.

fisticuff, *s.* murro; (*pl.*) briga a murros.

fistula, *s.* fístula.

fistular, *adj.* tubular.

fistulous, *adj.* cheio de fístulas.

fit, *s.* desmaio, ataque; capricho; veneta; corte ou talhe (de um fato ou vestido); ajuste, adaptação. 1) *by fits and starts,* a capricho, irregularmente, por acessos. 2) *if the fit takes me,* se me der na veneta. *adj.* (com *for*) apto, próprio, apropriado, justo; pronto a; capaz. *v.t. fitting, fitted.* ajustar, adaptar, acomodar; dispor, preparar, acertar; montar. talhar (um vestido, fato). *v.i.* convir, assentar, ficar bem (roupa); ajustar-se. 3) *to fit out,* equipar, armar, aprontar (um navio, etc.). 4) *fit up,* ajustar, adornar. 5) *if the cap fits,* se lhe assentar a carapuça.

fitch (es), *s.* escova ou brocha feita de pêlo de doninha; doninha.

fitchew, *s.* doninha.

fitful, *adj.* espasmódico; caprichoso; vacilante, intermitente.

fitfully, *adv.* caprichosamente; por acessos.

fitfulness, *s.* capricho.

fitly, *adv.* adequadamente, propriamente; convenientemente.

fitment, *s.* equipagem, aprestos; apropriação; peça de mobília.

fitness, *s.* propriedade, aptidão, adaptação, idoneidade, conveniência.

fitter, *s.* ajustador, adaptador; cortador (de fatos, vestidos); montador (de máquinas).

fitter, fittest, *comp.* e *sup.* de *fit.*

fitting, *adj.* próprio, adequado, conveniente. *s.* ajuste, encaixe, entalhe, corte (de vestido, etc.). 1) *fitting-out,* equipagem, aprestos; mobília. 2) *fitting-shop,* oficina para acertar as peças de uma máquina.

fittingly, *adv.* convenientemente.

fittings, *s.* guarnições; aprestos; ferragens; instalações.

five, *adj.* cinco.

fiver, *adj.* uma nota de cinco libras ou de cinco dólares.

fives, *s.* jogo da bola; alporcas nos cavalos; os cinco dedos.

fivefold, *adj.* quíntuplo.

fix, *v.t.* fixar, assentar; estabelecer, precisar;

determinar; terminar; concentrar a atenção; pôr em ordem. *v.i.* fixar residência; solidificar-se. 1) *to fix on, upon,* decidir, escolher. 2) *fix up,* arranjar. *s.* apuro, situação crítica, dilema.

fixable, *adj.* fixável; adaptável.

fixation, *s.* fixação, firmeza, estabilidade; coagulação.

fixative, *adj.* fixativo. *s.* mordente.

fixature, *s.* fixador (para o cabelo).

fixed, *adj.* fixo, estável, permanente, determinado, fixado.

fixedly, *adv.* fixamente.

fixedness, *s.* fixidez, firmeza, estabilidade; fixação.

fixer, *s.* fixador (de fotografia).

fixing, *s.* fixação, determinação, adaptação; *fixing solution,* fixador. (pl.) adornos, aprestos, acessórios.

fixity, ver *fixidness.*

fixture, *s.* o que está fixo; adorno; móveis fixos (no soalho ou na parede); data fixa para corrida, reunião, etc. (pl.) instalações.

fizz, *v.i.* assobiar; efervescer. *s.* assobio; efervescência.

fizzer, *s.* assobiador; o que efervesce.

fizzle, *v.i.* assobiar; *fizzle out,* dar fiasco. *s.* assobio; fiasco.

fiord, ver *fjord.*

flabbergast, *v.t.* causar espanto a, confundir alguém.

flabbilly, *adv.* frouxamente, debilmente.

flabbiness, *s.* frouxidão, placidez, moleza, debilidade.

flabby, *adj.* frouxo, mole, lasso.

flaccid, *adj.* frouxo, lasso, débil.

flaccidity, ver *flaccidness.*

flaccidly, *adv.* frouxamente, debilmente.

flaccidness, *s.* flacidez, moleza, lassidão, debilidade.

flag, bandeira, bandeirola; estandarte; pavilhão; espadana; laje. 1) *flag bearer,* porta-bandeira. 2) *flag-captain,* comandante do navio-almirante. 3) *flag-day,* festa da bandeira (correspondente à festa da flor). 4) *flag of distress,* bandeira a pedir socorro. 5) *flag of truce,* bandeira para parlamentar. 6) *flag-officer,* almirante, vice-almirante, contra-almirante ou comodoro. 7) *flag-lieutenant,* ajudante de almirante. 8) *flagship,* navio-almirante. 9) *flgastaff,* pau de bandeira, mastro. 10) *black flag,* pavilhão pirata; sinal de execução de sentença de morte. 11) *merchant flag,* bandeira mercante. 12) *pilot flag*, bandeira a pedir piloto. 13) *powder flag*, bandeira vermelha que indica que a bordo há explosivos. 14) *red flag*, sinal de perigo. 15) *white flag*, bandeira branca, sinal de amizade, de não hostilidade, de parlamentar, ou de rendição. 16) *yellow flag*, bandeira de quarentena. 17) *to lower ou strike the flag*, arriar a bandeira. 18) *flags fore and aft*, embandeiramento em arco. 19) *the flag at half mast high*, bandeira a meia haste. 20) *the fly and hoist of a flag*, o comprimento e a largura de uma bandeira. *v.i. e v.t. flagging, flagged,* pender, abater; enfraquecer; desanimar; estar lasso; enfeitar com bandeiras; fazer sinais com bandeiras; lajear, pavimentar.

flagellant, *adj.* e *s.* flagelante.

flagellate, *v.i.* flagelar.

flagellation, *s.* flagelação.

flagellator, *s.* flagelador.

flagelium, *s.* flagelo, açoite; vergôntea, rebento de planta.

flageolet, *s.* flageolé.

flaggin, *adj.* flácido, lânguido; flutuante; indeciso.

flaggy, *adj.* mole, flexível, fraco.

flagitious, *adj.* malvado, atroz, abominável.

flagitiously, *adv.* atrozmente.

flagitiousness, *s.* malvadez, perversidade, atrocidade.

flagon, *s.* garrafa de mesa com asa.

flagrancy, *s.* flagrância; notoriedade; escândalo; imprudência.

flagrant, *adj.* flagrante; notorio; escandaloso.

flagrantly, *adv.* notoriamente.

flagstone, *s.* laje.

flail, *s.* mangual. *v.t.* malhar cereais.

flair, *s.* olfacto; discernimento instintivo; gosto, tendência.

flake, *s.* floco; escama; lâmina; lasca (de pedra, etc.); cravo branco com estrias; chispa, centelha. *v.i.* formar (flocos, escamas ou lascas); cair em flocos.

flaky, *adj.* cheios de flocos ou escamas; em forma de escama.

flam, *s.* mentira, engano; mistificação.

flambeau, *s.* archote.

flamboyant, *adj.* extravagante; retumbante; flamejante.

flame, *s.* chama, fogo; ardor; paixão. amor; namoro. *v.t.* queimar. *v.i.* arder, incendiar-se, brilhar, inflamar-se.

flamen, *s.* flâmine.

flaming, *adj.* flamejante; ardente.

flamingo, *s.* flamingo.

flamy, *adj.* inflamado.

flange, *s.* beiral, borda, aba, rebordo; parte saliente; falange; manilha (de tubo). *v.t.* rebaixar, abater; colocar beirais, bordas ou abas; virar (uma aba).

flank, *s.* flanco, lado, ilharga. *v.t. e v.i.* flanquear, tomar flanco; fortificar os flancos.

flanker, *s.* flanco, espaço entre o baluarte e a cortina, em fortificações.

flannel, *s.* flanela de lã.

flannelette, *s.* flanela de algodão.

flannely, *adj.* feito de flanela.

flap, *s.* aba (do chapéu, casaco, etc.); lado, extremidade; saliência; lábios (de uma ferida); portinhola (de resbordo); palmada. 1) *flapdoodle*, disparate. 2) *printed on the flap*, impresso no verso. *v.i. flapping flapped*, dar palmadas; bater com as asas; pender; açoitar, bater o pano.

flapjack, *s.* pequeno bolo de farinha frito em gordura na sertã.

flapper, *s.* o que bate; ave nova (brava); rapariga quase desenvolvida; mãe.

flare, *s.* chama, fulgor, brilho; inclinação. 1) *flare-up*, cólera. *v.i.* brilhar, resplandecer; deslumbrar; ostentar vestuários ricos; projectar. 2) *to flare up*, encolerizar-se.

flaring, *adj.* deslumbrante.

flaringly, *adv.* de um modo deslumbrante; com ostentação.

flash (es), *s.* relâmpago, brilho; momento, instante; esguicho; borbotão de água. 1) *flash-wheel*, roda hidráulica. 2) *flash of the eye*, olhadela. 3) *a lighting flash*, relâmpago. 4) *flash in the pan*, brilho passageiro. 5) *flash of wit*, chiste. 6) *flash-light*, holofote; farol de relâmpagos; lâmpada eléctrica de mão. 7) *flash banknote*, nota falsa. *v.t. e v.i.* acender; queimar; fazer brilhar; cruzar ou passar como um relâmpago.

flashily, *adv.* superficialmente; de um modo pomposo.

flashiness, *s.* brilho passageiro.

flashing, *s.* centelha; *flashing-light*, farol de relâmpagos.

flashy, *adj.* superficial, insípido; brilhante mas transitório.

flask, *s.* frasco; *powder-flask*, polvorinho.

flasket, *s.* frasco pequeno, cesto chato.

flat, *s.* planície; baixio; banco de areia; coisa plana; chapa; pá de remo; barco chato; estrado, bailéu (de porão); andar ou parte de um andar de uma casa; bemol (mús.); mentecapto. *adj*. plano, liso, chato; positivo; categórico; insípido; monótono; aparente; desafinado (mús.). 1) *revolving flat*, chapa giratória. 2) *flat-boat*, barco de fundo chato. 3) *flat bottomed*, de fundo chato. 4) *flat ceiling*, forro de porão. 5) *flat coast*, costa rasa. 6) *flat-fish*, peixe achatado (solha, linguado, etc.). 7) *flat lie*, mentira manifesta. 8) *flat-nosed*, de nariz chato. 9) *flat wine*, vinho insípido. *v.t. flatting, flatted*, achatar, alisar.

flatly, *adv*. de um modo plano ou chato; redondamente, absolutamente.

flatness, *s*. lisura; insipidez.

flated, *pret. pp*. de *flat*.

flatten, *v.t*. aplanar, achatar; derrubar; deprimir; tornar insípido.

flatter, flattest, *pret*. e *pp*. de *flat*.

flatter, *v.t*. lisonjear, adular, exaltar. *v.i*. ser adulador. *s*. flauta, (assentador de ferreiro).

flatterer, *s*. adulador, lisonjeiro.

flatterring, *adj*. lisonjeiro.

flatteringly, *adv*. lisonjeiramente.

flattery (ies), *s*. lisonja, adulação.

flatting, *p. pr*. de *flat; flattingmill*, laminador.

flattish, *adj*. um tanto chato.

flatulence, *s*. flatulência; presunção.

flatulency, ver *flatulence*.

flatulent, *adj*. flatulento; pretensioso.

flatulently, *adv*. com flatulências; pretensiosamente.

flatus (es), *s*. flato, ventosidade, sopro.

flatways, *adj*. ou *adv*. sobre o chato, ou plano.

flatwise, ver *flatways*.

flaunt, *v.t*. pavonear. *v.i*. pavonear-se; agitar-se; tremular, ondular (bandeiras). *s*. ostentação.

flaunter, *s*. vaidoso.

flaunting, *adj*. vaidoso. *s*. pavonear(-se).

flautingly, *adv*. vaidosamente.

flautist, *s*. flautista.

flavorous, *adj*. saboroso.

flavour, *s*. sabor, gosto, aroma. *v.t*. condimentar, temperar.

flavoured, *adj*. saboroso.

flavouring, *s*. sainete.

flavourless, *adj*. insípido.

flaw, *s*. fenda, falha, defeito, choco (de fundição); rajada. *v.t*. fazer fendas; fazer imperfeito.

flawless, *adj*. sem fendas; perfeito, são.

flawlessly, *adv*. sem defeito.

flawlessness, *s*. perfeição

flawy, *adj*. imperfeito, defeituoso; tempestuoso; com chocos (fundição).

flax, *s*. linho (planta). 1) *flax-seed*, linhaça, semente de linho. 2) *flax comb*, carda. 3) *flax grower*, cultivador de linho.

flaxen, *adj*. de linho; loiro.

flaxy, ver *flaxen*.

flay, *v.t*. esfolar, pelar.

flayer, *s*. esfolador.

flea, pulga; *flea-bite*, picadela de pulga.

fleabane, *s*. pulicária.

fleam, *s*. lanceta para sangrar cavalos.

flèche, *s*. frecha, seta; remate em forma de pirâmide.

fleck, *v.t*. enodoar, manchar; salpicar com cores diversas. *s*. pinta, mancha, nódoa.

fleckless, *adj*. sem mancha.

flection, ver *flectional*.

flectional, *adj*. flexional; flexível; inclinado.

fled, *pret*. e *pp*. de *flee*.

fledge, *v.t*. fornecer de penas ou asa. *v.i*. ganhar penas ou asas.

fledged, *adj*. com penas; com asas; sazonado, maduro.

fledgeling, *s*. avezinha; pessoa inexperiente.

flee, *pret*. e *pp*. de *fled. v.t*. fugir de, evitar, escapar. *v.i*. fugir.

fleece, *s*. velo, pele de carneiro. *v.t*. tosquiar; despojar; cobrir com lã.

fleeced, *adj*. lanoso, lãzudo.

fleecer, *s*. tosquiador.

fleecy, *adj*. lanoso, lãzudo.

fleer, *s*. fugitivo; zombaria, escárnio, mofa. *v.t*. e *v.i*. zombar, escarnecer, mofar.

fleerer, *s*. escarnecedor.

fleering, *s*. escárnio. *s*. escarnecedor.

fleet, *s*. esquadra, armada, frota; enseada pouco funda; *pearling fleet*, flotilha para a apanha de pérolas. *adj*. rápido, veloz; pouco fundo. *v.i*. passar rapidamente; emendar (uma falha); tesar (enxárcia).

fleeting, *adj*. passageiro, transitório.

fleetingly, *adv*. rapidamente; de pouca dura.

fleetness, *s*. velocidade, ligeireza.

fleetly, ver *fleetingly*.

Fleming, *s*. flamengo.

Flemish, *s*. a língua flamenga, *adj*. flamengo.

flemish, *v.i*. agitar, mover (a cauda).

flench, flinch, flense, *v.t*. desmanchar; esquartejar (baleia); esfolar (foca).

flesh, *s*. carne; sensualidade; polpa de fruta. 1) *flesh-colour*, cor de carne. 2) *flesh diet*, dieta de carne. 3) *flesh-pots*, manjar, iguarias; símbolo de abundância. 4) *flesh-tint*, tinta cor de carne. 5) *flesh-wound*, ferida superficial. 6) *to gather flesh*, tomar carnes, criar gordura. 7) *to go the way of all flesh*, morrer. *v.t.* fartar; saciar (de carne); engordar; tirar a carne aos couros, descarnar. 8) *fleshing-knife*, cutelo embotado para raspar a carne dos couros.

fleshed, *adj.* carnudo.

fleshiness, *s.* gordura, corpulência.

fleshings, *s.* vestido leve cor de carne, usado justo ao corpo.

fleshless, *adj.* descarnado.

fleshliness, *s.* carnalidade.

fleshly, *adj.* carnal; corpóreo; sensual.

fleshy, *adj.* carnudo; polposo.

fletcher, *s.* fabricante de frechas.

fleur-de-lis, *s.* flor de lis.

flew, *prep.* de *fly*.

flex, *v.t.* dobrar, curvar.

flexibility, *s.* flexibilidade.

flexible, *adj.* flexível.

flexibleness, *s.* flexibilidade.

flexibly, *adv.* com flexibilidade.

flexion, *s.* flexão; curvatura.

flexional, *adj.* flexional; flexível.

flexor, *s.* flexor (músculo).

flexure, *s.* flexão, curvatura, inclinação.

flibbertigibbet, *s.* pessoa volúvel, caprichosa, frívola.

flick, *s.* chicotada; piparote. *v.i.* dar chicotadas leves; agitar.

flicker, *v.i.* adejar, tremular, vacilar, bruxulear. *s.* luz vacilante ou mortiça; picanço.

flickering, *s.* vacilação. *adj.* vacilante.

flier, *s.* voador, aviador; ave voadora, coisa veloz (navio, comboio, cavalo, etc.); volante; operação de Bolsa.

flight, *s.* voo (de ave, avião, etc.); fuga, rapidez, velocidade, espaço decorrido por uma bala ou por um avião; descarga, chuva de (flechas, etc.); pássaro; bando de aves; ímpeto; exaltação; rasgo (de imaginação); elevação (do pensamento). 1) *flight path*, linha de passagem de um avião. 2) *flight of steps*, série de degraus de escada. 3) *to take to flight*, fugir. 4) *to put to flight*, pôr em debandada.

flightly, *adv.* inconscientemente, levianamente.

flightiness, *s.* veleidade; versatilidade; inconstância; utopia.

flighty, *adj.* inconstante; caprichoso; utopista.

flim-flam, *s.* capricho, disparate; conversa oca; extravagância; partida, embuste.

flimsily, *adv.* sem consistência.

flimsiness, *s.* falta de consistência; fragilidade.

flimsy, *adj.* débil, inconsistente; delgado; fútil, frívolo. *s.* papel muito fino, papel de cópia; nota de banco.

flinch, *v.i.* titubear, vacilar; tergiversar; desistir; abster-se; *without flinching*, sem titubear.

flincher, *s.* o que vacila.

flinching, *adj.* vacilante.

flinchingly, *adv.* cobardemente.

flinders, *s.* estilhaços, fragmentos.

fling, *pret.* e *pp.* de flung *v.t.* arrojar, lançar, despedir, vibrar, derrubar; vencer. *v.i.* arremessar; escarnecer; mofar; dar saltos ou coices. 1) *fling away*, deitar fora. 2) *fling in one's face*, lançar em rosto. 3) *fling open*, abrir de repente. 4) *fling out*, arremessar com força; falar ou agir com violência. 5) *fling up*, abandonar. *s.* dança escocesa; salto; chufa.

flint, *s.* pederneira; coisa muito dura. 1) *flint-glass*, cristal da rocha. 2) *flint hearted*, cruel. 3) *flint-lock*, fuzil de pederneira. 4) *flint period*, Idade da Pedra.

flintily, *adv.* duramente, cruelmente.

flintiness, *s.* dureza, crueldade.

flinty, *adj.* pederneira; muito duro; empedernido; cruel.

flintstone, *s.* pederneira.

flip, *flipping, flipped. v.i.* tocar ao de leve; atirar (para o ar com um movimento do dedo polegar). *s.* sacudidela; bebida feita de cerveja, aguardente e açúcar.

flip-flap, *s.* sacudidela, cambalhota; espécie de carrossel.

flippancy, *s.* petulância; loquacidade, impertinência.

flippant, *adj.* petulante; loquaz.

flippantly, *adj.* loquazmente; de um modo petulante; com petulância.

flipper, *s.* barbatana; membro natatório (das focas, etc.); mão.

flirt, *s.* homem que dispensa atenções ou mulher que as recebe apenas por divertimento; coqueta; namoro; meneio. *v.t.* namorar (por distracção); menear-se; mofar.

flirtation, *s.* namoro por distracção; galanteio.

flirting, ver *flirtation*.

fli 167 **flo**

flirtingly, *adv.* de modo galanteador.

flit, flitting, flitted, *v.i.* voar, fugir; bater as asas; mudar de residência; emigrar.

flitch (es), *s.* manta de toucinho; posta de haibu; peixe chato. *v.t.* cortar (madeira ou haibu) em forma de posta.

flitter, *s.* andrajo, farrapo; lantejoula; emigrante. *v.t.* voar; esvoaçar; emigrar.

flitting, *s.* fuga; voo rápido.

flivver, *s.* automóvel barato.

float, *v.t.* e *v.i.* flutuar, boiar, pôr a nado; circular; emitir, pôr em circulação, inundar, alargar. s. flutuador; corpo flutuante, bóia; jangada; pá (de roda propulsora); carro para procissões ou espectáculos públicos; ribalta; *floatstone*, pedra que bóia na água.

floatable, *adj.* flutuável.

floatage, *s.* tudo o que flutua na água.

floatation, *s.* ver *flotation*.

floater, *s.* o que flutua.

floating, *adj.* flutuante; movimento; variável; circulante; pronto para uso. 1) *floating-bridge*, ponte flutuante. 2) *floating debt*, dívida flutuante. 3) *floating capital*, capital flutuante. 4) *floating dock*, doca flutuante. 5) *floating factory*, navio-oficina. 6) *floating policy*, apólice flutuante. 7) *floating population*, população flutuante. 8) *floating ribs*, costeletas separadas do esterno. 9) *floating stage*, jangada, cais flutuante.

flocculent, *adj.* semelhante a flocos (de lã, algodão, etc.).

flock, *s.* floco (de lã, algodão, etc.); tufo; manada, rebanho, bando, etc. *v.i.* reunir-se, congregar-se; caminhar em bandos. 1) *to flock together*, juntar-se. 2) *birds of a feather flock together*, diz-me com quem andas, dir-te-ei as manhas que tens.

flocky, *adj.* em flocos.

floe, *s.* massa de gelo flutuante.

flog, flogging, flogged, *v.t.* castigar, punir, açoitar.

flogging, *s.* açoite; sova.

flood, *s.* dilúvio, inundação; cheia; o mar; fluxo; maré; hemorragia interna. 1) *half-flood*, meia maré. 2) *flood-gate*, comporta. 3) *storm flood*, grande maré (por temporal). 4) *floodtide*, maré cheia, fluxo. *v.t.* inundar, alagar; ter hemorragia uterina.

flooding, *s.* hemorragia uterina; inundação.

floor, *s.* pavimento, soalho, cão; eira; andar (de casa); caverna (náut.); a parte do Parlamento ocupada pelos deputados ou senadores; (pl.) varengas (náut.). 1) *first*

second floor, primeiro, segundo andar. 2) *ground floor*, rés-do-chão. 3) *floor light*, janela ou vidro no soalho. 4) *floor-cloth*, oleado de corticite, linóleo, ou outro material para os soalhos. 5) *to take the floor*, tomar a palavra. *v.i.* soalhar, pavimentar; derrubar, estender, deitar ao chão; estender (num exame).

floorer, *s.* murro; forte pancada que faz derrubar; pergunta de exame que faz com que o aluno se «estenda».

flooring, *s.* material para pavimentos; chão, soalho; estrado.

flop, flopping, flopped, *v.t.* bater, sacudir as asas; deixar cair repentinamente. *v.i.* cair pesada e repentinamente; ir de encontro.

flora, *s.* flora.

floral, *adj.* floral.

florescence, *s.* florescência.

florescent, *adj.* florescente.

floret, *s.* florinha; flósculo.

floriate, *v.t.* decorar com desenhos florais.

floricultural, *adj.* relativo à floricultura.

floriculture, *s.* floricultura.

floriculturist, *s.* floricultor.

florid, *adj.* florido; ornado; ostentoso; corado.

floridly, *adv.* floridamente.

floridness, *s.* qualidade de ser florido.

floriferous, *adj.* florífero.

florin, *s.* florim.

florist, *s.* florista.

floruit, *s.* período, sem a data exacta do nascimento e morte, em que uma pessoa viveu.

floss, *s.* seda dos casulos; penugem; *floss-silk*, seda frouxa.

flossy, *adj.* seda frouxa.

flotation, *s.* flutuação; princípio de uma empresa comercial.

flotilla, *s.* flotilha.

flotsam, *s.* objectos flutuantes; destroços de naufrágio.

flounce, *s.* debrum, cairel; franjas das saias; movimento repentino do corpo; mergulho. *v.t.* guarnecer com franjas, debruar. *v.i.* mergulhar (na água ou lodo); agitar-se.

flounder, *s.* solha (peixe). *v.i.* patinhar ou espojar-se no lodo; lutar; ter dificuldade; estender-se (a falar).

floundering, *s.* acção de patinhar, ou espojar-se.

flour, *s.* farinha; *flour-mill*, moinho. *v.t.* enfarinhar; moer.

flourish, s. vigor; esplendor; rasgo de pena; floreio; ornamento; (mús.) prelúdio; *flourish of trumpts*, toque de trombetas. *v.t.* florescer, prosperar; jactar-se, florear (no falar, no escrever, etc.).

flourishingly, adv. prosperamente.

floury, adj. farinhento.

flout, s. mofa, escárnio, burla. *v.t.* e *v.i.* mofar, escarnecer, burlar.

flouting, s. mofa, escárnio. adj. escarnecedor.

floutingly, adv. insolentemente.

flow, s. corrente; fluxo, enchente, abundância; multidão. *v.i.* fluir, correr, dimanar; crescer a maré. 1) *to flow into*, desaguar. 2) *flow away*, deslizar, desaparecer.

flower, s. flor, planta em flor; adorno; beleza. 1) *eternal flower*, perpétuo. 2) *flower-bed*, canteiro de jardim. 3) *flower bud*, botão de flor. 4) *flower-girl*, florista. 5) *flower-garden*, jardim. 6) *flower leaf*, pétala. 7) *flowerpot*, vaso de flores. 8) *flower-piece*, pintura representando flores. 9) *flower stand*, jardineira. 10) *flower-show*, exposição de flores. 11) *flower-stalk*, pedúnculo. 12) *flowers of wine*, flor do vinho. *v.t.* e *v.i.* enfeitar (com figuras de flores); florescer.

flowerer, s. planta que só floresce em determinado tempo.

floweret, s. florinha.

flowerless, adj. sem flores,

flowering, s. floração.

flowery, adj. florido; poético.

flowing, adj. fluente, cheio. 1) *flowing garments*, vestidos que caem em dobras. s. fluxo. 2) *flowing sheet*, escota aventada (náut.). 3) *flowing wind*, vento de feição.

flowingly, adv. como uma torrente; abundantemente.

flowingness, s. influência; verbosidade.

flown, pp. de *fly*.

fluctuate, *v.i.* flutuar, ondear; vacilar, duvidar.

fluctuating, adj. flutuante; incerto.

fluctuation, s. flutuação.

flue, s. cano (da chaminé); tubo (de caldeira); conduta; cotão; abr. de *influenza*, neste sentido também se escreve «flu»; espécie de rede de pescar. *v.i.*, *v.t.* alargar abertura.

fluency, s. fluência; facilidade.

fluent, adj. fluente; eloquente.

fluently, adv. correntemente.

fluenteness, s. fluência.

fluff, s. cotão; penugem; lanugem. *v.t.* espa-

lhar, estender, cobrir com (cotão, penugem).

fluffiness, s. cobertura de penugem, lanugem ou penas.

fluffy, s. formado ou coberto de penugem, lanugem ou penas.

fluid, s. fluido; líquido; gás. adj. fluido.

fluidity, s. fluidez.

fluke, s. unha de âncora; cauda da baleia; parasita encontrado no fígado das ovelhas; solha, acaso; *by a fluke*, por milagre, por acaso.

flume, s. canal condutor de água para moinho, etc. ravina por onde passa uma torrente.

flummery, s. manjar branco; geleia de aveia; frioleira; lisonja.

flummox, *v.t.* confundir, desconcertar; atrapalhar.

flump, s. barulho, ruído, estrondo. *v.t.* e *v.i.* arremessar ou arremessar-se ao chão com violência.

flung, pret. e pp. de *to fling*.

flunkey, s. lacaio.

flunkeyism, s. servilismo.

fluor, s. flúor (mineral); estado líquido; menstruação.

fluorescence, s. fluorescência.

fluorescet, adj. fluorescente.

fluoric, adj. fluorídrico.

fluorite, s. fluorite, flúor.

fluorine, s. fluorina.

flurry, s. fluorina.

flurry, s. agitação, comoção; barulho; refrega (de vento). *v.t.* pret. pp. flurried, confundir, perturbar; atrapalhar.

flush, rubor, animação, emoção; voo rápido; fluxo rápido; abundância. adj. quente e pesado (tempo); vigoroso; abundante; rico; endinheirado; nivelado; à flor, à face. 1) *flush deck*, convés corrido. 2) *flush head*, cabeça à face (de rebite). 3) *he is flush with cash*, ele tem muito dinheiro. *v. t.* fazer enrubescer; inundar; levantar voo; excitar, nivelar. *v.i.* derramar-se, fluir, manar; enrubescer-se.

flushing, s. inundação; rubor.

fluster, *v.t.* aturdir (com bebidas alcoólicas). s. perturbação.

flute, s. flauta; estria, prega. *v.i.* acanelar, estriar; tocar flauta.

flutist, s. tocador de flauta.

fluting, s. estratagema; canelagem; estria.

flutter, s. alvoroço, agitação; palpitação. *v.t.*

agitar, pôr em confusão; palpitar. *v.i.*
alvoroçar-se.

flutterer, *s.* agitador.

fluty, *adj.* aflautado.

fluvial, *adj.* fluvial.

flux, *s.* fluxo; fusão; dissolvente.

fluxion, *s.* fluxo; proporção em que uma
quantidade aumente a sua grandeza (mat.);
method of fluxions, cálculo de Newton.

fly, *pret. flew, pp. flown. v.t.* fazer voar;
evadir; fugir de. *v.i.* voar, lançar-se,
precipitar-se; correr; saltar; fugir; escapar-
-se; desaparecer; atacar; arvorar (bandeira).
1) *to fly about,* saltar (o vento); voar de um
lado para o outro; espalhar-se. 2) *fly at,*
lançar-se sobre. 3) *fly away,* escapar-se;
levantar voo. 4) *fly from,* fugir de. 5) *fly into
a passion,* encolerizar-se. 6) *fly off,*
desaparecer. 7) *fly open,* abrir-se de
repente. 8) *fly out,* enfurecer-se. 9) *fly upon,*
atacar de repente. 10) *fly to arms,* recorrer
às armas. 11) *to fly a kite,* lançar um
papagaio (de papel). 12) *to fly to a flag,*
hastear uma bandeira. 13) *to let fly,* deixar
correr (um cabo); disparar. (pl. *flies*) *s.*
mosca; mosca artificial para a pesca; rosa-
-dos-ventos; cumprimento de bandeira
(náut.); cabriolé (nesta acepção o plural é
flys); lapela do casaco. 14) *fly-blow,* voo de
mosca. 15) *fly-fish,* pesca com moscas. 16)
fly leaf, folha em branco no princípio e no
fim de um livro. 17) *fly-line,* linha para
pescar com moscas artificiais. 18) *fly maker,*
o que faz moscas artificiais. 19) *fly-paper,*
papel mata-mosca. 20) *fly-trap,* mos-
queiro. 21) *fly wheel,* volante. 22) *fly on
wheel,* pessoa vaidosa. 23) *spanish fly,*
cantárida.

flying, *s.* voo; aviação. *adj.* voador; volante.
1) *flying-boat,* combinação de um avião e
um hidroavião. 2) *flying boom,* pau de giba.
3) *flying bridge,* ponte volante. 4) *flying fish,*
peixe-voador. 5) *flying ground,* aeródromo.
6) *flying jib,* giba. 7) *flying jib guy,* patarrás
da giba. 8) *flying kite,* vela alta. 9) *flying
machine,* avião. 10) *flying sail,* vela triangular sem estai.

foal, *s.* porto. *v.t.* parir (a égua).

foam, *s.* espuma; cachão; escarcéu. *v.t.* e
v.i. fazer espuma, espumar; fazer cachão;
ferver.

foamite, *s.* espumite.

foamy, *adj.* espumoso.

fob, fobbing, fobbed, *v.t.* meter no bolso;

iludir, dissimular. *s.* bolso de relógio;
engano; presumido.

focal, *adj.* focal.

focalise, *v.t.* focar, concentrar.

focus, *s.* foco. *pl. foci. v.t. focussing,
focussed,* focar.

fodder, *s.* forragem.

foe, *s.* inimigo, adversário.

foeman, *s.* inimigo de guerra.

foetal, *adj.* relativo ao feto.

foetid, *adj.* fétido; pútrido.

foetidly, *adv.* malcheiroso; fétido.

foetidness, *s.* fetidez, fedor.

foetus (es), *s.* feto.

fog, *s.* nevoeiro, névoa, cerração. 1) *fog-
bank,* nevoeiro espesso no mar. 2) *fog
bound,* preso pelo nevoeiro. 3) *fog-horn,*
sereia, busina. 4) *fog-signal,* sinal durante o
nevoeiro, como foguetões, etc. *v.t.* e *v.i.*
fogging, fogged, enovoar, obscurecer;
nevoar-se; enevoar-se; velar-se; obscu-
recer-se.

fogey, ver *fogy.*

foggily, *adv.* com névoas; obscuramente.

fogginess, *s.* nebulosidade.

foggy, *adj.* enevoado, cerrado (com
nevoeiro); confuso, indistinto.

fogy (ies), *s.* caturra; homem já muito velho
(em idade, ideias, ou costumes), bota-de-
-elástico.

fogyish, *adj.* antiquado, ronceiro.

fogyism, *s.* ronceirismo, caturrice.

foible, *s.* o fraco, o lado fraco.

foil, *s.* florete embolado; folha delgada de
metal; objecto que serve para realçar; pista,
rasto (de peça de caça); derrota, mau êxito.
v.t. realçar; frustrar.

foison, *s.* abundância.

foist, *v.t.* introduzir sub-repticiamente
cláusulas em documentos; impingir.

Fokker, *s.* avião de combate usado pelos
Alemães.

fold, *s.* dobra, prega; redil, curral, aprisco.
suf. para a formação de numerais multipli-
cativos. *v.t.* dobrar, pregar; enlaçar; envolver; encerrar; encurralar. *v.i.* dobrar-se,
encerrar-se.

foldage, *s.* direito de encurralar gado em
terra arável.

folder, *s.* dobrador.

folding, *adj.* dobradiço; flexível. 1) *folding-
machine,* dobradeira. 2) *folding door,* porta
de dois batentes. 3) *folding bed,* cama de
lona. 4) *folding table,* mesa dobradiça. *s.*

prega; acção de encurralar gado em terra arável.

foliage, s. folhagem.

foliate, adj. frondoso; folheado.

foliate, v.t. folhear; laminar, estanhar (espelhos).

foliation, s. folheatura; laminação, estanhadura; folheação; renovação das plantas.

foliferous, adj. folífero.

folio, s. infólio, página.

folk, s. povo, gente, nação, raça; (pl.) família; parentela. 1) *folk song*, canção popular, xácara. 2) *the old folks*, os meus ascendentes, os velhos da família. 3) *the little folks*, os meus meninos.

folcklore, s. tradições, crenças, costumes populares; folclore.

follicle, s. folículo.

follow, v.t. seguir, acompanhar; suceder; perseguir; imitar; obedecer; exercer uma profissão; compreender. v.i. seguir-se, resultar. 1) *as follows*, como se segue. 2) *follow my leader*, jogo em que cada parceiro faz o que faz o primeiro. 3) *to follow the plough*, ser lavrador. 4) *to follow suit*, jogar no mesmo naipe; conformar-se com a actuação de outrem, seguir-lhe o exemplo. 5) *to follow out*, continuar até ao fim. 6) *to follow up*, prosseguir, continuar persistentemente. 7) *to follow one's mind*, seguir a sua opinião. 8) *do you follow me?*, compreende-me? s. tacada mal dada no bilhar.

follower, s. sequaz, partidário; tambor de transmissão; roda ou peça que segue o movimento doutra. (pl.) partidários.

following, adj. seguinte, próximo; resultante; séquito, comitiva, carreira, profissão.

folly (ies), s. tolice, loucura.

foment, v.t. fomentar, instigar; dar fomentações.

fomentation, s. fomentação; fomento; excitação, instigação.

fond, s. amigo, apaixonada; afectuoso, terno; *to be fond of*, gostar de, ser amigo de.

fondant, s. bombom que se derrete na boca.

fondle, v.t. animar, acariciar.

fondler, s. acariciador.

fondling, s. mimalho.

fondly, adv. afectuosamente.

fondness, s., afecto, ternura, carinho, inclinação.

font, s. pia baptismal; receptáculo para água benta; depósito de combustível de lâmpada; (tip.), sortido completo de tipos de certa espécie.

fontal, adj. relativo a fonte ou a pia baptismal; oriundo.

food, s. alimento, comida; víveres. 1) *food-stuff*, matérias alimentícias. 2) *food-values*, propriedade nutritiva dos alimentos.

foodless, adj. sem víveres; estéril.

fool, s. tolo, néscio, louco; bobo; fruta escaldada ou cozida, misturada com nata ou açúcar. 1) *all fool's day*, primeiro de Abril, dia dos enganos. 2) *fool-hardy*, temerário. 3) *fool hardily*, temerariamente. 4) *fool-hardiness*, temeridade. 5) *fool's errand*, empresa estúpida e sem resultado. 6) *to play the fool*, fazer de bobo. 7) *to make a fool of*, escarnecer de. 8) *he has made a fool of himself*, ele deu-se ao desfrute. 9) *to live in a fool's paradise*, ignorar o perigo em que se está. v.t. e v.i. chasquear, zombar; divertir-se, brincar; fazer de doido; lograr. 10) *to fool away*, desperdiçar totalmente.

foolery (ies), s. tolice.

foolish, adj. tolo, néscio, tonto; *a foolish question requires no answer*, a palavras loucas, orelhas moucas.

foolishly, adv. tolamente.

foolishness, s. tontice, parvoíce, imprudência.

foolscap, s. gorro com campainhas, usado pelos bobos medievais; orelhas de burro, carapuça das crianças preguiçosas.

foot, s. pé (de animal), pé (medida); pé (de verso); pé (de mesa, cadeira, mastro, etc.); base; parte inferior (de uma página, de uma cruz, etc.); infantaria. pl. *feet*. 1) *at foot*, no fim de uma página. 2) *at the foot of the mountain*, no sopé da montanha. 3) *on foot*, a pé, de pé; activo, progressivo. 4) *foot-bath*, bacia dos pés, banho de pés. 5) *from head to foot*, dos pés à cabeça. 6) *foot band*, forro da esteira (náut.). 7) *footboard*, estribo da carruagem; pedal. 8) *footboy*, lacaio (rapaz). 9) *foot-bridge*, passadiço, ponte para peões. 10) *foot easer*, palmilha com mola de metal. 11) *foot-fall*, som do passo. 12) *foot-gear*, botas, peúgas, etc. 13) *foothold*, apoio para o pé. 14) *footlights*, ribalta. 15) *foot-note*, nota ao fundo de uma página. 16) *footman*, lacaio (adulto). 17) *foot mat*, capacho, coxim. 18) *footpad*, salteador, mas não a cavalo. 19) *fote-page*, lacaio. 20) *foot-path*, passeio (de rua); atalho. 21) *foot-passenger*, peão. 22) *foot-*

plate, plataforma da locomotiva. 23) *footpost*, correio a pé, mensageiro. 24) *footprint*, pegada. 25) *foot pavement*, passeio das ruas. 26) *foot-race*, corrida a pé. 27) *foot-rope*, estribo da verga. 28) *footrule*, medida de 12 polegadas. 29) *footsoldier*, soldado de infantaria. 30) *footsore*, com os pés doridos. 31) *footstalk*, pedúnculo. 32) *footstep*, pegada; passo. 33) *footstool*, escabelo, banquinho. 34) *foot stove*, esquentador para os pés. 35) *foot way*, caminho para peões. 36) *footwarmer*, aquecedor para os pés. 37) *foot worn*, cansado de andar. 38) *to set on foot*, começar, pôr me movimento. 39) *to put one's foot down*, protestar; pôr os pés à parede; recusar terminantemente. 40) *to put one's foot on it*, entregar uma coisa por indiscrição. *v.t.* pesar; percorrer; somar, escrever a soma em baixo; pôr pés (a meias, botas, etc.); pagar uma conta, custear. *v.i.* andar a pé, dançar; somar.

football, *s.* futebol.

footed, *adj.* que tem pés ou patas. 1) *four footed*, quadrúpede. 2) *cloven-foot*, de pata bifurcada.

footer, *s.* o jogo de futebol; que pessoa que anda a pé.

footgear, *s.* sapatos e meias, calçado.

footing, *s.* pé, base, fundamento, piso; passo; baile, dança; estado, condição; apoio para o pé; soma de uma coluna de números. 1) *on a war footing*, em pé de guerra. 2) *to be on equal footing*, estar em iguais condições.

foots, *s.* sedimentos, fezes, borra, pé.

foozle, *s.* indivíduo estúpido, caturra; tacada desastrada (golfe). *v.t.* fazer um jogo desastrado.

fop, *s.* peralvilho, fátuo.

fopling, ver *fop.*

foppery (ies), *s.* afectação no vestir, janotismo; fatuidade.

foppish, *adj.* afectado, vaidoso, adamado, fátuo.

foppish, *s.* fatuidade, vaidade.

for, *prep.* por, por causa de; durante, a favor de; em troca de; em busca de; para (lugar); para (aplicação); para (fim); 1) *for how long?*, por quanto tempo? 2) *for me ou as for me*, pelo que me diz respeito. 3) *for certain*, com certeza. 4) *for all that*, apesar disso. 5) *for all the world*, sem dúvida. 6) *for*

ever, para sempre. 7) *for short*, abreviando. 8) *good-bye for the present*, adeus, até logo. 9) *to go for a walk*, ir dar um passeio. 10) *I cannot do it for the life of me*, não posso fazê-lo por vida minha. *conj.* porque, pois que, porquanto.

forage, *s.* forragem; provisões. *v.t.* e *v.i.* saquear, roubar, forragear.

forager, *s.* forrageador.

foragin, *s.* forragem; *foraging party*, destacamento de forrageadores.

foramen, *s.* orifício, buraco, passagem.

foraminated, *adj.* com orifícios; poroso.

foray, *s.* correria, saque; pilhagem. *v.t.* saquear.

forbade, pret. de *forbid.*

forbear, *s.* antepassado. pret. *forbore*, *forborne*. *v.t.* e *v.i.* abster-se, deixar de, não usar; não mencionar; ter paciência; *bear and forbear*, sê paciente e tolerante.

forbearance, *s.* indulgência; clemência, paciência; abstenção.

forbearing, *adj.* paciente, indulgente.

forbearingly, *adv.* indulgentemente.

forbid, *pret.* forbad ou forbade. *pp.* forbidden. *v.t.* proibir, estorvar; *God forbid*, não permita Deus.

forbidding, *p. pr.* de *forbid* e *adj.* proibitivo, repelente, repugnante. *s.* proibição.

forbiddingly, *adv.* de um modo repelente.

forbore, *pret.* de *forbear.*

force, *s.* força, vigor; poder; motivo causa; coacção, violência; valor, importância; queda de água; força militar, tropa. 1) *in force*, em vigor, 2) *by main force*, à viva força. 3) *coming into force*, entrada em vigor (de lei, ou contrato). 4) *force-pump*, bomba premente. 5) *force and lifting pump*, bomba aspirante-premente. 6) *force-meat*, recheio de carne; salpicão. *v.t.* forçar, obrigar; constranger; meter à força; fazer amadurecer à força. 7) *force away*, obrigar a afastar-se. 8) *force back*, repelir, rechaçar. 9) *force down*, obrigar a baixar. 10) *force in*, introduzir à força; cravar. 11) *force out*, arrancar à força. 12) *force up*, obrigar a subir.

forced, *adj.* forçado, artificial.

forcedly, *adv.* de um modo forçado.

forcedness, *s.* constrangimento.

forceful, *adj.* forte, potente.

forceless, *adj.* fraco, débil.

forceps (es), *s.* fórceps.

forcer, *s.* êmbolo; o que força.

forcible, *adj.* forte, enérgico; de grande peso, concludente.

forcibleness, *s.* força, violência.,

forcibly, *adv.* violentamente, à força; *forcibly so,* forçosamente assim.

forcing, *s.* arte de obter flores ou frutos temporãos; frutos temporãos; clarificar o vinho. 1) *forcing house,* estufa (do jardim). 2) *forcing pump,* bomba premente. 3) *forcing box,* cortiço para onde se tira um enxame de abelhas. 4) *forcing pit,* estufim.

ford, *s.* vau. *v.t.* vadear.

fordable, *adj.* vadeável.

fordo, *pret. fordid. pp. fordone. v.t.* destruir, arruinar; esgotar; cansar.

fordone, *adj.* exausto.

fore, *adj.* anterior; dianteiro; à proa; de proa; do traquete. *adv.* anteriormente, diante, antes. *s.* mastro do traquete (náut.); a proa. 1) *fore and aft,* de proa a proa. 2) *fore-and-aft-rig,* armação latina. 3) *fore-and-aft-sails,* pano latino. 4) *fore body,* parte de vante, corpo da proa. 5) *fore boom,* retranca do traquete latino. 6) *fore bowline,* bolina do traquete. 7) *forecabin,* camarote (de navio) de 2.ª classe. 8) *fore course,* traquete. 9) *fore deck,* coberta da proa. 10) *fore foot,* pé da roda de proa. 11) *fore hatch,* escotilha da proa. 12) *fore hold,* porão da proa. 13) *forelock,* macho do leme. 14) *fore peak,* pique, alvaços da proa. 15) *fore rigging,* ovém do mastro do traquete. 16) *fore royal,* sobre a proa. 17) *fore royal back stay,* patarrás do sobre de proa. 18) *fore royal-yard,* verga do sobre de proa. 19) *fore skysail-stay,* estai do sobrinho de proa.

forearm, *s.* antebraço.

forearm, *v.t.* armar antecipadamente, premunir.

forebear, ver *forbear.*

forebode, *v.t.* prognosticar, pressagiar, pressentir.

foreboder, *s.* pressagiador.

foreboding, *s.* presságio, pressentimento.

forebodingly, *adv.* com pressentimento.

forecast, *s.* prognóstico, visão; projecto, plano, cálculo.

forecast, *v.t. e v.i.* projectar, planear; prognosticar, prever.

forecaster, *s.* previsor.

forecastle, *s.* castelo de proa; *forecastle-head,* coberta do castelo da proa.

forecited, *adj.* já mencionado.

foreclose, *v.t.* impedir, excluir.

foredate, *v.t.* antedatar.

foredoom, *v.t.* predestinar.

forefathers, *s.* antepassados, avoengos.

forefend, ver *forfend.*

forefinger, *s.* dedo indicador.

forefoot, *s.* pata dianteira.

forefront, *s.* parte mais adiantada, dianteira.

forego, *pret.* forewent, foregone. *v.t. e v.i.* preceder, adiantar-se a; ceder; renunciar a; privar-se de.

foregoer, *s.* precursor; predecessor; renunciante.

foregoing, *adj.* precedente.

foregone, *s.* decidido de antemão.

foreground, *s.* primeiro plano.

forehand, *s.* quarto dianteiro do cavalo. *adj.* prematuro, adiantado.

forehanded, *adj.* temporão; antecipado; previdente.

forehead, *s.* fronte; testa.

foreign, *adj.* estrangeiro; adventício; exótico; estranho; alheio. 1) *foreign-trade,* comércio externo. 2) *Foreign-Office,* Ministério dos Negócios Estrangeiros na Inglaterra. 3) *foreign policy,* política externa.

foreigner, *s.* estrangeiro; forasteiro.

forejudge, *v.t.* julgar de antemão.

forejudgment, *s.* prejuízo, juízo prévio,

foreknew, *pret.* de *foreknow.*

foreknow, *pret.* foreknew, pp. foreknown. *v.t.* prever, conhecer antecipadamente.

foreknowable, *adj.* que se pode prever.

foreknowledge, *s.* presciência.

foreknown, *pp.* de *foreknown.*

forel, *s.* espécie de pergaminho.

foreland, *s.* cabo, promontório, morro.

foreleg, *s.* perna da frente.

forelock, *s.* guedelha, topete; *take time by the forelock,* não deixes fugir a ocasião boa.

foreman, *s.* capataz, maioral, mestre (de oficina, etc.); regente; presidente de júri.

foremast, *s.* mastro do traquete, mastro de proa.

forementioned, *adj.* supracitado, supradito.

foremost, *adj.* primeiro, dianteiro; mais chegado da vante (náut.).

forenamed, *adj.* supradito; já mencionado.

forenoon, *s.* manhã; *fore watch,* quarto das 8 às 12 (náut.)

forensic, *adj.* forense.

fore-ordain, *v.t.* predestinar; predeterminar.

forepart, *s.* dianteira, princípio; proa de navio,

forereach, *v.t. e v.i.* navegar adiante de outro navio; ganhar barlavento.

forerum, *pret. foreran. pp. forerun. v.t.* preceder, adiantar-se a; anunciar.

forerunner, *s.* precursor; presságio, prognóstico.

foresaid, *adj.* supradito.

foresail, *s.* traquete.

foresee, *pret. foresaw.* pr. *foreseen. v.i.* prever.

foreseer, *s.* previsor; vidente.

foreshadow, *v.t.* escorçar (pint.).

foreshortening, *s.* escorço.

foreshow, *v.t.* mostrar antecipadamente; predizer.

foresight, *s.* previsão; prevenção; perspicácia; mira de arma.

foreskin, *s.* prepúcio.

forest, *s.* floresta, bosque, mata, selva.

forestal, *v.t.* antecipar, prevenir; açambarcar, monopolizar.

forestaller, *s.* açambarcador, monopolista.

forestalling, *s.* monopólio, açambarcamento.

forestay, *s.* estai do traquete.

forester, *s.* guarda-florestal; silvícola.

forestry, *s.* silvicultura.

foretaste, *s.* antegosto; *v.t.* antegostar.

foretell, *pret.* e *pp. de foretould. v.t.* predizer, profetizar.

foreteller, *s.* profeta.

foretelling, *s.* predição, profecia.

forethought, *s.* premeditação.

foretoken, *s.* sinal antecipado. v.t. dar sinais antecipadamente.

foretop, *s.* topete, carrapito; gávea do traquete (náut.). 1) *foretop gallant mast,* mastaréu do joanete de proa. 2) *foretop gallant sail,* vela do joanete de proa. 3) *foretop gallant-stay,* estai do mastaréu de joanete de proa. 4) *foretop gallant yard,* verga de joanete da proa. 5) *foretop sail,* velacho. 6) *foretop mast,* mastaréu do velacho.

forever, *adv.* sempre, para sempre. 1) *forever-more,* para todo o sempre. 2) *forever and a day* ou *fore ever and ever,* para sempre, eternamente.

forewarn, *v.t.* prevenir, advertir, visar; *forewarned, forearmed,* homem prevenido vale por dois.

forewarning, *s.* advertência, aviso, prevenção.

forewent, *pret.* de *forego.*

forewoman, *s.* presidente de um júri de mulheres; primeira oficial de costura (numa oficina de costura),

foreword, *s.* prefácio.

foreyard, *s.* verga do traquete.

forfeit, *s.* multa; pena; perda legal dos direitos, prenda de jogos; *game of forfeits,* jogo de prendas. *v.t.* perder o direito a uma coisa.

forfeitable, *adj.* confiscável.

forfeiture, *s.* confisco, multa, perda de algum direito.

forfend, *v.t.* prevenir, desviar; *God forfend,* Deus me livre.

forgather, *v.i.* associar-se.

forgave, *pret.* de *forgive.*

forge, *s.* forja, fornalha. 1) *forge-roll,* cilindro de laminar. *v.t.* forjar, falsificar; tramar. 2) *to forge off* ou *on over,* impelir. 3) *to forge ahead,* conservar a marcha; ganhar sobre outro navio.

forgeman, *s.* ferreiro.

forger, *s.* forjador, falsificador.

forget, *pret. forgot, forgotten. p. pr. forgetting. v.t.* esquecer, descurar, *v.i.* esquecer-se.

forgetful, *adj.* esquecido.

forgetfully, *adv.* negligentemente.

forgetfulness, *s.* esquecimento, negligência.

forget-me-not, *s.* miosótis.

forging, *s.* forja, forjadura, peça forjada.

forgivable, *adj.* perdoável.

forgive, *forgave, forgiven. v.t.* perdoar, remir.

forgiven, *pp.* de *forgive.*

forgiveness, *s.* perdão, remissão, indulgência, absolvição.

forgiving, *adj.* generoso, clemente.

forgo, *pret. forwent. pp. forgone. v.t.* e *v.i.* ceder, renunciar a, abandonar.

forgot, forgotten, *pret.* e *pp.* de *forget.*

fork, *s.* garfo; forcado, forquilha; bifurcação; confluência de um rio; ziguezague (raio). 1) *in fork,* em seco (mina). 2) *digging fork,* gadanha de cavar. 3) *pitch-fork,* forcado. 4) *tuning-fork,* diapasão, lamiré. 5) *dung-fork,* gadanho. *v.t.* remover com forcado; esgotar (mina); empolgar, filar. 6) *to fork out,* desembolsar dinheiro contra vontade.

forked, *adj.* bifurcado, bipartido, fendido; em ziguezague (raio).

forkedness, *s.* bifurcação.

forkiness, ver *forkedness.*

forky, ver *forked.*

forlorn, *adj.* abandonado, desemparado, perdido, esquecido; *forlorn-hope,* último recurso; destacamento de soldados para serviço perigoso.

forlornness, *s.* abandono.

form, *s.* forma, figura; modelo; modo, maneira, método, prática, ritual, formalidade, cerimónia; ordem, disposição; fórmula; molde, padrão, forma; porte, comportamento; aparição, sombra; banco; assento comprido; classe; cama de lebre; compasso de música. 1) *for form's sake*, pró-forma. 2) *in due form*, na devida forma. *v.t.* formar, conceber, compor, constituir. *v.i.* formar-se.

formal, *adj.* formal, metódico; cerimonioso; afectado.

formalism, *s.* formalismo.

formalist, *adj.* formalista.

formality (ies), *adj.* formalidade, cerimónia, etiqueta.

formalize, *v.t.* formalizar; fazer cerimonioso ou rígido.

formally, *adv.* formalmente.

format, *s.* formato.

formation, *s.* formação, disposição, arranjo; formação.

formative, *adj.* formativo.

forme, *s.* forma tipográfica já imposta na rama, pronta a entrar na máquina.

former, *adj.* anterior, primeiro, precedente, passado; *the former*, o primeiro mencionado (de dois). *s.* formador, autor, molde, matriz.

formerly, *adv.* antigamente.

formic, *adj.* fórmico.

formicant, *adj.* formigante.

formicary, *s.* formigueiro.

formication, *s.* formigueiro (na pele).

formidable, *adj.* formidável.

formidableness, *s.* pavor, horror.

formidably, *adv.* formidavelmente.

formless, *adj.* informe, disforme.

formlessness, *s.* informidade, deformidade.

formula, *s.* fórmula, receita.

formulary (ies), *s.* formulário. *adj.* formal, sujeito a fórmula.

formulate, *v.t.* formular.

formulize, *v.t.* e *v.i.* formalizar; formular.

fornicate, *v.i.* fornicar. *adj.* arqueado, abobadado.

fornicated, *adj.* abobadado; arqueado.

fornication, *s.* fornicação; arco, abóbada.

fornicato, *s.* fornicador.

forsake, *pret.* forsook, *pp.* forsaken. *v.t.* abandonar, desamparar, separar-se de; renegar.

forsaken, *pp.* de *forsake*.

forsaking, *s.* abandono.

forsook, *pret.* de *forsake*.

forsooth, *adv.* certamente.

forswear, *pret.* forswore, *pp.* forsworn. *v.t.* abjurar; *to forswear oneself*, perjurar.

fort, *s.* forte, castelo, fortaleza.

fortalice, *s.* fortim.

forte, *s.* o ponto forte; *that's not my forte*, isso não é o meu forte. *adj.* e *s.* forte (mús.).

forth, *adv.* adiante, fora, para fora, à vista, publicamente, até ao último; ao longe. 1) *and so forth*, e assim por diante. 2) *to come ou to go forth*, sair. 3) *from that day forth*, daquele dia em diante.

forthcoming, *adj.* próximo, futuro, que está a chegar.

forthright, *adj.* e *adv.* todo direito.

forthwith, *adv.* imediatamente.

fortieth, *s.* e *adj.* quadragésimo.

fortifiable, *adj.* fortificável.

fortification, *s.* fortificação; praça-forte; fortaleza; fortalecimento. (pl.) defesas.

fortified, *pret.* e *pp.* de *fortify*.

fortifier, *s.* fortificador; fortalecer.

fortify, *pret.* e *pp.* de *fortified. v.t.* fortificar, fortalecer, reforçar, corroborar. *v.i.* construir defesas.

fortitude, *s.* fortaleza; força de alma.

fortlet, *s.* fortim.

fortnight, *s.* quinzena. 1) *about a fortnight*, uns quinze dias. 2) *this day fortnight*, de hoje a quinze dias. 3) *a fortnight ago*, há quinze dias.

fortnightly (ies), *s.* quinzenário. *adj.* quinzenal. *adv.* quinzenalmente.

fortress, *s.* fortaleza, forte.

fortuitous, *adj.* fortuito, acidental, casual, eventual.

fortuitously, *adv.* fortuitamente.

fortuitousness, *s.* eventualidade, casualidade.

fortunate, *adj.* afortunado, venturoso, feliz, ditoso.

fortunately, *adv.* felizmente.

fortunateness, *s.* felicidade, dita, ventura.

fortune, *s,* fortuna, sorte, ventura, sina, destino; fortuna, riqueza, haveres. 1) *she told my fortune*, leu-me a sina. 2) *fortune-hunter*, o que anda à busca de esposa rica. 3) *fortune-book*, livro da sina. 4) *fortune-teller*, que lê a sina, adivinho. 5) *to make a fortune*, fazer fortuna. 6) *to marry a fortune*, casar com uma herdeira rica. 7) *to try one's fortune*, tentar a sua sorte.

fortuneless, adj. sem fortuna, sem bens.
forty, s. e adj. quarentena. 1) *the Forty*, Academia Francesa. 2) *the forties*, os anos entre 39 e 50. 3) *the roaring forties*, região tempestuosa do oceano entre os graus de latitude 39 e 50 (norte e sul).
forum, s. fórum, praça, foro, tribunal.
forward, adv. adiante, mais avante, para diante, de vante, para vante (náut.); em evidência. 1) *forward!*, para a frente! 2) *hence-forward*, de ora avante. 3) *from this time forward*, de hoje em diante. adj. adiantado, activo; oficioso; desembaraçado; empreendedor; presumido, atrevido. s. avançado (futebol). v.t. enviar, expedir, transmitir; fazer seguir; despachar; activar.
forwarder, s. agente de transportes.
forwarding, s. expedição, acto de expedir ou enviar; *fowarding agent*, expedidor.
forwardly, adv. anteriormente; descaradamente.
forwardness, s. adiantamento, progresso; desembaraço.
forwards, ver forward. adv.; *to go backward and forwards*, ir e vir.
forwent, pret. de forgo, ou forego.
foss, fosse, s. fosso.
fossick, v.i. ser importuno; procurar algum proveito.
fossil, s. fóssil.
fossiliferous, adj. fossilífero.
fossilist, s. paleontólogo.
fossilization, s. fossilização.
fossilize (ise) v.t. fossilizar, petrificar. v.i. fossilizar-se, petrificar-se.
foster, v.t. criar nutrir; alentar; encorajar, consolar. 1) *foster-brother*, ou *sister*, irmão ou irmã de leite, irmão ou irmã colaça. 2) *foster-child*, filho de leite. 3) *foster-father*, ou *mother*, pai ou mãe adoptiva. 5) *foster-nurse*, ama-de-leite.
fosterage, s. criação de uma criança alheia; consolador.
fostering, adj. benéfico, benfazejo.
fother, s. carga; peso (de diversas espécies). v.t. tapar uma fenda (por onde entra a água).
fought, pret. e pp. de fight.
foul, adj. sujo, porco, impuro, imundo; hediondo, fétido, viciado (ar); indecente; obsceno, vil, abominável; entocado (ferro); sujo (fundo do navio), carta de saúde (costa), atascado, entupido (cano, bomba, etc.); borrascoso (tempo); cheio de erros

(tip.). 1) *foul bill of health*, carta de saúde suja. 2) *foul-play ou dealing*, dolo, traição ou má-fé. 3) *foul-copy*, rascunho. 3) *foul language*, palavras injuriosas; linguagem obscena. 4) *foul-play*, acção incorrecta. 5) *foul mouthed*, pronto a injuriar, obsceno. 6) *foul-breath*, mau hálito. 7) *foul weather*, mau tempo. s. violação das regras estabelecidas nos jogos ou concursos; coisa suja; ferrugem. 8) *to run foul*, abordar um navio, abalroar. v.t. sujar, abalroar; violar as regras estabelecidas. v.i. sujar-se, enrascar-se; abalroar.
foulard, s. tecido de seda leve ou de seda e algodão; lenço de bolso feito desse tecido.
fouling, s. incrustações (no fundo do navio); abalroamento.
foully, adv. asquerosamente; vergonhosamente; infamante.
foulness, s. impureza; imundície, asquerosidade.
foumart, s. doninha.
found, pret. e pp. de find.
found, v.t. fundar, estabelecer, edificar, cimentar, instituir, assentar, fixar; fundir, derreter.
foundation, s. fundação; princípio, origem, erecção, estabelecimento, fundamento, base, apoio; alicerce; dotação (para estudos); razão de ser. 1) *foundation-school*, escola subvencionada. 2) *to lay the foundation-stone*, assentar a primeira pedra.
foundationer, s. pessoar subsidiada.
founder, s. fundador; inflamação de entrecasco dos cavalos; doença de animais. v.t. fazer soçobrar. v.i. ir a pique; fracassar, desaprumar; tropicar.
foundering, s. acto de ir a pique.
founding, s. fundição; acção de fundir.
foundling, s. criança exposta, exposto; *foundling hospital*, roda de hospício de expostos.
foundress, s. fundadora.
foundry (ies), s. fundição.
fount, ver fountain. s. (tip.) sortido completo de tipos de certa espécie.
fountain, s. fonte; repuxo; princípio, origem. 1) *fountain-head*, manancial, nascente. 2) *fountain-pen*, caneta de tinta permanente. 3) *fountain-play*, jogo de águas.
four, adj. e s. quatro. 1) *to go on all-fours*, andar de gatas, engatinhar. 2) *four-in-hand*, carruagem a quatro cavalos. 3) *four bladed*,

de quatro pás (náut.) 4) *four-footed*, quadrúpede. 5) *four-wheeled*, de quatro rodas.

four-fold, *adj.* quádruplo.

fourscore, oitenta, idade de oitenta anos.

foursome, *s.* jogo de golfe entre dois pares; aos quatro.

fourteen, *adj.* e *s.* catorze.

fourteenth, *s.* a *adj.* décimo quarto.

fourteenthly, *adv.* em décimo quarto lugar.

fourth, *s.* e *adj.* quarto, quarta parte; *fourth estate*, imprensa periódica, quarto estado.

fourthly, *adv.* em quarto lugar.

fowl, *s.* ave; ave doméstica; galo, galinha. (pl.) aves de capoeira. *v.i.* caçar aves.

fowler, *s.* criador de aves; passarinheiro.

fowling, *s.* caça de aves. 1) *fowling-piece*, espingarda caçadeira. 2) *fowling-net*, rede de caçar pássaros.

fox, *s.* raposa; velhaco; espertalhão. 1) *fox-brush*, rabo de raposa. 2) *fox-glove*, dedaleira, digital. 3) *fox-hound*, cão raposeiro. 4) *fox-hunting*, caça à raposa (com cães). 5) *fox-hunter*, caçador de raposas. 6) *fox-shark*, uma espécie de tubarão. 7) *fox-trap*, armadilha para apanhar raposas. 8) *foxtrot*, uma dança. *v.i.* proceder ardilosamente, dissimular; descolorar-se.

foxed, *adj.* com manchas escuras (como o papel mofado).

foxily, *adv.* com astúcia.

foxiness, *s.* astúcia.

foxish, *adj.* astuto, manhoso.

foxwood, *s.* madeira podre.

foxy, *adj.* velhaco, astuto, manhoso; azedo; descolorado.

foyer, *s.* sala de entrada, vestíbulo dos teatros.

fracas, *s.* desordem, rixa.

fraction, *s.* fractura, fragmento, fracção; quebrado.

fractional, *adj.* fraccionário.

fractious, *adj.* bulhento; brigão; irascível, mal-humorado.

fractiously, *adv.* de um modo bulhento.

fractiousness, *s.* carácter bulhento.

fracture, *s.* fractura, rotura, rompimento. *v.t.* fracturar, quebrar.

fragile, *adj.* frágil, quebradiço, débil.

fragilely, *adv.* fragilmente.

fragileness, *s.* fragilidade, debilidade.

fragility, ver *fragileness*.

fragmente, *s.* fragmento; estilhaço (de granada).

fragmental, *adj.* fragmentário.

fragmentary, *adj.* fragmentário; composto de fragmentos.

fragrance, *s.* fragrância, perfume, aroma.

fragrancy, ver *fragrance*.

fragrant, *adj.* fragrante.

fragrantly, *adv.* fragrantemente.

fragrantness, ver *fragrance*.

frail, *adj.* frágil, quebradiço, fraco, débil; incontinente. *adj.* caniço, cesta, canastra.

frailly, *adv.* fragilmente.

frailness, *s.* fragilidade, fraqueza.

frailty (ies), ver *frailness*.

frame, *v.t.* fabricar, formar; construir; armar; compor; ajustar; regular; dirigir; estabelecer; inventar; idear; traçar; estabelecer; inventar, idear, traçar; encaixilhar. *s.* composição, estrutura, forma, figura, construção; armação; esqueleto; bastidor; caixilho; moldura; banco de torneira; forma; disposição de espírito; caverna; ossada; cavername, baliza (náut.). 1) *frame bridge*, ponte de madeira. 2) *frame-saw*, serra de armar; serrote de arco. 3) *bracket frame*, baliza de luneta (náut.). 4) *cant frame*, baliza revirada. 5) *deep frame*, baliza reforçada. 6) *drawing frame*, laminador. 7) *frame floor*, caverna (náut.). 8) *photo frame*, caixilho de retrato. 9) *frame space*, vão da baliza. 10) *with* ou *right frame*, com boa disposição.

framer, fazedor, autor, criador, fabricante de moldes.

framework, *s.* armação; cavername.

framing, *s.* ossada (náut.); suportes, montantes.

franc, *s.* franco (moeda).

franchise, *s.* direito de voto; privilégio; isenção. *v.t.* conceder privilégios.

franchisement, *s.* liberação; imunidade; isenção.

Franciscan, *s.* franciscano.

francolin, *s.* francolim.

frangibility, *s.* frangibilidade.

frangible, *adj.* frágil, quebradiço, frangível.

frangibleness, ver *frangibility*.

frangipane, *s.* o jasmim-vermelho; perfume tirado desse jasmim.

frank, *adj.* franco, aberto, sincero; ingénuo; privilegiado, livre, isento. *v.t.* franquear; enviar franco de porte.

Frankenstein, *s.* invento prejudicial ao autor.

frankincense, s. incenso.

franklin, s. possuidor de terras, livre mas não de nascimento nobre (séc. XIV e XV).

frankly, adv. francamente, livremente.

frankness, s. franqueza, candura, sinceridade, ingenuidade.

frantic, adj. frenético.

frantically, adv. freneticamente.

franticness, s. frenesim, furor.

frap, frapping, frapped, v.t. rizar, reforçar as amarras de um navio.

fraternal, adj. fraternal.

fraternity, s. fraternidade, irmandade; grémio.

fraternization, s. fraternização.

fraternize, v.i. fraternizar, irmanar.

fratery, s. sala de capítulo de um mosteiro; fraternidade, convento (de frades).

fratricidal, adj. fratricida.

fratricide, s. fratricídio; fratricida.

fratry, ver fratery.

fraud, s. fraude, engano, logro.

fraudulence, s. fraude, engano, logro.

fraudulent, adj. fraudulento.

fraudulently, adj. fraudulentamente.

fraught, adj. (com with) carregado, cheio, atestado; acompanhado de.

fray, s. rixa, refrega, rasgão; lugar puído (no pano). v.i. atemorizar, esfregar, desgastar.

fraying, s. desgaste (por atrito).

frazil, s. gelo no leito de um regato.

freak, s. capricho, veleidade.

freakily, adv. caprichosamente.

freakiness, s. capricho, qualidade ou génio de caprichoso.

freakish, adj. caprichoso, excêntrico, extravagante.

freakishness, ver freakiness.

freckle, s. sarda. v.t. e v.i. ser ou tornar-se sardento.

freckly, adj. sardento.

freaky, ver freakish.

free, adj. livre, independente, forro; liberto, autónomo, desembaraçado, franco; folgado; atrevido; liberal, isento; dispensado; voluntário; discricionário; gratuito; inocente; galhardo, vivo, activo, desatado; público. adv. gratuitamente. 1) free agency, livre-arbítrio. 2) free and easy, à vontade. 3) free-born, ingénuo, livre de nascimento. 4) free goods, mercadorias isentas de direitos. 5) free-hand drawing, desenho à primeira vista. 6) free handed, com as mãos livres; generoso, liberal. 7) free-hearted, franco, aberto. 8) free-lance, soldado mercenário medieval. 9) free labour, trabalho livre. 10) free list, lista de artigos isentos de direitos. 11) free port, porto franco. 12) free pass, passe (em caminho de ferro). 13) free press, liberdade de imprensa. 14) free school, escola gratuita. 15) free-spoken, habituado a falar sem reserva; franco. 16) free-thinking, liberdade de pensamento. 17) free-tongued, linguareiro; maldizente. 18) free-trade, comércio com outras nações livre de quaisquer direitos. 19) free-trader, livre-cambista. 20) free-wheel, roda livre (da bicicleta). 21) cost free, livre de despesas. 22) free of charge, grátis. 23) delivered free, entrega no domicílio. 24) free on board, posto a bordo. 25) to wake free with, tratar sem cerimónia; usar de muita ou demasiada liberdade. 26) to set free, pôr em liberdade. v.t. libertar, livrar; resgatar, isentar; desembaraçar; desentupir; esgotar.

freeboard, s. bordo livre (distância entre o nível da água e a parte superior da coberta do navio).

freebooter, s. flibusteiro, pirata.

freedman, s. liberto; escravo emancipado.

freedom, s. liberdade pessoal, civil; independência; liberdade de acção; franqueza; familiaridade indevida; privilégio possuído por cidade ou corporação.

freehold, s. propriedade livre alodial.

freeholder, s. proprietário de terra livre e alodial.

freeing, pp. de free; freeing port, rebordo do convés (náut.).

freeman, s. homem livre.

freemanson, s. mação.

freemansonry, s. maçonaria.

freer, s. libertador.

freestone, s. grés. adj. de aparta-caroço (fruto).

freethinker, s. livre-pensador.

freewill, s. livre alvedrio.

freeze, pret. froze, pp. frozen. v.t. e v.i. gelar.

freezer, s. refrigerador, congelador; sorveteira.

freezing, adj. glacial, frigorífico. 1) freezing-machine, sorveteira. 2) freezing-point, ponto de congelação.

freight, v.t. fretar, descarregar. s. frete, carga; carregação. 1) dead-freight, frete por espaço não ocupado. 2) home ou home-ward freight, frete de retorno. 3) inward freight, frete à entrada. 4) outward freight, frete de saída. 5) out-and-home freight, frete de ida e volta. 6) *freight car*, vagão de mercadorias.

freightage, *s.* fretamento; fretagem; frete.

freighter, *s.* fretador, carregador.

freighting, *s.* fretagem.

fremitus, *s.* vibração; frémito.

French, *s.* a *adj.* língua francesa; francês. 1) *the french,* os franceses. 2) *french bean,* feijão (grão ou vagem). 3) *french leave,* despedida à francesa. 4) *french-like,* afrancesado. 5) *french roof,* mansarda. 6) *french window,* janela (que abre de alto a baixo, como uma porta).

frenchified, *pret.* e *pp.* de *frenchify.*

frenchify, *pret.* e *pp. frenchified. v.t.* afrancesar.

frenchily, *s.* qualidade ou condição de afrancesado.

Frenchman, *s.* francês. (pl.) *frenchmen.*

french-polish, *s.* vernis próprio para mobílias. *v.t.* envernizar (mobília).

frenchwoman, *s.* francesa.

frenchy, *adj.* afrancesado.

frenum, *s.* freio, ligamento membranoso (da língua, etc.).

frenzied, *adj.* frenético.

frenzy, *s.* frenesim, furor.

frequence, *s.* frequência.

frequency, ver *frequence.*

frequent, *v.t.* frequentar. *adj.* frequente.

frequentation, *s.* frequentação.

frequentative, *s.* e *adj.* frequentativo.

frequenteness, *s.* frequência.

frequenter, *s.* frequentador.

frequently, *adv.* frequentemente.

fresco, *s.* pintura a fresco. *pl. frescos* ou *frescoes. v.i.* pintar a fresco.

fresh, *adj.* fresco, novo, recém-chegado; refrigerante; puro (ar, água doce); louça (flor, planta); são, inexperto; presumido. 1) *fresh butter,* manteiga sem sal. 2) *fresh hand,* noviço. 3) *fresh water,* água doce. 4) *fresh wind,* vento fresco. *adv.* frescamente, recentemente. 5) *fresh-caught,* acabado de apanhar. 6) *fresh blown,* flor recém-aberta. *s.* enxurrada, corrente de água, aragem fresca; parte fresca do dia, do ano; fresco, fresca.

freshen, *v.t.* refrescar; refrigerar; tirar o sal. *v.i.* refrescar-se, avivar-se, tornar-se mais fresco.

fresher, *s.* caloro (de universidade).

freshet, *s,* cheia, inundação súbita; corrente de água doce.

freshly, *adv.* frescamente, recentemente.

freshman, *s.* primeiranista (universidade).

freshness, *s.* frescura, vigor.

freshwater, *adj.* água doce.

fret, fretting, fretted, *v.t.* esfregar; friccionar; desgastar; corroer; irritar; cinzelar; enfeitar com trabalhos em relevo. *v.i.* afligir-se, impacientar-se. *s.* fricção, desgaste, irritação, relevo, grega.

fretful, *adj.* aborrecido, mal-humorado; irritável, incómodo.

fretfully, *adv.* de mau humor.

fretfulness, *s.* mau humor.

fretted, *adj.* ornado de gregas (arq.)

fretting, *s.* impertinência, enfado, o amofinar-se. *adj.* corrosivo, que consome, impertinente.

friability, *s.* friabilidade.

friable, *adj.* friável.

friableness, *s.* ver *friability.*

friar, *s.* frade. 1) *friar's lantern,* fogo-fátuo. 2) *austin friar,* frade Agostinho. 3) *black friar,* dominicano. 4) *grey friar,* franciscano, 5) *white friar,* carmelita.

friary (ies), *s.* convento de frades.

fribble, *v.i.* divertir-se; escarnecer; vacilar. *adj.* vão, inútil, frívolo. *s.* pessoa frívola.

fribbler, *s.* escarnecedor.

fricandeau, *s.* fricandó.

fricassee, *s.* fricassé.

fricative, *adj.* fricativo. *s.* consoante fricativa.

friction, *s.* fricção, atrito. 1) *friction band,* freio de lâmina. 2) *friction roller,* cilindro de cadernal.

frictional, *adj.* produzido por fricção.

frictionless, *adj.* sem fricção.

Friday, *s.* sexta-feira. 1) *Good-friday,* Sexta-Feira Santa. 2) *friday-faced,* melancólico, desanimado.

fried, *pret.* e *pp.* de *fry.*

friend, *s.* amigo, companheiro; correligionário. 1) *attached friend,* prezado amigo. 2) *bosom-friend,* amigo íntimo. 3) *business friend,* correspondente. 4) *next friend,* pessoa que cede o seu nome para se intentar uma acção a favor de um menor ou demente. 5) *a worthy friend,* um amigo digno. 6) *friend at Court,* amigo influente. 7) *to make friends with one,* fazer as pazes; contrair amizade com alguém. 8) *a friend in need is a friend indeed,* os amigos conhecem-se nas ocasiões. 9) *short reckonings make long friends,* boas contas fazem bons amigos.

friendless, *adj.* sem amigos, desamparado.

friendlessness, *s.* desamparo.

friendliness, *s.* amizade, benevolência, simpatia.

friendly, *adj.* amigável, amistoso; serviçal, favorável, benévolo. *adv.* amigavelmente; *friendly society*, associação de socorros mútuos.

friendship, *s.* amizade.

frieze, *s.* ratina; friso.

frigate, *s.* fragat; *frigate bird*, rabo forcado, fragata (ave).

fright, *s.* susto; pessoa de aspecto grotesco. *v.t.* assustar.

frighten, *v.t.* assustar, espantar; amedrontar. 1) *to frighten away*, afugentar. 2) *to be frightened out of one's wits*, perder a cabeça.

frightful, *adj.* medonho, espantoso, horrendo, terrível.

frightfully, *adv.* espantosamente, terrivelmente.

frightfulness, *s.* horror, espanto.

frigid, *adj.* frígido, glacial; indiferente.

frigidity, *s.* frieza; frialdade; frigidez; indiferença.

frigidly, *adv.* frigidamente.

frigidness, ver *frigidity*.

frill, *s.* folhos (de peitilho de camisa).

frilling, ver *frill*.

fringe, *s.* franja, orla; guarnição; *fringe tree*, árvore da neve. *v.i.* pôr franjas.

fringeless, *adj.* sem franjas.

fringy, *adj.* com franjas.

frippery (ies), *s.* roupa velha; velharias; loja de adelo. *adj.* desprezível, frívolo.

frisette, *adj.* frisos ou caracóis de cabelo na testa; trança de cabelo.

frisk, *v.t.* saltar, brincar, pular, retouçar. *s.* brincadeira, salto.

frisker, *s.* brincalhão.

frisket, *s.* frasqueta de imprensa.

friskily, *adv.* alegremente.

friskiness, *s.* alegria, folia.

frisky, *adj.* alegre, brincalhão, travesso; fogoso (cavalo).

frit, *s.* frita, ingredientes para fazer vidro. *v.i.* derreter frita para fazer vidro.

frith, *s.* braço de mar; estuário.

fritillary (ies), *s.* fritilária.

fritter, *s.* posta de carne frita; fragmento, pedaço; rabanada. *v.t.* cortar em pedaços; picar carne para cozinhar; *to fritter away*, desperdiçar.

Fritz, *s.* soldado alemão (termo usado na grande guerra).

frivol, *v.t.* e *v.i.* dizer ou fazer coisas inúteis; gastar (dinheiro ou tempo) mal gasto.

frivolity, *s.* frivolidade, futilidade.

frivolous, *adj.* frívolo, fútil, vão, inútil, vão, vistoso mas sem valor.

frivolously, *adv.* frivolamente.

frivoulousness, ver *fivolity*.

frizz, frizzle, *v.t.* frisar, encrespar. *s.* friso ou anel de cabelo.

frizzy, frizzly, *adj.* frisado, encrespado.

fro, *adv.* de; atrás, para trás; *to and fro*, de um lado para o outro.

frock, *s.* vestido solto (de senhora ou de criança); hábito de frade; blusa de operário. *v.t.* ordenar.

frockcoat, *s.* sobrecasaca.

frog, *s.* rã; ranilha do cavalo; (pl.) alamares; desvios (nos carris de comboios); esperas. 1) *frog fish*, diabo marinho. 2) *frog hopper*, cigarrinha escumosa. 3) *frog mouth*, noitibó. 4) *frog-march*, levar um prisioneiro pelas pernas e pelos braços com a cara virada para baixo. 5) *frog-eater*, um francês. 6) *frog-in-the-throat*, rouquidão.

froggy (ies), *s.* rã pequena; um francês (por gostar muito de rãs). *adj.* abundante em rãs.

frolic, *p. pr.* frolicking, *pret.* e *pp.* frolicked. *v.i.* brincar, fazer travessuras. *s.* alegria, brincadeira. *adj.* parvalhão, travesso.

frolicsome, *adj.* brincalhão.

frolicsomeness, *s.* brincadeira.

from, *prep.* de, desde; da parte de; por causa de; conforme; sobre, acerca de. 1) *from above*, do alto, de cima. 2) *from among*, do meio de. 3) *from off*, de fora de. 4) *from out*, do fundo de; de dentro de. 5) *from nature*, do natural. 6) *from top to toe*, dos pés à cabeça. 7) *from time to time*, de quando em quando.

frond, *s.* fronde, copa de árvores.

front, *s.* frente, frontispício, fachada; área de combate; fronte, testa, cara; audácia, atrevimento; frontal do altar; frente do vestido; cano da bota. *adj.* fronteiro; dianteiro. *v.t.* olhar de frente, encarar. *v.i.* estar à frente na frente; fazer frente.

frontage, *s.* frontaria, extensão de uma frente; montra de loja.

frontal, *s.* frontal; frontão. *adj.* frontal, fronteiro, anterior.

frontier, *s.* fronteira, limite. *adj.* limítrofe;

frontiersman, habitante da fronteira, raiano; expedicionário.

frontispiece, *s.* frontispício, fachada.

frontless, *adj.* sem frente; sem vergonha; descarado.

frontlet, *s.* banda ou fita para usar na testa.

frost, *s.* geada. *v.t.* e *v.i.* gelar.

frostbite, *s.* o gelar-se alguma parte do corpo.

frostbitten, *adj.* queimado pela geada; gelado.

frostbound, *adj.* preso pela geada.

frostier, frostiest, *comp.* e *sup.* de *frosty.*

frostily, *adv.* com excessivo frio.

frostiness, *s.* frio excessivo.

frosting, *s.* clara de ovo e açúcar para cobrir doces.

frostwork, *s.* o rendilhado ou as figuras produzidas pela geada nos vidros das janelas, etc.

frosty, *adj.* gelado, glacial; indiferente; encanecido.

froth, *s.* espuma; palavras fúteis. *v.t.* e *v.i.* espumar; provocar espuma.

frothily, *adv.* com espuma, frivolamente.

frothiness, *s,* espumosidade, frivolidade.

frothy, *adj.* espumoso; frívolo, vão, inútil.

frou-frou, *s.* ruge-ruge, ruído produzido pelo roçar da seda.

frow, *s.* mulher holandesa.

froward, *adj.* teimoso, intratável, insolente.

frowardly, *adv.* insolentemente, indocilmente.

frowardness, *s.* insolência; indocilidade.

frown, *v.i.* franzir as sobrancelhas; olhar carrancudo. *s.* franzimento das sobrancelhas, olhar carrancudo.

frowning, *s.* olhar carrancudo. *adj.* carrancudo.

frowst, *s.* cheiro a mofo. *v.t.* e *v.i.* cheirar a mofo.

frowsty, *adj.* que cheira a mofo.

frowziness, *s.* mau cheiro; desalinho.

froze, *pret.* de *freeze.*

frozen, *pp.* de *freeze; frozen to death*, morto de frio.

fructiferous, *adj.* frutífero.

fructification, *s.* frutificação.

fructified, *pret.* e *pp.* de *fructify.*

fructify, *fructified. v.t. v.i.* frutificar; fertilizar.

fructuose, *s.* frutose.

fructuous, *adj.* frutífero; cheio de fruto; fértil.

frugal, *adj.* frugal, económico.

frugality, *s.* frugalidade, parcimónia; economia.

frugally, *adv.* frugalmente; economicamente.

friganess, ver *frugality.*

fruit, *s.* fruta; fruto, produto; proveito, utilidade. 1) *fruit-basket*, cesta para fruta. 2) *fruit-cake*, queque de corintos, etc. 3) *fruit-sugar*, glicose, levulose, frutose. 4) *stone fruit*, fruta de caroço. 5) *preserved fruit*, fruta de conserva. *v.i.* frutificar. *v.t.* fazer frutificar.

fruitage, *s.* frutas.

fruitarian, *s.* frutívoro.

fruiterer, *s.* fruteiro.

fruitful, *adj.* frutífero; fértil; fecundo; proveitoso.

fruitfully, *adv.* fertilmente.

fruitfulness, *s.* fertilidade, fecundidade.

fruitiness, *s.* cheiro ou gosto a fruta.

fruition, *s.* fruição; gozo.

fruitless, *adj.* infrutífero.

fruitlessly, *adv.* infrutuosamente.

fruitlessness, *s.* esterilidade.

fruity, *adj.* sabor ou cheiro a fruta; (vinho) que sabe a uva.

frumenty, *s.* manjar de trigo descascado cozido em leite e adubado com canela, açúcar, etc.

frump, *s.* velha rabugenta; mulher desalinhada.

frumpish, *adj.* rabugento; desalinhado.

frustrate, *v.t.* frustrar, privar.

frustration, *s.* frustração, contratempo, desapontamento.

frustrum, *s.* pedaço, fragmento; tronco de cone ou de pirâmide.

frutex, *s.* frútice.

fry, *pret.* e *pp.* fried *v.i.* e *v.t.* fritar; frigir. *s.* fritada; peixe miúdo; desova de peixe; multidão de coisas pequenas; *small fry*, coisas pequenas e insignificantes, crianças, etc.

frying, *p.* e *pr. de fry;* 1) *frying-pan*, frigideira. 2) *out of the frying-pan into the fire*, de mal para pior.

fuchsia, *s.* fúcsia, lágrimas (flor), brincos-de-princesa.

fucksine, *s.* fucsina.

fucus, *s.* fuco. pl. *fuci.*

fuddle, *v.t.* e *v.i.* embriagar, embriagar-se. *s.* bebedeira.

fuddler, *s.* ébrio.

fudge, *s.* embuste; palavrório. *v.t.* inventar uma história. *int.* Ora essa!

fuel, *s.* lenha, combustível; *patent-fuel*,

briquetes. *v.t.* alimentar o fogo. *v.i.* procurar combustíveis.

fug, *s.* bolor, cheiro a bolor.

fugacious, *adj.* fugaz, instável, transitório, efémero.

fugaciously, *adv.* fugazmente.

fugaciousness, ver *fugacity.*

fugacity, *s.* fugacidade.

fugitive, *s.* fugitivo, trânsfuga. *adj.* fugitivo, passageiro.

fugitively, *adv.* fugitivamente.

fugleman, *s.* chefe de fila (nos exercícios de soldados).

fugue, *s.* fuga.

fulcrum, *s.* fulcro, apoio, sustentáculo, suporte.

fulfil, *v.t.* cumprir, realizar, executar; encher, preencher.

fulfiller, *s.* cumpridor, executor.

fulfillement, *s,* cumprimento, desempenho, execução, realização.

fulgency, *s.* fulgor.

fulgent, *adj.* fulgente, brilhante.

fulgently, *adv.* brilhantemente.

fulgurate, *v.i.* fulgurar.

fulgurite, fulgurite.

fuliginous, *adj.* fuliginoso.

fuliginously, *adv.* fuliginosamente.

full, *adj.* cheio, completo, repleto, atestado; amplo; saciado; perfeito; inteiro; grávida. *adv.* inteiramente, em cheio; directamente. *s.* o mais alto; ponto ou grau; medida completa; lua cheia. *v.t.* ampliar, engrossar; pisoar. 1) *full admiral,* almirante. 2) *full and by,* aproveitando (o vento). 3) *at full speed,* a toda a velocidade. 4) *full band,* banda de música completa. 5) *full-blown,* cheio de vento; desabrochada (flor). 6) *full-blooded,* sanguíneo; vigoroso; de pura raça. 7) *full bound,* com encadernação inteira (livro). 8) *full brother,* irmão germano. 9) *full cargo,* carregamento completo. 10) *in full confidence,* com toda a confiança. 11) *full dress,* trajo de cerimónia; grande uniforme. 12) *full drive,* grande força ou velocidade. 13) *full eared,* com as espigas bem criadas (grãos). 14) *full eyed,* com os olhos salientes. 15) *full-faced,* cheio de rosto. 16) *full fledger,* completo, acabado. 17) *full-grown,* crescido, maduro. 18) *full-length,* de tamanho natural. 19) *full manned,* com a tripulação completa. 20) *full moon,* lua cheia. 21) *full rigged,* armado em galera. 22) *full of play,* brincalhão. 23) *full sea,* mar bravo. 24) *full sister,* irmã germana. 25) *full stop,* ponto final. 26) *full weight,* peso total. 27) *in full,* por extenso (escrita); por inteiro, sem redução, completo. 28) *full fifty summers,* bem cinquenta verões. 29) *to the full,* completamente. 30) *full many a flower is born to blush unseen,* mutíssimas flores nascem para desabrocharem sem ninguém as ver.

fullage, *s.* preço de pisoar.

fuller, *s.* assentador, pisoeiro.

fulling, *adv.* inteiramente.

fulmar, *s.* gaivota dos pólos.

fulminant, *s.* e *adj.* fulminante.

fulminate, *v.t.* e *v.i.* fulminar, fazer explodir; fulminar (excomunhão).

fulmination, *s.* fulminação, detonação; sentença eclesiástica condenatória.

fulminating, *adj.* fulminante.

fulminatory, *adj.* fulminatório.

fulness, *s.* plenitude.

fulsome, *adj.* baixo; servil; excessivo (em lisonja, adulação).

fulsomely, *adv.* de um modo grosseiro; servilmente.

fulsomeness, *s.* grosseria; servilismo; infâmia.

fulvous, *adj.* fulvo; amarelo tostado.

fumble, *v.t.* e *v.i.* tactear, apalpar; manusear; remexer; atirar uma bola desajeitadamente.

fumbler, *s.* pessoa desajeitada ou desastrada.

fume, *s.* fumo, gás; emanação; cólera; *fume of wine,* vapores do vinho. *v.t.* defumar, fumegar; incensar; perfumar; *v.i.* encolerizar-se; exalar vapores.

fumigate, *v.t.* fumigar, defumar, perfumar.

fumigation, *s.* fumigação.

fumigator, *s.* fumigador.

fun, *s.* gracejo, graça, chiste, brincadeira; divertimento. 1) *for fun* ou *in fun,* de brincadeira. 2) *like fun,* de uma maneira rápida. 3) *rare fun,* grande divertimento. 4) *had good fun,* diverti-me muito. 5) *to make fun of,* escarnecer de.

funambulist, *s.* funâmbulo.

function, *s.* função, ofício, ocupação; cerimónia religiosa; festa; função fisiológica.

functional, *adj.* funcional.

functionally, *adv.* de um modo funcional.

functionary (ies), *s.* e *adj.* funcionário.

fund, *s.* fundo, capital, (pl.) fundos públicos; dinheiro. 1) *fund-holder,* possuidor de fundos, capitalista. 2) *guaranty funds*, fundos de reserva. 3) *sinking funds*, fundos amortizáveis. *v.t.* empregar (dinheiro) em fundos; consolidar.

fundament, *s.* assento; nádegas.

fundamental, *adj.* fundamental. *s.* princípio fundamental.

fundamentality, *s.* fundamentalidade.

fundamentally, *adv.* fundamentalmente.

funded, *adj.* consolidado; empregado em fundos públicos; *funded debt*, dívida consolidada.

funding, *s.* consolidação de uma dívida flutuante; emprego de capital em fundos públicos.

fundless, *adj.* sem fundos, sem dinheiro.

funeral, *s.* funeral.

funereal, *adj.* fúnebre.

fungible, *adj.* que pode substituir, ou que pode ser substituído, que se pode pesar, ou contar; fungível.

fungoid, *adj.* fungiforme.

fungeous, *adj.* fungoso.

fungus, *s.* fungo; cogumelo; excrescência.

fungusy, *adj.* fungoso.

funicle, *s.* funículo; cordão umbilical.

funicular, *adj.* e *s.* funicular.

funiculus, ver *funicle.*

funk, *s.* medo, pânico; pessoa cobarde. *v.i.* hesitar; tremer de medo; mostrar cobardia; inspirar medo em. 1) *to put someone into a funk*, meter medo a alguém. 2) *to be in a fine funk*, aterrorizado. 3) *blue funk*, terror.

funkiness, *s.* timidez.

funky, *adj.* tímido.

funnel, *s.* funil; tubo; cano de guarda da chaminé. 1) *funnel cape*, guarda da chaminé. 2) *funnel cover* ou *hood*, tampa da chaminé. 3) *funnel guys*, ou *funnel shrouds* ou *funnel stays*, estais ou plumas da chaminé. 4) *funnel shaft*, poço de chaminé.

funnier, funniest, *comp.* e *sup.* de *funny.*

funnily, *adj.* de um modo engraçado.

funniness, *s.* divertimento, chiste.

funny, *adj.* engraçado, divertido, cómico, chistoso; raro, estranho.

fur, furring, furred, *v.t.* e *v.i.* forrar ou guarnecer de peles; cobrir-se de sarro; encrostar-se. *s.* peles (de animais para adorno); peliça; depósito, sarro, saburra, crosta; *fur-lined coat*, casaco de peles.

furbelow, *s.* folhos de saia; adorno.

furbish, *v.i.* lustrar, polir, brunir.

furcation, *s.* bifurcação.

furioso, *adj.* com muita força (mús.). *s.* um furioso.

furious, *adj.* furioso, irado.

furiously, *adv.* furiosamente.

furiousness, *s.* fúria.

furl, *v.t.* dobrar; ferrar as velas (náut.); *to furl round*, ferrar com tomadouro. *v.i.* enrolar-se, dobrar-se.

furling, *p. pr.* de *furl; furling line*, tomadouro.

furlong, *s.* medida linear inglesa de 1/8 milha.

furlough, *s.* baixa, licença, licenciamento; *sick furlough*, licença por doença.

furnace, *s.* forno; fornalha, caldeira de fogão de cozinha. 1) *blast furnace*, forno de alta tensão. 2) *furnace-bars*, grelhas da fornalha. 3) *furnace crown*, céu, tecto de fornalha.

furnish, *v.t.* fornecer, prover, sortir; guarnecer, mobilar; *furnished rooms*, quartos mobilados.

furnisher, *s.* fornecedor, provedor; decorador.

furnishings, *s.* artigos e acessórios (de uma casa, etc.).

furniture, *s.* mobília, móveis; adornos; equipamento; apresto. 1) *piece of furniture*, móvel, peça de mobília. 2) *furniture--brocker*, adeleiro.

furore, *s.* furor, admiração entusiástica.

furred, *pret.* e *pp.* de *fur; furred tongue*, língua grossa, saburrosa.

furrier, *p.* e *pr.* de *fur. s.* peles; sarro; crostas; reforço de madeira, embono (náut.).

furrow, *s.* sulco, rego do arado; estria; ranhura; ruga (da face). *v.t.* sulcar, abrir ranhuras ou estrias; enrugar.

forrowy, *adj.* com ranhuras, estrias, sulcos ou rugas.

furry, *adj.* coberto de peles, crosta ou sarro.

futher, *adj.* e *adv.* ulterior, adicional, ademais, além disso. 1) *and further*, ainda mais. 2) *till further orders*, até nova ordem. 3) *to wish one further*, desejar ver alguém pelas costas. *v.t.* promover, favorecer, facilitar.

furtherance, *s.* adiantamento, progresso, apoio, ajuda.

furtherer, *s.* promotor.

furthermore, *adv.* ademais, além de que, outrossim.

furthermost, *s.* o mais afastado, o mais remoto.

furthest, *adj.* e *adv.* o mais distante; muito remoto; extremo.

furtive, *adj.* furtivo.

furtively, *adj.* furtivamente.

furuncle, *s.* furúnculo.

fury (ies), *s.* fúria, furor, ira.

furze, *s.* tojo.

furzy, *adj.* coberto de tojo.

fuscous, *adj.* fusco, sombrio.

fuse, *v.t.* fundir, derreter, *v.i.* derreter-se. *s.* rastilho, mecha; fusível, espoleta.

fusee, *s.* isqueiro, acendalha; fósforo de cabeça grande; rastilho, mecha; fuso de relógio.

fuselage, *s.* armação (de um avião).

fusibility, *s.* fusibilidade.

fusible, *adj.* fusível.

fusil, *s.* espingarda de pederneira.

fusilier, *s.* fuzileiro.

fusillade, *s.* fuzilada.

fusing, *adj.* fundente; *fusing-point,* portão de fusão.

fusion, *s.* fusão, fundição, derretimento, união.

fusionist, *s.* fusionista.

fuss, *s.* bulha, barulho, reboliço. *v.i.* agitar-se, inquietar-se.

fusser, *s.* barulhento.

fussier, fussiest, *comp.* e sup. de *fussy.*

fussily, *adj.* com barulho.

fussiness, *s.* bulha, barulho.

fussy, *adj.* bulhento, inquieto, trapalhão, exigente.

fustian, *s.* fustão; discurso ou escrito bombástico; coisa sem valor, pretensiosa. *adj.* feito de fustão; bombástico.

fustic, *s.* pau amarelo usado em tinturaria.

fustigate, *v.t.* fustigar, açoitar.

fustigation, *s.* fustigação.

fustily, *adv.* com bolor.

fustiness, *s.* bolor.

fusty, *adj.* bolorento, mofento.

futile, *adj.* fútl, frívolo, inútil.

futilely, *adv.* futilmente.

futileness, *s.* futilidade.

futility, ver *futileness.*

futtock, *s.* caverna (de navio); ligação; braço de baliza (náut.); *futtock plate,* chapa das arreigadas.

future, *s.* e *adj.* futuro.

futurist, *s.* futurista.

futurity, *s.* futuro, porvir; futuridade; situação futura, existência depois da morte.

fuzz, *s.* cotão. *v.i.* levantar cotão; despegar-se em partículas diminutas com som sibilante (como a água dum ferro quente, etc.).

fuzzball, *s.* espécie de fungão, bexiga de lobo.

fuzzy, *adj.* coberto de cotão; semelhante a cotão; encrespado (cabelo).

fy, fye, *interj.* que vergonha!

G

g, sétima letra do alfabeto.

gab (gabbing, gabbed), *v.i.* tagarelar, palrar; *s.* tagarelice, garrulice. 1) *the gift of the gab,* o dom da palavra, loquacidade. 2) *stop your gab,* cala a boca.

gabardine, gaberdine, *s.* gabardina.

gabble, *v.i.* e *v.t.* tagarelar, galrar, papaguear; *s.* tagarelice, aranzal.

gabbler, *s.* palrador, tagarela.

gabby, *a.* loquaz, tagarela.

gable, *s.* empena (de parede); frontão; *gable window,* janela de empena.

gaby, *s.* simplório, papalvo.

gad (gadding, gadded), *v.i.* vadiar, vagabundear; *s.* estilete; punção; *gad!:* (interj.) caramba!

gadabout, *a.* e *s.* vadio, vagabundo.

gadder, *s.* vadio, vagabundo.

gadfly, *s.* moscardo.

gadget, *s.* engenhoca.

Gael, *s.* celta da Irlanda; escocês das montanhas.

gaff, *s.* arpão, fisga; caranguejha.

gaffer, *s.* velho, velhote; rústico.

gag (gagging, gagged), v.t. amordaçar; fazer calar; lograr; v.i. ter náuseas; s. mordaça; piada, bola.

gage, s. penhor, caução; desafio; v.t. dar em penhor, empenhar.

gagman, s. aquele que inventa piadas.

gaiety, gayety, s. alegria, jovialidade; atavios, ostentação.

gaily, gayly, adv. alegremente.

gain, s. ganho, lucro, proveito; v.t. ganhar, conseguir, obter; vencer, conquistar. 1) to gain the upper hand, prevalecer, vencer. 2) to gain ground, progredir; v.i. aumentar, melhorar, crescer.

gainable, a. acessível.

gainer, s. beneficiário.

gainful, a. lucrativo, vantajoso; ganancioso, interesseiro; adv. gainfully, vantajosamente.

gainless, a. desvantajoso, improfícuo.

gainly, a. belo, formoso.

gainsay, v.t. contradizer, disputar.

gait, s. modo de caminhar, passo, porte.

gaiter, s. polaina, botina.

gala, s. gala, festa. 1) in gala, em traje de gala. 2) gala day, dia de gala. 3) gala-dress, vestido de gala.

galactic, a. galáctico.

galantine, s. galantina.

galatea, s. espécie de cotim de riscas azuis e brancas.

galaxy, s. galáxia; reunião de pessoas notáveis.

galbanum, s. gálbano.

gale, s. rajada, ventania, temporal; acesso; estado de excitação; divertimento ruidoso; pagamento periódico de renda; hanging gale, rendas atrasadas.

galena, s. galena (min.).

Galician, a. e s. galego, galiziano.

Galilean, s. Galileu; a. relativo ao físico galileu.

galimatias, s. embrulhada, aranzel.

galipot, s. terebintina.

gall, s. fel; bílis; amargura; ódio; escoriação; excrescência. 1) gall-bladder, vesícula biliar. 2) gall duct, canal biliar; v.t. e v.i. esfolar, escoriar; irritar, mortificar.

gallant, a. galhardo, elegante, vistoso; grandioso, imponente; nobre; galante; s. galanteador; homem da moda; galã; v.t. e v.i. galantear, namorar; acompanhar, escoltar; adv. gallantly, com bravura; com galanteio.

gallantry, s. valentia, heroísmo; galantaria.

galleon, s. galeão.

gallery, s. galeria, tribuna, corredor, varanda; exposição de quadros.

galley, s. galera, galé; cozinha de navio. 1) galley-proof, prova de granel. 2) galley press, prelo das provas (imp.). 3) galley-slave, escravo das galés.

Gallic, s. gaulês, francês; a. gálico.

Gallican, s. e a. gaulês.

gallicism, s. galicismo.

gallicize, v.t. afrancesar.

gallinaceous, a. galináceo.

galling, a. mortificante, torturante.

gallipot, s. boião de farmácia.

gallium, s. gálio.

gallivant, v.i. vagabundear; galantear.

gallon, s. galão (medida).

gallon, s. galão; trança.

gallooned, a. agaloado.

gallop, s. galope; v.i. galopar.

gallopade, s. galope, galopada.

galloper, s. galopador; oficial às ordens (mil.).

gallows, s. forca, patíbulo. 1) gallows bird, pessoa que merce a forca. 2) gallows tree, forca.

gallstone, s. cálculo biliar.

galloot, s. pessoa desajeitada; labrego; recruta.

galop, s. galope (mus.).

galore, adv. em abundância, com fartura, muitíssimo.

galosh, s. galocha.

galvanic, a. galvânico.

galvanize, v.t. galvanizar; electrizar.

galyac, s. pele de cordeiro ou cabrito.

gam, s. bando de baleias.

gamashes, s. perneiras de montar.

gamb, gambe, s. perna (de animal).

gambade, s. salto de cavalo; cabriola.

gambit, s. gambito.

gamble, v.i. e v.t. jogar; apostar a dinheiro; arriscar.

gambler, s. jogador.

gambling, s. jogo; a. de jogo.

gambol (gambolling, gambolled), v.i. cabriolar; pular; fazer travessuras; s. cabriola, pulo; travessura.

game, s. jogo; partida; passatempo; brincadeira; artifício, projecto; zombaria; caça. 1) game-bag, bolsa de caçador. 2) game-cock, galo de combate. 3) game keeper, couteiro. 4) drawn game, partida nula de jogo. 5) little game, esperteza. 6) to *make game of*, mofar de; 7) *unfair game*, concorrência desleal; *a.* de caça, próprio para a caça; *v.t.* jogar.

gamely, *adv.* corajosamente, animosamente.

gameness, *s.* coragem, ânimo; resistência.

gamesome, *a.* alegre, jovial, travesso.

gamester, *s.* jogador batoteiro.

gamily, *adv.* corajosamente, animosamente.

gamin, *s.* garoto.

gaming, *s.* jogo, jogatina.

gamma, *s.* gama; terceira letra do alfabeto grego.

gammer, *s.* velha, velhota.

gammon, *s.* jogo de gamão; chasco, escárnio; balela, embuste; presunto; *v.t.* enganar, zombar; defumar carne.

gammoner, *s.* embusteiro, intrujão.

gamogenesis, *s.* (biol.) gamogénese, gamogenia.

gamp, *s.* guarda-chuva grande.

gamut, *s.* gama, escala de música.

gamy, *a.* abundante em caça; gosto ou sabor a caça; brigão; valente.

gander, *s.* ganso.

gang, *s.* grupo, malta; bando, brigada; quadrilha, destacamento; *gang-plank*, prancha de desembarque.

ganger, *s.* capataz.

ganglion, *s.* gânglio.

gangrene, *s.* gangrena.

gangster, *s.* bandido, malfeitor.

gangue, *s.* ganga.

gangway, *s.* passagem, corredor, coxia; prancha de desembarque; passadiço.

gannet, *s.* mergulhão, pato.

gantry, canteiro de adega.

gap, *s.* fenda, brecha; lacuna; hiato.

gape, *v.i.* bocejar; estar boquiaberto, embasbacar-se; *to gape at*, ficar boquiaberto diante de.

gapeseed, *s.* embasbacamento; coisa que embasbaca; prodígio, assombro.

gaping, *a.* hiante, escancarado; que boceja; boquiaberto.

garage, *s.* garagem; *v.t.* pôr ou guardar em garagem.

garb, *s.* vestido, traje, roupagem; aparência, aspecto; *v.t.* vestir, enroupar.

garbage, *s.* lixo, imundície; restos de cozinha.

garble, *v.t.* escolher, seleccionar; truncar, mutilar, deturpar; *s.* deturpação.

garbling, *s.* acto de escolher ou separar.

garboard, *s.* tabuado da quilha dum navio.

garboil, *s.* tumulto.

garden, *s.* jardim, quintal. 1) *garden-bed*, canteiro, talhão. 2) *garden-city*, cidade modelo. 3) *garden-stuff*, hortaliças, vegetais. 4) *garden nursery*, viveiro de plantas. 5) *kitchen garden*, horta. 6) *to lead someone up the garden path*, seduzir, engodar.

gardener, *s.* jardineiro, hortelão.

gardenia, *s.* gardénia.

gardening, *s.* jardinagem.

garefowl, *s.* corvo-marinho.

garfish, *s.* órfia, peixe-agulha.

gargantuan, *a.* gigantesco.

gargle, *s.* gargarejo; *v.t.* gargarejar.

gargling, *s.* gargarejo.

gargoyle, *s.* gárgula, goteira.

garish, *a.* vistoso, ostentoso, berrante; *adv. garishly*, berrantemente, deslumbrantemente.

garland, *s.* grinalda, coroa; palma, prémio pela vitória, galardão; colectânea de poesias, antologia; *v.t.* engrinaldar, coroar.

garlic, *s.* alho.

garlicky, *a.* com sabor a alho.

garment, *s.* peça de roupa, vestuário, veste.

garner, *s.* celeiro; *v.t.* enceleirar, armazenar.

garnet, *s.* granada (pedra); cor vermelho-granada; pequeno guindaste.

garnish, *v.t.* enfeitar, adornar; guarnecer; fornecer; notificar; *s.* enfeite, guarnição, adorno.

garnishee, *s.* pessoa intimada ou notificada judicialmente.

garnishment, *s.* adorno, ornamento; intimação judicial.

garniture, *s.* guarnição, adorno; armadura; acessórios.

garret, *s.* águas-furtadas, sótão; *garret-master*, operário que trabalha por conta própria.

garrison, *s.* guarnição militar; casquete, gorro de serviço; *v.t.* guarnecer; fortalecer; pôr guarnição. 1) *standing-garrison*, guarnição permanente. 2) *garrison artillery*, artilharia de praça.

garron, *s.* cavalo pequeno, garrano.

garrote, *s.* garrote; estrangulamento da vítima; *v.t.* garrotar, assaltar e estrangular.

garrulity, *s.* garrulice, loquacidade, tagarelice.

garrulous, *a.* gárrulo, palrador, tagarela, loquaz; *adv. garrulously*, com loquacidade.

garter, *s.* liga, jarreteira; *The Garter*, Ordem da Jarreteira.

garth, s. pátio; jardim.

gas, s. gás; bazófia, parlapatice; gasolina. 1) *gas-bag*, balão de gás, tagarela. 2) *gas-burner*, bico de gás. 3) *gas-coal*, carvão de gás. 4) *gas-fitting*, instalação de gás. 5) *gas heater*, fogão de gás. 6) gas-*mask*, máscara antigás. 7) *gas-jet*, bico de gás. 8) *gas-meter*, contador de gás. 9) *gas-pipe*, tubo de gás. 10) *gas-stove*, fogão a gás. 11) *gas well*, poço de onde sai gás natural. 12) *gas warfare*, guerra química; *v.t. (gassing, gassed)*, abastecer de gás; gasear; lançar gases contra o inimigo; tagarelar, bazofiar.

gascon, s. natural da Gasconha; fanfarrão.

gasconade, s. gasconada, fanfarronada; *v.i.* fanfarronar.

gaseous, a. gasoso; vaporoso.

gash, s. cutilada; *v.t.* acutilar, cortar.

gasholder, s. gasómetro.

gasify, *v.t.* e *v.i.* gaseificar, gasificar(-se).

gasoline, s. gasolina.

gasometer, s. gasómetro.

gasp, s. arfada, respiração convulsiva, arquejo; *v.t.* e *v.i.* arfar, respirar com dificuldade.

gasper, s. cigarro mata-ratos.

gasproof, a. à prova de gás.

gassiness, s. vaidade, verbosidade.

gassing, s. acção de gasear, lançar gases sobre.

gassy, a. impregnado de gás; enfatuado; verboso.

gastric, a. gástrico. 1) *gastric fever*, enterite. 2) *gastric juice*, suco gástrico.

gastritis, s. gastrite.

gastronomic, a. gastronómico.

gastronomist, s. gastrónomo.

gastronomy, s. gastronomia.

gasworks, s. fábrica de gás.

gate, s. portão, entrada; cancela, porta de cidade. 1) *flood-gate*, comporta. 2) *gatehouse*, casa de porteiro, casa numa muralha junto às portas da cidade. 3) *gatekeeper*, guarda-portão. 4) *gate-money*, pagamento de acesso a um recinto.

gateless, a. sem porta ou cancela.

gateway, s. passagem, entrada.

gather, *v.t.* juntar, reunir; concluir; franzir, fazer pregas; *v.i.* reunir-se, acumular-se, formar-se; aumentar, engrossar; s. prega, franzido.

gatherer, s. acolhedor, colector; *grape-gatherer*, vindimador.

gathering, s. acumulação; reunião; peditório, colecta; colheita; prega, franzido; abcesso.

gatling-gun, s. metralhadora.

gauche, a. canhoto; grosseiro, rústico, desajeitado.

gaucherie, s. grossaria, rusticidade, falta de tacto; inépcia.

gaud, s. enfeite, adorno; bugiganga; berloque.

gaudery, s. enfeites, adereços, arrebiques, ostentação.

gaudy, a. aparatoso, vistoso; pretensioso, arrebicado; *adv. gaudily,* ostentosamente.

gauge, gage, *v.t.* medir, calibrar; sondar; aferir; cobiçar; arquear; s. padrão (medida), regra de medir; calibre; bitola; diâmetro; indicador (de nível, de volume), instrumento para medir a capacidade de uma vasilha. 1) *broad gauge*, via larga (cam. de fer.). 2) *condenser gauge*, manómetro de vácuo. 3) *steam gauge*, manómetro. 4) *glass gauge*, tubo indicador de nível.

gauger, gager, s. medidor, aferidor, arqueador de navios.

gauging, s. arqueação.

Gaulish, a. gaulês.

gaunt, a. magro, ossudo, descarnado; triste, desolado; *adv. gauntly,* com magreza.

gauntlet, s. manopla; luva comprida de senhora; castigo militar. 1) *to take up the gauntlet*, aceitar o desafio. 2) *to run the gauntlet*, sujeitar-se à crítica.

gauze, s. gaze; névoa fina.

gauzy, a. fino, diáfano.

gavel, s. martelo de leiloeiro ou de juiz.

gavelkind, s. partilha das terras em parcelas iguais.

gawky, s. e a. parvo, desajeitado.

gay, a. alegre, jovial, de bom humor; festivo; vistoso; *adv. gayly,* alegremente.

gaze, *v.t.* contemplar; olhar fixamente; s. contemplação; olhar fixo.

gazebo, s. casa com grande terraço; mirante; belveder.

gazelle, s. gazela.

gazer, s. contemplador.

gazette, s. gazeta, jornal; *London Gazzette*, Diário do Governo Inglês; *v.t.* publicar no Diário do Governo.

gazing, s. contemplação; a. contemplador.

gazogene, s. gasogénio.

gean, s. cereja brava.

gear, s. engrenagem; aparelho de trans-missão; mecanismo; acessórios; roda dentada; volante; adorno; utensílios. 1) *gear wheel*, roda dentada de transmissão. 2) *connecting gear*, embraiagem. 3) *lifting gear*, elevador. 4) *starting gear*, mecanismo para pôr em movimento. 5) *steering gear*, volante, leme de navio. 6) *out of gear*, desengatado. 7) *top gear*, grande velocidade. 8) *low gear*, baixa velocidade, *v.t.* aparelhar; montar; engrenar; atrelar.

gearing, *s.* encaixe, engrenagem; transmissão de movimentos.

gearshift, *s.* mudança de velocidades; *gearshift lever*, alavanca de velocidades.

gecko, *s.* geco; lagarto.

gee, *s.* nome da letra G; cavalo; *interj.* chi!, arre!; *gee-up*, arre!, anda mais depressa!

geisha, *s.* gueixa.

gelatin, gelatine, *s.* gelatina.

gelatinize, *v.t.* e *v.i.* converter em gelatina; gelatinar(-se).

gelatinous, *s.* gelatinoso.

geld, *v.t.* castrar; *a.* castrado, estéril.

gelding, *s.* capão, animal castrado.

gelid, *a.* gélido, gelado; *adv. gelidly*, como gelo.

gelidity, *s.* gelidez.

gelignite, *s.* gelenhite.

gem, *s.* gema, jóia, pedra preciosa; *(gemming, gemmed), v.t.* adornar com pedras preciosas; adornar; rebentar (árvores).

geminate, *v.t.* germinar.

Gemini, *s.* Gémeos (const.).

gemmate, *v.i.* gemar, lançar rebentos; *a.* que tem rebentos, gemado.

gemmy, *a.* cheio de jóias.

gemot, *s.* comício, assembleia.

gendarm, *s.* gendarme, polícia.

gender, *s.* género; sexo.

genealogical, *a.* genealógico.

genealogize, *v.t.* estabelecer a genealogia; *v.i.* organizar genealogias.

genealogy, *s.* genealogia.

general, *s.* general; *a.* geral, comum; universal. 1) *general practitioner*, clínico geral. 2) *general servant*, criada para todo o serviço. 3) *the general reader*, o comum dos leitores. 4) *general head-quarters*, quartel-general. 5) *general of the army*, marechal.

generalissimo, *s.* generalíssimo.

generality, generalidade, a maior parte.

generalize, *v.t.* generalizar; inferir por indicação.

generally, geralmente, em geral.

general-purpose, *a.* de uso geral, para todos os fins.

generalship, *s.* generalato.

generate, *v.t.* gerar, procriar; produzir, causar.

generation, *s.* geração, prole.

generative, *a.* produtivo, procriador; gerador, produtor.

generator, *s.* gerador, criador; pai; gerador, dínamo (elect.).

generic, *a.* genérico; *adv. generically*, de modo genérico.

generosity, *s.* generosidade; liberdade.

generous, *a.* generoso, nobre; liberal, pródigo; *adv. generously*, generosamente.

genesis, *s.* Génesis, primeiro livro do Antigo Testamento; génese, geração, criação.

genet, *s.* gineto.

genetic, genetical, *a.* genético, relativo à genética.

genial, *a.* cordial, afável; benévolo; temperado, suave; *adv. genially*, cordialmente.

genial, *a.* relativo ao queixo.

geniality, *s.* cordialidade; suavidade.

genie, *s.* génio, espírito da mitologia maometana.

genista, *s.* genista; giesta.

genital, *a.* genital, sexual; (pl.) órgãos sexuais.

genius, *s.* génio, alto poder intelectual; espírito do bem ou do mal; espírito dos elementos.

genocide, *s.* genocídio, extermínio de um grupo político ou racial; genocida.

Genoese, *s.* e *a.* genovês.

genre, *s.* género, sorte, estilo.

gens, *s.* família nobre.

gent, *s.* abreviatura de *gentleman*.

genteel, *a.* gentil, urbano; elegante, fino, requintado; *adv. genteelly*, gentilmente.

gentian, *s.* genciana (bot.).

gentile, *a.* e *s.* gentio, pagão; gentílico.

gentility, *s.* nobreza, superioridade social; refinamento.

gentle, *s.* suave, brando, meigo; gentil, bem-nascido, digno; *the gentle sex*, o sexo fraco, as mulheres.

gentlefolk, gentlefolks, *s.* gente de posição; élite.

gentlehood, *s.* distinção; fidalguia.

gentleman, *s.* gentil-homem, fidalgo; cavalheiro. 1) *gentleman-at-arms*, cavaleiro da guarda de honra do monarca inglês. 2) *gentleman of fortune*, aventureiro. 3) *gentleman farmer*, proprietário agricultor que cultiva a terra por desporto. 4) *gentlemen's agreement*, acordo de honra.

gentlemanly, *a.* cavalheiresco, cortês, urbano, fidalgo.

gentleness, *s.* doçura, delicadeza.

gentlewoman, *s.* senhora, dama, fidalga.

gently, *adv.* suavemente, brandamente; pouco a pouco; *gently born*, bem-nascido, de nascimento nobre.

gentry, *s.* classe social elevada mas não nobre; classe média.

genuflect, *v.i.* genuflectir.

genuflection, *s.* genuflexão.

genuine, *a.* genuíno, puro, autêntico; natural, típico; *adv. genuinely*, genuinamente.

genus, *s.* género, classe.

geodetic, geodetical, *a.* geodésico, geodético.

geodimeter, *s.* geodímetro.

geographer, *s.* geógrafo.

geographic, geographical, *a.* geográfico; *geographical mile*, milha náutica; *adv. geographically*; geograficamente.

geography, *s.* geografia.

geoid, *s.* geóide.

geology, *s.* geologia.

geometer, *s.* geómetra.

geometric, geometrical, *s.* geométrico; *adv. geometrically*, geometricamente.

geometrician, *s.* geómetra; matemático.

geometry, *s.* geometria.

geomorphology, *s.* geomorfologia, estudo da forma da Terra.

geophagy, *s.* geofagia.

Georgian, *s.* jorgiano; estilo do tempo dos reis Jorges; habitante da Geórgia; *a.* georgiano.

georgic, *s.* geórgica (poema bucólico); *a.* agrícola, pastoral, bucólico.

geranium, *s.* gerânio, sardinheira.

gerent, *s.* administrador, gerente.

geriatrics, *s.* geriatria.

germ, *s.* germe, embrião; semente; bacilo; origem, princípio.

German, *s.* e *a.* alemão; a língua alemã.

germane, *a.* germano; apropriado, relativo a.

Germanic, *s.* germânico, alemão.

germanism, *s.* germanismo.

germanize, *v.i.* germanizar.

germanophile, *a.* e *s.* germanófilo.

germicide, *s.* germicida.

germinal, *a.* germinal; embrionário.

germinate, *v.i.* germinar; brotar.

germination, *s.* germinação.

gerrymander, *v.t.* falsificar o recenseamento político para favorecer eleitoralmente um partido; *s.* alteração do recenseamento político.

gerund, *s.* gerúndio.

gerundive, *s.* gerundivo.

gesso, *s.* gesso (molde de gesso).

gest, *s.* gesta, feito, façanha.

gestation, *s.* gestação; gravidez.

gestatorial, *a.* gestatório.

gesticulate, *v.t.* gesticular.

gesticulation, *s.* gesticulação.

gesture, *s.* gesto, aceno, acção.

get (getting, got), *v.t.* e *v.i.* adquirir, obter, alcançar, conquistar, ganhar, comprar, conseguir, arranjar. 1) *where did you got this hat?*, onde compraste este chapéu?. 2) *to get a prize*, ganhar um prémio. 3) *I got him a place*, arranjei-lhe um lugar; acostumar-se, contrair, habituar-se. 4) *to ger a bad habit*, contrair um mau costume; receber. 5) *he got his money*, ele recebeu o seu dinheiro; apanhar, agarrar. 6) *to get a fish*, apanhar um peixe; ter, possuir (com have). 7) *have you got a pen?*, tens uma caneta?; ser obrigado a (seguido dum infinito), persuadir, incitar (seguido dum infinito), mandar, ordenar (seguido dum particípio passado e este precedido dum substantivo); procriar. 8) *to get a child*, fazer um filho; trazer, buscar. 9) *go and get my pencil*, vai buscar o meu lápis; decorar, aprender. 10) *to get a lesson*, aprender uma lição, estudar; tornar-se, fazer-se; chegar (a um lugar, a um estado). 11) *the bus gets here at ten o'clock*, o autocarro chega às 10 horas. 12) *to get drunk*, embebedar-se; quando seguido dum adjectivo ou particípio passado, traduz-se pelo verbo de que é formado esse adjectivo ou particípio. 13) *to get warm*, aquecer. 14) *to get about*, tornar-se conhecido. 15) *to get above*, colocar-se acima de. 16) *to get abroad*, espalhar-se, divulgar-se. 17) *to get along*, progredir. 18) *to get ahead*, passar adiante. 19) *to get among*, misturar-se com. 20) *to get away*, ir-se, partir. 21) *to get away from*, escapar-se, fugir de. 22) *to get back*, voltar, recuperar. 23) *to get before*, prevenir, adiantar-se. 24) *to get behind*, penetrar. 25) *to get better*, melhorar. 26) *to get better of*, levar a melhor, vencer. 27) *to* *get done with*, acabar, pôr fim a. 28) *to get down*, descer, apear. 29) *to get into*, entrar, vestir, calçar. 30) *to get through*, passar, chegar ao destino. 31) *to get under*, passar sob, subjugar. 32) *to get underway*, pôr-se a caminho, preparar-se para partir. 33) *to get up*, levantar-se, tornar-se impetuoso (vento, fogo). 34) *get off!* ou *get away!* ou *get along with you!*, rua!, ponha-se lá fora!

get-at-able, *a.* alcançável, acessível.

getaway, *s.* partida, saída; largada; fuga.

getter, *s.* aquele que adquire; fazedor de fortunas.

getup, *s.* estrutura; estilo; acabamento.

gewgaw, *s.* bagatela, bugiganga; *a.* vistoso, ostentoso.

geyser, *s.* aparelho doméstico para aquecer água.

ghastly, *a.* pálido, lívido; cadavérico; medonho, horrível.

ghat, ghaut, *s.* garganta, desfiladeiro; cadeia de montanhas.

gherkin, *s.* pepino de conserva.

ghetto, *s.* bairro de judeus.

ghost, *s.* espectro, fantasma, alma penada, espírito; visão.

ghostly, *a.* espectral, fantasmagórico.

ghoul, *s.* vampiro.

ghoulish, *a.* vampiresco.

giant, *s.* gigante; *a.* gigantesco, colossal.

giantess, *s.* giganta.

gib, *s.* gato castrado; *s.* contra-chaveta.

gibber, *v.i.* tagarelar, falar atabalhoadamente.

gibberish, *s.* palavreado, fala rápida e inarticulada; *a.* ininteligível.

gibbet, *s.* forca, patíbulo; *v.t.* enforcar.

gibbon, *s.* gibão, macaco (Índia).

gibbosity, *s.* gibosidade; giba, saliência.

gibbous, *a.* giboso, corcunda.

gibe, jibe, *v.t.* e *v.i.* escarnecer, troçar; *s.* troça, remoque, zombaria.

giber, *s.* trocista.

giblet, *s.* miúdos de aves.

gibus, *s.* claque; chapéu de seda (de molas).

giddiness, *s.* vertigem, atordoamento; estouvamento, leviandade.

giddy, *a.* vertiginoso, volúvel, inconstante; atordoado; *adv.* *giddily*, vertiginosamente.

gift, *s.* presente, dádiva; dom, talento natural; *v.t.* doar, dotar. 1) *Christmas gift*, consoada. 2) *to have the gift of the gab*, falar pelos cotovelos.

gifted, *a.* dotado, prendado.

gig, *s.* cabriolé; fisga; arpéu; barco a remos ou de corridas; espantalho; coisa que gira; rapariga namoradeira.

gigantesque, *a.* gigantesco, titânico.

gigantic, *a.* gigantesco, titânico, enorme.

giggle, *v.i.* rir à socapa, rir sem motivo; *s.* riso abafado, risadinha.

giggling, *a.* que casquina; *adv.* *gigglingly*, casquinantemente.

giglet, *s.* rapariga estouvada.

gigolo, *s.* gigolo.

gigot, *s.* perna de carneiro.

gilbertian, *a.* jovial, prazenteiro.

gild (gilded, dilt), *v.t.* dourar, iluminar; *Gilded House*, Câmara dos Lordes.

gilder, *s.* dourador.

gilding, *s.* douramento, brilho, lustre; *a.* dourado.

gill, *s.* barranco, ravina; regato; guelra; papada; pequena medida para líquidos (1,42 dl); rapariga namoradeira.

gillie, *s.* jovem; criado.

gillyflower, *s.* goivo.

gilt, *s.* dourado; material para dourar; dinheiro; ladrão; *a.* dourado. 1) *gilt edge*, cercadura dourada. 2) *gilt edged papers*, títulos seguros, fundos públicos de inteira confiança.

gimbals, *s.* balanceiro (da bússola, cronómetro).

gimcrack, *s.* enfeite, bugiganga; mecanismo insignificante; *a.* vistoso, mas sem valor.

gimcrackery, *s.* bugigangas, quinquilharias.

gimlet, *s.* verruma.

gimp, *s.* galão, alamar.

gin, *s.* genebra, gin; armadilha de caça; descaroçador da semente do algodão. 1) *gin shop*, taverna. 2) *gin-rummy*, jogo de cartas. 3) *gin house*, lugar onde se separam as sementes do algodão; *(ginning, ginned)* *v.t.* apanhar em armadilha; descaroçar.

ginger, *s.* gengibre; raiz de gengibre.

gingerbread, *s.* pão de especiarias; adorno barato e de mau gosto; *a.* vistoso, vulgar.

gingerly, *adv.* cautelosamente, delicadamente.

gingersnap, *s.* bolo ou biscoito de gengibre.

gingival, *a.* gengival, das gengivas.

ginning, *s.* debulha; separação das sementes do algodão.

gip (gipping, gipped), *v.t.* estripar o peixe, limpar; *s.* cadela; criado; extorquidor.

gipsy, *s.* cigano; língua dos ciganos.

giraffe, s. girafa.

girandole, s. candelabro.

girasol, s. girassol.

gird, v.t. cingir, pôr à cintura; cercar, rodear, circundar; v.t. e v.i. (com at) troçar, zombar.

girder, s. trave, viga, barrote.

girding, s. cinto, faixa; acto de cingir.

girdle, s. cinto, cinturão; cinta; cintura; v.t. cingir, cercar.

girl, s. menina, rapariga.

girlhood, s. adolescência, mocidade (de rapariga).

girlish, a. menineiro, juvenil; feminino; adv. girlishly, ameninadamente.

girth, s. cilha; medida da cintura, perímetro; cinto, faixa; v.t. cingir, medir objecto redondo.

gist, s. ponto principal duma questão; substância.

give (gave, given), v.t. dar, doar; entregar; confiar; conceder; ceder; conferir; pagar; dar, empenhar (a palavra); oferecer; apresentar; relatar, produzir; sacrificar; desprender-se de; v.i. dar presentes ou esmolas; fazer donativos; dar de si; afrouxar, abrandar; ceder, recuar. 1) to give and take, dar ela por ela, fazer concessões. 2) to give away, transferir, alienar; divulgar um segredo. 3) to give back, devolver. 4) to give birth to, dar à luz, originar. 5) to give forth, around, divulgar, publicar. 6) to give ground, ceder, recuar. 7) to give in, ceder, dar-se por vencido. 8) to give like for like, pagar na mesma moeda. 9) to give lie to, desmentir. 10) to give odds, dar partido. 11) to give off, desistir; acabar. 12) to give oneself away, trair-se. 13) to give oneself to, render-se. 14) to give tit for tat, pagar na mesma moeda. 15) to give tongue, dar à língua. 16) to give up, desistir, entregar. 17) to give way, ceder, consentir; s. flexibilidade, elasticidade; acto de ceder.

given, a. dado, gratuito; propenso a.

giver, s. dador, doador.

giving, s. dom. 1) giving away, queda. 2) giving out, distribuição.

gizzard, s. moela de ave.

glabrous, a. glabro, liso, macio.

glacial, a. glacial.

glaciation, s. congelação.

glacier, s. geleira; glaciar.

glacis, s. esplanada; ladeira.

glad (gladding, gladdied) v.t. alegrar; a. contente, satisfeito; alegre.

gladden, v.t. alegrar; animar.

glade, s. clareira.

gladiator, s. gladiador.

gladiolus, s. gladíolo.

gladly, adv. alegremente; de bom grado.

gladness, s. alegria, prazer.

gladsome, a. alegre, contente; adv. gladsomely, alegremente.

gladstone, s. carruagem de luxo; gladstone-bag, mala de viagem.

glair, s. clara de ovo; v.t. cobrir com clara de ovo.

glairy, a. semelhante à clara de ovo; viscoso; pegajoso.

glamorous, a. enfeitiçador; encantador, maravilhoso.

glamour, s. feitiço, encanto.

glance, s. olhada, relance, vislumbre. 1) at first glance, à primeira vista; v.t. e v.i. olhar de soslaio, relancear; aludir; fazer alusões sarcásticas. 2) to glance off, desviar-se, mudar de assunto. 3) to glance over a book, folhear um livro.

glancingly, adv. de relance.

gland, s. glande, glândula.

glandular, a. glandular, adenoso.

glandule, s. glândula.

glare, v.i. brilhar, fulgurar, resplandecer; sobressair; olhar com ar feroz; olhar fixamente; s. brilho, resplendor; olhar penetrante.

glaring, a. brilhante, deslumbrante; evidente, notório; de olhar penetrante; adv. glaringly, manifestamente.

glass, s. vidro; vidraria; copo; bebida; espelho; termómetro; lente, lupa; (pl.) óculos; monóculo, luneta; v.t. envidraçar; espelhar; a. de vidro, vítreo.

glassfull, s. conteúdo de um copo.

glassy, a. vítreo; vidrado; cristalino.

glaucoma, s. glaucoma.

glaucous, a. glauco, verde-mar.

glaze, v.t. envidraçar; envernizar; acetinar (papel); lustrar; s. vidrado (da louça); lustre, brilho.

glazed, a. vidrado, envidraçado, acetinado.

glazer, s. vidreiro.

glazier, s. vidraceiro, colocador de vidraças.

glazing, s. arte de vidraceiro; enverniza-mento; polimento.

gleam, s. raio de luz; fulgor, cintilação; v.i. brilhar, cintilar.

gleaming, a. fulgurante; s. relâmpago; adv. gleamy, fulgurantemente.

glean, *v.t.* e *v.i.* respirar, recolher, rebuscar; compilar.

gleaning, *s.* respigo, rebusco.

glebe, *s.* terra, solo; campo.

glee, *s.* alegria; júbilo, prazer; canção; conjunto vocal.

gleeful, *a.* alegre, jovial; *adv. gleefully,* alegremente.

gleeman, *s.* trovador.

gleesome, *a.* alegre, gracioso.

gleet, *s.* gonorreia; pus; corrimento.

glen, *s.* vale estreito.

glib, *a.* liso, escorregadio; volúvel; *s.* madeixa de cabelo.

glide, *v.i.* deslizar, escorregar; planar; *s.* deslize.

glider, *s.* planador.

glim, *s.* luz, lanterna.

glimmer, *v.t.* alumiar, bruxulear; *s.* luz frouxa; reflexo; vislumbre.

glimmering, *s.* luz débil, claridade ténue; vaga ideia.

glimpse, *s.* lampejo, relance; luz débil; reflexo; prazer fugaz; *v.i.* olhar de relance; tremeluzir; *v.t.* fazer cintilar.

glint, *s.* cintilação, clarão, lampejo; brilho, lustre; *v.i.* cintilar, reflectir-se.

glisten, *v.i.* cintilar, faiscar, brilhar; *s.* cintilação, brilho.

glister, *v.i.* brilhar, luzir; *s.* brilho, esplendor.

glitter, *s.* brilho, lustre; *v.i.* brilhar, resplandecer.

glittering, *a.* cintilante, brilhante; *adv. glitteringly,* brilhantemente.

gloaming, *s.* crepúsculo.

gloat, *v.i.* olhar com satisfação maligna; olhar com volúpia.

global, *a.* global; mundial, universal.

globe, *s.* globo, esfera; *globe-trotter,* turista que percorre as principais zonas do Globo; *v.t.* e *v.i.* dar forma esférica.

globose, *a.* esférico.

globular, *a.* globular, esférico.

globule, *s.* glóbulo.

glomerate, *a.* aglomerado.

glomeration, *s.* conglomeração.

gloom, *s.* obscuridade, escuridão; melancolia; *v.i.* escurecer; *v.t.* entristecer; obscurecer.

gloomy, *a.* obscuro, sombrio; triste, lúgubre; *adv. gloomily,* obscuramente; tristemente.

gloria, *s.* glória (igr.), doxologia.

glorification, *s.* glorificação, apoteose.

glorify, *v.t.* glorificar, honrar.

glorious, *a.* glorioso; magnífico; soberbo.

glory, *v.i.* glorificar-se; orgulhar-se; *s.* glória, honra, fama; *to go to glory,* morrer.

gloss, *s.* lustro, brilho; verniz; falsa aparência; desculpa; *v.t.* e *v.i.* lustrar; polir; iludir com falsa aparência; entreter com desculpas.

glossary, *s.* glossário.

glosser, *s.* polidor; glossador.

glossy, *a.* lustroso, acetinado.

glottis, *s.* glote.

glottology, *s.* glossologia, linguística.

glove, *s.* luva. 1) *glove-fight,* luva de pugilista, boxe. 2) *glove money,* gratificação, gorjeta. 3) *to be hand in glove,* ser unha com carne. 4) *to throw down the glove,* desafiar. 5) *to take up the glove,* aceitar um desafio.

glover, *s.* luveiro.

glow, *v.i.* arder, luzir; resplandecer; incandescer-se; queimar(-se); *s.* calor; vermelhidão; paixão, ardor. 1) *she glowed with love,* ela arde de amor. 2) *in a glow,* corado, afogueado. 3) *glow-worm,* pirilampo.

glower, *v.t.* fitar, olhar ameaçadoramente; *s.* olhar ameaçador; cenho.

glowing, *a.* ardente; inflamado; *adv. glowingly,* ardentemente.

gloze, *v.i.* e *v.t.* adular; atenuar; encobrir; *s.* lisonja, adulação.

glucose, *s.* glicose.

glue, *s.* cola forte; grude; *v.t.* colar, grudar.

gluey, *a.* pegajoso, grudento, viscoso.

glum, *a.* sombrio, carrancudo, mal-humorado; *adv. glumly,* de modo mal-humorado.

glumpy, *a.* trombudo, carrancudo, amuado.

glumness, *s.* mau humor.

glut (glutting, glutted), *v.t.* saciar, fartar; *v.i.* devorar, tragar; *s.* fartura, excesso.

gluten, *s.* glúten.

glutenous, *a.* glutinoso, rico em glúten.

gluteus, *s.* glúteo, músculo glúteo.

glutinous, *a.* viscoso, pegajoso; *adv. glutinously,* dum modo pegajoso.

glutton, *s.* glutão, comilão; animal carnívoro.

gluttonize, *v.t.* e *v.i.* comer em excesso; devorar.

gluttonous, *a.* glutão, guloso, voraz; *adv. gluttonously,* vorazmente.

gluttony, *s.* gula.

glycerin, *s.* glicerina.

gnar, gnarr (gnarring, gnarred), *v.i.* rosnar.

gnarl, *v.i.* rosnar, grunhir; retorcer, deformar; *s.* nó (madeira).

gnarly, *a.* nodoso; torto, torcido.

gnash, *v.t.* e *v.i.* ranger (os dentes); *s.* o ranger de dentes.

gnat, *s.* mosquito; ninharia, coisa insignificante; *to strain at a gnat*, ser escrupuloso em coisas insignificantes.

gnaw, *v.t.* roer, morder, corroer.

gnawing, *s.* acto de roer; dor aguda no estômago; dores.

gnome, *s.* gnomo, diabrete.

gnomic, *a.* gnómico.

gnosis, *s.* gnose.

gnu, *s.* gnu, ruminante africano.

go (went, gone), *v.t.* e *v.i.* ir; andar, caminhar, marchar, partir, passar, dirigir-se a; conduzir; viajar; progredir; seguir, prosseguir; mudar (opinião, situação, lugar, tempo); desaparecer; participar; mover, funcionar; assentar; passar, decorrer (tempo); morrer; tornar-se; ser vendido; ser considerado; ser regulado; suportar. 1) *to go aboard*, embarcar. 2) *to go abroad*, viajar pelo estrangeiro. 3) *to go after*, seguir. 4) *to go against*, opor-se. 5) *to go ahead*, adiantar-se, prosseguir. 6) *to go along*, continuar. 7) *to go along with one*, acompanhar, estar de acordo. 8) *to go ashore*, encalhar. 9) *to go astray*, extraviar-se. 10) *to go asunder*, ir-se embora, desunir-se. 11) *to go at*, atacar. 12) *to go away*, ir-se embora. 13) *go away!*, rua!. 14) *to go back*, retirar-se, desistir, recuar. 15) *to go back from upon*, desdizer-se. 16) *to go before*. preceder. 17) *to go behind*, seguir alguém. 18) *to go between*, mediar, *(s.)* 19) *go between*, medianeiro. 20) *to go beyond*, exceder, abusar. 21) *to go by*, passar adiante, regular-se. 22) *to go by the worst*, ficar com o pior. 23) *to go down*, descer. 24) *to go for*, ir buscar; favorecer. 25) *to go forth*, publicar-se, sair à luz. 26) *to go into*, entrar (profissão, na política, etc.). 27) *to go on*, continuar. 28) *to go on the streets*, prostituir-se. 29) *to go out*, sair. 30) *to go out of the way*, desviar-se. 31) *to go over*, passar por cima. 32) *to go shares*, ir a meias, ser sócio. 33) *to go through*, concluir, levar a cabo. 34) *to go to law*, pôr acção judicial. 35) *to go to the bar*, advogar. 36) *to go to the bottom*, aprofundar. 37) *to go to the dogs*, arruinar-se. 38) *to go under*, falir, ser vencido. 39) *to go up and down*, andar errante. 40) *to go with child*, engravidar. 41) *to go without*, passar sem. 42) *to go without saying*, ser aceite como certo; *s.* (pl.) acto de ir; energia, ardor, actividade; estar na moda, uso; marcha, curso; pacto, convénio; oportunidade; êxito. 43) *at a go*, duma assentada, dum golpe. 44) *it is all the go*, é a grande moda. 45) *is it a go?*, estamos entendidos?. 46) *it is no go*, é inútil. 47) *on the go*, no activo.

goad, *s.* aguilhão, aguilhoada; *v.t.* aguilhoar; estimular.

go-ahead, *a.* empreendedor, enérgico.

goal, *s.* meta, fim; objectivo; golo (fut.).

goat, *s.* bode, cabra; *to get someone's goat*, enfurecer alguém.

goatee, *s.* pêra (barba no queixo).

goatherd, *s.* cabreiro.

goatish, *a.* caprino; libidinoso.

goatling, *s.* cabrito.

gob, *s.* escarro; *v.t.* e *v.i.* escarrar.

gobbet, *s.* naco, pedaço (de carne); fragmento.

gobble, *v.t.* e *v.i.* engolir, tragar, comer ruidosamente; gorgorejar como os perus.

gobbler, *s.* glutão; peru.

go-between, *s.* intermediário, medianeiro.

goblet, *s.* taça, copo de pé alto.

goblin, *s.* duende, diabrete.

go-by, *s.* desconsideração, evasiva.

go-cart, *s.* andadeira; carro de criança para aprender a andar.

god, *s.* deus; (com maiúsc.) Deus, o Senhor. 1) *god-fearing*, temente a Deus. 2) *godhead*, divindade. 3) *god-forsaken*, abandonado por deus; miserável. 4) *God's day*, domingo; dia do Corpo de Deus. 5) *God's penny*, esmola dada na igreja. 6) *for God's sake!*, por amor de Deus. 7) *God forbid!*, Deus me valha!. 8) *God save the King!*, Viva o Rei!; *v.t. (godding, godded)*, endeusar, tratar como um deus.

godchild, *s.* afilhado, afilhada.

goddaughter, *s.* afilhada.

goddess, *s.* deusa.

godfather, *s.* padrinho.

godless, *a.* infiel, ímpio, ateu; *adv. godlessly*, impiamente.

godly, *a.* piedoso, devoto.

godmother, *s.* madrinha.

dodown, *s.* armazém indiano ou chinês.

godparent, *s.* padrinho, madrinha; padrinhos (pl.).

godship, *s.* divindade, qualidade divina.

godson, s. afilhado.

goer, s. andador, passeante; *a good goer*, andarilho.

goffer, gopher, gauffer, v.t. frisar, encrespar, encanudar; s. instrumento para frisar.

go-getter, s. pessoa activa; fura-vidas.

goggle, v.i. arregalar, torcer os olhos; *goggle-eyed*, estrábico.

going, s. ida, partida; modo de vida (pl.); *goings-on*, leviandades.

goiter, s. papeira, bócio.

gold, s. ouro; dinheiro, riqueza; cor de ouro. 1) *gold-digger*: pesquisador de ouro. 2) *gold fever*, febre do ouro, da riqueza. 3) *goldfinch*, pintassilgo. 4) *gold-fish*, dourada. 5) *gold-wire*, fio de ouro. 6) *all is not gold that glitters*, nem tudo o que reluz é ouro.

golden, a. áureo, dourado; brilhante; louro; excelente. 1) *golden age*, período da mocidade, felicidade. 2) *golden calf*, bezerro de ouro. 3) *golden-mouthed*, eloquente. 4) *golden wedding*, bodas de ouro.

goldsmith, s. ourives.

golf, s. golfe.

golliwog, s. pessoa grotesca; espantalho.

gombeen, s. usura; *gombeen-man*, prestamista.

gondola, s. gôndola.

gondollier, s. gondoleiro.

gone, pp. de *go; a. gone*, perdido, arruinado, liquidado; morto, passado. 1) *far gone in years*, muito velho. 2) *a gone case*, um caso arrumado. 3) *a gone man*, um homem liquidado.

gong, s. gongo.

good, a. bom; genuíno; digno; útil. 1) *a good deal*, bastante, muito. 2) *good-afternoon*, boas tardes. 3) *good evening*, boa noite. 4) *good morning*, bom dia. 5) *good fellowship*, boa convivência. 6) *good for nothing*, inútil. 7) *Good Friday*, Sexta-Feira Santa. 8) *good gracious!*, Valha-me Deus!. 9) *good looking*, bem-parecido. 10) *good nature*, bondade. 11) *good-tempered*, com boa disposição. 12) *a good way*, muito longe. 13) *for good*, para sempre. 14) *for good and all*, finalmente. 15) *to be good at*, ser perito em. 16) *to have a good time*, divertir-se. 17) *the good people*, as fadas.

goodily, adv. ingenuamente.

goodliness, s. beleza, formosura.

goodness, s. bondade, benevolência, virtude; *Goodness!*, Meu Deus!

goods, s. mercadorias, géneros; haveres. 1) *green goods*, conto do vigário. 2) *dry goods*, modas e roupas. 3) *piece goods*, fazendas em peça.

goody, s. e a. bonacheirão, ingénuo; s. doce, gulodice.

goose, s. ganso; carne de ganso; bobo, tolo; *goose-flesh*, pele arrepiada, pele de galinha.

gooseberry, s. groselha.

gooseherd, s. guardador de gansos.

goosey, s. néscio, pacóvio, tolo.

gore, s. sangue, sangue derramado; peça de pano triangular; pedaço de terreno em forma de triângulo; v.t. cortar em forma de gomo; encornar; ferir com os chifres.

gorge, s. garganta, goela; desfiladeiro; v.t. engulir, tragar, saciar.

gorgeous, a. brilhante, vistoso, grandioso; *adv. gorgeously*, brilhantemente.

gorger, s. comilão, glutão.

gorilla, s. gorila; brutamontes.

gormandize, v.i. comer com voracidade; devorar; s. gula; o prazer da mesa.

gormandizer, s. glutão.

gorse, s. urze, tojo.

gory, a. ensanguentado; sangrento.

gosling, s. gansinho; pessoa inexperiente.

gospel, s. evangelho. 1) *the gospel*, a religião protestante. 2) *gospel truth*, verdade absoluta.

gossamer, s. teia de aranha; fio de teia de aranha; fio muito fino; tecido diáfano.

gossip, s. tagarelice; bisbilhotice; murmuração; v.i. tagarelar, cavaquear, bisbilhotar.

gossipy, a. tagarela, linguareiro.

Goth, s. Godo; bárbaro, vândalo.

Gothic, a. gótico; estilo gótico; língua dos godos.

gouache, s. guache.

gouge, s. goiva; entalhe, ranhura; v.t. cortar com uma goiva; arrancar; lograr.

gourd, s. abóbora; cabaça.

gourmand, s. guloso.

gourmet, s. gastrónomo.

gout, s. gota, artritismo.

govern, v.t. governar, dirigir, administrar; mandar; reger.

governess, s. governanta; perceptora.

government, s. governo, administração pública; autoridade; direcção; *government securities*, fundos públicos.

governor, s. governador; governante; patrão; pai; tutor.

governorship, s. governo.

gown, s. roupão; bata; *night gown*, camisa de dormir.

gownsman, s. o que usa toga, batina; universitário.

grab (grabbing, grabbed), v.t. agarrar, prender; tomar posse; arrebatar; s. acto de agarrar de repente; grampo.

grabble, v.i. tactear; procurar à apalpadelas; andar de gatas.

grace, s. graça, encanto; graça divina; título de honra. 1) *grace stroke*, golpe de misericórdia. 2) *to say graces*, rezar antes das refeições. 3) *the Graces*, as Graças (mit.).

graceful, a. gracioso; cortês; adv. *gracefully*, com graça.

graceless, a. desengraçado; perverso.

gracile, a. grácil, fino; delicado.

gracious, a. atraente, gracioso; encantador; benévolo; *good gracious!*, valha-me Deus!

gradation, s. gradação; matização; ordem; série; graduação.

grade, s. grau, classe, categoria; qualidade; ordem; declive; cruzamento de raças de animais; v.t. nivelar (rua, estrada), cruzar raças de animais.

gradient, s. declive; ladeira; rampa.

gradual, a. gradual; gradativo; adv. *gradually*, gradualmente.

graft, s. enxerto, rebento, garfo; v.t. enxertar; inserir.

grail, cálice; *Holy Grail*, Santo Gral.

grain, s. grão; semente, pevide; parcela muito pequena; v.t. granular.

grainy, a. com grânulos; granuloso.

gram, s. grão-de-bico.

gram, gramme, s. grama (peso).

grammar, s. gramática; *grammar school*, escola primária.

grammarian, s. gramático; línguista.

grammatical, a. gramatical; adv. *grammatically*, gramaticalmente.

granadilla, s. maracujá.

granary, s. celeiro.

grand, a. grande; grandioso; nobre, ilustre; grão. 1) *grand-duke*, grão-duque. 2) *grand opera*, ópera séria. 3) *grand piano*, piano de cauda.

grandchild, s. neto, neta.

granddaughter, s. neta.

grandee, s. magnata.

grandeur, s. grandeza, poder; magnificiência.

grandfather, s. avô.

grandiloquence, s. grandiloquência.

grandiloquent, a. grandiloquente; adv. *grandiloquently*, dum modo grandiloquente.

grandiose, a. grandioso, imponente; pomposo; adv. *grandiosely*, imponentemente.

grandparent, s. avô, avó.

grandson, s. neto.

grandstand, s. tribuna; exibicionismo.

grange, s. granja, herdade.

granger, s. granjeiro, agricultor.

granite, granito; firmeza, resistência; *to bite on granite*, malhar em ferro frio; perder tempo.

granny, grannie, s. avozinha; anciã.

grant, s. concessão, mercê, dádiva; v.t. conceder, dar; conferir; concordar; *to take for granted*, supor um facto como certo, garantido.

granular, a. granular; granuloso.

granulate, v.t. e v.i. granular(-se), tornar(-se) granuloso.

granule, s. grânulo.

grape, s. bago de uva; uvas; videira.

grapery, s. vinhedo, parreiral.

graph, s. gráfico, diagrama.

graphic, a. gráfico.

graphite, s. grafite.

grapnel, s. fateixa, pequena âncora.

grapple, s. acto de agarrar; pega, luta; v.t. e v.i. agarrar(-se), atracar-se.

grasp, s. acção de agarrar, ou de se apoderar; aperto; capacidade de compreender; v.t. agarrar; abraçar; compreender.

grasper, s. agarrador; pessoa ávida.

grasping, a. ávido, avarento.

grass, s. erva, pasto, relva.

grasshopper, s. gafanhoto.

grate, s. grade, grelha de fogão; v.t. esfregar; raspar; gradear.

grateful, a. agradecido, grato; agradável; adv. *gratefully*, reconhecidamente.

gratify, v.t. agradar, contentar, satisfazer, recompensar, premiar.

grating, a. grade, gradeamento; raspagem; a. áspero, irritante.

gratis, adv. grátis, de graça; a. gratuito.

gratitude, s. gratidão, reconhecimento.

gratuity, s. gratificação; gorjeta.

grave, s. sepultura, sepulcro; fossa; acento grave. 1) *grave clothes*, mortalha. 2) *graveyard*, cemitério. 3) *the pauper's grave*, a vala comum; a. grave, sério; difícil;

solene. *v.t.* (graved, graved ou graven), gravar, esculpir; fixar, arranjar.

gravel, *v.t.* cobrir de areia ou cascalho; macadamizar; *s.* cascalho.

graven, *a.* gravado, esculpido, impresso.

gravitation, *s.* gravitação, atracção dos corpos para o centro da Terra.

gravity, *s.* gravidade, seriedade; importância.

gravure, *s.* gravura.

gravy, *s.* molho; suco, *gravy-boat,* molheira; pechincha.

gray, grey, *a.* cinzento, pardo; grisalho; *s.* cor cinzenta; animal de cor cinzenta, pardo. 1) *gray friar,* frade franciscano. 2) *gray-haired,* encanecido, grisalho; *v.t.* e *v.i.* fazer(-se) cinzento, encanecido.

graybeard, *s.* homem de barba grisalha; velho, homem experiente.

grayish, greyish, *a.* acinzentado, pardacento.

graze, *v.t.* e *v.i.* pastar; pastorear; roçar, tocar de leve.

grazing, *s.* pastagem, pasto; *a.* que pasta.

grease, *s.* gordura, unto; substância oleosa ou gordurosa; *in pride of grease,* gordo, pronto para ser morto; *v.t.* engordurar, untar, lubrificar.

greasy, *a.* engraxado, gorduroso; sujo.

great, *a.* grande, volumoso; imenso, vasto; numeroso; excelente; importante; difícil; notório. 1) *great many,* muitos. 2) *greatcoat,* sobretudo, casacão. 3) *greathearted,* valente, corajoso. 4) *the great,* os poderosos. 5) *the great unwashed,* as classes operárias.

Great-Bear, *s.* Ursa Maior.

greatly, *adv.* muito; grandemente.

greatness, *s.* grandeza; majestade; nobreza; poder.

greed, *s.* voracidade, gula; cobiça, ambição.

greedy, *a.* voraz, insaciável; ambicioso; avarento; *adv. greedily,* vorazmente.

Greek, *s.* grego, finório, trapaceiro; *a.* grego, helénico.

green, *s.* cor verde; verdura; prado (pl.) hortaliça; *a.* verde; não maduro; inexperiente; vigoroso. 1) *green cop,* legumes 2) *green-eyed monster,* o ciúme. 3) *greenfinch,* verdelhão (ave). 4) *greengoose,* simplório. 5) *greenhouse,* estufa. 6) *greengage,* ameixa rainha-cláudia. 7) *greengrocer,* hortaliceiro. 8) *green table,* mesa de jogo; *v.t.* e *v.i.* pintar de verde; tornar-se verde; cobrir-se de verdura.

greenish, *s.* esverdeado.

greenness, *s.* cor verde; verdura; imaturidade; vitalidade.

greenwood, *s.* floresta.

greet, *v.t.* saudar, felicitar.

greeting, *s.* saudação, cumprimento.

gregarious, *a.* gregário.

gremlin, *s.* gnomo.

grenade, *s.* granada, bomba.

grenadier, *s.* granadeiro.

grid, *s.* grade, grelha.

griddle, *s.* sertã para assar bolos.

gridiron, *s.* grelha; rede; campo de futebol.

grief, *s.* pesar, dor, desgosto; luto; desastre.

grievance, *s.* motivo de queixa, queixa, ressentimento.

grieve, *v.t.* agravar, ofender; *v.i.* afligir-se, lamentar-se.

grievous, *a.* penoso, doloroso; cruel; *adv. grievously,* dum modo aflitivo; cruelmente.

griff, *s.* garra, grifo.

grill, *s.* grelha; carne assada na grelha; *v.t.* e *v.i.* grelhar, assar na grelha; atormentar (-se); *grillroom,* sala de restaurante cuja especialidade são os grelhados.

grim, *a.* feio, disforme, carrancudo.

grimace, *s.* careta, momice; *v.t.* fazer caretas; escarnecer.

grime, *s.* sugidade, fuligem; encardimento; *v.t.* sujar, encardir.

grimy, *a.* cheio de fuligem, imundo, porco; *adv. grimily,* porcamente.

grin (grinning, grinned), *v.i.* arreganhar os dentes, mostrar os dentes; *s.* arreganho de dentes; *broad grin,* riso escancarado.

grind, *v.t.* moer, triturar; pulverizar; afiar; oprimir; estudar com afinco; *s.* moagem; trabalho penoso; aluno estudioso.

grinder, *s.* moleiro; moinho; moedor; aluno aplicado; queixal (dente).

grip, *s.* aperto de mão; beliscadura; alça; tenaz; *v.t.* e *v.i.* (gripping, gripped), agarrar, segurar, agarrar-se com força.

gripe, *v.t.* afligir; fazer doer os intestinos; oprimir; *v.i.* sentir cólicas; resmungar; *s.* aflição; cólica; aborrecimento; cabo, alça.

grippe, *s.* gripe, *influenza.*

grist, *s.* grão para moer; *to bring grist to the mill,* levar água ao seu moinho.

gristle, *s.* cartilagem.

grit, *s.* areia; saibro; firmeza, fortaleza; *v.t.* e *v.i.* (gritting, gritted), cobrir ou encher de areia; ranger.

gritty, *a.* arenoso; saibroso; corajoso; persistente.

grizzled, *a.* grisalho, cinzento.

grizzly, *s.* urso pardo; *a.* grisalho.

groan, *s.* gemido, lamento; *v.t.* gemer, lamentar.

grocer, *s.* merceeiro; comerciante de secos e molhados.

grocery, *s.* mercearia; artigos de mercearia.

grog, *s.* grogue. 1) *grog-shop,* taberna. 2) *grog-blossom,* nariz avermelhado pelo consumo de álcool.

groggy, *a.* embriagado, cambaleante.

grogram, *s.* gorgorão.

groin, *s.* virilha; aresta.

groom, *s.* lacaio; moço de estrebaria; noivo.

groomsman, *s.* amigo do noivo, acompanhante do noivo.

groove, *s.* encaixe, entalhe, ranhura; rotina; *v.t.* encaixar, entalhar.

grope, *v.i.* e *v.t.* andar às apalpadelas; tactear.

gross, *a.* crasso; total; grosseiro; grosso; corpulento; ordinário; *s.* grosa; o grosso; por atacado; *adv. grossly,* dum modo grosseiro; completamente, por junto.

grotesque, *a.* grotesco.

grotto, *s.* gruta, antro.

ground, *s.* solo, terra; terreno; terras; região, território; base, fundamento; origem, causa; borras, sedimentos. 1) *there is no ground for alarm,* não há motivo para alarme; (pl.) borras. 2) *ground-auger,* sonda. 3) *ground game,* caça grossa. 4) *ground-hog,* marmota. 5) *classic ground,* lugar histórico. 6) *on the ground,* em terra. 7) *to hold one's ground,* manter-se firme. 8) *no grounds,* nenhuma ocasião; *v.t.* e *v.i.* fundar; pôr em terra; encalhar; instruir.

grounding, *s.* instrução elementar; encalhe (navio); conservação em terra.

groundling, *s.* espectador de plateia; animal que vive junto à terra; peixe de fundo; planta rasteira; pessoa vil, básica.

group, *s.* grupo; ordem; série; *v.t.* agrupar.

grouse, *s.* galo silvestre.

grove, *s.* bosque pequeno; alameda.

grovel (grovelling, grovelled), *v.i.* arrastar-se, rojar-se.

grovelling, *a.* rasteiro, vil.

grow (grew, grown), *v.t.* cultivar; produzir; *v.i.* crescer, aumentar, desenvolver-se, progredir; tornar-se, fazer-se; fixar-se. 1) *to grow flowers,* cultivar flores. 2) *she is growing old,* ela está a envelhecer. 3) *it is growing dark,* está a fazer-se noite.

growing, *s.* crescimento, desenvolvimento.

growl, *v.t.* e *v.i.* rosnar; resmungar, rezingar; *s.* rosnadela; resmungo.

growth, *s.* crescimento; progresso; aumento.

grub (grubbing, grubbed), *v.t.* e *v.i.* cavar, sachar, mourejar; *to grub up,* arrancar a erva ruim; *s.* larva; comida.

grubby, *a.* bichoso, bichado; sujo; desmazelado.

grudge, *v.t.* dar de má vontade, invejar, chorar; *v.i.* resmungar, mostrar má vontade; *s.* ressentimento, rancor.

gruel, *s.* papas de aveia; *to have ou get one's gruel,* ser castigado severamente; ser morto.

gruesome, *a.* horrível, horrendo, repelente.

gruff, *a.* rude, grosseiro; áspero (voz), rouco; *adv. gruffly,* asperamente; de mau modo.

grumble, *v.t.* resmungar, murmurar, queixar-se.

grumpy, *a.* mal-humorado, rabugento, irritadiço.

grunt, *v.t.* e *v.i.* grunhir; rosnar; queixar-se, gemer; *s.* grunhido, gemido.

guarantee, *s.* fiador; garantia; fiança; *v.t.* garantir, caucionar, assegurar.

guaranty, *s.* garantia, fiança.

guard, *v.t.* e *v.i.* guardar, vigiar, proteger; guardar-se, prevenir-se; *s.* guarda, vigilante, sentinela; defesa, protecção; resguardo; orla ou guarnição de um vestido. 1) *guard-house,* casa da guarda; prisão militar. 2) *guard-ring,* anilha. 3) *body guard,* guarda-costas. 4) *guard's van,* furgão.

guarded, *a.* cauteloso; *adv. guardedly:* cautelosamente.

guardian, *s.* guardião, guarda; tutor; *guardian angel,* anjo-da-guarda.

guardianship, *s.* tutela; tutoria; protecção; guarda.

guerdon, *s.* galardão, prémio.

guerrilla, *s.* guerrilha; guerrilheiro.

guess, *v.t.* e *v.i.* conjecturar, supor; adivinhar, acertar, imaginar, crer; *s.* conjectura, suspeita, suposição.

guest, *s.* hóspede, convidado; pensionista; *guest-house,* hospedaria.

guffaw, *s.* gargalhada; *v.t.* e *v.i.* rir-se às gargalhadas.

guindance, *s.* guia, governo, direcção; orientação.

guide, *v.t.* guiar, encaminhar, regular, ordenar; *s.* guia, mentor, director; *guide-book,* guia, roteiro.

guild, gild, s. corporação; associação; grémio; sindicato.

guile, s. engano, artifício.

guileful, a. astuto, manhoso, velhaco; adv. guilefully, insidiosamente.

guillotine, s. guilhotina; v.t. guilhotinar.

guilt, s. culpa, delito, crime; culpabilidade.

guiltless, s. inocente; adv. guiltlessly, inocentemente.

guinea, s. guinéu, unidade monetária de 21 xelins. 1) guinea-fowl, galinha-da-guiné. 2) guinea-pig, porquinho-da-índia.

guise, s. modo, maneira; pretexto.

guitar, s. violão.

gulch, s. ravina.

gulf, s. golfo; abismo.

gulfweed, s. sargaço.

gull, v.t. enganar, lograr, burlar; s. tolo, bobo crédulo.

gullet, s. esófago; garganta; canal para a água: desfiladeiro.

gullible, a. fácil de enganar, ingénuo.

gully, s. barranco; ravina.

gulp, v.t. tragar, engolir sofregamente; s. trago, golpe, gole.

gum (gumming, gummed), v.t. deitar goma, prender com goma; colar; s. gengiva; goma.

gummy, a. gumoso; viscoso.

gumption, s. senso prático; espírito empreendedor.

gun (gunning, gunned), descarregar (peça de artilharia); s. arma de fogo; peça de artilharia; rajada; son of a gun, pessoa desprezível.

gunboat, s. canhoneira.

gunfire, s. disparo de canhão; fogo de artilharia.

gunner, s. artilheiro; soldado de artilharia; caçador.

gunnery, s. artilharia.

gunpowder, s. pólvora.

gunshot, s. tiro de arma de fogo; ferimento por bala.

gunsmith, s. espingardeiro, armeiro.

gurge, s. remoinho; v.t. remoinhar.

gurgle, v.t. e v.i. borbotar; gorgolhar; s. gorgolejo, borbotão.

gush, v.t. e v.i. brotar; jorrar; emocionar-se; s. jorro; borbotão; emoção.

gusher, s. pessoa ou coisa que jorra; pessoa emotiva.

gust, s. pé-de-vento; rabanada; gosto; paixão.

gustation, s. gustação.

gusto, s. gosto, prazer, satisfação.

gusty, a. borrascoso; tempestuoso; violento; saboroso.

gut, s. tripa, intestino; v.t. (gutting, gutted), desentranhar, estripar. 1) large gut, intestino grosso. 2) small gut, intestino delgado. 3) greedy guts, comilão. 4) to have the guts to, ter coragem para.

gutter, s. goteira, calha; rego; valeta; sarjeta; gutter-child, filho da sarjeta, criança abandonada; v.i. escorrer, pingar.

guttural, a. gutural; s. som gutural; adv. gutturally, guturalmente.

guy, s. corda, cabo; sujeiro; pessoa ridícula.

guzzle, v.t. e v.i. entornar, beber em demasia; enfrascar-se.

guzzler, s. beberrão.

gymnasium, s. ginásio.

gymnast, s. ginasta; professor de ginástica.

gymnastics, s. ginástica.

gypsy, gipsy, s. cigano, zíngaro.

gyrate, a. enrolado, curvo; v.i. girar, dar voltas.

gyve, s. grilhão, ferro, algema; v.t. agrilhoar, algemar.

H

h, oitava letra do alfabeto.

haberdasher, s. capelista.

habile, a. hábil, competente, engenhoso.

habiliment, s. vestuário, traje.

habilitate, v.t. e v.i. habilitar(-se); equipar, apetrechar; aparelhar (mina).

habit, s. hábito, costume; feitio; hábito, vestido; v.t. vestir.

habitable, *a.* habitável; *adv. habitably,* de modo s ser habitável.

habitant, *s.* habitante.

habitat, *s.* habitat, habitáculo.

habitation, *s.* habitação; residência, domicílio.

habitual, *a.* habitual, costumeiro, usual; *adv. habitually,* habitualmente.

habituate, *v.t.* habituar, acostumar, familiarizar.

habitué, *s.* frequentador habitual.

hack, *v.t.* e *v.i.* fazer cortes em, cortar, entalhar; tossir secamente; dar caneladas (fut.); mutilar; *s.* cavalo de aluguer; mercenário; cutilada; tosse seca; grade. 1) *hack-hammer,* picareta. 2) *hack-writer,* escritor assalariado, escriba.

hackney, *s.* cavalo ou carruagem de aluguer; assalariado. *a.* de aluguer; gasto, banal; *v.t.* gastar pelo uso; banalizar.

haddock, *s.* espécie de bacalhau pequeno.

hades; *s.* morada dos mortos; Inferno.

haemorrhage, *s.* hemorragia.

haft, *s.* cabo (faca, punhal, navalha); *v.t.* encabar, pôr cabo em.

hag, *s.* bruxa, feiticeira; megera.

hagborn, *a.* nascido de uma bruxa.

haggard, *a.* conturbado, desvairado; pálido, macilento; selvagem, bravio.

haggish, *a.* muito feio, horrível.

haggle, *v.t.* cortar irregularmente, retalhar; incomodar; *v.i.* discutir, disputar, regatear; *s.* disputa, regateio.

hail, *s.* granizo, saraiva; grito, brado, saudação; *a.* familiar, íntimo; *v.t.* e *v.i.* saudar, aclamar; gritar, bradar, chamar; *interj.* salve!

hailstone, *s.* saraiva grossa, pedra de granizo.

hailstorm, *s.* tempestade de granizo.

hair, *s.* cabelo; pêlo; fio de cabelo; cabeleira. 1) *against the hair,* contra vontade. 2) *to keep one's hair,* manter-se calmo. 3) *not to turn a hair,* sem se impressionar.

hairbrush, *s.* escova de cabelo.

haircut, *s.* corte de cabelo.

hairdresser, *s.* cabeleireiro.

hairless, *a.* careca, calvo.

hairpin, *s.* gancho de cabelo.

hairy, *a.* peludo, cabeludo.

hake, *s.* abrótea; *v.t.* pescar.

halberd, *s.* alabarda.

halberdier, *s.* alabardeiro.

halcyon, *a.* calmo, tranquilo; *s.* alcião (ave).

hale, *v.t.* arrastar, levar à força; *a.* são, robusto, forte.

half, *s.* metade. 1) *half-a-crown,* meia coroa. 2) *half-a-dozen,* meia dúzia. 3) *half-back,* de defesa (fut.). 4) *half-boarder,* aluno semi-interno. 5) *half-blooded,* bastardo. 6) *half-bred,* mestiço. 7) *half-brother,* irmão consanguíneo. 8) *half-dead,* exausto. 9) *half-faced,* perfil. 10) *half-hose,* peúga. 11) *half-mourning,* meio luto. 12) *half-shot,* meio bêbedo. 13) *half-staff,* a meia haste. 14) *my better half,* minha cara-metade, minha mulher. 15) *he does nothing by halves,* ele é muito perfeito no que faz. 16) *half-a-loof is better than no bread,* é melhor pouco que nada.

halfhearted, *a.* indiferente, irresoluto.

halfpenny, *s.* meio péni.

halfway, *a.* mediano; parcial; *adv.* parcialmente.

halfwitted, *a.* tolo, imbecil.

halibut, *s.* halibu (peixe).

halitosis, *s.* mau hálito.

halitus, *s.* exalação; hálito.

hall, *s.* vestíbulo, átrio; corredor; edifício público; salão. 1) *hall-mark,* marca de contraste. 2) *hall-stand,* bengaleiro.

hallelujah, *s. interj.* aleluia!

halloo, *s.* e *interj.* grito para açular os cães; *v.t.* e *v.i.* gritar, açular os cães.

hallow, *v.t.* santificar, consagrar; *a.* santo.

Halloween, *s.* véspera do Dia de Todos os Santos; Dia das Bruxas (EUA).

hallucinate, *v.t.* alucinar.

hallucination, *s.* alucinação, visão.

hallucinatory, *a.* alucinatório; alucinante.

hallway, *s.* entrada; corredor.

halo, *s.* halo; auréola; prestígio; *v.t.* aureolar.

halt, *s.* alto, parada, paragem, estacionamento; *v.t.* e *v.i.* parar, deter, fazer parar; vacilar; *a.* coxo, manco.

halter, *s.* cabresto; corda para enforcar; coxo; haltere; *v.t.* encabrestar; amarrar (com corda).

halve, *v.t.* dividir em duas partes; mear; empatar.

ham, *s.* presunto; pernil de porco; curva da perna.

hamlet, *s.* aldeola, povoado.

hammer, *s.* martelo, malho; cão (arma de fogo). 1) *to bring to the hammer,* levar a leilão, pôr em praça. 2) *hammers and tongs,* com gana, com afinco; *v.t.* e *v.i.* martelar, malhar; trabalhar afincadamente.

hammock, *s.* rede de dormir; maca.

hamper, *s.* canastra; cesto grande; *v.t.* e *v.i.* embaraçar, dificultar; encestar.

hand, *s.* mão; posse, poder, autoridade: habitabilidade; auxílio; lado, direcção; ponteiro, indicador; jogador, parceiro; unidade linear; 1) *this child lives from hand to mouth*, esta criança vive ao deus-dará. 2) *in hands*, à disposição. 3) *to keep one´s hands in*, não perder a prática; *a.* de mão, manual; *v.t.* ajudar; passar; dar a mão; dar; guiar.

handbag, *s.* mala de mão.

handball, *s.* andebol.

handbill, *s.* impresso, boletim.

handbook, *s.* manual, compêndio.

handcuff, *s.* (pl.) algemas; *v.t.* algemar, manietar.

handfast, *s.* aperto de mão; pacto.

handful, *s.* punhado, mão-cheia; *by handfuls*, às mãos-cheias.

handgrip, *s.* agarradela; luta corpo a corpo.

handicap, *s.* desvantagem; obstáculo; *v.t.* embaraçar, pôr obstáculos.

handicraft, *s.* trabalho manual; mão-de-obra.

handicraftsman, *s.* artífice.

handiness, *s.* destreza; habilidade; facilidade de manobra.

handiwork, *s.* trabalho manual.

handkerchief, *s.* lenço; *to throw the handkerchief*, mostrar preferência.

handle, *v.t.* manusear, manejar; dirigir; deitar mãos a; *v.i.* trabalhar com as mãos; *s.* punho, manípulo, cabo; puxador; asa; manivela.

handless, *s.* maneta.

handling, *s.* manejo.

handmade, *a.* feito à mão; trabalhado à mão.

handsel, hansel, *s.* presente; presente de estreia; *v.t. (hanselling, hanselled),* estrear, iniciar.

handsome, *a.* formoso, belo, lindo; generoso; simpático; considerável; *handsome is that handsome does* (prov.), as aparências não contam, o que contam são as acções; *adv. handsomely,* primorosamente.

handwriting, *s.* escrita à mão; caligrafia.

handy, *a.* manual; manejável; cómodo, a jeito; hábil; desembaraçado, *handy-man*, faz-tudo.

hang, *v.t.* pendurar, suspender; levantar; enforcar; *v.i.* pender, cair; ser enforcado; ameaçar; agarrar-se (ao pescoço); esperar;

depender. 1) *to hang back*, hesitar. 2) *to hang fire*, suspender fogo. 3) *to hang upon*, olhar com afeição. 4) *time hangs heavily*, o tempo custa a passar.

hangar, *s.* hangar.

hangdog, *s.* indivíduo ordinário; *a.* de aspecto desprezível; tímido, acanhado.

hanger, *s.* carrasco, algoz; suspensor, suporte; cabide.

hanger-on, *s.* parasita, dependente; jantares, pendura.

hanging, *s.* enforcamento; *a.* suspenso; de suspensão; merecedor da forca. 1) *hanging face*, cara patibular. 2) *hanging matter*, caso de forca.

hangman, *s.* carrasco.

hang-nail, *s.* espigão das unhas.

hank, *s.* novelo, meada; arco; anilha; laçada, nó, volta.

hanker, *v.i.* ansiar, suspirar, desejar ardentemente.

hanky, *s.* lenço.

hanky-panky, *s.* escamoteação, zombaria; partida.

hap, *s.* acaso, sorte; *v.i. (happing, happed),* acontecer, suceder.

haphazard, *s.* acaso, casualidade, acidente; *a.* casual, acidental; *adv.* casualmente; ao acaso.

hapless, *a.* sem sorte, malfadado.

haply, *adv.* casualmente, por sorte; talvez.

happen, *v.i.* acontecer, suceder, ocorrer.

happening, *s.* acontecimento.

happily, *adv.* felizmente, por sorte; com felicidade.

happiness, *s.* felicidade, ventura.

happy, *a.* feliz, venturoso; contente, satisfeito.

happy-go-lucky, *a.* despreocupado, negligente.

harangue, *s.* arenga, discurso; *v.t.* e *v.i.* arengar, discursar.

harass, *v.t.* apoquentar, atormentar; cansar, fatigar; humilhar; hostilizar; *s.* estrago, distúrbio.

harbour, *s.* porto de abrigo; asilo; *vt.* abrigar, defender; *vi.* amparar-se.

hard, *a.* duro, sólido, firme; difícil, custoso; severo; opressivo; áspero, tosco; vigoroso. 1) *hard-cash*, dinheiro realizado. 2) *hard-gotten*, adquirido a custo. 3) *hard labour*, trabalho forçado. 4) *hard up*, com pouco dinheiro. 5) *hard by*, perto. 6) *to drink hard*, beber excessivamente. 7) *to grow hard*, endurecer. 8) *to be hard up*, estar em apuros; *adv.* diligentemente, afincadamente; muito; dificilmente.

harden, *v.t.* e *v.i.* endurecer(-se), solidificar (-se), consolidar(-se); fortalecer, enrijar; empedernir(-se); temperar (metal).

hardener, *s.* endurecedor.

hardhead, *s.* pessoa astuta, raposa-velha; cabeça-dura.

hardheaded, *a.* teimoso, obstinado; cabeça-firme; astuto.

hardhearted, *a.* insensível; cruel.

hardihood, *s.* audácia, temeridade; imprudência.

hardiness, *s.* ânimo; robustez, vigor.

hardly, *adv.* duramente, com dificuldade.

hardness, *s.* dureza, firmeza; severidade.

hardship, *s.* privação, penúria; trabalho incómodo; provação.

hardware, *s.* ferragens; conjunto dos vários elementos electrónicos que constituem o computador.

hardy, *a.* ousado, valente; temerário; robusto; resistente; *adv. hardily,* ousadamente, com vigor.

hare, *s.* lebre.

harebrained, *a.* leviano, volúvel, estouvado.

harem, *s.* harém.

haricot, *s.* feijão.

hark, *v.t.* e *v.i.* ouvir, escutar; *interj.* ouve! escuta!

harlequin, *s.* arlequim; palhaço.

harlot, *s.* prostituta, meretriz; *a.* lúbrico, devasso.

harm, *s.* dano, mal, prejuízo; *to mean no harm,* ter boas intenções; *v.t.* causar dano; danificar, prejudicar; ofender.

harmful, *a.* nocivo, prejudicial, daninho; *adv. harfully,* perniciosamente.

harmfulness, *s.* maldade, disposição nociva.

harmless, *a.* inofensivo, inocente; *adv. harmlessly,* inocentemente.

harmonic, *a.* harmónico, consonante; *s.* harmónico; som harmónico.

harmonica, *s.* harmónica, gaita-de-beiços.

harmonious, *a.* harmonioso; equilibrado.

harmonium, *s.* harmónio (mús.).

harmonize, *v.t.* harmonizar, tornar harmonioso, conciliar.

harmony, *s.* harmonia, concordância; harmonia (mús.).

harness, *s.* arreios; armadura; *to die in harness,* morrer a trabalhar.

harp, *s.* harpa; *vi.* tocar harpa, repetir de modo enfadonho.

harper, *s.* harpista.

harpoon, *s.* arpão.

harpsichord, *s.* cravo (mús.).

harpy, *s.* harpia; extorquidor, águia.

harridan, *s.* megera, bruxa, marafona.

harrow, *s.* grade; *v.t.* gradar, lacerar; *to be under the harrow,* estar em situação aflitiva.

harry, *v.t.* assolar, desvastar; esbulhar; perseguir, oprimir, atormentar.

harsh, *a.* áspero, desagradável; dissonante; rude; severo, rígido.

hart, *s.* veado.

harvest, *s.* colheita, ceifa; fruto, resultado. 1) *harvest home,* festa por ocasião das colheitas. 2) *harvest mouse,* rato das searas; *v.t.* e *v.i.* ceifar, colher.

harvester, *s.* ceifeiro; segadeira.

harvestman, *s.* ceifeiro.

has-been, *s.* pessoa que perdeu o seu antigo brilho ou grandeza; coisa do passado.

hash, *v.t.* picar, cortar em picadinho; misturar, confundir; *s.* picadinho, guisado; *to make a hash of,* estragar uma coisa, mutilar.

hashish, *s.* haxixe.

hasp, *s.* fecho de cadeado; broche; *v.t.* fechar com cadeado, abrochar.

hassock, *s.* tufo de ervas; almofada para ajoelhar.

haste, *s.* pressa, diligência, precipitação; *v.t.* e *v.i.* apressar-se; apressar.

hasten, *vt.* apressar, acelerar, activar; instigar, incitar; *v.i.* apressar-se, aviar-se; *to hasten to a place,* dirigir-se às pressas a um local.

hasty, *a.* apressado, rápido, diligente; vivo; violento; *hasty-pudding,* papas de farinha (trigo, aveia).

hat, *s.* chapéu. 1) *silk-hat,* chapéu alto. 2) *hat-tree,* cabide para chapéus. 3) *to knock into a cocked hat,* dar uma sova mestra. 4) *to send round the hat,* fazer colecta; *v.t. (hatting, hatted),* pôr chapéu, cobrir com chapéu.

hatable, *a.* odioso, detestável.

hatch, *s.* ninhada; saída da casca; manifestação; postigo; portinhola; quartel de escotilha; *under hatches,* no porão; decaído, humilhado (fig.); *v.t.* e *v.i.* chocar; sair da casca; fomentar; tramar; premeditar; traçar riscos, sombrear.

hatchery, s. incubadora, chocadeira.

hatchet, s. machadinha. 1) to bury the hatchet, pôr fim às hostilidades. 2) to dig up the hatchet, declarar guerra.

hate, v.t. e v.i. odiar, detestar, abominar; s. ódio, aversão.

hateful, a. odioso, detestável, abominável; adv. hatefully, abominavelmente.

hater, s. inimigo.

hatred, s. ódio, rancor, inimizade.

hatter, s. chapeleiro; as mad as a hatter, doido varrido.

hauberk, s. cota de malha.

haughty, a. soberbo, altivo, arrogante; adv. haughtily, arrogantemente.

haul, s. arrasto, arranco, puxão; v.t. e v.i. puxar, arrastar; transportar; alar; rondar; fazer caminho.

haunch, s. anca, quadril.

haunt, v.t. frequentar; visitar; obcecar, perseguir; a haunted house, uma casa assombrada; s. lugar frequentado; retiro; caverna, covil.

hautboy, hoboy, s. oboé (mús.); espécie de morango.

hauter, s. altivez, arrogância.

havana, s. charuto de Havana.

have, v.t. ter, possuir; querer; ter de; dever; tomar (comida, bebida). 1) you had better go, era melhor que fosses agora. 2) I had rather stay, eu preferia ficar. 3) what will you have?, o que é que toma? 4) I will have it so, quero que seja assim. 5) I had a dress made, mandei fazer um vestido. 6) to have someone on, rir-se de alguém. 7) to have someone up, processar alguém. 8) I have it, achei-o; consegui-o; entendi-o. 9) do well and have well, quem boa cama faz nela se deita. 10) she has on a beautiful coat, ela traz vestido um lindo casaco. 11) have done!, pára! acaba! 12) haves and have-nots, ricos e pobres.

haven, s. porto, enseada.

haversack, s. bornal; saco de provisões; mochila.

having, s. bens, fortuna, haveres; a. possuidor.

havoc, s. estrago, ruína, devastação; to play havoc with, fazer grandes estragos; v.t. assolar, destruir.

haw, s. baga de espinheiro; v.t. e v.i. falar embaraçadamente, gaguejar.

hawk, s. falcão; v.t. e v.i. caçar o falcão; vender géneros pelas ruas; apregoar; hawk-nose, nariz aquilino.

hawthorn, s. espinheiro branco.

hay, s. feno, palha; alfaia. 1) haycock, meda de feno. 2) hayfield, campo de feno. 3) hayfork, forcado. 4) to make hay while the sun shines, aproveitar a ocasião favorável. 5) between hay and grass, tarde demais para uma coisa. 6) look for a needle in ahaystack, procurar agulha em palheiro; v.t. fazer feno; alimentar com feno.

hazard, s. azar, sorte, acaso; risco, perigo; jogo de azar; at all hazards, a todos os riscos.

hazardous, a. arriscado; adv. hazardously, arriscadamente.

haze, s. nevoeiro, neblina; ofuscação mental; v.t. e v.i. enevoar, turvar; espantar; atormentar.

hazel, as. aveleira; hazelnut, avelã; a. cor de avelã, castanho-claro.

hazing, s. imposição de trabalho excessivo ou desnecessário; perseguição a caloiros; partidas.

hazy, a. enevoado, nebuloso; confuso, tonto.

he, pron. ele; s. homem; empregado para designar o macho de uma espécie. 1) he--goat, bode. 2) he-man, homem viril, másculo.

head, s. cabeça; chefe; ponta; título; fonte; nascente; juízo; assunto; proa; topo; unidade. 1) head and ears, completamente. 2) heads or tail, cara ou coroa. 3) to keep one's head, conservar a calma. 4) to loose one's head, perder a calma. 5) to be in debt head and ears, estar endividado até à raiz dos cabelos. 6) talk a person's head off, esgotar alguém de tanto falar. 7) head over heels, de pernas para o ar.

headache, s. dor de cabeça, enxaqueca.

headboard, s. cabeceira da cama.

headdress, s. toucado.

heading, s. título, cabeçalho.

headkerchief, s. lenço de cabeça.

headlight, s. farol; farol de automóvel.

headline, s. título, cabeçalho.

headlong, a. e adv. de cabeça para baixo; impensadamente.

headman, s. chefe (tribo, sociedade, grupo, etc.).

headmaster, s. director de colégio.

headmost, a. dianteiro, que vai na frente.

headoffice, s. sede, casa-mãe.

headpiece, s. capacete, chapéu.

headquarters, s. quartel-general; comando; sede.

headship, s. chefia; supremacia.

headstone, s. lápide mortuária.

headstrong, a. voluntarioso; obstinado; casmurro.

headwaters, s. nascente.

headwork, s. trabalho mental.

heady, a. impetuoso, violento; obstinado; embriagador (vinho); adv. headily, violentamente.

heal, v.t. e v.i. curar(-se); sarar; cicatrizar.

healing, a. curativo, medicinal; salutar.

health, s. saúde, sanidade; brinde, saudação.

healthful, a. saudável, sadio, são.

healthy, a. são, de boa saúde, saudável; adv. healthily, saudavelmente.

heap, s. montão, pinha; multidão; v.t. amontoar, acumular.

hear, v.t. e v.i. ouvir, escutar; ouvir dizer, atender a.

hearer, s. ouvinte.

hearing, s. audição; ouvido (sentido); acção de ouvir; audiência.

hearken, harken, v.i. escutar, prestar atenção; dar ouvidos.

hearsay, s. boato, rumor.

hearse, s. carro fúnebre; féretro.

heart, s. coração; peito, seio; interior (de qualquer coisa); coragem; alma; amor; sensibilidade; fertilidade (terra); naipe de copas. 1) heart and soul, com energia. 2) heart's ease, amor-perfeito (flor). 3) heart-throb, pulsação. 4) to have the heart in the mouth, excitar-se; falar com sentimento. 5) to have the heart to, ter coragem de. 6) faint heart never won fair lady, dos fracos não reza a história.

heartache, s. pesar, mágoa.

heartbreak, s. desgosto profundo.

heartbroken, a. prostrado pela dor.

heartburning, s. azedume, descontentamento, rancor, ódio, inveja.

hearten, v.t. e v.i. (também com up) animar(-se), encorajar(-se); alentar.

heartfelt, a. sincero, genuíno.

heart-free: a. de coração livre, disponível.

hearth, s. lar; lareira.

hearthrug, s. tapete grosso que se estende diante da lareira.

hearthstone, s. pedra da lareira.

heartily, adv. cordialmente, calorosamente.

heartiness, s. cordialidade; sinceridade.

heartsick, a. magoado, abatido, deprimido.

heartstrings, s. cordas da alma; afectos mais profundos.

hearty, a. sincero; cordial; caloroso; robusto; sadio.

heat, s. calor; veemência; cólera; cio; corrida. 1) heat-wave, onda de calor. 2) a dead heat, corrida sem vencedor; v.t. e v.i. aquecer; arde; inflamar.

heater, s. aquecedor.

heath, s. urze; charneca.

heathen, s. gentio, pagão, idólatra; adj. rude, bárbaro.

heather, s. urze (o mesmo que heath), heath-grass, urze.

heave, s. elevação; esforço para se levantar; arquejo; suspiro; ânsia de vómito; v.t. e v.i. erguer, levantar; içar; suspirar; arfar. 1) to heave a rope, puxar com corda. 2) to heave in sight, assomar, tornar-se visível.

heaven, s. céu, firmamento, 1) heaven-born, descido dos céus; dotado de qualidades. 2) for heaven's sake!, por amor de Deus!

heavenly, a. celeste, divino; adv. celestialmente; divinamente.

heavily, adv. pesadamente; lentamente; tristemente.

heavy, a. pesado; forte; duro; triste. 1) heavy-headed, estúpido. 2) heavy-laden, oprimido pela dor. 3) times hangs heavy, o tempo passa devagar.

heavyhearthed, a. pesaroso, triste.

heavyweight, s. peso-pesado (boxe).

Hebraic, a. hebraico, hebreu.

Hebraism, s. hebraísmo.

Hebrew, s. hebreu, judeu.

hecatom, s. hecatombe.

heckle, v.t. importunar, contrariar.

hectare, s. hectare.

hectic, a. febril; inquieto; desenfreado.

hedge, s. sebe; barreira; v.t. e v.i. cercar com sebes; obstruir, impedir. 1) to hedge in, fechar. 2) to hedge off, separar.

hedgehog, s. ouriço-cacheiro; porco-espinho.

heed, v.t. e v.i. atender, prestar atenção; considerar; s. cautela, cuidado.

heedless, a. desatento, distraído, descuidado, negligente; insensato.

heehaw, s. zurro; gargalhada ruidosa; v.t. zurrar como um burro.

heel, s. calcanhar; salto; tacão; pé (mastro, baliza, etc.). 1) heel-ball, bola de sebo (de sapateiro). 2) head over heels, às avessas. 3) to be at the heels of, colar-se às canelas de, seguir uma pessoa. 4) to show a clean pair of heels, dar aos calcanhares; v.t. e v.i.

colocar tacões em; ir no encalço; sapatear; tombar; adernar.

heeltap, s. capa, salto; resto de bebida deixado nos copos.

heifer, s. bezerra, novilha.

height, s. altura; altitude; extremo; auge; cúmulo.

heighten, v.t. erguer, levantar; realçar, aperfeiçoar; agravar.

heinous, a. odioso, atroz, abominável; adv. heinously, odiosamente, horrivelmente.

heir, s. herdeiro; sucessor.

heirdom, s. herança, direito de herança.

heirless, a. sem herdeiro.

heirloom, s. bens móveis herdados.

heirship, s. direito de sucessão; sucessão.

helicopter, s. helicóptero.

heliotrope, s. heliotrópio.

helium, s. hélio (quím.).

helix, s. hélice.

hell, s. inferno; qualquer lugar de vício ou de miséria; antro, espelunca.

hell-fire, s. fogo do inferno; ódio intenso; ressentimento.

hellion, s. demónio; pessoa endiabrada, peste.

hellish, a. infernal; diabólico; adv. hellishly, infernalmente.

hellkite, s. pessoa de crueldade diabólica; monstro.

hello, interj. e s. olá!; pronto!, está? (ao telefone).

helm, s. leme, governo; direcção; elmo; a hand to the helm, homem do leme; v.t. governar, dirigir.

helmet, s. elmo.

Helot, s. hilota; escravo, servo (com minús.).

helotism, s. escravidão, servidão.

help, s. ajuda, auxílio, socorro, protecção; criado auxiliar; to call for help, pedir ajuda, gritar por socorro; v.t. e v.i. ajudar, auxiliar, socorrer, amparar, proteger; evitar, impedir; servir.

helper, s. ajudante, auxiliar.

helpful, a. útil, prestável; proveitoso; adv. helpfully, de modo proveitoso.

helpless, a. desamparado, indefeso, impossibilitado; impotente; sem ânimo.

helpmate, s. companheiro; companheira; esposa, marido; assistente.

helve, s. cabo (de utensílio ou de arma).

Helvetic, a. helvético, suíço; s. suíço.

hem, s. bainha, debrum; (hemming, hem-med), v.t. fazer bainha, debruar; cercar; interj. hem!

hematoma, haematoma, s. hematoma (med.).

hematosis, haematosis, s. hematose (fisiol.).

hemisphere, s. hemisfério.

hemlock, s. cicuta; abeto do Canadá.

hemoglobin, s. hemoglobina (bioq.).

hemorrhage, haemorrhage, s. hemorragia.

hemorrhoids, haemorrhoids, s. hemorróidas.

hemp, s. cânhamo.

hemstitch, s. ponto aberto; bainha de ponto aberto; v.t. fazer ponto aberto.

hen, s. galinha; fêmea de aves. 1) brood hen, galinha choca. 2) hen-coop, capoeira. 3) turkey hen, perua. 5) hen-roost, poleiro.

hence, adv. daqui; por isso. 1) ten years hence, daqui a dez anos. 2) you can see it hence, pode vê-lo daqui. 3) her husband died, hence she needs a job, o marido dela morreu, por isso ela necessita de emprego.

henceforth, adv. de ora em diante, de hoje em diante, doravante.

henchman, s. escudeiro, pajem, criado.

hennery, s. galinheiro.

henpeck, v.t. dominar ou tiranizar (o marido).

hepatic, a. hepático.

hepatitis, s. hepatite (med.).

her, pron. oblíquo, 3ª pess. fem., a, lhe, a ela; a. poss. seu(s), sua(s), dela.

herald, s. arauto; precursor; v.t. anunciar, proclamar.

heraldic, a. heráldico.

heraldry, s. heráldica; brasões.

herb, s. erva, planta. 1) herb-doctor, herbanário. 2) sweet herbs, plantas odoríferas.

herbage, s. ervas, verdura.

herbal, a. herbáceo.

herbivorous, a. herbívoro.

herd, s. rebanho, manada; multidão, a ralé. 1) cow-herd, vaqueiro. 2) goat-herd, carneiro. 3) swine-herd, porqueiro. 4) sheep-herd, pastor. 5) the herd instinct, o instinto gregário; v.t. e v.i. andar ou reunir em rebanhos, manadas ou bandos.

herdsman, s. pastor, criador de gado.

here, adv. aqui; cá; para cá; presente! 1) here's to you, à sua saúde. 2) here below, cá na terra, nesta vida. 3) here lies, aqui jaz.

hereabout, adv. por aqui, aqui por perto.

hereafter, adv. mais adiante; doravante; s. futuro, um estado futuro.

hereat, adv. neste ponto, neste momento.

hereby, adv. por este meio, por estas palavras.

hereditary, a. hereditário; transmissível; adv. hereditarily, hereditariamente.

heredity, hereditariedade.

herein, adv. aqui; incluso.

hereinafter, adv. abaixo, adiante.

hereinbefore, adv. acima, atrás.

hereinto, adv. aqui, para dentro deste lugar.

hereof, adv. disto, deste; a este respeito.

hereon, adv. sobre isto, acerca disto.

heresy, s. heresia.

heretic, s. herege; a. herético.

heretical, a. herético; adv. heretically, hereticamente.

hereto, adv. até este tempo; anexo.

heretofore, adv. no passado, até agora.

hereunder, adv. abaixo disto, abaixo, em virtude disto.

hereunto, adv. (o mesmo que hereto) até agora.

hereupon, adv. nisto; em consequência disto; neste momento.

herewith, adv. com isto; junto.

heritage, s. herança.

heritance, s. herança; sucessão.

heritor, s. herdeiro.

hermetic, hermetical, a. hermético; adv. hermetically, hermeticamente.

hernia, s. hérnia (med.).

hero, s. herói; heroship, culto dos heróis.

heroic, heroical, a. heróico, corajoso; adv. heroically, heroicamente.

heroicomic, a. herói-cómico.

heroify, v.t. heroificar.

heroin, s. heroína, sedativo à base de morfina.

heroine, s. heroína; mulher heróica.

heroism, s. heroísmo; heroicidade.

heroize, v.t. heroificar; v.i. fazer-se herói.

heron, s. garça.

herpes, s. herpes (med.).

herring, s. arenque.

hers, pron. pess. abs. seu, sua, seus, suas (dela).

herself, pron. reflexo, ela mesma.

hesitate, v.i. hesitar, vacilar.

hesitating, a. hesitante, vacilante; adv. hesitatingly, hesitantemente.

hesitation, s. hesitação, vacilação; irresolução.

heterogeneous, a. heterogéneo; adv. heterogeneously, de modo heterogéneo.

heterosexual, a. e s. heterossexual.

hew, v.t. e v.i. cortar (em pedaços); talhar, desgastar, decepar.

hexagon, s. hexágono (geom.).

hexagonal, a. hexagonal.

hexameter, s. hexámetro (poes.).

hey, interj. eh! oh! hem! (alegria, surpresa, indignação).

heyday, interj. de alegria ou surpresa; s. auge; flor da idade; alegria; animação.

hiatus, s. greta, fenda; hiato; lacuna.

hibernate, v.i. hibernar.

hibernation, s. hibernação.

hiccup, hiccough, s. soluço; v.i. ter soluços.

hidden, pp. de hide; a. escondido, secreto, oculto.

hide, v.i. e v.t. esconder; esconder-se; açoitar, sovar; s. couro, pele de animal; medida de cerca de 120 acres. 1) to dress hides, curtir peles. 2) to warm one's hide, sacudir o pêlo a alguém. 3) hide-and seek, jogo das escondidas.

hidebound, a. com a pele junta aos ossos; com a casca junta à árvore de modo a estorvar o crescimento.

hideous, a. horrível, repugnante; adv. hideously, horrivelmente.

hideousness, s. horror; fealdade.

hidding, s. sova, pancadaria; acto de esconder; encobrimento. 1) hidding place, esconderijo. 2) to be in hidding, permanecer escondido.

hie, v.i. e refl. apressar-se, ir depressa; passar com rapidez.

hierarchical, a. hierárquico.

hierarchy, s. hierarquia.

hieratic, hieratical, a. hierático; sacerdotal.

higgle, v.i. regatear, disputar.

high, a. alto, elevado; eminente; difícil, árduo; altivo, arrogante, violento, zangado; forte, poderoso; solene; turbulento; pleno; adv. alto, altamente; de preço elevado; luxuosa-mente; s. ás de trunfo. 1) high and dry, encalhado a seco. 2) high and low, pessoas de todas as classes. 3) high art, trabalho artístico notável. 4) high blown, muito inchado. 5) high-born, de nascimento nobre. 6) high-bred, de raça (cavalos); bem-educado. 7) high-brow, intelectual. 9) high-colour, cor viva, berrante. 10) high-falutin, discurso pomposo e bombástico. 11) *high-farming*, cultura intensiva por meio de fertilizantes. 12) *high-flavoured*, muito picante. 13) *high-flying*, extravagante. 14) *high-flyer*, pessoa ambiciosa ou extravagante. 15) *high-going*, grau superior. 16) *high-life*, alta sociedade. 17) *high-mettled*, ardente, fogoso. 18) *high-pitched*, em tom alto; altivo. 19) *high-spirited*, animoso; fogoso. 20) *high-tide*, maré-alta. 21) *high--treason*, alta traição. 22) *high-water*, maré alta. 23) *high-water-mark*, o ponto mais alto da maré. 24) *Most High*, o Altíssimo.

higher, *a.* mais alto, superior.

highhanded: *a.* despótico; *adv.* highhandedly, despoticamente.

highland, *s.* região montanhosa, serrania.

Highlander, *s.* habitante da Alta Escócia.

highly, *adv.* altamente; muito; bem.

highness, *s.* elevação, altura; (com maiús.) alteza.

highway, *s.* estrada principal, auto-estrada.

highwayman, *s.* salteador de estrada.

hike, *v.i.* avançar com esforço; andar a pé; arrastar-se.

hilarious, *a.* hílare, alegre, jovial; *adv.* hilariously, hilariantemente.

hilarity, *s.* hilaridade; riso; alegria.

hill, *s.* colina, outeiro; monte, encosta.

hillman, *s.* habitante das colinas; montanhês.

hillock, *s.* pequena colina, montículo, cabeço.

hillside, *s.* encosta, vertente.

hilltop, *s.* cimo, cume.

hilly, *a.* colinoso, montanhoso.

hilt, *s.* punho, cabo (espada, punhal).

him, *pron. pess.* masc. 3ª pess. *sing.*, ele, lhe, o, aquele.

himself, *pron. pess. refl.*, masc., 3ª pess. sing., se, a si mesmo, ele mesmo, ele próprio.

hind, *s.* criado de lavoura; campónio, rústico; corça, cerva; *a.* posterior, traseiro.

hinder, *a.* posterior, traseiro; *v.t.* e *v.i.* impedir, pôr obstáculos, estorvar.

hindmost, *a.* o que está mais atrás, o mais afastado, o último.

hindrance, *s.* acto de impedir; impedimento, empecilho.

hinge, *s.* dobradiça, gonzo; ponto crítico; *v.i.* e *v.t.* girar, depender de; engonçar, pôr dobradiça.

hint, *s.* insinuação, alusão, referência; *v.t.* sugerir, insinuar, dar a entender.

hinterland, *s.* o interior do país, o sertão.

hip, *s.* quadril, anca. 1) *hip and thigh*, esmagadoramente, implacavelmente. 2) *to have up the hip*, levar vantagem a, dominar; *v.t.* *(hipping, hipped)*, desancar; deprimir, desalentar.

hip, hep, *s.* fruto da roseira brava; *interj.* hip, hip, hurrah!

hipbone, *s.* osso ilíaco.

hippodrome, *s.* hipódromo.

hippotamus, *s.* hipópotamo.

hire, *s.* aluguer; salário. 1) *hire-purchase*, venda a prazo; *v.t.* alugar; assalariar. 2) *hiring agreement*, contrato de arrendamento.

hirsute, *a.* hirsuto, peludo.

his, *a.* e *pron. poss.*, seu, sua, seus, suas, dele.

hiss, *v.i.* e *v.t.* assobiar; silvar; patear; *s.* assobio; silvo; pateada.

hissing, *a.* sibilante; o que assobia.

hist, *interj.* psiu!, caluda!, silêncio! *v.t.* mandar calar.

historian, *a.* historiador; cronista.

historic, *a.* histórico, famoso na história.

historical, *a.* histórico; pertencente ao passado; *adv.* historically, historicamente.

history, *s.* história.

hit (hitting, hit), *v.t.* topar, bater; atingir o alvo; alcançar. 1) *to hit the nail on the head*, pôr o dedo na ferida. 2) *to hit against*, dar contra alguma coisa. 3) *to hit upon*, achar, encontrar. 4) *to make a hit*, fazer sucesso; *s.* golpe, pancada; acerto; golpe feliz.

hit-and-run, *a.* bate e foge (motorista).

hitch, *s.* nó; dificuldade; *v.t.* e *v.i.* prender, agarrar; coxear; agarrar-se, acertar-se.

hither, *adv.* cá, para cá; *hither and thither*, de um lado para o outro.

hitherto, *adv.* até aqui, até agora.

hive, *s.* colmeia, cortiço; enxame; *v.t.* enxamear; pôr em cortiço.

hives, *s.* urticária.

hoar, *a.* encanecido; grisalho.

hoard, *s.* provisão, tesouro; *v.t.* acumular, entesourar, amontoar; *v.i.* juntar dinheiro, fazer mealheiro.

hoarfrost, *s.* geada.

hoarse, *a.* rouco; discordante.

hoarsen, *v.t.* e *v.i.* enrouquecer.

hoary, *a.* branco, encanecido; venerável.

hoax, *s.* engano, burla; *v.t.* enganar, lograr; pregar uma partida.

hobble, *v.i* e *v.t.* coxear, cambalear; embaraçar; *s.* manqueira; dificuldade.

hobby, *s.* passatempo favorito; mania; cavalinho de madeira (para criança).

hobgoblin, *s.* duende.

hobnail, *s.* prego de cabeça grossa; *v.t.* pregar.

hobo, *s.* trabalhador desempregado; vagabundo.

hock, *s.* jarrete (de cavalo); vinho branco do Reno.

hockey, *s.* hóquei.

hod, *s.* maçarico de pedreiro; vasilha para carvão.

hoe, *s.* enxada; *v.t.* e *v.i.* cavar, sachar.

hog, *s.* porco, suíno; homem vil.

hoggish, *a.* porcino, suíno; grosseiro.

hogshead, *s.* barril; casco.

hoist, *v.t.* erguer, içar.

hoity-toity, *a.* leviano, estouvado; brincalhão.

hokeypokey, *s.* sorvete barato vendido nas ruas.

hold, *v.t.* e *v.i.* segurar; manter; ter; caber; conter; defender; julgar; gozar; deter; conservar; celebrar; valer; durar; continuar; abaster-se; aderir; derivar. 1) *to hold aloof,* conservar-se afastado. 2) *to hold back,* reter; recuar. 3) *to hold down,* reter; baixar. 4) *to hold fast,* segurar firme. 5) *to hold forth,* falar em público. 6) *to hold good,* ser verdadeiro; valer. 7) *to hold in,* refrear-se, conter-se. 8) *to hold on,* segurar; continuar. 9) *to hold up,* levantar, erguer. 10) *hold on!,* pare!, *s.* presa; pega; asa; custódia; porão.

holder, *s.* detentor; possuidor; arrendatário; apoio, suporte. 1) *cigar-holder,* boquilha. 2) *landholder,* proprietário rural. 3) *shareholder,* accionista.

holding, *s.* posse; propriedade; arrendamento; títulos da bolsa; companhia que controla outras pela aquisição de acções.

holdup, *s.* assalto à mão armada; operação auto-stop.

hole, *s.* buraco, cavidade; caverna; situação difícil, dilema; *v.t.* e *v.i.* esburacar; meter em buraco; entrar num buraco.

holey, *a.* esburacado, furado.

holiday, *s.* dia santo, feriado; (pl.) férias.

holiness, *s.* santidade.

hollow, *a.* oco. cavo, cavado; surdo (som), abafado; falso; *s.* concavidade, cova, vale, depressão.

holly, *s.* azevinho; ramo de azevinho.

holocaust, *s.* holocausto.

holster, *s.* coldre.

holy, *s.* santo; sagrado; pio. 1) *Holy City,* Jerusalém; Meca. 2) *Holy Ghost,* o Espírito Santo. 3) *holy water,* água benta. 4) *Holy Writ,* a Sagrada Escritura.

homage, *s.* homenagem; respeito; *to pay homage,* prestar homenagem.

homager, *s.* vassalo.

home, *s.* casa, residência, morada; lar: família; pátria; terra natal; sede. *a.* doméstico, caseiro, familiar; nacional, interno, interior; *adv.* a casa, para casa; em casa; no país; à vontade; *v.t.* e *v.i.* alojar; ir para casa.

home-built, *a.* de construção caseira; de fabricação nacional.

homebred, *a.* criado em casa; doméstico; rude; inculto.

homeland, *s.* pátria, terra natal.

homeless, *a.* sem lar; desabrigado.

homelike, *a.* confortável; íntimo.

homely, *a.* simples, caseiro, despretensioso; grosseiro (feições), rude; *adv.* grosseiramente; simplesmente.

homemad, *a.* feito em casa.

homemaker, *s.* dona de casa.

homemaking, *s.* afazeres domésticos; lida da casa.

homesick, *a.* nostálgico; saudoso.

homestead, *s.* casa e os seus anexos; solar; quinta.

homesteader, *s.* proprietário.

homestretch, *s.* recta de chegada; meta.

homeward, *a.* em direcção à casa; de retorno; (pl.) *adv.* para a terra, para o seu país.

homey, *a.* caseiro; familiar.

homicide, *s.* homicídio; homicida.

homily, *s.* homilia, sermão.

homing, *a.* que volta a casa; residente; *homing pigeon,* pombo-correio.

homo, *s.* espécie humana.

homogeneous, *a.* homogéneo; uniforme.

hone, *s.* pedra de amolar; *v.t.* afiar, amolar.

honest, *a.* honesto, honrado, recto, sincero, franco; *to earn an honest penny,* ganhar a vida honradamente.

honesty, *s.* honestidade, honradez; sinceridade.

honey, *s.* mel; expressão de carinho; querido, querida; *a.* melífluo; doce; caro; precioso; *v.t.* adoçar; lisonjear.

honeybee, s. abelha produtora de mel, abelha doméstica.

honeycomb, s. favo de mel.

honeyed, a. doce, coberto de mel; melífluo.

honeymoon, s. lua-de-mel.

honeysuckle, s. madressilva.

honour, s. honra, veneração, honradez, dignidade; sinal de distinção; título de honra; v.t. honrar, estimar; aceitar e pagar no vencimento.

honourable, a. nobre, ilustre; louvável, meritório; respeitável; título honorífico.

honorarium, s. honorários.

honorary, a. honorário; honorífico; de honra.

hood, s. capuz, touca; tejadilho, capota; tampa, chapéu.

hoodoo, s. vodu; feitiço.

hoodwink, v.t. vendar, tapar os olhos a; cobrir, encobrir, ocultar; tapar os olhos; defraudar, enganar.

hoof, s. casco, pata de animal. 1) *hoof-beaten*, pisado pelos cavalos. 2) *to show the cloven hoof*, mostrar má disposição; revelar o carácter; v.i. andar devagar.

hook, s. gancho, anzol; v.t. e v.i. prender com gancho; engodar, fisgar.

hook-up, s. cadeia de rádio-emissoras.

hooligan, s. rufia, desordeiro.

hoop, s. arco, braçadeira; cinta.

hoot, v.i. e v.t. gritar, vaiar; soar, buzinar; s. apupo; pio do mocho.

hop (hopping, hopped), v.t. e v.i. pular, saltar; ir (morrer); s. pulo, salto; lúpulo; voo, travessia aérea.

hope, s. esperança; v.t. e v.i. esperar, ter esperança.

hopeful, a. esperançado, esperançoso; adv. *hopefully*, esperançadamente.

hopeless, a. desesperado; adv. *hopelessly*, sem esperança.

hopelessness, s. desesperança; inutilidade.

hopper, s. saltador; tremonha (de moinho); saco de sementeira.

horde, s. horda; bando, multidão.

horizon, s. horizonte.

horizontal, a. horizontal.

hormonal, a. hormonal.

horn, s. corno, chifre, antena de insecto; cornetim; trompa (de caça ou buzina de automóvel); v.t. encornar; dar chifradas.

horned, a. provido de chifres; cornudo.

hornet, s. vespão.

hornpipe, s. dança inglesa, muito popular entre os marinheiros; gaita-de-fole.

horny, a. córneo; feito de corno; caloso.

horologe, s. relógio.

horologer, s. relojoeiro.

horoscope, s. horóscopo; *to cast a horoscope*, tirar um horóscopo.

horrendous, a. horrendo, horrível, terrível.

horrible, a. horrível, terrível.

horrid, a. hórrido, horrendo, espantoso.

horrify, v.t. horrorizar, aterrar.

horror, s. horror, terror.

horse, s. cavalo; cavalete; cavalaria; soldado de cavalaria; burro (gír. escolar). 1) *horse-boy*: moço de estrebaria. 2) *horse-couper*, negociante de cavalos. 3) *horse-colt*, potro. 4) *horse-shoe*, ferradura. 5) *horse of state*, cavalo de luxo; v.t. e v.i. montar a cavalo; levar alguém às costas; pôr alguém às costas; fornecer cavalos.

horsed, a. montado.

horse-drawn, a. puxado a cavalo.

horseflesh, s. carne de cavalo.

horsehair, s. crina de cavalo.

horsejockey, s. jóquei.

horseman, s. cavaleiro, tratador de cavalos.

horsemanship, s. equitação.

horsemint, s. hortelã.

horseplay, s. brincadeira rude, gracejo de mau gosto.

horsepower, s. cavalo-vapor (mec.).

horsewhip, s. chicote.

horsewoman, s. cavaleira, amazona.

horticulture, s. horticultura.

hose, s. calções; meias; mangueira; tubo flexível.

hosiery, s. meias; artigos de malha; *hosiery-frame*, máquina de malhas.

hospice, s. hospício; lugar de abrigo e de hospedagem.

hospitable, a. hospitaleiro.

hospital, s. hospital.

hospitality, s. hospitalidade.

hospitalize, v.t. hospitalizar.

host, s. hóspede; hospedeiro; hoste, exército; hóstia sagrada.

hostage, s. refém.

hostel, s. estalagem, pousada.

hostelry, s. hospedaria, pousada.

hostess, hospedeira, anfitriã.

hostile, a. hostil, inimigo; adv. *hostilely*, hostilmente.

hostility, s. hostilidade.

hostler, s. moço de estrebaria, de estalagem; estalajadeiro.

hot, a. quente; fogoso; fervoroso; apaixonado; violento. 1) *to give it hot to someone*, castigar alguém severamente. 2) *to blow hot and cold*, virar a casaca constantemente. 3) *hot-stuff*, pessoa apaixonada ou destemida.

hotbed, *s.* canteiro de terra aquecida por estrume em fermentação; viveiro; *a hotbed vice*, foco de vício.

hot-blooded, *a.* excitável, fogoso; puro-sangue (cavalo).

hotel, *s.* hotel, hospedaria.

hotfoot, *adv.* a toda a pressa; à disparada; *v.i.* apressar-se.

hothead, *s.* pessoa impetuosa, espalha-brasas.

hotheaded, *a.* fogoso, precipitado, arrebatado, exaltado.

hothouse, *s.* estufa para plantas.

hound, *s.* cão de caça; sabujo; *pack of hounds*, matilha de cães. *v.t.* caçar com cães; açular.

hour, *s.* hora; tempo ou ocasião. 1) *hour-glass*, ampulheta. 2) *hour-hand*, ponteiro do relógio. 3) *to keep good hours*, deitar cedo e cedo erguer.

hourly, *s.* de todas as horas; *adv.* a cada hora.

house, *s.* casa, domicílio; casa comercial; família; teatro, auditório; câmara dum corpo lesgislativo. 1) *house-breaker*, assaltante. 2) *house dove*, pessoa caseira. 3) *house master*, dono da casa. 4) *house of Lords*, Câmara dos Pares. 5) *house of Commons*, Câmara dos Deputados. 6) *to have neither house nor home*, não ter eira nem beira; *v.t.* e *v.i.* residir, morar; hospedar; arrecadar; recolher; abrigar-se.

housebroken, *a.* domesticado.

household, *s.* casa, família, governo da casa.

householder, chefe de família; dono de casa.

housekeeper, *s.* dona de casa; governanta.

housekeeping, *s.* governo da casa, economia doméstica.

housemaid, *s.* empregada doméstica.

housetop, *s.* telhado; *to proclaim from the housetops*, anunciar aos quatro ventos.

housewarming, *s.* festa de inauguração duma casa nova.

housewife, *s.* mãe de família; dona de casa; caixa de costura.

housework, *s.* trabalho doméstico.

hovel, *s.* telheiro; cabana; casebre.

hover, *v.i.* pairar, flutuar; rondar, oscilar.

hovering, *a.* pairador, flutuante; hesitante.

how, *adv.* como, de que modo, quanto. 1) *how is your mother?* como está a sua mãe? 2) *how do you do?*, como está?. 3) *how far?* quanto dista? 4) *how long?* quanto tempo? 5) *how many?* quantos? 6) *how much?* quanto? 7) *how so?* como assim? 8) *how old are you?* que idade tem?

howbeit, *adv.* seja como for, não obstante.

however, *adv.* de qualquer maneira; *conj.* contudo, ainda que.

howl, *v.t.* e *v.i.* uivar; gemer; rugir; *s.* uivo; gemido, lamento; grito de raiva ou dor.

howsoever, *adv.* como quer que; por mais que.

hub, *s.* cubo de roda; eixo; *the hub of the Universe*, o centro do Universo.

hubbub, *s.* algazarra, alarido; desordem.

huckster, *s.* bufarinheiro; vendedor ambulante.

huddle, *v.i.* e *v.t.* acotovelar-se; amontoar; agrupar confusamente; vir em tropel; *s.* confusão, barafunda.

hue, *s.* cor, tinta, matiz; aspecto; grito; alarido; gritaria.

huff, *v.t.* ofender, insultar, melindrar; *v.i.* ofender-se, encolerizar-se; *s.* ataque de cólera, acesso de ira; arrogância; amuo.

huffish, *a.* impertinente, rabugento, irascível, arrogante.

huffy, *a.* rabugento, melindroso.

hug, *s.* abraço apertado; *v.t. (hugging, hugged),* abraçar, apertar nos braços.

huge, *a.* enorme, gigantesco, imenso; *adv.* hugely, enormemente.

hulk, *s.* navio velho e inútil; casco de navio; galé; coisa ou pessoa velha e tosca.

hull, *s.* casca, vagem; casco (navio); *v.t.* descascar, debulhar; atingir (navio) no casco.

hum (humming, hummed), *v.t.* e *v.i.* zumbir, zunir; cantarolar; estar em grande actividade; *s.* zumbido, zunido, sussurro; murmúrio.

human, *a.* humano; terreno, mundano; *s.* ser humano.

humane, *a.* humano, humanitário, benevolente.

humanist, *s.* e *a.* humanista.

humanitarian, *a.* e *s.* humanitário, filantropo.

humanity, *s.* humanidade, bondade.

humanize, *v.t.* e *v.i.* humanizar, civilizar.

humankind, s. género humano.

humble, a. humilde; modesto, despretensioso; v.t. humilhar, rebaixar.

humbug, s. fraude, logro; charlatão, embusteiro; v.t. enganar, mistificar; incomodar, importunar (fam.).

humdrum, a. monótono, enfadonho, maçudo; vulgar, imbecil; s. monotonia; vulgaridade; imbecilidade; pessoa maçadora.

humeral, a. umeral.

humerus, s. úmero, braço.

humid, a. húmido.

humidity, s. humidade.

humiliate, v.t. humilhar.

humiliation, s. humilhação, vexame.

humiliatory, a. humilhante, vexatório.

humility, s. humildade, modéstia.

hummingbird, s. beija-flor, colibri.

hummock, s. montículo, outeirinho.

humorist, s. humorista.

humorless, humourless, a. sem senso de humor, sensaborão.

humorous, a. chistoso; gracioso; caprichoso; adv. humorously, jocosamente, caprichosamente.

humorsome, a. caprichoso, petulante; fantasista, inconstante; mal-humorado.

humour, s. humor; índole, disposição; capricho, mania; when the humour takes him, quando se lhe dá na cabeça; v.t. aceder a, consentir em.

hump, s. giba, corcova, corcunda; v.t. e v.i. corcovar, dobrar; esforçar-se.

humpback, s. corcunda, corcova; pessoa corcunda.

humpbacked, a. corcovado.

humph, interj. safa! uf!

humpy, a. giboso, corcunda, corcovado.

humpy-dumpty, s. pessoa baixa e roliça; batoque.

humus, s. húmus.

Hun, s. huno; vândalo.

hunch, s. giba; murro, cotovelada; naco, pedaço grosso; v.t. e v.i. curvar-se, empurrar com o cotovelo.

hunchback, s. pessoa corcunda; corcunda.

hundred, a. e s. cem, cento, centena.

hundredfold, a. cêntuplo, cem vezes.

hundredth, a. e s. centésimo.

hundredwight, s. quintal (peso de 100 kg).

Hungarian, a. e s. húngaro.

hunger, s. fome; desejo ardente; sofreguidão; v.i. ter fome; ansiar por; v.t. esfomear, esfaimar. 1) hunger is the best auce, a fome é o melhor aperitivo. 2) to hunger into submission, submeter pela fome.

hungering, a. faminto, esfaimado; ávido, ansioso.

hungry, a. que tem fome; faminto; ávido, ansioso; que provoca fome, estimulante; pobre, estéril.

hunk, s. pedaço, naco.

hunks, es, s. avarento, sovina.

hunky, s. satisfatório, em bom estado; nome dado aos trabalhadores emigrantes jugoslavos ou húngaros.

hunt, v.t. e v.i. andar à caça; caçar, perseguir. 1) to hunt after, procurar, desejar com ardor. 2) to hunt up and down, procurar por toda a parte; s. caça, caçada, montaria; grupo de caçadores ou lugar onde decorre a caçada.

hunter, s. caçador; cavalo ou cão de caça.

hunting, s. caçada; a. da caça. 1) hunting-ground, campo de caça. 2) hunting-knife, faca de mato. 3) hunting match ou party, partida de caça.

huntress, s. caçadora.

huntsman, s. caçador.

huntsmanship, s. qualidades necessárias à condição de bom caçador.

hurdle, s. tapume de vimes ou varas; valado; cancela móvel; v.t. fechar com cancelas de vimes; fazer cercas de vimes.

hurl, v.t. atirar com violência; arremessar; s. tumulto, confusão.

hurler, s. o que atira ou arremessa; jogador do desporto "hurling".

hurley, s. jogo do hóquei ou bastão nele usado.

hurling, s. jogo da péla.

hurly-burly, s. tumulto, confusão, alvoroço.

hurrah, s. exclamação de alegria; interj. hurra!, viva!; v.t. e v.i. aclamar.

hurricane, s. furacão, tufão, vendaval.

hurry, s. pressa, precipitação, confusão; v.t. e v.i. apressar-se; acelerar; atropelar. 1) hurry up!, despache-se, avie-se. 2) to be in a hurry, estar com pressa.

hurst, s. montículo.

hurt, v.t. e v.i. magoar; ofender; prejudicar, fazer mal; doer; s. ferimento; lesão; dano; dor.

hurtful, a. prejudicial, nocivo, doloroso.

hurtle, v.t. arremessar; v.i. chocar-se, colidir.

hurtless, a. inofensivo.

husband, s. marido, esposo.

husbandman, s. agricultor, lavrador.

husbandry, s. administração da casa; economia; agricultura, lavoura.

hush, v.t. calar, silenciar, aquietar; v.i. calar-se, aquietar-se. s. silêncio, calada; *hush-money*, dinheiro com que se compra o silêncio de alguém.

hush-hush, a. secreto, feito em segredo.

husk, s. casca, vagem; v.t. descascar, debulhar.

huskiness, s. qualidade do que é cascudo; rouquidão.

husking, s. acção de descascar, debulha.

husky, a. cascudo, seco, áspero, rouco; adv. *huskily*, roucamente.

Husky, s. esquimó, língua esquimó.

hussy, s. rapariga ladina; sirigaita.

hustle, v.t. e v.i. empurrar, acotovelar rudemente; batalhar; s. atropelo.

hustler, s. fura-vidas.

hut, s. cabana, barraca; v.t. abarracar, aquartelar.

hutch, s. arca, cofre; v.t. entesourar.

huzza, interj. viva!

hyacinth, s. jacinto.

hybrid, a. e s. híbrido.

hybridize, v.t. e v.i. produzir híbridos; tornar-se híbrido; cruzar; miscigenizar.

hydrant, s. hidrante; boca de incêndio.

hydration, s. hidratação.

hydraulic, a. hidráulico.

hydraulics, s. hidráulica.

hydrogen, s. hidrogénio.

hydrophobia, s. hidrofobia.

hydroplane, s. hidroavião.

hydroscope, s. hidroscópio.

hydrostatics, s. hidrostática.

hyena, hyaena, s. hiena.

hygiene, s. higiene.

hygienic, a. higiénico, sanitário; adv. *hygienically*, higienicamente.

hygienist, s. higienista.

hymen, s. hímen; casamento, núpcias.

hymeneal, a. nupcial; s. canto nupcial.

hymn, s. hino, cântico de louvor; v.t. e v.i. celebrar em hino; cantar hinos.

hyperbole, s. hipérbole.

hyperbolic, a. hiperbólico; adv. *hyperbolically*, hiperbolicamente.

hypercritical, a. hipercrítico.

hypersensitive, a. hipersensível.

hyphen, s. hífen, traço de união; v.t. hifenizar, ligar com hífen.

hypnosis, s. hipnose.

hypnotic, a. e s. hipnótico; hipnotizado (indivíduo).

hypnotist, s. hipnotizador.

hypnotize, v.t. hipnotizar.

hypochondria, s. hipocondria (med.), melancolia.

hypochondriac, a. hipocondríaco (med.).

hypodrisy, s. hipocrisia; falsidade.

hipocrite, s. hipócrita; impostor.

hypocritical, a. hipócrita, falso; adv. *hipocritically*, hipocritamente.

hypothesis, s. hipótese; conjectura.

hypothetical, a. hipotético.

hysteretic, a. histerético (fis. e magn.).

hysteria, s. histeria, histerismo.

hysterical, histeric, a. histérico.

hysterics, s. crise histérica; histeria.

I

i, nona letra do alfabeto.

iamb, s. jambo.

iambic, a. jâmbico; s. jambo, verso jâmbico.

iambus, s. jambo.

Iberian, a. e s. ibero.

ibis, s. íbis (ave).

ice, s. gelo; sorvete; *to break the ice*, pôr a formalidade de lado; v.t. gelar; cobrir de gelo ou de açúcar cristalizado.

iceberg, s. icebergue, montanha de gelo flutuante.

icebound, a. bloqueado, retido ou obstruído pelo gelo.

icebox, s. geladeira, frigorífico.

ice-cream, s. sorvete.

iced, a. coberto de gelo; gelado; coberto com açúcar cristalizado.

Iceland, s. Islândia.

Icelander, s. islandês.

icicle, s. pingente de gelo; caramelo.

icily, adv. gelidamente.

iciness, s. gelidez, frigidez, frieza.

icing, s. crosta de açúcar ou merengue com que se cobre bolos; *adj.* coberto de açúcar.

icon, s. ícone, imagem sagrada.

iconolast, s. iconoclasta.

icy, *a.* frio, indiferente.

idea, s. ideia, s. ideia, conceito; concepção; propósito.

ideal, s. ideal, perfeição; *a.* ideal; mental; perfeito.

idealism, s. idealismo.

idealist, s. idealista; visionário; sonhador.

idealistic, idealistical, *a.* idealista, idealístico; *adv. idealistically,* idealisticamente.

idealize, *v.t.* idealizar, formar um ideal; sublimar.

ideate, *v.t.* idear, conceber, imaginar; evocar.

idem, *pron.* idem, o mesmo.

identical, identic, *a.* idêntico; *adv. identically,* identicamente.

identificable, *a.* identificável.

identification, s. identificação.

identify, *v.t.* identificar.

identity, s. identidade.

ideology, s. ideologia.

idiocrasy, s. idiossincrasia, idiocrasia.

idiocy, s. imbecilidade, idiotismo.

idiom, s. idioma, língua.

idiomatic, idiomatical, *a.* idiomático; vernáculo; *adv. idiomatically,* idiomaticamente.

idiosyncrasy, s. idiossincrasia; peculiaridade.

idiot, s. idiota; tolo, néscio; parvo.

idiotic, idiotical, *a.* idiota, idiótico; insensato, absurdo.

idiotism, s. idiotice, imbecilidade; idiotia.

idle, *a.* ocioso, preguiçoso, inútil; *v.t.* e *v.i.* mandriar, estar ocioso; desperdiçar; *adv. idly,* preguiçosamente.

idleness, s. preguiça; frivolidade.

idler, s. ocioso, preguiçoso, mandrião.

idol, s. ídolo.

idolater, s. idólatra; adorador.

idolatrize, *v.t.* e *v.i.* idolatrar, adorar; praticar a idolatria.

idolatry, s. idolatria.

idolize, *v.t.* idolatrar.

idyl, idyll, s. idílio.

idyllic, *a.* idílico.

if, *conj.* se, ainda que, suposto que, quando mesmo.

ignitable, ignitible, *a.* inflamável.

ignite, *v.t.* e *v.i.* inflamar(-se); acender(-se); pegar fogo.

ignition, s. ignição; combustão.

ignoble, *a.* ignóbil, desprezível, baixo.

ignominious, *a.* ignominioso, vergonhoso; desprezível.

ignominy, s. ignomínia; infâmia.

ignorance, s. ignorância; desconhecimento.

ignorant, *a.* ignorante, desconhecedor; *to be ignorant of,* ignorar, desconhecer; *adv. ignorantly,* ignorantemente.

ignore, *v.t.* ignorar, desconhecer; desprezar.

ileus, s. volvo, vólvulo (med.).

iliac, s. e *a.* ilíaco (anat.).

ill, *a.* doente; mau, ruim; s. mal, malícia; *adv.* mal; *to take ill,* levar a mal.

ill-advised, *a.* impensado, imprudente.

illation, s. ilação, conclusão.

ill-bred, *a.* malcriado, mal-educado.

illegal, *a.* ilegal, ilícito; *adv. illegally,* legalmente.

illegality, s. ilegalidade.

illegible, *a.* ilegível, indecifrável.

illegitimacy, s. ilegitimidade.

illegitimate, *a.* ilegítimo; ilegal; bastardo; desautorizado.

ill-fated, *a.* malfadado, desditoso.

ill-favored, ill-favoured, *a.* feio, desgracioso; desagradável.

ill-humored, ill-humoured, *a.* mal-humorado, zangado.

illicit, *a.* ilícito; ilegal; proibido.

illimitable, *a.* ilimitável, ilimitado, imenso.

illiteracy, s. falta de instrução; analfabetismo.

illiterate, *a.* e s. iletrado, ignorante, analfabeto.

ill-looking, *a.* feio; mal-encarado; que tem mau aspecto.

ill-mannered, *a.* mal-educado; grosseiro.

ill-natured, *a.* mal-humorado; rabugento; maldoso.

illness, s. doença, enfermidade.

illogical, *a.* ilógico; *adv. illogically,* ilogicamente.

ill-tempered, *a.* mal-humorado, de mau génio.

ill-treat, *v.t.* maltratar; insultar.

illume, *v.t.* iluminar, alumiar.

illuminate, *v.t.* iluminar; esclarecer.

illumination, s. iluminação; revelação; esclarecimento.

illumine, *v.t.* e *v.i.* iluminar-se; esclarecer; inspirar.

illuminism, s. iluminismo.

ill-use, *v.t.* maltratar; insultar.

illusion, s. ilusão.

illusive, illusory, a. ilusório, enganoso, falaz.

illustrate, v.t. ilustrar; esclarecer, exemplificar.

illustration, s. ilustração; exemplo.

illustrative, a. ilustrativo, elucidativo.

illustrator, s. ilustrador, desenhista.

illustrious, a. ilustre, nobre, célebre; adv. *Ilustriously,* ilustremente.

ill-wisher, a. adversário, inimigo.

illy, adv. mal.

image, s. imagem; figura; ideia.

imagery, s. imagens mentais; fantasias; figuras de retórica.

imaginable, a. imaginável, concebível; adv. *imaginably,* imaginavelmente.

imaginary, a. imaginário, irreal, fictício.

imagination, s. imaginação.

imagine, v.t. e v.i. imaginar, fantasiar; conceber; supor, pensar, conjecturar.

imbecile, a. e s. imbecil.

imbecility, s. imbecilidade.

imbibe, v.t. e v.i. absorver, chupar; embeber, assimilar (ideias); banhar, ensopar.

imbroglio, s. misturada; trapalhada, enredo.

imbrue, v.t. manchar, tingir, empapar (de sangue).

imbue, v.t. impregnar, embeber; inspirar (com sentimentos); imbuir.

imitable, a. imitável.

imitate, v.t. imitar, copiar.

imitation, s. imitação; cópia, reprodução; a. de imitação, artificial.

imitative, a. imitativo, imitador.

imitator, s. imitador.

immaculate, a. imaculado.

immaterial, a. imaterial, espiritual; insignificante.

immaterialize, v.t. imaterializar, espiritualizar.

immature, a. imaturo.

immaturity, s. imaturidade.

immeasurable, a. imensurável, imenso.

immediate, a. imediato; directo; pronto; *immediately,* imediatamente.

immedicable, a. imedicável; incurável.

immemorial, a. imemorial, antiquíssimo.

immense, a. imenso, infinito; enorme.

immensity, s. imensidade, imensidão; enormidade.

immensurable, a. imensurável.

immerge, v.t. mergulhar, imergir; v.i. afundar-se.

immerse, v.t. mergulhar, imergir, afundar; enterrar.

immersion, s. imersão, submersão, mergulho.

immigrant, a. e s. imigrante; imigrado.

immigrate, v.i. imigrar.

immigration, s. imigração.

imminent, a. iminente.

immobile, a. imóvel, fixo.

immobility, s. imobilidade, fixidez.

immobilize, v.t. imobilizar, fixar.

immoderate, a. imoderado, excessivo, exagerado; adv. *immoderately,* imoderadamente.

immoderation, s. imoderação, excesso.

immodest, a. imodesto, ousado, indecente; adv. *immodestly,* imodestamente.

immolate, v.t. imolar, sacrificar.

immoral, a. imoral; adv. *immorally,* imoralmente.

immorality, s. imoralidade.

immortal, a. imortal; adv. *immortally,* imortalmente.

immorality, s. imortalidade.

immortalize, v.t. imortalizar.

immovable, a. imóvel; inamovível.

immune, a. imune, imunizado; s. imune, pessoa imune.

immunity, s. imunidade, isenção.

immunize, v.t. imunizar.

immure, v.t. emparedar; encarcerar.

immutable, a. imutável, inalterável.

imp, s. rebento, filho; diabinho, diabrete.

impact, s. impacte, choque, colisão; v.t. embutir, fixar; comprimir.

impacted, a. encravado; incluso (dente).

impair, v.t. deteriorar, danificar, estragar; depreciar.

impale, v.t. empalar; espetar.

impalement, s. empalação.

impalpable, a. impalpável; intangível.

impart, v.t. dar, conceder; fazer saber, comunicar.

impartial, a. imparcial, justo.

impartiality, s. imparcialidade.

impassable, a. intransitável, impraticável.

impasse, s. impasse, beco sem saída, dificuldade.

impassible, a. impassível, insensível.

impassion, v.t. apaixonar, arrebatar.

impassionate, a. apaixonado, ardente, exaltado.

impassive, a. impassível, indiferente; calmo, sereno.

impatience, s. impaciência.

impatient, a. impaciente, irritável, inquieto, nervoso.

impavid, a. impávido, destemido.

impawn, v.t. penhorar, empenhar.

impeach, v.t. acusar, denunciar.

impeachment, s. acusação, denúncia.

impeccable, a. impecável; irrepreensível.

impeccant, a. sem pecado, inocente.

impede, v.t. impedir, estorvar, dificultar.

impedient, a. impediente, impeditivo; s. impedidor.

impediment, s. impedimento, estorvo, embaraço.

impeditive, a. impeditivo; obstrutivo.

impel (impelling, impelled), v.t. impelir; incitar.

impellent, a. e s. impulsor, instigador.

impend, v.i. impender, pender; ameaçar, estar iminente.

impendent, a. impendente, suspenso; ameaçador.

impenetrable, a. impenetrável; inacessível.

impenetrate, v.t. penetrar profundamente; repassar.

impenitent, a. impenitente; adv. impenitently, impenitentemente.

imperative, a. imperativo, imperioso; s. imperativo, ordem, imposição.

imperator, s. imperador.

imperceptible, a. imperceptível.

imperfect, a. imperfeito, defeituoso.

imperfection, s. imperfeição: defeito.

imperial, a. imperial; s. imperial; pêra no queixo.

imperialism, s. imperialismo.

imperialist, a. e s. imperialista.

imperil (imperilling, emperilled), v.t. pôr em perigo; arriscar.

imperious, a. imperioso, autoritário.

imperishable, a. imperecível, imorredouro.

imperium, s. império.

impermeable, a. impermeável, estanque.

impersonal, a. impessoal.

impersonate, v.t. personificar, simbolizar.

impersonation, s. personificação.

impertinent, a. impertinente.

imperturbable, a. imperturbável, impassível.

imperturbation, s. calma, serenidade.

impervious, a. intransitável, impenetrável; impermeável.

impetuous, a. impetuoso; impulsivo.

impetus, s. ímpeto, incentivo; estímulo.

impiety, s. impiedade.

impinge, v.i. chocar-se, colidir; infringir; ir de encontro a.

impious, a. ímpio.

impish, a. endiabrado, travesso.

implacable, a. implacável.

implead, v.t. e v.i. demandar, processar.

implement, s. instrumento.

implemental, a. eficaz.

implicate, v.t. envolver, implicar, enredar.

implication, s. implicação; enredo.

implicative, a. implicativo.

implicit, a. implícito; tácito; adv. implicitly, implicitamente.

implore, v.t. implorar, suplicar.

imploring, a. implorativo, suplicante; adv. imploringly, implorantemente.

imply, v.t. implicar, envolver; insinuar; significar.

impolite, a. descortês, grosseiro; adv. impolitely, grosseiramente.

import, v.t. importar; implicar, significar; ser de consequência; s. importância, consequência; significação.

importance, s. importância.

important, a. importante; adv. importantly, importantemente.

importation, s. importação.

importunate, a. importuno.

importune, v.t. e v.i. importunar; a. importuno, insistente.

impose, v.t. impor; impingir; tirar proveito de; enganar.

imposing, a. imponente, grandioso.

imposition, s. imposição; exigência; impostura.

impossibility, s. impossibilidade.

impossible, a. impossível.

impost, s. imposto.

impostor, s. impostor, embusteiro.

imposture, s. impostura, embuste.

impotence, s. impotência; incapacidade.

impotent, a. impotente; incapaz.

impoverish, v.t. empobrecer; arruinar.

imprecate, v.t. imprecar, invocar.

imprecation, s. imprecação, praga; invocação.

impregnable, a. fecundável.

impregnate, v.t. emprenhar, fecundar; impregnar.

impresario, s. empresário, (esp.) companhia teatral, etc.

impress, v.t. imprimir; impressionar, comover; recrutar (à força), requisitar; s.

impressão, estampagem; cunho, selo; recrutamento forçado; requisição.

impressible, *a.* impressionante; impressível; *adv. impressibly,* dum modo impressível.

impression, *s.* impressão, gravação; marca, sinal; mossa; ideia, recordação; edição, impressão.

impressionable, *a.* impressionável, sensível.

impressionism, *s.* impressionismo.

imprint, *v.t.* imprimir, estampar, marcar; *s.* impressão, marca, nome do editor.

imprision, *v.t.* prender, encarcerar.

imprisonment, *s.* prisão, detenção.

improbable, *a.* improvável; inverosímil; *adv. improbably,* improvavelmente.

improbity, *s.* improbidade; desonestidade.

impromptu, *adv.* e *a.* de improviso, improvisado; *s.* improviso, improvisação.

improper, *a.* impróprio, inconveniente; incorrecto; indecoroso.

impropriety, *s.* impropriedade; inexactidão; indecência.

improvable, *a.* aproveitável; que se pode melhorar.

improve, *v.t.* e *v.i.* aperfeiçoar(-se); melhorar.

improvement, *s.* melhoria, progresso; melhoramento; aumento.

improvident, *a.* imprevidente; negligente; impróvido.

improving, *a.* melhorador; que progride.

improvisation, *s.* improvisação; improviso.

improvise, *v.t.* e *v.i.* improvisar.

imprudent, *a.* imprudente, descuidado.

imprudence, impudency, *s.* descaramento, impertinência, atrevimento.

imprudent, *a.* descarado, desavergonhado; petulante, insolente.

impudicity, *s.* despudor, imodéstia.

impugn, *v.t.* impugnar, combater, contestar.

impuissant, *a.* impotente, fraco.

impulse, *s.* impulso.

impulsion, *s.* impulsão; ímpeto.

impulsive, *a.* impulsivo, impetuoso; *adv. impulsively,* impulsivamente.

impunity, *s.* impunidade.

impure, *a.* impuro; sujo; poluído; adulterado; lascivo, obsceno.

impurity, *s.* impureza, lascívia.

imputable, *a.* imputável, atribuível; *adv. imputably,* imputavelmente.

imputation, *s.* imputação; acusação.

imputative, *a.* imputado, atribuído; acusatório; *adv. imputatively,* por imputação.

impute, *v.t.* imputar, atribuir.

in, *prep.* em, por, a, de, durante (indicando tempo, lugar, modo). 1) *in time,* com tempo, a tempo. 2) *in two days,* dentro de dois dias, daqui a dois dias. 3) *in writing,* por escrito. 4) *in love,* apaixonado. 5) *in that,* porque. 6) *in earnest,* deveras. 7) *in cash,* com dinheiro, a dinheiro; a. interno. 8) *in-patient,* doente interno, internado em hospital; *adv.* dentro, em casa. 9) *you are in for it,* estás em maus lençóis. 10) *keep the boy in,* não deixes sair o rapaz; *s.* (pl.) partido que está no poder, 11) *the ins and outs,* entradas e saídas, cantos e recantos; pormenores.

inability, *s.* inaptidão; incapacidade.

inaccessible, *a.* inacessível; impenetrável; *adv. inaccessibly,* inacessivelmente.

inaccurate, *a.* inexacto, incorrecto.

inaction, *s.* inacção; inércia.

inactive, *a.* inactivo, ocioso; inerte.

inadequate, *a.* inadequado, inadaptado; impróprio.

inadmissible, *a.* inadmissível.

inadvertence, *s.* inadvertência, descuido, negligência.

inadvertent, *a.* desatento; descuidado; irreflectido.

inadvisable, *a.* desaconselhável; inoportuno.

inalienable, *a.* inalienável; *adv. inalienably,* inalienavelmente.

inalterable, *a.* inalterável; inabalável; *adv. inalterabilty,* inalteravelmente.

inane, *a.* oco, vazio, fútil; *s.* vácuo; *adv. inanely,* sem efeito.

inanimate, *a.* inanimado, sem vida; sem animação; *adv. inanimately,* desanimadamente.

inanition, *s.* inanidade; inanição.

inappetence, inappetency, *s.* indiferença; fastio.

inapplicable, *a.* inaplicável; impraticável; *adv. inapplicably,* impraticavelmente.

inappropriate, *a.* não apropriado, impróprio.

inapt, *a.* inapto; incompetente.

inaptitude, *s.* inaptidão, incapacidade.

inasmuch as, *conj.* visto que, considerando que, porquanto.

inattention, *s.* desatenção, inatenção; desconsideração.

inattentive, *a.* desatento; descortês; *adv. inattentively,* descuidadamente.

inaudible, *a.* inaudível; *adv. inaudibly,* inaudivelmente.

inaugural, *a.* inaugural, inaugurativo.

inaugurate, *v.t.* inaugurar, investir, instalar; iniciar.

inauguration, *s.* inauguração; posse, investidura; início, fundação.

inauspicious, *a.* de mau agouro, sinistro, nefasto, malfadado, infeliz; *adv. inauspiciously,* desgraçadamente, infelizmente.

inboard, *adv.* dentro (do interior dum navio), a bordo.

inborn, *a.* inato, ingénito.

inbred, *a.* congénito.

incalculable, *a.* incalculável; considerável; imprevisível.

incandescent, *a.* incandescente.

incantation, *s.* encantamento; magia.

incapable, *a.* incapaz; incompetente; *adv. incapably,* incompetentemente.

incapacious, *a.* limitado, acanhado; mentalmente deficiente.

incapacitate, *v.t.* incapacitar, impossibilitar, inabilitar.

incapacity, *s.* incapacidade; incompetência.

incarcerate, *v.t.* encarcerar, aprisionar.

incarnate, *a.* encarnado; personificado; *v.t.* e *v.i.* encarnar, revestir de carne; personificar.

incarnation, *s.* encarnação; personificação.

incase, *v.t.* encaixar, encaixotar; forrar.

incaution, *s.* descuido, imprudência.

incautious, *a.* incauto, descuidado, imprudente; *adv. incautiously,* incautamente.

incendiary, *a.* incendiário; revolucionário; *s.* incendiário, agitador.

incense, *s.* incenso; *incense-burner,* turíbulo; lisonja; *v.t.* incensar; exasperar, provocar.

incentive, *s.* incentivo, estímulo; *a.* incentivo, estimulante.

incept, *v.i.* começar, iniciar.

inception, *s.* princípio.

inceptive, *a.* incipiente, principiante.

incertitude, *s.* incerteza, dúvida; insegurança.

incessant, *a.* incessante, constante; repetido.

incest, *s.* incesto.

incestuous, *a.* incestuoso; *adv. incestuously,* incestuosamente.

inch, *s.* polegada (2,54 cm.); pequena quantidade. 1) *within an inch,* pouco mais ou menos. 2) *inch by inch,* pouco a pouco. 3) *give him an inch and he'll take mile,* se lhe dás o pé, tomar-te-á a mão; *v.t.* e *v.i.* avançar (aos poucos); medir polegadas.

incidence, *s.* incidência.

incident, *a.* incidente, possível, provável, eventual; *s.* incidente, acidente; ocorrência; casualidade.

incidental, *a.* incidental, casual; *adv. incidentally,* incidentalmente.

incinerate, *v.t.* incinerar, reduzir a cinzas; cremar.

incinerator, *s.* incinerador; forno de incineração.

incipient, *a.* incipiente; *adv. incipiently,* no começo.

incisive, *a.* incisivo; penetrante; mordaz; *adv. incisively,* incisivamente.

incisor, *s.* incisivo (dente).

incite, *v.t.* incitar, instigar, estimular.

inclement, *a.* inclemente, severo, cruel; *adv. inclemently,* inclementemente.

inclination, *s.* inclinação, tendência; declive.

incline, *s.* declive; *v.t.* e *v.i.* inclinar-se, pender, curvar, inclinar; *well inclined,* bem--intencionado.

inclose, *v.t.* cercar; incluir, conter.

inclosure, *s.* cercado, valado; cerca; conteúdo.

include, *v.t.* incluir, conter.

included, *a.* incluído, contido.

including, *a.* incluindo, compreendendo; incluso.

inclusion, *s.* inclusão; restrição.

inclusive, *a.* inclusivo; *inclusive charge:* preço sem extras, preço total; *adv. inclusively,* inclusivamente.

incognito, *a., adv.* e *s.* incógnito, desconhecido, disfarçado.

incoherence, *s.* incoerência.

incoherent, *a.* incoerente, desagregado.

incombustible, *a.* e *s.* incombustível.

income, *s.* renda, rendimento, receita.

incomer, *s.* recém-chegado; visitante; imigrante; intruso.

incommode, *v.t.* incomodar, aborrecer; estorvar.

incommunicable, *a.* incomunicável.

incomparable, *a.* incomparável; *adv. incomparably,* incomparavelmente.

incompatible, *a.* incompatível; *adv. incompatibly,* incompativelmente.

incompetence, incompetency, *s.* incompetência, incapacidade; insuficiência.

incompetent, *a.* incompetente, incapaz, inábil; *s.* pessoa incompetente, incapaz; *adv. incompetently,* incompetentemente.

incomplete, *a.* incompleto, inacabado, imperfeito; *adv. incompletly,* incompletamente.

incomprehensible, *a.* incompreensível; *adv. incomprehensibly,* incompreensivelmente.

incomprehension, *s.* incompreensão.

incomprehensive, *a.* incompreensivo.

inconceivable, *a.* inconcebível, inimaginável.

inconformity, *s.* inconformidade, desacordo, inconformismo.

incongruent, *a.* incongruente, incoerente; *adv. incongruently,* incoerentemente.

incongruity, *s.* incongruência, incoerência.

incongruous, *a.* incongruente, desproporcionado; *adv. incongruously,* incongruentemente.

inconsequence, *s.* inconsequência.

inconsequent, *a.* inconsequente; ilógico.

inconsiderable, *a.* insignificante, de pouca importância.

inconsiderate, *a.* inconsiderado; irreflectido.

inconsideration, *s.* inconsideração, inadvertência; indelicadeza.

inconsistence, inconsistency, *s.* inconsistência; incompatibilidade.

inconsistent, *a.* inconsistente; incompatível; inconsequente.

inconsolable, *a.* inconsolável, desconsolado.

inconstant, *a.* inconstante, volúvel; instável, irregular; *adv. inconstantly,* inconstantemente.

incontinent, *a.* incontinente; devasso, dissoluto; *adv. incontinently,* incontinentemente.

incontrovertible, *a.* incontestável, indiscutível.

inconvenient, *a.* incómodo; difícil; inconveniente; *adv. inconveniently,* inconvenientemente.

inconvertible, *a.* inconvertível.

incorporate, *a.* incorporado; unido; *v.t.* e *v.i.* incorporar; unir; formar grémio ou corpo; juntar-se, ligar-se.

incorporation, *s.* incorporação; associação.

incorrect, *a.* incorrecto, inconveniente; erróneo, inexacto; *adv. incorrectly,* incorrectamente.

incorrigible, *a.* e *s.* incorrigível, indócil; *adv. incorrigibly,* incorrigivelmente.

incorruptible, *a.* incorruptível; *adv. incorruptibly,* incorruptivelmente.

increase, *v.t.* e *v.i.* aumentar, acrescentar; crescer, multiplicar-se; *s.* aumento; lucro; crescimento; proliferação; prole, descendência, *on the increase,* aumentando.

incredible, *a.* incrível, inacreditável; *adv. incredibly,* incrivelmente.

incredulity, *s.* incredulidade, cepticismo.

increment, *s.* incremento, aumento, crescimento.

increscent, *a.* crescente.

incriminate, *v.t.* incriminar, acusar.

incrimination, *s.* acusação.

incrust, *v.t.* incrustar.

incrustation, *s.* incrustação; crosta.

incubate, *v.t.* e *v.i.* incubar, chocar.

incubation, *s.* incubação.

incubator, *s.* incubadora.

incubus, *s.* íncubo; pesadelo; opressor.

inculcate, *v.t.* inculcar, incutir.

inculpable, *a.* inculpável, inocente.

inculpate, *v.t.* e *v.i.* incriminar; acusar; censurar.

incult, *a.* inculto; rude, grosseiro.

incumbent, *a.* deitado, reclinado; obrigatório; *s.* beneficiado (ecles.), aquele que exerce cargo, titular; *adv. incumbently,* de modo obrigatório.

incur (incurring, incurred), *v.t.* ficar sujeito a; incorrer em; acarretar; suscitar.

incurable, *a.* incurável, irremediável; *s.* incurável; *adv. incurably,* incuravelmente.

incurious, *a.* descuidado, desatento; desinteressado; *adv. incuriously,* descuidadamente.

incurrence, *s.* incurso, acto de incorrer; responsabilidade.

incursion, *s.* incursão, invasão.

indebt, *v.t.* endividar, tornar devedor.

indebted, *a.* endividado; em dívida, devedor.

indebtedness, *s.* dívida, débito; obrigação.

indecency, *s.* indecência, imoralidade.

indecent, *a.* indecente, indecoroso, imoral; *adv. indecently,* indecentemente.

indecision, *s.* indecisão, irresolução, vacilação.

indecisive, *a.* indeciso, irresoluto, hesitante; incerto, duvidoso.

indecorous, *a.* indecoroso, impróprio, inconveniente; *adv. indecorously,* indecorosamente.

indecorum, *s.* inconveniência, indecoro.

indeed, *adv.* realmente, na verdade, de facto, deveras; *a friend in need is a friend indeed,* os amigos são para as ocasiões; *interj.* sim, será verdade!

indefatigable, *a.* infatigável, incansável.

indefeasible, *a.* indestrutível; irrevogável;

adv. *indefeasibly*, indestrutivelmente; irrevogavelmente.

indefensible, *a.* indefensável; indefeso; *adv. indefensibly,* dum modo indefeso.

indefinable, *a.* indefinível, indescritível; *s.* coisa indefinível; *adv. indefinably,* indefinidamente.

indefinite, *a.* indefinido, indeterminado; *adv. indefinitely,* indefinidamente.

indeliable, *a.* indelével; inapagável; *adv. indelibly,* indelevelmente.

indemnification, *s.* indemnização.

indemnify, *v.t.* indemnizar, ressarcir; imunizar.

indemnity, *s.* indemnidade, indemnização, ressarcimento.

indent, *s.* recorte dentado; impressão; encomenda, requisição; *v.t.* e *v.i.* recortar, dentear; amolgar; fazer uma requisição, uma encomenda do estrangeiro.

indentation, *s. s.* recorte dentado; amolgadela.

indenture, *s.* contrato, ajuste, pacto; carta de chamada.

independence, *s.* independência, libertação; abastança, renda própria.

independency, *s.* independência, autonomia; estado ou província independente.

independent, *a.* independente, livre; *s.* pessoa independente; *adv. independently,* independentemente.

indescribable, *a.* indescritível; indefinível; *adv. indescribably,* indescritivelmente.

indeterminate, *a.* indeterminado, incerto; indeciso; *adv. indeterminately,* indeterminadamente.

indetermination, *s.* indeterminação, irresolução.

index, *s.* índex, dedo índex; índice; indício; (mat.) expoente; indicador; lista de livros proibidos pela Igreja Católica; alidade do sextante (náut.).

Indian, *a.* e *s.* Indiano (da Índia); índio (da América). 1) *indian ink,* tinta-da-china. 2) *indian summer,* verão de S. Martinho.

indicate, *v.t.* indicar, designar, enunciar.

indication, *s.* indicação, sinal, sintoma; designação; menção; informação.

indicative, *a.* indicativo, indicador, designativo; *adv. indicatively,* indicativamente.

indicator, *s.* indicador; manómetro.

indict, *v.t.* denunciar, acusar; pronunciar.

indictable, *a.* sujeito a denúncia ou a processo.

indictment, *s.* acusação escrita.

indifference, *s.* indiferença; apatia; neutralidade.

indifferent, *a.* indiferente, desapegado, desinteressado; apático; neutro; *indifferently,* indiferentemente.

indigence, *s.* indigência, penúria, miséria.

indigene, indigen, *s.* indígena.

indegenous, *a.* indígena, autóctone, nativo.

indigent, *a.* indigente, pobre.

indigested, *a.* indigesto; mal digerido; não arranjado; disposto sem método.

indigestible, *a.* indigesto.

indigestion, *s.* indigestão; desarranjo.

indign, *a.* indigno; imerecido.

indignant, *a.* indignado, afrontado; *adv. indignantly,* indignadamente.

indignation, *s.* indignação.

indignity, *s.* indignidade; afronta, ultraje.

indigo, *s.* indigo, anil (planta, cor ou corante).

indirect, *a.* indirecto, sinuoso, tortuoso; dissimulado, enganoso, doloso; *adv. indirectly,* indirectamente.

indirectness, *s.* obliquidade; meio indirecto, rodeio.

indiscipline, *s.* indisciplina.

indiscreete, *s.* indiscreto, imprudente, irreflectido.

indiscretion, *s.* indiscrição, imprudência; deslize.

indiscriminate, *a.* indiscriminado, indistinto; promíscuo.

indispensable, *a.* indispensável; essencial.

indispose, *v.t.* indispor; inabilitar.

indisposition, *s.* indisposição, incómodo, mal-estar; aversão, animosidade.

indisputable, *a.* indisputável, incontestável; *adv. indisputably,* indisputavelmente.

indissoluble, *a.* indissolúvel, inseparável; *adv. indissolubly,* indissoluvelmente.

indistinct, *a.* indistinto, vago, obscuro; *adv. indistinctly,* indistintamente.

indistinguishable, *a.* indistinguível.

indite, *v.t.* compor, produzir, redigir.

individual, *a.* individual; particular; *s.* sujeito, pessoa, indivíduo; *adv. individually,* individualmente.

individualism, *s.* individualismo.

individualist, *a.* e *s.* individualista.

individuality, *s.* individualidade, personalidade.

individualize, *v.t.* individualizar, especificar.

indivisible, *a.* e *s.* indivisível; *adv. indivisibly,* indivisivelmente.

indocile, *a.* indócil, insubmisso, indisciplinado.

indocility, *s.* indocilidade.

indolence, *s.* indolência.

indolent, *a.* indolente; *adv. indolently,* indolentemente.

indomitable, *a.* invencível, indomável, inflexível.

indoor, *a.* interior; doméstico; feito portas a dentro.

indoors, *adv.* portas a dentro; ao abrigo.

indubitable, *a.* indubitável, certo; *adv. indubitably,* indubitavelmente.

induce, *v.t.* induzir, persuadir, instigar; ocasionar, provocar.

inducement, *s.* incentivo; motivo; pretexto.

induct, *v.t.* introduzir, instalar, dar posse.

inductile, *a.* indúctil.

induction, *s.* indução, instalação, introdução.

inductive, *a.* indutivo; *adv. inductively,* por indução.

inductor, *s.* instalador; indutor.

indulge, *v.t.* e *v.i.* favorecer, satisfazer, entregar-se a, gozar.

indulgence, *s.* indulgência, complacência; prorrogação, moratória (com.).

indulgent, *a.* indulgente, condescendente; *adv. indulgently,* indulgentemente.

indult, *s.* indulto.

indurate, *v.t.* e *v.i.* endurecer; endurecer-se, empedernir-se.

industrial, *a.* industrial; *s.* industrial, industriário; *adv. industrially,* industrialmente.

industrialize, *v.t.* industrializar.

industrious, *a.* industrioso, hábil, laborioso; *adv. industriously,* industriosamente.

industry, *s.* indústria; diligência; trabalho.

indwell, *v.t.* e *v.i.* residir, habitar, morar.

indweller, *s.* habitante, morador.

indwelling, *s.* residência; *a.* íntimo.

inearth, *v.t.* inumar, enterrar, sepultar.

inebriant, *a.* inebriante, embriagador; *s.* bebida inebriante.

inebriate, *a.* e *s.* embriagado; bêbedo, ébrio.

inebriation, inebriety, *s.* inebriamento, embriaguez; bebedeira; alcoolismo.

inedible, *a.* não comestível.

inedited, *a.* inédito, não publicado.

ineffable, *a.* inefável; *adv. ineffably,* inefavelmente.

ineffective, *a.* ineficaz, inútil, baldado.

ineffectual, *a.* ineficaz, infrutífero; fracassado; *adv. ineffectually,* baldadamente.

inefficiency, *s.* ineficiência; ineficácia.

inefficient, *a.* ineficiente, ineficaz; incapaz; *adv. inefficiently,* ineficientemente.

ineluctable, *a.* inelutável, inevitável, irresistível.

ineludible, *a.* iniludível.

inenarrable, *a.* inarrável.

inept, *a.* inepto; incapaz; inexperiente; absurdo; *adv. ineptly,* ineptamente.

inequality, *s.* desigualdade; irregularidade.

inequitable, *a.* iníquo, injusto.

inert, *a.* inerte, inactivo; indolente; *adv. inertly,* indolentemente.

inertia, *s.* inércia.

inestimable, *a.* inestimável; inapreciável, excelente.

inevitable, *a.* inevitável; *adv. inevitably,* inevitavelmente.

inexcusable, *a.* indesculpável, imperdoável.

inexhaustible, *a.* inesgotável; *adv. inexhaustibly,* inesgotavelmente.

inexistent, *a.* inexistente.

inexorable, *a.* inexorável, implacável; *adv. inexorably,* inexoravelmente.

inexpedient, *a.* impróprio; inconveniente, inoportuno.

inexpensive, *a.* barato, económico.

inexperience, *s.* inexperiência.

inexperienced, *a.* inexperiente, inábil.

inexpert, *a.* e *s.* imperito, inexperto, inábil.

inexplicable, *a.* inexplicável; incompreensível; *adv. inexplicably,* inexplicavelmente.

inexplicit, *a.* não explícito, não claro.

inexpressible, *a.* inexprimível, indizível; *adv. inexpressibly,* indiscritivelmente.

inexpressive, *a.* inexpressivo.

inextinguishable, *a.* inextinguível.

inextricable, *a.* inextricável, indeslindável, insolúvel; *adv. inextricably,* inextricavelmente.

infallible, *a.* infalível; certo; *s.* pessoa ou coisa infalível; *adv. infallibly,* infalivelmente.

infamize, *v.t.* infamar, desonrar; difamar.

infamous, *a.* infame, perverso, vergonhoso; *adv. infamously,* infamemente.

infamy, *s.* infâmia, desonra, ignomínia.

infancy, *s.* infância, meninice.

infant, *s.* infante, criança, menino, bebé; *a.* infante, infantil; tenro.

infanta, *s.* infanta (de sangue real português ou espanhol).

infante, *s.* infante (filho de rei, de Portugal ou Espanha).

infanticide, *s.* infanticídio; infanticida.

infantile, s. infantil, pueril.

infantine, a. infantil.

infantry, s. infantaria.

infatuate, v.t. enfatuar; inspirar uma paixão; transtornar a cabeça; a. enfatuado, loucamente apaixonado, embeiçado.

infatuation, s. paixão louca, enfatuação.

infect, v.t. infectar, infeccionar.

infection, s. infecção, contágio.

infectious, a. infecto, corruptor; adv. infectiously, por infecção.

infer (inferring, infered) v.t. e v.i. deduzir, inferir, concluir.

inference, s. inferência, dedução, conclusão.

inferior, a. e s. inferior, subalterno, secundário.

inferiority, a. inferioridade.

infernal, a. infernal; diabólico; abominável; adv. infernally, infernalmente.

inferno, s. inferno.

infertile, a. infértil, estéril.

infest, v.t. infestar; molestar.

infestation, s. infestação; invasão, praga.

infidel, a. e s. infiel, descrente.

infidelity, s. infidelidade, traição; adultério; descrença.

infiltrate, v.t. infiltrar; v.i. infiltrar-se.

infinite, a. infinito, ilimitado, sem fim, sem limite; s. o infinito; adv. infinitely, infinitamente.

infinitesimal, a. infinitesimal; adv. infinitesimally, num grau infinitesimal.

infinitive, a. e s. infinitivo; o modo infinito.

infinitude, s. infinidade; eternidade.

infinity, s. infinidade, imensidade.

infirm, a. débil, fraco, vacilante, enfermo.

infirmary, s. enfermaria, casa de saúde.

infirmity, s. enfermidade, doença; fraqueza, debilidade.

inflame, v.t. e v.i. inflamar, abrasar; provocar, irritar; inflamar-se.

inflammable, a. inflamável.

inflammation, s. inflamação.

inflammatory, a. inflamatório.

inflate, v.t. inflar, inchar.

inflation, s. inflação (esp. Fin.), inchação; orgulho.

inflator, s. assoprador, que faz inchar.

inflect, v.t. torcer; modular; dobrar, inflectir.

inflection, s. inflexão.

inflexible, a. inflexível.

inflict, v.t. infligir, impor, aplicar.

infliction, s. inflicção, aplicação; maçada; imposição.

inflow, a. afluxo, afluência, influxo.

influence, s. influência; ascendência; autoridade moral; v.t. influir, dirigir.

influent, a. influente; s. afluente.

influenza, s. influenza, gripe.

influx, s. afluência, afluxo; intromissão; desembocadura.

inform, a. informe, sem forma; disforme; v.t. informar, comunicar; ensinar; dar forma.

informal, a. não convencional; irregular; sem cerimónia; adv. informally, irregularmente, sem cerimónia.

informant, s. informante, informador; denunciante.

information, s. informação, notícia; conhecimento; esclarecimento; denúncia, acusação.

informative, a. informativo, informador.

informer, s. informador; delator.

infract, v.t. infringir, violar, quebrar, transgredir.

infraction, s. infracção.

infrequent, a. raro, pouco comum; adv. infrequently, infrequentemente.

infringe, v.t. infringir, violar, invadir.

infringement, s. infracção, violação.

infuriate, v.t. enfurecer, irritar; a. enfurecido, furioso.

infuse, v.t. infundir, inspirar; pôr de infusão.

infusion, s. infusão; inspiração; influência.

ingenious, a. engenhoso; inventivo; adv. ingeniously, engenhosamente.

ingenuity, s. ingenuidade, candura.

ingenuous, a. ingénuo, cândido, inocente; sincero; adv. ingenuously, ingenuamente.

ingenuity, s. ingenuidade, candura.

ingest, v.t. ingerir, engolir.

ingestion, s. ingestão.

inglorious, a. inglório; obscuro; adv. ingloriously, ingloriamente.

ingot, s. lingote, barra de metal.

ingrate, s. pessoa ingrata.

ingratiate, v.t. insinuar-se, ganhar as boas graças.

ingratiating, a. insinuante, cativante; adv. ingratiatingly, insinuantemente.

ingratitude, s. ingratidão.

ingredient, a. ingrediente, componente; s. ingrediente.

ingress, s. ingresso, entrada; acesso; ingress money, jóia.

ingression, s. entrada.

ingrown, a. inato, ingénito; encravada (unha).

ingulf, v.t. engolfar, abismar.

ingurgitate, v.t. e v.i. ingurgitar, devorar, engolir com sofreguidão.

inhabit, v.t. habitar; viver, morar em.

inhabitant, s. habitante, morador.

inhabitation, s. habitação.

inhalation, s. inalação; aspiração.

inhale, v.t. e v.i. inalar, aspirar, inspirar, absorver.

inharmonious, a. desarmonioso, dissonante, desafinado; adv. inharmoniously, desarmoniosamente.

inherence, inherency, s. inerência.

inherent, a. inerente, inato; adv. inherently, inerentemente.

inherit, v.t. herdar, receber em herança, suceder como herdeiro.

inheritance, s. herança; sucessão; posse.

inheritor, s. herdeiro.

inhibit, v.t. inibir, impedir, reprimir.

inhibition, s. inibição.

inhospitable, a. inóspito; adv. inhospitably, sem hospitabilidade.

inhuman, a. inumano, desumano; cruel, brutal.

inhumane, a. desumano, impiedoso; adv. inhumanely, desumanamente.

inhumanity, s. desumanidade, crueldade.

inimical, a. inimigo, hostil; adv. inimically, hostilmente.

inimitable, a. inimitável; adv. inimitably, inimitavelmente.

iniquitous, a. iníquo, injusto; adv. iniquitously, iniquamente.

iniquity, s. iniquidade, injustiça.

initial, a. inicial, incipiente; s. letra inicial; v.i. (initialling, initialled), assinar com iniciais, rubricar.

initiate, v.t. iniciar, tomar a iniciativa; v.i. iniciar-se.

initiation, s. iniciação; começo.

initiative, a. iniciativo, inicial; s. iniciativa.

inject, v.t. injectar.

injection, s. injecção.

injudicious, a. indiscreto, inconsiderado; adv. injudiciously, indiscretamente.

injuction, s. injunção, ordem, mandado, exortação.

injure, v.t. prejudicar, danificar, lesar; ofender.

injurious, a. prejudicial, nocivo, injusto; ofensivo; adv. injuriously, perniciosamente.

injury, s. dano, prejuízo; mal, agravo.

injustice, s. injustiça.

ink, s. tinta de escrever; indian ink, tinta-da--china; v.t. sujar com tinta; aplicar tinta.

inkling, s. insinuação, aviso, sugestão; suspeita.

inkwell, s. tinteiro.

inky, a. de tinta, preto como a tinta; manchado de tinta.

inlaid, a. embutido, marchetado.

inlay, v.t. embutir, marchetar; s. embutido, incrustação.

inlet, s. entrada, admissão; enseada, estreito.

inmate, s. morador, habitante; inquilino, companheiro de casa.

inmost, a. íntimo, recôndito.

inn, s. estalagem, hospedaria, hotel; taverna.

innards, s. entranhas, vísceras.

innate, a. inato, ingénito; adv. innately, dum modo ingénito.

inner, a. interno, interior, secreto, oculto.

innermost, a. o mesmo que inmost.

innholder, s. estalajadeiro.

inning, s. a vez de jogar; período de domínio ou de vida activa.

innkeeper, s. estalajadeiro, hospedeiro.

innocence, innocency, s. inocência, ingenuidade.

innocent, a. inocente; puro; ingénuo, crédulo; adv. innocently, inocentemente.

innocuous, a. inócuo, inofensivo; innocuously, inofensivamente.

innonimate, a. inominado, sem nome.

innovate, v.i. inovar, fazer inovações.

innovation, s. inovação, alteração, novidade.

innuendo, s. insinuação.

innumerable, a. inúmero, inumerável; adv. innumerably, inumeravelmente.

inobservance, s. distracção; inobservância.

inobservant, a. inobservante.

inoccupation, s. desocupação, ociosidade.

inoculation, s. inoculação; vacina.

inodorous, a. inodoro.

inoffensive, a. inofensivo; adv. inoffensively, inofensivamente.

inofficious, a. inoperante, ineficaz.

inoperative, a. inoperante; inactivo.

innoportune, a. inoportuno; adv. inopportunely, inoportunamente.

inordinate, a. irregular, desordenado; excessivo.

inorganic, a. inorgânico.

inquest, s. inquérito, investigação judicial.

inquietude, s. inquietação, desassossego.

inquiline, s. e a. inquilino, comensal.

inquire, v.t. e v.i. inquirir, perguntar, indagar, averiguar, investigar.

inquirer, s. inquiridor, investigador, examinador.

inquiry, s. investigação; exame; inquérito; *inquiry office*, agência de informações.

inquisition, s. inquisição (hist., com maiús.); inquisição, inquérito, investigação.

inquisitive, a. e s. curioso, perguntador; adv. *inquisitively*, com curiosidade.

inroad, s. incursão, correria, invasão, ataque.

inrush, s. irrupção, invasão.

insane, a. louco, doido, demente, insano; adv. *insanely*, loucamente.

insanity, s. loucura, insânia; psicose.

insatiable, a. insaciável; sôfrego, ávido; adv. *insatiably*, insaciavelmente.

inscribe, v.t. inscrever, gravar; registar; dedicar (livro).

inscription, s. inscrição; legenda; dedicatória; rótulo.

inscrutable, a. inescrutável, impenetrável; adv. *inscrutably*, impenetravelmente.

insect, s. insecto.

insecticide, s. insecticida.

insecurity, s. insegurança.

insensate, a. insensível, impiedoso; insensato, tolo.

insensible, a. insensível; inconsciente; apático, indiferente; adv. *insensibly*, insensivelmente.

inseparable, a. e s. inseparável.

insert, v.t. inserir, introduzir, colocar, meter; incluir, publicar.

insertion, s. inserção.

inshore, a. próximo da costa, costeiro.

inside, s. interior; conteúdo, forro; a. interior; adv. por dentro, dentro de, interiormente.

insidious, a. insidioso.

insight, s. discernimento; compreensão; vislumbre.

insignia, s. insígnia, emblema, distintivo.

insignificance, insignificancy, s. insignificância; bagatela.

insignificant, a. insignificante; adv. *insignificantly*, insignificantemente.

insinuate, v.t. insinuar, introduzir; v.i. insinuar-se.

insinuation, s. insinuação, sugestão indirecta.

insipid, a. insípido; monótono; adv. *insipidly*, insipidamente.

insist, v.i. e v.t. insistir, persistir, teimar; obstinar-se.

insistence, insistency, s. insistência, persistência.

insistent, a. insistente, persistente, teimoso; adv. *insistently*, insistentemente.

insolate, v.t. insolar, secar ao sol.

insolation, s. insolação.

insole, s. palmilha.

insolence, s. insolência; desfaçatez.

insolent, a. insolente, atrevido; s. insolente; adv. *insolently*, insolentemente.

insoluble, a. insolúvel; adv. *insolubly*, insoluvelmente.

insomnia, s. insónia.

insomnious, a. insone.

insomuch, adv. a tal ponto que, de modo que, de sorte que.

inspect, v.t. examinar, inspeccionar.

inspection, s. exame, inspecção.

inspector, s. inspector, fiscal.

inspiration, s. inspiração.

inspire, v.t. e v.i. inspirar; inalar; aspirar.

inspirit, v.t. animar, estimular, alegrar.

instability, s. instabilidade; insegurança; inconstância.

instable, a. instável.

install, instal (installing, installed), v.t. instalar, dar posse, colocar.

installation, s. instalação; montagem.

installment, instalment, s. instalação; prestação; prazo.

instance, s. instância; urgência, caso, ocasião, exemplo, modelo.

instant, s. instante, momento; a. urgente, instante; presente, do corrente; adv. *instantly*, imediatamente.

instantaneous, a. instantâneo; pronto, imediato; adv. *instantaneously*, instantaneamente.

instead, adv. em vez disso, em lugar disso; em vez de.

instep, s. peito do pé.

instigate, v.t. instigar, incitar, estimular.

instill, instil (instilling, instilled), v.t. infundir, inculcar; insinuar imperceptivelmente.

instinct, a. impregnado, imbuído; animado; movido; s. instinto.

instinctive, a. instintivo; natural, espontâneo; adv. *instinctively*, instintivamente.

institute, v.t. instituir; criar, fundar; estabelecer; s. instituto, estabelecimento; princípio elementar, preceito, norma.

institution, s. instituição; estabelecimento; instituto.

instruct, v.t. instruir, ensinar; doutrinar; dar instruções, mandar.

instruction, s. instrução, educação; (pl.) ordens, instruções.

instructive, a. instrutivo, educativo.

instructor, s. mestre, professor, instrutor.

instructress, s. instrutora.

instrument, s. instrumento; ferramenta.

instrumental, a. instrumental; adv. instrumentally, instrumentalmente.

instrumentalist, s. instrumentalista.

instrumentality, s. cooperação; meio, instrumento.

insubordinate, a. insubordinado, insubmisso.

insubordination, s. insubordinação.

insubstantial, a. insubstancial.

insufferable, a. insuportável; detestável.

insufficience, insufficiency, s. insuficiência; incapacidade.

insufficient, a. insuficiente; adv. insufficiently, insuficientemente.

insufflate, v.t. insuflar, soprar.

insufflator, s. insuflador (aparelho).

insular, a. insular; separado, isolado.

insulate, v.t. insular; isolar.

insulation, s. isolação.

insulin, s. insulina.

insult, s. insulto, injúria; v.t. insultar, injuriar, afrontar.

insuperable, a. insuperável; invencível; adv. insuperably, insuperavelmente.

insupportable, a. insuportável, intolerável; adv. insupportably, insuportavelmente.

insurance, s. seguro; life insurance, seguro de vida.

insurant, s. segurado.

insure, v.t. segurar.

insurgence, insurgency, s. insurreição, revolta.

insurgent, a. e s. insurgente, insurrecto, revoltoso.

insurmountable, a. insuperável, invencível.

insurrection, s. insurreição, sublevação.

insurrectionist, s. insurreccionista.

intact, a. intacto; ileso.

intake, s. entrada (de um fluido); depósito, fonte.

intangible, a. intangível, impalpável.

integrable, a. integrável.

integral, a. integral, inteiro, completo; s. o todo; adv. integrally, integralmente.

integrant, a. integrante, componente.

integrate, v.t. integrar; unificar.

integration, s. integração.

integrity, s. integridade; rectidão; pureza.

integument, s. tegumento; revestimento.

intellect, s. intelecto, entendimento, inteligência.

intellectual, a. intelectual; adv. intellectually, intelectualmente.

intelligence, s. inteligência, intelecto.

intelligent, a. inteligente; adv. intelligently, inteligentemente.

intelligible, a. inteligível, claro; adv. intelligibly, inteligivelmente.

intemperance, s. intemperança; excesso.

intemperate, a. imoderado, desmedido; adv. intemperately, desmedidamente.

intend, v.t. tencionar, pretender.

intendant, s. intendente, superintendente, director.

intense, a. intenso, extremo; adv. intensely, intensamente.

intensify, v.t. e v.i. intensificar(-se), aumentar, avivar(-se).

intensity, s. intensidade, veemência, tensão.

intensive, a. intensivo; adv. intensively, intensamente.

intent, a. atento, solícito; decidido; s. intenção, intento, fim.

intention, s. intenção, mira, propósito.

intentional, a. intencional; adv. intentionally, intencionalmente.

inter (interring, interred), v.t. enterrar, sepultar.

interaction, s. acção recíproca.

intercede, v.i. interceder, intervir, mediar.

intercept, v.t. interceptar, impedir, estorvar.

interception, s. intercepção.

intercession, s. intercessão, mediação.

intercessor, s. intercessor, medianeiro.

interchange, v.t. permutar, trocar, cambiar; v.i. alternar-se, revezar-se.

interchangeable, a. permutável; intercambiável.

intercourse, s. comércio, tráfego, trato, relações comerciais; coito; social intercourse, convívio social.

interdependent, a. interdependente.

interdict, s. interdito, interdição, proibição; v.t. interdizer, interditar, proibir.

interdiction, s. proibição.

interest, s. interesse, atenção, curiosidade; proveito, lucro, juros; v.t. interessar; impressionar.

interesting, a. interessante, atractivo.

interfere, v.i. intervir, intrometer-se, ingerir--se; colidir, chocar-se.

interference, s. interferência, intervenção, ingerência.

interfering, a. interferente; interveniente; oposto, contraditório.

interfuse, v.t. fundir, misturar.

interior, a. interior, interno; s. interior.

interject, v.t. interpor, meter de permeio.

interjection, s. interjeição; intervenção.

interlace, v.t. e v.i. entrelaçar, enlear; entrelaçar-se.

interlacement, s. entrelaçamento, entrete-cimento.

interlock, v.t. e v.i. apertar, abraçar; fixar; apertar-se.

interlocution, s. interlocução, conversação, diálogo.

interlocutor, s. interlocutor, interpelador.

interlope, v.i. intrometer-se, ingerir-se, imiscuir-se.

interloper, s. intruso, intrometido.

interlude, s. interlúdio; intervalo.

interlunar, a. interlunar.

intermarry, v.i. casarem-se vários membros das mesmas famílias ou raças.

intermeddle, v.i. intrometer-se, ingerir-se; v.t. misturar, entremisturar.

intermediary, a. e s. intermediário.

intermediate, a. e s. intermediário, inter-médio.

interment, s. enterro, funeral.

interminable, a. interminável.

intermingle, v.t. e v.i. misturar(-se); mis-turar, entremear.

intermission, s. intermissão, interrupção, intermitência.

intermit (intermitting, intermitted), v.t. e v.i. descontinuar, interromper, interromper--se.

intermittent, a. intermitente.

intermix, v.t. misturar, entremear.

intermixture, s. mistura.

internal, a. interno, interior.

international, a. internacional.

internationalize, v.t. internacionalizar.

interpellate, v.t. interpelar.

interpolate, v.t. interpolar, inserir.

interpolation, s. interpolação.

interpret, v.t. interpretar; traduzir; repre-sentar; tomar por.

interpreter, s. intérprete.

interrogate, v.t. interrogar; inquirir.

interrogation, s. interrogação; pergunta.

interrogative, a. interrogativo; adv. interro-gatively, interrogativamente.

interrupt, v.t. interromper, descontinuar; perturbar.

interruption, s. interrupção; suspensão.

intersect, v.t. e v.i. cortar, cruzar, atraves-sar, dividir; entrecortar-se, cruzar-se.

intersection, s. intersecção, cruzamento.

intersperse, v.t. espalhar, espargir, disse-minar.

interstate, a. interestadual.

interstice, s. interstício, intervalo.

intertwine, v.t. e v.i. entrelaçar, entrelaçar--se.

interval, s. intervalo, pausa; lacuna.

intervene, v.i. intervir, atravessar-se; sobrevir.

intervention, s. intervenção; mediação.

interview, s. entrevista, encontro.

interweave, v.t. e v.i. entrelaçar(-se), unir(-se).

intestinal, a. intestinal.

intestine, s. intestino. 1) *small intestine,* intestino delgado. 2) *large intestine,* intestino grosso.

intimate, v.t. anunciar, indicar, comunicar, dar a entender; s. amigo íntimo, confidente; a. íntimo, familiar.

intimation, s. notificação; aviso; indício, sinal.

intimidate, v.t. intimidar, amedrontar, coagir.

intimidation, s. intimidação.

intimity, s. intimidade, vida íntima; recolhi-mento.

intitule, v.t. intitular, denominar.

into, prep. em, dentro de, até ao interior. 1) *the water was changed into wine,* a água transformou-se em vinho. 2) *into the bargain,* ainda por cima.

intolerable, a. intolerável; adv. intolerably, intoleravelmente.

intolerant, a. e s. intolerante.

intonation, s. entoação.

intone, v.t. e v.i. entoar, cantar.

intoxicant, a. e s. enebriante, bebida embriagante.

intoxicate, v.t. embriagar; excitar; a. ébrio.

intoxication, s. intoxicação; embriaguez; exaltação, entusiasmo.

intractable, a. intratável; adv. intractably, intratavelmente.

intransigent, a. intransigente, irreconciliável, s. intransigente, radical; adv. intransigently, intransigentemente.

intransitive, a. intransitivo. s. verbo intran-sitivo.

intrench, *v.t.* sulcar, cortar; entrincheirar, ursupar.

intrenchment, *s.* entrincheiramento.

intrepid, *a.* intrépido, destemido, arrojado; *adv. intrepidly,* intrepidamente.

intrepidity, *s.* intrepidez, arrojo.

intricate, *a.* intrincado; *adv. intricately,* intrincadamente.

intrigant, *a.* intrigante.

intrigue, *v.t.* intrigar, tramar, fazer intrigas; *s.* enredo, intriga, trama; intriga amorosa.

intriguer, *s.* intrigante, intriguista; amante.

intrinsic, *a.* intrínseco, inerente; *adv. intrinsically,* intrinsecamente.

introduce, *v.t.* introduzir; apresentar (pessoa, projecto ou lei); divulgar.

introduction, *s.* introdução; apresentação; iniciação.

introspect, *v.i.* praticar a introspecção.

introspection, *s.* introspecção.

introspective, *a.* introspectivo.

introvert, *v.t.* e *v.i.* introverter(-se), recolher (-se), retrair(-se).

intrude, *v.t.* introduzir à força; meter, cravar; *v.i.* introduzir-se, intrometer-se, impor a sua presença.

intruder, *s.* intruso, intrometido.

intrusion, *s.* intrusão; invasão.

intrusive, *a.* intruso; *adv. intrusively,* intrusamente.

intuit, *v.t.* conhecer ou saber por intuição; *v.i.* intuir.

intuition, *s.* intuição.

intuitive, *a.* intuitivo; *adv. intuitively,* intuitivamente.

inundate, *v.t.* inundar.

inundation, *s.* inundação.

inure, *v.t.* habituar, acostumar.

inurement, *s.* hábito, costume, prática.

inutility, *s.* inutilidade.

invade, *v.t.* invadir; usurpar, violar, infringir (direitos).

invalid, *a.* não válido, nulo; *v.t.* e *v.i.* tornar inválido (por doença), tornar-se inválido, aposentar-se (por invalidez); *a.* inválido, doente.

invalidate, *v.t.* invalidar, inutilizar.

invaluable, *a.* inestimável, precioso.

invariable, *a.* invariável, constante; *adv. invariably,* invariavelmente.

invasion, *s.* invasão, incursão; violação.

invective, *s.* invectiva; *a.* invectivo, injurioso, agressivo.

inveigh, *v.i.* invectivar, injuriar.

inveigle, *v.t.* engodar, seduzir, enganar.

invent, *v.t.* inventar, forjar.

inventer, *s.* inventor.

invention, *s.* invenção; ficção, embuste.

inventive, *a.* inventivo, engenhoso; *adv. inventively,* engenhosamente.

inventory, *s.* inventário; balanço.

inverse, *s.* inverso; *a.* inverso, invertido.

inversion, *s.* inversão.

invert, *v.t.* inverter, transpor; *a.* invertido; *s.* invertido, homossexual.

invertebrate, *a.* e *s.* invertebrado.

inverter, *s.* inversor.

invest, *v.t.* vestir; investir; pôr dinheiro a render.

investigate, *v.t.* e *v.i.* investigar, inquirir, averiguar.

investigation, *s.* investigação, pesquisa; inquérito.

investiture, *s.* investidura, posse.

investment, *s.* investimento, aplicação de dinheiro; enroupamento; revestimento.

inveterate, *a.* inveterado, habitual; arraigado.

invidious, *a.* odioso, ofensivo, invejoso; *adv. invidiously,* odiosamente.

invigorate, *v.t.* robustecer, vigorizar, fortalecer.

invincible, *a.* invencível; *adv. invincibly,* invencivelmente.

inviolable, *a.* inviolável; *adv. inviolably,* inviolavelmente.

inviolate, *a.* inviolado, íntegro; *adv. inviolately,* invioladamente.

invisible, *a.* invisível; *adv. invisibly,* invisivelmente.

invitation, *s.* convite, solicitação.

invite, *v.t.* convidar; atrair.

inviting, *a.* convidativo; atraente, tentador; *invitingly,* convidativamente.

invocate, *v.t.* invocar, recorrer, solicitar.

invocation, *s.* invocação.

invoice, *s.* factura, remessa; *v.t.* facturar.

invoke, *v.t.* o mesmo que *invocate.*

involuntary, *a.* involuntário; *adv. involuntarily,* involuntariamente.

involve, *v.t.* envolver; embrulhar; implicar; comprometer; causar.

involved, *a.* envolvido.

involvement, *s.* envolvimento; enredo.

invulnerable, *a.* invulnerável; *adv. invulnerably,* de modo invulnerável.

inward, *a.* interior, interno, íntimo; *adv.* para dentro, por dentro, interiormente; *s.* o interior (pl.), entranhas.

inwardly, adv. interiormente; intimamente.

inwrought, a. lavrado, embutido; bordado.

iodide, iodid, s. (quím.) iodeto.

iodine, s. iodo.

ion, s. (fís. e quím.) ião.

ionian, a. e s. jónio.

ionic, a. jónico.

iota, s. jota, ponto; quantidade ínfima.

Iranian, a. e s. iraniano, persa.

Iraqi, Iraqian, a. e s. iraquiano.

irascible, a. irascível, colérico.

irate, a. irado, encolerizado.

ire, s. ira, cólera.

ireful, a. irado, colérico; adv. irefully, iradamente.

irenic, irenical, a. apaziguador, conciliador.

iridescence, s. iriação, cambiantes.

iridescent, a. iridescente, irisado; furta-cor.

iris, s. íris; arco-íris.

Irish, a. Irlandês; a língua irlandesa; an irish bull, uma calinada.

iron, s. ferro; ferro de engomar; (pl.) grilhões. 1) to have too many irons in the fire, fazer muitas coisas ao mesmo tempo. 2) to be in irons, estar a ferros; v.t. passar a ferro.

iron-gray, iron grey, a. cinzento-escuro.

ironical, ironic, a. irónico, sarcástico; adv. ironically, ironicamente.

irony, s. ironia.

irony, a. férreo, de ferro.

irradiate, v.t. irradiar, alumiar; animar; luzir.

irradiation, s. irradiação; brilho.

irrational, a. irracional; adv. irrationally, irracionalmente.

irreconcilable, a. irreconciliável; incompatível; adv. irreconcilably, irreconciliavelmente.

irrecoverable, a. irrecuperável; irremediável; adv. irrecoverably, irrecuperavelmente.

irredeemable, a. irremediável; adv. irredeemably, irremediavelmente.

irrefutable, a. irrefutável, incontestável; adv. rrefutably, irrefutavelmente.

irregular, a. irregular; desigual; adv. rregulary: irregularmente.

irregularity, s. irregularidade.

irrevelant, a. inadequado, descabido, despropositado; adv. irrelevantly, despropositadamente.

irreligious, a. irreligioso, ímpio, profano; adv. irreligiously, irreligiosamente.

irremediable, a. irremediável, incurável.

irreparable, a. irreparável; adv. irreparably, irreparavelmente.

irreproachable, a. irrepreensível; correcto; adv. irreproachably, irrepreensivelmente.

irresistible, a. irresistível; adv. irresistibly, irresistivelmente.

irresolution, s. irresolução, indecisão.

irrespective, a. independente de, sem levar em conta.

irresponsible, a. e s. irresponsável; adv. irresponsibly, irresponsavelmente.

irresponsive, a. insensível, indiferente; adv. irresponsively, sem corresponder.

irretrievable, a. irreparável, irrecuperável; adv. irretrievably, irreparavelmente.

irreverance, s. irreverência; desrespeito.

irreverent, a. irreverente; adv. irreverently, irreverentemente.

irrevocable, a. irrevogável, definitivo; adv. irrevocably, irrevogavelmente.

irrigate, v.t. irrigar; regar; aguar.

irrigation, s. irrigação; lavagem.

irritable, a. irritável, melindroso; adv. irritably, irritavelmente.

irritate, v.t. irritar; exasperar, encolerizar.

irritation, s. irritação; exasperação.

irruption, s. irrupção.

Islam, s. Islão; islamismo.

island, s. ilha.

isle, s. ilha; v.t. e v.i. transformar-se em ilha, insular(-se); pôr ou permanecer em ilha.

islet, s. ilhota, ilhéu.

isolate, v.t. isolar.

isolation, s. isolação.

isosceles, a. (geom.) isóscele.

Israeli, a. e s. israelita, habitante do Estado de Israel.

Israelite, s. israelita, judeu; a. israelita, judaico.

issuant, a. nascente.

issue, v.t. e v.i. sair, expedir, escoar, despachar; brotar; publicar; s. saída; escoadouro; fluxo, descarga (med.); fim, resultado; êxito, decisão; prole, sucessão; emissão (de notas, selos, etc.); edição; tiragem, impressão; without issue, sem sucessão.

issuer, s. emissor.

isthmus, s. istmo.

it, pron. pess. neutro da 3ª pess. do sing.; forma de sujeito ou compl. ele, ela, o, a, isto, isso; usado como sujeito de verbos impessoais, mas geralmente não é traduzido, ex. it rains: chove.

Italian, a. e s. Italiano.

italic, a. e s. itálico.

italicize, v.t. e v.i. imprimir em itálico.

itch, *s.* prurido, comichão; sarna; desejo veemente; *v.i.* prurir, desejar com veemência.

item, *s.* item, parágrafo, verba.

itemize, *v.t.* detalhar, especificar.

iterate, *v.t.* reiterar, repetir.

iteration, *s.* repetição.

itinerary, *s.* itinerário.

itself, *pron.* se; a si mesmo; o próprio; em si (forma reflexiva).

ivory, *s.* marfim; *pl.* dentes, dados, teclas de piano; *a.* de marfim, ebúrneo; *black ivory*, escravos africanos.

ivy, *s.* hera.

J

j, décima letra do alfabeto.

jabber, *s,* fala rápida e indistinta, algaravia, geringonça. *v.i.* e *v.t.* tagarelar, falar precipitadamente.

jabberer, *s.* tagarela, palrador, tartamudo.

jabiru, *s.* espécie de cegonha da América.

jaborandi, *s.* jaborandi, planta medicinal.

jacinth, *s.* jacinto; zircónio vermelho.

jack, *s.* qualquer instrumento que substitui um ajudante; alavanca; macaco para erguer pesos; companheiro; máquina para assar; macho (de alguns animais); lúcio; cavalete (dos serradores); bandeira de proa; odre; cota de malha; valete (nas cartas). 1) *jack boot*, bota de montar. 2) *jack-in-office*, empregado presumido e impertinente. 3) *jack-in-the-box*, títere, boneco movido por engonços. 4) *jack-in--the-green*, limpa-chaminés no primeiro de Maio, rodeado de arbustos verdes. 5) *jack ketch*, carrasco. 6) *jack-knife*, navalha de mola. 7) *jack-of-all-trades*, aprendiz de tudo e oficial de nada. 8) *jack-o'-lantern*, fogo--fátuo. 9) *jack-plane*, garlopa; desbastador. 10) *jack-pudding*, saltimbanco, palhaço, bobo. 11) *jack-rabbit*, lebre americana. 12) *jack sauce*, homem descarado. 13) *jack screw*, macaco de rosca. 14) *jack straw*, homem inútil. 15) *jack sprat*, sujeitinho. 16) *jack staff*, pau de bandeira. 17) *jack-tar*, marinheiro. 18) *jack towel*, toalha grossa e áspera. 19) *boot jack*, descalçadeira (tira--botas). 20) *fresh water jack*, marinheiro de água doce. 21) *every man jack*, todos sem excepção.

jackal, *s.* chacal.

jackanapes (es), *s.* impertinente; melquetre-fe, homem presumido (de sabedor e de fino).

jackass (es), *s.* burro, estúpido. 1) *laughing jackass*, alcião grande da Austrália. 2) *from jackass to jackass*, desde o amanhecer até ao escurecer.

jackdaw, *s.* gralha.

jacket, *s.* jaqueta; camisola; blusa; camisa de cilindro. 1) *cork jacket*, camisa-de--forças. 2) *to dust his jacket*, sacudir-lhe o pó, chegar-lhe a roupa ao pêlo.

jacketed, *adj.* jaqueta.

jacobean, *adj.* período de Jaime I da Inglaterra.

jacobin, *s.* frade dominicano; jacobino; pombo-de-capuz.

jacobinism, *s.* jacobinismo.

jacobite, *s.* e *adj.* jacobita, partidário de Jaime II e seus descendentes.

jacob's-ladder, *s.* escada de quebra-costas (náut.); planta.

jacobus, *s.* jacobo, moeda de ouro do tempo de Jaime I.

jactitation, *s.* agitação, inquietação.

jade, *s.* rocim; mulher vil; pedra nefrítica, jade. *v.t.* fatigar, maltratar. *v.i.* cansar-se, desanimar.

jadoo, *s.* seda artificial.

jaeger, *s.* caçador.

jag, *s.* corte, entalha; dente de serra; carga; bebedeira; piteira. *v.t. jagging, jagged*. dentear.

jagged, *adj.* dentado, irregular, recortado; escabroso.

jaggedly, *adv.* de maneira irregular, com saliências.

jaggedness, *s.* escabrosidade; o estado de denteado.

jagger, *s.* roda de latão, com a beira denteada, para cortar queques, etc.; bufarinheiro.

jaguar, *s.* jaguar.

jail, *s.* cárcere, cadeia. 1) *jail bird*, preso, cadastrado. 2) *jail-fever*, tifo.

jailer, *s.* carcereiro.

jalap, *s.* jalapa (planta).

jalousie, *s.* gelosia; persiana.

jam, *s.* geleia, compota; aperto. *jamming, jammed. v.t.* apertar, comprimir; calcar.

jammed, *adj.* mordida (corda).

jamaican, *adj.* da Jamaica.

jamb, *s.* umbral da porta; pano da chaminé.

jambok, *s.* chicote de couro de hipopótamo.

jamboree, *s.* celebração; comemoração; divertimento.

jangle, *v.t.* e *v.i.* altercar, disputar, soar discordantemente; fazer soar desagradavelmente.

jangler, *s.* altercador; tagarela.

jangling, *s.* altercação, som desagradável.

janitor, *s.* porteiro.

janizary (ies), *s.* janízaro.

jansenism, *s.* jansenismo.

jansenist, *s.* jansenista.

January, *s.* mês de Janeiro.

jap, *s.* e *adj.* japonês; a língua do Japão.

japan, *s.* charão; verniz do Japão; *japanning, japanned.* acharoar, envernizar; engraxar.

japanning, *s.* envernizamento.

jape, *s.* gracejo, partida. *v.t.* e *v.i.* mofar de; gracejar.

japhetic, *adj.* jafético.

japonica, *s.* camélia japónica; espécie de marmelo.

jar, *s.* vibração ruidosa; som discordante; choque; jarro; botija. 1) *on the jar ou ajar*, entreaberto. 2) *Leyden-jar*, garrafa de Leyde. *v.i. jarring, jarred,* discordar; altercar; ranger.

jardinière, *s.* jardineira, floreira.

jargon, *s.* algaravia, gíria, calão; zircónio.

jarrah, *s.* jarrá, ou mogno da Austrália,

jarring, *adj.* discordante. *s.* vibração; discordância, altercação.

jarringly, *adv.* discordantemente.

jarvey, *s.* cocheiro ou motorista de um veículo de carreira.

jasey, *s.* espécie de cabeleira feita de lã fiada.

jasmine, *s.* jasmim.

jasper, *s.* jaspe.

jaundice, *s.* icterícia.

jaundiced, *adj.* afectado de icterícia.

jaunt, *s.* pequena excursão, passeio. *v.i.* andar de um lugar para outro; passear; vaguear; saracotear.

jauntily, *adv.* airosamente, ligeiramente com graça.

jauntiness, *s.* ligeireza, garbo, elegância; bom modo.

jaunting, *adj.* que passeia; *jaunting-car*, veículo irlandês de duas rodas.

jaunty, *adj.* vistoso, airoso, garboso, gentil.

javan, *adj.* de Java.

javanese, *s.* javanês. habitante de Java. *adj.* javanês.

javelin, *s.* dardo de arremesso.

jaw, *s.* queixada, mandíbula; a boca; forquilha, boca (de lobo, de carangueja, etc.) garras, abismo; palavreado, gritaria; ralho. 1) *jaw fall*, depressão moral. 2) *jaw breaker*, palavra difícil de pronunciar. 3) *to hold one's jaw*, calar-se. *v.t.* e *v.i.* injuriar; ralhar; tagarelar.

jay, *s.* gaio (ave); palrador impertinente; simplório.

jazz, *s.* dança e música sincopada com origem nos negros dos EUA.; procedimento ruidoso grotesco. *v.i.* dançar o jazz; *jazz band*, banda de *jazz*.

jealous, *adj.* ciumento; desconfiado; suspeitoso; invejoso.

jealously, *adv.* com ciúme.

jealousness, *s.* ciúme, desconfiança.

jean, *s.* pano entrançado ou fustão.

jebusite, *s.* jebuseu.

jeer, *s.* zombaria, escárnio, mofa, motejo. *v.t.* e *v.i.* escarnecer, zombar, mofar.

jeerer, *s.* escarnecedor.

jeering, *adj.* escarnecedor, motejador. *s.* sarcasmo.

jeeringly, *adv.* por escárnio.

Jehovah, *s.* Jeová, Deus.

jehu, *s.* cocheiro, boleeiro.

jejune, *adj.* falto, desprovido; vazio, insípido; estéril, árido.

jejunely, *adv.* de um modo estéril.

jejuneness, *s.* carência, esterilidade; pobreza.

jejunum, *s.* jejuno.

jellied, *adj.* gelatinoso.

jellify, *v.t.* reduzir a geleia. *v.i.* reduzir-se a geleia.

jelly (ies), *s.* geleia, matéria gelatinosa; *jellyfish*, actínia.

jellygraph, *s.* copiógrafo, copiografia, reprodução por meio de uma massa gelatinosa. *v.t.* copiografar.

jemmy (ies), *s.* pé-de-cabra (de gatuno); cabeça de carneiro cozida; casacão.

jennet, s. cavalinho espanhol.

jenneting, s. uma variedade de maçã temporã.

jenny (ies), s. torno de máquina para fiar; *jenny-spinner*, típula. s. tacada (no jogo de bilhar).

jeopardize, v.t. arriscar, pôr em perigo; expor, comprometer.

jeopardous, adj. exposto a perigos.

jeopardy, s. perigo, risco.

jerboa, s. gerbo.

jeremiad, s. jeremiada.

Jericho, s. Jericó; *go to Jericho!*, Vá pentear macacos!

jerk, s. sacudidela, puxão, pancada, choque; salto; movimento espasmódico. v.t. sacudir, empuxar; arremessar; *jerked-beef*, carne salgada e seca ao sol.

jerker, s. verificador da alfândega.

jerkier, jerkiest, comp. e sup. de *jerky*.

jerkily, adv. aos empuxões.

jerkin, s. gibão (sem mangas).

jerkiness, s. a qualidade do que é espasmódico.

jerky, adj. espasmódico; caprichoso; impaciente.

jeroboam, s. grande tigela de metal; medida de oito garrafas.

jerry (ies), s. construção fraca, barata e feita à pressa; soldado alemão. 1) *jerry builder*, construtor de edifícios fracos e baratos; gaioleiro. 2) *jerry-building*, construção rápida de edifícios fracos e baratos.

jersey, s. camisola de lã; vaca ou boi da ilha de Jersey.

jess (ies), s. correia que se prendia à pernas do falcão; peia. v.t. prender às pernas do falcão; pear.

jessamine, s. jasmim.

jest, s. gracejo, brincadeira, chocarrice; joguete, alvo de zombaria; *in jest*, por brincadeira. v.i. gracejar, brincar, zombar.

jester, s. gracejador, brincalhão; bobo, truão, bufão.

jesting, s. gracejo, galhofa, chocarrice. adj. zombeteiro; *jesting-stock*, objecto de escárnio.

jestingly, adv. por brincadeira.

jesuit, s. jesuíta.

jesuitismo, s. jesuitismo.

jesuitic (al), adj. jesuítico.

jesuitically, adv. jesuiticamente.

Jesus, s. Jesus.

jet, s. azeviche; jacto; cano de saída. 1) *jet of water*, jacto de água. 2) *gas-jet*, bico de gás. 3) *jet-black*, negro como azeviche. 4) *jet pipe*, agulheta. 5) *jet-propeller-engine*, máquina de propulsão hidráulica. v.t. e v.i. jetting, jetted, arrojar, lançar; sair em jacto; pavonear-se; andar afectada ou arrogante-mente.

jetsam, s. alijamento de carga; a carga alijada e arrojada à praia.

jettison, ver *jetsam*.

jetton, s. ficha; ornamento para vestidos de senhora.

jetty (ies), s. molhe, quebra-mar, cais; saliência, protuberância. adj. de azeviche, negro.

jew, s. judeu. 1) *the wandering jew*, o judeu errante. 2) *jew's frank-incense*, benjoim. 3) *jew's pitch*, asfalto.

jewel, s. jóia, prenda; pedra preciosa. 1) *jewel block*, moitão do lais (náut.). 2) *jewel-case*, cofre para jóias. v.t. jewelling, jewelled, enfeitar com jóias.

jeweller, s. joalheiro.

jewellery, s. pedrarias, pedras preciosas; joalharia.

jewess (es), s. judia.

jewish, adj. judaico, de judeu.

jewishly, adv. à maneira dos judeus.

jewishness, s. a qualidade do que é judaico.

jewry, s. a judeia; judiaria; bairro dos judeus.

jew's-harp, s. berimbau.

jib, s. bujarrona; lança (de guindaste). 1) *jib-boom*, pau da bujarrona. 2) *flying-jib*, vela da giba. 3) *the cur of one's jib*, aparência pessoal. v.t. e v.i. jobbing, jobbed, mudar de lado a vela grande; mover-se irrequieta-mente; pegar-se (um cavalo).

jibe, s. e adj. ver *gibe*.

jiffy (ies), s. instante; *I'll be back in a jiffy*, in half a jiffy, venho já, já.

jig, s. giga, dança ou ária alegre; peça para guiar instrumentos cortantes; crivo. v.i. dançar uma giga.

jigger, s. o que dança gigas; qualquer utensílio que tem um movimento de vaivém, por exemplo um crivo para minerais; vela seca (de galera de 4 mastros); carro de carreira. 1) *jigger-mast*, mastro da ré de um navio de quatro mastros. 2) *jigger yard*, verga seca (de galera de quatro mastros).

jiggered, adj. frequentado pelos dançarinos de gigas; sacudido, agitado (como numa peneira); substituto, sem significação, de uma praga

jiggle, *v.t.* sacudir; estremecer; vacilar. *v.i.* menear-se, sacudir-se.

jigsaw, *s.* serra de vaivém.

jilt, *s.* namoradeira. *v.t.* namorar e enganar o namoro; *to be jilted,* ser abandonado pelo namoro.

Jim Crow, *s.* um preto; gincró, instrumento para endireitar ou dobrar barras de ferro ou carris pela pressão de parafuso.

jimjams, *s. delirium tremens.*

jimmy, *s.* pé-de-cabra (instr.)

jingle, *s.* tinido, retintim; correspondência de som (nas rimas). *v.t.* retinir, tinir, soar, rimar.

jingo, *s.* palavra usada na expressão «by jingo», praga mais ou menos inocente.

jingo, *s.* chauvinista.

jingoism, *s.* jingoísmo.

jink, *s.* volta rápida e enganadora; (pl.) *high jinks,* brincadeira ruidosa, pândega.

jinn, *s.* uma classe de espíritos na mitologia maometana.

jinricksha, *s.* pequeno carro de duas rodas puxado por homens.

jitney, *s.* moeda de 5 cêntimos; veículo a motor que transporta passageiros por baixo frete. *adj.* barato.

jo (es), *s.* namorado, namorada; querido, querida.

job, *s.* obra, bico de obra, de empreitada; remendo; negócio ou ocupação baixa e lucrativa; embuste; embrulhada. 1) *a bad job,* negócio infeliz. 2) *odd jobs,* bicos de obra ocasionais. 3) *by the job,* de empreitada. 4) *job-lot,* mercadorias várias vendidas num montão. 5) *job-master,* alquilador. *v.t.* e *v.i. jobbing, jobbed,* agiotar, alugar (ao mês, à semana); comprar e vender por junto; fazer bicos de obra. *s.* 6) *job's comforter,* o que agrava a miséria daquele que procura consolar. 7) *one od job's* comforters, ave de mau agoiro. 8) *job's post,* correio de más novas. 9) *as poor as Job's turkey,* extremamente pobre.

jobber, *s.* agiota, corretor; remendão; o que aluga cavalos ou caruagens; o que faz bicos de obra; enredador; *stock-jobber,* agiota.

jobbernowl, *s.* simplório, estúpido.

jobbery, *s.* agiotagem; meios ilícitos empregados para se conseguir algum fim particular.

jobbing, *p. pr.* de *job.* 1) *jobbing house,* firma comercial que compra e vende por junto. 2) *jobbing-man,* homem que se presta a todo o serviço.

jockey, *s.* negociante de cavalos; embusteiro; *jockey club,* associação para promover e dirigir corridas de cavalos. *v.t.* e *v.i.* burlar, defraudar, enganar.

jockeyship, *s.* ofício de *jockey.*

jocose, *s.* jocoso, espirituoso.

jocosely, *adv.* jocosamente.

jocoseness, *s.* jocosidade.

jocosity, *s.* jocosidade.

jocular, *adj.* jocoso, chistoso.

jocularity, *s.* jovialidade.

jocularly, *adv.* jovialmente.

jocund, *adj.* jocundo, jovial.

jocundity, *s.* alegria, jovialidade.

jocundly, *adv.* alegremente.

jocundness, *s.* alegria, jovialidade.

jodel, *joddeling, jodelled, v.t.* cantar em falsete (nas progressões harmónicas).

joe, *s.* moeda de prata de pouco valor; namorado, querido.

jog, *s.* sacudidela, pequeno empurrão; *jog trot,* meio trote, trote lento e sacudido. *v.i. jogging, jogged* (com *on* ou *along*) andar a meio trote; passear ou mover-se vagarosamente, arrastar-se.

jogger, *s.* o que anda lentamente.

joggle, *s.* entalhe ou encaixe (usado para juntar as pedras ou peças de madeira). *v.t. v.i.* sacudir ligeiramente; estremecer, vacilar.

John, S. João. 1) *John o'Nokes, John o' Styles,* fulano de tal. 2) *John Bull,* o povo Inglês. 3) *John Chinaman,* chinês, povo chinês.

john-dory (ies), *s.* dourada, peixe.

Johnian, *s.* membro do Colégio de S. João (Cambridge).

johnny (ies), *s.* diminutivo de John; um simplório ou sujeito em geral. 1) *johnny cake,* bolo de milho torrado. 2) *johnny raw,* um principiante. 3) *johnny Crapaud,* um francês. 4) *Johnny Armstrong,* força braçal.

johnsonese, *s.* o estilo de Johnson ou imitação dele.

Johnsonian, *adj.* próprio de Johnson.

join, *v.t.* e *v.i.* ligar, juntar; unir; associar; acrescentar, anexar; unir-se, associar-se; encontrar-se com; concordar; estar junto a; fazer uma costura de cabo (náut.). 1) *to join battle,* travar combate. 2) *to join a club,* entrar para uma clube. 3) *to join a ship*, embarcar como tripulante.

joiner, *s.* marceneiro.

joinery, *s.* marcenaria.

joining, *s.* união; costura (de cabo).

joint, *s.* articulação, junta; nó; união, ligação; bisagra; charneira; gonzo; quarto (de animal); encaixe; samblagem. 1) *out of joint*, deslocado, desconjuntado, 2) *to put a person's nose out of a joint*, suplantar alguém. *adj.* unido, combinado, associado, repartido, comum a muitos. 3) *joint account*, conta de participação. 4) *joint heir*, co--herdeiro. 5) *joint consent*, comum acordo. 6) *joint owner*, co-proprietário. 7) *joint sharer*, parceiro. 8) *joint-stock*, capital social. 9) *joint-stock company*, companhia por acções, sociedade anónima. 10) *joint--tenant*, co-proprietário de terras ou bens. *v.t.* e *v.i.* juntar, ligar, unir; unir-se por articulações, associar-se.

jointer, *s.* juntoira.

jointing, *s.* ligação.

jointly, *adv.* juntamente, unidamente; de acordo.

jointure, *s.* bens parafernais.

joist, *s.* viga, trave, barrote.

joke, *s.* gracejo; piada. 1) *to take* ou *to see a joke*, perceber a piada. 2) *to crack a joke*, dizer uma piada. 3) *to treat the matter as a joke*, não tomar uma coisa a sério. 4) *in joke*, por brincadeira. 5) *it was no joke*, não foi brincadeira. *v.t.* e *v.i.* gracejar, chalacear; divertir-se à custa de uma pessoa.

joker, *s.* gracejador, chocarreiro, chalaceador.

joking, *s.* brincadeira, gracejo. *adj.* gracejador, galhofeiro; *joking apart*, falando a sério.

jokingly, *adv.* por brincadeira.

jollification, *s.* festança, folia.

jollier, jolliest, *comp.* e *sup. jolly*

jollily, *adv.* alegremente.

jolliness, *s.* jovialidade, alegria, regozijo.

jollity (ies), *s.* alegria, regozijo, jovialidade.

jolly, *adj.* jovial, folgazão; excelente. *s.* soldado de marinha.

jollyboat, *s.* escaler.

jolt, *s.* balanço, solavanco. *v.t.* e *v.i.* dar balanços ou solavancos, sacudir, balançar.

jolting, *s.* balanço, solavanco.

joltingly, *adv.* aos solavancos.

Jonathan, *s.* alcunha do povo dos Estados Unidos de América do Norte.

jongleur, *s.* trovador; bufão.

jonguil, *s.* junquilho.

jorum, *s.* espécie de taça grande ou sem conteúdo.

joseph, *s.* antigo vestido de montar, amazona.

joss, *s.* ídolo chinês; *joss-stick*, pau de goma queimado como incenso diante do ídolo.

jostle, *v.t.* empurrar, impelir; acotovelar.

jot, jota; ponto; til. *v.t. jotting, jotted,* (com *down*), apontar, tomar notas, assentar.

jotting, *s.* nota, apontamento.

jougs, *s.* argola de ferro (para prender os condenados).

journal, *s.* jornal, diário; diário (livro); munhão. 1) *shft-journal*, munhão do eixo). 2) *end-journal*, munhão da cabeça.

journalism, *s.* jornalismo.

journalist, *s.* jornalista.

journalistic, *adj.* jornalístico.

journalize, *v.t.* e *v.i.* passar para o diário; escrever artigos para um jornal.

journey, *s.* jornada, viagem por terra; passagem, trajecto. *v.t.* jornadear, viajar por terra.

journeying, *s.* o viajar, viagem.

journeyman, *s.* mecânico; jornaleiro.

joust, *s.* justa, torneio. *v.i.* justar, correr em torneio.

jove, *s.* Júpiter; *by jove*, caramba!

jovial, *adj.* jovial, alegre, festivo.

joviality, *adv.* jovialidade.

jovially, *adv.* jovialmente.

jovialness, *s.* jovialidade.

jowl, *s.* cara, rosto, face; *cheek by jowl*, ao lado um do outro.

joy, *s.* alegria, prazer, júbilo, regozijo. 1) *joy-stick*, alavanca de marcha (de avião). 2) *I wish you joy*, congratulo-o. 3) *joyride*, passeio de automóvel de que uma pessoa se apossou por algum tempo. *v.t.* e *v.i.* alegrar-se, regozijar-se, alegrar.

joyful, *adj.* alegre, prazenteiro.

joyfully, *adv.* alegremente.

joyfulness, *s.* alegria, júbilo.

joyless, *adj.* triste, sem alegria.

joylessly, *adv.* tristemente.

joylessness, *s.* tristeza.

joyous, *adj.* alegre, jubiloso.

joyously, *adv.* alegremente.

joyousness, *s.* alegria, satisfação, júbilo.

jubilant, *adj.* que jubila, que exulta de alegria; triunfante.

jubilantly, *adv.* de maneira jubilosa.

jubilate, v.i. exultar-se, regozijar-se.

jubilation, s. júbilo.

jubilee, s. jubileu.

judaean, s. e adj. judeu.

judaic (al), adj. judaico.

judaically, adv. judaicamente, à maneira dos judeus.

Judaism, s. judaísmo.

Judaist, s. partidário do judaísmo.

judaize, v. i e v.t. judaizar.

judaizer, s. judaizante.

judean, adj. e s. judeu.

judge, s. juiz; árbitro; perito, conhecedor. 1) judge-advocate, promotor da justiça (num tribunal marcial). 2) judge's order, mandado judicial. v.t. e v.i. considerar; criticar; julgar; sentenciar; pensar, opinar. 3) as far as I can judge, na minha opinião.

judg(e)ment, s. juízo, critério, opinião; decisão, sentença. 1) judgment-day, dia de julgamento; Dia do Juízo Final. 3) judgementhall, tribunal de justiça. 4) judgement seat, cadeira do juiz.

judgeship, s. cargo de juiz.

judicature, s. judicatura; magistratura; tribunal.

judicial, adj. judicial. 1) judicial factor, administrador de bens, nomeado pelo tribunal. 2) judicial murder, sentença de morte legal mas injusta.

judicially, adv. judicialmente.

juduciary, adj. judiciário. s. judicatura, justiça.

judicious, adj. judicioso, prudente, discreto, sábio, racional.

judiciously, adv. judiciosamente.

judiciousness, s. juízo, perspicácia, discrição.

jug, s. jarro, cântaro, bilha; uma das notas do rouxinol (também se diz jug-jug). v.t. e v.i. jugging, jugged, estufar uma lebre; imitar o canto do rouxinol; encarcerar, engaiolar.

juggins (es), s. simplório.

juggle, s. ligeireza de mãos; impostura. v.i. fazer prestidigitação; enganar, iludir; fingir.

juggler, s. prestidigitador, escamoteador, impostor.

jugoslav, s. jugoslavo.

jugular, adj. jugular. s. veia jugular.

jugulate, v.t. jugular, decapitar, debelar.

juice, s. suco, sumo, chorume.

juiceless, adj. seco, sem sumo.

juicily, adv. de um modo sumarento.

juiciness, s. suculência.

juicy, adj. sucoso, sumarento.

jujitsu, s. jiu-jítsu.

jujube, s. açofeita.

julep, s. julepo.

Julian, adj. e s. juliano.

julienne, s. sopa juliana.

jumble, s. misturada, confusão, embrulhada; jumble-sale, bazar de caridade (de roupa usada). v.t. e v.i. embrulhar, confundir; confundir-se, revolver-se, confusamente.

jumbling, s. confusão, estrondo.

jumbo, s. um colosso; afamado elefante do Jardim Zoológico de Londres.

jump, s. salto; pulo; acaso; feliz encontro; vestido solto. 1) jump of a gun, coice de uma peça. v.t. e v.i. saltar; pular; cabriolar; transpor de um salto; galgar; levantar (caça); concordar, ajustar-se, convir. 2) to jump at, aceitar avidamente. 3) to jump out of one's skin, saltar de surpresa.

jumper, s. saltador; blusa de marinheiro; broca comprida.

jumping, adj. saltador, saltão. 1) jumping-jack, títere. 2) jumping-louse, saltão.

jun, abreviatura de júnior.

junction, s. junção; lugar de junção; entroncamento (caminho de ferro); derivação de circuito eléctrico; junction-dock, doca de ligação.

juncture, s. junção, união.

June, mês de Junho.

jungle, s. mato, matagal.

jungly, adj. cheio de matagais.

junior, adj. júnior, novo, mais novo. s. o mais moço. 1) junior to commander, oficial subalterno. 2) junior soph, segundanista da Universidade de Cambridge.

juniority, s. a qualidade de mais novo.

juniper, s. zimbro, junípero.

junk, s. junco (barco de vela chinês); massame desfeito, estopa; carne salgada fornecida aos navios para longas viagens; cesta; um bocado grosso (variante de chunk).

junker, s. jovem fidalgo alemão.

junket, s. acepipe, gulodice; requeijão misturado com nata e adoçado; festança; piquenique. v.t. e v.i. festejar, entreter; banquetear, tomar parte numa festança.

junketing, s. festa ou entretenimento alegre; comezaina.

junta, s. reunião, conselho, junta, assembleia.

junto, s. cabala, facção.

jupe, s. saia de cima.

jupon, *s.* saia de baixo, saiote.

jurat, *s.* jurado.

juridical, *adj.* jurídico.

juridically, *adv.* juridicamente.

jurisconsult, *s.* jurisconsulto, advogado, jurista.

jurisdiction, *s.* jurisdição, alçada.

jurisdictional, *adj.* jurisdicional.

jurisprudence, *s.* jurisprudência.

jurist, *s.* jurisconsulto.

juror, *s.* jurado.

jury (ies), *s.* júri. 1) *jury-box,* bancada dos jurados. 2) *jury process,* mandado de intimação a um júri. 3) *gentlemen of the jury,* os jurados.

juryman, *s.* jurado.

jus, *s.* jus, direito legal.

just, *adj.* justo; legítimo; exacto, conveniente; recto, imparcial. *adv.* justo, justamente, precisamente, quase, somente; logo. 1) *just as,* quando, no momento em que. 2) *just now,* agora mesmo. 3) *just by,* aqui perto. 4) *that's just it,* é isso, nem mais nem menos, tal qual, exacto. 5) *just as you please,* como você quiser. 6) *just so!,* isso mesmo! *s.* justa, torneio.

justice, justiça, rectidão, imparcialidade; juiz, magistrado. 1) *justice of the peace,* juiz de paz. 2) *to do justice to,* tratar bem; apreciar.

justiciar, *s.* administrador de justiça, juiz.

justiciary (ies), *s.* juiz; administrador de justiça. *adj.* relativo à administração de justiça; *high court of justice,* supremo tribunal criminal de justiça da Escócia.

justifiable, *adj.* justificável.

justifiableness, *s.* rectidão; possibilidade de ser justificado.

justifiably, *adv.* justificadamente, com justiça, com razão.

justification, *s.* justificação, defesa.

justificative, *adj.* justificativo.

justificatory, *adj.* justificativo.

justified, *pret.* e *pp.* de *justify.* *adj.* justificado.

justifier, *s.* justificador, justificante.

justify, *pret.* e *pp.* *justified.* *v.t.* justificar, provar em juizo, defender; absolver, perdoar; justificar; ajustar.

justly, *adv.* justamente, dignamente; rectamente, devidamente; exactamente, precisamente; de direito.

justness, *s.* justiça, equidade; precisão, rectidão, exactidão, propriedade; regularidade; primor.

jut, *s.* projecção, saliência; sacada. *v.i.* jutting, jutted, formar saliência; *jut-window,* janela saliente.

jute, *s.* juta, cânhamo-da-índia.

jutting, *adj.* saliente; arqueado; que faz sacada.

juvenescense, *s.* renovação da juventude.

juvenescent, *adj.* que rejuvenesce.

juvenile, *s.* pessoa nova, jovem. *adj.* juvenil, jovem.

juvenility, *s.* juventude, mocidade; vivacidade, ardor da mocidade.

juxtapose, *v.t.* justapor.

juxtaposition, s. justaposição.

K

k, décima primeira letra do alfabeto.

kaba, *s.* papagaio da Nova Zelândia.

kaffir, *s.* cafre; infile (entre os muçulmanos).

kailyard, *s.* horta.

kaiser, *s.* imperador (da Alemanha ou da Áustria)

kale, *s.* couve galega.

kaleidoscope, *s.* caleidoscópio.

kaleidoscopic, *adj.* caleidoscópico.

Kalends, *s.* calendas; *on the Greek calendas,* nunca, para as calendas gregas.

kangoroo, *s.* canguru.

kantian, *adj.* kantiano.

kantism, *s.* kantismo.

kantist, *s.* kantista.

kaolin, *s.* caulino.

kapok, *s.* sumaúma.

karroo, *s.* nome genérico dado aos planaltos estéreis da África do Sul.

katakana, *s.* um dos dois silabários da escrita japonesa.

katydid, *s.* espécie de cigarra comum nos Estados Unidos.

kayak, *s.* barco de pesca feito de peles de foca, usado na Gronelândia.

kea, *s.* papagaio da Nova Zelândia.

keckle, *v.i.* forrar um cabo (náut.).

kecling, *s.* forro de um cabo.

kedge, *s.* ancorote. *v.t.* rebocar; sirgar; alar sobre um ancorote.

kedgeree, *s.* prato de arroz na índia, preparado de modo especial.

keel, *s.* quilha; barco de fundo chato; pétalas interiores da corola de uma flor papilioná-cea; medida de peso para carvão (21 toneladas e meia). 1) *keel block,* picadeiro de quilha. 2) *bilge keel,* robalete. 3) *drop keel,* pastelão; quilha de arriar. 4) *scarfs of the keel,* juntas da quilha. *v.t.* e *v.i.* pôr uma quilha (numa embarcação); sulcar; mostrar a quilha; virar a quilha para cima, refrescar, arrefecer. 5) *to keel over,* voltar, soçobrar.

keelage, *s.* direitos de quilha, pagamento pelo direito de ancorar um navio num porto; quanto paga por esse direito.

keeled, *adj.* com quilha.

keeler, *s.* espécie de gamela ou selha; trabalhador de quilha ou barca.

keelhaul, *v.t.* passar por debaixo da quilha (castigo).

keelless, *adj.* sem quilha.

keelson, *s.* sobrequilha; *bilge-keelson,* sobrequilha lateral; escoa (em navios metálicos).

keen, *adj.* vivo, penetrante, perspicaz, fino; agudo; afiado; aguçado; mordaz; satírico; acerbo; ardente; fogoso; colérico, desa-brido, violento. 1) *keen sighted,* de vista perspicaz. 2) *keen appetite,* apetite devo-rador.

keenly, *adv.* agudamente, vivamente, subtilmente.

keeness, *s.* agudeza, subtileza (de fio de instrumento); viveza; anelo; ânsia; desejo veemente.

keep, *v.t. pret.* e *pp.* **kept.** 1) guardar; ter (para seu uso ou benefício); dirigir, administrar *(to keep a pub, a hotel);* guardar, olhar por, ter a responsabilidade de *(to keep a flock);* sustentar, proteger, alimentar *(to keep the parents);* prender, deter, fazer esperar *(what kept you there?);* obedecer a, observar, solenizar *(to keep the law, holidays);* presidir *(to keep a meeting);* anotar, registar, escriturar *(to keep account, records, etc.);* ter, possuir (para venda) *(do you keep tea?). v.i.* permanecer, continuar (numa condição, posição, acção, etc.), geralmente com gerúndio) *(to keep talking);* conservar-se; aguentar-se; durar *(salted meat and dried fruits keep a long time);* estar, permanecer, conservar-se *(keep quiet, silent);* residir; viver *(where do you keep?).* 1) *to keep oneself advised of,* conservar-se ao facto de. 2) *to keep an act,* defender tese (universidade). 3) *keep ahead,* conservar--se à proa. 4) *keep astern,* conservar-se à popa. 5) *keep asunder,* viver em desunião; manter separado; estar desunido. 6) *keep at arm's length,* evitar demasiada familiaridade. 7) *keep at it,* persistir numa coisa. 8) *keep at work,* não deixar o trabalho. 9) *keep away,* afastar, afastar-se; abster-se; conservar-se afastado; arribar. 10) *keep back,* reter, deter, impedir; ocultar; retardar; recuar, conservarei à parte. 11) *keep one's bed,* ficar de cama. 12) *keep body and soul together,* sustentar a vida. 13) *keep books,* ser guarda-livros. 14) *keep cash,* ser o caixa. 15) *keep company with,* acompanhar; estar frequentemente com; ter intimidade com. 16) *keep one's own counsel,* conservar a sua opinião. 17) *keep one's countenance,* conservar o seu sério. 18) *keep down a riot,* apaziguar um motim. 19) *keep an eye on,* vigiar cuidadosamente. 20) *keep fast,* conservar, segurar. 21) *keep one's feet,* não cair. 22) *keep from,* abster--se de, conservar-se à distância; ausentar--se; guardar; esconder; preservar; impedir (seguida de um gerúndio). 23) *keep good hours,* deitar e levantar cedo. 24) *keep one's ground,* manter-se firme. 25) *keep one's hand in,* conservar aptidão pela prática. 26) *keep house,* ter casa; dirigir os negócios da casa. 27) *keep to the house,* não sair de casa. 28) *keep one hungry,* fazer sofrer fome. 29) *keep in,* não sair de casa; ficar da parte de dentro. 30) *keep in with,* conservar as boas graças de. 31) *keep indoors,* conservar-se recolhido em casa. 32) *keep in shape,* conservar-se em forma. 33) *keep an intercourse by letters,* manter correspondência com alguém. 34) *keep the log*, conservar ou escriturar o diário de bordo. 35) *keep a look out*, estar de vigia. 36) *keep the luff*, meter-se de orça. 37) *keep off*, afastar-se, pôr-se ao largo (náut.), desanimar; estar separado ou afastado. 38) *keep the offing*, manter-se ao largo (náut.) 39) *keep on*, continuar, avançar, seguir, ficar em cima. 40) *keep one's balance*, manter o equilíbrio. 41) *keep one's word*, cumprir a palavra. 42) *keep oneself to oneself*, separar-se dos outros; não tomar conselhos com ninguém. 43) *keep open house*, ter casa franca. 44) *keep out*, conservar-se fora, impedir a entrada; pôr de fora; não querer entrar; afastar-se; rejeitar. 45) *keep out of sight*, esconder, esconder-se, estar oculto. 46) *keep out the cold*, defender-se do frio. 47) *keep the ball rolling*, tomar parte na conversa. 48) *keep the pot boilling*, ganhar a vida. 49) *keep the powder dry*, manter-se pronto para agir. 50) *keep sea*, aguentar (náut.). 51) *keep a shop*, ter ou dirigir um estabelecimento. 52) *keep one's temper*, ter calma, saber conter-se. 53) *keep term*, ter a frequência regular num trimestre (univ.). 54) *keep to*, guardar; observar; aderir; deter-se; limitar-se a. 55) *keep together*, permanecer ou fazer permanecer juntos. 56) *keep something ou someone under*, conter moderar, sujeitar, sugjugar. 57) *keep up*, sustentar-se; não desanimar; sustentar; manter; alimentar; guardar; conservar-se; conservar (o fogo, um estabelecimento); entreter; não se deitar. 58) *keep up with*, não se deixar exceder por alguém; acompanhar; seguir. 59) *keep watch*, fazer o quatro (náut.). 60) *keep within hail*, conservar-se à distância da voz. 61) *keep with the land*, cingir-se com a terra. 62) *keep her close!*, não arribar! 63) *keep her full!*, a todo o vento! 64) *keep stroke!*, remar juntos!. 65) *God keep you!*, Deus te guarde!. 66) *keep your head!*, conserve o sangue-frio! 67) *keep the fire in*, não deixes apagar o lume. 68) *keep your feet*, não caias. 69) *to be kept in*, ser retido (aluno) no colégio depois das horas da aula. 70) *keep good man campany, and you shall be of the number*, acompanha os bons, e serás um deles. *s.* guarda; protecção; sustento; torre de menagem; forte; capa de chumaceira; chapeleta (mec.). 71) *in good keep*, em bom estado.

keeper, *s.* guarda, defensor; carcereiro;

coiteiro. 1) *keeper of the Great Seal*, guarda-selo de el-rei. 2) *book-keeper*, guarda-caça. 3) *gamekeeper*, couteiro, guarda-caça. 4) *goal keeper*, guarda-redes (futebol). 5) *hotel keeper*, dono de hotel. 6) *shop keeper*, logista.

keeping, *s.* guarda; custódia; alimento; sustento; harmonia; ajuste.

keepsake, *s.* dádiva, lembrança; álbum (com peças literárias e gravuras).

keg, *s.* barril pequeno; barrica.

kelp, *s.* algas marinhas; soda ou cinza extraída de algas.

kelson, ver *keelson*.

kelt, *s.* celta; também se escreve *celt*.

keltic, *adj.* céltico.

kemp, *s.* pêlo grosseiro na lã.

ken, *s.* vista, alcance da vista. *v.t. kenning, kenned*, saber, conhecer; ver, reconhecer à distância.

kendal, *s.* pano grosso de lão.

kennel, *s.* sarjeta, valeta; casota; canil; matilha de cães; covil. *v.t.* e *v.i. kennelling, kennelled*, recolher ou recolher-se ao canil ou ao covil.

kennets, *s.* espécie de pano grosso do País de Gales.

kentledge, *s.* linguado de lastro (náut.).

kept, *pret.* e *pp.* de *keep*. *adj.* guardado, conservado, tido.

kerb, ver *curb*.

kerbstone, ver *curbstone*.

kerchief, *s.* lenço de cabeça; coifa.

kerchiefed, *adj.* toucado, coberto (com lenço).

kermes, *s.* quermesse.

kern, *s.* moinho de mão; sarilho; soldado ou camponês da Irlanda; o último feixe da colheita; festa da colheita; parte saliente de uma letra.

kernel, *s.* amêndoa; pevide; miolo; caroço; grão; núcleo.

kerosene, *s.* querosene.

kersey, *s,* pano grosso de lã.

kerseymere, *s.* casimira.

kertrel, *s.* francelho.

ketch (es), *s.* chalupa; carrasco do tempo de Jaime II.

ketchup, ver *catsup*.

kettle, *s.* caldeira; chaleira. 1) *a pretty kettle of fish*, uma bonita salgalhada. 2) *the pot calls the kettle black*, a panela disse para a sertã: «chega-te para lá, não me enfarrusques».

kettledrum, *s.* timbale; *kettledrum-drum*, reunião de senhoras; chá das cinco (onde antigamente se tocavam timbales).

kevel, *s.* cunho grande; escoteira (náut.).

key, *s.* chave; chaveta; manípulo; teclado; clave; fecho da abóbada (pedra); parcéis, recifes (náut.); cais. 1) *key bit,* palhetão, macho da chave. 2) *key bolt,* cavilha da chaveta. 3) *key cross,* chaveta. 4) *key-hole,* buraco de fechadura. 5) *key-note,* nota tónica. 6) *key rack,* chaveiro. 7) *key ring,* argola para chave. 8) *to strike a key-note,* dar o lamiré. 9) *to put under lock and key,* fechar a sete chaves. *v.t.* enchavetar; fechar com chaveta.

keyboard, *s.* teclado.

keyless, *adj.* sem chave; *keyless-watch,* relógio de corda pelo pé.

keystone, *s.* fecho de arco ou de abóbada, pedra angular.

khaki, *s.* caqui, pano leve muito usado para os uniformes.

khalifa, *s.* califa.

khan, *s.* cão, chefe; estalagem oriental.

khedive, *s.* quediva.

kiang, *s.* burro bravo.

kibe, frieira; doença na ranilha do cavalo.

kick, *s.* pontapé, couce; patada. 1) *kick-off,* pontapé de saída, num desafio de futebol. 2) *kick-up,* distúrbio. *v.t.* e *v.i.* escoucear, bater ou empurrar com o pé; dar pontapés. 3) *to kick the bucket,* esticar a canela, morrer. 4) *to kick up a row,* fazer grande barulho. 5) *to kick one's wheels,* esperar por muito tempo.

kicker, *s.* escoucear, o que dá pontapés ou couces.

kicking, *s.* escouço, acção de dar pontapés ou couces; violência.

kickshaw, *s.* ninharia, bagatela; fantasia ridícula; prato leve.

kid, *s.* cabrito; criança, garoto; gamelinha. pl. luvas ou sapatos de pele de cabrito. *v.t.* e *v.i. kidding, kidded,* parir cabritos; cobrir com pele de cabrito; enganar.

kiddle, *s.* pesqueira; represa de estacas, ou rede fixa (para apanhar peixes).

kiddling, *s.* cabritinho.

kidnap, *v.t. kidnapping, kidnapped,* raptar, sequestrar (crianças e mesmo adultos).

kidnapper, *s.* raptor (de crianças ou adultos).

kidnapping, *s.* sequestro, rapto (de crianças ou adultos).

kidney, *s.* rim; temperamento, disposição; espécie. 1) *of the same kidney,* da mesma natureza. 2) *kidney-bean,* feijão verde. 3) *kidney cotton,* uma espécie de algodão da América do Sul. 4) *kidney vetch,* vulnerária. 5) *kidney wort,* saxífraga.

kilderkin, *s.* meio barril (cerca de 80 litros).

kill, *v.t.* matar, neutralizar; acalmar; apaziguar; fascinar. *s.* riacho, arroio; acto de matar; animal morto.

killer, *s.* matador, assassino.

killing, *adj.* que mata. *s.* assassínio.

kiln, *s.* forno.

kilo, *s.* quilo.

kilogramme, *s.* quilograma.

kilolitre, *s.* quilolitro.

kilometre, *s.* quilómetro.

kilt, *s.* quilo; saiote escocês. *v.t.* arregaçar; franzir.

kimono, *s.* quimono.

kin, *s.* parentesco, parente; familiar; *next of kin,* parente próximo, mais chegado. *adj.* parente da mesma espécie ou natureza.

kincob, *s.* tecido de seda com fios de ouro ou prata, feito na Índia.

kind, *s.* género; espécie; casta; classe; qualidade, natureza; modo, maneira. 1) *in a kind,* de certo modo. 2) *in kind,* do mesmo modo; pagamento em géneros em vez de dinheiro. *adj.* benigno, bondoso, afável, amável. 3) *kind-hearted,* bondoso. 4) *kind-heartedly,* bondosamente. 5) *kind-heartedness,* bondade de coração.

kindergarten, *s.* escola para crianças em que se combina a instrução com o divertimento.

kindle, *v.t.* e *v.i.* acender, atear, inflamar, abarsar; abrasar-se, arder; animar-se.

kindler, *s.* incendiário; incitador; agitador.

kindlier, kindliest, *comp.* e *sup.* de *kindly.*

kindliness, *s.* bondade, benevolência; boa índole.

kindling, *s.* fogo, entusiasmo; material para acender o lume.

kindly, *adj.* afável, bondoso; benigno; suave; brando; carinhoso. *adv.* benignamente, afavelmente, com doçura; *kindly tell me,* faça o obséquio de me dizer.

kindness, *s.* bondade, benevolência, amabilidade.

kindred, *s.* parentesco, afinidade, parentes. *adj.* da mesma natureza ou carácter; congenial, parente.

kinemacolour, *s.* fita cinematográfica colorida.

kinematic (al), *adj.* cinemático, pertencente à cinemática.

kinematics, *s.* cinemática.

kinematograph, *s.* cinematógrafo.

kinetic, *s.* dinâmica.

king, *s.* rei. 1) *king-at-arms,* um dos principais arautos de Inglaterra. 2) *king-bird,* ave. 3) *king eagle,* águia real. 4) *king fern,* feto real. 5) *king gutter,* caleira principal. 6) *king hake,* peixe. 7) *king killer,* regicida. 8) *king monkey,* macaco. 9) *king mullet,* peixe. 10) *king nut,* árvore. 11) *king terrors,* morte. 12) *king's bench,* um dos tribunais superiores de Inglaterra. 13) *king's cushion,* assento feito pelo cruzamento das mãos de duas pessoas; cadeira de senhora. 14) *king's english,* inglês correcto. 15) *king's evidence,* testemunho de um réu contra os seus cúmplices. 16) *king's hood,* segundo estômago de um boi. 17) *king's scholar,* estudante subsidiado pelo rei; estudante de um instituto real. 18) *king's spear,* asfódelo. 19) *king's speech,* discurso da Coroa. 20) *king's tody,* ave do Brasil. 21) *king's yellow,* oiro-pigmento, jade. 22) *the tree kings* ou *the tree kings of Cologne,* os três reis do Oriente, Gaspar, Melchior e Baltazar. 23) *to wear the king's coat,* servir no exército. 24) *a one-eyed man is a king among the blind,* em terra de cegos quem tem olho é rei. 25) *God save the King,* Viva o rei.

kingcraft, *s.* arte de reinar.

kingcup, *s.* rainúnculo amarelo.

kingdom, *s.* reino, monarquia; reino (mineral, vegetal, animal).

kingfisher, *s.* alcião.

kinghood, *s.* realeza, soberania.

kingless, *adj.* sem rei.

kinglike, *adj.* real, régio; majestoso.

kinglier, kinliest, *comp.* e *sup.* de *kingly.*

kingliness, *s.* carácter, dignidade, ou majestade real.

kingly, *adj.* real, régio; majestoso.

kingship, *s.* majestade, dignidade real, realeza.

kink, *s.* volta de cabo; dobra, prega; tosse convulsa; *he's got a kink in the brain,* ele está com a telha. *v.t.* e *v.i.* fazer cocas (de cabo); torcer, tossir convulsivamente.

kinky, *adj.* com dobras ou pregas.

kinless, *adj.* sem parentes.

kinsfolk, *s.* parentela, parentes.

kinship, *s.* parentesco.

kinsman, *s.* parente.

kinswoman, *s.* parenta.

kiosk, *s.* quiosque.

kip, *s.* pele de animal (não curtida); hospedaria ordinária; cama.

kipper, *s.* salmão desovado; peixe curado ao fumo. *v.t.* curar peixe ao fumo.

kirk, *s.* igreja.

kirsch, *s.* cereja

kirschwasse, *s.* «kirsch».

kirtle, *s.* túnica, saiote; manto.

kismet, *s.* destino.

kiss, *s.* beijo, ósculo. *v.t.* e *v.i.* beijar; saudar com um beijo. 1) *to kiss farewell* to, dizer adeus enviando um beijo com a mão. 2) *kiss away,* fazer desaparecer (lágrimas, etc.) com beijos. 3) *kiss-me-quick,* espécie de plantas como a saxífraga, etc., espécie de touca usada na cabeça muito atrás; caracol usado na testa (pilha-rapazes).

kissing, *s.* beijo; acto de beijar; *kissing crust,* a parte da côdea de um pão que, ao cozer--se, pende para o lado e toca noutro.

kit, *s.* celha pequena; mochila de marinheiro, ou de soldado; conjunto de ferramentas de marinheiro, ou mecânico; estojo (de barbeiro, dentista ou cirurgião); rabeca de algibeira, cavaquinho; gatinho. 1) *kit bag,* saca forte para ferramentas dos marinheiros, mecânicos, etc. 2) *kit inspection,* revista da roupa.

kitcat, *s.* retrato de menos de meio corpo, mas incluindo as mãos; clube político dos «whigs» fundado com Jaime II.

kitchen, *s.* cozinha. 1) *kitchen-boy,* bicho da cozinha (rapaz). 2) *kitchen-garden,* horta. 3) *kitchen-maid,* criada de cozinha. 4) *kitchen range,* fogão de cozinha. 5) *kitchen-stuff,* material de cozinha, sobejos de cozinha. 6) *kitchen tackle,* trem de cozinha. 7) *soup kitchen,* sopa económica. 8) *travelling kitchen,* cozinha de campanha.

kitchener, *s.* cozinheiro-chefe; pessoa empregada na cozinha; fogão.

kite, *s.* milhano; papagaio de papel; papagaios (velas); *kiteflying,* o deitar papagaios de papel; negócio de papéis de crédito fictícios para levantar dinheiro.

kith, *s.* relações; amigos; *kith and kin,* pessoas conhecidas e parentes.

kitten, *s.* gatinho.

kittenish, *adj.* próprio de um gatinho; brincalhão.

kittiwake, s. espécie de gaivota com asas compridas.

kittle, adj. intratável; coceguento.

kiwi, s. quivi, ave da Nova Zelândia.

kleptomania, s. cleptomania, mania do roubo.

kleptomaniac, s. cleptomaníaco.

kloof, s. ravina; vale profundo e estreito na África do Sul.

knack, s. jeito; habilidade; brinquedo; expediente; ramerrão.

knacker, s. objecto que serve para bater. como: batente de porta, taramela, castanholas, etc.; fabricante de brinquedos; esfola, esfolador (negociante de cavalos velhos).

knag, s. nó da madeira; cavilha; raiz das pontas do veado.

knaggy, adj. nodoso; áspero; de carácter desigual; melancólico.

knap, v.t. knapping, knapped, partir, quebrar; estalar; britar. s. eminência; elevação.

knapper, s. britador.

knapsak, s. mochila de soldado; saco de campismo.

knapweed, s. grande centáurea.

knar, s. nó (de árvore).

knarry, adj. nodoso.

knave, s. patife, garoto, aventureiro; valete (nas cartas); amigalhote.

knavery (ies), s. velhacaria, picardia, travessura.

knavish, adj. travessa, travesso, brejeiro, malicioso.

knavishly, adv. velhacamente.

knavishness, s. velhacaria.

knead, v.t. amassar; unir, juntar.

kneader, s. amassador.

kneading, adj. que amassa; kneading-trough, amassadeira.

knee, s. joelho; curva ângulo. 1) housemaid's knee, higroma do joelho. 2) wooden knee, curva de madeira. 3) knee breeches, calções até aos joelhos. 4) knee-cap ou knee-pan, rótula do joelho. 5) knee-deep, até aos joelhos. 6) knee-joint, articulação do joelho. 7) knee piece, joelheira. 8) knee tribute, homenagem (prestada por genuflexão). 9) to bow the knee, submeter-se. v.t. e v.i. ajoelhar; cair de joelhos; criar joelheiras nas calças.

kneed, adj. geniculado.

kneel, pret. e pp. kneeded ou knelt. v.i. dobrar o joelho; ajoelhar-se.

kneeling, adj. de joelhos, ajoelhado. s. genuflexão.

knell, s. dobre de sinos. v.t. e v.i. dobrar o sino.

knelt, pret. e pp. de kneel.

knew, pret. de know.

knickerbocker, s. nova-iorquino. pl. calças de golfe; knickers, calção de homem ou calças de senhora, presas por baixo dos joelhos.

knick-knack, s. bagatela, ninharia, brinquedo.

knick-knackery, s. ninharias.

knife, s. faca, navalha, punhal. pl. knives. 1) carving-knife, faca de trinchar. 2) pocket-knife, canivete. 3) prunning-knife, podadeira. 4) pen-knife, canivete. 5) knife-board, tábua de limpar facas. 6) knife-edge, fio de uma faca; eixo de uma balança. 7) knife-grinder, amolador de facas e navalhas. 8) knife tray, faqueiro. 9) war to the knife, guerra sem tréguas, até à morte. v.t. apunhalar; procurar inutilizar, por um ataque traiçoeiro, as probabilidades de um candidato político.

knight, s. cavaleiro; campeão; cavalo (no xadrez); valete (nas cartas). 1) knight bachelor, cavaleiro que não pertence a nenhuma ordem titular. 2) knight-errant, cavaleiro andante. 3) knight of the shire, deputado por um condado. 4) knight of the shears, alfaiate. 5) knight service, serviço real a que era obrigado um cavaleiro feudatário. v.t. armar um cavaleiro.

knighthead, s. coluna da roda; apóstolo (náut.).

knighthood, s. cavalaria; dignidade de cavaleiro.

knightlier, knightliest, comp. e super. de knightly.

knightliness, s. porte ou deveres de um cavaleiro.

knightly, adj. cavaleiroso, próprio de cavaleiro. adv. cavaleirosamente.

knit, pret. e pp. knitted ou knit. v.t. e v.i. fazer renda ou meia; trabalhar a ponto de malha; enlaçar, unir; ligar, atar; contrair; to knit the eyebrows, franzir as sobrancelhas.

knitter, s. o que faz meia, renda ou malha.

knitting, s. junta, união, enlace, ponto de meia; obra (de ponto de meia). 1) knitting-needle, laçadeira, agulha para fazer meia. 2) knitting-sheath, estojo de agulhas.

knittle, s. amarra, cabo de atracar, gaxeta (náut.); agulheta; atacador.

knob, s. protuberância, corcova, inchaço duro; calo; castão; nó; botão, maçaneta; puxador de gaveta.

knobbiness, s. qualidade do que tem protuberâncias.

knobby, adj. nodoso; cheio de protuberâncias ou nós.

knock, s. golpe, pancada, toque. 1) knockabout man, homem útil, homem para todo o serviço. 2) knock down, que derruba, capaz de derrubar. 3) knock kneed, que tem joelhos que batem um contra o outro, a andar. 4) knock out, soco que inutiliza o adversário. v.t. e v.i. bater, chocar, encontrar-se chocando; impressionar. 5) to knock about, bater, desancar, vaguear; passar vida dissoluta. 6) knock against, ir de encontro; empurrar contra, topar, impelir contra. 7) knock away, afastar, fazer, retirar; bater sem cessar. 8) knock the bottom out of, inutilizar (argumento). 9) knock down, derrubar, vender, entregar o lanço num leilão; diminuir (preços); fazer sucumbir. 10) knock in, into, arrombar; enterrar, fazer entrar à força de pancadas. 11) knock into a cocked hat, chegar a um sujeito de forma a deixá-lo desfigurado, irreconhecível. 12) knock into the middle of next week, mandar para cascos de rolha. 13) knock off, cessar, parar (o trabalho); desistir; abater; deduzir; fazer cair; executar; fazer saltar com pancadas; quebrar. 14) knock on the head, tornar ineficaz, frustrar; espancar; matar às cacheiradas. 15) knock out, fazer sair à força de pancadas; vencer; submeter, inutilizar (no lanço de um leilão, ou por meio de murros). 16) knock out the eyes, vasar os olhos. 17) knock under, confessarse vencido; desistir. 18) knock up, acordar, levantar (batendo à porta); cansar; arruinar.

knocked, adj. quebrado por pancada.

knocker, s. o que bate; batente.

knocking, s. o bater, golpe, pancada; bulha, tumulto.

knoll, s. cume, colina, cabeço, outeirinho; dobre de finados. v.i. tocar o dobre de finados.

knop, s. botão de flor.

knot, s. nó, laçada, laço, vínculo; dificuldade, busílis; grupo, reunião; enredo; nó; milha náutica. 1) running knot ou slip knot, nó corredio. 2) knot-grass, grama (erva). v.t. e v.i. knotting, knotted, dar nós; atar, unir; fazer nós.

knottier, knottiest, comp. e sup. de knotty.

knottily, adv. intrincadamente.

knottiness, s. nodosidade; embaraço; dificuldade.

knotty, adj. nodoso; duro; difícil, intrincado.

knout, s. chicote para castigo, primitivamente usado na Rússia. v.t. chicotear.

know, pret. knew, pp. known. v.t. e v.i. conhecer, saber; distinguir; compreender. 1) to know again, reconhecer. 2) know by name, by sight, conhecer de nome, de vista. 3) know how, ter a informação ou conhecimento necessário. 4) know of, saber, perguntar, inquirir. 5) know the ropes, conhecer bem o assunto. 6) know what o'clock it is ou what's what, conhecer bem uma coisa; ter os olhos bem abertos. 7) to let know, dar parte, informar, comunicar. 8) to make known, tornar conhecido. 9) to know on which side one's bread is buttered, compreender muito bem onde está o seu interesse. 10) not that I know of, que eu saiba não. 11) as it is well known, segundo se diz. 12) ask and you will know, quem tem boca vai a Roma. 13) to be in the know, estar ao facto.

knowable, adj. que se pode saber ou conhecer, conhecível.

knower, s. conhecedor, sabedor; sábio.

knowing, adj. inteligente; sábio, instruído; hábil; fino; astucioso; chique, janota.

knowingly, adv. com conhecimento; intencionalmente; com finura; sagazmente.

knowingness, s. a qualidade de ser inteligente; esperteza.

knowledge, s. conhecimento, ciência, saber; erudição; inteligência, habilidade. 1) not to my knowledge, que eu saiba, não. 2) to the best of my knowledge and belief, conforme o que sei e tenho por mais certo.

know-nothing, s. ignorante chapado; membro de um partido americano que só reconhecia como americanos os nascidos na América ou de pais americanos.

known, pp. de know. adj. reconhecido, aberto, declarado; to make known, fazer saber, participar.

knuckle, s. nó dos dedos, junta, articulação; aresta viva; jarrete de vitela; presunto. 1) knuckle bones, jogo da pedrinha. 2) knuckle-duster, manápula de ferro. 3) knuckle joint, encaixe; juntura, articulação.

4) *knuckle rail*, cordão da popa. *v.i.* submeter-se, ceder; bater com os nós dos dedos (raro). 5) *to knuckle down*, empreender com vigor; submeter-se. 6) *knuckle under*, submeter-se.

knur, knur, *s.* nó de madeira.

knurl, *s.* protuberância, corcova, inchaço duro; nó; estria, serrilha. *v.t.* serrilhar.

kobold, s. duende das minas.

kodak, *s. v.t.* fotografar com «kodak».

Koh-i-noor, *s.* célebre diamante da Índia, que é agora propriedade da Coroa britânica.

khol-rabi, *s.* couve-rábano.

kola, *s.* cola; noz de cola.

koodoo, *s.* antílope africano com longas pontas em espiral.

kopek, *s.* copeque.

kopje, *s.* pequena colina.

koran, *s.* alcorão.

Koranic, *adj.* Alcorão.

kosher, *adj.* puro, limpo, (segundo a lei dos judeus). *s.* comida ou loja pura, limpa.

kotow, *s.* a cerimónia chinesa de se prostrar. *v.i.* cumprir essa cerimónia.

koumiss, *s.* o leite de égua fermentado pelos Tártaros.

kraal, *s.* aldeia ou cabana dos hotentotes.

kremlin, *s.* cidadela, especialmente a de Moscovo.

kreutzer, *s.* pequena moeda de cobre da Áustria, da Alemanha do Sul e da Polónia.

krypton, *s.* crípton (quím.).

kudos, *s.* crédito, fama.

Ku-Klux-Klan, *s.* sociedade secreta hostil aos negros formada nos EUA (principalmente nos estados do Sul) depois da guerra civil.

kümmel, *kümel* (licor).

kursaal, *s.* sala de visitas de um estabelecimento, balneário ou sanatório.

kyle, *s.* estreito entre duas ilhas.

kylo (es), *s.* boi ou vaca das Hébridas.

kyrie, *s. kyrie.*

L

l, décima segunda letra do alfabeto.

la, *s.* lá (mús.). *interj.* vede! eis aqui! eis aí! ah!

laager, *s.* acampamento (feito por um círculo de carros de bois chegados uns aos outros).

label, *s.* etiqueta; rótulo; letreiro; moldura saliente sobre uma janela gótica ou arco de um portal.

labial, *s.* letra labial. *adj.* labial.

labialize, *v.t.* labializar.

laboratory, *s.* laboratório.

laborious, *adj.* laborioso, trabalhador, diligente, industrioso.

labouriously, *adv.* laboriosamente.

laboriousness, *s.* trabalho; afã, diligência, dificuldade.

labour, *s.* trabalho; fadiga; esforço; lida; obra; dores de parto. 1) *hard labour*, trabalhos forçados. 2) *labour day*, dia dos operários (1.º de Maio na Europa e 1.ª segunda-feira de Setembro nos EUA). 3) *labour of love*, trabalho empreendido sem se olhar a qualquer recompensa. 4) *Labour Party*, Partido Trabalhista. *v.t.* e *v.i.*

trabalhar, executar, cultivar; afadigar-se, afanar-se; fatigar-se (o navio).

laboured, *adj.* trabalhado, elaborado.

labourer, *s.* operário jornaleiro.

labouring, *s.* trabalho, esforço, fadiga; cansaço (de um navio quando dá grandes balanços); *labouring class*, classe obreira.

laboursome, *adj.* saído para o mar (embarcação).

laburnum, *s.* cítiso dos Alpes; laburno.

labyrinth, *s.* labirinto.

labyrinthian, *adj.* labiríntico, intrincado, confuso.

labyrinthine, *adj.* labiríntico, intrincado, confuso.

lac, *s.* laca, goma-laca; cem mil rupias.

lace, *s.* atacador, cordão, laço; renda, galão, tira, fita colar, gargantilha; *lace piece*, talha-mar (náut.). *v.t.* atar, apertar com cordões; guarnecer com galões, fitas ou rendas; agaloar, acairelar; fazer uma cosedura (náut.); açoitar; aromatizar (leite, cerveja) com conhaque.

Lacedemonian, *s.* e *adj.* lacedemónio.
lacerate, *v.t.* dilacerar, rasgar, despedaçar.
lacerative, *adj.* que dilacera.
laceration, *s.* laceração.
laches, *s.* negligência, desleixo, demora indevida.
lachrymal, *adj.* lacrimal.
lachrymatory, *s.* lacrimatório; *lachrymatory- -shell*, granada com gases lacrimogéneos.
lachrymose, *adj.* lacrimoso.
lachrymosely, *adv.* de modo lacrimoso.
lacing, *s.* acto de atar; laço, cordão; passadeira; *lacing hole*, ilhó.
lack, *s.* falta, necessidade, carência. 1) *there's no lack of*, há abundância de. 2) *lack-a-day*, maldito dia!, dia aziago! 3) *lack lustre*, sem lustro ou brilho. *v.t.* e *v.i.* faltar, carecer, necessitar.
lackadaisical, *adj.* sentimental, lânguido, afectadamente pensativo.
lackey, *s.* lacaio. *v.t.* e *v.i.* servir como criado.
lacking, *adj.* (com *in*) falto de.
Laconian, *s.* e *adj.* lacónio.
laconic (al), *adj.* lacónico, breve, conciso.
laconically, *adv.* laconicamente.
laconism, *s.* laconismo.
lacquer, *adj.* laca, verniz; *lacquer work*, objectos de laca.
lacquerer, *s.* envernizador.
lacquering, *s.* envernizamento de laca; demão de verniz.
lacquey, ver *lackey*.
lacrose, *s.* o jogo nacional do Canadá.
lactate, *s.* lactato. *v.t.* e *v.i.* converter em leite; aleitar, amamentar.
lactation, *s.* lactação.
lactic, *adj.* láctico.
lactometer, *s.* lactómetro.
lacuna, *s.* lacuna, falta. Pl. *lacunae* ou *lacunas*.
lacunar, *s.* tecto abobadado.
lad, *s.* moço, rapaz.
ladder, *s.* escada de mão. 1) *ladder step*, degrau de escada. 2) *companion ladder*, escada de câmara; escada de tombadilho. 3) *side ladder*, escada de corda.
laddie, *s.* diminutivo de *lad*, rapazinho.
lade, *s.* canal; foz do rio; carga. *v.t. pp. ladded* ou *laden*, carregar; vazar, deitar fora; fazer água (embarcação).
laden, *adj.* carregado. 1) *laden in bulk*, com carga a granel (navio). 2) *deep laden*, abarrotado.

lading, *s.* carga, frete; *bill of lading*, conhecimento de embarque.
ladle, *s.* colherão ou pá.
ladleful, *s.* colherada.
lady (ies), *s.* senhora, dona de casa; esposa; título que se junta ao nome de uma senhora cujo marido não é de categoria inferior a cavaleiro ou cujo pai não é inferior a conde. 1) *lady chapel*, capela dedicada a Nossa Senhora, situada detrás do altar- -mor. 2) *lady in waiting*, dama da rainha ou princesa. 3) *lady killer*, galanteador, um D. João. 4) *lady-love*, amada, mulher querida; namorada. 5) *lady's-maid*, criada de senhora. 6) *lady's mantle*, pé-de-leão, planta. 7) *lady pupil*, aluna. 8) *faint heart never won fair lady*, dos fracos não reza a história. *9) Our Lady*, a Virgem Maria, Nossa Senhora.
ladybird, *s.* boi-de-deus, joaninha.
Ladyday, *s.* dia da Anunciação de Nossa Senhora (25 de Março).
ladylike, *adj.* senhoril, próprio de senhora, elegante, dedicado, distinto, preclaro.
ladyship, *s.* senhoria, senhora (tratamento de distinção).
lag, *s.* retardação de movimento (fís.); atraso; o que vem atrás; cobertura, revestimento (de cilindro, etc.). *adj.* retardado, demorado, último. *v.i. lagging, lagged*, ficar atrás, demorar-se; ir devagar; cobrir (um cilindro, um tambor, uma caldeira, etc.); mandar para a prisão.
lager-beer, *s.* uma qualidade de cerveja alemã.
laggard, *adj.* e *s.* retardatário, ronceiro, vagaroso.
lagger, *s.* ronceiro, retardatário.
lagging, *s.* cobertura, revestimento (de cadeira, etc.); material isolador. *adj.* lento, vagaroso, ronceiro.
lagoon, *s.* lagoa, laguna.
lah, *s.* a nota lá.
laic, *s.* e *adj.* leigo, secular.
laical, *adj.* leigo, secular.
laid, *pret.* e *pp.* de *lay. adj.* posto, colocado, deitado, estendido. 1) *new laid eggs*, ovos frescos. 2) *laid up*, desarmado, amarrado (navio); de cama, acamado.
lain, *pp.* de *lie*, estar deitado.
lair, *s.* covil; espaço para uma sepultura; lamaçal, paul.
laird, *s.* proprietário de terras, senhorio, fidalgo.

lairdship, *s.* propriedade.

laity, *s.* o estado secular; as pessoas leigas ou seculares.

lake, *s.* lago, charco; goma-laca; tinta (geralmente roxa); *lake dwellings*, habitações lacustres.

lakh, ver *lac.*

lam, *lamming, lammed v.t.* bater.

lama, *s.* lama, quadrúpede do Peru; sacerdote, monge ou monja do Tibete; lhama (tecido).

lamasery, *s.* mosteiro ou convento de lamas.

lamb, *s.* cordeiro. *v.i.* parir (a ovelha). 1) *the lamb of God*, o Cordeiro de Deus, Jesus Cristo. 2) *God tempers the wind to the shorn lamb*, Deus dá o frio conforme a roupa.

lambda, *s.* letra grega correspondente ao l.

lambency, *s.* a qualidade do que é ligeiro, movediço.

lambent, *adj.* ligeiro, que roça por, que toca ao de leve.

lambkin, *s.* cordeirinho.

lambrequin, *s.* sanefa.

lambskin, *s.* pelica; pele de cordeiro preparada com a lã.

lamb's-wool, *s.* lã fina; bebida feita de cerveja e polpa de maçãs assadas, com açúcar e aromas.

lame, *adj.* coxo, aleijado; imperfeito, defeituoso. 1) *lame excuse*, desculpa que não satisfaz. 2) *lame story*, história inverosímil, incompleta. v.t. estropiar, aleijar.

lamely, *adv.* imperfeitamente.

lameness, *s.* coxeadura; defeito; imperfeição.

lamella, *s.* lamela.

lamellar, *adj.* composto de lâminas, lamelar, laminar, lamiliforme.

lament, *s.* lamento, lamentação, queixa. *v.t.* e *v.i.* lamentar, deplorar, lamentar-se.

lamentable, *adj.* lamentável, deplorável, triste.

lamentably, *adv.* lamentavelmente.

lamentation, *s.* lamentação.

lamented, *adj.* chorado, deplorado, lastimado; *deep lamented friend*, muito chorado amigo.

lamenting, *s.* lamentação. *adj.* que se lamenta.

lamina, *s.* lâmina, chapa. *pl. laminae* ou *laminas.*

laminar, *adj.* laminar.

laminate, *v.t.* laminar.

laminated, *adj.* laminado.

laminating, *s.* laminação.

lamination, *s.* laminação.

Lammas, *s.* festa de frutos (1.º de Agosto).

lammargeier, *s.* grande abutre barbado.

lamp, *s.* lâmpada; candeia; candeeiro, candelabro. 1) *lamp burner*, bocal de candeeiro. 2) *lamp bracket*, porta-lanterna (de carro). 3) *lamp cotton*, mecha. 4) *lamp holder*, suporte de lâmpada. 5) *lamp post*, lampião; poste de lampião. 6) *lamp room*, casa das luzes. 7) *lamp shade*, quebra-luz. 8) *lamp wick*, torcida. 9) *blow lamp* ou *soldering lamp*, lâmpada de gasolina, maçarico. 10) *street lamp*, lampião da rua. 11) *night lamp*, lamparina.

lampas, *s.* lamparão; lampa, pano de seda e lã próprio para tapeçarias.

lampblack, *s.* fuligem, negro de fumo.

lampion, *s.* lampião.

lamplight, *s.* luz de lampião ou candeeiro.

lamplighter, *s.* o que acende os lampiões da rua.

lampoon, *s.* libelo difamatório; pasquim. *v.t.* satirizar, escrever pasquins.

lampooner, *s.* pasquineiro.

lamprey, *s.* lampreia.

Lancastrian, *adj.* lancastriano. *s.* habitante de Lancaster; partidário da casa de Lancaster na Guerra das duas Rosas.

lance, *s.* lança; *lance-corporal*, soldado que faz as vezes de cabo. *v.t.* ferir com a lança; lancetar.

lancer, *s.* lanceiro; o que lanceta; lanceiros (quadrilha).

lancet, *s.* lanceta; arco pontiagudo.

lancewood, *s.* árvore.

lancinating, *adj.* lancinante (dor).

lancing, *s.* lancetada; postigo em forma de lanceta,

land, *s.* terra, terreno; território, província, região; país, povo, nação; continente, terra firme; bens de raiz; sobreposição de chapas ou tábuas em sentido longitudinal. 1) *land-army*, trabalhos no campo. 2) *land-crab*, caranguejo que pode viver em terra. 3) *land-breeze*, brisa terrestre. 4) *land-girl*, rapariga que tomou parte nos serviços agrícolas durante a guerra. 5) *land-lubber*, apelido dado pelos marinheiros àqueles que o não são. 6) *land-owner*, proprietário de terras. 7) *land-shark*, ladrão de marinheiro. 8) *land surveying*, agrimensura. 9) *land surveyor*, agrimensor. 10) *land-tax*, imposto sobre bens de raiz. 11) *land waiter*, verificador da alfândega. 12) *to raise the land*, aproximar-se da terra (náut.). 13) *to make the land*, descobrir e aproximar-se da terra. 14) *land of cakes*, a Escócia. *v.t.* e *v.i.* desembarcar, descarregar; pôr em terra, trazer a terra, aterrar; arriar no convés.

landau, s. landó.

landed, pp. e adj. desembarcado; que é composto de terras; que tem terras.

landfall, s. herança em terras; primeira terra descoberta em viagem; aterragem.

landforce, s. exército de terra.

landgrabber, s. o que adquire terras por meios duros.

landgrabbing, s. a aquisição de terrenos por meios duros.

landgrave, s. landgrávio.

landgravine, s. landgrávia, condessa alemã.

landholder, s. fazendeiro, proprietário rural.

landing, s. desembarque; descarga; aterragem; desembarcadouro; patamar. 1) *landing charges*, despesas de descarga. 2) *landing-net*, rede pequena (para deitar em terra o peixe que se apanhou ao anzol), camaroeiro. 3) *landing place*, cais de desembarque. 4) *landing stage*, desembarcadouro flutuante.

landlady (ies), s. patroa; estalajadeira, proprietária, senhoria.

landlocked, adj. cercado de terras; resguardo do vento e das ondas pela terra.

landlord, s. proprietário; estalajadeiro; patrão; senhorio.

landlordism, s. autoridade, ou accção unida dos proprietários de terras.

landmark, s. marco, limite, baliza; reconhecimento.

landscape, s. paisagem.

landslide, s. desmoronamento (de uma encosta).

landslip, ver *landslide*.

landsman, s. o que vive em terra; soldado de terra; moço de viagem; homem que nunca embarcou.

landward, adv. para terra.

lanwind, s. brisa terrestre.

lane, s. rua estreita, beco, viela, quelha, congosta, azinhaga. 1) *blind lane*, beco sem saída. 2) *country lane*, azinhaga.

lang-syne, s. tempo há muito passado.

language, s. linguagem, língua, idioma. 1) *bad language*, linguagem vulgar, abusiva, ou profana. 2) *modern languages*, línguas modernas. 3) *living language*, língua viva.

languid, adj. lânguido, débil; lento; indolente.

languidly, adv. languidamente.

languidness, s. languidez, debilidade, desfalecimento.

languish, v.i. desfalecer, definhar, afrouxar; olhar com ternura.

languishing, adv. lânguido, desfalecido; requebrado.

languishingly, adv. languidamente, ternamente, de modo abatido.

languishment, s. languidez, abatimento, ternura (do olhar).

languor, s. langor, moleza.

languoropus, adj. lânguido, débil, exausto, desanimado, triste.

laniard, ver *lanyard*.

lank, adj. frouxo; magro, encolhido; liso; *lank hair*, cabelos lisos.

lankier, lankiest, comp. sup. de *lanky*.

lankily, adv. frouxamente.

lankness, s. frouxidão, magreza.

lanky, adj. frouxo, fraco, magro; alto e magro.

lanoline, s. lanolina.

lantern, s. lanterna, farol; lanternim. 1) *anchor lantern* ou *light*, farol de estai fundeado. 2) *dark lantern*, lanterna de furta-fogo. 3) *lantern jaws*, queixo-de-rabeca (pessoa muito magra). 4) *lantern-slides, lantern-views*, projecções luminosas.

lanyard, s. passadeira, correia, corda, arrida (cordel que prende os toldos às bordas dos escaleres).

Laodicean, s. e adj. tíbio ou indiferente em religião; habitante da Laodiceia.

lap, s. regaço; sobreposição (de tábuas ou chapas em sentido longitudinal); parte de uma casa sobreposta a outra; dobra, bainha, aba; volta completa de uma pista. 1) *earllap*, a ponta, o lóbulo da orelha. 2) *lap-dog*, cão de regaço. 3) *lap eared*, com as orelhas pendentes. 4) *lap joint*, junta sobreposta. 5) *lap strake*, tábua trincada (náut.). 6) *lap stone*, eixo de sapateiro. *v.t.* e *v.i. lapping, lapped*, dobrar, enrolar, embrulhar; sorver, lamber; beber como os cães e os gatos; encobrir; sobrepor; ficar sobreposto.

lapel, s. lapela.

lapful, s. arregaçada.

lapidary, s. lapidário. adj. lapidar; tumular.

lapidate, vt. lapidar, apedrejar.

lapidation, s. lapidação, apedrejamento.

lapis-lazuli, s. lápis-lazúli.

lapper, s. o que embrulha ou enrola; máquina de enrolar.

lappet, s. aba, pano, monco de peru; lanço de muro.

lappeted, adj. com abas, ou dobras.

lapse, s. queda, escorregadura, prescrição (foro); queda gradual; intervalo; lapso; falta; erro. v.i. passar, decorrer, decair, cair em erro; resvalar; caducar; prescrever.

lapsed, adj. descaído, caído, devoluto.

laputan, s. e adj. visionário.

lapwing, s. pavoncino.

lar, s. lar, divindade tutelar de uma casa, segundo os romanos. pl. lares.

larboard, s. bombordo.

larcenous, adj. ladrão.

larcenously, adv. à maneira de ladrão.

larceny (ies), s. furto, roubo.

larch, s. lárice ou larício.

lard, s. manteiga ou banha de porco; toucinho, unto. v.t. lardear; picar; engordar; misturar; larding-pin, lardeadeira.

larder, s. despensa.

lares, pl. de lar.

large, adj. grande, espaçoso; volumoso; corpulento; amplo, extenso, numeroso; populoso; vigoroso; liberal; generoso; favorável; largo (falando do vento). adv. com o vento; jactanciosamente. 1) large caliber, grosso calibre. 2) large-hearted, liberal. 3) large heartedness, liberalidade, magnanimidade. 4) large-minded, de vistas largas. 5) large of limb, membrudo. 6) at large, em liberdade, à vontade, sem constrangimento; em geral; em massa. 7) to go at large, ir em liberdade. 8) to sail large, largar as escotas, fazer-se ao largo.

largely, adv. grandemente, em grande parte, amplamente, literalmente.

largeness, s. grandeza, grossura, extensão, amplidão, liberalidade.

largess, s. dom, dádiva, presente.

larghetto, s. movimento na música mais pausado do que o adágio. adv. largamente.

largo, adj. largo, andamento musical muito pausado. adv. lento.

lariat, s. laço, corda.

lark, s. laberca, calhandra, cotovia; travessura, partida, brincadeira; to rise with the lark, levantar-se cedo. v.i. apanhar calhandras; fazer travessuras, dizer graçolas.

larkiness, s. qualidade de brincalhão ou travesso.

larkspur, s. esporas, planta.

larky, adj. brincalhão, travesso, folgazão; amigo de graçolas.

larrikin, adj. e s. desordeiro.

larum, s. alarme, rebate; relógio despertador.

larva, s. larva.

larval, adj. larval, próprio de larva.

laryngal, adj. laríngeo.

laryngeal, adj. laríngeo.

laryngitis, s. laringite.

laryngologist, s. laringólogo.

laryngology, s. laringologia.

laryngoscope, s. laringoscópio.

laryngoscopist, s. laringoscopia.

larynxes, s. laringe.

Lascar, s. láscar, marítimo da Índia Oriental.

lascivious, adj. lascivo, luxurioso, obsceno.

lasciviously, adv. lascivamente.

lasciviousness, s. lascívia, luxúria.

lash, s. látego, açoite, chicote, chicotada; ponta de látego; sarcasmo, invectiva; pestana. v.t. e v.i. açoitar, azorragar; satirizar, amarrar; atracar; fazer uma cosedura (náut.); fazer estalar o látego; bater contra. 1) to lash up, ferrar (náut.). 2) to lash oneself into a fury, enfurecer-se.

lasher, s. açoutador; cordas de amarração, cabos de ancoragem.

lashing, s. açoite, azorragada; arreatadura; peia; tomadouro; amarilho; cosedura (náut.). pl. abundância.

lass (es), s. moça, rapariga; aldeã; namorada.

lassie, diminutivo de lass, rapariguita.

lassitude, adj. debilidade, fraqueza, quebreira, cansaço, langor.

lasso, s. laço. vt. apanhar com o laço.

last, adj. último, passado. 1) last week, a semana passada. 2) the last but one, o penúltimo. 3) to be on one's last legs, estar no último apuro. 4) last but not least, o último mas não o menos importante. 5) the Last Supper, a Ceia de Quinta-Feira Santa. s. forma (de sapato); carga; lastro; fim, extremidade. 6) to breathe one's last, morrer. v.t. durar, permanecer, subsistir; conservar-se. adv. ultimamente, a última vez. 7) at last, por fim. 8) at long last, depois de muita demora. 9) to the last, até ao fim.

lastage, s. lastro, carregamento de lastro.

lasting, adj. duradouro, durável, permanente; constante.

lastingly, adv. perpetuamente, para sempre.

lastly, adv. por fim, em último lugar, finalmente.

Latakia, s. tabaco turco de primeira qualidade.

latch, s. aldrava, trinco, fecho; (pl.) presilhas dos cutelos; velas pequenas (náut.). v.t. fechar (com aldrava, trinco, etc.).

latchet, s. agulheta ou cordão de sapato; correia (de sandália, de sapato); trinco de fechadura.

latching, s. cosedura (de crescente de vela).

latchkey, s. chave de trinco.

late, adj. tardio, vagaroso, atrasado, demorado; remoto; recente, último; falecido há pouco. 1) of late years, nestes últimos anos. 2) to keep late hours, deitar-se ou recolher-se a casa a desoras. adv. tarde, fora de horas; há pouco, ultimamente. 3) of late, ultimamente. 4) better late than never, antes tarde do que nunca.

lateen, adj. latino. 1) lateen sail, vela latina (náut.) 2) lateen yard, antena. s. armação latina (náut.).

lately, adv. há pouco, recentemente.

latency, s. estado latente.

lateness, s. atraso, demora; o ser recente.

latent, adj. latente, escondido.

latently, adv. de um modo latente, ocultamente, secretamente.

later, adj. mais tardio, posterior, subsequente. adv. mais tarde.

lateral, adj. lateral, do lado.

laterally, adv. lateralmente

latest, sup. de late. adj. o último; o mais recente. 1) at the latest, o mais tardar. 2) latest thing out, última novidade.

latex, s. pl. latices ou latexes, látex, látice.

lath, s. ripa, sarrafo. v.i. cobrir com ripas ou sarrafos.

lathe, s. torno mecânico; lathe screw, fuso de torno.

lather, s. espuma (de sabão, ou a que é produzida por excessiva transpiração. como sucede, por exemplo, com os cavalos). v.t. e v.i. ensaboar, banhar, com espuma de sabão e água; espumar.

lathing, s. o acto ou processo de cobrir com ripas, cobertura de ripas; ripado.

lathy, adj. delgado, ténue, fraco.

Latin, s. latim. adj. latino.

latinism, s. latinismo.

latinist, s. latinista.

latinity, s. latinidade.

latinize, vt. e vi. latinizar, alatinar.

latish, adj. um tanto tardio, um tanto tarde.

latitude, s. latitude; extensão de significa-ção, acepção; excessiva liberdade, licença; campo (fig.). 1) horse latitudes, calmas do trópico de Câncer. 2) high latitudes, muito ao norte ou muito ao sul. 3) low latitudes, próximo do equador.

latitudinal, adj. latitudinal.

latitudinarian, s. latitudinário. adj. latitudinário, livre, sem limites.

latitudinarianism, s. os princípios dos latitudinários.

latria, s. latria.

latrine, s. latrina.

latter, adj. o último de dois, o mais recente; este, isto. 1) latter-day Saints, mórmones. 2) latter math, segunda sega da erva; sega do restolho.

latterly, adv. ultimamente, recentemente, há pouco, pouco depois.

lattice, s. gelosia, rótula, janela de grade.

latticed, adj. guarnecido de rótulas, engradado.

laud, s. louvor, elogio; auds, laudes. v.t. louvar, celebrar, elogiar.

laudable, adj. louvável; são, bom de saúde.

laudableness, s. qualidade do que é louvável.

laudably, louvavelmente, com honra.

laudenum, s. láudano.

laudatory, adj. laudatório. s. panegírico, elogio.

laugh, s. riso, risada, escárnio, mofa. 1) horse-laught, gargalhada. 2) silly laugh, riso tolo. v.t. e v.i. escarnecer, ridicularizar, rir; rir-se. 3) to laugh at, rir-se de, escarnecer. 4) laugh at a feather, rir-se sem razão. 5) laugh out ou aloud, rir às gargalhadas. 6) laugh down, fazer calar ridicularizando. 7) laugh one out of, fazer perder um hábito a alguém, ridicularizando-o. 8) laugh in one's sleeve, rir-se à socapa. 9) to laugh in any one's face, rir-se nas barbas ou bochechas de alguém. 10) laugh heartidly, rir a bom rir.

laughable, adj. risível, ridículo.

laughableness, s. qualidade de ser risível.

laughbly, adv. ridiculamente.

laugher, s. o que se ri, folgazão; motejador, zombador.

laughing, s. riso. adj. alegre, jovial; escarnecedor. 1) laughing-gas, gás hilariante. 2) laughing-jackass, alcião da Austrália. 3) laughing-stock, objecto de riso. 4) to burst with laughing, rebentar com riso. 5) to burst out laughing, desatar a rir; dar uma gargalhada.

laughingly, *adv.* alegremente, risivelmente.

laughter, *s.* riso, risada; *loud laughter,* gargalhada.

launce, *s.* uma espécie de enguia; lança; balança.

launch, *s.* lançamento de navio ao mar; lancha, chalupa. *v.t.* e *v.i.* lançar à água (navio); arremessar; deitar-se à água; encetar, dar princípio a um novo campo de acção; *he launched out into strong language,* desatou a empregar uma linguagem violenta.

launching, *s.* acção de lançar (à água, no mercado, etc.); bota-fora.

laundress, *s.* lavadeira.

laundry (ies), *s.* lavandaria; roupa para lavar. 1) *laundry-maid,* criada que cuida da roupa. 2) *laundry-man,* homem que trabalha numa lavandaria.

laureate, *v.t.* laurear; aplaudir, festejar.

laureate, *adj.* laureado; *poet laureate,* poeta laureado.

laureateship, *s.* dignidade de poeta laureado.

laurustinus (es), *s.* uma variedade de viburno.

lava, *s.* lava.

lavabo, *s.* lavabo, o acto do celebrante lavar os dedos durante a missa; lavatório.

lavatory (ies), *s.* lavatório; loção; retrete.

lave, *v.t.* e *v.i.* lavar, banhar; lavar-se.

lavender, *s.* alfazema.

laver, *s.* lavadouro, tina, bacia.

Lavinian, *s.* e *adj.* lavínio.

lavish, *adj.* pródigo, gastador, extravagante, profuso. *v.t.* dissipar, prodigalizar, desbaratar, sacrificar, desprezar.

lavishly, *adv.* prodigamente.

lavishness, *s.* profusão, desperdício, prodigalidade.

law, *s.* lei, estatuto, regra; constituição; jurisprudência; direito; foro; processo. 1) *law-abiding,* obediente à lei. 2) *law book,* livro de jurisprudência. 3) *law breaker,* transgressor das leis. 4) *law day,* dia de audiência. 5) *law giver,* legislador. 6) *law-Lord,* Par do Reino de jure. 7) *law-maker,* legislador. 8) *law making,* acto de legislar. 9) *law notices,* anúncios judiciais. 10) *lawsuit,* pleito, litígio, causa, acção, processo. 11) *to be law,* ter força de lei. 12) *to be at law,* estar em demanda. 13) *to go to law,* demandar, recorrer à justiça. 14) *to follow the law,* estudar direito. 15) *to take*

the law into one's own hands, fazer justiça por si mesmo. 16) *bye-law,* lei de uma cidade ou corporação particular; lei ou regulamento suplementar. 17) *brother-in-law,* cunhado. 18) *daughter-in-law,* nora. 19) *father-in-law,* sogro. 20) *son-in-law,* genro. 21) *mother-in-law,* sogra.

lawful, *adj.* legal, legítimo, lícito, válido.

lawfully, *adv.* legalmente; legitimamente.

lawless, *adj.* independente, não sujeito à lei; ilegal; ilegítimo; desordenado; bárbaro.

lawlessly, *adv.* ilegalmente, contra as leis; desordenadamente.

lawlessness, *s.* ilegalidade; desordem; desaforo.

lawn, *s.* relvado; prado; campo; planície; clareira nos matos; cambraia; dignidade de bispo anglicano.

lawn-mower, *s.* máquina para cortar relva.

lawn-tennis, *s.* ténis.

lawyer, *s.* advogado.

lax, *adj.* lasso, frouxo, solto; flácido; vago; fiarreico.

laxative, *s.* laxante. *adj.* laxativo.

laxativeness, *s.* propriedade laxativa.

laxity, *s.* lassidão, flacidez, relaxamento, afrouxamento, diarreia.

laxly, *adv.* frouxamente, sem concisão.

laxness, ver *laxity.*

lay, *s.* situação; camada; leito; aposta; campo de operações; medida de 800 jardas (em fabrico de linha); canto, balada, poema narrativo; concha de cabo (náut.). 1) *lay-days,* dias úteis de carga e descarga. 2) *over-lay-days,* estadia, dias de demora (de navio). *adj.* leigo, secular. 3) *lay-brother,* irmão leigo (de congregação religiosa). 4) *lay-reader,* leitor (na Igreja Anglicana). *v.t.* e *v.i. pret.* e *pp.* laid, pôr, colocar, estender, assentar (quilha, tábuas, etc.); deitar, aplicar; apontar; (uma peça de fogo); impor; mandar; ordenar; cochar (um cabo); acalmar, sossegar; projectar; apostar; acusar; apresentar; pôr ovos. 5) *to lay about,* bater como um cego, dar a torto e a direito. 6) *lay against,* acusar; estabelecer contra; pôr à conta de. 7) *lay alongside the quay,* atracar a um molhe. 8) *lay away,* deixar; pôr de lado; descartar-se de. 9) *lay bare open,* descobrir, patentear. 10) *lay before,* mostrar, apresentar, expor. 11) *lay by,* reservar, pôr de lado, guardar para a outra ocasião. 12) *lay claim,* reclamar, pretender. 13) *lay down,* assentar, estabelecer; pôr em baixo; registar; repousar; assentar a quilha de um navio; depor as armas; abandonar; pagar; reservar; pôr guarnições. 14) *lay fast ou by the heels*, encarcerar. 15) *lay great store upon*, avaliar muito. 16) *lay hands upon oneself*, suicidar-se. 17) *lay heads together*, consultar juntos, deliberar. 18) *lay hold*, aguentar. 19) *lay hold of*, pegar em, apossar-se de; atrair a atenção de; amontoar; meter; embarcar os remos. 20) *lay it on thick*, engraixar bem, lisonjear muito. 21) *lay off*, tirar e pôr de parte. 22) *lay on*, aplicar, colocar; bater; agir; voltar (um navio). 23) *lay it on*, pedir preço demasiado; fazer qualquer coisa como profisão. 24) *lay the odds*, apostar. 25) *lay open*, expor, descobrir. 26) *lay out*, dispor; preparar; plantar; desembolsar; gastar; exibir; amostrar; propor-se a fazer alguma coisa; espiar um ferro (náut.); sepultar. 27) *lay over*, cobrir; juntar; embutir. 28) *lay siege to*, sitiar, investir. 29) *lay to*, repreender, acusar; atacar, imputar; aplicar-se com vigor, diminuir (a marcha de um navio); pôr-se de capa; ancorar. 30) *lay to heart*, tomar a peito. 31) *lay together*, reunir; confrontar; comparar. 32) *lay to sleep* ou *rest*, sepultar. 33) *lay under*, sujeitar, subjugar. 34) *lay up*, acumular, guardar; fazer cair de cama; desarmar; fazer meter em prisão; meter um navio no dique. 35) *lay upon*, impor; infligir; oprimir. 36) *lay wail for*, armar ciladas a. 37) *lay waste*, devastar, assolar.

layer, *s.* apontador (de peça), assentador; galinha poedeira; leito, cama, camada (de terra, de tabuado, etc.), estrato; mergulhão, renovo, vergôntea. *v.t.* mergulhar (plantas).

layering, *s.* mergulhia.

laying, *s.* colocação; postura (de ovos); primeira camada de cal numa parede. 1) *laying down*, colocação de um navio de carreira; 2) *laying up*, armazenagem; desarmamento de um navio.

layman, *s.* leigo.

lazaretto, *s.* lazareto; armazém de víveres a bordo.

laze, *v.i.* viver na ociosidade.

lazier, laziest, *comp.* e *sup.* de *lazy*.

lazily, *adv.* preguiçosamentre

laziness, *s.* ociosidade, indolência, madraçaria, preguiça.

lazing, *adj.* preguiçoso, mandrião.

lazuli, *s.* lápis-lazúli.

lazulite, *s.* lazulite.

lazy, *adj.* preguiçoso, mandrião, vagaroso; 1) *a lazy devil*, ou *lazy bones*, um preguiçoso mandrião. 2) *lazy painter*, contra-boça de embarcação.

lb, lbs, abreviatura de «libra», 453 gramas, arrátel.

lea, *s.* prado, posto; planície ervosa; medida de filaça (para o linho é de 300 jardas = 274m²; para algodão e seda 120 j = 109,68m).

leach (es), *s.* lixívia, barrela, cinzas para lixívia; vasilha para a barrela; testa, guinda; trela. *v.t.* e *v.i* fazer lixívia ou barrela.

lead, *s.* chumbo; sonda (náut.); prumo; entrelinha; folhas de chumbo; primazia, primeiro lugar, dianteira; precedência; cabo de condutor; guia; comando; condução; mão (no jogo). 1) *lead line*, linha de sonda, de prumo. 2) *black lead*, grafite, plumbagina. 3) *cast of the lead*, prumada. 4) *lead pencil*, lápis. 5) *red lead*, vermelho de chumbo. *v.t.* e *v.i. pret.* e *pp.* led, conduzir, guiar, pilotar, levar, mandar, comandar, governar, preceder; induzir; passar; gastar, empregar; capitanear; mostrar o caminho; ser mão (no jogo); cobrir de chumbo. chumbar; entrelinhar. 6) *to lead astray*, desenca-minhar. 7) *lead back*, reconduzir. 8) *lead off*, ser o primeiro, começar primeiro. 9) *lead on a dance*, iludir; obrigar uma pessoa a fazer maiores esforços do que era preciso. 10) *lead out*, fazer sair. 11) *he lead me a hard life*, fazia-me levar uma vida penosa. 12) *to lead to*, conduzir a; ter por resultado, acarretar. 13) *lead by the nose*, levar ou trazer alguém pelo beiço.

leaden, *adj.* de chumbo, cor de chumbo, plúmbeo; pesado; vagaroso; estúpido.

Leadenhall, *s.* mercado de carne e aves em Londres.

leader, *s.* guia, condutor, chefe, comandante, caudilho, cabeça, regente (de orquestra); navio-testa; cavalo dianteiro; artigo de fundo de um jornal.

leaderette, *s.* pequeno artigo de fundo de um jornal.

leadership, *s.* direcção, chefia.

leading, *s.* direcção, condução. *adj.* principal; primeiro; condutor; de testa (náut.). 1) *leading article*, artigo de fundo. 2) *leading hand*, chefe (de operários). 3) *leading man*, chefe, notabilidade. 4) *leading men*, sumidades. 5) *leading press*, os principais jornais. 6) *leading question*, pergunta insidiosa. 7) *leading seaman*, gajeiro; cabo marinheiro. 8) *leading ship*, navio-testa. 9) *leading stocks*, fundos principais. 10) *leading strings*, andadeiras.

leaf, *s.* folha (de planta, de livro, de porta, de metal); aba (de mesa); caixilho, peça (de biombo); lâmina (de alça). pl. *leaves*. 1) *leaf-mould*, terriço de folhas. 2) *to take a leaf out of one's book*, seguir o exemplo de outrem. 3) *to turn over a new leaf*, comportar-se melhor, seguir vida nova. *v.t.* e *v.i.* desfolhar; lustrar (estofos); deitar folhas, cobrir-se de folhas.

leafless, *adj.* desfolhado.

leaflet, *s.* folhazinha; folha solta para distribuir; folíolo.

leafy, *adj.* folhudo, frondoso.

league, *s.* liga, aliança, confederação; união, associação; légua; *League of Nations*, Sociedade das Nações. *v.i.* ligar-se, aliar-se, confederar-se; mancomunar-se.

leaguer, *s.* confederado, conjurado; membro de uma liga.

leak, *s.* abertura, buraco, rombo; fuga (de água, de vapor, etc.). 1) *to spring a leak*, fazer ou abrir água. 2) *to cother a leak*, tapar um rombo. *v.i.* fazer água (náut.); verter, escoar, vazar, derramar-se; ter uma fuga; fugir, escapar. 3) *to leak out*, vir a público.

leakage, *s.* derrame, fuga (água, vapor, etc.); escoamento; desconto pelo líquido que se tiver escoado.

leakiness, *s.* o estado do que vaza.

leaking, *s.* escoamento.

leaky, *adj.* que vaza, que faz água; mal vedado, aberto, falador, linguareiro.

leal, *adj.* leal, fiel; *land o'the Leal*, o Paraíso.

lean, *s.* carne magra. *adj.* magro, chupado, enxuto; mesquinho, necessitado; improdutivo. *v.t.* e *v.i. pret.* e *pp.* leaned ou leant, inclinar, apoiar; apoiar-se; encostar-se, inclinar-se.

leaning, *adj.* inclinado. 1) *leaning staff*, bastão. 2) *leaning tower*, inclinada.

leanly, *adv.* magramente.

leanness, *s.* magreza; pobreza.

lean-to, *s.* alpendre ou edifício cujos suportes se encostam a outro edifício ou muro.

leap, *s.* salto, pulo; assalto; transição súbita; cesto, cesta; coito (dos animais); *leap in the*

dark, acto de que não se podem prever as consequências. *v.t.* e *v.i. pret.* e *pp.* leaped ou leapt, saltar, pular, transpor; cobrir (os animais).

leaping, *s.* salto; *leaping-horse*, volantim, cavalo de picaria.

leap-frog, *s.* jogo do eixo.

leap-year, *s.* ano bissexto.

learn, *v.t.* e *v.i. pret.* e *pp.* learned ou learnt, aprender; ensinar; instruir-se; informar-se.

learned, *adj.* douto, erudito, ilustrado; versado, entendido.

learnedly, *adv.* sabiamente, doutamente.

learnedness, *s.* erudição.

learner, *s.* aprendiz; caloiro; bisonho, noviço.

learning, *s.* saber, erudição.

lease, *s.* arrendamento; posse. *v.t.* e *v.i.* arrendar, alugar, respigar.

leasehold, *s.* arrendamento; terra arrendada. *adj.* arrendado.

leaseholder, *s.* arrendatário.

leash, *s.* trela, ajoujo, correia; três (um par e meio). *v.t.* atar, prender, ligar.

least, *a. sup.* de *little*, mínimo, o menor. *adv.* o menos. 1) *at least*, pelo menos. 2) *nor in the least*, de maneira nenhuma. 3) *least said is soonest mended*, quem muito fala pouco acerta.

leastways, *adv.* pelo menos; contudo.

leastwise, *adv.* leastways.

leat, *s.* calha que leva a água do moinho.

leather, *s.* couro, pele, cabedal. 1) *Morocco leather*, marroquim. 2) *patent leather*, couro envernizado. 3) *pump leather*, couro para anilhas (de bombas). 4) *leather bottle*, odre. 5) *leather cutter*, retalhista de couros. 6) *leather dresser*, acabador de couros. 7) *leather dressing*, acabamento de couros. 8) *leather jacket*, espécie de peixe; árvore da Austrália. *v.t.* e *v.i.* aplicar cabedal; curtir peles; bater; fazer qualquer coisa com muito barulho.

leatherette, *s.* pano ou papel imitando couro.

leatheriness, *s.* semelhança com o couro; rigidez.

leathern, *adj.* de couro.

leathery, *adj.* semelhante ao couro; rijo.

leave, *s.* licença, permissão; liberdade; despedida. 1) *sick leave*, de licença. 2) *by your leave with your leave*, com sua licença. 3) *to take leave*, despedir-se. 4) *to take French leave*, despedir-se à francesa. 5) *to take leave of one's senses*, endoidecer. *v.t.* e *v.i. pret.* e *pp. left,* deixar desamparar, abandonar; legar; separar-se de; sair de; desistir; renunciar a; cessar. 6) *to leave alone,* não perturbar. 7) *leave for,* pôr-se a caminho para. 8) *leave in the dark,* ocultar informação a alguém. 9) *leave in the lurch,* desamparar, abandonar. 10) *leave it at that,* abster-se de mais comentários. 11) *leave off,* cessar, acabar. 12) *leave out,* omitir, esquecer; deixar de lado; excluir.

leaved, *adj.* que tem folhas; guarnecido de obras; *a two-leaved door,* porta de dois batentes (folhas).

leaven, *s.* fermento, levedura. *v.t.* fermentar; levedar; corromper, viciar; imbuir.

leaves, *pl.* de *leaf.*

leaving, *s.* partida, saída; restos; desperdícios; resíduos.

lecherous, *adj.* luxurioso.

lecherously, *adv.* com luxúria, impudicamente.

lecherousness, *s.* luxúria.

lechery, *v. lecherousness.*

lectern, *s.* estante do coro.

lection, *s.* lição, leitura (bibliogr.); variação no texto de algum livro.

lector, *s.* leitura; discurso, sermão; lição, prelecção; repreensão. *v.t.* e *v.i.* ensinar, fazer prelecções; repreender, censurar.

lecture, *s.* prelecção, lição; discurso; sermão; repreensão. *v.t.* ensinar; preleccionar; repreender.

lecturer, *s.* leitor, prelector.

lectureship, *s.* ofício de leitor; cargo de prelector.

led, *pret.* e *pp.* de *lead; led horse,* cavalo de mão; cavalo disponível.

ledge, *s.* borda; saliência; braçola transversal; proeminência; recife, camada.

ledger, *s.* livro-mestre; pedra assente horizontalmente; lápide.

lee, *s.* sotavento. *pl.* fezes, borras. *s.* sotavento. 1) *lee-board,* tábua de abatimento. 2) *lee brails,* rizes de sotavento. 3) *lee gauge,* sotavento; o lado abrigado. 4) *lee helm,* leme de ló. 5) *lee side,* lado de sotavento. 6) *lee tack,* amura de revés. 7) *lee tide,* maré na mesma direcção do vento. 8) *under the lee,* a sotavento; abrigado do vento.

leech (es), *s.* sanguessuga; médico; guinda, testa; beira lateral da vela (náut.). *v.t.* aplicar sanguessugas; curar; tratar.

leek, *s.* alho-porro; o emblema nacional do País de Gales; *to eat the leek,* engolir, retractar as suas palavras.

leer, *s.* olhar de soslaio; olhar malicioso; compleição, cor; arco maleável pela acção do calor. *v.i.* olhar de soslaio, olhar maliciosamente.

leering, *s.* olhar. *adj.* de través; *aleering look,* olhar de través.

leeringly, *adv.* com olhar de soslaio ou malicioso.

lees, *s. pl.* fezes, borras, sedimento.

leet, *s.* lista de (candidatos para um cargo ou emprego); antigo tribunal inglês de justiça; o direito de funcionar o mesmo tribunal; *leet-days,* dias de despacho.

leetle, vulgarismo por *little.*

leeward, *s.* sotavento. *adj.* e *adv.* a sotavento.

leewardly, *adv.* que descai para sotavento.

leway, *s.* abatimento, declinação de derrota. 1) *to make leeway,* descair para sotavento, 2) *to make up leeway,* compensar o tempo perdido.

left, *s.* esquerda; esquerda (partido político). *adj.* esquerdo, à esquerda. *pret.* e *pp.* de *leave.* 1) *how much have you left?,* quanto (dinheiro) te resta? 2) *left-handed,* canhoto, desajeitado. 3) *left-handedness,* defeito de quem é canhoto; mau jeito. 4) *left-hander,* pancada dada com a mão esquerda; ataque repentino e inesperado. 5) *left off,* posto de parte, deixado de lado; já não usado. 6) *left turn!,* esquerda volver!

leftward, *adv.* para a esquerda; do lado esquerdo.

leg, *s.* perna; pata; pé; base; suporte; escora; borda; caminho andado (náut.) 1) *to find one's legs,* acostumar-se a. 2) *on one's last legs,* reduzido ao extremo. 3) *upon its legs,* numa posição independente. 4) *leg-bail,* fuga de prisão. 5) *leg-of-mutton sleeve,* manga (apertada no pulso, mas muito larga no resto). 6) *leg-of-mutton sail,* vela triangular do mastaréu.

legacy (ies), *s.* legado; legação; embaixada; *legacy duty,* imposto sobre legados.

legal, *adj.* legal, legítimo, válido.

legalism, *s.* legalismo

legalist, *s.* legalista

legality, *s.* legalidade.

legalization, *s.* legalização.

legalize (ise), *v.t.* legalizar.

legally, *adv.* legalmente.

legate, *s.* legado, embaixador.

legatee, s. legatário.

legatine, adj. referente a um legado do Papa.

legation, s. legação.

legatissimo, adv. muito unido, sem interrupção (mús.).

leg-bail, s. fuga da prisão; to give leg-bail, dever a fuga às suas próprias pernas.

leg-bye, s. um ponto ganho no «cricket» quando a bola, depois de dar no «batsman», passar pelo «wicket-keeper» sem que este a segure.

legend, s. lenda; legenda; inscrição; tabela.

legendary, adj. lendário; tradicional; romântico; fabuloso. s. colecção de lendas.

legendemain, s. ligeireza de mãos, prestidigitação.

legged, adj. que tem pernas.

legging, s. polaina.

leggy, adj. de pernas compridas e magras.

leghorn, s. variedade de galinhas; chapéu de palha.

legibility, s. qualidade de ser legível.

legible, adj. legível.

legibleness, s. ver legibility.

legibly, adv. legivelmente.

legion, s. legião, multidão.

legionary (ies), s. e adj. legionário.

legislate, v.i. legislar.

legislation, s. legislação.

legislative, adj. legislativo.

legislator, s. legislador.

legislature, s. legislatura; corpo legislativo.

legist, s. legista.

legitim, s. legítima (herança).

legitimacy, s. legitimidade.

legitimate, v.t. legitimar.

legitimate, adj. legítimo.

legitimately, adv. legitimamente.

legitimateness, s. legitimidade, legalidade.

legitimation, s. legitimação.

legitimist, s. legitimista.

legitimize (se), ver legitimate.

leguminous, adj. leguminoso.

leister, s. espécie de lança usada na pesca do salmão.

leisure, s. lazer, vagar, descanso, ócio, desocupação. 1) at leisure, livre; devagar; com sossego. 2) at your leisure, quando tiver tempo. 3) leisure hours, horas vagas.

leisured, adj. desocupado.

leisureliness, s. vagar.

leisurely, adv. com vagar, comodamente. adj. vagaroso.

leman, s. namoro; amante; concubina.

lemma, s. premissa de um silogismo; lema, assunto; emblema.

lemming, s. espécie de roedores do Norte da Europa.

lemna, s. lemna.

lemon, s. limão; cidra; limoeiro. 1) lemon-coloured, cor de limão. 2) lemon-juice, bebida feita com sumo de limão. 3) lemon-squash, limonada. 4) lemon-squezer, espremedor de limão.

lemonade, s. limonada.

lemur, s. lémure. (pl.) lémures; espíritos; espectros.

lend, v.t. pret. e pp. lent emprestar, proporcionar, dar, conceder, prestar; to lent a hand, ajudar.

lendable, adj. que se pode emprestar.

lender, s. emprestador.

lending, s. empréstimo.

length, s. comprimento, extensão; duração, amplificação de linguagem. 1) length over all, comprimento de fora a fora. 2) length of stroke, curso do êmbolo. 3) at length, afinal. 4) at full length, por extenso, completamente. 5) a full length picture ou portrait, retrato de corpo inteiro.

lengthen, v.t. e v.i. estender, alongar, prolongar, estirar; acrescentar; prolongar--se, alongar-se.

lengthening, s. prolongação, dilação.

lengthier, lenghtiest, comp. e sup. de lengthy.

lengthily, adv. dilatadamente.

lengthiness, s. comprimento, prolongação, dilatação.

lengthways, adv. longitudinalmente.

lengthwise, ver lengthways.

lengthy, adj. longo, dilatado.

lenience, s. lenidade.

lenient, adj. liniente, laxativo; suave, compassivo.

leniently, adv. de modo leniente; suavemente.

Leninism, s. leninismo, teoria ou regime socialista preconizado por Lenine.

lenitive, adj. e s. lenitivo.

lenity, s. lenidade, suavidade.

lens (es), s. lente (óptica).

lent, pret. e pp. de lend.

Lent, s. quaresma.

Lenten, adj. quaresmal.

lenticular, adj. lenticular.

lentil, s. lentilha.

lentisk, s, lentisco.

leonine, adj. leonino, poderoso; majestoso.

leopard, s. leopardo; Leopard's bane, dorónico.

leopardess, s. leoparda.

leper, s. leproso.

leprechaun, s. espírito doméstico muito serviçal que na Irlanda se julga aparecer de noite para se ocupar dos trabalhos de casa.

leprosy, s. lepra.

leprous, adj. leproso.

leprously, adv. como um leproso.

leprousness, s. o estado de leproso.

lepton, s. lepta, centésima parte de um dracma.

lesbian, adj. lésbio; erótico. s. dialecto ou natural de Lesbos.

lese-majesty, s. lesa-majestade.

lesion, s. lesão, ferida

less, comp. de little, menor. s. uma porção menos; o menor ou o mais novo; of two evils choose the less, de dois males o menor.

lessee, s. inquilino, arrendatário.

lessen, v.t. rebaixar, diminuir. v.i. rebaixar--se, deprimir-se.

lesser, adj. menor, inferior.

lesson, s. lição; repreensão, censura.

lessor, s. senhoria.

lest, conj. com medo de; a fim de que não; para que não.

let, p. pr. de letting, pret e pp. let. v.i. deixar, permitir, alugar, arrendar; fretar. 1) house to let, casa para alugar, arrendar, fretar. 2) to let alone, deixar só, deixar estar. 3) let be, parar, reparar, deixar estar. 4) let blood, sangrar. 5) let down, deixar cair; deixar morrer (fogos); abaixar, humilhar; alongar; amaciar (metais); deixar sair. 6) let down easy, mitigar (castigo, dor, etc.). 7) let in, deixar entrar, introduzir. 8) let into, deixar conhecer; inserir. 9) let go, largar (náut.). 10) let go amain, arriar redondo. 11) let loose, soltar. 12) let know, fazer saber, dar a conhecer. 13) let off, disparar; deixar fugir; desculpar; perdoar. 14) let on, divulgar; dizer; fingir. 15) let out, abrir a porta para; permitir a fuga; divulgar; estender; largar o pano (náut.); alugar. 16) let slip, permitir que suba. 17) I will let you of this time, por esta vez perdoo-te. 18) don't let the cat out of the bag, não deixes escapar coisa alguma (do segredo). 19) he was let off, ele foi absolvido. s. estorvo, obstáculo. adj. deixado; arredado.

lethal, adj. letal; mortal.

lethargic (al), adj. letárgico.

lethargically, adv. letargicamente.

lethargicalness, s. sonolência, adormecimento.

lethargy, s. letargia, letargo.

Lethe, s. Letes, rio infernal do esquecimento.

letter, s. letra; carta; diploma; garantia. pl. letras, cultura literária, literaturas. 1) letter-balance, pesa-cartas. 2) letter-book, copiador de cartas. 3) letter-box, caixa do correio. 4) letter-card, cartão que pode ser selado e fechado como carta. 5) letter-case, carteira; caixa tipográfica. 6) letter-file, aparelho para segurar cartas. 7) letter of attorney, procuração. 8) letter of credit, carta de crédito. 9) letter of licence, moratória. 10) letter of marque, carta de curso. 11) letter office, correio. 12) letter-paper, papel de carta. 13) letterpress, conteúdo de livro ilustrado além das ilustrações; o que se encontra impresso relativo às ilustrações. 14) letter scale, pesa-cartas. 15) letter-writer, memorista. 16) silent letters, letras mudas. 17) letters patent, privilégio de invenção. 18) man of letters, literato. v.t. pôr rótulos; estampar letras.

lettered, adj. letrado, erudito.

lettering, s. título, rótulo; impressão.

lettuce, s. alface.

leucocyte, s. leucócito.

leucopathy, s. leucopatia, albinismo.

levant, s. levante. adj. oriental.

Levanter, s. habitante do Levante; vento do Levante.

Levantine, adj. levantino. s. levantino (pano de seda).

levee, s. dique, represa.

levee, s. recepção (de homens somente pelo rei ou alta personalidade).

level, adj. plano, igual; liso, raso; horizontal; honrado, probo. 1) level-crossing, passagem de nível, cruzamento (de uma estrada com uma linha férrea). 2) to be level, estar ao nível de. 3) to make level, nivelar. 4) to do one's level best, fazer todo o possível. s. planície, superfície plana; piso; nível. 5) level line, linha de água; uniformidade, monotonia. v.t. levelling, levelled, nivelar, aplainar, arrasar; proporcionar, adaptar; assestar; arremessar; comparar; igualar. 6) to level to ou with the ground ou in the dust, arrasar. v.i. apontar (uma arma); nivelar.

leveller, s. nivelado; o que rejeita superioridade e quer reduzir tudo à igualdade.

levelling, s. nivelamento.

levelness, s. nível, igualdade.

lever, s. alavanca; pé-de-cabra; manivela;
espeque; *hand lever,* alavanca manual. *v.t.*
servir-se da alavanca ou manivela.

leverage, s. força da alavanca.

leveret, s. lebre pequena.

leviable, *adj.* taxável; a que se pode impor
tributo; susceptível de sofrer imposto.

leviathan, s. monstruosidade, coisa enorme
(como uma baleia, um navio enorme, etc.).

levied, *pret.* e *pp.* de *levy.*

levigate, *v.t.* levigar, moer.

levigation, s. pulverização.

levirate, s. obrigação de casar com a viúva
de um irmão (entre os judeus).

levitate, *v.t.* levitar; suspender no ar
(espiritismo).

levitation, s. acção de tornar leve; ligeireza;
levitação (espiritismo).

Levite, s. levita.

Levitic, *adj.* levítico.

Leviticus, s. *Levítico* (livro da Bíblia).

levity (ies), s. leveza; inconstância,
leviandade.

levy (ies), s. leva (de tropas); levantamento
(de dinheiro); cobrança. *v.t. pret.* e *pp.*
levied fazer levas (de soldados); recrutar;
impor (contribuições, multas, etc.); pôr
embargos.

lewd, *adj.* lascivo, licencioso.

lewdly, *adv.* licenciosamente.

lewdness, s. impudicícia.

lewis (es), s. luva (instrumento de ferro para
ajudar a levantar grandes pedras); *lewis-
gun,* espingarda de tiro rápido ou metralhadora.

lewisite, s. luisite, explosivo de grande
potência.

lexical, *adj.* lexicográfico.

lexicographer, s. lexicógrafo.

lexicography, s. lexicografia.

lexicon, s. léxico, dicionário.

liability (ies), s. perigo; risco; obrigação,
responsabilidade. *(pl.)* passivo (com.); *to
incur liabilities,* tornar-se responsável.

liable, *adj.* sujeito, exposto, responsável,
devedor.

liableness, s. responsabilidade

liaison, s. concubinato; ligação (de sons);
liaison officer, oficial de ligação entre duas
unidades.

liana, liane, cipó.

liar, s. mentiroso.

lias, s. lias.

liassic, *adj.* liássico.

libate, *v.t.* derramar (líquidos); libar, fazer
libações.

libation, s. libação.

libel, s. libelo; pasquim. *v.t.* e *v.i. libelling,
libelled,* difamar, caluniar.

libeller, s. libelista.

libelling, s. difamação.

libellous, *adv.* difamatório.

libellously, *adj.* de um modo difamatório.

liber, s. livro, registo; entrecasca.

liberal, *adj.* liberal, generoso, pródigo;
livre, franco; nobre; *Liberal Party,* Partido
Liberal.

liberalism, s. liberalismo.

liberality, s. liberalidade, generosidade,
magnificência.

liberalize (ise), *v.t.* liberalizar.

liberally, *adv.* liberalmente, generosamente.

liberate, *v.t.* libertar, liberar, livrar.

liberation, s. libertação, alforria.

liberator, s. libertador.

Liberian, s. e *adj.* liberiano.

libertinage, s. libertinagem.

libertinism, s. libertinagem.

libertine, *adj.* libertino. s. libertino; livre-pensador em matéria religiosa.

liberty (ies), s. liberdade; isenção, privilégio,
imunidade; licença, permissão. 1) *to set at
liberty,* pôr em liberdade. 2) *to take liberties,*
tomar muita confiança. 3) *liberty Bonds,*
títulos do governo para pagamento das
despesas da grande guerra (EUA).

libidinous, *adj.* libidinoso; desonesto.

libidinously, *adv.* libidinosamente,
lascivamente.

libidinousness, s. lascívia.

Libra, s. libra, Balança (ast.). abrv. 1b.

librarian, s. bibliotecário.

librarianship, s. cargo de bibliotecário.

library (ies), s. biblioteca, livraria.

librate, *v.t.* balancear, equilibrar.

libration, s. libração, balanço, equilíbrio.

librettist, s. autor de libretos.

libretto, s. libreto.

Libyan, s. e *adj.* líbio.

lice, s. plural de *louse.*

licence, s. licença, permissão, autorização;
despacho; liberdade excessiva. *v.t.*
autorizar; permitir, conceder um privilégio;
licenciar.

licensed, *adj.* encartado; habilitado; *licensed victualler,* vendedor autorizado (de vinhos, bebidas, comidas).

licensee, *s.* pessoa que obteve licença ou permissão.

licenser, *s.* o que dá licença.

licenciate, *s.* licenciado.

licentious, *adj.* licencioso.

licentiously, *adv.* licenciosamente.

licentiousness, *s.* licença, libertinagem.

lichen, *s.* líquen, musgo; doença de pele.

lichened, *adj.* coberto de líquenes.

lichenous, *adj.* como os líquenes.

lichgate, *s.* entrada alpendrada para um cemitério, onde o caixão espera até que chegue o padre.

Licinian, *s.* liciniano.

licit, *adj.* lícito, permitido.

licitly, *adv.* licitamente.

lick, *v.t.* lamber; chupar; retocar; bater; vencer; 1) *to lick the dust,* morder o pó. 2) *lick into shape,* dar a forma apropriada, amoldar. *s.* lambedura, acto de lamber; pancada; soco; terreno salgadiço.

licker, *s.* lambedor, lambão, glutão; lubrificador automático.

lickerish, *adj.* delicado, saboroso, apetitoso, delicioso.

lickerishness, *s.* delicadeza de paladar, delicioso.

licking, *s.* lambedura; pancada, chicotada; castigo.

licorice, liquorice, *s.* alcaçus.

lictor, *s.* lictor.

lid, *s.* tampa, coberta; portinhola; pálpebra; opérculo; *to put the lid on,* ser o cúmulo (de), exceder tudo.

lie, *s.* mentira, ficção, fábula. 1) *white lie,* mentirola. 2) *to give the lie to,* desmentir. *v.i. p. pr. lying, pret.* e *pp. lied* mentir. 3) *to lie in one's throat,* mentir pela gorja.

lie, *v.i. pret. lay pp. lain,* estar deitado, deitar-se; encostar-se, repousar; jazer; estar situado; permanecer. 1) *to lie at anchor,* estar ancorado. 2) *lie at the point of death,* estar moribundo. 3) *lie about,* estar espalhado. 4) *lie down,* deitar-se, jazer. 5) *lie in,* estar de parto. 6) *lie on* ou *upon,* ser obrigatório, pesar sobre; estar em caminho (náut.). 7) *lie over,* caducar, deixar de pagar (uma letra); ficar adiado. 8) *lie stick,* estar de cama. 9) *lie to,* estar à capa (náut.). 10) *to lie in the bed one has made,* sofrer as consequências dos seus actos. 11) *to lie in wait,* estar de emboscada. 12) *let sleeping dogs lie,* não acordes o cão que dorme. 13) *as far as in me lies,* quanto em mim couber. 14) *find out how the land lies,* orientar-se, rondar o terreno.

lief, *adj.* querido, amado (poét.). *adv.* de boa vontade, de bom agrado.

liege, *s.* senhor de feudo; soberano; vassalo; súbito. *adj.* feudatário, vassalo.

liegeman, *s.* vassalo.

lien, *s.* hipoteca, direito de retenção.

lier, *s.* pessoa que está deitada.

lieu, *s.* hipoteca, direito de retenção.

lieutenancy (ies), *s.* tenência; posto de tenente.

lieutenant, *s.* tenente; governador (de província). 1) *lieutenant-commander,* capitão-tenente. 2) *lieutenant-general,* tenente-general. 3) *lieutenant-governor,* governador de colónias. 4) *second lieutenant,* alferes. 5) *lord lieutenant,* vice-rei da Irlanda; governador permanente de um condado das Ilhas Britânicas.

life, *s.* vida; existência; modo de viver, conduta; biografia; vivacidade, movimento, ardor; mundo. *pl.* lives. 1) *life annuity,* renda vitalícia. 2) *life assurance,* seguro de vida. 3) *life-bell,* cinto de salvação. 4) *life-boat,* barco salva-vidas. 5) *life-buoy,* bóia de salvação. 6) *life class,* aula de desenho do natural (com pessoas). 7) *life-estate,* herdade com usufruto vitalício. 8) *life-guard,* guarda pessoal, constituída por soldados. 9) *life-giving,* vivificante. 10) *life insurance,* seguro de vida. 11) *life-interest* ou *rent,* renda vitalícia. 12) *life-jacket,* colete de salvação. 13) *life-line,* cabo de vaivém; redes de cordas nas bordas do navio. 14) *life-peer,* Par (do reino) vitalício. 15) *life-preserver,* aparelho de salvação, como cinto ou colete. 16) *life rocket,* foguetão porta-cabo. 17) *life-saving,* destinado a salvar a vida a náufragos. 18) *life-spring,* origem da vida. 19) *life stirring,* cheio de animação. 20) *early life,* mocidade. 21) *high life,* alta sociedade. 22) *for life,* por toda a vida. 23) *from life,* do natural. 24) *to the life,* ao vivo, ao natural (falando de pinturas). 25) *to make life a burden,* tornar a vida insuportável.

lifeless, *adj.* morto, inanimado; sem vida ou animação; desabitado.

lifelessly, *adv.* inanimado.

lifelessness, *s.* falta de vida ou de vigor.

lifelike, *adj.* que parece vivo, natural.

lifelong, *adj.* que dura a vida, vitalício.

lifer, *s.* o que é condenado a trabalhos forçados por toda a vida.

lifetime, *s.* curso da vida.

lift, *v.t.* e *v.i.* levantar, erguer, elevar; içar; desencalhar; exaltar; gabar; ensoberbecer; roubar, despojar; tentar erguer; levantar-se, subir. 1) *to lift ou the heel against*, tratar com insolência e desprezo. 2) *to lift up the voice*, levantar a voz, gritar. *s.* acção de levantar; esforço para levantar; elevador, ascensor; alça; amantilho (náut.). 3) *lift and force pump*, bomba aspirante-premente. 4) *to give one a lift*, ajudar alguém a levantar-se ou a levantar alguma coisa. 5) *a dead lift*, esforço inútil.

lifter, *s.* o que levanta, que eleva; ladrão.

lifting, *s.* acção de levantar; auxílio que se dá a alguém para que se levante. 1) *lifting apparatus*, aparelho de içar. 2) *lifting beam*, vega de içar. 3) *lifting gear*, elevador.

ligament, *s.* ligamento.

ligamental, *adj.* ligamentoso.

ligamentous, *adj.* ligamentoso.

ligation, *s.* ligação.

ligature, *s.* ligadura.

light, *s.* luz, claridade, clarão; resplendor; vela, candeeiro; lâmpada, farol; clarabóia, janela; o raiar da aurora; ponto de vista; aspecto; percepção; inteligência. 1) *light beacon*, baliza luminosa. 2) *light-boat*, barco-farol. 3) *light-keeper*, faroleiro. 3) *light room*, paiol das luzes. 4) *light-ship*, embarcação-farol. 5) *light wave*, onda de luz. 6) *anchor light*, luz de porto, luz de âncora. 7) *blue light*, facho de sinais. 8) *deck light*, olho-de-boi (náut.). 9) *moonlight*, luar. 10) *northern light*, aurora boreal. 11) *skylight*, clarabóia. 12) *to bring to light*, publicar. 13) *to turn on* ou *to switch on the light*, abrir a luz (eléct.). 14) *to turn off* ou *switch off the light*, apagar a luz (eléct.). *adj.* leve, ligeiro, lesto; alegre; volúvel, fútil; inconstante; mudável; leviano; claro, que tem uma claridade; brilhante; loiro; ruivo (cabelo), 15) *light airs*, brisas; quase calma. 16) *light blue*, azul-claro. 17) *light breeze*, aragem. 18) *light brain*, pessoa sem juízo. 19) *light draught*, calado mínimo. 20) *light-handed*, com tripulação reduzida. 21) *light-fingered*, ágil de mãos, hábil para furtar. 22) *light goods*, mercadorias leves. 23) *light hair*, cabelo loiro. 24) *light-headed*,

alegre, jovial. 25) *light-headedly*, estouvadamente. 26) *light-headness*, delírio. 27) *light-horsemen*, cavalaria ligeira. 28) *light-infantry*, infantaria ligeira. 29) *light literature*, literatura leve, novelas. 30) *light machine gun*, carabina-metralhadora (de tiro rápido). 31) *light-weight*, pessoa que não tem a média do peso (nos jogos). *v.t. pret.* e *pp. lighted* ou *lit*, acender, alumiar, iluminar. 32) *to light a fire*, acender lume. *v.i.* acender-se, atear-se; descer, poisar-se; dar com; encontrar por acaso; recair sobre; apear-se.

lighten, *v.t.* alumiar; aliviar. *v.i.* tornar-se leve; relampaguear.

lighter, *adj. comp.* de *light* mais ligeiro; mais claro. *s.* fragata, batelão; barcaça; acendedor.

lighterage, *s.* fragatagem, frete de fragata, barcagem.

lighterman, *s.* fragateiro.

lighthouse, *s.* farol (casa ou torre).

lighthousekeeper, *s.* faroleiro.

lighting, *s.* iluminação artificial.

lightless, *adj.* sem luz, obscuro.

lightly, *adv.* ligeiramente, levemente; facilmente; sem razão, sem motivo; alegremente; superficialmente; levianamente. 1) *to think lightly of*, fazer pouco caso de. 2) *lightly come lighly go*, dinheiros de sacristão cantando vêm cantando vão.

lightminded, *s.* volúvel, inconstante, doidivanas.

lightness, *s.* ligeireza; leviandade, frivolidade.

lightning, *s.* relâmpago; raio; faísca; centelha. 1) *lightning-arrester conductor* ou *rod*, pára-raios. 2) *lightning glance*, resplendor do relâmpago, impressão causada por ele. 3) *a flash of a lightning*, um relâmpago.

lights, *s. pl.* pulmões (dos animais); bofes.

lightsome, *adj.* alegre, claro.

lightsomely, *adj.* alegremente.

lightsomeness, *s.* claridade; alegria, regozijo.

ligneous, *adj.* lenhoso.

lignite, *s.* linhite (mineral).

lignum, *s.* ébano; *lignum-vitae*, gaiaco.

Ligurian, *s.* e *adj.* ligúrio.

like, *adj.* semelhante, parecido, igual; provável, verosímil; homogéneo; disposto para. *s.* igual, coisa igual ou parecida. *adv.* como, do mesmo modo que, semelhante a, igual. 1) *to do* ou *give like for like*, pagar na mesma moeda. 2) *like father like son*, tal pai tal filho. 3) *like master, like man*, tal amo tal criado. 4) *to look like*, parecer-se com. 5) *like manner*, do mesmo modo. 6) *to be as like as two peas*, parecer-se como duas gotas de água. 7) *to feel like*, estar disposto a fazer alguma coisa. *v.t.* e *v.i.* gostar de, desejar; estar contente com; querer; convir; achar conveniente. 8) *as you like*, como quiser. 9) *how do you like London?*, que tal lhe pareceu Londres?

likelihood, ver *likeliness*.

likelier, likeliest, *comp.* e *sup.* de *likely*.

likeliness, *s.* semelhança, verosimilhança, conformidade, probabilidade, boa aparência.

likely, *adj.* provável, verosímil, bem-parecido; agradável; de bom talhe; apto, idóneo, próprio para. 1) *it's likely to rain*, é provável que chova. 2) *he's likely to have forgotten*, é capaz de se ter esquecido. *adv.* provavelmente, verosimilmente.

likeminded, *adj.* da mesma opinião, de sentimentos idênticos.

liken, *v.t.* assemelhar, comparar.

likeness, *s.* semelhante; aparência, figura, ar; retrato.

likes, *s.* gostos.

likewise, *adv.* semelhantemente, do mesmo modo, também.

liking, *s.* inclinação, gosto, agrado, simpatia; prova, ensaio.

liliac, *s.* lilás. *adj.* cor de lilás.

liliceous, *adj.* liliáceo.

Liliputian, *s.* liliputiano.

lilt, *v.t.* e *v.i.* cantar (com melodia e ritmo); dançar. *s.* canto melodioso e rítmico.

lily, *s.* lírio, açucena. 1) *lily-livered*, cobarde. 2) *lily of the valley*, lírio do vale.

limb, *s.* membro (perna, braço, asa ou barbatana); pernada de árvore; braços da haste de cruz; saliência de monte; limbo (de astro, de instrumento); borda, orla, extremidade; um velhaco.

limbed, *adj.* com membros (geralmente usado em compostos, como *ling-limbed*).

limber, *adj.* flexível, brando. *s.* tábua de sobrequilha; carreta (das peças) *v.t.* engatar.

limberness, *s.* flexibilidade, facilidade, condescendência.

limbless, *adj.* privado de membros ou ramos.

limbo, *s.* limbo; prisão.

lime, *s.* cal; visco; lodo; lima (fruta), limeira; tília. 1) *lime-juice*, sumo de lima; remedio contra o escorbuto. 2) *lim-juicer*, marinheiro inglês. 3) *limelight*, luz de cálcio; ribalta. 4) *lime-pit*, pia (para curtir coiros); mina de pedra e cal. 5) *lime water*, água de cal (hidróxido de cálcio). 6) *lime wash*, aguada, água de cal para limpar as paredes. 7) *lime white*, cal desfeita. 8) *lime-twig*, varinha enviscada. 9) *quick lime*, cal viva. 10) *slaked lime*, cal apagada. *v.t.* enviscar; enredar; apanhar no laço; aplicar cal; adubar as terras com cal; cimentar.

limeklin, *s.* forno de cal.

limerick, *s.* limérico, verso mal feito.

limestone, *s.* pedra cálcaria.

limit, *s.* limite, termo, fim, fronteira; obstáculo; impedimento. *v.t.* limitar, determinar; restringir.

limitable, *adj.* que se pode limitar, restringível.

limitary, *adj.* limítrofe.

limitation, *s.* limitação, demarcação; restrição; prescrição.

limited, *adj.* limitado, restrito; *limited express train*, comboio só com carruagem de primeira classe.

limitedly, *adv.* limitadamente.

limitedness, *s.* ver *limitation*.

limitless, *adj.* sem limites, ilimitado.

limmer, *s.* falca de escada (náut.).

limn, *v.t.* pintar; iluminar; descrever; retratar.

limner, *s.* pintor, iluminador.

limning, *s.* pintura.

limous, *adj.* limoso, lodoso.

limousine, *s.* limusina.

limp, *s.* coxeadura, manqueira. *adj.* débil, flexível; brando, mole. *v.i.* coxear, manquejar.

limper, *s.* coxo.

limpet, *s.* lepa, lapa.

limpid, *s.* límpido, claro.

limpidity, *s.* limpidez, claridade, transparência.

limpidness, ver *limpidity*.

limping, *adj.* que coxeia, coxo. *s.* coxeadura.

limpingly, *adv.* coxeando.

limply, *adv.* debilmente.

limpness, *s.* debilidade.

limy, *adj.* calcário; viscoso.

linchpin, *s.* chaveta de ferro para segurar a roda do eixo.

lincolngreen, *s.* pano de cor verde muito viva.

lincrusta, *s.* lincrusta, espécie de linhagem com relevos para forrar paredes.

linden, *s.* tília.

line, *s.* linha; traço; perfil, contorno; linha (carreira de navegação); linha (férrea); frota mercante; equador; enfiamento; fila; limite; confim; carta pequena; ramo de actividade, linha de conduta; proceder, modo de comportar-se; (pl.) versos. 1) *base line*, linha de construção (desenho de navio); linha de serviço (no jogo de ténis). 2) *branch-line*, ramal (caminho de ferro). 3) *clean line*, linha fina. 4) *clothes-line*, corda em que se estende a roupa para secar. 5) *fighting-line*, linha de combate. 6) *straight line*, linha recta. 7) *trunk line*, linha principal. 8) *hard lines*, apuros, situação angustiosa. 9) *line-abreast*, linha (de esquadra). 10) *line keeper*, guarda-via. 11) *line of fire*, linha de fogo. 12) *line of sights*, linha de mira. 13) *line shafts*, linhas de eixo. 14) *first line transport*, trem de combate. 15) *ship of the line*, navio de linha que pode entrar em combate. 16) *to give line*, dar-lhe liberdade. *v.t.* traçar, riscar linhas, alinhar, pôr em fila; forrar, revestir, cobrir, guardar, guarnecer, debruar. *v.i.* estar em linha. 17) *furlined coat*, casaco forrado de peles.

lineage, *s.* linha, raça.

lineal, *adj.* linear, descendente.

lineally, *adv.* em linha recta.

lineament, *s.* lineamento; feição fisionómica, forma do rosto.

linear, *adj.* linear.

lineation, *s.* delineamento.

lined, *adj.* forrado.

lineman, *s.* guarda das linhas (de comboio, telégrafo, etc.).

linen, *s.* pano de linho, roupa branca. *adj.* feita de linho, pálido, branco, desmaiado. 1) *linen cambric*, cambraia de linho. 2) *linen draper*, fanqueiro. 3) *linen goods*, comércio de roupa branca. 4) *linen room*, rouparia. 5) *linen yarn*, fio de linho. 6) *bed linen*, roupa branca de cama, 7) *baby linen*, enxoval de criança.

liner, *s.* vapor de carreira, paquete; delineador; o que risca papel de música; calço; taco; casquilho; forro; camisa; forrador; *cylinder liner*, camisa de cilindro.

linesmank, *s.* soldado de regimento de linha; juiz de linha no futebol ou no ténis.

ling, *s.* urso, esteva; peixe semelhante ao bacalhau.

linger, *v.t.* e *v.i.* demorar-se; retardar; hesitar; estar doente por muito tempo; padecer; prolongar, diliatar, demorar.

lingerer, *s.* pessoa indolente; pessoa que padece; retardatário.

lingerie, *s.* roupa branca.

lingering, *adj.* lento, vagaroso, ronceiro; paciente. *s.* lentidão; demora; hesitação.

lingeringly, *adv.* lentamente, com demora; com hesitação.

lingo, *s.* girafa; algaravia, dialecto.

lingual, *s.* lingual, aparelho de meter na boca para ajudar a pronunciar certas vogais. *adj.* lingual.

lingually, *adv.* pronunciado com a língua.

linguist, *v.t.* e *s.* poliglota.

linguistic, *adj.* linguístico.

linguistics, *s.* linguística.

lining, *s.* forro, guarnecimento; guarnição (de chumaceira); forra de vela; parede interior.

link, *s.* anel de cadeia, elo; fuzil, tirante; sector, braçadeira; enlace; archote. 1) *link-boy* ou *man*, o que leva o archote na frente. 2) *bar link*, elo com estai. *v.t* ligar, encadear, unir. *v.i.* encadear-se, unir-se em matrimónio.

linking, *s.* amizade; união.

links, *s.* areal plano ou ondulado; campo de golfe.

linn, *s.* queda de água.

linaen, *s.* e *adj.* liniano.

linnet, *s.* pintarroxo; *green linnet*, verdelhão.

linoleum, *s.* linóleo.

linotype, *s.* linótipo.

linseed, *s.* linhaça. 1) *linseed-meal*, farinha de linhaça. 2) *linseed-oil*, óleo de linhaça. 3) *linseed-poultice*, cataplasma de linhaça.

linsey, *s.* uma espécie de barro (das minas); tecido de linho e lã.

linsey-woolsey, *adj.* feito de linho e lá. *s.* tecido de linho e lã.

linstock, *s.* morrão (de artilharia).

lint, *s.* fios de linho para feridas.

lintel, *s.* lintel, verga, padieira.

lion, *s.* leão; valente; herói; homem célebre; *pl.* lugares dignos de visita numa cidade. 1) *lion-hearted*, corajoso como um leão. 2) *lion-hunter*, caçador de leões. 3) *lion-like*, à maneira de leão. 4) *lion's provider*, nome popular para chacal; amigo humilde. 5) *lion's share*, a parte de leão. 6) *a lion in the way*, um perigo que tem de ser encarado e vencido. 7) *to beard the lion in his den*, arrostar com uma pessoa temida.

lioness, *s.* leoa.

lionize, *v.t.* tratar alguém com grande respeito; mostrar as coisas dignas de se ver numa cidade. *v.t.* visitar coisas de interesse.

lip, *s.* beiço; lábio; impertinência; borda, extremidade. 1) *lip-devotion*, devoção só de boca. 2) *lip-good*, bom nas palavras e não nas acções. 3) *lip-labour*, palavras vãs, de falsa cortesia. 4) *lip-reading*, interpretação do movimento dos lábios. 5) *lip-salve*, pomada para os lábios; palavras doces. 6) *lip-service*, ofício religioso sem devoção. 7) *to make, to put up a lip*, fazer tromba, fazer focinho. 8) *to smack one's lips*, fazer estalar os beiços. 9) *to hang on one's lips*, escutar reverentemente todas as palavras de alguém. 10) *none of your lip*, nada de palavras atrevidas, impertinentes. *v.t. lipping, lipped*, tocar com os lábios.

liquefaction, *s.* liquefacção.

liquefiable, *adj.* fusível, que se pode derreter.

liquefy, *pret.* e *pp. liquified. v.t.* liquefazer, derreter. *v.i.* liquefazer-se, derreter-se.

liqueur, *s.* licor, cordial.

liquid, *adj.* líquido; suave; doce; claro; *liquid assets* ou *securities*, valores realizáveis. *s.* líquido, substância líquida; bebida, beberagem.

liquidate, *v.t.* liquidar, saldar contas.

liquidation, *s.* liquidação.

liquidator, *s.* liquidatário.

liquidly, *adv.* liquidamente.

liquidness, *s.* liquidez.

liquor, *s.* bebida alcoólica; solução, banho. *v.i.* humedecer, untar.

liquorice, ver *licorice*.

lira, *s.* lira (moeda); *pl. lire* ou *liras*.

lisp, *v.t.* e *v.i.* balbuciar, ciciar, pronunciar mal. *s.* cicio.

lisper, *s.* pessoa que é ciciosa.

lisping, *adj.* cicioso, balbuciante.

lispingly, *adv.* falando como os ciciosos, balbuciando.

lisse, *s.* gaze de seda.

lissome, *adj.* ver *lithesome*.

lissomeness, ver *lithesomeness*.

list, *s.* lista, rol, registo; banda, ourela (do pano); tira; orla; inclinação (de navio); lista, filete, moldura; régua; limite (poét.); liça, arena; *army list*, almanaque do exército. *v.t.* registar, alistar, matricular; quotizar; dispor na arena; adornar; orlar; listrar; querenar;

escutar (poét.). *v.i.* alistar-se (para soldado); escorar; desejar.

listed, *adj.* listrado; quotizado.

listel, *s.* listel, filete.

listen, *v.t.* e *v.i.* escutar, atender.

listener, *s.* ouvinte, espião.

listening, *s.* acção de ouvir; *listening post*; posto de escuta.

listerine, *s.* listerina.

listerism, *s.* listerismo.

listing, *s.* ourela de pano; tira; sanefa; alistamento de soldados.

listless, *adj.* descuidado, indiferente, apático.

listlessly, *adv.* indiferentemente.

listlessness, *s.* descuido, indiferença, negligência, apatia.

lit, *pret.* e *pp.* de *light*.

litany, *s.* ladainha.

liter, *s.* litro.

literacy, *s.* capacidade de ler e escrever.

literal, *adj.* literal, recto, exacto.

literalness, *s.* sentido literal.

literalism, *s.* o sentido literal, positivismo.

literalist, *s.* pessoa escrupulosamente exacta; positivista.

literality, *s.* sentido literal; positivismo.

literally, *adv.* literalmente.

literalness, ver *literality*.

literary, *adj.* literário; versado em, ou devotado à literatura. 1) *literary property*, propriedade literária. 2) *literary man*, homem de letras.

literate, *s.* e *adj.* literato, douto.

literati, *s. pl.* literatos.

literatim, *adv.* literalmente.

literature, *s.* literatura; belas-letras; obras literárias; erudição.

litharge, *s.* litargírio.

lithe, *adj.* flexível, maleável, brando.

lithely, *adv.* de um modo flexível.

litheness, *s.* flexibilidade.

lither, *adj.* flexível, brando, maleável.

lithesome, *adj.* ágil, flexível.

lithesomeness, *s.* flexibilidade, brandura.

lithia, *s.* lítia.

lithic, *adj.* lítico.

lithium, *s.* lítio.

lithochromatic, *adj.* litocromático.

lithograph, *v.t.* e *v.i.* litografar. *s.* litografia (estampa).

lithographer, *s.* litógrafo.

litographic, *adj.* litográfico.

lithography, *s.* litografia.

lithontripic, *adj.* litotríptico. *s.* remédio litotríptico.

lithtype, *s.* litotipia. *v.t.* litotipar.

Lithuanian, *s.* e *adj.* lituano.

litigant, *s.* e *adj.* litigante.

litigate, *v.t.* e *v.i.* litigar.

litigation, *s.* litígio, pleito.

litigious, *adj.* litigioso, disputável; litigante; trapaceiro; caviloso.

litigiously, *adv.* litigiosamente.

litigiousness, *s.* inclinação para litígios; espírito trapaceiro.

litmus, *s.* musgo donde se extrai tinta azul.

litotes, *s.* litotes.

litre, *s.* litro.

litter, *s.* liteira, cama (de gato); retalhos, aparas; ninhada, barrigada (de animais); desordem, confusão. *v.t.* e *v.i.* parir (o animal); fazer a cama (aos animais); pôr em desordem, em confusão, espalhar, deixar objectos espalhados em todos os cantos.

little, *adj.* pouco, limitado; de pouca importância, insignificante; mesquinho; ruim. *s.* pouco, pouca coisa. *adv.* pouco, escassamente. 1) *a little one,* um menino. 2) *her little ones,* os seus filhos (pessoas ou animais). 3) *the little people,* os duendes. 4) *little by little,* a pouco e pouco. 5) *be it ever so little,* por pouco que seja.

littleness, *s.* pequenez, ninharia; ruindade, mesquinhez.

little-englander, *s.* oposicionista ao engrandecimento das colónias inglesas.

little-go, *s.* primeiro exame para bacharel.

littora, *s.* litora.

liturgic, *adj.* litúrgico.

liturgically, *adv.* liturgicamente.

liturgist, *s.* liturgista.

liturgy, *s.* liturgia.

lituus, *s.* lituo.

livable, *adj.* habitável; suportável; razoável.

live, *adj.* vivo; activo; eficaz; efectivo; útil; ardente, abrasador, brilhante. 1) *live coal,* brasa. 2) *live cartridge,* cartuxo com bala. 3) *live shell,* granada que ainda arde e pode explodir. 4) *live-stock,* animais domésticos. *v.t* e *v.i.* viver; existir, nutrir-se; passar a vida; habitar; residir; perpetuar-se. 5) *to live from hand to mouth,* viver dos ganhos de cada dia. 6) *to live down,* viver de maneira a esquecer ou fazer esquecer calúnia, mágoa, etc. 7) *to live up to,* viver em conformidade com. 8) *to live out,* sobreviver. 9) *to*

live in clover, viver regaladamente. 10) *to live on,* sustentar-se de. 11) *live and let live,* sê tolerante, vive e deixa viver.

lived, *adj.* da vida; de costumes, de maneira; 1) *long-lived,* de longa vida. 2) *low-lived,* de maus costumes. 3) *short-lived,* de curta duração.

livelier, liveliest, *comp. sup.* de *lively.*

liveliness, *s.* vida, agilidade, viveza, vivacidade; fermentação.

livelong, *adj.* longo; durável; eterno, inteiro; todo; *all the livelong day,* todo o santo dia.

lively, *adj.* vivo, animado, vigoroso, desembaraçado; que se levanta bem (navio). *adv.* vivamente.

liver, *s.* vivente; fígado; *liver-complaint,* doença de fígado.

livered, *adj.* que usa libré.

liverpudlian, *s.* habitante de Liverpul.

livery, *adj.* da consistência ou cor de fígado; irritável.

livery, *s.* libré, uniforme; aluguer de cocheira e sustento de cavalos; conjunto dos membros de uma corporação de Londres; *livery coach,* carruagem de aluguer.

liveryman, *s.* dono de cocheira de aluguer; membro da corporação de Londres chamada Libery Company; criado de libré.

lives, *pl.* de *life.* 3.ª pessoa *sing. ind. pres.* de *live.*

livid, *adj.* lívido; plúmbeo.

lividly, *adv.* lividamente.

lividness, *s.* lividez.

living, *s.* modo de viver ou de ganhar a vida; subsistência; vida, existência; benefício eclesiástico. 1) *the living,* os viventes, os vivos. 2) *plair living and high thinking,* vida frugal e filosófica. 3) *living-room,* sala de estar. *adj.* vivo, vigoroso; vivificante; evidente. 4) *living coals,* brasas. 5) *living wage,* salário (que permite ao operário viver com conforto). 6) *within living memory,* na memória da gente que ainda vive.

Livonian, *s.* e *adj.* livónio.

lixiviate, *v.i.* lixiviar.

lixiviated, *adj.* que contém lixívia.

lixiviation, *s.* lixiviação.

lizard, *s.* lagarto; sapatilho (naút.); caçoilo (náut.)

llama, *s.* lama.

Lloyd's, *s.* corporação de seguradores marítimos de Londres, *Lloyd's register,* lista alfabética anual dos navios classificados segundo a sua classe.

lo, *interj.* eis aí, vede!

loach, *s.* cadoz.

load, *s.* carga (de peça, de válvula, etc.); carregamento (de navio); peso; resistência; opressão; fardo. 1) *boat-load,* barcada. 2) *cart-load,* carroçada. 3) *load-draught,* calado. 4) *deep load-draught,* calado máximo. 5) *load line,* linha de água carregada. *v.t.* carregar; acumular; embaraçar; impedir. *v.i.* carregar, tomar carga.

loader, *s.* carregador.

loading, *s.* cargo (acto de carregar). 1) *loading-crane,* guincho de carga. 2) *loading days,* dias úteis de carga.

loadstone, *s.* magnetite.

loaf, *s.* um pão. *pl. loaves.* 1) *loaf-sugar,* açúcar em formas. *v.t.* e *v.i.* passar o tempo indolentemente. 2) *to loaf away,* mandriar, preguiçar. 3) *to loaf time away,* desperdiçar o tempo.

loafer, *s.* mandrião, preguiçoso.

loam, *s.* marga. *v.t.* untar ou cobrir com marga.

loaminess, *s.* natureza de marga.

loamy, *adj.* margoso.

loan, *s.* empréstimo (objecto, ou valor emprestado). *v.t.* emprestar; *loan-office,* caixa de crédito.

loath, *adj.* contrário a, relutante, que não tem vontade.

loathe, *v.t.* aborrecer, detestar. *v.i.* causar tédio; sentir desgosto ou aborrecimento.

loather, *s.* o que sente desgosto, tédio ou aborrecimento.

loathful, *adj.* cheio de tédio, enfastiado.

loathing, *s.* aborrecimento, desgosto, tédio, asco, repugnância. *adj.* repugnante, asqueroso.

loathingly, *adv.* com repugnância.

loathly, *adj.* detestável, nauseabundo. *adv.* contra vontade.

loathness, *s.* relutância.

loathsome, *adj.* repugnante, nauseabundo, asqueroso.

loathsomely, *adv.* asquerosamente.

loathsomeness, *s.* repugnância.

loaves, *pl.* de *loaf.*

lob, *s.* rústico, grosseirão. *v.t.* e *v.i. lobbing, lobbed,* andar, correr, mexer-se pesadamente, sem jeito ou devagar; atirar a bola vagarosamente.

lobby, *s.* vestíbulo, antecâmara; corredor; salão (de teatro); contra-paiol (náut,).

lobe, *s.* lobo.

lobed, *adj.* loboso.

lobelia, *s.* lobélia.

lobster, *s.* lagosta.

lobular, *adj.* lobular.

lobule, *s.* lóbulo.

local, *adj.* local; *local time,* a hora local.

locale, *s.* local.

localization, *s.* localização.

localism, *s.* apego a um lugar; bairrismo; idiotismo ou costume local.

locality, *s.* localidade.

localize, *v.t.* localizar.

locally, *adv.* localmente.

locate, *v.i.* pôr, situar.

located, *adj.* situado, sito.

location, *s.* colocação; situação; sítio; localidade.

locative, *s.* locativo.

loch, *s.* lago escocês; braço de mar muito estreito.

lock, *s.* fechadura; fecho; fechos de arma de fogo; comporta; canal entre duas comportas; represa; abraço apertado (em luta); cerca, valado; anel de cabelo; froco de lã; borla. 1) *lock bolt,* palhetão, lingueta, parafuso, freio. 2) *lock-jaw,* contracção espasmódica dos músculos do queixo. 3) *lock-nut,* contraporca. 4) *spring lock,* fechadura de mola. 5) *padlock,* loquete. 6) *under lock and key,* a sete chaves. 7) *lock washer,* anilha de pressão. *v.t.* fechar à chave; encerrar; apertar (nos braços); fazer represas (num canal); travar, apertar uma forma (tipográfica). *v.i.* fechar à chave. 8) *to lock in,* ou *up,* fechar, ter debaixo de chave. 9) *to lock one out,* fechar a porta a alguém para que não entre; diz-se também do patrão que não deixa trabalhar os operários, fechando-lhes a porta.

lockage, *s.* eclusa, comporta; desnivelamento de eclusa; taxa de eclusa.

locked, *adj.* fechado à chave; abrigado pela terra (náut.); apertado nos braços.

locker, *s.* compartimento (de bordo); caixão, paiol (náut.); gaveta com chave; armário. 1) *chain locker,* paiol de amarra. 2) *not a shot in the locker,* nem um vintém no bolso. 3) *Davy Jone's locker,* o mar, a sepultura dos afogados.

locket, *s.* colchete, broche; medalhão.

lockgate, *s.* porta de represa.

lock-jaw, locked-jaw, *s.* trismo, variedade de tétano.

lockout, *s.* greve de patrões.

lockram, s. estopa; *lockram jawed*, de rosto abatido.

locksmith, s. serralheiro.

lock-up, s. calabouço, aljube.

locomobile, s. locomóvel.

locomotion, s. locomoção.

locomotive, adj. locomotivo. s. locomotiva; *pl.* pernas.

locomotor, adj. locomotor.

locum-tenens, s. lugar-tenente.

locus, s. lugar. *pl. loci.*

locust, s. gafanhoto. 1) *locust bean*, alfarroba. 2) *locust-tree*, nome de diversas árvores, como a alfarrobeira.

locution, s. locução, frase.

locutory, s. locutório.

lode, s. filão.

lodestar, s. estrela do norte, estrela polar.

lodestones, s. pedra-íman.

lodge, v.t. alojar, recolher, hospedar; pôr, colocar; fixar; plantar; depositar dinheiro (em banco, etc,). v.i. residir, morar; alojar-se; hospedar-se. 1) *to lodge complaint against*, formular uma queixa contra alguém. 2) *lodge upon*, descer sobre, pousar (aves). s. casa da guarda; casa pequena, cubículo; cabana; covil; loja maçónica. 3) *porter's lodge*, quarto ou cubículo do porteiro.

lodgeable, adj. habitável, que pode servir para habitação.

lodgement, s. alojamento; colocação; depósito (bancário); amontoamento; entrincheiramento.

lodger, s. hóspede; inquilino; *lodger franchise*, direito de voto de certos inquilinos.

lodging, s. alojamento, pousada; hospedaria. 1) *lodging allowance*, subsídio de residência. 2) *private lodging*, quarto em casa particular. 3) *board and lodging*, cama e mesa.

lodginghouse, s. casa de hóspedes.

loft, s. sótão; celeiro, palheiro; pombal; bando de pombas; armazém; casa de arrecadação; casa das velas (náut.); *cock of the loft*, cabeça ou chefe de grupo.

loftily, adv. altivamente, pomposamente; em cima; no alto.

loftiness, s. altura, elevação; pompa; sublimidade; altivez; orgulho; majestade.

lofty, adj. alto, altíssimo, elevado, pomposo; sublime; grande; eminente; excelso; altivo, orgulhoso, soberbo.

log, s. acha, cepo, lenho; barrote; barquilha; logaritmo. 1) *log board*, tábua de barquilha. 2) *log-book*, livro da rota, diário de navegação. 3) *log-cabin* ou *hut*, cabana rústica, choça. 4) *log glass*, ampulheta. 5) *log-line*, linha de barquilha. 6) *log man*, lenheiro. 7) *log-rolling*, assistência mútua. 8) *log ship*, batel. 9) *log slate*, pedra das milhas (náut.). 10) *log mood*, pau-campeche. 11) *official log*, diário oficial (náut.). 12) *patent log*, barca patente, barca aperfeiçoada para indicar a distância percorrida pelo navio.

loganberry, s. fruto obtido pelo cruzamento da framboesa e amora da silva.

logarithm, s. logaritmo.

loggerhead, s. lorpa, estúpido; tartaruga marítima. 1) *at loggerheads*, em desacordo, em disputa. 2) *to fall, get* ou *to get to loggerheads*, vir às mãos.

logging, s. ocupação de rachador de lenha.

logic, s. lógica.

logical, adj. lógico, coerente, conforme as regras da lógica.

logically, adv. logicamente.

logican, s. lógico, o que ensina lógica.

logistic, adj. logístico. s. logística, cálculo algébrico. *pl.* ramo de ciência militar que trata de aquartelamento de tropas, etc.

logogram, s. logograma, sinal taquigráfico.

logomachist, s. logomaquista.

logomachy, s. logomaquia.

loin, s. lombo; *pl.* rins.

loiter, v.i. tardar-se, demorar-se. v.t. desperdiçar o tempo, vadiar.

loiterer, s. ocioso, preguiçoso, negligente, vagabundo.

loll, v.i. recostar-se, refastelar-se, estender-se, em atitude indolente. v.t. deitar a língua de fora.

loller, s. preguiçoso, indolente, ocioso, pessoa sem actividade.

lolling, s. o recostar-se indolentemente.

lollipop, s. caramelo.

londoner, s. londrino.

lone, adj. solitário, só, isolado, solteiro.

lonelier, loneliest, comp. e sup. de *lonely*.

loneliness, s. solidão, isolamento.

lonely, adj. solitário, só, abandonado; amante da solidão.

lonesome, adj. solitário, deserto; triste por causa da solidão; que evita a convivência social.

lonesomely, adv. solitariamente.

lonesomeness, *s.* estado ou qualidade do que está so.

long, *s.* longo, comprido, extenso; vagaroso, demorado; tedioso, ansioso. *adv.* a grande distância; muito; extenso; por muito tempo; durante, continuamente. *s.* muito tempo; sílaba longa; férias grandes. *v.i.* anelar, ansiar, suspirar por. 1) *long after,* muito depois. 2) *long-bow,* arco de mão. 3) *long cloth,* percal. 4) *long-clothes,* o primeiro vestido de uma criança. 5) *long-drawn,* lento, moroso, enfadonho. 6) *long dozen,* treze. 7) *long figure,* alto preço. 8) *long halt,* grande etapa. 9) *long home,* última morada, sepultura. 10) *long lifter,* alavanca de elevação. 11) *long-lived,* duradoiro. 12) *long-legged,* comprido de pernas; de grande pontal (náut.). 13) *long price,* preço incluindo direitos. 14) *Long Parliament,* parlamento eleito em 1640 e dissolvido em 1660. 15) *long primer,* tipo redondo (tip.). 16) *long shore man,* estivador, trabalhador de cais; fragateiro. 17) *long-sighted,* presbita. 18) *long-sightedness,* presbitia. 19) *long splice,* costura de laborar (náut.). 20) *long spun,* lento, enfadonho. 21) *long standing,* muito demorado; que existe há muito. 22) *long staple,* com filamentos compridos (algodão). 23) *long-suffering,* paciente. 24) *long-tailed,* cão de caça. 25) *long ton,* canhão comprido, = 2240 lbs = 1016,04 kg; ao passo que *short ton,* = 2,000 lbs = 907.20 kg. 26) *long-tongued,* linguareiro. 27) *long tried,* muito experimentado. 28) *a long way off,* a uma grande distância. 29) *long-winded,* longo, fastidioso. 30) *all day long,* o dia inteiro. 31) *before long,* em breve. 32) *to be long,* demorar-se. 33) *for long,* há muito tempo. 34) *so long as,* pelo tempo que, tanto tempo como. 35) *how long?,* quanto tempo? 36) *long live the King! the President!,* Viva o rei! o presidente! 37) *so long,* adeus! 38) *to draw the long bow,* pataratear. 39) *to go to one's long home,* morrer. 40) *in the long run,* no final de contas. 41) *that's the long and short of it,* é tudo quanto se pode e é preciso dizer-se acerca disso.

longboat, *s.* lancha; chalupa.

longer, *adj.* mais tempo; *no longer,* não é mais, já não. *s.* o que suspira por.

longeval, *adj.* longevo.

longevity, *s.* longevidade.

longhand, *s.* escrita por extenso.

longing, *s.* desejo veemente, anelo; ânsia. *adj.* ardente.

longingly, *adv.* veementemente.

longish, *adj.* um tanto longo.

longitude, *s.* longitude; *longitude in,* longitude de chegada (náut.).

longitudinal, *adj.* longitudinal. *s.* longarina (náut.).

longways, *adv.* longitudinalmente.

longwise, *v. longways.*

loo, *s.* lu, jogo de cartas. *v.t* dar capote ao jogo.

looby, *s.* tolo.

loof, *s.* ló (náut.).

loofah, *s.* lufa (bot.).

look, *v.t.* e *v.i.* ver, olhar, contemplar; esperar; ter cuidado; encarar; parecer-se. 1) *to look about,* olhar em volta; orientar-se. 2) *look about for,* procurar. 3) *look about one,* estar alerta. 4) *look after,* cuidar de. 5) *look ahead,* pensar no futuro. 6) *look alive,* mexer-se; aviar-se. 7) *look at,* considerar; ver. 8) *look at the bright side,* ver tudo cor-de-rosa. 9) *look at the other side,* ver o reverso da medalha. 10) *look daggers,* lançar olhares furiosos. 11) *look down,* abaixar os olhos; rebaixar o preço. 12) *look down on, upon,* considerar-se superior; olhar com desprezo. 13) *look for,* procurar; esperar. 14) *look forward to,* antecipar; contar com, esperar por. 15) *look ill,* ter cara de doente. 16) *look in,* fazer uma curta visita; entrar. 17) *look into,* examinar, considerar; tomar conhecimento de. 18) *look like,* parecer-se com. 19) *look up* ou *upon,* estimar, considerar; imaginar; olhar; ser mero espectador. 20) *look on to,* dar para (a rua, praça, etc.). 21) *look out,* olhar para fora; procurar; cuidar de; estar alerta. 22) *look out for,* olhar; procurar; cuidar de, estar preparado para. 23) *look out for,* olhar por (janela, vidros). 24) *look over,* examinar, rever, vigiar; passar por cima (perdoar). 25) *look sharp,* ser cuidadoso; aviar-se. 26) *look to,* cuidar de, velar; tomar a responsabilidade de. voltar-se para (como recurso). 27) *look through,* olhar através (janela, telescópio, etc.). percorrer, penetrar. 28) *look up,* levantar os olhos; recobrar ânimo; aumentar o preço; procurar (em livros); estar na alta (com.); visitar alguém. 29) *look up to,* venerar, ter esperança em alguém. 30) *look up and* *down*, examinar (alguém) dos pés à cabeça. 31) *look upon*, considerar. 32) *look well*, ter boa aparência. 33) *look sharp!*, Avie-se! 34) *look out!*, tenha cuidado! 35) *what are you looking at?*, para que estás a olhar? 36) *look before you leap!*, antes que cases, olha o que fazes! *s.* olhar, vista de olhos; ar, aspecto, semblante, aparência, ademanes. 37) *good looks*, beleza. 38) *sour look*, olhar triste. 39) *to cast a look*, lançar uma vista de olhos. *interj.* vê!, olha!

looker-on, *s.* espectador, contemplador.

looking, *s.* acção de olhar. 1) *good* ou *fine looking*, que tem boa figura. 2) *looking-glass*, espelho.

look-out, *s.* vigia, vigilância; guarita; atalaia. 1) *to be on the look-out*, estar de atalaia. 2) *look-out man*, vigia (homem).

loom, *s.* tear; braço de remo; miragem; presença; aparição. 1) *ribbon loom*, tear de cinta. 2) *power loom*, tear mecânico. *v.i.* assomar, aparecer; deformar-se (pela miragem), parecer grande ao longe; luzir, reluzir.

looming, *s.* miragem, reflexo especular (do mar); aparência exterior.

loon, *s.* basbaque, pateta; mergulhão (ave).

loony, *s.* velhaco; bobo; estúpido.

loop, *s.* olhal, presilha, aselha, ilhó, alça, cordão, alamar; curva; volta; clarabóia de igreja. 1) *loop-line*, desvio (em linha férrea). 2) *looping the loop*, dar uma volta completa no ar com um aparelho (avião, etc.). *v.t.* segurar com uma presilha. *v.i.* andar (fazendo curvas).

loophole, *s.* buraco, abertura; evasiva, tangente; seteira; canhoneira.

loopholed, *adj.* que tem seteiras; cheio de aberturas.

loose, *v.t.* desprender, desatar, largar (pano), aliviar, soltar; libertar. 1) *to loose one's hold*, soltar. *adj.* solto, livre, desatado; fraco, frouxo, folgado; vago, indeterminado; móvel; amplo; livre, licencioso; em liberdade; descuidado, negligente. 2) *loose morals*, costumes dissolutos. 3) *loose tooth*, dente abalado. 4) *to break loose*, escapar--se da prisão. 5) *to let loose*, soltar, pôr em liberdade. 6) *to have a srew loose*, não ter o juízo todo. 7) *to play fast and loose*, ignorar as suas obrigações. *s.* liberdade; soltura. 8) *to give loose to*, dar largas a.

loosely, *adv.* livremente; frouxamente; licenciosamente.

loosen, *v.t.* desprender, soltar, desatar, desligar; aliviar; abrandar; livrar; libertar; desembaraçar o ventre. *v.i.* desunir, desatar-se, soltar-se, separar-se.

looseness, *s.* frouxidão; relaxamento; liberdade, diarreia.

loosening, *adj.* laxante. *s.* laxação.

loot, *v.t.* saquear, pilhar; levar como despojo. *s.* despojo, pilhagem.

looter, *s.* saqueador.

lop, *v.t. lopping popped*, cortar a copa (das árvores), decotar, desbastar (as árvores). *v.i.* pender frouxamente. *s.* ramos cortados das árvores.

lope, *v.t.* e *v.i.* galopar; saltar. *s.* galope ou salto largo.

lop-eared, *adj.* que tem as orelhas caídas (cavalos).

lopper, *s.* podador.

lopping, *s.* poda; desbaste.

lop-sided, torto, mais pesado de um lado que do outro.

loquacious, *adj.* loquaz.

loquaciously, *adv.* loquazmente.

loquaciousness, *s.* loquacidade, tagarelice; picuinha.

lord, *s.* senhor, governador; marido; amo, dono. *v.t.* elevar à dignidade de lorde; governar, mandar. *v.i.* senhorear, dominar, mandar despoticamente; *to lord it over*, governar despoticamente.

Lord, *s.* Senhor; Deus; um grande, um magnate; Lorde (título). 1) *First Lord of the Admiralty*, ministro da Marinha. 2) *Lord Chamberlain*, camareiro-mor. 3) *Lord High Steward*, mordomo-mor. 4) *Lord Chief Justice*, presidente do Supremo Tribunal de Justiça da Inglaterra. 5) *Lord Lieutenant*, governador de um condado; governador civil. 6) *Lord Mayor*, presidente da câmara. 7) *Lord's Prayor*, Pai nosso. 8) *Lord's table*, altar da sagrada Eucaristia; Comunhão. 9) *Our Lord*, Nosso Senhor. 10) *House of Lords*, Câmara dos Pares. 11) *Lords spiritual*, bispos e arcebispos que têm assento na Câmara Alta. 12) *Lords temporal*, pares leigos.

lordliness, *s.* dignidade, senhorio, grandeza; altivez, orgulho.

lordling, *s.* fidalgote.

lordly, *adj.* senhoril, fidalgo, altivo, orgulhoso. adv. senhorilmente.

Lord's-day, *s.* domingo, dia do Senhor.

lordship, *s.* senhorio (terra do senhor);

domínio, poder; senhoria, excelência; *your lord*, vossa excelência.

Lord's supper, *s.* a Última Ceia; Sacramento da Eucaristia.

lore, *s.* erudição; lição.

lorgnette, *s.* binóculo de teatro; óculo de punho.

loricate, *v.t.* chapear, forrar de metal. *adj.* chapeado.

lorication, *s.* acção de chapear, forrar de metal.

loris, *s.* espécie de lémure.

lorn, *adj.* abandonado, desolado.

lorry, *s.* camião.

lory, *s.* arara.

losable, *adj.* fácil de perder.

lose, *pret.* e *pp.* de *lost v.t.* perder, desperdiçar, entregar à ignomínia ou à ruína; decair (náut.). *v.i.* perder-se, extraviar-se. 1) *to lose ground*, perder terreno. 2) *lose sight*, perder de vista. 3) *lose one's head*, perder a presença de espírito. 4) *lose one's way*, perder-se, andar perdido. 5) *lose one's temper*, perder as estribeiras, encolerizar-se. 6) *that stroke lost him many friends*, aquela acção fez-lhe perder muitos amigos.

loser, *s.* pessoa que perde; o que não logra o que deseja.

loss, *s.* perda, dano, privação; destruição; fracasso; quebra; desperdício. 1) *at a loss*, vender com prejuízo. 2) *dead loss*, perda total.

lost, *pret.* e *pp.* de *lose. adj.* perdido; frustrado; desperdiçado; desorientado; perplexo, extraviado; arruinado; condenado. 1) *lost to*, insensível a. 2) *lost-luggage office*, depósito de objectos perdidos ou encontrados.

lot, *s.* lote; sorte, fortuna, fado, destino; quota-parte, partilha, porção; grande quantidade, muito. 1) *a lot of money*, um dinheirão. 2) *to cast lots*, deitar sortes. 3) *he is a bad lot*, ele é um inútil. *v.t. lotting, lotted*, designar; dividir em lotes.

loth, *adj.* ver *loath*.

Lotahrio, *s.* galanteador; libertino.

lotion, *s.* loção.

lottery, *s.* lotaria, rifa.

lotus, *s.* lódão; *lotus eater*, indolente.

loud, *adj.* ruidoso, estrondoso, alto, forte, escandaloso; vistoso; grosseiro, vulgar, de mau gosto; urgente. 1) *to speak loud*, falar alto. 2) *loud laugh*, risada estrepitosa. 3)

loud speaker, altifalante (rádio). 4) *loud voice*, voz forte. 5) *loud woman*, mulher turbulenta; mulher de aparência equívoca. *adv.* ruidosamente, em voz alta.

loudly, *adv.* ruidosamente, vistosamente,

loudness, *s.* ruído, sonoridade; vulgaridade, mau gosto.

lough, *s.* lago; braço de mar.

louis, *s.* luís de ouro.

lounge, *v.i.* vadiar, preguiçar, mandriar, calacear; recostar-se, pôr-se à vontade. *s.* ociosidade; sesta, lugar onde se faz a sesta; preguiceira, sofá, divã; *lounging-room*, antecâmara.

lounger, *s.* madraço, ocioso.

lour, *v.i.* mostrar-se carrancudo.

louse, *s.* piolho. *pl. lice.* 1) *crab-louse*, piolho-ladro. 2) *dog louse*, carrapato. 3) *wood louse*, bicho-de-conta. 4) *louse wort*, estafiságria, erva piolheira.

louse, *v.t.* espiolhar.

lousiness, *s.* piolheira, o estado piolhoso.

lousy, *adj.* piolhoso; porco.

lout, *s.* estúpido, rústico; negligente. *v.i.* demorar-se, perder tempo.

loutish, *adj.* um tanto grosseiro, rústico ou rude.

loutishly, *adv.* grosseiramente.

loutishness, *s.* grossaria.

louver, *s.* lanternim com aberturas laterais para sair fumo; *louver-boards*, tábuas sobrepostas que deixam entrar o ar mas não a chuva.

lovable, *adj.* amável.

lovableness, *s.* amabilidade, atractivo.

lovage, *s.* ligústica.

love, *v.t.* amar, adorar, gostar de, ter inclinação ou afeição a. *v.i.* amar, estar enamorado; deleitar-se. *s.* amor, amizade, afeição; pessoa amada; galanteio. 1) *to make love*, namorar, cortejar. 2) *in love with*, namorado de. 3) *to fall in love*, enamorar-se. 4) *self-love*, amor-próprio. 5) *for love*, de graça, sem pagar. 6) *love-apple*, tomate. 7) *love all*, nada para ambas as partes (nos jogos). 8) *love-birds*, inseparáveis. 9) *love-feast*, ágape. 10) *love fit*, transporte de amor. 11) *love-in-idleness*, amor-perfeito. 12) *love-knot*, nó cego (sinal de amor). 13) *love lass*, namorada. 14) *love-letter*, carta de namorado. 15) *love-making*, galanteio. 16) *love-match*, casamento por amor. 17) *love-potion*, filtro. 18) *lovesick*, apaixonado, ferido de amor. 19) *love-song*, canção amorosa. 20) *love-token* ou *offering*, prenda de amor.

loveable, *adj.* amável.

loveableness, *s.* amabilidade.

lovebird, *s.* periquito.

loveless, *adj.* desamorável.

loveliness, *s.* amabilidade; encanto, beleza.

lovelorn, *adj.* sem amante.

lovely, *adj.* amável, formoso, agradável, ameno. *adv.* amavelmente, com amabilidade.

lover, *s.* amante, namorado, galanteador; querido, amigo; amador.

lovesome, *adj.* amável.

loving, *adj.* amante afectuoso, amoroso, terno, benigno; *loving-cup*, taça usada em banquetes, que passa de mão em mão.

lovingness, *s.* afeição, carinho, ternura, afabilidade.

low, *adj.* baixo; pequeno; profundo; humilde; barato; moderado; abatido, débil; fraco; desanimado; gravemente enfermo; vulgar; vil, ruim; servil; pobre; reverente, submisso. 1) *low-bred*, mal-educado. 2) *Low Countries*, Países Baixos. 3) *low expressions*, expressões vulgares. 4) *low Mass*, missa rezada. 5) *low-minded, low-thoughted*, ruim, que tem pensamentos baixos. 6) *low pressure*, baixa pressão. 7) *low spirited*, desanimado. 8) *Low Sunday*, domingo de Pascoela. 9) *low water*, vazante (de maré). 10) *in a low voice*, em voz baixa. 11) *in low spirits*, abatido. *adv.* baixo; barato; por baixo preço; profundamente; vilmente; submissamente; em voz baixa. *v.i.* mugir, balir. *s.* mugido, balido.

low-church, *s.* seita anglicana oposta ao ritualismo.

lower, *adj. comp.* de *low*, inferior, de baixo; de papa-figo; de gávea. 1) *lower band*, braçadeira. 2) *lower case*, caixa baixa (tip.). 3) *lower deck*, segunda coberta. 4) *lower mast*, mastro real. 5) *lower deck*, coberta inferior de um navio. 6) *lower shroud*, enxárcia real. 7) *lower studding sail*, varredoura. *v.t.* abaixar; descer, arriar; pôr mais baixo; humilhar; aviltar, rebaixar, diminuir. 8) *to lower the sails*, amainar as velas. *v.i.* baixar, minguar, diminuir-se; mostrar-se carrancudo; ameaçar; escurecer, toldar-se (o céu).

lowering, *adj.* sombrio, ameaçador; que desce.

loweringly, *adv.* de um modo ameaçador; nebulosamente.

lowermost, ou *lowest, adj.* o mais baixo; ínfimo.

lowing, *s.* mugido, balido.

lowland, *s.* terra baixa; *the lowlands*, terras baixas da Escócia.

lowlander, *s.* habitante de terras baixas.

lowlier, lowliest, *comp.* e *sup.* de *lowly*.

lowliness, *s.* humildade; baixeza, vileza, ruindade.

lowly, *adj.* humilde, submisso; baixo, abjecto. *adv.* humildemente, vilmente.

lowness, *s.* pequenez, baixeza; vileza; ruindade; humildade; abatimento, prostração; falta de meios; gravidade ou debilidade de som.

loyal, *s.* leal, fiel, constante.

loyalist, *s.* realista.

loyally, *adv.* lealmente.

loyalty, *s.* lealdade, fidelidade.

lozenge, *s.* losango; pastilha; *cough lozenges*, pastilhas para a tosse.

lubber, *s.* lapuz, tanso; rústico; um desastrado; marinheiro de água doce.

lubberly, *adj.* ronceiro; desastrado; vadio. *adv.* ronceiramente; toscamente.

lubricant, *adj.* lúbrico, escorregadio, lubrificante.

lubricate, *v.t.* lubrificar, amaciar, untar, tornar escorregado.

lubrication, *s.* lubrificação.

lubricator, *s.* lubrificador.

lubricity, *s.* lubricidade; lascívia; luxúria.

lubricous, *adj.* lúbrico, escorregadio; inconstante.

lucent, *adj.* luzente, brilhante.

lucerne, *s.* luzerna.

lucid, *adj.* lúcido, claro; transparente; brilhante; luminoso; *lucid intervals*, intervalos lúcidos.

lucidity, *s.* claridade, lucidez.

lucidly, *adv.* claramente.

lucidness, *s.* claridade, transparência; esplendor, resplendor.

Lucifer, *s.* Lúcifer; estrela de alva; o planeta Vénus.

lucifer, lucifer-match, *s.* fósforo de fricção.

lucigen, *s.* lucigénio, luz produzida por óleo e ar comprimido.

luck, *s.* acaso, casualidade; ventura, fortuna, felicidade; 1) *good luck*, fortuna, feliz acaso; felicidade. 2) *a run of bad luck*, um período de infelicidade. 3) *to be in luck*, estar com sorte. 4) *to try one's luck*, experimentar a sorte. 5) *to take pot luck*, comer o que haja, sem cerimónia.

luckier, luckiest, *comp.* e *sup.* de *lucky*

luckily, *adv.* por fortuna, felizmente, ditosamente. afortunadamente.

luckiness, *s.* felicidade, boa fortuna, boa sorte.

luckless, *adj.* desafortunado.

lucky, *adj.* afortunado, feliz, ditoso.

lucrative, *adj.* lucrativo, ganancioso.

lucratively, *adv.* lucrativamente.

lucre, *s.* lucro, proveito; ganância, usura.

lucubrate, *v.i.* lucubrar, trabalhar de noite.

lucubration, *s.* lucubração.

ludicrous, *adj.* burlesco, absurdo, jocoso, ridículo, cómico, caricato.

ludicrously, *adv.* ridiculamente, comicamente, burlescamente.

ludicrousness, *s.* qualidade do que é burlesco ou jocoso; jocosidade; extravagância.

luff, *s.* ló; barlavento; bolina; teque; amura; orçada; gurutil (de vela de estai), palma da mão. 1) *luff-tackle*, talha de gato, aparelho de bolinar. *v.t.* meter de ló, marear, bolinar; orçar. 2) *to keep the luff*, chegar-se ao vento.

luffing, *s.* orçada (náut.).

lug, *s.* coisa que se puxa com dificuldade; puxão; peso; orelha; coisa parecida com uma orelha; argola; asa. *v.t. lugging*, *lugged*, puxar com força; arrastar; alar; içar. 1) *to lug away ou off*, levar arrastado. 2) *to lug out*, fazer sair à força.

luggage, *s.* bagagem, trastes, tarecos; *excess luggage*, bagagem a mais do que a que se pode levar sem pagar.

lugger, *s.* lugre, barco de velas de pendão.

lugsail, *s.* vela latina quadrangular.

lugubrious, *adj.* lúgubre.

lugubriously, *adv.* de um modo lúgubre.

lugworm, *s.* biscalonga, arenícola, muito usada como isca.

lukewarm, *adj.* morno, tépido; indiferente, insensível.

lukewarmly, *adv.* friamente, indiferentemente.

lukewarmness, *s.* calor moderado; tibieza, indiferença.

lull, *v.t.* embalar; acalentar; acalmar; amainar; adormecer; mitigar; apaziguar. *s.* coisa que faz dormir; murmúrio, calma, calmaria.

lullaby, *s.* cantiga com que se adormece crianças; arrulho.

luller, *s.* pessoa que acalenta ou embala.

lumbago, *s.* lumbago.

lumbar, *adj.* lombar.

lumber, *s.* madeiramento, madeiras de construção, tábuas, tabuado; bordagem; trastes ou móveis velhos; coisa incómoda e de pouco valor. 1) *lumber-room*, quarto de arrumações. 2) *lumber-yard*, depósito de madeiras. *v.t.* amontoar trastes velhos. *v.i.* avançar com ruído surdo.

lumberman, *s.* negociante de madeiras.

luminary, *s.* luminar, astro.

luminiferous, *adj.* luminoso.

luminosity, *s.* luminosidade; intensidade da luz.

luminous, *adj.* luminoso.

luminously, *adv.* de um modo luminoso, luminosamente.

luminousness, *s.* resplendor, brilho, claridade, lucidez.

lump, *s.* massa informe, inchaço; conjunto; bocado. 1) *to sell by the lump*, vender por junto. 2) *in a lump*, por junto. 3) *lump sugar*, açúcar em pedra. v.t. amontoar; comprar ou vender por junto; ter de gramar. *v.i.* trabalhar, como estivador; amontoar-se, aglomerar-se, converter-se em massa.

lumper, *s.* estivador.

lumpily, *adv.* de um modo grumoso.

lumpiness, *s.* propriedade de ser grumoso.

lumping, *adj.* grande, pesado.

lumpish, *adj.* pesado, maciço; grosseiro, estúpido.

lumpishly, *adv.* pesadamente, grosseiramente, estupidamente.

lumpishness, *s.* qualidade do que é pesado; grosseria, estupidez.

lumpy, *adj.* grumoso.

lunacy, *s.* loucura intermitente.

lunar, *adj.* lunar; lunário; lunático de prata; *lunar caustic*, hidrato de prata.

lunate, *adj.* em forma de meia-lua.

lunated, ver *lunate*.

lunatic, *adj.* e *s.* lunático, alienado; *lunatic asylum*, manicómio.

lunation, *s.* lunação.

lunch, *s.* almoço. *v.t.* almoçar.

luncheon, *s.* almoço (de cerimónia).

lune, *s.* lúnula; lua; mania.

lunette, *s.* luneta (fresta semicircular); antolhos (para os cavalos).

lung, *s.* pulmão. (pl.). bofes, pulmões.

lunge, s. estocada, bote; investida, arremetida. v.i. dar um bote ou estocada; investir.

lunged, adj. que tem pulmões. pret. e pp. de lung.

lunule, s. lúnula.

lupercalia, s. pl. lupercais.

lupin, s. tremoço.

lupine, adj. lupino, do lobo; voraz; da família dos lobos e dos cães.

lupus, s. lúpus.

lurch, s. bordos; grande banda; balanço brusco, guinada; partida dobrada em alguns jogos; desamparo, abandono; dificuldade; to leave one in the lurch, abandonar alguém. v.i. enganar, trapacear; ganhar uma partida dobrada; inclinação repentina para o lado, fazer bordos.

lurcher, s. pessoa que está de emboscada; larápio; espia; cão que espreita a caça; glutão.

lurching, s. bordos (do navio em temporal); balanço rápido.

lure, s. chamariz, reclamo; laço para apanhar pássaros; isca; engano; engodo; atractivo; tentação. v.t. atrair, persuadir, induzir, tentar, engodar.

lurid, adj. lúgubre; fantástico; triste; pálido, lúrido; acobreado (céu).

luridly, adv. de um modo lúgubre.

lurk, v.i. ocultar-se, esconder-se, espiar.

lurker, s. espia, pessoa que está de emboscada.

lurking-place, s. esconderijo, emboscada.

luscious, adj. saboroso, muito suculento ou doce.

lusciously, adv. deliciosamente.

lusciousness, s. doçura extrema.

lush, adj. suculento; fresco e viçoso; fácil de lavrar; rico em vegetação.

Lusiads, s. lusíadas.

lust, s. desejo veemente, luxúria, lascívia. v.i. cobiçar; desejar; entregar-se à luxúria.

luster, s. lustre, brilho; candelabro; lustro, espaço de cinco anos.

lusterless, adj. sem brilho.

lustful, adj. luxurioso; sensual; voluptuoso, impudico; cobiçoso.

lustfully, adv. lascivamente.

lustfulness, s. lascívia, impudicícia; luxúria; cobiça.

lustier, lustiest, comp. e sup. de lusty.

lustly, adv. fortemente, vigorosamente, com força.

lustiness, s. vigor, robustez, louçania.

lustral, adj. lustral.

lustrate, v.t. lustrar, purificar.

lustration, s. lustração.

lustre, ver luster.

lustring, s. lustrina.

lustrous, adj. lustroso, brilhante,

lustrum, s. lustro (espaço de 5 anos); lustração, purificação.

lusty, adj. forte, robusto.

lute, s. alaúde; massa para vedar aparelhos. v.t. lutar, barrar de luto.

lutestring, s. corda de alaúde; lustrina; to speak in lutestring, falar com afectação.

Lutetian, adj. parisiense.

Lutheran, s. e adj. luterano.

lutheranism, s. luteranismo.

lutist, s. fabricante ou tocador de alaúde.

luxate, v.t. deslocar, desconjuntar.

luxation, s. luxação.

luxe, s. luxo.

luxuriance, s. exuberância, louçania, superabundância.

luxuriant, adj. exuberante, supérfluo, viçoso, luxuriante, frondoso; muito fértil.

luxuriantly, adv. exuberantemente.

luxuriate, v.i. vicejar, estar em plena fertilidade; crescer com exuberância; viver com luxo; jactar-se.

luxurious, adj. luxuoso, voluptuoso, exuberante.

luxuriously, adv. com louçania ou exuberância; voluptuosamente; luxuosamente, com fausto.

luxuriousness, s. luxo, fausto; voluptuosidade.

luxury, s. luxo, fausto, intemperança; manjar delicioso, delícia; to live in the lap of luxury, viver com muito conforto.

lyceum, s. liceu.

lychenis, s. licnic, pedra preciosa muito brilhante.

lycopodiam, s. licopódio.

Lycian, s. e adj. liciano.

lyddite, s. lidite (explosivo).

Lydian, s. e adj. lídio, da Lídia.

lye, s. líxivia.

lying, adj. falso, mentiroso; deitado, estendido; sito, situado. 1) lying in, parto; berço de criança. 2) a lying-in woman, uma parturiente. 3) a ship lying to, navio à vela, navio à capa. s. mentira, embuste.

lyingly, adv. mentirosamente, falsamente.

lymph, s. linfa. lymph-duct, vaso linfático.

lymphatic, adj. linfático; fleumático. s. vaso linfático.

lynch, v.t. linchar; julgar e castigar sem culpa formada; lynch-law, justiça pelas próprias mãos.

lynx, s. lince; lynx-eyed, que tem olhos de lince.

lyrate, adj. em forma de lira.

lyre, s. lira; lyre-bird, pássaro lira.

lyric, s. poema lírico. adj. lírico.

lyrical, s. lírico.

lyrist, s. tocador de lira; poeta lírico.

M

m, décima terceira letra do alfabeto.

ma, contrac. de mama, mamã.

ma`am, contrac. de madam, senhora.

macaroni, s. macarrão.

macerate, v.t. macerar.

maceration, s. maceração.

machination, s. maquinação, conjuração, trama.

machine, s. máquina; instrumento; veículo. 1) machine-made, feito à máquina. 2) machine-gun, metralhadora. 3) sewing-machine, máquina de costura; v.t. trabalhar com máquinas.

machinery, s. maquinismo; máquinas.

machinist, s. mecânico; maquinista.

mackerel, s. cavala (peixe).

mackintosh, s. casaco de borracha, impermeável.

macula, s. mácula, mancha.

maculate, v.t. macular, manchar; adj. manchado.

mad, adj. louco, doido, maníaco; distraído, perturbado. 1) like mad, furioso. 2) raving mad, doido-varrido. 3) drive somebody mad, levar alguém à loucura, enlouquecer alguém. 4) to run ou to go mad, enlouquecer; v.t. endoidecer, endoidar; exasperar; adv. madly, loucamente, furiosamente.

madam, s. senhora.

madame, s. madama.

madcap, adj. e s. estouvado, cabeça de vento.

madden, v.t. enlouquecer; v.i. tornar-se louco.

madding, adj. furioso, insensato; enlouquecido.

Madeira, s. vinho da Madeira.

mademoiselle, s. menina, rapariga solteira.

madhouse, s. hospital de alienados; casa de loucos.

madman, s. louco, maníaco.

madness, s. loucura.

madrigal, s. madrigal.

mag, s. pega; tagarela.

magazine, s. armazém; paiol de pólvora; revista (periódica); magazine gun ou rifle, espingarda de repetição.

magdalen, s. pecadora arrependida; prostituta regenerada.

mage, s. mago.

maggot, gusano; fantasia, capricho.

magie, s. magia; adj. mágico.

magical, adj. mágico, encantador; adv. magically, magicamente.

magician, s. mago, mágico.

magistrate, s. magistrado.

magistrature, s. magistratura.

magnanimous, adj. magnânimo, nobre; adv. magnanimously, magnanimamente.

magnate, s. magnate.

magnet, s. iman, magnete.

magnetic, al, adj. magnético; adv. magnetically, magneticamente.

magnetism, s. magnetismo.

magnetize, v.t. magnetizar; atrair.

magnificient, adj. magnificente, grandioso; adv. magnificiently, magnificentemente.

magnifico, s. magnífico, (título); to play the magnifico, dar-se ares.

magnify, v.t. ampliar, aumentar; exagerar.

magnitude, s. magnitude.

magnolia, s. magnólia (flor).

magpie, s. pega; pessoa tagarela.

Magus, s. mago.

Magyar, s. húngaro, língua húngara.

mahogany, s. mogno.

maid, s. donzela, menina; criada. 1) maid of

honour, dama de honor. 2) *oldmaid*, solteirona.

maiden, *s.* donzela, solteira; *adj.* virginal; virgem; solteira; intacto; *maiden name*, apelido de solteira; *adv. maidenly*, virginalmente.

maidenhood, *s.* virgindade.

mail, *s.* correio; correspondência; mala (do correio); *air mail*, correio aéreo; *v.t.* expedir; deitar no correio.

maim, *v.t.* mutilar, estropiar; *s.* mutilação.

maimed, *adj.* aleijado; estropiado.

main, *s.* oceano, alto mar; esforço, violência. 1) *with might and main*, com todas as forças; *adj.* principal, essencial; maior, grande. 2) *in the main*, no todo, em geral. 3) *by main force*, à viva força. 4) *to have an eye to the main chance*, cuidar dos seus interesses; *adv. mainly*, principalmente.

mainland, *s.* continente.

maintain, *v.t.* manter, sustentar, conservar.

maintainable, *adj.* defensável, sustentável.

maintainer, *s.* mantenedor; defensor; protector.

maintenance, *s.* manutenção, sustento; defesa.

maize, *s.* milho.

majestic, al, *adj.* majestoso; sublime, grande; *adv. majestically*, majestosamente.

majesty, *s.* majestade, poder.

major, *s.* major; *adj.* maior, principal.

majority, *s.* maioria; maioridade; *to join the great majority*, morrer.

majuscule, *adj.* e *s.* maiúsculo.

make, *v.t.* e *v.i.* criar; fazer, fabricar; construir; preparar, compor; produzir, completar; forçar, obrigar; preparar; perfazer, somar. 1) *one and one make two*, percorrer, atravessar; chegar a, avistar; ganhar, adquirir. 2) *to make a fortune*, concluir, pensar. 3) *what do you make of this?*, fazer-se, tornar-se. 4) *a good son makes a good father; to make at*, arremeter, atacar. 5) *to make against*, ser desfavorável, lutar contra. 6) *to make amends for*, compensar; remediar. 7) *to make away*, apressar. 8) *to make away with*, desfazer-se de; dissipar; matar. 9) *to make an end of*, acabar com. 10) *to make believe*, fingir. 11) *to make friends*, reconciliar-se. 12) *to make a figure*, fazer figura ridícula. 13) *to make fun of*, troçar de, rir-se de. 14) *to make good*, restituir; reparar; fazer valer. 15) *to make use of*, aproveitar. 17) *to make water*,

urinar. 18) *to make away*, progredir. *s.* forma, feitio, talhe, jeito; companheiro; fabrico; manufactura; produto.

make-believe, *s.* pretexto, pretensão; fingimento; *adj.* fictício; falso; *v.t.* pretender; fingir.

makeshift, *adj.* temporário, provisório, interino; *s.* substituto; paliativo.

make-up, *s.* conjunto, carácter, modo de ser; caracterização; cosmético; modo de pintar-se de modo teatral.

makeweight, *s.* contrapeso.

malachite, *s.* malaquite.

maladroit, *a.* desastrado; *adv. maladroitly*, desastradamente.

malady, *s.* doença.

mala fide, *adv.* de má-fé.

malaise, *s.* indisposição, mal-estar.

malaria, *s.* malária.

Malay, *s.* e *adj.* malaio.

malcontent, *a.* descontente.

male, *adj.* masculino, varão, macho; varonil; *male issue*, sucessão masculina; *s.* varão; macho.

malefactor, *s.* malfeitor.

malevolent, *adj.* malévolo, *adv. malevolently*, malevolamente.

malice, *s.* malícia, má intenção, picardia, ruindade.

malicious, *adj.* malicioso, ruim, velhaco; *adv. maliciously*, maliciosamente.

malign, *adj.* maligno, malicioso; daninho; *v.t.* invejar; prejudicar; caluniar; *adv. malignly*, malignamente.

malignant, *adj.* maligno, malévolo; perverso; nocivo; *s.* pessoa mal-intencionada, invejosa; *adv. malignantly*, malignamente.

malignity, *s.* malignidade, malícia, perversidade.

mall, *s.* maço, malho; alameda.

malleability, *s.* maleabilidade.

malleable, *adj.* maleável.

mallet, *s.* maço, macete, malho.

mallow, *s.* malva.

malmsey, *s.* malvazia.

malodorous, *adj.* malcheiroso; desagradável.

malt, *s.* malte; cerveja.

Maltese, *adj.* e *s.* maltês; *Maltese cross*, cruz de Malta.

maltreat, *v.t.* maltratar.

mamilla, *s.* bico do peito, mamilo.

mamma, *s.* mamã, mãe.

mammal, *s.* mamífero.

mammalla, *s. pl.* mamíferos.

mammalian, *adj.* mamífero.

mammoth, *s.* mamute; *adj.* enorme, gigantesco.

mammy, *s.* mãe, mamã; ama-de-leite.

man, *s.* homem; o género humano; varão; marido; peão (xadrez); criado; dama (jogo de damas); alguém, qualquer. 1) *man's estate,* virilidade. 2) *man Friday,* homem para todo o serviço. 3) *man-power,* número de homens aptos para o serviço militar, em tempo de guerra. 4) *man of straw,* testa-de-ferro. 5) *man alive!,* com a breca! 6) *play the man!,* tenha coragem! *v.t. (manning, manned)* tripular; equipar; armar; guarnecer; fortalecer.

manacle, *s.* manilha, grilheta; *pl.* algemas; *v.t.* manietar, algemar.

manage, *v.t.* e *v.i.* manejar; fazer andar ou funcionar; conduzir, manobrar, dirigir, administrar; operar, levar a cabo um assunto.

manageable, *adj.* maneável; manejável; dócil.

management, *s.* manejo, governo, direcção, administração; gerência; negociação; conduta; uso; destreza.

manager, *s.* administrador, director, empresário, gerente; *stage-manager,* empresário teatral.

man-at-arms, *s.* soldado.

mandarin, *s.* mandarim; tangerina.

mandate, *s.* mandato; ordem.

mandatory, *adj.* e *s.* mandatório; mandatário.

mandible, *s.* mandíbula.

mandolin, mandoline, *s.* bandolim.

mandrake, *s.* mandrágora.

mandrill, *s.* mandril (zool.).

mane, *s.* juba, crina.

manful, *adj.* bravo, valente; varonil; *adv. manfully,* varonilmente.

manganese, *s.* manganês.

mange, *s.* sarna; *adj. mangy,* sarnento.

manger, *s.* manjedoira; *a dog in the manger,* invejoso, que não goza nem deixa gozar.

mangily, *adv.* com sarna.

mangle, *s.* calandra; máquina de passar ou de espremer roupa; *v.t.* destroçar, mutilar, lacerar.

mango, *s.* manga, fruto da mangueira.

mangonel, *s.* catapulta.

mangrove, *s.* árvore dos trópicos.

manhood, *s.* natureza humana; virilidade.

mania, *s.* mania, loucura.

maniac, *s.* louco, maníaco.

maniacal, *adj.* maníaco; *adv. maniacally,* loucamente.

manicure, *s.* manicura; *v.t.* cuidar das mãos e unhas.

manifest, *s.* manifesto, declaração; *adj.* manifesto, claro; *v.t.* manifestar; expressar, declarar; demonstrar; *adv. manifestly,* manifestamente.

manifestation, *s.* manifestação, demonstração, declaração.

manifesto, *s.* manifesto, declaração, protesto público.

manifold, *adj.* múltiplo; muitos; vários; *s.* cópia ou duplicado; cano de várias aberturas; *v.t.* copiar, tirar cópias.

manikin, *s.* manequim.

manipulate, *v.t.* manipular, manejar.

manipulation, *s.* manipulação.

mankind, *s.* humanidade; os homens, o mundo.

manlike, *adj.* varonil.

manly, *adj.* varonil, valente, valoroso.

manna, *s.* maná.

manner, *s.* maneira, forma, modo; espécie, género; ar, porte; *pl.* urbanidade, delicadeza, conduta. 1) *she has no manners,* é uma malcriada. 2) *to the manners born,* acostumado desde o berço; *adv. mannerly,* cortesmente.

mannerism, *s.* maneirismo, afectação, pose.

mannerly, *adj.* cortês, polido, urbano.

mannish, *adj.* viril.

man-of-war, *s.* fisália (zool.).

manor, *s.* feudo, senhorio; fazenda.

manor-house, *s.* casa senhorial, solar.

manorial, *adj.* senhorial.

manse, *s.* granja, herdade; presbitério.

mansion, *s.* mansão.

manslaughter, *s.* homicídio.

man-slayer, *s.* homicida.

mansuetude, *s.* mansidão, docilidade.

mantel, mantelpiece, *s.* prateleira de fogão de sala; escarpa da chaminé.

mantle, *s.* manto, capa; *v.t.* e *v.i.* cobrir, tapar; disfarçar; encobrir-se; estender-se.

manual, *adj.* e *s.* manual; *adv. manually,* manualmente.

manufactory, *s.* fábrica, oficina, manufactura.

manufacture, *s.* indústria, fabricação; *v.t.* manufacturar, fabricar; *v.i.* ser fabricante.

manufacturer, *s.* fabricante, industrial.

manufacturing, *adj.* manufactor, industrial, fabril.

manumission, *s.* liberdade, alforria.

manumit (manumitting, manumitted), *v.t.* libertar, dar carta de alforria.

manure, *v.t.* estrumar, adubar as terras; *s.* estrume, adubo.

manuscript, *s.* manuscrito; *adj.* manuscrito.

many, *adj.* muitos, vários, diversos; um grande número. 1) *many a time*, mais de uma vez. 2) *many times*, muitas vezes, frequentemente. 3) *he was one to many for us*, foi mais esperto que nós. 4) *many-coloured*, multicolor. 5) *many-languaged*, poliglota. 6) *many-peopled*, composto ou habitado por vários povos; *s.* grande número; multidão.

map, *s.* mapa, carta geográfica; *v.t.* *(mapping, mapped)*, delinear mapas, traçar planos.

maple, *s.* ácer; bordo (árvore).

mar (marring, marred), *v.t.* estragar, manchar, desfigurar; frustrar, perturbar; corromper; *s.* mancha; injúria.

marathon, *s.* maratona.

marauder, *s.* rapinante; soldado que sem licença faz pilhagem.

marauding, *s.* pilhagem.

marble, *s.* mármore; berlinde.

marbling, *s.* mármore de imitação.

March, *s.* Março; *March mad*, muito excitado.

march, *s.* marcha; fronteira. 1) *a dead march*, marcha fúnebre; *v.t.* pôr em marcha; *v.i.* marchar, caminhar; estar fronteiriço, contíguo. 2) *to march in*, entrar. 3) *to march off*, partir. 4) *to march on*, caminhar, marchar. 5) *to march out*, sair; fazer sair. 6) *to march up*, avançar.

marchiness, *s.* marquesa.

Mardi gras, *s.* Terça-Feira Gorda.

mare, *s.* égua. 1) *mare's nest*, engano, logro. 2) *the grey mare is the better horse*, mulher que manda no marido. 3) *mare's-tail*, cavalinha (bot.).

margarine, *s.* margarina.

margin, *s.* margem, beira, orla; reserva, provisão; limite; *v.t.* pôr margem; marginar.

marginal, *adj.* marginal.

marginally, *adv.* marginalmente; à margem.

marginate, *adj.* marginado; *v.t.* marginar.

Marian, *adj.* mariano, relativo à Virgem Maria; relativo à rainha Maria Stuart; *s.* marianista, devoto da Virgem; partidário de Maria Stuart.

marigold, *s.* cravo de defunto.

marinade, *s.* escabeche.

marinate, *v.t.* marinar; pôr de escabeche.

marine, *adj.* marinho, naval, náutico; *s.* marinha; fuzileiro-naval.

mariner, *s.* marinheiro, marítimo.

marionette, *s.* títere, fantoche.

maritime, *adj.* marítimo, costeiro; náutico; naval.

marjoram, *s.* mangerona; *wild-marjoram*, orégão.

mark, *s.* marca; nota; prova; marco (moeda); alvo; sinal; distinção; *v.t.* notar; marcar; observar; caracterizar. 1) *to mark off*, separar. 2) *to mark out*, demarcar, destinar. 3) *to mark time*, marcar passo; *v.i.* marcar, assinalar; observar.

market, *s.* mercado; feira, praça; venda, tráfico. 1) *in the market*, no mercado; para venda. 2) *market rate*, preço de mercado. 3) *market-stand*, banca de praça. 4) *market money*, bolsa, mercado financeiro; *v.t.* e *v.i.* vender no mercado; mercar; negociar.

marksman, *s.* atirador (ao alvo); bom atirador.

markup, *s.* alta de preço.

marl, *s.* marna, marga; *v.t.* estrumar, adubar.

marline, *s.* merlim.

marmalade, *s.* compota (de laranja ou limão).

marmoset, *s.* sagui (símio).

marmot, *s.* marmota (roedor).

maroon, *s.* negro fugitivo; pessoa abandonada numa ilha; *adj.* castanho-avermelhado, cor de castanha; *v.t.* abandonar numa ilha; vadiar.

marquee, *s.* alpendre, marquise, toldo.

marquetry, *s.* embutido; mosaico.

marquis, *s.* marquês.

marriage, *s.* matrimónio, casamento; núpcias, boda; enlace.

marron, *s.* castanha.

marrow, *s.* medula, tutano; substância, essência; *spinal marrow*, espinhal medula.

marry, *v.t.* e *v.i.* casar(-se).

Mars, *s.* Marte.

marsh, *s.* pântano, lodaçal.

marshal, *s.* marechal; mestre-de-cerimónias; chefe de polícia; *v.t.* *(marshalling, marshalled)*, ordenar, disciplinar; pôr em ordem; dirigir.

marshalship, *s.* marechalato.

marshy, *adj.* pantanoso, palustre.

mart, *s.* empório; comércio; mercado, feira.

marten, *s.* pele de marta.

martial, *adj.* marcial, militar, bélico; *court-martial,* conselho de guerra. *adv. martially,* marcialmente.

martin, *s.* andorinha; gaivão.

martinet, *s.* oficial autoritário, austero, severo.

martyr, *s.* mártir; *v.t.* martirizar, torturar.

marvel, *s.* maravilha, prodígio; *v.t.* e *v.i. to marvel at,* maravilhar-se.

marvelous, *adj.* maravilhoso; *adv. marvellously,* maravilhosamente, às mil maravilhas.

marzipan, *s.* maçapão.

mascara, *s.* rímel.

mascot, *s.* mascote.

masculine, *adj.* masculino, varonil; macho; *s.* género masculino.

mash, *s.* mistura; massa (esp. farinha); malte; conquista amorosa; *v.t.* amassar; misturar; cortejar; fazer uma conquista amorosa. 1) *mashed potatoes,* puré de batata. 2) *to be mashed on,* estar babado por.

masher, *s.* triturador, *potato-masher:* passador (cul.); presumido a conquistador (gír.).

mashy, *adj.* misturado.

mask, *s.* máscara; caraça; disfarce, simulação; *v.t.* e *v.i.* mascarar-se, disfarçar-se.

masochism, *s.* masoquismo.

masochist, *s.* masoquista.

mason, *s.* pedreiro, canteiro; pedreiro-livre, mação.

masonic, *adj.* maçónico.

masonry, *s.* alvenaria; maçonaria (com maiúsc.).

masque, *s.* forma de representação teatral dos séculos XVI e XVII em que os actores usavam máscaras.

masquerade, *s.* mascarada, máscara, disfarce; baile de máscaras; *v.i.* disfarçar-se.

Mass, *s.* missa.

mass, *s.* massa, mistura; volume; multidão; *the masses,* as massas, o povo; *v.t.* e *v.i.* juntar(-se), reunir(-se), aglomerar(-se).

massacre, *s.* massacre; *v.t.* massacrar.

massage, *s.* massagem; *v.t.* fazer massagem.

massager, *s.* massagista.

massive, *adj.* maciço, pesado, compacto, sólido; *adv. massively,* maciçamente.

mast, *s.* mastro.

master, *s.* amo, senhor; mestre; chefe; *adj. magistral,* superior, principal; *v.t.* vencer, domar, governar, fazer-se senhor de, dominar; conhecer a fundo; executar com mestria; ser perito em; *v.i.* ser superior em alguma coisa.

masterdom, *s.* domínio, mando.

masterful, *adj.* imperioso, altivo, dominante; perito; *adv. masterfully,* imperiosamente, dominantemente.

masterly, *adj.* magistral; *adv.* magistralmente.

masterpiece, *s.* obra-prima.

mastership, *s.* domínio, governo, supremacia.

mastery, *s.* domínio, supremacia, poder; destreza, habilidade; vantagem, vitória.

masticate, *v.t.* mastigar, triturar.

mastiff, *s.* mastim (cão).

mastodon, *s.* mastodonte.

masturbate, *v.i.* masturbar-se.

masturbation, *s.* masturbação, onanismo.

mat, *s.* esteira, capacho; tecido com que se guarnecem as amarras; mate do metal; *v.t. (matting, matted),* esteirar, forrar, estofar; embaciar, deslustrar.

matador, *s.* matador (de toiros).

match, *s.* igual, semelhante; adversário, competidor; jogo, partida; fósforo; mecha; *v.t.* irmanar, emparelhar, casar; condizer com; igualar a; equiparar; competir com; *v.i.* combinar, condizer; irmanar-se, casar-se.

matchless, *adj.* incomparável, sem par, sem rival.

matchmaker, *s.* fabricante de fósforos; pessoa casamenteira.

matchwood, *s.* madeira própria para fósforos; lascas, cavacos.

mate, *s.* companheiro; marido, cônjuge; sócio, colega; mate (no xadrez); *v.t.* casar, unir, igualar; emparelhar; competir; dar cheque-mate no xadrez.

material, *s.* e *adj.* material; físico, corpóreo; substancial, importante; tecido, pano.

materialism, *s.* materialismo.

materialist, *s.* e *adj.* materialista.

materialistic, *adj.* materialístico.

materialize, *v.t.* e *v.i.* materializar, encarnar.

materiel, *s.* material, equipamento; material bélico.

maternal, *adj.* maternal, materno.

maternity, *s.* maternidade.

matey, *adj.* dado, afável.

mathematical, *adj.* matemático.

mathematics, *s.* matemática.

mathematician, *s.* matemático.

matinee, s. matiné, vesperal.

mating, s. acasalamento; união.

matins, mattins, s. matinas.

matriarch, s. matriarca.

matriarchy, s. matriarcado.

matriculate, v.t. e v.i. matricular, matricular--se; s. e adj. matriculado.

matriculation, s. matrícula.

matrimony, s. matrimónio.

matron, s. matrona; mãe de família; governanta; enfermeira-chefe.

matter, s. matéria; substância; assunto; coisas; negócios; importância; dificuldade; espaço. 1) it is no matter, não importa. 2) what is the matter?, de que se trata? 3) small matter, coisa de pouca importância. 4) matter of course, coisa de esperar, natural. 5) as a matter of fact, em verdade, o facto é que ...; v.i. importar, interessar, ter importância; fazer diferença.

matter-of-course, adj. natural, lógico, de esperar.

matter-of-fact, a. prosaico, positivo, prático; banal.

mattock, s. alvião.

mattrass, mattress, s. colchão.

maturation, s. amadurecimento, maturação.

mature, adj. maduro, sazonado; prudente; acabado, completo, perfeito; vencido, pagável (com.); v.t. amadurecer; v.i. amadurecer; vencer; terminar um prazo; adv. maturely, maduramente.

maturity, s. madureza; maturidade; idade madura; plenitude; vencimento (com.).

mauder, v.i. rosnar; murmurar, resmungar; andar com indiferença ou com moleza.

maudlin, adj. sentimental, chorão; embriagado.

maul, s. malho, marreta; v.t. malhar; espancar; criticar severamente.

mausoleum, s. mausoléu.

mauve, s. cor de malva, lilás.

mavis, s. tordo branco, tordo cantador.

maw, s. bucho, estômago (animais), papo, goela.

mawkish, adj. enjoativo; nauseabundo; insípido; adv. mawkishly, asquerosamente; de modo insípido.

maxillary, s. maxilar, osso maxilar; adj. maxilar.

maxim, s. máxima.

maximum, s. o máximo.

may, v.i. e aux. 3ª pess. sing. do pres. poder, ter permissão, ser possível, ser lícito ou

permitido. 1) it may be, pode ser. 2) may I?, posso?, é-me permitido?, dá licença?; forma orações optativas com o sujeito proposto. 3) may you arrive in time!, oxalá você chegue a tempo! 4) may God help you, que Deus o ajude! 5) may you live long and happy, viva você longos e felizes anos!

May, s. Maio; May-day: o 1º de Maio.

maybe, adv. talvez.

mayor, s. presidente de câmara municipal; prefeito.

mayoress, s. esposa do prefeito.

maze, s. labirinto, dédalo; segredo, perplexidade.

mazy, adj. complicado, confuso, perplexo.

me, pron. pess. me, mim, a mim; dear me!, valha-me Deus!

mead, s. hidromel; prado.

meadow, s. prado, campina.

meadowland, s. pradaria.

meager, meagre, adj. magro, descarnado, seco; escasso, estéril; adv. meagrely, magramente, esterilmente.

meal, s. refeição, repasto; alimento; farinha de milho.

mealtime, s. hora da comida.

mealy, adj. farináceo, farinhento.

mean, adj. humilde, inferior, pobre; baixo, vil, indigno, obscuro; mesquinho, insignificante; médio, intermédio. 1) mean-born, de nascimento humilde. 2) mean-spirited, desprezível, baixo; s. média; meio-termo; mediocridade; meio, recurso, método, forma. 3) the golden mean, moderação sensata. 4) by no means, de modo nenhum. 5) by foul means, à força. 6) to live on one's means, viver dos seus rendimentos; v.t. significar, querer dizer; pensar, ter em vista, tencionar, pretender. 7) to mean well to, ter boas intenções em relação a, ter importância para.

meander, s. meandro, labirinto; v.i. serpear, fazer meandros.

meaning, s. desígnio, propósito, intenção, significação; adj. expressivo, significativo; double-meaning, duplo sentido, ambiguidade; adv. meanningly, significativamente, intencionalmente.

meanly, adv. baixamente, vilmente; mediocremente.

meantime, adv. entretanto.

meanwhile, adv. entrementes, provisoriamente.

measles, s. sarampo.

measure, s. medida, medição; dimensão, tamanho, capacidade, extensão, quantidade, modelo; proporção, correspondência, compasso, metro, cadência; modo, grau; disposição, providência; meios, recursos; expediente; projecto; compasso (mús.). 1) *in some measure*, em parte. 2) *out of measure*, com excesso. 3) *to take measures*, tomar as medidas necessárias; *v.t.* medir; ajustar; proporcionar; graduar; estimar; avaliar; *v.i.* medir, tomar medida; ter de comprimento.

measured, adj. medido, calculado; uniforme, lento; limitado.

measurement, s. medição, dimensão, medida.

measurer, s. medidor.

meat, s. carne; alimento, comida. 1) *baked meat*, carne assada no forno. 2) *boiled meat*, cozido. 3) *broiled meat*, carne assada na grelha. 4) *stewed meat*, guisado. 5) *roasted meat*, assado. 6) *hashed meat*, *minced meat*, carne picada. 7) *fried meat*, carne frita. 8) *meat ball*, almôndega. 9) *meat spit*, espeto. 10) *to make meat of*, matar. 11) *one man's meat is another man's poison*, o que a um cura, a outro mata.

meatman, s. açougueiro, carniceiro.

meaty, adj. carnudo.

mechanic, adj. mecânico; s. artífice; mecânico.

mechanician, s. mecânico.

mechanics, s. mecânica.

mechanize, v.t. mecanizar.

medal, s. medalha.

medallion, s. medalhão.

meddle, v.i. meter-se, ingerir-se.

meddlesone, adj. intrometido, ingerido, metediço.

media, s. pl. de medium.

mediaeval, medieval, adj. medieval.

medial, adj. médio.

median, adj. mediano.

mediate, v.i. e v.t. mediar, intervir; adj. mediato, intermediário.

mediator, s. mediador; intercessor; árbitro.

medical, adj. médico, medicinal.

medicament, s. medicamento, remédio.

medicinal, adj. medicinal.

medicine, s. medicina; medicamento.

mediocre, adj. medíocre, vulgar.

mediocrity, s. mediocridade, mediania, vulgaridade.

meditate, v.t. meditar, idear, projectar, tramar, considerar; v.i. meditar, reflectir, cogitar.

meditation, s. meditação.

meditative, adj. meditativo, pensativo, contemplativo; adv. *meditatively*, contemplativamente.

Mediterranean, adj. e s. Mediterrâneo.

medium, s. médio, meio-termo; expediente; instrumento; atmosfera, ambiente; éter; médium (espiritismo); moeda; adj. mediano, intermédio; moderado.

medley, s. miscelânea, mistura, mixórdia; adj. misturado, confuso.

medulla, s. medula.

meed, s. prémio, galardão, recompensa.

meek, adj. manso, humilde, submisso, dócil, meigo; adv. *meekly*, mansamente, docilmente.

meekness, s. brandura, humildade, docilidade.

meet, v.t. encontrar, topar, achar; juntar, reunir; chocar com; convir em, satisfazer; saldar, honrar (com pagamento, etc.); afrontar; refutar, combater; ver, conhecer. 1) *I'm pleased to meet you*, muito prazer em conhecê-lo. 2) *to make both ends meet*, fazer coincidir a despesa com o rendimento. 3) *to meet a bill*, pagar no vencimento. 4) *to meet an obligation*, satisfazer um compromisso. 5) *till we meet again!*, até à próxima!; adj. apto, idóneo, próprio, conveniente; s. reunião, encontro, ponto de encontro.

meeting, s. encontro, entrevista, reunião; conferência; comício; duelo.

megaphone, s. megafone, porta-voz.

megrim, s. enxaqueca.

melancholic, adj. e s. melancólico, triste.

melancholy, s. melancolia, tristeza; adj. melancólico, deprimido, abatido.

melanin, s. melanina.

meld, v.t. e v.i. fundir(-se).

melee, s. recontro, refrega.

melioration, s. melhoramento, melhoria.

mellifluous, adj. melífluo.

mellow, adj. maduro, sazonado; doce, sumarento; mole, suave; melodioso; alegre (embriagado).

melodious, a. melodioso; adv. *melodiously*, melodiosamente.

melodrama, s. melodrama; dramalhão.

melodramatic, adj. melodramático.

melody, s. melodia; ária.

melon, s. melão; *water-melon,* melancia.

melt, *v.i.* e *v.t.* derreter-se, dissolver; abrandar; evaporar. 1) *to melt away,* gastar, dissipar. 2) *to melt into tears,* debulhar-se em lágrimas, desfazer-se em pranto. 3) *to melt something down,* derreter (fundir para aproveitar metal). 4) *to melt with,* enternecer(-se); s. fusão; material fundido.

melted, *adj.* derretido; comovido.

melting, *adj.* em fusão; que funde ou derrete; s. fusão, liquefacção; *melt-pot,* cadinho.

member, s. membro (do corpo); parte de um todo; membro, indivíduo, sócio.

membership, s. sociedade, confraria.

membrane, s. membrana.

membranous, *adj.* membranoso.

memento, s. memento, recordação, lembrança, memória.

memo, s. nota, apontamento, memorando.

memoir, s. memórias, livro de memórias, autobiografia.

memorable, *adj.* memorável, notável.

memorandum, s. memorando, nota.

memorial, *adj.* comemorativo; s. monumento comemorativo; memorial; nota.

memorialize, *v.t.* apresentar memorial ou petição; comemorar.

memorize, *v.t.* memorizar, registar, decorar.

memory, s. memória, recordação, reminiscência; fama, glória, monumento.

men, s. pl. de man; *many men many minds,* cada cabeça cada sentença.

menace, *v.t.* e *v.i.* ameaçar; s. ameaça.

menagerie, s. colecção de animais vivos; pátio de feras; jardim zoológico.

mend, *v.t.* reparar, consertar, remendar; corrigir, emendar, reforçar, remediar; *v.i.* corrigir-se, emendar-se; melhorar; restabelecer-se; s. reforma, emenda, melhoria.

mendacious, *adj.* mentiroso, embusteiro; *adv. mendaciously,* falsamente.

mendacity, s. falsidade, mentira, embuste.

mendicant, *adj.* e s. mendicante, mendigo, pobre.

menial, *adj.* doméstico; subalterno, servil; s. criado, lacaio.

meningitis, s. meningite.

menopause, s. (fisiol.) menopausa.

menses, s. pl. (fisiol.) menstruação, regras.

menstrual, *adj.* menstrual.

mensurable, *adj.* mensurável, medível.

mensuration, s. mensuração, medição; medida.

mental, *adj.* mental, intelectual.

mentality, s. mentalidade.

mentally, *adv.* mentalmente; intelectualmente.

mention, s. menção, alusão; *v.t.* mencionar, aludir, notar; *don't mention it,* não tem de quê.

mentionable, *adj.* mencionável; digno de menção.

mentor, s. mentor, conselheiro, guia.

menu, s. cardápio.

mercantile, *adj.* mercantil, mercante, comercial; *mercantile law,* código comercial.

mercantilism, s. mercantilismo.

mercenary, s. mercenário; *adj.* mercenário, interesseiro, venal.

mercer, s. comerciante de fazendas; capelista.

mercerize, *v.t.* mercerizar.

merchandise, s. mercadoria, géneros; *v.i.* comerciar, negociar.

merchant, *a.* comercial, mercantil; s. comerciante, mercador, negociante.

merchantman, s. navio mercante.

merchantship, s. navio mercante.

merciful, *adj.* misericordioso, benigno, clemente, compassivo.

merciless, *adj.* cruel, desalmado, implacável; *adv. mercilessly,* cruelmente, desapiedadamente.

Mercury, s. Mercúrio (planeta); mercúrio (quím.), azougue; planta; mensageiro.

mercy, s. misericórdia, clemência, piedade; mercê, graça, perdão.

mere, *adj.* mero, puro, simples; só; s. marco, limite, fronteira; lagoa.

merely, *adv.* meramente, somente, simplesmente.

meretricious, *adj.* meretrício, de meretriz.

merge, *v.t.* e *v.i.* fundir(-se), englobar(-se), incorporar(-se), dissolver(-se); ser absorvido; *the company merged into a larger one,* a companhia foi absorvida por uma maior.

mergence, s. fusão, absorção; desaparecimento.

merger, s. fusão (de sociedades, etc.).

meridian, s. meridiano; meio-dia; zénite, auge; *adj. meridiano,* relativo ao meio-dia; elevadíssimo.

meridional, s. meridional; *adv. meridionally,* meridionalmente.

meringue, s. merengue.

merit, s. mérito, virtude, excelência,

merecimento, prémio; *v.t.* merecer, ser digno de.

meritorious, *adj.* meritório, merecedor; *adv.* *meritoriously,* meritoriamente.

merl, merle, *s.* melro.

merlin, *s.* esmerilhão.

mermaid, *s.* sereia.

merman, *s.* tritão.

merry, *adj.* alegre, jovial, divertido; tocado, ligeiramente embriagado. 1) *to make merry over,* fazer troça de. 2) *merry andrew,* palhaço, bobo; *adv. merrily,* alegremente; jocosamente.

merry-go-round, *s.* carrossel.

merrymaker, *s.* folgazão.

mesh, *s.* malha (de rede, etc.); *pl.* malhas, rede, trama; *v.t.* enredar, apanhar com rede; *v.i.* enredar-se.

mesmerize, *v.t.* hipnotizar, magnetizar.

mesmerizer, *s.* magnetizador.

mesne, *adj.* médio, intermediário.

mess, *s.* ração; prato (de comida); rancho; chiqueiro; confusão, embrulhada; *v.t.* e *v.i.* dar de comer, dar rancho; desordenar, confundir; arranchar; fazer trapalhada.

message, *s.* mensagem, recado.

menssenger, *s.* mensageiro, arauto.

Messiah, *s.* Messias, Cristo.

metabolism, *s.* metabolismo.

metal, *s.* metal; liga; substância; material; vidro fundido; cascalho.

metallurgy, *s.* metalurgia.

metamorphosis, *s.* metamorfose, transformação, mudança.

metaphor, *s.* metáfora.

metaphysic, *s.* metafísico.

metaphysical, *adj.* metafísico, abstracto.

metaphysics, *s.* metafísica.

mete, *s.* meta, marco, limite; *v.t.* distribuir, repartir; medir.

meteor, *s.* meteoro.

meteorologist, *s.* meteorologista.

meteorology, *s.* meteorologia.

meter, metre, *s.* metro (em verso); metro (medida); medidor, contador.

meterage, *s.* medição.

method, *s.* método.

methodical, *adj.* metódico.

meticulous, *adj.* meticuloso; *adv. meticulously,* meticulosamente.

métier, *s.* profissão, ofício.

metric, *adj.* métrico.

Metro, *s.* metro, metropolitano.

metropolis, *s.* metrópole; centro, empório.

metropolitan, *adj.* metropolitano; metropolita, primaz.

mettle, *s.* brio, valor, coragem; vivacidade, fogo.

mew, *s.* miado; gaivota; gaiola, curral; *v.t.* engaiolar, encarcerar; *v.i.* miar.

mewing, *s.* mio, miado.

mewl, *v.i.* choramingar, lamuriar-se; *s.* choro de criança.

mewling, *s.* lamúria.

Mexican, *adj.* e *s.* mexicano.

mice, *s. pl.* de *mouse.*

microbe, *s.* micróbio; bactéria.

microcosm, *s.* microcosmo.

microfilm, *s.* microfilme.

micrometer, *s.* micrómetro.

microorganism, *s.* microrganismo.

microphone, *s.* microfone.

microscope, *s.* microscópio.

mid, *adj.* meio, médio.

midday, *s.* meio-dia; *adj.* do meio-dia; meridiano.

middle, *adj.* médio, intermediário; *s.* meio, metade, meado.

middleman, *s.* intermediário.

midge, *s.* mosquito, melga; pessoa pequena, nanico.

midget, *s.* anão, pigmeu.

midmost, *adj.* e *adv.* no meio; do meio.

midnight, *s.* meia-noite.

midnoon, *s.* meio-dia.

midst, *s.* meio, centro; *adv.* no meio, no centro; *prep.* entre.

midsummer, *s.* solstício do Verão; pleno Verão; *midsummer day,* dia de S. João.

midway, *s.* meio do caminho, metade do caminho; *adj.* situado a metade do caminho; entre; *adv.* no meio do caminho; a meio do caminho.

midwife, *s.* parteira.

mid-winter, *s.* solstício do Inverno, pleno Inverno.

mien, *s.* semblante, ar.

miff, *s.* mau humor; amuo, arrufo.

miffy, *adj.* arrufadiço, agastado, amuado; trombudo.

mig, migg, *s.* berlinde.

might, *s.* força, poder, pujança, prestígio.

mighty, *adj.* potente, forte, vigoroso; eficaz, importante; *adv.,* extremamente; *adv. mightily,* poderosamente.

migraine, *s.* enxaqueca.

migrant, *s.* e *adj.* migrante, migrador, migratório.

migrate, v.i. migrar, emigrar.

migration, s. migração, emigração.

migratory, adj. migratório.

milch, adj. leiteiro; milch-cow, vaca-leiteira.

mild, adj. suave, meigo; macio; adv. mildly, suavemente.

milden, v.t. e v.i. abrandar(-se), suavizar(-se).

mildew, s. míldio, oídio; v.t. e v.i. atacar, ser atacado de míldio.

mile, s. milha (medida equivalente a 1609 m).

mileage, s. comprimento ou distância em milhas; milhagem.

milestone, s. marco miliário.

militant, adj. militante, combatente; belicoso, guerreiro.

militarism, s. militarismo.

militarist, s. militarista.

military, adj. militar; s. milícia, tropa.

militate, v.i. militar.

militia, s. milícia; militiaman, miliciano.

milk, s. leite. 1) milk-and-water, insípido; vacilante. 2) milk-bag, úbere. 3) milk-food, lacticínio. 4) milk-white, branco como o leite; v.i. mungir, ordenhar, mamar; dar leite.

milker, s. ordenhador.

milkily, adv. de um modo leitoso.

milkmaid, s. leiteira.

milkman, s. leiteiro.

milksop, cobarde, maricas, banana.

milky, adj. lácteo, leitoso; Milky Way, Via Láctea.

mill, s. moinho; milésima parte do dólar. 1) millboard, cartão. 2) mill-dan, açude. 3) to go through the mill, saber alguma coisa por experiência. 4) to bring grist to the mill, levar água ao seu moinho; v.t. moer, pisar.

millenary, adj. milenário, milenar; s. milenário, milhar, milénio.

millennium, s. milénio.

miller, s. moleiro.

millet, s. milhete, milho miúdo.

milliard, s. mil milhões.

millimeter, millimetre, s. milímetro.

milliner, s. chapeleira, modista de chapéus.

millinery, s. chapelaria.

milling, s. moedura, moagem.

million, s. milhão.

millionaire, millionnaire, s. milionário.

millstone, s. mó; pedra de moinho.

milord, s. milorde.

mime, s. mimo; pantomima, farsa.

mimer, mimo, mímico.

mimic (mimicking, mimicked), v.t. imitar, copiar; parodiar; s. mimo, bobo; adj. mímico, burlesco.

mimicry, s. mimetismo; pantomima.

mince, v.t. cortar miudinho; picar; medir as palavras; adoçar; v.i. andar ou falar com ar afectado; s. afectação; picado (carne, etc.); mince-pie, pastel de carne.

mincemeat, s. picado de carne.

mincer, s. picador; máquina de picar; pessoa afectada.

mincing, adj. afectado, amaneirado; adv. mincingly, aos bocadinhos; com afectação.

mind, s. mente, entendimento, memória, espírito, vontade, intenção, resolução, desejo; pensamento, parecer; memória; opinião. 1) absence of mind, distracção. 2) of one mind, unânimes. 3) with one mind, unanimemente. 4) of sound mind, de perfeito juízo. 5) to be out of one's mind, estar doido. 6) to bear in mind, lembrar-se. 7) to make up one's mind, decidir-se. 8) to call to mind, trazer à memória. 9) to have in mind, ter em consideração. 10) to speak one's mind, falar francamente. 11) to have half a mind to, estar quase decidido. 12) to have something in mind, estar preocupado. 13) mind!, cuidado!; v.i. e v.t. notar, observar, considerar; cuidar; vigiar; estar atento; pôr-se em guarda; lembrar, recordar; atender; estar disposto a; importar-se. 14) mind your eye!, vê lá o que fazes!

minded, adj. inclinado, disposto.

mindful, adj. atento, observador, cuidadoso; adv. mindfully, atentamente.

mindless, s. descuidado, negligente; bronco.

mine, pron. pess. meu, minha, meus, minhas; s. mina, cavidade subterrânea; v.t. minar; destruir; extrair; v.i. explorar uma mina, sapar.

miner, s. mineiro; sapador.

mineral, s. mineral, minério; adj. mineral, inorgânico. 1) mineral-jelly, vaselina. 2) mineral-pitch, asfalto. 3) mineral-water, água mineral.

mineralogy, s. mineralogia.

mingle, v.t. misturar, juntar; confundir, matizar; v.i. misturar-se, juntar-se.

mingy, adj. sovina, mesquinho.

minimize, v.t. reduzir ao mínimo, minimizar; subestimar.

minimum, s. o mínimo; the minimum wage, o salário mínimo.

minion, s. amante, favorito; lacaio, agente, esbirro; adj. mimoso, delicado, bonito.

minister, s. ministro; sacerdote, clérigo; v.t. ministrar, dar; conferir, prover de, aplicar; v.i. atender, servir, oficiar.

ministerial, adj. ministerial.

ministration, s. administração; serviço, auxílio, fornecimento.

ministry, s. ministério, cargo; conselho de ministros; gabinete; clero.

mink, s. espécie de doninha ou a sua pele; vison.

minor, adj. e s. menor, mais pequeno, de menor idade; secundário, inferior.

minority, s. menoridade, minoria.

minster, s. igreja de mosteiro, catedral, basílica.

minstrel, s. menestrel, trovador, cantor.

mint, s. casa da moeda; fonte, tesouro, manacial; hortelã; v.t. cunhar moeda.

mintage, moedagem; cunho; moeda cunhada.

minuet, s. minuete.

minus, a. menos; sem; negativo; desprovido; falho.

minuscule, s. minúsculo, letra minúscula.

minute, s. minuto, momento, instante; minute-hand, ponteiro dos minutos.

minute, s. minuta, nota, apontamento; pl. acta; minute-book, agenda; v.t. minutar, anotar.

minute, adj. miúdo, diminuto, pequeno.

minutely, adj. que acontece de minuto a minuto; constante; adv. de minuto em minuto; todos os minutos.

minutia, s. minúcia, pormenor, insignificância.

minx, s. rapariga desenvolta ou galanteadora; atrevida; sirigaita.

miracle, s. milagre, prodígio.

miraculous, adj. milagroso, miraculoso.

mirage, s. miragem; ilusão.

mire, s. lodaçal, lamaçal, pântano; lodo, lama; v.t. e v.i. enlamear(-se); atascar-se em lama; to be in the mire, estar em apuros; meter-se em dificuldades.

mirror, s. espelho; exemplo, modelo; v.t. espelhar, reflectir.

mirth, s. alegria, gáudio, regozijo, hilaridade.

mirthful, adj. alegre, jovial, folgazão; hilariante, divertido; adv. mirthfully, jovialmente.

miry, adj. lamacento; pantanoso; lodoso.

misadventure, s. revés; contratempo, azar, infortúnio, desventura.

misanthrope, misanthropist, s. misantropo.

misanthropy, s. misantropia.

misapply, v.t. empregar mal, fazer mau uso de.

misapprehend, v.t. entender mal, compreender mal.

misbehave, v.i. portar-se ou conduzir-se mal.

misbehavior, misbehaviour, s. mau comportamento; mau procedimento.

misbelief, s. falsa crença, heresia.

miscalculate, v.t. e v.i. calcular mal.

miscall, v.t. dar nome errado a; injuriar, difamar.

miscarriage, s. mau êxito; fracasso; extravio.

miscarry, v.i. falhar, fracassar, malograr-se; extraviar-se.

miscellaneous, adj. misto, misturado; diverso.

miscellany, s. miscelânea, mistura, confusão.

mischance, s. contratempo, azar.

mischief, s. dano, mal, estrago; injúria.

mischievous, adj. daninho, nocivo; travesso, turbulento.

misconceive, v.t. e v.i. formar conceito erróneo, equivocar-se.

misconception, s. falso conceito; equívoco.

misconduct, v.t. conduzir, dirigir ou administrar mal; s. má conduta, mau procedimento.

misconstruction, s. interpretação falsa ou errónea.

misconstrue, v.t. interpretar mal; tomar em mau sentido.

miscreant, a. vil, torpe, perverso; s. patife, vilão, celerado, meliante.

misdeed, s. maldade, malfeitoria, crime.

misdemeanor, misdemeanour, s. delito leve, contravenção; mau procedimento.

misdirect, v.t. dirigir, orientar, endereçar mal.

misdoubt, v.t. duvidar (de); suspeitar de, desconfiar de; recear.

mise, s. acordo, pacto.

miser, s. avaro, avarento.

miserable, adj. miserável, pobre; infeliz, desditoso.

miserly, adj. avarento, sovina, somítico.

misery, s. aflição, angústia, sofrimento, tormento; miséria.

misfit, v.t. e v.i. ajustar mal; unir mal; não

encaixar bem; *s.* o que não assenta ou encaixa bem.

misfortune, *s.* infortúnio, desventura, desdita, desgraça.

misgiving, *s.* pressentimento, ansiedade, receio; desconfiança.

misgovern, *s. v.t.* governar mal, desgovernar, mal-governar.

misgovernment, *s.* desgoverno.

misguidance, *s.* extravio, direcção errada.

mishap, *s.* infortúnio, desventura, má sorte.

misinform, *v.t.* informar mal; enganar, iludir.

misinformation, *s.* informação falsa.

misinterpret, *v.t.* e *v.i.* interpretar mal.

misjudge, *v.t.* e *v.i.* julgar mal, fazer mau juízo, ter opinião errónea (de).

mislay, *v.t.* pôr em lugar ignorado, largar à toa; perder.

mislead, *v.t.* desencaminhar, transviar; corromper; iludir.

mismade, *adj.* malfeito, defeituoso.

mismake, *v.t.* fazer mal, executar mal, atamancar.

mismanage, *v.t.* e *v.i.* dirigir, gerir ou administrar mal.

mismanagement, *s.* má direcção; desgoverno.

misname, *v.t.* dar nome errado a.

misnomer, *s.* nome errado; erro de nome.

misplace, *v.t.* colocar mal; extraviar.

misplay, *s.* mau jogo, jogada errada; *v.t.* e *v.i.* jogar mal, errar no jogo.

misprint, *v.t.* e *v.i.* imprimir mal, imprimir com erros; *s.* erro tipográfico.

misprize, misprise, *v.t.* desprezar, desdenhar, subestimar.

mispronounce, *v.t.* pronunciar mal, pronunciar erradamente.

misquote, *v.t.* e *v.i.* citar erradamente.

misread, *v.t.* ler mal, enganar-se na leitura de, interpretar mal.

misrepresent, *v.t.* representar mal; desfigurar, deturpar.

misrepresentation, *s.* falsidade, embuste.

misrule, *v.t.* governar mal, desgovernar; *s.* mau governo; desordem, confusão.

miss, *s.* senhorita, jovem solteira; *v.t.* e *v.i.* falhar, errar; perder; ter saudades, sentir falta; frustrar-se; *to miss out,* omitir-se; falta, perda, erro, engano.

missal, *s.* missal; livro de missa.

missel, *s.* tordo.

misshape, *v.t.* formar mal; deformar, entortar.

misshapen, *adj.* deformado, disforme.

missile, *adj.* míssil, missivo; *s.* projéctil, arma de arremesso.

missing, *adj.* ausente, perdido, desaparecido, de que se não tem notícia; *to be missing,* faltar.

mission, *s.* missão, envio, comissão; destino; missão diplomática; missão religiosa.

missionary, *adj.* missionário, missioneiro; *s.* missionário, emissário.

missis, *s.* patroa, ama, senhora.

missive, *s.* missiva.

misspell, *v.t.* e *v.i.* escrever mal, soletrar mal.

misspend, *v.t.* dissipar, desperdiçar, esbanjar.

misstate, *v.t.* relatar mal uma questão; falsear.

misstatement, inexactidão; erro.

misstep, *s.* passo em falso; deslize.

missy, *s.* senhorinha, menina.

mist, *s.* neblina, bruma; *v.t.* e *v.i.* enevoar (-se); toldar(-se).

mistake (mistook, mistaken), *v.t.* compreender mal; trocar; *s.* equívoco, engano, erro; *and no mistake,* sem dúvida alguma, com toda a certeza.

mistaken, *adj.* enganado, equivocado; errado.

mistakenly, *adv.* erroneamente; erradamente.

mister, *s.* senhor (título); escrito usa-se a abreviatura Mr, que se pronuncia do mesmo modo.

mistletoe, *s.* visco (planta).

mistral, *s.* mistral, vento frio e seco que sopra no Mediterrâneo.

mistreat, *v.t.* maltratar, injuriar.

mistress, *s.* senhora, ama, patroa; amada; amante; mestra, professora; equivalente em português a senhora dona; escrito usa-se a abreviatura Mrs.

mistrust, *s.* desconfiança, suspeita; falta de confiança; *v.t.* e *v.i.* desconfiar, suspeitar, duvidar de

misty, *adj.* nevoento, brumoso; embaciado; *adv. mistily,* nubladamente.

misunderstand, *v.t.* e *v.i.* compreender mal, interpretar mal.

misunderstanding, *s.* má compreensão, má interpretação; equívoco, mal-entendido; desentendimento; disputa.

misuse, *s.* mau uso, mau emprego; abuso;

v.t. fazer mau uso; abusar de; maltratar, seviciar.

mite, *s.* traça, gorgulho; migalha; bocadinho.

miter, mitre, *s.* mitra; meia esquadria; ângulo de 45°.

mitigate, *v.t.* mitigar, moderar, atenuar, suavizar.

mitigation, *s.* mitigação.

mitten, *s.* mitene; luva sem dedos; manguito; *to give mitten,* acabar com o namoro; ser despedido do emprego.

mity, *adj.* coberto de traça; traçado.

mix, *v.t.* misturar, mesclar; incorporar, associar; *v.i.* misturar-se, confundir-se, tomar parte.

mixed, *adj.* misturado; misto; sortido; confuso.

mixer, *s.* misturador, batedeira; pessoa muito sociável.

mixture, *s.* mistura; mescla; preparado farmacêutico.

mix-up, *s.* confusão; tumulto, conflito.

mizzen, mizen, *s.* mezena; catita; vela de ré; *adj.* da mezena; da gata; *mizzen topsail,* gata.

moan, *s.* lamento, queixume, queixa, gemido; *v.i.* e *v.t.* lamentar(-se); carpir, gemer, lastimar(-se).

moat, *s.* fosso, vala; *v.t.* cercar de fosso ou vala.

mob, *s.* populaça, plebe, ralé; motim; touca de mulher; *v.t. (mobbing, mobbed);* aglomerar-se em torno de; cercar, assaltar, atacar.

mobbish, *adj.* turbulento, tumultuoso, anárquico.

mobile, *adj.* móvel, movediço; variável.

mobilize, *v.t.* mobilizar.

mobsman, *s.* gatuno; carteirista bem vestido.

mocassin, *s.* espécie de calçado em pele de gamo; mocassina.

mock, *adj.* falso, fingido, irrisório; *s.* mofa, escárnio; *v.t.* escarnecer, mofar, ridicularizar; *v.i.* (com *at*) zombar de; rir-se de.

mocker, *s.* escarnecedor.

mockery, *s.* escárnio.

mocking, *s.* zombaria, mofa; *adj.* escarnecedor, escarninho; *adv. mockingly,* por escárnio, em tom de mofa.

mode, *s.* modo, forma, maneira, método; moda, uso, costume; modo (de verbo).

model, *s.* modelo, exemplar, norma; figurino, modelo; *v.t.* e *v.i.* modelar, moldar; *adj.* modelar.

moderate, *v.t.* e *v.i. adj.* moderado, razoável; calmo, comedido; regular; módico; *v.t.* e *v.i.* moderar(-se), acalmar(-se); reprimir(-se), conter(-se).

moderation, *s.* moderação, comedimento, prudência, temperança.

moderator, *s.* moderador; árbitro, mediador.

modern, *adj.* moderno, novo, actual; *s.* modernista.

modernize, *v.t.* e *v.i.* modernizar-se, actualizar-se.

modest, *a.* modesto; simples, despretensioso; acanhado, reservado; módico, moderado.

modesty, *s.* modéstia, simplicidade; moderação, reserva, pudor, recato.

modicum, *s.* pitada; ração; pouco.

modification, *s.* modificação, alteração, variedade.

modify, *v.t.* modificar, alterar, variar.

modish, *adj.* à moda, na moda.

modiste, *s.* modista, costureira.

modulate, *v.t.* modular; *v.i.* modular, variar de tom.

modulation, *s.* modulação; suavização.

Mohammedan, *adj.* e *s.* maometano, muçulmano.

moiety, *s.* metade.

moil, *v.i.* labutar, cansar-se; *to toil and moil,* afanar-se; *s.* labuta, faina.

moist, *adj.* húmido, molhado.

moisten, *v.t.* e *v.i.* humedecer(-se), molhar.

moisture, *s.* humidade; sereno, orvalho.

molar, *adj.* molar, que mói, que tritura; relativo a massas; que actua por meio de massas; *s.* molar, queixal.

mold, mould, *s.* bolor, mofo; húmus; terra vegetal; matéria de que qualquer coisa é feita; molde; matriz, forma; modelo; *v.t.* e *v.i.* moldar, modelar; embolorar.

molder, moulder, *s.* molde; moldador; *v.i.* desfazer-se em pó; *v.t.* reduzir a pó, consumir.

molding, moulding, *s.* moldagem; modelação; feitio, forma; molde (objecto moldado).

moldy, mouldy, *adj.* bolorento, embolorado.

mole, *s.* mola; lunar; mancha; sinal congénito da pele; molhe, dique; toupeira; *to make a mountain of a mole-hill,* exagerar.

molecular, *adj.* molecular.

molecule, *s.* molécula; partícula.

molehill, *s.* montículo de terra levantado por uma toupeira ao cavar a toca; dificuldade insignificante.

molest, *v.t.* molestar, incomodar, atormentar.

moll, *s.* rapariga pouco decente; prostituta.

mollify, *v.t.* amolecer; suavizar, aliviar.

mollusc, mollusk, *s.* molusco.

molly, *s.* homem efeminado, maricas; molenga.

mollycoddle, *s.* mimalho, maricas; *v.t.* amimar, amimalhar.

molt, moult, *v.t.* e *v.i.* mudar (de penas, pêlo, pele), estar na muda; *s.* muda, mudança de pena, etc.

molten, *adj.* fundido; derretido.

moment, *s.* momento, instante; presentemente; época, período, fase; importância.

momentary, *adj.* momentâneo, instantâneo, rápido, breve.

momently, *adv.* de momento a momento, a todo o instante; constantemente; momentaneamente.

momentous, *adj.* momentoso, importante, grave.

monachal, *adj.* monacal, monástico.

monarch, *s.* monarca.

monarchal, *adj.* monárquico.

monarchist, *s.* monarquista.

monarchy, *s.* monarquia.

monastery, *s.* mosteiro, convento.

monastic, monastical, *adj.* monástico, monacal; conventual.

monasticism, *s.* monasticismo, vida monástica.

Monday, *s.* segunda-feira.

monetary, *adj.* monetário; pecuniário, financeiro.

money, *s.* dinheiro, moeda legal, papel-moeda; valores, fundos; riqueza, sistema monetário. 1) *to be hard up for money*, ter grande necessidade de dinheiro. 2) *to make money*, ganhar dinheiro. 3) *to put out money*, pôr dinheiro a juros. 4) *to run into money*, tornar-se dispendioso; *v.t.* cunhar moeda, fazer moeda; converter em moeda.

moneyed, *adj.* endinheirado, rico.

moneygrubber, *s.* pessoa gananciosa, avara.

moneylender, *s.* prestamista, agiota.

moneyless, *adj.* sem dinheiro.

monger, *s.* negociante.

Mongolian, *adj.* e *s.* mongol; mongólico; (med.) mongolóide.

mongolism, *s.* mongolismo.

mongrel, *s.* mestiço; planta ou animal cruzado; *adj.* mestiço, cruzado, atravessado, mulato.

moniker, monicker, *s.* marca (pessoal), sinal de identificação; alcunha.

monition, *s.* aviso.

monitor, *s.* monitor; instrutor, decurião, chefe de turma; monitor (couraçado de pequena velocidade); monitor de escuta; lagarto.

monk, *s.* monge, frade.

monkey, *s.* macaco, símio; *v.t.* macaquear; traquinar, brincar, fazer travessuras.

monkeyish, *adj.* simiesco, macacal.

monkood, *s.* monasticismo, vida monástica.

monocle, *s.* monóculo.

monogamy, *s.* monogamia.

monoglot, *s.* que fala apenas uma língua.

monograma, *s.* monograma.

monologue, *s.* monólogo.

monopolize, *v.t.* monopolizar.

monopoly, *s.* monopólio; cartel.

monosyllabic, *adj.* monossilábico; lacónico.

monosyllable, *s.* monossílabo.

monotheism, monoteísmo.

monotone, *s.* monotonia, insipidez; *adj.* monótono.

monotonous, *adj.* monótono, invariável, uniforme, tedioso, enfadonho; *adv. monotonously*, monotonamente.

monotony, *s.* monotonia, invariabilidade, insipidez.

monotype, *s.* monótipo; espécie única.

monovalent, *adj.* monovalente, univalente.

monsignor, *s.* monsenhor (catol.).

monsoon, *s.* monção; estação chuvosa.

monster, *s.* monstro; *adj.* monstro, enorme, colossal.

monstrance, *s.* ostensório, custódia.

monstrosity, *s.* monstruosidade; enormidade; absurdo.

monstrous, *adj.* monstruoso, disforme, horrendo; enorme, colossal; atroz, horrível, desalmado; absurdo; *adv. monstrously*, monstruosamente.

montage, *s.* montagem; sobreposição de imagens; truque.

month, *s.* mês; *month's mind*, missa do 30º dia.

monthly, *adj.* mensal; mensário; regras, menstruação (pl.); *adv.* uma vez por mês, mensalmente.

monument, *s.* monumento.

monumental, *adj.* monumental; comemorativo; grandioso.

mood, *s.* modo (de verbo); disposição de ânimo; génio; humor; (pl.) melancolia, mau humor, amuo.

moody, *adj.* mal-humorado, rabugento, amuado; taciturno; caprichoso. *adv.* *moodily,* caprichosamente; taciturnamente.

moon, *s.* Lua; mês lunar; luar; *v.t.* e *v.i.* vaguear; andar na lua.

moonbeam, *s.* raio de luar.

mooncalf, *s.* idiota, imbecil; monstro.

moonish, *adj.* caprichoso, inconstante; aluado, lunático.

moonlight, *s.* luar; *adj.* que se faz ao luar; nocturno; ao luar.

moonrise, *s.* o nascer da Lua.

moonset, *s.* o ocaso da Lua.

moonshine, *s.* luar; destino; disparate; quimera, devaneio; bebida alcoólica destilada ilegalmente.

moony, *adj.* semelhante à lua; lunar; redondo; sonhador; cismático, apatetado, distraído.

moor, *s.* charneca, terreno pantanoso; urzedo; matagal; mouro, negro; *moor-hen,* galinha-de-água; *v.t.* ancorar, amarrar, atracar.

mooring, *s.* amarração; (pl.) ancoradoiro.

moorish, moory, *adj.* pantanoso; mouro, mourisco.

moose, *s.* alce.

mop, *s.* esfregão, rodilha; careta; *v.t.* *(mopping, mopped)* limpar com o esfregão, esfregar, enxugar; caretear, fazer caretas.

mope, *v.t.* e *v.i.* aparvalhar, atordoar, andar apático; *s.* pessoa aparvalhada ou apática; (pl.) abatimento, desânimo.

moppet, *s.* criança, rapazelho.

moral, *adj.* moral, digno, virtuoso, casto; *s.* moral, moralidade; (pl.) costumes, conduta.

morality, *s.* moralidade, ética, bons costumes; virtude, rectidão; castidade, pureza; *morality play,* peça teatral da Idade Média na qual cada vício ou virtude era representado por um actor.

moralize, *v.t.* moralizar, edificar; *v.i.* moralizar, filosofar.

morass, *s.* pântano, lameiro, paul.

moray, *s.* moreia.

morbid, *adj.* mórbido, patológico, doentio.

morbity, *s.* morbidez.

mordacious, *adj.* mordaz, sarcástico, cáustico.

mordancy, *s.* mordacidade, causticidade.

more, *adj.* (comp. de *much* e de *many*), mais, em maior número, adicional; *adv.* mais, em maior grau.

moreover, *adv.* além disso, além de que; *conj.* bem como.

morgue, *s.* morgue, necrotério.

morning, *s.* manhã, alvorada. 1) *good morning,* bons dias! 2) *early in the morning,* de madrugada. 3) *adj.* da manhã, matinal, matutino. 4) *morning star,* estrela de alva.

Moroccan, *adj.* e *s.* marroquino.

morose, *adj.* mal-humorado, soturno, sombrio, taciturno, insociável; *adv.* *morosely,* taciturnamente, insociavelmente.

morphia, morphine, morphin, *s.* morfina.

morrow, *s.* dia seguinte, amanhã.

morse, *s.* morsa.

morsel, *s.* bocado, pedacinho, naco; petisco, guloseima, manjar.

mortal, *adj.* mortal, transitório; fatal; *s.* mortal, ser humano.

mortality, *s.* mortalidade, mortandade; género humano, humanidade.

mortally, *adv.* mortalmente; de morte.

mortar, *s.* almofariz, gral; morteiro; argamassa.

mortgage, *s.* hipoteca; *v.t.* hipotecar, empenhar.

mortgagee, *s.* credor hipotecário.

mortgagor, mortgager, *s.* devedor hipotecário.

mortician, *s.* armador; cangalheiro.

mortification, *s.* mortificação.

mortigy, *v.t.* mortificar; gangrenar; *v.i.* mortificar-se; gangrenar-se.

mortise, mortice, *s.* encaixe, entalhe; *v.t.* encaixar, entalhar.

mortuary, *s.* casa mortuária; necrotério; *adj.* mortuário, fúnebre.

mosaic, *s.* mosaico.

Moslem, *adj.* e *s.* muçulmano, maometano.

mosque, mosk, *s.* mesquita.

mosquito, *s.* mosquito.

moss, *s.* musgo.

mossy, *adj.* musgoso, musguento.

most, *adj.* (superl. de *much* e *many*); *s.* o mais, mais, a maior parte; *adv.* extremamente, mais, muito; *s.* o principal, a maior parte, o maior número. 1) *she is better than most,* ela é o máximo. 2) *to make the most of,* tirar o maior proveito de.

mostly, *adv.* pela maior parte, as mais das vezes, geralmente.

mote, *s.* grão de poeira; partícula; átomo; ponto.

motel, *s.* hotel de estrada, estalagem para automobilistas.

mother, s. mãe; causa, origem; religiosa; borra (do vinho, vinagre, etc.); adj. natural, nativo, nacional, materno. 1) grand-mother, avó. 2) great grand-mother, bisavó. 3) mother-country, pátria. 4) mother-tongue, língua materna. 5) mother-of-pearl, madrepérola; v.t. servir de mãe; perfilhar; v.i. criar borra (vinho, vinagre, etc.).

motherland, s. país de origem, terra-mãe, pátria.

motherless, adj. órfão de mãe, sem mãe.

motherly, adj. materno, maternal; adv. maternalmente.

mothy, adj. cheio de traças, traçado.

motif, s. motivo; tema, assunto.

motion, s. movimento, moção, mudança; meneio, ar; gesto; mecanismo, engrenagem; v.t. propor, aconselhar; v.i. fazer sinais; dar ordens por meio de gestos.

motionless, adj. imóvel, sem movimento, fixo; estupefacto, estarrecido.

motive, s. motivo; móbil, causa, razão; intuito; tema, assunto; adj. motor, motriz, motivo.

motivity, s. força motriz, motricidade.

motley, adj. matizado; mesclado; multicolor, diverso; s. policromia; traje de palhaço.

motor, s. motor, máquina motriz. 1) motorman, motorista. 2) motor-signal, sinal de trânsito nas estradas.

motoring, s. automobilismo.

motorist, s. motorista.

mottle, v.t. mosquear, sarapintar, pintalgar.

motto, s. mote, divisa, lema.

mouch, v.t. vadiar.

moucher, s. vadio, vagabundo.

mound, s. montículo.

mount, s. morro, monte, elevação; v.t. e v.i. montar a cavalo; subir, trepar; montar ou engastar de pedras preciosas; elevar-se; importar em.

mountain, s. montanha, serra.

mountaineer, s. montanhês, serrano.

mountainous, adj. montanhês, serrano.

mountebank, s. saltimbanco, charlatão.

mourn, v.t. lamentar, chorar, sentir pesar; v.i. lamentar-se, afligir-se; andar de luto.

mourner, s. dorido; pranteador, carpideira; pessoa enlutada.

mournful, a. pesaroso, magoado; choroso; lutuoso; adv. mournfully, tristemente, lutuosamente.

mournfulness, s. pesar, tristeza, sentimento.

mourning, s. lamento, dor, luto. 1)deep mourning, luto pesado. 2) to be in mourning, estar de luto. 3) to go into mourning, vestir-se de luto; adv. mourningly, tristemente.

mouse, s. rato; v.t. e v.i. caçar ratos.

mousetrap, s. ratoeira.

moustache, s. bigode.

mousy, adj. infestado de ratos; da cor do rato; semelhante ao rato.

mouth, s. boca; entrada, abertura; careta, trejeito; voz, fala; lábio, língua, goela; v.t. pronunciar, falar alto; mastigar, comer; abocanhar; v.t. vociferar, declamar.

mouthful, s. bocado; sorvo, gole.

mouthpiece, s. bocal, boquilha; intérprete, porta-voz.

mouthy, adj. grandiloquente, loquaz; maledicente, insultuoso.

move, v.t. mover, remover; mexer; transportar, colocar noutro lugar; sacudir, impelir; propor, persuadir, inclinar; comover; v.i. mover-se, agitar-se, transportar-se; andar, pôr-se em marcha; desalojar; mudar de residência; partir; s. movimento; mudança; proposta; acção, feito.

movement, s. movimento; deslocação, mudança de lugar; mecanismo; ritmo.

movie, s. cinema.

mow, s. meda de feno; v.t. (mowed, mown), segar, ceifar; enceleirar.

mower, s. ceifeiro, segador; máquina de ceifar.

much, adj. muito, grande, bastante, mais; abundante; s. muito, grande quantidade, abundância; adv. muito, excessivamente; quase, pouco mais ou menos. 1) as much, tanto. 2) as much as, tanto como. 3) as much more, mais. 4) how much?, quanto? 5) so much, tanto. 6) not so much as, nem sequer. 7) so much the better, tanto melhor. 8) so much the worse, tanto pior. 9) too much, demasiado. 10) much of a size, do mesmo tamanho. 11) to make much of, tratar com carinho, fazer caso de.

muck, s. esterco, estrume; porcaria; v.t. e v.i. sujar, emporcalhar; estrumar.

mucky, adj. lamacento, sujo, imundo.

mucus, s. muco, mucosidade.

mud, s. lama, lodo, vasa; mud-lark, garoto que vive nas margens dos rios; v.i. enlodar, enlamear.

muddily, adv. de modo turvo.

muddle, v.t. turvar, toldar; entontecer,

enevoar; embriagar; confundir; pôr em desordem; *s.* confusão, mixórdia.

muddy, *adj.* lamacento, lodoso, barrento.

muff, *s.* regalo (para as mãos); torpor; falta ou falha (em jogos); desajeitado; *v.t.* fazer alguma coisa sem habilidade.

muffin, *s.* bolo leve semelhante aos sonhos.

muffle, *v.t.* abafar, tapar, cobrir; *v.i.* rosnar, resmungar; *s.* amortecedor, abafador de som; embuço, luva.

muffler, *s.* cachecol; capuz; luva grossa.

mufti, *s.* traje civil; à paisana.

mug, *s.* caneca; cara; careta; pessoa estudiosa.

muggy, *adj.* abafado, sufocante.

mulatto, *s.* mulato; *adj.* mulato, amulatado.

mulberry, *s.* amora.

mulch, *v.t.* cobrir (as plantas, etc.) com palha e estrume; *s.* estrume e palha para cobrir plantas.

mulct, *v.t.* multar; *s.* multa.

mule, *s.* mula; pessoa teimosa; máquina de fiar algodão; *mule-jenny,* máquina de fiar.

muleteer, *s.* almocreve, arrieiro.

mulish, *adj.* teimoso, cabeçudo, obstinado.

mull, *v.i.* e *v.t.* aquecer e aromatizar bebidas; cogitar, meditar; afadigar-se em vão.

mullet, *s.* tainha, mugem; estrela, roseta.

mulligrubs, *s.* cólica intestinal; abatimento, melancolia.

multifarious, *adj.* vário, diverso, multiplicado, muito variado.

multiform, *adj.* multiforme.

multiple, *adj.* e *s.* múltiplo, múltiplice.

multiplication, *s.* multiplicação; aumento, proliferação.

multiplicity, *s.* multiplicidade, diversidade.

multiply, *v.t.* multiplicar; acumular; propagar; *v.i.* multiplicar-se; propagar-se; reproduzir-se.

multitude, *s.* multidão, turba, chusma; povo; legião.

mum, *interj.* caluda!, silêncio!, psiu!; *s.* espécie de cerveja forte; termo infantil para chamar a mãe; *adj.* calado, silencioso; *v.t.* e *v.i.* mascarar-se, disfarçar-se; guardar silêncio.

mumble, *v.t.* e *v.i.* murmurar, resmungar; mastigar com a boca fechada; mascar; *s.* murmúrio, resmungo.

mumbler, *s.* resmungão, murmurador.

mumbling, *adj.* murmurante; *adv.* *mumblingly,* falando por entre dentes, resmungando.

mummer, *s.* pantomineiro; mascarado.

mummery, *s.* mascarada, chocarrice; disfarce; hipocrisia.

mummy, *s.* múmia; mamã.

mump, *v.t.* resmungar; estar de mau humor; esmolar, mendigar.

mumpish, *adj.* mal-humorado, amuado, rabugento.

mumps, *s.* papeira; mau humor, mau modo.

munch, *v.t.* e *v.i.* mascar ruidosamente ou com a boca muito cheia.

mundane, *adj.* mundano; *adv.* *mundanely,* mundanamente.

municipal, *adj.* municipal; *municipal kitchen,* sopa económica.

municipality, *s.* município, municipalidade.

munificent, *adj.* munificente, liberal, pródigo; *adv.* *munificently,* munificentemente, liberalmente.

munition, *s.* munições, provisões, material de guerra.

mural, *adj.* mural, parietal; *s.* quadro mural, pintura mural.

murder, *s.* assassínio, homicídio; *v.t.* assassinar, matar.

murderer, *s.* assassino, homicida.

murderess, *s.* assassina.

murdering, *adj.* mortífero, homicida; *s.* assassínio.

murderous, *adj.* assassino, homicida, sanguinário, cruel; *adv.* *murderously,* cruelmente, desumanamente.

mure, *v.t.* murar, emparedar; fechar, enclausurar.

murk, *s.* escuridão, obscuridade.

murky, *adj.* obscuro, escuro.

murmur, *s.* murmúrio, rumor, sussurro; *v.t.* e *v.i.* murmurar, sussurrar, resmungar.

murphy, *s.* batata.

murrain, *s.* morrinha, gafeira.

muscle, *s.* músculo; força muscular.

muscular, *adj.* muscular, musculoso, vigoroso.

muse, *v.t.* e *v.i.* meditar, cismar, reflectir, cogitar; *s.* cisma, devaneio, meditação; musa, astro.

museful, *adj.* pensativo, cismador.

museum, *s.* museu.

mush, *s.* papa de farinha de milho; polpa; guarda-sol; sentimentalismo, pieguice.

mushroom, *s.* cogumelo, fungo; novo-rico.

mushy, *adj.* mole, sentimental, piegas, insípido.

music, *s.* música; melodia, harmonia; composição musical.

musical, *adj.* musical, harmonioso, melodioso; apreciador de música; *adv. musically,* musicalmente, harmoniosamente.

musician, *s.* músico.

musk, *s.* almíscar.

musket, *s.* mosquete.

musketeer, *s.* mosqueteiro.

musky, *adj.* almiscarado.

muslin, *s.* musselina, cassa.

muss, *s.* desordem, rixa.

mussel, *s.* mexilhão.

Mussulman, *s.* muçulmano.

must, *v. defect.,* dever, haver de, ter de, ser obrigado a, ser necessário. 1) *we must go,* temos de ir. 2) *it must be done at once,* é necessário fazer isso já; *adj.* obrigatório, impositivo. 3) *a must book,* um livro obrigatório; *s.* mosto, sumo de uva; bolor, bafio.

mustar, *s.* mostarda. 1) *mustard-gas,* gás de mostarda, gás venenoso. 2) *mustard-plaster,* cataplasma de mostarda.

muster, *v.t.* passar revista, formar, pôr em formatura; juntar, reunir; expor; *v.i.* formar, entrar na formatura; reunir-se, juntar-se; *s.* reunião, ajuntamento; chamada; revista; rol.

musty, *adj.* bolorento, bafiento, rançoso.

mutable, *adj.* mutável, mudável; instável; *adv. mutably,* instavelmente.

mutate, *v.t.* mudar, alterar.

mutation, *s.* mutação, variação, mudança.

mute, *adj.* mudo, silencioso, calado; *s.* mudo; *deaf-mute,* surdo-mudo; *adv. mutely,* mudamente.

muteness, *s.* mudez.

mutilate, *v.t.* mutilar, estropiar, aleijar.

mutilation, *s.* mutilação.

mutineer, *s.* amotinador, revoltoso, insubordinado.

mutinous, *adj.* rebelde, insubordinado; indomável; *adv. mutinously,* insubordinadamente, tumultuosamente.

mutiny, *s.* motim, revolta; *v.i.* insubordinar-se; amotinar-se.

mutism, *s.* mutismo, silêncio; mudez.

mutter, *v.i.* murmurar, resmungar, falar por entre dentes; *s.* murmuração.

muttering, *adj.* murmurante; resmungão; *adv. mutteringly,* resmungando, murmurando.

mutton, *s.* carne de carneiro. 1) *mutton-chop,* costeleta de carneiro. 2) *mutton-head,* pessoa estúpida. 3) *dead as mutton,* completamente morto.

mutual, *adj.* mútuo, mutual, recíproco; *adv. mutually,* mutuamente.

mutuality, *s.* reciprocidade.

muzz, *v.i.* vadiar, estar ocioso; *v.t.* atordoar, estupidificar, embebedar.

muzzle, *s.* focinho; açaimo, mordaça; *v.t.* açaimar, amordaçar, impor silêncio; *v.i.* cheirar, chegar com o focinho.

muzzy, *adj.* distraído, bêbedo.

myope, *s.* míope.

myopia, *s.* miopia.

myopic, *adj.* míope, curto de vista.

myosotis, *s.* miosótis.

myriad, *s.* miríade.

myrmidon, *s.* esbirro.

myrrh, *s.* mirra.

myrtle, *s.* mirto, murta.

myself, *pron. refl.* eu mesmo, me, a mim.

mysterious, *adj.* misterioso; *adv. mysteriously,* misteriosamente.

mystery, *s.* mistério; enigma.

mystic, *adj.* místico, simbólico; *s.* místico, pessoa que professa o misticismo.

mystical, *adj.* místico; simbólico; enigmático; *adv. mystically,* misticamente.

mysticism, *s.* misticismo.

mystification, *s.* mistificação, embuste.

mystify, *v.t.* mistificar, iludir.

myth, *s.* mito, fábula.

mythic, *adj.* mítico; *adv. mythically,* dum modo mítico.

mythologic, *adj.* mitológico.

mythology, *s.* mitologia.

N

n, décima quarta letra do alfabeto.

nab, *v.t. nabbing, nabbed,* prender, apanhar de súbito.

nabob, *s.* nababo; ricaço.

nacre, *s.* nácar, madrepérola.

nacreous, *adj.* nacarado.

nadir, *s.* nadir.

nag, *s.* garrano, sendeiro, rocim, cavalo pequeno. *v.t.* e *v.i.* nagging, nagged, atiçar, importunar, repreender; incomodar.

naiad, *s.* náiade.

nail, *s.* unha; garra; prego, cravo, tacha; décima parte da jarda. 1) *clout-nails,* pregos sem cabeça. 2) *wire-nails,* pontas-de-paris. 3) *nail-brush,* escova das unhas. 4) *nail-cleaner,* limpa-unhas. 5) *tooth and nail,* com unhas e dentes. 6) *on the nail,* já, neste instante. 7) *to have hit the nail on the head,* acertar, adivinhar. 8) *to drive a nail in one's coffin,* fazer alguma coisa que apresse a morte ou a ruína. *v.t.* pregar; tachonar; cravejar; encravar; guarnecer ou adornar com pregos. 9) *to nail a lie,* demonstrar que uma coisa é mentira. 10) *to nail down* ou *up,* condenar uma janela, porta, etc., pregando-a. 11) *to nail one's colours to the mast,* comprometer-se a ir até ao fim.

nailer, *s.* fabricante de pregos.

nailery, *s.* fábrica de pregos, pregaria.

naïve, *adj.* ingénuo, cândido.

naively, *adv.* candidamente, ingenuamente.

naked, *adj.* nu, despido; indigente; descoberto; indefeso; evidente, claro, manifesto; puro, simples. 1) *the naked truth,* a verdade nua e crua. 2) *stark naked,* nu, em pêlo. 3) *naked sword,* espada nua, desembainhada.

nakedly, *adv.* nuamente, meramente, simplesmente, claramente.

nakedness, *s.* nudez, desabrigo, evidência, simplicidade; falta ou carência (de adorno, etc.)

namby-pamby, *adj.* pretensioso, afectado, melindroso. *s.* afectação, coisa frívola, disparate.

name, *s.* nome; título, fama, opinião, reputação, crédito, autoridade, poder; representação; apodo. 1) *Christian name,* nome de baptismo. 2) *in God's name,* em nome de Deus; por amor de Deus. 3) *to call one names,* insultar, chamar nomes. 4) *of* ou *by the name,* chamado, nomeado. 5) *in the name of,* da parte de. *v.t.* nomear, apelidar, chamar, pôr nome, mencionar; proferir, especificar, eleger, designar, fixar. 6) *to name the day,* fixar a data para o casamento.

nameable, *adj.* que pode receber um nome.

nameless, *s.* anónimo, sem nome; desconhecido.

namely, *adv.* nomeadamente, particularmente; a saber.

namesake, *s.* homónimo.

naming, *s.* nomeação.

nankeen, *s.* nanquim (pano e tinta).

nanny, *s.* cabra.

nap, *s.* sono ligeiro, soneca, sesta; pêlo (do pano); lanugem (da fruta); um jogo de cartas. *v.t.* napping, napped, cardar. *v.i.* dormitar, estar desprevenido.

nape, *s.* nuca.

napery, *s.* toalhas de mesa e guardanapos.

naphtha, *adj.* nafta.

naphthalene, *s.* naftalina.

napkin, *s.* guardanapo; *napkin-ring,* argola de guardanapos.

napless, *adj.* liso, sem pêlo.

napoleon, *s.* napoleão (moeda).

napoleonic, *adj.* napoleónico.

napoo, *interj.* acabou!, foi-se!

napped, *adj.* peludo; cardado.

napper, *s.* dorminhoco; cardador; carda (do pano).

napiness, *s.* qualidade do que é felpudo.

napping, *s.* cardação.

nappy, *adj.* espumoso, forte; que faz dormir (vinho, cerveja); felpudo (pano).

narcissus, *s.* narciso.

narcotic, *adj.* narcótico, opiado; soporífico. *s.* narcótico, opiato.

narcotine, *s.* narcotina.

narcotism, *s.* narcotismo.

narcotist, *s.* narcotista.

narcotize, *v.t.* narcotizar.

nard, *s.* nardo.

narghile, *s.* narguilé, cachimbo turco.

narrate, *v.t.* narrar, relatar.

narration, *s.* narração, relação, resenha, narrativa.

narrative, *adj.* narrativo. *s.* narrativa, relatório, relação.

narratively, *adv.* narrativamente.

narrator, *s.* narrador.

narrow, *adj.* estreito, escasso, limitado; apertado; tacanho, mesquinho, avarento, escrupuloso. 1) *narrow bed,* sepultura. 2) *narrow circumstances,* circunstâncias apertadas; escassez de dinheiro. 3) *narrow escape,* via estreita (comboio). 4) *narrow minded,* tacanho. 5) *to have a narrow escape,* escapar por um triz. *s.* estreito, braço de mar; desfiladeiro. *v.t.* estreitar, contrair, reduzir, encolher; diminuir; limitar; coarctar; *v.i.* encolher-se,

coarctar; *v.i.* encolher-se, reduzir-se; andar com as patas muito juntas (cavalo).

narrowing, *s.* estreitamento; limitação.

narrowly, *adv.* estreitamente, apertadamente, reduzidamente, por pouco; mesquinhamente, de perto, estritamente.

narrowness, *s.* estreiteza, probreza, exiguidade; mesquinhez.

narthex, *s.* pórtico das igrejas antigas, separado por grade, para mulheres, penitentes e catecúmenos.

narwhal, narwal, *s.* narval.

nasal, *adj.* nasal. *s.* letra nasal; osso do nariz.

nasality, *s.* nasalidade.

nasalization, *s.* nasalização.

nasalize, *v.t.* nasalar.

nasally, *adv.* nasalmente.

nascent, *adj.* nascente.

nastily, *adv.* imundamente, asquerosamente; indecentemente.

nastiness, *s.* imundície, porcaria; obscenidade, vilania.

nasturtium, *s.* nastúrcio.

nasty, *adj.* sujo, porco, asqueroso, imundo; obsceno, desonesto, indecente, impuro; sórdido, desagradável; ofensivo, intratável; tempestuoso; *to play a nasty trick*, fazer uma brincadeira estúpida.

natal, *adj.* nativo; natal.

natation, *s.* natação.

natatorial, *adj.* natatório.

nation, *s.* nação, país, estado, povo, gente. 1) *law od nations*, direito das gentes. 2) *the most favoured nation*, a nação mais favorecida.

national, *adj.* nacional; geral, público; patriótico. 1) *national anthem*, hino nacional. 2) *national debt*, dívida pública. 3) *national gallery*, galeria nacional onde se expõem todos os quadros que são da nação. 4) *Grand National*, principal corrida de obstáculos realizada todos os anos, no mês de Março, no hipódromo de Aintree.

nationalism, *s.* nacionalismo, amor à pátria, patriotismo.

nationalist, *s.* nacionalista.

nationality, *s.* nacionalidade; nação; naturalidade.

nationalization, *s.* nacionalização.

nationalize, *v.t.* nacionalizar.

nationally, *adv.* nacionalmente.

native, *adj.* nativo, natural, indígena, oriun-dio, originário, vernáculo, pátrio. 1) *native inhabitants*, habitantes indígenas. 2) *native gold*, ouro nativo. 3) *native place*, terra natal. *s.* natural, indígena; produto nacional.

natively, *adv.* naturalmente, originariamente.

nativeness, *s.* estado natural; qualidade de nativo.

nativity, *s.* nascimento.

natran, *s.* natro, ou natrão.

natterjack, *s.* género de sapo britânico com risca amarela pelas costas abaixo.

nattily, *adv.* garbosamente.

nattiness, *s.* garbo, gentileza.

natty, *adj.* elegante, garboso.

natural, *adj.* natural, nativo, genuíno, ordinário; ilegítimo; natural; *natural philosophy*, física. *s.* bequadro; nota natural; idiota, simplório; natural de um país.

naturalism, *s.* naturalismo.

naturalist, *s.* naturalista.

naturalization, *s.* naturalização, aclimatação.

naturalize, *v.t.* naturalizar, habituar, aclimatar.

naturally, *adv.* naturalmente.

naturalness, *s.* naturalidade, ingenuidade, simplicidade, natural.

nature, *s.* natureza; natural, índole, génio, carácter, compleição, constituição; qualidade, espécie. 1) *freak of nature*, monstruosidade, aborto. 2) *from nature*, do natural. 3) *good-nature*, bondade, afabilidade. 4) to *relieve* ou *ease nature*, evacuar, obrar. 4) *to pay the debt of nature*, morrer.

natured, *adj.* de natureza. 1) *good-natured*, de boa índole, bonacheirão, afável, bondoso. 2) *ill-natured*, mal-humorado, perverso.

naught, *s.* nada; zero, a cifra (0). *adj.* de nenhum valor; *to set at naught*, desprezar.

naughtily, *adv.* com maldade, perversamente, iniquamente.

naughtiness, *s.* maldade, perversidade; travessura.

naughty, *adj.* desobediente, mau, travesso: preverso. 1) *naughty boy*, maroto. 2) *naughty trick*, velhacaria; patifaria.

nausea, *s.* náuseas.

nauseant, *adj.* nauseabundo. *s.* substância nauseabunda.

nauseate, *v.t.* causar aversão ou antipatia; aborrecer. *v.i.* ter, sentir náuseas; desgostar-se, aborrecer-se.

nauseous, *adj.* nauseabundo, asqueroso, repugnante.

nauseously, s. qualidade do que é nauseabundo; náusea; repugnância, aversão.

nautch, s. dança indiana.

nautical, s. náutico, marítimo. 1) *nautical office*, repartição de instrumentos náuticos. 2) *nautical mile*, milha náutica. 3) *nautical survey*, levantamento hidrográfico.

nautically, adv. como em náutica.

nautilus, s. náutilo, argonauta.

naval, adj. naval, da marinha. 1) *naval cadet*, oficial da marinha. 2) *naval tactics*, táctica naval, evoluções marítimas. 3) *naval stores*, apetrechos navais. 4) *naval yard*, estaleiro do Estado, arsenal da marinha.

nave, s. nave central (de igreja); cubo (de roda, de hélice).

navel, s. umbigo; centro; meio; parte inferior. adj. central 1) *navel orange*, laranja de umbigo. 2) *navel-string*, cordão umbilical.

navicular, adj. navicular, s. fossa navicular; osso navicular.

navigability, s. navegabilidade.

navigable, adj. navegável; *navigable waterway*, via navegável.

navigableness, s. navegabilidade.

navigate, v.t. e v.i. navegar, pilotar; comandar um navio.

navigation, s. navegação, náutica; pilotagem; marinha, naus. 1) *navigation act*, código marítimo. 2) *inland navigation*, navegação interior.

navigator, s. navegador.

navvy, s. cabouqueiro, escavador.

navy, s. esquadra; marinha; marinha de guerra, armada. 1) *navy department*, Ministério da Marinha. 2) *Secretary of the navy*, secretário ou ministro da Marinha. 3) *royal navy*, marinha real. 4) *navy list*, anuário da marinha. 5) *navy office*, administração central da marinha. 6) *navy-yard*, arsenal da marinha.

nawab, s. governador indígena, ou nobre na Índia; nababo.

nay, adv. não; não só; porém; demais a mais; por modo nenhum; pelo contrário, s. voto negativo ou contrário; desmentido; flauta egípcia.

Nazarene, adj. e s. nazareno.

naze, s. cabo, promontório.

neap, adj. baixo, íntimo, vazante, minguante (maré). s. águas mortas.

Neapolitan, s. e adj. napolitano.

near, prep. cerca de, imediato a, junto a, perto de, próximo a. adv. perto, próximo; quase. adj. próximo, chegado, contíguo, vizinho; parente; íntimo; mesquinho. 1) *near horse*, cavalo de sela. 2) *near relation*, parente próximo. 3) *near at hand*, à mão, perto. 4) *near side*, lado esquerdo (do cavalo). 5) *near-sighted*, míope. 6) *near-sightedness*, miopia. 7) *to draw near*, aproximar-se de 8) *quite near*, muito perto, contínuo. 9) *it's near upon ten*, são quase horas. 10) *those near and dear to you*, os que te são aparentados e queridos. v.t. aproximar. v.i. aproximar-se.

nearly, adv. perto, próximo, a pouca distância; miseravelmente, mesquinhamente; apertadamente; quase, pouco mais ou menos; aproximadamente.

nearness, s. proximidade, vizinhança; parentesco próximo; amizade íntima; afinidade; mesquinhez.

neat, a. limpo, asseado, primoroso, elegante, perfeito, nítido, claro; bovino. 1) *neat-handed*, destro; com mãos limpas. s. gado bovino. 2) *neat's leather*, couro de boi. 3) *neat's tongue*, língua de vaca.

neath, prep.; contr. de *beneath*, debaixo de.

neatly, adv. polidamente, primorosamente; limpamente; asseadamente; elegantemente; destramente.

neatness, s. asseio, limpeza; polidez, elegância, delicadeza, esmero.

neb, s. bico, ponta, nariz, extremidade; corrediça (téc.).

nebula, s. nebulosa; névoa nos olhos. Pl. *nebulae*.

nebular, adj. nebuloso.

nebulosity, s. nebulosidade.

nebulous, adj. nebuloso, nublado, confuso.

necessarily, adv. necessariamente, indispensavelmente.

necessariness, s. necessidade.

necessary, adj. necessário; forçoso; essencial, peremptório. s. necessário.(pl.) coisas necessárias, requisitos essenciais.

necessitate, vt. necessitar, obrigar, precisar.

necessitous, adj. necessitado, indigente, pobre.

necessitously, adv. pobremente.

necessitousness, s. necessidade, pobreza, indigência.

necessity, ies, s. necessidade, precisão, requisito indispensável; exigência; pobreza, indigência, penúria.

neck, s. pescoço, garganta, colo; gargalo; braço (de guitarra, rabeca, etc.); colarinho, istmo; desfiladeiro; punho da boca (náut.); delgado do remo. 1) *neck bush*, casquilho de bucim. 2) *neckcloth*, lenço do pescoço. 3) *neck yoke*, jugo de coleiras. 4) *neck of land*, língua de terra. 5) *neck of rollers*, juntas de cilindros. 6) *low-necked*, decotado. 7) *neck and crop*, tudo junto a um tempo. 8) *neck and neck*, com igual rapidez numa corrida. 9) *on the neck of* ou *over the neck of,* logo, imediatamente. 10) *neck or nothing*, tudo ou nada. 11) *to harden the neck*, tornar-se mais obstinado.

neckband, s. colarinho, tira de camisa.

necked, adj. que tem pescoço, de pescoço (delgado, etc.); (náut.) estalada ou dobrada (cavilha).

neckerchief, s. lenço do pescoço.

necklace, s. colar.

necklet, s. colar pequeno.

neck-tie, s. gravata.

neckwear, s. colarinhos e gravatas.

necrologic, adj. necrológico.

necrologist, s. necrólogo.

necrology, ies, s. necrologia.

necromancer, s. necromante, mago; bruxo.

necromancy, s. necromancia, feitiçaria.

necropolis, es, s. necrópole.

necropsy, s. autópsia.

necrosis, s. necrose.

nectar, s. néctar.

nectarean, adj. delicioso.

nectarine, s. pêssego careca.

nectary, s. nectário.

née, adj. (fr.) nascida. Usa-se para designar o apelido paterno de uma mulher casada como: *Mrs. Kate Brown, née Smith* (da família *Smith*).

need, s. necessidade, urgência; carência, falta; pobreza, miséria, indigência, coisa necessária. 1) *if need be*, se houver necessidade; se for preciso. 2) *in case of need*, em caso de necessidade. 3) *a friend in need, is a friend indeed*, os amigos conhecem-se nas ocasiões. *v.t.* necessitar, ter necessidade ou precisão de, requerer, exigir, carecer de. *v.i.* ser necessário, haver necessidade de.

needer, s. um necessitado.

needful, adj. necessário, indispensável, preciso.

needfully, adv. necessariamente.

needfulness, s. necessidade, precisão, pobreza, falta.

needier, neediest, comp. e sup. de *needy*.

needily, adv. pobremente.

neediness, s. indigência, pobreza, necessidade.

needle, s. agulha; agulha de marear, bússola; agulha, obelisco (arq.). 1) *needle of a dial*, agulha ou estilo dum relógio de sol. 2) *dipping needle*, agulha de inclinação. 3) *knitting-needle*, agulha de meia ou de malha. 4) *shepherd's needle*, agulha-de-pastor (planta). 5) *needle of a balance*, fiel de balança. 6) *crochet, darning needle*, agulha de croché, de cerzir. 7) *seaming-needle*, agulha para cozer. 8) *sewing-machine needle*, agulha de máquina de costura. 9) *needle-case*, agulheiro. 10) *needle-fish*, peixe-agulha. 11) *needle-shaped* ou *-pointed*, aguçado como o bico da agulha. 12) *needle-threader*, enfiador de agulhas. 13) *true as the needle to the pole*, leal, fidedigno. 14) *to seek a needle in a hay-stack*, procurar agulha em palheiro.

needleful, s. linha que se enfia de cada vez na agulha.

needler, s. agulheiro (que faz agulhas).

needless, adj. supérfluo, inútil.

needlessly, adv. inutilmente.

needlessness, s. superfluidade, inutilidade.

needlewoman, s. costureira.

needlework, s. trabalho feito à agulha; costura.

needn't, contr. de *need not*.

needs, adv. necessariamente.

needy, adj. indigente.

ne'er, contr. de *never*.

ne'er-do-well, s. pessoa inútil.

nefarious, adj. nefando, malvado, atroz, abominável.

nefariously, adv. abominavelmente.

nefariousness, s. abominação.

negation, s. negação, negativa.

negative, adj. negativo. s. negativa, denegação; veto, direito de recusar; negativo (fot.); electricidade negativa; *it was decided in the negative*, foi rejeitada a proposta. *v.t.* denegar, desaprovar, refutar, negar; opor-se a, votar contra.

negatively, adv. negativamente.

negativeness, s. negatividade.

neglect, s. descuido, negligência, omissão; desprezo, desdém, frieza, indiferença; desuso; *to fall into neglect*, cair em desuso. *v.t.* descuidar, desatender; olvidar, omitir, desprezar; negligenciar, não fazer caso.

neglecter, s. descuidado, negligente.

neglectful, adj. negligente, descuidado, preguiçoso.

neglectfully, adv. negligentemente.

neglectfulness, s. negligência, descuido.

négligé, adj. negligente, descuidado, preguiçoso. s. trajo caseiro.

negligence, s. negligência, descuido, desleixo; abandono.

negligent, adj. negligente.

negligently, adv. descuidadamente.

negligible, adj. desatendível, desprezível.

negotiability, s. negociabilidade.

negotiable, adj. negociável.

negotiate, vt. negociar, tratar; agenciar. v.i. levar a cabo uma negociação, negociar.

negotiation, s. negociação, negócio, transacção.

negotiator, s. negociador.

negress, as, s. negra.

negro, s. negro.

negrophile, s. negrófilo.

negrophobe, s. negrófobo.

negus, s. sangria (bebida); negus (nome dado ao monarca da Abissínia).

neigh, v.i. rinchar. s. rincho.

neighbour, s. vizinho; amigo (fam.). adj. vizinho, próximo. v.t. avizinhar, ser vizinho de.

neighbourhood, s. vizinhança, proximidade, imediação; cercanias, arredores.

neighbouring, adj. vizinho; da vizinhança próximo.

neighbourly, adj. de bom vizinho, urbano, atento, cortês. adv. como bom vizinho, civilmente.

neighing, s. rincho.

neither, adj. nenhum, nenhum dos dois. conj. nem (correlativo ordinário de nor): neither he nor she, nem ele nem ela; também não, nem sequer (depois de uma negação substitui-se por either). 1) neither will I do it, também não o farei. 2) nor I either, também eu não. pron. nenhum, nem um nem outro. 4) to have neither house or home, não ter eira nem beira. 5) He has neither honour nor honesty, ele não tem fé nem lei.

nem. con., por unanimidade (abrev. de nemine contradicente).

nenuphar, s. nenúfar, lírio-de-água (Castela speciosa).

neolithic, adj. neolítico.

neologize (-ise), vi. empregar neologismos.

neologism, s. neologismo.

neologist, s. neologista.

neon, s. néon, elemento gasoso que se encontra no ar.

neophyte, s. neófito.

nepenthe, s. droga que se supunha acalmar as dores; nepentes (planta).

nephew, s. sobrinho.

nephritis, s. nefrite.

nepotism, s. nepotismo.

Neptune, s. Neptuno (astro e deus); oceano (fig.).

neptunian, adj. neptuniano.

Nereid, s. nereida.

nerve, s. nervo, força, vigor, nervosidade, fibra; desfaçatez, descaro, pl. excitabilidade nervosa. v.t. dar vigor a, dar força; animar.

nerved, adj. vigoroso.

nerveless, adj. inerte; sem vigor.

nervine, s. remédio nervino. adj. nervino.

nervous, adj. nervoso; nervous-prostration, neurastenia.

nervously, adv. nervosamente.

nervousness, s. nervosidade, vigor, força; estado nervoso.

nervure, s. nervura; veia.

ness, s. promontório, cabo. suf. que serve para formar substantivos abstractos.

nest, s. ninho, ninhada; guarida, asilo, abrigo, covil; jogo, série. 1) nest of drawers or boxes, jogo de gavetas ou caixas. 2) crow's nest, cesto de vigia (náut.). v.t e v.i. aninhar, aninhar-se, fazer um ninho; buscar ninhos; alojar; estabelecer-se; colocar uma série de objectos uns dentro dos outros.

nest-egg, s. ovo natural ou artificial para atrair a galinha a pôr; endês.

nestle, v.t. abrigar, pôr num ninho, acariciar, afagar. v.i. aninhar-se, engaiolar-se; estar abrigado como num ninho.

nestling, s. passarinho, pintainho; filhote.

Nestorian, adj. e s. nestoriano.

net, s. rede, malha, laço. 1) net-braider, ou maker, fabricante de redes. 2) net-embroidery, bordado reticular. 3) net-work, renda, malha, retículo. 4) mosquito-net, mosquiteiro. v.t. netting, netted, prender ou colher com rede; tirar o produto líquido. v.i. lançar a rede, fazer redes.

net ou nett, adj. limpo; puro; líquido, livre de dedução. 1) nett produce, produto líquido. 2) nett profit, ou earnings, ganho ou benefício líquido.

nether, adj. inferior, mais baixo. 1) nether lip, lábio inferior. 2) nether garments, calças.

Netherlander, s. habitante dos Países Baixos.

nethermost, adj. o mais baixo (em situação).

netted, adj. coberto por uma rede; reticular; colhido com rede.

netting, s. rede (de gávea, gurupés, etc.); renda, obra de rede ou malha; trincheira; netting-needle, lançadeira (para fazer rede).

nettle, s. ortiga; amarra (náut.). v.t. picar com ortiga; irritar, exasperar, provocar; nettle-fever ou rash, urticária.

nettling, s. provocação, irritação; emenda de dois cabos (náut.).

neume, s. neuma (mús.)

neural, adj. neural.

neuralgia, s. nevralgia.

neuralgic, adj. nevrálgico.

neurasthenia, s. neurastenia.

neurasthenic, s. neurasténico.

neuritis, s. nevrite.

neurologist, s. neurologista, neurology, s. neurologia.

neuroma, s. neuroma.

neurosis, s. nevrose.

neurotic, adj. e s. nevrótico.

neuter, adj. e s. neutro.

neutral, adj. neutral, neutro; indefinido; pardacento ou azulado. s. neutral.

neutrality, s. neutralidade.

neutralization, s. neutralização.

neutralize, v.t. neutralizar.

neutrally, adv. neutralmente.

never, adv. nunca, jamais, de nenhum modo; nem. 1) never mind, não importa. 2) never so, por muito, ou por mais que; com never formam-se vários compostos, como: never-ceasing, never ending, contínuo sem fim, eterno; never-fading, incorruptível, indelével; never-failing, infalível. 3) better late than never, mais vale tarde do que nunca.

nevermore, adv. e conj. nunca, mais.

nevertheless, adv. não obstante, contudo, todavia.

new, adj. novo, fresco, recente, moderno, noviço, não acostumado, outro, diferente, distinto. 1) new year, ano novo. 2) new-year's day, dia de Ano Novo, primeiro dia do ano. 3) new year's gift, presente de ano novo. 4) new bread, pão fresco. 5) new-coined word, termo novo, palavra ultimamente inventada. 6) new-fangled, de nova invenção, da última moda. 7) new fashion, última moda. 8) new grown, recém-nascido,

recém-saído. 9) new-laid, posto, colocado ou estendido de fresco. 10) new-made, fresco, acabado de fazer. 11) new-married, recém-casado, 12) new-mown, cortado ou segado de fresco. 13) bran-new, novo em folha. 14) the New World, o Novo Mundo. adv. novamente, recentemente, de fresco, de novo.

newborn, s. recém-nascido.

newcomer, s. recém-chegado.

newel, s. pilar que sustenta os degraus da escada de caracol.

Newfoundlander, s. habitante da Terra Nova.

newish, adj. quase novo.

newly, adv. novamente, recentemente, há pouco; newly arrived, recém-chegado.

newness, s. novidade; inovação; falta de prática; início.

news, s. notícia, aviso, informação; notícias, novidades, novas; what is the news?, que há de novo?

news-agent, s. vendedor de jornais.

newsmonger, s. noveleiro, gazeteiro, porta-novas.

newspaper, s. diário, jornal, gazeta, periódico; papel de jornal; newspaper man, periodista, jornalista.

newsvendor, s. vendedor de jornais.

newsy, adj. noticioso.

newt, s. saramântiga.

Newtonian, adj. newtoniano.

next, adj. seguinte, próximo, imediato, contíguo, vizinho, sucessivo, futuro. 1) next ahead, navio de frente (em coluna). 2) the next day, o dia seguinte. adv. logo imediatamente, depois, em seguida. 3) next to impossible, quase impossível. 4) what next?, depois?, que se segue? pret. junto a, ao lado de.

nexus, s. nexo, laço, vínculo.

nib, s. bico, ponta, extremo; bico (de pena, de ave) (pl.) fragmentos de cacau ou de café. v.t. fazer ponta, aguçar, aparar (uma pena).

nibble, v.t. picar, morder; to nibble at, criticar, censurar. s. acção de morder, de dar uma dentada; roedura.

niblick, s. um dos tacos de golfe.

nice, adj. fino, agudo, subtil, delicado; diligente, solícito; circunspecto, cauto; exacto, escrupuloso; minucioso, pundonoroso; polido; primoroso; elegante, esmerado; agradável; delicioso; bonito, gentil, amável; a nice distinction, subtileza.

nicely, *adv.* com finura; delicadamente; primorosamente, subtilmente; muito bem.

niceness, *s.* finura, gentileza, amabilidade; delicadeza.

nicety, *s.* finura, delicadeza, primor, exactidão; esmero, subtileza. 1) *niceties of politics*, subtilezas da lógica; argúcias da política. 2) *niceties of honour*, pontos de honra. 3) *to a nicety*, com a maior precisão.

niche, *s.* nicho.

niched, adj. com nichos.

nick, *s.* talho, corte, entalhe; tarja; momento crítico; oportunidade; jogada favorável. 1) *old nick*, o diabo. 2) *in the nick of time*, no momento oportuno, a tempo. *v.t.* fazer cortes ou entalhes, tarjar; acertar, dar no alvo, chegar a tempo. *v.i.* corresponder, igualar-se, ser igual, fazer uma boa jogada.

nickel, *s.* níquel. *v.t.* niquelar.

nick-nack, *s.* frioleira, bagatela, ninharia.

nickname, *s.* alcunha, sobrenome. *v.t.* alcunhar.

nicotine, *s.* nicotina.

nidus, *s.* ninho (de insectos).

niece, *s.* sobrinha.

niello, *s.* nigela. *v.t.* nigelar.

nig, nigging, nigged, *v.t.* cortar a borda (de uma moeda, etc.) lavrar (a pedra). *s.* pedaço.

niggard, *adj.* e *s.* mesquinho, avarento, avaro, sórdido, miserável.

niggardish, *adj.* um tanto mesquinho ou avaro.

niggardliness, *s.* mesquinhez, avareza; miséria.

niggardly, *adj.* mesquinho, miserável. *adv.* mesquinhamente.

nigger, *s.* negro, negra; *nigger engine*, máquina rudemente construída.

niggle, *v.t.* enganar, burlar. *v.i.* ocupar-se em minúcias; gastar tempo com ninharias; meticuloso.

nigh, *prep.* próximo de; não longe de, junto a. *adv.* perto, imediato, quase; *to draw nigh*, aproximar-se. *adj.* próximo. vizinho; da esquerda (falando de cavalos); chegado, íntimo.

night, *s.* noite; trevas, obscuridade; cegueira; tristeza, aflição; morte. 1) *at night*, à noite. 2) *by night*, de noite, a coberto da noite. 3) *good night*, boas-noites. 4) *to-night*, esta noite. 5) *last night*, a noite passada, ontem à noite. 6) *Sunday night*, domingo à noite. 7) *night bell*, campainha para chamar de noite.

8) *night-bird*, ave nocturna. 9) *night-clothes, night-dress, night-gown, nightshirt, night rob*, traje de noite, camisa de dormir. 10) *night dew*, relento, sereno. 11) *night dog*, cão que caça de noite. 12) *night fall*, o cair da noite, o anoitecer. 13) *night fire*, fogo-fátuo. 14) *night latch, night clock*, fechadura de mola. 15) *night lamp, night light*, lamparina ou luz de noite. 16) *night-piece*, quadro ou cena nocturna. 16) *night rest*, repouso da noite. 17) *night robber*, ladrão nocturno. 18) *night school*, escola nocturna. 19) *night-soil*, lixo, conteúdo das latrinas. 20) *night-time*, noite. 21) *night walker*, sonâmbulo, noctívago. 22) *night-watchman*, ronda da noite. 23) *night-work*, serão.

nightingale, *s.* rouxinol.

nightly, *adv.* de noite, todas as noites. *adj.* nocturno.

nightmare, *s.* pesadelo.

nightshade, *s.* erva-moira.

nightward, *adj.* próximo da noite.

nightwatch, es, *s.* guarda-nocturno.

nihilism, *s.* niilismo.

nihilist, *s.* niilista.

nil, *s.* nada; faíscas, chispas.

nimble, *adj.* ligeiro, vivo, activo, ágil, veloz. 1) *nimble-fingered*, ligeiro de dedos. 2) *nimble-footed*, veloz no andar. 3) *nimble pinioned*, de voo rápido. 4) *nimble witted*, vivo, esperto, inteligente.

nimbleness, *s.* ligeireza, velocidade, actividade, agilidade; destreza.

nimbly, *adv.* ligeiramente, prontamente, agilmente.

nimbus, *s.* nimbo, auréola.

niminy-piminy, *adj.* afectado.

nincompoop, *s.* pateta, basbaque.

ninbe, *adj.* e *s.* nove; *the nine*, as nove musas.

ninefold, *adj.* nónuplo.

ninepin, *s.* papoula.

ninepins, *s.* jogo da bola (de nove paus).

ninescore, *adj.* e *s.* nove vezes vinte.

nineteen, *adj.* e *s.* dezanove.

nineteenth, *adj.* e *s.* décimo nono.

ninetieth, *adj.* e *s.* nonagésimo.

ninety, *adj.* e *s.* noventa.

ninny, es, *s.* simplório, parvo.

ninth, *adj.* nono. *s.* a nona parte; nona (mús.).

ninthly, *adv.* em nono lugar.

nip, *v.t.* nipping, nipped, *v.t.* beliscar, picar, arranhar; sujeitar; agarrar; prender;

enrascar; roçar; amichelar (náut.); morder; mordiscar; cortar; recortar; queimar (por geada); murchar. 1) *to nip in th bud*, ou *blossom*, cortar em flor, logo no início. 2) *to nip off*, cortar (a copa das árvores), despontar. s. unhada, beliscadura, dentada; pedaço, trago; dano repentino das plantas; coca; parte que roça; presa; prisão (náut.).

nipper, s. o que pica ou agarra; pinça; boca de alguns crustáceos; dente dianteiro do cavalo; pessoa satírica; pl. alicate; torquês; michelos.

nipping, s. arranhão, rasgão, mordedura. *adj.* picante, penetrante, mordaz, satírico; *nipping tool*, instrumento para fazer recortes.

nippingly, *adv.* mordazmente.

nipple, s. mamilo, bico do peito; bico de biberão; protuberância semelhante ao bico do peito; pequena elevação redonda (num monte); parte da culatra onde se coloca o cartucho; *nipple-wort*, lampsana (planta).

nippy, *adj.* picante; sarcástico.

nit, s. lêndea.

nitrate, s. nitrato.

nitre, s. nitro, salitre.

nitric, *adj.* nítrico.

nitrification, s. nitrificação.

nitrite, s. nitrite.

nitrogen, s. nitrogénio.

nitrogenous, *adj.* nitrógeno.

nitroglycerine, s. nitroglicerina.

nitrous, *adj.* nitroso, salitroso.

nitry, *adj.* nitroso.

nix, nixie, s. *nix*, génio das águas na mitologia alemã; nada. cal. sinal de que se aproxima um superior (entre estudantes, operários, etc).

no, *adv.* não. *adj.* nenhum, nenhuma, nenhuns, nenhumas. 1) *no one*, ninguém. 2) *no man's land*, terreno maninho; território discutível; terra-de-ninguém.

no, es, s. não; voto negativo.

no., *abrev.* de número.

nob, s. a cabeça; protuberância; nobre, pessoa de consideração.

nobbily, *adv.* ostentosamente.

nobbiness, s. ostentação.

nobble, *v.i.* impedir (as probabilidades de ganhar numa corrida); enganar.

nobby, *adj.* ostentoso, vistoso, taful.

nobiliary, *adj.* nobiliário.

nobility, s. nobreza, dignidade, grandeza, aristocracia.

noble, *adj.* nobre, ilustre, insigne, majestoso; generoso. s. nobre, aristocrata; moeda antiga. 1) *noble extraction*, origem nobre, sangue azul. 2) *noble metals*, metais nobres (ouro, prata, platina). 3) *noble minded*, de grande carácter. 4) *noble mindedness*, grandeza de carácter. 5) *to make noble*, enobrecer.

nobleman, s. fidalgo, nobre, titular do reino.

nobleness, s. nobreza, dignidade, grandeza, lustre, esplendor.

noblesse, s. nobreza, aristocracia.

noblewoman, s. mulher nobre, fidalga.

nobly, *adv.* nobremente; *nobly born*, de nascimento nobre.

nobody, ies, s. ninguém; nenhum; pessoa desprezível; *nobody else*, mais ninguém.

noctambulant, *adj.* noctâmbulo, sonâmbulo.

noctambulist, s. noctâmbulo, sonâmbulo.

noctambulism, s. noctambulismo, sonambulismo.

nocturnal, *adj.* nocturnal, nocturno.

nocturne, s. cena nocturna (pint.); nocturno (reza, mús.).

nod, *v.t. nodding, nodded,* mostrar, indicar (por sinal de cabeça). *v.i.* cabecear, inclinar a cabeça; dormitar. 1) *to nod assent,* acenar que sim. s. sinal, aceno (que se faz com a cabeça); inclinação de cabeça, saudação, reverência. 2) *land of nod*, o sono.

nodal, *adj.* nodos.

nodding, s. cabeceamento, saudação com a cabeça. *adj.* inclinado.

noddle, s. cabeça.

noddy, ies, s. alarve, estúpido; carro ligeiro de duas rodas; espécie de andorinha-do--mar.

node, s. protuberância, bossa; nó; nodo; tumor, dureza, nódulo; nodo (astron.); enredo, nó, trama (teat.)

nodose, *adj.* nodoso.

nodular, *adj.* nodular.

nodule, s. nódulo.

nodilous, *adj.* nodoso.

Noel, s. Natal; cântico do Natal.

nog, s. cavilha; bucha; cerveja forte; *eggnog*, caldo de rainha (de leite, ovos, açúcar e rum).

noggin, s. cubo; jarro.

nogging, s. tabique; escora.

nohow, *adv.* de nenhum modo, de modo algum.

noise, s. ruído, som; estrondo, barafunda; rumor, fama. v.t. divulgar, propalar; fazer bulha.

noiseful, adj. ruidoso, estrondoso.

noiseless, adj. sem ruído, tranquilo, calado, silencioso.

noiselessly, adv. silenciosamente.

noiselessness, s. silêncio.

noisette, s. uma variedade de roseira.

noisier, noisiest, comp. e sup. de noisy.

noisily, adv. ruidosamente.

noisiness, s. barafunda, estrépito, ruido, tumulto.

noisome, adj. nocivo, insalubre; asqueroso, fétido, desagradável.

noisomely, adv. de modo repugnante ou infecto.

noisomeness, s. mau cheiro; infecção; nojo.

noisy, adj. ruidoso, turbulento.

nolens volens, adv. ou por bem ou por mal.

nomad, adj. e s. nómada.

nomadic, adj. nómada.

nomadically, adv. nomadamente, como os nómadas.

nomenclature, s. nomenclatura.

nomic, adj. nómico.

nominal, adj. nominal; nominal partner, testa-de-ferro.

nominally, adv. nominalmente, nominativamente.

nominate, v.t. nomear, eleger, designar, mencionar.

nomination, s. nomeação, eleição, proposta.

nominative, s. e adj. nominativo.

nominator, s. nomeador.

nominee, s. o nomeado (para um emprego).

non, adv. não. 1) non-acceptance, falta de aceitação, recusa. 2) non-appearance, contumácia, rebeldia. 3) non-arrival, falta de chegada. 4) non-collegiate, não colegial. 5) non-combatant, não combatente. 6) non compliance, falta de condescendência. 7) non commissioned, que não tem patente oficial. 8) non-condutor, isolador. 9) non delivery, falta de entrega. 10) non-performance, falta de execução.

nonage, s. menoridade.

nonagenarian, adj. e s. nonagenário.

nonce, s. tempo presente, ocasião; for the nonce, por esta vez; para esta ocasião.

nonchalance, s. indiferença, indolência.

nonchalant, adj. indiferente, indolente.

nonconformist, s. não conformista (dissidente).

nonconformity, s. não conformidade (com a Igreja Anglicana).

noncontentious, adj. não contencioso.

nondescript, adj. não descritivo, não facilmente classificável, indescritível, raro, estrambótico. s. objecto curioso, raro e desconhecido.

none, s. nona (reza).

none, pron. ninguém, nenhum, nenhuma; nada. 1) none would be excepted, não se exceptuará pessoa alguma. 2) none of that, nada disso. 3) none of your business, não é nada consigo. adv. não, de nenhum modo. 4) he is none the better for it, nem por isso está melhor. 5) none the less, nem por isso menos. 6) the pay is none too high, o ordenado não é nada alto.

nones, s. pl. nonas.

nonetity, ies, s. o nada, a negação; pessoa ou coisa de nenhum valor; zero à esquerda.

nonilion, s. nonilião.

nonjuror, s. clérigo que não jurou fidelidade ao trono em 1688.

nonpareil, adj. sem par, incomparável, sem rival, sem igual. s. pessoa ou coisa de incomparável mérito; tipo miúdo, corpo 6.

nonplus, s. embaraço, perplexidade. v.t. confundir, embaraçar.

nonplussed, adj. confuso, embaraçado, sem saber o que há-se fazer.

nonsense, s. disparate, absurdo, ridículo, estúpido.

nonsensically, adv. absurdamente, tolamente.

nonsensicalness, s. insensatez, disparate, despropósito.

nonsuch, es, s. sem par, sem igual; modelo, planta denominada «Cruz de Malta».

nonsuit, s. desistência; abandono de acção; revelia. v.t. julgar à revelia. adj. abandonado à revelia.

noodle, s. simplório; basbaque; noodledom, conjunto de néscios.

nook, s. canto, ângulo, recanto, escaninho, esconderijo.

noon, s. meio-dia; meridiano, apogeu. 1) high noon, às doze em ponto. 2) at noon, ao meio-dia.

noonday, s. meio-dia, adj. meridional.

nooning, s. a sesta.

noontide, adj. meridional. s. meio-dia; apogeu; culminação.

noose, s. nó corredio, laço. v.t. apanhar num laço ou armadilha.

nor, *conj.* nem, não, partícula correlativa de *neither* ou *not*. 1) *neither you nor I*, nem tu nem eu. 2) *I did not go nor did I intend to*, não fui nem tive tenção de ir.

norma, *s.* norma, regra, modelo; lei; molde.

normal, *adj.* normal, regular, exemplar, perpendicular; *normal school*, escola normal.

normality, *s.* normalidade.

normalization, *s.* normalização.

normalize, *v.t.* normalizar, regularizar tornar normal

normally, *adv.* normalmente.

Norman, *adj.* e *s.* normando.

Norse, *adj.* escandinavo. *s.* antigo escandinavo; língua dos antigos escandinavos; *norseman*, homem do Norte, antigo escandinavo.

north, *s.* norte, setentrião. *adj.* setentrional, boreal, do norte. 1) *north pole*, pólo norte, pólo árctico. 2) *north by east*, norte, quarto nordeste. 3) *north by west*, norte, quarto noroeste. 4) *north star*, estrela polar, estrela do norte. 5) *north wind*, vento norte, o aquilão. *v.i.* ganhar norte; fazer-se norte (vento).

north-east, *s.* e *adj.* nordeste.

north-easter, *s.* nordeste (vento).

north-easterly, *adv.* que se dirige para nordeste.

north-eastern, *adj.* do nordeste; no nordeste.

north-eastward, *adv.* em direcção a nordeste.

norther, *s.* norte (vento).

northerly, *adj.* setentrional, boreal, do norte.

northern, *adj.* do norte; *northern lights*, aurora boreal.

northerner, *s.* habitante do norte.

northing, *s.* distância na direcção do norte.

northmost, *adj.* mais ao norte.

northward, *adv.* para norte.

north-west, *s.* e *adj.* noroeste.

north-wester, *s.* o noroeste (vento).

north-westerly, *adj.* que se dirige ou que vem de noroeste.

north-western, *adj.* pertencente ou situado a noroeste.

Norwegian, *s.* e *adj.* norueguês.

nose, *s.* nariz; focinho; bico de proa (náut.) olfacto; sagacidade; qualquer coisa parecida com um nariz, como: proa de um navio, bico ou boca (de cafeteira, jarro, etc.). 1) *nose-dive*, mergulho de um avião.

2) *nose-piece*, parte do microscópio onde se coloca a objectiva. 3) *nose-ring*, argola para conduzir os animais pelo focinho. 4) *flat nose*, nariz chato. 5) *pug nose*, nariz pequeno e arrebitado. 6) *Roman nose*, nariz aquilino. 7) *to count noses*, contar as pessoas. 8) *to follow one's nose*, seguir em linha recta. 9) *to lead by the nose*, conduzir ou governar alguém à sua vontade. 10) *to thrust the nose into*, intrometer-se, meter o nariz em, ser curioso. 11) *to put one's nose out of joint*, suplantar, vencer. 12) *to bleed at the nose*, deitar sangue pelo nariz. 13) *to blow one's nose*, assoar-se. 14) *to speak through the nose*, ser fanhoso. 15) *to turn up one's nose at*, olhar com desprezo. 16) *under one's nose*, nas barbas de alguém, na sua presença. 17) *he pokes his nose into everything*, ele mete o nariz onde não é chamado. *v.t.* e *v.i.* cheirar, encarar, afrontar; opor-se, fazer frente; blasonar. 18) *to nose out*, descobrir, averiguar.

noseband, *s.* focinheira (correia de cabeçada).

nosebleed, *s.* hemorragia nasal.

nosegay, *s.* ramalhete.

noseless, *adj.* desnarigado.

noser, *s.* forte vento ponteiro; murro no nariz.

nostalgia, *s.* nostalgia.

nostalgic, *adj.* nostálgico.

nostril, *s.* fossa nasal; venta.

nostrum, *s.* panaceia.

nosy, *adj.* narigudo, com grande nariz; mal-cheiroso, sensível a maus cheiros.

not, *adv.* não, nem, de maneira alguma. 1) *nor at all*, de modo algum. 2) *not to say*, por não dizer. 3) *not do much as*, nem sequer. 4) *I think not*, creio que não.

notability, ies, *s.* notabilidade, pessoa notável.

notable, *adj.* notável, memorável, digno de atenção; activo, laborioso; atento, cuidadoso, económico. *s.* pessoa notável ou eminente.

notableness, *s.* notabilidade.

notably, *adv.* notavelmente.

notarial, *adj.* de notário, feito perante notário.

notary, ies, *s.* notário, tabelião, escrivão público.

notation, *s.* notação, anotação; significação; notificação; numeração; escrita; anotação (arit., mús., quím., lóg.).

notch, *s.* entalhe, encaixe, corte, chanfradura; brecha; mossa, boca. *v.t.* entalhar, fazer cortaduras.

note, *s.* nota, marca, sinal; apontamento, memória; comunicação; nota diplomática; bilhete; missiva; escrito, observação; conhecimento; notícia, aviso; distinção, importância; nota (mús.); tom; vale; ordem de pagamento (com.). 1) *note-book*, agenda. 2) *note-paper*, papel de carta. 3) *note-worthy*, notável. 4) *bank note*, nota de banco. 5) *foot note*, nota de rodapé. 6) *half note*, mínima (mús.). 7) *whole note*, semibreve. 8) *note of hand* ou *promissory note*, promissória; obrigação de dívida. 9) *to take note*, tomar nota; notar. *v.t.* notar, marcar, distinguir; reparar, observar; advertir, tomar nota de; apontar, pôr por escrito; registar; protestar uma letra. 10) *to note an exception*, anotar nos autos a excepção que ponha uma das partes. 11) *note a bill*, apontar uma letra. 12) *note a protest*, protestar uma letra.

noted, *adj.* notável, distinto.

noteless, *adj.* obscuro, desconhecido.

nothing, *s.* nada, zero; ninharia; bagatela. 1) *that is nothing to me*, isso não é comigo. 2) *good for nothing*, que não presta para coisa alguma. 3) *next to nothing*, quase nada. 4) *to make nothing of*, importar-se pouco com, não tirar proveito de; não compreender. 5) *to come to nothing*, não dar resultado algum; ficar reduzido à miséria. 6) *for nothing*, por nada, gratuitamente. 7) *it's nothing like as good*, nem se lhe pode comparar. *adv.* de nenhum modo.

nothingness, *s.* nada, a não existência; ninharia.

notice, *s.* nota; observação; atenção; aviso, notícia, informe, advertência; anúncio; comunicação; menção; consideração; cortesia. 1) *law notices*, anúncios judiciários. 2) *worthy of notice*, digno de atenção ou de menção. 3) *notice to quit*, aviso de despejo. 4) *to gove notice*, avisar, fazer saber, informar, notificar. 5) *to take notice of*, fazer caso de, tomar conhecimento de. 6) *to give short notice*, conceder um curto prazo. 7) *at the shortest notice*, no momento, o mais depressa possível. *v.t.* notar, observar, olhar, reparar; atender a, cuidar de, aperceber-se de; tratar com atenção.

noticeable, *adj.* digno de atenção, notável, perceptível.

noticeably, *adv.* notavelmente, perceptivelmente.

notifiable, *adj.* que deve ser notificado.

notification, *s.* notificação, aviso, advertência, citação.

notify, *pret.* e *pp. notified, v.t.* notificar, noticiar, participar, advertir, avisar; informar; publicar.

notion, *s.* noção, conceito, percepção, ideia, pensamento, parecer, voto, entendimento, sentido; intenção; inclinação; capricho, novidade, bagatela.

notional, *adj.* imaginário, caprichoso.

notionally, *adv.* idealmente, mentalmente, imaginariamente.

notoriety, *s.* notariedade, evidência, publicidade.

notorious, *adj.* notório, conhecido, evidente desacreditado.

notoriously, *adv.* notoriamente.

notoriousness, *s.* notoriedade, publicidade.

notwithstanding, *adv.* não obstante, sem embargo. *prep.* apesar de, a despeito de. *conj.* ainda que, contudo, bem que, por mais que.

nougat, *s.* nogado.

noun, *s.* nome, substantivo.

nourish, *v.t.* nutrir, alimentar, sustentar; manter, abrigar, alentar, fomentar, criar, educar. *v.i.* nutrir-se.

nourishable, *adj.* que se pode nutrir ou fomentar.

nourisher, *s.* nutridor, nutritivo, alimentar.

nourishing, *adj.* nutritivo, substancial.

nourishment, *s.* alimento, sustento; nutrição; alimentação; pasto.

nous, *s.* mente, inteligência; senso comum.

novel, *adj.* novel, novo, original, recente, moderno. *s.* novela, romance.

novelist, *s.* novelista, romancista,

novelty, *s.* novidade, inovação.

November, *s.* Novembro.

novice, *s.* noviço, principiante, bisonho, neófito, novato.

noviciate, *s.* noviciado; noviço.

now, *adv.* agora, neste momento, actualmente, há pouco; já ora; depois disto, daqui a pouco; suposto isto; vamos! 1) *now and again now and then*, de vez em quando, de quando em vez, algumas vezes. 2) *before* ou *before now*, já anteriormente, dantes. 3) *but now*, agora mesmo, imediatamente, actualmente. 4) *how now?*, como?, que tal? 5) *until* ou *till now*, até agora, até este momento. 6) *now...now...*, já... já..., ora... ora..., alternativamente. 7) *now soft, now loud*, ora suave, ora estrepitoso. 8) *now! what do you think?*, vamos! que é que pensas?, o que te parece?. *conj.* mas, pois. 9) *now then*, pois bem. 10) *now that*, já que, agora que, posto que. *s.* actualidade, o momento actual.

nowadays, *adv.* nos nossos dias, hoje em dia, na actualidade.

noway, *adv.* de nenhum modo.

nowhere, *adv.* em parte alguma; *nowhere else*, em nenhuma outra parte.

nowise, *adv.* de nenhum modo.

noxious, *adj.* nocivo, daninho, pernicioso, insalubre.

noxiously, *adv.* perniciosamente, nocivamente.

noxiousness, *s.* nocividade.

noyau, *s.* licor aromatizado com amêndoas amargas.

nozzie, *s.* bico, extremidade; focinho; embocadura; agulheta de mangueira; tubo de descarga.

nuance, *s.* matiz, cambiante.

nubble, *s.* protuberância.

nubbly, *adj.* com protuberâncias.

nubile, *adj.* núbil.

nucleal, *adj.* nuclear.

nucleus, *s.* núcleo (de cometa, de guarnição); caroço.

nude, *adj.* nu; despido; nulo.

nudge, *v.t.* tocar com o cotovelo. *s.* toque ligeiro dado com o cotovelo.

nudity, *s.* estado de nudez.

nugatory, *adj.* nulo; fútil.

nugget, *s.* pepita, grão ou palheta de oiro.

nuisance, *s.* incómodo, tudo o que causa incómodo; moléstia; indecência, imundícies, prejuízo, dano, infracção. 1) *commit no nuisance*, é proibido verter águas ou depositar imundícies. 2) *what a nuisance!*, que aborrecimento!

null, *adj.* nulo, inválido, sem eficácia; zero. *v.t.* anular.

nullah, *s.* corrente, torrente; barranco.

nullification, *s.* anulação, invalidade.

nullify, *v.t. pret.* e *pp. nullifyed,* anular, invadir, ab-rogar.

nullity, *s.* nulidade; acto ou documento nulo e sem valor.

numb, *adj.* entorpecido; adormecido; paralisado; tolhido. *v.t.* tolher, paralisar, entorpecer.

number, *v.t.* numerar, contar, computar. *s.* número, algarismo; quantidade, colecção, multidão; número ou exemplar de periódico; *pl.* aritmética, ciência dos números; harmonia, cadência. 1) *back number*, número atrasado de um periódico; pessoa ou coisa antiquada. 2) *without number*, inumerável, sem-número.

numberer, *s.* numerador, contador.

numberless, *adj.* inumerável, infinito.

Numbers, *s.* Números, livro da Bíblia.

numbfish, *s.* torpedo (peixe).

numbly, *adv.* com entorpecimento.

numbness, *s.* torpor, entorpecimento, adormecimento.

numerable, *adj.* numerável.

numeral, *adj.* numeral, numerário, numérico. *s.* número, algarismo; nome ou adjectivo numeral (gram.). 1) *Roman number*, número romano. 2) *cardinal number*, número cardinal. 3) *ordinal number*, número ordinal. 4) *fractional number*, número quebrado ou fraccionário. 5) *multiplicative number*, numeral multiplicativo.

numeration, *s.* numeração.

numerator, *s.* contador; numerador.

numerical, *adj.* numérico,

numerous, *adj.* numeroso, copioso, abundante; harmonioso.

numerously, *adv.* numerosamente.

numerousness, *s.* numerosidade.

numismatic, *adj.* numismático,

numismatics, *s.* numismática.

numismatist, *s.* numismático.

numskilled, *adj.* parvo, lerdo.

numskull, *s.* parvo, bobo.

nun, *s.* monja, religiosa, freira; uma das várias espécies de aves, como: chapim, borracho, etc.

nunciature, *s.* nunciatura.

nuncio, *s.* núncio, enviado.

nunnery, *s.* convento de freiras.

nuptial, *adj.* nupcial, matrimonial, conjugal. 1) *nuptial son*, epitalâmio. 2) *nuptial plumage*, plumagem de uma ave durante a criação. *s. pl.* núpcias.

nurse, *s.* ama, aia, governanta, enfermeira, enfermeiro; protector; espécie de tubarão. 1) *wet nurse*, ama-de-leite. 2) *nurse-maid*, aia de crianças. 3) *nurse-pond*, viveiro, piscina. *v.t.* criar, amamentar, dar de mamar, alimentar, manter, abrigar, acariciar, cuidar, tratar de doentes; dar de mamar a uma criança, criar; amamentar-se.

nurselin, *s.* criança de peito.

nursery, *s.* quarto ou aposento destinado às crianças; criação, plantio, viveiro; criação, acto de criar. 1) *nursery-garden,* viveiro de plantas. 2) *nursery-maid,* aia de crianças. 3) *nursery tales,* contos para crianças.

nursing, *s.* criação, alimento. 1) *nursing-bottle,* biberão. 2) *nursing home,* casa de saúde.

nurture, *s.* alimentação; educação, criação; fomento. *v.t.* nutrir, alimentar, promover.

nut, *s.* noz, fruto parecido com a noz; porca de parafuso, botão; matriz; talão do arco do violino; petimetre. 1) *bolt and nut,* cavilha com porca. 2) *to be nuts on,* estar apaixonado por. 3) *to have a hard nut to crack,* ver-se em calças pardas.

nutarian, *s.* vegetariano; apologista das nozes como alimento.

nutate, *v.i.* nutar, oscilar.

nutation, *s.* nutação, oscilação; inclinação de cabeça.

nutbrown, *adj.* cor de castanha, acastanhado.

nutcracker, *s.* espécie de pega malhada de branco.

nutcrackers, *s.* quebra-nozes.

nuthatch, *s.* pica-pau.

nutmeg, *s.* noz-moscada.

nutrient, *s.* alimento nutritivo, nutrição. *adj.* nutritivo, nutriente.

nutriment, *s.* alimento, sustento.

nutrition, *s.* nutrição, alimentação; alimento.

nutritious, *adj.* nutritivo, alimentício, substancioso.

nutritiously, *adv.* de um modo nutritivo.

nutritiousness, *s.* nutrição.

nutritive, *adj.* nutritivo, substancioso.

nurshell, *s.* casca de noz; *in a nurshell,* em poucas palavras.

nutty, *adj.* abundante em nozes.

nux vomica, *s.* noz-vómica.

nymph, *s.* ninfa; mulher jovem, zagala; crisálida.

nymphlike, *adj.* como uma ninfa.

nymphomania, *s.* ninfomania.

O

o, décima quinta letra do alfabeto.

O, *interj.* ó! oh! oxalá! (para exprimir dor, surpresa, etc.).

oaf, *s.* idiota, imbecil.

oafish, *adj.* imbecil, estúpido, aparvalhado.

oak, *s.* carvalho, roble; madeira de carvalho. 1) *cork oak,* sobreiro. 2) *scarlet oak,* azinheira. 3) *oak-grove,* carvalhal.

oaken, *adj.* de carvalho.

oakum, *s.* estopa de calafetar; cordame.

oar, *s.* remo; *to lie on the oars,* cessar de remar; parar de trabalhar; *v.t.* remar.

oarlock, *s.* dispositivo onde se apoia o remo; forquilha.

oarsman, *s.* remador.

oasis, *s.* oásis.

oat, *s.* aveia; ; *to sow one´s wild oats,* entregar-se aos desvarios da juventude.

oatcake, *s.* bolo de aveia.

oaten, *adj.* de aveia.

oath, *s.* jura, juramento; praga, blasfémia. 1) *to take an oath,* prestar juramento. 2) *oath breaking,* perjúrio.

oatmeal, *s.* farinha de aveia; papas de aveia.

obduracy, *s.* obstinação, renitência, inexorabilidade.

obdurate, *adj.* obstinado, inexorável, insensível; *adv. obdurately,* obstinadamente.

obedience, *s.* obediência, submissão.

obedient, *adj.* obediente, dócil, submisso; *adv. obediently,* obedientemente.

obeisance, *s.* mesura, reverência, cortesia, vénia.

obelisk, *s.* obelisco.

obelus, *s.* óbelo, sinal ou cruz com que se assinalam passagens nos manuscritos.

obese, *adj.* obeso, gordo.

obesity, *s.* obesidade.

obey, *v.t.* obedecer; submeter-se a; cumprir.

obfuscate, *v.t.* ofuscar, obscurecer, toldar.

obit, s. óbito, exéquias, funerais.
obituary, adj. obituário, necrológico; s. necrologia; obituário, livro dos óbitos.
object, s. objecto, coisa, artigo; matéria; objectivo, fim, intento. 1) *object-glass*, objectiva. 2) *object-lesson*, lição prática; v.t. e v.i. objectar, opor(-se).
objection, s. objecção, oposição, reparo, dúvida, dificuldade; *to raise objections*, levantar dificuldades.
objectionable, adj. objectável, contestável; condenável.
objective, adj. objectivo; s. objectiva (lente); finalidade, meta.
objectivism, s. objectivismo.
objectivist, s. e adj. objectivista.
objectivity, s. objectividade; imparcialidade.
objectless, adj. sem objectivo, sem finalidade; vazio.
objector, s. impugnador, objector, opositor.
objurgate, v.t. objurgar, censurar, arguir.
oblation, s. oblação, oferenda.
obligate, adj. obrigado; v.t. obrigar.
obligation, s. obrigação; compromisso; dever.
obligatory, adj. obrigatório; adv. *obligatorily*, dum modo obrigatório.
oblige, vt. obrigar, forçar, constranger; obsequiar, agradar, condescender; agradecer; *I am much obliged to you*, estou-lhe muito reconhecido.
obliging, adj. obsequioso, cortês, prestável; adv. *obligingly*, obsequiosamente.
oblique, adj. oblíquo, inclinado; indirecto, evasivo; dissimulado; *oblique narration*, discurso indirecto; adv. *obliquely*, obliquamente,
obliquity, s. obliquidade; divergência; desvio.
obliterate, v.t. obliterar; apagar, suprimir; destruir.
oblivion, s. esquecimento, oblívio. 1) *to fall into oblivion*, cair no esquecimento, em desuso. 2) *act of oblivion*, amnistia.
oblivious, adj. esquecido, deslembrado; distraído; adv. *obliviously*, desmemoriadamente.
oblong, adj. oblongo, alongado, oblongado; s. figura oblonga.
obloquy, s. censura, maledicência; desonra, infâmia.
obnoxious, adj. desagradável, censurável, antipático, odioso; adv. *obnoxiously*, desagradavelmente.

oboe, s. oboé.
oboist, s. oboísta, tocador de oboé.
obscene, adj. obsceno, indecente, nojento; adv. *obscenely*, obscenamente.
obscenety, s. obscenidade; torpeza.
obscurantism, s. obscurantismo.
obscure, a. obscuro, sombrio; oculto; modesto, humilde; vago, indistinto; v.t. obscurecer, escurecer, toldar; suplantar; ocultar, esconder; adv. *obscurely*, obscuramente.
obscurity, s. obscuridade, escuridão, trevas, sombras; mediocridade.
obsequies, s. pl. exéquias, funeral.
obsequious, adj. servil, subserviente; adv. *obsequiously*, servilmente.
observable, adj. observável, perceptível; notável, digno de nota.
observance, s. observância, cumprimento; rito, costume, prática.
observant, adj. observador, perspicaz, reparador, atento; observante, obediente; adv. *observantly*, atenciosamente, atentamente.
observatory, s. observatório.
observe, v.t. observar, ver, olhar, notar, reparar, vigiar; examinar, estudar; acatar, cumprir; observar, fazer comentários.
observer, s. observador, espectador; comentador.
obsess, v.t. obsidiar, perseguir, assediar; obcecar.
obsession, s. obsessão, ideia fixa, mania.
obsessive, adj. obsessivo, obsessor.
obsolescent, adj. que se está a tornar antiquado ou obsoleto, envelhecido; adv. *obsolescently*, desusadamente.
obsolete, adj. obsoleto, antiquado; adv. *obsoletely*, dum modo obsoleto.
obstacle, s. obstáculo, barreira; impedimento, dificuldade.
obstetrician, s. obstetra, médico parteiro.
obstinacy, s. obstinação, teimosia, tenacidade.
obstinate, adj. obstinado, teimoso, voluntarioso; rebelde; adv. *obstinately*, obstinadamente.
obstruct, v.t. obstruir, entupir, tapar; dificultar, retardar; interromper.
obstruction, s. obstrução, impedimento, estorvo, obstáculo.
obtain, v.t. obter, adquirir, alcançar, granjear.
obtainable, adj. conseguível.
obtrude, v.t. fazer sair, expelir, expulsar; impor, introduzir à força.

obturate, *v.t.* obturar, tapar, obstruir.

obtuse, *adj.* obtuso; estúpido, bronco; *adv. obtusely,* obtusamente.

obverse, *adj.* invertido, reverso, correspondente; *s.* obverso, reverso.

obviate, *v.t.* obviar, prevenir, atalhar, evitar.

obvious, *adj.* óbvio, evidente, palpável; *adv. obviously,* obviamente, evidentemente.

occasion, *s.* ocasião, lance, caso, ocorrência, casualidade; acontecimento; motivo, razão; oportunidade; *v.t.* ocasionar, causar, dar lugar a; mover, excitar.

occasional, *adj.* ocasional; fortuito, casual, acidental; *adv. occasionally,* ocasionalmente.

occident, *s.* ocidente; oeste, poente.

occidental, *adj.* e *s.* ocidental; *adv. occidentally,* ocidentalmente.

occlude, *v.t.* fechar, tapar, obstruir.

occlusion, *s.* oclusão, obstrução.

occult, *adj.* oculto, secreto, misterioso; *s. the occult,* as ciências ocultas; *v.t.* e *v.i.* ocultar, encobrir, ocultar-se.

occultism, *s.* ocultismo.

occupancy, *s.* ocupação, posse.

occupant, *s.* ocupador, possuidor, inquilino, ocupante.

occupation, *s.* ocupação, posse; trabalho, tarefa, profissão, emprego.

occupy, *v.t.* ocupar; tomar posse de; morar em; habitar; arrendar; exercer, desempenhar.

occur (occurring, occurred), *v.i.* ocorrer, suceder, acontecer; acudir à mente; ser encontrado, encontrar-se.

occurrence, *s.* ocorrência; aparecimento; acontecimento, sucesso, incidente, facto.

ocean, *s.* oceano; mar.

oceanography, *s.* oceanografia.

ocher, ochre, *s.* ocre (terra ou cor; oca).

o'clock, *abrev.* de *on the clock; it is four o'clock,* são quatro horas.

octagon, *s.* octógono.

octagonal, *adj.* octogonal.

octave, *s.* oitava (mús., métr., liturg., esgrim.); grupo de oito.

octogenarian, *adj.* e *s.* octogenário, oitentão.

octopus, *s.* octópode; polvo.

ocular, *adj.* ocular, visual; *s.* ocular.

oculist, *s.* oculista.

odalisque, odalisk, *s.* odalisca.

odd, *a.* ímpar; tantos, excedente; casual; estranho, excêntrico, singular; desirmanado. 1) *odd-looking,* figura excêntrica. 2) *an odd name,* um nome estranho. 3) *at odd times,* de vez em quando.

oddity, *s.* singularidade, particularidade.

oddly, *adv.* estranhamente, singularmente.

oddment, *s.* parte ocasional; coisa supérflua; retalho, resto.

oddness, *s.* desigualdade, singularidade.

odds, *s.* diferença, desigualdade; vantagem; disputa; sobras. 1) *to be at odds,* disputar, questionar. 2) *to fight against odds,* lutar contra força superior.

ode, *s.* ode, poema lírico.

odeum, *s.* odeão, odéon.

odious, *adj.* odioso, execrável; repelente, repugnante; *adv. odiously,* odiosamente.

odium, *s.* ódio, repulsa.

odor, odour, *s.* cheiro, odor; aroma; reputação; sabor.

odoriferous, *adj.* cheiroso, perfumado, odorífero.

odorous, *adj.* odorífero; *adv. odorously,* aromaticamente.

odoured, *adj.* perfumado.

odourless, *adj.* sem perfume, inodoro.

Odyssey, *s.* Odisseia.

oestrum, oestrus, *s.* cio, paixão, frenesim.

of, *prep.* de. 1) *of the,* do, da, dos, das. 2) *I dreamt of you last night,* sonhei contigo a noite passada. 3) *I did this dress of myself,* fiz este vestido sozinha. 4) *of late,* ultimamente. 5) *he used to come of an afternoon,* ele vem à tarde.

off, *adj.* desocupado, livre; distante; *prep.* de, fora de. 1) *take the plates off the table,* levanta os pratos da mesa; distante. 2) *seven miles off shore,* a sete milhas de distância; *adv.* ao largo, distante, longe, para fora; *v.i.* 3) *to be off,* ir-se embora. 4) *well off,* estar bem de meios. 5) *to show off,* exibir-se. 6) *off with you!,* rua!.

offcast, off-cast, *adj.* rejeitado; proscrito; *s.* refugo; pária.

off-chace, *s.* probabilidade, possibilidade remota.

offend, *v.i.* ofender, pecar, transgredir; *v.t.* afrontar, enfadar, irritar, desgostar.

offender, *s.* ofensor; pecador; infractor; delinquente.

offense, *s.* ofensa, afronta.

offensive, *adj.* ofensivo, injurioso, ultrajante; *s.* ofensiva, ataque. *adv. offensively,* ofensivamente.

offer, *v.t.* oferecer, dar; apresentar, sacrificar,

imolar; *v.i.* oferecer-se, apresentar-se; *s.* oferta, oferecimento; promessa, convite; declaração; proposta.

offering, *s.* oferecimento, oferta, sacrifício; *burnt-offering,* holocausto.

offertory, *s.* ofertório, oferenda (missa).

off-hand, *adv.* de repente; sem preparação.

office, *s.* ofício, emprego, cargo; posto, colocação; departamento; repartição; escritório; oficina; dever, função. 1) *box office,* bilheteira (cinema, teatro). 2) *office hours,* horário de funcionamento. 3) *office hunter,* pretendente.

officeholder, *s.* funcionário público.

officer, *s.* oficial (mil.); funcionário graduado; agente da polícia.

official, *adj.* oficial; autorizado; *s.* oficial público, funcionário; provisor; juiz eclesiástico; *adv. oficially,* oficialmente.

officialdom, *s.* oficialismo, funcionalismo.

officialism, *s.* oficionalismo, burocracia.

officiant, *s.* (ecles.) oficiante, celebrante.

officiate, *v.t.* oficiar, celebrar; exercer funções oficiais; fazer as vezes de.

officious, *adj.* solícito, intrometido; oficioso; *adv. officiously,* oficiosamente.

offing, *s.* largo, mar alto (mas com terra à vista); *in the offing,* ao largo.

offish, *adj.* (fam.) arredio, arisco.

offprint, *s.* separata; *v.t.* publicar em separata.

offset, *s.* começo, renovo, vergôntea; balanço, compensação, equivalência, equivalente; desvio, deslocamento; palavra usada mundialmente para definir processo de impressão indirecta; *adj.* deslocado, descentrado; *v.t.* balançar, equiparar, compensar, contrapesar; terraplenar; *v.i.* partir, repelir.

offshoot, *s.* ramo, ramificação; rebento.

offshore, *adv.* para o largo, para o alto mar; a pouca distância de terra.

offspring, *s.* prole, descendência, fruto.

often, *adv.* muitas vezes, frequentemente, amiúde.

ogive, *s.* ogiva.

ogle, *v.t.* e *v.i.* deitar olhares de soslaio, amorosos; comer com os olhos; *s.* olhar de soslaio, amoroso, terno.

ogre, *s.* ogre, papão.

ogreish, ogrish, *adj.* como um ogre; medonho.

ogress, *s.* ogra, mulher do ogre.

oil, *s.* óleo; azeite; petróleo; *v.t.* olear; azeitar; lubrificar, untar; ungir; tornar liso, suave, agradável. 1) *to oil a person's palm,* subornar alguém. 2) *to burn the midnight oil,* queimar as pestanas a estudar, trabalhar até tarde. 3) *to strike oil,* encontrar um poço de petróleo, tornar-se rico de repente. 4) *to pour oil on troubled waters,* pacificar, deitar água na fervura.

oilcloth, *s.* oleado, encerado.

oilskin, *s.* tecido impermeável, oleado; roupa desse tipo.

oily, *adj.* oleoso, oleaginoso; gordurento, engordurado; bajulador, servil.

ointment, *s.* unguento, pomada, linimento.

O.K., *adj.* e *interj.* certo, correcto, aprovado, em ordem; está certo, está bem.

old, *adj.* velho, idoso, de idade. 1) *old bachelor,* solteirão. 2) *old Driver,* o demónio. 3) *old maid,* solteirona. 4) *old man,* pai, velhote, marido, chefe. 5) *old salt,* lobo do mar, marinheiro veterano. 6) *Old Glory,* a bandeira dos Estados Unidos.

olden, *adj.* antigo, passado; *the olden time,* o passado.

old-fashioned, *adj.* à moda antiga, antiquado, fora de moda.

oldish, *adj.* avelhentado, velhote.

old-line, *adj.* descendente de antiga linhagem; conservador.

oldster, *s.* (fam.) velho, pessoa de idade.

old-time, old-times, *adj.* antigo, dos tempos antigos.

old-timer, *s.* (fam.), morador antigo dum lugar; veterano; velharia.

old-world, *adj.* antigo; da Antiguidade; relativo ao Velho Continente.

olfaction, *s.* olfacto.

olfactory, *adj.* olfactivo, olfactório.

oligarch, *s.* oligarca.

oligarchic, oligarchical, *adj.* oligárquico.

oligarchy, *s.* oligarquia.

oligopoly, *s.* oligopólio (econ.), grupo de duas ou três empresas que controlam determinado mercado.

olive, *s.* azeitona, oliva. 1) *olive tree,* oliveira. 2) *olive green,* cor de azeitona; *adj.* oliváceo, azeitonado.

Olympic, *adj.* olímpico, olímpio; *olympic games:* Jogos Olímpicos; *s.* olimpiano, deus olímpico; participante nos jogos olímpicos.

omelet, omelette, *s.* omeleta.

omen, *s.* presságio, agoiro.

ominous, *adj.* ominoso, agoirento, nefasto, pressagioso.

omissible, adj. que se pode omitir, suprimível.

omission, s. omissão, supressão, exclusão; lacuna, falta, esquecimento.

omissive, adj. que omite, omissor; omisso, negligente.

omit (ommiting, ommited), v.t. omitir, passar por alto; suprimir, excluir, descuidar.

omnibus, s. ónibus (carruagem); omnibus book, selecção de obras dum autor a preços populares; adj. que compreende vários assuntos.

omnifarious, adj. de todos os géneros ou espécies.

omnipotence, s. omnipotência.

omnipotent, adj. e s. omnipotente, todo--poderoso; adv. omnipotently, omnipotente-mente.

omnipresent, adj. omnipresente, ubíquo.

omnipresence, s. omnipresença, ubiqui-dade.

omniscience, s. omnisciência; sabedoria; erudição.

omniscient, adj. e s. omnisciente; adv. omnisciently, omniscientemente.

omnivorous, adj. omnívoro; ávido, voraz, cobiçoso.

omoplate, s. omoplata.

on, prep. em, sobre, em cima; perto; a; ao; de; por; conforme; adv. por cima, sobre; adiante, progressivamente; sucessiva-mente; em marcha. 1) on and on, sem cessar. 2) on foot, a pé. 3) on no account, de modo nenhum; por nada. 4) on a sud-den, de repente, de improviso. 5) on one's own hook, por conta própria. 6) and so on, e assim por diante. 7) come on!, vamos!

onanism, s. onanismo, masturbação.

once, adv. uma vez; outrora; noutro tempo, antigamente. 1) once and for all, duma vez por todas, duma vez para sempre. 2) at once, ao mesmo tempo, duma vez, imediatamente. 3) all at once, de repente. 4) once more, mais uma vez. 5) once upon a time, noutro tempo, era uma vez; s. uma vez. 6) for this once, por esta vez.

oncology, s. oncologia, estudo dos tumores.

oncoming, adj. que se aproxima, próximo, iminente.

one, adj. um, um só; único; um tal; certo; igual; s. um, uma coisa só, a unidade, o número um; all at one, todos de acordo, concordes; pron. um, algum; alguém; aquele, aquela; qualquer; se.

oneness, s. unidade, singularidade; identidade.

oner, s. pessoa ou coisa notável; perito, craque.

onerous, adj. oneroso, opressivo, pesado; adv. onerously, onerosamente.

oneself, pron. se, si mesmo, a si próprio.

onesided, adj. unilateral; parcial, injusto; adv. onesidedly, imparcialmente.

onetime, adj. antigo; adv. outrora.

one-track, adj. de linha única (caminho de ferro); (fig.) acanhado, estreito.

one-way, adj. de sentido único, de uma só mão (estrada).

onion, s. cebola.

oniony, adj. com cheiro a cebola; seme-lhante à cebola.

onlooker, s. espectador, circunstante.

only, adj. único, só; singular, raro; adv. só, somente, unicamente, senão, não mais que; conj. mas, excepto; portanto.

onrush, s. investida, arremetida, assalto, carga.

onset, s. ataque, assalto, arremetida, investida; início, começo; at the first onset, logo à partida.

onshore, adj. dirigido para a praia, a terra; situado na praia.

onslaught, s. ataque ou assalto furioso; fúria, investida.

onus, s. ónus, carga, peso.

onward, onwards, adj. para a frente, avançado; adv. para diante, progressiva-mente.

onyx, s. ónix.

oodles, s. pl. grande quantidade; oodles of money, montes de dinheiro.

ooze, v.t. suar, destilar; v.i. manar, fluir, filtrar--se, gotejar; s. lama, lodo; destila-ção; infusão de substâncias taninosas para curtir coiros. adv. oozily, com lodo; gota a gota.

opacity, s. opacidade.

opal, s. opala.

opaque, adj. opaco; escuro, sombrio, fosco; impenetrável; obtuso, estúpido.

open, v.t. abrir (uma porta, caixa, carta, etc.), descobrir, destapar, despegar; franquear, abrir caminho, abrir ao público; iniciar, inaugurar, começar, dar princípio, estabele-cer; cortar, fender, rachar; romper; expor, manifestar, descobrir, revelar, explicar, aumentar; tornar acessível. 1) this door opens into the garden, esta porta dá para o

jardim; *adj.* aberto, franqueado; descoberto; livre, franco; descampado; desta-
pado; visível; disposto a, suceptível de;
pronto, preparado; patente, manifesto;
pendente. 2) *open-mouthed*, sôfrego; barulhento. 3) *open question*, questão pendente. 4) *open winter*, inverno suave. 5) *to
set open* ou *to throw open*, abrir de par em
par; *s.* claro; lugar aberto; campo raso; em
público.

open-eyed, *adj.* que tem os olhos abertos;
vigilante, atento; perspicaz.

openhanded, *adj.* de mãos abertas,
generoso, liberal.

openhearted, *adj.* de coração aberto,
sincero, franco; generoso.

opening, *s.* abertura, brecha, entrada; luz,
aberta; claro; galeria (de mina), começo,
princípio, prelúdio; abertura, oportunidade;
adj. que abre; de abertura; inicial, inaugural.

openly, *adv.* abertamente, francamente,
claramente, publicamente, em público.

open-minded, *adj.* compreensivo, receptivo,
despreocupado, razoável.

opera, *s.* ópera. 1) *grand opera,* ópera,
drama lírico. 2) *opera glasses,* binóculo de
teatro. 3) *opera hat,* chapéu de molas.

operate, *v.t.* fazer funcionar, governar, dirigir,
manejar; levar a cabo, efectuar; *v.i.* obrar,
operar, actuar, produzir efeito; influir, fazer
pressão; especular, jogar na bolsa.

operation, *s.* operação, função, acção,
efeito; procedimento, movimento, operação
(cir.); *operation order,* ordem de acção
(mil.).

operative, *s.* operário, trabalhador, obreiro;
artífice, maquinista.

operator, *s.* operador, agente, autor,
realizador; maquinista; telefonista; telegrafista; cirurgião; especulador; proprietário de
mina (EUA).

operetta, *s.* opereta.

opiate, *s.* opiato, narcótico; *adj.* opiato,
narcótico, soporífico; *v.t.* administrar ópio;
compor com ópio (farm.).

opine, *v.t.* e *v.i.* opinar, julgar; dar opinião.

opinion, *s.* opinião, modo de ver, juízo,
crença; parecer; conceito, ideia; reputação,
estimação.

opium, *s.* ópio; *opium poppy,* papoila
dormideira.

opossum, *s.* serigueia, gambá.

oppilate, *v.t.* (med.) opilar, obstruir.

opponency, *s.* oposição, antagonismo.

opponent, *adj.* oposto, contrário, adverso,
antagónico; *s.* antagonista, inimigo.

opportune, *adj.* oportuno; apropriado,
adequado, conveniente.

opportunism, *s.* oportunismo.

opportunist, *s.* e *adj.* oportunista.

opportunity, *s.* oportunidade, ocasião
favorável.

oppose, *v.t.* opor, contrapor; opor-se a,
combater, resistir a, contraditar, obstar.

opposed, *adj.* oposto, contrário; adverso,
hostil.

opposite, *adj.* fronteiro; oposto; adverso,
contrário, antagónico; outro, diferente; *s.*
antagonista; o oposto; o contrário; *adv.* em
frente, defronte; em sentido oposto;
contrariamente.

opposition, *s.* oposição, resistência;
contraste; contradição; aversão.

oppress, *v.t.* oprimir, angustiar, atormentar;
tiranizar, maltratar; dominar, subjugar.

oppression, *s.* opressão, tirania, despotismo; opressão de ânimo, fadiga.

oppressive, *adj.* opressivo, duro, cruel,
tirânico; *adv. oppressively,* opressivamente.

oppressor, *s.* opressor, tirano.

opprobrious, *adj.* ignominioso, infamante,
ultrajante.

opprobrium, *s.* ignomínia, infâmia, vergonha.

optic, *adj.* óptico, da vista; *s.* olho, vista.

optical, *adj.* óptico, visual, ocular.

optics, *s.* óptica.

optimate, *s.* e *adj.* aristocrata.

optimates, *s. pl.* magnates.

optimism, *s.* optimismo.

optimist, *s.* optimista.

optimistic, optimistical, *adj.* optimista.

optimum, *s.* e *adj.* óptimo, o mais favorável.

option, *s.* opção, escolha; direito de
escolher; preferência.

optional, *adj.* facultativo, não obrigatório;
adv. optionally, facultativamente, com
direito a escolha.

opulence, opulency, *s.* opulência, riqueza;
abundância.

opulent, *adj.* opulento, rico; abundante, farto;
fértil, produtivo.

opuscule, *s.* ópusculo.

or, *conj.* ou; quer; seja; *adv.* antes; *s.* oiro, cor
de oiro.

oracle, *s.* oráculo, profecia.

oracular, *adj.* oracular, profético; dogmático;
ambíguo; *adv. oracularly,* à maneira de
oráculo.

oral, adj. oral, verbal, falado; adv. orally, oralmente.

orang, orangutan, orangoutang, s. orangotango.

orange, s. laranja; cor de laranja; adj. pertencente às laranjas, alaranjado; orange wife, orange woman, vendedora de laranjas.

orangeade, s. laranjada.

oration, s. oração, alocução, discurso oratório.

orator, s. orador; peticionário, autor; suplicante.

oratorio, s. (mús.) oratória, concerto de música sacra; oratório, capela.

oratory, s. oratória, eloquência; oratório, capela, congregação (rel.).

orb, s. esfera, globo, astro; círculo, órbita; v.t. cercar, rodear; arredondar, formar círculo.

orbit, s. órbita; esfera, campo de acção.

orchard, s. pomar.

orchardist, orchardman, s. horticultor, pomareiro, pomicultor.

orchestra, s. orquestra.

orchestral, adj. orquestral, instrumental.

orchestrate, v.t. e v.i. orquestrar, instrumentar.

orchid, s. orquídea; cor lilás.

ordain, v.t. ordenar, mandar; decretar, instituir; ordenar (ecl.).

ordeal, s. ordálio (hist.); provação, prova, transe; exame, ensaio.

order, s. ordem; regra, método, regularidade; disposição, mandato, mandamento, ordenança, preceito; série, classe; pedido, encomenda (com.); sociedade, associação, ordem militar ou religiosa; condecoração honorífica; pl. (igr.) ordem sacerdotal, sacramento da ordem. 1) to take holy orders, receber as ordens, tornar-se sacerdote; v.t. ordenar; encomendar; dirigir, governar. 2) to order along, mandar avançar. 3) to order away, mandar embora; não deixar de mandar. 4) to order in, mandar entrar. 5) to order off, mandar retirar. 6) to order out, mandar sair, mandar pedir, mandar levar.

orderly, adv. metodicamente, em ordem; adj. ordenado, metódico, regular, bem arranjado; tranquilo; orderly officer, oficial de dia; s. impedido, ordenança (mil.); plantão, sentinela.

ordinal, adj. ordinal; relativo a uma ordem; s. número ordinal; ritual (igr.).

ordinance, s. ordenação; decreto, estatuto, lei, regulamento; rito, cerimónia de culto.

ordinary, adj. ordinário, comum, usual, corrente; ordinário, baixo, vulgar; s. o ordinário; autoridade que tem jurisdição permanente; juiz do Supremo Tribunal na Escócia; refeição a preço fixo, mesa redonda. 1) out of the ordinary, fora do comum. 2) in ordinary, no serviço activo; adv. ordinarily, ordinariamente, geralmente.

ordinate, s. (mat.) ordenada.

ordination, s. ordenação, determinação, prescrição; ordem, arranjo, classificação.

ordnance, s. material bélico, artilharia, canhões. 1) ordnance map, carta do estado maior; planta (duma cidade, etc.). 2) ordnance survey, levantamento topográfico.

ordure, s. esterco, estrume, excremento; obscenidade.

ore, s. minério; metal. 1) ore crusher, máquina de moer minério. 2) ore dressing, preparação mecânica de minérios.

organ, s. órgão, parte de um corpo; órgão, realejo; organ grinder, tocador de realejo.

organic, adj. orgânico; organizado; constitutivo; fundamental.

organism, s. organismo, ser vivo; estrutura orgânica; órgão.

organist, s. tocador de órgão, organista.

organization, s. organização; estrutura orgânica; constituição; organismo, sociedade; direcção, administração (de empresa, firma, etc.); organization chart, organigrama duma empresa.

organize, v.t. e v.i. organizar(-se), formar (-se), constituir(-se); dispor, arranjar; instituir, fundar, estabelecer.

orgasm, s. orgasmo.

orgiastic, adj. orgiástico, orgíaco.

orgy, s. orgia, bacanal.

oriel, s. sacada envidraçada, janela em ogiva; balcão coberto e envidraçado.

orient, s. oriental; levante; Ásia; adj. oriental, nascente; brilhante, resplandescente; v.t. e v.i. orientar(-se), nortear(-se); voltar-se para o Oriente.

oriental, adj. oriental, de leste; do Oriente, asiático. s. oriental, asiático.

orientate, v.t. e v.i. orientar(-se).

orifice, s. orifício, furo, buraco, abertura.

origan, s. orégão; manjerona.

origin, s. origem, princípio, nascença; causa, motivo; ascendência, família.

original, adj. original; primitivo, inicial,

primeiro; novo, inédito; próprio, pessoal; *original member,* sócio fundador; s. original, fonte, origem; modelo, protótipo; exemplar; pessoa excêntrica ou original.

originality, s. originalidade; autenticidade; excentricidade; personalidade.

originally, adv. originalmente; fundamentalmente; de origem; originariamente, a princípio.

originate, v.t. originar, dar origem a; iniciar; criar; v.i. originar-se, ter origem, provir, nascer, surgir, dimanar de.

origination, s. origem; iniciativa; criação, produção.

originative, adj. criador, produtor; inventivo; adv. *originatively,* causativamente.

oriole, s. oríolo, papa-figo (ave).

Orion, s. Oríon.

orison, s. oração, prece.

ornament, s. ornamento, adorno, enfeite; ornamentação, decoração; (pl. ecle.); paramento; condecoração, insígnia.

ornamental, adj. ornamental, decorativo; adv. *ornamentally,* ornamentalmente.

ornate, adj. ornado, adornado, ataviado; adv. *ornately,* ataviadamente.

ornithologist, s. ornitologista, ornitólogo.

ornithology, s. ornitologia, estudo das aves.

orotund, adj. sonoro, cheio, ressonante (voz); grandiloquente, empolado (estilo).

orphan, s. e adj. órfão; v.t. deixar alguém órfão.

orphanage, s. orfandade; orfanato.

orrery, s. planetário.

orthodox, s. ortodoxo; correcto, tradicional, convencional; adv. *orthodoxly,* de modo ortodoxo.

orthodoxy, s. ortodoxia.

orthopedic, adj. ortopédico.

oscillate, v.i. oscilar, balouçar; flutuar; vacilar, hesitar.

oscillation, s. oscilação, vibração, balanço; vacilação, hesitação.

oscular, adj. oral, relativo à boca.

osculate, v.t. e v.i. oscular, beijar; tocar por osculação (geom.).

osculation, s. ósculo, beijo; osculação (geom.).

osier, s. vime, vimeiro; adj. de vime.

osmose, v.t. difundir por osmose (quím.).

osmosis, s. osmose (fisic.-quím. e fisiol.).

osprey, s. águia-marinha.

osseous, adj. ósseo; ossificado.

ossification, s. ossificação.

ossify, v.t. e v.i. ossificar(-se).

ossuary, s. ossário, lugar onde se guardam os ossos.

osteal, adj. ósseo.

ostensible, adj. ostensivo, aparente; adv. *ostensibly,* ostensivamente.

ostensive, adj. ostensivo, que manifesta.

ostentation, ostentação, alarde, aparato, fausto.

ostentatious, adj. ostentoso, aparatoso, pretensioso; adv. *ostentatiously,* pomposamente

osteoma, s. osteoma, tumor dos ossos.

ostracism, s. ostracismo.

ostracize, v.t. condenar ao ostracismo, proscrever, desterrar.

ostrich, s. avestruz.

other, adj. outro, outra, outros, outras; restante, mais, adicional; *pron.* o outro, a outra; adv. (com *than*) mais que, outra coisa que não seja, diferentemente.

otherguess, adj. outro, de outra espécie, muito diferente; adv. de outro modo.

otherness, s. diferença, diversidade; outro ser, não-eu.

otherwhere, adv. algures, noutro lugar.

otherwise, adv. de outro modo, de outra maneira, diferentemente; aliás; adj. outro, diferente.

otherworldly, adj. transcendente; sobrenatural; místico, espiritual.

otic, adj. ótico, auricular, auditivo.

otitis, s. (med.) otite.

otter, s. lontra; pele de lontra.

Ottoman, adj. e s. otomano, turco.

ought, v. def. dever, ser necessário; convir, ser conveniente, ser muito possível; ter obrigação de. 1) *we ought to respect our parents,* temos a obrigação de respeitar os nossos pais. 2) *it ought to be so,* assim deve ser; adv. algo, alguma coisa; s. nada, zero.

ounce, s. onça (peso, medida); pitada; onça *(Felis uncia).*

our, pr. poss. conj. nosso, nossa, nossos, nossas; *we have done our work,* fizemos o nosso trabalho.

ours, pr. poss. abs. nosso, nossa, nossos, nossas; *this house of ours,* esta nossa casa.

ourself, pron. refl. nós mesmos; pl. *ourselves,* nós mesmos.

oust, v.t. desapossar, esbulhar; desalojar, despedir.

ouster, *s.* o que desaloja ou esbulha; esbulho, espoliação, despejo.

out, *adv.* e *prep.* fora; fora de casa; no estrangeiro; fora de moda; fora do lugar; fora do serviço; fora do poder; enganado; publicado, em público; muito. 1) *he is tired out,* ele está muito cansado, esgotado. 2) *the tickets are sold out,* os bilhetes foram inteiramente vendidos. 3) *before the day is out,* antes do dia terminar. 4) *the neighbours fell out,* os vizinhos estão zangados. 5) *out at the heels,* com os sapatos rotos. 6) *my money is out at interest,* o meu dinheiro está posto a juros. 7) *out of business,* retirado dos negócios. 8) *this dress is out of date,* este vestido está fora de moda. 9) *out of curiosity,* por curiosidade. 10) *out of friendship,* por amizade. 11) *out of joint,* deslocado. 12) *out of house and home,* sem eira nem beira. 13) *out of print,* edição esgotada. 14) *out of place,* deslocado, impróprio. 15) *out of spite,* por despique. 16) *out of touch,* em desacordo. 17) *to be all out,* fazer o possível, envidar todos os esforços. 18) *out of sight, out of mind,* longe da vista, longe do coração. 19) *out of the frying-pan into the fire,* de mal a pior, pior a emenda que o soneto; *interj.* Fora!. 20) *out with you!,* rua! 21) *out with it,* fale!, desembuche! *s.* exterior; distante; omissão, salto; *pl.* (pol.) a oposição; *v.t.* expulsar, desalojar; deitar fora; ser descoberto.

outbalance, *v.t.* pesar mais que, exceder em peso ou efeito.

outbid (outbidding, outbid), *v.t.* cobrir o lanço (leilões).

outbreak, *s.* erupção; ataque violento; paixão, tumulto.

outbreeding, *s.* cruzamento; acasalamento de indivíduos sem parentesco entre si.

outbuilding, *s.* edifício exterior, anexo.

outburst, *s.* explosão; assomo, transporte (de emoção).

outcast, *adj.* rejeitado, expulso, proscrito; *s.* pária.

outclass, *v.t.* exceder, ser superior.

outclassed, *adj.* excedido, desclassificado.

outcome, *s.* êxito, sucesso, resultado.

outcrossing, *s.* acasalamento de indivíduos da mesma raça.

outcry, *s.* clamor, alarido, tumulto, algazarra.

outdistance, *v.t.* ultrapassar, deixar para trás.

outdo (outdid, outdone), *v.t.* exceder, vencer.

outdone, *adj.* vencido, derrotado.

outdoor, *adj.* externo, exterior; para o exterior, para uso exterior; fora de casa, ao ar livre.

outdoors, *s.* o campo, o ar livre; *adv.* fora de casa, ao ar livre.

outer, *adj.* exterior, externo; *adv.* outerly, por fora, exteriormente.

outermost, *adj.* extremo, o mais exterior, o mais de fora.

outfield, *s.* campo aberto; parte do campo de jogo (basebol) que fica fora da demarcação.

outfielder, *s.* jogador colocado no *outfield.*

outfit, *s.* equipamento; bagagem; enxoval, roupa, traje; despesas de instalação, desembolso; *v.t.* (*outfitting, outfitted*), aviar, habilitar, prover.

outfitter, *s.* armador; fornecedor de navios, abastecedor.

outflank, *v.t.* flanquear, vencer, levar a melhor a.

outflow, *s.* jorro de água, fluxo; descarga, escoamento.

outgo, *s.* gasto, despesa; *v.t.* (*outwent, outgone*) exceder, superar.

outgoing, *adj.* que sai, que parte; cessante; *s.* saída, partida; (pl.) despesas.

outgrow (outgrew, outgrown), *v.t.* crescer mais que; crescer de mais; ser demasiado velho para; preceder, passar adiante.

outgrowth, *s.* excrescência; resultado, consequência.

outhouse, *s.* alpendre, telheiro; anexo; casinha privada.

outing, *s.* saída, caminhada, passeio; largo, mar alto.

outlast, *v.t.* exceder em duração, durar mais tempo que; durar mais de.

outlaw, *s.* bandido, foragido; criminoso; *v.t.* banir, proscrever.

outlawry, *s.* proscrição, banimento.

outlay, *s.* desembolso, gasto; *v.t.* gastar, desembolsar.

outlet, *s.* saída, passagem; desaguadouro, canal; *outlet valve,* válvula de descarga.

outlier, *s.* pessoa não residente no lugar onde trabalha ou vive, o que fica isolado.

outline, *s.* contorno, esboço, perfil; *v.t.* traçar, esboçar, delinear.

outlive, *v.t.* sobreviver a, viver ou durar mais que; sobreviver.

outlook, s. vigilância, observação; vista, panorama, perspectiva, probabilidade; v.t. ver mais longe que.

outlying, adj. distante, retirado; remoto.

outmaneuver, outmanoeuvre, v.t. manobrar melhor, exceder em manobra, em estratégia, superar em habilidade.

outmost, adj. o mesmo que outermost.

outnumber, v.t. exceder em número.

out-of-date, adj. antiquado, fora de moda.

outpace, v.t. passar adiante de, ultrapassar, deixar atrás.

outpour, s. jorro, jacto; v.t. jorrar, derramar a jorros.

outpouring, s. derramamento, efusão, explosão.

output, s. produção, rendimento; saída; o que é expelido pelos rins, pulmões ou pela pele.

outrage, v.t. ultrajar, injuriar; maltratar, violentar; s. afronta, ultraje.

outrageous, adj. ultrajante, injurioso, violento; adv. outrageously, ultrajosamente.

outré, adj. excêntrico, exagerado, arrebatado.

outreach, v.t. alcançar, ultrapassar; tomar a dianteira.

outride (outrode, outridden), v.t. ganhar a dianteira (a cavalo); resistir a, sair são e salvo. s. excursão, expedição.

outrider, s. batedor, picador.

outright, adj. sincero, fraco, aberto; adv. completamente, abertamente, sem reserva; logo, imediatamente.

outrun (outrunning, outrun), v.t. correr mais que outro; ultrapassar, exceder; escapar a.

outsell, v.t. vender mais que; vender mais caro.

outset, s. início, começo.

outshine, v.t. brilhar mais que; exceder em brilho, eclipsar.

outside, adj. exterior, externo, superficial, aparente; extremo; s. exterior, parte de fora, superfície, aparência; extremidade; adv. exteriormente, fora, por fora; prep. fora de, mais além de.

ousider, s. forasteiro, estranho; intruso.

outsize, s. tamanho extra; grandalhão, brutamontes; adj. (também outsized) tamanho maior que o normal; desmedido, desproporcionado.

outskirts, s. pl. orla, borda, limites; cercanias, arredores, subúrbios.

outspent, adj. esgotado, exausto.

outspoken, adj. franco, sincero; claro, aberto, directo.

outspread, v.t. e v.i. estender(-se), espalhar(-se), difundir(-se); adj. espalhado, difundido; s. expansão, extensão; desdobramento, dispersão.

outstand, v.t. resistir a, aguentar; demorar-se mais; sair do alinhamento.

outstanding, adj. saliente; pendente, não pago; outstanding bills, contas pendentes.

outstep (outstepping, outstepped), v.t. ultrapassar os limites.

outstretch, v.t. estender, espalhar; expandir, dilatar, alargar.

outward, adv. por fora, exteriormente; à vista, publicamente; para fora, para o exterior; adj. externo, exterior; dirigido ou voltado para fora; que sai; an outward ticket, passagem de ida; s. aparência exterior.

outwardly, adv. exteriormente.

outwards, adv. o mesmo que outward.

outweight, v.t. pesar mais.

outwit (outwitting, outwitted), v.t. exceder em astúcia; burlar, lograr.

outwork, v.t. trabalhar mais do que outro; s. obra exterior, obra avançada, trabalho feito fora da oficina ou de casa.

outworn, adj. gasto pelo uso.

ouzel, ousel, s. merlo.

oval, adj. oval, elíptico; s. oval.

ovarium, ovary, s. ovário (zool., bot. e anat.).

ovation, s. ovação; aclamação.

oven, s. forno. 1) oven-full, fornada. 2) oven-peel, pá do forno.

over, prep. sobre, em cima, por cima de; do outro lado de; além de; apesar de; entretanto, durante. 1) over the table, sobre a mesa. 2) over the road, do outro lado da estrada. 3) to sit over the fire, sentar à volta do lume. 4) to travel over Europe, viajar através da Europa; adv. do outro lado, ao lado, defronte, através; de cima a baixo; em cima; mais, além disso; dum extremo ao outro; completamente, inteiramente; acabado, terminado. 5) all over, por toda a parte, por todo o lado. 6) it is all over, acabou-se, terminou-se. 7) head over heels, apressadamente, sem reflectir. 8) over again, outra vez, mais uma vez. 9) over against, defronte. 10) over and over, repetidas vezes, vezes sem conta. 11) to be *over*, cessar, acabar. 12) *to hand over*, entregar. 13) *to run over*, transbordar; percorrer; rever; atropelar. 14) *to turn over*, voltar; *adj.* superior; excedente, excessivo; *s.* excesso, sobra, saldo; extra.

overact, *v.t.* exagerar; representar com exagero.

overage, *s.* excedente, sobras; *adj.* que ultrapassou determinado limite de idade.

over-all, *adj.* total, global; *adv.* a todos os respeitos.

overalls, *s.* fato-macaco.

overawe, *v.t.* intimidar, amedrontar.

overbalance, *v.t.* pesar mais que, exceder, fazer perder o equilíbrio; preponderar; levar vantagem; *s.* preponderância, vantagem.

overbalancing, *s.* excesso; preponderância.

overbear (overbore, overborne), *v.t.* subjugar, dominar, sujeitar; abater; reprimir; *v.i.* produzir frutos em demasia ou multiplicar-se demasiadamente.

overbearing, *adj.* despótico, tirânico, arrogante; *adv. overbearingly*, dum modo despótico ou arrogante.

overbid, *v.t.* cobrir o lanço, oferecer mais.

overboard, *adv.* ao mar, à água; *man overboard!*, homem ao mar!

overboil, *v.t.* ferver ou cozer de mais.

overburden, *v.t.* sobrecarregar; *s.* sobrecarga, excesso de peso.

overcast, *v.t.* escurecer, nublar, enevoar; chulear, cerzir; *adj.* enevoado, cerrado, encoberto (tempo).

overcasting, *s.* rebocadura (de parede); chuleio (cost.).

overcautious, *adj.* cauteloso de mais.

overcertify, *v.t.* visar (cheque) sem que exista saldo suficiente para o cobrir.

overcharge, *v.t.* sobrecarregar; exagerar; oprimir; carregar no preço, cobrar de mais; atestar, apinhar; *s.* sobrecarga, preço excessivo; extorsão.

overcloud, *v.t.* cobrir de nuvens; toldar; entristecer; *v.i.* enevoar-se.

overcoat, *s.* sobretudo, casacão.

overcome (overcame, overcome), *v.t.* vencer, derrotar; subjugar, submeter.

overcooked, *adj.* cozido, guisado ou assado em demasia.

overcrowd, *v.t.* superlotar, apinhar (com pessoas).

overdo (overdid, overdone), *v.t.* fazer mais do que o necessário; exagerar; esturrar; *v.i.* exceder-se, exceder os limites.

overdose, *s.* dose excessiva.

overdraft, overdraught, *s.* saque descoberto; ordem de pagamento superior aos fundos disponíveis.

overdraw (overdrew, overdrawn), *v.t.* sacar a descoberto; exceder o crédito; exagerar.

overdress, *v.t.* e *v.i.* vestir(-se) com aprumo exagerado; enfeitar(-se) em excesso; vestir(-se) de forma errada perante as ocasiões.

overdue, *adj.* vencido; fora de prazo (com.); atrasado (navio, comboio, etc.).

overestimate, *v.t.* sobrestimar, avaliar excessivamente; *s.* avaliação excessiva.

overfeed, *v.t.* dar de comer em excesso; fartar, saciar; *v.i.* superalimentar-se.

overflow, *v.t.* inundar, alagar; submergir; *v.i.* transbordar, extravasar-se; derramar-se; *s.* inundação, cheia; excesso, superabundância (fig.).

overfull, *adj.* repleto, transbordante.

overgild, *v.t.* durar.

overgrow (overgrew, overgrown), *v.t.* cobrir, atapetar, invadir (com plantas ou ervas); crescer de mais para a roupa; *v.i.* crescer ou desenvolver-se de mais.

overgrowth, *s.* crescimento ou desenvolvimento excessivo; superabundância; exuberância; vegetação exuberante.

overhand, *adj.* e *adv.* por baixo da mão; com a mão por cima da bola *(cricket)*, com a mão acima do ombro (basebol); *s.* superioridade; meia volta, laçada (náut.).

overhanded, *adj.* que tem excesso de operários.

overhang, *v.t.* sobressair, projectar; suspender, estar iminente, ameaçar; dar; olhar para; ficar sobranceiro; *v.i.* estar pendente ou suspenso; *s.* saliência, ressalto; aba do telhado; sacada.

overhardy, *adj.* temerário, arrojado, corajoso.

overhasty, *adj.* precipitado, irreflectido, impulsivo.

overhaul, *v.t.* rever, examinar; vistoriar, inspeccionar; beneficiar.

overhauling, *s.* vistoria, inspecção, exame, revista geral.

overhead, *adv.* em cima, por cima, por cima da cabeça, no alto, no andar de cima, cobrindo a cabeça; *adj.* situado no alto, aéreo, pendente, elevado, superior.

overhear, *v.t.* ouvir por casualidade, escutar conversa alheia.

overheat, *v.t.* aquecer demasiado; *s.* acção de requentar.

overhung, *adj.* lançado; apoiado num só lado.

overjoy, *v.t.* arrebatar.

overjoyed, *adj.* arrebatado, cheio de alegria, radiante.

overkind, *adj.* excessivamente carinhoso ou bom.

overlabor, overlabour, *v.t.* sobrecarregar de trabalho; aperfeiçoar de mais.

overlade, *v.t.* sobrecarregar.

overladen, *adj.* sobrecarregado.

overland, *adj.* por terra, caminho por via terrestre, por terra; *adv.* por terra.

overlap (overlapping, overlapped), *v.t.* sobrepor, cobrir, envolver; *v.i.* sobrepor-se, envolver-se; *s.* sobreposição, envoltório.

overlapping, *adj.* sobreposto; *s.* costura sobreposta; telhado, telheiro.

overlay, *v.t.* cobrir, revestir; dar uma camada de tinta; dourar, pratear; obscurecer, toldar; esmagar, sufocar; *s.* cobertura, capa, coberta, revestimento.

overlaying, *s.* cobertura, revestimento; coberta; camada; dourado, prateado.

overleaf, *adv.* no outro lado da página, no verso.

overlie (overlying, overlay, overlain), *v.t.* deitar-se por cima de, cobrir; sufocar com o seu peso.

overlive, *v.t.* e *v.i.* sobreviver.

overload, *v.t.* sobrecarregar, abarrotar; *s.* sobrecarga.

overlook, *v.t.* olhar do alto, ter vista para, dominar (com a vista); examinar, vigiar; passar por alto; fazer vista grossa, dissimular, tolerar, perdoar; esquecer; repassar, rever, olhar por alto; deitar mau--olhado.

overlooker, *s.* superintendente, inspector; chefe.

overlooking, *s.* inspecção, superinten-dência.

overlord, *s.* senhor supremo, soberano; *s.* acção de dominar.

overly, *adv.* demasiadamente, excessiva-mente.

overman, *s.* superintendente, capataz, inspector; árbitro; *v.t.* tripular navio com excesso de homens; colocar mais homens do que os necessários em determinado trabalho.

over-many, *adj.* demasiados, excessivos.

overmantel, *s.* prateleira dum fogão de sala.

overmaster, *v.t.* dominar.

overmatch, *v.t.* superar, vencer, derrotar.

overmuch, *adj.* demasiado, excessivo; *adv.* em demasia, de mais; *s.* excesso, exce-dente.

overnice, *adj.* escrupuloso; afectado; niquento, ultradelicado.

overnight, *adv.* na véspera, na noite anterior; durante a noite, toda a noite; *to stay overnight,* pernoitar; *s.* a noite anterior, a véspera; *adj.* que pernoita; nocturno.

overnumerous, *adj.* numerosíssimo, excessivo.

overpass, *v.t.* atravessar, transpor; superar, vencer; transgredir; exceder; olhar com indiferença; omitir.

overpast, *adj.* passado, remoto; desprezado, omitido.

overpay, *v.t.* pagar em excesso, repagar, compensar em demasia; *s.* sobrepaga, gratificação.

overpayment, *s.* paga excessiva.

overpeople, *v.t.* sobrepovoar.

overpersuade, *v.t.* fazer mudar de ideia, convencer, converter.

overpitched, *adj.* exagerado.

overplus, *s.* excedente, sobra, resto; excesso, superabundância.

overpopulate, *v.t.* sobrepovoar.

overpopulation, *s.* superpopulação.

overpopulous, *adj.* sobrepovoado, que tem excesso de população.

overpower, *v.t.* predominar, oprimir, subjugar, esmagar.

overpowering, *adj.* irresistível, esmagador.

overpraise, *v.t.* elogiar em demasia, imereci-damente.

overpress, *v.t.* afligir, oprimir; importunar, insistir vivamente.

overpressure, *s.* excesso de pressão; excesso de trabalho.

overprize, *v.t.* exagerar o valor de.

overproduction, *s.* superprodução.

overproof, *adj.* de alta graduação, que possui alto teor alcoólico.

overproud, *adj.* altivo ou orgulhoso de mais.

overrate, *v.t.* encarecer, exagera o valor de; sobrestimar, contar demasiado com.

overreach, *v.t.* estender ou alargar dema-siado; exceder ou ir mais além do que o necessário; vencer em rapidez ou astúcia;

alcançar-se (o cavalo); *she overreached
herself*, saiu-lhe o tiro pela culatra.

overrefined, *adj.* super-requintado.

override (overrode, overridden), *v.t.*
passar por cima, atropelar, calcar aos pés,
espezinhar; anular; tiranizar; repelir; fatigar
um cavalo.

overripe, *adj.* maduro de mais, passado
(fruto).

overrule, *v.t.* dominar, sujeitar, governar,
dirigir; rejeitar, revogar, indeferir.

overruler, *s.* dominador, senhor.

overrun (overrunning, overran), *v.t.*
invadir, infestar; ultrapassar os limites;
transbordar, extravasar; ser excessivo; *s.*
transbordamento; saldo, excedente.

oversea, overseas, *adj.* e *adv.* ultramarino,
além-mar, além dos mares.

oversee (oversaw, overseen), *v.t.*
inspeccionar, vigiar, observar, dominar com
a vista.

overseer, *s.* superintendente, intendente,
feitor, capataz.

overset, *v.t.* transtornar, perturbar, agitar;
derrubar, virar; subverter; *v.i.* virar-se; *s.*
queda, tombo, capotagem; subversão.

overshadow, *v.t.* ensombrar, obscurecer,
ofuscar.

overshoe, *s.* galocha.

oversight, *s.* inadvertência, engano, equívoco, descuido, lapso; vigilância, cuidado.

oversize, *s.* tamanho superior ao normal.

overslip, *v.t.* omitir, deixar passar, pular,
passar adiante.

overstate, *v.t.* exagerar.

overstatement, *s.* exagero.

overstep (overstepping, overstepped),
v.t. ultrapassar, transgredir, exceder-se.

overstrain, *v.t.* forçar de mais, puxar de
mais; danificar com o esforço; *v.i.* esforçar-
-se demasiado; *s.* tensão.

overstrung, *adj.* demasiado esticado;
hipersensível.

overstuff, *v.t.* encher de mais, abarrotar;
estofar de mais, estofar completamente.

oversupply, *v.t.* abastecer em demasia; *s.*
provisão excessiva; superabundância,
excesso.

overt, *adj.* aberto, público; claro, evidente.

overtake (overtook, overtaken), *v.t.*
alcançar, apanhar; apanhar em flagrante;
surpreender; terminar a tempo (tarefa).

overtax, *v.t.* sobrecarregar de impostos.

overthrow (overthrew, overthrown), *v.t.*

derrubar, deitar abaixo; demolir; derrocar;
destruir, derrotar, vencer; *s.* derrubamento;
derrota; deposição; destroço, ruína.

overtime, *s.* trabalho extraordinário, horas
extraordinárias; serão; *adv.* fora do tempo
estipulado.

overtly, *adv.* abertamente, manifestamente,
em público, às claras.

overture, *s.* proposta, declaração, insinuação; abertura (mús.).

overturn, *v.t.* voltar; subverter; deitar abaixo;
arruinar; emborcar; transtornar; *v.i.* virar,
tombar; capotar; *s.* queda, ruína; virada,
reviravolta.

overweigh, *v.t.* pesar mais que; prevalecer
ou predominar sobre; oprimir.

overweight, *s.* excesso de peso; peso
adicional; carga excessiva.

overwhelm, *v.t.* sepultar, soterrar;
submergir, confundir, afligir.

overwhelming, *adj.* opressivo, preponderante; irresistível, dominante.

overword, *s.* palavra ou expressão muito
repetida; estribilho, refrão.

overwork, *v.t.* fazer trabalhar em demasia,
escravizar; *v.i.* trabalhar demasiado; *s.*
trabalho feito fora das horas regulamenta-
res; trabalho excessivo.

overworn, *adj.* gasto pelo trabalho.

overwrought, *adj.* extenuado pelo trabalho;
muito agitado, sobreexcitado; muito elaborado, demasiadamente trabalhado.

oviparous, *adj.* (zool.) ovíparo.

ovoid, *adj.* e *s.* ovóide.

ovulate, *v.i.* (biol.) produzir ovos ou expeli-
-los do ovário.

ovulation, *s.* (biol.) ovulação.

ovule, *s.* (biol.) óvulo.

owe, *v.t.* dever; ser devedor a, ou de; estar
obrigado a. 1) *I owe money to my mother*,
devo dinheiro à minha mãe. 2) *to owe
some-one*, guardar rancor a alguém,
ter raiva a alguém; *v.i.* dever, estar endividado.

owing, *adj.* devido, que se deve; devido a,
atribuível a; *owing to*, por causa de, em
consequência de.

owl, coruja, mocho. 1) *barn-owl*, coruja das
torres. 2) *owl-light*, lusco-fusco.

owler, *s.* contrabandista.

owlet, *s.* corujinha.

own, *v.t.* possuir, ter, ser dono de; reconhecer como filho, reconhecer, confessar,
admitir; *adj.* próprio, particular, individual;

mesmo, verdadeiro, real. 1) *to be one's own man*, ser dono de si mesmo, ser independente. 2) *my own*, o que me pertence, aquilo que é meu; (também vocativo carinhoso) meu querido, minha querida. 3) I *want to have a house of my own*, quero ter casa própria.

owner, *s.* dono, proprietário, possuidor.

ownership, *s.* propriedade, domínio, posse.

ox, *s.* boi, pl. *oxen.*

oxeye, *s.* olho-de-boi; *oxeye daisy,* margarida dos prados.

oxidate, *v.t.* e *v.i.* oxidar(-se).

oxidation, *s.* oxidação.

oxide, *s.* óxido.

oxlip, *s.* (bot.) prímula, primavera-dos-jardins.

oxtail, *s.* rabo de boi, rabada; *oxtail soup,* sopa de rabo de boi.

oxygen, *s.* oxigénio.

oxygenize, oxygenate, *v.t.* (quím.) oxigenar; oxidar.

oyes, oyez, *interj.* ouçam!, atenção! (usada nos tribunais antes de comunicações importantes e repetida três vezes).

oyster, *s.* ostra; *oyster culture* ou *farming,* ostreicultura.

P

p, décima sexta letra do alfabeto.

pa, *s.* papá.

pabulum, *s.* pábulo, alimento, pasto, substância.

pace, *s.* passo, marcha, modo de andar, grau de celeridade; passo, andadura; passo (como medida de distância); estrado, tablado. 1) *pace-maker,* marcador de passo (em corrida). 2) *to keep pace with any one,* contender com, ou igualar alguém; andar tão depressa como outro. *v.t.* medir a passos, marcar passo; dirigir. *v.i.* passear, andar, andar a passo; ir a passo travado.

pacer, *s.* pessoa que marca o passo; cavalo que anda bem a passo.

pachyderm, *s.* paquiderme.

pachydermat, *s. pl.* paquiderme.

pachydermatous, *adj.* paquiderme.

pachymeter, *s.* paquímetro.

pacific, *adj.* pacífico, quieto, sossegado, tranquilo, pacato.

Pacific, *s.* o oceano Pacífico.

pacifically, *adv.* pacificamente.

pacification, *s.* pacificação, apaziguamento.

pacificatory, *adj.* pacificador, conciliador.

pacifier, *s.* pacificador, apaziguador.

pacifist, *s.* pacifista.

pacify, *v.t. pret.* e *pp. pacified,* pacificar, apaziguar, aquietar, acalmar, tranquilizar, conciliar.

pacing, *s.* passo, andadura.

pack, *s.* pacote, embrulho, fardo, mochila; baralho de cartas; banco de gelo (náut.); matilha de cães; bando, quadrilha. 1) *pack-animal,* besta de carga. 2) *pack cloth,* serapilheira. 3) *pack-ice,* massas de gelo flutuante. 4) *pack-saddle,* albardão. 5) *packthread,* fio para coser fardos. *v.t.* empacotar, enfardar; acougular, entulhar, atestar, acumular; despachar; enviar; carregar numa azêmola; levar ao ombro ou às costas; envolver um enfermo em lençóis molhados, cobrindo-o depois com mantas secas. *v.t.* empacotar, enfardar-se; guarnecer (junta êmbolo); formar uma massa compacta fugir, abalar. 6) *ground packs after a rain,* o terreno consolida-se depois da chuva. 7) *to pack off,* despachar. 8) *to send one packing,* mandar passear alguém.

package, *s.* fardo, pacote, enfardamento, embalagem.

packer, *s.* enfardador.

packet, *s.* pacote, fardo pequeno; vapor, paquete de carreira; mala, correio. *packet--boat,* paquete, correio marítimo. *v.i.* empacotar, enfardar, enfardelar.

packhorse, *s.* cavalo de carga.

packing, *s.* enfardamento, embalagem; empanque; recheio; enchimento; guarnição (de junta, de êmbolo). 1) *packing box* ou *case,* caixa de empacotamento. 2) *packing house,* estabelecimento onde se embarrilam conservas alimentícias. 3) *packing-needle,* agulha de enfardar.

pact, s. pacto, acordo, tratado, ajuste.

pad, s. almofada, coxim; defesa; calço; postiço, corselete, plastrão; salteador, ladrão de estrada. 1) *writing-pad*, bloco (de papel). 2) *calendar pad*, bloco de calendário. 3) *inking-pad*, almofada com tinta para carimbos. 4) *padlock*, cadeado, aloquete. *v.t. paddind, padded,* enchumaçar, acolchoar, aumentar (um livro) com material supérfluo; formar blocos de papel. *v.i.* levar postiços.

padding, s. chumaço.

paddle, *v.t.* e *v.i.* impelir, vogar, ou remar; manusear; apalpar, dar palmadinhas; patinhar, chapinhar. s. conduto; pá (de roda propulsora); remo de pá; pena de rodízio (dos moinhos). 1) *paddlebox*, tambor, caixa de rodas (dos vapores). 2) *paddle steamer,* ou *boat,* vapor de rodas.

paddler, s. remador.

paddock, s. tapada, parque, campo pequeno onde se guardam cavalos; espécie de sapo. 1) *paddock cheese*, aspárago. 2) *paddock pipe*, pimpinela. 3) *paddock stoll*, agárico (espécie de cogumelo).

paddy, s. pato americano; arroz com casca; um irlandês. adj. desprezível; *paddy field,* arrozal.

padlock, s. aloquete; cadeado. *v.i.* fechar a cadeado; fechar com aloquete.

padrone, s. patrão, mestre; alugador de realejos; pessoa que manda crianças pedir esmolas.

Paduam, s. e adj. paduano.

paen, s. péon, pé grego de quatro sílabas.

paeonic, adj. peónico.

pagan, s. e adj. pagão.

paganism, s. paganismo.

paganize, *v.t.* e *v.i.* paganizar, paganizar-se.

page, s. página, pajem, escudeiro, criado. *v.t.* paginar; servir de pajem.

pageant, s. cortejo cívico; fausto, pompa; espectáculo, aparato cénico.

pageantry, s. fausto, aparato.

paginal, adj. relativo a páginas.

paginate, *v.i.* paginar, folhear.

pagination, s. paginação.

paging, s. paginação.

pagoda, s. pagode; *pagoda-tree*, sófora, árvore.

paid, pret. e pp. de *pay.* 1) *paid up*, realizado (capital); liberada (acção). 2) *to be paid for upon delivery*, contra-reembolso.

pail, s. cuba, balde, tarro.

pailful, s. um balde cheio.

paillasse, s. palhaço, bobo.

paillette, s. lentejoula, palheta, pepita.

pain, *v.t.* afligir, doer, penar, angustiar, atormentar. s. pena, dor, tormento, sentimento; pena castigo. 1) *on pain of death*, sob pena de morte. pl. trabalho, esmero, incómodo, fadiga; ansiedade, inquietação, solicitude; dores de parto. 1) *to be in pain*, estar com muito cuidado; estar inquieto; doer, padecer. 2) *to be in pain all over*, doer todo o corpo. 3) *to be at the pains of*, dar-se ao trabalho de. 4) *to take great pains*, esmerar--se, afadigar-se.

pained, adj. aflito, doloroso, dorido.

painful, adj. dorido, aflito, atormentado; aflitivo, árduo, penoso, difícil, laborioso, trabalhoso.

painfully, adv. dolorosamente, penosamente, laboriosamente.

painfulness, s. dor, aflição, pena, trabalho, fadiga.

painless, adj. sem dor; fácil.

painlessly, adv. facilmente.

painlessness, s. ausência de dor.

painstaker, s. trabalhador, pessoa activa e laboriosa.

painstaking, adj. cuidadoso, esmerado, consciencioso.

paint, *v.t.* pintar, colorir; retratar ou copiar a cores. *v.i.* dedicar-se à pintura, pintar-se, arrebicar-se; descrever. s. pintura, tinta, cor, arrebique. 1) *coat of paint*, demão de tinta. 2) *paint-box*, caixa de tintas ou pinturas. 3) *paint-brush*, pincel, brocha. 4) *paint room*, paiol das tintas (náut.). 5) *paint tube*, tubo de tinta. 6) *oil-paints*, pinturas a óleo.

paintable, adj. que se pode pintar.

painter, s. pintor; boça, cabo, amarra de navio ou de lancha. 1) *house-painter*, pintor de casas. 2) *landscape painter*, paisagista, pintor de paisagens. 3) *painter's work*, pintura.

painting, s. pintura (arte e ofício); quadro ou pintura; descrição.

painty, adj. com muita tinta; sujo de tinta.

pair, s. par, parelha, junta; marido e mulher. casal. 1) *pair of shrouds*, encapeladura de enxárcia. 2) *a carriage and pair*, carruagem de dois cavalos. 3) *that's another pair of shoes*, isso é outra coisa (outro par de botas). *v.t.* emparelhar, ajuntar, igualar; casar. *v.i.* emparelhar-se, casar-se. 4) *to* *pair off*, sair da câmara antes da votação (dois deputados de opiniões contrárias).

pairing, *s.* acto de amparelhar; *pairingtime*, tempo de fazer criação (as aves).

pajamas, *s.* pijama.

pal, *s.* companheiro, amigalhote, confederado.

palace, *s.* palácio; *palace-car*, carruagem de comboio luxuosa.

paladin, *s.* paladino.

palaeographer, *s.* paleografia.

palaeolithic, *adj.* paleolítico.

palaeontology, *s.* paleontologia.

palaeotype, *s.* paleótipo.

palanquin, *s.* palanquim.

palatable, *adj.* gostoso, saboroso, apetitoso; agradável.

palatableness, *s.* sabor agradável.

palatably, *adv.* saborosamente.

palatal, *adj.* e *s.* palatal.

palatalization, *s.* palatalização.

palatalize, *v.t.* palatalizar.

palate, *s.* paladar; *nice palate*, gosto delicado.

palatial, *adj.* palacial.

palatinate, *s.* palatinado.

palatine, *adj.* palatino.

palaver, *s.* palavreado; lisonja; discussão. *v.t.* e *v.i.* palavrear.

palaverer, *s.* adulador.

pale, *adj.* pálido, descorado, claro, apagado. 1) *pale bull*, amarelo escuro. 2) *pale eyed*, de olhos sem brilho, que tem a vista turva. 3) *pale-face*, pessoa branca (nome que os índios dão aos brancos). 4) *pale faced*, de rosto pálido. 5) *pale green*, verde claro. 6) *pale hearted*, cobarde. 7) *pale wine*, vinho palhete. 8) *to grow pale* ou *to turn pale*, empalidecer. 9) *as pale as ashes*, pálido como a morte. *s.* estaca; paliçada; estacada; vala, limite, espaço cerrado; grémio, sociedade; pala do escudo. 10) *pale of the church*, grémio da igreja. *v.i.* guarnecer de paliçada, cercar, rodear, pôr pálido, fazer empalidecer, descorar. *v.i.* empalidecer, pôr-se pálido; perder a cor,

palely, *adv.* palidamente.

paleness, *s.* palidez.

paleographer, *s.* paleógrafo.

paleographic, *adj.* paleográfico.

paleography, *s.* paleografia.

paleolithic, *adj.* paleolítico.

paleontological, *s.* paleontológico.

paleontologist, *s.* paleontólogo.

paleontology, *s.* paleontologia.

paleotype, *s.* paleótipo.

paletot, *s.* paletó, sobretudo.

palette, *s.* paleta; *palette-knife*, espátula.

palfrey, *s.* palafrém.

palimpsest, *s.* palimpsesto.

palindrome, *s.* palavra ou verso ou frase que se lê da mesma maneira quer para a frente quer para trás.

paling, *s.* paliçada, estacada.

palinode, *s.* palinódia.

palisade, *s.* paliçada, estacada. *v.t.* cercar com paliçada.

palish, *adj.* macilento, um tanto pálido.

pall, *s.* pano mortuário; mortalha; o que causa aflição ou tristeza; pálio (de Arcebispo ou Papa); *pall-bearer*, o que pega nas bordas do caixão (nos enterros). *v.i.* evaporar, desvirtuar, tornar insípido; desalentar, saciar, fartar, desanimar. *v.i.* evaporar-se; tornar-se insípido; desalentar; saciar; fartar; desanimar. *v.i.* evaporar-se; tornar-se insípido; embotar os sentidos.

palladium, *s.* paládio; garantia, salvaguarda.

palladium, *s.* paládio (mineral).

pallet, *s.* cama pequena; cama de pobre; enxergão, paleta; instrumentos para dourar ou fazer inscrições nas capas dos livros.

palliate, *v.t.* paliar, aliviar; escusar; desculpar; encobrir.

palliation, *s.* paliação.

palliative, *adj.* e *s.* paliativo.

pallid, *adj.* pálido, descorado.

pallidly, *adv.* placidamente.

pallidness, *s.* palidez.

pallium, *s.* pálio; manto.

pall-mall, *s.* palamalha, jogo; Ministério da Guerra (na Rua Pall-Mall).

pallor, *s.* palidez.

palm, *s.* palma, palmeira; vitória, palma da mão, palmo (medida); pata da âncora; repuxo (náut.). 1) *palm-cabbage*, palmito. 2) *palm-oil*, óleo da palma. 3) *palm-sunday*, Domingo de Ramos. 4) *palm tree*, palmeira; palma. 5) *palm wine*, vinho de palmeira. 6) *to bear ou carry away* ou *off the palm*, levar a palma, a vitória. 7) *to have an itching palm*, prestar-se a suborno; ter a boca grande. *v.t.* empalmar; enganar, defraudar; manejar, manipular; cobrir de palmas. 8) *to palm off a thing*, livrar-se de uma coisa com falsos pretextos; impingir.

palma, *s.* palma (da mão).

palmar, *adj.* palmar.

palmate, adj. espalmado.

palmer, s. palmeiro, peregrino, romeiro (da Terra Santa; empalmador (no jogo das cartas).

palmetto, s. palmito.

palmhouse, s. jardim de inverno.

palmier, palmiest, comp. e sup. de palmy.

palmist, s. quiromante.

palmistry, s. quiromancia.

palmitine, s. palmitina.

palm-sunday, s. Domingo de Ramos.

palmy, adj. próspero, florescente; triunfal; palmar.

palmyra, s. palmeira da Índia.

palp, palpus, s. palpo.

palpability, s. qualidade do que é palpável; evidência.

palpable, adj. palpável, evidente, patente, óbvio.

palpably, adv. de modo palpável, claramente, evidentemente.

palpate, v.t. apalpar.

palpation, s. apalpação, apalpadela, toque.

palpitate, v.i. palpitar, latejar, bater.

palpitating, adj. palpitante.

palpitation, s. palpitação, latejo.

palsagrave, s. mordomo-mor de casa real.

palsied, adj. paralítico.

palsy, s. paralisia; ineficácia, apatia.

palter, v.i. simular, enganar, pregar partidas. v.t. desperdiçar, dissipar.

palterer, s. velhaco, trapaceiro.

paltrily, adv. mesquinhamente, desprezivelmente.

paltriness, s. mesquinhez, vileza.

paltry, adj. vil, miserável, mesquinho.

pam, s. valete de paus.

pampa, s. pampa, grande planície coberta de erva na América co Sul, principalmente na Argentina.

pamper, v.t. engordar; regalar; tratar com mimo; acariciar, deleitar.

pampered, adj. regalado, saciado.

pamperer, s. o que se sacia.

pampering, s. regalo, abundância; impresso.

pamphleteer, s. panfletário.

pan, s. panela, caçarola, caçoleta; chocolateira; chaleira; gamela; caçoleta de arma de fogo; quício, gonzo; crânio. 1) panhead, cabeça troncônica (náut.). 2) baking pan, torteira. 3) bed pan, aparadeira (para doentes). 4) brain-pan, crânio. 5) dripping--pan, pingadeira. 6) frying-pan, frigideira. 7) earthen pan, alguidar. 8) knee-pan, rótula.

9) salt-pan, salina. 10) stewing-pan, tacho, caçarola. 11) warming pan, esquentador, braseiro. 12) pan of a gunlock, caçoleta de escopeta. 13) out of the frying-pan into the fire, de mal para pior. v.i. panning, panned, separar o ouro; alcançar, lograr; cozer e servir em caçarola de barro. 14) to pan out, dar oiro (a terra ou areia); dar bom resultado.

panacea, s. panaceia.

panache, s. penacho, topete.

panama, s. panamá (chapéu).

Pan-American, adj. pan-americano.

Pan-Anglican, adj. pan-anglicano.

pancake, s. sonho (espécie de filhó); fragmento de gelo.

pancreas, s. pâncreas.

pancreatic, adj. pancreático.

Pandean, adj. do deus Pã.

pandect, s. tratado, compilação, digesto.

pandemic, adj. geral, comum, epidémico. s. epidemia.

pandemonium, s. pandemónio, inferno; barafunda.

pander, s. alcoviteiro. v.t. alcovitar.

pandora, s. pandora.

pane, s. vidro (de vidraça); quadrado (de madeira); crista (de malho); pena (de martelo); cara, lado, faceta.

paned, adj. composto de quadrados pequenos; que tem vidros, penas (martelo), facetas, etc.

panegyric, s. panegírico, apologia.

panegyric, adj. panegírico.

panegyrist, s. panegirista, encomiasta.

panel, s. painel, almofada (de porta, janela, etc.); caixotão (de tecto); pano (em vestido); xairel; espécie de cetim; face de uma pedra lavrada; lista dos jurados, o júri. v.i. panelling, panelled, almofadar (as portas, etc.); apainelar.

paneless, adj. sem vidros (janelas. etc.).

panful, s. uma caçarola cheia.

pang, s. angústia, dor, agonia, transe, tormento, pena. 1) in pangs, agonizante. 2) pangs of childbirth, dores de parto.

Pan-German, adj. pangermânico.

pangolin, s. pangelim.

panic, s. pânico, medo, terror, consternação; pânico comercial. adj. de terror, de pânico; panic-stricken, panic struck, possuído de terror.

panicky, adj. que produz pânico.

panicle, s. panícula.

panjandrum, *s.* alta personagem.

pannage, *s.* colheita de bolotas; sustento de porcos.

pannier, *s.* cabaz, cesto; parte da saia formando tufos nas ancas.

pannikin, *s.* copo de metal; bebida contida no mesmo.

panning, *s.* processo de separar o ouro ou minério da areia.

panoplied, *adj.* completamente armado.

panoply, *s.* panóplia.

panorama, *s.* panorama.

panoramic, *adj.* de panorama (quadro panorâmico; paisagem)

pansy, *s.* amor-perfeito (flor).

pant, *v.t.* e *v.i.* arquejar, ofegar; anelar; trepidar; palpitar; *o pant for ou after*, suspirar por, desejar com ânsia. *s.* palpitação.

pantaloon, *s.* arlequim, bobo. *pl.* calças, calções.

pantechnicon, *s.* pantécnicon.

pantheism, *s.* panteísmo.

pantheist, *s.* panteísta.

pantheistic, *s.* panteísta.

pantheon, *s.* panteão.

panther, *s.* pantera.

pantile, *s.* goteira, algeroz.

panting, *s.* palpitação.

pantingly, *adv.* com palpitações.

pantograph, *s.* pantógrafo.

pantographic, *adj.* pantográfico.

pantometer, *s.* pantómetro.

pantomine, *s.* pantomimo; pantomima.

pantomimic, *s.* pantomímico.

pantomimically, *adv.* com pantomimas.

pantomimist, *s.* pantomimo, pantomimeiro.

pantry, *s.* despensa, copa.

pants, *s. pl.* ceroulas, calças.

pap, *s.* teta; papa (alimentação de crianças); polpa (de frutos).

papa, *s.* papá.

papacy, *s.* papado.

papal, *adj.* papal, pontifical.

papalism, *s.* papismo.

papalist, *s.* papista.

papalize, *v.i.* adoptar e seguir a doutrina papal.

papaverous, *adj.* papaveráceo.

paper, *s.* papel; folha de papel; jornal, periódico, documento; demonstração; ensaio literário; valor, vela, letra ou ordem de pagamento; invólucro, pacote; cartas de valor, papéis; autos; bilhetes de borla (no teatro). 1) *a sheet of paper*, folha de papel. 2) *a quire of paper*, uma mão de papel. 3) *paper bag*, saca de papel. 4) *paper box*, caixa de cartão. 5) *paper-case*, papeleira. 6) *paper-clip*, prende-papéis. 7) *paper clamp*, instrumento para prender jornais. 8) *paper-currency*, papel-moeda. 9) *paper-cutter*, guilhotina, máquina de cortar papel. 10) *paper feeder*, aparelho para distribuir papéis numa máquina de impressão. 11) *paper-hanger*, artista que forra com papéis ou coloca papéis nas casas. 12) *paper-hanging*, arte de forrar paredes a papel. 13) *paper-hangings*, papel pintado para forrar salas. 14) *paper-knife*, faca de cortar papel. 15) *paper kite*, papagaio de papel. 16) *paper making*, fabrico de papel. 17) *paper-mill*, fábrica de papel. 18) *paper-money*, papel-moeda. 19) *paper pulp*, polpa para fabricar papel. 20) *paper reed*, papiro. 21) *paper scheme*, projecto fictício. 22) *paper-stainer*, fabricante de papel pintado. 23) *paper test*, aparelho para avaliar a resistência do papel. 24) *paper tube*, tubo de papelão. 25) *paper-weight*, pesa-papéis. 26) *brown-paper*, papel pardo. 27) *blotting-paper*, papel mata-borrão. 28) *emery-paper*, lixa de esmeril. 29) *filter paper*, papel de filtrar. 30) *fly paper*, papel da China. 31) *marbled paper*, papel jaspeado. 32) *note-paper*, papel de carta. 33) *tissue paper*, papel de seda. 34) *stamped paper*, papel selado. 35) *wall-paper*, papel de forrar paredes. 36) *test paper*, papel de ensaio. 37) *waste-paper*, papel de refugo. 38) *writing-paper*, papel de escrever. 39) *to put pen to paper*, começar a escrever. *v.t.* forrar de papel; dar muitos bilhetes de favor (no teatro).

papier-mâché, *s.* massa de papel (para caixas, bandejas).

papilla, *s.* papila, teta.

papillar, *adj.* parecido com papilas.

papillary, *adj.* papila, mamilar.

papist, *s.* papista.

papistic, *adj.* do papismo.

papoose, *s.* criança dos índios norte-americanos.

pappus, *s.* plúmula.

papyrus, *s.* papiro; papel de papiro.

par, *s.* equivalência; igualdade; nível; parágrafo; par. 1) *at par*, ao par. 2) *to be on a par with*, ser igual a, estar ao par de. 3) *par value*, valor ao par, ou nominal. 4) *above par,* a prémio. 5) *below par,* abaixo do par.

parabasis, *s.* parábase.

parable, *s.* parábola.

parabola, *s. (geom.)* parábola.

parabolic, *adj.* parabólico.

parachute, *s.* pára-quedas; cuba de segurança.

parachutist, *s.* pára-quedista.

Paraclete, *s.* Paracleto.

parade, *s.* parada, revista de tropas; procissão, cavalgada; passeio público; ostentação, pompa, alarde, gala, parada; *parade-ground,* praça de armas. *v.t.* e *v.i.* dispor em parada; passar revista; passear, cavalgar; fazer gala, alardear.

paradigm, *s.* paradigma, modelo, exemplo.

paradigmatic, *adj.* paradigmático, exemplar.

paradise, *s.* paraíso, éden, céu, paraíso; *to live in a fool's paradise,* ignorar o perigo em que se está.

paradisiac, *adj.* paradisíaco.

paradisiacal, *adj.* paradisíaco.

paradisic, *adj.* paradisíaco.

paradox, *s.* paradoxo.

paradoxical, *adj.* paradoxo.

paradoxicalness, *s.* carácter do que é paradoxal.

paraffin, *s.* parafina; *paraffin oil,* querosene.

paragon, *s.* modelo, exemplar, parangona (tipo de corpo 20).

paragraph, *v.t.* dividir em parágrafos. *s.* parágrafo.

parakeet, *s.* periquito.

parallax, *s.* paralaxe.

parallel, *adj.* paralelo; igual, semelhante. *s.* linha paralela; paralelo, comparação; semelhança, par igual, cópia. 1) *parallel of latitude,* paralelo, grau de latitude. 2) *parallel bars,* barras paralelas (de um ginásio). 3) *parallel motion,* paralelogramo articulado. 4) *parallel sailing,* navegação em longitude. 5) *parallel ruler,* régua para traçar linhas paralelas. *v.t.* ser paralelo, ou igual a, correr parelhas com; pôr em paralelo, comparar; assemelhar-se.

parallelepiped, *s.* paralelepípedo.

parallelogram, *s.* paralelograma.

paralyse, *v.t.* paralisar.

paralysis, *s.* paralisia.

paralytic, *s.* *adj.* paralítico.

parameter, *s.* parâmetro.

paramount, *adj.* superior, supremo.

paramoutly, *adv.* superiormente.

paramour, *s.* amante.

paranoia, *s.* paranóia.

parapet, *s.* varanda, peitoril; parapeito, baluarte.

parapeted, *adj.* com varanda ou parapeito.

paraphernalia, *s. pl.* atavios, adornos, ornamentos, galas, insígnias; bens parafernais.

paraphrase, *s.* paráfrase. *v.t.* parafrasear.

paraphrastic, *adj.* parafrástico.

paraplegia, *s.* paraplegia.

parasang, *s.* parassanga.

parasite, *s.* parasita.

parasitic, *adj.* parasítico.

parasitically, *adv.* à maneira de parasita.

parasol, *s.* sombrinha, chapéu-de-sol; um tipo de monoplanos.

paravane, *s.* caça-minas, aparelho que é rebocado por um navio para cortar as amarras das minas submersas.

parboil, *v.t.* cozer ligeiramente, dar uma fervura a.

parbuckle, *s.* virador; tira-vira. *v.t.* levantar ou baixar por meio de um virador.

parcel, *s.* pacote, embrulho; porção de quantidade, parcela; multidão; partida, remessa. 1) *parcel of ground,* lote de terreno. 2) *parcel post,* encomenda postal. 3) *part and parcel,* carne e osso. 4) *bill of parcels,* nota ou factura dos artigos comprados. *v.t. parcelling, parcelled,* dividir, distribuir, repartir, empacotar, percintar; vedar uma costura.

parcelling, *s.* percinta, pedaço de lona que se ata aos cabos para evitar que se gastem.

parcenary, *s.* herança indivisa.

parcener, *s.* co-herdeiro.

parch, *v.t.* secar, ressecar; tostar, queimar, abasar. *v.i.* tostar-se, queimar-se, abrasar-se.

parching, *adj.* abrasador, ardente.

parchment, *s.* pergaminho.

pard, *s.* leopardo; sócio.

pardon, *v.t.* perdoar, absolver; indultar, desculpar, dispensar. *s.* graça; absolvição, indulto; *I beg your pardon,* desculpe (forma de cortesia); como? quê? que diz?

pardonable, *adj.* perdoável.

pardonably, *adv.* desculpavelmente.

pardoner, *s.* perdoador.

pardoning, *s.* indulgente, que perdoa, clemente.

pare, *v.t.* aparar, cortar, recortar, descascar,

mondar (fruta); ralar, raspar, desbastar; aparelhar madeira; *to pare the nails,* cortar as unhas.

paregoric, *adj.* paregórico, calmante, anódino. *s.* elixir anódino.

parent, *s.* pai ou mãe; antepassado; autor, causa, origem. *adj.* paterno ou materno; *parent ship,* navio de apoio.

parentage, *s.* descendência.

parental, *adj.* paternal.

parentally, *adv.* paternalmente.

parenthesis, *s.* parênteses.

parenthetic, al, *adj.* parentético.

parenthetically, *adv.* parenteticamente.

parentless, *adj.* órfão.

parer, *s.* pessoa que corta ou apara; raspadeira.

parergon, *s.* parergo; ornato.

parget, *s.* reboco; gesso. *v.t.* rebocar (parede).

parhelion, *s.* parélio.

pariah, *s.* pária.

Parian, *adj.* pário, da ilha de Paros. *s.* porcelana fina.

parietal, *adj.* e *s.* parietal.

paring, *s.* aparas; raspas; casca, pele, refugo.

parish, *s.* paróquia, freguesia. *adj.* paroquial. 1) *parish council,* junta da paróquia. 2) *parish register,* registo paroquial. 3) *to go on the parish,* receber subsídio da paróquia.

parishioner, *s.* paroquiano.

Parisian, *adj.* e *s.* parisiense.

parisyllabic, *adj.* parissilábico.

parity, *s.* paridade, igualdade.

park, *s.* parque, jardim; campina, campo aberto; parque de artilharia. 1) *park-keeper,* guarda de parque. 2) *oyster-park,* área fechada para a cultura das ostras. *v.t.* meter em parque ou tapada.

parker, *s.* couteiro; guarda de parque.

parlance, *s.* linguagem, idioma, locução.

parley, *v.i.* parlamentar, discutir; conferenciar. *s.* conferência, prática, parlatório, negociação; *to beat ou sound a parley,* fazer ouvir o toque de parlamentar.

parliament, *s.* parlamento.

parliamentarian, *s.* parlamentário.

parliamentary, *adj.* parlamentar, do parlamento; *parliamentary train,* comboio barato, de operários.

parlour, *s.* pequena sala de visitas; *parlour--maid,* criada de sala.

parlous, *adj.* sagaz, vivo; chocareiro; perigoso.

parmesan, *s.* queijo de Parma. *adj.* parmesão.

Parnassian, *adj.* parnásio.

Parnassus, *s.* Parnaso.

parnellism, *s.* política de Parnell sobre a Irlanda.

parnellite, *s.* sequaz da política de Parnell.

parochial, *adj.* paroquial.

parochialism, *s.* administração de paróquia.

parochially, *adv.* por freguesias ou paróquias.

parodist, *s.* parodista.

parody, *s.* paródia. *v. pret. pp. parodied,* parodiar.

parole, *s.* palavra, promessa de honra de um prisioneiro de guerra; santo-e-senha; alegação ou alegado. *v.t.* pôr em liberdade sob palavra; afiançar.

paroxysm, *s.* paroxismo, acesso, agonia.

paroxysmal, *adj.* paroxismal, produzido por uma comoção.

paroxytone, *s.* paroxítono.

parquet, *s.* parquete.

parr, *s.* salmão pequeno.

parrel, *s.* ornamentos (de uma frente de fogão de sala); troça, enxertório (náut.). 1) *parrel rope,* bastardo de enxertório. 2) *parrel truck,* caçoilo (náut.).

parricidal, *adj.* parricidal.

parricide, *s.* parricida; parricídio.

parrot, *s.* papagaio; *parrot coal,* carvão que estala ao queimar-se.

parry, *v.t.* e *v.i. pret. pp. parried,* parar, esgrimir, desviar, parar o golpe. *s.* parada.

parrying, *s.* parada (esgr.).

parse, *v.t.* analisar gramaticalmente, logicamente.

parsimonious, *adj.* parco, frugal, parcimonioso, poupado.

parsimoniously, *adv.* com parcimónia,

parsimoniousness, *s.* parcimónia, economia.

parsimony, *s.* parcimónia.

parsing, *s.* análise gramatical, lógica.

parsley, *s.* salsa.

parsnip, *s.* cenoura branca.

parson, *s.* clérigo, sacerdote, cura, pároco, reitor.

parsonage, *s.* curato; presbitério.

part, *s.* parte, porção, pedaço, quinhão, fragmento; mambro; região, lugar, sítio, lado; papel (teat.); interesse, cuidado;

obrigação; dever, função; ofício; parte (mús.); entrega de uma publicação; risca de cabelo. pl. partes, habilidade, prendas pessoais, dotes. 1) *man of parts*, homem de talento. 2) *for my part*, quanto a mim, por minha parte. 3) *for the most part*, geralmente. 4) *to take one's part*, tomar o partido de alguém. 5) *part and parcel*, parte integrante, unha e carne. 6) *part of speech*, categoria gramatical. 7) *foreign parts*, países estrangeiros. 8) *do your part*, cumpra a sua obrigação. 9) *to play a part*, representar um papel. 10) *in good or ill part*, em boa ou má parte, por bem ou por mal. *v.t.* partir, repartir, distribuir; separar; desunir, dividir, romper, desprender, apartar; rebentar (cabo, amarra). 11) *to part the hair*, apartar o cabelo, fazer a risca. *v.i.* separar-se; desprender-se; saltar; safar-se; despedir-se; partir; ir, pôr-se a caminho; morrer. 12) *to part with*, desfazer-se de, alienar. 13) *to part from*, despedir-se, dizer adeus.

partake, *v.t. pret. partook, pp. partaken.* participar, partilhar; *to partake of with,* participar, tomar parte.

partaker, *s.* participante; cúmplice.

partaking, *s.* participação; combinação (para o mal).

parterre, *s.* tabuleiro de jardim; maciço de flores; plateia (teatr.).

parthenogenesis, *s.* partenogénese.

partial, *adj.* parcial; local; *partial to,* que gosta de.

partiality, *s.* parcialidade.

partially, *adv.* parcialmente, em parte, com parcialidade.

participant, *adj. e s.* participante, partícipe.

participate, *v.t. e v.i.* participar, tomar parte em.

participation, *s.* participação; parte, quinhão.

participator, *s.* participante.

participial, *adj.* participial.

participially, *adv.* participialmente.

participle, *s.* particípio.

particle, *s.* partícula.

parti-coloured, *adj.* de muitas cores.

particular, *adj.* particular, peculiar, especial; individual, privado, privativo; singular, extraordinário, notável; preciso, exacto, delicado, escrupuloso; minucioso, prolixo, pormenorizado, circunstanciado; raro, extravagante, estranho. *s.* particular,

particularidade, circunstância, pormenor; interesse próprio. *pl.* informações, pormenores. 1) *for further particulars*, para informações completas. 2) *to go into particulars*, narrar circunstanciadamente.

particularity, *s.* particularidade.

particularize, *v.t.* particularizar, pormenorizar.

particularly, *adv.* particularmente, especialmente.

parting, *s.* separação, divisão; partida, despedida, rompimento; bifurcação; risca do cabelo.

partisan, *s.* partidário; sequaz; partazana, alabarda.

partisanship, *s.* adesão cega a um partido.

partite, *adj.* dividido.

partition, *s.* partição, repartimento; divisão, separação; tabique; partilha; partitura (mús.); *partition wall*, tabique, parede meia. *v.t.* partir, dividir, separa; repartir, distribuir.

partitive, *adj.* partitivo; distributivo. *s.* partitivo.

partly, *adv.* em parte.

partner, *s.* sócio, associado; companheiro, companheira, par (na dança); camarada; consorte; cônjuge; interessado; participe; parceiro; enora; chaço, chapuz. 1) *head partner*, sócio principal. 2) *sleeping* ou *silent partner*, sócio comanditário. 3) *senior partner*, sócio chefe. *v.t.* associar-se.

partnership, *s.* sociedade, interesse social, associação, consórcio.

partook, *pret.* de *partake.*

partridge, *s.* perdiz.

parturition, *s.* parto.

party, *s.* partido, banda, bando; facção; parte; interessado; litigante; partícipe; partida; função; convite; sarau; reunião; destacamento, sujeito, indivíduo. 1) *party of pleasure* ou *pleasure party*, folguedo. 2) *evening party*, «soirée». 3) *hunting, fishing-party*, partida de caça, de pesca. 4) *riding party*, cavalgada. 5) *to join the party*, agregar-se à partida; filiar-se num partido. 6) *party-coloured*, mosqueado. 7) *party jury*, júri misto (de ingleses e estrangeiros). 8) *party-man*, partidário, homem de partido. 9) *party-wall*, parede meia. 10) *charter-party*, carta de fretamento.

parvenu, *s. e adj.* adventício.

pas, *s.* passo, dança; precedência.

paschal, *adj.* pascal.

pasha-cha, *s.* paxá.

pasquinade, s. pasquim, pasquinada.

pass, v.t. pret. e pp. passed ou past, passar, levar ou conduzir de um lugar para outro, transportar; cruzar; passar para outro lado, atravessar; transpor, passar, ir mais além do ponto determinado; aprovar (um projecto de lei); passar (a vida, o tempo, as horas, etc.): fazer um exame; transferir, transladar; exceder, superar; consentir; tolerar, fazer passar uma coisa por outra. v.i. passar, andar, caminhar, transitar por alguma parte; deslizar, correr passar (o tempo, etc.); cessar, dissipar-se, desvanecer-se ou acabar-se alguma coisa; morrer, ocorrer, acontecer, passar, ser admitida sem reparo (a moda, etc.); ser aprovado num exame; deixar de fazer, dar uma estocada; fazer um passe (esgr.); passar, deixar de fazer uma jogada. 1) pass away, gastar, consumir, dissipar; falecer. 2) pass by, dispensar, perdoar, omitir; passar perto de. 3) pass by in silence, passar em silêncio; passar por alto. 4) pass for, passar por, ser considerado ou reputado; passar, seguir o seu curso; dissipar-se. 5) pass on, entregar ao próximo, não parar; continuar; passar--se; suceder-se; formar juízo sobre. 6) pass up, subir. 7) pass upon, impingir, enganar ou abusar de alguém. 8) pass over, atravessar, cruzar; passar por alto, dispensar. 9) pass round, fazer circular. 10) pass through, passar por. 11) to pass one's word for another, empenhar a sua palavra por outro. 12) to come to pass, suceder, acontecer. 13) to let pass, deixar passar; não fazer caso, olvidar, perdoar. 14) to bring to pass, fazer suceder, efectuar. 15) to pass sentence ou judgement, sentenciar, julgar. 16) to pass muster, ser inspeccionado sem levar censura. s. passo, passagem, caminho, desfiladeiro, garganta, desembocadura; curso das águas; aprovação num exame, passe, licença, salvo-conduto, passaporte; bilhete de favor, estado, condição; passe de um magnetizador; estocada (esgr.) 17) pass book, livro de conta, livro denominado «razão»; caderneta de banco. 18) passkey, chave-mestra, gazua. 19) password, santo-e-senha, palavra de passe.

passable, adj. transitável; aceitável; it's passable, tolera-se, escapa.

passableness, s. praticabilidade.

passably, s. passagem, preço de passagem; passo, passada; trânsito; viagem, navegação, travessia; corredor, conduto (de vapor, etc.); trecho; ocorrência; acontecimento, incidente, episódio; encontro pessoal, lance, desafio; migração das aves. 1) passage home, viagem de volta. 2) passage out, viagem de ida.

passant, adj. passante (diz-se das figuras dos brasões).

passenger, s. passageiro, viajante, transeunte. 1) passenger train, comboio de passageiros. 2) saloon passenger, passageiro de primeira classe. 3) steerage passenger, o passageiro de terceira classe.

passe-pariut, s. "passepartout".

passer, s. pessoa que passa; perfurador (em cutelaria).

passer, s. pardal.

passer-by, s. transeunte.

passerine, adj. de pardal.

passibility, s. passibilidade.

passible, adj. passível.

passim, adv. aqui e ali.

passing, adj. que passa, passageiro, transitório, momentâneo. adv. eminentemente, perfeitamente, extremamente; muito. s. passo, passada; passagem; trânsito; morte; aprovação de um projecto de lei, 1) passing-bell, dobre de finados. 2) passing events, actualidades.

passion, s. paixão; ira, cólera, furor; passion--flower, martírio (flor).

passion, s. Paixão de Cristo. 1) passion-play, a representação da Paixão de Cristo. 2) passion sunday, Domingo da Paixão. 3) passion Week, Semana da Paixão.

passionate, adj. apaixonado; ardente; vivo; impetuoso, arrebatado.

passionately, adv. apaixonadamente; ardentemente, colericamente.

passionateness, s. veemência, impetuosidade, arrebatamento.

Passionist, s. membro de certa ordem religiosa.

passionless, adj. frio, impassível, insensível, sem paixões.

passive, adj. passivo; quieto; inactivo, inerte. s. voz passiva; passive obedience, obediência absoluta.

passively, adv. passivamente.

passivity, s. passividade; calma; paciência.

passman, s. o que passa no exame (sem classificação).

Passover, s. páscoa dos hebreus.

passport, s. passaporte.

password, s. palavra de passe, santo-e-
-senha.

past, adj. passado, transcorrido, último;
concluído, terminado; consumado. s. o
passado; antecedentes, história; pretérito.
1) *woman with a past,* mulher de maus
antecedentes. *prep.* mais de; depois de
(tempo), além de; fora de (lugar); fora de,
sem. 2) *past a doubt,* fora de dúvida. 3)
past bearing, insuportável; infecundo. 4)
past cure ou *recovery,* incurável. 5) *past
hope,* sem esperança. 6) *past dispute,*
incontestável, fora de dúvida.

paste, s. massa, pasta, grude, cola; imitação
de pedras preciosas. 1) *italian past,* massas
para sopas. 2) *past grain,* imitação de couro
para encadernações. *v.t.* colar, pegar. 3) *to
paste up,* afixar (um cartaz, etc.).

paste-board, s. cartão, papelão.

pastel, s. pastel (pintura ou desenho); erva-
-pastel.

pastelist, s. pastelista.

pastern, s. ranilha.

pasteurization, s. pasteurização, esterilização.

pasteurize, v.t. pasteurizar, esterilizar.

pastier, pastiest, comp. e sup. de *pasty.*

pastil, pastile, s. pastilha; pastel (pintura).

pastily, adj. de modo pastoso.

pastime, s. passatempo, diversão, recreação, entretenimento.

pastiness, s. qualidade de pastoso.

pastor, s. pastor espiritual, clérigo; estorni-
nho.

pastoral, adj. pastoril; pastoral. s. pastoral;
pastoral staff, báculo episcopal.

pastorale, s. pastoral (composição musical).

pastorate, s. cargo, dignidade, jurisdição de
pastor espiritual.

pastry, s. pastelaria.

pastrycook, s. pasteleiro.

pasturage, s. pastagem, pasto; apascentamento.

pasture, s. pasto; apascentamento. *v.t.*
pastar, apascentar, pastorear. *v.i.* pastar.

pasty, s. pastel de carne.

pasty, adj. da consistência da massa,
pastoso.

pat, s. alcunha de irlandês. adj. exacto,
oportuno, conveniente, próprio, apto, bom,
cómodo. s. carícia, pancadinha; ruído de
passos; pastilha. adv. justamente, convenientemente, *ad hoc,* oportunamente,

a propósito. *v.t. patting, patted,* acariciar,
passar a mão, dar uma pancadinha.

Patagonian, s. patagão.

patavinity, s. patavinidade, provincialismo.

patch, v.t. remendar; embutir; pôr sinais
postiços (no rosto). *v.i.* deitar remendos,
trabalhar em retalhos. s. remendo;
embutido; sinal postiço no rosto.

patchable, adj. remendável.

patcher, s. remendão.

patchily, adv. com remendos.

patching, s. acção de remendar, remendagem.

patchouli, s. patchouli, planta aromática;
perfume.

patchwork, s. obra de fancaria; remendo.

patchy, adj. com muitos remendos; semelhante à obra de fancaria.

pate, s. cabeça, sede da inteligência.

patella, s. patela, rótula do joelho; lapa
(marisco).

patellar, adj. patelar.

paten, s. patena (do cálice).

patent, adj. patente, manifesto, visível;
público. s. patente, privilégio, exclusivo;
privilégio de invenção; diploma, despacho,
título. 1) *patent fuel,* briquetes. 2) *patent
leather,* couro envernizado. 3) *patent right,*
direito de privilégio; monopólio. 4) *letters-
patent,* cartas patentes, privilégios
de invenção. *v.t.* obter uma patente
ou privilégio exclusivo; conceder um
privilégio.

patentable, adj. que pode ser objecto de
privilégio exclusivo.

patented, adj. concedido por alvará;
privilegiado.

patentee, s. privilegiado.

pater, s. pai.

paternal, adj. paternal, paterno.

paternally, adv. paternalmente.

paternity, s. paternidade.

paternoster, s. o pai-nosso; cada uma das
contas maiores de um rosário. 1) *paternoster line,* linha de pesca com uma série de
anzóis e chumbos em forma de contas. 2)
the devil's paternoster, uma praga rogada
entre os dentes.

path, s. senda, vereda; caminho; via; passo,
curso; conduta.

pathetic, adj. patético, terno, comovente,
sentimental.

pathetically, adv. pateticamente, ternamente.

patheticalness, s. qualidade do que é patético.

pathfinder, s. explorador; instrumento cirúrgico para exploração da uretra.

pathless, adj. intransitável.

pathlessness, s. ausência de caminhos.

pathologic, adj. patológico.

pathologist, s. patologista.

pathology, s. patologia.

pathos, s. patos; o patético, sentimento, ternura, compaixão.

pathway, s. senda, vereda.

patience, s. paciência, resignação, conformidade.

patient, adj. paciente, resignado; constante; tolerante. s. paciente, doente, cliente (med.).

patiently, adv. pacientemente.

patina, s. pátina.

patois, s. dialecto; algaravia.

patriarch, s. patriarca.

patriarchal, adj. patriarcal.

patriarchate, s. patriarcado.

patrician, adj. e s. patrício.

patriciate, s. aristocracia.

patrimonial, s. patrimonial.

patrimonially, adv. patrimonialmente, como património.

patrimony, s. património.

patriot, s. patriota.

patriotic, adj. patriótico.

patriotically, adv. patrioticamente.

patriotism, s. patriotismo; civismo; amor à pátria.

patristic, adj. patrístico, dos Padres da Igreja.

patrol, s. patrulha, ronda. v.t. e v.i. patrolling, patrolled, patrulhar, rondar; fazer a ronda.

patrology, s. patrologia.

patron, s. patrono, protector, defensor; padroeiro.

patronage, s. patrocínio, amparo; patrono, padroado.

patroness, s. protectora, advogada, padroeira.

patronize, v.t. patrocinar, proteger; apadrinhar; condescender com arrogância; ser freguês de.

patronizer, s. protector.

patronizing, adj. protector; condescendente.

patronizingly, adv. com condescendência.

patronless, adj. sem protecção, desamparo.

patronymic, s. e adj. patronímico.

patroon, s. proprietário de terras com privilégios.

patten, s. soco, tamanco; chinelas; soco, base, fundamento (arq.).

patter, v.i. fazer ruído compassado, tamborilar. 1) to patter with the feet, patear, sapatear. 2) to patter out, murmurar, falar entre dentes. s. sucessão de palmadinhas; tagarelice; murmuração.

patterer, s. murmurador, resmungão.

pattern, s. modelo, norma, exemplar, padrão, modelo, risco. v.t. copiar, imitar, servir de exemplo.

patty, s. pastelinho, torta, empada.

patulous, adj. aberto, entendido.

paucity, s. pouquidade, escassez.

paunch, s. barriga, abdómen; pança dos ruminantes; tecido para as amarras; paunch mat, defensa do coxim (do costado do navio).

pauper, s. pobre, indigente; a pauper's grave, vala comum.

pauperism, s. pauperismo.

pauperization, s. empobrecimento.

pauperize, v.t. depauperar, empobrecer.

pause, s. pausa, intervalo; hesitação. v.i. pausar, cessar, parar, deter-se, interromper-se; vacilar.

pausing, s. pausa, meditação, reflexão.

pausingly, adv. pausadamente.

pavan, s. pavana (dança).

pave, v.t. ladrilhar, lajear; to pave the way for, facilitar ou abrir caminho para.

pavé, s. pedra de calçada; calçada, rua, via pública.

pavement, s. pavimento, piso; passeio (da rua).

paver, s. calceteiro, ladrilhador.

paving, s. pavimento, piso (de rua), obra de calceteiro. 1) paving-beetle, maço de calceteiro. 2) paving brick, tijolo ou ladrilho. 3) paving-stone, pedra de calçada.

pavilion, s. pavilhão, barraca, tenda; torre pequena; estandarte, bandeira; pavilhão da orelha.

paw, s. garra; cat's paw, aragem, boca de lobo (náut.). v.t. e v.i. escavar a terra (o cavalo); dar patadas.

pawed, adj. que tem patas ou garras.

pawkiness, s. astúcia.

pawky, adj. astuto, velhaco, sagaz.

pawl, s. linguete (náut) v.t. e v.i. virar o linguete.

pawn, v.t. empenhar. s. penhor; peão (no xadrez); pawn-ticket, cautela de penhor.

pawnbroker, s. penhorista, prestamista.
pawnee, s. penhorista.
pawner, s. o que pede dinheiro sobre penhor.
pawnshop, s. casa de penhores.
pax, s. paz (na missa).
pay, v.i. pret. e pp. paid, pagar, saldar, satisfazer, custear, recompensar, desembolsar; sofrer uma pena ou castigo; alcatroar, embrear (náut.). v.i. pagar uma dívida; compensar, ser proveitoso. 1) to pay addresses to, cortejar, pretender para casamento. 2) pay attention, prestar atenção. 3) pay back, devolver, restituir. 4) pay by instalments, pagar em prestações. 5) pay a call, fazer uma visita. 6) pay compliments, apresentar cumprimentos; fazer as honras. 7) pay down, pagar à vista, pagar em moeda corrente. 8) pay for, pagar o que se compra; expiar, satisfazer. 9) pay in cash, pagar à vista. 10) pay in full, saldar. 11) pay off, pagar e despedir um empregado; descartar, pagar na mesma moeda. 12) pay off a ship, desarmar um navio. 13) pay on account, pagar à «boa conta». 14) pay the piper, carregar com a despesa e a responsabilidade de. 15) pay through the nose, ter de pagar preços exorbitantes. 16) pay one's respects, apresentar os seus respeitos. 17) pay one's way, não contrair dívidas. 18) pay a visit, fazer uma visita. 19) pay out a cable, arrear um cabo (náut.). 20) pay the seams of a ship, brear as costuras de um navio. 21) pay up, saldar uma dívida, liquidar. 22) to pay him in his own coin, pagar-lhe na mesma moeda. 23) to pay the debt of nature, morrer. 24) to pay for one's whistle, pagar caro um capricho. 25) there was the devil to pay, havia uns trabalhos de mil demónios. s. paga; salário, soldo, soldada, ordenado, estipêndio; pré; compensação; recompensa, equivalente; pena. 26) in the pay of, ao serviço de. 27) full pay, soldo por inteiro. 28) half pay, meio soldo. 29) pay-day, dia de pagamento. 30) pay-dirt, terra ou areia que dá uma quantidade apreciável de ouro. 31) pay-list ou -roll, relação, lista (para pagamentos). 32) pay sheet ou bill, folha de pagamentos (a operários, etc.).
payable, adj. pagável.
payee, s. sacador, portador (de cheque ou letra); pessoa a quem se paga.
payer, s. pagador, sacado.

paymaster, s. pagador, contador; comissário de marinha.
payment, s. paga, pagamento; recompensa; prémio. 1) payment in full, of all demands, saldo de conta. 2) payment on account, pagamento parcial. 3) cash payment, pagamento em moeda ou metal sonante. 4) on the payment of, mediante o pagamento de.
paynim, s. pagão.
pea, s. ervilha; unha (de âncora). 1) heat pea, chícharo. 2) canned peas, ervilhas em lata. 3) chick pea, gravanço, grão-de-bico. 4) sweet pea, ervilha de cheiro. 5) stick pea, ervilha de trepar. 6) pea jacket, jaquetão. 7) pea-green, verde-claro. 8) pea-gun, ou shooter, zarabatana. 9) pea-nut, amendoim. 10) pea shell, casca de ervilha. 11) pea soup, puré de ervilhas. 12) pea-souper, nevoeiro denso e amarelo. 13) pea weevil, gorgulho.
peace, s. paz; tranquilidade; silêncio, harmonia. interj. paz! silêncio!. 1) to keep the peace, não perturbar a paz pública. 2) to hold one's peace, guardar silêncio, calar-se. 3) justice of the peace, juiz de paz. 4) peace-offering, sacrifício propiciatório. 5) peace-officer, agente de força pública.
peaceable, adj. pacífico, pacato, sossegado.
peaceful, adj. calmo, sereno, tranquilo; pacífico.
peacefully, adv. serenamente, calmamente; pacificamente.
peacefulness, s. calma, tranquilidade, serenidade; paz.
peacemaker, s. pacificador, mediador.
peach, s. pêssego, pessegueiro; rapariga bonita, pêssega; peach-tree, pessegueiro. adj. cor de pêssego. v.i. delatar, denunciar, espiar.
peachy, adj. cor de pêssego; aveludado.
peacock, s. pavão. v.i. pavonear-se, exibir-se.
peacocky, adj. vaidoso, exibicionista.
peahen, s. pavoa.
peak, s. pico, cume, cimo; ponta afiada; cúspide; ponto culminante, máximo; parte mais estreita do porão (náut.); 1) peak-arch, arco em ogiva. v.t. (náut.) repicar, arvorar (remos); empinar a cauda. 2) to peak and pine, estiolar, enfraquecer, definhar.

peaked, *adj.* pontiagudo, acuminado, em ponta; magro, macilento, doentio.

peal, *s.* repique de sinos; conjunto de sinos; barulho, estrépito; rajada, salva; 1) *peal of laughter,* gargalhada; 2) *peal of thunder,* trovoada. *v.i.* e *v.t.* ressoar, entoar, tocar, repicar (os sinos).

peanut, *s.* amendoim.

pear, *s.* pêra, pereira.

pearl, *s.* pérola, gânulo, glóbulo. *adj.* relativo a pérola; perlado; perlífero: granulado. 1) *pearl-diver,* pescador de pérolas. 2) *pearl powder, pearl white,* cosmético para clarear a pele. *v.t.* perolar, perlar; granular; dar forma de pérola, dar brilho de pérola. *v.i.* tomar forma de pérola.

pearly, *adj.* relativo a pérolas, perlado, perolado; nacarado; puro, precioso; *pearl nautilus,* náutilo (zool.).

peasant, *s.* camponês, campónio, rústico, aldeão; lavrador.

peasantry, *s.* camponeses, classe camponesa, campesinato; rusticidade.

pease, *pl.* de pea.

peasecod, *s.* vagem ou casca de ervilha.

peat, *s.* turfa; *peat-bog,* turfeira.

peaty, *adj.* turfoso, turfento.

pebble, *s.* seixo, calhau; cristal de rocha (mineral.); variedade de ágata; couro granulado. *v.t.* apedrejar com seixos; pavimentar com cascalho; granular; dar superfície áspera a.

pebbly, *adj.* seixoso, coberto de cascalho.

pecan, *s.* espécie de nogueira norte-americana.

peccability, *s.* pecabilidade.

peccable, *adj.* pecável.

peccadillo, *s.; pl. dilloes;* pecadilho, falta leve.

peccant, *adj.* pecante, pecador; culpado, em falta; mórbido, insalubre (med.).

peccary, *s.* pecari (zool.).

peck, *s.* bicada, picada; marca de bicada; medida de capacidade para secos; porção, montão, grande quantidade; beijo rápido (coloq.) 1) *peck of troubles,* uma carga de trabalhos. *v.t.* bicar, debicar, dar bicadas; demolir com picareta; picar; 2) *to peck out,* arrancar com o bico; *v.i.* bicar, debicar; arreliar, implicar com, rezingar.

peckish, *adj.* com fome, esfomeado, com apetite.

pecten, *s.; pl. pectines.* Pente, pécten (dos olhos das aves e dos répteis).

pectin, *s.* pectina.

pectoral, *adj.* peitoral, pectoral, torácico. 1) *pectoral girdle, pectoral arch,* cintura escapular. 2) *pectoral lozenges,* rebuçados peitorais. *s.* peitoral, ornamento usado sobre o peito pelo sumo sacerdote judeu; peitoral.

peculate, *v.t.* e *v.i.* desviar (dinheiro), praticar o crime de peculato.

peculation, *s.* peculato, desvio de dinheiros públicos.

peculiar, *adj.* peculiar, próprio, característico; individual, pessoal, privativo, exclusivo, específico; estranho, esquisito. 1) *peculiar people,* o povo judeu, o povo eleito; 2) *Peculiar People,* seita religiosa. *s.* propriedade ou privilégio exclusivo; igreja ou paróquia independente da diocese a que pertence. 3) *Peculiar,* membro da seita Peculiar People.

peculiarity, *s.* peculiaridade, singularidade; excentricidade.

peculiarize, *v.t.* distinguir, caracterizar; particularizar.

peculiarly, *adv.* peculiarmente, especialmente; singularmente, estranhamente.

peculium, *s.* pecúlio.

pecuniary, *adj.* pecuniário, monetário; que implica pena pecuniária.

pedagog, *s.* o mesmo que *pedagogue.*

pedagogic, *adj.* pedagógico; professoral.

pedagogics, *s.* pedagogia.

pedagogism, pedagoguism, *s.* pedagogismo; pedantismo.

pedagogue, *s.* pedagogo.

pedagogy, *s.* pedagogia.

pedal, *adj.* pedal, podal, relativo ao pé.

pedal, *s.* pedal; *loud pedal,* primeiro pedal do piano. *adj.* relativo a pedal. *v.t.* e *v.i.* pedalar.

pedalist, *s.* ciclista.

pedant, *adj.* pedante; formalista.

pedantic, *adj.* pedante, pedantesco.

pedantry, *s.* pedantismo.

pedate, *adj.* provido de pés, pedífero; pediforme.

peddle, *v.t.* e *v.i.* ser vendedor ambulante, vender nas ruas; ocupar-se de ninharias, bisbilhotar, propagar boatos.

peddler, peddlar, *s.* bufarinheiro, vendedor ambulante; bisbilhoteiro; *peddler's French,* calão usado pelos gatunos.

peddlery, pedlary, s. ofício de vendedor ambulante.

peddling, adj. que vende nas ruas; mesquinho, insignificante; frívolo, fútil.

pederast, s. pederasta.

pedestal, s. pedestal; peanha; suporte; base. v.t. colocar em pedestal; realçar; glorificar.

pedestrian, adj. pedestre, relativo a marcha; prosaico, vulgar. s. pedestre, peão.

pedestrianism, s. pedestrianismo; vulgaridade.

pediatric, paedriatic, adj. pedriático.

pediatrician, paediatrician, s. pediatra, pediatro.

pediatrics, paediatrics, s. pediatria.

pediatrist, s. pediatra, pediatro.

pedicel, s. pedicelo; pedúnculo, pedículo.

pedicellate, adj. pedicelado.

pedicle, s. pedículo.

pedicular, adj. pedicular.

pediculate, adj. pediculado; s. peixe pediculado.

pediculosis, s. pediculose.

pediculous, adj. piolhoso, piolhento; pedicular.

pedicure, s. pedicuro; quiropodista.

pediform, adj. pediforme.

pedigree, s. genealogia, linhagem, estirpe, ascendência ilustre; origem.

pedigreed, adj. com árvore genealógica, com ascendência conhecida; com certificado de origem (os animais).

pediment, s. frontão.

pedipalp, s. pedipalpo.

pedology, s. pedologia, estudo dos solos.

peduncle, s. pedúnculo.

pedunculate, adj. pedunculado.

peek, v.i. olhar, espreitar, espiar. s. espreitadela, olhadela.

peel, v.t. e v.i. descascar, pelar; descamar, pelar-se; despir-se (coloq.); to keep one's eyes peeled, ter os olhos bem abertos; (av.) sair da formação. s. casca, pele (de fruta); pá de forno, pá de remo; pequena fortificação do séc. XVI na fronteira entre a Escócia e a Inglaterra.

peeler, s. descascador; agente da polícia.

peen, s. pena (de martelo); v.t. bater com a pena do martelo.

peep, s. pio, pipilo; olhadela, espreitadela; 1) the peep of dawn, o raiar da madrugada. 2) peep show, exibição de gravuras, fotografias ou objectos vistos através de uma lente colocada num pequeno orifício. 3) peep sight, alça de mira (em espingardas). v.i. piar, pipilar, guinchar, chilrear; espiar, espreitar; raiar, despontar; aparecer parcialmente; apontar; brotar (planta).

peeper, s. pessoa que espreita; avezinha; olho (coloq.).

peephole, s. buraco por onde se espreita.

peeping, adj. que espreita, curioso; que desabrocha; peeping Tom, bisbilhoteiro. s. acção de espreitar, espreitadela; pio, pipilo.

peer, s. par, igual, coisa ou pessoa que se iguala a outra; par do reino, nobre. 1) House of Peers, Câmara dos Lordes. 2) without peer, sem rival. v.t. e v.i. olhar atenta ou curiosamente, examinar, fitar, espreitar; entremostrar-se; despontar, raiar, aparecer. 3) to peer with, rivalizar com.

peerage, s. pariato; nobreza; nobiliário.

peeress, s. mulher nobre, esposa de um par do reino.

peerless, adj. sem par, sem rival, incomparável.

peerlessness, s. superioridade incontestável.

peeve, v.t. irritar, agastar.

peevish, adj. rabugento, rezingão, impertinente.

peevishly, adv. impertinentemente, caprichosamente.

peevishness, s. impertinência, rabugice; casmurrice.

peewee, s. pequerrucho.

peg, s. cavilha, prego ou cabide de madeira; pino; espigão; mola (de roupa); grau ou posição social (coloq.); pretexto ou desculpa para fazer qualquer coisa; perna de pau (cal.); bebida com brande e soda. 1) to take someone down a peg, humilhar alguém; 2) peg top, pião accionado por cordel. 3) peg-top trousers, calças de funil. v.t. e v.i. cavilhar, prender ou marcar com cavilhas; 4) to peg down, restringir; trabalhar arduamente, ser persistente; agredir com estaca, dar pontoadas.

pegnoir, s. penteador, roupão aberto de senhora.

pejorative, adj. pejorativo, depreciativo. s. termo pejorativo.

pekin, *s.* espécie de tecido de seda ornado de flores, fabricado na China.

Pekingese, Pekinese, *adj.* e *s.* pequinês.

pekoe, *s.* peco, tipo de chá preto.

pelage, pelagem, pêlo (dos animais).

Pelagian, *s.* pelagiano, relativo ao pelagianismo.

pelagic, *adj.* pelágico, oceânico.

pelargonium, *s.* pelargónio.

Pelasgian, *s.* pelasgo.

pelerine, *s.* pelerine.

pelf, *s.* saque, coisa roubada, dinheiro mal ganho; riquezas.

pelican, *s.* pelicano.

pelisse, *s.* peliça.

pellagra, *s.* pelagra.

pellet, *s.* pílula; bolinha feita com os dedos; grão de chumbo. *v.t.* bombardear com bolinhas de papel.

pellicle, *s.* película.

pellitory, *s.* parietária (bot.).

pell-mell, pellmell, *adv.* em desordem, desordenadamente; *adj.* confuso, tumultuoso; *s.* misturada, confusão, desordem.

pellucid, *adj.* transparente, diáfano, claro, cristalino.

pellucidity, *s.* transparência, limpidez, clareza.

pelmet, *s.* sanefa (de cortinado).

Peloponnesian, *adj.* e *s.* peloponésio.

pelota, *s.* pelota basca.

pelt, *s.* pele, peliça; couro não curtido; pancada, golpe; *at full pelt,* a toda a brida. *v.t.* e *v.i.* atirar pedras a, apedrejar; cobrir, crivar (de insultos); bater, malhar, martelar; fustigar (a chuva).

pelta, *s.* pelta, pequeno escudo.

peltate, *adj.* peltado.

peltry, *s.* pelaria, peles; couro.

pelvic, *adj.* pélvico; *pelvic girdle,* cintura pélvica.

pelvis, *s.* pélvis, pelve; bacia.

pemmican, pemican, *s.* espécie de bola de carne (entre os índios norte-americanos).

pen, *s.* curral, redil, cercado, galinheiro; prisão (cal.); gradeado para crianças (parque); cisne fêmea; pena, caneta, estilete; estilo, carreira literária; *pl.* rémiges. 1) *pen and ink drawing,* desenho feito à pena. 2) *pen compass,* tira--linhas. 3) *pen driver,* motorista profissional. 4) *pen feather,* rémige. 5) *pen*

name, pseudónimo. 6) *pen pal,* correspondente. 7) *fountain pen,* caneta de tinta permanente. *v.t.* escrever, redigir.

penal, *adj.* penal, punível; *penal servitude,* trabalhos forçados.

penalize, *v.t.* sujeitar a penalidade, atribuir penalidade; penalizar (desp.).

penalization, *s.* aplicação de uma pena; penalização (desp.).

penalty, *s.* pena, penalidade, multa; punição, castigo; desvantagem; *penalty-kick,* grande penalidade.

penance, *s.* penitência, castigo voluntário. *v.t.* impor penitência a; punir.

Penates, *s. pl.* penates.

pence, *pl.* de *penny.*

pencel, *s.* galhardete.

penchant, *s.* inclinação, propensão.

pencil, *s.* lápis; pincel fino de pintor; pintura, estilo de pintor; feixe luminoso; feixe de linhas convergentes; *propelling pencil,* lapiseira. *v.t.* lapisar, delinear, escrever a lápis; registar nome de cavalo no livro das apostas.

penciliform, *adj.* penicilado, peniciliforme; bem delimitado.

pendant, pendent, *s.* pendente, pingente, berloque, brinco; ornato pendente; lâmpada pendente; companheiro, par, complemento; coroa de mastro; flâmula, galhardete.

pendency, *s.* pendência, demora; suspensão.

pendent, *adj.* pendente, por decidir; suspenso, pendurado; inclinado.

pendentive, *s.* pendículo, pendurão (arq.).

pending, *adj.* pendente; que aguarda solução. *prep.* durante, no decorrer de, à espera de, até.

pendragon, *s.* príncipe, chefe supremo (bretão ou galês).

pendulate, *v.i.* pendular, oscilar; hesitar.

pendulous, *adj.* pêndulo, suspenso, pendente; oscilante; *pendulous motion,* movimento pendular.

pendulously, *adv.* de uma maneira pendente; de modo oscilante.

pendulum, *s.* pêndulo; 1) *pendulum wheel,* volante de relógio. 2) *the swing of the pendulum,* o movimento pendular (de qualquer coisa).

peneplain, peneplane, *s.* peneplanície.

penetrable, *adj.* penetrável; compreensível; sensível, impressionável.

penetralia, *s. pl.* penetrais; santuário, recesso, segredo, intimidade.

penetrant, *adj.* penetrante, penetrador; arguto, perspicaz.

penetrate, *v.t.* e *v.i.* penetrar, entrar em, furar, atravessar; repassar, impregnar; descobrir, compreender; introduzir-se.

penetrating, *adj.* penetrante, perfurante; pungente; comovente, impressionante; forte (cheiro); agudo (som); subtil, perspicaz.

penetration, *s.* penetração; discernimento; perspicácia, sagacidade.

penetrative, *adj.* penetrante, perfurante; agudo; pungente; sagaz, perspicaz.

pengo, *s.* pengo, antiga moeda húngara.

penguin, *s.* pinguim.

penholder, *s.* caneta, pena.

penial, *adj.* peniano.

penicillin, *s.* penicilina.

penicillium, *s.* penicílio, género de fungos.

peninsula, *s.* península; promontório.

penis, *s.* pénis.

penitence, *s.* penitência; arrependimento.

penitent, *s.* e *adj.* penitente; arrependido.

penitential, *adj.* penitencial, penitenciário. *s.* penitencial (ritual de penitências); penitente.

penitentiary, *s.* penitenciaria (tribunal pontifício); penitenciária (prisão); *Grand penitentiary,* penitenciário, cardeal que preside à penitenciaria em Roma. *adj.* penitencial, penitenciário.

penknife, *s.* canivete.

penman, *s.* calígrafo; escritor, autor.

penmanship, *s.* caligrafia.

penna, *s. pl. pennae.* pena de cobertura de ave.

pennant, *s.* flâmula, galhardete, bandeirola.

pennate, *adj.* emplumado, alado.

penniless, *adj.* pobre, sem cheta, sem vintém.

pennon, *s.* galhardete, flâmula; pendão.

Pennsylvania, *s.* Pensilvânia.

penny, *s. pl. pence* quando designa quantia; *pennies* quando designa moedas. Peni, a duodécima parte de um xelim, um dinheiro; quantia insignificante. 1) *penny a liner,* escritor barato. 2) *penny dreadful,* folhetim sensacionalista. 3) *penny wise,* económico nos gastos.

pennyroyal, *s.* poejo.

pennyweight, *s.* peso para metais e pedras preciosas (1,555 g).

pennyworth, *s.* valor de um péni; quantidade insignificante.

penologist, *s.* penologista, penalista.

penology, *s.* penologia, estudo ou tratado das penalidades.

pensile, *adj.* pênsil, suspenso, pendente; diz-se de ave que constrói ninho suspenso.

pension, *s.* pensão, tença; renda vitalícia, reforma; compensação ou retribuição paga por serviços prestados; 1) *pension fund,* caixa de pensões. *v.t.* conceder pensão a; pagar para que nos prestem certos serviços. 2) *to pension off,* aposentar, reformar.

pensionary, *s.* pensionário, pensionista; assalariado. *adj.* pensionário, relativo a pensão, reformado.

pensioner, *s.* o mesmo que *pensionary.*

pensive, *adj.* pensativo, meditativo; pesaroso, triste, melancólico.

pensiveness, *s.* melancolia; ar meditativo.

penstock, *s.* comporta; açude, represa; canalização de turbina hidráulica.

pent, *s. pret.* e *pp.* de *to pen* (encerrar); *adj.* encerrado, enclausurado, limitado; estreito, abafado.

pentacle, *s.* pentáculo, pentagrama; signo de Salomão.

pentad, *s.* grupo de cinco; lustro, quinquénio.

pentagon, *s.* pentágono.

pentagonal, *adj.* pentagonal.

pentagram, *s.* pentagrama, pentáculo.

pentahedral, *adj.* pentaédrico, pentaedral.

pentahedron, *s.* pentaedro.

pentarchy, *s.* pentarquia.

pentastich, *s.* estrofe ou poema pentástico.

pentathlon, *s.* pentatlo.

pentavalent, *adj.* pentavalente.

Pentecost, *s.* Pentecostes; festa do Espírito Santo.

penthouse, *s.* telheiro, alpendre; terraço; anexo de construção; toldo; habitação construída sobre a cobertura de um edifício de muitos andares.

pentose, *s.* pentose.

Pentothal Sodium, *s. Pentotal* (nome comercial de um anestésico e hipnótico chamado vulgarmente Soro da Verdade).

pentoxide, *s.* pentóxido.

penultimate, *adj.* penúltimo. *s.* penúltima sílaba de uma palavra. penumbra. *s.* penumbra.

penurious, *adj.* avaro, mesquinho, sovina; pobre, estéril.

penuriousness, *s.* avareza, mesquinhez.

penury, *s.* penúria, miséria, pobreza; escassez, míngua.

peon, *s.* (Índia) ordenança; mensageiro; criado; polícia indígena; (América do Sul) peão; jornaleiro; (México) devedor submetido ao seu credor até saldar a dívida; peão, soldado que combate a pé.

peonage, *s.* condição de peão; peonagem.

people, *s.* (com significado colectivo e verbo no plural) povo, comunidade, nação, raça, tribo; pessoas, seres humanos; eleitorado. *v.t.* povoar, encher de gente, encher de (animais, etc.); habitar, ocupar.

pep, *s.* vigor, ardor, brio, dinamismo. *v.t.* estimular, animar.

pepper, *s.* pimenta; pimenteira; pimentão. *v.t.* apimentar; salpicar, polvilhar; crivar de balas, metralhar; dar uma sova a alguém.

pepperbox, *s.* pimenteiro.

peppercorn, *s.* grão de pimenta; insignificância, ninharia.

peppermint, *s.* hortelã-pimenta.

peppery, *adj.* apimentado; ardente; picante; mordaz; irritadiço, irascível.

peppy, *adj.* vivo, ardente, enérgico, vigoroso.

pepsin, pepsine, *s.* pepsina.

peptic, *adj.* péptico, digestivo.

per, *prep.* por meio de, mediante, por.

peradventure, *adv.* talvez; por acaso. *s.* acaso, incerteza, dúvida.

perambulate, *v.t.* percorrer, atravessar, transitar, inspeccionar; *v.i.* perambular, vaguear.

perambulation, *s.* viagem de inspecção, visita de inspecção; demarcação de um território; perambular, vaguear.

perambulator, *s.* carrinho de criança; (agrim.) hodómetro.

percale, *s.* percal.

percaline, *s.* percalina.

perceivable, *adj.* perceptível, sensível; apreciável; inteligível.

perceive, *v.t.* perceber, sentir, ver, ouvir; observar, notar; apreender, aperceber-se.

percentage, *s.* percentagem; proporção.

percentile, *s.* percentil, dentil.

percept, *s.* objecto da percepção; produto mental da percepção.

perceptible, *adj.* perceptível, sensível; discernível.

perception, *s.* percepção; conhecimento, consciência.

perceptive, *adj.* perceptivo; inteligente.

perceptiveness, *s.* perceptividade, perceptibilidade.

perceptual, *adj.* relativo a percepção; perceptivo.

perch, poleiro; pouso de ave; posição elevada ou segura; medida inglesa de comprimento. *v.i.* pousar, empoleirar-se; *v.t.* empoleirar.

perchance, *adv.* acaso, porventura; talvez.

perchlorate, *s.* perclorato.

percipient, *adj.* perceptivo. *s.* aquele que percebe; pessoa dotada de percepção telepática.

percolate, *v.t.* e *v.i.* filtrar; passar, coar; infiltrar-se. *s.* (farm.) percolato.

percolation, *s.* infiltração, filtrage; (farm.) percolação.

percolator, *s.* máquina de passar café, cafeteira.

percuss, *v.t.* percutir.

percussion, *s.* percussão; choque, embate; 1) *percussion cap,* fulminante; 2) *percussion hammer,* cão, percutor.

perdition, *s.* perdição, danação, condenação eterna; ruína, destruição.

perdurable, *adj.* perdurável, duradouro; imperecível.

peregrinate, *v.i.* peregrinar, viajar.

peregrination, *s.* peregrinação, viagem.

peregrine, *s.* peregrino, viajante; estranho, exótico.

peremptory, *adj.* peremptório; terminante; essencial, indispensável; positivo, dogmático; imperioso, autoritário.

perennial, *adj.* perene, perenal; constante, incessante; eterno, perpétuo. *s.* planta perene.

perfect, *adj.* perfeito, impecável; rematado, concluído. *v.t.* completar, concluir; aperfeiçoar.

perfection, *s.* perfeição; acabamento; maturidade; excelência; primor, requinte, mestria.

perfectionism, *s.* perfeccionismo.

perfectionist, *s.* perfeccionista.

perfectly, *adv.* perfeitamente, completamente; com perfeição.

perfervid, *adj.* ardente, fogoso.
perfidious, *adj.* pérfido, desleal, traiçoeiro, falso.
perfidy, *s.* perfídia, deslealdade, falsidade.
perforate, *v.t.* perfurar, furar, brocar; penetrar; *v.i.* penetrar, atravessar furando.
perforate, perforated, *adj.* perfurado.
perforation, *s.* perfuração, furo; recorte dentado dos selos.
perforator, *s.* perfurador; broca.
perforce, *adv.* necessariamente, forçosamente.
perform, *v.t.* levar a cabo, cumprir, desempenhar, realizar, executar, efectuar; tocar (música); representar. *v.i.* executar, actuar, tocar, representar.
performance, *s.* cumprimento, desempenho, execução; acção, proeza; representação, actuação; função, espectáculo; rendimento.
performer, *s.* executante, realizador; artista.
perfume, *s.* perfume, aroma, fragância. *v.t.* perfumar, aromatizar.
perfumer, *s.* perfumador.
perfumery, *s.* perfumaria.
perfuse, *v.t.* aspergir, borrifar; orvalhar; cobrir tingindo.
pergola, *s.* pérgola, caramanchão.
perhaps, *adv.* talvez, porventura, por acaso.
periapt, *s.* amuleto, talismã.
pericardium, *s.* pericárdio.
pericarp, *s.* pericarpo.
pericranium, *s.* pericrânio; (joc.) crânio, cérebro, inteligência.
perigee, *s.* perigeu.
peril, *s.* perigo, risco. *v.t.* arriscar, pôr em perigo.
perilous, *adj.* perigoso, arriscado, aventuroso.
perilousness, *s.* perigo, risco, situação perigosa.
perimeter, *s.* perímetro, circunferência.
perimorph, *s.* cristal que encerra outro de espécie diferente.
perineum, *adj.* períneo, perineu.
period, *s.* período, ciclo; revolução; duração; fase, estádio; época, era, idade; *pl.* regras, menstruação; ponto, ponto final; *to put a period to,* pôr fim, pôr termo. *adj.* relativo a período ou época passada.
periodic, *adj.* periódico; intermitente; relativo a período gramatical.

periodical, *adj.* periódico; intermitente. *s.* publicação periódica.
periodicity, *s.* periodicidade; *(electr.)* frequência; posição na tabela periódica.
peripheral, *adj.* periférico; externo.
periphery, *s.* periferia; contorno; superfície externa.
periphrase, periphrasis, *s.* perífrase; circunlóquio.
periphrastic, *adj.* perifrástico.
perique, *s.* variedade de tabaco escuro.
periscope, *s.* periscópio.
perish, *v.i.* perecer, sucumbir, morrer, extinguir-se; *v.t.* corroer, deteriorar, estragar (o tempo).
perishable, *adj.* perecível, deteriorável.
perissodactyl, perissodactyle, *s.* e *adj.* perissodáctilo.
perissodactylous, *adj.* perissodáctilo.
peristome, *s.* perístomo.
peritoneum, peritonaeum, *s.* peritoneu.
peritonitis, *s.* peritonite.
periwig, *s.* cabeleira, peruca, capachinho.
perjure, *v.r.* perjurar; prestar falso depoimento.
perjured, *adj.* perjuro; culpado de falso testemunho.
perjurer, *s.* perjuro, pessoa culpada de falso testemunho.
perjury, *s.* perjúrio, falso juramento, falso testemunho em juízo.
perk, *v.i.* erguer a cabeça; empertigar-se, entesar-se; animar-se; pavonear-se; *v.t.* enfeitar; erguer, empertigar.
perkiness, *s.* presunção, arrogância, vaidade; vivacidade, atrevimento.
perky, *adj.* empertigado, presunçoso; atrevido; vivo, esperto.
perm, *s.* permanente, ondulação permanente.
permanence, *s.* permanência, estabilidade.
permanency, *s.* permanência; colocação ou emprego permanente.
permanent, *adj.* permanente, estável; fixo, inalterável, duradouro; *permanent wave,* ondulação permanente.
permanganate, *s.* permanganato.
permeability, *s.* permeabilidade.
permeable, *adj.* permeável; poroso.
permeate, *v.t.* permear, penetrar, repassar, impregnar, saturar. *v.i.* difundir-se.
permeation, *s.* penetração, impregnação.

permillage, s. permilagem (proporção relativamente a mil).

permissible, adj. permissível, lícito, admissível.

permit, v.t. permitir, autorizar, consentir em, admitir. s. permissão, licença, autorização escrita; alvará de licença.

permutable, adj. permutável.

permutation, s. permutação; transmutação.

permute, v.t. permutar; transpor.

pernicious, adj. pernicioso; ruim; fatal.

pernickety, adj. meticuloso; exigente; impertinente; delicado, melindroso.

perorate, v.i. perorar; rematar um discurso; arengar.

peroration, s. peroração, remate de discurso.

peroxide, s. peróxido; água oxigenada. v.t. oxigenar os cabelos.

perpend, s. perpianho, pedra de construção aparelhada que abrange toda a largura de uma parede. v.t. e v.i. ponderar, considerar.

perpendicular, adj. perpendicular; vertical; aprumado, teso; íngreme, alcantilado.

perpendicularity, s. perpendicularidade.

perpetrate, v.t. perpetrar, cometer, praticar acto condenável.

perpetration, s. perpetração; crime, acto condenável.

perpetual, adj. perpétuo, eterno; permanente; vitalício; contínuo, constante; que floresce todo o ano; s. planta perene.

perpetuance, s. perpetuação, perpetuidade.

perpetuate, v.t. perpetuar, eternizar, imortalizar.

perpetuation, s. perpetuação; acto de imortalizar.

perpetuity, s. perpetuidade; eternidade; coisa perpétua; posse perpétua; anuidade perpétua.

perplex, v.t. confundir, desconcertar, desorientar, aturdir, perturbar; complicar; enredar, embrulhar.

perplexed, adj. perplexo, confundido, desorientado, confuso.

perplexing, adj. desconcertante, desorientador.

perplexity, s. perplexidade, desorientação; complexidade.

perquisite, s. emolumento; lucro eventual; gorjeta ou gratificação habitual; remuneração; rendimento.

perron, escada exterior, escadaria.

perry, vinho de pêra.

persecute, v.t. perseguir; importunar, atormentar.

persecution, s. perseguição.

persecutor, s. perseguidor; opressor.

perseverance, s. perseverança, persistência, pertinácia.

persevere, v.i. perseverar, persistir, insistir.

persevering, adj. perseverante, persistente, pertinaz.

Persian, s. persa. adj. persa, pérsico, persiano; *persian blinds,* persianas.

persiennes, s. persianas.

persiflage, s. galhofa, chacota, troça.

persimm on, s. caqui (fruta); caquizeiro.

persist, v.i. persistir, perseverar, teimar, obstinar-se; insistir; permanecer, perdurar.

persistence, persistency, s. persistência, perseverança; perduração; teimosia, obstinação.

persistent, adj. persistente, perseverante, tenaz, pertinaz, obstinado; duradouro, permanente; contínuo, constante.

person, s. pessoa, indivíduo; individualidade; personalidade; ser humano; aparência, presença, figura.

personable, adj. bem-parecido, bem-apessoado, elegante.

personage, s. personagem; pessoa importante; pessoa.

personal, adj. pessoal, individual, particular, próprio; físico, corporal; 1) *personal effects,* objectos de uso pessoal; 2) *personal estate,* bens móveis. s. breve notícia ou anúncio de carácter pessoal.

personality, s. personalidade; individualidade; pessoa; alusão pessoal.

personalization, s. personalização, personificação.

personalize, v.t. personalizar; personificar.

personally, adv. pessoalmente, em pessoa, como pessoa.

personalty, s. pl. bens móveis.

personate, s. (bot.) personado.

personate, v.t. representar, fazer o papel de; fazer-se passar por outro; personificar, encarnar.

personification, s. personificação; encarnação.

personify, v.t. personificar, personalizar; encarnar; ser o tipo de.

personnel, s. pessoal, corpo de empregados; personnel officer, (mil.) ajudante.

perspective, s. perspectiva; vista, panorama. adj. perspectivo, relativo a perspectiva.

perspectively, adv. em perspectiva.

perspicacious, adj. perspicaz, sagaz.

perspicacity, s. perspicácia, sagacidade.

perspicuity, s. perspicuidade, clareza.

perspicuous, adj. perspícuo, claro, compreensível, evidente.

perspiration, s. transpiração, sudação; perspiração; suor.

perspiratory, adj. transpiratório; sudorífico; sudoríparo.

perspire, v.t. e v.i. transpirar, suar, perspirar; transudar.

persuadable, adj. persuadível. v.t. persuadir, convencer, fazer crer; induzir, aconselhar.

persuade, v.t. persuadir, convencer, fazer crer; induzir, aconselhar.

persuader, s. persuasor; pl. (gír.) esporas.

persuasible, adj. persuadível, persuasível.

persuasion, s. persuasão; poder de persuadir; convicção, opinião, crença, credo; seita, partido; (joc.) raça, género, nacionalidade, sexo; 1) a man of portuguese persuasion, um homem de nacionalidade portuguesa; 2) the male persuasion, o sexo masculino.

persuasive, adj. persuasivo, convincente. s. incentivo. adj. ousado, atrevido, petulante, insolente.

pertain, v.i. pertencer, tocar, dizer respeito, referir-se (com to).

pertinacious, adj. pertinaz, obstinado, tenaz, persistente.

pertinacity, s. pertinácia, obstinação, persistência.

pertinence, pertinency, s. pertinência, conveniência, interesse.

pertinent, adj. pertinente, apropriado; referente, relativo.

pertness, s. atrevimento, ousadia, insolência; vivacidade.

perturb, v.t. perturbar, transtornar, confundir; inquietar, incomodar.

perturbation, s. perturbação, desordem, confusão; inquietação, comoção.

pertussis, s. coqueluche.

peruke, s. peruca.

perusal, s. leitura atenta.

peruse, v.t. ler cuidadosa ou atentamente; estudar, examinar, escrutar.

peruvian, adj. peruviano, peruano.

pervade, v.t. difundir-se em, impregnar, saturar, penetrar, repassar.

pervasion, s. difusão, penetração, infiltração.

pervasive, adj. penetrante, difundido, difuso.

perverse, adj. que insiste no erro; perverso; corrupto; ruim, mau; caprichoso; voluntarioso; impertinente, birrento.

perversion, s. perversão; erro, desvio; corrupção.

perversity, s. perversidade, maldade, malvadez; obstinação; corrupção.

pervert, v.t. perverter; deturpar, desvirtuar, falsear, viciar; transtornar, corromper.

perverted, adj. pervertido; deturpado; perverso; depravado.

pervicacious, adj. pertinaz, contumaz, obstinado.

pervious, adj. pérvio; viável; acessível; penetrável; permeável; poroso.

perviousness, s. característica daquilo que é pérvio, que pode atravessar-se; permeabilidade; sensibilidade a.

pesky, adj. incómodo, desagradável, aborrecido, detestável.

pessimism, s. pessimismo.

pessimist, s. pessimista.

pessimistic, adj. pessimista.

pest, s. peste, praga (coisa, pessoa, ou animal incómodo ou nocivo); insecto nocivo; peste (epidemia).

pester, v.t. incomodar, aborrecer, importunar, apoquentar, atormentar.

pesterer, s. maçador, importuno.

pesthole, s. lugar empestado, foco de infecção.

pesthouse, s. hospital para doenças infecciosas.

pesticide, s. pesticida.

pestiferous, adj. pestífero, pernicioso, pestilento.

pestilence, s. pestilência, peste.

pestilent, adj. pestilento; pernicioso; incómodo, maçador, detestável.

pestle, s. pilão. v.t. e v.i. pilar, pisar no almofariz, moer, triturar.

pet, s. animal de estimação; querido, favorito; amuo, enfado; adj. favorito, mimado; *pet name,* nome carinhoso. *v.t.* acariciar, acarinhar, mimar.

petal, *s.* pétala.

petard, *s.* petardo.

petasos, petasus, *s.* pétaso; chapéu usado pelos gregos antigos; chapéu alado do deus Mercúrio.

peteman, *s.* (gír.) arrombador de cofres.

peter, *v.i. to peter out,* esgotar-se, acabar-se, secar; fracassar.

petiole, *s.* pecíolo.

petiolule, *s.* peciólulo.

petition, *s.* petição; requerimento; abaixo-assinado; pedido, súplica. solicitação. *v.t.* e *v.i.* rogar, pedir, solicitar, requerer; peticionar.

petitioner, *s.* peticionário; requerente.

petrel, *s.* petrel (ave).

petrification, *s.* petrificação.

petrify, *v.t.* e *v.i.* petrificar; empedernir; incrustar; imobilizar, paralisar.

petrine, *adj.* relativo ao apóstolo Pedro.

petroglyph, *s.* petróglifo.

petrol, *s.* gasolina. *v.r.* abastecer de gasolina.

petroleum, *s.* petróleo.

petrology, *s.* petrologia.

petronel, *s.* petrinal (arma de fogo dos sécs. XV e XVI).

petrous, *adj.* pétreo, rochoso.

petticoat, *s.* saia interior, saiote; *pl.* sexo feminino.

pettifog, *s. v.i.* chicanar.

pettifoger, *s.* chicaneiro, trapaceiro; advogado inferior; charlatão; rábula.

pettiness, *s.* insignificância, ninharia, mesquinhice.

pettish, *adj.* rabugento, birrento, implicativo, impertinente.

petishness, *s.* rabugice, impertinência.

pettitoes, *s. pl.* pés de porco; dedos dos pés (esp. de criança).

petty, *adj.* pequeno, insignificante, trivial, fútil; secundário, inferior; mesquinho; 1) *petty cash,* fundo para pequenos gastos; 2) *petty officer,* (náut.) oficial inferior.

petulance, *s.* rabugice, impaciência, mau humor, irritabilidade; petulância, insolência.

petulant, *adj.* rabugento, mal-humorado, irritadiço, impertinente; caprichoso; petulante, insolente.

petunia, *s.* petúnia.

petuntse, *s.* petunsé, terra branca usada no fabrico de porcelana na China.

pew, *s.* banco de igreja, lugar em igreja reservado para determinada família.

pewee, *s.* pequeno pássaro norte-americano.

pewit, *s.* (zool.) pavoncino, abibe.

pewter, *s.* peltre, liga de estanho e chumbo; vasilha de estanho; (cal.) prémio em dinheiro.

pewterer, *s.* fabricante de utensílios de estanho.

phaeton, *s.* faetonte; carruagem leve de quatro rodas.

phagocyte, *s.* fagócito.

phalange, phalanx, falange; linha de batalha; comuna socialista de cerca de 1800 pessoas no sistema de Fourier; grupo de pessoas unidas para qualquer fim.

phallic, *adj.* fálico.

phallicism, *s.* falicismo.

phallus, *s.* falo; pénis.

phantasm, *s.* fantasma, espectro, aparição; ilusão, ficção, fantasia; sombra, simulacro.

phantasma, *s. pl.* - *mata.* fantasia, visão, ilusão, sonho; fantasma, espectro, visão.

phantasmagoria, *s.* fantasmagoria.

phantasmagoric, *adj.* fantasmagórico.

phantasmal, phantasmic, *adj.* fantasmal, fantástico, ilusório, irreal; espectral.

phantasy, *s.* fantasia, imaginação; imagem mental; capricho.

phantom, *s.* fantasma, espectro; ilusão, aparição; sombra; *adj.* aparente, irreal, ilusório.

pharaoh, *s.* faraó.

pharaonic, *adj.* faraónico.

pharisaical, pharisaic, *adj.* farisaico; hipócrita.

pharmaceutical, pharmaceutic, *adj.* farmacêutico.

pharmaceutics, *s.* farmácia (arte farmacêutica).

pharmaceutist, *s.* farmacêutico, boticário.

pharmacology, *s.* farmacologia.

pharmacopoeia, *s.* farmacopeia.

pharmacy, *s.* farmácia; botica.

pharos, *s.* farol.

pharyngitis, *s.* faringite.

pharynx, *s.* faringe.

phase, *s.* fase, estádio; (electr.) fase; 1) *out of phase,* desfasado; 2) *two, three* *phase,* bifásica, trifásica; 3) *phase shift,* desfasagem.

phasis, *s. pl. phases.* fase *(também* astron.), aspecto.

pheasant, *s.* faisão.

phenazine, *s.* fenazina.

phenix, *s.* o mesmo que *phoenix.*

phenol, *s.* fenol, ácido fénico.

phenology, *s.* fenologia.

phenomena, *pl.* de *phenomenon.*

phenomenal, *adj.* fenomenal; extra-ordinário, prodigioso, insólito.

phenomenilism, phenomenism, *s.* fenomenismo.

phenomenology, *s.* fenomenologia.

phenomenon, *s. pl.* - mena. fenómeno; prodígio.

phenotype, *s.* fenótipo.

phi, *s. fi* (vigésima primeira letra do alfabeto grego.)

phial, *s.* frasco, garrafinha.

philander, *v.i.* namorar, namoriscar; galantear.

philanthropic, philanthropical, *adj.* filantropo, filantrópico, humanitário, altruísta.

philanthropist, *s.* filantropo.

philanthropy, *s.* filantropia, altruísmo, humanitarismo.

philatelist, *s.* filatelista.

philately, *s.* filatelia.

philarmonic, *adj.* filarmónico.

Philippians, *s.* Epístola de S. Paulo aos Filipenses.

philippic, *s.* filípica, discurso violento e injurioso, invectiva.

Philippine, *adj.* filipino, das ilhas Filipinas.

Philistine, *s.* filisteu. *adj.* filisteu: inculto, ignorante, prosaico.

philologer, philologian, philologist, *s.* filólogo; linguista.

philology, *s.* filologia; linguística.

philomel, *s.* filomela, nome poético do rouxinol.

philopena, *s.* filipina, jogo com uma amêndoa de dois caroços que obriga o recebimento ou pagamento de uma prenda.

philoprogenitiveness, *s.* filogenitura, amor à prole.

philosopher, *s.* filósofo.

philosophical, philosophic, *adj.* filosófico; racional; filósofo; sereno, judicioso.

philosophism, *s.* filosofismo, falsa filosofia; sofisma.

philosophize, *v.t.* e *v.i.* filosofar, fazer de filósofo.

philosophy, *s.* filosofia; serenidade, paciência.

philter, philtre, *s.* filtro, poção mágica.

phiz, *s.* cara, rosto, expressão.

phlebitis, *s.* flebite.

phlebotomy, *s.* flebotomia, sangria.

phlegm, *s.* fleuma, flegma; serenidade, impassibilidade; mucosidade, catarro, expectoração.

phlegmatic, *adj.* fleumático, calmo.

phlegmy, *adj.* mucoso, catarroso; fleumático.

phlogosis, *s.* flogose; inflamação; erisipela.

phobia, *s.* fobia.

Phoenician, *adj.* e *s.* fenício.

phoenix, phenix, *s.* (mit.) Fénix; modelo de excelência.

phonate, *v.i.* emitir a voz, produzir sons vocais.

phonation, *s.* fonação.

phone, *s.* fonema, som articulado; (fam.) telefone. *v.t.* e *v.i.* telefonar.

phoneme, *s.* fonema.

phonetic, *adj.* fonético.

phonetician, *s.* foneticista, fonetista.

phonetics, *s.* fonética.

phonic, *adj.* fónico, vocal; fonético; acústico, sonoro.

phonics, *s.* acústica; fonética.

phonogram, *s.* sinal que representa um som vocal; sinal taquigráfico; disco fonográfico.

phonograph, *s.* fonógrafo. *v.t.* gravar ou reproduzir sons fonograficamente.

phonographer, *s.* taquígrafo, estenógrafo.

phonography, *s.* fonografia, gravação fonográfica, uso do fonógrafo; estenografia.

phonology, *s.* fonologia.

phonometer, *s.* fonómetro.

phonometry, *s.* fonometria.

phonotypy, *s.* fonotipia, impressão com caracteres fonéticos.

phony, *adj.* falso, falsificado, suposto, duvidoso. *s.* falsificação, imitação; disfarce; nome falso; mentira; impostor.

phosphate, *s.* fosfato.

phosphite, *s.* fosfito.

phosphor, *s.* fósforo.

phosphoresce, *v.i.* fosforecer.

phosphorescence, *s.* fosforescência.

phosphorescent, *adj.* fosforescente.

phosphorism, *s.* fosforismo.

phosphorous, *adj.* fosforoso.

phosphorus, *s.* fósforo.

photo, *s.* foto, fotografia; *foto finish,* final de corrida decidido por foto. *v.t.* fotografar.

photochemistry, *s.* fotoquímica.

photochromy, *s.* fotocromia, fotografia a cores.

photoconductivity, *s.* fotocondutividade.

photodynamics, *s.* fotodinâmica.

photoelectric, *adj.* fotoeléctrico; *photoelectric cell,* célula fotoeléctrica.

photoemission, *s.* fotoemissão.

photoengraving, *s.* fotogravura.

photofilm, *s.* filme fotográfico.

photogenic, *adj.* fotogénico.

photograph, *s.* fotografia. *v.t.* e *v.i.* fotografar.

photographer, *s.* fotógrafo.

photographic, *adj.* fotográfico.

photography, *s.* fotografia (arte ou processo).

photogravure, *s.* fotogravura.

photolitho, photolithograph, *s.* fotolito.

photolithoprint, *s.* fotolitografia (processo).

photometry, *s.* fotometria.

photomicrography, *s.* fotomicrografia.

photomontage, *s.* fotomontagem, montagem fotográfica.

photon, *s.* fotão.

photophily, *s.* fotofilia.

photoplay, *s.* drama cinematográfico, filme.

photoprint, *s.* fotogravura.

photosensitive, *adj.* fotossensível.

photosphere, *s.* fotosfera.

photosynthesis, *s.* fotossíntese, função clorofilina.

phototelegraphy, *s.* fototelegrafia.

phototelescope, *s.* fototelescópio.

phototherapeutics, fototerapia.

phototopography, *s.* fototopografia.

phototropism, *s.* fototropismo.

phototube, *s.* célula fotoeléctrica.

phototypy, *s.* fototipia.

photozincography, *s.* fotozincografia.

phrase, *s.* expressão, frase; frase de sentido incompleto. *v.t.* expressar, exprimir; chamar, intitular; (mús.) dividir em frases.

phraseogram, *s.* sinal taquigráfico que representa uma frase ou locução.

phraseograph, *s.* frase ou locução representada por um único símbolo taquigráfico.

phraseological, *adj.* fraseológico, elocutório.

phraseology, *s.* fraseologia, linguagem, elocução, estilo.

phrasing, *s.* fraseado (também musical), fraseologia, estilo.

phrenetic, *adj.* frenético, exaltado, furioso.

phrenitis, *s.* delírio agudo; encefalite.

Phrygian, *adj.* e *s.* frígio.

phthisis, *s.* tísica, tuberculose pulmonar.

phut, *interj.* imitação do zunido de uma bala; na expressão *to go phut,* esvaziar--se, murchar, esmorecer, fracassar.

phylactery, *s.* filactério; ostentação da religiosidade, farisaísmo; amuleto, talismã.

phyletic, *adj.* filético, racial.

phylloid, *adj.* semelhante a folha, foliáceo, foliforme.

phyllome, *s.* (bot.) filoma, órgão foliáceo.

phylloxera, *s.* filoxera.

phylogeny, *s.* filogenia.

phylon, *s. pl. phyla.* Raça, tribo.

physic, *s.* medicina, ciência médica; arte de curar; remédio, medicamento; *v.t.* administrar um remédio a.

physical, *adj.* físico; (med.) somático.

physician, *s.* médico.

physicist, *s.* físico, pessoa versada em físico; naturalista; fisicista.

physics, *s.* física.

physiocrat, *s.* fisiocrata.

physiognomic, physiognomical, *adj.* fisionómico; característico.

physiognomist, *s.* fisionomista.

physiognomy, *s.* fisionomia, traços, feições, rosto, semblante; aspecto exterior; configuração.

physiography, *s.* fisiografia.

physiological, physiologic, *adj.* fisiológico.

physiologist, *s.* fisiólogo, fisiologista.

physiology, *s.* fisiologia.

physioterapy, *s.* fisioterapia.

physique, *s.* físico, compleição, corpo.

physostomous, *adj.* fisóstomo.

phytogenesis, phytogeny, *s.* fitogenia.

phytogenic, phytogenous, *adj.* fitogénio, de origem vegetal.

phytography, *s.* fitografia, botânica descritiva.

phytophagous, *adj.* fitófago, herbívoro.

pi, *s.* pi (letra grega e símbolo matemático).

piacular, *adj.* expiatório.

piaffer, *s.* piafé (movimento feito pelo cavalo ao bater com as patas no chão, sem andar.).

pianist, *s.* pianista.

piano, *s.* piano. *adv.* piano, suavemente.

piassava, piassaba, *s.* piaçava.

piaster, *s.* piastra.

piazza, *s.* praça; galeria coberta; varanda.

pica, *s.* tipo de corpo 12.

picaresque, *adj.* picaresco.

picaroon, *s.* tratante, velhaco; ladrão, pirata, corsário.

picayune, *s.* moeda de pouco valor; ninharia.

piccolo, *s.* flautim.

piceous, *adj.* píceo, relativo ao pez; cor de pez.

pick, *s.* picareta, picão; punção, furador; palito; movimento da lançadeira, fio de tecido; a parte melhor, escol; 1) *ice pick,* picador de gelo. *v.t.* picar, espicaçar; abrir buraco picando; palitar (os dentes); depenar aves; roer, descarnar; colher, apanhar (flores, etc.); apanhar com o bico, debicar; comer; escolher, seleccionar; 2) *to pick a bone,* roer um osso; 3) *to pick a hole in someone's reputation,* manchar a reputação de alguém; 4) *to pick a pocket,* roubar a carteira do bolso de alguém; 5) *to pick a quarrel,* provocar discussão; 6) *to pick off,* arrancar, abater os inimigos um por um; 7) *to pick out,* escolher, separar; distinguir com a vista ou com o ouvido; perceber, decifrar; colher informação; apanhar de ouvido (música); 8) *to pick up,* levantar, apanhar; receber passageiros; pegar (o motor); recobrar a saúde.

pickaback, *adv.* aos ombros, às costas; *to ride pickaback,* ser levado às costas, por alguém.

pickaninny, *s.* criança de cor; negrinho.

pickax, pickaxe, *s.* picareta, picão. *v.t.* e *v.i.* trabalhar a terra com picareta.

picked, *adj.* colhido; depenado; limpo; escolhido, seleccionado, selecto.

picker, *s.* pessoa que apanha, colhe, etc.; máquina debastadora de fibras; pessoa que trabalha com essa máquina;

descascadora, separadora; picareta, picão; ladrão, carteirista, gatuno; *pickers and stealers,* gatunos, larápios.

pickerel, *s.* lúcio (peixe).

picket, *s.* estaca; piqueta; pau de cerca; (mil.) piquete; grevista de piquete. *v.t.* segurar com estacas; pôr homens de piquete.

picking, *s.* colheita; pl. restos, sobras; lucros, proveitos.

pickle, *s.* salmoura para conservar carne, legumes, etc.; alimento conservado em salmoura ou vinagre; pl. condimentos vegetais conservados em vinagre, picles; banho de ácido para decapagem de metais; situação difícil, apuros; criança travessa. *v.t.* conservar em salmoura ou vinagre.

pickled, *adj.* (gír.) embriagado.

picklock, *s.* gazua, chave falsa; ladrão que usa uma gazua para entrar nas casas.

pickpocket, *s.* carteirista.

picksome, *adj.* impertinente.

pickup, *s.* captador sonoro, captador de som em gira-discos; captador de imagem em transmissor de televisão; carrinha para entregas rápidas; negócio de ocasião; pechincha; (desp.) escolha de campo; acto de apanhar a bola (no críquete); conhecimento de ocasião; aceleração (motor); *pickup circuit,* circuito de magnetização.

picnic, *s.* piquenique.

picot, *s.* picote.

Pict, *s.* picto, antigo habitante da Escócia.

pictogram, *s.* pictograma.

pictograph, *s.* pictorama; ideograma; inscrição ideográfica.

pictorial, *adj.* pictórico, pictural; pitoresco.

picture, *s.* pintura, quadro, tela; desenho; fotografia; gravura, figura, ilustração, estampa; retrato; imagem; filme cinematográfico; 1) *out of the picture,* fora de cogitação; 2) *picture house,* cinema; 3) *picture writing,* pictografia, ideografia; 4) *moving pictures,* cinema. *v.t.* pintar, desenhar, retratar; descrever; imaginar.

picturesque, *adj.* e *s.* pitoresco.

piddle, *v.i.* brincar; (fam.) urinar.

piddling, *adj.* insignificante, trivial.

pidgin, pigeon, *adj.* na expressão *pidgin English,* inglês adulterado usado como língua franca na China. *s.* ocupação, tarefa, interesse; *this is not my pidgin,* isto não é comigo.

pie, *s.* pastel, empada, *tarte;* pega (ave); confusão, embrulhada; *v.t.* baralhar.

piebald, *adj.* malhado de preto e branco; multicolor, sarapintado, pintalgado.

piece, *s.* peça, pedaço, fragmento, parte, porção, bocado; peça de fazenda; arma de fogo, peça de artilharia; moeda; barril de vinho; peça, pedra (de xadrez, damas, etc.); trabalho literário, trecho; peça teatral; composição musical; 1) *of a piece with,* de acordo com. 2) *to give someone a piece of one's mind,* dar uma opinião, dar uma repreensão. 3) *to go to pieces,* desfazer-se, desmoronar-se, sofrer colapso nervoso; *adj.* feito de várias peças, relativo a trabalho por peça; *v.t.* consertar, emendar, reparar, reconstruir. 4) *to piece on to,* ajustar a, encaixar em.

piecemeal, *adv.* aos pedaços, pouco a pouco, gradualmente; em pedaços; *adj.* feito gradualmente; fragmentário.

piecework, *s.* trabalho por peça, trabalho por tarefa.

piecrust, *s.* massa ou crosta de pastel ou empada.

pied, *adj.* sarapintado, pintalgado, malhado.

Piedmont, *s.* Piemonte; *adj.* situado no sopé de uma montanha.

Piedmontese, *adj.* e *s.* piemontês.

pieplant, *s.* ruibarbo das hortas.

pier, *s.* pegão de ponte; pilar, pilastra; molhe, quebra-mar, pontão; cais flutuante; pano de parede entre duas janelas; *pier table,* tremó, aparador que cobre o espaço entre duas paredes.

pierage, *s.* direitos de atracação.

pierce, *v.t.* furar, trespassar, apunhalar, perfurar; atravessar, penetrar; ferir (o ouvido). *v.i.* penetrar, abrir caminho, embrenhar-se.

piercing, *adj.* perfurante, penetrante, agudo.

piet, *s.* pega (ave).

pietism, *s.* pietismo; devoção; beatice, carolice.

pietist, *s.* pietista; devoto, beato, carola.

piety, *s.* piedade, religiosidade, devoção; fidelidade, lealdade, respeito, acto piedoso.

piezoelectricity, *s.* piezelectricidade.

piffle, *s.* baboseira, conversa fiada, tolice,

disparate. *v.i.* dizer disparates; ocupar-se de futilidades.

pig, *s.* porco, leitão; avarento, ganancioso; glutão; casmurro, cabeçudo; lingote de metal, gusa. 1) *pig iron,* ferro-gusa. 2) *wild pig,* javali. 3) *to buy a pig in a poke,* comprar nabos em saco.

pigboat, *s.* (gír.) submarino.

pigeon, *s.* pombo; simplório, trouxa. 1) *pigeon breast,* tórax quereniforme, deformidade causada pela proeminência do esterno. 2) *pigeon livered,* brando, pacífico. 3) *pigeon toed,* com as pontas dos pés voltadas para dentro.

pigeoneer, *s.* columbófilo.

pigeonhearted, *adj.* covarde.

pigeonhole, *s.* buraco de pombal; pequeno compartimento de móvel para papéis, etc. *v.t.* guardar em compartimento; pôr de lado, arquivar; ordenar.

pigeonry, *s.* pombal.

piggery, *s.* estabelecimento de criação de porcos; chiqueiro, pocilga; sordidez, avareza, egoísmo.

piggish, *adj.* porco, imundo, sórdido; avarento, mesquinho; teimoso; glutão; grosseiro.

pigheaded, *adj.* teimoso, obstinado, cabeçudo, estúpido.

pigment, *s.* pigmento.

pigmentary, *adj.* pigmentário.

pigmentation, *s.* pigmentação.

pignut, *s.* castanha-da-terra.

pigpen, *s.* pocilga, chiqueiro, curral de porcos.

pigskin, *s.* pele ou couro de porco; (gír.) sela de jóquei; (fam.) bola de futebol.

pigstick, *v.i.* caçar javali com chuço.

pigsty, *s.* pocilga, chiqueiro.

pigtail, *s.* rabicho, trança; tabaco em rolo.

pika, *s.* (zool.) pica.

pike, *s.* pique (lança antiga); pico de monte; cavilha, picareta; (zool.) lúcio; barreira onde se paga portagem. *v.t.* ferir com pique.

piker, *s.* sovina; tratante, caloteiro.

pilaster, *s.* pilastra.

pile, *s.* estaca; apoio de ponte; viga; monte de coisas, pilha, rima; pira (para a cremação de cadáveres); grande edifício, conjunto de grandes edifícios; pilha seca; pilha atómica; reverso de moeda; penugem, lanugem, pêlo macio; hemorróida. *v.t.* e *v.i.* prover de estacas; cravar estacas; amontoar; fazer uma rima de; empilhar; apinhar-se, acumular-se. 1) *to pile arms,* ensarilhar armas. 2) *to pile it on,* exagerar, dramatizar.

pileate, pileated, *adj.* cristado (ave).

piled, *adj.* felpudo.

pilfer, *v.t.* e *v.i.* furtar, roubar, surripiar.

pilferage, *s.* ratonice, furto insignificante.

pilferer, *s.* larápio, ratoneiro.

pilgarlic, *s.* careca; pobre-diabo.

pilgrim, *s.* peregrino, romeiro, viajante; *Pilgrim Fathers,* os puritanos ingleses emigrados que se estabeleceram na Nova Inglaterra em 1620.

pilgrimage, *s.* peregrinação, romagem.

piling, *s.* estacaria.

pill, *s.* pílula; (gír.) pessoa enfadonha. *v.t.* medicar com pílulas; (gír.) votar contra, rejeitar.

pillage, *s.* pilhagem, saque; *v.t.* e *v.i.* saquear, pilhar.

pillar, *s.* pilar, coluna, suporte. 1) *pillar box, pillar post,* marco de correio. 2) *from pillar to post,* de um lado para outro, de Herodes para Pilatos; *v.t.* sustentar ou reforçar com pilares.

pillbox, *s.* caixa para pílulas.

pillion, *s.* selim de mulher; assento traseiro de motociclo.

pillory, *s.* pelourinho. *v.t.* expor no pelourinho; expor ao sarcasmo público.

pillow, *s.* almofada, travesseiro; (mec.) chumaceira, mancal; *v.t.* descansar a cabeça em travesseiro.

pillowcase, *s.* fronha.

pilose, *adj.* piloso, peludo.

pilosity, *s.* pilosidade.

pilot, *s.* piloto; timoneiro; guia. 1) *pilot balloon,* balão sonda. 2) *pilot officer,* segundo-tenente aviador. 3) *to drop the pilot,* abandonar alguém que nos aconselha. *v.t.* pilotar, guiar, dirigir.

pilotage, *s.* pilotagem.

pilous, *adj.* piloso, peludo.

pilule, *s.* pílula pequena.

pimento, pimiento, *s.* pimentão doce.

pimola, *s.* azeitona recheada com pimentão doce.

pimp, *s.* alcoviteiro; proxeneta.

pimpernel, *s.* morrião; *scarlet pimpernel,* morrião escarlate.

pimple, *s.* espinha, borbulha.

pin, *s.* alfinete; broche; ninharia, insignificância; pino, cavilha, perno; cravelha (de

instrumento musical de cordas); estaca; bandeirinha indicadora de buraco no golfe; pequeno barril de 16 litros; *pin wheel,* cata-vento de papel; *v.t.* prender com alfinete; cravar, pregar, fixar; segurar, prender; encurralar; sujeitar.

pinafore, *s.* bibe.

pinaster, *s.* pinheiro-bravo.

pince-nez, *s.* luneta.

pincers, *s.* torquês, tenaz, pinça, alicate.

pinch, *v.t.* beliscar; apertar; prender com tenaz; afligir, atormentar, angustiar, oprimir; murchar, estiolar; extorquir; (gír.) furtar, roubar; (gír.) prender, deter; (náut.) cingir ao vento; *v.i.* apertar; economizar; diminuir, estreitar-se (o veio de minério). *s.* beliscão, beliscadura, aperto; momento crítico, apuro, situação de emergência; pressão, opressão, aflição; pitada; (gír.) furto, roubo; (gír.) prisão, detenção; visita inesperada da polícia, rusga.

pinchbeck, *s.* pechisbeque; imitação, jóia falsa. *adj.* feito de pechisbeque, falso; barato, vulgar.

pinched, *adj.* apertado, comprimido; contraído; encurralado.

pincushion, *s.* alfineteira, pregadeira de alfinetes.

pindling, *adj.* pequeno, franzino, frágil.

pine, *s.* pinheiro; pinho. 1) *pine groove, pinhal. 2) *pine nut,* pinha; *v.i.* definhar, consumir-se, enfraquecer, estiolar-se; decair; ansiar, anelar.

pineapple, *s.* ananás, abacaxi; (gír.) granada de mão.

pinery, *s.* plantação de abacaxis, ananasal.

pinfeather, *s.* pena nova.

pinfold, *s.* curral para gado extraviado. *v.t.* recolher gado.

ping, *s.* zunido, silvo; *v.i.* zunir, silvar, sibilar.

ping-pong, *s.* pingue-pongue, ténis de mesa.

pinguid, *adj.* oleoso, gorduroso.

pinhead, *s.* cabeça de alfinete; coisa insignificante; pessoa estúpida.

pinhole, *s.* furo; pontinho; buraco de cavilha.

pinion, *s.* pena de asa, rémige; (poét.) asa. *v.t.* cortar a ponta da asa a; amarrar os braços a, manietar, algemar; amarrar, prender.

pink, s. craveiro, cravo, cravina; cor-de-
-rosa; casaco vermelho de caçador de
raposas; caçador de raposas; perfeição,
apogeu, modelo; (zool.) leuciscus; simpatizante do comunismo; pigmento amarelado; embarcação de popa estreita; *adj.*
vermelho-pálido, rosado. *v.t.* ferir com
arma branca, apunhalar, trespassar;
picotar, pontilhar; recortar festões (em
pano); enfeitar.

pinkeye, s. conjuntivite aguda contagiosa.

pinnacle, s. pináculo; pico elevado; auge,
culminância; *v.t.* prover de pináculo;
servir de pináculo a; elevar.

pinnula, s. o mesmo que *pinnule.*

pinnule, s. pínula.

pinochle, pinocle, s. jogo de cartas.

pinpoint, *v.t.* localizar, apontar, determinar
com precisão.

pint, s. pinto, medida de capacidade para
líquidos igual a 56,825 centilitros, quartilho.

pintail, s. espécie de pato fluvial, arrabio.

pintle, s. cavilha; pino, espigão, engate de
canhão.

pinworm, s. oxiúro.

piny, *adj.* relativo relativo ou semelhante ao
pinheiro.

pioneer, s. pioneiro, desbravador, colonizador; precursor (mil.) sapador. *v.t.* e *v.i.*
desbravar, preparar caminho; explorar,
descobrir; guiar, conduzir.

pious, *adj.* pio, devoto, piedoso, religioso;
pious fraud, fraude piedosa.

pip, s. pevide, semente de maçã, pêra, laranja, etc.; doença das galinhas; gosma; pinta
(das cartas de jogar); estrela em uniforme
de oficial; (cal.) depressão nervosa, má
disposição, ira, cólera. *v.i.* piar, pipilar; (gír.)
morrer *v.t.* saír da casca (o pinto).

pipage, s. transporte em tubagem; tubagem,
canalização, encanamento.

pipe, s. tubo, cano; canto, pio; flauta; gaita de
foles; cachimbo, cachimbada; pl. vias
respiratórias; pipa; apito de bordo. 1) *pipe
clay,* argila plástica branca. 2) *pipe dream,*
sonho de ópio, esperança ilusória. *v.i.* tocar
flauta, gaita de foles, etc.; assobiar; silvar;
cantar (ave); falar com voz estridente. 3) *to
pipe down,* calar-se, silenciar; *v.t.* tocar
flauta ou gaita de foles; atrair ou conduzir
tocando flauta; enfeitar roupa com vivos;
colocar canos ou tubos; embarrilar; (bot.)
reproduzir por meio de estaca; arfar; fumar
cachimbo. 4) *to pipe one's eyes,* chorar.

pipeline, s. oleoduto, canalização para
transportar petróleo a longas distâncias.

piper, s. flautista; tocador de gaita de foles;
to pay the pipers, pagar as despesas.

pipette, pipet, s. pipeta.

piping, s. música de flauta ou gaita de foles;
apito, assobio, sibilo; canalização, cano,
tubo; vivos (enfeites de vestuário). *adj.*
relativo a flauta ou gaita de foles; que toca
flauta ou gaita de foles; agudo, sibilante,
aflautado, estridente; tranquilo, sereno; *the
piping times of peace,* a calma dos tempos
de paz.

piquant, *adj.* picante, pungente, mordente;
condimentado; estimulante, provocante.

pique, s. ressentimento, amuo; *v.t.* ofender,
melindrar, magoar, irritar; despertar
(interesse); *(av.)* picar sobre; *to pique
oneself up,* orgulhar-se de.

piquet, s. piquete, jogo de cartas.

piracy, s. pirataria, piratagem; plágio.

piragua, s. piroga.

pirate, s. pirata, corsário; plagiário, falsificador; *v.t.* e *v.i.* piratear; saquear, roubar,
pilhar; falsificar.

pirn, s. carretel, bobina.

pirogue, s. piroga.

pirouette, s. pirueta. *v.i.* fazer ou dar
piruetas.

piscatorial, piscatory, *adj.* piscatório.

piscicultural, *adj.* piscícola.

pisciculture, s. piscicultura.

pisciculturist, s. piscicultor.

pisciform, *adj.* pisciforme.

piscina, *pl. piscinae.* s. viveiro de peixes;
piscina onde, nas primeiras igrejas, o
sacerdote levava o cálice após a comunhão.

piscine, *adj.* písceo, relativo a peixes.

pishogue, s. bruxaria, feitiçaria; feitiço.

pisiforme, *adj.* pisiforme.

pismire, s. formiga.

piss, *v.i.* e *v.t.* mijar, urinar. s. mijo, urina.

pissed, *adj.* (pop.) embriagado.

pistachio, s. pistacho.

pistillate, *adj.* (bot.) pistilífero.

pistol, s. pistola; *pistol port,* janela de tiro.

pistole, s. pistola (antiga moeda espanhola).

pistoleer, s. pistoleiro.

piston, s. pistão, êmbolo.

pit, s. cova, fosso, escavação, poço de mina,
poço de elevador; fenda, abismo; sepultura,
túmulo; (teat.) segunda plateia; plateia;
(E.U.) recinto, na Bolsa, reservado a

determinadas mercadorias; pevide, caroço.
1) *pit-head*, poço de mina. 2) *pit-stall*,
cadeira de plateia. 3) *coal-pit*, hulheira. 4)
inspection-pit ou simplesmente *"pit"*, fosso
nas oficinas de mecânica para exame ou
reparação dos carros. 5) *orchestra-pit*, lugar
reservado à orquestra. 6) *turf-pit*, turfeira. 7)
to dig a pit for, passar uma rasteira ou
preparar uma armadilha a alguém. 8) *to fly
the pit*, abandonar o campo de batalha. *v.t.*
e *v.i.* colocar em buraco, enterrar, guardar
em silos; cavar, esburacar; marcar com
cicatrizes; incitar à luta (animais).

pita, *s.* pita, fibra das folhas de piteira; piteira.

pit-a-pat, *s.* tiquetaque, som palpitante.

pitch, *s.* piche; pez, breu; resina de pinheiro;
arremesso, lançamento; altura, grau,
intensidade, ponto extremo; altura de som,
diapasão; declive, grau de inclinação;
passo de hélice; quantidade de mercadoria
oferecida para venda; local onde um
vendedor ambulante exerce a sua actividade. 1) *pitch dark*, escuro como breu. *v.t.*
armar (tenda), instalar acampamento;
colocar, assentar, plantar; lançar, arremessar; entoar, indicar o tom; balouçar (o
navio); expor à venda; calcetar, pavimentar;
cobrir de pez, alcatroar. 2) *to pitch in*, deitar
mãos à obra; 3) *to pitch upon*, escolher ao
acaso.

pitchblende, *s.* pecheblenda.

pitcher, *s.* lançador (no basebol); cântaro,
bilha; vendedor ambulante com local de
venda fixo; (bot.) folha de planta insec-
tívora.

pitchfork, *s.* forquilha; diapasão. *v.t.* levantar
ou deslocar com uma forquilha; instalar à
força.

pitchy, *adj.* relativo a pez, píceo; resinoso;
negro.

piteous, *adj.* lastimoso, lastimável, deplorável.

piteousness, *s.* estado lamentável; compaixão, tristeza.

pitfall, *s.* alçapão; armadilha, cilada; perigo
oculto.

pith, *s.* medula de planta, de pena; tutano;
espinal medula; essência; força, energia;
importância, peso. *v.t.* matar animal cor-
tando a espinal medula.

pithy, *adj.* meduloso; vigoroso, enérgico,
incisivo, sentencioso.

pitiable, *adj.* lastimoso, lamentável, deplorável; miserável, mesquinho.

pitiful, *adj.* piedoso, compassivo; lamentável,
deplorável; insignificante, miserável,
desprezível.

pitifulness, *s.* piedade, compaixão, pena;
situação ou estado lamentável.

pitiless, *adj.* impiedoso, desapiedado, cruel.

pitman, *s.* mineiro.

pittance, *s.* salário ou mesada insignificante;
bagatela, ninharia, insignificância.

pitter-patter, *s.* tamborilar, tiquetaque.

pituitary, *s.* pituitária, hipófise.

pituitous, *adj.* pituitário.

pity, *s.* pena, piedade, dó, compaixão; *to take
pity on*, apiedar-se, ter pena de, perdoar.
v.t. ter pena de, apiedar-se, lamentar,
lastimar.

pitying, *adj.* compassivo, compadecido,
penalizado.

pivot, *s.* pivô, pino, perno, espigão, eixo,
articulação; (mil.) pião. *adj.* relativo a pivô;
articulado, giratório; central, fundamental.
v.t. prover de pivô, eixo ou espigão; girar,
rodar em torno de um ponto central.

pivotal, *adj.* relativo a pivô; central,
fundamental, principal.

pixilated, *adj.* (E.U. coloq.) amalucado;
excêntrico.

pixy, pixie, *s.* duende.

pizzle, *s.* vergalho de animal.

placability, *s.* placabilidade, serenidade,
clemência.

placable, *adj.* placável, aplacável, brando,
clemente.

placableness, *s.* o mesmo que *placability*.

placard, *s.* cartaz afixado nas paredes;
anúncio, letreiro.

placate, *v.t.* aplacar, apaziguar, conciliar.

placatory, placative, *adj.* apaziguador;
conciliador, calmante.

place, *s.* lugar, sítio, local, localidade;
situação, colocação; povoação; cargo,
posto, emprego; solar, mansão, herdade;
assento, lugar sentado; (mat.) casa
decimal. *v.t.* colocar, pôr, dispor, arranjar;
nomear para um cargo, encontrar colocação para; empregar, estabelecer; aplicar
(dinheiro); depositar; localizar; fixar.

placeman, *s.* funcionário público.

placement, *s.* colocação; arranjo, disposição; colocação da bola para o pontapé
livre.

placental, placentary, *adj.* placentário.

placentate, *adj.* provido de placenta.

placer, *s.* (geol.) plácer.

placet, *s.* voto favorável.

placid, *adj.* plácido, sereno, tranquilo, calmo.

placidity, *s.* placidez, serenidade, calma.

placket, *s.* bolso em saia ou vestido.

placoid, *adj.* placóide.

plagiarism, *s.* plágio, plagiato.

plagiarist, *s.* plagiador, plagiário.

plagiarize, *v.t.* e *v.i.* plagiar.

plagiary, *s.* plagiário, plagiador; plágio, plagiato.

plagiocephalic, *adj.* plagiocéfalo.

plagiotropism, *s.* plagiotropismo.

plague, *s.* praga, calamidade, flagelo, tormento; (fam.) maçada, aborrecimento; peste, epidemia; *the plague,* a peste bubónica. *v.t.* atormentar, afligir, flagelar; empestar, infectar; (fam.) perseguir, incomodar, irritar.

plaguesome, *adj.* importuno, maçador.

plaid, *s.* manta de lã escocesa em xadrez ou o tecido usado nestas mantas.

plain, *adj.* claro, evidente, manifesto; simples; inteligível; modesto, despretensioso, natural; vulgar, comum; franco, sincero; plano, liso; não colorido, a preto e branco; deselegante, feio. 1) *plain-chant, plain-song,* cantochão. 2) *the plain truth,* a pura verdade. 3) *plain-spoken,* franco, sincero. *s.* planície; campina. *adv.* claramente, com clareza.

plainsman, *s.* habitante da planície.

plaint, *s.* queixa, acusação.

plaintiff, *s.* (jur.) queixoso, autor de demanda judicial.

plaintive, *adj.* queixoso, lamentoso, lastimoso.

plaintiveness, *s.* tom lamentoso; lamentação, queixa, queixume.

plait, *s.* dobra, prega; *v.t.* dobrar, preguear.

plan, *s.* plano, desenho, traçado, planta; programa; projecto, desígnio, intenção; maneira de proceder; levantamento de terrenos. *v.t.* e *v.i.* planear, fazer planos; projectar; delinear; maquinar; tencionar.

planchet, *s.* peça de moeda não cunhada.

planchette, *s.* prancheta.

plane, *adj.* plano, raso, liso. 1) *plane-chart,* carta de marear. 2) *plane table,* prancheta. *s.* plano, superfície plana; plano, nível; avião, aeroplano; plaina. *v.t.* aplainar; nivelar, aplanar. *v.i.* planar; voar. 3) (bot.) planetree, plátano.

planer, *s.* aplainador, nivelador; *plaina mecânica.*

planet, *s.* planeta; *planet stricken,* aturdido, aterrado.

planetarium, *s.* planetário.

planetary, *adj.* planetário; terrestre; mundial; errante.

plangent, *adj.* plangente; vibrante, sonoro.

planish, *v.t.* aplainar.

planisphere, *s.* planisfério.

plank, *s.* prancha, tábua; plataforma. *v.t.* entabuar, assoalhar; (fam.) pagar.

planking, *s.* cobrir de pranchas; acção de assoalhar; forro de madeira.

plankton, *s.* plâncton.

planner, *s.* aquele que planeia; projectista, desenhista.

plano-concave, *adj.* plano-côncavo.

plano-convex, *adj.* plano-convexo.

planography, *s.* planografia; arte de desenhar planos.

planometry, *s.* planometria.

planospore, *s.* (biol.) planospório, zoospório.

plant, *s.* planta, vegetal; (pop.) erva; plantação; posição, atitude, postura; fábrica; maquinaria, aparelhagem; (cal.) embuste, vigarice, entrujice; (cal.) detective. 1) *plant-eating,* que se alimenta de plantas, fitófago. 2) *alternating-current plant,* instalação de corrente eléctrica. 3) *to lose plant,* murchar, secar. 4) *to miss plant,* não germinar. *v.t.* plantar, semear; cultivar; fixar, assentar, implantar; introduzir uma espécie animal numa região; fundar, criar; incutir ideia no espírito de alguém; assentar, acertar (um golpe); esconder produto de roubo; (cal.) maquinar, tramar.

plantain, *s.* tanchagem; espécie de banana.

plantar, *adj.* relativo à planta do pé.

plantation, *s.* plantação, fazenda; colonização, colónia.

planter, *s.* plantador, cultivador, agricultor.

plantigrade, *adj.* e *s.* plantígrado.

plaque, *s.* placa decorativa; condecoração, medalha; placa, mancha na pele.

plash, *v.t.* e *v.i.* entrelaçar ramos para fazer uma sebe; chapinhar; salpicar, borrifar. *s.* poça de água, charco; salpico.

plashy, *adj.* encharcado, lamacento, pantanoso.

plasm, *s.* (biol.) plasma; protoplasma, citoplasma.

plasma, *s.* (miner.) plasma, espécie de quartzo translúcido; plasma (do sangue, dos músculos).

plasmatic, *adj.* plásmico.
plasmic, *adj.* plásmico.
plasmolysis, *s.* plasmólise.
plaster, *s.* emplastro; reboco, estuque; gesso. *v.t.* rebocar, estucar; cobrir, revestir; cumular; pôr emplastro; colar, afixar; tratar (vinho) pelo sulfato de cálcio ou de potássio.
plasterer, *s.* rebocador, estucador; aquele que faz moldes ou modelos de gesso.
plastic, *adj.* plástico, formativo, modelador, criador; flexível, maleável; plástico, relativo a plástico. *s.* plástico, matéria plástica.
plasticity, *s.* plasticidade; flexibilidade.
plastics, *s.* plástico, matéria plástica. *adj.* relativo ou feito de plástico.
plastid, *s.* plastídio; célula.
plastron, *s.* plastrão, almofada de couro para proteger o peito contra os golpes de florete; peitilho.
plat, *s.* terreno, pedaço de terra, canteiro; (E.U.) mapa, plano; prato, manjar. *v.t.* fazer a planta de, cartografar.
platan, *s.* plátano.
plate, *s.* placa, chapa, lâmina, folha; lamela; lâmina, gravura, estampa; baixela, prataria; prato; armadura, couraça, revestimento de metal; (desp.) taça, corrida em que se ganha uma taça; (heráld.) besante de prata; (basebol) lugar do batedor. *v.t.* chapear; laminar; blindar.
plateau, *s.* planalto, altiplano, planura.
platelayer, *s.* colocador de carris.
platelet, *s.* plaqueta.
platen, *s.* platina; cilindro de máquina de escrever.
platform, *s.* plataforma; estrado, palanque, tribuna; terraço; cais, gare (nos caminhos de ferro).
plating, *s.* acção de chapear; revestimento com chapas de metal; blindagem; galvanização.
platinize, *v.t.* platinar.
platinum, *s.* platina; *platinum black,* negro de platina.
platitude, *s.* vulgaridade, trivialidade, lugar-comum.
platitudinarian, *s.* aquele que costuma dizer banalidades.
platitudinous, *adj.* vulgar, trivial, sensaborão.
platonic, *adj.* platónico.
platonism, *s.* platonismo.
platonist, *s.* platónico.

platoon, *s.* pelotão; roda, círculo social ou familiar.
platter, *s.* travessa.
platypus, *s.* ornitorrinco.
plaudit, *s.* aplauso.
plausible, *adj.* plausível, razoável, viável.
plausive, *adj.* laudatório, elogioso.
play, *v.t.* e *v.i.* brincar, folgar, foliar, divertir-se; comportar-se descuidadamente; jogar; tocar musica, executar; representar um papel, actuar, trabalhar no teatro ou no cinema; fazer de; agir, portar-se *(to play fair,* agir honestamente; *to play false or foul:* trair, lograr). 1) *to play into the hands of,* favorecer o adversário. 2) *to play upon,* tirar proveito de. 3) *to play up to,* contracenar com, adular, bajular, animar, encorajar. 4) *to play politics,* fazer de conta. 5) *to play the fool,* fazer-se de parvo. 6) *to play the races,* apostar nas corridas. 7) *to play someone or something against another,* colocar em posição ridícula. 8) *to play up,* troçar de, irritar, tirar proveito de. *s.* jogo, brincadeira, diversão; jogada; peça teatral; manejo de arma.
playboy, *s.* boémio, estroina.
player, *s.* jogador; actor; aquele que toca instrumento musical, executante; *player piano,* pianola.
playfellow, *s.* o mesmo que *playmate.*
playful, *adj.* brincalhão, folgazão, travesso.
playground, *s.* pátio de recreio, recreio.
playhouse, *s.* casa de espectáculos, teatro, cinema.
playing, *s.* jogo, brincadeira; execução (de música); representação, actuação; movimento (de peça de máquina); *playing card,* carta de jogar.
playmate, *s.* companheiro de folguedos.
play-off, *s.* partida de desempate.
plaything, *s.* brinquedo.
playwright, *s.* autor de peças teatrais, dramaturgo.
plaza, *s.* praça pública.
plea, *s.* alegação, argumento; desculpa, pretexto; pedido, apelo; (jur.) alegação, contestação (do réu), contrariedade; pleito, demanda, acção judicial.
pleach, *v.t.* entrançar, entrelaçar.
plead, *v.i.* e *v.t.* pleitear, litigiar, litigar; argumentar; defender, advogar (causa), alegar como desculpa, arguir. 1) *to plead against,* impugnar, argumentar contra. 2) *to plead for,* interceder por, implorar (perdão).

3) *to plead with a person for a thing,* insistir com alguém por alguma coisa. 4) *to plead guilty,* confessar-se culpado.

pleadable, *adj.* que pode ser defendido, litigável; alegável, justificável.

pleader, *s.* litigante; advogado.

pleading, *s.* patrocínio de causa em juízo; defesa; alegações; súplica. *adj.* que implora ou pede, suplicante.

pleasant, *adj.* agradável, aprazível, ameno, amável; alegre, divertido.

pleasantness, *s.* agradabilidade; amenidade, suavidade; encanto, amabilidade, afabilidade.

pleasantry, *s.* graça, dito espirituoso, gracejo; brincadeira.

please, *v.t.* e *v.i.* agradar, deleitar, satisfazer, aprazer a; achar conveniente. 1) *please your honour,* se apraz a V.Exa. 2) *please God,* se Deus quiser. 3) *take as many as you please,* tire quantos lhe aprouver. 4) *if you please,* se me dá licença, se faz favor, por favor. 5) *please,* por favor.

pleasing, *adj.* agradável, deleitável, grato, prazenteiro.

pleasurable, *adj.* agradável, satisfatório.

pleasure, *s.* prazer, deleite, gosto, divertimento, gozo, agrado, satisfação; alegria; desejo, vontade, ordem; 1) *what is your pleasure,* o que é que manda? 2) *at your pleasure,* como ou quando lhe aprouver. 3) *to take one's pleasure,* divertir-se. *v.t.* e *v.i.* agradar, dar prazer a, ter prazer, deleitar-se, gostar.

pleat, *s.* dobra, prega. *v.t.* dobrar, preguear.

plebe, *s.* (fam. E.U.) caloiro de academia militar.

plebeian, *s.* plebeu. *adj.* plebeu; vulgar, ordinário, grosseiro.

plebeianism, *s.* plebeísmo, vulgaridade.

plebiscite, *s.* plebiscito.

plectron, *s.* o mesmo que plectrum.

plectrum, *s.* (mús.) plectro, palheta.

pledge, *s.* penhor, garantia, caução, sinal, fiança; promessa, compromisso, voto, prova de amor, filho; brinde, saúde; promessa de abster-se de bebidas alcoólicas. 1) *to take out of pledge,* desempenhar. *v.t.* empenhar, caucionar, dar como garantia; comprometer, hipotecar. 2) *to pledge one's word,* dar a sua palavra brindar; beber à saúde.

pledger, *s.* aquele que empenha, penhora ou hipoteca .

pledget, *s.* pequena compressa para feridas.

plenary, *adj.* plenário; pleno, absoluto, completo.

plenipotent, *adj.* e *s.* o mesmo que *plenipotentiary.*

plenipotentiary, *adj.* e *s.* plenipotenciário.

plenitude, *s.* plenitude, totalidade; abundância.

plenteous, *adj.* abundante, copioso, profuso; fértil, opulento.

plentifulness, *s.* abundância; grande quantidade.

plenty, *adj.* abundante, numeroso. *s.* abundância, profusão, fartura, grande cópia; profusão. *adv.* bastante, muito, abundantemente.

plenum, *s.* espaço cheio de matéria; repleção, pletora; assembleia geral, sessão plenária; *plenum system,* sistema de ventilação de corrente de ar dirigida.

pleonasm, *s.* pleonasmo; redundância.

pleonastic, *adj.* pleonástico; supérfluo.

pleopod, *s.* pleópode, membro abdominal de crustáceo.

plesiosaurus, *s.* plesiossauro.

plethora, *s.* pletora, excesso, abundância.

pleura, *s.* pleura.

pleural, *adj.* pleural.

pleurisy, *s.* pleurisia.

pleuropneumonia, *s.* pleuropneumonia.

plexiform, *adj.* plexiforme, retiforme; complicado.

plexus, *s.* plexo; rede, entrelaçado, complexo, complicação.

pliable, *adj.* o mesmo que *pliant.*

pliancy, *s.* flexibilidade; docilidade.

pliant, *adj.* flexível, dobrável; dócil, maleável, influenciável; complacente.

plica, *s.* plica, dobra, prega; (med.) plica polónica, tricoma.

plicate, *adj.* plicado, dobrado, pregueado.

plication, *s.* plicação, franzimento; dobra.

plier, *s.* alicate.

plight, *s.* estado, situação, condição; apuro, aperto; compromisso, promessa solene. *v.t.* empenhar, comprometer; *to plight oneself to someone,* contratar casamento com alguém.

Plimsoil, *s.* (no plural) sapatos de lona com sola de borracha; *Plimsoil mark,* linha de flutuação.

plinth, *s.* plinto.

plod, *v.i.* e *v.t.* caminhar com dificuldade, arrastar-se; afadigar-se, labutar. *s.* caminhar penoso; labuta, faina, lida.

plodding, *adj.* laborioso, diligente, perseverante.

plop, *v.t.* e *v.i.* cair produzindo um som semelhante ao de um objecto que embate na água; *adv.* de chapa, produzindo o som "chape". *s.* chape; som de qualquer coisa a cair na água ou de rolha a saltar da garrafa.

plosive, *adj.* explosiva; *s.* consoante explosiva.

plot, *s.* porção de terreno, lote, nesga; (E.U.) planta, mapa, plano; conspiração, conluio, trama, intriga, maquinação; enredo. *v.t.* e *v.i.* levantar a planta de, cartografar; marcar, delimitar, assinalar num mapa; lotear; conspirar, tramar, maquinar.

plottage, *s.* área de pedaço de terra.

plotting, *s.* levantamento topográfico; registo ou representação gráfica; localização num mapa; loteamento; acto de conspirar, maquinação; *plotting paper,* papel milimétrico.

plough, *s.* arado, charrua; limpa-neves; guilhotina para papel; terra lavrada; reprovação, rejeição de candidato em exame; *(astron.)* a Ursa Maior. *v.t.* e *v.i.* arar, lavrar, arrancar ou levantar com arado; sulcar, fender; vincar, enrugar; reprovar em exame; avançar a custo.

poughable, *adj.* arável, cultivável.

plougher, *s.* lavrador.

ploughing, *s.* lavra, acção de lavrar; trabalho com o arado; sulco aberto pelo arado; reprovação em exame.

ploughshare, *s.* relha, ferro do arado.

plover, *s.* tarambola, lavandeira, pildra, tordeira-do-mar.

plow, *s., v.t.* e *v.i.* (E.U.), o mesmo que *plough.*

pluck, *v.t.* arrancar, colher, apanhar; dar um safanão a; sacudir; tanger (cordas de instrum. musical); depenar; (cal.) roubar, explorar; chumbar; *to pluck one's heart,* criar coragem. *s.* puxão, safanão; fressura, miúdos de animal morto; coragem ânimo; chumbo.

plucky, *adj.* corajoso, ousado, valente; resoluto.

plug, rolha, tampa, tampão, tarraxa, cavilha, cunha, bucha, obturador; cilindro de fechadura; obturação de dente; (fam.) propaganda, anúncio de rádio; (cal.) murro, soco; (elect.) tomada, ficha; (aut.) vela de ignição; cavalo velho ou inútil; livro difícil de vender; (cal.) cartola, chapéu alto. *v.t.* e *v.i.*

tapar, tamponar; meter uma cavilha; obturar dente; calar (fruta); esmurrar; anunciar, fazer propaganda; trabalhar com afinco, estafar-se.

plug-ugly, *s.* (E.U.) rufião, meliante.

plum, *s.* ameixa; uva passa; cor de ameixa; o melhor, nata; preciosidade. 1) *plum tree,* ameixeira. 2) *to get the plum,* ficar com a melhor parte.

plumage, *s.* plumagem.

plumate, *adj.* plumoso.

plumb, *s.* prumo; chumbada; (náut.) sonda; verticalidade; nível. 1) *out of plumb,* fora de prumo. 2) *plumb line,* fio de prumo; *adj.* vertical, a prumo; franco, sincero; *adv.* verticalmente, a prumo, a pique; directamente, exactamente; logo, imediatamente; (fam. E.U.) completamente, inteiramente; *v.t.* sondar com sonda, verificar a verticalidade com o fio de prumo; trabalhar como canalizador.

plumbeous, *adj.* plúmbeo.

plumber, *s.* canalizador; funileiro, latoeiro.

plumbing, *s.* trabalho de canalizador; sondagem.

plumbism, *s.* (med.) saturnismo, envenenamento pelo chumbo.

plumbless, *adj.* insondável.

plume, *s.* pena grande, pluma, penacho; prémio, galardão; *v.t.* enfeitar com plumas; alisar as penas; emplumar; *to plume oneself on,* vangloriar-se.

plumelet, *s.* peninha, pluminha, plúmula.

plummet, *s.* peso, contrapeso; chumbada; fio de prumo; prumo; sonda; nível; obstáculo, dificuldade. *v.i.* cair ou mergulhar na vertical.

plummy, *adj.* relativo a ameixas ou passas; (fam.) bom, gostoso, desejável, apetitoso, vantajoso.

plump, *adj.* roliço, cheio, rechonchudo. *v.t.* e *v.i.* arredondar, dilatar; engordar; inchar, arredondar-se, tornar-se rechonchudo; cair ou sentar-se pesadamente. *s.* baque, ruído surdo; (arc.) magote, grupo. *adv.* abruptamente; pesadamente; francamente.

plumper, *s.* chumaço para encher as bochechas; queda, tombo; voto dado a um só candidato; mentira, peta.

plumpness, *s.* gordura, obesidade, aspecto roliço; franqueza.

plumule, *s.* plúmula.

plumy, *adj.* plumoso; emplumado.

plunder, *v.t.* e *v.i.* saquear, pilhar, espoliar,

roubar; *s.* saque, pilhagem, roubo; extorsão; presa; (cal. E.U.) trastes, objectos de uso pessoal; (cal.) lucro, ganho.

plunderage, *s.* saque, pilhagem; desvio de mercadorias em navio; mercadorias roubadas.

plunderer, *s.* saqueador.

plunge, *s.* mergulho; imersão. 1) *to be put to a plunge,* ser posto numa situação delicada. 2) *to take the plunge,* aceitar correr o risco. *v.t.* e *v.i.* mergulhar, imergir, submergir; meter, cravar, enterrar; afundar; lançar-se, arremeter; entrar de rompante; (cal.) jogar arriscando grandes quantias.

plunger, *s.* mergulhador; especulador, jogador; soldado de cavalaria; (mec.) embolo, pistão.

plunk, *s.* pancada, ruído seco, som estrídulo; dólar. *v.t.* e *v.i.* produzir um ruído seco; atirar ou deixar cair pesadamente; golpear; cair pesadamente.

pluperfect, *adj.* e *s.* (gram.) mais-que--perfeito.

plural, *adj.* e *s.* plural.

pluralism, *s.* pluralismo; pluralidade; acumulação de benefícios eclesiásticos.

plurality, *s.* pluralidade, multiplicidade; multidão; acumulação de benefícios eclesiásticos, cargo ou benefício acumulado com outro; maioria; (E.U.) maioria relativa de votos.

pluralize, *v.t.* pluralizar, pôr no plural; *v.i.* acumular benefícios eclesiásticos.

plus, *prep.* mais, somado com, acrescido de. *adj.* positivo; de adição, adicional; *the plus sign,* o sinal + *s.* mais; o sinal +; quantidade positiva.

plus-four, *s. pl.* calções de golfe.

plush, *s.* pelúcia; (pl.) calças de pelúcia dos lacaios; (coloq. E.U.) elegância, prosperidade.

plutocracy, *s.* plutocracia.

plutonian, *adj.* plutónico; infernal.

plutonic, *adj.* plutónico, abissal.

plutonium, *s.* plutónio.

pluvial, *adj.* pluvial; chuvoso. *s.* pluvial, capa de asperges.

pluviometer, *s.* pluviómetro.

pluviometry, *s.* pluviometria.

pluvious, *adj.* pluvioso, chuvoso; pluvial.

ply, *v.t.* e *v.i.* manejar, brandir; aplicar-se a, ocupar-se de, trabalhar em, exercer; navegar em; importunar, assediar; estacionar à espera de clientes; entregar-se a; fazer

regularmente um percurso. *s.* dobra, prega; camada, espessura; capa, lona; cordão, fibra, fio; tendência, propensão. 1) *three ply,* com três fios, com três camadas; 2) *to take a ply,* habituar-se a, ter propensão para.

plyer, *s.* manejador; (pl.) alicate.

plywood, *s.* contraplacado.

pneuma, *s.* alma, espírito.

pneumatic, *adj.* pneumático; espiritual. 1) *pneumatic brake,* travão de ar comprimido. 2) *pneumatic raft,* balsa pneumática, pneu. *s.* pneumático, pneu; veículo provido de pneumáticos.

pneumatics, *s.* pneumática.

pneumatology, *s.* pneumatologia; doutrina do Espírito Santo; (fís.) pneumática.

pneumodynamics, *s.* pneumática.

pneumonia, *s.* pneumonia.

pneumonic, *adj.* pneumónico; (raro) pulmonar.

pneumonotomy, *s.* pneumotomia.

pneumothorax, *s.* pneumotórax.

poach, *v.t.* ferver, escaldar; espezinhar, pisar, calcar com os cascos, caçar ou pescar ilicitamente. *v.i.* soltar-se, tornar-se lamacenta; *to poach on,* invadir, penetrar em.

poacher, *s.* caçador furtivo.

pock, *s.* pústula.

pocket, *s.* bolso, algibeira, bolsa; cavidade; poço de ar; (bilhar) ventanilha; (Ingl.) circunscrição eleitoral dominada por uma só pessoa ou família. 1) *pocket money,* dinheiro de bolso, dinheiro para pequenas despesas. 2) *pocket veto,* veto de gaveta, retenção de projecto-lei. *v.t.* meter ao bolso, embolsar; apropriar-se de; esconder, reprimir (sentimentos); (bilhar) fazer entrar a bola numa das ventanilhas; (desp.) prejudicar adversário; dominar círculo eleitoral; 3) *to pocket an insult,* engolir um insulto.

pocketbook, *s.* agenda; carteira.

pocketknife, *s.* canivete.

pockmark, marca deixada pela varíola, bexiga.

pod, *s.* vagem de planta leguminosa, casca; casulo de bicho-da-seda; embocadura, mandril; pequeno bando de baleias ou focas. *v i.* produzir vagens; *v.t.* descascar (ervilhas, etc.).

podginess, *s.* gordura; aspecto rechonchudo.

podgy, adj. grosso, atarracado; gorducho.

podiatrist, s. pediatra, pedicuro.

podium, s. pódio.

poem, s. poema, poesia.

poet, s. poeta.

poetic, poetical, adj. poétlco.

poeticize, v.t. poetizar, tornar poético, versificar.

poetics, s. poética, arte poética.

poetize, v.i. e v.t. poetar, fazer versos, pôr em verso.

poetry, s. poesia.

pogrom, s. (do russo) pogrome, perseguição aos judeus.

poignancy, s. pungência; sabor picante; agudeza, mordacidade.

poignant, adj. pungente, penetrante; picante; mordaz; doloroso, lancinante.

point, s. ponto, sinal; ponto, sinal de pontuação; vírgula em número decimal; unidade de medida dos caracteres tipográficos, corpos de tipos. 1) 8-point type, tipo de corpo 8; objectivo, desígnio; ponta, extremidade aguçada; bico; vértice; cume; (mil.) patrulha de ponta; (pl.) agulhas (no caminho de ferro); acto de marrar (o cão de caça). 2) on point duty, no seu posto (o polícia). 3) points of the compass: rumos da rosa-dos-ventos. 4) to make a point, fazer questão de, insistir em. 5) to the point, a propósito. 6) to come to the point, falar sobre o assunto que interessa. 7) not to put too fine a point upon it, falar sem rodeios. v.t. e v.i. apontar, aguçar, afiar; (gram.) pontuar; realçar, salientar; revolver o solo com a ponta de uma pá; mostrar, aludir; ficar parado e atento (o cão de caça); rebocar; (med.) supurar, rebentar; (náut.) meter a vela nos rizes. 8) to point a moral, evidenciar a moral de uma história. 9) to point off, separar por meio de vírgulas. 10) to point out, realçar.

point-blank, adj. horizontal, à queima-roupa; (fig.) categórico, brusco. adv. horizontalmente; (fig.) francamente, desabridamente, categoricamente.

point-device, adj. correcto, exacto; adv. correctamente, com precisão.

pointed, adj. pontiagudo, terminado em ponta, aguçado; apropriado, oportuno; penetrante, mordaz; pronunciado, acentuado; evidente, flagrante; significativo, intencional; exacto, preciso; (arquit.) arco ogival, ogiva.

pointer, s. aquele que aponta; ponteiro, indicador; apontador; raça de cães de caça; (fam. E.U.) informação secreta, palpite; (pl. com maiúsc.) Guardas da Ursa Maior.

pointilism, s. pontilhismo.

pointless, adj. sem ponta, rombo; sem graça; despropositado, sem sentido.

poise, v.t. e v.i. equilibrar; estabilizar; suspender; equilibrar-se, pairar. s. equilíbrio; estabilidade; firmeza; postura, atitude; pausa, suspensão; indecisão.

poison, s. veneno, tóxico. 1) poison dogwood, poison elder, poison sumac: (bot.) espécie de sumagre venenoso. 2) poison pen, autor de cartas anónimas. v.t. envenenar, intoxicar; corromper, perverter.

poisonous, adj. venenoso, tóxico, peçonhento; maldoso, malicioso; corruptor.

poke, s. empurrão, cotovelada; espécie de canga para impedir que o animal atravesse as cercas; pala de chapéu. 1) to buy a pig in a poke, comprar nabos em saca. v.t. e v.i. acotovelar; aguilhoar; plcar, espicaçar, atiçar (fogo); empurrar, meter; abrir buraco com objecto pontiagudo; interferir, lntrometer-se. 2) to poke one's head, andar curvado. 3) to poke fun at, trocar de, gozar com. 4) to poke and pry, bisbilhotar.

poker, s. atiçador; instrumento para gravação em madeira; póquer (jogo de cartas); poker face, fisionomia impassível, inescrutável. v.t. gravar em madeira.

pokerwork, s. pirogravura.

poky, adj. pequeno, acanhado, apertado; miserável; mesquinho, insignificante.

polacre, polacca, s. polaca, tipo de navio com três mastros.

polar, adj. polar; dotado de polaridade, magnético; orientador; polar lights, aurora boreal.

polarity, s. polaridade.

polarization, s. polarização.

polarize, v.t. polarizar.

polder, s. pólder, região baixa conquistada ao mar por meio de diques.

pole, s. pólo; poste, mastro; pau, vara; varapau, estaca, baliza; vara de medir; medida de comprimento; timão, lança (de carro). 1) pole boat, barco manejado a vara. 2) pole-finder, busca-pólos. 3) pole vault, salto com vara. 4) up the poles, (coloq.) em apuros. v.t. prover de poste, vara, etc.; escorar com postes ou estacas; impelir barco com vara.

poleax, poleaxe, s. acha de armas; alabarda; machadinha. v.t. abater animal com machadinha; atacar com acha de armas.

polecat, s. furão bravo, toirão.

polemic, adj. polémico, controverso. s. polémica, controvérsia.

polemics, s. polémica.

polestar, s. estrela polar.

police, s. polícia; polícia de segurança pública. 1) police constable, police officer: agente da polícia, polícia. 2) police magistrate, juiz do tribunal da polícia. 3) police-state, estado totalitário. 4) police station, esquadra da polícia. v.t. policiar; fiscalizar; controlar.

policeman, s. polícia, agente da polícia.

policlinic, s. policlínica.

policy, s. política; diplomacia; sagacidade; astúcia; programa, orientação, método; apólice de seguro.

policyholder, s. segurado, portador de apólice de seguro.

poliomyelitis, s. poliomielite.

polish, s. polimento, polidura; lustre, verniz; acabamento; refinamento, distinção; graxa. v.t. polir, lustrar, alisar, dar brilho a; aperfeiçoar, retocar; refinar, educar, tornar elegante ou culto. 1) to polish off, acabar rapidamente, despachar. 2) to polish up, aperfeiçoar.

polite, adj. cortês, educado, urbano, gentil, delicado, bem-educado; refinado, culto, distinto.

politeness, s. delicadeza, educação, cortesia.

politic, adj. hábil, sagaz, diplomático; judicioso, conveniente; astuto, manhoso; polltico.

political, adj. político, relativo a política.

politician, s. político.

politicize, v.i. politilizar, tornar político, fazer política.

politics, s. política, opiniões políticas.

polity, s. governo, forma de governo, constituição política; estado, comunidade organizada.

polka, s. polca.

poll, s. cabeça, parte da cabeça coberta pelo cabelo; indivíduo, pessoa; capitação, imposto pago por cabeça; votação, eleição; lista eleitoral; escrutínio; assembleia de voto. v.t. e v.i. cortar o cabelo a; aparar a copa das árvores; votar; dar o voto a. 1) to

pole a vote for, votar a favor de. 2) he polled 20.000 votes, ele teve 20 000 votos a favor. adj. sem chifres.

pollack, pollock, s. espécie de pescada polaca.

pollard, s. animal sem chifres; árvore aparada.

pollen, s. pólen.

pollinate, v.t. polinizar.

pollination, s. polinização.

polling, adj. votante, que vota. s. acto de votar, votação, registo de votos; polling booth, cabina de voto.

pollute, v.t. poluir, manchar, sujar; corromper.

pollution, s. poluição; corrupção, impureza.

polo, s. pólo; water polo, pólo aquático.

polonaise, s. polonesa (dança).

poltrooll, s. e adj. poltrão, cobarde.

polychromatic, polychromic, adj. policromático; multicolor.

polychromy, s. policromia.

polyclinic, s. policlínica.

polygamist, s. polígamo, poligamista.

polygamous, adj. polígamo, poligâmico.

polygamy, s. poligamia.

polyglot, s. poliglota.

polygon, s. polígono.

polygonal, adj. poligonal.

polygraph, s. polígrafo.

polygynous, adj. políginio; (bot.) polígamo.

polygyny, s. poliginia, poligamia.

polyhedral, adj. poliédrico.

polyhedron, s. poliedro.

polymer, s. (quím.) polímero.

polymorph, s. organismo polimorfo ou cada uma das suas formas.

polymorphic, adj. polimórfico

polymorphism, s. polimorfismo.

Polynesian, s. e adj. polinésio.

polynuclear, adj. polinucelar.

polyp, s. pólipo.

polypary, s. polipeiro.

polyphagia, s. polifagia.

polyphagous, adj. polífago.

polyphase, adj. (elect.) polifásico.

polyphony, s. polifonia.

polypous, adj. poliposo.

polystyrene, s. (quim.) polistlreno.

polysylabic, adj. polissilábico.

polysylable, s. polissílabo.

polytechnic, s. e adj. politécnico.

polytheism, s. politeísmo.

polytheist, s. e adj. politeísta.

polyvalent, *adj.* polivalente.

pomace, *s.* pasta ou bagaço de maçãs.

pomaceous, *adj.* pomáceo, relativo a maçã.

pomade, *s.* pomada para o cabelo, brilhantina.

pome, *s.* pomo.

pomegranate, *s.* romã; romãzeira.

pomiculture, *s.* fruticultura, pomicultura.

pommel, pummel, *s.* botão do punho da espada, pomo; maçã, maçaneta; castão.

pomology, *s.* pomologia; fruticultura.

pomp, *s.* pompa, aparato, fausto.

pompon, *s.* pompom, borla.

pomposity, *s.* pomposidade, imponência; ostentação; linguagem empolada.

pompous, *adj.* pomposo, aparatoso, ostentoso; arrogante, pretensioso, afectado; empolado, bombástico.

pompousness, *s.* pompa, fausto, imponência.

poncho, *s.* poncho, capa.

pond, *s.* lago, charco, piscina; tanque. *v.t.* represar, acudar; *v.i.* formar lago.

pondel, *v.t.* e *v.i.* ponderar, reflectir, estudar, pensar.

ponderation, *s.* ponderação, apreciação; pesagem.

ponderous, *adj.* pesado, ponderoso; trabalhoso; enfadonho.

poniard, *s.* punhal, adaga. *v.t.* apunhalar.

pontiff, *s.* papa, sumo pontífice.

pontifical, *adj.* pontifical; relativo aos pontífices.

pontificate, *s.* pontificado, papado; episcopado. *v.i.* pontificar, celebrar missa.

pontify, *v.i.* pontificar, doutrinar.

ponton, *s.* (mil. E.U.) pontão.

pontoon, *s.* pontão; barcaça de fundo chato utilizada para formar uma ponte flutuante; jogo (vinte-e-um). *v.t.* atravessar rio por meio de ponte.

pony, *s.* pónei, cavalinho; copinho, cálice de bebida. *v.t.* (coloq. E.U.) pagar uma conta.

pooch, *s.* cachorrinho.

poodle, *s.* caniche.

pooh, *interj.* Ora! Basta! Balelas!

pooh-pooh, *v.t.* e *v.i.* manifestar desprezo, trocar; ridicularizar.

pool, *s.* poço, poça de água, lagoa, charco, lago, piscina; tanque; bolada; quantia apostada em certos jogos; variedade de bilhar; acordo entre empresas; *swimming pool,* piscina. *v.t.* abrir buraco em pedreira para introduzir uma cunha; minar; reunir num fundo comum; repartir entre si; explorar em comum.

poolroom, *s.* sala de apostas em corridas de cavalos.

poop, *s.* (náut.) popa, tombadilho; (coloq.) pateta, pacóvio, paspalhão. *v.t.* apanhar pela popa (vaga).

poor, *adj.* pobre, necessitado, miserável; deficiente, fraco; escasso, insuficiente; pouco produtivo (o solo) instisfatório, medíocre; desagradável; (fam.) coitado, pobre, infeliz. 1) *poor box,* caixa de esmolas em igreja. 2) *poor-spirited.* medroso, poltrão. 3) (E.U.) *poor white trash,* os brancos de baixa condição social.

poorhouse, *s.* asilo de indigentes.

poorly, *adv.* pobremente, miseravelmente; Insuficientemente, imperfeitamente, mal.

poorness, *s.* pobreza; insuficiência; improdutividade; imperfeição, Inferioridade, mesquinhez.

pop, *s.* estalo, estouro, estampido. 1) (coloq.) *in pop,* empenhado, no prego. *v.i.* e *v.t.* estourar, estalar, detonar; disparar arma. 2) *to pop up or down,* subir ou aparecer, descer ou desaparecer rapidamente. 3) *to pop upon,* deparar com alguém; por ou meter rapidamente; (coloq.) empenhar, por no prego. 4) *to pop up a question,* sair-se com uma pergunta. 5) *to pop the question,* fazer pedido de casamento.

popcorn, *s.* plpocas.

pope, *s.* papa; pope (da Igreja Ortodoxa).

popedom, *s.* papado.

popery, *s.* papísmo.

pop-eyed, *adj.* de olhos esbugalhados.

popgun, *s.* espingarda de ar comprimido.

popish, *adj.* (depr.) papista.

poplar, *s.* choupo.

poplin, *s.* popelina.

poppied, *adj.* coberto de papoilas; sonolento, sonífero.

poppy, *s.* papoila; dormideira.

poppycock, *s.* conversa fiada; balelas.

populace, *s.* populaça, povo, ralé.

popular, *adj.* popular; vulgar, comum; corrente, em moda; benquisto, estimado.

popularity, *s.* popularidade; estima, simpatia.

popularize, *v.t.* popularizar, vulgarizar, divulgar.

populate, *v.t.* povoar.

population, *s.* população; habitantes; povoamento.

populism, *s.* populismo.

populous, *adj.* populoso, muito povoado.

porcelain, *s.* porcelana.

porch, *s.* alpendre; varanda; *The Porch,* seita filosófica dos Estóicos.

porcupine, *s.* porco-espinho.

pore, *s.* poro. *v.i.* olhar, meditar, estudar atentamente.

porgy, *s.* pargo.

porism, *s.* (mat.) porisma.

pork, *s.* carne de porco.

porkpie, *s.* chapéu de feltro de copa chata e aba virada para cima.

pornography, *s.* pornografia.

porosity, *s.* porosidade.

porous, *adj.* poroso; permeável.

porousness, *s.* porosidade.

porpoise, *s.* toninha (espécie de golfinho).

porridge, *s.* papa de aveia.

port, *s.* porto; cidade com porto de mar; orifício, abertura; escotilha; canhoneira; vinho do Porto; porte, atitude; (náut.) bombordo; *adj.* portuário, relativo a porto; de bombordo, da esquerda. *v.t.* e *v.i.* transportar arma em diagonal inclinada para a esquerda; dirigir-se para bombordo.

portability, *s.* portabilidade.

portable, *adj.* portátil.

portage, *s.* porte, transporte, carregamento; frete; transporte de barcos ou mercadorias por terra, entre duas vias navegáveis; lugar por onde é feito esse transporte. *v.t.* transportar por terra.

portal, *s.* portal, portada; *adj.* (med.) porta; *portal vein,* veia porta.

portend, *v.t.* pressagiar, agourar, anunciar.

portent, *s.* presságio, agouro; portento, prodígio.

portentous, *adj.* agourento; portentoso, prodigioso, assombroso, maravilhoso.

porter, *s.* porteiro; carregador; (E.U.) empregado que faz serviço nas carruagens-cama dos comboios; tipo de cerveja preta.

porterhouse, *s.* taverna, cervejaria.

portfolio, *s.* pasta para documentos; pasta ministerial.

porthole, *s.* vigia.

portico, *s.* pórtico.

portiere, *s.* reposteiro.

portion, *s.* porção, quinhão, parte; pedaço; dote; destino, sorte; *v.t.* partilhar, distribuir; dar em dote, dotar.

portionless, *adj.* sem dote.

portmanteau, *s.* mala, mala de mão, maleta; *portmanteau-word,* palavra fantasiosa formada por elementos de outras duas.

portrait, *s.* retrato; tipo, imagem; descrição.

portraitist, *s.* retratista.

portray, *v.t.* retratar; pintar, descrever; representar.

portrayal, *s.* descrição; retrato, representação pictórica .

portress, *s.* fem. de *porter.*

Portuguese, *adj.* e *s.* português; *portuguese man-of-war,* caravela-portuguesa (espécie de medusa.)

pose, *v.t.* e *v.r.* colocar, pôr, dispor; posar, assumir determinada posição; dar-se ares, exibir-se; confundir, embaraçar; fazer pergunta, apresentar (problema); afirmar, emitir opiniões; *s.* pose, postura; atitude, afectação.

poser, *s.* pergunta desconcertante; enigma; pessoa afectada.

position, *s.* posição, postura, atitude; ponto de vista; lugar, colocação, localização; situação, circunstâncias; posição social, categoria; cargo, posto, emprego; tese, postulado. *v.t.* colocar, pôr em posição, posicionar.

positive, *adj.* positivo; expresso, explícito, categórico; certo, real, efectivo, concreto, incontestável; absoluto, incondicional; afirmativo; prático, realista; confiante, optimista; certo, que tem certeza; *I am positive that this is true. s.* positivo; quantidade positiva.

positivism, *s.* positivismo; certeza, convicção.

positivist, *s.* e *adj.* positivista.

posology, *s.* posologia.

posse, *s.* corpo, pelotão, bando de homens armados; turba; *posse comitatus,* força civil convocada pela autoridade para ajudar a manter a ordem, numa situação de emergência.

possess, *v.t.* possuir, ter, fruir, gozar, dispor de; apoderar-se do espírito de; *to possess oneself in patience,* armar-se de paciência.

possessed, *adj.* possesso.

possession, *s.* posse, possessão; propriedade, coisa possuída; fruição, gozo; (pl.) bens, haveres, património; possessões, colónias. 1) *in possession of,* de posse de. 2) *in the possession of,* em poder de.

possessive, *adj.* possessivo, relativo a

posse; dominador. s. (gram.) caso posses-sivo

possessor, s. possuidor; proprietário.

possessory, adj. possessório.

posset, s. bebida feita de leite quente coalhado.

possibility, s. possibilidade; probabilidade; potencialidade.

possible, adj. possível; potencial; praticável; concebível, razoável, admissível.

possum, s. forma abreviada de "opossum"; to play possum, fingir-se de doente.

post, s. poste, pilar, coluna; baliza, marco; estaca; esteio, suporte; camada compacta de arenito; posto, lugar; guarnição, forte; posta; correio; mala. postal; estação de correios; estafeta, mensageiro; determi-nado formato de papel. 1) post bag, saco postal. 2) post-card, cartão postal. 3) post-horse, cavalo de posta. 4) post-office, correio, estação de correios. 5) office-box, caixa postal. adv. pelo correio, com toda a rapidez, por expresso. 6) to travel post, viajar em mala-posta. v.t. e v.i. afixar; divulgar através de afixação; denunciar; afixar lista de nomes de alunos reprovados; cobrir de anúncios; postar, colocar; enviar pelo correio; viajar em mala-posta; (com.) passar lançamento do diário para o lívro--razão; (coloq.) pôr ao corrente. 7) to be posted to, (mil.) ser colocado em. 8) to be posted as captain, ser nomeado capitão.

postage, s. porte, franquia postal.

postal, adj. postal; postal-order, vale postal.

postcard, s. cartão-postal, bilhete postal.

postdate, v.t. pós-datar. s. pós-data.

postdiluvian, adj. pós-diluviano.

poster, s. afixador de cartazes; cartaz, anúncio.

posterior, adj. posterior, traseiro; ulterior. s. traseiro, assento, rabo.

posteriority, s. posterioridade, ulterioridade.

posterity, s. posteridade, os pósteros; descendência.

postern, s. porta traseira; entrada lateral.

postfix, s. sufixo.

post free, adj. com porte grátis; isento de porte.

posthumous, adj. póstumo.

postimpressionism, s. pós-impressionis-mo.

postlude, s. (mús.) poslúdio.

postman, s. carteiro.

postmark, s. carimbo postal.

postmaster, s. chefe dos correios.

post-mortem, adj. posterior a morte; relativo a autópsia. s. post-mortem examination, autópsia.

postoperative, adj. pós-operatório.

postponable, adj. adiável.

postpone, v.t. e v.i. adiar; postergar; pospor; protelar; subordinar, preterir; tardar, demorar.

postposition, s. posposição.

postscript, s. pós-escrito.

postulant, s. postulante, candidato.

postulate, s. postulado; condição essencial, requisito; v.t. e v.i. postular, exigir, recla-mar; tomar como postulado.

postulation, s. postulação, pedido, solicitação, exigência; postulado, pressu-posição.

posture, s. postura, atitude, posição, pose; estado, situação; atitude mental; posture-maker: contorcionista; v.t. e v.i. pôr em determinada posição; posar; assumir uma determinada atitude.

posy, adj. ramalhete de flores, bouquet; moto, frase inscrita em anel.

pot, s. pote, vaso; panela, tacho; cântaro; caneca; taça dada como prémio; aposta (no jogo). 1) tea-pot, bule. 2) melting pot, cadinho. 3) coffee pot, cafeteira. 4) to go to pot, arruinar-se. 5) pot lead, grafite. 6) pot shot, tiro fácil. 7) pot valliant, valente devido ao efeito do álcool. 8) pot walloper, eleitor que, em Inglaterra, tinha direito de voto na qualidade de dono da casa; v.t. pôr de conserva em pote; plantar em vaso; matar caça para comer; obter, conseguir; dar tiro de perto.

potable, adj. potável. s. pl. bebidas.

potash, s. potassa.

potass, s. potasse; potássio.

potassium, s. potássio.

potation, s. libação; bebida.

potato, s. batata.

potbellied, adj. barrigudo.

potency, s. potência, poder, força.

potent, adj. potente, poderoso, forte; convincente, de peso (um argumento).

potential, adj. potencial; virtual; latente; possível. s. potencial; (gram.) modo poten-cial.

potentiality, s. potencialidade.

pother, s. nuvem de pó, fumaça ou vapor; barulho, alvoroço, gritaria; v.t. e v.i. ator-mentar, perturbar, afligir, afligir-se.

pothole, s. caldeirão; buraco no pavimento de uma estrada.

pothouse, s. taverna.

pothunter, s. caçador que caça para comer; aquele que participa numa competição desportiva apenas motivado pelo prémio.

potion, s. poção; dose (de medicamento).

pottage, s. sopa, caldo.

potter, s. oleiro.

pottery, s. olaria, cerâmica; louça de barro.

potty, adj. trivial, insignificante; amalucado.

pouch, s. bolsa, sacola; algibeira. v.t. embolsar; engolir.

poulp, poulpe, s. polvo.

poulterer, s. criador ou negociante de aves de capoeira.

poultice, s. cataplasma.

poultry, s. aves de capoeira, aves domésticas.

pounce, s. pó fino usado antigamente para secar a tinta de escrever; garra de ave de rapina; acto de saltar sobre a presa; v.t. e v.i. agarrar; apoderar-se de; alisar com pedra-pomes; entrar de rompante.

pound, s. libra, unidade de peso equivalente a 453,59 g; libra esterlina (moeda Inglesa); depósito municipal para gado extraviado; depósito de mercadorias apreendidas; curral; canil; murro, golpe, pancada; v.t. e v.i. recolher gado extraviado; encerrar, prender; pisar, moer, triturar; golpear, esmurrar, bater; martelar; caminhar ou marchar pesadamente.

poundage, s. percentagem sobre os lucros totais de qualquer empreendimento comercial paga como salário ao pessoal; taxa a pagar pela guarda do gado no curral municipal.

pounder, s. triturador; pilão; almofariz; coisa que pesa uma libra.

pour, s. chuva torrencial, carga de água; acto de caminhar pesadamente; quantidade de metal fundido; v.t. e v.i. derramar, deitar, verter, vazar; coar, decantar; servir (bebida); chover torrencialmente; escoar--se, fluir, brotar, correr (com forth ou out).

pouring, adj. torrencial.

pout, s. nome vulgar de vários peixes; beicinho, trejeito feito com os lábios, careta; bico v.t. e v.i. fazer beicinho, mostrar má cara.

poverty, s. pobreza, miséria, penúria, destituição; escassez.

powder, s. pó; pólvora; pó-de-arroz; v.t. e v.i.

polvilhar, empoar; pulverizar, reduzir a pó; mosquear.

powdery, adj. pulverulento; poeirento; empoado.

power, s. poder; capacidade, faculdade; potência, energia, força; nação poderosa; domínio; influência, ascendência; poder de ampliação de uma lente; (mat.) potência, expoente; potencial, capacidade de trabalho de uma máquina; força motriz. 1) power driven, movido a motor. 2) power plant, central eléctrica. 3) power unit, unidade motriz. 4) a power of people, uma porção de gente. v.t. prover de energia.

powerboat, s. barco a motor.

powerful, adj. poderoso, forte, potente, possante, enérgico, pujante; intenso; influente.

powerhouse, s. casa das máquinas.

powerless, adj. impotente; ineficaz; incapaz; sem poderes.

pow-wow, s. feiticeiro ou curandeiro entre os índios norte-americanos; conferência entre Índios; conferência política; discussão ruidosa.

pox, s. sífilis: qualquer ﬔoença pustulosa ou eruptiva; varicela; varíola.

practicable, adj. praticável, exequível; viável.

practical, adj. prático; útil; practical joke, partida, brincadeira.

practice, s. prática; acto; acção; costume; exercício de uma profissão; clínica; clientela de advogado; regra, processo; target practice, exercícios de tiro.

practician, s. trabalhador; médico, clínico.

practise, v.t. e v.i. praticar, exercitar; treinar--se; exercer uma profissão; to practise on ou upon someone's credulity, explorar ou tirar proveito da credulidade de alguém.

practised, adj. experimentado, hábil.

practiser, s. aquele que pratica; prático, praticante.

practising, adj. que pratica; que exerce profissão, praticante; s. prática, acção de praticar; exercício.

practitioner, s. prático, profissional; médico general practitioner, médico de clínica geral.

praecocial, adj. precoce.

praenomen, s. prenome.

praetexta, s. pretexta, toga.

praetor, s. pretor.

praetorian, adj. pretoriano, pretorial.

pragmatic, *adj.* pragmático; prático; oficioso; dogmático.

pragmatism, *s.* pragmatismo.

pragmatist, *s.* pragamatista.

prairie, *s.* pradaria, campina; *prairie dog,* marmota.

praise, *s.* louvor, elogio; *v.t.* louvar, elogiar, gabar; exaltar, enaltecer.

praiseworthy, *adj.* louvável, digno de louvor.

pram, *s.* berço, carrinho de bebé.

prance, *v.i.* curvetear, empinar-se, obrigar o cavalo a empinar-se; fazer cabriolas; andar todo empertigado. *s.* cabriola; modo arrogante de caminhar.

prancing, *adj.* que faz cabriolas, que se empina, que se pavoneia ao andar.

prang, *v.t.* acertar em cheio; bombardear com êxito.

prank, *s.* travessura, partida, brincadeira; *v.t.* ornamentar, enfeitar, fazer travessuras.

prankish, *adj.* travesso, endiabrado, traquinas.

prat, *s.* traseiro, nádegas.

prate, *v.t.* e *v.i.* tagarelar, palrar. *s.* tagarelice, loquacidade.

prating, *adj.* loquaz, tagarela.

pratique, *s.* prática (licença de comunicar com um porto).

prattle, *v.t.* e *v.i.* tagarelar, palrar, murmurejar. *s.* tagarelice, conversa infantil.

prawn, *s.* camarão grande, gamba. *v.i.* pescar camarões.

praxis, *s.* praxe; uso, costume; exercício de gramática.

pray, *v.t.* e *v.i.* rezar, orar, suplicar, pedir, rogar.

prayer, *s.* aquele que reza; oração, prece, reza; súplica; rogo, pedido;

prayerfulness, *s.* devoção, piedade, religiosidade.

preach, *v.t.* e *v.i.* pregar, predicar; fazer sermões; dar conselhos; expor em prédica; preconizar, recomendar. 1) *to preach up,* elogiar, louvar. 2) *to preach down,* criticar, verberar, depreciar. *s.* sermão, predica.

preachify, *v.i.* pregar sermão, arengar, discursar enfadonhamente.

preaching, *s.* pregação, prédica; *adj.* pregador, predicante; admonitório.

preachment, *s.* prédica, sermão; exortação enfadonha.

preachy, *adj.* que gosta de pregar sermões.

preamble, *s.* preâmbulo, introdução, prefácio. *v.i.* fazer preâmbulo.

prearrange, *v.t.* dispor ou arranjar de antemão; preparar antecipadamente; combinar.

precarious, *adj.* precário, incerto, arriscado.

precatory, *adj.* precatório, rogatório.

precaution, *s.* precaução, medida de prevenção; cautela, previdência.

precautionary, *adj.* preventivo; cauteloso, precavido.

precede, *v.t.* e *v.i.* preceder, anteceder; ter precedência sobre; prevalecer a; precedence.

precedency, *s.* precedência, prioridade, anterioridade; primazia.

precedent, *adj.* precedente, anterior. *s.* precedente; exemplo.

preceding, *adj.* precedente, antecedente, anterior.

precent, *v.i.* dirigir um coro.

precentor, *s.* chantre, eclesiástico que dirige o coro numa colegiada.

precept, *s.* preceito, norma, regra, mandamento; máxima, instrução, ordem; ensinamento, doutrina; (jur.) ordem, mandado.

preceptor, *s.* professor, preceptor, mestre, mentor.

preceptorate, preceptorship, *s.* cargo de professor, preceptorado.

preceptress, *s. fem.,* preceptora.

pre-christian, *adj.* pré-cristão.

precinct, *s.* recinto, precinto; circuito; (E.U.) circunscrição eleitoral; *pl.* arredores.

preciosity, *s.* preciosismo, maneirismo.

precious, *adj.* precioso, valioso; caro, querido, estimado; refinado, amaneirado; afectado; *adv.* muito, extremamente.

preciousness, *s.* preciosidade; grande valor.

precipice, *s.* precipício, abismo; penhasco.

precipitance, *s.* precipitação, pressa excessiva; Irreflexão.

precipitate, *s.* precipitado; precipitação de chuva. *adj.* precipitado, rápido; irreflectido, impulsivo; súbito, abrupto. *v.t.* e *v.i.* precipitar; despenhar, derrubar, atirar; lançar, levar; apressar, antecipar, acelerar; precipitar-se.

precipitation, *s.* precipitação; queda; celeridade; pressa; irreflexão.

precipitous, *adj.* precipitoso, alcantilado, escarpado, ingreme; imprudente.

precis, *s.* sumárlo, resumo.

precise, *adj.* preciso, claro, definido; exacto, certo, justo, rigoroso; escrupuloso, meticuloso.

precision, s. precisão, exactidão.

precisionist, s. formalista; purista.

preclude, v.t. evitar, prevenir, impossibilitar, frustrar; impedir; obstruir, interceptar.

preclusion, s. prevenção; proibição, exclusão.

preclusive, adj. preventivo, impeditivo.

precocious, adj. precoce; prematuro, antecipado.

precociousness, s. precocidade.

precognition, s. conhecimento prévio; precognição; (jur. E.U.) interrogatório prévio das testemunhas para verificar se há fundamento para um julgamento.

preconceive, v.t. preconceber.

preconception, s. preconcepção, Ideia preconcebida; prejuízo, preconceito.

preconize, v.t. preconizar; elogiar publicamente; proclamar; fazer a preconização de (bispo)

precursor, s. precursor, anunciador; antecessor.

precursory, adj. precursor, anunciador; preliminar; prenunciador.

predate, v.t. pré-datar.

predator, s. predador.

predatory, adj. predatório; voraz.

predecease, v.t. e v.i. morrer antes de.

predecessor, s. predecessor; antepassado.

predestinate, v.t. predestinar, fadar. adj. predestinado, eleito.

predestination, s. predestinação, destino, fado.

predestine, v.t. predestinar, fadar, predeterminar.

predial, adj. rural, agrário; s. servo da gleba.

predicable, adj. predicável; afirmável. s. coisa afirmável.

predicament, s. predicamento, categoria; situação desagradável.

predicant, adj. predicante. s. predicante, pregador.

predicate, s. predicado; atributo, qualidade. v.t. afirmar; afirmar como verdadeiro ou existente; pressupor, implicar.

predication, s. afirmação; predicação.

predicatory, adj. relativo a prédica.

predict, v.t. predizer, profetizar, vaticinar.

prediction, s. predição; profecia.

predilection, s. predilecção, preferência.

predispose, v.t. predispor.

predisposition, s. predisposição, propensão.

predominance, s. predominância, preponderância.

predominant, adj. predominante, dominante, prevalecente.

predominate, v.t. predominar, prevalecer.

pre-empt, v.t. obter por preempção; apropriar-se antecipadamente de.

pre-emption, s. preempção; direito de preempção.

preen, v.t. alisar as penas com o bico; arranjar o pêlo; arranjar-se, enfeitar-se.

prefab, s. (fam.) casa pré-fabricada.

preface, s. prefácio; preâmbulo, prólogo, introdução; v.t. prefaciar; v.t. tecer conslderações preliminares.

prefect, s. prefeito (magistrado romano ou monitor nalguns colégios).

prefecture, s. prefeitura, divisão administrativa preliminar.

prelude, s. prelúdio, prólogo, princípio. v.t. e v.i. preludiar, prefaciar; preparar, introduzir.

prelusion, s. prelúdio, introdução.

premature, adj. prematuro; precipitado.

premeditate, v.t. e v.i. premeditar, planear, calcular.

premeditation, s. premeditação.

premier, adj. primeiro, principal; s. o primeiro-ministro.

premise, s. premissa; pl. imóveis, edifício, prédio, propriedade, local, recinto. v.t. e v.i. dizer, explicar de Início; estabelecer como premissas; prefaciar; pressupor, postular.

premium, s. prémio, recompensa com o fito de servir de estImulo; bonificação, prémio do seguro.

premolar, s. e adj. pré-molar.

premonish, v.t. premunir, avisar.

premonition, s. premonição, avIso; presságio, pressentimento.

premonitory, adj. premonitório.

prenotion, s. pré-noção, preconceito.

prenuptial, adj. antenupcial, pré-nupcial.

preoccupation, s. preocupação, inquietação; pré-ocupação.

preoccupied, adj. preocupado, inquieto; pré-ocupado.

preoccupy, v.t. preocupar, inquietar; pré-ocupar.

preordination, s. preordenação, predeterminação.

preparation, s. preparação, preparo; confecção, fabrico; pl. preparativos.

preparative, adj. preparativo, preparatório.

preparatory, adj. preparatório, preliminar,

introdutivo; (E.U.) que frequenta um curso de preparação. *s.* curso de preparação para escola superior.

prepare, *v.t.* preparar, aparelhar, aprestar, dispor, arranjar; estudar a lição, preparar--se.

prepared, *adj.* preparado, pronto.

prepay, *v.t.* pagar adiantadamente.

prepense, *adj.* premeditado, intencional.

preponderance, *s.* preponderância, predomínio, supremacia.

preponderant, *adj.* preponderante, predominante.

preponderation, *s.* o mesmo que *preponderance.*

preposition, *s.* (gram.) preposição.

prepositive, *adj.* (gram.) prepositivo. *s.* palavra prepositiva.

prepositor, *s.* monitor.

prepossess, *v.t.* imbuir, inspirar, dominar.

prepossessing, *adj.* cativante, simpático.

prepossession, *s.* prevenção, preconceito.

preposterous, *adj.* absurdo, despropositado.

preposterousness, *s.* absurdidade, despropósito.

prepotency, *s.* prepotência.

prepotent, *adj.* prepotente.

prepuce, *s.* prepúcio.

prerequisite, *adj.* necessário, indispensável. *s.* condição prévia, requisito Indispensável .

prerogative, *s.* prerrogativa, privilégio, regalia. *adj.* privilegiado.

presage, *s.* presságio, agouro, pressentimento, prognóstico; *v.t.* e *v.i.* pressagiar, augurar, predizer.

presbyter, *s.* presbítero.

presbyterate, *s.* presbitérlo; presbiterado.

Presbyterianism, *s.* presbiterianismo.

presbytry, *s.* presbitério; capela-mor; casa paroquial.

preschool, *s.* jardim infantil; *adj.* pré-escolar.

prescience, *s.* presciência, conhecimento do futuro.

prescient, *adj.* presciente; previdente.

prescind, *v.t.* e *v.i.* cercear, separar; abstralr; prescindir de.

prescribe, *v.t.* e *v.i.* prescrever, determinar, estabelecer; ordenar; receitar (medicamentos); passar uma receita (o médico); caducar; *to prescribe regulation,* impor regulamentos.

prescript, *s.* prescrição, ordem.

prescription, *s.* prescrição, receita médica.

presence, *s.* presença; comparecimento; porte, figura, aparência; *presence chamber,* sala de audiências de um soberano.

present, *adj.* presente, actual, vigente, corrente, em apreço, em discussão. *s.* o presente, tempo presente; presente, prenda. *v.t.* apresentar; mostrar; expor, submeter à consideração de; presentear, dar em presente, oferecer; proporcionar; apresentar na corte; apresentar-se, mostrar-se, aparecer; *to present arms,* apresentar armas.

presentable, *adj.* apresentável; ofertável.

presentation, *s.* apresentação; entrega; oferecimento; representação, espectáculo; (filos.) objecto de conhecimento; *on presentation,* à vista.

presentee, *s.* clérigo apresentado para um benefício; pessoa apresentada na corte.

presentiment, *s.* pressentimento, palpite.

presently, *adv.* dentro em pouco, logo, em breve; actualmente.

presentment, *s.* apresentação; acto de apresentar; representação; descrição; exposição; (jur.) declaração sob juramento feita pelo júri; representação ou queixa feita pelo bispo às autoridades paroquiais.

preservation, *s.* preservação, defesa; conservação, manutenção.

preservative, *adj.* preservativo, preservador; preventivo, profiláctico. *s.* preservativo (para a conservação de alimentos); salvaguarda, resguardo.

preserve, *v.t.* preservar, resguardar, proteger, defender; conservar, manter, guardar; pôr em conserva, fazer conservas (de fruta, etc.). *s.* conserva, compota; coutada, reserva de caça.

preside, *v.i.* presidir, governar, reinar; dirigir; assumir a presidência; *to preside at the piano,* ser o pianista.

presidency, *s.* presidência.

president, *s.* presidente; reitor de algumas universidades.

presidential, *adj.* presidencial.

presidentship, *s.* presidência.

presidiary, *adj.* presidiário, relativo a presídio; guarnecido de força militar.

presiding, *adj.* que preside.

presidium, *s.* presídio, forte, praça de guerra.

presignify, *v.t.* pressagiar.

press, *v.t.* e *v.i.* apertar, premir, comprimir, calcar, fazer pressão sobre; espremer;

empurrar, impelir; oprimir; perseguir, assediar; insistir com, instar; solicitar urgentemente; impor, impingir; exercer pressão;
urgir; recrutar à força para serviço público.
s. pressão, prensa, lagar, máquina de
impressão; premência, urgência; imprensa
(jornais, revistas, etc.); armário; *to have a
good press,* ser bem recebido pela crítica.

pressed, *adj.* comprimido, apertado; aflito,
em apuros; estampado; prensado; impresso.

presser, *s.* prensador; prensa.

pressgang, *s.* grupo de homens encarre-
gados de recrutar à força soldados ou
marinheiros.

pressing, *adj.* urgente, premente; insistente.

pressurage, *s.* prensagem (no lagar); mosto
resultante do bagaço prensado.

pressure, *s.* pressão; compressão; aperto;
opressão, aflição; premência, urgência;
(electr.) tensão; *pressure cooker,* panela de
pressão.

pressurize, *v.t.* pressurizar; pressionar.

presswork, *s.* impressão.

prestidigitation, *s.* prestidigitação, ilusionismo.

prestidigitator, *s.* prestidigitador, ilusionista.

prestige, *s.* prestígio; fama, renome; fascinação.

presumable, *adj.* presumível; provável.

presuming, *adj.* presumido, presunçoso.

presumption, *s.* presunção, suposição, conjectura, suspeita; pretensão,
arrogância.

presumptive, *adj.* presuntivo, presumível,
provável.

presumptuous, *adj.* presunçoso, presumido, convencido; arrogante; atrevido,
impertinente.

presuppose, *v.t.* pressupor, conjecturar;
implicar.

presupposition, *s.* pressuposição; pressuposto.

pretence, o mesmo que *pretense.*

pretend, *v.t.* fingir, simular, aparentar, fazer
de conta; pretender, aspirar a; intentar,
tentar; alegar.

pretended, *adj.* pretenso, suposto, falso,
fingido.

pretender, *s.* pretendente, candidato,
aspirante; simulador, hipócrita.

pretense, *s.* pretensão, aspiração, ambição;
presunção, ostentação; pretexto; aparência,
máscara, véu; fingimento.

pretension, *s.* pretensão, exigência,
reivindicação; presunção; alegação;
pretexto.

pretentious, *adj.* pretensioso, presunçoso,
arrogante, afectado.

preterhuman, *adj.* sobre-humano.

preterit, praterite, *adj.* e *s.* pretérito,
passado.

preterition, *s.* preterição, omissão.

pretermission, *s.* pretermissão, preterição,
omissão; interrupção.

pretermit, *v.t.* pretermitir, preterir, omitir;
interromper, suspender.

preternatural, *adj.* preternatural, sobrenatural; extraordinário.

pretext, *s.* pretexto, desculpa. *v.t.* pretextar,
alegar.

pretor, o mesmo que *praetor.*

prettify, *v.t.* alindar, tornar bonito, embonecar.

prettiness, *s.* lindeza, beleza, boniteza,
graça; enfeite, ornamento; estilo afectado.

pretty, *adj.* bonito, lindo, engraçado,
agradável; bastante, grande, considerável.
adv. bastante, razoavelmente. *s.* pessoa ou
coisa bonita; enfeite.

pretty-pretties, *s. pl.* enfeites, bugigangas;
ninharias.

prevail, *v.i.* prevalecer, preponderar, triunfar;
ser bem sucedido; predominar, ser mais
vulgar; *to prevail on ou upon someone,*
induzir, convencer alguém.

prevailing, *adj.* predominante, principal;
corrente, comum, dominante; superior,
vitorioso.

prevalence, *s.* predomínio; frequência.

prevalent, *adj.* predominante, corrente,
dominante; frequente; preponderante.

prevaricate, *v.i.* tergiversar, usar de
subterfúgios, mentir.

prevarication, *s.* tergiversão, mentira,
falsidade, evasiva.

prevent, *v.t.* prevenir, evitar, atalhar; impedir,
obstar.

prevention, *s.* prevenção, impedimento.

preventive, *adj.* preventivo, impeditivo;
profiláctico. *s.* medida preventiva;
preventivo.

preview, *s.* antestreia; apresentação
antecipada; *v.t.* ver ou apreciar em antes-
-treia.

previous, *adj.* prévio, anterior, antecedente,
precedente; apressado, precipitado;
previous to, antes de.

previse, *v.t.* prever, profetizar.

prevision, *s.* previsão; profecia.

prexy, *s.* (E.U.) director de faculdade.

prey, *s.* presa, vítima; pilhagem; *bird of prey,* ave de rapina. *v.t.* atacar, apresar, predar, dar caça a; rapinar, roubar, pilhar; atormentar, oprimir.

price, *s.* preço, custo; valor. *v.t.* apreçar, fixar o preço; cotar.

priceless, *adj.* inestimável, de valor incalculável; engraçadíssimo, delicioso.

prick, *s.* ponto, furo; picada, ferroada, alfinetada; escrúpulo, remorso; instrumento pontiagudo; aguilhão; espinho; pénis. *adj.* empinado, levantado. *v.t.* picar, pungir, aferroar, furar, perfurar; atormentar; esporear, incitar; marcar um desenho a pontilhado.

prickle, *s.* espinho, ponta, bico, ferrão; picada; *pl.* comichão. *v.t.* e *v.i.* picar, pungir, ferroar.

prickly, *adj.* espinhoso; picante, que pica; irritadiço; *prickly heat,* brotoeja.

pride, *s.* orgulho, soberba, arrogância, vaidade; altivez, brio; satisfação; ostentação, pompa. 1) *to take pride in,* orgulhar-se de. 2) *pride of the morning,* neblina matinal. *v.r.* orgulhar-se, vangloriar-se.

prideful, *adj.* orgulhoso, arrogante.

prier, *s.* bisbilhoteiro, curioso, indiscreto.

priest, *s.* sacerdote, padre. *v.t.* ordenar sacerdote.

priestess, *s.* sacerdotisa.

priesthood, *s.* sacerdócio; clero.

priestly, *adj.* sacerdotal, clerical, eclesiástico.

prig, *s.* pedante; pessoa presunçosa; (coloq.) gatuno. *v.t.* roubar.

priggery, *s.* pedantismo.

prim, *adj.* afectado, empertigado, formal; amaneirado; recatado. *v.t.* e *v.i.* assumir expressão afectada; embonecar; empertigar-se.

primacy, *s.* primazia; primado, dignidade de primaz; prioridade, superioridade.

primal, *adj.* primeiro, primordial; principal, fundamental.

primarily, *adv.* originariamente; antes de tudo, principalmente.

primary, *adj.* primário; original, primitivo; primordial; principal, fundamental. *s.* princípio fundamental; planeta primário; reunião prévia para a escolha dos candidatos a uma eleição; eleição

preliminar; (electr.) circuito indutor; rémige primária.

primate, *s.* primaz, arcebispo; primata.

primateship, *s.* primado, primazia.

prime, *s.* a melhor parte; começo, primórdios, aurora; primavera; vigor da juventude; plenitude, apogeu; (mat.) número primo; (mús.) tom fundamental. 1) *the prime of live,* a juventude. 2) *the prime of the moon,* a lua nova. 3) *the prime of the year,* a Primavera. *adj.* primeiro, primitivo; principal, fundamental; primário; de primeira qualidade. 4) *prime cost,* custo de produção. *v.t.* e *v.i.* escorvar, deitar pólvora na escorva; preparar para começar a trabalhar; instruir, industriar; espumar (uma caldeira a vapor).

primeness, *s.* excelência, qualidade superior.

primer, *s.* escorva; cápsula de cartucho; livro de leitura para ensinar as crianças a ler; cartilha; livro de orações.

primeval, *adj.* primevo, primitivo; antigo.

primitive, *adj.* primitivo; primevo, primordial; original, inicial; primária (cor). *s.* palavra primitiva, raiz; (mat.) primitiva.

primitivism, *s.* primitivismo.

primordial, *adj.* primordial; primitivo, original; primário, básico, fundamental.

primrose, *s.* Primavera, prímula. *adj.* amarelo-claro; florido, alegre; *the primrose path,* o caminho do prazer.

prince, *s.* príncipe; soberano.

princedom, *s.* principado.

princely, *adj.* principesco; nobre; magnífico, opulento.

princess, *s.* princesa.

principal, *adj.* principal; capital, cardeal; essencial, fundamental; (gram.) *the principal parts,* formas primitivas do verbo. *s.* chefe, superior; director; reitor; outorgante; trave mestra de telhado; principal responsável por um crime.

principality, *s.* principado, território governado por um príncipe.

principate, *s.* principado; dignidade imperial dos primeiros imperadores romanos.

principle, *s.* princípio; causa; origem; norma ou regra de conduta; postulado, axioma, verdade fundamental.

prink, *v.t.* e *v.i.* compor, alisar as penas; ataviar, enfeitar, enfeitar-se.

print, *s.* marca, impressão, sinal, vestígio; cunho, selo, sinete; chita, algodão estampado; impressão, letra de forma; impresso, folheto, publicação. 1) *in print,* impresso, publicado. 2) *out of print,* esgotado. 3) *print hand, print letters,* letra de imprensa. 4) *foot print,* pegada. *v.t.* e *v.i.* imprimir, gravar, estampar; marcar, deixar vestígio; aplicar molde a; publicar, dar à estampa; escrever em letra de imprensa.

printer, *s.* impressor; tipógrafo; máquina de imprimir; (fot.) copiador.

printery, *s.* estamparia; tipografia.

printing, *s.* gravação; estampagem de tecido; impressão, tipografia; *printing press,* prelo.

printworks, *s.* estamparia.

prior, *s.* prior; *adj.* anterior, precedente, prévio; *prior to,* antes de.

priorate, *s.* priorado.

prioress, *s.f.* priorisa.

priority, *s.* prioridade; anterioridade; precedência; preferência.

priory, *s.* priorado.

prism, *s.* prisma; *pl.* cores prismáticas.

prismatic, *adj.* prismático; vívido, brilhante, colorido; rômbico.

prison, *s.* prisão, cárcere, cadeia; detenção, reclusão. *v.t.* encarcerar.

prisoner, *s.* prisioneiro, detido, cativo; réu, acusado; *prisoner of State,* preso político.

prissy, *adj.* meticuloso, afectado, amaneirado.

pristine, *adj.* pristino, antigo, primitivo; incorrupto.

privacy, *s.* privacidade; isolamento, solidão; intimidade; segredo.

private, *adj.* privado, particular; pessoal, individual, íntimo; solitário; reservado, confidencial. *s.* soldado raso, recruta.

privateer, *s.* corsário.

privation, *s.* privação, ausência, carência, falta; penúria, miséria.

privative, *adj.* privativo.

privilege, *s.* privilégio, regalia, graça; direito, prerrogativa; patente. *v.t.* privilegiar, conceder privilégio; permitir; isentar, dispensar.

privy, *adj.* secreto, furtivo; oculto, escondido; conhecedor, informado, a par de; privado, particular. *s.* privada, latrina; (jur.) parte interessada.

prize, *v.t.* prezar, estimar, apreciar; capturar, apresar; arrombar. *s.* prémio, recompensa, galardão; presa, navio ou mercadorias apresadas; ponto de apoio das alavancas.

1) *to make prize of,* apresar. 2) *prize Court,* tribunal que decide sobre as presas marítimas. 3) *prize flighting,* boxe profissional.

prizeman, *s.* detentor de um prémio.

pro, *adv.* pró, a favor; *s.* voto ou votante favorável; argumento favorável; (fam.) profissional.

probability, *s.* probabilidade; verosimilhança, plausibilidade.

probable, *adj.* provável, presumível; verosímil, plausível; *probable cause,* (jur.) fundamento de uma acusação.

probate, *s.* (jur.) legitimação, aprovação (de testamento); cópia autenticada de testamento; *probate court,* tribunal de sucessões. *adj.* testamentário. *v.t.* aprovar, homologar.

probation, *s.* (jur.) liberdade condicional; período de prova, estágio; *probation officer,* funcionário encarregado de fiscalizar quem está sob liberdade condicional.

probationer, *s.* empregado em período de prova, estagiário, principiante, aprendiz; pessoa que se encontra em liberdade condicional.

probative, probatory, *adj.* que serve para experimentar ou para pôr à prova; probativo, probatório, comprovativo.

probe, *s.* sonda; sondagem, inquérito, sindicância. *v.t.* sondar; investigar, examinar, estudar; perfurar, penetrar.

probity, *s.* probidade, honradez, integridade.

problem, *s.* problema. *adj.* que constitui problema.

problematic, *adj.* problemático; difícil; discutível.

proboscidian, *adj.* e *s.* proboscídeo.

procedural, *adj.* (jur.) processual.

procedure, *s.* procedimento; (jur.) processo; método, actuação; ordem parlamentar.

proceed, *v.i.* prosseguir, continuar, avançar; proceder, originar-se, vir de. provir; instaurar processo; *to proceed to,* receber grau de. *s. pl.* produto, renda, lucro.

proceeding, *s.* procedimento, comportamento, conduta; acto, acção; transacção; *pl.* acta de assembleia; processo, acção; autos; *to institute legal proceedings,* instaurar processo.

process, *s.* processo, método; procedimento; operação, tratamento, manipulação; progresso, curso, continuação, andamento; (jur.) processo, acção judicial; (anat.) excrescência, apófise; (quim.) reacção;

(artes gráficas) processos fotomecânicos; *process printing*, impressão a três cores. *v.t.* processar; (jur.) instaurar processo judicial; submeter a processo industrial, tratar, preparar; pôr em conserva; revelar filme; reproduzir por processo fotomecânico. *v.i.* ir em procissão, desfilar.

procession, s. procissão, cortejo, desfile; *v.t.* percorrer em procissão.

processional, *adj.* processional. s. cântico de procissão.

processionist, s. participante em procissão.

proclaim, *v.t.* proclamar, anunciar, publicar, apregoar; declarar (guerra), anunciar oficialmente; proibir; proscrever.

proclamation, s. proclamação, publicação, declaração pública; promulgação; proscrição; édito.

proclivity, s. propensão, tendência.

proconsul, s. procônsul.

proconsulate, proconsulship, s. proconsulado.

procrastination, s. procrastinação, demora; adiamento.

procreate, *v.t.* procriar, gerar, criar, engendrar.

procreation, s. procriação, reprodução; formação.

proctology, s. proctologia.

proctor, s. solicitador, procurador (em tribunais eclesiásticos); inspector.

procumbent, *adj.* procumbente; deitado de bruços.

procuration, s. obtenção, aquisição; procuração, procuradoria, mandato; alcovitice.

procurator, s. procurador, agente, representante, delegado.

procure, *v.t.* obter, conseguir, adquirir, granjear; *v.i.* alcovitar.

procurement, s. obtenção, aquisição; instigação, maquinação; autorização.

procurer, s. aquele que obtém ou consegue, obtentor; alcoviteiro, proxeneta.

procuress, *s.f.* alcoviteira, proxeneta.

prod, s. picada, ferroada, estocada; cotovelada; ponta, instrumento pontiagudo, aguilhão, espeto, furador. *v.t.* aguilhoar, picar; espicaçar, incitar.

prodigal, *adj.* pródigo, esbanjador, perdulário; generoso, abundante, profuso; rico, fértil.

prodigality, s. prodigalidade, esbanjamento, desperdício; abundância, profusão.

prodigious, *adj.* prodigioso, extraordinário, fenomenal, maravilhoso; enorme, monstruoso.

prodigy, s. prodígio, portento; maravilha.

produce, s. produção, rendimento; produto, fruto; efeito, consequência, resultado; *raw produce,* produtos agrícolas. *v.t.* produzir, criar, gerar, fabricar, fazer; causar, motivar, ocasionar, provocar, originar; alegar, apresentar razões; exibir, mostrar.

producer, s. produtor; gerador, criador, autor.

product, s. produto; rendimento, produção; resultado, fruto, efeito.

production, s. produção, produto; criação, fabrico; apresentação, exibição.

productive, *adj.* produtivo, produtor, criador; fértil, fecundo; lucrativo, rendível.

productivity, s. produtividade, rendimento; fertilidade.

proem, s. proémio, prefácio, preâmbulo; prelúdio.

profanation, s. profanação, sacrilégio; abuso, aviltamento.

profanatory, *adj.* profanador, profano.

profane, *adj.* profano, secular, leigo, mundano, ímpio, blasfemo. *v.t.* profanar, violar, desrespeitar, macular.

profanity, s. profanidade, impiedade; blasfémia.

profess, *v.t.* professar, praticar, seguir, tomar o hábito de uma ordem religiosa, proferir votos solenes; anunciar, declarar, afirmar, confessar; manifestar, expressar; fingir, simular; ensinar como professor.

professed, *adj.* professo; declarado, manifesto; aparente, pretenso.

professedly, *adv.* declaradamente, ostensivamente.

profession, s. profissão; declaração solene; acto de professar, proferir votos solenes; profissão, ofício, carreira, ocupação, emprego.

professional, *adj.* e s. profissional.

professionalism, s. profissionalismo.

professor, s. professor; aquele que professa, que faz declaração pública.

professorate, professorship, s. professorado.

professoriate, s. corpo docente, professorado.

proffer, *v.t.* oferecer, dar, ofertar. s. oferecimento, oferta, proposta.

proficiency, *s.* proficiência, competência, perícia.

proficient, *adj.* proficiente, competente, hábil. *s.* perito, entendido.

profile, *s.* perfil, silhueta, contorno, corte transversal. *v.t.* perfilar, traçar o perfil de, delinear, contornar, dar perfil ou contorno a.

profit, *s.* proveito, lucro, benefício, vantagem, rendimento, ganho. *v.t.* e *v.i.* lucrar, ganhar, beneficiar, trazer vantagem, aproveitar a, favorecer, tirar partido.

profitable, *adj.* lucrativo, rendível; proveitoso, benéfico.

profitless, *adj.* inútil, infrutífero.

profligacy, *s.* desregramento, libertinagem, devassidão.

profligate, *adj.* e *s.* libertino, dissoluto, devasso.

profound, *adj.* profundo, fundo; sagaz, arguto, culto; recôndito; grande, intenso. *s.* profundidade, profundeza.

profundity, *s.* profundidade, profundeza; perspicácia, saber; intensidade.

profuse, *adj.* profuso, pródigo, generoso; abundante, copioso, exuberante; esbanjador.

profusion, *s.* profusão, prodigalidade; desperdício; abundância, exuberância.

prog, *s.* farnel, merenda.

progenitor, *s.* progenitor, antepassado; precursor, predecessor; original (de uma cópia).

progeniture, *s.* procriação; descendência.

progeny, *s.* progenitura, descendência; resultado, consequência.

progesterone, *s.* progesterona.

prognathism, *s.* prognatismo.

prognosis, *s.* prognóstico.

prognostic, *s.* prognóstico; agouro, presságio. *adj.* prognóstico, prenunciador.

prognosticate, *v.t.* prognosticar, vaticinar, predizer; prenunciar, agourar.

program, programme, *s.* programa; plano. *v.t.* programar, planear.

programmatic, *adj.* programático.

progress, *s.* progresso, avanço, marcha, progressão, curso; desenvolvimento, aperfeiçoamento. 1) *royal progress,* viagem de soberano. 2) *in progress,* em curso. *v.i.* progredir, desenvolver-se; avançar, adiantar-se, prosseguir.

progression, *s.* progressão, progresso, avanço, marcha; sequência, série, sucessão.

progressist, *s.* progressista.

pregressive, *adj.* progressivo; gradual; sucessivo, partidário do progresso, progressista.

progressivism, *s.* progressismo.

prohibit, *v.t.* proibir, interdizer, interditar, impedir.

prohibition, *s.* proibição, interdição; decreto proibitório; interdição legal do consumo de bebidas alcoólicas, proibicionismo; "Lei Seca".

prohibitionist, *s.* proibicionista, partidário da "Lei Seca".

prohibitory, *adj.* proibitivo.

project, *s.* projecto, plano, intento. *v.t.* e *v.i.* projectar, intentar, planear, delinear; projectar, arremessar, lançar; sobressair, ressaltar.

projectile, *s.* projéctil.

projection, *s.* projecção; arremesso, lançamento, ejecção; saliência, protuberância; planeamento, projecto.

projective, *adj.* projectivo.

projector, *s.* projector; holofote; aparelho de projecção; pessoa que faz planos, que projecta; especulador, vigarista.

prolapse, *s.* prolapso, queda. *v.i.* sofrer prolapso.

proletarian, *adj.* e *s.* proletário.

proletarianism, *s.* proletariado.

proletariat, proletariate, *s.* proletariado, a classe proletária.

proliferate, *v.t.* e *v.i.* proliferar, multiplicar-se.

proliferation, *s.* proliferação.

proliferous, *adj.* prolífero.

prolific, *adj.* prolífico, prolífero, fecundo, fértil, fecundo, abundante; inventivo, criativo.

prolix, *adj.* prolixo, longo, extenso, difuso, enfadonho; palavroso.

prolixity, *s.* prolixidade, extensão, verbosidade.

prolocutor, *s.* intérprete, interlocutor; presidente de assembleia.

prologue, *s.* prólogo.

prologuize, *v.i.* escrever um prólogo, fazer preceder de prólogo.

prolong, *v.t.* prolongar, alongar; aumentar, estender.

prolongation, *s.* prolongamento; continuação.

prolusion, *s.* prolusão, preâmbulo, preparação, tentativa preliminar; introdução.

promenade, s. passeio; (E.U., também prom) baile de estudantes. 1) *promenade concert,* concerto ao ar livre. 2) *promenade deck,* convés superior em navio de passageiros.

Promethean, adj. prometeico, relativo a Prometeu; audaz, original, criador.

prominence, s. proeminência, eminência, distinção, notoriedade, importância; saliencia, protuberância; outeiro.

prominent, adj. proeminente, saliente, protuberante; manifesto, patente; importante, ilustre, notável.

promiscuity, s. promiscuidade; mistura, confusão.

promiscuous, adj. promíscuo; misturado, confuso, indiscriminado.

promise, s. promessa, compromisso; palavra dada; cumprimento de promessa; indicação, sinal; esperança. v.t. e v.i. prometer, obrigar-se a, comprometer-se; assegurar, garantir, asseverar; ser prometedor.

promisee, s. (jur.) promissário.

promiser, s. promitente, promissor, aquele que fez uma promessa.

promising, adj. prometedor, promissor, esperançoso.

promisor, s. o mesmo que *promiser.*

promissory, adj. promissório, promissivo; *promissory note,* nota promissória.

promontory, s. promontório.

promote, v.t. promover, elevar a um posto; fomentar, estimular, animar; apoiar projecto de lei; fomentar a aprovação de.

promoter, s. promotor, patrocinador; fundador de empresas.

promotion, s. promoção, elevação a cargo superior; fomento, estímulo, desenvolvimento.

prompt, adj. pronto, activo, expedito, solícito; rápido, breve, imediato; pontual; para entrega imediata. adv. exacto, em ponto. s. prazo, termo, limite de tempo para pagamento; (teat.) indicação dada pelo ponto; lembrete, advertência. v.t. incitar, induzir, impelir; inspirar, sugerir; (teat.) servir de ponto a.

prompter, s. instigador, incitador; (teat.) ponto.

prompting, s. instigação, estímulo; sugestão.

promptitude, s. prontidão, solicitude, rapidez.

promulgate, v.t. promulgar, publicar, proclamar; propagar, disseminar.

prone, adj. inclinado, disposto, propenso, atreito; prostrado, de bruços, voltado para baixo; íngreme, inclinado, em declive.

prong, s. dente de garfo; ponta aguçada, pua; forcado; *prong hoe,* ancinho. v.t. perfurar, espetar; revolver a terra com forcado.

pronghorn, s. antilocabra.

pronominal, adj. pronominal.

pronoun, s. pronome.

pronounce, v.t. e v.i. pronunciar, proferir; proclamar, decretar, anunciar; pronunciar--se, manifestar-se.

pronouncement, s. declaração formal, afirmação, proclamação.

pronouncing, adj. pronúncia, acto de pronunciar; pronunciação, articulação; *pronouncing dictionary,* dicionário de pronúncia.

pronunciation, s. pronúncia, articulação; prosódia.

proof, s. prova, demonstração, evidência; ensaio, teste, experiência, verificação; graduação normal de bebidas alcoólicas; (quím.) tubo de ensaio; adj. à prova, resistente; imune; de graduação alcoólica normal. 1) *water-proof,* impermeável. 2) *fire-proof,* à prova de fogo. v.t. tornar resistente; impermeabilizar.

proofreader, s. revisor tipográfico.

prop, s. suporte, estaca, amparo, apoio; escora, esteio; (av. coloq.) o mesmo que *propeller;* (teat.) adereço; *prop-man,* aderecista. v.t. e v.i. apoiar, sustentar, estear, escorar, servir de suporte; estacar (o cavalo).

propaedeutic, adj. propedêutico.

propagable, adj. propagável, transmissível.

propaganda, s. propaganda.

propagandism, s. propagandismo.

propagandist, s. propagandista; (catól.) missionário da Congregação de Propaganda.

propagandize, v.t. propagandear, propagar, difundir, fazer propaganda.

propagate, v.t. e v.i. propagar, multiplicar; espalhar, disseminar, difundir; transmitir, conduzir; propagar-se.

propagation, s. propagação, multiplicação; disseminação, difusão; transmissão.

propane, s. propano.

propel, v.t. propulsinar, impelir, impulsionar, accionar, mover.

propeller, *s.* propulsor, impulsor, motor; hélice; *propeller shaft,* eixo de transmissão.

propense, *adj.* propenso, atreito, disposto.

propension, propensity, *s.* propensão, inclinação, tendência.

proper, *adj.* próprio; peculiar, particular, característico; apropriado, conveniente, oportuno; exacto, correcto; decente, respeitável; (coloq.) completo, perfeito, verdadeiro. 1) *he is a proper gentleman,* ele é um verdadeiro cavalheiro. 2) *proper-fraction,* fracção própria.

properly, *adv.* propriamente, particularmente; exactamente; adequadamente, correctamente, bem; (coloq.) muito, completamente.

property, *s.* propriedade; qualidade, atributo, característica; posses, direito de posse; imóvel, herdade; (teat. pl.) adereços; *property-man,* aderecista.

prophecy, *s.* profecia.

prophesy, *v.t.* e *v.i.* profetizar, predizer, vaticinar; falar sob inspiração divina.

prophet, *s.* profeta; vidente; defensor, adepto, advogado.

prophetess, *s.f.* profetisa.

prophetic, *adj.* profético; vaticinador.

prophylaxis, *s.* profilaxia.

propitiation, *s.* propiciação, apaziguamento; expiação, sacrifício.

propitious, *adj.* propício; favorável; próprio, adequado; auspicioso.

proponent, *s.* proponente.

proportion, *s.* proporção, relação, razão; (pl.) dimensões; parte, porção; harmonia, simetria, equilíbrio. *v.t.* proporcionar, harmonizar; adaptar.

proportional, *adj.* proporcional, proporcionado, em proporção, relativo; correspondente. *s.* (mat.) termo de uma proporção.

proportionate, *adj.* proporcionado, proporcional. *v.t.* proporcionar, harmonizar.

proposal, *s.* proposta, proposição, oferta; pedido de casamento.

propose, *v.t.* e *v.i.* propor, oferecer, apresentar, sugerir, expor; propor-se, tencionar; propor casamento.

proposition, *s.* proposta, proposição; oferecimento; plano, projecto; (coloq.) assunto, negócio, empresa; (mat.) proposição, teorema, problema.

propound, *v.t.* propor, apresentar, expor, sugerir.

proprietary, *s.* proprietário; (farm.) medicamento cuja fórmula é secreta; *proprietary name,* marca registada.

proprietor, *s.* proprietário, dono.

proprietorship, *s.* propriedade, condição de proprietário.

propriety, *s.* propriedade, adequação, conveniência, oportunidade; boas maneiras, decoro, decência; (pl.) conveniências, convenções sociais.

propulsion, *s.* propulsão; impulso.

propulsive, *adj.* propulsivo, propulsor, impulsor.

propylaeum, *s.* (arquit.) propileu.

prorate, *v.t.* e *v.i.* dividir proporcionalmente, ratear.

prorogation, *s.* suspensão das sessões parlamentares.

prorogue, *v.t.* suspender as sessões parlamentares.

prosaic, *adj.* prosaico; vulgar.

prosaism, *s.* prosaísmo; expressão prosaica.

prosaist, *s.* prosador.

proscenium, *s.* (teat.) proscénio.

proscribe, *v.t.* proscrever, exilar; condenar, rejeitar, proibir.

proscript, *s.* proscrito.

proscription, *s.* proscrição, desterro, exílio, banimento; interdição.

prose, *s.* prosa; prosaísmo; lengalenga, *adj.* escrito em prosa; prosaico, prático, trivial; enfadonho. *v.t.* e *v.i.* escrever em prosa; prosear, discursar de modo enfadonho.

prosecute, *v.t.* e *v.i.* prosseguir, continuar, levar a cabo, realizar; dedicar-se a, praticar; processar, proceder contra; submeter a processo judicial; sustentar em juízo; instaurar processo, promover acção penal.

prosecuting-attorney, *s.* promotor público.

prosecution, *s.* prossecução, prosseguimento; realização, execução; exercício, prática (de profissão); instauração de processo; acusação do Ministério Público.

prosecutor, *s.* prosseguidor; executor; autor de acção, querelante; promotor de justiça; *Public Prosecutor,* procurador da República; o Ministério Público.

proselyte, *s.* prosélito, convertido; *v.t.* e *v.i.* converter; fazer prosélitos.

proser, *s.* conversador ou escritor enfadonho.

prosiness, *s.* prosaísmo, vulgaridade.

prosody, *s.* métrica, ciência da versificação.

prospect, *s.* perspectiva, vista, panorama, paisagem; cena, espectáculo; situação; expectativa, esperança; amostra de minério. *v.t.* e *v.i.* pesquisar minério; explorar, sondar; prometer determinado rendimento.

prospective, *adj.* relativo ao futuro; em perspectiva, provável, possível, esperado.

prospector, *s.* pesquisador de minério; explorador.

prospectus, *s.* prospecto, folheto.

prosper, *v.i.* e *v.t.* prosperar, enriquecer, florescer, vingar, ser bem sucedido.

prosperity, *s.* prosperidade, fortuna, êxito, ventura, riqueza; florescimento, progresso.

prosperous, *adj.* próspero, florescente; bem sucedido, afortunado; feliz; auspicioso, favorável.

prostate, *s.* próstata.

prosthesis, *s.* prótese.

prostitute, *s.* prostituta, meretriz, *v.t.* prostituir; corromper, desonrar.

prostitution, *s.* prostituição; degradação, corrupção.

prostrate, *adj.* prostrado; deitado, estendido; abatido; derrotado, vencido; submisso, impotente; debilitado. *v.t.* prostrar; deitar por terra, derrubar, abater; derrotar, vencer, submeter; debilitar.

prostration, *s.* prostração, abatimento, debilidade; desânimo, impotência; subjugação.

prostyle, *s.* (arquit.) próstilo.

prosy, *adj.* prosaico, trivial; enfadonho, maçador.

protagonist, *s.* protagonista; herói.

protasis, *s.* prótase; primeira parte do período gramatical.

protect, *v.t.* proteger, defender, abrigar, presevar; patrocinar, apoiar; (comerc.) garantir o resgate de (letra, etc.).

protecting, *adj.* protector.

protection, *s.* protecção, defesa; salvaguarda, garantia, abrigo; patrocínio, apoio; salvo-conduto; (E.U.) certificado de cidadania americana; (econ.), proteccionismo.

protectionism, *s.* proteccionismo.

protective, *adj.* protector, que protege; preventivo; proteccionista; *protective custody,* prisão preventiva.

protector, *s.* protector, defensor, tutor, guarda, patrono; regente do reino; dispositivo de protecção.

protectorate, *s.* protectorado.

protectorship, *s.* protectorado, dignidade ou funções de protector; protecção, patrocínio; regência.

protectory, *s. s.* asilo de menores.

protégé, *s.* protegido, favorito.

protein, *s.* proteína.

protest, *s.* protesto; reclamação, objecção, queixa; declaração. *v.t.* e *v.i.* protestar; reclamar, objectar; declarar.

protestant, *s.* e *adj.* protestante.

protestantism, *s.* protestantismo, religião protestante.

protestation, *s.* protesto, declaração, juramento.

prothesis, *s.* o mesmo que *prosthesis.*

protocol, *s.* protocolo; minuta; cerimonial. *v.t.* e *v.i.* registar em acta, protocolizar.

proton, *s.* protão, próton.

protoplasm, *s.* protoplasma.

protoplast, *s.* protoplasta, o primeiro animal criado de cada espécie.

prototype, *s.* protótipo; arquétipo, modelo original.

protozoan, *s.* protozoário.

protract, *v.t.* protrair, prolongar, dilatar; retardar, adiar, protelar; (zool.) alongar para a frente; (agrim.) traçar a planta de.

protractile, *adj.* protráctil.

protractor, *s.* protractor, prolongador; retardador; (geom.) transferidor.

protrude, *v.t.* e *v.i.* tornar saliente, sair para fora; alongar; fazer saliência, sobressair, ser proeminente; aparecer, sair.

protrusion, *s.* acção de se projectar para fora; saliência, protuberância.

protrusive, *adj.* saliente, proeminente, protuberante; turbulento, buliçoso, importuno.

protuberance, protuberancy, *s.* protuberância, saliência, proeminência, bossa.

protuberant, *adj.* protuberante, saliente, proeminente.

protuberate, *v.t.* protuberar, salientar.

protyle, *s.* (filos.) prótilo, suposta matéria primordial de todos os corpos.

proud, *adj.* orgulhoso, altivo, soberbo, ufano, presunçoso, arrogante; admirável, esplêndido. 1) *to be proud of,* orgulhar-se de. *adv.* *(coloq.)* grandemente. 2) *you do me proud,* você enche-me de orgulho.

provable, *adj.* provável, demonstrável.

prove, *v.t.* e *v.i.* provar, comprovar, demonstrar; evidenciar, revelar; ensaiar, experimentar; submeter a uma prova, aprovar; revelar-se, resultar.

provenance, provenience, s. proveniência, origem.

proverb, s. provérbio, adágio. v.t. tornar proverbial.

proverbial, adj. proverbial; conhecido, notório.

proviant, s. provisões, mantimentos.

provide, v.t. e v.i. prover, munir, suprir, abastecer; fornecer, proporcionar; prover-se, munir-se; estipular (a lei); tomar providências para, providenciar, preparar-se para.

provided, adj. provido, munido; provided school, escola pública elementar sustentada pela autoridade local. conj. contanto que, desde que.

providence, s. providência, previdência, prudência; economia, poupança, parcimónia; (com maiúscula) a Divina Providência.

provident, adj. providente, previdente, prudente; económico, parcimonioso, poupado.

providential, adj. providencial; oportuno.

provider, s. provedor, provisor, abastecedor, fornecedor; lion's provider, chacal.

providing, conj. contanto que, desde que.

province, s. província; região, território; jurisdição; competência, incumbência; obrigação, função; campo, domínio, reino; (ecles.) arcebispado, território sob a jurisdição de um arcebispo.

provincial, adj. provincial; provinciano, rústico; local, estreito, limitado. s. provinciano.

provision, s. provisão, abastecimento, fornecimento; (pl.) provisões, mantimentos; víveres; providência, preparativo, medida; condição, cláusula, disposição. v.t. prover de mantimentos, aprovisionar.

provisional, adj. provisório, provisional, temporário.

provisioner, s. fornecedor de mantimentos.

provisory, adj. provisório, temporário; providente.

provocation, s. provocação, estímulo, incitamento, instigação; irritação; motivo, causa, pretexto.

provocative, adj. provocatório, provocador, incitador; provocante, insultuoso. s. incentivo; estimulante.

provoke, v.t. provocar, irritar, exasperar; excitar, instigar; tentar, despertar.

provoking, adj. provocante, irritante, provocador, provocatório.

provost, s. preboste; director ou reitor de certos colégios; presidente de municipalidade; designação genérica de antigos magistrados militares e civis 1) provost court, tribunal para o julgamento de delitos leves. 2) provost guard, destacamento de polícia militar.

prow, s. (náut.) proa. adj. (arc.) corajoso, valoroso.

prowess, s. bravura, coragem, heroísmo; acto de bravura, façanha, proeza.

prowl, v.t. e v.i. rondar em busca de presa; vaguear; andar furtivamente; prowl car, carro-patrulha.

prowler, s. vagabundo, gatuno.

proximate, adj. próximo, vizinho; íntimo; aproximado; imediato, logo a seguir.

proximity, s. proximidade, contiguidade, vizinhança; proximity of blood, parentesco.

proximo, adv. do próximo mês.

proxy, s. procuração; procurador; representante, substituto.

prude, s. mulher excessiva ou falsamente recatada.

prudence, s. prudência, ponderação; sensatez.

prudent, adj. prudente, cauteloso, ponderado.

prudery, s. recato excessivo, afectação de virtude.

prudish, adj. que afecta virtude; pudico; hipócrita.

prune, s. ameixa seca. v.t. podar, desbastar; suprimir.

pruning, s. poda.

prurience, s. prurido, comichão; lascívia.

pruriginous, adj. pruriginoso.

prurigo, s. prurigem, prurigo, prurido.

Prussian, s. e adj. prussiano.

pry, s. alavanca, pé-de-cabra. v.i. e v.t. espreitar, espiar; intrometer-se em, bisbilhotar.

psalm, s. salmo. v.i. recitar salmos.

psalmist, s. salmista.

psalmody, s. salmodia, arte de recitar salmos.

psalter, s. saltério, Livro dos Salmos de David.

psalterium, s. folhoso, terceiro estômago dos ruminantes.

psaltery, s. saltério, antigo instrumento musical.

pseudo, adj. pseudo, falso, pretenso.

pseudomorph, s. mineral pseudomorfo de outro.

pseudomorphism, s. pseudomorfismo, pseudomorfose.
pseudonym, s. pseudónimo.
psi, s. psi, letra grega.
psilanthropism, s. psilantropismo.
psoriasis, s. psoríase.
psyche, s. psique, alma, espírito, mente.
psychiatrist, s. psiquiatra.
psychiatry, s. psiquiatria.
psychic, adj. psíquico, mental; metapsíquico. s. médium, pessoa sensível a forças psíquicas.
psychics, s. psicologia.
psychoanalisis, s. psicanálise.
psychoanalist, s. psicanalista.
psychoanalyze, v.t. psicanalisar.
psychodynamics, s. psicodinâmica.
psychogenesis, s. psicogenia, psicogénese.
psychogenic, adj. psicogénico, de origem mental.
psychogram, s. psicograma.
psychological, adj. psicológico; mental.
psychologist, s. psicólogo.
psychology, s. psicologia.
psychometry, s. psicometria.
psychomotor, adj. psicomotor.
psychoneurosis, s. psiconeurose.
psychopath, s. psicopata.
psychopatic, adj. psicopático; s. psicopata.
psychopatist, s. psiquiatra.
psychopathology, s. psicopatologia.
psychopathy, s. psicopatia.
psychosis, s. psicose.
psychosomatic, adj. psicossomático.
psychosomatics, s. psicossomática.
psychotherapy, s. psicoterapia.
ptarmigan, s. ptármiga, lagópode, espécie de perdiz árctica.
PT boat, s. lancha-torpedeira.
pteridophyte, s. (bot.) pteridófito.
pterodactyl, s. (paleo.) pterodáctilo.
pterosaur, s. (paleo.) pterossauro.
ptisan, s. tisana.
ptolemaic, adj. ptolemaico.
pub, s. o mesmo que public house; bar, taverna.
puberty, s. puberdade.
pubes, s. púbis, região púbica.
pubescence, s. pubescência.
pubescent, adj. pubescente, púbere.
pubic, adj. púbico.
pubis, s. púbis, parte anterior dos ossos ilíacos.
public, adj. público; popular; comum, notório,

conhecido. 1) public house, hospedaria, taverna, bar, cervejaria. 2) public servant, funcionário público. 3) public spirit, patriotismo, civismo. 4) publics, acções de empresas públicas. s. público, audiência; povo.
publican, s. publicano, cobrador de impostos.
publication, s. publicação; promulgação; livro, prospecto.
publicist, s. publicista; jornalista.
publicity, s. publicidade; notoriedade; reclamo, propaganda.
publicize, v.t. publicitar, fazer propaganda de, anunciar.
public-spirited, adj. patriota, patriótico.
publish, v.t. publicar; promulgar; editar.
publisher, s. editor.
puce, adj. e s. cor de pulga.
puck, s. diabrete; disco de borracha usado no hóquei sobre gelo.
pucker, v.t. e v.i. franzir, enrugar, contrair. s. franzimento, ruga; careta.
puckery, adj. enrugado, franzido; ácido, adstringente.
puckish, adj. travesso, caprichoso.
pudding, s. pudim; chouriço, farinheira; pudding stone: (geol.) conglomerado.
puddle, s. pocinha de água; confusão, embrulhada; barro amassado. v.t. e v.i. enlamear, sujar (a água); amassar barro; chapinhar na lama.
pudency, s. pudor, recato.
pudendum, s. pl. (pudenda); partes pudendas, órgãos genitais externos; (sing.) vulva.
pudge, s. pessoa ou animal atarracado.
pudgy, adj. atarracado; rechonchudo.
puerile, adj. pueril, infantil; tolo, frívolo.
puerility, s. puerilidade, infantilidade; futilidade.
puff, s. sopro, baforada, respiração, lufada, bafo, jacto de vapor; espécie de bolo fofo; pompom, borla de pó-de-arroz; tufo, pufo, fofo; protuberância, inchaço; bolha; elogio exagerado, anúncio extravagante. 1) puff adder, serpente africana. 2) puff paste, massa folhada. v.i. e v.t. soprar, bufar, baforar; arquejar, ofegar; lufar; sair aos jactos; expelir, lançar jactos de; entufar, enfunar-se; licitar para elevar os preços (em leilão). 3) to puff out, extinguir com um sopro. 4) to puff up, inflar, entufar, enfunar; elogiar em excesso; envaidecer-se; fazer propaganda exagerada de; apregoar.

puffer, s. pessoa que faz anúncios extravagantes; indivíduo que faz elogios excessivos; pessoa que licita para provocar a subida dos lances em leilão; locomotiva a vapor.

puffin, s. papagaio-do-mar.

puffy, adj. que sopra em rajadas; ventoso; inchado, túmido; inflado, enfunado; balofo.

pug, s. dogue (raça de cães); criado de categoria superior à dos outros; raposa; pequena locomotiva; barro preparado para o fabrico de tijolos; (cal.) pugilista; pegada de animal. v.t. cobrir com argamassa; fazer barro; seguir pegadas de animal. v.t. cobrir com argamassa; fazer barro; seguir pegadas de animal.

puggaree, s. turbante; pano protector (de capacete colonial).

pugilism, s. pugilismo.

pugilist, s. pugilista.

pugnacious, adj. pugnaz, combativo, brigão.

pugnaciousness, pugnacity, s. pugnacidade, combatividade.

puisne, adj. mais novo, de categoria inferior; segundo, posterior, subalterno. s. juiz mais novo, de categoria inferior.

puissance, s. poder, força, pujança.

puissant, adj. poderoso, forte, potente.

puke, v.t. e v.i. vomitar. s. vómito.

pule, v.i. choramingar, lamuriar; pipilar.

pull, v.t. e v.i. puxar; tirar, arrastar; arrancar; extrair; atrair, obter; esticar; (cal.) prender, deter; (cal.) fazer uma rusga; (cal.) furtar, roubar; praticar, realizar (façanha); (tip.) tirar prova, imprimir; mover-se, deslocar; segurar o cavalo para o impedir de ganhar. 1) to pull a boat, fazer avançar um barco por meio de remos. 2) to pull a face, fazer uma careta. 3) to pull a fast one, enganar; to pull a long face: fazer uma expressão de desânimo. 4) to pull a yarn, contar uma história inverosímel. 5) to pull ahead, passar à frente. 6) to pull at a bottle, beber pela garrafa. 7) to pull back, puxar para trás, impedir de avançar. 8) to pull down, fazer descer, puxar para baixo, demolir, abater. 9) to pull in, entrar na estação (o comboio); prender, capturar. 10) to pull off, tirar, despir. 11) to pull on, vestir, calçar. 12) to pull one's weight, fazer o que se pode. 13) to pull oneself together, animar-se, controlar-se. 14) to pull over, encostar à berma. 15) to pull someone's leg, pregar uma partida a alguém, divertir-se à custa de alguém. 16) to pull something off, ser bem sucedido nalguma coisa. 17) to pull through, ser bem sucedido. 18) to pull up, deter-se, estacar. s. puxão, safanão; tracção, arrasto; trago, gole; remada; subida penosa, ladeira íngreme; puxador, maçaneta; cabo; (tip.) primeira prova; vantagem, influência.

pullback, s. obstáculo; revés.

puller, s. o que puxa; puxador; torquês.

pullet, s. franga, galinha nova.

pulley, s. roldana, polé; molinete; polia.

pull-over, s. camisola; adj. de enfiar pela cabeça. v.t. parar, encostando (o carro) à berma.

pullulate, v.i. pulular, brotar, germinar; multiplicar-se; abundar.

pull-up, s. estalagem, ponto de paragem para viajantes.

pulmonary, adj. pulmonar.

pulmonate, adj. e s. pulmonado.

pulp, s. polpa; pasta para o fabrico de papel.

pulpit, s. púlpito.

pulpiteer, s. pregador; v.i. pregar.

pulpy, adj. polposo, carnudo; mole, fofo.

pulsate, v.i. e v.t. pulsar, palpitar, bater, latejar; agitar (diamantes).

pulsatile, adj. pulsátil, palpitante; de percussão (instr. musical).

pulsation, s. pulsação, palpitação.

pulsator, s. (mec.) pulsador; bomba de vácuo.

pulsatory, adj. pulsativo, pulsátil, palpitante.

pulse, s. pulso, pulsação; vibração, onda luminosa ou sonora; batimento rítmico, cadência; (rádio) impulso; energia, vitalidade; grãos de leguminosas. v.t. (rádio) enviar, emitir através de impulsos.

pultaceous, adj. mole, pastoso.

pulverization, s. pulverização.

pulverize, v.t. e v.i. pulverizar; triturar; reduzir a pó; destruir, aniquilar; desintegrar-se.

pulverizer, s. pulverizador, vaporizador.

pulverulent, adj. pulverulento.

puma, s. puma, onça.

pumice, s. pómice, pedra-pomes; v.t. polir com pedra-pomes.

pummel, s. o mesmo que pommel.

pump, s. bomba (de água ou ar); sondagem; sapato leve de dança. v.t. e v.i. extrair por meio de bomba, aspirar; obter, arrancar informações, dar à bomba, bombear, trabalhar (o coração); to pump up, encher pneumáticos.

pumpernickel, *s.* pão integral.

pumpkin, *s.* abóbora.

punch, *s.* ponche (bebida); soco, murro; força, vigor, energia; punção, furador, sovela; polichinelo, personagem de teatro de fantoches. 1) *punch press,* prensa de estampar. 2) *punch-line* (teat.), deixa ou frase que provoca reacção forte. *v.t.* esmurrar, socar; picar; conduzir gado; furar, perfurar, picotar. 3) *punching ball,* bola de bater usada no treino dos pugilistas.

puncheon, *s.* espeque, escora; barrote.

punchinello, *s.* polichinelo, bobo.

punctate, *adj.* pontuado, pontilhado.

punctilious, *adj.* meticuloso; exigente; susceptível.

punctual, *adj.* pontual; exacto, preciso.

punctuality, *s.* pontualidade; exactidão.

punctuate, *v.t.* e *v.i.* pontuar (texto); interromper, entrecortar; destacar; usar sinais de pontuação.

puncture, *s.* punctura, perfuração, picada; furo, punção. *v.t.* e *v.i.* perfurar, picar, furar; furar-se (o pneu).

pundit, *s.* pândita; sábio, mestre.

pungency, *s.* pungência; mordacidade; sabor ou cheiro picante; agudeza.

Punic, *s.* e *adj.* púnico.

punish, *v.t.* e *v.i.* punir, castigar; consumir exageradamente.

punishment, *s.* punição, castigo, pena, penitência; maus tratos.

punitive, *adj.* punitivo.

punk, *s.* madeira podre ou determinados cogumelos que se desenvolvem na madeira que se utiliza para acender o lume; (arc.) prostituta. *adj.* ruim, sem valor, podre.

punnet, *s.* cestinho redondo.

punt, *s.* barco de fundo chato impelido com vara; ponto (em certos jogos de azar); pontapé dado na bola antes de ela chegar ao chão. *v.t.* e *v.i.* impelir barco com vara; chutar a bola antes de ela chegar ao chão; apostar, jogar.

punter, *s.* aquele que impele um barco com vara; apontador (em certos jogos de azar).

puny, *adj.* pequenino, fraco, débil, mesquinho.

pup, *s.* cachorro novo; cria de outros animais mamíferos; rapazola. 1) *in pup,* grávida (a cadela). 2) *to sell someone a pup,* vigarizar alguém. 3) *pup tent,* barraca de campanha.

pupa, *s.* pupa, crisálida.

pupation, *s.* estado de crisálida.

pupil, *s.* aluno, discípulo; pupila, menina do olho.

pupilage, pupillage, *s.* pupilagem, tutela, menoridade; período escolar.

pupillarity, *s.* impuberdade.

puppet, *s.* boneco, títere, fantoche, marioneta; *puppet player,* bonecreiro.

puppeteer, *s.* bonecreiro, titereiro.

puppetry, *s.* fantoches, fantochada, teatro de fantoches.

puppy, *s.* cachorrinho; jovem muito presumido, peralvilho.

purblind, *adj.* de visão limitada; obtuso, bronco, de vistas curtas.

purchase, *v.t.* comprar, adquirir; obter; içar por meio de roldana ou alavanca. *s.* compra, aquisição; rendimento anual de terras; vantagem, influência; alavanca, talha, cabrestante; relação entre braços de alavanca; transmissão por alavancas; ponto de apoio; *to take purchase on,* apoiar-se sobre.

purchaser, *s.* comprador.

purdah, *s.* cortina que, na Índia, serve para ocultar as mulheres aos estranhos; sistema de reclusão das mulheres de condição.

pure, *adj.* puro; claro, límpido; mero, simples.

purebred, *adj.* de puro sangue. *s.* puro-sangue.

purely, *adv.* puramente; simplesmente, meramente, unicamente; apenas; completamente.

pureness, *s.* pureza; limpidez; simplicidade; inocência.

purgation, *s.* purgação; purificação.

purgative, *adj.* purgativo, purgante; purificador. *s.* purgante, purga.

purgatory, *s.* (teol.) Purgatório. *adj.* purgatório, purificador.

purge, *v.t.* e *v.i.* purgar, purificar, depurar limpar, clarificar; expiar, resgatar, reabilitar--se; inocentar; expurgar; purgar-se, purificar-se. *s.* purgação, purga, purgante.

purification, *s.* purificação, purgação.

purify, *v.t.* e *v.i.* purificar(-se), purgar(-se), limpar(-se).

purism, *s.* purismo.

purist, *s.* purista.

puritan, *s.* e *adj.* puritano.

puritanism, *s.* puritanismo; austeridade, rigor, severidade.

purity, *s.* pureza; limpidez; inocência; castidade.

purl, *s.* canutilho, fio de ouro ou prata; picote,

ponto de renda; remoinho, ondulação; (fam.) tombo, queda; cerveja aquecida e misturada com gim. *v.t.* e *v.i.* debruar; orlar com picotes; inverter os pontos em costura; (fam.) derrubar; remoinhar, ondular, sussurrar (riacho); (fam.) virar-se.

purlieu, *s.* limites, confins; (pl.) arredores, cercanias; bairro miserável; coutada na orla de uma floresta.

purloin, *v.t.* roubar, furtar.

purple, *s.* roxo, a cor roxa; púrpura; veste purpúrea; dignidade real; cardinalato; posição elevada. *adj.* roxo, purpúreo; régio, real; rebuscado, pomposo. 1) *purple medic,* lucerna, alfafa. 2) *purple passage,* trecho brilhante de obra literária. *v.t.* e *v.i.* avermelhar-se, ficar roxo.

purplish, *adj.* arroxeado.

purport, *v.t.* significar, expressar; implicar, dar a entender; referir; parecer, denotar, indicar; passar por; *a message that purports to come from him,* uma mensagem que se supõe ser enviada por ele. *s.* propósito; teor, conteúdo, sentido, substância.

purpose, *s.* propósito, desígnio, intenção; objectivo, fim, finalidade; vontade, decisão; resultado, efeito, utilidade. 1) *on purpose,* de propósito. 2) *on purpose to,* para, a fim de. 3) *to the purpose,* apropositado, oportuno. *adv.* a propósito. *v.t.* propor-se, tencionar, pretender, ter em vista.

purposeful, *adj.* propositado, intencional, significativo; com uma finalidade.

purposive, *adj.* que tem uma finalidade, útil; intencional; decidido, resoluto.

purpure, *s.* (her.) púrpura.

purr, *v.i.* ronronar. *s.* ronronar de gato.

purse, *s.* bolsa, carteira; tesouro, erário. finanças; dinheiro, fundos; riqueza; colecta. 1) *purse bearer,* tesoureiro. 2) *purse net,* galeão (aparelho de pesca). *v.t.* e *v.i.* enrugar, franzir; embolsar.

purser, *s.* (mar.) comissário de bordo.

pursiness, *s.* fôlego curto, dispneia; corpulência, obesidade; arrogância.

pursuance, *s.* prossecução, prosseguimento; busca; execução, cumprimento; *in pursuance,* em conformidade com, em cumprimento de.

pursue, *v.t.* perseguir, acossar, ir no encalço de, dar caça a; prosseguir, continuar; adoptar; dedicar-se a (profissão, estudos, etc.), exercer (profissão).

pursuer, *s.* perseguidor.

pursuit, *s.* perseguição, caça; busca, procura: ocupação, actividade, profissão, estudo, investigação; *pursuit plane,* avião de combate, caça.

pursy, *adj.* dispneico, que tem o fôlego curto; gordo, obeso, corpulento; enrugado, franzido.

purulence, *s.* purulência; supuração; pus.

purulent, *adj.* purulento, supurante.

purvey, *v.t.* fornecer provisões; aprovisionar; actuar como fornecedor de alimentos.

purveyance, *s.* fornecimento, abastecimento; prerrogativa real de requisitar provisões a preço fixo.

purveyor, *s.* fornecedor, abastecedor.

purview, *s.* texto, corpo (de uma lei); propósito, intenção; alcance; extensão, esfera, âmbito; jurisdição, alçada; contemplação, consideração.

pus, *s.* pus.

push, *v.t.* empurrar, impelir; dar impulso a, fazer avançar; incitar, instigar; fazer pressão sobre, apertar, carregar; forçar, obrigar; impor, impingir; esforçar-se, lutar. 1) *to push roots,* lançar raízes. 2) *to push someone on,* incitar alguém. 3) *to push back,* repelir. 4) *to push one's way,* abrir caminho aos empurrões. 5) *to push through,* levar a cabo. *s.* impulso; empurrão; repelão; marrada; estocada; pressão; esforço; investida, avanço; energia, dinamismo; apuros.

pusher, *s.* aquele que empurra; impulsor, propulsor.

pushing, *adj.* activo, dinâmico, empreendedor; intrometido.

pushover, *s.* adversário desdenhável; pessoa que se convence facilmente.

pusillanimitty, *s.* pusilanimidade, covardia.

pusillanimous, *adj.* pusilânime, covarde.

puss, *s.* gato; rapariga.

pussy, *adj.* (med.) purulento.

pustular, *adj.* pustuloso, pustulento.

pustulate, *v.t.* e *v.i.* cobrir-se de pústulas; *adj.* pustulento.

pustulation, *s.* (med.) pustulação; pústula.

pustule, *s.* pústula.

put, *v.t.* e *v.i.* (*prt.* e *pp.* put) pôr, colocar, depositar; meter; lançar, atirar; expor, apresentar; propor; perguntar, submeter a; causar, motivar; prover, fornecer; depositar (num banco); calcular, avaliar; seguir (profissão). 1) *to put a question before him,* submeter um assunto à consideração dele;

2) *to put a horse to a fence,* fazer o cavalo saltar a vedação. 3) *to put someone on his oath,* exigir juramento a alguém. 4) *to put the clock forward,* adiantar o relógio. 5) *to put to death,* matar. 6) *to put away,* guardar. 7) *to put forth,* exercer; tornar público, publicar. 8) *to put forward,* pôr em evidência; sugerir, invocar; adiantar (o relógio). 9) *to put in an appearance,* aparecer, mostrar-se. 10) *to put off,* pôr passageiro em terra; adiar; tirar; despir; dissuadir. 11) *to put on,* vestir, calçar, pôr; afectar, fingir, aparentar; ganhar velocidade. 12) *to put on weight,* aumentar de peso, engordar. 13) *to put out,* expulsar, tirar; pôr fora de jogo; apagar (lume). 14) *to put oneself ou to,* esforçar-se por; investir dinheiro. 15) *to put through,* fazer ligação telefónica interurbana a. 16) *to put together,* reunir; montar; associar factos mentalmente. 17) *to put up,* erguer, levantar; levar à cena; aumentar; pôr em leilão. 18) *to put up a good flight,* lutar com energia. *s.* arremesso; opção de venda na Bolsa. *adj.* na expressão to stay put: ficar no lugar, ficar firme.

putative, *adj.* putativo, suposto.

putrefaction, *s.* putrefacção, apodrecimento, decomposição.

putrefactive, *adj.* pútrido.

putrefy, *v.t. e v.i.* putrefazer(-se), decompor-se, apodrecer.

putrescence, *s.* putrescência.

putrescent, *adj.* putrescente.

putrid, *adj.* pútrido; putrefacto, podre; corrompido; pestilento.

putridity, putridness, *s.* putridez, podridão.

putt, *s.* golpe seco dado em bola de golfe para a introduzir no buraco. *v.t. e v.i.* golpear a bola com esse fim.

putty, *s.* massa de vidraceiro, betume.

puzzle, *s.* confusão, perplexidade, embaraço; problema, enigma, quebra-cabeças. *v.t.* confundir, embaraçar, desorientar; *to puzzle out,* resolver, decifrar, encontrar a solução de.

puzzlement, *s.* perplexidade, desorientação.

puzzling, *adj.* embaraçoso, complicado, desconcertante.

pygmaean, pygmean, *adj.* anão, pigmeu, relativo aos pigmeus.

pygmy, pigmy, *s.* pigmeu; anão; elfo, duende.

pyic, *adj.* purulento.

pyjamas, *s.* pijama.

pylon, *s.* pilone, pórtico de templo egípcio.

pylorus, *s.* piloro.

pyrrhea, pyorrhoea, *s.* piorreia.

pyosis, *s.* piose, supuração.

pyoramid, *s.* pirâmide. *v.t.* dar forma de pirâmide.

pyramidal, pyramidical, pyramidic, *adj.* piramidal, relativo a pirâmide.

pyre, *s.* pira (funerária); fogueira.

pyretic, *adj.* pirético, febril.

pyrexia, *s.* pirexia, estado febril.

pyrexial, pyrexic, *adj.* pirético, febril.

pyrites, *s.* pirite.

pyrography, *s.* pirogravura.

pyromancy, *s.* piromancia.

pyromania, *s.* piromania.

pyromaniac, *s.* piromaníaco.

pyrometry, *s.* pirometria.

pyrophobia, *s.* pirofobia.

pyrosis, *s.* pirose, azia.

pyrotechnic, *adj.* pirotécnico; *pyrotechnic pistol,* pistola sinalizadora.

pyrotechnics, *s.* pirotecnia.

pyrotechnist, *s.* pirotécnico.

pyruvic, *adj.* (quím.) pirúvico.

Pythagorean, *adj. e s.* pitagórico.

Pythia, *s.* Pítia, sacerdotisa de Apolo, em Delfos.

Pythian, *adj.* pítio, relativo a Apolo.

python, *s.* pitão; serpente mitológica morta por Apolo; espírito, duende familiar.

pythoness, *s.* pitonisa; profetisa.

pyx, pix, *s.* píxide, vaso em que se guardam as hóstias consagradas; cofre em que se guardam as moedas destinadas a ensaio, na Casa da Moeda, em Londres.

pyxis, *s.* estojo, cofre pequeno, escrínio.

Q

q, décima sétima letra do alfabeto.

qua, *adv.* como, na qualidade de; *he presented her to us qua his fiancée*, ele apresentou-a como sua noiva.

quack, *v.t.* e *v.i.* grasnar; charlatanear; bazofiar; curar de modo empírico; *s.* grasnido de pato; *s.* e *adj.* charlatão, impostor, empírico, curandeiro.

quackery, *s.* charlatanismo.

quackish, *adj.* charlatanesco.

quacksalver, *s.* charlatão, curandeiro.

quad, *s. contr.* de *quadrat, quadrangle,* (fam.) quadra, pátio quadrangular; quatro gémeos.

quadragenarian, *adj.* e *s.* quadragenário, quarentão.

quadragesimal, *adj.* quadragesimal; composto de quarenta.

quadrangular, *adj.* quadrangular, quadrilateral.

quadrant, *s.* (geom. e astron.) quadrante; quarto de circulo.

quadrat, *s.* quadrado.

quadrate, *adj.* quadrado; conveniente, aplicável; *s.* quadrado, quadratura, rectângulo; *v.i.* quadrar-se, convir, condizer, ajustar-se.

quadratic, *adj.* quadrático; *s.* quadrática.

quadrature, *s.* quadratura; esquadro.

quadrilateral, *adj.* e *s.* quadrilateral; quadrilátero.

quadrille, *s.* quadrilha (dança); nome de antigo jogo de cartas.

quadrillion, *s.* quatrilião.

quadroon, *s.* quarteirão.

quadruped, *s.* e *adj.* quadrúpede.

quadruple, *s.* e *adj.* quádruplo; *v.t.* quadruplicar.

quadruplicate, *adj.* quadruplicado; *v.t.* quadruplicar.

quadruplication, *s.* quadruplicação.

quaff, *s.* trago, gole, copo; *v.t.* e *v.i.* beber a grandes tragos ou repetidamente; despejar o copo; escorropichar, emborcar.

quaffer, *s.* borracho, bêbedo.

quag, *s.* barranco; paul, pântano.

quaggy, *adj.* lodoso, pantanoso; mole, flácido.

quagmire, *s.* atoleiro, lameiro, charco.

quail, *v.i.* intimidar-se, encolher-se, recuar; *s.* codorniz.

quaint, *adj.* singular, esquisito, original; fino, exótico, gracioso.

quake, *v.i.* tremer, sacudir-se, estremecer, tiritar; *s.* tremor, estremecimento; (fam.) tremor de terra.

Quaker, *s.* quáquer, membro de seita religiosa que prega a simplicidade dos costumes, vestuário, etc.

quaking, *s.* tremor; *adj.* tremente.

qualification, *s.* qualificação, habilitação; requisito, condição.

qualified, *adj.* qualificado, habilitado, classificado; competente; restrito, condicional.

qualify, *v.t.* habilitar, tornar capaz; qualificar; diplomar; restringir, limitar, moderar; *v.i.* prepara-se, habilitar-se, qualificar-se.

qualitative, *adj.* qualitativo; *adv. qualitatively,* qualitativamente.

quality, *s.* qualidade, casta, categoria, classe; dote, prenda, virtude, propriedade; *man of quality,* homem distinto.

qualm, *s.* náusea, enjoo; tontura, vertigem; desmaio, desfalecimento; escrúpulo, remorso.

qualmish, *adj.* que se sente desfalecido; que tem náuseas; que sente escrúpulos ou remorsos; *adv. qualmishly.* nauseadamente; escrupulosamente.

quandary, *s.* perplexidade, dúvida, dilema, embaraço, incerteza.

quantic, *s.* quântico; *s.* (mat. e fis.) quântica.

quantify, *v.t.* quantificar, medir a quantidade.

quantitative, *adj.* quantitativo; *adv. quantitatively,* quantitativamente.

quantity, *s.* quantidade, grandeza; porção; número; abundância; massa, volume.

quantum, *s.* quantidade; parte; quinhão; total.

quarantine, *s.* quarentena, isolamento, observação, *v.t.* pôr de quarentena, de observação; isolar.

quarrel, *s.* disputa, altercação, contenda, rixa, briga, discórdia; *v.i. (quarreling, quarreled),* disputar, contender, brigar; abandonar, desviar-se; *to quarrel with bread and butter,* abandonar o emprego.

quarreling, s. disputas, contendas.

quarrelsome, adj. altercador, briguento, belicoso; adv. quarrelsomely, irascivelmente.

quarry, s. pedreira; caça, presa; quadro (de vidro, folha, telha, lousa); v.t. e v.i. extrair de pedreira; abrir pedreira.

quarrying, s. exploração de pedreiras.

quarryman, s. cabouqueiro, canteiro.

quart, s. (medida inglesa 1,11) quarto; quarta (posição em esgrima); quatro cartas do mesmo naipe.

quarter, s. quarto, quarta parte, quarteirão; medida de cereais (290 l); medida de peso (12,700 kg); trimestre; quarto de hora; quarto de tonelada; moeda de prata (quarto de dólar); quarto de lua; quarta (náut.); um dos pontos cardeais; bairro, sítio; fonte, procedência; residência, domicílio; alojamento (mil.); quartel; direcção. 1) to give no quarter to the enemy, não dar quartel ao inimigo. 2) to come to close quarters, chegar a vias de facto, lutar corpo a corpo; v.t. dividir em quartos; aquartelar, alojar hóspedes; v.i. aquartelar-se.

quarterage, s. soldo, salário, pensão trimestral.

quartered, adj. esquartejado, cortado em quatro; aquartelado; alojado.

quarterly, adj. trimestral; s. publicação trimestral; adv. trimestralmente.

quarternary, adj. quaternário; quadrilátero; s. período quaternário, quatro.

quartet, quartette, s. quarteto; quatro; quatro coisas da mesma espécie.

quartic, adj. do mesmo grau, ou da quarta ordem.

quartile, s. quartil (astrol.).

quarto, adj. em quarto; s. livro em quarto.

quartz, s. quartzo.

quash, v.t. sufocar, pôr fim a, subjugar, reprimir; anular, cancelar, revogar, arquivar (processo).

quasi, adv. como se; quase.

quater-centenary, s. quadricentenário.

quaternion, s. quaternião.

quatrain, s. quadra, quarteto, estrofe de quatro versos.

quatrillion, s. quatrilião.

quattrocentist, s. e adj. quatrocentista.

quaver, v.t. e v.i. tremer, vibrar; quavering out, dizer em voz trémula. trinar, gorjear; s. gorjeio, trinado; tremor da voz; vibração.

quavery, adj. trémulo (voz).

quay, s. cais, molhe, embarcadouro.

quayage, s. ancoragem, taxa de atracação; extensão do cais.

quean, s. mulher de má vida; rapariga descarada, sirigaita.

queasiness, s. indisposição de estômago, náuseas, enjoo.

queasy, adj. que tem vontade de vomitar; nauseabundo, nauseante; enjoado, fastiento; constrangido, escrupuloso; exigente, difícil.

queen, s. rainha, soberana; dama (jogo de cartas, damas e xadrez). 1) queen-bee. abelha-mestra. 2) queen dowager, rainha viúva; v.t. fazer rainha, coroar; v.i. fazer de rainha. 3) to queen it, governar como rainha.

queenlike, adj. à maneira de rainha.

queenly, adj. régio, próprio duma rainha, majestoso.

queer, adj. esquisito, estranho; suspeito, duvidoso; excêntrico; raro, original, s. (fam.) moeda falsa; v.t. comprometer, prejudicar; desconcertar, embatucar, levar à parede; adv. queerly, estranhamente.

quell, v.t. dominar, vencer, subjugar, reprimir, debelar, sufocar, esmagar.

quench, v.t. extinguir, apagar; amortecer; acalmar, conter; satisfazer, saciar (a sede); temperar (ferro); banhar em água, esfriar.

quenchable, adj. extinguível.

quencher, s. extintor; o que apaga, o que extingue; (gír.) bebida, trago.

quenchless, adj. inextinguível; insaciável.

querist, s. inquiridor; perguntador, curioso.

querulous, adj. queixoso, lamentoso; adv. querulously, queixosamente.

query, s. pergunta, dúvida; ponto de interrogação (como sinal de dúvida); v.t. perguntar, inquirir; v.i. fazer perguntas; expressar dúvidas.

quest, s. pesquisa, investigação, busca; v.i. procurar, indagar, investigar, dar caça.

question, s. pergunta, interrogação; questão; assunto; dúvida; interpelação; problema; debate, disputa; objecção; controvérsia. 1) list of questions, questionário. 2) the question is, o caso é. 3) out of question, fora de questão, nem pensar nisso. 4) to call someone into question, chamar alguém a prestar contas. 5) not a fair question, pergunta indiscreta; v.i. fazer perguntas, questionar.

questionable, adj. duvidoso, incerto,

discutível, contestável; suspeito, equívoco; *adv.* *questionably*, duvidosamente.

questionary, *s.* questionário.

questioner, *s.* inquiridor, interrogador.

questioning, *s.* acto de questionar ou perguntar.

questionless, *adj.* incontestável, indubitável.

questionnaire, *s.* questionário.

quetzal, *s.* curucui (ave); emblema nacional da Guatemala.

queue, *s.* rabicho; fila, fila de pessoas, cauda; *v.t.* entrançar, fazer rabo de cavalo; *v.i.* formar fila (com *up*); entrar na fila (com *on*).

quibble, *v.i.* usar trocadilhos; sofismar; *s.* trocadilho; sofisma; subterfúgio, evasiva.

quibbler, *s.* sofista; chicaneiro.

quick, *adj.* rápido, veloz, ligeiro, apressado, pronto; vivo, diligente, ágil, activo; fino, subtil; vivaz, ardente, esperto; disponível. 1) *quick-eyed*, olho-vivo, perspicaz. 2) *quick-sighted*, vista aguda, penetrante. 3) *quick-witted*, sagaz. 4) *to be quick about*, fazer qualquer coisa depressa. 5) *the quick and the dead*, os vivos e os mortos; *s.* vivo, carne viva. 6) *to bite one's nails to the quick*, roer as unhas até ao sabugo, roer as unhas até ficar em carne viva; *adv.* vivamente, velozmente.

quicken, *v.t.* dar vida, vivificar, avivar; estimular, animar; *v.i.* animar-se, reviver; agitar-se; mover-se com rapidez.

quickener, *s.* o que anima, que vivifica; princípio vivificante.

quickfiring, *adj.* de tiro rápido.

quick-freeze, *v.t.* submeter a congelação rápida.

quicklime, *s.* cal viva.

quickly, *adv.* rapidamente, prontamente, depressa.

quickness, *s.* vivacidade, esperteza, sagacidade, perspicácia; irritabilidade.

quicksand, *s.* areia movediça.

quickset, *s.* planta viva; espinheiro alvar; sebe de plantas vivas; *v.t.* cercar de sebe.

quickstep, *s.* passo dobrado (mús.); passo acelerado (mil.).

quicksticks, *s.* (fam.) num abrir e fechar de olhos.

quid, *s.* bocado de tabaco para mascar; libra esterlina (fam.); compensação; desforra; remoedura.

quiddity, *s.* essência duma coisa; subtileza, sofisma.

quidnunc, *s.* curioso, bisbilhoteiro.

quid pro quo, *s.* equívoco, disputa.

quiescence, quiescency, *s.* repouso, imobilidade, sossego.

quiescent, *adj.* quiescente, imóvel, inerte, inactivo, em repouso; *adv.* *quiescently*, inactivamente.

quiet, *adj.* tranquilo, sereno, calmo, sossegado, plácido, pacífico; manso; calado, silencioso; sério, discreto. 1) *she was dressed in quiet blue dress*, ela vestia um discreto vestido azul. 2) *be quiet*, fique quieto. 3) *keep quiet*, cale-se; *adv.* *quietly*, tranquilamente; *s.* tranquilidade, paz, sossego; calma, serenidade; *v.t.* aquietar, acalmar, tranquilizar; *v.i.* aquietar-se, acalmar-se, serenar.

quietness, *s.* o mesmo que *quietude*.

quietude, *s.* quietude, tranquilidade.

quietus, *s.* recibo de pagamento, quitação; descanso; morte.

quill, *s.* pena (de ave); tubo (de pena); tubo ou pena para escrever; pico, espinho, cerda; broca; tubo. 1) *quill-driver*, (aquele que trabalha com pena) escriturário, jornalista, escritor. 2) *the quill*, a profissão das letras; *v.t.* depenar, arrancar penas; encanudar, franzir.

quillings, *s. pl.* pregas encanudadas (roupa).

quilt, *s.* acolchoado, colcha, cobertor; *down quilt*, edredão; *v.t.* acolchoar, estofar.

quilter, *s.* estofador.

quilting, *s.* acção de acolchoar; *quilting-cotton*, algodão em pasta para acolchoar.

quinary, *adj.* quinário; quíntuplo.

quince, *s.* marmelo; *quince-tree*, marmeleiro.

quincentenary, *s.* quincentenário.

quindecennial, *adj.* relativo a 15 anos ou ao 15º aniversário; *s.* 15º aniversário.

quinine, quinin, quinina, *s.* (quím.) quinina; (farm.) quinino.

quinquagenarian, *adj. e s.* quinquagenário.

quinquagesima, *s.* quinquagésima.

quinquennial, *adj.* quinquenal; *s.* quinto aniversário.

quinquina, *s.* quinquina, quina.

quinsy, *s.* esquinência, amigdalite.

quint, *s.* quinta (mús.); cinco cartas do mesmo naipe; forma abreviada de *quintuple.*

quintal, *s.* quintal métrico (100 kg).

quinte, *s.* quinta (esgrima).

quintet, quintette, *s.* quinteto (mús.); grupo de cinco.

quintillion, *s.* quintilão.

quintuple, *adj.* quíntuplo; *v.t.* quintuplicar.

quintus, *s.* quinto, o que vem em quinto lugar.

quip, *s.* sarcasmo, ironia.

quire, *s.* coro (de igreja).

quirk, *s.* desvio, volta curta, curva; argúcia, subtileza, finura; evasiva, rodeio.

quirt, *s.* chicote de montar; *v.t.* chicotear.

quit (quitting, quitted ou **quit),** *v.t.* deixar, abandonar, desistir de, renunciar a; soltar, desocupar, sair de; pagar, satisfazer; cumprir o seu dever; isentar. 1) *quit you like a man,* porta-te como um homem. 2) *to give notice to quit,* avisar para que deixe uma casa. 3) *to quit work,* deixar o emprego. 4) *to quit scores,* pagar dívidas, ajustar as contas; *v.i.* desistir.

quite, *adv.* completamente, inteiramente; muito; *she is quite a beauty,* ela é uma beldade.

quits, *adj.* quite, quites; *now we are quits,* estamos quites agora.

quittance, *s.* quitação, pagamento; desforra, recompensa; recibo.

quitter, *s.* aquele que deixa, que desiste; cobarde; caloteiro.

quiver, *v.i.* tremer, estremecer, palpitar; agitar-se; *s.* tremor, estremecimento, palpitação; aljava.

quivering, *s.* tremor, estremecimento; *adj.* tremido.

quixotic, *adj.* quixotesco; *adv. quixotically,* de modo quixotesco.

quixotism, *s.* quixotismo.

quiz, *s.* pergunta embaraçosa ou absurda; trocista, troça; exame oral, interrogatório; mistificação, logro; *v.t. (quizzing, quizzed),* mistificar, lograr; fazer perguntas; olhar com curiosidade.

quizzical, *adj.* zombador, escarnecedor; excêntrico, esquisito; *adv. quizzically,* zombeteiramente.

quizzing, *s.* zombaria, motejo.

quod, *s.* prisão, cadeia; *v.t. e v.i. (quodding, quodded),* meter na cadeia.

quoin, *s.* canto, pedra angular; esquina, ângulo; cunha, calço; *v.t.* meter cunhas ou calços.

quoit, *s.* argola de ferro, malha, jogo do chinquilho ou malha; *v.t.* jogar a malha.

quondam, *adj.* antigo, de outros tempos, de outrora.

quorum, *s.* quórum; número suficiente de pessoas, necessário para que se realize uma assembleia.

quota, *s.* quota, quota-parte; quinhão; contribuição.

quotable, *adj.* citável, digno de citação; que se pode cotizar.

quotation, *s.* citação; cotação.

quote, *v.t.* citar; quotizar (com.).

quotha, *interj.* Deveras! Realmente! Apre!

quotidian, *adj.* quotidiano, diário.

quotient, *s.* quociente.

quoting, *s.* citação; cotação.

R

r, décima oitava letra do alfabeto.

rabbet, *v.t.* emalhatar, encaixar, fazer um entalhe; encaixe, ranhura, malhete, plaina de rebaixar.

rabbi, rabbin, *s.* rabino.

rabbit, *s.* coelho, pele de coelho. 1) *doe--rabbit,* coelha. 2) *rabbit nest,* toca de coelho. 3) *rabbit-warren,* ou *rabbit-hutch,* coelheira.

rabbitry, *s.* coelheira, recinto onde se criam coelhos.

rabble, *s.* turba, populaça, plebe, gentalha, ralé, multidão.

rabblement, *s.* tumulto, desordem.

rabid, *adj.* furioso, raivoso; rábido, hidrófobo; fanático, obstinado; *a rabid communist,* um comunista fanático.

rabidly, *adv.* furiosamente, com raiva.

rabidness, *s.* raiva, fúria.

rabies, *s.* raiva, hidrofobia.

race, *s.* corrida, carreira; competição, certame, regata; competência, decurso da vida; canal, estreito, escoadoiro; levada; aroma, sabor do vinho; raiz; raça; estirpe, casta, género; descendência, linhagem; gente, povo; origem, ascendência, classe, categoria, linhagem; espécie, laia. 1) *race-boat*, barco de corrida. 2) *race-course*, hipódromo; estádio. 3) *race cup*, prémio, taça. 4) *race ginger*, raiz de gengibre. 5) *race ground*, terreno de corridas. 6) *horse race*, corrida de cavalos. 7) *yacht race*, regata de iates; *adj.* de raça; racial. 8) *race riot*, conflito racial; *v.t.* e *v.i.* fazer correr depressa; mover aceleradamente; correr, competir; acelerar(-se). 9) *to race away*, perder dinheiro em corridas.

raceme, *s.* (bot.) cacho, racemo.

racemose, *adj.* racemoso; constituído por um cacho, racemo; que tem forma de cacho, racemiforme.

racer, *s.* corredor; cavalo, barco, etc.

racial, *adj.* racial; *adv. racially,* racialmente.

racism, *s.* racismo.

racist, *s.* racista.

rack, *s.* bastidor; lanceiro, cabide; armeiro; prateleira; grade de manjedoura; caniçada; nuvem passageira; tormenta, suplício. 1) *hat-rack,* chapeleira. 2) *letter-rack,* porta-cartas. 3) *towel-rack,* toalheiro. 4) *rack and pinion,* cremalheira; *v.t.* torturar; estirar, despedaçar, torcer, arrancar dinheiro por extorsão; oprimir, vexar; fechar ou cercar com grade; trasfegar vinho; (com *up*) encher a manjedoura; *v.i.* andar a trote; correr diante do vento (nuvens). 5) *to rack one's brains,* dar tratos ao juízo.

racket, *s.* barafunda, barulho, confusão; raqueta (de ténis ou para andar sobre a neve); (pl.) jogo da péla; folia, dissipação, patuscada; meio fraudulento para extorquir dinheiro; fazer bulha, alarido; extorquir dinheiro.

racketeer, *s.* escroque; membro de organização que extorque dinheiro por meios ilegais; contrabandista; explorador do mercado negro.

racketeering, *s.* actuação organizada dos "racketeers".

rackety, *adj.* ruidoso, estrondoso; *a rackety life,* vida dissoluta.

racking, *s.* tortura, suplício; lotação, trasfega; *adj.* atormentador; que anda a trote; *racking pain,* dor atroz.

racquet, *s.* raqueta.

racy, *adj.* rico, forte; aromático, espirituoso, picante; vivo, animado; de raça; *adv. racily,* de modo espirituoso, picante, animado, etc.

radar, *s.* radar.

radarman, *s.* operador de radar.

raddle, *s.* ocre vermelho, ocre sanguíneo; *v.t.* pintar de vermelho, pintar com ocre vermelho; trançar, entrelaçar.

radial, *adj.* radial.

radian, *s.* (geom.) radiano.

radiance, *s.* brilho, fulgor, radiância.

radiant, *adj.* radiante, luminoso, brilhante, resplandecente; deslumbrante; radiado (bot. e zool.); *s.* linha radial (geom.); foco luminoso; *adv. radiantly,* radiantemente.

radiate, *v.t.* e *v.i.* irradiar, iluminar, brilhar, cintilar.

radiated, *adj.* radiado (bot. e zool.); cheio de raios de luz.

radiation, *s.* irradiação; radiação.

radiator, *s.* radiador; irradiador; calorífero.

radical, *adj.* radical, essencial, fundamental; completo; básico; primário; extremo; *s.* radical (pol., quím., mat., gram.).

radicalism, *s.* radicalismo.

radically, *adv.* radicalmente, primariamente; extremamente, completamente.

radicalness, *s.* origem, natureza radical, fundamental.

radicate, *adj.* radicado.

radicle, *s.* radícula; (quím.) radical.

radio, *s.* rádio, radiograma; *v.t.* e *v.i.* difundir ou telegrafar pela rádio; radiografar; tratar pela rádio.

radio-active, *adj.* radioactivo.

radioactivity, *s.* radioactividade.

radiobroadcasting, *s.* radiodifusão, radiotransmissão.

radiochemistry, *s.* radioquímica, química dos corpos radioactivos.

radiogram, *s.* radiograma.

radiograph, *s.* radiografia; *v.t.* radiografar, tirar radiografia de.

radiographer, *s.* radiologista, radiógrafo.

radiography, *s.* radiografia.

radiologist, *s.* radiologista, radiólogo.

radiology, *s.* radiologia.

radiometer, *s.* radiómetro.

radiophone, *s.* radiofone.

radioscopy, *s.* radioscopia, exame por meio de raios X.

radiotelegraphy, *s.* radiotelegrafia.

radiotelephony, *s.* radiotelefonia, telefonia sem fios.

radiotherapy, *s.* radioterapia.

radiovision, *s.* radiovisão, televisão.

radish, *s.* rábano, rabanete.

radium, *s.* (quím.) rádio, radium.

radius, *s.* raio (geom.); esfera, circunferência; *radius of action*: raio de acção.

radix, *s.* raiz, origem, fonte; raiz (bot.).

raff, *s.* ralé, gentalha.

raffia, *s.* ráfia.

raffle, *s.* rifa, sorteio; restos, rebotalho; fragmentos, caliça; *v.t.* rifar, sortear; *v.i.* comprar bilhete de rifa.

raft, *s.* jangada, balsa, piroga; *v.t.* e *v.i.* transportar em jangada ou piroga, viajar em jangada ou piroga.

rafter, *s.* jangadeiro; barrote, viga.

rag, *s.* trapo, farrapo, frangalho; pessoa esfarrapada; capacho; bandeira, vela; jornal, periódico; cortina; pedra granulosa e grosseira. 1) *rag-baby*, boneca de trapos. 2) *rag-fair*, feira de roupa velha. 3) *rag-money*, papel moeda. 4) *she is always dressed with rags*, ela anda sempre vestida com farrapos, *v.t.* e *v.i. (ragging, ragged),* ralhar, censurar; atormentar, descompor; fazer algazarra (fam.).

ragamuffin, *s.* miserável, esfarrapado; bandalho, velhaco.

rage, *s.* raiva, ira, fúria; veemência, ardor, paixão, intensidade; voga, moda, coqueluche. 1) *she has a rage for shoes*, ela tem a mania dos sapatos. 2) *this new writer is the the rage*, este novo escritor faz furor; *v.i.* bramar, enfurecer-se, encolerizar-se; assolar (peste); devastar (tempestade); lavrar (incêndio).

rageful, *adj.* raivoso, furioso.

ragged, *adj.* áspero, desigual, irregular; defeituoso, imperfeito; nodoso, espinhoso; hirsuto, peludo; rouco, dissonante; roto, esfarrapado, andrajoso; *ragged school*, escola para crianças pobres; escola gratuita; *adv. raggedly*, andrajosamente; asperamente.

raging, *s.* raiva, ira, furor; *adj.* raivoso, furioso; *adv. ragingly*, furiosamente.

raglan, *s.* sobretudo largo.

ragman, *s.* trapeiro.

ragpicker, *s.* trapeiro.

ragstone, *s.* pedra de amolar, grés silicoso.

ragtag, *s.* gentalha, ralé.

raid, *s.* incursão; surpresa, invasão repentina, ataque súbito (mil.); *v.t.* invadir; fazer uma incursão.

raider, *s.* incursor, atacante, assaltante.

rail, *s.* barra, varão de grade; grade, balaustrada, varanda, parapeito, barreira, travessa; carril, caminho de ferro, trilho; galão, braçal (náut.); fracolim (ave). 1) *rail-*

chair, coxim. 2) *breast-rail*, parapeito. 3) *coat-rail*, cabide para casacos. 4) *to run off the rails*, descarrilar; *v.t.* cercar com grades ou parapeito; assentar trilhos em; transportar por via férrea; *v.i.* viajar por via férrea. 5) *to rail against*, injuriar; escarnecer de.

railer, *s.* insultador.

railing, *s.* balaustrada, parapeito, barreira; cerca, grade.

raillery, *s.* escárnio, chacota, mofa.

railroad, *s.* caminho de ferro, via férrea, ferrovia.

railway, *s.* caminho de ferro. 1) *railway crossing*, passagem de nível. 2) *railway porter,* carregador. 3) *railway rug*, manta de viagem.

raiment, *s.* vestuário, roupa, vestes.

rain, *s.* chuva; *v.i.* chover. 1) *it is raining cats and dogs*, chove a cântaros. 2) *rain or shine*, quer chova, quer faça sol; *v.t.* fazer chover; derramar copiosamente. 3) *it is pouring with rain*, chove a cântaros.

rainbow, *s.* arco-íris.

raincoat, *s.* impermeável, gabardina.

raindrop, *s.* gota de chuva.

rainfall, *s.* aguaceiro.

rainproof, *adj.* impermeável (à chuva); *v.t.* impermeabilizar.

rainstorm, *s.* tempestade, grande pancada de água.

rainy, *adj.* chuvoso, pluvioso, húmido.

raise, *v.t.* levantar, alçar; pôr em pé; elevar, erguer, suspender; erigir, construir; edificar; aumentar, subir, encarecer; engrandecer, exaltar; causar, ocasionar; produzir, criar; cultivar, educar; organizar, recrutar; recolher ou juntar (dinheiro); ressuscitar, vivificar, dar vida; pôr fim, abandonar. 1) *to raise a siege*, levantar um cerco. 2) *to raise a forbidding*, dar por finda uma proibição. 3) *to raise a row*, armar um chinfrim. 4) *to raise money on*, empenhar uma coisa. 5) *to raise the country*, sublevar o país. 6) *to raise a point*, levantar uma questão; fazer uma observação. 7) *to raise the curtain*, subir o pano (teatr.); *s.* aumento, subida.

raised, *adj.* levantado; em relevo.

raisin, *s.* passa de uva.

raja, rajah, *s.* rajá, príncipe de tribo hindu.

rake, *s.* ancinho; raspadura; inclinação; sacada da popa (náut.); libertino, debochado, *rake-dredge*, draga varredoura; *v.t.* raspar, limpar, juntar (com o ancinho); varrer; esquadrinhar, sondar, revolver;

cobrir com terra; *v.i.* passar com rapidez ou brusquidão; vadiar, levar vida devassa; inclinar-se; ter caimento (o mastro).

rake-off, *s.* lucro não merecido.

raker, *s.* raspadeira; esquadrinhador, explorador.

rakish, *adj.* libertino, dissoluto; que tem os mastros muito inclinados; *adv.* licenciosamente.

rally, *v.t.* reunir e reorganizar tropas; ridicularizar, zombar; reanimar; *v.i.* reorganizar-se, voltar à luta; reunir-se, refazer-se, reanimar-se; *s.* união ou reunião (de pessoas ou tropas dispersas); recuperação.

ram, *s.* carneiro; *aries* (signo); aríete hidráulico; maço (de calceteiro); *v.t. (ramming, rammed)* calcar; meter à força, atacar, cravar; assentar, atulhar.

Ramadam, *s.* Ramadão, mês em que o povo muçulmano pratica o jejum.

ramble, *v.t.* vaguear, errar, vadiar; divagar; dar voltas; *s.* passeio, excursão.

rambler, *s.* vagabundo, vadio; passeante; roseira trepadeira.

rambling, *adj.* errante, divagante; desconexo, incoerente; plantas rastejantes ou trepadeiras.

ramification, *s.* ramificação; ramagem; ramo; subdivisão.

ramiform, *adj.* ramiforme; ramificado.

ramify, *v.t.* e *v.i.* ramificar(-se), subdividir(-se).

rammer, *s.* maço de calceteiro; pilão; bate-estacas.

rammish, *adj.* fétido, malcheiroso.

ramose, *adj.* ramoso, ramalhudo.

ramp, *v.i.* e *v.t.* saltar, pular, brincar; trepar (bot.); cobrir com erva; subir ou descer um muro a diversos níveis; cobrar exorbitantemente; prover de rampa; *s.* pulo, salto; rampa, declive; preço exorbitante, vigarice.

rampage, *s.* alvoroço, agitação, tumulto; *v.i.* agitar-se; levantar um tumulto.

rampageous, *adj.* turbulento, tumultuoso; *adv. rampageously,* de modo turbulento.

rampancy, *s.* extravagância; exuberância; superabundância.

rampant, *adj.* exuberante, excessivo; predominante; agressivo, feroz, ameaçador; rampante (her.).

rampart, *s.* terrapleno, plataforma; muralha; baluarte; defesa, protecção; *v.t.* cercar com muralhas, proteger.

ramshackle, *adj.* desmoronado, em ruínas.

rance, *s.* mármore belga de cor vermelha salpicado de azul e branco.

ranch, *s.* rancho, fazenda (onde se cria gado); *v.t.* criar gado; espremer; dirigir uma fazenda de gado.

rancher, ranchman, *s.* fazendeiro, vaqueiro.

rancid, *adj.* rançoso, râncido; repugnante.

rancidity, *s.* ranço.

rancor, rancour, *s.* rancor, ódio, aversão.

rancorous, *adj.* rancoroso, vingativo.

rand, *s.* orla, margem, cordilheira.

random, *s.* acaso, desatino, desacerto. 1) *at random*, à toa, ao acaso; *adj.* fortuito; feito ao acaso, impensado, descuidado. 2) *random bullet*, bala perdida.

range, *v.t.* e *v.i.* alinhar, pôr em fila; colocar, classificar; percorrer, vaguear, errar; estender-se; passar junto de; estar ao nível de; estar na mesma altura; rastejar; costear; variar, flutuar; ter alcance (projéctil); *s.* fila, fileira; série, cadeia; classe, ordem; distância, extensão, espaço, curso, carreira; vasto terreno de pastagem; fogão de cozinha. 1) *range of mountains*, serrania, cordilheira. 2) *long-range fire*, tiro de longo alcance. 3) *range table*, tábua de tiro.

ranger, *s.* couteiro; guarda-florestal; (pl.) corpo de guarda montada; batedor; cão de busca.

rangy, *adj.* capaz de longas marchas; espaçoso, vasto; esguio, esgalgado.

rank, *s.* linha, fileira, fila; grau; graduação; qualidade, distinção, classe, ordem, esfera, posição, dignidade; as filas (mil.). 1) *the rank*, a tropa. 2) *she married a man of the rank*, ela casou com um fidalgo. 3) *in this school the poor take rank with the rich*, nesta escola os pobres estão lado a lado com os ricos; *adj.* luxuriante, viçoso, fértil, vigoroso; espesso; fétido; rançoso; consumado, acabado; grosseiro, ordinário; fundo, profundo; *v.t.* classificar, ordenar, colocar por graus, pôr em fila; ter um grau superior a (mil.); *v.i.* enfileirar-se; estar colocado; ter tal grau ou classificação; ser o mais graduado. 4) *to rank first*, ocupar o primeiro lugar.

ranker, *s.* soldado, praça; oficial prático, oficial que vem das fileiras.

rankle, *v.i.* inflamar-se, irritar-se, agravar-se; *to rankle in one's heart*, envenenar o espírito a uma pessoa.

rankly, *adv.* grosseiramente; rançosamente.

ransack, v.t. esquadrinhar, rebuscar, registar; explorar, roubar, saquear.

ransom, s. resgate; multa; v.t. resgatar; redimir.

rant, v.i. e v.t. usar de linguagem pomposa; declamar, arengar; disparatar, gritar; s. linguagem empolada; discurso extravagante; tirada, arenga, palavreado oco.

ranter, adj. declamador; energúmeno.

ranting, adj. afectado, bombástico; palavroso, ruidoso; disparatado; adv. rantingly, afectadamente.

ranunculus, s. ranúnculo.

rap, s. pancada seca; piparote; tapona; ninharia, bagatela; novelo de 120 jardas de linha; moeda de pouco valor; I don't care a rap, não me importa nada; v.t. e v.i. (rapping, rapped), bater com rapidez; dar uma pancada seca; falar com vivacidade; rudeza; praguejar.

rapacious, adj. rapace, ávido; adv. rapaciously, com rapacidade.

rapaciousness, rapacity, s. rapacidade.

rape, s. violação, estupro; rapto; extorsão; roubo; filtro para fazer vinagre, bagaço (de uva); rapazinho, nabo silvestre, colza; v.t. violar, desflorar, violentar.

rapid, adj. rápido, veloz; s. (pl.) rápido; a corrente (dum rio); adv. rapidly, rapidamente.

rapidity, s. rapidez, ligeireza; velocidade.

rapier, s. espadim.

rapine, s. rapina.

rapper, s. pessoa que bate à porta; batente, aldrava.

rapping, s. acto de bater (à porta, etc.).

rapprochement, s. aproximação, reconciliação.

rapscallion, s. biltre, velhaco.

rapt, adj. arrebatado, extasiado; absorto.

raptorial, adj. (zool.) de rapina; ave de rapina.

rapture, s. arroubo, êxtase, transporte, entusiasmo.

rapturous, adj. arrebatador, encantador.

rare, adj. raro, extraordinário, surpreendente, excelente, precioso; escasso, espalhado, disperso; invulgar; mal passado, meio cru (carne).

raree-show, s. curiosidade; espectáculo de feira.

rarefaction, s. rarefacção.

rarefactive, adj. rarefactivo, rarefaciente.

rarefy, v.t. rarefazer, rarear; v.i. rarefazer-se; estender-se, dilatar-se.

rarely, adv. raramente; excelentemente.

rareness, s. raridade; preciosidade.

rareripe, adj. precoce, prematuro.

rarity, s. raridade; preciosidade; escassez; excelência.

rascal, s. biltre, patife, velhaco, meliante; adj. vil desprezível.

rascalion, s. biltre, canalha.

rascality, s. patifaria, velhacaria, maroteira.

rascally, adj. velhaco, patife, baixo, ignóbil.

rash, adj. precipitado, urgente; arrebatado, temerário, irreflectido; s. borbulha; erupção; nettle rash, urticária; adv. rashly, precipitadamente.

rasher, s. talhada de toucinho ou presunto para fritar.

rashness, s. temeridade, audácia; leviandade, precipitação.

rasorial, adj. (zool.) galináceo.

rasp, s. grosa, raspador, lima; ruído estridente; v.t. raspar, limar com a grosa.

raspberry, s. framboesa.

rasping, adj. raspador; rascante, irritante; roufenho, áspero; s. raspagem, limalha.

raspy, adj. dissonante, áspero; irritadiço.

rasure, s. rasura.

rat, s. rato, ratazana; (gír.) vira-casaca (pol.); fura-greves; renegado. 1) to smell a rat, desconfiar, supeitar. 2) rat-trap, ratoeira; rats!: patetices; v.t. e v.i. (ratting, ratted), caçar ratos; trair um companheiro; virar a casaca; trabalhar por preço inferior ao fixado pelo sindicato.

ratability, s. capacidade para ser avaliado ou tributado.

ratable, rateable, adj. avaliável; tributável; adv. ratably, pro rata, proporcionalmente, por avaliação.

rate, s. razão; relação; proporção; preço, valor, taxa; variação; velocidade, marcha, andar; bitola, marcha; categoria, qualidade; modo maneira; contribuição local, imposto. 1) rate payer, contribuinte. 2) death rate, taxa de mortalidade. 3) at this rate she will soon became dismissed, por este andar será em breve despedida. 4) at any rate rate, we must tell him, de qualquer modo devemos dizer-lhe. 5) a first-rate ship, um navio de primeira classe; v.t. taxar, avaliar, apreciar; fixar ou pôr preço; classificar, dar categoria; aplicar taxa; v.i. valer, ser considerado ou avaliado em, estar classificado. 6) he was rated as manager director in that company, ele tinha o posto de administrador delegado naquela companhia.

rated, adj. taxado, tributado; avaliado, estimado.

rater, s. avaliador.

rathe, rath, adj. matinal; precoce; adv. cedo; pela manhã.

rather, adv. antes, talvez, mais exactamente, quiçá; muito; (em respostas, fam.) sem dúvida, claro, pudera, como não. 1) I would rather, I had rather, preferia, prefiro (seguido duma cláusula como objecto directo). 2) he gave himself up rather than be shot, preferiu entregar-se a ser morto. 3) this book is rather good, este livro é bastante bom.

raticide, s. raticida.

ratification, s. ratificação, confirmação.

ratify, v.t. ratificar, aprovar, sancionar.

ratin, s. veneno para ratos.

rating, s. classe, avaliação, classificação; tributo fixado; grau, posto (do marinheiro); descompostura, repreensão.

ratio, s. razão (mat.), proporção; índice, coeficiente.

ratiocinate, v.i. raciocinar.

ratiocination, s. raciocínio; dedução.

ration, s. ração; v.t. racionar.

rational, adj. racional, razoável; s. pessoa racional; adv. rationally, racionalmente.

rationale, s. análise racional; fundamento lógico.

rationalism, s. racionalismo.

rationalist, s. racionalista.

rationality, s. racionalidade; razão; tino.

rationalize, v.t. racionalizar; apresentar razões; v.i. raciocinar.

ratoon, s. rebento, renovo; v.i. rebrotar, vergontear.

ratsbane, s. veneno para ratos; arsénico branco.

rattan, s. rotim, rota; rattan chair, cadeira de palhinha.

ratten, v.t. e v.i. sabotar.

rattle, v.t. e v.i. matraquear; bater ou sacudir com ruído; aturdir; ribombar; vociferar, fazer alarido; ressoar, tagarelar; injuriar; s. estrondo, barulho, algazarra; tagarelice, palavreado; rufo (tambor), chocalho; tagarela; death rattle, estertor.

rattlebrained, rattleheaded, rattle-pated, adj. leviano, estouvado, doidivanas.

rattler, s. falador, palrador.

rattlesnake, s. cobra cascavel.

rattling, adj. vivo, surpreendente, alegre, retumbante; s. som rouco, soluço, estertor.

ratty, adj. ratinheiro; infestado de ratos; (gír.) mal vestido, maltrapilho; impaciente, rabugento.

raucity, s. rouquidão.

raucous, adj. rouco, rouquenho; adv. raucously, roucamente.

ravage, v.t. saquear, roubar; assolar, arruinar; s. devastação, ruína, estrago, destroço.

ravager, s. saqueador, assolador.

ravaging, s. assolação, devastação; adj. assolador, devastador.

rave, v.i. delirar; disparatar; vociferar, raivar; bramar; estrondear (o mar), entusiasmar-se, falar entusiasmadamente; she raves about her new job, ela está entusiasmada com o novo emprego; s. delírio, desvario, excitação; rugido (mar ou vento).

ravel, v.t. embaraçar, embrulhar; enredar, intrigar; desfazer; desfiar, desembrulhar; (com out) deslindar, esclarecer; v.i. (com out) desfiar-se, esfiapar-se, desmanchar-se; s. emaranhamento, nó; complicação; fiapo.

raven, s. corvo; adj. de cor negra e lustrosa; v.t. e v.i. rapinar; devorar, ser voraz; prender à força; desejar com avidez.

ravening, adj. rapace, rapinante; devorador.

ravenous, adj. rapace; ávido, sôfrego, voraz; faminto; adv. ravenously, vorazmente.

ravin, s. rapina (poét. e ret.); roubo, rapinagem; despojo.

ravine, s. ravina, barranco, garganta.

raving, s. devaneio, desvario, delírio; delirante; frenético; raving mad, doido-varrido; louco furioso.

ravish, v.t. arrebatar, encantar; raptar, violentar; extorquir.

ravisher, s. raptor; violador; arrebatador.

ravishing, adj. arrebatador, encantador; violador; s. rapto; adv. ravishingly, com arrebatamento; encantadoramente.

ravishment, s. rapto; violação, estupro; arrebatamento, êxtase.

raw, adj. cru; verde; em estado natural; bruto, em rama; fresco, novo, puro, sem confecção; novato, bisonho; rude, tosco; inculto, inexperiente; esfolado, em carne viva; frio, húmido (tempo). 1) raw-material, matéria-prima. 2) raw silk, seda crua; s. escoriação, esfoladura, chaga.

rawboned, adj. descarnado, magro.

rawhide, adj. feito de couro cru; s. couro, chicote.

rawish, adj. um tanto cru; com pouca experiência.

rawly, adv. cruamente; sem experiência.

rawness, s. crueza; qualidade de estar cru, frio ou húmido.

ray, s. raio (de luz, calor, etc.); linha recta, fila, risca; raia, (peixe); *X rays,* raios X; v.t. e v.i. irradiar, emitir raios, cintilar, fulgir; expor a radiação; raiar, riscar.

rayless, adj. sem raios; sombrio, opaco, fosco.

rayon, s. rayon, seda artificial.

raze, v.t. arrasar, derrubar; demolir; extirpar; apagar, anular.

razor, s. navalha de barba; (pl.) presas de javali. 1) *razor-blade,* lâmina de navalha de barba. 2) *razor-edge,* fio de navalha. 3) *razor shell,* navalha, lingueirão. 4) *safety razor,* gilete.

razorback, s. roqual (baleia).

razzia, s. razia, correria, incursão.

razzle, razzle-dazzle, s. (gír.) s. alvoroço, azáfama, farra.

re, s. ré (mús.); causa, litígio, acção; prep. a respeito de, com respeito a, em referência a (com.).

reach, v.t. alcançar, obter, conseguir, atingir, chegar a, tocar; apanhar, agarrar; estender, estirar; comunicar com, entrar em contacto com. 1) *we shall reach home tomorrow,* chegaremos a casa amanhã. 2) *reach me the salt,* passa-me o sal. 3) *our farm reaches the river,* a nossa quinta estende-se até ao rio; v.i. estender o braço, a mão; elevar-se; esforçar-se; s. extensão; poder, alcance, capacidade; astúcia, manha; troço de rio entre duas voltas.

reach-me-down, adj. (gír.) feito, comprado feito; em segunda mão; s. roupa de confecção.

react, v.i. reagir; contra-atacar (mil.); v.t. representar pela 2ª vez (uma peça).

reaction, s. reacção; contra-ataque (mil.).

reactionary, adj. e s. reaccionário.

reactive, adj. reactivo.

reactor, s. reactor.

read, v.t. ler, recitar; interpretar, decifrar, descobrir, compreender; estudar, aprender, ensinar, aconselhar, avisar. 1) *to read on to sleep,* adormecer (um pessoa) a ler; v.i. ler, estudar; dedicar-se à leitura ou ao estudo; estar concebido ou redigido (texto). 2) *to*

read aloud, ler em voz alta. 3) *to read law,* estudar direito. 4) *to read on,* prosseguir. 5) *to read out,* ler por alto; expulsar. 6) *to read through,* ler de fio a pavio. 7) *well read,* versado, instruído, erudito. 8) *I read her a lesson,* ralhei com ela; dei-lhe uma lição.

readable, adj. legível; agradável de ler; adv. *readably,* dum modo legível.

reader, s. leitor; recitador; revisor de provas; manual de leitura; professor.

readership, s. leitorado, cargo de leitor.

readily, adv. prontamente; com boa vontade; sem demora; facilmente.

readiness, s. disposição, boa vontade; prontidão, desembaraço.

reading, s. lição, leitura; conferência; estudo; interpretação dum texto; legenda; desempenho dum papel teatral; cultura literária; instrução; adj. de leitura. 1) *reading-room,* sala de leitura. 2) *worth reading,* digno de ser lido.

readjust, v.t. reajustar.

readjustment, s. reajustamento.

readmission, readmittance, s. readmissão.

readmit, v.t. readmitir.

ready, adj. pronto, preparado, disposto; inclinado, propenso; ágil, hábil, diligente; vivo, expedito; fácil, à mão, disponível; breve, curto; de contado, efectivo. 1) *ready money,* dinheiro de contado. 2) *ready payment,* pagamento imediato. 3) *ready witted,* atilado, sagaz. 4) *ready!,* carregar! (mil.).

reaffirm, v.t. reafirmar.

reagency, s. reacção.

reagent, s. (quím.) reagente, reactivo.

real, adj. real, verdadeiro, genuíno; propriedade imobiliária, imóvel; sincero; s. real, realidade; real, moeda espanhola.

realism, s. realismo.

realist, s. realista.

realistic, adj. realista; realístico; adv. *realistically,* realisticamente.

reality, s. realidade; objectividade; verdade.

realizable, adj. realizável.

realization, s. realização, concretização.

realize, v.t. realizar, efectuar, cumprir, levar a cabo; ganhar, render; compreender; *to realize the drift,* compreender o sentido.

realizing, adj. compreensivo, sagaz.

really, adv. realmente, efectivamente, de facto.

realm, s. reino; esfera, domínio.

realtor, s. corretor de imóveis.

realty, s. bens de raiz.

ream, s. resma; v.t. alargar (furo), escariar; desnatar (leite).

reamer, s. alargador, escariador; mandril; espremedor (laranjas, etc.); desnatador.

reanimate, v.t. reanimar.

reap, v.t. e v.i. segar, ceifar; colher; tirar proveito.

reaper, s. ceifeiro, segador; ceifeira (máquina).

reaping, s. ceifa, colheita; reaping-hook, foice.

reappear, v.i. reaparecer, tornar a aparecer.

reappearence, s. reaparição.

reappoint, v.t. nomear, designar de novo; restabelecer.

reappointment, s. nova nomeação; restabelecimento.

rear, s. retaguarda, fundo, costas, parte traseira. 1) to hang on the rear, ir na peugada. 2) to bring up the rear, fechar a marcha; adj. traseiro, último; v.t. erguer, levantar; erigir, construir; educar, criar; v.i. empinar-se.

rear-admiral, s. contra-almirante.

rear-guard, s. retaguarda.

rearm, v.t. rearmar.

rearmost, último da cauda.

rearrange, v.t. redistribuir, reagrupar; recompor; tornar a pôr em ordem.

rearrangement, s. acto de voltar a arranjar.

rearward, adj. dirigido para trás; retrospectivo; adv. para trás, atrás de; s. retaguarda, parte traseira.

reascend, v.t. e v.i. reascender; tornar a elevar-se.

reason, s. razão, motivo, causa; direito; entendimento, intuição; moderação. 1) to yield to reason, ceder à razão. 2) in reason, com direito; v.t. provar, arguir; persuadir; dissuadir; investigar; deduzir; discutir; v.i. raciocinar; argumentar, meditar, debater.

reasonable, razoável, racional; justo, módico, moderado; adv. reasonably, razoavelmente.

reasonableness, s. racionalidade; moderação; justiça, equidade.

reasoner, s. raciocinador.

reasoning, s. raciocínio; razões, argumentos.

reasonless, adj. irracional, incoerente, despropositado.

reassemble, v.t. e v.i. tornar a reunir-se; reagrupar-se; tornar a montar (mec.).

reassembly, s. reunião, reajuntamento; remontagem (mec.).

reassert, v.t. reafirmar.

reassess, v.r. reavaliar.

reassign, v.t. reencaminhar; transferir.

reassume, v.t. reassumir; recomeçar; revogar, anular.

reassurance, s. reafirmação; confiança restabelecida; resseguro.

reassure, v.t. tranquilizar; restituir a confiança; ressegurar.

reassuring, adj. tranquilizador; adv. reassuringly, de modo tranquilizador.

reave, v.t. (arc. e poét.) privar, despojar.

rebate, s. desconto, dedução, abatimento; redução, diminuição; v.t. e v.i. abater, deduzir, descontar.

rebel, s. e adj. rebelde, insurrecto; v.i. (rebelling, rebelled), rebelar-se, revoltar-se, sublevar-se.

rebellion, s. rebelião, revolta, sublevação, insurreição.

rebellious, adj. rebelde, revoltoso, sublevado, amotinado; adv. rebelliously, rebeldemente, com rebeldia.

rebind, v.t. reatar, amarrar novamente; encadernar de novo.

reabirth, s. renascimento; reencarnação.

reboant, adj. (poét.) reboante, ressoante.

reborn, adj. renascido, que renasce.

rebound, v.i. ressaltar, repinchar; repercutir; s. ressalto.

rebuff, s. desaire, vexame; repulsa, rejeitar; v.t. repelir, rejeitar.

rebuild, v.t. reconstruir, reedificar.

rebuke, v.t. repreender, verberar, censurar; s. repreensão, censura; adv. rebukingly, con censura.

rebus, s. enigma; charada; representação figurada de palavra ou frase.

rebut (rebutting, rebutted), v.t. refutar, contradizer; rechaçar.

rebuttable, adj. refutável.

rebuttal, s. refutação.

recalcitrant, adj. recalcitrante, obstinado.

recall, v.t. chamar de novo; recordar, relembrar; tocar a reunir; destituir dum cargo ou dum emprego; revogar, anular; recordação; toque de reunir; revogação.

recant, v.t. e v.i. retractar-se.

recantation, s. retractação.

recap (recapping, recapped), recauchutar; s. pneu recauchutado.

recapitulate, v.t. recapitular, resumir; epilogar.

recapitulation, s. recapitulação, resumo; epílogo.

recapitulative, recapitulatory, *adj.* recapitulativo.

recapture, *s.* recaptura; *v.t.* recapturar.

recast, *v.t.* refundir; reformar, refazer; *s.* remodelação.

recede, *v.i.* retroceder, recuar; retirar-se, afastar-se; desistir, desdizer-se; desviar-se, apartar-se; *v.t.* ceder novamente.

receipt, *s.* recibo, quitação; recepção, recebimento; receita; (pl.) ingressos, entradas, receitas. 1) *receipt book*, livro de despesas, rol. 2) *to acknowledge receipt*, acusar a recepção; *v.t.* e *v.i.* passar recibo.

receivable, *adj.* receptível, aceitável, admissível; a receber.

receive, *v.t.* receber, admitir; acolher, hospedar; aceitar; apanhar, captar; conter, suportar, suster.

receiving, *s.* recepção.

recency, *adj.* qualidade daquilo que é recente; novidade, data recente.

recension, *s.* revisão; exame; recensão.

recent, *adj.* recente, moderno; novo, fresco; *adv. recently*, recentemente.

receptacle, *s.* receptáculo, recipiente.

reception, *s.* recepção, recebimento; acolhimento. 1) *reception-room*, sala de recepção. 2) *reception-desk*, balcão da recepção.

receptive, *adj.* receptivo.

receptivity, *s.* receptividade.

recess, *s.* recesso, retiro; nicho, alcova; esconderijo; suspensão (do trabalho); férias do parlamento; retirada, partida; *v.t.* abrigar, ocultar; apartar, afastar; fazer um retiro; abrir nicho numa parede.

recession, *s.* recesso, retirada, desistência.

recessional, *adj.* relativo a férias parlamentares; *recessional hymn*, hino cantado depois do ofício divino.

recharge, *v.t.* recarregar.

recherché, *adj.* aquilo que é muito procurado, desejado ou solicitado.

recidivism, *s.* reincidência.

recidivist, *s.* reincidente.

recidivous, *adj.* reincidente.

recipe, *s.* receita; fórmula.

recipient, *s.* recipiente; receptor; *adj.* recebedor, receptivo.

reciprocal, *adj.* recíproco; mútuo; correspondente; *adv. reciprocally*, reciprocamente.

reciprocate, *v.t.* reciprocar, permutar; corresponder; retribuir.

reciprocation, *s.* reciprocidade; correspondência mútua.

reciprocity, *s.* reciprocidade.

recital, *s.* relação, narração; exposição; récita, concerto.

recitation, *s.* recitação, declamação.

recitative, *adj.* recitativo, narrativo; *s.* recitativo (mús.).

recite, *v.t.* e *v.i.* referir, narrar, relatar; recitar, declamar.

reciter, *s.* recitador, narrador.

reck, *v.t.* e *v.i.* fazer caso de; importar-se, inquietar-se. 1) *to reck of*, ligar importância. 2) *it recks me not*, pouco me importa.

reckless, *adj.* descuidado, negligente; temerário, estouvado; *adv. recklessly*, indiferentemente.

reckon, *v.t.* e *v.i.* contar, numerar, calcular, avaliar, estimar, supor, crer. 1) *to reckon for*, pagar. 2) *I reckon on you*, confio em ti, conto contigo. 3) *after I shall reckon with you*, depois ajusto contas contigo, faço contas contigo.

reckoner, *s.* calculador, calculista; *ready-rackoner*, livro de cálculos feitos.

reckoning, *s.* cálculo; conta; ajuste de contas.

reclaim, *v.t.* reclamar, reivindicar; reformar, reconduzir, regenerar; *s.* reclamação; regeneração.

reclaimable, *adj.* que se pode reclamar, emendar ou reformar.

reclaimer, *adj.* reclamante.

reclamation, *s.* reclamação.

recline, *v.t.* e *v.i.* reclinar(-se); recostar(-se), encostar(-se); repousar.

recluse, *adj.* recluso; solitário; *s.* recluso, eremita.

reclusion, *s.* reclusão.

recognition, *s.* reconhecimento; confissão.

recognizable, *adj.* reconhecível; *adv. recognizably*, de modo reconhecível; reconhecidamente.

recognizance, *s.* reconhecimento; obrigação contraída.

recognize, *v.t.* reconhecer, admitir, conceder; examinar de novo; divisar; confessar; saudar.

recoil, *v.i.* recuar, retroceder; rechaçar; dar coice (arma de fogo); recair; *s.* recuo; coice (arma de fogo); refluxo; repugnância; temor.

recollect, *v.t.* e *v.i.* recordar, lembrar(-se) de; recolher, reunir.

recollected, *adj.* calmo, sereno; recordado, lembrado.

recollection, s. lembrança, recordação, memória.

recommence, v.t. recomeçar.

recommend, v.t. recomendar; aconselhar; encomendar, encarregar.

recommendable, adj. recomendável; digno de elogio.

recommendation, s. recomendação; conselho, sugestão.

recommendatory, adj. recomendatório, recomendativo.

recommit, v.t. tornar a cometer; tornar a pôr na prisão; reenviar (projecto-lei) a uma comissão parlamentar.

recompense, v.t. recompensar, compensar; s. recompensa, compensação.

recompose, v.t. recompor; reorganizar; refazer; recombinar (quím.).

reconcentrate, v.t. e v.i. reconcentrar(-se).

reconcilable, adj. reconciliável; compatível; adv. reconcilably, compativelmente.

reconcile, v.t. reconciliar, compor, conciliar, harmonizar, concordar; conformar-se, resignar-se.

reconciliation, s. reconciliação, conciliação, ajuste; concordância; expiação.

reconciliatory, adj. reconciliatório, conciliador.

recondite, adj. recôndito, oculto, secreto; profundo.

recondition, v.t. recondicionar; restaurar, renovar; reeducar, modificar.

reconduct, v.t. reconduzir.

reconnaissance, reconnoissance, s. reconhecimento, exame minucioso, inspecção.

reconquer, v.t. reconquistar.

reconquest, s. reconquista.

reconsider, v.t. reconsiderar.

reconsideration, s. reconsideração; revisão.

reconstitute, v.t. reconstituir, reformar, reorganizar.

reconstitution, s. reconstituição, reorganização.

reconstruct, v.t. reedificar, reconstruir, restabelecer.

reconstruction, s. reedificação, restabelecimento.

reconvey, v.t. e v.i. transportar de novo; reconduzir.

record, v.t. registar, inscrever; arquivar; recordar, fixar na memória; gravar; s. registo, acta, anais; ficha, folha de serviços; antecedentes; memória, monumento;

recorde (desporto); disco (fonográfico); to break the record, bater o recorde.

recordable, adj. registável.

recorder, s. registador; arquivista; oficial do registo; juiz municipal; contador (mec.); gravador (fonográfico); flautim (mús.).

recorship, s. juizado municipal.

recount, s. recontagem, nova contagem; v.t. recontar; referir, relatar.

re-count, v.t. recontar, contar novamente.

recountment, s. narração minuciosa.

recoup, s. desquite, separação; dedução de parte de quantia; v.t. deduzir, reter para indemnizar; reparar; desquitar-se.

recourse, s. recurso, remédio.

recover, v.t. tornar a cobrir ou tapar; recobrir; recobrar, recuperar; reaver; desempenhar, resgatar; restabelecer, curar; v.i. restabelecer-se, recobrar a saúde; ganhar uma causa (justiça).

recoverable, adj. curável; recuperável; reparável.

recovery, s. recuperação; cobrança; resgate, restabelecimento; cura.

recreant, adj. e s. falso, desleal; traidor; cobarde; adv. recreantly, falsamente, com deslealdade.

recreate, v.t. recrear, deleitar; v.i. recrear-se, divertir-se.

re-create, v.t. recriar, tornar a criar; reconstituir.

recreation, s. recreio, recreação, divertimento; diversão.

re-creation, s. recriação.

recreative, adj. recreativo, agradável, deleitoso.

recrement, s. escória, refugo.

recriminate, v.t. e v.i. recriminar.

recrimination, s. recriminação.

recriminative, recriminatory, adj. recriminatório, recriminador.

recriminator, s. recriminador.

recrudesce, v.t. recrudescência.

recrudescence, s. recrudescência.

recrudescent, adj. recrudescente.

recruit, v.t. e v.i. alistar, recrutar; restabelecer, reparar forças, refazer(-se); s. recruta, principiante.

recruitment, s. recrutamento.

rectangle, s. rectângulo.

rectangular, adj. rectangular.

rectifiable, adj. rectificável.

rectification, s. rectificação, correcção, emenda; refinação (quím.).

rectify, *v.t.* rectificar, corrigir, emendar; refinar (quím.).

rectilineal, *adj.* rectilíneo.

rectilinear, *adj.* rectilíneo.

rectitude, *s.* rectidão, correcção; integridade.

recto, *adj.* recto, direito; igual; justo.

rector, *s.* reitor, pároco; prior; reitor de universidade.

rectorate, *s.* reitorado, reitoria.

rectory, *s.* reitoria; presbitério.

rectum, *s.* recto (anat.).

recumbence, *s.* repouso, inactividade.

recumbent, *adj.* deitado; ocioso, inactivo; *adv. recumbently*, ociosamente.

recuperate, *v.t.* recuperar, recobrar; *v.i.* restabelecer-se.

recuperation, *s.* recuperação.

recuperative, *adj.* recuperativo; restaurador, revigorante.

recur (recurring, recurred), *v.i.* recordar-se, ocorrer, vir à memória; voltar, tornar a um assunto; recorrer a; suceder.

recurrence, *s.* volta, renovação; repetição; recurso; retorno, reversão; recordação.

recurrent, *adj.* que reaparece, periódico, cíclico; recorrente.

recusant, *adj.* e *s.* dissidente, o que recusa obediência; não conformista.

recuse, *v.t.* rejeitar; não aceitar a autoridade.

red, *adj.* vermelho, encarnado; revolucionário, anárquico; *s.* cor vermelha ou encarnada; cor de sangue; ocre. 1) *brick red*, cor de tijolo. 2) *deep red*, vermelho vivo, escarlate. 3) *red bird*, cardeal (ave). 4) *red haired*, ruivo. 5) *red-handed*, mãos ensanguentadas, em flagrante. 6) *red-hot*, acérrimo, em brasa. 7) *red wine*, vinho tinto. 8) *to turn red*, corar; *v.t.* corar; pintar de vermelho.

redact, *v.t.* redigir; editar.

redaction, *s.* redacção.

redactor, *s.* redactor.

redden, *v.t.* avermelhar; *v.i.* ruborizar-se, corar.

reddish, *adj.* avermelhado.

reddishness, *s.* vermelhidão.

redecorate, *v.t.* decorar de novo.

redeem, *v.t.* remir; amortizar; resgatar; remir do pecado; reparar; cumprir promessa; salvar; expiar.

redeemable, *adj.* remível, resgatável.

redeemer, *s.* redentor; (com maiúsc.) o Redentor.

redeliver, *v.t.* restituir; devolver.

redemand, *v.t.* pedir a devolução de; reclamar de novo.

redemption, *s.* redenção; resgate; libertação; amortização de uma dívida; *this man is a criminal without redemption*, este homem é um criminoso irrecuperável.

redemptive, *adj.* que redime ou resgata; redentor.

redevelop, *v.t.* virar.

redevelopment, *s.* viragem.

redintegrate, *v.t.* reintegrar, restabelecer, restaurar.

redirect, *v.t.* dirigir de novo; *adj.* instado (foro).

redness, *s.* vermelhidão.

redolence, *s.* perfume, aroma.

redolent, *adj.* perfumado, aromático, odorífero.

redouble, *v.t.* redobrar, aumentar; repetir; reiterar; *v.i.* redobrar-se, reduplicar-se.

redoubt, *s.* reduto (de fortaleza).

redoubtable, *adj.* terrível, temível; formidável.

redound, *v.i.* redundar, resultar; recair; contribuir; *the benefits will redound to us*, os benefícios recaem sobre nós.

redress, *v.t.* endireitar; reparar, compensar; remediar; aliviar, consolar; *to redress the balance*, restabelecer o equilíbrio; *v.t.* e *v.i.* vestir, ou vestir-se de novo; arranjar de novo.

redskin, *s.* pele-vermelha.

red-tape, *s.* oficialismo; formalidades excessivas.

reduce, *v.t.* reduzir, diminuir, minorar, rebaixar, abreviar; sujeitar, submeter.

reduction, *s.* redução; rebaixa, diminuição; *reduction to the ranks*, baixa a soldado.

redundance, redundancy, *s.* redundância, excesso; pleonasmo.

redundant, *adj.* redundante, excessivo, supérfluo; *adv. redundantly*, redundantemente.

reduplicate, *v.t.* reduplicar, redobrar, repetir, multiplicar; *adj.* duplicado, duplo.

reduplication, *s.* reduplicação, repetição.

re-echo, *v.i.* e *v.t.* responder, repercutir; ressoar; *s.* eco repetido.

reed, *s.* cana, junco; haste; palheta; flauta, gaita rústica; flecha, dardo; poesia bucólica.

reedify, *v.t.* reconstruir.

reedit, *v.t.* reeditar, reproduzir.

reedy, *adj.* cheio de canas; caniçoso; juncoso; feito de cana ou de junco; fraco como uma cana, fino, delgado, frágil; fino, esganiçado.

reef, s. recife, escolho, baixio; filão, veio; banco de areia; rizes (náut.); *to take in a reef,* rizar uma vela; proceder com cautela (fig.); *v.t.* rizar (vela); recolher (pás das rodas).

reefy, adj. cheio de escolhos.

reek, s. fumo, vapor, exalação; *v.t.* encher de fumo; defumar; exalar vapores; *v.i.* fumegar, cheirar mal, tresandar; *you reek of tobacco,* tresandas a tabaco.

reeky, adj. fumegante, fumarento; cheio de fumo; enegrecido; malcheiroso.

reel, s. carretel, bobina, carrete, sarilho, dobadoura; tambor; torniquete; *v.t.* dobar; *v.i.* girar, andar à roda; cambalear; vacilar.

re-elect, *v.t.* reeleger.

re-election, s. reeleição.

re-elegible, adj. reelegível.

reeling, adj. cambaleando (ébrio).

re-enact, *v.t.* ordenar de novo; restabelecer.

re-enactment, s. restabelecimento (de lei).

re-engage, *v.t.* contratar; readmitir ao serviço; recomeçar.

re-engagement, s. renovação; readmissão.

re-enter, *v.t.* entrar de novo, reentrar.

re-entrance, s. reentrada, volta; readmissão.

re-entrant, adj. reentrante.

re-establish, *v.t.* restabelecer, restaurar, reconstituir, reinstalar.

re-establishment, s. restabelecimento, restauração.

reeve, s. presidente do conselho de vila ou aldeia; fêmea do pássaro, cavaleiro (v. *ruff*); *v.t.* abrir caminho por.

re-examination, s. acto de examinar de novo.

re-export, *v.t.* reexportar.

re-exportation, s. reexportação.

refashion, *v.t.* remodelar, refazer.

refection, s. refeição.

refectory, s. refeitório.

refer (referring, referred), *v.t.* referir, remeter, enviar; dirigir, encaminhar; atribuir; entregar, apresentar; submeter; *v.i.* referir--se, aludir, remeter-se; dizer respeito, concernir; recorrer, consultar.

referable, adj. que se pode referir.

referee, s. árbitro, avaliador, perito; procurador nomeado pelo tribunal, juiz.

reference, s. referência; alusão, relação, menção, nota; referências, recomendação; abonador; pedido de informação. 1) *reference number,* número de ordem. 2) *in reference,* com relação a.

referendum, s. referendo; plebiscito.

referential, adj. referente, relativo; alusivo.

refill, *v.t.* reencher, reabastecer; s. reenchimento, carga.

refine, *v.t.* refinar, apurar, purificar; polir, corrigir, aperfeiçoar, requintar; *v.i.* refinar--se, polir-se, aprimorar-se; *to be refined,* ser muito cortês, bem-educado.

refined, adj. refinado, purificado; polido, aperfeiçoado; apurado, fino.

refinement, s. refinamento; cortesia, requinte; cultura, refinação; *over refinement,* afectação.

refiner, s. refinador.

refinery, s. refinaria.

refining, s. refinação; afinagem.

refit (refitting, refitted), *v.t.* reparar, consertar, compor, reabilitar; equipar de novo.

refitting, s. reparação.

reflect, *v.t.* e *v.i.* reflectir, repercutir; (com *on* ou *upon*) deslustrar, recair, trazer descrédito a, prejudicar a; meditar, reflectir, pensar.

reflecting, adj. reflectivo, pensador; reflector; *adv: reflectingly,* com reflexão; com censura.

reflection, s. reflexão, meditação; censura, injúria, mancha.

reflective, adj. reflectivo, meditativo, meditabundo; reflexivo (gram.); *adv. reflectively,* reflectidamente.

reflex, s. reflexo; imagem, representação, efeito; adj. reflexo, reflectido; introspectivo.

reflexible, adj. reflexível.

reflexive, adj. reflexivo.

refloat, *v.t.* desencalhar (navio).

reflorescence, reflorescimento, reflorescência.

reflow, *v.i.* refluir.

refluent, adj. refluente.

reflux, s. refluxo, vazante.

reforest, *v.t.* e *v.i.* reflorestar.

reforestation, s. reflorestamento.

reform, *v.t.* reformar, emendar, corrigir; regenerar; *v.i.* emendar-se, corrigir-se, regenerar-se; s. reforma, melhoramento; *reform school,* reformatório.

reformation, s. reforma; (com maiúsc.) Reforma, movimento religioso do séc. XVI.

reformative, adj. reformativo.

reformatory, s. reformatório, casa de correcção; adj. reformatório.
reformer, s. reformador.
reformist, s. reformista.
refract, v.t. refranger, refractar.
refracted, adj. refracto.
refractive, adj. refractivo.
refractor, s. refractor.
refractory, adj. refractário, teimoso, obstinado.
refragable, adj. impugnável, refutável, contestável.
refrain, v.t. refrear, conter, reprimir, moderar, reter; v.i. refrear-se, abster-se; s. refrão, estribilho.
refresh, v.t. refrescar; renovar, revigorar; repousar, descansar, restaurar; animar; v.i. refrescar-se; reparar as forças.
refresher, s. reanimador, revigorante, tónico; refresco, bebida (fam.); honorários adicionais ao advogado quando se protela a causa.
refreshing, adj. restabelecedor, animador.
refreshment, s. refresco, merenda; revigoramento, restauração de forças; refrigério, conforto.
refrigerant, adj. refrigerante; s. refrigerante, refresco.
refrigerate, v.t. refrigerar, refrescar.
refrigeration, s. refrigeração.
refrigerator, s. refrigerador, geladeira, frigorífico.
refuel, v.t. e v.i. rebastecer(-se) de combustível.
refuge, s. refúgio, abrigo; amparo, protecção; recurso, subterfúgio; v.t. e v.i. proteger, dar asilo; abrigar(-se).
refugee, s. refugiado, exilado.
refulgence, s. refulgência, esplendor.
refulgent, adj. refulgente.
refund, v.t. restituir, reintegrar, reembolsar; consolidar uma dívida.
refundable, adj. restituível.
refurbish, v.t. brunir, polir de novo.
refurnish, v.t. fornecer, abastecer de novo.
refusable, adj. recusável.
refusal, s. recusa, negativa, desaire; rejeição.
refuse, v.t. e v.i. recusar, negar, rejeitar; opor-se, negar-se; v.t. fundir, refundir, tornar a fundir.
refutability, s. impugnabilidade.
refutable, adj. impugnável, refutável.
refutation, s. refutação, impugnação.

refute, v.t. refutar, contradizer, impugnar.
regain, v.t. recobrar, recuperar, voltar a ganhar.
regal, adj. real, régio; sumptuoso.
regale, v.t. regalar, festejar; recrear, deleitar; s. banquete, festim.
regality, s. realeza; regalia, privilégio real.
regard, v.t. observar, examinar; olhar, fitar, mirar; considerar, respeitar; estimar, prezar; dizer respeito; s. olhar; aspecto, aparência; atenção, consideração; respeito, estima. 1) *I have always had regard for your opinion,* sempre respeitei a tua opinião; (pl.) cumprimentos, lembranças. 2) *with my best regards,* com os meus melhores cumprimentos. 3) *with regard to,* com respeito a.
regardant, adj. observador, vigilante, atento.
regardful, adj. atento, cuidadoso; respeitador, atencioso; adv. *regardfully,* atentamente.
regarding, prep. relativamente a; com respeito a.
regardless, adj. indiferente, descuidado, negligente.
regatta, s. regata.
regency, s. regência.
regeneracy, s. regeneração, estado do que foi regenerado.
regenerate, v.t. regenerar, reformar, reabilitar, corrigir; reproduzir; v.i. regenerar-se, reabilitar-se, emendar-se; reproduzir-se, tornar a formar-se; adj. regenerado.
regeneration, s. regeneração, renovação; restauração, reconstituição, reabilitação; renascimento.
regenerative, adj. regenerativo, regenerador.
regenerator, s. regenerador, recuperador.
regent, adj. regente; *prince regent,* príncipe regente; s. regente; governador.
regentship, s. regência.
regicidal, adj. regicida.
regicide, s. regicida; regicídio.
regild, v.t. redourar, tornar a dourar.
regime, régime, s. regime.
regiment, s. regimento.
regimental, adj. regimental; s. (pl.) uniforme, farda.
region, s. região, território, país; distrito, comarca, lugar.
regional, adj. regional.
register, s. registo, inscrição, matrícula; lista, arquivo, protocolo; registador, indicador, contador; registo, cartório; v.t. registar,

inscrever, matricular; indicar, marcar; *v.i.* inscrever-se, matricular-se.

registered, registado, inscrito, matriculado.

registrar, *s.* registador.

registrary, *adj.* registador, arquivista.

registration, *s.* registo, acto de registar, assento; inscrição.

regnant, *adj.* reinante.

regorge, *v.t.* vomitar, lançar; regurgitar.

regrant, *v.t.* reconceder; renovar a concessão de; *s.* renovação de concessão.

regress, *s.* regresso, retorno; *v.i.* regressar, voltar.

regression, *s.* regresso.

regressive, *adj.* regressivo.

regret, *s.* pesar, sentimento, tristeza; arrependimento; *v.i. (regretting, regretted),* sentir, lamentar; arrepender-se.

regretful, *adj.* pesaroso; arrependido; saudoso; *adv. regretfully,* com pesar.

regrettable, *adj.* lamentável, sensível; *adv. regrettably,* lamentavelmente.

regular, *adj.* regular; normal, harmonioso, simétrico; uniforme; ordenado, metódico; formal, mediano; soldado de linha; trabalhador permanente; cliente habitual; *adv.* regularmente, bastante, muito; *adv. regularly,* regularmente.

regularize, *v.t.* regularizar; uniformizar.

regulate, *v.t.* regular, reger, governar; regulamentar; regularizar; regular, ajustar; moderar.

regulation, *s.* regulação, regulamento, ordem, regra, regime.

regulative, *adj.* regulador.

regulator, *s.* (elect. e mec.) regulador; guia.

regurgitate, *v.t.* e *v.i.* regurgitar, vomitar.

rehabilitate, *v.t.* reabilitar; reintegrar.

rehabilitation, *s.* reabilitação.

rehear, *v.t.* ouvir segunda vez.

rehearsal, *s.* ensaio.

rehearse, *v.t.* e *v.i.* ensaiar (teat.); repetir; recitar; *v.i.* ensaiar, recitar.

reign, *v.t.* reinar, imperar; predominar, prevalecer; estar na moda; *s.* reino, reinado.

reigning, *adj.* reinante, actual, predominante.

reimburse, *v.t.* reembolsar.

reimbursement, reembolso.

reimport, *v.t.* reimportar.

reimpose, *v.t.* impor de novo.

reimpression, *s.* reimpressão, reedição.

rein, *s.* rédea; (fig.) governo, direcção; *v.t.* guiar, conduzir cavalo; governar; conter,

refrear; *I must rein in this boy,* tenho de refrear este rapaz; puxar pela rédea; deter.

reincarnate, *v.t.* e *v.i.* reencarnar.

reinforce, *v.t.* reforçar.

reinforced, *adj.* reforçado; *reinforced cement,* cimento armado, betão.

reinforcement, *s.* reforço.

reins, *s.* rins, região renal; entranhas; rédeas.

reinstall, *v.t.* instalar de novo.

reinstalement, *s.* nova instalação.

reinsure, *v.t.* ressegurar.

reinsurance, *v.t.* resseguro.

reintegrate, *v.t.* reintegrar, restabelecer, restaurar; *adj.* reintegrado, restabelecido; renovado.

reinveste, *v.t.* reinvestir, reinverter (capitais).

reinvestment, *s.* reinvestimento, reinversão (de capitais).

reinvigorate, *v.t.* revigorar, fortalecer, reanimar.

reissue, *s.* reedição; nova edição ou emissão; *v.t.* reeditar, tornar a emitir.

reiterate, *v.t.* reiterar; *adv. reiteratedly,* reiteradamente, repetidas vezes.

reiteration, *s.* reiteração; repetição.

reject, *v.t.* rejeitar, recusar; repudiar.

rejection, *s.* rejeição, exclusão; repudiação.

rejector, *s.* pessoa que rejeita ou recusa.

rejoice, *v.t.* alegrar; rejubilar, regozijar; *v.i.* regozijar-se, congratular-se.

rejoicing, *s.* júbilo, regozijo; festa, festejo, comemoração; *adj.* jubiloso, festivo, alegre; *adv. rejoicingly,* jubilosamente.

rejoin, *v.t.* reunir-se com, tornar a juntar-se; *v.i.* reunir; retorquir; treplicar.

rejoinder, *s.* resposta, réplica; tréplica (for.).

rejuvenate, *v.t.* rejuvenescer, remoçar.

rejuvenation, *s.* rejuvenescimento.

rekindle, *v.t.* reacender.

relapse, *v.i.* recair; reincidir; *s.* recaída; recidiva (med.).

relate, *v.t.* relatar, referir, contar, narrar; *v.i.* (com to) relacionar-se com, tocar, referir.

related, *adj.* conexo; relativo a; aparentado com.

relater, *s.* relator, narrador.

relation, *s.* relação, conexão; correspondência; referência, alusão; comunicação, trato; parente; ligação; (pl.) parentela.

relationship, *s.* parentesco, afinidade.

relative, *adj.* relativo; *s.* parente; pronome relativo; *adv. relatively,* relativamente.

relax, *s.* descanso; *v.t.* relaxar, afrouxar, abrandar, moderar, ceder; *v.i.* relaxar-se, afrouxar; comedir-se, espairecer, distrair-se.

relaxation, s. relaxação, relaxamento; abrandamento; repouso, distração.

relaxing, adj. calmo, repousante.

relay, s. posta, muda (de cavalos); substituição; v.t. mudar os cavalos; substituir; repor; tornar a deitar; reapontar (artilh.)

release, v.t. libertar, livrar, liberar; soltar, largar, desprender, desamarrar; desobrigar; she released her fiancé from their engagement, ela desobrigou o noivo do compromisso que tinham; permissão (venda, publicação, etc.); renunciar, s. libertação, desobrigação, exoneração; licença; lançamento, largada; recibo, quitação.

re-lease, tornar a arrendar, renovar arrendamento.

relegate, v.t. exilar, banir, desterrar, proscrever.

relegation, s. exílio, desterro, degredo.

relent, v.i. aplacar-se, abrandar-se, enternecer-se; ceder, afrouxar.

relentless, adj. implacável, inexorável; adv. relentlessly, desapiedadamente.

relevance, relevancy, s. pertinência, aplicabilidade.

relevant, adj. pertinente, aplicável; adv. relevantly, pertinentemente.

reliable, adj. seguro, sólido, de confiança; adv. reliably, confiadamente.

reliance, s. confiança.

reliant, adj. confiado.

relic, s. relíquia.

relict, viúva.

relief, s. alívio, desafogo, lenitivo, refrigério, consolo; acção de render uma sentinela; sentinela que rende outra; reparação, compensação; relevo, realce, saliência. 1) indoor relief, socorro aos indigentes numa casa de caridade. 2) outdoor relief, socorro ao domicílio. 3) relief map, mapa em relevo.

relier, s. aquele que confia.

relieve, v.t. socorrer, aliviar, consolar; remediar; isentar, exonerar, mitigar, suavizar; realçar, pôr em relevo; render (guarda ou sentinela); reparar, fazer justiça.

relieving, adj. consolador, mitigador.

religion, s. religião.

religionism, s. beatice, devoção excessiva.

religionist, s. beato, fanático.

religiosity, s. religiosidade.

religious, adj. religioso, devoto; consciente; s. religioso, religiosa, padre, freira; adv. religiously, religiosamente.

relinquish, v.t. abandonar, deixar, desistir de, renunciar a, abrir mão de; soltar, largar.

reliquary, s. relicário.

relish, s. gosto, sabor agradável; pitada, condimento; apetite, prazer, gozo; v.t. saborear, apreciar; v.i. saber bem, ter bom gosto, ser saboroso.

relishable, adj. gostoso, saboroso.

reload, carregar de novo; s. recarga.

reluctance, s. repugnância, relutância.

reluctant, adj. relutante, hesitante, mal-disposto, repugnante; adv. reluctantly, relutantemente, contravontade.

relume, v.t. reacender.

relumine, v.t. o mesmo que o anterior.

rely, v.i. fiar-se em, confiar em, contar com (com on ou up).

remain, v.t. ficar, permanecer, persistir, morar; conservar-se; s. resto, sobra; restos mortais (pl.).

remainder, s. resto, restante; adj. resto, remanescente.

remains, s. restos; relíquias; obras póstumas; restos mortais.

remake, v.t. refazer.

remand, v.t. mandar voltar, reenviar; s. prisioneiro reencarcerado.

remandment, s. acção de encarcerar de novo; ordem de reencarceramento.

remark, v.t. observar, advertir; notar, perceber, reparar em; comentar; s. observação, reparo, advertência, nota.

remarkable, adj. notável, extraordinário, singular.

remarriage, s. novo casamento, segundas núpcias.

remarry, v.t. e v.i. tornar a casar; desposar em segundas núpcias.

remediable, adj. remediável, reparável, curável; adv. remediably, de modo remediável.

remedy, s. remédio, medicamento; recurso; curar, remediar, reparar; prevenir; atalhar.

remember, v.t. recordar, lembrar-se; ter presente; fazer uma menção; remember me to them, dê-lhes lembranças minhas; v.i. recordar-se.

remembrance, s. memória, retentiva, recordação; lembrança, comemoração.

remind, s. recordar, lembrar; avisar; I must remind you of your homework, tenho de lembrar-te dos trabalhos de casa.

reminder, s. lembrança, sinal; advertência.

reminisce, v.t. relembrar.

reminiscence, s. reminiscência; pl. memórias.

reminiscent, adj. recordativo, rememorativo.

remise, s. cocheira; carruagem de aluguer; cedência; v.t. abandonar, entregar, ceder a.

remiss, adj. remisso, negligente, descuidado, lento.

remissible, adj. remissível, perdoável.

remission, s. remissão, perdão, absolvição; redução, mitigação, remessa; adv. remissly, brandamente, negligentemente.

remit (remitting, remitted), remeter, enviar; remitir, perdoar, relevar; abrandar, afrouxar, diminuir; adiar, protelar; v.i. abrandar-se, acalmar-se; esmorecer; fazer remessas; diminuir; s. remessa, envio.

remittal, s. remissão, perdão; relevação, suspensão.

remittence, remittency, s. remitência; remessa (dinheiro); letra de câmbio.

remittent, adj. remitente; s. remitente; remittent fever, febre remitente.

remitter, s. remetente; pessoa que perdoa ou absolve.

remnant, s. remanescente.

remodel (remodelling, remodelled), remodelar, refazer, reconstruir.

remodelling, s. remodelação.

remonstrance, s. protesto, queixa, advertência, admoestação; custódia.

remonstrant, adj. que protesta; reclamante, opositor; s. queixoso, reclamante.

remonstrate, v.i. protestar; queixar-se; admoestar.

remorse, s. remorso, compunção.

remorseful, adj. cheio de remorsos; arrependido; adv. remorsefully, arrependidamente.

remorseless, s. sem remorsos, cruel; adv. remorselessly, cruelmente.

remote, adj. remoto, retirado, isolado; alheio, estranho; leve, vago; to live remote, viver longe, isolado; adv. remotely, remotamente.

remotion, s. afastamento, retirada, remoção; distância, solidão.

remould, v.t. tornar a moldar, remodelar.

remount, v.t. tornar a subir, reascender; tornar a montar; s. remonta, cavalo de muda.

removability, s. amovibilidade.

removable, adj. amovível; transportável; retirável.

remove, v.t. remover, retirar, afastar, desviar; demitir; eliminar; extirpar, fazer desaparecer, assassinar, matar; (na passiva) ser substituído; the cheese was removed by chocolat cake, depois do queijo veio bolo de chocolate; v.i. mudar-se, mudar de domicílio; s. transferência, mudança, remoção; grau, passo; prato; partida.

removed, adj. distante, afastado.

remunerate, v.t. e v.i. s. remunerar, recompensar, compensar, pagar.

remuneration, s. remuneração, paga, salário, recompensa.

remunerative, adj. remunerativo; compensador, lucrativo.

Renaissance, s. Renascimento, renascença; adj. do renascimento, renascentista.

renal, adj. renal.

rename, v.t. renomear, rebaptizar; dar novo nome a; tornar a mencionar.

renascence, s. renascimento, renascença.

renascent, adj. renascente.

rend, v.t. rasgar, fender; arrancar, dilacerar; dividir; v.i. rasgar-se; fender-se, rachar(-se); s. rasgão; costura (do navio).

render, v.t. entregar, devolver, restituir, causar, ocasionar; dar, prestar, render; tornar; dispensar (ajuda); representar, pintar, descrever; interpretar, executar, tocar (mús.); traduzir; derreter; clarificar.

rendering, s. entrega; dom, dádiva; tradução, versão; interpretação; pintura; expressão; reboco.

rendezvous, s. entrevista, reunião; ponto de encontro.

rendition, s. rendição; tradução, versão; interpretação.

renegade, s. renegado, apóstata, traidor, vira-casaca; adj. renegado; traiçoeiro; v.i. renegar a sua fé, partido, etc.

renege, renegue, v.t. renegar; v.i. negar-se.

renew, v.t. e v.i. renovar(-se); reformar; reatar.

renewable, adj. renovável.

renewal, s. renovação, restauração, reforma.

rennet, s. coalho, coalheira; reineta (maçã).

renouce, v.t. renunciar a; renegar, abandonar, abdicar.

renouncement, s. renúncia.

renovate, v.t. renovar, refazer; restaurar; purificar.

renovation, s. renovação.

renown, s. renome, fama; v.t. afamar, tornar célebre.

renowned, adj. afamado, célebre.

rent, s. renda, arrendamento, aluguer. 1) rent day, dia de pagar a renda; v.t. arrendar, dar de arrendamento. 2) he rents his tenants low, ele cobra rendas baixas aos inquilinos; v.i. ser arrendado ou alugado.

rental, s. renda, rendimento, arrendamento; adj. relativo a renda, rendimento.

renter, s. arrendatário; rendeiro.

renunciation, s. renúncia, renunciação.

reoccupation, s. reocupação.

reoccupy, v.t. reocupar.

reopen, v.i. reabrir.

reopening, s. reabertura.

reorganization, s. reorganização.

reorganize, v.t. reorganizar.

rep, s. repes (tecido); verso ou texto decorado; libertino, pessoa de pouca moral.

repaint, v.t. repintar; s. repintura; restauro.

repair, v.t. restaurar, reparar, fazer reparações, compor, consertar, remediar; recompensar, indemnizar; restabelecer; v.i. ir, dirigir-se, encaminhar-se, acorrer; s. reparo, restauração; habitação, guarida; ida, saída; frequência.

repairman, s. consertador.

reparable, adj. reparável, remediável; adv. reparably, de modo reparável.

reparation, s. reparação, indemnização, compensação; conserto, compostura.

reparative, adj. reparatório; reparador, restaurador.

repartee, s. réplica, resposta pronta, agudeza.

repartition, s. repartição, distribuição, divisão.

repass, v.t. e v.i. repassar, tornar a passar.

repassage, s. acto de repassar, nova passagem.

repast, s. repasto, refeição, comida.

repatriate, v.t. e v.i. repatriar-se.

repave, v.t. recalçar, tornar a pavimentar.

repay, v.t. repagar, recompensar, reembolsar, restituir, reintegrar, indemnizar; pagar na mesma moeda; retribuir.

repayable, adj. reparável.

repayment, s. pagamento, devolução; retribuição; recompensa.

repeal, v.t. revogar, anular, abolir; s. revogação, anulação.

repeat, v.t. repetir, reiterar; ensaiar; recitar; s. repetição.

repeated, adj. repetido; adv. repeatedly, repetidamente.

repeating, adj. repetidor, repetente; de repetição.

repel (repelling, repelled), v.t. repelir, rebater; resistir, expulsar; ser repelente, repulsivo.

repellent, adj. repelente, repulsivo; impermeável; s. tela impermeável.

repent, v.t. e v.i. arrepender-se; adj. (bot.) rastejante, rasteiro.

repentance, s. arrependimento, contrição.

repentant, adj. arrependido; adv. repentantly, arrependidamente, contritamente.

repenting, s. arrependimento.

repeople, v.t. repovoar.

repeopling, s. repovoação.

repercussion, s. repercussão.

repertoire, s. repertório.

repertory, s. repertório, repositório, compilação.

repetend, s. refrão, estribilho.

repetition, s. repetição, reiteração.

repetitive, adj. de repetição.

repine, v.i. arrepender-se, lamentar-se, queixar-se; murmurar.

repining, s. pesar, desgosto; lamentação; murmuração; adj. descontente, impaciente, lamentoso, queixoso; adv. repiningly, de modo pesaroso.

replace, v.t. repor, recolocar; devolver, restituir, reembolsar; restabelecer.

replaceable, adj. substituível, renovável.

replacement, s. substituição, reposição.

replant, v.t. replantar; reinstalar.

replenish, v.t. reencher, reabastecer, atestar; acabar, completar; v.i. prover-se, encher-se.

replete, adj. repleto, cheio.

repletion, s. repleção; saciedade.

replevin, s. reivindicação.

replica, s. duplicado, cópia exacta, réplica.

replicate, replicated, adj. replicativo; dobrado sobre si mesmo; v.t. repetir, fazer cópia de; dobrar para trás.

replication, s. réplica; resposta; eco; cópia, reprodução; acto de copiar.

replier, s. o que responde, replicador.

reply, v.t. e v.i. responder, retorquir, redarguir; s. resposta, réplica, contestação.

report, v.t. informar, relatar; referir, contar, dar parte, manifestar; divulgar, delatar, denunciar, ressoar; v.i. apresentar informes; apresentar-se; fazer reportagem; s. relatório, notícia, informação; rumor, boato;

fama, reputação; estampido; *flying report*, boato que corre.

reporter, *s.* repórter, correspondente; informador.

reporting, *s.* relatório, reportagem.

repose, *v.t.* e *v.i.* descansar, repousar, reclinar; depositar confiança em; assentar, basear(-se); *s.* repouso, descanso; sono; paz, serenidade.

reposeful, *adj.* repousado, sossegado, calmo, sereno; *adv. reposefully,* repousadamente.

repository, *s.* repositório, armazém, depósito.

repoussé, *adj.* repelido.

reprehend, *v.t.* repreender, ralhar.

reprehension, *s.* repreensão, censura.

represent, *v.t.* representar, simbolizar, descrever, retratar, apresentar; expor; fazer as vezes de; apresentar de novo.

representation, *s.* representação; retrato, figura, pintura, desenho; imagem; símbolo, sinal; conceito, representação teatral.

representative, *adj.* representativo; *s.* representante; delegado.

repress, subjugar, reprimir, sufocar, recalcar.

represser, *s.* repressor.

repression, *s.* repressão; recalque.

repressive, *adj.* repressivo, repressor; *adv. repressively,* repressivamente.

reprieve, v.t. suspender a execução duma pena; conceder moratória; aliviar; *s.* suspensão da execução duma pena; moratória.

reprimand, *s.* repreensão, reprimenda, admoestação; *v.t.* repreender, corrigir, admoestar.

reprint, *v.t.* reimprimir, reeditar; *s.* reimpressão, reedição.

reprisal, *s.* represália.

reproach, *v.t.* censurar, acusar, exprobrar, condenar; *s.* censura, acusação, exprobração; vitupério, vergonha.

reproachable, *adj.* repreensível.

reproachful, *adj.* injurioso, degradante; condenável; *adv. reproachfully,* censuravelmente.

reprobate, *adj.* e *s.* réprobo; pessoa sem princípios; depravado, patife; *v.t.* reprovar, condenar.

reprobation, *s.* reprovação, condenação.

reproduce, *v.t.* reproduzir.

reproducer, *s.* reprodutor, pessoa ou coisa que reproduz.

reproductive, *adj.* reprodutivo.

reproof, *s.* reprovação, censura, repreensão.

reprovable, *adj.* reprovável, censurável, condenável; *adv. reprovably,* de modo reprovável.

reproval, *s.* reprovação.

reprove, *v.t.* reprovar, censurar, ralhar, repreender.

reprovingly, *adv.* em tom de censura.

reptile, *s.* réptil; *adj.* rastejante, reptante; vil, desprezível.

reptilian, *adj.* relativo à classe dos répteis; *s.* réptil.

republic, *s.* república.

republican, *adj.* e *s.* republicano.

republicanism, *s.* republicanismo.

republish, *v.t.* republicar, reeditar.

repudiate, *v.t.* repudiar; rejeitar, repelir; divorciar-se; não reconhecer.

repudiation, *s.* repúdio; rejeição; negação de dívida.

repugn, *v.t.* repugnar, opor-se.

repugnance, repugnancy, *s.* repugnância; aversão, antipatia, nojo, asco.

repugnant, *adj.* repugnante, oposto a, incompatível; *adv. repugnantly,* com repugnância.

repulse, *s.* repulsa, repulsão, repugnância.

repulsion, *s.* repulsão; repugnância.

repulsive, *adj.* repulsivo, repelente, repugnante, asqueroso, nojento; *adv. repulsively,* de modo repulsivo.

repurchase, *v.t.* readquirir; *s.* reaquisição.

reputable, *adj.* considerado, reputável, respeitável; digno, meritório; *adv. reputably,* reputadamente, meritoriamente.

reputation, *s.* reputação, crédito, renome; respeitabilidade.

repute, *v.t.* reputar, estimar, considerar, ter na conta de; *s.* reputação, bom nome, renome; *he is a good man by repute,* ele é um bom homem ao que dizem.

reputed, *adj.* reputado; *adv. reputedly,* supostamente, segundo a opinião geral.

request, *s.* pedido, petição, solicitação; instância, reclamação; requisição, requerimento. 1) *request book,* livro de reclamações. 2) *at the request of,* a pedido de. 3) *in request,* pedido, procurado, solicitado; *v.t.* pedir, rogar, solicitar; requerer.

requiem, *s.* descanso, réquiem; *requiem mass,* missa de réquiem.

require, *v.t.* requerer, reclamar, solicitar, pedir; exigir, necessitar.

requirement, s. pedido, requerimento, exigência, necessidade; (pl.) qualidades pretendidas. *adj.* necessário, requerido, preciso, indispensável; s. requisito.

requisition, s. pedido, requisição; requisito, condição; *v.t.* requisitar; fazer pedido; pedir, exigir; utilizar; convocar.

requital, s. retorno, paga, satisfação, compensação; vingança.

requiter, s. recompensador.

reremouse, s. morcego.

res, s. coisa.

rescind, *v.t.* rescindir, anular.

rescission, s. rescisão, anulação, abolição.

rescuable, *adj.* resgatável.

rescue, *v.t.* socorrer, salvar, valer a; resgatar; s. socorro, resgate, salvação.

research, s. pesquisa, investigação; busca, procura; *v.i.* pesquisar, fazer pesquisas.

researcher, s. pesquisador.

reseat, *v.t.* reassentar, repor, recolocar.

resell, *v.t.* revender.

resemblance, s. parecença, semelhança, similaridade.

resemble, *v.t.* parecer-se, assemelhar-se.

resend, *v.t.* reenviar.

resent, *v.t.* ressentir, ressentir-se de, ofender-se com.

resentful, *adj.* ressentido, ofendido, despeitado; rancoroso, vingativo; *resentfully,* ressentidamente.

resentment, s. ressentimento, indignação, despeito, rancor.

reservation, s. reserva, reservação; restrição.

reserve, *v.t.* reservar, guardar, reter, conservar, excluir; s. reserva; restrição; excepção; comedimento, cautela, sigilo; lugar reservado para um fim específico, limitação.

reserved, *adj.* reservado; circunspecto, retraído; *adv. reservedly,* reservadamente.

reservoir, s. reservatório, tanque; depósito (água, gás, etc.).

reset (resetting, reset), *v.t.* engastar, montar; reajustar; receber objectos roubados; s. engaste, montagem.

resetter, s. receptador.

reside, *v.i.* residir, morar, viver.

residence, s. residência, habitação; permanência; vivenda.

resident, *adj.* residente, morador permanente; s. habitante; ministro residente; *the english residents,* a colónia inglesa.

residential, *adj.* residencial.

residual, *adj.* residual.

residue, s. resíduo, resto.

residuum, s. resíduo, resto, desperdício.

resign, *v.t.* resignar, demitir-se, renunciar a.

re-sign, *v.t.* reassinar, assinar de novo.

resignation, s. pedido de demissão, renúncia; demissão; abandono; resignação, submissão.

resigned, *adj.* resignado, conformado, submisso; *adv. resignedly,* resignadamente.

resigning, *adj.* demissionário.

resilience, s. elasticidade.

resilient, *adj.* elástico.

resin, s. resina.

resinous, *adj.* resinoso.

resist, *v.t.* e *v.i.* resistir, repelir; opor-se, impedir; negar-se; aguentar, suportar.

resistance, s. resistência; oposição, obstáculo, reacção.

resistant, *adj.* resistente.

resoluble, *adj.* resolúvel.

resolute, *adj.* resoluto, determinado, firme, constante; *adv. resolutely,* resolutamente.

resolution, s. resolução, determinação, decisão, firmeza; propósito; solução; decomposição (de forças).

resolvable, *adj.* resolúvel.

resolve, *v.t.* e *v.i.* resolver(-se), decidir(-se); concordar; analisar; dar solução, desvanecer; s. propósito, acordo.

resolved, *adj.* resolvido, decidido, determinado.

resonance, s. ressonância.

resonant, *adj.* ressonante.

resort, *v.i.* recorrer a; lançar mão de, fazer uso de, empregar; ir, dirigir-se, frequentar; s. recurso, refúgio; concurso, concorrência; covil, caverna; mola. 1) *last resort,* último recurso. 2) *seaside resort,* estância balnear.

resound, *v.t.* repetir, fazer ecoar; apregoar; *v.i.* ressoar, ter ressonância, ter fama.

resounding, s. ressonância; *adj.* ressonante; *she has a resounding family name,* ela tem um ressonante apelido.

resource, s. recurso, meio; (pl.) recursos.

resourceful, *adj.* com bastantes meios; engenhoso.

respect, *v.t.* respeitar, venerar, estimar; acatar, observar, guardar; dizer respeito a; s. respeito, atenção, veneração, consideração, estima; acatamento; relação, referência; (pl.) cumprimentos. 1) *in other respects,* por outra parte. 2) *in respect that,* desde que, visto que. 3) *without respect to*, sem levar em conta.

respectability, *s.* respeitabilidade; crédito, decência.

respectable, *adj.* respeitável, estimável, acreditado; considerável; *adv. respectably*, respeitavelmente.

respectful, *adj.* respeitoso; *adv. respectfully*, respeitosamente.

respecting, *prep.* com respeito a, relativamente.

respective, *adj.* respectivo, relativo; individual.

respectively, *adv.* respectivamente.

respirable, *adj.* respirável.

respiration, *s.* respiração.

respirator, *s.* respirador.

respiratory, *adj.* respiratório.

respire, *v.i.* respirar; aspirar (ar); exalar; viver, manifestar.

respite, *s.* espera, pausa, folga, descanso; adiamento, prazo, prorrogação; *v.t.* dar folga a; suspender, adiar.

resplendence, resplendency, *s.* resplandescência, esplendor.

resplendent, *adj.* resplandescente, esplendoroso, fulgurante; *adv. resplendently*, de modo esplendoroso.

respond, *v.i.* responder, replicar; reagir; ajustar-se; *s.* responso, resposta.

respondent, *adj.* correspondente a; *s.* defensor, responsável, fiador.

response, *s.* resposta, réplica; reacção.

responsibility, *s.* responsabilidade; dever, obrigação, encargo; solvência.

responsible, *adj.* responsável; de responsabilidade; solvente.

responsive, *adj.* que responde, que corresponde, correspondente.

rest, *s.* descanso, repouso, folga, inacção; paz, tranquilidade; apoio, base, suporte; resto, sobra; os outros; tudo o mais; fundos de reserva. 1) *at rest*, em paz. 2) *to be laid to rest*, ser enterrado; *v.t.* e *v.i.* descansar, repousar, dormir, folgar, jazer, morrer; cessar, parar; estar em paz; pousar; apoiar-se, contar com; depender de; apoiar, encostar, colocar. 3) *to rest on promises*, fiar-se em promessas.

restaurant, *s.* restaurante.

restful, *adj.* repousado, sossegado, tranquilo; *adv. restfully*, tranquilamente.

resting, *s.* descanso; *adj.* de descanso.

restitution, *s.* restituição, devolução; reparação, indemnização; recuperação; elasticidade (fís.).

restive, *adj.* rebelde, teimoso, obstinado, inquieto; *adv. restively*, impacientemente.

restless, adj. inquieto, impaciente, desassossegado; *adv. restlessy*, desassossegadamente.

restorable, *adj.* restaurável; restituível.

restoration, *s.* restauração, renovação; reabilitação; reintegração (posto, lugar); restituição.

restorative, *adj.* restaurativo, restaurador; *s.* restaurador.

restore, *v.t.* restaurar, reparar, consertar; reconstruir; reedificar; devolver, restituir.

restorer, *s.* restaurador.

restrain, *v.t.* refrear, reprimir, conter, coibir, impedir, limitar, reter.

restrainable, *adj.* restringível.

restrained, *adj.* reprimido, contido; discreto, reservado; *adv. restrainedly*, restritamente; contidamente.

restrainer, *s.* repressor.

restraint, *s.* repressão, sujeição, restrição; coerção; coibição.

restrict, *v.t.* restringir, limitar.

restricted, *adj.* restrito, limitado; reservado.

restriction, s. restrição, limitação.

restrictive, *adj.* restritivo, limitativo.

result, *v.i.* resultar, originar-se, provir, proceder, decorrer; *s.* resultado; efeito, consequência.

resultant, *adj.* e *s.* resultante.

resume, *v.t.* resumir, recapitular; retomar; recomeçar, reatar, recuperar.

résumé, *s.* resumo, sumário, recapitulação.

resumption, *s.* ressunção, retomada, recuperação, recobro; reatamento, prossecução.

resurge, *v.i.* ressurgir.

resurgence, *s.* ressurgência, ressurgimento.

resurrect, *v.t.* ressuscitar, exumar (fam.).

ressurection, *s.* ressurreição, renovação, restabelecimento; (com maiúsc.) Ressurreição do Senhor.

ressuscitate, *v.t.* e *v.i.* ressuscitar, renascer, reviver.

resuscitation, *s.* ressurreição, renascimento, renovamento.

retail, *s.* retalho, venda a retalho, revenda; *v.t.* vender a retalho; revender; relatar com minúcia.

retain, *v.t.* reter, conservar, guardar, manter; contratar, assalariar, ajustar; *v.i.* estar ajustado ou contratado; *retaining wall*, parede mestra.

retainable, *adj.* ajustável, retível.

retainer, *s.* retentor; aderente, partidário; dependente, cliente, servidor; (jur.) retenção da posse; sinal pago a advogado, custas, etc.

retake (retook, retaken), *v.t.* retomar.

retaliate, *v.t.* e *v.i.* retaliar.

retaliation, *s.* retaliação; desforra; *by way of retaliation*, como represália.

retaliatory, *adj.* retaliativo.

retard, *v.t.* retardar, atrasar, demorar, deter, diferir, adiar; *s.* atraso, demora.

retardation, *s.* retardamento, atraso, demora, delonga.

retardment, *s.* retardamento, demora.

retention, *s.* retenção; conservação; memória.

retentive, *adj.* retentivo; *adv. retentively*, retentivamente.

reticence, *s.* reticência.

reticent, *adj.* reticente; reservado.

retina, *s.* retina.

retinue, *s.* séquito, comitiva, cortejo.

retire, *v.i.* retirar-se, ir-se; retroceder, voltar atrás; retirar-se (vida activa ou profissional); recolher-se; reformar-se; retrair-se; separar-se; ausentar-se; *v.t.* recolher, retirar da circulação; *s.* toque de retirada.

retired, *adj.* retirado, afastado; aposentado; retraído, solitário, isolado; *adv. retiredly*, retiradamente.

retirement, *s.* retiro, refúgio; reforma, aposentação; retirada; isolamento, solidão.

retiring, *adj.* retraído, recatado; modesto, reservado; referente à reforma; *retiring allowance*, pensão de reforma.

retort, *v.t.* redarguir, retorquir; *s.* resposta incisiva, réplica mordaz; retorta, destilador.

retouch, *v.t.* retocar, aperfeiçoar.

retoucher, *s.* retocador.

retrace, *v.t.* remontar a; voltar à origem; rever, reconstituir, reler, recordar, percorrer com os olhos ou com a mente; desandar, retroceder; referir de novo.

retract, *v.t.* e *v.i.* retrair, encolher; retirar, renegar; retractar(-se).

retractation, *s.* retractação, desmentido.

retreat, *s.* retirada, afastamento; retiro, refúgio, abrigo; *v.i.* retirar-se; bater em retirada; refugiar-se; retrair-se.

retrench, *v.t.* cercear, reduzir, restringir, cortar (despesas), economizar; (mil.) entrincheirar.

retrenchement, *s.* cerceamento, economia; entrincheiramento.

retribution, *s.* retribuição, recompensa; retaliação; punição, castigo.

retributive, retributory, *adj.* retribuidor; punitivo; vingador.

retrievable, *adj.* recuperável; reparável; *adv. retrievably*, dum modo reparável.

retrieve, *v.t.* recuperar, reaver, recobrar; reaver; reparar, remediar, restabelecer; ir buscar, trazer (caça abatida).

retriever, *s.* cão de busca; recuperador.

retroactive, *adj.* retroactivo; *adv. retroactively*, dum modo retroactivo.

retrocession, *s.* retrocesso.

retrograde, *adj.* retrógrado; *v.i.* retroceder.

retrogressive, *adj.* retrógrado.

retrospection, *s.* retrospecção.

retrospective, *adj.* retrospectivo.

return, *v.i.* voltar, regressar, tornar, retornar; reverter; responder, replicar; entregar, devolver, restituir; corresponder, pagar, retribuir; reenviar; recompensar; agradecer (um favor, etc.); render, produzir; eleger, nomear (pol.); reflectir (luz, som, etc.); ecoar; *s.* regresso, volta; vinda, chegada; paga, recompensa, retribuição; resposta, réplica; restituição, devolução, reembolso; lucro; lista, relatório; troco; eleição; *pl.* tábuas estatísticas; resultados de eleição; receitas (com.). 1) *return ticket*, bilhete de ida e volta. 2) *return match*, segundo desafio, desafio de desempate. 3) *by return of mail*, na volta do correio.

returnable, *adj.* restituível; reversível.

reunion, *s.* reunião; tertúlia; reconciliação.

reunite, *v.t.* reunir, juntar; reconciliar; *v.i.* reunir-se, juntar-se.

reveal, *v.t.* revelar, divulgar.

revealable, *adj.* revelável.

revealer, *s.* revelador.

reveille, *s.* toque de alvorada (mil.).

revel (revelling, revelled), *v.i.* folgar, andar na farra, divertir-se; *s.* prazer, folia, pândega.

revelation, *s.* revelação.

reveller, *s.* folgazão, folião, farrista.

revelry, *s.* festa, folguedo, festança, folia.

revenge, *v.t.* e *v.i.* vingar, vingar-se, desforrar-se; *s.* vingança, desforra.

revengeful, *adj.* vingativo; *adv. revengefully*, vingativamente.

revenue, *s.* renda, rendimento, receita; rendimentos públicos; direitos alfândegários; fisco; entrada, proventos; tesouro, fazenda pública.

reverberate, *v.t.* e *v.i.* reverberar, repercutir; ecoar, retinir; reflectir-se; retumbar.

reverberation, *s.* reverberação; eco; reflexão.

revere, *v.t.* reverenciar, venerar, honrar, acatar.

reverence, *s.* reverência, respeito, veneração; reverência (tratamento eclesiástico); *to pay reverence*, prestar homenagem; *v.t.* reverenciar, respeitar.

reverend, *adj.* reverendo, venerável; *s.* reverendo, padre, pastor.

reverent, *adj.* reverente, submisso, humilde.

reverential, *adj.* reverencial, respeitoso.

reverie, *s.* devaneio, fantasia.

reversal, *s.* inversão.

reverse, *v.t.* inverter; virar, revirar, dar a volta a; trocar, transpor; modificar totalmente; (jur.) revogar, anular; *adj.* reverso, inverso, oposto, contrário; *s.* o contrário, o oposto, revés; inversão; mudança.

reversible, *adj.* reversível, revogável; de duas faces (tecido, reacção química).

reversion, *s.* reversão.

revert, *v.i.* retroceder, voltar; reverter (jur.).

revertible, *adj.* reversível.

review, *v.t.* rever, examinar, revistar, passar revista; analisar; *s.* revista, inspecção; revista (publicação); parada (mil.).

reviewer, *s.* revisor; redactor; comentador; crítico.

revile, *v.t.* ultrajar, injuriar; *s.* ultraje; injúria.

reviler, *s.* insultador.

reviling, *adj.* injurioso; *s.* injúria; *adv.* revilingly, injuriosamente.

revise, *v.t.* rever, reler, repassar, corrigir; *s.* revisão, revista, segunda prova; *second revise,* terceira prova.

reviser, *s.* revisor, corrector de provas.

revision, *s.* revisão.

revival, *s.* renascimento, restauração; renovação; representação de obras antigas (teat.).

revivalist, *s.* revivalista; envangelizador, pregador que percorre um país tentando despertar a fé.

revive, *v.t.* ressuscitar, renovar, restaurar; despertar, excitar; *v.i.* reviver, ressuscitar; reanimar-se; voltar a si; renascer.

reviver, *s.* restaurador, reanimador; bebida estimulante.

revivify, *v.t.* revivificar; fazer reviver; *v.i.* restabelecer, reviver.

revocable, *adj.* revocável.

revocation, *s.* revocação, revogação.

revoke, *v.t.* revogar, abolir, cancelar, anular; *v.i.* negar-se (em jogos de cartas); *s.* renúncia (no jogo).

revolt, *v.i.* revoltar-se, amotinar-se; *v.t.* revolucionar; repugnar; *s.* revolta, sublevação, rebelião.

revolting, *adj.* repugnante, revoltante.

revolution, *s.* revolução; mudança radical; rotação, volta, giro; ciclo.

revolutionary, *adj.* e *s.* revolucionário.

revolutionize, *v.t.* revolucionar, sublevar.

revolve, *v.t.* rodar, girar, dar voltas; ponderar maduramente; *v.i.* voltear, revolver, fazer girar; meditar, discorrer.

revolver, *s.* revólver.

revolving, *adj.* giratório.

revulsion, *s.* revulsão; reacção (med.); reviravolta; mudança violenta.

reward, *v.t.* recompensar, premiar; remunerar; gratificar; retribuir; *s.* recompensa, prémio; retribuição, gratificação.

rewarder, *s.* recompensador, remunerador, gratificador.

rewrite (rewrote, rewritten), *v.t.* tornar a escrever.

rhapsody, *s.* rapsódia.

rhea, *s.* avestruz da América do Sul.

rhetoric, *s.* retórica.

rhetorical, *adj.* retórico.

rhetorician, *s.* retórico.

rheum, *s.* reuma, catarro, expectoração.

rheumatic, *adj.* reumático; *s.* reumático (pessoa que sofre de reumatismo); dores reumáticas.

rheumatism, *s.* reumatismo.

rheumy, *adj.* catarroso; húmido; rameloso.

rhino, *s.* dinheiro, bago (fam.).

rhinoceros, *s.* rinoceronte.

rhinologist, *s.* rinologista, rinólogo.

rhinology, *s.* rinologia.

rhododendron, *s.* redodendro (bot.).

rhubarb, *s.* ruibarbo.

rhyme, *s.* rima; *v.t.* rimar; *without rhyme or reason*, sem tom nem som.

rhythm, *s.* ritmo, cadência, compasso; harmonia; periodicidade.

rhythmic, *adj.* rítmico; *adv.* rhythmically, compassadamente.

rib, *s.* costela; friso, aresta, veio; borda saliente; nervura duma folha; vareta de guarda-chuva; viga; *v.t. (ribbing, ribbed),* marcar com listas ou filetes; guarnecer de nervuras; raiar; sulcar, enrugar; *ribs of a ship*, costado dum navio.

ribald, *adj.* ribaldo, obsceno, lascivo; *s.* homem grosseiro, dissoluto.

ribaldry, *s.* linguagem obscena, grosseira; irreverência.

riband, *s.* o mesmo que *ribbon*.

ribble-rabble, *s.* ralé, escumalha, gentalha.

ribbon, *s.* fita; faixa, cinta, banda; pl. rédeas; *v.t.* enfeitar com fitas; enastrar.

rice, *s.* arroz. 1) *rice-field*, arrozal. 2) *rice-paper*, papel de arroz ou da China. 3) *rice pudding*, arroz doce.

rich, *adj.* rico, opulento, precioso, valioso, de valor, sumptuoso; abundante; copioso, generoso; fértil; divertido, impagável; cor viva; *adv. richly*, ricamente.

riches, *s.* riquezas, opulência, bens.

richness, *s.* riqueza.

rick, *s.* meda, pilha.

rickets, *s.* raquitismo.

rickety, *adj.* raquítico.

ricochet, *s.* ricochete, fogo de ressalto; *v.t.* atingir de ricochete; *v.i.* ricochetear.

rid (ridding, rid), *v.t.* desembaraçar, livrar, safar; despojar; *adj.* livre, desembaraçado. 1) *to get ride of*, desembaraçar-se, livrar-se. 2) *to be rid of*, estar livre de.

riddance, *s.* acto de libertar-se ou desembaraçar-se de um mal, perigo; *good riddance*, bons ventos o levem! Tanto melhor!

riddle, *s.* enigma, adivinha, charada; mistério; peneira grossa, ciranda, joeira; *v.t.* cirandar, joeirar, peneirar; crivar; *they died riddled with bullets*, morreram crivados de balas; decifrar, resolver; *v.i.* falar por enigmas.

ride (rode, ridden), (rid, rid), cavalgar, montar; andar (de carro, de bicicleta, etc.); flutuar, vogar; manejar um cavalo; rodar, funcionar (mec.). 1) *to ride away*, partir. 2) *to ride back*, voltar. 3) *to ride by*, passar. 4) *to ride down*, tratar mal; atropelar. 5) *to ride hard*, ir muito depressa. 6) *to ride out*, sobreviver. 7) *to ride past*, passar adiante. 8) *to ride through*, atravessar. 9) *to ride to the tide*, lutar contra a corrente. 10) *to ride well*, ser bom cavaleiro; *s.* passeio (a cavalo, de carro, de bicicleta, etc.); trajecto, percurso; sela de montar.

rider, *s.* cavaleiro; ciclista; amansador de cavalos; caixeiro-viajante; folha adicional que se junta a um manuscrito; codicilo, apostila.

ridge, *v.t.* sulcar, abrir regos, estriar, encrespar (a água); *s.* aresta, saliência, estria, ruga; crista, espinhaço, cumeada; recife, escolho.

ridgy, *adj.* rugoso; sulcado, estriado; acidentado.

ridicule, *s.* ridículo, ridicularia; *v.i.* ridicularizar.

ridiculous, *adj.* ridículo, grotesco, risível; *adv. ridiculously*, ridiculamente.

riding, *s.* passeio a cavalo ou de carro; cavalgada; equitação; divisão administrativa do condado de York. 1) *ridingcoat*, casaco de montar. 2) *riding-habit*, trajo de amazona. 3) *riding-light*, luz de âncora. 4) *riding-school*, picadeiro, escola de equitação.

rife, *adj.* abundante, numeroso, predominante; *adv. rifely*, abundantemente.

riff-raff, *s.* canalha, plebe; rebotalho, refugo.

rifle, *v.t.* roubar, pilhar; subtrair; esquadrinhar, varejar; estriar, raiar; atirar com espingarda; *s.* fuzil, carabina, espingarda. 1) *rifle-pit*, trincheira para atiradores. 2) *magazine rifle*, espingarda de repetição.

rifleman, *s.* carabineiro.

rifler, *s.* ladrão, saqueador.

rift, *s.* fenda, racha, abertura; *v.t.* fender, rachar, dividir; *v.i.* rebentar; rachar-se; partir-se.

rig (rigging, rigged), *v.t.* e *v.i.* aparelhar; equipar (navio); ataviar, enfeitar; vestir-se; provocar alta ou baixa (no mercado financeiro); prover, guarnecer; enroupar, enfarpelar; *s.* aparelho; roupa, roupagem; equipamento, maquinaria; trapaça, fraude; açambarcamento; *to run a rig*, pregar uma partida.

rigger, *s.* armador (náut.).

rigging, *s.* aparelho, cordame.

right, *adj.* direito, recto, justo; honesto, sincero; correcto, certo; verdadeiro; conveniente, próprio, legítimo, natural; direito (contrário de esquerdo); são, sensato; direito (contrário de avesso). 1) *right angle*, ângulo recto. 2) *right angled*, rectangular. 3) *right-hand man*, braço direito, o homem de confiança. 4) *right handed*, destro, hábil, manhoso. 5) *right minded*, recto, honrado. 6) *the right heir*, o herdeiro legítimo. 7) *to make right*, corrigir; arranjar. 8) *right ahead*, sempre a direito; *adv.* rectamente, justamente, exactamente, perfeitamente; com razão; em linha recta, directamente; imediatamente, agora mesmo. 9) *right along*, sem parar; *s.* direito; equidade; razão; verdade; domínio, título; poder, autoridade; privilégio, regalia; mão direita; direito (oposto ao esquerdo e ao avesso); *v.t.* fazer justiça; endireitar, pôr em ordem; corrigir, ajustar; adriçar (náut.); *interj.* bem! muito bem!

righteous, *adj.* justo, recto; honrado; *adv. righteously,* rectamente, justamente, honradamente.

rightful, *adj.* justo, equitativo, legítimo; *adv. rightfully,* legalmente, legitimamente, justamente.

rightly, *adv.* justamente, exactamente.

rightness, *s.* rectidão, justiça.

rightwards, *adv.* à direita.

rigid, *adj.* rígido, teso, inflexível; severo, rigoroso; *adv. rigidly,* rigidamente; inflexivelmente.

rigidity, *s.* rigidez, inflexibilidade; rigor, severidade.

rigor, *s.* rigor; rigidez; calafrio; *rigor mortis,* rigidez cadavérica.

rigorous, *adj.* rigoroso; *adv. rigorously,* rigorosamente; severamente.

rill, *s.* ribeiro, regato.

rim, *s.* borda, canto, margem; rebordo; arco, aro; pestana, sobrancelha; *rim of a wheel,* aro de roda.

rime, *s.* geada; rima, verso, poesia; greta, fenda; degrau de escada de mão; *v.t.* versificar, compor versos; *v.i.* rimar, harmonizar-se; gear.

rimy, *adj.* geoso, coberto de geada; *rimy morning,* manhã de geada.

rind, *s.* cortiça; casca de árvore; pele do presunto; *v.t.* descascar, pelar.

rinderpest, *s.* morrinha.

ring, *s.* anel, argola; arco, aro, coroa, virola, banda, cinta, anilha; bracelete, colar; roda, círculo (de pessoas ou coisas); circo, arena; cerne, olheiras; som, toque de campainha; repique dos sinos; timbre; rumor, clamor, ruído, estrondo; tablado de pugilismo; anete de âncora. 1) *ring-finger,* dedo anular. 2) *wedding ring,* aliança de casamento. 3) *ear-ring,* brinco; *v.t.* cercar, rodear, circundar, cingir; colocar anel, aro em; cortar em rodelas; *v.i.* andar em círculos, voltear.

ring (rang, rung), *v.t.* e *v.i.* soar, ressoar, tinir, retinir; tocar (sino, sineta, campainha); repicar; tocar para chamar, para pedir alguma coisa; zumbir; vibrar, ecoar, repercutir. 1) *the world shall ring of Churchill's deeds,* os feitos de Churchill hão-de repercutir-se em todo o mundo. 2) *to ring true,* parecer sincero. 3) *to ring false,* soar falso. 4) *ring off!,* desliga o telefone! 5) *to ring up,* telefonar; anunciar, proclamar.

ringleader, *s.* chefe, cabeça (em motins), cabecilha.

ringlet, *s.* anel, pequena argola; anel de cabelo.

ringmaster, *s.* director de circo.

rink, *s.* pista de gelo para patinar; campo de patinagem para hóquei.

rinse, *v.t.* lavar, limpar, enxaguar.

rinsing, *s.* lavagem, enxaguamento.

riot, *s.* tumulto, revolta; excesso; *v.t.* armar motim, fazer barulho; viver de modo dissoluto.

rioter, *s.* amotinador; dissoluto.

riotous, *adj.* turbulento, desenfreado; devasso; *adv. riotously,* desenfreadamente.

rip (ripping, ripped), *v.t.* (com *up, open, off*) rasgar, romper, partir, rachar; descoser; soltar; (com *out* ou *away*) cortar, arrancar, destroçar; (com *up*) sondar, estudar a fundo, descobrir; *v.i.* rasgar-se, fender-se, romper-se; *s.* rasgão, abertura, racha; raspador (instrumento).

riparian, *adj.* ribeirinho.

ripe, *adj.* maduro, sazonado; feito, acabado, pronto, preparado; oportuno. *adv. ripely,* maduramente; a propósito.

ripen, *v.t.* e *v.i.* amadurecer.

ripeness, *s.* maturação.

ripple, *v.t.* e *v.i.* encapelar, ondear, agitar (a água); cardar (o linho); agitar-se, encapelar-se; murmurar; *s.* ondulação, encapeladura; murmúrio (de água, de um regato); carda.

rippling, *s.* ondulação, borbotão; o ripar (o linho).

ripply, *adj.* com ondulação.

rise (rose, risen), *v.i.* subir, ascender, elevar-se, levantar-se, erguer-se; suspender; nascer ou surgir (o sol); nascer, brotar; sublevar-se, amotinar-se; armar, suscitar (disputa, etc.); inchar, aumentar de volume; encher (maré); encarecer, subir de preço; pôr-se à altura de. 1) *to rise to one's feet,* pôr-se em pé. 2) *to rise up,* levantar-se; *s.* levantamento, elevação; subida (da maré, temperatura, barómetro, etc.); o nascer, o brotar; subida (preços); cheia (rio, etc.);

fonte, origem, causa; acesso (a um grau); elevação da voz. 3) *to take a rise out of a person*, baixar a crista a alguém.

risen, *adj.* levantado.

risible, *adj.* risível.

rising, *adj.* nascente; que se levanta ou sobe; crescente, saliente; novo; próspero; *s.* subida, ascensão, levantamento; insurreição; levedura, fermento.

risk, *s.* risco, perigo; acaso (jogo); *to run a risk*, correr perigo; *v.t.* arriscar, aventurar, expor.

risky, *adj.* perigoso, arriscado; imprudente, temerário.

rissole, *s.* almôndega.

rite, *s.* rito, cerimónia.

ritual, *adj.* e *s.* ritual, cerimonial.

rival, *adj.* rival, contrário; *s.* rival, antagonista, competidor; *v.t.* *rivalling, rivalled*, competir, emular, rivalizar com.

rivalry, *s.* rivalidade, competição.

rive (rived, riven), *v.t.* e *v.i.* rachar(-se), fender(-se); *s.* racha, fenda.

river, *s.* rio. 1) *river-head*, nascente dum rio. 2) *river-bed*, leito dum rio. 3) *river-horse*, hipopótamo; *s.* rachador.

riverside, *s.* e *adj.* margem do rio.

rivet, *s.* cravo, prego, gato (em loiça); pl. rebites; *v.t.* *(riveting, riveted)*, revirar, arrebitar; assegurar, afiançar; cravar, fixar.

riveter, *s.* cravador.

riveting, *s.* cravação; rebitagem.

rivulet, *s.* regato, arroio, fio de água.

road, *s.* caminho, via, estrada, passagem, curso, viagem; pl. enseada, baía. 1) *on the road*, a caminho, viajando, em digressão. 2) *beaten road*, caminho trilhado. 3) *cross road*, encruzilhada. 4) *high road*, estrada nacional. 5) *rail road*, caminho de ferro. 6) *road net*, rede rodoviária. 7) *to take the road*, fazer-se salteador.

roadbook, *s.* roteiro rodoviário.

roadway, *s.* auto-estrada.

roam, *v.t.* e *v.i.* vaguear, vagabundear; *s.* vida errante.

roamer, *s.* vadio, vagabundo.

roan, *adj.* ruão, sabino; *s.* cavalo ruão; ruço.

roar, *v.i.* rugir, bramar, mugir, roncar, berrar; troar (canhão); *s.* rugido, bramido, mugido; estampido, estrondo; grito, berro.

roast, *v.t.* assar; torrar, tostar; calcinar; ridicularizar (fam.); *adj.* assado; tostado. 1) *roast meat*, assado. 2) *roast beef*, carne assada, rosbife; *s.* carne assada, assado.

roaster, *s.* assador, grelhador.

roasting, *s.* acto de assar; calcinação; zombaria, troça (fam.).

rob (robbing, robbed), roubar, furtar; pilhar, saquear.

robber, *s.* ladrão, salteador.

robbery, *s.* roubo, furto, pilhagem.

robe, *s.* manto, túnica, roupão; toga, veste; *v.t.* e *v.i.* vestir, enverga trajo cerimonial.

roble, *s.* carvalho da Califórnia.

robust, *adj.* robusto, forte; grosseiro; *adv.* robustly, robustamente.

rock, *s.* rocha, penha, penhasco, rochedo; recife, escolho; solidez, defesa, amparo. 1) *rock-crystal*, cristal de rocha. 2) *rock-drill*, perfurador. 3) *rock-island*, ilhéu. 4) *rock-oil*, petróleo. 5) *rock-salt*, sal-gema; *v.t.* agitar, baloiçar, embalar; acalmar, sossegar; rocar (no xadrez); *v.i.* oscilar, tremer, balançar--se.

rocker, *s.* embaladeira (berço, cadeira de baloiço); oscilador, balancim.

rocket, *s.* foguete, foguetão.

rocking, *s.* acção de embalar; balanço, baloiço; *rocking chair*, cadeira de baloiço.

rocky, *adj.* cheio de penhascos, rochas ou rochedos; de rocha; endurecido, empedernido.

rod, *s.* vara, varinha; bastão, bordão; barra, haste, tirante; varinha de condão; cana de pesca; varão de cortina; vara de medir; correcção; disciplina, castigo; linhagem, raça. 1) *to give the rod*, açoitar, dar açoites. 2) *spare the rod and spoil the child*, quem poupa o pau estraga a criança.

rodent, *adj.* e *s.* roedor.

roe, *s.* cabrito-montês; *roe-deer*, cerva, corça; ovas de peixe.

rogation, *s.* rogação, ladainha; *rogation week*, semana das ladainhas.

rogue, *s.* velhaco, patife, maroto, manganão.

roguery, *s.* patifaria, maroteira.

roguish, *adj.* velhaco, mau; travesso, gaiato; *adv.* roguishly, velhacamente; gaiatamente.

roil, *v.t.* turbar, turvar (líquido); perturbar, molestar, vexar.

roily, *adj.* turvo, agitado.

roister, *v.i.* fanfarronar, bazofiar; bulhar.

roistering, *adj.* bulhento.

roisting, *s.* bravata, bulha.

role, *s.* papel, parte (teat.).

roll, *v.t.* fazer girar; rolar, voltear, rodar; revolver; enrolar; enroscar; laminar, estirar, cilindrar, alisar, aplanar; envolver, enfaixar;

cilindrar; rufar, fazer rufar (o tambor); fazer vibrar (a língua); revolver os olhos; rebolar; bambolear-se; encrespar-se (as ondas); encarquilhar-se. 1) *to roll about*, rodar, andar de cá para lá. 2) *to roll up*, enrolar. 3) *to roll in money*, nadar em dinheiro; *s.* rolo; lista, rol, catálogo, matrícula, registo; cilindro; rufar (de tambor); balanço (de navio); troar (do canhão, do trovão); novelo. 4) *to call the roll*, fazer a chamada.

roller, *s.* rolo, cilindro; o que aplana ou alisa; tambor, calandra; onda, faixa, ligadura; patim.

rollick, *v.i.* fazer travessuras.

rollicking, *adj.* jovial, brincalhão; engraçado.

rolling, *adj.* rolante; ondulado; agitado; *rolling pin*, rolo de massa.

Roman, *adj.* e *s.* romano; católico romano; papal.

Romance, *adj.* românico, romance, neo-latino; línguas românicas.

romance, *s.* romance, novela, conto; fábula, romança; *v.i.* inventar, forjar, fazer romance.

romancer, *s.* romancista; visionário, fantasista.

romanism, *s.* romanismo, doutrina da Igreja Católica Romana.

romantic, *adj.* romântico, romanesco; sentimental; *adv. romantically*, romantica-mente.

romanticism, *s.* romanticismo.

romanticist, *s.* romântico, romanticista.

romp, *s.* rapariga travessa, brincalhona; graça pesada; brinquedo barulhento; *v.i.* traquinar, brincar violenta ou ruidosamente.

rompish, *adj.* brincalhão, travesso, estouvado.

rood, *s.* cruz, crucifixo; medida agrária (1/4 de acre).

roof, *s.* tecto, telhado, abóbada; céu (poét.); tejadilho (automóvel); casa, habitação. 1) *flat roof*, terraço. 2) *tile-roof*, telhado. 3) *roof-tile*, telha. 4) *french roof*, mansarda; *v.t.* telhar, pôr tecto; abrigar.

rook, *s.* gralha; torre (no xadrez); trapaceiro, batoteiro; *v.t.* e *v.i.* roubar, fazer trapaça (no jogo, no preço).

room, *s.* quarto, sala, aposento; lugar, espaço, sítio; casa; acomodação, aloja-mento; ocasião, oportunidade; motivo, razão. 1) *they have room for dispute*, eles têm motivo para discórdia. 2) *there is no room for doubt*, não há dúvida possível. 3)

cloack room: depósito de bagagens. 4) *powder room*, paiol de pólvora. 5) *room mate*, companheiro de quarto. 6) *to give room*, dar lugar, deixar passar. 7) *to make room*, abrir caminho. 8) *to leave the room*, retirar-se.

roomer, *s.* navio muito grande.

roomily, *adv.* espaçosamente, amplamente.

roomy, *adj.* espaçoso, amplo.

roost, *s.* poleiro; galinheiro; quarto de dormir, cama; choco (fig.); lugar de descanso; *v.i.* empoleirar-se; descansar.

rooster, *s.* galo.

root, *s.* raiz; nota fundamental; fonte, origem, princípio. 1) *root and branch*, completa-mente. 2) *to take root*, criar raízes; *v.t.* e *v.i.* arraigar-se, implantar, enraizar. 3) *to root up*, arrancar pela raiz; desenraizar.

rooted, *adj.* radical, enraizado; *adv. rootedly*, radicalmente, fixamente.

rootlet, *s.* radícula.

rooty, *adj.* cheio de raízes, radicoso.

rope, *s.* corda, corcel, cabo; enforcamento; fiada, fieira (de pérolas); cordame, maçame; réstia de cebolas; intestinos (dos pássaros). 1) *rope-ladder*, escada de corda. 2) *rope maker*, cordoeiro. 3) *on the high rope*, altivo, arrogante. 4) *to know the ropes*, saber a quantas anda. 5) *to give a person rope*, dar plena liberdade a uma pessoa; *v.t.* atar, amarrar; apanhar com laço; entralhar (vela); enganar; *v.i.* fazer enfiaduras; torcer-se em forma de corda. 6) *to rope in*, seduzir.

roper, *s.* cordoeiro.

ropery, *s.* cordoaria.

rosary, *s.* rosário, terço; roseiral.

rose, *s.* rosa, roseira; roseta; cor-de-rosa; rosa de agulha náutica; ralo de regador; florão. 1) *rose-bush*, roseira. 2) *cabbage rose*, rosas de toucado. 3) *rose-window*, rosácea. 4) *tea-rose*, rosa-chá. 5) *to speak under the rose*, falar em surdina, em segredo.

roseate, *adj.* rosado; róseo; cheio de rosas.

rose-bud, *s.* botão de rosa.

rosemary, *s.* rosmaninho.

rosette, *s.* roseta; florão.

rose-water, *s.* água de rosas.

rosin, *s.* resina.

rosiness, *s.* cor rosada.

roster, *s.* lista de oficiais e soldados; ordem de serviço (mil.).

rostrum, *s.* tribuna, púlpito; rostro; esporão.

rosy, *adj.* róseo, rosado; em forma de rosa; feito de rosas; agradável, risonho; optimista.

rot (rotting, rotted), *v.t.* e *v.i.* apodrecer, estragar-se, decompor-se; decair, definhar; transtornar, arreliar; *s.* podridão; putrefacção; caruncho, morrinha; tolice, disparate (fam.).

rotary, *adj.* rotativo, rotatório, giratório.

rotate, *v.t.* e *v.i.* rodar, girar, fazer girar; dar voltas; alternar, revezar.

rotation, *s.* rotação, turno, alternativa, volta; *in rotation*, por turnos.

rote, *s.* o que se aprende de cor; *to learn by rote*, aprender de cor; rotina.

rotten, *adj.* podre, putrefacto, carunchoso, fétido.

rotteness, *s.* podridão.

rotund, *adj.* rotundo, redondo, circular, esférico.

rotunda, *s.* rotunda.

rotundity, *s.* rotundidade.

rouble, *s.* rublo (moeda).

rouge, *s.* carmim, cosmético para as faces; *adj.* vermelho, encarnado; *v.t.* e *v.i.* pintar o rosto, arrebicar, usar rouge.

rough, *adj.* áspero, desigual, tosco; rude, grosseiro; tempestuoso, encapelado; imperfeito, descuidado; insolente, arrogante; desagradável, rouco; desconfortável; inculto, bronco; mal acabado; aproximativo, estimativo. 1) *rough and ready*, feito às três pancadas. 2) *rough-cast*, reboco; esboço. 3) *rough calculation*, cálculo, estimativa. 4) *rough diamond*, diamante bruto. 5) *rough draught*, rascunho. 6) *rough estimate*, orçamento aproximado. 7) *rough passage*, má travessia. 8) *rough words*, palavras grosseiras. 9) *to ride rough-shod*, impor-se com arrogância; *s.* estado bruto; rude; mariola, biltre; sem polimento; pl. gentalha, ralé; *v.t.* tornar áspero, tosco, escabroso; domar, amansar, domesticar. 10) *to rough it*, levar vida dura, passar trabalhos; irritar; *adv.* rudemente, toscamente.

roughly, *adv.* asperamente, bruscamente, rudemente.

roughness, *s.* aspereza, rudeza; grosseria; tempestade, borrasca.

roulette, *s.* roleta (jogo); rodízio.

Roumanian, *adj.* e *s.* romeno.

round, *s.* redondo, esférico, circular, cilíndrico; rotundo, arredondado, cheio; sonoro; grande; liberal, amplo; franco, claro, sincero, liso, positivo, ingénuo; rápido, vivo, acelerado; justo, honrado; fluente; inteiro, completo. 1) *round assertion*, afirma-ção categórica. 2) *round sum*, soma redonda. 3) *round-shouldered*, espadaúdo. 4) *round trip ticket*, bilhete de ida e volta; *s.* círculo, roda, esfera; rotação, volta; giro; rodela; degrau (de escada); assalto (esgrima, boxe); rota, caminho; dança de roda. 5) *to fire a round*, disparar uma descarga. 6) *officer of the round*, oficial da ronda; *adv.* em roda, ao redor, circularmente. 7) *all round*, completo, em torno. 8) *to bring round*, restabelecer duma doença. 9) *to came round*, recobrar os sentidos; dar uma volta; *prep.* à volta de; em torno de; do princípio ao fim; *v.t.* arredondar; fazer redondo; andar à roda de; voltear, cercar; cingir; acabar, aperfeiçoar; dar a volta a; *v.i.* arredondar-se, fazer-se redondo; aperfeiçoar-se; dar voltas; rondar. 10) *to round on*, voltar-se contra, atacar. 11) *to round out*, encher-se. 12) *to round up*, orçar. 13) *to round a cape*, dobrar um cabo.

rondabout, *adj.* indirecto, com rodeios, evasivo; desviado; *s.* roda de dança.

roundel, *s.* melodia, canção; dança em círculo.

Roundhead: *s.* "cabeças-redondas", alcunha que se dava aos puritanos no tempo de Carlos I de Inglaterra (hist.).

roundish, *adj.* arredondado.

roundly, *adv.* completamente; francamente, sem rodeios; redondamente.

roundness, *s.* redondeza, rotundidade; franqueza.

rouse, *v.t.* despertar, acordar; animar, excitar, estimular, activar; levantar a caça; *v.i.* levantar-se, animar-se, mover-se, excitar-se.

rouser, *s.* despertador; incitador; embuste, mentira (fam.).

rousing, *adj.* que desperta, estimulante, excitante; grande, violento; *adv.* rousingly, de modo excitante; violentamente, fortemente.

rout, *s.* derrota, destroço; turba, tropel; chusma, horda, malta; séquito, comitiva; tumulto, confusão; debandada; *v.t.* derrotar, desbaratar, destroçar, debandar, dispersar; descobrir, desencavar; *v.i.* foçar, remexer, bisbilhotar.

route, *s.* caminho, rumo, rota; estrada, via, trajecto; itinerário, marcha.

routine, *s.* rotina, hábito.

rove, *v.i.* vaguear, percorrer, errar; *v.t.* desfiar; encarretar; torcer o fio, fiar por grosso; cardar; *s.* vagabundo; passeio; correria; mecha; fiado.

rover, *s.* vagabundo, ladrão; nómada; pirata; alvo de archeiro.

roving, *s.* preparação para a tecelagem do algodão; mecha; vida errante; *adj.* vagabundo, errante.

row, *s.* fileira, fila, fiada, linha, ordem, carreira; passeio em bote; remadura; *v.i.* remar, vogar; conduzir barco de remos; armar remos.

row, *s.* bulha, tumulto, rixa, algazarra; repreensão; *v.i.* armar um tumulto; repreender, censurar.

rowdy, *adj.* barulhento, desordeiro, bulhento; *adv. rowdily,* desordeiramente.

rower, *s.* remador.

rowing, *s.* acção de remar; desporto do remo.

rowlock, *s.* (náut.) forqueta, tolete.

royal, *adj.* real, régio; majestoso, nobre, magnânimo; excelente; papel de grande formato para escrever ou imprensa; mastaréu volante.

royalist, *s.* realista; monárquico.

royalty, *s.* realeza, soberania real; direito de autor; regalia; membro da família real.

rub (rubbing, rubbed), *v.t.* e *v.i.* esfregar; friccionar; raspar; roçar; coçar, irritar, incomodar; ser desagradável. 1) *to rub along,* viver em apuros. 2) *to rub away,* esfregar continuamente. 3) *to rub in,* lixar, alisar esfregando. 4) *to rub out,* apagar; *s.* fricção, atrito; polimento; embaraço, obstáculo; sarcasmo, chasco. 5) *there is the rub,* aí é que a porca torce o rabo.

rubber, *s.* borracha; apagador; raspador, alisador, grosa; pastilha elástica; *pl.* galochas; *adj.* feito de borracha.

rubbish, *s.* entulho, caliça, lixo; refugo, farrapos; ninharia, futilidade.

rubbishy, *adj.* sem valor.

rubble, *s.* pedregulho, cascalho, seixos; entulho; *rubble-work,* alvenaria de pedra bruta.

rubbly, *adj.* pedregoso.

rubicund, *adj.* rubicundo, corado, rubro.

rubric, *adj.* rubro, vermelho, encarnado; *s.* rubrica.

ruby, *s.* rubim; carmim, cor de vermelho vivo; *adj.* vermelho; da cor do rubim.

ruck, rucle, *s.* prega, vinco, dobra, ruga; *v.t.* vincar, dobrar, amarrotar; *v.i.* enrugar-se, preguear-se.

ruction, *s.* tumulto.

rudd, *s.* ruivo (peixe).

rudder, *s.* leme (náut.); governo, guia, orientador; *main piece of a rudder,* madre do leme.

ruddiness, *s.* vermelhidão.

ruddy, *adj.* vermelho, rubro, rosado; *v.t.* corar, tingir de vermelho.

rude, *adj.* rude, ordinário, rústico, grosseiro; tosco; arrogante; *adv. rudely,* rudemente, toscamente, grosseiramente.

rudeness, *s.* grosseria, rudeza, crueza, insolência.

rudiment, *s.* rudimento, princípio, elemento; embrião, germe.

rudimental, *adj.* rudimentar; elementar.

rue, *v.t.* e *v.i.* chorar, lastimar, lamentar, sentir mágoa; arrepender-se, pagar; *s.* arruda; arrependimento, pesar.

rueful, *adj.* lamentável, lastimável, triste, deplorável; *adv: ruefully,* tristemente, deploravelmente.

ruff, *s.* golinha, rufo, adorno de pescoço; colar de penas de algumas aves; perca (peixe); rufo (tambor); *v.t.* e *v.i.* rufar o tambor; trunfar no jogo de cartas; pôr em desordem.

ruffian, *s.* rufião, biltre, arruaceiro; *adj.* brutal, desalmado, cruel.

ruffle, *v.t.* franzir, frisar, fazer pregar, fazer tufos em; desordenar; amarrotar; incomodar, irritar; rufar o tambor; franzir-se; enrugar-se; agitar-se; incomodar-se; encrespar-se; *s.* rufo, folho, franzido; irritação, agastamento.

rug, *s.* tapete; burel; manta de viagem.

rugged, *adj.* áspero, abrupto, escarpado, rude, tosco, bruto; inculto, bronco; desmedido; ríspido; carrancudo; forte, vigoroso, robusto; *adv. ruggedly,* rudemente, asperamente, severamente.

ruin, *s.* ruína, queda, decadência; bancarrota, destruição; degradação, perdição; *pl.* ruínas; resíduos, restos, vestígios; *v.t.* arruinar, destruir; empobrecer; seduzir, perder; *v.i.* cair em ruínas, arruinar-se.

ruination, *s.* arruinamento, perdição.

ruined, *adj.* arruinado, em ruínas; falido; desonrado, perdido.

ruinous, *adj.* ruinoso, desastroso, funesto; arruinado, em ruínas; *adv. ruinously,* ruinosamente.

rulable, adj. que pode governar-se, dirigir-se.

rule, s. regra, norma, preceito, cânone, regulamento; guia, método, modelo, medida; mando, domínio, poder, autoridade. 1) to bear rule, mandar, governar; régua (de carpinteiro); auto, parecer dum tribunal; risca, filete. 2) as a rule, usualmente. 3) by rule, por regulamento; v.t. e v.i. governar, reger, dirigir, dominar, controlar; fazer riscas ou linhas, traçar com régua. 4) to rule over, reinar.

ruler, s. governador; legislador; regente; régua.

ruling, s. acção dum governante; decisão, disposição regulamentar; adj. dominante, predominante.

rum, s. rum, aguardente de melaço; pessoa ou coisa estranha; adj. estranho, singular, esquisito; a rum customer, um cliente perigoso; adv. rumly, de modo estranho, de modo surpreendente.

rumble, v.t. e v.i. retumbar, rugir, roncar, ressoar; s. rumor, ruído prolongado; estrondo; parte traseira dum carro.

rumbler, s. o que faz ruído surdo e contínuo.

rumbling, adj. que faz estrondo; s. estrondo, ruído; the rumbling of thunder, ribombar do trovão.

ruminant, adj. e s. ruminante; meditativo.

ruminate, v.t. e v.i. ruminar; meditar.

rumination, s. ruminação; meditação.

rummage, s. busca, revolvimento, revista; transtorno, desordem; v.t. e v.i. explorar, esquadrinhar, procurar, revolver, pôr em desordem.

rummer, s. copo grande, copázio.

rummy, adj. relativo a rum; estranho, extravagante; engraçado.

rumour, s. rumor; boato; v.t. divulgar, espalhar; fazer correr um boato.

rumourer, s. boateiro.

rump, s. rabadela, rabadilha; garupa, anca, alcatra; traseiro; resto, remanescente.

rumple, v.t. amarrotar, enrugar; s. ruga, prega, dobra, vinco.

rumpus, s. balbúrdia, motim, banzé.

run (running, ran, run), v.i. e v.t. correr; mover-se rapidamente; fazer correr; ir depressa; voar; andar; apressar-se; fugir; trabalhar (uma máquina, relógio, etc.); disputar, competir; dirigir (um negócio); candidatar-se (a eleição); estender-se de um ponto a outro; expor-se a, incorrer em; seguir. 1) things must run their course, as coisas devem seguir o seu curso; romper,

forçar. 2) to run the shellfish close season, romper o defeso do marisco; inclinar-se, apreciar; examinar. 3) this movie runs for two hours, este filme dura duas horas. 4) to run about, andar de um lado para outro. 5) to run after, suspirar por, correr atrás de. 6) to run down, deixar de funcionar. 7) to run goods into a country, fazer contrabando. 8) to run in, prender; correr em, para; convir. 9) to run into, correr para, precipitar-se, lançar-se; encontrar-se com, chocar. 10) to run off, sair, partir apressadamente. 11) to run on, continuar, prosseguir, ir adiante. 13) to run over, derramar-se, transbordar; examinar rapidamente; passar por cima, atropelar. 14) to run through, gastar, dissipar; atravessar. 15) to run up, levantar, içar; construir rapidamente. 16) the story runs that, reza a história. 17) my contract with that company ran for two years, o meu contrato com essa companhia durou dois anos; s. corrida, carreira, curso; corrida aos bancos; marcha, batida, caça; volta, excursão, viagem; derrota; continuação, duração; série de representações duma peça; fio do discurso; vontade, gosto. 18) in the long run, no fim de contas. 19) a run of bad luck, um período de infelicidade. 20) the common run, a generalidade dos homens; adj. extraído; despejado, esvaziado, derramado, derretido.

runagate, s. renegado; fugitivo, desertor.

runaway, s. fugitivo, desertor; fuga, rapto; adj. fugitivo, desertor; runaway matcher, casamento que se segue a um rapto.

runnel, s. regato, ribeirinho.

runner, s. corredor; peão, andarilho; correio, mensageiro; agente da polícia; fugitivo; maquinista; agente corretor; contrabandista (fam.); passadeira, corredor, trilho; rebento, vergôntea; pequeno navio de mercadorias. 1) blockade runner, forçador de bloqueio. 2) scarlet runner, feijão trepador, feijão vermelho.

running, s. funcionamento; fluxo; direcção, administração, gerência. 1) to take up the running, assumir o comando; carreira, corrida, curso; adj. corredor, corrente, corredio; consecutivo; a vencer (com.). 2) running days, dias consecutivos estipulados num contrato, dias correntes. 3) running title, título de página. 4) running water, água corrente. 5) to be in the running, competir com esperança na vitória.

rupee, s. rupia (moeda).

rupture, s. ruptura, rompimento; desavença; fenda, brecha; hérnia, quebradura; v.t. romper, partir, quebrar, rebentar, fracturar; cortar, dissolver; produzir hérnia em; v.i. romper-se, partir-se, rebentar-se.

rural, adj. rural, campestre, rústico, agrícola; adv. rurally, ruralmente.

ruse, s. ardil, astúcia, manha.

rusé, adj. astuto, manhoso.

rush, s. arremetida, investida, assalto, ímpeto; pressa, fúria, precipitação; torrente, tropel; assédio; luta, briga; junco, caniço, verga; ninharia, bagatela. 1) rush-bottomed, com assento em verga. 2) rush mat, esteira de junco. 3) rush on the bank, corrida ao banco. 4) it is not worth a rush, não vale nada; v.i. arrojar-se, arremessar-se, precipitar-se, lançar-se; v.t. empurrar, activar, acelerar; despachar prontamente; precipitar, abrir à força. 5) to rush in, entrar de roldão, de rompante. 6) to rush in upon, surpreender. 7) to rush out, sair precipitadamente.

rusher, s. pessoa que se precipita, que se arremessa; jogador de futebol que conduz a bola para o campo do adversário.

rushing, s. correria, arremetida, ímpeto; adj. impetuoso, precipitado.

rusk, s. biscoito, rosca, pão duro.

russet, adj. vermelho, avermelhado; rústico, grosseiro; russet leather, coiro vermelho; s. cor avermelhada; trajo de camponês; maçã de inverno; coiro avermelhado.

russety, adj. moreno, triguiero.

Russian, s. e adj. russo.

rust, s. bolor, mofo, ferrugem; rança, alforra; rust coloured, da cor da ferrugem; ócio; v.i.

enferrujar-se; criar mofo ou ranço; entorpecer; embotar; v.t. enferrujar; embotar; enfraquecer o espírito.

rustic, adj. rústico, rural, agrário; campesino, aldeão; sincero, simples; inculto, grosseiro; s. camponês, rústico, campónio; rustically, rusticamente.

rusticate, v.t. rusticar, ruralizar; mandar para o campo; ir viver para o campo; expulsar duma universidade; v.i. passar uma temporada no campo, ir para o campo; rusticar-se.

rustication, s. vida no campo.

rusticity, s. rusticidade; simplicidade; rudeza.

rustiness, enferrujamento; falta de uso.

rustle, v.t. e v.i. sussurrar; rugir (a seda); murmurar; s. sussurro, zunido, ruído.

rustler, s. homem activo e empreendedor.

rustless, adj. sem ferrugem; desenferrujado.

rustling, adj. sussurrante, murmurante; s. sussurro, murmúrio, ruído.

rusty, adj. bolorento, rançoso, ferrugento; entorpecido; broco.

rut (rutting, rutted), v.t. sulcar, abrir carris; v.i. bramar, estar com o cio; s. carril, sulco; cio, brama; costume, hábito arraigado, rotina; rutting-time, época do cio.

ruth, s. compaixão.

ruthful, adj. compassivo, misericordioso; adv. ruthfully, compadecidamente.

ruthless, adj. cruel, desapiedado, insensível; adv. ruthlessly, desapiedadamente.

ruttish, adj. lascivo.

rutty, adj. cheio de sulcos.

rye, s. centeio; uísque de centeio; rye-grass, erva dos prados.

S

s, décima nona letra do alfabeto.

Sabaism, s. sabeísmo; adoração dos astros.

Sabaoth, s. exércitos, hostes; Lord of Sabaoth, Senhor dos Exércitos.

Sabbath, s. sábado; dia de descanso; dia de culto entre os judeus.

saber, sabre, s. sabre de cavalaria; sabre; v.t. acutilar.

sable, s. marta zibelina; pele de marta; cor negra; adj. negro, triste.

sabot, s. tamanco, soco.

sabotage, s. sabotagem.

sac, s. saco, bolsa, cavidade.

saccharine, s. sacarina; adj. sacarino.

sacerdotal, adj. sacerdotal; adv. sacerdotally, sacerdotalmente.

sack, s. saco, saca; saque; pilhagem; nome dado a alguns vinhos brancos generosos de Espanha; bata de mulher; despedida; *v.t.* ensacar; saquear; despedir alguém; *I give him the sack*, despedi-o.

sacker, s. saqueador, ensacador.

sackful, s. sacada; saco cheio.

sacral, *adj.* sacro, sagrado, ritual; sacro, relativo ao osso sacro (anat.).

sacrament, s. sacramento; *The Sacrament,* a eucaristia.

sacramental, *adj.* sacramental.

sacramentarian, s. sacramentário.

sacred, *adj.* sagrado, sacro, consagrado, santo; inviolável; *adv. sacredly,* sagradamente, santamente.

sacredness, s. santidade, inviolabilidade.

sacrifice, s. sacrifício; imolação; *v.t.* sacrificar; imolar; *v.i.* oferecer em sacrifício.

sacrilege, s. sacrilégio; profanação.

sacrilegious, *adj.* sacrílego; *adv. sacrilegiously,* sacrilegamente.

sacrilegist, s. sacrílego.

sacristan, s. sacristão.

sacristy, s. sacristia.

sacrosanct, *adj.* sacrossanto.

sacrum, s. sacro (anat.).

sad, *adj.* triste, pensativo; abatido; sombrio; melancólico; desagradável; *in sad earnest,* seriamente, deveras, a valer.

sadden, *v.t.* e *v.i.* entristecer(-se), afligir(-se), magoar(-se); escurecer.

saddle, s. sela, selim. 1) *pack saddle,* albarda. 2) *saddle of mutton,* lombo de carneiro. 3) *saddle roof,* telhado de duas águas. 4) *in the saddle,* a cavalo. *v.t.* selar, albardar; carregar.

saddleback, s. outeiro em forma de sela; cavalo cilhão; espécie de gaivota.

saddlebag, s. alforge; bolsa de sela.

saddlecloth, s. chairel, manta.

saddler, s. seleiro.

saddlery, s. selaria.

sadism, s. sadismo.

sadist, s. e *adj.* sádico, sadista; *adv. sadistically,* sadicamente.

sadness, s. tristeza, melancolia, abatimento.

safari, s. expedição de caça.

safe, *adj.* ileso, salvo, intacto; leal, seguro, digno; s. cofre, caixa-forte; guarda-comida. 1) *safe and sound,* são e salvo. 2) *safe keeping,* guarda, depósito, custódia. 3) *safe conduct,* salvo-conduto.

safeblowing, s. arrombamento de cofre por explosão.

safebreaker, s. arrombador de cofres.

safeguard, s. salvaguarda, ressalva, protecção; defesa; salvo-conduto; escolta, guarda; *v.t.* salvaguardar, proteger, defender, ressalvar, assegurar.

safekeeping, s. custódia, guarda, protecção, preservação.

safelight, s. quebra-luz.

safely, *adv.* a salvo, em segurança, são e salvo; sem risco.

safety, s. segurança, salvamento; incolumidade; isenção de dano, de perda ou ofensa. 1) *safety-belt,* cinto de segurança. 2) *safety-match,* fósforo amorfo. 3) *safety-pin,* alfinete de segurança.

saffron, s. açafrão.

sag (sagging, sagged), *v.i.* vergar, pender, curvar; dar de si; sucumbir; baixar, descair; s. inclinação, dobra, curva, descaída.

saga, s. saga; narrativa; contos antigos da Escandinávia.

sagacious, *adj.* sagaz, perspicaz, agudo, arguto, astuto; *adv. sagaciously,* sagazmente.

sagacity, s. sagacidade, perspicácia; astúcia.

sage, s. salva (bot.); sábio; *adj.* sábio, atilado, ajuizado, prudente. *adv. sagely,* prudentemente.

sageness, s. sabedoria, prudência, juízo.

sago, s. sagu.

sagy, *adj.* temperado com salva.

sail, s. vela (de navio ou de moinho); pano de vela; navio; passeio de barco. 1) *under full sail,* a toda a vela. 2) *to set sail,* desfraldar as velas. 3) *to shorten sail,* encolher a vela. 4) *to take the wind out of one's sails,* privar uma pessoa duma vantagem; *v.i.* e *v.t.* fazer-se à vela, pôr-se a caminho, sair para o mar, velejar; singrar; viajar; ir embarcado; deslizar, passar; manobrar um navio, navegar, atravessar à vela. 5) *to sail down,* descer (um rio, uma corrente).

sailboat, s. veleiro.

sailcloth, s. lona.

sailer, s. barco à vela ligeiro.

sailing, s. navegação, náutica; marcha do navio; mareação; partida, largada; *sailing match,* regata à vela.

sailor, s. marinheiro.

saint, s. santo; (abreviatura St.); santa.

sainted, *adj.* santo, virtuoso; sagrado.

sainthood, s. santidade; hagiologia.

saintly, *adj*. santo, de santo; piedoso, devoto.

saintship, *s*. santidade.

sake, *s*. causa, razão; fim, propósito; respeito, consideração. 1) *for my sake*, por minha causa. 2) *for God's sake*, por amor de Deus. 3) *for the sake of appearances*, para salvar as aparências.

salacious, *adj*. lascivo.

salacity, *s*. lascívia.

salad, *s*. salada. 1) *salad dish*, saladeira. 2) *salad-dressing*, molho de salada. 3) *to dress salad*, temperar.

salamender, *s*. salamandra.

salaried, *adj*. assalariado.

salary, *s*. salário.

sale, *s*. venda; venda em hasta pública; leilão; mercado. 1) *on sale*, à venda. 2) *for sale*, vende-se. 3) *sale by auction*, venda em leilão.

saleable, *adj*. vendável.

saleratus, *s*. bicarbonato de sódio.

salesman, *s*. vendedor.

salience, *s*. saliência.

salient, *adj*. saliente; proeminente; *s*. ângulo saliente.

salification, *s*. salificação, salinagem.

salify, *v.t*. salificar.

saline, *s*. salina; *adj*. salino.

salinity, *s*. sanilidade.

saliva, *s*. saliva.

salivate, *v.t*. salivar.

salivation, *s*. salivação.

sallow, *adj*. pálido, macilento, lívido; *s*. espécie de salgueiro.

sally, *s*. saída, surtida; arranco, arrancada, acesso, repente; dito, réplica; excursão, passeio; *sally-port*, porta falsa por onde se efectuam saídas; *v.t*. sair, fazer uma surtida; sair repentinamente.

salmon, *s*. salmão; *salmon trout*, truta salmonada.

salmonete, *s*. salmonete.

salon, *s*. sala de visitas, salão.

saloon, *s*. salão, sala grande; câmara principal de vapor; carruagem-salão; taberna; automóvel-salão; salão de barbeiro; salão de 1ª classe.

salt, *s*. sal; sabor, gosto; espírito, agudeza; lobo do mar, marinheiro experimentado. 1) *in salt*, conservado em salmoura. 2) *to eat some-one's salt*, gozar a hospitalidade de alguém; *adj*. salgado; picante; caro, dispendioso; impudico. 3) *salt-work*, salinas. 4)

above the salt, entre os convidados mais distintos; *v.t*. salgar.

saltpeter, saltpetre, *s*. salitre.

salty, *adj*. salgado, picante; chistoso.

salubrious, *adj*. salubre, saudável.

salutation, *s*. saudação.

salute, *s*. saudação; continência; salva; *v.t*. saudar; beijar; salvar (mil.).

saluting, *s*. salva (mil.).

salvable, *adj*. salvável.

salvage, *s*. salvamento; salvados; sucata; *v.t*. salvar (material); recuperar.

salvation, *s*. salvação, redenção.

salve, *s*. unguento, pomada; auxílio, remédio; *v.t*. aplicar ou curar com unguento ou pomada; auxiliar, remediar.

salver, *s*. salva, bandeja; curandeiro; salvador.

same, *adj*. mesmo; igual, idêntico; *pron*. o mesmo. 1) *it's all the same to me*, é-me indiferente, tanto me faz. 2) *at the same time*, contudo, ao mesmo tempo. 3) *the very same man*, o próprio homem.

sameness, *s*. identidade; semelhança; monotonia.

sample, *s*. amostra; exemplo, modelo; espécimen; *v.t*. dar amostra; tirar amostra de; provar; exemplificar.

sampler, *s*. amostra; bordado realizado como amostra; o que dá amostras.

sanatorium, *s*. sanatório.

sanctification, *s*. santificação.

sanctified, *adj*. santificado, santo, sagrado; purificado.

sanctify, *v.t*. santificar.

sanction, *s*. sanção, lei, decreto; ratificação; pena; *v.t*. sancionar, ratificar; autorizar.

sanctity, *s*. santidade.

sanctuary, *s*. santuário; abrigo, refúgio.

sand, *s*. areia; (pl.) areal; força de carácter; momentos de vida. 1) *sand bank*, banco de areia. 2) *sand glass*, ampulheta. 3) *sand hill*, duna. 4) *sand paper*, lixa. 5) *to build on the sand*, fazer castelos no ar; *v.t*. cobrir de areia; arear, esfregar com areia.

sandal, *s*. sandália, alpercata; *sandal wood*, pau de sândalo.

sandpiper, *s*. pintão (ave).

sandstone, *s*. pedra arenosa.

sandwich, *s*. sanduiche; *v.t*. colocar entre duas camadas.

sandy, *adj*. arenoso, saibroso; solto; ruivo; alcunha dos escoceses.

sane, *adj*. são de espírito, sensato; *adv*. *sanely*, sãmente.

saneness, s. sanidade.

sang-froid, s. sangue frio; serenidade.

sanguinary, adj. sanguinário; adv. sanguinarily, sanguinariamente.

sanguine, adj. sanguíneo; cor de sangue; ardente; confiado; adv. sanguinely, ardentemente; confiadamente.

sanguineous, adj. sanguíneo.

sanitarian, adj. sanitário; s. higienista.

sanitarium, s. sanatório.

sanitary, adj. sanitário.

sanitation, s. saneamento; higiene.

sanitize, v.t. sanear.

sanity, s. razão.

Santa Claus, s. Pai Natal.

sap (sapping, sapped), v.t. sapar, minar, solapar; v.i. fazer trabalho de sapa; avançar minando; ser muito aplicado; s. sapa (mil.); seiva; aluno estudioso.

sapid, adj. saboroso, gostoso.

sapidity, s. sabor, gosto.

sapience, s. sapiência.

sapient, adj. sábio, sapiente; adv. sapiently, sabiamente.

sapless, adj. sem seiva; seco.

saponification, s. saponificação.

saponify, v.t. e v.i. saponificar.

sapor, s. sabor, gosto.

sapper, s. sapador (mil.).

sapphire, s. safira.

sappiness, s. abundância de seiva; sentimentalismo.

sappy, adj. cheio de seiva; suculento; terno, sentimental.

saraband, s. sarabanda.

Saracen, s. sarraceno; saracen corn, trigo mourisco.

sarcasm, s. sarcasmo.

sarcastic, adj. sarcástico; adv. sarcastically, sarcasticamente, dum modo sarcástico.

sarcenet, s. tafetá.

sarcoma, s. sarcoma.

sarcomatous, adj. sarcomatoso.

sarcophagus, s. sarcófago.

sard, s. sárdio (pedra preciosa).

sardine, s. sardinha de conserva.

sardonic, adj. sardónico; adv. sardonically, sardonicamente.

sargasso, s. sargaço.

sarigue, s. sarigueia.

sark, s. camisa; mortalha.

salsaparilla, s. salsaparrilha.

sash, s. faixa, banda, cinta; caixilho, vidraça; sash window, janela de guilhotina.

Satan, s. Satanás, Satã.

satanic, adj. satânico.

satchel, s. sacola; bolsa de colegial; malinha.

sate, v.t. saciar, fartar.

sateen, s. cetineta.

satellite, s. satélite.

satiable, adj. saciável.

satiate, v.t. saciar, satisfazer; adj. farto, cheio, saciado.

satiation, s. acto de saciar; saciedade.

satiety, s. saciedade.

satin, s. cetim; adj. de cetim, acetinado.

satinity, adj. acetinado, de cetim.

satire, s. sátira.

satiric, adj. satírico; adv. satirically, satiricamente.

satirize, v.t. satirizar.

satisfaction, s. satisfação; adv. satisfactorily, satisfatoriamente.

satisfactory, adj. satisfatório.

satisfy, v.t. e v.i. satisfazer, contentar; recompensar; pagar.

satrap, s. sátrapa.

satrapy, s. satrapia.

saturable, adj. saturável.

saturate, v.t. saturar.

saturation, s. saturação.

Saturday, s. sábado.

saturnine, adj. saturnino, fleumático, melancólico.

satyr, s. sátiro; pessoa devassa.

satyric, adj. satírico; devasso.

sauce, s. molho; imprudência, descaramento. 1) sauce boat, molheira. 2) hunger is the best sauce, a fome é o melhor aperitivo; v.t. deitar molho, adubar; tratar uma pessoa imprudentemente ou com atrevimento (pop.).

saucer, s. pires.

saucy, adj. atrevido, descarado.

saunter, v.i. vaguear; andar dum lado para o outro ociosamente; saracotear.

saurel, s. chicharro.

saurian, adj. sáurio.

sausage, s. salsicha, linguiça, chouriço.

savage, adj. e s. selvagem; adv. savagely: selvaticamente.

savageness, s. selvajaria, ferocidade.

savagery, s. o mesmo que savageness.

savannah, s. savana.

savant, s. sábio.

save, s. economia; coisa poupada; v.t. salvar, poupar, economizar; aproveitar, guardar;

evitar; reservar; *God save the King!*, Viva o Rei! *v.i.* fazer economias. *prep.* excepto, salvo; *conj.* a não ser que.

saver, *s.* libertador; economizador.

saving, *s.* economia; salvamento; salvação; (pl.) economia; *savings-bank*, caixa económica; *adj.* económico; frugal; salutar; *prep.* excepto, com excepção; *adv. savingly,* economicamente.

savingness, *s.* economia.

saviour, *s.* salvador.

savory, *s.* segurelha (bot.).

savour, *s.* sabor, gosto; odor, perfume, cheiro; nome, reputação; interesse, graça, *a girl without savour,* uma rapariga sem graça, sem interesse; *v.t.* saborear, provar; cheirar com prazer; *v.i.* (com *of*) saber, ter gosto; cheirar; sugerir, lembrar.

savourless, *adj.* sem sabor, insípido.

savoury, *adj.* saboroso, apetitoso, delicioso; *adv.* saborosamente, com gosto.

savoy, *s.* couve lombarda.

saw, *s.* serra, serrote; rifão, provérbio, adágio. 1) *hack-saw*, serrote para metal. 2) *hand-saw*, serrote. 3) *meat-saw*, serrote para cortar ossos. 4) *old-saw*, história antiga. 5) *saw-horse*, cavalete de serrador; *v.t.* serrar; *v.i.* ser serrado.

sawbones, *s.* médico cirurgião (gír.).

sawder, *s.* adulação.

sawdust, *s.* serradura.

sawer, *s.* serrador.

sawfish, *s.* peixe-serra.

sawmill, *s.* serraria, oficina de serração; engenho para serrar.

Sawney, *s.* um escocês.

sawyer, *s.* serrador.

Saxon, *s.* e *adj.* saxão.

saxophone, *s.* saxofone.

saxophonist, *s.* saxofonista.

say, *v.t.* e *v.i.* dizer, falar, contar, recitar; declarar, afirmar; mostrar, indicar; experimentar, ensaiar. 1) *to say over again*, repetir. 2) *it is said*, diz-se. 3) *that is to say*, por outras palavras, isto é. 4) *I say!*: escute! olhe!; *s.* palavra, afirmação; discurso; deixa; vez de falar; qualidade de seda. 5) *to have one's say*, expressar a sua opinião. 6) *she has had her say*, ela disse o que tinha a dizer.

saying, *s.* ditado, provérbio, adágio; *as the saying goes*, como diz o ditado.

scab, *s.* crosta (de ferida); ronha, sarna; biltre; fura-greves; operário que não segue a orientação do sindicato; *v.i.*

(scabbing, scabbed), encrostar, criar crosta, cicatrizar; trabalhar contra a orientação do sindicato.

scabbard, *s.* bainha de sabre ou espada, etc.

scabbed, *adj.* ranhoso, sarnento.

scabbies, *s.* sarna.

scabbious, *adj.* sarnento, sarnoso; escabioso; ronhento; *s.* escabiosa (bot.).

scabbrous, *adj.* escabroso.

scad, *s.* chicharro, carapau grande; *pl.* dinheiro, grande quantidade (gír. americ.).

scaffold, *s.* andaime, tablado; patíbulo, cadafalso; *v.t.* construir andaime, patíbulo ou tablado.

scaffolding, *s.* material para andaimes ou tablados; andaime.

scalable, *adj.* qualidade do que é escalável.

scald, *v.t.* escaldar, queimar; escalfar; esquentar; *v.i.* escaldar-se; *s.* escaldadura, escaldo, escaldão, queimadura; tinha; caspa. *(scalled), adj.* tinhoso; casposo; vil, miserável; *scalled-head*, tinha.

scalder, *s.* recipiente em que se escalda.

scalding, *s.* escaldadura; coisas escaldadas.

scale, *s.* prato de balança; balança; libra (signo); escama; caspa; ferrugem ou incrustações; lâmina ou folha delgada; escala; escada de mão; proporção; escalada. 1) *a pair of scales*, uma balança. 2) *scale beam*, braço de balança; *v.t.* e *v.i.* escamar(-se); descascar(-se); raspar; pesar, avaliar, medir; escalar, trepar; subir gradualmente.

scaled, *adj.* escamoso; escamado; escalado.

scaleless, *adj.* sem escamas.

scaling, *s.* escalada; escamadura; *scaling ladder*, escada de bombeiro.

scall, *s.* tinha.

scallion, *s.* cebolinha; chalota; alho-porro.

scallop, *s.* pectúnculo, concha; recorte; bico; adorno de roupa; *v.t.* recortar, fazer recortes em; assar ostras.

scalp, *s.* couro cabeludo; pericrânio; banco de ostras; *v.t.* tirar o couro cabeludo; esfolar; vender por preços superiores aos da tabela.

scalpel, *s.* escalpelo, bisturi (cir.).

scalper, *s.* o que esfola ou tira o couro cabeludo; máquina para cortar as pontas dos cereais.

scaly, *adj.* escamoso; esfoliado; incrustado; infestado de piolhos (planta); vil, ruim (gír.).

scamp, *s.* velhaco, patife; *v.i.* trabalhar de modo apressado ou desleal.

scamper, s. fuga apressada; aquele que trabalha de modo desleal; *v.i.* fugir apressadamente; escapar-se.

scan (scanning, scanned), *v.t.* esquadrinhar, examinar com cuidado; escrutar, medir versos; correr os olhos por (fam.); s. olhar perscrutador, exame atento; alcance de visão ou de entendimento.

scandal, s. escândalo; opróbrio; difamação.

scandalize, *v.t.* escandalizar; ofender, chocar; dar escândalo.

scandalmonger, s. maledicente, difamador.

scandalous, *adj.* escandaloso; difamatório; *adv. scandalously,* escandalosamente.

Scandinavian, *adj.* e s. escandinavo.

scansion, s. escanção (métr.), medida.

scant, *adj.* escasso, parco; estreito, limitado; deficiente; *adv.* escassamente; apenas, a custo; s. escassez; falta, míngua; *v.t.* e *v.i.* limitar; invejar, escassear.

scantly, *adv.* escassamente.

scantness, s. escassez, pequenez, insuficiência.

scanting, s. quantidade pequena; amostra, modelo.

scanty, *adj.* escasso, parco; limitado; avarento, mesquinho.

scape, s. escapo (bot.); fuste de coluna (arq.); canhão (de ave pequena); antena (de insecto); fuga, evasão.

scapegoat, s. bode expiatório.

scapegrace, s. velhaco, mandrião.

scaphander, s. escafandro.

scapula, s. omoplata.

scapular, *adj.* escapular.

scar, s. cicatriz; marca ou sinal; gilvaz; mancha (na reputação); *v.t.* e *v.i.* (scarring, scarred), marcar com cicatriz, cicatrizar.

scarab, s. escaravelho.

scarce, *adj.* escasso, raro; *adv.* apenas, mal; *to make oneself scarce,* fugir, ausentar-se voluntariamente; desaparecer.

scarcely, *adv.* apenas, mal, com dificuldade.

scarcity, s. escassez; penúria; insuficiência.

scare, s. susto, sobressalto, pânico; *v.t.* assustar, amedrontar, afugentar.

scarecrow, s. espantalho.

scarf, s. lenço para pescoço; manta; faixa; camilha.

scarlatina, s. escarlatina.

scarlet, *adj.* escarlate, *scarlet fever,* escarlatina; s. cor escarlate.

scary, *adj.* assustador, alarmante; medroso, assustadiço.

scarp, s. escarpa, declive; banda; *v.t.* fazer escarpa; cortar em declive.

scathe, s. dano, estrago; *v.t.* estragar, danificar, destruir.

scatheful, *adj.* destrutivo.

scatheless, *adj.* são e salvo, incólume, intacto.

scathing, *a.* destruidor; fulminante, ardente, abrasador; *adv. scathingly,* dum modo fulminante, abrasador.

scatter, *v.t.* espalhar, dispersar; derramar; dissipar; semear; *v.i.* espalhar-se, dispersar-se, dissipar-se.

scavenger, s. varredor de ruas; animal que se alimenta de carne putrefacta.

scena, s. cena; monólogo (em drama).

scene, s. cena; *side-scene,* bastidor; s. perspectiva, vista, paisagem; cenário.

scenic, *adj.* cénico; *adv. scenically,* cenicamente.

scenographer, s. cenógrafo.

scenographic, *a.* cenográfico.

scenography, s. cenografia.

scent, s. cheiro, olfacto; faro; perfume; fragância; pista, rasto; *to put off the scent,* despistar; *v.t.* e *v.i.* cheirar, perfumar; suspeitar.

scented, *adj.* perfumado.

scentful, *adj.* cheiroso, perfumado; que fareja bem, com bom olfacto.

scentless, *adj.* sem cheiro, inodoro; que não possui olfacto; sem faro.

sceptic, *adj.* e s. céptico.

sceptical, *adj.* céptico; desconfiado; *adv. sceptically,* cepticamente.

scepticism, s. cepticismo.

sceptre, s. ceptro.

schedule, s. lista, catálogo; horário; inventário; *v.t.* fixar, marcar dia e hora; estabelecer itinerário; incluir numa lista.

schema, s. esquema; plano, esboço, sinopse; quadro, diagrama.

schematic, *adj.* esquemático; *adv. scematically,* esquematicamente.

scheme, s. plano, projecto, desígnio; planta, esquema, modelo; diagrama; sistema, disposição; ardil, artifício; *v.t.* e *v.i.* formar um plano, projectar; esboçar, urdir, intrigar.

schemer, s. o que faz projectos; maquinador; intrigante.

schism, s. cisma.

schismatic, s. cismático; *adv. schismatically,* cismaticamente.

schist, s. xisto.

schistose, *adj.* xistoso.

scholar, *s.* escolar, estudante, aluno; homem erudito, sábio, literato, aluno sustentado pelas universidades em Inglaterra; *classical scholar,* helenista, humanista.

scholarly, *adj.* erudito, sábio, douto; *adv.* eruditamente.

scholarship, *s.* erudição, saber; bolsa de estudo.

scholastic, *adj.* escolástico.

school, *s.* escola, aula; colégio, classe; cardume de peixes. 1) *boarding school,* internato. 2) *school-fellow,* condiscípulo. 3) *school-master,* mestre-escola; *v.t.* e *v.i.* ensinar, educar; repreender, disciplinar; formar; nadar em cardumes.

schoolhouse, *s.* escola (prédio).

schooling, *s.* instrução, ensino; preço de ensino.

schoolman, *s.* filósofo ou teólogo da Idade Média.

schoolmate, *s.* companheiro de escola.

scooner, *s.* escuna, goleta, palhabote (náut.), *common schooner,* iate; copo grande, copázio (amer.).

sciatica, *s.* (med.) ciática.

science, *s.* ciência, conhecimento, sabedoria; habilidade, perícia.

scientific, *adj.* científico; *adv. scientifically,* cientificamente.

scientist, *s.* cientista, sábio.

scintillant, *a.* cintilante, faiscante.

scintillate, *v.i.* cintilar, chispar.

scintillation, *s.* cintilação.

scion, *s.* rebento, renovo, enxerto; filho, descendente; garfo (também *cion*).

scirrhous, *adj.* cirroso, duro, endurecido.

scission, *s.* cissão, corte.

scissor, *v.t.* cortar com tesoura; recortar; *s.* tesoura (pl.).

scissure, *s.* cissura, fenda, racha.

sclerosis, *s.* esclerose.

sclerotic, *s.* esclerótica; *adj.* esclerótico.

scobs, *s.* limalha; raspas, aparas; serradura.

scoff, *s.* escárnio, chacota, zombaria; remoque; *v.t.* e *v.i.* escarnecer, zombar, mofar.

scoffer, *s.* escarnecedor.

scoffing, *adj.* zombateiro, escarninho; *s.* escárnio, zombaria; *adv. scoffingly,* por escárnio.

scold, *s.* mulher rabugenta; *v.t.* e *v.i.* ralhar, censurar, repreender.

scolding, *s.* ralhos, repreensão; *adj.* ralhador, rabugento; vituperativo.

scomber, *s.* cavala.

sconce, *s.* baluarte, fortim; elmo; cabeça, cocuruto; miolos, juízo; pequena multa, penalidade; aplique, candelabro de parede; *v.t.* multar; proteger com fortim; abrigar; fortificar.

scone, *s.* bolo leve de farinha de trigo ou cevada, assado na chapa.

scoop, *s.* pá côncava; colher, alcatruz; concavidade; escavação; concha; lucro, fatia, negócio, pechincha; *v.t.* esvaziar, esgotar; tirar com concha; cavar, escavar; (fam.) apropriar-se de, ganhar; (gír. jornal). publicar.

scooper, *s.* cavador, escavador.

scoot, *v.t.* dar às pernas, correr.

scooter, *s.* pequeno veículo de quatro rodas; patinete, lambreta.

scope, *s.* alcance, campo, raio, esfera de acção; intento, fim, propósito; liberdade, desafogo; *to have free scope,* ter carta branca.

scorch, *v.t.* e *v.i.* queimar, chamuscar, tostar, torrar; magoar com palavras; queimar-se, torrar-se; andar de automóvel a alta velocidade.

scorching, *adj.* abrasador, ardente.

score, *s.* corte, entalhe; sinal, marca, risco; cava de leme; vinte, vintena; número de pontos feitos pelos jogadores de certos jogos; consideração, respeito, razão, motivo. 1) *on the score of,* com motivo de; fundamentado em; em consideração a. 2) *to go off at score,* começar animadamente. 3) *to pay off old scores,* saldar antigos agravos. 4) *what is the score?,* qual é a pontuação? (jogo); *v.t.* fazer uma incisão; riscar, gravar; lançar em conta; marcar pontos em jogos; pôr em música; orquestrar. 5) *to score a success,* obter um triunfo.

scorer, *s.* mancador, contador.

scoria, *s.* escória (geol. e metal.).

scoring, *adj.* que marca.

scorn, *s.* desdém, escárnio; *v.t.* desprezar, desdenhar, escarnecer; *v.i.* mofar, fazer escárnio.

scornful, *adj.* desdenhoso; *adv. scornfully,* com desdém, insolentemente.

scornfulness, *s.* desprezo, desdém.

scorpion, *s.* escorpião, lacrau.

scot, *s.* escocês.

scotch, *adj.* escocês; *s.* o escocês (dialecto); os escoceses; aguardente dos escoceses;

incisão; calço, escora; *v.t.* fazer incisões; ferir de ligeiro; picar pedra; escorar.

Scotchman, *adj.* escocês.

scot-free, *adj.* isento de pagamento; impune; ileso.

scotticism, *s.* idiotismo escocês.

scottish, *adj.* escocês.

scoundrel, *s.* maroto, biltre, canalha.

scour, *v.t.* esfregar, limpar, tirar as nódoas; branquear; purgar; percorrer, explorar, bater; livrar de; desentupir; *s.* esfregação, polimento, limpeza; desobstrução mediante jorro de água; diarreia.

scourer, *s.* o que limpa esfregando; esfregão; vagabundo.

scourge, *s.* açoite, flagelo; castigo, aflição; *v.t.* açoitar, castigar.

scourging, *s.* flagelação, castigo.

scouring, *s.* esfrega; branqueamento; diarreia; exploração, batida.

scout, *s.* escoteiro; explorador, batedor, sentinela avançada; criado dos colégios da Universidade de Oxford; avião pequeno e rápido; *v.i.* e *v.t.* ir à descoberta, explorar; vigiar de perto; desdenhar, desprezar.

scouting, *s.* reconhecimento.

scow, *s.* barco de fundo chato.

scowl, *v.i.* e *v.t.* fazer carranca; fazer um ar ameaçador; *s.* carranca; ar carrancudo.

scrabble, *s.* garatuja, arranhão; *v.t.* garatujar, arranhar.

scramble, *s.* esforço; contenda; acção de trepar; *v.i.* trepar; rastejar; fazer esforços para conseguir; fritar ovos.

scrambling, *adj.* espalhado, disperso; *s.* luta renhida para a posse duma coisa; acção de trepar ou de arrastar.

scrap, *s.* pedaço, bocado, fragmento; migalhas, sobras; *scrap-book*, livro para guardar extractos; álbum; *v.t. (scrapping, scrapped)* deitar fora, deitar no lixo, pôr de parte; brigar, discutir.

scrape, *v.t.* e *v.i.* raspar, arranhar um instrumento; tocar mal; juntar aos poucos. 1) *to scrape along,* ir vivendo. 2) *to get into a scrape,* meter-se em trabalhos. 3) *to scrape out,* apagar raspando; *s.* embaraço, aperto, dificuldade; ruído de raspar. 4) *scrape-penny,* avarento, sovina.

scraper, *s.* raspa; raspador; mau rabequista.

scraping, *s.* raspadura; economias; *adj.* que raspa; sovina.

scratch, *s.* arranhadura, esfoladura; raspadura, unhada; linha, risca; linha de partida numa corrida; *v.t.* e *v.i.* arranhar; coçar; raspar; riscar; esgaravatar; *adj.* feito ao acaso ou às pressas.

scratchings, *s.* torresmos.

scratchy, *adj.* rabiscado, garatujado.

scraw, *s.* torrão.

scrawl, *s.* garatujas, rabiscos; *v.t.* e *v.i.* garatujar, rabiscar.

scream, *v.i.* gritar, dar guinchos; guinchar; *s.* grito, pio; guincho.

screech, *s.* grito agudo e repentino; *v.i.* dar um grito agudo e repentino; guinchar.

screechy, *adj.* agudo e áspero.

screed, *s.* retalho, pedaço, arenga, tirada; rasgão, rotura.

screen, *s.* biombo, guarda-vento; pára-fogo; sanefa; ciranda, protecção; quadro branco onde se faz incidir a imagem dum objecto; *v.t.* abrigar, cirandar, esconder.

screw, *s.* parafuso, rosca; hélice; torcedura; maço de tabaco, chá, etc., com as pontas torcidas; avarento; (fam.) salário, ordenado. 1) *cork-screw,* saca-rolhas. 2) *female-screw,* porca de parafuso. 3) *screw-key,* chave-inglesa. 4) *to have a screw loose,* ter pouco juízo; ter um parafuso solto; *v.t.* e *v.i.* aparafusar, atarraxar; apertar, torcer, girar, comprimir; ser avarento. 5) *to screw out,* fazer sair à força; arrancar uma confissão. 6) *to screw up,* excitar.

screwed, *adj.* em forma de parafuso; com torcidos; ébrio.

screwer, *s.* pessoa ou coisa que aparafusa; opressor; forreta.

screwing, *adj.* exigente; apertado.

scribble, *s.* rabisco, escrita mal feita, garatujo; *v.t.* e *v.i.* escrever com desleixo; escrevinhar; cardar lã.

scribe, *s.* escrevente, amanuense, escriturário; escrivão, escriba; escrevinhar, registar, marcar, riscar.

scrimmage, *s.* escaramuça; contenda.

scrimp, *v.t.* encurtar, estreitar, apertar; economizar; *adj.* curto, escasso; contraído; económico em excesso.

scrimping, *s.* economia, frugalidade.

scrip, *s.* cédula, escrito; certificado provisório, escrito de acções ou de fundos subscritos ou distribuídos; bolsa, alforge.

script, *s.* escrita, manuscrito; letra redonda.

scripture, *s.* escritura.

Scripture, *s.* a Sagrada Escritura.

scrivener, *s.* escrivão, amanuense; notário.

scroll, *s.* rolo de papel ou pregaminho; rascunho; lista, inventário; espiral.

scrounge, *v.t.* e *v.i.* apropriar-se de coisas alheias.

scrub, *s.* mato, arbusto pequeno; vassoura gasta, toco; *adj.* reles, vil, desprezível; *v.t.* *(scrubbing, scrubbed)* esfregar, desencardir; trabalhar com afinco.

scrubber, *s.* esfregão, escova de esfregar; vassoura rija; máquina para lavar couro depois de curtido.

scrubbing, *s.* escova de esfrega; esfrega.

scrubby, *adj.* pequeno e desprezível; enfezado; miserável; coberto de mato; (fam.) insignificante, sem valor.

scruff, *s.* nuca.

scrunch, *v.t.* esmagar.

scruple, *s.* escrúpulo, dúvida; *v.i.* ter escrúpulos, duvidar, hesitar.

scrupulous, *adj.* escrupuloso, consciencioso; *adv. escrupulously,* escrupulosamente.

scrutineer, *s.* escrutador; escrutinador.

scrutinize, *v.t.* examinar cuidadosamente ou com crítica; investigar; escrutar.

scrutiny, *s.* escrutínio, pesquisa.

scud, *s.* carreira rápida; nuvens soltas impelidas pelo vento; fuga precipitada; pancada, palmada; *v.i.* fugir, voar ou deslizar rapidamente.

scuff, *v.t.* e *v.i.* caminhar arrastando os pés; arrastar, roçar.

scuffle, *s.* briga, rixa, tumulto; *v.i.* lutar corpo a corpo, confusamente; brigar.

scuffler, *s.* altercador.

scull, *s.* crânio; remo pequeno e leve; barquinho; *v.t.* e *v.i.* impelir um barco com remos pequenos; gingar um barco.

scullery, *s.* copa de cozinha.

scullion, *s.* ajudante de cozinha; lavador de pratos; sujeito desprezível.

sculptor, *s.* escultor.

sculpture, *s.* escultura; *v.t.* esculpir, talhar, cinzelar.

scum, *s.* escuma; refugo, resíduos; (fig.) ralé, escumalha; *v.t. (scumming, scummed),* escumar.

scummer, *s.* escumadeira.

scummy, *adj.* escumoso.

scupper, *s.* embornal (náut.).

scurf, *s.* caspa; tinha; crosta; escória; truta salmonada.

scurfy, *adj.* casposo, tinhoso.

scurrility, *s.* linguagem grosseira, indecente; graça pesada; insolência.

scurrilous, *adj.* grosseiro, rude, obsceno; *adv. scurrilously,* grosseiramente.

scurry, *v.i.* fugir precipitadamente, apressar-se; *s.* fuga apressada, pressa.

scurvy, *adj.* vil, miserável; atacado de escorbuto; *s.* escorbuto; *adv. scurvily,* vilmente, grosseiramente.

scut, *s.* pequena cauda.

scutcheon, *s.* escudo de armas, escudete.

scuttle, *s.* paneiro, alcofa, cabaz, cesto; escotilha; corrida apressada, passo acelerado; *v.t.* e *v.i.* correr apressadamente, fugir; meter a pique um navio.

scythe, foice grande; *v.t.* ceifar.

sea, *s.* mar, oceano; vaga, golpe de mar; *adj.* marítimo, naval. 1) *sea dog,* marinheiro experimentado, lobo do mar; tubarão pequeno; foca. 2) *sea farm,* viveiro de moluscos. 3) *sea maid,* sereia. 4) *sea robber,* pirata. 5) *sea rose,* anémona. 6) *sea run,* migração de peixes para o mar. 7) *sea tossed,* agitado pelo mar. 8) *sea-wolf,* leão-marinho; corsário. 9) *main sea,* alto mar, o oceano. 10) *to go to sea,* fazer-se marinheiro. 11) *to put to sea,* fazer-se ao mar.

seaboard, *s.* costa, litoral.

seafarer, *s.* marinheiro; navegante.

seafaring, *s.* profissão marítima; *adj.* de marinheiro, de navegante.

seagoing, *adj.* de alto mar.

seal, *s.* selo, sinete, chancela; sigilo; seladura; penhor; foca, pele de foca. 1) *under seal,* selado. 2) *under my hand and seal,* assinado e selado por mim; *v.i.* e *v.t.* selar, chancelar; firmar, estabelecer; fechar com lacre; completar; pescar focas.

sealing, *s.* confirmação por meio de selo; pesca das focas.

sealskin, *s.* pele de foca.

seam, *s.* costura, cicatriz, sutura; veia, filão; banha, unto; medida de oito alqueires; *v.t.* fazer uma costura, coser, juntar; marcar com cicatriz.

seaman, *s.* marinheiro, marítimo; (pl.) marinhagem; *ordinary seaman,* marinheiro de 2ª classe.

seamanship, *s.* arte de marinheiro; marinhagem; marinharia.

seamstress, *s.* costureira.

seamy, *adj.* que tem costuras; avesso; *seamy-side,* o pior lado duma coisa.

seance, *s.* sessão.

seaplane, *s.* hidrovião.

sear, *v.t.* queimar, tostar; secar; murchar,

fanar; tornar insensível; *adj.* seco, murcho; árido.

search, *v.t.* buscar, procurar, esquadrinhar; investigar; *v.i.* introduzir-se. 1) *search for*, procurar; *s.* pesquisa, procura, exame, investigação; busca. 2) *search-warrant*, ordem para se dar busca a uma casa.

searcher, *s.* pesquisador, examinador; empregado de alfândega.

searching, *adj.* penetrante; completo; investigador; *s.* procura, busca, pesquisa.

seascape, *s.* quadro representando cena marítima.

seashore, *s.* praia, litoral.

seasick, *adj.* enjoado.

seaside, *s.* praia, beira-mar.

season, *s.* estação; época; quadra; oportunidade, tempo próprio; tempero, adubo. 1) *dull season*, estação morta. 2) *in due season*, no tempo devido. 3) *open season*, tempo de caça. 4) *close season*, defeso; *v.t.* temperar, adubar; aclimatar; amadurecer; secar madeira; *v.i.* amadurecer; acostumar-se.

seasonable, *a.* oportuno, favorável; *adv.* *seasonably*, oportunamente, a tempo.

seasonal, *adj.* pertencente às estações, das estações.

seasoning, *s.* adubo, condimento; sal; acto de temperar; aclimatação.

seat, *s.* assento, banco; fundilhos (das calças); sítio, posição, lugar; fixo; base, carlinga; sede, capital, residência; *v.t.* assentar; colocar em assentos; pôr fundilhos; *this room will seat two thousand*, esta sala tem lugar para duas mil.

seatings, *s.* assento (mec.).

seaward, *adj.* ao largo, ao mar; *adv.* em direcção ao mar.

sebaceous, *adj.* sebáceo.

secede, *v.i.* ir-se embora; apartar-se.

seceding, *s.* apartamento, separação; *adj.* separatista.

secession, *s.* apartamento, separação; *War of Secession*, Guerra da Secessão, guerra civil dos Estados Unidos.

seclude, *v.t.* apartar, excluir.

seclusion, *s.* separação, exclusão; retiro.

second, *s.* segundo, instante, padrinho (de duelo); defensor; ajuda; braço direito; segunda (mús.); *adj.* segundo; inferior; outro. 1) *the second best*, o melhor depois do primeiro. 2) *second sight*, conhecimento do futuro. 3) *on second thoughts*,

reconsiderando. 4) *to be second to none*, não ser inferior a ninguém; *v.t.* seguir, auxiliar, apoiar, apadrinhar.

secondary, *adj.* secundário; subalterno; segundo.

secondly, *adv.* secundariamente, em segundo lugar.

secrecy, *s.* segredo, reserva; mistério, retiro.

secret, *s.* segredo; *in secret*, em segredo, secretamente; *adj.* secreto, oculto; reservado.

secretary, *s.* secretário, amanuense; ministro do governo; secretária. 1) *Secretary of War*, ministro da Guerra. 2) *Secretary of the Navy*, Ministro da Marinha. 3) *Home Secretary*, Ministro do Interior.

secretaryship, *s.* secretariado.

secrete, *v.t.* ocultar, esconder, encobrir; secretar, segregar; *adv. secretly*, secretamente.

secretion, *s.* secreção.

secretive, *adj.* reservado, calado; secretório; *adv. secretively*, reservadamente.

secretness, *s.* segredo, sigilo; fidelidade de guardar segredo.

sect, *s.* seita; doutrina.

sectarian, *s.* e *adj.* sectário; fanático.

sectary, *s.* sectário, cismático; fanático.

section, *s.* secção, divisão, corte; parte, porção; artigo, parágrafo; *section of defense*, sector de defesa.

sectional, *adj.* seccional; regional, local.

sector, *s.* sector; compasso de proporção.

secular, *adj.* secular; profano, mundano; temporal; *s.* secular, leigo.

secularist, *s.* mundano; o que defende a separação da educação e religião.

secure, *adj.* seguro, livre de perigo; descuidado, tranquilo; forte, firme; *v.t.* assegurar, garantir, salvar, proteger; prender, consolidar; amarrar; segurar; guardar, pôr em segurança; apossar-se de; *adv. securely*, seguramente; tranquilamente.

secureness, *s.* segurança; confiança.

security, *s.* segurança; protecção, defesa; certeza; confiança; garantia, penhor, fiança, depósito; título; fiador; *pl.* títulos públicos, valores, obrigações; *to stand security*, ser fiador, afiançar.

sedate, *adj.* sereno, sossegado, tranquilo; sério; *adv. sedately*, tranquilamente.

sedateness, *s.* serenidade, tranquilidade.

sedative, *s.* e *adj.* sedativo, calmante.

sedentary, *adj.* sedentário; *adv. sedentarily,* sedentariamente.

sediment, *s.* sedimento.

sedimentation, *s.* sedimentação.

sedition, *v.t.* sedição, tumulto.

seditious, *adj.* sedicioso, revoltoso, amotinado, incorrecto; *adv. seditiously,* sediciosamente.

seduce, *v.t.* seduzir, enganar, desencaminhar, desonrar.

seducement, *s.* sedução.

seducer, *s.* sedutor.

seduction, *s.* sedução.

seductive, *adj.* sedutor, enganador; atraente; *adv. seductively,* de modo sedutor.

sedulous, *adj.* diligente, assíduo, cuidadoso; *adv. sedulously,* assiduamente.

see (saw, seen), *v.t.* olhar, ver; perceber; reparar, observar; descobrir, distinguir; inquirir, indagar, informar-se; considerar, examinar; visitar, frequentar; acompanhar, escoltar. 1) *to see a person home,* acompanhar alguém a casa. 2) *to see one off,* ir à despedida de alguém; *s.* sé, catedral; sede episcopal. 3) *Holy See,* Santa Sé.

seed, *s.* semente; grão; pevide; gérmen, origem, causa. 1) *seed bud,* botão, gérmen. 2) *seed oil,* óleo de linhaça. 3) *seed time,* tempo de sementeira; *v.t.* e *v.i.* semear, fazer a sementeira.

seeded, *adj.* semeado; espigado.

seeder, *s.* semeador; máquina de semear.

seedless, *adj.* sem semente.

seedling, *s.* planta nova.

seedly, *adj.* cheio de sementes; espigado; surrado; miserável.

seek, *v.t.* e *v.i.* procurar, buscar, pesquisar; pretender, ambicionar; perguntar. 1) *to seek after,* buscar, procurar, investigar. 2) *to seek for,* andar a procurar; esforçar-se por. 3) *to seek of,* solicitar. 4) *to seek out,* procurar por toda a parte; seguir a pista. 5) *to seek a needle in a stack hay,* procurar agulha em palheiro.

seeking, *s.* busca, pesquisa.

seem, *v.i.* parecer; parecer-se; aparentar; *it seems,* diz-se.

seeming, *s.* aparência; parecer; *adj.* aparente; imaginário; parecido; *adv. seemingly,* aparentemente.

seemliness, *s.* decoro, decência; graça, formusura.

seemly, *adj.* decente, decoroso, conveniente,

próprio; *adv.* convenientemente, decentemente.

seep, *v.i.* coar-se, filtrar-se, vazar-se.

seer, *s.* vidente; profeta.

seesaw, *s.* vaivém, balanço, vibração; *adj.* de vaivém, de balanço; *v.i.* balançar-se.

seethe, *v.t.* e *v.i.* ferver; fazer ferver; estar agitado; *to seethe over,* deitar por fora ao ferver.

seether, *s.* caldeira, panela.

seething, *s.* fervura; *adj.* fervente.

segment, *s.* segmento.

segregate, *adj.* segregado; *v.t.* e *v.i.* segregar, separar, segregar-se.

segregation, *s.* segregação, separação.

seine, *s.* rede de arrasto; *v.t.* e *v.i.* pescar com rede de arrastar.

seize, *v.t.* agarrar, apanhar; apoderar-se de; prender, capturar; amarrar (um cabo); sequestrar; fazer uma cozedura; embargar.

seized, *adj.* agarrado; embargado; amarrado; sequestrado.

seizer, *s.* apreensor, embargante; sequestrador.

seizin, *s.* posse; coisa possuída.

seizing, *s.* tomada de posse; ligadura; cozedura.

seizure, *s.* acto de agarrar; apreensão; prisão; embargo; sequestro.

seldom, *adv.* raramente.

select, *v.t.* escolher, optar por; *adj.* selecto.

selection, *s.* selecção, escolha.

selective, *adj.* selectivo.

selenium, *s.* silénio.

self, *s.* pessoa, indivíduo. 1) *Your royal self,* Vossa real pessoa; *pref.* mesmo, mesma, próprio, própria. 2) *myself,* a minha pessoa, eu mesmo. 3) *self abasement,* consciência de inferioridade. 4) *self-moving,* automático. 5) *self assumption,* presunção. 6) *self-defense,* legítima defesa. 7) *self-educated,* que se instruiu a si mesmo. 8) *self-made man,* homem que venceu na vida pelos seus meios. 9) *self-sacrifice,* abnegação. 10) *self-willed,* obstinado. 11) *self-wise,* vaidoso.

selfish, *adj.* interesseiro, egoísta; vaidoso; *adv. selfishly,* interesseiramente, por egoísmo.

selfishness, *s.* egoísmo.

selfsame, *adj.* idêntico, próprio, mesmo.

selfwill, *s.* obstinação.

sell, *v.t.* vender, comerciar; burlar, atraiçoar; *v.i.* vender-se, ser vendável. 1) *to sell at* *auction,* vender em hasta pública. 2) *to sell off,* liquidar. 3) *to sell on credit,* vender fiado. 4) *to sell to the highest bidder,* vender pela melhor oferta. 5) *to sell wholesale,* vender por atacado; *s.* engano, logro.

seller, *s.* vendedor.

selling, *s.* venda; *selling out,* venda forçada.

selvage, selvedge, *s.* orla, ourela.

selves, *s. pl.* de *self.*

semaphore, *s.* semáforo.

semblance, *s.* semelhança, aparência exterior; semblante; imagem; ficção.

semen, *s.* sémen; semente.

semester, *s.* semestre escolar.

semi, *pref.* semi, metade; meio.

semiannual, *adj.* semianual.

semicircle, *s.* semicírculo.

semicircular, *adj.* semicircular.

semicolon, *s.* ponto e vírgula.

semimonthly, *adj.* quinzenal; *s.* revista quinzenal.

seminal, *adj.* seminal.

seminary, *s.* seminário; *adj.* seminal.

Semite, *s.* semita.

Semitic, *adj.* e *s.* semítico.

semiweekly, *adj.* bissemanal; *s.* publicação bissemanal.

sempstress, *s.* costureira.

senary, *a.* senário.

senate, *s.* senado; corpo legislativo.

senator, *s.* senador.

senatorial, *adj.* senatorial.

senatus, *s.* antigo senado romano.

send, *v.t.* e *v.i.* mandar, enviar, expedir, despachar, remeter; emitir, arrojar; produzir; espalhar, propagar; conceder, dar; acontecer. 1) *to send away,* despedir, mandar embora. 2) *to send back,* devolver. 3) *to send forth,* despachar. 4) *to send off,* ou *to send on,* expedir. 5) *to send out,* despedir; exalar. 6) *to send word,* mandar recado.

sender, *s.* remetente.

send-off, *s.* despedida; partida.

senile, *adj.* senil, caduco.

senility, *s.* senilidade, velhice.

senior, *s.* sénior, ancião; decano; chefe de casa comercial; sócio mais antigo; *adj.* sénior, mais velho; decano.

seniority, *s.* antiguidade, ancianidade.

sensation, *s.* sensação; excitação.

sensational, *adj.* sensacional; excitante; *adv. sensationally,* de modo sensacional, excitante.

sensationalism, *s.* sensacionalismo.

sense, *s.* sentido (faculdade ou percepção sensitiva); mente, inteligência; razão; sensação; sentimento; sentido; significado, interpretação; sentido; direcção (geom); engenho, agudeza; *common sense,* senso comum.

senseless, *adj.* insensível; néscio; sem sentido, disparatado; *adv. senselessly,* insensatamente.

senselessness, *s.* insensatez; tolice.

sensibility, *s.* sensibilidade.

sensible, *adj.* sensível; razoável; sensato, judicioso; convencido; *adv. sensibly,* sensivelmente.

sensitive, *adj.* sensitivo; sensível; impressionável; terno, sentido; *adv. sensitively,* sensivelmente, com sentimento.

sensitize, *v.t.* sensibilizar.

sensorial, *adj.* sensório.

sensory, *adj.* e *s.* sensório.

sensual, *adj.* sensual, carnal, lascivo, voluptuoso; *adv. sensually,* sensualmente.

sensualism, *s.* sensualismo, sensualidade.

sensuality, *s.* sensualidade, voluptuosidade, lascívia.

sensuous, *adj.* patético, terno, sensível, apaixonado; *adv. sensuously,* apaixonadamente.

sentence, *s.* oração (gram.); sentença, condenação (for.); máxima, dito; opinião, parecer, frase; *v.t.* sentenciar; condenar.

sententious, *adj.* sentencioso, conceituoso; *adv. sententiously,* sentenciosamente.

sentient, *adj.* sensível; *s.* ente sensível; *adv. sentiently,* sensivelmente.

sentiment, *s.* sentimento, afecto, simpatia; modo de sentir; opinião.

sentimental, *adj.* sentimental, terno, sensível.

sentimentalism, *s.* sentimentalismo.

sentimentality, *s.* sentimentalidade.

sentry, *s.* sentinela; *sentry box,* guarita.

sepal, *s.* sépala.

separable, *adj.* separável; *adv. separably,* de modo que pode separar-se.

separate, *adj.* separado; desunido, distinto, diferente; *v.t.* separar, desunir; dividir; apartar; *adv. separately,* separadamente.

separation, *s.* separação, desunião, divisão.

separatism, *s.* separatismo.

separatist, *s.* separatista.

separator, *s.* separador.

September, *s.* Setembro.

septic, *adj.* céptico, putrefactivo.

septicemia, *s.* septicemia.

septime, s. sétima (posição em esgrima).

septuagenarian, adj. e s. septuagenário.

sepulchral, adj. sepulcral.

sepulchre, s. sepulcro.

sepulture, s. sepultura.

sequel, s. sequela; ilação; êxito.

sequence, s. sequência, série, continuação; ilação, efeito, consequência; modulação (mús.).

sequester, v.t. separar, apartar; sequestrar.

sequestrate, v.t. confiscar, sequestrar.

seraglio, s. serralho, harém.

seraphic, adj. seráfico, angélico; adv. seraphically, seraficamente.

Serb, adj. e s. sérvio.

Serbian, adj. e s. sérvio.

sere, adj. seco, árido; seguro, salvo; separado; s. unha, garra (de ave).

serenade, s. serenata; v.t. fazer serenatas.

serene, adj. sereno, tranquilo; Most serene, sereníssimo (título); adv. serenely, serenamente.

serenity, adj. serenidade, sossego, tranquilidade, paz.

serf, s. servo, escravo; hilota.

serfdom, s. escravidão; hilotismo.

sergeant, s. sargento; advogado de primeira classe; esbirro.

serial, adj. disposto em série; s. publicação periódica; fascículo.

series, s. série, sucessão; enlace, união.

seringa, s. seringueira, árvore da borracha.

serious, adj. sério, circunspecto, sério, sincero; adv. seriously, seriamente.

sermon, s. sermão; admoestação, exortação.

serpent, s. serpente; serpentário (astr.).

serpentine, adj. serpentino, tortuoso; s. serpentina (canhão antigo); serpentária (bot.); The Serpentine, o lago ornamental de Hyde Park, em Londres.

serrate, adj. dentado (em serra).

serration, s. recorte dentado.

serum, s. soro.

servant, s. criado, criada, servo, servidor; empregado; officer's servant, impedido, ordenança.

serve, v.t. e v.i. servir, estar empregado em; servir, ser de utilidade, prestar; tratar; servir à mesa; exercer um cargo; bastar, ser suficiente; satisfazer; obsequiar; pagar, compensar; servir de, fazer as vezes de; prestar culto; apresentar formalmente (for.). 1) to serve an office, desempenhar um cargo. 2) to serve one a trick, pregar uma partida. 3) to serve one's ends, servir para todos os fins. 4) to serve one's time, ser aprendiz. 5) to serve time, cumprir uma condenação numa prisão. 6) to serve a warrant, intimar ou executar uma ordem de prisão. 7) to serve up, servir uma iguaria. 8) serve you right!, é bem feito!

server, s. servidor; criado de mesa; bandeja; ajudante de missa; aquele que atira a bola de ténis.

service, s. serviço; préstimo, utilidade; obséquio; ofício divino; homenagem, uso, vantagem; serviço de mesa; baixela; obediência, respeito; lona para forrar cabos. 1) at your service, à sua disposição. 2) it is of no service, não presta para nada. 3) to see service, servir no exército ou na marinha. 4) civil service, funcionalismo público; adj. de serviço; v.t. prestar serviços a, atender, servir; consertar, fazer reparos em.

serviceable, adj. serviçal, oficioso, útil, prestável; adv. serviceably, utilmente.

servile, adj. servil, baixo, humilde; adulador; adv. servilely, servilmente.

servility, s. servilismo; baixeza; servidão.

serving, adj. servente; s. forro de cabos (náut.). 1) serving-maid, criada. 2) serving--man, criado.

servitor, s. servidor, ajudante, assistente; partidário.

servitude, s. servidão; escravidão; trabalho forçado; dependência.

sesame, s. sésamo, gergelim.

session, s. sessão; reunião, assembleia; in session, em sessão, reunido, em exercício.

set (setting, set), v.t. e v.i. assentar; pôr, colocar; fixar; estabelecer; ajustar; pôr para chocar; endireitar; engastar (pedras preciosas); dar, oferecer; acertar (relógio); armar (laço); assinar; fixar-se; dirigir-se; inclinar-se; pôr-se (o Sol); endurecer (cimento, gesso, etc.). 1) to set a bone, recolocar um osso deslocado. 2) to set aside, pôr de parte. 3) to set sail, largar uma vela. 4) to set a hen, deitar uma galinha. 5) to set about, começar, principiar. 6) to set back, recuar, fazer retroceder. 7) to set down, mencionar, citar; determinar; assentar por escrito; apear-se; imputar, atribuir. 8) to set forth, expor, manifestar; realçar; estabelecer, regular; partir, ir-se. 9) to set forward, avançar, adiantar-se, impelir, encorajar. 10) to set free, libertar. 11) to set off, partir, pôr-se a andar; realçar.

12) *to set in,* começar. 13) *to set on,* instigar, animar; pôr-se a caminho. 14) *to set on fire,* incendiar, pegar fogo. 15) *to set one's mind on,* resolver-se, decidir-se. 16) *to set out,* publicar, declarar, manifestar; expor; partir; deitar ao mar uma embarcação. 17) *to set right,* colocar bem, rectificar. 18) *to set together,* comparar, confrontar. 19) *to set up,* erigir, levantar; arvorar; exaltar, armar. 20) *to set up for,* dar-se pelo que não é. 21) *to set up for oneself,* estabelecer-se por conta própria; *adj.* fixo, imóvel; firme, constante; estabelecido, determinado, resolvido; simétrico; feito, montado, engastado. 22) *set smile,* sorriso fixo; *s.* aparelho; colecção; grupo; posição; colocação; direcção, curso, movimento, tendência; ocaso, o pôr do Sol; decoração (teat.); partida (desportos); adaptação (vestuário). 23) *set of horses,* parelha de cavalos. 24) *set of teeth,* dentadura. 25) *tea-set,* serviço de chá.

setback, *s.* retrocesso; revés, contrariedade; contracorrente.

set-down, *s.* reprimenda.

set-off, *s.* compensação; contrapeso; adorno; realce.

sette, *s.* canapé.

setter, *s.* cão perdigueiro; espião.

settle, *v.t.* e *v.i.* colocar, pôr, assentar; decidir, acabar, pôr fim a; saldar, pagar (a conta); colonizar, povoar; acalmar; sossegar; instituir; arranjar, ajustar; repousar, acalmar-se, tranquilizar-se; fixar-se, estabelecer-se; decidir-se, determinar-se; fixar-se (vento, tempo); afundar-se, assentar no fundo. 1) *to settle accounts,* ajustar contas. 2) *to settle down,* fixar-se, estabelecer-se; recompor-se. 3) *to settle disputes,* vencer dificuldades. 4) *to settle down to dinner,* para jantar. 5) *to settle matters,* decidir assuntos. 6) *to settle upon,* cair sobre, precipitar-se; dar em dote, determinar uma pensão; *s.* cadeira, assento, banco comprido.

settled, *adj.* fixo, firme, inalterável; constante; *settled fair,* consolidado; casado; sério; povoado, colonizado.

settlement, *s.* acordo, ajuste; dote; sedimento, depósito; colonização, povoamento, colónia; fixação, estabelecimento, pagamento, saldo; posse; *act of settlement,* lei de sucessão ao trono.

settler, *s.* colono, povoador.

settling, *s.* estabelecimento, fixação; borra, sedimento.

settlor, *s.* doador (jur.).

setup, *s.* porte, aspecto, aprumo.

seven, *adj.* e *s.* sete; *the seven deadly sins,* os sete pecados mortais.

sevenfold, *adj.* séptulo; *adv.* sete vezes.

sevenscore, *adj.* cento e quarenta.

seventeen, *s.* e *adj.* dezassete.

seventeenth, *s.* e *adj.* décimo sétimo.

seventh, *adj.* sétimo; *s.* um sétimo (mús.); *adv.* seventhly, em sétimo lugar.

seventy, *s.* e *adj.* setenta.

sever, *v.t.* e *v.i.* separar, desunir; arrancar com violência; desfazer; separar-se, partir-se.

severable, *adj.* separável.

several, *adj.* diversos, vários, alguns; diferente, diverso, distinto; *pron.* vários; cada um em particular.

severance, *s.* separação; rompimento.

severe, *adj.* severo, austero; violento, forte; difícil, rigoroso; *adv. severely,* severamente; rigorosamente.

severety, *s.* severidade, rigor, opressão, crueldade; rigorismo, seriedade.

sew, *v.t.* e *v.i.* coser. 1) *to be sewed up,* estar encalhado (navio); estar arruinado. 2) *to sew on a button,* pregar um botão.

sewage, *s.* imundícies; esgotos.

sewer, *s.* pessoa que cose; cano de esgoto.

sewing, *s.* costura; *sewing machine,* máquina de costura.

sex, *s.* sexo; *irrespective of sex,* indistinção de sexo.

sexagenarian, *s.* sexagenário.

sexagesima, *s.* sexagésima.

sexless, *s.* assexuado, neutro.

sext, *s.* sexta (hora canónica).

sextan, *adj.* de seis em seis dias.

sextant, *s.* sextante.

sextet, *s.* sexteto (mús.).

sextillion, *s.* sextilhão.

sexton, *s.* sacristão; coveiro.

sexual, *adj.* sexual.

sexuality, *s.* sexualidade.

sexually, *adv.* sexualmente.

shabbily, *adv.* andrajosamente, miseravelmente, mesquinhamente.

shabbiness, *s.* desalinho, vileza, baixeza, miséria.

shabby, *s.* usado, gasto; esfarrapado, vil, mesquinho.

shackle, *v.t.* encadear, algemar, pôr grilhões, travar; estorvar, embaraçar; *s.* algema, grilheta; travão; impedimento; manilha, braga.

shad, s. sável.

shaddock, s. toranja.

shade, s. sombra, escuridão; lugar escuro; graduação de cor; fantasma; ilusão; pequena quantidade; imagem; quebra-luz.

shadeless, adj. sem sombra.

shadily, adv. com sombra.

shadiness, s. sombra, opacidade; qualidade de estar à sombra, ou coberto com a sombra.

shading, s. sombreado; acção de cobrir com sombra.

shadow, s. sombra, escuridão, protecção, parte sombreada (pint.); imagem reflectida; traço, vestígio; v.t. assombrar, sombrear, matizar; representar imperfeitamente; v.i. escurecer-se; mudar gradualmente de cor.

shadowless, adj. sem sombra.

shadowy, adj. escuro, sombrio; tenebroso, vago, indefinido; alegórico.

shady, adj. opaco, escuro, sombrio; sombreado, umbroso.

shaft, s. frecha, dardo, seta, arma de arremesso; fuste de coluna, agulha, capitel de torre; veio, eixo, fuso (mec.); haste de âncora; lança, varal (de carro); poço de mina, túnel de forno de chaminé. 1) air shaft, ventilador. 2) crank shaft, veio motor.

shafting, s. jogo de eixos e correias; veios, transmissões (mec.); adj. de transmissão.

shag, s. pelúcia, riço; felpa; pêlo áspero; corvo marinho; v.t. (shagging, shagged) eriçar, tornar felpudo; tornar áspero; cobrir com vegetação áspera.

shagged, adj. felpudo, peludo, hirsuto; adv. shaggily, dum modo hirsuto.

shaggy, adj. felpudo, hirsuto; áspero; escabroso.

shagreen, s. lixa.

shah, s. xá, designação nacional do rei da Pérsia.

shake (shook, shaken), v.t. sacudir, menear, abanar, abalar, agitar, mover, mexer, lançar, arrojar, arremessar; debilitar; desanimar; fazer vacilar; apertar a mão; trinar uma nota (mús.); v.i. estremecer; trepidar; vacilar, titubear; trinar, gargantear (mús.); dar um aperto de mão; bater o pano (náut.). 1) to shake off, sacudir; desembaraçar-se de. 2) to shake one's head, sacudir a cabeça em sinal de reprovação. 3) to shake to pieces, sacudir qualquer coisa até a

fazer em pedaços. 4) to shake up, sacudir; remover; s. sacudidura; agitação; meneio; vibração; aperto de mão; trinado; calafrio de febre; racha da madeira; aduela; pl. vasilhame vazio; coisa sem importância.

shaker, s. pessoa ou coisa que abala, que faz tremer; batedor.

Shakespearian, adj. relativo a Shakespeare, shakespeariano.

shakily, dum modo trémulo ou vacilante.

shakiness, s. qualidade de ser trémulo ou vacilante.

shaking, s. sacudimento, sacudidura; meneio; vibração; tremura, estremecimento; insegurança.

shakings, s. desperdícios.

shaky, adj. abalado, trémulo, vacilante; movediço; fendido, estalado; com falta de crédito (com.).

shale, s. argila xistosa.

shall, v. aux. serve para formar o futuro nas primeiras pessoas *(I, we)*; v. principal: dever, ser obrigado a; antigamente era usado em todas as pessoas na forma afirmativa, mas hoje nas segundas e terceiras significa: promessa, obrigação ou ameaça; na forma interrogativa o seu significado é totalmente diferente: nas primeiras e terceiras pessoas, consulta a pessoa a quem se dirige de quem depende a realização de determinada acção: *shall we go?*, vamos embora?, *shall I open the door?*, quer que eu abra a porta?; nas segundas pessoas, também consulta a pessoas com quem se fala, no sentido de saber a sua intenção de praticar determinada acção: *shall you go to the party?*, vais à festa?

shallop, s. chalupa.

shallot, s. chalota.

shallow, adj. baixo, pouco profundo; superficial, trivial, frívolo; insípido; néscio, parvo. 1) shallow-brained, estouvado, cabeça no ar. 2) shallow water, fundos baixos; s. baixio (náut.); v.t. fazer uma coisa de modo superficial.

shallowness, s. pouca profundidade; aparência; superficialidade.

shaly, adj. argiloso; xistoso.

sham, v.t. e v.i. (shamming, shammed), simular, fingir; lograr, enganar, fazer crer; trapacear; s. falsa aparência, pretexto; fingimento, engano, impostura; adj. fingido, suposto, simulado, dissimulado; postiço.

shamble, *v.i.* andar com dificuldade arrastando os pés; *s.* passo vacilante; o arrastar de pés.

shambles, *s. pl.* açougue, matadouro; carnificina.

shame, *s.* vergonha, pejo; ignomínia, desonra. 1) *for shame!,* que vergonha! 2) *shame on you,* que vergonha!, devia ter vergonha! *v.t.* envergonhar; desonrar; *v.i.* envergonhar-se.

shameful, *adj.* vergonhoso; indecente, indecoroso, ignominioso; *adv. shamefully,* vergonhosamente; ignominiosamente; escandalosamente; indecentemente.

shamefulness, *s.* vergonha, ignomínia.

shameless, *adj.* desavergonhado, descarado.

shamelessness, *s.* impudência; descaramento.

shammer, *s.* trapaceiro.

shampoo, *s.* loção para a lavagem do cabelo; *v.t.* lavar o cabelo.

shamrock, *s.* trevo branco, emblema da Irlanda.

shamy, *s.* camurça, pele de camurça.

shank, *s.* perna, o osso ou cana da perna; haste (mec.); cabo; cana, canudo; tronco; *to ride shank's mare,* ir a pé.

shanked, *adj.* que tem perna ou haste.

shanty, *s.* cabana, choça.

shape, *s.* forma, figura, talhe, contorno, aspecto, configuração; imagem, modelo, exemplar, norma, molde, padrão; maneira; modo. 1) *to put an idea into shape,* exteriorizar uma ideia. 2) *to take shape,* assumir uma forma; *v.t.* e *v.i. (shaped, shapen),* formar, dar forma, figurar, proporcionar; ajustar, igualar, cortar, talhar; imaginar, conceber.

shapeless, *adj.* informe, disforme, desproporcionado; em bruto.

shapelessness, *s.* deformidade, irregularidade, desproporção.

shapeliness, *s.* simetria, proporção, beleza.

shapely, *adj.* simétrico, proporcionado, bem informado; trabalhado.

shaper, *s.* conformador; máquina de talhar.

share, *s.* parte, porção, cota, acção (com.); participação, interesse; relha (do arado). 1) *to hold a share,* possuir uma acção. 2) *to go shares in,* ter partes iguais em; *v.t.* e *v.i.* dividir, repartir, distribuir; participar, tomar parte em.

shareholder, *s.* accionista.

sharer, *s.* repartidor; partícipe.

sharing, *s.* divisão; *profit sharing,* divisão de lucros, participação de lucros.

shark, *s.* tubarão; ladrão, gatuno, tunante, fraude; *v.t.* e *v.i.* furtar, gatunar.

sharp, *adj.* agudo, aguçado, cortante, afiado, penetrante, incisivo, fino, perspicaz, vivo, astuto, manhoso; mordaz, picante; severo, rígido; violento; ardente, fogoso; desabrido (no falar); vigilante, atento; distinto, definido. 1) *sharp-nosed,* nariz pontiagudo; de olfacto apurado. 2) *sharp-set,* ávido, ansioso. 3) *sharp-sighted,* de olhar penetrante; perspicaz. 4) *sharp-visaged,* de rosto afilado; *s.* sustenido (mús.); agulha comprida e fina; espadachim; som agudo; *adv.* exactamente, pontualmente. 5) *at six sharp,* às seis em ponto; *v.t.* afiar, aguçar, elevar meio tom (mús.); *v.i.* cantar ou tocar mais alto que o som devido; enganar, trapacear.

sharpen, *v.t.* afiar, aguçar, amolar; excitar, irritar; *v.i.* aguçar-se; azedar-se.

sharpener, *s.* amolador.

sharper, *s.* gatuno, velhaco; caloteiro; *cards-sharper,* batoteiro.

sharply, *adv.* com fio ou ponta; vivamente.

sharpness, *s.* agudeza; fineza de formas; subtileza; mordacidade; rigor; inclemência (no tempo).

shatter, *v.t.* despedaçar, esmigalhar; estragar; quebrantar (saúde); *v.i.* despedaçar-se; *shatter-brained,* estouvado.

shattery, *adj.* frágil, quebradiço.

shave, *v.t.* barbear, aparar, raspar; roçar, tocar de leve; acepilhar, aplainar; extorquir; *v.i.* barbear-se; levar a melhor parte; *s.* acto de barbear ou aparar; escapar por um triz; *that was a close shave,* foi escapar por um triz.

shaver, *s.* barbeiro; ladrão; interesseiro.

shaving, *s.* acto de barbear ou de raspar; raspas; raspadura; aparas de carpinteiro.

shawl, *s.* xaile, manta.

shawm, *s.* oboé.

she, *pren. pess.* ela; fêmea (dos animais). 1) *she-ass,* jumenta. 2) *she cat,* gata. 3) *she-devil,* diaba.

sheaf, *s.* feixe, molho, gavela; *v.t.* enfeixar, fazer molhos.

shear, *v.t.* tosquiar; tosar; aparar; cortar o cabelo; *s.* tosquia, tosquiadela.

shearer, *s.* tosquiador; tosador.

shearing, *s.* pêlo de lã tosquiada; *shearing time,* tempo da tosquia.

shears, *s.* tesouras de tosquia.

sheath, *s.* bainha (lâmina, espada, faca, etc.); estojo; vagem.

sheathe, *v.t.* embainhar, meter na bainha; forrar (navio); cobrir com algo que proteja.

sheave, *s.* roldana, moitão.

shed, *v.t.* *(shedding, shed),* derramar, entornar, verter, espalhar, vazar; deixar cair, desprender, largar; mudar; *v.i.* mudar (as penas, pele, etc.); *s.* alpendre; telheiro; barraca, cabana; secadouro.

shedder, *s.* derramador; animal que muda (pele ou penas).

shedding, *s.* derramamento; o que desprende; muda (de pele ou penas).

sheen, *s.* resplendor, brilho, lustre.

sheeny, *adj.* lustroso.

sheep, *s.* ovelhas, carneiro; ovelha; parvo, simplório; pele de carneiro. 1) *sheep-cote, fold-pen,* curral, redil. 2) *sheep-walk,* pastagem para ovelhas. 3) *sheep's-eye,* olhar terno, amoroso, modesto; 4) *black--sheep,* ovelha ronhosa numa família.

sheepish, *adj.* acanhado, envergonhado, tímido; *adv. sheepishly,* tímidamente.

sheepishness, *s.* timidez, acanhamento.

sheer, *adj.* puro, claro, consumado; completo, sem mistura; ligeiro, fino, delgado (tec.); escarpado; *adv.* dum golpe, completamente; *s.* arrufo, arrufada; desvio dum navio; *v.i.* desviar-se do rumo; dar guinadas; escabecear; *to sheer off,* fugir, separar-se; folgar as espias; largar.

sheering, *s.* desvio, balanço (náut.); fuga.

sheers, *s. pl.* cábrea (náut.); tesouras (variante de *shears).*

sheet, *s.* folha (de papel); lençol; lâmina; extensão (de água, gelo); escota. 1) *sheet--anchor,* âncora mestra. 2) *sheet-pilling,* pilotagem; 3) *to be three sheets in the wind,* estar a meio pau (ébrio); *v.t.* embrulhar; amortalhar; estender em lâminas ou folhas.

sheeting, *s.* pano para lençóis; metal laminado.

shelf, *s.* prateleira, estante; descanso; banco de areia; baixio; *to put* ou *to lay on the shelf,* pôr de parte.

shell, *s.* casca (de noz, avelã, ovo); concha; casco; vagem; armação, arcaboiço; cápsula; bomba, granada; barco para regata. 1) *shell-fish,* marisco. 2) *shell-proof,* à prova de bomba. 3) *shell-shock,* depressão nervosa causada pelo horror da guerra; *v.t.* e *v.i.* descascar(-se); mudar a pele; lascar;

bombardear. 4) *to shell out,* pagar, dar dinheiro (fam.).

shellac, *v.t. (shellacking, shellacked),* envernizar com goma-laca; *s.* goma-laca em folhas.

sheller, *s.* descascador.

shelling, *s.* descascamento; acto de descascar; bombardeamento.

shelly, *adj.* escamoso; coberto de conchas.

shelter, *s.* abrigo; resguardo, guarida, protecção; *v.t.* pôr ao abrigo ou a coberto; resguardar, acolher, proteger, encobrir; *v.i.* resguardar-se, pôr-se em seguro.

shelterless, *adj.* desamparado, sem abrigo, desabrigado.

shelve, *v.t.* pôr numa estante; prover de estantes; pôr de parte (fig.). *v.i.* inclinar-se, estar em declive.

shelvy, *adj.* inclinado, cheio de escolhos (náut.).

shepherd, *s.* pastor, zagal; pastor de almas (fig.); *shepherd's crook,* cajado.

shepherdess, *s.* pastora.

sherbet, *s.* sorvete.

sherd, *s.* caco, tijolo.

sheriff, *s.* xerife, corregedor.

sherry, *s.* vinho de Xerez.

shibboleth, *s.* palavra que serve de santo-e--senha.

shield, *s.* escudo, broquel; égide, amparo; resguardo, defesa; defensor; escudo de armas; *shield-bearer,* escudeiro; *v.t.* escudar, cobrir com escudo; amparar, defender, proteger.

shift, *v.t.* e *v.i.* mudar, transferir, remover; desviar, alterar; mover-se, mudar-se; mudar de direcção, de roupa; ganhar a vida; usar de frases equívocas. 1) *to shift about,* girar. 2) *to shift for oneself,* ganhar a vida sozinho. 3) *to shift off,* adiar. 4) *to shift one off,* desembaraçar-se de alguém.

shiftable, *adj.* mudável.

shifter, *s.* desviador (mec.); mentiroso, trapaceiro.

shiftiness, *s.* astúcia, velhacaria.

shifting, *s.* mudança; astúcia, artifício, expediente; *adj.* mudável, volante, móvel; astuto, velhaco; *shifting spanner,* chave-inglesa.

shiftless, *adj.* desamparado, sem recursos, sem camisa.

shifty, *adj.* abundante em recursos; astuto, velhaco.

shilling, *s.* xelim; *to take the King's shilling,* alistar-se no exército.

shimmer, *v.i.* vacilar, tremular (a luz), brilhar; *s.* luz vacilante, trémula.

shin, *s.* canela da perna; *v.t.* e *v.i.* (*shinning, shinned*), trepar; dar caneladas; subir agarrando-se com as pernas.

shinbone, *s.* tíbia.

shine, *v.i.* luzir, reluzir, brilhar, resplandecer, sobressair, distinguir-se; *v.t.* dar lustro (aos sapatos); *s.* brilho, claridade, lustre, resplendor. 1) *to take the shine out of a person,* eclipsar uma pessoa, excedê-la. 2) *to shine up to,* esforçar-se por agradar a alguém, engraxar alguém.

shiner, *s.* o que brilha.

shingle, *s.* seixo, pedrinha; sarrafo, ripa; letreiro, chapa (de médico), advogado, etc.); *v.t.* ripar, cobrir com ripas.

shingly, *adj.* coberto de seixos.

shining, *adj.* brilhante, resplandecente; *s.* esplendor, lustre, brilho.

shiny, *adj.* cintilante, brilhante.

ship, *s.* navio, embarcação, nau, barco. 1) *ship agent,* agente marítimo. 2) *ship boat,* escaler, bote, lancha. 3) *ship biscuit,* bolacha. 4) *ship boy,* grumete. 5) *ship-chandler,* fornecedor de navios. 6) *ship fever,* tifo. 7) *shipload,* carregamento. 8) *ship's log book,* diário de bordo; *v.t.* (*shipping, shipped*), embarcar, receber a bordo; transportar, remeter; expedir (com.); tripular; armar, montar (o leme, os remos, etc.); *v.i.* embarcar. 9) *to ship a sea,* receber uma vaga. 10) *to ship a crew,* contratar uma tripulação.

shipboard, *s.* bordo do navio; *to go on shipboard,* embarcar.

shipmaster, *s.* capitão do navio.

shipmate, *s.* companheiro de navio.

shipment, *s.* embarque, carregamento; remessa.

shipper, *s.* armador de navio, expedidor; carregador.

shipping, *s.* marinha mercante, navegação; navios, embarcações; embarque; *adj.* naval, marítimo, da marinha mercante; *ship intelligence,* notícias marítimas.

shipshape, *adj.* bem arranjado, ordenado.

shipwreck, *s.* naufrágio; desastre, ruína; *v.t.* naufragar.

shipwright, *s.* construtor naval; mestre construtor.

shipyard, *s.* estaleiro.

shire, *s.* condado, distrito; *shire-horse,* cavalo corpulento.

shirk, *v.t.* e *v.i.* esquivar-se; mostrar-se desentendido; faltar a; *s.* o que se esquiva a qualquer coisa.

shirt, *s.* camisa de homem; camisa de senhora com colarinho e punhos de engomar; revestimento de forno; *shirt-bosom ou front,* peito de camisa.

shiver, *s.* estremecimento, calafrio; pedaço, fragmento; roldana (náut.) *v.i.* tiritar, tremer; agitar-se; fazer-se em pedaços; estalar-se; *v.t.* romper; despedaçar.

shivering, *s.* estremecimento, arrepiamento, arrepio, calafrio; *adj.* que treme; *adv. shiveringly,* com calafrios.

shivery, *adj.* trémulo, quebradiço.

shoal, *s.* baixio, parcel, banco de areia, multidão, ajuntamento; cardume; *adj.* baixo, pouco fundo; *v.t.* e *v.i.* diminuir em profundidade; diminuir o fundo; ajuntar-se.

shock, *s.* choque, encontro, colisão; encontrão, recontro, combate; surpresa, susto; sobressalto, comoção, prostração nervosa; traumatismo; ofensa; monte de molhos de trigo; cabelo ou pêlo abundante; *shock-absorver,* amortecedor; *adj.* felpudo, lãzudo, peludo; *v.t.* e *v.i.* chocar, ofender, horrorizar; chocar-se, encontrar-se; fazer molhos de trigo.

shockhead, *adj.* com cabelo ou pêlo espesso.

shocking, *adj.* de mau gosto, irritante, ofensivo; horrível; *adv. shockingly,* chocantemente, escandalosamente.

shoddy, *adj.* de lã artificial; falso, aparente; *s.* imitação de lã.

shoe, *s.* sapato, calçado; ferradura; sapato ou calço de carruagem; descanso, almofada. 1) *shoe-horn,* calçadeira. 2) *it is quite another pair of shoes,* isso é outro par de botas. 3) *to die in one's shoes,* morrer na forca. 4) *to put the shoe on the right foot,* enfiar a carapuça a alguém. 5) *to know where the shoe pinches,* saber onde aperta o sapato; *v.t.* calçar, ferrar.

shoeing, *s.* acto de calçar ou ferrar.

shoeless, *adj.* descalço; desferrado.

shoe-maker, *s.* sapateiro.

shoer, *s.* ferrador.

shoot, *v.t.* e *v.i.* atirar, disparar, descarregar; ferir ou matar com arma de fogo; arremessar; lançar; aplainar; atravessar, passar rapidamente; fotografar, filmar (uma cena); dar um tiro; arremessar-se, passar rapidamente; fotografar, filmar (uma cena); dar um tiro; arremessar-se, passar rapidamente; brotar, germinar; latejar; sobressair. 1) *to shoot an arrow,* disparar uma seta. 2) *to shoot dice,* jogar dados. 3) *to shoot forth,* brotar, germinar; lançar-se, arremessar-se. 4) *to shoot up,* crescer, brotar. 5) *my legs are shooting,* as minhas pernas estão a latejar; *s.* rebento novo, renovo; tiro; passador; conduta, calha; rápido de rio.

shooter, *s.* atirador.

shooting, *s.* caça com espingarda; tiro; picada, dor aguda; *shooting star,* estrela-cadente.

shop, *s.* loja, estabelecimento, oficina; escola, colégio. 1) *shop-boy,* marçano. 2) *shop-walker,* vigilante de loja. 3) *shop-window,* montra. 4) *to come to the wrong shop,* enganar-se na porta; *v.i. (shopping, shopped),* ir às compras; fazer compras.

shopper, *s.* comprador.

shopping, acto de ir às compras.

shop-lifter, *s.* ladrão que rouba numa loja.

shopman, *s.* logista, caixeiro.

shorage, *s.* direitos de praia.

shore, *s.* praia, costa, terra, margem, borda; *to go on shore,* ir a terra; *v.t.* escorar; levar a terra.

shoreward, *adv.* em direcção à praia.

shoring, *s.* escoramento.

short, *adj.* curto, breve, reduzido, a breve prazo; resumido, pequeno, baixo; escasso, limitado, insuficiente, inadequado, próximo, perto. 1) *at short sight,* pagável depois de apresentado. 2) *to be short of,* estar longe de. 3) *to cut short,* cortar a palavra; abreviar. 4) *to fall short,* ser inferior. 5) *to make short of,* resolver rapidamente uma dificuldade. 6) *to make short work of,* dispor de, destruir ou consumir depressa. 7) *to take short,* cortar a palavra a alguém. 8) *short allowance,* meia-ração. 9) *short commons,* pouca quantidade de comida. 10) *short-handed,* que carece de mão de obra. 11) *short-lived,* passageiro, de passagem. 12) *short shipment,* mercadoria não embarcada. 13) *short sight,* miopia; falta de perspicácia. 14) *short witted,* pobre de espírito; *s.* sumário, resumo; substância; sílaba ou vogal breve; défice; *pl.* farelo misturado com farinha grossa; calções.

shortage, *s.* défice; falta (numa encomenda).

shortcoming, *s.* defeito, omissão, falta.

shorthand, *s.* taquigrafia, estenografia; *adj.* taquigráfico.

shortly, *adv.* brevemente, de caminho; em resumo.

shortness, *s.* brevidade, concisão; pequenez, curteza; deficiência.

shot, *s.* golpe, pancada, tiro de arma de fogo; projéctil; carga, bala; chumbo de arma; granada; distância de tiro; pontaria; bom atirador; jogada; escote, quota-parte. 1) *a bad shot,* má pontaria ou desacerto no adivinhar. 2) *I will have a shot at it,* vou tentar fazê-lo. 3) *snapshot,* instantâneo. 4) *a shot in the locker,* uma última reserva (de dinheiro ou comida, etc.); *v.t.* carregar com bala, chumbo ou granada; tornar muito pesado; *adj.* morto a tiro; ferido por um tiro.

shoulder, *s.* ombro, espádua; quarto dianteiro; parte saliente. 1) *shoulder blade,* omoplata. 2) *straight from the shoulder,* com toda a franqueza. 3) *to turn a cold shoulder,* com indiferença; mostrar indiferença; *v.t.* pôr, carregar ao ombro; olhar por cima do ombro; assumir (responsabilidade, trabalho); meter ombros; empurrar com violência.

shout, *s.* brado, grito (de alegria, de aplauso ou de exultação), exclamação, aclamação. 1) *shouts of laughter,* gargalhadas; *v.t.* e *v.i.* gritar, exclamar, dar vivas. 2) *to shout out,* gritar muito.

shouter, *s.* gritador, o que aplaude.

shouting, *s.* gritaria; aclamação; *adj.* que grita.

shove, *s.* empurrão, impulso; *v.t.* e *v.i.* empurrar, afastar, impelir. 1) *to shove along,* empurrar; fazer avançar. 2) *to shove away,* afastar, repelir; desviar. 3) *to shove from,* empurrar, afastar aos empurrões. 4) *to shove off,* deitar fora. 5) *to shove out,* fazer sair. 6) *to shove the queer,* passar dinheiro falso.

shovel, *s.* pá de ferro; *v.t. (shovelling, shoveled)* tirar ou amontoar com pá.

shovelfull, *s.* pazada.

show (showed, shown), *v.t.* mostrar, manifestar, fazer; ver, provar, demonstrar; indicar, explicar; justificar. *v.i.* parecer, ter aparência de; dar mostras de, aparecer, mostrar-se. 1) *to show in ou into,* mandar entrar; introduzir alguém nalguma parte. 2) *to show off,* descobrir, fazer; ostentar. 3) *to show out,* acompanhar à porta; expulsar de casa. 4) *to show up,* fazer subir, desmascarar; descobrir uma fraude. 5) *to show a clean pair of heels,* fugir, abalar; *s.* exibição, exposição, espectáculo; ostentação, pompa;

manifestação, aparência; pretexto; empresa, organização. 6) *to run the show*, dirigir a empresa. 7) *in open show*, publicamente. 8) *to vote by show of hands*, votar por mãos levantadas.

shower, *s.* o que mostra, mostrador; aguaceiro; chuveiro; cópia; abundância; *v.t.* derramar; distribuir liberalmente; *v.i.* chover, cair um aguaceiro.

showery, *adj.* chuvoso.

showily, *adv.* vistosamente, ostentosamente.

showy, *adj.* pomposo, vistoso.

shred (shredding, shredded), *v.t.* picar, retalhar, cortar em pedaços ou tiras; *s.* tira, pedaço, retalho; fragmento, partícula.

shreded, *adj.* retalhado.

shrew, *s.* víbora (mulher de mau feitio).

shrewd, *adj.* astuto, perspicaz, sagaz, fino; agudo, cortante; *adv. shrewdly,* astutamente; cortantemente.

shrewdness, *s.* sagacidade, perspicácia, finura, astúcia.

shrewish, *adj.* gritador, ralhador, gritante.

shriek, *s.* berro, grito, guincho; *v.i.* gritar, berrar.

shrift, *s.* confissão; absolvição.

shrike, *s.* esmerilhão.

shrill, *adj.* agudo (som), penetrante; *v.i.* produzir um som agudo e penetrante, guinchar, chiar.

shrimp, *s.* camarão; anão; homem pequeno (fam.); *v.i.* encurtar, encolher.

shrine, *s.* relicário, urna; santuário; ermida.

shrink (shrank, shrunk, shrunken), *v.i.* encolher-se, contrair-se, diminuir; abater; sucumbir; fugir dum perigo. 1) *to shrink away,* desaparecer gradualmente; fugir. 2) *to shrink up,* estreitar, estreitar-se; encolher-se; *s.* contracção; encolhimento; arrepiamento.

shrinkage, *s.* contracção, encolhimento; redução, diminuição.

shrinkingly, *adv.* encolhendo-se; retrocedendo.

shrive, *v.t.* e *v.i.* confessar, ouvir de confissão; confessar-se.

shrivel (shrivelling, shrivelled), *v.t.* enrugar, franzir, dobrar, encolher; estreitar; *v.t.* enrugar-se, franzir-se, encolher-se.

shriver, *s.* confessor.

shroud, *s.* mortalha; guarida, abrigo, amparo, protecção; *v.i.* amortalhar; cobrir; abrigar; defender, proteger, ocultar; esgalhar, desbastar; *v.i.* refugiar-se, ocultar-se.

shrub, *s.* arbusto; limonada de rum.

shrubbery, *s.* arbustos, bosquete.

shrubby, *adj.* semelhante a um arbusto; cheio de arbustos.

shrug (shrugging, shrugged), *v.t.* encolher, contrair; *v.i.* encolher os ombros; *s.* encolhimento de ombros.

shuck, *s.* casca, vagem, pele, concha; *v.t.* descascar, tirar a pele; tirar a concha à ostra; *not worth shucks,* que nada vale.

shudder, *v.i.* estremecer, tremer de medo; *s.* estremecimento, tremor.

shuffle, *s.* confusão; mistura; evasiva, escusa, artifício; fraude; arrasto de pés; *v.t.* e *v.i.* misturar, baralhar; confundir; pôr em desordem, enredar; iludir; desviar, repelir; esquivar; arrastar os pés. 1) *to shuffle of,* fugir duma dificuldade; sair de embaraços; desembaraçar-se de. 2) *to shuffle off,* fugir duma dificuldade; sair de embaraços; desembaraçar-se de. 3) *to shuffle off a fault to another,* lançar a culpa a outro.

shuffler, *s.* embusteiro, trapaceiro.

shuffling, *s.* subterfúgio, evasiva; confusão; andar irregular; o arrastar dos pés; *shuffling fellow,* chicaneiro.

shun (shunning, shunned), *v.t.* e *v.i.* evitar, fugir; retrair-se.

shunt, *v.t.* desviar, passar duma via para a outra (cam. de ferro); colocar derivações; colocar a corrente de derivações (elec.), iludir; mudar de curso ou de opinião; *s.* desvio; derivação (elec.).

shut (shutting, shut), *v.t.* fechar, cerrar, tapar, obstruir, vedar; *v.i.* fechar-se. 1) *to shut close,* fechar bem. 2) *to shut from,* excluir. 3) *to shut off,* excluir; impedir a entrada; cortar; interceptar. 4) *to shut up,* fechar completamente; calar-se; terminar; condenar; aprisionar. 5) *shut up!,* cale a boca!; *s.* acção de fechar; termo; fim; tampa, tapador; *adj.* cerrado, fechado. 6) *to get shut of,* desembaraçar-se de.

shuter, *s.* o que fecha; postigo, porta da janela; obturador (fot.). *v.t.* cobrir com postigos.

shutting, *s.* acto de fechar; *shutting out,* exclusão.

shuttle, *s.* lançadeira (tecel.).

shy, *adj.* tímido, assustadiço; reservado, cauteloso; esquivo, arisco; recatado, envergonhado; *v.i.* e *v.t.* esquivar-se, afastar-se, recuar, desviar-se; assustar-se; fazer desviar; lançar; arrojar; *s.* sobressalto;

acto de lançar; prova; *adv. shyly,* timidamente; reservadamente; com dissimulação.

shyness, *s.* timidez; reserva.

sibilant, *adj.* sibilante.

sibilation, *s.* sibilo, assobio, silvo.

sibyl, *s.* sibila.

sibyline, *adj.* sibilino.

sick, *adj.* mal, doente, enfermo; com náuseas. 1) *sick of,* cansado; farto de. 2) *sick head-ache,* enxaqueca com náuseas. 3) *sick leave,* licença por doença. 4) *sick-ward,* enfermaria. 5) *the sick,* os doentes. 6) *to fall sick,* adoecer. 7) *to be sick at heart,* ter o coração trespassado pela dor. 8) *to be sick for,* suspirar.

sicken, *v.t.* enfermar; fazer adoecer, cair doente; cansar-se; ter náuseas; desmaiar.

sickening, *adj.* nauseabundo, repugnante, asqueroso.

sickish, *adj.* adoentado, indisposto; nauseabundo.

sickle, *s.* foice.

sickly, *adj.* achacoso, doentio, lânguido, débil; *adv.* debilmente, com achaques.

sickness, *s.* doença, moléstia, enfermidade, indisposição, mal; náusea.

sicknurse, *s.* enfermeira.

side, *s.* lado, ilharga, flanco, costado; margem, borda; fracção, partido, parte, bordo, costado (do navio); bando; amurada; face, cara, aspecto; laço de parentesco; ares pretensiosos; *adj.* lateral; oblíquo. 1) *right side,* lado direito; lado bom. 2) *wrong side,* avesso (de tecido). 3) *side-arms,* armas portáteis, armas brancas. 4) *side-show,* exposição, exibição. 5) *to take sides with,* pôr-se do lado de; tomar partido por; *adj.* lateral, de lado; oblíquo; secundário. 6) *side glance,* olhar de soslaio; *v.t.* e *v.i.* tomar o partido de alguém; estar ao lado de; combinar; igualar.

sideboard, *s.* aparador.

sideface, *s.* perfil.

sidelong, *adj.* lateral, de lado; oblíquo; *adv.* lateralmente.

sidereal, *adj.* sideral, astral.

sidesman, *s.* assistente, ajudante.

sidewalk, *s.* passeio (da rua); calçada.

sideward(s), *adv.* de lado.

sideways, *adv.* de lado, obliquamente, através.

siding, *s.* desvio (de caminho de ferro); via lateral.

sidle, *v.i.* ir de lado, andar de lado; tomar o partido de alguém.

siege, *s.* sítio, cerco, assédio; assento; *to raise siege,* levantar um cerco.

siesta, *s.* sesta, sono da sesta.

sieve, *s.* peneira, joeira, crivo; ciranda.

sift, *v.t.* peneirar, joeirar, crivo, cirandar; examinar, esquadrinhar; aprofundar, sondar; dividir, separar; *to sift out,* investigar.

sifter, *s.* o que peneira; esquadrinhador; peneira, crivo.

sifting, *s.* acção de peneirar; exame.

sigh, *s.* suspiro; *v.i.* suspirar; *v.t.* lamentar.

sight, *s.* vista; visão; faculdade de ver; cena, espectáculo; aspecto; opinião, parecer; pontaria; visor; alçar de mira; abertura de mira. 1) *a sight of people,* uma multidão de gente. 2) *out of sight,* longe da vista; sem igual. 3) *to lose sight of,* perder de vista, não reparar em; *v.t.* avistar; fazer pontaria.

sighted, *adj.* assinalado; *short-sighted,* curto de vista.

sighting, *s.* pontaria.

sightless, *adj.* falho de vista; cego.

sightliness, *s.* elegância; aparência vistosa.

sightly, *adj.* agradável à vista, belo.

sign, *s.* sinal; indício; sintoma; tabuleta; insígnia; rubrica; signo do zodíaco; simbolo; vestígio; *the sign of the cross,* o sinal da cruz; *v.t.* firmar, rubricar, assinar; assinalar; marcar; representar, significar; fazer sinais; pôr uma marca.

signal, *s.* sinal, aviso; *adj.* notável, insigne, assinalado, memorável. 1) *signal failure,* fracasso total. 2) *signal station,* casa dos sinais de bordo. 3) *signal torch,* facho de sinais; *v.t.* e *v.i. (signalling, signalled):* fazer sinais, indicar.

signalize, *v.t.* assinalar, singularizar, particularizar.

signaller, *s.* sinaleiro.

signalling, *s.* transmissão de sinais.

signalman, *s.* sinaleiro.

signatory, *s.* signatário; assinante.

signature, *s.* assinatura; sinal, marca, prova.

signboard, *s.* tábua de sinais; tabuleta.

signer, *s.* signatário.

signet, *s.* sinete, selo.

significance, *s.* significação, expressão; significado; importância, ênfase.

significant, *adj.* significativo, expressivo, importante; *adv. significantly,* dum modo significativo.

signify, *v.t.* significar, expressar, manifestar,

dar a entender; representar, denotar; simbolizar; importar, valer; *v.t.* importar, ser significativo.

signor, *s.* senhor.

silence, *s.* silêncio; *interj.* silêncio!; *silence gives consent,* quem cala consente; *v.t.* impor silêncio, mandar ou fazer calar; sossegar; calar uma bateria.

silent, *adj.* silencioso; mudo; calado; taciturno; tranquilo, sossegado; quieto; *silent partner,* sócio comanditário.

silex, *s.* silex, sílice.

silhouetta, *s.* silhueta.

silica, *s.* sílica.

silicate, *s.* silicato.

silicated, *adj.* combinado com sílica.

silicon, *s.* silicone.

silk, *s.* seda. 1) *raw silk,* seda crua. 2) *silk cotton,* seda vegetal; *adj.* de seda.

silken, *adj.* de seda; sedoso; brando, suave.

silkiness, *s.* brandura, suavidade; efeminação.

silkworm, *s.* bicho-da-seda.

silky, *adj.* de seda; sedoso; macio, suave, lustroso.

sill, *s.* soleira; peitoril.

silly, *adj.* tolo, parvo, imbecil; estúpido, imprudente; absurdo, ridículo; *adv. sillily,* tolamente.

silt, *s.* lodo, lama, limo; aluvião, depósito sedimentar; *v.t.* e *v.i.* obstruir com lodo; assorear-se.

silting, *s.* assoreamento.

silty, *adj.* lodoso, sedimento.

silvan, *adj.* selvoso, cheio de bosques; silvestre; rústico, rural.

silver, *s.* prata; moedas de prata (com.); dinheiro; baixela de prata, prataria, cor de prata; *adj.* de prata, relativo a prata; prateado; argentino (também de som); eloquente; *v.t.* pratear; argentear; estanhar.

silverly, *adv.* como prata; com som argentino.

silvern, *adj.* (arc.) de prata; argentino.

silversmith, *s.* ourives de prata.

silverware, *s.* baixela de prata; prataria.

silvery, *adj.* prateado, argênteo; melodioso.

similar, *adj.* semelhante, parecido, homogéneo.

similarity, *s.* semelhança, conformidade, homogeneidade.

simile, *s.* comparação, analogia.

similitude, *s.* similitude, comparação, semelhança.

simper, *s.* sorriso tolo ou pretensioso; *v.t.* sorrir-se tolamente.

simpering, *s.* sorriso afectado.

simple, *adj.* simples, puro, fácil; ingénuo, cândido; néscio; insignificante; vulgar; *s.* simples, pessoa de condição humilde; ignorante, simplório; elemento.

simple-hearted, *adj.* franco, sincero.

simpleton, *s.* simplório.

simplicity, *s.* simplicidade, clareza, naturalidade; modéstia, singeleza; ignorância; rusticidade; ingenuidade.

simplify, *v.t.* simplificar.

simplism, *s.* simplismo.

simply, *adv.* simplesmente; meramente; verdadeiramente; tolamente.

simulacre, *s.* simulacro, imagem; representação, semelhança.

simulate, *v.t.* simular, fingir, aparentar.

simulation, *s.* simulação, dissimulação; imitação.

simultaneous, *adj.* simultâneo; *adv. simultaneously,* simultaneamente.

sin, *s.* pecado, culpa, maldade; transgressão, falta, ofensa; *deadly* ou *mortal sin,* pecado mortal; *v.i. (sinning, sinned),* pecar, faltar; errar.

sinapism, *s.* sinapismo.

since, *adv.* desde, desde então; há (tempo passado); *it is a month since,* há um mês; *prep.* desde, depois de; *conj.* desde que; já que, porque.

sincere, *adj.* sincero, franco, aberto; real, verdadeiro, genuíno; *adv. sincerely,* sinceramente.

sincerity, *s.* sinceridade.

sinew, *v.i.* fortalecer; *s.* tendão; músculo; nervo; fortaleza; força.

sinewy, *adj.* nervoso; forte, robusto.

sinful, *adj.* pecaminoso; *adv. sinfully,* pecaminosamente.

sinfulness, *s.* maldade, corrupção; má conduta.

sing (sang, sung), *v.t.* e *v.i.* cantar; murmurar (a água); gorjear (as aves); zumbir (os ouvidos). 1) *to sing out,* apregoar. 2) *to sing small,* falar em tom humilde; desempenhar papel secundário.

singe, *v.t.* chamuscar; danificar, prejudicar; *s.* chamuscada.

singeing, *s.* chamusco.

singer, *s.* cantor, cantora; chamuscador.

singing, *s.* canto. 1) *singing boy,* menino de coro. 2) *a singing bird,* uma ave canora.

single, adj. único, só, singular; simples; singelo; solteiro; solteira; puro, incorrupto. 1) single blessedness, o estado de solteiro. 2) single life, celibato. 3) not a single one, nem um sequer; v.t. escolher, distinguir, preferir (com out); s. jogo com uma pessoa de cada lado.

singleness, s. singeleza; sinceridade; unidade.

singleton, s. uma única carta dum naipe na mão dum jogador.

singular, adj. singular, único; estranho, peculiar; s. o singular (gram.).

sinister, adj. sinistro, funesto; de mau agoiro; adv. sinistrally, sinistramente.

sink (sank, sunk), v.t. afundar, meter a pique, submergir, mergulhar; fundear, sumir, afundar, escavar, abrir poço; humilhar, rebaixar; desbaratar, arruinar; ocultar, esconder; investir (capital); penetrar; descer, diminuir; absorver, chupar; to sink on one's knees, cair de joelhos; s. fundo do porão; cano de esgoto; pia, lavatório, latrina.

sinker, s. chumbo (de pesca); o que afunda ou submerge.

sinking, s. acto de submergir; abatimento; desmoronamento.

sinless, adj. impecável, isento de pecado; puro, santo; adv. sinlessly, dum modo impecável.

sinner, pecador, pecadora.

sinology, s. sinologia.

sinuosity, s. sinuosidade, meandro.

sinuous, adj. sinuoso, tortuoso.

sinus, s. enseada, baía; cavidade.

sip (sipping, sipped), v.t. beberricar; chupar, absorver; s. sorvo.

siphon, s. sifão; v.t. e v.i. extrair um líquido por meio de sifão.

sir, s. senhor, cavalheiro.

sire, s. pai, progenitor; macho dos animais; tratamento dado ao rei.

siren, s. sereia; mulher que fascina; sereia (de vapor, de automóvel, etc.); sereia, espécie de anfíbio; adj. fascinador.

sirloin, s. lombo de vaca.

siskin, s. verdilhão (ave).

sister, s. irmã; freira; sister-in-law, cunhada; adj. da mesma espécie; v.t. tratar como irmã.

sisterly, adj. fraternal, próprio de irmã.

sit (sitting, sat, sat), v.t. e v.i. sentar-se; assentar-se; estar sentado; empoleirar-se; reunir-se para deliberar; chocar; incubar; presidir, dar audiência; residir; ter assento no parlamento; montar bem; assentar, ajustar. 1) to sit by, sentar-se junto ou ao lado de. 2) to sit down, assentar-se; iniciar um cerco. 3) to sit up, velar, passar a noite. 4) to sit upon a person, oprimir uma pessoa, humilhar uma pessoa.

site, s. sítio, lugar; situação, postura; building sites, terrenos para construção.

sitter, s. o que está sentado; o que faz retratar-se; ave no choco.

sitting, s. acção de sentar-se; posição de quem está sentado; assento; assentada; audiência; sessão (para retrato); choco.

situate, adj. situado.

situation, s. situação; posição, condição; ofício, emprego; out of situation, desempregado.

six, adj. e s. seis; sena.

sixteen, adj. e s. dezasseis.

sixteenth, adj. e s. décimo sexto; adv. sixteenthly, em décimo sexto lugar.

sixth, adj. e s. sexto; a sexta parte.

sixty, adj. e s. sessenta.

size, s. tamanho, capacidade; bitola, calibre; estatura; classe; grandeza; craveira; ração, cola; v.t. e v.i. medir, classificar; calibrar; colar; julgar, formar uma opinião (fam.).

sized, adj. calibrado; de (tal) tamanho; que tem cola na sua composição. 1) middle sized, de estatura mediana. 2) full sized, de corpo inteiro (fot.).

sizzle, s. som sibilante; calor excessivo; v.t. e v.i. chiar, chamuscar(-se).

skate, s. patim; arraia (peixe); roller-skate, patim de rodas; v.t. patinar.

skater, s. patinador.

skating, s. patinagem.

skein, s. meada; confusão, enredo (fig.); bando de aves a voar.

skeleton, s. esqueleto; armação; ossada; esboço, esquema; skeleton key, chave-mestra.

skelter, v.i. andar apressado; s. pressa.

sketch, s. esboço, rascunho, borrão; v.t. esboçar, desenhar.

sketchable, adj. próprio para ser esboçado ou desenhado; adv. sketchily, em esboço.

sketchy, adj. da natureza dum esboço; esboçado; incompleto.

skew, s. desvio; engano; olhar estrábico; adj. oblíquo, esguelhado.

skewer, s. espeto de pau; florete; v.t. espetar.

ski, s. esqui; v.i. andar de esqui.

skid, s. travão, sapata, peia, calce, calço; v.t. (skidding, skidded), calçar, pegar de zorra, resvalar.

skiff, s. esquife, charuto (barco).

skiffer, s. patrão; capitão dum navio pequeno.

skilful, adj. destro, hábil; adv. skilfully, habilmente.

skill, s. perícia, habilidade, destreza, perícia.

skilled, adj. perito, hábil, destro.

skillet, s. caçarola.

skilly, s. sopa muito aguada.

skim, s. o acto de escumar; escuma. 1) skim milk, leite desnatado; v.t. e v.i. (skimming, skimmed), escumar; desnatar; roçar; focar ao de leve; passar à lima; deslizar, resvalar. 2) to skim over, resvalar; roçar; folhear um livro; tocar ao de leve uma questão.

skimmer, s. escumadeira, coadeira; ave aquática.

skimmings, s. pl. escumado.

skimp, v.t. e v.i. economizar; restringir; ser tacanho; fazer as coisas com imperfeição.

skimpiness, s. economia; mesquinhez; imperfeição.

skimping, adj. económico, poupado; mesquinho; imperfeito.

skin, s. pele, coiro, casca; casco; querena; forro; camisa de vela (náut.). 1) skindeep, superficial. 2) skin-tight, apertado como uma luva. 3) by the skin of one's teeth, por um triz; v.t. e v.i. (skinning, skinned), tirar a pele; esfolar; cobrir com pele; cobrir-se de pele.

skinflint, s. sovina, miserável.

skinner, s. esfolador, peleiro.

skinning, s. forro.

skinny, adj. magro, descarnado.

skip, s. salto, pulo; omissão duma parte; cubo, alcatruz (nas minas); v.t. e v.i. (skipping, skipped), pular, saltar, passar por alto, omitir.

skipper, s. capitão de navio.

skipping, s. acção de saltar; skipping-rope, corda de saltar.

skirmish, s. escaramuça, luta, rixa; v.i. escaramuçar.

skirmisher, s. escaramuçador.

skirmishing, s. escaramuças.

skirt, s. saia; aba, fralda; extremidade, orla, borda; skirts of a town, arredores duma cidade; v.t. e v.i. ladear; orlar; guarnecer, debruar; cingir; confinar.

skit, s. ataque satírico ou sarcástico;

pasquim, panfleto; seringa de pau de salgueiro (brinquedo).

skittish, adj. volúvel, leviano; atrevido, desavergonhado; apressado; medroso, espantadiço (cavalo); adv. skittishly, caprichosamente; levianamente.

skittishness, s. leviandade.

skive, v.t. cortar; aparar; polir.

skiver, s. máquina para aparar couro; coiro para encadernar.

skulk, v.i. esconder-se, esquivar-se, escapar--se.

skull, s. crânio; caveira; cérebro; inteligência; skull and crossbones, caveira com duas tíbias cruzadas, símbolo da morte.

skunk, s. doninha fedorenta; pessoa vil, pulha.

sky, s. céu, firmamento, abóbada celeste; tempo, atmosfera. 1) sky-blue, azul celeste. 2) sky-line, horizonte; v.t. levantar ao ar.

skyish, adj. semelhante ao céu; próximo do céu; elevado.

skylark, s. cotovia, calhandra; v.i. fazer travessuras.

skylight, s. clarabóia; escotilha (náut.).

skyward, adv. em direcção ao céu.

slab, s. prancha, tábua; placa, chapa; laje; v.t. (slabbing, slabbed), cortar (tábuas, lajes, etc.); adj. viscoso.

slabby, adj. babado; viscoso.

slack, adj. frouxo, bambo; descuidado; inactivo; slack-water, água estagnada; s. parte bamba duma corda; período de inactividade; carvão miúdo; v.i. e v.t. afrouxar; moderar; diminuir; enfraquecer(-se); adv. dum modo frouxo; insuficientemente.

sackly, adv. frouxamente.

slackness, s. frouxidão, lassidão; indolência, negligência.

slag, s. escória, escumalha; adv. slaggy, pertencente à escória.

slake, v.t. e v.i. apagar(-se), extinguir(-se); saciar; caldear (a cal).

slam, v.t. e v.i. fechar(-se) com violência; atirar com força; dar capote (no jogo); s. acção de fechar(-se) violentamente; to make a grand slam, ganhar todas as vazas.

slander, s. calúnia; difamação; v.t. difamar, caluniar.

slanderer, s. caluniador, difamador.

slandering, s. calúnia, maledicência, difamação; adj. maldizente, caluniador.

slanderous, adj. calunioso; adv. slanderously, caluniosamente.

slang, s. gíria, calão; tira estreita de terra; fantochada; v.t. e v.i. ralhar; injuriar empregando calão; adv. slangily, com palavras vulgares ou ofensivas.

slangy, adj. de natureza do calão; que emprega o calão.

slant, s. declive, obliquidade; plano inclinado; ponto de vista, opinião; esguelha; adj. oblíquo, de esguelha, inclinado; v.t. e v.i. obliquar, inclinar.

slanting, adj. inclinado, oblíquo, de viés; s. obliquidade; declive; adv. slatingly, oblíquamente; de esguelha.

slantwise, adv. obliquamente; de soslaio.

slap, s. palmada, sopapo; v.t. (slapping, slapped), dar palmadas ou pancadas; adv. de repente, de súbito; com pancada súbita.

slap-bang, adv. violentamente, de repente.

slapdash, adv. de repente, duma vez; ao acaso; adj. descuidado, feito ao acaso.

slapping, adj. muito rápido, muito grande; óptimo.

slash, s. cutilada; golpe ao acaso; corte; clareira; v.t. e v.i. acutilar, dar cutiladas em; açoitar; criticar; fazer cortes (salários, preços, etc.).

slat, s. lasca; tabuinha; pancada súbita e violenta.

slate, s. ardósia, loisa; lista de candidatos; programa dum partido; v.t. cobrir com ardósia; assentar uma loisa; pôr num programa; criticar com severidade.

slattern, s. mulher desmazelada.

slatternly, adv. negligentemente, desalinhadamente; adj. porco, desalinhado.

slaughter, s. matança, carnificina, mortandade; slaughter-house, açougue; v.t. matar, trucidar.

slaughterer, s. matador, magarefe.

slaughterous, adj. mortífero; slaughterously, de modo mortífero.

slave, s. escravo, servo; v.i. trabalhar como escravo; moirejar.

slaver, s. negreiro; navio negreiro; baba; v.t. e v.i. babar(-se); sujar com baba.

slavery, s. escravidão; adj. baboso.

slavey, s. criada.

Slavic, adj. eslavo.

slavish, adj. servil, baixo; adv. slavishly, servilmente.

slavishness, s. servilismo; escravidão; baixeza.

slay (slew, slain), v.t. matar; s. pente de tecelão.

slayer, s. assassino, matador.

sleazy, adj. delgado, franzino.

sledge, s. trenó; malho; v.t. e v.i. transportar ou viajar de trenó.

sleek, adj. liso, polido; brando, suave; insinuante; fingido; v.t. alisar, lustrar; suavizar, acalmar; deslizar; adv. skeekly, brandamente; dum modo insinuante.

sleeky, adj. suave, liso; manhoso.

sleep, s. sono, descanso, repouso. 1) to go to sleep, adormecer. 2) to put to sleep, adormecer (alguém); v.t. dormir, descansar, repousar. 3) to sleep away, dissipar, desperdiçar tempo dormindo. 4) to sleep over, consultar o travesseiro. 5) to sleep upon, não fazer caso de; descuidar-se. 6) we did not sleep a wink, não pregámos olho.

sleeper, s. o que dorme; dorminhoco; viga, barrote, dormente.

sleepily, adv. com sonolência.

sleepiness, s. sonolência.

sleeping, s. sono, descanso; adj. que serve para dormir, soporífero. 1) sleeping-draught, poção soporífera, calmante. 2) sleeping-partner, sócio comanditário. 3) sleeping-room, dormitório.

sleepless, adj. falto de sono, insone; adv. sleeplessly, sem sono.

sleeplessness, s. insónia.

sleepy, adj. sonolento, letárgico.

sleet, s. geada, chuva com neve ou saraiva.

sleety, adj. de chuva e neve.

sleeve, s. manga; camisa (mec.). 1) sleeve-band, punho. 2) to laugh in the sleeve, rir-se à sucapa. 3) to wear one's heart on one's sleeve, ter o coração na boca; ser desbocado.

sleeved, adj. com mangas.

sleeveless, adj. sem mangas; sem pretexto.

sleight, s. habilidade, perícia; ardil, artifício; sleight of hands, prestidigitação.

slender, adj. delgado; esbelto; esguio; débil; inadequado; escasso, pequeno, insuficiente; adv. slenderly, de modo escasso, insuficiente.

sleuth, s. detective; sleuth-hound, cão de caça, sabujo.

slice, s. fatia, talhada, tira, posta, rodinha; camada; espátula; escumadeira; batida errada na bola (no golfe); v.t. cortar em fatias; partir, dividir; jogar na direcção errada.

slicer, s. talhador; o que talha; faca larga e chata; instrumento para lapidar.

slick, *adj.* macio, escorregadio; insincero, cínico; simples; *adv.* directamente, completamente.

slide, *v.i. e v.t.* resvalar, escorregar, deslizar; passar gradualmente dum estado para outro; fazer deslizar; *s.* acção de deslizar; escorrega; plano inclinado; desmoronamento; travessa (para cabelo). 1) *slide rule,* régua de cálculo. 2) *slide valve,* válvula distribuidora.

slider, *s.* o que escorrega; cursor.

sliding, *s.* escorregadela, escorregamento, deslizamento; lapso; *adj.* corredio, volúvel; de cursor; *sliding door,* porta de correr.

slight, *s.* indiferença; descuido, desprezo; desconsideração, desfeita; *to make slight of,* fazer pouco caso de; *adj.* ligeiro, leve, insignificante, fútil; desdenhoso; *v.t.* desprezar, desdenhar; descuidar.

slighting, *s.* menosprezo. desdém; descuido; *adj.* desdenhoso; *adv. slightingly,* com desprezo.

slightly, *adv.* com desprezo.

slim, *adj.* magro, delgado, esguio, franzino; insignificante, ténue.

slime, *s.* lama, limo, lodo; *v.t. e v.i.* enlamear, enlodar.

slimy, *adj.* viscoso, pegajoso, glutinoso; limoso, lodoso; escorregadio; *adv. slimily,* viscosamente.

sling, *s.* funda (para atirar pedras); tiro de funda; boldrié; cabo (de guindar); atadura; estropo (náut.); *v.t. e v.i.* atirar com a funda; arremessar; suspender; pôr a tiracolo; atar.

slink, *v.i.* escapulir-se, safar-se; *v.i.* parir prematuramente, abortar; *s.* parto prematuro; criança ilegítima.

slip, *s.* escorregadela; lapso; falta; recuo da hélice; tira; trela; plano inclinado; estaca; enxerto; linguado (imp.); *v.t. e v.i. (slipping, slipped),* fazer deslizar, introduzir secretamente; omitir; saltar; desatar, livrar-se de; parir prematuramente; deslizar, resvalar; deslocar-se; escapar-se; cair em falta. 1) *to slip down,* deixar-se cair. 2) *to slip off,* soltar. 3) *to slip out,* escapar-se à sorrelfa; deslocar um osso. 4) *to slip one's clothes on,* vestir-se depressa.

slipknot, *s.* nó corredio.

slipper, *s.* chinela; avental de criança.

slippery, *adj.* escorregadio; movediço; incerto.

slipping, *s.* deslize.

slippy, *adj.* escorregadio; incerto, instável.

slipshod, *adj.* o que traz os sapatos cambados; desmazelado.

slipslop, *s.* zurrapa; composição fraca.

slipway, *s.* plano inclinado; pista onde um avião levanta voo.

slit, *s.* racha, fenda; *v.t. (slitting, slitted)* rachar, fender; rachar-se.

slither, *v.i.* resvalar, escorregar; *s.* pedra solta; entulho; dinheiro falso.

slithery, *adj.* escorregadio.

sliver, *s.* fatia, posta; lasca; torçal, mecha; esgalho, ramo; *v.t. e v.i.* rachar; cortar em tiras.

slobber, *v.t. e v.i.* babar, babar-se; sujar de baba; *s.* baba.

sloe, *s.* ameixa brava.

slogan, *s.* lema, mote.

sloop, *s.* chalupa; corveta.

slop, *v.i. e v.t.* transbordar; derramar, sujar; *s.* (pl.) água suja; alimento líquido (sopa, leite, etc.), roupa mal feita e barata; *to live on slops,* estar a meia dieta.

slope, *s.* declive; talude; vertente; rampa; escarpa; *v.t. e v.i.* esguelhar, obliquar; inclinar; desaparecer, fugir.

sloping, *adj.* oblíquo; em declive, inclinado; *adv. slopingly,* de esguelha, com declive.

sloppy, *adj.* molhado e sujo; lamacento; descuidado.

slosh, *s.* lama mole; neve meio derretida; massa oleosa para lubrificar; *v.i.* patinhar em lama; andar vagarosamente.

sloshy, *adj.* lamacento.

slot, *s.* pista, rasto; barra; ferrolho; ranhura; *v.t. (slotting, slotted),* abrir ranhuras; ajustar numa ranhura.

sloth, *s.* preguiça, indolência, lentidão; preguiça (zool.).

slothful, *adj.* preguiçoso, indolente, inactivo; *adv. slothfully,* indolentemente.

slouch, *s.* postura ou andar relaxado; inclinação do corpo; pessoa grosseira; *v.i.* andar curvado; ter um aspecto rústico; *v.t.* virar a aba para baixo.

slough, *s.* lamaçal, pântano, estado de depressão mental; pele que a serpente muda; crosta de chaga; tecido morto; *v.t. e v.i.* separar; mudar a pele (a serpente).

sloughy, *adj.* lamacento; que tem crosta.

sloven, *s.* homem desalinhado.

slovenliness, *s.* desalinho, falta de asseio; porcaria.

slovenly, *adj.* desalinhado, porco; *adv.* porcamente.

slow, *adj.* vagaroso, lento, tardio; estúpido; *my watch is slow,* o meu relógio está atrasado; *v.t.* diminuir a velocidade; *adv. slowly,* vagarosamente.

slowness, *s.* lentidão, vagar.

slue, *v.t.* torcer, retroceder (náut.).

slug, *s.* lesma; mandrião; mono; pedaço de metal, pepita.

sluggard, *s.* madraço.

sluggish, *adj.* indolente, preguiçoso; inerte; *adv. sluggishly,* lentamente; indolentemente.

sluice, *s.* comporta; saída; canal artificial; masseira, calha; *v.t.* abrir a comporta; lavar com jorro de água; derramar.

slum, *s.* bairro pobre e sujo; bairro de barracas; *v.i.* visitar os bairros pobres.

slumber, *s.* sono ligeiro, sonolência; repouso; *v.i.* dormitar, estar descuidado.

slumberer, *s.* dorminhoco.

slumbering, acção de dormitar; *adj.* sonolento.

slump, *s.* queda, baixa repentina em preços; declínio súbito, colapso, fracasso; diminuição de interesse num assunto; *v.i.* cair bruscamente, tombar; baixar subitamente (preço); fracassar, frustrar-se.

slur (slurring, slurred), *v.t.* escrever ou pronunciar indistintamente, mascarrar, borrar; passar por alto, omitir; manchar, enganar; modular (mús.); *s.* mancha na reputação; reparo, observação.

slush, *s.* lama; neve meio derretida; graxa para lubrificação; sebo.

slushy, *adj.* lamacento; mole; lamechas (fig.).

sluttish, *adj.* porco, desmazelado.

sly, *adj.* astuto, manhoso; falso, dissimulado; *on the sly,* pela calada; *adv. slyly,* astutamente, dissimuladamente; pela calada.

slyness, *s.* astúcia, manha.

smack, *s.* sabor, gosto; cheiro, aroma; noção, laivos, vestígios; tintura; som agudo, estalido; beijo estalado, beijoca; palmada; sumaca (barco); *v.t.* beijocar; bater, dar palmadas; *to smack the lips,* fazer estalar os lábios, mostrar satisfação; *v.i.* saber, ter sabor; cheirar; dar estalos com a boca.

smacker, *s.* beijoca.

small, *adj.* pequeno, miúdo, baixo, curto, pouco; mesquinho; débil, brando, obscuro. 1) *small-clothes,* calções. 2) *small-fry,* peixinhos; gente miúda; coisas pequenas. 3) *small hours,* as primeiras horas depois da meia-noite. 4) *small-pox,* varíola. 5) *small* *wares,* artigos miúdos (botões, agulhas, linhas, etc.). 6) *in a small way,* com pequeno capital ou sortimento; em pequena escala; sem ostentação. 7) *to think small beer of,* ter fraca opinião de; *s.* parte estreita de qualquer coisa; *pl.* calções; exame preliminar; *adv.* em tom baixo, suavemente.

smallage, *s.* aipo silvestre.

smallish, *adj.* um tanto pequeno.

smallness, *s.* pequenez; insignificância.

smalt, *s.* esmalte.

smart, *adj.* vivo, activo; esperto; bem vestido, elegante, à moda; picante, mordaz; *be smart!,* depressa!; *s.* dor pungente, aflição; *v.i.* sentir dor; arder, doer; torcer-se; *adv. smartly,* de modo pungente; elegantemente.

smarten, *v.t.* tornar elegante; aformosear, embelezar, picar.

smartness, *s.* agudeza, viveza, astúcia; elegância.

smash, *s.* rompimento, quebra, falência; refresco de conhaque com açúcar; *to go to smash,* ir para a ruína; *v.t.* e *v.i.* quebrar, arrombar; despedaçar; falir.

smasher, *s.* o que esmaga; coisa extraordinária.

smashing, *adj.* que serve para esmagar ou despedaçar; irresistível; extraordinário; muito activo (fam.).

smatter, *v.i.* falar ou saber superficialmente; *s.* tintura; leve noção.

smatterer, *s.* pedante, pretensioso no falar.

smear, *s.* substância untuosa; nódoa de gordura; termo ofensivo; *v.t.* untar, sujar, lambuzar.

smeary, *adj.* untuoso, gorduroso; viscoso.

smell, *s.* cheiro, olfacto; faro; aroma, perfume; mau cheiro, fedor; *v.t. (smelled, smelt)* farejar, cheirar, perceber, descobrir. 1) *to smell a rat,* suspeitar; *v.i.* cheirar. 2) *to smell of,* cheirar a.

smelliness, *s.* mau cheiro, cheiro activo.

smelling, *s.* acção de cheirar; o olfacto. 1) *smelling-bottle,* frasco de perfume; *adj.* que cheira, cheiroso. 2) *sweet smelling,* odorífero, cheiroso. 3) *foul smelling,* fedorento.

smelly, *adj.* malcheiroso.

smelt, *s.* salmonete; *v.t.* fundir (metais).

smelter, *s.* fundidor.

smelting, *s.* fusão. 1) *smelting-furnace,* forno de alta pressão. 2) *smelting-pot,* cadinho.

smile, *s.* sorriso; favor, graça; *v.i.* sorrir; favorecer, ser propício; mostrar desprezo.

smiling, *adj.* risonho; alegre; *adv. smilingly,* sorrindo, dum modo risonho.

smirch, *s.* mancha, nódoa, farrusca, mascarra; *v.t.* sujar, manchar; rebaixar, desonrar.

smirk, *s.* sorriso afectado; *v.i.* sorrir com afectação.

smite, *v.t.* e *v.i. (smote, smitten),* bater, golpear; ferir, castigar; arruinar, destruir; afligir, excitar; chocar-se, ir de encontro a; *s.* pancada, golpe; tentativa.

smith, *s.* ferreiro; forjador de metais. 1) *goldsmith,* ourives. 2) *locksmith,* serralheiro. 3) *smith's fire,* forja.

smithery, *s.* ferraria; forja, obra de ferreiro.

smock, *s.* bata de mulher; avental abotoado; blusa comprida de camponês.

smoke, *s.* fumo; fumaça, fumarada. 1) *no smoke without fire,* não há fumo sem fogo. 2) *to have a smoke,* fumar, dar uma fumada; *v.i.* e *v.t.* fumegar; fumar; defumar; farejar, descobrir; (com *out*) expulsar por meio de fumo. 3) *to smoke dry,* secar ao fumeiro.

smoker, *s.* fumador.

smoking, *s.* acção de fumar. 1) *smoking--room,* sala de fumo. 2) *smoking-jacket,* casaco de cerimónia.

smoky, *adj.* fumarento; fumegante; sujo de fumo; *adv. smokily,* com fumo, fumegando.

smooth, *adj.* liso, polido; plano, igual; suave, brando, manso, tranquilo; regular, uniforme; cortês, afável; insinuante; adulador. 1) *smoothfaced,* sem barba; imberbe. 2) *smooth-tongued,* melífluo; *v.t.* aplanar, polir; alisar; facilitar, abrandar; *adv. smoothly,* suavemente; regularmente.

smoothness, *s.* lisura, igualdade; suavidade, brandura.

smother, *v.t.* sufocar, abafar; suprimir; *v.i.* estar sufocado.

smudge, *s.* mancha, nódoa; tisna; fumo sufocante; *v.t.* manchar, tisnar, enegrecer; *adv. smudgily,* dum modo sujo.

smudginess, *s.* sujidade; negrura.

smudgy, *adj.* tisnado, sujo; fumegante.

smug, *adj.* presumido; asseado.

smuggle, *v.t.* passar contrabando.

smuggler, *s.* contrabandista.

smuggling, *s.* contrabando.

smugly, *adv.* elegantemente, afectadamente.

smugness, *s.* janotice; afectação no trajar; presunção.

smut, *s.* tisna, farrusca, mancha; linguagem obscena; *v.t.* mascarrar; enfarruscar; manchar.

smutty, *adj.* enfarruscado; mascarrado; obsceno; *adv. smuttily,* sujamente; indecentemente.

snack, *s.* refeição ligeira; bocado.

snaffle, *s.* bridão; *v.t.* refrear, conter, agarrar pelo bridão.

snag, *s.* protuberância, saliência, nó de madeira; tronco à tona da água que estorva a navegação.

snagged, *adj.* nodoso; cheio de troncos.

snail, *s.* caracol; pessoa lerda; *snail-pace,* a passo de caracol.

snake, *s.* cobra, serpente; *rattle-snake,* cobra cascavel; *v.t.* enrolar uma corda em espiral.

snaky, *adj.* serpentino; cheio de serpentes; enganador.

snap, *s.* quebra repentina dum objecto; ruído repentino; estalo; mola; energia; refeição ligeira, dentada; *(snapping, snapped) v.i.* morder, abocanhar; quebrar, partir; rachar; agarrar; dar um estalo; interromper, cortar a palavra a alguém.

snappish, *adj.* mordaz; arisco; respondão; teimoso; *adv. snappishly,* mordazmente; asperamente.

snapshot, *s.* tiro rápido; instantâneo (fot.).

snare, *s.* laço, armadilha, artimanha; *v.t.* enredar, emaranhar; apanhar no laço.

snarl, *s.* rosnadura; rixa; nó, fio enredado; nó da madeira; *v.i.* rosnar, resmungar; *v.t.* enredar, emaranhar, confundir.

snarling, *adj.* que rosna; rabugento; raivoso.

snarly, *adj.* enredoso, insidioso.

snatch, *s.* apanhadura; arrebatamento; bocadito; um momento; refeição ligeira; *by snatches,* com intervalos; aos saltos; por capricho; *v.t.* agarrar, apanhar com precipitação; *v.i.* arrebatar, esforçar-se por.

snatcher, *s.* o que arrebata; ladrão.

sneak, *s.* homem vil, delator, gatuno; *v.i.* ir ou vir à sorrelfa; portar-se com vileza; rastejar; delatar; *v.i.* furtar; *a soapy sneak,* um engraxador (delator).

sneaking, *adj.* covarde; vil, desprezível; ordinário; furtivo, encoberto; *adv. sneakingly,* vilmente, rasteiramente.

sneaky, *adj.* baixo, vil; oculto.

sneer, *s.* olhar ou riso de desprezo; escárnio; *v.i.* olhar ou falar com desprezo; escarnecer, mofar, chacotear.

sneerer, *s.* chacoteador, escarnecedor, trocista.

sneering, adj. escarnecedor; s. acção de rir com desprezo; adv. sneeringly, com desdém.

sneeze, s. espirro; v.i. espirrar; desdenhar; to sneeze at, fazer pouco caso.

snicker, s. riso sufocado; v.i. rir-se de modo abafado.

sniff, s. olfacto; aspiração; fungadela; v.t. aspirar; v.i. fungar, sorver o monco.

sniffle, s. fungadela; v.t. fungar, choramingar.

sniffy, adj. desdenhoso, altaneiro; ligeiramente malcheiroso.

snip, v.t. tesourar, cortar com tesoura; v.i. dar tesouradas; to snip up, retalhar; s. tesourada; pedaço; retalho.

snipe, s. narceja; v.t. e v.i. ir caçar narcejas; atirar sobre o inimigo dum lugar escondido.

snipper, s. o que corta com tesoura; alfaiate; snipper-snapper, pessoa insignificante.

snippet, s. recorte, pequeno retalho, pequena porção.

snippety, adj. trivial, insignificante.

snivel, s. ranho; monco; sentimento hipócrita; v.i. choramingar.

sniveller, s. chorão, choramingas; ranhoso, moncoso.

snivelling, adj. ranhoso, choroso; s. acção de choramingar ou deitar monco.

snively, adj. choroso, ranhoso.

snob, s. snobe, pretensioso.

snobbery, s. snobismo.

snobbish, adj. próprio do que tem pretensões a aristocrata; adv. snobbishly, snobemente.

snobbism, s. snobismo.

snooze, s. soneca, sesta. v.i. dormir uma soneca, dormitar.

snore, s. ronco; v.i. ressonar, roncar.

snoring, s. ronco.

snort, s. bufo, ronco, resfôlego; v.t. e v.i. resfolegar, bufar.

snot, s. monco.

snotty, adj. nevoso; moncoso.

snout, s. focinho; nariz (fam.); tromba de elefante; bico.

snouted, adj. focinhudo.

snouty, adj. parecido com um focinho.

snow, s. neve, nevada; inverno; embarcação; v.t. e v.i. cobrir de neve, nevar.

snowdrift, s. montículo de neve feito pela acção do vento.

snowy, adj. nevoso; níveo; puro, imaculado.

snub, s. repreensão; desprezo; desconsideração; descortesia; adj. chato e arrebitado

(o nariz); v.t. (snubbing, snubbed), acolher mal, tratar com aspereza, repelir, mostrar má cara; humilhar intencionalmente.

snuff, s. morrão; coto de vela; tabaco em pó; rapé; cheiro; enfado; v.t. e v.i. aspirar, cheirar, sorver pelo nariz; espevitar; tomar rapé; to snuff out, espevitar.

snuffer, s. tabaquista; espevitador; pl. espevitadeira, espevitador.

snuffle, s. som fanhoso; pl. catarro nasal; v.i. falar fanhoso; respirar pelo nariz.

snuffy, adj. que cheira a rapé; dado ao uso do rapé; sujo de rapé.

snug, adj. agasalhado; aconchegado; confortável; apertado; em ordem; v.t. ajustar, acomodar; estar a gosto.

snuggery, s. retiro confortável; aposento particular; reservado.

snuggle, v.i. aninhar-se, aconchegar-se.

snugly, adv. comodamente.

snugness, s. aconchego.

so, adv. desta maneira, assim; portanto; tão, tanto, de tal modo; também, de igual modo, o, isso, aquilo (para evitar a repetição duma palavra ou frase); assim, bem; conj. contanto que, no caso de. 1) so?, deveras?, de verdade? 2) so so, assim, assim. 3) so as to, de maneira a. 4) so that, de maneira a que. 5) so then, de modo que. 6) so much as, tanto como; ao menos. 7) so be it, assim seja. 8) and so on ou forth, e assim por diante, etc. 9) so far, até aqui. 10) or so, mais ou menos. 11) quite so, isso mesmo; exacto. 12) so do I!, também eu! 13) Mr. So and so, fulano.

soak, s. acção de embeber, de empapar; borrachão; orgia; v.t. e v.i. embeber; pôr de molho, impregnar; infiltrar; estar ensopado.

soaker, s. borrachão; o que embebe.

soaking, s. acção de embeber; o ficar-se ensopado com a chuva; adj. que molha completamente.

soaky, adj. ensopado, cheio de água.

so-and-so, s. pessoa indeterminada ou imaginária; fulano.

soap, s. sabão. 1) soap-ball, sabonete. 2) soap suds, água de sabão, saponária. 3) soft soap, sabão mole; adulação, lisonja; v.t. ensaboar; lisonjear.

soapy, adj. saponáceo; cheio de sabão; brando, mole; adulador (fam.).

soar, s. voo elevado; rasgo; ascensão; alcance (da imaginação); v.i. voar muito alto; remontar-se; sublimar-se.

sob, s. soluço, suspiro; v.i. (sobbing, sobbed), soluçar; suspirar.

sobbing, s. soluços.

sober, adj. sóbrio, moderado, discreto; prudente, sensato, sério; sereno; modesto; sombrio, de cor apagada; não ébrio; sober-minded, desapaixonado; sereno; v.t. desembriagar; sossegar; v.i. tornar-se sóbrio, moderado; adv. soberly, sobriamente; com moderação.

so-called, adj. assim chamado, pseudo, suposto.

soccer, s. futebol.

sociability, s. sociabilidade.

sociable, adj. sociável, comunicativo, dado; urbano, polido; s. carro com dois assentos, um em frente do outro; espécie de side-car; cadeira de espaldar em forma de S; adv. sociably, socialmente; sociavelmente.

social, adj. social, sociável; afável; gregário; adv. socially, socialmente.

socialism, s. socialismo.

socialist, s. socialista.

sociality, s. sociabilidade; gregarismo.

society, s. sociedade.

sociology, s. sociologia.

sock, s. meia curta, peúga; soco, golpe; v.t. socar, golpear.

socker, s. futebol.

socket, s. encaixe, o receptáculo ou pé em que se encaixa qualquer coisa. 1) the socket of the eye, órbita do olho. 2) the socket of a tooth, alvéolo do dente.

sod, s. torrão, turfa; adj. relvoso; v.t. cobrir com relva; the old sod, a pátria.

soda, s. soda; soda-water, água saturada de ácido carbónico.

sodden, adj. molhado, empapado.

sodium, s. sódio (metal).

sodomy, s. sodomia.

soever, adv. por, por mais que seja; emprega-se sempre que se queira alargar o sentido de who, what, where, how, etc.

sofa, s. sofá, canapé.

soft, s. pessoa tola, mole; adj. brando, suave, mole; macio, terno; afável; manso; efeminado, fraco; sibilante (gram.); doce (água); adv. devagarinho; sossegadamente; interj. devagar!, suspenda!, pare!. 1) soft eggs, ovos quentes. 2) soft soap, lisonja. 3) to have a soft place in one's head, ter a cabeça fraca.

soften, v.t. abrandar; suavizar, mitigar;

enternecer; efeminar; v.i. abrandar-se, amolecer, enternecer-se.

softening, adj. emoliente; s. brandura, enternecimento, suavidade; soft of the brain, amolecimento cerebral.

softly, adv. devagarinho, suavemente; ternamente, em voz baixa.

softness, s. brandura, suavidade; afabilidade; efeminação.

softy, s. pessoa tola.

soggy, adj. húmido, encharcado.

soil, s. solo, terra arável; região; país; sujidade, espojadouro; porcaria; mancha; esterco, estrume. 1) native soil, terra natal; v.t. e v.i. sujar; manchar; estrumar; sujar-se. 2) to refuse to soil one's hands, recusar-se a fazer trabalho desonroso.

soiling, s. acção de sujar ou de estrumar; alimentar gado em curral.

soirée, s. sarau.

sojourn, s. residência temporária; v.i. residir temporariamente.

sol, s. sol; sol (mús.); oiro (her.); Febo.

solace, s. consolação, alívio; v.t. confortar; consolar; aliviar.

solar, adj. solar.

solder, s. solda; v.t. soldar.

soldier, s. soldado, militar; v.i. servir o exército, ir como soldado.

soldiery, s. soldadesca.

sole, s. planta do pé, sola; sola de calçado; linguado (peixe); adj. só, sozinho; único; solteiro; exclusivo; v.t. deitar solas; adv. solely, unicamente.

solemn, adj. solene; majestoso; adv. solemnly, solenemente.

solemnity, s. solenidade.

solemnization, s. solenização, celebração.

solemnize, v.t. solenizar, celebrar solenemente.

sol-fa, s. solfejo; v.t. solfejar.

solfeggio, s. solfejo.

solicit, v.t. solicitar, pedir, rogar; importunar; induzir.

solicitation, s. solicitação; instigação.

solicitor, s. solicitador, procurador; pretendente.

solicitous, adj. solícito, ansioso, diligente; adv. solicitously, solicitamente.

solicitude, s. solicitude, ansiedade, cuidado.

solid, s. sólido; adj. sólido, compacto; maciço, duro; firme.

solidarity, s. solidariedade.

solidification, s. solidificação.

solidify, *v.t.* solidificar.

solidity, *s.* solidez, consistência, firmeza.

solidness, *s.* solidez, consistência, firmeza; dureza.

soliloquy, *s.* solilóquio.

solitaire, *s.* solitário; paciência, jogo de cartas jogado por uma só pessoa; ermitão; *adv.* solitariamente.

solitary, *s.* solitário, ermitão, *adj.* só, sozinho; solitário.

solitude, *s.* solidão; vida solitária.

solo, *s.* solo (mús. e jogo).

soloist, *s.* solista.

so-long, *int.* adeus.

solstice, *s.* solstício.

solubility, *s.* solubilidade.

soluble, *adj.* solúvel.

solution, *s.* solução, resolução; explicação, esclarecimento; separação, ruptura; solução (fís., quím., med.); solução de borracha.

solvability, *s.* solvabilidade.

solvable, *adj.* dissolúvel, solúvel; explicável; solvente; pagável.

solve, *v.t.* resolver, solver, dissolver; explicar; pagar.

solvency, *s.* solvência, solvabilidade.

solvent, *adj.* solvível; solvente, solúvel; dissolutivo; *s.* dissolvente.

somatic, *adj.* somático.

sombre, *adj.* sombrio, escuro; triste, melancólico; *adv. sombrely,* sombriamente.

sombreness, *s.* escuridão; tristeza, melancolia.

some, *adj.* algum, alguma, alguns, algumas; certo (bastante); uns, umas (mais ou menos). 1) *some twelve persons were at that party,* estavam umas doze pessoas nessa festa; *pron.* algum, alguma, alguns, algumas; uma porção; uma parte. 2) *someone:* alguém, uma certa pessoa; *suf.* para formar adjectivos de substantivos ou doutros adjectivos: *lonesome, quarrelsome,* etc.

somebody, *s.* alguém, pessoa importante; *pron.* alguém.

somehow, *adv.* de alguma forma; seja como for.

someone, *pron.* alguém.

somersault, *s.* cambalhota, salto mortal; *v.i.* dar cambalhotas, dar saltos mortais.

something, *s.* alguma coisa; *adv.* um tanto, algo; *knock me something off,* faça-me um desconto (no preço).

sometime, *adv.* nalguma ocasião; antigamente.

sometimes, *adv.* algumas vezes, de vez em quando.

somewhat, *adv.* um tanto, algo; *s.* alguma coisa.

somewhere, *adv.* algures.

somnambulism, *s.* sonambulismo.

somnambulist, *s.* sonâmbulo.

somniferous, *a.* sonífero.

somnolent, *adj.* sonolento; *adv. somnolently,* com sonolência.

son, *s.* filho. 1) *son-in-law,* genro. 2) *godson,* afilhado. 4) *grandson,* neto. 5) *stepson,* enteado.

sonant, *s.* letra sonante; *adj.* sonante, sonoro.

sonata, *s.* sonata.

song, *s.* canto; canção; bagatela. 1) *an old song,* uma bagatela. 2) *to sing the same song,* repetir a mesma coisa.

songster, *s.* cantor; ave canora.

songstress, *s.* cantora.

sonnet, *s.* soneto.

sonny, *s.* filhinho.

sonority, *s.* sonoridade.

sonorous, *adj.* sonoro.

sonship, *s.* filiação.

soon, *adv.* depressa, em pouco tempo; cedo; prontamente; de boa vontade; *as soon as,* logo que.

sooner, *comp.* de *soon;* mais depressa; antes, melhor; *the sooner the better;* quanto antes, melhor.

soonest, *sup.* de *soon; at the soonest,* quanto antes; o mais cedo.

soot, *s.* fuligem; *v.t.* cobrir com fuligem.

sooth, *s.* verdade, realidade; *adj.* verdadeiro; *adv.* na verdade.

soothe, *v.t.* acalmar, aliviar; adular, lisonjear.

soothing, *adj.* calmante, acariciador; *s.* mitigação; adulação; *adv. soothingly,* com doçura, em tom acariciador.

soothsayer, *s.* adivinho, profeta.

sooty, *adj.* fuliginoso.

sop, *s.* sopa; suborno, presente; *milksop,* rapaz ou homem sem energia; *v.t.* *(sopping, sopped),* ensopar, embeber.

sophism, *s.* sofisma.

sophist, *s.* sofista; chicaneiro.

sophistic, *adj.* sofístico.

sophisticate, *v.t.* sofismar, falsificar, adulterar.

sophistry, *s.* sofisma.

soporific, *adj.* soporífero; *s.* sedativo.

soppy, *adj.* ensopado, embebido.

soprano, *s.* soprano.

sorbet, *s.* sorvete.

sorcerer, *s.* feiticeiro, bruxo.

sorceress, *s.* feiticeira, bruxa.

sorcery, *s.* bruxaria.

sordid, *adj.* sórdido, baixo, vil; mesquinho; imundo, avarento; *adv. sordidly,* sordidamente.

sordidness, *s.* baixeza, mesquinhez; avareza.

sordino, *s.* surdina.

sore, *s.* ferida, chaga, dor, pena, desgosto; *adj.* doente; ferido; doloroso; dorido; magoado, penalizado; sensível, melindroso; *adv.* dolorosamente; excessivamente.

soreness, *s.* dor; ulceração; intensidade da dor.

sorrel, *s.* azeda (erva); alazão (cavalo); cor de canela; *adj.* alazão.

sorrily, *adv.* mal, lastimosamente.

sorriness, *s.* tristeza, pesar, lástima; baixeza, vileza.

sorrow, *s.* mágoa, aflição, dor, pesar, sentimento, infortúnio; *hang sorrow!,* leve o diabo a tristeza!; *v.i.* sentir pena, afligir-se, entristecer-se.

sorrowful, *adj.* pesaroso, aflito, doloroso; lastimoso, desconsolado.

sorrowing, *adj.* angustiado, contristado; *s.* aflição, tristeza; lastimação. *adv. sorrowingly,* angustiadamente.

sorry, *adj.* pesaroso; aflito, desconsolado; pobre, miserável, desgraçado; vil, desprezível; *a sorry excuse,* uma fraca desculpa.

sort, *s.* sorte, classe, género, espécie, qualidade, condição, maneira, modo, forma; tipo ou letra. 1) *in a sort,* de certo modo. 2) *out of sorts,* descontente; indisposto; infeliz; *v.t.* classificar, dividir em grupos; sortear; ordenar, arranjar; convir a.

sorter, *s.* classificador.

sortie, *s.* saída, surtida (mil.).

sortilege, *s.* sortilégio.

sorting, *adj.* escolha, distribuição; sorteio.

so-so, *adj.* assim-assim, nem mau nem bom; regular, sofrível.

sot, *s.* estúpido, ignorante; bêbedo.

sottish, *adj.* tolo; bêbedo; *adv. sottishly,* estupidamente.

souffle, *s.* sopro, murmúrio, sussurro.

sough, *s.* suspiro; escoadouro; sarjeta; *v.t.* suspirar, sussurrar.

soul, *s.* alma, espírito, essência; vida; pessoa, habitante. 1) *all soul's day,* dia de finados. 2) *upon my soul,* na minha consciência. 3) *not a soul will go,* ninguém irá.

soulless, *adj.* desalmado; sem sentimentos; desumano; insípido, desinteressante.

sound, *s.* som, ruído; sonda; estuário; bexiga natatória do peixe; *adj.* são, bom, inteiro; escorreito; ileso; perfeito; saudável, forte; correcto; ortodoxo; seguro, certo; sólido; completo; solvente (com.); *safe and sound,* são e salvo; *v.t.* sondar (com sonda); sondar, examinar; auscultar; tocar, tanger; celebrar, publicar, cantar, entoar; *v.i.* soar, ressoar; espalhar-se, divulgar-se; tocar para chamar; *adv.* profundamente.

sounding, *adj.* sonoro, sonante; *s.* sonda, sondagem.

soundly, *adv.* sãmente, vigorosamente; firmemente.

soundness, *s.* sanidade, saúde; vigor, firmeza; ortodoxia.

soup, *s.* sopa. 1) *soap-ladle,* colher ou concha de sopa. 2) *you are in the soup,* estás em apuros.

soupçon, *s.* suspeita.

soupy, *adj.* parecido com sopa.

sour, *adj.* azedo, ácido, picante, áspero; *v.t.* e *v.i.* azedar(-se); avinagrar(-se); irritar(-se).

source, *s.* fonte, manancial; origem, causa, princípio.

sourdine, *s.* surdina (mús.).

sourish, *adj.* um tanto azedo.

sourly, *adv.* asperamente; com azedume.

sourness, *s.* acidez; azedume; aspereza.

souse, *s.* salmoura, escabeche; conserva de porco (orelhas e pés); bebedeira, beberrão; mergulho; *v.i.* mergulhar; dar um mergulho; encharcar-se; embebedar-se; *to souse upon,* lançar-se sobre; cair sobre; atacar com violência; *adv.* de chofre; pesadamente.

soutane, *s.* sotaina, batina (de padre).

south, *s.* sul, meio-dia; o vento sul; *adj.* meridional, sul, austral; *south sea,* oceano Pacífico; *adv.* para o sul.

southerly, *adj.* meridional; do sul; *adv.* para o sul, ao sul.

southern, *adj.* do sul, meridional, austral; sulino.

southerner, *s.* habitante do sul.

southernmost, *sup.* de *southern,* o mais chegado a sul.

southing, *s.* tendência para o sul; *adj.* que se dirige para sul.

southward, southwards, adv. para o sul, rumo ao sul; adj. situado no sul; s. região do sul.

south-west, s. e adj. sudoeste.

souvenir, s. lembrança.

sovereign, s. soberano, rei ou rainha; soberano, libra esterlina; adj. soberano, eficaz.

sovereignty, s. soberania.

soviet, s. soviete.

sow, s. porca; v.t. e v.i. (sowed, sown), semear, espalhar; fazer a sementeira; to sow the wind and to reap the whirlwind, semear ventos e colher tempestades.

soy, s. soja.

spa, s. estância de águas.

space, s. espaço, lugar, volume; distância; extensão; período; intervalo; alojamento; câmara; v.t. espaçar.

spacing, s. distância; vão.

spacious, adj. espaçoso, vasto; adv. spaciously, espaçosamente.

spaciousness, s. capacidade, extensão, amplitude.

spade, s. pá, enxada; espadas (cartas de jogar); spade-work, trabalho pesado; v.t. cavar com enxada.

spall, s. pedaço, lasca; v.t. e v.i. tirar lascas; rachar.

span, s. palmo; instante, momento; corda dum arco; junta (de bois); parelha (de cavalos); arco de ponte; v.t. medir aos palmos; alcançar; abarcar, amarar, atar; v.i. contradizer; aparelhar cavalos; seguir por etapas.

spangle, s. lantejoula; v.t. ornar de lantejoulas; v.i. brilhar.

Spaniard, s. espanhol (o habitante).

spaniel, s. sabujo; adulador desprezível.

Spanish, s. espanhol, língua espanhola; adj. espanhol.

spank, s. palmada; v.t. dar palmadas; v.i. ir depressa.

spanking, adj. que anda a passo ligeiro; apressado; vigoroso.

spanner, s. mediador; o que mede; chave de porcas, chave-inglesa; travessão de ponte.

spar, s. espato; vara, antena; vergôntea; pugilato; luta de galos; v.i. (sparring, sparred), andar ao soco; discutir.

spare, v.t. poupar, economizar; dispensar, isentar; passar sem; conceder, dar; perdoar; livrar de; adj. poupado, frugal; escasso; magro; supérfluo; de sobra, de

reserva; sobresselente; disponível. 1) spare room, quarto de hóspedes. 2) spare time, tempo livre.

spareness, s. magreza, escassez; frugalidade, economia.

sparing, adj. escasso; poupado; frugal; misericordioso; adv. sparingly, escassamente; cautelosamente.

spark, s. faísca, chispa, centelha; casquilho; amante; v.i. lançar faíscas; fazer de casquilho; galantear.

sparkle, s. centelha, chispa; v.i. cintilar, faiscar; espumar (vinho); v.t. lançar faíscas.

sparkler, s. diamante (fam.).

sparklet, s. faiscazinha.

sparkling, adj. cintilante, espumoso. 1) sparkling eyes, olhos brilhantes. 2) sparkling wine, vinho espumoso.

sparrow, s. pardal.

sparse, adj. escasso, disseminado, disperso, ralo; adv. sparsely, dum modo escasso; dispersamente.

sparseness, s. rareza, pouca densidade; dispersão.

spasm, s. espasmo.

spasmodic, adj. espasmódico, convulsivo.

spat, s. molusco novo; polaina; palmada; desavença, rixa; v.i. dar palmadas; questionar, discutir.

spate, s. enchente dum rio após uma chuvada.

spatial, adj. do espaço.

spatter, s. salpico; v.t. salpicar, manchar; difamar.

spatula, s. espátula.

spawn, s. ovas; prole; v.t. e v.i. produzir; parir; desovar.

speak, v.t. e v.i. (spoke, spoken), falar, dizer; exprimir-se; conversar; discursar; dirigir-se a; declarar; indicar, revelar. 1) to speak out, falar sem rodeios; falar com clareza. 2) to speak well of, ser indício favorável.

speaker, s. falador, orador, relator; presidente da Câmara dos Deputados.

speaking, s. discurso; adj. falante.

spear, s. lança; arpão de pesca; v.t. matar com lança.

spearman, s. lanceiro.

special, adj. especial, notável; distinto; extra; privativo; particular; s. pessoa ou coisa destinada a um fim especial; comboio especial; tiragem de jornal extraordinária; adv. specially, especialmente.

specialism, s. especialidade.

speciality, s. especialidade.
specialization, s. especialização.
specialize, v.t. especializar.
specie, s. dinheiro contado; moeda metálica.
species, s. espécie; classe, género, variedade; imagem, noção, ideia.
specific, adj. específico, definido; s. medicamento específico.
specification, s. especificação; coisa especificada; caderno de encargos.
specify, v.t. especificar, determinar, pormenorizar.
specimen, s. amostra, exemplar, espécime.
specious, adj. plausível; adv. speciously, plausivelmente.
speck, s. mancha, malha; lugar, sinal; pontinha; átomo; v.t. manchar, macular.
speckless, adj. imaculado; impecável, perfeitamente limpo.
spectable, s. espectáculo, exibição.
spectacular, adj. espectacular; aparatoso.
spectador, s. espectador.
spectral, adj. espectral.
spectre, s. espectro.
spectrum, s. espectro.
specular, adj. especular, relativo a espelho; reflector.
speculate, v.i. especular; meditar, reflectir, considerar.
speculation, s. especulação; meditação.
speculative, adj. especulativo; ideal, teórico, especulador.
speculator, s. contemplador; especulador (com.).
speculum, s. espelho, espéculo; mirante.
speech, s. fala, palavra; linguagem, idioma; oração, discurso, conferência, dissertação. 1) to make a speech, fazer um discurso. 2) after-dinner speech, brinde.
speechless, adj. mudo; estupefacto.
speed, s. rapidez, velocidade, prontidão, pressa; bom êxito; to make speed, apressar-se; v.i. apressar-se; ter êxito; ser bem sucedido; despachar; expedir; adiantar, aviar; favorecer, ajudar; despedir; adv. speedily, rapidamente.
speediness, s. prontidão; rapidez, pressa, diligência.
speedy, adj. ligeiro, rápido, expedito, apressado, veloz.
spell, s. encanto, feitiço, bruxaria; turno, terno, partido de gente; intervalo, descanso; turno; temporada, período curto; ataque

(doença); by spells, por turnos, alternadamente; v.t. e v.i. (spalled, spelt), enfeitiçar; significar, substituir; soletrar.
spellbound, adj. enfeitiçado; fascinado.
speller, s. o que soletra.
spelling, s. soletração; ortografia; spelling-book, cartilha.
spelter, s. zinco.
spence, s. despensa.
spend, v.t. e v.i. gastar; desperdiçar; passar (férias); gastar-se; fazer despesas; deitar ovas.
spender, s. gastador.
spendthrift, s. pródigo, gastador.
spent, adj. perdido; gasto, esgotado.
sperm, s. esperma; sémen; ovas; sperm-whale, cachalote.
spermaceti, s. esparmacete.
spew, v.t. e v.i. vomitar, lançar.
sphere, s. esfera, globo; alçada; campo definido; posição social; astro.
spheric, adj. esférico.
spherics, s. geometria e trigonometria esféricas.
spice, s. especiaria; sabor; sainete, cheiro aromático; v.t. adubar, temperar.
spicery, s. especiarias; qualidade do que é picante (no pl.).
spick-and-span, adj. novinho em folha; apurado; alinhado.
spicy, adj. temperado com especiarias, condimentado; aromático; adv. spicily, condimentadamente.
spider, s. aranha; frigideira, caçarola; spider-crab, santola.
spiffing, adj. excelente (fam.); adv. spiffingly, excelentemente.
spiffy, adj. asseado, janota.
spifflicate, v.t. sufocar, matar; bater, sovar; confundir (fam.).
spigot, s. espiche, torneira; macho; dente, espiga.
spike, s. espiga, espigão; ponta; escápula; cavilha; torno; v.t. pregar, encravar.
spiky, adj. pontudo; pontiagudo.
spill, s. queda, tombo; derramamento; cavilha, hastilha; chuvada; bátega de água; v.t. entornar, derramar; espalhar; cuspir do carro; desperdiçar; esvaziar; v.i. derramar-se; perder-se, desperdiçar-se.
spin, s. giro, volta; passeio ou corrida rápida; v.t. (spinning, spun), fiar, entrançar; prolongar, protelar, dilatar; adiar, reprovar (em exame); fazer girar; v.i. fiar, sair em fio;

rodar, girar; andar depressa! *to spin out,* prolongar fastidiosamente.

spinach, *s.* espinafre.

spinal, *adj.* espinhal, espinal.

spindle, *s.* fuso, bilro; veio; eixo; carretel; haste comprida; *v.i.* criar talo.

spindly, *adj.* de comprimento e finura desproporcionados.

spine, *s.* espinha dorsal; espinho.

spined, *adj.* que tem espinhos ou espinha dorsal.

spinner, *s.* fiandeiro, fiandeira; máquina de fiar.

spinning, *s.* fiação; manobra de avião; *spinning-frame,* tear.

spinous, *adj.* espinhoso.

spiral, *s.* e *adj.* espiral; *adv. spirally,* em espiral.

spire, *s.* agulha (de torre); cúspide; junco, caniço; ponto mais alto.

spirit, *s.* espírito, alma; ânimo, energia; génio, talento; humor; motivo; significado verdadeiro; influência; álcool, bebidas espirituosas; *v.t.* animar, encorajar; (com *away* ou *off*) arrebatar, raptar, levar misteriosamente.

spirited, *adj.* vivo, fogoso, animoso; *adv. spiritedly,* animosamente.

spiritism, *s.* espiritismo.

spiritist, *s.* espírita.

spiritual, *adj.* espiritual; *adv. spiritually,* espiritualmente.

spirituous, *adj.* espirituoso; *adv. spirituously,* espirituosamente.

spiry, *adj.* alto, esguio, adelgaçado.

spit, *s.* saliva, cuspo; *v.i. (spitting, spat),* cuspir, escarrar.

spit, *v.t. (spitting, spitted),* espetar, atravessar; *s.* espeto, assador; ponta de terra.

spitch-cock, *s.* enguia aberta e assada na grelha; *v.t.* abrir uma enguia e assá-la na grelha.

spite, *s.* rancor, ódio, despeito. 1) *in spite of,* apesar de. 2) *out of spite,* em despique; *v.t.* agastar, mortificar, vexar, irritar.

spiteful, *adj.* rancoroso, vingativo; malévolo, maligno; *adv. spitefully,* rancorosamente.

spitefulness, *s.* rancor, malignidade.

spittle, *s.* cuspo, saliva, escarro.

spittoon, *s.* escarradeira.

splash, *s.* salpico de lama; chape; *v.t.* enlamear, salpicar; *v.i.* chafurdar, chapinhar.

splash-board, *s.* guarda-lamas (de carro).

splashy, *adj.* enlameado, molhado.

splatter, *v.i.* esparrinhar, chapinhar.

splay, *s.* alargamento (arq.); largura, abertura; *v.t.* estender, desdobrar; abrir (com *out*), deslocar; afunilar; *v.i.* alargar-se, desdobrar-se, afunilar-se; inclinar-se; *adj.* achatado, virado para fora, torto; desajeitado.

splayfoot, *s.* pé chato.

spleen, *s.* baço (anat.); rancor, mau humor; melancolia.

spleenful, *adj.* mal-humorado, taciturno, impertinente, colérico.

splendent, *adj.* magnífico; ilustre; reluzente.

splendid, *adj.* esplêndido, magnífico, grandioso; brilhante, glorioso; *adv. splendidly,* esplendidamente.

splendour, *s.* esplendor.

splenetic, *adj.* rabugento, melancólico, mal-humorado.

splice, *v.t.* ajustar, juntar, casar; fazer costura em cabos; *s.* emenda, junção, costura; casamento (fam.).

splint, *s.* lasca, hastilha, estilhaço; tala; esquírola; *v.t.* pôr em talas.

splinter, *s.* lasca, estilhaço; *v.t.* e *v.i.* desfazer em lascas; despedaçar(-se).

split, *s.* fenda, greta, racha; quebra; divisão, rompimento; rasgão; *v.t.* e *v.i. (splitting, split),* fender(-se), rachar(-se), partir(-se), dividir(-se); desunir(-se); promover discórdia.

splitting, *adj.* o que faz gretar; o que causa a sensação de quebrar; *a splitting headache,* aguda dor de cabeça.

splotch, *s.* mancha; grande nódoa.

splotchy, *adj.* manchado.

splutter, *s.* barulho, barafunda, confusão; azáfama; *v.t.* e *v.i.* balbuciar; falar lançando perdigotos; cuspir.

spoffish, *adj.* azafamado.

spoil, *s.* saque, roubo, despojo, pilhagem; presa; ruína, dano; perdição; *v.t.* estragar, inutilizar; corromper; despojar, saquear; *spoil-sport,* desmancha-prazeres; *v.i.* inutilizar-se, estragar-se.

spoilage, *s.* estragos.

spoiler, *s.* espoliador, ladrão; estragador.

spoke, *s.* raio de roda; degrau duma escada; travão de roda; malagueta do leme; *to put a spoke in someone's wheel,* contrariar os planos de uma pessoa.

spokesman, *s.* porta-voz, interlocutor, orador, representante.

spoliation, *s.* saque, pilhagem; espoliação; esbulho, extorsão, roubo.

sponge, s. esponja; banho ou limpeza com esponja; massa levedada; parasita, chupista; *sponge-cake,* pão-de-ló; *v.t.* limpar com esponja; viver à custa alheia; embeber-se.

spongy, adj. esponjoso; embebido; poroso; bêbedo.

sponsor, s. padrinho, madrinha; fiador; fomentador; patrocinador; defensor; *v.t.* apadrinhar; patrocinar; promover; ser fiador de.

spontaneity, s. espontaneidade.

spontaneous, adj. espontâneo.

spoof, *v.t.* burlar, intrujar, enganar.

spook, s. fantasma, aparição.

spookish, adj. fantástico; que é frequentado por fantasmas.

spooky, adj. próprio dum fantasma; mal--assombrado.

spool, s. carretel, bobina; *v.t.* enrolar em carretel; bobinar.

spoon, s. colher; apaixonado, baboso; *to be spoons on,* estar completamente apaixonado; *v.t.* apanhar com colher; *v.i.* estar todo babado, apaixonado.

spoonful, s. colherada.

spoonily, adv. de modo lamecha.

spoony, adj. tolo, lamecha, baboso, sentimental; s. simplório, tolo.

spoor, s. rasto, pista, trilha, faro; *v.t.* e *v.i.* farejar, fariscar.

sporadic, adj. esporádico, raro, acidental, isolado; incomum; adv. *sporadically,* esporadicamente.

sport, s. desporto, divertimento, passatempo, diversão; brincadeira, mofa. 1) *in sport,* por brincadeira. 2) *to be a good sport,* saber perder bem (no jogo); ser bom companheiro; *v.t.* ostentar, fazer alarde de; divertir; *v.i.* divertir-se, brincar, zombar.

sporting, s. desporto; adj. desportivo; próprio do desporto; que se diverte.

sportive, adj. desportivo; brincalhão, alegre, galhofeiro; adv. *sportively,* desportivamente, dum modo brincalhão.

sportsman, s. desportista; que se dedica ao desporto; bom perdedor.

sportsmanship, s. prática do desporto; espírito desportista; habilidade desportiva.

spot, s. sítio, lugar, ponto; local; nódoa, mancha, borrão; *on the spot,* imediatamente no local; no acto; *v.t. (spotting, spotted),* manchar; corromper; (fam.) localizar, reconhecer, notar.

spotless, adj. sem mancha; imaculado; adv. *spotlessly,* sem mancha.

spotlessness, s. pureza; imaculabilidade.

spotty, adj. cheio de manchas.

spouse, s. esposo, esposa.

spout, s. cano, tubo; goteira; bica, torneira; repuxo, dala; bico do bule; *v.t.* e *v.i.* esguichar; (gír.) penhorar, empenhar; jorrar; discursar, arengar.

sprain, *v.t.* torcer (tornozelo, pulso, etc.), dar um jeito; s. torcedura, mau jeito, entorse.

sprat, s. petinga; arenque pequeno.

sprawl, s. trambolhão; *v.i.* estender-se ao comprido; espojar-se.

spray, s. espuma do mar; borrifo; pulverizador, vaporizador; *v.t.* borrifar, pulverizar.

spread, *v.t.* e *v.i.* espalhar(-se); estender (-se); derramar; untar com; pôr a mesa; distribuir; difundir(-se), divulgar(-se); desenrolar(-se). 1) *to spread abroad,* divulgar. 2) *to spread apart,* abrir(-se), separar (-se); s. expansão, difusão, desenvolvimento; festa, festim; envergadura da vela; cobertor, toalha de mesa; adj. estendido.

spreading, adj. expansivo, extensivo.

sprig, s. vergôntea, renovo, pimpolho; jovem; prego sem cabeça; *v.t.* enfeitar com ramos; bordar ramos em.

sprightliness, s. alegria, vivacidade.

sprightly, adj. alegre, esperto, vivo.

spring, s. Primavera; origem, nascente, fonte; salto, pulo; elasticidade. 1) *hot springs,* termas. 2) *spring-board,* trampolim. 3) *spring tides,* águas vivas; *v.t. (sprang, sprung),* fazer levantar (a caça); fazer saltar (mina); abrir fenda; *v.i.* brotar, rebentar, saltar, nascer de repente; estalar. 4) *to spring at,* saltar sobre. 5) *to spring forth,* crescer, sair; precipitar-se.

springe, s. armadilha, laço.

springily, adv. com elasticidade.

springing, s. elasticidade; crescença; rebento.

sprinkle, s. borrifo; *v.t.* borrifar, aspergir, regar, derramar, baptizar; *v.i.* chuviscar, cair em gotas.

sprinkler, s. o que borrifa; borrifador; extintor de incêndios.

sprinkling, s. aspersão, rega, borrifo; um pouco, laivos.

sprint, s. corrida pedestre; corrida de velocidade; esforço intenso; *v.i.* correr com velocidade; correr uma distância determinada.

sprinter, s. corredor de velocidade.

sprite, s. espírito, sombra, fantasma, duende, fada.

sprout, s. renovo, grelo; *v.t.* grelar, brotar, germinar.

spruce, s. abeto; *adj.* asseado, janota, catita, elegante; *v.t.* e *v.i.* vestir(-se), enfeitar(-se), ajanotar(-se); *adv. sprucely,* com extremo ou afectado asseio, janotice.

spruceness, s. garbo, asseio, elegância; afectação no trajar.

spry, *adj.* vivo, vigoroso, ágil.

spryness, s. agilidade, vivacidade.

spume, s. espuma; *v.i.* espumar.

spunk, s. madeira podre; isca; faísca; brio, coragem.

spunky, *adj.* brioso, corajoso.

spur, s. espora, esporão; aguilhão, estímulo; raiz principal duma árvore; escora, travessa; pontão; *v.t. (spurring, spurred),* esporear; aguilhoar, instigar, estimular; *v.i.* apertar o passo.

spurious, *adj.* espúrio, ilegítimo, bastardo, adulterado; *adv. spuriously,* falsamente, adulteradamente, de modo espúrio.

spurn, *v.t.* expulsar, repelir; desdenhar, menosprezar; s. rejeição.

spurred, *adj.* esporeado, com esporões.

spurt, *v.i.* e *v.t.* esguichar, jorrar, surgir, empregar um esforço repentino; s. esguicho, jorro, arranco; esforço máximo; explosão colérica.

sputter, s. baba, perdigoto; *v.t.* e *v.i.* falar cuspindo; falar depressa e indistintamente.

sputum, s. cuspo, saliva.

spy, s. espia, espião; *v.t.* e *v.i.* espiar, vigiar, observar; avistar, descortinar. 1) *to spy out,* descobrir. 2) *to spy into,* examinar de perto.

squab, s. borracho, pombo pequeno; pessoa atarracada; pequena almofada; sofá com estofo espesso; *adj.* implume; rechonchudo; atarracado; *adv.* pesadamente; *v.t.* estofar; *v.i.* cair pesadamente.

squabble, s. disputa, rixa, altercação; *v.i.* disputar, altercar.

squabbler, s. altercador.

squad, s. esquadra (de soldados).

squadron, s. esquadrão de cavalaria; batalhão; esquadra (náut.).

squalid, *adj.* esquálido, sujo, imundo, miserável; *adv. squalidly,* esqualidamente.

squalidness, s. imundície.

squall, s. grito agudo; borrasca; aguaceiro; pé-de-vento; *v.i.* dar gritos agudos.

squally, *adj.* borrascoso.

squalor, s. esqualidez, sujidade, sordidez.

squama, s. escama; bráctea.

squamous, *adj.* escamoso.

squander, *v.t.* dissipar, desperdiçar, malbaratar; dispersar.

squanderer, s. gastador, dissipador, pródigo.

square, s. quadrado; praça, largo; esquadria, esquadro; nível, igualdade, conformidade; *adj.* quadrado, quadrangular; em esquadria; exacto, perfeito; recto, justo, imparcial. 1) *square dance,* quadrilha. 2) *square dealing,* boa fé. 3) *square meal,* refeição completa. 4) *square sails,* velas redondas (náut.). 5) *square toes,* maneirismos; pessoa cheia de nove-horas; *v.t.* quadrar, enquadrar; ajustar; acomodar; saldar (com.); medir; *v.i.* quadrar, convir, ficar bem; *adv.* em forma quadrada; exactamente; *adv. squarely,* em forma quadrada; honradamente; exactamente, firmemente.

squash, s. abóbora; queda repentina dum corpo mole que se esborracha; coisa mole; aperto; polpa; *v.t.* e *v.i.* esmagar, comprimir, espremer; esborrachar-se.

squashy, *adj.* mole, húmido; polposo.

squat, *v.i.* agachar-se; acocorar-se; estabelecer-se clandestinamente; s. acocoramento, agachamento; *adj.* agachado, acocorado; atarracado; rechonchudo.

squatter, s. o que se agacha; colono intruso.

squawk, s. grasnido; (fam.) protesto, queixa; goraz americano; *v.i.* e *v.t.* grasnar, soltar gritos ásperos; (fam.) protestar, guinchar.

squeak, s. grito agudo e repentino; guincho; grunhido; chiado; *v.i.* e *v.t.* grunhir, guinchar, gritar; chiar; (fam.) trair um segredo.

squeaker, s. o que guincha; avezinha.

squeaking, *adj.* gritante; penetrante; agudo.

squeaky, *adj.* de som áspero.

squeal, s. grito alto e agudo; *v.i.* soltar grito alto e agudo; ser delator, denunciador.

squealer, s. gritador; delator.

squeamish, *adj.* delicado, melindroso, enjoado, enfastiado; *adv. squeamishly,* delicadamente; de modo enjoado.

squeeze, s. aperto, apertão; compressão; impressão (dum desenho, esboço, etc.); abraço; *v.t.* apertar, abraçar, comprimir, espremer, oprimir; *v.i.* entrar ou sair apertando.

squeezer, s. o que aperta, o que espreme, espremedor.

squeich, v.t. e v.i. esmagar; impor silêncio; ficar esmagado; s. pancada forte, queda pesada.

squib, busca-pé; sátira; remoque; v.t. e v.i. lançar busca-pés; satirizar; atirar remoques.

squid, s. lula; calamar; anzol giratório.

squiffer, s. concertina.

squiffy, adj. um pouco toldado, ébrio.

squint, s. olhar vesgo; estrabismo; v.t. e v.i. entortar os olhos; olhar de maneira vesga.

squinting, s. estrabismo.

squire, s. escudeiro; cavaleiro; morgado; proprietário rural; juiz de paz (nos E.U.A.).

squirm, v.i. serpear; trepar.

squirrel, s. esquilo.

squirt, s. seringa; seringada, esguichadela.

squish, s. marmelada; compota de laranja.

stab, s. punhalada; estocada, golpe; injúria, ofensa; v.t. (stabbing, stabbed), apunhalar, injuriar.

stability, s. estabilidade, permanência; solidez, firmeza.

stable, s. estábulo; cavalariça, estrebaria; adj. estável, firme, permanente, durável, constante, sólido; v.t. encurralar; firmar, consolidar; firmar; v.i. viver em cavalariça.

stably, adv. firmemente.

stack, s. meda, pilha, montão (de feno, trigo, lenha, etc.); pilha de carvão; chaminé; cano de chaminé; estante de livros; v.t. empilhar, amontoar.

stadium, s. estádio.

staff, s. estado-maior dum exército, ou pessoal duma empresa; bordão, esteio, apoio; bastão de mando; báculo; pau de bandeira, cabo dum instrumento; braço (de violino, de violoncelo); vara de ofício; vara de medir; estância; estrofe.

stage, s. palco, estrado, prancha, tablado; andaime; teatro; pousada, estação, muda; progresso, período, fase, jornada; grau, degrau; andaime; diligência, mala-posta; v.t. pôr em cena; representar.

stager, s. cavalo de diligência; pessoa muito experiente.

stagger, s. vacilação, cambaleio; mania, loucura; vertigem; v.t. fazer vacilar, fazer cambalear; causar vertigens; abalar; v.i. cambalear, vacilar; começar a ceder; começar a duvidar; hesitar.

staging, s. andaime; tablado; encenação.

stagnancy, s. estagnação.

stagnant, adj. estagnante; adv. stagnantly, dum modo estagnante.

stagnate, v.i. estagnar-se.

stagnation, s. estagnação.

stagy, adj. teatral; adv. stagily, teatralmente.

staid, adj. grave, sério.

staidness, s. gravidade, seriedade, sobriedade.

stain, s. mancha, mácula; tinta, tintura; desonra, deslustre; v.t. manchar; tingir, colorir; difamar.

stainer, s. o que mancha; difamador; tintureiro.

staining, s. tintura; coloração.

stainless, adj. limpo, imaculado.

stair, s. degrau; pl. escadas, escadaria. 1) stairrods, varões para as passadeiras. 2) winding stairs, escada de caracol.

staircase, s. escada; lanço de escada.

staith, s. cais de descarga.

stake, s. estaca, poste; pelourinho, aposta; entrada, parada (no jogo); bigorna; risco, contingência; v.t. pôr estacas, apoiar; estacar; apostar; arriscar; to stake all, arriscar tudo.

stalactite, s. estalactite.

stalagmite, s. estalagmite.

stale, adj. velho, sediço, rançoso; safado, gasto; antiquado; deteriorado; s. engodo, isca; bobo, incauto; sedutor, atractivo; urina de gado; v.t. tornar velho ou sediço; v.i. urinar; adv. stalely, de velho; com ranço.

staleness, s. velhice; rancidez.

stalk, s. talo, haste, cana; pé, tronco; andar altivo; pé (de copo) chaminé de fábrica.

stalky, adj. duro ou parecido com uma haste.

stall, s. estrebaria; barraca, tenda; quiosque; v.t. encurralar; atascar; v.i. atolar-se; residir, morar; butcher's stall, açougue, talho.

stallion, s. garanhão.

stalwart, adj. forte, valente, rijo; corajoso; leal; resoluto; adv. stalwartly, valentemente.

stammer, s. gaguez; v.i. gaguejar; balbuciar.

stamp, s. selo, estampilha, timbre, cunho; marca, impressão; estampa, imagem; carácter; casta; máquina de moer; stamp paper, papel selado; v.t. e v.i. estampar, marcar, imprimir, selar, cunhar; moer, pisar, calcar; sapatear, patear; v.i. bater com força com o pé no chão.

stampede, s. fuga motivada por pânico; v.i. fugir devido a pânico.

stamper, s. estampador, impressor; pilão.

stamperer, s. gago.

stamping, *s.* estampilhagem; estampagem.

stance, *s.* sítio, local, estância; postura, posição.

stanch, *adj.* constante, fiel, zeloso; são, forte, firme, sólido; *v.t.* e *v.i.* estancar, esgotar, vedar.

stanchion, *s.* escora, pontalete; balaústre; pau de toldo.

stand, *v.t.* e *v.i.* pôr de pé, colocar; suportar; aguentar, tolerar. 1) *I cannot stand him,* não o suporto; estar sujeito ou exposto a; fazer as despesas, pagar; estar de pé; levantar-se; colocar em posição vertical; persistir, resistir; juntar; ter de altura; fornecer; defender; ajudar, manter; manter-se fiel a; representar; apoiar; ser candidato; estar em; custar. 2) *to stand off,* permanecer afastado; não concordar. 3) *to stand upon,* insistir em; estar em cima. 4) *to stand on end,* ter-se de pé; permancer de pé; eriçar-se (o cabelo). 5) *to stand out,* ser proeminente; sobressair-se; resistir. 6) *to stand over,* ser adiado; ser transferido. 7) *to stand to,* manter (a palavra, promessa, etc.). 8) *it stands to reason,* é razoável, é lógico; *s.* lugar, posto, estante, mesinha; pedestal; parada, pausa, alto; estação, ponto culminante, termo; estrado, plataforma. 9) *cruet-stand,* galheteiro. 10) *music-stand,* estante para música; coreto. 11) *standpoint,* ponto de vista. 12) *grand-stand,* arquibancada.

standard, *s.* marca, norma, tipo, modelo, padrão; regra fixa; poste, escora, coluna, suporte; curva de construção; estandarte; *adj.* de marca, normal; oficial, legal, clássico.

standardization, *s.* normalização; uniformização; produção por séries.

standardize, *v.t.* uniformizar, normalizar; construir segundo um modelo.

standing, *s.* posição, reputação, crédito; duração, antiguidade; classe, categoria; sítio; paragem; *adj.* permanente, fixo, durável, constante; erecto, de pé; estagnado; parado; erguido. 1) *standing orders,* ordens permanentes. 2) *of long standing,* de longa data.

standish, *s.* escrivaninha.

standstill, *s.* pausa, paralisação; *these works are at a standstill,* estas obras estão paralisadas.

standup, *adj.* direito.

stannic, *adj.* de estanho.

stannous, *adj.* que contém estanho.

stanza, *s.* estância (poes.).

staple, *s.* gato de ferro; chapa onde entra a lingueta da fechadura; empório, mercado; mola de prender papéis; produto principal duma região; matéria bruta; fibra (de algodão ou lã); *adj.* principal; indispensável; de uso corrente; estabelecido.

star, *s.* estrela, astro; destino; sorte, fado; estrelinha; asterisco; cruz; insígnia; actor ou actriz principal; mancha branca na frente dum cavalo, vaca, etc. 1) *shooting star,* estrela-cadente. 2) *star-gazer,* astrólogo. 3) *stars-spangled,* semeado de estrelas. 4) *the star-and-stripes,* a bandeira dos E.U.A.; *v.t.* *(starring, starred),* semear ou ornar de estrelas.

starboard, *s.* estibordo; *v.i.* guinar para estibordo.

starch, *s.* amido, fécula, goma; rigidez, formalidade; *adj.* teso, duro, rígido, formal; *v.t.* engomar.

starched, *adj.* engomado; teso, duro.

starchy, *adj.* teso, engomado; afectado.

stare, *s.* olhar fixo; pasmo; *v.t.* e *v.i.* fitar, encarar; olhar com espanto ou insolentemente; saltar à vista; ser evidente; *to stare in the face,* olhar fixamente alguém; aparecer à frente de alguém.

staring, *adj.* fito, fixo; espantado, admirado; *s.* o acto de fitar; *adv.* *staringly,* fixamente.

stark, *adj.* rígido, teso; completo, chapado; *adv.* completamente; *stark mad,* doido-varrido.

starless, *adj.* sem estrelas.

starlight, *adj.* iluminado pelas estrelas.

starry, *adj.* estrelado, constelado.

start, *v.i.* e *v.t.* saltar, pular; partir, seguir viagem; começar, principiar; deslocar-se, pôr-se em marcha; pôr em marcha (motor); sobressaltar-se; originar-se; entrar numa competição; suscitar, dar origem; empreender; ter a intenção de; dar sinal de partida para; começar a funcionar; levantar a caça; *s.* começo, princípio; ímpeto, impulso, arranco; vantagem (corrida); *by fits and starts,* aos arrancos, irregularmente.

starter, *s.* iniciador; iniciador de marcha; instrumento para pôr em movimento; cão que levanta a caça; aquele que dá o sinal de partida.

startle, *v.t.* assustar, espantar; *v.i.* sobressaltar-se, estremecer.

startling, *adj.* aterrador, assustador.

starvation, *s.* fome, inanição; miséria.

starve, *v.i.* e *v.t.* morrer de fome; matar à fome; vencer pela fome; enfraquecer.

starveling, *s.* animal morto de fome; planta estiolada; *adj.* faminto; estiolado.

state, *s.* estado, condição, situação, classe, ordem; Estado (pol.); pompa, fausto, aparato, gala; poder civil, governo. 1) *state house,* palácio do Governo. 2) *married--state,* matrimónio. 3) *single-state,* celibato. 4) *in state,* estar exposto (cadáver em câmara ardente); *v.t.* declarar, expor; relatar, narrar detalhadamente; estabelecer; fixar.

stated, *adj.* estabelecido, fixado.

stateliness, *s.* grandeza, fausto; altivez, dignidade.

stately, *adj.* majestoso, grandioso, sublime; soberbo, altivo.

statement, *s.* declaração; ajuste; exposição, relatório, resumo, narração; relato; extracto de conta (com.); balanço (com.).

statesman, *s.* estadista.

statesmanlike, *adj.* próprio dum estadista; *adv.* statesmanly, dum modo próprio dum estadista.

statesmanship, *s.* qualidade dum estadista; habilidade política.

static, *adj.* estático; *adv.* statically, de modo estático.

statics, *s.* estática.

station, *s.* sítio, posto, lugar assinado; condição social; esquadra (da polícia); depósito de carvão; pouso, estância. 1) *he enjoys a good station in life,* ele desfruta duma boa posição social. 2) *station master,* chefe de estação. 3) *stations of the cross,* via-sacra; *v.t.* postar, colocar; nomear para um lugar ou posto.

stationary, *adj.* estacionário.

stationer, *s.* dono de papelaria; *stationer's hall,* associação de livreiros.

stationery, *s.* artigos de escritório.

statistic, *adj.* estatístico; *adv. statistically,* dum modo estatístico.

statistics, *s.* estatística.

statue, *s.* estátua, imagem.

statuette, *s.* estatueta.

statutory, *adj.* estabelecido por lei ou estatuto, legal.

staunch, *adj.* firme, fiel, seguro, sólido; são, forte; *adv. staunchly,* firmemente.

staunchness, *s.* firmeza, solidez.

stave, *s.* aduela; estância, estrofe (poes.); *v.t.* (*staved, stove*), partir aduelas; arrombar;

pôr aduelas; afastar com pau; ir à pressa; *to stave off,* repelir; adiar, demorar.

stay, *s.* estada, residência, demora; parada; estadia; suspensão (processo judicial); obstáculo, estorvo; escora; apoio, suporte; *pl.* espartilho, corpete. 1) *stay-at-home,* pessoa caseira. 2) *to be in stays,* ter o vento pela proa; *v.t.* parar, permanecer; deter-se, demorar-se; ficar no mesmo lugar; hospedar-se (fam.); esperar; confiar. 3) *to stay away,* estar ausente. 4) *to stay up,* velar, não se deitar. 5) *it has come to stay,* deve ser considerado permanente.

stead, *s.* lugar, sítio, auxílio, ajuda. 1) *instead of stead,* em lugar de. 2) *in good stead,* servir, prestar, ser útil.

steadfast, *adj.* constante, firme, determinado; *adv. steadfastly,* com firmeza.

steady, *adj.* firme, fixo, seguro, constante; decidido; sóbrio; *v.t.* portar-se bem (o navio), dar pouco balanço, estar calmo; *adv. steadily,* firmemente, seguramente.

steak, *s.* talhada, posta; bife.

steal, *v.t.* e *v.i.* (*stole, stolen*), roubar, tirar; retirar clandestinamente; surripiar. 1) *to steal along,* passar em silêncio. 2) *to steal away,* escapar-se, escapulir-se. 3) *to steal into,* entrar furtivamente. 4) *to steal forth,* sair furtivamente. 5) *to steal upon,* surpreender; *s.* furto, roubo.

stealer, *s.* ladrão, gatuno.

stealing, *s.* furto, roubo; *adj.* ladrão, gatuno.

stealth, *s.* reserva, procedimento secreto.

stealthy, *adj.* furtivo, secreto, escondido, clandestino; *adv. stealthily,* furtivamente, clandestinamente.

steam, *s.* vapor, exalação; energia, força; espírito; *by steam,* a vapor; *v.i.* e *v.t.* exalar vapor; evaporar-se; mover a vapor; viajar a vapor; cozer a vapor.

steamer, *s.* navio ou veículo a vapor; bomba de vapor para incêndios; recipiente para se pôr qualquer coisa a vapor.

steamy, *adj.* constante de, parecido com; cheio de vapor.

stearin, *s.* estearina.

steed, *s.* cavalo, corcel, ginete; *to shut the stable-door, after the steed stolen,* casa roubada, trancas à porta.

steel, *s.* aço; instrumento de aço; armas brancas; dureza extrema; *adj.* de aço; feito de aço; *v.t.* acerar; revestir de aço; endurecer; *to steel oneself against,* fortalecer-se contra.

steeliness, dureza de aço; inflexibilidade, dureza.

steely, *adj.* acerado, feito de aço; parecido com aço.

steelyard, *s.* balança romana.

steep, *s.* precipício; despenhadeiro; *adj.* escarpado, precipitoso; difícil; excessivo; *v.t.* ensopar, molhar; saturar; pôr em infusão.

steeping, *s.* acção de demolhar; *steeping tub ou vat,* vasilha onde se demolha.

steeple, *s.* torre, campanário.

steeply, *adv.* escarpadamente; em declive.

steer, *s.* novilho; *v.t.* governar, dirigir; *v.i.* navegar; obedecer ao leme; *to steer clear of scrapes,* evitar embaraços.

steerage, *s.* governo, direcção; alojamento dos passageiros de 3ª classe; antecâmara (náut.).

steerer, *s.* timoneiro.

steering, *s.* governo, direcção; *steering wheel,* roda do leme; roda do leme.

steersman, *s. v. steerer.*

stele, *s.* coluna, padrão; marco miliário.

stellar, *adj.* astral.

stem, *s.* talo, caule, tronco, pé, pedúnculo, haste; estoma; roda de proa; proa; raiz (de palavra); *v.t. (stemming, stemmed),* fazer frente a, resistir; cortar, vencer a corrente; deter; inscrever.

stench, *s.* fedor.

stencil, *s.* modelo, padrão; estampilha (chapa de metal para gravar); *stencil paper,* papel encerado para tirar cópias; *v.t. (stencilling, stencilled),* estampilhar; gravar.

stenographer, *s.* estenógrafo, estenógrafa; taquígrafo.

stenography, *s.* estenografia, taquigrafia.

stentorian, *s.* estentório.

step, *s.* passo, passada; degrau; medida; maneira de andar; pegada; carlinga (náut.); *pl.* diligências, meios. 1) *door-step,* soleira da porta. 2) *to take a step,* dar um passo, tomar uma medida; *v.t. (stepping, stepped),* pôr ou assentar o pé; fixar um mastro; v.i. dar um passo, andar, caminhar. 3) *to step aside,* desviar-se. 4) *to step back,* retroceder. 5) *to step forth,* avançar. 6) *to step on,* pôr o pé, calcar. 7) *to step over,* atravessar; passar por cima.

step-brother, *s.* filho do padrasto ou madrasta.

step-child, *s.* enteado, enteada.

step-daughter, *s.* enteada.

step-father, *s.* padrasto.

step-ladder, *s.* escadote.

step-mother, *s.* madrasta.

steppe, *s.* estepe.

stepping, *s.* acção de andar, trotar, dançar.

step-sister, *s.* filha do padrasto ou madrasta.

step-son, *s.* enteado.

steroscope, *s.* estereoscópio.

sterile, *adj.* estéril, infecundo.

sterility, *s.* esterilidade.

sterilization, *s.* esterilização.

sterilize, *v.t.* esterilizar.

sterling, *adj.* puro, genuíno, verdadeiro; *s.* libra esterlina.

stern, *s.* popa (náut.); painel da popa; rabo de animal; ré; *adj.* severo, áspero, duro, carrancudo; *the sterner sex,* o sexo forte; *adv. sternly,* duramente, austeramente.

sternness, *s.* severidade, dureza, rigor; ar carrancudo.

sternum, *s.* esterno (anat.).

stethoscopic, *s.* estetoscópio.

stevedore, *s.* estivador.

stew, *s.* estufado, guisado; ansiedade; arrelia; lupanar; viveiro, tanque; pessoa muito estudiosa; *v.t.* guisar, estufar; *v.i.* cozer-se em vaso tapado; estar arreliado; estudar muito.

steward, *s.* dispenseiro; administrador (de terras); comissário de bordo; criado de mesa.

stewardess, *s.* hospedeira de bordo; criada de bordo.

stewarship, *s.* cargo de dispenseiro; intendência.

stick, *s.* pau, vara, vareta; palito; bengala; estocada; pessoa estúpida e teimosa; pau, verga (náut.); demora; dúvida, vacilação. 1) *broom stick,* pau de vassoura. 2) *to cut one's stick,* pisgar-se; *v.t.* cravar, enterrar, pregar; introduzir, aderir; prender; apunhalar, matar; afixar; confundir. 3) *stick no bills,* afixação proibida; *v.i.* estar preso; aderir; fixar-se, deter-se; vacilar; atolar-se; meter-se em sarilhos. 4) *to stick by,* sustentar; apoiar. 5) *to stick close,* manter-se juntos. 6) *to stick out,* recusar; sobressair. 7) *to be stuck on,* estar apaixonado. 8) *to stick pigs,* caçar javalis.

stickily, *adv.* com adesão.

sticking, *adj.* saliente; pegajoso; adesivo.

stick-in-the-mud, *adj.* e *s.* diz-se de pessoa atrasada, retrógrada ou sem iniciativa.

stickle, *v.t.* criar dificuldades; levantar

objecções; disputar; discutir; opor-se; fazer questão; s. ponta aguda; espinho.

sticky, adj. tenaz; viscoso; pegajoso.

stiff, adj. duro, teso, firme, obstinado; rígido, direito; formal, inflexível; adv. stiffly, tesamente, duramente, rigorosamente.

stiffen, v.t. e v.i. enrijar, endurecer, reforçar, consolidar; obstinar-se; endurecer-se.

stiffener, s. chumaço; contraforte.

stiffening, s. endurecimento; consolidação.

stiffness, s. rigidez, dureza; obstinação; rigor; consistência.

stifle, adj. sufocante; s. sufocação.

stigma, s. estigma, ferrete.

stigmatize, v.t. estigmatizar.

stile, s. degraus ou qualquer outra coisa, além da cancela, para dar passagem de um cercado a outro.

still, s. sossego, silêncio; tranquilidade; alambique; adj. sossegado, silencioso, quieto; constante, contínuo; calmo; não espumoso (vinho); inanimado, morto; v.i. acalmar, sossegar, deter, parar; destilar; calar, fazer calar; adv. ainda, sempre; conj. todavia, ainda assim; adv. stilly, silenciosamente.

still-born, adj. nascido morto.

stilletto, s. estilete.

stillness, s. silêncio, sossego; tranquilidade.

stiller, s. apaziguador.

stilling, s. destilação; acto de apaziguar; canteiro de adega; still-room, s. laboratório de destilação; despensa.

stilt, s. uma perna de pau; pl. andas.

stilted, adj. elevado em andas; afectado, inchado; empolado.

stimulant, adj. e s. estimulante.

stimulate, v.t. estimular, excitar.

stimulation, s. estimulação, excitação.

stimulative, adj. estimulante; s. estimulante, estímulo.

stimulus, estímulo, estimulante, incentivo.

sting, s. aguilhão, ferrão, picada; remorso; dor aguda; vigor; v.t. e v.i. picar, aguilhoar, dar ferroadas; doer; ter remorsos.

stinginess, s. mesquinhez, avareza, sordidez.

stingy, adj. sovina, mesquinho, avarento; escasso, reduzido; adv. stingily, mesquinhamente, avaramente.

stink, s. fedor; v.i. (stank, stunk), cheirar mal, feder, ter má reputação.

stint, v.t. e v.i. limitar, restringir; ser económico; s. limite, restrição; quinhão, porção.

stipend, s. estipêndio, salário.

stipulate, v.t. e v.i. estipular, contratar, fixar condições.

stipulation, s. estipulação, contrato.

stipulator, s. estipulador.

stir, s. tumulto, reboliço, algazarra; movimento, excitação; comoção; (stirring, stirred), agitar, mover, mexer, sacudir, despertar; irritar, excitar, incitar, instigar, suscitar. 1) stir your stumps, mexe-te!; v.i. mexer-se; estar levantado (da cama). 2) to stir up, avivar, despertar.

stirabout, s. pessoa activa; papas de aveia.

stirps, s. estirpe; família.

stirrer, s. agitador; batedor.

stirring, s. movimento, incitamento; adj. activo; buliçoso; agitado; instigador; estimulante, excitante.

stirrup, s. estribo.

stitch, s. ponto (de costura): pontada; dor aguda; malha. 1) a stitch in time saves nine, um passo dado a tempo vale por nove; v.t. e v.i. dar pontos, coser, alinhavar. 2) to stitch up, remendar.

stitching, s. pontos; costura.

stithy, s. bigorna; forja.

stock, s. tronco, cepo; tolo, néscio; cabo (de ferramenta); cepo de âncora; enxerto; cavalo; acções; linhagem, estirpe, raça; gado; fundos públicos; sortimento; provisão; capital, fundo; caldo; estoque de mercadorias; lote; pescoçinho (gravata); pl. fundos, fazendas; tronco com olhais (instrumento de tortura). 1) stockfish, bacalhau seco. 2) stock holder, accionista. 3) stock taking, inventário. 4) stock-in-trade, toda a provisão dum logista. 5) to lay in a stock, fazer uma provisão. 6) to take stock, avaliar; fazer inventário; v.t. prover, fornecer, abastecer; acumular; guarnecer.

stockade, s. estacada; v.t. fortificar com paliçadas.

stocking, s. meia; a blue stocking, mulher pedante.

stock-taking, s. inventariação, o acto de inventariar.

stocky, adj. grosso, atarracado.

stockyard, s. matadouro.

stodgy, adj. indigesto; pesado; recheado, atulhado; atarracado; enfadonho, insípido.

stoic, adj. e s. estóico; adv. stoically, estoicamente.

stoicism, s. estoicismo.

stoke, v.i. atiçar o lume; fazer fogo.

stokehold, *s.* casa de caldeiras.

stokehole, *s.* porta de fornalha.

stoker, *s.* fogueiro.

stole, *s.* estola.

stolid, *adj.* estólido; impassível.

stolidity, *s.* estolidez.

stomach, *s.* estômago; desejo; brio, coragem, cólera; *v.t.* suportar, aturar.

stomachic, *adj.* estomacal; *s.* medicamento para o estômago.

stone, *s.* pedra; caroço (de fruta); peso de 14 arráteis; pedra (cálculo); pedra preciosa; testículo (fam.). 1) *arch-stone,* aduela, pedra de arco da abóbada. 2) *load-stone,* íman. 3) *millstone,* mó. 4) *stone-pine,* pinheiro manso. 5) *stone-pit,* pedreira; *v.t.* apedrejar; tirar os caroços; revestir de pedras; endurecer.

stonemason, *s.* pedreiro.

stony, *adj.* pedregoso; duro, insensível; empedernido; *adv. stonily,* insensivelmente.

stood, *s.* meda (de trigo, centeio, etc.) feita no campo da ceifa.

stool, *s.* banco, mocho, tamborete, base, suporte; *pl.* câmaras.

stoop, *s.* inclinação, acção de curvar-se ou debruçar-se; submissão; abatimento; condescendência; descida, arremesso de ave de rapina sobre a presa; cantil para beber; suporte, escora; telheiro, varanda; *v.t.* e *v.i.* abaixar, inclinar; dobrar; debruçar--se; sujeitar-se, humilhar-se; arremessar-se sobre a presa.

stop, *s.* paragem, pausa, interrupção, suspensão; espera, batente; obstrução, embaraço, impedimento; repressão; ponto (gram.); fiador, linguete (mec.). 1) *full stop,* ponto final. 2) *stop-gap,* expediente de ocasião. 3) *dead stop,* paragem total; *v.i. (stopping, stopped)* fazer alto, parar; ficar por algum tempo, hospedar-se. 4) *to stop short,* estacar, parar; parar de repente. 5) *stop!,* basta!; *v.t.* deter, suspender, demorar, tapar, obstruir; obturar (dente). 6) *to stop up,* tapar, obstruir.

stoppage, *s.* acção de impedir, de interceptar; interrupção; paragem, suspensão; arresto; obstáculo; estrangulamento (med.).

stopper, *s.* o que faz parar; batoque, rolha; boça; bicha; bojão; *v.t.* aboçar, tapar.

stopping, *s.* paragem; obturação, enchimento.

storage, *s.* armazenagem; preço de armazenagem.

store, *s.* abundância, provisão; armazém; depósito; fornecimento; loja, estabelecimento; *pl.* aprestos, víveres, provisões, munições, armazém. 1) *in store,* de reserva. 2) *to set store by,* estimar muito; *v.t.* abastecer, fornecer, sortir; amontoar, acumular, armazenar.

storey, *s.* andar (de casa).

storeyed, *adj.* que tem andares; *a four-storeyed house,* uma casa de quatro andares.

storiette, *s.* historieta, conto.

storing, *s.* armazenagem.

stork, *s.* cegonha.

storm, *s.* temporal, tempestade; tormenta, borrasca; comoção; tumulto; calamidade; ímpeto, ataque, assalto. 1) *to take by storm,* tomar de assalto; fascinar, impressionar favoravelmente. 2) *to raise* ou *stir up a storm,* provocar desordens; *v.t.* assaltar, tomar de assalto; *v.i.* tempestear; irritar-se, zangar com violência.

stormy, *adj.* tempestuoso, tormentoso; violento; apaixonado; *adv. stormily,* tempes-tuosamente, furiosamente.

story, *s.* história, narração; relatório; anedota, conto, enredo; argumento; mentir; andar (duma casa). 1) *as the story goes,* segundo se diz. 2) *storyteller,* contador de histórias; mentiroso, mexeriqueiro. 3) *cock and bull story,* história da carochinha; *v.t.* historiar.

stout, *adj.* robusto, forte, corpulento; valente, intrépido, esforçado; *s.* cerveja preta muito forte; *adv. stoutly,* vigorosamente, intrepida-mente.

stoutness, *s.* corpulência, força, robustez; intrepidez.

stovaine, *s.* anestésico.

stove, *s.* estufa, calorífero, esquentador; *stove-pipe,* tubo de aquecimento.

stow, *v.t.* colocar, meter; guardar, arrumar; esconder, encerrar; estivar.

stowage, *s.* armazenagem; arrumação, estiva.

stowed, *adj.* arrumado; estivado.

stower, *s.* estivador.

strabismus, *s.* estrabismo.

straggle, *v.i.* errar, vaguear; afastar-se do corpo principal.

straggler, *s.* vagabundo, errante; soldado extraviado; pessoa que anda perdida das outras.

straggly, *adj.* que se estende ou desvia.

straight, *adj.* direito, recto, desempenado; justo, exacto, correcto: franco; seguido; *s.*

pista direita (corridas); *adv.* imediatamente; em linha recta; *straight on,* a direito.

straighten, *v.t.* endireitar; arranjar, pôr em ordem.

straightforward, *adj.* recto, direito; honesto, honrado; franco; *adv. straightforwardly,* em linha recta; francamente.

straightway, *adv.* imediatamente; perda de tempo.

strain, *s.* tensão, esforço violento, puxão; repelão; resistência; contorção, torcedura; estilo, tom, som; ária, verso; disposição, raça, descendência, linhagem; *v.t.* e *v.i.* forçar, torcer, retorcer; deformar-se; esticar; desligar; desconjuntar-se, esmerar-se; filtrar, coar; *to strain every nerve,* fazer todos os esforços.

strained, *adj.* fatigado; solto; forçado; desmedido; filtrado.

strainer, *s.* coador, passador, filtro; ralo de aspiração.

straining, *s.* tensão, esforço; filtragem.

strait, *adj.* difícil, estreito; rigoroso; mesquinho; *strait-jacket,* camisa-de-forças; *s.* estreito; garganta, desfiladeiro; apuro, aperto, dificuldade.

straiten, *v.t.* estreitar, apertar, encolher; pôr em dificuldades.

strand, *s.* margem, praia, costa; toro de corda, cordão; pernada; *v.t.* e *v.i.* encalhar, dar à costa; partir um dos fios duma corda.

stranding, *s.* encalhe (na costa).

strange, *adj.* estranho, singular; desconhecido, estrangeiro; desconhecido; acanhado; inexperiente; *adv. stangely,* estranhamente.

stranger, *s.* estranho, desconhecido, estrangeiro; o que ignora alguma coisa.

strangle, *v.t.* estrangular, afogar, sufocar; *v.i.* morrer estrangulado.

strangling, *s.* estrangulamento.

strangulate, *v.t.* estrangular.

strap, *s.* correia, tira, alça; precinta; presilha; assentador de navalhas; *v.t.* apertar com uma correia; açoitar com correia; afiar navalha.

strapping, *s.* correia (tec.); *adj.* corpulento.

stratagem, *s.* estratagema.

strategic, *adj.* estratégico.

strategy, *s.* estratégia.

strath, *s.* vale extenso; ribeira.

stratum, *s.* estrato, camada.

stratus, *s.* estratos (nuvens).

straw, *s.* palha; ninharia. 1) *man of straw,* testa-de-ferro, homem pouco importante. 2) *to pick straws,* mandriar, estar ocioso.

strawberry, *s.* morango, morangueiro, medronho; *strawberry-tree,* medronheiro.

stray, *s.* extravio; um extraviado; um desgarrado; *adj.* extraviado; *v.i.* extraviar-se, desgarrar-se; perder-se, desviar-se.

streak, *s.* lista, raia; raio de luz; cor e aparência dum mineral quando se raspa; veia, rasgo de talento; vestígio, leve, característico; costura, percinta (náut.); *v.t.* listrar, mosquear.

streaky, *adj.* raiado, listrado.

stream, *s.* corrente (de água, ou luz); jorro; fluxo, caudal, rio; arroio, fonte; *v.t.* e *v.i.* correr, jorrar; estender-se.

streamlet, *s.* riacho, regato.

street, *s.* rua.

strength, *s.* força, vigor, robustez, virilidade; energia, eficácia; poder, potência; fortaleza, firmeza, resistência, intensidade; veemência; força ou forças militares; *on the strength of,* baseado em.

strengthen, *v.t.* fortalecer, dar ânimo; infundir brio; confirmar; *v.i.* fortalecer-se.

strengthening, *s.* reforço, consolidação; resistência.

strenuous, *a.* estrénuo, enérgico, forte; persistente, tenaz; *adv. strenuously,* energicamente.

stress, *s.* força, pressão; violência; acento tónico; ênfase; peso, importância; resistência; *v.t.* sujeitar à tensão; insistir; dar importância a; dar ênfase.

stretch, *s.* estiramento, dilatação, esforço; luta; alcance, extensão, trecho, distância; tirada, intervalo; assentada; bordo, bordada (náut.); elasticidade; *v.t.* estender, estirar, expandir; entesar, esticar; exagerar; violentar, torcer, forçar; *v.i.* alargar-se, estender-se, dar de si.

stretching, *s.* estiramento; entesadura; dilatação; alongamento.

strew, *v.t. (strewed, strewn),* espalhar, espargir; derramar, semear; salpicar, polvilhar; juncar.

stria, *s.* estria; sulcos (em conchas, minerais e plantas).

striate, *adj.* estriado.

striated, *adj.* marcado com estrias.

stricken, *adj.* atacado, acometido de ou por.

strict, *adj.* estrito, exacto, rigoroso, escrupuloso; regular; restrito, limitado; rígido, íntimo; *adv. strictly,* estritamente, rigorosamente.

strictness, s. exactidão, pontualidade; rigor, severidade.

stricture, s. crítica, observação; censura.

stride, s. passo largo; v.t. (strode, stridden), montar, cavalgar; galgar; andar a passos largos.

strident, adj. estridente, estrídulo; adv. stridently, estridentemente.

strife, s. contenda, disputa.

strike, v.t. e v.i. (struck, stricken), colidir, dar bofetadas, bater, atacar, golpear, ferir; infligir, concluir (um negócio); riscar (um fósforo); cunhar, cravar, enfiar; tocar, soar; impressionar, surpreender; fulminar; encontrar; arriar (bandeira); levantar, desarmar (tenda); cancelar; ocorrer (ideia); assumir (postura, atitude); fazer greve; ir, prosseguir; incidir, reflectir; avançar ou passar depressa. 1) to strike at, atacar, acometer. 2) to strike off, arrancar, separar, cortar; cance-lar; partir. 3) to strike out, fazer sair batendo; fazer sair faísca duma pedra; inventar, imaginar; cancelar; tomar uma resolução; arrojar-se. 4) to strike through, atravessar, trespassar; fazer-se sentir. 5) to strike up, começar, iniciar. 6) to strike a match, riscar um fósforo. 7) to strike blind, cegar repentinamente. 8) to strike one's attention, atrair a atenção de alguém; s. golpe; greve; achado (de petróleo, mina, etc.). 9) on strike, em greve.

striker, s. grevista; o que bate ou fere.

striking, adj. conspícuo, notável; espantoso, surpreendente; extraordinário.

string, s. fio, cordel, barbante, atilho; fibra, nervo, tendão; corda de instrumento; réstia; série, fileira, fila; v.t. encordar; enfiar, afinar, esticar; tirar fios; v.i. estender-se em linha; formar-se em fios.

stringed, adj. encordado; enfiado.

stringency, s. aperto, apuro, forte, pressão.

stringent, adj. severo, rigoroso, urgente; adj. stringently, rigorosamente.

stringy, adj. fibroso; tenaz, duro.

strip, s. tira, faixa, barreta; proveta; v.t. (stripping, stripped), despir, desnudar, desaparelhar, desguarnecer; descascar, esburgar; esbulhar, roubar; cortar em tiras; v.i. despir-se; soltar-se, moer (uma rosca); to strip off, despir.

stripe, s. raia, lista, barra, tira; franja, galão; galão de oficial; vergão; classe, género; v.t. listrar.

stripling, s. mancebo, rapaz, jovem.

stripper, s. esbulhador, espoliador.

stripy, adj. listrado.

stroke, s. golpe, pancada; toque; ataque apopléctico; tentativa, esforço; badaladas do relógio; pincelada; remada; tacada; rasgo; influência; êxito. 1) she arrived on the stroke of two, ela chegou ao bater das duas horas. 2) sun stroke, insolação; v.t. acariciar, afagar; esfregar.

strokesman, s. remador.

stroll, s. passeio vagaroso; giro; v.i. passear descansadamente; vaguear.

stroller, s. vagabundo; passeante; actor ambulante.

strong, adj. forte, vigoroso, robusto, possante; musculoso; impetuoso, ardente; sólido; eficaz, activo; enérgico, determinado, resoluto; indigesto. 1) strong-box, cofre-forte. 2) strong bodied wine, vinho encorpado. 3) strong set, bem composto, sólido; adv. strongly, fortemente, vigorosamente.

stronghold, s. forte, fortaleza, praça-forte.

strongish, adj. um tanto forte.

strongminded, adj. de espírito forte; de crença arreigada.

strongmindedness, s. fortaleza de espírito.

strop, v.t. (stropping, stropped), assentar o fio à navalha; s. assentador de navalhas.

strophe, s. estrofe.

structure, s. estrutura, construção; edifício; organização.

struggle, s. esforço, luta, contenda; agonia; to struggle for life, lutar pela vida; v.i. esforçar-se, debater-se, lutar; contorcer-se.

strum, v.t. e v.i. (strumming, strummed), tocar mal um instrumento de corda, arranhar; ralo de aspiração.

strumpet, s. prostituta; adj. de prostituta; lascivo; v.t. prostituir.

strut (strutting, strutted), v.i. empertigar-se, pavonear-se; v.t. reforçar com escoras; sustentar com vigas ou barras; s. andar empertigado; vigamento; barrote, suporte, escora.

strutter, s. pessoa empertigada.

strutting, adj. empertigado, pomposo; adv. struttingly, empertigadamente.

stub, s. toco de árvore; cepo; fragmento, resto; ponta de cigarro, charuto, etc.); talão, canhoto (livro de cheques, etc.); v.t. (stubbing, stubbed) arrancar pela raiz; limpar o campo de toros; dar uma pancada por acidente.

stubbed, *adj.* decepado, reduzido a toco; curto, grosso, atarracado.

stubble, *s.* restolho; barba ou pêlo de barba hirsuta; cabelo espetado.

stubbly, *adj.* coberto de restolhos; curto, eriçado (cabelo, barba).

stucco, *s.* estuque.

stuck, *adj.* vaidoso, presumido; embeiçado, entusiasmado.

stuck-up, *adj.* presunçoso, convencido; insolente.

stud, *v.t.* *(studding, studded),* guarnecer de pregos; pregar pregos ou tachas; semear, salpicar; *s.* manada de cavalos; botão de camisa; barrote, tronco; prego de cabeça grande.

student, *s.* estudante, aluno.

studentship, *s.* a qualidade de ser estudante; bolsa de estudos.

studio, *s.* *atelier* de artista; estúdio.

studious, *adj.* estudioso, aplicado, diligente; *adv. studiously,* estudiosamente.

study, *v.t.* e *v.i.* estudar, investigar, examinar; *s.* estudo; gabinete de estudo; *to be in a brown study,* pensar na morte da bezerra.

stuff, *s.* matéria, material, substância; estofo, tecido; essência, remédio; bagatela, tolice, coisa sem valor. 1) *household stuff,* mobília. 2) *silly stuff,* tolices; *v.t.* e *v.i.* encher, atestar; obstruir; fartar; rechear; empalhar; embalsamar; empanturrar-se.

stuffing, *s.* recheio; material para estofos.

stuffy, *adj.* abafado; mal ventilado.

stum, *v.t.* avivar (vinho) pela adição de mosto; enxofrar; *s.* mosto; sumo de uva; mistela.

stumble, *s.* tropeção, topada; embaraço, estorvo, erro, desatino; *v.i.* tropeçar, errar; dar um passo em falso; cambalear; gaguejar; vacilar; *v.t.* fazer tropeçar, embaraçar.

stumbler, *adj.* o que tropeça.

stump, *s.* tronco, cepo, toco; coto; arnela; um dos três paus do *wicket,* no jogo do *cricket;* plataforma ou estrado para orador; *v.t.* e *v.i.* truncar; tirar os toros (de terreno); deixar abaixo o *wicket* no jogo do *cricket;* desafiar; deitar abaixo; fazer discursos políticos ou improvisados; esfumar; *v.i.* coxear.

stumpy, *adj.* cheio de cepos; atarracado, baixote.

stun, *v.t. (stunning, stunned),* aturdir, estontear, ensurdecer, espantar; *s.* choque ou pancada que atordoa; atordoamento; assombro.

stunning, *adj.* atordoador, atordoante; assombroso; extraordinário, formidável (gír.); *adv. stunningly,* dum modo notável.

stunt, *v.t.* tolher o desenvolvimento, enfezar; *v.i.* realizar proezas, fazer acrobacias; *s.* proeza, acrobacia, pirueta; parada no crescimento; criatura enfezada.

stupe, *s.* compressa.

stupefaction, *s.* estupefacção.

stupefy, *v.t.* estupificar.

stupendous, *adj.* estupendo, assombroso; *adv. stupendously,* estupendamente.

stupi, *adj.* estúpido; *adv. stupidly,* estupidamente.

stupidity, *s.* estupidez.

stupor, *s.* estupor, entorpecimento, letargia; assombro, pasmo.

sturdy, *adj.* forte, vigoroso, robusto; resoluto, determinado; *adv. sturdily,* firmemente, tenazmente.

sturgeon, *s.* esturjão.

stutter, *s.* gaguez, hesitação em falar; *v.i.* gaguejar, hesitar em falar.

stutterer, *s.* gago, tartamudo.

sty, *s.* pocilga, chiqueiro; antro, covil; (também *stye,* terçol).

stygian, *adj.* infernal.

style, *s.* estilo, dicção; linguagem; modo, maneira; moda; expressão, execução; título; buril; estilete; *v.t.* intitular, nomear.

stylet, *s.* estilete.

stylish, *adj.* elegante, à moda, vistoso, brilhante; *adv: stylishly,* elegantemente.

stylist, *s.* estilista.

suasion, *s.* suasão, persuasão; conselho.

suasive, *adj.* suasório, suasivo.

suave, *adj.* suave, harmonioso; *suarely,* suavemente.

suaveness, *s.* suavidade.

suavity, *s.* suavidade.

sub, *s.* substituído; subordinado.

subaltern, *s.* e *adj.* subalterno.

subclass, *s.* subclasse.

subconscious, *adj.* subconsciente; *adv. subconsciously,* subconscientemente.

subcutaneous, *s.* subcutâneo.

subdivide, *v.t.* subdividir; *v.i.* subdividir-se, separar-se.

subdivision, *s.* subdivisão.

subdominant, *s.* subdominante.

subduable, *adj.* domável.

subdue, *v.t.* subjugar, sujeitar, conquistar; domar, suavizar.

subduer, *s.* subjugador.

subjacent, *adj.* subjacente.

subject, *s.* súbdito; vassalo; matéria, assunto, tópico; *adj.* sujeito, submetido; exposto; subordinado; subserviente; *v.t.* sujeitar, submeter; subordinar.

subjection, *s.* sujeição, dependência; vassalagem, jugo.

subjective, *adj.* subjectivo; *adv. subjectively,* subjectivamente.

subjectivity, *s.* subjectividade.

subjoin, *v.t.* acrescentar.

subjugate, *v.t.* subjugar.

subjugation, *s.* sujeição, dependência, jugo.

subjugator, *s.* subjugador.

subjunctive, *adj.* subjuntivo; *adj.* de modo subjuntivo.

sublease, *s.* sublocação.

sublessee, *s.* sublocatário.

sublessor, *s.* sublocador.

sublet (subletting, subletted), *v.t.* sublocar, subarrendar.

sublimate, *s.* sublimado.

sublimation, *s.* sublimação.

sublime, *s.* o sublime; *adj.* sublime, elevado; majestoso; *v.t.* exaltar, sublimar; purificar; *adv. sublimely,* sublimemente.

sublimity, *s.* sublimidade.

submarine, *s.* e *adj.* submarino.

submerge, *v.t.* imergir, submergir; *v.i.* submergir-se.

submergence, *s.* submersão.

submission, *s.* submissão.

submissive, *adj.* submisso; *adv. submissively,* submissamente.

submit, *v.t. (submitting, submitted),* submeter; apresentar; *v.i.* submeter-se, sujeitar-se.

subordinate, *s.* e *adj.* subordinado, inferior; *v.t.* subordinar.

subordination, *s.* suborno.

subordinative, *adj.* subordinativo.

suborn, *v.t.* subornar.

suborner, *s.* subornador.

subscribe, *v.t.* e *v.i.* subscrever; firmar; assinar (jornal).

subscriber, *s.* subscritor; assinante.

subscript, *adj.* subscrito.

subscription, *s.* subscrição.

subsequence, *s.* subsequência.

subsequent, *adj.* subsequente.

subserve, *v.t.* servir; ser útil; ajudar; favorecer.

subservience, *s.* subserviência.

subservient, *adj.* subserviente; *adv. subserviently,* subservientemente.

subside, *v.i.* acalmar; cessar, assentar; depositar-se no fundo.

subsidence, *s.* calma, derrocada; baixa; precipitação (quím.).

subsidiary, *s.* ajudante; *adj.* subsidiário.

subsidize, *v.t.* subsidiar; subvencionar.

subsidy, *s.* subsídio, subvenção.

subsist, *v.i.* subsistir, durar; conservar-se, sustentar-se, manter-se; *v.t.* alimentar, manter.

subsistence, *s.* subsistência; existência; qualidade, inerente.

subsoil, *s.* subsolo.

substance, *s.* substância; essência; material; substancioso, real; considerável; nutritivo.

substantiate, *v.t.* comprovar, justificar, estabelecer.

substantival, *adj.* relativo a um substantivo.

substantive, *s.* e *adj.* substantivo, nome; *adv. substantively,* substantivamente.

substitute, *s.* e *adj.* substituto; *v.t.* substituir.

substitution, *s.* substituição.

substratum, *s.* substrato.

substructure, *s.* subestrutura.

subtenancy, *s.* sublocação.

subtenant, *s.* sublocatário.

subtend, *v.t.* estender por baixo; subestender.

subterfuge, *s.* subterfúgio.

subterranean, *adj.* subterrâneo.

subtile, *adj.* subtil, astuto; ténue; fino, delicado; *adv. subtilely,* subtilmente.

subtilize, *v.t.* discorrer com subtileza.

subtilty, *s.* subtileza.

subtle, *adj.* subtil, fino, astuto; delgado, fino; *adv. subtly,* subtilmente, engenhosamente.

subtract, *v.t.* subtrair.

subtraction, *s.* subtracção.

subtropical, *adj.* subtropical.

suburb, *s.* subúrbio.

suburban, *adj.* suburbano.

subvariety, *s.* subvariedade.

subvention, *s.* subvenção, subsídio, ajuda.

subversion, *s.* subversão.

subversive, *adj.* subversivo.

subvert, *v.t.* subverter.

subway, *s.* caminho subterrâneo.

succedaneous, *adj.* sucedâneo.

succedaneum, *s.* sucedâneo, substituto.

succeed, *v.t.* suceder, seguir-se a outro; ser o sucessor de, substituir; *v.i.* ser bem sucedido; ter êxito; conseguir.

succeeding, *adj.* sucessivo; seguinte.

success, *s.* êxito; bom êxito; sucesso, triunfo.

successful, *adj.* feliz, afortunado; *adv. successfully,* com sucesso.

succession, *s.* sucessão, seguimento; movimentos sucessivos; descendência; linhagem; direito de herança.

successive, *adj.* sucessivo; *adv. successively,* sucessivamente.

successor, *s.* sucessor.

succint, *adj.* sucinto, conciso, breve, lacónico; *adv. succinctly,* sucintamente.

succory, *s.* chicória (bot.)

succour, *v.t.* socorrer, ajudar, auxiliar; *s.* socorro, ajuda, auxílio.

succulence, *s.* suculência.

succulent, *adj.* suculento; *adv. succulently,* suculentamente.

succumb, *v.i.* sucumbir.

succursal, (com.); capela; *adj.* sucursal, subsidiário.

such, *adj.* tal, semelhante, igual, aquele, aquela; *such a thing,* uma tal coisa; *pron.* tal, aquele, aquela, aqueles, aquelas; o, a, os, as, aquele; que, o que, aqueles que, os que, qualquer que.

such-and-such, *pron.* este ou aquele, algum.

suck, *s.* sucção, acção de mamar; chupadura; leite que as crias chupam; pequena bebida; *v.t.* e *v.i.* chuchar, chupar; sorver, sugar, absorver; esgotar; aspirar; mamar. 1) *to suck out,* dar à bomba; esgotar. 2) *to suck up,* tragar. 3) *to suck up to,* bajular, agradar; *s.* sucção; chupada; mamada. 4) *to give suck to,* dar de mamar.

sucker, *s.* chupador; êmbolo; renovo; ventosa; leitão; pessoa estúpida; beberrão; chupista.

sucking, *adj.* que ainda mama; novo e inexperiente; *sucking bottle,* mamadeira.

suckle, *s.* peito, teta; *v.t.* amamentar.

suckling, *s.* criança de peito; cria de leite.

suction, *s.* sucção, aspiração.

sudden, *adj.* repentino, súbito, improvisado; apressado, imprevisto; *on a sudden,* de repente; *adv. suddenly,* repentinamente.

sudorific, *s.* e *adj.* sudorífico.

suds, *s.* água de sabão; espuma; *to be in suds,* estar em maus lençóis.

sue, *v.t.* e *v.i.* citar, processar, demandar; accionar; solicitar; cortejar.

suet, *s.* sebo.

suety, *adj.* seboso.

suffer, *v.t.* e *v.i.* sofrer; tolerar; permitir; padecer.

sufferance, *s.* sofredor; tolerância, permissão.

sufferer, *s.* sofredor, pessoa que padece; *to be a sufferer by,* ser vítima de.

suffering, *s.* sofrimento, padecimento; *adj.* sofredor, doente.

suffice, *v.i.* bastar; ser suficiente, chegar; *v.t.* satisfazer.

sufficiency, *s.* suficiência; o suficiente.

sufficient, *adj.* suficiente, bastante; apto, competente, idóneo; *adv. sufficiently,* suficientemente.

suffix, *s.* sufixo; *v.t.* acrescentar um sufixo.

suffocate, *v.t.* e *v.i.* sufocar(-se), asfixiar (-se); apagar um fogo.

suffocation, *s.* sufocação.

suffrage, *s.* voto; assentimento; sufrágio.

suffragist, *s.* sufragista; o que advoga o direito de voto para as mulheres.

suffuse, *v.t.* estender, derramar, difundir, cobrir.

suffusion, *s.* sufusão; derramamento.

sugar, *s.* açúcar; lisonja; *sugar loaf,* pão de açúcar; *v.t.* adoçar, polvilhar de açúcar.

sugared, *adj.* açucarado.

sugariness, *s.* doçura.

sugary, *adj.* açucarado, adoçado, lisonjeiro.

suggest, *v.t.* sugerir, alvitrar.

suggestion, *s.* sugestão, insinuação, inspiração, alvitre; instigação; incitamento.

suggestive, *adj.* sugestivo.

suicidal, *adj.* suicida.

suing, *s.* o acto de processar; solicitação; galanteio.

suit, *s.* processo (for.); petição; série, jogo, sortimento; colecção; fato completo; galanteio; naipe. 1) *to bring a suit,* intentar uma acção, demandar. 2) *to follow suit,* jogar do mesmo naipe; imitar outro. 3) *dress-suit,* fato de cerimónia; *v.i.* ajustar; assentar bem; agradar; adaptar, acomodar; *v.i.* convir, corresponder; ajustar-se.

suitable, *adj.* conveniente, adequado, próprio, apropriado; *adv. suitably,* convenientemente.

suite, *s.* série; jogo; séquito; acompanhamento; sequela; *a suite of rooms,* vários quartos ligados entre si.

suiting, *s.* tecido para fatos; fazenda.

suitor, *s.* demandante, parte autora num processo; litigante; pretendente, candidato.

sulk, *s.* mau humor, enfado; *v.i.* estar de mau humor; *adv. sulkily,* de mau humor.

sulky, *adj.* rabugento; que está de trombas.

sullen, *adj.* taciturno, soturno; sombrio, casmurro, cabeçudo, teimoso; malévolo; rabugento, colérico; *adv. sullenly,* de mau humor; iradamente, taciturnamente.

sully, *v.t.* manchar, empanar; *v.i.* manchar-se.

sulphate, *s.* sulfato.

sulphide, *s.* sulfureto.

sulphur, *s.* enxofre.

sulphurate, *v.t.* sulfurar; enxofrar.

sulphureous, *adj.* sulfuroso.

sulphuretted, *adj.* sulfuretado.

sulphuric, *adj.* sulfúrico.

sulphurous, *adj.* sulfuroso.

sultan, *s.* sultão.

sultanate, *s.* autoridade ou jurisdição dum sultão.

sultry, *adj.* muito quente e opressivo; pesado, abafado, sufocante; *adv. sultrily,* duma maneira opressiva ou abafada.

sum, *v.t. (summing, summed),* somar; *to sum up,* resumir; recapitular; *s.* soma, total; quantia, importância; sumário.

summary, *s.* sumário, resumo, compêndio; *adj.* sumário, breve; *adv. summarily,* sumàriamente.

summation, *s.* soma; agregado; resumo; somatório.

summer, *s.* Verão, estio; viga mestra; *v.i.* veranear.

summerlike, *adv.* de modo estival.

summerly, *adj.* estival.

summery, *adj.* relativo ao estio; parecido com o estio.

summit, *s.* cume, topo, alto; sumidade, zénite.

summon, *v.t.* chamar, mandar chamar; convocar; citar; citar.

summoner, *s.* o que cita ou intima; oficial de justiça.

sumpter, *s.* azêmola, besta de carga.

sumptuary, *adj.* sumptuário.

sumptuous, *adj.* sumptuoso, esplêndido, magnífico; opíparo; *adv. sumptuously,* sumptuosamente.

sun, *s.* sol, soalheira; *v.t. (sunning, sunned),* expor aos raios de sol; aquecer-se ao sol.

sunbeam, *s.* raio de sol.

sunburn, *s.* queimadura solar.

sunburnt, *adj.* queimado pelo sol.

sunday, *s.* domingo; *adj.* domingueiro, dominical.

sunder, *v.i.* separar, dividir.

sundries, *s. pl.* miscelâneas, acessórios.

sundry, *adj.* vários, diversos.

sunflower, *s.* girassol.

sunk, *adj.* afundado.

sunless, *adj.* sem sol, sombrio.

sunlight, *s.* luz do sol.

sunlike, *adj.* parecido com o sol.

sunlit, *adj.* iluminado pelo sol.

sunniness, *s.* soalheira; brilho; disposição radiante.

sunny, *adj.* soalheiro, radiante, brilhante, iluminado pelo sol; alegre, risonho.

sunrise, *s.* nascer do Sol.

sunset, *s.* pôr do Sol.

sunshade, *s.* sombrinha.

sunshiny, *adj.* cheio de sol.

sunstroke, *s.* insolação.

sup (supping, supped), *v.t.* sorver, beber aos goles; *v.i.* cear; *s.* gole, trago.

super, *s.* actor supranumerário; pessoa sem importância ou indesejável.

superable, *adj.* superável.

superabundance, *s.* superabundância.

superabundant, *adj.* superabundante; *adv. superabundantly,* superabundantemente.

superadd, *v.t.* acrescentar.

superb, *adj.* soberbo, magnífico; excelente; *adv. superbly,* magnificamente.

supercargo, *s.* sobrecarga; comissário (encarregado de carga).

supercilious, *adj.* altivo, soberbo, arrogante; *adv. superciliously,* arrogantemente.

superficial, *adj.* superficial; *adv. superficially,* superficialmente.

superficiality, *s.* superficialidade.

superficies, *s.* superfície.

superfluous, *adj.* supérfluo; *adv. superfluously,* superfluamente.

superimpose, *v.t.* sobrepor.

superimposition, *s.* sobreposição.

superintend, *v.t.* e *v.i.* superintender; fiscalizar, dirigir.

superintendence, *s.* superintendência, direcção.

superintendent, *s.* superintendente.

superior, *s.* e *adj.* superior.

superiority, *s.* superioridade.

superlative, *s.* e *adj.* superlativo.

superman, *s.* super-homem.

supernatural, *adj.* sobrenatural; *adv. supernaturally,* sobrenaturalmente.

supernumerary, *adj.* e *s.* supranumerário.

superpose, *v.t.* sobrepor.

superposition, *s.* sobreposição.

superscribe, *v.t.* sobrescrever; escrever no alto ou no exterior.

supersede, *v.t.* substituir; inutilizar; invalidar; pôr de lado.

superstition, *s.* superstição.

superstitious, *adj.* supersticioso.

supervise, *v.t.* superintender, fiscalizar, inspeccionar, dirigir.

supervision, *s.* supervisão, inspecção, fiscalização.

supervisor, *s.* supervisor, superintendente.

supine, *adj.* deitado de costas; negligente; inactivo, indolente; *adv. supinely,* de costas; negligentemente.

supper, *s.* ceia.

supplant, *v.t.* suplantar.

supple, *adj.* flexível, brando.

supplement, *s.* suplemento; *v.t.* suprir, preencher, acrescentar.

supplemental, *adj.* suplementar.

supplementary, *adj.* suplementar.

suppleness, *s.* flexibilidade; complacência.

suppliance, *s.* suplicação.

suppliant, *s.* e *adj.* suplicante.

supplicate, *v.t.* suplicar.

supplicatingly, *adv.* suplicantemente.

supplication, *s.* súplica, rogo, suplicação, petição.

supplicatory, *adj.* suplicatório.

supply, *v.t.* suprir; fornecer, completar, proporcionar; prover; abastecer; preencher; *s.* suprimento; provisão, fornecimento, abastecimento; pl. *supplies,* víveres, materiais; munições, recursos; subsídios.

support, *v.t.* sustentar, escorar, manter, prover; suportar, ajudar, patrocinar; *s.* sustentação; apoio, sustentáculo; sustento, manutenção; defesa, protecção.

supportable, *adj.* suportável, tolerável, sustentável.

supporter, *s.* aquele que apoia ou suporta; apoio, sustentáculo; escora; aderente, partidário.

suppose, *v.t.* supor, imaginar, presumir, admitir.

supposition, *s.* suposição.

supposititious, *adj.* falso, espúrio; *adv. supposititiously,* de modo suposto; imaginariamente.

suppress, *v.t.* suprimir; abafar; conter; reprimir; omitir.

suppression, *s.* supressão.

suppurate, *v.i.* supurar.

suppuration, *s.* supuração.

supremay, *s.* supremacia.

supreme, *adj.* supremo; *adv. supremely,* supremamente.

surcharge, *s.* sobrecarga; *v.t.* sobrecarregar.

surcoat, *s.* sobretudo.

surdity, *s.* surdez.

sure, *s.* seguro, firme, certo, infalível; *adv.* certamente, firmemente; *adv. surely,* certamente.

sureness, *s.* certeza; segurança.

surety, *s.* certeza, confiança; fiança, garantia, caução; fiador; *to be surety for,* ser fiador de.

suretyship, *s.* fiança, caução, garantia.

surf, *s.* ressaca, rebentação.

surgeon, *s.* cirurgião.

surgery, *s.* cirurgia.

surgical, *adj.* cirúrgico.

surgy, *s.* grosso.

surlily, *adv.* de mau humor, grosseiramente, indolentemente.

surliness, *s.* grosseria, mau humor, insolência.

surly, *adj.* áspero, rude, grosseiro, insolente; tempestuoso.

surmise, *s.* suspeita, conjectura, desconfiança; apreensão; *v.t.* e *v.i.* conjecturar, supor, desconfiar, suspeitar.

surmount, *v.t.* passar por cima, sobrepujar; encimar.

surmountable, *adj.* superável.

surname, *s.* sobrenome, apelido, cognome, alcunha; *v.t.* apelidar, alcunhar; cognominar.

surpass, *v.t.* exceder, ultrapassar.

surpassable, *adj.* excedível.

surpassing, *adj.* superior, exímio; *adv. surpassingly,* transcendentalmente.

surplice, *s.* sobrepeliz (ecles.).

surplus, *s.* o excedente.

surprise, *s.* surpresa; *v.t.* surpreender.

surprising, *adj.* surpreendente; maravilhoso; inesperado; *adv. surprisingly,* surpreendentemente.

surrenders, *s.* rendição, entrega; cessão de bens; renúncia; *v.t.* entregar, render; renunciar a; ceder, resignar; *v.i.* render-se.

surreptitious, *adj.* sub-reptício; *adv. surreptitiously,* sub-repticiamente.

surrogate, *s.* substituto, delegado de juiz eclesiástico; testamenteiro dativo.

surround, *v.t.* cercar, circundar, rodear.

surrounding, *adj.* circunvizinho, que circunda; *s. pl.* arredores, arrabaldes; meio, ambiente.

surtax, *s.* sobretaxa.

surtout, *s.* sobretudo; sobrecasaca.

surveillance, *s.* vigilância.

survey, *s.* perspectiva, vista; inspecção; exame; vistoria; descrição; levantamento duma planta; *engine survey,* vigilância duma máquina; *v.t.* ver, inspeccionar, examinar, vistoriar; levantar plantas; fazer hidrografia.

surveying, *s.* hidrografia; agrimensura.

surveyor, *s.* superintendente; agrimensor; inspector; hidrógrafo.

survival, *s.* sobrevivência; sobrevivente.

survive, *v.t.* e *v.i.* sobreviver.

survivor, *s.* sobrevivente.

susceptibility, *s.* susceptibilidade, delicadeza.

susceptible, *adj.* susceptível; delicado, melindroso; *adj. susceptibly,* dum modo susceptível.

suspect, *s.* pessoa suspeita; *v.t.* e *v.i.* suspeitar, desconfiar.

suspend, *v.t.* suspender, pendurar; interromper temporariamente; adiar.

suspender, *s.* o que suspende; *pl.* suspensórios.

suspense, *s.* suspensão, interrupção; incerteza, ansiedade.

suspension, *s.* suspensão.

suspicion, *s.* suspeita, desconfiança; pequena quantidade.

suspicious, *adj.* suspeitoso, desconfiado; *adv. suspiciously,* suspeitosamente.

sustain, *v.i.* sustentar, aguentar, suster, manter; ajudar, sofrer (avaria, perda).

sustainable, *adj.* sustentável.

sustainer, *s.* sustentador; sustentáculo.

sustenance, sustentação, sustento, alimento; sustentáculo.

sustentation, *s.* sustentação, manutenção.

suture, sutura, juntura, costura.

suzerain, *s.* senhor feudal; suserano.

suzerainty, *s.* soberania.

swab (swabbing, swabbed), *v.i.* limpar ou enxugar com um esfregão; *s.* esfregão; pessoa desajeitada.

swabber, *s.* o que limpa com esfregão; varredor.

swaddle, *v.t.* enfaixar; pôr fraldas.

swaddling-clothes, *s.* cueiros, fraldas para crianças de mama.

swag, *s.* (fam.) tudo o que se obtém pelo roubo; saque, pilhagem; bagagem, trouxa.

swage, *s.* instrumento usado para fazer molduras em chapas de ferro; *v.t.* e *v.i.* aliviar, estampar (metal).

swagger, *s.* modo insolente, bazófia; bravata; fanfarronice; *v.i.* bazofiar; bambolear--se; andar em atitude arrogante.

swaggerer, *s.* fanfarrão; pimpão.

swaggering, *s.* fanfarronada, bravata; *adj.* arrogante, pimpão; jactancioso; *adv. swaggeringly,* com fanfarronice.

swain, *s.* jovem camponês; namorado rústico; pretendente.

swallow, *s.* andorinha; garganta; voracidade; deglutição; capacidade de engolir, trago, bocado; *v.t.* engolir, tragar; absorver; ocupar; abismar, engolfar, esgotar; *one swallow does not make a summer,* nem um dedo faz mão, nem uma andorinha faz verão.

swamp, *s.* pântano, brejo; *v.t.* meter ou afundar num pântano; meter em dificuldades; *v.i.* encher-se de água.

swampiness, *s.* estado pantanoso.

swampy, *adj.* pantanoso, atoladiço, brejoso.

swan, *s.* cisne; colo de cisne; tubo de descarga.

swank, *adj.* flexível, ágil.

swanky, *s.* zurrapa; cerveja ordinária; jovem desembaraçado.

swap (swapping, swapped), *v.t.* trocar, permutar; *s.* troca, permuta, barganha.

sward, *s.* relva; pele, coiro; *v.t.* relvar, arrelvar.

swarm, *s.* enxame; formigueiro; multidão; colmeia; *v.i.* enxamear, pulular; abundar; trepar por uma árvore; *v.t.* criar em enxames; encher, apinhar.

swarthy, *adj.* trigueiro, moreno, escuro; *adv. swarthily,* de cor morena.

swash, *v.t.* e *v.i.* chapinhar; bater de encontro; bravatear; esparrinhar (na água); *s.* bravata, fanfarronada; o chapinhar da água.

swashbuckler, *s.* fanfarrão, espadachim; mata-sede.

swashing, *adj.* de fanfarrão.

swastika, *s.* cruz suástica.

swat, *v.t.* esmagar, bater.

swathe, *v.t.* enfaixar.

sway, *s.* o manejo duma arma; balanço; agitação; influência, poder; *v.t.* manejar; inclinar para um lado; influir, governar; *v.i.* pender, inclinar-se, oscilar; governar, ter influência.

swear (swore, sworn), *v.t.* e *v.i.* jurar;

blsfemar, praguejar; juramentar; fazer jurar; prometer sobre juramento.

swearer, s. o que jura; blasfemador; praguejador.

swearing, s. juramento; blasfémia.

sweat, s. suor; trabalho, fadiga; v.i. suar, transpirar; afadigar-se; sofrer; v.t. fazer suar; obrigar a trabalhar por pouco dinheiro.

sweater, s. pessoa que transpira muito; patrão explorador; camisola grossa de lã.

sweatiness, s. suor.

sweating, s. suor.

sweaty, adj. suado; coberto de suor; trabalhoso.

Swede, s. sueco, natural da Suécia; nabo sueco.

Swedish, adj. sueco; s. língua sueca.

sweep (swept, swept), v.t. varrer, vasculhar, dragar; passar rapidamente por cima; remar; rocegar; levar impetuosamente, arrebatar; assolar, desvastar; v.i. passar impetuosamente. 1) to sweep away, arrebatar; arrastar tudo; s. varredura, vassourada; extensão; andar ou movimento majestoso; alcance, campo (fig.) arrasto (rede); assolação: remada; limpa-chaminés. 2) sweep-net, rede varredoura.

sweeper, s. varredor, limpa-chaminés.

sweeping, adj. vasto, compreensivo; arrebatador; radical.

sweepstake, s. moda de apostar nas corridas de cavalos; o que ganha em todos os jogos.

sweet, s. doçura; termo de carinho; parte doce de alguma coisa; doce, bombom; adj. doce, saboroso; belo, lindo; gentil; suave, meigo, agradável. 1) to be sweet on, estar apaixonado por. 2) to have a sweet tooth, gostar das coisas doces. 3) sweet oil, azeite de azeitona. 4) sweet temper, amabilidade, afabilidade.

sweeten, v.t. adoçar; açucarar; abrandar, suavizar, mitigar; v.i. adoçar-se.

sweetheart, s. namorado, namorada; querido, querida (vocativo).

sweetmeat, s. compota, doce; fruto cristalizado.

sweetness, s. doçura; suavidade, delicadeza.

sweety, s. confeito.

swell, s. aumento de volume ou tamanho, inchaço; elevação (do mar); ondulação; um crescendo e diminuindo de som (mús.); disposição dum órgão para aumentar ou diminuir a intensidade do som; elevação gradual do terreno; janota, peralta; all the swells of the place, a sociedade elegante do lugar; v.i. (swollen, swollen), inchar, intumescer; boiar; avolumar-se; pavonear-se; encolerizar-se; elevar-se; v.t. inchar, bojar, distender; engrossar, aumentar, avolumar.

swelling, s. inchaço, tumor; elevação (das ondas); estuação; adj. inchado, empolado.

swelter, v.i. abafar, sufocar; transpirar muito; v.t. sufocar, oprimir, abafar.

swerve, s. desvio; v.i. desviar-se (da linha, dever ou costume); vaguear, errar.

swift, adj. veloz, rápido; ágil, vivo; pronto; s. gavião; corrente (de rio); dobadoura; adv. rapidamente, velozmente; prontamente; swift-footed, de pé leve.

swiftly, adv. ligeiramente, rapidamente.

swiftness, s. rapidez, velocidade, presteza, prontidão.

swig (swigging, swigged), v.t. esticar uma corda; castrar, beber com sofreguidão; v.i. beber dum gole, beber de mais; s. trago; bêbado.

swill, s. grande trago; lavadura de cozinha; lavagem; v.t. e v.i. (com out) banhar, lavar, enxaguar, beber e grandes tragos, embriagar-se.

swim (swam, swum), v.i. e v.t. nadar; flutuar, boiar; deslizar; transbordar; ter vertigens, sentir-se tonto; atravessar a nado; s. natação; tendência; bexiga dos peixes.

swimmer, s. nadador.

swimming, s. natação; nado, nadadura; flutuação; tontura, vertigem; adj. que nada, nadador; flutuante; próprio para nadar; natatório; banhado, inundado; tonto, estonteado. 1) swimming-pool, piscina de natação. 2) swimming bladder, bexiga natatória.

swimmingly, adv. facilmente, sem dificuldade; deslizando.

swindle, v.t. lograr, burlar, espoliar por fraude; calotear; trapacear; s. logro, trapaça.

swindler, s. escroque, burlista, cavalheiro de indústria, trapaceiro.

swindling, s. burla, trapaça; adj. fraudulento, trapaceiro.

swine, s. porco, varrão. 1) wild swine, javali. 2) sea swine, golfinho. 3) do not cast pearls before swine, não deites pérolas a porcos.

swineherd, s. porqueiro.

swing, vt. e vi. balançar(-se), oscilar; fazer

oscilar; girar, fazer girar; brandir, vibrar, ser enforcado; *s.* balanço, oscilação; compasso, ritmo; espaço percorrido; andar desembaraçado; livre curso; *in full swing,* em plena actividade.

swipe, *s.* pancada violenta; *v.t.* dar uma pancada violenta; roubar, furtar (gír.) *pl.* cerveja má ou estragada; cerveja fraca.

swirl, *vi.* passar rapidamente ou remoinhando; *s.* remoinho de água ou de vento; salto dum peixe.

Swiss, *s.* e *adj.* suíço.

switch, *s.* vara flexível; açoite; cabelo postiço; comutador, interruptor (elect.), agulha (via férrea); mudança de uma coisa para outra; chibatada, chicotada; *v.t.* e *v.i.* chibatar, açoitar; sacudir, agitar; mudar-se, desviar-se; interromper; comutar (elect.). 1) *to switch on the light,* acender a luz. 2) *to switch off the light,* apagar a luz.

switchboard, *s.* quadro de distribuição.

swivel, *s.* argola ou elo móvel; *v.t.* e *v.i.* girar sobre um eixo.

swizzle, *v.i.* beber em excesso; *s.* bebida composta.

swoon, *s.* desmaio; *v.i.* desmaiar, desfalecer.

swooning, *s.* desmaio.

swoop, *s.* descida da ave de rapina sobre a presa; *v.t.* apanhar no ar; *v.i.* descer rapidamente.

swop (swopping, swopped), *v.i.* trocar; *s.* troca.

sword, *s.* espada. 1) *to put to fire and sword,* pôr a ferro e fogo. 2) *sword-play,* esgrima.

swordfish, *s.* peixe-espada.

sybarite, *s.* sibarita.

sycamine, *s.* amoreira.

syce, *s.* criado, criado montado; escudeiro.

sycophancy, *s.* delação; servilismo.

sycophant, *s.* adulador, bajulador, servil.

syllabic, *adj.* silábico.

syllable, *s.* sílaba; *v.t.* exprimir por sílabas; proferir, articular.

syllogism, *s.* silogismo.

sylph, *s.* silfo, sílfide.

sylvan, *adj.* silvestre, selvático.

symbol, *s.* símbolo, emblema, abreviatura, letra; credo (teol.).

symbolic, *adj.* simbólico, figurativo; *adv.* symbolically, simbolicamente.

symbolism, *s.* simbolismo.

symbolization, *s.* simbolização.

symbolize, *v.t.* e *v.i.* simbolizar.

symbology, *s.* simbologia.

symetric, *adj.* simétrico; *adv. symmetrically,* simetricamente.

symmetry, *s.* simetria.

sympathetic, *adj.* simpático; compassivo.

sympathize, *vi.* compadecer-se, condoer-se, ser compassivo.

sympathy, *s.* compaixão, comiseração; simpatia (med.).

symphonic, *adj.* sinfónico.

symphony, *s.* sinfonia.

symposium, *s.* banquete, festim; reunião em que se discute determinado assunto; conjunto de opiniões sobre determinado assunto.

symptom, *s.* sintoma, sinal.

symtomatic, *adj.* sintomático.

synagogue, *s.* sinagoga.

synchronism, *s.* sincronismo.

synchronization, *s.* sincronização.

synchronize, *v.t.* sincronizar; *v.i.* ser síncrono.

synchronous, *adj.* síncrono.

syncopate, *v.t.* sincopar.

syncope, *s.* síncope.

syndic, *s.* síndico.

syndicalism, *s.* sindicalismo.

syndicalist, *s.* sindicalista.

syndicate, *s.* sindicato; *v.t.* e *v.i.* sindicar.

syne, *s.* tempo há muito passado.

synodic, al, *adj.* sinódico; *adv. synodically,* sinodicamente.

synonym, sinónimo.

synopsis, *s.* sinopse.

syntactic, *adj.* sintáctico.

syntax, *s.* sintaxe.

synthesis, *s.* síntese.

syphilis, *s.* sífilis.

syphilitic, *adj.* sifilítico.

syphon, *s.* sifão, tubo; *v.t.* tirar por meio de sifão.

Syriac, *adj.* e *s.* siríaco.

Syrian, *adj.* e *s.* sírio.

syringe, *s.* seringa; *v.t.* seringar.

syrup, *s.* xarope.

system, *s.* sistema.

systematic, al, *adj.* sistemático; *adv.* sistematicamente.

systematization, *s.* sistematização.

systematize, *v.t.* reduzir a sistema, sistematizar.

systole, *s.* sístole.

systolic, *adj.* sistólico.

T

t, vigésima letra do alfabeto.

tab, s. apêndice; aba; ponta, presilha, alça. 1) *ear-tab,* orelheira, aba de certos gorros que cobre as orelhas. 2) *to keep tabs on,* vigiar, controlar.

tabby, s. tabi, espécie de tafetá engelhado. *tabby-cat,* gato doméstico, gato malhado; solteirona, mexeriqueira; espécie de traça; variedade de cimento.

table, s. mesa; tábua; tabela, índice, lista; superfície plana de uma pedra preciosa lapidada; cada uma das metades do tabuleiro de gamão; *(arquit.)* painel; *(geol.)* camada horizontal. 1) *to lay on the table,* adiar indefinidamente a discussão de um projecto. 2) *to turn the tables,* inverter as posições. 3) *table leaf,* tábua sobressalente de mesa. 4) *table-linen,* roupa de mesa. *v.t.* pôr na mesa (carta de jogar); pagar; organizar em tabela; apresentar projecto ao Parlamento.

tableau, s. quadro, pintura.

tablecloth, s. toalha de mesa.

tableland, s. planalto.

tablespoon, s. colher de sopa.

tablet, s. tabuinha, lâmina de marfim ou de madeira onde se grava inscrição; tabuleta; bloco de papel para notas; pastilha, comprimido; barra de chocolate.

tableware, s. utensílios de mesa (roupa, talheres).

tabloid, s. jornal pequeno com muitas gravuras e pouco texto; comprimido, pastilha.

taboo, tabu, s. tabu; proibição; *adj.* tabu, proíbido; sagrado, inviolável. *v.t.* declarar tabu, proibir, excluir.

tabular, *adj.* tabular; relativo ou em forma de quadro, tábua, tabela; laminar.

tabulate, *adj.* tabular, laminar. *v.t.* dispor em tabela, em quadro.

tabulator, s. tabulador (de máquina de escrever).

tachogram, s. tacografia.

tachograph, s. tacógrafo.

tachometer, s. taquímetro.

tachycardia, s. taquicardia.

tachygraph, s. texto taquigrafado; taquígrafo.

tachygrapher, s. taquígrafo; estenógrafo.

tachygraphy, s. taquigrafia; estenografia.

tachymetry, s. taqueometria.

tacit, *adj.* tácito, implícito, subentendido.

taciturn, *adj.* taciturno, calado.

tack, s. tacha (prego pequeno de cabeça achatada); (pl.) alinhavos; (náut.) amura; (fig.) comida. *v.t.* e *v.i.* pregar com taxas; alinhavar; (fig.) ligar, unir; virar de bordo (o navio); mudar de rumo; bordejar.

tackle, s. talha, aparelho de navio; cordame; roldana, guincho, molinete; apetrechos, aparelhagem; acto de agarrar o adversário (especialmente no futebol); jogador de futebol americano. *v.t.* e *v.i.* segurar ou fixar com talhas; atacar um problema ou uma tarefa; engalfinhar-se com um adversário; deter jogador; arrear, atrelar cavalo; *to tackle to,* deitar mãos à obra.

tacky, *adj.* pegajoso; mal vestido, desalinhado, trapalhão.

tact, s. tacto, diplomacia.

tactful, *adj.* que tem tacto, diplomata; insinuante.

tactic, s. táctica; método, expediente; estratégia.

tactical, *adj.* táctico; hábil, habilidoso.

tactician, s. táctico, estratego.

tactics, s. táctica; estratégia; diplomacia; meio, método.

tactile, *adj.* táctil, tangível, palpável.

tactless, *adj.* com falta de tacto, desajeitado, indelicado.

tadpole, s. girino.

taenia, tenia, s. ténia, solitária; (anat.) faixa estreita de tecido nervoso; fita que os antigos gragos usavam no cabelo; (arquit.) listel.

taffeta, s. tafetá.

taffy, *adj.* caramelo.

tag, s. etiqueta, rótulo; farrapo; ponta solta;

madeixa de cabelos; puxadeira de bota; ponta da cauda de animal; resto; apêndice; penduricalho; frase batida; refrão de canção; fim da fala do actor, deixa. 1) *tag-day*, dia de colecta para uma instituição beneficente. 2) *tag and rag*, gentalha, ralé; *v.t.* e *v.i.* pôr etiqueta em, etiquetar, rotular; encher de citações ou frases feitas; fazer rimar; cortar a lã emaranhada ao carneiro; enfeitar com penduricalhos; salpicar, mosquear; seguir alguém de perto.

tail, *s.* cauda, rabo; apêndice; aba de casaco; trança de cabelos, rabicho; traseira, retaguarda; cabo comprido (de pá, ancinho, etc.); reverso de moeda; bicha, fila de pessoas; comitiva; (pl.) casaca; (jur.) limitação de propriedade, propriedade vinculada; (mús.) haste de nota; (tip.) pé de página; 1) *to turn tail*, virar as costas, fugir. 2) *tails up*, bem disposto. 3) *tail-coat*, fraque. *adj.* da cauda, de popa; de trás, traseiro, posterior, último; (jur.) vinculado. 4) *tail-gate*, comporta de descarga. 5) *tail-plane*, (av.) estabilizador. 6) *tail-wind*, vento de cauda, vento de popa. *v.t.* e *v.i.* colocar cauda ou rabo em; caminhar na cauda, seguir no fim, ir atrás de; cortar a cauda a; puxar pelo rabo a; amarrar pela extremidade; acrescentar, juntar, emendar; cortar as pontas a um fruto; seguir de perto, perseguir; formar bicha ou fila. 7) *to tail off, to tail away*, ir no fim da cauda; afastar-se. 8) *to tail on*, seguir na cauda. 9) *to tail to the tide*, virar-se consoante os movimentos da maré. 10) *to tail up*, (av.) picar de frente.

tailing, *s.* acto de guarnecer de cauda; *(pl.)* resíduos, refugo, escória.

tailless, *adj.* sem cauda; anuro.

taillight, *s.* farolim traseiro; luz de cauda (de comboio ou avião).

tailor, *s.* alfaiate. *v.t.* talhar, fazer roupa por medida; adaptar, acomodar.

tailorbird, *s.* pássaro-alfaiate.

tailored, *adj.* talhado por alfaiate; feito por medida; feito por encomenda; *a well tailored man*, um homem bem vestido.

tailpiece, *s.* parte terminal, ponta, remate; vinheta.

tain, *s.* folha de estanho.

taint, *s.* mancha, nódoa; defeito; tara; sinal; infecção, corrupção; *v.t.* e *v.i.* infectar, corromper; contaminar(-se); apodrecer, alterar-se; manchar, macular; sujar.

taintless, *adj.* imaculado; puro.

take, *s.* quantidade recolhida; receita; pescaria; caçada; (cin.) tomada de vistas. *v.t.* e *v.i.* *(took, taken)* tomar, pegar, apanhar, agarrar, segurar; tomar, capturar, conquistar; prender, aprisionar; apreender; apoderar-se de; (na voz passiva), ser tomado de, ser acometido de, ter ataque; comer, tomar (uma peça de xadrez, etc.); apanhar, surpreender; atrair, prender; cativar, encantar; atingir, acertar em; tomar, comer, beber; tomar, acolher, admitir; alugar, arrendar; assumir (forma, carácter), adoptar; prestar juramento; fazer voto de, encarregar-se de, desempenhar; tomar, escolher; tomar, ocupar (espaço); requerer, necessitar; tirar, obter; receber; aceitar; seguir (conselho); sofrer, submeter-se a; aguentar; compreender, perceber; comparar, confrontar; levar, conduzir, transportar; tirar, extrair, arrancar; subtrair, deduzir; arrebatar, matar. 1) *he was taken by a strong fever*, foi acometido de um febrão. 2) *to take someone of guard*, apanhar alguém desprevenido. 3) *to take someone a blow*, acertar um golpe em alguém. 4) *deuce take him*, diabos o levem! 5) *to take into one's service*, tomar a seu serviço. 6) *to take a seat for a concert*, reservar um lugar para um concerto. 7) *to take the throne*, apoderar-se do trono, subir ao trono. 8) *to take legal advice*, consultar um advogado. 9) *to take a bus*, tomar um autocarro. 10) *to take advantage of*, aproveitar-se de, tirar partido de. 11) *to take a walk*, dar um passeio. 12) *to take into account*, levar em conta. 13) *to take leave*, despedir-se. 14) *to take notice of*, reparar em. 15) *to take upon onself*, assumir a responsabilidade. 16) *to take one's seat*, sentar-se. 17) *to take along*, levar consigo. 18) *to take amiss*, levar a mal, ofender-se com. 19) *to take back*, reaver, recuperar; retirar (o que se disse). 20) *to take out*, levar ou conduzir para fora. 21) *to take over*, suceder a; assumir a direcção de. 22) *to take up residence*, fixar residência. 23) *to take up the gauntlet*, aceitar o desafio. 24) *to take after his father*, saír ao pai. 25) *to take to one's heels*, fugir, dar às de vila-diogo. 26) *to take up with*, associar-se, ligar-se a.

takedown, *adj.* desmontável; *s.* humilhação, vexame, afronta; máquina desmontável.

take-in, *s.* logro, burla, impostura; impostor.

take-off, s. partida, descolagem; imitação, paródia, caricatura.

taking, s. tomada, captura, apreensão; produto de caçada ou pescaria; agitação, perturbação; (pl.) receitas; adj. cativante, atraente; infeccioso, contagioso.

talaria, s. talares (sandálias aladas de Mercúrio).

talc, s. talco.

talcum, s. talcum-powder, pó de talco.

tale, s. conto, história; fábula; mentira, falsidade; intriga, mexerico; to tell tales, contar mentiras.

talebearing, adj. mexeriqueiro, intriguista. s. mexerico, intriga.

talent, s. talento, vocação; talento (moeda e unidade de peso da antiguidade); inteligência.

talented, adj. talentoso, dotado.

taler, thaler, s. táler (antiga moeda alemã de prata).

tales, s. (jur.) convocação de jurados suplentes; lista dos mesmos.

taleteller, s. contador de histórias; mexeriqueiro.

talipes, s. (med.) talipe, pé torto.

talisman, s. talismã.

talk, s. conversa, conversação, cavaqueira; fala; boato, rumor; dialecto, maneira de falar. 1) the talk of the town, assunto de falatório da cidade. 2) small talk, conversa fiada. 3) talking film, filme sonoro; v.t. e v.i. fa-lar, conversar, discorrer, tagarelar, cavaquear; bisbilhotar. 4) to talk back, retrucar, rebater. 5) to talk round, discutir longamente um assunto sem chegar a uma conclusão. 6) to talk through one's hat, dizer disparates. 7) to talk oneself hoarse, enrouquecer de tanto falar. 8) to talk someone into doing something, convencer alguém a fazer qualquer coisa. 9) to talk turkey, falar desabridamente. 10) to talk up, discutir, divulgar.

talkative, adj. loquaz, tagarela, falador.

talkativeness, s. loquacidade, verbosidade; tagarelice.

talkee-talkee, s. tagarelice; algaraviada.

talker, s. conversador, falador.

talkie, s. filme sonoro; cinema sonoro.

talking, s. fala, conversa. 1) talking to, repri-menda, repreensão; adj. falante, falador; tagarela; sonoro (filme). 2) talking-machine, fonógrafo.

tall, adj. alto, de estatura elevada; grande;

esguio, comprido; (coloq.) extravagante, excessivo, jactancioso. 1) tall-talk, gaba-rolice. 2) tall story, patranha. 3) to talk tall, gabar-se, vangloriar-se.

tallage, talliage, s. antigo imposto pago pelo rendeiro ao senhor feudal.

tallith, s. talete, espécie de xaile dos judeus.

tallow, s. sebo. v.t. ensebar.

tallowy, adj. sebáceo, sebento, seboso; gordurento.

tally, s. talha, vara na qual se fazem entalhes para marcar quantidades; contagem feita através de entalhes ou marcas; entalho, incisão ou marca usada em contagem; marcação, contagem, conta; grupo; série, lote; etiqueta, rótulo; duplicado, réplica, reprodução. 1) tally shop, loja de venda a prestações. 2) tally wife, amante. 3) to answer in tally to, corresponder exac-tamente a. 4) to buy goods by the tally, comprar mercadorias à dúzia, à vintena, ao cento, etc. v.t. e v.i. contar, calcular, marcar; corresponder a; ajustar-se a; etiquetar, rotular.

Talmud, s. Talmude.

talon, s. garra, presa de ave de rapina, unha comprida; monte (em jogos de cartas); saliência da lingueta que é pressionada pela chave

talus, s. (anat.) astrágalo; tornozelo, artelho; rampa, escarpa.

tam, s. espécie de gorro escocês com borla.

tamale, s. prato mexicano feito com carne picada e pimenta.

tamandua, tamandu, s. tamanduá.

tamarind, s. tamarindo.

tamarisk, s. (bot.) tamargueira, tamariz.

tambour, s. tambor, caixa, bombo; bastidor de bordar; pano bordado em bastidor; peixe-tambor.

tambourin, s. tamborim, tambor comprido usado na Provença; dança provençal.

tambourine, s. pandeiro, pandeireta.

tame, adj. manso, doméstico; dócil; inofen-sivo; servil; insípido, desenxabido; cultivado (planta, terreno); tame-cat, dependente, pau-mandado; v.t. domar, domesticar; humilhar, abater, dominar; suavizar.

tameless, adj. indomável, selvagem.

tamp, v.t. embuchar; carregar ou calcar carga explosiva; pisar, bater com maço ou pilão; tamped asphalt, asfalto prensado.

tamper, s. calcadeira; soquete; indivíduo que coloca buchas em cargas explosivas. v.t.

interferir; mexer em; intrometer-se; forçar; alterar ilegalmente; adulterar; falsificar; violar (urna eleitoral) corromper, desencaminhar; perverter; subornar.

tampon, s. tampão. v.t. tamponar.

tamponade, tamponage, s. (cir.) tamponamento.

tan, s. curtume (matéria com que se curte); tanino; cor castanho-amarelada; bronzeado; desperdícios de cascas de curtume; abreviatura de tangente. v.t. e v.i. curtir; tostar, bronzear-se; (cal.) sovar, desancar; adj. bronzeado, moreno, trigueiro, castanho-amarelado.

tanbark, s. casca de curtume.

tandem, adv. um atrás do outro, em fila (relativamente ao modo de atrelar cavalos); s. tandem (bicicleta de dois lugares).

tang, s. espiga (extremidade de uma ferramenta que se encaixa no cabo); travo, sabor picante; cheiro penetrante; vestígio, indício; som metálico ou agudo; tom; sotaque; v.t. e v.i. soar, ressoar.

tangency, s. tangência.

tangent, s. e adj. tangente.

tangential, adj. tangencial; divergente, errático, desordenado; superficial.

tangerine, s. tangerina.

tangibility, s. tangibilidade; realidade.

tangible, adj. tangível, palpável; real; (jur.) corpóreo; (pl.) bens corpóreos.

tangle, v.t. e v.i. emaranhar(-se), enredar(-se), enlear, embaraçar; apanhar em laço ou armadilha; complicar(-se). s. entrelaçamento, enredo; confusão, complicação, meada; sargaços.

tangleberry, s. espécie de mirtilo.

tania, s. inhame.

tank, s. tanque, tina, cuba, reservatório, cisterna, angibe; piscina; tanque, carro de combate; v.t. armazenar em tanque ou reservatório.

tankage, s. armazenagem em tanques; capacidade de um tanque; (agric.) resíduos animais usados como adubo ou como alimento para animais.

tankard, s. caneca de cerveja (geralmente de estanho).

tanker, s. navio-cisterna, petroleiro.

tannage, s. curtimento, curtume.

tannate, s. tanato.

tanner, s. curtidor.

tannery, s. loja ou fábrica de curtumes.

tannin, s. tanino.

tantalize, v.t. tantalizar, atormentar.

tantalizing, adj. tantalizante, torturante, desesperador.

tantamount, adj. equivalente; to be tantamount to, equivaler a, importar em, ser o mesmo que.

tantrum, s. acesso de cólera; zanga, fúria.

Taoism, s. tauismo.

tap, s. batida leve, pancadinha; remendo em sola de calçado; torneira, bica; tarugo; espicho; macho de atarraxar; (elect.) tomada; espécie de bebida. 1) *tap bond,* título de dívida pública de emissão ilimitada. 2) *tap borer,* verruma. 3) *tap dancing,* sapateado. 4) *tap house,* casa de bebidas, taberna; v.t. e v.i. bater levemente; pôr remendo em calçado; extrair líquido de reservatório; espichar torneira em barril; abrir, perfurar; roscar; sangrar (árvore); fazer derivação em fio eléctrico; interceptar mensagem radiotelefónica; roubar; introduzir.

tape, s. fita, tira, nastro; fita métrica. v.t. atar, prender, enrolar, isolar com fita; medir com fita métrica.

taper, s. vela estreita de cera, círio; candeia, lamparina; forma afilada, afunilamento; flecha de torre; adj. afilado, afusado, afunilado, piramidal, cónico. v.t. e v.i. afilar(-se), estreitar(-se); diminuir gradualmente.

tapering, adj. afilado, aguçado, afusado.

tapestry, s. tapeçaria.

tapeworm, s. ténia, solitária.

tapper, s. manipulador telegráfico, transmissor.

taproom, s. bar, taberna.

tapster, s. taberneiro.

tar, s. alcatrão; marujo, marinheiro; to have a touch of the tar brush, ter sangue negro; adj. de alcatrão. v.t. alcatroar.

tarantula, s. tarântula.

tardiness, s. lentidão, indolência, vagar; demora, falta de pontualidade.

tardy, adj. lento, vagaroso, moroso, indolente; tardio, atrasado, retardado; relutante.

tare, s. tara, peso do recipiente; (bibl.) joio. v.t. tarar.

target, s. alvo; objectivo, objecto; tarja, escudo pequeno e redondo. 1) *target date,* (mil.) data prevista para o início de uma operação. 2) *target range,* linha de tiro.

tariff, s. tarifa; direitos de importação. v.t. tarifar, tabelar.

tarmac, s. estrada ou pista de aeródromo revestida de macadame alcatroado.

tarnish, v.t. e v.i. embaçar, embaciar(-se); manchar; perder o brilho. s. embaciamento, perda de brilho; deslustre; mancha.

tarpaulin, s. lona encerada, encerado; toldo de lona; chapéu de pano encerado usado pelo marinheiros.

tarragon, s. estragão.

tarry, adj. de alcatrão; alcatroado; enfarruscado.

tarry, v.t. e v.i. esperar, aguardar; tardar, atrasar-se, demorar-se; s. demora, permanência.

tarsus, s. tarso; tornozelo; társio (cartilagem da pálpebra).

tart, adj. ácido, azedo, acre; pungente, cáustico, mordaz. s. tarte, pastel, empada; (coloq.) moça, rapariga leviana.

tartan, s. tecido de lã axadrezado usado pelos escoceses das Terras Altas; manto feito desse tecido com o padrão distintivo de um clã; qualquer tecido axadrezado; (náut.) tartana, embarcação comprida de um só mastro usada no Mediterrâneo.

tartar, s. tártaro, depósito deixado pelo vinho no interior das vasilhas; pedra dos dentes.

Tartar, adj. tártaro, relativo à Tartária; s. tártaro, natural da Tartária; pessoa violenta ou irascível.

tartlet, s. tarte pequena.

task, s. tarefa, trabalho, incumbência; empreendimento, empreitada; dever escolar; task force, (mil.) unidade encarregada de missão especial; v.t. impor tarefa, incumbir de uma missão; encarregar; sobrecarregar, exigir demasiado de.

tassel, s. borla; pendão; bandeira do milho. v.t. e v.i. guarnecer com borlas; tirar o pendão ao milho; criar pendão (o milho).

taste, s. gosto, sabor, paladar; prova (acto de provar); amostra; predilecção, gosto, propensão; bom gosto, elegância. 1) there is no accounting for tastes, gostos não se discutem. 2) add salt to taste, pôr sal a gosto; v.t. e v.i. provar, tomar o gosto de; sentir gosto de; saborear; experimentar, provar; saber a.

tasteful, adj. de bom gosto, requintado, artístico.

tasteless, adj. sensaborão, sem sabor, insípido; sem paladar; sem graça; deselegante.

taster, s. provador; copinho usado pelos provadores de vinho.

tasty, adj. saboroso, apaladado, gostoso; de bom gosto.

tatou, s. tatu.

tatter, s. farrapo, trapo, (pl.) andrajos. v.t. e v.i. esfarrapar(-se).

tatterdemalion, s. indivíduo esfarrapado; maltrapilho.

tattle, v.t. e v.i. tagarelar, taramelar; mexericar, bisbilhotar, dar com a língua nos dentes. s. tagarelice.

tattler, s. tagarela, mexeriqueiro; bisbilhoteiro; (zool.) maçarico.

tattoo, s. toque de recolher; tatú, espectáculo militar, geralmente à noite, com acompanhamento de música; tatuagem; tamborilar de dedos. v.t. tatuar.

tau, s. tau (letra grega).

taunt, s. insulto; censura; escárnio. v.t. censurar, insultar, escarnecer, fazer observações insultuosas sobre; he taunted him with poverty, lançou-lhe em cara a sua pobreza. adj. (náut.) alto, demasiado alto (o mastro).

taupe, s. cor da pele da toupeira, cinzento-amarelado.

taurine, adj. taurino, bovino.

tauromachy, s. tauromaquia.

taut, adj. esticado, retesado, teso; arrumado, em ordem.

tauten, v.t. e v.i. esticar(-se), retesar(-se).

tautology, s. tautologia.

tavern, s. taberna, botequim.

taverner, s. taberneiro.

taw, s. jogo do berlinde; v.t. curtir peles com pedra-ume.

tawdry, adj. vistoso, de mau gosto, berrante, espalhafatoso; s. ornamentos espalhafatosos.

tawny, adj. castanho-amarelado, fulvo, trigueiro.

tax, s. taxa, imposto, tributo; peso, ónus; esforço. 1) tax sale, leilão de bens por falta de pagamento dos impostos; v.t. lançar impostos, tributar, taxar; exigir esforço de; forçar, sobrecarregar; (jur.) avaliar custas de um processo. 2) to tax someone's patience, pôr à prova a paciência de alguém.

taxation, s. tributação, lançamento de impostos; imposto; taxação.

taxcollector, s. cobrador de impostos.

taxi, s. Abreviatura de Taxicab; taxi-girl, mulher empregada em bares para dançar com os clientes a tanto por dança. v.i. andar de táxi; (av.) rolar pela pista.

taxicab, *s.* táxi, automóvel de praça, carro de aluguer.

taxidermist, *s.* taxidermista, embalsamador.

taxidermy, *s.* taxidermia.

taximeter, *s.* taxímetro.

taxonomy, *s.* taxonomia.

taxpayer, *s.* o contribuinte (aquele que paga impostos).

tea, *s.* chá. 1) *tea-party,* festa ou lanche em que se serve chá. 2) *tea wagon,* carrinho de chá.

teach, *v.t.* e *v.i.* (pret. e pp. *taught*) ensinar, instruir, leccionar, dar lições a; explicar.

teacher, *s.* professor, mestre, instrutor, preceptor.

teaching, *s.* ensino, educação, ensinamento, doutrina.

teak, *s.* (bot.) teca.

teal, *s.* (zool.) cerceta, marreco.

team, *s.* equipa; turma; grupo; parelha, junta de bois; *v.t.* atrelar, jungir; *to team up with,* associar-se com, trabalhar em conjunto com.

teamster, *s.* condutor de uma junta de bois.

teapot, *s.* bule.

teapoi, *s.* mesinha de chá.

tear, *s.* lágrima, gota.

tear, *s.* rasgão, pedaço rasgado; rotura; fúria, cólera. 1) *tear and wear,* desgaste. 2) *to go off on a tear,* ir para a farra; *v.t.* e *v.i.* (pret. *tore,* pp. *torn*) rasgar(-se), despedaçar(-se), dilacerar(-se); romper(-se); arrancar violentamente; arremessar-se, correr precipitadamente.

teardrop, *s.* lágrima.

tearful, *adj.* lacrimoso, choroso; triste.

tearing, *adj.* dilacerante; violento, furioso; impetuoso.

tearless, *adj.* sem lágrimas; secos, enxutos (os olhos).

tease, *s.* pessoa arreliadora, provocador. *v.t.* arreliar, irritar, provocar; cardar a lã.

teaser, *s.* arreliador, provocador: cardador.

teasing, *adj.* irritante, arreliador, importuno.

teaspoon, *s.* colher de chá.

teat, *s.* teta, mama.

tec, *s.* (cal.) detective.

technic, *s.* técnica.

technical, *adj.* técnico; *technical sargeant,* primeiro-sargento.

technician, *s.* técnico; especialista, perito.

technique, *s.* técnica.

technocracy, *s.* tecnocracia.

technocratic, *adj.* tecnocrático.

technological, technologic, *adj.* tecnológico.

technologist, *s.* tecnólogo.

technology, *s.* tecnologia.

tectonic, *adj.* tectónico.

tectonics, *s.* tectónica.

tectrix, *s.* tectriz, pena que cobre a base das rémiges e das rectrizes das aves.

teddy-bear, *s.* ursinho de pelúcia.

tedious, *adj.* entediante, aborrecido, enfadonho, cansativo.

tedium, *s.* tédio, aborrecimento, enfado.

teem, *v.i.* e *v.t.* abundar, estar cheio, pulular, proliferar, formigar; vazar, descarregar, despejar.

teeming, *adj.* prolífico, fértil, produtivo; cheio, apinhado; abundante, pululante.

teen, *adj.* idade compreendida entre os 13 e os 19 anos.

teeny, *adj.* o mesmo que *tiny.*

teepee, *s.* o mesmo que *tepee.*

teeter, *s.* baloiço; oscilação; *v.t.* e *v.i.* balouçar, fazer oscilar ou vacilar; hesitar.

teethe, *v.i.* criar dentes, começar a ter dentes.

teething, *s.* dentição, nascimento dos dentes.

teetotal, *adj.* total, completo, inteiro; abstémio, antialcoólico; relativo à abstemia.

teetotaler, teewtotaller, teetotalist, *s.* abstémio.

teetotalism, *s.* abstemia, abstenção de bebidas alcoólicas.

tegmen, *s.* tegumento; cobertura, revestimento.

tegument, *s.* tegumento.

teil, *s.* tília.

telecast, *s.* transmissão de televisão; *v.t.* e *v.i.* transmitir por televisão.

telecomunication, *s.* telecomunicação.

telegenic, *adj.* telegénico.

telegram, *s.* telegrama.

telegraph, *s.* telégrafo, aparelho telegráfico; semáforo; (desp.) quadro que marca os resultados; *v.t.* e *v.i.* telegrafar; fazer sinais.

telegraphic, *adj.* telegráfico; lacónico, conciso.

telegraphist, *s.* telegrafista.

telegraphy, *s.* telegrafia.

telekinesis, *s.* telecinesia.

telemetry, *s.* telemetria.

teleology, *s.* teleologia.

teleosaurus, *s.* (paleo.) teleossáurio.

teleost, teleostan, *s.* teleósteo.

telepathic, *adj.* telepático.
telepathist, *s.* telepata.
telepathy, *s.* telepatia.
telephone, *s.* telefone; *v.t.* e *v.i.* telefonar.
telephonic, *adj.* telefónico.
telephonograph, *s.* telefonógrafo.
telephony, *s.* telefonia.
telephoto, *adj.* telefotográfico; *telephoto lens,* teleobjectiva.
telephotography, *s.* telefotografia.
telescope, *s.* telescópio; óculo de longo alcance; *v.t.* e *v.i.* encaixar(-se) uns nos outros como as partes de um óculo de longo alcance.
telescopic, *adj.* telescópico.
telescopy, *s.* telescopia.
teletape, *s.* teletipo.
teletypewriter, *s.* teletipo, tipotelégrafo.
teleview, *v.t.* e *v.i.* ver na televisão; ser espectador de televisão.
televiewer, *s.* espectador de televisão, telespectador.
television, *s.* televisão; *television set,* televisor, aparelho de televisão.
televisor, *s.* televisor, aparelho de televisão.
tell, *v.t.* e *v.i.* dizer, contar, narrar, referir, declarar; revelar, expor, comunicar, informar; determinar, saber, distinguir; mandar, ordenar. 1) *to tell the difference,* perceber a diferença. 2) *that tells a tale,* isso é significativo. 3) *to tell off,* distinguir, separar (de um todo); ralhar, dar uma repreensão; ser mandado. 4) *we can never tell,* nunca se sabe.
teller, *s.* contador, narrador, relator; escrutinador de votos; caixa de um banco.
telling, *s.* narração, relação; contagem; *beyond all telling,* inexprimível; *adj.* eficaz; forte, notável; expressivo.
telltale, *s.* mexeriqueiro, intriguista; delator; indício, sinal; *adj.* denunciador, revelador, indicador; *telltale lamp,* (elect.) lâmpada-piloto.
tellurian, *adj.* telúrico, terrestre.
tellurium, *s.* telúrio.
telly, *s.* (fam.) televisão; televisor.
telophase, *s.* telófase, telocinese.
telotype, *s.* teletipo.
telpher, telfer, *s.* e *adj.* teleférico.
telpherage, telferage, *s.* transporte por via aérea (especialmente eléctrico).
Telugu, *s.* télego, telinga, dialecto da Índia meridional.
temerarious, *adj.* temerário.

temerity, *s.* temeridade.
temper, *v.t.* temperar (aço, etc.); misturar; moderar, abrandar, amenizar; (mús.) temperar, afinar; *v.i.* temperar-se (o metal). *s.* têmpera; mistura, consistência; índole, temperamento; disposição; calma; moderação, serenidade; *to lose one's temper,* zangar-se, perder as estribeiras.
tempera, *s.* pintura à têmpera.
temperament, *s.* temperamento, índole, carácter.
temperamental, *adj.* temperamental; nervoso, sensível, caprichoso.
temperance, *s.* temperança, moderação; abstinência; *temperance hotel,* hotel onde não se servem bebidas alcoólicas.
temperate, *adj.* temperado; moderado; sóbrio, abstémio; ameno.
temperature, *s.* temperatura.
tempered, *adj.* temperado, moderado.
tempest, *s.* tempestade, temporal.
tempestuous, *adj.* tempestuoso; tumultuoso.
Templar, *s.* e *adj.* templário.
template, *s.* gabarito; padrão, escantilhão.
temple, *s.* templo; igreja: (anat.) fronte, têmpora; (tecel.) tempereiro.
templet, *s.* o mesmo que *template.*
tempo, *s.* (mús.) tempo, andamento, movimento; ritmo.
temporal, *adj.* temporal; secular, leigo; civil; terreno, mundano. *s.* temporalidade; osso temporal.
temporality, *s.* temporalidade.
temporalty, *s.* a classe dos leigos; (pl.) temporalidade, bens temporais.
temporary, *adj.* temporário, transitório, provisório.
temporize, *v.i.* temporizar, contemporizar.
tempt, *v.t.* tentar, seduzir, atrair; incitar, instigar; convencer ou tentar convencer; pôr à prova, experimentar.
temptation, *s.* tentação; sedução; ímpeto.
tempter, *s.* tentador.
tempting, *adj.* tentador, sedutor, convidativo.
ten, *adj.* e *s.* dez, o número dez; dezena.
tenable, *adj.* defensável, sustentável; que pode ser defendido, mantido ou ocupado por determinado tempo.
tenace, *s.* (no *whist* ou no *bridge*) combinação de duas cartas de grande valor e do mesmo naipe na mão de um jogador.
tenacious, *adj.* tenaz, firme; persistente, pertinaz, obstinado; viscoso; *to be*

tenacious of one's rights, ser cioso dos seus direitos.

tenacity, *s.* tenacidade, firmeza; persistência, obstinação; viscosidade.

tenancy, *s.* posse de bens imóveis; arrendamento; propriedade arrendada; período de arrendamento; *tenancy at will,* arrendamento de imóvel sem prazo determinado.

tenant, *s.* arrendatário, inquilino, rendeiro; (jur.) possuidor de imóvel; morador, ocupante. *v.t.* ser locatário de; ocupar, habitar.

tenantable, *adj.* arrendável.

tenantless, *adj.* sem inquilino, desocupado, devoluto.

tenantry, *s.* conjunto dos rendeiros ou inquilinos; arrendamento.

tend, *v.t.* e *v.i.* vigiar, guardar, tomar conta de, zelar; servir, atender; tender, ter tendência, propender, inclinar-se; dirigir-se, encaminhar-se; (náut.) vigiar navio ancorado.

tendance, *s.* cuidado; vigilância.

tendency, *s.* tendência, inclinação, propensão; direcção.

tendentious, tendencious, *adj.* tendencioso.

tender, *s.* encarregado, guarda, vigia; navio auxiliar; (cam. de fer.) tênder; proposta; dinheiro oferecido em pagamento; *v.t* e *v.i.* oferecer, apresentar, propor; oferecer dinheiro em pagamento; concorrer à adjudicação de uma obra; *adj.* tenro, brando, macio; fraco, frágil, delicado; imaturo; suave, brando; meigo afectuoso; sensível, impressionável; cauteloso, prudente; (náut.) doce de borda.

tenderfoot, *s.* (E.U. cal.) imigrante recém-chegado e não habituado à vida dura de uma região agreste; recém-chegado, principiante, novato.

tenderhearted, *adj.* sensível, terno, compassivo.

tenderloin, *s.* lombo de vaca ou porco; (com maiúsculas) zona de diversões nocturnas de uma grande cidade.

tenderness, *s.* ternura; delicadeza, fragilidade; sensibilidade; qualidade da carne tenra.

tendon, *s.* tendão.

tendril, *s.* gavinha; anel de cabelo.

tenebrous, *adj.* tenebroso.

tenement, *s.* (jur.) prazo foreiro; bens imóveis; residência; apartamento; *tenement house,* casa de apartamentos de aluguer.

tenet, *s.* princípio, doutrina, dogma; opinião.

tenfold, *adj.* décuplo; *adv.* dez vezes mais.

tenner, *s.* nota de dez libras.

tennis, *s.* ténis.

tenon, *s.* respiga, espiga; (carp.) macho; cavilha, pino.

tenor, *s.* teor, conteúdo: curso, tendência, sistema; índole, carácter; (mús.) tenor.

tenpin, *s.* cada um dos pinos do jogo de "tenpins".

tenpins, *s.* espécie de "bowling" jogado com dez pinos.

tense, *adj.* tenso; teso, esticado, retesado; nervoso, excitado; *v.t.* e *v.i.* retesar(-se); *s.* tempo de verbo.

tensile, *adj.* relativo a tensão ou tracção; dúctil, extensível.

tensimeter, *s.* tensímetro.

tension, *s.* tensão; pressão; retesamento; nervosismo, ansiedade; (electr.) tensão, voltagem, potencial; tracção.

tensity, *s.* tensão, retesamento.

tensive, *adj.* tensivo, que provoca tensão.

tensor, *s.* (anat.) tensor.

tent, *s.* tenda, barraca; pavilhão; variedade de vinho tinto espanhol; mecha introduzida em ferida ou fenda natural para a conservar aberta; *v.t.* e *v.i.* alojar em tendas; acampar, viver em tenda; introduzir mecha em ferida.

tentacle, *s.* tentáculo.

tentacular, *adj.* tentacular.

tentative, *s.* tentativa, experiência; *adj.* experimental; hesitante; hipotético.

tentatively, *adv.* a título experimental, experimentalmente.

tenth, *s.* e *adj.* décimo.

tenuity, *s.* tenuidade, finura, delgadeza; leveza, rarefacção; debilidade; escassez.

tenuous, *adj.* ténue; fino, delgado; leve, rarefeito; ligeiro, vago, subtil.

tenure, *s.* posse; (jur.) título de posse; ocupação, uso, gozo; título, autoridade; domínio.

tepee, *s.* tipi, tenda cónica usada pelos índios norte-americanos.

tepid, *adj.* tépido, morno.

tepidity, *s.* tepidez.

teraphim, *s. pl.* terafins, imagens dos primitivos deuses domésticos dos judeus.

teratology, *s.* teratologia.

terce, *s.* terça, hora canónica.

tercel, tercelet, s. terço (falcão macho usado na falcoaria).

tercentenary, s. e adj. tricentenário.

tercet, s. terceto.

terebinthine, s. terebintina.

tergal, s. tergal, dorsal.

tergiversate, v.i. tergiversar; virar as costas; apostatar; (coloq.) virar a casaca.

tergiversation, s. tergiversação; apostasia; mudança de partido; evasiva, rodeio.

tergum, s. dorso.

term, s. termo, limite, fim, meta, conclusão; período, tempro, prazo, duração; data de vencimento; período lectivo; condição; termo, palavra; pl. relações pessoais. 1) *short term,* a curto prazo. 2) *long term,* a longo prazo. 3) *for term of life,* vitaliciamente. 4) *limited term life insurance,* seguro por prazo limitado. 5) *what are your terms?,* quais são as vossas condições? 6) *to be on bad terms with someone,* estar de más relações com. 7) *to come to terms,* chegar a acordo; v.t. chamar, denominar, designar; qualificar.

termagant, s. virago, megera; adj. turbulento, desordeiro.

termer, s. aquele que cumpre pena na prisão.

terminable, adj. terminável, limitado, finito; (jur.) amortizável.

terminal, adj. terminal; final; extremo; limítrofe; trimestral; *terminal value* (mat.), forma mais simples de uma expressão; s. terminal, extremidade, limite.

terminally, adv. trimestralmente.

terminate, v.t. e v.i. terminar, concluir, acabar; rematar; limitar; adj. (mat.) finito.

terminative, adj. terminativo, conclusivo, final.

terminator, s. pessoa que termina alguma coisa; exterminador; (astron.) linha divisória entre a parte iluminada e a não iluminada de um astro.

terminology, s. terminologia, nomenclatura.

terminus, s. fim, meta; extremidade, limite; término; marco, baliza; estação terminal.

termite, s. térmita, formiga-branca.

termor, s. (jur.) foreiro.

tern, s. andorinha-do-mar; terno, trio, terceto.

ternary, adj. ternário; terciário.

ternion, s. terno, trio, tríade.

Terpsichorean, adj. relativo a Terpsícore, relativo à dança.

terrace, s. terraço; socalco, terrapleno; fila de casas no topo de uma colina; v.t. dispor em socalcos.

terracota, s. terracota; cor vermelho--acastanhada.

terrain, s. terreno.

terrane, s. (geol.) terreno.

terraneous, adj. (bot.) terrestre.

terrapin, s. variedade de tartaruga de água doce.

terraqueous, adj. terráqueo.

terrarium, s. viveiro de animais terrestres.

terrene, adj. terreno, terrestre; mundano; s. terreno, terra.

terrestrial, adj. terrestre, terreno, terrícola; mundano; s. terrícola.

terrible, adj. terrível; espantoso; formidável.

terricolous, adj. (zool.) terrícola; (bot.) terrestre.

terrier, s. raça de cães; (ingl.) soldado do exército territorial; inventário dos bens de raiz.

terrific, adj. terrífico, terrível; espantoso, formidável.

terrify, v.t. aterrar, aterrorizar, apavorar.

terrigenous, adj. terrígeno; autóctone.

territorial, adj. territorial; local, regional; *territorial aristocracy,* aristocracia rural.

territorialism, s. territorialismo.

territory, s. território; região, distrito.

terror, s. terror, pavor, medo; *terror stricken,* apavorado, aterrorizado.

terrorism, s. terrorismo.

terrorist, s. terrorista.

terrorize, v.t. aterrorizar, aterrar, amedrontar.

terse, adj. sóbrio, conciso e elegante (estilo).

tertian, s. e adj. (med.) terçã.

tertiary, adj. e s. terciário.

tervalent, adj. trivalente.

tesselate, v.t. cobrir de mosaico; embutir.

tesselation, s. mosaico; colocação de mosaicos.

tessera, s. peça de mosaico, tessela; téssera, placa de metal ou marfim usada na antiga Roma como bilhete de entrada.

test, s. teste, ensaio, prova, exame, verificação; padrão, bitola, craveira; reagente; concha (de molusco); profissão de fé, juramento. 1) *to put to the test,* pôr à prova. 2) *to take the Test,* prestar o juramento previsto no Test Act, lei de 1672, para quem era designado para um cargo público. 3) *test pilot,* piloto de ensaios. 4) *test tube,* tubo de ensaio; v.t. pôr à prova, ensaiar, experimentar, verificar; examinar, analisar.

testa, s. concha, carapaça (de invertebrado).

testacean, s. e adj. testácio.

testacy, s. (júr.) situação da pessoa que deixa testamento.

testament, s. testamento.

testamentary, adj. testamentário, testamental.

testate, s. pessoa que deixa testamento válido; adj. que deixou testamento válido.

testator, s. (júr.) testador.

tester, s. analista; verificador, examinador; aparelho de ensaio; dossel, baldaquim; moeda cunhada na época de Henrique VIII.

testicle, s. testículo.

testification, s. testificação; testemunho, depoimento.

testifier, s. testificador, testemunha.

testify, v.t. e v.i. testemunhar, atestar, testificar; declarar, prestar declarações; demonstrar, indicar.

testimonial, s. atestado, certificado, carta de recomendação; dádiva em sinal de reconhecimento.

testimony, s. testemunho, depoimento; declarações; prova, comprovação; (bibl.) o Decálogo; (pl.) as Escrituras.

testis, s. testículo.

testosterone, s. testosterona.

testy, adj. irascível, rabugento, impertinente.

tetanic, adj. tetânico.

tetanus, s. tétano.

tetchy, adj. rabugento, impertinente.

tether, s. corda, corrente, trela.

tetrachloride, s. tetracloreto.

tetrad, s. (biol.) tétrade.

tetragonal, adj. tetragonal, quadrangular; quaternário.

tetragram, s. tetragrama, palavra de quatro letras.

tetralogy, s. tetralogia, conjunto de quatro dramas.

tetrarch, s. tetrarca.

tetrasyllable, s. tetrassílabo.

tetravalent, adj. quadrivalente.

tetter, s. designação de várias doenças de pele (eczema, herpes, etc.).

Teuton, s. teutão (membro de uma antiga raça germânica); adj. teutónico, germânico.

teutonic, adj. teutónico, germânico. s. (ling.) teutónico.

teutonism, s. teutonismo; crença na superioridade da raça alemã.

text, s. texto; assunto, tema; church text, letra gótica.

textbook, s. compêndio.

textile, s. têxtil, fibra têxtil, tecido; adj. têxtil, relativo a tecidos.

textual, adj. textual, literal.

textuary, adj. textual.

texture, s. textura; estrutura; constituição; teia, urdidura.

textureless, adj. sem textura, amorfo.

Thai, Tai, s. e adj. tailandês.

thalamus, s. (anat.) tálamo.

thalassic, adj. talássico, marinho.

thallus, s. (bot.) talo.

than, conj. que; do que; de; se não; que não. 1) he is richer than me, ele é mais rico do que eu. 2) a man better informed than no one, um homem mais bem informado que ninguém. 3) he would rather go to hell than stay here, preferia ir para o Inferno que ficar aqui. 4) he couldn't be any other than himself, não podia ser outro se não ele. 5) no sooner said than done, dito e feito.

thane, s. guerreiro anglo-saxão de categoria inferior à nobreza.

thank, s. (geralmente no pl.) agradecimento, graças; v.t. agradecer; thank you, obrigado.

thankful, adj. agradecido, grato, reconhecido.

thankfulness, s. gratidão, reconhecimento.

thankless, adj. ingrato, mal-agradecido.

thanksgiving, s. acção de graças; agradecimento; (E.U.) Thanksgiving Day, Dia de Acção de Graças.

thankworthy, adj. digno de reconhecimento, meritório, louvável.

that, adj. e pron. (pl. those) esse, aquele; isso, aquilo. 1) at that moment, nesse momento. 2) and that's that, e pronto! 3) don't talk to me about that man!, não me fales desse homem! 4) is that you?, és tu? 5) that is, isto é; pron. rel. que, o qual (substituído em muitos casos por who ou wich). 6) the present that I gave you, o presente que te dei; adv. tão, a tal ponto, de tal modo. 7) I was that tired, I went to sleep rightaway, estava tão cansado que adormeci logo; conj. que, para que, a fim de que, porque. 8) he died that we might live, ele morreu para que pudéssemos viver.

thatch, s. cobertura de colmo, telhado de colmo; (cal.) cabeleireira; v.t. cobrir de colmo.

thatching, s. colmo.

thaumaturge, thaumaturgist, *s.* taumaturgo.

thaw, *s.* degelo; descongelação; *v.t.* e *v.i.* descongelar, derreter; liquefazer-se; abrandar, enternecer(-se).

the, *art. def.* o, a, os, as; *adv.* quanto mais, tanto mais; quanto, tanto; nessa proporção. 1) *all the better,* tanto melhor. 2) *the sooner the better,* quanto mais cedo melhor.

theanthropism, *s.* teantropia; antropomorfismo.

thearchy, *s.* governo exercido por Deus ou outra divindade.

theater, theatre, *s.* teatro; anfiteatro; cena; arte dramática; *movie theatre,* sala de cinema.

theatrical, *adj.* teatral; cénico; dramático, aparatoso.

theatrics, *s.* arte cénica.

Theban, *s.* e *adj.* tebano.

theca, *s.* (bot.) teca.

thee, *pron.* (arc. ou poét.) te, ti; a ti, tigo.

theft, *s.* roubo, furto.

their, *adj.* seu, sua, seus, suas, deles, delas.

theirs, *pron.* seu, seus, sua, suas, deles, delas; o seu, a sua, os seus, as suas, o deles, o delas, os deles, as delas.

theism, *s.* teísmo.

theist, *s.* e *adj.* teísta.

them, *pron. pess. compl.* 3.ª pes. *pl.* os, as, lhes, a eles, a elas, eles, elas; *adj. dem.* (dial.) esses, aqueles.

thematic, *adj.* temático.

theme, *s.* tema; matéria, assunto, tópico; exercício escolar; composição, ensaio.

themselves, *pron. refl.* se; a si mesmos, a si mesmas; eles mesmos, elas mesmas; *by themselves,* sozinhos.

then, *adv.* então, nessa ocasião, naquele tempo; depois, a seguir; seguidamente, em seguida; *conj.* então, nesse caso, portanto; *adj.* de então, desse tempo. *s.* então, esse tempo. 1) *before then,* antes disso, antes desse tempo. 2) *by then,* a essa hora, nessa altura.

thence, *adv.* daí, por esse motivo, por consequência; desse lugar.

thenceforth, thenceforward, *adv.* desde então, daí em diante.

theocracy, *s.* teocracia.

theocrat, *s.* teocrata.

theocratic, *adj.* teocrático.

theologian, *s.* teólogo.

theological, *adj.* teológico.

theology, *s.* teologia.

theopathy, *s.* êxtase religioso.

theophany, *s.* teofania.

theorem, *s.* teorema.

theorethical, *adj.* teórico.

theorethics, *s.* teórica, parte teórica de uma ciência.

theorist, *s.* teórico.

theorize, *v.i.* teorizar; especular.

theory, *s.* teoria; hipótese, conjectura.

theosophy, *s.* teosofia.

therapeutic(al), *adj.* terapêutico; curativo.

therapeutics, *s.* terapêutica.

therapeutist, therapist, *s.* terapeuta; médico.

therapy, *s.* terapia; tratamento médico; terapêutica.

there, *adv.* aí, ali, lá, acolá, além, nesse ou naquele lugar. 1) *there and then,* ali e naquele momento. 2) *here and there,* por aqui e por ali, em vários lugares. 3) *to be all there,* ter juízo, ser atilado. 4) *there and back,* ida e volta. 5) *to get there,* chegar lá, ser bem sucedido. 6) *in there,* lá dentro, ali dentro. 7) *up there,* ali ou lá em cima. 8) *over there,* ali, acolá, além, do outro lado; *s.* esse lugar, lá; *interj.* aí tem! aí está! ora toma! pronto!

thereabouts, *s.* nos arredores; nas redondezas; aproximadamente, cerca de; por aí.

thereafter, *adv.* depois disso, posteriormente.

thereby, *adv.* por esse meio, desse modo, assim; (arc.) perto dali; a esse respeito.

therefore, *adv.* por conseguinte, consequentemente, por esse motivo, portanto.

thereinafter, *adv.* mais adiante, mais abaixo (em documentos).

thereinbefore, *adv.* mais acima, mais atrás (em documentos).

thereupon, *adv.* depois disso, logo a seguir; após o que; sobre isso.

therianthropic, *adj.* que combina a forma humana e animal.

therm, *s.* pequena caloria; unidade calorífica usada no fornecimento de gás de iluminação (em Inglat.).

thermae, *s. pl.* termas.

thermal, *adj.* térmico, termal.

thermic, *adj.* térmico, relativo ao calor.

thermionics, *s.* estudo dos fenómenos termiónicos.

thermobarometer, *s.* termobarómetro.

thermochesmitry, s. termoquímica.
thermodynamic (al), adj. termodinâmico.
thermodynamics, s. termodinâmica.
thermoelectricity, s. termoelectricidade.
thermogenesis, s. termogénese.
thermograph, s. termógrafo.
thermometer, s. termómetro.
thermometry, s. termometria.
thermos, s. thermos-bottle, termo, garrafa-termo.
thermostat, s. termóstato.
thermostatics, s. termostática.
thermotropism, s. termotropismo.
theroid, adj. teróide, bestial, animalesco.
therology, s. mamologia, estudo dos mamíferos.
thesaurus, s. léxico, enciclopédia, repositório.
these, adj. e pron. pl. de this.
thesis, pl. theses, s. tese; tema, composição, ensaio; postulado.
Thessalian, s. e adj. tessálico, relativo à Tessália.
Thessalonian, s. e adj. tessalonicense, relativo à Tessalónica.
theta, s. teta (letra grega).
theurgist, s. teurgo, teurgista.
theurgy, s. teurgia, teurgismo; intervenção divina, milagre.
thew, s. (geralmente no pl.) músculo, tendão; força, vigor.
thewy, adj. musculoso, vigoroso.
they, pron. eles, elas; os, as, aqueles, aquelas; usado como sujeito indeterminado: they say, dizem, diz-se; they who, aqueles que.
thick, adj. grosso, espesso; denso; compacto, cerrado; numeroso, abundante; cheio, apinhado; rouco, com voz pouco clara; lodoso, turvo; familiar, íntimo. 1) a layer two inches thick, uma camada com duas polegadas de espessura. 2) the street was thick with people, a rua estava apinhada de gente. 3) to be thick with someone, ser íntimo de alguém. 4) the weather is thick, o tempo está nublado; adv. espessamente, em grossa camada; densamente; copiosamente, abundantemente. 5) to lay it on thick, exceder-se; s. parte mais grossa ou mais espessa; o mais denso, o mais espesso, auge, apogeu, centro, ponto principal; (coloq.) indivíduo estúpido.
thick-and-thin, adj. leal, constante, firme.

thicken, v.t. e v.i. engrossar(-se), espessar(-se), cerrar(-se); encher(-se), aumentar; turvar(-se), toldar(-se).
thickening, s. engrossamento, espessamento.
thicket, s. bosque cerrado, mata; moita, matagal.
thickhead, adj. estúpido, bronco; teimoso.
thickness, s. grossura, espessura; abundância; densidade, consistência; turvação, aspecto lodoso; rouquidão.
thickset, s. souto, moita, sebe cerrada; adj. denso, compacto, cerrado; atarracado.
thick-skulled, adj. estúpido, bronco.
thief, s. ladrão, gatuno, larápio.
thieve, v.t. e v.i. roubar, furtar.
thievery, s. ladroagem, ladroeira; roubalheira, roubo, furto.
thievish, adj. furtivo, dissimulado; desonesto.
thievishness, s. tendência para o roubo.
thigh, s. coxa.
thighbone, s. osso da coxa, fémur.
thimble, s. dedal; casquilho; (náut.) sapatilho.
thimblerig, s. jogo em que se esconde uma bolinha debaixo de um de três dedais para que se tente adivinhar em qual deles se encontra.
thimbleweed, s. designação de algumas espécies de anémonas norte-americanas.
thin, adj. fino, delgado; magro, esguio; franzino, delicado; fraco, pobre, escasso, ralo (por exemplo, o cabelo); pouco consistente, aguado, diluído, rarefeito; superficial, ligeiro; transparente (discussão); adv. finamente, escassamente; insuficientemente; v.t. e v.i. adelgaçar; emagrecer; rarear, escassear; clarear, espaçar; reduzir(-se), diminuir; enfraquecer; diluir(-se), rarefazer(-se).
thine, pron. (arc.) teu, tua, teus, tuas; o teu, a tua, os teus, as tuas.
thing, s. coisa; objecto; ser, criatura. 1) living thing, ser vivo. 2) poor thing!, coitado! 3) I am not quite the thing, não estou lá grande coisa, não estou muito bem disposto.
thingamabob, thingumabob, thingamy, thingummy, thingamajig, s. fulano, pessoa ou coisa cujo nome não ocorre.
think, v.t. e v.i. (prt. e pp. "thought") pensar, julgar, crer, considerar, achar; tencionar, esperar; resolver, decidir; inventar, conceber; reflectir, meditar; ter determinada

opinião. 1) *to think highly of someone*, ter alguém em grande conta. 2) *to think no harm*, não suspeitar de nada; agir sem má intenção. 3) *I think so*, acho que sim.

thinkable, *adj.* concebível, imaginável, possível.

thinker, *s.* pensador.

thinking, *adj.* pensante, racional; reflectido, ponderado.

thinner, *s.* dissolvente volátil usado na composição dos vernizes.

thionic, *adj.* (quím.) tiónico, relativo ao enxofre.

thionine, *s.* tionina.

third, *adj.* terceiro; de terceira classe; *third rate*, de terceira ordem, inferior; *s.* terço, a terça parte; terceiro; (mús.) terça, terceira.

thirdly, *adv.* em terceiro lugar.

thirst, *s.* sede; ânsia, avidez, cobiça.

thirsty, *adj.* sequioso, sedento, que tem sede; ansioso, ávido; *to feel thirsty*, ter sede.

thirteen, *adj.* e *s.* treze.

thirteenth, *adj.* e *s.* décimo terceiro.

thirtieth, *adj.* e *s.* trigésimo.

thirty, *adj.* e *s.* trinta. 1) *thirty second note*, (mús.) fusa. 2) *the thirties*, a casa dos trinta; os anos trinta.

thirtyfold, *adj.* trinta vezes maior; *adv.* trinta vezes mais.

this, *adj.* este, esta. *pron.* isto. *adv.* assim, tão... como isto.

thistle, *s.* cardo.

thistledown, *s.* lanugem do cardo.

thither, *adv.* para lá, para aí, naquela direcção; *adj.* de lá.

thitherto, *adv.* até então.

thomism, *s.* tomismo.

thong, *s.* correia, tira de couro; *v.t.* pôr correia em; prender com correias; açoitar com correia.

thoracic, *adj.* torácico.

thorax, *s.* tórax.

thorium, *s.* tório.

thorn, *s.* espinho; espinheiro; abrolho; (fig.) tormento, aflição; *to sit on thorns*, estar sobre brasas.

thornback, *s.* (zool.) raia pregada.

thorny, *adj.* espinhoso; difícil, doloroso; aflitivo.

thorough, *adj.* completo, perfeito; acabado, consumado; profundo, minucioso, exaustivo; intenso.

thoroughbred, *adj.* de puro sangue; *s.* puro--sangue (especialmente o cavalo).

thoroughfare, *s.* via de comunicação; via pública; estrada; artéria, rua; trânsito; *no throughfare*, trânsito cortado.

thoroughness, *s.* perfeição; minúcia; eficiência.

thoroughpaced, *adj.* totalmente adestrado (o cavalo); consumado, completo.

thorp(e), *s.* aldeia, lugar, povoado.

those, *pl.* de *that*.

thou, *pron.* (arc. e poét.) tu. *v.t.* tratar por tu.

though, *conj.* embora, se bem que, apesar de, posto que; *as though*, como se; *adv.* porém, contudo, todavia.

thought, *pret.* e *pp.* de *to think*. *s.* pensamento; reflexão; atenção, consideração; ideia, noção, conceito; tenção, intenção; opinião; *on second thoughts*, pensando melhor.

thoughtful, *adj.* pensativo; profundo; cheio de ideias; ponderado, previdente; atencioso, cortês.

thoughtfulness, *s.* meditação, reflexão; ponderação; amabilidade, cortesia, atenção.

thoughtless, *adj.* irreflectido, imprudente; impulsivo, estouvado; descortês.

thousand, *adj.* e *s.* mil, milhar.

thousandth, *adj.* e *s.* milésimo.

thousanfold, *adj.* multiplicado por mil, mil vezes maior; *adv.* mil vezes mais.

Thracian, *adj.* e *s.* trácio.

thrall, *s.* (arc.) servo, escravo; escravidão; *adj.* escravizado. *v.t.* escravizar.

thralldom, *s.* escravidão, servidão.

thrash, *v.t.* e *v.i.* debulhar, malhar; açoitar, sovar, bater, zurzir; agitar, sacudir; *s.* debulha; agitação; batidas; surra, sova.

thrasher, *s.* debulhadora; debulhador; batedor; (zool.) variedade de tordo americano.

thrashing, *s.* surra, sova.

thread, *s.* fio, linha; filamento, fibra; cabelo; réstia (de luz); espiral de parafuso; *v.t.* e *v.i.* enfiar (agulha, colar, etc.); raiar de fios diferentes; riscar; passar por, atravessar, abrir caminho com dificuldade; enroscar parafuso; enroscar-se.

threadbare, *adj.* coçado, no fio, surrado; andrajoso, miserável.

thready, *adj.* filiforme, capilar; fino, delgado.

threat, *s.* ameaça; prenúncio, sinal.

threaten, *v.t.* e *v.i.* ameaçar; pôr em perigo; indicar, prenunciar; estar iminente.

threatening, *adj.* ameaçador.

three, *adj.* e *s.* três. 1) *three cornered,* triangular. 2) *three-phase,* (elect.) trifásico. 3) *three point landing,* (av.) aterragem com a cauda caída.

threefold, *adj.* triplo, triplicado; *adv.* três vezes mais, triplamente.

three-quarter, *s.* jogador de râguebi.

threescore, *adj.* sessenta.

threesome, *adj.* triplo, composto de três; *s.* grupo de três pessoas; trio, trinca; jogo para três pessoas.

thresh, *v.* e *s.* o mesmo que trash.

threshing, *s.* debulha, malha; *threshing-machine,* debulhadora.

threshold, *s.* limiar, soleira; entrada, começo, início.

threw, *pret.* de to throw.

thrice, *adv.* três vezes; triplamente.

thrift, *s.* economia, parcimónia, poupança.

thrifty, *adj.* económico, poupado; viçoso, próspero.

thrill, *s.* emoção forte, frémito, arrepio; sensação, impressão; excitação; tremor, palpitação; *v.t.* e *v.i.* arrebatar, entusiasmar; excitar; emocionar; impressionar; vibrar, estremecer.

thriller, *s.* o que faz vibrar; filme ou livro emocionante.

thrilling, *adj.* emocionante, excitante, impressionante, sensacional; palpitante.

thrive, *v.i.* prt. *"trove"* florescer, prosperar, ser bem sucedido; viçoso.

throat, *s.* garganta; passagem estreita; (cal.) pescoço, gasganete. 1) *to lie in one's throat,* mentir descaradamente. 2) *throat seizing,* (náut.), punho da boca; *v.t.* acanelar, goivar.

throaty, *adj.* gutural, rouco.

throb, *s.* palpitação, latejo; *v.i.* palpitar, pulsar, latejar.

throbbing, *adj.* palpitante, latejante.

throe, *s.* espasmo, guinada, dor violenta; convulsão; (pl.) dores de parto; *v.i.* angustiar-se.

thrombosis, *s.* trombose.

thrombus, *s.* trombo, coágulo sanguíneo.

throne, *s.* trono; *pl.* (teol.) tronos; *to come to the throne,* subir ao trono; *v.t.* e *v.i.* entronizar(-se).

throng, *s.* multidão, turba, ajuntamento; *v.t.* e *v.i.* apinhar, atravancar; empurrar, acotevelar-se.

throttle, *s.* garganta, goela; (mec.) válvula reguladora de pressão; estrangulador; *v.t.* e *v.i.* esganar, estrangular; sufocar; afogar (o automóvel).

through, *prep.* através de, pelo meio de, por; de um extremo a outro; durante; por causa de; por intermédio de; *adv.* de ponta a ponta, até ao fim; completamente, inteiramente. 1) *wet through,* completamente molhado. 2) *through and through,* de lado a lado, de fio a pavio. 3) *are you through?,* já acabou? *adj.* que vai de lado a lado; contínuo; directo (comboio, camioneta, etc.).

throughout, *adv.* completamente, totalmente, inteiramente, do princípio ao fim; *prep.* de uma ponta a outra de; por toda a parte de; em todo, por todo, durante todo.

throve, *pret.* de to thrive.

throw, *v.t.* e *v.i.* prt. threw; pp. thrown. lançar, atirar, arremessar, deitar, projectar; lançar ao chão, derrubar; ter cria, parir; despejar; torcer fio, fiar; jogar (dados); moldar na roda do oleiro; (mec.) mover uma alavanca. 1) *to throw away,* deitar fora, rejeitar (oportunidade). 2) *to throw back,* lançar de volta, devolver; atrasar, retardar. 3) *to throw down,* deitar ao chão, derrubar. 4) *to throw off,* lançar fora, desfazer-se de; improvisar. 5) *to throw out,* lançar fora, expelir; ganhar galhos ou folhas novas; sugerir. 6) *to throw up,* lançar para cima, erguer; vomitar; realçar; dar-se por vencido. 7) *to throw a chest,* fazer peito, enfunar o peito. 8) *to throw the book at someone,* castigar alguém com a pena máxima; *s.* lançamento, arremesso; aventura, risco, acto de derrubar o adversário; (geol.) deslocamento vertical produzido por uma falha; (mec.) passeio de excêntrico, percurso de êmbolo; bola lançada irregularmente no críquete. 9) *a stone's throw,* a pequena distância.

throwaway, *s.* folheto de propaganda.

throwback, *s.* regresso ao passado, recuo, regressão; reversão a um tipo ancestral; atavismo.

thrum, *s.* cadilhos; pedaço de fio, franja; (mús.) som monótono; (náut.) mialhar; *v.t.* e *v.i.* franjar; arranhar, ferir as cordas de um instrumento musical; tamborilar.

thrush, *s.* tordo; (med.) afta; inflamação da ranilha dos cascos do cavalo:

thrust, *s.* empurrão, puxão, impulso; golpe com instrumento de ponta, estocada, facada; ataque, assalto, incursão; (mec.)

impulso, tracção, pressão; (geol.) falha de pressão; *v.t.* e *v.i.* empurrar, impelir; introduzir, meter; enfiar; mergulhar; impor; encaixar; introduzir-se; trespassar; golpear com instrumento de ponta; introduzir-se, meter-se à força. 1) *to thrust back*, rechaçar, repelir. 2) *to thrust one's way*, abrir caminho à força. 3) *to thrust oneself into something*, meter-se à força em alguma coisa.

thud, *s.* golpe, pancada, baque.

thug, *s.* tugue, membro de uma seita indiana de assassinos; bandido, assassino, rufião.

thulium, *s.* (quim.) túlio.

thumb, *s.* polegar. 1) *Tom Thumb*, o Pequeno Polegar. 2) *thumb index*, índice alfabético; *v.t.* manusear; folhear (livro); dedilhar (instrumento musical). 3) *to thumb a ride*, pedir boleia.

thump, *s.* choque, baque, golpe, batida, pancada; paulada; *v.t.* e *v.i.* golpear, bater em, esmurrar, sovar, espancar; caminhar pesadamente.

thunder, *s.* trovão; estrondo; *v.i.* e *v.t.* trovejar; atroar, ribombar, retumbar; bradar, clamar, berrar.

thunderbolt, *s.* raio; ameaça tremenda; algo fulminante e terrível.

thundering, *adj.* trovejante, ribombante, atroador; enorme, tremendo, fulminante; *adv.* enormemente, extremamente; invulgarmente.

thunderous, *adj.* trovejante, atroador; de trovoada.

thunderstorm, *s.* trovoada.

thunderstruck, thunderstricken, *adj.* fulminado, atingido por um raio; estupefacto, assombrado.

thursday, *s.* quinta-feira.

thus, *adv.* assim, deste modo, desta maneira, portanto, por conseguinte, por isso, consequentemente; tão. 1) *thus far*, até aqui. 2) *thus much*, tanto, esse tanto.

thwart, *s.* (náut.) bancada, banco do remador; *v.t.* frustrar, impedir, contrariar, opor-se a; *adj.* transversal, atravessado; adverso; *adv.* de través, transversalmente; *prep.* através de, transversalmente a.

thwart-ship, *adj.* transversal; através do navio.

thy, *adj.* (arc.) teu, tua, teus, tuas.

thylacine, *s.* tilacino, lobo da Austrália.

thyme, *s.* tomilho.

thymol, *s.* timol.

thyreoid, *adj.* e *s.* o mesmo que *thyroid*.

thyroid, *s.* tiróide; *adj.* tiróideo.

thyroidectomy, *s.* tiroidectomia.

thyrse, *s.* (bot.) tirso.

thyself, *pron.* (arc.) te, a ti mesmo.

tiara, *s.* tiara.

tibetan, *s.* e *adj.* tibetano.

tibia, *s.* tíbia.

tick, *s.* tiquetaque; batida leve; palpitação, pulsação; (coloq.) momento, instante; carrapato, carraça; capa de colchão ou travesseiro; (coloq.) crédito. 1) *to buy on tick*, comprar a crédito; *v.i.* e *v.t.* fazer tiquetaque; marcar o tempo; marcar com um pequeno sinal, conferir; conceder crédito. 2) *to tick someone off*, repreender alguém.

ticker, *s.* (coloq.) relógio, coração; telégrafo impressor.

ticket, *s.* bilhete, entrada, passagem; rótulo, etiqueta; (E.U.) lista de candidatos de um partido político; (cal. mil.) licença. 1) *ticket collector*, revisor. 2) *ticket of leave*, liberdade condicional concedida a preso que já cumpriu parte da pena; *v.t.* etiquetar, rotular.

tickle, *s.* cócegas, comichão; *v.t.* e *v.i.* fazer ou ter cócegas; fazer ou ter comichão; tocar ao de leve; agradar, divertir, deliciar.

tickler, *s.* aquele ou aquilo que faz cócegas; questão embaraçosa, problema; livro ou caderno de apontamentos; pena usada para fazer cócegas; (elect.) bobina de reacção.

ticklish, *adj.* coceguento; sensível, susceptível, comichoso, irritadiço; delicado, melindroso.

ticktack, *s.* tiquetaque; sinais de código usados pelos *bookmakers*.

tidal, *adj.* de maré(s), relativo a maré(s). 1) *tidal harbour*, porto de marés. 2) *tidal wave*, onda da maré; macaréu.

tidbit, *s.* petisco, guloseima; iguaria.

tide, *s.* maré; corrente, curso, tendência; época, estação; ocasião. 1) *tide rode*, (náut.) aproado à maré; *v.i.* e *v.t.* subir como a maré; ir com a maré, aproveitar a maré. 2) *to tide someone over a difficulty*, ajudar alguém a vencer uma dificuldade. 3) *to tide over*, vencer, ultrapassar dificuldade; superar.

tideland, *s.* marisma, terreno que fica alagado na praia-mar.

tideway, *s.* canal de maré.

tidiness, s. asseio, arrumação, arranjo.

tidy, adj. asseado, limpo, bem arranjado; considerável, regular; v.t. e v.i. arrumar, arranjar. s. coberta bordada para os braços de uma poltrona; *street tidy,* cesto de papéis de rua.

tie, v.t. e v.i. atar, amarrar, dar laço em; ligar, unir, prender, vincular; sujeitar, restringir; empatar (jogo, prova, etc.). 1) *to tie up with,* asociar-se, ligar-se, unir-se a. 2) *to tie the knot,* dar o nó, casar; s. gravata; fio, cordão, atilho; corda, corrente; laço, ligação, vínculo; empate, igualdade; travessão, tirante (em construções); (náut.) amantilho, ostaga; (mús.) ligadura. 3) *tie-rod, (*autom.) coluna de direcção.

tier, s. fila, renque, fileira; bancada; camada; v.t. dispor em filas ou em camadas; *to tier up,* empilhar.

tierce, s. terça parte de uma pipa, medida de capacidade inglesa; terça, hora canónica.

tiff, s. trago, gole; amuo, arrufo, pequena desavença; v.t. e v.i. bebericar; amuar; (Índia) almoçar.

tiffany, s. gaze de seda.

tiffin, s. (Índia) almoço leve.

tiger, s. tigre; criado de libré; *tiger-cat,* gato--bravo.

tigerish, adj. tigrino, cruel, feroz.

tighrope, s. corda ou arame esticado onde trabalham os artistas de circo.

tight, adj. apertado, estreito, justo; estanque, impermeável; compacto; tenso, esticado; rigoroso; escasso (o dinheiro); difícil; avarento, sovina; (coloq.) embriagado; *tight squeeze,* situação difícil, aperto; adv. firme, firmemente, com firmeza; hermeticamente; apertadamente.

tighten, v.t. e v.i. apertar; comprimir; firmar; esticar; endurecer; cerrar-se, comprimir-se, estreitar-se.

tightfisted, adj. sovina, avarento.

tightly, adv. apertadamente, cerradamente; rigorosamente, severamente; firmemente, fortemente.

tightness, s. impermeabilidade; tensão; aperto, constrição (coloq.) embriaguez; escassez (de dinheiro).

tights, s. meias de senhora; fato de malha justo ao corpo usado pelos acrobatas.

tigress, s. fem. de *tiger.*

tilbury, s. tílburi, carruagem leve de dois lugares puxada por um cavalo.

tilde, s. til (sinal ortográfico).

tile, s. telha, ladrilho, azulejo; chapéu alto, cartola; v.t. telhar, ladrilhar.

tiler, s. assentador de telhas ou de ladrilhos; porteiro de loja maçónica.

till, prep. até; conj. até que; enquanto não; v.t. e v.i. cultivar, lavrar; s. gaveta de caixa registadora; conglomerado argiloso de origem glaciária.

tillage, s. cultivo, amanho (do solo); agricultura, lavoura; terra cultivada.

tiller, s. agricultor, lavrador; rebento de planta; (náut.) cana do leme.

tilt, v.t. e v.i. inclinar(-se), pender, enviesar; cobrir com toldo; enristar (lança); tomar parte em torneios; s. justa, torneio; combate, disputa; carga de lança; toldo; tenda; inclinação, declive, encosta; pendor; martelo de forja; *at full tilt,* a toda a brida.

tilth, s. amanho, cultivo da terra, lavoura.

timbal, s. (mús.) timbale.

timbale, s. espécie de empada.

timber, s. madeira; madeiramento, madeira de construção; floresta, mata; árvores; viga, prancha, vigamento; (náut.) baliza; (her.) timbre; (coloq.) perna de pau. 1) *timber and a half hitch,* (náut.) volta da ribeira e meia volta. 2) *timber sow,* caruncho. 3) *timber toe,* perna de pau. 4) *timber wolf,* lobo cinzento norte-americano. 5) *shiver my timbers!,* Diabos me levem! v.t. guarnecer ou revestir de madeira; colocar vigas.

timbering, s. madeiramento, vigamento; escora, traves, vigas de madeira; madeira de construção.

timberman, s. madeireiro.

timberyard, s. depósito de madeiras.

timbre, s. timbre.

timbrel, s. pandeiro, adufe.

time, s. tempo; duração, período; prazo; horas; momento; oportunidade, ocasião; época; pena (de prisão); (mús.) compasso, ritmo; vez. 1) *what time is it?,* que horas são? 2) *once upon a time,* era uma vez. 3) *to have a good time,* divertir-se. 4) *for the time being,* por enquanto. 5) *from time to time,* de vez em quando. 6) *in time,* a tempo. 7) *in good time,* a seu tempo. 8) *in no time,* num instante; adj. relativo ao tempo, temporal, horário; com a prazo. 9) *time-book,* livro de ponto. 10) *time deposit,* depósito bancário a prazo; v.t. e v.i. calcular o tempo ou o momento para; calcular a duração de; cronometrar; regular (relógio); marcar o compasso de; harmonizar-se.

time-honoured, *adj.* consagrado pelo tempo; venerável, venerando.

timekeeper, *s.* apontador das horas de trabalho dos operários.

timeless, *adj.* intemporal; eterno; inoportuno.

timely, *adj.* oportuno, conveniente.

time-out, *s.* intervalo; suspensão, interrupção.

timepiece, *s.* relógio, cronómetro; relógio de mesa.

timer, *s.* cronometrista; *full-timer,* empregado que trabalha a tempo inteiro.

timerserver, *s.* contemporizador; oportunista; pessoa servil, bajulador.

timetable, *s.* horário.

timeworn, *adj.* desgastado pelo tempo; velho.

timid, *s.* e *adj.* tímido.

timidity, *s.* timidez.

timing, *s.* acto de regular ou de ajustar o tempo; escolha do momento; sincronização.

timorous, *adj.* timorato, tímido, assustadiço.

timpanist, *s.* (mús.) timbaleiro.

tin, *s.* estanho; folha-de-flandres; lata; (cal.) dinheiro. 1) *tin foil,* folha de estanho. 2) *tin hat,* capacete de soldado. 3) *tin plater,* estanhador; *v.t.* estanhar, revestir de estanho; enlatar.

tinct, *adj.* tinto, tingido; *s.* tinta, cor.

tincture, *s.* tintura; vestígios, laivos; matiz, coloração; *v.t.* tingir, colorir; impregnar.

tinder, *s.* mecha.

tine, *s.* dente (de garfo, ancinho, etc.); ponta da armação do veado.

tinea, *s.* (med.) tinha.

ting, *s.* tinido, som de campainha ou sineta; *v.i.* tilintar, tinir.

tinge, *s.* matiz, cambiante, tom; laivos, sabor, vestígios; *v.t.* tingir, colorir, matizar; dar determinado sabor a; impregnar; misturar com pequena quantidade de outra substância.

tingle, *v.i.* e *v.t.* formigar, sentir formigueiros, picar, arder; tinir, zunir, vibrar; *s.* formigueiro, picada; ardor; tinido, zunido.

tininess, *s.* pequenez.

tinker, *s.* latoeiro, funileiro; remendão; faz-tudo; remendo, arranjo mal feito; *v.t.* e *v.i.* exercer um ofício sem perceber do assunto; remendar, atamancar.

tinkle, *s.* tinido; *v.i.* e *v.t.* tilintar, retinir; tanger; tocar campainha; anunciar tilintando.

tinning, *s.* estanhagem.

tinny, *adj.* estanífero, relativo ao estanho; metálico (sons ou cores).

tin-plate, *s. v.t.* estanhar.

tinsel, *s.* ouropel, falso brilho; lantejoula; *adj.* com brilho falso, aparatoso; *v.t.* enfeitar com ouropel.

tinsmith, *s.* latoeiro, funileiro.

tint, *s.* tinta, tinto; cambiante; sombreado; *v.t.* matizar, tingir, colorir.

tintinnabulation, *s.* repique de sino, tilintar de campainha.

tinware, *s.* utensílios feitos de folha-de-flandres.

tiny, *adj.* pequenino, minúsculo.

tip, *s.* ponta, extremidade, bico, ápice; cimo, cume; batida leve; gorjeta; informação; conselho; sugestão, palpite; inclinação; depósito de lixo. 1) *tip-truck,* camião de báscula; *v.t.* e *v.i.* colocar ponta em, guarnecer com ponteira; inclinar, virar, entornar, despejar; derrubar, fazer cair; bater ao de leve; erguer (o chapéu em saudação); gratificar, dar gorjeta; dar informações, ou palpites; avisar; (cal.) atirar, dar. 2) *tip us a song,* cante-nos qualquer coisa. 3) *tip us a coin,* atire-nos uma moeda.

tippet, *s.* palatina, estola de pele.

tipple, *v.t.* bebericar; *v.i.* beber habitualmente; *s.* bebida alcoólica.

tippy, *adj.* que se inclina facilmente, instável.

tipstaff, *s. pl. tipstaves;* meirinho, oficial de justiça; vara de justiça.

tipster, *s.* aquele que dá informações confidenciais sobre corridas de cavalos, cotações da bolsa, etc.

tipsy, *adj.* ébrio, tocado, tonto; vacilante, cambaleante; enviesado.

tiptoe, *s.* ponta dos pés; *to be on tiptoes,* estar em pontas dos pés; estar ansioso; *adv.* nas pontas dos pés; ansiosamente; *v.t.* andar nas pontas dos pés.

tiptop, *s.* cume, cimo, topo; auge, apogeu; o melhor; *adj.* o melhor, supremo; excelente; *adv.* optimamente, excelentemente.

tirade, *s.* invectiva, diatribe; discurso longo, tirada, arenga.

tire, *s.* pneu, pneumático; (arc.) atavio, roupagem; penteado, toucado; *v.t.* e *v.i.* cansar, fatigar, extenuar, esgotar; aborrecer, importunar; fartar, entediar; *(arc.)* ataviar, pentear; *tiring room,* camarim, quarto de vestir.

tired, *adj.* cansado, fatigado; farto.

tiredness, *s.* cansaço, fadiga; enfado, aborrecimento.

tireless, *adj.* incansável, infatigável; sem aro, sem pneumático.

tiresome, *adj.* cansativo, fatigante; aborrecido, enfadonho; irritante.

tirewoman, *s.* criada de senhora, açafata.

tiro, *s.* tiro.

tirocinium, *s.* tirocínio, aprendizagem.

'tis, contracção de *"it is"*.

tisane, *s.* tisana.

tissue, *s.* tecido; (fig.) conjunto, série, encadeamento.

tit, *s.* (zool.) petinha, sombria; chapim, cachapim; (arc.) cavalo pequeno, pileca; (fam.) mamilo, teta; *tit for tat,* olho por olho; dente por dente.

titan, *s.* titã.

titanic, *adj.* titânico; colossal, gigantesco; (quím.) titânico, relativo ao titânio.

titaniferous, *adj.* titanífero.

titanium, *s.* (quím.) titânio.

titbit, *s.* petisco, guloseima, pitéu.

tithable, *adj.* sujeito ao dízimo.

tithe, *s.* dízimo; a décima parte; pequeno tributo; *v.t.* pagar ou cobrar o dízimo.

tither, *s.* cobrador de dízimos.

titilate, *v.t.* titilar, fazer cócegas; excitar agradavelmente; deleitar.

titillation, *s.* titilação, cócegas; excitação agradável.

titivate, tittivate, *v.t. e v.i.* enfeitar(-se), ataviar(-se).

title, *s.* título; epígrafe; rótulo; distinção honorífica; documento comprobatório de um direito; direito; quantidade de ouro contida numa liga; denominação, tratamento. 1) *title-role,* papel principal. 2) *title deed,* título de propriedade; *v.t.* intitular, dar título a.

titled, *adj.* titular, que tem título de nobreza.

titmouse, *s.* (zool.) chapim, cachapim.

titter, *v.i.* rir à socapa; *s.* riso abafado.

tittle, *s.* pequeno traço feito com pena, pontinho; partícula, parte minúscula; pormenor.

tittle-tattle, *s.* tagarelice, falatório; *v.t.* tagarelar, mexericar.

titular, *adj.* titular; nominal; *titular saint,* santo padroeiro de uma igreja; *s.* bispo titular; santo padroeiro.

tmesis, *s.* (gram.) tmese.

to, *prep.* a; para; com o fim de; a fim de; em direcção a; com; por; de; até; antes; de acordo com; em comparação com; ao som de; pertencente a; (quando precede um infinito, não se traduz.) 1) *to a certain degree,* até certo grau. 2) *to my surprise,* para minha surpresa. 3) *to my knowledge,* tanto quanto saiba. 4) *to my remberance,* segundo me lembro. 5) *to the south of,* a sul de. 6) *a quarter to ten,* um quarto para as dez. 7) *add some sugar to your coffee,* ponha açúcar no café. 8) *ambassador to que Queen of England,* embaixador junto da rainha de Inglaterra. 9) *face to face,* cara a cara, frente a frente. 10) *from begining to end,* do princípio ao fim. 11) *from nine to five,* das nove às cinco. 12) *he is cousin to the Queen,* ele é primo da rainha. 13) *sentenced to death,* condenado à morte. 14) *so to say,* por assim dizer. 15) *the road to Lisbon,* a estrada para Lisboa. 16) *the way to freedom,* o caminho da liberdade. 17) *true to life,* fiel à realidade. 18) *to burn to ashes,* reduzir a cinzas. 19) *to eat oneself to death,* morrer devido a excesso de comida. 20) *to go to sleep,* adormecer. 21) *to march to the sound of music,* marchar ao som de música. 22) *here is to you!,* à sua saúde!. 23) *I told him to come, but he didn't want to,* disse-lhe que viesse mas ele não quis. 24) *that is all there is to it,* é tudo quanto há a respeito disso. 25) *that is not to my liking,* isso não me agrada. 26) *there was not a sound to be heard,* não se ouvia absolutamente nada. 27) *this is nothing to what it might be,* isto não é nada comparado com o que podia ser. 28) *to arms!,* às armas! 29) *what is that to you?,* que lhe interessa isto?. 30) *what are we to do?,* que havemos de fazer? 31) *the worse is yet to come,* o pior ainda está para vir; *adv.* para a frente; para a posição normal; na posição devida; a si, à consciência. 32) *to and fro,* de um lado para o outro. 33) *to come to senses, to come to oneself,* recobrar os sentidos. 34) *to turn to with a will,* pôr-se ao trabalho com vontade. 35) *the door is to,* a porta está encostada. 36) *the ship is moored to,* o navio está ancorado em direcção ao vento. 37) *he put on his hat back to front,* ele pôs o chapéu virado ao contrário.

toad, *s.* sapo; pessoa detestável; *toad eater,* bajulador.

toadflax, *s.* (bot.) linária.

toady, *adj.* bajulador, adulador; *v.t.* e *v.i.* bajular, adular.

toast, *s.* torrada; brinde, saúde; *v.t.* torrar; tostar(-se); brindar à saúde de.

toaster, *s.* torradeira.

tobacco, *s.* tabaco.

tobacconism, *s.* tabagismo.

tobacconist, *s.* vendedor de tabaco; *tobacconist's shop*, tabacaria.

toboggan, *s.* tobogã, espécie de trenó para escorregar na neve.

toby, *s.* caneca para cerveja em forma de velhote com chapéu tricórnio; charuto ordinário.

tocology, *s.* tocologia, obstetrícia.

tocsin, *s.* toque a rebate; o repicar do sino.

today, *adv.* hoje; hoje em dia, actualmente; *s.* hoje, o dia de hoje; a actualidade.

toddle, *v.i.* e *v.t.* caminhar vacilantemente; dar os primeiros passos; andar despreocupadamente; *s.* andar cambaleante; passos vacilantes.

toddler, *s.* criança que dá os primeiros passos.

to-do, *s.* azáfama, agitação, balbúrdia.

toe, *s.* dedo do pé; ponta do pé; ponta da meia; bico do sapato; parte anterior de casco de animal; extremidade da cabeça de taco de golfe. 1) *from top to toes*, da cabeça aos pés. 2) *to turn up one's toes*, morrer, esticar o pernil; *v.t.* e *v.i.* pôr biqueira em calçado; (desp.) tocar com a ponta dos pés na linha de partida; dar pontapé em; pregar um prego obliquamente. 3) *to toe the line*, conformar-se com as ordens recebidas. 4) *to toe in*, virar as pontas dos pés para dentro ao caminhar.

toed, *adj.* com determinado número ou forma de dedos dos pés: *four-toed animal*, um animal com quatro dedos dos pés.

tofee, *s.* caramelo.

toga, *s.* toga.

together, *adv.* juntos, juntamente, em companhia, em grupo; um com o outro; um ao outro; simultaneamente; ao mesmo tempo; seguidamente; ininterruptamente. 1) *to act together*, agir de comum acordo. 2) *I worked eight hours together*, trabalhei oito horas a fio.

toggery, *s.* roupas, vestuário.

toil, *s.* lida, labuta, estafa; *pl.* armadilha, laço; *v.i.* labutar, lidar, trabalhar duramente, mourejar; avançar penosamente.

toiler, *s.* trabalhador, mourejador.

toilet, *s.* trajo, vestido, fato, indumentária; acto de vestir-se e arranjar-se; toucador; casa de banho. 1) *toilet paper*, papel higiénico. 2) *toilet soap*, sabonete. 3) *to make one's toilet*, arranjar-se, vestir-se.

toilsome, *adj.* penoso, trabalhoso, árduo, difícil.

token, *s.* sinal, indício; símbolo, prova, testemunho, penhor; moeda emitida, outrora por bancos, de valor nominal muito superior ao valor real. 1) *a token payment*, pagamento simbólico de dívida. 2) *by the same token*, por isso, também. 3) *by token of*, conforme, em consideração de. 4) *in token of, as a token of*, em sinal de, como prova de.

told, *pret.* e *pp.* de *tell*.

tolerable, *adj.* tolerável, suportável; sofrível, regular; suficiente.

tolerance, *s.* tolerância; paciência, indulgência.

tolerant, *adj.* tolerante, paciente.

tolerate, *v.t.* tolerar; suportar, admitir.

toleration, *s.* tolerância religiosa.

toll, *s.* portagem, taxa paga pela utilização de ponte ou estrada; tributo; toque do sino, toque a finados, dobre. 1) *toll bar*, barreira da portagem. 2) *toll call*, chamada telefónica interurbana. 3) *to take toll of*, levar uma parte de. 4) *the toll of the roads*, a mortalidade das estradas; *v.t.* e *v.i.* tocar a finados; dobrar (sino); pagar ou cobrar portagem.

tollable, *adj.* sujeito ao pagamento de portagem.

tollgate, *s.* barreira de portagem.

tollkeeper, *s.* portageiro, guarda de portagem.

tom, *s.* macho de alguns animais.

tomahawk, *s.* machado de guerra dos índios norte-americanos.

tomato, *s.* tomate.

tomb, *s.* túmulo, sepultura, sepulcro; *v.t.* sepultar, enterrar.

tomboy, *s.* maria-rapaz.

tombstone, *s.* pedra tumular, laje, lápide.

tomcat, *s.* gato macho.

tome, *s.* tomo, volume; livro.

tomentum, *s.* tomento.

tomfool, *s.* e *adj.* toleirão, paspalhão.

tommy, *s.* salário pago em géneros; soldado britânico; refeição que o trabalhador leva consigo; pão, naco de pão.

tomography, *s.* tomografia.

tomorrow, adv. e s. amanhã.

tom-tom, s. tantã, espécie de tambor oriental; gongo.

ton, s. tonelada.

tonality, s. tonalidade.

tone, s. tom; som; timbre; entoação, inflexão; pronúncia, sotaque; espírito, carácter, característica; tendência geral, estilo; vigor, saúde; tónus, tonicidade; acento tónico; (mús.) intervalo de segunda; v.t. e v.i. entoar; dar tom a; tonificar; (mús.) afinar; harmonizar-se com. 1) to tone down, suavizar(-se), atenuar(-se). 2) to tone up, levantar o tom a, fortalecer. 3) that hat does not tone with your dress, esse chapéu não combina com o teu vestido.

tongs, s. pl. tenaz, pinça.

tongue, s. língua; fala, linguagem; língua, idioma; lingueta; badalo (de sino); fiel de balança; (carp.) macho; língua de terra, península. 1) tongue bone, osso hióide. 2) tongue pie, descompostura. 3) to hold one's tongue, calar-se. 4) to speak with one's tongue in one's cheek, falar com malícia ou com ironia. 5) to wag one's tongue, dar com a língua nos dentes; v.t. e v.i. tocar com a ponta da língua; tocar instrumento de sopro utilizando a língua.

tongue-tie, s. (med.) língua presa, encurtamento do freio da língua.

tonic, s. tónico; (mús.) tónica; adj. tónico; revigorante, fortificante, estimulante, tonificante.

tonight, adv. esta noite, hoje à noite; s. esta noite.

tonnage, s. tonelagem; direitos cobrados por tonelada.

tonner, s. navio com determinada tonelagem.

tonsil, s. amígdala.

tonsilitis, s. amigdalite.

tonsure, s. tonsura; corte de cabelo dos clérigos que deixa calvo o alto da cabeça; coroa de padre ou monge; v.t. tonsurar.

tonus, s. (med.) tónus; tonicidade; espasmo tónico.

too, adv. também, igualmente; demasiado, de mais, excessivo; muito, extremamente. 1) this car is too expensive, este carro é demasiado caro. 2) I am a student too, também sou estudante. 3) I know him too well, conheço-o bem de mais.

tool, s. ferramenta, utensílio; instrumento; joguete (nas mãos de alguém); v.t. trabalhar com ferramenta; gravar a ferro quente; conduzir uma carruagem.

toot, s. toque breve de sereia, buzina, etc.; v.t. e v.i. tocar (corneta, etc.) produzindo sons breves; buzinar, tocar, apitar; cantar (o galo silvestre e outras aves).

tooth, s. pl. teeth. dente; paladar, gosto; to have a sweet tooth, gostar de coisas doces; v.t. dentar; v.i. engrenar-se.

toothache, s. dor de dentes.

toothbrush, s. escova de dentes.

toothfull, s. dedal (de bebida).

toothless, adj. desdentado, sem dentes.

toothpick, s. palito.

tootle, v.i. produzir sons breves e suaves (em flauta); flautear.

tootsy, s. pé (em linguagem infantil).

top, s. alto, cimo, cume, topo. crista; ponto mais alto; parte melhor; parte de cima; cabeço; ponta; tejadilho de carro; tampa; tampo; cabeceira da mesa; copa (das árvores); (náut.) gávea, cesto da gávea; pião, piorra, carapeta. 1) from top to bottom, de alto a baixo. 2) on the top of, além de, ademais de. 3) top boots, botas de montar, botas altas. 4) top hat, chapéu alto; v.t. cobrir, encimar, coroar, rematar; chegar ao topo; estar à frente de; dominar; exceder, ser superior a; cortar a parte de cima a; podar; (náut.) desamantilhar; (quím.) extrair a parte mais volátil de. 5) to be of the top a class, ser o melhor da turma. 6) the ship topped the sea, o barco elevou-se com a vaga. 7) he tops 200 pounds, ele tem cem quilos de peso. 8) he topped his dinner with a glass of Port, rematou o jantar com um cálice de Porto; 9) to top up, acabar de encher.

topaz, s. topázio.

top-drawer, adj. de primeira ordem; da mais alta estirpe; excelente.

toper, s. bêbedo, ébrio.

topic, s. tópico; tema, assunto.

topical, adj. local; corrente; relativo a assuntos locais; tópico. 1) a topical allusion, alusão a assuntos conhecidos. 2) topical film, filme de actualidades.

toplofty, adj. altivo, altaneiro.

topman, s. (náut.) gajeiro, vigia de gávea.

topmast, s. mastaréu da gávea.

topographer, s. topógrafo.

topographic(al), adj. topográfico.

topography, s. topografia.

topology, s. topologia.

toponym, s. topónimo.

toponymic(al), adj. toponímico.

toponymy, s. toponímia.

topper, s. chapéu alto; coisa formidável; camaradão.

topping, s. poda, corte; poupa de ave; cobertura; adj. excelente, de categoria superior; avantajado, altaneiro.

topple, v.i. e v.t. cair, tombar, ruir, desabar; descambar; pender, ameaçar cair; deitar abaixo, fazer cair.

topsail, s. (náut.) gávea.

torah, tora, s. Tora, nome hebreu do livro da Lei de Moisés.

torch, s. archote, tocha, facho.

tore, pret. de tear.

toreador, s. toureiro.

torment, s. tormento, tortura, suplício, sofrimento; v.t. atormentar, torturar, afligir.

tormentor, s. torturador, atormentador; carrasco; garfo grande utilizado para tirar a carne dos caldeirões; (cin.) anteparo anti--sonoro.

torn, pp. de tear.

tornado, s. tornado, tufão.

torose, adj. toroso; nodoso; musculado, vigoroso.

torpedo, s. torpedo. 1) torpedo boat, torpedeiro. 2) torpedo boat destroyer, contratorpedeiro; v.t. torpedear; destruir, arruinar.

torpid, adj. entorpecido, dormente, letárgico; inerte, apático; estúpido, obtuso; s. pl. regatas da Páscoa em Oxford.

torpidness, s. entorpecimento, apatia.

torpor, s. torpor, entorpecimento, letargia; apatia.

torporific, adj. entorpecedor; paralisante.

torquate, s. (zool.) torcaz.

torque, s. esforço de torção, momento de torção; colar de metal torcido, usado pelos Gauleses.

torrefaction, s. torrefacção.

torrefy, v.t. torrefazer.

torrent, s. torrente; avalancha.

torrential, adj. torrencial; caudaloso; impetuoso.

torrid, adj. tórrido, escaldante, abrasador.

torsion, s. torção.

torso, s. torso, tronco do corpo humano; estátua mutilada.

torticollis, s. torcicolo.

tortoise, s. tartaruga terrestre; cágado.

tortuosity, s. tortuosidade, sinuosidade.

tortuous, adj. tortuoso, sinuoso; ardiloso.

torture, s. tortura; suplício, tormento, aflição; sofrimento; v.t. torturar, atormentar, supliciar; desvirtuar, distorcer, deturpar o sentido de.

torturer, s. torturador; algoz, carrasco.

torturing, adj. torturante, atormentador.

torus, s. (arq., geom. e bot.) toro.

Tory, s. tóri, membro do partido conservador inglês.

toss, v.t. e v.i. atirar ao ar, lançar; tirar à sorte com moeda; arremessar; sacudir, abanar; perturbar, inquietar; discutir; encrespar-se, encapelar-se (o mar); debater-se, torcer-se, lançar-se. 1) to toss oars, arvorar remos. 2) to toss off, beber apressadamente. 3) to toss out of a room, precipitar-se para fora do quarto. 4) to toss about in one's sleep, remexer-se durante o sono; s. sacudidela, meneio, balanço, agitação; lançamento; distância a que se pode lançar alguma coisa; acto de atirar a cabeça para trás em sinal de desdém ou enfado; aposta.

tossup, s. sorteio atirando moeda ao ar; questão duvidosa.

total, adj. total, inteiro, integral, completo; s. total, soma; v.t. e v.i. somar, totalizar, montar a, subir a importar em.

totalitarian, adj. totalitário; s. totalitarista.

totalitarianism, s. totalitarismo.

totality, s. totalidade.

totalize, v.t. totalizar.

totem, s. totem.

totter, v.i. vacilar, cambalear; ameaçar ruína, oscilar.

tottering, adj. vacilante, cambaleante, trôpego; instável.

toucan, s. tucano.

touch, s. toque; acto de tocar; tacto; apalpadela; ligação, contacto; pequena quantidade, pontinha, pitada; vislumbre, laivo; pincelada; pontada (de dor); remoque, indirecta; prova; toque, contraste; habilidade artística, vocação. 1) to be in touch with someone, estar em contacto com alguém. 2) to put to touch, pôr à prova. 3) to make a touch, pedir dinheiro emprestado; v.t. e v.i. tocar, tocar em; pegar, apalpar; manusear; estar em contacto com, pôr em contacto com; alcançar com a mão; estar contíguo a; ensaiar com pedra-de-toque; bater levemente em; dedilhar; temperar, suavizar; comparar-se com; receber dinheiro; (cal.) furtar; aludir a, referir-se a; dizer respeito a; atingir ligeiramente; afectar; manchar, macular, sujar; impressionar, causar abalo a, sensibilizar. 4) *to touch up,* retocar, aperfeiçoar.

touchback, *s.* determinada jogada no futebol americano.

touchdown, *s.* ponto marcado pelo jogador de futebol americano no decurso de determinada jogada.

touching, *adj.* comovente, tocante.

touchline, *s. (rugby)* linha lateral.

touchstone, *s.* pedra-de-toque; maneira de avaliar, critério; teste.

touchy, *adj.* susceptível, sensível; niquento; irascível.

tough, *adj.* rijo, forte, duro, robusto; rude, violento; teimoso, pertinaz, persistente; difícil, árduo; *s.* desordeiro, brigão.

toughen, *v.t.* e *v.i.* enrijar(-se), fortalecer (-se), endurecer.

toupee, *s.* postiço, cabeleira, capachinho.

tour, *s.* volta, excursão, passeio, viagem de recreio; digressão; *v.t.* e *v.i.* viajar, percorrer, passear.

tourism, *s.* turismo.

tourist, *s.* turista.

tourmaline, *s.* (min.) turmalina.

tournament, *s.* torneio, justa; certame.

tourney, *s.* justa, torneio.

tourniquet, *s.* torniquete.

tousle, *v.t.* desgrenhar, esguedelhar, despentear; maltratar, amarrotar; *s.* cabelo desalinhado, guedelha.

tout, *v.t.* angariar ou aliciar clientes; espiar (treinos de cavalos de corrida); fornecer informações confidenciais; *s.* corretor, angariador; informador clandestino.

tow, *v.t.* rebocar, levar a reboque; *s.* reboque; embarcação rebocada; cabo de reboque.

towage, *s.* reboque.

toward, *adj.* dócil, condescendente; apto; próximo.

towards, *prep.* para, em direcção a, na direcção de; relativamente a; a respeito de; voltado para; a fim de, com o fim de; próximo, perto.

towboat, *s.* rebocador.

towel, *s.* toalha; *to throw in the towell,* dar-se por vencido; *v.t.* e *v.i.* secar(-se), enxugar (-se).

tower, *s.* torre, torreão, campanário; cidadela, fortaleza; *v.i.* elevar-se, erguer-se, estar sobranceiro a; destacar-se, salientar-se.

towering, *adj.* alto, altaneiro, alteroso; grande, proeminente, superior; furioso, arrebatado.

towline, *s.* cabo de reboque.

town, *s.* cidade, vila, burgo. 1) *town council,* conselho municipal. 2) *town hall,* câmara municipal.

township, *s.* distrito, concelho, divisão administrativa de condado; paróquia; *(austral.)* povoação.

townsman, *s.* cidadão, citadino.

toxemia, *s.* toxemia.

toxic, *adj.* tóxico, venenoso.

toxication, *s.* intoxicação, envenenamento.

toxicity, *s.* toxicidade.

toxicologist, *s.* toxicólogo.

toxicology, *s.* toxicologia.

toxin, *s.* toxina.

toxophilite, *s.* atirador com arco, praticante de tiro com arco.

toy, *s.* brinquedo, boneco; bugiganga, ninharia; passatempo; *v.i.* brincar, divertir-se, entreter-se.

trace, *s.* rasto, vestígio, pista, pegada, indício; desenho, traçado, plano; sombra, pequena quantidade; tirante (de carruagem). 1) *in the traces,* atrelado. 2) *to kick over the traces,* rebelar-se: *v.t.* traçar, delinear, esboçar, planear; decalcar, copiar por cima; registar; seguir o rasto de; localizar; remontar à origem de; investigar, descobrir, encontrar; encontrar rastos, vestígios ou sinais de. 3) *to trace back to,* remontar a.

tracer, *s.* investigador; desenhador; tira-linhas; projéctil luminoso.

trachea, *s.* traqueia.

tracheitis, *s.* traqueíte.

tracheotomy, *s.* traqueotomia.

trachoma, *s.* tracoma.

tracing, *s.* investigação; decalque, cópia; esboço, desenho, plano; traço; *tracing paper,* papel de engenheiro, papel transparente próprio para decalques.

track, *s.* rasto, pista; pegadas; esteira; carril; marca, sinal vestígio; trilho; vereda; trajecto, trajectória, rota; sequência; linha férrea; pista de corridas. 1) *the tracks,* as corridas de atletismo. 2) *off the tracks,* descarrilado. 3) *on the track of,* na pista de. 4) *to cover one's tracks,* despistar, esconder o que se faz. 5) *to keep track of,* acompanhar os factos que se desenvolvem, manter-se a par. 6) *track rope,* sirga; *v.t.* e *v.i.* seguir o rasto ou a pista de;

encontrar, apanhar, capturar; seguir, perseguir; acompanhar o curso de; percorrer; sirgar (barco); deixar pegadas; ter determinada largura; estar em alinhamento.

trackage, s. vias férreas; extensão das vias férreas; taxa cobrada por uma companhia ferroviária pela utilização das suas linhas.

tracker, s. batedor, perseguidor.

trackless, adj. que não deixa vestígios; sem caminhos nem carreiros; ínvio.

tract, s. tracto, extensão de terreno; (anat.) tracto, conjunto de órgãos que desempenham a mesma função; opúsculo, brochura, folhete.

tractable, adj. tratável, dócil; maleável.

traction, s. tracção.

tractor, s. tractor; avião com hélices à frente.

trade, s. ofício, mister, arte, profissão; profissão de mercador, comércio; tráfico; freguesia, clientela; negócio, transacção, troca. 1) *trade barriers,* barreiras comerciais. 2) *trade gap,* défice na balança comercial. 3) *trade mark,* marca de fábrica, marca registada. 4) *trade-show,* antestreia. 5) *trade winds,* ventos alísios. 6) *home trade,* comércio interno. 7) *trade price,* preço de fábrica (para venda aos retalhistas). 8) *to be in trade,* seguir um ofício. 9) *to sell to the trade,* vender por atacado; v.t. e v.i. comerciar, negociar, trocar. 10) *to trade on someone,* aproveitar-se de alguém.

trader, s. comerciante, negociante, traficante; navio mercante.

tradesman, s. comerciante; lojista.

trade-union, s. sindicato.

trade-unionism, s. sindicalismo.

trade-unionist, s. sindicalista; operário sindicalizado.

trading, s. comércio, actividade comercial; negócio. 1) *trading post,* feitoria. 2) *trading stamp,* vale oferecido como bónus por certas empresas e que pode ser trocado por mercadorias. 3) *trading vessel,* navio mercante.

tradition, s. tradição.

traditional, adj. tradicional.

traditionalism, s. tradicionalismo.

traditionalist, s. e adj. tradicionalista.

traduce, v.t. difamar, caluniar.

traducement, s. difamação, calúnia.

traducer, s. caluniador.

traffic, s. tráfego, movimento, trânsito; tráfico, comércio; compra e venda; *traffic light,* sinal de tráfego, semáforo; v.i. e v.t. comerciar, negociar, traficar.

trafficker, s. negociante; traficante.

tragedian, s. actor de tragédia.

tragedienne, s. actriz de tragédia.

tragedy, s. tragédia; desgraça.

tragic, adj. trágico, de tragédia; dramático; funesto, terrível; lamentável.

tragicomedy, s. tragicomédia.

tragicomic, adj. tragicómico.

trail, s. rasto, esteira, pista; pegada; trilho, caminho; carreiro; faro; fila, linha; cauda de vestido; (artilh.) conteira; v.t. e v.i. seguir o rasto de; arrastar(-se); puxar pelo chão; trilhar; caminhar com dificuldade; rastejar; trepar; deixar rasto; avançar em fila. 1) *to trail along,* arrastar-se. 2) *to trail arms,* suspender armas. 3) *to trail one's dress,* arrastar o vestido.

trailer, s. pessoa que segue o rasto de; reboque; planta trepadeira; excertos de um filme utilizados para o promover; filme de apresentação.

train, s. comboio; cauda (de vestido, cometa, etc.); comitiva, séquito; cortejo; procissão; série, sequência; fileira, fiada; rastilho. 1) *train-dress,* vestido de cauda. 2) *train oil,* óleo de baleia. 3) *train of gears,* jogo de engrenagens. 4) *train work,* sistema de engrenagens. 5) *by fast train,* em grande velocidade. 6) *to be in train,* estar pronto, estar na devida ordem. 7) *war brings many evils in its train,* a guerra traz muitos males atrás de si; v.t. e v.i. treinar; preparar; exercitar; instruir; adestrar; (bot.) orientar o crescimento de uma planta; dispor em latada; podar; apontar, dirigir; (coloq.) viajar de comboio. 8) *to train down,* perder peso fazendo exercício. 9) *to train off,* sair enviesado (o tiro).

training, s. treino; exercício; instrução; educação, preparação, adestramento; (artilh.) direcção; cultivo de plantas em latadas; *training-ship,* navio-escola.

trait, s. traço, toque, penada; feição, característica; piada, remoque.

traitor, s. traidor.

traitorous, adj. traiçoeiro, traidor, pérfido, desleal.

traitress, adj. traidora.

traject, v.t. transmitir.

trajectory, s. trajectória.

tram, s. carro eléctrico, eléctrico; vagoneta

usada nas minas; *v.t.* e *v.i.* andar de eléctrico; transportar em vagonetas.

tramcar, *s.* carro eléctrico, eléctrico; vagoneta de mina.

tramline, *s.* linha de eléctrico.

trammel, *s.* tresmalho, designação de várias redes de pesca; peia ou trava para ensinar o cavalo a andar a passo; obstáculo, impedimento; cabide sobre a lareira para pendurar as panelas; espécie de calibre para ajustar peças de máquinas; compasso para traçar elipses; *v.t.* apanhar na rede, enredar; obstar, impedir, estorvar.

tramontane, *adj.* e *s.* tramontano, transmontano.

tramp, *s.* vagabundo, pedinte, mendigo, vadio; longa caminhada a pé; passada; navio sem carreira regular; chapa de ferro para proteger a sola do calçado quando se utiliza o pé para ajudar a cavar; *to be on the tramp,* vagabundear; *v.i.* e *v.t.* caminhar pesadamente; andar a pé; vagabundear, errar; pisar, espezinhar; palmilhar.

trample, *v.t.* e *v.i.* calcar aos pés, pisar, atropelar, espezinhar, esmagar; andar pesadamente; tiranizar; *to trample on* ou *upon,* pisar, calcar aos pés, menosprezar, oprimir; *s.* ruído de passos; tropel; acto de calcar aos pés.

tramroad, tramway, *s.* linha férrea de mina; linha de eléctrico.

trance, *s.* transe, êxtase; arrebatamento, arroubo; estupor; estado cataléptico ou hipnótico.

tranquil, *adj.* tranquilo, calmo.

tranquillity, *s.* tranquilidade, calma.

tranquillize, *v.t.* e *v.i.* tranquilizar(-se), acalmar(-se), serenar, sossegar.

tranquillizer, *s.* tranquilizante, calmante.

tranquillizing, *adj.* tranquilizante, calmante.

transact, *v.t.* e *v.i.* levar a cabo, realizar, efectuar (negócio), transaccionar, negociar.

transaction, *s.* negociação, execução, realização; transacção; negócio, operação; (no pl.) acta, relatório.

transactor, *s.* negociador, transaccionador.

transalpine, *adj.* transalpino.

transceiver, *s.* transmissor-receptor.

transcend, *v.t.* e *v.i.* transcender, exceder, superar, ser transcendente; distinguir-se, salientar-se.

transcendence, *s.* transcendência.

transcendent, *adj.* transcendente; excelente, superior, sublime.

transcendental, *adj.* transcendental; para além da experiência humana; idealista; vago, obscuro.

transcontinental, *adj.* transcontinental.

transcribe, *v.t.* transcrever, copiar.

transcriber, *s.* transcritor; copista.

transcript, *s.* transcrito, cópia, traslado; reprodução, imitação.

transcription, *s.* transcrição; cópia.

transect, *v.t.* cortar transversalmente.

transection, *s.* corte transversal.

transept, *s.* transepto.

transeunt, *adj.* transitivo.

transfer, *v.t.* e *v.i.* transferir, trasladar, transportar, mudar; transmitir, trespassar; fazer transbordo, mudar de um transporte para outro; *s.* transferência, transladação, transporte; pessoa ou coisa transferida; bilhete de transbordo; decalcomania; ordem de transferência de títulos; cessão de direitos; trespasse; *transfer ink,* tinta litográfica.

transferable, *adj.* transferível; transmitível.

transferee, *s.* (jur.) cessionário.

transference, *s.* transferência, transladação, transmissão.

transferor, *s.* (jur.) transferente, cedente.

transfiguration, *s.* transfiguração; transformação, metamorfose.

transfigure, *v.t.* transfigurar, transformar; glorificar, idealizar.

transfix, *v.t.* atravessar, trespassar; transfixar; espetar; pregar ao chão, paralisar; petrificar.

transfixion, *s.* transfixação.

transform, *v.t.* e *v.i.* transformar(-se); converter, mudar; metamorfosear.

transformation, *s.* transformação; alteração, modificação; metamorfose; cabeleira postiça de senhora.

transformer, *s.* pessoa ou coisa que (se) transforma; (elect.) transformador.

transformism, *s.* transformismo.

transfuse, *v.t.* transfundir, transvasar, passar de um recipiente para outro; repassar; fazer transfusão de sangue.

transfusion, *s.* transfusão; transvasamento; transmissão.

transgress, *v.t.* e *v.i.* transgredir, infringir, violar, desobedecer a; ultrapassar, transpor, exceder limite; pecar.

transgression, *s.* transgressão, infracção; desobediência; delito, crime, pecado.

transgressor, *s.* transgressor, infractor; delinquente, criminoso; pecador.

transhumance, *s.* transumância.

transience, *s.* transitoriedade.

transient, *adj.* transitório, passageiro, breve; temporário; momentâneo; (mús.) de passagem.

transilient, *adj.* descontínuo, que salta repentinamente de uma coisa para outra.

transistor, *s.* transístor.

transit, *s.* trânsito, passagem, viagem, transporte; trajecto, trajectória, rota; *v.t.* e *v.i.* transitar, passar por, atravessar, fazer girar.

transition, *s.* transição, passagem, mudança.

transitional, *adj.* de transição, intermédio, intermediário.

transitive, *adj.* e *s.* transitivo.

transitory, *adj.* transitório, temporário, passageiro; breve, momentâneo.

translate, *v.t.* traduzir; verter; transladar, transferir; interpretar, explicar; transformar; (Bíblia) subir aos céus; retransmitir (telegrama).

translation, *s.* tradução, versão; traslado, transporte, transferência; interpretação; transformação; (mec.) translação; retransmissão automática de telegrama.

translator, *s.* tradutor; (cal.) sapateiro que reforma calçado velho; repetidor de aparelho telegráfico.

translucence, *s.* translucidez; transparência.

translucent, *adj.* translúcido; transparente.

transmarine, *adj.* ultramarino.

transmigration, *s.* transmigração; migração.

transmission, *s.* transmissão; transferência; propagação.

transmit, *v.t.* transmitir; enviar; passar a; propagar; comunicar; legar; emitir.

transmitter, *s.* transmissor; estação emissora.

transmontane, *adj.* e *s.* transmontano, tramontano.

transmutable, *adj.* transmutável, transformável, convertível.

transmutation, *s.* transmutação; transformação; alteração; conversão.

transmute, *v.t.* transmutar, transformar, converter.

transmuter, *s.* transmutador.

transom, *s.* travessa, travessão; bandeira de porta ou janela.

transonic, *adj.* supersónico.

transparency, *s.* transparência; translucidez; sinceridade; clareza; quadro, letreiro, anúncio ou desenho iluminado por transparência; diapositivo.

transparent, *adj.* transparente; diáfano; claro, evidente; sincero, simples.

transpicuous, *adj.* transparente; claro, evidente, compreensível.

transpierce, *v.t.* trespassar; perfurar.

transpiration, *s.* transpiração.

transpiratory, *adj.* transpiratório.

transpire, *v.t.* e *v.i.* transpirar; exalar; espalhar-se, divulgar-se.

transplant, *s.* transplante; enxerto; *v.t.* transplantar; transferir, trasladar.

transplantation, *s.* transplantação; enxerto.

transport, *s.* transporte; arrebatamento, rapto; *v.t.* transportar; extasiar, enlevar, arrebatar.

transportable, *adj.* transportável; punível com a pena de desterro.

transportation, *s.* transporte, condução; bilhete, passe; desterro, degredo.

transpose, *v.t.* transpor.

transposition, *s.* transposição; transporte.

transshipment, *s.* transbordo.

transude, *v.i.* transudar; exsudar.

transvaluation, *s.* transposição de valores.

transversal, *adj.* transversal, transverso; oblíquo; *s.* (geom.) transversal; artéria ou músculo transversal.

transverse, *adj.* transverso, transversal, atravessado; *s.* transverso, transversal *(músculo);* (geom.) eixo maior.

trap, *s.* armadilha, laço; cilada, ardil; escotilha; carro leve de duas rodas; sifão; (geol.) trape; aparelho para lançar pombos de barro no tiro ao alvo. 1) *trap door,* alçapão. 2) *mouse trap,* ratoeira; *v.t.* e *v.i.* apanhar em armadilha; pôr armadilhas; colocar sifão; aparelhar cavalo.

trapeze, *s.* trapézio.

trapezium, *s.* (geom. e anat.) trapézio.

trapper, *s.* pessoa que prepara ou caça com armadilhas.

trapping, *s.* (pl.) arreios.

traprock, *s.* (geol.) trape.

trapshooting, *s.* tiro aos pratos.

trash, *s.* lixo, refugo, escória; galhos de árvore cortados; coisa ordinária ou mal feita; ralé, gentalha; *v.t.* limpar; podar (árvores); deitar fora, rejeitar.

trashy, *adj.* ordinário, inferior, desprezível, insignificante, inútil.

trauma, *s.* trauma; lesão, ferimento, choque.

traumatic, *adj.* traumático.

traumatism, *s.* traumatismo.

traumatize, *v.t.* traumatizar, ferir.

travel, *s.* viagem; jornada; curso, percurso; avanço, jogo, andamento; *v.i.* e *v.t.* viajar, fazer viagem; andar, mover-se, avançar, propagar-se; percorrer; deslocar-se; atravessar; trabalhar como caixeiro-viajante.

traveler, traveller, *s.* viajante; caixeiro--viajante; guindaste rolante; cursor.

travelling, *adj.* viajante, ambulante, itinerante; rolante, móvel, próprio para viagem.

travelogue, *s.* narrativa ilustrada de viagem.

traverse, *adj.* atravessado, traverso, transversal; *s.* travessa, travessão; coisa transversal; degrau de escada de mão; travessia, passagem; galeria transversal de comunicação em igreja; movimento lateral; (jur.) contestação negativa, objecção legal; (náut.) rota em ziguezague; (geom.) linha transversal; *v.t.* e *v.i.* atravessar, cruzar, percorrer; estar atravessado; examinar, estudar; contrariar, opor-se a, impedir; mover lateralmente, caminhar de lado; girar sobre eixo vertical; aplainar madeira; apontar (canhão).

traverser, *s.* o que atravessa; (jur.) contestante.

travesty, *s.* imitação grotesca, caricatura; *v.t.* parodiar, caricaturizar.

trawl, *s.* rede de arrasto; *trawl boat,* traineira, barco de arrasto.

trawler, *s.* pescador de arrasto; traineira, barco de arrasto.

tray, *s.* bandeja, tabuleiro, salva; tina.

treacherous, *adj.* traiçoeiro, traidor, desleal.

treachery, *s.* traição, perfídia, deslealdade.

treacle, *s.* melaço.

tread, *s.* passo; andar, passada; modo de andar; piso de degrau; trilho (de roda); apoio para os pés; parte da sola que assenta no chão; cicatrícula (no ovo); *v.i.* e *v.t. prt. trod, pp. trodden,* pisar; calcar com os pés, esmagar; caminhar em, palmilhar, trilhar; andar. 1) *to tread a valse,* dançar uma valsa. 2) *to tread down,* calcar com os pés, espezinhar. 3) *to tread in someone's footsteps,* seguir as pisadas de alguém. 4) *to tread lightly,* agir prudentemente. 5) *to tread out,* apagar fogo com os pés. 6) *to tread the boards,* pisar o palco.

treadle, *s.* pedal; *v.i.* pedalar.

treason, *s.* traição; deslealdade.

treasure, *s.* tesouro; riqueza; preciosidade; *v.t.* ter em grande conta; guardar como preciosidade, prezar; entesourar.

treat, *s.* regalo, prazer, gosto; festa ou divertimento (especialmente oferecido a crianças); convite para comer ou beber. 1) *that is my treat,* quem paga sou eu, sou eu que ofereço. 2) *to stand treat,* pagar a festa, pagar a despesa; *v.t.* e *v.i.* tratar, tratar de; considerar, encarar; acolher, festejar, obsequiar; negociar, parlamentar. 3) *to treat with the enemy,* negociar com o inimigo. 4) *to treat of,* tratar de, discorrer sobre, discutir (assunto). 5) *he treated me to a glass of Port,* ele obsequiou-me com um cálice de vinho do Porto, ele ofereceu-me um cálice de vinho do Porto.

treatise, *s.* tratado.

treatment, *s.* tratamento; trato, acolhimento.

treaty, *s.* tratado; acordo, convénio, pacto. 1) *to be in treaty with someone for something,* negociar alguma coisa com alguém. 2) *treaty port,* porto aberto em virtude de um tratado;

treble, *adj.* triplo, tríplice; triplicado; (mús.) próprio de soprano, agudo; *s.* triplo; (mús.) tiple, soprano.

trebuchet, *s.* trabuco, catapulta; balança para pequenos pesos.

tree, *s.* árvore; mastro, poste, viga; madeira; (arc.) cruz; patíbulo, forca. 1) *up a tree,* em apuros, encurralado. 2) *tree-toad,* rela. 3) *in the green tree,* quando tudo corre bem; *v.t.* fazer subir a uma árvore; encurralar; meter sapato em forma.

trefoil, *s.* trevo.

trek, *s.* viagem, jornada em carro de bois; *v.i.* viajar em carro de bois; puxar carro de bois.

tremble, *v.i.* tremer, estremecer, tiritar; agitar-se, vibrar, trepidar, vacilar; *s.* tremor, tremura, frémito, vibração; *all of a tremble,* todo a tremer.

trembling, *adj.* trémulo, tremente; agitado, ansioso, receoso; vacilante.

trembly, *adj.* trémulo.

tremendous, *adj.* tremendo, terrível, espantoso; formidável, enorme.

tremor, *s.* tremor, tremura; estremecimento; agitação; vibração, trepidação.

tremulous, *adj.* trémulo; trepidante; receoso; tímido; vacilante.

trench, *s.* fosso, vala, valado; trincheira; sulco, ruga, cicatriz. 1) *trench coat,* impermeável; *v.t.* e *v.i.* abrir fosso, vala ou rego; lavrar em sulcos paralelos; cortar, talhar; rodear de trincheiras, entrincheirar(-se); abrir caminho cavando fossos ou valas; invadir, usurpar; raiar, aproximar-se de. 2) *to trench upon someone's rights,* usurpar os direitos de alguém. 3) *his ideias trench on heresy,* as ideias dele roçam a heresia.

trenchancy, *s.* vigor, energia; mordacidade; argúcia.

trenchant, *adj.* cortante; agudo, arguto; incisivo, enérgico; mordaz.

trencher, *s.* aquele que abre valas ou regos; tábua de cortar carne, pão, etc.; (arc.) os prazeres da mesa.

trend, *s.* direcção, rumo, orientação; tendência, corrente; *v.i.* ter ou tomar determinada direcção, tender, inclinar-se para, propender.

trepan, *s.* (cir.) trépano; *v.t.* trepanar, fazer a operação do trépano; atrair, seduzir, enganar.

trepidation, *s.* trepidação.

trespass, *v.i.* transgredir; ofender; invadir propriedade alheia; *s.* transgressão, delito, crime, falta, ofensa; violação; violação de propriedade alheia.

trespasser, *s.* infractor, transgressor; invasor de propriedade alheia.

trestle, *s.* cavalete; tripé; armação de mesa.

trews, *s. pl.* calças justas de tecido axadrezado.

trey, *s.* três, terno (nas cartas ou no dominó).

triable, *adj.* que se pode experimentar, experimental; (jur.) que pode ser julgado.

triad, *s.* tríade, trio; trindade.

triagonal, *adj.* triangular.

trial, *s.* experiência, ensaio, prova, teste, verificação; tentativa, esforço; provação, infortúnio, flagelo; (jur.) julgamento, processo. 1) *trial and error,* método das tentativas. 2) *trial judge,* juiz de primeira instância. 3) *civil trial,* acção civil. 4) *on trial,* à experiência. 5) *to be on trial,* estar a ser julgado. 6) *trial flight,* voo de ensaio.

triangle, *s.* triângulo; esquadro; (mús.) ferrinhos.

triangular, *adj.* triangular.

triangulate, *adj.* triangulado; *v.t.* triangular.

triangulation, *s.* triangulação.

triarchy, *s.* triarquia; triunvirato.

tribal, *adj.* tribal, de tribo.

tribalism, *s.* tribalismo.

tribasic, *adj.* (quím.) tribásico.

tribe, *s.* tribo.

tribesman, *s.* membro de uma tribo.

tribulation, *s.* tribulação, adversidade, aflição; opressão.

tribunal, *s.* tribunal; foro; assento de juiz.

tribunate, *s.* tribunado; cargo de tribuno.

tribune, *s.* tribuno, magistrado da Roma antiga; tribuna; trono episcopal; púlpito.

tributary, *adj.* tributário, que paga tributo; afluente; *s.* tributário, contribuinte; rio afluente.

tribute, *s.* tributo; imposto; contribuição; louvor, homenagem; *to pay tribute to,* render homenagem a.

trice, *v.t.* (náut.) alar, içar; *s.* ápice, instante.

tricentenary, tricentennial, *adj.* e *s.* tricentenário.

trichina, *s.* (zool.) triquina.

trichloride, *s.* (quím.) tricloreto.

trichoid, *adj.* tricóide, capilar, capiliforme.

trichord, *adj.* (mús.) tricorde; *s.* (mús.) tricórdio.

trick, *s.* truque, artifício, estratagema, ardil; tramóia, trapaça, embuste, proeza, habilidade; maneirismo, tique; partida, travessura; turno de trabalho; vaza (em jogos de cartas). 1) *to play a trick on someone,* pregar uma partida a alguém. 2) *to do the trick,* dar resultado, resolver o assunto. 3) *conjuring tricks,* truques de prestidigitação; *v.t.* e *v.i.* enganar, lograr; defraudar; pregar partidas; apanhar de surpresa; decepcionar. 4) *to trick out,* vestir, enfeitar. 5) *to trick someone into doing something,* induzir alguém a fazer alguma coisa.

tricker, *s.* embusteiro, trapaceiro.

trickery, *s.* velhacaria, embuste, trapaça, fraude, artifício.

tricking, *adj.* impostura, velhacaria, fraude; ornamentação, decoração.

trickish, *adj.* manhoso, ardiloso; difícil, espinhoso, arriscado.

trickle, *s.* fio de água; pingo; lágrima; *v.t.* e *v.i.* escorrer, correr em fio, escoar(-se), gotejar; *to trickle out,* divulgar-se, tornar-se conhecido a pouco e pouco.

trickster, *s.* trapaceiro, embusteiro.

tricksy, *adj.* enfeitado, ataviado; alinhado, elegante; travesso; brincalhão; astuto, manhoso; enganoso; difícil.

tricky, *adj.* manhoso, ardiloso, desonesto; astuto; difícil, espinhoso; delicado, arriscado; complicado.

triclinic, *adj.* triclínico.

tricorn, s. tricórnio; adj. tricorne.
tricornered, adj. triangular, que tem três cantos.
tricycle, s. triciclo.
trident, s. tridente.
tridentate, adj. tridentado, tridente.
tridimensional, adj. tridimensional.
tried, pret. e pp. de to try; adj. experimentado; fiel, leal.
triennial, adj. trienal.
triennium, s. triénio.
trier, s. aquele que experimenta, ensaia ou tenta; juiz.
trierarch, s. trierarca.
trifid, adj. trífido; tridentado.
trifle, s. bagatela, ninharia, futilidade, insignificância; pequena quantidade; sobremesa feita com pão-de-ló; peltre, liga de estanho e chumbo; v.i. e v.t. brincar, gracejar, perder tempo; troçar de; desperdiçar, esbanjar.
trifler, s. brincalhão; pessoa leviana ou fútil.
trifling, adj. frívolo, fútil, leviano; insignificante; s. conversa banal; trivialidade, futilidade.
trig, adj. elegante, bem vestido; janota; são, sadio, forte; s. calço de roda; (cal.) trigonometria. v.t. vestir bem; escorar; calçar roda.
trigeminal, adj. e s. (anat.) trigémeo.
trigger, s. gatilho. 1) to be quick on the trigger, de resposta pronta, impetuoso. 2) trigger happy, que gosta de apertar o gatilho.
triggerfish, s. (zool.) cangulo, xaputa.
trigonometry, s. trigonometria.
trigonous, adj. trígono, triangular.
trigram, s. grupo de três letras que representam um único som.
trike, s. (fam.) triciclo.
trilateral, adj. trilateral, trilátero.
trilemma, s. trilema.
trilith, s. (arqueol.) trílito, anta.
trilling, s. trilado, trinado; (pl.) trigémeos.
trillion, s. (Ingl.) trilião; (E.U.) bilião.
trilogy, s. trilogia.
trim, s. roupa, traje, vestuário, atavios; aprumo, garbo, alinho; bom estado, boa condição, boa forma; corte de cabelo; (náut.) condições de navegabilidade; equilíbrio do navio; arrumação da carga, estiva. 1) in a good trim, numa boa linha de água; v.t. e v.i. arranjar, pôr em ordem, arrumar, alinhar, preparar; enfeitar, ador-

nar, orlar; aparar; podar; desbastar; avivar, atear (o fogo); (fam.) castigar, repreender, ralhar; equilibrar (barco) arrumando a carga; levar a melhor, derrotar; ser oportunista; equilibrar (balança); equilibrar-se (o navio); conciliar opiniões contrárias. 2) to trim by the head, (náut.) afocinhar à proa. 3) to trim someone's jacket, dar uma tareia a alguém; adj. arranjado, em boa ordem, arrumado; elegante, bem vestido, asseado; em boas condições.
trimensual, trimestral, adj. trimestral, trimensal.
trimester, s. trimestre.
trimmer, s. estivador; aquele que enfeita ou guarnece; máquina ou aparelho de podar; oportunista; pl. tesoura de aparar.
trimming, s. acto de arrumar, preparar, guarnecer, etc.; ornamento, enfeite; arrumação da carga no porão do navio; estiva; equilíbrio longitudinal do navio; pl. acompanhamentos de um prato; (pl.) aparas, raspas, limalha; (fam.) sova, derrota, repreensão; trimming tab, (av.) compensador do plano de comando.
trimonthly, adj. trimensal, trimestral.
trinary, adj. ternário.
trine, adj. trino, tríplice; (astrol.) que está em trígono; favorável, auspicioso; s. trígono; tríade, trindade.
tringle, s. varão de cortina; pequena moldura quadrada.
trinity, s. trindade; tríade; trio; Trinity Sunday, Festa da Santíssima Trindade.
trinket, s. jóia de pequeno valor; berloque, bugiganga; quinquilharia.
trio, s. trio, terceto.
triode, s. (elect.) tríodo.
trioxide, s. trióxido.
trip, s. viagem, excursão, jornada; modo de caminhar agilmente; tropeção, topada, passo em falso; erro, deslize, falta; (mec.) desengate, disparo; trip-hammer, martinete de báscula, martelão; v.i. e v.t. saltitar, andar ou dançar com passos leves e curtos; tropeçar; viajar; errar, enganar-se, prevaricar; rasteirar; obstruir, atrapalhar; (mec.) desengatar, disparar; (náut.) arrancar do fundo; empinar (verga), guindar.
tripartite, adj. tripartido, tríplice, triplo; em três vias (documento).
tripartition, s. tripartição.
tripe, s. estômago de boi usado como

alimento, tripas, dobrada; (cal.) disparate, porcaria.

tripedal, *adj.* trípode.

triplane, *s. (av.)* triplano.

triple, *adj.* triplo, tríplice, triplicado. 1) *triple crown*, tiara papal. 2) *triple time*, compasso ternário; *s.* triplo; tríade, grupo de três; *v.t.* e *v.i.* triplicar, ser o triplo de.

triplet, *s.* trinca, terno, trio; trigémeo; (mús.) grupo de três notas com o valor de duas.

triplex, *adj.* triplo, tríplice; *s.* vidro triplex; (mús.) compasso ternário.

triplicate, *s.* triplicado; *adj.* triplo, tríplice; *v.t.* triplicar.

triply, *adv.* triplamente, três vezes, três vezes mais.

tripod, *s.* tripeça, tripé; mesa de três pés.

tripos, *s.* exame para obter título de bacharel com distinção, na Universidade de Cambridge.

tripper, *s.* excursionista, turista; dançarino, pessoa que anda com passinhos miúdos e rápidos.

tripping, *adj.* ágil, saltitante, leve, ligeiro; pecador, prevaricador.

triptych, *s.* tríptico.

tripudiate, *v.i.* tripudiar, dançar de alegria, exultar.

trisect, *v.t.* dividir em três partes, trissecar.

trisection, *s.* divisão em três partes; trissecação.

trismus, *s.* (med.) trismo.

trisyllabic(al), *adj.* trissílabo, trissilábico.

trisyllable, *s.* trissílabo.

trite, *adj.* velho, cediço, gasto, usado; banal, trivial.

triteness, *s.* trivialidade, banalidade.

triton, *s.* (zool.) tritão; (quím.) tríton.

triturate, *v.t.* triturar, moer, esmagar.

trituration, *s.* trituração, esmagamento.

triumph, *s.* triunfo; vitória, sucesso, êxito; exultação, regozijo; *v.i.* triunfar, vencer, prevalecer, ser bem sucedido, vingar; exultar, regozijar-se.

triumphal, *adj.* triunfal.

triumphant, *adj.* triunfante, vitorioso; exultante.

triumvirate, *s.* triunvirato, triunvirado; trio.

triune, *adj.* trino e uno, três num só; *triune Godhead*, divindade trina e una; Trindade.

triunity, *s.* trindade.

trivalent, *adj.* trivalente.

trivet, *s.* trempe (suporte para tachos e panelas); tripé; mesas de três pernas; *right as a trivet*, de perfeita saúde.

trivia, *s. pl.* ninharias.

trivial, *adj.* trivial, banal, insignificante, superficial; não científico; específico (em contraposição a "genérico").

triviality, *s.* trivialidade, banalidade, insignificância.

triweekly, *adj.* trissemanal; *adv.* três vezes por semana.

trochilus, *s.* (zool.) tróquilo.

trochlea, *s.* (anat.) tróclea.

trod, *pret.* e *pp.* de *to tead.*

trodden, *pp.* de *to tread.*

troglodyte, *s.* troglodita.

troll, *s.* espécie de rondó (canção); linha usada na pesca ao corrico; ser sobrenatural, duende, gigante; *v.t.* e *v.i.* cantar em rondó (canção); cantarolar; pescar ao corrico; fazer circular (objecto).

trolley, *s.* carro leve de vendedor ambulante; vagoneta sobre carris; carro eléctrico; mesinha com rodas; variedade de renda; *v.t.* e *v.i.* conduzir ou viajar em carro eléctrico.

trollop, *s.* mulher desmazelada; rameira, prostituta.

trombone, *s.* trombone.

troop, *s.* grupo, bando, magote; manada, rebanho; companhia de actores; (mil.) esquadrão de cavalaria; (pl.) tropas, forças militares. 1) *troop-carrier*, avião de transporte de tropas. 2) *troop horse*, cavalo do exército; *v.i.* reunir-se, aglomerar-se; mover-se em bando; marchar, desfilar; associar-se. 3) *to troop the colours*, saudar a bandeira; *v.t.* formar em esquadrões (regimento).

trooper, *s.* soldado de cavalaria; (austral.) soldado da polícia montada; (E.U.) soldado da polícia estadual; cavalo do exército; (coloq.) pára-quedista.

trope, *s.* tropo, figura de retórica.

trophy, *s.* troféu; prémio; despojo de guerra; medalha, taça ganha como prémio.

tropic, *s.* trópico; (pl.) trópicos, regiões tropicais; *adj.* tropical; quente; (fig.) apaixonado.

tropical, *adj.* tropical, relativo aos trópicos; quente; ardente, apaixonado; metafórico.

tropism, *s.* tropismo.

tropologic(al), *adj.* tropológico, figurado, metafórico.

tropology, *s.* tropologia; linguagem figurada; tratado sobre os tropos.

troposphere, *s.* troposfera.

trot, *s.* trote; passo rápido e certo; faina, actividade, lida; criança pequena que dá os primeiros passos; velha, megera; *v.i.* e *v.t.* trotar, andar a trote, caminhar depressa; fazer o cavalo andar a trote; percorrer distância a trote; apresentar pessoa ou coisa para ser admirada.

troth, *s.* fé, fidelidade; verdade; palavra dada; promessa. 1) *to plight one's troth,* dar a sua palavra. 2) *in troth,* em verdade, na verdade.

trothplight, *s.* esponsais, contrato de casamento; *adj.* prometido em casamento; empenhada (a palavra); *v.t.* prometer casamento a; prometer em casamento.

trotter, *s.* cavalo de trote; pessoa que anda rapidamente; (pl.) pés de porco.

troubadour, *s.* trovador.

trouble, *s.* perturbação, inquietação, preocupação, problema, aflição, tormento, sarilho, angústia, aborrecimento, contratempo, dificuldade, mal, distúrbio; trabalho, incómodo; enfermidade, doença; defeito, avaria. 1) *to take the trouble to,* dar-se ao trabalho de. 2) *to be worth the trouble,* valer o esforço. 3) *to put someone to great trouble,* dar muito trabalho a alguém. 4) *what is the trouble?,* o que é que se passa? 5) *no trouble at all!,* não dá trabalho nenhum! 6) *keep out of trouble!,* não arranjes sarilhos! 7) *to be in trouble,* estar metido em sarilhos, estar em apuros, estar com dificuldades; *v.t.* e *v.i.* incomodar(-se), perturbar, aborrecer, importunar, inquietar, preocupar, atormentar, afligir; agitar, revolver (águas); esforçar-se, dar-se ao trabalho de.

troublemaker, *s.* desordeiro, brigão, arruaceiro.

troublesome, *adj.* aborrecido, perturbador, incómodo; importuno; penoso, maçador.

troubling, *adj.* perturbador, inquietante, incómodo.

trough, *s.* tina comprida e estreita onde se põe a comida ou a água para os animais; comedouro, bebedouro; cuba (para lavar minério); cocho (tabuleiro para transportar argamassa); tina, cuba, alguidar; algeroz, calha; leito de curso de água; (náut.) cavado, depressão entre duas ondas; (geol.) sinclinal.

trounce, *v.t.* surrar, espancar, açoitar, sovar; derrotar.

troupe, *s.* trupe, companhia de actores, grupo de saltimbancos.

trousers, *s. pl.* calças.

trousseau, *s.* enxoval de noiva.

trout, *s.* truta.

trow, *v.t.* e *v.i.* crer, acreditar, pensar, supor.

trowel, *s.* colher de trolha ou de pedreiro; pá pequena de jardim.

troy, *s.* sistema de pesos empregado para ouro e prata; *troy-ounce* = 31,103 g.

truant, *s.* e *adj.* vadio, gazeteiro, cábula.

truce, *s.* trégua, armistício.

truck, *s.* camião, camioneta de carga; (cam. de ferro) vagão de carga; carro de mão de duas, três ou quatro rodas; jogo das rodas em carruagem de comboio; (náut.) disco de madeira no topo do mastro para içar bandeira; troca, permuta, pagamento em géneros; trato, negócio; miudezas, bugigangas; *v.t.* e *v.i.* transportar em camião; trocar, permutar.

truckage, *s.* transporte em camião; frete.

trucker, *s.* aquele que troca ou permuta; motorista de camião.

truckle, *s.* rodinha, rodízio; *v.i.* ceder, submeter-se, sujeitar-se.

truckling, *adj.* submisso, servil.

truckman, *s.* transportador em camião; motorista de camião.

truculence, *s.* truculência, ferocidade, crueldade.

truculent, *adj.* truculento, cruel, feroz, bárbaro; rude, violento.

trudge, *v.i.* e *v.t.* caminhar penosamente, arrastar-se; percorrer a pé. *s.* grande caminhada, estirão.

true, *adj.* verdadeiro, certo; verídico; autêntico, genuíno, real; puro; correcto, exacto; bem ajustado, bem centrado, bem afinado. 1) *it is true,* é verdade. 2) *true bill,* (jur.) veredicto de júri de instrução. 3) *true blue,* fiel, leal. 4) *true born,* autêntico, de raça pura. 5) *true north,* norte geográfico. 6) *true ribs,* costelas verdadeiras. 7) *true time,* hora solar média. 8) *to come true,* realizar--se, concretizar-se; *adv.* verdadeiramente, na verdade, sinceramente; de facto; exactamente; bem. 9) *to aim true,* apontar bem. 10) *tell me true,* diga-me sinceramente; *v.t.* ajustar, rectificar, desempenar.

truelove, *s.* namorado, bem-amado;

truelove-knot, espécie de laço, símbolo do amor fiel.

trueness, *s.* verdade; veracidade; fidelidade; exactidão.

truffle, *s.* trufa.

truism, *s.* truísmo; banalidade, lugar-comum.

trull, *s.* meretriz, rameira.

truly, *adv.* realmente, de facto; na verdade; sinceramente; fielmente; com exactidão.

trump, *s.* trunfo, naipe de trunfo; boa pessoa, amigo; (arc.) trombeta. 1) *to put someone to his trumps,* reduzir alguém a uma situação muito difícil, apertar com alguém. 2) *to turn up trumps,* sair-se melhor do que se esperava, ter sorte; *v.t.* e *v.i.* cortar com trunfo; vencer, superar. 3) *to trump up,* forjar, arquitectar, inventar; jogar trunfo; (arc.) trombetear.

trumpery, *s.* adereços sem valor, ouropel; bugigangas; refugo; tolice, baboseira; *adj.* vistoso, ordinário; ilusório; superficial.

trumpet, *s.* trombeta; clarim; corneta; porta-voz; barrido de elefante; *v.i.* tombetear, apregoar ao som da trombeta.

trumpeter, *s.* trombeteiro; pregoeiro; propagandista; variedade de cisne selvagem; variedade de pombo doméstico.

truncate, *v.t.* truncar, mutilar; *adj.* truncado, mutilado.

truncation, *s.* truncamento.

truncheon, *s.* bastão de polícia, cassetete.

trundle, *s.* rodinha, rodízio; zorra, carro de rodas baixas; cama de rodízios; *v.t.* e *v.i.* rolar; fazer andar sobre rodízios; revolver, girar; bolar (no críquete).

trunk, *s.* tronco (de árvore, homem, etc.); tromba; baú, mala, arca; calha de madeira; clarabóia; (pl.) bragas (calções largos usados no séc. XVI); (pl.) calções usados na prática de desportos ou na praia; *(arquit.)* fuste de coluna. 1) *trunk call,* telefonema inter-urbano. 2) *trunk drawers,* ceroulas curtas. 3) *trunk piston,* êmbolo de tronco; *v.t.* separar (minério).

truss, *s.* asna; suporte do tecto; armação; feixe, molho; fardo de palha (17,452 kg); medida para feno seco: funda para hérnia. 1) *truss bridge,* ponte com armação metálica. 2) *truss frame,* rede metálica; *v.t.* reforçar com suportes; sustentar, firmar com vigas cruzadas; amarrar, atar. 3) *to truss up,* atar num feixe, fazer um molho de.

trust, *s.* confiança, fé, crença; esperança;

pessoa em quem se confia; crédito; responsabilidade, encargo, obrigação, dever; custódia, guarda, cuidado; (jur.) depósito, fideicomisso, bens confiados à guarda de alguém; consórcio, cartel. 1) *to hold property in trust,* administrar propriedades de outra pessoa. 2) *to sell on trust,* vender a crédito. 3) *trust territory,* território colocado sob curadoria; *v.t.* e *v.i.* confiar em, ter fé em, acreditar em; entregar, cometer; deixar à guarda de; encarregar confiadamente; esperar, contar, acreditar; fiar-se em; vender a crédito.

trustee, *s.* depositário, fiduciário, curador; mandatário; depositário; administrador; provedor; membro do conselho de administração de uma fundação.

trusteeship, *s.* curadoria; administração de bens dos quais se é depositário.

trustful, *adj.* confiante, confiado, esperançoso.

trustfulness, *s.* confiança.

trusting, *adj.* confiante, confiado.

trustworthy, *adj.* digno de confiança; fiel, leal; fidedigno, exacto.

trusty, *adj.* digno de confiança, leal, fiel, seguro; *s.* pessoa de confiança; preso que, nos E.U., goza de privilégios especiais.

truth, *s.* verdade; veracidade, sinceridade; autenticidade; fidelidade (a um modelo); exactidão; realidade, facto; ajustamento; *the wheel is out of truth,* a roda está desajustada.

truthful, *adj.* verídico, verdadeiro, sincero.

truthfulness, *s.* veracidade; autenticidade; boa fé; exactidão.

truthless, *adj.* falso; infiel, desleal.

try, *s.* ensaio, experiência, prova, tentativa; ensaio no râguebi. 1) *to have a try,* experimentar; *v.t.* e *v.i.* experimentar, ensaiar; tentar, fazer uma tentativa; procurar, conseguir; pôr em prática; (jur.) julgar, actuar como juiz; cansar, fatigar; pôr à prova; afligir, submeter a provação. 2) *to try out,* experimentar, pôr à prova; purificar, refinar (gorduras, óleos). 3) *to try back,* voltar atrás.

trying, *adj.* penoso, difícil, duro; fatigante; exasperante.

tryout, *s.* prova, teste.

trypanosoma, *s.* tripanossoma.

tryst, *s.* (arc.) encontro marcado, entrevista, compromisso; *v.t.* marcar encontro.

tsar, *s.* czar.

tsardom, *s.* domínio de um czar, czarismo.

tsarevich, *s.* czareviche, filho do czar.

tsarina, *s.* czarina.

tsarism, *s.* czarismo.

tsetse, *s.* tsé-tsé, mosca africana responsável pela doença do sono.

tub, *s.* tina, selha, cuba, dorna; tonel, barril; banheira, (cal.) batoque, pessoa gorda e atarracada.

tuba, *s.* tuba.

tubal, *adj.* (anat.) tubário.

tubate, *adj.* tubular, tubulado.

tubby, *adj.* atarracado, corpulento.

tube, *s.* tubo, cano; bisnaga; canal, conduta, (anat.) trompa; (med.) sonda; (mús.) tubo de instrumento de sopro; (Londres) metropolitano; *v.t.* pôr tubos ou canos em; fazer a tubagem de.

tuber, *s.* tubérculo; (anat.) tubérculo, protuberância, excrescência; túbera.

tuberculate, *adj.* tuberculado, tubercular.

tuberculize, *v.t.* tuberculizar.

tuberculosis, *s.* tuberculose.

tuberculous, *adj.* tuberculoso; tuberculado.

tuberose, *s.* (bot.) tuberosa, angélica.

tuberosity, *s.* tuberosidade.

tuberous, *adj.* tuberoso, nodoso.

tubiform, *adj.* tubiforme.

tubing, *s.* fabrico de tubos; tubos, canos; tubagem, canalização.

tubular, *adj.* tubular, tubiforme; cilíndrico; brônquio (respiração).

tubule, *s.* tubo pequeno.

tubulous, *adj.* tubuloso.

tuck, *s.* refego, prega, dobra; (náut.) parte traseira do navio onde as tábuas do costado se encontram; (cal.) comida; (arc.) toque de trombetas, rufar de tambores. 1) *tuck net,* rede com que se recolhem os peixes da rede maior; *v.t.* e *v.i.* arregaçar, arrepanhar; preguear, fazer pregas; dobrar, fazer dobra (de lençol); aconchegar pessoa na cama; guardar, enfiar, meter; franzir-se, contrair-se; (cal.) empanturrar-se. 2) *to tuck up,* (cal.) enforcar criminoso.

tucker, *s.* lenço usado ao pescoço pelas mulheres; gola postiça de vestido; *v.t.* (E.U.) cansar, fatigar.

tuesday, *s.* terça-feira.

tufa, *s.* (geol.) tufo calcário.

tuff, *s.* (geol.) tufo vulcânico.

tuft, *s.* tufo (de pêlos, penas, ervas, etc.), borla, penacho, poupa; feixe, molho; moita; pêra (barba em bico); estudante univer-

sitário com título de nobreza; (anat.) glomérulo de capilares; *v.t.* guarnecer ou enfeitar com borla, tufo, etc.;

tufted, *adj.* guarnecido de tufo, borla, penacho, etc.; agrupado em moitas.

tufty, *adj.* enfeitado com tufos ou borlas; espesso.

tug, *s.* puxão, empurrão; esforço violento, trabalho; corda ou cabo com que se puxa alguma coisa; *tug of war,* jogo em que as extremidades de uma corda são puxadas por duas equipas para avaliar qual a equipa mais forte; *v.t.* e *v.i.* puxar com força; arrastar; rebocar; dar puxões ou empurrões; labutar, lutar.

tugboat, *s.* rebocador.

tuition, *s.* ensino, instrução, educação; custo do ensino; honorários de professor.

tulip, *s.* túlipa.

tulle, *s.* tule.

tumble, *s.* tombo, queda, trambolhão; salto acrobático; desordem, confusão; *v.i.* e *v.t.* cair, dar trambolhão; tombar; derrubar; mover-se desordenadamente; agitar-se, revolver-se; dar saltos acrobáticos, dar cambalhotas; atirar ao chão; pôr em desordem, desarrumar. 1) *to tumble home,* (cal.) ir para a cama. 2) *to tumble in one's thoughts,* debater-se com os seus pensamentos. 3) *to tumble in,* encaixar peça em outra.

tumbler, *s.* copo de vidro sem pé; acrobata; gatilho de espingarda; raça de pombo; tranqueta de fechadura; boneco teimoso; *tumbler gear,* mecanismo de inversão.

tumbrel, tumbril, *s.* carro ou carroça de duas rodas.

tumefacient, *adj.* tumefaciente.

tumefaction, *s.* tumefacção.

tumefy, *v.t.* e *v.i.* tumefazer(-se).

tumescent, *adj.* túmido, tumescente.

tumid, *adj.* túmido, intumescido, inchado; protuberante, saliente (fig.) pomposo, bombástico; cheio, repleto.

tummy, *s.* barriga, barriguinha.

tumor, tumour, *s.* tumor.

tumular, *adj.* tumular.

tumult, *s.* tumulto, agitação, alvoroço; confusão.

tumultuary, *adj.* tumultuário.

tumultuous, *adj.* tumultuoso, agitado, turbulento; ruidoso; tempestuoso.

tumulus, *s.* (arqueol.) túmulo.

tun, *s.* tonel; antiga medida de capacidade

equivalente a 955 litros; *v.t.* guardar em tonel.

tuna, *s.* atum.

tundra, *s.* tundra.

tune, *s.* melodia, ária, música, cantiga; afinação, harmonia, concordância; disposição, veia, humor. 1) *out of tune,* desafinado, em discordância. 2) *in tune,* afinado, harmonioso. 3) *to change one's tune,* mudar de tom, mudar de linguagem. 4) *he payed to the tune of 10.000 pounds!,* pagou a quantia de 10 000 libras! (dá a noção de que a quantia é exorbitante); *v.t.* e *v.i.* afinar; adaptar, harmonizar, ajustar; entoar, cantar; (rád.) sintonizar. 5) *to tune up,* regular (motor). 6) *to tune in,* sintonizar uma estação de rádio.

tuneful, *adj.* melodioso, musical, harmonioso.

tuneless, *adj.* desafinado, desarmonioso, dissonante; silencioso (o instrumento musical).

tuner, *s.* afinador; sintonizador.

tungsten, *s.* (quím.) tungsténio.

tungus, *adj.* relativo aos Tungus ou Tunguses; *s.* (ling.) tungúsio.

tunic, *s.* túnica.

tuning, *s.* afinação; sintonização; *tuning fork,* diapasão.

tunnel, *s.* túnel; galeria; *v.t.* e *v.i.* abrir um túnel, escavar passagem subterrânea.

tup, *s.* carneiro; peso de martelo-pilão.

tuppence, *s.* (coloq.) o mesmo que *twopence.*

turban, *s.* turbante; chapéu de mulher ou criança, sem aba.

turbid, *adj.* turvo, opaco, lodoso, toldado; perturbado, confuso, obscuro.

turbidity, *s.* turvação; aspecto turvo ou toldado.

turbine, *s.* turbina.

turbojet, *adj.* turbojacto.

turbo-propeller, *adj.* turbopropulsor.

turbulence, *s.* turbulência, agitação.

turbulent, *adj.* turbulento; rebelde, desordeiro; agitado, perturbado; tumultuoso.

turco, *s.* soldado argelino de infantaria.

turd, *s.* (cal.) monte de excrementos.

tureen, *s.* terrina.

turf, *s.* relva, relvado; torrão; turfa; *the turf,* as corridas de cavalos; *v.t.* arrelvar; (cal.) deitar fora.

turfy, *adj.* relvado, coberto de relva; relvoso; turfoso; relativo às corridas de cavalos.

turgescence, *s.* turgescência.

turgescent, *adj.* turgescente, túrgido.

turgid, *adj.* túrgido, inchado, túmido; empolado.

turgor, *s.* turgescência.

Turk, *s.* turco, otomano.

turkey, *s.* peru.

Turkish, *adj.* e *s.* turco.

Turkman, *s.* turcomano, natural da República Turcomana.

turmeric, *s.* curcuma, açafrão-da-índia.

turmoil, *s.* agitação, tumulto, desordem, inquietação; *v.t.* agitar, perturbar.

turn, *s.* volta, giro, rotação, movimento circular, revolução; curva, ângulo; desvio, mudança de direcção; viragem, reviravolta; mudança, alteração; vez, ocasião, turno; oportunidade; favor, serviço, acção boa ou má que se faz a alguém; troca; dança, número de variedades; passeio, giro, volta; maneira de ser; tendência, queda, propensão; objectivo, propósito; forma, feitio; expressão, estilo, arranjo de frase; interpretação; choque, susto, surpresa; pl. menstruação. 1) *turn and turn about,* alternadamente. 2) *turn bench,* torno de torneiro. 3) *turn bridge,* ponte giratória. 4) *turn of life,* a menopausa, mudança de idade. 5) *land turn,* (náut.) brisa da terra. 6) *right about turn,* (mil.) meia volta, direita! 7) *the milk is on the turn,* o leite está quase a azedar; *v.t.* e *v.i.* girar, andar à volta; rodar, virar, voltar, virar do avesso; mudar, modificar(-se); vir a ser, revelar-se; desviar, mudar de direcção; inverter; dirigir, volver; tornear, trabalhar no torno; empregar, usar, aplicar; rodear, contornar; dobrar; passar de; transtornar, desarranjar; sentir tonturas; azedar, coalhar; aperfeiçoar; reverter; traduzir; transformar, converter; fazer uma curva (estrada, rio, etc.); revoltar-se; revolver, rodopiar; recorrer, virar-se para; tornar-se. 8) *to turn about,* fazer meia volta. 9) *to turn adrift,* abandonar. 10) *to turn aside,* desviar, mudar de direcção. 11) *to turn back,* repelir; recusar; devolver; voltar para trás. 12) *to turn off,* desligar. 13) *to turn on,* ligar. 14) *to turn out,* expulsar, pôr na rua; virar para fora; fabricar, produzir; apagar; aparecer, surgir; ter como resultado, vir a ser. 15) *to turn over,* voltar(-se); mudar de posição; entregar, transferir; revolver no pensamento, ponderar. 16) *to turn up,* virar, voltar ou dobrar para cima;

desenterrar, pôr a descoberto. 17) *to turn colour*, mudar de cor. 18) *to turn down the bed*, abrir a cama. 19) *to turn out well*, ser bem sucedido. 20) *to turn something to account*, aproveitar, tirar proveito de alguma coisa. 21) *to turn tail*, fugir. 22) *to turn the tables on someone*, virar o feitiço contra o feiticeiro. 23) *he hasn't turned up yet*, ele ainda não apareceu. 24) *to turn to work*, começar a trabalhar.

turnabout, *s.* viravolta.

turnback, *s.* dobra (de lençol).

turning, *s.* trabalho de torno; tornearia, arte de tornear; curva, volta, ângulo; cruzamento (de estradas); *adj.* relativo ao trabalho de torno; giratório, rotativo.

turnip, *s.* nabo.

turnout, *s.* reunião, assembleia; afluência; séquito; greve; (cam. fer.) ramal, desvio de linha; produção (industrial); resultados de eleição.

turnover, *s.* reviravolta; trambolhão; volteio (de acrobata); volume de negócios; restruturação, renovação de pessoal; saída de mercadoria; (polít.) transferência de votos de um partido para outro; artigo de jornal que passa de uma página para outra; espécie de empada em forma de meia-lua; dobra de sobrescrito.

turnpike, *s.* torniquete, molinete; barreira de portagem.

turnscrew, *s.* chave de parafusos.

turnsole, *s.* girassol.

turnstone, *s.* (zool.) maçarico.

turpentine, *s.* terebintina.

turpitude, *s.* torpeza, vilania, indignidade, infâmia.

turquoise, *s.* turquesa.

turret, *s.* torreão; (mec.) revólver, espera de revólver.

turtle, *s.* tartaruga; *to turn turtle,* (náut.) virar de quilha para cima.

turves, *pl.* de *turf.*

Tuscan, *adj.* e *s.* toscano.

tush, *s.* dente canino de cavalo; interj. ora! ora essa!

tusk, *s.* presa (de elefante, javali, etc.); dente comprido e saliente, colmilho.

tusker, *s.* elefante ou javali de grandes presas.

tussis, *s.* tosse.

tussle, *s.* luta, contenda, disputa; *v.i.* lutar, pelejar, contender.

tussock, *s.* moita, tufo; madeixa.

tut, *interj.* ora! ora essa!

tutelage, *s.* tutela, tutoria, guarda, protecção; ensino, educação.

tutelar(y), *adj.* tutelar, protector, padroeiro.

tutor, *s.* tutor; preceptor, professor particular; professor que orienta um pequeno grupo de estudantes; *v.t.* e *v.i.* tutelar, ser tutor de; ensinar, educar; disciplinar; orientar; admoestar, repreender; estudar com professor particular.

tutorage, *s.* tutela, tutoria, preceptorado; cargo ou honorários de professor universitário.

tutorial, *adj.* preceptorial; relativo a tutor.

tutorship, *s.* tutela; preceptorado; ensino, educação.

tuxedo, *s.* "smoking", casaco de cerimónia.

twaddle, *v.i.* tagarelar, dizer tolices; *s.* tagarelice, conversa tola; disparates, asneiras, tolices.

twang, *s.* som agudo e penetrante; zunido; voz nasalada e fanhosa; sotaque característico de uma região; *v.t.* e *v.i.* produzir um som agudo ou metálico; fazer ressoar; arranhar (instrumento de cordas); falar com voz fanhosa.

twattle, *v.i.* e *v.t.* o mesmo que *twaddle.*

tweak, *s.* puxão, torcegão, torcedura, beliscão; (coloq.) astúcia, artimanha; *v.t.* dar puxão, torcer; beliscar.

tweed, *s.* tecido de lã com fios de várias cores para fatos de homem.

tweedledum and tweedledee, *s.* coisas que só divergem no nome; personagens de *Alice no País das Maravilhas.*

tweet, *s.* chilreio, pipilar; *v.i.* chilrear, pipilar.

tweezer, *s.* pinça pequena; *v.t.* arrancar com pinça.

twelfth, *adj.* duodécimo, décimo segundo; *Twelfth night,* Festa de Reis; *s.* duodécimo.

twelfthtide, *s.* Festa de Reis.

twelve, *adj.* e *s.* doze.

twentieth, *adj.* e *s.* vigésimo.

twenty, *adj.* e *s.* vinte.

twice, *adv.* duas vezes.

twicer, *s.* (tip.) compositor-impressor.

twiddle, *s.* volta, giro; *v.t.* e *v.i.* girar (especialmente os polegares); agitar-se, estremecer, palpitar.

twig, *s.* raminho, galho, rebento; (anat.) pequena ramificação de vaso sanguíneo ou de nervo; varinha mágica, varinha de vedor; *to hop the twig,* (coloq.) morrer; *v.t.,* (coloq.) compreender, perceber; observar; avistar.

twilight, s. crepúsculo; média luz, penumbra; adj. crepuscular; sombrio; primitivo.

twill, s. sarja.

twin, s. e adj. gémeo; v.t. e v.i. dar à luz gémeos; acasalar, juntar; unir(-se); igualar (-se).

twine, s. fio torcido; cordão, barbante, guita; voluta, rosca, espira; tortuosidade, rodeio; liana; v.t. e v.i. entrançar; entrelaçar; tecer; enroscar(-se), enrolar(-se); enlaçar, cingir; serpentear.

twiner, s. máquina de torcer fio.

twinge, s. pontada, ferroada, picada; v.t. dar pontadas ou ferroadas; espicaçar.

twink, s. piscar de olhos; v.i. cintilar.

twinkle, s. piscadela, pestanejo; cintilação; brilho; vislumbre; movimento rápido; in the twink of an eye, num abrir e fechar de olhos; v.i. e v.t. piscar, pestanejar; cintilar, tremeluzir, brilhar, faiscar; mover-se rapidamente de um lado para outro; aparecer e desaparecer; piscar os olhos; dardejar (luz).

twinkling, s. piscadela; cintilação; momento, instante.

twinned, adj. geminado.

twinning, s. parto de gémeos; união, ligação; hemitropia.

twirl, s. rotação, giro, rodopio, volta; v.t. e v.i. girar, rodopiar, rodear; torcer(-se), enrolar (-se); lançar a bola (no basebol).

twist, s. acto de torcer, torcedura; torção; flexão; (fís.) esforço de torção; curva, volta, desvio; fio torcido, trança, torçal, retrós; fumo em espiral; pão de forma torcida, regueifa; cartucho de papel com as pontas torcidas; variedade de tabaco grosseiro; tendência, queda, propensão; pecularidade, mania; deformação; inclinação das estrias em arma de fogo; (coloq.) apetite; mistura de bebidas; dança moderna (anos 60); efeito dado à bola (basebol, bilhar, etc.); v.t. e v.i. torcer(-se), enrolar(-se); tecer; entrançar; entrelaçar; retorcer; enroscar (-se), espiralar; contorcer(-se); entortar (-se); deformar; girar, rodopiar; confundir, desorientar; deturpar, desvirtuar; serpentear; revolver(-se); virar(-se); desviar(-se); dar efeito à bola (no basebol, críquete, bilhar, etc.); dançar o twist.

twister, s. cordoeiro; aparelho de torcer; remoinho de pó, ciclone; parte interna da coxa de cavaleiro; bola lançada com efeito.

twit, s. censura, reprimenda; crítica; v.t. censurar, criticar, acusar, lançar em cara.

twitch, s. puxão, safanão; crispação, contracção; beliscão; convulsão, espasmo; v.t. e v.i. puxar, repuxar, dar safanão a; beliscar; contrair(-se), crispar(-se), contorcer (-se).

twitter, s. chilreio, pipilar; algaraviada; alvoroço; v.i. chilrear, pipilar; falar excitadamente.

two, adj. e s. dois, duas. 1) in two twos, num abrir e fechar de olhos. 2) to put two and two together, tirar conclusões, somar dois e dois. 3) two cleft, bífido. 4) two fisted, (coloq.) viril, vigoroso. 5) two step, dança de ritmo vivo.

twofold, adj. duplo, dual; duplicado, dobrado, duas vezes maior; adv. duplamente, duas vezes mais.

twopence, s. dois "pence", moeda desse valor.

tycoon, s. grande magnate do mundo dos negócios.

tying, adj. que prende, pesado, difícil; vinculativo; s. acto de prender; nó, laço.

tymbal, s. o mesmo que timbal.

tympan, s. tímpano; membrana esticada.

tympanic, adj. timpânico.

tympanist, s. timpanista, tocador de tímpano.

tympanites, s. (anat.) timpanismo, timpanite.

tympanitis, s. (med.) timpanite, otite média.

typal, adj. típico, característico; simbólico; tipográfico.

type, s. tipo; modelo, padrão, exemplo; símbolo, emblema; sinal, marca; espécie, género, classe, categoria; (tip.) tipo. 1) type setter, máquina de compor, compositor. 2) to set type, (tip.) compor; v.t. e v.i. escrever à máquina, dactilografar; ser o tipo de, tipificar.

typescript, s. documento dactilografado.

typewrite, v.t. e v.i. escrever à máquina, dactilografar.

typewiter, s. máquina de escrever.

typewriting, s. dactilografia.

typhlology, s. tiflologia, estudo da cegueira.

typhoid, adj. tifóide, tífico. 1) typhoid bacillus, bacilo tífico. 2) typhoid fever, febre tifóide.

typhoon, s. tufão.

typhus, s. tifo.

typic, adj. típico.

typical, adj. típico, característico; representativo; simbólico.

typification, s. tipificação.

typify, *v.t.* tipificar; ser o tipo de; representar; exemplificar.

typist, *s.* dactilógrafo.

typo, *s.* (tip.) tipógrafo.

typographer, *s.* tipógrafo, impressor.

typographic(al), *adj.* tipográfico.

typography, *s.* tipografia.

tyrannic(al), *adj.* tirânico, despótico; inflexível; cruel, opressivo.

tyrannize, *v.i.* tiranizar, proceder como tirano, governar tiranicamente.

tyrannous, *adj.* tirânico, despótico; inflexível; cruel, opressivo.

tyranny, *s.* tirania; despotismo.

tyrant, *s.* tirano; déspota.

tyre, *s.* o mesmo que *tire*.

Tyrian, *adj.* e *s.* tírio.

tyro, tiro, *s.* principiante, noviço, aprendiz.

tyrolean, *adj.* e *s.* tirolês.

tzar, *s.* o mesmo que czar.

U

u, vigésima primeira letra do alfabeto.

ubiety, *s.* ubicação; facto de ocupar uma posição no espaço.

ubiquitous, *adj.* ubíquo.

ubiquity, *s.* ubiquidade.

udal, *s.* (jur.) usucapião.

udder, *s.* úbere, teta (de vaca).

udometer, *s.* udómetro, pluviómetro.

ugliness, *s.* fealdade.

ugly, *adj.* feio; disforme, horrendo, medonho, repulsivo, revoltante; desagradável.

uitlander, *s.* estrangeiro (na África do Sul).

Ukrainian, *adj.* e *s.* ucraniano.

ukulele, *s.* espécie de guitarra havaiana.

ulcer, *s.* úlcera, chaga.

ulcerate, *v.t.* e *v.i.* ulcerar(-se).

ulceration, *s.* ulceração; úlcera.

ulcerous, *adj.* ulceroso, ulcerado.

ulna, (anat. e zool.), cúbito.

ulotrichous, *adj.* ulótrico (diz-se das raças que têm o cabelo crespo).

ulster, *s.* espécie de sobretudo de Inverno.

Ulster, *s.* província do Norte da Irlanda.

ulterior, *adj.* ulterior, posterior, futuro; inconfessado, oculto.

ultimate, *adj.* último, derradeiro, supremo; final; fundamental, básico; máximo; *s.* princípio fundamental.

ultimatum, *s.* ultimato.

ultimo, *adj.* do mês passado, do mês findo.

ultra, *adj.* e *s.* extremista, radical; *pref.* ultra.

ultraism, *s.* radicalismo, extremismo.

ultramarine, *adj.* e *s.* ultramarino.

ultramicroscope, *s.* ultramicroscópio.

ultramicroscopy, *s.* ultramicroscopia.

ultramontane, *adj.* e *s.* ultramontano, transmontano; transalpino.

ultrared, *adj.* infravermelho.

ultraviolet, *adj.* ultravioleta.

ululant, *adj.* ululante, uivante; lamentoso.

ululate, *v.i.* ulular, uivar; lamentar-se.

umbel, *s.* (bot.) umbela.

umbellate(d), *adj.* umbelado, umbelífero.

umber, *s.* umbra, ocre, terra-de-siena; (zool.) umbla (espécie de salmão); *adj.* cor de umbra, fusco, escuro; *v.t.* colorir ou tingir com umbra.

umbilical, *adj.* umbilical.

umbilicate(d), *adj.* umbilicado.

umbilicus, *s.* umbigo.

umbiliform, *adj.* que tem a forma de umbigo; umbilicado.

umbles, *s.* miúdos de veado.

umbra, *s.* (astron.) sombra.

umbrage, *s.* ressentimento; despeito; sombra; (arc.) traço, suspeita. 1) *to give umbrage to,* melindrar, ofender. 2) *to take umbrage at,* ofender-se, ressentir-se.

umbrageous, *adj.* umbroso, sombrio; melindroso, susceptível; desconfiado.

umbrella, *s.* guarda-chuva; guarda-sol; (mil.

av.) cobertura aérea; (zool.) umbrela (de medusa); *umbrella bird,* pavão do mato.

umbrian, *s.* e *adj.* umbriano, úmbrico.

umpirage, *s.* arbitragem.

umpire, *s.* árbitro, juiz; *v.t.* e *v.i.* arbitrar.

umpteen, *adj.* (coloq.) muitos, vários, um monte de, uma data de.

un, *pron.* (coloq.) um, uma pessoa; *that is a good un!,* essa é boa!

unabashed, *adj.* que não se perturba, imperturbável; ousado; descarado.

unable, *adj.* incapaz, que não pode ou não consegue; inábil, incompetente; impossibilitado.

unabridged, *adj.* não abreviado, integral.

unaccommodated, *adj.* desprovido, destituído, privado.

unaccountable, *adj.* inexplicável; estranho; misterioso; *unaccountable for something,* não responsável por alguma coisa.

unaccounted for, *adj.* que não teve explicação, sem explicação, sem esclarecimento.

unaccustomed, *adj.* desacostumado, desusado; extraordinário; não habituado.

unaffected, *adj.* desafectado, simples, singelo, natural; sincero, genuíno; impassível; não afectado.

unanimity, *s.* unanimidade.

unanimous, *adj.* unânime.

unappealable, *adj.* inapelável; (jur.) sem apelação, irrecorrível.

unapt, *adj.* inapto, inepto; impróprio; descabido.

unarm, *v.t.* desarmar.

unarmed, *adj.* desarmado; indefeso.

unasked, *adj.* não convidado, não solicitado; espontâneo.

unattached, *adj.* desligado, desprendido, solto; descomprometido, livre.

unattended, *adj.* desacompanhado, sozinho; não vigiado; não tratado; não atendido.

unau, *s.* (zool.) preguiça-real.

unavailable, *adj.* indisponível; inútil, ineficaz, inutilizável.

unavoidable, *adj.* inevitável.

unavowed, *adj.* inconfessado.

unaware, *adj.* que ignora, que desconhece; alheio, inconsciente.

unawareness, *s.* desconhecimento, ignorância.

unawares, *adv.* inopinadamente, inesperadamente, de surpresa.

unbag, *v.t.* tirar de um saco, desensacar.

unbaked, *adj.* cru, não cozido: imperfeito, incompleto.

unbalance, *v.t.* desequilibrar.

unbearable, *adj.* insuportável, insustentável, intolerável.

unbecoming, *adj.* inconveniente, impróprio; que fica mal.

unbegotten, *adj.* ingénito.

unbelief, *s.* descrença, incredulidade.

unbelievable, *adj.* incrível, inacreditável.

unbeliever, *s.* descrente, incrédulo, céptico.

unbelieving, *adj.* incrédulo, descrente.

unbend, *v.t.* e *v.i.* distender(-se), endireitar (-se), afrouxar; desdobrar; desenrugar (a testa); estender; suavizar-se.

unbending, *adj.* inflexível; firme; teso, rígido.

unbeseeming, *adj.* inconveniente, impróprio; de mau gosto.

unbidden, *adj.* não convidado; espontâneo.

unbigoted, *adj.* tolerante, liberal.

unbind, *v.t.* desamarrar, desatar, libertar, soltar, liberar.

unbitted, *adj.* sem freio, desenfreado.

unblemished, *adj.* imaculado, puro, sem mancha.

unblessed, unblest, *adj.* não abençoado; maldito, amaldiçoado; infortunado; ímpio, profano.

unbodied, *adj.* incorpóreo; desencarnado.

unbolt, *v.t.* desaferrolhar, abrir, desaparafusar.

unbolted, *adj.* desaferrolhado, aberto; *unbolted flour,* farinha não peneirada.

unborn, *adj.* por nascer, nasciturno: futuro, vindouro.

unbosom, *v.t.* confessar, revelar, abrir-se, desabafar.

unbound, *adj.* libertado; livre, solto; não encadernado.

unbounded, *adj.* ilimitado, infinito, sem limites.

unbrace, *v.t.* destar, desprender; distender; enfraquecer.

unbraid, *v.t.* desentrançar.

unbred, *adj.* mal-educado, sem educação.

unbridle, *v.t.* tirar o freio a, desenfrear.

unbuckle, *v.t.* desafivelar; abrir, desapertar.

unburden, *v.t.* descarregar, aliviar; desbafar, revelar, confessar.

uncanny, *adj.* misterioso, fantástico, sobrenatural; perigoso; violento.

unceasing, *adj.* incessante, contínuo.

uncertain, *adj.* incerto, duvidoso; indeterminado, indefinido; vago; problemático; inconstante; que não tem certeza; indeciso.

uncertainty, *s.* incerteza, dúvida; indecisão; ambiguidade; precariedade.

unchallengeable, *adj.* incontestável.

unchangeable, *adj.* imutável, inalterável.

unchanged, *adj.* inalterado; intacto.

unchanging, *adj.* imutável, invariável, contante.

unchaste, *adj.* libertino, lascivo, impuro; incontinente.

unchurch, *v.t.* excomungar.

uncial, *adj.* uncial; *s.* letra uncial, escrita em caracteres unciais.

unciform, *adj.* unciforme; *s.* osso unciforme.

uncinate, *adj.* uncinado, unciforme.

uncircumcised, *adj.* não circuncidado, incircunciso.

uncivil, *adj.* descortês, incivil; rude, grosseiro; incivilizado.

uncivilized, *adj.* incivilizado; bárbaro, inculto.

unclad, *adj.* sem roupas, despido.

uncle, *s.* tio; (cal.) prestamista. 1) *Uncle Sam,* os Estados Unidos ou o seu governo. 2) *to talk to someone like a Dutch Uncle,* repreender alguém com brandura.

unclean, *adj.* imundo, sujo; impuro.

unclench, *v.t.* e *v.i.* abrir(-se); abrir à força; desprender, arrancar (da mão, etc.).

unclose, *v.t.* e *v.t.* abrir(-se); revelar; descobrir.

uncock, *v.t.* desengatilhar.

uncoil, *v.t.* e *v.i.* desenrolar(-se), estender (-se).

uncomely, *adj.* inconveniente, impróprio, inadequado; indecoroso; feio, deselegante.

uncomfortable, *adj.* desconfortável, incómodo; desagradável; lamentável; constrangedor; embaraçado, constrangido, contrafeito; indisposto.

uncommon, *adj.* incomum, invulgar, desusado; singular, raro; notável, extraordinário.

unconcerned, *adj.* indiferente, despreocupado, tranquilo, impassível; negligente; desinteressado; não envolvido, imparcial.

unconfessed, *adj.* inconfesso, não declarado, oculto.

unconformable, *adj.* em desacordo, discordante; discrepante, incoerente; incompatível; insubmisso.

unconformity, *s.* discordância; desacordo, divergência, discrepância.

uncongenial, *adj.* incompatível; não favorável; hostil; antipático; desagradável.

unconquered, *adj.* invicto, não conquistado.

unconscientious, *adj.* pouco consciencioso, negligente.

unconscionable, *adj.* irracional, despropositado; imoderado; excessivo; grandessíssimo, rematado, perfeito; sem consciência, pouco escrupuloso.

unconscious, *adj.* inconsciente; ignorante; desconhecedor; sem sentidos, desmaiado; sem querer, involuntário; *s.* o inconsciente.

unconsequential, *adj.* inconsequente.

unconstraint, *s.* liberdade, naturalidade, espontaneidade.

uncord, *v.t.* desamarrar, desatar.

uncork, *v.t.* desarrolhar, tirar a rolha a, abrir garrafa; (coloq.) manifestar, dar vazão.

uncorrected, *adj.* não corrigido; impune.

uncorrupted, *adj.* incorrupto, íntegro.

uncountable, *adj.* incontável, inumerável; inestimável.

uncouple, *v.t.* separar; desengatar; desemparelhar; desembraiar; desatrelar.

uncouth, *adj.* estranho, insólito, misterioso, maravilhoso; curioso, singular, esquisito; desajeitado, rústico, tosco; pedante; agreste, selvagem.

uncover, *v.t.* e *v.i.* descobrir; pôr a descoberto; desvendar, revelar, divulgar; destapar; descobrir-se, tirar o chapéu.

unction, *s.* unção; acto de ungir; unguento; bálsamo; fervor; entusiasmo afectado; maneiras untuosas, obsequiosidade.

unctuosity, *s.* untuosidade, oleosidade; melifluidade.

unctuous, *adj.* untuoso, oleoso; gordo, rico (o solo); moldável; fervoroso; melífluo.

uncultivated, *adj.* não cultivado, inculto, maninho; rústico, grosseio, incivilizado.

uncurbed, *adj.* desenfreado, incontido.

uncurl, *v.t.* e *v.i.* desencaracolar(-se), desfrisar; desenrolar(-se), desenvolver(-se).

undamaged, *adj.* ileso, incólume; intacto; sem avarias.

undaunted, *adj.* destemido, audaz, intrépido.

undeceive, *v.t.* desenganar, desiludir.

undecipherable, *adj.* indecifrável, ilegível, incompreensível.

undecked, *adj.* sem ornamentos; (náut.) sem convés.

undeclinable, *adj.* indeclinável; irrecusável.

undefensible, *adj.* indefensável.

undefiled, *adj.* sem mácula, puro, casto; impoluto.

undemonstrative, *adj.* reservado, retraído, comedido.

undeniable, *adj.* inegável.

undependable, *adj.* com que não se pode contar; que não inspira confiança.

under, *prep.* sob, debaixo de, abaixo de, por baixo de; ao abrigo de, sob a protecção de; sob as ordens de; sob o peso de; sob pena de; em menos de; com menos de; inferior a; segundo, conforme; em, dentro de (classe, categoria). 1) *under cover,* abrigado. 2) *under oath,* sob juramento. 3) *under lock and key,* a sete chaves. 4) *to be under age,* ser menor. 5) *to serve under,* servir sob as ordens de. 6) *he did it all in under one hour,* ele fez tudo em menos de uma hora. 7) *under pretense of ignorance,* pretextando ignorância; *adv.* por baixo, debaixo; submerso; em sujeição; insuficientemente. 8) *to keep under,* manter em sujeição; *adj.* inferior; subordinado; deficiente; insuficiente.

underact, *v.t.* e *v.i.* (teat.) representar mal ou insatisfatoriamente.

underbid, *v.t. pret.* e *pp. bid,* oferecer menos do que outra pessoa, oferecer menos que o valor real.

underbred, *adj.* pouco educado, vulgar; mestiço.

underbrush, *s.* vegetação rasteira.

undercharge, *v.t.* cobrar menos do que o valor real; *s.* subcarga (de arma de fogo).

undercover, *adj.* secreto, furtivo; *under-cover man,* espião.

undercroft, *s.* cripta, galeria subterrânea.

undercurrent, *s.* corrente submarina; corrente subterrânea; corrente oculta de opinião.

undercut, *v.t.* (conjuga-se como *cut*) cortar por baixo, escavar pela base, minar; esculpir em relevo; suplantar concorrente vendendo por menor preço; rebater a bola com a mão por baixo (no ténis); *s.* corte feito por baixo; golpe dado de baixo para cima (no boxe).

underdog, *s.* aquele que sai vencido numa luta; oprimido, pobre diabo.

underdone, *adj.* mal cozido, mal passado.

underestimate, *v.t.* subestimar, depreciar.

underfeed, *adj.* subnutrido, subalimentado.

underfoot, *adv.* sob os pés, aos pés, debaixo dos pés.

undergarment, *s.* peça de roupa interior.

undergo, *v.t.* (conjuga-se como *go*) sofrer, passar por, ser submetido a.

underground, *adv.* debaixo da terra, sob o solo, no subsolo; às escondidas, em segredo; enterrado; *adj.* subterrâneo; secreto, oculto, furtivo; *s.* o subsolo, as entranhas da terra; subterrâneo, passagem subterrânea; caminho de ferro subterrâneo, metro.

undergrowth, *s.* vegetação rasteira.

underhand, *adj.* secreto, clandestino, furtivo; dissimulado; ardiloso, fraudulento; discreto.

underlay, *v.t.* e *v.i.* (*pret.* e *pp. underlaid*) sustentar; forrar, reforçar; *s.* (tip.) forro que se coloca por baixo do tipo para alteá-lo.

underlease, *s.* subarrendamento.

underlet, *v.t.* (conjuga-se como *let*) sublugar; alugar a preço excessivamente baixo.

underlie, *v.t.* (conjuga-se como *lie*) estar exposto ou sujeito a; sofrer castigo; estar debaixo de; estar subjacente a; sustentar, suportar; formar a base; inspirar.

underline, *v.t.* sublinhar; pôr em destaque.

underlinen, *s.* roupa branca, roupa interior.

underling, *s.* subordinado, subalterno.

underlying, *adj.* subjacente; oculto, encoberto; básico.

undermost, *adj.* o mais baixo, o ínfimo, o último, o inferior.

underneath, *adv.* abaixo, em baixo, por baixo. *prep.* sob, em baixo de, abaixo de, debaixo de, por baixo de; sob o poder de, dominado por; sob o disfarce de; oculto por; *adj.* inferior; situado em baixo; *s.* parte inferior, face inferior.

underpay, *v.t. prt.* e *pp. underpaid;* pagar ou remunerar insuficientemente.

underplot, *s.* acção ou trama secundário (de peça teatral), intriga, episódio.

underprop, *v.t.* (conjuga-se como *prof*) escorar, firmar com escoras.

underrate, *v.t.* subestimar, não dar o devido valor a, menosprezar.

undersecretary, *s.* subsecretário.

undersign, *v.t.* subscrever, assinar.

undersigned, *adj.* assinado; *s.* abaixo--assinado.

undersized, *adj.* mais pequeno do que o normal.

undersong, *s.* refrão, estribilho; sentido profundo, sentido oculto.

understand, *v.t.* e *v.i.* (conjuga-se como *stand*), compreender, entender, perceber;

ser informado; conhecer; julgar; pensar; inferir; interpretar; subentender.

understandable, *adj.* compreensível.

understanding, *s.* entendimento, inteligência, intelecto; compreensão; discernimento; conhecimento; interpretação; acordo, harmonia, concórdia; *adj.* inteligente; compreensivo.

understate, *v.t.* e *v.i.* expor (factos) de modo incompleto; não dizer toda a verdade a respeito de; atenuar, mitigar, diminuir.

understatement, *s.* exposição incompleta; atenuação.

understood, *pret.* e *pp.* de *understand; adj.* compreendido, entendido; combinado.

understudy, *s.* substituto de actor.

undertake, *v.t.* (conjuga-se como *take*), empreender, intentar; encarregar-se de, tomar a seu cargo, incumbir-se de, comprometer-se a; afirmar, prometer, garantir; (arc.) travar combate com; *v.i.* ser fiador, responsabilizar-se.

undertaker, *s.* empreiteiro; empresário; agente funerário, cangalheiro.

undertaking, *s.* empreendimento, empresa; promessa, garantia; negócio de agente funerário.

undertenant, *s.* sublocatário, subarrendatário.

undertow, *s.* ressaca, recuo das ondas.

undervalue, *v.t.* avaliar em menos do que o valor real, depreciar, menosprezar; desprezar.

underwear, *s.* roupa interior.

underworld, *s.* submundo; inferno, mundo dos mortos; mundo do crime e da marginalidade.

underwrite, *v.t.* e *v.i.* (conjuga-se como *write*); escrever em baixo, assinar, subscrever (apólice de seguro); confirmar, apoiar; (fin.) comprometer-se a subscrever acções de determinada empresa; dedicar-se ao negócio de seguros.

underwriter, *s.* segurador; inspector de seguros; subscritor de acções de uma empresa.

undeserved, *adj.* imerecido, injusto.

undesirable, *adj.* indesejável, inconveniente.

undeviating, *adj.* firme, perseverante, imutável.

undies, *s. pl.* (coloq.) roupa interior.

undiminished, *adj.* sem diminuição; inquebrantável, indomável.

undine, *s.* ondina.

undiscovered, *adj.* por descobrir, não descoberto, oculto, desconhecido, inexplorado; sem explicação.

undisguised, *adj.* indisfarçável, franco, sincero.

undismayed, *adj.* impávido, intrépido.

undissembled, *adj.* sincero, genuíno; franco, evidente.

undisturbed, *adj.* não perturbado; calmo, tranquilo, sereno; impassível.

undivided, *adj.* indiviso, inteiro; ininterrupto, inseparável.

undo, *v.t.* (conjuga-se como *do*); desatar, desabotoar, desprender, abrir; resolver, decifrar; desfazer, desmanchar; anular, invalidar; arruinar.

undone, *adj.* desatado, aberto, desabotoado; perdido, arruinado; por fazer, por acabar.

undoubtedly, *adv.* indubitavelmente, incontestavelmente, com toda a certeza, sem dúvida alguma.

undraw, *v.t.* (conjuga-se como *draw*); abrir (a cortina).

undress, *v.t.* e *v.i.* despir(-se), desenfaixar, tirar ligaduras.

undue, *adj.* não vencido, por vencer (letra); indevido, impróprio; desmedido, excessivo, exagerado.

undulate, *v.i.* e *v.t.* ondular, ondear.

undulate, *adj.* ondulado.

undulatory, *adj.* ondulatório; ondulante.

unduly, *adv.* indevidamente; ilegitimamente; injustificadamente; excessivamente, desmedidamente.

unearned, *adj.* imerecido.

unearth, *v.t.* desenterrar, exumar; descobrir, revelar.

unearthly, *adj.* sobrenatural, fantástico, irreal; pavoroso, medonho; extraterreno; celestial, sublime.

unease, *s.* constrangimento, mal-estar; perturbação.

uneasy, *adj.* contrafeito, constrangido, que não está à vontade; ansioso, apreensivo, nervoso; incómodo, desconfortável.

unemotional, *adj.* calmo, frio; amorfo.

unemployed, *adj.* não aproveitado; inactivo; desempregado, sem trabalho.

unemployment, *s.* desemprego.

unending, *adj.* sem fim, interminável; eterno.

unequal, *adj.* desigual; irregular; desproporcionado; variável, inconstante; insuficiente, incapaz, inferior, que não está à altura de; parcial, injusto.

unequaled, adj. sem igual, sem rival, inigualável.

unequitable, adj. iníquo, injusto.

unequivocal, adj. inequívoco, evidente, claro.

unerring, adj. infalível.

uneven, adj. desigual, irregular; acidentado, desnivelado, assimétrico, torto; ímpar (número).

uneventful, adj. monótono, rotineiro.

unexampled, adj. sem exemplo, sem precedentes, sem paralelo, único.

unexceptionable, adj. irrepreensível, inatacável, perfeito.

unexpected, adj. inesperado, imprevisto.

unfair, adj. injusto; desleal; desonesto; parcial; falso.

unfaithful, adj. infiel, desleal; traidor; desonesto; inexacto.

unfaltering, adj. firme, que não vacila.

unfashioned, adj. não modelado, tosco.

unfasten, v.t. e v.i. desatar, desprender, desapertar; soltar, desabotoar, abrir.

unfeather, v.t. depenar.

unfit, adj. impróprio, inadequado, inapto; v.t. incapacitar, tornar inapto.

unfitness, s. incapacidade, inaptidão; desvantagem; mau estado de saúde.

unflagging, adj. persistente, inquebrantável.

unfleshly, adj. incorpóreo, imaterial, espiritual.

unfold, v.t. e v.i. desdobrar(-se), estender (-se), abrir(-se); revelar(-se), expor, exibir; ostentar; manifestar; esclarecer; desenrolar, desembrulhar; desenvolver-se.

unforeseen, adj. imprevisto, inopinado.

unforgettable, adj. inesquecível.

unforgivable, adj. imperdoável.

unforgiving, adj. implacável, rancoroso.

unfortunate, adj. infortunado, infeliz; lamentável.

unfounded, adj. infundado, sem fundamento, improcedente, não fundado.

unfriendly, adj. hostil, pouco amistoso; desfavorável, adverso.

unfrock, v.t. tirar o hábito a, destituir (ecles.); *to unfrock oneself,* despir o hábito.

unfruitful, adj. estéril, improdutivo; infrutífero.

unfurl, v.t. e v.i. desfraldar(-se) (bandeiras).

ungainly, adj. desajeitado, deselegante.

ungenerous, adj. pouco generoso, mesquinho; avaro.

unglue, v.t. e v.i. descolar(-se).

ungodly, adj. ímpio; medonho, terrível.

ungovernable, adj. ingovernável, incontrolável; indomável, bravio.

ungracious, adj. desagradável, ingrato; mal visto; pouco atraente; descortês, indelicado.

ungrateful, adj. ingrato, mal-agradecido; estéril.

ungual, adj. (anat.) e (zool.) ungueal.

unguarded, adj. desprotegido; vulnerável.

unguent, s. unguento.

unguiculate, adj. unguiculado.

unguis, s. (zool. e bot.) unha; (anat.) únguis, osso lacrimal.

ungula, s. (zool.) unha; (geom.) tronco de cone.

ungulate, adj. e s. (zool.) ungulado.

unhallow, v.t. profanar.

unhand, v.t. largar, soltar.

unhandy, adj. incómodo, inconveniente, difícil de manejar; desajeitado.

unhappy, adj. infeliz, descontente, triste; mal sucedido, malogrado; funesto.

unharmed, adj. ileso, incólume.

unhealthy, adj. doente, enfermo; doentio, enfermiço; insalubre.

unheard, adj. inaudito; desconhecido; não ouvido.

unheeding, adj. desatento, descuidado, negligente.

unhinge, v.t. tirar dos gonzos, desengonçar; transtornar, desequilibrar.

unholiness, s. carácter profano; impiedade.

unholy, adj. ímpio, profano; pecaminoso; terrível, medonho.

unhouseled, adj. que não recebeu a eucaristia.

unicorn, s. unicórnio.

unicycle, s. monociclo.

unideaed, adj. destituído de ideias, estúpido, frívolo.

unification, s. unificação.

unifier, s. unificador.

unifilar, adj. unifilar.

uniform, adj. uniforme, homogéneo, igual, regular; constante, coerente; semelhante; s. uniforme, farda; v.t. uniformizar.

uniformed, adj. fardado.

uniformity, s. uniformidade, homogeneidade; coerência; monotonia.

unify, v.t. unificar, unir.

unimaginable, adj. inimaginável, inconcebível.

unimaginative, adj. sem imaginação, prosaico.

uni

uni

unimpaired, *adj.* não enfraquecido; ileso, intacto.

unimpeachable, *adj.* irrepreensível, inatacável; inquestionável.

unimpeded, *adj.* desimpedido.

unimportance, *s.* insignificância, trivialidade; pouca importância.

unimportant, *adj.* insignificante, sem importância.

uninfected, *adj.* incontaminado, não contagiado.

uninflected, *adj.* sem flexão; não flexivo.

uninhabitable, *adj.* inabitável.

uninhabited, *adj.* desabitado, inabitado.

unintelligible, *adj.* ininteligível, incompreensível.

unintended, *adj.* involuntário.

unintentional, *adj.* não intencional, involuntário.

uninteresting, *adj.* desinteressante.

unintermitted, *adj.* ininterrupto.

uninviting, *adj.* pouco convidativo, pouco atraente.

union, *s.* união, junção; fusão, combinação, coligação; federação, confederação; associação, casamento; sindicato; hospício, asilo; parte de bandeira com emblema de união ou confederação. 1) *union down,* bandeira a meia haste. 2) *Union Jack,* bandeira do Reino Unido.

unionism, *s.* sindicalismo.

unionist, *s.* sindicalista; (E.U.) indivíduo que, durante a guerra da secessão, era contrário a esta.

unionize, *v.t.* unir, unificar, confederar; sindicalizar.

unique, *adj.* único, ímpar, sem igual, inimitável, incomparável, singular; extraordinário, notável.

unison, *s.* uníssono, unissonância; acordo, harmonia, consonância.

unisonous, unisonal, unisonant, *adj.* uníssono, unissonante.

unit, *s.* unidade.

Unitarianism, *s.* (teol.) unitarismo.

unitary, *adj.* unitário; indiviso, integral; uniforme.

unite, *v.t.* e *v.i.* unir(-se), reunir(-se), combinar(-se), ligar(-se); casar(-se); aderir.

united, *adj.* unido, ligado, reunido; conjugado, combinado.

unitism, *s.* (filos.) monismo.

unity, *s.* unidade; unicidade; uniformidade; união, concórdia, harmonia; unificação.

univalent, *adj.* univalente, monovalente.

univalve, *adj.* e *s. adj.* (zool.) univalve.

universal, *adj.* universal, geral; total; *s.* (lóg.) proposição universal.

universalism, *s.* (teol.) universalismo.

universality, *s.* universalidade.

universalize, *v.t.* universalizar; generalizar.

universe, *s.* universo, cosmo; mundo.

university, *s.* universidade.

injust, *adj.* injusto.

unjustifiable, *adj.* injustificável.

unkempt, *adj.* despenteado, desgrenhado; desalinhado, desleixado; rude.

unkind, *adj.* rude, grosseiro, indelicado; duro, cruel.

unkindly, *adv.* indelicadamente, com rudeza; *adj.* indelicado, rude, grosseiro.

unknit, *v.t.* e *v.i.* (conjuga-se como *knit*) desfazer(-se), desfiar(-se), desmalhar; desenrugar (a testa); afrouxar; separar(-se); destruir.

unknowable, *adj.* incognoscível; impenetrável, insondável.

unknown, *adj.* desconhecido, ignorado; estranho; inexplorado.

unlaboured, *adj.* inculto (terreno); fácil, simples, natural.

unlace, *v.t.* desapertar; desatar, desamarrar; aliviar.

unlash, *v.t.* desatar, soltar.

unlawful, *adj.* ilegal, ilegítimo, ilícito.

unleaded, *adj.* sem chumbo; (tip.) desentrelinhado, sem entrelinhas, compacto.

unlearn, *v.t.* (conjuga-se como *learn*), desaprender, esquecer.

unleash, *v.t.* tirar a trela, desatrelar.

unleavened, *adj.* não levedado, ázimo.

unless, *conj.* a não ser que, a menos que, salvo se, se não, excepto quando.

unlettered, *adj.* iletrado, analfabeto; sem letras.

unlike, *adj.* diferente, diverso, distinto; dissemelhante; não parecido; contrário à índole de; *pre.* e *adv.* ao contrário de; de modo diferente a; diferentemente de.

unlikeky, *adv.* improvável, inverosímil.

unlikeness, *s.* diferença, dissemelhança, diversidade.

unlimited, *adj.* ilimitado; sem restrições.

unlive, *v.t.* anular (o passado), desfazer.

unload, *v.t.* descarregar; desembarcar; aliviar da carga; libertar-se de, desfazer-se de.

unlock, *v.t.* abrir com chave, abrir a

fechadura; desapertar; desprender; revelar, desvendar.

unlodge, v.t. desalojar.

unloose(n), v.t. afrouxar, desapertar; soltar.

unlucky, adj. azarado, sem sorte; infeliz; malfadado; desastrado; lamentável; agourento.

unmake, v.t. (conjuga-se como make), desfazer, anular, destruir; alterar; rebaixar, demitir; arruinar.

unman, v.t. (conjuga-se como man), desvirilizar, efeminar; tirar o ânimo a; desanimar, deprimir, desumanizar; (mil.) desguarnecer.

unmanlike, adj. desumano; impróprio do homem.

unmanly, adj. impróprio ou indigno do homem; degradante; efeminado.

unmanned, adj. desvirilizado; não tripulado; desguarnecido; despovoado.

unmannerly, adj. grosseiro, indelicado, malcriado.

unmarried, adj. solteiro.

unmask, v.t. e v.i. desmascarar(-se), tirar a máscara; revelar; descobrir.

unmatched, adj. único, sem par.

unmeant, adj. não intencional.

unmeasurable, adj. incomensurável, imenso, vasto.

unmentionable, adj. que não se pode mencionar ou dizer.

unmerciful, adj. desapiedado, implacável, cruel.

unmew, v.t. libertar, soltar.

unmistakable, adj. inconfundível, inequívoco; claro, evidente.

unmoral, adj. amoral.

unmorality, s. amoralidade.

unmovable, adj. imóvel, fixo; inalterável; inabalável.

unmuzzle, v.t. tirar o açaime a.

unnamable, unnameable, adj. indescritível; horrível.

unnamed, adj. inominado, sem nome.

unnatural, adj. antinatural; desnaturado; perverso, anormal; monstruoso, contranatura; afectado, artificial.

unnecessary, adj. desnecessário, escusado, dispensável.

unneighbourly, adj. impróprio de bom vizinho; pouco amável, descortês.

unnerve, v.t. enervar; debilitar; desencorajar.

unnest, v.t. tirar do ninho, desalojar.

unnoticed, adj. despercebido.

unobservant, adj. desatento, distraído.

unobserved, adj. despercebido, sem ser notado.

unobstructed, adj. desimpedido, desobstruído, livre.

unobtrusive, adj. discreto, moderado, comedido.

unoffending, adj. inofensivo.

unorthodox, adj. heterodoxo.

unowned, adj. sem dono; não reconhecido.

unpack, v.t. e v.i. desfazer (as malas); desempacotar, desembrulhar; esvaziar, descarregar.

unpalatable, adj. desagradável ao paladar, repulsivo, intragável; amargo.

unpardonable, adj. imperdoável.

unparliamentary, adj. contrário às regras parlamentares.

unpaved, adj. sem pavimento, não pavimentado.

unpen, v.t. (conjuga-se como pen), tirar do curral.

unpeople, v.t. despovoar.

unperceived, adj. não percebido, inobservado.

unpick, v.t. descoser, tirar os pontos (de costura).

unpile, v.t. desempilhar.

unpleasant, adj. desagradável.

unplowed, adj. não cultivado, inculto, baldio.

unpolitic, adj. impolítico; inoportuno.

unpolluted, adj. impoluto.

unpopular, adj. impopular.

unprecedented, adj. sem precedente, inaudito, inédito.

unprepared, adj. não preparado; desprevenido.

unprepossessing, adj. pouco atraente, pouco simpático.

unpretentious, adj. despretensioso, simples, modesto.

unprintable, adj. impublicável; inconveniente.

unprofessional, adj. pouco profissional.

unprovided, adj. desprovido, destituído; desprevenido; unprovided for, sem recursos.

unpublished, adj. não publicado; inédito.

unpunished, adj. impune.

unquailing, adj. destemido.

unqualified, adj. não habilitado, inapto; incondicional, sem reservas.

unquestionable, adj. inquestionável.

unquestioning, adj. incondicional.

unquotable, adj. que não pode citar-se.

unquote, *v.t.* e *v.i.* fechar as aspas, pôr fim a citação.

unravel, *v.t.* e *v.i.* desenredar(-se), desembaraçar; desfiar(-se) (tecido); esclarecer, decifrar.

unreadable, *adj.* ilegível.

unreal, *adj.* irreal, imaginário, fictício, ideal.

unreasonable, *adj.* irracional; insensato, despropositado; absurdo.

unreasoning, *adj.* irracional, ilógico; impulsivo, temperamental, irreflectido.

unreel, *v.t.* e *v.i.* desenrolar(-se).

unrein, *v.t.* dar rédea larga a.

unrelated, *adj.* não aparentado, não relacionado; desconexo.

unreliable, *adj.* indigno de confiança; volúvel; duvidoso; precário, falível.

unreserved, *adj.* franco, expansivo, extrovertido; sem restrições; ilimitado; não reservado.

unrestraint, *s.* desenvoltura, desembaraço, ausência de constrangimento.

unriddle, *v.t.* decifrar, resolver.

unrighteous, *adj.* iníquo, injusto; perverso.

unroll, *v.t.* e *v.i.* desenrolar(-se), estender (-se).

unruly, *adj.* desregrado, indisciplinado, turbulento, rebelde.

unsafe, *adj.* inseguro.

unsaid, *adj.* não dito.

unsatisfactory, *adj.* insatisfatório.

unsatisfied, *adj.* insatisfeito.

unsavoury, *adj.* desagradável; repugnante; nojento; malcheiroso; indecente, detestável; insípido.

unsay, *v.t.* (conjuga-se como *say*) desdizer, retirar o que se disse.

unscale, *v.t.* escamar, tirar as escamas a.

unscientific, *adj.* não científico.

unscrew, *v.t.* e *v.i.* desaparafusar(-se).

unseam, *v.t.* descoser; abrir, rasgar.

unseasonable, *adj.* inoportuno, extemporâneo; impróprio, despropositado; fora da época.

unseeing, *adj.* que não vê, cego; distraído.

unseemly, *adj.* inconveniente, impróprio, indecente; feio; *adv.* indecorosamente.

unseen, *adj.* não visto; invisível.

unsew, *v.t.* (conjuga-se como *sew*) descoser.

unshaken, *adj.* firme, não abalado; imóvel.

unshaped, *adj.* informe, disforme.

unsheathe, *v.t.* desembainhar.

unshod, *adj.* desferrado (o cavalo).

unshoe, *v.t.* desferrar (o cavalo); descalçar.

unsightly, *adj.* feio, disforme; desagradável à vista.

unsigned, *adj.* não assinado, sem assinatura.

unsmiling, *adj.* sério, sisudo.

unsociable, *adj.* insociável, reservado; solitário, misantropo.

unsocial, *adj.* insocial, antissocial.

unsoiled, *adj.* limpor, sem mácula, puro.

unsolvable, *adj.* insolúvel.

unsound, *adj.* doente, doentio; mórbido; insalubre; mau, perverso, corrupto; insano: infundado, incorrecto, erróneo; frouxo, frágil, instável; estragado, em mau estado; leve (sono).

unsounded, *adj.* insondado; (fon.) mudo, que não se pronuncia.

unstable, *adj.* instável; inseguro; variável; volúvel; vacilante.

unstaid, *adj.* leviano, frívolo, inconstante; indeciso; incerto.

unsteady, *adj.* instável, inseguro; trémulo; inconstante, volúvel; irregular, variável; libertino.

unsteel, *v.t.* amolecer, abrandar, suavizar.

unstick, *v.t.* (conjuga-se como *stick*) descolar, despegar; desatolar.

unstop, *v.t.* (conjuga-se como *stop*) desarrolhar, destapar, abrir; desobstruir, limpar.

unsuccessful, *adj.* mal sucedido, fracassado; infrutífero, malogrado.

unsuccessfully, *adj.* infrutiferamente, em vão, debalde, inutilmente.

unsuitable, *adj.* inadequado, impróprio, inconveniente; inoportuno; incompatível.

unsummed, *adj.* incalculado, incontável.

unsure, *adj.* inseguro; que não merece confiança; duvidoso, incerto; que não tem certeza.

unsurpassable, *adj.* insuperável, inultrapassável.

unsurpassed, *adj.* não ultrapassado; sem igual.

unsuspected, *adj.* insuspeito; desconhecido, ignorado.

untameable, *adj.* indomável; bravio; arisco.

untamed, *adj.* indomado; selvagem, bravio; insubmisso.

untargle, *v.t.* desenredar, desembaraçar, desemaranhar.

untemper, *v.t.* destemperar (metal).

unthinkable, *adj.* impensável, inconcebível.

unthinking, *adj.* irreflectido, precipitado; descuidado, imprudente; irracional.

unthoughtful, adj. irreflectido, leviano, estouvado; desatento.

unthought-of, adj. imprevisto, inesperado; desconhecido, esquecido.

unthread, v.t. desenfiar (agulha): abrir caminho por, sair de labirinto.

unthrone, v.t. destronar.

untie, v.t. e v.i. (conjuga-se como *tie*), desatar(-se), desapertar(-se); soltar, desprender; deslindar, esclarecer.

until, prep. até; conj. até que.

untile, v.t. destelhar, tirar as telhas a.

untilable, adj. incultivável, improdutivo (solo).

unto, prep. (poét. e arc.) o mesmo que *to*, excepto antes de um infinito.

untold, adj. não contado, não revelado, por contar, por dizer; incontável, incalculável, imenso.

untomb, v.t. exumar, desenterrar.

untouchables, s. pl. *the Untouchables:* os intocáveis (na Índia).

untoward, adj. calamitoso, fatídico, sinistro; desagradável, inconveniente; teimoso, rebelde, insubmisso; intratável.

untraceable, adj. cuja pista não se pode seguir ou encontrar; insondável, impenetrável; incompreensível.

untrammeled, adj. sem entraves, desobstruído, livre.

untrod, untrodden, adj. não pisado; inexplorado.

untrue, adj. falso, inexacto, erróneo; contrário à verdade; (mec.) gasto, imperfeito, deformado; descentrado.

untrustful, adj. desconfiado, suspeitoso.

untruth, s. falsidade, mentira, inexactidão; deslealdade, desonestidade.

untruthul, adj. falso, mentiroso, erróneo.

unusable, adj. inutilizável.

unused, adj. desabituado, não habituado; abandonado, desocupado.

unusual, adj. incomum, invulgar, desusado; insólito, raro; notável, extraordinário.

unvarnished, adj. não envernizado; tosco, rústico; simples, natural.

unveil, v.t. e v.i. tirar o véu, descobrir(-se); revelar(-se).

unveiled, adj. não velado, sem véu; indisfarçável.

unversed, adj. não versado, ignorante.

unvoiced, adj. não expressado; (fon.) surdo (consoante).

unwarranted, adj. desautorizado, sem autorização; injustificado; não garantido, sem garantia; não comprovado.

unwary, adj. incauto, descuidado, imprevidente.

unwearying, adj. que não cansa; incansável; persistente.

unwed, adj. solteiro.

unwell, adj. indisposto, adoentado.

unwholesome, adj. insalubre, doentio; prejudicial; corrupto.

unwieldy, adj. desajeitado; pesadão; de manejo difícil.

unwilling, adj. relutante, sem vontade.

unwillingly, adv. de má vontade, com relutância, a contragosto.

unwise, adj. imprudente, insensato.

unwittingly, adv. inconscientemente, inadvertidamente.

unworldly, adj. extraterreno, espiritual; desinteressado.

unworthiness, s. indignidade; desmerecimento.

unworthy, adj. indigno; desprezível; sem mérito; *unworthy of respect,* que não merece respeito.

unwrap, v.t. (conjuga-se como *wrap*), desembrulhar, abrir.

unwrinkle, v.t. desenrugar, alisar.

unwritten, adj. não escrito, em branco; oral, tradicional; *unwritten law* (jur.) direito consuetudinário.

unwrought, adj. não trabalhado, em bruto.

unyielding, adj. duro, tenaz; inflexível, firme.

up, adv. em cima, no alto; para cima, para o alto; até ao ponto de origem; até determinado grau; por completo, completamente; em actividade; em lugar de relevo; com segurança, com vantagem; em posição vertical, de pé; levantado, acordado; acima do horizonte; terminado, no fim; de parte, de lado; (náut.) para barlavento; a alto preço; versado, instruído. 1) *up to now,* até agora. 2) *up to standard,* completamente bom, conforme às regras. 3) *all the way up,* até ao cimo. 4) *from eight years up,* a partir dos 8 anos. 5) *to be up,* estar levantado, estar a pé. 6) *to be up in years,* ter uma idade avançada. 7) *to be up to anything,* ser capaz de tudo. 8) *to keep up with,* acompanhar ou alguma coisa, manter-se a par. 9) *to eat up,* comer tudo, comer até ao fim. 10) *to burn up,* arder até ao fim. 11) *to come up to someone,* chegar ao pé de alguém, dirigir-se a alguém. 12) *to* *catch up,* alcançar. 13) *to feel up to,* sentir-se capaz de. 14) *to go up,* subir. 15) *to go up in price,* subir de preço. 16) *to live up to one's income,* gastar consoante o que se ganha. 17) *to stand up,* pôr-se em pé, levantar-se. 18) *to stir up,* mexer, agitar. 19) *to throw up,* atirar ao ar. 20) *to be up on oneself,* ser presunçoso. 21) *to be well up in history,* ser muito versado em história. 22) *it is all up with him,* ele está liquidado. 23) *that is up to you,* isso é contigo. 24) *to live up to expectations,* corresponder às expectativas. 25) *my leave is up,* a minha licença chegou ao fim. 26) *speak up,* desembuche! 27) *steam is up,* a pressão é grande. 28) *the sun is up,* o sol já nasceu. 29) *the tide is up,* a maré subiu. 30) *there is something up,* aconteceu alguma coisa. 31) *time is up:* está na hora. 32) *what's up?,* que se passa?. 33) *up and down,* para cima e para baixo; *prep.* no cimo de; sobre; para cima de; contra, em direcção contrária a; para o interior de; ao longo de. 34) *to climb up a rope,* trepar por uma corda. 35) *to sail up a river,* navegar por um rio acima. 36) *to walk up a street:* subir uma rua. 37) *the smoke goes up the chimney,* o fumo sobe pela chaminé. 38) *three miles up country,* três milhas par o interior; 39) *up the wind,* contra o vento. 40) *up hill and down dales,* por montes e vales; *adj.* ascendente; que se dirige para o interior ou para cima; que se dirige para a capital. 41) *up train,* comboio que se dirige para a capital. *s.* 42) *ups and downs,* altos e baixos; *v.t.* e *v.i.* *pret.* e *pp. upped;* erguer(-se), levantar(-se); *interj.* acima! upa! vamos! de pé!

upbraid, *v.t.* censurar, repreender; lançar em rosto; reprovar.

upbraiding, *s.* censura, repreensão; acto de exprobrar. *adj.* reprovador.

upbringing, *s.* educação, criação.

upcast, *s.* deslocamento para cima; corrente de ar ascendente (em mina); poço de ventilação; *adj.* lançado para cima, voltado para cima; *with upcast eyes,* com os olhos em alvo.

upcountry, *adj.* do interior; *s.* interior de um país.

updraft, *s.* corrente de ar ascendente.

upend, *v.t.* e *v.i.* pôr(-se) em pé ou a prumo; empinar(-se).

upgrade, *s.* inclinação, rampa, subida; *to be on the upgrade,* estar a melhorar; subir (preços). *adv.* para cima.

upgrowth, *s.* crescimento, desenvolvimento; excrescência, afloramento.

upheaval, *s.* elevação da crosta terrestre; erupção; convulsão social, sublevação.

uphill, *s.* subida, encosta; *adj.* elevado; ascendente, íngreme; *adv.* para cima, monte acima.

upholster, *v.t.* estofar, acolchoar; guarnecer de tapeçarias.

upholsterer, *s.* estofador.

upland, *s.* região montanhosa; terreno elevado; *adj.* elevado, montanhoso; das montanhas; montês; do interior, distante.

uplift, *s.* elevação, levantamento; melhoria; *v.t.* erguer, levantar; enaltecer.

upon, *prep.* o mesmo que *on.*

upper, *adj.* superior; de cima; mais elevado; mais alto. 1) *Upper house:* Câmara Alta, Câmara dos Pares. 2) *Upper Nile,* Alto Nilo. 3) *upper case,* (tip.) caixa alta. 4) *upper crust,* (coloq.) alta sociedade. 5) *upper keyboard,* teclado do piano que corresponde à mão direita. 6) *the upper ten,* a aristocracia. 7) *upper hand,* vantagem, superioridade, primazia. 8) *to get the upper hand,* suplantar, levar a melhor, prevalecer; *s.* gáspeas; parte do calçado que fica acima da sola; polainitos. 9) *to be on one's uppers,* ter as solas completamente gastas, estar na penúria.

uppercut, *s.* golpe curto dirigido de baixo para cima (boxe).

uppermost, *adj.* mais elevado, mais alto; supremo; predominante; *adv.* para cima; no ponto mais alto; em primeiro lugar; *to say whatever comes uppermost,* dizer a primeira coisa que vem à cabeça.

upraise, *v.t.* erguer, levantar.

uprear, *v.t.* erguer, levantar; erigir; enaltecer; educar.

upright, *adj.* vertical, erecto, aprumado, teso; em pé, a prumo; honrado, recto, honesto, íntegro; *s.* viga ou pilar vertical; montante; pé-direito; postes de baliza; verticalidade, prumo; *adv.* direito, em posição vertical.

uprise, *v.i.* levantar-se, erguer-se, elevar-se; surgir; subir; *s.* subida, elevação; ascensão; nascimento (do sol).

uprising, *s.* insurreição, revolta; nascer (do sol); acto de levantar da cama.

uproar, *s.* tumulto, alvoroço, rebuliço; gritaria, algazarra.

uproot, *v.t.* desenraizar; extirpar.

upset, *v.t.* e *v.i.* (conjuga-se como *set*) virar, voltar, derrubar, tombar, entornar; transtornar; perturbar, agitar, afligir, aborrecer; indispor; *adj.* virado, derrubado; perturbado, aflito, agitado transtornado; indisposto; erguido, erecto; fixo.

upshot, *s.* resultado final, conclusão; desfecho; limite; essência; *in the upshot,* finalmente, em conclusão.

upside-down, *adv.* de pernas para o ar; em desordem; ao contrário; *adj.* invertido, de pernas para o ar, ao contrário.

upsilon, *s.* hipsilo, ipsilon (letra grega).

upspring, *v.i.* (conjuga-se como *spring*) saltar para cima, levantar-se de um salto; nascer, surgir; crescer; *s.* salto para cima; origem, nascimento, desenvolvimento.

upstairs, *adv.* em cima, para cima, no andar superior, para o andar superior; *adj.* relativo ao andar superior.

upstanding, *adj.* erecto, aprumado, direito, em pé; recto, íntegro; fixo (salário).

upstart, *s.* novo-rico, arrivista; pessoa arrogante; impostor; *adj.* próprio de novo rico; arrogante; recente, moderno; *v.i.* levantar-se de um salto, pôr-se em pé; surgir, nascer.

upstate, *adj.* do interior do estado; do norte do estado; *s.* interior ou parte setentrional de um estado.

upstream, *adv.* rio acima; a montante.

up-to-date, *adj.* actualizado, moderno, à moda.

upward, *adv.* para cima, acima, para o alto; para a nascente; para o interior ou para o centro de um país; mais; *he owes me upward of one thousand pounds,* ele deve-me mais de mil libras; *adj.* voltado ou dirigido para cima; ascendente.

upwind, *adv.* contra o vento.

uranium, *s.* urânio.

urban, *adj.* urbano, citadino.

urbane, *adj.* urbano, cortês, delicado, gentil.

urbanity, *s.* urbanidade, civilidade, cortesia.

urbanize, *v.t.* urbanizar.

urchin, *s.* garoto, fedelho, diabrete; garoto de rua; (zool.) ouriço-do-mar.

urea, *s.* ureia.

ureter, *s.* (anat.) ureter.

urethra, *s.* uretra.

urethroscopy, *s.* uretroscopia.

urge, *s.* anseio; impulso, ímpeto; necessidade; *v.t.* e *v.i.* forçar; insistir, instar, insti-gar; acelerar, apressar; alegar; advertir; insistir com; exortar, atiçar, estimular.

urgency, *s.* urgência, premência.

urgent, *adj.* urgente, premente; insistente, que insiste ou insta.

urgently, *adv.* urgentemente, com urgência; com insistência, insistentemente.

uric, *adj.* úrico.

urinal, *s.* urinol, mictório.

urinary, *adj.* urinário.

urinate, *v.t.* urinar.

urination, *s.* micção.

urine, *s.* urina.

urn, *s.* urna; espécie de samovar.

urolith, *s.* urólito, cálculo urinário.

urologist, *s.* urologista.

urology, *s.* urologia.

ursine, *adj.* ursino.

urticaria, *s.* urticária.

urticate, *v.t.* e *v.i.* urticar; irritar.

urtication, *s.* urticação.

Uruguayan, *adj.* e *s.* uruguaio.

us, *pron.* a nós. 1) *with us,* connosco. 2) *it is us,* somos nós.

usable, *adj.* utilizável.

usage, *s.* uso, emprego; costume; tratamento, trato; manuseio.

usance, *s. (comerc.)* prazo concedido para o pagamento de letras de câmbio estrangeiras.

use, *s.* uso, emprego, utilização; modo de usar; consumo (de alimentos, etc.); hábito, costume, prática; utilidade, função, serventia; benefício, vantagem; conveniência; fim, objectivo. 1) *what is the use of that?,* para que serve isso? *v.t.* usar, utilizar, empregar, utilizar-se de, servir-se de; proceder com, mostrar; aproveitar; gastar, consumir. 2) *to use someone ill,* tratar mal alguém. 3) *to use up,* gastar inteiramente, consumir, esgotar.

used, *adj.* usado, utilizado, em segunda mão; gasto; usual, habitual; acostumado, habituado.

useful, *adj.* útil, vantajoso, proveitoso; (coloq.) eficiente, capaz, competente.

useless, *adj.* inútil, imprestável; infrutífero; incapaz, inábil; (coloq.) abatido, indisposto.

user, *s.* utente; (jur.) usufrutuário.

usher, *s.* porteiro, arrumador (num teatro, cinema, etc.); oficial de diligências; (cal.) mestre-escola; *v.t.* acompanhar, conduzir, introduzir, preceder, anunciar.

usual, adj. habitual, usual, costumeiro; vulgar.
usually, adv. usualmente, habitualmente, geralmente, vulgarmente.
usucapion, s. (jur.) usucapião.
usufruct, s. (jur.) usufruto; v.t. usufruir, ter o usufruto de.
usufructuary, s. (jur.) usufrutuário.
usurer, s. usurário, agiota; prestamista.
usurious, adj. usurário, relativo a usura.
usurp, v.t. usurpar; apropriar-se de, invadir.
usurpation, s. usurpação.
usury, s. usura; agiotagem.
Utahan, s. natural ou habitante do estado de Utah.
utensil, s. utensílio; ferramenta.
uterine, adj. uterino.
uterus, s. útero.
utilitarian, adj. utilitário; s. partidário do utilitarismo.
utilitarianism, s. (filo.) utilitarismo.
utility, s. utilidade; proveito, vantagem, benefício; empresa de utilidade pública, serviço público. 1) *public utilities,* serviços de utilidade pública. 2) *utility actor,* actor que desempenha pequenos papéis. 3) *utility room,* copa.

utilize, v.t. utilizar, utilizar-se de; aproveitar, tirar proveito de.
utmost, adj. extremo, mais distante, mais elevado, mais avançado; máximo; s. extremo, limite, último grau; máximo possível.
utopia, s. utopia.
utopian, adj. utópico; s. utopista, visionário.
utopianism, s. utopismo.
utricle, s. (anat. bot. e zool.) utrículo.
utter, adj. completo, total, absoluto, extremo; v.t. pronunciar, proferir, dizer; expressar; emitir; pôr em circulação, passar (dinheiro falso).
utterance, s. elocução, expressão oral, fala, dom da palavra; pronúncia, dicção; declaração; emissão (de dinheiro falso).
utterly, adv. completamente, inteiramente, totalmente; terminantemente, categoricamente.
uttermost, adj. e s. o mesmo que utmost.
uvula, s. úvula.
uvular, adj. uvular.
uxorious, adj. excessivamente dependente da mulher, dominado pela mulher.
uxoriousness, s. afeição excessiva pela mulher.

V

v, vigésima segunda letra do alfabeto.
vacancy, s. vácuo, vazio; lugar vago.
vacant, adj. vazio; vago, devoluto; distraído; descuidado, ocioso; fútil; *vacant mind,* espírito despreocupado; adv. *vacantly,* negligente.
vacate, v.t. vagar, deixar vago; abandonar; invalidar, revogar.
vacation, s. férias; descanso; anulação, revogação (for.).
vaccinate, v.t. vacinar.
vaccination, s. vacinação, vacina.
vaccine, s. vacina; adj. vacum.
vacillate, v.i. vacilar.
vacillating, adj. titubeante, vacilante; *vacilantingly,* vacilantemente.
vacuity, s. vacuidade.

vacuous, adj. vácuo, vazio, desocupado; fátuo, mentecapto.
vacuum, s. vácuo, vazio. 1) *vacuum brake,* freio pneumático. 2) *vacuum cleaner,* aspirador.
vagabond, s. e adj. vagabundo.
vagabondage, s. vagabundagem.
vagary, s. capricho, veneta, extravagância.
vagina, s. vagina (anat.).
vaginal, adj. vaginal.
vagrancy, s. vida errante; madraçaria.
vagrant, s. vagabundo; adj. vagabundo, errante.
vague, adj. vago, indefenido; adv. *vaguely,* vagamente.
vagueness, s. indeterminação; incerteza.
vail, s. gorjeta (no pl.); v.t. abaixar em sinal de respeito; tirar; v.i. ceder, render-se.

vain, *adj.* vão, vaidoso, presunçoso; inútil, frívolo; orgulhoso. *in vain,* em vão, debalde, *adv. vainly,* vãmente, inutilmente.

vainglorious, *adj.* vanglorioso, orgulhoso; *adv. vaingloriously,* vangloriosamente.

vainness, *s.* vaidade, presunção; futilidade; inutilidade.

valance, *s.* sanefa (de cama), rodapé; *v.t.* decorar com sanefa ou rodapé.

vale, *s.* vale (poét.).

valediction, *s.* despedida, adeus.

valence, *s.* valência (quím.).

valentine, *s.* valentino, namorado ou namorada que se escolhe no dia de S. Valentim (14 de Fevereiro).

valerian, *s.* valeriana (bot.).

valet, *s.* criado, pajem; *v.t.* ser criado ou pajem.

valiant, *s.* valente, bravo; esforçado, valoroso; *adv. valiantly,* valentemente, valorosamente.

valid, *adj.* válido, forte, poderoso; *adv. validly,* validamente.

validate, *v.t.* validar, tornar válido; confirmar.

validation, *s.* validação.

validity, *s.* validade.

validness, *s.* validez, força.

valise, *s.* maleta.

Valkyr, Valkyria, ie, *s.* valquíria.

valley, *s.* vale.

valorous, *adj.* valoroso; *adv. valorously,* valorosamente.

valour, *s.* valor, brio, valentia, ânimo, intrepidez.

valuable, *adj.* valioso, estimável, apreciável, precioso.

valuation, *s.* avaliação.

value, *v.t.* avaliar, taxar, estimar; apreciar, prezar; *s.* valor, preço; apreço, estimação; *to set great value on,* fazer grande caso de.

valued, *adj.* estimado, avaliado.

valueless, *adj.* sem valor, sem préstimo, insignificante.

valuer, *s.* avaliador, perito.

valve, *s.* válvula; distribuidor. 1) *delivery valve,* válvula de compressão. 2) *valve gear,* aparelho de marcha.

valvular, *adj.* valvular.

vamose, *v.t.* sair, partir, ir-se (fam.).

vamp, *s.* gáspea de sapato; remendo, tomba; mulher aventureira, *v.t.* remendar, atrair agir como vamp.

vamper, *s.* remendão.

vampire, *s.* vampiro.

van, *s.* carroça; vagão; furgão; crivo, ciranda; *v.t.* (*vanning, vanned*), transportar em carroça ou vagão.

vandal, *adj.* vandálico; *s.* vândalo, destruidor; *adv. vaingloriously,* vangloriosamente.

vandalism, *s.* vandalismo.

vane, *s.* cata-vento, grimpa; pínula.

vaned, *adj.* com cata-ventos.

vanguard, *s.* vanguarda.

vanilla, *s.* baunilha.

vanish, *v.i.* desaparecer, dissipar-se, desvanecer-se.

vanity, *s.* vaidade, presunção.

vanquish, *v.t.* vencer, conquistar, domar, subjugar, superar.

vanquishable, *adj.* vencível, conquistável.

vanquisher, *s.* vencedor, conquistador.

vantage, *s.* vantagem, lucro, proveito; superioridade; ocasião favorável; ponto ganho no ténis.

vapid, *adj.* evaporado, que perdeu a força; insípido, desenxabido; *adv. vapidly,* dum modo insípido.

vapidity, *s.* insipidez, sansaboria.

vaporization, *s.* vaporização.

vaporiza, *v.t.* evaporar-se.

vaporizer, *s.* vaporizador.

vaporosity, *s.* estado do que é vaporoso.

vaporous, *adj.* vaporoso; etéreo; quimérico.

vapour, *s.* vapor, exalação, nuvem ligeira; gás; fluido, hálito; vaidade, presunção, soberba, arrogância; *pl.* melancolia; *v.i.* evaporar-se, dissipar-se; converter-se em vapor, bazofiar; *v.t.* evaporar, exalar.

vapoury, *adj.* vaporoso; melancólico; rabugento; impertinente.

variability, *s.* variabilidade, inconstância.

variable, *adj.* variável, mudável, volúvel, inconstante; *s.* o que varia; quantidade variável (mat.); *adv. variably,* variavelmente.

variance, *s.* variação; desacordo, desavença, desinteligência; *to be at variance,* estar em desacordo.

variant, *adj.* variante; vário, diverso; variável; *s.* variante, variação.

variation, *s.* variação, diferença, declinação magnética.

varicella, *s.* varicela.

varices, *s. pl.* de *varix.*

varicose, *adj.* varicoso.

varied, *adj.* variado; diverso.

variegate, *v.t.* variegar, mosquear, matizar; variar, diversificar.

variegation, *s.* variegação, diversidade de cores; matiz.

variety, s. variedade, diversidade de cores; matiz.

variety, s. variedade, diversidade, diferença, variação, mudança; variabilidade; *variety theatre,* teatro de variedades.

variola, s. varíola, bexigas.

various, adj. vário, diverso, variado; inconsciente; variegado; adv. *variously,* variadamente, diversamente.

varix, s. variz.

varlet, s. lacaio, pajem; velhaco, maroto.

varnish, s. verniz; v.t. envernizar; vidrar (loiça); encobrir.

varnisher, s. envernizador.

varnishing, s. envernizamento.

varsity, s. universidade (abrev. fam.).

vary, v.t. variar, mudar, diversificar; v.i. variar, mudar-se; discordar; desviar-se (agulha magnética).

vascular, adj. vascular.

vascularity, s. vascularidade.

vase, s. vaso, jarrão; cálice (bot.).

vaseline, s. vaselina.

vassal, s. vassalo, súbdito; adj. tributário.

vassalage, s. vassalagem.

vast, adj. vasto, grande, amplo, extenso, imenso; s. vastidão; adv. *vastly,* vastamente, imensamente.

vasteness, s. grande extensão; enormidade, imensidade.

vasty, adj. vasto, imenso.

vat, s. tina, dorna, cuba; v.t. *(vatting, vatted),* pôr em tinas ou dornas.

vatful, s. capacidade de conteúdo da tina.

vault, s. abóbada; adega; caverna; espelunca; túmulo, sepulcro; salto; v.t. abobadar; v.i. saltar, pular, voltear; curvar, arquear.

vaulter, s. o que salta; atleta de salto com vara.

vaunt, s. vaidade, jactância, ostentação; vi. gabar-se, gloriar-se, bazofiar, jactar-se; v.t. exaltar, louvar.

veal, s. carne de vitela. 1) *bob-veal,* carne de vitela muito tenra. 2) *veal-cutlet,* costeleta de vitela.

vector, s. raio vector (mat.).

vedette, s. vedeta (mil.).

veer, vt. e vi. virar, voltar, mudar; arrear, largar (náut.); rondar ao direito (vento); *veer away,* arrear.

vegetable, s. vegetal, planta; pl. hortaliças.

vegetal, adj. e s. vegetal.

vegetarian, s. e adj. vegetariano.

vegetarianism, s. vegetarianismo.

vegetate, v.i. vegetar.

vegetation, s. vegetação.

vegetative, adj. vegetativo.

vehemence, s. veemência, impetuosidade, força, ardor.

vehement, adj. veemente, impetuoso, forte; *vehemently,* veementemente.

vehicle, s. veículo, carruagem.

vehicular, adj. pertencente ou relativo a veículo.

veil, s. véu; banda, faixa; disfarce, pretexto, máscara; v.t. cobrir com véu; tecido próprio para véus.

vein, s. veia, estro; filão; nervura; v.i. encher de veias; jaspear; pintar fingindo mármore.

veined, adj. com veias; com nervuras; variegado.

veinless, adj. sem veias; sem nervuras.

veiny, adj. venoso.

velar, adj. velar, relativo ao véu (anat.).

veloce, adj. veloz (mús.).

velocípede, s. velocípede.

velocity, s. velocidade.

velvet, s. veludo; adj. de veludo, aveludado.

velveted, adj. aveludado.

velvety, adj. aveludado.

venal, adj. venal, mercenário; adv. *venally,* venalmente.

venality, s. venalidade.

vend, v.t. vender.

vendee, s. comprador.

vendetta, s. vingança pessoal.

vendor, s. vendedor.

vendue, s. venda em leilão.

veneer, v.t. embutir, entalhar, folhear; s. embutido, folheado; capa exterior, aparência.

venerable, adj. venerável, respeitável; adv. *venerably,* veneravelmente.

venerate, v.t. venerar, respeitar, reverenciar.

veneration, s. veneração, respeito, acatamento.

venerator, s. verenador.

venereal, adj. venéreo.

venery, s. montaria, caçada.

venge, v.t. vingar.

vengeance, s. vingança.

vengeful, adj. vingativo; adv. *vengefully,* vingativamente.

venial, adj. venial, desculpável, perdoável; adv. *venially,* venialmente.

venialness, s. venialidade.

venom, s. veneno, peçonha.

venomed, adj. envenenado.

venomous, *adj.* venenoso, peçonhento; maligno; *adv. venomously,* venenosamente.
venous, *adj.* venoso.
vent, *s.* abertura, saída, passagem, respiradouro; escape; cano de chaminé; ouvido de peça; desafogo; *v.t.* exalar, dar saída, dar curso; descarregar; desabafar; tornar conhecido; *v.i.* cheirar, farejar; ter ventilação.
ventilate, *v.t.* ventilar, arejar, abanar; discutir.
ventilation, *s.* ventilação; discussão.
ventilator, *s.* ventilador.
ventricle, *s.* ventrículo.
ventricular, *adj.* ventricular.
ventriloquist, *s.* ventríloquo.
ventriloquy, *s.* ventriloquismo.
venture, *s.* aventura, risco, perigo; especulação comercial; *at a venture,* ao acaso; *v.t.* e *v.i.* aventurar(-se); arriscar(-se), atrever-se, ousar.
venturer, *s.* aventureiro.
venturesome, *adj.* atrevido, empreendedor, arriscado; *adv. venturesomely,* atrevidamente, arrojadamente.
venturesomeness, *s.* temeridade, arrojo.
venturous, *adj.* ousado, atrevido; *adv. venturously,* ousadamente.
veracious, *adj.* verdadeiro, verídico; *adv. veraciously,* veridicamente.
veracity, *s.* veracidade.
veranda, *s.* varanda, pórtico, galeria.
verb, *s.* verbo, (gram.).
verbal, *adj.* verbal, de viva voz; literal; *adv. verbally,* verbalmente.
verbalism, *s.* expressão, observação oral.
verbalist, *s.* verbalista.
verbatim, *adv.* literalmente.
verbena, *s.* verbena (bot.).
verbiage, *s.* verbosidade.
verbose, *adj.* verboso, loquaz; *adv. verbosely,* com loquacidade.
verboseness, *s.* verbosidade, loquacidade.
verbosity, *s.* verbosidade.
verdancy, *s.* verdura; inexperiência.
verdant, *adj.* verde; verdejante, fresco; inocente, simples, inexperiente; *adv. verdantly,* com verdura, sem experiência.
verdict, *s.* veredicto, decisão do júri.
verdigris, *s.* verdete.
verdure, *s.* verdura, vegetação.
verge, *s.* vara (insígnia); alçada, jurisdição; extremidade, borda, fim, margem, limite, orla; fuste de coluna (arq.); *upon the verge of,* à beira de; *v.i.* aproximar-se de; tender, inclinar, pender, dirigir-se.
verger, *s.* meirinho, oficial de justiça; bedel.
verifiable, *adj.* verificável.
verification, *s.* verificação.
verifier, *s.* verificador.
verify, *v.t.* verificar, provar; averiguar, examinar; cumprir, executar (promessa); afirmar, confirmar sob juramento (for.); acreditar.
veritable, *adj.* verdadeiro, genuíno, real; *adv. veritably,* verdadeiramente.
verity, *s.* verdade; veracidade.
vermeil, *s.* prata dourada.
vermicelly, *s.* aletria.
vermicide, *adj.* vermicida.
vermiform, *adj.* vermiforme.
vermilion, *s.* vermelhão; *v.t.* tingir de vermelho, corar.
vermin, *s.* animal nocivo, insecto; praga; parasitas; (fig.) ralé, canalha.
verminous, *adj.* verminoso.
vermouth, *s.* vermute.
vernacular, *adj.* vernáculo, nacional; *s.* idioma nacional, língua materna.
vernal, *adj.* da primavera; vernal; *adv. vernally,* vernalmente.
verruca, *s.* verruga.
versant, *adj.* versado, experimentado; *s.* declive, vertente.
versatile, *adj.* versátil, mutável; inconstante; flexível; *adv. versatilely,* versatilmente; inconstantemente.
versatility, *s.* versatilidade.
verse, *s.* verso, poesia; estrofe, estância.
versed, *adj.* versado, douto, experimentado.
versicle, *s.* versículo.
versification, *s.* versificação, metrificação.
versifier, *s.* versificador, rimador.
versify, *v.t.* e *v.i.* versificar, versejar.
version, *s.* versão, tradução; modo de contar um facto; variante.
verso, *s.* verso (de página).
versus, *prep.* contra (for.).
vertebra, *s.* vértebra.
vertebral, *adj.* vertebral; *s.* artéria vertebral; animal vertebrado.
vertebrate, *adj.* vertebrado; *s.* animal vertebrado.
vertebration, *s.* formação de vértebras.
vertical, *adj.* vertical; *adv. vertically,* verticalmente.
vertiginous, *adj.* vertiginoso; rotatório.
vertigo, *s.* vertigem.

vervain, s. verbena (bot.).

verve, s. entusiamo, energia, estro.

very, adv. muito; very much, muitíssimo; adj. verdadeiro, mesmo, próprio.

vesicle, s. vesícula.

vesper, s. véspera, tarde, o anoitecer; pl. vésperas (igr.).

vespertine, adj. vespertino.

vespiary, s. vespeiro, toca de vespas.

vessel, s. embarcação, navio; recipiente, vaso, vasilha.

vest, s. camisola; colete; jaqueta antiga; traje; v.t. e v.i. vestir, revestir; dar posse, investir; colocar, pôr; vestir-se; vir de direito; to vest with power, investir de autoridade; conferir poder a.

vestal, adj. vestal; virgem; virginal, casta; s. vestal, virgem.

vestibular, adj. vestibular.

vestibule, s. vestíbulo, átrio, pórtico.

vestige, s. vestígio, pegada.

vestment, s. veste, vestido, vestimenta, fato.

vestry, s. sacristia.

vesture, s. vestidos, vestimenta, cobertura; v.t. vestir.

vet, s. veterano (fam.); veterinário.

veteran, adj. e s. veterano.

veterinary, adj. e s. veterinário.

veto, v.t. vetar, proibir; pôr o veto; recusar a aprovação; s. veto, proibição.

vex, v.t. vexar, aborrecer, molestar, incomodar, enfadar, irritar; discutir, debater; agitar, perturbar.

vexation, s. vexação, aborrecimento, irritação; vexame, incómodo.

vexatious, adj. vexatório; enfadonho, molesto; penoso, triste; adv. vexatiously, penosamente, de modo vexatório.

vexed, adj. vexado, incomodado; a vexed question, questão muito debatida.

vexing, adj. vexatório; enfadonho.

via, s. via, caminho, estrada; prep. pela via de, por.

viable, adj. capaz de conservar a vida (diz-se dum recém-nascido).

viaduct, s. viaduto.

vial, s. redoma; frasco.

viand, s. vianda, carne; pl. comida, provisões, vitualhas.

vibrate, v.t. vibrar, agitar, brandir, mover; v.i. oscilar, vibrar.

vibration, s. vibração, trepidação.

vibrator, s. vibrador.

vibratory, adj. vibratório, oscilatório.

vicar, s. vicário; cura; vicar of Bray, vira--casacas.

vicarage, s. vicariato.

vicarial, adj. vigarial, de vigário.

vicarious, adj. vigarial, deputado, delegado, substituto; adv. vicariously, como vigário; como delegado.

vice, s. vício, defeito, falta; maldade, imoralidade, depravação; prep. em lugar de; pref. correspondente a "vice" em português.

vice-admiral, s. vice-almirante.

vice-chairman, s. vice-presidente.

vice-chancellor, s. vice-chanceler.

vice-consul, s. vice-cônsul.

vice-consulate, s. vice-consulado.

vice-gerent, s. vice-gerente.

vice-president, s. vice-presidente.

vice-principal, s. subgerente; vice-director.

viceroy, s. vice-rei.

vicinity, s. vizinhança, proximidade.

vicious, adj. vicioso, defeituoso, imperfeito, corrompido; vicious animal: animal traiçoeiro; viciously, viciosamente.

viciousness, s. vício, corrupção; furor; violência.

vicissitude, s. vicissitude.

victim, s. vítima.

victimize, v.t. vitimar.

victor, s. vencedor, triunfador; senhor; árbitro.

victoria, s. vitória (carruagem); vitória (raça de pombos).

victorious, adj. vitorioso; adv. victoriously, vitoriosamente.

victory, s. vitória.

victual, s. (geralmente no pl.) alimentos, víveres; v.t. suprir de víveres, abastecer; v.i. abastecer-se.

victualler, s. fornecedor.

vide, v. imper. vide, veja, veja-se, vede.

videlicet, adv. a saber, isto é.

vie, v.i. competir, disputar, desafiar, rivalizar.

view, s. vista; aspecto; paisagem, panorama; inspecção, exame; opinião, parecer; propósito, intento; percepção; perspectiva. 1) in view of, em vista de. 2) on view, em exposição. 3) with a view to, com o propósito de; v.t. examinar, ver, observar, averiguar, investigar.

viewpoint, s. ponto de vista.

vigil, s. vigília, vela; to keep vigil, velar.

vigilance, s. vigilância, cuidado, desvelo.

vigilant, adj. vigilante; adv. vigilantly, vigilantemente.

vigorous, adj. vigoroso, forte, potente, robusto; adv. vigorously, vigorosamente.

vigour, s. vigor, força, energia, actividade.

viking, s. antigo pirata escandinavo.

vile, adj. vil, baixo, desprezível, indigno; malvado, perverso, ruim. adv. vilely, vilmente.

vileness, s. vileza, baixeza, mesquinhez, pequenez.

vilifier, s. difamador, caluniador.

vilify, v.t. aviltar, difamar.

villa, s. casa de campo.

village, s. aldeia, burgo; adj. de aldeia.

villager, s. aldeão, aldeã.

villain, s. vilão; servo, camponês.

villainous, adj. baixo, vil, velhaco; malvado, repugnante.

villainy, s. vilania, perversidade, maldade.

vim, s. força; energia; vitalidade; flexibilidade.

vincible, adj. vencível.

viculum, s. vínculo.

vindicable, adj. sustentável, justificável.

vindicate, v.t. justificar, manter, sustentar; reivindicar.

vindication, s. justificação, defesa.

vindicative, adj. justificativo; vingativo.

vindicator, s. defensor.

vindictive, adj. justificativo; vingativo; adv. vindictively, vingativamente.

vine, s. vinha, videira; trepadeira; parreira.

vinegar, s. vinagre.

vinegary, adj. avinagrado.

vineyard, s. vinha, vinhedo.

viniculture, s. vinicultura.

vint, v.t. fazer ou produzir vinho.

vintage, s. vindima.

vintager, s. vindimador.

vintner, s. taberneiro; negociante de vinhos.

viny, adj. que tem vinhas.

viol, s. instrumento medieval semelhante ao violino.

viola, s. viola.

violable, adj. violável.

violate, v.t. violar, transgredir; violentar.

violation, s. violação; violentação.

violator, s. violador, transgressor; esturpador.

violence, s. violência, impetuosidade, força, veemência.

violent, adj. violento, impetuoso, arrebatado; severo, duro; adv. violently, violentamente.

violet, adj. violeta (flor).

violin, s. violino, rabeca; composto venenoso (quím.).

violinist, s. violinista.

violoncellist, s. violoncelista.

violoncello, s. violoncelo.

viper, s. víbora.

virago, s. virago.

virgin, s. virgem, donzela, virgo (ast.); adj. virginal, casto, puro.

virginal, adj. virginal; s. espineta.

virginity, s. virgindade.

viridescent, adj. esverdeado.

viridity, s. verdura, verdor.

virile, adj. viril, varonil.

virility, s. virilidade.

virtual, adj. virtual, eficaz; virtually, virtualmente.

virtue, s. virtude; poder, eficácia; mérito, excelência; valor.

virtuous, adj. virtuoso; casto; bravo, corajoso; adj. virtuously, virtuosamente.

virtuousness, s. virtude.

virulence, s. virulência, veneno; malignidade.

virulent, adj. virulento; adv. virulently, com virulência.

virus, s. vírus.

vis, s. força, potência.

visage, s. rosto, semblante, face, aspecto.

viscera, s. pl. vísceras.

visceral, adj. visceral, visceroso.

viscid, adj. viscoso, pegajoso.

viscidity, s. viscosidade.

viscosity, s. viscosidade.

viscount, s. visconde.

viscountess, s. viscondessa.

viscounty, s. viscondado.

viscous, adj. viscoso, pegajoso.

viscousness, s. viscosidade.

visé, v.t. visar, referendar; s. visto.

visibility, s. visibilidade.

visible, adj. visível, claro, evidente, manifesto; externo; adv. visibly, visivelmente.

visibleness, s. visibilidade.

Visigoth, s. visigodo.

vision, s. visão; a vista; fantasma, aparição; v.t. visionar, imaginar.

visional, adj. de visão; visionário; adv. visionally, visionariamente, com visão.

visionary, s. visionário, sonhador; adj. visionário, ilusório.

visit, v.t. visitar, ir ver; v.t. fazer visitas, ir de visita; s. visita; reconhecimento.

visitant, s. visitante, visitador; visita, hóspede.

visitation, s. visita, visitação; inspecção; reconhecimento; castigo, graça.

visitor, s. visita, hóspede; visitador, inspector.

visor, s. visor, máscara.

visual, adj. visual; adv. visually, visualmente.

visualization, s. visualização, visualidade.

vital, adj. vital, essencial; adv. vitally, vitalmente.

vitality, s. vitalidade.

vitalize, v.t. vitalizar, dar vida; animar, reanimar.

vitamines, s. pl. vitaminas.

vitiate, v.t. viciar, corromper.

vitiation, s. viciação, depravação, corrupção; invalidação.

vitiator, s. viciador.

viteous, adj. vítreo; vidroso, vidrento.

vitrify, v.t. e v.i. vitrificar-se.

vitriol, s. vitríolo, ácido sulfúrico.

vituperate, v.i. vituperar.

vituperation, s. vituperação, vitupério.

vituperator, s. vituperador.

vivace, adv. apressadamente.

vivacious, adj. vivo, esperto; adv. vivaciously, com vivacidade.

vivacity, s. vivacidade.

viva voce, adv. de viva voz.

vivid, adj. vívido, vivo, esperto: intenso, veemente; adv. vividly, vividamente, vivamente.

vividness, s. vivacidade, brilho; actividade.

vivification, s. vivificação.

vivify, v.t. vivificar.

viviparous, adj. vivíparo.

vivisect, v.t. e v.i. dissecar um animal vivo.

vivisection, s. vivissecção, dissecação dum animal vivo.

vivisectionist, s. vivisseccionista.

vixen, s. raposa; víbora, mulher de mau génio; mulher turbulenta.

vixenish, adj. com características de pessoa de mau génio.

vizier, s. vizir.

vocable, s. vocábulo, termo.

vocabulary, s. vocabulário.

vocal, adj. vocal, de voz; adv. vocally, vocalmente.

vocalic, adj. vocálico.

vocalism, s. vocalização.

vocalist, s. vocalista; cantor, cantora.

vocalization, s. vocalização.

vocalize, v.t. vocalizar.

vocation, s. vocação.

vocational, adj. relativo à vocação ou inclinação; adv. vocationally, com vocação, ou inclinação.

vocative, s. e adj. vocativo.

vociferate, v.i. vociferar.

vociferation, s. vociferação.

vociferous, adj. vociferante; adv. vociferously, ruidosamente.

vodka, s. vodca.

vogue, s. voga, fama, reputação, moda; in vogue, na moda, em voga.

voice, s. voz, som, palavra; opinião, voto; o que fala em nome de outro; voz do verbo (gram.); v.t. expressar, proclamar, publicar, divulgar; v.i. vociferar, gritar.

voiced, adj. com voz, sonante (diz-se de certas consoantes).

voiceless, adj. sem voz, mudo; adv. voicelessly, silenciosamente.

voicing, s. acto de se tornar vocal, ou de dar voto.

void, adj. vazio, oco, desocupado, deserto, vago; vacante; nulo, desprovido, falto (com of); vão, ilusório; v.t. anular, invalidar; despejar, desocupar; evacuar; vomitar.

voidable, adj. anulável; que pode vomitar-se ou evacuar-se.

voidance, s. anulação; vacatura; expulsão; evacuação; subterfúgio, evasiva; fingimento.

voidness, s. vácuo, vacuidade; nulidade; invalidade.

volant, s. volante; adj. voador; mudável; rápido, ágil.

volatile, adj. volátil, subtil, fugaz, volúvel, inconstante; passageiro, transitório; s. animal alado.

volatilization, s. volatilização.

volatilize, v.t. e v.i. volatilizar(-se).

volcanic, adj. vulcânico.

volcano, s. vulcão.

volley, s. descarga; salva (de artilharia); aclamação, grito de alegria; v.t. e v.i. dar uma descarga.

volt, s. volt (elect.).

voltage, s. voltagem (elect.).

voltaic, adj. voltaico; galvânico.

voltameter, s. voltímetro.

volte, s. movimento rápido ou salto.

volte-face, s. mudança.

volubility, s. volubilidade.

voluble, adj. volúvel; adv. volubly, voluvelmente.

volume, s. volume (livro); volume, tamanho, quantidade.

volumeter, s. volúmetro.

voluminous, adj. volumoso, copioso, difuso,

dilatado; *adv. voluminously,* volumosamente; extensamente.

voluntary, *adj.* voluntário; *s.* caprichoso; solo de órgão durante ofício religioso; acção voluntária.

volunteer, *s.* e *adj.* voluntário; *v.t.* e *v.i.* oferecer-se para fazer uma coisa; servir de voluntário.

voluptuary, *s.* pessoa voluptuosa; sibarita.

voluptuous, *adj.* voluptuoso; *adv. voluptuously,* voluptuosamente.

volute, *s.* voluta.

vomit, *s.* vómito, vomitório; *v.t.* e *v.i.* vomitar; lançar violentamente.

vomiting, *s.* vómito.

voracious, *adj.* voraz; *adv. voraciously,* vorazmente.

voracity, *s.* voracidade.

vortex, *s.* turbilhão, remoinho.

vortical, *adj.* circular, de redor; que faz remoinho; *adv. vortically,* com remoinho.

votaress, *s.* devota.

votary, *s.* devoto, partidário.

vote, *s.* voto, sufrágio; *v.t.* e *v.i.* votar, eleger, decidir, deliberar.

voteless, *adj.* sem direito a voto.

voter, *s.* votante.

votive, *adj.* votivo; comemorativo; votado a; *votive medal,* medalha comemorativa.

vouch, *v.t.* chamar como testemunha, atestar; confirmar, afirmar, assegurar, garantir, sustentar; verificar; *v.i.* dar testemunho, testemunhar; *s.* afirmação, testemunho.

voucher, *s.* responsável, fiador; testemunho, prova, título, documento; recibo, certidão; garantia.

vouchsafe, *v.t.* conceder, permitir; *v.i.* condescender, dignar-se.

vow, *s.* voto, promessa solene; *v.t.* votar, dedicar, consagrar, fazer voto; *v.i.* fazer votos, jurar, protestar.

vowel, *s.* vogal (gram.).

vox, *s.* voz (mús.).

voyage, *s.* viagem, travessia; *v.t.* viajar.

voyager, *s.* viajante.

vulcanite, *s.* vulcanite.

vulcanization, *s.* vulcanização.

vulcanize, *v.t.* vulcanizar.

vulgar, *adj.* vulgar, comum, trivial, ordinário; baixo, grosseiro; *s.* vulgo, plebe, gentalha; *adv. vulgarly,* vulgarmente, grosseiramente.

vulgarism, *s.* vulgarismo, expressão baixa, grosseira.

vulgarity, *s.* vulgaridade, grosseria.

vulgarization, *s.* vulgarização.

vulgarize, *v.t.* vulgarizar.

vulgarizer, *s.* vulgarizador.

vulnerability, *s.* vulnerabilidade.

vulnerable, *adj.* vulnerável.

vulpine, *adj.* vulpino, astuto.

vulture, *s.* abutre.

vulturine, *s.* e *adj.* de abutre, rapace.

vulturous, *adj.* de abutre.

vulva, *s.* vulva.

vying, *s.* desafio (em corridas, etc.).

W

w, vigésima terceira letra do alfabeto.

wacky, *adj.* doido, maluco; ridículo.

wad, *s.* chumaço, enchimento; bola de papel; (coloq.) maço de notas enroladas; bola de papel; bucha de espingarda; *v.t.* enchumaçar, estofar, acolchoar; enrolar em bola; pôr bucha, apertar com bucha.

wadding, *s.* chumaço, enchimento, estofo.

waddle, *v.i.* andar bamboleando-se, gingar; *s.* andar bamboleante.

waddy, *s.* maça de guerra ou clava dos indígenas australianos.

wade, *v.t.* e *v.i.* andar com dificuldade na água, na lama, na neve, etc.; patinhar, chapinhar; avançar com dificuldade; passar a vau; *s.* acto de passar a vau, vadeação, vau.

wader, *s.* aquele que anda na água; ave pernalta; *pl.* botas de água.

wadi, *s. uade, uadi, uede* (designação dos rios intermitentes do Norte de África).

wafer, *s.* espécie de filhó; hóstia, pastilha; disco adesivo usado para fechar cartas ou outros documentos.

waffle, s. espécie de bolo chato com um desenho especial; v.t. falar sem parar.

waft, v.t. e v.i. impelir ou levar suavemente pela água ou pelo ar; soprar; atirar beijos; fazer flutuar ou deslizar; deslizar com suavidade; vogar; s. aragem, sopro de vento; baforada; fragrância passageira; bater de asas; aceno de mão; (náut.) sinal com bandeira.

wag, v.t. e v.i. agitar, abanar, balancear, oscilar; menear(-se); (coloq.) ir embora, retirar-se; viajar, andar; fazer gazeta. 1) how wags the world?, que tal vão as coisas? 2) to let the world wag, deixar correr o marfim. 3) to wag one's finger at someone, advertir alguém com o dedo.

wage, s. (geralm. no pl.) salário, ordenado, paga; recompensa, preço; v.t. empreender; travar (batalha).

wager, s. aposta; parada, dinheiro apostado; v.t. apostar, jogar, arriscar.

wagerer, s. apostador.

waggery, s. brincadeira, travessura, gracejo, partida.

waggish, adj. brincalhão, gaiateiro, divertido.

waggle, v.t. e v.i. abanar(-se), sacudir(-se), menear(-se), agitar(-se); manejar.

waggly, adj. meneante, coleante; oscilante.

wag(g)on, s. carroça, carro; vagão aberto. 1) wagon-train, comboio de abastecimento. 2) tea-wagon, carrinho de chá.

wag(g)oner, s. condutor de carro; The Wagoner, (astrol.) o Auriga, o Cocheiro.

wag(g)onette, s. breque.

wagtail, s. (zool.) lavandisca, alvéola.

waif, s. coisa abandonada, objecto sem dono; coisa lançada à praia pelo mar; pessoa sem casa; vagabundo; criança abandonada; (jur.) objectos roubados e abandonados durante a fuga; waifs and stays, crianças sem lar.

wail, s. lamento, lamúria; choro, gemido, queixume, vagido; v.t. e v.i. lamentar(-se), chorar, prantear, lastimar(-se), gemer, queixar-se.

wailful, adj. lamentoso, pesaroso, dorido.

wailing, adj. lamentoso, choroso, que se queixa ou geme; s. lamento, lamúria, choro; queixume; vagido; Wailling Wall, Muro das Lamentações.

wain, s. carro, carroça; Arthur's Wain, Charle's Wain, The Wain, a Ursa Maior.

wainscot, s. lambril, lambrim.

waist, s. cintura, cinta; corpete; espartilho; (náut.) parte do convés entre os castelos.

waistband, s. cós; cinto, faixa.

waistcoat, s. colete.

waistline, s. cintura, linha da cinta.

wait, v.i. e v.t. esperar, aguardar, estar à espera de; (coloq.) adiar, protelar, atrasar; servir (espec. à mesa); (arc.) escoltar, acompanhar; seguir de perto; to wait on, servir alguém, ser criado de alguém; s. espera, acto de esperar; demora; cilada, emboscada; (pl.) grupo de pessoas que, no Natal, andam a cantar de casa em casa.

waiter, s. criado de mesa; salva, bandeja; dumb waiter, aparador (móvel).

waiting, s. espera, acto de esperar; serviço; acto de servir à mesa. 1) waiting room, sala de espera. 2) lady in waiting, dama de honor, dama de companhia. 3) waiting maid, criada de senhora. 4) officer in waiting, oficial de serviço.

waitress, s. criada de mesa.

waive, v.t. renunciar a, prescindir de, pôr de parte; adiar, protelar.

wake, s. vigília, vigia, vela; (Irl.) velório; (náut.) esteira, rasto de navio; v.i. e v.t. despertar, acordar, estar acordado; animar(-se); estimular; evocar; reviver, ressuscitar; perturbar (silêncio); fazer ressoar, atroar; (Irl.) velar (defunto).

wakeful, adj. desperto, acordado; insone; passada em claro (noite); vigilante, alerta.

wakefulness, s. vigília, insónia.

wakeless, adj. profundo (sono).

waken, v.t. e v.i. despertar, acordar; tornar (-se) activo ou vigilante; animar(-se); estimular; provocar, evocar.

wakening, s. despertar.

wale, s. vergão, vinco; textura; (náut.) cintas; v.t. avergoar, fazer vergões em.

walk, s. caminhada, passeio, volta; passo, marcha; andar, modo de andar; procedimento; alameda, avenida; caminho habitual de uma pessoa que anda a pé; distância percorrida a pé; profissão, ocupação; v.i. e v.t. caminhar, andar, andar a pé, passear; andar a passo; percorrer a pé; andar sobre; levar, conduzir, acompanhar. 1) to walk into, entrar. 2) to walk off, retirar-se, sair. 3) to walk away, afastar-se, sair. 4) to walk away with, levar consigo. 5) to walk over, ganhar por falta de competidores. 6) to walk out, saír. 7) to walk the dog, passear o cão. 8) to walk someone home, levar ou acompanhar alguém a casa. 9) *to walk the hospitals,* estagiar nos hospitais. 10) *to walk the boards,* pisar o palco, ser actor.

walkie-talkie, *s.* rádio portátil.

walking, *s.* acto de andar a pé; marcha, caminhada; passeio a pé; andar, modo de andar; caminho; procedimento; *adj.* que anda a pé, caminhante; ambulante.

walkover, *s.* vitória por desistência dos competidores; vitória fácil.

walk-up, *s.* edifício de apartamentos sem elevador.

walkway, *s.* passadiço.

walky-talky, *s.* o mesmo que *walkie-talkie.*

wall, *s.* parede, muro, muralha. 1) *to give someone the wall,* ceder, por cortesia, o lado de dentro da calçada; *adj.* mural, de parede. 2) *wall clock,* relógio de parede. 3) *wall rock,* rocha onde se encontra um filão; *v.t.* murar; emparedar.

wallaby, *s.* espécie de canguru.

wallaroo, *s.* canguru gigante.

wallet, *s.* carteira de bolso; pequeno estojo.

walleyed, *s.* que sofre de estrabismo divergente; zarolho; que tem os olhos arregalados.

wallflower, *s.* goivo amarelo; rapariga que não arranja par num baile.

wallonian, *s.* e *adj.* valão.

wallop, *s.* pancada forte, paulada; *v.i.* e *v.t.* mover-se desajeitadamente; rolar, espernear; ferver ruidosamente; surrar, sovar, espancar, desancar.

walloping, *s.* sova, surra, tareia.

wallow, *s.* chafurdeiro, lamaçal; chafurdice; *v.i.* chafurdar, espojar-se, rebolar-se, chapinhar; nadar; encapelar-se (vaga); jorrar.

wallpaper, *s.* papel de parede.

walnut, *s.* nogueira; noz; madeira de nogueira.

walrus, *s.* morsa.

waltz, *s.* valsa; *v.i.* valsar, dançar a valsa.

wan, *adj.* pálido, descorado, lívido; abatido, doentio, lânguido; escuro, sombrio; *v.i.* empalidecer.

wand, *s.* varinha, vara, bastão; ceptro; batuta; ponteiro; alvo para exercícios de arco.

wander, *v.i.* e *v.t.* vaguear, errar, viajar, passear; divagar, devanear, delirar; serpentear (rio); desviar-se, afastar-se; transviar-se, perder-se; percorrer, atravessar.

wanderer, *s.* viajante, caminhante, nómada, vagabundo, andarilho, peregrino.

wandering, *s.* vagabundagem; viagem; peregrinação; passeio; desvio, afastamento; divagação, devaneio; *adj.* errante, vagabundo, nómada; móvel, inconstante, incerto; sinuoso; delirante.

wane, *v.i.* minguar, diminuir; declinar, decair; aproximar-se do fim; empalidecer.

waness, *s.* palidez.

wangle, *v.i.* e *v.t.* livrar-se, desembaraçar-se; manobrar; sacudir, abanar; adulterar, falsificar; *s.* manobra, tramóia.

wanly, *adv.* palidamente, languidamente.

want, *s.* falta, carência, deficiência, escassez; penúria, privação; necessidade; *v.t.* e *v.i.* querer, desejar; requerer, exigir; ter falta de, não ter, carecer de, ter necessidade de, precisar de; sofrer privações.

wanting, *adj.* que falta, que se faz esperar, ausente, inexistente; insuficiente, deficiente, em falta; carente, desprovido, destituído; *to be wanting to one's duty,* não estar à altura do seu dever.

wanton, *adj.* brincalhão, folgazão, travesso; caprichoso; licencioso, lascivo, devasso; injustificado, gratuito; brutal, insolente, impiedoso; imoderado, extravagante, pródigo; (poét.) luxuriante, viçoso; *s.* pessoa libertina; criança travessa; *to play the wanton,* brincar; namoriscar; *v.i.* e *v.t.* brincar; comportar-se lascivamente; exceder-se; vadiar; esbanjar.

wapiti, *s.* espécie de veado norte-americano.

war, *s.* guerra, conflito, batalha. 1) *War Department (E.U.),* Ministério da Guerra. 2) *War Office* (Inglat.), Ministério da Guerra; *v.i.* e *v.t.* guerrear, fazer guerra; lutar, combater. 3) *to war down,* derrotar, submeter pela guerra.

warble, *s.* gorjeio, trinado, chilreio; larva de insecto; *v.t.* e *v.i.* gorjear, chilrear, trinar; murmurar, murmurejar; cantar.

warbler, *s.* cantor; ave canora.

ward, *s.* guarda, vigilância; custódia, protecção, tutela; pupilo, protegido; enfermaria; secção, divisão, ala; divisão administrativa de cidade; (arc.); pátio interior de castelo; *v.t.* guardar, proteger; aparar, desviar, evitar (golpe).

warden, *s.* director; administrador; governador; guardião, guarda.

warder, *s.* sentinela; carcereiro, guarda de prisão; guarda.

wardress, s. feminino de warder.

wardrobe, s. guarda-fato; guarda-roupa.

wardroom, s. sala dos oficiais dum navio de guerra.

wardship, s. tutela, protecção.

ware, s. produtos manufacturados; utensílios de uso diário; (pl.) mercadorias, produtos; louça, porcelana.

warehouse, s. armazém, depósito.

warfare, s. campanha, operações militares; guerra; luta, conflito.

warhead, s. ogiva de combate (de torpedo).

warily, adv. com cuidado, cautelosamente.

wariness, s. cautela, prudência.

warlike, adj. marcial, militar; guerreiro, bélico; hostil.

warlock, s. feiticeiro, mago, bruxo.

warm, adj. morno, tépido, quente, aquecido; cordial, franco, sincero, afável; caloroso; fervoroso; acalorado, ardente; to get warm, aquecer(-se); v.t. e v.i. aquecer(-se), esquentar; excitar; animar-se, entusiasmar--se.

warmhearted, adj. afectuoso, bondoso, afável.

warmish, adj. tépido.

warmness, s. tepidez; calor.

warmth, s. calor moderado, tepidez; ardor, vivacidade, fervor; entusiasmo; cordialidade; excitação.

warn, v.t. avisar, prevenir, advertir; informar; to warn someone away, off or from a place, avisar alguém para que se afaste de um lugar.

warning, s. aviso, advertência; conselho; notificação; alerta, alarme; to give a month's warning, despedir alguém com um mês de antecedência.

warp, s. urdidura, urdume; empenamento, arqueamento, deformação; aberração; (náut.) espia; v.t. e v.i. empenar, torcer, entorar, trabalhar, curvar; deformar; perverter; (tecel.) urdir.

warrant, s. autorização, ordem, permissão; justificação, razão, fundamento; testemunha; prova; garantia; ordem de pagamento; (jur.) mandato, ordem por escrito; v.t. justificar; autorizar; garantir; afiançar, responder por; atestar, confirmar.

warrantable, adj. autorisável, justificável.

warrantee, s. (jur.) aquele que recebe uma garantia.

warrantor, s. (jur.) aquele que presta garantia.

warranty, s. garantia de vendedor; justificação, fundamento.

warren, s. coutada, parque; coelheira.

warrener, s. couteiro.

warring, adj. em guerra; rival, contrário, oposto, incompatível.

warrior, s. guerreiro.

wart, s. verruga; wart hog, javali africano.

warty, adj. verrugoso.

warworn, adj. devastado pela guerra.

wary, adj. cauteloso, prudente, ponderado; desconfiado.

wash, v.t. e v.i. lavar(-se), banhar; limpar; molhar, inundar; levar, arrastar; cobrir com uma demão de tinta ou verniz; revestir com uma camada de ouro ou prata. 1) to wash out, rejeitar. 2) to wash down, acompanhar, engolir alimentos com bebida. 3) to wash ashore, lançar à praia, dar à costa. 4) to wash away, to wash down, ser desgastado pela água, sofrer erosão; s. lavagem; roupa lavada ou para lavar; (fig.) sensaboria, lengalenga; loção; ligeira camada de tinta; esfregaço; agitação das águas, marulho, embate das vagas; água levantada pelos remos; terreno alagadiço, pântano; vau (de estuário); aluvião; (av.) esteira, sulco; adj. lavável. 5) wash sale, venda fictícia de títulos para influenciar o mercado.

washable, adj. lavável.

washed-out, adj. desbotado; abatido, debilitado, desanimado; exausto.

washer, s. máquina de lavar; (mec.) anilha.

washhouse, s. lavandaria.

washing, s. lavagem, limpeza, ablução; banho; roupa para lavar, roupa suja; erosão, desgaste pela água; metal obtido pela lavagem de minério; washing machine, máquina de lavar.

washout, s. erosão, desmoronamento do leito de uma estrada provocado por inundação; (coloq.) fracasso total.

washroom, s. lavabo; quarto de banho de hotel.

washstand, s. lavatório.

washtub, s. tina para lavar roupa.

washy, adj. aguado, ralo, desenxabido; fraco, débil, difuso.

wasp, s. vespa.

waspish, adj. semelhante a vespa; que tem a cintura fina; irritadiço, susceptível; melindroso, rabugento; rancoroso.

wastage, s. quebra, perda, desperdício, desgaste.

waste, s. ermo, solidão; terra inculta, baldio; extensão, imensidade; desperdício, perda, esbanjamento; abundância; desgaste, declínio; resíduos, restos; sucata, lixo; *adj.* deserto, ermo, desabitado, inóspito, agreste; estéril, árido; inculto; vazio; sombrio, tétrico; inútil; perdido, excedente; *to lay waste,* devastar, assolar; *v.t.* e *v.i.* gastar (-se), consumir(-se), destruir; definhar, debilitar, abater; desperdiçar, esbanjar, perder(-se).

wasteful, *adj.* esbanjador, perdulário; devastador, destrutivo.

wasteness, s. desolação; improdutividade, esterilidade.

waster, s. gastador, esbanjador, pródigo; devastador; artigo com defeito de fabrico; (coloq.) vadio, inútil.

wasting, *adj.* destruidor, devastador; debilitante.

wastrel, gastador, esbanjador, perdulário; libertino; vadio, vagabundo; criança abandonada; artigo defeituoso; refugo.

watch, s. relógio; vigília, vela; vigilância, guarda; ronda; quarto de sentinela. 1) *to keep watch,* estar de guarda, guardar. 2) *watch and ward,* vigilância constante. 3) *watch guard,* corrente de relógio; *v.i.* e *v.t.* vigiar, velar, estar atento; montar guarda; observar, espreitar, prestar atenção a; atentar em; cuidar de; esperar, aguardar. 4) *to watch for,* esperar, estar à espera. 5) *to watch over,* zelar por, cuidar de. 6) *watch it!* tem cuidado!

watchdog, s. cão de guarda.

watcher, s. vigilante, guarda, vigia, sentinela.

watchful, *adj.* vigilante, alerta; observador, atento; esperto; cauteloso, prudente; desperto, de vigília.

watchhouse, s. casa da guarda.

watchmaker, s. relojoeiro.

watchtower, s. torre de vigia.

water, s. água. 1) *high, low water,* maré alta, maré baixa. 2) *in low waters,* em maré de baixo, em situação difícil. 3) *to make waters, to pass waters,* verter águas, urinar; *adj.* de água, relativo a água; hidráulico, hídrico; aquático; fluvial, marítimo. 4) *water bath,* banho-maria. 5) *Water Bearer,* (astron.) Aquário. 6) *water blister,* bolha na pele. 7) *water brake,* travão hidráulico. 8) *water brash,* azia. 9) *water carrier,* aguadeiro. 10) *water closet,* sanita, retrete.

11) *water colour,* aguarela. 12) *water gap,* passagem de um curso de água por uma garganta entre duas montanhas. 13) *water hen,* galinha de água. 14) *water lily,* nenúfar. 15) *water sick,* (agric.) saturado de água; *v.t.* e *v.i.* molhar, regar; dar de beber a, dessedentar(-se); banhar, irrigar; aguar, diluir, misturar água a; encher-se de água, salivar; lacrimejar. 16) *to water down,* atenuar, diluir.

waterfall, s. catarata, queda de água, cascata.

waterfowl, s. ave aquática.

wateriness, s. aquosidade; humidade; insipidez.

watering, s. 1) *watering place,* bebedouro, aguada. 2) *watering can,* regador.

waterish, *adj.* aguado, aquoso, diluído; fraco; insípido; húmido, vaporoso.

waterlogged, *adj.* alagado, saturado de água, encharcado.

watermelon, s. melancia.

waterproof, *adj.* impermeável, à prova de água; *v.t.* impermeabilizar.

waterside, s. margem de rio, lago, etc.; beira-mar; *adj.* ribeirinho.

waterspout, s. bica, gárgula; (meteor.) tromba de água.

watertight, *adj.* estanque, impermeável; explícito, inequívoco.

waterway, s. via navegável; canal.

waterwork, s. repuxo, chafariz; oficina hidráulica; *to turn on the waterworks,* chorar, abrir a torneira.

watery, *adj.* aguado; diluído, fraco, pálido; insípido, desenxabido; fluido; húmido; pantanoso; chuvoso; choroso.

wattle, s. armação de vergas; latada, estacaria de varas; caniçada; vergas, vimes; barbela de galinha; *v.t.* amarrar com vimes; cercar com vimes; cobrir com entrançado de varas; entrançar, entrelaçar (vimes).

waul, *v.i.* soltar grito agudo; miar (o gato), vagir.

wave, s. onda, vaga; ondulação, ondeado, sinuosidade; aceno, sinal feito com a mão; gesto; oscilação; afluência, maré; *v.i.* e *v.t.* ondular, ondear; drapejar, agitar(-se), oscilar; acenar, agitar a mão; abanar, brandir, vibrar; acenar a, fazer sinal com a mão a; *to wave aside,* pôr de lado, rejeitar.

waver, *v.i.* hesitar, vacilar; ceder terreno, recuar; ondular; tremer, vibrar; flutuar; s. hesitação; tremor.

wavering, *adj.* hesitante, vacilante; oscilante.

wavy, *adj.* ondulado, ondeado, cheio de ondas, agitado; sinuoso, ondulante; vacilante; instável.

wax, *s.* cera; cerúmen; lacre; acesso de cólera, fúria. 1) *wax cloth,* encerado, oleado. 2) *wax tree,* árvore da cera; *v.t.* encerar.

wax, *v.i.* crescer (a lua); aumentar, engrandecer(-se), prosperar; tornar-se, fazer-se.

waxberry, *s.* árvore da cera ou o seu fruto.

waxen, *adj.* de cera, céreo; encerado, polido, brilhante; plástico, moldável; pálido; impressionável.

waxwing, *s.* (zool.) âmpelis.

waxy, *adj.* de cera, ceroso, ceráceo; viscoso, adesivo, pegajoso; mole, moldável, impressionável; encerado; irritadiço.

way, *s.* caminho, via, estrada; rua, avenida, alameda; passagem; rumo, rota; direcção, sentido, lado; caminhada, viagem; carreira; impulso, velocidade, ímpeto, andamento; seguimento; percurso, trajectória; distância; modo, maneira, método, meio, processo, jeito; vontade, desejo; costume, hábito, moda, tendência, maneira de ser, mania; natureza, género, espécie; ramo de actividade, negócio, profissão; nível de vida; estado, situação, condição; meios, possibilidade; *pl.* carreira de construção de navios. 1) *way in,* entrada. 2) *way out,* saída. 3) *to clear the way,* desobstruir o caminho. 4) *to stand in the way,* atrapalhar, estorvar. 5) *either way,* de uma maneira ou de outra. 6) *to be on one's way, to be on the way,* ir a caminho. 7) *on the way back:,* de regresso, de volta, ao voltar. 8) *to make one's way,* fazer carreira, progredir. 9) *to gather way,* ganhar velocidade. 10) *to go a long way,* percorrer uma grande distância. 11) *way of life, way of living,* modo de vida. 12) *to get one's own way,* conseguir o que se quer. 13) *to change one's ways,* mudar de hábitos. 14) *in some ways,* sob certos aspectos. 15) *to go the way off all flesh, of all the nature,* pagar o tributo à natureza, morrer. 16) *where there is a will, there is a way,* querer é poder. 17) *to be in the family way,* estar grávida. 18) *to be in a great way,* estar agitado. 19) *by the way,* a propósito; de caminho, de passagem. 20) *by way of,* por via de; para servir de. 21) *out of the way,* longe, distante, remoto; inconveniente, impróprio. 22) *to get out of the way,* sair da

frente, tirar do caminho, afastar(-se). 23) *to go out of one's way to do something,* dar-se o trabalho de fazer alguma coisa. 24) *to know one's way about,* saber orientar-se numa localidade. 25) *to make way,* abrir caminho; avançar, progredir. 26) *to pay one's way,* fazer frente às despesas. 27) *under way,* a caminho, em movimento, em andamento. 28) *to lead the way,* ir à frente, liderar. 29) *way train,* comboio que pára em quase todas as estações. 30) *ways and means,* meios, recursos.

waybill, *s.* guia de marcha.

wayfarer, *s.* viajante, caminhante.

wayfaring, *s.* viagem ou viagens, jornada(s), peregrinação; *adj.* viajante, viandante.

waygoing, *s.* partida, despedida; *adj.* que parte; *waygoing crop,* (jur.) colheita que o rendeiro tem o direito de levar consigo ao terminar o arrendamento.

waylay, *v.t.* (conjuga-se como *lay*) armar emboscada; atacar de surpresa.

waylayer, *s.* assaltante emboscado.

wayward, *adj.* desobediente, obstinado; intratável, caprichoso; errante, inconstante, instável.

we, *pron.* nós.

weak, *adj.* fraco, débil, frágil, delicado, debilitado; brando, maleável; indeciso, vacilante; medíocre, insuficiente.

weaken, *v.t.* e *v.i.* enfraquecer(-se), debilitar, diminuir, reduzir, atenuar, fraquejar.

weakling, *s.* pessoa ou animal fraco; *adj.* fraco, débil.

weakness, *s.* fraqueza, debilidade.

weal, *s.* bem-estar, felicidade, prosperidade.

weald, *s.* região florestal do Sudeste de Inglaterra.

wealth, *s.* riqueza; bens, fortuna; abundância, fartura, exuberância: saúde, bem-estar, prosperidade.

wealthy, *adj.* rico, abastado; próspero, florescente, saudável.

wean, *v.t.* desmamar; desacostumar, desabituar; afastar, apartar, emancipar; *to wean someone from a habit,* curar alguém de um hábito.

weanling, *s.* criança ou animal recém-desmamado.

weapon, *s.* arma; *pl.* armas, armamento.

weaponless, *adj.* desarmado, sem armas; indefeso.

wear, *s.* uso, acto de usar; artigos próprios para determinado uso; artigos de vestuário;

desgaste, estragos, deterioração causada pelo uso; durabilidade, resistência. 1) *men's wear,* roupas para homem. 2) *clothes for summer wear,* roupas de Verão; *v.t.* e *v.i. pret.* wore, *pp.* worn; usar, vestir(-se), trazer; ter, andar com, mostrar, ostentar; gastar(-se), consumir, desgastar, apagar, deteriorar; fatigar, cansar, debilitar, esgotar; enfraquecer, debilitar, declinar, definhar; resistir ao uso, ser durável, durar; (náut.) virar em roda. 3) *to wear down,* gastar, consumir ou diminuir devido ao uso, ao atrito, etc.. 4) *to wear off,* usar(-se), gastar (-se), desaparecer, enfraquecer. 5) *to wear out,* gastar, deteriorar, desgastar pelo uso; cansar, estafar. 6) *to wear well,* durar, ser durável ou resistente. 7) *to wear one'sheart on one's sleeve,* ter o coração nas mãos. 8) *to wear the King's coat,* servir no exército.

wearily, *adv.* com enfado; com fadiga.

weariness, *s.* cansaço, fadiga; desgaste; tédio, enfado.

wearing, *adj.* fatigante, cansativo; desgastante, sujeito a atrito; de uso.

wearisome, *adj.* enfadonho, aborrecido; cansativo.

weary, *adj.* cansado, fatigado, exausto; abatido; farto, enfastiado, aborrecido; *v.t.* e *v.i.* cansar(-se), fatigar(-se); entediar(-se), aborrecer(-se).

weasel, *s.* doninha.

weather, *s.* tempo, estado atmosférico; clima; (náut.) barlavento. 1) *to keep one's weather eye open,* estar alerta, precaver-se. 2) *under the weather,* (coloq.) adoentado, indisposto, em apuros. 3) *weather bound,* retido pelo mau tempo. 4) *weather deck,* (náut.) convés corrido. 5) *weather forecast,* previsão meteorológica. 6) *weather strip,* fita isoladora usada para cafetar portas ou janelas. 7) *weather vane,* cata-vento. 8) *weather wise,* hábil a prever o tempo; *v.t.* e *v.i.* expor ao ar; aguentar ou resistir a tempestade; superar, vencer (dificuldades); suportar a acção do tempo; desgastar-se pela acção do tempo; (náut.) pôr-se a barlavento de, dobrar cabo.

weatherboarding, *s.* tábuas sobrepostas que servem de telhado.

weathercock, *s.* cata-vento, ventoinha, grimpa.

weathered, *adj.* descorado, desgastado pela acção do tempo; (arquit.) inclinado para dar escoamento às águas.

weatherglass, *s.* barómetro.

weathering, *s.* alteração, descoloração, desgaste pela acção do tempo; inclinação a fim de dar escoamento à água.

weatherman, *s.* meteorologista.

weave, *v.t.* e *v.i.* tecer, entrelaçar(-se), entrançar(-se); entremear; urdir, criar, compor; ter o ofício de tecelão; avançar dando voltas.

weaver, *s.* tecelão.

web, *s.* teia, tecido; rede, trama, conjunto, série, sistema; membrana interdigital; folha de serra; bobina, rolo de papel contínuo; braço (de manivela); *web-footed,* palmípede; *v.t.* envolver com teia; cercar, rodear; enredar; unir os dedos com membrana.

webbed, *adj.* palmípede; provido de membrana interdigital.

wed, *v.t.* e *v.i.* casar(-se), desposar; unir, juntar, ligar.

wedding, *s.* casamento, boda, núpcias, união, enlace.

wedge, *s.* cunha, calço; chaveta; *v.t.* rachar com cunha, calçar com cunha, meter cunha em; introduzir à força, entalar, encravar.

wedlock, *s.* matrimónio, casamento, vida conjugal.

wednesday, *s.* quarta-feira.

wee, *adj.* pequenino, minúsculo; *the wee folk,* as fadas.

weed, *s.* erva daninha; pessoa ou coisa prejudicial; (fam.) tabaco, charuto; sinal de luto; *v.t.* limpar de ervas daninhas, mondar; extirpar, eliminar.

weeder, *s.* mondador; sacho, sachola.

weedy, *adj.* daninho, inútil; cheio de ervas daninhas.

week, *s.* semana.

week-end, *s.* fim de semana.

weekly, *adv.* semanalmente, uma vez por semana; *adj.* semanal, hebdomadário; *s.* semanário, publicação semanal.

weep, *v.i.* e *v.t. pret.* e *pp.* wept; chorar, prantear, carpir, lastimar, lamentar; verter (lágrimas); exsudar, gotejar.

weeper, *s.* carpideira; fumo, canhão branco usado no punho da manga, em sinal de luto; véu de viúva.

weeping, *adj.* que chora, choroso; gotejante; pendente; *weeping willow,* (bot.) chorão; *s.* choro, pranto; exsudação.

weever, *s.* (zool.) peixe-aranha.

weevil, *s.* gorgulho.

weft, *s.* (tecel.) trama; tecido.

weigh, *v.t.* e *v.i.* pesar, ter peso; suspender; levantar âncora, levantar ferro; ponderar, considerar. 1) *to weigh down*, exceder em peso; oprimir; vergar pelo peso. 2) *to weigh in*, averiguar o peso do jóquei antes da corrida. 3) *to weigh up*, elevar, fazer subir pela força do peso; *s.* pesagem.

weight, *s.* peso; gravidade; importância; ponderação; consequência. 1) *by weight*, a peso. 2) *balance weight*, contrapeso. 3) *net weight*, peso líquido. 4) *stamped weight*, peso aferido. 5) *weight of metal*, peso total de metal atirado numa descarga das peças de um navio; *v.i.* pôr peso em, carregar com peso, lastrar; sobrecarregar, oprimir; dar peso a; ponderar.

weighty, *adj.* pesado; denso; de peso, importante, sério; influente; opressivo, penoso.

weir, *s.* represa, açude; caniçada para pesca.

weird, *adj.* estranho; esquisito; misterioso, fantástico, sobrenatural; fatídico; *Weird Sisters,* as Três Parcas; bruxas; *s.* destino, fado, sorte.

welcome, *adj.* bem-vindo, bem recebido; grato, agradável. 1) *you are welcome to do it*, tenho muito gosto em que o faça, convido-o a fazê-lo. 2) *you are welcome*, não tem de quê (resposta a um agradecimento); *s.* boas-vindas, recepção cordial, acolhimento; *v.t.* dar as boas-vindas, receber ou saudar alguém; acolhimento.

weld, *v.t.* soldar; caldear; unir, fundir, consolidar; *s.* solda, soldadura, caldeamento; (bot.) lírio-dos-tintureiros.

welding, *s.* solda; caldeamento.

weldment, *s.* soldadura, soldagem.

weldor, *s.* soldador.

welfare, *s.* bem-estar, saúde; felicidade; prosperidade; *welfare institution*, instituição de beneficência.

welkin, *s.* (poét.) céu.

well, *s.* poço; fonte, nascente; (náut.) arca de bomba; porão (num barco); vão no centro de uma escadaria; cavidade; remoinho. 1) *well deck*, (náut.) parte do convés entre os castelos. 2) *well room*, sala em que se distribui a água das fontes minerais. 3) *well head*, mãe-d`água; *v.i.* manar, brotar, nascer. 4) *to well up*, crescer, avolumar-se.

well, *adj.* bom, de boa saúde; satisfatório; feliz; conveniente, próprio; vantajoso, útil; em boas relações; *adv.* bem; muito; favoravelmente; convenientemente; completamente; devidamente. 1) *well done!*, muito bem, bravo! 2) *well met!*, bons olhos o vejam! 3) *as well as*, tão bem como; tão ... como, tanto ... como, não só ... mas também; 4) *just as well*, igualmente bem. 5) *well accomplished*, consumado, perfeito. 6) *well acquainted*, bem relacionado. 7) *well doing*, beneficência. 8) *well mannered*, com boas maneiras, educado. 9) *to be well off*, ser rico, estar vem na vida. 10) *to be well up in*, ser muito versado em. 11) *it may well be that ...*, é bem possível que; *interj.* bem! Bom! Ora! 12) *well then!*, Então! Bem, pois bem!

well-to-do, *adj.* próspero, abastado.

welsh, welch, *v.t.* e *v.i.* fugir sem pagar as apostas.

Welsh, *adj.* e *s.* galês.

welt, *s.* orla, debrum; vira de calçado; vinco, vergão; *v.t.* debruar; pôr vira em calçado; açoitar.

welter, *v.i.* espojar-se, chafurdar, rebolar-se; agitar-se, alvoroçar-se, encapelar-se (o mar); estar em tumulto; *s.* confusão; agitação, tumulto; *welter weight*, peso adicional imposto a cavalos de corridas.

wen, *s.* lobinho, tumor, quisto.

wench, *s.* moça, rapariga; criada; camponesa; meretriz; *v.i.* frequentar prostitutas.

wend, *v.t.* e *v.i.* encaminhar-se, dirigir-se.

went, *pret.* de *go.*

wept, *pret.* de *weep.*

werewolf, *s.* lobisomem.

west, *s.* oeste, ocidente, poente; *adj.* ocidental, de oeste.

wester, *v.i.* dirigir-se para oeste; declinar (o sol); *s.* vento de oeste.

westerly, *adj.* de oeste, ocidental; *adv.* em direcção a oeste, para oeste.

western, *adj.* ocidental, de oeste, proveniente do oeste; *s.* filme sobre o Oeste americano.

wasterner, *s.* habitante do Ocidente, ocidental.

westernmost, *adj.* o mais ocidental.

westward, *adv.* para oeste, em direcção a oeste; *adj.* situado a oeste, ocidental; voltado para oeste.

wet, *adj.* molhado, húmido; chuvoso; *wet blanket*, desmancha-prazeres; *s.* humidade; tempo chuvoso; orvalho, relento; aquele que é contrário à Lei Seca; trago de bebida. *v.t.* e *v.i.* molhar(-se), humedecer(-se).

wetness, s. humidade, lentura.

whack, v.t. golpear; derrotar; repartir, partilhar, dividir; s. golpe, pancada; varada, bengalada; parte, quinhão; to take a whack at, experimentar.

whacker, s. coisa ou pessoa muito grande; grande mentira.

whale, s. baleia; whale bone, barba de baleia; v.i. pescar baleias; v.t. espancar, vergastar.

whaleboat, s. baleeira.

whaler, s. baleeiro; baleeira; pescador de baleias.

whang, v.t. e v.i. bater com força, espancar; ressoar, zunir; s. pancada, golpe.

wharf, s. desembarcadouro, cais, molhe; muralha; v.t. colocar ou descarregar no cais; atracar.

wharfage, s. acostagem, direitos pagos pela utilização de um cais.

what, pron. interr. que; o quê? que coisa? 1) what are you saying?, que dizes? 2) what do you call that flower?, como se chama aquela flor? 3) what is this for?, para que serve isto? 4) what next?, que se segue? 5) what else?, que mais? 6) what for?, para quê? pron. relat. o que, aquilo que, a coisa que, as coisas que; 7) to give someone what for (coloq.): castigar alguém; adj. relat. o, a, os, as, aquele ou aquela que, aqueles ou aquelas que; 8) give me what help you can, dê-me a ajuda que puder; adj. inter. qual? que? que espécie de? quão grande? 9) what countries have you visited?, que países visitou? conj. que; adv. em parte; em que; 10) what by ignorance, what by fear, em parte por ignorância, em parte por medo; s. coisa, objecto; interj. que! como!

whatever, pron. e adj. qualquer coisa que, tudo o que, o que quer que, seja o que for; por mais que.

whatnot, s. estante, papeleira.

whatsoever, pron. e adj. forma enfática de whatever.

wheal, s. vergão, estria; (med.) pápula.

wheat, s. trigo.

wheaten, adj. de trigo.

wheedle, v.t. enganar com lisonjas, seduzir, engodar, adular.

wheel, s. roda; bicicleta, triciclo; rotação, revolução; volta; cambalhota. 1) steering wheel, volante, leme. 2) on wheels, sobre rodas, facilmente; v.t. e v.i. rodar, girar, voltear; virar(-se), voltar(-se); mover-se em círculo; empurrar veículo de rodas; andar de bicicleta, pedalar.

wheelbarrow, s. carrinho de mão.

wheeler, s. o que roda ou faz rodar; carro de rodas.

wheelhouse, s. (náut.) casa do leme.

wheeze, v.i. respirar com dificuldade, arfar.

wheezy, adj. ofegante, asmático; sibilante, roufenho.

whelk, s. espinha, pústula; búzio.

whelm, v.t. submergir, soterrar; oprimir, esmagar.

whelp, s. cachorro; cria de alguns animais ferozes; v.i. parir.

when, adv. conj. quando, no momento em que, logo que; ao passo que, embora, conquanto.

whence, adv. donde, de que lugar, de que fonte, como, de que modo, por isso.

whencesoever, adv. e conj. donde quer que, seja donde for que.

whenever, adv. e conj. em qualquer tempo que, sempre que, todas as vezes que, quando.

where, adv. onde, em que, em que lugar; aonde, para onde.

whereabout, adv. e conj. perto ou próximo; onde, perto de que? a respeito de que?

whereabouts, s. paradeiro; adv. perto, próximo, onde?

whereas, conj. considerando que, atendendo a que; quando, enquanto, ao passo que.

whereat, adv. a que, ao qual, para o qual; no qual, em que, onde; ao que, por causa do que.

whereby, adv. pelo qual, por meio do qual, de acordo com o qual, junto ao qual.

wherefore, adv. e conj. porquê? por que razão? para quê? pelo qual, em consequência do qual; por isso, por consequência; s. razão, motivo, causa.

wherefrom, adv. donde? de que, do qual; donde, de que lugar?

wherein, adv. em que, em que ponto; no qual, onde.

whereinto, adv. a que, ao qual, em que, no qual.

whereof, adv. de que, do que, de que?

whereon, adv. sobre que, em que; sobre o qual, no qual.

wheresoever, adv. e conj. onde quer que, em qualquer parte que, seja onde for que; a onde quer que.

whereto, *adv.* a que, para quê? aonde, para onde? ao qual, a que.

whereupon, *adv.* sobre quê, a respeito de quê? sobre o qual, no qual, em que; ao que, em consequência do que, e então.

wherever, *adv.* e *conj.* onde quer que, em qualquer parte que, seja onde for que; aonde quer que; em qualquer caso que; sempre que.

wherewith(al), *adv.* com que, com o qual, por meio do qual; com quê?

wherry, *s.* bote, barco; *v.t.* e *v.i.* transportar em bote.

whet, *v.t.* afiar, aguçar, amolar; estimular, excitar; *s.* estimulante, estímulo; aperitivo.

whetter, *s.* amolador.

whether, *conj.* e *adv.* se; quer ... quer; ou ... ou; *whether or no,* em todo o caso; *pron. rel.* e *int.* qual dos dois.

whetstone, *s.* pedra de amolar.

whey, *s.* soro de leite coalhado.

which, *adj. int.* qual, quais, qual ou quais dos, que (indica escolha); *adj. rel.* o qual, os quais, que, esse(s); *pron. int.* qual, quais; *pron. rel.* que, o qual, os quais, o que, cujo.

whichever, *adj.* e *pron.* qualquer que, quaisquer que, seja qual for, qualquer.

whiff, *s.* sopro, baforada, lufada; espécie de bote de corrida; *v.t.* lançar baforadas; soprar.

whiffle, *v.i.* e *v.i.* soprar, bafejar; mudar (o vento), virar, girar rodar; divagar (o pensamento); palpitar, bruxulear; *s.* aragem.

whiffler, *s.* pessoa frívola e volúvel; ventoinha; (hist.) batedor que ia à frente de um cortejo.

whig, *s.* membro de um partido político surgido após a revolução de 1688 e que foi substituído em meados do séc. XIX pelos Liberais.

whiggery, *s.* princípios dos "whigs".

while, *s.* tempo, espaço de tempo; *conj.* enquanto; ainda que, embora; *v.t.* passar, entreter o tempo.

whilst, *conj.* o mesmo que *while.*

whim, *s.* capricho, fantasia, extravagância; espécie de sarilho ou cabrestante accionado por cavalos para fazer subir o carvão do fundo da mina.

whimper, *s.* lamúria, choradeira; *v.i.* e *v.t.* choramingar, lamuriar-se.

whimperer, *s.* choramingão, choramingas.

whimsical, *adj.* caprichoso, extravagante.

whimzy, *adj.* caprichoso, volúvel; *s.* capricho, extravagância, veneta.

whin, *s.* urze, tojo.

whine, *v.i.* e *v.t.* queixar-se, lamuriar, gemer, lamentar-se; ganir (o cão); *s.* queixume, lamento, gemido; ganido (do cão).

whining, *adj.* lamentoso, lamuriento, gemebundo.

whinny, *v.i.* e *v.t.* relinchar; *s.* relincho.

whinstone, *s.* designação de certos tipos de rochas duras.

whip, *s.* chicote, açoite, vergasta; cocheiro; *(Parl. Inglês)* chefe de bancada com a função de garantir a presença dos membros do seu grupo parlamentar nas votações. 1) *to have the wip hand of,* ter vantagem sobre, dominar; *v.t.* chicotear, vergastar, açoitar; castigar; mover, agarrar ou puxar súbita e vigorosamente, arrebatar; pescar com isco artificial; enrolar, revestir com fio; bater natas, claras, etc. 2) *to ship off or away,* escorraçar ou expulsar com chicotadas ou à força; *v.i.* mover-se rapidamente ou com agilidade.

whippet, *s.* cão treinado para corridas.

whipping, *s.* flagelação, vergastadas. 1) *whipping boy,* menino que era educado com um príncipe e recebia os castigos em lugar dele; bode-expiatório. 2) *whipping post,* pelourinho.

whipsaw, *s.* serra braçal para cortar madeira nos dois sentidos.

whipster, *s.* criança; fedelho.

whir, *s.* zumbido, zunzum, sussurro, zunido, chiado; *v.i.* zumbir, zunir, sussurrar, chiar; esvoaçar.

whirl, *s.* remoinho, turbilhão, vórtice; giro, volteio, rodopio; corropio, precipitação, confusão, tumulto; *v.i.* e *v.t.* girar, rodar, rodopiar, remoinhar; precipitar-se, lançar-se, arremessar.

whirlabout, *s.* volteio, rodopio, turbilhão.

whirlpool, *s.* remoinho de água, voragem.

whirlwind, *s.* remoinho de vento; furacão, tufão.

whish, *v.i.* zunir, sibilar; farfalhar.

whisk, *s.* movimento rápido, sopro repentino; tufo de pêlos; batedor de ovos; *v.t.* e *v.i.* mover-se rapidamente, arremessar-se; levar, carregar, tirar rapidamente; bater (ovos, natas, etc.); dar uma escovadela a; brandir, agitar, sacudir.

whisker, *s.* (pl.) bigodes; *side whiskers,* suíças.

whisky, whiskey, s. uísque; antiga carruagem de duas rodas.

whisper, s. sussurro, murmúrio; cochicho, segredo, rumor; v.t. e v.i. murmurar, sussurrar, segredar; cochichar, bisbilhotar.

whispering, adj. murmurante, sussurrante; bisbilhoteiro, maledicente; s. murmúrio, sussurro; rumor.

whist, s. jogo de cartas.

whistle, s. assobio, apito; silvo, zunido; chamado; (coloq.) garganta, boca; v.i. e v.t. assobiar; sibilar; zunir; apitar; piar (algumas aves). 1) *let him go whistle,* ele que se lixe. 2) *to whistle for,* desejar em vão.

whistling, adj. que assobia, sibilante.

whit, s. porção mínima, pouquinho.

white, s. branco, brancura, alvura; clara de ovo; branco do olho, esclerótica; homem ou mulher branca; (pl. med.) flores brancas, leucorreia; adj. branco, alvo; pálido, descorado; inocente; feliz. 1) *white feather,* sinal de cobardia. 2) *white horses,* ondas de crista branca. 3) *white lead,* alvaiade de chumbo. 4) *white lie,* mentira inocente. 5) *white-livered,* pálido; covarde. 6) *white slaver,* traficante de escravas brancas. 7) *white war,* guerra económica. 8) *white whale,* beluga.

white-collar, s. empregado de escritório.

whitewash, s. cal para caiar, leite de cal, caiação; falso colorido, falsa aparência, cosmético; v.t. caiar; encobrir as faltas; reabilitar.

whitewing, s. pessoa que usa uniforme branco.

wither, adv. aonde, para onde; a que, ao qual; até que onde, até onde, até quando, com que fim, para quê? s. destino.

whiting, s. pescada marlonga; cré, branco de gesso; *whiting pout,* faneca.

whitish, adj. esbranquiçado.

whitsunday, s. Domingo de Pentecostes.

whittle, v.t. e v.i. cortar, aparar, desbastar, entalhar, esculpir (madeira); s. faca de trinchar.

whity, s. esbranquiçado.

whiz, v.t. e v.i. zunir, sibilar, zumbir; passar zunindo, fazer zunir, vibrar com força; s. zunido, zumbido, silvo.

who, pron. rel. e int. que, quem, o qual, a qual, os quais, as quais, aquele ou aquela que, aqueles ou aquelas que.

whodunit, s. (E.U.) novela ou filme policial.

whoever, pron. rel. com significado indefinido, quem quer que, todo aquele que, seja quem for, qualquer.

whole, adj. todo, total, completo, inteiro; são, intacto, ileso; s. o todo, o total, totalidade, conjunto. 1) *as a whole,* como um todo, em conjunto. 2) *in whole,* no todo, totalmente, inteiramente. 3) *on the whole,* de um modo geral, em geral.

wholeheartedly, adv. sinceramente, de todo o coração.

wholeness, s. integridade, unidade, perfeição.

wholesale, s. venda por atacado; adj. por atacado, por junto, extenso.

wholesaler, s. vendedor por atacado.

wholesome, adj. são, saudável, sadio, higiénico; salutar, benéfico; favorável; seguro, que não é perigoso.

wholesomeness, s. salubridade; sanidade; condições higiénicas, segurança.

wholly, adv. inteiramente, por completo; absolutamente; exclusivamente.

whom, pron. rel. e int. complemento de *who,* que, quem, o qual, a qual, os quais, as quais.

whoop, s. grito, algazarra; expressão de entusiasmo; v.i. e v.t. gritar; apupar, vaiar; piar (o mocho); *whipping cough,* tosse convulsa.

whop, v.t. sovar, surrar, espancar; v.i. deixar-se cair, atirar-se.

whopper, s. coisa enorme, colosso; grande mentira.

whore, s. prostituta; v.i. prostituir-se.

whoredom, s. prostituição, devassidão.

whorish, adj. devasso, libertino.

whorl, s. (bot.) verticilo; espira, voluta.

whorled, adj. espiralado; (bot.) verticilado.

whortleberry, s. uva-do-monte.

whose, caso possessivo do pron. rel. e int. *who,* do qual, da qual, dos quais, das quais, de quem, cujo, cuja, cujos, cujas; é também utilizado como caso possessivo de *which.*

whoso, pron. rel. indef. quem quer que seja, todo aquele que, seja quem for.

why, adv. porquê? por que razão? conj. porque; interj. ora! ora essa! como! s. o porquê, causa, motivo.

wick, s. mecha, pavio, torcida.

wicked, adj. mau, perverso, malvado; feio, imoral; prejudicial; desagradável, repulsivo.

wicker, s. vime.

wicket, s. postigo, portinhola; cancela; (críquete) meta formada por três postes paralelos sobre os quais assentam, duas travessas horizontais; tempo durante o qual o batedor defende a meta.

wide, *adj.* largo; vasto, amplo, espaçoso, grande; aberto, escancarado; extenso, geral, variado; liberal, tolerante; remoto, desviado; *wide ball,* (críquete) bola que passa fora do alcance do batedor; *s.* extensão, vastidão, amplitude; largura; *adv.* longe, a grande distância, amplamente, por toda a parte; muito, com grande distância.

widely, *adv.* amplamente, largamente; grandemente, muito.

widen, *v.t.* e *v.i.* alargar(-se), ampliar(-se), estender(-se), aumentar.

widgeon, *s.* pato marreco.

widow, *s.* viúva; *v.t.* enviuvar, tornar viúvo; privar, despojar.

widower, *s.* viúvo.

widowhood, *s.* viuvez.

width, *s.* largura; amplitude, vastidão, extensão; tolerância.

wield, *v.t.* empunhar, brandir, manejar; dominar, exercer domínio sobre.

wieldy, *adj.* manejável, dirigível.

wife, *s.* esposa, mulher.

wifehood, *s.* condição de esposa, estado de casada.

wig, *s.* cabeleira postiça, capachinho, chinó, peruca; *v.t.* pôr peruca em; repreender, ralhar.

wigging, *s.* repreensão, descompostura.

wiggle, *v.t.* e *v.i.* menear(-se), sacudir(-se), agitar(-se); serpear; *s.* meneio, sacudidela.

wiggly, *adj.* serpeante, coleante; tortuoso.

wight, *s.* criatura, ser, ente; *adj.* bravo, valente; forte, ágil.

wigwag, *v.t.* e *v.i.* agitar(-se), sacudir(-se), menear(-se); (mil. e náut.) sinalizar, enviar sinais; *s.* (mil. náut.) sinalização através de bandeirola ou lanterna; mensagem.

wild, *adj.* selvagem, bravo, bravio, silvestre; feroz; deserto, ermo, inóspito; inculto, agreste, árido; simples, rústico, espontâneo; incivilizado, bárbaro; rebelde; em desordem, desordenado; violento, tempestuoso; tumultuoso, desenfreado; impetuoso, ardente, apaixonado; travesso, barulhento; desregrado, dissoluto; irritado, encolerizado, furioso; fantástico, extravagante, insensato; ao acaso, à sorte. 1) *to run wild,* viver uma vida desregrada; voltar ao estado selvagem. 2) *to sow one's wild oats,* fazer as extravagâncias próprias da mocidade;

adv. ao acaso, à toa; irreflectidamente, incoerentemente; descontroladamente; *s.* região selvagem e inculta; ermo.

wildcat, *s.* gato selvagem, gato montês; lince; *adj.* estouvado, inseguro, insensato; ilegítimo, ilícito.

wildebeest, *s.* gnu.

wilder, *v.t.* e *v.i.* extraviar(-se), perder(-se), desencaminhar; desorientar, aturdir.

wilderness, *s.* vastidão selvagem, região inculta, deserto, ermo, selva; imensidão, vastidão.

wildfire, *s.* fogo-fátuo; relâmpago sem trovão.

wilding, *s.* planta bravia; *adj.* selvagem, silvestre, bravio.

wildly, *adv.* insensatamente, loucamente; desregradamente; tumultuosamente; furiosamente, impetuosamente, desordenadamente; extremamente; espontaneamente; selvaticamente; rudemente.

wildness, *s.* estado selvagem; rusticidade, espontaneidade; selvajaria, ferocidade, brutalidade; rebeldia; licenciosidade; ardor, veemência, impetuosidade; insensatez; loucura.

wile, *s.* astúcia, manha, ardil, estratagema; *v.t.* atrair, iludir.

will, *s.* vontade; arbítrio; desejo; intenção, propósito; testamento. 1) *at will,* à vontade, onde ou quando se quiser, à disposição. 2) *with a will,* resolutamente; *v.t.* querer, determinar, decidir; tencionar fazer; controlar, persuadir; dispor ou deixar em testamento, legar; *v.i.* querer; exercer a sua vontade. 3) *God willing,* se Deus quiser.

will, *v.* auxiliar do futuro; pret. *would.* na 1ª pessoa exprime vontade, intenção ou determinação, sendo a futuridade expressa nessa pessoa por *shall.* Na 2ª e 3ª pessoas *will* exprime apenas futuridade ou certeza, perdendo a ideia de vontade, intenção ou desejo. *would* aparece na formação do *conj.* e cond. e também se emprega em frases optativas, tendo, neste último caso, a força de verbo independente.

willed, *adj.* determinado pela vontade, voluntário; que tem vontade.

willful, *adj.* voluntário, intencional, propositado, deliberado; voluntarioso, obstinado.

willies, *s. pl.* nervosismo; *to get the willies,* ficar com nervoso miudinho.

willing, *adj.* disposto, pronto; condescendente, complacente, indulgente, dócil; solícito; voluntário.

willingly, *adv.* de boa vontade, com gosto.

willingness, *s.* disposição, boa vontade; voluntariedade.

will-o'-the-wisp, *s.* fogo-fátuo; pessoa misteriosa de paradeiro incerto; *adj.* fantástico, misterioso.

willow, *s.* salgueiro; bastão de críquete; máquina de limpar algodão, lã, etc.

willy-nilly, *adv.* de boa ou má vontade.

wilt, *v.i.* e *v.t.* murchar; esmorecer; encolher (-se).

wilt, 2ª pessoa do sing. do pres. ind. de *will* (v. aux. do futuro).

wily, *adj.* manhoso, astuto, ardiloso, matreiro.

wimble, *s.* verruma; *v.t.* verrumar, perfurar.

wimple, *s.* touca de freira; flâmula, galhardete; *v.t.* cobrir com touca; velar, pôr véu em; *v.i.* ondear, encrespar-se ligeiramente.

win, *pret.* e *pp.* won. *v.t.* e *v.i.* ganhar, adquirir, alcançar, conseguir, obter, lograr; persuadir, induzir, atrair, arrastar, cativar, conquistar; prevalecer; conseguir, chegar, passar. 1) *to win someone over,* converter alguém ao seu partido. 2) *to win the field,* alcançar a vitória. 3) *to win one's way,* avançar, progredir; *s.* vitória.

wince, *v.i.* encolher-se, tremer, recuar; melindrar-se; *s.* estremecimento.

winch, *s.* manivela; guincho; carreto.

wind, *s.* vento, ventania; ar, sopro, bafo; respiração, hálito; insignificância; cheiro. 1) *wind bound,* retido por ventos contrários. 2) *wind chest,* reservatório, num órgão, para o vento produzido pelo fole. 3) *wind egg,* ovo não fecundado. 4) *wind instrument,* instrumento de sopro. 5) *wind rose,* rosa-dos-ventos. 6) *wind side,* o lado de onde vem o vento. 7) *wind tight,* impermeável ao vento. 8) *to take the wind of,* pôr-se a barlavento de. 9) *to get wind of,* farejar, vir a saber. 10) *to break wind,* aliviar os gases intestinais. 11) *on a wind,* (náut.) à bolina. 12) *to have the wind up:* assustar-se. 13) *to sail close to the wind,* navegar à bolina, cingido ao vento; quase ultrapassar os limites da decência. *v.t.* aventar, arejar, ventilar; farejar; tirar o fôlego a; descansar para recobrar o fôlego; tocar instrumento de sopro; buzinar, soprar.

wind, *s.* curva, volta, sinuosidade; empenamento; *v. pret.* e *pp.* wound. *v.t.* Enrolar, dobrar; torcer, retorcer; dar corda a; dirigir; seguir as voltas de; içar por meio de cabrestante; envolver, enredar; virar a proa de (navio). 1) *to wind off,* desenrolar. 2) *to wind up,* enrolar completamente. 3) *to wind one's way,* insinuar-se; *v.i.* dar voltar, serpear, serpentear; enroscar-se; insinuar-se; empenar (a madeira). 4) *to wind up,* concluir, terminar; entrar em liquidação (empresa).

windage, *s.* deslocamento de ar produzido por projéctil; desvio do projéctil devido ao vento; folga.

windbreak, *s.* quebra-vento.

wind-broken, *adj.* asmático.

winded, *adj.* ventilado; esbaforido.

winder, *s.* dobadeira, dobador; dobadoura; manivela de sarilho; chave de relógio; degrau de escada de caracol.

windfall, *s.* fruta caída da árvore; ganho ou vantagem inesperada.

windflaw, *s.* pé-de-vento; rajada.

windflower, *s.* anémona.

windily, *adv.* com vento; agitado pelo vento; tempestuosamente; futilmente.

windiness, *s.* carácter ventoso; flatulência; presunção.

winding, *s.* volta, curva, dobra; rodeio, meandro, sinuosidade; (tecel.) dobagem; espira, esquina, ângulo, canto; enrolamento, bobinagem. 1) *in winding,* empenado. 2) *winding stair,* escada de caracol. 3) *winding of the voice,* inflexão da voz; 4) *windings and turnings,* voltas e reviravoltas; *adj.* sinuoso, tortuoso; enrolado, torcido; em espiral.

windmill, *s.* moinho de vento.

window, *s.* janela; tampa; postigo; montra; *window shopping,* ver as montras.

windowpane, *s.* vidraça.

windward, *s.* (náut.) barlavento, lado de onde sopra o vento; *adv.* a barlavento, para barlavento; *adj.* de barlavento, situado a barlavento.

windy, *adj.* ventoso, tempestuoso; relativo ao vento; volúvel; flatulento; pomposo, empolado; vão, oco.

wine, *s.* vinho; sumo fermentado de certos frutos; *wine cellar,* adega; *v.t.* servir vinho a; *v.i.* beber vinho.

wineskin, *s.* odre de vinho.

wing, *s.* asa; voo; ala; flanco; bastidor; orelha (de sofá). 1) *to take wing,* levantar voo. 2) *on the wing,* em pleno voo, em movimento, em marcha; *v.t.* alar, dar asas a; atravessar voando; ferir na asa; transportar pelo ar; *v.i.* voar.

winged, *adj.* alado, com asas; veloz, rápido; elevado; ferido na asa.

winglet, *s.* asinha.

wingspread, *s.* envergadura das asas.

wink, *v.i.* e *v.t.* piscar os olhos; pestanejar; cintilar; *s.* piscadela, piscar de olhos; abrir e fechar de olhos, instante.

winner, *s.* vencedor.

winning, *s.* vitória; ganhos, lucros; galeria de mina de carvão; *adj.* vencedor, vitorioso; premiado; cativante, sedutor.

winningly, *adv.* encantadoramente, sedutoramente.

winnow, *v.t.* e *v.i.* joeirar, cirandar; investigar; soprar, bater com as asas.

winsome, *adj.* encantador, sedutor, atraente; alegre.

winter, *s.* inverno; *adj.* invernoso, invernal; *winter sleep,* hibernação; *v.i.* invernar, hibernar, passar o Inverno; *v.t.* conservar durante o Inverno.

winterer, *s.* invernante.

wintergreen, *s.* (bot.) pírola.

winterly, *adj.* invernal, invernoso, de Inverno; frio.

wintry, *adj.* invernoso, próprio do Inverno; frio, gélido; desolado, brumoso, sombrio.

winy, *adj.* vinoso, avinhado.

wipe, *v.t.* enxugar, secar; limpar. 1) *to wipe off, out ou away,* apagar, riscar, eliminar. 2) *to wipe someone's eye,* antecipar-se a alguém; *v.i.* dar uma pancada, desferir um golpe; *s.* limpeza, enxugo; pancada, palmada; gracejo.

wire, *s.* arame; fio metálico; fio eléctrico; corda (de instrumento musical); telegrama. 1) *barbed wire,* arame farpado. 2) *to pull the wires,* mexer os cordelinhos; *v.t.* e *v.i.* prover de arame; prender com arame; instalar fios eléctricos; telegrafar.

wiredraw, *v.t.* fiar (metal), puxar à fieira; estirar, alongar, prolongar, dar corda; refinar.

wiredrawn, *adj.* estirado, alongado; subtil, refinado.

wireless, *adj.* sem fios; radiofónico; *s.* radiotelegrafia, radiotelefonia; rádio; receptor de rádio.

wire-wove, *adj.* feito de tecido metálico.

wiring, *s.* colocação de arames; instalação eléctrica.

wiry, *adj.* de arame; metálico; magro, teso; vigoroso.

wisdom, *s.* sabedoria, sensatez, bom senso,

juízo; ciência, saber; *wisdom tooth,* dente do siso.

wise, *adj.* sábio, sensato, prudente, judicioso; sagaz, experiente, esperto; sério, grave. 1) *wise man,* mago; *v.t.* e *v.i.* informar, ser informado, pôr-se a par; avisar; tornar(-se) esperto. *s.* modo, maneira, forma. 2) *in no wise,* de modo algum.

wisecrack, *s.* piada, gracejo.

wish, *s.* desejo, anseio, aspiração, ambição; *pl.* votos de felicidade, cumprimentos; *v.t.* e *v.i.* desejar, ansiar, querer; apetecer; cobiçar; *I wish I could!,* quem me dera!

wishful, *adj.* desejoso, ansioso.

wishfully, *adv.* ansiosamente, vivamente, ardentemente, impacientemente.

wish-wash, *s.* bebida aguada, água chilra; sensaboria.

wisp, *s.* molho, punhado, trouxa; torcida; escova; pedaço, fragmento, lasca, tira, farrapo; madeixa (de cabelo); coisa ou pessoa pequenina; *v.t.* torcer, enrolar.

wist, *pret.* de *to wit.*

wistful, *adj.* anelante, ansioso; cobiçoso, ávido, sôfrego; atento, pensativo, melancólico.

wistfulness, *s.* avidez, anelo.

wit, *s.* espírito, agudeza de espírito; engenho, aptidão, destreza; finura, sagacidade, inteligência; imaginação, juízo, razão; *pl.* juízo, razão, sentido. 1) *out of one's wits,* fora de si, louco. 2) *the five wits,* os cinco sentidos. 3) *to live by one's wits,* viver de expedientes; 4) *to lose one's wits,* perder o juízo; *v.t.* e *v.i. indic. pres.* wot; *pret.* e *pp.* wist; ter conhecimento de, perceber; *loc. conj. to wit,* isto é, a saber.

witch, *s.* bruxa, feiticeira; *v.t.* enfeitiçar.

witchcraft, *s.* feitiçaria, bruxaria; sortilégio.

witchery, *s.* feitiçaria, bruxaria, bruxedo, sortilégio.

witching, *s.* feitiçaria, bruxaria; *adj.* mágico; fascinante, sedutor.

witenagemot, *s.* (hist.) conselho nacional dos anglo-saxões.

with, *prep.* com, com respeito a, para com, por, de, contra, a, em, entre.

withal, *adv.* demais, além disso, além de que; também, por outro lado; juntamente com, ao mesmo tempo; *prep.* com.

withdraw, (conjuga-se como *draw*) *v.t.* e *v.i.* retirar(-se), tirar; afastar(-se), apartar(-se), ir embora, ausentar-se; recolher-se.

withdrawal, *s.* retirada, retiro, afastamento.

withe, s. vime, verga.

wither, v.t. e v.i. murchar, secar, definhar, mirrar, estiolar(-se); decair, declinar; debilitar; fulminar.

withering, adj. que murcha; decadente; fulminante, devastador.

withers, s. pl. cernelha.

withhold, v.t. (conjuga-se como hold) conter; deter, reter; impedir, estorvar; recusar.

within, prep. dentro de, adentro, no interior de, em; da parte de dentro, no espaço de, à distância de; ao alcance de; por pouco; desde, daqui a; cerca de; adv. dentro, interiormente, em casa. 1) from within, de dentro. 2) within a while, dentro em pouco, brevemente.

without, prep. sem; desprovido de; fora de. 1) to do ou to go without, passar sem, dispensar; adv. fora, de fora, por fora, fora de casa, exteriormente. 2) from without, de fora; conj. a menos que, se não, a não ser que, excepto, salvo.

whithoutdoors, adv. fora de casa, ao ar livre; no estrangeiro.

withstand, v.t. e v.i. (conjuga-se como stand) resistir a, suportar, opor-se (a); contrariar.

witless, adj. insensato, tonto; estúpido; inconsciente.

witling, s. pessoa que procura ter graça; pedante.

witness, s. testemunha; testemunho; prova, confirmação; espectador. 1) eye witness, testemunha ocular. 2) in witness whereof, (jur.) em fé do que. 3) to bear witness to, prestar testemunho, testemunhar. 4) to call to witness, invocar como testemunha. 5) witness stand, banco das testemunhas; v.t. e v.i. testemunhar, atestar, assinar como testemunha; provar, revelar; presenciar, assistir, ser testemunha de; prestar testemunho, depor.

witted, adj. espirituoso, inteligente. 1) quick witted, perspicaz. 2) dull witted, lento de compreensão, simplório.

witticism, s. dito espirituoso, graça, chiste.

witting, adj. consciente.

wittingly, adv. conscientemente; intencionadamente.

wittol, s. marido que finge ignorar as infidelidades da esposa.

witty, adj. espirituoso; gracioso.

wizard, s. mago, mágico, feiticeiro.

wizardry, s. magia, feitiçaria.

wizen, v.i. murchar, secar, mirrar; adj. engelhado, mirrado.

woad, s. isátis.

woad, adj. tingido com tinta extraída do isátis.

wobble, v.i. vacilar, balançar-se, cambalear; s. balouço, bamboleio, oscilação.

wobbler, s. aquele que vacila ou cambaleia; (mec.) excêntrico.

wobbling, adj. vacilante, cambaleante, oscilante, trémulo.

wobbly, adj. vacilante, trémulo.

woe, s. pesar, mágoa, dor; aflição; calamidade, infortúnio. 1) woe is me!, ai de mim!. 2) woe be to, maldito seja!. 3) woe worth the day!, maldito seja o dia!

woebegone, adj. abatido, desanimado; miserável.

woeful, adj. pesaroso, aflito; desgraçado; deplorável, lastimoso; mesquinho.

woesome, adj. o mesmo que woeful.

woke, pret. de wake.

woken, pp. de wake.

wold, s. planície; charneca, descampado.

wolf, s. lobo; larva destruidora de vários escaravelhos. 1) to hold a wolf by the ears, estar em apuros. 2) to keep the wolf from the door, evitar a fome; v.t. devorar.

wolfish, adj. lupino, de lobo; feroz, cruel; voraz.

wolfram, s. volfrâmio.

wolves, pl. de wolf.

woman, s. mulher.

womanhood, s. condição de mulher, feminilidade; o sexo feminino.

womanish, adj. mulheril, mulherengo; efeminado.

womanize, v.t. efeminar.

womankind, s. as mulheres, o sexo feminino.

womanlike, adj. feminino, próprio de mulher.

womanly, adj. mulheril, mulherengo, de mulher, efeminado; adv. como mulher, femininamente.

womb, s. útero; ventre, seio, entranhas.

wombat, s. vombate.

women, pl. de woman.

womenfolk, s. mulheres, mulherio.

won, pret. e pp. de win.

wonder, s. maravilha, prodígio, milagre; admiração, surpresa, assombro, espanto. 1) it is no wonder, não admira. 2) for a wonder, excepcionalmente. 3) wonder-stricken, atónito, pasmado. 4) wonder-worker, pessoa que faz prodígios, taumaturgo; *v.i.* e *v.t.* admirar-se, surpreender-se, espantar-se, maravilhar-se, surpreender-se com, estranhar; perguntar a si próprio, interrogar-se, desejar saber.

wonderful, *adj.* maravilhoso, admirável, surpreendente, assombroso, prodigioso, extraordinário, fantástico, extraordinário.

wondering, *adj.* admirado, maravilhado, surpreendido, espantado, atónito.

wonderland, *s.* país das maravilhas, reino das fadas.

wonderment, *s.* admiração, surpresa, espanto, pasmo; maravilha, prodígio.

wonderworck, *s.* maravilha, prodígio, milagre.

wondrous, *adj.* extraordinário, maravilhoso, portentoso, admirável, prodigioso.

wont, *adj.* acostumado, habituado; *s.* hábito, costume; uso, usança, tradição; *v.t.* acostumar, habituar; *v.i.* costumar, estar habituado.

wonted, *adj.* habitual, costumeiro, usual; acostumado, habituado.

woo, *v.t.* cortejar, fazer a corte a, namorar, pedir em casamento; procurar, perseguir, pretender; solicitar, convidar, instar com.

wood, *s.* madeira, pau, lenha; bosque, floresta, mata; barril, pipa. 1) *fire wood,* lenha. 2) *wood pigeon,* pombo bravo. 3) *wood tick,* caruncho. 4) *wood winds,* (mús.) instrumentos de sopro de madeira; *v.t.* e *v.i.* arborizar; abastecer(-se) de lenha.

woodbin, *s.* depósito de lenha.

woodchuck, *s.* espécie de marmota norte- -americana.

woodcock, *s.* galinhola.

woodcut, *s.* gravura em madeira, xilografia.

woodcutter, *s.* lenhador; xilógrafo.

wooded, *adj.* arborizado.

wooden, *adj.* de madeira, de pau; grosseiro, tosco; duro, rígido.

woodenheaded, *adj.* estúpido, bronco.

woodenware, *s.* utensílios domésticos de madeira.

woodiness, *s.* consistência ou aparência lenhosa.

woodland, *s.* região florestal, florestas, bosques; *adj.* florestal; silvestre.

woodlander, *s.* habitante das florestas.

woodman, *s.* guarda-florestal; lenhador.

woodpecker, *s.* pica-pau.

woodprint, *s.* xilografia.

woodsman, *s.* habitante das florestas, homem do mato; lenhador, madeireiro.

woodwaxwn, *s.* giesta.

woodworker, *s.* carpinteiro.

woodworm, *s.* caruncho, bicho-da-madeira.

woody, *adj.* lenhoso; de madeira; coberto de arvoredo; silvestre.

wooer, *s.* pretendente, namorado.

wool, *s.* lã; fio de lã; fazenda de lã; lanugem. 1) *against the wool,* contra o pêlo. 2) *wool bearing,* lanígero. 3) *wool grease,* gordura de lã, lanolina. 4) *wool hall,* bolsa ou mercado da lã. 5) *wool stapler,* negociante de lã.

woolen, *adj.* de lã, lanoso; *s.* tecido de lã.

wollgrower, *s.* criador de gado lanígero.

wooly, *adj.* lanoso, lanífero, lanígero; de lã, coberto de lã; crespo (cabelo); rouca (voz); indeciso, confuso; *s.* peça de roupa de lã.

woorali, *s.* curare.

woozy, *adj.* tonto, confuso; embriagado.

wop, *s.* termo depreciativo com que se designam os imigrantes oriundos da Europa Meridional.

word, *s.* palavra, termo, vocábulo; lingua- gem; mensagem, recado; dito, sentença; *pl.* palavras, expressão verbal; letra de canção. 1) *by word of mouth,* verbalmente. 2) *upon my word,* palavra de honra. 3) *at a word,* sem delongas. 4) *in a word,* em suma. 5) *word accent,* acento tónico. 6) *to send word to,* mandar recado a. 7) *to leave word,* deixar recado. 8) *to put or to say a good word for,* interceder a favor de alguém. 9) *to have words with someone,* discutir com alguém. 10) *a word to the wise is enough,* a bom entendedor meia palavra basta. 11) *words are but wind,* palavras leva-as o vento; *v.t.* expressar, exprimir, enunciar; redigir; escrever; instar com palavras.

wordbook, *s.* glossário; libreto (de ópera).

wordiness, *s.* verbosidade.

wording, *s.* fraseado, redacção, enunciação.

wordless, *adj.* sem palavras; mudo.

wordy, *adj.* verboso, palavroso.

wore, *pret.* de *wear.*

work, *s.* trabalho; ocupação, ofício, emprego; labor, tarefa; obra, acto; efeito; *pl.* obras; livro, poema, composição, pintura, etc.; fábrica, oficina; engrenagem, mecanismo. 1) *at work,* ocupado, a trabalhar. 2) *to get to work,* começar a trabalhar. 3) *to give someone the works,* dar uma tareia a alguém. 4) *to make short work of,* dar cabo de, livrar-se de. 5) *work shy,* preguiçoso;

v.t. e *v.i. pret.* e *pp.* worked ou wrought. trabalhar; operar, funcionar; fabricar, manufacturar, elaborar; produzir efeito; mover, accionar; manobrar; efectuar; causar; manipular, manejar; talhar; impelir; investigar, estudar; resolver (um problema); ocupar-se; ser eficaz. 6) *to work in,* encaixar. 7) *to work into,* penetrar em. 8) *to work off,* descarregar; livrar-se de; concluir. 9) *to work out,* calcular total; esgotar; fazer exercício. 10) *to work upon,* influenciar; 11) *to work up,* trabalhar, lavrar; transformar (pelo trabalho); desenvolver (um assunto); aperfeiçoar; formar, criar; excitar, provocar, incitar. 12) *to work through,* penetrar, atravessar. 13) *to work loose,* soltar-se, ter folga (peça de máquina). 14) *to work one's will,* realizar o seu desejo. 15) *to work wonders,* fazer maravilhas. 16) *wrought-up state,* estado de excitação, nervosismo.

workable, *adj.* trabalhável; viável; explorável (mina).

workaday, *adj.* próprio dos dias de trabalho; diário; rotineiro, comum.

worker, *s.* trabalhador, operário; artífice.

workhouse, *s.* asilo para pobres, albergue; casa de correcção.

working, *s.* obra, trabalho, operação; funcionamento, movimento; manobra; fermentação; exploração (de mina); tiragem; influência; agitação; desenvolvimento; *adj.* que trabalha; que funciona; prático, eficaz; de trabalho; activo; agitado. 1) *in working order,* pronto para funcionar. 2) *working capital,* capital produtivo. 3) *working parts,* partes móveis de uma máquina.

workless, *adj.* sem trabalho, desempregado.

workman, *s.* trabalhador, operário; artífice, artesão.

workmanlike, *adv.* próprio de bom trabalhador; hábil; perfeito, bem acabado; primoroso.

workmanship, *s.* obra, trabalho; artefacto; manufactura; habilidade.

workout, *s.* (coloq.) teste, prova, exercício.

workshop, *s.* oficina.

world, *s.* mundo, universo, cosmo, terra, globo terrestre; abundância, infinidade. 1) *the great world,* a alta sociedade. 2) *world-old,* velho como o mundo. 3) *world series,* campeonato mundial. 4) *world-wide,* espalhado por todo o mundo, universal. 5) *all the world,* toda a gente, o mundo inteiro;

6) *for all the world,* por nada deste mundo; em todos os aspectos. 7) *to be all the world for someone,* ser tudo para alguém. 8) *how in the world...?,* como é que...?. 9) *to let the world slide,* deixar correr o marfim. 10) *I have a world of things to tell you,* tenho um monte de coisas para te contar. 11) *I would give the world to know,* daria tudo para saber.

worldling, *s.* pessoa mundana.

worldly, *adj.* terreno, temporal, profano, secular; mundano, carnal; frívolo; experiente; *adv.* de forma mundana, mundanamente; temporalmente.

worm, *s.* verme, minhoca, lombriga; bicho, larva; rosca de parafuso; (quim.) serpentina; saca-trapo (extractor de bucha de arma de fogo). 1) *worm-eaten,* roído da traça, carunchoso. 2) *wormgearing,* engrenagem de rosca. 3) *worm-pipe,* serpentina. 4) *glow-worm,* pirilampo. 5) *silk-worm,* bicho-da-seda. 6) *the worm of conscience,* o remorso; *v.t.* e *v.i.* insinuar-se, introduzir-se; rastejar, serpear; minar; arrancar segredo ardilosamente; tirar bucha de arma de fogo; (náut.) engaiar. 7) *to worm oneself into favour,* insinuar-se. 8) *to worm one's way,* avançar lenta ou tortuosamente.

wormwood, *s.* (bot.) absinto.

wormy, *adj.* verminal, vermicular; bichoso, bichento; roído pelas traças, carcomido; antiquado, decrépito; verminoso; rasteiro, vil, nojento; servil.

worm, *pp.* de *wear. adj.* gasto, usado, coçado; cansado, exausto, fatigado.

worried, *adj.* inquieto, preocupado, incomodado.

worry, *s.* inquietação, cuidado, preocupação; mordedura, acto de atacar a dentadas (o cão); *v.t.* e *v.i.* afligir(-se), preocupar(-se), atormentar; maçar; dilacerar, morder, sacudir com os dentes, maltratar. 1) *to worry along,* ir vivendo, apesar das dificuldades. 2) *I should worry,* (E.U.) pouco me importa.

worse, *adj.* e *adv. (comp. de bad, badly, evil* ou *ill).* Pior, em pior situação, em pior estado. 1) *so much the worse,* tanto pior. 2) *worse and worse,* cada vez pior. 3) *to get, to grow worse,* piorar. 4) *to go from bad to worse,* ir de mal a pior.

worsen, *v.t.* e *v.i.* piorar.

worship, *s.* adoração, culto, veneração;

respeito; respeito, deferência; honra, dignidade, mérito; excelência; *Your Worship,* Vossa Excelência; *v.t.* e *v.i.* adorar, venerar; idolatrar; prestar culto.

worshipful, *adj.* venerável, respeitável, venerando; venerador, reverente, adorador.

worshipfulness, *s.* venerabilidade, respeitabilidade.

worst, *adj.* e *adv. (sup. de bad, badly, evil* ou *ill).* o pior, a parte pior; da pior maneira; *v.t.* vencer, derrotar, levar a melhor sobre.

worsted, *s.* tecido ou fio de lã torcida.

wort, *s.* planta, erva; cerveja ainda não fermentada.

worth, *s.* mérito, importância, consideração; excelência; valor, custo, praço; riqueza, bens; *adj.* digno, merecedor; que tem o valor de , que vale; equivalente a. 1) *to be worth,* valer, ter, possuir. 2) *to be worth of,* ser digno de, merecer. 3) *to be worth a lot of money,* ser muito rico. 4) *it is worth seeing,* digno de se ver. 5) *it is worth nothing,* não vale nada. 6) *to be worth while,* valer a pena. 7) *he is worth a million,* ele tem bens no valor de um milhão.

worthiness, *s.* valor, mérito, dignidade, excelência.

worthless, *adj.* sem valor, inútil; indigno, desprezível.

worthy, *adj.* digno, estimável, honrado, respeitável, excelente; meritório; digno de, merecedor; *s.* pessoa ilustre; sumidade.

wot, *pres. indic.* de *wit.*

would, *pret.* e *condic.* de *will.*

would-be, *adj.* que pretende ser, que tem pretensões a, aspirante a; pretenso, suposto.

wound, *pret.* e *pp.* de *wind.*

wound, *s.* ferida, ferimento, lesão; golpe; ofensa. *v.t.* ferir, magoar; ofender.

wounded, *adj.* ferido

wounless, *adj.* ileso, incólume.

wove, *pret.* de *weave.*

woven, *pp.* de *weave.*

wowser, *s.* puritano, moralista, fanático.

wrack, *s.* alga marinha, sargaço; ruína; nuvens levadas pelo vento.

wraith, *s.* espectro, fantasma, aparição.

wrangle, *s.* altercação, disputa, questão; *v.i.* altercar, discutir.

wrangler, *s.* altercador, disputador; estudante que *(na Univ. de Cambridge)* obteve distinção em matemáticas; (E.U.) vaqueiro.

wrap, *v.t.* e *v.i.* envolver, embrulhar,

agasalhar; rodear, envolver; ocultar; cobrir, revestir; conter, encerrar; absorver, mergulhar; dobrar, enrolar; sobrepor-se; *s.* agasalho, coberta, manta, abafo.

wrapper, *s.* cobertura, capa; invólucro; cinta para jornais ou revistas; roupão de senhora.

wrapping, *s.* acto de envolver, embrulhar ou cobrir; invólucro; *wrapping paper,* papel de embrulho.

wrath, *s.* ira, raiva, cólera.

wrathful, *adj.* irado, encolerizado, furioso, raivoso.

wreak, *v.t.* descarregar, dar curso a, saciar; infligir; vingar.

wreath, *s.* coroa (de flores), grinalda, festão; anel, espiral.

wreathe, *v.t.* e *v.i.* entrelaçar, fazer ou guarnecer de grinaldas; enrolar, torcer, enroscar; contrair, enrugar.

wreck, *s.* destroços, restos de naufrágio, salvados; navio naufragado; ruína, destruição; *v.t.* e *v.i.* naufragar; dar à costa; afundar-se; ir a pique; arruinar(-se), perder(-se).

wreckage, *s.* destroços, escombros, ruínas, restos; naufrágios; destruição.

wrecker, *s.* o que causa naufrágios; arruinador, destruidor; salvador ou salteador de naufrágios; barco de socorro; demolidor.

wrecking, *s.* salvamento de navios naufragados; demolição de edifícios; acto de provocar naufrágios; *adj.* de socorro, de salvamento.

wren, *s.* (zool.) carriça.

wrench, *s.* repelão, puxão; torção, torcedura; deslocação; entorse; chave de porcas, chave-inglesa; *v.t.* torcer ou puxar com força; retorcer, forçar; arrancar, arrebatar; deslocar, distender; alterar, deturpar, perverter.

wrest, *s.* torção, torcedura; puxão, safanão; chave de afinar pianos; *wrest-pin,* cravelha (de piano); *v.t.* tirar à força, arrancar; torcer, retorcer; extorquir, usurpar, arrebatar; forçar, deturpar, perverter.

wrestle, *s.* luta corpo a corpo; luta, contenda; *v.t.* e *v.i.* lutar corpo a corpo, travar combate de luta greco-romana; lutar, contender, combater; engalfinhar-se com.

wrestling, *s.* luta corpo a corpo, luta greco-romana.

wretch, *s.* infeliz, desgraçado, miserável; patife, canalha, vilão.

wretched, *adj.* infeliz, desgraçado, miserável; lamentável, deplorável; insignificante, mesquinho; desprezível, vil; mau, perverso; péssimo.

wrick, *s.* entorse; mau jeito.

wrier, *comp.* e *supr.* de **wry.**

wriggle, *s.* meneio, coleio; sinuosidade; *v.t.* e *v.i.* retorcer-se; menear-se; mexer, revolver; insinuar-se; *to wriggle out of,* escapar-se de.

wriggly, *adj.* que se retorce, coleante, sinuoso, tortuoso.

wright, *s.* artífice, artesão, carpinteiro.

wring, *s.* acto de torcer, torcedura; aperto; *v.t.* pret. e *pp.* wrung. torcer, retorcer, apertar; espremer; puxar; arrancar, tirar ou arrancar à força; extorquir; forçar, obrigar; atormentar, torturar; desvirtuar, perverter.

wringer, *s.* espremedor; máquina de espremer roupa.

wrinkle, *s.* ruga, vinco, prega, dobra; ondulação; ardil, truque, estratagema; informação secreta, palpite; *v.t.* e *v.i.* enrugar(-se), franzir(-se), encarquilhar(-se); contrair-se, encrespar(-se); preguear(-se).

wrinkly, *adj.* rugoso, enrugado.

wrist, *s.* pulso; punho.

wrisband, *s.* punho de camisa.

wristlet, *s.* pulseira, bracelete; algema.

writ, *s.* (bibl.) escrito, escritura; (jur.) mandado, ordem; intimação judicial.

write, *v.t.* e *v.i.* pret. wrote, *pp.* written. escrever; redigir; inscrever; dizer por carta, mandar notícias por escrito; compor (música). 1) *to write down,* tomar nota, assentar, anotar. 2) *to write out,* copiar, transcrever, passar a limpo; escrever por extenso. 3) *to write up,* descrever por extenso; louvar, ou elogiar por escrito; pôr em dia (livro de contabilidade). 4) *to write a cheque,* passar um cheque. 5) *to write a good hand,* ter boa letra.

writer, *s.* escritor, autor; literato; redactor; *the present writer,* o signatário.

write-up, *s.* (E.U.) reportagem; artigo elogioso.

writhe, *s.* contorção; estremecimento; *v.t.* e *v.i.* torcer(-se), retorcer(-se), contorcer(-se); enrolar(-se), enroscar(-se).

writhen, *adj.* torcido, contorcido; enrolado, enroscado; entrelaçado.

writing, *s.* escrita, acto de escrever; escrito, manuscrito; letra, caligrafia; estilo, obra literária, livro; artigo; documento escrito; inscrição; texto. 1) *in writing,* por escrito. 2) *in my own writing,* pelo meu próprio punho. 3) *to put to writing,* pôr por escrito. 4) *writing desk,* escrivaninha. 5) *the Sacred Writings,* as Sagradas Escrituras.

written, *pret.* de **write;** *adj.* escrito.

wrong, *adj.* errado, incorrecto; errôneo; inexacto; injusto, mau; falso; impróprio, inoportuno, indevido; ilegal, ilegítimo; equivocado, enganado. 1) *wrong note,* (mús.) nota falsa. 2) *wrong side out,* do avesso. 3) *to be wrong,* estar enganado, não ter razão. 4) *on the wrong side of forty,* para lá dos quarenta anos. 5) *to be wrong in the head,* não regular bem da cabeça. 6) *what is wrong with you?,* o que é que tens? *s.* mal, prejuízo, dano; erro, engano; falsidade; injustiça, injúria. 7) *to complain of one's wrongs,* queixar-se das injustiças sofridas. 8) *to be in the wrong,* não ter razão. 9) *to put someone in the wrong,* lançar as culpas a alguém, tirar a razão a alguém; *adv.* mal; erradamente, incorrectamente, indevidamente; falsamente; injustamente. 10) *to do wrong,* proceder mal. 11) *to go wrong,* enganar-se no caminho, transviar-se; cair em erro, errar; dar mau resultado, não resultar, gorar-se. 12) *to lead somebody wrong,* induzir alguém em erro; desencaminhar alguém; *v.t.* prejudicar, fazer mal, lesar; ofender, injuriar; ser injusto com, tratar injustamente; defraudar; seduzir (uma mulher).

wrongdoer, *s.* pessoa que pratica o mal; malfeitor; pecador.

wrongful, *adj.* injusto; nocivo; ilegal.

wrongheaded, *adj.* teimoso, obstinado, birrento.

wrongly, *adv.* erradamente; mal; injustamente.

wrongness, *s.* injustiça, maldade; erro, falsidade, inexactidão.

wrote, *pret.* de **write.**

wrought, *pp.* de **work.** *adj.* trabalhado; lavrado, talhado; forjado; bordado; manufacturado.

wrung, *pret.* e *pp.* de **wring.**

wry, *adj.* torto, torcido, dobrado; enviesado, de esguelha, oblíquo; errado, aberrante; deformado, pervertido, perverso; *to make a wry mouth,* torcer a boca, fazer uma careta de desagrado; *v.t.* e *v.i.* torcer(-se), contorcer(-se); entortar.

wryly, *adv.* de esguelha; retorcidamente.

wryneck, *s.* torcicolo; aquele que tem um torcicolo; (zool.) papa-formigas (ave).

wryness, *s.* contorção; deformação; assimetria.

X

x, vigésima quarta letra do alfabeto.
xanthus, *s.* xanto; espécie de mineral.
xenogamy, *s.* xenogamia.
Xmas, *s. abrev.* de Christmas.
X-rays, *s. pl.* raios X.

xylographe, *s.* gravado em madeira.
xylographer, *s.* xilógrafo.
xylography, *s.* xilografia.
xylonite, *s.* celulóide.
xylophone, *s.* xilofone.

Y

y, vigésima quinta letra do alfabeto.
yacht, *s.* iate, barco de recreio; *v.i.* navegar em iate.
yachting, *s.* desporto náutico; navegação em iate; acção de viajar em iate.
yachtsman, *s.* proprietário ou timoneiro dum iate.
yah, *interj.* exclamação de desagrado.
yahoo, *s.* selvagem.
yak, *s.* iaque, ruminante da Ásia.
yam, *s.* inhame.
Yankee, *s.* e *adj.* americano do norte (fam.); nome dado aos americanos pelos estrangeiros.
yap, *v.i. (yapping, yapped),* ladrar, ganir; chalrear; *s.* cão pequeno, cachorrinho; latido.
yard, *v.i.* encurralar, aprisionar; fechar em pátio; *s.* curral, pátio; cercado; estaleiro; verga; vara, jarda (medida inglesa = 0,m914); vara de medir. 1) *dock-yard,* arsenal do porto, estaleiro. 2) *to brace the yards,* bracejar as vergas.

yarrow, *s.* (bot.) mil-em-rama.
yashmak, *s.* véu usado pelas mulheres muçulmanas.
yataghan, *s.* adaga, alfange.
yaw, *s.* guinada (náut.); *v.t.* e *v.i.* guinar, elevar-se, erguer-se; espumar.
yawl, *s.* iole, bote, chalupa.
yawn, *v.i.* bocejar; ficar com a boca aberta; suspirar; *s.* bocejo; abertura; voragem.
ye, antiga forma gráfica de imprimir *the.*
yea, *adv.* certamente; na verdade; *s.* voto afirmativo; *yea or nay,* sim ou não.
yean, *v.i.* parir (a ovelha).
yeanling, *s.* cordeirinho.
year, *s.* ano; *pl.* anos, idade, velhice. 1) *by the year,* por ano, ao ano. 2) *every other year,* de dois em dois anos. 3) *leap year,* ano bissexto. 4) *man in years,* ancião, homem de idade avançada.
yearbook, *s.* anuário.
yearling, *adj.* dum ano; *s.* animal com um ano.
yearly, *adj.* anual; *adv.* anualmente, todos os anos.

yearn, *v.i.* anelar, desejar vivamente, suspirar por; estar saudoso.

yearning, *s.* saudade, anelo, aspiração, lembrança viva; *adv. yearningly,* saudosamente.

yeast, *s.* levedura, fermento; espuma.

yeaty, *adj.* fermentício; buliçoso.

yell, *v.t.* e *v.i.* vociferar, gritar, bramir, soltar gritos ferozes; *s.* alarido, grito, bramido, grito feroz, ou de guerra; *college yell,* grito peculiar que serve de identificação aos estudantes de cada escola.

yellow, *adj.* amarelo. 1) *yellow boy,* dinheiro ou ouro. 2) *yellow leaf,* velhice; *s.* cor amarela.

yellowish, *adj.* amarelado.

yellowishness, *s.* cor amarelada.

yellowy, *adj.* amarelo, amarelado.

yelp, *v.i.* latir, ganir; *s.* latido, ganido.

yelping, *s.* latido, ganido; *adj.* que está a latir, a ganir.

yen, *s.* iene, moeda japonesa.

yeoman, *s.* proprietário; lavrador abastado; burguês; despenseiro; oficial da Casa Real de Inglaterra; membro da guarda nacional (Inglaterra); *Yeoman of the Guard:* archeiro do palácio.

yeomanry, *s.* os lavradores ricos; guarda particular do rei (arc. inglês).

yes, sim, certamente.

yester, *adj.* de ontem; passado, último.

yesterday, *s.* ontem; *the day before yesterday,* anteontem.

yet, *adj.* contudo, ainda, todavia; por ora; por enquanto; eventualmente. 1) *as yet,* todavia; até agora; ainda. 2) *not yet,* ainda não; *conj.* contudo, não obstante; mas; ainda assim.

yew, *s.* teixo.

yewen, *adj.* de teixo.

yield, *v.t.* produzir; ceder; devolver, restituir, entregar; conceder; *v.i.* render-se, ser útil; cair; sujeitar-se, submeter-se.

yielding, *adj.* que se rende, que condescende; dócil.

yodel, *v.t.* e *v.i. (yodelling, yodelled),* cantar modulando a voz rapidamente desde o tom natural ao falsete; *s.* modo de cantar dos tiroleses.

yo-ho, *interj.* olhe! ali!

yoke, *s.* jugo, canga; junta de bois; parelha; par; *(fig.)* opressão, escravidão; cana do leme; *yoke-fellow,* camarada; esposa; *v.t.* jungir, pôr a canga em; emparelhar; subjugar, sujeitar, oprimir; encadear, reprimir, conter.

yokel, *s.* rústico, camponês.

yolk, *s.* gema de ovo; unto, gordura.

yon, *adj.* e *adv.* aquele, aquela, aqueles, aquelas (que se vêem ao longe); ali, acolá, além.

yore, *adv.* outrora, antigamente.

you, *pren. pess.* tu, vós, vossa mercê, V. Exª., V. Srª., te, a ti, a você, a V. Exª., etc.

young, *adj.* jovem, novo, moço, juvenil, novato, inexperiente; *s.* a mocidade; as crias dos animais; *with young,* prenhe, cheia.

younger, *adj.* mais novo.

youngest, *adj.* o mais novo.

youngish, *adj.* um tanto novo.

youngling, *s.* cria.

youngly, *adv.* em tenra idade; cedo.

youngster, *s.* jovem, rapaz.

younker, *s.* mancebo, jovem.

your, *pron. pess. conj.* o teu, a tua, o vosso, a vossa, os vossos, as vossas, etc.; de você, de V. Srª., de V. Exª.

yours, *pron. poss. abs.* o teu, a tua, os teus, as tuas, o vosso, a vossa, os vossos, as vossas, etc; *I am yours,* sou todo vosso; fico ao seu dispor.

yourself, *pron. reflex.* tu mesmo, vós mesmo; *pl. yourselves,* vós mesmos.

youth, *s.* juventude, mocidade; um jovem; a juventude, os jovens.

youthful, *adj.* juvenil, jovem, moço; *adv. youthfully,* juvenilmente.

yowl, *s.* uivo, grito longo, choroso ou funesto; *v.i.* uivar, dar grito longo e melancólico.

yule, yuletide, *s.* Natal, tempo de Natal.

Z

z, vigésima sexta letra do alfabeto.
zany, *s.* palhaço, bobo; *v.t.* imitar, macaquear.
zeal, *s.* zelo; fervor, ardor, paixão.
zealot, *s.* entusiasta, partidário acérrimo,
  fanático.
zealotry, *s.* fanatismo.
zealous, *adj.* zeloso, entusiasta;
zealously, *adj.* zelosamente, apaixonadamente, com paixão, com ardor.
zealousness, *s.* ardor, zelo, entusiasmo.
zebra, *s.* zebra.
zenith, *s.* zénite, apogeu.
zeppelin, *s.* zepelim.
zero, *s.* zero, cifra; nada.
zest, *s.* deleite, gosto; sabor; casquinha (de
  limão, laranja, etc.); *v.t.* dar gosto ou sabor;
  temperar com casquinhas de limão, etc.
zeta, *s.* zeta.
zeugma, *s.* zeugma.
zigzag, *v.t.* e *v.i.* ir em ziguezagues; fazer
  ziguezagues; *adj.* serpentino, ondulado, em
  ziguezagues.
zigzagging, *s.* direcção tortuosa, em
  ziguezagues.
zimotic, *adj.* azimótico.

zinc, *s.* zinco; *v.t.* cobrir com zinco.
zincky, *adj.* de zinco.
zinco, *s.* zinco.
zither, *s.* cítara.
zodiac, *s.* zodíaco, circuito.
zodiacal, *adj.* zodiacal.
zoic, *adj.* que contém fósseis.
zonal, *adj.* pertencente a uma zona; *adv.*
  zonally, com zonas.
zone, *s.* zona; faixa, cinta.
zoned, *adj.* de cinta, que tem faixa.
Zoo, *s.* jardim zoológico.
zoographer, *s.* zoógrafo.
zoography, *s.* zoografia.
zooks, *int.* por Deus!
zoolite, *s.* zoólito.
zoological, *adj.* zoológico; *adv.* zoologi-
  camente.
zoologist, *s.* zoólogo.
zoology, *s.* zoologia.
zoon, *s.* produto de um ovo fertilizado.
zootomist, *s.* zootomista; *adj.* zoótico (geol.).
zounds, *interj.* irra! por Deus!.
Zulu, *adj.* e *s.* zulo.
zymosis, *s.* zimose.
zymotic, *adj.* zimótico.